THE GRASS WITHERETH, THE FLOWER FADETH, BUT THE
WORD OF OUR GOD SHALL STAND FOR EVER.

—ISAIAH **40:8**

Presented to

_____

BY _____

_____

ON THE OCCASION OF

_____

_____

DATE _____

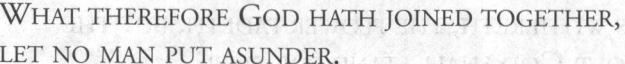

WHAT THEREFORE GOD HATH JOINED TOGETHER,
LET NO MAN PUT ASUNDER.

—MARK 10:9

Marriage

_____

AND _____

WERE UNITED IN MARRIAGE ON
_____

AT _____

BY _____

WITNESSED BY _____

MAID OF HONOR _____

BEST MAN _____

ATTENDANTS _____
_____
_____
_____
_____

LO, CHILDREN ARE AN HERITAGE
OF THE LORD.

—PSALM 127:3

Births

NAME _____ DATE _____

BIRTHPLACE _____

NAME _____ DATE _____

BIRTHPLACE _____

NAME _____ DATE _____

BIRTHPLACE _____

NAME _____ DATE _____

BIRTHPLACE _____

NAME _____ DATE _____

BIRTHPLACE _____

NAME _____ DATE _____

BIRTHPLACE _____

ONE LORD,
ONE FAITH,
ONE BAPTISM.
—EPHESIANS 4:5

Baptisms

_____

WAS BAPTIZED ON _____

AT _____

BY _____

_____

WAS BAPTIZED ON _____

AT _____

BY _____

_____

WAS BAPTIZED ON _____

AT _____

BY _____

_____

WAS BAPTIZED ON _____

AT _____

BY _____

GOD HATH BOTH RAISED UP THE LORD,
AND WILL ALSO RAISE US UP
BY HIS OWN POWER.
—1 CORINTHIANS 6:14

Deaths

NAME _____ DATE _____

NAME _____ DATE _____

NAME _____ DATE _____

NAME _____ DATE _____

NAME _____ DATE _____

NAME _____ DATE _____

NAME _____ DATE _____

The Family Tree

Husband

NAME _____ BIRTHPLACE _____ DATES

BROTHERS AND SISTERS

PARENTS

FATHER

NAME

BIRTHPLACE   DATES

MOTHER

NAME

BIRTHPLACE   DATES

GRANDPARENTS

PATERNAL

GRANDFATHER

BIRTHPLACE   DATES

GRANDMOTHER

BIRTHPLACE   DATES

MATERNAL

GRANDFATHER

BIRTHPLACE   DATES

GRANDMOTHER

BIRTHPLACE   DATES

GREAT-GRANDPARENTS

PATERNAL

GRANDFATHER'S FATHER

BIRTHPLACE   DATES

GRANDFATHER'S MOTHER

BIRTHPLACE   DATES

GRANDMOTHER'S FATHER

BIRTHPLACE   DATES

GRANDMOTHER'S MOTHER

BIRTHPLACE   DATES

MATERNAL

GRANDFATHER'S FATHER

BIRTHPLACE   DATES

GRANDFATHER'S MOTHER

BIRTHPLACE   DATES

GRANDMOTHER'S FATHER

BIRTHPLACE   DATES

GRANDMOTHER'S MOTHER

BIRTHPLACE   DATES

Wife

NAME   BIRTHPLACE   DATES

BROTHERS AND SISTERS

PARENTS

FATHER	MOTHER
NAME	NAME
BIRTHPLACE DATES	BIRTHPLACE DATES

GRANDPARENTS

PATERNAL	MATERNAL
GRANDFATHER	GRANDFATHER
BIRTHPLACE DATES	BIRTHPLACE DATES
GRANDMOTHER	GRANDMOTHER
BIRTHPLACE DATES	BIRTHPLACE DATES

GREAT-GRANDPARENTS

PATERNAL	MATERNAL
GRANDFATHER'S FATHER	GRANDFATHER'S FATHER
BIRTHPLACE DATES	BIRTHPLACE DATES
GRANDFATHER'S MOTHER	GRANDFATHER'S MOTHER
BIRTHPLACE DATES	BIRTHPLACE DATES
GRANDMOTHER'S FATHER	GRANDMOTHER'S FATHER
BIRTHPLACE DATES	BIRTHPLACE DATES
GRANDMOTHER'S MOTHER	GRANDMOTHER'S MOTHER
BIRTHPLACE DATES	BIRTHPLACE DATES

O GIVE THANKS UNTO THE LORD; FOR HE IS
GOOD: FOR HIS MERCY ENDURETH FOR EVER.
—PSALM 118:29

Special memories

EVENT

PLACE   DATE

EVENT

PLACE   DATE

EVENT

PLACE   DATE

EVENT

PLACE   DATE

EVENT

PLACE   DATE

Crossings
Devotional Bible

Crossings
Devotional Bible

CrossAmerica Books
Crossings Book Club, Garden City, New York

Crossings Devotional Bible
© 2001 Crossings™ Book Club
All rights reserved

CrossAmerica Books is an imprint and trademark
pending on behalf of Crossings Book Club

Notes and features © 2000 by Rolf Zettersten. All rights reserved.

Notes and features contained in this Bible have been adapted from *Parents Resource Bible*
(Tyndale House Publishers)

Design by Monica Elias.

ISBN 0-7394-1747-9

Printed in the United States of America

CONTENTS

ALPHABETICAL BOOK LISTING

Editorial Team

Executive Editor
Rolf Zettersten

Managing Editor
Dr. Bruce B. Barton

Project Editors
Kathryn S. Stinnette
Daryl J. Lucas

Reviewers
Dr. Walter Elwell, theological
    review committee chairman
Dr. R. K. Harrison,
    Old Testament
Dr. Leon Morris,
    New Testament
Dr. John Trent, family
    counseling review
    committee chairman
Dr. Ralph H. Earle
Dr. Bill Retts
Dr. Scott Collier
Dr. Gary Rosberg

Writers

Book Introductions
Mark Fackler

Breaking Free
Dr. John Trent

Family Life Articles
Bylines included with
    each article

Biblical Profiles
Daryl J. Lucas

Family Traditions
Marlee Alex

Worship in Your Home
Dr. V. Gilbert Beers

Devotional Moments
William Bonikowsky
Kimberley Converse
Jack Crabtree
Phil Craven
Betsy Rossen Elliot
Mark Fackler
Rev. Dietrich Gruen
Carole Newing Johnson
Rev. Kent Keller
Daryl J. Lucas
Linda S. Vanderzalm
Rev. Neil Wilson
Rev. Len Woods

Welcome and Introduction

Welcome to the *Crossings Devotional Bible*, which was created with you, our member, in mind. This Bible contains the complete text of the authorized *King James Bible*, plus seven extra features designed to help you apply God's Word to your life.

Following Christ in the details of our lives presents both challenges and opportunities. Our goal with this Bible is to provide you with help for the challenges, and illumination for the opportunities. We've included articles written by authors you can trust—including James Dobson, Jerry Jenkins, Dennis Rainey, Steve Arterburn, Bill Hybels, John Trent, Josh McDowell, and many more. From family life to issues of personal development, they will show you how the Bible speaks to every need in every age.

There are many ways to get the most out of your *Crossings Devotional Bible*. Read the **Devotional Moments** as a personal meditation time. Use the **Worship in Your Home** and **Family Traditions** ideas to create more meaningful family times. Use the **Biblical Profiles** and **Breaking Free** articles as the basis for more in-depth Bible study. And all the special elements can be used as a topical resource, to refer to when the need arises. We hope your time in God's Word will be truly enriched by the additional elements contained in this special edition.

Notes and features contained in this edition have been adapted from *Parents Resource Bible* (Tyndale House Publishers). A detailed description of the features in this Bible begins on page xi.

Features of the
Crossings Devotional Bible

Book Introductions
The book introductions highlight the major themes of each book of the Bible from the perspective of how they speak to us today.

Breaking Free
Written by best-selling author John Trent, "Breaking Free" articles help us break negative behavior learned from the past. Sample topics are: learning to take responsibility instead of shifting blame (page 471) and breaking free of unfulfilled intimacy (page 1716).

Contributors' Articles
There are more than fifty of these articles written by leading Christians on all aspects of family life, such as sexuality, sibling rivalry, coping with family illness, infertility, and honoring children—to name just a few. Authors include Dr. James Dobson (page 851), Bill and Lynne Hybels (page 1712), Max Lucado (page 1482), Josh McDowell (page 835), and Joni Eareckson Tada (page 1772).

Biblical Profiles
Key figures in the Bible and their significance are described in the biblical profiles. Each one includes lessons we can learn from their experiences. The first one appears on page 12.

Family Traditions
These articles show you how to build traditions into various aspects of family living. A few examples: traditions of everyday love (page 1871), baptism traditions (page 1579), nurturing mother/daughter-in-law relationships (page 436), and traditions for two (page 1762).

Worship in Your Home
Here you'll find lots of ideas for making devotions and worship a vital, meaningful part of your spiritual life. Try "Devotions with a Seasonal Theme" (page 16) or "Good Food and Devotions Make

Good Companions" (page 1718). And don't miss "When *Not* to Have Family Devotions" (page 1705).

Devotional Moments
Hundreds of applications of individual passages of Scripture to your daily life appear throughout the Bible text. Topics include anger, friendship, money, teamwork, and worry, plus many more.

Indexes
Each special feature is indexed in the back of the Bible for easy reference to the topics you're interested in.

The Old Testament

GENESIS

Purpose
To record God's creation
of the world and his
desire to have a people
set apart to worship him

Author
Moses

To Whom Written
The people of Israel

Date Written
1450–1410 B.C.

Setting
The region presently
known as the Middle
East

Key Verses
"So God created man in
his own image, in the
image of God created he
him; male and female
created he them" (1:27).
"Now the Lord had said
unto Abram . . . I will
make of thee a great
nation, and I will bless
thee, and make thy
name great; and thou
shalt be a blessing "
(12:1-2).

Key People
Adam, Eve, Noah, Abra-
ham, Sarah, Isaac, Re-
bekah, Jacob, Joseph

Y ou spent *how much* for those shoes?"
"You never listen to me!!"
"Mom! Jenny won't share!"

No family is perfect. Family members always seem to find something to fight about—from finances to seating arrangements in the car. Painful memories of past conflicts wedge their way into present relationships. Inside the family, a person's faith is tested more than anywhere else, and family conflict is part of that testing.

In that regard, the book of Genesis is reassuring. Cain and Abel fought over who was God's favorite. Lot took advantage of his uncle Abraham's generosity. Rebekah and Leah, sisters, enviously contested with one another in a race to bear children. Jacob stole from his brother Esau (helped along in his deceitful ways by a mother playing favorites). And Joseph's brothers sold him into slavery.

The list of family problems profiled in Genesis fits right in with family life today: sibling rivalry, favoritism, blame-shifting, even incest and adultery. The Bible doesn't shy away from presenting people and families as they really were—faults included. God uses these honest portrayals of family problems to warn us of potential pitfalls and to encourage us to choose his way instead.

As you meet the families introduced in Genesis, look for similarities to your family. See if you recognize any of your own character and tendencies. Take comfort in the fact that others have also experienced the struggles you face. Then learn from these families and determine to make the right choices.

1

¹In the beginning God created the heaven and the earth. ²And the earth was without form, and void; and darkness *was* upon the face of the deep. And the Spirit of God moved upon the face of the waters.

³And God said, Let there be light: and there was light. ⁴And God saw the light, that *it was* good: and God divided the light from the darkness. ⁵And God called the light Day, and the darkness he called Night. And the evening[a] and the morning were the first day.

⁶And God said, Let there be a firmament[b] in the midst of the waters, and let it divide the waters from the waters. ⁷And God made the firmament, and divided the waters which *were* under the firmament from the waters which *were* above the firmament: and it was so. ⁸And God called the firmament Heaven. And the evening and the morning were the second day.

⁹And God said, Let the waters under the heaven be gathered together unto one place, and let the dry *land* appear: and it was so. ¹⁰And God called the dry *land* Earth; and the gathering together of the waters called he Seas: and God saw that *it was* good. ¹¹And God said, Let the earth bring forth grass[c], the herb yielding seed, *and* the fruit tree yielding fruit after his kind, whose seed *is* in itself, upon the earth: and it was so. ¹²And the earth brought forth grass, *and* herb yielding seed after his kind, and the tree yielding fruit, whose seed *was* in itself, after his kind: and God saw that *it was* good. ¹³And the evening and the morning were the third day.

¹⁴And God said, Let there be lights in the firmament of the heaven to divide the day[d] from the night; and let them be for signs, and for seasons, and for days, and years: ¹⁵And let them be for lights in the firmament of the heaven to give light upon the earth: and it was so. ¹⁶And God made two great lights; the greater light to rule the day[e], and the lesser light to rule the night: *he made* the stars also. ¹⁷And God set them in the firmament of the heaven to give light upon the earth, ¹⁸And to rule over the day and over the night, and to divide the light from the darkness: and God saw that *it was* good. ¹⁹And the evening and the morning were the fourth day.

²⁰And God said, Let the waters bring forth abundantly the moving creature that hath life, and fowl *that* may fly above the earth in the open firmament of heaven. ²¹And God created great whales, and every living creature that moveth, which the waters brought forth abundantly, after their kind, and every winged fowl after his kind: and God saw that *it was* good. ²²And God blessed them, saying, Be fruitful, and multiply, and fill the waters in the seas, and let fowl multiply in the earth.

---

[a] And the evening . . . : Heb. And the evening was, and the morning was
[b] firmament: Heb. expansion
[c] grass: Heb. tender grass
[d] the day . . . : Heb. between the day and between the night
[e] to rule the day . . . : Heb. for the rule of the day, etc.

²³And the evening and the morning were the fifth day.

²⁴And God said, Let the earth bring forth the living creature after his kind, cattle, and creeping thing, and beast of the earth after his kind: and it was so. ²⁵And God made the beast of the earth after his kind, and cattle after their kind, and every thing that creepeth upon the earth after his kind: and God saw that *it was* good.

²⁶And God said, Let us make man in our image, after our likeness: and let them have dominion over the fish of the sea, and over the fowl of the air, and over the cattle, and over all the earth, and over every creeping thing that creepeth upon the earth. ²⁷So God created man in his *own* image, in the image of God created he him; male and female created he them. ²⁸And God blessed them, and God said unto them, Be fruitful, and multiply, and replenish the earth, and subdue it: and have dominion over the fish of the sea, and over the fowl of the air, and over every living thing that moveth[f] upon the earth.

²⁹And God said, Behold, I have given you every herb bearing[g] seed, which *is* upon the face of all the earth, and every tree, in the which *is* the fruit of a tree yielding seed; to you it shall be for meat. ³⁰And to every beast of the earth, and to every fowl of the air, and to every thing that creepeth upon the earth, wherein *there is* life[h], *I have given* every green herb for meat: and it was so.

³¹And God saw every thing that he had made, and, behold, *it was* very good. And the evening and the morning were the sixth day.

2

¹Thus the heavens and the earth were finished, and all the host of them. ²And on the seventh day God ended his work which he had made; and he rested on the seventh day from all his work which he had made. ³And God blessed the seventh day, and sanctified it: because that in it he had rested from all his work which God created[a] and made.

⁴These *are* the generations of the heavens and of the earth when they were created, in the day that the LORD God made the earth and the heavens, ⁵And every plant of the field before it was in the earth, and every herb of the field before it grew: for the LORD God had not caused it to rain upon the earth, and *there was* not a man to till the ground. ⁶But there went up a mist from the earth, and watered the whole face of the ground. ⁷And the LORD God formed man *of* the dust of the ground, and breathed into his nostrils the breath of life; and man became a living soul.

⁸And the LORD God planted a garden eastward in Eden; and there he put the man whom he had formed. ⁹And out of the ground made the LORD God to grow every tree that is pleasant to the sight, and good for food; the tree of life also in the midst of the garden, and the tree of knowledge of good and evil. ¹⁰And a river went out of

---

f moveth: Heb. creepeth
g bearing . . . : Heb. seeding seed
h life: Heb. a living soul
a created . . . : Heb. created to make

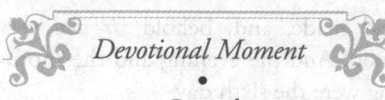

Devotional Moment
•
Growth

2:18-24 God said, "It is not good that the man should be alone," so he created Eve as a perfect coworker for the task he had given Adam. In the work God has called each of us to do, we also need the support of others and we find them in family relationships. Family members can be the first ones we turn to when we need help or support. When you have a difficult or challenging task facing you, don't turn inward; turn to family relationships—including relationships within your church family—for the help and support you need.

Eden to water the garden; and from thence it was parted, and became into four heads. ¹¹The name of the first *is* Pison: that *is* it which compasseth the whole land of Havilah, where *there is* gold; ¹²And the gold of that land *is* good: there *is* bdellium and the onyx stone. ¹³And the name of the second river *is* Gihon: the same *is* it that compasseth the whole land of Ethiopia^b. ¹⁴And the name of the third river *is* Hiddekel: that *is* it which goeth toward^c the east of Assyria. And the fourth river *is* Euphrates. ¹⁵And the LORD God took the man^d, and put him into the garden of Eden to dress it and to keep it.

¹⁶And the LORD God commanded the man, saying, Of every tree of the garden thou mayest freely eat: ¹⁷But of the tree of the knowledge of good and evil, thou shalt not eat of it: for in the day that thou eatest thereof thou shalt surely^e die.

¹⁸And the LORD God said, *It is* not good that the man should be alone; I will make him an help meet^f for him. ¹⁹And out of the ground the LORD God formed every beast of the field, and every fowl of the air; and brought *them* unto Adam^g to see what he would call them: and whatsoever Adam called every living creature, that *was* the name thereof. ²⁰And Adam gave^h names to all cattle, and to the fowl of the air, and to every beast of the field; but for Adam there was not found an help meet for him.

²¹And the LORD God caused a deep sleep to fall upon Adam, and he slept: and he took one of his ribs, and closed up the flesh instead thereof; ²²And the rib, which the LORD God had taken from man, made^i he a woman, and brought her unto the man. ²³And Adam said, This *is* now bone of my bones, and flesh of my flesh: she shall be called Woman^j, because she was taken out of Man. ²⁴Therefore shall a man leave his father and his mother, and shall cleave unto his wife: and they shall be one flesh.

---

^b Ethiopia: Heb. Cush
^c toward . . . : or, eastward to Assyria
^d the man: or, Adam
^e thou shalt surely . . . : Heb. dying thou shalt die
^f meet . . . : Heb. as before him
^g Adam: or, the man
^h gave: Heb. called
^i made: Heb. built
^j Woman: Heb. Isha

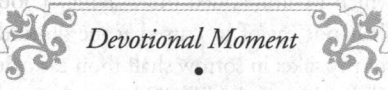

Devotional Moment

Faithfulness

2:24 In God's plan for marriage, the man and woman become one person. Such an intense commitment and joining binds the two together in a way that cuts off all options for "retreat" or "bailing out" when the going gets rough, but in such a way that the relationship doesn't smother the individual needs of each person. Are you committed to your marriage partner in a way that cuts off all options for retreat? If so, you are prepared to weather the storms that can break apart many less committed marriages.

²⁵And they were both naked, the man and his wife, and were not ashamed.

3

¹Now the serpent was more subtil than any beast of the field which the LORD God had made. And he said unto the woman, Yea[a], hath God said, Ye shall not eat of every tree of the garden? ²And the woman said unto the serpent, We may eat of the fruit of the trees of the garden: ³But of the fruit of the tree which *is* in the midst of the garden, God hath said, Ye shall not eat of it, neither shall ye touch it, lest ye die. ⁴And the serpent said unto the woman, Ye shall not surely die: ⁵For God doth know that in the day ye eat thereof, then your eyes shall be opened, and ye shall be as gods, knowing good and evil. ⁶And when the woman saw that the tree *was* good for food, and that it *was*

pleasant[b] to the eyes, and a tree to be desired to make *one* wise, she took of the fruit thereof, and did eat, and gave also unto her husband with her; and he did eat. ⁷And the eyes of them both were opened, and they knew that they *were* naked; and they sewed fig leaves together, and made themselves aprons[c]. ⁸And they heard the voice of the LORD God walking in the garden in the cool[d] of the day: and Adam and his wife hid themselves from the presence of the LORD God amongst the trees of the garden.

⁹And the LORD God called unto Adam, and said unto him, Where *art* thou? ¹⁰And he said, I heard thy voice in the garden, and I was afraid, because I *was* naked; and I hid myself.

¹¹And he said, Who told thee that thou *wast* naked? Hast thou eaten of the tree, whereof I commanded thee that thou shouldest not eat? ¹²And the man

Devotional Moment

Unity

3:12-13, 17 When Adam admitted his sin, he tried to blame his personal failing on Eve (and on God as well). Like any unit made up of interdependent parts, the family needs unity and cohesiveness for strength. But pointing the finger of blame at others or dodging personal responsibility for sins or mistakes can shatter unity and destroy cohesiveness. Don't blame your failings on other family members. Instead, confess your shortcomings and lean on each other for strength to recover from wrong choices or sinful failings.

---

[a] Yea . . . : Heb. Yea, because, etc.
[b] pleasant: Heb. a desire
[c] aprons: or, things to gird about
[d] cool: Heb. wind

said, The woman whom thou gavest *to be* with me, she gave me of the tree, and I did eat. ¹³And the LORD God said unto the woman, What *is* this *that* thou hast done? And the woman said, The serpent beguiled me, and I did eat.

¹⁴And the LORD God said unto the serpent, Because thou hast done this, thou *art* cursed above all cattle, and above every beast of the field; upon thy belly shalt thou go, and dust shalt thou eat all the days of thy life: ¹⁵And I will put enmity between thee and the woman, and between thy seed and her seed; it shall bruise thy head, and thou shalt bruise his heel.

¹⁶Unto the woman he said, I will greatly multiply thy sorrow and thy conception; in sorrow thou shalt bring forth children; and thy desire *shall be* to thy husband, and he shall rule over thee.

¹⁷And unto Adam he said, Because thou hast hearkened unto the voice of thy wife, and hast eaten of the tree, of which I commanded thee, saying, Thou shalt not eat of it: cursed *is* the ground for thy sake; in sorrow shalt thou eat *of* it all the days of thy life; ¹⁸Thorns also and thistles shall it bring forth to thee; and thou shalt eat the herb of the field; ¹⁹In the sweat of thy face shalt thou eat bread, till thou return unto the ground; for out of it wast thou taken: for dust thou *art*, and unto dust shalt thou return.

²⁰And Adam called his wife's name Eve^e; because she was the mother of all living.

²¹Unto Adam also and to his wife did the LORD God make coats of skins, and clothed them.

²²And the LORD God said, Behold, the man is become as one of us, to know good and evil: and now, lest he put forth his hand, and take also of the tree of life, and eat, and live for ever: ²³Therefore the LORD God sent him forth from the garden of Eden, to till the ground from whence he was taken. ²⁴So he drove out the man; and he placed at the east of the garden of Eden Cherubims, and a flaming sword which turned every way, to keep the way of the tree of life.

4

¹And Adam knew Eve his wife; and she conceived, and bare Cain^a, and said, I have gotten a man from the LORD. ²And she again bare his brother Abel^b. And Abel was a keeper of sheep, but Cain was a tiller of the ground.

³And in process^c of time it came to pass, that Cain brought of the fruit of the ground an offering unto the LORD. ⁴And Abel, he also brought of the firstlings of his flock^d and of the fat thereof. And the LORD had respect unto Abel and to his offering: ⁵But unto Cain and to his offering he had not respect. And Cain was very wroth, and his countenance fell.

⁶And the LORD said unto Cain, Why art thou wroth? and why is thy countenance fallen? ⁷If thou doest well, shalt thou not be accepted^e? and if

---

^e Eve: Heb. Chavah: that is Living
^a Cain: that is Gotten, or, Acquired
^b Abel: Heb. Hebel
^c in process . . . : Heb. at the end of days
^d flock: Heb. sheep, or, goats
^e be accepted: or, have the excellency

Leaving Before Cleaving

by John Trent

Couples stand at the altar with great expectations of a loving, lasting relationship. Yet without realizing it, many are setting themselves up for deep hurt and disappointment. The trouble begins when they fail to practice a biblical necessity—truly leaving home as a prerequisite to cleaving to their spouse (Gen. 2:24).

There are several steps any couple can take—no matter how long they have been married—to leave home.

First, *work at establishing a peer relationship with your parents.* This isn't always easy. But genuine growth means graduating from childlike ways of responding to others—even to our parents.

It is hard to break patterns from the past. In most Christian homes, parents rightfully (and biblically) start with a vertical power structure. Dad and Mom are on top, and the children are on the bottom. But in the healthiest homes, as the children grow older, the power base shifts. By adulthood, there should be a horizontal sharing of power—a side-by-side friendship in which great respect is given the parents and yet great responsibility and independence are handed to the children. This does not deny honor to a parent (which is another command from Scripture); rather, it affirms it. Shifting the power base merely recognizes that preteen children are called to obey, whereas adult children are called to honor.

Building a peer relationship with parents can begin with something as simple as going Dutch for dinner instead of having Mom and Dad pay. It can also mean saying no to them when appropriate, not equating every one of your vacations with "a visit to the relatives," or simply asking them to talk with you on an adult level.

Second, *take a long, honest look at your past.* Your past influences you. And your spouse sees that most acutely. But how do you begin to tackle the past?

One exercise you can do as a couple is to gather as many old family photos as possible. Over a long afternoon or evening, discuss why the situations in the pictures were photographed. Take note of who was always in the pictures and who was left out. What memories, patterns, or emotions emerge as you view your life through the years?

We may be uncomfortable with this exercise because it can bring to the surface feelings we have avoided for years. Perhaps we will see all over again how favored our sister was or how all the photos featured the athlete of the family, not the band member. Perhaps your father was never in the picture because he rarely took time to be with you.

Whatever the pictures reveal, the truth of John 8:32 needs to be your guide: "And ye shall know the truth, and the truth shall make you free." For those with a background full of hurt, it is only by honestly facing their past that they will ever be free from its control.

For some, such a process may involve a skilled Christian counselor. The Scriptures tell us to "hear counsel, and receive instruction, that thou mayest be wise in thy latter end" (Prov. 19:20). You are not weak or foolish to seek help.

Third, *be careful not to equate leaving home with simply doing the opposite of what your parents say.* Sometimes doing the opposite can be profitable. There is a form of financial investing called "contrarian theory," which says that when everyone else is selling, you buy, or when everyone else is bailing out of a plunging market, you dive in.

In personal relationships, both two-year-olds and teenagers often adopt this strategy when dealing with parents. Saying "Don't touch the stove!" to a two-year-old often entices him to do that very thing. "Clean up your room!" can cause a teenager to throw another layer of clothes on the floor. However, as adults, doing the opposite of what our parents say simply to establish our independence does not work.

Many parents have a child whose quest for independence has meant tossing aside parental values for the sake of striking out on his or her own. But in a healthy peer relationship, we should evaluate our parents' counsel to see how it squares with Scripture and common sense—and then honor their advice if we can. That makes for healthy leaving and joyous cleaving.

DIGGING DEEPER

1. How did Esau, the wayward son of Isaac and Rebekah, separate himself from his parents and the traditions of his ancestors? What was the result? See Genesis 25:27–26:35; Jeremiah 49:7-19; Hebrews 12:15-17.

2. What struggles did Jesus face in "leaving" those who knew him only as a child? Look at Mark 3:31-35; Luke 4:16-30; John 2:1-4.

3. What advice does the apostle Paul offer that might help an adult leave his or her parents? See 1 Corinthians 13:11; Philippians 3:13-14; 1 Timothy 4:12.

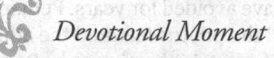

Devotional Moment
•
Relationships
4:6-7 Cain was angry, but God said he could be filled with joy if he would do what he should. The Bible teaches that obedience to God's will leads to happiness, but Cain tried to make his own path and was bitterly disappointed. The family functions in a way that God ordained in Scripture. Whether you are a father or mother, child or adult, in-law or blood relation, uncle or aunt, joy comes from fulfilling your God-given role in the family to the best of your ability. Within your family relationships, your face can be bright with joy if you will build the relationships you've been given.

Where *is* Abel thy brother? And he said, I know not: *Am* I my brother's keeper? ¹⁰And he said, What hast thou done? the voice of thy brother's blood[f] crieth unto me from the ground. ¹¹And now *art* thou cursed from the earth, which hath opened her mouth to receive thy brother's blood

Devotional Moment
•
Siblings
4:8-10 Cain lured his brother out to a deserted field where he attacked and killed him. What a contrast to the loving, supportive, encouraging way God intended brotherly relationships to function! Brothers and sisters should support and encourage each other. Cain's envy and jealousy drove him to murder his brother. In contrast, Christ's love and compassion for us as his brothers and sisters led him to give up his own life for our sake. God wants us to model our relationships after him, who the Bible says is even closer than a brother (Prov. 18:24). Make sure your actions toward your siblings show this kind of love.

thou doest not well, sin lieth at the door. And unto thee *shall be* his desire, and thou shalt rule over him.

⁸And Cain talked with Abel his brother: and it came to pass, when they were in the field, that Cain rose up against Abel his brother, and slew him.

⁹And the LORD said unto Cain,

f blood: Heb. bloods

from thy hand; ¹²When thou tillest the ground, it shall not henceforth yield unto thee her strength; a fugitive and a vagabond shalt thou be in the earth.

¹³And Cain said unto the LORD, My punishment *is* greater than I can bear. ¹⁴Behold, thou hast driven me out this day from the face of the earth; and from thy face shall I be hid; and I shall be a fugitive and a vagabond in the earth; and it shall come to pass, *that* every one that findeth me shall slay me. ¹⁵And the LORD said unto him, Therefore whosoever slayeth Cain, vengeance shall be taken on him sevenfold. And the LORD set a mark upon Cain, lest any finding him should kill him.

¹⁶And Cain went out from the presence of the LORD, and dwelt in the land of Nod, on the east of Eden. ¹⁷And Cain knew his wife; and she conceived, and bare Enoch[g]: and he builded a city, and called the name of the city, after the name of his son, Enoch. ¹⁸And unto Enoch was born Irad: and Irad begat Mehujael: and Mehujael begat Methusael: and Methusael begat Lamech[h].

¹⁹And Lamech took unto him two wives: the name of the one *was* Adah, and the name of the other Zillah. ²⁰And Adah bare Jabal: he was the father of such as dwell in tents, and *of such as have* cattle. ²¹And his brother's name *was* Jubal: he was the father of all such as handle the harp and organ. ²²And Zillah, she also bare Tubalcain, an instructer of every artificer in brass and iron: and the sister of Tubalcain *was* Naamah.

²³And Lamech said unto his wives, Adah and Zillah, Hear my voice; ye wives of Lamech, hearken unto my speech: for I have slain a man to my wounding, and a young man to my hurt. ²⁴If Cain shall be avenged sevenfold, truly Lamech seventy and sevenfold.

²⁵And Adam knew his wife again; and she bare a son, and called his name Seth[i]: For God, *said she,* hath appointed me another seed instead of Abel, whom Cain slew. ²⁶And to Seth, to him also there was born a son; and he called his name Enos[j]: then began men to call upon the name of the LORD.

5

¹This *is* the book of the generations of Adam. In the day that God created man, in the likeness of God made he him; ²Male and female created he them; and blessed them, and called their name Adam, in the day when they were created. ³And Adam lived an hundred and thirty years, and begat *a son* in his own likeness, after his image; and called his name Seth: ⁴And the days of Adam after he had begotten Seth were eight hundred years: and he begat sons and daughters: ⁵And all the days that Adam lived were nine hundred and thirty years: and he died.

⁶And Seth lived an hundred and five years, and begat Enos[a]: ⁷And Seth lived after he begat Enos eight hundred and seven years, and begat sons and daughters: ⁸And all the days of Seth were nine hundred and twelve years: and he died. ⁹And Enos lived

---

g Enoch: Heb. Chanoch

h Lamech: Heb. Lemech

i Seth: Heb. Sheth: that is Appointed, or, Put

j Enos: Heb. Enosh

a Enos: Heb. Enosh

Adam

We don't usually think of Adam as a father. But among the facts the Bible records about Adam we find the statement "And the days of Adam after he had begotten Seth were eight hundred years: and he begat sons and daughters" (Gen. 5:4). While we don't know much about Adam, we do know that he continued to produce children over the span of eight centuries. Adam and Eve must have had an enormous family!

Should we judge Adam's fathering on the basis of how his children turned out? One son (Abel) became a shepherd and pleased God. One (Cain) murdered his brother Abel. And another (Seth) was the image of his father in every way; Eve considered him a replacement for Abel. Other than that, we know little about Adam's children. God's Word says nothing about any of his other sons or many daughters, except the fact that theirs was the first generation of people born into sin.

More telling clues show up a few generations later, when Noah walked the earth. By then, society was so filled with sin and violence that God was sorry he had made them and flooded the earth.

We will never know exactly what kind of father Adam was. But it's clear that along the way his main challenge to raising his children proved to be sin itself, not how to help his children get ahead in life. Are you passing on your faith to your children? Are you teaching them how to pray, study the Bible, and worship? In the end, those are the skills they will need most.

LESSONS FROM ADAM AS A FATHER

Children grow up and become their own people. Abel and Cain both came from the same gene pool. Adam and Eve reared both. Yet their individual personalities were as different as two people can be.

Sin can wreck families. Adam began sinless. Yet even Adam saw the effect of sin on his children. It wasn't long before his descendants formed a society we would recognize today, filled with sin and violence.

The challenge of fathering goes beyond merely producing sons and daughters. Teaching individual children to love and obey God means more than having a prestigious name.

ninety years, and begat Cainan[b]: ¹⁰And Enos lived after he begat Cainan eight hundred and fifteen years, and begat sons and daughters: ¹¹And all the days of Enos were nine hundred and five years: and he died. ¹²And Cainan lived seventy years, and begat Mahalaleel[c]: ¹³And Cainan lived after he begat Mahalaleel eight hundred and forty years, and begat sons and daughters: ¹⁴And all the days of Cainan were nine hundred and ten years: and he died. ¹⁵And Mahalaleel lived sixty and five years, and begat Jared[d]: ¹⁶And Mahalaleel lived after he begat Jared eight hundred and thirty years, and begat sons and daughters: ¹⁷And all the days of Mahalaleel were eight hundred ninety and five years: and he died. ¹⁸And Jared lived an hundred sixty and two years, and he begat Enoch: ¹⁹And

Jared lived after he begat Enoch eight hundred years, and begat sons and daughters: ²⁰And all the days of Jared were nine hundred sixty and two years: and he died.

²¹And Enoch lived sixty and five years, and begat Methuselah[e]: ²²And Enoch walked with God after he begat Methuselah three hundred years, and begat sons and daughters: ²³And all the days of Enoch were three hundred sixty and five years: ²⁴And Enoch walked with God: and he *was* not; for God took him.

²⁵And Methuselah lived an hundred eighty and seven years, and begat Lamech: ²⁶And Methuselah lived after he begat Lamech[f] seven hundred eighty and two years, and begat sons and daughters: ²⁷And all the days of Methuselah were nine hundred sixty and nine years: and he died.

²⁸And Lamech lived an hundred eighty and two years, and begat a son: ²⁹And he called his name Noah[g], saying, This *same* shall comfort us concerning our work and toil of our hands, because of the ground which the LORD hath cursed. ³⁰And Lamech lived after he begat Noah five hundred ninety and five years, and begat sons and daughters: ³¹And all the days of Lamech were seven hundred seventy and seven years: and he died. ³²And Noah was five hundred years old: and Noah begat Shem, Ham, and Japheth.

6

¹And it came to pass, when men began to multiply on the face of the earth, and

---

ᵇ Cainan: Heb. Kenan
ᶜ Mahalaleel: Gr. Maleleel
ᵈ Jared: Heb. Jered
ᵉ Methuselah: Gr. Mathusala
ᶠ Lamech: Heb. Lemech
ᵍ Noah: Gr. Noe: that is Rest, or, Comfort

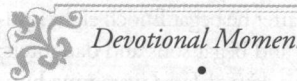

Devotional Moment
•

Forgiveness

6:1-4 God saw that people were wholly evil, yet he gave them time to mend their ways. We probably don't see our relatives or friends as wholly evil, but they often fail or fall short of our expectations. That can lead to disappointment which fuels anger and resentment and finally a bitter grudge. When others fail or disappoint us, even when it happens again and again, it is important to give them the time and opportunity to change—first by talking it out with them if they are responsive, and then by letting *them* mend their ways. Realize that you cannot control their behaviors, feelings, or attitudes. Growing together takes time. Allowing time and opportunity for that growth creates healthy relationships.

daughters were born unto them, ²That the sons of God saw the daughters of men that they *were* fair; and they took them wives of all which they chose.

³And the LORD said, My spirit shall not always strive with man, for that he also *is* flesh: yet his days shall be an hundred and twenty years.

⁴There were giants in the earth in those days; and also after that, when the sons of God came in unto the daughters of men, and they bare *children* to them, the same *became* mighty men which *were* of old, men of renown.

⁵And GOD saw that the wickedness of man *was* great in the earth, and *that* every imagination of the thoughts of his heart *was* only evil continually.

⁶And it repented the LORD that he had made man on the earth, and it grieved him at his heart. ⁷And the LORD said, I will destroy man whom I have created from the face of the earth; both man, and beast, and the creeping thing, and the fowls of the air; for it repenteth me that I have made them.

⁸But Noah found grace in the eyes of the LORD. ⁹These *are* the generations of Noah: Noah was a just man *and* perfect^a in his generations, *and* Noah walked with God. ¹⁰And Noah begat three sons, Shem, Ham, and Japheth.

¹¹The earth also was corrupt before God, and the earth was filled with violence. ¹²And God looked upon the earth, and, behold, it was corrupt; for all flesh had corrupted his way upon the earth.

¹³And God said unto Noah, The end of all flesh is come before me; for the earth is filled with violence through them; and, behold, I will destroy them with the earth^b. ¹⁴Make thee an ark of gopher wood; rooms^c shalt thou make in the ark, and shalt pitch it within and without with pitch. ¹⁵And this *is the fashion* which thou shalt make it *of:* The length of the ark *shall be* three hundred cubits, the breadth of it fifty cubits, and the height of it thirty cubits. ¹⁶A window shalt thou make to the ark, and in a cubit shalt thou finish it above; and the door of the ark shalt thou set in the side thereof; *with* lower, second, and third *stories* shalt thou make it. ¹⁷And, behold, I, even I, do bring a flood of waters upon the earth, to destroy all flesh, wherein *is* the breath of life, from under heaven; *and* every

---

^a perfect: or, upright
^b with the earth: or, from the earth
^c rooms: Heb. nests

thing that *is* in the earth shall die. ¹⁸But with thee will I establish my covenant; and thou shalt come into the ark, thou, and thy sons, and thy wife, and thy sons' wives with thee. ¹⁹And of every living thing of all flesh, two of every *sort* shalt thou bring into the ark, to keep *them* alive with thee; they shall be male and female. ²⁰Of fowls after their kind, and of cattle after their kind, of every creeping thing of the earth after his kind, two of every *sort* shall come unto thee, to keep *them* alive. ²¹And take thou unto thee of all food that is eaten, and thou shalt gather *it* to thee; and it shall be for food for thee, and for them. ²²Thus did Noah; according to all that God commanded him, so did he.

7

¹And the LORD said unto Noah, Come thou and all thy house into the ark; for thee have I seen righteous before me in this generation. ²Of every clean beast thou shalt take to thee by sevens^a, the male and his female: and of beasts that *are* not clean by two, the male and his female. ³Of fowls also of the air by sevens^b, the male and the female; to keep seed alive upon the face of all the earth. ⁴For yet seven days, and I will cause it to rain upon the earth forty days and forty nights; and every living substance that I have made will I destroy^c from off the face of the earth. ⁵And Noah did according unto all that the LORD commanded him. ⁶And

Noah *was* six hundred years old when the flood of waters was upon the earth. ⁷And Noah went in, and his sons, and his wife, and his sons' wives with him, into the ark, because of the waters of the flood. ⁸Of clean beasts, and of beasts that *are* not clean, and of fowls, and of every thing that creepeth upon the earth, ⁹There went in two and two unto Noah into the ark, the male and the female, as God had commanded Noah. ¹⁰And it came to pass after seven days, that the waters of the flood were upon the earth.

¹¹In the six hundredth year of Noah's life, in the second month, the seventeenth day of the month, the same day were all the fountains of the great deep broken up, and the windows^d of heaven were opened. ¹²And the rain was upon the earth forty days and forty nights.

¹³In the selfsame day entered Noah, and Shem, and Ham, and Japheth, the sons of Noah, and Noah's wife, and the three wives of his sons with them, into the ark; ¹⁴They, and every beast after his kind, and all the cattle after their kind, and every creeping thing that creepeth upon the earth after his kind, and every fowl after his kind, every bird of every sort^e. ¹⁵And they went in unto Noah into the ark, two and two of all flesh, wherein *is* the breath of life. ¹⁶And they that went in, went in male and female of all flesh, as God had commanded him: and the LORD shut him in.

¹⁷And the flood was forty days

---

^a by sevens: Heb. seven seven
^b by sevens: Heb. seven seven
^c destroy: Heb. blot out
^d windows: or, floodgates
^e sort: Heb. wing

Worship
in Your Home

DEVOTIONS WITH A SEASONAL THEME
While the earth remaineth, seedtime and harvest, and cold and heat, and summer and winter, and day and night shall not cease. Genesis 8:22

Each expression of a season is an opportunity to point to the Creator who made that expression. These may be in formal devotional times, or informal times.

For formal devotional times, collect seasonal pictures. You can use them at seasonal devotion time to talk about the wonder of this seasonal masterpiece—leaves, pumpkins, snowflakes, ice, flowering trees.

I'm content in each of these times to reinforce the one central theme—the Lord God made them all. He is the Creator. He says, "I love you" with each of these beautiful expressions that he made.

You may want to add "living object lessons" to your devotions—colored leaves, a little pumpkin or squash, an icicle, a flower. As it graces the table where you sit, you have an object that demonstrates your discussion.

Of course, informal devotions are a natural for seasonal themes. As you walk through the autumn woods, talk about the God who made them. As you smell flowers near the house, marvel that he could bring those beautiful things from little seeds or brown bulbs.

Seasons remind us of the One who made them all. What opportunities to praise him and honor him and talk about him as you interact with seasonal glories—through pictures, objects, or a walk through the seasonal wonders.

upon the earth; and the waters increased, and bare up the ark, and it was lift up above the earth. ¹⁸And the waters prevailed, and were increased greatly upon the earth; and the ark went upon the face of the waters. ¹⁹And the waters prevailed exceedingly upon the earth; and all the high hills, that *were* under the whole heaven, were covered. ²⁰Fifteen cubits upward did the waters prevail; and the mountains were covered.

²¹And all flesh died that moved upon the earth, both of fowl, and of cattle, and of beast, and of every creeping thing that creepeth upon the earth, and every man: ²²All in whose nostrils *was* the breath[f] of life, of all that *was* in the dry *land*, died. ²³And every living substance was destroyed which was upon the face of the ground, both man, and cattle, and the creeping things, and the fowl of the heaven; and they were destroyed from the earth: and Noah only remained *alive*, and they that *were* with him in the ark. ²⁴And the waters prevailed upon the earth an hundred and fifty days.

8

¹And God remembered Noah, and every living thing, and all the cattle that *was* with him in the ark: and God made a wind to pass over the earth, and the waters asswaged; ²The fountains also of the deep and the windows of heaven were stopped, and the rain from heaven was restrained; ³And the waters returned from off the earth continually[a]:

---

[f] the breath . . . : Heb. the breath of the spirit of life
[a] continually: Heb. in going and returning

and after the end of the hundred and fifty days the waters were abated.

⁴And the ark rested in the seventh month, on the seventeenth day of the month, upon the mountains of Ararat. ⁵And the waters decreased[b] continually until the tenth month: in the tenth *month*, on the first *day* of the month, were the tops of the mountains seen.

⁶And it came to pass at the end of forty days, that Noah opened the window of the ark which he had made: ⁷And he sent forth a raven, which went forth to[c] and fro, until the waters were dried up from off the earth. ⁸Also he sent forth a dove from him, to see if the waters were abated from off the face of the ground; ⁹But the dove found no rest for the sole of her foot, and she returned unto him into the ark, for the waters *were* on the face of the whole earth: then he put forth his hand, and took her, and pulled her in unto him into the ark. ¹⁰And he stayed yet other seven days; and again he sent forth the dove out of the ark; ¹¹And the dove came in to him in the evening; and, lo, in her mouth *was* an olive leaf pluckt off: so Noah knew that the waters were abated from off the earth. ¹²And he stayed yet other seven days; and sent forth the dove; which returned not again unto him any more.

¹³And it came to pass in the six hundredth and first year, in the first *month*, the first *day* of the month, the waters were dried up from off the earth: and Noah removed the covering of the ark, and looked, and, behold, the face of the ground was dry. ¹⁴And in the second month, on the seven and twentieth day of the month, was the earth dried.

¹⁵And God spake unto Noah, saying, ¹⁶Go forth of the ark, thou, and thy wife, and thy sons, and thy sons' wives with thee. ¹⁷Bring forth with thee every living thing that *is* with thee, of all flesh, *both* of fowl, and of cattle, and of every creeping thing that creepeth upon the earth; that they may breed abundantly in the earth, and be fruitful, and multiply upon the earth. ¹⁸And Noah went forth, and his sons, and his wife, and his sons' wives with him: ¹⁹Every beast, every creeping thing, and every fowl, *and* whatsoever creepeth upon the earth, after their kinds[d], went forth out of the ark.

²⁰And Noah builded an altar unto the LORD; and took of every clean beast, and of every clean fowl, and offered burnt offerings on the altar. ²¹And the LORD smelled a sweet[e] savour; and the LORD said in his heart, I will not again curse the ground any more for man's sake; for the imagination of man's heart *is* evil from his youth; neither will I again smite any more every thing living, as I have done. ²²While the earth remaineth, seedtime and harvest, and cold and heat, and summer and winter, and day and night shall not cease.

9

¹And God blessed Noah and his sons, and said unto them, Be fruitful, and

---

[b] decreased . . . : Heb. were in going and decreasing
[c] to . . . : Heb. in going forth and returning
[d] kinds: Heb. families
[e] a sweet . . . : Heb. a savour of rest or, satisfaction

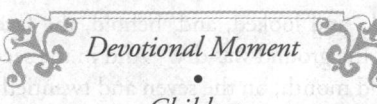

Devotional Moment
•
Children

9:1 God blessed Noah and his sons and told them to have many children. The Bible teaches that children are a blessing from the Lord, but they are also a blessing on the earth. Every child born into a home that honors and worships God is potentially one who causes others to recognize and honor God and so bring his continued and expanding blessing on the world. Do you see children as God's way to bless others? God does.

multiply, and replenish the earth. ²And the fear of you and the dread of you shall be upon every beast of the earth, and upon every fowl of the air, upon all that moveth *upon* the earth, and upon all the fishes of the sea; into your hand are they delivered. ³Every moving thing that liveth shall be meat for you; even as the green herb have I given you all things. ⁴But flesh with the life thereof, *which is* the blood thereof, shall ye not eat. ⁵And surely your blood of your lives will I require; at the hand of every beast will I require it, and at the hand of man; at the hand of every man's brother will I require the life of man. ⁶Whoso sheddeth man's blood, by man shall his blood be shed: for in the image of God made he man. ⁷And you, be ye fruitful, and multiply; bring forth abundantly in the earth, and multiply therein.

⁸And God spake unto Noah, and to his sons with him, saying, ⁹And I, behold, I establish my covenant with you, and with your seed after you; ¹⁰And with every living creature that *is* with you, of the fowl, of the cattle, and of every beast of the earth with you; from all that go out of the ark, to every beast of the earth. ¹¹And I will establish my covenant with you; neither shall all flesh be cut off any more by the waters of a flood; neither shall there any more be a flood to destroy the earth.

¹²And God said, This *is* the token of the covenant which I make between me and you and every living creature that *is* with you, for perpetual generations: ¹³I do set my bow in the cloud, and it shall be for a token of a covenant between me and the earth. ¹⁴And it shall come to pass, when I bring a cloud over the earth, that the bow shall be seen in the cloud: ¹⁵And I will remember my covenant, which *is* between me and you and every living creature of all flesh; and the waters shall no more become a flood to destroy all flesh. ¹⁶And the bow shall be in the cloud; and I will look upon it, that I may remember the everlasting covenant between God and every living creature of all flesh that *is* upon the earth. ¹⁷And God said unto Noah, This *is* the token of the covenant, which I have established between me and all flesh that *is* upon the earth.

¹⁸And the sons of Noah, that went forth of the ark, were Shem, and Ham, and Japheth: and Ham *is* the father of Canaanᵃ. ¹⁹These *are* the three sons of Noah: and of them was the whole earth overspread. ²⁰And Noah began *to be* an husbandman, and he planted a vineyard: ²¹And he drank of the wine, and was drunken; and he was uncovered within his tent. ²²And Ham, the father of Canaan, saw the nakedness of his fa-

---

ᵃ Canaan: Heb. Chenaan

ther, and told his two brethren without. ²³And Shem and Japheth took a garment, and laid *it* upon both their shoulders, and went backward, and covered the nakedness of their father; and their faces *were* backward, and they saw not their father's nakedness.

²⁴And Noah awoke from his wine, and knew what his younger son had done unto him. ²⁵And he said, Cursed *be* Canaan; a servant of servants shall he be unto his brethren. ²⁶And he said, Blessed *be* the LORD God of Shem; and Canaan shall be his servant[b]. ²⁷God shall enlarge[c] Japheth, and he shall dwell in the tents of Shem; and Canaan shall be his servant.

²⁸And Noah lived after the flood three hundred and fifty years. ²⁹And all the days of Noah were nine hundred and fifty years: and he died.

10

¹Now these *are* the generations of the sons of Noah, Shem, Ham, and Japheth: and unto them were sons born after the flood. ²The sons of Japheth; Gomer, and Magog, and Madai, and Javan, and Tubal, and Meshech, and Tiras. ³And the sons of Gomer; Ashkenaz, and Riphath, and Togarmah. ⁴And the sons of Javan; Elishah, and Tarshish, Kittim, and Dodanim[a]. ⁵By these were the isles of the Gentiles divided in their lands; every one after his tongue, after their families, in their nations.

⁶And the sons of Ham; Cush, and Mizraim, and Phut, and Canaan. ⁷And the sons of Cush; Seba, and Havilah, and Sabtah, and Raamah, and Sabtecha: and the sons of Raamah; Sheba, and Dedan. ⁸And Cush begat Nimrod: he began to be a mighty one in the earth. ⁹He was a mighty hunter before the LORD: wherefore it is said, Even as Nimrod the mighty hunter before the LORD. ¹⁰And the beginning of his kingdom was Babel[b], and Erech, and Accad, and Calneh, in the land of Shinar. ¹¹Out of that land went forth Asshur, and builded Nineveh, and the city Rehoboth, and Calah, ¹²And Resen between Nineveh and Calah: the same *is* a great city. ¹³And Mizraim begat Ludim, and Anamim, and Lehabim, and Naphtuhim, ¹⁴And Pathrusim, and

---

[b] his servant: or, servant to them
[c] enlarge: or, persuade
[a] Dodanim: or, as some read it, Rodanim
[b] Babel: Gr. Babylon

Casluhim, (out of whom came Philistim,) and Caphtorim.

¹⁵And Canaan begat Sidon° his firstborn, and Heth, ¹⁶And the Jebusite, and the Amorite, and the Girgasite, ¹⁷And the Hivite, and the Arkite, and the Sinite, ¹⁸And the Arvadite, and the Zemarite, and the Hamathite: and afterward were the families of the Canaanites spread abroad. ¹⁹And the border of the Canaanites was from Sidon, as thou comest to Gerar, unto Gazaᵈ; as thou goest, unto Sodom, and Gomorrah, and Admah, and Zeboim, even unto Lasha. ²⁰These *are* the sons of Ham, after their families, after their tongues, in their countries, *and* in their nations.

²¹Unto Shem also, the father of all the children of Eber, the brother of Japheth the elder, even to him were *children* born. ²²The children of Shem; Elam, and Asshur, and Arphaxadᵉ, and Lud, and Aram. ²³And the children of Aram; Uz, and Hul, and Gether, and Mash. ²⁴And Arphaxad begat Salahᶠ; and Salah begat Eber. ²⁵And unto Eber were born two sons: the name of one *was* Pelegᵍ; for in his days was the earth divided; and his brother's name *was* Joktan. ²⁶And Joktan begat Almodad, and Sheleph, and Hazarmaveth, and Jerah, ²⁷And Hadoram, and Uzal, and Diklah, ²⁸And Obal, and Abimael, and Sheba, ²⁹And Ophir, and

Havilah, and Jobab: all these *were* the sons of Joktan. ³⁰And their dwelling was from Mesha, as thou goest unto Sephar a mount of the east. ³¹These *are* the sons of Shem, after their families, after their tongues, in their lands, after their nations. ³²These *are* the families of the sons of Noah, after their generations, in their nations: and by these were the nations divided in the earth after the flood.

11

¹And the whole earth was of one languageᵃ, and of one speech. ²And it came to pass, as they journeyed from the east, that they found a plain in the land of Shinar; and they dwelt there. ³And they saidᵇ one to another, Go to, let us make brick, and burn them throughly. And they had brick for stone, and slime had they for morter. ⁴And they said, Go to, let us build us a city and a tower, whose top *may reach* unto heaven; and let us make us a name, lest we be scattered abroad upon the face of the whole earth.

⁵And the LORD came down to see the city and the tower, which the children of men builded. ⁶And the LORD said, Behold, the people *is* one, and they have all one language; and this they begin to do: and now nothing will be restrained from them, which they have imagined to do. ⁷Go to, let us go down, and there confound their language, that they may not understand

---

ᶜ Sidon: Heb. Tzidon
ᵈ Gaza: Heb. Azzah
ᵉ Arphaxad: Heb. Arpachshad
ᶠ Salah: Heb. Shelah
ᵍ Peleg: that is Division
ᵃ language: Heb. lip.
ᵇ they said . . . : Heb. a man said to his neighbour

one another's speech. ⁸So the LORD scattered them abroad from thence upon the face of all the earth: and they left off to build the city. ⁹Therefore is the name of it called Babelᶜ; because the LORD did there confound the language of all the earth: and from thence did the LORD scatter them abroad upon the face of all the earth.

¹⁰These *are* the generations of Shem: Shem *was* an hundred years old, and begat Arphaxad two years after the flood: ¹¹And Shem lived after he begat Arphaxad five hundred years, and begat sons and daughters. ¹²And Arphaxad lived five and thirty years, and begat Salah: ¹³And Arphaxad lived after he begat Salah four hundred and three years, and begat sons and daughters. ¹⁴And Salah lived thirty years, and begat Eber: ¹⁵And Salah lived after he begat Eber four hundred and three years, and begat sons and daughters. ¹⁶And Eber lived four and thirty years, and begat Pelegᵈ: ¹⁷And Eber lived after he begat Peleg four hundred and thirty years, and begat sons and daughters. ¹⁸And Peleg lived thirty years, and begat Reu: ¹⁹And Peleg lived after he begat Reu two hundred and nine years, and begat sons and daughters. ²⁰And Reu lived two and thirty years, and begat Serugᵉ: ²¹And Reu lived after he begat Serug two hundred and seven years, and begat sons and daughters. ²²And Serug lived thirty years, and begat Nahor: ²³And Serug lived after he begat Nahor two hundred years, and begat sons and daughters.

²⁴And Nahor lived nine and twenty years, and begat Terahᶠ: ²⁵And Nahor lived after he begat Terah an hundred and nineteen years, and begat sons and daughters. ²⁶And Terah lived seventy years, and begat Abram, Nahor, and Haran.

²⁷Now these *are* the generations of Terah: Terah begat Abram, Nahor, and Haran; and Haran begat Lot. ²⁸And Haran died before his father Terah in the land of his nativity, in Ur of the Chaldees. ²⁹And Abram and Nahor took them wives: the name of Abram's wife *was* Sarai; and the name of Nahor's wife, Milcah, the daughter of Haran, the father of Milcah, and the father of Iscah. ³⁰But Sarai was barren; she *had* no child. ³¹And Terah took Abram his son, and Lot the son of Haran his son's son, and Sarai his daughter in law, his son Abram's wife; and they went forth with them from Ur of the Chaldees, to go into the land of Canaan; and they came unto Haran, and dwelt there. ³²And the days of Terah were two hundred and five years: and Terah died in Haran.

12

¹Now the LORD had said unto Abram, Get thee out of thy country, and from thy kindred, and from thy father's house, unto a land that I will shew thee: ²And I will make of thee a great nation, and I will bless thee, and make thy name great; and thou shalt be a blessing: ³And I will bless them that bless thee, and curse him that curseth

---

ᶜ Babel: that is, Confusion
ᵈ Peleg: Gr. Phalec
ᵉ Serug: Gr. Saruch
ᶠ Terah: Gr. Thara

thee: and in thee shall all families of the earth be blessed.

⁴So Abram departed, as the LORD had spoken unto him; and Lot went with him: and Abram *was* seventy and five years old when he departed out of Haran. ⁵And Abram took Sarai his wife, and Lot his brother's son, and all their substance that they had gathered, and the souls that they had gotten in Haran; and they went forth to go into the land of Canaan; and into the land of Canaan they came.

⁶And Abram passed through the land unto the place of Sichem, unto the plain of Moreh. And the Canaanite *was* then in the land. ⁷And the LORD appeared unto Abram, and said, Unto thy seed will I give this land: and there builded he an altar unto the LORD, who appeared unto him. ⁸And he removed from thence unto a mountain on the east of Bethel, and pitched his tent, *having* Bethel on the west, and Hai on the east: and there he builded an altar unto the LORD, and called upon the name of the LORD. ⁹And Abram journeyed, going on still toward the south.

¹⁰And there was a famine in the land: and Abram went down into Egypt to sojourn there; for the famine *was* grievous in the land. ¹¹And it came to pass, when he was come near to enter into Egypt, that he said unto Sarai his wife, Behold now, I know that thou *art* a fair woman to look upon: ¹²Therefore it shall come to pass, when the Egyptians shall see thee, that they shall say, This *is* his wife: and they will kill me, but they will save thee alive. ¹³Say, I pray thee, thou *art* my sister: that it may be well with me for thy sake; and my soul shall live because of thee.

¹⁴And it came to pass, that, when Abram was come into Egypt, the Egyptians beheld the woman that she *was* very fair. ¹⁵The princes also of Pharaoh saw her, and commended her before Pharaoh: and the woman was taken into Pharaoh's house. ¹⁶And he entreated Abram well for her sake: and he had sheep, and oxen, and he asses, and menservants, and maidservants, and she asses, and camels. ¹⁷And the LORD plagued Pharaoh and his house with great plagues because of Sarai Abram's wife. ¹⁸And Pharaoh called Abram, and said, What *is* this *that* thou hast done unto me? why didst thou not tell me that she *was* thy wife? ¹⁹Why saidst thou, She *is* my sister? so I might have taken her to me to wife: now therefore behold thy wife, take *her*, and go thy way. ²⁰And Pharaoh commanded *his* men concerning him: and they sent him away, and his wife, and all that he had.

13

¹And Abram went up out of Egypt, he, and his wife, and all that he had, and Lot with him, into the south. ²And Abram *was* very rich in cattle, in silver, and in gold. ³And he went on his journeys from the south even to Bethel, unto the place where his tent had been at the beginning, between Bethel and Hai; ⁴Unto the place of the altar, which he had made there at the first: and there Abram called on the name of the LORD.

⁵And Lot also, which went with Abram, had flocks, and herds, and tents. ⁶And the land was not able to bear them, that they might dwell together: for their substance was great, so that they could not dwell together. ⁷And there was a strife between the herdmen of Abram's cattle and the herdmen of Lot's cattle: and the

Devotional Moment

•

Stubbornness

13:5-9 Both Abram and his nephew Lot became very wealthy in terms of servants, livestock, and possessions. In fact, the sheer size of their flocks and herds brought them and their herdsmen into a fierce territorial battle. The two groups were too stubborn to give an inch until Abram made the first move, giving the younger man first choice of the land. Sometimes we can be stubborn as well, prolonging arguments and even endangering others, until someone makes the first move toward resolving matters. The next time you "stick to your principles," make sure stubbornness isn't the reason. Respectfully listen to the other person's case, and try to find a solution that works for both of you.

Canaanite and the Perizzite dwelled then in the land. ⁸And Abram said unto Lot, Let there be no strife, I pray thee, between me and thee, and between my herdmen and thy herdmen; for we *be* brethrenᵃ. ⁹*Is* not the whole land before thee? separate thyself, I pray thee, from me: if *thou wilt take* the left hand, then I will go to the right; or if *thou depart* to the right hand, then I will go to the left.

¹⁰And Lot lifted up his eyes, and beheld all the plain of Jordan, that it *was* well watered every where, before the LORD destroyed Sodom and Gomorrah, *even* as the garden of the LORD, like the land of Egypt, as thou comest unto Zoar. ¹¹Then Lot chose him all the plain of Jordan; and Lot journeyed east: and they separated themselves the one from the other. ¹²Abram dwelled in the land of Canaan,

and Lot dwelled in the cities of the plain, and pitched *his* tent toward Sodom. ¹³But the men of Sodom *were* wicked and sinners before the LORD exceedingly.

¹⁴And the LORD said unto Abram, after that Lot was separated from him, Lift up now thine eyes, and look from the place where thou art northward, and southward, and eastward, and westward: ¹⁵For all the land which thou seest, to thee will I give it, and to thy seed for ever. ¹⁶And I will make thy seed as the dust of the earth: so that if a man can number the dust of the earth, *then* shall thy seed also be numbered. ¹⁷Arise, walk through the land in the length of it and in the breadth of it; for I will give it unto thee. ¹⁸Then Abram removed *his* tent, and came and dwelt in the plainᵇ of Mamre,

Devotional Moment

•

Moving

13:12 Lot had his choice of land and decided in favor of the then-lush plains of the Jordan River. He was swayed by the material benefits of the area and ignored the notorious reputation of his neighbors, the people of Sodom, a group throughout history synonymous with immorality. People today say that the three most important factors in choosing a home are location, location, and location. We must consider the nonmaterial elements of any location and the effect our choices will have on our own and our children's ability to follow God, because the people we live near will influence us. The community spirit, emotional climate, and potential for a support system must go into the decision to rent or buy a home.

ᵃ brethren: Heb. men brethren
ᵇ plain: Heb. plains

which *is* in Hebron, and built there an altar unto the LORD.

14

¹And it came to pass in the days of Amraphel king of Shinar, Arioch king of Ellasar, Chedorlaomer king of Elam, and Tidal king of nations; ² *That these* made war with Bera king of Sodom, and with Birsha king of Gomorrah, Shinab king of Admah, and Shemeber king of Zeboiim, and the king of Bela, which is Zoar. ³All these were joined together in the vale of Siddim, which is the salt sea. ⁴Twelve years they served Chedorlaomer, and in the thirteenth year they rebelled. ⁵And in the fourteenth year came Chedorlaomer, and the kings that *were* with him, and smote the Rephaims in Ashteroth Karnaim, and the Zuzims in Ham, and the Emims in Shaveh Kiriathaim, ⁶And the Horites in their mount Seir, unto Elparan[a], which *is* by the wilderness. ⁷And they returned, and came to Enmishpat, which *is* Kadesh, and smote all the country of the Amalekites, and also the Amorites, that dwelt in Hazezontamar. ⁸And there went out the king of Sodom, and the king of Gomorrah, and the king of Admah, and the king of Zeboiim, and the king of Bela (the same *is* Zoar;) and they joined battle with them in the vale of Siddim; ⁹With Chedorlaomer the king of Elam, and with Tidal king of nations, and Amraphel king of Shinar, and Arioch king of Ellasar; four kings with five. ¹⁰And the vale of Siddim *was full of* slimepits; and the kings of

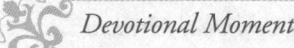

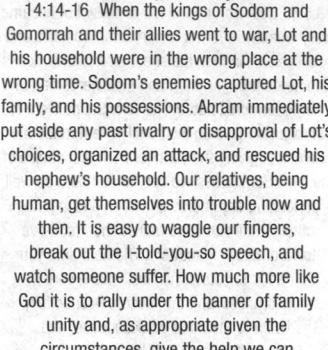

Devotional Moment
•
Family Unity
14:14-16 When the kings of Sodom and Gomorrah and their allies went to war, Lot and his household were in the wrong place at the wrong time. Sodom's enemies captured Lot, his family, and his possessions. Abram immediately put aside any past rivalry or disapproval of Lot's choices, organized an attack, and rescued his nephew's household. Our relatives, being human, get themselves into trouble now and then. It is easy to waggle our fingers, break out the I-told-you-so speech, and watch someone suffer. How much more like God it is to rally under the banner of family unity and, as appropriate given the circumstances, give the help we can. The speeches can come later—if at all.

Sodom and Gomorrah fled, and fell there; and they that remained fled to the mountain. ¹¹And they took all the goods of Sodom and Gomorrah, and all their victuals, and went their way. ¹²And they took Lot, Abram's brother's son, who dwelt in Sodom, and his goods, and departed.

¹³And there came one that had escaped, and told Abram the Hebrew; for he dwelt in the plain of Mamre the Amorite, brother of Eshcol, and brother of Aner: and these *were* confederate with Abram. ¹⁴And when Abram heard that his brother was taken captive, he armed[b] his trained *servants*, born in his own house, three hundred and eighteen, and pursued *them* unto Dan. ¹⁵And he divided himself against them, he and his servants, by night, and smote them, and pursued them unto

[a] Elparan: or, The plain of Paran
[b] armed: or, led forth

Hobah, which *is* on the left hand of Damascus. ¹⁶And he brought back all the goods, and also brought again his brother Lot, and his goods, and the women also, and the people.

¹⁷And the king of Sodom went out to meet him after his return from the slaughter of Chedorlaomer, and of the kings that *were* with him, at the valley of Shaveh, which *is* the king's dale. ¹⁸And Melchizedek king of Salem brought forth bread and wine: and he *was* the priest of the most high God. ¹⁹And he blessed him, and said, Blessed *be* Abram of the most high God, possessor of heaven and earth: ²⁰And blessed be the most high God, which hath delivered thine enemies into thy hand. And he gave him tithes of all.

²¹And the king of Sodom said unto Abram, Give me the persons^c, and take the goods to thyself. ²²And Abram said to the king of Sodom, I have lift up mine hand unto the LORD, the most high God, the possessor of heaven and earth, ²³That I will not *take* from a thread even to a shoelatchet, and that I will not take any thing that *is* thine, lest thou shouldest say, I have made Abram rich: ²⁴Save only that which the young men have eaten, and the portion of the men which went with me, Aner, Eshcol, and Mamre; let them take their portion.

15

¹After these things the word of the LORD came unto Abram in a vision, saying, Fear not, Abram: I *am* thy shield, *and* thy exceeding great reward.

²And Abram said, Lord GOD, what wilt thou give me, seeing I go

---

Devotional Moment
•
Childlessness

15:2-3 When the Lord told Abram that he would receive many blessings, Abram was hardly in a receptive mood. His and Sarai's childlessness was all that he could see. Many couples today feel this despair, the result of any one of many factors such as delaying starting a family and the difficulties of adoption. They see nothing but the child they cannot have. If God has entrusted you with children, be sensitive to your childless friends and relatives. And when you feel tempted to complain about the trials of parenthood, remember that some people long to have such problems.

---

childless, and the steward of my house *is* this Eliezer of Damascus? ³And Abram said, Behold, to me thou hast given no seed: and, lo, one born in my house is mine heir. ⁴And, behold, the word of the LORD *came* unto him, saying, This shall not be thine heir; but he that shall come forth out of thine own bowels shall be thine heir. ⁵And he brought him forth abroad, and said, Look now toward heaven, and tell the stars, if thou be able to number them: and he said unto him, So shall thy seed be. ⁶And he believed in the LORD; and he counted it to him for righteousness.

⁷And he said unto him, I *am* the LORD that brought thee out of Ur of the Chaldees, to give thee this land to inherit it. ⁸And he said, Lord GOD, whereby shall I know that I shall inherit it? ⁹And he said unto him, Take me an heifer of three years old, and a she goat of three years old, and a ram of three years old, and a turtledove, and a young

---

^c persons: Heb. souls

pigeon. ¹⁰And he took unto him all these, and divided them in the midst, and laid each piece one against another: but the birds divided he not. ¹¹And when the fowls came down upon the carcases, Abram drove them away.

¹²And when the sun was going down, a deep sleep fell upon Abram; and, lo, an horror of great darkness fell upon him. ¹³And he said unto Abram, Know of a surety that thy seed shall be a stranger in a land *that is* not theirs, and shall serve them; and they shall afflict them four hundred years; ¹⁴And also that nation, whom they shall serve, will I judge: and afterward shall they come out with great substance. ¹⁵And thou shalt go to thy fathers in peace; thou shalt be buried in a good old age. ¹⁶But in the fourth generation they shall come hither again: for the iniquity of the Amorites *is* not yet full.

¹⁷And it came to pass, that, when the sun went down, and it was dark, behold a smoking furnace, and a burningᵃ lamp that passed between those pieces. ¹⁸In the same day the LORD made a covenant with Abram, saying, Unto thy seed have I given this land, from the river of Egypt unto the great river, the river Euphrates: ¹⁹The Kenites, and the Kenizzites, and the Kadmonites, ²⁰And the Hittites, and the Perizzites, and the Rephaims, ²¹And the Amorites, and the Canaanites, and the Girgashites, and the Jebusites.

16

¹Now Sarai Abram's wife bare him no children: and she had an handmaid, an Egyptian, whose name *was* Hagar. ²And Sarai said unto Abram, Behold now, the

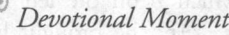

Devotional Moment
•
Trusting God

16:1-3 God had promised Abram and his wife, Sarai, that they would have a son and many other descendants. Abram believed this promise, but trusting in God to deliver became more difficult as time went by. Abram's peers would have accepted Sarai's solution as customary, but as God's child Abram was taking matters into his own hands, ignoring God's power to work. When frustration tempts you to take matters into your own hands, recall some of God's promises that took a long time but did eventually come true. Use that memory to fortify your trust that God is still at work.

LORD hath restrained me from bearing: I pray thee, go in unto my maid; it may be that I may obtain children by her. And Abram hearkened to the voice of Sarai. ³And Sarai Abram's wife took Hagar her maid the Egyptian, after Abram had dwelt ten years in the land of Canaan, and gave her to her husband Abram to be his wife. ⁴And he went in unto Hagar, and she conceived: and when she saw that

Devotional Moment
•
Responsibility

16:8 Hagar answered only the first question, for that was all she knew, that she was running away from Sarai. Hagar took responsibility for her actions, though she had options: she could have made excuses for herself, she could have blamed Sarai for her predicament, or she could have lied about her plans. Most people don't realize that there are always more options. Develop the practice of brainstorming more options before evaluating them or deciding prematurely that there is no way out.

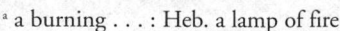

ᵃ a burning . . . : Heb. a lamp of fire

she had conceived, her mistress was despised in her eyes. ⁵And Sarai said unto Abram, My wrong *be* upon thee: I have given my maid into thy bosom; and when she saw that she had conceived, I was despised in her eyes: the LORD judge between me and thee. ⁶But Abram said unto Sarai, Behold, thy maid *is* in thy hand; do to her as it pleaseth thee. And when Sarai dealt hardly with her, she fled from her face.

⁷And the angel of the LORD found her by a fountain of water in the wilderness, by the fountain in the way to Shur. ⁸And he said, Hagar, Sarai's maid, whence camest thou? and whither wilt thou go? And she said, I flee from the face of my mistress Sarai. ⁹And the angel of the LORD said unto her, Return to thy mistress, and submit thyself under her hands.

¹⁰And the angel of the LORD said unto her, I will multiply thy seed exceedingly, that it shall not be numbered for multitude. ¹¹And the angel of the LORD said unto her, Behold, thou *art* with child, and shalt bear a son, and shalt call his name Ishmael[a]; because the LORD hath heard thy affliction. ¹²And he will be a wild man; his hand *will be* against every man, and every man's hand against him; and he shall dwell in the presence of all his brethren. ¹³And she called the name of the LORD that spake unto her, Thou God seest me: for she said, Have I also here looked after

him that seeth me? ¹⁴Wherefore the well was called Beerlahairoi[b]; behold, *it is* between Kadesh and Bered.

¹⁵And Hagar bare Abram a son: and Abram called his son's name, which Hagar bare, Ishmael. ¹⁶And Abram *was* fourscore and six years old, when Hagar bare Ishmael to Abram.

17

¹And when Abram was ninety years old and nine, the LORD appeared to Abram, and said unto him, I *am* the Almighty God; walk before me, and be thou perfect[a]. ²And I will make my covenant between me and thee, and will multiply thee exceedingly. ³And Abram fell on his face: and God talked with him, saying,

⁴As for me, behold, my covenant *is* with thee, and thou shalt be a father of many[b] nations. ⁵Neither shall thy name any more be called Abram, but thy name shall be Abraham[c]; for a father of many nations have I made thee. ⁶And I will make thee exceeding fruitful, and I will make nations of thee, and kings shall come out of thee.

⁷And I will establish my covenant between me and thee and thy seed after thee in their generations for an everlasting covenant, to be a God unto thee, and to thy seed after thee. ⁸And I will give unto thee, and to thy seed after thee, the land wherein thou art a stranger, all the land of Canaan, for an everlasting possession; and I will be their God. ⁹And

---

[a] Ishmael: that is, God shall hear
[b] Beerlahairoi: that is, The well of him that liveth and seeth me
[a] perfect: or, upright, or, sincere
[b] many . . . : Heb. multitude of nations
[c] Abraham: that is, Father of a great multitude

God said unto Abraham, Thou shalt keep my covenant therefore, thou, and thy seed after thee in their generations. [10]This *is* my covenant, which ye shall keep, between me and you and thy seed after thee; Every man child among you shall be circumcised. [11]And ye shall circumcise the flesh of your foreskin; and it shall be a token of the covenant betwixt me and you. [12]And he that is eight[d] days old shall be circumcised among you, every man child in your generations, he that is born in the house, or bought with money of any stranger, which *is* not of thy seed. [13]He that is born in thy house, and he that is bought with thy money, must needs be circumcised: and my covenant shall be in your flesh for an everlasting covenant. [14]And the uncircumcised man child whose flesh of his foreskin is not circumcised, that soul shall be cut off from his people; he hath broken my covenant.

[15]And God said unto Abraham, As for Sarai thy wife, thou shalt not call her name Sarai, but Sarah[e] *shall* her name *be.* [16]And I will bless her, and give thee a son also of her: yea, I will bless her, and she shall be *a mother* of nations; kings of people shall be of her. [17]Then Abraham fell upon his face, and laughed, and said in his heart, Shall *a child* be born unto him that is an hundred years old? and shall Sarah, that is ninety years old, bear? [18]And Abraham said unto God, O that Ishmael might live before thee! [19]And God said, Sarah thy wife shall bear thee a son indeed; and thou shalt call his name Isaac: and I will establish my covenant with him

for an everlasting covenant, *and* with his seed after him. [20]And as for Ishmael, I have heard thee: Behold, I have blessed him, and will make him fruitful, and will multiply him exceedingly; twelve princes shall he beget, and I will make him a great nation. [21]But my covenant will I establish with Isaac, which Sarah shall bear unto thee at this set time in the next year. [22]And he left off talking with him, and God went up from Abraham.

[23]And Abraham took Ishmael his son, and all that were born in his house, and all that were bought with his money, every male among the men of Abraham's house; and circumcised the flesh of their foreskin in the selfsame day, as God had said unto him. [24]And Abraham *was* ninety years old and nine, when he was circumcised in the flesh of his foreskin. [25]And Ishmael his son *was* thirteen years old, when he was circumcised in the flesh of his foreskin. [26]In the selfsame day was Abraham circumcised, and Ishmael his son. [27]And all the men of his house, born in the house, and bought with money of the stranger, were circumcised with him.

18

[1]And the LORD appeared unto him in the plains of Mamre: and he sat in the tent door in the heat of the day; [2]And he lift up his eyes and looked, and, lo, three men stood by him: and when he saw *them,* he ran to meet them from the tent door, and bowed himself toward the ground, [3]And said, My Lord, if now I have found favour in thy sight, pass

---

[d] he that is eight . . . : Heb. a son of eight days
[e] Sarah: that is Princess

28

Devotional Moment

Hospitality

18:2-5 On a hot summer's afternoon, Abraham saw three men approaching the tent where he sat. Immediately he welcomed them, urging them to rest and refresh themselves. By his kindness he provided one of the clearest examples of selfless hospitality—hospitality that meets another person's needs instead of advancing one's own reputation. Today, we have the same opportunity to be hospitable hosts instead of entertainers concerned with setting the perfect table in an immaculate home. What practical steps can you take (for example, in meal planning and housecleaning) to enjoy your guests and meet their needs?

not away, I pray thee, from thy servant: ⁴Let a little water, I pray you, be fetched, and wash your feet, and rest yourselves under the tree: ⁵And I will fetch a morsel of bread, and comfort ye your hearts; after that ye shall pass on: for therefore are ye come to your servant. And they said, So do, as thou hast said. ⁶And Abraham hastened into the tent unto Sarah, and said, Make ready quickly three measures of fine meal, knead *it*, and make cakes upon the hearth. ⁷And Abraham ran unto the herd, and fetcht a calf tender and good, and gave *it* unto a young man; and he hasted to dress it. ⁸And he took butter, and milk, and the calf which he had dressed, and set *it* before them; and he stood by them under the tree, and they did eat.

⁹And they said unto him, Where *is* Sarah thy wife? And he said, Behold, in the tent. ¹⁰And he said, I will certainly return unto thee according to the time of life; and, lo, Sarah thy wife shall have a son. And Sarah heard *it* in the tent

door, which *was* behind him. ¹¹Now Abraham and Sarah *were* old *and* well stricken in age; *and* it ceased to be with Sarah after the manner of women. ¹²Therefore Sarah laughed within herself, saying, After I am waxed old shall I have pleasure, my lord being old also? ¹³And the LORD said unto Abraham, Wherefore did Sarah laugh, saying, Shall I of a surety bear a child, which am old? ¹⁴Is any thing too hard for the LORD? At the time appointed I will return unto thee, according to the time of life, and Sarah shall have a son. ¹⁵Then Sarah denied, saying, I laughed not; for she was afraid. And he said, Nay; but thou didst laugh.

¹⁶And the men rose up from thence, and looked toward Sodom: and Abraham went with them to bring them on the way. ¹⁷And the LORD said, Shall I hide from Abraham that thing which I do; ¹⁸Seeing that Abraham shall surely become a great and mighty nation, and all the nations of

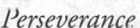

Devotional Moment

Perseverance

18:14 Sarah and Abraham's three visitors turned out to be messengers from the Lord, telling them that their long wait for a child was coming to an end. Sarah laughed skeptically at the news, but the Lord's message to persevere in trusting the divine promise was repeated. Perseverance is not a common quality today, as companies consider only short-range consequences of policies and television shows resolve family crises in thirty minutes. Perhaps you and your spouse face relational or financial problems that seem to drag on with no end in sight. Keep your sense of humor, but don't laugh as Sarah laughed. Persevere in trusting God.

the earth shall be blessed in him? ¹⁹For I know him, that he will command his children and his household after him, and they shall keep the way of the LORD, to do justice and judgment; that the LORD may bring upon Abraham that which he hath spoken of him. ²⁰And the LORD said, Because the cry of Sodom and Gomorrah is great, and because their sin is very grievous; ²¹I will go down now, and see whether they have done altogether according to the cry of it, which is come unto me; and if not, I will know. ²²And the men turned their faces from thence, and went toward Sodom: but Abraham stood yet before the LORD.

²³And Abraham drew near, and said, Wilt thou also destroy the righteous with the wicked? ²⁴Peradventure there be fifty righteous within the city: wilt thou also destroy and not spare the place for the fifty righteous that *are* therein? ²⁵That be far from thee to do

after this manner, to slay the righteous with the wicked: and that the righteous should be as the wicked, that be far from thee: Shall not the Judge of all the earth do right? ²⁶And the LORD said, If I find in Sodom fifty righteous within the city, then I will spare all the place for their sakes. ²⁷And Abraham answered and said, Behold now, I have taken upon me to speak unto the Lord, which *am but* dust and ashes: ²⁸Peradventure there shall lack five of the fifty righteous: wilt thou destroy all the city for *lack of* five? And he said, If I find there forty and five, I will not destroy *it.* ²⁹And he spake unto him yet again, and said, Peradventure there shall be forty found there. And he said, I will not do *it* for forty's sake. ³⁰And he said *unto him,* Oh let not the Lord be angry, and I will speak: Peradventure there shall thirty be found there. And he said, I will not do *it,* if I find thirty there. ³¹And he said, Behold now, I have taken upon me to speak unto the Lord: Peradventure there shall be twenty found there. And he said, I will not destroy *it* for twenty's sake. ³²And he said, Oh let not the Lord be angry, and I will speak yet but this once: Peradventure ten shall be found there. And he said, I will not destroy *it* for ten's sake. ³³And the LORD went his way, as soon as he had left communing with Abraham: and Abraham returned unto his place.

19

¹And there came two angels to Sodom at even; and Lot sat in the gate of Sodom: and Lot seeing *them* rose up to meet them; and he bowed himself with his face toward the ground; ²And he said, Behold now, my lords, turn in, I

pray you, into your servant's house, and tarry all night, and wash your feet, and ye shall rise up early, and go on your ways. And they said, Nay; but we will abide in the street all night. ³And he pressed upon them greatly; and they turned in unto him, and entered into his house; and he made them a feast, and did bake unleavened bread, and they did eat.

⁴But before they lay down, the men of the city, *even* the men of Sodom, compassed the house round, both old and young, all the people from every quarter: ⁵And they called unto Lot, and said unto him, Where *are* the men which came in to thee this night? bring them out unto us, that we may know them. ⁶And Lot went out at the door unto them, and shut the door after him, ⁷And said, I pray you, brethren, do not so wickedly. ⁸Behold now, I have two daughters which have not known man; let me, I pray you, bring them out unto you, and do ye to them as *is* good in your eyes: only unto these men do nothing; for therefore came they under the shadow of my roof. ⁹And they said, Stand back. And they said *again*, This one *fellow* came in to sojourn, and he will needs be a judge: now will we deal worse with thee, than with them. And they pressed sore upon the man, *even* Lot, and came near to break the door. ¹⁰But the men put forth their hand, and pulled Lot into the house to them, and shut to the door. ¹¹And they smote the men that *were* at the door of the house with blindness, both small and great: so that they wearied themselves to find the door.

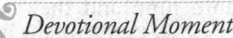

Devotional Moment

Priorities

19:8 How could any father give his daughters to be ravished by a mob of perverts, just to protect two strangers? Although it was the custom of the day to protect guests at any cost, this terrible suggestion reveals how deeply Sodom's twisted values had infiltrated Lot's life. Whatever Lot's motives, he did not have God's priorities. Does your family pay a price for commitments you've made or priorities you have embraced? Make sure you don't compromise the well-being of your loved ones for the sake of another less important priority. If necessary, adjust your commitments and schedule to protect and respect the family God has entrusted to you.

¹²And the men said unto Lot, Hast thou here any besides? son in law, and thy sons, and thy daughters, and whatsoever thou hast in the city, bring *them* out of this place: ¹³For we will destroy this place, because the cry of them is waxen great before the face of the LORD; and the LORD hath sent us to destroy it. ¹⁴And Lot went out, and spake unto his sons in law, which married his daughters, and said, Up, get you out of this place; for the LORD will destroy this city. But he seemed as one that mocked unto his sons in law.

¹⁵And when the morning arose, then the angels hastened Lot, saying, Arise, take thy wife, and thy two daughters, which are here[a]; lest thou be consumed in the iniquity of the city. ¹⁶And while he lingered, the men laid hold upon his hand, and upon the hand of his wife, and upon the hand of his two daughters; the LORD being

---

[a] are here: Heb. are found

merciful unto him: and they brought him forth, and set him without the city. ¹⁷And it came to pass, when they had brought them forth abroad, that he said, Escape for thy life; look not behind thee, neither stay thou in all the plain; escape to the mountain, lest thou be consumed. ¹⁸And Lot said unto them, Oh, not so, my Lord: ¹⁹Behold now, thy servant hath found grace in thy sight, and thou hast magnified thy mercy, which thou hast shewed unto me in saving my life; and I cannot escape to the mountain, lest some evil take me, and I die: ²⁰Behold now, this city *is* near to flee unto, and it *is* a little one: Oh, let me escape thither, (*is* it not a little one?) and my soul shall live. ²¹And he said unto him, See, I have accepted thee^b concerning this thing also, that I will not overthrow this city, for the which thou hast spoken. ²²Haste thee, escape thither; for I cannot do any thing till thou be come thither. Therefore the name of the city was called Zoar^c. ²³The sun was risen^d upon the earth when Lot entered into Zoar.

²⁴Then the LORD rained upon Sodom and upon Gomorrah brimstone and fire from the LORD out of heaven; ²⁵And he overthrew those cities, and all the plain, and all the inhabitants of the cities, and that which grew upon the ground. ²⁶But his wife looked back from behind him, and she became a pillar of salt.

²⁷And Abraham gat up early in the morning to the place where he stood

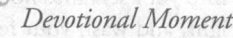

Devotional Moment
·
Singleness
19:30-38 Lot lived with his two single daughters, their fiancés having perished in the destruction of Sodom and Gomorrah (see 19:14). They became desperate to marry and have children, to the point of committing incest. Fear of singleness still grips many people, male and female alike. The church must be careful not to so elevate marriage as the most desirable state so that it becomes the only goal of life. What can you do to honor the single members of your family or church?

before the LORD: ²⁸And he looked toward Sodom and Gomorrah, and toward all the land of the plain, and beheld, and, lo, the smoke of the country went up as the smoke of a furnace. ²⁹And it came to pass, when God destroyed the cities of the plain, that God remembered Abraham, and sent Lot out of the midst of the overthrow, when he overthrew the cities in the which Lot dwelt.

³⁰And Lot went up out of Zoar, and dwelt in the mountain, and his two daughters with him; for he feared to dwell in Zoar: and he dwelt in a cave, he and his two daughters. ³¹And the firstborn said unto the younger, Our father *is* old, and *there is* not a man in the earth to come in unto us after the manner of all the earth: ³²Come, let us make our father drink wine, and we will lie with him, that we may preserve seed of our father. ³³And they made their father drink wine that night: and the firstborn went in, and lay

---

^b thee: Heb. thy face
^c Zoar: that is, Little
^d risen: Heb. gone forth

A Little Hospitality

by Doris Greig

Whenever I'm suddenly called upon to invite someone into my home or extend hospitality in another way, I'm reminded of Abraham.

Abraham had a servant's heart, asking three complete strangers to rest in the shade of a tree and bringing water to bathe their feet (Gen. 18:4). Then he ran back to his tent and had Sarah prepare food while he selected a fine calf for the meal. Abraham gave these strangers his very best.

Sharing our homes with friends and strangers can be a joy. But unfortunately, having people over is often one of the first things we neglect when we feel rushed, tired, or out of sorts.

Here are some practical ideas on how to show hospitality and bring glory to God without feeling frazzled:

1. Accept interruptions as a God-given part of his plan and rejoice in opportunities to serve him through these interruptions.

2. Try to keep your house clean by training the whole family to put away things when they finish using them. Many times it's the clutter that discourages us from extending hospitality to others. Find a system that works for you and other members of your family, encouraging all to pitch in.

3. Don't compare yourself to other homemakers. Decide on housekeeping standards that suit *your* home and family.

4. Get a long extension cord for your telephone—or a cordless phone—so you can accomplish a variety of chores and still talk with someone who needs you. I have managed to polish silver, mend, iron clothes, clean kitchen cupboards, and even exercise while talking on the phone.

5. Cook meals for company in advance and freeze them.

6. Simplify your household as much as possible by adding storage shelves and other conveniences that help reduce clutter.

7. Get your children to help prepare the home for guests. Many books in the library offer tips on how to involve young ones.

Helpful hints for times when you entertain:

1. Pray together before guests arrive, asking God to bless them through you and your interactions. It is more important to pray than to clean your house to immaculate perfection or to arrange the food elaborately on the table. As you pray, the Lord will prepare your heart and your guests for the blessing he wants to give.

2. When you find a menu that is easy to prepare, one that can be done ahead, put it down on a recipe card. Keep a note of who you serve the menu to. If you have a separate file for this type of menu planning, your entertaining will be much simpler to plan, leaving you more relaxed.

3. Don't apologize for how your house looks, drawing attention to problem areas. Welcome your guests with joy and they will not see all the flaws. Remember, most people don't come to see your house; they come to see you!

4. This may seem like a simple, logical suggestion, but a lot of people don't do it: Turn off the television or radio when your guests arrive. Enjoy listening undistractedly to the people who come to see you. Learn to be a good listener.

5. Concentrate on enjoying your guests. You do not need to serve a gourmet meal.

Sometimes you may just want to invite people over for coffee, tea, and dessert, and afterward have a time for talking, playing games, working puzzles, or relaxing in some other way.

6. Consider inviting families to join you at a park for a picnic breakfast or barbecue. It's a relaxed setting in which the food can be kept simple and you don't have to worry about your house. Some of my fondest memories are of breakfasts and barbecues with neighbors and friends in a nearby park. I'm sure our children enjoyed those relaxed times as much as the parents did.

7. If you live in a small apartment or a single room, you can entertain by preparing a meal and taking it to your "guest's" house.

8. If you do not have a home in which to entertain, you can always invite someone to a restaurant for a piece of pie and a cup of coffee, practicing hospitality in the way you extend your friendship.

To build a hospitable home takes courage, planning, and Christ's power. But it's well worth the effort for all the blessing that can come to your guests and your own family. Besides, you never know when—like Abraham—you may find yourself entertaining angels! (Heb. 13:2)

DIGGING DEEPER

1. There's more than one way to show hospitality. Compare the two different approaches described in Luke 10:38-42.

2. Why is it a good idea to extend hospitality to more than just friends and family? See Leviticus 19:34; Luke 14:12-14.

3. What kinds of hospitality can you offer besides entertaining guests in your home? Matthew 25:31-36; Luke 10:25-37.

with her father; and he perceived not when she lay down, nor when she arose. [34]And it came to pass on the morrow, that the firstborn said unto the younger, Behold, I lay yesternight with my father: let us make him drink wine this night also; and go thou in, *and* lie with him, that we may preserve seed of our father. [35]And they made their father drink wine that night also: and the younger arose, and lay with him; and he perceived not when she lay down, nor when she arose. [36]Thus were both the daughters of Lot with child by their father. [37]And the firstborn bare a son, and called his name Moab: the same *is* the father of the Moabites

unto this day. [38]And the younger, she also bare a son, and called his name Benammi: the same *is* the father of the children of Ammon unto this day.

20

[1]And Abraham journeyed from thence toward the south country, and dwelled between Kadesh and Shur, and sojourned in Gerar. [2]And Abraham said of Sarah his wife, She *is* my sister: and Abimelech king of Gerar sent, and took Sarah.

[3]But God came to Abimelech in a dream by night, and said to him, Behold, thou *art but* a dead man, for the woman which thou hast taken; for she *is* a man's[a]

---

[a] a man's . . . : Heb. married to an husband

wife. ⁴But Abimelech had not come near her: and he said, Lord, wilt thou slay also a righteous nation? ⁵Said he not unto me, She *is* my sister? and she, even she herself said, He *is* my brother: in the integrity^b of my heart and innocency of my hands have I done this. ⁶And God said unto him in a dream, Yea, I know that thou didst this in the integrity of thy heart; for I also withheld thee from sinning against me: therefore suffered I thee not to touch her. ⁷Now therefore restore the man *his* wife; for he *is* a prophet, and he shall pray for thee, and thou shalt live: and if thou restore *her* not, know thou that thou shalt surely die, thou, and all that *are* thine.

⁸Therefore Abimelech rose early in the morning, and called all his servants, and told all these things in their ears: and the men were sore afraid. ⁹Then Abimelech called Abraham, and said unto him, What hast thou done unto us? and what have I offended thee, that thou hast brought on me and on my kingdom a great sin? thou hast done deeds unto me that ought not to be done. ¹⁰And Abimelech said unto Abraham, What sawest thou, that thou hast done this thing? ¹¹And Abraham said, Because I thought, Surely the fear of God *is* not in this place; and they will slay me for my wife's sake. ¹²And yet indeed *she is* my sister; she *is* the daughter of my father, but not the daughter of my mother; and she became my wife. ¹³And it came to pass, when God caused me to wander from my father's house, that I said unto her, This *is* thy kindness which thou shalt shew unto me; at every place whither we shall come, say of me, He *is* my brother.

¹⁴And Abimelech took sheep, and oxen, and menservants, and womenservants, and gave *them* unto Abraham, and restored him Sarah his wife. ¹⁵And Abimelech said, Behold, my land *is* before thee: dwell where it pleaseth thee. ¹⁶And unto Sarah he said, Behold, I have given thy brother a thousand *pieces* of silver: behold, he *is* to thee a covering of the eyes, unto all that *are* with thee, and with all *other*: thus she was reproved. ¹⁷So Abraham prayed unto God: and God healed Abimelech, and his wife, and his maidservants; and they bare *children*. ¹⁸For the LORD had fast closed up all the wombs of the house of Abimelech, because of Sarah Abraham's wife.

21

¹And the LORD visited Sarah as he had said, and the LORD did unto Sarah as he had spoken. ²For Sarah conceived, and bare Abraham a son in his old age, at the set time of which God had spoken to him. ³And Abraham called the name of his son that was born unto him, whom Sarah bare to him, Isaac. ⁴And Abraham circumcised his son Isaac being eight days old, as God had commanded him. ⁵And Abraham was an hundred years old, when his son Isaac was born unto him. ⁶And Sarah said, God hath made me to laugh, *so that* all that hear will laugh with me. ⁷And she said, Who would have said unto Abraham, that Sarah should have given children suck? for I have born *him* a son in his

^b integrity: or, simplicity, or, sincerity

Devotional Moment
•
Old Age

21:1-7 God did the impossible: Isaac was born when Abraham was a hundred years old and Sarah was ninety (see 17:17). They could have reasonably expected life to slow down, yet suddenly they had a bouncing baby boy to care for! Plans for their golden years took quite a turn—imagine what reactions the new family must have encountered. God can and does intervene at any age for any person, including those who assume their productive years are over. Energies and priorities may change, but commitment to the Lord must remain strong. In what ways does your nuclear and extended family honor its oldest members?

old age. ⁸And the child grew, and was weaned: and Abraham made a great feast the *same* day that Isaac was weaned.

⁹And Sarah saw the son of Hagar the Egyptian, which she had born unto Abraham, mocking. ¹⁰Wherefore she said unto Abraham, Cast out this bondwoman and her son: for the son of this bondwoman shall not be heir with my son, *even* with Isaac. ¹¹And the thing was very grievous in Abraham's sight because of his son. ¹²And God said unto Abraham, Let it not be grievous in thy sight because of the lad, and because of thy bondwoman; in all that Sarah hath said unto thee, hearken unto her voice; for in Isaac shall thy seed be called. ¹³And also of the son of the bondwoman will I make a nation, because he *is* thy seed.

¹⁴And Abraham rose up early in the morning, and took bread, and a bottle of water, and gave *it* unto Hagar, putting *it* on her shoulder, and the child, and sent her away: and she departed, and wandered in the wilderness of Beersheba. ¹⁵And the water was spent in the bottle, and she cast the child under one of the shrubs. ¹⁶And she went, and sat her down over against *him* a good way off, as it were a bowshot: for she said, Let me not see the death of the child. And she sat over against *him*, and lift up her voice, and wept. ¹⁷And God heard the voice of the lad; and the angel of God called to Hagar out of heaven, and said unto her, What aileth thee, Hagar? fear not; for God hath heard the voice of the lad where he *is*. ¹⁸Arise, lift up the lad, and hold him in thine hand; for I will make him a great nation. ¹⁹And God opened her eyes, and she saw a well of water; and she went, and filled the bottle with water, and gave the lad drink. ²⁰And God was with the lad; and he grew, and dwelt in the wilderness, and became an archer. ²¹And he dwelt in the wilderness of Paran: and his mother took him a wife out of the land of Egypt.

²²And it came to pass at that time, that Abimelech and Phichol the chief captain of his host spake unto Abraham, saying, God *is* with thee in all that thou doest: ²³Now therefore swear unto me here by God that thou wilt not deal falsely with me, nor with my son, nor with my son's son: *but* according to the kindness that I have done unto thee, thou shalt do unto me, and to the land wherein thou hast sojourned. ²⁴And Abraham said, I will swear. ²⁵And Abraham reproved Abimelech because of a well of water, which Abimelech's servants had violently taken away. ²⁶And Abimelech said, I wot not who hath done this thing: neither didst thou tell me, neither yet heard I *of it*, but to day.

²⁷And Abraham took sheep and oxen, and gave them unto Abimelech; and both of them made a covenant. ²⁸And Abraham set seven ewe lambs of the flock by themselves. ²⁹And Abimelech said unto Abraham, What *mean* these seven ewe lambs which thou hast set by themselves? ³⁰And he said, For *these* seven ewe lambs shalt thou take of my hand, that they may be a witness unto me, that I have digged this well. ³¹Wherefore he called that place Beersheba[a]; because there they sware both of them. ³²Thus they made a covenant at Beersheba: then Abimelech rose up, and Phichol the chief captain of his host, and they returned into the land of the Philistines.

³³And *Abraham* planted a grove[b] in Beersheba, and called there on the name of the LORD, the everlasting God. ³⁴And Abraham sojourned in the Philistines' land many days.

22

¹And it came to pass after these things, that God did tempt Abraham, and said unto him, Abraham: and he said, Behold, *here* I am.[a] ²And he said, Take now thy son, thine only *son* Isaac, whom thou lovest, and get thee into the land of Moriah; and offer him there for a burnt offering upon one of the mountains which I will tell thee of.

³And Abraham rose up early in the morning, and saddled his ass, and took two of his young men with him, and Isaac his son, and clave the wood for the

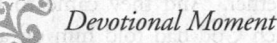

Devotional Moment
•
Fathering
22:1 The account here is stark: God tested and called; Abraham replied. The patriarch and his God had walked together many years, and the son that God had promised was now a fine young boy. The time had come for a test of the father, determining whether his faith and obedience were strong enough. Today's fathers face many tests. Some may even feel that God is unfair to them. But our heavenly Father does not intend to vex earthly fathers. Rather, he wants to strengthen their faith and sharpen their obedience so that their sons and daughters may be guided and nurtured. May our response to God's call always be "Yes, Lord?" rather than "Why me?" In what ways is God strengthening you as a father?

burnt offering, and rose up, and went unto the place of which God had told him. ⁴Then on the third day Abraham lifted up his eyes, and saw the place afar off. ⁵And Abraham said unto his young men, Abide ye here with the ass; and I and the lad will go yonder and worship, and come again to you. ⁶And Abraham took the wood of the burnt offering, and laid *it* upon Isaac his son; and he took the fire in his hand, and a knife; and they went both of them together. ⁷And Isaac spake unto Abraham his father, and said, My father: and he said, Here *am* I, my son. And he said, Behold the fire and the wood: but where *is* the lamb[b] for a burnt offering? ⁸And Abraham said, My son, God will provide himself a lamb for a burnt offering: so they went both of

---

[a] Beersheba: that is, The well of the oath
[b] grove: or, tree
[a] Behold . . . : Heb. Behold me
[b] lamb: or, kid

them together. ⁹And they came to the place which God had told him of; and Abraham built an altar there, and laid the wood in order, and bound Isaac his son, and laid him on the altar upon the wood. ¹⁰And Abraham stretched forth his hand, and took the knife to slay his son.

¹¹And the angel of the LORD called unto him out of heaven, and said, Abraham, Abraham: and he said, Here *am* I. ¹²And he said, Lay not thine hand upon the lad, neither do thou any thing unto him: for now I know that thou fearest God, seeing thou hast not withheld thy son, thine only *son* from me. ¹³And Abraham lifted up his eyes, and looked, and behold behind *him* a ram caught in a thicket by his horns: and Abraham went and took the ram,

---

Devotional Moment

•

Family Purpose

22:17-18 Because he obeyed God concerning Isaac, Abraham was blessed beyond his wildest imagination. But the blessings were not the material riches some people associate with the word *blessings*. God had in mind a rich family heritage of countless descendants and a continuity of purpose through history—the purpose of blessing all the nations of the earth. Though the effects of our obedience may not reach as far as Abraham's, we can still be assured that God has a purpose for our families. Other people can be blessed by our devotion to God, can become Christians through our witness, and benefit from our creative output or even our career choices. For what purposes do you think your family was created?

---

and offered him up for a burnt offering in the stead of his son. ¹⁴And Abraham called the name of that place Jehovahjirehᶜ: as it is said *to* this day, In the mount of the LORD it shall be seen.

¹⁵And the angel of the LORD called unto Abraham out of heaven the second time, ¹⁶And said, By myself have I sworn, saith the LORD, for because thou hast done this thing, and hast not withheld thy son, thine only *son*: ¹⁷That in blessing I will bless thee, and in multiplying I will multiply thy seed as the stars of the heaven, and as the sand which *is* upon the sea shoreᵈ; and thy seed shall possess the gate of his enemies; ¹⁸And in thy seed shall all the nations of the earth be blessed; because thou hast obeyed my voice. ¹⁹So Abraham returned unto his young men, and they rose up and went together to Beersheba; and Abraham dwelt at Beersheba.

²⁰And it came to pass after these things, that it was told Abraham, saying, Behold, Milcah, she hath also born children unto thy brother Nahor; ²¹Huz his firstborn, and Buz his brother, and Kemuel the father of Aram, ²²And Chesed, and Hazo, and Pildash, and Jidlaph, and Bethuel. ²³And Bethuel begat Rebekahᵉ: these eight Milcah did bear to Nahor, Abraham's brother. ²⁴And his concubine, whose name *was* Reumah, she bare also Tebah, and Gaham, and Thahash, and Maachah.

23

¹And Sarah was an hundred and seven and twenty years old: *these were* the

---

ᶜ Jehovahjireh: that is, The Lord will see, or, provide
ᵈ shore: Heb. lip
ᵉ Rebekah: Gr. Rebecca

years of the life of Sarah. ²And Sarah died in Kirjatharba; the same *is* Hebron in the land of Canaan: and Abraham came to mourn for Sarah, and to weep for her.

³And Abraham stood up from before his dead, and spake unto the sons of Heth, saying, ⁴I *am* a stranger and a sojourner with you: give me a possession of a buryingplace with you, that I may bury my dead out of my sight. ⁵And the children of Heth answered Abraham, saying unto him, ⁶Hear us, my lord: thou *art* a mighty[a] prince among us: in the choice of our sepulchres bury thy dead; none of us shall withhold from thee his sepulchre, but that thou mayest bury thy dead. ⁷And Abraham stood up, and bowed himself to the people of the land, *even* to the children of Heth. ⁸And he communed with them, saying, If it be

your mind that I should bury my dead out of my sight; hear me, and intreat for me to Ephron the son of Zohar, ⁹That he may give me the cave of Machpelah, which he hath, which *is* in the end of his field; for as much[b] money as it is worth he shall give it me for a possession of a buryingplace amongst you. ¹⁰And Ephron dwelt among the children of Heth: and Ephron the Hittite answered Abraham in the audience[c] of the children of Heth, *even* of all that went in at the gate of his city, saying, ¹¹Nay, my lord, hear me: the field give I thee, and the cave that *is* therein, I give it thee; in the presence of the sons of my people give I it thee: bury thy dead. ¹²And Abraham bowed down himself before the people of the land. ¹³And he spake unto Ephron in the audience of the people of the land, saying, But if thou *wilt give it*, I pray thee, hear me: I will give thee money for the field; take *it* of me, and I will bury my dead there. ¹⁴And Ephron answered Abraham, saying unto him, ¹⁵My lord, hearken unto me: the land *is worth* four hundred shekels of silver; what *is* that betwixt me and thee? bury therefore thy dead.

¹⁶And Abraham hearkened unto Ephron; and Abraham weighed to Ephron the silver, which he had named in the audience of the sons of Heth, four hundred shekels of silver, current *money* with the merchant. ¹⁷And the field of Ephron, which *was* in Machpelah, which *was* before Mamre, the field, and the cave which *was* therein, and all the trees that *were* in the field,

---

[a] a mighty . . . : Heb. a prince of God
[b] as much . . . : Heb. full money
[c] audience: Heb. ears

that *were* in all the borders round about, were made sure ¹⁸Unto Abraham for a possession in the presence of the children of Heth, before all that went in at the gate of his city. ¹⁹And after this, Abraham buried Sarah his wife in the cave of the field of Machpelah before Mamre: the same *is* Hebron in the land of Canaan. ²⁰And the field, and the cave that *is* therein, were made sure unto Abraham for a possession of a burying-place by the sons of Heth.

24

¹And Abraham was old, *and* well stricken in age: and the LORD had blessed Abraham in all things. ²And Abraham said unto his eldest servant of his house, that ruled over all that he had, Put, I pray thee, thy hand under my thigh: ³And I will make thee swear by the LORD, the God of heaven, and the God of the earth, that thou shalt not take a wife unto my son of the daughters of the Canaanites, among whom I dwell: ⁴But thou shalt go unto my country, and to my kindred, and take a wife unto my son Isaac. ⁵And the servant said unto him, Peradventure the woman will not be willing to follow me unto this land: must I needs bring thy son again unto the land from whence thou camest? ⁶And Abraham said unto him, Beware thou that thou bring not my son thither again. ⁷The LORD God of heaven, which took me from my father's house, and from the land of my kindred, and which spake unto me, and that sware unto me, saying, Unto thy seed will I give this land; he shall send his angel before thee, and thou shalt take a wife unto my son from thence. ⁸And if the woman will not be willing to follow thee, then thou shalt be clear from this my oath: only bring not my son thither again. ⁹And the servant put his hand under the thigh of Abraham his master, and sware to him concerning that matter.

¹⁰And the servant took ten camels of the camels of his master, and departed; for all the goods of his master *were* in his hand: and he arose, and went to Mesopotamia, unto the city of Nahor. ¹¹And he made his camels to kneel down without the city by a well of water at the time of the evening, *even* the time that women go out to draw *water.* ¹²And he said, O LORD God of my master Abraham, I pray thee, send me good speed this day, and shew kindness unto my master Abraham. ¹³Behold, I stand *here* by the well of water; and the daughters of the men of the city come out to draw water: ¹⁴And let it come to pass, that the damsel to whom I shall say, Let down thy pitcher, I pray thee, that I may drink; and she shall say, Drink, and I will give thy camels drink also: *let the same be* she *that* thou hast appointed for thy servant Isaac; and thereby shall I know that thou hast shewed kindness unto my master. ¹⁵And it came to pass, before he had done speaking, that, behold, Rebekah came out, who was born to Bethuel, son of Milcah, the wife of Nahor, Abraham's brother, with her pitcher upon her shoulder. ¹⁶And the damsel *was* very[a] fair to look upon, a virgin, neither had any man known her: and she went down to the well, and filled her pitcher,

---

[a] very . . . : Heb. good of countenance

and came up. ¹⁷And the servant ran to meet her, and said, Let me, I pray thee, drink a little water of thy pitcher. ¹⁸And she said, Drink, my lord: and she hasted, and let down her pitcher upon her hand, and gave him drink. ¹⁹And when she had done giving him drink, she said, I will draw *water* for thy camels also, until they have done drinking. ²⁰And she hasted, and emptied her pitcher into the trough, and ran again unto the well to draw *water*, and drew for all his camels. ²¹And the man wondering at her held his peace, to wit whether the LORD had made his journey prosperous or not. ²²And it came to pass, as the camels had done drinking, that the man took a golden earring[b] of half a shekel weight, and two bracelets for her hands of ten *shekels* weight of gold; ²³And said, Whose daughter *art* thou? tell me, I pray thee: is there room *in* thy father's house for us to lodge in? ²⁴And she said unto him, I *am* the daughter of Bethuel the son of Milcah, which she bare unto Nahor. ²⁵She said

moreover unto him, We have both straw and provender enough, and room to lodge in. ²⁶And the man bowed down his head, and worshipped the LORD. ²⁷And he said, Blessed *be* the LORD God of my master Abraham, who hath not left destitute my master of his mercy and his truth: I *being* in the way, the LORD led me to the house of my master's brethren. ²⁸And the damsel ran, and told *them of* her mother's house these things.

²⁹And Rebekah had a brother, and his name *was* Laban: and Laban ran out unto the man, unto the well. ³⁰And it came to pass, when he saw the earring and bracelets upon his sister's hands, and when he heard the words of Rebekah his sister, saying, Thus spake the man unto me; that he came unto the man; and, behold, he stood by the camels at the well. ³¹And he said, Come in, thou blessed of the LORD; wherefore standest thou without? for I have prepared the house, and room for the camels. ³²And the man came into the house: and he ungirded his camels, and gave straw and provender for the camels, and water to wash his feet, and the men's feet that *were* with him. ³³And there was set *meat* before him to eat: but he said, I will not eat, until I have told mine errand. And he said, Speak on. ³⁴And he said, I *am* Abraham's servant. ³⁵And the LORD hath blessed my master greatly; and he is become great: and he hath given him flocks, and herds, and silver, and gold, and menservants, and maidservants, and camels, and asses. ³⁶And Sarah my master's wife bare a son to my master when she was old: and unto him hath he given all that

---

[b] earring: or, jewel for the forehead

Rebekah

In Rebekah's time the highest honor a woman could receive came from having children. Imagine her mounting despair, then, as she watched year after year go by—childless. Isaac pleaded with God for a child.

Twenty years passed before Rebekah finally became pregnant, and then she had twins! She named one child Esau, after his prominent red hair, and the other Jacob, after his tenacious hold on his brother's heel as they were born. The two parents each had a favorite: "Isaac loved Esau, because he did eat of *his* venison: but Rebekah loved Jacob" (Gen. 25:28).

In an effort to help Jacob steal Esau's blessing, Rebekah schemed against both Isaac and Esau, in league with Jacob. After twenty years of childlessness, perhaps it is understandable that her favoritism toward Jacob became such an all-consuming passion. Still, Rebekah was a grown woman; her scheming can only be called immature.

Rebekah's favoritism had disastrous effects. Esau came to hate Jacob, and Jacob had to run for his life. From her interactions with Jacob we can infer that Rebekah and Isaac did not make decisions together well. (We know of only one other decision Isaac and Rebekah made together—allowing Jacob to leave home and go to live with her brother Laban. But even in this, their reasons were quite different: Rebekah was rescuing Jacob from Esau's anger, while Isaac thought he was keeping Jacob from marrying a pagan girl, as his brother had done.) As far as we know, Rebekah never saw her favorite son again.

he hath. ³⁷And my master made me swear, saying, Thou shalt not take a wife to my son of the daughters of the Canaanites, in whose land I dwell: ³⁸But thou shalt go unto my father's house, and to my kindred, and take a wife unto my son. ³⁹And I said unto my master, Peradventure the woman will not follow me. ⁴⁰And he said unto me, The LORD, before whom I walk, will send his angel with thee, and prosper thy way; and thou shalt take a wife for my son of my kindred, and of my father's house: ⁴¹Then shalt thou be clear from *this* my oath, when thou comest to my kindred; and if they give not thee *one*, thou shalt be clear from my oath. ⁴²And I came this day unto the well, and said, O LORD God of my master Abraham, if now thou do prosper my way which I go: ⁴³Behold, I stand by the well of water; and it shall come to pass, that when the virgin cometh forth to draw *water*, and I

Devotional Moment
•
Thankfulness

24:48 As soon as Abraham's servant found a wife for Isaac, he offered thanks to God. When we first fall in love and get engaged our attitude is thankfulness also; we are grateful for God's provision. As time goes on we may forget God's leading in the choice of a spouse, especially as we get to know him or her better. Hurts come along with the joys. Confess those hurts to your spouse and seek to resolve your conflicts, experiencing God's and their forgiveness. Ask God for help to see your spouse through the same loving eyes you had when you began your relationship. Then thank God for your mate, God's provision for you.

---

say to her, Give me, I pray thee, a little water of thy pitcher to drink; ⁴⁴And she say to me, Both drink thou, and I will also draw for thy camels: *let* the same *be* the woman whom the LORD hath appointed out for my master's son. ⁴⁵And before I had done speaking in mine heart, behold, Rebekah came forth with her pitcher on her shoulder; and she went down unto the well, and drew *water*: and I said unto her, Let me drink, I pray thee. ⁴⁶And she made haste, and let down her pitcher from her *shoulder*, and said, Drink, and I will give thy camels drink also: so I drank, and she made the camels drink also. ⁴⁷And I asked her, and said, Whose daughter *art* thou? And she said, The daughter of Bethuel, Nahor's son, whom Milcah bare unto him: and I put the earring upon her face, and the bracelets upon her hands. ⁴⁸And I bowed down my head, and worshipped the LORD, and blessed the LORD God of my master Abraham, which had led me in the right way to take my master's brother's daughter unto his son. ⁴⁹And now if ye will deal kindly and truly with my master, tell me: and if not, tell me; that I may turn to the right hand, or to the left. ⁵⁰Then Laban and Bethuel answered and said, The thing proceedeth from the LORD: we cannot speak unto thee bad or good. ⁵¹Behold, Rebekah *is* before thee, take *her*, and go, and let her be thy master's son's wife, as the LORD hath spoken. ⁵²And it came to pass, that, when Abraham's servant heard their words, he worshipped the LORD, *bowing himself* to the earth. ⁵³And the servant brought forth jewels^c of silver, and jewels of gold, and raiment, and gave

---

^c jewels: Heb. vessels

Devotional Moment

•

Comfort

24:67 Rebekah did not know Isaac very well; they had just met and were newly married. She had not known his mother and could not share in any of his memories of her. And she had just traveled many miles from her home and left behind her own family; she probably felt homesick. How could she possibly comfort her new husband? We don't have to have lived through other people's experiences to be a help to them in their grief. Sometimes all they need is a listening ear. Even when we ourselves have needs, we can comfort them just by being there. The next time someone in trouble needs comfort, just sit down together, put an arm around the slumped shoulders, and listen.

---

them to Rebekah: he gave also to her brother and to her mother precious things. ⁵⁴And they did eat and drink, he and the men that *were* with him, and tarried all night; and they rose up in the morning, and he said, Send me away unto my master. ⁵⁵And her brother and her mother said, Let the damsel abide with us *a few* days, at the least ten; after that she shall go. ⁵⁶And he said unto them, Hinder me not, seeing the LORD hath prospered my way; send me away that I may go to my master. ⁵⁷And they said, We will call the damsel, and enquire at her mouth. ⁵⁸And they called Rebekah, and said unto her, Wilt thou go with this man? And she said, I will go. ⁵⁹And they sent away Rebekah their sister, and her nurse, and Abraham's servant, and his men. ⁶⁰And they blessed Rebekah, and said unto her, Thou *art* our sister, be thou *the mother* of thousands of millions, and let thy seed

possess the gate of those which hate them. ⁶¹And Rebekah arose, and her damsels, and they rode upon the camels, and followed the man: and the servant took Rebekah, and went his way.

⁶²And Isaac came from the way of the well Lahairoi; for he dwelt in the south country. ⁶³And Isaac went out to meditate^d in the field at the eventide: and he lifted up his eyes, and saw, and, behold, the camels *were* coming. ⁶⁴And Rebekah lifted up her eyes, and when she saw Isaac, she lighted off the camel. ⁶⁵For she *had* said unto the servant, What man *is* this that walketh in the field to meet us? And the servant *had* said, It *is* my master: therefore she took a vail, and covered herself. ⁶⁶And the servant told Isaac all things that he had done. ⁶⁷And Isaac brought her into his mother Sarah's tent, and took Rebekah, and she became his wife; and he loved her: and Isaac was comforted after his mother's *death*.

25

¹Then again Abraham took a wife, and her name *was* Keturah. ²And she bare him Zimran, and Jokshan, and Medan, and Midian, and Ishbak, and Shuah. ³And Jokshan begat Sheba, and Dedan. And the sons of Dedan were Asshurim, and Letushim, and Leummim. ⁴And the sons of Midian; Ephah, and Epher, and Hanoch, and Abida, and Eldaah. All these *were* the children of Keturah. ⁵And Abraham gave all that he had unto Isaac. ⁶But unto the sons of the concubines, which Abraham had, Abraham gave gifts, and sent them away from Isaac his son, while he yet lived,

---

^d to meditate: or, to pray

eastward, unto the east country. ⁷And these *are* the days of the years of Abraham's life which he lived, an hundred threescore and fifteen years. ⁸Then Abraham gave up the ghost, and died in a good old age, an old man, and full *of years*; and was gathered to his people. ⁹And his sons Isaac and Ishmael buried him in the cave of Machpelah, in the field of Ephron the son of Zohar the Hittite, which *is* before Mamre; ¹⁰The field which Abraham purchased of the sons of Heth: there was Abraham buried, and Sarah his wife.

¹¹And it came to pass after the death of Abraham, that God blessed his son Isaac; and Isaac dwelt by the well Lahairoi. ¹²Now these *are* the generations of Ishmael, Abraham's son, whom Hagar the Egyptian, Sarah's handmaid, bare unto Abraham: ¹³And these *are* the names of the sons of Ishmael, by their names, according to their generations: the firstborn of Ishmael, Nebajoth; and Kedar, and Adbeel, and Mibsam, ¹⁴And Mishma, and Dumah, and Massa, ¹⁵Hadar*, and Tema, Jetur, Naphish, and Kedemah: ¹⁶These *are* the sons of Ishmael, and these *are* their names, by their towns, and by their castles; twelve princes according to their nations. ¹⁷And these *are* the years of the life of Ishmael, an hundred and thirty and seven years: and he gave up the ghost and died; and was gathered unto his people. ¹⁸And they dwelt from Havilah unto Shur, that *is* before Egypt, as thou goest toward Assyria: *and* he died^b in the presence of all his brethren.

¹⁹And these *are* the generations of

> ### Devotional Moment
> •
> ### Sibling Rivalry
> 25:22-24 "I can't endure this!" Rebekah said while her two sons fought inside her. Most mothers say this *after* the children are born, not while they are still in the womb. As parents we experience the whining, the fighting, the competition, and all aspects of sibling rivalry. Yet Rebekah set a good example: "She went to enquire of the Lord." Competition among siblings will always challenge parents. Let it challenge you too—to the point of prayer. God gave Rebekah the insights she needed (v. 23); he will give you insight as well.

Isaac, Abraham's son: Abraham begat Isaac: ²⁰And Isaac was forty years old when he took Rebekah to wife, the daughter of Bethuel the Syrian of Padanaram, the sister to Laban the Syrian. ²¹And Isaac intreated the LORD for his wife, because she *was* barren: and the LORD was intreated of him, and Rebekah his wife conceived. ²²And the children struggled together within her; and she said, If *it be* so, why *am* I thus? And she went to enquire of the LORD. ²³And the LORD said unto her, Two nations *are* in thy womb, and two manner of people shall be separated from thy bowels; and *the one* people shall be stronger than *the other* people; and the elder shall serve the younger. ²⁴And when her days to be delivered were fulfilled, behold, *there were* twins in her womb. ²⁵And the first came out red, all over like an hairy garment; and they called his name Esau. ²⁶And after that came his brother out, and his hand took hold on Esau's heel; and his name

---

ª Hadar: or, Hadad
ᵇ died: Heb. fell

was called Jacob: and Isaac *was* three-score years old when she bare them. ²⁷And the boys grew: and Esau was a cunning hunter, a man of the field; and Jacob *was* a plain man, dwelling in tents. ²⁸And Isaac loved Esau, because he did eat of *his* venison: but Rebekah loved Jacob.

²⁹And Jacob sod pottage: and Esau came from the field, and he *was* faint: ³⁰And Esau said to Jacob, Feed me, I pray thee, withᶜ that same red *pottage*; for I *am* faint: therefore was his name called Edom. ³¹And Jacob said, Sell me this day thy birthright. ³²And Esau said, Behold, I *am* at the point to die: and what profit shall this birthright do to me? ³³And Jacob said, Swear to me this day; and he sware unto him: and he sold his birthright unto Jacob. ³⁴Then Jacob gave Esau bread and pottage of lentils; and he did eat and drink, and rose up, and went his way: thus Esau despised *his* birthright.

26

¹And there was a famine in the land, beside the first famine that was in the days of Abraham. And Isaac went unto Abimelech king of the Philistines unto Gerar. ²And the LORD appeared unto him, and said, Go not down into Egypt; dwell in the land which I shall tell thee of: ³Sojourn in this land, and I will be with thee, and will bless thee; for unto thee, and unto thy seed, I will give all these countries, and I will perform the oath which I sware unto Abraham thy father; ⁴And I will make thy seed to multiply as the stars of heaven, and will give unto thy seed all these countries; and in thy seed shall all the nations of

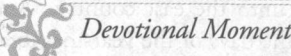

Devotional Moment
•
Modeling

26:7-10 Abraham had been a sterling example to his son Isaac in many ways, particularly when they had gone to the mountain in full faith that God could raise the dead (see 22:1-14 for the story). But Abraham was not perfect, and Isaac learned some bad habits as well, as Abraham's lie to King Abimelech about Sarah (20:1-4) repeated itself in Isaac's similar lie about Rebekah. Each of us as parents has flaws which our children observe. We'd like them to see just the good we do and imitate that alone. But we are a package deal and our children will imitate the bad as well as the good. Before you act, ask whether you would want your children to follow your example. Chances are that someday they will.

the earth be blessed; ⁵Because that Abraham obeyed my voice, and kept my charge, my commandments, my statutes, and my laws.

⁶And Isaac dwelt in Gerar: ⁷And the men of the place asked *him* of his wife; and he said, She *is* my sister: for he feared to say, *She is* my wife; lest, *said he*, the men of the place should kill me for Rebekah; because she *was* fair to look upon. ⁸And it came to pass, when he had been there a long time, that Abimelech king of the Philistines looked out at a window, and saw, and, behold, Isaac *was* sporting with Rebekah his wife. ⁹And Abimelech called Isaac, and said, Behold, of a surety she *is* thy wife: and how saidst thou, She *is* my sister? And Isaac said unto him, Because I said, Lest I die for her. ¹⁰And Abimelech said, What *is* this thou hast done unto us? one of the people might

---

ᶜ with . . . : Heb. with that red, with that red pottage

lightly have lien with thy wife, and thou shouldest have brought guiltiness upon us. [11]And Abimelech charged all *his* people, saying, He that toucheth this man or his wife shall surely be put to death.

[12]Then Isaac sowed in that land, and received[a] in the same year an hundredfold: and the LORD blessed him. [13]And the man waxed great, and went[b] forward, and grew until he became very great: [14]For he had possession of flocks, and possession of herds, and great store of servants[c]: and the Philistines envied him. [15]For all the wells which his father's servants had digged in the days of Abraham his father, the Philistines had

Devotional Moment

•

Problem Solving

26:17-22 Isaac had no doubt that God would provide for his family and enable them to settle in the land. And because he trusted in God's provision, he had peace about his circumstances and, in turn, he could be at peace with his neighbors. Instead of being hostile and defensive when his well was stolen, he dug another well—and yet another. When relationships within your family turn sour, look for other solutions rather than attacking or blaming someone. Trust that God, in his sovereignty, has a way out for all concerned. Then do your part in contributing to a new course of action, trusting God to change the attitudes of the other people involved.

stopped them, and filled them with earth. [16]And Abimelech said unto Isaac, Go from us; for thou art much mightier than we. [17]And Isaac departed thence, and pitched his tent in the valley of Gerar, and dwelt there. [18]And Isaac digged again the wells of water, which they had digged in the days of Abraham his father; for the Philistines had stopped them after the death of Abraham: and he called their names after the names by which his father had called them. [19]And Isaac's servants digged in the valley, and found there a well of springing[d] water. [20]And the herdmen of Gerar did strive with Isaac's herdmen, saying, The water *is* ours: and he called the name of the well Esek[e]; because they strove with him. [21]And they digged another well, and strove for that also: and he called the name of it Sitnah[f]. [22]And he removed from thence, and digged another well; and for that they strove not: and he called the name of it Rehoboth[g]; and he said, For now the LORD hath made room for us, and we shall be fruitful in the land. [23]And he went up from thence to Beersheba. [24]And the LORD appeared unto him the same night, and said, I *am* the God of Abraham thy father: fear not, for I *am* with thee, and will bless thee, and multiply thy seed for my servant Abraham's sake. [25]And he builded an altar there, and called upon the name of the

---

[a] received: Heb. found
[b] went . . . : Heb. went going
[c] servants: or, husbandry
[d] springing: Heb. living
[e] Esek: that is, Contention
[f] Sitnah: that is, Hatred
[g] Rehoboth: that is Room

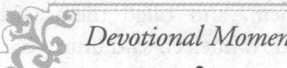

Devotional Moment

•

Expectations

26:34-35 Esau's marriage to two of the local girls shocked his parents. Before Rebekah and Isaac's marriage, their parents had arranged to bring them together under God's direction and approval (see 24:50-51). Naturally they expected the same for Esau. Yet Esau had his own plans. What are your expectations for your children? Be careful not to hold on to these expectations so tightly that you become embittered if they don't materialize. When children do not become all we imagined for them, let us maintain a loving relationship and choose not to become bitter.

LORD, and pitched his tent there: and there Isaac's servants digged a well.

²⁶Then Abimelech went to him from Gerar, and Ahuzzath one of his friends, and Phichol the chief captain of his army. ²⁷And Isaac said unto them, Wherefore come ye to me, seeing ye hate me, and have sent me away from you? ²⁸And they said, We saw^h certainly that the LORD was with thee: and we said, Let there be now an oath betwixt us, *even* betwixt us and thee, and let us make a covenant with thee; ²⁹That thou wilt do us no hurt, as we have not touched thee, and as we have done unto thee nothing but good, and have sent thee away in peace: thou *art* now the blessed of the LORD. ³⁰And he made them a feast, and they did eat and drink. ³¹And they rose up betimes in the morning, and sware one to another: and Isaac sent them away, and they departed from him

in peace. ³²And it came to pass the same day, that Isaac's servants came, and told him concerning the well which they had digged, and said unto him, We have found water. ³³And he called it Shebahⁱ: therefore the name of the city *is* Beersheba unto this day.

³⁴And Esau was forty years old when he took to wife Judith the daughter of Beeri the Hittite, and Bashemath the daughter of Elon the Hittite: ³⁵Which were a grief^j of mind unto Isaac and to Rebekah.

27

¹And it came to pass, that when Isaac was old, and his eyes were dim, so that he could not see, he called Esau his eldest son, and said unto him, My son: and he said unto him, Behold, *here am* I. ²And he said, Behold now, I am old, I know not the day of my death: ³Now therefore take, I pray thee, thy weapons, thy quiver and thy bow, and go out to the field, and take^a me *some* venison; ⁴And make me savoury meat, such as I love, and bring *it* to me, that I may eat; that my soul may bless thee before I die. ⁵And Rebekah heard when Isaac spake to Esau his son. And Esau went to the field to hunt *for* venison, *and* to bring *it.*

⁶And Rebekah spake unto Jacob her son, saying, Behold, I heard thy father speak unto Esau thy brother, saying, ⁷Bring me venison, and make me savoury meat, that I may eat, and bless thee before the LORD before my death. ⁸Now therefore, my son, obey my voice accord-

---

^h We saw . . . : Heb. Seeing we saw
ⁱ Shebah: That is, an oath
^j a grief . . . : Heb. bitterness of spirit
^a take: Heb. hunt

ing to that which I command thee. ⁹Go now to the flock, and fetch me from thence two good kids of the goats; and I will make them savoury meat for thy father, such as he loveth: ¹⁰And thou shalt bring it to thy father, that he may eat, and that he may bless thee before his death. ¹¹And Jacob said to Rebekah his mother, Behold, Esau my brother is a hairy man, and I am a smooth man: ¹²My father peradventure will feel me, and I shall seem to him as a deceiver; and I shall bring a curse upon me, and not a blessing. ¹³And his mother said unto him, Upon me be thy curse, my son: only obey my voice, and go fetch me them. ¹⁴And he went, and fetched, and brought them to his mother: and his mother made savoury meat, such as his father loved. ¹⁵And Rebekah took goodly[b] raiment of her eldest son Esau, which were with her in the house, and put them upon Jacob her younger son: ¹⁶And she put the skins of the kids of the goats upon his hands, and upon the smooth of his neck: ¹⁷And she gave the savoury meat and the bread, which she had prepared, into the hand of her son Jacob.

¹⁸And he came unto his father, and said, My father: and he said, Here am I; who art thou, my son? ¹⁹And Jacob said unto his father, I am Esau thy firstborn; I have done according as thou badest me: arise, I pray thee, sit and eat of my venison, that thy soul may bless me. ²⁰And Isaac said unto his son, How is it that thou hast found it so quickly, my son? And he said, Because the LORD thy God brought it to me[c]. ²¹And Isaac said unto Jacob, Come near, I pray thee, that I may

feel thee, my son, whether thou be my very son Esau or not. ²²And Jacob went near unto Isaac his father; and he felt him, and said, The voice is Jacob's voice, but the hands are the hands of Esau. ²³And he discerned him not, because his hands were hairy, as his brother Esau's hands: so he blessed him. ²⁴And he said, Art thou my very son Esau? And he said, I am. ²⁵And he said, Bring it near to me, and I will eat of my son's venison, that my soul may bless thee. And he brought it near to him, and he did eat: and he brought him wine, and he drank. ²⁶And his father Isaac said unto him, Come near now, and kiss me, my son. ²⁷And he came near, and kissed him: and he smelled the smell of his raiment, and blessed him, and said, See, the smell of my son is as the smell of a field which the LORD hath blessed: ²⁸Therefore God give thee of the dew of heaven, and the fatness of the earth, and plenty of corn and wine: ²⁹Let people serve thee, and nations bow down to thee: be lord over thy brethren, and let thy mother's sons bow down to thee: cursed be every one that curseth thee, and blessed be he that blesseth thee.

³⁰And it came to pass, as soon as Isaac had made an end of blessing Jacob, and Jacob was yet scarce gone out from the presence of Isaac his father, that Esau his brother came in from his hunting. ³¹And he also had made savoury meat, and brought it unto his father, and said unto his father, Let my father arise, and eat of his son's venison, that thy soul may bless me. ³²And Isaac his father said unto him, Who art thou? And he said, I am thy son, thy firstborn Esau. ³³And Isaac

---

[b] goodly: Heb. desirable
[c] to me: Heb. before me

trembled^d very exceedingly, and said, Who? where *is* he that hath taken venison, and brought *it* me, and I have eaten of all before thou camest, and have blessed him? yea, *and* he shall be blessed. ³⁴And when Esau heard the words of his father, he cried with a great and exceeding bitter cry, and said unto his father, Bless me, *even* me also, O my father. ³⁵And he said, Thy brother came with subtilty, and hath taken away thy blessing. ³⁶And he said, Is not he rightly named Jacob^e? for he hath supplanted me these two times: he took away my birthright; and, behold, now he hath taken away my blessing. And he said, Hast thou not reserved a blessing for me? ³⁷And Isaac answered and said unto Esau, Behold, I have made him thy lord, and all his brethren have I given to him for servants; and with corn and wine have I sustained^f him: and what shall I do now unto thee, my son? ³⁸And Esau said unto his father, Hast thou but one blessing, my father? bless me, *even* me also, O my father. And Esau lifted up his voice, and wept. ³⁹And Isaac his father answered and said unto him, Behold, thy dwelling shall be the fatness^g of the earth, and of the dew of heaven from above; ⁴⁰And by thy sword shalt thou live, and shalt serve thy brother; and it shall come to pass when thou shalt have the dominion, that thou shalt break his yoke from off thy neck.

⁴¹And Esau hated Jacob because of the blessing wherewith his father blessed him: and Esau said in his heart, The

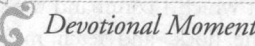

Devotional Moment

•

Blessing

27:33-37 The firstborn son in a Hebrew family was entitled to many blessings and privileges not given to the other children. His birthright entitled him to a double portion of the inheritance and the eventual position of family leader. Jacob, the second born, cheated Esau out of these rights, and Esau sorely missed and grieved his lost blessings. In chapter 24 we read about the joy that family blessings brought to Rebekah. In this example we see the bitterness and pain caused by withholding the blessing from a child. Parents' words are tremendously important to the self-esteem of a child. Words shape what a child believes he or she can be and do. As a parent, give blessings freely.

days of mourning for my father are at hand; then will I slay my brother Jacob. ⁴²And these words of Esau her elder son were told to Rebekah: and she sent and called Jacob her younger son, and said unto him, Behold, thy brother Esau, as touching thee, doth comfort himself, *purposing* to kill thee. ⁴³Now therefore, my son, obey my voice; and arise, flee thou to Laban my brother to Haran; ⁴⁴And tarry with him a few days, until thy brother's fury turn away; ⁴⁵Until thy brother's anger turn away from thee, and he forget *that* which thou hast done to him: then I will send, and fetch thee from thence: why should I be deprived also of you both in one day? ⁴⁶And Rebekah said to Isaac, I am weary of my life because of the daughters of Heth: if

^d trembled . . . : Heb. trembled with a great trembling greatly
^e Jacob: that is, A supplanter
^f sustained: or, supported
^g the fatness: or, of the fatness

Jacob take a wife of the daughters of Heth, such as these *which are* of the daughters of the land, what good shall my life do me?

28

¹And Isaac called Jacob, and blessed him, and charged him, and said unto him, Thou shalt not take a wife of the daughters of Canaan. ²Arise, go to Padanaram, to the house of Bethuel thy mother's father; and take thee a wife from thence of the daughters of Laban thy mother's brother. ³And God Almighty bless thee, and make thee fruitful, and multiply thee, that thou mayest be a multitudeᵃ of people; ⁴And give thee the blessing of Abraham, to thee, and to thy seed with thee; that thou mayest inherit the land wherein thou art a stranger, which God gave unto Abraham. ⁵And Isaac sent away Jacob: and he went to Padanaram unto Laban, son of Bethuel the Syrian, the brother of Rebekah, Jacob's and Esau's mother.

⁶When Esau saw that Isaac had blessed Jacob, and sent him away to Padanaram, to take him a wife from thence; and that as he blessed him he gave him a charge, saying, Thou shalt not take a wife of the daughters of Canaan; ⁷And that Jacob obeyed his father and his mother, and was gone to Padanaram; ⁸And Esau seeing that the daughters of Canaan pleasedᵇ not Isaac his father; ⁹Then went Esau unto Ishmael, and took unto the wives which he had Mahalathᶜ the daughter of Ishmael Abraham's son, the sister of Nebajoth, to be his wife.

¹⁰And Jacob went out from Beersheba, and went toward Haranᵈ. ¹¹And he lighted upon a certain place, and tarried there all night, because the sun was set; and he took of the stones of that place, and put *them for* his pillows, and lay down in that place to sleep. ¹²And he dreamed, and behold a ladder set up on the earth, and the top of it reached to heaven: and behold the angels of God ascending and descending on it. ¹³And, behold, the LORD stood above it, and said, I *am* the LORD God of Abraham thy father, and the God of Isaac: the land whereon thou liest, to thee will I give it, and to thy seed; ¹⁴And thy seed shall be as the dust of the earth, and thou shalt spread abroad to the west, and to the east, and to the north, and to the south: and in thee and in thy seed shall all the families of the earth be blessed. ¹⁵And, behold, I *am* with thee, and will keep thee in all *places* whither thou goest, and will bring thee again into this land; for I will not leave thee, until I have done *that* which I have spoken to thee of.

¹⁶And Jacob awaked out of his sleep, and he said, Surely the LORD is in this place; and I knew *it* not. ¹⁷And he was afraid, and said, How dreadful *is* this place! this *is* none other but the house of God, and this *is* the gate of heaven. ¹⁸And Jacob rose up early in the morning, and took the stone that he had put *for* his pillows, and set it up *for*

ᵃ a multitude . . . : Heb. an assembly of people
ᵇ pleased . . . : Heb. were evil in the eyes, etc
ᶜ Mahalath: or, Bashemath
ᵈ Haran: Gr. Charran

Where Most Heartache Begins: The Lost Blessing

"Bless me, even me also, O my father." Genesis 27:34

Can you feel the anguish in the words, "Bless me, even me also"? Perhaps today you feel like Esau. For whatever reason, you didn't receive your parents' blessing—their love, warm touch, verbal praise, or unconditional acceptance. As a result, you may feel anger, resentment, or a heartfelt loneliness.

While missing this key biblical concept is often the deepest cause of past emotional hurts, *you can break free from missed blessing.* In fact, in this and the other "Breaking Free" articles in this Bible, you'll see passage after passage, tool after tool, for helping you overcome the hurt and build new, loving, lasting relationships!

To begin with, here are two specific things you can do to begin the healing process and make sure a pattern of "withholding the blessing" isn't passed down in your own relationships.

1. Become a student of your own parents' past. For most people who grow up without the "blessing," it isn't because their parents are "terrible" people. Rather, it's because their own parents never received it from *their* parents.

Often, taking the time to understand our parents' personal history can bring to light many factors around why a parent didn't give us the blessing. As a result, we can often gain a compassion, freedom, and desire to forgive we may never have thought possible.

Take Don, for example. His father abandoned his family when Don was just two months old and didn't make contact again until he was in college. Even then, times with his father were angry and uncomfortable. Never once did he feel he had received his father's "blessing."

Filled with anger and hurt, Don had a long talk with a great-uncle, someone who, for the first time, was able to fill him in on his father's past . . . a terrible history of verbal and emotional abuse. While his own father wouldn't talk about it, that uncle shared how the cruelty he'd experienced as a child had left Don's dad cut off from his feelings, afraid of intimacy, and uncomfortable with any show of warmth or affection.

While understanding these factors didn't change his father's reactions, it changed Don. For it explained why his father didn't "bless" him. It wasn't because of Don's lack of value, but because of his father's own hurt and background.

You can increase compassion and decrease anger toward a parent who never blessed you by understanding his or her past.

2. Look to your heavenly Father and spiritual family for help. As a Christian, you receive a spiritual family. Paul told Timothy, "Rebuke not an elder, but intreat him as a father; and the younger men as brethren; the elder women as mothers; the younger as sisters, with all purity" (1 Tim. 5:1-2).

While some of us may never receive our earthly parents' blessing, we can receive the hugs, verbal affirmation, and unconditional acceptance of a loving family through our church and Christian friends.

Many people find that a "spiritual father" or "spiritual mother" will give them the blessing that their parents did not. In a healthy, Bible-centered church, you can find re-parenting, emotional support, and acceptance that can help wash away hurts from the past and set up positive patterns for the future.

---

a pillar, and poured oil upon the top of it. ¹⁹And he called the name of that place Bethelᵉ: but the name of that city *was called* Luz at the first. ²⁰And Jacob vowed a vow, saying, If God will be with me, and will keep me in this way that I go, and will give me bread to eat, and raiment to put on, ²¹So that I come again to my father's house in peace; then shall the LORD be my God: ²²And this stone, which I have set *for* a pillar, shall be God's house: and of all that thou shalt give me I will surely give the tenth unto thee.

29

¹Then Jacob went on his journey, and came into the land of the people of the east. ²And he looked, and behold a well in the field, and, lo, there *were* three flocks of sheep lying by it; for out of that well they watered the flocks: and a great stone *was* upon the well's mouth. ³And thither were all the flocks gathered: and they rolled the stone from the well's mouth, and watered the sheep, and put the stone again upon the well's

mouth in his place. ⁴And Jacob said unto them, My brethren, whence *be* ye? And they said, Of Haran *are* we. ⁵And he said unto them, Know ye Laban the son of Nahor? And they said, We know *him.* ⁶And he said unto them, *Is* he well? And they said, *He is* well: and, behold, Rachel his daughter cometh with the sheep. ⁷And he said, Lo, *it is* yet high day, neither *is it* time that the cattle should be gathered together: water ye the sheep, and go *and* feed *them.* ⁸And they said, We cannot, until all the flocks be gathered together, and *till* they roll the stone from the well's mouth; then we water the sheep.

⁹And while he yet spake with them, Rachel came with her father's sheep: for she kept them. ¹⁰And it came to pass, when Jacob saw Rachel the daughter of Laban his mother's brother, and the sheep of Laban his mother's brother, that Jacob went near, and rolled the stone from the well's mouth, and watered the flock of Laban his mother's brother. ¹¹And Jacob kissed Rachel, and lifted up his voice, and wept. ¹²And Jacob told

---

ᵉ Bethel: that is, The house of God

53

Rachel that he *was* her father's brother, and that he *was* Rebekah's son: and she ran and told her father. [13]And it came to pass, when Laban heard the tidings[a] of Jacob his sister's son, that he ran to meet him, and embraced him, and kissed him, and brought him to his house. And he told Laban all these things. [14]And Laban said to him, Surely thou *art* my bone and my flesh. And he abode with him the space[b] of a month.

[15]And Laban said unto Jacob, Because thou *art* my brother, shouldest thou therefore serve me for nought? tell me, what *shall* thy wages *be?* [16]And Laban had two daughters: the name of the elder *was* Leah, and the name of the younger *was* Rachel. [17]Leah *was* tender eyed; but Rachel was beautiful and well favoured. [18]And Jacob loved Rachel; and said, I will serve thee seven years for Rachel thy younger daughter. [19]And Laban said, *It is* better that I give her to thee, than that I should give her to another man: abide with me. [20]And Jacob served seven years for Rachel; and they seemed unto him *but* a few days, for the love he had to her. [21]And Jacob said unto Laban, Give *me* my wife, for my days are fulfilled, that I may go in unto her. [22]And Laban gathered together all the men of the place, and made a feast. [23]And it came to pass in the evening, that he took Leah his daughter, and brought her to him; and he went in unto her. [24]And Laban gave unto his daughter Leah Zilpah his maid *for* an handmaid. [25]And it came to pass, that in the morning, behold, it

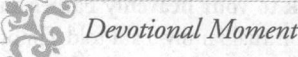

Devotional Moment

Love

29:18-28 Jacob worked seven long years to receive his bride, his love, his Rachel. Yet the years "seemed unto him but a few days." When Laban demanded seven more years, Jacob demonstrated his love with commitment, action, and sacrifice by working another seven years. Jacob surely didn't enjoy those long years of working and waiting. Yet he persisted because he was in love with Rachel, and love does not count the convenience or cost. That's the kind of love that holds families together. How can you demonstrate such love to your spouse, your children, and your parents?

was Leah: and he said to Laban, What *is* this thou hast done unto me? did not I serve with thee for Rachel? wherefore then hast thou beguiled me? [26]And Laban said, It must not be so done in our country[c], to give the younger before the firstborn. [27]Fulfil her week, and we will give thee this also for the service which thou shalt serve with me yet seven other years. [28]And Jacob did so, and fulfilled her week: and he gave him Rachel his daughter to wife also. [29]And Laban gave to Rachel his daughter Bilhah his handmaid to be her maid. [30]And he went in also unto Rachel, and he loved also Rachel more than Leah, and served with him yet seven other years.

[31]And when the LORD saw that Leah *was* hated, he opened her womb: but Rachel *was* barren. [32]And Leah conceived, and bare a son, and she called his name Reuben[d]: for she said, Surely

[a] tidings: Heb. hearing
[b] the space . . . : Heb. a month of days
[c] country: Heb. place
[d] Reuben: that is, See a son

the LORD hath looked upon my afflic-tion; now therefore my husband will love me. ³³And she conceived again, and bare a son; and said, Because the LORD hath heard that I *was* hated, he hath therefore given me this *son* also: and she called his name Simeonᵉ. ³⁴And she conceived again, and bare a son; and said, Now this time will my hus-band be joined unto me, because I have born him three sons: therefore was his name called Leviᶠ. ³⁵And she conceived again, and bare a son: and she said, Now will I praise the LORD: therefore she called his name Judahᵍ; and left bearing.

30

¹And when Rachel saw that she bare Ja-cob no children, Rachel envied her sis-ter; and said unto Jacob, Give me chil-dren, or else I die. ²And Jacob's anger was kindled against Rachel: and he said, *Am* I in God's stead, who hath withheld from thee the fruit of the womb? ³And she said, Behold my maid Bilhah, go in unto her; and she shall bear upon my knees, that I may also have children by her. ⁴And she gave him Bilhah her handmaid to wife: and Jacob went in unto her. ⁵And Bilhah con-ceived, and bare Jacob a son. ⁶And Rachel said, God hath judged me, and hath also heard my voice, and hath given me a son: therefore called she his name Danᵃ. ⁷And Bilhah Rachel's maid

conceived again, and bare Jacob a sec-ond son. ⁸And Rachel said, With greatᵇ wrestlings have I wrestled with my sis-ter, and I have prevailed: and she called his name Naphtali. ⁹When Leah saw that she had left bearing, she took Zil-pah her maid, and gave her Jacob to wife. ¹⁰And Zilpah Leah's maid bare Ja-cob a son. ¹¹And Leah said, A troop cometh: and she called his name Gadᶜ. ¹²And Zilpah Leah's maid bare Jacob a second son. ¹³And Leah said, Happy am I, for the daughters will call me blessed: and she called his name Asher.

¹⁴And Reuben went in the days of wheat harvest, and found mandrakes in the field, and brought them unto his mother Leah. Then Rachel said to

---

Devotional Moment

Adult Children

30:1-3 Jacob's response to his wife Rachel's infertility was quite different from his father's (Isaac's) reaction to Rebekah's infertility. Isaac prayed for his wife; Jacob "flew into a rage." Isaac had been a good example to Jacob, yet that didn't prevent Jacob from being his own unique person once he was an adult. Parents of adult children sometimes ask themselves, "Where did we go wrong?" But we must remember that once our children grow up, they are responsible for making their own choices. You may grieve over some of your children's actions, but don't take responsibility for what your adult children do. They are accountable to God.

ᵉ Simeon: that is, Hearing
ᶠ Levi: that is, Joined
ᵍ Judah: that is, Praise
ᵃ Dan: that is, Judging
ᵇ great . . . : Heb. wrestlings of God
ᶜ Gad: that is, A troop, or, company

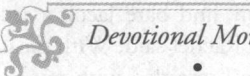

Devotional Moment

Waiting

30:22-24 When Rachel first realized that she, unlike her sister Leah, was not going to have a child, she became frantic and angry. Jealous of her sister, she went so far as to give her servant Bilhah to Jacob so she could have a child through her. But then Leah stopped having children, and she gave *her* servant to Jacob. Back and forth they volleyed, all because of jealousy. They could not bear to wait for God's timing. Sometimes God doesn't answer our prayers in our time frame. Whether your desire is for a child, a new job, a new home, or something else, pray and wait for God's timing. Your reaction to the delay shows how much you trust God. Meanwhile, thank him and praise him for bringing all good gifts in their perfect time.

Leah, Give me, I pray thee, of thy son's mandrakes. ¹⁵And she said unto her, *Is it* a small matter that thou hast taken my husband? and wouldest thou take away my son's mandrakes also? And Rachel said, Therefore he shall lie with thee to night for thy son's mandrakes. ¹⁶And Jacob came out of the field in the evening, and Leah went out to meet him, and said, Thou must come in unto me; for surely I have hired thee with my son's mandrakes. And he lay with her that night. ¹⁷And God hearkened unto Leah, and she conceived, and bare Jacob the fifth son. ¹⁸And Leah said, God hath given me my hire, because I have given my maiden to my husband: and she called his name Issachar^d. ¹⁹And Leah conceived again,

and bare Jacob the sixth son. ²⁰And Leah said, God hath endued me *with* a good dowry; now will my husband dwell with me, because I have born him six sons: and she called his name Zebulun^e. ²¹And afterwards she bare a daughter, and called her name Dinah^f. ²²And God remembered Rachel, and God hearkened to her, and opened her womb. ²³And she conceived, and bare a son; and said, God hath taken away my reproach: ²⁴And she called his name Joseph^g; and said, The LORD shall add to me another son.

²⁵And it came to pass, when Rachel had born Joseph, that Jacob said unto Laban, Send me away, that I may go unto mine own place, and to my country. ²⁶Give *me* my wives and my children, for whom I have served thee, and

Devotional Moment

Home Sweet Home

30:30 Jacob wanted to establish his own household, independent of Laban, but Laban resisted. Jacob did not need to "move out" so much as he needed to establish his own home; his own household identity. In tough times it may be helpful for newlyweds to depend on their parents; once the new couple leaves home, it is also good to keep close ties. But there must come a time when a man leaves his parents and cleaves to his wife, both materially and emotionally. Have you given your family a home they can call their own? As your family grows, focus your energies on establishing family traditions, vacations, and rituals that you and your family enjoy alone.

---

^d Issachar: that is, An hire
^e Zebulun: that is, Dwelling: Gr. Zabulon
^f Dinah: that is Judgment
^g Joseph: that is, Adding

Releasing Your Child

by Carol Kuykendall

While coming out of church one Sunday morning, I ran into my friend Sue. Her eyes suddenly filled with tears when I asked how she was doing.

"I know this sounds silly, but my 'baby' started kindergarten this week and I feel sad . . . like this is the beginning of the end," she confessed. "I can't stand the thought of our kids leaving home someday."

"I understand," I told her, because I used to dread that painful thought as a young mother. I remember vividly my own feelings of sadness the day the big yellow school bus swallowed up my "baby" and lumbered down the road toward kindergarten.

The story of Jacob and Laban in Genesis 29–31 illustrates two orderly steps that we can apply to the process of releasing children. Jacob, son of Isaac and Rebekah, traveled four hundred miles to Haran from his home in search of a wife. There he became part of his uncle Laban's family for twenty years, a time of preparation and labor, before establishing his own family and independence.

A time to prepare. God gives us the structure of family and a time to rear our children, preparing them to cope on their own in the world. Just as Jacob spent twenty years with Laban, working to earn two wives and a flock of animals, so our children live within our family structures for about eighteen years, earning their independence. During this period, both children and parents undergo a process of change and growth. Children enter our families at birth as totally helpless and dependent little babies. We do everything they need—feed, dress, change, bathe, burp, and protect them. When they are toddlers, we tell them what to do and when to do it. Yet by the time they leave home, they should be totally independent and able to care for themselves. This means that during those eighteen years, we engage in an orderly process of transferring responsibility and control from us to them. In doing so, we build their confidence in their ability to make decisions and to think for themselves. A two-year-old chooses his shirt from the drawer; a sixteen-year-old chooses a new sweater at the store, based on her budget and her needs.

Increased freedom brings increased responsibility. A seventh grader depends on his parents for transportation after a school dance. They are still responsible for getting him home at a certain time. But a sixteen-year-old starting to drive suddenly realizes she is responsible for getting herself home before her curfew. As she nears the point of leaving home, she realizes that the person in charge of me . . . is me.

A time to let go. After laboring for his father-in-law and earning his independence, Jacob knew it was time to be off on his own, with his own family. Laban finally consented, though reluctantly.

I know that feeling. As Derek, our oldest, began considering his choices for college, he felt drawn to those far away from home. "Please don't go," my heart cried, but I knew my resistant response was aimed more at meeting my needs than his.

As his high school graduation approached, I gathered up all his school photos, from preschool straight through to his senior portrait, and pasted them in order on a piece of poster board that I hung in the front hall. The collage showed the dramatic progression of a little boy growing into a man, which helped me sort through my feelings about his leaving. The child I longed to cuddle and hold on to was the chubby little preschool cherub who still needed my protection. But the finished product—the picture of the eighteen-year-old senior— had a look of grown-up confidence and eagerness. I didn't want to hold on to that person. I wanted to applaud his achievement of maturity and cheer him on as he tested his wings. He was ready—and now I was ready—to embark on an exciting new chapter in the life of our family.

As I hugged my friend Sue on the steps of the church that morning, I tried to reassure her. "Trust God," I offered simply. "He will prepare both you and your children, and when it is time, you will be ready. For now, don't let your worries rob you of enjoying today's irretrievable moments."

DIGGING DEEPER

1. In Ecclesiastes 3, the preacher assures us "to every thing there is a season" and then lists several examples. Which pertain to the orderly process of releasing our children—and how?

2. In Psalm 127:3 the psalmist refers to children as a reward. Some of us subtly see our children as our *possessions*. What is the difference?

3. Abraham longed for his son Isaac for many years. No wonder his son became the idol of his heart. What did God intend Abraham to learn about "letting go" on Mount Moriah (Gen. 22)?

let me go: for thou knowest my service which I have done thee. ²⁷And Laban said unto him, I pray thee, if I have found favour in thine eyes, *tarry: for* I have learned by experience that the LORD hath blessed me for thy sake. ²⁸And he said, Appoint me thy wages, and I will give *it*. ²⁹And he said unto him, Thou knowest how I have served thee, and how thy cattle was with me. ³⁰For *it was* little which thou hadst before I *came*, and it is *now* increased[h] unto a multitude; and the LORD hath blessed thee since my coming: and now when shall I provide for mine own house also? ³¹And he said, What shall I give thee? And Jacob said, Thou shalt not give me any thing: if thou wilt do this thing for me, I will again feed *and* keep thy flock: ³²I will pass through all thy flock to day, removing from thence all the speckled and spotted cattle, and all the brown cattle among the sheep, and the spotted and speckled among the goats: and *of such* shall be my hire. ³³So shall my righteousness answer for me in time[i] to come, when it shall come for my hire before thy face: every one that *is* not speckled and spotted among the goats, and brown among the sheep, that shall be counted stolen with me. ³⁴And Laban said, Behold, I would it might be according to thy word. ³⁵And he removed that day the he goats that were ringstraked and spotted, and all the she goats that were speckled and spotted, *and* every one that had *some* white in it, and all the brown among the sheep, and gave *them* into the hand of his sons. ³⁶And he set three days' journey betwixt himself and Jacob: and Jacob fed the rest of Laban's flocks.

---

[h] increased: Heb. broken forth
[i] in time . . . : Heb. to morrow

³⁷And Jacob took him rods of green poplar, and of the hazel and chesnut tree; and pilled white strakes in them, and made the white appear which *was* in the rods. ³⁸And he set the rods which he had pilled before the flocks in the gutters in the watering troughs when the flocks came to drink, that they should conceive when they came to drink. ³⁹And the flocks conceived before the rods, and brought forth cattle ringstraked, speckled, and spotted. ⁴⁰And Jacob did separate the lambs, and set the faces of the flocks toward the ringstraked, and all the brown in the flock of Laban; and he put his own flocks by themselves, and put them not unto Laban's cattle. ⁴¹And it came to pass, whensoever the stronger cattle did conceive, that Jacob laid the rods before the eyes of the cattle in the gutters, that they might conceive among the rods. ⁴²But when the cattle were feeble, he put *them* not in: so the feebler were Laban's, and the stronger Jacob's. ⁴³And the man increased exceedingly, and had much cattle, and maidservants, and menservants, and camels, and asses.

31

¹And he heard the words of Laban's sons, saying, Jacob hath taken away all that *was* our father's; and of *that* which *was* our father's hath he gotten all this glory. ²And Jacob beheld the countenance of Laban, and, behold, it *was* not toward him as beforeª. ³And the LORD said unto Jacob, Return unto the land of thy fathers, and to thy kindred; and I will be

---

Devotional Moment

•

Jealousy

31:1-3 Laban created a lot of problems by the way he raised his children: He taught them to be jealous of each other. From watching him, they learned how to use other people. As long as they had the advantage, everything ran smoothly. Then Jacob began to prosper, and they felt threatened. Jealousy can divide families more thoroughly than almost any other force. When jealousy strikes, ask yourself what you can learn from the person you envy. Pray for that person and thank God for his or her giftedness. Turn feelings of jealousy into a personal challenge.

---

with thee. ⁴And Jacob sent and called Rachel and Leah to the field unto his flock, ⁵And said unto them, I see your father's countenance, that it *is* not toward me as before; but the God of my father hath been with me. ⁶And ye know that with all my power I have served your father. ⁷And your father hath deceived me, and changed my wages ten times; but God suffered him not to hurt me. ⁸If he said thus, The speckled shall be thy wages; then all the cattle bare speckled: and if he said thus, The ringstraked shall be thy hire; then bare all the cattle ringstraked. ⁹Thus God hath taken away the cattle of your father, and given *them* to me. ¹⁰And it came to pass at the time that the cattle conceived, that I lifted up mine eyes, and saw in a dream, and, behold, the ramsᵇ which leaped upon the cattle *were* ringstraked, speckled, and grisled. ¹¹And the angel of God spake unto me in a dream, *saying*, Jacob: And I said, Here *am* I. ¹²And he said, Lift up now thine eyes, and see, all the rams

---

ª as before: Heb. as yesterday and the day before
ᵇ rams: or, he goats

which leap upon the cattle *are* ringstraked, speckled, and grisled: for I have seen all that Laban doeth unto thee. ¹³I *am* the God of Bethel, where thou anointedst the pillar, *and* where thou vowedst a vow unto me: now arise, get thee out from this land, and return unto the land of thy kindred. ¹⁴And Rachel and Leah answered and said unto him, *Is there* yet any portion or inheritance for us in our father's house? ¹⁵Are we not counted of him strangers? for he hath sold us, and hath quite devoured also our money. ¹⁶For all the riches which God hath taken from our father, that *is* ours, and our children's: now then, whatsoever God hath said unto thee, do.

¹⁷Then Jacob rose up, and set his sons and his wives upon camels; ¹⁸And he carried away all his cattle, and all his goods which he had gotten, the cattle of his getting, which he had gotten in Padanaram, for to go to Isaac his father in the land of Canaan. ¹⁹And Laban went to shear his sheep: and Rachel had stolen the images[c] that *were* her father's. ²⁰And Jacob stole away unawares[d] to Laban the Syrian, in that he told him not that he fled. ²¹So he fled with all that he had; and he rose up, and passed over the river, and set his face *toward* the mount Gilead. ²²And it was told Laban on the third day that Jacob was fled. ²³And he took his brethren with him, and pursued after him seven days' journey; and they overtook him in the mount Gilead. ²⁴And God came to Laban the Syrian in a dream by night, and said unto him, Take heed that thou speak not to Jacob either good or bad.

²⁵Then Laban overtook Jacob. Now Jacob had pitched his tent in the mount: and Laban with his brethren pitched in the mount of Gilead. ²⁶And Laban said to Jacob, What hast thou done, that thou hast stolen away unawares to me, and carried away my daughters, as captives *taken* with the sword? ²⁷Wherefore didst thou flee away secretly, and steal away from me; and didst not tell me, that I might have sent thee away with mirth, and with songs, with tabret, and with harp? ²⁸And hast not suffered me to kiss my sons and my daughters? thou hast now done foolishly in *so* doing. ²⁹It is in the power of my hand to do you hurt: but the God of your father spake unto me yesternight, saying, Take thou heed that thou speak not to Jacob either good or bad. ³⁰And now, *though* thou wouldest needs be gone, because thou sore longedst after thy father's house, *yet* wherefore hast thou stolen my gods? ³¹And Jacob answered and said to Laban, Because I was afraid: for I said, Peradventure thou wouldest take by force thy daughters from me. ³²With whomsoever thou findest thy gods, let him not live: before our brethren discern thou what *is* thine with me, and take *it* to thee. For Jacob knew not that Rachel had stolen them. ³³And Laban went into Jacob's tent, and into Leah's tent, and into the two maidservants' tents; but he found *them* not. Then went he out of Leah's tent, and entered into Rachel's tent. ³⁴Now Rachel had taken the images, and put them in the camel's furniture, and sat upon them.

---

[c] images: Heb. teraphim
[d] unawares . . . : Heb. the heart of Laban

And Laban searched^e all the tent, but found *them* not. ³⁵And she said to her father, Let it not displease my lord that I cannot rise up before thee; for the custom of women *is* upon me. And he searched, but found not the images.

³⁶And Jacob was wroth, and chode with Laban: and Jacob answered and said to Laban, What *is* my trespass? what *is* my sin, that thou hast so hotly pursued after me? ³⁷Whereas thou hast searched^f all my stuff, what hast thou found of all thy household stuff? set *it* here before my brethren and thy brethren, that they may judge betwixt us both. ³⁸This twenty years *have* I *been* with thee; thy ewes and thy she goats have not cast their young, and the rams of thy flock have I not eaten. ³⁹That which was torn *of beasts* I brought not unto thee; I bare the loss of it; of my hand didst thou require it, *whether* stolen by day, or stolen by night. ⁴⁰*Thus* I was; in the day the drought consumed me, and the frost by night; and my sleep departed from mine eyes. ⁴¹Thus have I been twenty years in thy house; I served thee fourteen years for thy two daughters, and six years for thy cattle: and thou hast changed my wages ten times. ⁴²Except the God of my father, the God of Abraham, and the fear of Isaac, had been with me, surely thou hadst sent me away now empty. God hath seen mine affliction and the labour of my hands, and rebuked *thee* yesternight.

⁴³And Laban answered and said unto Jacob, *These* daughters *are* my daughters, and *these* children *are* my children, and *these* cattle *are* my cattle, and all that thou seest *is* mine: and what can I do this day unto these my daughters, or unto their children which they have born? ⁴⁴Now therefore come thou, let us make a covenant, I and thou; and let it be for a witness between me and thee. ⁴⁵And Jacob took a stone, and set it up *for* a pillar. ⁴⁶And Jacob said unto his brethren, Gather stones; and they took stones, and made an heap: and they did eat there upon the heap. ⁴⁷And Laban called it Jegarsahadutha^g: but Jacob called it Galeed. ⁴⁸And Laban said, This heap *is* a witness between me and thee this day. Therefore was the name of it called Galeed; ⁴⁹And Mizpah^h; for he said, The LORD watch between me and thee, when we are absent one from another. ⁵⁰If thou shalt afflict my daughters, or if thou shalt take *other* wives beside my daughters, no man *is* with us; see, God *is* witness betwixt me and thee. ⁵¹And Laban said to Jacob, Behold this heap, and behold *this* pillar, which I have cast betwixt me and thee; ⁵²This heap *be* witness, and *this* pillar *he* witness, that I will not pass over this heap to thee, and that thou shalt not pass over this heap and this pillar unto me, for harm. ⁵³The God of Abraham, and the God of Nahor, the God of their father, judge betwixt us. And Jacob sware by the fear of his father Isaac. ⁵⁴Then Jacob offered^i sacrifice upon the mount,

---

^e searched: Heb. felt
^f searched: Heb. felt
^g Jegarsahadutha: that is, The heap of witness, Chaldee
^h Mizpah: that is, A beacon, or, watchtower
^i offered . . . : or, killed beasts

and called his brethren to eat bread: and they did eat bread, and tarried all night in the mount. ⁵⁵And early in the morning Laban rose up, and kissed his sons and his daughters, and blessed them: and Laban departed, and returned unto his place.

32

¹And Jacob went on his way, and the angels of God met him. ²And when Jacob saw them, he said, This *is* God's host: and he called the name of that place Mahanaim^a.

³And Jacob sent messengers before him to Esau his brother unto the land of Seir, the country^b of Edom. ⁴And he commanded them, saying, Thus shall ye speak unto my lord Esau; Thy servant Jacob saith thus, I have sojourned with Laban, and stayed there until now: ⁵And I have oxen, and asses, flocks, and menservants, and womenservants: and I have sent to tell my lord, that I may find grace in thy sight. ⁶And the messengers returned to Jacob, saying, We came to thy brother Esau, and also he cometh to meet thee, and four hundred men with him. ⁷Then Jacob was greatly afraid and distressed: and he divided the people that *was* with him, and the flocks, and herds, and the camels, into two bands; ⁸And said, If Esau come to the one company, and smite it, then the other company which is left shall escape.

⁹And Jacob said, O God of my father Abraham, and God of my father Isaac, the LORD which saidst unto me,

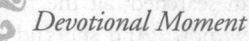

Devotional Moment
•
Reconciliation
32:3, 9-12 Jacob had just ended an extremely stressful time of living twenty years with his father-in-law; now he had to face his estranged brother Esau. This was the same brother he had cheated out of a birthright and blessing twenty years before. The last Jacob had heard, Esau wanted to kill him. Jacob had dreaded leaving Laban, but he was terrified about meeting his brother. So Jacob adopted two important strategies: (1) He sent a friendly and hopeful message to Esau; and (2) he prayed as hard as he could. When we get angry at each other, remember: (1) A cooling-off period often helps; (2) to begin the peacemaking, someone has to take initiative to break the ice; (3) we must include God in every part of our family life, even the hard times.

Return unto thy country, and to thy kindred, and I will deal well with thee: ¹⁰I am not worthy of the least of all the mercies, and of all the truth, which thou hast shewed unto thy servant; for with my staff I passed over this Jordan; and now I am become two bands. ¹¹Deliver me, I pray thee, from the hand of my brother, from the hand of Esau: for I fear him, lest he will come and smite me, *and* the mother with^c the children. ¹²And thou saidst, I will surely do thee good, and make thy seed as the sand of the sea, which cannot be numbered for multitude.

¹³And he lodged there that same night; and took of that which came to his hand a present for Esau his brother; ¹⁴Two hundred she goats, and twenty he goats, two hundred ewes, and twenty

^a Mahanaim: that is, Two hosts, or, camps
^b country: Heb. field
^c with: Heb. upon

rams, ¹⁵Thirty milch camels with their colts, forty kine, and ten bulls, twenty she asses, and ten foals. ¹⁶And he delivered *them* into the hand of his servants, every drove by themselves; and said unto his servants, Pass over before me, and put a space betwixt drove and drove. ¹⁷And he commanded the foremost, saying, When Esau my brother meeteth thee, and asketh thee, saying, Whose *art* thou? and whither goest thou? and whose *are* these before thee? ¹⁸Then thou shalt say, *They be* thy servant Jacob's; it *is* a present sent unto my lord Esau: and, behold, also he *is* behind us. ¹⁹And so commanded he the second, and the third, and all that followed the droves, saying, On this manner shall ye speak unto Esau, when ye find him. ²⁰And say ye moreover, Behold, thy servant Jacob *is* behind us. For he said, I will appease him with the present that goeth before me, and afterward I will see his face; peradventure he will accept of me^d. ²¹So went the present over before him: and himself lodged that night in the company. ²²And he rose up that night, and took his two wives, and his two womenservants, and his eleven sons, and passed over the ford Jabbok. ²³And he took them, and sent them over the brook, and sent over that he had.

²⁴And Jacob was left alone; and there wrestled a man with him until the breaking^e of the day. ²⁵And when he saw that he prevailed not against him, he touched the hollow of his thigh; and the hollow of Jacob's thigh was out of joint, as he wrestled with him. ²⁶And he said, Let me go, for the day breaketh. And he said, I will not let thee go, except thou bless me. ²⁷And he said unto him, What *is* thy name? And he said, Jacob. ²⁸And he said, Thy name shall be called no more Jacob, but Israel^f: for as a prince hast thou power with God and with men, and hast prevailed. ²⁹And Jacob asked *him*, and said, Tell *me*, I pray thee, thy name. And he said, Wherefore *is* it *that* thou dost ask after my name? And he blessed him there. ³⁰And Jacob called the name of the place Peniel^g: for I have seen God face to face, and my life is preserved. ³¹And as he passed over Penuel the sun rose upon him, and he halted upon his thigh. ³²Therefore the children of Israel eat not *of* the sinew which shrank, which *is* upon the hollow of the thigh, unto this day: because he touched the hollow of Jacob's thigh in the sinew that shrank.

33

¹And Jacob lifted up his eyes, and looked, and, behold, Esau came, and with him four hundred men. And he divided the children unto Leah, and unto Rachel, and unto the two handmaids. ²And he put the handmaids and their children foremost, and Leah and her children after, and Rachel and Joseph hindermost. ³And he passed over before them, and bowed himself to the ground seven times, until he came near to his brother. ⁴And Esau ran to meet him, and embraced him, and fell

---

^d of me: Heb. my face
^e breaking . . . : Heb. ascending of the morning
^f Israel: that is, A prince of God
^g Peniel: that is, The face of God

Devotional Moment

Forgiveness

33:1-11 Imagine how surprised Jacob must have felt when he finally met Esau face-to-face. Esau had a legitimate grudge against his brother over land and money. Yet he forgave Jacob, and the two restored their relationship. Even in close families, conflicts over money or territory can divide deeply. These kinds of conflicts can go on for years if the cycle of anger is not broken. When family conflicts do not involve physical or sexual abuse, be willing to restore the relationship with one who has offended you.

on his neck, and kissed him: and they wept.

⁵And he lifted up his eyes, and saw the women and the children; and said, Who *are* those with thee? And he said, The children which God hath graciously given thy servant. ⁶Then the handmaidens came near, they and their children, and they bowed themselves. ⁷And Leah also with her children came near, and bowed themselves: and after came Joseph near and Rachel, and they bowed themselves. ⁸And he said, What *meanest* thou by all this drove[a] which I met? And he said, *These are* to find grace in the sight of my lord. ⁹And Esau said, I have enough, my brother; keep that thou hast unto thyself. ¹⁰And Jacob said, Nay, I pray thee, if now I have found grace in thy sight, then receive

my present at my hand: for therefore I have seen thy face, as though I had seen the face of God, and thou wast pleased with me. ¹¹Take, I pray thee, my blessing that is brought to thee; because God hath dealt graciously with me, and because I have enough[b]. And he urged him, and he took *it.* ¹²And he said, Let us take our journey, and let us go, and I will go before thee. ¹³And he said unto him, My lord knoweth that the children *are* tender, and the flocks and herds with young *are* with me: and if men should overdrive them one day, all the flock will die. ¹⁴Let my lord, I pray thee, pass over before his servant: and I will lead on softly, according as the cattle that goeth before me and the children be able to endure, until I come unto my lord unto Seir. ¹⁵And Esau said, Let me now leave[c] with thee *some* of the folk that *are* with me. And he said, What needeth it? let me find grace in the sight of my lord.

¹⁶So Esau returned that day on his way unto Seir. ¹⁷And Jacob journeyed to Succoth[d], and built him an house, and made booths for his cattle: therefore the name of the place is called Succoth. ¹⁸And Jacob came to Shalem, a city of Shechem[e], which *is* in the land of Canaan, when he came from Padanaram; and pitched his tent before the city. ¹⁹And he bought a parcel of a field, where he had spread his tent, at the hand of the children of Hamor[f],

---

[a] What . . . : Heb. What is all this band to thee?
[b] enough: Heb. all things
[c] leave: Heb. set, or, place
[d] Succoth: that is, Booths
[e] Shechem: Gr. Sychem
[f] Hamor: Gr. Emmor

Shechem's father, for an hundred pieces of money. ²⁰And he erected there an altar, and called it Elelohe-Israel⁸.

34

¹And Dinah the daughter of Leah, which she bare unto Jacob, went out to see the daughters of the land. ²And when Shechem the son of Hamor the Hivite, prince of the country, saw her, he took her, and lay with her, and defiled her. ³And his soul clave unto Dinah the daughter of Jacob, and he loved the damsel, and spake kindly⁴ unto the damsel. ⁴And Shechem spake unto his father Hamor, saying, Get me this damsel to wife. ⁵And Jacob heard that he had defiled Dinah his daughter: now his sons were with his cattle in the field: and Jacob held his peace until they were come.

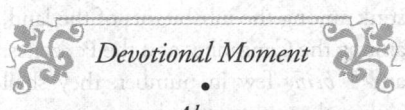

Devotional Moment

Abuse

34:1-4 If Shechem had really loved Dinah, he would have treated her with respect. Instead, he selfishly satisfied his own craving, violating Dinah and dishonoring her family. Sexual abuse is one of the ugliest crimes a person can commit against another. It takes away something priceless without that person's permission. It doesn't just hurt the other person's body; it also wounds the spirit and mind in ways that may never heal. People learn to respect others, or not to respect others, in the home. They learn it from the way Mom and Dad treat each other, from the way they treat their children, and from the way they let their children treat each other. Let respect for one another be an unbreakable rule in your home.

⁶And Hamor the father of Shechem went out unto Jacob to commune with him. ⁷And the sons of Jacob came out of the field when they heard *it*: and the men were grieved, and they were very wroth, because he had wrought folly in Israel in lying with Jacob's daughter; which thing ought not to be done. ⁸And Hamor communed with them, saying, The soul of my son Shechem longeth for your daughter: I pray you give her him to wife. ⁹And make ye marriages with us, *and* give your daughters unto us, and take our daughters unto you. ¹⁰And ye shall dwell with us: and the land shall be before you; dwell and trade ye therein, and get you possessions therein. ¹¹And Shechem said unto her father and unto her brethren, Let me find grace in your eyes, and what ye shall say unto me I will give. ¹²Ask me never so much dowry and gift, and I will give according as ye shall say unto me: but give me the damsel to wife. ¹³And the sons of Jacob answered Shechem and Hamor his father deceitfully, and said, because he had defiled Dinah their sister: ¹⁴And they said unto them, We cannot do this thing, to give our sister to one that is uncircumcised; for that *were* a reproach unto us: ¹⁵But in this will we consent unto you: If ye will be as we *be*, that every male of you be circumcised; ¹⁶Then will we give our daughters unto you, and we will take your daughters to us, and we will dwell with you, and we will become one people. ¹⁷But if ye will not hearken unto us, to be circumcised; then will we take our daughter, and we will be gone.

---

⁸ Elelohe-Israel: that is God the God of Israel
ᵃ kindly . . . : Heb. to the heart of the damsel

Devotional Moment

Temper

34:24-31 In defending Dinah's honor, Levi and Simeon went way beyond revenge. They went to the point of senseless killing, pillaging, and kidnapping—all in the name of "justice." Many, many innocent people suffered because of their uncontrolled anger and pent-up frustration. Their father Jacob eventually cursed them (see 49:5-7). When family members are hurt, it is easy to feel strongly about defending them. And in many cases we may be called to defend them (as in Prov. 31:8-9). But our anger must never become an outlet for unbridled rage. When you feel the need to defend someone, be angry—but control how you respond.

---

¹⁸And their words pleased Hamor, and Shechem Hamor's son. ¹⁹And the young man deferred not to do the thing, because he had delight in Jacob's daughter: and he *was* more honourable than all the house of his father. ²⁰And Hamor and Shechem his son came unto the gate of their city, and communed with the men of their city, saying, ²¹These men *are* peaceable with us; therefore let them dwell in the land, and trade therein; for the land, behold, *it is* large enough for them; let us take their daughters to us for wives, and let us give them our daughters. ²²Only herein will the men consent unto us for to dwell with us, to be one people, if every male among us be circumcised, as they *are* circumcised. ²³*Shall* not their cattle and their substance and every beast of theirs *be* ours? only let us consent unto them, and they will dwell with us. ²⁴And unto Hamor and unto Shechem his son hearkened all that

went out of the gate of his city; and every male was circumcised, all that went out of the gate of his city.

²⁵And it came to pass on the third day, when they were sore, that two of the sons of Jacob, Simeon and Levi, Dinah's brethren, took each man his sword, and came upon the city boldly, and slew all the males. ²⁶And they slew Hamor and Shechem his son with the edge[b] of the sword, and took Dinah out of Shechem's house, and went out. ²⁷The sons of Jacob came upon the slain, and spoiled the city, because they had defiled their sister. ²⁸They took their sheep, and their oxen, and their asses, and that which *was* in the city, and that which *was* in the field, ²⁹And all their wealth, and all their little ones, and their wives took they captive, and spoiled even all that *was* in the house. ³⁰And Jacob said to Simeon and Levi, Ye have troubled me to make me to stink among the inhabitants of the land, among the Canaanites and the Perizzites: and I *being* few in number, they shall gather themselves together against me, and slay me; and I shall be destroyed, I and my house. ³¹And they said, Should he deal with our sister as with an harlot?

35

¹And God said unto Jacob, Arise, go up to Bethel, and dwell there: and make there an altar unto God, that appeared unto thee when thou fleddest from the face of Esau thy brother. ²Then Jacob said unto his household, and to all that *were* with him, Put away the strange gods that *are* among you, and be clean, and change your garments: ³And let us arise, and go up to Bethel; and I will make

---

[b] edge: Heb. mouth

there an altar unto God, who answered me in the day of my distress, and was with me in the way which I went. ⁴And they gave unto Jacob all the strange gods which *were* in their hand, and *all their* earrings which *were* in their ears; and Jacob hid them under the oak which *was* by Shechem. ⁵And they journeyed: and the terror of God was upon the cities that *were* round about them, and they did not pursue after the sons of Jacob.

⁶So Jacob came to Luz, which *is* in the land of Canaan, that *is*, Bethel, he and all the people that *were* with him. ⁷And he built there an altar, and called the place Elbethelª: because there God appeared unto him, when he fled from the face of his brother. ⁸But Deborah Rebekah's nurse died, and she was buried beneath Bethel under an oak: and the name of it was called Allonbachuthᵇ. ⁹And God appeared unto Jacob again, when he came out of Padanaram, and blessed him. ¹⁰And God said unto him, Thy name *is* Jacob: thy name shall not be called any more Jacob, but Israel shall be thy name: and he called his name Israel. ¹¹And God said unto him, I *am* God Almighty: be fruitful and multiply; a nation and a company of nations shall be of thee, and kings shall come out of thy loins; ¹²And the land which I gave Abraham and Isaac, to thee I will give it, and to thy seed after thee will I give the land. ¹³And God went up from him in the place where he talked with him. ¹⁴And Jacob set up a pillar in the place where he talked with him, *even* a pillar of stone: and he poured a drink offering thereon, and he poured oil thereon. ¹⁵And Jacob called the name of the place where God spake with him, Bethel.

¹⁶And they journeyed from Bethel; and there was but a littleᶜ way to come to Ephrath: and Rachel travailed, and she had hard labour. ¹⁷And it came to pass, when she was in hard labour, that the midwife said unto her, Fear not; thou shalt have this son also. ¹⁸And it came to pass, as her soul was in departing, (for she died) that she called his name Benoniᵈ: but his father called him Benjamin. ¹⁹And Rachel died, and was buried in the way to Ephrath, which *is* Bethlehem. ²⁰And Jacob set a pillar upon her grave: that *is* the pillar of Rachel's grave unto this day.

²¹And Israel journeyed, and spread his tent beyond the tower of Edar. ²²And it came to pass, when Israel dwelt in that land, that Reuben went and lay with Bilhah his father's concubine: and Israel

---

ª Elbethel: that is, The God of Bethel
ᵇ Allonbachuth: that is, The oak of weeping
ᶜ a little . . . : Heb. a little piece of ground
ᵈ Benoni: that is, The son of my sorrow

heard *it*. Now the sons of Jacob were twelve: ²³The sons of Leah; Reuben, Jacob's firstborn, and Simeon, and Levi, and Judah, and Issachar, and Zebulun: ²⁴The sons of Rachel; Joseph, and Benjamin: ²⁵And the sons of Bilhah, Rachel's handmaid; Dan, and Naphtali: ²⁶And the sons of Zilpah, Leah's handmaid; Gad, and Asher: these *are* the sons of Jacob, which were born to him in Padanaram. ²⁷And Jacob came unto Isaac his father unto Mamre, unto the city of Arbah, which *is* Hebron, where Abraham and Isaac sojourned. ²⁸And the days of Isaac were an hundred and fourscore years. ²⁹And Isaac gave up the ghost, and died, and was gathered unto his people, *being* old and full of days: and his sons Esau and Jacob buried him.

36

¹Now these *are* the generations of Esau, who *is* Edom. ²Esau took his wives of the daughters of Canaan; Adah the daughter of Elon the Hittite, and Aholibamah the daughter of Anah the daughter of Zibeon the Hivite; ³And Bashemath Ishmael's daughter, sister of Nebajoth. ⁴And Adah bare to Esau Eliphaz; and Bashemath bare Reuel; ⁵And Aholibamah bare Jeush, and Jaalam, and Korah: these *are* the sons of Esau, which were born unto him in the land of Canaan. ⁶And Esau took his wives, and his sons, and his daughters, and all the persons[a] of his house, and his cattle, and all his beasts, and all his substance, which he had got in the land of Canaan; and went into the country from the face of his brother Jacob. ⁷For their riches were more than that they might dwell together; and the land wherein they were strangers could not bear them because of their cattle. ⁸Thus dwelt Esau in mount Seir: Esau *is* Edom.

⁹And these *are* the generations of Esau the father of the Edomites[b] in mount Seir: ¹⁰These *are* the names of Esau's sons; Eliphaz the son of Adah the wife of Esau, Reuel the son of Bashemath the wife of Esau. ¹¹And the sons of Eliphaz were Teman, Omar, Zepho[c], and Gatam, and Kenaz. ¹²And Timna was concubine to Eliphaz Esau's son; and she bare to Eliphaz Amalek: these *were* the sons of Adah Esau's wife. ¹³And these *are* the sons of Reuel; Nahath, and Zerah, Shammah, and Mizzah: these were the sons of Bashemath Esau's wife. ¹⁴And these were the sons of Aholibamah, the daughter of Anah the daughter of Zibeon, Esau's wife: and she bare to Esau Jeush, and Jaalam, and Korah. ¹⁵These *were* dukes of the sons of Esau: the sons of Eliphaz the firstborn *son* of Esau; duke Teman, duke Omar, duke Zepho, duke Kenaz, ¹⁶Duke Korah, duke Gatam, *and* duke Amalek: these *are* the dukes *that came* of Eliphaz in the land of Edom; these *were* the sons of Adah. ¹⁷And these *are* the sons of Reuel Esau's son; duke Nahath, duke Zerah, duke Shammah, duke Mizzah: these *are* the dukes *that came* of Reuel in the land of Edom; these *are* the sons of Bashemath Esau's wife. ¹⁸And these *are* the sons of Aholibamah Esau's wife; duke Jeush, duke Jaalam, duke Korah:

---

[a] persons: Heb. souls
[b] the Edomites: Heb. Edom
[c] Zepho: or, Zephi

these *were* the dukes *that came* of Aholibamah the daughter of Anah, Esau's wife. ¹⁹These *are* the sons of Esau, who *is* Edom, and these *are* their dukes.

²⁰These *are* the sons of Seir the Horite, who inhabited the land; Lotan, and Shobal, and Zibeon, and Anah, ²¹And Dishon, and Ezer, and Dishan: these *are* the dukes of the Horites, the children of Seir in the land of Edom. ²²And the children of Lotan were Hori and Hemam^d; and Lotan's sister *was* Timna. ²³And the children of Shobal *were* these; Alvan^e, and Manahath, and Ebal, Shepho, and Onam. ²⁴And these *are* the children of Zibeon; both Ajah, and Anah: this *was that* Anah that found the mules in the wilderness, as he fed the asses of Zibeon his father. ²⁵And the children of Anah *were* these; Dishon, and Aholibamah the daughter of Anah. ²⁶And these *are* the children of Dishon; Hemdan^f, and Eshban, and Ithran, and Cheran. ²⁷The children of Ezer *are* these; Bilhan, and Zaavan, and Akan^g. ²⁸The children of Dishan *are* these; Uz, and Aran. ²⁹These *are* the dukes *that came* of the Horites; duke Lotan, duke Shobal, duke Zibeon, duke Anah, ³⁰Duke Dishon, duke Ezer, duke Dishan: these *are* the dukes *that came* of Hori, among their dukes in the land of Seir.

³¹And these *are* the kings that reigned in the land of Edom, before there reigned any king over the children of Israel. ³²And Bela the son of Beor reigned in Edom: and the name of his city *was* Dinhabah. ³³And Bela died, and Jobab the son of Zerah of Bozrah reigned in his stead. ³⁴And Jobab died, and Husham of the land of Temani reigned in his stead. ³⁵And Husham died, and Hadad the son of Bedad, who smote Midian in the field of Moab, reigned in his stead: and the name of his city *was* Avith. ³⁶And Hadad died, and Samlah of Masrekah reigned in his stead. ³⁷And Samlah died, and Saul of Rehoboth *by* the river reigned in his stead. ³⁸And Saul died, and Baalhanan the son of Achbor reigned in his stead. ³⁹And Baalhanan the son of Achbor died, and Hadar reigned in his stead: and the name of his city *was* Pau; and his wife's name *was* Mehetabel, the daughter of Matred, the daughter of Mezahab. ⁴⁰And these *are* the names of the dukes *that came* of Esau, according to their families, after their places, by their names; duke Timnah, duke Alvah^h, duke Jetheth, ⁴¹Duke Aholibamah, duke Elah, duke Pinon, ⁴²Duke Kenaz, duke Teman, duke Mibzar, ⁴³Duke Magdiel, duke Iram: these *be* the dukes of Edom, according to their habitations in the land of their possession: he *is* Esau the father of the Edomites^i.

37

¹And Jacob dwelt in the land wherein his father was a stranger, in the land of Canaan. ²These *are* the generations of Ja-

---

^d Hemam: or, Homam
^e Alvan: or, Alian
^f Hemdan: or, Amram
^g Akan: or, Jakan
^h Alvah: or, Aliah
^i the Edomites: Heb. Edom

cob. Joseph, *being* seventeen years old, was feeding the flock with his brethren; and the lad *was* with the sons of Bilhah, and with the sons of Zilpah, his father's wives: and Joseph brought unto his father their evil report. ³Now Israel loved Joseph more than all his children, because he *was* the son of his old age: and he made him a coat of *many* colours[a]. ⁴And when his brethren saw that their father loved him more than all his brethren, they hated him, and could not speak peaceably unto him.

⁵And Joseph dreamed a dream, and he told *it* his brethren: and they hated him yet the more. ⁶And he said unto them, Hear, I pray you, this dream which I have dreamed: ⁷For, behold, we *were* binding sheaves in the field, and, lo, my sheaf arose, and also stood upright; and, behold, your sheaves stood round about, and made obeisance to my sheaf. ⁸And his brethren said to him, Shalt thou indeed reign over us? or shalt thou indeed have dominion over us? And they hated him yet the more for his dreams, and for his words. ⁹And he dreamed yet another dream, and told it his brethren, and said, Behold, I have dreamed a dream more; and, behold, the sun and the moon and the eleven stars made obeisance to me. ¹⁰And he told *it* to his father, and to his brethren: and his father rebuked him, and said unto him, What *is* this dream that thou hast dreamed? Shall I and thy mother and thy brethren indeed come to bow down ourselves to thee to the earth? ¹¹And his brethren envied him; but his father observed the saying.

¹²And his brethren went to feed their father's flock in Shechem. ¹³And Israel said unto Joseph, Do not thy brethren feed *the flock* in Shechem? come, and I will send thee unto them. And he said to him, Here *am I*. ¹⁴And he said to him, Go, I pray thee, see[b] whether it be well with thy brethren, and well with the flocks; and bring me word again. So he sent him out of the vale of Hebron, and he came to Shechem. ¹⁵And a certain man found him, and, behold, *he was* wandering in the field: and the man asked him, saying, What seekest thou? ¹⁶And he said, I seek my brethren: tell me, I pray thee, where they feed *their flocks*. ¹⁷And the man said, They are departed hence; for I heard them say, Let us go to Dothan. And Joseph went after his brethren, and found them in Dothan. ¹⁸And when they saw him afar off, even before he came near unto them, they conspired against him to slay him.

---

[a] colours: or, pieces

[b] see . . . : Heb. see the peace of thy brethren, etc

¹⁹And they said one to another, Behold, this dreamerᶜ cometh. ²⁰Come now therefore, and let us slay him, and cast him into some pit, and we will say, Some evil beast hath devoured him: and we shall see what will become of his dreams. ²¹And Reuben heard *it*, and he delivered him out of their hands; and said, Let us not kill him. ²²And Reuben said unto them, Shed no blood, *but* cast him into this pit that *is* in the wilderness, and lay no hand upon him; that he might rid him out of their hands, to deliver him to his father again.

²³And it came to pass, when Joseph was come unto his brethren, that they stript Joseph out of his coat, *his* coat of *many* coloursᵈ that *was* on him; ²⁴And they took him, and cast him into a pit: and the pit *was* empty, *there was* no water in it. ²⁵And they sat down to eat bread: and they lifted up their eyes and looked, and, behold, a company of Ishmeelites came from Gilead with their camels bearing spicery and balm and myrrh, going to carry *it* down to Egypt. ²⁶And Judah said unto his brethren, What profit *is it* if we slay our brother, and conceal his blood? ²⁷Come, and let us sell him to the Ishmeelites, and let not our hand be upon him; for he *is* our brother *and* our flesh. And his brethren were content. ²⁸Then there passed by Midianites merchantmen; and they drew and lifted up Joseph out of the pit, and sold Joseph to the Ishmeelites for twenty *pieces* of silver: and they brought Joseph into Egypt. ²⁹And Reuben returned unto the pit; and, behold, Joseph *was* not in the pit; and he

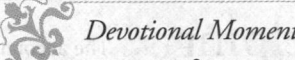

Devotional Moment

•

Lying

37:28, 31-32 Joseph's brothers covered their guilt by selling Joseph and then convincing their father he had been killed by wild animals. What they didn't realize was how hard it would be to keep their secret hidden. One lie requires others. As soon as you lie you have to keep track of everything you say, afraid someone may find out the truth. Honesty is priceless. Make honesty a top priority, and protect those who tell embarrassing truths from being ridiculed or mocked.

rent his clothes. ³⁰And he returned unto his brethren, and said, The child *is* not; and I, whither shall I go?

³¹And they took Joseph's coat, and killed a kid of the goats, and dipped the coat in the blood; ³²And they sent the coat of *many* colours, and they brought *it* to their father; and said, This have we found: know now whether it *be* thy son's coat or no. ³³And he knew it, and said, *It is* my son's coat; an evil beast hath devoured him; Joseph is without doubt rent in pieces. ³⁴And Jacob rent his clothes, and put sackcloth upon his loins, and mourned for his son many days. ³⁵And all his sons and all his daughters rose up to comfort him; but he refused to be comforted; and he said, For I will go down into the grave unto my son mourning. Thus his father wept for him. ³⁶And the Midianites sold him into Egypt unto Potiphar, an officerᵉ of Pharaoh's, *and* captain of the guard.

ᶜ dreamer: Heb. master of dreams

ᵈ colours: or, pieces

ᵉ officer: Heb. eunuch: but the word doth signify not only eunuchs, but also chamberlains, courtiers, and officers

Helping Children Love Each Other

by Joyce Milburn

The account of Joseph, his coat, his dreams, and his brothers is one that has intrigued people for centuries. Why did Jacob show such distinct favoritism to Joseph? Why did Joseph tell his brothers of his prophetic dreams, knowing how much they hated him? How could eleven brothers mutually decide to be so cruel to their teenage sibling? How could their parents have let things get so bad?

Perhaps we are intrigued by Joseph's story because it is so familiar. What parent of more than one child *hasn't* seen sibling rivalry in action?

Scripture contains abundant examples of people who could not get along with their brothers or sisters. Beginning with Cain and Abel, the very first pair of brothers, we move through Old Testament history to read of conflict after conflict: Isaac and Ishmael, Jacob and Esau, Rachel and Leah, Joseph and his brothers, David's children, and many more. The ideal is brotherly *love*, not brotherly *conflict*.

What can parents do? Quite a few things.

Set the example. Do you bicker and quibble over money, in-laws, job, and household stresses? Are you a contentious person who has to take on every salesclerk, or one who has a knack for alienating others over trivia? Are you able to say to your children that you would like to see them follow your example in getting along with others? Practice accepting irritations as a part of life. Learn to laugh about them, and try not to sweat the small stuff. You'll find that your children become more flexible and adaptable as well.

Meet your children's needs for time and attention. Children often fight and bicker with one another simply to grab their parents' attention and get them involved. A child who feels secure about his place in his parents' priorities is less likely to fight constantly.

Do not show favoritism. Yes, we all sometimes enjoy one child more than another, or have one child that seems to be more disaster-prone than the others. And because of differences in age, interests, abilities, and other factors, most parents don't want to treat all children identically. But we can treat them with fairness, and they will usually recognize that fact.

Look at others you know who are children of God. We have not all had identical, cookie-cutter lives, and the events that mark our lives are hardly equal. Yet we are each still aware of God's abundant, personal love. We need to remember that just as God is not a respecter of persons, he gave us each of our children to be loved fully, individually, and abundantly, the same way he loves us.

See yourself as a full-time teacher. Take advantage of every teachable moment. Deuteronomy 6:6-9 instructs us to spend time with our children, sharing and discussing God's principles as they apply to daily life. Don't be afraid to exert your parental authority and stop your children when you find them being hurtful or unkind to others or expressing negative attitudes.

In many homes, parents are reluctant to take action when their children do something wrong. Some say that children must express themselves no matter what; if the self-expression turns out to be ugly, too bad. They believe they must not stifle children.

Don't do that to your children. You're their teacher, remember? This is why they have parents. Just as their physical growth will not be completed for a number of years, they are also in the process of growing mentally, emotionally, and spiritually. You wouldn't hesitate to act if their physical growth needed intervention; why hesitate to help them grow in other ways as well? Teach them not to fight.

I'm tempted to speculate on why Jacob raised his sons the way he did. One safe conclusion is that everyone makes mistakes and we can learn from them. Appropriate behavior rarely comes naturally; it is the product of a consistent, godly example and much patient instruction. Your kids need you to be involved in the process. Will you invest the time?

DIGGING DEEPER

1. List some of the qualities of our heavenly Father that would be desirable for parents to have. Which of these qualities have been easy or difficult for your children to see in you?

2. According to 1 John 2:3-11, what conclusion can we draw about a person who truly hates his brother? Why isn't it reasonable to expect a child to be loving all the time? Where does love come from? (See 1 John 4:7-8.)

3. Romans 12:7-21 contains instructions for Christians. How can these help siblings locked in sibling rivalry?

38

¹And it came to pass at that time, that Judah went down from his brethren, and turned in to a certain Adullamite, whose name *was* Hirah. ²And Judah saw there a daughter of a certain Canaanite, whose name *was* Shuah; and he took her, and went in unto her. ³And she conceived, and bare a son; and he called his name Er. ⁴And she conceived again, and bare a son; and she called his name Onan. ⁵And she yet again conceived, and bare a son; and called his name Shelah: and he was at Chezib, when she bare him. ⁶And Judah took a wife for Er his firstborn, whose name *was* Tamar. ⁷And Er, Judah's firstborn, was wicked in the sight of the LORD; and the LORD slew him. ⁸And Judah said unto Onan, Go in unto thy brother's wife, and marry her, and raise up seed to thy brother. ⁹And Onan knew that the seed should not be his; and it came to pass, when he went in unto his brother's wife, that he spilled *it* on the ground, lest that he should give seed to his brother. ¹⁰And the thing which he did displeased[a] the LORD: wherefore he slew him also. ¹¹Then said Judah to Tamar his daughter in law, Remain a widow at thy father's house, till Shelah my son be grown: for he said, Lest peradventure he die also, as his brethren *did.* And Tamar went and dwelt in her father's house.

¹²And in process[b] of time the daughter of Shuah Judah's wife died; and Judah was comforted, and went up unto his sheepshearers to Timnath, he and his friend Hirah the Adullamite. ¹³And it was told Tamar, saying, Behold thy father in law goeth up to Timnath to shear his sheep. ¹⁴And she put her widow's garments off from her, and covered her with a vail, and wrapped herself, and sat in an

---

[a] displeased . . . : Heb. was evil in the eyes of the Lord
[b] in process . . . : Heb. the days were multiplied

open^c place, which *is* by the way to Timnath; for she saw that Shelah was grown, and she was not given unto him to wife. ¹⁵When Judah saw her, he thought her *to be* an harlot; because she had covered her face. ¹⁶And he turned unto her by the way, and said, Go to, I pray thee, let me come in unto thee; (for he knew not that she *was* his daughter in law.) And she said, What wilt thou give me, that thou mayest come in unto me? ¹⁷And he said, I will send *thee* a kid^d from the flock. And she said, Wilt thou give *me* a pledge, till thou send *it?* ¹⁸And he said, What pledge shall I give thee? And she said, Thy signet, and thy bracelets, and thy staff that *is* in thine hand. And he gave *it* her, and came in unto her, and she conceived by him. ¹⁹And she arose, and went away, and laid by her vail from her, and put on the garments of her widowhood. ²⁰And Judah sent the kid by the hand of his friend the Adullamite, to receive *his* pledge from the woman's hand: but he found her not. ²¹Then he asked the men of that place, saying, Where *is* the harlot, that *was* openly^e by the way side? And they said, There was no harlot in this *place.* ²²And he returned to Judah, and said, I cannot find her; and also the men of the place said, *that* there was no harlot in this *place.* ²³And Judah said, Let her take *it* to her, lest we be shamed^f: behold, I sent this kid, and thou hast not found her.

²⁴And it came to pass about three months after, that it was told Judah, saying, Tamar thy daughter in law hath played the harlot; and also, behold, she *is* with child by whoredom. And Judah said, Bring her forth, and let her be burnt. ²⁵When she *was* brought forth, she sent to her father in law, saying, By the man, whose these *are, am* I with child: and she said, Discern, I pray thee, whose *are* these, the signet, and bracelets, and staff. ²⁶And Judah acknowledged *them,* and said, She hath been more righteous than I; because that I gave her not to Shelah my son. And he knew her again no more. ²⁷And it came to pass in the time of her travail, that, behold, twins *were* in her womb. ²⁸And it came to pass, when she travailed, that *the one* put out *his* hand: and the midwife took and bound upon his hand a scarlet thread, saying, This came out first. ²⁹And it came to pass, as he drew back his hand, that, behold, his brother came out: and she said, How hast thou broken forth? *this* breach *be* upon thee: therefore his name was called Pharez. ³⁰And afterward came out his brother, that had the scarlet thread upon his hand: and his name was called Zarah.

39

¹And Joseph was brought down to Egypt; and Potiphar, an officer of Pharaoh, captain of the guard, an Egyptian, bought him of the hands of the Ishmeelites, which had brought him down thither. ²And the LORD was with Joseph, and he was a prosperous man; and he was in the house of his master the Egyptian. ³And his master

---

^c an open . . . : Heb. the door of eyes, or, of Enajim
^d a kid: Heb. a kid of the goats
^e openly: or, in Enajim
^f be shamed: Heb. become a contempt

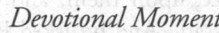

Devotional Moment
•
Adultery

39:8-12 Potiphar's wife hounded Joseph day after day. Joseph forcefully refused to defraud his master or to sin against God. Then he took steps to avoid Potiphar's wife altogether, refusing even to be in the same room with her. Happily married couples rarely seek out temptation to commit adultery. Rather, the temptation comes from unexpected places or at unexpected times. Don't deliberately place yourself in situations that could invite such temptation. Avoid people and settings that could lead to danger. And if anyone begins harassing you or pressures you to be unfaithful, resist to the full extent available to you. Then tell someone you trust so that he or she can hold you—and perhaps the other person as well—accountable. Do all you can to protect your God-given marriage.

saw that the LORD *was* with him, and that the LORD made all that he did to prosper in his hand. ⁴And Joseph found grace in his sight, and he served him: and he made him overseer over his house, and all *that* he had he put into his hand. ⁵And it came to pass from the time *that* he had made him overseer in his house, and over all that he had, that the LORD blessed the Egyptian's house for Joseph's sake; and the blessing of the LORD was upon all that he had in the house, and in the field. ⁶And he left all that he had in Joseph's hand; and he knew not ought he had, save the bread which he did eat. And Joseph was *a* goodly *person*, and well favoured.

⁷And it came to pass after these things, that his master's wife cast her eyes upon Joseph; and she said, Lie with me. ⁸But he refused, and said unto his master's wife, Behold, my master wotteth not what *is* with me in the house, and he hath committed all that he hath to my hand; ⁹*There is* none greater in this house than I; neither hath he kept back any thing from me but thee, because thou *art* his wife: how then can I do this great wickedness, and sin against God? ¹⁰And it came to pass, as she spake to Joseph day by day, that he hearkened not unto her, to lie by her, *or* to be with her. ¹¹And it came to pass about this time, that *Joseph* went into the house to do his business; and *there was* none of the men of the house there within. ¹²And she caught him by his garment, saying, Lie with me: and he left his garment in her hand, and fled, and got him out.

¹³And it came to pass, when she saw that he had left his garment in her hand, and was fled forth, ¹⁴That she called unto the men of her house, and spake unto them, saying, See, he hath brought in an Hebrew unto us to mock us; he came in unto me to lie with me, and I cried with a loud[a] voice: ¹⁵And it came to pass, when he heard that I lifted up my voice and cried, that he left his garment with me, and fled, and got him out. ¹⁶And she laid up his garment by her, until his lord came home. ¹⁷And she spake unto him according to these words, saying, The Hebrew servant, which thou hast brought unto us, came in unto me to mock me: ¹⁸And it came to pass, as I lifted up my voice and cried, that he left his garment with me, and fled out.

¹⁹And it came to pass, when his master heard the words of his wife, which she spake unto him, saying, Af-

---

[a] loud: Heb. great

ter this manner did thy servant to me; that his wrath was kindled. ²⁰And Joseph's master took him, and put him into the prison, a place where the king's prisoners *were* bound: and he was there in the prison. ²¹But the LORD was with Joseph, and shewed[b] him mercy, and gave him favour in the sight of the keeper of the prison. ²²And the keeper of the prison committed to Joseph's hand all the prisoners that *were* in the prison; and whatsoever they did there, he was the doer *of it.* ²³The keeper of the prison looked not to any thing *that was* under his hand; because the LORD was with him, and *that* which he did, the LORD made *it* to prosper.

40

¹And it came to pass after these things, *that* the butler of the king of Egypt and *his* baker had offended their lord the king of Egypt. ²And Pharaoh was wroth against two *of* his officers, against the chief of the butlers, and against the chief of the bakers. ³And he put them in ward in the house of the captain of the guard, into the prison, the place where Joseph *was* bound. ⁴And the captain of the guard charged Joseph with them, and he served them: and they continued a season in ward.

⁵And they dreamed a dream both of them, each man his dream in one night, each man according to the interpretation of his dream, the butler and the baker of the king of Egypt, which *were* bound in the prison. ⁶And Joseph came in unto them in the morning,

and looked upon them, and, behold, they *were* sad. ⁷And he asked Pharaoh's officers that *were* with him in the ward of his lord's house, saying, Wherefore look[a] ye *so* sadly to day? ⁸And they said unto him, We have dreamed a dream, and *there is* no interpreter of it. And Joseph said unto them, *Do* not interpretations *belong* to God? tell me *them,* I pray you. ⁹And the chief butler told his dream to Joseph, and said to him, In my dream, behold, a vine *was* before me; ¹⁰And in the vine *were* three branches: and it *was* as though it budded, *and* her blossoms shot forth; and the clusters thereof brought forth ripe grapes: ¹¹And Pharaoh's cup *was* in my hand: and I took the grapes, and pressed them into Pharaoh's cup, and I gave the cup into Pharaoh's hand. ¹²And Joseph said unto him, This *is* the interpretation of it: The three branches *are* three days: ¹³Yet within three days shall Pharaoh lift up thine head, and restore thee unto thy place: and thou shalt deliver Pharaoh's cup into his hand, after the former manner when thou wast his butler. ¹⁴But think[b] on me when it shall be well with thee, and shew kindness, I pray thee, unto me, and make mention of me unto Pharaoh, and bring me out of this house: ¹⁵For indeed I was stolen away out of the land of the Hebrews: and here also have I done nothing that they should put me into the dungeon. ¹⁶When the chief baker saw that the interpretation was good, he said unto Joseph, I also *was* in my dream, and,

---

[b] shewed . . . : Heb. extended kindness unto him
[a] look . . . : Heb. are your faces evil?
[b] think . . . : Heb. remember me with thee

behold, *I had* three white^c baskets on my head: ¹⁷And in the uppermost basket *there was* of all manner of bakemeats^d for Pharaoh; and the birds did eat them out of the basket upon my head. ¹⁸And Joseph answered and said, This *is* the interpretation thereof: The three baskets *are* three days: ¹⁹Yet within three days shall Pharaoh lift up thy head from off thee, and shall hang thee on a tree; and the birds shall eat thy flesh from off thee.

²⁰And it came to pass the third day, *which was* Pharaoh's birthday, that he made a feast unto all his servants: and he lifted up the head of the chief butler and of the chief baker among his servants. ²¹And he restored the chief butler unto his butlership again; and he gave the cup into Pharaoh's hand: ²²But he hanged the chief baker: as Joseph had interpreted to them. ²³Yet did not the chief butler remember Joseph, but forgat him.

41

¹And it came to pass at the end of two full years, that Pharaoh dreamed: and, behold, he stood by the river. ²And, behold, there came up out of the river seven well favoured kine and fatfleshed; and they fed in a meadow. ³And, behold, seven other kine came up after them out of the river, ill favoured and leanfleshed; and stood by the *other* kine upon the brink of the river. ⁴And the ill favoured and leanfleshed kine did eat up the seven well favoured and fat kine. So Pharaoh awoke. ⁵And he slept and

dreamed the second time: and, behold, seven ears of corn came up upon one stalk, rank^a and good. ⁶And, behold, seven thin ears and blasted with the east wind sprung up after them. ⁷And the seven thin ears devoured the seven rank and full ears. And Pharaoh awoke, and, behold, *it was* a dream. ⁸And it came to pass in the morning that his spirit was troubled; and he sent and called for all the magicians of Egypt, and all the wise men thereof: and Pharaoh told them his dream; but *there was* none that could interpret them unto Pharaoh.

⁹Then spake the chief butler unto Pharaoh, saying, I do remember my faults this day: ¹⁰Pharaoh was wroth with his servants, and put me in ward in the captain of the guard's house, *both* me and the chief baker: ¹¹And we dreamed a dream in one night, I and he; we dreamed each man according to the interpretation of his dream. ¹²And *there was* there with us a young man, an Hebrew, servant to the captain of the guard; and we told him, and he interpreted to us our dreams; to each man according to his dream he did interpret. ¹³And it came to pass, as he interpreted to us, so it was; me he restored unto mine office, and him he hanged. ¹⁴Then Pharaoh sent and called Joseph, and they brought him hastily out of the dungeon: and he shaved *himself*, and changed his raiment, and came in unto Pharaoh. ¹⁵And Pharaoh said unto Joseph, I have dreamed a dream, and *there is* none that can interpret it: and I have heard say of thee, *that* thou canst

---

^c white: or, full of holes
^d bakemeats . . . : Heb. meat of Pharaoh, the work of a baker, or, cook
^a rank: Heb. fat

understand a dream to interpret it. ¹⁶And Joseph answered Pharaoh, saying, *It is* not in me: God shall give Pharaoh an answer of peace.

¹⁷And Pharaoh said unto Joseph, In my dream, behold, I stood upon the bank of the river: ¹⁸And, behold, there came up out of the river seven kine, fatfleshed and well favoured; and they fed in a meadow: ¹⁹And, behold, seven other kine came up after them, poor and very ill favoured and leanfleshed, such as I never saw in all the land of Egypt for badness: ²⁰And the lean and the ill favoured kine did eat up the first seven fat kine: ²¹And when they had eaten them up, it could not be known that they had eaten them; but they *were* still ill favoured, as at the beginning. So I awoke. ²²And I saw in my dream, and, behold, seven ears came up in one stalk, full and good: ²³And, behold, seven ears, withered[b], thin, *and* blasted with the east wind, sprung up after them: ²⁴And the thin ears devoured the seven good ears: and I told *this* unto the magicians; but *there was* none that could declare *it* to me. ²⁵And Joseph said unto Pharaoh, The dream of Pharaoh *is* one: God hath shewed Pharaoh what he *is* about to do. ²⁶The seven good kine *are* seven years; and the seven good ears *are* seven years: the dream *is* one. ²⁷And the seven thin and ill favoured kine that came up after them *are* seven years; and the seven empty ears blasted with the east wind shall be seven years of famine. ²⁸This *is* the thing which I have spoken unto Pharaoh: What God *is* about to do he sheweth unto Pharaoh. ²⁹Behold, there come seven years of great plenty throughout all the land of Egypt: ³⁰And there shall arise after them seven years of famine; and all the plenty shall be forgotten in the land of Egypt; and the famine shall consume the land; ³¹And the plenty shall not be known in the land by reason of that famine following; for it *shall be* very grievous[c]. ³²And for that the dream was doubled unto Pharaoh twice; *it is* because the thing *is* established[d] by God, and God will shortly bring it to pass.

³³Now therefore let Pharaoh look out a man discreet and wise, and set him over the land of Egypt. ³⁴Let Pharaoh do *this*, and let him appoint officers[e] over the land, and take up the fifth part of the land of Egypt in the seven plenteous years. ³⁵And let them gather all the food of those good years that come, and lay up corn under the hand of Pharaoh, and let them keep food in the cities. ³⁶And that food shall be for store to the land against the seven years of famine, which shall be in the land of Egypt; that the land perish[f] not through the famine. ³⁷And the thing was good in the eyes of Pharaoh, and in the eyes of all his servants. ³⁸And Pharaoh said unto his servants, Can we find *such a one* as this *is*, a man in whom the Spirit of God *is*? ³⁹And

---

[b] withered: or, small

[c] grievous: Heb. heavy

[d] established . . . : or, prepared of God

[e] officers: or, overseers

[f] perish . . . : Heb. be not cut off

Pharaoh said unto Joseph, Forasmuch as God hath shewed thee all this, *there is* none so discreet and wise as thou *art*: ⁴⁰Thou shalt be over my house, and according unto thy word shall all my people be ruledᵍ: only in the throne will I be greater than thou. ⁴¹And Pharaoh said unto Joseph, See, I have set thee over all the land of Egypt. ⁴²And Pharaoh took off his ring from his hand, and put it upon Joseph's hand, and arrayed him in vestures of fine linen, and put a gold chain about his neck; ⁴³And he made him to ride in the second chariot which he had; and they cried before him, Bow the knee: and he made him *ruler* over all the land of Egypt. ⁴⁴And Pharaoh said unto Joseph, I *am* Pharaoh, and without thee shall no man lift up his hand or foot in all the land of Egypt. ⁴⁵And Pharaoh called Joseph's name Zaphnathpaaneahʰ; and he gave him to wife Asenath the daughter of Potipherah priest of On. And Joseph went out over *all* the land of Egypt.

⁴⁶And Joseph *was* thirty years old when he stood before Pharaoh king of Egypt. And Joseph went out from the presence of Pharaoh, and went throughout all the land of Egypt. ⁴⁷And in the seven plenteous years the earth brought forth by handfuls. ⁴⁸And he gathered up all the food of the seven years, which were in the land of Egypt, and laid up the food in the cities: the food of the field, which *was* round about every city, laid he up in the same. ⁴⁹And Joseph gathered corn as the sand of the sea, very much, until he left numbering; for *it was* without number. ⁵⁰And unto Joseph were born two sons before the years of famine came, which Asenath the daughter of Potipherah priestⁱ of On bare unto him. ⁵¹And Joseph called the name of the firstborn Manassehʲ: For God, *said he*, hath made me forget all my toil, and all my father's house. ⁵²And the name of the second called he Ephraimᵏ: For God hath caused me to be fruitful in the land of my affliction. ⁵³And the seven years of plenteousness, that was in the land of Egypt, were ended. ⁵⁴And the seven years of dearth began to come, according as Joseph had said: and the dearth was in all lands; but in all the land of Egypt there was bread. ⁵⁵And when all the land of Egypt was famished, the people cried to Pharaoh for bread: and Pharaoh said unto all the Egyptians, Go unto Joseph; what he saith to you, do. ⁵⁶And the famine was over all the face of the earth: And Joseph opened all the storehousesˡ, and sold unto the Egyptians; and the famine waxed sore in the land of Egypt. ⁵⁷And all countries came into Egypt to Joseph for to buy *corn*; because that the famine was *so* sore in all lands.

ᵍ be ruled: Heb. be armed, or, kiss

ʰ Zaphnathpaaneah: which in the Coptic signifies, A revealer of secrets, or, The man to whom secrets are revealed

ⁱ priest: or, prince

ʲ Manasseh: that is, Forgetting

ᵏ Ephraim: that is, Fruitful

ˡ all the storehouses: Heb. all wherein was

42

[1]Now when Jacob saw that there was corn in Egypt, Jacob said unto his sons, Why do ye look one upon another? [2]And he said, Behold, I have heard that there is corn in Egypt: get you down thither, and buy for us from thence; that we may live, and not die. [3]And Joseph's ten brethren went down to buy corn in Egypt. [4]But Benjamin, Joseph's brother, Jacob sent not with his brethren; for he said, Lest peradventure mischief befall him. [5]And the sons of Israel came to buy *corn* among those that came: for the famine was in the land of Canaan. [6]And Joseph *was* the governor over the land, *and* he *it was* that sold to all the people of the land: and Joseph's brethren came, and bowed down themselves before him *with* their faces to the earth.

[7]And Joseph saw his brethren, and he knew them, but made himself strange unto them, and spake roughly[a] unto them; and he said unto them, Whence come ye? And they said, From the land of Canaan to buy food. [8]And Joseph knew his brethren, but they knew not him. [9]And Joseph remembered the dreams which he dreamed of them, and said unto them, Ye *are* spies; to see the nakedness of the land ye are come. [10]And they said unto him, Nay, my lord, but to buy food are thy servants come. [11]We *are* all one man's sons; we *are* true *men*, thy servants are no spies. [12]And he said unto them, Nay, but to see the nakedness of the land ye are come. [13]And they said, Thy servants *are* twelve brethren, the sons of one

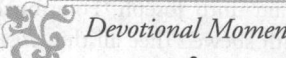

Devotional Moment

Growth

42:15 Because of his brothers' prior treachery, Joseph decided to put his siblings to the test. He ordered them to bring Benjamin back to Egypt. This was the ultimate test of brotherly love. How would they react? Were their hearts as coldhearted and cruel as before? Would they display remorse over their previous sin? Joseph was looking for evidence of change. No matter what has transpired in your family in the *past*, the fact is that God can change hearts in the *present*, and give you a brighter *future* together! If you have been guilty of mistreating a family member, seek forgiveness and then make a concerted effort to show love, kindness, and concern. If you have been the victim of cruelty, pray for God to work in your situation, seek counsel, and then watch what happens.

man in the land of Canaan; and, behold, the youngest *is* this day with our father, and one *is* not. [14]And Joseph said unto them, That *is it* that I spake unto you, saying, Ye *are* spies: [15]Hereby ye shall be proved: By the life of Pharaoh ye shall not go forth hence, except your youngest brother come hither. [16]Send one of you, and let him fetch your brother, and ye shall be kept in prison, that your words may be proved, whether *there be any* truth in you: or else by the life of Pharaoh surely ye *are* spies. [17]And he put them all together into ward three days. [18]And Joseph said unto them the third day, This do, and live; *for* I fear God: [19]If ye *be* true *men*, let one of your brethren be bound in the house of your prison: go ye, carry corn for the famine of your houses: [20]But bring your youngest brother unto

---

[a] roughly . . . : Heb. hard things with them

me; so shall your words be verified, and ye shall not die. And they did so.

²¹And they said one to another, We *are* verily guilty concerning our brother, in that we saw the anguish of his soul, when he besought us, and we would not hear; therefore is this distress come upon us. ²²And Reuben answered them, saying, Spake I not unto you, saying, Do not sin against the child; and ye would not hear? therefore, behold, also his blood is required. ²³And they knew not that Joseph understood *them*; for he spake unto them by an interpreter. ²⁴And he turned himself about from them, and wept; and returned to them again, and communed with them, and took from them Simeon, and bound him before their eyes. ²⁵Then Joseph commanded to fill their sacks with corn, and to restore every man's money into his sack, and to give them provision for the way: and thus did he unto them. ²⁶And they laded their asses with the corn, and departed thence. ²⁷And as one of them opened his sack to give his ass provender in the inn, he espied his money; for, behold, it *was* in his sack's mouth. ²⁸And he said unto his brethren, My money is restored; and, lo, *it is* even in my sack: and their heart failed[b] *them*, and they were afraid, saying one to another, What *is* this *that* God hath done unto us?

²⁹And they came unto Jacob their father unto the land of Canaan, and told him all that befell unto them; saying, ³⁰The man, *who is* the lord of the land, spake roughly[c] to us, and took us for spies of the country. ³¹And we said

unto him, We *are* true *men*; we are no spies: ³²We *be* twelve brethren, sons of our father; one *is* not, and the youngest *is* this day with our father in the land of Canaan. ³³And the man, the lord of the country, said unto us, Hereby shall I know that ye *are* true *men*; leave one of your brethren *here* with me, and take *food for* the famine of your households, and be gone: ³⁴And bring your youngest brother unto me: then shall I know that ye *are* no spies, but *that* ye *are* true *men: so* will I deliver you your brother, and ye shall traffick in the land. ³⁵And it came to pass as they emptied their sacks, that, behold, every man's bundle of money *was* in his sack: and when *both* they and their father saw the bundles of money, they were afraid. ³⁶And Jacob their father said unto them, Me have ye bereaved *of my children:* Joseph *is* not, and Simeon *is* not, and ye will take Benjamin *away:* all these things are against me. ³⁷And Reuben spake unto his father, saying, Slay my two sons, if I bring him not to thee: deliver him into my hand, and I will bring him to thee again. ³⁸And he said, My son shall not go down with you; for his brother is dead, and he is left alone: if mischief befall him by the way in the which ye go, then shall ye bring down my gray hairs with sorrow to the grave.

43

¹And the famine *was* sore in the land. ²And it came to pass, when they had eaten up the corn which they had brought out of Egypt, their father said unto them, Go

---

[b] failed . . . : Heb. went forth
[c] roughly . . . : Heb. with us hard things

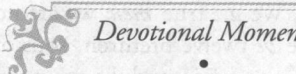

Devotional Moment
•
Leadership

43:9 When faced with the prospect of losing another brother and seeing his father's heart broken even further, Judah boldly stepped forward and agreed to look out for Benjamin's safety. The marks of a leader include a willingness to take on serious responsibilities and a determination to keep one's commitments no matter what the cost. In difficult situations, do you tend to sit back and wait for others to act, or do you take initiative? Can others count on you to fulfill your responsibilities? Think of one unpleasant responsibility or task in your home that no one else seems eager to do—such as doing laundry, fixing the car, discussing a problem with another family member—and tackle it today.

again, buy us a little food. ³And Judah spake unto him, saying, The man did solemnly protest unto us, saying, Ye shall not see my face, except your brother *be* with you. ⁴If thou wilt send our brother with us, we will go down and buy thee food: ⁵But if thou wilt not send *him*, we will not go down: for the man said unto us, Ye shall not see my face, except your brother *be* with you. ⁶And Israel said, Wherefore dealt ye *so* ill with me, *as* to tell the man whether ye had yet a brother? ⁷And they said, The man asked* us straitly of our state, and of our kindred, saying, *Is* your father yet alive? have ye *another* brother? and we told him according to the tenor of these words: could we certainly know that he would say, Bring your brother down? ⁸And Judah said unto Israel his father, Send the lad with me, and

we will arise and go; that we may live, and not die, both we, and thou, *and* also our little ones. ⁹I will be surety for him; of my hand shalt thou require him: if I bring him not unto thee, and set him before thee, then let me bear the blame for ever: ¹⁰For except we had lingered, surely now we had returned this second time.

¹¹And their father Israel said unto them, If *it must be* so now, do this; take of the best fruits in the land in your vessels, and carry down the man a present, a little balm, and a little honey, spices, and myrrh, nuts, and almonds: ¹²And take double money in your hand; and the money that was brought again in the mouth of your sacks, carry *it* again in your hand; peradventure it *was* an oversight: ¹³Take also your brother, and arise, go again unto the man: ¹⁴And God Almighty give you mercy before the man, that he may send away your other brother, and Benjamin. If ᵇ I be bereaved *of my children*, I am bereaved.

¹⁵And the men took that present, and they took double money in their hand, and Benjamin; and rose up, and went down to Egypt, and stood before Joseph. ¹⁶And when Joseph saw Benjamin with them, he said to the ruler of his house, Bring *these* men home, and slayᶜ, and make ready; for *these* men shall dine with me at noon. ¹⁷And the man did as Joseph bade; and the man brought the men into Joseph's house. ¹⁸And the men were afraid, because they were brought into Joseph's house; and they said, Because of the money that was returned in our sacks at the first

---

ᵃ asked . . . : Heb. asking asked us
ᵇ If . . . : or, And I, as I have been, etc
ᶜ slay: Heb. kill a killing

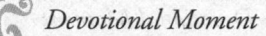

Devotional Moment

•

Heritage

43:23 Joseph's terrified brothers tried to explain their confusing situation to Joseph's steward, certain they would be accused of stealing the royal silver. The steward told them not to worry, attributing their good fortune to "your God, and the God of your father." How *ironic* that the covenant people of God had to be reminded of his sovereignty by one who probably did not even know God. How *encouraging* the steward's words are to us. When we consistently trust God with our circumstances, other people—especially our children and our children's children— see the hand of God on our lives. Voice your trust in God, and your children will learn to trust him too.

time are we brought in; that he may seek occasion against us, and fall upon us, and take us for bondmen, and our asses. ¹⁹And they came near to the steward of Joseph's house, and they communed with him at the door of the house, ²⁰And said, O sir, we came indeed down at the first time to buy food: ²¹And it came to pass, when we came to the inn, that we opened our sacks, and, behold, *every* man's money *was* in the mouth of his sack, our money in full weight: and we have brought it again in our hand. ²²And other money have we brought down in our hands to buy food: we cannot tell who put our money in our sacks. ²³And he said, Peace *be* to you, fear not: your God, and the God of your father, hath given you treasure in your sacks: I had^d your money. And he brought Simeon out unto them. ²⁴And the man brought the

men into Joseph's house, and gave *them* water, and they washed their feet; and he gave their asses provender. ²⁵And they made ready the present against Joseph came at noon: for they heard that they should eat bread there.

²⁶And when Joseph came home, they brought him the present which *was* in their hand into the house, and bowed themselves to him to the earth. ²⁷And he asked them of *their* welfare^e, and said, Is your father well, the old man of whom ye spake? Is he yet alive? ²⁸And they answered, Thy servant our father *is* in good health, he *is* yet alive. And they bowed down their heads, and made obeisance. ²⁹And he lifted up his eyes, and saw his brother Benjamin, his mother's son, and said, Is this your younger brother, of whom ye spake unto me? And he said, God be gracious unto thee, my son. ³⁰And Joseph made haste; for his bowels did yearn upon his brother: and he sought *where* to weep; and he entered into *his* chamber, and wept there. ³¹And he washed his face, and went out, and refrained himself, and said, Set on bread. ³²And they set on for him by himself, and for them by themselves, and for the Egyptians, which did eat with him, by themselves: because the Egyptians might not eat bread with the Hebrews; for that *is* an abomination unto the Egyptians. ³³And they sat before him, the firstborn according to his birthright, and the youngest according to his youth: and the men marvelled one at another. ³⁴And he took *and sent* messes unto them from before him: but Benjamin's

^d I had . . . : Heb. your money came to me
^e welfare: Heb. peace

mess was five times so much as any of theirs. And they drank, and were merry with him.

44

¹And he commanded the steward of his house, saying, Fill the men's sacks *with* food, as much as they can carry, and put every man's money in his sack's mouth. ²And put my cup, the silver cup, in the sack's mouth of the youngest, and his corn money. And he did according to the word that Joseph had spoken. ³As soon as the morning was light, the men were sent away, they and their asses. ⁴*And* when they were gone out of the city, *and* not *yet* far off, Joseph said unto his steward, Up, follow after the men; and when thou dost overtake them, say unto them, Wherefore have ye rewarded evil for good? ⁵*Is* not this *it* in which my lord drinketh, and whereby indeed he divineth*ª*? ye have done evil in so doing. ⁶And he overtook them, and he spake unto them these same words. ⁷And they said unto him, Wherefore saith my lord these words? God forbid that thy servants should do according to this thing: ⁸Behold, the money, which we found in our sacks' mouths, we brought again unto thee out of the land of Canaan: how then should we steal out of thy lord's house silver or gold? ⁹With whomsoever of thy servants it be found, both let him die, and we also will be my lord's bondmen. ¹⁰And he said, Now also *let* it *be* according unto your words: he with whom it is found shall be my servant; and ye shall be blameless. ¹¹Then they speedily took down every man his sack

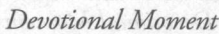

Devotional Moment
•
Maturity

44:16-34 Joseph carefully orchestrated a whole chain of events to make it appear as if Benjamin had stolen the Pharaoh's precious cup. Joseph figured that the ensuing confrontation would show once and for all whether his older brothers would stand up for their sibling, or whether they would abandon Benjamin as they had done to Joseph years before. Judah's moving plea for mercy, his heartfelt concern for his father, and his willingness to serve as a substitute for his accused brother brought Joseph to tears. Judah was not the same callous man who had once suggested selling Joseph into slavery; over the years he had become a caring and sensitive son and brother. Can your family see you changing and growing into what God wants you to be? Have the humility to let them see progress.

to the ground, and opened every man his sack. ¹²And he searched, *and* began at the eldest, and left at the youngest: and the cup was found in Benjamin's sack. ¹³Then they rent their clothes, and laded every man his ass, and returned to the city. ¹⁴And Judah and his brethren came to Joseph's house; for he *was* yet there: and they fell before him on the ground. ¹⁵And Joseph said unto them, What deed *is* this that ye have done? wot ye not that such a man as I can certainly divine*ᵇ*? ¹⁶And Judah said, What shall we say unto my lord? what shall we speak? or how shall we clear ourselves? God hath found out the iniquity of thy servants: behold, we *are* my lord's servants, both we, and *he* also with whom the cup is found. ¹⁷And he said, God forbid that I should do so: *but* the man in whose

---

ª divineth: or, maketh trial?
ᵇ divine: or, make trial?

hand the cup is found, he shall be my servant; and as for you, get you up in peace unto your father.

[18]Then Judah came near unto him, and said, Oh my lord, let thy servant, I pray thee, speak a word in my lord's ears, and let not thine anger burn against thy servant: for thou *art* even as Pharaoh. [19]My lord asked his servants, saying, Have ye a father, or a brother? [20]And we said unto my lord, We have a father, an old man, and a child of his old age, a little one; and his brother is dead, and he alone is left of his mother, and his father loveth him. [21]And thou saidst unto thy servants, Bring him down unto me, that I may set mine eyes upon him. [22]And we said unto my lord, The lad cannot leave his father: for *if* he should leave his father, *his father* would die. [23]And thou saidst unto thy servants, Except your youngest brother come down with you, ye shall see my face no more. [24]And it came to pass when we came up unto thy servant my father, we told him the words

---

Devotional Moment

•

Honoring Parents

44:19-33 Judah's appeal for Benjamin's release was based on his desire to spare his father Jacob further grief. The loss of Joseph years before had devastated Jacob enough; Judah knew that the loss of another favorite son could very well kill his father. Consequently he decided to do *anything* to avoid that prospect—even remain in Egypt as Joseph's slave. Honoring one's parents means thinking about how events will affect them and then being willing to go to great lengths to spare them unnecessary emotional pain. How can you honor your parents?

---

of my lord. [25]And our father said, Go again, *and* buy us a little food. [26]And we said, We cannot go down: if our youngest brother be with us, then will we go down: for we may not see the man's face, except our youngest brother *be* with us. [27]And thy servant my father said unto us, Ye know that my wife bare me two *sons*: [28]And the one went out from me, and I said, Surely he is torn in pieces; and I saw him not since: [29]And if ye take this also from me, and mischief befall him, ye shall bring down my gray hairs with sorrow to the grave. [30]Now therefore when I come to thy servant my father, and the lad *be* not with us; seeing that his life is bound up in the lad's life; [31]It shall come to pass, when he seeth that the lad *is* not *with us*, that he will die: and thy servants shall bring down the gray hairs of thy servant our father with sorrow to the grave. [32]For thy servant became surety for the lad unto my father, saying, If I bring him not unto thee, then I shall bear the blame to my father for ever. [33]Now therefore, I pray thee, let thy servant abide instead of the lad a bondman to my lord; and let the lad go up with his brethren. [34]For how shall I go up to my father, and the lad *be* not with me? lest peradventure I see the evil that shall come on my father.

45

[1]Then Joseph could not refrain himself before all them that stood by him; and he cried, Cause every man to go out from me. And there stood no man with him, while Joseph made himself known unto his brethren. [2]And he wept[a] aloud: and the Egyptians and the house of

---

[a] wept . . . : Heb. gave forth his voice in weeping

Devotional Moment

•

Trust

45:4-8 When Joseph revealed himself to his brothers, he also revealed a remarkable attitude of trust. Three times in his brief statement he emphasized the fact that *God* was the one who had sent him to Egypt. No doubt his brothers were shocked to hear him exclaim, "It was not you that sent me hither, but God." We often blame others for personal difficulties. But in looking *around* for scapegoats to blame we forget to look *up* to the God who orchestrates the events of our lives for his own glory and purposes—and for our own good (see Rom. 8:28). Try to look at family difficulties from God's perspective. Sometimes just remembering that he's in control can give us the faith we need to hang in there one more day.

Pharaoh heard. ³And Joseph said unto his brethren, I *am* Joseph; doth my father yet live? And his brethren could not answer him; for they were troubled[b] at his presence. ⁴And Joseph said unto his brethren, Come near to me, I pray you. And they came near. And he said, I *am* Joseph your brother, whom ye sold into Egypt. ⁵Now therefore be not grieved, nor angry with yourselves, that ye sold me hither: for God did send me before you to preserve life. ⁶For these two years *hath* the famine *been* in the land: and yet *there are* five years, in the which *there shall* neither *be* earing nor harvest. ⁷And God sent me before you to preserve[c] you a posterity in the earth, and to save your lives by a great deliverance. ⁸So now *it was* not you *that* sent me hither, but God: and he hath made me a father to Pharaoh, and lord of all his house, and a ruler throughout all the land of Egypt. ⁹Haste ye, and go up to my father, and say unto him, Thus saith thy son Joseph, God hath made me lord of all Egypt: come down unto me, tarry not: ¹⁰And thou shalt dwell in the land of Goshen, and thou shalt be near unto me, thou, and thy children, and thy children's children, and thy flocks, and thy herds, and all that thou hast: ¹¹And there will I nourish thee; for yet *there are* five years of famine; lest thou, and thy household, and all that thou hast, come to poverty. ¹²And, behold, your eyes see, and the eyes of my brother Benjamin, that *it is* my mouth that speaketh unto you. ¹³And ye shall tell my father of all my glory in Egypt, and of all that ye have seen; and ye shall haste and bring down my father hither. ¹⁴And he fell upon his brother Benjamin's neck, and wept; and Benjamin wept upon his neck. ¹⁵Moreover he kissed all his brethren, and wept upon them: and after that his brethren talked with him.

¹⁶And the fame thereof was heard in Pharaoh's house, saying, Joseph's brethren are come: and it pleased[d] Pharaoh well, and his servants. ¹⁷And Pharaoh said unto Joseph, Say unto thy brethren, This do ye; lade your beasts, and go, get you unto the land of Canaan; ¹⁸And take your father and your households, and come unto me: and I will give you the good of the land of Egypt, and ye shall eat the fat of the land. ¹⁹Now thou art commanded, this do ye; take you wagons out of the land of Egypt for your little ones, and for

---

[b] troubled: or, terrified
[c] to preserve . . . : Heb. to put for you a remnant
[d] pleased . . . : Heb. was good in the eyes of Pharaoh

Devotional Moment

Fighting

45:24 Why did Joseph say this? Probably for several reasons: (1) He knew his brothers' history of friction; (2) he thought they might spend much of the trip home blaming each other for the events that had transpired over the years; (3) he wanted them to focus on the joy of their family's reunion; (4) he may have realized that traveling together (even in ideal circumstances) creates unusual stress on families. If your family is struggling with strife—whatever the cause—try concentrating on what you appreciate about each other rather than first focusing on your individual differences. Take time to affirm someone in your family.

your wives, and bring your father, and come. ²⁰Also regard^e not your stuff; for the good of all the land of Egypt *is* yours. ²¹And the children of Israel did so: and Joseph gave them wagons, according to the commandment^f of Pharaoh, and gave them provision for the way. ²²To all of them he gave each man changes of raiment; but to Benjamin he gave three hundred *pieces* of silver, and five changes of raiment. ²³And to his father he sent after this *manner*; ten asses laden^g with the good things of Egypt, and ten she asses laden with corn and bread and meat for his father by the way. ²⁴So he sent his brethren away, and they departed: and he said unto them, See that ye fall not out by the way.

²⁵And they went up out of Egypt, and came into the land of Canaan unto Jacob their father, ²⁶And told him, saying, Joseph *is* yet alive, and he *is* gover-nor over all the land of Egypt. And Jacob's heart fainted, for he believed them not. ²⁷And they told him all the words of Joseph, which he had said unto them: and when he saw the wagons which Joseph had sent to carry him, the spirit of Jacob their father revived: ²⁸And Israel said, *It is* enough; Joseph my son *is* yet alive: I will go and see him before I die.

46

¹And Israel took his journey with all that he had, and came to Beersheba, and offered sacrifices unto the God of his father Isaac. ²And God spake unto Israel in the visions of the night, and said, Jacob, Jacob. And he said, Here *am* I. ³And he said, I *am* God, the God of thy father: fear not to go down into Egypt; for I will there make of thee a great nation: ⁴I will go down with thee into Egypt; and I will also surely bring thee up *again*: and Joseph shall put his hand upon thine eyes.

Devotional Moment

Moving

46:1-7 At Joseph's invitation, Jacob packed up and moved his entire clan—approximately seventy folks (see 46:27)—from Hebron down to Egypt. The great patriarch must have had some reservations about leaving the land of his father Isaac and grandfather Abraham. Verses 3-4 inform us that God came to Jacob in a vision and spoke words of comfort to him. Moving is never an easy undertaking. Yet despite the pervasive stress that accompanies a move, we can find peace by remembering that God will lead us, care for us, and meet our every need.

---

^e regard . . . : Heb. let not your eye spare, etc
^f commandment: Heb. mouth
^g laden . . . : Heb. carrying

⁵And Jacob rose up from Beersheba: and the sons of Israel carried Jacob their father, and their little ones, and their wives, in the wagons which Pharaoh had sent to carry him. ⁶And they took their cattle, and their goods, which they had gotten in the land of Canaan, and came into Egypt, Jacob, and all his seed with him: ⁷His sons, and his sons' sons with him, his daughters, and his sons' daughters, and all his seed brought he with him into Egypt. ⁸And these *are* the names of the children of Israel, which came into Egypt, Jacob and his sons: Reuben, Jacob's firstborn. ⁹And the sons of Reuben; Hanoch, and Phallu, and Hezron, and Carmi. ¹⁰And the sons of Simeon; Jemuelª, and Jamin, and Ohad, and Jachin, and Zohar, and Shaul the son of a Canaanitish woman. ¹¹And the sons of Levi; Gershonᵇ, Kohath, and Merari. ¹²And the sons of Judah; Er, and Onan, and Shelah, and Pharez, and Zerah: but Er and Onan died in the land of Canaan. And the sons of Pharez were Hezron and Hamul. ¹³And the sons of Issachar; Tola, and Phuvah, and Jobᶜ, and Shimron. ¹⁴And the sons of Zebulun; Sered, and Elon, and Jahleel. ¹⁵These *be* the sons of Leah, which she bare unto Jacob in Padanaram, with his daughter Dinah: all the souls of his sons and his daughters *were* thirty and three. ¹⁶And the sons of Gad; Ziphionᵈ, and Haggi, Shuni, and Ezbon, Eri, and Arodi, and Areli. ¹⁷And the sons of Asher; Jimnah, and Ishuah, and Isui, and Beriah, and Serah their sister: and the sons of Beriah; Heber, and Malchiel. ¹⁸These *are* the sons of Zilpah, whom Laban gave to Leah his daughter, and these she bare unto Jacob, *even* sixteen souls. ¹⁹The sons of Rachel Jacob's wife; Joseph, and Benjamin. ²⁰And unto Joseph in the land of Egypt were born Manasseh and Ephraim, which Asenath the daughter of Potipherah priestᵉ of On bare unto him. ²¹And the sons of Benjamin *were* Belah, and Becher, and Ashbel, Gera, and Naaman, Ehiᶠ, and Rosh, Muppim, and Huppim, and Ard. ²²These *are* the sons of Rachel, which were born to Jacob: all the souls *were* fourteen. ²³And the sons of Dan; Hushimᵍ. ²⁴And the sons of Naphtali; Jahzeel, and Guni, and Jezer, and

---

Devotional Moment

•

Family Reunion

46:30 The reunion between Jacob and Joseph made both men weep. The aging father had found his long-lost, thought-to-be-dead son. Jacob could rest assured that God's covenant promises were still intact. Visits with relatives can help get "unfinished business" done. Imagine the sense of loss Joseph and Jacob would have felt if their reunion had never taken place. Think about your own family. Are there "long-lost" relatives with whom you need to gather? The energy and expense required for such a reunion may be great, but the emotional dividends you will receive are well worth the investment.

ª Jemuel: or, Nemuel
ᵇ Gershon: or, Gershom
ᶜ Phuvah, and Job: or, Puah, and Jashub
ᵈ Ziphion: or, Zephon
ᵉ priest: or, prince
ᶠ Ehi: or, Ahiram
ᵍ Hushim: or, Shuham

Shillem. ²⁵These *are* the sons of Bilhah, which Laban gave unto Rachel his daughter, and she bare these unto Jacob: all the souls *were* seven. ²⁶All the souls that came with Jacob into Egypt, which came out of his loins^h, besides Jacob's sons' wives, all the souls *were* threescore and six; ²⁷And the sons of Joseph, which were born him in Egypt, *were* two souls: all the souls of the house of Jacob, which came into Egypt, *were* threescore and ten.

²⁸And he sent Judah before him unto Joseph, to direct his face unto Goshen; and they came into the land of Goshen. ²⁹And Joseph made ready his chariot, and went up to meet Israel his father, to Goshen, and presented himself unto him; and he fell on his neck, and wept on his neck a good while. ³⁰And Israel said unto Joseph, Now let me die, since I have seen thy face, because thou *art* yet alive. ³¹And Joseph said unto his brethren, and unto his father's house, I will go up, and shew Pharaoh, and say unto him, My brethren, and my father's house, which *were* in the land of Canaan, are come unto me; ³²And the men *are* shepherds, for their trade hath been to feed cattle; and they have brought their flocks, and their herds, and all that they have. ³³And it shall come to pass, when Pharaoh shall call you, and shall say, What *is* your occupation? ³⁴That ye shall say, Thy servants' trade hath been about cattle from our youth even until now, both we, *and* also our fathers: that ye may dwell in the land of Goshen; for

every shepherd *is* an abomination unto the Egyptians.

47

¹Then Joseph came and told Pharaoh, and said, My father and my brethren, and their flocks, and their herds, and all that they have, are come out of the land of Canaan; and, behold, they *are* in the land of Goshen. ²And he took some of his brethren, *even* five men, and presented them unto Pharaoh. ³And Pharaoh said unto his brethren, What *is* your occupation? And they said unto Pharaoh, Thy servants *are* shepherds, both we, *and* also our fathers. ⁴They said moreover unto Pharaoh, For to sojourn in the land are we come; for thy servants have no pasture for their flocks; for the famine *is* sore in the land of Canaan: now therefore, we pray thee, let thy servants dwell in the land of Goshen. ⁵And Pharaoh spake unto Joseph, saying, Thy father and thy brethren are come unto thee: ⁶The land of Egypt *is* before thee; in the best of the land make thy father and brethren to dwell; in the land of Goshen let them dwell: and if thou knowest *any* men of activity among them, then make them rulers over my cattle. ⁷And Joseph brought in Jacob his father, and set him before Pharaoh: and Jacob blessed Pharaoh. ⁸And Pharaoh said unto Jacob, How^a old *art* thou? ⁹And Jacob said unto Pharaoh, The days of the years of my pilgrimage *are* an hundred and thirty years: few and evil have the days of the years of my life been, and have not attained unto the days of the

---

^h loins: Heb. thigh
^a How . . . : Heb. How many are the days of the years of thy life?

years of the life of my fathers in the days of their pilgrimage. ¹⁰And Jacob blessed Pharaoh, and went out from before Pharaoh. ¹¹And Joseph placed his father and his brethren, and gave them a possession in the land of Egypt, in the best of the land, in the land of Rameses, as Pharaoh had commanded. ¹²And Joseph nourished his father, and his brethren, and all his father's household, with bread, according^b to *their* families.

¹³And *there was* no bread in all the land; for the famine *was* very sore, so that the land of Egypt and *all* the land of Canaan fainted by reason of the famine. ¹⁴And Joseph gathered up all the money that was found in the land of Egypt, and in the land of Canaan, for the corn which they bought: and Joseph brought the money into Pharaoh's house. ¹⁵And when money failed in the land of Egypt, and in the land of Canaan, all the Egyptians came unto Joseph, and said, Give us bread: for why should we die in thy presence? for the money faileth. ¹⁶And Joseph said, Give your cattle; and I will give you for your cattle, if money fail. ¹⁷And they brought their cattle unto Joseph: and Joseph gave them bread *in exchange* for horses, and for the flocks, and for the cattle of the herds, and for the asses: and he fed^c them with bread for all their cattle for that year. ¹⁸When that year was ended, they came unto him the second year, and said unto him, We will not hide *it* from my lord, how that our money is spent; my lord also hath our herds of cattle; there is not ought left in the sight of my lord, but our bodies, and our lands: ¹⁹Wherefore shall we die before thine eyes, both we and our land? buy us and our land for bread, and we and our land will be servants unto Pharaoh: and give *us* seed, that we may live, and not die, that the land be not desolate. ²⁰And Joseph bought all the land of Egypt for Pharaoh; for the Egyptians sold every man his field, because the famine prevailed over them: so the land became Pharaoh's. ²¹And as for the people, he removed them to cities from *one* end of the borders of Egypt even to the *other* end thereof. ²²Only the land of the priests^d bought he not; for the priests had a portion *assigned them* of Pharaoh, and did eat their portion which Pharaoh gave them: wherefore they sold not their lands. ²³Then Joseph said unto the people, Behold, I have bought you this day and your land for Pharaoh: lo, *here is* seed for you, and ye shall sow the land. ²⁴And it shall come to pass in the increase, that ye shall give the fifth *part* unto Pharaoh, and four parts shall be your own, for seed of the field, and for your food, and for them of your households, and for food for your little ones. ²⁵And they said, Thou hast saved our lives: let us find grace in the sight of my lord, and we will be Pharaoh's servants. ²⁶And Joseph made it a law over the land of Egypt unto this day, *that* Pharaoh should have the fifth *part*, except the land of the priests^e only, *which* became not Pharaoh's.

²⁷And Israel dwelt in the land of Egypt, in the country of Goshen; and

---

^b according . . . : or, as a little child is nourished: Heb. according to the little ones

^c fed . . . : Heb. led them

^d priests: or, princes

^e priests: or, princes

Devotional Moment
•
Death of Parents

47:27-31 When Jacob sensed that his death was imminent, he called for Joseph in order to make the necessary funeral arrangements. Joseph promised to grant his father's request to be buried back in Canaan in the cave of Machpelah (see 50:12-13). It is important for us to find out our parents' final wishes; it is even more important to carry out those desires if at all possible. By honoring their last requests, we honor them. Find out your parents' final wishes, if you can.

they had possessions therein, and grew, and multiplied exceedingly. ²⁸And Jacob lived in the land of Egypt seventeen years: so the whole age of Jacob was an hundred forty and seven years. ²⁹And the time drew nigh that Israel must die: and he called his son Joseph, and said unto him, If now I have found grace in thy sight, put, I pray thee, thy hand under my thigh, and deal kindly and truly with me; bury me not, I pray thee, in Egypt: ³⁰But I will lie with my fathers, and thou shalt carry me out of Egypt, and bury me in their buryingplace. And he said, I will do as thou hast said. ³¹And he said, Swear unto me. And he sware unto him. And Israel bowed himself upon the bed's head.

48

¹And it came to pass after these things, that *one* told Joseph, Behold, thy father *is* sick: and he took with him his two sons, Manasseh and Ephraim. ²And *one* told Jacob, and said, Behold, thy son Joseph cometh unto thee: and Israel strengthened himself, and sat upon the bed. ³And Jacob said unto Joseph, God Almighty appeared unto me at Luz in the land of Canaan, and blessed me, ⁴And said unto me, Behold, I will make thee fruitful, and multiply thee, and I will make of thee a multitude of people; and will give this land to thy seed after thee *for* an everlasting possession. ⁵And now thy two sons, Ephraim and Manasseh, which were born unto thee in the land of Egypt before I came unto thee into Egypt, *are* mine; as Reuben and Simeon, they shall be mine. ⁶And thy issue, which thou begettest after them, shall be thine, *and* shall be called after the name of their brethren in their inheritance. ⁷And as for me, when I came from Padan, Rachel died by me in the land of Canaan in the way, when yet *there was* but a little way to come unto Ephrath: and I buried her there in the way of Ephrath; the same *is* Bethlehem.

⁸And Israel beheld Joseph's sons, and said, Who *are* these? ⁹And Joseph said unto his father, They *are* my sons, whom God hath given me in this *place*. And he said, Bring them, I pray thee, unto me, and I will bless them. ¹⁰Now the eyes of Israel were dim[a] for age, so *that* he could not see. And he brought them near unto him; and he kissed them, and embraced them. ¹¹And Israel said unto Joseph, I had not thought to see thy face: and, lo, God hath shewed me also thy seed. ¹²And Joseph brought them out from between his knees, and he bowed himself with his face to the earth. ¹³And Joseph took them both, Ephraim in his right hand toward Israel's left hand, and Manasseh in his left hand toward Israel's right hand, and

---

[a] dim: Heb. heavy

Devotional Moment
•
Prayer

48:11 God not only orchestrated events so that father and son were reunited, he also provided Jacob with the added blessing of getting to embrace Joseph's sons—his previously unknown grandchildren! That is the kind of God we serve—a loving heavenly Father who delights in blessing his children with good gifts. The apostle Paul asserted that God "is able to do exceeding abundantly above all that we ask or think" (Eph. 3:20). What family situation have you decided is impossible? What relationship have you written off as dead and gone? God may be about to surprise you with a blessing beyond your wildest dreams. Don't give up hope!

brought *them* near unto him. ¹⁴And Israel stretched out his right hand, and laid *it* upon Ephraim's head, who *was* the younger, and his left hand upon Manasseh's head, guiding his hands wittingly; for Manasseh *was* the first-

Devotional Moment
•
Birth Order

48:9-20 Just as Abraham had blessed the younger Isaac rather than Ishmael, and Isaac had blessed Jacob instead of his older brother Esau, now Jacob unexpectedly blessed Ephraim over Manasseh. In the spiritual realm it matters not when or where or how you were *born*. The real issue is how you *live*. What is your character like? Don't become obsessed with your birth order, your family's customs, or your own inadequacies. Focus instead on being faithful and available. And with your own children, make sure you affirm each one individually, recognizing the unique personalities and abilities of each.

born. ¹⁵And he blessed Joseph, and said, God, before whom my fathers Abraham and Isaac did walk, the God which fed me all my life long unto this day, ¹⁶The Angel which redeemed me from all evil, bless the lads; and let my name be named on them, and the name of my fathers Abraham and Isaac; and let them grow^b into a multitude in the midst of the earth. ¹⁷And when Joseph saw that his father laid his right hand upon the head of Ephraim, it displeased^c him: and he held up his father's hand, to remove it from Ephraim's head unto Manasseh's head. ¹⁸And Joseph said unto his father, Not so, my father: for this *is* the firstborn; put thy right hand upon his head. ¹⁹And his father refused, and said, I know *it,* my son, I know *it:* he also shall become a people, and he also shall be great: but truly his younger brother shall be greater than he, and his seed shall become a multitude^d of nations. ²⁰And he blessed them that day, saying, In thee shall Israel bless, saying, God make thee as Ephraim and as Manasseh: and he set Ephraim before Manasseh. ²¹And Israel said unto Joseph, Behold, I die: but God shall be with you, and bring you again unto the land of your fathers. ²²Moreover I have given to thee one portion above thy brethren, which I took out of the hand of the Amorite with my sword and with my bow.

49

¹And Jacob called unto his sons, and said, Gather yourselves together, that I may

---

^b grow: Heb. as fishes do increase
^c displeased . . . : was evil in his eyes
^d multitude: Heb. fulness

Breaking Free from Hurt

But Joseph told them, "Fear not: for am I in the place of God? But as for you, ye thought evil against me; but God meant it unto good, to bring to pass, as it is this day, to save much people alive. Now therefore fear ye not: I will nourish you, and your little ones. And he comforted them, and spake kindly unto them." Genesis 50:19-21

I f anyone had grounds for bitterness over the treatment he had received from his family, it was Joseph. He faced jealousy and scorn from his brothers, and finally came close to death at their hands. Following the death of their father, Joseph's brothers knew what his "natural" reaction could have been.

"Now that their father was dead, they said, Joseph will peradventure hate us, and will certainly requite us all the evil which we did unto him." (Gen. 50:15). And they came to him in fear and trembling.

What was Joseph's response? When we look closely at how he answered his brothers, we can see three important tools we can use in breaking a negative cycle.

1. "Fear not: for am I in the place of God?" (50:19). Joseph knew something that helped keep him from bitterness: the fact that God would be their judge. As it says in 1 Samuel 2:10, "The adversaries of the Lord shall be broken to pieces; out of heaven shall he thunder upon them: the Lord shall judge the ends of the earth."

Instead of wasting time and emotional energy judging and condemning his brothers, Joseph left them in the hands of a God who judges each person's actions impartially. If you're tempted to seek revenge or let bitterness stake a claim in your thoughts, think of Joseph. He bypassed all the negative physical and emotional by-products of a life filled with hate, by placing others' final judgment in God's hands.

2. ". . . ye thought evil against me" (50:20). A second important tool for breaking past cycles is to be honest in dealing with the hurt others have caused us. Joseph didn't sugarcoat the truth. His brothers had hurt him deeply, and their act was indeed cruel and evil.

Denying the truth never leads to the freedom that facing the truth brings. Joseph didn't gloss over the past to make his brothers feel better, but neither did he dwell on what they'd done.

3. "But God meant it unto good, to bring to pass . . . to save much people alive." (50:20). Joseph saw clearly that every trial comes with some type of benefit. Counselors call this "reframing." Joseph knew that God, in his own time, can bring some good in our lives from even an evil act. Romans 8:28 testifies to this truth: "We know that all things work together for good to them that love God."

Think of the negative experiences you have had. What positive lessons have those experiences taught you? What positive circumstances did they force upon your life? What unexpected good came about as an indirect result? For example, some people who grow up in a single-parent home learn responsibility more quickly than others and are consequently more mature. Or perhaps losing a job can cause a person to hit bottom and see his or her need for Christ.

There is tremendous power in seeing that, in spite of the genuine pain, grieving, and heartache in negative experiences, God can and does bring good from trials.

Breaking free from hurt means (1) allowing God to judge those who hurt us, (2) being truthful about what happened in our past, and (3) looking for positive benefits in our negative experience. With God's help, the cycle of hurt *can* be broken.

---

tell you *that* which shall befall you in the last days. ²Gather yourselves together, and hear, ye sons of Jacob; and hearken unto Israel your father. ³Reuben, thou *art* my firstborn, my might, and the beginning of my strength, the excellency of dignity, and the excellency of power: ⁴Unstable as water, thou shalt not excel; because thou wentest up to thy father's bed; then defiledst thou *it*: he went up to my couch.

⁵Simeon and Levi *are* brethren; instruments[a] of cruelty *are in* their habitations. ⁶O my soul, come not thou into their secret; unto their assembly, mine honour, be not thou united: for in their anger they slew a man, and in their self-will they digged down a wall. ⁷Cursed *be* their anger, for *it was* fierce; and their wrath, for it was cruel: I will divide them in Jacob, and scatter them in Israel.

⁸Judah, thou *art he* whom thy brethren shall praise: thy hand *shall be* in the neck of thine enemies; thy father's children shall bow down before thee. ⁹Judah *is* a lion's whelp: from the prey, my son, thou art gone up: he stooped down, he couched as a lion, and as an old lion; who shall rouse him up? ¹⁰The sceptre shall not depart from Judah, nor a lawgiver from between his feet, until Shiloh come; and unto him *shall* the gathering of the people *be*. ¹¹Binding his foal unto the vine, and his ass's colt unto the choice vine; he washed his garments in wine, and his clothes in the blood of grapes: ¹²His eyes *shall be* red with wine, and his teeth white with milk.

¹³Zebulun shall dwell at the haven of the sea; and he *shall be* for an haven of ships; and his border *shall be* unto Zidon. ¹⁴Issachar *is* a strong ass couching down between two burdens: ¹⁵And he saw that rest *was* good, and the land that *it was* pleasant; and bowed his shoulder to bear, and became a servant unto tribute. ¹⁶Dan shall judge his people, as one of the tribes of Israel. ¹⁷Dan shall be a serpent by the way, an adder[b] in the path, that biteth the horse heels,

---

[a] instruments . . . : or, their swords are weapons of violence
[b] an adder: Heb. an arrow snake

Devotional Moment

Character

49:3-12 Jacob informed Reuben that, despite his position of being the eldest son, and despite his natural gifts and abilities, he would not receive the privileges usually granted to the firstborn. The reason for this pronouncement? Years earlier Reuben had slept with Bilhah, one of his father's concubines (see 35:22). Jacob then rebuked Simeon and Levi for their violence, and awarded the position of leadership to Judah, his fourth son. It is possible to withhold rewards from our children without withholding love and acceptance. Do your kids understand that wrong behavior costs something? Are you teaching them that disobedience now will cause them to forfeit special privileges in the future? Help them learn this truth when they are young, and they may avoid the painful lesson that the oldest sons of Jacob had to learn later in life.

---

so that his rider shall fall backward. ¹⁸I have waited for thy salvation, O LORD. ¹⁹Gad, a troop shall overcome him: but he shall overcome at the last. ²⁰Out of Asher his bread *shall be* fat, and he shall yield royal dainties. ²¹Naphtali *is* a hind let loose: he giveth goodly words.

²²Joseph *is* a fruitful bough, *even* a fruitful bough by a well; *whose* branchesᶜ run over the wall: ²³The archers have sorely grieved him, and shot *at him*, and hated him: ²⁴But his bow abode in strength, and the arms of his hands were made strong by the hands of the mighty *God* of Jacob; (from thence *is* the shepherd, the stone of Israel:) ²⁵*Even* by the God of thy father, who shall help thee; and by the Almighty, who shall bless thee with blessings of heaven above, blessings of the deep that lieth under, blessings of the breasts, and of the womb: ²⁶The blessings of thy father have prevailed above the blessings of my progenitors unto the utmost bound of the everlasting hills: they shall be on the head of Joseph, and on the crown of the head of him that was separate from his brethren. ²⁷Benjamin shall ravin *as* a wolf: in the morning he shall devour the prey, and at night he shall divide the spoil.

²⁸All these *are* the twelve tribes of Israel: and this *is it* that their father spake unto them, and blessed them; every one according to his blessing he blessed them. ²⁹And he charged them, and said unto them, I am to be gathered unto my people: bury me with my fathers in the cave that *is* in the field of Ephron the Hittite, ³⁰In the cave that *is* in the field of Machpelah, which *is* before Mamre, in the land of Canaan, which Abraham bought with the field of Ephron the Hittite for a possession of a buryingplace. ³¹There they buried Abraham and Sarah his wife; there they buried Isaac and Rebekah his wife; and there I buried Leah. ³²The purchase of the field and of the cave that *is* therein *was* from the children of Heth. ³³And when Jacob had made an end of commanding his sons, he gathered up his feet into the bed, and yielded up the ghost, and was gathered unto his people.

50

¹And Joseph fell upon his father's face, and wept upon him, and kissed him. ²And Joseph commanded his servants

---

ᶜ branches: Heb. daughters

the physicians to embalm his father: and the physicians embalmed Israel. ³And forty days were fulfilled for him; for so are fulfilled the days of those which are embalmed: and the Egyptians mourned[a] for him threescore and ten days. ⁴And when the days of his mourning were past, Joseph spake unto the house of Pharaoh, saying, If now I have found grace in your eyes, speak, I pray you, in the ears of Pharaoh, saying, ⁵My father made me swear, saying, Lo, I die: in my grave which I have digged for me in the land of Canaan, there shalt thou bury me. Now therefore let me go up, I pray thee, and bury my father, and I will come again. ⁶And Pharaoh said, Go up, and bury thy father, according as he made thee swear.

⁷And Joseph went up to bury his father: and with him went up all the servants of Pharaoh, the elders of his house, and all the elders of the land of Egypt, ⁸And all the house of Joseph, and his brethren, and his father's house: only their little ones, and their flocks, and their herds, they left in the land of Goshen. ⁹And there went up with him both chariots and horsemen: and it was a very great company. ¹⁰And they came to the threshingfloor of Atad, which *is* beyond Jordan, and there they mourned with a great and very sore lamentation: and he made a mourning for his father seven days. ¹¹And when the inhabitants of the land, the Canaanites, saw the mourning in the floor of Atad, they said, This *is* a grievous mourning to the Egyptians: where-

fore the name of it was called Abelmizraim[b], which *is* beyond Jordan. ¹²And his sons did unto him according as he commanded them: ¹³For his sons carried him into the land of Canaan, and buried him in the cave of the field of Machpelah, which Abraham bought with the field for a possession of a buryingplace of Ephron the Hittite, before Mamre. ¹⁴And Joseph returned into Egypt, he, and his brethren, and all that went up with him to bury his father, after he had buried his father.

¹⁵And when Joseph's brethren saw that their father was dead, they said, Joseph will peradventure hate us, and will certainly requite us all the evil which we did unto him. ¹⁶And they sent a messenger unto Joseph, saying, Thy father did command before he died, saying, ¹⁷So shall ye say unto Joseph, Forgive, I pray thee now, the trespass of thy brethren, and their sin; for they did unto thee evil: and now, we pray thee, forgive the trespass of the servants of the God of thy father. And Joseph wept when they spake unto him. ¹⁸And his brethren also went and fell down before his face; and they said, Behold, we *be* thy servants. ¹⁹And Joseph said unto them, Fear not: for *am* I in the place of God? ²⁰But as for you, ye thought evil against me; *but* God meant it unto good, to bring to pass, as *it is* this day, to save much people alive. ²¹Now therefore fear ye not: I will nourish you, and your little ones. And he comforted them, and spake kindly[c] unto them.

²²And Joseph dwelt in Egypt, he,

---

[a] mourned: Heb. wept
[b] Abelmizraim: that is, The mourning of the Egyptians
[c] kindly . . . : Heb. to their hearts

and his father's house: and Joseph lived an hundred and ten years. [23]And Joseph saw Ephraim's children of the third *generation*: the children also of Machir the son of Manasseh were brought up upon Joseph's knees. [24]And Joseph said unto his brethren, I die: and God will surely visit you, and bring you out of this land unto the land which he sware to Abra-

ham, to Isaac, and to Jacob. [25]And Joseph took an oath of the children of Israel, saying, God will surely visit you, and ye shall carry up my bones from hence. [26]So Joseph died, *being* an hundred and ten years old: and they embalmed him, and he was put in a coffin in Egypt.

EXODUS

Purpose
To record the events of Israel's deliverance from Egypt and development as a nation

Author
Moses

Date Written
1450–1410 B.C., approximately the same as Genesis

Where Written
In the wilderness during Israel's wanderings, somewhere in the Sinai Peninsula

Setting
Egypt. God's people, once highly favored in the land, are now slaves. A God of great miracles is about to set them free.

Key Verses
"I have surely seen the affliction of my people . . . I will send thee unto Pharaoh . . . to bring forth my people the children of Israel out of Egypt" (3:7-10).

Key People
Moses, Miriam, Pharaoh, Pharaoh's daughter, Jethro, Aaron, Joshua, Bezalel

Key Places
Egypt, Goshen, Nile River, Land of Midian, Red Sea, Sinai Peninsula, Mount Sinai

Special Features
Exodus relates more miracles than any other Old Testament book and is noted for containing the Ten Commandments.

The appearance of a rental truck in a neighbor's driveway has become as familiar a summer tradition as Little League and lawn mowing.

"Those poor people," we say. "All that packing to do. All those boxes. All that basement junk to haul!"

Children say, "I'll miss my friend."

Grandparents say, "We'll miss them all."

The bright side of moving is, of course, new beginnings: new friends, job, house, church. Maybe a better salary. Maybe nicer schoolteachers. Maybe a new mountain to look at, or lake to fish in. Hey, moving can be an adventure.

In the Exodus, no children missed friends and no grandparents said good-bye to children. Everyone moved together. Everybody left their basement junk behind. Every step out of Egypt was new, often dangerous, always risky. And the people had their share of flat tires on the highway, from a sea that threatened to wash out their dreams to golden idols that offended their God.

To make this an unforgettable move, God revealed himself in new ways to the Hebrew people: as deliverer, helper, law-giver, and judge. God wanted to be worshiped in new ways, too. This was to be a new start with the heart as well as the feet. "Walking by faith" was a daily adventure for these pioneers.

Discover the trials, hardships, and happiness of "starting over" in the book about "getting out and getting moving."

1

¹Now these *are* the names of the children of Israel, which came into Egypt; every man and his household came with Jacob. ²Reuben, Simeon, Levi, and Judah, ³Issachar, Zebulun, and Benjamin, ⁴Dan, and Naphtali, Gad, and Asher. ⁵And all the souls that came out of the loins[a] of Jacob were seventy souls: for Joseph was in Egypt *already*. ⁶And Joseph died, and all his brethren, and all that generation. ⁷And the children of Israel were fruitful, and increased abundantly, and multiplied, and waxed exceeding mighty; and the land was filled with them.

⁸Now there arose up a new king over Egypt, which knew not Joseph. ⁹And he said unto his people, Behold, the people of the children of Israel *are* more and mightier than we: ¹⁰Come on, let us deal wisely with them; lest they multiply, and it come to pass, that, when there falleth out any war, they join also unto our enemies, and fight against us, and *so* get them up out of the land. ¹¹Therefore they did set over them taskmasters to afflict them with their burdens. And they built for Pharaoh treasure cities, Pithom and Raamses. ¹²But the more they afflicted them, the more they multiplied and grew. And they were grieved because of the children of Israel. ¹³And the Egyptians made the children of Israel to serve with rigour: ¹⁴And they made their lives bitter with hard bondage, in morter, and in brick, and in all manner of service in the field: all their service, wherein they made them serve, *was* with rigour.

> **Devotional Moment**
> •
> *Abortion/Adoption*
> **1:15-21** The reason Shiphrah and Puah refused to participate in a systematic program of infanticide is that they "feared God" (v. 17). If we fear God and believe that each human being bears the image of God, we too—like the Hebrew midwives—will take a stand against the slaughter of innocent, helpless children. Prayerfully consider what role God would have you play in the fight for life, whether that means merely supporting an organization that protects children, helping an unwed mother, counseling teenagers, serving as foster parents, or even adopting a child.

¹⁵And the king of Egypt spake to the Hebrew midwives, of which the name of the one *was* Shiphrah, and the name of the other Puah: ¹⁶And he said, When ye do the office of a midwife to the Hebrew women, and see *them* upon the stools; if it *be* a son, then ye shall kill him: but if it *be* a daughter, then she shall live. ¹⁷But the midwives feared God, and did not as the king of Egypt commanded them, but saved the men children alive. ¹⁸And the king of Egypt called for the midwives, and said unto them, Why have ye done this thing, and have saved the men children alive? ¹⁹And the midwives said unto Pharaoh, Because the Hebrew women *are* not as the Egyptian women; for they *are* lively, and are delivered ere the midwives come in unto them. ²⁰Therefore God dealt well with the midwives: and the people multiplied, and waxed very mighty. ²¹And it came to pass, because the midwives feared God, that he made them houses. ²²And Pharaoh charged all his people, saying, Every son that is born ye shall

---
[a] loins: Heb. thigh

cast into the river, and every daughter ye shall save alive.

2

[1]And there went a man of the house of Levi, and took *to wife* a daughter of Levi. [2]And the woman conceived, and bare a son: and when she saw him that he *was a* goodly *child,* she hid him three months. [3]And when she could not longer hide him, she took for him an ark of bulrushes, and daubed it with slime and with pitch, and put the child therein; and she laid *it* in the flags by the river's brink. [4]And his sister stood afar off, to wit what would be done to him.

[5]And the daughter of Pharaoh came down to wash *herself* at the river; and her maidens walked along by the river's side; and when she saw the ark among the flags, she sent her maid to fetch it. [6]And when she had opened *it,* she saw the child: and, behold, the babe wept. And she had compassion on him, and said, This *is one* of the Hebrews' children. [7]Then said his sister to Pharaoh's daughter, Shall I go and call to thee a nurse of the Hebrew women, that she may nurse the child for thee? [8]And Pharaoh's daughter said to her, Go. And the maid went and called the child's mother. [9]And Pharaoh's daughter said unto her, Take this child away, and nurse it for me, and I will give *thee* thy wages. And the woman took the child, and nursed it. [10]And the child grew, and she brought him unto Pharaoh's daughter, and he became her son. And she called his name Moses[a]: and she said, Because I drew him out of the water.

[11]And it came to pass in those days, when Moses was grown, that he went out unto his brethren, and looked on their burdens: and he spied an Egyptian smiting an Hebrew, one of his brethren. [12]And he looked this way and that way, and when he saw that *there was* no man, he slew the Egyptian, and hid him in the sand. [13]And when he went out the second day, behold, two men of the Hebrews strove together: and he said to him that did the wrong, Wherefore smitest thou thy fellow? [14]And he said, Who made thee a prince[b] and a judge over us? intendest thou to kill me, as thou killedst the Egyptian? And Moses feared, and said, Surely this thing is known. [15]Now when Pharaoh heard this thing, he sought to slay Moses. But Moses fled from the face of Pharaoh, and dwelt in the land of Midian: and he sat down by a well.

[16]Now the priest[c] of Midian had

Devotional Moment

•

Adoption

2:3 Moses' mother chose to give him up for adoption rather than see her child destroyed. Under the murderous edict of Pharaoh, she had few options. But God affirmed her decision when Pharaoh's daughter found him and allowed a Hebrew woman, who turned out to be Moses' own mother, to be the baby's wet nurse. This baby grew up to lead the Israelite slaves out of Egypt. In God's sovereign care, Moses' adoption spared not only Moses' life, but also, eighty years later, the lives of millions of Israelites as well. Consider how God might use you to save a life by adoption.

---

[a] Moses: that is, Drawn out
[b] a prince: Heb. a man, a prince
[c] priest: or, prince

seven daughters: and they came and drew *water*, and filled the troughs to water their father's flock. ¹⁷And the shepherds came and drove them away: but Moses stood up and helped them, and watered their flock. ¹⁸And when they came to Reuel[d] their father, he said, How *is it that* ye are come so soon to day? ¹⁹And they said, An Egyptian delivered us out of the hand of the shepherds, and also drew *water* enough for us, and watered the flock. ²⁰And he said unto his daughters, And where *is* he? why *is* it *that* ye have left the man? call him, that he may eat bread. ²¹And Moses was content to dwell with the man: and he gave Moses Zipporah his daughter. ²²And she bare *him* a son, and he called his name Gershom[e]: for he said, I have been a stranger in a strange land.

²³And it came to pass in process of time, that the king of Egypt died: and the children of Israel sighed by reason of the bondage, and they cried, and their cry came up unto God by reason of the bondage. ²⁴And God heard their groaning, and God remembered his covenant with Abraham, with Isaac, and with Jacob. ²⁵And God looked upon the children of Israel, and God had respect unto *them*.

3

¹Now Moses kept the flock of Jethro his father in law, the priest of Midian: and he led the flock to the backside of the desert, and came to the mountain of God, *even* to Horeb. ²And the angel of the LORD appeared unto him in a flame of fire out of the midst of a bush:

and he looked, and, behold, the bush burned with fire, and the bush *was* not consumed. ³And Moses said, I will now turn aside, and see this great sight, why the bush is not burnt. ⁴And when the LORD saw that he turned aside to see, God called unto him out of the midst of the bush, and said, Moses, Moses. And he said, Here *am* I. ⁵And he said, Draw not nigh hither: put off thy shoes from off thy feet, for the place whereon thou standest *is* holy ground. ⁶Moreover he said, I *am* the God of thy father, the God of Abraham, the God of Isaac, and the God of Jacob. And Moses hid his face; for he was afraid to look upon God.

⁷And the LORD said, I have surely seen the affliction of my people which *are* in Egypt, and have heard their cry by reason of their taskmasters; for I know their sorrows; ⁸And I am come down to deliver them out of the hand of the

---

[d] Reuel: called also Jethro, or, Jether
[e] Gershom: that is, A stranger here

Egyptians, and to bring them up out of that land unto a good land and a large, unto a land flowing with milk and honey; unto the place of the Canaanites, and the Hittites, and the Amorites, and the Perizzites, and the Hivites, and the Jebusites. ⁹Now therefore, behold, the cry of the children of Israel is come unto me: and I have also seen the oppression wherewith the Egyptians oppress them. ¹⁰Come now therefore, and I will send thee unto Pharaoh, that thou mayest bring forth my people the children of Israel out of Egypt.

¹¹And Moses said unto God, Who *am* I, that I should go unto Pharaoh, and that I should bring forth the children of Israel out of Egypt? ¹²And he said, Certainly I will be with thee; and this *shall be* a token unto thee, that I have sent thee: When thou hast brought forth the people out of Egypt, ye shall serve God upon this mountain. ¹³And Moses said unto God, Behold, *when* I come unto the children of Israel, and shall say unto them, The God of your fathers hath sent me unto you; and they shall say to me, What *is* his name? what shall I say unto them? ¹⁴And God said unto Moses, I AM THAT I AM: and he said, Thus shalt thou say unto the children of Israel, I AM hath sent me unto you. ¹⁵And God said moreover unto Moses, Thus shalt thou say unto the children of Israel, The LORD God of your fathers, the God of Abraham, the God of Isaac, and the God of Jacob, hath sent me unto you: this *is* my name for ever, and this *is* my memorial unto all generations.

¹⁶Go, and gather the elders of Israel together, and say unto them, The LORD God of your fathers, the God of Abraham, of Isaac, and of Jacob, appeared unto me, saying, I have surely visited you, and *seen* that which is done to you in Egypt: ¹⁷And I have said, I will bring you up out of the affliction of Egypt unto the land of the Canaanites, and the Hittites, and the Amorites, and the Perizzites, and the Hivites, and the Jebusites, unto a land flowing with milk and honey. ¹⁸And they shall hearken to thy voice: and thou shalt come, thou and the elders of Israel, unto the king of Egypt, and ye shall say unto him, The LORD God of the Hebrews hath met with us: and now let us go, we beseech thee, three days' journey into the wilderness, that we may sacrifice to the LORD our God. ¹⁹And I am sure that the king of Egypt will not let you go, noᵃ, not by a mighty hand. ²⁰And I will stretch out my hand, and smite Egypt with all my wonders which I will do in the midst thereof: and after that he will let you go. ²¹And I will give this people favour in the sight of the Egyptians: and it shall come to pass, that, when ye go, ye shall not go empty: ²²But every woman shall borrow of her neighbour, and of her that sojourneth in her house, jewels of silver, and jewels of gold, and raiment: and ye shall put *them* upon your sons, and upon your daughters; and ye shall spoil the Egyptiansᵇ.

4

¹And Moses answered and said, But, behold, they will not believe me, nor

---

ᵃ no . . . : or, but by strong hand
ᵇ the Egyptians: or, Egypt

Jochebed
(Moses' Mother)

How much courage does it take to protect a newborn child from murderers? Fortunately, most of us will never know. Moses' mother, a Levite woman named Jochebed, knew all too well.

Because the Egyptians feared the growing Hebrew nation, Pharaoh ordered that all male babies born to Hebrew women be thrown into the Nile River. Jochebed could not let it happen. When she gave birth, she hid her newborn son. The risks she took defy common sense. But then she had faith in God. Perhaps the greatest test of that faith came when it became impossible to hide Moses any longer, only three months later. How difficult it must have been for her to leave him among the riverbank reeds in a waterproofed basket.

Jochebed counted on God. She could have despaired when the Pharaoh issued his edict. She could have rationalized the difficulty of hiding her baby and handed him over to be drowned. She could have cursed God for allowing such terrible circumstances to afflict her. But she did none of those things. Instead she did what she could in full belief that God existed and would take care of her and her child. And God did.

Jochebed's story spans only ten verses (Exod. 2:1-10), verses which don't even mention her name. But the little we are told inspires us. She risked all for her child's life, believing that God would rescue him, and her faith paid off. A mother's heart has many reasons to fear—each one an opportunity to step out in faith.

LESSONS FROM JOCHEBED AS A MOTHER

God values life and honors parents who do. Jochebed went to extraordinary lengths to preserve her baby's life. We should do the same with our children.

Parenting takes courage. Having children generates a steady stream of unexpected circumstances and frightening surprises. The only way to confront these with confidence is to draw courage from God.

Caring for children requires sacrifice. Caring for Moses required his mother to make many, many sacrifices—sacrifices of time, safety, economy, security, and comfort. We should be willing to pay the price that properly caring for children involves.

We must balance prayer and faith with action. Jochebed didn't merely pray and wait for a miracle. She did everything in her power to protect her baby.

Even "unwanted" children should be given a chance to live. Many childless couples wait desperately for a chance to adopt a child.

hearken unto my voice: for they will say, The LORD hath not appeared unto thee. ²And the LORD said unto him, What *is* that in thine hand? And he said, A rod. ³And he said, Cast it on the ground. And he cast it on the ground, and it became a serpent; and Moses fled from before it. ⁴And the LORD said unto Moses, Put forth thine hand, and take it by the tail. And he put forth his hand, and caught it, and it became a rod in his hand: ⁵That they may believe that the LORD God of their fathers, the God of Abraham, the God of Isaac, and the God of Jacob, hath appeared unto thee. ⁶And the LORD said furthermore unto him, Put now thine hand into thy bosom. And he put his hand into his bosom: and when he took it out, behold, his hand *was* leprous as snow. ⁷And he said, Put thine hand into thy bosom again. And he put his hand into his bosom again; and plucked it out of his bosom, and, behold, it was turned again as his *other* flesh. ⁸And it shall come to pass, if they will not believe thee, neither hearken to the voice of the first sign, that they will believe the voice of the latter sign. ⁹And it shall come to pass, if they will not believe also these two signs, neither hearken unto thy voice, that thou shalt take of the water of the river, and pour *it* upon the dry *land*: and the water which thou takest out of the river shall become blood upon the dry *land*.

¹⁰And Moses said unto the LORD, O my Lord, I *am* not eloquentª, neither heretofore, nor since thou hast spoken unto thy servant: but I *am* slow of speech, and of a slow tongue. ¹¹And the LORD

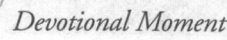

> ### Devotional Moment
> •
> ### Self-Esteem
> 4:10-17 Moses tried to avoid living up to what God created and called him to be—a spokesman for God. Perhaps Moses thought his response showed humility, but in fact he disparaged rather than exalted God's creative role, as God pointed out. God promised to be with him and to bolster his confidence with the help of his brother Aaron. God wants us to believe that we can do whatever he has given us to do in life, however impossible it may seem, if we will rely on him and others for help. When you are in over your head in your family role as spouse, parent, or child, don't let low self-esteem stop you from acting. Keep your faith and ask God for help.

said unto him, Who hath made man's mouth? or who maketh the dumb, or deaf, or the seeing, or the blind? have not I the LORD? ¹²Now therefore go, and I will be with thy mouth, and teach thee what thou shalt say. ¹³And he said, O my Lord, send, I pray thee, by the hand *of him whom* thou wilt send. ¹⁴And the anger of the LORD was kindled against Moses, and he said, *Is* not Aaron the Levite thy brother? I know that he can speak well. And also, behold, he cometh forth to meet thee: and when he seeth thee, he will be glad in his heart. ¹⁵And thou shalt speak unto him, and put words in his mouth: and I will be with thy mouth, and with his mouth, and will teach you what ye shall do. ¹⁶And he shall be thy spokesman unto the people: and he shall be, *even* he shall be to thee instead of a mouth, and thou shalt be to him instead of God. ¹⁷And thou shalt take this rod in thine hand, wherewith thou shalt do signs.

ª eloquent: Heb. a man or words

¹⁸And Moses went and returned to Jethro[b] his father in law, and said unto him, Let me go, I pray thee, and return unto my brethren which *are* in Egypt, and see whether they be yet alive. And Jethro said to Moses, Go in peace. ¹⁹And the LORD said unto Moses in Midian, Go, return into Egypt: for all the men are dead which sought thy life. ²⁰And Moses took his wife and his sons, and set them upon an ass, and he returned to the land of Egypt: and Moses took the rod of God in his hand. ²¹And the LORD said unto Moses, When thou goest to return into Egypt, see that thou do all those wonders before Pharaoh, which I have put in thine hand: but I will harden his heart, that he shall not let the people go. ²²And thou shalt say unto Pharaoh, Thus saith the LORD, Israel *is* my son, *even* my firstborn: ²³And I say unto thee, Let my son go, that he may serve me: and if thou refuse to let him go, behold, I will slay thy son, *even* thy firstborn.

²⁴And it came to pass by the way in the inn, that the LORD met him, and sought to kill him. ²⁵Then Zipporah took a sharp stone, and cut off the foreskin of her son, and cast *it* at his feet, and said, Surely a bloody husband *art* thou to me. ²⁶So he let him go: then she said, A bloody husband *thou art*, because of the circumcision. ²⁷And the LORD said to Aaron, Go into the wilderness to meet Moses. And he went, and met him in the mount of God, and kissed him. ²⁸And Moses told Aaron all the words of the LORD who had sent him, and all the signs which he had commanded him. ²⁹And Moses and Aaron went and gathered together all the elders of the children of Israel: ³⁰And Aaron spake all the words which the LORD had spoken unto Moses, and did the signs in the sight of the people. ³¹And the people believed: and when they heard that the LORD had visited the children of Israel, and that he had looked upon their affliction, then they bowed their heads and worshipped.

5

¹And afterward Moses and Aaron went in, and told Pharaoh, Thus saith the LORD God of Israel, Let my people go, that they may hold a feast unto me in the wilderness. ²And Pharaoh said, Who *is* the LORD, that I should obey his voice to let Israel go? I know not the LORD, neither will I let Israel go.

³And they said, The God of the Hebrews hath met with us: let us go, we pray thee, three days' journey into the desert, and sacrifice unto the LORD

Devotional Moment

Values

5:1-23 The Pharaoh and his Egyptian taskmasters did not share Hebrew values or priorities. Egypt had many gods, whereas the Hebrews believed in the one Lord God. With no knowledge of or respect for the God of Israel, Pharaoh would not listen to his slaves' request for time off to worship. Likewise, non-Christian employers, when confronted with our values, may ignore our request for time off for worship, or family leave time when the need arises. First we must give a good account of ourselves at work, even under harsh conditions. Next we must expect that they will not agree or respect our spiritual values, but in all cases we must maintain our commitment to God and speak up for his values.

---

[b] Jethro: Heb. Jether

our God; lest he fall upon us with pestilence, or with the sword. ⁴And the king of Egypt said unto them, Wherefore do ye, Moses and Aaron, let the people from their works? get you unto your burdens. ⁵And Pharaoh said, Behold, the people of the land now *are* many, and ye make them rest from their burdens. ⁶And Pharaoh commanded the same day the taskmasters of the people, and their officers, saying, ⁷Ye shall no more give the people straw to make brick, as heretofore: let them go and gather straw for themselves. ⁸And the tale of the bricks, which they did make heretofore, ye shall lay upon them; ye shall not diminish *ought* thereof: for they *be* idle; therefore they cry, saying, Let us go *and* sacrifice to our God. ⁹Let there more work be laid upon the men, that they may labour therein; and let them not regard vain words.

¹⁰And the taskmasters of the people went out, and their officers, and they spake to the people, saying, Thus saith Pharaoh, I will not give you straw. ¹¹Go ye, get you straw where ye can find it: yet not ought of your work shall be diminished. ¹²So the people were scattered abroad throughout all the land of Egypt to gather stubble instead of straw. ¹³And the taskmasters hasted *them*, saying, Fulfil your works, *your* daily tasks, as when there was straw. ¹⁴And the officers of the children of Israel, which Pharaoh's taskmasters had set over them, were beaten, *and* demanded, Wherefore have ye not fulfilled your task in making brick both yesterday and to day, as heretofore?

¹⁵Then the officers of the children of Israel came and cried unto Pharaoh, saying, Wherefore dealest thou thus with thy servants? ¹⁶There is no straw given unto thy servants, and they say to us, Make brick: and, behold, thy servants *are* beaten; but the fault *is* in thine own people. ¹⁷But he said, Ye *are* idle, *ye are* idle: therefore ye say, Let us go *and* do sacrifice to the LORD. ¹⁸Go therefore now, *and* work; for there shall no straw be given you, yet shall ye deliver the tale of bricks. ¹⁹And the officers of the children of Israel did see *that* they *were* in evil *case*, after it was said, Ye shall not minish *ought* from your bricks of your daily task. ²⁰And they met Moses and Aaron, who stood in the way, as they came forth from Pharaoh: ²¹And they said unto them, The LORD look upon you, and judge; because ye have made our savour to be abhorred in the eyes of Pharaoh, and in the eyes of his servants, to put a sword in their hand to slay us. ²²And Moses returned unto the LORD, and said, Lord, wherefore hast thou *so* evil entreated this people? why *is* it *that* thou hast sent me? ²³For since I came to Pharaoh to speak in thy name, he hath done evil to this people; neither hast thou delivered thy people at all.

6

¹Then the LORD said unto Moses, Now shalt thou see what I will do to Pharaoh: for with a strong hand shall he let them go, and with a strong hand shall he drive them out of his land. ²And God spake unto Moses, and said unto him, I *am* the LORD*a*: ³And I appeared unto Abraham, unto Isaac, and

---

a the LORD: or, JEHOVAH

Devotional Moment
•
Hope

6:6-12 When God said yes to the Hebrews, promising deliverance from Egyptian slavery to become God's own people, those who were too discouraged to believe took that promise as hollow, even a hoax. When they had previously attempted to rectify their situation, they had received even heavier burdens to bear. Sometimes we too hear God say, "Yes, I will" and find it hard to believe because our present family circumstances bear no relation to that future hope. Financial setbacks, postponed plans, and lingering difficulties can make us either *bitter* or *better*. It all depends on whether we trust God and take hope in him, or focus on our own overwhelming situation.

unto Jacob, by *the name of* God Almighty, but by my name JEHOVAH was I not known to them. ⁴And I have also established my covenant with them, to give them the land of Canaan, the land of their pilgrimage, wherein they were strangers. ⁵And I have also heard the groaning of the children of Israel, whom the Egyptians keep in bondage; and I have remembered my covenant. ⁶Wherefore say unto the children of Israel, I *am* the LORD, and I will bring you out from under the burdens of the Egyptians, and I will rid you out of their bondage, and I will redeem you with a stretched out arm, and with great judgments: ⁷And I will take you to me for a people, and I will be to you a God: and ye shall know that I *am* the LORD your God, which bringeth you out from under the burdens of the Egyptians. ⁸And I will bring you in unto the land, concerning the which I did swear[b] to give it to Abraham, to Isaac, and to Jacob; and I will give it you for an heritage: I *am* the LORD. ⁹And Moses spake so unto the children of Israel: but they hearkened not unto Moses for anguish[c] of spirit, and for cruel bondage.

¹⁰And the LORD spake unto Moses, saying, ¹¹Go in, speak unto Pharaoh king of Egypt, that he let the children of Israel go out of his land. ¹²And Moses spake before the LORD, saying, Behold, the children of Israel have not hearkened unto me; how then shall Pharaoh hear me, who *am* of uncircumcised lips? ¹³And the LORD spake unto Moses and unto Aaron, and gave them a charge unto the children of Israel, and unto Pharaoh king of Egypt, to bring the children of Israel out of the land of Egypt.

¹⁴These *be* the heads of their fathers' houses: The sons of Reuben the firstborn of Israel; Hanoch, and Pallu, Hezron, and Carmi: these *be* the families of Reuben. ¹⁵And the sons of Simeon; Jemuel, and Jamin, and Ohad, and Jachin, and Zohar, and Shaul the son of a Canaanitish woman: these *are* the families of Simeon. ¹⁶And these *are* the names of the sons of Levi according to their generations; Gershon, and Kohath, and Merari: and the years of the life of Levi *were* an hundred thirty and seven years. ¹⁷The sons of Gershon; Libni, and Shimi, according to their families. ¹⁸And the sons of Kohath; Amram, and Izhar, and Hebron, and Uzziel: and the years of the life of Ko-

---

[b] swear: Heb. lift up my hand
[c] anguish: Heb. shortness, or, straitness

hath *were* an hundred thirty and three years. ¹⁹And the sons of Merari; Mahali and Mushi: these *are* the families of Levi according to their generations. ²⁰And Amram took him Jochebed his father's sister to wife; and she bare him Aaron and Moses: and the years of the life of Amram *were* an hundred and thirty and seven years. ²¹And the sons of Izhar; Korah, and Nepheg, and Zichri. ²²And the sons of Uzziel; Mishael, and Elzaphan, and Zithri. ²³And Aaron took him Elisheba, daughter of Amminadab, sister of Naashon, to wife; and she bare him Nadab, and Abihu, Eleazar, and Ithamar. ²⁴And the sons of Korah; Assir, and Elkanah, and Abiasaph: these *are* the families of the Korhites. ²⁵And Eleazar Aaron's son took him *one* of the daughters of Putiel to wife; and she bare him Phinehas: these *are* the heads of the fathers of the Levites according to their families. ²⁶These *are* that Aaron and Moses, to whom the LORD said, Bring out the children of Israel from the land of Egypt according to their armies. ²⁷These *are* they which spake to Pharaoh king of Egypt, to bring out the children of Israel from Egypt: these *are* that Moses and Aaron. ²⁸And it came to pass on the day *when* the LORD spake unto Moses in the land of Egypt, ²⁹That the LORD spake unto Moses, saying, I *am* the LORD: speak thou unto Pharaoh king of Egypt all that I say unto thee. ³⁰And Moses said before the LORD, Behold, I *am* of uncircumcised lips, and how shall Pharaoh hearken unto me?

7

¹And the LORD said unto Moses, See, I have made thee a god to Pharaoh: and Aaron thy brother shall be thy prophet. ²Thou shalt speak all that I command thee: and Aaron thy brother shall speak unto Pharaoh, that he send the children of Israel out of his land. ³And I will harden Pharaoh's heart, and multiply my signs and my wonders in the land of Egypt. ⁴But Pharaoh shall not hearken unto you, that I may lay my hand upon Egypt, and bring forth mine armies, *and* my people the children of Israel, out of the land of Egypt by great judgments. ⁵And the Egyptians shall know that I *am* the LORD, when I stretch forth mine hand upon Egypt, and bring out the children of Israel from among them. ⁶And Moses and Aaron did as the LORD commanded them, so did they. ⁷And Moses *was* fourscore years old, and Aaron fourscore and three years old, when they spake unto Pharaoh.

⁸And the LORD spake unto Moses and unto Aaron, saying, ⁹When Pharaoh shall speak unto you, saying, Shew a miracle for you: then thou shalt say unto Aaron, Take thy rod, and cast *it* before Pharaoh, *and* it shall become a serpent. ¹⁰And Moses and Aaron went

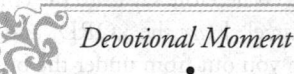

Devotional Moment

Retirement

7:6-7 Moses and Aaron were old enough to retire; instead they started a second career as diplomats and elder statesmen, negotiating the release of their Hebrew kindred. For Moses, this new assignment of service began at age eighty. We should view aging not as a sad decline toward retirement and uselessness, but as an opportunity to take on a new job—that of mentoring those mature enough to listen. Make a list of the people you would like to "lead out of Egypt." How can you serve as their elder statesman?

in unto Pharaoh, and they did so as the LORD had commanded: and Aaron cast down his rod before Pharaoh, and before his servants, and it became a serpent. ¹¹Then Pharaoh also called the wise men and the sorcerers: now the magicians of Egypt, they also did in like manner with their enchantments. ¹²For they cast down every man his rod, and they became serpents: but Aaron's rod swallowed up their rods. ¹³And he hardened Pharaoh's heart, that he hearkened not unto them; as the LORD had said.

¹⁴And the LORD said unto Moses, Pharaoh's heart *is* hardened, he refuseth to let the people go. ¹⁵Get thee unto Pharaoh in the morning; lo, he goeth out unto the water; and thou shalt stand by the river's brink against he come; and the rod which was turned to a serpent shalt thou take in thine hand. ¹⁶And thou shalt say unto him, The LORD God of the Hebrews hath sent me unto thee, saying, Let my people go, that they may serve me in the wilderness: and, behold, hitherto thou wouldest not hear. ¹⁷Thus saith the LORD, In this thou shalt know that I *am* the LORD: behold, I will smite with the rod that *is* in mine hand upon the waters which *are* in the river, and they shall be turned to blood. ¹⁸And the fish that *is* in the river shall die, and the river shall stink; and the Egyptians shall lothe to drink of the water of the river. ¹⁹And the LORD spake unto Moses, Say unto Aaron, Take thy rod, and stretch out thine hand upon the waters of Egypt, upon their streams, upon their rivers, and upon their ponds, and upon all their pools* of water, that they may become

blood; and *that* there may be blood throughout all the land of Egypt, both in *vessels of* wood, and in *vessels of* stone. ²⁰And Moses and Aaron did so, as the LORD commanded; and he lifted up the rod, and smote the waters that *were* in the river, in the sight of Pharaoh, and in the sight of his servants; and all the waters that *were* in the river were turned to blood. ²¹And the fish that *was* in the river died; and the river stank, and the Egyptians could not drink of the water of the river; and there was blood throughout all the land of Egypt. ²²And the magicians of Egypt did so with their enchantments: and Pharaoh's heart was hardened, neither did he hearken unto them; as the LORD had said. ²³And Pharaoh turned and went into his house, neither did he set his heart to this also. ²⁴And all the Egyptians digged round about the river for water to drink; for they could not drink of the water of the river. ²⁵And seven days were fulfilled, after that the LORD had smitten the river.

8

¹And the LORD spake unto Moses, Go unto Pharaoh, and say unto him, Thus saith the LORD, Let my people go, that they may serve me. ²And if thou refuse to let *them* go, behold, I will smite all thy borders with frogs: ³And the river shall bring forth frogs abundantly, which shall go up and come into thine house, and into thy bedchamber, and upon thy bed, and into the house of thy servants, and upon thy people, and into thine ovens, and into thy kneadingtroughsᵃ: ⁴And the frogs

---

ᵃ pools . . . : Heb. gathering of their waters
ᵃ kneadingtroughs: or, dough

shall come up both on thee, and upon thy people, and upon all thy servants. ⁵And the LORD spake unto Moses, Say unto Aaron, Stretch forth thine hand with thy rod over the streams, over the rivers, and over the ponds, and cause frogs to come up upon the land of Egypt. ⁶And Aaron stretched out his hand over the waters of Egypt; and the frogs came up, and covered the land of Egypt. ⁷And the magicians did so with their enchantments, and brought up frogs upon the land of Egypt. ⁸Then Pharaoh called for Moses and Aaron, and said, Intreat the LORD, that he may take away the frogs from me, and from my people; and I will let the people go, that they may do sacrifice unto the LORD. ⁹And Moses said unto Pharaoh, Glory[b] over me: when shall I intreat for thee, and for thy servants, and for thy people, to destroy the frogs from thee and thy houses, *that* they may remain in the river only? ¹⁰And he said, To morrow[c]. And he said, *Be it* according to thy word: that thou mayest know that *there is* none like unto the LORD our God. ¹¹And the frogs shall depart from thee, and from thy houses, and from thy servants, and from thy people; they shall remain in the river only. ¹²And Moses and Aaron went out from Pharaoh: and Moses cried unto the LORD because of the frogs which he had brought against Pharaoh. ¹³And the LORD did according to the word of Moses; and the frogs died out of the houses, out of the villages, and out of the fields. ¹⁴And they gathered them together upon heaps: and the land stank. ¹⁵But when Pharaoh saw that there was respite, he hardened his heart, and hearkened not unto them; as the LORD had said.

¹⁶And the LORD said unto Moses, Say unto Aaron, Stretch out thy rod, and smite the dust of the land, that it may become lice throughout all the land of Egypt. ¹⁷And they did so; for Aaron stretched out his hand with his rod, and smote the dust of the earth, and it became lice in man, and in beast; all the dust of the land became lice throughout all the land of Egypt. ¹⁸And the magicians did so with their enchantments to bring forth lice, but they could not: so there were lice upon man, and upon beast. ¹⁹Then the magicians said unto Pharaoh, This *is* the finger of God: and Pharaoh's heart was hardened, and he hearkened not unto them; as the LORD had said.

²⁰And the LORD said unto Moses, Rise up early in the morning, and stand before Pharaoh; lo, he cometh forth to the water; and say unto him, Thus saith the LORD, Let my people go, that they may serve me. ²¹Else, if thou wilt not let my people go, behold, I will send swarms[d] *of flies* upon thee, and upon thy servants, and upon thy people, and into thy houses: and the houses of the Egyptians shall be full of swarms *of flies*, and also the ground whereon they *are*. ²²And I will sever in that day the land of Goshen, in which my people dwell, that no swarms *of flies* shall be there; to the end thou mayest know that I *am*

---

[b] Glory . . . : or, Have this honour over me, etc

[c] To morrow: or, Against to morrow

[d] swarms . . . : or, a mixture of noisome beasts, etc

Devotional Moment

Compromise

8:25-29 Pharaoh urged the Hebrews to sacrifice nearby. Moses insisted that they needed to go three days' journey into the wilderness, exactly as God had commanded. We can and should compromise on matters of style or personal preference, but not on matters in which God has given a clear command. Choose your battles carefully. Conflict goes hand in hand with family living, so be willing to negotiate when something less than a biblical command is at stake. If you do, you'll have more credibility when needing to enforce a clear command from God.

the LORD in the midst of the earth. ²³And I will put a division^e between my people and thy people: to morrow shall this sign be. ²⁴And the LORD did so; and there came a grievous swarm *of flies* into the house of Pharaoh, and *into* his servants' houses, and into all the land of Egypt: the land was corrupted^f by reason of the swarm *of flies.* ²⁵And Pharaoh called for Moses and for Aaron, and said, Go ye, sacrifice to your God in the land. ²⁶And Moses said, It is not meet so to do; for we shall sacrifice the abomination of the Egyptians to the LORD our God; lo, shall we sacrifice the abomination of the Egyptians before their eyes, and will they not stone us? ²⁷We will go three days' journey into the wilderness, and sacrifice to the LORD our God, as he shall command us. ²⁸And Pharaoh said, I will let you go, that ye may sacrifice to the LORD your God in the wilderness; only ye shall not go very far away: intreat for me. ²⁹And

Moses said, Behold, I go out from thee, and I will intreat the LORD that the swarms *of flies* may depart from Pharaoh, from his servants, and from his people, to morrow: but let not Pharaoh deal deceitfully any more in not letting the people go to sacrifice to the LORD. ³⁰And Moses went out from Pharaoh, and intreated the LORD. ³¹And the LORD did according to the word of Moses; and he removed the swarms *of flies* from Pharaoh, from his servants, and from his people; there remained not one. ³²And Pharaoh hardened his heart at this time also, neither would he let the people go.

9

¹Then the LORD said unto Moses, Go in unto Pharaoh, and tell him, Thus saith the LORD God of the Hebrews, Let my people go, that they may serve me. ²For if thou refuse to let *them* go,

Devotional Moment

Perseverance

9:1 Moses was told repeatedly to "go unto" Pharaoh (Exod. 3:10; 7:15; 8:1, 20; 10:1). Each time, Moses held out hope for change. Each time, Pharaoh's hard heart proved disappointing. Moses' remarkable patience and perseverance with Pharaoh encourages all of us who must deal with difficult family members to persevere if the matter is important. If you have young children, stubborn teenagers, or ornery relatives who clash with you again and again, choose your battle carefully but persevere. If the stakes matter, it's often better to suffer through the conflict than to back down and let foolishness get the upper hand.

---

^e a division: Heb. a redemption
^f corrupted: or, destroyed

and wilt hold them still, ³Behold, the hand of the LORD is upon thy cattle which *is* in the field, upon the horses, upon the asses, upon the camels, upon the oxen, and upon the sheep: *there shall be* a very grievous murrain. ⁴And the LORD shall sever between the cattle of Israel and the cattle of Egypt: and there shall nothing die of all *that is* the children's of Israel. ⁵And the LORD appointed a set time, saying, To morrow the LORD shall do this thing in the land. ⁶And the LORD did that thing on the morrow, and all the cattle of Egypt died: but of the cattle of the children of Israel died not one. ⁷And Pharaoh sent, and, behold, there was not one of the cattle of the Israelites dead. And the heart of Pharaoh was hardened, and he did not let the people go.

⁸And the LORD said unto Moses and unto Aaron, Take to you handfuls of ashes of the furnace, and let Moses sprinkle it toward the heaven in the sight of Pharaoh. ⁹And it shall become small dust in all the land of Egypt, and shall be a boil breaking forth *with* blains upon man, and upon beast, throughout all the land of Egypt. ¹⁰And they took ashes of the furnace, and stood before Pharaoh; and Moses sprinkled it up toward heaven; and it became a boil breaking forth *with* blains upon man, and upon beast. ¹¹And the magicians could not stand before Moses because of the boils; for the boil was upon the magicians, and upon all the Egyptians. ¹²And the LORD hardened the heart of Pharaoh, and he hearkened not unto them; as the LORD had spoken unto Moses.

¹³And the LORD said unto Moses, Rise up early in the morning, and stand before Pharaoh, and say unto him, Thus saith the LORD God of the Hebrews, Let my people go, that they may serve me. ¹⁴For I will at this time send all my plagues upon thine heart, and upon thy servants, and upon thy people; that thou mayest know that *there is* none like me in all the earth. ¹⁵For now I will stretch out my hand, that I may smite thee and thy people with pestilence; and thou shalt be cut off from the earth. ¹⁶And in very deed for this *cause* have I raised thee up, for to shew *in* thee my power; and that my name may be declared throughout all the earth. ¹⁷As yet exaltest thou thyself against my people, that thou wilt not let them go? ¹⁸Behold, to morrow about this time I will cause it to rain a very grievous hail, such as hath not been in Egypt since the foundation thereof even until now. ¹⁹Send therefore now, *and* gather thy cattle, and all that thou hast in the field; *for upon* every man and beast which shall be found in the field, and shall not be brought home, the hail shall come down upon them, and they shall die. ²⁰He that feared the word of the LORD among the servants of Pharaoh made his servants and his cattle flee into the houses: ²¹And he that regardedª not the word of the LORD left his servants and his cattle in the field.

²²And the LORD said unto Moses, Stretch forth thine hand toward heaven, that there may be hail in all the land of Egypt, upon man, and upon beast, and upon every herb of the field,

ª regarded . . . : Heb. set not his heart unto

throughout the land of Egypt. ²³And Moses stretched forth his rod toward heaven: and the LORD sent thunder and hail, and the fire ran along upon the ground; and the LORD rained hail upon the land of Egypt. ²⁴So there was hail, and fire mingled with the hail, very grievous, such as there was none like it in all the land of Egypt since it became a nation. ²⁵And the hail smote throughout all the land of Egypt all that *was* in the field, both man and beast; and the hail smote every herb of the field, and brake every tree of the field. ²⁶Only in the land of Goshen, where the children of Israel *were*, was there no hail. ²⁷And Pharaoh sent, and called for Moses and Aaron, and said unto them, I have sinned this time: the LORD *is* righteous, and I and my people *are* wicked. ²⁸Intreat the LORD (for *it is* enough) that there be no *more* mighty[b] thunderings and hail; and I will let you go, and ye shall stay no longer. ²⁹And Moses said unto him, As soon as I am gone out of the city, I will spread abroad my hands unto the LORD; *and* the thunder shall cease, neither shall there be any more hail; that thou mayest know how that the earth *is* the LORD'S. ³⁰But as for thee and thy servants, I know that ye will not yet fear the LORD God. ³¹And the flax and the barley was smitten: for the barley *was* in the ear, and the flax *was* bolled. ³²But the wheat and the rie were not smitten: for they *were* not grown up. ³³And Moses went out of the city from Pharaoh, and spread abroad his hands unto the LORD: and the thunders and hail ceased, and the rain was not poured upon the earth. ³⁴And when Pharaoh saw that the rain and the hail and the thunders were ceased, he sinned yet more, and hardened his heart, he and his servants. ³⁵And the heart of Pharaoh was hardened, neither would he let the children of Israel go; as the LORD had spoken by Moses[c].

10

¹And the LORD said unto Moses, Go in unto Pharaoh: for I have hardened his heart, and the heart of his servants, that I might shew these my signs before him: ²And that thou mayest tell in the ears of thy son, and of thy son's son, what things I have wrought in Egypt, and my signs which I have done among them; that ye may know how that I *am* the LORD. ³And Moses and Aaron came in unto Pharaoh, and said unto him, Thus saith the LORD God of the Hebrews, How long wilt thou refuse to

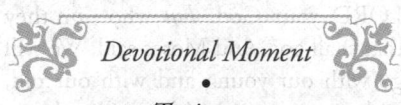

Devotional Moment

•

Testimony

10:2 The story of God's delivering the Israelites out of Egypt would become a testimony to God's power and love for his people that they could tell to their children and grandchildren. These testimonies would become the foundation of their children's faith. How has God worked in your life? Share with your family how God answers your prayers and meets your needs. Celebrate together how he works in your family. Recounting God's goodness together will form the foundation of your children's faith as they grow and eventually leave home.

---

[b] mighty . . . : Heb. voices of God
[c] by Moses: Heb. by the hand of Moses

humble thyself before me? let my people go, that they may serve me. ⁴Else, if thou refuse to let my people go, behold, to morrow will I bring the locusts into thy coast: ⁵And they shall cover the faceᵃ of the earth, that one cannot be able to see the earth: and they shall eat the residue of that which is escaped, which remaineth unto you from the hail, and shall eat every tree which groweth for you out of the field: ⁶And they shall fill thy houses, and the houses of all thy servants, and the houses of all the Egyptians; which neither thy fathers, nor thy fathers' fathers have seen, since the day that they were upon the earth unto this day. And he turned himself, and went out from Pharaoh. ⁷And Pharaoh's servants said unto him, How long shall this man be a snare unto us? let the men go, that they may serve the LORD their God: knowest thou not yet that Egypt is destroyed? ⁸And Moses and Aaron were brought again unto Pharaoh: and he said unto them, Go, serve the LORD your God: *but* whoᵇ *are* they that shall go? ⁹And Moses said, We will go with our young and with our old, with our sons and with our daughters, with our flocks and with our herds will we go; for we *must hold* a feast unto the LORD. ¹⁰And he said unto them, Let the LORD be so with you, as I will let you go, and your little ones: look *to it*; for evil *is* before you. ¹¹Not so: go now ye *that are* men, and serve the LORD; for that ye did desire. And they were driven out from Pharaoh's presence.

¹²And the LORD said unto Moses, Stretch out thine hand over the land of Egypt for the locusts, that they may come up upon the land of Egypt, and eat every herb of the land, *even* all that the hail hath left. ¹³And Moses stretched forth his rod over the land of Egypt, and the LORD brought an east wind upon the land all that day, and all *that* night; *and* when it was morning, the east wind brought the locusts. ¹⁴And the locusts went up over all the land of Egypt, and rested in all the coasts of Egypt: very grievous *were they*; before them there were no such locusts as they, neither after them shall be such. ¹⁵For they covered the face of the whole earth, so that the land was darkened; and they did eat every herb of the land, and all the fruit of the trees which the hail had left: and there remained not any green thing in the trees, or in the herbs of the field, through all the land of Egypt. ¹⁶Then Pharaoh calledᶜ for Moses and Aaron in haste; and he said, I have sinned against the LORD your God, and against you. ¹⁷Now therefore forgive, I pray thee, my sin only this once, and intreat the LORD your God, that he may take away from me this death only. ¹⁸And he went out from Pharaoh, and intreated the LORD. ¹⁹And the LORD turned a mighty strong west wind, which took away the locusts, and castᵈ them into the Red sea; there remained not one locust in all the coasts of Egypt. ²⁰But the LORD hardened Pharaoh's heart, so

---

ᵃ face: Heb. eye
ᵇ who . . . : Heb. who and who, etc
ᶜ called: Heb. hastened to call
ᵈ cast: Heb. fastened

that he would not let the children of Israel go.

²¹And the LORD said unto Moses, Stretch out thine hand toward heaven, that there may be darkness over the land of Egypt, even darkness *which* may be felt. ²²And Moses stretched forth his hand toward heaven; and there was a thick darkness in all the land of Egypt three days: ²³They saw not one another, neither rose any from his place for three days: but all the children of Israel had light in their dwellings. ²⁴And Pharaoh called unto Moses, and said, Go ye, serve the LORD; only let your flocks and your herds be stayed: let your little ones also go with you. ²⁵And Moses said, Thou must give us^c also sacrifices and burnt offerings, that we may sacrifice unto the LORD our God. ²⁶Our cattle also shall go with us; there shall not an hoof be left behind; for thereof must we take to serve the LORD our God; and we know not with what we must serve the LORD, until we come thither. ²⁷But the LORD hardened Pharaoh's heart, and he would not let them go. ²⁸And Pharaoh said unto him, Get thee from me, take heed to thyself, see my face no more; for in *that* day thou seest my face thou shalt die. ²⁹And Moses said, Thou hast spoken well, I will see thy face again no more.

11

¹And the LORD said unto Moses, Yet will I bring one plague *more* upon Pharaoh, and upon Egypt; afterwards he will let you go hence: when he shall let *you* go, he shall surely thrust you out hence altogether. ²Speak now in the ears of the people, and let every man borrow of his neighbour, and every woman of her neighbour, jewels of silver, and jewels of gold. ³And the LORD gave the people favour in the sight of the Egyptians. Moreover the man Moses *was* very great in the land of Egypt, in the sight of Pharaoh's servants, and in the sight of the people.

⁴And Moses said, Thus saith the LORD, About midnight will I go out into the midst of Egypt: ⁵And all the firstborn in the land of Egypt shall die, from the firstborn of Pharaoh that sitteth upon his throne, even unto the firstborn of the maidservant that *is* behind the mill; and all the firstborn of beasts. ⁶And there shall be a great cry throughout all the land of Egypt, such as there was none like it, nor shall be like it any more. ⁷But against any of the children of Israel shall not a dog move his tongue, against man or beast: that ye may know how that the LORD doth put a difference between the Egyptians and Israel. ⁸And all these thy servants shall come down unto me, and bow down themselves unto me, saying, Get thee out, and all the people that follow^a thee: and after that I will go out. And he went out from Pharaoh in a great anger. ⁹And the LORD said unto Moses, Pharaoh shall not hearken unto you; that my wonders may be multiplied in the land of Egypt. ¹⁰And Moses and Aaron did all these wonders before Pharaoh: and the LORD hardened Pharaoh's heart, so that he would not

---

^c us: Heb. into our hands
^a that follow . . . : Heb. that is at thy feet

let the children of Israel go out of his land.

12

¹And the LORD spake unto Moses and Aaron in the land of Egypt, saying, ²This month *shall be* unto you the beginning of months: it *shall be* the first month of the year to you. ³Speak ye unto all the congregation of Israel, saying, In the tenth *day* of this month they shall take to them every man a lamb^a, according to the house of *their* fathers, a lamb for an house: ⁴And if the household be too little for the lamb, let him and his neighbour next unto his house take *it* according to the number of the souls; every man according to his eating shall make your count for the lamb. ⁵Your lamb shall be without blemish, a male of the first year: ye shall take *it* out from the sheep, or from the goats: ⁶And ye shall keep it up until the fourteenth day of the same month: and the whole assembly of the congregation of Israel shall kill it in^b the evening. ⁷And they shall take of the blood, and strike *it* on the two side posts and on the upper door post of the houses, wherein they shall eat it. ⁸And they shall eat the flesh in that night, roast with fire, and unleavened bread; *and* with bitter *herbs* they shall eat it. ⁹Eat not of it raw, nor sodden at all with water, but roast *with* fire; his head with his legs, and with the purtenance thereof. ¹⁰And ye shall let nothing of it remain until the morning;

and that which remaineth of it until the morning ye shall burn with fire. ¹¹And thus shall ye eat it; *with* your loins girded, your shoes on your feet, and your staff in your hand; and ye shall eat it in haste: it *is* the LORD'S passover. ¹²For I will pass through the land of Egypt this night, and will smite all the firstborn in the land of Egypt, both man and beast; and against all the gods^c of Egypt I will execute judgment: I *am* the LORD. ¹³And the blood shall be to you for a token upon the houses where ye *are*: and when I see the blood, I will pass over you, and the plague shall not be upon you to destroy^d *you*, when I smite the land of Egypt. ¹⁴And this day shall be unto you for a memorial; and ye shall keep it a feast to the LORD throughout your generations; ye shall keep it a feast by an ordinance for ever. ¹⁵Seven days shall ye eat unleavened bread; even the first day ye shall put away leaven out of your houses: for whosoever eateth leavened bread from the first day until the seventh day, that soul shall be cut off from Israel. ¹⁶And in the first day *there shall be* an holy convocation, and in the seventh day there shall be an holy convocation to you; no manner of work shall be done in them, save *that* which every man^e must eat, that only may be done of you. ¹⁷And ye shall observe *the feast of* unleavened bread; for in this selfsame day have I brought your armies out of the land of Egypt: therefore shall ye observe

---

^a lamb: or, kid
^b in . . . : Heb. between the two evenings
^c gods: or, princes
^d to destroy . . . : Heb. for a destruction
^e man: Heb. soul

this day in your generations by an ordinance for ever. [18]In the first *month*, on the fourteenth day of the month at even, ye shall eat unleavened bread, until the one and twentieth day of the month at even. [19]Seven days shall there be no leaven found in your houses: for whosoever eateth that which is leavened, even that soul shall be cut off from the congregation of Israel, whether he be a stranger, or born in the land. [20]Ye shall eat nothing leavened; in all your habitations shall ye eat unleavened bread.

[21]Then Moses called for all the elders of Israel, and said unto them, Draw out and take you a lamb[f] according to your families, and kill the passover. [22]And ye shall take a bunch of hyssop, and dip *it* in the blood that *is* in the bason, and strike the lintel and the two side posts with the blood that *is* in the bason; and none of you shall go out at the door of his house until the morning. [23]For the LORD will pass through to smite the Egyptians; and when he seeth the blood upon the lintel, and on the two side posts, the LORD will pass over the door, and will not suffer the destroyer to come in unto your houses to smite *you*. [24]And ye shall observe this thing for an ordinance to thee and to thy sons for ever. [25]And it shall come to pass, when ye be come to the land which the LORD will give you, according as he hath promised, that ye shall keep this service. [26]And it shall come to pass, when your children shall say unto you, What mean ye by this service?

[27]That ye shall say, It *is* the sacrifice of the LORD'S passover, who passed over the houses of the children of Israel in Egypt, when he smote the Egyptians, and delivered our houses. And the people bowed the head and worshipped. [28]And the children of Israel went away, and did as the LORD had commanded Moses and Aaron, so did they.

[29]And it came to pass, that at midnight the LORD smote all the firstborn in the land of Egypt, from the firstborn of Pharaoh that sat on his throne unto the firstborn of the captive that *was* in the dungeon[g]; and all the firstborn of cattle. [30]And Pharaoh rose up in the night, he, and all his servants, and all the Egyptians; and there was a great cry in Egypt; for *there was* not a house where *there was* not one dead. [31]And he called for Moses and Aaron by night, and said, Rise up, *and* get you forth from among my people, both ye and the children of Israel; and go, serve the LORD, as ye have said. [32]Also take your flocks and your herds, as ye have said, and be gone; and bless me also. [33]And the Egyptians were urgent upon the people, that they might send them out of the land in haste; for they said, We *be* all dead *men*. [34]And the people took their dough before it was leavened, their kneadingtroughs[h] being bound up in their clothes upon their shoulders. [35]And the children of Israel did according to the word of Moses; and they borrowed of the Egyptians jewels of silver, and jewels of gold, and raiment: [36]And the LORD gave the people favour in

[f] lamb: or, kid
[g] dungeon: Heb. house of the pit
[h] kneadingtroughs: or, dough

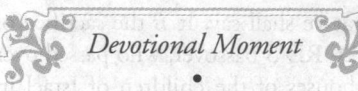

Devotional Moment

•

Hospitality

12:48-49 Some people criticize organized religion for acting as a barrier between people: Jews vs. Christians, Catholics vs. Protestants, denomination vs. denomination, etc. But God instructed his people to look for ways to *include* foreigners in their observance of the Passover. He didn't tell them to forget the standards that made them his holy people; the foreign guests were still required to fulfill the law. But God gave a clear principle: look for ways to draw outsiders in, not for ways to exclude them.

the sight of the Egyptians, so that they lent unto them *such things as they required.* And they spoiled the Egyptians.

³⁷And the children of Israel journeyed from Rameses to Succoth, about six hundred thousand on foot *that were* men, beside children. ³⁸And a mixed[i] multitude went up also with them; and flocks, and herds, *even* very much cattle. ³⁹And they baked unleavened cakes of the dough which they brought forth out of Egypt, for it was not leavened; because they were thrust out of Egypt, and could not tarry, neither had they prepared for themselves any victual. ⁴⁰Now the sojourning of the children of Israel, who dwelt in Egypt, *was* four hundred and thirty years. ⁴¹And it came to pass at the end of the four hundred and thirty years, even the selfsame day it came to pass, that all the hosts of the LORD went out from the land of Egypt. ⁴²It *is* a night[j] to be much ob-

served unto the LORD for bringing them out from the land of Egypt: this *is* that night of the LORD to be observed of all the children of Israel in their generations.

⁴³And the LORD said unto Moses and Aaron, This *is* the ordinance of the passover: There shall no stranger eat thereof: ⁴⁴But every man's servant that is bought for money, when thou hast circumcised him, then shall he eat thereof. ⁴⁵A foreigner and an hired servant shall not eat thereof. ⁴⁶In one house shall it be eaten; thou shalt not carry forth ought of the flesh abroad out of the house; neither shall ye break a bone thereof. ⁴⁷All the congregation of Israel shall keep[k] it. ⁴⁸And when a stranger shall sojourn with thee, and will keep the passover to the LORD, let all his males be circumcised, and then let him come near and keep it; and he shall be as one that is born in the land: for no uncircumcised person shall eat thereof. ⁴⁹One law shall be to him that is homeborn, and unto the stranger that sojourneth among you. ⁵⁰Thus did all the children of Israel; as the LORD commanded Moses and Aaron, so did they. ⁵¹And it came to pass the selfsame day, *that* the LORD did bring the children of Israel out of the land of Egypt by their armies.

13

¹And the LORD spake unto Moses, saying, ²Sanctify unto me all the firstborn, whatsoever openeth the womb among the children of Israel, *both* of man and of

---

[i] a mixed . . . : Heb. a great mixture
[j] a night . . . : Heb. a night of observations
[k] keep . . . : Heb. do it

Family Traditions

Telling Stories to the Family

EXODUS 12–15

A candle glows from a brass holder on the table. Susan picks up the long feather next to it and tickles her baby brother under the chin.

"Dad, where are you?" she calls excitedly. "Come on!"

It is the evening before Passover, the most important religious holiday on the Jewish calendar. In this Denver, Colorado, family the celebration starts with a simple ritual involving Father and all the children. Holding the flickering candle and feather, they go from corner to corner in every room of the house looking for crumbs of bread, the ones Mother symbolically left for them to find after her thorough spring cleaning.

At last, on the kitchen windowsill, the crumbs are found, swept by the feather into a piece of paper, taken outside, and burned; the house is pronounced free from yeast and impurities.

The Passover feast to follow the next day will recount the climactic final plague God inflicted on the ancient Egyptians, killing the firstborn in every family while passing over Hebrew households. For the messianic Jewish family, it is a way of teaching about the greatest story of all—the story of God's love and the redemption of his people through the blood of Jesus Christ.

Just as the celebration of Passover provides a time and context to retell Hebrew stories, Christian families can create personalized ways and times to retell their stories of God's intervention in hard times, marking forever the places of God's redemptive love.

Did your family go through a desert this year? Or did you stand at the edge of a Red Sea and witness the water parting? Do you remember the tears or laughter? the astonishment you saw on each other's face when God changed everything? These are the milestones you want to remember.

Why not write down the events that have taught your family about God? What crises have you faced? What did you pray at the time? How did you find comfort and guidance? How did God meet your needs? What wonderful surprises did he bring out of the hardship? Record the stories however you like—make a tape recording, write them down, or annotate a photo album. Get different family members' versions.

The point is to tell and retell the stories, until, in a sense, they become family testimonies. Just as the Israelites sang to the Lord on the far banks of the Red Sea, putting their crossing into words and music of praise to God, our stories honor God and give us another way to praise him in families.

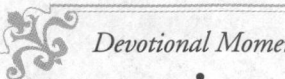

Devotional Moment

•

Celebrations

13:8-10 If people from a culture unfamiliar with the Bible spent Christmas with your family, what would they observe? Colored lights, plastic Santas, trees with pretty packages underneath? Or next Easter: chocolate bunnies, decorated eggs, new clothes for the children? Would your guests understand that there are real, historical, flesh-and-blood events behind the festivities? Children start out just like such foreigners. They don't grasp the significance of these and other religious holidays any more than you did when you were a young child. Explain your celebrations to your children. To do otherwise risks losing their meaning, or missing the chance to teach your children something important.

beast: it *is* mine. ³And Moses said unto the people, Remember this day, in which ye came out from Egypt, out of the house of bondageᵃ; for by strength of hand the LORD brought you out from this *place*: there shall no leavened bread be eaten. ⁴This day came ye out in the month Abib. ⁵And it shall be when the LORD shall bring thee into the land of the Canaanites, and the Hittites, and the Amorites, and the Hivites, and the Jebusites, which he sware unto thy fathers to give thee, a land flowing with milk and honey, that thou shalt keep this service in this month. ⁶Seven days thou shalt eat unleavened bread, and in the seventh day *shall be* a feast to the LORD. ⁷Unleavened bread shall be eaten seven days; and there shall no leavened bread be seen with thee, neither shall there be leaven seen with thee in all thy quarters. ⁸And thou shalt shew thy son in that day,

saying, *This is done* because of that *which* the LORD did unto me when I came forth out of Egypt. ⁹And it shall be for a sign unto thee upon thine hand, and for a memorial between thine eyes, that the LORD'S law may be in thy mouth: for with a strong hand hath the LORD brought thee out of Egypt. ¹⁰Thou shalt therefore keep this ordinance in his season from year to year.

¹¹And it shall be when the LORD shall bring thee into the land of the Canaanites, as he sware unto thee and to thy fathers, and shall give it thee, ¹²That thou shalt set apart unto the LORD all that openeth the matrix, and every firstling that cometh of a beast which thou hast; the males *shall be* the LORD'S. ¹³And every firstling of an ass thou shalt redeem with a lambᵇ; and if thou wilt not redeem it, then thou shalt break his neck: and all the firstborn of man among thy children shalt thou redeem. ¹⁴And it shall be when thy son asketh thee in time to come, saying, What *is* this? that thou shalt say unto him, By strength of hand the LORD brought us out from Egypt, from the house of bondage: ¹⁵And it came to pass, when Pharaoh would hardly let us go, that the LORD slew all the firstborn in the land of Egypt, both the firstborn of man, and the firstborn of beast: therefore I sacrifice to the LORD all that openeth the matrix, being males; but all the firstborn of my children I redeem. ¹⁶And it shall be for a token upon thine hand, and for frontlets between thine eyes: for by strength of hand the LORD brought us forth out of Egypt.

¹⁷And it came to pass, when

ᵃ bondage: Heb. servants
ᵇ lamb: or, kid

Pharaoh had let the people go, that God led them not *through* the way of the land of the Philistines, although that *was* near; for God said, Lest peradventure the people repent when they see war, and they return to Egypt: ¹⁸But God led the people about, *through* the way of the wilderness of the Red sea: and the children of Israel went up harnessed ͨ out of the land of Egypt. ¹⁹And Moses took the bones of Joseph with him: for he had straitly sworn the children of Israel, saying, God will surely visit you; and ye shall carry up my bones away hence with you. ²⁰And they took their journey from Succoth, and encamped in Etham, in the edge of the wilderness. ²¹And the LORD went before them by day in a pillar of a cloud, to lead them the way; and by night in a pillar of fire, to give them light; to go by day and night: ²²He took not away the pillar of the cloud by day, nor the pillar of fire by night, *from* before the people.

14

¹And the LORD spake unto Moses, saying, ²Speak unto the children of Israel, that they turn and encamp before Pihahiroth, between Migdol and the sea, over against Baalzephon: before it shall ye encamp by the sea. ³For Pharaoh will say of the children of Israel, They *are* entangled in the land, the wilderness hath shut them in. ⁴And I will harden Pharaoh's heart, that he shall follow after them; and I will be honoured upon Pharaoh, and upon all his host; that the Egyptians may know that I *am* the LORD. And they did so.

⁵And it was told the king of Egypt that the people fled: and the heart of Pharaoh and of his servants was turned against the people, and they said, Why have we done this, that we have let Israel go from serving us? ⁶And he made ready his chariot, and took his people with him: ⁷And he took six hundred chosen chariots, and all the chariots of Egypt, and captains over every one of them. ⁸And the LORD hardened the heart of Pharaoh king of Egypt, and he pursued after the children of Israel: and the children of Israel went out with an high hand. ⁹But the Egyptians pursued after them, all the horses *and* chariots of Pharaoh, and his horsemen, and his army, and overtook them encamping by the sea, beside Pihahiroth, before Baalzephon.

¹⁰And when Pharaoh drew nigh, the children of Israel lifted up their eyes, and, behold, the Egyptians marched after them; and they were sore afraid: and the children of Israel cried out unto the LORD. ¹¹And they said unto Moses, Because *there were* no graves in Egypt, hast thou taken us away to die in the wilderness? wherefore hast thou dealt thus with us, to carry us forth out of Egypt? ¹²*Is* not this the word that we did tell thee in Egypt, saying, Let us alone, that we may serve the Egyptians? For *it had been* better for us to serve the Egyptians, than that we should die in the wilderness. ¹³And Moses said unto the people, Fear ye not, stand still, and see the salvation of the LORD, which he will shew to you to day: for the Egyptians whom ye have seen to day, ye shall see them again no

---

ͨ harnessed: or, by five in a rank

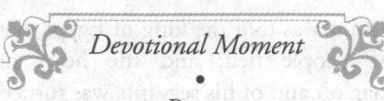

Devotional Moment

•

Prayer

14:15 God heard the cries of his people and saw the courageous stand taken by his chosen leader, Moses. He did not need to see anything more or to be persuaded to act on their behalf; he had promised to deliver them from the Egyptians, and now the time had come. He had done his part, miraculously parting the Red Sea. Now he wanted them to do their part, to step into the dry seabed. God wants us to pray, but there comes a time when we should start moving as well. As you pray, ask how you can act on the needs you bring before God.

was a cloud and darkness *to them*, but it gave light by night *to these*: so that the one came not near the other all the night. ²¹And Moses stretched out his hand over the sea; and the LORD caused the sea to go *back* by a strong east wind all that night, and made the sea dry *land*, and the waters were divided. ²²And the children of Israel went into the midst of the sea upon the dry *ground*: and the waters *were* a wall unto them on their right hand, and on their left. ²³And the Egyptians pursued, and went in after them to the midst of the sea, *even* all Pharaoh's horses, his chariots, and his horsemen. ²⁴And it came to pass, that in the morning watch the LORD looked unto the host of the Egyptians through the pillar of fire and of the cloud, and troubled the host of the Egyptians, ²⁵And took off their chariot wheels, that they drave them heavily: so that the Egyptians said, Let us flee from the face of Israel; for the LORD fighteth for them against the Egyptians. ²⁶And the LORD said unto Moses, Stretch out thine hand over the sea, that the waters may come again upon the Egyptians, upon their chariots, and upon their horsemen. ²⁷And Moses stretched forth his hand over the sea, and the sea returned to his strength when the morning appeared; and the Egyptians fled against it; and the LORD overthrew^a the Egyptians in the midst of the sea. ²⁸And the waters returned, and covered the chariots, and the horsemen, *and* all the host of Pharaoh that came into the sea after them; there remained not so much as

more for ever. ¹⁴The LORD shall fight for you, and ye shall hold your peace.

¹⁵And the LORD said unto Moses, Wherefore criest thou unto me? speak unto the children of Israel, that they go forward: ¹⁶But lift thou up thy rod, and stretch out thine hand over the sea, and divide it: and the children of Israel shall go on dry *ground* through the midst of the sea. ¹⁷And I, behold, I will harden the hearts of the Egyptians, and they shall follow them: and I will get me honour upon Pharaoh, and upon all his host, upon his chariots, and upon his horsemen. ¹⁸And the Egyptians shall know that I *am* the LORD, when I have gotten me honour upon Pharaoh, upon his chariots, and upon his horsemen. ¹⁹And the angel of God, which went before the camp of Israel, removed and went behind them; and the pillar of the cloud went from before their face, and stood behind them: ²⁰And it came between the camp of the Egyptians and the camp of Israel; and it

---

^a overthrew: Heb. shook off

one of them. [29]But the children of Israel walked upon dry *land* in the midst of the sea; and the waters *were* a wall unto them on their right hand, and on their left. [30]Thus the LORD saved Israel that day out of the hand of the Egyptians; and Israel saw the Egyptians dead upon the sea shore. [31]And Israel saw that great work[b] which the LORD did upon the Egyptians: and the people feared the LORD, and believed the LORD, and his servant Moses.

15

[1]Then sang Moses and the children of Israel this song unto the LORD, and spake, saying, I will sing unto the LORD, for he hath triumphed gloriously: the horse and his rider hath he thrown into the sea. [2]The LORD *is* my strength and song, and he is become my salvation: he *is* my God, and I will prepare him an habitation; my father's God, and I will exalt him. [3]The LORD *is* a man of war: the LORD *is* his name. [4]Pharaoh's chariots and his host hath he cast into the sea: his chosen captains also are drowned in the Red sea. [5]The depths have covered them: they sank into the bottom as a stone. [6]Thy right hand, O LORD, is become glorious in power: thy right hand, O LORD, hath dashed in pieces the enemy. [7]And in the greatness of thine excellency thou hast overthrown them that rose up against thee: thou sentest forth thy wrath, *which* consumed them as stubble. [8]And with the blast of thy nostrils the waters were gathered together, the floods stood

upright as an heap, *and* the depths were congealed in the heart of the sea. [9]The enemy said, I will pursue, I will overtake, I will divide the spoil; my lust shall be satisfied upon them; I will draw my sword, my hand shall destroy[a] them. [10]Thou didst blow with thy wind, the sea covered them: they sank as lead in the mighty waters. [11]Who *is* like unto thee, O LORD, among the gods[b]? who *is* like thee, glorious in holiness, fearful *in* praises, doing wonders? [12]Thou stretchedst out thy right hand, the earth swallowed them. [13]Thou in thy mercy hast led forth the people *which* thou hast redeemed: thou hast guided *them* in thy strength unto thy holy habitation. [14]The people shall hear, *and* be afraid: sorrow shall take hold on the inhabitants of Palestina. [15]Then the dukes of Edom shall be amazed; the mighty men of Moab, trembling shall take hold upon them; all the inhabitants of Canaan shall melt away. [16]Fear and dread shall fall upon them; by the greatness of thine arm they shall be *as* still as a stone; till thy people pass over, O LORD, till the people pass over, *which* thou hast purchased. [17]Thou shalt bring them in, and plant them in the mountain of thine inheritance, *in* the place, O LORD, *which* thou hast made for thee to dwell in, *in* the Sanctuary, O Lord, *which* thy hands have established. [18]The LORD shall reign for ever and ever. [19]For the horse of Pharaoh went in with his chariots and with his horsemen into the sea, and the LORD brought again the waters of the

---

[b] work: Heb. hand
[a] destroy: or, repossess
[b] gods: or, mighty ones?

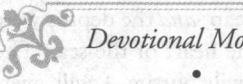

Devotional Moment
•
Obedience

15:26 Obedience brings God's blessing, and disobedience brings his punishment. Sometimes his responses have taken supernatural forms, as in the parting of the Red Sea. Other times they have been built into the fabric of everyday life, as in this case, where adherence to God's laws (dietary and otherwise) would keep the Israelites free of certain diseases and immoral religious practices common to that part of the world. God's rules cause us to live in harmony with this world of his design. Look for object lessons—natural and supernatural—to help understand that obedience to him is the best possible life-style.

sea upon them; but the children of Israel went on dry *land* in the midst of the sea. ²⁰And Miriam the prophetess, the sister of Aaron, took a timbrel in her hand; and all the women went out after her with timbrels and with dances. ²¹And Miriam answered them, Sing ye to the LORD, for he hath triumphed gloriously; the horse and his rider hath he thrown into the sea.

²²So Moses brought Israel from the Red sea, and they went out into the wilderness of Shur; and they went three days in the wilderness, and found no water. ²³And when they came to Marah^c, they could not drink of the waters of Marah, for they *were* bitter: therefore the name of it was called Marah. ²⁴And the people murmured against Moses, saying, What shall we drink? ²⁵And he cried unto the LORD; and the LORD shewed him a tree, *which* when he had cast into the waters, the waters were made sweet: there he

made for them a statute and an ordinance, and there he proved them, ²⁶And said, If thou wilt diligently hearken to the voice of the LORD thy God, and wilt do that which is right in his sight, and wilt give ear to his commandments, and keep all his statutes, I will put none of these diseases upon thee, which I have brought upon the Egyptians: for I *am* the LORD that healeth thee. ²⁷And they came to Elim, where *were* twelve wells of water, and threescore and ten palm trees: and they encamped there by the waters.

16

¹And they took their journey from Elim, and all the congregation of the children of Israel came unto the wilderness of Sin, which *is* between Elim and Sinai, on the fifteenth day of the second month after their departing out of the land of Egypt. ²And the whole congregation of the children of Israel murmured against Moses and Aaron in the wilderness: ³And the

Devotional Moment
•
Complaining

16:2 Even after God had miraculously brought the Israelites out of Egypt, parted the Red Sea, and destroyed Pharaoh's army, they still doubted his ability to meet their needs. Rather than encourage each other with recollections of God's faithfulness, they complained. Many parents feel that their children complain about everything. But adults do it too. The next time something annoys you, first ask what you can do to contribute to a solution. Instead of complaining, remember the many ways God has met your needs and promised never to leave you (see Heb. 13:5).

^c Marah: that is Bitterness

children of Israel said unto them, Would to God we had died by the hand of the LORD in the land of Egypt, when we sat by the flesh pots, *and* when we did eat bread to the full; for ye have brought us forth into this wilderness, to kill this whole assembly with hunger. ⁴Then said the LORD unto Moses, Behold, I will rain bread from heaven for you; and the people shall go out and gather a certain rate every day, that I may prove them, whether they will walk in my law, or no. ⁵And it shall come to pass, that on the sixth day they shall prepare *that* which they bring in; and it shall be twice as much as they gather daily. ⁶And Moses and Aaron said unto all the children of Israel, At even, then ye shall know that the LORD hath brought you out from the land of Egypt: ⁷And in the morning, then ye shall see the glory of the LORD; for that he heareth your murmurings against the LORD: and what *are* we, that ye murmur against us? ⁸And Moses said, *This shall be*, when the LORD shall give you in the evening flesh to eat, and in the morning bread to the full; for that the LORD heareth your murmurings which ye murmur against him: and what *are* we? your murmurings *are* not against us, but against the LORD. ⁹And Moses spake unto Aaron, Say unto all the congregation of the children of Israel, Come near before the LORD: for he hath heard your murmurings. ¹⁰And it came to pass, as Aaron spake unto the whole congregation of the children of Israel, that they looked toward the wilderness, and, behold, the glory of the LORD appeared in the cloud. ¹¹And the LORD spake unto Moses, saying, ¹²I have heard the murmurings of the children of Israel: speak unto them, saying, At even ye shall eat flesh, and in the morning ye shall be filled with bread; and ye shall know that I *am* the LORD your God.

¹³And it came to pass, that at even the quails came up, and covered the camp: and in the morning the dew lay round about the host. ¹⁴And when the dew that lay was gone up, behold, upon the face of the wilderness *there lay* a small round thing, *as* small as the hoar frost on the ground. ¹⁵And when the children of Israel saw *it*, they said one to another, It *is* manna: for they wist not what it *was*. And Moses said unto them, This *is* the bread which the LORD hath given you to eat. ¹⁶This *is* the thing which the LORD hath commanded, Gather of it every man according to his eating, an omer for every man, *according to* the number of your persons; take ye every man for *them* which *are* in his tents. ¹⁷And the children of Israel did so, and gathered, some more, some less. ¹⁸And when they did mete *it* with an omer, he that gathered much had nothing over, and he that gathered little had no lack; they gathered every man according to his eating. ¹⁹And Moses said, Let no man leave of it till the morning. ²⁰Notwithstanding they hearkened not unto Moses; but some of them left of it until the morning, and it bred worms, and stank: and Moses was wroth with them. ²¹And they gathered it every morning, every man according to his eating: and when the sun waxed hot, it melted.

²²And it came to pass, *that* on the sixth day they gathered twice as much bread, two omers for one *man*: and all the rulers of the congregation came and told Moses. ²³And he said unto them, This *is that* which the LORD hath said,

To morrow *is* the rest of the holy sabbath unto the LORD: bake *that* which ye will bake *to day*, and seethe that ye will seethe; and that which remaineth over lay up for you to be kept until the morning. ²⁴And they laid it up till the morning, as Moses bade: and it did not stink, neither was there any worm therein. ²⁵And Moses said, Eat that to day; for to day *is* a sabbath unto the LORD: to day ye shall not find it in the field. ²⁶Six days ye shall gather it; but on the seventh day, *which is* the sabbath, in it there shall be none. ²⁷And it came to pass, *that* there went out *some* of the people on the seventh day for to gather, and they found none. ²⁸And the LORD said unto Moses, How long refuse ye to keep my commandments and my laws? ²⁹See, for that the LORD hath given you the sabbath, therefore he giveth you on the sixth day the bread of two days; abide ye every man in his place, let no man go out of his place on the seventh day. ³⁰So the people rested on the seventh day. ³¹And the house of Israel called the name thereof Manna: and it *was* like coriander seed, white; and the taste of it *was* like wafers *made* with honey.

³²And Moses said, This *is* the thing which the LORD commandeth, Fill an omer of it to be kept for your generations; that they may see the bread wherewith I have fed you in the wilderness, when I brought you forth from the land of Egypt. ³³And Moses said unto Aaron, Take a pot, and put an omer full of manna therein, and lay it up before the LORD, to be kept for your generations. ³⁴As the LORD commanded Moses, so Aaron laid it up before the Testimony, to be kept. ³⁵And the children of Israel did eat manna forty years, until they came to a land inhabited; they did eat manna, until they came unto the borders of the land of Canaan. ³⁶Now an omer *is* the tenth *part* of an ephah.

17

¹And all the congregation of the children of Israel journeyed from the wilderness of Sin, after their journeys, according to the commandment of the LORD, and pitched in Rephidim: and *there was* no water for the people to drink. ²Wherefore the people did chide with Moses, and said, Give us water that we may drink. And Moses said unto them, Why chide ye with me? wherefore do ye tempt the LORD? ³And the people thirsted there for water; and the people murmured against Moses, and said, Wherefore *is* this *that* thou hast brought us up out of Egypt, to kill us and our children and our cattle with thirst? ⁴And Moses cried unto the LORD, saying, What shall I do unto this people? they be almost ready to stone me. ⁵And the LORD said unto Moses, Go on before the people, and take with thee of the elders of Israel; and thy rod, wherewith thou smotest the river, take in thine hand, and go. ⁶Behold, I will stand before thee there upon the rock in Horeb; and thou shalt smite the rock, and there shall come water out of it, that the people may drink. And Moses did so in the sight of the elders of Israel. ⁷And he called the name of the place Massahᵃ, and Meribah, because of the chiding of the children of Israel, and because they

---

ᵃ Massah: that is, Temptation

tempted the LORD, saying, Is the LORD among us, or not?

[8]Then came Amalek, and fought with Israel in Rephidim. [9]And Moses said unto Joshua[b], Choose us out men, and go out, fight with Amalek: to morrow I will stand on the top of the hill with the rod of God in mine hand. [10]So Joshua did as Moses had said to him, and fought with Amalek: and Moses, Aaron, and Hur went up to the top of the hill. [11]And it came to pass, when Moses held up his hand, that Israel prevailed: and when he let down his hand, Amalek prevailed. [12]But Moses' hands *were* heavy; and they took a stone, and put *it* under him, and he sat thereon; and Aaron and Hur stayed up his hands, the one on the one side, and the other on the other side; and his hands were steady until the going down of the sun. [13]And Joshua discomfited Amalek and his people with the edge of the sword. [14]And the LORD said unto Moses, Write this *for* a memorial in a book, and rehearse *it* in the ears of Joshua: for I will utterly put out the remembrance of Amalek from under heaven. [15]And Moses built an altar, and called the name of it Jehovahnissi[c]: [16]For he said, Because the LORD hath sworn *that* the LORD *will have* war with Amalek from generation to generation.

18

[1]When Jethro, the priest of Midian, Moses' father in law, heard of all that God had done for Moses, and for Israel his people, *and* that the LORD had brought Israel out of Egypt; [2]Then Jethro, Moses' father in law, took Zipporah, Moses' wife, after he had sent her back, [3]And her two sons; of which the name of the one *was* Gershom[a]; for he said, I have been an alien in a strange land: [4]And the name of the other *was* Eliezer[b]; for the God of my father, *said he, was* mine help, and delivered me from the sword of Pharaoh: [5]And Jethro, Moses' father in law, came with his sons and his wife unto Moses into the wilderness, where he encamped at the mount of God: [6]And he said unto Moses, I thy father in law Jethro am come unto thee, and thy wife, and her two sons with her.

[7]And Moses went out to meet his father in law, and did obeisance, and kissed him; and they asked each other of *their* welfare[c]; and they came into

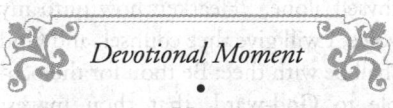

Devotional Moment

•

Unity

17:10-13 If Aaron and Hur had not come along and held up Moses' arms, the Israelites would have been defeated. Do we not do the same thing to our parents and elder relations every time we criticize them? Instead of coming alongside and offering assistance and encouragement, we "shoot the wounded," and everybody loses. Elder members of our families, especially parents, need our support.

[b] Joshua: called Jesus
[c] Jehovahnissi: that is, The LORD my banner
[a] Gershom: that is A stranger there
[b] Eliezer: that is, My God is an help
[c] welfare: Heb. peace

the tent. ⁸And Moses told his father in law all that the LORD had done unto Pharaoh and to the Egyptians for Israel's sake, *and* all the travail that had come^d upon them by the way, and *how* the LORD delivered them. ⁹And Jethro rejoiced for all the goodness which the LORD had done to Israel, whom he had delivered out of the hand of the Egyptians. ¹⁰And Jethro said, Blessed *be* the LORD, who hath delivered you out of the hand of the Egyptians, and out of the hand of Pharaoh, who hath delivered the people from under the hand of the Egyptians. ¹¹Now I know that the LORD *is* greater than all gods: for in the thing wherein they dealt proudly *he was* above them. ¹²And Jethro, Moses' father in law, took a burnt offering and sacrifices for God: and Aaron came, and all the elders of Is-

---

Devotional Moment

In-Laws

18:8-11 Moses and his father-in-law Jethro had a unique relationship. They showed obvious warmth and respect toward each other: Moses greeted Jethro warmly, and then the two went in Moses' tent to talk, just like old friends. Word had reached Jethro of how God had used Moses in extraordinary ways (18:1), and he was undoubtedly very proud of his son-in-law. In the end Jethro praised God, proclaiming him "greater than any other god." Relationships with in-laws don't have to be strained. But whether they are or not, show respect to extended family. Your relationship with them may be one way God shows his glory to an unbelieving relative.

---

rael, to eat bread with Moses' father in law before God.

¹³And it came to pass on the morrow, that Moses sat to judge the people: and the people stood by Moses from the morning unto the evening. ¹⁴And when Moses' father in law saw all that he did to the people, he said, What *is* this thing that thou doest to the people? why sittest thou thyself alone, and all the people stand by thee from morning unto even? ¹⁵And Moses said unto his father in law, Because the people come unto me to enquire of God: ¹⁶When they have a matter, they come unto me; and I judge between one^e and another, and I do make *them* know the statutes of God, and his laws. ¹⁷And Moses' father in law said unto him, The thing that thou doest *is* not good. ¹⁸Thou wilt surely wear away, both thou, and this people that *is* with thee: for this thing *is* too heavy for thee; thou art not able to perform it thyself alone. ¹⁹Hearken now unto my voice, I will give thee counsel, and God shall be with thee: Be thou for the people to God-ward, that thou mayest bring the causes unto God: ²⁰And thou shalt teach them ordinances and laws, and shalt shew them the way wherein they must walk, and the work that they must do. ²¹Moreover thou shalt provide out of all the people able men, such as fear God, men of truth, hating covetousness; and place *such* over them, *to be* rulers of thousands, *and* rulers of hundreds, rulers of fifties, and rulers of tens: ²²And let them judge the people at all seasons: and it shall be, *that* every

---

^d come . . . : Heb. found them
^e one . . . : Heb. a man and his fellow

great matter they shall bring unto thee, but every small matter they shall judge: so shall it be easier for thyself, and they shall bear *the burden* with thee. ²³If thou shalt do this thing, and God command thee *so,* then thou shalt be able to endure, and all this people shall also go to their place in peace. ²⁴So Moses hearkened to the voice of his father in law, and did all that he had said. ²⁵And Moses chose able men out of all Israel, and made them heads over the people, rulers of thousands, rulers of hundreds, rulers of fifties, and rulers of tens. ²⁶And they judged the people at all seasons: the hard causes they brought unto Moses, but every small matter they judged themselves. ²⁷And Moses let his father in law depart; and he went his way into his own land.

19

¹In the third month, when the children of Israel were gone forth out of the land of Egypt, the same day came they *into* the wilderness of Sinai. ²For they were departed from Rephidim, and were come *to* the desert of Sinai, and had pitched in the wilderness; and there Israel camped before the mount. ³And Moses went up unto God, and the LORD called unto him out of the mountain, saying, Thus shalt thou say to the house of Jacob, and tell the children of Israel; ⁴Ye have seen what I did unto the Egyptians, and *how* I bare you on eagles' wings, and brought you unto myself. ⁵Now therefore, if ye will obey my voice indeed, and keep my covenant, then ye shall be a peculiar treasure unto me above all people: for all the earth *is* mine: ⁶And ye shall be unto me a kingdom of priests, and an holy nation. These *are* the words which thou shalt speak unto the children of Israel. ⁷And Moses came and called for the elders of the people, and laid before their faces all these words which the LORD commanded him. ⁸And all the people answered together, and said, All that the LORD hath spoken we will do. And Moses returned the words of the people unto the LORD.

⁹And the LORD said unto Moses, Lo, I come unto thee in a thick cloud, that the people may hear when I speak with thee, and believe thee for ever. And Moses told the words of the people unto the LORD. ¹⁰And the LORD said unto Moses, Go unto the people, and sanctify them to day and to morrow, and let them wash their clothes, ¹¹And be ready against the third day: for the third day the LORD will come down in the sight of all the people upon mount Sinai. ¹²And thou shalt set bounds unto the people round about, saying, Take heed to yourselves, *that ye* go *not* up

into the mount, or touch the border of it: whosoever toucheth the mount shall be surely put to death: [13]There shall not an hand touch it, but he shall surely be stoned, or shot through; whether *it be* beast or man, it shall not live: when the trumpet[a] soundeth long, they shall come up to the mount. [14]And Moses went down from the mount unto the people, and sanctified the people; and they washed their clothes. [15]And he said unto the people, Be ready against the third day: come not at *your* wives.

[16]And it came to pass on the third day in the morning, that there were thunders and lightnings, and a thick cloud upon the mount, and the voice of the trumpet exceeding loud; so that all the people that *was* in the camp trembled. [17]And Moses brought forth the people out of the camp to meet with God; and they stood at the nether part of the mount. [18]And mount Sinai was altogether on a smoke, because the LORD descended upon it in fire: and the smoke thereof ascended as the smoke of a furnace, and the whole mount quaked greatly. [19]And when the voice of the trumpet sounded long, and waxed louder and louder, Moses spake, and God answered him by a voice. [20]And the LORD came down upon mount Sinai, on the top of the mount: and the LORD called Moses *up* to the top of the mount; and Moses went up. [21]And the LORD said unto Moses, Go down, charge[b] the people, lest they break through unto the LORD to gaze, and many of them perish. [22]And let the priests also, which

come near to the LORD, sanctify themselves, lest the LORD break forth upon them. [23]And Moses said unto the LORD, The people cannot come up to mount Sinai: for thou chargedst us, saying, Set bounds about the mount, and sanctify it. [24]And the LORD said unto him, Away, get thee down, and thou shalt come up, thou, and Aaron with thee: but let not the priests and the people break through to come up unto the LORD, lest he break forth upon them. [25]So Moses went down unto the people, and spake unto them.

20

[1]And God spake all these words, saying, [2]I *am* the LORD thy God, which have brought thee out of the land of Egypt, out of the house of bondage[a]. [3]Thou shalt have no other gods before me. [4]Thou shalt not make unto thee any graven image, or any likeness *of any thing* that *is* in heaven above, or that *is* in the earth beneath, or that *is* in the water under the earth: [5]Thou shalt not bow down thyself to them, nor serve them: for I the LORD thy God *am* a jealous God, visiting the iniquity of the fathers upon the children unto the third and fourth *generation* of them that hate me; [6]And shewing mercy unto thousands of them that love me, and keep my commandments. [7]Thou shalt not take the name of the LORD thy God in vain; for the LORD will not hold him guiltless that taketh his name in vain. [8]Remember the sabbath day, to keep it holy. [9]Six days shalt thou labour, and do all thy work:

---

[a] trumpet: or, cornet
[b] charge: Heb. contest
[a] bondage: Heb. servants

¹⁰But the seventh day *is* the sabbath of the LORD thy God: *in it* thou shalt not do any work, thou, nor thy son, nor thy daughter, thy manservant, nor thy maidservant, nor thy cattle, nor thy stranger that *is* within thy gates: ¹¹For *in* six days the LORD made heaven and earth, the sea, and all that in them *is*, and rested the seventh day: wherefore the LORD blessed the sabbath day, and hallowed it.

¹²Honour thy father and thy mother: that thy days may be long upon the land which the LORD thy God giveth thee. ¹³Thou shalt not kill. ¹⁴Thou shalt not commit adultery. ¹⁵Thou shalt not steal. ¹⁶Thou shalt not bear false witness against thy neighbour. ¹⁷Thou shalt not covet thy neighbour's house, thou shalt not covet thy neighbour's wife, nor his manservant, nor his maidservant, nor his ox, nor his ass, nor any thing that *is* thy neighbour's.

¹⁸And all the people saw the thunderings, and the lightnings, and the noise of the trumpet, and the mountain smoking: and when the people saw *it*, they removed, and stood afar off. ¹⁹And they said unto Moses, Speak thou with us, and we will hear: but let not God speak with us, lest we die. ²⁰And Moses said unto the people, Fear not: for God is come to prove you, and that his fear may be before your faces, that ye sin not. ²¹And the people stood afar off, and Moses drew near unto the thick darkness where God *was*.

²²And the LORD said unto Moses, Thus thou shalt say unto the children of Israel, Ye have seen that I have talked with you from heaven. ²³Ye shall not make with me gods of silver, neither shall ye make unto you gods of gold. ²⁴An altar of earth thou shalt make unto me, and shalt sacrifice thereon thy burnt offerings, and thy peace offerings, thy sheep, and thine oxen: in all places where I record my name I will come unto thee, and I will bless thee. ²⁵And if thou wilt make me an altar of stone, thou shalt not build[b] it of hewn stone: for if thou lift up thy tool upon it, thou hast polluted it. ²⁶Neither shalt thou go up by steps unto mine altar, that thy nakedness be not discovered thereon.

21

¹Now these *are* the judgments which thou shalt set before them. ²If thou buy an Hebrew servant, six years he shall serve: and in the seventh he shall go out free for nothing. ³If he came in by himself[a], he shall go out by himself: if he

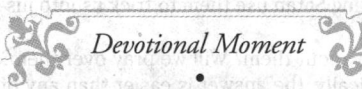

Devotional Moment

Adultery

20:14 God's prohibition against adultery cut across practices that Israel and other ancient cultures accepted as normal. In most cultures of that time, women had few rights and were treated in some ways like slaves. Many men thought nothing of having sexual relations with more than one woman, whether they were married or not. God instituted a higher view of women and sexual relations. Just as God's relationship with his people was a holy agreement (covenant) not to be violated, so too is the relationship between husband and wife. Marriage is a holy bond. We should not take it lightly.

---

b build . . . : Heb. build them with hewing
a by himself: Heb. with his body

The Price of Infidelity

by Jerry B. Jenkins

Infidelity. What a genteel word for the act it describes. Such a word goes down easier than "violating trust," "breaking marriage vows," "being unfaithful," "sleeping around," "fornicating," or "committing adultery" (Exod. 20:14). But using a mild word for sin doesn't change its repugnance.

Marital infidelity devastates those it affects. I have heard countless stories of the chaos caused by adultery, including those of both a senior pastor and an assistant pastor. One man left notes for his friends and associates, praising God for his "new love that is so wonderful, the Lord has to be in it." Another friend tried to convince me that the relationship breaking up both his and his girlfriend's marriages was "in the center of God's will."

I've been acquainted with enough such men to see their defenses coming a mile away. The typical one suddenly begins to portray his wife—this woman we all know as a wonderful person, though not perfect, maybe a bit dull, maybe harried and overworked, maybe not as dazzling as when they married—as a monster. Usually he blames it all on his wife. This from a man who is no prize himself, yet who has justified breaking the law of God so clearly stated in Exodus 20:14.

The snare is lust. Even a man with as perfect a wife as he could want is vulnerable to a senseless seeking after that which would destroy him and his family. If he does not fear his own potential and build hedges around himself and his marriage, he heads for disaster.

Even a Christian with an open mind about divorce says and means at his wedding that he is pledging himself to his spouse forever. He may later forget it or decide it was merely archaic formality, but there's no way around it: His vows were legal, sacred, and moral. When he commits adultery—when he violates the commandment found in this verse—he breaks his promise.

A complex litany of events takes place between the vows and the adultery. And it behooves those who want to remain pure to examine those events, expose them for what they are, and either avoid letting them happen or avoid letting Satan use them to trick us into justifying our sin.

Once we have identified them, what will we do about them? Will we pray over them? Resolve to conquer them? Turn over a new leaf? Ironically, the answer is easier than any of those options.

God does not expect us to win, to gain the victory, to succeed by the sheer force of our will, our conscience, or our determination. Rather, 2 Timothy 2:22 says we are to run, to flee, to get out, to get away. Why? While Exodus 20:14 prohibits adultery, Matthew 5:28 tells us that if a man so much as looks at a woman lustfully, he has already committed adultery with her in his heart.

Clearly we are stronger at some times than at others. So what is the solution when temptation rages? If we are weak and have not taken precautions, if we have not applied preventive medicine, we have already failed. The only answer is to plan, to anticipate danger, to plot the way of escape. The time to build hedges is before the enemy attacks.

The general guidelines are quite simple:

Avoid tempting situations. What do you need to guard yourself against? Pornography? Questionable media? Flirting? Inappropriate touching? Spending time alone with someone you shouldn't? Make a list of clear dangers for you, and covenant with God and your spouse that you will never go near them.

Build your marriage. Proverbs 3:3 says, "Let not mercy and truth forsake thee: bind them about thy neck; write them upon the table of thine heart." Every day, think of at least one loving act you can do for your spouse, and do it. Treat him or her lovingly, patiently, and kindly. And remember not to neglect your spouse's sexual needs. Touch each other and show affection often (Prov. 5:15-20).

Be afraid of infidelity. Run scared from it. Avoid tempting situations and pour everything into building your marriage. Your marriage, and the kingdom, will be the better for it.

DIGGING DEEPER
   1. Read 1 Corinthians 10:13 and think about the importance of escape from temptation. When is escape easiest? Most difficult?
   2. How seriously does God take adultery? Read Leviticus 20:10.
   3. What can a person who has committed adultery do (John 8:3-11)?

were married, then his wife shall go out with him. ⁴If his master have given him a wife, and she have born him sons or daughters; the wife and her children shall be her master's, and he shall go out by himself. ⁵And if the servant shall plainly say, I love my master, my wife, and my children; I will not go out free: ⁶Then his master shall bring him unto the judges; he shall also bring him to the door, or unto the door post; and his master shall bore his ear through with an aul; and he shall serve him for ever. ⁷And if a man sell his daughter to be a maidservant, she shall not go out as the menservants do. ⁸If she please*ᵇ* not her master, who hath betrothed her to himself, then shall he let her be redeemed: to sell her unto a strange nation he shall have no power, seeing he hath dealt deceitfully with her. ⁹And if he have betrothed her unto his son, he shall deal with her after the manner of daughters.

¹⁰If he take him another *wife*; her food, her raiment, and her duty of marriage, shall he not diminish. ¹¹And if he do not these three unto her, then shall she go out free without money.

¹²He that smiteth a man, so that he die, shall be surely put to death. ¹³And if a man lie not in wait, but God deliver *him* into his hand; then I will appoint thee a place whither he shall flee. ¹⁴But if a man come presumptuously upon his neighbour, to slay him with guile; thou shalt take him from mine altar, that he may die. ¹⁵And he that smiteth his father, or his mother, shall be surely put to death. ¹⁶And he that stealeth a man, and selleth him, or if he be found in his hand, he shall surely be put to death. ¹⁷And he that curseth*ᶜ* his father, or his mother, shall surely be put to death. ¹⁸And if men strive together, and one smite another*ᵈ* with a stone, or with *his* fist, and he die not, but keepeth *his*

ᵇ please . . . : Heb. be evil in the eyes of, etc
ᶜ curseth: or, revileth
ᵈ another: or, his neighbour

133

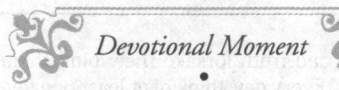

Devotional Moment
•
Discipline

21:23-25 God gave this instruction not to show us how to take revenge, but to guide judges (see 18:13-26). It set a limit on what kind of retribution could serve as punishment for a crime against another person: The punishment should not exceed the crime. This kept people from escalating conflicts beyond the original offense. Parenting involves disciplining children almost daily. Set a limit on how far your discipline can go. Make the consequences fit the crime.

bed: ¹⁹If he rise again, and walk abroad upon his staff, then shall he that smote *him* be quit: only he shall pay *for* the loss of his time, and shall cause *him* to be thoroughly healed. ²⁰And if a man smite his servant, or his maid, with a rod, and he die under his hand; he shall be surely punishedᵉ. ²¹Notwithstanding, if he continue a day or two, he shall not be punished: for he *is* his money.

²²If men strive, and hurt a woman with child, so that her fruit depart *from her*, and yet no mischief follow: he shall be surely punished, according as the woman's husband will lay upon him; and he shall pay as the judges *determine*. ²³And if *any* mischief follow, then thou shalt give life for life, ²⁴Eye for eye, tooth for tooth, hand for hand, foot for foot, ²⁵Burning for burning, wound for wound, stripe for stripe. ²⁶And if a man smite the eye of his servant, or the eye of his maid, that it perish; he shall let him go free for his eye's sake. ²⁷And if he smite out his manservant's tooth, or his maidservant's tooth; he shall let him go free for his tooth's sake. ²⁸If an ox gore a man or a woman, that they die: then the ox shall be surely stoned, and his flesh shall not be eaten; but the owner of the ox *shall be* quit. ²⁹But if the ox were wont to push with his horn in time past, and it hath been testified to his owner, and he hath not kept him in, but that he hath killed a man or a woman; the ox shall be stoned, and his owner also shall be put to death. ³⁰If there be laid on him a sum of money, then he shall give for the ransom of his life whatsoever is laid upon him. ³¹Whether he have gored a son, or have gored a daughter, according to this judgment shall it be done unto him. ³²If the ox shall push a manservant or a maidservant; he shall give unto their master thirty shekels of silver, and the ox shall be stoned. ³³And if a man shall open a pit, or if a man shall dig a pit, and not cover it, and an ox or an ass fall therein; ³⁴The owner of the pit shall make *it* good, *and* give money unto the owner of them; and the dead *beast* shall be his. ³⁵And if one man's ox hurt another's, that he die; then they shall sell the live ox, and divide the money of it; and the dead *ox* also they shall divide. ³⁶Or if it be known that the ox hath used to push in time past, and his owner hath not kept him in; he shall surely pay ox for ox; and the dead shall be his own.

22

¹If a man shall steal an ox, or a sheepᵃ, and kill it, or sell it; he shall restore five oxen for an ox, and four sheep for a sheep. ²If a thief be found breaking up,

ᵉ punished: Heb. avenged
ᵃ or a sheep: or, or a goat

and be smitten that he die, *there shall no blood be shed* for him. ³If the sun be risen upon him, *there shall be* blood *shed* for him; *for* he should make full restitution; if he have nothing, then he shall be sold for his theft. ⁴If the theft be certainly found in his hand alive, whether it be ox, or ass, or sheep; he shall restore double. ⁵If a man shall cause a field or vineyard to be eaten, and shall put in his beast, and shall feed in another man's field; of the best of his own field, and of the best of his own vineyard, shall he make restitution. ⁶If fire break out, and catch in thorns, so that the stacks of corn, or the standing corn, or the field, be consumed *therewith*; he that kindled the fire shall surely make restitution.

⁷If a man shall deliver unto his neighbour money or stuff to keep, and it be stolen out of the man's house; if the thief be found, let him pay double. ⁸If the thief be not found, then the master of the house shall be brought unto the judges, *to see* whether he have put his hand unto his neighbour's goods. ⁹For all manner of trespass, *whether it be* for ox, for ass, for sheep, for raiment, or for any manner of lost thing, which *another* challengeth to be his, the cause of both parties shall come before the judges; *and* whom the judges shall condemn, he shall pay double unto his neighbour. ¹⁰If a man deliver unto his neighbour an ass, or an ox, or a sheep, or any beast, to keep; and it die, or be hurt, or driven away, no man seeing *it*: ¹¹ *Then* shall an oath of the LORD be between them both, that he hath not put his hand unto his neighbour's

goods; and the owner of it shall accept *thereof*, and he shall not make *it* good. ¹²And if it be stolen from him, he shall make restitution unto the owner thereof. ¹³If it be torn in pieces, *then* let him bring it *for* witness, *and* he shall not make good that which was torn. ¹⁴And if a man borrow *ought* of his neighbour, and it be hurt, or die, the owner thereof *being* not with it, he shall surely make *it* good. ¹⁵But if the owner thereof *be* with it, he shall not make *it* good: if it *be* an hired *thing*, it came for his hire.

¹⁶And if a man entice a maid that is not betrothed, and lie with her, he shall surely endow her to be his wife. ¹⁷If her father utterly refuse to give her unto him, he shall pay[b] money according to the dowry of virgins. ¹⁸Thou shalt not suffer a witch to live. ¹⁹Whosoever lieth with a beast shall surely be put to death. ²⁰He that sacrificeth unto *any* god, save unto the LORD only, he shall be utterly destroyed. ²¹Thou shalt neither vex

---

Devotional Moment

The Poor

22:21-27 Most people have family who can help them out in a pinch. But not everyone—some are widows or orphans, with no family at all, or with no one to help them out when they are short on resources. God wants us to defend and take care of people who have no family. How do you feel when someone collecting for a charity knocks on your door, when you pass a beggar on the street, or when your church announces the need for a special offering? Leave room in your family budget for generosity to people outside your immediate kin. Be a family to those who have none.

---

[b] pay: Heb. weigh

a stranger, nor oppress him: for ye were strangers in the land of Egypt. ²²Ye shall not afflict any widow, or fatherless child. ²³If thou afflict them in any wise, and they cry at all unto me, I will surely hear their cry; ²⁴And my wrath shall wax hot, and I will kill you with the sword; and your wives shall be widows, and your children fatherless.

²⁵If thou lend money to *any of* my people *that is* poor by thee, thou shalt not be to him as an usurer, neither shalt thou lay upon him usury. ²⁶If thou at all take thy neighbour's raiment to pledge, thou shalt deliver it unto him by that the sun goeth down: ²⁷For that *is* his covering only, it *is* his raiment for his skin: wherein shall he sleep? and it shall come to pass, when he crieth unto me, that I will hear; for I *am* gracious. ²⁸Thou shalt not revile the gods^c, nor curse the ruler of thy people. ²⁹Thou shalt not delay *to offer* the first of thy ripe fruits, and of thy liquors: the firstborn of thy sons shalt thou give unto me. ³⁰Likewise shalt thou do with thine oxen, *and* with thy sheep: seven days it shall be with his dam; on the eighth day thou shalt give it me. ³¹And ye shall be holy men unto me: neither shall ye eat *any* flesh *that is* torn of beasts in the field; ye shall cast it to the dogs.

23

¹Thou shalt not raise^a a false report: put not thine hand with the wicked to be an unrighteous witness. ²Thou shalt not

---

> ### Devotional Moment
> •
> #### Integrity
> 23:1-3 Within any family, the pressure to be untruthful can become enormous. Circumstances often arise when one or more family members want to hear another say something in particular; you (and perhaps they) know the truth will only disappoint. Yet dishonesty, even in small matters—and especially among family members—erodes trust. The only way to *build* trust is to tell the truth—even if it may disappoint. The next time you are tempted to lie to your spouse or your children to please them, ask whether the short-term gain is really worth it.

---

follow a multitude to *do* evil; neither shalt thou speak^b in a cause to decline after many to wrest *judgment*: ³Neither shalt thou countenance a poor man in his cause. ⁴If thou meet thine enemy's ox or his ass going astray, thou shalt surely bring it back to him again. ⁵If thou see the ass of him that hateth thee lying under his burden, and wouldest forbear to help him, thou shalt surely help with him. ⁶Thou shalt not wrest the judgment of thy poor in his cause. ⁷Keep thee far from a false matter; and the innocent and righteous slay thou not: for I will not justify the wicked. ⁸And thou shalt take no gift: for the gift blindeth the wise^c, and perverteth the words of the righteous. ⁹Also thou shalt not oppress a stranger: for ye know the heart^d of a stranger, seeing ye were strangers in the land of Egypt.

---

^c gods: or, judges
^a raise: or, receive
^b speak: Heb. answer
^c the wise: Heb. the seeing
^d heart: Heb. soul

¹⁰And six years thou shalt sow thy land, and shalt gather in the fruits thereof: ¹¹But the seventh *year* thou shalt let it rest and lie still; that the poor of thy people may eat: and what they leave the beasts of the field shall eat. In like manner thou shalt deal with thy vineyard, *and* with thy oliveyardᵉ. ¹²Six days thou shalt do thy work, and on the seventh day thou shalt rest: that thine ox and thine ass may rest, and the son of thy handmaid, and the stranger, may be refreshed. ¹³And in all *things* that I have said unto you be circumspect: and make no mention of the name of other gods, neither let it be heard out of thy mouth. ¹⁴Three times thou shalt keep a feast unto me in the year. ¹⁵Thou shalt keep the feast of unleavened bread: (thou shalt eat unleavened bread seven days, as I commanded thee, in the time appointed of the month Abib; for in it thou camest out from Egypt: and none shall appear before me empty:) ¹⁶And the feast of harvest, the firstfruits of thy labours, which thou hast sown in the field: and the feast of ingathering, *which is* in the end of the year, when thou hast gathered in thy labours out of the field. ¹⁷Three times in the year all thy males shall appear before the Lord GOD. ¹⁸Thou shalt not offer the blood of my sacrificeᶠ with leavened bread; neither shall the fat of my sacrifice remain until the morning. ¹⁹The first of the firstfruits of thy land thou shalt bring into the house of the LORD thy God. Thou shalt not seethe a kid in his mother's milk.

²⁰Behold, I send an Angel before

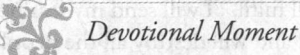

Devotional Moment
•
Idolatry

23:24-26 Human beings have a natural bent toward worship. Creation shouts to everyone that God exists. And God himself stamps the fact on our consciousness. But our sinful nature feels attracted to many substitutes. Consider the damage that the more popular gods—money, power, and sex—have done to families. Many good things make bad gods. We must put God first in our relationships, our family life, our work, and in everything we do if we are to have harmony at home.

thee, to keep thee in the way, and to bring thee into the place which I have prepared. ²¹Beware of him, and obey his voice, provoke him not; for he will not pardon your transgressions: for my name *is* in him. ²²But if thou shalt indeed obey his voice, and do all that I speak; then I will be an enemy unto thine enemies, and an adversaryᵍ unto thine adversaries. ²³For mine Angel shall go before thee, and bring thee in unto the Amorites, and the Hittites, and the Perizzites, and the Canaanites, the Hivites, and the Jebusites: and I will cut them off. ²⁴Thou shalt not bow down to their gods, nor serve them, nor do after their works: but thou shalt utterly overthrow them, and quite break down their images. ²⁵And ye shall serve the LORD your God, and he shall bless thy bread, and thy water; and I will take sickness away from the midst of thee. ²⁶There shall nothing cast their young, nor be barren, in thy land: the number of thy

---

ᵉ oliveyard: or, olive trees
ᶠ sacrifice: or, feast
ᵍ an adversary . . . : or, I will afflict them that afflict thee

days I will fulfil. ²⁷I will send my fear before thee, and will destroy all the people to whom thou shalt come, and I will make all thine enemies turn their backsʰ unto thee. ²⁸And I will send hornets before thee, which shall drive out the Hivite, the Canaanite, and the Hittite, from before thee. ²⁹I will not drive them out from before thee in one year; lest the land become desolate, and the beast of the field multiply against thee. ³⁰By little and little I will drive them out from before thee, until thou be increased, and inherit the land. ³¹And I will set thy bounds from the Red sea even unto the sea of the Philistines, and from the desert unto the river: for I will deliver the inhabitants of the land into your hand; and thou shalt drive them out before thee. ³²Thou shalt make no covenant with them, nor with their gods. ³³They shall not dwell in thy land, lest they make thee sin against me: for if thou serve their gods, it will surely be a snare unto thee.

24

¹And he said unto Moses, Come up unto the LORD, thou, and Aaron, Nadab, and Abihu, and seventy of the elders of Israel; and worship ye afar off. ²And Moses alone shall come near the LORD: but they shall not come nigh; neither shall the people go up with him. ³And Moses came and told the people all the words of the LORD, and all the judgments: and all the people answered with one voice, and said, All the words which the LORD hath said will we do. ⁴And Moses wrote all the words of the LORD, and rose up early in the morning, and builded an altar under the hill, and twelve pillars, according to the twelve tribes of Israel. ⁵And he sent young men of the children of Israel, which offered burnt offerings, and sacrificed peace offerings of oxen unto the LORD. ⁶And Moses took half of the blood, and put *it* in basons; and half of the blood he sprinkled on the altar. ⁷And he took the book of the covenant, and read in the audience of the people: and they said, All that the LORD hath said will we do, and be obedient. ⁸And Moses took the blood, and sprinkled *it* on the people, and said, Behold the blood of the covenant, which the LORD hath made with you concerning all these words.

⁹Then went up Moses, and Aaron, Nadab, and Abihu, and seventy of the elders of Israel: ¹⁰And they saw the God of Israel: and *there was* under his feet as it were a paved work of a sapphire stone, and as it were the body of heaven in *his* clearness. ¹¹And upon the nobles of the children of Israel he laid not his hand: also they saw God, and did eat and drink.

¹²And the LORD said unto Moses, Come up to me into the mount, and be there: and I will give thee tables of stone, and a law, and commandments which I have written; that thou mayest teach them. ¹³And Moses rose up, and his minister Joshua: and Moses went up into the mount of God. ¹⁴And he said unto the elders, Tarry ye here for us, until we come again unto you: and, behold, Aaron and Hur *are* with you: if any man have any matters to do, let him come unto them. ¹⁵And Moses

---

ʰ backs: Heb. neck

went up into the mount, and a cloud covered the mount. ¹⁶And the glory of the LORD abode upon mount Sinai, and the cloud covered it six days: and the seventh day he called unto Moses out of the midst of the cloud. ¹⁷And the sight of the glory of the LORD *was* like devouring fire on the top of the mount in the eyes of the children of Israel. ¹⁸And Moses went into the midst of the cloud, and gat him up into the mount: and Moses was in the mount forty days and forty nights.

25

¹And the LORD spake unto Moses, saying, ²Speak unto the children of Israel, that they bring me an offering: of every man that giveth it willingly with his heart ye shall take my offering. ³And this *is* the offering[a] which ye shall take of them; gold, and silver, and brass, ⁴And blue, and purple, and scarlet, and fine linen, and goats' *hair*, ⁵And rams' skins dyed red, and badgers' skins, and shittim wood, ⁶Oil for the light, spices

---

Devotional Moment
•
Tithing

25:1-7 We often focus on how little we can give and still meet God's "minimum requirements." Yet God wants to receive gifts only from everyone who "giveth it willingly with his heart" (v. 2). God is not greedy; he already has all he needs. He merely wants us to show that we love him, to prove it to ourselves. Giving should be an opportunity for you to show your love for God. Your generosity should be genuine, not a mere duty.

---

for anointing oil, and for sweet incense, ⁷Onyx stones, and stones to be set in the ephod, and in the breastplate. ⁸And let them make me a sanctuary; that I may dwell among them. ⁹According to all that I shew thee, *after* the pattern of the tabernacle, and the pattern of all the instruments thereof, even so shall ye make *it*.

¹⁰And they shall make an ark *of* shittim wood: two cubits and a half *shall be* the length thereof, and a cubit and a half the breadth thereof, and a cubit and a half the height thereof. ¹¹And thou shalt overlay it with pure gold, within and without shalt thou overlay it, and shalt make upon it a crown of gold round about. ¹²And thou shalt cast four rings of gold for it, and put *them* in the four corners thereof; and two rings *shall be* in the one side of it, and two rings in the other side of it. ¹³And thou shalt make staves *of* shittim wood, and overlay them with gold. ¹⁴And thou shalt put the staves into the rings by the sides of the ark, that the ark may be borne with them. ¹⁵The staves shall be in the rings of the ark: they shall not be taken from it. ¹⁶And thou shalt put into the ark the testimony which I shall give thee. ¹⁷And thou shalt make a mercy seat *of* pure gold: two cubits and a half *shall be* the length thereof, and a cubit and a half the breadth thereof. ¹⁸And thou shalt make two cherubims *of* gold, *of* beaten work shalt thou make them, in the two ends of the mercy seat. ¹⁹And make one cherub on the one end, and the other cherub on the other end: *even* of the mercy seat shall ye make the cherubims on the two ends thereof.

---

[a] offering: or, heave offering

²⁰And the cherubims shall stretch forth *their* wings on high, covering the mercy seat with their wings, and their faces *shall look* one to another; toward the mercy seat shall the faces of the cherubims be. ²¹And thou shalt put the mercy seat above upon the ark; and in the ark thou shalt put the testimony that I shall give thee. ²²And there I will meet with thee, and I will commune with thee from above the mercy seat, from between the two cherubims which *are* upon the ark of the testimony, of all *things* which I will give thee in commandment unto the children of Israel.

²³Thou shalt also make a table *of* shittim wood: two cubits *shall be* the length thereof, and a cubit the breadth thereof, and a cubit and a half the height thereof. ²⁴And thou shalt overlay it with pure gold, and make thereto a crown of gold round about. ²⁵And thou shalt make unto it a border of an hand breadth round about, and thou shalt make a golden crown to the border thereof round about. ²⁶And thou shalt make for it four rings of gold, and put the rings in the four corners that *are* on the four feet thereof. ²⁷Over against the border shall the rings be for places of the staves to bear the table. ²⁸And thou shalt make the staves *of* shittim wood, and overlay them with gold, that the table may be borne with them. ²⁹And thou shalt make the dishes thereof, and spoons thereof, and covers thereof, and bowls thereof, to cover withal: *of* pure gold shalt thou make them. ³⁰And thou shalt set upon the table shewbread before me alway.

³¹And thou shalt make a candlestick *of* pure gold: *of* beaten work shall the candlestick be made: his shaft, and his branches, his bowls, his knops, and his flowers, shall be of the same. ³²And six branches shall come out of the sides of it; three branches of the candlestick out of the one side, and three branches of the candlestick out of the other side: ³³Three bowls made like unto almonds, *with* a knop and a flower in one branch; and three bowls made like almonds in the other branch, *with* a knop and a flower: so in the six branches that come out of the candlestick. ³⁴And in the candlestick *shall be* four bowls made like unto almonds, *with* their knops and their flowers. ³⁵And *there shall be* a knop under two branches of the same, and a knop under two branches of the same, and a knop under two branches of the same, according to the six branches that proceed out of the candlestick. ³⁶Their knops and their branches shall be of the same: all it *shall be* one beaten work *of* pure gold. ³⁷And thou shalt make the seven lamps thereof: and they shall lightᵇ the lamps thereof, that they may give light over against it. ³⁸And the tongs thereof, and the snuffdishes thereof, *shall be of* pure gold. ³⁹*Of* a talent of pure gold shall he make it, with all these vessels. ⁴⁰And look that thou make *them* after their pattern, which was shewed thee in the mount.

26

¹Moreover thou shalt make the tabernacle *with* ten curtains *of* fine twined linen, and blue, and purple, and scarlet: *with* cherubims of cunningᵃ work shalt thou

---

ᵇ shall light: or, shall cause to ascend
ᵃ of cunning . . . : Heb. the work of a cunning workman, or, embroiderer

make them. ²The length of one curtain *shall be* eight and twenty cubits, and the breadth of one curtain four cubits: and every one of the curtains shall have one measure. ³The five curtains shall be coupled together one to another; and *other* five curtains *shall be* coupled one to another. ⁴And thou shalt make loops of blue upon the edge of the one curtain from the selvedge in the coupling; and likewise shalt thou make in the uttermost edge of *another* curtain, in the coupling of the second. ⁵Fifty loops shalt thou make in the one curtain, and fifty loops shalt thou make in the edge of the curtain that *is* in the coupling of the second; that the loops may take hold one of another. ⁶And thou shalt make fifty taches of gold, and couple the curtains together with the taches: and it shall be one tabernacle.

⁷And thou shalt make curtains *of* goats' *hair* to be a covering upon the tabernacle: eleven curtains shalt thou make. ⁸The length of one curtain *shall be* thirty cubits, and the breadth of one curtain four cubits: and the eleven curtains *shall be all* of one measure. ⁹And thou shalt couple five curtains by themselves, and six curtains by themselves, and shalt double the sixth curtain in the forefront of the tabernacle. ¹⁰And thou shalt make fifty loops on the edge of the one curtain *that is* outmost in the coupling, and fifty loops in the edge of the curtain which coupleth the second. ¹¹And thou shalt make fifty taches of brass, and put the taches into the loops, and couple the tentᵇ together, that it may be one. ¹²And the remnant that remaineth of the curtains of the tent, the half curtain that remaineth, shall hang over the backside of the tabernacle. ¹³And a cubit on the one side, and a cubit on the other side of that which remaineth in the length of the curtains of the tent, it shall hang over the sides of the tabernacle on this side and on that side, to cover it. ¹⁴And thou shalt make a covering for the tent *of* rams' skins dyed red, and a covering above *of* badgers' skins.

¹⁵And thou shalt make boards for the tabernacle *of* shittim wood standing up. ¹⁶Ten cubits *shall be* the length of a board, and a cubit and a half *shall be* the breadth of one board. ¹⁷Two tenonsᶜ *shall there be* in one board, set in order one against another: thus shalt thou make for all the boards of the tabernacle. ¹⁸And thou shalt make the boards for the tabernacle, twenty boards on the south side southward. ¹⁹And thou shalt make forty sockets of silver under the twenty boards; two sockets under one board for his two tenons, and two sockets under another board for his two tenons. ²⁰And for the second side of the tabernacle on the north side *there shall be* twenty boards: ²¹And their forty sockets *of* silver; two sockets under one board, and two sockets under another board. ²²And for the sides of the tabernacle westward thou shalt make six boards. ²³And two boards shalt thou make for the corners of the tabernacle in the two sides. ²⁴And they shall be coupledᵈ together beneath, and they shall be coupled together above the head of it unto one ring: thus shall it be for them both; they shall be for the

---

ᵇ tent: or, covering
ᶜ tenons: Heb. hands
ᵈ coupled: Heb. twinned

two corners. ²⁵And they shall be eight boards, and their sockets *of* silver, sixteen sockets; two sockets under one board, and two sockets under another board. ²⁶And thou shalt make bars *of* shittim wood; five for the boards of the one side of the tabernacle, ²⁷And five bars for the boards of the other side of the tabernacle, and five bars for the boards of the side of the tabernacle, for the two sides westward. ²⁸And the middle bar in the midst of the boards shall reach from end to end. ²⁹And thou shalt overlay the boards with gold, and make their rings *of* gold *for* places for the bars: and thou shalt overlay the bars with gold. ³⁰And thou shalt rear up the tabernacle according to the fashion thereof which was shewed thee in the mount.

³¹And thou shalt make a vail *of* blue, and purple, and scarlet, and fine twined linen of cunning work: with cherubims shall it be made: ³²And thou shalt hang it upon four pillars of shittim *wood* overlaid with gold: their hooks *shall be of* gold, upon the four sockets of silver. ³³And thou shalt hang up the vail under the taches, that thou mayest bring in thither within the vail the ark of the testimony: and the vail shall divide unto you between the holy *place* and the most holy. ³⁴And thou shalt put the mercy seat upon the ark of the testimony in the most holy *place*. ³⁵And thou shalt set the table without the vail, and the candlestick over against the table on the side of the tabernacle toward the south: and thou shalt put the table on the north side. ³⁶And thou shalt make an hanging for the door of the tent, *of* blue, and purple, and scarlet, and fine twined linen, wrought with needlework. ³⁷And thou shalt make for the hanging five pillars *of* shittim *wood*, and overlay them

with gold, *and* their hooks *shall be of* gold: and thou shalt cast five sockets of brass for them.

27

¹And thou shalt make an altar *of* shittim wood, five cubits long, and five cubits broad; the altar shall be foursquare: and the height thereof *shall be* three cubits. ²And thou shalt make the horns of it upon the four corners thereof: his horns shall be of the same: and thou shalt overlay it with brass. ³And thou shalt make his pans to receive his ashes, and his shovels, and his basons, and his fleshhooks, and his firepans: all the vessels thereof thou shalt make *of* brass. ⁴And thou shalt make for it a grate of network *of* brass; and upon the net shalt thou make four brasen rings in the four corners thereof. ⁵And thou shalt put it under the compass of the altar beneath, that the net may be even to the midst of the altar. ⁶And thou shalt make staves for the altar, staves *of* shittim wood, and overlay them with brass. ⁷And the staves shall be put into the rings, and the staves

shall be upon the two sides of the altar, to bear it. ⁸Hollow with boards shalt thou make it: as it was shewed thee in the mount, so shall they make *it*.

⁹And thou shalt make the court of the tabernacle: for the south side southward *there shall be* hangings for the court *of* fine twined linen of an hundred cubits long for one side: ¹⁰And the twenty pillars thereof and their twenty sockets *shall be of* brass; the hooks of the pillars and their fillets *shall be of* silver. ¹¹And likewise for the north side in length *there shall be* hangings of an hundred *cubits* long, and his twenty pillars and their twenty sockets *of* brass; the hooks of the pillars and their fillets *of* silver. ¹²And *for* the breadth of the court on the west side *shall be* hangings of fifty cubits: their pillars ten, and their sockets ten. ¹³And the breadth of the court on the east side eastward *shall be* fifty cubits. ¹⁴The hangings of one side *of the gate shall be* fifteen cubits: their pillars three, and their sockets three. ¹⁵And on the other side *shall be* hangings fifteen *cubits*: their pillars three, and their sockets three. ¹⁶And for the gate of the court *shall be* an hanging of twenty cubits, *of* blue, and purple, and scarlet, and fine twined linen, wrought with needlework: *and* their pillars *shall be* four, and their sockets four. ¹⁷All the pillars round about the court *shall be* filleted with silver; their hooks *shall be of* silver, and their sockets *of* brass. ¹⁸The length of the court *shall be* an hundred cubits, and the breadth fifty[a] every where, and the height five cubits *of* fine twined linen, and their sockets *of* brass. ¹⁹All the vessels of the tabernacle in all the service thereof, and all the pins thereof, and all the pins of the court, *shall be of* brass.

²⁰And thou shalt command the children of Israel, that they bring thee pure oil olive beaten for the light, to cause the lamp to burn[b] always. ²¹In the tabernacle of the congregation without the vail, which *is* before the testimony, Aaron and his sons shall order it from evening to morning before the LORD: *it shall be* a statute for ever unto their generations on the behalf of the children of Israel.

28

¹And take thou unto thee Aaron thy brother, and his sons with him, from among the children of Israel, that he may minister unto me in the priest's office, *even* Aaron, Nadab and Abihu, Eleazar and Ithamar, Aaron's sons. ²And thou shalt make holy garments for Aaron thy brother for glory and for beauty. ³And thou shalt speak unto all

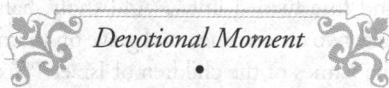

Devotional Moment
•
Competency
28:3 In his instructions about the clothing that the High Priest and his sons were to wear, God told Moses to commission tailors with special skills. God gives skill to every person he creates. As children grow, they become increasingly concerned with their competence. They want to know, "Am I good at anything?" Yes they are. Don't overlook the importance of telling them how God has gifted them. Notice what they do well and find satisfying, and point it out to them—in positive, affirming ways. This will not only help them gain confidence in themselves, but (more importantly) help them acknowledge and appreciate God's goodness.

---

[a] fifty . . . : Heb. fifty by fifty
[b] to burn: Heb. to ascend up

that *are* wise hearted, whom I have filled with the spirit of wisdom, that they may make Aaron's garments to consecrate him, that he may minister unto me in the priest's office. ⁴And these *are* the garments which they shall make; a breastplate, and an ephod, and a robe, and a broidered coat, a mitre, and a girdle: and they shall make holy garments for Aaron thy brother, and his sons, that he may minister unto me in the priest's office. ⁵And they shall take gold, and blue, and purple, and scarlet, and fine linen.

⁶And they shall make the ephod *of* gold, *of* blue, and *of* purple, *of* scarlet, and fine twined linen, with cunning work. ⁷It shall have the two shoulderpieces thereof joined at the two edges thereof; and *so* it shall be joined together. ⁸And the curious girdle of the ephod, which *is* upon it, shall be of the same, according to the work thereof; *even of* gold, *of* blue, and purple, and scarlet, and fine twined linen. ⁹And thou shalt take two onyx stones, and grave on them the names of the children of Israel: ¹⁰Six of their names on one stone, and *the other* six names of the rest on the other stone, according to their birth. ¹¹With the work of an engraver in stone, *like* the engravings of a signet, shalt thou engrave the two stones with the names of the children of Israel: thou shalt make them to be set in ouches of gold. ¹²And thou shalt put the two stones upon the shoulders of the ephod *for* stones of memorial unto the children of Israel: and Aaron shall bear their names before the LORD upon his two shoulders for a memorial.

¹³And thou shalt make ouches *of* gold; ¹⁴And two chains *of* pure gold at the ends; *of* wreathen work shalt thou make them, and fasten the wreathen chains to the ouches.

¹⁵And thou shalt make the breastplate of judgment with cunning work; after the work of the ephod thou shalt make it; *of* gold, *of* blue, and *of* purple, and *of* scarlet, and *of* fine twined linen, shalt thou make it. ¹⁶Foursquare it shall be *being* doubled; a span *shall be* the length thereof, and a span *shall be* the breadth thereof. ¹⁷And thou shalt set[a] in it settings of stones, *even* four rows of stones: *the first* row *shall be* a sardius, a topaz, and a carbuncle: *this shall be* the first row. ¹⁸And the second row *shall be* an emerald, a sapphire, and a diamond. ¹⁹And the third row a ligure, an agate, and an amethyst. ²⁰And the fourth row a beryl, and an onyx, and a jasper: they shall be set in gold in their inclosings[b]. ²¹And the stones shall be with the names of the children of Israel, twelve, according to their names, *like* the engravings of a signet; every one with his name shall they be according to the twelve tribes. ²²And thou shalt make upon the breastplate chains at the ends *of* wreathen work *of* pure gold. ²³And thou shalt make upon the breastplate two rings of gold, and shalt put the two rings on the two ends of the breastplate. ²⁴And thou shalt put the two wreathen *chains* of gold in the two rings *which are* on the ends of the breastplate. ²⁵And *the other* two ends of the two wreathen *chains* thou shalt fasten in the two ouches, and put *them* on the shoulder-

---

[a] set . . . : Heb. fill in it fillings of stone
[b] inclosings: Heb. fillings

pieces of the ephod before it. ²⁶And thou shalt make two rings of gold, and thou shalt put them upon the two ends of the breastplate in the border thereof, which *is* in the side of the ephod inward. ²⁷And two *other* rings of gold thou shalt make, and shalt put them on the two sides of the ephod underneath, toward the forepart thereof, over against the *other* coupling thereof, above the curious girdle of the ephod. ²⁸And they shall bind the breastplate by the rings thereof unto the rings of the ephod with a lace of blue, that *it* may be above the curious girdle of the ephod, and that the breastplate be not loosed from the ephod. ²⁹And Aaron shall bear the names of the children of Israel in the breastplate of judgment upon his heart, when he goeth in unto the holy *place*, for a memorial before the LORD continually. ³⁰And thou shalt put in the breastplate of judgment the Urim and the Thummim; and they shall be upon Aaron's heart, when he goeth in before the LORD: and Aaron shall bear the judgment of the children of Israel upon his heart before the LORD continually.

³¹And thou shalt make the robe of the ephod all *of* blue. ³²And there shall be an hole in the top of it, in the midst thereof: it shall have a binding of woven work round about the hole of it, as it were the hole of an habergeon, that it be not rent. ³³And *beneath* upon the hem[c] of it thou shalt make pomegranates *of* blue, and *of* purple, and *of* scarlet, round about the hem thereof; and bells of gold between them round about: ³⁴A golden bell and a pomegranate, a golden bell and a pomegranate, upon the hem of the robe round about. ³⁵And it shall be upon Aaron to minister: and his sound shall be heard when he goeth in unto the holy *place* before the LORD, and when he cometh out, that he die not. ³⁶And thou shalt make a plate *of* pure gold, and grave upon it, *like* the engravings of a signet, HOLINESS TO THE LORD. ³⁷And thou shalt put it on a blue lace, that it may be upon the mitre; upon the forefront of the mitre it shall be. ³⁸And it shall be upon Aaron's forehead, that Aaron may bear the iniquity of the holy things, which the children of Israel shall hallow in all their holy gifts; and it shall be always upon his forehead, that they may be accepted before the LORD. ³⁹And thou shalt embroider the coat of fine linen, and thou shalt make the mitre *of* fine linen, and thou shalt make the girdle *of* needlework.

⁴⁰And for Aaron's sons thou shalt make coats, and thou shalt make for them girdles, and bonnets shalt thou make for them, for glory and for beauty. ⁴¹And thou shalt put them upon Aaron thy brother, and his sons with him; and shalt anoint them, and consecrate[d] them, and sanctify them, that they may minister unto me in the priest's office. ⁴²And thou shalt make them linen breeches to cover their nakedness; from the loins even unto the thighs they shall reach: ⁴³And they shall be upon Aaron, and upon his sons, when they come in unto the tabernacle of the congregation, or when they come

---

[c] hem: or, skirts
[d] consecrate . . . : Heb. fill their hand

near unto the altar to minister in the holy *place*; that they bear not iniquity, and die: *it shall be* a statute for ever unto him and his seed after him.

29

¹And this *is* the thing that thou shalt do unto them to hallow them, to minister unto me in the priest's office: Take one young bullock, and two rams without blemish, ²And unleavened bread, and cakes unleavened tempered with oil, and wafers unleavened anointed with oil: *of* wheaten flour shalt thou make them. ³And thou shalt put them into one basket, and bring them in the basket, with the bullock and the two rams. ⁴And Aaron and his sons thou shalt bring unto the door of the tabernacle of the congregation, and shalt wash them with water. ⁵And thou shalt take the garments, and put upon Aaron the coat, and the robe of the ephod, and the ephod, and the breastplate, and gird him with the curious girdle of the ephod: ⁶And thou shalt put the mitre upon his head, and put the holy crown upon the mitre. ⁷Then shalt thou take the anointing oil, and pour *it* upon his head, and anoint him. ⁸And thou shalt bring his sons, and put coats upon them. ⁹And thou shalt gird them with girdles, Aaron and his sons, and put[a] the bonnets on them: and the priest's office shall be theirs for a perpetual statute: and thou shalt consecrate Aaron and his sons. ¹⁰And thou shalt cause a bullock to be brought before the tabernacle of the congregation: and Aaron and his sons shall put their hands

upon the head of the bullock. ¹¹And thou shalt kill the bullock before the LORD, *by* the door of the tabernacle of the congregation. ¹²And thou shalt take of the blood of the bullock, and put *it* upon the horns of the altar with thy finger, and pour all the blood beside the bottom of the altar. ¹³And thou shalt take all the fat that covereth the inwards, and the caul[b] *that is* above the liver, and the two kidneys, and the fat that *is* upon them, and burn *them* upon the altar. ¹⁴But the flesh of the bullock, and his skin, and his dung, shalt thou burn with fire without the camp: it *is* a sin offering. ¹⁵Thou shalt also take one ram; and Aaron and his sons shall put their hands upon the head of the ram. ¹⁶And thou shalt slay the ram, and thou shalt take his blood, and sprinkle *it* round about upon the altar. ¹⁷And thou shalt cut the ram in pieces, and wash the inwards of him, and his legs, and put *them* unto his pieces, and unto his head. ¹⁸And thou shalt burn the whole ram upon the altar: it *is* a burnt offering unto the LORD: it *is* a sweet savour, an offering made by fire unto the LORD. ¹⁹And thou shalt take the other ram; and Aaron and his sons shall put their hands upon the head of the ram. ²⁰Then shalt thou kill the ram, and take of his blood, and put *it* upon the tip of the right ear of Aaron, and upon the tip of the right ear of his sons, and upon the thumb of their right hand, and upon the great toe of their right foot, and sprinkle the blood upon the altar round about. ²¹And thou shalt take of the blood that *is* upon the altar, and of

---

[a] put: Heb. bind
[b] the caul: it seemeth by anatomy, and the Hebrew doctors, to be the midriff

the anointing oil, and sprinkle *it* upon Aaron, and upon his garments, and upon his sons, and upon the garments of his sons with him: and he shall be hallowed, and his garments, and his sons, and his sons' garments with him. ²²Also thou shalt take of the ram the fat and the rump, and the fat that covereth the inwards, and the caul *above* the liver, and the two kidneys, and the fat that *is* upon them, and the right shoulder; for it *is* a ram of consecration: ²³And one loaf of bread, and one cake of oiled bread, and one wafer out of the basket of the unleavened bread that *is* before the LORD: ²⁴And thou shalt put all in the hands of Aaron, and in the hands of his sons; and shalt waveᶜ them *for* a wave offering before the LORD. ²⁵And thou shalt receive them of their hands, and burn *them* upon the altar for a burnt offering, for a sweet savour before the LORD: it *is* an offering made by fire unto the LORD. ²⁶And thou shalt take the breast of the ram of Aaron's consecration, and wave it *for* a wave offering before the LORD: and it shall be thy part. ²⁷And thou shalt sanctify the breast of the wave offering, and the shoulder of the heave offering, which is waved, and which is heaved up, of the ram of the consecration, *even* of *that* which *is* for Aaron, and of *that* which is for his sons: ²⁸And it shall be Aaron's and his sons' by a statute for ever from the children of Israel: for it *is* an heave offering: and it shall be an heave offering from the children of Israel of the sacrifice of their peace offerings, *even* their heave offering unto the LORD. ²⁹And the holy garments of Aaron shall be his sons' after him, to be anointed therein, and to be consecrated in them. ³⁰*And* that sonᵈ that is priest in his stead shall put them on seven days, when he cometh into the tabernacle of the congregation to minister in the holy *place.* ³¹And thou shalt take the ram of the consecration, and seethe his flesh in the holy place. ³²And Aaron and his sons shall eat the flesh of the ram, and the bread that *is* in the basket, *by* the door of the tabernacle of the congregation. ³³And they shall eat those things wherewith the atonement was made, to consecrate *and* to sanctify them: but a stranger shall not eat *thereof,* because they *are* holy. ³⁴And if ought of the flesh of the consecrations, or of the bread, remain unto the morning, then thou shalt burn the remainder with fire: it shall not be eaten, because it *is* holy. ³⁵And thus shalt thou do unto Aaron, and to his sons, according to all *things* which I have commanded thee: seven days shalt thou consecrate them. ³⁶And thou shalt offer every day a bullock *for* a sin offering for atonement: and thou shalt cleanse the altar, when thou hast made an atonement for it, and thou shalt anoint it, to sanctify it. ³⁷Seven days thou shalt make an atonement for the altar, and sanctify it; and it shall be an altar most holy: whatsoever toucheth the altar shall be holy.

³⁸Now this *is that* which thou shalt offer upon the altar; two lambs of the first year day by day continually. ³⁹The one lamb thou shalt offer in the morning; and the other lamb thou shalt offer

---

ᶜ shalt wave: or, shalt shake to and fro
ᵈ that son: Heb. he of his sons

at even: ⁴⁰And with the one lamb a tenth deal of flour mingled with the fourth part of an hin of beaten oil; and the fourth part of an hin of wine *for* a drink offering. ⁴¹And the other lamb thou shalt offer at even, and shalt do thereto according to the meat offering of the morning, and according to the drink offering thereof, for a sweet savour, an offering made by fire unto the LORD. ⁴²*This shall be* a continual burnt offering throughout your generations *at* the door of the tabernacle of the congregation before the LORD: where I will meet you, to speak there unto thee. ⁴³And there I will meet with the children of Israel, and *the tabernacle* shall be sanctified by my glory. ⁴⁴And I will sanctify the tabernacle of the congregation, and the altar: I will sanctify also both Aaron and his sons, to minister to me in the priest's office. ⁴⁵And I will dwell among the children of Israel,

---

Devotional Moment

•

Absentee Parent

29:45-46 God promised to live among the people of Israel, to know them and to be known by them. And today he lives in all his people through his Holy Spirit. God is not an absentee parent. God wants us to imitate him. Children need not only "quality time" with their parents, but "quantity time" as well. It is not easy, with our busy schedules, to give much time to anything. But we can find time to do what we want to do. Let's copy God's example and "live among" our family. Put time with kids on your list of nonnegotiables.

---

and will be their God. ⁴⁶And they shall know that I *am* the LORD their God, that brought them forth out of the land of Egypt, that I may dwell among them: I *am* the LORD their God.

30

¹And thou shalt make an altar to burn incense upon: *of* shittim wood shalt thou make it. ²A cubit *shall be* the length thereof, and a cubit the breadth thereof; foursquare shall it be: and two cubits *shall be* the height thereof: the horns thereof *shall be* of the same. ³And thou shalt overlay it with pure gold, the topᵃ thereof, and the sides thereof round about, and the horns thereof; and thou shalt make unto it a crown of gold round about. ⁴And two golden rings shalt thou make to it under the crown of it, by the two cornersᵇ thereof, upon the two sides of it shalt thou make *it*; and they shall be for places for the staves to bear it withal. ⁵And thou shalt make the staves *of* shittim wood, and overlay them with gold. ⁶And thou shalt put it before the vail that *is* by the ark of the testimony, before the mercy seat that *is* over the testimony, where I will meet with thee. ⁷And Aaron shall burn thereon sweet incenseᶜ every morning: when he dresseth the lamps, he shall burn incense upon it. ⁸And when Aaron lightethᵈ the lamps at even, he shall burn incense upon it, a perpetual incense before the LORD throughout your generations. ⁹Ye shall offer no strange incense thereon, nor burnt sac-

---

ᵃ top: Heb. roof
ᵇ corners: Heb. ribs
ᶜ sweet incense: Heb. incense of spices
ᵈ lighteth: or setteth up: Heb. causeth to ascend

rifice, nor meat offering; neither shall ye pour drink offering thereon. ¹⁰And Aaron shall make an atonement upon the horns of it once in a year with the blood of the sin offering of atonements: once in the year shall he make atonement upon it throughout your generations: it *is* most holy unto the LORD.

¹¹And the LORD spake unto Moses, saying, ¹²When thou takest the sum of the children of Israel after their number°, then shall they give every man a ransom for his soul unto the LORD, when thou numberest them; that there be no plague among them, when *thou* numberest them. ¹³This they shall give, every one that passeth among them that are numbered, half a shekel after the shekel of the sanctuary: (a shekel *is* twenty gerahs:) an half shekel *shall be* the offering of the LORD. ¹⁴Every one that passeth among them that are numbered, from twenty years old and above, shall give an offering unto the LORD. ¹⁵The rich shall not give moreᶠ, and the poor shall not give less than half a shekel, when *they* give an offering unto the LORD, to make an atonement for your souls. ¹⁶And thou shalt take the atonement money of the children of Israel, and shalt appoint it for the service of the tabernacle of the congregation; that it may be a memorial unto the children of Israel before the LORD, to make an atonement for your souls.

¹⁷And the LORD spake unto Moses, saying, ¹⁸Thou shalt also make a laver *of* brass, and his foot *also of* brass, to wash *withal:* and thou shalt put it be-

tween the tabernacle of the congregation and the altar, and thou shalt put water therein. ¹⁹For Aaron and his sons shall wash their hands and their feet thereat: ²⁰When they go into the tabernacle of the congregation, they shall wash with water, that they die not; or when they come near to the altar to minister, to burn offering made by fire unto the LORD: ²¹So they shall wash their hands and their feet, that they die not: and it shall be a statute for ever to them, *even* to him and to his seed throughout their generations.

²²Moreover the LORD spake unto Moses, saying, ²³Take thou also unto thee principal spices, of pure myrrh five hundred *shekels*, and of sweet cinnamon half so much, *even* two hundred and fifty *shekels*, and of sweet calamus two hundred and fifty *shekels*, ²⁴And of cassia five hundred *shekels*, after the shekel of the sanctuary, and of oil olive an hin: ²⁵And thou shalt make it an oil of holy ointment, an ointment compound after the art of the apothecaryᵍ: it shall be an holy anointing oil. ²⁶And thou shalt anoint the tabernacle of the congregation therewith, and the ark of the testimony, ²⁷And the table and all his vessels, and the candlestick and his vessels, and the altar of incense, ²⁸And the altar of burnt offering with all his vessels, and the laver and his foot. ²⁹And thou shalt sanctify them, that they may be most holy: whatsoever toucheth them shall be holy. ³⁰And thou shalt anoint Aaron and his sons, and consecrate them, that *they* may minister unto me

---

ᵉ their number: Heb. them that are to be numbered
ᶠ give more: Heb. multiply
ᵍ apothecary: or, perfumer

in the priest's office. ³¹And thou shalt speak unto the children of Israel, saying, This shall be an holy anointing oil unto me throughout your generations. ³²Upon man's flesh shall it not be poured, neither shall ye make *any other* like it, after the composition of it: it *is* holy, *and* it shall be holy unto you. ³³Whosoever compoundeth *any* like it, or whosoever putteth *any* of it upon a stranger, shall even be cut off from his people. ³⁴And the LORD said unto Moses, Take unto thee sweet spices, stacte, and onycha, and galbanum; *these* sweet spices with pure frankincense: of each shall there be a like *weight:* ³⁵And thou shalt make it a perfume, a confection after the art of the apothecary, tempered[h] together, pure *and* holy: ³⁶And thou shalt beat *some* of it very small, and put of it before the testimony in the tabernacle of the congregation, where I will meet with thee: it shall be unto you most holy. ³⁷And *as for* the perfume which thou shalt make, ye shall not make to yourselves according to the composition thereof: it shall be unto thee holy for the LORD. ³⁸Whosoever shall make like unto that, to smell thereto, shall even be cut off from his people.

31

¹And the LORD spake unto Moses, saying, ²See, I have called by name Bezaleel the son of Uri, the son of Hur, of the tribe of Judah: ³And I have filled him with the spirit of God, in wisdom,

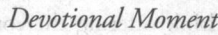

Devotional Moment
•
Child Rearing

31:1-5 God himself gave Bezalel his artistic ability. But no one would have discovered Bezalel's skill if he had sat sipping wine in his tent or spent his time hanging out at the chariot races. As he used his abilities in the Tabernacle project, his unique giftedness flourished. God gifts *every* person with creative skill. Unfortunately, television watching takes no creative skill at all. What are some ways you can give your children opportunities to use their creative skills? God has certainly gifted them—let them put it to use!

and in understanding, and in knowledge, and in all manner of workmanship, ⁴To devise cunning works, to work in gold, and in silver, and in brass, ⁵And in cutting of stones, to set *them,* and in carving of timber, to work in all manner of workmanship. ⁶And I, behold, I have given with him Aholiab, the son of Ahisamach, of the tribe of Dan: and in the hearts of all that are wise hearted I have put wisdom, that they may make all that I have commanded thee; ⁷The tabernacle of the congregation, and the ark of the testimony, and the mercy seat that *is* thereupon, and all the furniture[a] of the tabernacle, ⁸And the table and his furniture[b], and the pure candlestick with all his furniture, and the altar of incense, ⁹And the altar of burnt offering with all his furniture[c], and the laver and his foot, ¹⁰And the cloths of service, and the holy garments for Aaron the priest,

[h] tempered . . . : Heb. salted
[a] furniture: Heb. vessels
[b] furniture: Heb. vessels
[c] furniture: Heb. vessels

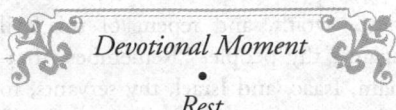

Devotional Moment
•
Rest

31:12-17 God considered it immensely important that Israel follow the pattern he set in creation—six days of work, one day of rest. It would remind them of God's relationship with them and give them a chance to recharge their batteries, so to speak (see 23:12). So important was this that the penalty for working on the Sabbath was death. Plan now to put on the brakes one day a week. Protect that time from work intrusions, and make it a day to enjoy.

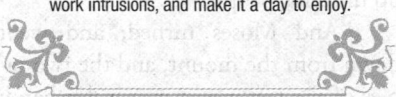

and the garments of his sons, to minister in the priest's office, ¹¹And the anointing oil, and sweet incense for the holy *place*: according to all that I have commanded thee shall they do.

¹²And the LORD spake unto Moses, saying, ¹³Speak thou also unto the children of Israel, saying, Verily my sabbaths ye shall keep: for it *is* a sign between me and you throughout your generations; that *ye* may know that I *am* the LORD that doth sanctify you. ¹⁴Ye shall keep the sabbath therefore; for it *is* holy unto you: every one that defileth it shall surely be put to death: for whosoever doeth *any* work therein, that soul shall be cut off from among his people. ¹⁵Six days may work be done; but in the seventh *is* the sabbath of rest, holy[d] to the LORD: whosoever doeth *any* work in the sabbath day, he shall surely be put to death. ¹⁶Wherefore the children of Israel shall keep the sabbath, to observe the sabbath throughout their generations, *for* a perpetual covenant. ¹⁷It *is* a sign between me and the children of Israel for ever: for *in* six days the LORD made heaven and earth, and on the seventh day he rested, and was refreshed. ¹⁸And he gave unto Moses, when he had made an end of communing with him upon mount Sinai, two tables of testimony, tables of stone, written with the finger of God.

32

¹And when the people saw that Moses delayed to come down out of the mount, the people gathered themselves together unto Aaron, and said unto him, Up, make us gods, which shall go before us; for *as for* this Moses, the man that brought us up out of the land of Egypt, we wot not what is become of him. ²And Aaron said unto them, Break off the golden earrings, which *are* in the ears of your wives, of your sons, and of your daughters, and bring *them* unto me. ³And all the people brake off the golden earrings which *were* in their ears, and brought *them* unto Aaron. ⁴And he received *them* at their hand, and fashioned it with a graving tool, after he had made it a molten calf: and they said, These *be* thy gods, O Israel, which brought thee up out of the land of Egypt. ⁵And when Aaron saw *it*, he built an altar before it; and Aaron made proclamation, and said, To morrow *is* a feast to the LORD. ⁶And they rose up early on the morrow, and offered burnt offerings, and brought peace offerings; and the people sat down to eat and to drink, and rose up to play.

⁷And the LORD said unto Moses, Go, get thee down; for thy people, which thou broughtest out of the land

[d] holy: Heb. holiness

of Egypt, have corrupted *themselves*. ⁸They have turned aside quickly out of the way which I commanded them: they have made them a molten calf, and have worshipped it, and have sacrificed thereunto, and said, These *be* thy gods, O Israel, which have brought thee up out of the land of Egypt. ⁹And the LORD said unto Moses, I have seen this people, and, behold, it *is* a stiff-necked people: ¹⁰Now therefore let me alone, that my wrath may wax hot against them, and that I may consume them: and I will make of thee a great nation. ¹¹And Moses besought the LORDª his God, and said, LORD, why doth thy wrath wax hot against thy people, which thou hast brought forth out of the land of Egypt with great power, and with a mighty hand? ¹²Wherefore should the Egyptians speak, and say, For mischief did he bring them out, to slay them in the mountains, and to consume them from the face of the earth? Turn from thy fierce wrath, and repent of this evil against thy people. ¹³Remember Abraham, Isaac, and Israel, thy servants, to whom thou swarest by thine own self, and saidst unto them, I will multiply your seed as the stars of heaven, and all this land that I have spoken of will I give unto your seed, and they shall inherit *it* for ever. ¹⁴And the LORD repented of the evil which he thought to do unto his people.

¹⁵And Moses turned, and went down from the mount, and the two tables of the testimony *were* in his hand: the tables *were* written on both their sides; on the one side and on the other *were* they written. ¹⁶And the tables *were* the work of God, and the writing *was* the writing of God, graven upon the tables. ¹⁷And when Joshua heard the noise of the people as they shouted, he said unto Moses, *There is* a noise of war in the camp. ¹⁸And he said, *It is* not the voice of *them that* shout for mastery, neither *is it* the voice of *them that* cry for being overcome: *but* the noise of *them that* sing do I hear. ¹⁹And it came to pass, as soon as he came nigh unto the camp, that he saw the calf, and the dancing: and Moses' anger waxed hot, and he cast the tables out of his hands, and brake them beneath the mount. ²⁰And he took the calf which they had made, and burnt *it* in the fire, and ground *it* to powder, and strawed *it* upon the water, and made the children of Israel drink *of it*.

²¹And Moses said unto Aaron, What did this people unto thee, that thou hast brought so great a sin upon them? ²²And Aaron said, Let not the

---

Devotional Moment

Prayer

32:11-14 God was angry with his people, and understandably so. But Moses, their patient leader, pleaded on their behalf, and God listened. Moses' prayer made a difference. When God hears you pray for others, he listens. What greater protection can you offer than that? Don't forget to schedule time for prayer each day. And if it gets crowded out by interruptions, simply stop in the middle of your day and take five minutes and pray. Certainly no heartfelt prayer for your loved ones will be wasted.

ª the LORD: Heb. the face of the LORD

anger of my lord wax hot: thou knowest the people, that they *are set* on mischief. ²³For they said unto me, Make us gods, which shall go before us: for *as for* this Moses, the man that brought us up out of the land of Egypt, we wot not what is become of him. ²⁴And I said unto them, Whosoever hath any gold, let them break *it* off. So they gave *it* me: then I cast it into the fire, and there came out this calf. ²⁵And when Moses saw that the people *were* naked; (for Aaron had made them naked unto *their* shame among their enemies^b:) ²⁶Then Moses stood in the gate of the camp, and said, Who *is* on the LORD'S side? *let him come* unto me. And all the sons of Levi gathered themselves together unto him. ²⁷And he said unto them, Thus saith the LORD God of Israel, Put every man his sword by his side, *and* go in and out from gate to gate throughout the camp, and slay every man his brother, and every man his companion, and every man his neighbour. ²⁸And the children of Levi did according to the word of Moses: and there fell of the people that day about three thousand men. ²⁹For Moses^c had said, Consecrate yourselves to day to the LORD, even every man upon his son, and upon his brother; that he may bestow upon you a blessing this day.

³⁰And it came to pass on the morrow, that Moses said unto the people, Ye have sinned a great sin: and now I will go up unto the LORD; peradventure I shall make an atonement for your sin. ³¹And Moses returned unto the LORD, and said, Oh, this people have sinned a great sin, and have made them gods of gold. ³²Yet now, if thou wilt forgive their sin—; and if not, blot me, I pray thee, out of thy book which thou hast written. ³³And the LORD said unto Moses, Whosoever hath sinned against me, him will I blot out of my book. ³⁴Therefore now go, lead the people unto *the place* of which I have spoken unto thee: behold, mine Angel shall go before thee: nevertheless in the day when I visit I will visit their sin upon them. ³⁵And the LORD plagued the people, because they made the calf, which Aaron made.

33

¹And the LORD said unto Moses, Depart, *and* go up hence, thou and the people which thou hast brought up out of the land of Egypt, unto the land which I sware unto Abraham, to Isaac, and to Jacob, saying, Unto thy seed will I give it: ²And I will send an angel before thee; and I will drive out the Canaanite, the Amorite, and the Hittite, and the Perizzite, the Hivite, and the Jebusite: ³Unto a land flowing with milk and honey: for I will not go up in the midst of thee; for thou *art* a stiffnecked people: lest I consume thee in the way. ⁴And when the people heard these evil tidings, they mourned: and no man did put on him his ornaments. ⁵For the LORD had said unto Moses, Say unto the children of Israel, Ye *are* a stiffnecked people: I will come up into the midst of thee in a moment, and

---

^b their enemies: Heb. those that rose up against them
^c For Moses . . . : or, And Moses said, Consecrate yourselves to day to the LORD, because every man hath been against his brother, etc

consume thee: therefore now put off thy ornaments from thee, that I may know what to do unto thee. ⁶And the children of Israel stripped themselves of their ornaments by the mount Horeb.

⁷And Moses took the tabernacle, and pitched it without the camp, afar off from the camp, and called it the Tabernacle of the congregation. And it came to pass, *that* every one which sought the LORD went out unto the tabernacle of the congregation, which *was* without the camp. ⁸And it came to pass, when Moses went out unto the tabernacle, *that* all the people rose up, and stood every man *at* his tent door, and looked after Moses, until he was gone into the tabernacle. ⁹And it came to pass, as Moses entered into the tabernacle, the cloudy pillar descended, and stood *at* the door of the tabernacle, and *the LORD* talked with Moses. ¹⁰And all the people saw the cloudy pillar stand *at* the tabernacle door: and all the people rose up and worshipped, every man *in* his tent door. ¹¹And the LORD spake unto Moses face to face, as a man speaketh unto his friend. And he turned again into the camp: but his servant Joshua, the son of Nun, a young man, departed not out of the tabernacle.

¹²And Moses said unto the LORD, See, thou sayest unto me, Bring up this people: and thou hast not let me know whom thou wilt send with me. Yet thou hast said, I know thee by name, and thou hast also found grace in my sight. ¹³Now therefore, I pray thee, if I have found grace in thy sight, shew me now thy way, that I may know thee, that I may find grace in thy sight: and consider that this nation *is* thy people.

¹⁴And he said, My presence shall go *with thee*, and I will give thee rest. ¹⁵And he said unto him, If thy presence go not *with me*, carry us not up hence. ¹⁶For wherein shall it be known here that I and thy people have found grace in thy sight? *is it* not in that thou goest with us? so shall we be separated, I and thy people, from all the people that *are* upon the face of the earth. ¹⁷And the LORD said unto Moses, I will do this thing also that thou hast spoken: for thou hast found grace in my sight, and I know thee by name. ¹⁸And he said, I beseech thee, shew me thy glory. ¹⁹And he said, I will make all my goodness pass before thee, and I will proclaim the name of the LORD before thee; and will be gracious to whom I will be gracious, and will shew mercy on whom I will shew mercy. ²⁰And he said, Thou canst not see my face: for there shall no man see me, and live. ²¹And the LORD said, Behold, *there is* a place by me, and thou shalt stand upon a rock: ²²And it shall come to pass, while my glory passeth by, that I will put thee in a clift of the rock, and will cover thee with my hand while I pass by: ²³And I will take away mine hand, and thou shalt see my back parts: but my face shall not be seen.

34

¹And the LORD said unto Moses, Hew thee two tables of stone like unto the first: and I will write upon *these* tables the words that were in the first tables, which thou brakest. ²And be ready in the morning, and come up in the morning unto mount Sinai, and present thyself there to me in the top of the mount. ³And no man shall come up

with thee, neither let any man be seen throughout all the mount; neither let the flocks nor herds feed before that mount. ⁴And he hewed two tables of stone like unto the first; and Moses rose up early in the morning, and went up unto mount Sinai, as the LORD had commanded him, and took in his hand the two tables of stone.

⁵And the LORD descended in the cloud, and stood with him there, and proclaimed the name of the LORD. ⁶And the LORD passed by before him, and proclaimed, The LORD, The LORD God, merciful and gracious, longsuffering, and abundant in goodness and truth, ⁷Keeping mercy for thousands, forgiving iniquity and transgression and sin, and that will by no means clear *the guilty*; visiting the iniquity of the fathers upon the children, and upon the children's children, unto the third and to the fourth *generation*. ⁸And Moses made haste, and bowed his head toward the earth, and worshipped. ⁹And he said, If now I have found grace in thy sight, O Lord, let my

Lord, I pray thee, go among us; for it *is* a stiffnecked people; and pardon our iniquity and our sin, and take us for thine inheritance.

¹⁰And he said, Behold, I make a covenant: before all thy people I will do marvels, such as have not been done in all the earth, nor in any nation: and all the people among which thou *art* shall see the work of the LORD: for it *is* a terrible thing that I will do with thee. ¹¹Observe thou that which I command thee this day: behold, I drive out before thee the Amorite, and the Canaanite, and the Hittite, and the Perizzite, and the Hivite, and the Jebusite. ¹²Take heed to thyself, lest thou make a covenant with the inhabitants of the land whither thou goest, lest it be for a snare in the midst of thee: ¹³But ye shall destroy their altars, break their images[a], and cut down their groves: ¹⁴For thou shalt worship no other god: for the LORD, whose name *is* Jealous, *is* a jealous God: ¹⁵Lest thou make a covenant

---

ᵃ images: Heb. statues

with the inhabitants of the land, and they go a whoring after their gods, and do sacrifice unto their gods, and *one* call thee, and thou eat of his sacrifice; [16]And thou take of their daughters unto thy sons, and their daughters go a whoring after their gods, and make thy sons go a whoring after their gods. [17]Thou shalt make thee no molten gods.

[18]The feast of unleavened bread shalt thou keep. Seven days thou shalt eat unleavened bread, as I commanded thee, in the time of the month Abib: for in the month Abib thou camest out from Egypt. [19]All that openeth the matrix *is* mine; and every firstling among thy cattle, *whether* ox or sheep[b], *that is male.* [20]But the firstling of an ass thou shalt redeem with a lamb[c]: and if thou redeem *him* not, then shalt thou break his neck. All the firstborn of thy sons thou shalt redeem. And none shall appear before me empty. [21]Six days thou shalt work, but on the seventh day thou shalt rest: in earing time and in harvest thou shalt rest. [22]And thou shalt observe the feast of weeks, of the firstfruits of wheat harvest, and the feast of ingathering at the year's end[d]. [23]Thrice in the year shall all your men children appear before the Lord GOD, the God of Israel. [24]For I will cast out the nations before thee, and enlarge thy borders: neither shall any man desire thy land, when thou shalt go up to appear before the LORD thy God thrice in the year. [25]Thou shalt not offer the blood of my sacrifice with leaven; neither shall the

sacrifice of the feast of the passover be left unto the morning. [26]The first of the firstfruits of thy land thou shalt bring unto the house of the LORD thy God. Thou shalt not seethe a kid in his mother's milk. [27]And the LORD said unto Moses, Write thou these words: for after the tenor of these words I have made a covenant with thee and with Israel.

[28]And he was there with the LORD forty days and forty nights; he did neither eat bread, nor drink water. And he wrote upon the tables the words of the covenant, the ten commandments[e]. [29]And it came to pass, when Moses came down from mount Sinai with the two tables of testimony in Moses' hand, when he came down from the mount, that Moses wist not that the skin of his face shone while he talked with him. [30]And when Aaron and all the children of Israel saw Moses, behold, the skin of his face shone; and they were afraid to come nigh him. [31]And Moses called unto them; and Aaron and all the rulers of the congregation returned unto him: and Moses talked with them. [32]And afterward all the children of Israel came nigh: and he gave them in commandment all that the LORD had spoken with him in mount Sinai. [33]And *till* Moses had done speaking with them, he put a vail on his face. [34]But when Moses went in before the LORD to speak with him, he took the vail off, until he came out. And he came out, and spake unto the children

[b] sheep: or, kid
[c] lamb: or, kid
[d] year's end: Heb. revolution of the year
[e] commandments: Heb. words

of Israel *that* which he was commanded. ³⁵And the children of Israel saw the face of Moses, that the skin of Moses' face shone: and Moses put the vail upon his face again, until he went in to speak with him.

35

¹And Moses gathered all the congregation of the children of Israel together, and said unto them, These *are* the words which the LORD hath commanded, that *ye* should do them. ²Six days shall work be done, but on the seventh day there shall be to you an holy day, a sabbath of rest to the LORD: whosoever doeth work therein shall be put to death. ³Ye shall kindle no fire throughout your habitations upon the sabbath day. ⁴And Moses spake unto all the congregation of the children of Israel, saying, This *is* the thing which the LORD commanded, saying, ⁵Take ye from among you an offering unto the LORD: whosoever *is* of a willing heart, let him bring it, an offering of the LORD; gold, and silver, and brass, ⁶And blue, and purple, and scarlet, and

---

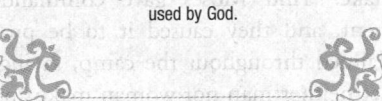

Devotional Moment

Competency

35:10, 25-26, 30-35 God commanded the Israelites to build a Tabernacle, and the people responded by using their many and various skills. These skills, from metal smithing to construction to sewing, and the items they produced, were gifts to God. We all have strengths and abilities that can be given to God. While some may be impressive or appear uniquely religious, all can bring glory to and be used by God.

---

fine linen, and goats' *hair*, ⁷And rams' skins dyed red, and badgers' skins, and shittim wood, ⁸And oil for the light, and spices for anointing oil, and for the sweet incense, ⁹And onyx stones, and stones to be set for the ephod, and for the breastplate. ¹⁰And every wise hearted among you shall come, and make all that the LORD hath commanded; ¹¹The tabernacle, his tent, and his covering, his taches, and his boards, his bars, his pillars, and his sockets, ¹²The ark, and the staves thereof, *with* the mercy seat, and the vail of the covering, ¹³The table, and his staves, and all his vessels, and the shewbread, ¹⁴The candlestick also for the light, and his furniture, and his lamps, with the oil for the light, ¹⁵And the incense altar, and his staves, and the anointing oil, and the sweet incense, and the hanging for the door at the entering in of the tabernacle, ¹⁶The altar of burnt offering, with his brasen grate, his staves, and all his vessels, the laver and his foot, ¹⁷The hangings of the court, his pillars, and their sockets, and the hanging for the door of the court, ¹⁸The pins of the tabernacle, and the pins of the court, and their cords, ¹⁹The cloths of service, to do service in the holy *place*, the holy garments for Aaron the priest, and the garments of his sons, to minister in the priest's office.

²⁰And all the congregation of the children of Israel departed from the presence of Moses. ²¹And they came, every one whose heart stirred him up, and every one whom his spirit made willing, *and* they brought the LORD'S offering to the work of the tabernacle of the congregation, and for all his service, and for the holy garments. ²²And they

came, both men and women, as many as were willing hearted, *and* brought bracelets, and earrings, and rings, and tablets, all jewels of gold: and every man that offered *offered* an offering of gold unto the LORD. ²³And every man, with whom was found blue, and purple, and scarlet, and fine linen, and goats' *hair*, and red skins of rams, and badgers' skins, brought *them*. ²⁴Every one that did offer an offering of silver and brass brought the LORD'S offering: and every man, with whom was found shittim wood for any work of the service, brought *it*. ²⁵And all the women that were wise hearted did spin with their hands, and brought that which they had spun, *both* of blue, and of purple, *and* of scarlet, and of fine linen. ²⁶And all the women whose heart stirred them up in wisdom spun goats' *hair*. ²⁷And the rulers brought onyx stones, and stones to be set, for the ephod, and for the breastplate; ²⁸And spice, and oil for the light, and for the anointing oil, and for the sweet incense. ²⁹The children of Israel brought a willing offering unto the LORD, every man and woman, whose heart made them willing to bring for all manner of work, which the LORD had commanded to be made by the hand of Moses.

³⁰And Moses said unto the children of Israel, See, the LORD hath called by name Bezaleel the son of Uri, the son of Hur, of the tribe of Judah; ³¹And he hath filled him with the spirit of God, in wisdom, in understanding, and in knowledge, and in all manner of workmanship; ³²And to devise curious works, to work in gold, and in silver, and in brass, ³³And in the cutting of stones, to set *them*, and in carving of wood, to make any manner of cunning work. ³⁴And he hath put in his heart that he may teach, *both* he, and Aholiab, the son of Ahisamach, of the tribe of Dan. ³⁵Them hath he filled with wisdom of heart, to work all manner of work, of the engraver, and of the cunning workman, and of the embroiderer, in blue, and in purple, in scarlet, and in fine linen, and of the weaver, *even* of them that do any work, and of those that devise cunning work.

36

¹Then wrought Bezaleel and Aholiab, and every wise hearted man, in whom the LORD put wisdom and understanding to know how to work all manner of work for the service of the sanctuary, according to all that the LORD had commanded. ²And Moses called Bezaleel and Aholiab, and every wise hearted man, in whose heart the LORD had put wisdom, *even* every one whose heart stirred him up to come unto the work to do it: ³And they received of Moses all the offering, which the children of Israel had brought for the work of the service of the sanctuary, to make it *withal*. And they brought yet unto him free offerings every morning. ⁴And all the wise men, that wrought all the work of the sanctuary, came every man from his work which they made; ⁵And they spake unto Moses, saying, The people bring much more than enough for the service of the work, which the LORD commanded to make. ⁶And Moses gave commandment, and they caused it to be proclaimed throughout the camp, saying, Let neither man nor woman make any

more work for the offering of the sanctuary. So the people were restrained from bringing. ⁷For the stuff they had was sufficient for all the work to make it, and too much.

⁸And every wise hearted man among them that wrought the work of the tabernacle made ten curtains *of* fine twined linen, and blue, and purple, and scarlet: *with* cherubims of cunning work made he them. ⁹The length of one curtain *was* twenty and eight cubits, and the breadth of one curtain four cubits: the curtains *were* all of one size. ¹⁰And he coupled the five curtains one unto another: and *the other* five curtains he coupled one unto another. ¹¹And he made loops of blue on the edge of one curtain from the selvedge in the coupling: likewise he made in the uttermost side of *another* curtain, in the coupling of the second. ¹²Fifty loops made he in one curtain, and fifty loops made he in the edge of the curtain which *was* in the coupling of the second: the loops held one *curtain* to another. ¹³And he made fifty taches of gold, and coupled the curtains one unto another with the taches: so it became one tabernacle.

¹⁴And he made curtains *of* goats' *hair* for the tent over the tabernacle: eleven curtains he made them. ¹⁵The length of one curtain *was* thirty cubits, and four cubits *was* the breadth of one curtain: the eleven curtains *were* of one size. ¹⁶And he coupled five curtains by themselves, and six curtains by themselves. ¹⁷And he made fifty loops upon the uttermost edge of the curtain in the coupling, and fifty loops made he upon the edge of the curtain which coupleth the second. ¹⁸And he made fifty taches *of* brass to couple the tent together, that it might be one. ¹⁹And he made a covering for the tent *of* rams' skins dyed red, and a covering *of* badgers' skins above *that*. ²⁰And he made boards for the tabernacle *of* shittim wood, standing up. ²¹The length of a board *was* ten cubits, and the breadth of a board one cubit and a half. ²²One board had two tenons, equally distant one from another: thus did he make for all the boards of the tabernacle. ²³And he made boards for the tabernacle; twenty boards for the south side southward: ²⁴And forty sockets of silver he made under the twenty boards; two sockets under one board for his two tenons, and two sockets under another board for his two tenons. ²⁵And for the other side of the tabernacle, *which is* toward the north corner, he made twenty boards, ²⁶And their forty sockets of silver; two sockets under one board, and two sockets under another board. ²⁷And for the sides of the tabernacle westward he made six boards. ²⁸And two boards made he for the corners of the tabernacle in the two sides. ²⁹And they were coupledᵃ beneath, and coupled together at the head thereof, to one ring: thus he did to both of them in both the corners. ³⁰And there were eight boards; and their sockets *were* sixteen sockets of silver, under every board two sockets. ³¹And he made bars of shittim wood; five for the boards of the one side of the tabernacle, ³²And five bars for the boards of the other side of the tabernacle, and five bars for the boards of the tabernacle for the sides westward. ³³And

---

ᵃ coupled: Heb. twinned

he made the middle bar to shoot through the boards from the one end to the other. ³⁴And he overlaid the boards with gold, and made their rings of gold to be places for the bars, and overlaid the bars with gold.

³⁵And he made a vail of blue, and purple, and scarlet, and fine twined linen: with cherubims made he it of cunning work. ³⁶And he made thereunto four pillars of shittim wood, and overlaid them with gold: their hooks were of gold; and he cast for them four sockets of silver. ³⁷And he made an hanging for the tabernacle door of blue, and purple, and scarlet, and fine twined linen, of needlework^b; ³⁸And the five pillars of it with their hooks: and he overlaid their chapiters and their fillets with gold: but their five sockets were of brass.

37

¹And Bezaleel made the ark of shittim wood: two cubits and a half was the length of it, and a cubit and a half the breadth of it, and a cubit and a half the height of it: ²And he overlaid it with pure gold within and without, and made a crown of gold to it round about. ³And he cast for it four rings of gold, to be set by the four corners of it; even two rings upon the one side of it, and two rings upon the other side of it. ⁴And he made staves of shittim wood, and overlaid them with gold. ⁵And he put the staves into the rings by the sides of the ark, to bear the ark. ⁶And he made the mercy seat of pure gold: two cubits and a half was the length thereof, and one cubit and a half the breadth thereof. ⁷And he made two cherubims of gold, beaten out of one piece made he them, on^a the two ends of the mercy seat; ⁸One cherub on the end^b on this side, and another cherub on the other end on that side: out of the mercy seat made he the cherubims on the two ends thereof. ⁹And the cherubims spread out their wings on high, and covered with their wings over the mercy seat, with their faces one to another; even to the mercy seatward were the faces of the cherubims.

¹⁰And he made the table of shittim wood: two cubits was the length thereof, and a cubit the breadth thereof, and a cubit and a half the height thereof: ¹¹And he overlaid it with pure gold, and made thereunto a crown of gold round about. ¹²Also he made thereunto a border of an handbreadth round about; and made a crown of gold for the border thereof round about. ¹³And he cast for it four rings of gold, and put the rings upon the four corners that were in the four feet thereof. ¹⁴Over against the border were the rings, the places for the staves to bear the table. ¹⁵And he made the staves of shittim wood, and overlaid them with gold, to bear the table. ¹⁶And he made the vessels which were upon the table, his dishes, and his spoons, and his bowls, and his covers to cover^c withal, of pure gold. ¹⁷And he made the candlestick of

---

^b of needlework: Heb. the work of a needleworker or, embroiderer
^a on . . . : or, out of, etc
^b on the end: or, out of, etc
^c to cover . . . : or, to pour out withal

pure gold: *of* beaten work made he the candlestick; his shaft, and his branch, his bowls, his knops, and his flowers, were of the same: [18]And six branches going out of the sides thereof; three branches of the candlestick out of the one side thereof, and three branches of the candlestick out of the other side thereof: [19]Three bowls made after the fashion of almonds in one branch, a knop and a flower; and three bowls made like almonds in another branch, a knop and a flower: so throughout the six branches going out of the candlestick. [20]And in the candlestick *were* four bowls made like almonds, his knops, and his flowers: [21]And a knop under two branches of the same, and a knop under two branches of the same, and a knop under two branches of the same, according to the six branches going out of it. [22]Their knops and their branches were of the same: all of it *was* one beaten work *of* pure gold. [23]And he made his seven lamps, and his snuffers, and his snuffdishes, *of* pure gold. [24]*Of* a talent of pure gold made he it, and all the vessels thereof.

[25]And he made the incense altar *of* shittim wood: the length of it *was* a cubit, and the breadth of it a cubit; *it was* foursquare; and two cubits *was* the height of it; the horns thereof were of the same. [26]And he overlaid it with pure gold, *both* the top of it, and the sides thereof round about, and the horns of it: also he made unto it a crown of gold round about. [27]And he made two rings of gold for it under the crown thereof, by the two corners of it, upon the two sides thereof, to be places for the staves to bear it withal. [28]And he made the staves *of* shittim wood, and overlaid them with gold. [29]And he made the holy anointing oil, and the pure incense of sweet spices, according to the work of the apothecary.

38

[1]And he made the altar of burnt offering *of* shittim wood: five cubits *was* the length thereof, and five cubits the breadth thereof; *it was* foursquare; and three cubits the height thereof. [2]And he made the horns thereof on the four corners of it; the horns thereof were of the same: and he overlaid it with brass. [3]And he made all the vessels of the altar, the pots, and the shovels, and the basons, *and* the fleshhooks, and the firepans: all the vessels thereof made he *of* brass. [4]And he made for the altar a brasen grate of network under the compass thereof beneath unto the midst of it. [5]And he cast four rings for the four ends of the grate of brass, *to be* places for the staves. [6]And he made the staves *of* shittim wood, and overlaid them with brass. [7]And he put the staves into the rings on the sides of the altar, to bear it withal; he made the altar hollow with boards. [8]And he made the laver *of* brass, and the foot of it *of* brass, of the lookingglasses[a] of *the women* assembling, which assembled *at* the door of the tabernacle of the congregation.

[9]And he made the court: on the south side southward the hangings of the court *were of* fine twined linen, an hundred cubits: [10]Their pillars *were* twenty, and their brasen sockets twenty; the hooks of the pillars and their fillets

---

[a] lookingglasses: or, brasen glasses

were of silver. ¹¹And for the north side *the hangings were* an hundred cubits, their pillars *were* twenty, and their sockets of brass twenty; the hooks of the pillars and their fillets *of* silver. ¹²And for the west side *were* hangings of fifty cubits, their pillars ten, and their sockets ten; the hooks of the pillars and their fillets *of* silver. ¹³And for the east side eastward fifty cubits. ¹⁴The hangings of the one side *of the gate were* fifteen cubits; their pillars three, and their sockets three. ¹⁵And for the other side of the court gate, on this hand and that hand, *were* hangings of fifteen cubits; their pillars three, and their sockets three. ¹⁶All the hangings of the court round about *were* of fine twined linen. ¹⁷And the sockets for the pillars *were of* brass; the hooks of the pillars and their fillets *of* silver; and the overlaying of their chapiters *of* silver; and all the pillars of the court *were* filleted with silver. ¹⁸And the hanging for the gate of the court *was* needlework, *of* blue, and purple, and scarlet, and fine twined linen: and twenty cubits *was* the length, and the height in the breadth *was* five cubits, answerable to the hangings of the court. ¹⁹And their pillars *were* four, and their sockets *of* brass four; their hooks *of* silver, and the overlaying of their chapiters and their fillets *of* silver. ²⁰And all the pins of the tabernacle, and of the court round about, *were of* brass.

²¹This is the sum of the tabernacle, *even* of the tabernacle of testimony, as it was counted, according to the commandment of Moses, *for* the service of the Levites, by the hand of Ithamar, son to Aaron the priest. ²²And Bezaleel the son of Uri, the son of Hur, of the tribe of Judah, made all that the LORD commanded Moses. ²³And with him *was* Aholiab, son of Ahisamach, of the tribe of Dan, an engraver, and a cunning workman, and an embroiderer in blue, and in purple, and in scarlet, and fine linen. ²⁴All the gold that was occupied for the work in all the work of the holy *place*, even the gold of the offering, was twenty and nine talents, and seven hundred and thirty shekels, after the shekel of the sanctuary. ²⁵And the silver of them that were numbered of the congregation *was* an hundred talents, and a thousand seven hundred and threescore and fifteen shekels, after the shekel of the sanctuary: ²⁶A bekah for every man[b], *that is,* half a shekel, after the shekel of the sanctuary, for every one that went to be numbered, from twenty years old and upward, for six hundred thousand and three thousand and five hundred and fifty *men.* ²⁷And of the hundred talents of silver were cast the sockets of the sanctuary, and the sockets of the vail; an hundred sockets of the hundred talents, a talent for a socket. ²⁸And of the thousand seven hundred seventy and five shekels he made hooks for the pillars, and overlaid their chapiters, and filleted them. ²⁹And the brass of the offering *was* seventy talents, and two thousand and four hundred shekels. ³⁰And therewith he made the sockets to the door of the tabernacle of the congregation, and the brasen altar, and the brasen grate for it, and all the vessels of the altar, ³¹And the sockets of the court round about, and the sockets of the court gate, and all the

---

[b] every man: Heb. a poll

pins of the tabernacle, and all the pins of the court round about.

39

¹And of the blue, and purple, and scarlet, they made cloths of service, to do service in the holy *place*, and made the holy garments for Aaron; as the LORD commanded Moses. ²And he made the ephod *of* gold, blue, and purple, and scarlet, and fine twined linen. ³And they did beat the gold into thin plates, and cut *it into* wires, to work *it* in the blue, and in the purple, and in the scarlet, and in the fine linen, *with* cunning work. ⁴They made shoulderpieces for it, to couple *it* together: by the two edges was it coupled together. ⁵And the curious girdle of his ephod, that *was* upon it, *was* of the same, according to the work thereof; *of* gold, blue, and purple, and scarlet, and fine twined linen; as the LORD commanded Moses. ⁶And they wrought onyx stones inclosed in ouches of gold, graven, as signets are graven, with the names of the children of Israel. ⁷And he put them on the shoulders of the ephod, *that they should be* stones for a memorial to the children of Israel; as the LORD commanded Moses. ⁸And he made the breastplate *of* cunning work, like the work of the ephod; *of* gold, blue, and purple, and scarlet, and fine twined linen. ⁹It was foursquare; they made the breastplate double: a span *was* the length thereof, and a span the breadth thereof, *being* doubled. ¹⁰And they set in it four rows of stones: *the first* row *was* a sardius[a], a topaz, and a carbuncle: this *was* the first row. ¹¹And the second row, an emerald, a sapphire, and a diamond. ¹²And the third

row, a ligure, an agate, and an amethyst. ¹³And the fourth row, a beryl, an onyx, and a jasper: *they were* inclosed in ouches of gold in their inclosings. ¹⁴And the stones *were* according to the names of the children of Israel, twelve, according to their names, *like* the engravings of a signet, every one with his name, according to the twelve tribes. ¹⁵And they made upon the breastplate chains at the ends, *of* wreathen work *of* pure gold. ¹⁶And they made two ouches *of* gold, and two gold rings; and put the two rings in the two ends of the breastplate. ¹⁷And they put the two wreathen chains of gold in the two rings on the ends of the breastplate. ¹⁸And the two ends of the two wreathen chains they fastened in the two ouches, and put them on the shoulderpieces of the ephod, before it. ¹⁹And they made two rings of gold, and put *them* on the two ends of the breastplate, upon the border of it, which *was* on the side of the ephod inward. ²⁰And they made two *other* golden rings, and put them on the two sides of the ephod underneath, toward the forepart of it, over against the *other* coupling thereof, above the curious girdle of the ephod. ²¹And they did bind the breastplate by his rings unto the rings of the ephod with a lace of blue, that it might be above the curious girdle of the ephod, and that the breastplate might not be loosed from the ephod; as the LORD commanded Moses. ²²And he made the robe of the ephod *of* woven work, all *of* blue. ²³And *there was* an hole in the midst of the robe, as the hole of an habergeon, *with* a band round about the hole, that it should not rend. ²⁴And they made upon the hems of the robe pome-

---

[a] sardius: or, ruby

granates *of* blue, and purple, and scarlet, *and* twined *linen.* ²⁵And they made bells *of* pure gold, and put the bells between the pomegranates upon the hem of the robe, round about between the pomegranates; ²⁶A bell and a pomegranate, a bell and a pomegranate, round about the hem of the robe to minister *in*; as the LORD commanded Moses. ²⁷And they made coats *of* fine linen *of* woven work for Aaron, and for his sons, ²⁸And a mitre *of* fine linen, and goodly bonnets *of* fine linen, and linen breeches *of* fine twined linen, ²⁹And a girdle *of* fine twined linen, and blue, and purple, and scarlet, *of* needlework; as the LORD commanded Moses. ³⁰And they made the plate of the holy crown *of* pure gold, and wrote upon it a writing, *like to* the engravings of a signet, HOLINESS TO THE LORD. ³¹And they tied unto it a lace of blue, to fasten *it* on high upon the mitre; as the LORD commanded Moses.

³²Thus was all the work of the tabernacle of the tent of the congregation finished: and the children of Israel did according to all that the LORD commanded Moses, so did they. ³³And they brought the tabernacle unto Moses, the tent, and all his furniture, his taches, his boards, his bars, and his pillars, and his sockets, ³⁴And the covering of rams' skins dyed red, and the covering of badgers' skins, and the vail of the covering, ³⁵The ark of the testimony, and the staves thereof, and the mercy seat, ³⁶The table, *and* all the vessels thereof, and the shewbread, ³⁷The pure candlestick, *with* the lamps thereof, *even with* the lamps to be set in order, and all the vessels thereof, and the oil for light, ³⁸And the golden al-

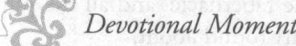

Devotional Moment

Obedience

39:32 God's people carefully obeyed his instructions for the Tabernacle because every detail had significance to its function and purpose. Every command God has given us, no matter how insignificant it may seem, has a purpose. Do you obey God's commands, even in the seemingly insignificant areas of your life? While you may be meticulously honest when you fill out your tax return, do you fudge with the truth to get out of an inconvenient volunteer assignment? Obeying God's command to be honest applies to *all* situations. Focus on obeying God in *every* detail, big and small.

tar, and the anointing oil, and the sweet[b] incense, and the hanging for the tabernacle door, ³⁹The brasen altar, and his grate of brass, his staves, and all his vessels, the laver and his foot, ⁴⁰The hangings of the court, his pillars, and his sockets, and the hanging for the court gate, his cords, and his pins, and all the vessels of the service of the tabernacle, for the tent of the congregation, ⁴¹The cloths of service to do service in the holy *place*, and the holy garments for Aaron the priest, and his sons' garments, to minister in the priest's office. ⁴²According to all that the LORD commanded Moses, so the children of Israel made all the work. ⁴³And Moses did look upon all the work, and, behold, they had done it as the LORD had commanded, even so had they done it: and Moses blessed them.

40

¹And the LORD spake unto Moses, saying, ²On the first day of the first

---

ᵇ the sweet . . . : Heb. the incense of sweet spices

month shalt thou set up the tabernacle of the tent of the congregation. ³And thou shalt put therein the ark of the testimony, and cover the ark with the vail. ⁴And thou shalt bring in the table, and set in order the things that are to be set in order upon it; and thou shalt bring in the candlestick, and light the lamps thereof. ⁵And thou shalt set the altar of gold for the incense before the ark of the testimony, and put the hanging of the door to the tabernacle. ⁶And thou shalt set the altar of the burnt offering before the door of the tabernacle of the tent of the congregation. ⁷And thou shalt set the laver between the tent of the congregation and the altar, and shalt put water therein. ⁸And thou shalt set up the court round about, and hang up the hanging at the court gate. ⁹And thou shalt take the anointing oil, and anoint the tabernacle, and all that *is* therein, and shalt hallow it, and all the vessels thereof: and it shall be holy. ¹⁰And thou shalt anoint the altar of the burnt offering, and all his vessels, and sanctify the altar: and it shall be an altar most holyᵃ. ¹¹And thou shalt anoint the laver and his foot, and sanctify it. ¹²And thou shalt bring Aaron and his sons unto the door of the tabernacle of the congregation, and wash them with water. ¹³And thou shalt put upon Aaron the holy garments, and anoint him, and sanctify him; that he may minister unto me in the priest's office. ¹⁴And thou shalt bring his sons, and clothe them with coats: ¹⁵And thou shalt anoint them, as thou didst anoint their father, that they may minister unto me in the priest's office: for their anointing shall

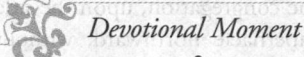

Devotional Moment

•

Traditions

40:14-15 Special ceremonial washing, anointing, and clothing symbolically set apart Aaron and his sons for service to the Lord and his people and became a permanent heritage for Aaron's family. A Christian family has an important legacy of faith to pass on as well. Giving the gift of Jesus—not merely presents—at Christmas, giving Thanksgiving dinner to a needy family, and celebrating your children's "Christian" birthdays can all leave an unforgettable and Christ-honoring legacy for your children. What traditions do you observe in your family? Consider how you can use Bible reading, prayer, or other Christ-centered activities in birthday celebrations, holidays, and other special occasions to pass on your faith.

surely be an everlasting priesthood throughout their generations.

¹⁶Thus did Moses: according to all that the LORD commanded him, so did he. ¹⁷And it came to pass in the first month in the second year, on the first *day* of the month, *that* the tabernacle was reared up. ¹⁸And Moses reared up the tabernacle, and fastened his sockets, and set up the boards thereof, and put in the bars thereof, and reared up his pillars. ¹⁹And he spread abroad the tent over the tabernacle, and put the covering of the tent above upon it; as the LORD commanded Moses. ²⁰And he took and put the testimony into the ark, and set the staves on the ark, and put the mercy seat above upon the ark: ²¹And he brought the ark into the tabernacle, and set up the vail of the covering, and covered the ark of the testimony; as the LORD commanded Moses. ²²And he put the table in the

---

ᵃ most holy: Heb. holiness of holinesses

tent of the congregation, upon the side of the tabernacle northward, without the vail. ²³And he set the bread in order upon it before the LORD; as the LORD had commanded Moses. ²⁴And he put the candlestick in the tent of the congregation, over against the table, on the side of the tabernacle southward. ²⁵And he lighted the lamps before the LORD; as the LORD commanded Moses. ²⁶And he put the golden altar in the tent of the congregation before the vail: ²⁷And he burnt sweet incense thereon; as the LORD commanded Moses. ²⁸And he set up the hanging *at* the door of the tabernacle. ²⁹And he put the altar of burnt offering *by* the door of the tabernacle of the tent of the congregation, and offered upon it the burnt offering and the meat offering; as the LORD commanded Moses. ³⁰And he set the laver between the tent of the congregation and the altar, and put water there, to wash *withal.* ³¹And Moses and Aaron and his sons washed their hands and their feet thereat: ³²When

they went into the tent of the congregation, and when they came near unto the altar, they washed; as the LORD commanded Moses. ³³And he reared up the court round about the tabernacle and the altar, and set up the hanging of the court gate. So Moses finished the work.

³⁴Then a cloud covered the tent of the congregation, and the glory of the LORD filled the tabernacle. ³⁵And Moses was not able to enter into the tent of the congregation, because the cloud abode thereon, and the glory of the LORD filled the tabernacle. ³⁶And when the cloud was taken up from over the tabernacle, the children of Israel went onwardᵇ in all their journeys: ³⁷But if the cloud were not taken up, then they journeyed not till the day that it was taken up. ³⁸For the cloud of the LORD *was* upon the tabernacle by day, and fire was on it by night, in the sight of all the house of Israel, throughout all their journeys.

ᵇ went onward: Heb. journeyed

LEVITICUS

Purpose
A handbook for the Levites outlining their priestly duties in worship, and a guidebook of holy living for the Hebrews

Author
Moses

Date Written
1445–1444 B.C.

Setting
At the foot of Mount Sinai. God is teaching the Israelites how to live as holy people.

Key Verse
"Ye shall be holy: for I the Lord your God am holy." (19:2).

Key People
Moses, Aaron, Nadab, Abihu, Eleazar, Ithamar

Key Place
Mount Sinai

Special Feature
Holiness is mentioned more times (152) than in any other book of the Bible.

Nobody loves rules. Children resent anti-snacking rules (but enjoy a dinner-time appetite); teenagers argue over curfews (but appreciate a good night's rest before the next day's soccer practice); adults wince at the tangle of tax regulations they face every spring (but demand good schools, roads, mosquito abatement, and other amenities that tax monies buy). Hardly anyone loves rules, but we all like the benefits that good rules bring.

In Leviticus, God gives enough rules to fill a bookshelf. The list covers everything from temple worship to infectious diseases, Day of Atonement to day of marriage. All these rules had a purpose—to give holiness a chance with the new Hebrew nation, God's chosen people.

What rules govern your family life? Who can bend them or ignore them? Who sits as family judge, jury, and prison warden? Most important, what's the real purpose of all those rules?

As you read the rules and regulations governing this big new family (the Israelites) consider whether that rule would help (or hurt) you today. Would your heart be more open to God's voice with (or without) the rules that once governed a homeless nation camped at the base of Mount Sinai? Which of these rules would help you make better choices? Solve problems with children? Lead to a happier "lights out" at the end of the day? Wince if you must, but follow God's guidelines. Then enjoy the benefits.

1

¹And the LORD called unto Moses, and spake unto him out of the tabernacle of the congregation, saying, ²Speak unto the children of Israel, and say unto them, If any man of you bring an offering unto the LORD, ye shall bring your offering of the cattle, *even* of the herd, and of the flock.

³If his offering *be* a burnt sacrifice of the herd, let him offer a male without blemish: he shall offer it of his own voluntary will at the door of the tabernacle of the congregation before the LORD. ⁴And he shall put his hand upon the head of the burnt offering; and it shall be accepted for him to make atonement for him. ⁵And he shall kill the bullock before the LORD: and the priests, Aaron's sons, shall bring the blood, and sprinkle the blood round about upon the altar that *is by* the door of the tabernacle of the congregation. ⁶And he shall flay the burnt offering, and cut it into his pieces. ⁷And the sons of Aaron the priest shall put fire upon the altar, and lay the wood in order upon the fire: ⁸And the priests, Aaron's sons, shall lay the parts, the head, and the fat, in order upon the wood that *is* on the fire which *is* upon the altar: ⁹But his inwards and his legs shall he wash in water: and the priest shall burn all on the altar, *to be* a burnt sacrifice, an offering made by fire, of a sweet savour unto the LORD.

¹⁰And if his offering *be* of the flocks, *namely,* of the sheep, or of the goats, for a burnt sacrifice; he shall bring it a male without blemish. ¹¹And he shall kill it on the side of the altar northward before the LORD: and the priests, Aaron's sons, shall sprinkle his blood round about upon the altar. ¹²And he shall cut it into his pieces, with his head and his fat: and the priest shall lay them in order on the wood that *is* on the fire which *is* upon the altar: ¹³But he shall wash the inwards and the legs with water: and the priest shall bring *it* all, and burn *it* upon the altar: it *is* a burnt sacrifice, an offering made by fire, of a sweet savour unto the LORD. ¹⁴And if the burnt sacrifice for his offering to the LORD *be* of fowls, then he shall bring his offering of turtledoves, or of young pigeons. ¹⁵And the priest shall bring it unto the altar, and wring off his head, and burn *it* on the altar; and the blood thereof shall be wrung out at the side of the altar: ¹⁶And he shall pluck away his crop with his feathersᵃ, and cast it beside the altar on the east part, by the place of the ashes: ¹⁷And he shall cleave it with the wings thereof, *but* shall not divide *it* asunder: and the priest shall burn it upon the altar, upon the wood that *is* upon the fire: it *is* a burnt sacrifice, an offering made by fire, of a sweet savour unto the LORD.

Devotional Moment
•
Why Sacrifices?

1:2-3 Animal sacrifices may be difficult to explain to children who love animals and have pets. If your children ask about them, use the opportunity to point out how serious sin is, and how much God loves us. You can explain that (1) to sin means to disobey God; (2) sin makes us guilty of a horrible crime against God; and (3) we should be glad and thankful that Jesus died once and for all, so that we can be forgiven and no more animals have to die for our sin.

ᵃ his feathers: or, the filth thereof

2

¹And when any will offer a meat offering unto the LORD, his offering shall be *of* fine flour; and he shall pour oil upon it, and put frankincense thereon: ²And he shall bring it to Aaron's sons the priests: and he shall take thereout his handful of the flour thereof, and of the oil thereof, with all the frankincense thereof; and the priest shall burn the memorial of it upon the altar, *to be* an offering made by fire, of a sweet savour unto the LORD: ³And the remnant of the meat offering *shall be* Aaron's and his sons': *it is* a thing most holy of the offerings of the LORD made by fire. ⁴And if thou bring an oblation of a meat offering baken in the oven, *it shall be* unleavened cakes of fine flour mingled with oil, or unleavened wafers anointed with oil. ⁵And if thy oblation *be* a meat offering *baken* in a panª, it shall be *of* fine flour unleavened, mingled with oil. ⁶Thou shalt part it in pieces, and pour oil thereon: it *is* a meat offering. ⁷And if thy oblation *be* a meat offering *baken* in the fryingpan, it shall be made *of* fine flour with oil. ⁸And thou shalt bring the meat offering that is made of these things unto the LORD: and when it is presented unto the priest, he shall bring it unto the altar. ⁹And the priest shall take from the meat offering a memorial thereof, and shall burn *it* upon the altar: *it is* an offering made by fire, of a sweet savour unto the LORD. ¹⁰And that which is left of the meat offering *shall be* Aaron's and his sons': *it is* a thing most holy of the offerings of the LORD made by fire.

¹¹No meat offering, which ye shall bring unto the LORD, shall be made with leaven: for ye shall burn no leaven, nor any honey, in any offering of the LORD made by fire. ¹²As for the oblation of the firstfruits, ye shall offer them unto the LORD: but they shall not be burntᵇ on the altar for a sweet savour. ¹³And every oblation of thy meat offering shalt thou season with salt; neither shalt thou suffer the salt of the covenant of thy God to be lacking from thy meat offering: with all thine offerings thou shalt offer salt. ¹⁴And if thou offer a meat offering of thy firstfruits unto the LORD, thou shalt offer for the meat offering of thy firstfruits green ears of corn dried by the fire, *even* corn beaten out of full ears. ¹⁵And thou shalt put oil upon it, and lay frankincense thereon: it *is* a meat offering. ¹⁶And the priest shall burn the memorial of it, *part* of the beaten corn thereof, and *part* of the oil thereof, with all the frankincense thereof: *it is* an offering made by fire unto the LORD.

3

¹And if his oblation *be* a sacrifice of peace offering, if he offer *it* of the herd; whether *it be* a male or female, he shall offer it without blemish before the LORD. ²And he shall lay his hand upon the head of his offering, and kill it *at* the door of the tabernacle of the congregation: and Aaron's sons the priests shall sprinkle the blood upon the altar round about. ³And he shall offer of the sacrifice of the peace offering an offering made by fire unto the LORD; the fatª that covereth the in-

---

ª in a pan: or, on a flat plate, or, slice
ᵇ be burnt: Heb. ascend
ª fat: or, suet

Devotional Moment

Thankfulness

3:1 The peace offering symbolized the giver's attitude of thanksgiving and gratitude for what God had done. It also symbolized the relationship between the giver and God—the fellowship that had been established. What a joyful offering this must have been, this celebration of finite people's relationship with their mighty, infinite Creator! Since Christ became our complete sacrifice for sin, we no longer have to sacrifice an animal as a peace offering, yet God still desires an attitude of thankfulness for what he has done for us. A family that regularly offers thanks to the Lord will benefit from the positive attitude and atmosphere thanksgiving creates. Make thanksgiving a regular part of your family prayer and conversation.

wards, and all the fat that *is* upon the inwards, ⁴And the two kidneys, and the fat that *is* on them, which *is* by the flanks, and the caul[b] above the liver, with the kidneys, it shall he take away. ⁵And Aaron's sons shall burn it on the altar upon the burnt sacrifice, which *is* upon the wood that *is* on the fire: *it is* an offering made by fire, of a sweet savour unto the LORD.

⁶And if his offering for a sacrifice of peace offering unto the LORD *be* of the flock; male or female, he shall offer it without blemish. ⁷If he offer a lamb for his offering, then shall he offer it before the LORD. ⁸And he shall lay his hand upon the head of his offering, and kill it before the tabernacle of the congregation: and Aaron's sons shall sprinkle the blood thereof round about upon the altar. ⁹And he shall offer of the sacrifice of the peace offering an offering made by fire unto the LORD; the fat thereof,

and the whole rump, it shall he take off hard by the backbone; and the fat that covereth the inwards, and all the fat that *is* upon the inwards, ¹⁰And the two kidneys, and the fat that *is* upon them, which *is* by the flanks, and the caul above the liver, with the kidneys, it shall he take away. ¹¹And the priest shall burn it upon the altar: *it is* the food of the offering made by fire unto the LORD. ¹²And if his offering *be* a goat, then he shall offer it before the LORD. ¹³And he shall lay his hand upon the head of it, and kill it before the tabernacle of the congregation: and the sons of Aaron shall sprinkle the blood thereof upon the altar round about. ¹⁴And he shall offer thereof his offering, *even* an offering made by fire unto the LORD; the fat that covereth the inwards, and all the fat that *is* upon the inwards, ¹⁵And the two kidneys, and the fat that *is* upon them, which *is* by the flanks, and the caul above the liver, with the kidneys, it shall he take away. ¹⁶And the priest shall burn them upon the altar: *it is* the food of the offering made by fire for a sweet savour: all the fat *is* the LORD'S. ¹⁷*It shall be* a perpetual statute for your generations throughout all your dwellings, that ye eat neither fat nor blood.

4

¹And the LORD spake unto Moses, saying, ²Speak unto the children of Israel, saying, If a soul shall sin through ignorance against any of the commandments of the LORD *concerning things* which ought not to be done, and shall do against any of them: ³If the priest that is anointed do sin according

---

[b] caul . . . : or, midriff over the liver, and over the kidneys

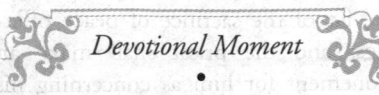

Devotional Moment

•

Discipline

4:1-2 When the Israelites deliberately disobeyed God, the law required them to offer guilt sacrifices to God for forgiveness. But God also made provision for those sins that they committed *unintentionally* or in a moment of weakness. Though such sins required a sacrifice, the purpose of the offering was to make the Israelites aware of the sin so they would not commit it again. In disciplining children, we need to make a distinction between willful disobedience and immaturity or ignorance. While discipline should be swift and fair when our children willfully disobey us, a child who errs because of ignorance or immaturity will benefit more from being patiently shown the right way than from being disciplined. We need to exercise the same mercy with our children that God shows to us.

to the sin of the people; then let him bring for his sin, which he hath sinned, a young bullock without blemish unto the LORD for a sin offering. ⁴And he shall bring the bullock unto the door of the tabernacle of the congregation before the LORD; and shall lay his hand upon the bullock's head, and kill the bullock before the LORD. ⁵And the priest that is anointed shall take of the bullock's blood, and bring it to the tabernacle of the congregation: ⁶And the priest shall dip his finger in the blood, and sprinkle of the blood seven times before the LORD, before the vail of the sanctuary. ⁷And the priest shall put *some* of the blood upon the horns of the altar of sweet incense before the LORD, which *is* in the tabernacle of the congregation; and shall pour all the blood of the bullock at the bottom of the altar of the burnt offering, which *is at* the door of the tabernacle of the congregation. ⁸And he shall take off from it all the fat of the bullock for the sin offering; the fat that covereth the inwards, and all the fat that *is* upon the inwards, ⁹And the two kidneys, and the fat that *is* upon them, which *is* by the flanks, and the caul above the liver, with the kidneys, it shall he take away, ¹⁰As it was taken off from the bullock of the sacrifice of peace offerings: and the priest shall burn them upon the altar of the burnt offering. ¹¹And the skin of the bullock, and all his flesh, with his head, and with his legs, and his inwards, and his dung, ¹²Even the whole bullock shall he carry forth without ᵃ the camp unto a clean place, where the ashes are poured out, and burn him on the wood with fire: where the ashes are poured out shall he be burnt.

¹³And if the whole congregation of Israel sin through ignorance, and the thing be hid from the eyes of the assembly, and they have done *somewhat against* any of the commandments of the LORD *concerning things* which should not be done, and are guilty; ¹⁴When the sin, which they have sinned against it, is known, then the congregation shall offer a young bullock for the sin, and bring him before the tabernacle of the congregation. ¹⁵And the elders of the congregation shall lay their hands upon the head of the bullock before the LORD: and the bullock shall be killed before the LORD. ¹⁶And the priest that is anointed shall bring of the bullock's blood to the tabernacle of the congre-

ᵃ without . . . : Heb. to without the camp

gation: ¹⁷And the priest shall dip his finger *in some* of the blood, and sprinkle *it* seven times before the LORD, *even* before the vail. ¹⁸And he shall put *some* of the blood upon the horns of the altar which *is* before the LORD, that *is* in the tabernacle of the congregation, and shall pour out all the blood at the bottom of the altar of the burnt offering, which *is at* the door of the tabernacle of the congregation. ¹⁹And he shall take all his fat from him, and burn *it* upon the altar. ²⁰And he shall do with the bullock as he did with the bullock for a sin offering, so shall he do with this: and the priest shall make an atonement for them, and it shall be forgiven them. ²¹And he shall carry forth the bullock without the camp, and burn him as he burned the first bullock: it *is* a sin offering for the congregation.

²²When a ruler hath sinned, and done *somewhat* through ignorance *against* any of the commandments of the LORD his God *concerning things* which should not be done, and is guilty; ²³Or if his sin, wherein he hath sinned, come to his knowledge; he shall bring his offering, a kid of the goats, a male without blemish: ²⁴And he shall lay his hand upon the head of the goat, and kill it in the place where they kill the burnt offering before the LORD: it *is* a sin offering. ²⁵And the priest shall take of the blood of the sin offering with his finger, and put *it* upon the horns of the altar of burnt offering, and shall pour out his blood at the bottom of the altar of burnt offering. ²⁶And he shall burn all his fat upon the altar, as

the fat of the sacrifice of peace offerings: and the priest shall make an atonement for him as concerning his sin, and it shall be forgiven him.

²⁷And if any one[b] of the common people sin through ignorance, while he doeth *somewhat against* any of the commandments of the LORD *concerning things* which ought not to be done, and be guilty; ²⁸Or if his sin, which he hath sinned, come to his knowledge: then he shall bring his offering, a kid of the goats, a female without blemish, for his sin which he hath sinned. ²⁹And he shall lay his hand upon the head of the sin offering, and slay the sin offering in the place of the burnt offering. ³⁰And the priest shall take of the blood thereof with his finger, and put *it* upon the horns of the altar of burnt offering, and shall pour out all the blood thereof at the bottom of the altar. ³¹And he shall take away all the fat thereof, as the fat is taken away from off the sacrifice of peace offerings; and the priest shall burn *it* upon the altar for a sweet savour unto the LORD; and the priest shall make an atonement for him, and it shall be forgiven him. ³²And if he bring a lamb for a sin offering, he shall bring it a female without blemish. ³³And he shall lay his hand upon the head of the sin offering, and slay it for a sin offering in the place where they kill the burnt offering. ³⁴And the priest shall take of the blood of the sin offering with his finger, and put *it* upon the horns of the altar of burnt offering, and shall pour out all the blood thereof at the bottom of the altar: ³⁵And he shall take away all the fat thereof, as the fat of the lamb is taken away from

[b] any one: Heb. any soul

the sacrifice of the peace offerings; and the priest shall burn them upon the altar, according to the offerings made by fire unto the LORD: and the priest shall make an atonement for his sin that he hath committed, and it shall be forgiven him.

5

¹And if a soul sin, and hear the voice of swearing, and *is* a witness, whether he hath seen or known *of it*, if he do not utter *it*, then he shall bear his iniquity. ²Or if a soul touch any unclean thing, whether *it be* a carcase of an unclean beast, or a carcase of unclean cattle, or the carcase of unclean creeping things, and *if* it be hidden from him; he also shall be unclean, and guilty. ³Or if he touch the uncleanness of man, whatsoever uncleanness *it be* that a man shall be defiled withal, and it be hid from him; when he knoweth *of it*, then he shall be guilty. ⁴Or if a soul swear, pronouncing with *his* lips to do evil, or to do good, whatsoever *it be* that a man shall

---

Devotional Moment
•
Promises

5:4 Breaking a promise is sin—even if it is a foolish promise to begin with. As Christians, we need to consider carefully before we make a promise, because we would be foolish to promise something that we haven't a serious intention of fulfilling, and even more foolish if keeping that promise would lead to sin. How trustworthy is your word? When you tell your wife you'll get to that project next week, or promise the kids you'll take them skating after work, can they count on you to follow through on your word? Keeping promises starts with the little things at home. Be a promise keeper others can count on.

---

pronounce with an oath, and it be hid from him; when he knoweth *of it*, then he shall be guilty in one of these. ⁵And it shall be, when he shall be guilty in one of these *things*, that he shall confess that he hath sinned in that *thing*: ⁶And he shall bring his trespass offering unto the LORD for his sin which he hath sinned, a female from the flock, a lamb or a kid of the goats, for a sin offering; and the priest shall make an atonement for him concerning his sin.

⁷And if he be not able to bring a lamb, then he shall bring for his trespass, which he hath committed, two turtledoves, or two young pigeons, unto the LORD; one for a sin offering, and the other for a burnt offering. ⁸And he shall bring them unto the priest, who shall offer *that* which *is* for the sin offering first, and wring off his head from his neck, but shall not divide *it* asunder: ⁹And he shall sprinkle of the blood of the sin offering upon the side of the altar; and the rest of the blood shall be wrung out at the bottom of the altar: it *is* a sin offering. ¹⁰And he shall offer the second *for* a burnt offering, according to the manner ᵃ: and the priest shall make an atonement for him for his sin which he hath sinned, and it shall be forgiven him. ¹¹But if he be not able to bring two turtledoves, or two young pigeons, then he that sinned shall bring for his offering the tenth part of an ephah of fine flour for a sin offering; he shall put no oil upon it, neither shall he put *any* frankincense thereon: for it *is* a sin offering. ¹²Then shall he bring it to the priest, and the priest shall take his handful of it, *even* a

---

ᵃ manner: or, ordinance

memorial thereof, and burn *it* on the altar, according to the offerings made by fire unto the LORD: it *is* a sin offering. [13] And the priest shall make an atonement for him as touching his sin that he hath sinned in one of these, and it shall be forgiven him: and *the remnant* shall be the priest's, as a meat offering.

[14] And the LORD spake unto Moses, saying, [15] If a soul commit a trespass, and sin through ignorance, in the holy things of the LORD; then he shall bring for his trespass unto the LORD a ram without blemish out of the flocks, with thy estimation by shekels of silver, after the shekel of the sanctuary, for a trespass offering: [16] And he shall make amends for the harm that he hath done in the holy thing, and shall add the fifth part thereto, and give it unto the priest: and the priest shall make an atonement for him with the ram of the trespass offering, and it shall be forgiven him. [17] And if a soul sin, and commit any of these things which are forbidden to be done by the commandments of the LORD; though he wist *it* not, yet is he guilty, and shall bear his iniquity. [18] And he shall bring a ram without blemish out of the flock, with thy estimation, for a trespass offering, unto the priest: and the priest shall make an atonement for him concerning his ignorance wherein he erred and wist *it* not, and it shall be forgiven him. [19] It *is* a trespass offering: he hath certainly trespassed against the LORD.

6

[1] And the LORD spake unto Moses, saying, [2] If a soul sin, and commit a tres-

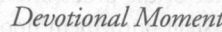

Devotional Moment
•
Making Amends

6:1-7 Under God's law, an Israelite who stole and kept something that belonged to a neighbor had to ask forgiveness of that neighbor and of God, and then pay back more than what had been stolen. Solving a conflict that results from sin usually involves making restitution. Children should learn to respect and care for what belongs to others and that not doing so will cost them something. If your daughter borrows her sister's blouse without asking and ruins it, she should have to replace it. If your son breaks something that belongs to a neighbor, have him fix or replace it rather than just apologize. Having your children make amends (as well as expressing their sorrow as long as it is genuine) for wronging others will go a long way toward making them thoughtful, responsible adults.

pass against the LORD, and lie unto his neighbour in that which was delivered him to keep, or in fellowship[a], or in a thing taken away by violence, or hath deceived his neighbour; [3] Or have found that which was lost, and lieth concerning it, and sweareth falsely; in any of all these that a man doeth, sinning therein: [4] Then it shall be, because he hath sinned, and is guilty, that he shall restore that which he took violently away, or the thing which he hath deceitfully gotten, or that which was delivered him to keep, or the lost thing which he found, [5] Or all that about which he hath sworn falsely; he shall even restore it in the principal, and shall add the fifth part more thereto, *and* give it unto him to whom it appertaineth, in the day[b] of his trespass offering. [6] And he shall bring his trespass of-

---

[a] in fellowship: or, in dealing

[b] in the day . . . : or, in the day of his being found guilty: Heb. in the day of his trespass

fering unto the LORD, a ram without blemish out of the flock, with thy estimation, for a trespass offering, unto the priest: ⁷And the priest shall make an atonement for him before the LORD: and it shall be forgiven him for any thing of all that he hath done in trespassing therein.

⁸And the LORD spake unto Moses, saying, ⁹Command Aaron and his sons, saying, This *is* the law of the burnt offering: It *is* the burnt offering, because of the burning upon the altar all night unto the morning, and the fire of the altar shall be burning in it. ¹⁰And the priest shall put on his linen garment, and his linen breeches shall he put upon his flesh, and take up the ashes which the fire hath consumed with the burnt offering on the altar, and he shall put them beside the altar. ¹¹And he shall put off his garments, and put on other garments, and carry forth the ashes without the camp unto a clean place. ¹²And the fire upon the altar shall be burning in it; it shall not be put out: and the priest shall burn wood on it every morning, and lay the burnt offering in order upon it; and he shall burn thereon the fat of the peace offerings. ¹³The fire shall ever be burning upon the altar; it shall never go out.

¹⁴And this *is* the law of the meat offering: the sons of Aaron shall offer it before the LORD, before the altar. ¹⁵And he shall take of it his handful, of the flour of the meat offering, and of the oil thereof, and all the frankincense which *is* upon the meat offering, and shall burn *it* upon the altar *for* a sweet savour, *even* the memorial of it, unto the LORD. ¹⁶And the remainder thereof shall Aaron and his sons eat: with un-leavened bread shall it be eaten in the holy place; in the court of the tabernacle of the congregation they shall eat it. ¹⁷It shall not be baken with leaven. I have given it *unto them for* their portion of my offerings made by fire; it *is* most holy, as *is* the sin offering, and as the trespass offering. ¹⁸All the males among the children of Aaron shall eat of it. *It shall be* a statute for ever in your generations concerning the offerings of the LORD made by fire: every one that toucheth them shall be holy. ¹⁹And the LORD spake unto Moses, saying, ²⁰This *is* the offering of Aaron and of his sons, which they shall offer unto the LORD in the day when he is anointed; the tenth part of an ephah of fine flour for a meat offering perpetual, half of it in the morning, and half thereof at night. ²¹In a pan it shall be made with oil; *and when it is* baken, thou shalt bring it in: *and* the baken pieces of the meat offering shalt thou offer *for* a sweet savour unto the LORD. ²²And the priest of his sons that is anointed in his stead shall offer it: *it is* a statute for ever unto the LORD; it shall be wholly burnt. ²³For every meat offering for the priest shall be wholly burnt: it shall not be eaten.

²⁴And the LORD spake unto Moses, saying, ²⁵Speak unto Aaron and to his sons, saying, This *is* the law of the sin offering: In the place where the burnt offering is killed shall the sin offering be killed before the LORD: it *is* most holy. ²⁶The priest that offereth it for sin shall eat it: in the holy place shall it be eaten, in the court of the tabernacle of the congregation. ²⁷Whatsoever shall touch the flesh thereof shall be holy: and when there is sprinkled of the

blood thereof upon any garment, thou shalt wash that whereon it was sprinkled in the holy place. ²⁸But the earthen vessel wherein it is sodden shall be broken: and if it be sodden in a brasen pot, it shall be both scoured, and rinsed in water. ²⁹All the males among the priests shall eat thereof: it *is* most holy. ³⁰And no sin offering, whereof *any* of the blood is brought into the tabernacle of the congregation to reconcile *withal* in the holy *place*, shall be eaten: it shall be burnt in the fire.

7

¹Likewise this *is* the law of the trespass offering: it *is* most holy. ²In the place where they kill the burnt offering shall they kill the trespass offering: and the blood thereof shall he sprinkle round about upon the altar. ³And he shall offer of it all the fat thereof; the rump, and the fat that covereth the inwards, ⁴And the two kidneys, and the fat that *is* on them, which *is* by the flanks, and the caul *that is* above the liver, with the kidneys, it shall he take away: ⁵And the priest shall burn them upon the altar *for* an offering made by fire unto the LORD: it *is* a trespass offering. ⁶Every male among the priests shall eat thereof: it shall be eaten in the holy place: it *is* most holy. ⁷As the sin offering *is*, so *is* the trespass offering: there *is* one law for them: the priest that maketh atonement therewith shall have it. ⁸And the priest that offereth any man's burnt offering, *even* the priest shall have to himself the skin of the burnt offering which he hath offered. ⁹And all the meat offering that is baken

in the oven, and all that is dressed in the fryingpan, and in the pan*, shall be the priest's that offereth it. ¹⁰And every meat offering, mingled with oil, and dry, shall all the sons of Aaron have, one *as much* as another.

¹¹And this *is* the law of the sacrifice of peace offerings, which he shall offer unto the LORD. ¹²If he offer it for a thanksgiving, then he shall offer with the sacrifice of thanksgiving unleavened cakes mingled with oil, and unleavened wafers anointed with oil, and cakes mingled with oil, of fine flour, fried. ¹³Besides the cakes, he shall offer *for* his offering leavened bread with the sacrifice of thanksgiving of his peace offerings. ¹⁴And of it he shall offer one out of the whole oblation *for* an heave offering unto the LORD, *and* it shall be the priest's that sprinkleth the blood of the peace offerings. ¹⁵And the flesh of the sacrifice of his peace offerings for thanksgiving shall be eaten the same day that it is offered; he shall not leave any of it until the morning. ¹⁶But if the sacrifice of his offering *be* a vow, or a voluntary offering, it shall be eaten the same day that he offereth his sacrifice: and on the morrow also the remainder of it shall be eaten: ¹⁷But the remainder of the flesh of the sacrifice on the third day shall be burnt with fire. ¹⁸And if *any* of the flesh of the sacrifice of his peace offerings be eaten at all on the third day, it shall not be accepted, neither shall it be imputed unto him that offereth it: it shall be an abomination, and the soul that eateth of it shall bear his iniquity. ¹⁹And the flesh that toucheth any unclean *thing* shall not be

---

ª in the pan: or, on the flat plate or, slice

eaten; it shall be burnt with fire: and as for the flesh, all that be clean shall eat thereof. ²⁰But the soul that eateth *of* the flesh of the sacrifice of peace offerings, that *pertain* unto the LORD, having his uncleanness upon him, even that soul shall be cut off from his people. ²¹Moreover the soul that shall touch any unclean *thing, as* the uncleanness of man, or *any* unclean beast, or any abominable unclean *thing*, and eat of the flesh of the sacrifice of peace offerings, which *pertain* unto the LORD, even that soul shall be cut off from his people. ²²And the LORD spake unto Moses, saying, ²³Speak unto the children of Israel, saying, Ye shall eat no manner of fat, of ox, or of sheep, or of goat. ²⁴And the fat of the beast that dieth of itself, and the fat of that which is torn with beasts[b], may be used in any other use: but ye shall in no wise eat of it. ²⁵For whosoever eateth the fat of the beast, of which men offer an offering made by fire unto the LORD, even the soul that eateth *it* shall be cut off from his people. ²⁶Moreover ye shall eat no manner of blood, *whether it be* of fowl or of beast, in any of your dwellings. ²⁷Whatsoever soul *it be* that eateth any manner of blood, even that soul shall be cut off from his people. ²⁸And the LORD spake unto Moses, saying, ²⁹Speak unto the children of Israel, saying, He that offereth the sacrifice of his peace offerings unto the LORD shall bring his oblation unto the LORD of the sacrifice of his peace offerings. ³⁰His own hands shall bring the offerings of the LORD made by fire, the fat with the breast, it shall he bring, that the

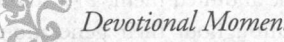

Devotional Moment

Rituals

7:37-38 Practicing these rituals and understanding the purpose or meaning behind them helped to draw the people closer to God. With these reminders, the people would not easily forget God or what he had done for them. We need to explain the importance of Communion and baptism to our children, and try to keep these rituals from becoming dry or meaningless to them. Are there any rituals at your church that *you* don't understand? Learn about them. Then, take time at meals or on trips to and from church to explain the ones your children don't understand.

breast may be waved *for* a wave offering before the LORD. ³¹And the priest shall burn the fat upon the altar: but the breast shall be Aaron's and his sons'. ³²And the right shoulder shall ye give unto the priest *for* an heave offering of the sacrifices of your peace offerings. ³³He among the sons of Aaron, that offereth the blood of the peace offerings, and the fat, shall have the right shoulder for *his* part. ³⁴For the wave breast and the heave shoulder have I taken of the children of Israel from off the sacrifices of their peace offerings, and have given them unto Aaron the priest and unto his sons by a statute for ever from among the children of Israel.

³⁵This *is the portion* of the anointing of Aaron, and of the anointing of his sons, out of the offerings of the LORD made by fire, in the day *when* he presented them to minister unto the LORD in the priest's office; ³⁶Which the LORD commanded to be given them of the children of Israel, in the

---

[b] beast . . . : Heb. carcase

day that he anointed them, *by* a statute for ever throughout their generations. ³⁷This *is* the law of the burnt offering, of the meat offering, and of the sin offering, and of the trespass offering, and of the consecrations, and of the sacrifice of the peace offerings; ³⁸Which the LORD commanded Moses in mount Sinai, in the day that he commanded the children of Israel to offer their oblations unto the LORD, in the wilderness of Sinai.

8

¹And the LORD spake unto Moses, saying, ²Take Aaron and his sons with him, and the garments, and the anointing oil, and a bullock for the sin offering, and two rams, and a basket of unleavened bread; ³And gather thou all the congregation together unto the door of the tabernacle of the congregation. ⁴And Moses did as the LORD commanded him; and the assembly was gathered together unto the door of the tabernacle of the congregation. ⁵And Moses said unto the congregation, This *is* the thing which the LORD commanded to be done. ⁶And Moses brought Aaron and his sons, and washed them with water. ⁷And he put upon him the coat, and girded him with the girdle, and clothed him with the robe, and put the ephod upon him, and he girded him with the curious girdle of the ephod, and bound *it* unto him therewith. ⁸And he put the breastplate upon him: also he put in the breastplate the Urim and the Thummim. ⁹And he put the mitre upon his head; also upon the mitre, *even* upon his forefront, did he put the golden plate, the holy crown; as the LORD commanded Moses. ¹⁰And Moses took the anointing oil, and anointed the tabernacle and all that *was* therein, and sanctified them. ¹¹And he sprinkled thereof upon the altar seven times, and anointed the altar and all his vessels, both the laver and his foot, to sanctify them. ¹²And he poured of the anointing oil upon Aaron's head, and anointed him, to sanctify him. ¹³And Moses brought Aaron's sons, and put coats upon them, and girded them with girdles, and put bonnets ᵃ upon them; as the LORD commanded Moses.

¹⁴And he brought the bullock for the sin offering: and Aaron and his sons laid their hands upon the head of the bullock for the sin offering. ¹⁵And he slew *it*; and Moses took the blood, and put *it* upon the horns of the altar round about with his finger, and purified the altar, and poured the blood at the bottom of the altar, and sanctified it, to make reconciliation upon it. ¹⁶And he took all the fat that *was* upon the inwards, and the caul *above* the liver, and the two kidneys, and their fat, and Moses burned *it* upon the altar. ¹⁷But the bullock, and his hide, his flesh, and his dung, he burnt with fire without the camp; as the LORD commanded Moses. ¹⁸And he brought the ram for the burnt offering: and Aaron and his sons laid their hands upon the head of the ram. ¹⁹And he killed *it*; and Moses sprinkled the blood upon the altar round about. ²⁰And he cut the ram into pieces; and Moses burnt the head, and the pieces, and the fat. ²¹And he washed

---

ᵃ put bonnets: Heb. bound bonnets

the inwards and the legs in water; and Moses burnt the whole ram upon the altar: it *was* a burnt sacrifice for a sweet savour, *and* an offering made by fire unto the LORD; as the LORD commanded Moses. ²²And he brought the other ram, the ram of consecration: and Aaron and his sons laid their hands upon the head of the ram. ²³And he slew *it*; and Moses took of the blood of it, and put *it* upon the tip of Aaron's right ear, and upon the thumb of his right hand, and upon the great toe of his right foot. ²⁴And he brought Aaron's sons, and Moses put of the blood upon the tip of their right ear, and upon the thumbs of their right hands, and upon the great toes of their right feet: and Moses sprinkled the blood upon the altar round about. ²⁵And he took the fat, and the rump, and all the fat that *was* upon the inwards, and the caul *above* the liver, and the two kidneys, and their fat, and the right shoulder: ²⁶And out of the basket of unleavened bread, that *was* before the LORD, he took one unleavened cake, and a cake of oiled bread, and one wafer, and put *them* on the fat, and upon the right shoulder: ²⁷And he put all upon Aaron's hands, and upon his sons' hands, and waved them *for* a wave offering before the LORD. ²⁸And Moses took them from off their hands, and burnt *them* on the altar upon the burnt offering: they *were* consecrations for a sweet savour: it *is* an offering made by fire unto the LORD. ²⁹And Moses took the breast, and waved it *for* a wave offering before the LORD: *for* of the ram of consecration it was Moses' part; as the LORD commanded Moses. ³⁰And Moses took of the anointing oil, and of the blood which *was* upon the altar, and sprinkled *it* upon Aaron, *and* upon his garments, and upon his sons, and upon his sons' garments with him; and sanctified Aaron, *and* his garments, and his sons, and his sons' garments with him.

³¹And Moses said unto Aaron and to his sons, Boil the flesh *at* the door of the tabernacle of the congregation: and there eat it with the bread that *is* in the basket of consecrations, as I commanded, saying, Aaron and his sons shall eat it. ³²And that which remaineth of the flesh and of the bread shall ye burn with fire. ³³And ye shall not go out of the door of the tabernacle of the congregation *in* seven days, until the days of your consecration be at an end: for seven days shall he consecrate you. ³⁴As he hath done this day, *so* the LORD hath commanded to do, to make an atonement for you. ³⁵Therefore shall ye abide *at* the door of the tabernacle of the congregation day and night seven days, and keep the charge of the LORD, that ye die not: for so I am commanded. ³⁶So Aaron and his sons did all things which the LORD commanded by the hand of Moses.

9

¹And it came to pass on the eighth day, *that* Moses called Aaron and his sons, and the elders of Israel; ²And he said unto Aaron, Take thee a young calf for a sin offering, and a ram for a burnt offering, without blemish, and offer *them* before the LORD. ³And unto the children of Israel thou shalt speak, saying, Take ye a kid of the goats for a sin offering; and a calf and a lamb, *both* of the first year, without blemish, for a burnt offering; ⁴Also a bullock and a ram for

peace offerings, to sacrifice before the LORD; and a meat offering mingled with oil: for to day the LORD will appear unto you. [5]And they brought *that* which Moses commanded before the tabernacle of the congregation: and all the congregation drew near and stood before the LORD. [6]And Moses said, This *is* the thing which the LORD commanded that ye should do: and the glory of the LORD shall appear unto you. [7]And Moses said unto Aaron, Go unto the altar, and offer thy sin offering, and thy burnt offering, and make an atonement for thyself, and for the people: and offer the offering of the people, and make an atonement for them; as the LORD commanded.

[8]Aaron therefore went unto the altar, and slew the calf of the sin offering, which *was* for himself. [9]And the sons of Aaron brought the blood unto him: and he dipped his finger in the blood, and put *it* upon the horns of the altar, and poured out the blood at the bottom of the altar: [10]But the fat, and the kidneys, and the caul above the liver of the sin offering, he burnt upon the altar; as the LORD commanded Moses. [11]And the flesh and the hide he burnt with fire without the camp. [12]And he slew the burnt offering; and Aaron's sons presented unto him the blood, which he sprinkled round about upon the altar. [13]And they presented the burnt offering unto him, with the pieces thereof, and the head: and he burnt *them* upon the altar. [14]And he did wash the inwards and the legs, and burnt *them* upon the burnt offering on the altar. [15]And he brought

the people's offering, and took the goat, which *was* the sin offering for the people, and slew it, and offered it for sin, as the first. [16]And he brought the burnt offering, and offered it according to the manner [a]. [17]And he brought the meat offering, and took[b] an handful thereof, and burnt *it* upon the altar, beside the burnt sacrifice of the morning. [18]He slew also the bullock and the ram *for* a sacrifice of peace offerings, which *was* for the people: and Aaron's sons presented unto him the blood, which he sprinkled upon the altar round about, [19]And the fat of the bullock and of the ram, the rump, and that which covereth *the inwards,* and the kidneys, and the caul *above* the liver: [20]And they put the fat upon the breasts, and he burnt the fat upon the altar: [21]And the breasts and the right shoulder Aaron waved *for* a wave offering before the LORD; as Moses commanded. [22]And Aaron lifted up his hand toward the people, and blessed them, and came down from offering of the sin offering, and the burnt offering, and peace offerings.

[23]And Moses and Aaron went into the tabernacle of the congregation, and came out, and blessed the people: and the glory of the LORD appeared unto all the people. [24]And there came a fire out from before the LORD, and consumed upon the altar the burnt offering and the fat: *which* when all the people saw, they shouted, and fell on their faces.

10

[1]And Nadab and Abihu, the sons of Aaron, took either of them his censer,

---

[a] manner: or, ordinance
[b] took . . . : Heb. filled his hand out of it

Devotional Moment

•

Honoring God

10:1-2 As priests, Aaron's sons had the important responsibility of offering sacrifices to the Lord. But over time they grew callous to God's holiness and blatantly disobeyed God's instructions for the sacrifice, inviting swift and severe punishment. God is patient and kind, but he is also holy. He wants us to approach him, but not flippantly. Pray together at mealtime, bedtime, and on other occasions with proper respect for who God is. Show by example that we must respect our holy God.

and put fire therein, and put incense thereon, and offered strange fire before the LORD, which he commanded them not. ²And there went out fire from the LORD, and devoured them, and they died before the LORD.

³Then Moses said unto Aaron, This *is it* that the LORD spake, saying, I will be sanctified in them that come nigh me, and before all the people I will be glorified. And Aaron held his peace. ⁴And Moses called Mishael and Elzaphan, the sons of Uzziel the uncle of Aaron, and said unto them, Come near, carry your brethren from before the sanctuary out of the camp. ⁵So they went near, and carried them in their coats out of the camp; as Moses had said. ⁶And Moses said unto Aaron, and unto Eleazar and unto Ithamar, his sons, Uncover not your heads, neither rend your clothes; lest ye die, and lest wrath come upon all the people: but let your brethren, the whole house of Israel, bewail the burning which the LORD hath kindled. ⁷And ye shall not go out from the door of the tabernacle of the con-

gregation, lest ye die: for the anointing oil of the LORD *is* upon you. And they did according to the word of Moses.

⁸And the LORD spake unto Aaron, saying, ⁹Do not drink wine nor strong drink, thou, nor thy sons with thee, when ye go into the tabernacle of the congregation, lest ye die: *it shall be* a statute for ever throughout your generations: ¹⁰And that ye may put difference between holy and unholy, and between unclean and clean; ¹¹And that ye may teach the children of Israel all the statutes which the LORD hath spoken unto them by the hand of Moses.

¹²And Moses spake unto Aaron, and unto Eleazar and unto Ithamar, his sons that were left, Take the meat offering that remaineth of the offerings of the LORD made by fire, and eat it without leaven beside the altar: for it *is* most holy: ¹³And ye shall eat it in the holy place, because it *is* thy due, and thy sons' due, of the sacrifices of the LORD made by fire: for so I am commanded. ¹⁴And the wave breast and heave shoulder shall ye eat in a clean place; thou, and thy sons, and thy daughters with thee: for *they be* thy due, and thy sons' due, *which* are given out of the sacrifices of peace offerings of the children of Israel. ¹⁵The heave shoulder and the wave breast shall they bring with the offerings made by fire of the fat, to wave *it for* a wave offering before the LORD; and it shall be thine, and thy sons' with thee, by a statute for ever; as the LORD hath commanded. ¹⁶And Moses diligently sought the goat of the sin offering, and, behold, it was burnt: and he was angry with Eleazar

and Ithamar, the sons of Aaron *which were* left *alive*, saying, [17]Wherefore have ye not eaten the sin offering in the holy place, seeing it *is* most holy, and *God* hath given it you to bear the iniquity of the congregation, to make atonement for them before the LORD? [18]Behold, the blood of it was not brought in within the holy *place*: ye should indeed have eaten it in the holy *place*, as I commanded. [19]And Aaron said unto Moses, Behold, this day have they offered their sin offering and their burnt offering before the LORD; and such things have befallen me: and *if* I had eaten the sin offering to day, should it have been accepted in the sight of the LORD? [20]And when Moses heard *that*, he was content.

11

[1]And the LORD spake unto Moses and to Aaron, saying unto them, [2]Speak unto the children of Israel, saying, These *are* the beasts which ye shall eat among all the beasts that *are* on the earth. [3]Whatsoever parteth the hoof, and is clovenfooted, *and* cheweth the cud, among the beasts, that shall ye eat. [4]Nevertheless these shall ye not eat of them that chew the cud, or of them that divide the hoof: *as* the camel, because he cheweth the cud, but divideth not the hoof; he *is* unclean unto you. [5]And the coney, because he cheweth the cud, but divideth not the hoof; he *is* unclean unto you. [6]And the hare, because he cheweth the cud, but divideth not the hoof; he *is* unclean unto you. [7]And the swine, though he divide the hoof, and be clovenfooted, yet he cheweth not the cud; he *is* unclean to you. [8]Of their flesh shall ye not eat,

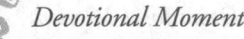

> ### Devotional Moment
> •
> #### Temptation
> 11:8 God had forbidden the people to eat certain meats, either for health reasons or because the animals were associated with pagan religious practices. To minimize temptation, God forbade them even to touch the meat. Temptation often overcomes us when we allow ourselves to push the limits, rationalizing that we are keeping the letter of the law. Watching movies or reading books that fill your mind with lewd or obscene images only flirts with temptation. Is there a temptation in your life that you like to touch even though you haven't eaten it yet? Flee from it; don't set an example of compromise.

and their carcase shall ye not touch; they *are* unclean to you.

[9]These shall ye eat of all that *are* in the waters: whatsoever hath fins and scales in the waters, in the seas, and in the rivers, them shall ye eat. [10]And all that have not fins and scales in the seas, and in the rivers, of all that move in the waters, and of any living thing which *is* in the waters, they *shall be* an abomination unto you: [11]They shall be even an abomination unto you; ye shall not eat of their flesh, but ye shall have their carcases in abomination. [12]Whatsoever hath no fins nor scales in the waters, that *shall be* an abomination unto you. [13]And these *are they which* ye shall have in abomination among the fowls; they shall not be eaten, they *are* an abomination: the eagle, and the ossifrage, and the ospray, [14]And the vulture, and the kite after his kind; [15]Every raven after his kind; [16]And the owl, and the night hawk, and the cuckow, and the hawk after his kind, [17]And the little owl, and the cor-

morant, and the great owl, ¹⁸And the swan, and the pelican, and the gier eagle, ¹⁹And the stork, the heron after her kind, and the lapwing, and the bat. ²⁰All fowls that creep, going upon *all* four, *shall be* an abomination unto you. ²¹Yet these may ye eat of every flying creeping thing that goeth upon *all* four, which have legs above their feet, to leap withal upon the earth; ²²*Even* these of them ye may eat; the locust after his kind, and the bald locust after his kind, and the beetle after his kind, and the grasshopper after his kind. ²³But all *other* flying creeping things, which have four feet, *shall be* an abomination unto you. ²⁴And for these ye shall be unclean: whosoever toucheth the carcase of them shall be unclean until the even. ²⁵And whosoever beareth *ought* of the carcase of them shall wash

Devotional Moment

Worship

11:24-25 Any Israelite who touched something that God had declared unclean became unclean and could not participate in worship until he or she became clean again. God wants us to be prepared when we come to worship him. In order to do so, we need to approach God in a proper frame of mind. Are Sunday mornings a frantic attempt for your family to get in the mood to worship? Your attitude and actions throughout the week all affect that Sunday morning routine. Establish a pattern of daily worship preparation for your family. It may be as simple as having family devotions and prayer times, keeping each other accountable for having personal devotions, or confessing personal failings to each other. Whatever you do, begin today, as a family, to prepare for Sunday every day. Create a family atmosphere that makes going to church enjoyable.

his clothes, and be unclean until the even. ²⁶*The carcases* of every beast which divideth the hoof, and *is* not cloven-footed, nor cheweth the cud, *are* unclean unto you: every one that toucheth them shall be unclean. ²⁷And whatsoever goeth upon his paws, among all manner of beasts that go on *all* four, those *are* unclean unto you: whoso toucheth their carcase shall be unclean until the even. ²⁸And he that beareth the carcase of them shall wash his clothes, and be unclean until the even: they *are* unclean unto you. ²⁹These also *shall be* unclean unto you among the creeping things that creep upon the earth; the weasel, and the mouse, and the tortoise after his kind, ³⁰And the ferret, and the chameleon, and the lizard, and the snail, and the mole. ³¹These *are* unclean to you among all that creep: whosoever doth touch them, when they be dead, shall be unclean until the even. ³²And upon whatsoever *any* of them, when they are dead, doth fall, it shall be unclean; whether *it be* any vessel of wood, or raiment, or skin, or sack, whatsoever vessel *it be*, wherein *any* work is done, it must be put into water, and it shall be unclean until the even; so it shall be cleansed. ³³And every earthen vessel, whereinto *any* of them falleth, whatsoever *is* in it shall be unclean; and ye shall break it. ³⁴Of all meat which may be eaten, *that* on which *such* water cometh shall be unclean: and all drink that may be drunk in every *such* vessel shall be unclean. ³⁵And every *thing* whereupon *any part* of their carcase falleth shall be unclean; *whether it be* oven, or ranges for pots, they shall be broken down: *for they are* unclean, and shall be unclean unto you.

³⁶Nevertheless a fountain or pit, *wherein there is* plenty of water, shall be clean: but that which toucheth their carcase shall be unclean. ³⁷And if *any part* of their carcase fall upon any sowing seed which is to be sown, it *shall be* clean. ³⁸But if *any* water be put upon the seed, and *any part* of their carcase fall thereon, it *shall be* unclean unto you. ³⁹And if any beast, of which ye may eat, die; he that toucheth the carcase thereof shall be unclean until the even. ⁴⁰And he that eateth of the carcase of it shall wash his clothes, and be unclean until the even: he also that beareth the carcase of it shall wash his clothes, and be unclean until the even. ⁴¹And every creeping thing that creepeth upon the earth *shall be* an abomination; it shall not be eaten. ⁴²Whatsoever goeth upon the belly, and whatsoever goeth upon *all* four, or whatsoever hath more feet among all creeping things that creep upon the earth, them ye shall not eat; for they *are* an abomination.

⁴³Ye shall not make yourselves abominable with any creeping thing that creepeth, neither shall ye make yourselves unclean with them, that ye should be defiled thereby. ⁴⁴For I *am* the LORD your God: ye shall therefore sanctify yourselves, and ye shall be holy; for I *am* holy: neither shall ye defile yourselves with any manner of creeping thing that creepeth upon the earth. ⁴⁵For I *am* the LORD that bringeth you up out of the land of Egypt, to be your God: ye shall therefore be holy, for I *am* holy. ⁴⁶This *is* the law of the beasts, and of the fowl, and of every living creature that moveth in the waters, and of every creature that creepeth upon the earth: ⁴⁷To make a difference between the unclean and the clean, and between the beast that may be eaten and the beast that may not be eaten.

12

¹And the LORD spake unto Moses, saying, ²Speak unto the children of Israel, saying, If a woman have conceived seed, and born a man child: then she shall be unclean seven days; according to the days of the separation for her infirmity shall she be unclean. ³And in the eighth day the flesh of his foreskin shall be circumcised. ⁴And she shall then continue in the blood of her purifying three and thirty days; she shall touch no hallowed thing, nor come into the sanctuary, until the days of her purifying be fulfilled. ⁵But if she bear a maid child, then she shall be unclean two weeks, as in her separation: and she shall continue in the blood of her purifying threescore and six days.

⁶And when the days of her purifying are fulfilled, for a son, or for a daughter, she shall bring a lamb of the firstᵃ year for a burnt offering, and a young pigeon, or a turtledove, for a sin offering, unto the door of the tabernacle of the congregation, unto the priest: ⁷Who shall offer it before the LORD, and make an atonement for her; and she shall be cleansed from the issue of her blood. This *is* the law for her that hath born a male or a female. ⁸And if she be not able to bring a lamb, then she shall bring two turtles, or two young pigeons; the one for the burnt offering, and the other for a sin offer-

---

ᵃ of the first . . . : Heb. a son of his year

ing: and the priest shall make an atonement for her, and she shall be clean.

13

¹And the LORD spake unto Moses and Aaron, saying, ²When a man shall have in the skin of his flesh a rising ᵃ, a scab, or bright spot, and it be in the skin of his flesh *like* the plague of leprosy; then he shall be brought unto Aaron the priest, or unto one of his sons the priests: ³And the priest shall look on the plague in the skin of the flesh: and *when* the hair in the plague is turned white, and the plague in sight *be* deeper than the skin of his flesh, it *is* a plague of leprosy: and the priest shall look on him, and pronounce him unclean. ⁴If the bright spot *be* white in the skin of his flesh, and in sight *be* not deeper than the skin, and the hair thereof be not turned white; then the priest shall shut up *him that hath* the plague seven days: ⁵And the priest shall look on him the seventh day: and, behold, *if* the plague in his sight be at a stay, *and* the plague spread not in the skin; then the priest shall shut him up seven days more: ⁶And the priest shall look on him again the seventh day: and, behold, *if* the plague be somewhat dark, *and* the plague spread not in the skin, the priest shall pronounce him clean: it *is but* a scab: and he shall wash his clothes, and be clean. ⁷But if the scab spread much abroad in the skin, after that he hath been seen of the priest for his cleansing, he shall be seen of the priest again: ⁸And *if* the priest see that, behold, the scab spreadeth in the skin, then the priest

shall pronounce him unclean: it *is* a leprosy. ⁹When the plague of leprosy is in a man, then he shall be brought unto the priest; ¹⁰And the priest shall see *him*: and, behold, *if* the rising *be* white in the skin, and it have turned the hair white, and *there be* quick ᵇ raw flesh in the rising; ¹¹It *is* an old leprosy in the skin of his flesh, and the priest shall pronounce him unclean, and shall not shut him up: for he *is* unclean. ¹²And if a leprosy break out abroad in the skin, and the leprosy cover all the skin of *him that hath* the plague from his head even to his foot, wheresoever the priest looketh; ¹³Then the priest shall consider: and, behold, *if* the leprosy have covered all his flesh, he shall pronounce *him* clean *that hath* the plague: it is all turned white: he *is* clean. ¹⁴But when raw flesh appeareth in him, he shall be unclean. ¹⁵And the priest shall see the raw flesh, and pronounce him to be unclean: *for* the raw flesh *is* unclean: it *is* a leprosy. ¹⁶Or if the raw flesh turn again, and be changed unto white, he shall come unto the priest; ¹⁷And the priest shall see him: and, behold, *if* the plague be turned into white; then the priest shall pronounce *him* clean that *hath* the plague: he *is* clean.

¹⁸The flesh also, in which, *even* in the skin thereof, was a boil, and is healed, ¹⁹And in the place of the boil there be a white rising, or a bright spot, white, and somewhat reddish, and it be shewed to the priest; ²⁰And if, when the priest seeth it, behold, it *be* in sight lower than the skin, and the hair thereof be turned white; the priest shall pronounce

---

ᵃ rising: or, swelling
ᵇ quick . . . : Heb. the quickening of living flesh

him unclean: it *is* a plague of leprosy broken out of the boil. ²¹But if the priest look on it, and, behold, *there be* no white hairs therein, and *if* it *be* not lower than the skin, but *be* somewhat dark; then the priest shall shut him up seven days: ²²And if it spread much abroad in the skin, then the priest shall pronounce him unclean: it *is* a plague. ²³But if the bright spot stay in his place, *and* spread not, it *is* a burning boil; and the priest shall pronounce him clean. ²⁴Or if there be *any* flesh, in the skin whereof *there is* a hot‹ burning, and the quick *flesh* that burneth have a white bright spot, somewhat reddish, or white; ²⁵Then the priest shall look upon it: and, behold, *if* the hair in the bright spot be turned white, and it *be in* sight deeper than the skin; it *is* a leprosy broken out of the burning: wherefore the priest shall pronounce him unclean: it *is* the plague of leprosy. ²⁶But if the priest look on it, and, behold, *there be* no white hair in the bright spot, and it *be* no lower than the *other* skin, but *be* somewhat dark; then the priest shall shut him up seven days: ²⁷And the priest shall look upon him the seventh day: *and* if it be spread much abroad in the skin, then the priest shall pronounce him unclean: it *is* the plague of leprosy. ²⁸And if the bright spot stay in his place, *and* spread not in the skin, but it *be* somewhat dark; it *is* a rising of the burning, and the priest shall pronounce him clean: for it *is* an inflammation of the burning. ²⁹If a man or woman have a plague upon the head or the beard; ³⁰Then the priest shall see the plague: and, behold, if it *be* in sight deeper than the skin; *and there be* in it a yellow thin hair; then the priest shall pronounce him unclean: it *is* a dry scall, *even* a leprosy upon the head or beard. ³¹And if the priest look on the plague of the scall, and, behold, it *be* not in sight deeper than the skin, and *that there is* no black hair in it; then the priest shall shut up *him that hath* the plague of the scall seven days: ³²And in the seventh day the priest shall look on the plague: and, behold, *if* the scall spread not, and there be in it no yellow hair, and the scall *be* not in sight deeper than the skin; ³³He shall be shaven, but the scall shall he not shave; and the priest shall shut up *him that hath* the scall seven days more: ³⁴And in the seventh day the priest shall look on the scall: and, behold, *if* the scall be not spread in the skin, nor *be* in sight deeper than the skin; then the priest shall pronounce him clean: and he shall wash his clothes, and be clean. ³⁵But if the scall spread much in the skin after his cleansing; ³⁶Then the priest shall look on him: and, behold, if the scall be spread in the skin, the priest shall not seek for yellow hair; he *is* unclean. ³⁷But if the scall be in his sight at a stay, and *that* there is black hair grown up therein; the scall is healed, he *is* clean: and the priest shall pronounce him clean.

³⁸If a man also or a woman have in the skin of their flesh bright spots, *even* white bright spots; ³⁹Then the priest shall look: and, behold, *if* the bright spots in the skin of their flesh *be* darkish white; it *is* a freckled spot *that* groweth in the skin; he *is* clean. ⁴⁰And the man whose hair is fallen off his head, he *is* bald; yet *is* he clean. ⁴¹And he that hath his hair fallen off from the

---

‹ a hot . . . : Heb. a burning of fire

part of his head toward his face, he *is* forehead bald: *yet is* he clean. ⁴²And if there be in the bald head, or bald forehead, a white reddish sore; it *is* a leprosy sprung up in his bald head, or his bald forehead. ⁴³Then the priest shall look upon it: and, behold, *if* the rising of the sore *be* white reddish in his bald head, or in his bald forehead, as the leprosy appeareth in the skin of the flesh; ⁴⁴He is a leprous man, he *is* unclean: the priest shall pronounce him utterly unclean; his plague *is* in his head. ⁴⁵And the leper in whom the plague *is*, his clothes shall be rent, and his head bare, and he shall put a covering upon his upper lip, and shall cry, Unclean, unclean. ⁴⁶All the days wherein the plague *shall be* in him he shall be defiled; he *is* unclean: he shall dwell alone; without the camp *shall* his habitation *be*.

⁴⁷The garment also that the plague of leprosy is in, *whether it be* a woollen garment, or a linen garment; ⁴⁸Whether *it be* in the warp, or woof; of linen, or of woollen; whether in a skin, or in any thing made of skin; ⁴⁹And if the plague be greenish or reddish in the garment, or in the skin, either in the warp, or in the woof, or in any thing⁴ of skin; it *is* a plague of leprosy, and shall be shewed unto the priest: ⁵⁰And the priest shall look upon the plague, and shut up *it that hath* the plague seven days: ⁵¹And he shall look on the plague on the seventh day: if the plague be spread in the garment, either in the warp, or in the woof, or in a skin, *or* in any work that is made of skin; the plague *is* a fretting leprosy; it *is* unclean. ⁵²He shall therefore burn that garment, whether warp or woof, in woollen or in linen, or any thing of skin, wherein the plague is: for it *is* a fretting leprosy; it shall be burnt in the fire. ⁵³And if the priest shall look, and, behold, the plague be not spread in the garment, either in the warp, or in the woof, or in any thing of skin; ⁵⁴Then the priest shall command that they wash *the thing* wherein the plague *is*, and he shall shut it up seven days more: ⁵⁵And the priest shall look on the plague, after that it is washed: and, behold, *if* the plague have not changed his colour, and the plague be not spread; it *is* unclean; thou shalt burn it in the fire; it *is* fret inward, *whether* it *be* bare within or without. ⁵⁶And if the priest look, and, behold, the plague *be* somewhat dark after the washing of it; then he shall rend it out of the garment, or out of the skin, or out of the warp, or out of the woof: ⁵⁷And if it appear still in the garment, either in the warp, or in the woof, or in any thing of skin; it *is* a spreading *plague*: thou shalt burn that wherein the plague *is* with fire. ⁵⁸And the garment, either warp, or woof, or whatsoever thing of skin *it be*, which thou shalt wash, if the plague be departed from them, then it shall be washed the second time, and shall be clean. ⁵⁹This *is* the law of the plague of leprosy in a garment of woollen or linen, either in the warp, or woof, or any thing of skins, to pronounce it clean, or to pronounce it unclean.

14

¹And the LORD spake unto Moses, saying, ²This shall be the law of the leper in the day of his cleansing: He

---

⁴ thing: Heb. vessel, or, instrument

shall be brought unto the priest: ³And the priest shall go forth out of the camp; and the priest shall look, and, behold, *if* the plague of leprosy be healed in the leper; ⁴Then shall the priest command to take for him that is to be cleansed two birds[a] alive *and* clean, and cedar wood, and scarlet, and hyssop: ⁵And the priest shall command that one of the birds be killed in an earthen vessel over running water: ⁶As for the living bird, he shall take it, and the cedar wood, and the scarlet, and the hyssop, and shall dip them and the living bird in the blood of the bird *that was* killed over the running water: ⁷And he shall sprinkle upon him that is to be cleansed from the leprosy seven times, and shall pronounce him clean, and shall let the living bird loose into the open field. ⁸And he that is to be cleansed shall wash his clothes, and shave off all his hair, and wash himself in water, that he may be clean: and after that he shall come into the camp, and shall tarry abroad out of his tent seven days. ⁹But it shall be on the seventh day, that he shall shave all his hair off his head and his beard and his eyebrows, even all his hair he shall shave off: and he shall wash his clothes, also he shall wash his flesh in water, and he shall be clean.

¹⁰And on the eighth day he shall take two he lambs without blemish, and one ewe lamb of the first year without blemish, and three tenth deals of fine flour *for* a meat offering, mingled with oil, and one log of oil. ¹¹And the priest that maketh *him* clean shall present the man that is to be made clean, and those things, before the LORD, *at* the door of the tabernacle of the congregation: ¹²And the priest shall take one he lamb, and offer him for a trespass offering, and the log of oil, and wave them *for* a wave offering before the LORD: ¹³And he shall slay the lamb in the place where he shall kill the sin offering and the burnt offering, in the holy place: for as the sin offering *is* the priest's, *so is* the trespass offering: it *is* most holy: ¹⁴And the priest shall take *some* of the blood of the trespass offering, and the priest shall put *it* upon the tip of the right ear of him that is to be cleansed, and upon the thumb of his right hand, and upon the great toe of his right foot: ¹⁵And the priest shall take *some* of the log of oil, and pour *it* into the palm of his own left hand: ¹⁶And the priest shall dip his right finger in the oil that *is* in his left hand, and shall sprinkle of the oil with his finger seven times before the LORD: ¹⁷And of the rest of the oil that *is* in his hand shall the priest put upon the tip of the right ear of him that is to be cleansed, and upon the thumb of his right hand, and upon the great toe of his right foot, upon the blood of the trespass offering: ¹⁸And the remnant of the oil that *is* in the priest's hand he shall pour upon the head of him that is to be cleansed: and the priest shall make an atonement for him before the LORD. ¹⁹And the priest shall offer the sin offering, and make an atonement for him that is to be cleansed from his uncleanness; and afterward he shall kill the burnt offering: ²⁰And the priest shall offer the burnt offering and the meat offering upon the altar: and the priest shall make an

---

[a] birds: or, sparrows

atonement for him, and he shall be clean.

²¹And if he *be* poor, and cannot get so much; then he shall take one lamb *for* a trespass offering to be waved, to make an atonement for him, and one tenth deal of fine flour mingled with oil for a meat offering, and a log of oil; ²²And two turtledoves, or two young pigeons, such as he is able to get; and the one shall be a sin offering, and the other a burnt offering. ²³And he shall bring them on the eighth day for his cleansing unto the priest, unto the door of the tabernacle of the congregation, before the LORD. ²⁴And the priest shall take the lamb of the trespass offering, and the log of oil, and the priest shall wave them *for* a wave offering before the LORD: ²⁵And he shall kill the lamb of the trespass offering, and the priest shall take *some* of the blood of the trespass offering, and put *it* upon the tip of the right ear of him that is to be cleansed, and upon the thumb of his right hand, and upon the great toe of his right foot: ²⁶And the priest shall pour of the oil into the palm of his own left hand: ²⁷And the priest shall sprinkle with his right finger *some* of the oil that *is* in his left hand seven times before the LORD: ²⁸And the priest shall put of the oil that *is* in his hand upon the tip of the right ear of him that is to be cleansed, and upon the thumb of his right hand, and upon the great toe of his right foot, upon the place of the blood of the trespass offering: ²⁹And the rest of the oil that *is* in the priest's hand he shall put upon the head of him that is to be cleansed, to make an atonement

for him before the LORD. ³⁰And he shall offer the one of the turtledoves, or of the young pigeons, such as he can get; ³¹*Even* such as he is able to get, the one *for* a sin offering, and the other *for* a burnt offering, with the meat offering: and the priest shall make an atonement for him that is to be cleansed before the LORD. ³²This *is* the law *of him* in whom *is* the plague of leprosy, whose hand is not able to get *that which pertaineth* to his cleansing.

³³And the LORD spake unto Moses and unto Aaron, saying, ³⁴When ye be come into the land of Canaan, which I give to you for a possession, and I put the plague of leprosy in a house of the land of your possession; ³⁵And he that owneth the house shall come and tell the priest, saying, It seemeth to me *there is* as it were a plague in the house: ³⁶Then the priest shall command that they empty[b] the house, before the priest go *into it* to see the plague, that all that *is* in the house be not made unclean: and afterward the priest shall go in to see the house: ³⁷And he shall look on the plague, and, behold, *if* the plague *be* in the walls of the house with hollow strakes, greenish or reddish, which in sight *are* lower than the wall; ³⁸Then the priest shall go out of the house to the door of the house, and shut up the house seven days: ³⁹And the priest shall come again the seventh day, and shall look: and, behold, *if* the plague be spread in the walls of the house; ⁴⁰Then the priest shall command that they take away the stones in which the plague *is*, and they shall cast them into an unclean place

[b] empty: or, prepare

without the city: ⁴¹And he shall cause the house to be scraped within round about, and they shall pour out the dust that they scrape off without the city into an unclean place: ⁴²And they shall take other stones, and put *them* in the place of those stones; and he shall take other morter, and shall plaister the house. ⁴³And if the plague come again, and break out in the house, after that he hath taken away the stones, and after he hath scraped the house, and after it is plaistered; ⁴⁴Then the priest shall come and look, and, behold, *if* the plague be spread in the house, it *is* a fretting leprosy in the house: it *is* unclean. ⁴⁵And he shall break down the house, the stones of it, and the timber thereof, and all the morter of the house; and he shall carry *them* forth out of the city into an unclean place. ⁴⁶Moreover he that goeth into the house all the while that it is shut up shall be unclean until the even. ⁴⁷And he that lieth in the house shall wash his clothes; and he that eateth in the house shall wash his clothes. ⁴⁸And if the priest shall come in, and look *upon it,* and, behold, the plague hath not spread in the house, after the house was plaistered: then the priest shall pronounce the house clean, because the plague is healed. ⁴⁹And he shall take to cleanse the house two birds, and cedar wood, and scarlet, and hyssop: ⁵⁰And he shall kill the one of the birds in an earthen vessel over running water: ⁵¹And he shall take the cedar wood, and the hyssop, and the scarlet, and the living bird, and dip them in the blood of the slain bird, and in the running water, and sprinkle the house seven times:

⁵²And he shall cleanse the house with the blood of the bird, and with the running water, and with the living bird, and with the cedar wood, and with the hyssop, and with the scarlet: ⁵³But he shall let go the living bird out of the city into the open fields, and make an atonement for the house: and it shall be clean.

⁵⁴This *is* the law for all manner of plague of leprosy, and scall, ⁵⁵And for the leprosy of a garment, and of a house, ⁵⁶And for a rising, and for a scab, and for a bright spot: ⁵⁷To teach when *it is* unclean, and when *it is* clean: this *is* the law of leprosy.

15

¹And the LORD spake unto Moses and to Aaron, saying, ²Speak unto the children of Israel, and say unto them, When any man hath a running issue out of his flesh, *because of* his issue he *is* unclean. ³And this shall be his uncleanness in his issue: whether his flesh run with his issue, or his flesh be stopped from his issue, it *is* his uncleanness. ⁴Every bed, whereon he lieth that hath the issue, is unclean: and every thing[a], whereon he sitteth, shall be unclean. ⁵And whosoever toucheth his bed shall wash his clothes, and bathe *himself* in water, and be unclean until the even. ⁶And he that sitteth on *any* thing whereon he sat that hath the issue shall wash his clothes, and bathe *himself* in water, and be unclean until the even. ⁷And he that toucheth the flesh of him that hath the issue shall wash his clothes, and bathe *himself* in water, and be unclean until the even. ⁸And if he

---

[a] thing: Heb. vessel

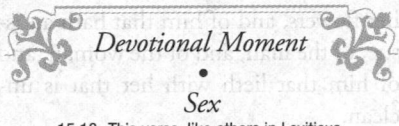

that hath the issue spit upon him that is clean; then he shall wash his clothes, and bathe *himself* in water, and be unclean until the even. ⁹And what saddle soever he rideth upon that hath the issue shall be unclean. ¹⁰And whosoever toucheth any thing that was under him shall be unclean until the even: and he that beareth *any of* those things shall wash his clothes, and bathe *himself* in water, and be unclean until the even. ¹¹And whomsoever he toucheth that hath the issue, and hath not rinsed his hands in water, he shall wash his clothes, and bathe *himself* in water, and be unclean until the even. ¹²And the vessel of earth, that he toucheth which hath the issue, shall be broken: and every vessel of wood shall be rinsed in water. ¹³And when he that hath an issue is cleansed of his issue; then he shall number to himself seven days for his cleansing, and wash his clothes, and bathe his flesh in running water, and shall be clean. ¹⁴And on the eighth day he shall take to him two turtledoves, or two young pigeons, and come before the LORD unto the door of the tabernacle of the congregation, and give them unto the priest: ¹⁵And the priest shall offer them, the one *for* a sin offering, and the other *for* a burnt offering; and the priest shall make an atonement for him before the LORD for his issue.

¹⁶And if any man's seed of copulation go out from him, then he shall wash all his flesh in water, and be unclean until the even. ¹⁷And every garment, and every skin, whereon is the seed of copulation, shall be washed with water, and be unclean until the even. ¹⁸The woman also with whom man shall lie *with* seed of copulation, they shall *both* bathe *themselves* in water, and be unclean until the even.

¹⁹And if a woman have an issue, *and* her issue in her flesh be blood, she shall be put apart seven days: and whosoever toucheth her shall be unclean until the even. ²⁰And every thing that she lieth upon in her separation shall be unclean: every thing also that she sitteth upon shall be unclean. ²¹And whosoever toucheth her bed shall wash his clothes, and bathe *himself* in water, and be unclean until the even. ²²And whosoever toucheth any thing that she sat upon shall wash his clothes, and bathe *himself* in water, and be unclean until the even. ²³And if it *be* on *her* bed, or on any thing whereon she sitteth, when he toucheth it, he shall be unclean until the even. ²⁴And if any man lie with her at all, and her flowers be upon him, he shall be unclean seven days; and all the bed whereon he lieth shall be unclean. ²⁵And if a woman have an issue of her blood many days out of the time of her separation, or if it run beyond the time of her separation; all the days of the issue of her uncleanness shall be as the days of her separation: she *shall be* unclean. ²⁶Every bed whereon she lieth all the days of her issue shall be unto her as the bed of her separation: and whatsoever she sitteth upon shall be unclean, as the unclean-

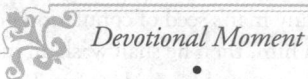

Devotional Moment

•

Sexual Purity

15:32-33 God is concerned about health, the dignity of the person, the dignity of the body, and the dignity of the sexual experience. His commands call people to avoid unhealthy practices and promote healthy ones. To wash was the physical health response, to be purified or cleansed was the spiritual dignity response. This shows God's high regard for sex and sexuality. In our day, sex has been degraded by publicity; it has become public domain, not private celebration. God calls us to have a high regard for sex, both in good health and purity.

ness of her separation. ²⁷And whosoever toucheth those things shall be unclean, and shall wash his clothes, and bathe *himself* in water, and be unclean until the even. ²⁸But if she be cleansed of her issue, then she shall number to herself seven days, and after that she shall be clean. ²⁹And on the eighth day she shall take unto her two turtles, or two young pigeons, and bring them unto the priest, to the door of the tabernacle of the congregation. ³⁰And the priest shall offer the one *for* a sin offering, and the other *for* a burnt offering; and the priest shall make an atonement for her before the LORD for the issue of her uncleanness. ³¹Thus shall ye separate the children of Israel from their uncleanness; that they die not in their uncleanness, when they defile my tabernacle that *is* among them. ³²This *is* the law of him that hath an issue, and *of him* whose seed goeth from him, and is defiled therewith; ³³And of her that is sick of

her flowers, and of him that hath an issue, of the man, and of the woman, and of him that lieth with her that is unclean.

16

¹And the LORD spake unto Moses after the death of the two sons of Aaron, when they offered before the LORD, and died; ²And the LORD said unto Moses, Speak unto Aaron thy brother, that he come not at all times into the holy *place* within the vail before the mercy seat, which *is* upon the ark; that he die not: for I will appear in the cloud upon the mercy seat. ³Thus shall Aaron come into the holy *place*: with a young bullock for a sin offering, and a ram for a burnt offering. ⁴He shall put on the holy linen coat, and he shall have the linen breeches upon his flesh, and shall be girded with a linen girdle, and with the linen mitre shall he be attired: these *are* holy garments; therefore shall he wash his flesh in water, and *so* put them on.

⁵And he shall take of the congregation of the children of Israel two kids of the goats for a sin offering, and one ram for a burnt offering. ⁶And Aaron shall offer his bullock of the sin offering, which *is* for himself, and make an atonement for himself, and for his house. ⁷And he shall take the two goats, and present them before the LORD *at* the door of the tabernacle of the congregation. ⁸And Aaron shall cast lots upon the two goats; one lot for the LORD, and the other lot for the scapegoatª. ⁹And Aaron shall bring the goat upon which the LORD'S lot fellᵇ, and

---

ª scapegoat: Heb. Azazel
ᵇ fell: Heb. went up

offer him *for* a sin offering. ¹⁰But the goat, on which the lot fell to be the scapegoat, shall be presented alive before the LORD, to make an atonement with him, *and* to let him go for a scapegoat into the wilderness. ¹¹And Aaron shall bring the bullock of the sin offering, which *is* for himself, and shall make an atonement for himself, and for his house, and shall kill the bullock of the sin offering which *is* for himself: ¹²And he shall take a censer full of burning coals of fire from off the altar before the LORD, and his hands full of sweet incense beaten small, and bring *it* within the vail: ¹³And he shall put the incense upon the fire before the LORD, that the cloud of the incense may cover the mercy seat that *is* upon the testimony, that he die not: ¹⁴And he shall take of the blood of the bullock, and sprinkle *it* with his finger upon the mercy seat eastward; and before the mercy seat shall he sprinkle of the blood with his finger seven times.

¹⁵Then shall he kill the goat of the sin offering, that *is* for the people, and bring his blood within the vail, and do with that blood as he did with the blood of the bullock, and sprinkle it upon the mercy seat, and before the mercy seat: ¹⁶And he shall make an atonement for the holy *place*, because of the uncleanness of the children of Israel, and because of their transgressions in all their sins: and so shall he do for the tabernacle of the congregation, that remaineth[c] among them in the midst of their uncleanness. ¹⁷And there shall be no man in the tabernacle of the con-gregation when he goeth in to make an atonement in the holy *place*, until he come out, and have made an atonement for himself, and for his household, and for all the congregation of Israel. ¹⁸And he shall go out unto the altar that *is* before the LORD, and make an atonement for it; and shall take of the blood of the bullock, and of the blood of the goat, and put *it* upon the horns of the altar round about. ¹⁹And he shall sprinkle of the blood upon it with his finger seven times, and cleanse it, and hallow it from the uncleanness of the children of Israel.

²⁰And when he hath made an end of reconciling the holy *place*, and the tabernacle of the congregation, and the altar, he shall bring the live goat: ²¹And Aaron shall lay both his hands upon the head of the live goat, and confess over him all the iniquities of the children of Israel, and all their transgressions in all their sins, putting them upon the head of the goat, and shall send *him* away by the hand of a fit[d] man into the wilderness: ²²And the goat shall bear upon him all their iniquities unto a land not inhabited: and he shall let go the goat in the wilderness. ²³And Aaron shall come into the tabernacle of the congregation, and shall put off the linen garments, which he put on when he went into the holy *place*, and shall leave them there: ²⁴And he shall wash his flesh with water in the holy place, and put on his garments, and come forth, and offer his burnt offering, and the burnt of-

[c] remaineth: Heb. dwelleth
[d] a fit . . . : Heb. a man of opportunity

193

Breaking Free from the "Scapegoat" Role in the Family

Cast lots upon the two goats; one lot for the Lord, and the other lot for the scapegoat. And Aaron shall bring the goat upon which the Lord's lot fell, and offer him for a sin offering. But the scapegoat shall be presented alive before the Lord, to make an atonement with him, and to let him go for a scapegoat into the wilderness. Leviticus 16:8-10

For the Old Testament Jews, a special ceremony took place every year on the Day of Atonement. The ceremony worked like this: Two goats were chosen by lots, one to be sacrificed, the other to become a scapegoat. Aaron, the High Priest, would gather all the people together and lay his hands on the scapegoat's head. In doing so, he was giving them a symbolic picture that all the sins of the nation had been transferred to the animal. The goat was then driven outside the camp and forced into the wilderness to die.

This poor animal's sacrifice foreshadowed an even greater sacrifice. When Jesus was led outside the city to be crucified, God the Father placed our sins upon him and he became our "scapegoat" and our lamb of sacrifice (Rom. 3:25; Heb. 10:10).

For Israel of old, having one animal symbolically "carry" the sins of the whole nation was a powerful event. Unfortunately, some families today carry on a similar practice in an unhealthy way.

Just like the scapegoats of old, some children grow up bearing the brunt of all their family's problems. Often they "carry" the blame for all family problems, and are often discarded and even driven away from those they love.

Take Gretta for example. As a baby, she had a terrible respiratory problem that made it hard for her to sleep for longer than a few hours at a time. She would cry for hours, and her mother was soon overwhelmed by all the care she required night and day.

Her father began to avoid coming home at night. And on one such night he was killed in an automobile accident.

Gretta's mother took the news terribly hard. As a way of dealing with the pain, she began blaming Gretta for all her problems.

Children who become the scapegoat of a family long for the love and acceptance they have never received. Often they can act out their low self-worth in outbursts of anger or rebellion. They know deep inside the injustice of being singled out and pushed away from the family, and their frustrations can find their way into behavioral problems.

While there was a redeeming nature to the Old Testament scapegoat, there isn't for a family scapegoat. They bear problems beyond their age or ability to understand until much damage has been done. And their attempts at reaching out to their family for nurturing only lead to greater and greater rejection.

How can you begin to "break free" if you've grown up in a family that designated you "scapegoat"?

Gretta finally discovered that there was one safe place where she could always take her needs for unconditional love and acceptance: her relationship with Jesus Christ. In his love she found unconditional acceptance (Rom. 8:38-39; John 10:1-18; Heb. 13:5). In his power she found the strength to be joyful in spite of her circumstances (Phil. 4:11-14; 1 Pet. 1:6-9). Through a relationship with him, she found a spiritual family at church that loved her unconditionally, and from him she received the peace she had never found before (John 16:33).

Now, whenever Gretta finds herself feeling angry with her parents or brothers and sisters, she remembers that an unhealthy, unfair system doesn't have to define her worth. She's even developed a compassion for her mother that has allowed her to pray for her with genuine concern.

God has already provided the ultimate sacrifice for our sins. He doesn't ask us to make more. And neither does he honor the "sacrifice" of one person in a home who has been singled out to carry all family problems or shame. For all of us who know God, we have the freedom to be in the role God has reserved for us: *beloved child.*

fering of the people, and make an atonement for himself, and for the people. ²⁵And the fat of the sin offering shall he burn upon the altar. ²⁶And he that let go the goat for the scapegoat shall wash his clothes, and bathe his flesh in water, and afterward come into the camp. ²⁷And the bullock *for* the sin offering, and the goat *for* the sin offering, whose blood was brought in to make atonement in the holy place, shall *one* carry forth without the camp; and they shall burn in the fire their skins, and their flesh, and their dung. ²⁸And he that burneth them shall wash his clothes, and bathe his flesh in water, and afterward he shall come into the camp.

²⁹And *this* shall be a statute for ever unto you: *that* in the seventh month, on the tenth *day* of the month, ye shall afflict your souls, and do no work at all, *whether it be* one of your own country, or a stranger that sojourneth among you: ³⁰For on that day shall *the priest* make an atonement for you, to cleanse you, *that* ye may be clean from all your sins before the LORD. ³¹It *shall be* a sabbath of rest unto you, and ye shall afflict your souls, by a statute for ever. ³²And the priest, whom he shall anoint, and whom he shall consecrateᵉ to minister in

ᵉ consecrate: Heb. fill his hand

the priest's office in his father's stead, shall make the atonement, and shall put on the linen clothes, *even* the holy garments: ³³And he shall make an atonement for the holy sanctuary, and he shall make an atonement for the tabernacle of the congregation, and for the altar, and he shall make an atonement for the priests, and for all the people of the congregation. ³⁴And this shall be an everlasting statute unto you, to make an atonement for the children of Israel for all their sins once a year. And he did as the LORD commanded Moses.

17

¹And the LORD spake unto Moses, saying, ²Speak unto Aaron, and unto his sons, and unto all the children of Israel, and say unto them; This *is* the thing which the LORD hath commanded, saying, ³What man soever *there be* of the house of Israel, that killeth an ox, or lamb, or goat, in the camp, or that kill-

---

Devotional Moment
•
Rules

17:5 God set careful rules for sacrificing to keep the Israelites' attention on him. The rules kept the sacrifice rituals from becoming haphazard and meaningless and protected the people from falling into the heathen worship practices around them. As believers, we need to understand that God's rules establish boundaries to protect us from harm much like a parent's rules about curfews and dating protect children from making careless mistakes. As a fence frees a horse to run safely within the bounds of its pasture, God's rules—rather than limit us—free us to live within their boundaries. Thank God for his boundaries, and remind one another of the benefits they bring.

---

eth *it* out of the camp, ⁴And bringeth it not unto the door of the tabernacle of the congregation, to offer an offering unto the LORD before the tabernacle of the LORD; blood shall be imputed unto that man; he hath shed blood; and that man shall be cut off from among his people: ⁵To the end that the children of Israel may bring their sacrifices, which they offer in the open field, even that they may bring them unto the LORD, unto the door of the tabernacle of the congregation, unto the priest, and offer them *for* peace offerings unto the LORD. ⁶And the priest shall sprinkle the blood upon the altar of the LORD *at* the door of the tabernacle of the congregation, and burn the fat for a sweet savour unto the LORD. ⁷And they shall no more offer their sacrifices unto devils, after whom they have gone a whoring. This shall be a statute for ever unto them throughout their generations. ⁸And thou shalt say unto them, Whatsoever man *there be* of the house of Israel, or of the strangers which sojourn among you, that offereth a burnt offering or sacrifice, ⁹And bringeth it not unto the door of the tabernacle of the congregation, to offer it unto the LORD; even that man shall be cut off from among his people.

¹⁰And whatsoever man *there be* of the house of Israel, or of the strangers that sojourn among you, that eateth any manner of blood; I will even set my face against that soul that eateth blood, and will cut him off from among his people. ¹¹For the life of the flesh *is* in the blood: and I have given it to you upon the altar to make an atonement for your souls: for it *is* the blood *that* maketh an atonement for the soul. ¹²Therefore I said unto the children of Israel, No soul of you shall eat

blood, neither shall any stranger that sojourneth among you eat blood. ¹³And whatsoever man *there be* of the children of Israel, or of the strangers that sojourn among you, which hunteth and catcheth any beast or fowl that may be eaten; he shall even pour out the blood thereof, and cover it with dust. ¹⁴For *it is* the life of all flesh; the blood of it *is* for the life thereof: therefore I said unto the children of Israel, Ye shall eat the blood of no manner of flesh: for the life of all flesh *is* the blood thereof: whosoever eateth it shall be cut off. ¹⁵And every soul that eateth that which died ͣ *of itself,* or that which was torn *with beasts, whether it be* one of your own country, or a stranger, he shall both wash his clothes, and bathe *himself* in water, and be unclean until the even: then shall he be clean. ¹⁶But if he wash *them* not, nor bathe his flesh; then he shall bear his iniquity.

18

¹And the LORD spake unto Moses, saying, ²Speak unto the children of Israel, and say unto them, I am the LORD your God. ³After the doings of the land of Egypt, wherein ye dwelt, shall ye not do: and after the doings of the land of Canaan, whither I bring you, shall ye not do: neither shall ye walk in their ordinances. ⁴Ye shall do my judgments, and keep mine ordinances, to walk therein: I *am* the LORD your God. ⁵Ye shall therefore keep my statutes, and my judgments: which if a man do, he shall live in them: I *am* the LORD.

⁶None of you shall approach to any that is near ͣ of kin to him, to uncover *their* nakedness: I *am* the LORD. ⁷The nakedness of thy father, or the nakedness of thy mother, shalt thou not uncover: she *is* thy mother; thou shalt not uncover her nakedness. ⁸The nakedness of thy father's wife shalt thou not uncover: it *is* thy father's nakedness. ⁹The nakedness of thy sister, the daughter of thy father, or daughter of thy mother, *whether she be* born at home, or born abroad, *even* their nakedness thou shalt not uncover. ¹⁰The nakedness of thy son's daughter, or of thy daughter's daughter, *even* their nakedness thou shalt not uncover: for theirs *is* thine own nakedness. ¹¹The nakedness of thy father's wife's daughter, begotten of thy father, she *is* thy sister, thou shalt not uncover her nakedness. ¹²Thou shalt not uncover the nakedness of thy father's sister: she *is* thy father's near kinswoman. ¹³Thou shalt not uncover the nakedness of thy mother's sister: for she *is* thy mother's near kinswoman. ¹⁴Thou shalt not uncover the nakedness of thy father's brother, thou shalt not approach to his wife: she *is* thine aunt. ¹⁵Thou shalt not uncover the nakedness of thy daughter in law: she *is* thy son's wife; thou shalt not uncover her nakedness. ¹⁶Thou shalt not uncover the nakedness of thy brother's wife: it *is* thy brother's nakedness. ¹⁷Thou shalt not uncover the nakedness of a woman and her daughter, neither shalt thou take her son's daughter, or her daughter's daughter, to uncover her nakedness; *for* they *are* her near kinswomen: it *is* wickedness. ¹⁸Neither shalt thou take a wife ͤ to her sister, to vex *her,*

ͣ that which died . . . : Heb. a carcase
ͣ near . . . : Heb. remainder of his flesh
ͤ a wife . . . : or, one wife to another

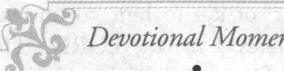

to uncover her nakedness, beside the other in her life *time*.

¹⁹Also thou shalt not approach unto a woman to uncover her nakedness, as long as she is put apart for her uncleanness. ²⁰Moreover thou shalt not lie carnally with thy neighbour's wife, to defile thyself with her. ²¹And thou shalt not let any of thy seed pass through *the fire* to Molech ͨ, neither shalt thou profane the name of thy God: I *am* the LORD. ²²Thou shalt not lie with mankind, as with womankind: it *is* abomination. ²³Neither shalt thou lie with any beast to defile thyself therewith: neither shall any woman stand before a beast to lie down thereto: it *is* confusion. ²⁴Defile not ye yourselves in any of these things: for in all these the nations are defiled which I cast out before you: ²⁵And the land is defiled:

therefore I do visit the iniquity thereof upon it, and the land itself vomiteth out her inhabitants. ²⁶Ye shall therefore keep my statutes and my judgments, and shall not commit *any* of these abominations; *neither* any of your own nation, nor any stranger that sojourneth among you: ²⁷(For all these abominations have the men of the land done, which *were* before you, and the land is defiled;) ²⁸That the land spue not you out also, when ye defile it, as it spued out the nations that *were* before you. ²⁹For whosoever shall commit any of these abominations, even the souls that commit *them* shall be cut off from among their people. ³⁰Therefore shall ye keep mine ordinance, that *ye* commit not *any one* of these abominable customs, which were committed before you, and that ye defile not yourselves therein: I *am* the LORD your God.

19

¹And the LORD spake unto Moses, saying, ²Speak unto all the congregation of the children of Israel, and say unto them, Ye shall be holy: for I the LORD your God *am* holy. ³Ye shall fear every man his mother, and his father, and keep my sabbaths: I *am* the LORD your God. ⁴Turn ye not unto idols, nor make to yourselves molten gods: I *am* the LORD your God. ⁵And if ye offer a sacrifice of peace offerings unto the LORD, ye shall offer it at your own will. ⁶It shall be eaten the same day ye offer it, and on the morrow: and if ought remain until the third day, it shall be burnt in the fire. ⁷And if it be eaten at all on the third day, it *is* abom-

---

ͨ Molech: Gr. Moloch

inable; it shall not be accepted. [8]Therefore *every one* that eateth it shall bear his iniquity, because he hath profaned the hallowed thing of the LORD: and that soul shall be cut off from among his people. [9]And when ye reap the harvest of your land, thou shalt not wholly reap the corners of thy field, neither shalt thou gather the gleanings of thy harvest. [10]And thou shalt not glean thy vineyard, neither shalt thou gather *every* grape of thy vineyard; thou shalt leave them for the poor and stranger: I *am* the LORD your God.

[11]Ye shall not steal, neither deal falsely, neither lie one to another. [12]And ye shall not swear by my name falsely, neither shalt thou profane the name of thy God: I *am* the LORD. [13]Thou shalt not defraud thy neighbour, neither rob *him*: the wages of him that is hired shall not abide with thee all night until the morning. [14]Thou shalt not curse the deaf, nor put a stumblingblock before the blind, but shalt fear thy God: I *am* the LORD. [15]Ye shall do no unrighteousness in judgment: thou shalt not respect the person of the poor, nor honour the person of the mighty: *but* in righteousness shalt thou judge thy neighbour. [16]Thou shalt not go up and down *as* a talebearer among thy people: neither shalt thou stand against the blood of thy neighbour: I *am* the LORD. [17]Thou shalt not hate thy brother in thine heart: thou shalt in any wise rebuke thy neighbour, and not suffer sin upon him. [18]Thou shalt not avenge, nor bear any grudge against the children of thy people, but

thou shalt love thy neighbour as thyself: I *am* the LORD.

[19]Ye shall keep my statutes. Thou shalt not let thy cattle gender with a diverse kind: thou shalt not sow thy field with mingled seed: neither shall a garment mingled of linen and woollen come upon thee. [20]And whosoever lieth carnally with a woman, that *is* a bondmaid, betrothed[a] to an husband, and not at all redeemed, nor freedom given her; she shall be scourged; they shall not be put to death, because she was not free. [21]And he shall bring his trespass offering unto the LORD, unto the door of the tabernacle of the congregation, *even* a ram for a trespass offering. [22]And the priest shall make an atonement for him with the ram of the trespass offering before the LORD for his sin which he hath done: and the sin which he hath done shall be forgiven him. [23]And when ye shall come into the land, and shall have planted all manner of trees for food, then ye shall count the fruit thereof as uncircumcised: three years shall it be as uncircumcised unto you: it shall not be eaten of. [24]But in the fourth year all the fruit thereof shall be holy[b] to praise the LORD *withal*. [25]And in the fifth year shall ye eat of the fruit thereof, that it may yield unto you the increase thereof: I *am* the LORD your God. [26]Ye shall not eat *any thing* with the blood: neither shall ye use enchantment, nor observe times. [27]Ye shall not round the corners of your heads, neither shalt thou mar the corners of thy beard. [28]Ye shall not make any cuttings in your flesh for the dead, nor print any

---

[a] betrothed . . . : or, abused by any: Heb. reproached by (or, for) man
[b] holy . . . : Heb. holiness of praises to the LORD

marks upon you: I *am* the LORD. ²⁹Do not prostitute^c thy daughter, to cause her to be a whore; lest the land fall to whoredom, and the land become full of wickedness.

³⁰Ye shall keep my sabbaths, and reverence my sanctuary: I *am* the LORD. ³¹Regard not them that have familiar spirits, neither seek after wizards, to be defiled by them: I *am* the LORD your God. ³²Thou shalt rise up before the hoary head, and honour the face of the old man, and fear thy God: I *am* the LORD. ³³And if a stranger sojourn with thee in your land, ye shall not vex^d him. ³⁴*But* the stranger that dwelleth with you shall be unto you as one born among you, and thou shalt love him as thyself; for ye were strangers in the land of Egypt: I *am* the LORD your God. ³⁵Ye shall do no unrighteousness in judgment, in meteyard, in weight, or in

measure. ³⁶Just balances, just weights^e, a just ephah, and a just hin, shall ye have: I *am* the LORD your God, which brought you out of the land of Egypt. ³⁷Therefore shall ye observe all my statutes, and all my judgments, and do them: I *am* the LORD.

20

¹And the LORD spake unto Moses, saying, ²Again, thou shalt say to the children of Israel, Whosoever *he be* of the children of Israel, or of the strangers that sojourn in Israel, that giveth *any* of his seed unto Molech; he shall surely be put to death: the people of the land shall stone him with stones. ³And I will set my face against that man, and will cut him off from among his people; because he hath given of his seed unto Molech, to defile my sanctuary, and to profane my holy name. ⁴And if the peo-

---

^c prostitute: Heb. profane
^d vex: or, oppress
^e weights: Heb. stones

ple of the land do any ways hide their eyes from the man, when he giveth of his seed unto Molech, and kill him not: ⁵Then I will set my face against that man, and against his family, and will cut him off, and all that go a whoring after him, to commit whoredom with Molech, from among their people. ⁶And the soul that turneth after such as have familiar spirits, and after wizards, to go a whoring after them, I will even set my face against that soul, and will cut him off from among his people. ⁷Sanctify yourselves therefore, and be ye holy: for I *am* the LORD your God. ⁸And ye shall keep my statutes, and do them: I *am* the LORD which sanctify you. ⁹For every one that curseth his father or his mother shall be surely put to death: he hath cursed his father or his mother; his blood *shall be* upon him.

¹⁰And the man that committeth adultery with *another* man's wife, *even he* that committeth adultery with his neighbour's wife, the adulterer and the adulteress shall surely be put to death. ¹¹And the man that lieth with his father's wife hath uncovered his father's nakedness: both of them shall surely be put to death; their blood *shall be* upon them. ¹²And if a man lie with his daughter in law, both of them shall surely be put to death: they have wrought confusion; their blood *shall be* upon them. ¹³If a man also lie with mankind, as he lieth with a woman, both of them have committed an abomination: they shall surely be put to death; their blood *shall be* upon them. ¹⁴And if a man take a wife and her mother, it *is* wickedness: they shall be burnt with fire, both he and they; that there be no wickedness among you. ¹⁵And if a man lie with a beast, he shall surely be put to death: and ye shall slay the beast. ¹⁶And if a woman approach unto any beast, and lie down thereto, thou shalt kill the woman, and the beast: they shall surely be put to death; their blood *shall be* upon them. ¹⁷And if a man shall take his sister, his father's daughter, or his mother's daughter, and see her nakedness, and she see his nakedness; it *is* a wicked thing; and they shall be cut off in the sight of their people: he hath uncovered his sister's nakedness; he shall bear his iniquity. ¹⁸And if a man shall lie with a woman having her sickness, and shall uncover her nakedness; he hath discovered[a] her fountain, and she hath uncovered the fountain of her blood: and both of them shall be cut off from among their people. ¹⁹And thou shalt not uncover the nakedness of thy mother's sister, nor of thy father's sister: for he uncovereth[b] his near kin: they shall bear their iniquity. ²⁰And if a man shall lie with his uncle's wife, he hath uncovered his uncle's nakedness: they shall bear their sin; they shall die childless. ²¹And if a man shall take his brother's wife, it *is* an unclean thing: he hath uncovered his brother's nakedness; they shall be childless.

²²Ye shall therefore keep all my statutes, and all my judgments, and do them: that the land, whither I bring you to dwell therein, spue you not out. ²³And ye shall not walk in the manners of the

---

ᵃ discovered: Heb. made naked
ᵇ uncovereth: Heb. hath made naked

nation, which I cast out before you: for they committed all these things, and therefore I abhorred them. ²⁴But I have said unto you, Ye shall inherit their land, and I will give it unto you to possess it, a land that floweth with milk and honey: I *am* the LORD your God, which have separated you from *other* people. ²⁵Ye shall therefore put difference between clean beasts and unclean, and between unclean fowls and clean: and ye shall not make your souls abominable by beast, or by fowl, or by any manner of living thing that creepeth^c on the ground, which I have separated from you as unclean. ²⁶And ye shall be holy unto me: for I the LORD *am* holy, and have severed you from *other* people, that ye should be mine. ²⁷A man also or woman that hath a familiar spirit, or that is a wizard, shall surely be put to death: they shall stone them with stones: their blood *shall be* upon them.

21

¹And the LORD said unto Moses, Speak unto the priests the sons of Aaron, and say unto them, There shall none be defiled for the dead among his people: ²But for his kin, that is near unto him, *that is*, for his mother, and for his father, and for his son, and for his daughter, and for his brother, ³And for his sister a virgin, that is nigh unto him, which hath had no husband; for her may he be defiled. ⁴*But* he shall not defile himself, *being* a chief man among his people, to profane himself. ⁵They shall not make baldness upon their head, neither shall they shave off the corner of their beard, nor make any

cuttings in their flesh. ⁶They shall be holy unto their God, and not profane the name of their God: for the offerings of the LORD made by fire, *and* the bread of their God, they do offer: therefore they shall be holy. ⁷They shall not take a wife *that is* a whore, or profane; neither shall they take a woman put away from her husband: for he *is* holy unto his God. ⁸Thou shalt sanctify him therefore; for he offereth the bread of thy God: he shall be holy unto thee: for I the LORD, which sanctify you, *am* holy. ⁹And the daughter of any priest, if she profane herself by playing the whore, she profaneth her father: she shall be burnt with fire.

¹⁰And *he that is* the high priest among his brethren, upon whose head the anointing oil was poured, and that is consecrated to put on the garments, shall not uncover his head, nor rend his clothes; ¹¹Neither shall he go in to any dead body, nor defile himself for his father, or for his mother; ¹²Neither shall he go out of the sanctuary, nor profane the sanctuary of his God; for the crown of the anointing oil of his God *is* upon him: I *am* the LORD. ¹³And he shall take a wife in her virginity. ¹⁴A widow, or a divorced woman, or profane, *or* an harlot, these shall he not take: but he shall take a virgin of his own people to wife. ¹⁵Neither shall he profane his seed among his people: for I the LORD do sanctify him. ¹⁶And the LORD spake unto Moses, saying, ¹⁷Speak unto Aaron, saying, Whosoever *he be* of thy seed in their generations that hath *any* blemish, let him not approach to offer the bread^a

---

^c creepeth: or, moveth
^a bread: or, food

of his God. [18]For whatsoever man *he be* that hath a blemish, he shall not approach: a blind man, or a lame, or he that hath a flat nose, or any thing superfluous, [19]Or a man that is brokenfooted, or brokenhanded, [20]Or crookbackt, or a dwarf[b], or that hath a blemish in his eye, or be scurvy, or scabbed, or hath his stones broken; [21]No man that hath a blemish of the seed of Aaron the priest shall come nigh to offer the offerings of the LORD made by fire: he hath a blemish; he shall not come nigh to offer the bread of his God. [22]He shall eat the bread of his God, *both* of the most holy, and of the holy. [23]Only he shall not go in unto the vail, nor come nigh unto the altar, because he hath a blemish; that he profane not my sanctuaries: for I the LORD do sanctify them. [24]And Moses told *it* unto Aaron, and to his sons, and unto all the children of Israel.

22

[1]And the LORD spake unto Moses, saying, [2]Speak unto Aaron and to his sons, that they separate themselves from the holy things of the children of Israel, and that they profane not my holy name *in those things* which they hallow unto me: I *am* the LORD. [3]Say unto them, Whosoever *he be* of all your seed among your generations, that goeth unto the holy things, which the children of Israel hallow unto the LORD, having his uncleanness upon him, that soul shall be cut off from my presence: I *am* the LORD. [4]What man

soever of the seed of Aaron *is* a leper, or hath a running issue; he shall not eat of the holy things, until he be clean. And whoso toucheth any thing *that is* unclean *by* the dead, or a man whose seed goeth from him; [5]Or whosoever toucheth any creeping thing, whereby he may be made unclean, or a man of whom he may take uncleanness, whatsoever uncleanness he hath; [6]The soul which hath touched any such shall be unclean until even, and shall not eat of the holy things, unless he wash his flesh with water. [7]And when the sun is down, he shall be clean, and shall afterward eat of the holy things; because it *is* his food. [8]That which dieth of itself, or is torn *with beasts*, he shall not eat to defile himself therewith: I *am* the LORD. [9]They shall therefore keep mine ordinance, lest they bear sin for it, and die therefore, if they profane it: I the LORD do sanctify them.

[10]There shall no stranger eat *of* the holy thing: a sojourner of the priest, or an hired servant, shall not eat *of* the holy thing. [11]But if the priest buy *any* soul with[a] his money, he shall eat of it, and he that is born in his house: they shall eat of his meat. [12]If the priest's daughter also be *married* unto a stranger[b], she may not eat of an offering of the holy things. [13]But if the priest's daughter be a widow, or divorced, and have no child, and is returned unto her father's house, as in her youth, she shall eat of her father's meat: but there shall no stranger eat thereof. [14]And if a man eat *of* the holy thing unwittingly, then

---

[b] a dwarf: or, too slender
[a] with . . . : Heb. with the purchase of his money
[b] a stranger: Heb. a man a stranger

he shall put the fifth *part* thereof unto it, and shall give *it* unto the priest with the holy thing. [15]And they shall not profane the holy things of the children of Israel, which they offer unto the LORD; [16]Or suffer them to bear the iniquity of trespass, when they eat their holy things: for I the LORD do sanctify them.

[17]And the LORD spake unto Moses, saying, [18]Speak unto Aaron, and to his sons, and unto all the children of Israel, and say unto them, Whatsoever *he be* of the house of Israel, or of the strangers in Israel, that will offer his oblation for all his vows, and for all his freewill offerings, which they will offer unto the LORD for a burnt offering; [19]*Ye shall offer* at your own will a male without blemish, of the beeves, of the sheep, or of the goats. [20]*But* whatsoever hath a blemish, *that* shall ye not offer: for it shall not be acceptable for you. [21]And whosoever offereth a sacrifice of peace offerings unto the LORD to accomplish *his* vow, or a freewill offering in beeves or sheep[c], it shall be perfect to be accepted; there shall be no blemish therein. [22]Blind, or broken, or maimed, or having a wen, or scurvy, or scabbed, ye shall not offer these unto the LORD, nor make an offering by fire of them upon the altar unto the LORD. [23]Either a bullock or a lamb[d] that hath any thing superfluous or lacking in his parts, that mayest thou offer *for* a freewill offering; but for a vow it shall not be accepted. [24]Ye shall not offer unto the LORD that which is bruised, or crushed, or broken,

or cut; neither shall ye make *any offering thereof* in your land. [25]Neither from a stranger's hand shall ye offer the bread of your God of any of these; because their corruption *is* in them, *and* blemishes *be* in them: they shall not be accepted for you. [26]And the LORD spake unto Moses, saying, [27]When a bullock, or a sheep, or a goat, is brought forth, then it shall be seven days under the dam; and from the eighth day and thenceforth it shall be accepted for an offering made by fire unto the LORD. [28]And *whether it be* cow or ewe[e], ye shall not kill it and her young both in one day. [29]And when ye will offer a sacrifice of thanksgiving unto the LORD, offer *it* at your own will. [30]On the same day it shall be eaten up; ye shall leave none of it until the morrow: I *am* the LORD. [31]Therefore shall ye keep my commandments, and do them: I *am* the LORD. [32]Neither shall ye profane my holy name; but I will be hallowed among the children of Israel: I *am* the LORD which hallow you, [33]That brought you out of the land of Egypt, to be your God: I *am* the LORD.

23

[1]And the LORD spake unto Moses, saying, [2]Speak unto the children of Israel, and say unto them, *Concerning* the feasts of the LORD, which ye shall proclaim *to be* holy convocations, *even* these *are* my feasts. [3]Six days shall work be done: but the seventh day *is* the sabbath of rest, an holy convocation; ye shall do no work *therein*: it *is* the sab-

---

[c] sheep: or, goats
[d] lamb: or, kid
[e] ewe: or, she goat

bath of the LORD in all your dwellings.

⁴These *are* the feasts of the LORD, *even* holy convocations, which ye shall proclaim in their seasons. ⁵In the fourteenth *day* of the first month at even *is* the LORD'S passover. ⁶And on the fifteenth day of the same month *is* the feast of unleavened bread unto the LORD: seven days ye must eat unleavened bread. ⁷In the first day ye shall have an holy convocation: ye shall do no servile work therein. ⁸But ye shall offer an offering made by fire unto the LORD seven days: in the seventh day *is* an holy convocation: ye shall do no servile work *therein*. ⁹And the LORD spake unto Moses, saying, ¹⁰Speak unto the children of Israel, and say unto them, When ye be come into the land which I give unto you, and shall reap the harvest thereof, then ye shall bring a sheaf ᵃ of the firstfruits of your harvest unto the priest: ¹¹And he shall wave the sheaf before the LORD, to be accepted for you: on the morrow after the sabbath the priest shall wave it. ¹²And ye shall offer that day when ye wave the sheaf an he lamb without blemish of the first year for a burnt offering unto the LORD. ¹³And the meat offering thereof *shall be* two tenth deals of fine flour mingled with oil, an offering made by fire unto the LORD *for* a sweet savour: and the drink offering thereof *shall be* of wine, the fourth *part* of an hin. ¹⁴And ye shall eat neither bread, nor parched corn, nor green ears, until the selfsame day that ye have brought an offering unto your God: *it shall be* a statute for ever throughout your generations in all your dwellings.

¹⁵And ye shall count unto you from the morrow after the sabbath, from the day that ye brought the sheaf of the wave offering; seven sabbaths shall be complete: ¹⁶Even unto the morrow after the seventh sabbath shall ye number fifty days; and ye shall offer a new meat offering unto the LORD. ¹⁷Ye shall bring out of your habitations two wave loaves of two tenth deals: they shall be of fine flour; they shall be baken with leaven; *they are* the firstfruits unto the LORD. ¹⁸And ye shall offer with the bread seven lambs without blemish of the first year, and one young bullock, and two rams: they shall be *for* a burnt offering unto the LORD, with their meat offering, and their drink offerings, *even* an offering made by fire, of sweet savour unto the LORD. ¹⁹Then ye shall sacrifice one kid of the goats for a sin offering, and two lambs of the first year for a sacrifice of peace offerings. ²⁰And the priest shall wave them with the bread of the firstfruits *for* a wave offering before the LORD, with the two lambs: they shall be holy to the LORD for the priest. ²¹And ye shall proclaim on the selfsame day, *that* it may be an holy convocation unto you: ye shall do no servile work *therein: it shall be* a statute for ever in all your dwellings throughout your generations. ²²And when ye reap the harvest of your land, thou shalt not make clean riddance of the corners of thy field when thou reapest, neither shalt thou gather any gleaning of thy harvest: thou shalt leave them unto the poor, and to the stranger: I *am* the LORD your God.

ᵃ sheaf: or, handful: Heb. omer

²³And the LORD spake unto Moses, saying, ²⁴Speak unto the children of Israel, saying, In the seventh month, in the first *day* of the month, shall ye have a sabbath, a memorial of blowing of trumpets, an holy convocation. ²⁵Ye shall do no servile work *therein*: but ye shall offer an offering made by fire unto the LORD. ²⁶And the LORD spake unto Moses, saying, ²⁷Also on the tenth *day* of this seventh month *there shall be* a day of atonement: it shall be an holy convocation unto you; and ye shall afflict your souls, and offer an offering made by fire unto the LORD. ²⁸And ye shall do no work in that same day: for it *is* a day of atonement, to make an atonement for you before the LORD your God. ²⁹For whatsoever soul *it be* that shall not be afflicted in that same day, he shall be cut off from among his people. ³⁰And whatsoever soul *it be* that doeth any work in that same day, the same soul will I destroy from among his people. ³¹Ye shall do no manner of work: *it shall be* a statute for ever throughout your generations in all your dwellings. ³²It *shall be* unto you a sabbath of rest, and ye shall afflict your souls: in the ninth *day* of the month at even, from even unto even, shall ye celebrate[b] your sabbath.

³³And the LORD spake unto Moses, saying, ³⁴Speak unto the children of Israel, saying, The fifteenth day of this seventh month *shall be* the feast of tabernacles *for* seven days unto the LORD. ³⁵On the first day *shall be* an holy convocation: ye shall do no servile work *therein*. ³⁶Seven days ye shall offer an offering made by fire unto the LORD: on the eighth day shall be an holy convoca-

tion unto you; and ye shall offer an offering made by fire unto the LORD: it *is* a solemn assembly; *and* ye shall do no servile work *therein*. ³⁷These *are* the feasts of the LORD, which ye shall proclaim *to be* holy convocations, to offer an offering made by fire unto the LORD, a burnt offering, and a meat offering, a sacrifice, and drink offerings, every thing upon his day: ³⁸Beside the sabbaths of the LORD, and beside your gifts, and beside all your vows, and beside all your freewill offerings, which ye give unto the LORD. ³⁹Also in the fifteenth day of the seventh month, when ye have gathered in the fruit of the land, ye shall keep a feast unto the LORD seven days: on the first day *shall be* a sabbath, and on the eighth day *shall be* a sabbath. ⁴⁰And ye shall take you on the first day the boughs of goodly trees, branches of palm trees, and the boughs of thick trees, and willows of the brook; and ye shall rejoice before the LORD your God seven days. ⁴¹And ye shall keep it a feast unto the LORD seven days in the year. *It shall be* a statute for ever in your generations: ye shall celebrate it in the seventh month. ⁴²Ye shall dwell in booths seven days; all that are Israelites born shall dwell in booths: ⁴³That your generations may know that I made the children of Israel to dwell in booths, when I brought them out of the land of Egypt: I *am* the LORD your God. ⁴⁴And Moses declared unto the children of Israel the feasts of the LORD.

24

¹And the LORD spake unto Moses, saying, ²Command the children of Is-

[b] celebrate: Heb. rest

rael, that they bring unto thee pure oil olive beaten for the light, to cause the lamps to burn continually. ³Without the vail of the testimony, in the tabernacle of the congregation, shall Aaron order it from the evening unto the morning before the LORD continually: *it shall be* a statute for ever in your generations. ⁴He shall order the lamps upon the pure candlestick before the LORD continually. ⁵And thou shalt take fine flour, and bake twelve cakes thereof: two tenth deals shall be in one cake. ⁶And thou shalt set them in two rows, six on a row, upon the pure table before the LORD. ⁷And thou shalt put pure frankincense upon *each* row, that it may be on the bread for a memorial, *even* an offering made by fire unto the LORD. ⁸Every sabbath he shall set it in order before the LORD continually, *being taken* from the children of Israel by an everlasting covenant. ⁹And it shall be Aaron's and his sons'; and they shall eat it in the holy place: for it *is* most holy unto him of the offerings of the LORD made by fire by a perpetual statute.

¹⁰And the son of an Israelitish woman, whose father *was* an Egyptian, went out among the children of Israel: and this son of the Israelitish *woman* and a man of Israel strove together in the camp; ¹¹And the Israelitish woman's son blasphemed the name *of the LORD,* and cursed. And they brought him unto Moses: (and his mother's name *was* Shelomith, the daughter of Dibri, of the tribe of Dan:) ¹²And they put him in ward, that the mind of the LORD might be shewed them. ¹³And the LORD spake unto Moses, saying,

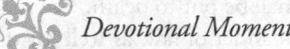

Devotional Moment
•
Swearing
24:11 In the heat of a fight, an Egyptian boy living with the Israelites swore using God's name. God's severe punishment served as a dramatic reminder of how seriously God meant his command not to use his name in vain (Exod. 20:7). God's name stands for all that he is—holiness and righteousness. For it to be used in a common or vile manner is like a bride dressed in her wedding splendor walking the streets as a prostitute. Guard your own language, and teach your children at a young age to use God's name reverently. And when guests use God's name in vain, don't be afraid to tell them, "We don't say 'God' that way in our house."

¹⁴Bring forth him that hath cursed without the camp; and let all that heard *him* lay their hands upon his head, and let all the congregation stone him. ¹⁵And thou shalt speak unto the children of Israel, saying, Whosoever curseth his God shall bear his sin. ¹⁶And he that blasphemeth the name of the LORD, he shall surely be put to death, *and* all the congregation shall certainly stone him: as well the stranger, as he that is born in the land, when he blasphemeth the name *of the LORD,* shall be put to death. ¹⁷And he that killethª any man shall surely be put to death. ¹⁸And he that killeth a beast shall make it good; beast for beast. ¹⁹And if a man cause a blemish in his neighbour; as he hath done, so shall it be done to him; ²⁰Breach for breach, eye for eye, tooth for tooth: as he hath caused a blemish in a man, so shall it be done to him *again.* ²¹And he that killeth a beast, he shall restore it: and he that killeth a

---

ª killeth . . . : Heb. smiteth the life of a man

man, he shall be put to death. [22]Ye shall have one manner of law, as well for the stranger, as for one of your own country: for I *am* the LORD your God. [23]And Moses spake to the children of Israel, that they should bring forth him that had cursed out of the camp, and stone him with stones. And the children of Israel did as the LORD commanded Moses.

25

[1]And the LORD spake unto Moses in mount Sinai, saying, [2]Speak unto the children of Israel, and say unto them, When ye come into the land which I give you, then shall the land keep[a] a sabbath unto the LORD. [3]Six years thou shalt sow thy field, and six years thou shalt prune thy vineyard, and gather in the fruit thereof; [4]But in the seventh year shall be a sabbath of rest unto the land, a sabbath for the LORD: thou shalt neither sow thy field, nor prune thy vineyard. [5]That which groweth of its own accord of thy harvest thou shalt not reap, neither gather the grapes of thy vine undressed: *for* it is a year of rest unto the land. [6]And the sabbath of the land shall be meat for you; for thee, and for thy servant, and for thy maid, and for thy hired servant, and for thy stranger that sojourneth with thee, [7]And for thy cattle, and for the beast that *are* in thy land, shall all the increase thereof be meat.

[8]And thou shalt number seven sabbaths of years unto thee, seven times seven years; and the space of the seven sabbaths of years shall be unto thee forty and nine years. [9]Then shalt thou cause the trumpet of the jubile[b] to sound on the tenth *day* of the seventh month, in the day of atonement shall ye make the trumpet sound throughout all your land. [10]And ye shall hallow the fiftieth year, and proclaim liberty throughout *all* the land unto all the inhabitants thereof: it shall be a jubile unto you; and ye shall return every man unto his possession, and ye shall return every man unto his family. [11]A jubile shall that fiftieth year be unto you: ye shall not sow, neither reap that which groweth of itself in it, nor gather *the grapes* in it of thy vine undressed. [12]For it *is* the jubile; it shall be holy unto you: ye shall eat the increase thereof out of the field. [13]In the year of this jubile ye shall return every man unto his possession. [14]And if thou sell ought unto thy neighbour, or buyest *ought* of thy neighbour's hand, ye shall not oppress one another: [15]According to the number of years after the jubile thou shalt buy of thy neighbour, *and* according unto the number of years of the fruits he shall sell unto thee: [16]According to the multitude of years thou shalt increase the price thereof, and according to the fewness of years thou shalt diminish the price of it: for *according* to the number *of the years* of the fruits doth he sell unto thee. [17]Ye shall not therefore oppress one another; but thou shalt fear thy God: for I *am* the LORD your God. [18]Wherefore ye shall do my statutes, and keep my judgments, and do them; and ye shall dwell in the land in safety. [19]And the land shall yield her

---

[a] keep: Heb. rest
[b] of the jubile: Heb. loud of sound

fruit, and ye shall eat your fill, and dwell therein in safety. [20]And if ye shall say, What shall we eat the seventh year? behold, we shall not sow, nor gather in our increase: [21]Then I will command my blessing upon you in the sixth year, and it shall bring forth fruit for three years. [22]And ye shall sow the eighth year, and eat *yet* of old fruit until the ninth year; until her fruits come in ye shall eat *of* the old *store*.

[23]The land shall not be sold for ever[c]: for the land *is* mine; for ye *are* strangers and sojourners with me. [24]And in all the land of your possession ye shall grant a redemption for the land. [25]If thy brother be waxen poor, and hath sold away *some* of his possession, and if any of his kin come to redeem it, then shall he redeem that which his brother sold. [26]And if the man have none to redeem it, and himself[d] be able to redeem it; [27]Then let him count the

years of the sale thereof, and restore the overplus unto the man to whom he sold it; that he may return unto his possession. [28]But if he be not able to restore *it* to him, then that which is sold shall remain in the hand of him that hath bought it until the year of jubile: and in the jubile it shall go out, and he shall return unto his possession. [29]And if a man sell a dwelling house in a walled city, then he may redeem it within a whole year after it is sold; *within* a full year may he redeem it. [30]And if it be not redeemed within the space of a full year, then the house that *is* in the walled city shall be established for ever to him that bought it throughout his generations: it shall not go out in the jubile. [31]But the houses of the villages which have no wall round about them shall be counted as the fields of the country: they may be redeemed, and they shall go out in the jubile. [32]Notwithstanding the cities of the Levites, *and* the houses of the cities of their possession, may the Levites redeem at any time. [33]And if a man purchase of the Levites, then the house that was sold, and the city of his possession, shall go out in *the year of* jubile: for the houses of the cities of the Levites *are* their possession among the children of Israel. [34]But the field of the suburbs of their cities may not be sold; for it *is* their perpetual possession. [35]And if thy brother be waxen poor, and fallen in decay with thee; then thou shalt relieve him: *yea, though he be* a stranger, or a sojourner; that he may live with thee. [36]Take thou no usury of him, or increase: but fear thy God; that thy

---

Devotional Moment
•
Stewardship

25:23 The Israelites' land and possessions did not really belong to them. God owned it all and had given it to them only as a trust. This freed them from the materialism—worry, greed, ambition—that comes with ownership, and challenged them to be good stewards of God's property. Your spouse, children, and possessions have been entrusted to you, their steward. They have been given to you to glorify God. Treasure and cultivate what God has given you, but hold it in an open hand. Take a moment right now to give back to God what is already his. Treat everything you have as a trust from God. And acknowledge God's ownership in prayer every day.

---

[c] for ever: or, to be quite cut off: Heb. for cutting off
[d] himself . . . : Heb. his hand hath attained and found sufficiency

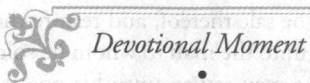

Devotional Moment
•
Poor Relatives

25:35-37 God commanded the Israelites to care for any relatives who became poor—even if it was costly. The family unit is precious to God, and was created for our benefit. When one member is in trouble, we aren't to judge why it happened or expect the government to take care of him. God tells us to take responsibility for meeting his needs and getting him back on his feet. If such were the practice in our society, homelessness would be virtually wiped out. Is anyone in your extended family in financial need? Don't wait for someone else to do something. Do what you can to meet that person's needs.

brother may live with thee. ³⁷Thou shalt not give him thy money upon usury, nor lend him thy victuals for increase. ³⁸I *am* the LORD your God, which brought you forth out of the land of Egypt, to give you the land of Canaan, *and* to be your God.

³⁹And if thy brother *that dwelleth* by thee be waxen poor, and be sold unto thee; thou shalt not compel[e] him to serve as a bondservant: ⁴⁰*But* as an hired servant, *and* as a sojourner, he shall be with thee, *and* shall serve thee unto the year of jubile: ⁴¹And *then* shall he depart from thee, *both* he and his children with him, and shall return unto his own family, and unto the possession of his fathers shall he return. ⁴²For they *are* my servants, which I brought forth out of the land of Egypt: they shall not be sold as[f] bondmen. ⁴³Thou shalt not rule over him with

rigour; but shalt fear thy God. ⁴⁴Both thy bondmen, and thy bondmaids, which thou shalt have, *shall be* of the heathen that are round about you; of them shall ye buy bondmen and bondmaids. ⁴⁵Moreover of the children of the strangers that do sojourn among you, of them shall ye buy, and of their families that *are* with you, which they begat in your land: and they shall be your possession. ⁴⁶And ye shall take them as an inheritance for your children after you, to inherit *them for* a possession; they shall be your bondmen for ever: but over your brethren the children of Israel, ye shall not rule one over another with rigour. ⁴⁷And if a sojourner or stranger wax rich[g] by thee, and thy brother *that dwelleth* by him wax poor, and sell himself unto the stranger *or* sojourner by thee, or to the stock of the stranger's family: ⁴⁸After that he is sold he may be redeemed again; one of his brethren may redeem him: ⁴⁹Either his uncle, or his uncle's son, may redeem him, or *any* that is nigh of kin unto him of his family may redeem him; or if he be able, he may redeem himself. ⁵⁰And he shall reckon with him that bought him from the year that he was sold to him unto the year of jubile: and the price of his sale shall be according unto the number of years, according to the time of an hired servant shall it be with him. ⁵¹If *there be* yet many years *behind*, according unto them he shall give again the price of his redemption out of the money that he was bought for. ⁵²And if there remain but few years unto the

---

[e] compel . . . : Heb. serve thyself with him with the service, etc
[f] as . . . : Heb. with the sale of a bondman
[g] wax rich . . . : Heb. his hand obtain, etc

year of jubile, then he shall count with him, *and* according unto his years shall he give him again the price of his redemption. [53]*And* as a yearly hired servant shall he be with him: *and the other* shall not rule with rigour over him in thy sight. [54]And if he be not redeemed in these[h] *years*, then he shall go out in the year of jubile, *both* he, and his children with him. [55]For unto me the children of Israel *are* servants; they *are* my servants whom I brought forth out of the land of Egypt: I *am* the LORD your God.

26

[1]Ye shall make you no idols nor graven image, neither rear you up a standing image, neither shall ye set up *any* image of stone in your land, to bow down unto it: for I *am* the LORD your God. [2]Ye shall keep my sabbaths, and reverence my sanctuary: I *am* the LORD. [3]If ye walk in my statutes, and keep my commandments, and do them; [4]Then I will give you rain in due season, and the land shall yield her increase, and the trees of the field shall yield their fruit. [5]And your threshing shall reach unto the vintage, and the vintage shall reach unto the sowing time: and ye shall eat your bread to the full, and dwell in your land safely. [6]And I will give peace in the land, and ye shall lie down, and none shall make *you* afraid: and I will rid[a] evil beasts out of the land, neither shall the sword go through your land. [7]And ye shall chase your enemies, and they shall fall before you by the sword. [8]And five of you shall chase an hundred, and an hundred of you shall put ten thousand to flight: and your enemies shall fall before you by the sword. [9]For I will have respect unto you, and make you fruitful, and multiply you, and establish my covenant with you. [10]And ye shall eat old store, and bring forth the old because of the new. [11]And I will set my tabernacle among you: and my soul shall not abhor you. [12]And I will walk among you, and will be your God, and ye shall be my people. [13]I *am* the LORD your God, which brought you forth out of the land of Egypt, that ye should not be their bondmen; and I have broken the bands of your yoke, and made you go upright.

[14]But if ye will not hearken unto me, and will not do all these commandments; [15]And if ye shall despise my statutes, or if your soul abhor my judgments, so that ye will not do all my commandments, *but* that ye break my covenant: [16]I also will do this unto you; I will even appoint over you terror, consumption, and the burning ague, that shall consume the eyes, and cause sorrow of heart: and ye shall sow your seed in vain, for your enemies shall eat it. [17]And I will set my face against you, and ye shall be slain before your enemies: they that hate you shall reign over you; and ye shall flee when none pursueth you. [18]And if ye will not yet for all this hearken unto me, then I will punish you seven times more for your sins. [19]And I will break the pride of your power; and I will make your heaven as iron, and your earth as brass: [20]And your strength shall be spent in vain: for

---

[h] in these . . . : or, by these means
[a] rid: Heb. cause to cease

your land shall not yield her increase, neither shall the trees of the land yield their fruits. ²¹And if ye walk contrary[b] unto me, and will not hearken unto me; I will bring seven times more plagues upon you according to your sins. ²²I will also send wild beasts among you, which shall rob you of your children, and destroy your cattle, and make you few in number; and your *high* ways shall be desolate. ²³And if ye will not be reformed by me by these things, but will walk contrary unto me; ²⁴Then will I also walk contrary unto you, and will punish you yet seven times for your sins. ²⁵And I will bring a sword upon you, that shall avenge the quarrel of *my* covenant: and when ye are gathered together within your cities, I will send the pestilence among you; and ye shall be delivered into the hand of the enemy. ²⁶*And* when I have broken the staff of your bread, ten women shall bake your bread in one oven, and they shall deliver *you* your bread again by weight: and ye shall eat, and not be satisfied. ²⁷And if ye will not for all this hearken unto me, but walk contrary unto me; ²⁸Then I will walk contrary unto you also in fury; and I, even I, will chastise you seven times for your sins. ²⁹And ye shall eat the flesh of your sons, and the flesh of your daughters shall ye eat. ³⁰And I will destroy your high places, and cut down your images, and cast your carcases upon the carcases of your idols, and my soul shall abhor you. ³¹And I will make your cities waste, and bring your sanctuaries unto desolation, and I will not smell the savour of your

sweet odours. ³²And I will bring the land into desolation: and your enemies which dwell therein shall be astonished at it. ³³And I will scatter you among the heathen, and will draw out a sword after you: and your land shall be desolate, and your cities waste. ³⁴Then shall the land enjoy her sabbaths, as long as it lieth desolate, and ye *be* in your enemies' land; *even* then shall the land rest, and enjoy her sabbaths. ³⁵As long as it lieth desolate it shall rest; because it did not rest in your sabbaths, when ye dwelt upon it. ³⁶And upon them that are left *alive* of you I will send a faintness into their hearts in the lands of their enemies; and the sound of a shaken[c] leaf shall chase them; and they shall flee, as fleeing from a sword; and they shall fall when none pursueth. ³⁷And they shall fall one upon another, as it were before a sword, when none pursueth: and ye shall have no power to stand before your enemies. ³⁸And ye shall perish among the heathen, and the land of your enemies shall eat you up. ³⁹And they that are left of you shall pine away in their iniquity in your enemies' lands; and also in the iniquities of their fathers shall they pine away with them.

⁴⁰If they shall confess their iniquity, and the iniquity of their fathers, with their trespass which they trespassed against me, and that also they have walked contrary unto me; ⁴¹And *that* I also have walked contrary unto them, and have brought them into the land of their enemies; if then their uncircumcised hearts be humbled, and they then accept of the punishment of their iniq-

---

b contrary . . . : or, at all adventures with me
c shaken: Heb. driven

uity: ⁴²Then will I remember my covenant with Jacob, and also my covenant with Isaac, and also my covenant with Abraham will I remember; and I will remember the land. ⁴³The land also shall be left of them, and shall enjoy her sabbaths, while she lieth desolate without them: and they shall accept of the punishment of their iniquity: because, even because they despised my judgments, and because their soul abhorred my statutes. ⁴⁴And yet for all that, when they be in the land of their enemies, I will not cast them away, neither will I abhor them, to destroy them utterly, and to break my covenant with them: for I *am* the LORD their God. ⁴⁵But I will for their sakes remember the covenant of their ancestors, whom I brought forth out of the land of Egypt in the sight of the heathen, that I might be their God: I *am* the LORD. ⁴⁶These *are* the statutes and judgments and laws, which the LORD made between him and the children of Israel in mount Sinai by the hand of Moses.

27

¹And the LORD spake unto Moses, saying, ²Speak unto the children of Israel, and say unto them, When a man shall make a singular vow, the persons *shall be* for the LORD by thy estimation. ³And thy estimation shall be of the male from twenty years old even unto sixty years old, even thy estimation shall be fifty shekels of silver, after the shekel of the sanctuary. ⁴And if it *be* a female, then thy estimation shall be thirty shekels. ⁵And if *it be* from five years old even unto twenty years old, then thy estimation shall be of the male twenty shekels, and for the female ten shekels.

Devotional Moment

Promises

27:9-10 God made many promises to the Israelites—and fulfilled every one. In turn he asked that they take their promises to him just as seriously, even if they turned out to be costly. As Christians we need to honor the promises we've made to God. Are there any promises you need to act on today? Did you vow to love your wife or husband? Did you dedicate your children to God, promising to raise them to know him? Did you commit to God a certain percentage of your income, whatever that income might be? Guard against taking any promises lightly.

---

⁶And if *it be* from a month old even unto five years old, then thy estimation shall be of the male five shekels of silver, and for the female thy estimation *shall be* three shekels of silver. ⁷And if *it be* from sixty years old and above; if *it be* a male, then thy estimation shall be fifteen shekels, and for the female ten shekels. ⁸But if he be poorer than thy estimation, then he shall present himself before the priest, and the priest shall value him; according to his ability that vowed shall the priest value him. ⁹And if *it be* a beast, whereof men bring an offering unto the LORD, all that *any man* giveth of such unto the LORD shall be holy. ¹⁰He shall not alter it, nor change it, a good for a bad, or a bad for a good: and if he shall at all change beast for beast, then it and the exchange thereof shall be holy. ¹¹And if *it be* any unclean beast, of which they do not offer a sacrifice unto the LORD, then he shall present the beast before the priest: ¹²And the priest shall value it, whether it be good or bad: as thou valuest it, *who*

art the priest, so shall it be. ¹³But if he will at all redeem it, then he shall add a fifth *part* thereof unto thy estimation.

¹⁴And when a man shall sanctify his house *to be* holy unto the LORD, then the priest shall estimate it, whether it be good or bad: as the priest shall estimate it, so shall it stand. ¹⁵And if he that sanctified it will redeem his house, then he shall add the fifth *part* of the money of thy estimation unto it, and it shall be his. ¹⁶And if a man shall sanctify unto the LORD *some part* of a field of his possession, then thy estimation shall be according to the seed thereof: an homer of barley seed *shall be valued* at fifty shekels of silver. ¹⁷If he sanctify his field from the year of jubile, according to thy estimation it shall stand. ¹⁸But if he sanctify his field after the jubile, then the priest shall reckon unto him the money according to the years that remain, even unto the year of the jubile, and it shall be abated from thy estimation. ¹⁹And if he that sanctified the field will in any wise redeem it, then he shall add the fifth *part* of the money of thy estimation unto it, and it shall be assured to him. ²⁰And if he will not redeem the field, or if he have sold the field to another man, it shall not be redeemed any more. ²¹But the field, when it goeth out in the jubile, shall be holy unto the LORD, as a field devoted; the possession thereof shall be the priest's. ²²And if *a man* sanctify unto the LORD a field which he hath bought, which *is* not of the fields of his possession; ²³Then the priest shall reckon unto him the worth of thy estimation, *even* unto the year of the jubile: and he shall give thine estimation in that day, *as* a holy thing unto the LORD. ²⁴In the year of the jubile the field shall return unto him of whom it was bought, *even* to him to whom the possession of the land *did belong.* ²⁵And all thy estimations shall be according to the shekel of the sanctuary: twenty gerahs shall be the shekel.

²⁶Only the firstling of the beasts, which should be the LORD'S firstling, no man shall sanctify it; whether *it be* ox, or sheep: it *is* the LORD'S. ²⁷And if *it be* of an unclean beast, then he shall redeem *it* according to thine estimation, and shall add a fifth *part* of it thereto: or if it be not redeemed, then it shall be sold according to thy estimation. ²⁸Notwithstanding no devoted thing, that a man shall devote unto the LORD of all that he hath, *both* of man and beast, and of the field of his possession, shall be sold or redeemed: every devoted thing *is* most holy unto the LORD. ²⁹None devoted, which shall be devoted of men, shall be redeemed; *but* shall surely be put to death. ³⁰And all the tithe of the land, *whether* of the seed of the land, *or* of the fruit of the tree, *is* the LORD'S: *it is* holy unto the LORD. ³¹And if a man will at all redeem *ought* of his tithes, he shall add thereto the fifth *part* thereof. ³²And concerning the tithe of the herd, or of the flock, *even* of whatsoever passeth under the rod, the tenth shall be holy unto the LORD. ³³He shall not search whether it be good or bad, neither shall he change it: and if he change it at all, then both it and the change thereof shall be holy; it shall not be redeemed. ³⁴These *are* the commandments, which the LORD commanded Moses for the children of Israel in mount Sinai.

NUMBERS

Purpose
To tell the story of how the people of Israel prepared to enter the Promised Land, how they sinned and were punished, and how they prepared to try again

Author
Moses

To Whom Written
The people of Israel

Date Written
1450–1410 B.C.

Setting
The vast desert of the Sinai region, as well as lands just south and east of Canaan

Key Verses
"Those men . . . who have not hearkened to my voice . . . shall not see the land which I sware unto their fathers" (14:22-23).

Key People
Moses, Aaron, Miriam, Joshua, Caleb, Eleazar, Korah, Balaam

Key Places
Mount Sinai, Promised Land (Canaan), Kadesh-barnea, Mount Hor, plains of Moab

When many politicians and preachers get up to talk, most people tune to another frequency. Nothing against the speaker. It's just a common habit to tune out someone who wants his or her words to get through to us. Mothers who give advice to teenage children know the feeling.

But when an animal, especially a dull-witted donkey, starts to speak—well, listeners tune in fast. Who can ignore an animal who speaks with polished diction?

The book of Numbers documents the thirty-nine-year wilderness wanderings of the Israelites. God's plan was to lead them in the quick victory of Canaan, the Promised Land. But the people said, in effect, "Catch that action later!" A donkey who spoke to a pagan prophet helped the people recover their wits and their courage, but too late for the generation that escaped Egypt. Only their children saw Canaan; the promise had passed to the young in faith.

Next time your children go deaf at the sound of advice or admonition, ask them what they'd do if their kitten looked up from the milk dish and said, "Listen, buster, sweep the lint from between your ears and pay attention to your mother." Or if the snapping turtle in the shoe box popped his head from under that shell with, "On my scale, dude, your mom's advice is awesome!"

While reading Numbers, remember how deeply God desires for his Word to reach you. Catch God's frequency early and keep it tuned in, lest the spiders in your closet start a sermon.

1

¹And the LORD spake unto Moses in the wilderness of Sinai, in the tabernacle of the congregation, on the first *day* of the second month, in the second year after they were come out of the land of Egypt, saying, ²Take ye the sum of all the congregation of the children of Israel, after their families, by the house of their fathers, with the number of *their* names, every male by their polls; ³From twenty years old and upward, all that are able to go forth to war in Israel: thou and Aaron shall number them by their armies. ⁴And with you there shall be a man of every tribe; every one head of the house of his fathers. ⁵And these *are* the names of the men that shall stand with you: of *the tribe of* Reuben; Elizur the son of Shedeur. ⁶Of Simeon; Shelumiel the son of Zurishaddai. ⁷Of Judah; Nahshon the son of Amminadab. ⁸Of Issachar; Nethaneel the son of Zuar. ⁹Of Zebulun; Eliab the son of Helon. ¹⁰Of the children of Joseph: of Ephraim; Elishama the son of Ammihud: of Manasseh; Gamaliel the son of Pedahzur. ¹¹Of Benjamin; Abidan the son of Gideoni. ¹²Of Dan; Ahiezer the son of Ammishaddai. ¹³Of Asher; Pagiel the son of Ocran. ¹⁴Of Gad; Eliasaph the son of Deuelᵃ. ¹⁵Of Naphtali; Ahira the son of Enan. ¹⁶These *were* the renowned of the congregation, princes of the tribes of their fathers, heads of thousands in Israel.

¹⁷And Moses and Aaron took these men which are expressed by *their* names: ¹⁸And they assembled all the congregation together on the first *day* of the second month, and they declared their pedigrees after their families, by the house of their fathers, according to the number of the names, from twenty years old and upward, by their polls. ¹⁹As the LORD commanded Moses, so he numbered them in the wilderness of Sinai. ²⁰And the children of Reuben, Israel's eldest son, by their generations, after their families, by the house of their fathers, according to the number of the names, by their polls, every male from twenty years old and upward, all that were able to go forth to war; ²¹Those that were numbered of them, *even* of the tribe of Reuben, *were* forty and six thousand and five hundred. ²²Of the children of Simeon, by their generations, after their families, by the house of their fathers, those that were numbered of them, according to the number of the names, by their polls, every male from twenty years old and upward, all that were able to go forth to war; ²³Those that were numbered of them, *even* of the tribe of Simeon, *were* fifty and nine thousand and three hundred. ²⁴Of the children of Gad, by their generations, after their families, by the house of their fathers, according to the number of the names, from twenty years old and upward, all that were able to go forth to war; ²⁵Those that were numbered of them, *even* of the tribe of Gad, *were* forty and five thousand six hundred and fifty. ²⁶Of the children of Judah, by their generations, after their families, by the house of their fathers, according to the number of the names, from twenty years old and upward, all that were able to go forth to war;

ᵃ Deuel: also called, Reuel

²⁷Those that were numbered of them, *even* of the tribe of Judah, *were* threescore and fourteen thousand and six hundred. ²⁸Of the children of Issachar, by their generations, after their families, by the house of their fathers, according to the number of the names, from twenty years old and upward, all that were able to go forth to war; ²⁹Those that were numbered of them, *even* of the tribe of Issachar, *were* fifty and four thousand and four hundred. ³⁰Of the children of Zebulun, by their generations, after their families, by the house of their fathers, according to the number of the names, from twenty years old and upward, all that were able to go forth to war; ³¹Those that were numbered of them, *even* of the tribe of Zebulun, *were* fifty and seven thousand and four hundred. ³²Of the children of Joseph, *namely,* of the children of Ephraim, by their generations, after their families, by the house of their fathers, according to the number of the names, from twenty years old and upward, all that were able to go forth to war; ³³Those that were numbered of them, *even* of the tribe of Ephraim, *were* forty thousand and five hundred. ³⁴Of the children of Manasseh, by their generations, after their families, by the house of their fathers, according to the number of the names, from twenty years old and upward, all that were able to go forth to war; ³⁵Those that were numbered of them, *even* of the tribe of Manasseh, *were* thirty and two thousand and two hundred. ³⁶Of the children of Benjamin, by their generations, after their families, by the house of their fathers, according to the number of the names, from twenty years old and up-ward, all that were able to go forth to war; ³⁷Those that were numbered of them, *even* of the tribe of Benjamin, *were* thirty and five thousand and four hundred. ³⁸Of the children of Dan, by their generations, after their families, by the house of their fathers, according to the number of the names, from twenty years old and upward, all that were able to go forth to war; ³⁹Those that were numbered of them, *even* of the tribe of Dan, *were* threescore and two thousand and seven hundred. ⁴⁰Of the children of Asher, by their generations, after their families, by the house of their fathers, according to the number of the names, from twenty years old and upward, all that were able to go forth to war; ⁴¹Those that were numbered of them, *even* of the tribe of Asher, *were* forty and one thousand and five hundred. ⁴²Of the children of Naphtali, throughout their generations, after their families, by the house of their fathers, according to the number of the names, from twenty years old and upward, all that were able to go forth to war; ⁴³Those that were numbered of them, *even* of the tribe of Naphtali, *were* fifty and three thousand and four hundred.

⁴⁴These *are* those that were numbered, which Moses and Aaron numbered, and the princes of Israel, *being* twelve men: each one was for the house of his fathers. ⁴⁵So were all those that were numbered of the children of Israel, by the house of their fathers, from twenty years old and upward, all that were able to go forth to war in Israel; ⁴⁶Even all they that were numbered were six hundred thousand and three thousand and five hundred and fifty.

⁴⁷But the Levites after the tribe of

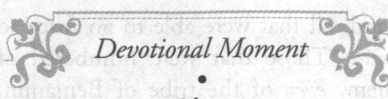

Devotional Moment
•
Plans

1:54 The people of Israel had completed their census as God had commanded them. They also set apart the tribe of Levi for the work of the Tabernacle, people who would have much of the spiritual responsibility for the rest of the Israelites. God knew that they would function best with this division of labor, and his people obeyed the directions given through Moses. God also knows how your family can function at its best. Reading and following scriptural principles, listening to sound advice, and being aware of what works best for your household— all these can help in both day-to-day situations and long-term decisions. Follow God's methods, knowing that he has the best in mind for your family, and be open to his changes in the future.

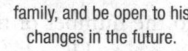

their fathers were not numbered among them. ⁴⁸For the LORD had spoken unto Moses, saying, ⁴⁹Only thou shalt not number the tribe of Levi, neither take the sum of them among the children of Israel: ⁵⁰But thou shalt appoint the Levites over the tabernacle of testimony, and over all the vessels thereof, and over all things that *belong* to it: they shall bear the tabernacle, and all the vessels thereof; and they shall minister unto it, and shall encamp round about the tabernacle. ⁵¹And when the tabernacle setteth forward, the Levites shall take it down: and when the tabernacle is to be pitched, the Levites shall set it up: and the stranger that cometh nigh shall be put to death. ⁵²And the children of Israel shall pitch their tents, every man by his own camp, and every man by his own standard, throughout their hosts. ⁵³But the Levites shall pitch round about the tabernacle of testimony, that there be no wrath upon the congregation of the children of Israel: and the Levites shall keep the charge of the tabernacle of testimony. ⁵⁴And the children of Israel did according to all that the LORD commanded Moses, so did they.

2

¹And the LORD spake unto Moses and unto Aaron, saying, ²Every man of the children of Israel shall pitch by his own standard, with the ensign of their father's house: far off about the tabernacle of the congregation shall they pitch. ³And on the east side toward the rising of the sun shall they of the standard of the camp of Judah pitch throughout their armies: and Nahshon the son of Amminadab *shall be* captain of the children of Judah. ⁴And his host, and those that were numbered of them, *were* threescore and fourteen thousand and six hundred. ⁵And those that do pitch next unto him *shall be* the tribe of Issachar: and Nethaneel the son of Zuar *shall be* captain of the children of Issachar. ⁶And his host, and those that were numbered thereof, *were* fifty and four thousand and four hundred. ⁷*Then* the tribe of Zebulun: and Eliab the son of Helon *shall be* captain of the children of Zebulun. ⁸And his host, and those that were numbered thereof, *were* fifty and seven thousand and four hundred. ⁹All that were numbered in the camp of Judah *were* an hundred thousand and fourscore thousand and six thousand and four hundred, throughout their armies. These shall first set forth. ¹⁰On the south side *shall be* the standard of the camp of Reuben according to their armies: and the captain of the children of Reuben *shall be* Elizur the son of

Shedeur. [11]And his host, and those that were numbered thereof, *were* forty and six thousand and five hundred. [12]And those which pitch by him *shall be* the tribe of Simeon: and the captain of the children of Simeon *shall be* Shelumiel the son of Zurishaddai. [13]And his host, and those that were numbered of them, *were* fifty and nine thousand and three hundred. [14]Then the tribe of Gad: and the captain of the sons of Gad *shall be* Eliasaph the son of Reuel[a]. [15]And his host, and those that were numbered of them, *were* forty and five thousand and six hundred and fifty. [16]All that were numbered in the camp of Reuben *were* an hundred thousand and fifty and one thousand and four hundred and fifty, throughout their armies. And they shall set forth in the second rank. [17]Then the tabernacle of the congregation shall set forward with the camp of the Levites in the midst of the camp: as they encamp, so shall they set forward, every man in his place by their standards. [18]On the west side *shall be* the standard of the camp of Ephraim according to their armies: and the captain of the sons of Ephraim *shall be* Elishama the son of Ammihud. [19]And his host, and those that were numbered of them, *were* forty thousand and five hundred. [20]And by him *shall be* the tribe of Manasseh: and the captain of the children of Manasseh *shall be* Gamaliel the son of Pedahzur. [21]And his host, and those that were numbered of them, *were* thirty and two thousand and two hundred. [22]Then the tribe of Benjamin: and the captain of the sons of Benjamin *shall be* Abidan the son of Gideoni. [23]And his host, and

those that were numbered of them, *were* thirty and five thousand and four hundred. [24]All that were numbered of the camp of Ephraim *were* an hundred thousand and eight thousand and an hundred, throughout their armies. And they shall go forward in the third rank. [25]The standard of the camp of Dan *shall be* on the north side by their armies: and the captain of the children of Dan *shall be* Ahiezer the son of Ammishaddai. [26]And his host, and those that were numbered of them, *were* threescore and two thousand and seven hundred. [27]And those that encamp by him *shall be* the tribe of Asher: and the captain of the children of Asher *shall be* Pagiel the son of Ocran. [28]And his host, and those that were numbered of them, *were* forty and one thousand and five hundred. [29]Then the tribe of Naphtali: and the captain of the children of

---

Devotional Moment
•
Obedience

2:34 With the results of the census close at hand, God organized Moses and the tribal leaders. He told them where and how to camp under the banners and standards of each tribe. This also determined the way that they set out on their continuing journey, obeying the God who had first brought them out of Egypt. Obedience to God must be foundational both at home and in the way each of us sets out into the world each day. Is your home a refuge where listening to and following God is the rule rather than the exception? Do your children see you applying this same rule of life in your dealings at work, at church, in your extended family, and in the community? Remember, God wants us to obey him so he can protect us.

---

[a] Reuel: also called, Deuel

Naphtali *shall be* Ahira the son of Enan. ³⁰And his host, and those that were numbered of them, *were* fifty and three thousand and four hundred. ³¹All they that were numbered in the camp of Dan *were* an hundred thousand and fifty and seven thousand and six hundred. They shall go hindmost with their standards. ³²These *are* those which were numbered of the children of Israel by the house of their fathers: all those that were numbered of the camps throughout their hosts *were* six hundred thousand and three thousand and five hundred and fifty. ³³But the Levites were not numbered among the children of Israel; as the LORD commanded Moses. ³⁴And the children of Israel did according to all that the LORD commanded Moses: so they pitched by their standards, and so they set forward, every one after their families, according to the house of their fathers.

3

¹These also *are* the generations of Aaron and Moses in the day *that* the LORD spake with Moses in mount Sinai. ²And these *are* the names of the sons of Aaron; Nadab the firstborn, and Abihu, Eleazar, and Ithamar. ³These *are* the names of the sons of Aaron, the priests which were anointed, whom he consecrated to minister in the priest's office. ⁴And Nadab and Abihu died before the LORD, when they offered strange fire before the LORD, in the wilderness of Sinai, and they had no children: and Eleazar and Ithamar ministered in the priest's office in the sight of Aaron their father. ⁵And the LORD spake unto Moses, saying, ⁶Bring the tribe of Levi near, and present them before Aaron

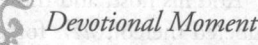

Devotional Moment
•
The Approachable God

3:10 Only Aaron and his sons served as priests—anyone else even entering the inner sanctuary had to be put to death, according to God's commandment. Though we worship the same all-powerful God, now each one of us *can* approach him without fear of punishment. The New Testament tells us we may walk into the very Holy of Holies because of the blood of Jesus (Heb. 10:19). In your prayers this week, thank God for welcoming us.

the priest, that they may minister unto him. ⁷And they shall keep his charge, and the charge of the whole congregation before the tabernacle of the congregation, to do the service of the tabernacle. ⁸And they shall keep all the instruments of the tabernacle of the congregation, and the charge of the children of Israel, to do the service of the tabernacle. ⁹And thou shalt give the Levites unto Aaron and to his sons: they *are* wholly given unto him out of the children of Israel. ¹⁰And thou shalt appoint Aaron and his sons, and they shall wait on their priest's office: and the stranger that cometh nigh shall be put to death. ¹¹And the LORD spake unto Moses, saying, ¹²And I, behold, I have taken the Levites from among the children of Israel instead of all the firstborn that openeth the matrix among the children of Israel: therefore the Levites shall be mine; ¹³Because all the firstborn *are* mine; *for* on the day that I smote all the firstborn in the land of Egypt I hallowed unto me all the firstborn in Israel, both man and beast: mine shall they be: I *am* the LORD. ¹⁴And the LORD spake unto

Moses in the wilderness of Sinai, saying, [15]Number the children of Levi after the house of their fathers, by their families: every male from a month old and upward shalt thou number them. [16]And Moses numbered them according to the word[a] of the LORD, as he was commanded. [17]And these were the sons of Levi by their names; Gershon, and Kohath, and Merari. [18]And these *are* the names of the sons of Gershon by their families; Libni, and Shimei. [19]And the sons of Kohath by their families; Amram, and Izehar, Hebron, and Uzziel. [20]And the sons of Merari by their families; Mahli, and Mushi. These *are* the families of the Levites according to the house of their fathers. [21]Of Gershon *was* the family of the Libnites, and the family of the Shimites: these *are* the families of the Gershonites. [22]Those that were numbered of them, according to the number of all the males, from a month old and upward, *even* those that were numbered of them *were* seven thousand and five hundred. [23]The families of the Gershonites shall pitch behind the tabernacle westward. [24]And the chief of the house of the father of the Gershonites *shall be* Eliasaph the son of Lael. [25]And the charge of the sons of Gershon in the tabernacle of the congregation *shall be* the tabernacle, and the tent, the covering thereof, and the hanging for the door of the tabernacle of the congregation, [26]And the hangings of the court, and the curtain for the door of the court, which *is* by the tabernacle, and by the altar round about, and the cords of it for all the service thereof. [27]And of Kohath *was* the family of the Amramites, and the family of the Izeharites, and the family of the Hebronites, and the family of the Uzzielites: these *are* the families of the Kohathites. [28]In the number of all the males, from a month old and upward, *were* eight thousand and six hundred, keeping the charge of the sanctuary. [29]The families of the sons of Kohath shall pitch on the side of the tabernacle southward. [30]And the chief of the house of the father of the families of the Kohathites *shall be* Elizaphan the son of Uzziel. [31]And their charge *shall be* the ark, and the table, and the candlestick, and the altars, and the vessels of the sanctuary wherewith they minister, and the hanging, and all the service thereof. [32]And Eleazar the son of Aaron the priest *shall be* chief over the chief of Levites, *and have* the oversight of them that keep the charge of the sanctuary. [33]Of Merari *was* the family of the Mahlites, and the family of the Mushites: these *are* the families of Merari. [34]And those that were numbered of them, according to the number of all the males, from a month old and upward, *were* six thousand and two hundred. [35]And the chief of the house of the father of the families of Merari *was* Zuriel the son of Abihail: *these* shall pitch on the side of the tabernacle northward. [36]And *under* the custody and charge of the sons of Merari *shall be* the boards of the tabernacle, and the bars thereof, and the pillars thereof, and the sockets thereof, and all the vessels thereof, and all that serveth thereto, [37]And the pillars of the court round about, and their sockets, and their pins,

---

[a] word: Heb. mouth

and their cords. ³⁸But those that encamp before the tabernacle toward the east, *even* before the tabernacle of the congregation eastward, *shall be* Moses, and Aaron and his sons, keeping the charge of the sanctuary for the charge of the children of Israel; and the stranger that cometh nigh shall be put to death. ³⁹All that were numbered of the Levites, which Moses and Aaron numbered at the commandment of the LORD, throughout their families, all the males from a month old and upward, *were* twenty and two thousand.

⁴⁰And the LORD said unto Moses, Number all the firstborn of the males of the children of Israel from a month old and upward, and take the number of their names. ⁴¹And thou shalt take the Levites for me (I *am* the LORD) instead of all the firstborn among the children of Israel; and the cattle of the Levites instead of all the firstlings among the cattle of the children of Israel. ⁴²And Moses numbered, as the LORD commanded him, all the firstborn among the children of Israel. ⁴³And all the firstborn males by the number of names, from a month old and upward, of those that were numbered of them, were twenty and two thousand two hundred and threescore and thirteen. ⁴⁴And the LORD spake unto Moses, saying, ⁴⁵Take the Levites instead of all the firstborn among the children of Israel, and the cattle of the Levites instead of their cattle; and the Levites shall be mine: I *am* the LORD. ⁴⁶And for those that are to be redeemed of the two hundred and threescore and thirteen of the firstborn of the children of Israel, which are more than the Levites; ⁴⁷Thou shalt even take five

shekels apiece by the poll, after the shekel of the sanctuary shalt thou take *them*: (the shekel *is* twenty gerahs:) ⁴⁸And thou shalt give the money, wherewith the odd number of them is to be redeemed, unto Aaron and to his sons. ⁴⁹And Moses took the redemption money of them that were over and above them that were redeemed by the Levites: ⁵⁰Of the firstborn of the children of Israel took he the money; a thousand three hundred and threescore and five *shekels*, after the shekel of the sanctuary: ⁵¹And Moses gave the money of them that were redeemed unto Aaron and to his sons, according to the word of the LORD, as the LORD commanded Moses.

4

¹And the LORD spake unto Moses and unto Aaron, saying, ²Take the sum of the sons of Kohath from among the sons of Levi, after their families, by the house of their fathers, ³From thirty years old and upward even until fifty years old, all that enter into the host, to do the work in the tabernacle of the congregation. ⁴This *shall be* the service of the sons of Kohath in the tabernacle of the congregation, *about* the most holy things: ⁵And when the camp setteth forward, Aaron shall come, and his sons, and they shall take down the covering vail, and cover the ark of testimony with it: ⁶And shall put thereon the covering of badgers' skins, and shall spread over *it* a cloth wholly of blue, and shall put in the staves thereof. ⁷And upon the table of shewbread they shall spread a cloth of blue, and put thereon the dishes, and the spoons, and the bowls, and coversᵃ to

---

ᵃ cover . . . : or, pour out withal

cover withal: and the continual bread shall be thereon: [8]And they shall spread upon them a cloth of scarlet, and cover the same with a covering of badgers' skins, and shall put in the staves thereof. [9]And they shall take a cloth of blue, and cover the candlestick of the light, and his lamps, and his tongs, and his snuff-dishes, and all the oil vessels thereof, wherewith they minister unto it: [10]And they shall put it and all the vessels thereof within a covering of badgers' skins, and shall put *it* upon a bar. [11]And upon the golden altar they shall spread a cloth of blue, and cover it with a covering of badgers' skins, and shall put to the staves thereof: [12]And they shall take all the instruments of ministry, wherewith they minister in the sanctuary, and put *them* in a cloth of blue, and cover them with a covering of badgers' skins, and shall put *them* on a bar: [13]And they shall take away the ashes from the altar, and spread a purple cloth thereon: [14]And they shall put upon it all the vessels thereof, wherewith they minister about it, *even* the censers, the flesh-hooks, and the shovels, and the basons[b], all the vessels of the altar; and they shall spread upon it a covering of badgers' skins, and put to the staves of it. [15]And when Aaron and his sons have made an end of covering the sanctuary, and all the vessels of the sanctuary, as the camp is to set forward; after that, the sons of Kohath shall come to bear *it*: but they shall not touch *any* holy thing, lest they die. These *things are* the burden of the sons of Kohath in the tabernacle of the congregation. [16]And to the office of Eleazar the son of Aaron the priest *per-taineth* the oil for the light, and the sweet incense, and the daily meat offer-ing, and the anointing oil, *and* the over-sight of all the tabernacle, and of all that therein *is*, in the sanctuary, and in the vessels thereof. [17]And the LORD spake unto Moses and unto Aaron, saying, [18]Cut ye not off the tribe of the families of the Kohathites from among the Levites: [19]But thus do unto them, that they may live, and not die, when they approach unto the most holy things: Aaron and his sons shall go in, and ap-point them every one to his service and to his burden: [20]But they shall not go in to see when the holy things are covered, lest they die.

[21]And the LORD spake unto Moses, saying, [22]Take also the sum of the sons of Gershon, throughout the houses of their fathers, by their families; [23]From thirty years old and upward un-til fifty years old shalt thou number them; all that enter in to perform[c] the service, to do the work in the taberna-cle of the congregation. [24]This *is* the ser-vice of the families of the Gershonites, to serve, and for burdens[d]: [25]And they shall bear the curtains of the tabernacle, and the tabernacle of the congregation, his covering, and the covering of the badgers' skins that *is* above upon it, and the hanging for the door of the taber-nacle of the congregation, [26]And the hangings of the court, and the hanging for the door of the gate of the court, which *is* by the tabernacle and by the

---

[b] basons: or, bowls
[c] to perform . . . : Heb. to war the warfare
[d] burdens: or, carriage

altar round about, and their cords, and all the instruments of their service, and all that is made for them: so shall they serve. ²⁷At the appointment᷾ of Aaron and his sons shall be all the service of the sons of the Gershonites, in all their burdens, and in all their service: and ye shall appoint unto them in charge all their burdens. ²⁸This *is* the service of the families of the sons of Gershon in the tabernacle of the congregation: and their charge *shall be* under the hand of Ithamar the son of Aaron the priest. ²⁹As for the sons of Merari, thou shalt number them after their families, by the house of their fathers; ³⁰From thirty years old and upward even unto fifty years old shalt thou number them, every one that entereth into the service᷾, to do the work of the tabernacle of the congregation. ³¹And this *is* the charge of their burden, according to all their service in the tabernacle of the congrega-

tion; the boards of the tabernacle, and the bars thereof, and the pillars thereof, and sockets thereof, ³²And the pillars of the court round about, and their sockets, and their pins, and their cords, with all their instruments, and with all their service: and by name ye shall reckon the instruments of the charge of their burden. ³³This *is* the service of the families of the sons of Merari, according to all their service, in the tabernacle of the congregation, under the hand of Ithamar the son of Aaron the priest.

³⁴And Moses and Aaron and the chief of the congregation numbered the sons of the Kohathites after their families, and after the house of their fathers, ³⁵From thirty years old and upward even unto fifty years old, every one that entereth into the service, for the work in the tabernacle of the congregation: ³⁶And those that were numbered of them by their families were two thousand seven hundred and fifty. ³⁷These *were* they that were numbered of the families of the Kohathites, all that might do service in the tabernacle of the congregation, which Moses and Aaron did number according to the commandment of the LORD by the hand of Moses. ³⁸And those that were numbered of the sons of Gershon, throughout their families, and by the house of their fathers, ³⁹From thirty years old and upward even unto fifty years old, every one that entereth into the service, for the work in the tabernacle of the congregation, ⁴⁰Even those that were numbered of them, throughout their families, by the house of their fathers, were two thousand and

---

᷾ appointment: Heb. mouth
᷾ service: Heb. warfare

six hundred and thirty. ⁴¹These *are* they that were numbered of the families of the sons of Gershon, of all that might do service in the tabernacle of the congregation, whom Moses and Aaron did number according to the commandment of the LORD. ⁴²And those that were numbered of the families of the sons of Merari, throughout their families, by the house of their fathers, ⁴³From thirty years old and upward even unto fifty years old, every one that entereth into the service, for the work in the tabernacle of the congregation, ⁴⁴Even those that were numbered of them after their families, were three thousand and two hundred. ⁴⁵These *be* those that were numbered of the families of the sons of Merari, whom Moses and Aaron numbered according to the word of the LORD by the hand of Moses. ⁴⁶All those that were numbered of the Levites, whom Moses and Aaron and the chief of Israel numbered, after their families, and after the house of their fathers, ⁴⁷From thirty years old and upward even unto fifty years old, every one that came to do the service of the ministry, and the service of the burden in the tabernacle of the congregation, ⁴⁸Even those that were numbered of them, were eight thousand and five hundred and fourscore. ⁴⁹According to the commandment of the LORD they were numbered by the hand of Moses, every one according to his service, and according to his burden: thus were they numbered of him, as the LORD commanded Moses.

5

¹And the LORD spake unto Moses, saying, ²Command the children of Israel, that they put out of the camp

every leper, and every one that hath an issue, and whosoever is defiled by the dead: ³Both male and female shall ye put out, without the camp shall ye put them; that they defile not their camps, in the midst whereof I dwell. ⁴And the children of Israel did so, and put them out without the camp: as the LORD spake unto Moses, so did the children of Israel. ⁵And the LORD spake unto Moses, saying, ⁶Speak unto the children of Israel, When a man or woman shall commit any sin that men commit, to do a trespass against the LORD, and that person be guilty; ⁷Then they shall confess their sin which they have done: and he shall recompense his trespass with the principal thereof, and add unto it the fifth *part* thereof, and give *it* unto *him* against whom he hath trespassed. ⁸But if the man have no kinsman to recompense the trespass unto, let the trespass be recompensed unto the LORD, *even* to the priest; beside the ram of the atonement, whereby an atonement shall be made for him. ⁹And every offering[a] of all the holy things of the children of Israel, which they bring unto the priest, shall be his. [10]And every man's hallowed things shall be his: whatsoever any man giveth the priest, it shall be his.

[11]And the LORD spake unto Moses, saying, [12]Speak unto the children of Israel, and say unto them, If any man's wife go aside, and commit a trespass against him, [13]And a man lie with her carnally, and it be hid from the eyes of her husband, and be kept close, and she be defiled, and *there be* no witness against her, neither she be taken *with the manner*; [14]And the spirit of jealousy come upon him, and he be jealous of his wife, and she be defiled: or if the spirit of jealousy come upon him, and he be jealous of his wife, and she be not defiled: [15]Then shall the man bring his wife unto the priest, and he shall bring her offering for her, the tenth *part* of an ephah of barley meal; he shall pour no oil upon it, nor put frankincense thereon; for it *is* an offering of jealousy, an offering of memorial, bringing iniquity to remembrance. [16]And the priest shall bring her near, and set her before the LORD: [17]And the priest shall take holy water in an earthen vessel; and of the dust that is in the floor of the tabernacle the priest shall take, and put *it* into the water: [18]And the priest shall set the woman before the LORD, and uncover the woman's head, and put the offering of memorial in her hands, which *is* the jealousy offering: and the priest shall have in his hand the bitter water that causeth the curse: [19]And the priest shall charge her by an oath, and say unto the woman, If no man have lain with thee, and if thou hast not gone aside to uncleanness *with another* instead of thy husband, be thou free from this bitter water that causeth the curse: [20]But if thou hast gone aside *to another* instead of thy husband, and if thou be defiled, and some man have lain with thee beside thine husband: [21]Then the priest shall charge the woman with an oath of cursing, and the priest shall say unto the woman, The LORD make thee a curse and an oath among thy people, when the LORD doth make thy thigh to rot[b], and thy belly to swell; [22]And this water that causeth the curse shall go into thy bowels, to make *thy* belly to swell, and *thy* thigh to rot: And the woman shall say, Amen, amen. [23]And the priest shall write these curses in a book, and he shall blot *them* out with the bitter water: [24]And he shall cause the woman to drink the bitter water that causeth the curse: and the water that causeth the curse shall enter into her, *and become* bitter. [25]Then the priest shall take the jealousy offering out of the woman's hand, and shall wave the offering before the LORD, and offer it upon the altar: [26]And the priest shall take an handful of the offering, *even* the memorial thereof, and burn *it* upon the altar, and afterward shall cause the woman to drink the water. [27]And when he hath made her to drink the water, then it shall come to pass, *that*, if she be defiled, and have done trespass against her husband, that the

---

[a] offering: or, heave offering
[b] rot: Heb. fall

water that causeth the curse shall enter into her, *and become* bitter, and her belly shall swell, and her thigh shall rot: and the woman shall be a curse among her people. ²⁸And if the woman be not defiled, but be clean; then she shall be free, and shall conceive seed. ²⁹This *is* the law of jealousies, when a wife goeth aside *to another* instead of her husband, and is defiled; ³⁰Or when the spirit of jealousy cometh upon him, and he be jealous over his wife, and shall set the woman before the LORD, and the priest shall execute upon her all this law. ³¹Then shall the man be guiltless from iniquity, and this woman shall bear her iniquity.

6

¹And the LORD spake unto Moses, saying, ²Speak unto the children of Israel, and say unto them, When either man or woman shall separate *themselves* to vow a vow of a Nazarite, to separate[a] *themselves* unto the LORD: ³He shall separate *himself* from wine and strong drink, and shall drink no vinegar of wine, or vinegar of strong drink, neither shall he drink any liquor of grapes, nor eat moist grapes, or dried. ⁴All the days of his separation[b] shall he eat nothing that is made of the vine tree, from the kernels even to the husk. ⁵All the days of the vow of his separation there shall no razor come upon his head: until the days be fulfilled, in the which he separateth *himself* unto the LORD, he shall be holy, *and* shall let the locks of the hair

---

Devotional Moment
•
Devotion to God

6:1ff. God instituted the Nazarite vow for people who wanted to devote some time exclusively to serving him. This vow could be taken for as few as thirty days or for a lifetime. It was voluntary, with one exception—parents could take the vow for their young children, making them Nazarites for life. The purpose of the Nazarite vow was to raise up a group of leaders devoted completely to God. Though we don't take Nazarite vows today, and rarely are children dedicated to full-time service before birth, we can learn from the intense commitment that these families had. Do our children understand complete devotion to God?

---

of his head grow. ⁶All the days that he separateth *himself* unto the LORD he shall come at no dead body. ⁷He shall not make himself unclean for his father, or for his mother, for his brother, or for his sister, when they die: because the consecration[c] of his God *is* upon his head. ⁸All the days of his separation he *is* holy unto the LORD. ⁹And if any man die very suddenly by him, and he hath defiled the head of his consecration; then he shall shave his head in the day of his cleansing, on the seventh day shall he shave it. ¹⁰And on the eighth day he shall bring two turtles, or two young pigeons, to the priest, to the door of the tabernacle of the congregation: ¹¹And the priest shall offer the one for a sin offering, and the other for a burnt offering, and make an atonement for him, for that he sinned by the dead, and

---

[a] to separate . . . : or, to make themselves Nazarites
[b] separation: or, Nazariteship
[c] consecration: Heb. separation

shall hallow his head that same day. [12]And he shall consecrate unto the LORD the days of his separation, and shall bring a lamb of the first year for a trespass offering: but the days that were before shall be lost[d], because his separation was defiled. [13]And this *is* the law of the Nazarite, when the days of his separation are fulfilled: he shall be brought unto the door of the tabernacle of the congregation: [14]And he shall offer his offering unto the LORD, one he lamb of the first year without blemish for a burnt offering, and one ewe lamb of the first year without blemish for a sin offering, and one ram without blemish for peace offerings, [15]And a basket of unleavened bread, cakes of fine flour mingled with oil, and wafers of unleavened bread anointed with oil, and their meat offering, and their drink offerings. [16]And the priest shall bring *them* before the LORD, and shall offer his sin offering, and his burnt offering: [17]And he shall offer the ram *for* a sacrifice of peace offerings unto the LORD, with the basket of unleavened bread: the priest shall offer also his meat offering, and his drink offering. [18]And the Nazarite shall shave the head of his separation *at* the door of the tabernacle of the congregation, and shall take the hair of the head of his separation, and put *it* in the fire which *is* under the sacrifice of the peace offerings. [19]And the priest shall take the sodden shoulder of the ram, and one unleavened cake out of the basket, and one unleavened wafer, and shall put *them* upon the hands of the

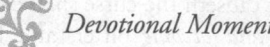

Devotional Moment

Blessing Children

6:24-26 The Israelites had followed God's words to the letter; the Tabernacle was set up and ready for dedication. God wanted to bless his people, and he gave words to Moses, who in turn entrusted them to the priests, Aaron and his sons. The beautiful blessing has endured through the millennia: "The Lord bless thee, and keep thee. . . ." As a parent or other special adult in a young person's life, you can bless your children as well. Consider making this passage (or another that's meaningful to you) a regular part of mealtime devotions or bedtime. For older children, writing the words in a letter may be a more natural way to communicate your care and your hopes.

Nazarite, after *the hair of* his separation is shaven: [20]And the priest shall wave them *for* a wave offering before the LORD: this *is* holy for the priest, with the wave breast and heave shoulder: and after that the Nazarite may drink wine. [21]This *is* the law of the Nazarite who hath vowed, *and of* his offering unto the LORD for his separation, beside *that* that his hand shall get: according to the vow which he vowed, so he must do after the law of his separation.

[22]And the LORD spake unto Moses, saying, [23]Speak unto Aaron and unto his sons, saying, On this wise ye shall bless the children of Israel, saying unto them, [24]The LORD bless thee, and keep thee: [25]The LORD make his face shine upon thee, and be gracious unto thee: [26]The LORD lift up his countenance upon thee, and give thee peace. [27]And they shall put my name

[d] be lost: Heb. fall

upon the children of Israel; and I will bless them.

7

¹And it came to pass on the day that Moses had fully set up the tabernacle, and had anointed it, and sanctified it, and all the instruments thereof, both the altar and all the vessels thereof, and had anointed them, and sanctified them; ²That the princes of Israel, heads of the house of their fathers, who *were* the princes of the tribes, and were over them that were numbered, offered: ³And they brought their offering before the LORD, six covered wagons, and twelve oxen; a wagon for two of the princes, and for each one an ox: and they brought them before the tabernacle. ⁴And the LORD spake unto Moses, saying, ⁵Take *it* of them, that they may be to do the service of the tabernacle of the congregation; and thou shalt give them unto the Levites, to every man according to his service. ⁶And Moses took the wagons and the oxen, and gave them unto the Levites. ⁷Two wagons and four oxen he gave unto the sons of Gershon, according to their service: ⁸And four wagons and eight oxen he gave unto the sons of Merari, according unto their service, under the hand of Ithamar the son of Aaron the priest. ⁹But unto the sons of Kohath he gave none: because the service of the sanctuary belonging unto them *was that* they should bear upon their shoulders.

¹⁰And the princes offered for dedicating of the altar in the day that it was anointed, even the princes offered their offering before the altar. ¹¹And the LORD said unto Moses, They shall offer their offering, each prince on his day, for the dedicating of the altar. ¹²And he that offered his offering the first day was Nahshon the son of Amminadab, of the tribe of Judah: ¹³And his offering *was* one silver charger, the weight thereof *was* an hundred and thirty *shekels*, one silver bowl of seventy shekels, after the shekel of the sanctuary; both of them *were* full of fine flour mingled with oil for a meat offering: ¹⁴One spoon of ten *shekels* of gold, full of incense: ¹⁵One young bullock, one ram, one lamb of the first year, for a burnt offering: ¹⁶One kid of the goats for a sin offering: ¹⁷And for a sacrifice of peace offerings, two oxen, five rams, five he goats, five lambs of the first year: this *was* the offering of Nahshon the son of Amminadab. ¹⁸On the second day Nethaneel the son of Zuar, prince of Issachar, did offer: ¹⁹He offered *for* his offering one silver charger, the weight whereof *was* an hundred and thirty *shekels*, one silver bowl of seventy shekels, after the shekel of the sanctuary; both of them full of fine flour mingled with oil for a meat offering: ²⁰One spoon of gold of ten *shekels*, full of incense: ²¹One young bullock, one ram, one lamb of the first year, for a burnt offering: ²²One kid of the goats for a sin offering: ²³And for a sacrifice of peace offerings, two oxen, five rams, five he goats, five lambs of the first year: this *was* the offering of Nethaneel the son of Zuar. ²⁴On the third day Eliab the son of Helon, prince of the children of Zebulun, *did offer:* ²⁵His offering *was* one silver charger, the weight whereof *was* an hundred and thirty *shekels*, one silver bowl of seventy shekels, after the shekel of the sanctuary; both of them full of fine flour mingled with oil for a meat

offering: ²⁶One golden spoon of ten *shekels*, full of incense: ²⁷One young bullock, one ram, one lamb of the first year, for a burnt offering: ²⁸One kid of the goats for a sin offering: ²⁹And for a sacrifice of peace offerings, two oxen, five rams, five he goats, five lambs of the first year: this *was* the offering of Eliab the son of Helon. ³⁰On the fourth day Elizur the son of Shedeur, prince of the children of Reuben, *did offer*: ³¹His offering *was* one silver charger of the weight of an hundred and thirty *shekels*, one silver bowl of seventy shekels, after the shekel of the sanctuary; both of them full of fine flour mingled with oil for a meat offering: ³²One golden spoon of ten *shekels*, full of incense: ³³One young bullock, one ram, one lamb of the first year, for a burnt offering: ³⁴One kid of the goats for a sin offering: ³⁵And for a sacrifice of peace offerings, two oxen, five rams, five he goats, five lambs of the first year: this *was* the offering of Elizur the son of Shedeur. ³⁶On the fifth day Shelumiel the son of Zurishaddai, prince of the children of Simeon, *did offer*: ³⁷His offering *was* one silver charger, the weight whereof *was* an hundred and thirty *shekels*, one silver bowl of seventy shekels, after the shekel of the sanctuary; both of them full of fine flour mingled with oil for a meat offering: ³⁸One golden spoon of ten *shekels*, full of incense: ³⁹One young bullock, one ram, one lamb of the first year, for a burnt offering: ⁴⁰One kid of the goats for a sin offering: ⁴¹And for a sacrifice of peace offerings, two oxen, five rams, five he goats, five lambs of the first year: this *was* the offering of Shelumiel the son of Zurishaddai. ⁴²On the sixth day Eliasaph the son of Deuel,

prince of the children of Gad, *offered*: ⁴³His offering *was* one silver charger of the weight of an hundred and thirty *shekels*, a silver bowl of seventy shekels, after the shekel of the sanctuary; both of them full of fine flour mingled with oil for a meat offering: ⁴⁴One golden spoon of ten *shekels*, full of incense: ⁴⁵One young bullock, one ram, one lamb of the first year, for a burnt offering: ⁴⁶One kid of the goats for a sin offering: ⁴⁷And for a sacrifice of peace offerings, two oxen, five rams, five he goats, five lambs of the first year: this *was* the offering of Eliasaph the son of Deuel. ⁴⁸On the seventh day Elishama the son of Ammihud, prince of the children of Ephraim, *offered*: ⁴⁹His offering *was* one silver charger, the weight whereof *was* an hundred and thirty *shekels*, one silver bowl of seventy shekels, after the shekel of the sanctuary; both of them full of fine flour mingled with oil for a meat offering: ⁵⁰One golden spoon of ten *shekels*, full of incense: ⁵¹One young bullock, one ram, one lamb of the first year, for a burnt offering: ⁵²One kid of the goats for a sin offering: ⁵³And for a sacrifice of peace offerings, two oxen, five rams, five he goats, five lambs of the first year: this *was* the offering of Elishama the son of Ammihud. ⁵⁴On the eighth day *offered* Gamaliel the son of Pedahzur, prince of the children of Manasseh: ⁵⁵His offering *was* one silver charger of the weight of an hundred and thirty *shekels*, one silver bowl of seventy shekels, after the shekel of the sanctuary; both of them full of fine flour mingled with oil for a meat offering: ⁵⁶One golden spoon of ten *shekels*, full of incense: ⁵⁷One young bullock, one ram, one lamb of the first year, for a burnt offering: ⁵⁸One kid of the goats for a sin offering: ⁵⁹And for a sacrifice of peace offerings, two oxen, five rams, five he goats, five lambs of the first year: this *was* the offering of Gamaliel the son of Pedahzur. ⁶⁰On the ninth day Abidan the son of Gideoni, prince of the children of Benjamin, *offered*: ⁶¹His offering *was* one silver charger, the weight whereof *was* an hundred and thirty *shekels*, one silver bowl of seventy shekels, after the shekel of the sanctuary; both of them full of fine flour mingled with oil for a meat offering: ⁶²One golden spoon of ten *shekels*, full of incense: ⁶³One young bullock, one ram, one lamb of the first year, for a burnt offering: ⁶⁴One kid of the goats for a sin offering: ⁶⁵And for a sacrifice of peace offerings, two oxen, five rams, five he goats, five lambs of the first year: this *was* the offering of Abidan the son of Gideoni. ⁶⁶On the tenth day Ahiezer the son of Ammishaddai, prince of the children of Dan, *offered*: ⁶⁷His offering *was* one silver charger, the weight whereof *was* an hundred and thirty *shekels*, one silver bowl of seventy shekels, after the shekel of the sanctuary; both of them full of fine flour mingled with oil for a meat offering: ⁶⁸One golden spoon of ten *shekels*, full of incense: ⁶⁹One young bullock, one ram, one lamb of the first year, for a burnt offering: ⁷⁰One kid of the goats for a sin offering: ⁷¹And for a sacrifice of peace offerings, two oxen, five rams, five he goats, five lambs of the first year: this *was* the offering of Ahiezer the son of Ammishaddai. ⁷²On the eleventh day Pagiel the son of Ocran, prince of the children of Asher, *offered*: ⁷³His offering *was* one silver

charger, the weight whereof *was* an hundred and thirty *shekels*, one silver bowl of seventy shekels, after the shekel of the sanctuary; both of them full of fine flour mingled with oil for a meat offering: ⁷⁴One golden spoon of ten *shekels*, full of incense: ⁷⁵One young bullock, one ram, one lamb of the first year, for a burnt offering: ⁷⁶One kid of the goats for a sin offering: ⁷⁷And for a sacrifice of peace offerings, two oxen, five rams, five he goats, five lambs of the first year: this *was* the offering of Pagiel the son of Ocran. ⁷⁸On the twelfth day Ahira the son of Enan, prince of the children of Naphtali, *offered*: ⁷⁹His offering *was* one silver charger, the weight whereof *was* an hundred and thirty *shekels*, one silver bowl of seventy shekels, after the shekel of the sanctuary; both of them full of fine flour mingled with oil for a meat offering: ⁸⁰One golden spoon of ten *shekels*, full of incense: ⁸¹One young bullock, one ram, one lamb of the first year, for a burnt offering: ⁸²One kid of the goats for a sin offering: ⁸³And for a sacrifice of peace offerings, two oxen, five rams, five he goats, five lambs of the first year: this *was* the offering of Ahira the son of Enan. ⁸⁴This *was* the dedication of the altar, in the day when it was anointed, by the princes of Israel: twelve chargers of silver, twelve silver bowls, twelve spoons of gold: ⁸⁵Each charger of silver *weighing* an hundred and thirty *shekels*, each bowl seventy: all the silver vessels *weighed* two thousand and four hundred *shekels*, after the shekel of the sanctuary: ⁸⁶The golden spoons *were* twelve, full of incense, *weighing* ten *shekels* apiece, after the shekel of the sanctuary: all the gold of the spoons *was* an hundred and twenty *shekels.* [87]All the oxen for the burnt offering *were* twelve bullocks, the rams twelve, the lambs of the first year twelve, with their meat offering: and the kids of the goats for sin offering twelve. [88]And all the oxen for the sacrifice of the peace offerings *were* twenty and four bullocks, the rams sixty, the he goats sixty, the lambs of the first year sixty. This *was* the dedication of the altar, after that it was anointed. [89]And when Moses was gone into the tabernacle of the congregation to speak with him [a], then he heard the voice of one speaking unto him from off the mercy seat that *was* upon the ark of testimony, from between the two cherubims: and he spake unto him.

8

[1]And the LORD spake unto Moses, saying, [2]Speak unto Aaron, and say unto him, When thou lightest the lamps, the seven lamps shall give light over against the candlestick. [3]And Aaron did so; he lighted the lamps thereof over against the candlestick, as the LORD commanded Moses. [4]And this work of the candlestick *was of* beaten gold, unto the shaft thereof, unto the flowers thereof, *was* beaten work: according unto the pattern which the LORD had shewed Moses, so he made the candlestick.

[5]And the LORD spake unto Moses, saying, [6]Take the Levites from among the children of Israel, and cleanse them. [7]And thus shalt thou do unto them, to cleanse them: Sprinkle water of purifying upon them, and let them shave [a] all their flesh, and let them wash their clothes, and *so* make themselves clean. [8]Then let them take a young bullock with his meat offering, *even* fine flour mingled with oil, and another young bullock shalt thou take for a sin offering. [9]And thou shalt bring the Levites before the tabernacle of the congregation: and thou shalt gather the whole assembly of the children of Israel together: [10]And thou shalt bring the Levites before the LORD: and the children of Israel shall put their hands upon the Levites: [11]And Aaron shall offer [b] the Levites before the LORD *for* an offering of the children of Israel, that they may execute the service of the LORD. [12]And the Levites shall lay their hands upon the heads of the bullocks: and thou shalt offer the one *for* a sin offering, and the other *for* a burnt offering, unto the LORD, to make an atonement for the Levites. [13]And thou shalt set the Levites before Aaron, and before his sons, and offer them *for* an offering unto the LORD. [14]Thus shalt thou separate the Levites from among the children of Israel: and the Levites shall be mine. [15]And after that shall the Levites go in to do the service of the tabernacle of the congregation: and thou shalt cleanse them, and offer them *for* an offering. [16]For they *are* wholly given unto me from among the children of Israel; instead of such as open every womb, *even* *instead of* the firstborn of all the children of Israel, have I taken them unto me.

---

[a] with him: that is, with God
[a] let them shave . . . : Heb. let them cause a razor to pass over, etc
[b] offer: Heb. wave

[17]For all the firstborn of the children of Israel *are* mine, *both* man and beast: on the day that I smote every firstborn in the land of Egypt I sanctified them for myself. [18]And I have taken the Levites for all the firstborn of the children of Israel. [19]And I have given the Levites *as* a gift[c] to Aaron and to his sons from among the children of Israel, to do the service of the children of Israel in the tabernacle of the congregation, and to make an atonement for the children of Israel: that there be no plague among the children of Israel, when the children of Israel come nigh unto the sanctuary. [20]And Moses, and Aaron, and all the congregation of the children of Israel, did to the Levites according unto all that the LORD commanded Moses concerning the Levites, so did the children of Israel unto them. [21]And the Levites were purified, and they washed their clothes; and Aaron offered them *as* an offering before the LORD; and Aaron made an atonement for them to cleanse them. [22]And after that went the Levites in to do their service in the tabernacle of the congregation before Aaron, and before his sons: as the LORD had commanded Moses concerning the Levites, so did they unto them. [23]And the LORD spake unto Moses, saying, [24]This *is it* that *belongeth* unto the Levites: from twenty and five years old and upward they shall go in to wait upon the service of the tabernacle of the congregation: [25]And from the age of fifty years they shall cease[d] waiting upon the service *thereof,* and shall serve

no more: [26]But shall minister with their brethren in the tabernacle of the congregation, to keep the charge, and shall do no service. Thus shalt thou do unto the Levites touching their charge.

9

[1]And the LORD spake unto Moses in the wilderness of Sinai, in the first month of the second year after they were come out of the land of Egypt, saying, [2]Let the children of Israel also keep the passover at his appointed season. [3]In the fourteenth day of this month, at even[a], ye shall keep it in his appointed season: according to all the rites of it, and according to all the ceremonies thereof, shall ye keep it. [4]And Moses spake unto the children of Israel, that they should keep the passover. [5]And they kept the passover on the fourteenth day of the first month at even in the wilderness of Sinai: according to all that the LORD commanded Moses, so did the children of Israel. [6]And there were certain men, who were defiled by the dead body of a man, that they could not keep the passover on that day: and they came before Moses and before Aaron on that day: [7]And those men said unto him, We *are* defiled by the dead body of a man: wherefore are we kept back, that we may not offer an offering of the LORD in his appointed season among the children of Israel? [8]And Moses said unto them, Stand still, and I will hear what the LORD will command concerning you. [9]And the LORD spake unto Moses,

---

[c] a gift: Heb. given
[d] cease . . . . : Heb. return from the warfare of the service
[a] at even: Heb. between the two evenings

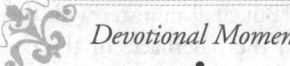

Devotional Moment

•

Compromising Faith

9:6-12 Two years out of Egypt, an issue arose over Passover. Some Israelites could not celebrate on the appointed day because they were ceremonially unclean, having touched a dead body. God directed Moses to have them— and those who had been away on a journey— celebrate it exactly one month later. God often graciously provides alternatives for us when we fail to meet his requirements. But just as some Israelites could perhaps have headed off the problem by staying away from a dead body for the appointed time or rescheduling a journey, we must avoid compromising situations as well. What Saturday activities make it more difficult to get to church the next day? What TV shows or reading material make it difficult to keep your thoughts pure? Know yourself, that you may better know the Lord.

saying, [10]Speak unto the children of Israel, saying, If any man of you or of your posterity shall be unclean by reason of a dead body, or *be* in a journey afar off, yet he shall keep the passover unto the LORD. [11]The fourteenth day of the second month at even they shall keep it, *and* eat it with unleavened bread and bitter *herbs.* [12]They shall leave none of it unto the morning, nor break any bone of it: according to all the ordinances of the passover they shall keep it. [13]But the man that *is* clean, and is not in a journey, and forbeareth to keep the passover, even the same soul shall be cut off from among his people: because he brought not the offering of the LORD in his appointed season, that man shall bear his sin. [14]And if a stranger shall sojourn among you, and will keep the passover unto the LORD; according to the ordinance of the passover, and according to the manner thereof, so shall

he do: ye shall have one ordinance, both for the stranger, and for him that was born in the land.

[15]And on the day that the tabernacle was reared up the cloud covered the tabernacle, *namely,* the tent of the testimony: and at even there was upon the tabernacle as it were the appearance of fire, until the morning. [16]So it was alway: the cloud covered it *by day,* and the appearance of fire by night. [17]And when the cloud was taken up from the tabernacle, then after that the children of Israel journeyed: and in the place where the cloud abode, there the children of Israel pitched their tents. [18]At the commandment of the LORD the children of Israel journeyed, and at the commandment of the LORD they pitched: as long as the cloud abode upon the tabernacle they rested in their tents. [19]And when the cloud tarried long upon the tabernacle many days, then the children of Israel kept the charge of the LORD, and journeyed not. [20]And *so* it was, when the cloud was a few days upon the tabernacle; according to the commandment of the LORD they abode in their tents, and according to the commandment of the LORD they journeyed. [21]And *so* it was, when the cloud abode from even unto the morning, and *that* the cloud was taken up in the morning, then they journeyed: whether *it was* by day or by night that the cloud was taken up, they journeyed. [22]Or *whether it were* two days, or a month, or a year, that the cloud tarried upon the tabernacle, remaining thereon, the children of Israel abode in their tents, and journeyed not: but when it was taken up, they journeyed. [23]At the commandment of the

LORD they rested in the tents, and at the commandment of the LORD they journeyed: they kept the charge of the LORD, at the commandment of the LORD by the hand of Moses.

10

¹And the LORD spake unto Moses, saying, ²Make thee two trumpets of silver; of a whole piece shalt thou make them: that thou mayest use them for the calling of the assembly, and for the journeying of the camps. ³And when they shall blow with them, all the assembly shall assemble themselves to thee at the door of the tabernacle of the congregation. ⁴And if they blow *but* with one *trumpet*, then the princes, *which are* heads of the thousands of Israel, shall gather themselves unto thee. ⁵When ye blow an alarm, then the camps that lie on the east parts shall go forward. ⁶When ye blow an alarm the second time, then the camps that lie on the south side shall take their journey: they shall blow an alarm for their journeys. ⁷But when the congregation is to be gathered together, ye shall blow, but ye shall not sound an alarm. ⁸And the sons of Aaron, the priests, shall blow with the trumpets; and they shall be to you for an ordinance for ever throughout your generations. ⁹And if ye go to war in your land against the enemy that oppresseth you, then ye shall blow an alarm with the trumpets; and ye shall be remembered before the LORD your God, and ye shall be saved from your enemies. ¹⁰Also in the day of your gladness, and in your solemn days, and in the beginnings of your months, ye shall blow with the trumpets over your burnt offerings, and over the sacrifices of your peace offerings; that they may be to you for a memorial before your God: I *am* the LORD your God.

¹¹And it came to pass on the twentieth *day* of the second month, in the second year, that the cloud was taken up from off the tabernacle of the testimony. ¹²And the children of Israel took their journeys out of the wilderness of Sinai; and the cloud rested in the wilderness of Paran. ¹³And they first took their journey according to the commandment of the LORD by the hand of Moses. ¹⁴In the first *place* went the standard of the camp of the children of Judah according to their armies: and over his host *was* Nahshon the son of Amminadab. ¹⁵And over the host of the tribe of the children of Issachar *was* Nethaneel the son of Zuar. ¹⁶And over the host of the tribe of the children of Zebulun *was* Eliab the son of Helon. ¹⁷And the tabernacle was taken down; and the sons of Gershon and the sons of Merari set forward, bearing the tabernacle. ¹⁸And the standard of the camp of Reuben set forward according to their armies: and over his host *was* Elizur the son of Shedeur. ¹⁹And over the host of the tribe of the children of Simeon *was* Shelumiel the son of Zurishaddai. ²⁰And over the host of the tribe of the children of Gad *was* Eliasaph the son of Deuel. ²¹And the Kohathites set forward, bearing the sanctuary: and *the other* did set up the tabernacle against they came. ²²And the standard of the camp of the children of Ephraim set forward according to their armies: and over his host *was* Elishama the son of Ammihud. ²³And over the host of the tribe of the children of Manasseh *was* Gamaliel the son of Pedahzur. ²⁴And over the host of the tribe of the children of Benjamin

was Abidan the son of Gideoni. ²⁵And the standard of the camp of the children of Dan set forward, *which was* the rereward of all the camps throughout their hosts: and over his host *was* Ahiezer the son of Ammishaddai. ²⁶And over the host of the tribe of the children of Asher *was* Pagiel the son of Ocran. ²⁷And over the host of the tribe of the children of Naphtali *was* Ahira the son of Enan. ²⁸Thus were ᵃ the journeyings of the children of Israel according to their armies, when they set forward.

²⁹And Moses said unto Hobab, the son of Raguel the Midianite, Moses' father in law, We are journeying unto the place of which the LORD said, I will give it you: come thou with us, and we will do thee good: for the LORD hath spoken good concerning Israel. ³⁰And he said unto him, I will not go; but I will depart to mine own land, and to my kindred. ³¹And he said, Leave us not, I pray thee; forasmuch as thou knowest how we are to encamp in the wilderness, and thou mayest be to us instead of eyes. ³²And it shall be, if thou go with us, yea, it shall be, that what goodness the LORD shall do unto us, the same will we do unto thee. ³³And they departed from the mount of the LORD three days' journey: and the ark of the covenant of the LORD went before them in the three days' journey, to search out a resting place for them. ³⁴And the cloud of the LORD *was* upon them by day, when they went out of the camp. ³⁵And it came to pass, when the ark set forward, that Moses

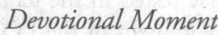

Devotional Moment
•
Expressing Appreciation
10:29-32 The Israelites were ready to leave Sinai, continuing their exodus. Moses asked Hobab, his brother-in-law, to join them, but the Midianite said he would return home. Moses finally convinced Hobab to stay by affirming his in-law's scouting abilities and familiarity with desert life. Telephone companies, florists, and greeting card companies all encourage us to do likewise: express our appreciation for others. Some people think they are building a person's character by withholding kind words, but Scripture is clear in its instruction that we encourage one another (see Rom. 1:11-12 and 1 Thess. 5:11). Is there someone in your life—spouse, child, in-law, parent, neighbor—who has gone too long without hearing your words of honest appreciation?

said, Rise up, LORD, and let thine enemies be scattered; and let them that hate thee flee before thee. ³⁶And when it rested, he said, Return, O LORD, unto the many thousandsᵇ of Israel.

11

¹And *when* the people complainedᵃ, it displeased the LORD: and the LORD heard *it*; and his anger was kindled; and the fire of the LORD burnt among them, and consumed *them that were* in the uttermost parts of the camp. ²And the people cried unto Moses; and when Moses prayed unto the LORD, the fire was quenched. ³And he called the name of the place Taberahᵇ: because the fire of the LORD burnt among them.

⁴And the mixt multitude that *was*

ᵃ Thus: Heb. These
ᵇ many thousands: Heb. ten thousand thousands
ᵃ complained: or, were as it were complainers
ᵇ Taberah: that is, A burning

among them fell a lusting: and the children of Israel also wept again, and said, Who shall give us flesh to eat? ⁵We remember the fish, which we did eat in Egypt freely; the cucumbers, and the melons, and the leeks, and the onions, and the garlic: ⁶But now our soul *is* dried away: *there is* nothing at all, beside this manna, *before* our eyes. ⁷And the manna *was* as coriander seed, and the colour thereof as the colour of bdellium. ⁸*And* the people went about, and gathered *it*, and ground *it* in mills, or beat *it* in a mortar, and baked *it* in pans, and made cakes of it: and the taste of it was as the taste of fresh oil. ⁹And when the dew fell upon the camp in the night, the manna fell upon it. ¹⁰Then Moses heard the people weep throughout their families, every man in the door of his tent: and the anger of the LORD was kindled greatly; Moses also was displeased. ¹¹And Moses said unto the LORD, Wherefore hast thou afflicted thy servant? and wherefore have I not found favour in thy sight, that thou layest the burden of all this people

Devotional Moment
Complaining

11:1, 11-15 The Lord fed his people each day, as he had promised, but they were getting tired of the limited menu. When they complained about having only manna, the Lord became very angry. Moses in turn complained to the Lord about the burden of carrying and providing for all the people. We too can prove the truth of the old saying, Misery loves company. But grumbling does not help us; honestly praying about our concerns accomplishes much more because God cares about our needs. Turn your gripes into prayers.

upon me? ¹²Have I conceived all this people? have I begotten them, that thou shouldest say unto me, Carry them in thy bosom, as a nursing father beareth the sucking child, unto the land which thou swarest unto their fathers? ¹³Whence should I have flesh to give unto all this people? for they weep unto me, saying, Give us flesh, that we may eat. ¹⁴I am not able to bear all this people alone, because *it is* too heavy for me. ¹⁵And if thou deal thus with me, kill me, I pray thee, out of hand, if I have found favour in thy sight; and let me not see my wretchedness.

¹⁶And the LORD said unto Moses, Gather unto me seventy men of the elders of Israel, whom thou knowest to be the elders of the people, and officers over them; and bring them unto the tabernacle of the congregation, that they may stand there with thee. ¹⁷And I will come down and talk with thee there: and I will take of the spirit which *is* upon thee, and will put *it* upon them; and they shall bear the burden of the people with thee, that thou bear *it* not thyself alone. ¹⁸And say thou unto the people, Sanctify yourselves against to morrow, and ye shall eat flesh: for ye have wept in the ears of the LORD, saying, Who shall give us flesh to eat? for *it was* well with us in Egypt: therefore the LORD will give you flesh, and ye shall eat. ¹⁹Ye shall not eat one day, nor two days, nor five days, neither ten days, nor twenty days; ²⁰But even a whole month, until it come out at your nostrils, and it be loathsome unto you: because that ye have despised the LORD which *is* among you, and have wept before him, saying, Why came we forth out of Egypt? ²¹And Moses said,

The people, among whom I *am, are* six hundred thousand footmen; and thou hast said, I will give them flesh, that they may eat a whole month. ²²Shall the flocks and the herds be slain for them, to suffice them? or shall all the fish of the sea be gathered together for them, to suffice them? ²³And the LORD said unto Moses, Is the LORD'S hand waxed short? thou shalt see now whether my word shall come to pass unto thee or not.

²⁴And Moses went out, and told the people the words of the LORD, and gathered the seventy men of the elders of the people, and set them round about the tabernacle. ²⁵And the LORD came down in a cloud, and spake unto him, and took of the spirit that *was* upon him, and gave *it* unto the seventy elders: and it came to pass, *that*, when the spirit rested upon them, they prophesied, and did not cease. ²⁶But there remained two *of the* men in the camp, the name of the one *was* Eldad, and the name of the other Medad: and the spirit rested upon them; and they *were* of them that were written, but went not out unto the tabernacle: and they prophesied in the camp. ²⁷And there ran a young man, and told Moses, and said, Eldad and Medad do prophesy in the camp. ²⁸And Joshua the son of Nun, the servant of Moses, *one* of his young men, answered and said, My lord Moses, forbid them. ²⁹And Moses said unto him, Enviest thou for my sake? would God that all the LORD'S people were prophets, *and* that the

LORD would put his spirit upon them! ³⁰And Moses gat him into the camp, he and the elders of Israel.

³¹And there went forth a wind from the LORD, and brought quails from the sea, and let *them* fall by the camp, as it were a day's^c journey on this side, and as it were a day's journey on the other side, round about the camp, and as it were two cubits *high* upon the face of the earth. ³²And the people stood up all that day, and all *that* night, and all the next day, and they gathered the quails: he that gathered least gathered ten homers: and they spread *them* all abroad for themselves round about the camp. ³³And while the flesh *was* yet between their teeth, ere it was chewed, the wrath of the LORD was kindled against the people, and the LORD smote the people with a very great plague. ³⁴And he called the name of that place Kibrothhattaavah^d: because there they buried the people that lusted. ³⁵*And* the people journeyed from Kibrothhattaavah unto Hazeroth; and abode at Hazeroth.

12

¹And Miriam and Aaron spake against Moses because of the Ethiopian^a woman whom he had married: for he had married an Ethiopian woman. ²And they said, Hath the LORD indeed spoken only by Moses? hath he not spoken also by us? And the LORD heard *it*. ³(Now the man Moses *was* very meek, above all the men which *were* upon the face of the earth.)

---

^c as it were a day's . . . : Heb. as it were the way of a day
^d Kibrothhattaavah: that is, The graves of lust
^a Ethiopian: or, Cushite

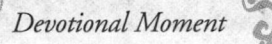

Devotional Moment

•

Disagreements

12:1-2 Miriam and Aaron had traveled with their brother, Moses, for years since their escape from Egypt. Suddenly they banded together against him, criticizing him for marrying a Cushite. But the real cause of their feelings was evidently envy of Moses' leadership. People often create smoke screens to hide their true motives. When as a parent you are called on to settle disputes between your children, make sure you listen and try to determine the root cause of the disagreement. Behind a simple argument may lie something else.

⁴And the LORD spake suddenly unto Moses, and unto Aaron, and unto Miriam, Come out ye three unto the tabernacle of the congregation. And they three came out. ⁵And the LORD came down in the pillar of the cloud, and stood *in* the door of the tabernacle, and called Aaron and Miriam: and they both came forth. ⁶And he said, Hear now my words: If there be a prophet among you, *I* the LORD will make myself known unto him in a vision, *and* will speak unto him in a dream. ⁷My servant Moses *is* not so, who *is* faithful in all mine house. ⁸With him will I speak mouth to mouth, even apparently, and not in dark speeches; and the similitude of the LORD shall he behold: wherefore then were ye not afraid to speak against my servant Moses? ⁹And the anger of the LORD was kindled against them; and he departed.

¹⁰And the cloud departed from off the tabernacle; and, behold, Miriam *became* leprous, *white* as snow: and Aaron looked upon Miriam, and, behold, *she was* leprous. ¹¹And Aaron said unto Moses, Alas, my lord, I beseech thee, lay not the sin upon us, wherein we have done foolishly, and wherein we have sinned. ¹²Let her not be as one dead, of whom the flesh is half consumed when he cometh out of his mother's womb. ¹³And Moses cried unto the LORD, saying, Heal her now, O God, I beseech thee. ¹⁴And the LORD said unto Moses, If her father had but spit in her face, should she not be ashamed seven days? let her be shut out from the camp seven days, and after that let her be received in *again*. ¹⁵And Miriam was shut out from the camp seven days: and the people journeyed not till Miriam was brought in *again*. ¹⁶And afterward the people removed from Hazeroth, and pitched in the wilderness of Paran.

13

¹And the LORD spake unto Moses, saying, ²Send thou men, that they may search the land of Canaan, which I give unto the children of Israel: of every tribe of their fathers shall ye send a man, every one a ruler among them. ³And Moses by the commandment of the LORD sent them from the wilderness of Paran: all those men *were* heads of the children of Israel. ⁴And these *were* their names: of the tribe of Reuben, Shammua the son of Zaccur. ⁵Of the tribe of Simeon, Shaphat the son of Hori. ⁶Of the tribe of Judah, Caleb the son of Jephunneh. ⁷Of the tribe of Issachar, Igal the son of Joseph. ⁸Of the tribe of Ephraim, Oshea the son of Nun. ⁹Of the tribe of Benjamin, Palti the son of Raphu. ¹⁰Of the tribe of Zebulun, Gaddiel the son of Sodi. ¹¹Of the tribe of Joseph, *namely*, of the tribe

Miriam

Many people know that Pharaoh's daughter pulled the baby Moses from the Nile River. But it was Moses' big sister Miriam who diplomatically suggested to Pharaoh's daughter that she get a woman to nurse him—Moses' own mother. Because of Miriam's initiative, the baby Moses survived and his mother got to care for him.

Many years later Miriam served alongside her younger brother in leading the nation of Israel out of slavery in Egypt. Though Miriam was older than Moses, she lived in Moses' shadow. Her younger brother held the high-profile spot in God's plan, and Miriam found that difficult to take. Miriam's secondary role eventually became a bitter pill as she allowed herself to grow jealous of Moses' position.

Miriam was a world-class sister by many counts, but it is easy to understand—and identify with—the fact that she and Aaron eventually said, "Hath the Lord indeed spoken only by Moses? hath he not spoken also by us?" (See Num. 12:1-2.) And where was Miriam when Aaron condoned the Israelites' carousing around the golden calf? The Bible doesn't say she helped Aaron, but she apparently didn't protest either. Miriam and Aaron both struggled with their brother's success.

Miriam helped her brother lead the nation, supporting Moses at almost every turn. The Bible even calls her a "prophetess" (Exod. 15:20). But her relationship with her younger brother exposed her deepest flaws. What do your sibling relationships show about you? Examine how you feel toward those who have been successful; then praise them, support them, and thank God for the role he has given you to fill.

of Manasseh, Gaddi the son of Susi. [12]Of the tribe of Dan, Ammiel the son of Gemalli. [13]Of the tribe of Asher, Sethur the son of Michael. [14]Of the tribe of Naphtali, Nahbi the son of Vophsi. [15]Of the tribe of Gad, Geuel the son of Machi. [16]These *are* the names of the men which Moses sent to spy out the land. And Moses called Oshea the son of Nun Jehoshua. [17]And Moses sent them to spy out the land of Canaan, and said unto them, Get you up this *way* southward, and go up into the mountain: [18]And see the land, what it *is*; and the people that dwelleth therein, whether they *be* strong or weak, few or many; [19]And what the land *is* that they dwell in, whether it *be* good or bad; and what cities *they be* that they dwell in, whether in tents, or in strong holds; [20]And what the land *is*, whether it *be* fat or lean, whether there be wood therein, or not. And be ye of good courage, and bring of the fruit of the land. Now the time *was* the time of the firstripe grapes.

[21]So they went up, and searched the land from the wilderness of Zin unto Rehob, as men come to Hamath. [22]And they ascended by the south, and came unto Hebron; where Ahiman, Sheshai, and Talmai, the children of Anak, *were*. (Now Hebron was built seven years before Zoan in Egypt.) [23]And they came unto the brook[a] of Eshcol, and cut down from thence a branch with one cluster of grapes, and they bare it between two upon a staff; and *they brought* of the pomegranates,

and of the figs. [24]The place was called the brook[b] Eshcol, because of the cluster of grapes which the children of Israel cut down from thence. [25]And they returned from searching of the land after forty days.

[26]And they went and came to Moses, and to Aaron, and to all the congregation of the children of Israel, unto the wilderness of Paran, to Kadesh; and brought back word unto them, and unto all the congregation, and shewed them the fruit of the land. [27]And they told him, and said, We came unto the land whither thou sentest us, and surely it floweth with milk and honey; and this *is* the fruit of it. [28]Nevertheless the people *be* strong that dwell in the land, and the cities *are* walled, *and* very great: and moreover we saw the children of Anak there. [29]The Amalekites dwell in the land of the south: and the Hittites, and the Jebusites, and the Amorites, dwell in the mountains: and the Canaanites dwell by the sea, and by the coast of Jordan. [30]And Caleb stilled the people before Moses, and said, Let us go up at once, and possess it; for we are well able to overcome it. [31]But the men that went up with him said, We be not able to go up against the people; for they *are* stronger than we. [32]And they brought up an evil report of the land which they had searched unto the children of Israel, saying, The land, through which we have gone to search it, *is* a land that eateth up the inhabitants thereof; and all the people that we saw in it *are* men[c]

[a] brook: or, valley
[b] brook: or, valley
[c] men . . . : Heb. men of statures

Devotional Moment

•

When They Complain

13:32–14:4 Moses (like many parents) must have grown very weary of the constant whining and complaining of his "children"—the people of Israel. Whining is a childish and indirect attempt to make others rescue us from a difficult situation or help us avoid responsibility. Encourage your children to be direct in communicating their desires, rather than trying to manipulate people. Patiently listen and acknowledge the difficulty of the task, but don't rescue them. Provide support, encouragement, and direction so they will learn to persevere.

of a great stature. ³³And there we saw the giants, the sons of Anak, *which come* of the giants: and we were in our own sight as grasshoppers, and so we were in their sight.

14

¹And all the congregation lifted up their voice, and cried; and the people wept that night. ²And all the children of Israel murmured against Moses and against Aaron: and the whole congregation said unto them, Would God that we had died in the land of Egypt! or would God we had died in this wilderness! ³And wherefore hath the LORD brought us unto this land, to fall by the sword, that our wives and our children should be a prey? were it not better for us to return into Egypt? ⁴And they said one to another, Let us make a captain, and let us return into Egypt.

⁵Then Moses and Aaron fell on their faces before all the assembly of the congregation of the children of Israel.

⁶And Joshua the son of Nun, and Caleb the son of Jephunneh, *which were* of them that searched the land, rent their clothes: ⁷And they spake unto all the company of the children of Israel, saying, The land, which we passed through to search it, *is* an exceeding good land. ⁸If the LORD delight in us, then he will bring us into this land, and give it us; a land which floweth with milk and honey. ⁹Only rebel not ye against the LORD, neither fear ye the people of the land; for they *are* bread for us: their defence^a is departed from them, and the LORD *is* with us: fear them not. ¹⁰But all the congregation bade stone them with stones. And the glory of the LORD appeared in the tabernacle of the congregation before all the children of Israel.

¹¹And the LORD said unto Moses, How long will this people provoke me? and how long will it be ere they believe me, for all the signs which I have shewed among them? ¹²I will smite them with the pestilence, and disinherit them, and will make of thee a greater nation and mightier than they. ¹³And Moses said unto the LORD, Then the Egyptians shall hear *it,* (for thou broughtest up this people in thy might from among them;) ¹⁴And they will tell *it* to the inhabitants of this land: *for* they have heard that thou LORD *art* among this people, that thou LORD art seen face to face, and *that* thy cloud standeth over them, and *that* thou goest before them, by day time in a pillar of a cloud, and in a pillar of fire by night. ¹⁵Now *if* thou shalt kill *all* this people as one man, then the nations which

---

^a defence: Heb. shadow

have heard the fame of thee will speak, saying, ¹⁶Because the LORD was not able to bring this people into the land which he sware unto them, therefore he hath slain them in the wilderness. ¹⁷And now, I beseech thee, let the power of my Lord be great, according as thou hast spoken, saying, ¹⁸The LORD *is* long-suffering, and of great mercy, forgiving iniquity and transgression, and by no means clearing *the guilty*, visiting the iniquity of the fathers upon the children unto the third and fourth *generation.* ¹⁹Pardon, I beseech thee, the iniquity of this people according unto the greatness of thy mercy, and as thou hast forgiven this people, from Egypt even until now.

²⁰And the LORD said, I have pardoned according to thy word: ²¹But *as* truly *as* I live, all the earth shall be filled with the glory of the LORD. ²²Because all those men which have seen my glory, and my miracles, which I did in Egypt and in the wilderness, and have tempted me now these ten times, and have not hearkened to my voice; ²³Surely they shall not see the land which I sware unto their fathers, neither shall any of them that provoked me see it: ²⁴But my servant Caleb, because he had another spirit with him, and hath followed me fully, him will I bring into the land whereinto he went; and his seed shall possess it. ²⁵(Now the Amalekites and the Canaanites dwelt in the valley.) To morrow turn you, and get you into the wilderness by the way of the Red sea. ²⁶And the LORD spake unto Moses and unto Aaron, saying,

²⁷How long *shall I bear with* this evil congregation, which murmur against me? I have heard the murmurings of the children of Israel, which they murmur against me. ²⁸Say unto them, *As truly as* I live, saith the LORD, as ye have spoken in mine ears, so will I do to you: ²⁹Your carcases shall fall in this wilderness; and all that were numbered of you, according to your whole number, from twenty years old and upward, which have murmured against me, ³⁰Doubtless ye shall not come into the land, *concerning* which I sware^b to make you dwell therein, save Caleb the son of Jephunneh, and Joshua the son of Nun. ³¹But your little ones, which ye said should be a prey, them will I bring in, and they shall know the land which ye have despised. ³²But *as for* you, your carcases, they shall fall in this wilderness. ³³And your children shall wander^c in the wilderness forty years, and bear your whoredoms, until your carcases be wasted in the wilderness. ³⁴After the number of the days in which ye searched the land, *even* forty days, each day for a year, shall ye bear your iniquities, *even* forty years, and ye shall know my breach of promise. ³⁵I the LORD have said, I will surely do it unto all this evil congregation, that are gathered together against me: in this wilderness they shall be consumed, and there they shall die.

³⁶And the men, which Moses sent to search the land, who returned, and made all the congregation to murmur against him, by bringing up a slander upon the land, ³⁷Even those men that

---

ᵇ sware: Heb. lifted up my hand
ᶜ wander: or, feed

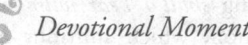

did bring up the evil report upon the land, died by the plague before the LORD. ³⁸But Joshua the son of Nun, and Caleb the son of Jephunneh, *which were* of the men that went to search the land, lived *still.* ³⁹And Moses told these sayings unto all the children of Israel: and the people mourned greatly. ⁴⁰And they rose up early in the morning, and gat them up into the top of the mountain, saying, Lo, we *be here,* and will go up unto the place which the LORD hath promised: for we have sinned. ⁴¹And Moses said, Wherefore now do ye transgress the commandment of the LORD? but it shall not prosper. ⁴²Go not up, for the LORD *is* not among you; that ye be not smitten before your enemies. ⁴³For the Amalekites and the Canaanites *are* there before you, and ye shall fall by the sword: because ye are turned away from the LORD, therefore the LORD will not be with you. ⁴⁴But they presumed to go up unto the hill top: nevertheless the ark of the covenant of the LORD, and Moses, departed not out of the camp. ⁴⁵Then the Amalekites came down, and the Canaanites which dwelt in that hill, and smote them, and discomfited them, *even* unto Hormah.

15

¹And the LORD spake unto Moses, saying, ²Speak unto the children of Israel, and say unto them, When ye be come into the land of your habitations, which I give unto you, ³And will make an offering by fire unto the LORD, a burnt offering, or a sacrifice in performing^a a vow, or in a freewill offering, or in your solemn feasts, to make a sweet savour unto the LORD, of the herd, or of the flock: ⁴Then shall he that offereth his offering unto the LORD bring a meat offering of a tenth deal of flour mingled with the fourth *part* of an hin of oil. ⁵And the fourth *part* of an hin of wine for a drink offering shalt thou prepare with the burnt offering or sacrifice, for one lamb. ⁶Or for a ram, thou shalt prepare *for* a meat offering two tenth deals of flour mingled with the third *part* of an hin of oil. ⁷And for a drink offering thou shalt offer the third *part* of an hin of wine, *for* a sweet savour unto the LORD. ⁸And when thou preparest a bullock *for* a burnt offering, or *for* a sacrifice in performing a vow, or peace offerings unto the LORD: ⁹Then shall he bring with a bullock a meat offering of three tenth deals of flour mingled with half an hin of oil. ¹⁰And thou shalt bring for a

---

^a performing: Heb. separating

drink offering half an hin of wine, *for* an offering made by fire, of a sweet savour unto the LORD. [11]Thus shall it be done for one bullock, or for one ram, or for a lamb, or a kid. [12]According to the number that ye shall prepare, so shall ye do to every one according to their number. [13]All that are born of the country shall do these things after this manner, in offering an offering made by fire, of a sweet savour unto the LORD. [14]And if a stranger sojourn with you, or whosoever *be* among you in your generations, and will offer an offering made by fire, of a sweet savour unto the LORD; as ye do, so he shall do. [15]One ordinance *shall be both* for you of the congregation, and also for the stranger that sojourneth *with you*, an ordinance for ever in your generations: as ye *are*, so shall the stranger be before the LORD. [16]One law and one manner shall be for you, and for the stranger that sojourneth with you. [17]And the LORD spake unto Moses, saying, [18]Speak unto the children of Israel, and say unto them, When ye come into the land whither I bring you, [19]Then it shall be, that, when ye eat of the bread of the land, ye shall offer up an heave offering unto the LORD. [20]Ye shall offer up a cake of the first of your dough *for* an heave offering: as *ye do* the heave offering of the threshingfloor, so shall ye heave it. [21]Of the first of your dough ye shall give unto the LORD an heave offering in your generations.

[22]And if ye have erred, and not observed all these commandments, which the LORD hath spoken unto Moses, [23]*Even* all that the LORD hath commanded you by the hand of Moses, from the day that the LORD commanded *Moses*, and henceforward among your generations; [24]Then it shall be, if *ought* be committed by ignorance without the knowledge of the congregation, that all the congregation shall offer one young bullock for a burnt offering, for a sweet savour unto the LORD, with his meat offering, and his drink offering, according to the manner, and one kid of the goats for a sin offering. [25]And the priest shall make an atonement for all the congregation of the children of Israel, and it shall be forgiven them; for it *is* ignorance: and they shall bring their offering, a sacrifice made by fire unto the LORD, and their sin offering before the LORD, for their ignorance: [26]And it shall be forgiven all the congregation of the children of Israel, and the stranger that sojourneth among them; seeing all the people *were* in ignorance. [27]And if any soul sin through ignorance, then he shall bring a she goat of the first year for a

---

Devotional Moment

Oops!

15:30-31 Outward behavior is important; so is inward motivation. Here God gave radically different instructions for dealing with unintentional and intentional sin. The same principle applies to family life. A child who accidentally breaks a lamp or spills his drink should be treated much differently from the child who does so in willful defiance. God is a good Father. We are wise to remember how he distinguishes between unintentional and intentional disobedience, and apply that to the way we deal with children.

sin offering. ²⁸And the priest shall make an atonement for the soul that sinneth ignorantly, when he sinneth by ignorance before the LORD, to make an atonement for him; and it shall be forgiven him. ²⁹Ye shall have one law for him that sinneth[b] through ignorance, *both for* him that is born among the children of Israel, and for the stranger that sojourneth among them.

³⁰But the soul that doeth *ought* presumptuously[c], *whether he be* born in the land, or a stranger, the same reproacheth the LORD; and that soul shall be cut off from among his people. ³¹Because he hath despised the word of the LORD, and hath broken his commandment, that soul shall utterly be cut off; his iniquity *shall be* upon him. ³²And while the children of Israel were in the wilderness, they found a man that gathered sticks upon the sabbath day. ³³And they that found him gathering sticks brought him unto Moses and Aaron, and unto all the congregation. ³⁴And they put him in ward, because it was not declared what should be done to him. ³⁵And the LORD said unto Moses, The man shall be surely put to death: all the congregation shall stone him with stones without the camp. ³⁶And all the congregation brought him without the camp, and stoned him with stones, and he died; as the LORD commanded Moses.

³⁷And the LORD spake unto Moses, saying, ³⁸Speak unto the children of Israel, and bid them that they make them fringes in the borders of their garments throughout their generations, and that they put upon the fringe of the borders a ribband of blue: ³⁹And it shall be unto you for a fringe, that ye may look upon it, and remember all the commandments of the LORD, and do them; and that ye seek not after your own heart and your own eyes, after which ye use to go a whoring: ⁴⁰That ye may remember, and do all my commandments, and be holy unto your God. ⁴¹I *am* the LORD your God, which brought you out of the land of Egypt, to be your God: I *am* the LORD your God.

16

¹Now Korah, the son of Izhar, the son of Kohath, the son of Levi, and Dathan and Abiram, the sons of Eliab, and On, the son of Peleth, sons of Reuben, took *men:* ²And they rose up before Moses, with certain of the children of Israel, two hundred and fifty princes of the assembly, famous in the congregation, men of renown: ³And they gathered themselves together against Moses and against Aaron, and said unto them, *Ye take* too much upon you, seeing all the congregation *are* holy, every one of them, and the LORD *is* among them: wherefore then lift ye up yourselves above the congregation of the LORD? ⁴And when Moses heard *it*, he fell upon his face: ⁵And he spake unto Korah and unto all his company, saying, Even to morrow the LORD will shew who *are* his, and *who is* holy; and will cause *him* to come near unto him: even *him* whom he hath chosen will he cause to

---

[b] sinneth: Heb. doth
[c] presumptuously: Heb. with an high hand

come near unto him. ⁶This do; Take you censers, Korah, and all his company; ⁷And put fire therein, and put incense in them before the LORD to morrow: and it shall be *that* the man whom the LORD doth choose, he *shall be* holy: *ye take* too much upon you, ye sons of Levi. ⁸And Moses said unto Korah, Hear, I pray you, ye sons of Levi: ⁹*Seemeth it but* a small thing unto you, that the God of Israel hath separated you from the congregation of Israel, to bring you near to himself to do the service of the tabernacle of the LORD, and to stand before the congregation to minister unto them? ¹⁰And he hath brought thee near *to him*, and all thy brethren the sons of Levi with thee: and seek ye the priesthood also? ¹¹For which cause *both* thou and all thy company *are* gathered together against the LORD: and what *is* Aaron, that ye murmur against him?

¹²And Moses sent to call Dathan and Abiram, the sons of Eliab: which said, We will not come up: ¹³*Is it* a small thing that thou hast brought us up out of a land that floweth with milk and honey, to kill us in the wilderness, except thou make thyself altogether a prince over us? ¹⁴Moreover thou hast not brought us into a land that floweth with milk and honey, or given us inheritance of fields and vineyards: wilt thou put out the eyes of these men? we will not come up. ¹⁵And Moses was very wroth, and said unto the LORD, Respect not thou their offering: I have not taken one ass from them, neither have I hurt one of them. ¹⁶And Moses said unto Korah, Be thou and all thy company before the LORD, thou, and they, and Aaron, to morrow: ¹⁷And take

every man his censer, and put incense in them, and bring ye before the LORD every man his censer, two hundred and fifty censers; thou also, and Aaron, each *of you* his censer. ¹⁸And they took every man his censer, and put fire in them, and laid incense thereon, and stood in the door of the tabernacle of the congregation with Moses and Aaron. ¹⁹And Korah gathered all the congregation against them unto the door of the tabernacle of the congregation: and the glory of the LORD appeared unto all the congregation. ²⁰And the LORD spake unto Moses and unto Aaron, saying, ²¹Separate yourselves from among this congregation, that I may consume them in a moment. ²²And they fell upon their faces, and said, O God, the God of the spirits of all flesh, shall one man sin, and wilt thou be wroth with all the congregation?

²³And the LORD spake unto Moses, saying, ²⁴Speak unto the congregation, saying, Get you up from about the tabernacle of Korah, Dathan, and

Devotional Moment

Revenge

16:22-35 How do you respond when someone wrongs you or tries to discredit you? If you get angry or resentful, join the crowd. Those are typical responses to abrasive or abusive behavior. Moses and Aaron were angry and indignant with Korah and his crowd. Even so, they did not let their anger overrule their judgment. They even pled with God *not* to punish all the people for the sins of a few! It is all right to be angry at times. But it is best to let God take care of retribution.

Abiram. ²⁵And Moses rose up and went unto Dathan and Abiram; and the elders of Israel followed him. ²⁶And he spake unto the congregation, saying, Depart, I pray you, from the tents of these wicked men, and touch nothing of theirs, lest ye be consumed in all their sins. ²⁷So they gat up from the tabernacle of Korah, Dathan, and Abiram, on every side: and Dathan and Abiram came out, and stood in the door of their tents, and their wives, and their sons, and their little children. ²⁸And Moses said, Hereby ye shall know that the LORD hath sent me to do all these works; for *I have* not *done them* of mine own mind. ²⁹If these men die the common death of all men, or if they be visited after the visitation of all men; *then* the LORD hath not sent me. ³⁰But if the LORD make ᵃ a new thing, and the earth open her mouth, and swallow them up, with all that *appertain* unto them, and they go down quick into the pit; then ye shall understand that these men have provoked the LORD. ³¹And it came to pass, as he had made an end of speaking all these words, that the ground clave asunder that *was* under them: ³²And the earth opened her mouth, and swallowed them up, and their houses, and all the men that *appertained* unto Korah, and all *their* goods. ³³They, and all that *appertained* to them, went down alive into the pit, and the earth closed upon them: and they perished from among the congregation. ³⁴And all Israel that *were* round about them fled at the cry of them: for they said, Lest the earth swallow us up *also.*

³⁵And there came out a fire from the LORD, and consumed the two hundred and fifty men that offered incense. ³⁶And the LORD spake unto Moses, saying, ³⁷Speak unto Eleazar the son of Aaron the priest, that he take up the censers out of the burning, and scatter thou the fire yonder; for they are hallowed. ³⁸The censers of these sinners against their own souls, let them make them broad plates *for* a covering of the altar: for they offered them before the LORD, therefore they are hallowed: and they shall be a sign unto the children of Israel. ³⁹And Eleazar the priest took the brasen censers, wherewith they that were burnt had offered; and they were made broad *plates for* a covering of the altar: ⁴⁰*To be* a memorial unto the children of Israel, that no stranger, which *is* not of the seed of Aaron, come near to offer incense before the LORD; that he be not as Korah, and as his company: as the LORD said to him by the hand of Moses.

⁴¹But on the morrow all the congregation of the children of Israel murmured against Moses and against Aaron, saying, Ye have killed the people of the LORD. ⁴²And it came to pass, when the congregation was gathered against Moses and against Aaron, that they looked toward the tabernacle of the congregation: and, behold, the cloud covered it, and the glory of the LORD appeared. ⁴³And Moses and Aaron came before the tabernacle of the congregation. ⁴⁴And the LORD spake unto Moses, saying, ⁴⁵Get you up from among this congregation, that I may consume them as in a moment. And they fell upon their faces. ⁴⁶And Moses

---

ᵃ make . . . : Heb. create a creature

said unto Aaron, Take a censer, and put fire therein from off the altar, and put on incense, and go quickly unto the congregation, and make an atonement for them: for there is wrath gone out from the LORD; the plague is begun. ⁴⁷And Aaron took as Moses commanded, and ran into the midst of the congregation; and, behold, the plague was begun among the people: and he put on incense, and made an atonement for the people. ⁴⁸And he stood between the dead and the living; and the plague was stayed. ⁴⁹Now they that died in the plague were fourteen thousand and seven hundred, beside them that died about the matter of Korah. ⁵⁰And Aaron returned unto Moses unto the door of the tabernacle of the congregation: and the plague was stayed.

17

¹And the LORD spake unto Moses, saying, ²Speak unto the children of Israel, and take of every one of them a rod according to the house of *their* fathers, of all their princes according to the house of their fathers twelve rods: write thou every man's name upon his rod. ³And thou shalt write Aaron's name upon the rod of Levi: for one rod *shall be* for the head of the house of their fathers. ⁴And thou shalt lay them up in the tabernacle of the congregation before the testimony, where I will meet with you. ⁵And it shall come to pass, *that* the man's rod, whom I shall choose, shall blossom: and I will make to cease from me the murmurings of the children of Israel, whereby they murmur against you. ⁶And Moses spake unto the children of Israel, and every one of their princes gave him a rodᵃ apiece, for each prince one, according to their fathers' houses, *even* twelve rods: and the rod of Aaron *was* among their rods. ⁷And Moses laid up the rods before the LORD in the tabernacle of witness.

⁸And it came to pass, that on the morrow Moses went into the tabernacle of witness; and, behold, the rod of Aaron for the house of Levi was budded, and brought forth buds, and bloomed blossoms, and yielded almonds. ⁹And Moses brought out all the rods from before the LORD unto all the children of Israel: and they looked, and took every man his rod. ¹⁰And the LORD said unto Moses, Bring Aaron's rod again before the testimony, to be kept for a token against the rebelsᵇ; and thou shalt quite take away their murmurings from me, that they die not. ¹¹And Moses did *so*: as the LORD commanded him, so did he. ¹²And the children of Israel spake unto Moses, saying, Behold, we die, we perish, we all perish. ¹³Whosoever cometh any thing near unto the tabernacle of the LORD shall die: shall we be consumed with dying?

18

¹And the LORD said unto Aaron, Thou and thy sons and thy father's house with thee shall bear the iniquity of the sanctuary: and thou and thy sons with thee shall bear the iniquity of your priesthood. ²And thy brethren also of the tribe of Levi, the tribe of thy father, bring

---

ᵃ a rod . . . : Heb. a rod for one prince, a rod for one prince
ᵇ rebels: Heb. children of rebellion

thou with thee, that they may be joined unto thee, and minister unto thee: but thou and thy sons with thee *shall minister* before the tabernacle of witness. ³And they shall keep thy charge, and the charge of all the tabernacle: only they shall not come nigh the vessels of the sanctuary and the altar, that neither they, nor ye also, die. ⁴And they shall be joined unto thee, and keep the charge of the tabernacle of the congregation, for all the service of the tabernacle: and a stranger shall not come nigh unto you. ⁵And ye shall keep the charge of the sanctuary, and the charge of the altar: that there be no wrath any more upon the children of Israel. ⁶And I, behold, I have taken your brethren the Levites from among the children of Israel: to you *they are* given *as* a gift for the LORD, to do the service of the tabernacle of the congregation. ⁷Therefore thou and thy sons with thee shall keep your priest's office for every thing of the altar, and within the vail; and ye shall serve: I have given your priest's office *unto you* as a service of gift: and the stranger that cometh nigh shall be put to death.

⁸And the LORD spake unto Aaron, Behold, I also have given thee the charge of mine heave offerings of all the hallowed things of the children of Israel; unto thee have I given them by reason of the anointing, and to thy sons, by an ordinance for ever. ⁹This shall be thine of the most holy things, *reserved* from the fire: every oblation of theirs, every meat offering of theirs, and every sin offering of theirs, and every trespass offering of theirs, which they shall render unto me, *shall be* most holy for thee and for thy

sons. ¹⁰In the most holy *place* shalt thou eat it; every male shall eat it: it shall be holy unto thee. ¹¹And this *is* thine; the heave offering of their gift, with all the wave offerings of the children of Israel: I have given them unto thee, and to thy sons and to thy daughters with thee, by a statute for ever: every one that is clean in thy house shall eat of it. ¹²All the best ᵃ of the oil, and all the best of the wine, and of the wheat, the firstfruits of them which they shall offer unto the LORD, them have I given thee. ¹³*And* whatsoever is first ripe in the land, which they shall bring unto the LORD, shall be thine; every one that is clean in thine house shall eat *of* it. ¹⁴Every thing devoted in Israel shall be thine. ¹⁵Every thing that openeth the matrix in all flesh, which they bring unto the LORD, *whether it be* of men or beasts, shall be thine: nevertheless the firstborn of man shalt thou surely redeem, and the firstling of unclean beasts shalt thou redeem. ¹⁶And those that are to be redeemed from a month old shalt thou redeem, according to thine estimation, for the money of five shekels, after the shekel of the sanctuary, which *is* twenty gerahs. ¹⁷But the firstling of a cow, or the firstling of a sheep, or the firstling of a goat, thou shalt not redeem; they *are* holy: thou shalt sprinkle their blood upon the altar, and shalt burn their fat *for* an offering made by fire, for a sweet savour unto the LORD. ¹⁸And the flesh of them shall be thine, as the wave breast and as the right shoulder are thine. ¹⁹All the heave offerings of the holy things, which the children of Israel offer unto the LORD, have I given thee, and thy sons and thy daughters with thee, by

---

ᵃ best: Heb. fat

a statute for ever: it *is* a covenant of salt for ever before the LORD unto thee and to thy seed with thee.

²⁰And the LORD spake unto Aaron, Thou shalt have no inheritance in their land, neither shalt thou have any part among them: I *am* thy part and thine inheritance among the children of Israel. ²¹And, behold, I have given the children of Levi all the tenth in Israel for an inheritance, for their service which they serve, *even* the service of the tabernacle of the congregation. ²²Neither must the children of Israel henceforth come nigh the tabernacle of the congregation, lest they bear sin, and die[b]. ²³But the Levites shall do the service of the tabernacle of the congregation, and they shall bear their iniquity: *it shall be* a statute for ever throughout your generations, that among the children of Israel they have no inheritance. ²⁴But the tithes of the children of Israel, which they offer *as* an heave offering unto the LORD, I have

given to the Levites to inherit: therefore I have said unto them, Among the children of Israel they shall have no inheritance. ²⁵And the LORD spake unto Moses, saying, ²⁶Thus speak unto the Levites, and say unto them, When ye take of the children of Israel the tithes which I have given you from them for your inheritance, then ye shall offer up an heave offering of it for the LORD, *even* a tenth *part* of the tithe. ²⁷And *this* your heave offering shall be reckoned unto you, as though *it were* the corn of the threshingfloor, and as the fulness of the winepress. ²⁸Thus ye also shall offer an heave offering unto the LORD of all your tithes, which ye receive of the children of Israel; and ye shall give thereof the LORD'S heave offering to Aaron the priest. ²⁹Out of all your gifts ye shall offer every heave offering of the LORD, of all the best[c] thereof, *even* the hallowed part thereof out of it. ³⁰Therefore thou shalt say unto them, When ye have heaved the best[d] thereof from it, then it shall be counted unto the Levites as the increase of the threshingfloor, and as the increase of the winepress. ³¹And ye shall eat it in every place, ye and your households: for it *is* your reward for your service in the tabernacle of the congregation. ³²And ye shall bear no sin by reason of it, when ye have heaved from it the best of it: neither shall ye pollute the holy things of the children of Israel, lest ye die.

Devotional Moment

Tithing

18:25-26 God's law required everyone to tithe. Even the Levites, whose income came from the tithes of others, were to give 10 percent of *that* to the Lord. Tithing is one of the ways God reminds us that everything we have comes from him, and that we must not be overly possessive or materialistic with his gifts. Do you model good stewardship of your resources for your family? If you want your children to learn to tithe, don't keep *your* tithing a secret. Show them how by your example, and discuss your giving as a family. Encourage your children to tithe their resources as well.

19

¹And the LORD spake unto Moses and unto Aaron, saying, ²This *is* the ordi-

^b and die: Heb. to die
^c best: Heb. fat
^d best: Heb. fat

nance of the law which the LORD hath commanded, saying, Speak unto the children of Israel, that they bring thee a red heifer without spot, wherein *is* no blemish, *and* upon which never came yoke: [3]And ye shall give her unto Eleazar the priest, that he may bring her forth without the camp, and *one* shall slay her before his face: [4]And Eleazar the priest shall take of her blood with his finger, and sprinkle of her blood directly before the tabernacle of the congregation seven times: [5]And *one* shall burn the heifer in his sight; her skin, and her flesh, and her blood, with her dung, shall he burn: [6]And the priest shall take cedar wood, and hyssop, and scarlet, and cast *it* into the midst of the burning of the heifer. [7]Then the priest shall wash his clothes, and he shall bathe his flesh in water, and afterward he shall come into the camp, and the priest shall be unclean until the even. [8]And he that burneth her shall wash his clothes in water, and bathe his flesh in water, and shall be unclean until the even. [9]And a man *that is* clean shall gather up the ashes of the heifer, and lay *them* up without the camp in a clean place, and it shall be kept for the congregation of the children of Israel for a water of separation: it *is* a purification for sin. [10]And he that gathereth the ashes of the heifer shall wash his clothes, and be unclean until the even: and it shall be unto the children of Israel, and unto the stranger that sojourneth among them, for a statute for ever.

[11]He that toucheth the dead body of any man[a] shall be unclean seven days. [12]He shall purify himself with it on the third day, and on the seventh day he shall be clean: but if he purify not himself the third day, then the seventh day he shall not be clean. [13]Whosoever toucheth the dead body of any man that is dead, and purifieth not himself, defileth the tabernacle of the LORD; and that soul shall be cut off from Israel: because the water of separation was not sprinkled upon him, he shall be unclean; his uncleanness *is* yet upon him. [14]This *is* the law, when a man dieth in a tent: all that come into the tent, and all that *is* in the tent, shall be unclean seven days. [15]And every open vessel, which hath no covering bound upon it, *is* unclean. [16]And whosoever toucheth one that is slain with a sword in the open fields, or a dead body, or a bone of a man, or a grave, shall be unclean seven days. [17]And for an unclean *person* they shall take of the ashes[b] of the burnt heifer of purification for sin, and running water shall be put thereto in a vessel: [18]And a clean person shall take hyssop, and dip *it* in the water, and sprinkle *it* upon the tent, and upon all the vessels, and upon the persons that were there, and upon him that touched a bone, or one slain, or one dead, or a grave: [19]And the clean *person* shall sprinkle upon the unclean on the third day, and on the seventh day: and on the seventh day he shall purify himself, and wash his clothes, and bathe himself in water, and shall be clean at even. [20]But the man that shall be unclean, and shall not purify himself, that soul shall be cut off from among the congregation, because he hath defiled the sanctuary of the LORD: the water of

---

[a] man: Heb. soul of man
[b] ashes: Heb. dust

Eleazar

Eleazar was the son of Aaron, the High Priest of Israel and Moses' brother. As Eleazar grew up, Moses and Aaron trained him, along with his three brothers, in the priestly office. Though Aaron had his own moments of public failure (such as when he helped the people construct a golden calf-idol; see Exod. 32), he was a powerful and important person in Israel. He advised and helped Moses lead Israel through the wilderness and to the Promised Land. Eleazar grew up in that shadow.

With a pedigree like that, perhaps we naturally expect "greatness" from Eleazar. Like father, like son, right? Not always. Two of Eleazar's brothers (Nadab and Abihu) died for disobeying one of God's direct commands (Lev. 10:1-3). In the aftermath, Eleazar (and his other brother, Ithamar) angered Moses for failing to sacrifice properly (see Lev. 10:16-18). Eleazar wasn't perfect.

Yet when the time came for Aaron to die, God told Moses and Aaron to pass the mantel on to Eleazar (Num. 20:23-29). The simple ceremony they conducted on Mount Hor tells us nothing of Eleazar's thoughts or feelings about taking his father's place. He simply put on Aaron's priestly garments, attended his father's death, and went back down the mountain with Moses.

Eleazar was made High Priest in his father's place—difficult shoes to step into. Eleazar did well. He helped lead the Israelites into the Promised Land, serving with distinction alongside Joshua. He also became a capable spokesman. All in all, he was an adequate successor.

LESSONS FROM ELEAZAR AS A SON

Some children can and do fill their parents' shoes well. Eleazar did. His three brothers did not.

It takes time to learn a parent's trade. Eleazar learned his priestly duties from Aaron himself (not from a nanny) over many years. And those years included some failure.

We must step into our adult roles when the time comes. Once Eleazar was ready to assume Aaron's role as High Priest, he took over those duties. The time for childish dependence was over.

separation hath not been sprinkled upon him; he *is* unclean. ²¹And it shall be a perpetual statute unto them, that he that sprinkleth the water of separation shall wash his clothes; and he that toucheth the water of separation shall be unclean until even. ²²And whatsoever the unclean *person* toucheth shall be unclean; and the soul that toucheth *it* shall be unclean until even.

20

¹Then came the children of Israel, *even* the whole congregation, into the desert of Zin in the first month: and the people abode in Kadesh; and Miriam died there, and was buried there. ²And there was no water for the congregation: and they gathered themselves together against Moses and against Aaron. ³And the people chode with Moses, and spake, saying, Would God that we had died when our brethren died before the LORD! ⁴And why have ye brought up the congregation of the LORD into this wilderness, that we and our cattle should die there? ⁵And wherefore have ye made us to come up out of Egypt, to bring us in unto this evil place? it *is* no place of seed, or of figs, or of vines, or of pomegranates; neither *is* there any water to drink. ⁶And Moses and Aaron went from the presence of the assembly unto the door of the tabernacle of the congregation, and they fell upon their faces: and the glory of the LORD appeared unto them. ⁷And the LORD spake unto Moses, saying, ⁸Take the rod, and gather thou the assembly together, thou, and Aaron thy brother, and speak ye unto the rock before their eyes; and it shall give forth his water, and thou shalt bring forth to them water out of the rock: so thou shalt give the congregation and their beasts drink. ⁹And Moses took the rod from before the LORD, as he commanded him. ¹⁰And Moses and Aaron gathered the congregation together before the rock, and he said unto them, Hear now, ye rebels; must we fetch you water out of this rock? ¹¹And Moses lifted up his hand, and with his rod he smote the rock twice: and the water came out abundantly, and the congregation drank, and their beasts *also*. ¹²And the LORD spake unto Moses and Aaron, Because ye believed me not, to sanctify me in the eyes of the children of Israel, therefore ye shall not bring this congregation into the land which I have given them. ¹³This *is* the water of Meribahª; because the children of Israel strove with the LORD, and he was sanctified in them.

¹⁴And Moses sent messengers from

Devotional Moment

Denial

20:3-5 They had spent forty years in the wilderness as a result of their own sins, and yet there were still many who wanted to blame it all on Moses and Aaron. It is always easier to blame someone else than to face our own sinfulness; it is also always wrong. Until we accept the responsibility for our own wrong choices, we cannot confess, repent, and come to grips with them. Children need to see that their parents can admit when they are wrong and then ask forgiveness from God and each other. They will then find it easier to do so themselves.

ª Meribah: that is, Strife

Kadesh unto the king of Edom, Thus saith thy brother Israel, Thou knowest all the travail that hath befallen[b] us: [15]How our fathers went down into Egypt, and we have dwelt in Egypt a long time; and the Egyptians vexed us, and our fathers: [16]And when we cried unto the LORD, he heard our voice, and sent an angel, and hath brought us forth out of Egypt: and, behold, we *are* in Kadesh, a city in the uttermost of thy border: [17]Let us pass, I pray thee, through thy country: we will not pass through the fields, or through the vineyards, neither will we drink *of* the water of the wells: we will go by the king's *high* way, we will not turn to the right hand nor to the left, until we have passed thy borders. [18]And Edom said unto him, Thou shalt not pass by me, lest I come out against thee with the sword. [19]And the children of Israel said unto him, We will go by the high way: and if I and my cattle drink of thy water, then I will pay for it: I will only, without *doing* any thing *else*, go through on my feet. [20]And he said, Thou shalt not go through. And Edom came out against him with much people, and with a strong hand. [21]Thus Edom refused to give Israel passage through his border: wherefore Israel turned away from him.

[22]And the children of Israel, *even* the whole congregation, journeyed from Kadesh, and came unto mount Hor. [23]And the LORD spake unto Moses and Aaron in mount Hor, by the coast of the land of Edom, saying,

[24]Aaron shall be gathered unto his people: for he shall not enter into the land which I have given unto the children of Israel, because ye rebelled against my word[c] at the water of Meribah. [25]Take Aaron and Eleazar his son, and bring them up unto mount Hor: [26]And strip Aaron of his garments, and put them upon Eleazar his son: and Aaron shall be gathered *unto his people*, and shall die there. [27]And Moses did as the LORD commanded: and they went up into mount Hor in the sight of all the congregation. [28]And Moses stripped Aaron of his garments, and put them upon Eleazar his son; and Aaron died there in the top of the mount: and Moses and Eleazar came down from the mount. [29]And when all the congregation saw that Aaron was dead, they mourned for Aaron thirty days, *even* all the house of Israel.

21

[1]And *when* king Arad the Canaanite, which dwelt in the south, heard tell that Israel came by the way of the spies; then he fought against Israel, and took *some* of them prisoners. [2]And Israel vowed a vow unto the LORD, and said, If thou wilt indeed deliver this people into my hand, then I will utterly destroy their cities. [3]And the LORD hearkened to the voice of Israel, and delivered up the Canaanites; and they utterly destroyed them and their cities: and he called the name of the place Hormah[a].

[4]And they journeyed from mount

---

[b] befallen . . . : Heb. found us
[c] word: Heb. mouth
[a] Hormah: that is, Utter destruction

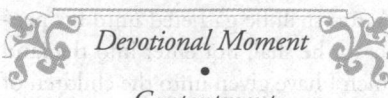

Hor by the way of the Red sea, to compass the land of Edom: and the soul of the people was much discouraged[b] because of the way. ⁵And the people spake against God, and against Moses, Wherefore have ye brought us up out of Egypt to die in the wilderness? for *there is* no bread, neither *is there any* water; and our soul loatheth this light bread. ⁶And the LORD sent fiery serpents among the people, and they bit the people; and much people of Israel died. ⁷Therefore the people came to Moses, and said, We have sinned, for we have spoken against the LORD, and against thee; pray unto the LORD, that he take away the serpents from us. And Moses prayed for the people. ⁸And the LORD said unto Moses, Make thee a fiery serpent, and set it upon a pole: and it shall come to pass, that every one that is bitten, when he looketh upon it, shall live. ⁹And

Moses made a serpent of brass, and put it upon a pole, and it came to pass, that if a serpent had bitten any man, when he beheld the serpent of brass, he lived.

¹⁰And the children of Israel set forward, and pitched in Oboth. ¹¹And they journeyed from Oboth, and pitched at Ijeabarim[c], in the wilderness which *is* before Moab, toward the sunrising. ¹²From thence they removed, and pitched in the valley of Zared. ¹³From thence they removed, and pitched on the other side of Arnon, which *is* in the wilderness that cometh out of the coasts of the Amorites: for Arnon *is* the border of Moab, between Moab and the Amorites. ¹⁴Wherefore it is said in the book of the wars of the LORD, What he did in the Red sea, and in the brooks of Arnon, ¹⁵And at the stream of the brooks that goeth down to the dwelling of Ar, and lieth[d] upon the border of Moab. ¹⁶And from thence *they went* to Beer: that *is* the well whereof the LORD spake unto Moses, Gather the people together, and I will give them water. ¹⁷Then Israel sang this song, Spring up, O well; sing ye unto it: ¹⁸The princes digged the well, the nobles of the people digged it, by *the direction of* the lawgiver, with their staves. And from the wilderness *they went* to Mattanah: ¹⁹And from Mattanah to Nahaliel: and from Nahaliel to Bamoth: ²⁰And from Bamoth *in* the valley, that *is* in the country[e] of Moab, to the top of Pisgah, which looketh toward Jeshimon.

---

[b] discouraged: or, grieved: Heb. shortened
[c] Ijeabarim: or, heaps of Abarim
[d] lieth: Heb. leaneth
[e] country: Heb. field

²¹And Israel sent messengers unto Sihon king of the Amorites, saying, ²²Let me pass through thy land: we will not turn into the fields, or into the vineyards; we will not drink *of* the waters of the well: *but* we will go along by the king's *high* way, until we be past thy borders. ²³And Sihon would not suffer Israel to pass through his border: but Sihon gathered all his people together, and went out against Israel into the wilderness: and he came to Jahaz, and fought against Israel. ²⁴And Israel smote him with the edge of the sword, and possessed his land from Arnon unto Jabbok, even unto the children of Ammon: for the border of the children of Ammon *was* strong. ²⁵And Israel took all these cities: and Israel dwelt in all the cities of the Amorites, in Heshbon, and in all the villages[f] thereof. ²⁶For Heshbon *was* the city of Sihon the king of the Amorites, who had fought against the former king of Moab, and taken all his land out of his hand, even unto Arnon. ²⁷Wherefore they that speak in proverbs say, Come into Heshbon, let the city of Sihon be built and prepared: ²⁸For there is a fire gone out of Heshbon, a flame from the city of Sihon: it hath consumed Ar of Moab, *and* the lords of the high places of Arnon. ²⁹Woe to thee, Moab! thou art undone, O people of Chemosh: he hath given his sons that escaped, and his daughters, into captivity unto Sihon king of the Amorites. ³⁰We have shot at them; Heshbon is perished even unto Dibon, and we have laid them waste even unto Nophah, which *reacheth* unto Medeba.

³¹Thus Israel dwelt in the land of the Amorites. ³²And Moses sent to spy out Jaazer, and they took the villages thereof, and drove out the Amorites that *were* there. ³³And they turned and went up by the way of Bashan: and Og the king of Bashan went out against them, he, and all his people, to the battle at Edrei. ³⁴And the LORD said unto Moses, Fear him not: for I have delivered him into thy hand, and all his people, and his land; and thou shalt do to him as thou didst unto Sihon king of the Amorites, which dwelt at Heshbon. ³⁵So they smote him, and his sons, and all his people, until there was none left him alive: and they possessed his land.

22

¹And the children of Israel set forward, and pitched in the plains of Moab on this side Jordan *by* Jericho. ²And Balak the son of Zippor saw all that Israel had done to the Amorites. ³And Moab was sore afraid of the people, because they *were* many: and Moab was distressed because of the children of Israel. ⁴And Moab said unto the elders of Midian, Now shall this company lick up all *that are* round about us, as the ox licketh up the grass of the field. And Balak the son of Zippor *was* king of the Moabites at that time. ⁵He sent messengers therefore unto Balaam the son of Beor to Pethor, which *is* by the river of the land of the children of his people, to call him, saying, Behold, there is a people come out from Egypt: behold, they cover the face[a] of the earth, and they abide over against me: ⁶Come now therefore, I pray thee,

f villages: Heb. daughters
a face: Heb. eye

curse me this people; for they *are* too mighty for me: peradventure I shall prevail, *that* we may smite them, and *that* I may drive them out of the land: for I wot that he whom thou blessest *is* blessed, and he whom thou cursest is cursed. ⁷And the elders of Moab and the elders of Midian departed with the rewards of divination in their hand; and they came unto Balaam, and spake unto him the words of Balak. ⁸And he said unto them, Lodge here this night, and I will bring you word again, as the LORD shall speak unto me: and the princes of Moab abode with Balaam. ⁹And God came unto Balaam, and said, What men *are* these with thee? ¹⁰And Balaam said unto God, Balak the son of Zippor, king of Moab, hath sent unto me, *saying*, ¹¹Behold, *there is* a people come out of Egypt, which covereth the face of the earth: come now, curse me them; peradventure I shall be able to overcome them, and drive them out. ¹²And God said unto Balaam, Thou shalt not go with them; thou shalt not curse the people: for they *are* blessed. ¹³And Balaam rose up in the morning, and said unto the princes of Balak, Get you into your land: for the LORD refuseth to give me leave to go with you. ¹⁴And the princes of Moab rose up, and they went unto Balak, and said, Balaam refuseth to come with us.

¹⁵And Balak sent yet again princes, more, and more honourable than they. ¹⁶And they came to Balaam, and said to him, Thus saith Balak the son of Zippor, Let nothing, I pray thee, hinder thee from coming unto me: ¹⁷For I will promote thee unto very great honour, and I will do whatsoever thou sayest unto me: come therefore, I pray thee, curse me this people. ¹⁸And Balaam answered and said unto the servants of Balak, If Balak would give me his house full of silver and gold, I cannot go beyond the word of the LORD my God, to do less or more. ¹⁹Now therefore, I pray you, tarry ye also here this night, that I may know what the LORD will say unto me more. ²⁰And God came unto Balaam at night, and said unto him, If the men come to call thee, rise up, *and* go with them; but yet the word which I shall say unto thee, that shalt thou do. ²¹And Balaam rose up in the morning, and saddled his ass, and went with the princes of Moab.

²²And God's anger was kindled because he went: and the angel of the LORD stood in the way for an adversary against him. Now he was riding upon his ass, and his two servants *were* with him. ²³And the ass saw the angel of the LORD standing in the way, and his sword drawn in his hand: and the ass turned aside out of the way, and went into the field: and Balaam smote the ass, to turn her into the way. ²⁴But the angel of the LORD stood in a path of the vineyards, a wall *being* on this side, and a wall on that side. ²⁵And when the ass saw the angel of the LORD, she thrust herself unto the wall, and crushed Balaam's foot against the wall: and he smote her again. ²⁶And the angel of the LORD went further, and stood in a narrow place, where *was* no way to turn either to the right hand or to the left. ²⁷And when the ass saw the angel of the LORD, she fell down under Balaam: and Balaam's anger was kindled, and he smote the ass with a staff. ²⁸And the LORD opened the mouth of the ass, and she said unto Balaam, What have I done unto thee,

Devotional Moment
·
Humility

22:29 The Bible is filled with examples of the warning found in Proverbs 16:18: "Pride goeth before destruction, and an haughty spirit before a fall." Instead of expressing gratitude for this miraculous intervention from God, Balaam wanted to kill the donkey for causing him to look foolish. How much better it would have been for Balaam to respond with gratitude and humility! The next time someone points out something you need to change, remember Balaam. Then swallow your pride, admit your need, and thank the person for helping you learn.

that thou hast smitten me these three times? ²⁹And Balaam said unto the ass, Because thou hast mocked me: I would there were a sword in mine hand, for now would I kill thee. ³⁰And the ass said unto Balaam, *Am* not I thine ass, upon which thou hast ridden ever since *I was* thine unto this day? was I ever wont to do so unto thee? And he said, Nay. ³¹Then the LORD opened the eyes of Balaam, and he saw the angel of the LORD standing in the way, and his sword drawn in his hand: and he bowed down his head, and fell flat on his face. ³²And the angel of the LORD said unto him, Wherefore hast thou smitten thine ass these three times? behold, I went out to withstand thee, because *thy* way is perverse before me: ³³And the ass saw me, and turned from me these three times: unless she had turned from me, surely now also I had slain thee, and saved her alive. ³⁴And Balaam said unto the angel of the LORD, I have sinned; for I knew not that thou stoodest in the

way against me: now therefore, if it displease thee, I will get me back again. ³⁵And the angel of the LORD said unto Balaam, Go with the men: but only the word that I shall speak unto thee, that thou shalt speak. So Balaam went with the princes of Balak.

³⁶And when Balak heard that Balaam was come, he went out to meet him unto a city of Moab, which *is* in the border of Arnon, which *is* in the utmost coast. ³⁷And Balak said unto Balaam, Did I not earnestly send unto thee to call thee? wherefore camest thou not unto me? am I not able indeed to promote thee to honour? ³⁸And Balaam said unto Balak, Lo, I am come unto thee: have I now any power at all to say any thing? the word that God putteth in my mouth, that shall I speak. ³⁹And Balaam went with Balak, and they came unto Kirjathhuzoth[b]. ⁴⁰And Balak offered oxen and sheep, and sent to Balaam, and to the princes that *were* with him. ⁴¹And it came to pass on the morrow, that Balak took Balaam, and brought him up into the high places of Baal, that thence he might see the utmost *part* of the people.

23

¹And Balaam said unto Balak, Build me here seven altars, and prepare me here seven oxen and seven rams. ²And Balak did as Balaam had spoken; and Balak and Balaam offered on *every* altar a bullock and a ram. ³And Balaam said unto Balak, Stand by thy burnt offering, and I will go: peradventure the LORD will come to meet me: and whatsoever he sheweth me I will tell thee. And he went to an high place. ⁴And God met Balaam:

---

[b] Kirjathhuzoth: or, a city of streets

Breaking the Power
of a "Curse"

This was Balaam's message: "Balak the king of Moab hath brought me from Aram, out of the mountains of the east, saying, 'Come, curse me Jacob, and come, defy Israel.'" Numbers 23:7

I n Old Testament times, there was tremendous power behind a curse. Balaam was a sorcerer who was hired by the king of Moab to curse God's people, the Israelites. But on his way to carry out his task, a mighty angel and a talking donkey changed his mind (see Num. 22).

While many have seen humor in God using a donkey to foil Balaam's plans, there was nothing funny about what he set out to do. Cursing someone can hold terrible power. And unfortunately, the negative cycle some people have to break today is one of growing up under a curse.

Take Dan, for example. He grew up with an alcoholic father who lived to torment him. His most graphic memory was of a time when he was only eight years old and had done something to upset his mother. She had called his father at work and told him of Dan's poor behavior. When Dan saw his father's car pull into the driveway after work that day, he ran up to greet him with a big smile.

Without a word, his father got out of the car and knocked him unconscious with one punch. Nearly thirty years later, Dan can still remember regaining consciousness and hearing his father uttering terrible curses on him.

Or take Rachel. Her father treated her to an even crueler curse by exposing her to satanism and terrible horror stories and films from the time she was very young. In fact, his favorite nickname for her was "demon daughter."

When Rachel first came in for counseling, she was in her twenties. She was tall and stunning in appearance, but there was one thing you soon noticed about her if you saw her more than once: She always dressed in black. With all the darkness she felt in her heart, she refused to wear anything but that one color, painted by her father across her mind and heart.

Nothing had the power to break a curse in Old Testament times except the greater power of a blessing. That's just what happened with Balaam, and that's what can happen for anyone who labors under a curse today.

Deuteronomy 23 contains a list of people to be excluded from the assembly of Israel. It says: "An Ammonite or Moabite shall not enter into the congregation of the Lord; even to their tenth generation. . . . because they hired against thee Balaam the son of Beor of Pethor of Mesopotamia, to curse thee." (vv. 3-4).

Balaam's curse was a powerful weapon, yet one that was defeated by an even greater power: "Nevertheless the Lord thy God would not hearken unto Balaam; but the Lord thy God turned the curse into a blessing unto thee, because the Lord thy God loved thee." (Deut. 23:5).

If you've grown up under the curse of a verbally or physically abusive parent or other relative, you're not trapped forever as a victim. God offers a way of escape and a blessing that carries even greater positive power to affect your life.

Today Rachel still has her black dresses, but they're stuffed in the back of a closet filled with bright colors. She keeps them as a reminder of the curse she felt she was once under and the freedom she now feels in Christ who brought springtime to her soul.

One key verse that has helped Rachel and many others is Jeremiah 29:11. If you feel as if you're laboring under damaging words or actions, memorize this verse and allow its truth and power to push aside those destructive words, just as God brushed aside Balaam's curse:

"For I know the thoughts that I think toward you, saith the Lord, thoughts of peace, and not of evil, to give you an expected end."

---

and he said unto him, I have prepared seven altars, and I have offered upon *every* altar a bullock and a ram. ⁵And the LORD put a word in Balaam's mouth, and said, Return unto Balak, and thus thou shalt speak. ⁶And he returned unto him, and, lo, he stood by his burnt sacrifice, he, and all the princes of Moab. ⁷And he took up his parable, and said, Balak the king of Moab hath brought me from Aram, out of the mountains of the east, *saying*, Come, curse me Jacob, and come, defy Israel. ⁸How shall I curse, whom God hath not cursed? or how shall I defy, *whom* the LORD hath not defied? ⁹For from the top of the rocks I see him, and from the hills I behold him: lo, the people shall dwell alone, and shall not be reckoned among the nations. ¹⁰Who can count the dust of Jacob, and

the number of the fourth *part* of Israel? Let me die the death of the righteous, and let my last end be like his! ¹¹And Balak said unto Balaam, What hast thou done unto me? I took thee to curse mine enemies, and, behold, thou hast blessed *them* altogether. ¹²And he answered and said, Must I not take heed to speak that which the LORD hath put in my mouth?

¹³And Balak said unto him, Come, I pray thee, with me unto another place, from whence thou mayest see them: thou shalt see but the utmost part of them, and shalt not see them all: and curse me them from thence. ¹⁴And he brought him into the field of Zophim, to the top of Pisgahª, and built seven altars, and offered a bullock and a ram on *every* altar. ¹⁵And he said unto Balak, Stand

---

ª Pisgah: or, the hill

here by thy burnt offering, while I meet *the LORD* yonder. ¹⁶And the LORD met Balaam, and put a word in his mouth, and said, Go again unto Balak, and say thus. ¹⁷And when he came to him, behold, he stood by his burnt offering, and the princes of Moab with him. And Balak said unto him, What hath the LORD spoken? ¹⁸And he took up his parable, and said, Rise up, Balak, and hear; hearken unto me, thou son of Zippor: ¹⁹God *is* not a man, that he should lie; neither the son of man, that he should repent: hath he said, and shall he not do *it?* or hath he spoken, and shall he not make it good? ²⁰Behold, I have received *commandment* to bless: and he hath blessed; and I cannot reverse it. ²¹He hath not beheld iniquity in Jacob, neither hath he seen perverseness in Israel: the LORD his God *is* with him, and the shout of a king *is* among them. ²²God brought them out of Egypt; he hath as it were the strength of an unicorn. ²³Surely *there is* no enchantment against Jacob, neither *is there* any divination against Israel: according to this time it shall be said of Jacob and of Israel, What hath God wrought! ²⁴Behold, the people shall rise up as a great lion, and lift up himself as a young lion: he shall not lie down until he eat *of* the prey, and drink the blood of the slain. ²⁵And Balak said unto Balaam, Neither curse them at all, nor bless them at all. ²⁶But Balaam answered and said unto Balak, Told not I thee, saying, All that the LORD speaketh, that I must do? ²⁷And Balak said unto Balaam, Come, I pray thee, I will bring thee unto another place; peradventure it will please God that thou mayest curse me them

from thence. ²⁸And Balak brought Balaam unto the top of Peor, that looketh toward Jeshimon. ²⁹And Balaam said unto Balak, Build me here seven altars, and prepare me here seven bullocks and seven rams. ³⁰And Balak did as Balaam had said, and offered a bullock and a ram on *every* altar.

24

¹And when Balaam saw that it pleased the LORD to bless Israel, he went not, as at other times, to seek ᵃ for enchantments, but he set his face toward the wilderness. ²And Balaam lifted up his eyes, and he saw Israel abiding *in his tents* according to their tribes; and the spirit of God came upon him. ³And he took up his parable, and said, Balaam the son of Beor hath said, and the man whose eyes are open hath said: ⁴He hath said, which heard the words of God, which saw the vision of the Almighty, falling *into a trance,* but having his eyes open: ⁵How goodly are thy tents, O Jacob, *and* thy tabernacles, O Israel! ⁶As the valleys are they spread forth, as gardens by the river's side, as the trees of lign aloes which the LORD hath planted, *and* as cedar trees beside the waters. ⁷He shall pour the water out of his buckets, and his seed *shall be* in many waters, and his king shall be higher than Agag, and his kingdom shall be exalted. ⁸God brought him forth out of Egypt; he hath as it were the strength of an unicorn: he shall eat up the nations his enemies, and shall break their bones, and pierce *them* through with his arrows. ⁹He couched, he lay down as a lion, and as a great lion: who shall stir him up? Blessed

ᵃ to seek . . . : Heb. to the meeting of

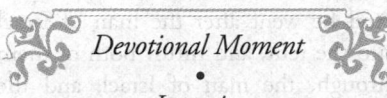

Devotional Moment

Integrity

24:10-14 Balaam was not always a model of pure motives and integrity, but in this instance he did what was right. Though tempted by Balak's offer of wealth and honor, Balaam refused to speak falsely in God's name. If you have not already experienced the temptation to put a selfish goal or reward above God's truth, you will, and so will your children. Help them learn from Balaam's example—good example, in this case—that it does not pay to give up your integrity for money or the praise of other people.

is he that blesseth thee, and cursed *is* he that curseth thee.

¹⁰And Balak's anger was kindled against Balaam, and he smote his hands together: and Balak said unto Balaam, I called thee to curse mine enemies, and, behold, thou hast altogether blessed *them* these three times. ¹¹Therefore now flee thou to thy place: I thought to promote thee unto great honour; but, lo, the LORD hath kept thee back from honour. ¹²And Balaam said unto Balak, Spake I not also to thy messengers which thou sentest unto me, saying, ¹³If Balak would give me his house full of silver and gold, I cannot go beyond the commandment of the LORD, to do *either* good or bad of mine own mind; *but* what the LORD saith, that will I speak? ¹⁴And now, behold, I go unto my people: come *therefore, and* I will advertise thee what this people shall do to thy people in the latter days.

¹⁵And he took up his parable, and said, Balaam the son of Beor hath said, and the man whose eyes are open hath said: ¹⁶He hath said, which heard the words of God, and knew the knowledge of the most High, *which* saw the vision of the Almighty, falling *into a trance*, but having his eyes open: ¹⁷I shall see him, but not now: I shall behold him, but not nigh: there shall come a Star out of Jacob, and a Sceptre shall rise out of Israel, and shall smiteᵇ the corners of Moab, and destroy all the children of Sheth. ¹⁸And Edom shall be a possession, Seir also shall be a possession for his enemies; and Israel shall do valiantly. ¹⁹Out of Jacob shall come he that shall have dominion, and shall destroy him that remaineth of the city. ²⁰And when he looked on Amalek, he took up his parable, and said, Amalek *was* the first of the nationsᶜ; but his latter end *shall be* that he perish for ever. ²¹And he looked on the Kenites, and took up his parable, and said, Strong is thy dwellingplace, and thou puttest thy nest in a rock. ²²Nevertheless the Keniteᵈ shall be wasted, until Asshur shall carry thee away captive. ²³And he took up his parable, and said, Alas, who shall live when God doeth this! ²⁴And ships *shall come* from the coast of Chittim, and shall afflict Asshur, and shall afflict Eber, and he also shall perish for ever. ²⁵And Balaam rose up, and went and returned to his place: and Balak also went his way.

25

¹And Israel abode in Shittim, and the people began to commit whoredom

ᵇ smite . . . : or, smite through the princes of
ᶜ the nations: the nations that warred against Israel
ᵈ the Kenite: Heb. Kain

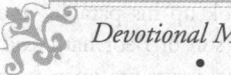

Devotional Moment

•

Compromise

25:1 The temptation to compromise your principles comes in many forms. Money, promotion, security, and sex are a few of the most common enticements. For the Israelites, it meant contaminating the worship of the true God with elements of other, pagan religions. For us, it can take more subtle forms, like materialism, lust, ambition, etc. In any case, flirting with a false god is like keeping toxic waste in the house: over time, it is very destructive to you and your loved ones. You cannot indulge sinful desires and still maintain a vibrant relationship with the true God.

with the daughters of Moab. ²And they called the people unto the sacrifices of their gods: and the people did eat, and bowed down to their gods. ³And Israel joined himself unto Baalpeor: and the anger of the LORD was kindled against Israel. ⁴And the LORD said unto Moses, Take all the heads of the people, and hang them up before the LORD against the sun, that the fierce anger of the LORD may be turned away from Israel. ⁵And Moses said unto the judges of Israel, Slay ye every one his men that were joined unto Baalpeor.

⁶And, behold, one of the children of Israel came and brought unto his brethren a Midianitish woman in the sight of Moses, and in the sight of all the congregation of the children of Israel, who *were* weeping *before* the door of the tabernacle of the congregation. ⁷And when Phinehas, the son of Eleazar, the son of Aaron the priest, saw *it*, he rose up from among the congregation, and took a javelin in his hand;

⁸And he went after the man of Israel into the tent, and thrust both of them through, the man of Israel, and the woman through her belly. So the plague was stayed from the children of Israel. ⁹And those that died in the plague were twenty and four thousand. ¹⁰And the LORD spake unto Moses, saying, ¹¹Phinehas, the son of Eleazar, the son of Aaron the priest, hath turned my wrath away from the children of Israel, while he was zealous for my sake among them, that I consumed not the children of Israel in my jealousy. ¹²Wherefore say, Behold, I give unto him my covenant of peace: ¹³And he shall have it, and his seed after him, *even* the covenant of an everlasting priesthood; because he was zealous for his God, and made an atonement for the children of Israel. ¹⁴Now the name of the Israelite that was slain, *even* that was slain with the Midianitish woman, *was* Zimri, the son of Salu, a prince of a chiefª house among the Simeonites. ¹⁵And the name

Devotional Moment

•

Anger

25:10-11 Phinehas acted on God's behalf, for God's high moral honor, when he killed the couple engaged in immoral sexual activity. God rewarded Phinehas' passion for his honor by granting him peace. Many events stir up anger in us; only a few warrant our retribution. Regaining God's high moral honor is one of these, yet we often seek revenge only when our social status or pride has suffered. Don't major in the minors. Keep anger under control so you can act to uphold God's honor.

ª chief . . . : Heb. house of a father

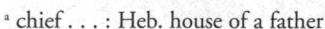

of the Midianitish woman that was slain *was* Cozbi, the daughter of Zur; he *was* head over a people, *and* of a chief house in Midian. ¹⁶And the LORD spake unto Moses, saying, ¹⁷Vex the Midianites, and smite them: ¹⁸For they vex you with their wiles, wherewith they have beguiled you in the matter of Peor, and in the matter of Cozbi, the daughter of a prince of Midian, their sister, which was slain in the day of the plague for Peor's sake.

26

¹And it came to pass after the plague, that the LORD spake unto Moses and unto Eleazar the son of Aaron the priest, saying, ²Take the sum of all the congregation of the children of Israel, from twenty years old and upward, throughout their fathers' house, all that are able to go to war in Israel. ³And Moses and Eleazar the priest spake with them in the plains of Moab by Jordan *near* Jericho, saying, ⁴ *Take the sum of the people*, from twenty years old and upward; as the LORD commanded Moses and the children of Israel, which went forth out of the land of Egypt.

⁵Reuben, the eldest son of Israel: the children of Reuben; Hanoch, *of whom cometh* the family of the Hanochites: of Pallu, the family of the Palluites: ⁶Of Hezron, the family of the Hezronites: of Carmi, the family of the Carmites. ⁷These *are* the families of the Reubenites: and they that were numbered of them were forty and three thousand and seven hundred and thirty. ⁸And the sons of Pallu; Eliab. ⁹And the sons of Eliab; Nemuel, and Dathan, and Abiram. This *is that* Dathan and Abiram, *which were* famous in the congregation, who strove against Moses and against Aaron in the company of Korah, when they strove against the LORD: ¹⁰And the earth opened her mouth, and swallowed them up together with Korah, when that company died, what time the fire devoured two hundred and fifty men: and they became a sign. ¹¹Notwithstanding the children of Korah died not. ¹²The sons of Simeon after their families: of Nemuel[a], the family of the Nemuelites: of Jamin, the family of the Jaminites: of Jachin, the family of the Jachinites: ¹³Of Zerah[b], the family of the Zarhites: of Shaul, the family of the Shaulites. ¹⁴These *are* the families of the Simeonites, twenty and two thousand and two hundred. ¹⁵The children of Gad after their families: of Zephon[c], the family of the Zephonites: of Haggi, the family of the Haggites: of Shuni, the family of the Shunites: ¹⁶Of Ozni[d], the family of the Oznites: of Eri, the family of the Erites: ¹⁷Of Arod[e], the family of the Arodites: of Areli, the family of the Arelites. ¹⁸These *are* the families of the children of Gad according to those that were numbered of them, forty thousand and five hundred. ¹⁹The sons of Judah

---

[a] Nemuel: also called, Jemuel
[b] Zerah: also called, Zohar
[c] Zephon: also called, Ziphion
[d] Ozni: or, Ezbon
[e] Arod: also called, Arodi

were Er and Onan: and Er and Onan died in the land of Canaan. ²⁰And the sons of Judah after their families were; of Shelah, the family of the Shelanites: of Pharez, the family of the Pharzites: of Zerah, the family of the Zarhites. ²¹And the sons of Pharez were; of Hezron, the family of the Hezronites: of Hamul, the family of the Hamulites. ²²These *are* the families of Judah according to those that were numbered of them, threescore and sixteen thousand and five hundred. ²³*Of* the sons of Issachar after their families: *of* Tola, the family of the Tolaites: of Pua^f, the family of the Punites: ²⁴Of Jashub^g, the family of the Jashubites: of Shimron, the family of the Shimronites. ²⁵These *are* the families of Issachar according to those that were numbered of them, threescore and four thousand and three hundred. ²⁶*Of* the sons of Zebulun after their families: of Sered, the family of the Sardites: of Elon, the family of the Elonites: of Jahleel, the family of the Jahleelites. ²⁷These *are* the families of the Zebulunites according to those that were numbered of them, threescore thousand and five hundred. ²⁸The sons of Joseph after their families *were* Manasseh and Ephraim. ²⁹Of the sons of Manasseh: of Machir, the family of the Machirites: and Machir begat Gilead: of Gilead *come* the family of the Gileadites. ³⁰These *are* the sons of Gilead: *of* Jeezer^h, the family of the Jeezerites: of Helek, the family of the Helekites: ³¹And *of* Asriel, the family of the Asrielites: and *of* Shechem, the family of the Shechemites: ³²And *of* Shemida, the family of the Shemidaites: and *of* Hepher, the family of the Hepherites. ³³And Zelophehad the son of Hepher had no sons, but daughters: and the names of the daughters of Zelophehad *were* Mahlah, and Noah, Hoglah, Milcah, and Tirzah. ³⁴These *are* the families of Manasseh, and those that were numbered of them, fifty and two thousand and seven hundred. ³⁵These *are* the sons of Ephraim after their families: of Shuthelah, the family of the Shuthalhites: of Becherⁱ, the family of the Bachrites: of Tahan, the family of the Tahanites. ³⁶And these *are* the sons of Shuthelah: of Eran, the family of the Eranites. ³⁷These *are* the families of the sons of Ephraim according to those that were numbered of them, thirty and two thousand and five hundred. These *are* the sons of Joseph after their families. ³⁸The sons of Benjamin after their families: of Bela, the family of the Belaites: of Ashbel, the family of the Ashbelites: of Ahiram^j, the family of the Ahiramites: ³⁹Of Shupham^k, the family of the Shuphamites: of Hupham, the family of the Huphamites. ⁴⁰And the sons of Bela were Ard^l and Naaman: *of Ard,* the family of the Ardites: *and* of Naaman, the family of the Naamites. ⁴¹These *are* the

---

^f Pua: or, Phuvah
^g Jashub: or, Job
^h Jeezer: also called Abiezer
ⁱ Becher: also called, Bered
^j Ahiram: also called, Ehi, or, Aharah
^k Shupham . . . Hupham: also called, Muppim and Huppim
^l Ard: also called, Addar

sons of Benjamin after their families: and they that were numbered of them *were* forty and five thousand and six hundred. [42]These *are* the sons of Dan after their families: of Shuham[m], the family of the Shuhamites. These *are* the families of Dan after their families. [43]All the families of the Shuhamites, according to those that were numbered of them, *were* threescore and four thousand and four hundred. [44]*Of* the children of Asher after their families: of Jimna, the family of the Jimnites: of Jesui, the family of the Jesuites: of Beriah, the family of the Beriites. [45]Of the sons of Beriah: of Heber, the family of the Heberites: of Malchiel, the family of the Malchielites. [46]And the name of the daughter of Asher *was* Sarah. [47]These *are* the families of the sons of Asher according to those that were numbered of them; *who were* fifty and three thousand and four hundred. [48]*Of* the sons of Naphtali after their families: of Jahzeel, the family of the Jahzeelites: of Guni, the family of the Gunites: [49]Of Jezer, the family of the Jezerites: of Shillem[n], the family of the Shillemites. [50]These *are* the families of Naphtali according to their families: and they that were numbered of them *were* forty and five thousand and four hundred. [51]These *were* the numbered of the children of Israel, six hundred thousand and a thousand seven hundred and thirty.

[52]And the LORD spake unto Moses, saying, [53]Unto these the land shall be divided for an inheritance according to the number of names. [54]To many thou shalt give the more[o] inheritance, and to few thou shalt give the less inheritance: to every one shall his inheritance be given according to those that were numbered of him. [55]Notwithstanding the land shall be divided by lot: according to the names of the tribes of their fathers they shall inherit. [56]According to the lot shall the possession thereof be divided between many and few.

[57]And these *are* they that were numbered of the Levites after their families: of Gershon, the family of the Gershonites: of Kohath, the family of the Kohathites: of Merari, the family of the Merarites. [58]These *are* the families of the Levites: the family of the Libnites, the family of the Hebronites, the family of the Mahlites, the family of the Mushites, the family of the Korathites. And Kohath begat Amram. [59]And the name of Amram's wife *was* Jochebed, the daughter of Levi, whom *her mother* bare to Levi in Egypt: and she bare unto Amram Aaron and Moses, and Miriam their sister. [60]And unto Aaron was born Nadab, and Abihu, Eleazar, and Ithamar. [61]And Nadab and Abihu died, when they offered strange fire before the LORD. [62]And those that were numbered of them were twenty and three thousand, all males from a month old and upward: for they were not numbered among the children of Israel, because there was no inheritance given them among the children of Israel.

---

[m] Shuham: or, Hushim
[n] Shillem: also called, Shallum
[o] give the more . . . . : Heb. multiply his inheritance

⁶³These *are* they that were numbered by Moses and Eleazar the priest, who numbered the children of Israel in the plains of Moab by Jordan *near* Jericho. ⁶⁴But among these there was not a man of them whom Moses and Aaron the priest numbered, when they numbered the children of Israel in the wilderness of Sinai. ⁶⁵For the LORD had said of them, They shall surely die in the wilderness. And there was not left a man of them, save Caleb the son of Jephunneh, and Joshua the son of Nun.

27

¹Then came the daughters of Zelophehad, the son of Hepher, the son of Gilead, the son of Machir, the son of Manasseh, of the families of Manasseh the son of Joseph: and these *are* the names of his daughters; Mahlah, Noah, and Hoglah, and Milcah, and Tirzah. ²And they stood before Moses, and before Eleazar the priest, and before the princes and all the congregation, *by* the door of the tabernacle of the congregation, saying, ³Our father died in the wilderness, and he was not in the company of them that gathered themselves together against the LORD in the company of Korah; but died in his own sin, and had no sons. ⁴Why should the name of our father be done away from among his family, because he hath no son? Give unto us *therefore* a possession among the brethren of our father. ⁵And Moses brought their cause before the LORD. ⁶And the LORD spake unto Moses, saying, ⁷The daughters of Zelophehad speak right: thou shalt surely give them a possession of an inheritance among their father's brethren; and thou shalt cause the inheritance of their father to pass unto them. ⁸And thou shalt speak unto the children of Israel, saying, If a man die, and have no son, then ye shall cause his inheritance to pass unto his daughter. ⁹And if he have no daughter, then ye shall give his inheritance unto his brethren. ¹⁰And if he have no brethren, then ye shall give his inheritance unto his father's brethren. ¹¹And if his father have no brethren, then ye shall give his inheritance unto his kinsman that is next to him of his family, and he shall possess it: and it shall be unto the children of Israel a statute of judgment, as the LORD commanded Moses.

¹²And the LORD said unto Moses, Get thee up into this mount Abarim, and see the land which I have given unto the children of Israel. ¹³And when thou hast seen it, thou also shalt be gathered unto thy people, as Aaron thy brother was gathered. ¹⁴For ye rebelled against my commandment in the desert

---

Devotional Moment

Inheritance

27:3-4 Up to this point, the Hebrew law gave sons alone the right to inherit. The daughters of Zelophehad, having no brothers, came to Moses to ask for their father's possessions. God told Moses that if a man died without sons, his inheritance would go to his daughters (27:8). But the daughters could keep it only if they married within their own tribe, probably so the territorial lines would remain intact (36:5-12). Many people don't think through the issues related to inheritance because they have so little to pass on, but parents and children should talk through the issues so that everyone has a clear understanding before the parents' death. Those decisions should be put in writing to make everything clear.

Devotional Moment

Children and Responsibility

27:15-20 God commanded Moses to hold a public meeting to present Joshua as God's new leader. Joshua was given authority because he had been proven trustworthy and faithful to God during years of testing and training in the wilderness. Sometimes parents withhold responsibility from children, fearing that they are not ready for it or that they will be crushed by early failures. But signs of maturity need to be rewarded with new responsibilities. Knowing when to pass on responsibilities takes discernment. But when a child shows signs of maturity, don't hesitate to train him or her by giving the child new responsibilities and duties. Your whole family will benefit.

of Zin, in the strife of the congregation, to sanctify me at the water before their eyes: that *is* the water of Meribah in Kadesh in the wilderness of Zin.

¹⁵And Moses spake unto the LORD, saying, ¹⁶Let the LORD, the God of the spirits of all flesh, set a man over the congregation, ¹⁷Which may go out before them, and which may go in before them, and which may lead them out, and which may bring them in; that the congregation of the LORD be not as sheep which have no shepherd. ¹⁸And the LORD said unto Moses, Take thee Joshua the son of Nun, a man in whom *is* the spirit, and lay thine hand upon him; ¹⁹And set him before Eleazar the priest, and before all the congregation; and give him a charge in their sight. ²⁰And thou shalt put *some* of thine honour upon him, that all the congregation

of the children of Israel may be obedient. ²¹And he shall stand before Eleazar the priest, who shall ask *counsel* for him after the judgment of Urim before the LORD: at his word shall they go out, and at his word they shall come in, *both* he, and all the children of Israel with him, even all the congregation. ²²And Moses did as the LORD commanded him: and he took Joshua, and set him before Eleazar the priest, and before all the congregation: ²³And he laid his hands upon him, and gave him a charge, as the LORD commanded by the hand of Moses.

28

¹And the LORD spake unto Moses, saying, ²Command the children of Israel, and say unto them, My offering, *and* my bread for my sacrifices made by fire, *for* a sweet[a] savour unto me, shall ye observe to offer unto me in their due season. ³And thou shalt say unto them, This *is* the offering made by fire which ye shall offer unto the LORD; two lambs of the first year without spot day by day[b], *for* a continual burnt offering. ⁴The one lamb shalt thou offer in the morning, and the other lamb shalt thou offer at even[c]; ⁵And a tenth *part* of an ephah of flour for a meat offering, mingled with the fourth *part* of an hin of beaten oil. ⁶*It is* a continual burnt offering, which was ordained in mount Sinai for a sweet savour, a sacrifice made by fire unto the LORD. ⁷And the drink offering thereof *shall be* the fourth *part* of an hin for the one lamb:

---

^a a sweet . . . : Heb. a savour of my rest
^b day by day: Heb. in a day
^c at even: Heb. between the two evenings

in the holy *place* shalt thou cause the strong wine to be poured unto the LORD *for* a drink offering. ⁸And the other lamb shalt thou offer at even: as the meat offering of the morning, and as the drink offering thereof, thou shalt offer *it*, a sacrifice made by fire, of a sweet savour unto the LORD.

⁹And on the sabbath day two lambs of the first year without spot, and two tenth deals of flour *for* a meat offering, mingled with oil, and the drink offering thereof: ¹⁰*This is* the burnt offering of every sabbath, beside the continual burnt offering, and his drink offering. ¹¹And in the beginnings of your months ye shall offer a burnt offering unto the LORD; two young bullocks, and one ram, seven lambs of the first year without spot; ¹²And three tenth deals of flour *for* a meat offering, mingled with oil, for one bullock; and two tenth deals of flour *for* a meat offering, mingled with oil, for one ram; ¹³And a several tenth deal of flour mingled with oil *for* a meat offering unto one lamb; *for* a burnt offering of a sweet savour, a sacrifice made by fire unto the LORD. ¹⁴And their drink offerings shall be half an hin of wine unto a bullock, and the third *part* of an hin unto a ram, and a fourth *part* of an hin unto a lamb: this *is* the burnt offering of every month throughout the months of the year. ¹⁵And one kid of the goats for a sin offering unto the LORD shall be offered, beside the continual burnt offering, and his drink offering.

¹⁶And in the fourteenth day of the first month *is* the passover of the LORD. ¹⁷And in the fifteenth day of this month *is* the feast: seven days shall unleavened bread be eaten. ¹⁸In the first day *shall be* an holy convocation; ye shall do no manner of servile work *therein*: ¹⁹But ye shall offer a sacrifice made by fire *for* a burnt offering unto the LORD; two young bullocks, and one ram, and seven lambs of the first year: they shall be unto you without blemish: ²⁰And their meat offering *shall be of* flour mingled with oil: three tenth deals shall ye offer for a bullock, and two tenth deals for a ram; ²¹A several tenth deal shalt thou offer for every lamb, throughout the seven lambs: ²²And one goat *for* a sin offering, to make an atonement for you. ²³Ye shall offer these beside the burnt offering in the morning, which *is* for a continual burnt offering. ²⁴After this manner ye shall offer daily, throughout the seven days, the meat of the sacrifice made by fire, of a sweet savour unto the LORD: it shall be offered beside the continual burnt offering, and his drink offering. ²⁵And on the seventh day ye shall have an holy convocation; ye shall do no servile work. ²⁶Also in the day of the firstfruits, when ye bring a new meat offering unto the LORD, after your weeks *be out*, ye shall have an holy convocation; ye shall do no servile work: ²⁷But ye shall offer the burnt offering for a sweet savour unto the LORD; two young bullocks, one ram, seven lambs of the first year; ²⁸And their meat offering of flour mingled with oil, three tenth deals unto one bullock, two tenth deals unto one ram, ²⁹A several tenth deal unto one lamb, throughout the seven lambs; ³⁰*And* one kid of the goats, to make an atonement for you. ³¹Ye shall offer *them* beside the continual burnt offering, and his meat offer-

ing, (they shall be unto you without blemish) and their drink offerings.

29

¹And in the seventh month, on the first *day* of the month, ye shall have an holy convocation; ye shall do no servile work: it is a day of blowing the trumpets unto you. ²And ye shall offer a burnt offering for a sweet savour unto the LORD; one young bullock, one ram, *and* seven lambs of the first year without blemish: ³And their meat offering *shall be of* flour mingled with oil, three tenth deals for a bullock, *and* two tenth deals for a ram, ⁴And one tenth deal for one lamb, throughout the seven lambs: ⁵And one kid of the goats *for* a sin offering, to make an atonement for you: ⁶Beside the burnt offering of the month, and his meat offering, and the daily burnt offering, and his meat offering, and their drink offer-

---

Devotional Moment

Holidays

29:1 God designated certain feasts and holidays for the Israelites to put aside their everyday routine—the work, the deadlines, the house projects, and the other demands of living—and focus on him. During these times the people devoted themselves to remembering God's deeds. Many families take vacations together to rest and relax, and that's good. Yet we also need "vacations" that observe and celebrate God's place in our lives. Make your celebrations of Christmas, Easter, and other "holy days" opportunities to remember God's deeds together. Start and keep traditions that your family can observe together—not only around Christmas, but also during other sacred holidays. These observances will draw everyone closer to God—and draw your family closer to each other as an extra benefit.

---

ings, according unto their manner, for a sweet savour, a sacrifice made by fire unto the LORD. ⁷And ye shall have on the tenth *day* of this seventh month an holy convocation; and ye shall afflict your souls: ye shall not do any work *therein*: ⁸But ye shall offer a burnt offering unto the LORD *for* a sweet savour; one young bullock, one ram, *and* seven lambs of the first year; they shall be unto you without blemish: ⁹And their meat offering *shall be of* flour mingled with oil, three tenth deals to a bullock, *and* two tenth deals to one ram, ¹⁰A several tenth deal for one lamb, throughout the seven lambs: ¹¹One kid of the goats *for* a sin offering; beside the sin offering of atonement, and the continual burnt offering, and the meat offering of it, and their drink offerings.

¹²And on the fifteenth day of the seventh month ye shall have an holy convocation; ye shall do no servile work, and ye shall keep a feast unto the LORD seven days: ¹³And ye shall offer a burnt offering, a sacrifice made by fire, of a sweet savour unto the LORD; thirteen young bullocks, two rams, *and* fourteen lambs of the first year; they shall be without blemish: ¹⁴And their meat offering *shall be of* flour mingled with oil, three tenth deals unto every bullock of the thirteen bullocks, two tenth deals to each ram of the two rams, ¹⁵And a several tenth deal to each lamb of the fourteen lambs: ¹⁶And one kid of the goats *for* a sin offering; beside the continual burnt offering, his meat offering, and his drink offering. ¹⁷And on the second day *ye shall offer* twelve young bullocks, two rams, fourteen lambs of the first year without spot: ¹⁸And their meat offering and their

drink offerings for the bullocks, for the rams, and for the lambs, *shall be* according to their number, after the manner: ¹⁹And one kid of the goats *for* a sin offering; beside the continual burnt offering, and the meat offering thereof, and their drink offerings. ²⁰And on the third day eleven bullocks, two rams, fourteen lambs of the first year without blemish; ²¹And their meat offering and their drink offerings for the bullocks, for the rams, and for the lambs, *shall be* according to their number, after the manner: ²²And one goat *for* a sin offering; beside the continual burnt offering, and his meat offering, and his drink offering. ²³And on the fourth day ten bullocks, two rams, *and* fourteen lambs of the first year without blemish: ²⁴Their meat offering and their drink offerings for the bullocks, for the rams, and for the lambs, *shall be* according to their number, after the manner: ²⁵And one kid of the goats *for* a sin offering; beside the continual burnt offering, his meat offering, and his drink offering. ²⁶And on the fifth day nine bullocks, two rams, *and* fourteen lambs of the first year without spot: ²⁷And their meat offering and their drink offerings for the bullocks, for the rams, and for the lambs, *shall be* according to their number, after the manner: ²⁸And one goat *for* a sin offering; beside the continual burnt offering, and his meat offering, and his drink offering. ²⁹And on the sixth day eight bullocks, two rams, *and* fourteen lambs of the first year without blemish: ³⁰And their meat offering and their drink offerings for the bullocks, for the rams, and for the lambs, *shall be*

according to their number, after the manner: ³¹And one goat *for* a sin offering; beside the continual burnt offering, his meat offering, and his drink offering. ³²And on the seventh day seven bullocks, two rams, *and* fourteen lambs of the first year without blemish: ³³And their meat offering and their drink offerings for the bullocks, for the rams, and for the lambs, *shall be* according to their number, after the manner: ³⁴And one goat *for* a sin offering; beside the continual burnt offering, his meat offering, and his drink offering. ³⁵On the eighth day ye shall have a solemn assembly: ye shall do no servile work *therein*: ³⁶But ye shall offer a burnt offering, a sacrifice made by fire, of a sweet savour unto the LORD: one bullock, one ram, seven lambs of the first year without blemish: ³⁷Their meat offering and their drink offerings for the bullock, for the ram, and for the lambs, *shall be* according to their number, after the manner: ³⁸And one goat *for* a sin offering; beside the continual burnt offering, and his meat offering, and his drink offering. ³⁹These *things* ye shall do*ᵃ* unto the LORD in your set feasts, beside your vows, and your freewill offerings, for your burnt offerings, and for your meat offerings, and for your drink offerings, and for your peace offerings. ⁴⁰And Moses told the children of Israel according to all that the LORD commanded Moses.

30

¹And Moses spake unto the heads of the tribes concerning the children of Israel, saying, This *is* the thing which the

---

ᵃ do: or, offer

LORD hath commanded. [2]If a man vow a vow unto the LORD, or swear an oath to bind his soul with a bond; he shall not break[a] his word, he shall do according to all that proceedeth out of his mouth.

[3]If a woman also vow a vow unto the LORD, and bind herself by a bond, *being* in her father's house in her youth; [4]And her father hear her vow, and her bond wherewith she hath bound her soul, and her father shall hold his peace at her: then all her vows shall stand, and every bond wherewith she hath bound her soul shall stand. [5]But if her father disallow her in the day that he heareth; not any of her vows, or of her bonds wherewith she hath bound her soul, shall stand: and the LORD shall forgive her, because her father disallowed her. [6]And if she had at all an husband, when she vowed[b], or uttered ought out of her lips, wherewith she bound her soul; [7]And her husband heard *it,* and held his peace at her in the day that he heard *it:* then her vows shall stand, and her bonds wherewith she bound her soul shall stand. [8]But if her husband disallowed her on the day that he heard *it;* then he shall make her vow which she vowed, and that which she uttered with her lips, wherewith she bound her soul, of none effect: and the LORD shall forgive her. [9]But every vow of a widow, and of her that is divorced, wherewith they have bound their souls, shall stand against her. [10]And if she vowed in her husband's house, or bound her soul by a bond with an oath; [11]And her husband heard *it,* and held his peace at her,

and disallowed her not: then all her vows shall stand, and every bond wherewith she bound her soul shall stand. [12]But if her husband hath utterly made them void on the day he heard *them; then* whatsoever proceeded out of her lips concerning her vows, or concerning the bond of her soul, shall not stand: her husband hath made them void; and the LORD shall forgive her. [13]Every vow, and every binding oath to afflict the soul, her husband may establish it, or her husband may make it void. [14]But if her husband altogether hold his peace at her from day to day; then he establisheth all her vows, or all her bonds, which *are* upon her: he confirmeth them, because he held his peace at her in the day that he heard *them.* [15]But if he shall any ways make them void after that he hath heard *them;* then he shall bear her iniquity. [16]These *are* the statutes, which the LORD commanded Moses, between a man and his wife, between the father and his daughter, *being yet* in her youth in her father's house.

31

[1]And the LORD spake unto Moses, saying, [2]Avenge the children of Israel of the Midianites: afterward shalt thou be gathered unto thy people. [3]And Moses spake unto the people, saying, Arm some of yourselves unto the war, and let them go against the Midianites, and avenge the LORD of Midian. [4]Of every tribe a thousand, throughout all the tribes of Israel, shall ye send to the war. [5]So there were delivered out of the

---

[a] break: Heb. profane
[b] she vowed: Heb. her vows were upon her

thousands of Israel, a thousand of *every* tribe, twelve thousand armed for war. [6]And Moses sent them to the war, a thousand of *every* tribe, them and Phinehas the son of Eleazar the priest, to the war, with the holy instruments, and the trumpets to blow in his hand.

[7]And they warred against the Midianites, as the LORD commanded Moses; and they slew all the males. [8]And they slew the kings of Midian, beside the rest of them that were slain; *namely*, Evi, and Rekem, and Zur, and Hur, and Reba, five kings of Midian: Balaam also the son of Beor they slew with the sword. [9]And the children of Israel took *all* the women of Midian captives, and their little ones, and took the spoil of all their cattle, and all their flocks, and all their goods. [10]And they burnt all their cities wherein they dwelt, and all their goodly castles, with fire. [11]And they took all the spoil, and all the prey, *both* of men and of beasts. [12]And they brought the captives, and the prey, and the spoil, unto Moses, and Eleazar the priest, and unto the congregation of the children of Israel, unto the camp at the plains of Moab, which *are* by Jordan *near* Jericho.

[13]And Moses, and Eleazar the priest, and all the princes of the congregation, went forth to meet them without the camp. [14]And Moses was wroth with the officers of the host, *with* the captains over thousands, and captains over hundreds, which came from the battle[a]. [15]And Moses said unto them, Have ye saved all the women alive? [16]Behold, these caused the children of Israel, through the counsel of Balaam, to commit trespass against the LORD in the matter of Peor, and there was a plague among the congregation of the LORD. [17]Now therefore kill every male among the little ones, and kill every woman that hath known man by lying with him[b]. [18]But all the women children, that have not known a man by lying with him, keep alive for yourselves. [19]And do ye abide without the camp seven days: whosoever hath killed any person, and whosoever hath touched any slain, purify *both* yourselves and your captives on the third day, and on the seventh day. [20]And purify all *your* raiment, and all that is made of skins, and all work of goats' *hair*, and all things made of wood. [21]And Eleazar the priest said unto the men of war which went to the battle, This *is* the ordinance of the law which the LORD commanded Moses; [22]Only the gold, and the silver, the brass, the iron, the tin, and the lead, [23]Every thing that may abide the fire, ye shall make *it* go through the fire, and it shall be clean: nevertheless it shall be purified with the water of separation: and all that abideth not the fire ye shall make go through the water. [24]And ye shall wash your clothes on the seventh day, and ye shall be clean, and afterward ye shall come into the camp.

[25]And the LORD spake unto Moses, saying, [26]Take the sum of the prey that was taken, *both* of man and of beast, thou, and Eleazar the priest, and the chief fathers of the congregation: [27]And divide the prey into two

---

[a] battle: Heb. host of war
[b] him: Heb. a male

parts; between them that took the war upon them, who went out to battle, and between all the congregation: [28]And levy a tribute unto the LORD of the men of war which went out to battle: one soul of five hundred, *both* of the persons, and of the beeves, and of the asses, and of the sheep: [29]Take *it* of their half, and give it unto Eleazar the priest, *for* an heave offering of the LORD. [30]And of the children of Israel's half, thou shalt take one portion of fifty, of the persons, of the beeves, of the asses, and of the flocks[c], of all manner of beasts, and give them unto the Levites, which keep the charge of the tabernacle of the LORD. [31]And Moses and Eleazar the priest did as the LORD commanded Moses. [32]And the booty, *being* the rest of the prey which the men of war had caught, was six hundred thousand and seventy thousand and five thousand sheep, [33]And threescore and twelve thousand beeves, [34]And threescore and one thousand asses, [35]And thirty and two thousand persons in all, of women that had not known man by lying with him. [36]And the half, *which was* the portion of them that went out to war, was in number three hundred thousand and seven and thirty thousand and five hundred sheep: [37]And the LORD'S tribute of the sheep was six hundred and threescore and fifteen. [38]And the beeves *were* thirty and six thousand; of which the LORD'S tribute *was* threescore and twelve. [39]And the asses *were* thirty thousand and five hundred; of which the LORD'S tribute *was* threescore and one. [40]And the persons *were* sixteen thousand; of which the LORD'S tribute *was* thirty and two persons. [41]And Moses gave the tribute, *which was* the LORD'S heave offering, unto Eleazar the priest, as the LORD commanded Moses. [42]And of the children of Israel's half, which Moses divided from the men that warred, [43](Now the half *that pertained unto* the congregation was three hundred thousand and thirty thousand *and* seven thousand and five hundred sheep, [44]And thirty and six thousand beeves, [45]And thirty thousand asses and five hundred, [46]And sixteen thousand persons;) [47]Even of the children of Israel's half, Moses took one portion of fifty, *both* of man and of beast, and gave them unto the Levites, which kept the charge of the tabernacle of the LORD; as the LORD commanded Moses.

[48]And the officers which *were* over thousands of the host, the captains of thousands, and captains of hundreds, came near unto Moses: [49]And they said unto Moses, Thy servants have taken the sum of the men of war which *are* under our charge[d], and there lacketh not one man of us. [50]We have therefore brought an oblation for the LORD, what every man hath gotten[e], of jewels of gold, chains, and bracelets, rings, earrings, and tablets, to make an atonement for our souls before the LORD. [51]And Moses and Eleazar the priest took the gold of them, *even* all wrought jew-

---

[c] flocks: or, goats
[d] charge: Heb. hand
[e] gotten: Heb. found

els. ⁵²And all the gold of the offering^f that they offered up to the LORD, of the captains of thousands, and of the captains of hundreds, was sixteen thousand seven hundred and fifty shekels. ⁵³(*For* the men of war had taken spoil, every man for himself.) ⁵⁴And Moses and Eleazar the priest took the gold of the captains of thousands and of hundreds, and brought it into the tabernacle of the congregation, *for* a memorial for the children of Israel before the LORD.

32

¹Now the children of Reuben and the children of Gad had a very great multitude of cattle: and when they saw the land of Jazer, and the land of Gilead, that, behold, the place *was* a place for cattle; ²The children of Gad and the children of Reuben came and spake unto Moses, and to Eleazar the priest,

and unto the princes of the congregation, saying, ³Ataroth, and Dibon, and Jazer, and Nimrah^a, and Heshbon, and Elealeh, and Shebam, and Nebo, and Beon, ⁴*Even* the country which the LORD smote before the congregation of Israel, *is* a land for cattle, and thy servants have cattle: ⁵Wherefore, said they, if we have found grace in thy sight, let this land be given unto thy servants for a possession, *and* bring us not over Jordan. ⁶And Moses said unto the children of Gad and to the children of Reuben, Shall your brethren go to war, and shall ye sit here? ⁷And wherefore discourage ye the heart of the children of Israel from going over into the land which the LORD hath given them? ⁸Thus did your fathers, when I sent them from Kadeshbarnea to see the land. ⁹For when they went up unto the valley of Eshcol, and saw the land, they discouraged the heart of the children of Israel, that they should not go into the land which the LORD had given them. ¹⁰And the LORD'S anger was kindled the same time, and he sware, saying, ¹¹Surely none of the men that came up out of Egypt, from twenty years old and upward, shall see the land which I sware unto Abraham, unto Isaac, and unto Jacob; because they have not wholly^b followed me: ¹²Save Caleb the son of Jephunneh the Kenezite, and Joshua the son of Nun: for they have wholly followed the LORD. ¹³And the LORD'S anger was kindled against Israel, and he made them wander in the wilderness forty years, until all the generation, that

---

^f offering: Heb. heave offering
^a Nimrah: also called, Bethnimrah
^b wholly . . . : Heb. fulfilled after me

had done evil in the sight of the LORD, was consumed. ¹⁴And, behold, ye are risen up in your fathers' stead, an increase of sinful men, to augment yet the fierce anger of the LORD toward Israel. ¹⁵For if ye turn away from after him, he will yet again leave them in the wilderness; and ye shall destroy all this people.

¹⁶And they came near unto him, and said, We will build sheepfolds here for our cattle, and cities for our little ones: ¹⁷But we ourselves will go ready armed before the children of Israel, until we have brought them unto their place: and our little ones shall dwell in the fenced cities because of the inhabitants of the land. ¹⁸We will not return unto our houses, until the children of Israel have inherited every man his inheritance. ¹⁹For we will not inherit with them on yonder side Jordan, or forward; because our inheritance is fallen to us on this side Jordan eastward. ²⁰And Moses said unto them, If ye will do this thing, if ye will go armed before the LORD to war, ²¹And will go all of you armed over Jordan before the LORD, until he hath driven out his enemies from before him, ²²And the land

---

Devotional Moment

Teamwork

32:16-19 After Moses' words of correction, the two tribes agreed to fulfill their obligation to God and to the other ten tribes. They would cross the Jordan to fight with the others as a team. The nature of teamwork lies in everyone working together until each member receives his or her portion. Think of your family as a team. Encourage each person to look out for the others and keep helping until everyone has what he or she needs.

---

be subdued before the LORD: then afterward ye shall return, and be guiltless before the LORD, and before Israel; and this land shall be your possession before the LORD. ²³But if ye will not do so, behold, ye have sinned against the LORD: and be sure your sin will find you out. ²⁴Build you cities for your little ones, and folds for your sheep; and do that which hath proceeded out of your mouth. ²⁵And the children of Gad and the children of Reuben spake unto Moses, saying, Thy servants will do as my lord commandeth. ²⁶Our little ones, our wives, our flocks, and all our cattle, shall be there in the cities of Gilead: ²⁷But thy servants will pass over, every man armed for war, before the LORD to battle, as my lord saith.

²⁸So concerning them Moses commanded Eleazar the priest, and Joshua the son of Nun, and the chief fathers of the tribes of the children of Israel: ²⁹And Moses said unto them, If the children of Gad and the children of Reuben will pass with you over Jordan, every man armed to battle, before the LORD, and the land shall be subdued before you; then ye shall give them the land of Gilead for a possession: ³⁰But if they will not pass over with you armed, they shall have possessions among you in the land of Canaan. ³¹And the children of Gad and the children of Reuben answered, saying, As the LORD hath said unto thy servants, so will we do. ³²We will pass over armed before the LORD into the land of Canaan, that the possession of our inheritance on this side Jordan *may be* ours. ³³And Moses gave unto them, *even* to the children of Gad, and to the children of Reuben, and unto half the tribe of Manasseh the son

of Joseph, the kingdom of Sihon king of the Amorites, and the kingdom of Og king of Bashan, the land, with the cities thereof in the coasts, *even* the cities of the country round about. [34]And the children of Gad built Dibon, and Ataroth, and Aroer, [35]And Atroth, Shophan, and Jaazer[c], and Jogbehah, [36]And Bethnimrah[d], and Bethharan, fenced cities: and folds for sheep. [37]And the children of Reuben built Heshbon, and Elealeh, and Kirjathaim, [38]And Nebo, and Baalmeon, (their names being changed,) and Shibmah: and gave[e] other names unto the cities which they builded. [39]And the children of Machir the son of Manasseh went to Gilead, and took it, and dispossessed the Amorite which *was* in it. [40]And Moses gave Gilead unto Machir the son of Manasseh; and he dwelt therein. [41]And Jair the son of Manasseh went and took the small towns thereof, and called them Havothjair. [42]And Nobah went and took Kenath, and the villages thereof, and called it Nobah, after his own name.

33

[1]These *are* the journeys of the children of Israel, which went forth out of the land of Egypt with their armies under the hand of Moses and Aaron. [2]And Moses wrote their goings out according to their journeys by the commandment of the LORD: and these *are* their journeys according to their goings out. [3]And they departed from Rameses in the first month, on the fifteenth day of the first month; on the morrow after the passover the children of Israel went out with an high hand in the sight of all the Egyptians. [4]For the Egyptians buried all *their* firstborn, which the LORD had smitten among them: upon their gods also the LORD executed judgments. [5]And the children of Israel removed from Rameses, and pitched in Succoth. [6]And they departed from Succoth, and pitched in Etham, which *is* in the edge of the wilderness. [7]And they removed from Etham, and turned again unto Pihahiroth, which *is* before Baalzephon: and they pitched before Migdol. [8]And they departed from before Pihahiroth, and passed through the midst of the sea into the wilderness, and went three days' journey in the wilderness of Etham, and pitched in Marah. [9]And they removed from Marah, and came unto Elim: and in Elim *were* twelve fountains of water, and threescore and ten palm trees; and they pitched there. [10]And they removed from Elim, and encamped by the Red sea. [11]And they removed from the Red sea, and encamped in the wilderness of Sin. [12]And they took their journey out of the wilderness of Sin, and encamped in Dophkah. [13]And they departed from Dophkah, and encamped in Alush. [14]And they removed from Alush, and encamped at Rephidim, where was no water for the people to drink. [15]And they departed from Rephidim, and pitched in the wilderness of Sinai. [16]And they removed from the desert of

---

[c] Jaazer: also called, Jazer
[d] Bethnimrah: also called, Nimrah
[e] gave . . . : Heb. they called by names the names of the cities

Sinai, and pitched at Kibrothhattaavah[a]. [17]And they departed from Kibrothhattaavah, and encamped at Hazeroth. [18]And they departed from Hazeroth, and pitched in Rithmah. [19]And they departed from Rithmah, and pitched at Rimmonparez. [20]And they departed from Rimmonparez, and pitched in Libnah. [21]And they removed from Libnah, and pitched at Rissah. [22]And they journeyed from Rissah, and pitched in Kehelathah. [23]And they went from Kehelathah, and pitched in mount Shapher. [24]And they removed from mount Shapher, and encamped in Haradah. [25]And they removed from Haradah, and pitched in Makheloth. [26]And they removed from Makheloth, and encamped at Tahath. [27]And they departed from Tahath, and pitched at Tarah. [28]And they removed from Tarah, and pitched in Mithcah. [29]And they went from Mithcah, and pitched in Hashmonah. [30]And they departed from Hashmonah, and encamped at Moseroth. [31]And they departed from Moseroth, and pitched in Benejaakan. [32]And they removed from Benejaakan, and encamped at Horhagidgad. [33]And they went from Horhagidgad, and pitched in Jotbathah. [34]And they removed from Jotbathah, and encamped at Ebronah. [35]And they departed from Ebronah, and encamped at Eziongaber. [36]And they removed from Eziongaber, and pitched in the wilderness of Zin, which is Kadesh. [37]And they removed from Kadesh, and pitched in mount Hor, in the edge of the land of Edom. [38]And Aaron the priest went up into mount Hor at the commandment of the LORD, and died there, in the fortieth year after the children of Israel were come out of the land of Egypt, in the first *day* of the fifth month. [39]And Aaron *was* an hundred and twenty and three years old when he died in mount Hor. [40]And king Arad the Canaanite, which dwelt in the south in the land of Canaan, heard of the coming of the children of Israel. [41]And they departed from mount Hor, and pitched in Zalmonah. [42]And they departed from Zalmonah, and pitched in Punon. [43]And they departed from Punon, and pitched in Oboth. [44]And they departed from Oboth, and pitched in Ijeabarim[b], in the border of Moab. [45]And they departed from Iim, and pitched in Dibongad. [46]And they removed from Dibongad, and encamped in Almondiblathaim. [47]And they removed from Almondiblathaim, and pitched in the mountains of Abarim, before Nebo. [48]And they departed from the mountains of Abarim, and pitched in the plains of Moab by Jordan *near* Jericho. [49]And they pitched by Jordan, from Bethjesimoth *even* unto Abelshittim[c] in the plains of Moab.

[50]And the LORD spake unto Moses in the plains of Moab by Jordan *near* Jericho, saying, [51]Speak unto the children of Israel, and say unto them, When ye are passed over Jordan into the land of Canaan; [52]Then ye shall drive out all the inhabitants of the land

---

[a] Kibrothhattaavah: that is, the graves of lust
[b] Ijeabarim: or, heaps of Abarim
[c] Abelshittim: or, the plains of Shittim

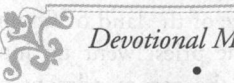

Devotional Moment
•
Idolatry

33:52 God warned his people to destroy all the idols of the people living in the land they were about to enter. If the Israelites did not destroy all aspects of idolatry, they would not fully appreciate the land that God gave them. Most of us feel too sophisticated to bow down before literal idols. However, we fashion idols in our lives with our time and attention, as surely as if we'd carved or cast them. Anything that takes the place of God in our heart—whether it be a career, prestige, money, a nice home, or our reputation—has become our idol. Does your family have an idol—some thing or priority that everyone allows to take God's place? If so, admit it to God. Then renew your commitment to worship only him.

from before you, and destroy all their pictures, and destroy all their molten images, and quite pluck down all their high places: ⁵³And ye shall dispossess *the inhabitants* of the land, and dwell therein: for I have given you the land to possess it. ⁵⁴And ye shall divide the land by lot for an inheritance among your families: *and* to the more ye shall give the more[d] inheritance, and to the fewer ye shall give the less inheritance: every man's *inheritance* shall be in the place where his lot falleth; according to the tribes of your fathers ye shall inherit. ⁵⁵But if ye will not drive out the inhabitants of the land from before you; then it shall come to pass, that those which ye let remain of them *shall be* pricks in your eyes, and thorns in your sides, and shall vex you in the land wherein ye dwell. ⁵⁶Moreover it

shall come to pass, *that* I shall do unto you, as I thought to do unto them.

34

¹And the LORD spake unto Moses, saying, ²Command the children of Israel, and say unto them, When ye come into the land of Canaan; (this *is* the land that shall fall unto you for an inheritance, *even* the land of Canaan with the coasts thereof:) ³Then your south quarter shall be from the wilderness of Zin along by the coast of Edom, and your south border shall be the outmost coast of the salt sea eastward: ⁴And your border shall turn from the south to the ascent of Akrabbim, and pass on to Zin: and the going forth thereof shall be from the south to Kadeshbarnea, and shall go on to Hazaraddar, and pass on to Azmon: ⁵And the border shall fetch a compass from Azmon unto the river of Egypt, and the goings out of it shall be at the sea. ⁶And *as for* the western border, ye shall even have the great sea for a border: this shall be your west border. ⁷And this shall be your north border: from the great sea ye shall point out for you mount Hor: ⁸From mount Hor ye shall point out *your border* unto the entrance of Hamath; and the goings forth of the border shall be to Zedad: ⁹And the border shall go on to Ziphron, and the goings out of it shall be at Hazarenan: this shall be your north border. ¹⁰And ye shall point out your east border from Hazarenan to Shepham: ¹¹And the coast shall go down from Shepham to Riblah, on the east side of Ain; and the border shall descend, and shall reach unto the side

---

[d] give the more . . . : Heb. multiply his inheritance

of the sea[a] of Chinnereth eastward: [12]And the border shall go down to Jordan, and the goings out of it shall be at the salt sea: this shall be your land with the coasts thereof round about. [13]And Moses commanded the children of Israel, saying, This *is* the land which ye shall inherit by lot, which the LORD commanded to give unto the nine tribes, and to the half tribe: [14]For the tribe of the children of Reuben according to the house of their fathers, and the tribe of the children of Gad according to the house of their fathers, have received *their inheritance*; and half the tribe of Manasseh have received their inheritance: [15]The two tribes and the half tribe have received their inheritance on this side Jordan *near* Jericho eastward, toward the sunrising.

[16]And the LORD spake unto Moses, saying, [17]These *are* the names of the men which shall divide the land unto you: Eleazar the priest, and Joshua the son of Nun. [18]And ye shall take one prince of every tribe, to divide the land by inheritance. [19]And the names of the men *are* these: Of the tribe of Judah, Caleb the son of Jephunneh. [20]And of the tribe of the children of Simeon, Shemuel the son of Ammihud. [21]Of the tribe of Benjamin, Elidad the son of Chislon. [22]And the prince of the tribe of the children of Dan, Bukki the son of Jogli. [23]The prince of the children of Joseph, for the tribe of the children of Manasseh, Hanniel the son of Ephod. [24]And the prince of the tribe of the children of Ephraim, Kemuel the son of Shiphtan. [25]And the prince of the tribe of the children of Zebulun, Elizaphan the son of Parnach. [26]And the prince of the tribe of the children of Issachar, Paltiel the son of Azzan. [27]And the prince of the tribe of the children of Asher, Ahihud the son of Shelomi. [28]And the prince of the tribe of the children of Naphtali, Pedahel the son of Ammihud. [29]These *are they* whom the LORD commanded to divide the inheritance unto the children of Israel in the land of Canaan.

35

[1]And the LORD spake unto Moses in the plains of Moab by Jordan *near* Jericho, saying, [2]Command the children of Israel, that they give unto the Levites of the inheritance of their possession cities to dwell in; and ye shall give *also* unto the Levites suburbs for the cities round about them. [3]And the cities shall they have to dwell in; and the suburbs of them shall be for their cattle, and for their goods, and for all their beasts. [4]And the suburbs of the cities, which ye shall give unto the Levites, *shall reach* from the wall of

---

Devotional Moment

Parents as Partners

34:16-29 God appointed Joshua and Eleazar to divide up the land, but he also appointed men from each tribe to act as representatives for the individual tribes. This would guard against possible misunderstandings or unfairnesses. To be fair, parents also need input from others, particularly from each other, but also from the children. As a leader of your family, rely on input from others. Work as a team. Make sure everyone's viewpoint receives attention before making a decision that may affect others.

---

[a] side of the sea: Heb. shoulder of the sea

the city and outward a thousand cubits round about. ⁵And ye shall measure from without the city on the east side two thousand cubits, and on the south side two thousand cubits, and on the west side two thousand cubits, and on the north side two thousand cubits; and the city *shall be* in the midst: this shall be to them the suburbs of the cities. ⁶And among the cities which ye shall give unto the Levites *there shall be* six cities for refuge, which ye shall appoint for the manslayer, that he may flee thither: and to them ye shall add forty and two cities. ⁷*So* all the cities which ye shall give to the Levites *shall be* forty and eight cities: them *shall ye give* with their suburbs. ⁸And the cities which ye shall give *shall be* of the possession of the children of Israel: from *them that have* many ye shall give many; but from *them that have* few ye shall give few: every one shall give of his cities unto the Levites according to his inheritance which he inheriteth.

⁹And the LORD spake unto Moses, saying, ¹⁰Speak unto the children of Israel, and say unto them, When ye be come over Jordan into the land of Canaan; ¹¹Then ye shall appoint you cities to be cities of refuge for you; that the slayer may flee thither, which killeth any person at unawares. ¹²And they shall be unto you cities for refuge from the avenger; that the manslayer die not, until he stand before the congregation in judgment. ¹³And of these cities which ye shall give six cities shall ye have for refuge. ¹⁴Ye shall give three cities on this side Jordan, and three cities shall ye give in the land of Canaan, *which* shall be cities of refuge. ¹⁵These six cities shall be a refuge, *both* for the children of Israel, and for the stranger, and for the sojourner among them: that every one that killeth any person unawares may flee thither. ¹⁶And if he smite him with an instrument of iron, so that he die, he *is* a murderer: the murderer shall surely be put to death. ¹⁷And if he smite him with throwing a stone, wherewith he may die, and he die, he *is* a murderer: the murderer shall surely be put to death. ¹⁸Or *if* he smite him with an hand weapon of wood, wherewith he may die, and he die, he *is* a murderer: the murderer shall surely be put to death. ¹⁹The revenger of blood himself shall slay the murderer: when he meeteth him, he shall slay him. ²⁰But if he thrust him of hatred, or hurl at him by laying of wait, that he die; ²¹Or in enmity smite him with his hand, that he die: he that smote *him* shall surely be put to death; *for* he *is* a murderer: the revenger of blood shall slay the murderer, when he meeteth him. ²²But if he thrust him suddenly without enmity, or have cast

upon him any thing without laying of wait, ²³Or with any stone, wherewith a man may die, seeing *him* not, and cast *it* upon him, that he die, and *was* not his enemy, neither sought his harm: ²⁴Then the congregation shall judge between the slayer and the revenger of blood according to these judgments: ²⁵And the congregation shall deliver the slayer out of the hand of the revenger of blood, and the congregation shall restore him to the city of his refuge, whither he was fled: and he shall abide in it unto the death of the high priest, which was anointed with the holy oil. ²⁶But if the slayer shall at any time come without the border of the city of his refuge, whither he was fled; ²⁷And the revenger of blood find him without the borders of the city of his refuge, and the revenger of blood kill the slayer; he shall not be guilty of blood: ²⁸Because he should have remained in the city of his refuge until the death of the high priest: but after the death of the high priest the slayer shall return into the land of his possession. ²⁹So these *things* shall be

for a statute of judgment unto you throughout your generations in all your dwellings. ³⁰Whoso killeth any person, the murderer shall be put to death by the mouth of witnesses: but one witness shall not testify against any person *to cause him* to die. ³¹Moreover ye shall take no satisfaction for the life of a murderer, which *is* guilty[a] of death: but he shall be surely put to death. ³²And ye shall take no satisfaction for him that is fled to the city of his refuge, that he should come again to dwell in the land, until the death of the priest. ³³So ye shall not pollute the land wherein ye *are*: for blood it defileth the land: and the land cannot be cleansed of the blood that is shed therein, but by the blood of him that shed it. ³⁴Defile not therefore the land which ye shall inhabit, wherein I dwell: for I the LORD dwell among the children of Israel.

36

¹And the chief fathers of the families of the children of Gilead, the son of Machir, the son of Manasseh, of the families of the sons of Joseph, came near, and spake before Moses, and before the princes, the chief fathers of the children of Israel: ²And they said, The LORD commanded my lord to give the land for an inheritance by lot to the children of Israel: and my lord was commanded by the LORD to give the inheritance of Zelophehad our brother unto his daughters. ³And if they be married to any of the sons of the *other* tribes of the children of Israel, then shall their inheritance be taken from the inheritance of our fathers, and shall

---

Devotional Moment

•

Fairness

35:33 God provided six Cities of Refuge for those in Israel who were guilty of manslaughter (unintentional killing), cities where they could find safety from vengeful relatives and receive a fair trial. This provision demonstrates God's mercy and concern for justice. Do you have a "safe place" in your home? Always consider the motives and make a distinction between intentional hurts and unintended ones, including the breaking of a toy or prized possession.

---

[a] guilty . . . : Heb. faulty to die

be put to the inheritance of the tribe whereunto they are received: so shall it be taken from the lot of our inheritance. ⁴And when the jubile of the children of Israel shall be, then shall their inheritance be put unto the inheritance of the tribe whereunto they are received: so shall their inheritance be taken away from the inheritance of the tribe of our fathers.

⁵And Moses commanded the children of Israel according to the word of the LORD, saying, The tribe of the sons of Joseph hath said well. ⁶This *is* the thing which the LORD doth command concerning the daughters of Zelophehad, saying, Let them marry[a] to whom they think best; only to the family of the tribe of their father shall they marry. ⁷So shall not the inheritance of the children of Israel remove from tribe to tribe: for every one of the children of Israel shall keep[b] himself to the inheritance of the tribe of his fathers. ⁸And every daughter, that possesseth an inheritance in any tribe of the children of Israel, shall be wife unto one of the family of the tribe of her father, that the children of Israel may enjoy every man the inheritance of his fathers. ⁹Neither shall the inheritance remove from *one* tribe to another tribe; but every one of the tribes of the children of Israel shall keep himself to his own inheritance. ¹⁰Even as the LORD commanded Moses, so did the daughters of Zelophehad: ¹¹For Mahlah, Tirzah, and Hoglah, and Milcah, and Noah, the daughters of Zelophehad, were married unto their father's brothers' sons: ¹²*And* they were married into the families of the sons of Manasseh the son of Joseph, and their inheritance remained in the tribe of the family of their father. ¹³These *are* the commandments and the judgments, which the LORD commanded by the hand of Moses unto the children of Israel in the plains of Moab by Jordan *near* Jericho.

---

[a] marry: Heb. be wives
[b] keep . . . : Heb. cleave to the, etc

DEUTERONOMY

Purpose
To remind the people of what God has done and encourage them to rededicate their lives to him

Author
Moses (except for the final summary which was probably written by Joshua after Moses' death)

To Whom Written
Israel (the new generation entering the Promised Land)

Date Written
About 1407 B.C.

Setting
The east side of the Jordan River, in view of the Promised Land

Key Verse
"The Lord thy God, he is God, the faithful God" (7:9).

Key People
Moses, Joshua

Key Places
The valley of the Arabah in Moab, east of the Jordan River

Most of us have boxes full of photographs—kindergarten classmates, old boyfriends, parents, siblings, friends. Now camcorders and digital cameras are recording every holiday and birthday. The scrapbook of our life is heavy on visuals and light on words, apart from captions.

But why not a scrapbook of words? Why shouldn't parents record for later reading the early bedtime stories they told the child, the first bedside prayers, the sweet words of aging grandparents, the baptism sermon, the talk on dating, the thoughts they tried to share on the wedding day, and finally, at the end—perhaps with a grown child's help—words of faith and hope as a parent's or grandparent's vision turns toward heaven. Why not?

In a sense, that's what we have in Deuteronomy—a book in which Moses records how God loved the people all along, forgave their mistakes, kept them from hunger, and will lead them to Canaan when Moses is gone. It's a scrapbook of faith, a word book, vivid and strong—the head of a family saying to his children, "God is the Rock. Don't be afraid."

Some of Moses' words repeat parts of earlier Bible books. No problem; we can use the reminder. Always Moses' words ring with the call to trust, obey, and follow God in joy: timely advice from a father in the faith.

1

¹These *be* the words which Moses spake unto all Israel on this side Jordan in the wilderness, in the plain over against the Red[a] *sea*, between Paran, and Tophel, and Laban, and Hazeroth, and Dizahab. ²(*There are* eleven days' *journey* from Horeb by the way of mount Seir unto Kadeshbarnea.) ³And it came to pass in the fortieth year, in the eleventh month, on the first *day* of the month, *that* Moses spake unto the children of Israel, according unto all that the LORD had given him in commandment unto them; ⁴After he had slain Sihon the king of the Amorites, which dwelt in Heshbon, and Og the king of Bashan, which dwelt at Astaroth in Edrei: ⁵On this side Jordan, in the land of Moab, began Moses to declare this law, saying, ⁶The LORD our God spake unto us in Horeb, saying, Ye have dwelt long enough in this mount: ⁷Turn you, and take your journey, and go to the mount of the Amorites, and unto all *the places* nigh[b] thereunto, in the plain, in the hills, and in the vale, and in the south, and by the sea side, to the land of the Canaanites, and unto Lebanon, unto the great river, the river Euphrates. ⁸Behold, I have set[c] the land before you: go in and possess the land which the LORD sware unto your fathers, Abraham, Isaac, and Jacob, to give unto them and to their seed after them.

⁹And I spake unto you at that time, saying, I am not able to bear you myself alone: ¹⁰The LORD your God hath multiplied you, and, behold, ye *are* this day as the stars of heaven for multitude. ¹¹(The LORD God of your fathers make you a thousand times so many more as ye *are*, and bless you, as he hath promised you!) ¹²How can I myself alone bear your cumbrance, and your burden, and your strife? ¹³Take[d] you wise men, and understanding, and known among your tribes, and I will make them rulers over you. ¹⁴And ye answered me, and said, The thing which thou hast spoken *is* good *for us* to do. ¹⁵So I took the chief of your tribes, wise men, and known, and made[e] them heads over you, captains over thousands, and captains over hundreds, and captains over fifties, and captains over tens, and officers among your tribes. ¹⁶And I charged your judges at that time, saying, Hear *the causes* between your brethren, and judge righ-

---

Devotional Moment

Teamwork

1:9-13 Jethro's wise advice to delegate some of his responsibility (Exod. 18:13-27) convinced Moses to share the workload with other leaders. Do you have a tendency to try to do everything yourself? Do you feel overwhelmed by your responsibilities? Why not ask your family members for help? Set aside a time when everyone pitches in to tackle the family to-do list. You can follow this with a special lunch or fun activity. Involving children will make them feel needed. And in carrying out their tasks they may begin to discover and develop their own God-given abilities.

---

[a] the Red . . . : or, Zuph
[b] all . . . : Heb. all his neighbours
[c] set: Heb. given
[d] Take: Heb. Give
[e] made: Heb. gave

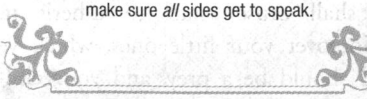

Devotional Moment
•
Fair-mindedness

1:14-18 Moses carefully chose those who would help him judge disputes. He sought wise, respected, fair-minded, courageous, humble people. The key was *fair-mindedness*. God is just, and he wants his people to be just. Do all you can to ensure that disputes in your home are judged fairly. Take a few moments to grade yourself in how fair-minded you are, and then ask God to show you how to be a fair-minded leader at home. And whenever a dispute erupts, make sure *all* sides get to speak.

teously between *every* man and his brother, and the stranger *that is* with him. [17]Ye shall not respect[f] persons in judgment; *but* ye shall hear the small as well as the great; ye shall not be afraid of the face of man; for the judgment *is* God's: and the cause that is too hard for you, bring *it* unto me, and I will hear it. [18]And I commanded you at that time all the things which ye should do.

[19]And when we departed from Horeb, we went through all that great and terrible wilderness, which ye saw by the way of the mountain of the Amorites, as the LORD our God commanded us; and we came to Kadeshbarnea. [20]And I said unto you, Ye are come unto the mountain of the Amorites, which the LORD our God doth give unto us. [21]Behold, the LORD thy God hath set the land before thee: go up *and* possess *it*, as the LORD God of thy fathers hath said unto thee; fear not, neither be discouraged. [22]And ye

came near unto me every one of you, and said, We will send men before us, and they shall search us out the land, and bring us word again by what way we must go up, and into what cities we shall come. [23]And the saying pleased me well: and I took twelve men of you, one of a tribe: [24]And they turned and went up into the mountain, and came unto the valley of Eshcol, and searched it out. [25]And they took of the fruit of the land in their hands, and brought *it* down unto us, and brought us word again, and said, It is a good land which the LORD our God doth give us. [26]Notwithstanding ye would not go up, but rebelled against the commandment of the LORD your God: [27]And ye murmured in your tents, and said, Because the LORD hated us, he hath brought us forth out of the land of Egypt, to deliver us into the hand of the Amorites, to destroy us. [28]Whither shall we go up? our brethren have discouraged[g] our

Devotional Moment
•
Faith

1:22 When the Israelite spies returned with a glowing report of the land but a disturbing report about the size of the enemy Canaanites, the Israelites faced a true test of their faith in God. Despite God's power and promise, they lost all confidence that he could act. What does your example teach your children about faith in God? Do they see you become overwhelmed by the problems of life? Or do they see you trust in God's power and promise to care for your family? Model openness—tell your family about an area that seems overwhelming, and ask them to pray with you for God's help.

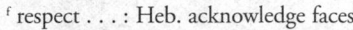

[f] respect . . . : Heb. acknowledge faces
[g] discouraged: Heb. melted

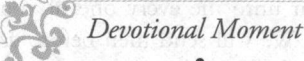

Devotional Moment

•

Problems

1:27-28 The more the Israelites concentrated on their problems, the less they believed in God's promise. Before long, the fearful Israelites were even speculating that God *hated* them! What caused such a complete collapse in confidence? The people of God focused on what *seemed to be true* rather than on what God had said was true. Ultimately, they despaired. If you are facing a serious challenge, try to look at the situation from God's perspective. Then trust in God, resisting the urge to dwell on your problems. Make the conscious effort to remember God's promise to help you.

heart, saying, The people *is* greater and taller than we; the cities *are* great and walled up to heaven; and moreover we have seen the sons of the Anakims there. ²⁹Then I said unto you, Dread not, neither be afraid of them. ³⁰The LORD your God which goeth before you, he shall fight for you, according to all that he did for you in Egypt before your eyes; ³¹And in the wilderness, where thou hast seen how that the LORD thy God bare thee, as a man doth bear his son, in all the way that ye went, until ye came into this place. ³²Yet in this thing ye did not believe the LORD your God, ³³Who went in the way before you, to search you out a place to pitch your tents *in*, in fire by night, to shew you by what way ye should go, and in a cloud by day. ³⁴And the LORD heard the voice of your words, and was wroth, and sware, saying, ³⁵Surely there shall not one of these men of this evil generation see that

good land, which I sware to give unto your fathers, ³⁶Save Caleb the son of Jephunneh; he shall see it, and to him will I give the land that he hath trodden upon, and to his children, because he hath wholly^h followed the LORD. ³⁷Also the LORD was angry with me for your sakes, saying, Thou also shalt not go in thither. ³⁸*But* Joshua the son of Nun, which standeth before thee, he shall go in thither: encourage him: for he shall cause Israel to inherit it. ³⁹Moreover your little ones, which ye said should be a prey, and your children, which in that day had no knowledge between good and evil, they shall go in thither, and unto them will I give it, and they shall possess it. ⁴⁰But *as for* you, turn you, and take your journey into the wilderness by the way of the Red sea. ⁴¹Then ye answered and said unto me, We have sinned against the LORD, we will go up and fight, according to all that the LORD our God commanded us. And when ye had girded on every man his weapons of war, ye were ready to go up into the hill. ⁴²And the LORD said unto me, Say unto them, Go not up, neither fight; for I *am* not among you; lest ye be smitten before your enemies. ⁴³So I spake unto you; and ye would not hear, but rebelled against the commandment of the LORD, and wentⁱ presumptuously up into the hill. ⁴⁴And the Amorites, which dwelt in that mountain, came out against you, and chased you, as bees do, and destroyed you in Seir, *even* unto Hormah. ⁴⁵And ye returned and wept before the LORD; but the

---

^h wholly . . . : Heb. fulfilled to go after
ⁱ went . . . : Heb. ye were presumptuous, and went up

LORD would not hearken to your voice, nor give ear unto you. ⁴⁶So ye abode in Kadesh many days, according unto the days that ye abode *there*.

2

¹Then we turned, and took our journey into the wilderness by the way of the Red sea, as the LORD spake unto me: and we compassed mount Seir many days. ²And the LORD spake unto me, saying, ³Ye have compassed this mountain long enough: turn you northward. ⁴And command thou the people, saying, Ye *are* to pass through the coast of your brethren the children of Esau, which dwell in Seir; and they shall be afraid of you: take ye good heed unto yourselves therefore: ⁵Meddle not with them; for I will not give[a] you of their land, no, not so much as a foot breadth; because I have given mount Seir unto Esau *for* a possession. ⁶Ye shall buy meat of them for money, that ye may eat; and ye shall also buy water of them for money, that ye may drink. ⁷For the LORD thy God hath blessed thee in all the works of thy hand: he knoweth thy walking through this great wilderness: these forty years the LORD thy God *hath been* with thee; thou hast lacked nothing.

⁸And when we passed by from our brethren the children of Esau, which dwelt in Seir, through the way of the plain from Elath, and from Eziongaber, we turned and passed by the way of the wilderness of Moab. ⁹And the LORD said unto me, Distress[b] not the Moabites, neither contend with them in battle: for I will not give thee of their land *for* a possession; because I have given Ar unto the children of Lot *for* a possession. ¹⁰The Emims dwelt therein in times past, a people great, and many, and tall, as the Anakims; ¹¹Which also were accounted giants, as the Anakims; but the Moabites call them Emims. ¹²The Horims also dwelt in Seir beforetime; but the children of Esau succeeded[c] them, when they had destroyed them from before them, and dwelt in their stead; as Israel did unto the land of his possession, which the LORD gave unto them. ¹³Now rise up, *said I*, and get you over the brook[d] Zered. And we went over the brook Zered. ¹⁴And the space in which we came from Kadeshbarnea, until we were come over the brook[e] Zered, *was* thirty and eight years; until all the generation of the men of war were wasted out from among the host, as the LORD sware unto them. ¹⁵For indeed the hand of the LORD was against them, to destroy them from among the host, until they were consumed. ¹⁶So it came to pass, when all the men of war were consumed and dead from among the people, ¹⁷That the LORD spake unto me, saying, ¹⁸Thou art to pass over through Ar, the coast of Moab, this day: ¹⁹And *when* thou comest nigh over against the children of Ammon, distress them not, nor meddle with them: for I

---

[a] no . . . : Heb. even to the treading of the sole of the foot
[b] Distress . . . : or, Use no hostility against Moab
[c] succeeded: Heb. inherited
[d] brook: or, valley
[e] brook: or, valley

will not give thee of the land of the children of Ammon *any* possession; because I have given it unto the children of Lot *for* a possession. [20](That also was accounted a land of giants: giants dwelt therein in old time; and the Ammonites call them Zamzummims[f]; [21]A people great, and many, and tall, as the Anakims; but the LORD destroyed them before them; and they succeeded them, and dwelt in their stead: [22]As he did to the children of Esau, which dwelt in Seir, when he destroyed the Horims from before them; and they succeeded them, and dwelt in their stead even unto this day: [23]And the Avims which dwelt in Hazerim, *even* unto Azzah, the Caphtorims, which came forth out of Caphtor, destroyed them, and dwelt in their stead.) [24]Rise ye up, take your journey, and pass over the river Arnon: behold, I have given into thine hand Sihon the Amorite, king of Heshbon, and his land: begin[g] to possess *it*, and contend with him in battle. [25]This day will I begin to put the dread of thee and the fear of thee upon the nations *that are* under the whole heaven, who shall hear report of thee, and shall tremble, and be in anguish because of thee. [26]And I sent messengers out of the wilderness of Kedemoth unto Sihon king of Heshbon with words of peace, saying, [27]Let me pass through thy land: I will go along by the high way, I will neither turn unto the right hand nor to the left. [28]Thou shalt sell me meat for money, that I may eat; and give me water for money, that I may drink: only I will pass through on my feet; [29](As the children of Esau which dwell in Seir, and the Moabites which dwell in Ar, did unto me;) until I shall pass over Jordan into the land which the LORD our God giveth us. [30]But Sihon king of Heshbon would not let us pass by him: for the LORD thy God hardened his spirit, and made his heart obstinate, that he might deliver him into thy hand, as *appeareth* this day. [31]And the LORD said unto me, Behold, I have begun to give Sihon and his land before thee: begin to possess, that thou mayest inherit his land. [32]Then Sihon came out against us, he and all his people, to fight at Jahaz. [33]And the LORD our God delivered him before us; and we smote him, and his sons, and all his people. [34]And we took all his cities at that time, and utterly destroyed the men[h], and the women, and the little ones, of every city, we left none to remain: [35]Only the cattle we took for a prey unto ourselves, and the spoil of the cities which we took. [36]From Aroer, which *is* by the brink of the river of Arnon, and *from* the city that *is* by the river, even unto Gilead, there was not one city too strong for us: the LORD our God delivered all unto us: [37]Only unto the land of the children of Ammon thou camest not, *nor* unto any place of the river Jabbok, nor unto the cities in the mountains, nor unto whatsoever the LORD our God forbad us.

3

[1]Then we turned, and went up the way to Bashan: and Og the king of Bashan came out against us, he and all his peo-

---

[f] Zamzummims: also called, Zuzims

[g] begin . . . : Heb. begin, possess

[h] the men . . . : Heb. every city of men, and women, and little ones

ple, to battle at Edrei. [2]And the LORD said unto me, Fear him not: for I will deliver him, and all his people, and his land, into thy hand; and thou shalt do unto him as thou didst unto Sihon king of the Amorites, which dwelt at Heshbon. [3]So the LORD our God delivered into our hands Og also, the king of Bashan, and all his people: and we smote him until none was left to him remaining. [4]And we took all his cities at that time, there was not a city which we took not from them, threescore cities, all the region of Argob, the kingdom of Og in Bashan. [5]All these cities *were* fenced with high walls, gates, and bars; beside unwalled towns a great many. [6]And we utterly destroyed them, as we did unto Sihon king of Heshbon, utterly destroying the men, women, and children, of every city. [7]But all the cattle, and the spoil of the cities, we took for a prey to ourselves. [8]And we took at that time out of the hand of the two kings of the Amorites the land that *was* on this side Jordan, from the river of Arnon unto mount Hermon; [9](*Which* Hermon the Sidonians call Sirion; and the Amorites call it Shenir;) [10]All the cities of the plain, and all Gilead, and all Bashan, unto Salchah and Edrei, cities of the kingdom of Og in Bashan. [11]For only Og king of Bashan remained of the remnant of giants; behold, his bedstead *was* a bedstead of iron; *is* it not in Rabbath of the children of Ammon? nine cubits *was* the length thereof, and four cubits the breadth of it, after the cubit of a man.

[12]And this land, *which* we possessed at that time, from Aroer, which *is* by the river Arnon, and half mount Gilead, and the cities thereof, gave I unto the Reubenites and to the Gadites. [13]And the rest of Gilead, and all Bashan, *being* the kingdom of Og, gave I unto the half tribe of Manasseh; all the region of Argob, with all Bashan, which was called the land of giants. [14]Jair the son of Manasseh took all the country of Argob unto the coasts of Geshuri and Maachathi; and called them after his own name, Bashanhavothjair, unto this day. [15]And I gave Gilead unto Machir. [16]And unto the Reubenites and unto the Gadites I gave from Gilead even unto the river Arnon half the valley, and the border even unto the river Jabbok, *which is* the border of the children of Ammon; [17]The plain also, and Jordan, and the coast *thereof,* from Chinnereth even unto the sea of the plain, *even* the salt sea, under Ashdothpisgah[a] eastward. [18]And I commanded you at that time, saying, The LORD your God hath given you this land to possess it: ye shall pass over armed before your brethren the children of Israel, all *that are* meet[b] for the war. [19]But your wives, and your little ones, and your cattle, (*for* I know that ye have much cattle,) shall abide in your cities which I have given you; [20]Until the LORD have given rest unto your brethren, as well as unto you, and *until* they also possess the land which the LORD your God hath given them beyond Jordan: and *then* shall ye return every man unto his possession, which I have given you.

[21]And I commanded Joshua at that

---

[a] Ashdothpisgah; or, the springs of Pisgah, or, the hill
[b] meet . . . : Heb. sons of power

time, saying, Thine eyes have seen all that the LORD your God hath done unto these two kings: so shall the LORD do unto all the kingdoms whither thou passest. ²²Ye shall not fear them: for the LORD your God he shall fight for you. ²³And I besought the LORD at that time, saying, ²⁴O Lord GOD, thou hast begun to shew thy servant thy greatness, and thy mighty hand: for what God *is there* in heaven or in earth, that can do according to thy works, and according to thy might? ²⁵I pray thee, let me go over, and see the good land that *is* beyond Jordan, that goodly mountain, and Lebanon. ²⁶But the LORD was wroth with me for your sakes, and would not hear me: and the LORD said unto me, Let it suffice thee; speak no more unto me of this matter. ²⁷Get thee up into the top of Pisgahᶜ, and lift up thine eyes westward, and northward, and southward, and eastward, and behold *it* with thine eyes: for thou shalt not go over this Jordan. ²⁸But charge Joshua, and encourage him, and strengthen him: for he shall go over before this people, and he shall cause them to inherit the land which thou shalt see. ²⁹So we abode in the valley over against Bethpeor.

4

¹Now therefore hearken, O Israel, unto the statutes and unto the judgments, which I teach you, for to do *them*, that ye may live, and go in and possess the land which the LORD God of your fathers giveth you. ²Ye shall not add unto the word which I command you, neither shall ye diminish *ought* from it,

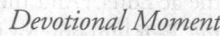

Devotional Moment

•

Life-Style

4:6 Obedience to God's laws would result in at least two benefits: (1) God's people would enjoy God's blessing (see 4:3-4); and (2) they would demonstrate to the unbelieving nations around them the wisdom of following God's standards. Though times have changed, God still expects us to obey him, and for the same reasons. Is obedience to the revealed will of God a priority for you? Can your friends and neighbors visit your home and see a positive difference? A pleasant, friendly home is a great advertisement for the difference that Christ can make.

that ye may keep the commandments of the LORD your God which I command you. ³Your eyes have seen what the LORD did because of Baalpeor: for all the men that followed Baalpeor, the LORD thy God hath destroyed them from among you. ⁴But ye that did cleave unto the LORD your God *are* alive every one of you this day. ⁵Behold, I have taught you statutes and judgments, even as the LORD my God commanded me, that ye should do so in the land whither ye go to possess it. ⁶Keep therefore and do *them*; for this *is* your wisdom and your understanding in the sight of the nations, which shall hear all these statutes, and say, Surely this great nation *is* a wise and understanding people. ⁷For what nation *is there* so great, who *hath* God so nigh unto them, as the LORD our God *is* in all *things that* we call upon him *for*? ⁸And what nation *is there* so great, that hath statutes and judgments *so* righteous as all this law, which I set before

---

ᶜ Pisgah: or, the hill

you this day? ⁹Only take heed to thyself, and keep thy soul diligently, lest thou forget the things which thine eyes have seen, and lest they depart from thy heart all the days of thy life: but teach them thy sons, and thy sons' sons; ¹⁰*Specially* the day that thou stoodest before the LORD thy God in Horeb, when the LORD said unto me, Gather me the people together, and I will make them hear my words, that they may learn to fear me all the days that they shall live upon the earth, and *that* they may teach their children. ¹¹And ye came near and stood under the mountain; and the mountain burned with fire unto the midstᵃ of heaven, with darkness, clouds, and thick darkness. ¹²And the LORD spake unto you out of the midst of the fire: ye heard the voice of the words, but saw no similitude; onlyᵇ *ye heard* a voice. ¹³And he declared unto you his covenant, which he commanded you to perform, *even* ten commandments; and he wrote them upon two tables of stone. ¹⁴And the LORD commanded me at that time to teach you statutes and judgments, that ye might do them in the land whither ye go over to possess it. ¹⁵Take ye therefore good heed unto yourselves; for ye saw no manner of similitude on the day *that* the LORD spake unto you in Horeb out of the midst of the fire: ¹⁶Lest ye corrupt *yourselves*, and make you a graven image, the similitude of any figure, the likeness of male or female, ¹⁷The likeness of any beast that *is* on the earth, the likeness of any winged

fowl that flieth in the air, ¹⁸The likeness of any thing that creepeth on the ground, the likeness of any fish that *is* in the waters beneath the earth: ¹⁹And lest thou lift up thine eyes unto heaven, and when thou seest the sun, and the moon, and the stars, *even* all the host of heaven, shouldest be driven to worship them, and serve them, which the LORD thy God hath dividedᶜ unto all nations under the whole heaven. ²⁰But the LORD hath taken you, and brought you forth out of the iron furnace, *even* out of Egypt, to be unto him a people of inheritance, as *ye are* this day. ²¹Furthermore the LORD was angry with me for your sakes, and sware that I should not go over Jordan, and that I should not go in unto that good land, which the LORD thy God giveth thee *for* an inheritance: ²²But I must die in this land, I must not go over Jordan: but ye shall go over, and possess that good land. ²³Take heed unto yourselves, lest ye forget the covenant of the LORD your God, which he made with you, and make you a graven image, *or* the likeness of any *thing*, which the LORD thy God hath forbidden thee. ²⁴For the LORD thy God *is* a consuming fire, *even* a jealous God. ²⁵When thou shalt beget children, and children's children, and ye shall have remained long in the land, and shall corrupt *yourselves*, and make a graven image, *or* the likeness of any *thing*, and shall do evil in the sight of the LORD thy God, to provoke him to anger: ²⁶I call heaven and earth to witness against you this

ᵃ midst: Heb. heart
ᵇ only . . . : Heb. save a voice
ᶜ divided: or, imparted

day, that ye shall soon utterly perish from off the land whereunto ye go over Jordan to possess it; ye shall not prolong *your* days upon it, but shall utterly be destroyed. ²⁷And the LORD shall scatter you among the nations, and ye shall be left few in number among the heathen, whither the LORD shall lead you. ²⁸And there ye shall serve gods, the work of men's hands, wood and stone, which neither see, nor hear, nor eat, nor smell. ²⁹But if from thence thou shalt seek the LORD thy God, thou shalt find *him*, if thou seek him with all thy heart and with all thy soul. ³⁰When thou art in tribulation, and all these things are come upon thee, *even* in the latter days, if thou turn to the LORD thy God, and shalt be obedient unto his voice; ³¹(For the LORD thy God *is* a merciful God;) he will not forsake thee, neither destroy thee, nor forget the covenant of thy fathers which he sware unto them. ³²For ask now of the days that are past, which were before thee, since the day that God created man upon the earth, and *ask* from the one side of heaven unto the other, whether there hath been *any such thing* as this great thing *is*, or hath been heard like it? ³³Did *ever* people hear the voice of God speaking out of the midst of the fire, as thou hast heard, and live? ³⁴Or hath God assayed to go *and* take him a nation from the midst of *another* nation, by temptations, by signs, and by wonders, and by war, and by a mighty hand, and by a stretched out arm, and by great terrors, according to all that the LORD your God did for you in Egypt before your eyes? ³⁵Unto thee it was shewed, that thou mightest know that the LORD he *is* God; *there is* none else

beside him. ³⁶Out of heaven he made thee to hear his voice, that he might instruct thee: and upon earth he shewed thee his great fire; and thou heardest his words out of the midst of the fire. ³⁷And because he loved thy fathers, therefore he chose their seed after them, and brought thee out in his sight with his mighty power out of Egypt; ³⁸To drive out nations from before thee greater and mightier than thou *art*, to bring thee in, to give thee their land *for* an inheritance, as *it is* this day. ³⁹Know therefore this day, and consider *it* in thine heart, that the LORD he *is* God in heaven above, and upon the earth beneath: *there is* none else. ⁴⁰Thou shalt keep therefore his statutes, and his commandments, which I command thee this day, that it may go well with thee, and with thy children after thee, and that thou mayest prolong *thy* days upon the earth, which the LORD thy God giveth thee, for ever.

⁴¹Then Moses severed three cities on this side Jordan toward the sunrising; ⁴²That the slayer might flee thither, which should kill his neighbour unawares, and hated him not in times past; and that fleeing unto one of these cities he might live: ⁴³*Namely*, Bezer in the wilderness, in the plain country, of the Reubenites; and Ramoth in Gilead, of the Gadites; and Golan in Bashan, of the Manassites. ⁴⁴And this *is* the law which Moses set before the children of Israel: ⁴⁵These *are* the testimonies, and the statutes, and the judgments, which Moses spake unto the children of Israel, after they came forth out of Egypt, ⁴⁶On this side Jordan, in the valley over against Bethpeor, in the land of Sihon king of the Amorites, who dwelt at

Heshbon, whom Moses and the children of Israel smote, after they were come forth out of Egypt: ⁴⁷And they possessed his land, and the land of Og king of Bashan, two kings of the Amorites, which *were* on this side Jordan toward the sunrising; ⁴⁸From Aroer, which *is* by the bank of the river Arnon, even unto mount Sion, which *is* Hermon, ⁴⁹And all the plain on this side Jordan eastward, even unto the sea of the plain, under the springs of Pisgah.

5

¹And Moses called all Israel, and said unto them, Hear, O Israel, the statutes and judgments which I speak in your ears this day, that ye may learn them, and keep[a], and do them. ²The LORD our God made a covenant with us in Horeb. ³The LORD made not this covenant with our fathers, but with us, *even* us, who *are* all of us here alive this day. ⁴The LORD talked with you face to face in the mount out of the midst of the fire, ⁵(I stood between the LORD and you at that time, to shew you the word of the LORD: for ye were afraid by reason of the fire, and went not up into the mount;) saying,

⁶I *am* the LORD thy God, which brought thee out of the land of Egypt, from the house of bondage[b]. ⁷Thou shalt have none other gods before me. ⁸Thou shalt not make thee *any* graven image, *or* any likeness *of any thing* that *is* in heaven above, or that *is* in the earth beneath, or that *is* in the waters beneath the earth: ⁹Thou shalt not bow down thyself unto them, nor serve them: for I the LORD thy God *am* a jealous God, visiting the iniquity of the fathers upon the children unto the third and fourth *generation* of them that hate me, ¹⁰And shewing mercy unto thousands of them that love me and keep my commandments. ¹¹Thou shalt not take the name of the LORD thy God in vain: for the LORD will not hold *him* guiltless that taketh his name in vain. ¹²Keep the sabbath day to sanctify it, as the LORD thy God hath commanded thee. ¹³Six days thou shalt labour, and do all thy work: ¹⁴But the seventh day *is* the sabbath of the LORD thy God: *in it* thou shalt not do any work, thou, nor thy son, nor thy daughter, nor thy manservant, nor thy maidservant, nor thine ox, nor thine ass, nor any of thy cattle, nor thy stranger that *is* within thy gates; that thy manservant and thy maidservant may rest as well as thou. ¹⁵And remember that thou wast a servant in the land of Egypt, and *that* the LORD thy God brought thee out thence through a mighty hand and by a stretched out arm: therefore the LORD thy God commanded thee to keep the sabbath day. ¹⁶Honour thy father and thy mother, as the LORD thy God hath commanded thee; that thy days may be prolonged, and that it may go well with thee, in the land which the LORD thy God giveth thee. ¹⁷Thou shalt not kill. ¹⁸Neither shalt thou commit adultery. ¹⁹Neither shalt thou steal. ²⁰Neither shalt thou bear false witness against thy neighbour. ²¹Neither shalt thou desire thy neighbour's wife, neither shalt thou covet thy neighbour's house, his field,

[a] keep . . . : Heb. keep to do them
[b] bondage: Heb. servants

Devotions in the Home

by Stuart & Jill Briscoe

Moses charged all Israel to reverence the Lord and love him with all their heart, soul, and might (6:5). But how was this going to happen? As Moses told the people, it was a matter of them teaching their children (vv.7-9). They were to teach their children what they themselves had learned and knew of God.

Nothing has changed. That is still the way it should be done. But how?

Teach the facts. Like the parents in Moses' time, modern parents need to be sure their children are learning the *facts about the Lord.* Children need to know he is as concerned about today's kids as he was about the young people in Egypt; that he has shown his love for them in offering redemption through Christ, the Lamb of God, just as he redeemed the Israelites through the blood of the Passover lamb. They should be told that his provision for our daily needs is as real as his provision of manna in the wilderness. In other words, today's kids, who love stories, need to be exposed to the stories of the Bible so they can learn the facts about the Lord's unique and gracious presence—his provision and person.

Show the way. There is more to teaching children, however, than just telling them the facts about God and his work in history. Our children need to be taught how to exercise personal faith in him, too. There is no person better suited to this task than a loving parent.

A child needs to be shown how to respond to life as a child of God. A child who observes love in action at home is much more likely to respond in love to the Lord than a child who sees only tension. Likewise, a youngster who has been well-disciplined in everyday matters is better able to learn obedience to the Lord than a young person who has never been held accountable for his actions.

Moses said the Lord's commandments should be tied on fingers, worn on foreheads, and written on doorposts (vv.8-9). In other words, God wants his commands to determine what we do, what we think, and how we treat one another everywhere we live and work. This living out of his commandments is crucial to our children's training because they take cues from our example.

Formal devotions. Some families do very little together, making formal devotional times difficult to schedule. Others make the mistake of setting idealistic and inflexible goals that only cause tension and prove counterproductive.

Where's the balance? Here are a few suggestions.

1. Make the spiritual nurture of children a priority.

2. Don't divorce spiritual nurture from everyday living. Let children see, love, and understand discipline around the home.

3. Live out a life-style of *loving obedience to the Lord* in front of the kids.

4. Be authentic. Talk openly about the Lord without shame, but avoid dragging religion into everything just to appear spiritual.

5. Spend time daily teaching your kids, but keep it within limits—theirs, not yours!

6. Use materials that interest them. Get a translation of the Bible that they can understand and feel comfortable using.

7. Be flexible about time and place for family devotions, particularly as kids get older.

8. If possible, pray with your kids every day.

There are two pitfalls to avoid: doing too much, and doing too little. A little sensitivity to your kids will enable you to avoid both.

While some parents don't try hard enough to develop their children's knowledge of

God, others try too hard and end up pushing their children to respond before they're ready. So parents must be deliberate in teaching, while being sensitive to their children. Otherwise, they may miss their children's spiritual searchings, or lead them further along than God has prepared them to go, only bewildering them. Alert parents realize that the spiritual development of their children is God's work, while sometimes he graciously allows us to be agents of his working. Keep yourself ready to be used by God for such opportunities.

DIGGING DEEPER

1. What must a parent avoid doing if he or she hopes to draw sons and daughters to the Lord? See Ephesians 6:4.

2. Children love stories. How can this help you in your task of teaching God's Word to your children? See Psalm 78:1-7.

3. How can your family's involvement in a church help you raise your children in the faith? For examples, see Nehemiah 3:12; Acts 16:33-34; Romans 16:5; 1 Corinthians 16:15.

Devotional Moment

Contentment

5:21 God commanded the Israelites not to *envy* their neighbors. Envious people are never satisfied. They cannot enjoy anything because they care only about what they *don't* have. The solution to envy is contentment. Spend some time listing the ways God has blessed your life. See how many blessings you can thank God for.

---

or his manservant, or his maidservant, his ox, or his ass, or any *thing* that *is* thy neighbour's. ²²These words the LORD spake unto all your assembly in the mount out of the midst of the fire, of the cloud, and of the thick darkness, with a great voice: and he added no more. And he wrote them in two tables of stone, and delivered them unto me.

²³And it came to pass, when ye heard the voice out of the midst of the darkness, (for the mountain did burn with fire,) that ye came near unto me, *even* all the heads of your tribes, and your elders; ²⁴And ye said, Behold, the LORD our God hath shewed us his glory and his greatness, and we have heard his voice out of the midst of the fire: we have seen this day that God doth talk with man, and he liveth. ²⁵Now therefore why should we die? for this great fire will consume us: if we hear[c] the voice of the LORD our God any more, then we shall die. ²⁶For who *is there of* all flesh, that hath heard the voice of the living God speaking out of the midst of the fire, as we *have*, and lived? ²⁷Go thou near, and hear all that the LORD our God shall say: and speak thou unto us all that the LORD our God shall speak unto thee; and we will hear *it*, and do *it*. ²⁸And the LORD heard the voice of your words, when ye spake unto me; and the LORD said unto me, I have heard the voice of the words of this people, which they have spoken unto thee: they have well said all that they have spoken. ²⁹O that there were such an heart in them, that they

---

c hear: Heb. add to hear

would fear me, and keep all my commandments always, that it might be well with them, and with their children for ever! [30]Go say to them, Get you into your tents again. [31]But as for thee, stand thou here by me, and I will speak unto thee all the commandments, and the statutes, and the judgments, which thou shalt teach them, that they may do *them* in the land which I give them to possess it. [32]Ye shall observe to do therefore as the LORD your God hath commanded you: ye shall not turn aside to the right hand or to the left. [33]Ye shall walk in all the ways which the LORD your God hath commanded you, that ye may live, and *that it may be* well with you, and *that* ye may prolong *your* days in the land which ye shall possess.

6

[1]Now these *are* the commandments, the statutes, and the judgments, which the LORD your God commanded to teach you, that ye might do *them* in the land whither ye go[a] to possess it: [2]That thou mightest fear the LORD thy God, to keep all his statutes and his commandments, which I command thee, thou, and thy son, and thy son's son, all the days of thy life; and that thy days may be prolonged. [3]Hear therefore, O Israel, and observe to do *it*, that it may be well with thee, and that ye may increase mightily, as the LORD God of thy fathers hath promised thee, in the land that floweth with milk and honey.

[4]Hear, O Israel: The LORD our God *is* one LORD: [5]And thou shalt love the LORD thy God with all thine heart, and with all thy soul, and with all

---

Devotional Moment

•

Teaching Children

6:7 In their quest to train their children in God's ways, the Israelites were to take advantage of every teachable moment: during conversations at home, while traveling together, at bedtime, and early in the day. Kids are not always open-minded during the times we set aside for religious instruction. Your most meaningful conversation with a son or daughter may take place on a trip to the hardware store, at the mall, during a morning jog together, or while giving a back rub. Ask God to make you sensitive to times when your children are open to spiritual conversation . . . and, if it's still possible, start while they're young.

---

thy might. [6]And these words, which I command thee this day, shall be in thine heart: [7]And thou shalt teach them diligently unto thy children, and shalt talk of them when thou sittest in thine house, and when thou walkest by the way, and when thou liest down, and when thou risest up. [8]And thou shalt bind them for a sign upon thine hand, and they shall be as frontlets between thine eyes. [9]And thou shalt write them upon the posts of thy house, and on thy gates. [10]And it shall be, when the LORD thy God shall have brought thee into the land which he sware unto thy fathers, to Abraham, to Isaac, and to Jacob, to give thee great and goodly cities, which thou buildedst not, [11]And houses full of all good *things*, which thou filledst not, and wells digged, which thou diggedst not, vineyards and olive trees, which thou plantedst not; when thou shalt have eaten and be full; [12]*Then* beware lest thou forget the

---

[a] go: Heb. pass over

Family Traditions

Teaching the Commands of the Lord

DEUTERONOMY 6

It seems as if small children are always thirsty, whether at bedtime, during play, or en route to some destination. While frequent trips to the kitchen faucet may bother some parents, thirst is a healthy sign. Little bodies need lots of liquid.

In a similar way, when children thirst for God, it's because of basic nutritional needs of the spirit. Your children have this need just as surely as they need water.

Many family traditions can grow out of young ones' need for spiritual water. Some families have regular, formal devotions at the dinner table. Readings and discussions of some portion of God's Word can easily become a regular part of an established family mealtime. Other families include devotions in a more informal way: warbling Bible verses to the tune of radio hits or pausing to pray for individuals' needs as kids walk out the door one by one, shouting after them, "I love you, and pray for me today, too!"

You can also encourage honest questions about truth over schoolbooks and homework (while silently rethinking your own pat answers). While small children may readily listen to your explanations, remember that teens learn best from a parent who will *listen,* not necessarily talk, and be honest about his or her own faith struggles. "We can't just hand children a set of do's and don'ts," says Christian novelist Frank Peretti. "We should encourage them to be really curious about life, faith, and ideas."

Teaching by example is also crucial. Daily, let kids catch you being honest, kind, and sacrificial. Doing the right thing doesn't have to be heroic, but it does need to be consistent.

Bedtime is sometimes the thirstiest moment of all. As your children are growing up, you can put age-appropriate Bibles, devotional books, and blank books for journaling on their bedside table. The time before the light goes out can be mealtime for any child's soul. Also make yourself available at this crucial time—to talk, pray, and discuss the day's events with your children. Don't become so preoccupied with your own end-of-the-day concerns that you can't hear a tired cry for counsel.

There are few convenient times to talk over a child's spiritual probing. But Jesus promised that if "whosoever shall give to drink unto one of these little ones a cup of cold water only . . . he shall in no wise lose his reward" (Matt. 10:42).

LORD, which brought thee forth out of the land of Egypt, from the house of bondage[b]. ¹³Thou shalt fear the LORD thy God, and serve him, and shalt swear by his name. ¹⁴Ye shall not go after other gods, of the gods of the people which *are* round about you; ¹⁵(For the LORD thy God *is* a jealous God among you) lest the anger of the LORD thy God be kindled against thee, and destroy thee from off the face of the earth. ¹⁶Ye shall not tempt the LORD your God, as ye tempted *him* in Massah.

¹⁷Ye shall diligently keep the commandments of the LORD your God, and his testimonies, and his statutes, which he hath commanded thee. ¹⁸And thou shalt do *that which is* right and good in the sight of the LORD: that it may be well with thee, and that thou mayest go in and possess the good land which the LORD sware unto thy fathers, ¹⁹To cast out all thine enemies from before thee, as the LORD hath spoken. ²⁰*And* when thy son asketh thee in time to come, saying, What *mean* the testimonies, and the statutes, and the judgments, which the LORD our God hath commanded you? ²¹Then thou shalt say unto thy son, We were Pharaoh's bondmen in Egypt; and the LORD brought us out of Egypt with a mighty hand: ²²And the LORD shewed signs and wonders, great and sore[c], upon Egypt, upon Pharaoh, and upon all his household, before our eyes: ²³And he brought us out from thence, that he might bring us in, to give us the land which he sware unto our fathers. ²⁴And the LORD commanded us to do all these statutes, to fear the LORD our God, for our good always, that he might preserve us alive, as *it is* at this day. ²⁵And it shall be our righteousness, if we observe to do all these commandments before the LORD our God, as he hath commanded us.

7

¹When the LORD thy God shall bring thee into the land whither thou goest to possess it, and hath cast out many nations before thee, the Hittites, and the Girgashites, and the Amorites, and the Canaanites, and the Perizzites, and the Hivites, and the Jebusites, seven nations greater and mightier than thou; ²And when the LORD thy God shall deliver them before thee; thou shalt smite them, *and* utterly destroy them; thou shalt make no covenant with them, nor shew mercy unto them: ³Neither shalt thou make marriages with them; thy daughter thou shalt not give unto his son, nor his daughter shalt thou take unto thy son. ⁴For they will turn away thy son from following me, that they may serve other gods: so will the anger of the LORD be kindled against you, and destroy thee suddenly. ⁵But thus shall ye deal with them; ye shall destroy their altars, and break down their images[a], and cut down their groves, and burn their graven images with fire. ⁶For thou *art* an holy people unto the LORD thy God: the LORD thy God hath chosen thee to be a special people

---

[b] bondage: Heb. bondmen or, servants
[c] sore: Heb. evil
[a] their images: Heb. their statues, or, pillars

unto himself, above all people that *are* upon the face of the earth. [7]The LORD did not set his love upon you, nor choose you, because ye were more in number than any people; for ye *were* the fewest of all people: [8]But because the LORD loved you, and because he would keep the oath which he had sworn unto your fathers, hath the LORD brought you out with a mighty hand, and redeemed you out of the house of bondmen, from the hand of Pharaoh king of Egypt. [9]Know therefore that the LORD thy God, he *is* God, the faithful God, which keepeth covenant and mercy with them that love him and keep his commandments to a thousand generations; [10]And repayeth them that hate him to their face, to destroy them: he will not be slack to him that hateth him, he will repay him to his face. [11]Thou shalt therefore keep the commandments, and the statutes, and the judgments, which I command thee this day, to do them.

[12]Wherefore it shall come to pass, if [b] ye hearken to these judgments, and keep, and do them, that the LORD thy God shall keep unto thee the covenant and the mercy which he sware unto thy fathers: [13]And he will love thee, and bless thee, and multiply thee: he will also bless the fruit of thy womb, and the fruit of thy land, thy corn, and thy wine, and thine oil, the increase of thy kine, and the flocks of thy sheep, in the land which he sware unto thy fathers to give thee. [14]Thou shalt be blessed above all people: there shall not be male or female barren among you, or among your cattle. [15]And the LORD will take away from thee all sickness, and will put none of the evil diseases of Egypt, which thou knowest, upon thee; but will lay them upon all *them* that hate thee. [16]And thou shalt consume all the people which the LORD thy God shall deliver thee; thine eye shall have no pity upon them: neither shalt thou serve their gods; for that *will be* a snare unto thee. [17]If thou shalt say in thine heart, These nations *are* more than I; how can I dispossess them? [18]Thou shalt not be afraid of them: *but* shalt well remember what the LORD thy God did unto Pharaoh, and unto all Egypt; [19]The great temptations which thine eyes saw, and the signs, and the wonders, and the mighty hand, and the stretched out arm, whereby the LORD thy God brought thee out: so shall the LORD thy God do unto all the people of whom thou art afraid. [20]Moreover the LORD thy God will send the hornet among them, until they that are left, and hide themselves from thee, be destroyed. [21]Thou shalt not be affrighted at them: for the LORD thy God *is* among you, a mighty God and terrible. [22]And the LORD thy God will put out those nations before thee by little and little: thou mayest not consume them at once, lest the beasts of the field increase upon thee. [23]But the LORD thy God shall deliver them unto thee, and shall destroy them with a mighty destruction, until they be destroyed. [24]And he shall deliver their kings into thine hand, and thou shalt destroy their name from under heaven: there shall no man be able to stand before thee, until thou have destroyed them. [25]The graven

[b] if: Heb. because

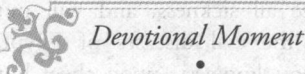

Devotional Moment

Instant Changes?

7:21-24 When God gave the Promised Land to the people of Israel, he told them they would still have to conquer the land little by little. He knew they couldn't handle everything at once. Sometimes children want responsibilities or privileges before they can handle them. Parents need to help them receive, a little at a time, what might otherwise overwhelm them. Think through chores and responsibilities. Then think through privileges, curfew, and allowances and spread them over the grades in school, first through twelfth. Show your children how they can have more privileges year by year by keeping up with responsibilities.

images of their gods shall ye burn with fire: thou shalt not desire the silver or gold *that is* on them, nor take *it* unto thee, lest thou be snared therein: for it *is* an abomination to the LORD thy God. ²⁶Neither shalt thou bring an abomination into thine house, lest thou be a cursed thing like it: *but* thou shalt utterly detest it, and thou shalt utterly abhor it; for it *is* a cursed thing.

8

¹All the commandments which I command thee this day shall ye observe to do, that ye may live, and multiply, and go in and possess the land which the LORD sware unto your fathers. ²And thou shalt remember all the way which the LORD thy God led thee these forty years in the wilderness, to humble thee, *and* to prove thee, to know what *was* in thine heart, whether thou wouldest keep his commandments, or no. ³And he humbled thee, and suffered thee to

hunger, and fed thee with manna, which thou knewest not, neither did thy fathers know; that he might make thee know that man doth not live by bread only, but by every *word* that proceedeth out of the mouth of the LORD doth man live. ⁴Thy raiment waxed not old upon thee, neither did thy foot swell, these forty years. ⁵Thou shalt also consider in thine heart, that, as a man chasteneth his son, *so* the LORD thy God chasteneth thee. ⁶Therefore thou shalt keep the commandments of the LORD thy God, to walk in his ways, and to fear him. ⁷For the LORD thy God bringeth thee into a good land, a land of brooks of water, of fountains and depths that spring out of valleys and hills; ⁸A land of wheat, and barley, and vines, and fig trees, and pomegranates; a land of oil[a] olive, and honey; ⁹A land wherein thou shalt eat bread without scarceness, thou shalt not lack any *thing* in it; a land whose stones *are* iron, and out of whose hills thou mayest dig brass. ¹⁰When thou hast eaten and art full, then thou shalt bless the LORD thy God for the good land which he hath given thee. ¹¹Beware that thou forget not the LORD thy God, in not keeping his commandments, and his judgments, and his statutes, which I command thee this day: ¹²Lest *when* thou hast eaten and art full, and hast built goodly houses, and dwelt *therein*; ¹³And *when* thy herds and thy flocks multiply, and thy silver and thy gold is multiplied, and all that thou hast is multiplied; ¹⁴Then thine heart be lifted up, and thou forget the LORD thy

---

[a] of oil . . . : Heb. of olive tree of oil

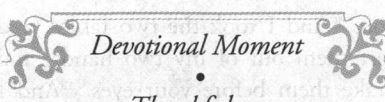

God, which brought thee forth out of the land of Egypt, from the house of bondage; ¹⁵Who led thee through that great and terrible wilderness, *wherein were* fiery serpents, and scorpions, and drought, where *there was* no water; who brought thee forth water out of the rock of flint; ¹⁶Who fed thee in the wilderness with manna, which thy fathers knew not, that he might humble thee, and that he might prove thee, to do thee good at thy latter end; ¹⁷And thou say in thine heart, My power and the might of *mine* hand hath gotten me this wealth. ¹⁸But thou shalt remember the LORD thy God: for *it is* he that giveth thee power to get wealth, that he may establish his covenant which he sware unto thy fathers, as *it is* this day. ¹⁹And it shall be, if thou do at all forget the LORD thy God, and walk after other gods, and serve them, and worship them, I testify against you this day that ye shall surely perish. ²⁰As the nations which the LORD destroyeth before your face, so shall ye perish; because ye would not be obedient unto the voice of the LORD your God.

9

¹Hear, O Israel: Thou *art* to pass over Jordan this day, to go in to possess nations greater and mightier than thyself, cities great and fenced up to heaven, ²A people great and tall, the children of the Anakims, whom thou knowest, and *of whom* thou hast heard *say*, Who can stand before the children of Anak! ³Understand therefore this day, that the LORD thy God *is* he which goeth over before thee; *as* a consuming fire he shall destroy them, and he shall bring them down before thy face: so shalt thou drive them out, and destroy them quickly, as the LORD hath said unto thee. ⁴Speak not thou in thine heart, after that the LORD thy God hath cast them out from before thee, saying, For my righteousness the LORD hath brought me in to possess this land: but for the wickedness of these nations the LORD doth drive them out from before thee. ⁵Not for thy righteousness, or for the uprightness of thine heart, dost thou go to possess their land: but for the wickedness of these nations the LORD thy God doth drive them out from before thee, and that he may perform the word which the LORD sware unto thy fathers, Abraham, Isaac, and Jacob. ⁶Understand therefore, that the LORD thy God giveth thee not this good land to possess it for thy righteousness; for thou *art* a stiffnecked people. ⁷Remember, *and* forget not, how thou provokedst the LORD thy God to wrath in the wilderness: from the day that thou didst depart out of the land of Egypt, until ye came unto

this place, ye have been rebellious against the LORD. ⁸Also in Horeb ye provoked the LORD to wrath, so that the LORD was angry with you to have destroyed you. ⁹When I was gone up into the mount to receive the tables of stone, *even* the tables of the covenant which the LORD made with you, then I abode in the mount forty days and forty nights, I neither did eat bread nor drink water: ¹⁰And the LORD delivered unto me two tables of stone written with the finger of God; and on them *was written* according to all the words, which the LORD spake with you in the mount out of the midst of the fire in the day of the assembly. ¹¹And it came to pass at the end of forty days and forty nights, *that* the LORD gave me the two tables of stone, *even* the tables of the covenant. ¹²And the LORD said unto me, Arise, get thee down quickly from hence; for thy people which thou hast brought forth out of Egypt have corrupted *themselves*; they are quickly turned aside out of the way which I commanded them; they have made them a molten image. ¹³Furthermore the LORD spake unto me, saying, I have seen this people, and, behold, it *is* a stiffnecked people: ¹⁴Let me alone, that I may destroy them, and blot out their name from under heaven: and I will make of thee a nation mightier and greater than they. ¹⁵So I turned and came down from the mount, and the mount burned with fire: and the two tables of the covenant *were* in my two hands. ¹⁶And I looked, and, behold, ye had sinned against the LORD your God, *and* had made you a molten calf: ye had turned aside quickly out of the way which the LORD had commanded you. ¹⁷And I took the two tables, and cast them out of my two hands, and brake them before your eyes. ¹⁸And I fell down before the LORD, as at the first, forty days and forty nights: I did neither eat bread, nor drink water, because of all your sins which ye sinned, in doing wickedly in the sight of the LORD, to provoke him to anger. ¹⁹For I was afraid of the anger and hot displeasure, wherewith the LORD was wroth against you to destroy you. But the LORD hearkened unto me at that time also. ²⁰And the LORD was very angry with Aaron to have destroyed him: and I prayed for Aaron also the same time. ²¹And I took your sin, the calf which ye had made, and burnt it with fire, and stamped it, *and* ground *it* very small, *even* until it was as small as dust: and I cast the dust thereof into the brook that descended out of the mount. ²²And at Taberah, and at Massah, and at Kibrothhattaavah, ye provoked the LORD to wrath. ²³Likewise when the LORD sent you from Kadeshbarnea, saying, Go up and possess the land which I have given you; then ye rebelled against the commandment of the LORD your God, and ye believed him not, nor hearkened to his voice. ²⁴Ye have been rebellious against the LORD from the day that I knew you. ²⁵Thus I fell down before the LORD forty days and forty nights, as I fell down *at the first*; because the LORD had said he would destroy you. ²⁶I prayed therefore unto the LORD, and said, O Lord GOD, destroy not thy people and thine inheritance, which thou hast redeemed through thy greatness, which thou hast brought forth out of Egypt with a mighty hand.

²⁷Remember thy servants, Abraham, Isaac, and Jacob; look not unto the stubbornness of this people, nor to their wickedness, nor to their sin: ²⁸Lest the land whence thou broughtest us out say, Because the LORD was not able to bring them into the land which he promised them, and because he hated them, he hath brought them out to slay them in the wilderness. ²⁹Yet they *are* thy people and thine inheritance, which thou broughtest out by thy mighty power and by thy stretched out arm.

10

¹At that time the LORD said unto me, Hew thee two tables of stone like unto the first, and come up unto me into the mount, and make thee an ark of wood. ²And I will write on the tables the words that were in the first tables which thou brakest, and thou shalt put them in the ark. ³And I made an ark *of* shittim wood, and hewed two tables of stone like unto the first, and went up into the mount, having the two tables in mine hand. ⁴And he wrote on the tables, according to the first writing, the ten commandmentsᵃ, which the LORD spake unto you in the mount out of the midst of the fire in the day of the assembly: and the LORD gave them unto me. ⁵And I turned myself and came down from the mount, and put the tables in the ark which I had made; and there they be, as the LORD commanded me. ⁶And the children of Israel took their journey from Beeroth of the children of Jaakan to Mosera: there Aaron died, and there he was buried; and Eleazar his son ministered in the priest's office in his stead. ⁷From thence they journeyed unto Gudgodah; and from Gudgodah to Jotbath, a land of rivers of waters. ⁸At that time the LORD separated the tribe of Levi, to bear the ark of the covenant of the LORD, to stand before the LORD to minister unto him, and to bless in his name, unto this day. ⁹Wherefore Levi hath no part nor inheritance with his brethren; the LORD *is* his inheritance, according as the LORD thy God promised him. ¹⁰And I stayed in the mount, according to the firstᵇ time, forty days and forty nights; and the LORD hearkened unto me at that time also, *and* the LORD would not destroy thee. ¹¹And the LORD said unto me, Arise, takeᶜ *thy* journey before the people, that they may go in and possess the land, which I sware unto their fathers to give unto them.

¹²And now, Israel, what doth the LORD thy God require of thee, but to fear the LORD thy God, to walk in all his ways, and to love him, and to serve the LORD thy God with all thy heart and with all thy soul, ¹³To keep the commandments of the LORD, and his statutes, which I command thee this day for thy good? ¹⁴Behold, the heaven and the heaven of heavens *is* the LORD'S thy God, the earth *also*, with all that therein *is*. ¹⁵Only the LORD had a delight in thy fathers to love them, and he chose their seed after them, *even* you above all people, as *it is* this day. ¹⁶Cir-

---

ᵃ commandments: Heb. words
ᵇ first . . . : or, former days
ᶜ take . . . : Heb. go in journey

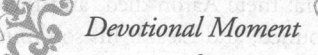

Devotional Moment
•
Stubborn Children

10:16 Moses finished his description of God's expectations for his people by pointing out one of their biggest problems: stubbornness. They did not listen to God, obey him, love him, or worship him (vv. 12-13). They forgot everything he had done for them in the past (v. 15). Children are often described as strong-willed. Where do they learn it? It is partly human nature, but they also learn it from their parents. Demonstrate humility toward God and a willingness to do what he says, and your strong-willed children will have an example to follow in complying with *your* wishes.

cumcise therefore the foreskin of your heart, and be no more stiffnecked. ¹⁷For the LORD your God *is* God of gods, and Lord of lords, a great God, a mighty, and a terrible, which regardeth not persons, nor taketh reward: ¹⁸He doth execute the judgment of the fatherless and widow, and loveth the stranger, in giving him food and raiment. ¹⁹Love ye therefore the stranger: for ye were strangers in the land of Egypt. ²⁰Thou shalt fear the LORD thy God; him shalt thou serve, and to him shalt thou cleave, and swear by his name. ²¹He *is* thy praise, and he *is* thy God, that hath done for thee these great and terrible things, which thine eyes have seen. ²²Thy fathers went down into Egypt with threescore and ten persons; and now the LORD thy God hath made thee as the stars of heaven for multitude.

11

¹Therefore thou shalt love the LORD thy God, and keep his charge, and his statutes, and his judgments, and his commandments, alway. ²And know ye this day: for *I speak* not with your children which have not known, and which have not seen the chastisement of the LORD your God, his greatness, his mighty hand, and his stretched out arm, ³And his miracles, and his acts, which he did in the midst of Egypt unto Pharaoh the king of Egypt, and unto all his land; ⁴And what he did unto the army of Egypt, unto their horses, and to their chariots; how he made the water of the Red sea to overflow them as they pursued after you, and *how* the LORD hath destroyed them unto this day; ⁵And what he did unto you in the wilderness, until ye came into this place; ⁶And what he did unto Dathan and Abiram, the sons of Eliab, the son of Reuben: how the earth opened her mouth, and swallowed them up, and their households, and their tents, and all the substanceᵃ that *was* in their possession, in the midst of all Israel: ⁷But your eyes have seen all the great acts of the LORD which he did.

⁸Therefore shall ye keep all the commandments which I command you this day, that ye may be strong, and go in and possess the land, whither ye go to possess it; ⁹And that ye may prolong *your* days in the land, which the LORD sware unto your fathers to give unto them and to their seed, a land that floweth with milk and honey. ¹⁰For the land, whither thou goest in to possess it, *is* not as the land of Egypt, from whence ye came out, where thou sowedst thy seed, and wateredst *it* with

---

ᵃ substance . . . : or, living substance which followed them

thy foot, as a garden of herbs: ¹¹But the land, whither ye go to possess it, *is* a land of hills and valleys, *and* drinketh water of the rain of heaven: ¹²A land which the LORD thy God careth for: the eyes of the LORD thy God *are* always upon it, from the beginning of the year even unto the end of the year. ¹³And it shall come to pass, if ye shall hearken diligently unto my commandments which I command you this day, to love the LORD your God, and to serve him with all your heart and with all your soul, ¹⁴That I will give *you* the rain of your land in his due season, the first rain and the latter rain, that thou mayest gather in thy corn, and thy wine, and thine oil. ¹⁵And I will send^b grass in thy fields for thy cattle, that thou mayest eat and be full. ¹⁶Take heed to yourselves, that your heart be not deceived, and ye turn aside, and serve other gods, and worship them; ¹⁷And *then* the LORD'S wrath be kindled against you, and he shut up the heaven, that there be no rain, and that the land yield not her fruit; and *lest* ye perish quickly from off the good land which the LORD giveth you.

¹⁸Therefore shall ye lay up these my words in your heart and in your soul, and bind them for a sign upon your hand, that they may be as frontlets between your eyes. ¹⁹And ye shall teach them your children, speaking of them when thou sittest in thine house, and when thou walkest by the way, when thou liest down, and when thou risest up. ²⁰And thou shalt write them upon the door posts of thine house, and upon thy gates: ²¹That your days may be multiplied, and the days of your children, in the land which the LORD sware unto your fathers to give them, as the days of heaven upon the earth. ²²For if ye shall diligently keep all these commandments which I command you, to do them, to love the LORD your God, to walk in all his ways, and to cleave unto him; ²³Then will the LORD drive out all these nations from before you, and ye shall possess greater nations and mightier than yourselves. ²⁴Every place whereon the soles of your feet shall tread shall be yours: from the wilderness and Lebanon, from the river, the river Euphrates, even unto the uttermost sea shall your coast be. ²⁵There shall no man be able to stand before you: *for* the LORD your God shall lay the fear of you and the dread of you upon all the land that ye shall tread upon, as he hath said unto you.

²⁶Behold, I set before you this day a blessing and a curse; ²⁷A blessing, if ye obey the commandments of the LORD your God, which I command you this day: ²⁸And a curse, if ye will not obey the commandments of the LORD your God, but turn aside out of the way which I command you this day, to go after other gods, which ye have not known. ²⁹And it shall come to pass, when the LORD thy God hath brought thee in unto the land whither thou goest to possess it, that thou shalt put the blessing upon mount Gerizim, and the curse upon mount Ebal. ³⁰*Are* they not on the other side Jordan, by the way where the sun goeth down, in the land of the Canaanites, which dwell in the champaign over against Gilgal,

---

^b send: Heb. give

beside the plains of Moreh? [31]For ye shall pass over Jordan to go in to possess the land which the LORD your God giveth you, and ye shall possess it, and dwell therein. [32]And ye shall observe to do all the statutes and judgments which I set before you this day.

12

[1]These *are* the statutes and judgments, which ye shall observe to do in the land, which the LORD God of thy fathers giveth thee to possess it, all the days that ye live upon the earth. [2]Ye shall utterly destroy all the places, wherein the nations which ye shall possess[a] served their gods, upon the high mountains, and upon the hills, and under every green tree: [3]And ye shall overthrow[b] their altars, and break their pillars, and burn their groves with fire; and ye shall hew down the graven images of their gods, and destroy the names of them out of that place. [4]Ye shall not do so unto the LORD your God.

[5]But unto the place which the LORD your God shall choose out of all your tribes to put his name there, *even* unto his habitation shall ye seek, and thither thou shalt come: [6]And thither ye shall bring your burnt offerings, and your sacrifices, and your tithes, and heave offerings of your hand, and your vows, and your freewill offerings, and the firstlings of your herds and of your flocks: [7]And there ye shall eat before the LORD your God, and ye shall rejoice in all that ye put your hand unto, ye and your households, wherein the LORD thy God hath blessed thee. [8]Ye shall not do after all *the things* that we do here this day, every man whatsoever *is* right in his own eyes. [9]For ye are not as yet come to the rest and to the inheritance, which the LORD your God giveth you. [10]But *when* ye go over Jordan, and dwell in the land which the LORD your God giveth you to inherit, and *when* he giveth you rest from all your enemies round about, so that ye dwell in safety; [11]Then there shall be a place which the LORD your God shall choose to cause his name to dwell there; thither shall ye bring all that I command you; your burnt offerings, and your sacrifices, your tithes, and the heave offering of your hand, and all your choice[c] vows which ye vow unto the LORD: [12]And ye shall rejoice before

---

Devotional Moment

Priority: Worship

12:4-5 Because God's people lived among pagans who practiced do-your-own-religion-anywhere-you-want-to, God had to train them in the right way to worship. He wanted unity, understanding, and order when people worshiped him. So he told them to worship together in one place. Today, many people want to invent their own personal religion. While God's Word gives us some freedom in worship, we do not have the freedom to treat God any way we like. Worship needs to be regular, respectful, and orderly, as well as heartfelt. Individuals and families ought to set aside specific times and places for worshiping God. Where and how often does your family worship God? Make getting to church each week a top priority.

---

[a] possess: or, inherit
[b] overthrow: Heb. break down
[c] your choice . . . : Heb. the choice of your vows

the LORD your God, ye, and your sons, and your daughters, and your menservants, and your maidservants, and the Levite that *is* within your gates; forasmuch as he hath no part nor inheritance with you. ¹³Take heed to thyself that thou offer not thy burnt offerings in every place that thou seest: ¹⁴But in the place which the LORD shall choose in one of thy tribes, there thou shalt offer thy burnt offerings, and there thou shalt do all that I command thee. ¹⁵Notwithstanding thou mayest kill and eat flesh in all thy gates, whatsoever thy soul lusteth after, according to the blessing of the LORD thy God which he hath given thee: the unclean and the clean may eat thereof, as of the roebuck, and as of the hart. ¹⁶Only ye shall not eat the blood; ye shall pour it upon the earth as water. ¹⁷Thou mayest not eat within thy gates the tithe of thy corn, or of thy wine, or of thy oil, or the firstlings of thy herds or of thy flock, nor any of thy vows which thou vowest, nor thy freewill offerings, or heave offering of thine hand: ¹⁸But thou must eat them before the LORD thy God in the place which the LORD thy God shall choose, thou, and thy son, and thy daughter, and thy manservant, and thy maidservant, and the Levite that *is* within thy gates: and thou shalt rejoice before the LORD thy God in all that thou puttest thine hands unto. ¹⁹Take heed to thyself that thou forsake not the Levite as long as thou livest upon the earth. ²⁰When the LORD thy God shall enlarge thy border, as he hath promised thee, and thou shalt say, I will eat flesh, because thy soul longeth to eat flesh; thou mayest eat flesh, whatsoever thy soul lusteth after. ²¹If the place which the LORD thy God hath chosen to put his name there be too far from thee, then thou shalt kill of thy herd and of thy flock, which the LORD hath given thee, as I have commanded thee, and thou shalt eat in thy gates whatsoever thy soul lusteth after. ²²Even as the roebuck and the hart is eaten, so thou shalt eat them: the unclean and the clean shall eat *of* them alike. ²³Only be sure that thou eat not the blood: for the blood *is* the life; and thou mayest not eat the life with the flesh. ²⁴Thou shalt not eat it; thou shalt pour it upon the earth as water. ²⁵Thou shalt not eat it; that it may go well with thee, and with thy children after thee, when thou shalt do *that which is* right in the sight of the LORD. ²⁶Only thy holy things which thou hast, and thy vows, thou shalt take, and go unto the place which the LORD shall choose: ²⁷And thou shalt offer thy burnt offerings, the flesh and the blood, upon the altar of the LORD thy God: and the blood of thy sacrifices shall be poured out upon the altar of the LORD thy God, and thou shalt eat the flesh. ²⁸Observe and hear all these words which I command thee, that it may go well with thee, and with thy children after thee for ever, when thou doest *that which is* good and right in the sight of the LORD thy God. ²⁹When the LORD thy God shall cut off the nations from before thee, whither thou goest to possess them, and thou succeedest[d] them, and dwellest in their land; ³⁰Take heed to thyself that thou be not snared by following them, after that they be de-

---

[d] succeedest . . . : Heb. inheritest, or, possessest them

stroyed from before thee; and that thou enquire not after their gods, saying, How did these nations serve their gods? even so will I do likewise. ³¹Thou shalt not do so unto the LORD thy God: for every abomination to the LORD, which he hateth, have they done unto their gods; for even their sons and their daughters they have burnt in the fire to their gods. ³²What thing soever I command you, observe to do it: thou shalt not add thereto, nor diminish from it.

13

¹If there arise among you a prophet, or a dreamer of dreams, and giveth thee a sign or a wonder, ²And the sign or the wonder come to pass, whereof he spake unto thee, saying, Let us go after other gods, which thou hast not known, and let us serve them; ³Thou shalt not hearken unto the words of that prophet, or that dreamer of dreams: for the LORD your God proveth you, to know whether ye love the LORD your God with all your heart and with all your soul. ⁴Ye shall walk after the LORD your God, and fear him, and keep his commandments, and obey his voice, and ye shall serve him, and cleave unto him. ⁵And that prophet, or that dreamer of dreams, shall be put to death; because he hath spoken to turnᵃ *you* away from the LORD your God, which brought you out of the land of Egypt, and redeemed you out of the house of bondage, to thrust thee out of the way which the LORD thy God commanded thee to walk in. So shalt thou put the evil away from the midst of thee.

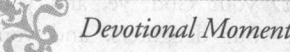

Devotional Moment

Loyalty

13:5-11 Just because people love you or are dear to you does not mean they will always tell you what is right. God told his people not to listen to anyone, even a close relative, who might lead them away from him. Family loyalty is important, but it must have limits. Best friends or relatives who urge us to disobey God become our worst enemies when they lead us astray. We need to say no to anyone who tells us to do something God says is wrong. Likewise, we must teach our children to have their own convictions. Study the Bible together so you can learn what God's will is.

⁶If thy brother, the son of thy mother, or thy son, or thy daughter, or the wife of thy bosom, or thy friend, which *is* as thine own soul, entice thee secretly, saying, Let us go and serve other gods, which thou hast not known, thou, nor thy fathers; ⁷*Namely*, of the gods of the people which *are* round about you, nigh unto thee, or far off from thee, from the *one* end of the earth even unto the *other* end of the earth; ⁸Thou shalt not consent unto him, nor hearken unto him; neither shall thine eye pity him, neither shalt thou spare, neither shalt thou conceal him: ⁹But thou shalt surely kill him; thine hand shall be first upon him to put him to death, and afterwards the hand of all the people. ¹⁰And thou shalt stone him with stones, that he die; because he hath sought to thrust thee away from the LORD thy God, which brought thee out of the land of Egypt, from the house of bondageᵇ. ¹¹And all

---

ᵃ to turn . . . : Heb. revolt against the LORD
ᵇ bondage: Heb. bondmen

Israel shall hear, and fear, and shall do no more any such wickedness as this is among you.

¹²If thou shalt hear *say* in one of thy cities, which the LORD thy God hath given thee to dwell there, saying, ¹³*Certain* men, the children[c] of Belial, are gone out from among you, and have withdrawn the inhabitants of their city, saying, Let us go and serve other gods, which ye have not known; ¹⁴Then shalt thou enquire, and make search, and ask diligently; and, behold, *if it be* truth, *and* the thing certain, *that* such abomination is wrought among you; ¹⁵Thou shalt surely smite the inhabitants of that city with the edge of the sword, destroying it utterly, and all that *is* therein, and the cattle thereof, with the edge of the sword. ¹⁶And thou shalt gather all the spoil of it into the midst of the street thereof, and shalt burn with fire the city, and all the spoil thereof every whit, for the LORD thy God: and it shall be an heap for ever; it shall not be built again. ¹⁷And there shall cleave nought of the cursed thing to thine hand: that the LORD may turn from the fierceness of his anger, and shew thee mercy, and have compassion upon thee, and multiply thee, as he hath sworn unto thy fathers; ¹⁸When thou shalt hearken to the voice of the LORD thy God, to keep all his commandments which I command thee this day, to do *that which is* right in the eyes of the LORD thy God.

14

¹Ye *are* the children of the LORD your God: ye shall not cut yourselves, nor make any baldness between your eyes for the dead. ²For thou *art* an holy people unto the LORD thy God, and the LORD hath chosen thee to be a peculiar people unto himself, above all the nations that *are* upon the earth. ³Thou shalt not eat any abominable thing. ⁴These *are* the beasts which ye shall eat: the ox, the sheep, and the goat, ⁵The hart, and the roebuck, and the fallow deer, and the wild goat, and the pygarg, and the wild ox, and the chamois. ⁶And every beast that parteth the hoof, and cleaveth the cleft into two claws, *and* cheweth the cud among the beasts, that ye shall eat. ⁷Nevertheless these ye shall not eat of them that chew the cud, or of them that divide the cloven hoof; *as* the camel, and the hare, and the coney: for they chew the cud, but divide not the hoof; *therefore* they *are* unclean unto you. ⁸And the swine, because it divideth the hoof, yet cheweth not the cud, it *is* unclean unto you: ye shall not eat of their flesh, nor touch their dead carcase. ⁹These ye shall eat of all that *are* in the waters: all that have fins and scales shall ye eat: ¹⁰And whatsoever hath not fins and scales ye may not eat; it *is* unclean unto you. ¹¹*Of* all clean birds ye shall eat. ¹²But these *are they* of which ye shall not eat: the eagle, and the ossifrage, and the ospray, ¹³And the glede, and the kite, and the vulture after his kind, ¹⁴And every raven after his kind, ¹⁵And the owl, and the night hawk, and the cuckow, and the hawk after his kind, ¹⁶The little owl, and the great owl, and the swan, ¹⁷And the pelican, and the gier eagle, and the cormorant, ¹⁸And the stork, and the heron after her kind, and

---

[c] the children . . . : or, naughty men

the lapwing, and the bat. ¹⁹And every creeping thing that flieth *is* unclean unto you: they shall not be eaten. ²⁰*But* of all clean fowls ye may eat. ²¹Ye shall not eat *of* any thing that dieth of itself: thou shalt give it unto the stranger that *is* in thy gates, that he may eat it; or thou mayest sell it unto an alien: for thou *art* an holy people unto the LORD thy God. Thou shalt not seethe a kid in his mother's milk.

²²Thou shalt truly tithe all the increase of thy seed, that the field bringeth forth year by year. ²³And thou shalt eat before the LORD thy God, in the place which he shall choose to place his name there, the tithe of thy corn, of thy wine, and of thine oil, and the firstlings of thy herds and of thy flocks; that thou mayest learn to fear the LORD thy God always. ²⁴And if the way be too long for thee, so that thou art not able to carry it; *or* if the place be too far from thee, which the LORD thy

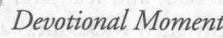

Devotional Moment

Whose Money?

14:22-23 God instructed his people to give back to him the first or best one-tenth of everything he gave them. Tithing was a clear way of showing that God came first in their lives. Tithing can still serve the same purpose. Is it really *our money*, or merely a manifestation of the time and abilities God has given us? Tithing allows us to thank and trust God at the same time. We thank him by giving, and we trust him by making him more important than other claims on the money. Tithing also requires that we become good stewards of the way we spend the rest of what he has given us.

Devotional Moment

Radical Relief

14:28-29 Usually, the tithe collected in Israel was used to provide for God's priests and Levites. But every third year, the money was given to the poor. What an amazing approach to welfare! God counts it a gift to him when we give to those who don't have enough. And giving should be more personal than just putting an offering in the plate at church. We should always be aware of ways in which we can serve and help those around us in direct ways. Are there any families in your neighborhood that your family could help by sharing your tithe? How can you give some portion for relief of poor and starving people?

God shall choose to set his name there, when the LORD thy God hath blessed thee: ²⁵Then shalt thou turn *it* into money, and bind up the money in thine hand, and shalt go unto the place which the LORD thy God shall choose: ²⁶And thou shalt bestow that money for whatsoever thy soul lusteth after, for oxen, or for sheep, or for wine, or for strong drink, or for whatsoever thy soul desireth[a]: and thou shalt eat there before the LORD thy God, and thou shalt rejoice, thou, and thine household, ²⁷And the Levite that *is* within thy gates; thou shalt not forsake him; for he hath no part nor inheritance with thee. ²⁸At the end of three years thou shalt bring forth all the tithe of thine increase the same year, and shalt lay *it* up within thy gates: ²⁹And the Levite, (because he hath no part nor inheritance with thee,) and the stranger, and the fatherless, and the widow, which *are* within thy gates, shall

---

[a] desireth: Heb. asketh of thee

come, and shall eat and be satisfied; that the LORD thy God may bless thee in all the work of thine hand which thou doest.

15

¹At the end of *every* seven years thou shalt make a release. ²And this *is* the manner of the release: Every creditor[a] that lendeth *ought* unto his neighbour shall release *it*; he shall not exact *it* of his neighbour, or of his brother; because it is called the LORD'S release. ³Of a foreigner thou mayest exact *it* again: but *that* which is thine with thy brother thine hand shall release; ⁴Save[b] when there shall be no poor among you; for the LORD shall greatly bless thee in the land which the LORD thy God giveth thee *for* an inheritance to possess it: ⁵Only if thou carefully hearken unto the voice of the LORD thy God, to observe to do all these commandments which I command thee this day. ⁶For the LORD thy God blesseth thee, as he promised thee: and thou shalt lend unto many nations, but thou shalt not borrow; and thou shalt reign over many nations, but they shall not reign over thee. ⁷If there be among you a poor man of one of thy brethren within any of thy gates in thy land which the LORD thy God giveth thee, thou shalt not harden thine heart, nor shut thine hand from thy poor brother: ⁸But thou shalt open thine hand wide unto him, and shalt surely lend him sufficient for his need, *in that* which he wanteth. ⁹Beware that there be not a thought[c] in thy wicked heart, saying, The seventh year, the year of release, is at hand; and thine eye be evil against thy poor brother, and thou givest him nought; and he cry unto the LORD against thee, and it be sin unto thee. ¹⁰Thou shalt surely give him, and thine heart shall not be grieved when thou givest unto him: because that for this thing the LORD thy God shall bless thee in all thy works, and in all that thou puttest thine hand unto. ¹¹For the poor shall never cease out of the land: therefore I command thee, saying, Thou shalt open thine hand wide unto thy brother, to thy poor, and to thy needy, in thy land.

¹²*And* if thy brother, an Hebrew man, or an Hebrew woman, be sold unto thee, and serve thee six years; then in the seventh year thou shalt let him go free from thee. ¹³And when thou sendest him out free from thee, thou shalt not let him go away empty: ¹⁴Thou shalt furnish him liberally out of thy flock, and out of thy floor, and out of thy winepress: *of that* wherewith the LORD thy God hath blessed thee thou shalt give unto him. ¹⁵And thou shalt remember that thou wast a bondman in the land of Egypt, and the LORD thy God redeemed thee: therefore I command thee this thing to day. ¹⁶And it shall be, if he say unto thee, I will not go away from thee; because he loveth thee and thine house, because he is well with thee; ¹⁷Then thou shalt take an aul, and thrust *it* through his ear unto the door, and he shall be thy ser-

---

[a] creditor: Heb. master of the lending of his hand
[b] Save . . . : or, To the end that there be no poor among you
[c] thought: Heb. word

vant for ever. And also unto thy maid-servant thou shalt do likewise. [18]It shall not seem hard unto thee, when thou sendest him away free from thee; for he hath been worth a double hired servant *to thee*, in serving thee six years: and the LORD thy God shall bless thee in all that thou doest.

[19]All the firstling males that come of thy herd and of thy flock thou shalt sanctify unto the LORD thy God: thou shalt do no work with the firstling of thy bullock, nor shear the firstling of thy sheep. [20]Thou shalt eat *it* before the LORD thy God year by year in the place which the LORD shall choose, thou and thy household. [21]And if there be *any* blemish therein, *as if it be* lame, or blind, *or have* any ill blemish, thou shalt not sacrifice it unto the LORD thy God. [22]Thou shalt eat it within thy gates: the unclean and the clean *person shall eat it* alike, as the roebuck, and as the hart. [23]Only thou shalt not eat the blood thereof; thou shalt pour it upon the ground as water.

16

[1]Observe the month of Abib, and keep the passover unto the LORD thy God: for in the month of Abib the LORD thy God brought thee forth out of Egypt by night. [2]Thou shalt therefore sacrifice the passover unto the LORD thy God, of the flock and the herd, in the place which the LORD shall choose to place his name there. [3]Thou shalt eat no leavened bread with it; seven days shalt thou eat unleavened bread therewith, *even* the bread of affliction; for thou camest forth out of the land of Egypt in haste: that thou mayest remember the day when thou camest forth out of the land of Egypt all the days of thy life. [4]And there shall be no leavened bread seen with thee in all thy coast seven days; neither shall there *any thing* of the flesh, which thou sacrificedst the first day at even, remain all night until the morning. [5]Thou mayest not sacrifice[a] the passover within any of thy gates, which the LORD thy God giveth thee: [6]But at the place which the LORD thy God shall choose to place his name in, there thou shalt sacrifice the passover at even, at the going down of the sun, at the season that thou camest forth out of Egypt. [7]And thou shalt roast and eat *it* in the place which the LORD thy God shall choose: and thou shalt turn in the morning, and go unto thy tents. [8]Six days thou shalt eat unleavened bread: and on the seventh day *shall be* a solemn assembly to the LORD thy God: thou shalt do no work *therein*. [9]Seven weeks shalt thou number unto thee: begin to number the seven weeks from *such time as* thou beginnest *to put* the sickle to the corn. [10]And thou shalt keep the feast of weeks unto the LORD thy God with a tribute[b] of a freewill offering of thine hand, which thou shalt give *unto the LORD thy God*, according as the LORD thy God hath blessed thee: [11]And thou shalt rejoice before the LORD thy God, thou, and thy son, and thy daughter, and thy

---

[a] sacrifice: or, kill
[b] a tribute: or, sufficiency

manservant, and thy maidservant, and the Levite that *is* within thy gates, and the stranger, and the fatherless, and the widow, that *are* among you, in the place which the LORD thy God hath chosen to place his name there. ¹²And thou shalt remember that thou wast a bondman in Egypt: and thou shalt observe and do these statutes. ¹³Thou shalt observe the feast of tabernacles seven days, after that thou hast gathered in thy corn^c and thy wine: ¹⁴And thou shalt rejoice in thy feast, thou, and thy son, and thy daughter, and thy manservant, and thy maidservant, and the Levite, the stranger, and the fatherless, and the widow, that *are* within thy gates. ¹⁵Seven days shalt thou keep a solemn feast unto the LORD thy God in the place which the LORD shall choose: because the LORD thy God shall bless thee in all thine increase, and in all the works of thine hands, therefore thou shalt surely rejoice. ¹⁶Three times in a year shall all thy males appear before the LORD thy God in the place which he shall choose; in the feast of unleavened bread, and in the feast of weeks, and in the feast of tabernacles: and they shall not appear before the LORD empty: ¹⁷Every man *shall give* as he is able, according to the blessing of the LORD thy God which he hath given thee.

¹⁸Judges and officers shalt thou make thee in all thy gates, which the LORD thy God giveth thee, throughout thy tribes: and they shall judge the people with just judgment. ¹⁹Thou shalt not wrest judgment; thou shalt not respect persons, neither take a gift: for a gift doth blind the eyes of the wise, and pervert the words^d of the righteous. ²⁰That which is altogether just shalt thou follow, that thou mayest live, and inherit the land which the LORD thy God giveth thee. ²¹Thou shalt not plant thee a grove of any trees near unto the altar of the LORD thy God, which thou shalt make thee. ²²Neither shalt thou set thee up *any* image^e; which the LORD thy God hateth.

17

¹Thou shalt not sacrifice unto the LORD thy God *any* bullock, or sheep^a, wherein is blemish, *or* any evilfavouredness: for that *is* an abomination unto the LORD thy God. ²If there be found among you, within any of thy gates which the LORD thy God giveth thee, man or woman, that hath wrought wickedness in the sight of the LORD thy God, in transgressing his covenant, ³And hath gone and served other gods, and worshipped them, either the sun, or moon, or any of the host of heaven, which I have not commanded; ⁴And it be told thee, and thou hast heard *of it*, and enquired diligently, and, behold, *it be* true, *and* the thing certain, *that* such abomination is wrought in Israel: ⁵Then shalt thou bring forth that man or that woman, which have committed

---

^c corn . . . : Heb. floor, and thy winepress
^d words: or, matters
^e image: or, statue, or, pillar
^a sheep: or, goat

that wicked thing, unto thy gates, *even* that man or that woman, and shalt stone them with stones, till they die. ⁶At the mouth of two witnesses, or three witnesses, shall he that is worthy of death be put to death; *but* at the mouth of one witness he shall not be put to death. ⁷The hands of the witnesses shall be first upon him to put him to death, and afterward the hands of all the people. So thou shalt put the evil away from among you.

⁸If there arise a matter too hard for thee in judgment, between blood and blood, between plea and plea, and between stroke and stroke, *being* matters of controversy within thy gates: then shalt thou arise, and get thee up into the place which the LORD thy God shall choose; ⁹And thou shalt come unto the priests the Levites, and unto the judge that shall be in those days, and enquire; and they shall shew thee the sentence of judgment: ¹⁰And thou shalt do according to the sentence, which they of that place which the LORD shall choose shall shew thee; and thou shalt observe to do according to all that they inform thee: ¹¹According to the sentence of the law which they shall teach thee, and according to the judgment which they shall tell thee, thou shalt do: thou shalt not decline from the sentence which they shall shew thee, *to* the right hand, nor *to* the left. ¹²And the man that will do presumptuously, and will not hearken unto the priest that standeth to minister there before the LORD thy God, or unto the judge, even that man shall die: and thou shalt put away the evil from Israel. ¹³And all the people shall hear, and fear, and do no more presumptuously.

¹⁴When thou art come unto the land which the LORD thy God giveth thee, and shalt possess it, and shalt dwell therein, and shalt say, I will set a king over me, like as all the nations that *are* about me; ¹⁵Thou shalt in any wise set *him* king over thee, whom the LORD thy God shall choose: *one* from among thy brethren shalt thou set king over thee: thou mayest not set a stranger over thee, which *is* not thy brother. ¹⁶But he shall not multiply horses to himself, nor cause the people to return to Egypt, to the end that he should multiply horses: forasmuch as the LORD hath said unto you, Ye shall henceforth return no more that way. ¹⁷Neither shall he multiply wives to himself, that his heart turn not away: neither shall he greatly multiply to himself silver and gold. ¹⁸And it shall be, when he sitteth upon the throne of his kingdom, that he shall write him a copy of this law in a book out of *that which is* before the priests the Levites: ¹⁹And it shall be with him, and he shall read therein all the days of his life: that he may learn to fear the LORD his God, to keep all the words of this law and these statutes, to do them: ²⁰That his heart be not lifted up above his brethren, and that he turn not aside from the commandment, *to* the right hand, or *to* the left: to the end that he may prolong *his* days in his kingdom, he, and his children, in the midst of Israel.

18

¹The priests the Levites, *and* all the tribe of Levi, shall have no part nor inheritance with Israel: they shall eat the offerings of the LORD made by fire, and his inheritance. ²Therefore shall

Devotional Moment

Serving the Servers

18:1-8 In Israel, an entire tribe called the Levites was set apart for special service to God. They were not to own land or be employed. Their lives were to be available to God. The rest of the people were told that part of their offerings and sacrifices was to be given to the Levites for their personal use. Today, those who minister in church receive some of the funds that are given in offerings. But small gifts, notes of encouragement, and special meals are also important ways that church members can honor those who serve them in worship. In what ways could you thank a faithful pastor or wise teacher in the church you attend? Start today to bless those who bless you.

they have no inheritance among their brethren: the LORD *is* their inheritance, as he hath said unto them. ³And this shall be the priest's due from the people, from them that offer a sacrifice, whether *it be* ox or sheep; and they shall give unto the priest the shoulder, and the two cheeks, and the maw. ⁴The firstfruit *also* of thy corn, of thy wine, and of thine oil, and the first of the fleece of thy sheep, shalt thou give him. ⁵For the LORD thy God hath chosen him out of all thy tribes, to stand to minister in the name of the LORD, him and his sons for ever. ⁶And if a Levite come from any of thy gates out of all Israel, where he sojourned, and come with all the desire of his mind unto the place which the LORD shall choose; ⁷Then he shall minister in the name of the LORD his God, as all his brethren the Levites *do*, which stand there before the LORD. ⁸They shall

have like portions to eat, beside that which cometh of the sale of his patrimony.

⁹When thou art come into the land which the LORD thy God giveth thee, thou shalt not learn to do after the abominations of those nations. ¹⁰There shall not be found among you *any one* that maketh his son or his daughter to pass through the fire, *or* that useth divination, *or* an observer of times, or an enchanter, or a witch, ¹¹Or a charmer, or a consulter with familiar spirits, or a wizard, or a necromancer. ¹²For all that do these things *are* an abomination unto the LORD: and because of these abominations the LORD thy God doth drive them out from before thee. ¹³Thou shalt be perfectª with the LORD thy God. ¹⁴For these nations, which thou shalt possessᵇ, hearkened unto observers of times, and unto diviners: but as for thee, the LORD thy God hath not suffered thee so *to do*.

¹⁵The LORD thy God will raise up unto thee a Prophet from the midst of thee, of thy brethren, like unto me; unto him ye shall hearken; ¹⁶According to all that thou desiredst of the LORD thy God in Horeb in the day of the assembly, saying, Let me not hear again the voice of the LORD my God, neither let me see this great fire any more, that I die not. ¹⁷And the LORD said unto me, They have well *spoken that* which they have spoken. ¹⁸I will raise them up a Prophet from among their brethren, like unto thee, and will put my words in his mouth; and he shall speak unto them all that I shall com-

---

ª perfect: or, upright, or, sincere
ᵇ possess: or, inherit

mand him. ¹⁹And it shall come to pass, *that* whosoever will not hearken unto my words which he shall speak in my name, I will require *it* of him. ²⁰But the prophet, which shall presume to speak a word in my name, which I have not commanded him to speak, or that shall speak in the name of other gods, even that prophet shall die. ²¹And if thou say in thine heart, How shall we know the word which the LORD hath not spoken? ²²When a prophet speaketh in the name of the LORD, if the thing follow not, nor come to pass, that *is* the thing which the LORD hath not spoken, *but* the prophet hath spoken it presumptuously: thou shalt not be afraid of him.

19

¹When the LORD thy God hath cut off the nations, whose land the LORD thy

---

Devotional Moment

•

Safe Ground

19:2-7 God had a practical solution for the problem of revenge: He told the people to create Cities of Refuge, where a person accused of a crime could be safe until he or she was determined to be guilty or innocent. Every family needs to have clear rules about blame, revenge, and discipline. Children need to know they will have an opportunity to explain an accident. They need to know that revenge is not an acceptable way to resolve problems in the family. And they need to understand that when guilt is established, appropriate discipline will follow. What are the rules for crimes, accidents, and corrective discipline in your family? Guarantee each other's safety until the whole story can be told.

God giveth thee, and thou succeedest[a] them, and dwellest in their cities, and in their houses; ²Thou shalt separate three cities for thee in the midst of thy land, which the LORD thy God giveth thee to possess it. ³Thou shalt prepare thee a way, and divide the coasts of thy land, which the LORD thy God giveth thee to inherit, into three parts, that every slayer may flee thither. ⁴And this *is* the case of the slayer, which shall flee thither, that he may live: Whoso killeth his neighbour ignorantly, whom he hated not in time past; ⁵As when a man goeth into the wood with his neighbour to hew wood, and his hand fetcheth a stroke with the axe to cut down the tree, and the head[b] slippeth from the helve, and lighteth upon his neighbour, that he die; he shall flee unto one of those cities, and live: ⁶Lest the avenger of the blood pursue the slayer, while his heart is hot, and overtake him, because the way is long, and slay[c] him; whereas he *was* not worthy of death, inasmuch as he hated him not in time past. ⁷Wherefore I command thee, saying, Thou shalt separate three cities for thee. ⁸And if the LORD thy God enlarge thy coast, as he hath sworn unto thy fathers, and give thee all the land which he promised to give unto thy fathers; ⁹If thou shalt keep all these commandments to do them, which I command thee this day, to love the LORD thy God, and to walk ever in his ways; then shalt thou add three cities more for thee, beside these three: ¹⁰That innocent blood be not shed in thy land,

---

[a] succeedest: Heb. inheritest, or, possessest

[b] head: Heb. iron

[c] slay . . . : Heb. smite him in life

which the LORD thy God giveth thee *for* an inheritance, and *so* blood be upon thee. ¹¹But if any man hate his neighbour, and lie in wait for him, and rise up against him, and smite him mortally[d] that he die, and fleeth into one of these cities: ¹²Then the elders of his city shall send and fetch him thence, and deliver him into the hand of the avenger of blood, that he may die. ¹³Thine eye shall not pity him, but thou shalt put away *the guilt of* innocent blood from Israel, that it may go well with thee.

¹⁴Thou shalt not remove thy neighbour's landmark, which they of old time have set in thine inheritance, which thou shalt inherit in the land that the LORD thy God giveth thee to possess it. ¹⁵One witness shall not rise up against a man for any iniquity, or for any sin, in any sin that he sinneth: at the mouth of two witnesses, or at the mouth of three witnesses, shall the mat-

ter be established. ¹⁶If a false witness rise up against any man to testify against him *that which is* wrong; ¹⁷Then both the men, between whom the controversy *is*, shall stand before the LORD, before the priests and the judges, which shall be in those days; ¹⁸And the judges shall make diligent inquisition: and, behold, *if* the witness *be* a false witness, *and* hath testified falsely against his brother; ¹⁹Then shall ye do unto him, as he had thought to have done unto his brother: so shalt thou put the evil away from among you. ²⁰And those which remain shall hear, and fear, and shall henceforth commit no more any such evil among you. ²¹And thine eye shall not pity; *but* life *shall go* for life, eye for eye, tooth for tooth, hand for hand, foot for foot.

20

¹When thou goest out to battle against thine enemies, and seest horses, and chariots, *and* a people more than thou, be not afraid of them: for the LORD thy God *is* with thee, which brought thee up out of the land of Egypt. ²And it shall be, when ye are come nigh unto the battle, that the priest shall approach and speak unto the people, ³And shall say unto them, Hear, O Israel, ye approach this day unto battle against your enemies: let not your hearts faint[a], fear not, and do not tremble, neither be ye terrified because of them; ⁴For the LORD your God *is* he that goeth with you, to fight for you against your enemies, to save you. ⁵And the officers shall speak unto the people, saying, What

Devotional Moment

Discipline

19:16-19 The law required false witnesses to receive the punishment they thought would be inflicted on the person they accused. This was a sure way to discourage people from falsely accusing each other. The same principle works in families. When children lie about their siblings to get them in trouble, they should receive the same correction they sought for the other. They will soon learn that false accusations can painfully backfire. Parents who enforce this principle in their families teach their children about honesty and justice while enhancing peace in the home.

---

[d] mortally: Heb. in life
[a] faint: Heb. be tender

man *is there* that hath built a new house, and hath not dedicated it? let him go and return to his house, lest he die in the battle, and another man dedicate it. ⁶And what man *is he* that hath planted a vineyard, and hath not *yet* eaten^b of it? let him *also* go and return unto his house, lest he die in the battle, and another man eat of it. ⁷And what man *is there* that hath betrothed a wife, and hath not taken her? let him go and return unto his house, lest he die in the battle, and another man take her. ⁸And the officers shall speak further unto the people, and they shall say, What man *is there that is* fearful and fainthearted? let him go and return unto his house, lest his brethren's heart faint^c as well as his heart. ⁹And it shall be, when the officers have made an end of speaking unto the people, that they shall make captains of the armies to lead^d the people.

¹⁰When thou comest nigh unto a city to fight against it, then proclaim peace unto it. ¹¹And it shall be, if it make thee answer of peace, and open unto thee, then it shall be, *that* all the people *that is* found therein shall be tributaries unto thee, and they shall serve thee. ¹²And if it will make no peace with thee, but will make war against thee, then thou shalt besiege it: ¹³And when the LORD thy God hath delivered it into thine hands, thou shalt smite every male thereof with the edge of the sword: ¹⁴But the women, and the little ones, and the cattle, and all that is in the city, *even* all the spoil thereof, shalt thou take^e unto thyself; and thou shalt eat the spoil of thine enemies, which the LORD thy God hath given thee. ¹⁵Thus shalt thou do unto all the cities *which are* very far off from thee, which *are* not of the cities of these nations. ¹⁶But of the cities of these people, which the LORD thy God doth give thee *for* an inheritance, thou shalt save alive nothing that breatheth: ¹⁷But thou shalt utterly destroy them; *namely*, the Hittites, and the Amorites, the Canaanites, and the Perizzites, the Hivites, and the Jebusites; as the LORD thy God hath commanded thee: ¹⁸That they teach you not to do after all their abominations, which they have done unto their gods; so should ye sin against the LORD your God. ¹⁹When thou shalt besiege a city a long time, in making war against it to take it, thou shalt not destroy the trees thereof by forcing an axe against them: for thou mayest eat of them, and thou shalt not cut them down (for the tree of the field *is* man's *life*) to employ *them* in the siege: ²⁰Only the trees which thou knowest that they *be* not trees for meat, thou shalt destroy and cut them down; and thou shalt build bulwarks against the city that maketh war with thee, until it be subdued.

21

¹If *one* be found slain in the land which the LORD thy God giveth thee to possess it, lying in the field, *and* it be not known who hath slain him: ²Then thy

---

^b eaten . . . : Heb. made it common
^c faint: Heb. melt
^d to lead . . . : Heb. to be in the head of the people
^e take: Heb. spoil

elders and thy judges shall come forth, and they shall measure unto the cities which *are* round about him that is slain: ³And it shall be, *that* the city *which is* next unto the slain man, even the elders of that city shall take an heifer, which hath not been wrought with, *and* which hath not drawn in the yoke; ⁴And the elders of that city shall bring down the heifer unto a rough valley, which is neither eared nor sown, and shall strike off the heifer's neck there in the valley: ⁵And the priests the sons of Levi shall come near; for them the LORD thy God hath chosen to minister unto him, and to bless in the name of the LORD; and by their word° shall every controversy and every stroke be *tried*: ⁶And all the elders of that city, *that are* next unto the slain *man*, shall wash their hands over the heifer that is beheaded in the valley: ⁷And they shall answer and say, Our hands have not shed this blood, neither have our eyes seen *it*. ⁸Be merciful, O LORD, unto thy people Israel, whom thou hast redeemed, and lay not innocent blood unto thy people of Israel's charge. And the blood shall be forgiven them. ⁹So shalt thou put away the *guilt of* innocent blood from among you, when thou shalt do *that which is* right in the sight of the LORD.

¹⁰When thou goest forth to war against thine enemies, and the LORD thy God hath delivered them into thine hands, and thou hast taken them captive, ¹¹And seest among the captives a beautiful woman, and hast a desire unto her, that thou wouldest have her to thy wife; ¹²Then thou shalt bring her home to thine house; and she shall shave her head, and pareᵇ her nails; ¹³And she shall put the raiment of her captivity from off her, and shall remain in thine house, and bewail her father and her mother a full month: and after that thou shalt go in unto her, and be her husband, and she shall be thy wife. ¹⁴And it shall be, if thou have no delight in her, then thou shalt let her go whither she will; but thou shalt not sell her at all for money, thou shalt not make merchandise of her, because thou hast humbled her.

¹⁵If a man have two wives, one beloved, and another hated, and they have born him children, *both* the beloved and the hated; and *if* the firstborn son be hers that was hated: ¹⁶Then it shall be, when he maketh his sons to inherit *that* which he hath, *that* he may not make the son of the beloved firstborn before the son of the hated, *which is indeed* the firstborn: ¹⁷But he shall acknowledge the son of the hated *for* the firstborn, by giving him a double portion of all that he hath: for he *is* the beginning of his strength; the right of the firstborn *is* his.

¹⁸If a man have a stubborn and rebellious son, which will not obey the voice of his father, or the voice of his mother, and *that*, when they have chastened him, will not hearken unto them: ¹⁹Then shall his father and his mother lay hold on him, and bring him out unto the elders of his city, and unto the gate of his place; ²⁰And they shall say unto the elders of his city, This our son *is* stubborn and rebellious, he will not obey our voice; *he is* a glutton, and a drunkard. ²¹And all the men of his city

---

ᵃ word: Heb. mouth
ᵇ pare: or, suffer to grow: Heb. make, or, dress

shall stone him with stones, that he die: so shalt thou put evil away from among you; and all Israel shall hear, and fear. ²²And if a man have committed a sin worthy of death, and he be to be put to death, and thou hang him on a tree: ²³His body shall not remain all night upon the tree, but thou shalt in any wise bury him that day; (for he that is hanged *is* accursedᶜ of God;) that thy land be not defiled, which the LORD thy God giveth thee *for* an inheritance.

22

¹Thou shalt not see thy brother's ox or his sheep go astray, and hide thyself from them: thou shalt in any case bring them again unto thy brother. ²And if thy brother *be* not nigh unto thee, or if thou know him not, then thou shalt bring it unto thine own house, and it shall be with thee until thy brother seek after it, and thou shalt restore it to him again. ³In like manner shalt thou do with his ass; and so shalt thou do with his raiment; and with all lost thing of thy brother's, which he hath lost, and thou hast found, shalt thou do likewise: thou mayest not hide thyself. ⁴Thou shalt not see thy brother's ass or his ox fall down by the way, and hide thyself from them: thou shalt surely help him to lift *them* up again.

⁵The woman shall not wear that which pertaineth unto a man, neither shall a man put on a woman's garment: for all that do so *are* abomination unto the LORD thy God. ⁶If a bird's nest chance to be before thee in the way in any tree, or on the ground, *whether they be* young ones, or eggs, and the dam sitting upon the young, or upon the eggs, thou shalt not take the dam with the young: ⁷*But* thou shalt in any wise let the dam go, and take the young to thee; that it may be well with thee, and *that* thou mayest prolong *thy* days. ⁸When thou buildest a new house, then thou shalt make a battlement for thy roof, that thou bring not blood upon thine house, if any man fall from thence. ⁹Thou shalt not sow thy vineyard with divers seeds: lest the fruit of thy seedᵃ which thou hast sown, and the fruit of thy vineyard, be defiled. ¹⁰Thou shalt not plow with an ox and an ass together. ¹¹Thou shalt not wear a garment of divers sorts, *as* of woollen and linen together. ¹²Thou shalt make thee fringes upon the four quartersᵇ of thy vesture, wherewith thou coverest *thyself.*

Devotional Moment

Faithfulness

22:13-30 God regards faithfulness between marriage partners as very important. The law specified severe punishments for a variety of sexual sins and crimes. This severity shows how important sexual purity is to God. Having sex only with one's spouse helps maintain the life and health of those individuals, of the family, and of the nation. Sexual misbehavior has the potential to destroy lives and may affect many of your relationships and your family. Recognize the danger of misusing God's beautiful gift of sex, and commit to following his pattern, for your own health and for the sake of all those you love.

ᶜ accursed . . . : Heb. the curse of God
ᵃ fruit of thy seed: Heb. fulness of the seed
ᵇ quarters: Heb. wings

¹³If any man take a wife, and go in unto her, and hate her, ¹⁴And give occasions of speech against her, and bring up an evil name upon her, and say, I took this woman, and when I came to her, I found her not a maid: ¹⁵Then shall the father of the damsel, and her mother, take and bring forth *the tokens of* the damsel's virginity unto the elders of the city in the gate: ¹⁶And the damsel's father shall say unto the elders, I gave my daughter unto this man to wife, and he hateth her; ¹⁷And, lo, he hath given occasions of speech *against her*, saying, I found not thy daughter a maid; and yet these *are the tokens of* my daughter's virginity. And they shall spread the cloth before the elders of the city. ¹⁸And the elders of that city shall take that man and chastise him; ¹⁹And they shall amerce him in an hundred *shekels* of silver, and give *them* unto the father of the damsel, because he hath brought up an evil name upon a virgin of Israel: and she shall be his wife; he may not put her away all his days. ²⁰But if this thing be true, *and the tokens of* virginity be not found for the damsel: ²¹Then they shall bring out the damsel to the door of her father's house, and the men of her city shall stone her with stones that she die: because she hath wrought folly in Israel, to play the whore in her father's house: so shalt thou put evil away from among you. ²²If a man be found lying with a woman married to an husband, then they shall both of them die, *both* the man that lay with the woman, and the woman: so shalt thou put away evil from Israel. ²³If a damsel *that is* a virgin be betrothed unto an husband, and a man find her in the city, and lie with her; ²⁴Then ye shall bring them both out unto the gate of that city, and ye shall stone them with stones that they die; the damsel, because she cried not, *being* in the city; and the man, because he hath humbled his neighbour's wife: so thou shalt put away evil from among you. ²⁵But if a man find a betrothed damsel in the field, and the man force[c] her, and lie with her: then the man only that lay with her shall die: ²⁶But unto the damsel thou shalt do nothing; *there is* in the damsel no sin *worthy* of death: for as when a man riseth against his neighbour, and slayeth him, even so *is* this matter: ²⁷For he found her in the field, *and* the betrothed damsel cried, and *there was* none to save her. ²⁸If a man find a damsel *that is* a virgin, which is not betrothed, and lay hold on her, and lie with her, and they be found; ²⁹Then the man that lay with her shall give unto the damsel's father fifty *shekels* of silver, and she shall be his wife; because he hath humbled her, he may not put her away all his days. ³⁰A man shall not take his father's wife, nor discover his father's skirt.

23

¹He that is wounded in the stones, or hath his privy member cut off, shall not enter into the congregation of the LORD. ²A bastard shall not enter into the congregation of the LORD; even to his tenth generation shall he not enter into the congregation of the LORD. ³An Ammonite or Moabite shall not enter into the congregation of the

---

[c] force: or, take strong hold of

LORD; even to their tenth generation shall they not enter into the congregation of the LORD for ever: ⁴Because they met you not with bread and with water in the way, when ye came forth out of Egypt; and because they hired against thee Balaam the son of Beor of Pethor of Mesopotamia, to curse thee. ⁵Nevertheless the LORD thy God would not hearken unto Balaam; but the LORD thy God turned the curse into a blessing unto thee, because the LORD thy God loved thee. ⁶Thou shalt not seek their peace nor their prosperity[a] all thy days for ever. ⁷Thou shalt not abhor an Edomite; for he *is* thy brother: thou shalt not abhor an Egyptian; because thou wast a stranger in his land. ⁸The children that are begotten of them shall enter into the congregation of the LORD in their third generation.

⁹When the host goeth forth against thine enemies, then keep thee from every wicked thing. ¹⁰If there be among you any man, that is not clean by reason of uncleanness that chanceth him by night, then shall he go abroad out of the camp, he shall not come within the camp: ¹¹But it shall be, when evening cometh on, he shall wash *himself* with water: and when the sun is down, he shall come into the camp *again*. ¹²Thou shalt have a place also without the camp, whither thou shalt go forth abroad: ¹³And thou shalt have a paddle upon thy weapon; and it shall be, when thou wilt ease thyself abroad, thou shalt dig therewith, and shalt turn back and cover that which cometh from thee:

¹⁴For the LORD thy God walketh in the midst of thy camp, to deliver thee, and to give up thine enemies before thee; therefore shall thy camp be holy: that he see no unclean[b] thing in thee, and turn away from thee.

¹⁵Thou shalt not deliver unto his master the servant which is escaped from his master unto thee: ¹⁶He shall dwell with thee, *even* among you, in that place which he shall choose in one of thy gates, where it liketh him best: thou shalt not oppress him. ¹⁷There shall be no whore[c] of the daughters of Israel, nor a sodomite of the sons of Israel. ¹⁸Thou shalt not bring the hire of a whore, or the price of a dog, into the house of the LORD thy God for any vow: for even both these *are* abomination unto the LORD thy God. ¹⁹Thou shalt not lend upon usury to thy brother; usury of money, usury of victuals, usury of any thing that is lent upon usury: ²⁰Unto a stranger thou mayest lend upon usury; but unto thy brother thou shalt not lend upon usury: that the LORD thy God may bless thee in all that thou settest thine hand to in the land whither thou goest to possess it. ²¹When thou shalt vow a vow unto the LORD thy God, thou shalt not slack to pay it: for the LORD thy God will surely require it of thee; and it would be sin in thee. ²²But if thou shalt forbear to vow, it shall be no sin in thee. ²³That which is gone out of thy lips thou shalt keep and perform; *even* a freewill offering, according as thou hast vowed unto the LORD thy God, which

---

[a] prosperity: Heb. good
[b] unclean . . . : Heb. nakedness of any thing
[c] whore: or, sodomitess

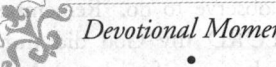

thou hast promised with thy mouth. ²⁴When thou comest into thy neighbour's vineyard, then thou mayest eat grapes thy fill at thine own pleasure; but thou shalt not put *any* in thy vessel. ²⁵When thou comest into the standing corn of thy neighbour, then thou mayest pluck the ears with thine hand; but thou shalt not move a sickle unto thy neighbour's standing corn.

24

¹When a man hath taken a wife, and married her, and it come to pass that she find no favour in his eyes, because he hath found some^a uncleanness in her: then let him write her a bill of divorcement, and give *it* in her hand, and send her out of his house. ²And when she is departed out of his house, she may go and be another man's *wife*. ³And *if* the latter husband hate her, and write her a bill of divorcement, and giveth *it* in her hand, and sendeth her out of his house; or if the latter husband die,

Devotional Moment
•
Marriage and Divorce
24:1-4 The law regulated divorce because God did not want it to become a normal way of life. The law permitted divorce only because the people's hearts were hard. God's design for marriage is for one person to be faithful and committed to a single partner as a reflection of the character and nature of God. If you are married, commit yourself wholeheartedly to your spouse (as long as your spouse is not abusive). If you are divorced, don't waste time wallowing in guilt; instead, look on any future marriage with an eye toward a lasting commitment.

Devotional Moment
•
Marriage
24:5 Israel's law freed a newly married man from military service or any community responsibilities that would separate him from his wife during their first year of marriage. This gave the couple time to bond, helping create a healthy and committed relationship. Families are the building blocks of society. The commitment and unity of the marriage partners holds the family together. God-following couples, whether newlyweds or seasoned veterans, can strengthen their families by taking time to build their relationship with each other.

which took her *to be* his wife; ⁴Her former husband, which sent her away, may not take her again to be his wife, after that she is defiled; for that *is* abomination before the LORD: and thou shalt not cause the land to sin, which the LORD thy God giveth thee *for* an inheritance.

⁵When a man hath taken a new wife, he shall not go out to war, neither shall he be charged with any business: *but* he shall be free at home one year, and shall cheer up his wife which he hath taken. ⁶No man shall take the nether or the upper millstone to pledge: for he taketh *a man's* life to pledge. ⁷If a man be found stealing any of his brethren of the children of Israel, and maketh merchandise of him, or selleth him; then that thief shall die; and thou shalt put evil away from among you. ⁸Take heed in the plague of leprosy, that thou observe diligently, and do according to all that the priests the Levites shall teach you: as I commanded them,

---

^a some . . . : Heb. matter of nakedness

so ye shall observe to do. ⁹Remember what the LORD thy God did unto Miriam by the way, after that ye were come forth out of Egypt. ¹⁰When thou dost lend[b] thy brother any thing, thou shalt not go into his house to fetch his pledge. ¹¹Thou shalt stand abroad, and the man to whom thou dost lend shall bring out the pledge abroad unto thee. ¹²And if the man be poor, thou shalt not sleep with his pledge: ¹³In any case thou shalt deliver him the pledge again when the sun goeth down, that he may sleep in his own raiment, and bless thee: and it shall be righteousness unto thee before the LORD thy God.

¹⁴Thou shalt not oppress an hired servant that is poor and needy, whether he be of thy brethren, or of thy strangers that are in thy land within thy gates: ¹⁵At his day thou shalt give him his hire, neither shall the sun go down upon it; for he is poor, and setteth[c] his heart upon it: lest he cry against thee unto the LORD, and it be sin unto thee. ¹⁶The fathers shall not be put to death for the children, neither shall the children be put to death for the fathers: every man shall be put to death for his own sin. ¹⁷Thou shalt not pervert the judgment of the stranger, nor of the fatherless; nor take a widow's raiment to pledge: ¹⁸But thou shalt remember that thou wast a bondman in Egypt, and the LORD thy God redeemed thee thence: therefore I command thee to do this thing. ¹⁹When thou cuttest down thine harvest in thy field, and hast forgot a sheaf in the field, thou shalt not go again to fetch it: it shall be for the stranger, for the fatherless, and for the widow: that the LORD thy God may bless thee in all the work of thine hands. ²⁰When thou beatest thine olive tree, thou shalt not go over the boughs again: it shall be for the stranger, for the fatherless, and for the widow. ²¹When thou gatherest the grapes of thy vineyard, thou shalt not glean it afterward[d]: it shall be for the stranger, for the fatherless, and for the widow. ²²And thou shalt remember that thou wast a bondman in the land of Egypt: therefore I command thee to do this thing.

25

¹If there be a controversy between men, and they come unto judgment, that the judges may judge them; then they shall justify the righteous, and condemn the wicked. ²And it shall be, if the wicked man be worthy to be beaten, that the judge shall cause him to lie down, and to be beaten before his face, according to his fault, by a certain number. ³Forty stripes he may give him, and not exceed: lest, if he should exceed, and beat him above these with many stripes, then thy brother should seem vile unto thee. ⁴Thou shalt not muzzle the ox when he treadeth out the corn.

⁵If brethren dwell together, and one of them die, and have no child, the wife of the dead shall not marry without unto a stranger: her husband's brother shall go in unto her, and take her to him to wife, and perform the duty of an husband's brother unto her.

---

[b] lend . . . : Heb. lend the loan of any thing to, etc
[c] setteth . . . : Heb. lifteth his soul unto it
[d] afterward: Heb. after thee

⁶And it shall be, *that* the firstborn which she beareth shall succeed in the name of his brother *which is* dead, that his name be not put out of Israel. ⁷And if the man like not to take his brother's wife, then let his brother's wife go up to the gate unto the elders, and say, My husband's brother refuseth to raise up unto his brother a name in Israel, he will not perform the duty of my husband's brother. ⁸Then the elders of his city shall call him, and speak unto him: and *if* he stand *to it,* and say, I like not to take her; ⁹Then shall his brother's wife come unto him in the presence of the elders, and loose his shoe from off his foot, and spit in his face, and shall answer and say, So shall it be done unto that man that will not build up his brother's house. ¹⁰And his name shall be called in Israel, The house of him that hath his shoe loosed. ¹¹When men strive together one with another, and the wife of the one draweth near for to deliver her husband out of the hand of him that smiteth him, and putteth forth her hand, and taketh him by the secrets: ¹²Then thou shalt cut off her hand, thine eye shall not pity *her.*

¹³Thou shalt not have in thy bag divers weights, a great and a small. ¹⁴Thou shalt not have in thine house divers measures, a great and a small. ¹⁵*But* thou shalt have a perfect and just weight, a perfect and just measure shalt thou have: that thy days may be lengthened in the land which the LORD thy God giveth thee. ¹⁶For all that do such things, *and* all that do unrighteously, *are* an abomination unto the LORD thy God. ¹⁷Remember what Amalek did unto thee by the way, when ye were come forth out of Egypt; ¹⁸How he met thee by the way, and smote the hindmost of thee, *even* all *that were* feeble behind thee, when thou *wast* faint and weary; and he feared not God. ¹⁹Therefore it shall be, when the LORD thy God hath given thee rest from all thine enemies round about, in the land which the LORD thy God giveth thee *for* an inheritance to possess it, *that* thou shalt blot out the remembrance of Amalek from under heaven; thou shalt not forget *it.*

26

¹And it shall be, when thou *art* come in unto the land which the LORD thy God giveth thee *for* an inheritance, and possessest it, and dwellest therein; ²That thou shalt take of the first of all the fruit of the earth, which thou shalt bring of thy land that the LORD thy God giveth thee, and shalt put *it* in a basket, and shalt go unto the place which the LORD thy God shall choose to place his name there. ³And thou shalt go unto the priest that shall be in those days, and say unto him, I profess this day unto the LORD thy God, that I am come unto the country which the LORD sware unto our fathers for to give us. ⁴And the priest shall take the basket out of thine hand, and set it down before the altar of the LORD thy God. ⁵And thou shalt speak and say before the LORD thy God, A Syrian ready to perish *was* my father, and he went down into Egypt, and sojourned there with a few, and became there a nation, great, mighty, and populous: ⁶And the Egyptians evil entreated us, and afflicted us, and laid upon us hard bondage: ⁷And when we cried unto the LORD God of our fathers, the LORD

heard our voice, and looked on our affliction, and our labour, and our oppression: ⁸And the LORD brought us forth out of Egypt with a mighty hand, and with an outstretched arm, and with great terribleness, and with signs, and with wonders: ⁹And he hath brought us into this place, and hath given us this land, *even* a land that floweth with milk and honey. ¹⁰And now, behold, I have brought the firstfruits of the land, which thou, O LORD, hast given me. And thou shalt set it before the LORD thy God, and worship before the LORD thy God: ¹¹And thou shalt rejoice in every good *thing* which the LORD thy God hath given unto thee, and unto thine house, thou, and the Levite, and the stranger that *is* among you.

¹²When thou hast made an end of tithing all the tithes of thine increase the third year, *which is* the year of tithing, and hast given *it* unto the Levite, the stranger, the fatherless, and the widow, that they may eat within thy gates, and be filled; ¹³Then thou shalt say before the LORD thy God, I have brought away the hallowed things out of *mine* house, and also have given them unto the Levite, and unto the stranger, to the fatherless, and to the widow, according to all thy commandments which thou hast commanded me: I have not transgressed thy commandments, neither have I forgotten *them*: ¹⁴I have not eaten thereof in my mourning, neither have I taken away *ought* thereof for *any* unclean *use*, nor given *ought* thereof for the dead: *but* I have hearkened to the voice of the LORD my God, *and* have done according to all that thou hast com-

manded me. ¹⁵Look down from thy holy habitation, from heaven, and bless thy people Israel, and the land which thou hast given us, as thou swarest unto our fathers, a land that floweth with milk and honey.

¹⁶This day the LORD thy God hath commanded thee to do these statutes and judgments: thou shalt therefore keep and do them with all thine heart, and with all thy soul. ¹⁷Thou hast avouched the LORD this day to be thy God, and to walk in his ways, and to keep his statutes, and his commandments, and his judgments, and to hearken unto his voice: ¹⁸And the LORD hath avouched thee this day to be his peculiar people, as he hath promised thee, and that *thou* shouldest keep all his commandments; ¹⁹And to make thee high above all nations which he hath made, in praise, and in name, and in honour; and that thou mayest be an holy people unto the LORD thy God, as he hath spoken.

27

¹And Moses with the elders of Israel commanded the people, saying, Keep all the commandments which I command you this day. ²And it shall be on the day when ye shall pass over Jordan unto the land which the LORD thy God giveth thee, that thou shalt set thee up great stones, and plaister them with plaister: ³And thou shalt write upon them all the words of this law, when thou art passed over, that thou mayest go in unto the land which the LORD thy God giveth thee, a land that floweth with milk and honey; as the LORD God of thy fathers hath promised thee. ⁴Therefore it shall be

when ye be gone over Jordan, *that* ye shall set up these stones, which I command you this day, in mount Ebal, and thou shalt plaister them with plaister. ⁵And there shalt thou build an altar unto the LORD thy God, an altar of stones: thou shalt not lift up *any* iron *tool* upon them. ⁶Thou shalt build the altar of the LORD thy God of whole stones: and thou shalt offer burnt offerings thereon unto the LORD thy God: ⁷And thou shalt offer peace offerings, and shalt eat there, and rejoice before the LORD thy God. ⁸And thou shalt write upon the stones all the words of this law very plainly. ⁹And Moses and the priests the Levites spake unto all Israel, saying, Take heed, and hearken, O Israel; this day thou art become the people of the LORD thy God. ¹⁰Thou shalt therefore obey the voice of the LORD thy God, and do his commandments and his statutes, which I command thee this day.

¹¹And Moses charged the people the same day, saying, ¹²These shall stand upon mount Gerizim to bless the people, when ye are come over Jordan; Simeon, and Levi, and Judah, and Issachar, and Joseph, and Benjamin: ¹³And these shall stand upon mount Ebal to curse*ᵃ*; Reuben, Gad, and Asher, and Zebulun, Dan, and Naphtali. ¹⁴And the Levites shall speak, and say unto all the men of Israel with a loud voice, ¹⁵Cursed *be* the man that maketh *any* graven or molten image, an abomination unto the LORD, the work of the hands of the craftsman, and putteth *it* in *a* secret *place*. And all the people shall answer and say, Amen. ¹⁶Cursed *be*

he that setteth light by his father or his mother. And all the people shall say, Amen. ¹⁷Cursed *be* he that removeth his neighbour's landmark. And all the people shall say, Amen. ¹⁸Cursed *be* he that maketh the blind to wander out of the way. And all the people shall say, Amen. ¹⁹Cursed *be* he that perverteth the judgment of the stranger, fatherless, and widow. And all the people shall say, Amen. ²⁰Cursed *be* he that lieth with his father's wife; because he uncovereth his father's skirt. And all the people shall say, Amen. ²¹Cursed *be* he that lieth with any manner of beast. And all the people shall say, Amen. ²²Cursed *be* he that lieth with his sister, the daughter of his father, or the daughter of his mother. And all the people shall say, Amen. ²³Cursed *be* he that lieth with his mother in law. And all the people shall say, Amen. ²⁴Cursed *be* he that smiteth his neighbour secretly. And all the people shall say, Amen. ²⁵Cursed *be* he that taketh reward to slay an innocent person. And all the people shall say, Amen. ²⁶Cursed *be* he that confirmeth not *all* the words of this law to do them. And all the people shall say, Amen.

28

¹And it shall come to pass, if thou shalt hearken diligently unto the voice of the LORD thy God, to observe *and* to do all his commandments which I command thee this day, that the LORD thy God will set thee on high above all nations of the earth: ²And all these blessings shall come on thee, and overtake thee, if thou shalt hearken unto the voice of the LORD thy God. ³Blessed *shalt* thou *be*

ᵃ to curse: Heb. for a cursing

in the city, and blessed *shalt* thou *be* in the field. [4]Blessed *shall be* the fruit of thy body, and the fruit of thy ground, and the fruit of thy cattle, the increase of thy kine, and the flocks of thy sheep. [5]Blessed *shall be* thy basket and thy store[a]. [6]Blessed *shalt* thou *be* when thou comest in, and blessed *shalt* thou *be* when thou goest out. [7]The LORD shall cause thine enemies that rise up against thee to be smitten before thy face: they shall come out against thee one way, and flee before thee seven ways. [8]The LORD shall command the blessing upon thee in thy storehouses[b], and in all that thou settest thine hand unto; and he shall bless thee in the land which the LORD thy God giveth thee. [9]The LORD shall establish thee an holy people unto himself, as he hath sworn unto thee, if thou shalt keep the commandments of the LORD thy God, and walk in his ways. [10]And all people of the earth shall see that thou art called by the name of the LORD; and they shall be afraid of thee. [11]And the LORD shall make thee plenteous in goods[c], in the fruit of thy body, and in the fruit of thy cattle, and in the fruit of thy ground, in the land which the LORD sware unto thy fathers to give thee. [12]The LORD shall open unto thee his good treasure, the heaven to give the rain unto thy land in his season, and to bless all the work of thine hand: and thou shalt lend unto many nations, and thou shalt not borrow. [13]And the LORD shall make thee the head, and not the tail; and thou shalt be above only, and

thou shalt not be beneath; if that thou hearken unto the commandments of the LORD thy God, which I command thee this day, to observe and to do *them*: [14]And thou shalt not go aside from any of the words which I command thee this day, *to* the right hand, or *to* the left, to go after other gods to serve them.

[15]But it shall come to pass, if thou wilt not hearken unto the voice of the LORD thy God, to observe to do all his commandments and his statutes which I command thee this day; that all these curses shall come upon thee, and overtake thee: [16]Cursed *shalt* thou *be* in the city, and cursed *shalt* thou *be* in the field. [17]Cursed *shall be* thy basket and thy store. [18]Cursed *shall be* the fruit of thy body, and the fruit of thy land, the increase of thy kine, and the flocks of thy sheep. [19]Cursed *shalt* thou *be* when thou comest in, and cursed *shalt* thou *be* when thou goest out. [20]The LORD shall send upon thee cursing, vexation, and rebuke, in all that thou settest thine hand unto for to do, until thou be destroyed, and until thou perish quickly; because of the wickedness of thy doings, whereby thou hast forsaken me. [21]The LORD shall make the pestilence cleave unto thee, until he have consumed thee from off the land, whither thou goest to possess it. [22]The LORD shall smite thee with a consumption, and with a fever, and with an inflammation, and with an extreme burning, and with the sword[d], and with blasting, and with mildew; and they shall pursue

---

[a] store: or, dough, or, kneadingtroughs
[b] storehouses: or, barns
[c] in goods: or, for good
[d] sword: or, drought

thee until thou perish. ²³And thy heaven that *is* over thy head shall be brass, and the earth that is under thee *shall be* iron. ²⁴The LORD shall make the rain of thy land powder and dust: from heaven shall it come down upon thee, until thou be destroyed. ²⁵The LORD shall cause thee to be smitten before thine enemies: thou shalt go out one way against them, and flee seven ways before them: and shalt be removed[e] into all the kingdoms of the earth. ²⁶And thy carcase shall be meat unto all fowls of the air, and unto the beasts of the earth, and no man shall fray *them* away. ²⁷The LORD will smite thee with the botch of Egypt, and with the emerods, and with the scab, and with the itch, whereof thou canst not be healed. ²⁸The LORD shall smite thee with madness, and blindness, and astonishment of heart: ²⁹And thou shalt grope at noonday, as the blind gropeth in darkness, and thou shalt not prosper in thy ways: and thou shalt be only oppressed and spoiled evermore, and no man shall save *thee.* ³⁰Thou shalt betroth a wife, and another man shall lie with her: thou shalt build an house, and thou shalt not dwell therein: thou shalt plant a vineyard, and shalt not gather the grapes thereof. ³¹Thine ox *shall be* slain before thine eyes, and thou shalt not eat thereof: thine ass *shall be* violently taken away from before thy face, and shall not be restored to thee: thy sheep *shall be* given unto thine enemies, and thou shalt have none to rescue *them.* ³²Thy sons and thy daughters *shall be* given unto another people, and thine eyes shall look, and fail *with long-*

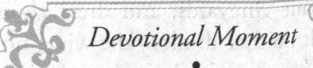

Devotional Moment

Evil

28:33-34 God warned the Israelites that a final consequence of refusing to follow his ways would be madness as they witnessed the horrible outcome of their sinful choices. Even though this curse was directed at ungodly people, evil in the world can drive believers nearly mad, too, as we wonder why so much evil exists in the world, and why its consequences fall so heavily upon us. Acquiring God's perspective on evil assures us that one day God will bring an end to all evil in the world. Study the Bible to develop that perspective. The illumination of God's Holy Spirit will safeguard your family against the maddening effects of evil.

ing for them all the day long: and *there shall be* no might in thine hand. ³³The fruit of thy land, and all thy labours, shall a nation which thou knowest not eat up; and thou shalt be only oppressed and crushed alway: ³⁴So that thou shalt be mad for the sight of thine eyes which thou shalt see. ³⁵The LORD shall smite thee in the knees, and in the legs, with a sore botch that cannot be healed, from the sole of thy foot unto the top of thy head. ³⁶The LORD shall bring thee, and thy king which thou shalt set over thee, unto a nation which neither thou nor thy fathers have known; and there shalt thou serve other gods, wood and stone. ³⁷And thou shalt become an astonishment, a proverb, and a byword, among all nations whither the LORD shall lead thee. ³⁸Thou shalt carry much seed out into the field, and shalt gather *but* little in; for the locust shall consume it. ³⁹Thou

---

[e] removed: Heb. for a removing

shalt plant vineyards, and dress *them,* but shalt neither drink *of* the wine, nor gather *the grapes;* for the worms shall eat them. ⁴⁰Thou shalt have olive trees throughout all thy coasts, but thou shalt not anoint *thyself* with the oil; for thine olive shall cast *his fruit.* ⁴¹Thou shalt beget sons and daughters, but thou shalt not enjoy them; for they shall go into captivity. ⁴²All thy trees and fruit of thy land shall the locust consume*f*. ⁴³The stranger that *is* within thee shall get up above thee very high; and thou shalt come down very low. ⁴⁴He shall lend to thee, and thou shalt not lend to him: he shall be the head, and thou shalt be the tail.

⁴⁵Moreover all these curses shall come upon thee, and shall pursue thee, and overtake thee, till thou be destroyed; because thou hearkenedst not unto the voice of the LORD thy God, to keep his commandments and his statutes which he commanded thee: ⁴⁶And they shall be upon thee for a sign and for a wonder, and upon thy seed for ever. ⁴⁷Because thou servedst not the LORD thy God with joyfulness, and with gladness of heart, for the abundance of all *things;* ⁴⁸Therefore shalt thou serve thine enemies which the LORD shall send against thee, in hunger, and in thirst, and in nakedness, and in want of all *things:* and he shall put a yoke of iron upon thy neck, until he have destroyed thee. ⁴⁹The LORD shall bring a nation against thee from far, from the end of the earth, *as swift* as the eagle flieth; a nation whose tongue thou shalt not understand*g*; ⁵⁰A nation of fierce*h* countenance, which shall not regard the person of the old, nor shew favour to the young: ⁵¹And he shall eat the fruit of thy cattle, and the fruit of thy land, until thou be destroyed: which *also* shall not leave thee *either* corn, wine, or oil, *or* the increase of thy kine, or flocks of thy sheep, until he have destroyed thee. ⁵²And he shall besiege thee in all thy gates, until thy high and fenced walls come down, wherein thou trustedst, throughout all thy land: and he shall besiege thee in all thy gates throughout all thy land, which the LORD thy God hath given thee. ⁵³And thou shalt eat the fruit of thine own body*i*, the flesh of thy sons and of thy daughters, which the LORD thy God hath given thee, in the siege, and in the straitness, wherewith thine enemies shall distress thee: ⁵⁴*So that* the man *that is* tender among you, and very delicate, his eye shall be evil toward his brother, and toward the wife of his bosom, and toward the remnant of his children which he shall leave: ⁵⁵So that he will not give to any of them of the flesh of his children whom he shall eat: because he hath nothing left him in the siege, and in the straitness, wherewith thine enemies shall distress thee in all thy gates. ⁵⁶The tender and delicate woman among you, which would not adventure to set the sole of her foot upon the

---

f consume: or, possess
g understand: Heb. hear
h of fierce . . . : Heb. strong of face
i body: Heb. belly

ground for delicateness and tenderness, her eye shall be evil toward the husband of her bosom, and toward her son, and toward her daughter, ⁵⁷And toward her young oneʲ that cometh out from between her feet, and toward her children which she shall bear: for she shall eat them for want of all *things* secretly in the siege and straitness, wherewith thine enemy shall distress thee in thy gates. ⁵⁸If thou wilt not observe to do all the words of this law that are written in this book, that thou mayest fear this glorious and fearful name, THE LORD THY GOD; ⁵⁹Then the LORD will make thy plagues wonderful, and the plagues of thy seed, *even* great plagues, and of long continuance, and sore sicknesses, and of long continuance. ⁶⁰Moreover he will bring upon thee all the diseases of Egypt, which thou wast afraid of; and they shall cleave unto thee. ⁶¹Also every sickness, and every plague, which *is* not written in the book of this law, them will the LORD bringᵏ upon thee, until thou be destroyed. ⁶²And ye shall be left few in number, whereas ye were as the stars of heaven for multitude; because thou wouldest not obey the voice of the LORD thy God. ⁶³And it shall come to pass, *that* as the LORD rejoiced over you to do you good, and to multiply you; so the LORD will rejoice over you to destroy you, and to bring you to nought; and ye shall be plucked from off the land whither thou goest to possess it. ⁶⁴And the LORD shall scatter thee among all people, from the one end of the earth even unto the other; and there thou shalt serve other gods, which neither thou nor thy fathers have known, *even* wood and stone. ⁶⁵And among these nations shalt thou find no ease, neither shall the sole of thy foot have rest: but the LORD shall give thee there a trembling heart, and failing of eyes, and sorrow of mind: ⁶⁶And thy life shall hang in doubt before thee; and thou shalt fear day and night, and shalt have none assurance of thy life: ⁶⁷In the morning thou shalt say, Would God it were even! and at even thou shalt say, Would God it were morning! for the fear of thine heart wherewith thou shalt fear, and for the sight of thine eyes which thou shalt see. ⁶⁸And the LORD shall bring thee into Egypt again with ships, by the way whereof I spake unto thee, Thou shalt see it no more again: and there ye shall be sold unto your enemies for bondmen and bondwomen, and no man shall buy *you.*

29

¹These *are* the words of the covenant, which the LORD commanded Moses to make with the children of Israel in the land of Moab, beside the covenant which he made with them in Horeb. ²And Moses called unto all Israel, and said unto them, Ye have seen all that the LORD did before your eyes in the land of Egypt unto Pharaoh, and unto all his servants, and unto all his land; ³The great temptations which thine eyes have seen, the signs, and those great miracles: ⁴Yet the LORD hath not given you

---

ʲ young one: Heb. afterbirth
ᵏ bring: Heb. cause to ascend

an heart to perceive, and eyes to see, and ears to hear, unto this day. ⁵And I have led you forty years in the wilderness: your clothes are not waxen old upon you, and thy shoe is not waxen old upon thy foot. ⁶Ye have not eaten bread, neither have ye drunk wine or strong drink: that ye might know that I *am* the LORD your God. ⁷And when ye came unto this place, Sihon the king of Heshbon, and Og the king of Bashan, came out against us unto battle, and we smote them: ⁸And we took their land, and gave it for an inheritance unto the Reubenites, and to the Gadites, and to the half tribe of Manasseh. ⁹Keep therefore the words of this covenant, and do them, that ye may prosper in all that ye do.

¹⁰Ye stand this day all of you before the LORD your God; your captains of your tribes, your elders, and your officers, *with* all the men of Israel, ¹¹Your little ones, your wives, and thy stranger that *is* in thy camp, from the hewer of thy wood unto the drawer of thy water: ¹²That thou shouldest enter[a] into covenant with the LORD thy God, and into his oath, which the LORD thy God maketh with thee this day: ¹³That he may establish thee to day for a people unto himself, and *that* he may be unto thee a God, as he hath said unto thee, and as he hath sworn unto thy fathers, to Abraham, to Isaac, and to Jacob. ¹⁴Neither with you only do I make this covenant and this oath; ¹⁵But with *him* that standeth here with us

this day before the LORD our God, and also with *him* that *is* not here with us this day: ¹⁶(For ye know how we have dwelt in the land of Egypt; and how we came through the nations which ye passed by; ¹⁷And ye have seen their abominations, and their idols[b], wood and stone, silver and gold, which *were* among them:) ¹⁸Lest there should be among you man, or woman, or family, or tribe, whose heart turneth away this day from the LORD our God, to go *and* serve the gods of these nations; lest there should be among you a root that beareth gall[c] and wormwood; ¹⁹And it come to pass, when he heareth the words of this curse, that he bless himself in his heart, saying, I shall have peace, though I walk in the imagination[d] of mine heart, to add drunkenness to thirst: ²⁰The LORD will not spare him, but then the anger of the LORD and his jealousy shall smoke against that man, and all the curses that are written in this book shall lie upon him, and the LORD shall blot out his name from under heaven. ²¹And the LORD shall separate him unto evil out of all the tribes of Israel, according to all the curses of the covenant that are written in this book of the law: ²²So that the generation to come of your children that shall rise up after you, and the stranger that shall come from a far land, shall say, when they see the plagues of that land, and the sicknesses which the LORD hath laid upon it; ²³*And that* the whole land thereof *is*

---

[a] enter: Heb. pass
[b] idols: Heb. dungy gods
[c] gall: or, a poisonous herb
[d] imagination: or, stubbornness

brimstone, and salt, *and* burning, *that* it is not sown, nor beareth, nor any grass groweth therein, like the overthrow of Sodom, and Gomorrah, Admah, and Zeboim, which the LORD overthrew in his anger, and in his wrath: ²⁴Even all nations shall say, Wherefore hath the LORD done thus unto this land? what *meaneth* the heat of this great anger? ²⁵Then men shall say, Because they have forsaken the covenant of the LORD God of their fathers, which he made with them when he brought them forth out of the land of Egypt: ²⁶For they went and served other gods, and worshipped them, gods whom they knew not, and *whom* he had not given unto them: ²⁷And the anger of the LORD was kindled against this land, to bring upon it all the curses that are written in this book: ²⁸And the LORD rooted them out of their land in anger, and in wrath, and in great indignation, and cast them into another land, as *it is* this day. ²⁹The secret *things belong* unto the LORD our God: but those *things which are* revealed *belong* unto us and to our children for ever, that *we* may do all the words of this law.

30

¹And it shall come to pass, when all these things are come upon thee, the blessing and the curse, which I have set before thee, and thou shalt call *them* to mind among all the nations, whither the LORD thy God hath driven thee, ²And shalt return unto the LORD thy God, and shalt obey his voice according to all that I command thee this day, thou and thy children, with all thine heart, and with all thy soul; ³That then the LORD thy God will turn thy cap-

Devotional Moment
•
Mercy

30:1-6 God promised restoration to all who would repent and return to him, even after they had experienced the curses of rejecting his way. He promised to bring the repentant ones back, even from the most distant lands. The return route to God stays open to every one of his children, and God's offer of restoration still stands. Similarly, parents should clearly show their children how to be restored. After an errant child has been disciplined and repents of the wrongful behavior, hugs, loving words, and forgiveness can help to restore closeness. Parents can also model restoration and forgiveness between each other— an example that will teach the children to do the same.

tivity, and have compassion upon thee, and will return and gather thee from all the nations, whither the LORD thy God hath scattered thee. ⁴If *any* of thine be driven out unto the outmost *parts* of heaven, from thence will the LORD thy God gather thee, and from thence will he fetch thee: ⁵And the LORD thy God will bring thee into the land which thy fathers possessed, and thou shalt possess it; and he will do thee good, and multiply thee above thy fathers. ⁶And the LORD thy God will circumcise thine heart, and the heart of thy seed, to love the LORD thy God with all thine heart, and with all thy soul, that thou mayest live. ⁷And the LORD thy God will put all these curses upon thine enemies, and on them that hate thee, which persecuted thee. ⁸And thou shalt return and obey the voice of the LORD, and do all his commandments which I command thee this day. ⁹And the LORD thy God will make thee plenteous in every work of thine hand, in the fruit of thy body, and in the fruit of thy cattle, and in the fruit of thy land, for good: for the LORD will again rejoice over thee for good, as he rejoiced over thy fathers: ¹⁰If thou shalt hearken unto the voice of the LORD thy God, to keep his commandments and his statutes which are written in this book of the law, *and* if thou turn unto the LORD thy God with all thine heart, and with all thy soul.

¹¹For this commandment which I command thee this day, it *is* not hidden from thee, neither *is* it far off. ¹²It *is* not in heaven, that thou shouldest say, Who shall go up for us to heaven, and bring it unto us, that we may hear it, and do it? ¹³Neither *is* it beyond the sea, that thou shouldest say, Who shall go over the sea for us, and bring it unto us, that we may hear it, and do it? ¹⁴But the word *is* very nigh unto thee, in thy mouth, and in thy heart, that thou mayest do it.

¹⁵See, I have set before thee this day life and good, and death and evil; ¹⁶In that I command thee this day to love the LORD thy God, to walk in his ways, and to keep his commandments and his statutes and his judgments, that thou mayest live and multiply: and the LORD thy God shall bless thee in the land whither thou goest to possess it. ¹⁷But if thine heart turn away, so that thou wilt not hear, but shalt be drawn away, and worship other gods, and serve them; ¹⁸I denounce unto you this day, that ye shall surely perish, *and that* ye shall not prolong *your* days upon the land, whither thou passest over Jordan to go to possess it. ¹⁹I call heaven and earth to record this day against you, *that* I have set before you life and death,

blessing and cursing: therefore choose life, that both thou and thy seed may live: ²⁰That thou mayest love the LORD thy God, *and* that thou mayest obey his voice, and that thou mayest cleave unto him: for he *is* thy life, and the length of thy days: that thou mayest dwell in the land which the LORD sware unto thy fathers, to Abraham, to Isaac, and to Jacob, to give them.

31

¹And Moses went and spake these words unto all Israel. ²And he said unto them, I *am* an hundred and twenty years old this day; I can no more go out and come in: also the LORD hath said unto me, Thou shalt not go over this Jordan. ³The LORD thy God, he will go over before thee, *and* he will destroy these nations from before thee, and thou shalt possess them: *and* Joshua, he shall go over before thee, as the LORD hath said. ⁴And the LORD shall do unto them as he did to Sihon and to Og, kings of the Amorites, and unto the land of them, whom he destroyed. ⁵And the LORD shall give them up before your face, that ye may do unto them according unto all the commandments which I have commanded you.

⁶Be strong and of a good courage, fear not, nor be afraid of them: for the LORD thy God, he *it is* that doth go with thee; he will not fail thee, nor forsake thee. ⁷And Moses called unto Joshua, and said unto him in the sight of all Israel, Be strong and of a good courage: for thou must go with this people unto the land which the LORD hath sworn unto their fathers to give them; and thou shalt cause them to inherit it. ⁸And the LORD, he *it is* that doth go before thee; he will be with thee, he will not fail thee, neither forsake thee: fear not, neither be dismayed.

⁹And Moses wrote this law, and delivered it unto the priests the sons of Levi, which bare the ark of the covenant of the LORD, and unto all the elders of Israel. ¹⁰And Moses commanded them, saying, At the end of *every* seven years, in the solemnity of the year of release, in the feast of taber-

---

Devotional Moment

•

Child Rearing

31:10-13 Everyone in Israel learned to respect the Lord by hearing the law. Few parental tasks outweigh the importance of making sure children hear the Word of God. It is almost impossible to start at too early an age. Even very young children like to hear Bible stories, and infants can enjoy lullabies sung from the many Psalms that are set to music. And when children hear God's Word read by their parents, they see that their parents love the Word. It can also plant the seed of faith that Romans 10:17 says comes from listening to the Good News. Make regular Bible reading a part of your family devotions at meals or bedtime.

---

nacles, ¹¹When all Israel is come to appear before the LORD thy God in the place which he shall choose, thou shalt read this law before all Israel in their hearing. ¹²Gather the people together, men, and women, and children, and thy stranger that *is* within thy gates, that they may hear, and that they may learn, and fear the LORD your God, and observe to do all the words of this law: ¹³And *that* their children, which have not known *any thing*, may hear, and learn to fear the LORD your God, as long as ye live in the land whither ye go over Jordan to possess it.

¹⁴And the LORD said unto Moses, Behold, thy days approach that thou must die: call Joshua, and present yourselves in the tabernacle of the congregation, that I may give him a charge. And Moses and Joshua went, and presented themselves in the tabernacle of the congregation. ¹⁵And the LORD appeared in the tabernacle in a pillar of a cloud: and the pillar of the cloud stood over the door of the tabernacle. ¹⁶And the LORD said unto Moses, Behold, thou shalt sleepᵃ with thy fathers; and this people will rise up, and go a whoring after the gods of the strangers of the land, whither they go *to be* among them, and will forsake me, and break my covenant which I have made with them. ¹⁷Then my anger shall be kindled against them in that day, and I will forsake them, and I will hide my face from them, and they shall be devoured, and many evils and troubles shall befallᵇ them; so that they will say in that day, Are not these evils come upon us, because our God *is* not among us?

ᵃ sleep: Heb. lie down
ᵇ befall: Heb. find

¹⁸And I will surely hide my face in that day for all the evils which they shall have wrought, in that they are turned unto other gods. ¹⁹Now therefore write ye this song for you, and teach it the children of Israel: put it in their mouths, that this song may be a witness for me against the children of Israel. ²⁰For when I shall have brought them into the land which I sware unto their fathers, that floweth with milk and honey; and they shall have eaten and filled themselves, and waxen fat; then will they turn unto other gods, and serve them, and provoke me, and break my covenant. ²¹And it shall come to pass, when many evils and troubles are befallen them, that this song shall testify against^c them as a witness; for it shall not be forgotten out of the mouths of their seed: for I know their imagination which they go about, even now, before I have brought them into the land which I sware.

²²Moses therefore wrote this song the same day, and taught it the children of Israel. ²³And he gave Joshua the son of Nun a charge, and said, Be strong and of a good courage: for thou shalt bring the children of Israel into the land which I sware unto them: and I will be with thee. ²⁴And it came to pass, when Moses had made an end of writing the words of this law in a book, until they were finished, ²⁵That Moses commanded the Levites, which bare the ark of the covenant of the LORD, saying, ²⁶Take this book of the law, and put it in the side of the ark of the covenant of the LORD your God, that it may be there for a witness against thee. ²⁷For I know thy rebellion, and

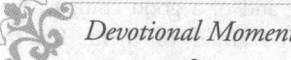

Devotional Moment
•
Rebellion

31:27-29 Moses warned that if the people were defiant while he was still alive, they would surely become even more rebellious after he was gone. An unchecked spirit of rebellion would lead to even greater defiance. If young children learn that they can disobey without consequence, they can become characteristically rebellious as they grow up. To encourage your children to be responsive to God, be sure that you set clear standards, make discipline swift and fair, and train children in the Word of God.

thy stiff neck: behold, while I am yet alive with you this day, ye have been rebellious against the LORD; and how much more after my death? ²⁸Gather unto me all the elders of your tribes, and your officers, that I may speak these words in their ears, and call heaven and earth to record against them. ²⁹For I know that after my death ye will utterly corrupt *yourselves*, and turn aside from the way which I have commanded you; and evil will befall you in the latter days; because ye will do evil in the sight of the LORD, to provoke him to anger through the work of your hands. ³⁰And Moses spake in the ears of all the congregation of Israel the words of this song, until they were ended.

32

¹Give ear, O ye heavens, and I will speak; and hear, O earth, the words of my mouth. ²My doctrine shall drop as the rain, my speech shall distil as the dew, as the small rain upon the tender

---

^c against: Heb. before

herb, and as the showers upon the grass: ³Because I will publish the name of the LORD: ascribe ye greatness unto our God. ⁴*He is* the Rock, his work *is* perfect: for all his ways *are* judgment: a God of truth and without iniquity, just and right *is* he. ⁵They have corrupted themselves, their spot *is* not *the spot* of his children: *they are* a perverse and crooked generation. ⁶Do ye thus requite the LORD, O foolish people and unwise? *is* not he thy father *that* hath bought thee? hath he not made thee, and established thee?

⁷Remember the days of old, consider the years of many[a] generations: ask thy father, and he will shew thee; thy elders, and they will tell thee. ⁸When the most High divided to the nations their inheritance, when he separated the sons of Adam, he set the bounds of the people according to the number of the children of Israel. ⁹For the LORD'S portion *is* his people; Jacob *is* the lot[b] of his inheritance. ¹⁰He found him in a desert land, and in the waste howling wilderness; he led him about, he instructed him, he kept him as the apple of his eye. ¹¹As an eagle stirreth up her nest, fluttereth over her young, spreadeth abroad her wings, taketh them, beareth them on her wings: ¹²So the LORD alone did lead him, and *there was* no strange god with him. ¹³He made him ride on the high places of the earth, that he might eat the increase of the fields; and he made him to suck honey out of the rock, and

oil out of the flinty rock; ¹⁴Butter of kine, and milk of sheep, with fat of lambs, and rams of the breed of Bashan, and goats, with the fat of kidneys of wheat; and thou didst drink the pure blood of the grape.

¹⁵But Jeshurun waxed fat, and kicked: thou art waxen fat, thou art grown thick, thou art covered *with fatness*; then he forsook God *which* made him, and lightly esteemed the Rock of his salvation. ¹⁶They provoked him to jealousy with strange *gods*, with abominations provoked they him to anger. ¹⁷They sacrificed unto devils, not to God; to gods whom they knew not, to new *gods that* came newly up, whom your fathers feared not. ¹⁸Of the Rock *that* begat thee thou art unmindful, and hast forgotten God that formed thee.

¹⁹And when the LORD saw *it*, he abhorred[c] *them*, because of the provoking of his sons, and of his daughters. ²⁰And he said, I will hide my face from them, I will see what their end *shall be*: for they *are* a very froward generation, children in whom *is* no faith. ²¹They have moved me to jealousy with *that which is* not God; they have provoked me to anger with their vanities: and I will move them to jealousy with *those which are* not a people; I will provoke them to anger with a foolish nation. ²²For a fire is kindled in mine anger, and shall burn[d] unto the lowest hell, and shall consume the earth with her increase, and set on fire the founda-

---

[a] many . . . : Heb. generation and generation
[b] lot: Heb. cord
[c] abhorred: or, despised
[d] shall burn: or, hath burned

tions of the mountains. ²³I will heap mischiefs upon them; I will spend mine arrows upon them. ²⁴ *They shall be* burnt with hunger, and devoured with burning heatᵉ, and with bitter destruction: I will also send the teeth of beasts upon them, with the poison of serpents of the dust. ²⁵The sword without, and terror withinᶠ, shall destroy both the young man and the virgin, the suckling *also* with the man of gray hairs.

²⁶I said, I would scatter them into corners, I would make the remembrance of them to cease from among men: ²⁷Were it not that I feared the wrath of the enemy, lest their adversaries should behave themselves strangely, *and* lest they should say, Our hand *is* high, and the LORD hath not done all this. ²⁸For they *are* a nation void of counsel, neither *is* there any understanding in them. ²⁹O that they were wise, *that* they understood this, *that* they would consider their latter end! ³⁰How should one chase a thousand, and two put ten thousand to flight, except their Rock had sold them, and the LORD had shut them up? ³¹For their rock *is* not as our Rock, even our enemies themselves *being* judges. ³²For their vine *is* of the vineᵍ of Sodom, and of the fields of Gomorrah: their grapes *are* grapes of gall, their clusters *are* bitter: ³³Their wine *is* the poison of dragons, and the cruel venom of asps. ³⁴*Is* not this laid up in store with me, *and* sealed up among my treasures? ³⁵To me *belongeth* vengeance, and recompence; their foot shall slide in *due* time: for the day of their calamity *is* at hand, and the things that shall come upon them make haste. ³⁶For the LORD shall judge his people, and repent himself for his servants, when he seeth that *their* powerʰ *is* gone, and *there is* none shut up, or left. ³⁷And he shall say, Where *are* their gods, *their* rock in whom they trusted, ³⁸Which did eat the fat of their sacrifices, *and* drank the wine of their drink offerings? let them rise up and help you, *and* be your protection.

³⁹See now that I, *even* I, *am* he, and *there is* no god with me: I kill, and I make alive; I wound, and I heal: neither *is there any* that can deliver out of my hand. ⁴⁰For I lift up my hand to heaven, and say, I live for ever. ⁴¹If I whet my glittering sword, and mine hand take hold on judgment; I will render vengeance to mine enemies, and will reward them that hate me. ⁴²I will make mine arrows drunk with blood, and my sword shall devour flesh; *and that* with the blood of the slain and of the captives, from the beginning of revenges upon the enemy. ⁴³Rejoiceⁱ, O ye nations, *with* his people: for he will avenge the blood of his servants, and will render vengeance to his adversaries, and will be merciful unto his land, *and* to his people.

⁴⁴And Moses came and spake all the words of this song in the ears of the people, he, and Hosheaʲ the son of Nun. ⁴⁵And Moses made an end of speaking all

---

ᵉ heat: Heb. coals
ᶠ within: Heb. from the chambers
ᵍ of the vine: or, worse than the vine
ʰ power: Heb. hand
ⁱ Rejoice . . . : or, Praise his people, ye nations: or, Sing ye
ʲ Hoshea: or, Joshua

these words to all Israel: ⁴⁶And he said unto them, Set your hearts unto all the words which I testify among you this day, which ye shall command your children to observe to do, all the words of this law. ⁴⁷For it *is* not a vain thing for you; because it *is* your life: and through this thing ye shall prolong *your* days in the land, whither ye go over Jordan to possess it. ⁴⁸And the LORD spake unto Moses that selfsame day, saying, ⁴⁹Get thee up into this mountain Abarim, *unto* mount Nebo, which *is* in the land of Moab, that *is* over against Jericho; and behold the land of Canaan, which I give unto the children of Israel for a possession: ⁵⁰And die in the mount whither thou goest up, and be gathered unto thy people; as Aaron thy brother died in mount Hor, and was gathered unto his people: ⁵¹Because ye trespassed against me among the children of Israel at the waters of Meribah-Kadesh, in the wilderness of Zin; because ye sanctified me not in the midst of the children of Israel. ⁵²Yet thou shalt see the land before *thee*; but thou shalt not go thither unto the land which I give the children of Israel.

33

¹And this *is* the blessing, wherewith Moses the man of God blessed the children of Israel before his death. ²And he said, The LORD came from Sinai, and rose up from Seir unto them; he shined forth from mount Paran, and he came with ten thousands of saints: from his right hand *went* a fiery[a] law for them. ³Yea, he loved the people; all his saints *are* in thy hand: and they sat down at thy feet; *every one* shall receive of thy words. ⁴Moses commanded us a law, *even* the inheritance of the congregation of Jacob. ⁵And he was king in Jeshurun, when the heads of the people *and* the tribes of Israel were gathered together.

⁶Let Reuben live, and not die; and let *not* his men be few. ⁷And this *is the blessing* of Judah: and he said, Hear, LORD, the voice of Judah, and bring him unto his people: let his hands be sufficient for him; and be thou an help *to him* from his enemies.

⁸And of Levi he said, *Let* thy Thummim and thy Urim *be* with thy holy one, whom thou didst prove at Massah, *and with* whom thou didst strive at the waters of Meribah; ⁹Who said unto his father and to his mother, I have not seen him; neither did he acknowledge his brethren, nor knew his own children: for they have observed thy word, and kept thy covenant. ¹⁰They shall teach[b] Jacob thy judgments, and Israel thy law: they shall put incense before thee, and whole burnt sacrifice upon thine altar. ¹¹Bless, LORD, his substance, and accept the work of his hands: smite through the loins of them that rise against him, and of them that hate him, that they rise not again.

¹²*And* of Benjamin he said, The beloved of the LORD shall dwell in safety by him; *and the LORD* shall cover him all the day long, and he shall dwell between his shoulders. ¹³And of Joseph he said, Blessed of the LORD *be* his land, for the precious things of heaven, for the dew, and for the deep

---

[a] a fiery . . . : Heb. a fire of law
[b] They shall teach: or, Let them teach

that coucheth beneath, ¹⁴And for the precious fruits *brought forth* by the sun, and for the precious things put forth by the moon, ¹⁵And for the chief things of the ancient mountains, and for the precious things of the lasting hills, ¹⁶And for the precious things of the earth and fulness thereof, and *for* the good will of him that dwelt in the bush: let *the blessing* come upon the head of Joseph, and upon the top of the head of him *that was* separated from his brethren. ¹⁷His glory *is like* the firstling of his bullock, and his horns *are like* the horns of unicorns^c: with them he shall push the people together to the ends of the earth: and they *are* the ten thousands of Ephraim, and they *are* the thousands of Manasseh.

¹⁸And of Zebulun he said, Rejoice, Zebulun, in thy going out; and, Issachar, in thy tents. ¹⁹They shall call the people unto the mountain; there they shall offer sacrifices of righteousness: for they shall suck *of* the abundance of the seas, and *of* treasures hid in the sand. ²⁰And of Gad he said, Blessed *be* he that enlargeth Gad: he dwelleth as a lion, and teareth the arm with the crown of the head. ²¹And he provided the first part for himself, because there, *in* a portion of the lawgiver, *was he* seated^d; and he came with the heads of the people, he executed the justice of the LORD, and his judgments with Israel.

²²And of Dan he said, Dan *is* a lion's whelp: he shall leap from Bashan. ²³And of Naphtali he said, O Naphtali,

satisfied with favour, and full with the blessing of the LORD: possess thou the west and the south. ²⁴And of Asher he said, *Let* Asher *be* blessed with children; let him be acceptable to his brethren, and let him dip his foot in oil. ²⁵Thy shoes^e *shall be* iron and brass; and as thy days, *so shall* thy strength *be.*

²⁶*There is* none like unto the God of Jeshurun, *who* rideth upon the heaven in thy help, and in his excellency on the sky. ²⁷The eternal God *is thy* refuge, and underneath *are* the everlasting arms: and he shall thrust out the enemy from before thee; and shall say, Destroy *them.* ²⁸Israel then shall dwell in safety alone: the fountain of Jacob *shall be* upon a land of corn and wine; also his heavens shall drop down dew. ²⁹Happy *art* thou, O Israel: who *is* like unto thee, O people saved by the LORD, the shield of thy help, and who *is* the sword of thy excellency! and thine enemies shall be found liars unto thee; and thou shalt tread upon their high places.

34

¹And Moses went up from the plains of Moab unto the mountain of Nebo, to the top of Pisgah^a, that *is* over against Jericho. And the LORD shewed him all the land of Gilead, unto Dan, ²And all Naphtali, and the land of Ephraim, and Manasseh, and all the land of Judah, unto the utmost sea, ³And the south, and the plain of the valley of Jericho, the city of palm trees, unto Zoar. ⁴And the LORD said unto him, This *is* the

---

^c unicorns: Heb. an unicorn
^d seated: Heb. cieled
^e Thy shoes: or, Under thy shoes
^a Pisgah: or, the hill

land which I sware unto Abraham, unto Isaac, and unto Jacob, saying, I will give it unto thy seed: I have caused thee to see *it* with thine eyes, but thou shalt not go over thither.

⁵So Moses the servant of the LORD died there in the land of Moab, according to the word of the LORD. ⁶And he buried him in a valley in the land of Moab, over against Bethpeor: but no man knoweth of his sepulchre unto this day. ⁷And Moses *was* an hundred and twenty years old when he died: his eye was not dim, nor his natural force abated. ⁸And the children of Israel wept for Moses in the plains of Moab thirty days: so the days of weeping *and* mourning for Moses were ended.

⁹And Joshua the son of Nun was full of the spirit of wisdom; for Moses had laid his hands upon him: and the children of Israel hearkened unto him, and did as the LORD commanded Moses. ¹⁰And there arose not a prophet since in Israel like unto Moses, whom the LORD knew face to face, ¹¹In all the signs and the wonders, which the LORD sent him to do in the land of Egypt to Pharaoh, and to all his servants, and to all his land, ¹²And in all that mighty hand, and in all the great terror which Moses shewed in the sight of all Israel.

JOSHUA

Purpose
To give the history of Israel's conquest of the Promised Land

Author
Joshua, except for the ending which may have been written by the High Priest Phinehas, an eyewitness to the events recounted there

Setting
Canaan, also called the Promised Land, which occupied the same general geographical territory of modern-day Israel

Key Verse
"Within three days ye shall pass over this Jordan, to go in to possess the land, which the Lord your God giveth you. . . ." (1:11).

Key People
Joshua, Rahab, Achan, Phinehas, Eleazar

Key Places
Jericho, Ai, Mount Ebal, Mount Shiloh, Shechem

Special Feature
Of over a million people who left Egypt, Joshua and Caleb were the only two who lived to enter the Promised Land.

The most popular TV families never encountered a Jericho. Sure, Ozzie and Harriet had problems, and the Cleavers had their moments of stress, but moments only. "Problems" of the half-hour-comedy variety are all solvable in twenty-two minutes or less. And somehow we've come to expect quick and easy solutions to all of our problems, too.

But Scripture would indicate otherwise. Consider Joshua, for instance. When Joshua assumed leadership of the wandering nation, his first problem was a whopper. There is nothing quick and easy about his life. Joshua woke up for his first day on the job and faced Jericho.

How many Jerichos confront us today? We invent new terms every week to describe them. News magazines alternate between cover stories on natural disasters, political intrigue, and family dysfunctions. New books on stress are so plentiful that soon we'll have a "reading syndrome" to deal with trying to keep abreast of the flow of information. Most real families face tougher problems than TV families ever dreamed of; very few family problems heal in twenty-two minutes or less.

That's why faith is still a "banner headline" issue. Joshua would have been crushed without it—nailed in his first campaign, if not by the citizens of Jericho, then by his own extended family. All of us—fathers and mothers, grandparents and teenagers need faith, too. Family wellness depends on it; family leadership requires it.

How do we learn faith? Count the lessons in this book. Gain the courage that Joshua discovered. Face your Jerichos from a new position of strength.

1

¹Now after the death of Moses the servant of the LORD it came to pass, that the LORD spake unto Joshua the son of Nun, Moses'minister, saying, ²Moses my servant is dead; now therefore arise, go over this Jordan, thou, and all this people, unto the land which I do give to them, *even* to the children of Israel. ³Every place that the sole of your foot shall tread upon, that have I given unto you, as I said unto Moses. ⁴From the wilderness and this Lebanon even unto the great river, the river Euphrates, all the land of the Hittites, and unto the great sea toward the going down of the sun, shall be your coast. ⁵There shall not any man be able to stand before thee all the days of thy life: as I was with Moses, *so* I will be with thee: I will not fail thee, nor forsake thee. ⁶Be strong and of a good courage: for unto this people shalt thou divide for an inheritance the land, which I sware unto their fathers to give them. ⁷Only be thou strong and very courageous, that thou mayest observe to do according to all the law, which Moses my servant commanded thee: turn not from it *to* the right hand or *to* the left, that thou mayest prosperª whithersoever thou goest. ⁸This book of the law shall not depart out of thy mouth; but thou shalt meditate therein day and night, that thou mayest observe to do according to all that is written therein: for then thou shalt make thy way prosperous, and then thou shalt have good success. ⁹Have not I commanded thee? Be strong and of a good courage; be not afraid, neither be thou dismayed: for the

Devotional Moment

Family Unity

1:12-15 Not all of Israel's twelve tribes wanted to live together on the same side of the Jordan River. Reuben, Gad, and the half-tribe of Manasseh wanted their own space east of the Jordan. Joshua accommodated this request with one stipulation: The twelve tribes must band together against a common enemy to assure everyone's welfare. Then and only then could each tribe go its own way. Extended families and blended families are like that, too. We may live apart physically, or even emotionally, but we need to come together to manage a crisis or defeat a common enemy. Don't let the enemy—whether an illness, a disability, loss of job or spouse, or even an unjust system—defeat you. Instead, band together and help one another whenever the need arises.

LORD thy God *is* with thee whithersoever thou goest.

¹⁰Then Joshua commanded the officers of the people, saying, ¹¹Pass through the host, and command the people, saying, Prepare you victuals; for within three days ye shall pass over this Jordan, to go in to possess the land, which the LORD your God giveth you to possess it. ¹²And to the Reubenites, and to the Gadites, and to half the tribe of Manasseh, spake Joshua, saying, ¹³Remember the word which Moses the servant of the LORD commanded you, saying, The LORD your God hath given you rest, and hath given you this land. ¹⁴Your wives, your little ones, and your cattle, shall remain in the land which Moses gave you on this side Jordan; but ye shall pass before your brethren armedᵇ, all

---

ª prosper: or, do wisely
ᵇ armed: Heb. marshalled by five

Taking First Steps

"As I was with Moses, so I will be with thee: I will not fail thee, nor forsake thee." Joshua 1:5

A woman fears commitment so much that she breaks her engagement just before the wedding—just as she's done twice before. Or a man knows he needs his degree, yet his fear of failure blocks him from ever applying. A couple's marriage is in deep trouble, but neither partner picks up the phone to call a pastor or counselor before it's too late.

What holds us back from making needed changes? For many, two factors must be overcome if a negative cycle is to be broken and new ground won, and Joshua can teach us a great deal about them.

1. Joshua did not fear the unfamiliar. For nearly forty years, Joshua had wandered in the desert with a nation that had paid a high price for its unbelief. God had already told this stiff-necked generation that the land was theirs for the taking. But in Numbers 13–14, only two men, Joshua and Caleb, had listened to the Lord and encouraged the people to take the land. Joshua was all set to go forward toward a new challenge. But what about the people of Israel? When they were presented with the challenge, they wanted to go *back*—back into slavery, back into oppression and bondage. "Let us make a captain," they said, "and let us return into Egypt" (14:4).

Why would *anyone* want to return to a painful, hurtful past? Because it's so *familiar*. For many people, especially those from a difficult background, the old familiar pain they've felt is more tolerable than the unknown pain that comes from making changes. Put in even more graphic terms, the writer of Proverbs tells us, "As a dog returneth to his vomit, so a fool returneth to his folly" (Prov. 26:11). As bad as the past may be, if we are without the courage to change, we will return to it.

Yet there is hope.

2. Joshua drew strength to change from a well of security. Joshua listened to what God said about his future and drew strength from those words. The tremendous inner security he felt enabled him to make changes.

Joshua had heard of God's words to Moses, "Certainly I will be with thee" (Exod. 3:12). When Moses passed the mantle of leadership to Joshua, the Lord added to that security by speaking directly to Joshua: "As I was with Moses, so I will be with thee. I will not fail thee, nor forsake thee. Be strong and of a good courage . . . be not afraid, neither be thou dismayed: for the Lord thy God is with thee whithersoever thou goest" (Josh. 1:5-6, 9).

Like Joshua, when we're faced with big challenges and stretching new responsibilities, we don't have to fall back into a hurtful, familiar past. We can listen to God's words of strength and security and take that first step to move ahead.

What is the forward step that you fear taking? Is it a conversation with a son or daughter? A new relationship? The repair of a failing marriage? Positive change can happen if you will draw strength from your inner well of security in God.

Here's how to do it. First, write down the first step you need to take toward the positive change you fear. Perhaps it is "Tell John I want to talk to him" or "Call Susan and invite her over." Second, read and think about Joshua 1:9 over and over for a week. Third, take the step you wrote down. Risky? Yes. But remember that you, like Joshua, can take this risk because you have God Almighty on your side. Everyone who is a Christian—even if he or she has missed words of security in the past—can bank on Jesus' words. "God has said, 'I will never leave thee, nor forsake thee.' That is why we can say without any doubt or fear, 'The Lord is my Helper, and I will not fear what man shall do unto me' " (Heb. 13:5-6).

What step forward do you need to make today?

---

the mighty men of valour, and help them; ¹⁵Until the LORD have given your brethren rest, as *he hath given* you, and they also have possessed the land which the LORD your God giveth them: then ye shall return unto the land of your possession, and enjoy it, which Moses the LORD'S servant gave you on this side Jordan toward the sunrising.

¹⁶And they answered Joshua, saying, All that thou commandest us we will do, and whithersoever thou sendest us, we will go. ¹⁷According as we hearkened unto Moses in all things, so will we hearken unto thee: only the LORD thy God be with thee, as he was with Moses. ¹⁸Whosoever *he be* that doth rebel against thy commandment, and will not hearken unto thy words in all that thou commandest him, he shall be put to death: only be strong and of a good courage.

2

¹And Joshua the son of Nun sent^a out of Shittim two men to spy secretly, saying, Go view the land, even Jericho. And they went, and came into an harlot's house, named Rahab, and lodged there. ²And it was told the king of Jericho, saying, Behold, there came men in hither to night of the children of Israel to search out the country. ³And the king of Jericho sent unto Rahab, saying, Bring forth the men that are come to thee, which are entered into thine house: for they be come to search out all the country. ⁴And the woman took the two men, and hid them, and said thus, There came men unto me, but I wist not whence they *were*: ⁵And it

---

^a sent: or, had sent

came to pass *about the time* of shutting of the gate, when it was dark, that the men went out: whither the men went I wot not: pursue after them quickly; for ye shall overtake them. ⁶But she had brought them up to the roof of the house, and hid them with the stalks of flax, which she had laid in order upon the roof. ⁷And the men pursued after them the way to Jordan unto the fords: and as soon as they which pursued after them were gone out, they shut the gate.

⁸And before they were laid down, she came up unto them upon the roof; ⁹And she said unto the men, I know that the LORD hath given you the land, and that your terror is fallen upon us, and that all the inhabitants of the land faint[b] because of you. ¹⁰For we have heard how the LORD dried up the water of the Red sea for you, when ye came out of Egypt; and what ye did unto the two kings of the Amorites, that *were* on the other side Jordan, Sihon and Og, whom ye utterly destroyed. ¹¹And as soon as we had heard *these things*, our hearts did melt, neither did there remain any more courage in any man, because of you: for the LORD your God, he *is* God in heaven above, and in earth beneath. ¹²Now therefore, I pray you, swear unto me by the LORD, since I have shewed you kindness, that ye will also shew kindness unto my father's house, and give me a true token: ¹³And *that* ye will save alive my father, and my mother, and my brethren, and my sisters, and all that they have, and deliver our lives from death. ¹⁴And the men answered her, Our life for yours, if ye utter not this our business. And it shall be, when the LORD hath given us the land, that we will deal kindly and truly with thee. ¹⁵Then she let them down by a cord through the window: for her house *was* upon the town wall, and she dwelt upon the wall. ¹⁶And she said unto them, Get you to the mountain, lest the pursuers meet you; and hide yourselves there three days, until the pursuers be returned: and afterward may ye go your way. ¹⁷And the men said unto her, We *will be* blameless of this thine oath which thou hast made us swear. ¹⁸Behold, *when* we come into the land, thou shalt bind this line of scarlet thread in the window which thou didst let us down by: and thou shalt bring[c] thy father, and thy mother, and thy brethren, and all thy father's household, home unto thee. ¹⁹And it shall be, *that* whosoever shall go out of the doors of thy house into the street, his blood *shall be* upon his head, and we *will be* guiltless: and whosoever shall be with thee in the house, his blood *shall be*

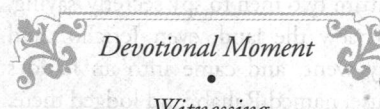

Devotional Moment

Witnessing

2:9-13 Rahab was an unlikely convert to the God of Israel. She was a pagan and a prostitute, living behind enemy lines. Yet God calls all kinds of people to himself, even those like Rahab. We should not limit God with our preconceived notions of who will come to faith. An illicit lifestyle, criminal record, or shoddy appearance will not keep people out of the Kingdom. Only lack of faith will. So share your faith openly and honestly. Witnessing to one of these unlikely converts could produce another Rahab for God's Kingdom.

ᵇ faint: Heb. melt
ᶜ bring: Heb. gather

on our head, if *any* hand be upon him. ²⁰And if thou utter this our business, then we will be quit of thine oath which thou hast made us to swear. ²¹And she said, According unto your words, so *be* it. And she sent them away, and they departed: and she bound the scarlet line in the window.

²²And they went, and came unto the mountain, and abode there three days, until the pursuers were returned: and the pursuers sought *them* throughout all the way, but found *them* not. ²³So the two men returned, and descended from the mountain, and passed over, and came to Joshua the son of Nun, and told him all *things* that befell them: ²⁴And they said unto Joshua, Truly the LORD hath delivered into our hands all the land; for even all the inhabitants of the country do faint^d because of us.

3

¹And Joshua rose early in the morning; and they removed from Shittim, and came to Jordan, he and all the children of Israel, and lodged there before they passed over. ²And it came to pass after three days, that the officers went through the host; ³And they commanded the people, saying, When ye see the ark of the covenant of the LORD your God, and the priests the Levites bearing it, then ye shall remove from your place, and go after it. ⁴Yet there shall be a space between you and it, about two thousand cubits by measure: come not near unto it, that ye may know the way by which ye must go: for ye have not passed *this* way heretofore^a. ⁵And Joshua said unto the people, Sanctify yourselves: for to morrow the LORD will do wonders among you. ⁶And Joshua spake unto the priests, saying, Take up the ark of the covenant, and pass over before the people. And they took up the ark of the covenant, and went before the people.

⁷And the LORD said unto Joshua, This day will I begin to magnify thee in the sight of all Israel, that they may know that, as I was with Moses, *so* I will be with thee. ⁸And thou shalt command the priests that bear the ark of the covenant, saying, When ye are come to the brink of the water of Jordan, ye shall stand still in Jordan. ⁹And Joshua said unto the children of Israel, Come hither, and hear the words of the LORD your God. ¹⁰And Joshua said, Hereby ye shall know that the living God *is* among you, and *that* he will without fail drive out from before you the Canaanites, and the Hittites, and the Hivites, and the Perizzites, and the Girgashites, and the Amorites, and the Jebusites. ¹¹Behold, the ark of the covenant of the Lord of all the earth passeth over before you into Jordan. ¹²Now therefore take you twelve men out of the tribes of Israel, out of every tribe a man. ¹³And it shall come to pass, as soon as the soles of the feet of the priests that bear the ark of the LORD, the Lord of all the earth, shall rest in the waters of Jordan, *that* the waters of Jordan shall be cut off *from* the waters that come down from above; and they shall stand upon an heap. ¹⁴And it came to

---

^d faint: Heb. melt
^a heretofore: Heb. since yesterday, and the third day

Devotional Moment
·
Leadership

3:11-14 As Israel prepared to cross the Jordan River to claim the Promised Land, God went with them in the Ark of the Covenant, but Joshua and his men bore responsibility for moving the people forward. So it is with parenting. You must lead your children in the development of their faith. The steps you take (or don't take) will make a difference. If you want your spouse or children to pray, *you* pray. If you want them to follow God's Word, let them see *you* reading it. If you want them to have faith in God, don't *you* be consumed with worry every time something goes wrong. Every step forward you take will move the whole family forward.

the LORD spake unto Joshua, saying, ²Take you twelve men out of the people, out of every tribe a man, ³And command ye them, saying, Take you hence out of the midst of Jordan, out of the place where the priests' feet stood firm, twelve stones, and ye shall carry them over with you, and leave them in the lodging place, where ye shall lodge this night. ⁴Then Joshua called the twelve men, whom he had prepared of the children of Israel, out of every tribe a man: ⁵And Joshua said unto them, Pass over before the ark of the LORD your God into the midst of Jordan, and take ye up every man of you a stone upon his shoulder, according unto the number of the tribes of the children of Israel: ⁶That this may be a sign among you, *that* when your children ask *their fathers* in time to come, saying, What *mean* ye by these stones? ⁷Then ye shall answer them, That the waters of Jordan were cut off before the ark of the covenant of the LORD; when it passed over Jordan, the waters of Jordan were cut off: and these stones shall be for a

pass, when the people removed from their tents, to pass over Jordan, and the priests bearing the ark of the covenant before the people; ¹⁵And as they that bare the ark were come unto Jordan, and the feet of the priests that bare the ark were dipped in the brim of the water, (for Jordan overfloweth all his banks all the time of harvest,) ¹⁶That the waters which came down from above stood *and* rose up upon an heap very far from the city Adam, that *is* beside Zaretan: and those that came down toward the sea of the plain, *even* the salt sea, failed, *and* were cut off: and the people passed over right against Jericho. ¹⁷And the priests that bare the ark of the covenant of the LORD stood firm on dry ground in the midst of Jordan, and all the Israelites passed over on dry ground, until all the people were passed clean over Jordan.

4

¹And it came to pass, when all the people were clean passed over Jordan, that

Devotional Moment
·
Remembering

4:2-7, 21-24 Joshua's team was on the go and eager to conquer the Promised Land when God urged them to take time out to remember his powerful work with a memorial of twelve stones taken from the Jordan River. Performing countless tasks and pursuing lifetime goals—even godly ones—can divert us from remembering God's part. He wants us to interrupt our life in the fast lane and remember him, memorialize his work, and record the great things he has done. In your memories of human events, remember God's almighty hand.

memorial unto the children of Israel for ever. [8]And the children of Israel did so as Joshua commanded, and took up twelve stones out of the midst of Jordan, as the LORD spake unto Joshua, according to the number of the tribes of the children of Israel, and carried them over with them unto the place where they lodged, and laid them down there. [9]And Joshua set up twelve stones in the midst of Jordan, in the place where the feet of the priests which bare the ark of the covenant stood: and they are there unto this day.

[10]For the priests which bare the ark stood in the midst of Jordan, until every thing was finished that the LORD commanded Joshua to speak unto the people, according to all that Moses commanded Joshua: and the people hasted and passed over. [11]And it came to pass, when all the people were clean passed over, that the ark of the LORD passed over, and the priests, in the presence of the people. [12]And the children of Reuben, and the children of Gad, and half the tribe of Manasseh, passed over armed before the children of Israel, as Moses spake unto them: [13]About forty thousand prepared[a] for war passed over before the LORD unto battle, to the plains of Jericho. [14]On that day the LORD magnified Joshua in the sight of all Israel; and they feared him, as they feared Moses, all the days of his life. [15]And the LORD spake unto Joshua, saying, [16]Command the priests that bear the ark of the testimony, that they come up out of Jordan. [17]Joshua therefore commanded the priests, say-

ing, Come ye up out of Jordan. [18]And it came to pass, when the priests that bare the ark of the covenant of the LORD were come up out of the midst of Jordan, and the soles of the priests' feet were lifted up unto the dry land, that the waters of Jordan returned unto their place, and flowed over all his banks, as they did before. [19]And the people came up out of Jordan on the tenth day of the first month, and encamped in Gilgal, in the east border of Jericho.

[20]And those twelve stones, which they took out of Jordan, did Joshua pitch in Gilgal. [21]And he spake unto the children of Israel, saying, When your children shall ask their fathers in time to come, saying, What mean these stones? [22]Then ye shall let your children know, saying, Israel came over this Jordan on dry land. [23]For the LORD your God dried up the waters of Jordan from before you, until ye were passed over, as the LORD your God did to the Red sea, which he dried up from before us, until we were gone over: [24]That all the people of the earth might know the hand of the LORD, that it is mighty: that ye might fear the LORD your God for ever[b].

5

[1]And it came to pass, when all the kings of the Amorites, which were on the side of Jordan westward, and all the kings of the Canaanites, which were by the sea, heard that the LORD had dried up the waters of Jordan from before the children of Israel, until we were passed over, that their heart melted, neither

[a] prepared: or, ready armed
[b] for ever: Heb. all days

Setting up
Memorial Markers to a
Changed Life

*"When your children ask . . . What mean ye by these stones? Then
ye shall answer them, That the waters of Jordan were cut off before
the ark of the covenant of the Lord . . . These stones shall be for a
memorial unto the children of Israel for ever."* Joshua 4:6-7

J oshua's first act of leadership involved a seemingly impossible task. God commanded
him to enter and take the Promised Land. Yet before him lay an impassible barrier to
moving an entire army: the Jordan River in springtime. Undeterred, in faith Joshua
stepped out in front of his people—and God rolled back the waters so they could pass.

Before Joshua moved on, he stopped and set up something that would stand for ages:
a memorial marker to the people of Israel that they could look to as a reminder of this miracle. This is something that we can do today to help break past, negative cycles.

Dawn had been involved in immorality as a teen, and even after she came to Christ
she could never truly accept God's forgiveness for her past sins. She felt unworthy, even
unlovable, because of her past. After years of concentrating on growing in Christ, Dawn
finally fell in love and married a wonderful man in her church. Yet on the first night of
their honeymoon, she sat in tears in their hotel room. She had not stayed pure before
marriage, and she couldn't shake the pain and shame she felt—that is, until her husband
did something that changed her life.

Dawn's husband knew of her feelings of guilt, and he decided that before they began
their sexual relationship, they needed a "memorial marker" to what God had truly done
for both of them. As his new bride sat on the bed, he came out with a basin of warm water and a towel. And as Jesus had done with Peter, Dawn's husband washed her feet, as a
symbol of what God had done for her soul.

Dawn was so moved, she broke into fresh sobs. As she experienced the humbling act
of having her feet washed, for the first time in her Christian life she truly understood and
accepted God's forgiveness. Since then she has never doubted that reality.

When the accuser of Dawn's soul tries to make her feel ashamed of her past now, Dawn
recalls the symbolic memorial marker that her husband provided her on their wedding
night. It still reminds her of a biblical truth: Her sins were washed away at the cross.

Setting up a personal memorial marker to an expression of God's love has made tremendous healing possible to many, many people. One man lost his business because of the illegal dealings of a partner—and found a way to lose the gripping anger he felt as well. On a sheet of paper, he wrote down all his feelings and hurts toward this other man. Then with his pastor present, he burned the paper—an expression of his need to be honest about his feelings, and yet let go of the rage he felt inside and move on to walk in newness of life.

Another man's father was killed in battle on D day plus 1, in Normandy. The thought of his father's grave half a world away had always been the source of his emotional hurts and unfulfilled longings. But in the course of counseling, he was encouraged to make a trip to that hated grave. Once there, he read a letter written by his uncle, a letter telling of the love his father was never able to express to him personally. Today, thoughts of that grave evoke positive emotions as he remembers the time he honestly came to grips with the loss of his father.

If you've had trouble moving away from hurts in the past, consider something many others have found helpful. Provide yourself (or another) with a memorial marker to God's faithfulness. Whether it's a card, a symbolic action, or something else, it can give you a powerful picture of the fact you are a new creature . . . full of God's love and potential for good.

---

was there spirit in them any more, because of the children of Israel. ²At that time the LORD said unto Joshua, Make thee sharp[a] knives, and circumcise again the children of Israel the second time. ³And Joshua made him sharp[b] knives, and circumcised the children of Israel at the hill of the foreskins. ⁴And this *is* the cause why Joshua did circumcise: All the people that came out of Egypt, *that were* males, *even* all the men of war, died in the wilderness by the way, after they came out of Egypt. ⁵Now all the people that came out were circumcised: but all the people *that were* born in the wilderness by the way as they came forth out of Egypt, *them* they had not circumcised. ⁶For the children of Israel walked forty years in the wilderness, till all the people *that were* men of war, which came out of Egypt, were consumed, because they obeyed not the voice of the LORD: unto whom the LORD sware that he would not shew them the land, which the LORD sware unto their fathers that he would give us, a land that floweth with milk and honey. ⁷And their children, *whom* he raised up in their stead, them Joshua circumcised: for they were uncircumcised, because they had not circumcised them by the way. ⁸And it came to pass, when they had done circumcising all the people, that they abode in their places in the camp, till they were whole. ⁹And the LORD said unto Joshua, This day have I rolled away the reproach of Egypt from off

---

[a] sharp . . . : or, knives of flints
[b] sharp . . . : or, knives of flints

you. Wherefore the name of the place is called Gilgal[c] unto this day.

[10]And the children of Israel encamped in Gilgal, and kept the passover on the fourteenth day of the month at even in the plains of Jericho. [11]And they did eat of the old corn of the land on the morrow after the passover, unleavened cakes, and parched *corn* in the selfsame day. [12]And the manna ceased on the morrow after they had eaten of the old corn of the land; neither had the children of Israel manna any more; but they did eat of the fruit of the land of Canaan that year.

[13]And it came to pass, when Joshua was by Jericho, that he lifted up his eyes and looked, and, behold, there stood a man over against him with his sword drawn in his hand: and Joshua went unto him, and said unto him, *Art* thou for us, or for our adversaries? [14]And he said, Nay; but *as* captain[d] of the host of the LORD am I now come. And Joshua fell on his face to the earth, and did worship, and said unto him, What saith my lord unto his servant? [15]And the captain of the LORD'S host said unto Joshua, Loose thy shoe from off thy foot; for the place whereon thou standest *is* holy. And Joshua did so.

6

[1]Now Jericho was straitly shut up because of the children of Israel: none went out, and none came in. [2]And the LORD said unto Joshua, See, I have given into thine hand Jericho, and the king thereof, *and* the mighty men of valour. [3]And ye shall compass the city, all *ye* men of war, *and* go round about the city once. Thus shalt thou do six days. [4]And seven priests shall bear before the ark seven trumpets of rams' horns: and the seventh day ye shall compass the city seven times, and the priests shall blow with the trumpets. [5]And it shall come to pass, that when they make a long *blast* with the ram's horn, *and* when ye hear the sound of the trumpet, all the people shall shout with a great shout; and the wall of the city shall fall down flat[a], and the people shall ascend up every man straight before him.

[6]And Joshua the son of Nun called the priests, and said unto them, Take up the ark of the covenant, and let seven priests bear seven trumpets of rams' horns before the ark of the LORD. [7]And he said unto the people, Pass on, and compass the city, and let him that is armed pass on before the ark of the LORD. [8]And it came to pass, when Joshua had spoken unto the people, that the seven priests bearing the seven trumpets of rams' horns passed on before the LORD, and blew with the trumpets: and the ark of the covenant of the LORD followed them. [9]And the armed men went before the priests that blew with the trumpets, and the rereward[b] came after the ark, *the priests* going on, and blowing with the trumpets. [10]And Joshua had com-

---

[c] Gilgal: that is Rolling
[d] captain: or, prince
[a] flat: Heb. under it
[b] rereward: Heb. gathering host

manded the people, saying, Ye shall not shout, nor make any noise[c] with your voice, neither shall *any* word proceed out of your mouth, until the day I bid you shout; then shall ye shout. [11]So the ark of the LORD compassed the city, going about *it* once: and they came into the camp, and lodged in the camp. [12]And Joshua rose early in the morning, and the priests took up the ark of the LORD. [13]And seven priests bearing seven trumpets of rams' horns before the ark of the LORD went on continually, and blew with the trumpets: and the armed men went before them; but the rereward came after the ark of the LORD, *the priests* going on, and blowing with the trumpets. [14]And the second day they compassed the city once, and returned into the camp: so they did six days. [15]And it came to pass on the seventh day, that they rose early about the dawning of the day, and compassed the city after the same manner seven times: only on that day they compassed the city seven times. [16]And it came to pass at the seventh time, when the priests blew with the trumpets, Joshua said unto the people, Shout; for the LORD hath given you the city.

[17]And the city shall be accursed[d], *even* it, and all that *are* therein, to the LORD: only Rahab the harlot shall live, she and all that *are* with her in the house, because she hid the messengers that we sent. [18]And ye, in any wise keep *yourselves* from the accursed thing, lest ye make *yourselves* accursed[e], when ye take of the accursed thing, and make the camp of Israel a curse, and trouble it. [19]But all the silver, and gold, and vessels of brass and iron, *are* consecrated[f] unto the LORD: they shall come into the treasury of the LORD. [20]So the people shouted when *the priests* blew with the trumpets: and it came to pass, when the people heard the sound of the trumpet, and the people shouted with a great shout, that the wall fell down flat[g], so that the people went up into the city, every man straight before him, and they took the city. [21]And they utterly destroyed all that *was* in the city, both man and woman, young and old, and ox, and sheep, and ass, with the edge of the sword. [22]But Joshua had said unto the two men that had spied out the country, Go into the harlot's house, and bring out thence the woman, and all that she hath, as ye sware unto her. [23]And the young men that were spies went in, and brought out Rahab, and her father, and her mother, and her brethren, and all that she had; and they brought out all her kindred[h], and left them without the camp of Israel. [24]And they burnt the city with fire, and all that *was* therein: only the silver, and the gold, and the vessels of brass and of iron, they put into the treasury of the house of the LORD. [25]And Joshua saved Rahab the harlot alive, and her fa-

---

[c] any noise . . . : Heb. your voice to be heard
[d] accursed: or, devoted
[e] accursed: or, devoted
[f] consecrated: Heb. holiness
[g] flat: Heb. under it
[h] kindred: Heb. families

ther's household, and all that she had; and she dwelleth in Israel *even* unto this day; because she hid the messengers, which Joshua sent to spy out Jericho. ²⁶And Joshua adjured *them* at that time, saying, Cursed *be* the man before the LORD, that riseth up and buildeth this city Jericho: he shall lay the foundation thereof in his firstborn, and in his youngest *son* shall he set up the gates of it. ²⁷So the LORD was with Joshua; and his fame was *noised* throughout all the country.

7

¹But the children of Israel committed a trespass in the accursed thing: for Achan^a, the son of Carmi, the son of Zabdi, the son of Zerah, of the tribe of Judah, took of the accursed thing: and the anger of the LORD was kindled against the children of Israel. ²And Joshua sent men from Jericho to Ai, which *is* beside Bethaven, on the east side of Bethel, and spake unto them, saying, Go up and view the country. And the men went up and viewed Ai. ³And they returned to Joshua, and said unto him, Let not all the people go up; but let about two or three thousand men go up and smite Ai; *and* make not all the people to labour thither; for they *are but* few. ⁴So there went up thither of the people about three thousand men: and they fled before the men of Ai. ⁵And the men of Ai smote of them about thirty and six men: for they chased them *from* before the gate *even* unto Shebarim, and smote them in the

going down: wherefore the hearts of the people melted, and became as water.

⁶And Joshua rent his clothes, and fell to the earth upon his face before the ark of the LORD until the eventide, he and the elders of Israel, and put dust upon their heads. ⁷And Joshua said, Alas, O Lord GOD, wherefore hast thou at all brought this people over Jordan, to deliver us into the hand of the Amorites, to destroy us? would to God we had been content, and dwelt on the other side Jordan! ⁸O Lord, what shall I say, when Israel turneth their backs^b before their enemies! ⁹For the Canaanites and all the inhabitants of the land shall hear *of it,* and shall environ us round, and cut off our name from the earth: and what wilt thou do unto thy great name?

¹⁰And the LORD said unto Joshua, Get thee up; wherefore liest^c thou thus upon thy face? ¹¹Israel hath sinned, and

---

Devotional Moment

•

Humility

7:6 Israel's defeat by tiny Ai stood in contrast to their stunning victory over the fortress city of Jericho. Unexpected defeat was disorienting and humiliating to the Israelites. Confused and contrite, they turned to God for guidance and renewal. The most humbling experiences often come right after heady successes. When you experience defeat in your role as a husband or wife, parent or child, examine yourself before God and allow him to point out any hidden sin that may be responsible. Staying humble before God gives him the opportunity he longs for to work in your life and your family's life.

^a Achan: also called, Achar
^b backs: Heb. necks
^c liest: Heb. fallest

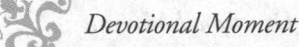

Devotional Moment

•

Hidden Sin

7:11 God called Israel to sanctify themselves because the whole nation needed to understand the importance of acknowledging wrongdoing for what it is. Achan had not only taken things that God had wanted destroyed; he had also lied about it. Attempting to cover up sin can be a destructive problem in families. Perhaps the most grotesque example is physical or sexual abuse, but even covering up smaller offenses is wrong. It is our secrets that destroy us.

If there is a hidden sin festering under the surface in your family, bring it out in the open and deal with it before it does more damage—or destroys the entire family.

they have also transgressed my covenant which I commanded them: for they have even taken of the accursed thing, and have also stolen, and dissembled also, and they have put *it* even among their own stuff. ¹²Therefore the children of Israel could not stand before their enemies, *but* turned *their* backs before their enemies, because they were accursed: neither will I be with you any more, except ye destroy the accursed from among you. ¹³Up, sanctify the people, and say, Sanctify yourselves against to morrow: for thus saith the LORD God of Israel, *There is* an accursed thing in the midst of thee, O Israel: thou canst not stand before thine enemies, until ye take away the accursed thing from among you. ¹⁴In the morning therefore ye shall be brought according to your tribes: and it shall be, *that* the tribe which the LORD taketh shall come according to the families

thereof; and the family which the LORD shall take shall come by households; and the household which the LORD shall take shall come man by man. ¹⁵And it shall be, *that* he that is taken with the accursed thing shall be burnt with fire, he and all that he hath: because he hath transgressed the covenant of the LORD, and because he hath wrought folly[d] in Israel.

¹⁶So Joshua rose up early in the morning, and brought Israel by their tribes; and the tribe of Judah was taken: ¹⁷And he brought the family of Judah; and he took the family of the Zarhites: and he brought the family of the Zarhites man by man; and Zabdi was taken: ¹⁸And he brought his household man by man; and Achan, the son of Carmi, the son of Zabdi, the son of Zerah, of the tribe of Judah, was taken. ¹⁹And Joshua said unto Achan, My son, give, I pray thee, glory to the LORD God of Israel, and make confession unto him; and tell me now what thou hast done; hide *it* not from me. ²⁰And Achan answered Joshua, and said, Indeed I have sinned against the LORD God of Israel, and thus and thus have I done: ²¹When I saw among the spoils a goodly Babylonish garment, and two hundred shekels of silver, and a wedge[e] of gold of fifty shekels weight, then I coveted them, and took them; and, behold, they *are* hid in the earth in the midst of my tent, and the silver under it. ²²So Joshua sent messengers, and they ran unto the tent; and, behold, *it was* hid in his tent, and the silver under it. ²³And they took them out of the

---

[d] folly: or, wickedness
[e] wedge: Heb. tongue

357

midst of the tent, and brought them unto Joshua, and unto all the children of Israel, and laid them out before the LORD. ²⁴And Joshua, and all Israel with him, took Achan the son of Zerah, and the silver, and the garment, and the wedge of gold, and his sons, and his daughters, and his oxen, and his asses, and his sheep, and his tent, and all that he had: and they brought them unto the valley of Achor. ²⁵And Joshua said, Why hast thou troubled us? the LORD shall trouble thee this day. And all Israel stoned him with stones, and burned them with fire, after they had stoned them with stones. ²⁶And they raised over him a great heap of stones unto this day. So the LORD turned from the fierceness of his anger. Wherefore the name of that place was called, The valley of Achor[f], unto this day.

8

¹And the LORD said unto Joshua, Fear not, neither be thou dismayed: take all the people of war with thee, and arise, go up to Ai: see, I have given into thy hand the king of Ai, and his people, and his city, and his land: ²And thou shalt do to Ai and her king as thou didst unto Jericho and her king: only the spoil thereof, and the cattle thereof, shall ye take for a prey unto yourselves: lay thee an ambush for the city behind it. ³So Joshua arose, and all the people of war, to go up against Ai: and Joshua chose out thirty thousand mighty men of valour, and sent them away by night. ⁴And he commanded them, saying, Behold, ye shall lie in wait against the city,

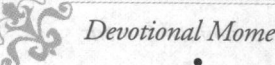

Devotional Moment

Failure

8:1-2 Despite Israel's failure to conquer Ai the first time, God gave them a second chance. He told Joshua how to root out the problem that had caused their defeat and prepare to fight again. This time, God promised, they would win and even get a share of the booty. We all experience failure in our relationships with parents, children, siblings, or other relatives. Sometimes we have disagreements. Yet we must learn, as Joshua did, to pray, make adjustments, and start again. Relationships within the home take work. Keep working at the relationships in your family despite the temporary setbacks you will inevitably experience.

even behind the city: go not very far from the city, but be ye all ready: ⁵And I, and all the people that *are* with me, will approach unto the city: and it shall come to pass, when they come out against us, as at the first, that we will flee before them, ⁶(For they will come out after us) till we have drawn[a] them from the city; for they will say, They flee before us, as at the first: therefore we will flee before them. ⁷Then ye shall rise up from the ambush, and seize upon the city: for the LORD your God will deliver it into your hand. ⁸And it shall be, when ye have taken the city, *that* ye shall set the city on fire: according to the commandment of the LORD shall ye do. See, I have commanded you. ⁹Joshua therefore sent them forth: and they went to lie in ambush, and abode between Bethel and Ai, on the west side of Ai: but Joshua lodged that night among the people. ¹⁰And Joshua rose up

---

[f] Achor: that is, Trouble
[a] drawn: Heb. pulled

early in the morning, and numbered the people, and went up, he and the elders of Israel, before the people to Ai. ¹¹And all the people, *even the people* of war that *were* with him, went up, and drew nigh, and came before the city, and pitched on the north side of Ai: now *there was* a valley between them and Ai. ¹²And he took about five thousand men, and set them to lie in ambush between Bethel and Ai, on the west side of the city. ¹³And when they had set the people, *even* all the host that *was* on the north of the city, and their liers in wait on the west of the city, Joshua went that night into the midst of the valley. ¹⁴And it came to pass, when the king of Ai saw *it*, that they hasted and rose up early, and the men of the city went out against Israel to battle, he and all his people, at a time appointed, before the plain; but he wist not that *there were* liers in ambush against him behind the city. ¹⁵And Joshua and all Israel made as if they were beaten before them, and fled by the way of the wilderness. ¹⁶And all the people that *were* in Ai were called together to pursue after them: and they pursued after Joshua, and were drawn away from the city. ¹⁷And there was not a man left in Ai or Bethel, that went not out after Israel: and they left the city open, and pursued after Israel. ¹⁸And the LORD said unto Joshua, Stretch out the spear that *is* in thy hand toward Ai; for I will give it into thine hand. And Joshua stretched out the spear that *he had* in his hand toward the city. ¹⁹And the ambush arose quickly out of their place, and they ran as soon as he had stretched out his hand: and they entered into the city, and took it, and hasted and set the city on fire. ²⁰And when the men of Ai looked behind them, they saw, and, behold, the smoke of the city ascended up to heaven, and they had no power[b] to flee this way or that way: and the people that fled to the wilderness turned back upon the pursuers. ²¹And when Joshua and all Israel saw that the ambush had taken the city, and that the smoke of the city ascended, then they turned again, and slew the men of Ai. ²²And the other issued out of the city against them; so they were in the midst of Israel, some on this side, and some on that side: and they smote them, so that they let none of them remain or escape.

²³And the king of Ai they took alive, and brought him to Joshua. ²⁴And it came to pass, when Israel had made an end of slaying all the inhabitants of Ai in the field, in the wilderness wherein they chased them, and when they were all fallen on the edge of the sword, until they were consumed, that all the Israelites returned unto Ai, and smote it with the edge of the sword. ²⁵And *so* it was, *that* all that fell that day, both of men and women, *were* twelve thousand, *even* all the men of Ai. ²⁶For Joshua drew not his hand back, wherewith he stretched out the spear, until he had utterly destroyed all the inhabitants of Ai. ²⁷Only the cattle and the spoil of that city Israel took for a prey unto themselves, according unto the word of the LORD which he commanded Joshua. ²⁸And Joshua burnt Ai, and made it an heap for ever, *even* a desolation unto this day. ²⁹And the king of Ai he hanged on a tree until even-

---

b power: Heb. hand

tide: and as soon as the sun was down, Joshua commanded that they should take his carcase down from the tree, and cast it at the entering of the gate of the city, and raise thereon a great heap of stones, *that remaineth* unto this day.

³⁰Then Joshua built an altar unto the LORD God of Israel in mount Ebal, ³¹As Moses the servant of the LORD commanded the children of Israel, as it is written in the book of the law of Moses, an altar of whole stones, over which no man hath lift up *any* iron: and they offered thereon burnt offerings unto the LORD, and sacrificed peace offerings. ³²And he wrote there upon the stones a copy of the law of Moses, which he wrote in the presence of the children of Israel. ³³And all Israel, and their elders, and officers, and their judges, stood on this side the ark and on that side before the priests the Levites, which bare the ark of the covenant of the LORD, as well the stranger, as he that was born among them; half of them over against mount Gerizim, and half of them over against mount Ebal; as Moses the servant of the LORD had commanded before, that they should bless the people of Israel. ³⁴And afterward he read all the words of the law, the blessings and cursings, according to all that is written in the book of the law. ³⁵There was not a word of all that Moses commanded, which Joshua read not before all the congregation of Israel, with the women, and the little ones, and the strangers that were conversant among them.

9

¹And it came to pass, when all the kings which *were* on this side Jordan, in the hills, and in the valleys, and in all the coasts of the great sea over against Lebanon, the Hittite, and the Amorite, the Canaanite, the Perizzite, the Hivite, and the Jebusite, heard *thereof;* ²That they gathered themselves together, to fight with Joshua and with Israel, with one accord ᵃ.

³And when the inhabitants of Gibeon heard what Joshua had done unto Jericho and to Ai, ⁴They did work wilily, and went and made as if they had been ambassadors, and took old sacks upon their asses, and wine bottles, old, and rent, and bound up; ⁵And old shoes and clouted upon their feet, and old garments upon them; and all the bread of their provision was dry *and* mouldy. ⁶And they went to Joshua unto the camp at Gilgal, and said unto him, and to the men of Israel, We be come from a far country: now therefore make ye a league with us. ⁷And the men of Israel said unto the Hivites, Peradventure ye dwell among us; and how shall we make a league with you? ⁸And they said unto Joshua, We *are* thy servants. And Joshua said unto them, Who *are* ye? and from whence come ye? ⁹And they said unto him, From a very far country thy servants are come because of the name of the LORD thy God: for we have heard the fame of him, and all that he did in Egypt, ¹⁰And all that he did to the two kings of the Amorites, that *were* beyond Jordan, to Sihon king of Heshbon, and to Og king of Bashan, which *was* at Ashtaroth. ¹¹Wherefore

---

ᵃ accord: Heb. mouth

our elders and all the inhabitants of our country spake to us, saying, Take victuals with you[b] for the journey, and go to meet them, and say unto them, We *are* your servants: therefore now make ye a league with us. [12]This our bread we took hot *for* our provision out of our houses on the day we came forth to go unto you; but now, behold, it is dry, and it is mouldy: [13]And these bottles of wine, which we filled, *were* new; and, behold, they be rent: and these our garments and our shoes are become old by reason of the very long journey. [14]And the men[c] took of their victuals, and asked not *counsel* at the mouth of the LORD.

[15]And Joshua made peace with them, and made a league with them, to let them live: and the princes of the congregation sware unto them. [16]And it came to pass at the end of three days after they had made a league with them, that they heard that they *were* their neighbours, and *that* they dwelt among them. [17]And the children of Israel journeyed, and came unto their cities on the third day. Now their cities *were* Gibeon, and Chephirah, and Beeroth, and Kirjathjearim. [18]And the children of Israel smote them not, because the princes of the congregation had sworn unto them by the LORD God of Israel. And all the congregation murmured against the princes. [19]But all the princes said unto all the congregation, We have sworn unto them by the LORD God of Israel: now therefore we may not touch them. [20]This we will do to them; we will even let them live, lest wrath be upon

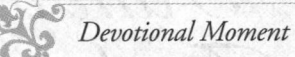

Devotional Moment
•
Promises
9:19-20 These Gibeonites tricked Joshua into thinking they were a faraway people, with whom a pledge of mutual defense would be prudent. This proved to be a big mistake. Vows, however rashly taken, are not invalidated by false premises or faulty reasoning. A couple pledged in marriage may not be all that they represent themselves to be, yet their marriage vow is nonetheless valid. You may be deceived on a loan guarantee, but that promise is nonetheless binding. Remember the lesson of Joshua and the Gibeonites and do not make pledges lightly, especially to children or a spouse.

us, because of the oath which we sware unto them. [21]And the princes said unto them, Let them live; but let them be hewers of wood and drawers of water unto all the congregation; as the princes had promised them.

[22]And Joshua called for them, and he spake unto them, saying, Wherefore have ye beguiled us, saying, We *are* very far from you; when ye dwell among us? [23]Now therefore ye *are* cursed, and there shall none of you be freed from being bondmen, and hewers of wood and drawers of water for the house of my God. [24]And they answered Joshua, and said, Because it was certainly told thy servants, how that the LORD thy God commanded his servant Moses to give you all the land, and to destroy all the inhabitants of the land from before you, therefore we were sore afraid of our lives because of you, and have done this thing. [25]And now, behold, we *are* in

---

[b] with you: Heb. in your hand
[c] the men . . . : or, they received the men by reason of their victuals

Family Traditions

A Tradition of Prayer

JOSHUA 10:7-14

What can parents do to live courageously in a fearful world? How can moms and dads confront the forces of evil from the doorstep of their home? And what can parents do to help change that world—to make it a better place for all families to live in?

God has given us a means to fight—not merely to defend ourselves, but to march, to chase, to destroy without mercy all powers that stand against our efforts to follow God in this world.

"But wait," you say, "I'm working hard enough just trying to survive— to raise happy children, be a good spouse, participate in my church. Where am I going to find the strength to fight against the evils of the world?"

It all starts with prayer. An established tradition of prayer.

One busy homemaker taped a picture of Jesus inside one of her kitchen cupboards. Whenever she wanted to pray, she opened the cupboard door, pulled a chair up in front of it, and laid her worn Bible open on the counter. Her children learned to respect those times of private intercession.

Another busy mom took whatever moments her toddlers would give her, however brief, to throw her apron over her head and pray for their world.

A husband and wife knelt together in their bedroom to pray each morning before leaving for work. Day after day, year after year, they made prayer as much a part of their morning routine as getting dressed.

Sandwiched between such prayers, of course, you will have fighting of a different kind to do—wrestling with shades of gray over how to discipline or guide children, sticking to decisions that none of your kids want to go along with, retreating from commitments that threaten to overwhelm you, expressing opinions about school policies, and many others. Those battles are important, no doubt, but remember that prayer is where many of them are decided.

"Prayer is an indispensable ingredient in challenging the strongholds of evil," writes noted Christian author Karen Mains. Every prayer is a step forward against the gates of hell. Joshua 10:14 says that "the Lord fought for Israel," and when we pray, this truth will be written across our lives, too.

thine hand: as it seemeth good and right unto thee to do unto us, do. ²⁶And so did he unto them, and delivered them out of the hand of the children of Israel, that they slew them not. ²⁷And Joshua made^d them that day hewers of wood and drawers of water for the congregation, and for the altar of the LORD, even unto this day, in the place which he should choose.

10

¹Now it came to pass, when Adonizedek king of Jerusalem had heard how Joshua had taken Ai, and had utterly destroyed it; as he had done to Jericho and her king, so he had done to Ai and her king; and how the inhabitants of Gibeon had made peace with Israel, and were among them; ²That they feared greatly, because Gibeon *was* a great city, as one of the royal^a cities, and because it *was* greater than Ai, and all the men thereof *were* mighty. ³Wherefore Adonizedek king of Jerusalem sent unto Hoham king of Hebron, and unto Piram king of Jarmuth, and unto Japhia king of Lachish, and unto Debir king of Eglon, saying, ⁴Come up unto me, and help me, that we may smite Gibeon: for it hath made peace with Joshua and with the children of Israel. ⁵Therefore the five kings of the Amorites, the king of Jerusalem, the king of Hebron, the king of Jarmuth, the king of Lachish, the king of Eglon, gathered themselves together, and went up, they and all their hosts, and encamped before Gibeon, and made war against it. ⁶And the men

of Gibeon sent unto Joshua to the camp to Gilgal, saying, Slack not thy hand from thy servants; come up to us quickly, and save us, and help us: for all the kings of the Amorites that dwell in the mountains are gathered together against us.

⁷So Joshua ascended from Gilgal, he, and all the people of war with him, and all the mighty men of valour. ⁸And the LORD said unto Joshua, Fear them not: for I have delivered them into thine hand; there shall not a man of them stand before thee. ⁹Joshua therefore came unto them suddenly, *and* went up from Gilgal all night. ¹⁰And the LORD discomfited them before Israel, and slew them with a great slaughter at Gibeon, and chased them along the way that goeth up to Bethhoron, and smote them to Azekah, and unto Makkedah. ¹¹And it came to pass, as they fled from before Israel, *and* were in the going down to Bethhoron, that the LORD cast down great stones from heaven upon them unto Azekah, and they died: *they were* more which died with hailstones than *they* whom the children of Israel slew with the sword. ¹²Then spake Joshua to the LORD in the day when the LORD delivered up the Amorites before the children of Israel, and he said in the sight of Israel, Sun, stand thou still upon Gibeon; and thou, Moon, in the valley of Ajalon. ¹³And the sun stood still, and the moon stayed, until the people had avenged themselves upon their enemies. *Is* not this written in the book of Jasher^b? So

---

^d made: Heb. gave, or, delivered to be
^a royal . . . : Heb. cities of the kingdom
^b Jasher: or, the upright?

the sun stood still in the midst of heaven, and hasted not to go down about a whole day. ¹⁴And there was no day like that before it or after it, that the LORD hearkened unto the voice of a man: for the LORD fought for Israel.

¹⁵And Joshua returned, and all Israel with him, unto the camp to Gilgal. ¹⁶But these five kings fled, and hid themselves in a cave at Makkedah. ¹⁷And it was told Joshua, saying, The five kings are found hid in a cave at Makkedah. ¹⁸And Joshua said, Roll great stones upon the mouth of the cave, and set men by it for to keep them: ¹⁹And stay ye not, *but* pursue after your enemies, and smite the hindmost of them; suffer them not to enter into their cities: for the LORD your God hath delivered them into your hand. ²⁰And it came to pass, when Joshua and the children of Israel had made an end of slaying them with a very great slaughter, till they were consumed, that the rest *which* remained of them entered into fenced cities. ²¹And all the people returned to the camp to Joshua at Makkedah in peace: none moved his tongue against any of the children of Israel. ²²Then said Joshua, Open the mouth of the cave, and bring out those five kings unto me out of the cave. ²³And they did so, and brought forth those five kings unto him out of the cave, the king of Jerusalem, the king of Hebron, the king of Jarmuth, the king of Lachish, *and* the king of Eglon. ²⁴And it came to pass, when they brought out those kings unto Joshua, that Joshua called for all the men of Israel, and said unto the captains of the men of war which went with him, Come near, put your feet upon the

Devotional Moment

•

Challenge

10:25 For Joshua, the odds were never even; the playing field was never level. Against his pagan adversaries he threw citizen-soldiers who had zeal but little training. Always forging beachheads against entrenched defenders, Joshua faced morale trouble, supply-route problems, and often overwhelming enemy numbers. Yet one thing gave Joshua the ability to face it all: his supreme confidence in and devotion to God. Joshua believed in victory because God had ordered the march. If you are frustrated with problems, turn each hassle into a challenge. Pray, believe, and do what you can, but rest in the fact that God is in control, not you. Let God sweep your fears away. God has led you to this point for a purpose. So what if the odds are against you?

necks of these kings. And they came near, and put their feet upon the necks of them. ²⁵And Joshua said unto them, Fear not, nor be dismayed, be strong and of good courage: for thus shall the LORD do to all your enemies against whom ye fight. ²⁶And afterward Joshua smote them, and slew them, and hanged them on five trees: and they were hanging upon the trees until the evening. ²⁷And it came to pass at the time of the going down of the sun, *that* Joshua commanded, and they took them down off the trees, and cast them into the cave wherein they had been hid, and laid great stones in the cave's mouth, *which remain* until this very day.

²⁸And that day Joshua took Makkedah, and smote it with the edge of the sword, and the king thereof he utterly destroyed, them, and all the souls that *were* therein; he let none remain: and he did to the king of

Makkedah as he did unto the king of Jericho. ²⁹Then Joshua passed from Makkedah, and all Israel with him, unto Libnah, and fought against Libnah: ³⁰And the LORD delivered it also, and the king thereof, into the hand of Israel; and he smote it with the edge of the sword, and all the souls that *were* therein; he let none remain in it; but did unto the king thereof as he did unto the king of Jericho. ³¹And Joshua passed from Libnah, and all Israel with him, unto Lachish, and encamped against it, and fought against it: ³²And the LORD delivered Lachish into the hand of Israel, which took it on the second day, and smote it with the edge of the sword, and all the souls that *were* therein, according to all that he had done to Libnah. ³³Then Horam king of Gezer came up to help Lachish; and Joshua smote him and his people, until he had left him none remaining. ³⁴And from Lachish Joshua passed unto Eglon, and all Israel with him; and they encamped against it, and fought against it: ³⁵And they took it on that day, and smote it with the edge of the sword, and all the souls that *were* therein he utterly destroyed that day, according to all that he had done to Lachish. ³⁶And Joshua went up from Eglon, and all Israel with him, unto Hebron; and they fought against it: ³⁷And they took it, and smote it with the edge of the sword, and the king thereof, and all the cities thereof, and all the souls that *were* therein; he left none remaining, according to all that he had done to Eglon; but destroyed it utterly, and all the souls that *were* therein. ³⁸And Joshua returned, and all Israel with him, to Debir; and fought against it: ³⁹And he took

it, and the king thereof, and all the cities thereof; and they smote them with the edge of the sword, and utterly destroyed all the souls that *were* therein; he left none remaining: as he had done to Hebron, so he did to Debir, and to the king thereof; as he had done also to Libnah, and to her king. ⁴⁰So Joshua smote all the country of the hills, and of the south, and of the vale, and of the springs, and all their kings: he left none remaining, but utterly destroyed all that breathed, as the LORD God of Israel commanded. ⁴¹And Joshua smote them from Kadeshbarnea even unto Gaza, and all the country of Goshen, even unto Gibeon. ⁴²And all these kings and their land did Joshua take at one time, because the LORD God of Israel fought for Israel. ⁴³And Joshua returned, and all Israel with him, unto the camp to Gilgal.

11

¹And it came to pass, when Jabin king of Hazor had heard *those things*, that he sent to Jobab king of Madon, and to the king of Shimron, and to the king of Achshaph, ²And to the kings that *were* on the north of the mountains, and of the plains south of Chinneroth, and in the valley, and in the borders of Dor on the west, ³*And to* the Canaanite on the east and on the west, and *to* the Amorite, and the Hittite, and the Perizzite, and the Jebusite in the mountains, and *to* the Hivite under Hermon in the land of Mizpeh. ⁴And they went out, they and all their hosts with them, much people, even as the sand that *is* upon the sea shore in multitude, with horses and chariots very many. ⁵And when all these kings were met together, they

came and pitched together at the waters of Merom, to fight against Israel. [6]And the LORD said unto Joshua, Be not afraid because of them: for to morrow about this time will I deliver them up all slain before Israel: thou shalt hough their horses, and burn their chariots with fire. [7]So Joshua came, and all the people of war with him, against them by the waters of Merom suddenly; and they fell upon them. [8]And the LORD delivered them into the hand of Israel, who smote them, and chased them unto great Zidon[a], and unto Misrephothmaim, and unto the valley of Mizpeh eastward; and they smote them, until they left them none remaining. [9]And Joshua did unto them as the LORD bade him: he houghed their horses, and burnt their chariots with fire.

[10]And Joshua at that time turned back, and took Hazor, and smote the king thereof with the sword: for Hazor beforetime was the head of all those kingdoms. [11]And they smote all the souls that *were* therein with the edge of the sword, utterly destroying *them*: there was not any left to breathe: and he burnt Hazor with fire. [12]And all the cities of those kings, and all the kings of them, did Joshua take, and smote them with the edge of the sword, *and* he utterly destroyed them, as Moses the servant of the LORD commanded. [13]But *as for* the cities that stood still in their strength, Israel burned none of them, save Hazor only; *that* did Joshua burn. [14]And all the spoil of these cities, and

the cattle, the children of Israel took for a prey unto themselves; but every man they smote with the edge of the sword, until they had destroyed them, neither left they any to breathe.

[15]As the LORD commanded Moses his servant, so did Moses command Joshua, and so did Joshua; he left[b] nothing undone of all that the LORD commanded Moses. [16]So Joshua took all that land, the hills, and all the south country, and all the land of Goshen, and the valley, and the plain, and the mountain of Israel, and the valley of the same; [17]*Even* from the mount[c] Halak, that goeth up to Seir, even unto Baalgad in the valley of Lebanon under mount Hermon: and all their kings he took, and smote them, and slew them. [18]Joshua made war a long time with all those kings. [19]There was not a city that made peace with the children of Israel, save the Hivites the inhabitants of Gibeon: all *other* they took in battle. [20]For it was of the LORD

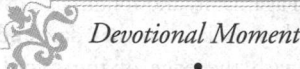

Devotional Moment

Long Haul

11:15 Joshua did *everything* God asked. Don't think that it was easy—Joshua had a hard life. Yet he was faithful to God's way. Parenting is very difficult work also. Parents can easily feel intimidated by the challenge, whether because of continual exhaustion, sickness, poor schools, endless questions, challenge to authority, or whatever. You can persevere by asking God each day for strength to stay in the battle. With God's help, it *is* possible to keep going. Difficult, yes. But certainly not impossible.

---

[a] great Zidon: or, Zidonrabbah
[b] left . . . : Heb. removed nothing
[c] the mount . . . : or, the smooth mountain

Devotional Moment
•
Spiritual Growth

11:18 Joshua did not conquer Canaan in a day. He was at it for seven years and more—struggling, learning, growing, trying, and praying. Spiritual growth is a process, too. We do not conquer all our Jerichos in a day. We learn to know God through years of daily prayer and with small steps of trust that add up to Joshua-like faith. Your life is God's ongoing project. Give growth a chance.

to harden their hearts, that they should come against Israel in battle, that he might destroy them utterly, *and* that they might have no favour, but that he might destroy them, as the LORD commanded Moses. ²¹And at that time came Joshua, and cut off the Anakims from the mountains, from Hebron, from Debir, from Anab, and from all the mountains of Judah, and from all the mountains of Israel: Joshua destroyed them utterly with their cities. ²²There was none of the Anakims left in the land of the children of Israel: only in Gaza, in Gath, and in Ashdod, there remained. ²³So Joshua took the whole land, according to all that the LORD said unto Moses; and Joshua gave it for an inheritance unto Israel according to their divisions by their tribes. And the land rested from war.

12

¹Now these *are* the kings of the land, which the children of Israel smote, and possessed their land on the other side Jordan toward the rising of the sun, from the river Arnon unto mount Hermon, and all the plain on the east: ²Sihon king of the Amorites, who dwelt in Heshbon, *and* ruled from Aroer, which *is* upon the bank of the river Arnon, and from the middle of the river, and from half Gilead, even unto the river Jabbok, *which is* the border of the children of Ammon; ³And from the plain to the sea of Chinneroth on the east, and unto the sea of the plain, *even* the salt sea on the east, the way to Bethjeshimoth; and from the south^a, under Ashdothpisgah: ⁴And the coast of Og king of Bashan, *which was* of the remnant of the giants, that dwelt at Ashtaroth and at Edrei, ⁵And reigned in mount Hermon, and in Salcah, and in all Bashan, unto the border of the Geshurites and the Maachathites, and half Gilead, the border of Sihon king of Heshbon. ⁶Them did Moses the servant of the LORD and the children of Israel smite: and Moses the servant of the LORD gave it *for* a possession unto the Reubenites, and the Gadites, and the half tribe of Manasseh. ⁷And these *are* the kings of the country which Joshua and the children of Israel smote on this side Jordan on the west, from Baalgad in the valley of Lebanon even unto the mount Halak, that goeth up to Seir; which Joshua gave unto the tribes of Israel *for* a possession according to their divisions; ⁸In the mountains, and in the valleys, and in the plains, and in the springs, and in the wilderness, and in the south country; the Hittites, the Amorites, and the Canaanites, the Perizzites, the Hivites, and the Jebusites: ⁹The king of Jericho, one; the

---

^a the south: or, Teman

king of Ai, which *is* beside Bethel, one; ¹⁰The king of Jerusalem, one; the king of Hebron, one; ¹¹The king of Jarmuth, one; the king of Lachish, one; ¹²The king of Eglon, one; the king of Gezer, one; ¹³The king of Debir, one; the king of Geder, one; ¹⁴The king of Hormah, one; the king of Arad, one; ¹⁵The king of Libnah, one; the king of Adullam, one; ¹⁶The king of Makkedah, one; the king of Bethel, one; ¹⁷The king of Tappuah, one; the king of Hepher, one; ¹⁸The king of Aphek, one; the king of Lasharon^b, one; ¹⁹The king of Madon, one; the king of Hazor, one; ²⁰The king of Shimronmeron, one; the king of Achshaph, one; ²¹The king of Taanach, one; the king of Megiddo, one; ²²The king of Kedesh, one; the king of Jokneam of Carmel, one; ²³The king of Dor in the coast of Dor, one; the king of the nations of Gilgal, one; ²⁴The king of Tirzah, one: all the kings thirty and one.

13

¹Now Joshua was old *and* stricken in years; and the LORD said unto him, Thou art old *and* stricken in years, and there remaineth yet very much land to be possessed. ²This *is* the land that yet remaineth: all the borders of the Philistines, and all Geshuri, ³From Sihor, which *is* before Egypt, even unto the borders of Ekron northward, *which* is counted to the Canaanite: five lords of the Philistines; the Gazathites, and the Ashdothites, the Eshkalonites, the Gittites, and the Ekronites; also the Avites: ⁴From the south, all the land of

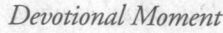

Devotional Moment

•

Aging Gracefully

13:1 God gave Joshua quite an agenda for someone approaching retirement age. But no worry. Joshua knew the source of his energy: the power of God. Older women and men, especially grandmothers and grandfathers, have important responsibilities, maybe even (as Joshua had) special missions suited just for them. Growing old doesn't have to mean becoming useless. Keep doing what God has given you to do in service to him, whether that be full-time ministry, teaching Sunday school, or merely talking about God as you play with children. God provides us with all we need to do his work.

the Canaanites, and Mearah^a that *is* beside the Sidonians, unto Aphek, to the borders of the Amorites: ⁵And the land of the Giblites, and all Lebanon, toward the sunrising, from Baalgad under mount Hermon unto the entering into Hamath. ⁶All the inhabitants of the hill country from Lebanon unto Misrephothmaim, *and* all the Sidonians, them will I drive out from before the children of Israel: only divide thou it by lot unto the Israelites for an inheritance, as I have commanded thee.

⁷Now therefore divide this land for an inheritance unto the nine tribes, and the half tribe of Manasseh, ⁸With whom the Reubenites and the Gadites have received their inheritance, which Moses gave them, beyond Jordan eastward, *even* as Moses the servant of the LORD gave them; ⁹From Aroer, that *is* upon the bank of the river Arnon, and the city that *is* in the midst of the river, and all the plain of Medeba unto Dibon; ¹⁰And

---

^b Lasharon: or, Sharon
^a Mearah: or, the cave

all the cities of Sihon king of the Amorites, which reigned in Heshbon, unto the border of the children of Ammon; ¹¹And Gilead, and the border of the Geshurites and Maachathites, and all mount Hermon, and all Bashan unto Salcah; ¹²All the kingdom of Og in Bashan, which reigned in Ashtaroth and in Edrei, who remained of the remnant of the giants: for these did Moses smite, and cast them out. ¹³Nevertheless the children of Israel expelled not the Geshurites, nor the Maachathites: but the Geshurites and the Maachathites dwell among the Israelites until this day. ¹⁴Only unto the tribe of Levi he gave none inheritance; the sacrifices of the LORD God of Israel made by fire *are* their inheritance, as he said unto them. ¹⁵And Moses gave unto the tribe of the children of Reuben *inheritance* according to their families. ¹⁶And their coast was from Aroer, that *is* on the bank of the river Arnon, and the city that *is* in the midst of the river, and all the plain by Medeba; ¹⁷Heshbon, and all her cities that *are* in the plain; Dibon, and Bamothbaal^b, and Bethbaalmeon, ¹⁸And Jahazah, and Kedemoth, and Mephaath, ¹⁹And Kirjathaim, and Sibmah, and Zarethshahar in the mount of the valley, ²⁰And Bethpeor, and Ashdothpisgah^c, and Bethjeshimoth, ²¹And all the cities of the plain, and all the kingdom of Sihon king of the Amorites, which reigned in Heshbon, whom Moses smote with the princes of Midian, Evi, and Rekem, and Zur, and Hur, and Reba, *which were* dukes of Sihon, dwelling in the country.

²²Balaam also the son of Beor, the soothsayer^d, did the children of Israel slay with the sword among them that were slain by them. ²³And the border of the children of Reuben was Jordan, and the border *thereof.* This *was* the inheritance of the children of Reuben after their families, the cities and the villages thereof. ²⁴And Moses gave *inheritance* unto the tribe of Gad, *even* unto the children of Gad according to their families. ²⁵And their coast was Jazer, and all the cities of Gilead, and half the land of the children of Ammon, unto Aroer that *is* before Rabbah; ²⁶And from Heshbon unto Ramathmizpeh, and Betonim; and from Mahanaim unto the border of Debir; ²⁷And in the valley, Betharam, and Bethnimrah, and Succoth, and Zaphon, the rest of the kingdom of Sihon king of Heshbon, Jordan and *his* border, *even* unto the edge of the sea of Chinnereth on the other side Jordan eastward. ²⁸This *is* the inheritance of the children of Gad after their families, the cities, and their villages. ²⁹And Moses gave *inheritance* unto the half tribe of Manasseh: and *this* was *the possession* of the half tribe of the children of Manasseh by their families. ³⁰And their coast was from Mahanaim, all Bashan, all the kingdom of Og king of Bashan, and all the towns of Jair, which *are* in Bashan, threescore cities: ³¹And half Gilead, and Ashtaroth, and Edrei, cities of the kingdom of Og in Bashan, *were pertaining* unto the children of Machir the son of Manasseh, *even* to the one half of the children of Machir by their families. ³²These *are the*

---

^b Bamothbaal . . . : or, the high places of Baal, and house of Baalmeon
^c Ashdothpisgah: or, springs of Pisgah, or, the hill
^d soothsayer: or, diviner

countries which Moses did distribute for inheritance in the plains of Moab, on the other side Jordan, by Jericho, eastward. ³³But unto the tribe of Levi Moses gave not *any* inheritance: the LORD God of Israel *was* their inheritance, as he said unto them.

14

¹And these *are the countries* which the children of Israel inherited in the land of Canaan, which Eleazar the priest, and Joshua the son of Nun, and the heads of the fathers of the tribes of the children of Israel, distributed for inheritance to them. ²By lot *was* their inheritance, as the LORD commanded by the hand of Moses, for the nine tribes, and *for* the half tribe. ³For Moses had given the inheritance of two tribes and an half tribe on the other side Jordan: but unto the Levites he gave none inheritance among them. ⁴For the children of Joseph were two tribes, Manasseh and Ephraim: therefore they gave no part unto the Levites in the land, save cities to dwell *in,* with their suburbs for their cattle and for their substance. ⁵As the LORD commanded Moses, so the children of Israel did, and they divided the land.

⁶Then the children of Judah came unto Joshua in Gilgal: and Caleb the son of Jephunneh the Kenezite said unto him, Thou knowest the thing that the LORD said unto Moses the man of God concerning me and thee in Kadeshbarnea. ⁷Forty years old *was* I when Moses the servant of the LORD sent me from Kadeshbarnea to espy out the land; and I brought him word again as *it was*

in mine heart. ⁸Nevertheless my brethren that went up with me made the heart of the people melt: but I wholly followed the LORD my God. ⁹And Moses sware on that day, saying, Surely the land whereon thy feet have trodden shall be thine inheritance, and thy children's for ever, because thou hast wholly followed the LORD my God. ¹⁰And now, behold, the LORD hath kept me alive, as he said, these forty and five years, even since the LORD spake this word unto Moses, while *the children of* Israel wandered[a] in the wilderness: and now, lo, I *am* this day fourscore and five years old. ¹¹As yet I *am as* strong this day as *I was* in the day that Moses sent me: as my strength *was* then, even so *is* my strength now, for war, both to go out, and to come in. ¹²Now therefore give me this mountain, whereof the LORD spake in that day; for thou heardest in that day how the Anakims *were* there, and *that* the cities *were* great *and* fenced: if so be the LORD *will be* with me, then I shall be able to drive them out, as the LORD said. ¹³And Joshua blessed him, and gave unto Caleb the son of Jephunneh Hebron for an inheritance. ¹⁴Hebron therefore became the inheritance of Caleb the son of Jephunneh the Kenezite unto this day, because that he wholly followed the LORD God of Israel. ¹⁵And the name of Hebron before *was* Kirjatharba; *which Arba was* a great man among the Anakims. And the land had rest from war.

15

¹*This* then was the lot of the tribe of the children of Judah by their families; *even*

---

[a] wandered: Heb. walked

to the border of Edom the wilderness of Zin southward *was* the uttermost part of the south coast. ²And their south border was from the shore of the salt sea, from the bay* that looketh southward: ³And it went out to the south side to Maalehacrabbim, and passed along to Zin, and ascended up on the south side unto Kadeshbarnea, and passed along to Hezron, and went up to Adar, and fetched a compass to Karkaa: ⁴*From thence* it passed toward Azmon, and went out unto the river of Egypt; and the goings out of that coast were at the sea: this shall be your south coast. ⁵And the east border *was* the salt sea, *even* unto the end of Jordan. And *their* border in the north quarter *was* from the bay of the sea at the uttermost part of Jordan: ⁶And the border went up to Bethhogla, and passed along by the north of Betharabah; and the border went up to the stone of Bohan the son of Reuben: ⁷And the border went up toward Debir from the valley of Achor, and so northward, looking toward Gilgal, that *is* before the going up to Adummim, which *is* on the south side of the river: and the border passed toward the waters of Enshemesh, and the goings out thereof were at Enrogel: ⁸And the border went up by the valley of the son of Hinnom unto the south side of the Jebusite; the same *is* Jerusalem: and the border went up to the top of the mountain that *lieth* before the valley of Hinnom westward, which *is* at the end of the valley of the giants northward: ⁹And the border was drawn from the top of the hill unto the fountain of the water of Nephtoah, and went out to the cities of mount

Ephron; and the border was drawn to Baalah, which *is* Kirjathjearim: ¹⁰And the border compassed from Baalah westward unto mount Seir, and passed along unto the side of mount Jearim, which *is* Chesalon, on the north side, and went down to Bethshemesh, and passed on to Timnah: ¹¹And the border went out unto the side of Ekron northward: and the border was drawn to Shicron, and passed along to mount Baalah, and went out unto Jabneel; and the goings out of the border were at the sea. ¹²And the west border *was* to the great sea, and the coast *thereof.* This *is* the coast of the children of Judah round about according to their families.

¹³And unto Caleb the son of Jephunneh he gave a part among the children of Judah, according to the commandment of the LORD to Joshua, *even* the city* of Arba the father of Anak, which *city is* Hebron. ¹⁴And Caleb drove thence the three sons of Anak, Sheshai, and Ahiman, and Talmai, the children of Anak. ¹⁵And he went up thence to the inhabitants of Debir: and the name of Debir before *was* Kirjathsepher. ¹⁶And Caleb said, He that smiteth Kirjathsepher, and taketh it, to him will I give Achsah my daughter to wife. ¹⁷And Othniel the son of Kenaz, the brother of Caleb, took it: and he gave him Achsah his daughter to wife. ¹⁸And it came to pass, as she came *unto him,* that she moved him to ask of her father a field: and she lighted off *her* ass; and Caleb said unto her, What wouldest thou? ¹⁹Who answered, Give me a blessing; for thou hast given me a

---

ᵃ bay: Heb. tongue
ᵇ the city . . . : or, Kirjatharba

south land; give me also springs of water. And he gave her the upper springs, and the nether springs.

²⁰This *is* the inheritance of the tribe of the children of Judah according to their families. ²¹And the uttermost cities of the tribe of the children of Judah toward the coast of Edom southward were Kabzeel, and Eder, and Jagur, ²²And Kinah, and Dimonah, and Adadah, ²³And Kedesh, and Hazor, and Ithnan, ²⁴Ziph, and Telem, and Bealoth, ²⁵And Hazor, Hadattah, and Kerioth, *and* Hezron, which *is* Hazor, ²⁶Amam, and Shema, and Moladah, ²⁷And Hazargaddah, and Heshmon, and Bethpalet, ²⁸And Hazarshual, and Beersheba, and Bizjothjah, ²⁹Baalah, and Iim, and Azem, ³⁰And Eltolad, and Chesil, and Hormah, ³¹And Ziklag, and Madmannah, and Sansannah, ³²And Lebaoth, and Shilhim, and Ain, and Rimmon: all the cities *are* twenty and nine, with their villages: ³³*And* in the valley, Eshtaol, and Zoreah, and Ashnah, ³⁴And Zanoah, and Engannim, Tappuah, and Enam, ³⁵Jarmuth, and Adullam, Socoh, and Azekah, ³⁶And Sharaim, and Adithaim, and Gederah, and Gederothaimᶜ; fourteen cities with their villages: ³⁷Zenan, and Hadashah, and Migdalgad, ³⁸And Dilean, and Mizpeh, and Joktheel, ³⁹Lachish, and Bozkath, and Eglon, ⁴⁰And Cabbon, and Lahmam, and Kithlish, ⁴¹And Gederoth, Bethdagon, and Naamah, and Makkedah; sixteen cities with their villages: ⁴²Libnah, and Ether, and Ashan, ⁴³And Jiphtah, and Ashnah, and Nezib, ⁴⁴And Keilah, and Achzib, and Mareshah; nine cities with their vil-

lages: ⁴⁵Ekron, with her towns and her villages: ⁴⁶From Ekron even unto the sea, all that *lay* nearᵈ Ashdod, with their villages: ⁴⁷Ashdod with her towns and her villages, Gaza with her towns and her villages, unto the river of Egypt, and the great sea, and the border *thereof*: ⁴⁸And in the mountains, Shamir, and Jattir, and Socoh, ⁴⁹And Dannah, and Kirjathsannah, which *is* Debir, ⁵⁰And Anab, and Eshtemoh, and Anim, ⁵¹And Goshen, and Holon, and Giloh; eleven cities with their villages: ⁵²Arab, and Dumah, and Eshean, ⁵³And Janumᵉ, and Bethtappuah, and Aphekah, ⁵⁴And Humtah, and Kirjatharba, which *is* Hebron, and Zior; nine cities with their villages: ⁵⁵Maon, Carmel, and Ziph, and Juttah, ⁵⁶And Jezreel, and Jokdeam, and Zanoah, ⁵⁷Cain, Gibeah, and Timnah; ten cities with their villages: ⁵⁸Halhul, Bethzur, and Gedor, ⁵⁹And Maarath, and Bethanoth, and Eltekon; six cities with their villages: ⁶⁰Kirjathbaal, which *is* Kirjathjearim, and Rabbah; two cities with their villages: ⁶¹In the wilderness, Betharabah, Middin, and Secacah, ⁶²And Nibshan, and the city of Salt, and Engedi; six cities with their villages. ⁶³As for the Jebusites the inhabitants of Jerusalem, the children of Judah could not drive them out: but the Jebusites dwell with the children of Judah at Jerusalem unto this day.

16

¹And the lot of the children of Joseph fellᵃ from Jordan by Jericho, unto the water of Jericho on the east, to the wilderness that goeth up from Jericho

---

ᶜ and Gederothaim: or, or Gederothaim
ᵈ near: Heb. by the place of
ᵉ Janum: or, Janus
ᵃ fell: Heb. went forth

throughout mount Bethel, ²And goeth out from Bethel to Luz, and passeth along unto the borders of Archi to Ataroth, ³And goeth down westward to the coast of Japhleti, unto the coast of Bethhoron the nether, and to Gezer: and the goings out thereof are at the sea. ⁴So the children of Joseph, Manasseh and Ephraim, took their inheritance.

⁵And the border of the children of Ephraim according to their families was *thus*: even the border of their inheritance on the east side was Atarothaddar, unto Bethhoron the upper; ⁶And the border went out toward the sea to Michmethah on the north side; and the border went about eastward unto Taanathshiloh, and passed by it on the east to Janohah; ⁷And it went down from Janohah to Ataroth, and to Naarath, and came to Jericho, and went out at Jordan. ⁸The border went out from Tappuah westward unto the river Kanah; and the goings out thereof were at the sea. This *is* the inheritance of the tribe of the children of Ephraim by their families. ⁹And the separate cities for the children of Ephraim *were* among the inheritance of the children of Manasseh, all the cities with their villages. ¹⁰And they drave not out the Canaanites that dwelt in Gezer: but the Canaanites dwell among the Ephraimites unto this day, and serve under tribute.

17

¹There was also a lot for the tribe of Manasseh; for he *was* the firstborn of Joseph; *to wit*, for Machir the firstborn

of Manasseh, the father of Gilead: because he was a man of war, therefore he had Gilead and Bashan. ²There was also *a lot* for the rest of the children of Manasseh by their families; for the children of Abiezer[a], and for the children of Helek, and for the children of Asriel, and for the children of Shechem, and for the children of Hepher, and for the children of Shemida: these *were* the male children of Manasseh the son of Joseph by their families. ³But Zelophehad, the son of Hepher, the son of Gilead, the son of Machir, the son of Manasseh, had no sons, but daughters: and these *are* the names of his daughters, Mahlah, and Noah, Hoglah, Milcah, and Tirzah. ⁴And they came near before Eleazar the priest, and before Joshua the son of Nun, and before the princes, saying, The LORD commanded Moses to give us an inheritance among our brethren. Therefore according to the commandment of the LORD he gave them an inheritance among the brethren of their father. ⁵And there fell ten portions to Manasseh, beside the land of Gilead and Bashan, which *were* on the other side Jordan; ⁶Because the daughters of Manasseh had an inheritance among his sons: and the rest of Manasseh's sons had the land of Gilead.

⁷And the coast of Manasseh was from Asher to Michmethah, that *lieth* before Shechem; and the border went along on the right hand unto the inhabitants of Entappuah. ⁸*Now* Manasseh had the land of Tappuah: but Tappuah on the border of Manasseh *belonged* to the children of Ephraim;

ᵃ Abiezer: also called, Jeezer

⁹And the coast descended unto the river Kanahᵇ, southward of the river: these cities of Ephraim *are* among the cities of Manasseh: the coast of Manasseh also *was* on the north side of the river, and the outgoings of it were at the sea: ¹⁰Southward *it was* Ephraim's, and northward *it was* Manasseh's, and the sea is his border; and they met together in Asher on the north, and in Issachar on the east. ¹¹And Manasseh had in Issachar and in Asher Bethshean and her towns, and Ibleam and her towns, and the inhabitants of Dor and her towns, and the inhabitants of Endor and her towns, and the inhabitants of Taanach and her towns, and the inhabitants of Megiddo and her towns, *even* three countries. ¹²Yet the children of Manasseh could not drive out *the inhabitants of* those cities; but the Canaanites would dwell in that land. ¹³Yet it came to pass, when the children of Israel were waxen strong, that they put the Canaanites to tribute; but did not utterly drive them out.

¹⁴And the children of Joseph spake unto Joshua, saying, Why hast thou given me *but* one lot and one portion to inherit, seeing I *am* a great people, forasmuch as the LORD hath blessed me hitherto? ¹⁵And Joshua answered them, If thou *be* a great people, *then* get thee up to the wood *country*, and cut down for thyself there in the land of the Perizzites and of the giantsᶜ, if mount Ephraim be too narrow for thee. ¹⁶And the children of Joseph said, The hill is not enough for us: and all the Canaanites that dwell in the land of the valley have chariots of iron, *both they* who *are* of Bethshean and her towns, and *they* who *are* of the valley of Jezreel. ¹⁷And Joshua spake unto the house of Joseph, *even* to Ephraim and to Manasseh, saying, Thou *art* a great people, and hast great power: thou shalt not have one lot *only*: ¹⁸But the mountain shall be thine; for it *is* a wood, and thou shalt cut it down: and the outgoings of it shall be thine: for thou shalt drive out the Canaanites, though they have iron chariots, *and* though they *be* strong.

18

¹And the whole congregation of the children of Israel assembled together at Shiloh, and set up the tabernacle of the congregation there. And the land was subdued before them.

²And there remained among the children of Israel seven tribes, which had not yet received their inheritance. ³And Joshua said unto the children of Israel, How long *are* ye slack to go to possess the land, which the LORD God of your fathers hath given you? ⁴Give out from among you three men for *each* tribe: and I will send them, and they shall rise, and go through the land, and describe it according to the inheritance of them; and they shall come *again* to me. ⁵And they shall divide it into seven parts: Judah shall abide in their coast on the south, and the house of Joseph shall abide in their coasts on the north. ⁶Ye shall therefore describe the land *into* seven parts, and bring *the description* hither to me, that I may cast lots for you here before the LORD our

---

ᵇ river Kanah: or, brook of reeds
ᶜ giants: or, Rephaims

Devotional Moment

•

Needless Delay

18:3-6 Joshua's question had a bite to it. Listening between the lines, the tribal leaders might have heard, "Time's up, lazybones. No more excuses, no more delays, no more procrastination. Get moving, now!" Christians undertaking big projects do well to prepare, to plan, to pray; rushing headlong into projects can be a cover for carelessness. But there comes a time for action. Sometimes leaders of families need to hear a "get moving" order, and sometimes they need to give one. Show your children the action side of life by setting an example of *doing* God's will, not just talking about it.

God. ⁷But the Levites have no part among you; for the priesthood of the LORD *is* their inheritance: and Gad, and Reuben, and half the tribe of Manasseh, have received their inheritance beyond Jordan on the east, which Moses the servant of the LORD gave them. ⁸And the men arose, and went away: and Joshua charged them that went to describe the land, saying, Go and walk through the land, and describe it, and come again to me, that I may here cast lots for you before the LORD in Shiloh. ⁹And the men went and passed through the land, and described it by cities into seven parts in a book, and came *again* to Joshua to the host at Shiloh. ¹⁰And Joshua cast lots for them in Shiloh before the LORD: and there Joshua divided the land unto the children of Israel according to their divisions.

¹¹And the lot of the tribe of the children of Benjamin came up according to their families: and the coast of their lot came forth between the children of Judah and the children of Joseph. ¹²And their border on the north side was from Jordan; and the border went up to the side of Jericho on the north side, and went up through the mountains westward; and the goings out thereof were at the wilderness of Bethaven. ¹³And the border went over from thence toward Luz, to the side of Luz, which *is* Bethel, southward; and the border descended to Atarothadar, near the hill that *lieth* on the south side of the nether Bethhoron. ¹⁴And the border was drawn *thence*, and compassed the corner of the sea southward, from the hill that *lieth* before Bethhoron southward; and the goings out thereof were at Kirjathbaal, which *is* Kirjathjearim, a city of the children of Judah: this *was* the west quarter. ¹⁵And the south quarter *was* from the end of Kirjathjearim, and the border went out on the west, and went out to the well of waters of Nephtoah: ¹⁶And the border came down to the end of the mountain that *lieth* before the valley of the son of Hinnom, *and* which *is* in the valley of the giants on the north, and descended to the valley of Hinnom, to the side of Jebusi on the south, and descended to Enrogel, ¹⁷And was drawn from the north, and went forth to Enshemesh, and went forth toward Geliloth, which *is* over against the going up of Adummim, and descended to the stone of Bohan the son of Reuben, ¹⁸And passed along toward the side over against Arabahª northward, and went down unto Arabah: ¹⁹And the border passed along to the side of Bethhoglah north-

---

ª Arabah: or, the plain

ward: and the outgoings of the border were at the north bay[b] of the salt sea at the south end of Jordan: this *was* the south coast. ²⁰And Jordan was the border of it on the east side. This *was* the inheritance of the children of Benjamin, by the coasts thereof round about, according to their families. ²¹Now the cities of the tribe of the children of Benjamin according to their families were Jericho, and Bethhoglah, and the valley of Keziz, ²²And Betharabah, and Zemaraim, and Bethel, ²³And Avim, and Parah, and Ophrah, ²⁴And Chepharhaammonai, and Ophni, and Gaba; twelve cities with their villages: ²⁵Gibeon, and Ramah, and Beeroth, ²⁶And Mizpeh, and Chephirah, and Mozah, ²⁷And Rekem, and Irpeel, and Taralah, ²⁸And Zelah, Eleph, and Jebusi, which *is* Jerusalem, Gibeath, *and* Kirjath; fourteen cities with their villages. This *is* the inheritance of the children of Benjamin according to their families.

19

¹And the second lot came forth to Simeon, *even* for the tribe of the children of Simeon according to their families: and their inheritance was within the inheritance of the children of Judah. ²And they had in their inheritance Beersheba, or Sheba, and Moladah, ³And Hazarshual, and Balah, and Azem, ⁴And Eltolad, and Bethul, and Hormah, ⁵And Ziklag, and Bethmarcaboth, and Hazarsusah, ⁶And Bethlebaoth, and Sharuhen; thirteen cities and their villages: ⁷Ain, Remmon, and Ether, and Ashan; four cities and their villages: ⁸And all the villages that *were* round about these cities to Baalathbeer, Ramath of the south. This *is* the inheritance of the tribe of the children of Simeon according to their families. ⁹Out of the portion of the children of Judah *was* the inheritance of the children of Simeon: for the part of the children of Judah was too much for them: therefore the children of Simeon had their inheritance within the inheritance of them.

¹⁰And the third lot came up for the children of Zebulun according to their families: and the border of their inheritance was unto Sarid: ¹¹And their border went up toward the sea, and Maralah, and reached to Dabbasheth, and reached to the river that *is* before Jokneam; ¹²And turned from Sarid eastward toward the sunrising unto the border of Chislothtabor, and then goeth out to Daberath, and goeth up to Japhia, ¹³And from thence passeth on along on the east to Gittahhepher, to Ittahkazin, and goeth out to Remmonmethoar to Neah; ¹⁴And the border compasseth it on the north side to Hannathon: and the outgoings thereof are in the valley of Jiphthahel: ¹⁵And Kattath, and Nahallal, and Shimron, and Idalah, and Bethlehem: twelve cities with their villages. ¹⁶This *is* the inheritance of the children of Zebulun according to their families, these cities with their villages.

¹⁷*And* the fourth lot came out to Issachar, for the children of Issachar according to their families. ¹⁸And their border was toward Jezreel, and Chesulloth, and Shunem, ¹⁹And Hapharaim,

---

and Shion, and Anaharath, ²⁰And Rabbith, and Kishion, and Abez, ²¹And Remeth, and Engannim, and Enhaddah, and Bethpazzez; ²²And the coast reacheth to Tabor, and Shahazimah, and Bethshemesh; and the outgoings of their border were at Jordan: sixteen cities with their villages. ²³This *is* the inheritance of the tribe of the children of Issachar according to their families, the cities and their villages.

²⁴And the fifth lot came out for the tribe of the children of Asher according to their families. ²⁵And their border was Helkath, and Hali, and Beten, and Achshaph, ²⁶And Alammelech, and Amad, and Misheal; and reacheth to Carmel westward, and to Shihorlibnath; ²⁷And turneth toward the sunrising to Bethdagon, and reacheth to Zebulun, and to the valley of Jiphthahel toward the north side of Bethemek, and Neiel, and goeth out to Cabul on the left hand, ²⁸And Hebron, and Rehob, and Hammon, and Kanah, *even* unto great Zidon; ²⁹And *then* the coast turneth to Ramah, and to the strong city Tyre[a]; and the coast turneth to Hosah; and the outgoings thereof are at the sea from the coast to Achzib: ³⁰Ummah also, and Aphek, and Rehob: twenty and two cities with their villages. ³¹This *is* the inheritance of the tribe of the children of Asher according to their families, these cities with their villages.

³²The sixth lot came out to the children of Naphtali, *even* for the children of Naphtali according to their families. ³³And their coast was from Heleph, from Allon to Zaanannim, and Adami,

Nekeb, and Jabneel, unto Lakum; and the outgoings thereof were at Jordan: ³⁴And *then* the coast turneth westward to Aznothtabor, and goeth out from thence to Hukkok, and reacheth to Zebulun on the south side, and reacheth to Asher on the west side, and to Judah upon Jordan toward the sunrising. ³⁵And the fenced cities *are* Ziddim, Zer, and Hammath, Rakkath, and Chinnereth, ³⁶And Adamah, and Ramah, and Hazor, ³⁷And Kedesh, and Edrei, and Enhazor, ³⁸And Iron, and Migdalel, Horem, and Bethanath, and Bethshemesh; nineteen cities with their villages. ³⁹This *is* the inheritance of the tribe of the children of Naphtali according to their families, the cities and their villages.

⁴⁰*And* the seventh lot came out for the tribe of the children of Dan according to their families. ⁴¹And the coast of their inheritance was Zorah, and Eshtaol, and Irshemesh, ⁴²And Shaalabbin, and Ajalon, and Jethlah, ⁴³And Elon, and Thimnathah, and Ekron, ⁴⁴And Eltekeh, and Gibbethon, and Baalath, ⁴⁵And Jehud, and Beneberak, and Gathrimmon, ⁴⁶And Mejarkon, and Rakkon, with the border before[b] Japho. ⁴⁷And the coast of the children of Dan went out *too little* for them: therefore the children of Dan went up to fight against Leshem, and took it, and smote it with the edge of the sword, and possessed it, and dwelt therein, and called Leshem, Dan, after the name of Dan their father. ⁴⁸This *is* the inheritance of the tribe of the children of Dan according to their families, these cities with their villages.

⁴⁹When they had made an end of

---

[a] Tyre: Heb. Tzor
[b] before: or, over against

377

dividing the land for inheritance by their coasts, the children of Israel gave an inheritance to Joshua the son of Nun among them: ⁵⁰According to the word of the LORD they gave him the city which he asked, *even* Timnathserah in mount Ephraim: and he built the city, and dwelt therein. ⁵¹These *are* the inheritances, which Eleazar the priest, and Joshua the son of Nun, and the heads of the fathers of the tribes of the children of Israel, divided for an inheritance by lot in Shiloh before the LORD, at the door of the tabernacle of the congregation. So they made an end of dividing the country.

20

¹The LORD also spake unto Joshua, saying, ²Speak to the children of Israel, saying, Appoint out for you cities of refuge, whereof I spake unto you by the hand of Moses: ³That the slayer that killeth *any* person unawares *and* unwittingly may flee thither: and they shall be your refuge from the avenger of blood. ⁴And when he that doth flee unto one of those cities shall stand at the entering of the gate of the city, and shall declare his cause in the ears of the elders of that city, they shall take him into the city unto them, and give him a place, that he may dwell among them. ⁵And if the avenger of blood pursue after him, then they shall not deliver the slayer up into his hand; because he smote his neighbour unwittingly, and hated him not beforetime. ⁶And he shall dwell in that city, until he stand before the congregation for judgment, *and* until the death of the high priest

that shall be in those days: then shall the slayer return, and come unto his own city, and unto his own house, unto the city from whence he fled.

⁷And they appointed[a] Kedesh in Galilee in mount Naphtali, and Shechem in mount Ephraim, and Kirjatharba, which *is* Hebron, in the mountain of Judah. ⁸And on the other side Jordan by Jericho eastward, they assigned Bezer in the wilderness upon the plain out of the tribe of Reuben, and Ramoth in Gilead out of the tribe of Gad, and Golan in Bashan out of the tribe of Manasseh. ⁹These were the cities appointed for all the children of Israel, and for the stranger that sojourneth among them, that whosoever killeth *any* person at unawares might flee thither, and not die by the hand of the avenger of blood, until he stood before the congregation.

21

¹Then came near the heads of the fathers of the Levites unto Eleazar the priest, and unto Joshua the son of Nun, and unto the heads of the fathers of the tribes of the children of Israel; ²And they spake unto them at Shiloh in the land of Canaan, saying, The LORD commanded by the hand of Moses to give us cities to dwell in, with the suburbs thereof for our cattle. ³And the children of Israel gave unto the Levites out of their inheritance, at the commandment of the LORD, these cities and their suburbs. ⁴And the lot came out for the families of the Kohathites: and the children of Aaron the priest, *which were* of the Levites, had by lot out

---

ª appointed: Heb. sanctified

of the tribe of Judah, and out of the tribe of Simeon, and out of the tribe of Benjamin, thirteen cities. [5]And the rest of the children of Kohath *had* by lot out of the families of the tribe of Ephraim, and out of the tribe of Dan, and out of the half tribe of Manasseh, ten cities. [6]And the children of Gershon *had* by lot out of the families of the tribe of Issachar, and out of the tribe of Asher, and out of the tribe of Naphtali, and out of the half tribe of Manasseh in Bashan, thirteen cities. [7]The children of Merari by their families *had* out of the tribe of Reuben, and out of the tribe of Gad, and out of the tribe of Zebulun, twelve cities. [8]And the children of Israel gave by lot unto the Levites these cities with their suburbs, as the LORD commanded by the hand of Moses.

[9]And they gave out of the tribe of the children of Judah, and out of the tribe of the children of Simeon, these cities which are *here* mentioned[a] by name, [10]Which the children of Aaron, *being* of the families of the Kohathites, *who were* of the children of Levi, had: for theirs was the first lot. [11]And they gave them the city[b] of Arba the father of Anak, which *city is* Hebron, in the hill *country* of Judah, with the suburbs thereof round about it. [12]But the fields of the city, and the villages thereof, gave they to Caleb the son of Jephunneh for his possession. [13]Thus they gave to the children of Aaron the priest Hebron with her suburbs, *to be* a city of refuge for the slayer; and Libnah with her suburbs, [14]And Jattir with her suburbs, and Eshtemoa with her suburbs, [15]And Holon[c] with her suburbs, and Debir with her suburbs, [16]And Ain[d] with her suburbs, and Juttah with her suburbs, *and* Bethshemesh with her suburbs; nine cities out of those two tribes. [17]And out of the tribe of Benjamin, Gibeon with her suburbs, Geba[e] with her suburbs, [18]Anathoth with her suburbs, and Almon[f] with her suburbs; four cities. [19]All the cities of the children of Aaron, the priests, *were* thirteen cities with their suburbs. [20]And the families of the children of Kohath, the Levites which remained of the children of Kohath, even they had the cities of their lot out of the tribe of Ephraim. [21]For they gave them Shechem with her suburbs in mount Ephraim, *to be* a city of refuge for the slayer; and Gezer with her suburbs, [22]And Kibzaim with her suburbs, and Bethhoron with her suburbs; four cities. [23]And out of the tribe of Dan, Eltekeh with her suburbs, Gibbethon with her suburbs, [24]Aijalon with her suburbs, Gathrimmon with her suburbs; four cities. [25]And out of the half tribe of Manasseh, Tanach with her suburbs, and Gathrimmon with her suburbs; two cities. [26]All the cities *were* ten with their suburbs for the families of the children of Kohath that remained. [27]And unto the children of

---

[a] mentioned: Heb. called
[b] the city . . . : or, Kirjatharba
[c] Holon: also called, Hilen
[d] Ain: also called, Ashan
[e] Geba: also called, Gaba
[f] Almon: also called, Alemeth

Gershon, of the families of the Levites, out of the *other* half tribe of Manasseh *they gave* Golan in Bashan with her suburbs, *to be* a city of refuge for the slayer; and Beeshterah with her suburbs; two cities. ²⁸And out of the tribe of Issachar, Kishon with her suburbs, Dabareh with her suburbs, ²⁹Jarmuth with her suburbs, Engannim with her suburbs; four cities. ³⁰And out of the tribe of Asher, Mishal with her suburbs, Abdon with her suburbs, ³¹Helkath with her suburbs, and Rehob with her suburbs; four cities. ³²And out of the tribe of Naphtali, Kedesh in Galilee with her suburbs, *to be* a city of refuge for the slayer; and Hammothdor with her suburbs, and Kartan with her suburbs; three cities. ³³All the cities of the Gershonites according to their families *were* thirteen cities with their suburbs. ³⁴And unto the families of the children of Merari, the rest of the Levites, out of the tribe of Zebulun, Jokneam with her suburbs, and Kartah with her suburbs, ³⁵Dimnah with her suburbs, Nahalal with her suburbs; four cities. ³⁶And out of the tribe of Reuben, Bezer with her suburbs, and Jahazah with her suburbs, ³⁷Kedemoth with her suburbs, and Mephaath with her suburbs; four cities. ³⁸And out of the tribe of Gad, Ramoth in Gilead with her suburbs, *to be* a city of refuge for the slayer; and Mahanaim with her suburbs, ³⁹Heshbon with her suburbs, Jazer with her suburbs; four cities in all. ⁴⁰So all the cities for the children of Merari by their families, which were remaining of the families of the Levites, were *by* their lot twelve cities. ⁴¹All the cities of the Levites within the possession of the children of Israel *were* forty and eight cities with

their suburbs. ⁴²These cities were every one with their suburbs round about them: thus *were* all these cities.

⁴³And the LORD gave unto Israel all the land which he sware to give unto their fathers; and they possessed it, and dwelt therein. ⁴⁴And the LORD gave them rest round about, according to all that he sware unto their fathers: and there stood not a man of all their enemies before them; the LORD delivered all their enemies into their hand. ⁴⁵There failed not ought of any good thing which the LORD had spoken unto the house of Israel; all came to pass.

22

¹Then Joshua called the Reubenites, and the Gadites, and the half tribe of Manasseh, ²And said unto them, Ye have kept all that Moses the servant of the LORD commanded you, and have obeyed my voice in all that I commanded you: ³Ye have not left your brethren these many days unto this day, but have kept the charge of the com-

---

Devotional Moment

Tenacity

22:1-4 Everyone can admire the tenacity of these tribes. They were fighting for land that they would never occupy—for the sake of the nation and in response to God's commands. Parenting includes many God-given tasks that appear to benefit everyone *but* the parents. Though there is apparently nothing in it for them, God still calls them to change the diapers, give a hug to a heartbroken five-year-old, or remind their teenager of the upcoming history test. In many ways such acts are like conquering land you will never live on. Stick to your mission. God will be pleased.

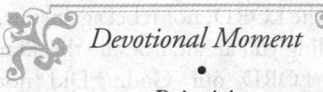

Devotional Moment

Priorities

22:5 Joshua wanted the people to remember to worship, to cultivate the inner life of devotion and prayer. Their tendency would be to forget, in their busyness, what really mattered. Today's families are like that, too. Parents face demands—from the PTA to the church missions committee. Children can feel the overload from homework, sports, music, youth group, and on and on. Joshua would say, "In all your service, in all your activity, take time to worship, to pray, to listen to God." If your home is like Grand Central Station, make sure there's a chapel in it.

mandment of the LORD your God. ⁴And now the LORD your God hath given rest unto your brethren, as he promised them: therefore now return ye, and get you unto your tents, *and* unto the land of your possession, which Moses the servant of the LORD gave you on the other side Jordan. ⁵But take diligent heed to do the commandment and the law, which Moses the servant of the LORD charged you, to love the LORD your God, and to walk in all his ways, and to keep his commandments, and to cleave unto him, and to serve him with all your heart and with all your soul. ⁶So Joshua blessed them, and sent them away: and they went unto their tents. ⁷Now to the *one* half of the tribe of Manasseh Moses had given *possession* in Bashan: but unto the *other* half thereof gave Joshua among their brethren on this side Jordan westward. And when Joshua sent them away also unto their tents, then he blessed them, ⁸And he spake unto them, saying, Re-

turn with much riches unto your tents, and with very much cattle, with silver, and with gold, and with brass, and with iron, and with very much raiment: divide the spoil of your enemies with your brethren. ⁹And the children of Reuben and the children of Gad and the half tribe of Manasseh returned, and departed from the children of Israel out of Shiloh, which *is* in the land of Canaan, to go unto the country of Gilead, to the land of their possession, whereof they were possessed, according to the word of the LORD by the hand of Moses.

¹⁰And when they came unto the borders of Jordan, that *are* in the land of Canaan, the children of Reuben and the children of Gad and the half tribe of Manasseh built there an altar by Jordan, a great altar to see to. ¹¹And the children of Israel heard say, Behold, the children of Reuben and the children of Gad and the half tribe of Manasseh have built an altar over against the land of Canaan, in the borders of Jordan, at the passage of the children of Israel. ¹²And when the children of Israel heard *of it*, the whole congregation of the children of Israel gathered themselves together at Shiloh, to go up to war against them. ¹³And the children of Israel sent unto the children of Reuben, and to the children of Gad, and to the half tribe of Manasseh, into the land of Gilead, Phinehas the son of Eleazar the priest, ¹⁴And with him ten princes, of each chief ᵃ house a prince throughout all the tribes of Israel; and each one *was* an head of the house of their fathers among the thousands of Israel. ¹⁵And they came unto the children

---

ᵃ chief . . . : Heb. house of the father

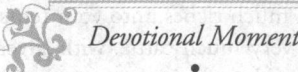

Devotional Moment
•
Conflict

22:11-34   Israel could have plunged into barbaric civil war—a world of hurt and pain and bloodshed—over nothing more than false charges and misperceptions. Fortunately, cooler heads prevailed, and the fact-finding team cleared the air. When your teenager misses curfew, is your head of steam such that no fact-finding is possible—with punishment rolling like a mighty locomotive on a downgrade? When your siblings miss a child's birthday, or your mother cancels a baby-sitting promise, do you quickly attack with angry words? Take a lesson from the ten tribes of Israel: Get all the facts instead of blowing your top. Make sure the conflict is a real one, not just a misunderstanding.

of Reuben, and to the children of Gad, and to the half tribe of Manasseh, unto the land of Gilead, and they spake with them, saying, ¹⁶Thus saith the whole congregation of the LORD, What trespass *is* this that ye have committed against the God of Israel, to turn away this day from following the LORD, in that ye have builded you an altar, that ye might rebel this day against the LORD? ¹⁷*Is* the iniquity of Peor too little for us, from which we are not cleansed until this day, although there was a plague in the congregation of the LORD, ¹⁸But that ye must turn away this day from following the LORD? and it will be, *seeing* ye rebel to day against the LORD, that to morrow he will be wroth with the whole congregation of Israel. ¹⁹Notwithstanding, if the land of your possession *be* unclean, *then* pass ye over unto the land of the possession of the LORD, wherein the LORD'S tabernacle dwelleth, and take possession among us: but rebel not

against the LORD, nor rebel against us, in building you an altar beside the altar of the LORD our God. ²⁰Did not Achan the son of Zerah commit a trespass in the accursed thing, and wrath fell on all the congregation of Israel? and that man perished not alone in his iniquity.

²¹Then the children of Reuben and the children of Gad and the half tribe of Manasseh answered, and said unto the heads of the thousands of Israel, ²²The LORD God of gods, the LORD God of gods, he knoweth, and Israel he shall know; if *it be* in rebellion, or if in transgression against the LORD, (save us not this day,) ²³That we have built us an altar to turn from following the LORD, or if to offer thereon burnt offering or meat offering, or if to offer peace offerings thereon, let the LORD himself require *it*; ²⁴And if we have not *rather* done it for fear of *this* thing, saying, In time to come your children might speak unto our children, saying, What have ye to do with the LORD God of Israel? ²⁵For the LORD hath made Jordan a border between us and you, ye children of Reuben and children of Gad; ye have no part in the LORD: so shall your children make our children cease from fearing the LORD. ²⁶Therefore we said, Let us now prepare to build us an altar, not for burnt offering, nor for sacrifice: ²⁷But *that* it *may be* a witness between us, and you, and our generations after us, that we might do the service of the LORD before him with our burnt offerings, and with our sacrifices, and with our peace offerings; that your children may not say to our children in time to come, Ye have no part in the LORD. ²⁸Therefore said we, that it shall be,

when they should *so* say to us or to our generations in time to come, that we may say *again*, Behold the pattern of the altar of the LORD, which our fathers made, not for burnt offerings, nor for sacrifices; but it *is* a witness between us and you. ²⁹God forbid that we should rebel against the LORD, and turn this day from following the LORD, to build an altar for burnt offerings, for meat offerings, or for sacrifices, beside the altar of the LORD our God that *is* before his tabernacle.

³⁰And when Phinehas the priest, and the princes of the congregation and heads of the thousands of Israel which *were* with him, heard the words that the children of Reuben and the children of Gad and the children of Manasseh spake, it pleased[b] them. ³¹And Phinehas the son of Eleazar the priest said unto the children of Reuben, and to the children of Gad, and to the children of Manasseh, This day we perceive that the LORD *is* among us, because ye have not committed this trespass against the LORD: now[c] ye have delivered the children of Israel out of the hand of the LORD. ³²And Phinehas the son of Eleazar the priest, and the princes, returned from the children of Reuben, and from the children of Gad, out of the land of Gilead, unto the land of Canaan, to the children of Israel, and brought them word again. ³³And the thing pleased the children of Israel; and the children of Israel blessed God, and did not intend to go up against them in battle, to destroy the land wherein the children of Reuben and Gad dwelt. ³⁴And the children of Reuben and the children of Gad called the altar *Ed*: for it *shall be* a witness between us that the LORD *is* God.

23

¹And it came to pass a long time after that the LORD had given rest unto Israel from all their enemies round about, that Joshua waxed old *and* stricken[a] in age. ²And Joshua called for all Israel, *and* for their elders, and for their heads, and for their judges, and for their officers, and said unto them, I am old *and* stricken in age: ³And ye have seen all that the LORD your God hath done unto all these nations because of you; for the LORD your God *is* he that hath fought for you. ⁴Behold, I have divided unto you by lot these nations that remain, to be an inheritance for your tribes, from Jordan, with all the nations that I have cut off, even unto the great sea westward[b]. ⁵And the LORD your God, he shall expel them from before you, and drive them from out of your sight; and ye shall possess their land, as the LORD your God hath promised unto you. ⁶Be ye therefore very courageous to keep and to do all that is written in the book of the law of Moses, that ye turn not aside therefrom *to* the right hand or *to* the left; ⁷That ye come not among these nations, these that remain among you; neither make mention of the name of their gods, nor cause to swear *by them*, neither serve them, nor

---

b pleased . . . : Heb. was good in their eyes
c now: Heb. then
a stricken . . . : Heb. come into days
b westward: Heb. at the sunset

bow yourselves unto them: [8]But cleave[c] unto the LORD your God, as ye have done unto this day. [9]For the LORD[d] hath driven out from before you great nations and strong: but *as for* you, no man hath been able to stand before you unto this day. [10]One man of you shall chase a thousand: for the LORD your God, he *it is* that fighteth for you, as he hath promised you.

[11]Take good heed therefore unto yourselves[e], that ye love the LORD your God. [12]Else if ye do in any wise go back, and cleave unto the remnant of these nations, *even* these that remain among you, and shall make marriages with them, and go in unto them, and they to you: [13]Know for a certainty that the LORD your God will no more drive out *any of* these nations from before you; but they shall be snares and traps unto you, and scourges in your sides, and thorns in your eyes, until ye perish from off this good land which the LORD your God hath given you. [14]And, behold, this day I *am* going the way of all the earth: and ye know in all your hearts and in all your souls, that not one thing hath failed of all the good things which the LORD your God spake concerning you; all are come to pass unto you, *and* not one thing hath failed thereof. [15]Therefore it shall come to pass, *that* as all good things are come upon you, which the LORD your God promised you; so shall the LORD bring upon you all evil things, until he have destroyed you from off this good land which the LORD your God hath given you. [16]When ye have trans-gressed the covenant of the LORD your God, which he commanded you, and have gone and served other gods, and bowed yourselves to them; then shall the anger of the LORD be kindled against you, and ye shall perish quickly from off the good land which he hath given unto you.

24

[1]And Joshua gathered all the tribes of Israel to Shechem, and called for the elders of Israel, and for their heads, and for their judges, and for their officers; and they presented themselves before God. [2]And Joshua said unto all the people, Thus saith the LORD God of Israel, Your fathers dwelt on the other side of the flood in old time, *even* Terah, the father of Abraham, and the father of Nachor: and they served other gods. [3]And I took your father Abraham from the other side of the flood, and led him throughout all the land of Canaan, and multiplied his seed, and gave him Isaac. [4]And I gave unto Isaac Jacob and Esau: and I gave unto Esau mount Seir, to possess it; but Jacob and his children went down into Egypt. [5]I sent Moses also and Aaron, and I plagued Egypt, according to that which I did among them: and afterward I brought you out. [6]And I brought your fathers out of Egypt: and ye came unto the sea; and the Egyptians pursued after your fathers with chariots and horsemen unto the Red sea. [7]And when they cried unto the LORD, he put darkness between you and the Egyptians, and brought the

[c] But cleave . . . : or, For if ye will cleave, etc
[d] For the LORD . . . : or, Then the LORD will drive
[e] yourselves: Heb. your souls

sea upon them, and covered them; and your eyes have seen what I have done in Egypt: and ye dwelt in the wilderness a long season. ⁸And I brought you into the land of the Amorites, which dwelt on the other side Jordan; and they fought with you: and I gave them into your hand, that ye might possess their land; and I destroyed them from before you. ⁹Then Balak the son of Zippor, king of Moab, arose and warred against Israel, and sent and called Balaam the son of Beor to curse you: ¹⁰But I would not hearken unto Balaam; therefore he blessed you still: so I delivered you out of his hand. ¹¹And ye went over Jordan, and came unto Jericho: and the men of Jericho fought against you, the Amorites, and the Perizzites, and the Canaanites, and the Hittites, and the Girgashites, the Hivites, and the Jebusites; and I delivered them into your hand. ¹²And I sent the hornet before you, which drave them out from before you, *even* the two kings of the Amorites; *but* not with thy sword, nor with thy bow. ¹³And I have given you a land for which ye did not labour, and cities which ye built not, and ye dwell in them; of the vineyards and oliveyards which ye planted not do ye eat. ¹⁴Now therefore fear the LORD, and serve him in sincerity and in truth: and put away the gods which your fathers served on the other side of the flood, and in Egypt; and serve ye the LORD.

¹⁵And if it seem evil unto you to serve the LORD, choose you this day whom ye will serve; whether the gods which your fathers served that *were* on the other side of the flood, or the gods of the Amorites, in whose land ye dwell: but as for me and my house, we will

> ### Devotional Moment
> •
> #### Life-Style
> 24:15 Here is one of the most dramatic family declarations in the Bible: Joshua testifies to the commitments and choices that place his family among God's larger family. It is both a statement of belief and a promise: "We *will* serve the Lord." Joshua sent a big message to the people that day. He did not claim perfection or problem-free kids; he did not boast a model marriage. But he did declare to all the people his first loyalty. Dare you imitate Joshua? Would your kids confirm it? Your spouse support it? Your life-style accommodate it? Consider your family's first loyalty.

serve the LORD. ¹⁶And the people answered and said, God forbid that we should forsake the LORD, to serve other gods; ¹⁷For the LORD our God, he *it is* that brought us up and our fathers out of the land of Egypt, from the house of bondage, and which did those great signs in our sight, and preserved us in all the way wherein we went, and among all the people through whom we passed: ¹⁸And the LORD drave out from before us all the people, even the Amorites which dwelt in the land: *therefore* will we also serve the LORD; for he *is* our God. ¹⁹And Joshua said unto the people, Ye cannot serve the LORD: for he *is* an holy God; he *is* a jealous God; he will not forgive your transgressions nor your sins. ²⁰If ye forsake the LORD, and serve strange gods, then he will turn and do you hurt, and consume you, after that he hath done you good. ²¹And the people said unto Joshua, Nay; but we will serve the LORD. ²²And Joshua said unto the people, Ye *are* witnesses against yourselves that ye have chosen you the LORD, to serve him. And they said, *We are* witnesses. ²³Now therefore put away, *said he*, the strange gods which *are* among you, and incline your heart unto the LORD God of Israel. ²⁴And the people said unto Joshua, The LORD our God will we serve, and his voice will we obey. ²⁵So Joshua made a covenant with the people that day, and set them a statute and an ordinance in Shechem. ²⁶And Joshua wrote these words in the book of the law of God, and took a great stone, and set it up there under an oak, that *was* by the sanctuary of the LORD. ²⁷And Joshua said unto all the people, Behold, this stone shall be a witness unto us; for it hath heard all the words of the LORD which he spake unto us: it shall be therefore a witness unto you, lest ye deny your God. ²⁸So Joshua let the people depart, every man unto his inheritance.

²⁹And it came to pass after these things, that Joshua the son of Nun, the servant of the LORD, died, *being* an hundred and ten years old. ³⁰And they buried him in the border of his inheritance in Timnathserah, which *is* in mount Ephraim, on the north side of the hill of Gaash. ³¹And Israel served the LORD all the days of Joshua, and all the days of the elders that overlived[a] Joshua, and which had known all the works of the LORD, that he had done for Israel. ³²And the bones of Joseph, which the children of Israel brought up out of Egypt, buried they in Shechem, in a parcel of ground which Jacob bought of the sons of Hamor the father of Shechem for an hundred pieces of silver: and it became the inheritance of the children of Joseph. ³³And Eleazar the son of Aaron died; and they buried him in a hill *that pertained to* Phinehas his son, which was given him in mount Ephraim.

---

[a] overlived . . . : Heb. prolonged their days after Joshua

JUDGES

Purpose
To show that God's judgment against sin—and his forgiveness of sin for those who repent—are equally certain.

Author
Probably Samuel

Setting
The land of Canaan, later called Israel. God had helped the Israelites conquer Canaan, which had been inhabited by a host of wicked nations. But they were in danger of losing this Promised Land because they compromised their convictions and disobeyed God.

Key Verse
"In those days there was no king in Israel, but every man did that which was right in his own eyes" (17:6).

Key People
Othniel, Ehud, Deborah, Gideon, Abimelech, Jephthah, Samson, Delilah

Special Feature
Records Israel's first civil war.

Wax museums around the world tell the stories of the bizarre, sometimes hideous personalities who have walked the earth. These wax museums usually include weirdos of considerable distinction.

Each of us knows an oddball character or two. Some families have had pirates among their number. Maybe some of your neighbors have gold rush forty-niners or Florida swampland speculators as uncles and aunts (great or great-great). Daredevils who scale the sides of skyscrapers are *somebody's* children.

Judges is full of odd and original personalities. Technically this book is the history of Israel from the death of Joshua to Saul's kingship. But read as drama, Judges is like going to a circus—or sometimes a horror show. Violence plays its ugly role here. Romance casts a net around these lives. Pain and loss pervade every story.

Yet a profound purpose is woven through the stories: God made a people for a special life together—for true worship, for true witness. That's the heart of Judges—finding truth in a waxy world. That's why Gideon and Deborah and Samson are people we all should know.

As you read about the heroes and villains of Israel's past, remember that God loved them, led them, and listened to their prayers—just as God does when you pray, imperfect as you are.

1

¹Now after the death of Joshua it came to pass, that the children of Israel asked the LORD, saying, Who shall go up for us against the Canaanites first, to fight against them? ²And the LORD said, Judah shall go up: behold, I have delivered the land into his hand. ³And Judah said unto Simeon his brother, Come up with me into my lot, that we may fight against the Canaanites; and I likewise will go with thee into thy lot. So Simeon went with him. ⁴And Judah went up; and the LORD delivered the Canaanites and the Perizzites into their hand: and they slew of them in Bezek ten thousand men. ⁵And they found Adonibezek in Bezek: and they fought against him, and they slew the Canaanites and the Perizzites. ⁶But Adonibezek fled; and they pursued after him, and caught him, and cut off his thumbs and his great toes. ⁷And Adonibezek said, Threescore and ten kings, having their thumbsᵃ and their great toes cut off, gathered *their meat* under my table: as I have done, so God hath requited me. And they brought him to Jerusalem, and there he died. ⁸Now the children of Judah had fought against Jerusalem, and had taken it, and smitten it with the edge of the sword, and set the city on fire.

⁹And afterward the children of Judah went down to fight against the Canaanites, that dwelt in the mountain, and in the south, and in the valleyᵇ. ¹⁰And Judah went against the Canaanites that dwelt in Hebron: (now the name of Hebron before *was* Kirjatharba:) and they slew Sheshai, and Ahiman, and Talmai. ¹¹And from thence he went against the inhabitants of Debir: and the name of Debir before *was* Kirjathsepher: ¹²And Caleb said, He that smiteth Kirjathsepher, and taketh it, to him will I give Achsah my daughter to wife. ¹³And Othniel the son of Kenaz, Caleb's younger brother, took it: and he gave him Achsah his daughter to wife. ¹⁴And it came to pass, when she came *to him*, that she moved him to ask of her father a field: and she lighted from off *her* ass; and Caleb said unto her, What wilt thou? ¹⁵And she said unto him, Give me a blessing: for thou hast given me a south land; give me also springs of water. And Caleb gave her the upper springs and the nether springs. ¹⁶And the children of the Kenite, Moses' father in law, went up out of the city of palm trees with the children of Judah into the wilderness of Judah, which *lieth* in the south of Arad; and they went and dwelt among the people. ¹⁷And Judah went with Simeon his brother, and they slew the Canaanites that inhabited Zephath, and utterly destroyed it. And the name of the city was called Hormah. ¹⁸Also Judah took Gaza with the coast thereof, and Askelon with the coast thereof, and Ekron with the coast thereof. ¹⁹And the LORD was with Judah; and he drave out *the inhabitants of* the mountain; but could not drive out the inhabitants of the valley, because they had chariots of iron. ²⁰And they gave Hebron unto Caleb, as Moses said: and he expelled thence the three sons of Anak.

ᵃ their thumbs . . . : Heb. the thumbs of their hands and of their feet
ᵇ valley: or, low country

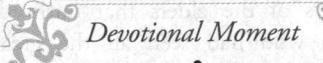

Devotional Moment
•
Promises

1:20 Caleb tasted the joy of knowing our promise-keeping God when he rode into Hebron. This event did not necessarily mean much to the nation of Israel, but it certainly meant a great deal to Caleb, who was one of the only Israelites to believe God's promise years earlier (see Num. 13:30). This event proved to Caleb that his life was really in God's hands. Do you want to feel the joy Caleb felt? Then open your eyes to the sure promises of God.

²¹And the children of Benjamin did not drive out the Jebusites that inhabited Jerusalem; but the Jebusites dwell with the children of Benjamin in Jerusalem unto this day. ²²And the house of Joseph, they also went up against Bethel: and the LORD *was* with them. ²³And the house of Joseph sent to descry Bethel. (Now the name of the city before *was* Luz.) ²⁴And the spies saw a man come forth out of the city, and they said unto him, Shew us, we pray thee, the entrance into the city, and we will shew thee mercy. ²⁵And when he shewed them the entrance into the city, they smote the city with the edge of the sword; but they let go the man and all his family. ²⁶And the man went into the land of the Hittites, and built a city, and called the name thereof Luz: which *is* the name thereof unto this day. ²⁷Neither did Manasseh drive out *the inhabitants of* Bethshean and her towns, nor Taanach and her towns, nor the inhabitants of Dor and her towns, nor the inhabitants of Ibleam and her towns, nor the inhab-

itants of Megiddo and her towns: but the Canaanites would dwell in that land. ²⁸And it came to pass, when Israel was strong, that they put the Canaanites to tribute, and did not utterly drive them out. ²⁹Neither did Ephraim drive out the Canaanites that dwelt in Gezer; but the Canaanites dwelt in Gezer among them. ³⁰Neither did Zebulun drive out the inhabitants of Kitron, nor the inhabitants of Nahalol; but the Canaanites dwelt among them, and became tributaries. ³¹Neither did Asher drive out the inhabitants of Accho, nor the inhabitants of Zidon, nor of Ahlab, nor of Achzib, nor of Helbah, nor of Aphik, nor of Rehob: ³²But the Asherites dwelt among the Canaanites, the inhabitants of the land: for they did not drive them out. ³³Neither did Naphtali drive out the inhabitants of Bethshemesh, nor the inhabitants of Bethanath; but he dwelt among the Canaanites, the inhabitants of the land: nevertheless the inhabitants of Bethshemesh and of Bethanath became tributaries unto them. ³⁴And the Amorites forced the children of Dan into the mountain: for they would not suffer them to come down to the valley: ³⁵But the Amorites would dwell in mount Heres in Aijalon, and in Shaalbim: yet the hand of the house of Joseph prevailed,ᶜ so that they became tributaries. ³⁶And the coast of the Amorites *was* from the going up to Akrabbim, from the rock, and upward.

2

¹And an angelᵃ of the LORD came up from Gilgal to Bochim, and said, I

ᶜ prevailed: Heb. was heavy
ᵃ angel: or, messenger

Devotional Moment
Conformity

2:2-3 Time and time again, the Israelites became enticed by Canaanite ways and readily abandoned God's law. Often you'll flinch to read what the people brought on themselves. You may say, "How foolish! I'll never make *their* mistakes." It is easy to say and hard to do. Many, many people disregard God and seem to get along fine. The temptation is to blend right in—to be just like every other parent, every other teenager, every other family. Don't do it! "Be not conformed to this world: but be ye transformed by the renewing of your mind" that honors God (Rom. 12:2).

made you to go up out of Egypt, and have brought you unto the land which I sware unto your fathers; and I said, I will never break my covenant with you. ²And ye shall make no league with the inhabitants of this land; ye shall throw down their altars: but ye have not obeyed my voice: why have ye done this? ³Wherefore I also said, I will not drive them out from before you; but they shall be *as thorns* in your sides, and their gods shall be a snare unto you. ⁴And it came to pass, when the angel of the LORD spake these words unto all the children of Israel, that the people lifted up their voice, and wept. ⁵And they called the name of that place Bochim[b]: and they sacrificed there unto the LORD.

⁶And when Joshua had let the people go, the children of Israel went every man unto his inheritance to possess the land. ⁷And the people served the LORD all the days of Joshua, and all the days of the elders that outlived[c] Joshua, who had seen all the great works of the LORD, that he did for Israel. ⁸And Joshua the son of Nun, the servant of the LORD, died, *being* an hundred and ten years old. ⁹And they buried him in the border of his inheritance in Timnathheres, in the mount of Ephraim, on the north side of the hill Gaash. ¹⁰And also all that generation were gathered unto their fathers: and there arose another generation after them, which knew not the LORD, nor yet the works which he had done for Israel. ¹¹And the children of Israel did evil in the sight of the LORD, and served Baalim: ¹²And they forsook the LORD God of their fathers, which brought them out of the land of Egypt, and followed other gods, of the gods of the people that *were* round about them, and bowed themselves unto them, and provoked the LORD to anger. ¹³And they forsook the LORD, and served Baal and Ashtaroth. ¹⁴And the anger of the LORD was hot against Israel, and

Devotional Moment
Teaching Faith

2:10 Whose responsibility was it to keep Israel's next generation on track with God? The children needed teachers of the faith. God gave that job to parents and elders (Deut. 4:9). Everything a child learns about God must be taught by someone. If you have children, take their spiritual learning seriously. If you're an elder, support the teaching function. Pass on your faith to the next generation.

---

[b] Bochim: that is, Weepers
[c] outlived: Heb. prolonged days after

he delivered them into the hands of spoilers that spoiled them, and he sold them into the hands of their enemies round about, so that they could not any longer stand before their enemies. ¹⁵Whithersoever they went out, the hand of the LORD was against them for evil, as the LORD had said, and as the LORD had sworn unto them: and they were greatly distressed. ¹⁶Nevertheless the LORD raised up judges, which delivered[d] them out of the hand of those that spoiled them. ¹⁷And yet they would not hearken unto their judges, but they went a whoring after other gods, and bowed themselves unto them: they turned quickly out of the way which their fathers walked in, obeying the commandments of the LORD; *but* they did not so. ¹⁸And when the LORD raised them up judges, then the LORD was with the judge, and delivered them out of the hand of their enemies all the days of the judge: for it repented the LORD because of their groanings by reason of them that oppressed them and vexed them. ¹⁹And it came to pass, when the judge was dead, *that* they returned, and corrupted[e] *themselves* more than their fathers, in following other gods to serve them, and to bow down unto them; they ceased not from their own doings, nor from their stubborn way. ²⁰And the anger of the LORD was hot against Israel; and he said, Because that this people hath transgressed my covenant which I commanded their fathers, and have not hearkened unto my voice; ²¹I

also will not henceforth drive out any from before them of the nations which Joshua left when he died: ²²That through them I may prove Israel, whether they will keep the way of the LORD to walk therein, as their fathers did keep *it*, or not. ²³Therefore the LORD left[f] those nations, without driving them out hastily; neither delivered he them into the hand of Joshua.

3

¹Now these *are* the nations which the LORD left, to prove Israel by them, *even* as many *of Israel* as had not known all the wars of Canaan; ²Only that the generations of the children of Israel might know, to teach them war, at the least such as before knew nothing thereof; ³*Namely*, five lords of the Philistines, and all the Canaanites, and the Sidonians, and the Hivites that dwelt in mount Lebanon, from mount Baalhermon unto the entering in of Hamath. ⁴And they were to prove Israel by them, to know whether they would hearken unto the commandments of the LORD, which he commanded their fathers by the hand of Moses. ⁵And the children of Israel dwelt among the Canaanites, Hittites, and Amorites, and Perizzites, and Hivites, and Jebusites: ⁶And they took their daughters to be their wives, and gave their daughters to their sons, and served their gods. ⁷And the children of Israel did evil in the sight of the LORD, and forgat the LORD their God, and served Baalim and the groves.

---

d delivered: Heb. saved
e corrupted . . . : or, were corrupt
f left: or, suffered

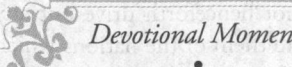

Devotional Moment
•
Relationships

3:5-6 The people of Israel failed to realize how greatly relationships influence a person's walk with God. Should Christians today have only Christian friends? Should children have overnights only with Sunday school playmates? Should dinner guests all meet the test for deacons and elders? No, such isolation is more a sign of insecurity than robust faith. But relationships do shape us, and people who would grow close to God must nurture friendships with others who share the same Christian goals and values. Because marriage is an intimate bond, single Christians would be wise to limit their courting to other believers. Pray for the future marriage of each of your children, as this is one of the most important decisions they will ever make.

⁸Therefore the anger of the LORD was hot against Israel, and he sold them into the hand of Chushanrishathaim king of Mesopotamia^a: and the children of Israel served Chushanrishathaim eight years. ⁹And when the children of Israel cried unto the LORD, the LORD raised up a deliverer^b to the children of Israel, who delivered them, *even* Othniel the son of Kenaz, Caleb's younger brother. ¹⁰And the Spirit of the LORD came upon him, and he judged Israel, and went out to war: and the LORD delivered Chushanrishathaim king of Mesopotamia into his hand; and his hand prevailed against Chushanrishathaim. ¹¹And the land had rest forty years. And Othniel the son of Kenaz died.

¹²And the children of Israel did evil again in the sight of the LORD: and the LORD strengthened Eglon the king of Moab against Israel, because they had done evil in the sight of the LORD. ¹³And he gathered unto him the children of Ammon and Amalek, and went and smote Israel, and possessed the city of palm trees. ¹⁴So the children of Israel served Eglon the king of Moab eighteen years. ¹⁵But when the children of Israel cried unto the LORD, the LORD raised them up a deliverer, Ehud the son of Gera, a Benjamite^c, a man lefthanded: and by him the children of Israel sent a present unto Eglon the king of Moab. ¹⁶But Ehud made him a dagger which had two edges, of a cubit length; and he did gird it under his raiment upon his right thigh. ¹⁷And he brought the present unto Eglon king of Moab: and Eglon *was* a very fat man. ¹⁸And when he had made an end to offer the present, he sent away the people that bare the present. ¹⁹But he himself turned again from the quarries^d that *were* by Gilgal, and said, I have a secret errand unto thee, O king: who said, Keep silence. And all that stood by him went out from him. ²⁰And Ehud came unto him; and he was sitting in a summer^e parlour, which he had for himself alone. And Ehud said, I have a message from God unto thee. And he arose out of *his* seat. ²¹And Ehud put forth his left hand, and took the dagger from his right thigh, and

---

^a Mesopotamia: Heb. Aramnaharaim
^b deliverer: Heb. saviour
^c a Benjamite: or, the son of Jemini
^d quarries: or, graven images
^e a summer . . . : Heb. a parlour of cooling

thrust it into his belly: ²²And the haft also went in after the blade; and the fat closed upon the blade, so that he could not draw the dagger out of his belly; and the dirt ᶠ came out. ²³Then Ehud went forth through the porch, and shut the doors of the parlour upon him, and locked them. ²⁴When he was gone out, his servants came; and when they saw that, behold, the doors of the parlour *were* locked, they said, Surely he covereth ᵍ his feet in his summer chamber. ²⁵And they tarried till they were ashamed: and, behold, he opened not the doors of the parlour; therefore they took a key, and opened *them*: and, behold, their lord *was* fallen down dead on the earth. ²⁶And Ehud escaped while they tarried, and passed beyond the quarries, and escaped unto Seirath. ²⁷And it came to pass, when he was come, that he blew a trumpet in the mountain of Ephraim, and the children of Israel went down with him from the mount, and he before them. ²⁸And he said unto them, Follow after me: for the LORD hath delivered your enemies the Moabites into your hand. And they went down after him, and took the fords of Jordan toward Moab, and suffered not a man to pass over. ²⁹And they slew of Moab at that time about ten thousand men, all lustyʰ, and all men of valour; and there escaped not a man. ³⁰So Moab was subdued that day under the hand of Israel. And the land had rest fourscore years.

³¹And after him was Shamgar the son of Anath, which slew of the Philistines six hundred men with an ox goad: and he also delivered Israel.

4

¹And the children of Israel again did evil in the sight of the LORD, when Ehud was dead. ²And the LORD sold them into the hand of Jabin king of Canaan, that reigned in Hazor; the captain of whose host *was* Sisera, which dwelt in Harosheth of the Gentiles. ³And the children of Israel cried unto the LORD: for he had nine hundred chariots of iron; and twenty years he mightily oppressed the children of Israel.

⁴And Deborah, a prophetess, the wife of Lapidoth, she judged Israel at that time. ⁵And she dwelt under the palm tree of Deborah between Ramah and Bethel in mount Ephraim: and the children of Israel came up to her for judgment. ⁶And she sent and called Barak the son of Abinoam out of Kedeshnaphtali, and said unto him, Hath not the LORD God of Israel commanded, *saying*, Go and draw toward mount Tabor, and take with thee ten thousand men of the children of Naphtali and of the children of Zebulun? ⁷And I will draw unto thee to the river Kishon Sisera, the captain of Jabin's army, with his chariots and his multitude; and I will deliver him into thine hand. ⁸And Barak said unto her, If thou wilt go with me, then I will go: but if thou wilt not go with me, *then* I will not go. ⁹And she said, I will surely go with thee: notwithstanding the journey that thou takest shall not be for thine hon-

---

ᶠ the dirt . . . : or, it came out at the buttocks
ᵍ covereth . . . : or, doeth his easement
ʰ lusty: Heb. fat

our; for the LORD shall sell Sisera into the hand of a woman. And Deborah arose, and went with Barak to Kedesh.

¹⁰And Barak called Zebulun and Naphtali to Kedesh; and he went up with ten thousand men at his feet: and Deborah went up with him. ¹¹Now Heber the Kenite, *which was* of the children of Hobab the father in law of Moses, had severed himself from the Kenites, and pitched his tent unto the plain of Zaanaim, which *is* by Kedesh. ¹²And they shewed Sisera that Barak the son of Abinoam was gone up to mount Tabor. ¹³And Sisera gathered together[a] all his chariots, *even* nine hundred chariots of iron, and all the people that *were* with him, from Harosheth of the Gentiles unto the river of Kishon. ¹⁴And Deborah said unto Barak, Up; for this *is* the day in which the LORD hath delivered Sisera into thine hand: is not the LORD gone out before thee? So Barak went down from mount Tabor, and ten thousand men after him. ¹⁵And the LORD discomfited Sisera, and all *his* chariots, and all *his* host, with the edge of the sword before Barak; so that Sisera lighted down off *his* chariot, and fled away on his feet. ¹⁶But Barak pursued after the chariots, and after the host, unto Harosheth of the Gentiles: and all the host of Sisera fell upon the edge of the sword; *and* there was not a man[b] left.

¹⁷Howbeit Sisera fled away on his feet to the tent of Jael the wife of Heber the Kenite: for *there was* peace between Jabin the king of Hazor and the house of Heber the Kenite. ¹⁸And Jael went out to meet Sisera, and said unto him, Turn in, my lord, turn in to me; fear not. And when he had turned in unto her into the tent, she covered him with a mantle[c]. ¹⁹And he said unto her, Give me, I pray thee, a little water to drink; for I am thirsty. And she opened a bottle of milk, and gave him drink, and covered him. ²⁰Again he said unto her, Stand in the door of the tent, and it shall be, when any man doth come and enquire of thee, and say, Is there any man here? that thou shalt say, No. ²¹Then Jael Heber's wife took a nail of the tent, and took[d] an hammer in her hand, and went softly unto him, and smote the nail into his temples, and fastened it into the ground: for he was fast asleep and weary. So he died. ²²And, behold, as Barak pursued Sisera, Jael came out to meet him, and said unto him, Come, and I will shew thee the man whom thou seekest. And when he came into her *tent,* behold, Sisera lay dead, and the nail *was* in his temples. ²³So God subdued on that day Jabin the king of Canaan before the children of Israel. ²⁴And the hand of the children of Israel prospered[e], and prevailed against Jabin the king of Canaan, until they had destroyed Jabin king of Canaan.

5

¹Then sang Deborah and Barak the son of Abinoam on that day, saying, ²Praise

---

[a] together: Heb. by cry, or, proclamation
[b] a man: Heb. unto one
[c] mantle: or, rug, or, blanket
[d] and took: Heb. and put
[e] prospered . . . : Heb. going went and was hard

ye the LORD for the avenging of Israel, when the people willingly offered themselves. ³Hear, O ye kings; give ear, O ye princes; I, *even* I, will sing unto the LORD; I will sing *praise* to the LORD God of Israel. ⁴LORD, when thou wentest out of Seir, when thou marchedst out of the field of Edom, the earth trembled, and the heavens dropped, the clouds also dropped water. ⁵The mountains melted^a from before the LORD, *even* that Sinai from before the LORD God of Israel.

⁶In the days of Shamgar the son of Anath, in the days of Jael, the highways were unoccupied, and the travellers^b walked through byways. ⁷ *The inhabitants of* the villages ceased, they ceased in Israel, until that I Deborah arose, that I arose a mother in Israel. ⁸They chose new gods; then *was* war in the gates: was there a shield or spear seen among forty thousand in Israel? ⁹My heart *is* toward the governors of Israel, that offered themselves willingly among the people. Bless ye the LORD. ¹⁰Speak^c, ye that ride on white asses, ye that sit in judgment, and walk by the way. ¹¹ *They that are delivered* from the noise of archers in the places of drawing water, there shall they rehearse the righteous acts of the LORD, *even* the righteous acts *toward the inhabitants* of his villages in Israel: then shall the people of the LORD go down to the gates.

¹²Awake, awake, Deborah: awake, awake, utter a song: arise, Barak, and lead thy captivity captive, thou son of Abinoam. ¹³Then he made him that remaineth have dominion over the nobles among the people: the LORD made me have dominion over the mighty. ¹⁴Out of Ephraim *was there* a root of them against Amalek; after thee, Benjamin, among thy people; out of Machir came down governors, and out of Zebulun they that handle^d the pen of the writer. ¹⁵And the princes of Issachar *were* with Deborah; even Issachar, and also Barak: he was sent on foot^e into the valley. For the divisions of Reuben *there were* great thoughts of heart. ¹⁶Why abodest thou among the sheepfolds, to hear the bleatings of the flocks? For the divisions of Reuben *there were* great searchings of heart. ¹⁷Gilead abode beyond Jordan: and why did Dan remain in ships? Asher continued on the sea shore^f, and abode in his breaches. ¹⁸Zebulun and Naphtali *were* a people *that* jeoparded^g their lives unto the death in the high places of the field. ¹⁹The kings came *and* fought, then fought the kings of Canaan in Taanach by the waters of Megiddo; they took no gain of money. ²⁰They fought from heaven; the stars in their courses^h fought against Sisera. ²¹The river of Kishon swept them away, that ancient river, the river Kishon. O

---

^a melted: Heb. flowed
^b travellers: Heb. walkers of paths
^c Speak: or, Meditate
^d handle: Heb. draw with
^e foot: Heb. his feet
^f shore: or, port
^g jeoparded: Heb. exposed to reproach
^h courses: Heb. paths

my soul, thou hast trodden down strength. ²²Then were the horsehoofs broken by the means of the pransings[i], the pransings of their mighty ones. ²³Curse ye Meroz, said the angel of the LORD, curse ye bitterly the inhabitants thereof; because they came not to the help of the LORD, to the help of the LORD against the mighty.

²⁴Blessed above women shall Jael the wife of Heber the Kenite be, blessed shall she be above women in the tent. ²⁵He asked water, *and* she gave *him* milk; she brought forth butter in a lordly dish. ²⁶She put her hand to the nail, and her right hand to the workmen's hammer; and with the hammer she smote Sisera, she smote off his head, when she had pierced and stricken through his temples. ²⁷At her feet he bowed, he fell, he lay down: at her feet he bowed, he fell: where he bowed, there he fell down dead. ²⁸The mother of Sisera looked out at a window, and cried through the lattice, Why is his chariot *so* long in coming? why tarry the wheels of his chariots? ²⁹Her wise ladies answered her, yea, she returned answer[j] to herself, ³⁰Have they not sped? have they *not* divided the prey; to every[k] man a damsel *or* two; to Sisera a prey of divers colours, a prey of divers colours of needlework, of divers colours of needlework on both sides, *meet* for the necks of *them that take* the spoil? ³¹So let all thine enemies perish, O LORD: but *let* them that love him

be as the sun when he goeth forth in his might. And the land had rest forty years.

6

¹And the children of Israel did evil in the sight of the LORD: and the LORD delivered them into the hand of Midian seven years. ²And the hand of Midian prevailed[a] against Israel: *and* because of the Midianites the children of Israel made them the dens which *are* in the mountains, and caves, and strong holds. ³And *so* it was, when Israel had sown, that the Midianites came up, and the Amalekites, and the children of the east, even they came up against them; ⁴And they encamped against them, and destroyed the increase of the earth, till thou come unto Gaza, and left no sustenance for Israel, neither sheep, nor ox, nor ass. ⁵For they came up with their cattle and their tents, and they came as grasshoppers for multitude; *for* both they and their camels were without number: and they entered into the land to destroy it. ⁶And Israel was greatly impoverished because of the Midianites; and the children of Israel cried unto the LORD.

⁷And it came to pass, when the children of Israel cried unto the LORD because of the Midianites, ⁸That the LORD sent a prophet[b] unto the children of Israel, which said unto them, Thus saith the LORD God of Israel, I brought you up from Egypt, and

---

[i] pransings: or, tramplings, or, plungings
[j] answer: Heb. her words
[k] every . . . : Heb. the head of a man
[a] prevailed: Heb. was strong
[b] a prophet: Heb. a man a prophet

brought you forth out of the house of bondage; [9]And I delivered you out of the hand of the Egyptians, and out of the hand of all that oppressed you, and drave them out from before you, and gave you their land; [10]And I said unto you, I *am* the LORD your God; fear not the gods of the Amorites, in whose land ye dwell: but ye have not obeyed my voice.

[11]And there came an angel of the LORD, and sat under an oak which *was* in Ophrah, that *pertained* unto Joash the Abiezrite: and his son Gideon[c] threshed wheat by the winepress, to hide *it* from the Midianites. [12]And the angel of the LORD appeared unto him, and said unto him, The LORD *is* with thee, thou mighty man of valour. [13]And Gideon said unto him, Oh my Lord, if the LORD be with us, why then is all this befallen us? and where *be* all his miracles which our fathers told us of, saying, Did not the LORD bring us up from Egypt? but now the LORD hath forsaken us, and delivered us into the hands of the Midianites. [14]And the LORD looked upon him, and said, Go in this thy might, and thou shalt save Israel from the hand of the Midianites: have not I sent thee? [15]And he said unto him, Oh my Lord, wherewith shall I save Israel? behold, my family[d] *is* poor in Manasseh, and I *am* the least in my father's house. [16]And the LORD said unto him, Surely I will be with thee, and thou shalt smite the Midianites as one man. [17]And he said unto him, If now I have found grace in thy sight, then shew me a sign that thou talkest with me. [18]Depart not hence, I pray thee, until I come unto thee, and bring forth my present[e], and set *it* before thee. And he said, I will tarry until thou come again. [19]And Gideon went in, and made ready a kid[f], and unleavened cakes of an ephah of flour: the flesh he put in a basket, and he put the broth in a pot, and brought *it* out unto him under the oak, and presented *it*. [20]And the angel of God said unto him, Take the flesh and the unleavened cakes, and lay *them* upon this rock, and pour out the broth. And he did so. [21]Then the angel of the LORD put forth the end of the staff that *was* in his hand, and touched the flesh and the unleavened cakes; and there rose up fire out of the rock, and consumed the flesh and the unleavened cakes. Then the angel of the LORD departed out of his sight. [22]And when Gideon perceived that he *was* an angel of the LORD, Gideon said, Alas, O

Devotional Moment

Crisis

6:22-27 At this time of crisis, Gideon could have focused on his perception that God was against them, or he could have ignored God's desires altogether. Instead, after his initial hesitation, Gideon acted in faith. Because all of us face times of crisis, we need such faith, too—faith that looks to God for strength and acts with courage against all obstacles.

---

[c] Gideon: Gr. Gedeon
[d] my family . . . : Heb. my thousand is the meanest
[e] present: or, meat offering
[f] a kid: Heb. a kid of the goats

Lord GOD! for because I have seen an angel of the LORD face to face. ²³And the LORD said unto him, Peace *be* unto thee; fear not: thou shalt not die. ²⁴Then Gideon built an altar there unto the LORD, and called it Jehovah-shalom^g: unto this day it *is* yet in Ophrah of the Abiezrites.

²⁵And it came to pass the same night, that the LORD said unto him, Take thy father's young bullock, even the second bullock of seven years old, and throw down the altar of Baal that thy father hath, and cut down the grove that *is* by it: ²⁶And build an altar unto the LORD thy God upon the top of this rock^h, in the ordered place, and take the second bullock, and offer a burnt sacrifice with the wood of the grove which thou shalt cut down. ²⁷Then Gideon took ten men of his servants, and did as the LORD had said unto him: and *so* it was, because he feared his father's household, and the men of the city, that he could not do *it* by day, that he did *it* by night. ²⁸And when the men of the city arose early in the morning, behold, the altar of Baal was cast down, and the grove was cut down that *was* by it, and the second bullock was offered upon the altar *that was* built. ²⁹And they said one to another, Who hath done this thing? And when they enquired and asked, they said, Gideon the son of Joash hath done this thing. ³⁰Then the men of the city said unto Joash, Bring out thy son, that

he may die: because he hath cast down the altar of Baal, and because he hath cut down the grove that *was* by it. ³¹And Joash said unto all that stood against him, Will ye plead for Baal? will ye save him? he that will plead for him, let him be put to death whilst *it is yet* morning: if he *be* a god, let him plead for himself, because *one* hath cast down his altar. ³²Therefore on that day he called him Jerubbaalⁱ, saying, Let Baal plead against him, because he hath thrown down his altar.

³³Then all the Midianites and the Amalekites and the children of the east were gathered together, and went over, and pitched in the valley of Jezreel. ³⁴But the Spirit of the LORD came^j upon Gideon, and he blew a trumpet; and Abiezer was gathered after him. ³⁵And he sent messengers throughout all Manasseh; who also was gathered^k after him: and he sent messengers unto Asher, and unto Zebulun, and unto Naphtali; and they came up to meet them. ³⁶And Gideon said unto God, If thou wilt save Israel by mine hand, as thou hast said, ³⁷Behold, I will put a fleece of wool in the floor; *and* if the dew be on the fleece only, and *it be* dry upon all the earth *beside*, then shall I know that thou wilt save Israel by mine hand, as thou hast said. ³⁸And it was so: for he rose up early on the morrow, and thrust the fleece together, and wringed the dew out of the fleece, a bowl full of water. ³⁹And Gideon said unto God, Let

---

^g Jehovahshalom: that is, The LORD send peace
^h rock: Heb. strong place
ⁱ Jerubbaal: that is, Let Baal plead
^j came . . . : Heb. clothed
^k gathered: Heb. called

not thine anger be hot against me, and I will speak but this once: let me prove, I pray thee, but this once with the fleece; let it now be dry only upon the fleece, and upon all the ground let there be dew. ⁴⁰And God did so that night: for it was dry upon the fleece only, and there was dew on all the ground.

7

¹Then Jerubbaal, who *is* Gideon, and all the people that *were* with him, rose up early, and pitched beside the well of Harod: so that the host of the Midianites were on the north side of them, by the hill of Moreh, in the valley. ²And the LORD said unto Gideon, The people that *are* with thee *are* too many for me to give the Midianites into their hands, lest Israel vaunt themselves against me, saying, Mine own hand hath saved me. ³Now therefore go to, proclaim in the ears of the people, saying, Whosoever *is* fearful and afraid, let him return and depart early from mount Gilead. And there returned of the people twenty and two thousand; and there remained ten thousand. ⁴And the LORD said unto Gideon, The people *are* yet *too* many; bring them down unto the water, and I will try them for thee there: and it shall be, *that* of whom I say unto thee, This shall go with thee, the same shall go with thee; and of whomsoever I say unto thee, This shall not go with thee, the same shall not go. ⁵So he brought down the people unto the water: and the LORD said unto Gideon, Every one that lappeth of the water with his tongue, as a dog lappeth, him shalt thou set by himself; likewise every one that boweth down upon his knees to drink. ⁶And the number of them that lapped, *putting* their hand to their mouth, were three hundred men: but all the rest of the people bowed down upon their knees to drink water. ⁷And the LORD said unto Gideon, By the three hundred men that lapped will I save you, and deliver the Midianites into thine hand: and let all the *other* people go every man unto his place. ⁸So the people took victuals in their hand, and their trumpets: and he sent all *the rest of* Israel every man unto his tent, and retained those three hundred men: and the host of Midian was beneath him in the valley.

⁹And it came to pass the same night, that the LORD said unto him, Arise, get thee down unto the host; for I have delivered it into thine hand. ¹⁰But if thou fear to go down, go thou with Phurah thy servant down to the host: ¹¹And thou shalt hear what they say; and afterward shall thine hands be strengthened to go down unto the host. Then went he down with Phurah his servant unto the outside of the armed menᵃ that *were* in the host. ¹²And the Midianites and the Amalekites and all the children of the east lay along in the valley like grasshoppers for multitude; and their camels *were* without number, as the sand by the sea side for multitude. ¹³And when Gideon was come, behold, *there was* a man that told a dream unto his fellow, and said, Behold, I dreamed a dream, and, lo, a cake of barley bread tumbled into the host of Midian, and came unto a tent, and smote it that it fell, and overturned it,

---

ᵃ armed men: or, ranks by five

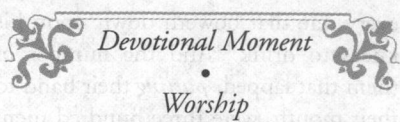

Devotional Moment

Worship

7:15 After Gideon heard the Midianite soldier's dream and interpretation, his first response was worship. Terrific idea! We should develop a bent for worship—anytime, anywhere—as a first response to life's great moments. When your son walks the high school stage to receive his diploma, when your daughter walks the church aisle to receive her husband, remember Gideon's response. When your wife of twenty years takes your hand on a moonlit night, when a long-lost friend calls to reconnect, remember Gideon's response. Whether unusual or ordinary—all circumstances are prime opportunities to worship God.

that the tent lay along. ¹⁴And his fellow answered and said, This *is* nothing else save the sword of Gideon the son of Joash, a man of Israel: *for* into his hand hath God delivered Midian, and all the host. ¹⁵And it was *so*, when Gideon heard the telling of the dream, and the interpretation[b] thereof, that he worshipped, and returned into the host of Israel, and said, Arise; for the LORD hath delivered into your hand the host of Midian.

¹⁶And he divided the three hundred men *into* three companies, and he put a trumpet[c] in every man's hand, with empty pitchers, and lamps within the pitchers. ¹⁷And he said unto them, Look on me, and do likewise: and, behold, when I come to the outside of the camp, it shall be *that*, as I do, so shall ye do. ¹⁸When I blow with a trumpet, I and all that *are* with me, then blow ye the trumpets also on every side of all the camp, and say, *The sword* of the LORD, and of Gideon. ¹⁹So Gideon, and the hundred men that *were* with him, came unto the outside of the camp in the beginning of the middle watch; and they had but newly set the watch: and they blew the trumpets, and brake the pitchers that *were* in their hands. ²⁰And the three companies blew the trumpets, and brake the pitchers, and held the lamps in their left hands, and the trumpets in their right hands to blow *withal*: and they cried, The sword of the LORD, and of Gideon. ²¹And they stood every man in his place round about the camp: and all the host ran, and cried, and fled. ²²And the three hundred blew the trumpets, and the LORD set every man's sword against his fellow, even throughout all the host: and the host fled to Bethshittah in Zererath, *and* to the border of Abelmeholah, unto Tabbath.

²³And the men of Israel gathered themselves together out of Naphtali, and out of Asher, and out of all Manasseh, and pursued after the Midianites. ²⁴And Gideon sent messengers throughout all mount Ephraim, saying, Come down against the Midianites, and take before them the waters unto Bethbarah and Jordan. Then all the men of Ephraim gathered themselves together, and took the waters unto Bethbarah and Jordan. ²⁵And they took two princes of the Midianites, Oreb and Zeeb; and they slew Oreb upon the rock Oreb, and Zeeb they slew at the winepress of Zeeb, and pursued Midian, and brought the heads

---

[b] interpretation: Heb. breaking
[c] a trumpet . . . : Heb. trumpets in the hand of all of them

of Oreb and Zeeb to Gideon on the other side Jordan.

8

¹And the men of Ephraim said unto him, Why hast thou served us thus, that thou calledst us not, when thou wentest to fight with the Midianites? And they did chide with him sharply. ²And he said unto them, What have I done now in comparison of you? *Is* not the gleaning of the grapes of Ephraim better than the vintage of Abiezer? ³God hath delivered into your hands the princes of Midian, Oreb and Zeeb: and what was I able to do in comparison of you? Then their angerᵃ was abated toward him, when he had said that.

⁴And Gideon came to Jordan, *and* passed over, he, and the three hundred men that *were* with him, faint, yet pursuing *them.* ⁵And he said unto the men of Succoth, Give, I pray you, loaves of bread unto the people that follow me; for they *be* faint, and I am pursuing after Zebah and Zalmunna, kings of Midian. ⁶And the princes of Succoth said, *Are* the hands of Zebah and Zalmunna now in thine hand, that we should give bread unto thine army? ⁷And Gideon said, Therefore when the LORD hath delivered Zebah and Zalmunna into mine hand, then I will tearᵇ your flesh with the thorns of the wilderness and with briers. ⁸And he went up thence to Penuel, and spake unto them likewise: and the men of Penuel answered him as the men of Succoth had answered *him.* ⁹And he spake also unto the men of Penuel, saying, When I come again in peace, I will break down this tower. ¹⁰Now Zebah and Zalmunna *were* in Karkor, and their hosts with them, about fifteen thousand *men,* all that were left of all the hosts of the children of the east: for there fell an hundred and twenty thousand men that drew sword. ¹¹And Gideon went up by the way of them that dwelt in tents on the east of Nobah and Jogbehah, and smote the host: for the host was secure. ¹²And when Zebah and Zalmunna fled, he pursued after them, and took the two kings of Midian, Zebah and Zalmunna, and discomfitedᶜ all the host. ¹³And Gideon the son of Joash returned from battle before the sun *was up,* ¹⁴And caught a young man of the men of Succoth, and enquired of him: and he describedᵈ unto him the princes of

---

Devotional Moment

•

Serving

8:1-3 The Ephraimites were upset because Gideon had not included them in the main battle. Ephraim's leaders worried that the spotlight was pointing elsewhere. Stardom was eluding them. But a successful campaign against Midian required lots of anonymous heroics—hard work behind the lines. For most families, the least glamorous chores (like dishwashing, laundry sorting, bike-tire puncture patching) are the last to get done. Surprise your family this week. Help make your home happier from the bottom up. Try (cheerfully) doing the chores that only God will see and headline writers will never notice.

ᵃ anger: Heb. spirit
ᵇ tear: Heb. thresh
ᶜ discomfited: Heb. terrified
ᵈ described: Heb. writ

Succoth, and the elders thereof, *even* threescore and seventeen men. ¹⁵And he came unto the men of Succoth, and said, Behold Zebah and Zalmunna, with whom ye did upbraid me, saying, *Are* the hands of Zebah and Zalmunna now in thine hand, that we should give bread unto thy men *that are* weary? ¹⁶And he took the elders of the city, and thorns of the wilderness and briers, and with them he taughtᵉ the men of Succoth. ¹⁷And he beat down the tower of Penuel, and slew the men of the city.

¹⁸Then said he unto Zebah and Zalmunna, What manner of men *were they* whom ye slew at Tabor? And they answered, As thou *art*, so *were* they; each one resembledᶠ the children of a king. ¹⁹And he said, They *were* my brethren, *even* the sons of my mother: *as* the LORD liveth, if ye had saved them alive, I would not slay you. ²⁰And he said unto Jether his firstborn, Up, *and* slay them. But the youth drew not his sword: for he feared, because he *was* yet a youth. ²¹Then Zebah and Zalmunna said, Rise thou, and fall upon us: for as the man *is, so is* his strength. And Gideon arose, and slew Zebah and Zalmunna, and took away the ornamentsᵍ that *were* on their camels' necks.

²²Then the men of Israel said unto Gideon, Rule thou over us, both thou, and thy son, and thy son's son also: for thou hast delivered us from the hand of Midian. ²³And Gideon said unto them, I will not rule over you, neither shall my son rule over you: the LORD shall rule over you. ²⁴And Gideon said unto them, I would desire a request of you, that ye would give me every man the earrings of his prey. (For they had golden earrings, because they *were* Ishmaelites.) ²⁵And they answered, We will willingly give *them*. And they spread a garment, and did cast therein every man the earrings of his prey. ²⁶And the weight of the golden earrings that he requested was a thousand and seven hundred *shekels* of gold; beside ornaments, and collarsʰ, and purple raiment that *was* on the kings of Midian, and beside the chains that *were* about their camels' necks. ²⁷And Gideon made an ephod thereof, and put it in his city, *even* in Ophrah: and all Israel went thither a whoring after it: which thing became a snare unto Gideon, and to his house. ²⁸Thus was Midian subdued before the children of Israel, so that they lifted up their heads no more. And the country was in quietness forty years in the days of Gideon.

²⁹And Jerubbaal the son of Joash went and dwelt in his own house. ³⁰And Gideon had threescore and ten sons of his body begotten: for he had many wives. ³¹And his concubine that *was* in Shechem, she also bare him a son, whose name he calledⁱ Abimelech. ³²And Gideon the son of Joash died in a good old age, and was buried in the sepulchre of Joash his father, in Ophrah of the Abiezrites. ³³And it came to pass,

---

ᵉ taught: Heb. made to know
ᶠ resembled . . . : Heb. according to the form, etc
ᵍ ornaments: or, ornaments like the moon
ʰ collars: or, sweet jewels
ⁱ called: Heb. set

Devotional Moment

Temptation

8:31 Though he had "many wives," Gideon succumbed to an age-old temptation: to have a secret lover. Little did Gideon know that it was trouble, not love, he was making in her bed because of the child they would have. Today, given the strength of sexual attraction and the media environment that reminds us of it constantly, it's a spiritual challenge to stay faithful to a spouse, or to refrain from sexual adventures if unmarried. Focus on pleasing God, who made you so special, and restrain your desires with a prayer—and a renewed commitment to live with the partner God has given you (see Prov. 4). And if you think you may struggle with sexual addiction, seek out a counselor. Your family's stability and security depends on it.

as soon as Gideon was dead, that the children of Israel turned again, and went a whoring after Baalim, and made Baalberith their god. ³⁴And the children of Israel remembered not the LORD their God, who had delivered them out of the hands of all their enemies on every side: ³⁵Neither shewed they kindness to the house of Jerubbaal, *namely*, Gideon, according to all the goodness which he had shewed unto Israel.

9

¹And Abimelech the son of Jerubbaal went to Shechem unto his mother's brethren, and communed with them, and with all the family of the house of his mother's father, saying, ²Speak, I pray you, in the ears of all the men of Shechem, Whether *is* better ᵃ for you, either that all the sons of Jerubbaal, *which are* threescore and ten persons, reign over you, or that one reign over you? remember also that I *am* your bone and your flesh. ³And his mother's brethren spake of him in the ears of all the men of Shechem all these words: and their hearts inclined to follow ᵇ Abimelech; for they said, He *is* our brother. ⁴And they gave him threescore and ten *pieces* of silver out of the house of Baalberith, wherewith Abimelech hired vain and light persons, which followed him. ⁵And he went unto his father's house at Ophrah, and slew his brethren the sons of Jerubbaal, *being* threescore and ten persons, upon one stone: notwithstanding yet Jotham the youngest son of Jerubbaal was left; for he hid himself. ⁶And all the men of Shechem gathered together, and all the house of Millo, and went, and made Abimelech king, by the plain ᶜ of the pillar that *was* in Shechem.

⁷And when they told *it* to Jotham, he went and stood in the top of mount Gerizim, and lifted up his voice, and cried, and said unto them, Hearken unto me, ye men of Shechem, that God may hearken unto you. ⁸The trees went forth *on a time* to anoint a king over them; and they said unto the olive tree, Reign thou over us. ⁹But the olive tree said unto them, Should I leave my fatness, wherewith by me they honour God and man, and go ᵈ to be promoted over the trees? ¹⁰And the trees said to

---

ᵃ Whether . . . : Heb. What is good? whether, etc
ᵇ to follow: Heb. after
ᶜ plain: or, oak
ᵈ go . . . : or, go up and down for other trees

the fig tree, Come thou, *and* reign over us. [11]But the fig tree said unto them, Should I forsake my sweetness, and my good fruit, and go to be promoted over the trees? [12]Then said the trees unto the vine, Come thou, *and* reign over us. [13]And the vine said unto them, Should I leave my wine, which cheereth God and man, and go to be promoted over the trees? [14]Then said all the trees unto the bramble[e], Come thou, *and* reign over us. [15]And the bramble said unto the trees, If in truth ye anoint me king over you, *then* come *and* put your trust in my shadow: and if not, let fire come out of the bramble, and devour the cedars of Lebanon. [16]Now therefore, if ye have done truly and sincerely, in that ye have made Abimelech king, and if ye have dealt well with Jerubbaal and his house, and have done unto him according to the deserving of his hands; [17](For my father fought for you, and adventured[f] his life far, and delivered you out of the hand of Midian: [18]And ye are risen up against my father's house this day, and have slain his sons, threescore and ten persons, upon one stone, and have made Abimelech, the son of his maidservant, king over the men of Shechem, because he *is* your brother;) [19]If ye then have dealt truly and sincerely with Jerubbaal and with his house this day, *then* rejoice ye in Abimelech, and let him also rejoice in you: [20]But if not, let fire come out from Abimelech, and devour the men of Shechem, and the house of Millo; and

let fire come out from the men of Shechem, and from the house of Millo, and devour Abimelech. [21]And Jotham ran away, and fled, and went to Beer, and dwelt there, for fear of Abimelech his brother.

[22]When Abimelech had reigned three years over Israel, [23]Then God sent an evil spirit between Abimelech and the men of Shechem; and the men of Shechem dealt treacherously with Abimelech: [24]That the cruelty *done* to the threescore and ten sons of Jerubbaal might come, and their blood be laid upon Abimelech their brother, which slew them; and upon the men of Shechem, which aided[g] him in the killing of his brethren. [25]And the men of Shechem set liers in wait for him in the top of the mountains, and they robbed all that came along that way by them: and it was told Abimelech. [26]And Gaal the son of Ebed came with his brethren, and went over to Shechem: and the men of Shechem put their confidence in him. [27]And they went out into the fields, and gathered their vineyards, and trode *the grapes*, and made merry[h], and went into the house of their god, and did eat and drink, and cursed Abimelech. [28]And Gaal the son of Ebed said, Who *is* Abimelech, and who *is* Shechem, that we should serve him? *is* not *he* the son of Jerubbaal? and Zebul his officer? serve the men of Hamor the father of Shechem: for why should we serve him? [29]And would to God this people

---

[e] bramble: or, thistle
[f] adventured . . . : Heb. cast his life
[g] aided . . . : Heb. strengthened his hands to kill
[h] merry: or, songs

were under my hand! then would I remove Abimelech. And he said to Abimelech, Increase thine army, and come out. ³⁰And when Zebul the ruler of the city heard the words of Gaal the son of Ebed, his anger was kindledⁱ. ³¹And he sent messengers unto Abimelech privilyʲ, saying, Behold, Gaal the son of Ebed and his brethren be come to Shechem; and, behold, they fortify the city against thee. ³²Now therefore up by night, thou and the people that *is* with thee, and lie in wait in the field: ³³And it shall be, *that* in the morning, as soon as the sun is up, thou shalt rise early, and set upon the city: and, behold, *when* he and the people that *is* with him come out against thee, then mayest thou do to them as thou shalt find occasion. ³⁴And Abimelech rose up, and all the people that *were* with him, by night, and they laid wait against Shechem in four companies. ³⁵And Gaal the son of Ebed went out, and stood in the entering of the gate of the city: and Abimelech rose up, and the people that *were* with him, from lying in wait. ³⁶And when Gaal saw the people, he said to Zebul, Behold, there come people down from the top of the mountains. And Zebul said unto him, Thou seest the shadow of the mountains as *if they were* men. ³⁷And Gaal spake again and said, See there come people down by the middleᵏ of the land, and another company come along by the plain of Meonenim. ³⁸Then said Zebul unto him, Where *is* now thy mouth, wherewith thou saidst, Who *is* Abimelech, that we should serve him? *is* not this the people that thou hast despised? go out, I pray now, and fight with them. ³⁹And Gaal went out before the men of Shechem, and fought with Abimelech. ⁴⁰And Abimelech chased him, and he fled before him, and many were overthrown *and* wounded, *even* unto the entering of the gate. ⁴¹And Abimelech dwelt at Arumah: and Zebul thrust out Gaal and his brethren, that they should not dwell in Shechem. ⁴²And it came to pass on the morrow, that the people went out into the field; and they told Abimelech. ⁴³And he took the people, and divided them into three companies, and laid wait in the field, and looked, and, behold, the people *were* come forth out of the city; and he rose up against them, and smote them. ⁴⁴And Abimelech, and the company that *was* with him, rushed forward, and stood in the entering of the gate of the city: and the two *other* companies ran upon all *the people* that *were* in the fields, and slew them. ⁴⁵And Abimelech fought against the city all that day; and he took the city, and slew the people that *was* therein, and beat down the city, and sowed it with salt. ⁴⁶And when all the men of the tower of Shechem heard *that*, they entered into an hold of the house of the god Berith. ⁴⁷And it was told Abimelech, that all the men of the tower of Shechem were gathered together. ⁴⁸And Abimelech gat him up to mount Zalmon, he and all the people that *were* with him; and

---

ⁱ kindled: or, hot
ʲ privily: Heb. craftily or, to Tormah
ᵏ middle: Heb. navel

Abimelech took an axe in his hand, and cut down a bough from the trees, and took it, and laid *it* on his shoulder, and said unto the people that *were* with him, What ye have seen me do[1], make haste, *and* do as I *have done.* [49]And all the people likewise cut down every man his bough, and followed Abimelech, and put *them* to the hold, and set the hold on fire upon them; so that all the men of the tower of Shechem died also, about a thousand men and women.

[50]Then went Abimelech to Thebez, and encamped against Thebez, and took it. [51]But there was a strong tower within the city, and thither fled all the men and women, and all they of the city, and shut *it* to them, and gat them up to the top of the tower. [52]And Abimelech came unto the tower, and fought against it, and went hard unto the door of the tower to burn it with fire. [53]And a certain woman cast a piece of a millstone upon Abimelech's head, and all to brake his skull. [54]Then he called hastily unto the young man his armourbearer, and said unto him, Draw thy sword, and slay me, that men say not of me, A woman slew him. And his young man thrust him through, and he died. [55]And when the men of Israel saw that Abimelech was dead, they departed every man unto his place. [56]Thus God rendered the wickedness of Abimelech, which he did unto his father, in slaying his seventy brethren: [57]And all the evil of the men of Shechem did God render upon their heads: and upon them came the curse of Jotham the son of Jerubbaal.

10

[1]And after Abimelech there arose to defend[a] Israel Tola the son of Puah, the son of Dodo, a man of Issachar; and he dwelt in Shamir in mount Ephraim. [2]And he judged Israel twenty and three years, and died, and was buried in Shamir. [3]And after him arose Jair, a Gileadite, and judged Israel twenty and two years. [4]And he had thirty sons that rode on thirty ass colts, and they had thirty cities, which are called Havothjair[b] unto this day, which *are* in the land of Gilead. [5]And Jair died, and was buried in Camon.

[6]And the children of Israel did evil again in the sight of the LORD, and served Baalim, and Ashtaroth, and the gods of Syria, and the gods of Zidon, and the gods of Moab, and the gods of the children of Ammon, and the gods of the Philistines, and forsook the LORD, and served not him. [7]And the anger of the LORD was hot against Israel, and he sold them into the hands of the Philistines, and into the hands of the children of Ammon. [8]And that year they vexed and oppressed[c] the children of Israel: eighteen years, all the children of Israel that *were* on the other side Jordan in the land of the Amorites, which *is* in Gilead. [9]Moreover the children of Ammon passed over Jordan to fight

---

[1] me do: Heb. I have done
[a] defend: or, deliver: Heb. save
[b] Havothjair: or, the villages of Jair
[c] oppressed: Heb. crushed

also against Judah, and against Benjamin, and against the house of Ephraim; so that Israel was sore distressed.

¹⁰And the children of Israel cried unto the LORD, saying, We have sinned against thee, both because we have forsaken our God, and also served Baalim. ¹¹And the LORD said unto the children of Israel, *Did* not *I deliver you* from the Egyptians, and from the Amorites, from the children of Ammon, and from the Philistines? ¹²The Zidonians also, and the Amalekites, and the Maonites, did oppress you; and ye cried to me, and I delivered you out of their hand. ¹³Yet ye have forsaken me, and served other gods: wherefore I will deliver you no more. ¹⁴Go and cry unto the gods which ye have chosen; let them deliver you in the time of your tribulation. ¹⁵And the children of Israel said unto the LORD, We have sinned: do thou unto us whatsoever seemeth^d good unto thee; deliver us only, we pray thee, this day. ¹⁶And they put away the strange^e gods from among them, and served the LORD: and his soul was grieved for the misery of Israel. ¹⁷Then the children of Ammon were gathered together, and encamped in Gilead. And the children of Israel assembled themselves together, and encamped in Mizpeh. ¹⁸And the people *and* princes of Gilead said one to another, What man *is he* that will begin to fight against the children of Ammon? he shall be head over all the inhabitants of Gilead.

11

¹Now Jephthah^a the Gileadite was a mighty man of valour, and he *was* the son of an harlot: and Gilead begat Jephthah. ²And Gilead's wife bare him sons; and his wife's sons grew up, and they thrust out Jephthah, and said unto him, Thou shalt not inherit in our father's house; for thou *art* the son of a strange woman. ³Then Jephthah fled from^b his brethren, and dwelt in the land of Tob: and there were gathered vain men to Jephthah, and went out with him.

⁴And it came to pass in process of time, that the children of Ammon made war against Israel. ⁵And it was so, that when the children of Ammon made war against Israel, the elders of Gilead went to fetch Jephthah out of

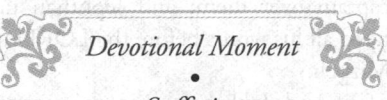

Devotional Moment

•

Suffering

11:1-2 Jephthah did not deserve such name-calling from his half brothers. Father Gilead was the culprit, after all. Jephthah was merely the natural consequence of Gilead's night with a prostitute. Nonetheless, his brothers' taunts forced Jephthah out of town. But they also made him strong. Suffering always hurts; it can also build the soul and fortify the character. If you're the victim, let suffering point your angry eyes to God, who gives us hope. When you're hurting, let the pain be a window to God's never-failing promises.

---

^d seemeth . . . : Heb. is good in thine eyes
^e strange . . . : Heb. gods of strangers
^a Jephthah: called Jephthae
^b from: Heb. from the face

the land of Tob: [6]And they said unto Jephthah, Come, and be our captain, that we may fight with the children of Ammon. [7]And Jephthah said unto the elders of Gilead, Did not ye hate me, and expel me out of my father's house? and why are ye come unto me now when ye are in distress? [8]And the elders of Gilead said unto Jephthah, Therefore we turn again to thee now, that thou mayest go with us, and fight against the children of Ammon, and be our head over all the inhabitants of Gilead. [9]And Jephthah said unto the elders of Gilead, If ye bring me home again to fight against the children of Ammon, and the LORD deliver them before me, shall I be your head? [10]And the elders of Gilead said unto Jephthah, The LORD be witness[c] between us, if we do not so according to thy words. [11]Then Jephthah went with the elders of Gilead, and the people made him head and captain over them: and Jephthah uttered all his words before the LORD in Mizpeh.

[12]And Jephthah sent messengers unto the king of the children of Ammon, saying, What hast thou to do with me, that thou art come against me to fight in my land? [13]And the king of the children of Ammon answered unto the messengers of Jephthah, Because Israel took away my land, when they came up out of Egypt, from Arnon even unto Jabbok, and unto Jordan: now therefore restore those lands again peaceably. [14]And Jephthah sent messengers again unto the king of the children of Ammon: [15]And said unto him, Thus saith Jephthah, Israel took not away the land of Moab, nor the land of the children of Ammon: [16]But when Israel came up from Egypt, and walked through the wilderness unto the Red sea, and came to Kadesh; [17]Then Israel sent messengers unto the king of Edom, saying, Let me, I pray thee, pass through thy land: but the king of Edom would not hearken thereto. And in like manner they sent unto the king of Moab: but he would not consent: and Israel abode in Kadesh. [18]Then they went along through the wilderness, and compassed the land of Edom, and the land of Moab, and came by the east side of the land of Moab, and pitched on the other side of Arnon, but came not within the border of Moab: for Arnon was the border of Moab. [19]And Israel sent messengers unto Sihon king of the Amorites, the king of Heshbon; and Israel said unto him, Let us pass, we pray thee, through thy land into my place. [20]But Sihon trusted not Israel to pass through his coast: but Sihon gathered all his people together, and pitched in Jahaz, and fought against Israel. [21]And the LORD God of Israel delivered Sihon and all his people into the hand of Israel, and they smote them: so Israel possessed all the land of the Amorites, the inhabitants of that country. [22]And they possessed all the coasts of the Amorites, from Arnon even unto Jabbok, and from the wilderness even unto Jordan. [23]So now the LORD God of Israel hath dispossessed the Amorites from before his people Israel, and shouldest thou possess it? [24]Wilt not

---

[c] witness . . . : Heb. the hearer between us

thou possess that which Chemosh thy god giveth thee to possess? So whomsoever the LORD our God shall drive out from before us, them will we possess. ²⁵And now *art* thou any thing better than Balak the son of Zippor, king of Moab? did he ever strive against Israel, or did he ever fight against them, ²⁶While Israel dwelt in Heshbon and her towns, and in Aroer and her towns, and in all the cities that *be* along by the coasts of Arnon, three hundred years? why therefore did ye not recover *them* within that time? ²⁷Wherefore I have not sinned against thee, but thou doest me wrong to war against me: the LORD the Judge be judge this day between the children of Israel and the children of Ammon. ²⁸Howbeit the king of the children of Ammon hearkened not unto the words of Jephthah which he sent him.

²⁹Then the Spirit of the LORD came upon Jephthah, and he passed over Gilead, and Manasseh, and passed over Mizpeh of Gilead, and from Mizpeh of Gilead he passed over *unto* the children of Ammon. ³⁰And Jephthah vowed a vow unto the LORD, and said, If thou shalt without fail deliver the children of Ammon into mine hands, ³¹Then it shall be, that whatsoever^d cometh forth of the doors of my house to meet me, when I return in peace from the children of Ammon, shall surely be the LORD'S, and I will offer it up for a burnt offering. ³²So Jephthah passed over unto the children

of Ammon to fight against them; and the LORD delivered them into his hands. ³³And he smote them from Aroer, even till thou come to Minnith, *even* twenty cities, and unto the plain^e of the vineyards, with a very great slaughter. Thus the children of Ammon were subdued before the children of Israel. ³⁴And Jephthah came to Mizpeh unto his house, and, behold, his daughter came out to meet him with timbrels and with dances: and she *was his* only child; beside her he had neither son nor daughter. ³⁵And it came to pass, when he saw her, that he rent his clothes, and said, Alas, my daughter! thou hast brought me very low, and thou art one of them that trouble me: for I have opened my mouth unto the LORD, and I cannot go back. ³⁶And she said unto him, My father, *if* thou hast opened thy mouth unto the LORD, do to me according to that which hath proceeded out of thy mouth; forasmuch as the LORD hath taken vengeance for thee of thine enemies, *even* of the children of Ammon. ³⁷And she said unto her father, Let this thing be done for me: let me alone two months, that I may go up^f and down upon the mountains, and bewail my virginity, I and my fellows. ³⁸And he said, Go. And he sent her away *for* two months: and she went with her companions, and bewailed her virginity upon the mountains. ³⁹And it came to pass at the end of two months, that she returned unto her father, who did with her *according* to his vow which he had

---

^d whatsoever . . . : Heb. that which cometh forth, which shall come forth
^e the plain: or, Abel
^f go up . . . : Heb. go and go down

vowed: and she knew no man. And it was a custom[g] in Israel, [40]*That* the daughters of Israel went yearly[h] to lament the daughter of Jephthah the Gileadite four days in a year.

12

[1]And the men of Ephraim gathered themselves together, and went northward, and said unto Jephthah, Wherefore passedst thou over to fight against the children of Ammon, and didst not call us to go with thee? we will burn thine house upon thee with fire. [2]And Jephthah said unto them, I and my people were at great strife with the children of Ammon; and when I called you, ye delivered me not out of their hands. [3]And when I saw that ye delivered *me* not, I put my life in my hands, and passed over against the children of Am-

mon, and the LORD delivered them into my hand: wherefore then are ye come up unto me this day, to fight against me? [4]Then Jephthah gathered together all the men of Gilead, and fought with Ephraim: and the men of Gilead smote Ephraim, because they said, Ye Gileadites *are* fugitives of Ephraim among the Ephraimites, *and* among the Manassites. [5]And the Gileadites took the passages of Jordan before the Ephraimites: and it was *so,* that when those Ephraimites which were escaped said, Let me go over; that the men of Gilead said unto him, *Art* thou an Ephraimite? If he said, Nay; [6]Then said they unto him, Say now Shibboleth: and he said Sibboleth: for he could not frame to pronounce *it* right. Then they took him, and slew him at the passages of Jordan: and there fell at that time of the Ephraimites forty and two thousand. [7]And Jephthah judged Israel six years. Then died Jephthah the Gileadite, and was buried in *one of* the cities of Gilead.

[8]And after him Ibzan of Bethlehem judged Israel. [9]And he had thirty sons, and thirty daughters, *whom* he sent abroad, and took in thirty daughters from abroad for his sons. And he judged Israel seven years. [10]Then died Ibzan, and was buried at Bethlehem. [11]And after him Elon, a Zebulonite, judged Israel; and he judged Israel ten years. [12]And Elon the Zebulonite died, and was buried in Aijalon in the country of Zebulun. [13]And after him Abdon the son of Hillel, a Pirathonite, judged Israel. [14]And he had forty sons and thirty nephews[a],

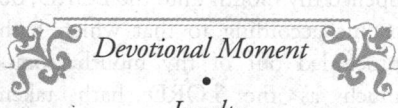

Devotional Moment

Insults

12:1-4 Some insults need to be addressed: racial slurs, ethnic jabs, smearing of a reputation. Other insults—the kind we tell children to ignore—simply call for thick-skinned self-assurance. Jephthah let himself get upset needlessly over the second kind, and lots of people suffered as a result. Families that can tell the difference between good-natured, healthy conflict and cruel, demeaning behavior can handle both. Has your family learned both how to laugh and how to resolve conflict—even laughing together when things go wrong—without piling up the hurt? If possible, take courses in communication skills or family therapy. The peace and harmony are worth it.

---

[g] custom: or, ordinance
[h] yearly: Heb. from year to year
[a] nephews: Heb. sons' sons

that rode on threescore and ten ass colts: and he judged Israel eight years. ¹⁵And Abdon the son of Hillel the Pirathonite died, and was buried in Pirathon in the land of Ephraim, in the mount of the Amalekites.

13

¹And the children of Israel did evilᵃ again in the sight of the LORD; and the LORD delivered them into the hand of the Philistines forty years. ²And there was a certain man of Zorah, of the family of the Danites, whose name *was* Manoah; and his wife *was* barren, and bare not. ³And the angel of the LORD appeared unto the woman, and said unto her, Behold now, thou *art* barren, and bearest not: but thou shalt conceive, and bear a son. ⁴Now therefore beware, I pray thee, and drink not wine nor strong drink, and eat not any unclean *thing*: ⁵For, lo, thou shalt conceive, and bear a son; and no razor shall

---

Devotional Moment

•

Dedicated to God

13:5 Samson was to be a Nazarite—a person who took a vow to be set apart for God's service. Samson's parents made the vow for him. A Nazarite vow was sometimes temporary, but in Samson's case, it was for life. As a Nazarite, Samson could not cut his hair, touch a dead body, or drink anything containing alcohol. Today, we need to dedicate ourselves to God, and to raise our children to have a strong sense of dedication of their lives to God—to help them see themselves as enlisted in God's service in whatever vocation they pursue.

---

come on his head: for the child shall be a Nazarite unto God from the womb: and he shall begin to deliver Israel out of the hand of the Philistines. ⁶Then the woman came and told her husband, saying, A man of God came unto me, and his countenance *was* like the countenance of an angel of God, very terrible: but I asked him not whence he *was*, neither told he me his name: ⁷But he said unto me, Behold, thou shalt conceive, and bear a son; and now drink no wine nor strong drink, neither eat any unclean *thing*: for the child shall be a Nazarite to God from the womb to the day of his death.

⁸Then Manoah intreated the LORD, and said, O my Lord, let the man of God which thou didst send come again unto us, and teach us what we shall do unto the child that shall be born. ⁹And God hearkened to the voice of Manoah; and the angel of God came again unto the woman as she sat in the field: but Manoah her husband *was* not with her. ¹⁰And the woman made haste, and ran, and shewed her husband, and said unto him, Behold, the man hath appeared unto me, that came unto me the *other* day. ¹¹And Manoah arose, and went after his wife, and came to the man, and said unto him, *Art* thou the man that spakest unto the woman? And he said, I *am*. ¹²And Manoah said, Now let thy words come to pass. How shall we orderᵇ the child, and *how* shall we do unto him? ¹³And the angel of the LORD said unto Manoah, Of all that I said unto the woman let her beware. ¹⁴She may not eat of any *thing* that

---

ᵃ did evil . . . : Heb. added to commit, etc
ᵇ How shall we order . . . : Heb. What shall be the manner of the, etc

cometh of the vine, neither let her drink wine or strong drink, nor eat any unclean *thing*: all that I commanded her let her observe.

¹⁵And Manoah said unto the angel of the LORD, I pray thee, let us detain thee, until we shall have made ready a kid for thee.ᶜ ¹⁶And the angel of the LORD said unto Manoah, Though thou detain me, I will not eat of thy bread: and if thou wilt offer a burnt offering, thou must offer it unto the LORD. For Manoah knew not that he *was* an angel of the LORD. ¹⁷And Manoah said unto the angel of the LORD, What *is* thy name, that when thy sayings come to pass we may do thee honour? ¹⁸And the angel of the LORD said unto him, Why askest thou thus after my name, seeing it *is* secretᵈ? ¹⁹So Manoah took a kid with a meat offering, and offered *it* upon a rock unto the LORD: and *the angel* did wondrously; and Manoah and his wife looked on. ²⁰For it came to pass, when the flame went up toward heaven from off the altar, that the angel of the LORD ascended in the flame of the altar. And Manoah and his wife looked on *it*, and fell on their faces to the ground. ²¹But the angel of the LORD did no more appear to Manoah and to his wife. Then Manoah knew that he *was* an angel of the LORD. ²²And Manoah said unto his wife, We shall surely die, because we have seen God. ²³But his wife said unto him, If the LORD were pleased to kill us, he would not have received a burnt offer-

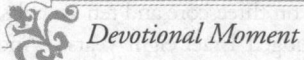

Devotional Moment

•

Preparing the Young

13:25 God blessed Samson with ferocious energy, self-confidence, and strength of will. Naturally, young Samson bounced with eager anticipation when he saw his tribe's army strut and step. Parents do well to help their children define and reach goals, based on their special abilities. Parents of gifted children need to prepare them for unusual service and teach them to regard their giftedness as a responsibility to serve God and people. Notice your children's unique gifts, and give them opportunities to develop each one.

ing and a meat offering at our hands, neither would he have shewed us all these *things*, nor would as at this time have told us *such things* as these.

²⁴And the woman bare a son, and called his name Samson: and the child grew, and the LORD blessed him. ²⁵And the Spirit of the LORD began to move him at times in the campᵉ of Dan between Zorah and Eshtaol.

14

¹And Samson went down to Timnath, and saw a woman in Timnath of the daughters of the Philistines. ²And he came up, and told his father and his mother, and said, I have seen a woman in Timnath of the daughters of the Philistines: now therefore get her for me to wife. ³Then his father and his mother said unto him, *Is there* never a woman among the daughters of thy brethren, or among all my people, that

---

ᶜ for thee: Heb. before thee
ᵈ secret: or, wonderful
ᵉ the camp . . . : Heb. Mahanehdan

thou goest to take a wife of the uncircumcised Philistines? And Samson said unto his father, Get her for me; for she pleaseth me well. ⁴But his father and his mother knew not that it *was* of the LORD, that he sought an occasion against the Philistines: for at that time the Philistines had dominion over Israel. ⁵Then went Samson down, and his father and his mother, to Timnath, and came to the vineyards of Timnath: and, behold, a young lion roaroed against[a] him. ⁶And the Spirit of the LORD came mightily upon him, and he rent him as he would have rent a kid, and *he had* nothing in his hand: but he told not his father or his mother what he had done. ⁷And he went down, and talked with the woman; and she pleased Samson well. ⁸And after a time he returned to take her, and he turned aside to see the carcase of the lion: and, behold, *there was* a swarm of bees and honey in the carcase of the lion. ⁹And he took thereof in his hands, and went on eating, and came to his father and mother, and he gave them, and they did eat: but he told not them that he had taken the honey out of the carcase of the lion.

¹⁰So his father went down unto the woman: and Samson made there a feast; for so used the young men to do. ¹¹And it came to pass, when they saw him, that they brought thirty companions to be with him. ¹²And Samson said unto them, I will now put forth a riddle unto you: if ye can certainly declare it

me within the seven days of the feast, and find *it* out, then I will give you thirty sheets[b] and thirty change of garments: ¹³But if ye cannot declare *it* me, then shall ye give me thirty sheets[c] and thirty change of garments. And they said unto him, Put forth thy riddle, that we may hear it. ¹⁴And he said unto them, Out of the eater came forth meat, and out of the strong came forth sweetness. And they could not in three days expound the riddle. ¹⁵And it came to pass on the seventh day, that they said unto Samson's wife, Entice thy husband, that he may declare unto us the riddle, lest we burn thee and thy father's house with fire: have ye called us to take that we have? *is it* not *so*? ¹⁶And Samson's wife wept before him, and said, Thou dost but hate me, and lovest me not: thou hast put forth a riddle unto the children of my people, and hast not told *it* me. And he said unto her, Behold, I have not told *it* my father nor my mother, and shall I tell *it* thee? ¹⁷And she wept before him the seven[d] days, while their feast lasted: and it came to pass on the seventh day, that he told her, because she lay sore upon him: and she told the riddle to the children of her people. ¹⁸And the men of the city said unto him on the seventh day before the sun went down, What *is* sweeter than honey? and what *is* stronger than a lion? And he said unto them, If ye had not plowed with my heifer, ye had not found out my riddle. ¹⁹And the Spirit of the LORD came

---

[a] against . . . : Heb. in meeting him
[b] sheets: or, shirts
[c] sheets: or, shirts
[d] the seven . . . : or, the rest of the seven days

Samson's Parents
(Manoah and his wife)

We don't know how long Manoah and his wife lived with childlessness, but in a place and time when having no children could mean having no one to care for you in old age, barrenness had material as well as emotional implications.

The announcement by the Angel surely came as a great surprise to Manoah and his wife since they were physically unable to conceive. Make no mistake—Samson would be a miracle baby, in the literal sense. And God had special plans for Samson from the very beginning.

For Manoah and his wife, along with the usual challenges of parenting came the knowledge that Samson was to be dedicated to God's service. Manoah had only one request: "O my Lord . . . teach us what we shall do unto the child that shall be born" (Judg. 13:8). They feared God and wanted to obey the Lord's instructions, so they raised Samson as God had instructed them. He grew up a Nazirite, and God used him to deliver the Israelite nation from its enemies, the Philistines. Their special son was an only child.

Childlessness is a painful reality for many couples. Most of those who can't conceive would rather have the option. To live without it can be quite difficult. When the privilege of parenting has been denied us, we should pray for God's help to protect us from depression and envy. When God brings along a miracle baby, we can pray, as did Manoah, that God would teach us how to bring up the child who is to be born.

upon him, and he went down to Ashkelon, and slew thirty men of them, and took their spoil^c, and gave change of garments unto them which expounded the riddle. And his anger was kindled, and he went up to his father's house. ²⁰But Samson's wife was *given* to his companion, whom he had used as his friend.

15

¹But it came to pass within a while after, in the time of wheat harvest, that Samson visited his wife with a kid; and he said, I will go in to my wife into the chamber. But her father would not suffer him to go in. ²And her father said, I verily thought that thou hadst utterly hated her; therefore I gave her to thy companion: *is* not her younger sister fairer than she? take her, I pray thee, instead of her. ³And Samson said concerning them, Now shall I be more blameless than the Philistines, though I do them a displeasure. ⁴And Samson went and caught three hundred foxes, and took firebrands^a, and turned tail to tail, and put a firebrand in the midst between two tails. ⁵And when he had set the brands on fire, he let *them* go into the standing corn of the Philistines, and burnt up both the shocks, and also the standing corn, with the vineyards *and* olives. ⁶Then the Philistines said, Who hath done this? And they answered, Samson, the son in law of the Timnite, because he had taken his wife, and given her to his companion. And the Philistines came up, and burnt her and

her father with fire. ⁷And Samson said unto them, Though ye have done this, yet will I be avenged of you, and after that I will cease. ⁸And he smote them hip and thigh with a great slaughter: and he went down and dwelt in the top of the rock Etam.

⁹Then the Philistines went up, and pitched in Judah, and spread themselves in Lehi. ¹⁰And the men of Judah said, Why are ye come up against us? And they answered, To bind Samson are we come up, to do to him as he hath done to us. ¹¹Then three thousand men of Judah went^b to the top of the rock Etam, and said to Samson, Knowest thou not that the Philistines *are* rulers over us? what *is* this *that* thou hast done unto us? And he said unto them, As they did unto me, so have I done unto them. ¹²And they said unto him, We are come down to bind thee, that we may deliver thee into the hand of the Philistines. And Samson said unto them, Swear unto me, that ye will not fall upon me yourselves. ¹³And they spake unto him, saying, No; but we will bind thee fast, and deliver thee into their hand: but surely we will not kill thee. And they bound him with two new cords, and brought him up from the rock. ¹⁴*And* when he came unto Lehi, the Philistines shouted against him: and the Spirit of the LORD came mightily upon him, and the cords that *were* upon his arms became as flax that was burnt with fire, and his bands loosed^c from off his hands. ¹⁵And he

---

^c spoil: or, apparel

^a firebrands: or, torches

^b went: Heb. went down

^c loosed: Heb. were melted

found a new[d] jawbone of an ass, and put forth his hand, and took it, and slew a thousand men therewith. [16]And Samson said, With the jawbone of an ass, heaps upon heaps, with the jaw of an ass have I slain a thousand men. [17]And it came to pass, when he had made an end of speaking, that he cast away the jawbone out of his hand, and called that place Ramathlehi[e].

[18]And he was sore athirst, and

Devotional Moment

•

Depression

15:18 Because life is never perfect, most people find good reasons to be melancholy. Samson had bouts with sadness, too, sometimes as an aftermath to anger, sometimes following euphoria over a victory. Whatever the cause, depression troubles many people. It can ruin a lifetime, or just a day. It can dampen great success or embitter after great loss. It can be an overly intense response to a real but manageable problem.

If you are depressed, seek out the cures that God has so graciously provided for us: his love, prayer, counseling, support from other Christians, medical intervention, or whatever is needed. All these forms of help are gifts of God; there is no reason to feel guilty for needing them.

And if you are a parent, it is important to let children know that occasional depression is a normal part of life. Don't tell children to "snap out of it" when they're down. What they may need is God's love, straight from you in the form of a hug, a listening ear, or reassurance of your support. Even God's people get depressed . . . and that's why we have each other.

---

called on the LORD, and said, Thou hast given this great deliverance into the hand of thy servant: and now shall I die for thirst, and fall into the hand of the uncircumcised? [19]But God clave an hollow place that *was* in the jaw, and there came water thereout; and when he had drunk, his spirit came again, and he revived: wherefore he called the name thereof Enhakkore[f], which *is* in Lehi unto this day. [20]And he judged Israel in the days of the Philistines twenty years.

16

[1]Then went Samson to Gaza, and saw there an harlot[a], and went in unto her. [2]*And it was told* the Gazites, saying, Samson is come hither. And they compassed *him* in, and laid wait for him all night in the gate of the city, and were quiet all the night, saying, In the morning, when it is day, we shall kill him. [3]And Samson lay till midnight, and arose at midnight, and took the doors of the gate of the city, and the two posts, and went away with them, bar[b] and all, and put *them* upon his shoulders, and carried them up to the top of an hill that *is* before Hebron.

[4]And it came to pass afterward, that he loved a woman in the valley of Sorek, whose name *was* Delilah. [5]And the lords of the Philistines came up unto her, and said unto her, Entice him, and see wherein his great strength *lieth*, and by what *means* we may prevail against him, that we may bind him

---

[d] new: Heb. moist

[e] Ramathlehi: that is, the lifting up of the jawbone, or, casting away of the jawbone

[f] Enhakkore: that is, the well of him that called or, cried

[a] harlot: Heb. a woman an harlot

[b] bar . . . : Heb. with the bar

Samson

Though the macho image takes a lot of official heat, in practice we reward it and expect it of men. "Real" men take charge. We tell our sons to fight back and not to be wimps. We admire physically strong and healthy athletes. We talk up being meek and gentle in church, but the world rewards tough and brash.

If ever a man embodied the macho image, it was Samson. He was strong, aggressive, and arrogant. He bragged freely. And he treated women like things.

Samson's strength came from God, but he forgot that. He treated Delilah like a toy because he thought too much of himself—or, more accurately, too much of what God had made him.

Samson brings us straight to the problem many men have with pride. The temptation to impress women is as much a part of the macho act as acting tough itself. But men who do so are in danger of treating women like things. Samson never used his strength *against* Delilah; he never abused her. But he didn't treat her with respect, either.

Give credit to God for every good quality you have and every good turn your life takes. Don't let God's good work in you become an excuse for belittling others. Have respect for God and for women. Samson had his strengths—his courage delivered his people from a cruel, oppressive enemy nation. Yet his brazen, arrogant attitude has no place among God's people, least of all the ones who lead a home.

LESSONS FROM SAMSON AS A MAN

Success comes from God. Be humble about what you do well.

It is possible to follow God and still forget your priorities. Samson lost his perspective when everything was going well.

You can tell a lot from how a man treats his wife. Beware of trying to impress or prove something to her.

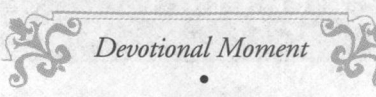

Devotional Moment

•

Beware

16:4-16 Shrewd Delilah knew she had caught Samson in the vice of sexual desire and that she would get his secret in due time. All who experience the power of sexual attraction know something of Samson's problem. Sexual intimacy causes enormous repercussions in emotions, expectations, and commitments. The temptation to isolate the act from marriage is as old as human hormones and as recent as last night's prime-time TV. For Samson, sex outside of God's will led to pain, humiliation, and death. Because our sexuality is so powerful, we need God's help to control it. Our part is to avoid needless temptations, maintain accountability with a friend if possible, and seek counseling should desires get out of control.

to afflict[c] him: and we will give thee every one of us eleven hundred *pieces* of silver. ⁶And Delilah said to Samson, Tell me, I pray thee, wherein thy great strength *lieth*, and wherewith thou mightest be bound to afflict thee. ⁷And Samson said unto her, If they bind me with seven green[d] withs that were never dried, then shall I be weak, and be as another man. ⁸Then the lords of the Philistines brought up to her seven green[e] withs which had not been dried, and she bound him with them. ⁹Now *there were* men lying in wait, abiding with her in the chamber. And she said unto him, The Philistines *be* upon thee, Samson. And he brake the withs, as a thread of tow is broken when it toucheth[f] the fire. So his strength was

not known. ¹⁰And Delilah said unto Samson, Behold, thou hast mocked me, and told me lies: now tell me, I pray thee, wherewith thou mightest be bound. ¹¹And he said unto her, If they bind me fast with new ropes that never were occupied, then shall I be weak, and be as another man. ¹²Delilah therefore took new ropes, and bound him therewith, and said unto him, The Philistines *be* upon thee, Samson. And *there were* liers in wait abiding in the chamber. And he brake them from off his arms like a thread. ¹³And Delilah said unto Samson, Hitherto thou hast mocked me, and told me lies: tell me wherewith thou mightest be bound. And he said unto her, If thou weavest the seven locks of my head with the web. ¹⁴And she fastened *it* with the pin, and said unto him, The Philistines *be* upon thee, Samson. And he awaked out of his sleep, and went away with the pin of the beam, and with the web. ¹⁵And she said unto him, How canst thou say, I love thee, when thine heart *is* not with me? thou hast mocked me these three times, and hast not told me wherein thy great strength *lieth*. ¹⁶And it came to pass, when she pressed him daily with her words, and urged him, *so* that his soul was vexed[g] unto death; ¹⁷That he told her all his heart, and said unto her, There hath not come a razor upon mine head; for I *have been* a Nazarite unto God from my mother's womb: if I be shaven, then my strength

---

[c] afflict: or, humble
[d] green . . . : or, new cords: Heb. moist
[e] green . . . : or, new cords: Heb. moist
[f] toucheth: Heb. smelleth
[g] vexed: Heb. shortened

will go from me, and I shall become weak, and be like any *other* man.

¹⁸And when Delilah saw that he had told her all his heart, she sent and called for the lords of the Philistines, saying, Come up this once, for he hath shewed me all his heart. Then the lords of the Philistines came up unto her, and brought money in their hand. ¹⁹And she made him sleep upon her knees; and she called for a man, and she caused him to shave off the seven locks of his head; and she began to afflict him, and his strength went from him. ²⁰And she said, The Philistines *be* upon thee, Samson. And he awoke out of his sleep, and said, I will go out as at other times before, and shake myself. And he wist not that the LORD was departed from him. ²¹But the Philistines took him, and put out[h] his eyes, and brought him down to Gaza, and bound him with fetters of brass; and he did grind in the prison house.

²²Howbeit the hair of his head began to grow again after[i] he was shaven. ²³Then the lords of the Philistines gathered them together for to offer a great sacrifice unto Dagon their god, and to rejoice: for they said, Our god hath delivered Samson our enemy into our hand. ²⁴And when the people saw him, they praised their god: for they said, Our god hath delivered into our hands our enemy, and the destroyer of our country, which slew many of us. ²⁵And it came to pass, when their hearts were merry, that they said, Call for Samson, that he may make us sport. And they called for Samson out of the prison house; and he made them[j] sport: and they set him between the pillars. ²⁶And Samson said unto the lad that held him by the hand, Suffer me that I may feel the pillars whereupon the house standeth, that I may lean upon them. ²⁷Now the house was full of men and women; and all the lords of the Philistines *were* there; and *there were* upon the roof about three thousand men and women, that beheld while Samson made sport. ²⁸And Samson called unto the LORD, and said, O Lord GOD, remember me, I pray thee, and strengthen me, I pray thee, only this once, O God, that I may be at once avenged of the Philistines for my two eyes. ²⁹And Samson took hold of the two middle pillars upon which the house stood, and on which it was borne up, of the one with his right hand, and of the other with his left. ³⁰And Samson said, Let me die with the Philistines. And he bowed himself with *all his* might; and the house fell upon the lords, and upon all the people that *were* therein. So the dead which he slew at his death were more than *they* which he slew in his life. ³¹Then his brethren and all the house of his father came down, and took him, and brought *him* up, and buried him between Zorah and Eshtaol in the buryingplace of Manoah his father. And he judged Israel twenty years.

17

¹And there was a man of mount Ephraim, whose name *was* Micah. ²And he said unto his mother, The eleven hundred

---

[h] put out: Heb. bored out
[i] after . . . : or, as when he was shaven
[j] them: Heb. before them

shekels of silver that were taken from thee, about which thou cursedst, and spakest of also in mine ears, behold, the silver *is* with me; I took it. And his mother said, Blessed *be thou* of the LORD, my son. ³And when he had restored the eleven hundred *shekels* of silver to his mother, his mother said, I had wholly dedicated the silver unto the LORD from my hand for my son, to make a graven image and a molten image: now therefore I will restore it unto thee. ⁴Yet he restored the money unto his mother; and his mother took two hundred *shekels* of silver, and gave them to the founder, who made thereof a graven image and a molten image: and they were in the house of Micah. ⁵And the man Micah had an house of gods, and made an ephod, and teraphim, and con-secrated ᵃ one of his sons, who became his priest. ⁶In those days *there was* no king in Israel, *but* every man did *that which was* right in his own eyes.

⁷And there was a young man out of Bethlehemjudah of the family of Judah, who *was* a Levite, and he sojourned there. ⁸And the man departed out of the city from Bethlehemjudah to sojourn where he could find *a place*: and he came to mount Ephraim to the house of Micah, as he journeyed. ⁹And Micah said unto him, Whence comest thou? And he said unto him, I *am* a Levite of Bethlehemjudah, and I go to sojourn where I may find *a place*. ¹⁰And Micah said unto him, Dwell with me, and be unto me a father and a priest, and I will give thee ten *shekels* of sil-ver by the year, and a suit ᵇ of apparel, and thy victuals. So the Levite went in. ¹¹And

the Levite was content to dwell with the man; and the young man was unto him as one of his sons. ¹²And Micah conse-crated the Levite; and the young man be-came his priest, and was in the house of Micah. ¹³Then said Micah, Now know I that the LORD will do me good, seeing I have a Levite to *my* priest.

18

¹In those days *there was* no king in Israel: and in those days the tribe of the Danites sought them an inheritance to dwell in; for unto that day *all their* inheritance had not fallen unto them among the tribes of Israel. ²And the children of Dan sent of their family five men from their coasts, men of valour, from Zorah, and from Eshtaol, to spy out the land, and to search it; and they said unto them, Go, search the land: who when they came to mount Ephraim, to the house of Micah, they lodged there. ³When they *were* by the house of Micah, they knew the voice of the young man the Levite: and they turned in thither, and said unto him, Who brought thee hither? and what makest thou in this *place*? and what hast thou here? ⁴And he said unto them, Thus and thus dealeth Micah with me, and hath hired me, and I am his priest. ⁵And they said unto him, Ask counsel, we pray thee, of God, that we may know whether our way which we go shall be prosperous. ⁶And the priest said unto them, Go in peace: before the LORD *is* your way wherein ye go.

⁷Then the five men departed, and came to Laish ᵃ, and saw the people that

---

ᵃ consecrated: Heb. filled the hand
ᵇ a suit . . . : or, a double suit, etc: Heb. an order of garments
ᵃ Laish: called elsewhere, called Leshom

were therein, how they dwelt careless, after the manner of the Zidonians, quiet and secure; and *there was* no magistrate in the land, that might put *them* to shame in *any* thing; and they *were* far from the Zidonians, and had no business with *any* man. ⁸And they came unto their brethren to Zorah and Eshtaol: and their brethren said unto them, What *say* ye? ⁹And they said, Arise, that we may go up against them: for we have seen the land, and, behold, it *is* very good: and *are* ye still? be not slothful to go, *and* to enter to possess the land. ¹⁰When ye go, ye shall come unto a people secure, and to a large land: for God hath given it into your hands; a place where *there is* no want of any thing that *is* in the earth. ¹¹And there went from thence of the family of the Danites, out of Zorah and out of Eshtaol, six hundred men appointed^b with weapons of war. ¹²And they went up, and pitched in Kirjathjearim, in Judah: wherefore they called that place Mahanehdan unto this day: behold, *it is* behind Kirjathjearim. ¹³And they passed thence unto mount Ephraim, and came unto the house of Micah.

¹⁴Then answered the five men that went to spy out the country of Laish, and said unto their brethren, Do ye know that there is in these houses an ephod, and teraphim, and a graven image, and a molten image? now therefore consider what ye have to do. ¹⁵And they turned thitherward, and came to the house of the young man the Levite, *even* unto the house of Micah, and saluted^c him. ¹⁶And the six hundred men ap-

pointed with their weapons of war, which *were* of the children of Dan, stood by the entering of the gate. ¹⁷And the five men that went to spy out the land went up, *and* came in thither, *and* took the graven image, and the ephod, and the teraphim, and the molten image: and the priest stood in the entering of the gate with the six hundred men *that were* appointed with weapons of war. ¹⁸And these went into Micah's house, and fetched the carved image, the ephod, and the teraphim, and the molten image. Then said the priest unto them, What do ye? ¹⁹And they said unto him, Hold thy peace, lay thine hand upon thy mouth, and go with us, and be to us a father and a priest: *is it* better for thee to be a priest unto the house of one man, or that thou be a priest unto a tribe and a family in Israel? ²⁰And the priest's heart was glad, and he took the ephod, and the teraphim, and the graven image, and went in the midst of the people. ²¹So they turned and departed, and put the little ones and the cattle and the carriage before them. ²²*And* when they were a good way from the house of Micah, the men that *were* in the houses near to Micah's house were gathered together, and overtook the children of Dan. ²³And they cried unto the children of Dan. And they turned their faces, and said unto Micah, What aileth thee, that thou comest with such a company? ²⁴And he said, Ye have taken away my gods which I made, and the priest, and ye are gone away: and what have I more? and what *is* this *that* ye say unto me, What aileth thee? ²⁵And the children of Dan said

---

^b appointed: Heb. girded
^c saluted . . . : Heb. asked him of peace

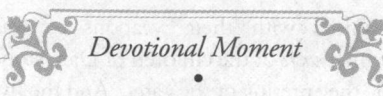

Devotional Moment

•

Success

18:27 The battle was short and brutal—a textbook victory. The Danite band had accurate intelligence, the element of surprise, and the will to win. By any measure except one, this was a triumph.

We tend to measure success by salaries, perks, seniority, honors, varsity letters, grades, and academic degrees. But none of these necessarily reflects the one quality the Danite invaders lacked: a personal relationship with God. The truly successful person first and foremost asks God to guide his or her actions, tempers ambition with the desire to serve and obey God, and displays integrity in the way he or she treats people. And all this shows up most vividly in the home.

unto him, Let not thy voice be heard among us, lest angry[d] fellows run upon thee, and thou lose thy life, with the lives of thy household. ²⁶And the children of Dan went their way: and when Micah saw that they *were* too strong for him, he turned and went back unto his house.

²⁷And they took *the things* which Micah had made, and the priest which he had, and came unto Laish, unto a people *that were* at quiet and secure: and they smote them with the edge of the sword, and burnt the city with fire. ²⁸And *there was* no deliverer, because it *was* far from Zidon, and they had no business with *any* man; and it was in the valley that *lieth* by Bethrehob. And they built a city, and dwelt therein. ²⁹And they called the name of the city Dan, after the name of Dan their father, who was born

unto Israel: howbeit the name of the city *was* Laish at the first. ³⁰And the children of Dan set up the graven image: and Jonathan, the son of Gershom, the son of Manasseh, he and his sons were priests to the tribe of Dan until the day of the captivity of the land. ³¹And they set them up Micah's graven image, which he made, all the time that the house of God was in Shiloh.

19

¹And it came to pass in those days, when *there was* no king in Israel, that there was a certain Levite sojourning on the side of mount Ephraim, who took to him a concubine[a] out of Bethlehemjudah. ²And his concubine played the whore against him, and went away from him unto her father's house to Bethlehemjudah, and was there four whole months. ³And her husband arose, and went after her, to speak friendly[b] unto her, *and* to bring her again, having his servant with him, and a couple of asses: and she brought him into her father's house: and when the father of the damsel saw him, he rejoiced to meet him. ⁴And his father in law, the damsel's father, retained him; and he abode with him three days: so they did eat and drink, and lodged there. ⁵And it came to pass on the fourth day, when they arose early in the morning, that he rose up to depart: and the damsel's father said unto his son in law, Comfort[c] thine heart with a morsel of bread, and afterward go your way.

---

[d] angry: Heb. bitter of soul
[a] a concubine: Heb. a woman a concubine, or, a wife a concubine
[b] friendly . . . : Heb. to her heart
[c] Comfort: Heb. Strengthen

⁶And they sat down, and did eat and drink both of them together: for the damsel's father had said unto the man, Be content, I pray thee, and tarry all night, and let thine heart be merry. ⁷And when the man rose up to depart, his father in law urged him: therefore he lodged there again. ⁸And he arose early in the morning on the fifth day to depart: and the damsel's father said, Comfort thine heart, I pray thee. And they tarried until afternoonᵈ, and they did eat both of them. ⁹And when the man rose up to depart, he, and his concubine, and his servant, his father in law, the damsel's father, said unto him, Behold, now the day drawethᵉ toward evening, I pray you tarry all night: behold, the day groweth to an end, lodge here, that thine heart may be merry; and to morrow get you early on your way, that thou mayest go home. ¹⁰But the man would not tarry that night, but he rose up and departed, and came over againstᶠ Jebus, which is Jerusalem; and there were with him two asses saddled, his concubine also was with him. ¹¹And when they were by Jebus, the day was far spent; and the servant said unto his master, Come, I pray thee, and let us turn in into this city of the Jebusites, and lodge in it. ¹²And his master said unto him, We will not turn aside hither into the city of a stranger, that is not of the children of Israel; we will pass over to Gibeah. ¹³And he said unto his servant, Come, and let us draw near to one of these places to lodge all night, in Gibeah, or in Ramah. ¹⁴And they passed on and went their way; and the sun went down upon them when they were by Gibeah, which belongeth to Benjamin. ¹⁵And they turned aside thither, to go in and to lodge in Gibeah: and when he went in, he sat him down in a street of the city: for there was no man that took them into his house to lodging.

¹⁶And, behold, there came an old man from his work out of the field at even, which was also of mount Ephraim; and he sojourned in Gibeah: but the men of the place were Benjamites. ¹⁷And when he had lifted up his eyes, he saw a wayfaring man in the street of the city: and the old man said, Whither goest thou? and whence comest thou? ¹⁸And he said unto him, We are passing from Bethlehemjudah toward the side of mount Ephraim; from thence am I: and I went to Bethlehemjudah, but I am now going to the house of the LORD; and there is no man that receivethᵍ me to house. ¹⁹Yet there is both straw and provender for our asses; and there is bread and wine also for me, and for thy handmaid, and for the young man which is with thy servants: there is no want of any thing. ²⁰And the old man said, Peace be with thee; howsoever let all thy wants lie upon me; only lodge not in the street. ²¹So he brought him into his house, and gave provender unto the asses: and they washed their feet, and did eat and drink.

ᵈ until afternoon: Heb. till the day declined
ᵉ draweth: Heb. is weak
ᶠ over against: Heb. to over against
ᵍ receiveth: Heb. gathereth

²²*Now* as they were making their hearts merry, behold, the men of the city, certain sons of Belial, beset the house round about, *and* beat at the door, and spake to the master of the house, the old man, saying, Bring forth the man that came into thine house, that we may know him. ²³And the man, the master of the house, went out unto them, and said unto them, Nay, my brethren, *nay*, I pray you, do not *so* wickedly; seeing that this man is come into mine house, do not this folly. ²⁴Behold, *here is* my daughter a maiden, and his concubine; them I will bring out now, and humble ye them, and do with them what seemeth good unto you: but unto this man do not so vile[h] a thing. ²⁵But the men would not hearken to him: so the man took his concubine, and brought her forth unto them; and they knew her, and abused her all the night until the morning: and when the day began to spring, they let her go. ²⁶Then came the woman in the dawning of the day, and fell down at the door of the man's house where her lord *was*, till it was light. ²⁷And her lord rose up in the morning, and opened the doors of the house, and went out to go his way: and, behold, the woman his concubine was fallen down *at* the door of the house, and her hands *were* upon the threshold. ²⁸And he said unto her, Up, and let us be going. But none answered. Then the man took her *up* upon an ass, and the man rose up, and gat him unto his place. ²⁹And when he was come into his house, he took a knife, and laid hold on his concubine, and divided her, *together* with her bones, into twelve pieces, and sent her into all the coasts of Israel. ³⁰And it was so, that all that saw it said, There was no such deed done nor seen from the day that the children of Israel came up out of the land of Egypt unto this day: consider of it, take advice, and speak *your minds*.

20

¹Then all the children of Israel went out, and the congregation was gathered together as one man, from Dan even to Beersheba, with the land of Gilead, unto the LORD in Mizpeh. ²And the chief of all the people, *even* of all the tribes of Israel, presented themselves in the assembly of the people of God, four hundred thousand footmen that drew sword. ³(Now the children of Benjamin heard that the children of Israel were gone up to Mizpeh.) Then said the children of Israel, Tell *us*, how was this wickedness? ⁴And the Levite[a], the husband of the woman that was slain, answered and said, I came into Gibeah that *belongeth* to Benjamin, I and my concubine, to lodge. ⁵And the men of Gibeah rose against me, and beset the house round about upon me by night, *and* thought to have slain me: and my concubine have they forced[b], that she is dead. ⁶And I took my concubine, and cut her in pieces, and sent her throughout all the country of the inheritance of Israel: for they have committed lewdness and folly in Israel. ⁷Behold, ye *are* all children of Israel; give here your ad-

---

[h] so vile . . . : Heb. the matter of this folly
[a] the Levite: Heb. the man the Levite
[b] forced: Heb. humbled

vice and counsel. ⁸And all the people arose as one man, saying, We will not any *of us* go to his tent, neither will we any *of us* turn into his house. ⁹But now this *shall be* the thing which we will do to Gibeah; *we will go up* by lot against it; ¹⁰And we will take ten men of an hundred throughout all the tribes of Israel, and an hundred of a thousand, and a thousand out of ten thousand, to fetch victual for the people, that they may do, when they come to Gibeah of Benjamin, according to all the folly that they have wrought in Israel. ¹¹So all the men of Israel were gathered against the city, knit together as one man.

¹²And the tribes of Israel sent men through all the tribe of Benjamin, saying, What wickedness *is* this that is done among you? ¹³Now therefore deliver *us* the men, the children of Belial, which *are* in Gibeah, that we may put them to death, and put away evil from Israel. But the children of Benjamin would not hearken to the voice of their brethren the children of Israel: ¹⁴But the children of Benjamin gathered themselves together out of the cities unto Gibeah, to go out to battle against the children of Israel. ¹⁵And the children of Benjamin were numbered at that time out of the cities twenty and six thousand men that drew sword, beside the inhabitants of Gibeah, which were numbered seven hundred chosen men. ¹⁶Among all this people *there were* seven hundred chosen men lefthanded; every one could sling stones at an hair *breadth*, and not miss. ¹⁷And the men of Israel, beside Benjamin, were numbered four hundred thousand men that drew sword: all these *were* men of war.

¹⁸And the children of Israel arose, and went up to the house of God, and asked counsel of God, and said, Which of us shall go up first to the battle against the children of Benjamin? And the LORD said, Judah *shall go up* first. ¹⁹And the children of Israel rose up in the morning, and encamped against Gibeah. ²⁰And the men of Israel went out to battle against Benjamin; and the men of Israel put themselves in array to fight against them at Gibeah. ²¹And the children of Benjamin came forth out of Gibeah, and destroyed down to the ground of the Israelites that day twenty and two thousand men. ²²And the people the men of Israel encouraged themselves, and set their battle again in array in the place where they put themselves in array the first day. ²³(And the children of Israel went up and wept before the LORD until even, and asked counsel of the LORD, saying, Shall I go up again to battle against the children of Benjamin my brother? And the LORD said, Go up against him.) ²⁴And the children of Israel came near against the children of Benjamin the second day. ²⁵And Benjamin went forth against them out of Gibeah the second day, and destroyed down to the ground of the children of Israel again eighteen thousand men; all these drew the sword.

²⁶Then all the children of Israel, and all the people, went up, and came unto the house of God, and wept, and sat there before the LORD, and fasted that day until even, and offered burnt offerings and peace offerings before the LORD. ²⁷And the children of Israel enquired of the LORD, (for the ark of the covenant of God *was* there in those days, ²⁸And Phinehas, the son of Eleazar, the

son of Aaron, stood before it in those days,) saying, Shall I yet again go out to battle against the children of Benjamin my brother, or shall I cease? And the LORD said, Go up; for to morrow I will deliver them into thine hand. ²⁹And Israel set liers in wait round about Gibeah. ³⁰And the children of Israel went up against the children of Benjamin on the third day, and put themselves in array against Gibeah, as at other times. ³¹And the children of Benjamin went out against the people, *and* were drawn away from the city; and they began to smite^c of the people, *and* kill, as at other times, in the highways, of which one goeth up to the house of God, and the other to Gibeah in the field, about thirty men of Israel. ³²And the children of Benjamin said, They *are* smitten down before us, as at the first. But the children of Israel said, Let us flee, and draw them from the city unto the highways. ³³And all the men of Israel rose up out of their place, and put themselves in array at Baaltamar: and the liers in wait of Israel came forth out of their places, *even* out of the meadows of Gibeah. ³⁴And there came against Gibeah ten thousand chosen men out of all Israel, and the battle was sore: but they knew not that evil *was* near them. ³⁵And the LORD smote Benjamin before Israel: and the children of Israel destroyed of the Benjamites that day twenty and five thousand and an hundred men: all these drew the sword.

³⁶So the children of Benjamin saw that they were smitten: for the men of Israel gave place to the Benjamites, because they trusted unto the liers in wait which they had set beside Gibeah. ³⁷And the liers in wait hasted, and rushed upon Gibeah; and the liers in wait drew *themselves* along^d, and smote all the city with the edge of the sword. ³⁸Now there was an appointed sign^e between the men of Israel and the liers in wait, that they should make a great flame with smoke rise up out of the city. ³⁹And when the men of Israel retired in the battle, Benjamin began to smite^f *and* kill of the men of Israel about thirty persons: for they said, Surely they are smitten down before us, as *in* the first battle. ⁴⁰But when the flame began to arise up out of the city with a pillar of smoke, the Benjamites looked behind them, and, behold, the flame of the city ascended up to heaven. ⁴¹And when the men of Israel turned again, the men of Benjamin were amazed: for they saw that evil was come^g upon them. ⁴²Therefore they turned *their backs* before the men of Israel unto the way of the wilderness; but the battle overtook them; and them which *came* out of the cities they destroyed in the midst of them. ⁴³*Thus* they inclosed the Benjamites round about, *and* chased them, *and* trode them down with ease^h over against Gibeah toward the sunrising. ⁴⁴And there fell of Benjamin eighteen thousand men; all these *were* men

---

^c to smite . . . : Heb. to smite of the people wounded as at, etc
^d drew . . . : or, made a long sound with the trumpet
^e sign: or, time
^f to smite . . . : Heb. to smite the wounded
^g was come . . . : Heb. touched them
^h with ease . . . : or, from Menuchah, etc

of valour. ⁴⁵And they turned and fled toward the wilderness unto the rock of Rimmon: and they gleaned of them in the highways five thousand men; and pursued hard after them unto Gidom, and slew two thousand men of them. ⁴⁶So that all which fell that day of Benjamin were twenty and five thousand men that drew the sword; all these *were* men of valour. ⁴⁷But six hundred men turned and fled to the wilderness unto the rock Rimmon, and abode in the rock Rimmon four months. ⁴⁸And the men of Israel turned again upon the children of Benjamin, and smote them with the edge of the sword, as well the men of *every* city, as the beast, and all that came to handⁱ: also they set on fire all the cities that they came to.

21

¹Now the men of Israel had sworn in Mizpeh, saying, There shall not any of us give his daughter unto Benjamin to wife. ²And the people came to the house of God, and abode there till even before God, and lifted up their voices, and wept sore; ³And said, O LORD God of Israel, why is this come to pass in Israel, that there should be to day one tribe lacking in Israel? ⁴And it came to pass on the morrow, that the people rose early, and built there an altar, and offered burnt offerings and peace offerings. ⁵And the children of Israel said, Who *is there* among all the tribes of Israel that came not up with the congregation unto the LORD? For they had made a great oath concerning him that came not up to the LORD to Mizpeh, saying, He shall

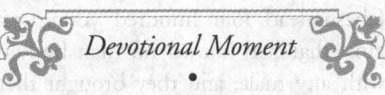

Devotional Moment
•
Reconciliation
21:2-4, 15 Many years of war and killing had created huge rifts between the tribes. Now the Israelites grieved the division of their larger family. As they grieved they looked to God and asked him for help in reconciliation. Although the cause of such family breaks today is rarely as serious as murder, the gap still leaves people feeling lonely and angry. Tragically, grown children and their parents may not speak to each other for years. Yet bitter, separated families can be reconciled with God's help. Don't sweep the division and hurts under the rug—openly acknowledge them and ask God for his help.

surely be put to death. ⁶And the children of Israel repented them for Benjamin their brother, and said, There is one tribe cut off from Israel this day. ⁷How shall we do for wives for them that remain, seeing we have sworn by the LORD that we will not give them of our daughters to wives? ⁸And they said, What one *is there* of the tribes of Israel that came not up to Mizpeh to the LORD? And, behold, there came none to the camp from Jabeshgilead to the assembly. ⁹For the people were numbered, and, behold, *there were* none of the inhabitants of Jabeshgilead there. ¹⁰And the congregation sent thither twelve thousand men of the valiantest, and commanded them, saying, Go and smite the inhabitants of Jabeshgilead with the edge of the sword, with the women and the children. ¹¹And this *is* the thing that ye shall do, Ye shall utterly destroy every male, and every woman that hath lain^a by man. ¹²And they found among the inhabitants of

---

ⁱ came to hand: Heb. was found
^a hath lain . . . : Heb. knoweth the lying with man

Jabeshgilead four hundred young[b] virgins, that had known no man by lying with any male: and they brought them unto the camp to Shiloh, which *is* in the land of Canaan. [13]And the whole congregation sent *some* to speak[c] to the children of Benjamin that *were* in the rock Rimmon, and to call peaceably unto them. [14]And Benjamin came again at that time; and they gave them wives which they had saved alive of the women of Jabeshgilead: and yet so they sufficed them not. [15]And the people repented them for Benjamin, because that the LORD had made a breach in the tribes of Israel.

[16]Then the elders of the congregation said, How shall we do for wives for them that remain, seeing the women are destroyed out of Benjamin? [17]And they said, *There must be* an inheritance for them that be escaped of Benjamin, that a tribe be not destroyed out of Israel. [18]Howbeit we may not give them wives of our daughters: for the children of Israel have sworn, saying, Cursed *be* he that giveth a wife to Benjamin. [19]Then they said, Behold, *there is* a feast of the LORD in Shiloh yearly[d] *in a place* which *is* on the north side of Bethel, on the east side of the highway that goeth up from Bethel to Shechem, and on the south of Lebonah. [20]Therefore they commanded the children of Benjamin, saying, Go and lie in wait in the vineyards; [21]And see, and, behold, if the daughters of Shiloh come out to dance in dances, then come ye out of the vineyards, and catch you every man

> ### Devotional Moment
> •
> ### Leadership
> 21:25 The people abandoned the laws that God gave to Moses because no human leaders served as law enforcers. While it's always best to have leaders to hold people accountable, there may be some life situations in which leaders are absent. If you come from a family with weak or absent authority figures, ask God to lead you personally with his Word and by Jesus' example. Don't fall into either extreme: becoming a tyrant or continuing the cycle in your own family of everyone doing whatever he or she thinks is right.

his wife of the daughters of Shiloh, and go to the land of Benjamin. [22]And it shall be, when their fathers or their brethren come unto us to complain, that we will say unto them, Be favourable[e] unto them for our sakes: because we reserved not to each man his wife in the war: for ye did not give unto them at this time, *that* ye should be guilty. [23]And the children of Benjamin did so, and took *them* wives, according to their number, of them that danced, whom they caught: and they went and returned unto their inheritance, and repaired the cities, and dwelt in them. [24]And the children of Israel departed thence at that time, every man to his tribe and to his family, and they went out from thence every man to his inheritance. [25]In those days *there was* no king in Israel: every man did *that which was* right in his own eyes.

---

[b] young . . . : Heb. young women virgins
[c] to speak . . . : Heb. and spake and called
[d] yearly: Heb. from year to year
[e] Be favourable . . . : or, Gratify us in them

RUTH

Names carry meanings. What names today connote intelligence? Strength of character? Beauty? Toughness? We build such associations in many ways, but mostly through stories. Stories create impressions about a person's character based only on a name.

What's your image of a "Ruth"? What qualities do you expect from a person so named? Would you vote for a Ruth? marry a Ruth? name a child Ruth?

You are about to read an ancient Hebrew story about an obscure non-Hebrew woman whose name carries world-class associations. Note her character well. Cultivate her strength. Imagine her struggles and pain. Refresh yourself in the simplicity of her virtues. Note the aura of happiness that surrounds her. God made her life and those she touched remarkable examples of redemption and fulfillment.

What traits will your loved ones associate with your name—high hopes? lofty goals? strong finish? a God-blessed life amid human pain and loss?

The legacy of a good name is hard to measure.

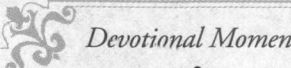

Devotional Moment
•
Appreciation

1:8 Naomi had every reason to cling to Ruth and Orpah. After all, she had no one else in the world to help her; she was a poor widow with a bleak future. But rather than make these two women feel obligated to care for her, she released them with words of appreciation. She thanked them for their help and expressed hope that God would bless them for their kindness.

Many people have difficulty expressing appreciation; the words get stuck in their hearts and never go beyond good intentions. Have you expressed your appreciation to a loved one recently? Do it today!

1

¹Now it came to pass in the days when the judges ruled[a], that there was a famine in the land. And a certain man of Bethlehemjudah went to sojourn in the country of Moab, he, and his wife, and his two sons. ²And the name of the man *was* Elimelech, and the name of his wife Naomi, and the name of his two sons Mahlon and Chilion, Ephrathites of Bethlehemjudah. And they came into the country of Moab, and continued there. ³And Elimelech Naomi's husband died; and she was left, and her two sons. ⁴And they took them wives of the women of Moab; the name of the one *was* Orpah, and the name of the other Ruth: and they dwelled there about ten years. ⁵And Mahlon and Chilion died also both of them; and the woman was left of her two sons and her husband.

⁶Then she arose with her daughters in law, that she might return from the country of Moab: for she had heard in the country of Moab how that the LORD had visited his people in giving them bread. ⁷Wherefore she went forth out of the place where she was, and her two daughters in law with her; and they went on the way to return unto the land of Judah. ⁸And Naomi said unto her two daughters in law, Go, return each to her mother's house: the LORD deal kindly with you, as ye have dealt with the dead, and with me. ⁹The LORD grant you that ye may find rest, each *of you* in the house of her husband. Then she kissed them; and they lifted up their voice, and wept. ¹⁰And they said unto her, Surely we will return with thee unto thy people. ¹¹And Naomi said, Turn again, my daughters: why will ye go with me? *are* there yet *any more* sons in my womb, that they may be your husbands? ¹²Turn again, my daughters, go *your way*; for I am too old to have an husband. If I should say, I have hope, *if* I should have an husband also to night, and should also bear sons; ¹³Would ye tarry[b] for them till they were grown? would ye stay for them from having husbands? nay, my daughters; for it grieveth me much for your sakes that the hand of the LORD is gone out against me. ¹⁴And they lifted up their voice, and wept again: and Orpah kissed her mother in law; but Ruth clave unto her. ¹⁵And she said, Behold, thy sister in law is gone back unto her people, and unto her gods: return thou after thy sister in law. ¹⁶And Ruth said, Intreat[c] me

---

[a] ruled: Heb. judged
[b] tarry: Heb. hope
[c] Intreat . . . : or, Be not against me

not to leave thee, *or* to return from following after thee: for whither thou goest, I will go; and where thou lodgest, I will lodge: thy people *shall be* my people, and thy God my God: [17]Where thou diest, will I die, and there will I be buried: the LORD do so to me, and more also, *if ought* but death part thee and me. [18]When she saw that she was stedfastly minded to go with her, then she left speaking unto her.

[19]So they two went until they came to Bethlehem. And it came to pass, when they were come to Bethlehem, that all the city was moved about them, and they said, *Is* this Naomi? [20]And she said unto them, Call me not Naomi[d], call me Mara: for the Almighty hath dealt very bitterly with me. [21]I went out full, and the LORD hath brought me home again empty: why *then* call ye me Naomi, seeing the LORD hath testified against me, and the Almighty hath afflicted me? [22]So

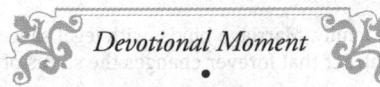

Devotional Moment

Bitterness

1:19-21 "Is it really Naomi?" the women who grew up with her asked in disbelief. Perhaps the circumstances of an embittered life had left their mark on her face as well as on her perception of herself, on her emotions, and on her view of the future. Naomi even wanted to change her name from Naomi, meaning "pleasant," to Mara, meaning "bitter." Bitterness affects every part of us, even when we try to hide it or ignore it; it shows on our countenance and in our attitudes. If you are bitter about something, release your bitterness to God. He can help you deal with your anger and loss. Pray for a new perspective that sees the future in terms of what God can do.

Worship
in Your Home

PARENTS NEED CHILDREN— AND THEIR PRAYERS, TOO!

Ruth said, "Whither thou goest, I will go: and where thou lodgest, I will lodge: thy people shall be my people, and thou God my God."
Ruth 1:16

Parents often try to look strong when they are weak. They try to put on a good face when life behind that facade is crumbling. We've all done it.

The irony is that parents have needs. If parents aren't vulnerable to their growing children, the kids won't even think to pray for Mom or Dad.

Ruth knew how vulnerable Naomi was—how life had crumbled around her. Knowing that, Ruth wanted to be there to help.

What kinds of weaknesses can we parents share with our growing children? What will help them pray intelligently but not cave in under the pressure of parental burdens?

It's not as hard as you might imagine. When you are sick, why not let your children know and ask for their prayers? If you lose a job, why not let the children share in the adventure of seeking a new one? Don't dwell on the insecurities, lest the child feel a burden too great to bear, but dwell on the simple need. Are you short of money, in need of something special, or have a concern? Why not share it together?

Develop a prayer partnership with your children—both ways. Only you can judge what your child, at a certain age, can bear. But share it and pray together.

---

[d] Naomi: that is, Pleasant

In-Laws

by Howard Hendricks

When a man and woman are joined together in marriage, the newly formed family changes everyone involved. Since women have a natural tendency to move toward close personal involvements, in-laws often pose problems for them. But from the book of Ruth comes a story of positive instruction, a case history "duet" of a mother and daughter-in-law who played beautiful counterpoint melodies.

During the time of the judges, Elimelech and Naomi took their two sons from Bethlehem to Moab, at least fifty miles from their homeland, in an effort to survive. Facing famine in Judah, they sought the lush green meadowlands of Moab. But Elimelech died, and his sons grew up to marry young Moabite women.

When her sons, Mahlon and Chilion, died, Naomi was destitute. News that the famine in Bethlehem was over prompted her to return home. Both of the young widows chose to stay with Naomi and return with her to Bethlehem.

Apparently Naomi's daily life showed kindness and caring that bridged their many differences. In the tragedy of losing Elimelech, and then Mahlon and Chilion, Naomi and her daughters-in-law clung to each other. Surely Ruth and Orpah saw Naomi's faith in the way she coped; despite the loss of her family and financial income, she retained confidence in her God.

At some point during the journey, Naomi changed her mind about bringing her daughters-in-law and urged them to return to their own family homes in Moab. Orpah decided to return to her home, but Ruth steadfastly clung to Naomi and in so doing illustrated an in-law relationship that stands as a model for blending two families into one.

The story of Ruth and Naomi raises four cautions for newly blended families and reminds us of four possibilities for in-law relationships.

Cautions for newly blended families. 1. A new in-law will change the family balance and routine. When a grown child marries, the decision making shifts to the next generation, and the balance of power begins to shift.

2. A new in-law will change the status of the family. Marriage binds, with legal sanction. Community recognition finalizes a marriage contract that forever changes the status of a family. Nothing is ever quite the same again.

3. The newcomer will have to undergo a kind of trial. Most often the newcomer is unknown to everyone else. This is especially true in modern society, because young adults can move far away from home before marrying. The in-law's probation will show whether he or she measures up to family expectations.

4. A new in-law will be a competitor for the support and resources of the family he or she marries into. Other family members may resent this competition unless the newcomer agrees to assume certain responsibilities within the family.

Possibilities for in-law relationships. 1. If the new in-law earns everyone's trust, a new sense of family will develop. The newcomer becomes accepted by everyone else, and everyone is drawn to the newest member and develops a sense of loyalty to him or her.

2. If everyone is committed to biblical values, many wrong choices can be avoided. In Naomi's case, a strong faith in God who cares and provides produced harmony in her home. The teaching of God's truth to children and reinforcement during the growing-up years make the selection of a marriage partner a natural extension of the family way.

3. If the family learns to treat strangers with hospitality, disarm conflicts, and deal

with error and nonconformity, it will build a solid foundation for later marriages. Naomi's code of conduct spoke to the whole community. This affected the kind of marriage Ruth eventually had.

4. If the child can break emotional ties with the parents, the transition will go smoothly. Transferring allegiance and love from a parent to a spouse promotes normal growth. But this happens only when parents freely release children.

Families were instituted by God; they form the basic unit of any society, and their stability determines the fate of any nation. Ultimate responsibility for pleasant and friendly families rests with parents who, like Naomi, pave the path by modeling gentle acceptance and clear vision for their children.

DIGGING DEEPER
1. Read the story of a son whose choice of marriage partners did not fit the family way (Gen. 26:34-35; 27:46; 28:6-9).
2. Why did God forbid his chosen people to marry foreigners? See 1 Kings 11:2. Compare this with 2 Corinthians 6:14-17.
3. What insights can you gain from the in-law relationships described in Exodus 2:21-22; 29:26; Mark 1:29-31?

Naomi returned, and Ruth the Moabitess, her daughter in law, with her, which returned out of the country of Moab: and they came to Bethlehem in the beginning of barley harvest.

2

[1] And Naomi had a kinsman of her husband's, a mighty man of wealth, of the family of Elimelech; and his name *was* Boaz[a]. [2] And Ruth the Moabitess said unto Naomi, Let me now go to the field, and glean ears of corn after *him* in whose sight I shall find grace. And she said unto her, Go, my daughter. [3] And she went, and came, and gleaned in the field after the reapers: and her hap[b] was to light on a part of the field *belonging* unto Boaz, who *was* of the kindred of Elimelech.

[4] And, behold, Boaz came from Bethlehem, and said unto the reapers, The LORD *be* with you. And they answered him, The LORD bless thee. [5] Then said Boaz unto his servant that was set over the reapers, Whose damsel *is* this? [6] And the servant that was set over the reapers answered and said, It *is* the Moabitish damsel that came back with Naomi out of the country of Moab: [7] And she said, I pray you, let me glean and gather after the reapers among the sheaves: so she came, and hath continued even from the morning until now, that she tarried a little in the house. [8] Then said Boaz unto Ruth, Hearest thou not, my daughter? Go not to glean in another field, neither go from hence, but abide here fast by my maidens: [9] *Let* thine eyes *be* on the field

---

[a] Boaz: Gr. Booz
[b] hap . . . : Heb. hap happened

Devotional Moment

Protection

2:8-9, 22 If ever there was a vulnerable and unprotected person, it was Ruth. In fact, Ruth had three strikes against her: She was a widow, she was poor, and she was a foreigner (a Moabite woman living in the land of Judah). As a widow, she had no husband to protect and provide for her. Being poor, she had to humble herself and pick up the leftover grain in the fields. And as a foreigner, she had few of the rights citizens enjoyed. But God provided for her protection through the actions of Boaz. At some time in our lives we all need protection. This is one reason God gives us families. In your family, look out for one another as God-given guardians.

that they do reap, and go thou after them: have I not charged the young men that they shall not touch thee? and when thou art athirst, go unto the vessels, and drink of *that* which the young men have drawn. ¹⁰Then she fell on her face, and bowed herself to the ground, and said unto him, Why have I found grace in thine eyes, that thou shouldest take knowledge of me, seeing I *am* a stranger? ¹¹And Boaz answered and said unto her, It hath fully been shewed me, all that thou hast done unto thy mother in law since the death of thine husband: and *how* thou hast left thy father and thy mother, and the land of thy nativity, and art come unto a people which thou knewest not heretofore. ¹²The LORD recompense thy work, and a full reward be given thee of the LORD God of Israel, under whose wings thou art come to trust. ¹³Then she said, Let me find favour in thy sight, my lord; for

that thou hast comforted me, and for that thou hast spoken friendly unto thine handmaid, though I be not like unto one of thine handmaidens. ¹⁴And Boaz said unto her, At mealtime come thou hither, and eat of the bread, and dip thy morsel in the vinegar. And she sat beside the reapers: and he reached her parched *corn*, and she did eat, and was sufficed, and left. ¹⁵And when she was risen up to glean, Boaz commanded his young men, saying, Let her glean even among the sheaves, and reproachᶜ her not: ¹⁶And let fall also *some* of the handfuls of purpose for her, and leave *them*, that she may glean *them*, and rebuke her not.

¹⁷So she gleaned in the field until even, and beat out that she had gleaned: and it was about an ephah of barley. ¹⁸And she took *it* up, and went into the city: and her mother in law saw what she had gleaned: and she brought forth, and gave to her that she had reserved after she was sufficed. ¹⁹And her mother in law said unto her, Where hast thou gleaned to day? and where wroughtest thou? blessed be he that did take knowledge of thee. And she shewed her mother in law with whom she had wrought, and said, The man's name with whom I wrought to day *is* Boaz. ²⁰And Naomi said unto her daughter in law, Blessed *be* he of the LORD, who hath not left off his kindness to the living and to the dead. And Naomi said unto her, The man *is* near of kin unto us, one of our next kinsmen. ²¹And Ruth the Moabitess said, He said unto me also, Thou shalt keep fast by my young men, until they have ended all

ᶜ reproach . . . : Heb. shame her not

Naomi and Ruth

From the beginning, Naomi's story is not just about her, but about her sons and their wives as well—most notably, her daughter-in-law Ruth.

When Naomi set out to return to Judah, she took her two widowed daughters-in-law with her. Later, however, Naomi stopped and insisted that Ruth and Orpah not further burden their lives with her troubles. Naomi tried not to invade their lives.

Make no mistake about her state of mind, though. Note her words to Ruth and Orpah in 1:13 and later to the townspeople of Bethlehem, where she was from: " 'Call me not Naomi, call me Mara' (Naomi means 'pleasant'; Mara means 'bitter') 'for the Almighty hath dealt very bitterly with me' " (1:20). She was hardly pleasant to be around.

Nevertheless, Ruth did not resent Naomi's presence. Her devotion is the kind that we could scarcely dare to hope for in a relative brought into the family through marriage. When Naomi first suggested that Ruth try to woo Boaz, Ruth replied, "All that thou sayest unto me I will do" (3:5). Quite a statement to make to anyone—especially your mother-in-law.

We must not deny that both Ruth and Naomi were extraordinary women. Unpretentious, kind, selfless, unimposing, self-effacing—they both had the character to make a great relationship. But should that discourage us from aiming so high? Not at all! Ruth and Naomi had a wonderful relationship because each went out of her way to put the other first. If we would be that kind to *our* in-laws, wouldn't it make a difference?

LESSONS FROM RUTH AND NAOMI AS IN-LAWS

An in-law can become a close friend. Ruth and Naomi devoted themselves to each other. They helped each other. They looked out for each other's best interests. They became good friends. Don't let the stereotype of in-law relationships sour yours. Work and pray toward being a help and support to your in-laws. Perhaps God will grant you a new or even closer friendship.

Widowhood does not have to be lonely. Why Ruth dedicated herself so wholeheartedly to Naomi remains a mystery. Somewhere along the way she decided to devote herself to Naomi, to allow nothing to separate them. In short, she made a commitment to that relationship. Both Naomi and Ruth were widows, but they had each other.

God brings new family members for a purpose. God used Ruth to heal Naomi's bitterness. God used Naomi to take care of Ruth. They helped each other. You and your in-laws can do the same.

Family Traditions

Nurturing Mother/Daughter-in-law Relationships

RUTH

Inga met her daughter-in-law to be, Judy, for the first time on her doorstep and greeted her with the one English word she knew well: "Congratulations!"

From that moment on Inga spoke not another word of Judy's language. Judy had to learn Inga's mother tongue, Danish, as well as her culture in order to develop a relationship with her.

Learning to speak your mother-in-law's language is a major step to creating happy traditions for your own emerging family. How can you create a loving, trusting relationship like that of Ruth and Naomi?

Get to know your mother-in-law in her own element. Spend time with her in the places where she's at her best, for that is how you'll learn her secrets and win her loyalty. Inga demonstrated her love for her family by spending hours in the kitchen preparing perfect meals. She was proud of her gravy recipe, which she had developed after decades of cooking. Knowing this was important to her, Judy spent numerous afternoons in Inga's small kitchen admiring her work and trying to learn the secret of her sauces. It was the highest compliment Judy could pay.

Show respect for your mother-in-law's life history. Ask to see photographs from her childhood: her parents, their work, her siblings. Learn about her family's customs and traditions. Also, she can tell you anecdotes from your husband's childhood that he never will. Sometimes asking about a prized possession will bring her memories to the surface.

Inga always had candles on the table and linen napkins at every place. Judy began to imitate her graceful table settings, especially when Inga was visiting.

Go the extra mile to show consideration for the things you know your mother-in-law appreciates. Older women often enjoy little luxuries reminiscent of their youth, things and customs they set aside to raise their family—an afternoon tea party, a book about life in her childhood, or a walk in a city rose garden. When you visit, bring home-baked cookies or a cake to share, the latest snapshots of the kids, a new kitchen gadget or small practical item for her sewing basket. Participate in the games she likes, the walks she enjoys, and meeting her neighbors and friends.

Like Naomi's, Inga's life was not easy. With each baby boy she had, her friends would try to cheer her by saying, "Don't worry—the girls will come later." They never did. Instead, Judy became her girl, reaping the benefit of Inga's years of loving labor. You, too, can strive to be the "missing child" in your mother-in-law's life.

my harvest. ²²And Naomi said unto Ruth her daughter in law, *It is* good, my daughter, that thou go out with his maidens, that they meet⁴ thee not in any other field. ²³So she kept fast by the maidens of Boaz to glean unto the end of barley harvest and of wheat harvest; and dwelt with her mother in law.

3

¹Then Naomi her mother in law said unto her, My daughter, shall I not seek rest for thee, that it may be well with thee? ²And now *is* not Boaz of our kindred, with whose maidens thou wast? Behold, he winnoweth barley to night in the threshingfloor. ³Wash thyself therefore, and anoint thee, and put thy raiment upon thee, and get thee down to the floor: *but* make not thyself known unto the man, until he shall have done eating and drinking. ⁴And it shall be, when he lieth down, that thou shalt mark the place where he shall lie,

---

Devotional Moment

Humility

3:1-5 "All that thou sayest unto me I will do," Ruth responded to Naomi's instructions. Having the humility to accept wise counsel reflects maturity and personal security. Wise people seek counsel; foolish people reject advice. We must strive to be wise. Whether someone's suggestion involves a mundane matter (such as how to get to the store) or a serious decision (such as getting marriage counseling), have the humility to adopt good ideas when they come along.

---

and thou shalt go in, and uncover⁴ his feet, and lay thee down; and he will tell thee what thou shalt do. ⁵And she said unto her, All that thou sayest unto me I will do.

⁶And she went down unto the floor, and did according to all that her mother in law bade her. ⁷And when Boaz had eaten and drunk, and his heart was merry, he went to lie down at the end of the heap of corn: and she came softly, and uncovered his feet, and laid her down. ⁸And it came to pass at midnight, that the man was afraid, and turned⁵ himself: and, behold, a woman lay at his feet. ⁹And he said, Who *art* thou? And she answered, I *am* Ruth thine handmaid: spread therefore thy skirt over thine handmaid; for thou *art* a near kinsman. ¹⁰And he said, Blessed *be* thou of the LORD, my daughter: *for* thou hast shewed more kindness in the latter end than at the beginning, inasmuch as thou followedst not young men, whether poor or rich. ¹¹And now, my daughter, fear not; I will do to thee all that thou requirest: for all the city⁵ of my people doth know that thou *art* a virtuous woman. ¹²And now it is true that I *am thy* near kinsman: howbeit there is a kinsman nearer than I. ¹³Tarry this night, and it shall be in the morning, *that* if he will perform unto thee the part of a kinsman, well; let him do the kinsman's part: but if he will not do the part of a kinsman to thee, then will I do the part of a kins-

---

⁴ meet . . . : or, fall upon thee
ᵃ uncover: or, lift up the clothes that are on
ᵇ turned: or, took hold on
ᶜ city: Heb. gate

man to thee, *as* the LORD liveth: lie down until the morning.

¹⁴And she lay at his feet until the morning: and she rose up before one could know another. And he said, Let it not be known that a woman came into the floor. ¹⁵Also he said, Bring the vail[d] that *thou hast* upon thee, and hold it. And when she held it, he measured six *measures* of barley, and laid *it* on her: and she went into the city. ¹⁶And when she came to her mother in law, she said, Who *art* thou, my daughter? And she told her all that the man had done to her. ¹⁷And she said, These six *measures* of barley gave he me; for he said to me, Go not empty unto thy mother in law. ¹⁸Then said she, Sit still, my daughter, until thou know how the matter will fall: for the man will not be in rest, until he have finished the thing this day.

4

¹Then went Boaz up to the gate, and sat him down there: and, behold, the kinsman of whom Boaz spake came by; unto whom he said, Ho, such a one! turn aside, sit down here. And he turned aside, and sat down. ²And he took ten men of the elders of the city, and said, Sit ye down here. And they sat down. ³And he said unto the kinsman, Naomi, that is come again out of the country of Moab, selleth a parcel of land, which *was* our brother Elimelech's: ⁴And I thought[a] to advertise thee, saying, Buy *it* before the inhabitants, and before the elders of my people. If thou wilt redeem *it*, redeem *it*: but if thou wilt not redeem *it*, *then* tell

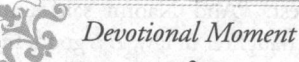

me, that I may know: for *there is* none to redeem *it* beside thee; and I *am* after thee. And he said, I will redeem *it*. ⁵Then said Boaz, What day thou buyest the field of the hand of Naomi, thou must buy *it* also of Ruth the Moabitess, the wife of the dead, to raise up the name of the dead upon his inheritance. ⁶And the kinsman said, I cannot redeem *it* for myself, lest I mar mine own inheritance: redeem thou my right to thyself; for I cannot redeem *it*. ⁷Now this *was the manner* in former time in Israel concerning redeeming and concerning changing, for to confirm all things; a man plucked off his shoe, and gave *it* to his neighbour: and this *was* a testimony in Israel. ⁸Therefore the kinsman said unto Boaz, Buy *it* for thee. So he drew off his shoe.

---

[d] vail: or, sheet, or, apron
[a] I thought . . . : Heb. I said, I will reveal in thine ear

Devotional Moment

•

Love Finds a Way

4:9-10 Boaz didn't really want Elimelech's property; he wanted to marry Ruth and to take care of her. But he loved Ruth enough to pay the price, both literally and figuratively, to do so. Boaz's love was not just an overwhelming feeling of adoration; it was a decision, a choice of selfless devotion. Loving a person often requires sacrifice. As the honeymoon fades into a memory, more mundane matters may put our loving feelings to the test. Children, too, can test their parents' love in countless ways. Are you willing to pay the price and love them despite the absence of feelings to motivate you?

⁹And Boaz said unto the elders, and *unto* all the people, Ye *are* witnesses this day, that I have bought all that *was* Elimelech's, and all that *was* Chilion's and Mahlon's, of the hand of Naomi. ¹⁰Moreover Ruth the Moabitess, the wife of Mahlon, have I purchased to be my wife, to raise up the name of the dead upon his inheritance, that the name of the dead be not cut off from among his brethren, and from the gate of his place: ye *are* witnesses this day. ¹¹And all the people that *were* in the gate, and the elders, said, *We are* witnesses. The LORD make the woman that is come into thine house like Rachel and like Leah, which two did build the house of Israel: and do thou worthily in Ephratah, and be famous in Bethlehem: ¹²And let thy house be like the house of Pharez, whom Tamar bare unto Judah, of the seed which the LORD shall give thee of this young woman.

¹³So Boaz took Ruth, and she was his wife: and when he went in unto her, the LORD gave her conception, and she bare a son. ¹⁴And the women said unto Naomi, Blessed *be* the LORD, which hath not left[b] thee this day without a kinsman, that his name may be famous in Israel. ¹⁵And he shall be unto thee a restorer of *thy* life, and a nourisher of thine old age: for thy daughter in law, which loveth thee, which is better to thee than seven sons, hath born him. ¹⁶And Naomi took the child, and laid it in her bosom, and became nurse unto it. ¹⁷And the women her neighbours gave it a name, saying, There is a son born to Naomi; and they called his name Obed: he *is* the father of Jesse, the father of David. ¹⁸Now these *are* the generations of Pharez: Pharez begat Hezron, ¹⁹And Hezron begat Ram, and Ram begat Amminadab, ²⁰And Amminadab begat Nahshon, and Nahshon begat Salmon[c], ²¹And Salmon begat Boaz, and Boaz begat Obed, ²²And Obed begat Jesse, and Jesse begat David.

---

[b] left . . . : Heb. caused to cease unto thee
[c] Salmon: or, Salmah

FIRST SAMUEL

Purpose
To record the life of Samuel, Israel's last judge; the reign and decline of Saul, the first king; and the choice and preparation of David, Israel's greatest king

Author
Unknown

Setting
The book begins in the days of the judges and describes Israel's transition from a theocracy (led by God) to a monarchy (led by a king).

Key Verses
"Hearken unto the voice of the people in all that they say unto thee: for they have not rejected thee, but they have rejected me, that I should not reign over them . . . and show them the manner of the king that shall reign over them" (8:7, 9).

Key People
Eli, Hannah, Samuel, Saul, Jonathan, David

Toyland, toyland, wonderful girl and boy land" begins a well-known song about the carefree days of childhood. But the song's last line is ominous, a warning almost, a lament: "Once you pass its borders, you can never return again."

Children grow; toy cars give way to gas-guzzling, horn-honking, four-on-the-floor "wheels." Nations pass through stages; people seek leadership they can trust. When the people of Israel grew tired of corrupt priests and judges, they demanded a king—partly to be like other nations (peer pressure), partly to recover law and order through centralized power. God agreed, knowing that the appointment of a king would create a heavy barrier of bureaucracy between him and the people.

Nonetheless, like a parent who helps a child through adolescence, God guides the Israelites toward the reign of Saul and then David. The passage is rough, but the future holds promise, especially with the young shepherd king who has music in his heart for God. Eli, Samuel, and Jonathan play major roles in the passage, too.

Reading 1 Samuel can lead to important conversations on friendship (What's a good friend like? How do you find one? Become one?), courage (What giants threaten you? Does fear or faith prompt your response?), and growing up (Why do Eli's children go bad while Jesse's kids prosper?). If you're crossing borders in your life, the lessons of 1 Samuel can help keep you close to God.

1

¹Now there was a certain man of Ramathaimzophim, of mount Ephraim, and his name *was* Elkanah, the son of Jeroham, the son of Elihu, the son of Tohu, the son of Zuph, an Ephrathite: ²And he had two wives; the name of the one *was* Hannah, and the name of the other Peninnah: and Peninnah had children, but Hannah had no children. ³And this man went up out of his city yearly[a] to worship and to sacrifice unto the LORD of hosts in Shiloh. And the two sons of Eli, Hophni and Phinehas, the priests of the LORD, *were* there. ⁴And when the time was that Elkanah offered, he gave to Peninnah his wife, and to all her sons and her daughters, portions: ⁵But unto Hannah he gave a worthy[b] portion; for he loved Hannah: but the LORD had shut up her womb. ⁶And her adversary also provoked[c] her sore, for to make her fret, because the LORD had shut up her womb. ⁷And *as* he did so year by year, when[d] she went up to the house of the LORD, so she provoked her; therefore she wept, and did not eat. ⁸Then said Elkanah her husband to her, Hannah, why weepest thou? and why eatest thou not? and why is thy heart grieved? *am* not I better to thee than ten sons?

⁹So Hannah rose up after they had eaten in Shiloh, and after they had drunk. Now Eli the priest sat upon a seat by a post of the temple of the LORD.

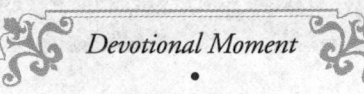

Devotional Moment
•
Husbands

1:8 Questions that begin with *why* can be particularly irritating! Elkanah asked Hannah several *why* questions in a row: Why was she crying? Why wouldn't she eat? Why was she so listless? His attempt at a joke only made matters worse. Husbands and fathers, take note: Elkanah shows us how *not* to help a hurting wife or daughter. A sensitive man will not besiege a woman with questions about why she feels the way she does; nor will he insist that she hurry up and get over her sadness; nor will he joke that he's all she needs, so why doesn't she stop crying? Listen to your wife and ask her what she needs. Perhaps she needs a hug, a gentle answer, help with solving a problem, or for you to cry with her. If you learn no other family-living skill, learn this one.

¹⁰And she *was* in bitterness of soul, and prayed unto the LORD, and wept sore. ¹¹And she vowed a vow, and said, O LORD of hosts, if thou wilt indeed look on the affliction of thine handmaid, and remember me, and not forget thine handmaid, but wilt give unto thine handmaid a man[e] child, then I will give him unto the LORD all the days of his life, and there shall no razor come upon his head. ¹²And it came to pass, as she continued[f] praying before the LORD, that Eli marked her mouth. ¹³Now Hannah, she spake in her heart; only her lips moved, but her voice was not heard: therefore Eli thought she had been drunken. ¹⁴And Eli said unto her, How

---

ª yearly: Heb. from year to year
ᵇ worthy: or, double
ᶜ provoked: Heb. angered
ᵈ when . . . : or, from the time that she, etc: Heb. from her going up
ᵉ a man . . . : Heb. seed of men
ᶠ continued . . . : Heb. multiplied to pray

Eli

LESSONS FROM ELI AS A FATHER

Rearing children takes conscious intervention in your kids' lives. Perhaps Eli hoped Hophni and Phinehas would learn God's ways from their mother or merely by watching him. While setting the example is certainly important, it doesn't do the whole job. We must also consciously and explicitly teach our children.

Dad makes a difference. We don't hear about the failure of Hophni and Phinehas's mother. We hear about how Eli failed. Your talks, your time, and your presence make a difference, Dad.

Professional success is not your only responsibility. Eli was High Priest of all Israel and a judge for forty years, but he still had a God-given responsibility to rear his sons. We, too, are responsible for our children's upbringing.

Loving your children without disciplining them is really loving yourself. It would have taken self-sacrifice for Eli to intervene in his sons' lives while there was still time. The same is true for us.

Dads, don't miss Eli. He has shown us how *not* to do it. This highly successful man failed miserably as a father, largely because he did not discipline his children.

Eli's sons, Hophni and Phinehas, evidently learned nothing of Eli's love of God. Though they served as priests in the Temple, they bullied the worshipers and stole meat that should have been sacrificed as burnt offerings to God. They also seduced young women who came to the Temple (see 1 Sam. 2:13-17, 22). As their father and as High Priest, Eli had a double responsibility—and duty—to discipline them. He simply did not. If 1 Samuel 1–4 is representative of his fathering habits, he didn't even try beyond mentioning that he opposed their behavior (see 1 Sam. 2:23-25).

Why did Eli fail as a dad? Because he cared more for his sons than for God, and the Lord said: "Wherefore . . . honourest thy sons above me, to make yourselves fat with the chiefest of all the offerings of Israel my people?" (1 Sam. 2:29).

Dads, it bears repeating: Don't miss Eli. It does no good to delegate your responsibility to discipline your children. Don't give it to Mom, to the school system, or to day-care. No one but you can keep your Hophni and Phinehas in line. Do it for their sakes and for yours.

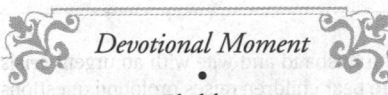

Devotional Moment

•

Children

1:10-16 Did Hannah want a child for the wrong reasons? We don't know. If someone who can't have a child prays just like Hannah, will she have a baby? We don't know that either. We do know that Hannah reached a point where she no longer wanted a child for herself, but wondered if she might become the mother of a child who could be God's servant. She gave up ownership of her baby before he was even conceived! God allows us to be parents for many good reasons, but keeping our children is not one of them. Be good stewards of your kids—you have them for only a short time. Hannah's prayer can help you remember to whom your children really belong. Have your children ever heard you giving them back to God in prayer?

long wilt thou be drunken? put away thy wine from thee. ¹⁵And Hannah answered and said, No, my lord, I *am* a woman of a sorrowful[g] spirit: I have drunk neither wine nor strong drink, but have poured out my soul before the LORD. ¹⁶Count not thine handmaid for a daughter of Belial: for out of the abundance of my complaint[h] and grief have I spoken hitherto. ¹⁷Then Eli answered and said, Go in peace: and the God of Israel grant *thee* thy petition that thou hast asked of him. ¹⁸And she said, Let thine handmaid find grace in thy sight. So the woman went her way, and did eat, and her countenance was no more *sad.*

¹⁹And they rose up in the morning early, and worshipped before the LORD, and returned, and came to their house to Ramah: and Elkanah knew Hannah his wife; and the LORD remembered her. ²⁰Wherefore it came to pass, when the time was come about after Hannah had conceived, that she bare a son, and called his name Samuel, *saying,* Because I have asked him of the LORD. ²¹And the man Elkanah, and all his house, went up to offer unto the LORD the yearly sacrifice, and his vow. ²²But Hannah went not up; for she said unto her husband, *I will not go up* until the child be weaned, and *then* I will bring him, that he may appear before the LORD, and there abide for ever. ²³And Elkanah her husband said unto her, Do what seemeth thee good; tarry until thou have weaned him; only the LORD establish his word. So the woman abode, and gave her son suck until she weaned him. ²⁴And when she had weaned him, she took him up with her, with three bullocks, and one ephah of flour, and a bottle of wine, and brought him unto the house of the LORD in Shiloh: and the child *was* young. ²⁵And they slew a bullock, and brought the child to Eli. ²⁶And she said, Oh my lord, *as* thy soul liveth, my lord, I *am* the woman that stood by thee here, praying unto the LORD. ²⁷For this child I prayed; and the LORD hath given me my petition which I asked of him: ²⁸Therefore also I have lent him to the LORD; as long as he liveth he shall be lent to the LORD. And he worshipped the LORD there.

2

¹And Hannah prayed, and said, My heart rejoiceth in the LORD, mine horn is exalted in the LORD: my

---

[g] of a sorrowful . . . : Heb. hard of spirit
[h] complaint: or, meditation

Redeeming Infertility

by Beth Spring

Infertility can present a husband and wife with an urgent crisis of faith. Being unable to bear children raises profound questions about the purpose of a marriage, the worth of the marriage partners, and their sense of belonging in the church community.

The account of Hannah and Elkanah in 1 Samuel 1 is the most detailed description in the Bible of the grief of barrenness. Hannah's handling of her grief can teach us a great deal.

Whose fault is it, anyway?

Perhaps the most difficult question facing infertile couples is whether God *causes* or *allows* their condition. In the New Testament, the apostle Paul had a physical affliction from which he prayed to be healed (2 Cor. 12:7-9). In his sovereign plan for Paul's life, God allowed Satan to bring this "messenger" so Paul could learn to rely on God (12:7). "My grace is sufficient for thee," God told Paul (12:9).

God is our ally, not our enemy. Satan is our enemy. God has plans to teach and develop us through our difficult circumstances.

Only God sees the whole picture. It may be that he allows our condition for reasons we can't possibly imagine. The first step in redeeming infertility is therefore to trust that God has *allowed* it (but not *caused* it) because he loves us.

Will we ever conceive?

Bargaining with God is one of the stages many infertile couples pass through on their way toward resolution. In 1 Samuel 1:11, this appears to be what Hannah was doing: "And she vowed a vow, and said, 'O Lord of hosts, if thou wilt indeed look on the affliction of thine handmaid, and . . . give unto thine handmaid a man child, then I will give him unto the Lord all the days of his life.' "

We don't know whether God granted Hannah a child because of her vow. We can bargain with God if we want to, but ultimately we must realize that all we are and have belongs to God, even the children we so desperately want.

Why do the righteous suffer?

If Hannah was not being punished, then how could she begin to make sense of her suffering? She was overcome with sorrow, anger, and grief to such an extent that she could not function normally.

For Christians who are settled in their faith before they encounter infertility, childlessness may serve to refine their relationship with God. God calls us to become increasingly Christlike, and that sometimes involves pain. Moreover, recognizing our ultimate goal of becoming more like Christ reminds us that marriage and childbearing are not our only purpose in life. Having children is *not* essential for our attaining maturity in Christ, our having value in the Christian community, or even our having value as people.

We must also recognize that suffering may occur simply as a consequence of living in a fallen world. The foremost biblical example of this is Job. His ordeal, his interactions with well-meaning but thoughtless friends, and his responses to God can be a source of tremendous comfort to infertile couples. Job did not understand what he endured, but we have the benefit of knowing, from Job 1, that his pain was brought on by Satan. God is not the author of evil.

Redeeming infertility.
As painful as infertility can be, it is one way God can expand a couple's capacity for compassion and faith. Once their grief has run its course and they begin to accept their situation, they may be able to meet needs around them that they might not otherwise notice. If a childless couple can turn their sense of longing for children over to God, their desires may find an outlet in the church, where young people are always needing adult mentors, teachers, youth workers, friends, and confidants.

Infertility can also be redeemed through physical or emotional healing and—as in Hannah's case—the experience of parenting. It is not wrong for infertile couples to ask others to pray for them and to pray themselves about a resolution, but they must remain open to receiving an answer on God's terms.

Finally, God can redeem infertility by restoring calm after the storm. After a couple's emotions, marital relations, and spiritual life have been shaken by childlessness, an internal rebuilding and rearranging can come as a husband and wife begin to pray for God's peace.

DIGGING DEEPER
    1. How would you describe Hannah's attitude? In what way did she blame God or herself? What did she do with her feelings of hurt? Check 1 Samuel 1:7-11.
    2. What meaning does Romans 8:28 hold for an infertile couple?
    3. What can you learn about redeeming infertility from other biblical examples? See Genesis 15–21, 30; Judges 13; Luke 1.

---

mouth is enlarged over mine enemies; because I rejoice in thy salvation. *²There is* none holy as the LORD: for *there is* none beside thee: neither *is there* any rock like our God. ³Talk no more so exceeding proudly; let *not* arrogancy[a] come out of your mouth: for the LORD *is* a God of knowledge, and by him actions are weighed. ⁴The bows of the mighty men *are* broken, and they that stumbled are girded with strength. ⁵*They that were* full have hired out themselves for bread; and *they that were* hungry ceased: so that the barren hath born seven; and she that hath many children is waxed feeble. ⁶The LORD killeth, and maketh alive: he bringeth down to the grave, and bringeth up.

⁷The LORD maketh poor, and maketh rich: he bringeth low, and lifteth up. ⁸He raiseth up the poor out of the dust, *and* lifteth up the beggar from the dunghill, to set *them* among princes, and to make them inherit the throne of glory: for the pillars of the earth *are* the LORD'S, and he hath set the world upon them. ⁹He will keep the feet of his saints, and the wicked shall be silent in darkness; for by strength shall no man prevail. ¹⁰The adversaries of the LORD shall be broken to pieces; out of heaven shall he thunder upon them: the LORD shall judge the ends of the earth; and he shall give strength unto his king, and exalt the horn of his anointed.

ᵃ arrogancy: Heb. hard

¹¹And Elkanah went to Ramah to his house. And the child did minister unto the LORD before Eli the priest. ¹²Now the sons of Eli *were* sons of Belial; they knew not the LORD. ¹³And the priests' custom with the people *was, that,* when any man offered sacrifice, the priest's servant came, while the flesh was in seething, with a fleshhook of three teeth in his hand; ¹⁴And he struck *it* into the pan, or kettle, or caldron, or pot; all that the fleshhook brought up the priest took for himself. So they did in Shiloh unto all the Israelites that came thither. ¹⁵Also before they burnt the fat, the priest's servant came, and said to the man that sacrificed, Give flesh to roast for the priest; for he will not have sodden flesh of thee, but raw. ¹⁶And *if* any man said unto him, Let them not fail to burn the fat presently[b], and *then* take *as much* as thy soul desireth; then he would answer him, *Nay;* but thou shalt give *it me* now: and if not, I will take *it* by force. ¹⁷Wherefore the sin of the young men was very great before the LORD: for men abhorred the offering of the LORD. ¹⁸But Samuel ministered before the LORD, *being* a child, girded with a linen ephod. ¹⁹Moreover his mother made him a little coat, and brought *it* to him from year to year, when she came up with her husband to offer the yearly sacrifice. ²⁰And Eli blessed Elkanah and his wife, and said, The LORD give thee seed of this woman for the loan[c]

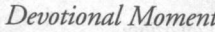

Devotional Moment
•
On-the-Job Training
2:18-21 Samuel grew up in the temple as Eli's protégé. Despite Samuel's young age, he served God right alongside his elder teacher, learning by doing as much as by watching or hearing. Children don't need to grow up before they can honor God and serve him. Let them help you with family devotions, Easter and Christmas preparations, or choosing a church. When children feel included in such important "adult" responsibilities, they learn more than a few developmental skills. They begin to learn what it means to have a personal relationship with God and to serve him.

which is lent to the LORD. And they went unto their own home. ²¹And the LORD visited Hannah, so that she conceived, and bare three sons and two daughters. And the child Samuel grew before the LORD. ²²Now Eli was very old, and heard all that his sons did unto all Israel; and how they lay with the women that assembled[d] *at* the door of the tabernacle of the congregation. ²³And he said unto them, Why do ye such things? for I hear of your evil dealings by all this people. ²⁴Nay, my sons; for *it is* no good report that I hear: ye make the LORD'S people to transgress[e]. ²⁵If one man sin against another, the judge shall judge him: but if a man sin against the LORD, who shall intreat for him? Notwithstanding they hearkened not unto the voice of their father, because the LORD would slay them. ²⁶And

---

[b] presently: Heb. as on the day
[c] loan . . . : or, petition which she asked, etc
[d] assembled: Heb. assembled by troops
[e] transgress: or, cry out

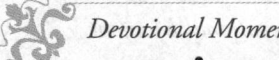

Devotional Moment

•

Warnings

2:25 Eli should have disciplined his sons, but didn't. As a result, they continued brazenly in their sin until they received the ultimate punishment: death. Wise and loving parents don't enjoy disciplining their children, but they know that loving correction may actually keep their children from much greater harm. Children must learn to obey because otherwise the habit of disobedience will someday mature into full-blown rebellion against God. No loving parent wants that. Set boundaries for your children. It is a wonderful way to say, "I love you."

the child Samuel grew on, and was in favour both with the LORD, and also with men. ²⁷And there came a man of God

Devotional Moment

•

Growing Up

2:26 Samuel was growing up in more ways than one. Just as the natural process of physical growth was taking place, Samuel was becoming more mature in his faith and obedience to God. Most Christian parents want to give their children the proper elements for both kinds of growth. While physical growth is obvious for all to see, we sometimes grow impatient when we cannot see spiritual growth quite so readily. As your children grow up, remember that spiritual growth is a *process*. It will take time and many failures for them to reach maturity. Do not nag or get down on your kids—especially teenagers—for their shortcomings. Rather, encourage them to take the next step from where they are now. Celebrate their little successes, no matter how small those victories seem to you or to other relatives.

unto Eli, and said unto him, Thus saith the LORD, Did I plainly appear unto the house of thy father, when they were in Egypt in Pharaoh's house? ²⁸And did I choose him out of all the tribes of Israel *to be* my priest, to offer upon mine altar, to burn incense, to wear an ephod before me? and did I give unto the house of thy father all the offerings made by fire of the children of Israel? ²⁹Wherefore kick ye at my sacrifice and at mine offering, which I have commanded *in my* habitation; and honourest thy sons above me, to make yourselves fat with the chiefest of all the offerings of Israel my people? ³⁰Wherefore the LORD God of Israel saith, I said indeed *that* thy house, and the house of thy father, should walk before me for ever: but now the LORD saith, Be it far from me; for them that honour me I will honour, and they that despise me shall be lightly esteemed. ³¹Behold, the days come, that I will cut off thine arm, and the arm of thy father's house, that there shall not be an old man in thine house. ³²And thou shalt see an enemy^f *in my* habitation, in all *the wealth* which *God* shall give Israel: and there shall not be an old man in thine house for ever. ³³And the man of thine, *whom* I shall not cut off from mine altar, *shall be* to consume thine eyes, and to grieve thine heart: and all the increase of thine house shall die in the flower of their age. ³⁴And this *shall be* a sign unto thee, that shall come upon thy two sons, on Hophni and Phinehas; in one day they shall die both of them. ³⁵And I will raise me up a faithful priest, *that* shall do ac-

^f an enemy . . . : or, the affliction of the tabernacle, for all the wealth which God would have given Israel

cording to *that* which *is* in mine heart and in my mind: and I will build him a sure house; and he shall walk before mine anointed for ever. ³⁶And it shall come to pass, *that* every one that is left in thine house shall come *and* crouch to him for a piece of silver and a morsel of bread, and shall say, Putᵍ me, I pray thee, into one of the priests' offices, that I may eat a piece of bread.

3

¹And the child Samuel ministered unto the LORD before Eli. And the word of the LORD was precious in those days; *there was* no open vision. ²And it came to pass at that time, when Eli *was* laid down in his place, and his eyes began to wax dim, *that* he could not see; ³And ere the lamp of God went out in the temple of the LORD, where the ark of God *was*, and Samuel was laid down *to sleep*; ⁴That the LORD called Samuel: and he answered, Here *am* I. ⁵And he ran unto Eli, and said, Here *am* I; for thou calledst me. And he said, I called not; lie down again. And he went and lay down. ⁶And the LORD called yet again, Samuel. And Samuel arose and went to Eli, and said, Here *am* I; for thou didst call me. And he answered, I called not, my son; lie down again. ⁷Now Samuel did not yet know the LORD, neither was the word of the LORD yet revealed unto him. ⁸And the LORD called Samuel again the third time. And he arose and went to Eli, and said, Here *am* I; for thou didst call me. And Eli perceived that the LORD had called the child. ⁹Therefore Eli said unto Samuel, Go, lie down: and it shall

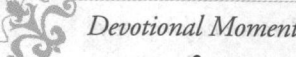

Devotional Moment
•
Listening

3:10 Television, radio, phone calls, people talking . . . We are so surrounded by noise that the idea of waiting quietly and listening to God seems foreign to many of us. And yet this is what young Samuel was doing in the Temple as God spoke to him. Even though the message he received was hardly pleasant, it was important that Samuel hear it and understand it so he could fill the role God wanted him to play as prophet to the people. Is there a place and time where you can—without distraction—listen to God by reading the Bible and praying? Carving out such a niche will help you learn about and understand the role God has for you.

be, if he call thee, that thou shalt say, Speak, LORD; for thy servant heareth. So Samuel went and lay down in his place. ¹⁰And the LORD came, and stood, and called as at other times, Samuel, Samuel. Then Samuel answered, Speak; for thy servant heareth.

¹¹And the LORD said to Samuel, Behold, I will do a thing in Israel, at which both the ears of every one that heareth it shall tingle. ¹²In that day I will perform against Eli all *things* which I have spoken concerning his house: when I begin, I will also make an end. ¹³For I have told him that I will judge his house for ever for the iniquity which he knoweth; because his sons made themselves vile, and he restrained them not. ¹⁴And therefore I have sworn unto the house of Eli, that the iniquity of Eli's house shall not be purged with sacrifice nor offering for ever. ¹⁵And Samuel lay until the morning, and opened the doors of the house of the

---

ᵍ Put: Heb. Join

LORD. And Samuel feared to shew Eli the vision. ¹⁶Then Eli called Samuel, and said, Samuel, my son. And he answered, Here *am* I. ¹⁷And he said, What *is* the thing that *the LORD* hath said unto thee? I pray thee hide *it* not from me: God do so to thee, and more also[a], if thou hide *any* thing from me of all the things that he said unto thee. ¹⁸And Samuel told him every whit, and hid nothing from him. And he said, It *is* the LORD: let him do what seemeth him good.

¹⁹And Samuel grew, and the LORD was with him, and did let none of his words fall to the ground. ²⁰And all Israel from Dan even to Beersheba knew that Samuel *was* established[b] *to be* a prophet of the LORD. ²¹And the LORD appeared again in Shiloh: for the LORD revealed himself to Samuel in Shiloh by the word of the LORD.

4

¹And the word of Samuel came to all Israel. Now Israel went out against the Philistines to battle, and pitched beside Ebenezer: and the Philistines pitched in Aphek. ²And the Philistines put themselves in array against Israel: and when they joined[a] battle, Israel was smitten before the Philistines: and they slew of the army in the field about four thousand men. ³And when the people were come into the camp, the elders of Israel said, Wherefore hath the LORD smit-

ten us to day before the Philistines? Let us fetch[b] the ark of the covenant of the LORD out of Shiloh unto us, that, when it cometh among us, it may save us out of the hand of our enemies. ⁴So the people sent to Shiloh, that they might bring from thence the ark of the covenant of the LORD of hosts, which dwelleth *between* the cherubims: and the two sons of Eli, Hophni and Phinehas, *were* there with the ark of the covenant of God. ⁵And when the ark of the covenant of the LORD came into the camp, all Israel shouted with a great shout, so that the earth rang again. ⁶And when the Philistines heard the noise of the shout, they said, What *meaneth* the noise of this great shout in the camp of the Hebrews? And they understood that the ark of the LORD was come into the camp. ⁷And the Philistines were afraid, for they said, God is come into the camp. And they said, Woe unto us! for there hath not been such a thing heretofore[c]. ⁸Woe unto us! who shall deliver us out of the hand of these mighty Gods? these *are* the Gods that smote the Egyptians with all the plagues in the wilderness. ⁹Be strong, and quit[d] yourselves like men, O ye Philistines, that ye be not servants unto the Hebrews, as they have been to you: quit yourselves like men, and fight.

¹⁰And the Philistines fought, and Israel was smitten, and they fled every man into his tent: and there was a very

---

[a] more also: so add
[b] established: or, faithful
[a] they joined . . . : Heb. the battle was spread
[b] fetch: Heb. take unto us
[c] heretofore: Heb. yesterday, or, the third day
[d] quit . . . : Heb. be men

Family Traditions

Baby Dedication Customs

1 SAMUEL 1:1–2:10

Since the praises recorded by godly mothers like Sarah and Hannah, customs have developed to celebrate and remember the birthdays of children. Here are some ideas for developing a few customs of your own.

Journaling. Before the baby is born, begin a journal for him or her and commit to write on a regular basis after the baby is born. It will be difficult to keep it up with a child (or children) vying for your time and attention, so get it started before the birth. Adding entries once a month for the first three years is a good pace. Stay flexible, though—with several children you may be keeping several journals going.

A Baby Shower. A baby shower is not only a time of supplying clothes and accessories for the new family member, but of reassuring parents that this child is part of a larger group—people who will love and look out for his or her parents as well.

Decorating the House. Family and neighbors can help decorate with banners draped across the front door, messages of congratulations in the front yard, garlands of greenery around the new parents' entrance-way, or pink or blue ribbons tied here and there.

Current Events. Thoughtful friends may clip newspaper headlines of the baby's birthday, record the day's hit songs and an interview with the new mom, or videotape the trip home.

Scripture Verses. Choose a Scripture verse for the new child and have it written in calligraphy and framed along with his or her name.

A Prayer Diary. A mother might keep a prayer diary for her child, recording petitions to God concerning crises, praise to him for joy and festivity, and Bible passages that are meaningful to her as she raises her child. In this diary she may note the dates of her child's first prayer, of salvation, and of baptism. She may also note the names of people who are spiritual influences in his or her life.

A Formal Dedication. Enlist a friend to take photographs of baby's dedication or christening. Then make a scrapbook of that day to enjoy as the child grows; include the church program, a wisp of hair, any cards you receive, Scriptures quoted, and the name and address of the pastor.

Once you've caught the spirit of celebrating your baby, it will likely continue through all the big and little events of the years to come. Eventually, your child will begin to follow the way you celebrate and join the fun in planning festivities for younger siblings.

great slaughter; for there fell of Israel thirty thousand footmen. ¹¹And the ark of God was taken; and the two sons of Eli, Hophni and Phinehas, were slainᵉ.

¹²And there ran a man of Benjamin out of the army, and came to Shiloh the same day with his clothes rent, and with earth upon his head. ¹³And when he came, lo, Eli sat upon a seat by the wayside watching: for his heart trembled for the ark of God. And when the man came into the city, and told it, all the city cried out. ¹⁴And when Eli heard the noise of the crying, he said, What *meaneth* the noise of this tumult? And the man came in hastily, and told Eli. ¹⁵Now Eli was ninety and eight years old; and his eyes were dimᶠ, that he could not see. ¹⁶And the man said unto Eli, I *am* he that came out of the army, and I fled to day out of the army. And he said, What is there done, my son? ¹⁷And the messenger answered and said, Israel is fled before the Philistines, and there hath been also a great slaughter among the people, and thy two sons also, Hophni and Phinehas, are dead, and the ark of God is taken. ¹⁸And it came to pass, when he made mention of the ark of God, that he fell from off the seat backward by the side of the gate, and his neck brake, and he died: for he was an old man, and heavy. And he had judged Israel forty years.

¹⁹And his daughter in law, Phinehas' wife, was with child, *near* to be delivered^g: and when she heard the tidings that the ark of God was taken, and that her father in law and her husband were dead, she bowed herself and travailed; for her pains came upon her. ²⁰And about the time of her death the women that stood by her said unto her, Fear not; for thou hast born a son. But she answered not, neither did she regard *it.* ²¹And she named the child Ichabodʰ, saying, The glory is departed from Israel: because the ark of God was taken, and because of her father in law and her husband. ²²And she said, The glory is departed from Israel: for the ark of God is taken.

5

¹And the Philistines took the ark of God, and brought it from Ebenezer unto Ashdod. ²When the Philistines took the ark of God, they brought it into the house of Dagon, and set it by Dagon. ³And when they of Ashdod arose early on the morrow, behold, Dagon *was* fallen upon his face to the earth before the ark of the LORD. And they took Dagon, and set him in his place again. ⁴And when they arose early on the morrow morning, behold, Dagon *was* fallen upon his face to the ground before the ark of the LORD; and the head of Dagon and both the palms of his hands *were* cut off upon the threshold; only *the stump of* Dagon was left to him. ⁵Therefore neither the priests of Dagon, nor any that come into Dagon's house, tread on the

---

ᵉ were slain: Heb. died
ᶠ were dim: Heb. stood
ᵍ be delivered: or, cry out
ʰ Ichabod: that is, Where is the glory? or, There is no glory

threshold of Dagon in Ashdod unto this day.

⁶But the hand of the LORD was heavy upon them of Ashdod, and he destroyed them, and smote them with emerods, *even* Ashdod and the coasts thereof. ⁷And when the men of Ashdod saw that *it was* so, they said, The ark of the God of Israel shall not abide with us: for his hand is sore upon us, and upon Dagon our god. ⁸They sent therefore and gathered all the lords of the Philistines unto them, and said, What shall we do with the ark of the God of Israel? And they answered, Let the ark of the God of Israel be carried about unto Gath. And they carried the ark of the God of Israel about *thither.* ⁹And it was *so,* that, after they had carried it about, the hand of the LORD was against the city with a very great destruction: and he smote the men of the city, both small and great, and they had emerods in their secret parts. ¹⁰Therefore they sent the ark of God to Ekron. And it came to pass, as the ark of God came to Ekron, that the Ekronites cried out, saying, They have brought about the ark of the God of Israel to us, to slay us and our people. ¹¹So they sent and gathered together all the lords of the Philistines, and said, Send away the ark of the God of Israel, and let it go again to his own place, that it slay us not,ᵃ and our people: for there was a deadly destruction throughout all the city; the hand of God was very heavy there. ¹²And the men that died not were smitten with the emerods:

and the cry of the city went up to heaven.

6

¹And the ark of the LORD was in the country of the Philistines seven months. ²And the Philistines called for the priests and the diviners, saying, What shall we do to the ark of the LORD? tell us wherewith we shall send it to his place. ³And they said, If ye send away the ark of the God of Israel, send it not empty; but in any wise return him a trespass offering: then ye shall be healed, and it shall be known to you why his hand is not removed from you. ⁴Then said they, What *shall be* the trespass offering which we shall return to him? They answered, Five golden emerods, and five golden mice, *according to* the number of the lords of the Philistines: for one plague *was* on youᵃ all, and on your lords. ⁵Wherefore ye shall make images of your emerods, and images of your mice that mar the land; and ye shall give glory unto the God of Israel: peradventure he will lighten his hand from off you, and from off your gods, and from off your land. ⁶Wherefore then do ye harden your hearts, as the Egyptians and Pharaoh hardened their hearts? when he had wrought wonderfullyᵇ among them, did they not let the people go, and they departed? ⁷Now therefore make a new cart, and take two milch kine, on which there hath come no yoke, and tie the kine to the cart, and bring their calves home from them: ⁸And take the ark of the

---

ᵃ us not . . . : Heb. me not, and my
ᵃ you: Heb. them
ᵇ wonderfully: or, reproachfully

LORD, and lay it upon the cart; and put the jewels of gold, which ye return him *for* a trespass offering, in a coffer by the side thereof; and send it away, that it may go. ⁹And see, if it goeth up by the way of his own coast to Bethshemesh, *then* he hath done us this great evil: but if not, then we shall know that *it is* not his hand *that* smote us: it *was* a chance *that* happened to us.

¹⁰And the men did so; and took two milch kine, and tied them to the cart, and shut up their calves at home: ¹¹And they laid the ark of the LORD upon the cart, and the coffer with the mice of gold and the images of their emerods. ¹²And the kine took the straight way to the way of Bethshemesh, *and* went along the highway, lowing as they went, and turned not aside *to* the right hand or *to* the left; and the lords of the Philistines went after them unto the border of Bethshemesh. ¹³And *they of* Bethshemesh *were* reaping their wheat harvest in the valley: and they lifted up their eyes, and saw the ark, and rejoiced to see *it.* ¹⁴And the cart came into the field of Joshua, a Bethshemite, and stood there, where *there was* a great stone: and they clave the wood of the cart, and offered the kine a burnt offering unto the LORD. ¹⁵And the Levites took down the ark of the LORD, and the coffer that *was* with it, wherein the jewels of gold *were*, and put *them* on the great stone: and the men of Bethshemesh offered burnt offerings and sacrificed sacrifices the same day unto the LORD. ¹⁶And when the five lords of the Philistines had seen *it*, they returned to Ekron the same day. ¹⁷And these *are* the golden emerods which the Philistines re-turned *for* a trespass offering unto the LORD; for Ashdod one, for Gaza one, for Askelon one, for Gath one, for Ekron one; ¹⁸And the golden mice, *according to* the number of all the cities of the Philistines *belonging* to the five lords, *both* of fenced cities, and of country villages, even unto the greatᶜ *stone of* Abel, whereon they set down the ark of the LORD: *which stone remaineth* unto this day in the field of Joshua, the Bethshemite.

¹⁹And he smote the men of Bethshemesh, because they had looked into the ark of the LORD, even he smote of the people fifty thousand and threescore and ten men: and the people lamented, because the LORD had smitten *many* of the people with a great slaughter. ²⁰And the men of Bethshemesh said, Who is able to stand before this holy LORD God? and to whom shall he go up from us? ²¹And they sent messengers to the inhabitants of Kirjathjearim, saying, The Philistines have brought again the ark of the LORD; come ye down, *and* fetch it up to you.

7

¹And the men of Kirjathjearim came, and fetched up the ark of the LORD, and brought it into the house of Abinadab in the hill, and sanctified Eleazar his son to keep the ark of the LORD. ²And it came to pass, while the ark abode in Kirjathjearim, that the time was long; for it was twenty years: and all the house of Israel lamented after the LORD.

³And Samuel spake unto all the house of Israel, saying, If ye do return unto the LORD with all your hearts,

---

ᶜ great . . . : or, great stone

then put away the strange gods and Ashtaroth from among you, and prepare your hearts unto the LORD, and serve him only: and he will deliver you out of the hand of the Philistines. ⁴Then the children of Israel did put away Baalim and Ashtaroth, and served the LORD only. ⁵And Samuel said, Gather all Israel to Mizpeh, and I will pray for you unto the LORD. ⁶And they gathered together to Mizpeh, and drew water, and poured *it* out before the LORD, and fasted on that day, and said there, We have sinned against the LORD. And Samuel judged the children of Israel in Mizpeh.

⁷And when the Philistines heard that the children of Israel were gathered together to Mizpeh, the lords of the Philistines went up against Israel. And when the children of Israel heard *it*, they were afraid of the Philistines. ⁸And the children of Israel said to Samuel, Cease* not to cry unto the LORD our God for us, that he will save us out of the hand of the Philistines. ⁹And Samuel took a sucking lamb, and offered *it for* a burnt offering wholly unto the LORD: and Samuel cried unto the LORD for Israel; and the LORD heardᵇ him. ¹⁰And as Samuel was offering up the burnt offering, the Philistines drew near to battle against Israel: but the LORD thundered with a great thunder on that day upon the Philistines, and discomfited them; and they were smitten before Israel. ¹¹And the men of Israel went out of Mizpeh, and pursued the Philistines,

and smote them, until *they came* under Bethcar. ¹²Then Samuel took a stone, and set *it* between Mizpeh and Shen, and called the name of it Ebenezerᶜ, saying, Hitherto hath the LORD helped us.

¹³So the Philistines were subdued, and they came no more into the coast of Israel: and the hand of the LORD was against the Philistines all the days of Samuel. ¹⁴And the cities which the Philistines had taken from Israel were restored to Israel, from Ekron even unto Gath; and the coasts thereof did Israel deliver out of the hands of the Philistines. And there was peace between Israel and the Amorites. ¹⁵And Samuel judged Israel all the days of his life. ¹⁶And he went from year to year in circuitᵈ to Bethel, and Gilgal, and Mizpeh, and judged Israel in all those places. ¹⁷And his return *was* to Ramah; for there *was* his house; and there he judged Israel; and there he built an altar unto the LORD.

8

¹And it came to pass, when Samuel was old, that he made his sons judges over Israel. ²Now the name of his firstborn was Joel; and the name of his second, Abiah: *they were* judges in Beersheba. ³And his sons walked not in his ways, but turned aside after lucre, and took bribes, and perverted judgment.

⁴Then all the elders of Israel gathered themselves together, and came to Samuel unto Ramah, ⁵And said unto him, Behold, thou art old, and thy sons

---

ª Cease . . . : Heb. Be not silent from us from crying
ᵇ heard: or, answered
ᶜ Ebenezer: that is, The stone of help
ᵈ in circuit: Heb. and he circuited

Devotional Moment

•

Like Father?

8:3 "And his sons walked not in his ways, but turned aside after lucre, and took bribes, and perverted judgment." What an epitaph for Samuel's sons! Though Samuel had been a righteous man, his sons Joel and Abijah were anything but that. You can't fully control how your children turn out, but you can give lots of time and energy to your parenting. Be available to your kids, talk with them when they have problems, and help them understand God's Word. It won't guarantee that your kids grow up perfect, but it will all make a difference in how much of your faith they adopt and shape into their own.

walk not in thy ways: now make us a king to judge us like all the nations. ⁶But the thing displeasedᵃ Samuel, when they said, Give us a king to judge us. And Samuel prayed unto the LORD. ⁷And the LORD said unto Samuel, Hearken unto the voice of the people in all that they say unto thee: for they have not rejected thee, but they have rejected me, that I should not reign over them. ⁸According to all the works which they have done since the day that I brought them up out of Egypt even unto this day, wherewith they have forsaken me, and served other gods, so do they also unto thee. ⁹Now therefore hearkenᵇ unto their voice: howbeit yet protest solemnly unto them, and shew them the manner of the king that shall reign over them. ¹⁰And Samuel told all the words of the LORD unto the people that asked of

him a king. ¹¹And he said, This will be the manner of the king that shall reign over you: He will take your sons, and appoint *them* for himself, for his chariots, and *to be* his horsemen; and *some* shall run before his chariots. ¹²And he will appoint him captains over thousands, and captains over fifties; and *will set them* to ear his ground, and to reap his harvest, and to make his instruments of war, and instruments of his chariots. ¹³And he will take your daughters *to be* confectionaries, and *to be* cooks, and *to be* bakers. ¹⁴And he will take your fields, and your vineyards, and your oliveyards, *even* the best *of them*, and give *them* to his servants. ¹⁵And he will take the tenth of your seed, and of your vineyards, and give to his officersᶜ, and to his servants. ¹⁶And

Devotional Moment

•

Prayer

8:5, 19-22 God's people have always lived under a different set of rules. One of the key distinctives for Israel was that, unlike other nations, they were to have no earthly king; God himself was to be their ruler. While that seems like a reasonable arrangement to us, the Israelites grew unhappy with it. First they asked for judges; then they asked for a king. God finally told Samuel to give them what they wanted. Just as God had predicted, it solved none of their problems but, in fact, created new ones. When we pray, we need to remember that God knows better than we do what is in our best interest. Sometimes when God allows us to have what we ask for, we find out that it is not good for us.

ᵃ displeased: Heb. as evil in the eyes of
ᵇ hearken . . . : or, obey
ᶜ officers: Heb. eunuchs

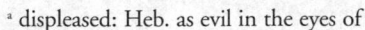

he will take your menservants, and your maidservants, and your goodliest young men, and your asses, and put *them* to his work. ¹⁷He will take the tenth of your sheep: and ye shall be his servants. ¹⁸And ye shall cry out in that day because of your king which ye shall have chosen you; and the LORD will not hear you in that day. ¹⁹Nevertheless the people refused to obey the voice of Samuel; and they said, Nay; but we will have a king over us; ²⁰That we also may be like all the nations; and that our king may judge us, and go out before us, and fight our battles. ²¹And Samuel heard all the words of the people, and he rehearsed them in the ears of the LORD. ²²And the LORD said to Samuel, Hearken unto their voice, and make them a king. And Samuel said unto the men of Israel, Go ye every man unto his city.

9

¹Now there was a man of Benjamin, whose name *was* Kish, the son of Abiel, the son of Zeror, the son of Bechorath, the son of Aphiah, a Benjamiteᵃ, a mighty man of power. ²And he had a son, whose name *was* Saul, a choice young man, and a goodly: and *there was* not among the children of Israel a goodlier person than he: from his shoulders and upward *he was* higher than any of the people.

³And the asses of Kish Saul's father were lost. And Kish said to Saul his son, Take now one of the servants with thee,

and arise, go seek the asses. ⁴And he passed through mount Ephraim, and passed through the land of Shalisha, but they found *them* not: then they passed through the land of Shalim, and *there they were* not: and he passed through the land of the Benjamites, but they found *them* not. ⁵*And* when they were come to the land of Zuph, Saul said to his servant that *was* with him, Come, and let us return; lest my father leave *caring* for the asses, and take thought for us. ⁶And he said unto him, Behold now, *there is* in this city a man of God, and *he is* an honourable man; all that he saith cometh surely to pass: now let us go thither; peradventure he can shew us our way that we should go. ⁷Then said Saul to his servant, But, behold, *if* we go, what shall we bring the man? for the bread is spentᵇ in our vessels, and *there is* not a present to bring to the man of God: what have we? ⁸And the servant answered Saul again, and said, Behold, I haveᶜ here at hand the fourth part of a shekel of silver: *that* will I give to the man of God, to tell us our way. ⁹(Beforetime in Israel, when a man went to enquire of God, thus he spake, Come, and let us go to the seer: for *he that is* now *called* a Prophet was beforetime called a Seer.) ¹⁰Then said Saul to his servant, Well saidᵈ; come, let us go. So they went unto the city where the man of God *was*.

¹¹*And* as they went up the hillᵉ to the city, they found young maidens go-

---

ᵃ a Benjamite: or, the son of a man of Jemini
ᵇ is spent . . . : Heb. is gone out of, etc
ᶜ I have . . . : Heb. there is found in my hand
ᵈ Well said: Heb. Thy word is good
ᵉ the hill . . . : Heb. in the ascent of the city

ing out to draw water, and said unto them, Is the seer here? [12]And they answered them, and said, He is; behold, *he is* before you: make haste now, for he came to day to the city; for *there is* a sacrifice[f] of the people to day in the high place: [13]As soon as ye be come into the city, ye shall straightway find him, before he go up to the high place to eat: for the people will not eat until he come, because he doth bless the sacrifice; *and* afterwards they eat that be bidden. Now therefore get you up; for about this time[g] ye shall find him. [14]And they went up into the city: *and* when they were come into the city, behold, Samuel came out against them, for to go up to the high place. [15]Now the LORD had told[h] Samuel in his ear a day before Saul came, saying, [16]To morrow about this time I will send thee a man out of the land of Benjamin, and thou shalt anoint him *to be* captain over my people Israel, that he may save my people out of the hand of the Philistines: for I have looked upon my people, because their cry is come unto me. [17]And when Samuel saw Saul, the LORD said unto him, Behold the man whom I spake to thee of! this same shall reign over my people.

[18]Then Saul drew near to Samuel in the gate, and said, Tell me, I pray thee, where the seer's house *is*. [19]And Samuel answered Saul, and said, I *am* the seer: go up before me unto the high place; for ye shall eat with me to day, and to morrow I will let thee go, and will tell thee all that *is* in thine heart. [20]And as for thine asses that were lost three[i] days ago, set not thy mind on them; for they are found. And on whom *is* all the desire of Israel? *Is it* not on thee, and on all thy father's house? [21]And Saul answered and said, *Am* not I a Benjamite, of the smallest of the tribes of Israel? and my family the least of all the families of the tribe of Benjamin? wherefore then speakest thou so[j] to me? [22]And Samuel took Saul and his servant, and brought them into the parlour, and made them sit in the chiefest place among them that were bidden, which *were* about thirty persons. [23]And Samuel said unto the cook, Bring the portion which I gave thee, of which I said unto thee, Set it by thee. [24]And the cook took up the shoulder, and *that* which *was* upon it, and set *it* before Saul. And *Samuel* said, Behold that which is left[k]! set *it* before thee, *and* eat: for unto this time hath it been kept for thee since I said, I have invited the people. So Saul did eat with Samuel that day. [25]And when they were come down from the high place into the city, *Samuel* communed with Saul upon the top of the house. [26]And they arose early: and it came to pass about the spring of the day, that Samuel called Saul to the top of the house, saying, Up, that I may send thee away. And Saul arose, and

---

[f] sacrifice: or, feast
[g] this time: Heb. to day
[h] told . . . : Heb. revealed the ear of Samuel
[i] three . . . : Heb. to day three days
[j] so . . . : Heb. according to this word
[k] left: or, reserved

they went out both of them, he and Samuel, abroad. ²⁷ *And* as they were going down to the end of the city, Samuel said to Saul, Bid the servant pass on before us, (and he passed on,) but stand thou still a while¹, that I may shew thee the word of God.

10

¹Then Samuel took a vial of oil, and poured *it* upon his head, and kissed him, and said, *Is it* not because the LORD hath anointed thee *to be* captain over his inheritance? ²When thou art departed from me to day, then thou shalt find two men by Rachel's sepulchre in the border of Benjamin at Zelzah; and they will say unto thee, The asses which thou wentest to seek are found: and, lo, thy father hath left the care^a of the asses, and sorroweth for you, saying, What shall I do for my son? ³Then shalt thou go on forward from thence, and thou shalt come to the plain of Tabor, and there shall meet thee three men going up to God to Bethel, one carrying three kids, and another carrying three loaves of bread, and another carrying a bottle of wine: ⁴And they will salute^b thee, and give thee two *loaves* of bread; which thou shalt receive of their hands. ⁵After that thou shalt come to the hill of God, where *is* the garrison of the Philistines: and it shall come to pass, when thou art come thither to the city, that thou shalt meet a company of prophets coming down from the high place with a psaltery, and a tabret, and a pipe, and a harp, before them; and they shall prophesy: ⁶And the Spirit of the LORD will come upon thee, and thou shalt prophesy with them, and shalt be turned into another man. ⁷And let it be, when these signs are come unto thee, *that* thou do as occasion serve thee; for God *is* with thee. ⁸And thou shalt go down before me to Gilgal; and, behold, I will come down unto thee, to offer burnt offerings, *and* to sacrifice sacrifices of peace offerings: seven days shalt thou tarry, till I come to thee, and shew thee what thou shalt do.

⁹And it was *so*, that when he had turned his back^c to go from Samuel, God gave him another heart: and all those signs came to pass that day. ¹⁰And when they came thither to the hill, behold, a company of prophets met him; and the Spirit of God came upon him, and he prophesied among them. ¹¹And it came to pass, when all that knew him beforetime saw that, behold, he prophesied among the prophets, then the people said one^d to another, What *is* this *that* is come unto the son of Kish? *Is* Saul also among the prophets? ¹²And one of the same place answered and said, But who *is* their father? Therefore it became a proverb, *Is* Saul also among the prophets? ¹³And when he had made an end of prophesying, he came to the high place. ¹⁴And Saul's uncle said unto him and to his

---

¹ a while: Heb. to day
^a care: Heb. business
^b salute . . . : Heb. ask thee of peace
^c back: Heb. shoulder
^d one . . . : Heb. a man to his neighbour

servant, Whither went ye? And he said, To seek the asses: and when we saw that *they were* no where, we came to Samuel. ¹⁵And Saul's uncle said, Tell me, I pray thee, what Samuel said unto you. ¹⁶And Saul said unto his uncle, He told us plainly that the asses were found. But of the matter of the kingdom, whereof Samuel spake, he told him not.

¹⁷And Samuel called the people together unto the LORD to Mizpeh; ¹⁸And said unto the children of Israel, Thus saith the LORD God of Israel, I brought up Israel out of Egypt, and delivered you out of the hand of the Egyptians, and out of the hand of all kingdoms, *and* of them that oppressed you: ¹⁹And ye have this day rejected your God, who himself saved you out of all your adversities and your tribulations; and ye have said unto him, *Nay,* but set a king over us. Now therefore present yourselves before the LORD by your tribes, and by your thousands. ²⁰And when Samuel had caused all the tribes of Israel to come near, the tribe of Benjamin was taken. ²¹When he had caused the tribe of Benjamin to come near by their families, the family of Matri was taken, and Saul the son of Kish was taken: and when they sought him, he could not be found. ²²Therefore they enquired of the LORD further, if the man should yet come thither. And the LORD answered, Behold, he hath hid himself among the stuff. ²³And they ran and fetched him thence: and when he stood among the people, he was higher than any of the people from his shoulders and upward. ²⁴And Samuel said to all the people, See ye him whom the LORD hath chosen, that *there is* none like him among all the people? And all the people shouted, and said, God save the king. ²⁵Then Samuel told the people the manner of the kingdom, and wrote *it* in a book, and laid *it* up before the LORD. And Samuel sent all the people away, every man to his house. ²⁶And Saul also went home to Gibeah; and there went with him a band of men, whose hearts God had touched. ²⁷But the children of Belial said, How shall this man save us? And they despised him, and brought him no presents. But he held his peace.

11

¹Then Nahash the Ammonite came up, and encamped against Jabeshgilead: and all the men of Jabesh said unto Nahash, Make a covenant with us, and we will serve thee. ²And Nahash the Ammonite answered them, On this *condition* will I make *a covenant* with you, that I may thrust out all your right eyes, and lay it *for* a reproach upon all Israel. ³And the elders of Jabesh said unto him, Give us seven days' respite, that we may send messengers unto all the coasts of Israel: and then, if *there be* no man to save us, we will come out to thee. ⁴Then came the messengers to Gibeah of Saul, and told the tidings in the ears of the people: and all the people lifted up their voices, and wept.

⁵And, behold, Saul came after the herd out of the field; and Saul said, What *aileth* the people that they weep? And they told him the tidings of the men of Jabesh. ⁶And the Spirit of God came upon Saul when he heard those tidings, and his anger was kindled greatly. ⁷And he took a yoke of oxen, and hewed them in pieces, and sent

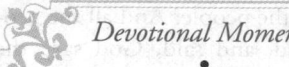

Devotional Moment

•

Anger

11:6-11 Most people think of anger as a negative, destructive force. Angry *behavior* often is, but angry *feelings* can have the positive effect of telling us what's important to us and moving us to take action against a circumstance or pattern of behavior that should be changed. Here, Saul's anger came from God's Holy Spirit and served as the catalyst to prepare the people for battle—and ultimate victory—against a wicked enemy.

Within families, it is easy to get angry over trivial matters, such as whose turn it is to take out the trash, a sibling's annoying habit, or a preschooler's relentless negativism. When you feel angry, let your anger tell you what's important to you. If something needs to be changed, then direct your feelings toward finding a solution, *not* blowing up. Your home will be a safer, more peaceful place if you will learn to admit your feelings, listen to your anger, and control your responses for the good of all.

them throughout all the coasts of Israel by the hands of messengers, saying, Whosoever cometh not forth after Saul and after Samuel, so shall it be done unto his oxen. And the fear of the LORD fell on the people, and they came out with one consent. [8]And when he numbered them in Bezek, the children of Israel were three hundred thousand, and the men of Judah thirty thousand. [9]And they said unto the messengers that came, Thus shall ye say unto the men of Jabeshgilead, To morrow, by *that time* the sun be hot, ye shall have help[a]. And the messengers came and shewed *it* to the men of Jabesh; and they were glad. [10]Therefore the men of Jabesh said, To morrow we will come out unto you, and ye shall

do with us all that seemeth good unto you. [11]And it was *so* on the morrow, that Saul put the people in three companies; and they came into the midst of the host in the morning watch, and slew the Ammonites until the heat of the day: and it came to pass, that they which remained were scattered, so that two of them were not left together.

[12]And the people said unto Samuel, Who *is* he that said, Shall Saul reign over us? bring the men, that we may put them to death. [13]And Saul said, There shall not a man be put to death this day: for to day the LORD hath wrought salvation in Israel. [14]Then said Samuel to the people, Come, and let us go to Gilgal, and renew the kingdom there. [15]And all the people went to Gilgal; and there they made Saul king before the LORD in Gilgal; and there they sacrificed sacrifices of peace offerings before the LORD; and there Saul and all the men of Israel rejoiced greatly.

Devotional Moment

•

Affirmation

11:14-15 Occasionally we hear about a couple renewing their wedding vows. Why? Were the original vows no longer valid? Were they somehow inadequate or out of date? No—the husband and wife simply want to say again in front of family and friends how much they love and appreciate each other. That is what Samuel and the people did for Saul at Gilgal. They said to him, in front of God and each other, that they were glad that God had made Saul their king, and then they had a big celebration. Why not look for ways to affirm your love and appreciation of your spouse and children?

---

[a] help: or, deliverance

12

¹And Samuel said unto all Israel, Behold, I have hearkened unto your voice in all that ye said unto me, and have made a king over you. ²And now, behold, the king walketh before you: and I am old and grayheaded; and, behold, my sons *are* with you: and I have walked before you from my childhood unto this day. ³Behold, here I *am*: witness against me before the LORD, and before his anointed: whose ox have I taken? or whose ass have I taken? or whom have I defrauded? whom have I oppressed? or of whose hand have I received *any* bribe[a] to blind mine eyes therewith? and I will restore it you. ⁴And they said, Thou hast not defrauded us, nor oppressed us, neither hast thou taken ought of any man's hand. ⁵And he said unto them, The LORD *is* witness against you, and his anointed *is* witness this day, that ye have not found ought in my hand. And they answered, *He is* witness.

⁶And Samuel said unto the people, *It is* the LORD that advanced[b] Moses and Aaron, and that brought your fathers up out of the land of Egypt. ⁷Now therefore stand still, that I may reason with you before the LORD of all the righteous acts of the LORD, which he did to you and to your fathers. ⁸When Jacob was come into Egypt, and your fathers cried unto the LORD, then the LORD sent Moses and Aaron, which brought forth your fathers out of Egypt, and made them dwell in this place. ⁹And when they forgat the LORD their God, he sold them into the hand of Sisera, captain of the host of Hazor, and into the hand of the Philistines, and into the hand of the king of Moab, and they fought against them. ¹⁰And they cried unto the LORD, and said, We have sinned, because we have forsaken the LORD, and have served Baalim and Ashtaroth: but now deliver us out of the hand of our enemies, and we will serve thee. ¹¹And the LORD sent Jerubbaal, and Bedan, and Jephthah, and Samuel, and delivered you out of the hand of your enemies on every side, and ye dwelled safe. ¹²And when ye saw that Nahash the king of the children of Ammon came against you, ye said unto me, Nay; but a king shall reign over us: when the LORD your God *was* your king. ¹³Now therefore behold the king whom ye have chosen, *and* whom ye have desired! and, behold, the LORD hath set a king over you. ¹⁴If ye will fear the LORD, and serve him, and obey his voice, and not rebel against the commandment[c] of the LORD, then shall

---

Devotional Moment

•

Consequences

12:10, 14, 19-25 Serving the Lord is not something that we should do only on Sunday mornings. Following God has implications for the way we live every part of our lives. The Israelites got into serious trouble whenever they forgot about their special relationship with God that set them apart. Their carelessness with worship led to problems in other areas. What we believe about God, how we worship him, and how we relate that to the rest of life is critical for us.

---

[a] bribe: Heb. ransom
[b] advanced: or, made

both ye and also the king that reigneth over you continue following the LORD your God: ¹⁵But if ye will not obey the voice of the LORD, but rebel against the commandment of the LORD, then shall the hand of the LORD be against you, as *it was* against your fathers.

¹⁶Now therefore stand and see this great thing, which the LORD will do before your eyes. ¹⁷*Is it* not wheat harvest to day? I will call unto the LORD, and he shall send thunder and rain; that ye may perceive and see that your wickedness *is* great, which ye have done in the sight of the LORD, in asking you a king. ¹⁸So Samuel called unto the LORD; and the LORD sent thunder and rain that day: and all the people greatly feared the LORD and Samuel. ¹⁹And all the people said unto Samuel, Pray for thy servants unto the LORD thy God, that we die not: for we have added unto all our sins *this* evil, to ask us a king. ²⁰And Samuel said unto the people, Fear not: ye have done all this wickedness: yet turn not aside from following the LORD, but serve the LORD with all your heart; ²¹And turn ye not aside: for *then should ye go* after vain *things*, which cannot profit nor deliver; for they *are* vain. ²²For the LORD will not forsake his people for his great name's sake: because it hath pleased the LORD to make you his people. ²³Moreover as for me, God forbid that I should sin against the LORD in ceasing to pray for you: but I will teach you the good and the right way: ²⁴Only fear the LORD, and serve him in truth with all your heart: for consider how great *things*

he hath done for you. ²⁵But if ye shall still do wickedly, ye shall be consumed, both ye and your king.

13

¹Saul reigned one year; and when he had reigned two years over Israel, ²Saul chose him three thousand *men* of Israel; *whereof* two thousand were with Saul in Michmash and in mount Bethel, and a thousand were with Jonathan in Gibeah of Benjamin: and the rest of the people he sent every man to his tent. ³And Jonathan smote the garrison of the Philistines that *was* in Geba^a, and the Philistines heard *of it*. And Saul blew the trumpet throughout all the land, saying, Let the Hebrews hear. ⁴And all Israel heard say *that* Saul had smitten a garrison of the Philistines, and *that* Israel also was had in abomination with the Philistines. And the people were called together after Saul to Gilgal. ⁵And the Philistines gathered themselves together to fight with Israel, thirty thousand chariots, and six thousand horsemen, and people as the sand which *is* on the sea shore in multitude: and they came up, and pitched in Michmash, eastward from Bethaven. ⁶When the men of Israel saw that they were in a strait, (for the people were distressed,) then the people did hide themselves in caves, and in thickets, and in rocks, and in high places, and in pits. ⁷And *some of* the Hebrews went over Jordan to the land of Gad and Gilead. As for Saul, he *was* yet in Gilgal, and all the people followed^b him trembling.

---

^c commandment: Heb. mouth
^a Geba: or, the hill
^b followed . . . : Heb. trembled after him

⁸And he tarried seven days, according to the set time that Samuel *had appointed*: but Samuel came not to Gilgal; and the people were scattered from him. ⁹And Saul said, Bring hither a burnt offering to me, and peace offerings. And he offered the burnt offering. ¹⁰And it came to pass, that as soon as he had made an end of offering the burnt offering, behold, Samuel came; and Saul went out to meet him, that he might salute^c him. ¹¹And Samuel said, What hast thou done? And Saul said, Because I saw that the people were scattered from me, and *that* thou camest not within the days appointed, and *that* the Philistines gathered themselves together at Michmash; ¹²Therefore said I, The Philistines will come down now upon me to Gilgal, and I have not made supplication unto the LORD: I forced myself therefore, and offered a burnt offering. ¹³And Samuel said to Saul, Thou hast done foolishly: thou hast not kept the commandment of the LORD thy God, which he commanded thee: for now would the LORD have established thy kingdom upon Israel for ever. ¹⁴But now thy kingdom shall not continue: the LORD hath sought him a man after his own heart, and the LORD hath commanded him *to be* captain over his people, because thou hast not kept *that* which the LORD commanded thee.

¹⁵And Samuel arose, and gat him up from Gilgal unto Gibeah of Benjamin. And Saul numbered the people *that were* present^d with him, about six

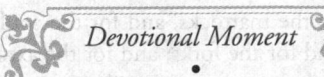

Devotional Moment

Foolishness

13:13-14 If you are sometimes tempted to believe that the end justifies the means, take a close look at Saul. This renegade king, preparing for battle against the Philistines, decided to offer a sacrifice to God. Offering a sacrifice was not wrong; the problem was that Saul was not the right person to do it. Saul was a king, not a priest, and therefore was not authorized to offer sacrifices (see Num. 18). Rather than be patient and do it God's way, he tried a shortcut and paid a high price. For Saul's disobedience, God took the throne away from him and his descendants. If God seems to be taking his time addressing your needs, be patient and beware of the temptation to meet them in your own way.

hundred men. ¹⁶And Saul, and Jonathan his son, and the people *that were* present^e with them, abode in Gibeah of Benjamin: but the Philistines encamped in Michmash. ¹⁷And the spoilers came out of the camp of the Philistines in three companies: one company turned unto the way *that leadeth to* Ophrah, unto the land of Shual: ¹⁸And another company turned the way *to* Bethhoron: and another company turned *to* the way of the border that looketh to the valley of Zeboim toward the wilderness. ¹⁹Now there was no smith found throughout all the land of Israel: for the Philistines said, Lest the Hebrews make *them* swords or spears: ²⁰But all the Israelites went down to the Philistines, to sharpen every man his share, and his coulter, and his axe, and his mattock. ²¹Yet they had a

---

^c salute: Heb. bless
^d present: Heb. found
^e present: Heb. found

file[f] for the mattocks, and for the coulters, and for the forks, and for the axes, and to sharpen the goads. 22So it came to pass in the day of battle, that there was neither sword nor spear found in the hand of any of the people that *were* with Saul and Jonathan: but with Saul and with Jonathan his son was there found. 23And the garrison[g] of the Philistines went out to the passage of Michmash.

14

1Now it came to pass upon a day, that Jonathan the son of Saul said unto the young man that bare his armour, Come, and let us go over to the Philistines' garrison, that *is* on the other side. But he told not his father. 2And Saul tarried in the uttermost part of Gibeah under a pomegranate tree which *is* in Migron: and the people that *were* with him *were* about six hundred men; 3And Ahiah[a], the son of Ahitub, Ichabod's brother, the son of Phinehas, the son of Eli, the LORD'S priest in Shiloh, wearing an ephod. And the people knew not that Jonathan was gone. 4And between the passages, by which Jonathan sought to go over unto the Philistines' garrison, *there was* a sharp rock on the one side, and a sharp rock on the other side: and the name of the one *was* Bozez, and the name of the other Seneh. 5The forefront[b] of the one *was* situate northward over against Michmash, and the other southward over against Gibeah. 6And Jonathan

said to the young man that bare his armour, Come, and let us go over unto the garrison of these uncircumcised: it may be that the LORD will work for us: for *there is* no restraint to the LORD to save by many or by few. 7And his armourbearer said unto him, Do all that *is* in thine heart: turn thee; behold, I *am* with thee according to thy heart. 8Then said Jonathan, Behold, we will pass over unto *these* men, and we will discover ourselves unto them. 9If they say thus unto us, Tarry[c] until we come to you; then we will stand still in our place, and will not go up unto them. 10But if they say thus, Come up unto us; then we will go up: for the LORD hath delivered them into our hand: and this *shall be* a sign unto us. 11And both of them discovered themselves unto the garrison of the Philistines: and the Philistines said, Behold, the Hebrews come forth out of the holes where they had hid themselves. 12And the men of the garrison answered Jonathan and his armourbearer, and said, Come up to us, and we will shew you a thing. And Jonathan said unto his armourbearer, Come up after me: for the LORD hath delivered them into the hand of Israel. 13And Jonathan climbed up upon his hands and upon his feet, and his armourbearer after him: and they fell before Jonathan; and his armourbearer slew after him. 14And that first slaughter, which Jonathan and his armourbearer made, was about twenty men,

---

[f] a file: Heb. a file with mouths
[g] garrison: or, standing camp
[a] Ahiah: called Ahimelech
[b] forefront: Heb. tooth
[c] Tarry: Heb. Be still

within as it were an[d] half acre of land, *which* a yoke *of oxen might plow.* [15]And there was trembling in the host, in the field, and among all the people: the garrison, and the spoilers, they also trembled, and the earth quaked: so it was a very great trembling.

[16]And the watchmen of Saul in Gibeah of Benjamin looked; and, behold, the multitude melted away, and they went on beating down *one another.* [17]Then said Saul unto the people that *were* with him, Number now, and see who is gone from us. And when they had numbered, behold, Jonathan and his armourbearer *were* not *there.* [18]And Saul said unto Ahiah, Bring hither the ark of God. For the ark of God was at that time with the children of Israel. [19]And it came to pass, while Saul talked unto the priest, that the noise[e] that *was* in the host of the Philistines went on and increased: and Saul said unto the priest, Withdraw thine hand. [20]And Saul and all the people that *were* with him assembled[f] themselves, and they came to the battle: and, behold, every man's sword was against his fellow, *and there was* a very great discomfiture. [21]Moreover the Hebrews *that* were with the Philistines before that time, which went up with them into the camp *from the country* round about, even they also *turned* to be with the Israelites that *were* with Saul and Jonathan. [22]Likewise all the men of Israel which had hid themselves in mount Ephraim, *when* they heard that the Philistines fled, even they also followed hard after them in the battle. [23]So the

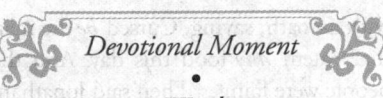

Devotional Moment
•
Words

14:24-30 Perhaps you've heard someone say that it is better to remain silent and be thought a fool than to open your mouth and remove all doubt. Too bad no one passed this wisdom on to King Saul. He not only did many foolish and impulsive things, he also made a lot of rash statements that cost him dearly. In his pride and desire to avenge himself on the Philistines, Saul uttered a foolish curse, and it almost cost him the life of his son and the loyalty of his troops. Do yourself and your family a favor: Weigh your words carefully, and teach your children how to do the same. Few effects are harder to undo than the harm caused by hastily spoken words.

LORD saved Israel that day: and the battle passed over unto Bethaven.

[24]And the men of Israel were distressed that day: for Saul had adjured the people, saying, Cursed *be* the man that eateth *any* food until evening, that I may be avenged on mine enemies. So none of the people tasted *any* food. [25]And all *they of* the land came to a wood; and there was honey upon the ground. [26]And when the people were come into the wood, behold, the honey dropped; but no man put his hand to his mouth: for the people feared the oath. [27]But Jonathan heard not when his father charged the people with the oath: wherefore he put forth the end of the rod that *was* in his hand, and dipped it in an honeycomb, and put his hand to his mouth; and his eyes were enlightened. [28]Then answered one of the people, and said, Thy father straitly charged the people

---

[d] an . . . : or, half a furrow of an acre of land
[e] noise: or, tumult
[f] assembled . . . : Heb. were cried together

with an oath, saying, Cursed *be* the man that eateth *any* food this day. And the people were faint[g]. [29]Then said Jonathan, My father hath troubled the land: see, I pray you, how mine eyes have been enlightened, because I tasted a little of this honey. [30]How much more, if haply the people had eaten freely to day of the spoil of their enemies which they found? for had there not been now a much greater slaughter among the Philistines? [31]And they smote the Philistines that day from Michmash to Aijalon: and the people were very faint. [32]And the people flew upon the spoil, and took sheep, and oxen, and calves, and slew *them* on the ground: and the people did eat *them* with the blood. [33]Then they told Saul, saying, Behold, the people sin against the LORD, in that they eat with the blood. And he said, Ye have transgressed[h]: roll a great stone unto me this day. [34]And Saul said, Disperse yourselves among the people, and say unto them, Bring me hither every man his ox, and every man his sheep, and slay *them* here, and eat; and sin not against the LORD in eating with the blood. And all the people brought every man his ox with him[i] that night, and slew *them* there. [35]And Saul built an altar unto the LORD: the same was the first altar that he built unto the LORD.

[36]And Saul said, Let us go down after the Philistines by night, and spoil them until the morning light, and let us not leave a man of them. And they said,

Do whatsoever seemeth good unto thee. Then said the priest, Let us draw near hither unto God. [37]And Saul asked counsel of God, Shall I go down after the Philistines? wilt thou deliver them into the hand of Israel? But he answered him not that day. [38]And Saul said, Draw ye near hither, all the chief[j] of the people: and know and see wherein this sin hath been this day. [39]For, *as* the LORD liveth, which saveth Israel, though it be in Jonathan my son, he shall surely die. But *there was* not a man among all the people *that* answered him. [40]Then said he unto all Israel, Be ye on one side, and I and Jonathan my son will be on the other side. And the people said unto Saul, Do what seemeth good unto thee. [41]Therefore Saul said unto the LORD God of Israel, Give[k] a perfect *lot*. And Saul and Jonathan were taken: but the people escaped. [42]And Saul said, Cast *lots* between me and Jonathan my son. And Jonathan was taken. [43]Then Saul said to Jonathan, Tell me what thou hast done. And Jonathan told him, and said, I did but taste a little honey with the end of the rod that *was* in mine hand, *and,* lo, I must die. [44]And Saul answered, God do so and more also: for thou shalt surely die, Jonathan. [45]And the people said unto Saul, Shall Jonathan die, who hath wrought this great salvation in Israel? God forbid: *as* the LORD liveth, there shall not one hair of his head fall to the ground; for he hath wrought

---

[g] faint: or, weary
[h] transgressed: or, dealt treacherously
[i] with him: Heb. in his hand
[j] chief: Heb. corners
[k] Give . . . : or, Shew the innocent

with God this day. So the people rescued Jonathan, that he died not. ⁴⁶Then Saul went up from following the Philistines: and the Philistines went to their own place.

⁴⁷So Saul took the kingdom over Israel, and fought against all his enemies on every side, against Moab, and against the children of Ammon, and against Edom, and against the kings of Zobah, and against the Philistines: and whithersoever he turned himself, he vexed *them*. ⁴⁸And he gathered¹ an host, and smote the Amalekites, and delivered Israel out of the hands of them that spoiled them. ⁴⁹Now the sons of Saul were Jonathan, and Ishui, and Melchishua: and the names of his two daughters *were these*; the name of the firstborn Merab, and the name of the younger Michal: ⁵⁰And the name of Saul's wife *was* Ahinoam, the daughter of Ahimaaz: and the name of the captain of his host *was* Abnerᵐ, the son of Ner, Saul's uncle. ⁵¹And Kish *was* the father of Saul; and Ner the father of Abner *was* the son of Abiel. ⁵²And there was sore war against the Philistines all the days of Saul: and when Saul saw any strong man, or any valiant man, he took him unto him.

15

¹Samuel also said unto Saul, The LORD sent me to anoint thee *to be* king over his people, over Israel: now therefore hearken thou unto the voice of the words of the LORD. ²Thus saith the LORD of hosts, I remember *that*

which Amalek did to Israel, how he laid *wait* for him in the way, when he came up from Egypt. ³Now go and smite Amalek, and utterly destroy all that they have, and spare them not; but slay both man and woman, infant and suckling, ox and sheep, camel and ass. ⁴And Saul gathered the people together, and numbered them in Telaim, two hundred thousand footmen, and ten thousand men of Judah. ⁵And Saul came to a city of Amalek, and laid wait in the valley. ⁶And Saul said unto the Kenites, Go, depart, get you down from among the Amalekites, lest I destroy you with them: for ye shewed kindness to all the children of Israel, when they came up out of Egypt. So the Kenites departed from among the Amalekites. ⁷And Saul smote the Amalekites from Havilah *until* thou comest to Shur, that *is* over against Egypt. ⁸And he took Agag the king of the Amalekites alive, and utterly destroyed all the people with the edge of the sword. ⁹But Saul and the people spared Agag, and the best of the sheep, and of the oxen, and of the fatlingsᵃ, and the lambs, and all *that was* good, and would not utterly destroy them: but every thing *that was* vile and refuse, that they destroyed utterly.

¹⁰Then came the word of the LORD unto Samuel, saying, ¹¹It repenteth me that I have set up Saul *to be* king: for he is turned back from following me, and hath not performed my commandments. And it grieved Samuel; and he cried unto the LORD all night. ¹²And when Samuel rose early to meet Saul in

---

¹ gathered . . . : or, wrought mightily
ᵐ Abner: Heb. Abiner
ᵃ fatlings: or, second sort

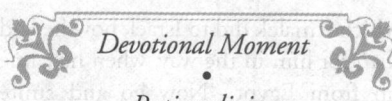

Devotional Moment

Rationalizing

15:13-15 Most of us are reluctant to confess our own disobedience. Saul certainly was. When Samuel confronted him about his sin (failing to *completely destroy* the Amalekites and their property as God had commanded him), Saul first tried to shift the blame to his soldiers. Then he said that even though they had kept the best of the livestock, they only did it so they could offer them in sacrifice to the Lord. That sounds very spiritual, but it was really a rationalization for not doing what God had said. Saul again provides an excellent example of what *not* to do: disobey God and then try to cover it up. Children are experts at rationalizing! Help your kids avoid Saul's mistake by demonstrating a proper attitude toward your own shortcomings. Let them see you admit your mistakes, repent, and go on.

the morning, it was told Samuel, saying, Saul came to Carmel, and, behold, he set him up a place, and is gone about, and passed on, and gone down to Gilgal. ¹³And Samuel came to Saul: and Saul said unto him, Blessed *be* thou of the LORD: I have performed the commandment of the LORD. ¹⁴And Samuel said, What *meaneth* then this bleating of the sheep in mine ears, and the lowing of the oxen which I hear? ¹⁵And Saul said, They have brought them from the Amalekites: for the people spared the best of the sheep and of the oxen, to sacrifice unto the LORD thy God; and the rest we have utterly destroyed. ¹⁶Then Samuel said unto Saul, Stay, and I will tell thee what the LORD hath said to me this night. And he said unto him, Say on. ¹⁷And Samuel said, When thou *wast* little in thine own sight, *wast* thou not *made* the head of the tribes of Israel,

and the LORD anointed thee king over Israel? ¹⁸And the LORD sent thee on a journey, and said, Go and utterly destroy the sinners the Amalekites, and fight against them until they be consumed. ¹⁹Wherefore then didst thou not obey the voice of the LORD, but didst fly upon the spoil, and didst evil in the sight of the LORD? ²⁰And Saul said unto Samuel, Yea, I have obeyed the voice of the LORD, and have gone the way which the LORD sent me, and have brought Agag the king of Amalek, and have utterly destroyed the Amalekites. ²¹But the people took of the spoil, sheep and oxen, the chief of the things which should have been utterly destroyed, to sacrifice unto the LORD thy God in Gilgal. ²²And Samuel said, Hath the LORD *as great* delight in burnt offerings and sacrifices, as in obeying the voice of the LORD? Behold, to obey *is* better than sacrifice, *and* to hearken than the fat of rams. ²³For rebellion *is as* the sin of witchcraft[b], and stubbornness *is as* iniquity and idolatry. Because thou hast rejected the word of the LORD, he hath also rejected thee from *being* king.

²⁴And Saul said unto Samuel, I have sinned: for I have transgressed the commandment of the LORD, and thy words: because I feared the people, and obeyed their voice. ²⁵Now therefore, I pray thee, pardon my sin, and turn again with me, that I may worship the LORD. ²⁶And Samuel said unto Saul, I will not return with thee: for thou hast rejected the word of the LORD, and the LORD hath rejected thee from being king over Israel. ²⁷And as Samuel turned about to go away, he laid hold upon the skirt of his

---

[b] witchcraft: Heb. divination

mantle, and it rent. ²⁸And Samuel said unto him, The LORD hath rent the kingdom of Israel from thee this day, and hath given it to a neighbour of thine, *that is* better than thou. ²⁹And also the Strengthᶜ of Israel will not lie nor repent: for he *is* not a man, that he should repent. ³⁰Then he said, I have sinned: *yet* honour me now, I pray thee, before the elders of my people, and before Israel, and turn again with me, that I may worship the LORD thy God. ³¹So Samuel turned again after Saul; and Saul worshipped the LORD.

³²Then said Samuel, Bring ye hither to me Agag the king of the Amalekites. And Agag came unto him delicately. And Agag said, Surely the bitterness of death is past. ³³And Samuel said, As thy sword hath made women childless, so shall thy mother be childless among women. And Samuel hewed Agag in pieces before the LORD in Gilgal. ³⁴Then Samuel went to Ramah; and Saul went up to his house to Gibeah of Saul. ³⁵And Samuel came no more to see Saul until the day of his death: nevertheless Samuel mourned for Saul: and the LORD repented that he had made Saul king over Israel.

16

¹And the LORD said unto Samuel, How long wilt thou mourn for Saul, seeing I have rejected him from reigning over Israel? fill thine horn with oil, and go, I will send thee to Jesse the Bethlehemite: for I have provided me a king among his sons. ²And Samuel said, How can I go? if Saul hear *it*, he will kill

me. And the LORD said, Take an heifer with theeᵃ, and say, I am come to sacrifice to the LORD. ³And call Jesse to the sacrifice, and I will shew thee what thou shalt do: and thou shalt anoint unto me *him* whom I name unto thee. ⁴And Samuel did that which the LORD spake, and came to Bethlehem. And the elders of the town trembled at his coming, and said, Comest thou peaceably? ⁵And he said, Peaceably: I am come to sacrifice unto the LORD: sanctify yourselves, and come with me to the sacrifice. And he sanctified Jesse and his sons, and called them to the sacrifice.

⁶And it came to pass, when they were come, that he looked on Eliabᵇ, and said, Surely the LORD'S anointed *is* before him. ⁷But the LORD said unto

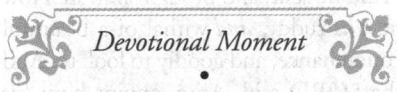

Devotional Moment

Appearances

16:6-7 Adolescents find it difficult to remember that a person's worth is not determined by his or her appearance. In a culture (like ours) that worships physical beauty, it is hard to remember that what really makes a person valuable lies below the surface. Samuel faced this struggle when looking for a successor to Saul. Saul was tall, handsome, and impressive; apparently Samuel thought the next king should be, too. But God chose a young shepherd named David because of his character. We judge by appearances; God judges the heart. Help those in your family to cultivate inner beauty and appreciate it in others by praising acts of kindness and generosity, recognizing accomplishments that don't require beauty, and avoiding putting down others for how they dress or present themselves.

ᶜ Strength: or, Eternity, or, Victory
ᵃ with thee: Heb. in thine hand
ᵇ Eliab: called Elihu

Samuel, Look not on his countenance, or on the height of his stature; because I have refused him: for *the LORD seeth* not as man seeth; for man looketh on the outward appearance, but the LORD looketh on the heart. ⁸Then Jesse called Abinadab, and made him pass before Samuel. And he said, Neither hath the LORD chosen this. ⁹Then Jesse made Shammahᶜ to pass by. And he said, Neither hath the LORD chosen this. ¹⁰Again, Jesse made seven of his sons to pass before Samuel. And Samuel said unto Jesse, The LORD hath not chosen these. ¹¹And Samuel said unto Jesse, Are here all *thy* children? And he said, There remaineth yet the youngest, and, behold, he keepeth the sheep. And Samuel said unto Jesse, Send and fetch him: for we will not sit downᵈ till he come hither. ¹²And he sent, and brought him in. Now he *was* ruddy, *and* withal of a beautiful countenance, and goodly to look to. And the LORD said, Arise, anoint him: for this *is* he. ¹³Then Samuel took the horn of oil, and anointed him in the midst of his brethren: and the Spirit of the LORD came upon David from that day forward. So Samuel rose up, and went to Ramah.

¹⁴But the Spirit of the LORD departed from Saul, and an evil spirit from the LORD troubledᵉ him. ¹⁵And Saul's servants said unto him, Behold now, an evil spirit from God troubleth thee. ¹⁶Let our lord now command thy servants, *which are* before thee, to seek out a man, *who is* a cunning player on an harp: and it shall come to pass, when the evil spirit from God is upon thee, that he shall play with his hand, and thou shalt be well. ¹⁷And Saul said unto his servants, Provide me now a man that can play well, and bring *him* to me. ¹⁸Then answered one of the servants, and said, Behold, I have seen a son of Jesse the Bethlehemite, *that is* cunning in playing, and a mighty valiant man, and a man of war, and prudent in mattersᶠ, and a comely person, and the LORD *is* with him. ¹⁹Wherefore Saul sent messengers unto Jesse, and said, Send me David thy son, which *is* with the sheep. ²⁰And Jesse took an ass *laden* with bread, and a bottle of wine, and a kid, and sent *them* by David his son unto Saul. ²¹And David came to Saul, and stood before him: and he loved him greatly; and he became his armourbearer. ²²And Saul sent to Jesse, saying, Let David, I pray thee, stand before me; for he hath found favour in my sight. ²³And it came to pass, when the *evil* spirit from God was upon Saul, that David took an harp, and played with his hand: so Saul was refreshed, and was well, and the evil spirit departed from him.

17

¹Now the Philistines gathered together their armies to battle, and were gathered together at Shochoh, which *belongeth* to Judah, and pitched between Shochoh and Azekah, in Ephesdammimª. ²And Saul and the men of Israel were gathered

---

ᶜ Shammah: Shimeah, also called, Shimma
ᵈ down: Heb. round
ᵉ troubled: or, terrified
ᶠ matters: or, speech
ª Ephesdammim: or, the coast of Dammim, called Pasdammim

Shouldering Responsibility versus Shifting Blame

" 'Wherefore then didst thou not obey the voice of the Lord, but didst fly upon the spoil, and didst evil in the sight of the Lord?' And Saul said unto Samuel, 'Yea, I have obeyed the voice of the Lord . . . but the people took of the spoil, sheep and oxen . . . to sacrifice unto the Lord.' " 1 Samuel 15:19-21

One mark of someone who breaks free of negative behavior is the ability to shoulder responsibility rather than shift blame to someone else. Adam shifted the blame in the garden. And in the passage above, Saul does the same thing. According to him, he's not responsible for his sin—the troops are.

Some of us think it's not our problem we've been fired from so many jobs—it's *all those lousy bosses* out there. It's not our fault our children won't come to visit now that they're grown—it's *their mother* who poisoned their minds.

If we're serious about breaking past cycles, we must face the truth. We must become more interested in being Christlike than in shifting blame.

Why was it so easy for Saul—and for us today—to blame others? In many cases, it's because we're more concerned about the image we present to others than being responsible people.

Are you more concerned about image management than authentic living? Here are three questions to help you answer that question and assess your level of responsibility.

1. Are you great at beginning spiritual commitments . . . but terrible at finishing them? Saul started well. In fact, in 1 Samuel 11:6 we learn that the "Spirit of God came upon Saul." Yet near the end of his life, he sought counsel from a witch (1 Sam. 28:7-8)! What a slide! Maintaining his image as king became so important to Saul that he was willing to do *anything*—except take responsibility for his failures—to keep it from getting tarnished.

2. Does the fear of losing others' approval "force" you into increased compromise? Because Saul looked to the crowd, and not to God, to define himself, he was in deep trouble when "the people were scattered from him" (1 Sam. 13:8). He panicked and offered a sacrifice when he shouldn't have. Taking responsibility may mean going against the crowd, refusing to sacrifice our morals or clear biblical commands to please them.

3. Is your repentance simply disappointment over getting caught rather than sorrow over the acts you've committed? One mark of irresponsibility is reacting with anger over getting caught instead of heartbreak over the fact that we sinned. Not feeling legitimate guilt for our wrongs is a clear indication of avoiding responsibility for our actions. There is an antidote to irresponsibility. It comes in the form of a loving God who hates sin, but who always stands ready to forgive: "If we confess our sins, he is faithful and just to forgive us our sins, and to cleanse us from all unrighteousness" (1 John 1:9).

Of his attempt to cover up his sins of adultery and murder, King David recalled, "When I kept silence, my bones waxed old through my roaring all the day long" (Ps. 32:3). The antidote to his denying responsibility for the hurt he'd caused?

"I acknowledged my sin unto thee . . . I said, I will confess my transgressions unto the Lord; and thou forgavest the iniquity of my sin" (Ps. 32:5).

Taking responsibility is something that Saul rarely did . . . but *you* can. If you've been stuck in a pattern of blaming your teacher, coach, parents, spouse, ex-spouse, boss, children, or even God for all your problems, you need to do as David did. Take responsibility for your actions, admit your wrongs, receive God's forgiveness and cleansing, and then walk forward in a new path.

---

together, and pitched by the valley of Elah, and set the battle in array against the Philistines. ³And the Philistines stood on a mountain on the one side, and Israel stood on a mountain on the other side: and *there was* a valley between them. ⁴And there went out a champion out of the camp of the Philistines, named Goliath, of Gath, whose height *was* six cubits and a span. ⁵And *he had* an helmet of brass upon his head, and he *was* armed^b with a coat of mail; and the weight of the coat *was* five thousand shekels of brass. ⁶And *he had* greaves of brass upon his legs, and a target^c of brass between his shoulders. ⁷And the staff of his spear *was* like a weaver's beam; and his spear's head *weighed* six hundred shekels of iron: and one bearing a shield went before him. ⁸And he stood and cried unto the armies of Is-

rael, and said unto them, Why are ye come out to set *your* battle in array? *am* not I a Philistine, and ye servants to Saul? choose you a man for you, and let him come down to me. ⁹If he be able to fight with me, and to kill me, then will we be your servants: but if I prevail against him, and kill him, then shall ye be our servants, and serve us. ¹⁰And the Philistine said, I defy the armies of Israel this day; give me a man, that we may fight together. ¹¹When Saul and all Israel heard those words of the Philistine, they were dismayed, and greatly afraid.

¹²Now David *was* the son of that Ephrathite of Bethlehemjudah, whose name *was* Jesse; and he had eight sons: and the man went among men *for* an old man in the days of Saul. ¹³And the three eldest sons of Jesse went *and* followed Saul to the battle: and the names

---

^b armed: Heb. clothed
^c target: or, gorget

of his three sons that went to the battle *were* Eliab the firstborn, and next unto him Abinadab, and the third Shammah. ¹⁴And David *was* the youngest: and the three eldest followed Saul. ¹⁵But David went and returned from Saul to feed his father's sheep at Bethlehem. ¹⁶And the Philistine drew near morning and evening, and presented himself forty days. ¹⁷And Jesse said unto David his son, Take now for thy brethren an ephah of this parched *corn*, and these ten loaves, and run to the camp to thy brethren; ¹⁸And carry these ten cheesesᵈ unto the captain of *their* thousand, and look how thy brethren fare, and take their pledge. ¹⁹Now Saul, and they, and all the men of Israel, *were* in the valley of Elah, fighting with the Philistines. ²⁰And David rose up early in the morning, and left the sheep with a keeper, and took, and went, as Jesse had commanded him; and he came to the trenchᵉ, as the host was going forth to the fight, and shouted for the battle. ²¹For Israel and the Philistines had put the battle in array, army against army. ²²And David left his carriageᶠ in the hand of the keeper of the carriage, and ran into the army, and came and saluted his brethren. ²³And as he talked with them, behold, there came up the champion, the Philistine of Gath, Goliath by name, out of the armies of the Philistines, and spake according to the same words: and David heard *them*. ²⁴And all the men of Israel, when they saw the man, fled from him, and were

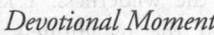

Devotional Moment

•

Sibling Rivalry

17:28-29 Sibling rivalries are often intense—and irrational. Young David, seeking to take a stand for God, began asking questions about why no one had stood up to Goliath. While the other soldiers answered him, David's oldest brother, Eliab, became angry. Like many older brothers, Eliab was annoyed by David's presence and initiative, even though David's intentions were good. When your children squabble, help them see the issue at stake. Are they at odds over prized possessions, cherished territory, interpretation of some rule, or just differences in personal style? Help them negotiate and resolve the conflict before resentment grows.

sore afraid. ²⁵And the men of Israel said, Have ye seen this man that is come up? surely to defy Israel is he come up: and it shall be, *that* the man who killeth him, the king will enrich him with great riches, and will give him his daughter, and make his father's house free in Israel. ²⁶And David spake to the men that stood by him, saying, What shall be done to the man that killeth this Philistine, and taketh away the reproach from Israel? for who *is* this uncircumcised Philistine, that he should defy the armies of the living God? ²⁷And the people answered him after this manner, saying, So shall it be done to the man that killeth him. ²⁸And Eliab his eldest brother heard when he spake unto the men; and Eliab's anger was kindled against David, and he said, Why camest thou down hither? and with whom hast thou left those few

---

ᵈ cheeses: Heb. cheeses of milk
ᵉ trench: or, place of the carriage
ᶠ his carriage: Heb. the vessels from upon him

sheep in the wilderness? I know thy pride, and the naughtiness of thine heart; for thou art come down that thou mightest see the battle. ²⁹And David said, What have I now done? *Is there* not a cause? ³⁰And he turned from him toward another, and spake after the same manner⁸: and the people answered him again after the former manner.

³¹And when the words were heard which David spake, they rehearsed *them* before Saul: and he sentʰ for him. ³²And David said to Saul, Let no man's heart fail because of him; thy servant will go and fight with this Philistine. ³³And Saul said to David, Thou art not able to go against this Philistine to fight with him: for thou *art but* a youth, and he a man of war from his youth. ³⁴And David said unto Saul, Thy servant kept his father's sheep, and there came a lion, and a bear, and took a lambⁱ out of the flock: ³⁵And I went out after him, and smote him, and delivered *it* out of his mouth: and when he arose against me, I caught *him* by his beard, and smote him, and slew him. ³⁶Thy servant slew both the lion and the bear: and this uncircumcised Philistine shall be as one of them, seeing he hath defied the armies of the living God. ³⁷David said moreover, The LORD that delivered me out of the paw of the lion, and out of the paw of the bear, he will deliver me out of the hand of this Philistine. And Saul said unto David,

Go, and the LORD be with thee. ³⁸And Saul armed Davidʲ with his armour, and he put an helmet of brass upon his head; also he armed him with a coat of mail. ³⁹And David girded his sword upon his armour, and he assayed to go; for he had not proved *it*. And David said unto Saul, I cannot go with these; for I have not proved *them*. And David put them off him.

⁴⁰And he took his staff in his hand, and chose him five smooth stones out of the brookᵏ, and put them in a shepherd's bag which he had, even in a scrip; and his sling *was* in his hand: and he drew near to the Philistine. ⁴¹And the Philistine came on and drew near unto David; and the man that bare the shield *went* before him. ⁴²And when the Philistine looked about, and saw David, he disdained him: for he was *but* a youth, and ruddy, and of a fair countenance. ⁴³And the Philistine said unto David, *Am* I a dog, that thou comest to me with staves? And the Philistine cursed David by his gods. ⁴⁴And the Philistine said to David, Come to me, and I will give thy flesh unto the fowls of the air, and to the beasts of the field. ⁴⁵Then said David to the Philistine, Thou comest to me with a sword, and with a spear, and with a shield: but I come to thee in the name of the LORD of hosts, the God of the armies of Israel, whom thou hast defied. ⁴⁶This day will the LORD deliverˡ thee into mine hand;

---

⁸ manner: Heb. word
ʰ sent . . . : Heb. took him
ⁱ lamb: or, kid
ʲ armed David . . . : Heb. clothed David with his clothes
ᵏ brook: or, valley
ˡ deliver . . . : Heb. shut thee up

and I will smite thee, and take thine head from thee; and I will give the carcases of the host of the Philistines this day unto the fowls of the air, and to the wild beasts of the earth; that all the earth may know that there is a God in Israel. ⁴⁷And all this assembly shall know that the LORD saveth not with sword and spear: for the battle *is* the LORD'S, and he will give you into our hands.

⁴⁸And it came to pass, when the Philistine arose, and came and drew nigh to meet David, that David hasted, and ran toward the army to meet the Philistine. ⁴⁹And David put his hand in his bag, and took thence a stone, and slang *it,* and smote the Philistine in his forehead, that the stone sunk into his forehead; and he fell upon his face to the earth. ⁵⁰So David prevailed over the Philistine with a sling and with a stone, and smote the Philistine, and slew him; but *there was* no sword in the hand of David. ⁵¹Therefore David ran, and stood upon the Philistine, and took his sword, and drew it out of the sheath thereof, and slew him, and cut off his head therewith. And when the Philistines saw their champion was dead, they fled. ⁵²And the men of Israel and of Judah arose, and shouted, and pursued the Philistines, until thou come to the valley, and to the gates of Ekron. And the wounded of the Philistines fell down by the way to Shaaraim, even unto Gath, and unto Ekron. ⁵³And the children of Israel returned from chasing after the Philistines, and they spoiled their tents. ⁵⁴And David took the head of the Philistine, and brought it to Jerusalem; but he put his armour in his tent. ⁵⁵And when Saul saw David go forth against the Philistine, he said unto Abner, the captain of the host, Abner, whose son *is* this youth? And Abner said, *As* thy soul liveth, O king, I cannot tell. ⁵⁶And the king said, Enquire thou whose son the stripling *is.* ⁵⁷And as David returned from the slaughter of the Philistine, Abner took him, and brought him before Saul with the head of the Philistine in his hand. ⁵⁸And Saul said to him, Whose son *art* thou, *thou* young man? And David answered, I *am* the son of thy servant Jesse the Bethlehemite.

18

¹And it came to pass, when he had made an end of speaking unto Saul, that the soul of Jonathan was knit with the soul of David, and Jonathan loved him as his own soul. ²And Saul took him that day, and would let him go no more home to his father's house. ³Then Jonathan and David made a covenant, because he loved him as his own soul. ⁴And Jonathan stripped himself of the robe that *was* upon him, and gave it to

Devotional Moment

Friendship

18:1-4 Friendships like David and Jonathan's are sorely missed in our fast-paced, disposable society. Closer than many brothers, their mutual commitment to God and unconditional love for one another overcame vast differences in background—David a junior shepherd, Jonathan an experienced war veteran and heir apparent to the throne of Israel. Who of us would not benefit from such a bond? Yet close friendships do not come easily. To build strong friendships, strive to *be* a loyal friend. Take the initiative to explore common interests with others and spend time with them.

David, and his garments, even to his sword, and to his bow, and to his girdle. ⁵And David went out whithersoever Saul sent him, *and* behaved himself wisely: and Saul set him over the men of war, and he was accepted in the sight of all the people, and also in the sight of Saul's servants.

⁶And it came to pass as they came, when David was returned from the slaughter of the Philistineᵃ, that the women came out of all cities of Israel, singing and dancing, to meet king Saul, with tabrets, with joy, and with instruments of musick. ⁷And the women answered *one another* as they played, and said, Saul hath slain his thousands, and David his ten thousands. ⁸And Saul was very wroth, and the saying displeased him;ᵇ and he said, They have ascribed unto David ten thousands, and to me they have ascribed *but* thousands: and *what* can he have more but the kingdom? ⁹And Saul eyed David from that day and forward. ¹⁰And it came to pass on the morrow, that the evil spirit from God came upon Saul, and he prophesied in the midst of the house: and David played with his hand, as at other times: and *there was* a javelin in Saul's hand. ¹¹And Saul cast the javelin; for he said, I will smite David even to the wall *with it.* And David avoided out of his presence twice.

¹²And Saul was afraid of David, because the LORD was with him, and was departed from Saul. ¹³Therefore Saul removed him from him, and made him his captain over a thousand; and he

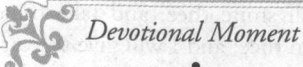

Devotional Moment

Domestic Abuse

18:8-14 Saul was jealous, angry, suspicious, fearful, raving mad, and wildly abusive toward David. Saul threw more than emotional daggers; he threw deadly spears (18:10-12; 19:9-10; 20:30-34). Once David recognized Saul's problem, he left the scene for safety's sake. Then he rebuilt his life, with God's help, to accomplish his life's purpose. Saul illustrates the savage side of human nature. If you grew up with or now live with an abusive person, do not retaliate or try to appease the person. Establish boundaries for yourself and seek help and a safe location where you can rebuild your life.

went out and came in before the people. ¹⁴And David behaved himself wisely in all his ways; and the LORD *was* with him. ¹⁵Wherefore when Saul saw that he behaved himself very wisely, he was afraid of him. ¹⁶But all Israel and Judah loved David, because he went out and came in before them. ¹⁷And Saul said to David, Behold my elder daughter Merab, her will I give thee to wife: only be thou valiantᶜ for me, and fight the LORD'S battles. For Saul said, Let not mine hand be upon him, but let the hand of the Philistines be upon him. ¹⁸And David said unto Saul, Who *am* I? and what *is* my life, *or* my father's family in Israel, that I should be son in law to the king? ¹⁹But it came to pass at the time when Merab Saul's daughter should have been given to David, that she was given unto Adriel the Meholathite to wife. ²⁰And Michal

---

ᵃ Philistine: or, Philistines
ᵇ displeased him: Heb. was evil in his eyes
ᶜ valiant: Heb. a son of valour

Saul's daughter loved David: and they told Saul, and the thing pleased him.[d] [21]And Saul said, I will give him her, that she may be a snare to him, and that the hand of the Philistines may be against him. Wherefore Saul said to David, Thou shalt this day be my son in law in *the one of* the twain. [22]And Saul commanded his servants, *saying*, Commune with David secretly, and say, Behold, the king hath delight in thee, and all his servants love thee: now therefore be the king's son in law. [23]And Saul's servants spake those words in the ears of David. And David said, Seemeth it to you *a* light *thing* to be a king's son in law, seeing that I *am* a poor man, and lightly esteemed? [24]And the servants of Saul told him, saying, On this manner spake David. [25]And Saul said, Thus shall ye say to David, The king desireth not any dowry, but an hundred foreskins of the Philistines, to be avenged of the king's enemies. But Saul thought to make David fall by the hand of the Philistines. [26]And when his servants told David these words, it pleased David well to be the king's son in law: and the days were not expired[e]. [27]Wherefore David arose and went, he and his men, and slew of the Philistines two hundred men; and David brought their foreskins, and they gave them in full tale to the king, that he might be the king's son in law. And Saul gave him Michal his daughter to wife. [28]And Saul saw and knew that the LORD *was* with David, and *that* Michal Saul's daughter loved him. [29]And Saul was yet the more afraid of David; and Saul became David's enemy continually. [30]Then the princes of the Philistines went forth: and it came to pass, after they went forth, *that* David behaved himself more wisely than all the servants of Saul; so that his name was much set by[f].

19

[1]And Saul spake to Jonathan his son, and to all his servants, that they should kill David. [2]But Jonathan Saul's son delighted much in David: and Jonathan told David, saying, Saul my father seeketh to kill thee: now therefore, I pray thee, take heed to thyself until the morning, and abide in a secret *place*, and hide thyself: [3]And I will go out and stand beside my father in the field where thou *art*, and I will commune with my father of thee; and what I see, that I will tell thee. [4]And Jonathan spake good of David unto Saul his father, and said unto him, Let not the king sin against his servant, against David; because he hath not sinned against thee, and because his works *have been* to thee-ward very good: [5]For he did put his life in his hand, and slew the Philistine, and the LORD wrought a great salvation for all Israel: thou sawest *it*, and didst rejoice: wherefore then wilt thou sin against innocent blood, to slay David without a cause? [6]And Saul hearkened unto the voice of Jonathan: and Saul sware, *As* the LORD liveth, he shall not be slain. [7]And Jonathan called David, and

---

[d] pleased him: Heb. was right in his eyes
[e] expired: Heb. fulfilled
[f] set by: Heb. precious

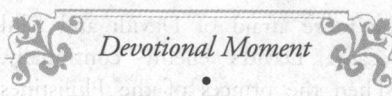

Devotional Moment

•

No Cover-Up

19:1-7; 20:1-15 Jonathan tried to deflect some of Saul's anger away from David and agreed to help David. When Jonathan, too, suffered Saul's wrath, he acted immediately to protect David (20:30-40). Jonathan did all he could to help his friend escape Saul's wrath. Jonathan had his eyes wide open about his father's problem. Sometimes relatives of a person with a drinking or drug addiction become *codependent*. That is, they minimize, deny, and delude themselves about the true nature of the sick person's addictive behavior. Their codependence becomes part of the problem, as it prevents the offender from getting help. If you have a family member with a drinking problem or some other addiction, be like Jonathan—take steps to confront the problem and to protect innocent members of the family from harm.

Jonathan shewed him all those things. And Jonathan brought David to Saul, and he was in his presence, as in times past.

⁸And there was war again: and David went out, and fought with the Philistines, and slew them with a great slaughter; and they fled from him.ᵃ ⁹And the evil spirit from the LORD was upon Saul, as he sat in his house with his javelin in his hand: and David played with *his* hand. ¹⁰And Saul sought to smite David even to the wall with the javelin; but he slipped away out of Saul's presence, and he smote the javelin into the wall: and David fled, and escaped that night.

¹¹Saul also sent messengers unto David's house, to watch him, and to slay him in the morning: and Michal David's wife told him, saying, If thou save not thy life to night, to morrow thou shalt be slain. ¹²So Michal let David down through a window: and he went, and fled, and escaped. ¹³And Michal took an imageᵇ, and laid *it* in the bed, and put a pillow of goats' *hair* for his bolster, and covered *it* with a cloth. ¹⁴And when Saul sent messengers to take David, she said, He *is* sick. ¹⁵And Saul sent the messengers *again* to see David, saying, Bring him up to me in the bed, that I may slay him. ¹⁶And when the messengers were come in, behold, *there was* an image in the bed, with a pillow of goats' *hair* for his bolster. ¹⁷And Saul said unto Michal, Why hast thou deceived me so, and sent away mine enemy, that he is escaped? And Michal answered Saul, He said unto me, Let me go; why should I kill thee?

¹⁸So David fled, and escaped, and came to Samuel to Ramah, and told him all that Saul had done to him. And he and Samuel went and dwelt in Naioth. ¹⁹And it was told Saul, saying, Behold, David *is* at Naioth in Ramah. ²⁰And Saul sent messengers to take David: and when they saw the company of the prophets prophesying, and Samuel standing *as* appointed over them, the Spirit of God was upon the messengers of Saul, and they also prophesied. ²¹And when it was told Saul, he sent other messengers, and they prophesied likewise. And Saul sent messengers again the third time, and they prophesied also. ²²Then went he also to Ramah, and came to a great well

---

ᵃ him: Heb. his face
ᵇ image: Heb. teraphim

478

that *is* in Sechu: and he asked and said, Where *are* Samuel and David? And *one* said, Behold, *they be* at Naioth in Ramah. ²³And he went thither to Naioth in Ramah: and the Spirit of God was upon him also, and he went on, and prophesied, until he came to Naioth in Ramah. ²⁴And he stripped off his clothes also, and prophesied before Samuel in like manner, and lay down naked all that day and all that night. Wherefore they say, *Is* Saul also among the prophets?

20

¹And David fled from Naioth in Ramah, and came and said before Jonathan, What have I done? what *is* mine iniquity? and what *is* my sin before thy father, that he seeketh my life? ²And he said unto him, God forbid; thou shalt not die: behold, my father will do nothing either great or small, but that he will shew^a it me: and why should my father hide this thing from me? it *is* not *so.* ³And David sware moreover, and said, Thy father certainly knoweth that I have found grace in thine eyes; and he saith, Let not Jonathan know this, lest he be grieved: but truly *as* the LORD liveth, and *as* thy soul liveth, *there is* but a step between me and death. ⁴Then said Jonathan unto David, Whatsoever thy soul desireth, I will even do *it* for thee. ⁵And David said unto Jonathan, Behold, to morrow *is* the new moon, and I should not fail to sit with the king at

meat: but let me go, that I may hide myself in the field unto the third *day* at even. ⁶If thy father at all miss me, then say, David earnestly asked *leave* of me that he might run to Bethlehem his city: for *there is* a yearly sacrifice^b there for all the family. ⁷If he say thus, *It is* well; thy servant shall have peace: but if he be very wroth, *then* be sure that evil is determined by him. ⁸Therefore thou shalt deal kindly with thy servant; for thou hast brought thy servant into a covenant of the LORD with thee: notwithstanding, if there be in me iniquity, slay me thyself; for why shouldest thou bring me to thy father?

⁹And Jonathan said, Far be it from thee: for if I knew certainly that evil were determined by my father to come upon thee, then would not I tell it thee? ¹⁰Then said David to Jonathan, Who shall tell me? or what *if* thy father answer thee roughly? ¹¹And Jonathan said unto David, Come, and let us go out into the field. And they went out both of them into the field. ¹²And Jonathan said unto David, O LORD God of Israel, when I have sounded^c my father about to morrow any time, *or* the third *day,* and, behold, *if there be* good toward David, and I then send not unto thee, and shew it thee; ¹³The LORD do so and much more to Jonathan: but if it please my father *to do* thee evil, then I will shew^d it thee, and send thee away, that thou mayest go in peace: and the LORD be with thee, as he hath been with my father. ¹⁴And thou shalt not

---

^a shew . . . : Heb. uncover mine ear
^b sacrifice: or, feast
^c sounded: Heb. searched
^d shew . . . : Heb. uncover thine ear

Devotional Moment
•
Vows

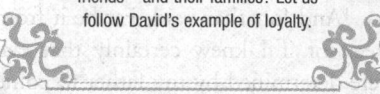

20:12-17, 42 David promised a loyalty to Jonathan that went far beyond traditional friendship. He extended unconditional loyalty even to *future* generations of Saul's household. To seal this vow, David and Jonathan swore an oath of friendship. David went to great personal expense to make good on this vow when, years later, he sought out and took in Mephibosheth, the sole surviving member of Saul's family (2 Sam. 9).

Not many people today take their vows as seriously as David did. Self-interest, rather than sacrifice, governs most relationships. When have you kept a family promise that inconvenienced you? What other sacrifices are you willing to make for your family and friends—and their families? Let us follow David's example of loyalty.

only while yet I live shew me the kindness of the LORD, that I die not: ¹⁵But *also* thou shalt not cut off thy kindness from my house for ever: no, not when the LORD hath cut off the enemies of David every one from the face of the earth. ¹⁶So Jonathan made^e *a covenant* with the house of David, *saying*, Let the LORD even require *it* at the hand of David's enemies. ¹⁷And Jonathan caused David to swear again, because he loved him: for he loved him as he loved his own soul. ¹⁸Then Jonathan said to David, To morrow *is* the new moon: and thou shalt be missed, because thy seat will be empty^f. ¹⁹And *when* thou hast stayed three days, *then* thou shalt go down quickly^g, and come to the place where thou didst hide thyself when the business was *in hand*, and shalt remain by the stone Ezel. ²⁰And I will shoot three arrows on the side *thereof*, as though I shot at a mark. ²¹And, behold, I will send a lad, *saying*, Go, find out the arrows. If I expressly say unto the lad, Behold, the arrows *are* on this side of thee, take them; then come thou: for *there is* peace to thee, and no hurt^h; *as* the LORD liveth. ²²But if I say thus unto the young man, Behold, the arrows *are* beyond thee; go thy way: for the LORD hath sent thee away. ²³And *as touching* the matter which thou and I have spoken of, behold, the LORD *be* between thee and me for ever.

²⁴So David hid himself in the field: and when the new moon was come, the king sat him down to eat meat. ²⁵And the king sat upon his seat, as at other times, *even* upon a seat by the wall: and Jonathan arose, and Abner sat by Saul's side, and David's place was empty. ²⁶Nevertheless Saul spake not any thing that day: for he thought, Something hath befallen him, he *is* not clean; surely he *is* not clean. ²⁷And it came to pass on the morrow, *which was* the second *day* of the month, that David's place was empty: and Saul said unto Jonathan his son, Wherefore cometh not the son of Jesse to meat, neither yesterday, nor to day? ²⁸And Jonathan answered Saul, David earnestly asked *leave* of me *to go* to Bethlehem: ²⁹And he said, Let me go, I pray thee; for our family hath a sacrifice in the city; and my brother, he hath

---

^e made: Heb. cut

^f empty: Heb. missed

^g quickly: or, diligently: Heb. greatly

^h no hurt: Heb. not any thing

commanded me *to be there*: and now, if I have found favour in thine eyes, let me get away, I pray thee, and see my brethren. Therefore he cometh not unto the king's table. ³⁰Then Saul's anger was kindled against Jonathan, and he said unto him, Thou son of the perverse rebellious *woman*, do not I know that thou hast chosen the son of Jesse to thine own confusion, and unto the confusion of thy mother's nakedness? ³¹For as long as the son of Jesse liveth upon the ground, thou shalt not be established, nor thy kingdom. Wherefore now send and fetch him unto me, for he shall surely die. ³²And Jonathan answered Saul his father, and said unto him, Wherefore shall he be slain? what hath he done? ³³And Saul cast a javelin at him to smite him: whereby Jonathan knew that it was determined of his father to slay David. ³⁴So Jonathan arose from the table in fierce anger, and did eat no meat the second day of the month: for he was grieved for David, because his father had done him shame.

³⁵And it came to pass in the morning, that Jonathan went out into the field at the time appointed with David, and a little lad with him. ³⁶And he said unto his lad, Run, find out now the arrows which I shoot. *And* as the lad ran, he shot an arrow beyond[i] him. ³⁷And when the lad was come to the place of the arrow which Jonathan had shot, Jonathan cried after the lad, and said, *Is not the arrow beyond thee?* ³⁸And Jonathan cried after the lad, Make

speed, haste, stay not. And Jonathan's lad gathered up the arrows, and came to his master. ³⁹But the lad knew not any thing: only Jonathan and David knew the matter. ⁴⁰And Jonathan gave his artillery[j] unto his lad, and said unto him, Go, carry *them* to the city. ⁴¹*And* as soon as the lad was gone, David arose out of *a place* toward the south, and fell on his face to the ground, and bowed himself three times: and they kissed one another, and wept one with another, until David exceeded. ⁴²And Jonathan said to David, Go in peace, forasmuch as we have sworn both of us in the name of the LORD, saying, The LORD be between me and thee, and between my seed and thy seed for ever. And he arose and departed: and Jonathan went into the city.

21

¹Then came David to Nob to Ahimelech[a] the priest: and Ahimelech was afraid at the meeting of David, and said unto him, Why *art* thou alone, and no man with thee? ²And David said unto Ahimelech the priest, The king hath commanded me a business, and hath said unto me, Let no man know any thing of the business whereabout I send thee, and what I have commanded thee: and I have appointed *my* servants to such and such a place. ³Now therefore what is under thine hand? give *me* five *loaves of* bread in mine hand, or what there is present[b]. ⁴And the priest answered David, and said, *There is* no com-

---

[i] beyond . . . : Heb. to pass over him
[j] artillery: Heb. instruments
[a] Ahimelech: also called, called Ahiah
[b] present: Heb. found

Soul-Mate Friendships: Rare and Precious

by Dee Brestin

While we are likely to have many friends pass through our lives, soul mates are exceptional. Whereas lovers are knit together in body, soul mates—or *second selves*—are knit together in soul. In 1 Samuel 20 we see, through David and Jonathan, why soul mates are so precious.

Finding a soul mate. Though friends can be found by being friendly, soul mates are unique. You *discover* soul mates. Often it seems you meet by chance, but as in the case of David and Jonathan, it is not chance at all, but the providence of God. You will have to pray, and you may have to wait months or even years for an answer—but when God knows the time is right, he will help you discover a "second self."

Jonathan, like David, stood alone among his peers because of his strong faith. Like David, he had taken on the Philistines, who had defamed God's name (compare 1 Sam. 14 with 1 Sam. 17). The very first day they met, Jonathan saw David as a soul mate and committed himself to him, showing a vulnerability that is little known among men (1 Sam. 18:1-4).

Differences between men and women. Most men do not have soul mates of their own gender. Men find it very difficult to make themselves vulnerable, especially to other men. Richard Cohen, a columnist for the *Washington Post*, put it like this: "My friends have no friends. They are men . . . and men, I have come to believe, cannot or will not have real friends. They have something else—companions, buddies, pals, chums . . . but no one when it comes to saying how they feel—especially how they hurt."

Women are not only more comfortable with connection but often err on the side of being *too* connected. Little girls, for example, are territorial and often treacherous to a third little girl who tries to break into their circle of two. Even Christian women, who should know better, can be reluctant to divide their cozy Bible study group or to welcome newcomers. Rather than finding their security in God, they find it in relationships—and sometimes cling to them in an unhealthy way.

Spiritual maturity leads to changes in the friendships of both women and men. As women mature and learn to find their security in Christ, they become less grasping. They are less apt to smother a friend and more willing to open their circle. In contrast, as men mature in Christ, they become less threatened by intimacy. A few even grow to the point of being like Christ, who, in the Garden of Gethsemane, shared his feelings with his friends, asked them for help, and even wept.

David and Jonathan were exceptionally mature in their faith, and this obviously affected their friendship. Not only do they give an example to men of what is possible for their friendships, but they serve as a model to both men and women on how to preserve these precious friendships in the face of great obstacles.

Keeping a soul-mate friendship. Most soul mates can overcome the obstacles of stress and distance. However, there is an obstacle that can destroy even soul-mate friendships, and that is the feeling that your soul mate has betrayed you. Sooner or later, most soul mates are going to experience this, for we all have feet of clay.

Over the years Marilyn and Shelly found great comfort and strength in their friendship. But one day Shelly made herself vulnerable and asked if Marilyn thought she was making some mistakes as a mother. Marilyn jumped in without prayer and was far too harsh.

Later, Marilyn felt bad and apologized. But Shelly had been wounded and was unwilling to trust Marilyn again. She stopped calling and was cool whenever Marilyn called her.

While they both nursed their hurt feelings, the friendship covenant they had made years before, based on that of David and Jonathan in 1 Samuel 20, haunted them. One day when Marilyn had a bad cold and was feeling sorry for herself, Shelly appeared at her door with a casserole. They wept and forgave each other. Today their friendship is stronger than ever.

Soul-mate friendships are rare and precious. Pray for them. Trust God for them. Nurture them. And above all, honor the deep level of trust they bring.

DIGGING DEEPER

1. What is the value of a promise? the danger? Read Ecclesiastes 5:1-7.

2. What can we learn from David and Jonathan's example of friendship even when the two were separated by distance? See 1 Samuel 20:41-42 and 23:15-18.

3. How did David keep his promise to Jonathan? See 2 Samuel 9.

---

mon bread under mine hand, but there is hallowed bread; if the young men have kept themselves at least from women. ⁵And David answered the priest, and said unto him, Of a truth women *have been* kept from us about these three days, since I came out, and the vessels of the young men are holy, and *the bread is* in a manner common, yea,ᶜ though it were sanctified this day in the vessel. ⁶So the priest gave him hallowed *bread*: for there was no bread there but the shewbread, that was taken from before the LORD, to put hot bread in the day when it was taken away. ⁷Now a certain man of the servants of Saul *was* there that day, detained before the LORD; and his name *was* Doeg, an Edomite, the chiefest of the herdmen that *belonged* to Saul. ⁸And David said unto Ahimelech, And is there not here under thine hand spear or sword? for I have neither brought my

sword nor my weapons with me, because the king's business required haste. ⁹And the priest said, The sword of Goliath the Philistine, whom thou slewest in the valley of Elah, behold, it *is here* wrapped in a cloth behind the ephod: if thou wilt take that, take *it*: for *there is* no other save that here. And David said, *There is* none like that; give it me.

¹⁰And David arose, and fled that day for fear of Saul, and went to Achish the king of Gath. ¹¹And the servants of Achish said unto him, *Is* not this David the king of the land? did they not sing one to another of him in dances, saying, Saul hath slain his thousands, and David his ten thousands? ¹²And David laid up these words in his heart, and was sore afraid of Achish the king of Gath. ¹³And he changed his behaviour before them, and feigned himself mad in their hands, and scrabbledᵈ on the doors of the gate,

---

ᶜ yea . . . : or, especially when this day there is other sanctified in the vessel
ᵈ scrabbled: or, made marks

and let his spittle fall down upon his beard. ¹⁴Then said Achish unto his servants, Lo, ye see the man is mad*: wherefore *then* have ye brought him to me? ¹⁵Have I need of mad men, that ye have brought this *fellow* to play the mad man in my presence? shall this *fellow* come into my house?

22

¹David therefore departed thence, and escaped to the cave Adullam: and when his brethren and all his father's house heard *it*, they went down thither to him. ²And every one *that was* in distress, and every one that *was* in debt, and every one *that was* discontented, gathered themselves unto him; and he became a captain over them: and there were with him about four hundred men. ³And David went thence to Mizpeh of Moab: and he said unto the

---

Devotional Moment
•
Family Ties

22:1-4 David, himself an outlaw, gathered fellow outlaws, malcontents, misfits, and even family members to form a motley crew that became his power base. Some of these eventually became his "mighty men" of valor. He needed them, as much as they needed him, to help him become king. Before that could happen, however, David's parents also needed a safe place to stay, so David appealed to the king of Moab. As David seized an available opportunity to care for his parents, despite living on the run and far from home, so also should we. Care for your parents when it is in your power to do so, even if you live far from home.

---

king of Moab, Let my father and my mother, I pray thee, come forth, *and be* with you, till I know what God will do for me. ⁴And he brought them before the king of Moab: and they dwelt with him all the while that David was in the hold. ⁵And the prophet Gad said unto David, Abide not in the hold; depart, and get thee into the land of Judah. Then David departed, and came into the forest of Hareth.

⁶When Saul heard that David was discovered, and the men that *were* with him, (now Saul abode in Gibeah under a tree* in Ramah, having his spear in his hand, and all his servants *were* standing about him;) ⁷Then Saul said unto his servants that stood about him, Hear now, ye Benjamites; will the son of Jesse give every one of you fields and vineyards, *and* make you all captains of thousands, and captains of hundreds; ⁸That all of you have conspired against me, and *there is* none that sheweth* me that my son hath made a league with the son of Jesse, and *there is* none of you that is sorry for me, or sheweth unto me that my son hath stirred up my servant against me, to lie in wait, as at this day? ⁹Then answered Doeg the Edomite, which was set over the servants of Saul, and said, I saw the son of Jesse coming to Nob, to Ahimelech the son of Ahitub. ¹⁰And he enquired of the LORD for him, and gave him victuals, and gave him the sword of Goliath the Philistine. ¹¹Then the king sent to call Ahimelech the priest, the son of Ahitub, and all his father's house, the priests that *were* in

---

ᵉ is mad: or, playeth the mad man
ᵃ tree . . . : or, grove in a high place
ᵇ sheweth . . . : Heb. uncovereth mine ear

Nob: and they came all of them to the king. ¹²And Saul said, Hear now, thou son of Ahitub. And he answered, Here I *am*, my lord. ¹³And Saul said unto him, Why have ye conspired against me, thou and the son of Jesse, in that thou hast given him bread, and a sword, and hast enquired of God for him, that he should rise against me, to lie in wait, as at this day? ¹⁴Then Ahimelech answered the king, and said, And who *is so* faithful among all thy servants as David, which is the king's son in law, and goeth at thy bidding, and is honourable in thine house? ¹⁵Did I then begin to enquire of God for him? be it far from me: let not the king impute *any* thing unto his servant, *nor* to all the house of my father: for thy servant knew nothing of all this, less*ᶜ* or more. ¹⁶And the king said, Thou shalt surely die, Ahimelech, thou, and all thy father's house. ¹⁷And the king said unto the footmen*ᵈ* that stood about him, Turn, and slay the priests of the LORD; because their hand also *is* with David, and because they knew when he fled, and did not shew it to me. But the servants of the king would not put forth their hand to fall upon the priests of the LORD. ¹⁸And the king said to Doeg, Turn thou, and fall upon the priests. And Doeg the Edomite turned, and he fell upon the priests, and slew on that day fourscore and five persons that did wear a linen ephod. ¹⁹And Nob, the city of the priests, smote he with the edge of the sword, both men and women, children and sucklings, and oxen, and asses, and sheep, with the edge of the sword. ²⁰And one of the sons of Ahim-

elech the son of Ahitub, named Abiathar, escaped, and fled after David. ²¹And Abiathar shewed David that Saul had slain the LORD'S priests. ²²And David said unto Abiathar, I knew *it* that day, when Doeg the Edomite *was* there, that he would surely tell Saul: I have occasioned *the death* of all the persons of thy father's house. ²³Abide thou with me, fear not: for he that seeketh my life seeketh thy life: but with me thou *shalt be* in safeguard.

23

¹Then they told David, saying, Behold, the Philistines fight against Keilah, and they rob the threshingfloors. ²Therefore David enquired of the LORD, saying, Shall I go and smite these Philistines? And the LORD said unto David, Go, and smite the Philistines, and save Keilah. ³And David's men said unto him, Behold, we be afraid here in Judah: how much more then if we come to Keilah against the armies of the Philistines? ⁴Then David enquired of the LORD yet again. And the LORD answered him and said, Arise, go down to Keilah; for I will deliver the Philistines into thine hand. ⁵So David and his men went to Keilah, and fought with the Philistines, and brought away their cattle, and smote them with a great slaughter. So David saved the inhabitants of Keilah. ⁶And it came to pass, when Abiathar the son of Ahimelech fled to David to Keilah, *that* he came down *with* an ephod in his hand. ⁷And it was told Saul that David was come to Keilah. And Saul said,

---

ᶜ less . . . : Heb. little or great
ᵈ footmen: or, guard: Heb. runners

God hath delivered him into mine hand; for he is shut in, by entering into a town that hath gates and bars. ⁸And Saul called all the people together to war, to go down to Keilah, to besiege David and his men. ⁹And David knew that Saul secretly practised mischief against him; and he said to Abiathar the priest, Bring hither the ephod. ¹⁰Then said David, O LORD God of Israel, thy servant hath certainly heard that Saul seeketh to come to Keilah, to destroy the city for my sake. ¹¹Will the men of Keilah deliver me up into his hand? will Saul come down, as thy servant hath heard? O LORD God of Israel, I beseech thee, tell thy servant. And the LORD said, He will come down. ¹²Then said David, Will the men of Keilah deliver[a] me and my men into the hand of Saul? And the LORD said, They will deliver *thee* up. ¹³Then David and his men, *which were* about six hundred, arose and departed out of Keilah, and went whithersoever they could go. And it was told Saul that David was escaped from Keilah; and he forbare to go forth.

¹⁴And David abode in the wilderness in strong holds, and remained in a mountain in the wilderness of Ziph. And Saul sought him every day, but God delivered him not into his hand. ¹⁵And David saw that Saul was come out to seek his life: and David *was* in the wilderness of Ziph in a wood. ¹⁶And Jonathan Saul's son arose, and went to David into the wood, and strengthened his hand in God. ¹⁷And he said unto him, Fear not: for the hand of Saul my

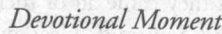

Devotional Moment

•

Loyalty and Priorities

23:16-18 Jonathan was Saul's own son, yet he promised David protection from Saul, loyal service when David became king, and encouragement in obeying God. Jonathan's loyalty to God's kingdom exceeded his loyalty to Saul; his own personal welfare meant even less to him. In a similar way, David passed up opportunities to kill Saul because he respected the Lord's will in choosing Saul to be king (24:4-7; 26:8-11). Sometimes following the Lord requires us to overrule family tradition or personal preference. Our commitment to God needs to take priority over our family ties and our own interests.

father shall not find thee; and thou shalt be king over Israel, and I shall be next unto thee; and that also Saul my father knoweth. ¹⁸And they two made a covenant before the LORD: and David abode in the wood, and Jonathan went to his house.

¹⁹Then came up the Ziphites to Saul to Gibeah, saying, Doth not David hide himself with us in strong holds in the wood, in the hill of Hachilah, which *is* on the south of Jeshimon? ²⁰Now therefore, O king, come down according to all the desire of thy soul to come down; and our part *shall be* to deliver him into the king's hand. ²¹And Saul said, Blessed *be* ye of the LORD; for ye have compassion on me. ²²Go, I pray you, prepare yet, and know and see his place where his haunt[b] is, *and* who hath seen him there: for it is told me *that* he dealeth very subtilly. ²³See therefore, and take knowledge of all the

---

[a] deliver: Heb. shut up
[b] haunt . . . : Heb. foot shall be

lurking places where he hideth himself, and come ye again to me with the certainty, and I will go with you: and it shall come to pass, if he be in the land, that I will search him out throughout all the thousands of Judah. ²⁴And they arose, and went to Ziph before Saul: but David and his men *were* in the wilderness of Maon, in the plain on the south of Jeshimon. ²⁵Saul also and his men went to seek *him.* And they told David: wherefore he came down into a rock, and abode in the wilderness of Maon. And when Saul heard *that*, he pursued after David in the wilderness of Maon. ²⁶And Saul went on this side of the mountain, and David and his men on that side of the mountain: and David made haste to get away for fear of Saul; for Saul and his men compassed David and his men round about to take them. ²⁷But there came a messenger unto Saul, saying, Haste thee, and come; for the Philistines have invadedᶜ the land. ²⁸Wherefore Saul returned from pursuing after David, and went against the Philistines: therefore they called that place Selahammahlekothᵈ. ²⁹And David went up from thence, and dwelt in strong holds at Engedi.

24

¹And it came to pass, when Saul was returned from followingᵃ the Philistines, that it was told him, saying, Behold, David *is* in the wilderness of Engedi. ²Then Saul took three thousand chosen men out of all Israel, and went to seek David and his men upon the rocks of the wild goats. ³And he came to the sheepcotes by the way, where *was* a cave; and Saul went in to cover his feet: and David and his men remained in the sides of the cave. ⁴And the men of David said unto him, Behold the day of which the LORD said unto thee, Behold, I will deliver thine enemy into thine hand, that thou mayest do to him as it shall seem good unto thee. Then David arose, and cut off the skirt of Saul'sᵇ robe privily. ⁵And it came to pass afterward, that David's heart smote him, because he had cut off Saul's skirt. ⁶And he said unto his men, The LORD forbid that I should do this thing unto my master, the LORD'S anointed, to stretch forth mine hand against him, seeing he *is* the anointed of the LORD. ⁷So David stayedᶜ his servants with these words, and suffered them not to rise against Saul. But Saul rose up out of the cave, and went on *his* way. ⁸David also arose afterward, and went out of the cave, and cried after Saul, saying, My lord the king. And when Saul looked behind him, David stooped with his face to the earth, and bowed himself.

⁹And David said to Saul, Wherefore hearest thou men's words, saying, Behold, David seeketh thy hurt? ¹⁰Behold, this day thine eyes have seen how that the LORD had delivered thee to day into mine hand in the cave: and

---

ᶜ invaded . . . : Heb. spread themselves upon, etc
ᵈ Selahammahlekoth: that is, The rock of divisions
ᵃ following: Heb. after
ᵇ Saul's . . . : Heb. the robe which was Saul's
ᶜ stayed: Heb. cut off

some bade *me* kill thee: but *mine eye* spared thee; and I said, I will not put forth mine hand against my lord; for he *is* the LORD'S anointed. [11]Moreover, my father, see, yea, see the skirt of thy robe in my hand: for in that I cut off the skirt of thy robe, and killed thee not, know thou and see that *there is* neither evil nor transgression in mine hand, and I have not sinned against thee; yet thou huntest my soul to take it. [12]The LORD judge between me and thee, and the LORD avenge me of thee: but mine hand shall not be upon thee. [13]As saith the proverb of the ancients, Wickedness proceedeth from the wicked: but mine hand shall not be upon thee. [14]After whom is the king of Israel come out? after whom dost thou pursue? after a dead dog, after a flea. [15]The LORD therefore be judge, and judge between me and thee, and see, and plead my cause, and deliver[d] me out of thine hand.

[16]And it came to pass, when David had made an end of speaking these words unto Saul, that Saul said, *Is* this thy voice, my son David? And Saul lifted up his voice, and wept. [17]And he said to David, Thou *art* more righteous than I: for thou hast rewarded me good, whereas I have rewarded thee evil. [18]And thou hast shewed this day how that thou hast dealt well with me: forasmuch as when the LORD had delivered[e] me into thine hand, thou killedst me not. [19]For if a man find his enemy, will he let him go well away? wherefore

the LORD reward thee good for that thou hast done unto me this day. [20]And now, behold, I know well that thou shalt surely be king, and that the kingdom of Israel shall be established in thine hand. [21]Swear now therefore unto me by the LORD, that thou wilt not cut off my seed after me, and that thou wilt not destroy my name out of my father's house. [22]And David sware unto Saul. And Saul went home; but David and his men gat them up unto the hold.

25

[1]And Samuel died; and all the Israelites were gathered together, and lamented him, and buried him in his house at Ramah. And David arose, and went down to the wilderness of Paran.

[2]And *there was* a man in Maon, whose possessions[a] *were* in Carmel; and the man *was* very great, and he had three thousand sheep, and a thousand goats: and he was shearing his sheep in Carmel. [3]Now the name of the man *was* Nabal; and the name of his wife Abigail: and *she was* a woman of good understanding, and of a beautiful countenance: but the man *was* churlish and evil in his doings; and he *was* of the house of Caleb. [4]And David heard in the wilderness that Nabal did shear his sheep. [5]And David sent out ten young men, and David said unto the young men, Get you up to Carmel, and go to Nabal, and greet[b] him in my name: [6]And thus shall ye say to him that liveth *in prosperity*, Peace *be* both to thee, and

---

[d] deliver: Heb. judge
[e] delivered: Heb. shut up
[a] possessions: or, business
[b] greet . . . : Heb. ask him in my name of peace

peace *be* to thine house, and peace *be* unto all that thou hast. ⁷And now I have heard that thou hast shearers: now thy shepherds which were with us, we hurtᶜ them not, neither was there ought missing unto them, all the while they were in Carmel. ⁸Ask thy young men, and they will shew thee. Wherefore let the young men find favour in thine eyes: for we come in a good day: give, I pray thee, whatsoever cometh to thine hand unto thy servants, and to thy son David. ⁹And when David's young men came, they spake to Nabal according to all those words in the name of David, and ceasedᵈ. ¹⁰And Nabal answered David's servants, and said, Who *is* David? and who *is* the son of Jesse? there be many servants now a days that break away every man from his master. ¹¹Shall I then take my bread, and my water, and my fleshᵉ that I have killed for my shearers, and give *it* unto men, whom I know not whence they *be*?

¹²So David's young men turned their way, and went again, and came and told him all those sayings. ¹³And David said unto his men, Gird ye on every man his sword. And they girded on every man his sword; and David also girded on his sword: and there went up after David about four hundred men; and two hundred abode by the stuff. ¹⁴But one of the young men told Abigail, Nabal's wife, saying, Behold, David sent messengers out of the wilderness to salute our master; and he railedᶠ on them. ¹⁵But the men *were* very good unto us, and we were not hurtᵍ, neither missed we any thing, as long as we were conversant with them, when we were in the fields: ¹⁶They were a wall unto us both by night and day, all the while we were with them keeping the sheep. ¹⁷Now therefore know and consider what thou wilt do; for evil is determined against our master, and against all his household: for he *is such* a son of Belial, that *a man* cannot speak to him.

¹⁸Then Abigail made haste, and took two hundred loaves, and two bottles of wine, and five sheep ready dressed, and five measures of parched

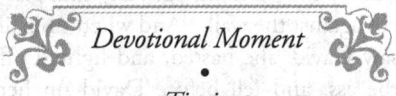

Devotional Moment

•

Timing

25:17-35 If it were not for Abigail's bold, selfless initiatives in keeping the peace, her husband and his men would have been killed outright. She solved the immediate problem with David by taking matters into her own hands, even though it meant taking responsibility for her husband's actions. Once the emergency had subsided, she bided her time, waited to bring up the touchy subject when Nabal was sober, and let the Lord act justly in due course. Abigail shows us that timing is important in resolving problems and conflicts. There is a time for quiet and a time to speak out; a time to act and a time to wait (see 25:36-42). The next time you need to discuss a delicate issue with a family member, think about the timing, pray for a good time to speak, and wait for God's leading to discern that time.

ᶜ hurt: Heb. shamed
ᵈ ceased: Heb. rested
ᵉ flesh: Heb. slaughter
ᶠ railed . . . : Heb. flew upon them
ᵍ hurt: Heb. shamed

corn, and an hundred clusters of raisins, and two hundred cakes of figs, and laid *them* on asses. ¹⁹And she said unto her servants, Go on before me; behold, I come after you. But she told not her husband Nabal. ²⁰And it was *so, as* she rode on the ass, that she came down by the covert of the hill, and, behold, David and his men came down against her; and she met them. ²¹Now David had said, Surely in vain have I kept all that this *fellow* hath in the wilderness, so that nothing was missed of all that *pertained* unto him: and he hath requited me evil for good. ²²So and more also do God unto the enemies of David, if I leave of all that *pertain* to him by the morning light any that pisseth against the wall. ²³And when Abigail saw David, she hasted, and lighted off the ass, and fell before David on her face, and bowed herself to the ground, ²⁴And fell at his feet, and said, Upon me, my lord, *upon* me *let this* iniquity *be*: and let thine handmaid, I pray thee, speak in thine audience[h], and hear the words of thine handmaid. ²⁵Let not my lord, I pray thee, regard[i] this man of Belial, *even* Nabal: for as his name *is*, so *is* he; Nabal *is* his name, and folly *is* with him: but I thine handmaid saw not the young men of my lord, whom thou didst send. ²⁶Now therefore, my lord, *as* the LORD liveth, and *as* thy soul liveth, seeing the LORD hath withholden thee from coming to *shed* blood, and from avenging[j] thyself with thine

own hand, now let thine enemies, and they that seek evil to my lord, be as Nabal. ²⁷And now this blessing[k] which thine handmaid hath brought unto my lord, let it even be given unto the young men that follow my lord. ²⁸I pray thee, forgive the trespass of thine handmaid: for the LORD will certainly make my lord a sure house; because my lord fighteth the battles of the LORD, and evil hath not been found in thee *all* thy days. ²⁹Yet a man is risen to pursue thee, and to seek thy soul: but the soul of my lord shall be bound in the bundle of life with the LORD thy God; and the souls of thine enemies, them shall he sling out, *as out* of the middle of a sling. ³⁰And it shall come to pass, when the LORD shall have done to my lord according to all the good that he hath spoken concerning thee, and shall have appointed thee ruler over Israel; ³¹That this shall be no grief[l] unto thee, nor offence of heart unto my lord, either that thou hast shed blood causeless, or that my lord hath avenged himself: but when the LORD shall have dealt well with my lord, then remember thine handmaid.

³²And David said to Abigail, Blessed *be* the LORD God of Israel, which sent thee this day to meet me: ³³And blessed *be* thy advice, and blessed *be* thou, which hast kept me this day from coming to *shed* blood, and from avenging myself with mine own hand. ³⁴For in very deed, *as* the LORD God of

---

[h] audience: Heb. ears
[i] regard: Heb. lay it to his heart
[j] avenging . . . : Heb. saving thyself
[k] blessing: or, present
[l] no grief: Heb. no staggering, or, stumbling

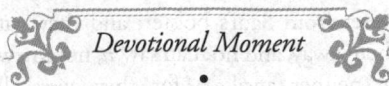

Israel liveth, which hath kept me back from hurting thee, except thou hadst hasted and come to meet me, surely there had not been left unto Nabal by the morning light any that pisseth against the wall. ³⁵So David received of her hand *that* which she had brought him, and said unto her, Go up in peace to thine house; see, I have hearkened to thy voice, and have accepted thy person.

³⁶And Abigail came to Nabal; and, behold, he held a feast in his house, like the feast of a king; and Nabal's heart *was* merry within him, for he *was* very drunken: wherefore she told him nothing, less or more, until the morning light. ³⁷But it came to pass in the morning, when the wine was gone out of Nabal, and his wife had told him these things, that his heart died within him, and he became *as* a stone. ³⁸And it came to pass about ten days *after*, that the LORD smote Nabal, that he died.

³⁹And when David heard that Nabal was dead, he said, Blessed *be* the LORD, that hath pleaded the cause of my reproach from the hand of Nabal, and hath kept his servant from evil: for the LORD hath returned the wickedness of Nabal upon his own head. And David sent and communed with Abigail, to take her to him to wife. ⁴⁰And when the servants of David were come to Abigail to Carmel, they spake unto her, saying, David sent us unto thee, to take thee to him to wife. ⁴¹And she arose, and bowed herself on *her* face to the earth, and said, Behold, *let* thine handmaid *be* a servant to wash the feet of the servants of my lord. ⁴²And Abigail hasted, and arose, and rode upon an ass, with five damsels of hers that went after her^m; and she went after the messengers of David, and became his wife. ⁴³David also took Ahinoam of Jezreel; and they were also both of them his wives. ⁴⁴But Saul had given Michal his daughter, David's wife, to Phalti^n the son of Laish, which *was* of Gallim.

26

¹And the Ziphites came unto Saul to Gibeah, saying, Doth not David hide himself in the hill of Hachilah, *which is* before Jeshimon? ²Then Saul arose, and went down to the wilderness of Ziph, having three thousand chosen men of Israel with him, to seek David in the wilderness of Ziph. ³And Saul pitched in the hill of Hachilah, which *is* before Jeshimon, by the way. But David abode in the wilderness, and he saw that Saul came after him into the wilderness.

---

^m after her: Heb. at her feet
^n Phalti: Phaltiel

⁴David therefore sent out spies, and understood that Saul was come in very deed. ⁵And David arose, and came to the place where Saul had pitched: and David beheld the place where Saul lay, and Abner the son of Ner, the captain of his host: and Saul lay in the trenchᵃ, and the people pitched round about him.

⁶Then answered David and said to Ahimelech the Hittite, and to Abishai the son of Zeruiah, brother to Joab, saying, Who will go down with me to Saul to the camp? And Abishai said, I will go down with thee. ⁷So David and Abishai came to the people by night: and, behold, Saul lay sleeping within the trench, and his spear stuck in the ground at his bolster: but Abner and the people lay round about him. ⁸Then said Abishai to David, God hath deliveredᵇ thine enemy into thine hand this day: now therefore let me smite him, I pray thee, with the spear even to the earth at once, and I will not *smite* him the second time. ⁹And David said to Abishai, Destroy him not: for who can stretch forth his hand against the LORD'S anointed, and be guiltless? ¹⁰David said furthermore, *As* the LORD liveth, the LORD shall smite him; or his day shall come to die; or he shall descend into battle, and perish. ¹¹The LORD forbid that I should stretch forth mine hand against the LORD'S anointed: but, I pray thee, take thou now the spear that *is* at his bolster, and the cruse of water, and let us go. ¹²So David took the spear and the cruse of water from Saul's bolster; and they gat them away, and no man saw *it*, nor knew *it*, neither awaked: for they *were* all asleep; because a deep sleep from the LORD was fallen upon them.

¹³Then David went over to the other side, and stood on the top of an hill afar off; a great space *being* between them: ¹⁴And David cried to the people, and to Abner the son of Ner, saying, Answerest thou not, Abner? Then Abner answered and said, Who *art* thou *that* criest to the king? ¹⁵And David said to Abner, *Art* not thou a *valiant* man? and who *is* like to thee in Israel? wherefore then hast thou not kept thy lord the king? for there came one of the people in to destroy the king thy lord. ¹⁶This thing *is* not good that thou hast done. *As* the LORD liveth, ye *are* worthy to dieᶜ, because ye have not kept your master, the LORD'S anointed. And now see where the king's spear *is*, and the cruse of water that *was* at his bolster. ¹⁷And Saul knew David's voice, and said, *Is* this thy voice, my son David? And David said, *It is* my voice, my lord, O king. ¹⁸And he said, Wherefore doth my lord thus pursue after his servant? for what have I done? or what evil *is* in mine hand? ¹⁹Now therefore, I pray thee, let my lord the king hear the words of his servant. If the LORD have stirred thee up against me, let him acceptᵈ an offering: but if *they be* the children of men, cursed *be* they before the LORD; for they have driven me out this day from abiding in the inheritance of the LORD, saying, Go, serve

---

ᵃ trench: or, midst of his carriages
ᵇ delivered: Heb. shut up
ᶜ worthy to die: Heb. the sons of death
ᵈ accept: Heb. smell

Devotional Moment
•
True Confessions?

26:17-24 Saul's confession of wrongdoing was too insincere to be trusted, even by one as desperate to resolve their conflict as David (see 27:1). Saul was paying mere lip service to his repentance in an effort to make David show himself. It was all a game of deception. Words of confession ("I was wrong") can heal and restore broken family relationships when spoken from the heart and demonstrated in actions. But watch out for confessions that someone uses only to make you vulnerable to another wrong or to avoid painful consequences. There is no value in pretending that everything is all right when in fact it is not.

other gods. ²⁰Now therefore, let not my blood fall to the earth before the face of the LORD: for the king of Israel is come out to seek a flea, as when one doth hunt a partridge in the mountains.

²¹Then said Saul, I have sinned: return, my son David: for I will no more do thee harm, because my soul was precious in thine eyes this day: behold, I have played the fool, and have erred exceedingly. ²²And David answered and said, Behold the king's spear! and let one of the young men come over and fetch it. ²³The LORD render to every man his righteousness and his faithfulness: for the LORD delivered thee into *my* hand to day, but I would not stretch forth mine hand against the LORD'S anointed. ²⁴And, behold, as thy life was much set by this day in mine eyes, so let my life be much set by in the eyes of the LORD, and let him deliver me out of

all tribulation. ²⁵Then Saul said to David, Blessed *be* thou, my son David: thou shalt both do great *things*, and also shalt still prevail. So David went on his way, and Saul returned to his place.

27

¹And David said in his heart, I shall now perishª one day by the hand of Saul: *there is* nothing better for me than that I should speedily escape into the land of the Philistines; and Saul shall despair of me, to seek me any more in any coast of Israel: so shall I escape out of his hand. ²And David arose, and he passed over with the six hundred men that *were* with him unto Achish, the son of Maoch, king of Gath. ³And David dwelt with Achish at Gath, he and his men, every man with his household, *even* David with his two wives, Ahinoam the Jezreelitess, and Abigail the Carmelitess, Nabal's wife. ⁴And it was told Saul that David was fled to Gath: and he sought no more again for him. ⁵And David said unto Achish, If I have now found grace in thine eyes, let them give me a place in some town in the country, that I may dwell there: for why should thy servant dwell in the royal city with thee? ⁶Then Achish gave him Ziklag that day: wherefore Ziklag pertaineth unto the kings of Judah unto this day. ⁷And the time^b that David dwelt in the country of the Philistines was a full year and four months.

⁸And David and his men went up, and invaded the Geshurites, and the Gezrites^c, and the Amalekites: for those

---

ª perish: Heb. be consumed
ᵇ the time: Heb. the number of days
ᶜ Gezrites: or, Gerzites

nations were of old the inhabitants of the land, as thou goest to Shur, even unto the land of Egypt. ⁹And David smote the land, and left neither man nor woman alive, and took away the sheep, and the oxen, and the asses, and the camels, and the apparel, and returned, and came to Achish. ¹⁰And Achish said, Whither[d] have ye made a road to day? And David said, Against the south of Judah, and against the south of the Jerahmeelites, and against the south of the Kenites. ¹¹And David saved neither man nor woman alive, to bring *tidings* to Gath, saying, Lest they should tell on us, saying, So did David, and so *will be* his manner all the while he dwelleth in the country of the Philistines. ¹²And Achish believed David, saying, He hath made his people Israel utterly[e] to abhor him; therefore he shall be my servant for ever.

28

¹And it came to pass in those days, that the Philistines gathered their armies together for warfare, to fight with Israel. And Achish said unto David, Know thou assuredly, that thou shalt go out with me to battle, thou and thy men. ²And David said to Achish, Surely thou shalt know what thy servant can do. And Achish said to David, Therefore will I make thee keeper of mine head for ever. ³Now Samuel was dead, and all Israel had lamented him, and buried him in Ramah, even in his own city. And Saul had put away those that had familiar spirits, and the wizards, out of the land. ⁴And the Philistines gathered themselves to-

gether, and came and pitched in Shunem: and Saul gathered all Israel together, and they pitched in Gilboa. ⁵And when Saul saw the host of the Philistines, he was afraid, and his heart greatly trembled. ⁶And when Saul enquired of the LORD, the LORD answered him not, neither by dreams, nor by Urim, nor by prophets.

⁷Then said Saul unto his servants, Seek me a woman that hath a familiar spirit, that I may go to her, and enquire of her. And his servants said to him, Behold, *there is* a woman that hath a familiar spirit at Endor. ⁸And Saul disguised himself, and put on other raiment, and he went, and two men with him, and they came to the woman by night: and he said, I pray thee, divine unto me by the familiar spirit, and bring me *him* up, whom I shall name unto thee. ⁹And the woman said unto him, Behold, thou knowest what Saul hath done, how he hath cut off those that have familiar spirits, and the wizards, out of the land: wherefore then layest thou a snare for my life, to cause me to die? ¹⁰And Saul sware to her by the LORD, saying, *As* the LORD liveth, there shall no punishment happen to thee for this thing. ¹¹Then said the woman, Whom shall I bring up unto thee? And he said, Bring me up Samuel. ¹²And when the woman saw Samuel, she cried with a loud voice: and the woman spake to Saul, saying, Why hast thou deceived me? for thou *art* Saul. ¹³And the king said unto her, Be not afraid: for what sawest thou? And the woman said unto Saul, I saw gods ascending out of the earth. ¹⁴And

---

[d] Whither . . . : or, Did you not make a road, etc
[e] utterly . . . : Heb. to stink

he said unto her, What form *is* he of? And she said, An old man cometh up; and he *is* covered with a mantle. And Saul perceived that it *was* Samuel, and he stooped with *his* face to the ground, and bowed himself.

[15]And Samuel said to Saul, Why hast thou disquieted me, to bring me up? And Saul answered, I am sore distressed; for the Philistines make war against me, and God is departed from me, and answereth me no more, neither by prophets[a], nor by dreams: therefore I have called thee, that thou mayest make known unto me what I shall do. [16]Then said Samuel, Wherefore then dost thou ask of me, seeing the LORD is departed from thee, and is become thine enemy? [17]And the LORD hath done to him[b], as he spake by me: for the LORD hath rent the kingdom out of thine hand, and given it to thy neighbour, *even* to David: [18]Because thou obeyedst not the voice of the LORD, nor executedst his fierce wrath upon Amalek, therefore hath the LORD done this thing unto thee this day. [19]Moreover the LORD will also deliver Israel with thee into the hand of the Philistines: and to morrow *shalt* thou and thy sons *be* with me: the LORD also shall deliver the host of Israel into the hand of the Philistines.

[20]Then Saul fell[c] straightway all along on the earth, and was sore afraid, because of the words of Samuel: and there was no strength in him; for he had eaten no bread all the day, nor all the night. [21]And the woman came unto Saul, and saw that he was sore troubled, and said unto him, Behold, thine handmaid hath obeyed thy voice, and I have put my life in my hand, and have hearkened unto thy words which thou spakest unto me. [22]Now therefore, I pray thee, hearken thou also unto the voice of thine handmaid, and let me set a morsel of bread before thee; and eat, that thou mayest have strength, when thou goest on thy way. [23]But he refused, and said, I will not eat. But his servants, together with the woman, compelled him; and he hearkened unto their voice. So he arose from the earth, and sat upon the bed. [24]And the woman had a fat calf in the house; and she hasted, and killed it, and took flour, and kneaded *it*, and did bake unleavened bread thereof: [25]And she brought *it* before Saul, and before his servants; and they did eat. Then they rose up, and went away that night.

29

[1]Now the Philistines gathered together all their armies to Aphek: and the Israelites pitched by a fountain which *is* in Jezreel. [2]And the lords of the Philistines passed on by hundreds, and by thousands: but David and his men passed on in the rereward with Achish. [3]Then said the princes of the Philistines, What *do* these Hebrews *here*? And Achish said unto the princes of the Philistines, *Is* not this David, the servant of Saul the king of Israel, which hath been with me these days, or these years, and I have found no fault in him since he fell *unto me* unto this day? [4]And

---

[a] by prophets: Heb. by the hand of prophets
[b] to him: or, for himself
[c] fell . . . : Heb. made haste, and fell with the fulness of his stature

the princes of the Philistines were wroth with him; and the princes of the Philistines said unto him, Make this fellow return, that he may go again to his place which thou hast appointed him, and let him not go down with us to battle, lest in the battle he be an adversary to us: for wherewith should he reconcile himself unto his master? *should it* not *be* with the heads of these men? [5] *Is* not this David, of whom they sang one to another in dances, saying, Saul slew his thousands, and David his ten thousands?

[6]Then Achish called David, and said unto him, Surely, *as* the LORD liveth, thou hast been upright, and thy going out and thy coming in with me in the host *is* good in my sight: for I have not found evil in thee since the day of thy coming unto me unto this day: nevertheless the lords[a] favour thee not. [7]Wherefore now return, and go in peace, that thou displease[b] not the lords of the Philistines. [8]And David said unto Achish, But what have I done? and what hast thou found in thy servant so long as I have been with thee unto this day, that I may not go fight against the enemies of my lord the king? [9]And Achish answered and said to David, I know that thou *art* good in my sight, as an angel of God: notwithstanding the princes of the Philistines have said, He shall not go up with us to the battle. [10]Wherefore now rise up early in the morning with thy master's servants that are come with thee: and as soon

as ye be up early in the morning, and have light, depart. [11]So David and his men rose up early to depart in the morning, to return into the land of the Philistines. And the Philistines went up to Jezreel.

30

[1]And it came to pass, when David and his men were come to Ziklag on the third day, that the Amalekites had invaded the south, and Ziklag, and smitten Ziklag, and burned it with fire; [2]And had taken the women captives, that *were* therein: they slew not any, either great or small, but carried *them* away, and went on their way. [3]So David and his men came to the city, and, behold, *it was* burned with fire; and their wives, and their sons, and their daughters, were taken captives. [4]Then David and the people that *were* with him lifted up their voice and wept, until they had no more power to weep. [5]And David's two wives were taken captives, Ahinoam the Jezreelitess, and Abigail the wife of Nabal the Carmelite. [6]And David was greatly distressed; for the people spake of stoning him, because the soul of all the people was grieved[a], every man for his sons and for his daughters: but David encouraged himself in the LORD his God.

[7]And David said to Abiathar the priest, Ahimelech's son, I pray thee, bring me hither the ephod. And Abiathar brought thither the ephod to David. [8]And David enquired at the LORD, saying, Shall I pursue after this

---

[a] the lords . . . : Heb. thou art not good in the eyes of the lords
[b] displease . . . : Heb. do not evil in the eyes of the lords
[a] grieved: Heb. bitter

he said, I *am* a young man of Egypt, servant to an Amalekite; and my master left me, because three days agone I fell sick. ¹⁴We made an invasion *upon* the south of the Cherethites, and upon *the coast* which *belongeth* to Judah, and upon the south of Caleb; and we burned Ziklag with fire. ¹⁵And David said to him, Canst thou bring me down to this company? And he said, Swear unto me by God, that thou wilt neither kill me, nor deliver me into the hands of my master, and I will bring thee down to this company. ¹⁶And when he had brought him down, behold, *they were* spread abroad upon all the earth, eating and drinking, and dancing, because of all the great spoil that they had taken out of the land of the Philistines, and out of the land of Judah. ¹⁷And David smote them from the twilight even unto the evening of the next day: and there escaped not a man of them, save four hundred young men, which rode upon camels, and fled. ¹⁸And David recovered all that the Amalekites had carried away: and David rescued his two wives. ¹⁹And there was nothing lacking to them, neither small nor great, neither sons nor daughters, neither spoil, nor any *thing* that they had taken to them: David recovered all. ²⁰And David took all the flocks and the herds, *which* they drave before those *other* cattle, and said, This *is* David's spoil.

²¹And David came to the two hundred men, which were so faint that they could not follow David, whom they had made also to abide at the brook Besor: and they went forth to meet David, and to meet the people that *were* with him: and when David came near to the

Devotional Moment
Leadership

30:1-20 David and his men could hardly believe their eyes when they arrived home. Grieved at losing their wives and children to a band of raiders, they all wept uncontrollably. No doubt their grief was mixed with guilt for not returning sooner to intercept the marauders and prevent the disaster. David's men were so upset that they directed their anger at David, their leader. David wisely took strength from the Lord and wasted no time mobilizing everyone to rescue their loved ones.

Preschoolers throw tantrums because you didn't cut their sandwich right; grade-schoolers take you to task for being unfair; teenagers point the finger for the ride you failed to give. Every parent at some time will be blamed for events beyond his control. Rather than take these attacks personally, take strength from the Lord and lead everyone toward a peaceful solution.

troop? shall I overtake them? And he answered him, Pursue: for thou shalt surely overtake *them,* and without fail recover *all.* ⁹So David went, he and the six hundred men that *were* with him, and came to the brook Besor, where those that were left behind stayed. ¹⁰But David pursued, he and four hundred men: for two hundred abode behind, which were so faint that they could not go over the brook Besor. ¹¹And they found an Egyptian in the field, and brought him to David, and gave him bread, and he did eat; and they made him drink water; ¹²And they gave him a piece of a cake of figs, and two clusters of raisins: and when he had eaten, his spirit came again to him: for he had eaten no bread, nor drunk *any* water, three days and three nights. ¹³And David said unto him, To whom *belongest* thou? and whence *art* thou? And

people, he saluted[b] them. [22]Then answered all the wicked men and *men of Belial*, of those[c] that went with David, and said, Because they went not with us, we will not give them *ought* of the spoil that we have recovered, save to every man his wife and his children, that they may lead *them* away, and depart. [23]Then said David, Ye shall not do so, my brethren, with that which the LORD hath given us, who hath preserved us, and delivered the company that came against us into our hand. [24]For who will hearken unto you in this matter? but as his part *is* that goeth down to the battle, so *shall* his part *be* that tarrieth by the stuff: they shall part alike. [25]And it was *so* from that day forward[d], that he made it a statute and an ordinance for Israel unto this day. [26]And when David came to Ziklag, he sent of the spoil unto the elders of Judah, *even* to his friends, saying, Behold a present[e] for you of the spoil of the enemies of the LORD; [27]To *them* which *were* in Bethel, and to *them* which *were* in south Ramoth, and to *them* which *were* in Jattir, [28]And to *them* which *were* in Aroer, and to *them* which *were* in Siphmoth, and to *them* which *were* in Eshtemoa, [29]And to *them* which *were* in Rachal, and to *them* which *were* in the cities of the Jerahmeelites, and to *them* which *were* in the cities of the Kenites, [30]And to *them* which *were* in Hormah, and to

them which *were* in Chorashan, and to *them* which *were* in Athach, [31]And to *them* which *were* in Hebron, and to all the places where David himself and his men were wont to haunt.

31

[1]Now the Philistines fought against Israel: and the men of Israel fled from before the Philistines, and fell down slain[a] in mount Gilboa. [2]And the Philistines followed hard upon Saul and upon his sons; and the Philistines slew Jonathan, and Abinadab, and Malchishua, Saul's sons. [3]And the battle went sore against Saul, and the archers[b] hit him; and he was sore wounded of the archers. [4]Then said Saul unto his armourbearer, Draw thy sword, and thrust me through therewith; lest these uncircumcised come and thrust me through, and abuse[c] me. But his armourbearer would not; for he was sore afraid. Therefore Saul took a sword, and fell upon it. [5]And when his armourbearer saw that Saul was dead, he fell likewise upon his sword, and died with him. [6]So Saul died, and his three sons, and his armourbearer, and all his men, that same day together. [7]And when the men of Israel that *were* on the other side of the valley, and *they* that *were* on the other side Jordan, saw that the men of Israel fled, and that Saul and his sons were dead, they forsook the cities, and fled; and the Philistines came and dwelt in them.

---

[b] saluted . . . : or, asked them how they did
[c] those: Heb. men
[d] forward: Heb. and forward
[e] present: Heb. blessing
[a] slain: or, wounded
[b] and the archers: Heb. and the shooters, men with bows
[c] abuse . . . : or, mock me

⁸And it came to pass on the morrow, when the Philistines came to strip the slain, that they found Saul and his three sons fallen in mount Gilboa. ⁹And they cut off his head, and stripped off his armour, and sent into the land of the Philistines round about, to publish *it in* the house of their idols, and among the people. ¹⁰And they put his armour in the house of Ashtaroth: and they fastened his body to the wall of Bethshan. ¹¹And when the inhabitants of Jabeshgilead heard of that which the Philistines had done to Saul; ¹²All the valiant men arose, and went all night, and took the body of Saul and the bodies of his sons from the wall of Bethshan, and came to Jabesh, and burnt them there. ¹³And they took their bones, and buried *them* under a tree at Jabesh, and fasted seven days.

SECOND SAMUEL

Purpose
To record the history of David's reign, including his effective leadership under God; the personal qualities he possessed that pleased God; and the fact that he was an imperfect leader of an imperfect kingdom, foreshadowing Christ who will be the ideal leader of a new and perfect kingdom (chap. 7)

Author
Unknown. Some have suggested that Nathan's son Zabud may have been the author (1 Kings 4:5). The book also includes the writings of Nathan and Gad (1 Chron. 29:29).

Date Written
930 B.C.; written soon after David's reign, 1050–970 B.C.

Setting
The land of Israel under David's rule

Key Verse
"David perceived that the Lord had established him king over Israel, and that he had exalted his kingdom for his people Israel's sake" (5:12).

Special Features
This book was named after the prophet who anointed David and guided him in godly living.

"Get a grip!"

The phrase is often directed to a person of promise and prestige who is courting disaster: a musician who's becoming an alcoholic; a doctor whose job stress is affecting her judgment; a father who comes down like a tyrant on his children.

The story of David in 2 Samuel is a series of highs and lows, super achievements, and stupid decisions. David, the great winner, reckless to defend God's name against the Philistines, singer and dancer, horseman, general, and poet. David the adulterer, the mastermind of murder, blind to his son's rebelliousness. Rape and killing invade his own family. His favorite son goes to war against him.

What a mix of vice and virtue! What a life to keep together! No wonder God sends special people with a message for David: "Get a grip!"

When your children run roughshod over values you've tried to instill, when arguments start to crack your marriage, when grief and loss make your spirit sick—remember God's love for David; remember David's heart for God.

When your spouse flashes that loving smile, when clients double your commissions—remember God as David did, in joy and song.

The sea breeze of life is warm at noon and stormy by evening. On your sail through 2 Samuel, remember your anchor and relish the winds and the waves.

1

¹Now it came to pass after the death of Saul, when David was returned from the slaughter of the Amalekites, and David had abode two days in Ziklag; ²It came even to pass on the third day, that, behold, a man came out of the camp from Saul with his clothes rent, and earth upon his head: and *so* it was, when he came to David, that he fell to the earth, and did obeisance. ³And David said unto him, From whence comest thou? And he said unto him, Out of the camp of Israel am I escaped. ⁴And David said unto him, How*ᵃ* went the matter? I pray thee, tell me. And he answered, That the people are fled from the battle, and many of the people also are fallen and dead; and Saul and Jonathan his son are dead also. ⁵And David said unto the young man that told him, How knowest thou that Saul and Jonathan his son be dead? ⁶And the young man that told him said, As I happened by chance upon mount Gilboa, behold, Saul leaned upon his spear; and, lo, the chariots and horsemen followed hard after him. ⁷And when he looked behind him, he saw me, and called unto me. And I answered, Here *am* I.ᵇ ⁸And he said unto me, Who *art* thou? And I answered him, I *am* an Amalekite. ⁹He said unto me again, Stand, I pray thee, upon me, and slay me: for anguishᶜ is come upon me, because my life *is* yet whole in me. ¹⁰So I stood upon him, and slew him, because I was sure that he could not live

after that he was fallen: and I took the crown that *was* upon his head, and the bracelet that *was* on his arm, and have brought them hither unto my lord.

¹¹Then David took hold on his clothes, and rent them; and likewise all the men that *were* with him: ¹²And they mourned, and wept, and fasted until even, for Saul, and for Jonathan his son, and for the people of the LORD, and for the house of Israel; because they were fallen by the sword. ¹³And David said unto the young man that told him, Whence *art* thou? And he answered, I *am* the son of a stranger, an Amalekite. ¹⁴And David said unto him, How wast thou not afraid to stretch forth thine hand to destroy the LORD'S anointed? ¹⁵And David called one of the young men, and said, Go near, *and* fall upon him. And he smote him that he died. ¹⁶And David said unto him, Thy blood *be* upon thy head; for thy mouth hath testified against thee, saying, I have slain the LORD'S anointed.

¹⁷And David lamented with this lamentation over Saul and over Jonathan his son: ¹⁸(Also he bade them teach the children of Judah *the use of* the bow: behold, *it is* written in the book of Jasherᵈ.) ¹⁹The beauty of Israel is slain upon thy high places: how are the mighty fallen! ²⁰Tell *it* not in Gath, publish *it* not in the streets of Askelon; lest the daughters of the Philistines rejoice, lest the daughters of the uncircumcised triumph. ²¹Ye mountains of Gilboa, *let there be* no dew, neither *let*

ᵃ How . . . : Heb. What was, etc
ᵇ Here . . . : Heb. Behold me
ᶜ anguish . . . : or, my coat of mail (or, my embroidered coat) hindereth me, that my, etc
ᵈ of Jasher: or, of the upright

there be rain, upon you, nor fields of offerings: for there the shield of the mighty is vilely cast away, the shield of Saul, *as though he had* not *been* anointed with oil. ²²From the blood of the slain, from the fat of the mighty, the bow of Jonathan turned not back, and the sword of Saul returned not empty. ²³Saul and Jonathan *were* lovely and pleasant^c in their lives, and in their death they were not divided: they were swifter than eagles, they were stronger than lions. ²⁴Ye daughters of Israel, weep over Saul, who clothed you in scarlet, with *other* delights, who put on ornaments of gold upon your apparel. ²⁵How are the mighty fallen in the midst of the battle! O Jonathan, *thou wast* slain in thine high places. ²⁶I am distressed for thee, my brother Jonathan: very pleasant hast thou been unto me: thy love to me was wonderful, passing the love of women. ²⁷How are the mighty fallen, and the weapons of war perished!

2

¹And it came to pass after this, that David enquired of the LORD, saying, Shall I go up into any of the cities of Judah? And the LORD said unto him, Go up. And David said, Whither shall I go up? And he said, Unto Hebron. ²So David went up thither, and his two wives also, Ahinoam the Jezreelitess, and Abigail Nabal's wife the Carmelite. ³And his men that *were* with him did David bring up, every man with his household: and they dwelt in the cities of Hebron. ⁴And the men of Judah came, and there they anointed David king over the house of Judah. And they told David, saying, *That* the men of Jabeshgilead *were they* that buried Saul. ⁵And David sent messengers unto the men of Jabeshgilead, and said unto them, Blessed *be* ye of the LORD, that ye have shewed this kindness unto your lord, *even* unto Saul, and have buried him. ⁶And now the LORD shew kindness and truth unto you: and I also will requite you this kindness, because ye have done this thing. ⁷Therefore now let your hands be strengthened, and be ye valiant: for your master Saul is dead, and also the house of Judah have anointed me king over them.

⁸But Abner the son of Ner, captain of Saul's host^a, took Ishbosheth the son of Saul, and brought him over to Mahanaim; ⁹And made him king over Gilead, and over the Ashurites, and over Jezreel, and over Ephraim, and over Benjamin, and over all Israel. ¹⁰Ishbosheth Saul's son *was* forty years old when he began to reign over Israel, and reigned two years. But the house of Judah followed David. ¹¹And the time^b that David was king in Hebron over the house of Judah was seven years and six months. ¹²And Abner the son of Ner, and the servants of Ishbosheth the son of Saul, went out from Mahanaim to Gibeon. ¹³And Joab the son of Zeruiah, and the servants of David, went out, and met together^c by the pool of

---

^c pleasant: or, sweet
^a Saul's host: Heb. the host which was Saul's
^b time: Heb. number of days
^c together: Heb. them together

Gibeon: and they sat down, the one on the one side of the pool, and the other on the other side of the pool. ¹⁴And Abner said to Joab, Let the young men now arise, and play before us. And Joab said, Let them arise. ¹⁵Then there arose and went over by number twelve of Benjamin, which *pertained* to Ishbosheth the son of Saul, and twelve of the servants of David. ¹⁶And they caught every one his fellow by the head, and *thrust* his sword in his fellow's side; so they fell down together: wherefore that place was called Helkathhazzurim^d, which *is* in Gibeon. ¹⁷And there was a very sore battle that day; and Abner was beaten, and the men of Israel, before the servants of David.

¹⁸And there were three sons of Zeruiah there, Joab, and Abishai, and Asahel: and Asahel *was as* light of foot^e as a wild roe. ¹⁹And Asahel pursued after Abner; and in going he turned not to the right hand nor to the left from following Abner. ²⁰Then Abner looked behind him, and said, *Art* thou Asahel? And he answered, I *am.* ²¹And Abner said to him, Turn thee aside to thy right hand or to thy left, and lay thee hold on one of the young men, and take thee his armour^f. But Asahel would not turn aside from following of him. ²²And Abner said again to Asahel, Turn thee aside from following me: wherefore should I smite thee to the ground? how then should I hold up my face to Joab thy brother? ²³Howbeit he refused to turn aside: wherefore Abner with the hinder end of the spear smote him under the fifth *rib*, that the spear came out behind him; and he fell down there, and died in the same place: and it came to pass, *that* as many as came to the place where Asahel fell down and died stood still. ²⁴Joab also and Abishai pursued after Abner: and the sun went down when they were come to the hill of Ammah, that *lieth* before Giah by the way of the wilderness of Gibeon.

²⁵And the children of Benjamin gathered themselves together after Abner, and became one troop, and stood on the top of an hill. ²⁶Then Abner called to Joab, and said, Shall the sword devour for ever? knowest thou not that it will be bitterness in the latter end? how long shall it be then, ere thou bid the people return from following their brethren? ²⁷And Joab said, *As* God liveth, unless thou hadst spoken, surely then in the morning the people had gone up every one from following his brother. ²⁸So Joab blew a trumpet, and all the people stood still, and pursued after Israel no more, neither fought they any more. ²⁹And Abner and his men walked all that night through the plain, and passed over Jordan, and went through all Bithron, and they came to Mahanaim. ³⁰And Joab returned from following Abner: and when he had gathered all the people together, there lacked of David's servants nineteen men and Asahel. ³¹But the servants of David had smitten of Benjamin, and of Abner's men, *so that* three hundred and threescore men died. ³²And they took up Asahel, and buried him in the sepul-

---

^d Helkathhazzurim: that is, The field of strong men
^e of foot: Heb. of his feet
^f armour: or, spoil

chre of his father, which *was in* Bethlehem. And Joab and his men went all night, and they came to Hebron at break of day.

3

¹Now there was long war between the house of Saul and the house of David: but David waxed stronger and stronger, and the house of Saul waxed weaker and weaker. ²And unto David were sons born in Hebron: and his firstborn was Amnon, of Ahinoam the Jezreelitess; ³And his second, Chileabª, of Abigail the wife of Nabal the Carmelite; and the third, Absalom the son of Maacah the daughter of Talmai king of Geshur; ⁴And the fourth, Adonijah the son of Haggith; and the fifth, Shephatiah the son of Abital; ⁵And the sixth, Ithream, by Eglah David's wife. These were born to David in Hebron. ⁶And it came to pass, while there was war between the house of Saul and the house of David, that Abner made himself strong for the house of Saul.

⁷And Saul had a concubine, whose name *was* Rizpah, the daughter of Aiah: and *Ishbosheth* said to Abner, Wherefore hast thou gone in unto my father's concubine? ⁸Then was Abner very wroth for the words of Ishbosheth, and said, *Am* I a dog's head, which against Judah do shew kindness this day unto the house of Saul thy father, to his brethren, and to his friends, and have not delivered thee into the hand of David, that thou chargest me to day with a fault concerning this woman? ⁹So do God to Abner, and more also,

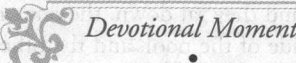

Devotional Moment
•
Relationships

3:2-5; 5:13-16 David took numerous wives despite the divine command against it in Deuteronomy 17:17. The sad results of his marital mix-ups—murder, rebellion, and greed—are recorded in 2 Samuel 13-19 and 1 Kings 1-2. Though laws today prohibit people from having more than one spouse, couples still face friction and hurt feelings when there are divided loyalties. Is your marriage suffering because of an excessive devotion to a hobby, a job, a friendship, a club involvement, church activities, or some other commitment? Ask God for the wisdom to evaluate your affections objectively and then for the courage to change what needs changing. You may need to ask a friend to hold you accountable for changes necessary in the best interests of your family.

except, as the LORD hath sworn to David, even so I do to him; ¹⁰To translate the kingdom from the house of Saul, and to set up the throne of David over Israel and over Judah, from Dan even to Beersheba. ¹¹And he could not answer Abner a word again, because he feared him. ¹²And Abner sent messengers to David on his behalf, saying, Whose *is* the land? saying *also*, Make thy league with me, and, behold, my hand *shall be* with thee, to bring about all Israel unto thee. ¹³And he said, Well; I will make a league with thee: but one thing I require of thee, that is b, Thou shalt not see my face, except thou first bring Michal Saul's daughter, when thou comest to see my face. ¹⁴And David sent messengers to Ishbosheth Saul's son, saying, Deliver *me* my wife

---

ª Chileab: or, Daniel
b that is: Heb. saying

Michal, which I espoused to me for an hundred foreskins of the Philistines. ¹⁵And Ishbosheth sent, and took her from *her* husband, *even* from Phaltiel^c the son of Laish. ¹⁶And her husband went with her along weeping behind her to Bahurim. Then said Abner unto him, Go, return. And he returned. ¹⁷And Abner had communication with the elders of Israel, saying, Ye sought for David in times^d past *to be* king over you: ¹⁸Now then do *it*: for the LORD hath spoken of David, saying, By the hand of my servant David I will save my people Israel out of the hand of the Philistines, and out of the hand of all their enemies. ¹⁹And Abner also spake in the ears of Benjamin: and Abner went also to speak in the ears of David in Hebron all that seemed good to Israel, and that seemed good to the whole house of Benjamin. ²⁰So Abner came to David to Hebron, and twenty men with him. And David made Abner and the men that *were* with him a feast. ²¹And Abner said unto David, I will arise and go, and will gather all Israel unto my lord the king, that they may make a league with thee, and that thou mayest reign over all that thine heart desireth. And David sent Abner away; and he went in peace.

²²And, behold, the servants of David and Joab came from *pursuing* a troop, and brought in a great spoil with them: but Abner *was* not with David in Hebron; for he had sent him away, and he was gone in peace. ²³When Joab and all the host that *was* with him were

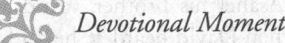

Devotional Moment

Revenge

3:26-30 Several events led to this violent incident: (1) King Saul's death splintered the nation of Israel into two warring factions—those loyal to Ishbosheth, a son of Saul, and those loyal to David; (2) during that fighting, Abner, Ishbosheth's top military leader, killed Asahel, one of David's high officers, in self-defense; (3) Abner later offered terms of peace to David; (4) Joab, Asahel's brother, jeopardized the prospect for peace by killing Abner to avenge his brother's death. Since this murder had the potential to spark renewed fighting, David responded in a harsh manner. The lesson for us is clear: We must resist the urge to seek revenge. If someone has wronged you or one of your family members, let God deal with that individual in his own time.

come, they told Joab, saying, Abner the son of Ner came to the king, and he hath sent him away, and he is gone in peace. ²⁴Then Joab came to the king, and said, What hast thou done? behold, Abner came unto thee; why *is* it *that* thou hast sent him away, and he is quite gone? ²⁵Thou knowest Abner the son of Ner, that he came to deceive thee, and to know thy going out and thy coming in, and to know all that thou doest. ²⁶And when Joab was come out from David, he sent messengers after Abner, which brought him again from the well of Sirah: but David knew *it* not. ²⁷And when Abner was returned to Hebron, Joab took him aside in the gate to speak with him quietly^e, and smote him there under the fifth *rib*, that he died, for the

---

^c Phaltiel: also called, Phalti
^d in times . . . : Heb. both yesterday and the third day
^e quietly: or, peaceably

blood of Asahel his brother. ²⁸And afterward when David heard *it*, he said, I and my kingdom *are* guiltless before the LORD for ever from the blood^f of Abner the son of Ner: ²⁹Let it rest on the head of Joab, and on all his father's house; and let there not fail^g from the house of Joab one that hath an issue, or that is a leper, or that leaneth on a staff, or that falleth on the sword, or that lacketh bread. ³⁰So Joab and Abishai his brother slew Abner, because he had slain their brother Asahel at Gibeon in the battle. ³¹And David said to Joab, and to all the people that *were* with him, Rend your clothes, and gird you with sackcloth, and mourn before Abner. And king David *himself* followed the bier^h. ³²And they buried Abner in Hebron: and the king lifted up his voice, and wept at the grave of Abner; and all the people wept. ³³And the king lamented over Abner, and said, Died Abner as a fool dieth? ³⁴Thy hands *were* not bound, nor thy feet put into fetters: as a man falleth before wickedⁱ men, *so* fellest thou. And all the people wept again over him. ³⁵And when all the people came to cause David to eat meat while it was yet day, David sware, saying, So do God to me, and more also, if I taste bread, or ought else, till the sun be down. ³⁶And all the people took notice *of it*, and it pleased them^j: as whatsoever the king did pleased all the people. ³⁷For all the people and all Israel understood that day that it was not of the king to slay Abner the son of Ner. ³⁸And the king said unto his servants, Know ye not that there is a prince and a great man fallen this day in Israel? ³⁹And I *am* this day weak^k, though anointed king; and these men the sons of Zeruiah *be* too hard for me: the LORD shall reward the doer of evil according to his wickedness.

4

¹And when Saul's son heard that Abner was dead in Hebron, his hands were feeble, and all the Israelites were troubled. ²And Saul's son had two men *that were* captains of bands: the name of the one *was* Baanah, and the name of the other^a Rechab, the sons of Rimmon a Beerothite, of the children of Benjamin: (for Beeroth also was reckoned to Benjamin: ³And the Beerothites fled to Gittaim, and were sojourners there until this day.) ⁴And Jonathan, Saul's son, had a son *that was* lame of *his* feet. He was five years old when the tidings came of Saul and Jonathan out of Jezreel, and his nurse took him up, and fled: and it came to pass, as she made haste to flee, that he fell, and became lame. And his name *was* Mephibosheth^b. ⁵And the sons of Rimmon the

---

^f blood: Heb. bloods
^g fail: Heb. be cut off
^h bier: Heb. bed
ⁱ wicked . . . : Heb. children of iniquity
^j pleased them: Heb. was good in their eyes
^k weak: Heb. tender
^a other: Heb. second
^b Mephibosheth: or, Meribbaal

Devotional Moment

Children

4:4 In an accidental fall, Mephibosheth, a five-year-old grandson of Saul, suffered a crippling injury (and this right on the heels of losing his father, Jonathan—1 Sam. 31:2). Somehow Mephibosheth endured, and later in life he became a beloved member of King David's extended family. This is a good reminder that no matter what limitations, disabilities, weaknesses, or faults our children have, each one is a gift from the Lord. God carefully designs each of us to bring him glory. Instead of focusing on our children's disabilities or short-comings, we should concentrate on their strengths and positive traits and be liberal with encouragement.

Beerothite, Rechab and Baanah, went, and came about the heat of the day to the house of Ishbosheth, who lay on a bed at noon. ⁶And they came thither into the midst of the house, *as though* they would have fetched wheat; and they smote him under the fifth *rib*: and Rechab and Baanah his brother escaped. ⁷For when they came into the house, he lay on his bed in his bed-chamber, and they smote him, and slew him, and beheaded him, and took his head, and gat them away through the plain all night. ⁸And they brought the head of Ishbosheth unto David to Hebron, and said to the king, Behold the head of Ishbosheth the son of Saul thine enemy, which sought thy life; and the LORD hath avenged my lord the king this day of Saul, and of his seed.

⁹And David answered Rechab and Baanah his brother, the sons of Rimmon the Beerothite, and said unto them, *As* the LORD liveth, who hath redeemed my soul out of all adversity,

¹⁰When one told me, saying, Behold, Saul is dead, thinking to have brought good tidings, I took hold of him, and slew him in Ziklag, who *thought* that I would have given him a reward for his tidings: ¹¹How much more, when wicked men have slain a righteous person in his own house upon his bed? shall I not therefore now require his blood of your hand, and take you away from the earth? ¹²And David commanded his young men, and they slew them, and cut off their hands and their feet, and hanged *them* up over the pool in Hebron. But they took the head of Ishbosheth, and buried *it* in the sepulchre of Abner in Hebron.

5

¹Then came all the tribes of Israel to David unto Hebron, and spake, saying, Behold, we *are* thy bone and thy flesh. ²Also in time past, when Saul was king over us, thou wast he that leddest out and broughtest in Israel: and the LORD said to thee, Thou shalt feed my people Israel, and thou shalt be a captain over Israel. ³So all the elders of Israel came to the king to Hebron; and king David made a league with them in Hebron before the LORD: and they anointed David king over Israel. ⁴David *was* thirty years old when he began to reign, *and* he reigned forty years. ⁵In Hebron he reigned over Judah seven years and six months: and in Jerusalem he reigned thirty and three years over all Israel and Judah.

⁶And the king and his men went to Jerusalem unto the Jebusites, the inhabitants of the land: which spake unto David, saying, Except thou take away the blind and the lame, thou shalt not

come in hither: thinking[a], David cannot come in hither. [7]Nevertheless David took the strong hold of Zion: the same *is* the city of David. [8]And David said on that day, Whosoever getteth up to the gutter, and smiteth the Jebusites, and the lame and the blind, *that are* hated of David's soul, *he shall be chief and captain.* Wherefore they said, The blind and the lame shall not come into the house. [9]So David dwelt in the fort, and called it the city of David. And David built round about from Millo and inward. [10]And David went[b] on, and grew great, and the LORD God of hosts *was* with him.

[11]And Hiram king of Tyre sent messengers to David, and cedar trees, and carpenters, and masons[c]: and they built David an house. [12]And David perceived that the LORD had established him king over Israel, and that he had exalted his kingdom for his people Israel's sake. [13]And David took *him* more concubines and wives out of Jerusalem, after he was come from Hebron: and there were yet sons and daughters born to David. [14]And these *be* the names of those that were born unto him in Jerusalem; Shammua, and Shobab, and Nathan, and Solomon, [15]Ibhar also, and Elishua, and Nepheg, and Japhia, [16]And Elishama, and Eliada, and Eliphalet.

[17]But when the Philistines heard that they had anointed David king over Israel, all the Philistines came up to seek David; and David heard *of it*, and went down to the hold. [18]The Philistines also came and spread themselves in the valley of Rephaim. [19]And David enquired of the LORD, saying, Shall I go up to the Philistines? wilt thou deliver them into mine hand? And the LORD said unto David, Go up: for I will doubtless deliver the Philistines into thine hand. [20]And David came to Baalperazim[d], and David smote them there, and said, The LORD hath broken forth upon mine enemies before me, as the breach of waters. Therefore he called the name of that place Baalperazim. [21]And there they left their images, and David and his men burned[e] them. [22]And the Philistines came up yet again, and spread themselves in the valley of Rephaim. [23]And when David enquired of the LORD, he said, Thou shalt not go up; *but* fetch a compass behind them, and come upon them over against the mulberry trees. [24]And let it be, when thou hearest the sound of a going in the tops of the mulberry trees, that then thou shalt bestir thyself: for then shall the LORD go out before thee, to smite the host of the Philistines. [25]And David did so, as the LORD had commanded him; and smote the Philistines from Geba[f] until thou come to Gazer.

6

[1]Again, David gathered together all *the* chosen *men* of Israel, thirty thousand.

---

[a] thinking . . . : or, saying David shall not, etc
[b] went . . . : Heb. went, going and growing
[c] masons: Heb. hewers of the stone of the wall
[d] Baalperazim: that is, the plain of breaches
[e] burned . . . : or, took them away
[f] Geba: also called, Gibeon

²And David arose, and went with all the people that *were* with him from Baale of Judah, to bring up from thence the ark of God, whose name is called by the name of the LORD of hosts that dwelleth *between* the cherubims. ³And they set[a] the ark of God upon a new cart, and brought it out of the house of Abinadab that *was* in Gibeah: and Uzzah and Ahio, the sons of Abinadab, drave the new cart. ⁴And they brought it out of the house of Abinadab which *was* at Gibeah, accompanying[b] the ark of God: and Ahio went before the ark. ⁵And David and all the house of Israel played before the LORD on all manner of *instruments made of* fir wood, even on harps, and on psalteries, and on timbrels, and on cornets, and on cymbals.

⁶And when they came to Nachon's threshingfloor, Uzzah put forth *his hand* to the ark of God, and took hold of it; for the oxen shook *it*. ⁷And the anger of the LORD was kindled against Uzzah; and God smote him there for *his* error[c]; and there he died by the ark of God. ⁸And David was displeased, because the LORD had made[d] a breach upon Uzzah: and he called the name of the place Perezuzzah to this day. ⁹And David was afraid of the LORD that day, and said, How shall the ark of the LORD come to me? ¹⁰So David would not remove the ark of the LORD unto him into the city of David: but David carried it aside into the house of Obededom the Gittite. ¹¹And the ark of the LORD continued in the house of Obededom the Gittite three months: and the LORD blessed Obededom, and all his household.

¹²And it was told king David, saying, The LORD hath blessed the house of Obededom, and all that *pertaineth* unto him, because of the ark of God. So David went and brought up the ark of God from the house of Obededom into the city of David with gladness. ¹³And it was *so*, that when they that bare the ark of the LORD had gone six paces, he sacrificed oxen and fatlings. ¹⁴And David danced before the LORD with all *his* might; and David *was* girded with a linen ephod. ¹⁵So David and all the house of Israel brought up the ark of the LORD with shouting, and with the sound of the trumpet. ¹⁶And as the ark of the LORD came into the city of David, Michal Saul's daughter looked through a window, and saw king David leaping and dancing before the LORD; and she despised him in her heart. ¹⁷And they brought in the ark of the LORD, and set it in his place, in the midst of the tabernacle that David had pitched[e] for it: and David offered burnt offerings and peace offerings before the LORD. ¹⁸And as soon as David had made an end of offering burnt offerings and peace offerings, he blessed the people in the name of the LORD of hosts. ¹⁹And he dealt among all the people, *even* among the whole multitude of Israel, as well to the

---

[a] set: Heb. made to ride
[b] accompanying: Heb. with
[c] error: or, rashness
[d] made: Heb. broken
[e] pitched: Heb. stretched

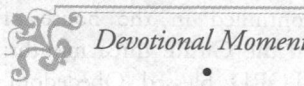

Devotional Moment

•

Values

6:20-22 Why did Michal feel humiliated by David's actions? Apparently she placed great value on how she appeared to others and what others thought of her and her husband. Michal totally missed the significant reason for David's celebration—the fact that God was now present again among his people! David, in contrast, was more concerned with what was right and what God thought than with how "respectable" he appeared. His passionate love for God and his commitment to worship far outweighed any concerns about looking foolish. Which kind of values are you teaching and modeling in your family—Michal's or David's? Ask God for the courage to do what is right, no matter how foolish it may appear to others.

women as men, to every one a cake of bread, and a good piece *of flesh*, and a flagon *of wine*. So all the people departed every one to his house.

²⁰Then David returned to bless his household. And Michal the daughter of Saul came out to meet David, and said, How glorious was the king of Israel to day, who uncovered himself to day in the eyes of the handmaids of his servants, as one of the vain fellows shamelessly[f] uncovereth himself! ²¹And David said unto Michal, *It was* before the LORD, which chose me before thy father, and before all his house, to appoint me ruler over the people of the LORD, over Israel: therefore will I play before the LORD. ²²And I will yet be more vile than thus, and will be base in

mine own sight: and of the[g] maidservants which thou hast spoken of, of them shall I be had in honour. ²³Therefore Michal the daughter of Saul had no child unto the day of her death.

7

¹And it came to pass, when the king sat in his house, and the LORD had given him rest round about from all his enemies; ²That the king said unto Nathan the prophet, See now, I dwell in an house of cedar, but the ark of God dwelleth within curtains. ³And Nathan said to the king, Go, do all that *is* in thine heart; for the LORD *is* with thee.

⁴And it came to pass that night, that the word of the LORD came unto Nathan, saying, ⁵Go and tell my servant[a] David, Thus saith the LORD, Shalt thou build me an house for me to dwell in? ⁶Whereas I have not dwelt in *any* house since the time that I brought up the children of Israel out of Egypt, even to this day, but have walked in a tent and in a tabernacle. ⁷In all *the places* wherein I have walked with all the children of Israel spake I a word with any of the tribes of Israel, whom I commanded to feed my people Israel, saying, Why build ye not me an house of cedar? ⁸Now therefore so shalt thou say unto my servant David, Thus saith the LORD of hosts, I took thee from the sheepcote, from following[b] the sheep, to be ruler over my people, over Israel: ⁹And I was with thee whithersoever thou wentest, and have cut off all

---

[f] shamelessly: or, openly
[g] of the . . . : or, of the handmaids of my servants
[a] my servant . . . : Heb. to my servant, to David
[b] from following: Heb. from after

Nathan

You need a friend. Not just someone who sees you at church every week, or who shares your interest in sports. You need someone who is unimpressed with your position at work, who checks up on you and can tell if you're glossing over the bad news, and who would intervene if you started to neglect your responsibilities.

Nathan was a prophet, but he was also David's loyal *friend*. When David wanted to build a temple, he told Nathan, and Nathan gave him some advice (2 Sam. 7:2-17). When David received the news that his baby would suffer because of his adultery with Bathsheba, Nathan comforted him with the news that God had forgiven him. And when Adonijah tried to usurp the throne from David, Nathan was one of the few who alerted the queen mother and remained loyal to King David (1 Kings 1:8-45).

But Nathan is also the one who had the thankless job of confronting King David with his sins of adultery and murder. Nathan shared God's point of view at a time when David couldn't see it for himself. And he did it with tact. Nathan's friendship involved a concern for *David*, not only a concern for David's reputation or power base.

"Faithful are the wounds of a friend; but the kisses of an enemy are deceitful" the Bible says (Prov. 27:6).

Don't underestimate the importance of a friend like Nathan. Pray for such a friend—for you, your spouse, and your kids.

LESSONS FROM NATHAN AS A TRUE FRIEND

True friends are a gift from God. It's clear that God sent Nathan to serve a special purpose in David's life. He was a valuable part of God's plan for David. Pray that God will send such people into your life.

We need friends who will tell us the truth. You probably know many people. How many of them would alert you to a problem in your life? Sent by God, Nathan did not let David's sins go but exposed them—a valuable service that only a true friend can perform.

People who offer you hard advice and criticism are not always your enemies. Beware of friends who never have a bad thing to say about you.

Families need outside, objective truth and guidance lest they become victims of their own rationalizations. Sometimes family members help each other deny the truth. A true friend will not be duped.

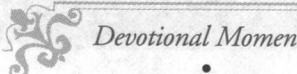

Devotional Moment

•

Loving Discipline

7:13-16 Often overlooked in God's covenant promise to David is the statement in verse 14 that God and David's descendants would enjoy an intimate Father-son relationship. What comfort we find in this! What does it mean that God is our Father? Part of the answer is right here: loving discipline (vv. 14-15). Because God loves us, he corrects us when we do what is wrong. Punishing children in anger or without a loving purpose is brutality. But indulging their every wish or never disciplining them only invites them to equate wrong with right. Strive for a balance in the way you rear your children.

thine enemies out of thy sight, and have made thee a great name, like unto the name of the great *men* that *are* in the earth. ¹⁰Moreover I will appoint a place for my people Israel, and will plant them, that they may dwell in a place of their own, and move no more; neither shall the children of wickedness afflict them any more, as beforetime, ¹¹And as since the time that I commanded judges *to be* over my people Israel, and have caused thee to rest from all thine enemies. Also the LORD telleth thee that he will make thee an house. ¹²And when thy days be fulfilled, and thou shalt sleep with thy fathers, I will set up thy seed after thee, which shall proceed out of thy bowels, and I will establish his kingdom. ¹³He shall build an house for my name, and I will stablish the throne of his kingdom for ever. ¹⁴I will be his father, and he shall be my son. If he commit iniquity, I will chasten him with the rod of men, and with the stripes of the children of men: ¹⁵But my

mercy shall not depart away from him, as I took *it* from Saul, whom I put away before thee. ¹⁶And thine house and thy kingdom shall be established for ever before thee: thy throne shall be established for ever. ¹⁷According to all these words, and according to all this vision, so did Nathan speak unto David.

¹⁸Then went king David in, and sat before the LORD, and he said, Who *am* I, O Lord GOD? and what *is* my house, that thou hast brought me hitherto? ¹⁹And this was yet a small thing in thy sight, O Lord GOD; but thou hast spoken also of thy servant's house for a great while to come. And *is* this the manner^c of man, O Lord GOD? ²⁰And what can David say more unto thee? for thou, Lord GOD, knowest thy servant. ²¹For thy word's sake, and according to thine own heart, hast thou done all these great things, to make thy servant know *them.* ²²Wherefore thou art great, O LORD God: for *there is* none like thee, neither *is there any* God beside

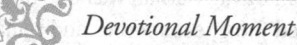

Devotional Moment

•

Prayer

7:18-29 Evident in David's prayer was a sense of awe and wonder. He was truly amazed that the sovereign Lord of the universe would show him such favor. Nevertheless, he boldly reminded God of his covenant promise and requested further blessings. We ought to exhibit the same thankful, adoring attitude in our prayers. And we should not be reluctant to ask our heavenly Father to bless our homes. What pressing need does your family have right now? Look to the one who controls all things, the one whose Word is trustworthy, the one who loves to give good things to those who serve him!

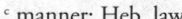

---

^c manner: Heb. law

thee, according to all that we have heard with our ears. ²³And what one nation in the earth *is* like thy people, *even* like Israel, whom God went to redeem for a people to himself, and to make him a name, and to do for you great things and terrible, for thy land, before thy people, which thou redeemedst to thee from Egypt, *from* the nations and their gods? ²⁴For thou hast confirmed to thyself thy people Israel *to be* a people unto thee for ever: and thou, LORD, art become their God. ²⁵And now, O LORD God, the word that thou hast spoken concerning thy servant, and concerning his house, establish *it* for ever, and do as thou hast said. ²⁶And let thy name be magnified for ever, saying, The LORD of hosts *is* the God over Israel: and let the house of thy servant David be established before thee. ²⁷For thou, O LORD of hosts, God of Israel, hast revealed[d] to thy servant, saying, I will build thee an house: therefore hath thy servant found in his heart to pray this prayer unto thee. ²⁸And now, O Lord GOD, thou *art* that God, and thy words be true, and thou hast promised this goodness unto thy servant: ²⁹Therefore now let it please thee to bless the house of thy servant, that it may continue for ever before thee: for thou, O Lord GOD, hast spoken *it*: and with thy blessing let the house of thy servant be blessed for ever.

8

¹And after this it came to pass, that David smote the Philistines, and sub-dued them: and David took Methegammah[a] out of the hand of the Philistines. ²And he smote Moab, and measured them with a line, casting them down to the ground; even with two lines measured he to put to death, and with one full line to keep alive. And *so* the Moabites became David's servants, *and* brought gifts. ³David smote also Hadadezer[b], the son of Rehob, king of Zobah, as he went to recover his border at the river Euphrates. ⁴And David took from him a thousand *chariots*, and seven hundred horsemen, and twenty thousand footmen: and David houghed all the chariot *horses*, but reserved of them *for* an hundred chariots. ⁵And when the Syrians of Damascus came to succour Hadadezer king of Zobah, David slew of the Syrians two and twenty thousand men. ⁶Then David put garrisons in Syria of Damascus: and the Syrians became ser-

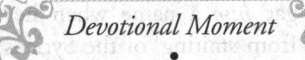

Devotional Moment

•

Fairness

8:15 David was a successful king because he ruled with justice and a keen sense of fairness. He resisted the pressure to show favoritism, opting instead to do what was fair to everyone. Are you marked by this same spirit of impartiality? Can others count on you to look at situations objectively and to make decisions that take into account the interests of all? Think back over the conversations, activities, and encounters of the previous week. In what ways might your words, actions, or responses have been more fair?

---

[d] revealed: Heb. opened the ear
[a] Methegammah: or, the bridle of Ammah
[b] Hadadezer: or, Hadarezer

vants to David, *and* brought gifts. And the LORD preserved David whithersoever he went. ⁷And David took the shields of gold that were on the servants of Hadadezer, and brought them to Jerusalem. ⁸And from Betah, and from Berothai, cities of Hadadezer, king David took exceeding much brass.

⁹When Toi king of Hamath heard that David had smitten all the host of Hadadezer, ¹⁰Then Toi sent Joramᶜ his son unto king David, to salute him, and to bless him, because he had fought against Hadadezer, and smitten him: for Hadadezer had wars with Toi. And *Joram* brought with him vessels of silver, and vessels of gold, and vessels of brass: ¹¹Which also king David did dedicate unto the LORD, with the silver and gold that he had dedicated of all nations which he subdued; ¹²Of Syria, and of Moab, and of the children of Ammon, and of the Philistines, and of Amalek, and of the spoil of Hadadezer, son of Rehob, king of Zobah. ¹³And David gat *him* a name when he returned from smitingᵈ of the Syrians in the valley of salt, *being* eighteen thousand *men.* ¹⁴And he put garrisons in Edom; throughout all Edom put he garrisons, and all they of Edom became David's servants. And the LORD preserved David whithersoever he went.

¹⁵And David reigned over all Israel; and David executed judgment and justice unto all his people. ¹⁶And Joab the son of Zeruiah *was* over the host; and

Jehoshaphat the son of Ahilud *was* recorderᵉ; ¹⁷And Zadok the son of Ahitub, and Ahimelech the son of Abiathar, *were* the priests; and Seraiah *was* the scribeᶠ; ¹⁸And Benaiah the son of Jehoiada *was over* both the Cherethites and the Pelethites; and David's sons were chief rulersᵍ.

9

¹And David said, Is there yet any that is left of the house of Saul, that I may shew him kindness for Jonathan's sake? ²And *there was* of the house of Saul a servant whose name *was* Ziba. And when they had called him unto David, the king said unto him, *Art* thou Ziba? And he said, Thy servant *is he.* ³And the

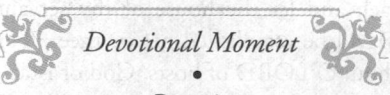

Devotional Moment
•
Promises

9:1 David could have followed the customs of his day and sought to destroy the remaining members of his rival's family (that is, Saul's household). But years before, he had promised Jonathan, Saul's son and David's best friend, that he would treat his descendants with love and kindness (1 Sam. 20:14-17). Here David went to great lengths to find any surviving relatives of Saul so that he could keep his word. What an example to us! We all make promises, especially to family members. How seriously do you take yours? If you are unsure, ask your family to grade you in the area of promise keeping. Such an exercise may be painful, but it also may help you begin to build better, more trusting relationships at home!

ᶜ Joram: also called, Hadoram
ᵈ smiting: Heb. his smiting
ᵉ recorder: or, remembrancer, or, writer of chronicles
ᶠ scribe: or, secretary
ᵍ chief rulers: or, princes

king said, *Is* there not yet any of the house of Saul, that I may shew the kindness of God unto him? And Ziba said unto the king, Jonathan hath yet a son, *which is* lame on *his* feet. ⁴And the king said unto him, Where *is* he? And Ziba said unto the king, Behold, he *is* in the house of Machir, the son of Ammiel, in Lodebar. ⁵Then king David sent, and fetched him out of the house of Machir, the son of Ammiel, from Lodebar. ⁶Now when Mephibosheth^a, the son of Jonathan, the son of Saul, was come unto David, he fell on his face, and did reverence. And David said, Mephibosheth. And he answered, Behold thy servant! ⁷And David said unto him, Fear not: for I will surely shew thee kindness for Jonathan thy father's sake, and will restore thee all the land of Saul thy father; and thou shalt eat bread at my table continually. ⁸And he bowed himself, and said, What *is* thy servant, that thou shouldest look upon such a dead dog as I *am*?

⁹Then the king called to Ziba, Saul's servant, and said unto him, I have given unto thy master's son all that pertained to Saul and to all his house. ¹⁰Thou therefore, and thy sons, and thy servants, shall till the land for him, and thou shalt bring in *the fruits*, that thy master's son may have food to eat: but Mephibosheth thy master's son shall eat bread alway at my table. Now Ziba had fifteen sons and twenty servants. ¹¹Then said Ziba unto the king, According to all that my lord the king hath commanded his servant, so shall thy servant do. As for Mephibosheth, *said the king*,

he shall eat at my table, as one of the king's sons. ¹²And Mephibosheth had a young son, whose name *was* Micha. And all that dwelt in the house of Ziba *were* servants unto Mephibosheth. ¹³So Mephibosheth dwelt in Jerusalem: for he did eat continually at the king's table; and was lame on both his feet.

10

¹And it came to pass after this, that the king of the children of Ammon died, and Hanun his son reigned in his stead. ²Then said David, I will shew kindness unto Hanun the son of Nahash, as his father shewed kindness unto me. And David sent to comfort him by the hand of his servants for his father. And David's servants came into the land of the children of Ammon. ³And the princes of the children of Ammon said unto Hanun their lord, Thinkest^a thou that David doth honour thy father, that he hath sent comforters unto thee? hath not David *rather* sent his servants unto thee, to search the city, and to spy it out, and to overthrow it? ⁴Wherefore Hanun took David's servants, and shaved off the one half of their beards, and cut off their garments in the middle, *even* to their buttocks, and sent them away. ⁵When they told *it* unto David, he sent to meet them, because the men were greatly ashamed: and the king said, Tarry at Jericho until your beards be grown, and *then* return.

⁶And when the children of Ammon saw that they stank before David, the children of Ammon sent and hired the Syrians of Bethrehob, and the Syri-

---

^a Mephibosheth: also called Meribbaal
^a Thinkest . . . : Heb. In thy eyes doth David

Family Traditions

Adoption: A Special Kind of Miracle

2 SAMUEL 9

"Thy master's son shall eat bread always at my table" (2 Sam. 9:10). Children are a gift from God, to be sure, but that gift can come in many different ways. One of those ways is adoption. Each adopted child is a miracle with his or her own special history.

Here are some ways to build unique traditions around the adoption of your child and his or her growing up:

Compile a list of famous people who were adopted. Record the spiritual influences in their lives, the crises they overcame, and what they are most remembered for. Present this to the adopted child on a special birthday, perhaps at twelve or thirteen.

Write down the story of the child's adoption. Tell all about the emotions you had, the highs and lows of the process. Weave in as many facts as you know about the child's birth and natural ancestry, including ethnic heritage. Then record your own ancestry, and show how Jesus' ancestry was traced back to King David through Joseph, his "adoptive" father.

Celebrate the day of adoption each year as well as your child's birthday. Make a scrapbook together, adding to it each year on that day photos, souvenirs, programs, or postcards of places and events you attended together.

Keep duplicates of your child's school photographs and other prized snapshots as he or she grows up. If as an adult your child chooses to locate his or her birth parents, you can present these as a way of giving back some of the precious history gifted to you.

If a natural-born child comes along after you adopt, involve your adopted child in the ups and downs of the pregnancy. Let your child listen to the baby's heartbeat and bring you a footstool to prop up your legs when you're tired. Talk about how God knows us from the moment of conception.

Nurture relationships with other families who have adopted children or parents who are adopted themselves. These relationships will serve as a kind of support to you. Any kind of unexpected emotions, questions, or problems can usually be minimized or processed through sharing them with someone who understands.

Begin from early on to emphasize to your child that "adopted means loved." Equate adoption with warm, positive feelings, good choices, and value added to the family.

ans of Zoba, twenty thousand footmen, and of king Maacah a thousand men, and of Ishtob[b] twelve thousand men. [7]And when David heard of *it*, he sent Joab, and all the host of the mighty men. [8]And the children of Ammon came out, and put the battle in array at the entering in of the gate: and the Syrians of Zoba, and of Rehob, and Ishtob, and Maacah, *were* by themselves in the field. [9]When Joab saw that the front of the battle was against him before and behind, he chose of all the choice *men* of Israel, and put *them* in array against the Syrians: [10]And the rest of the people he delivered into the hand of Abishai his brother, that he might put *them* in array against the children of Ammon. [11]And he said, If the Syrians be too strong for me, then thou shalt help me: but if the children of Ammon be too strong for thee, then I will come and help thee. [12]Be of good courage, and let us play the men for our people, and for the cities of our God: and the LORD do that which seemeth him good. [13]And Joab drew nigh, and the people that *were* with him, unto the battle against the Syrians: and they fled before him. [14]And when the children of Ammon saw that the Syrians were fled, then fled they also before Abishai, and entered into the city. So Joab returned from the children of Ammon, and came to Jerusalem.

[15]And when the Syrians saw that they were smitten before Israel, they gathered themselves together. [16]And Hadarezer sent, and brought out the Syrians that *were* beyond the river[c]: and they came to Helam; and Shobach the captain of the host of Hadarezer *went* before them. [17]And when it was told David, he gathered all Israel together, and passed over Jordan, and came to Helam. And the Syrians set themselves in array against David, and fought with him. [18]And the Syrians fled before Israel; and David slew *the men of* seven hundred chariots of the Syrians, and forty thousand horsemen[d], and smote Shobach the captain of their host, who died there. [19]And when all the kings *that were* servants to Hadarezer saw that they were smitten before Israel, they made peace with Israel, and served them. So the Syrians feared to help the children of Ammon any more.

11

[1]And it came to pass, after the year was expired, at the time when kings go forth *to battle*, that David sent Joab, and his servants with him, and all Israel; and they destroyed the children of Ammon, and besieged Rabbah. But David tarried still at Jerusalem. [2]And it came to pass in an eveningtide, that David arose from off his bed, and walked upon the roof of the king's house: and from the roof he saw a woman washing herself; and the woman *was* very beautiful to look upon. [3]And David sent and enquired after the woman. And *one* said, *Is* not this Bathsheba[a], the daughter of Eliam,

---

[b] Ishtob: or, the men of Tob
[c] the river: that is, Euphrates
[d] horsemen: also called, footmen
[a] Bathsheba: or, Bathshuah

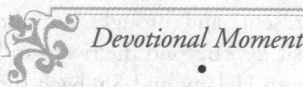

Devotional Moment

•

Adultery

11:1-5 How different events *could* have been if only David had actively avoided this temptation. He could have gone out with his troops, immediately looked away and left his rooftop perch upon seeing Bathsheba, or contacted Nathan or another godly friend for support during his struggle with lust. Unfortunately, David decided to entertain the temptation, and he paid for this choice the rest of his life.

If we fail to learn from David's tragic sin, we are extremely foolish. We need to avoid obvious temptations altogether. Whenever we unexpectedly find ourselves in dangerous situations, we need to flee. If we find ourselves thinking about sinning, we need to call on God and our friends to hold us accountable and give us strength. And if we have fallen into sin, we need to make use of the people available to help us—Christian friends, a church small group, a Twelve-Step group, or perhaps a marriage and family therapist.

from the king. ⁹But Uriah slept at the door of the king's house with all the servants of his lord, and went not down to his house. ¹⁰And when they had told David, saying, Uriah went not down unto his house, David said unto Uriah, Camest thou not from *thy* journey? why *then* didst thou not go down unto thine house? ¹¹And Uriah said unto David, The ark, and Israel, and Judah, abide in tents; and my lord Joab, and the servants of my lord, are encamped in the open fields; shall I then go into mine house, to eat and to drink, and to lie with my wife? *as* thou livest, and *as* thy soul liveth, I will not do this thing. ¹²And David said to Uriah, Tarry here to day also, and to morrow I will let thee depart. So Uriah abode in Jerusalem that day, and the morrow. ¹³And when David had called him, he did eat and drink before him; and he

the wife of Uriah the Hittite? ⁴And David sent messengers, and took her; and she came in unto him, and he lay with her; for she was purified from her uncleanness: and she returned unto her house. ⁵And the woman conceived, and sent and told David, and said, I *am* with child.

⁶And David sent to Joab, *saying*, Send me Uriah the Hittite. And Joab sent Uriah to David. ⁷And when Uriah was come unto him, David demanded *of him* how Joab^b did, and how the people did, and how the war prospered. ⁸And David said to Uriah, Go down to thy house, and wash thy feet. And Uriah departed out of the king's house, and there followed^c him a mess *of meat*

Devotional Moment

•

Abuse of Authority

11:6-27 David seriously abused his regal power and position in the aftermath of his sin. First he ordered Uriah (Bathsheba's husband) home from battle in an attempt to make it look as if Bathsheba had conceived by her husband. When that plan failed, David conspired to have Uriah killed in battle. Finally, once Uriah was dead, David took Bathsheba as his own wife. Such manipulation, deception, and selfishness was an absolute misuse of authority. Every attempt to use authority—political, parental, or work-related—to control or exploit others is a grave sin against God. Guard against using your authority inappropriately; never set arbitrary rules merely to show your power.

^b how Joab . . . : Heb. of the peace of, etc
^c followed . . . : Heb. went out after him

made him drunk: and at even he went out to lie on his bed with the servants of his lord, but went not down to his house.

¹⁴And it came to pass in the morning, that David wrote a letter to Joab, and sent *it* by the hand of Uriah. ¹⁵And he wrote in the letter, saying, Set ye Uriah in the forefront of the hottest^d battle, and retire ye from him, that he may be smitten, and die. ¹⁶And it came to pass, when Joab observed the city, that he assigned Uriah unto a place where he knew that valiant men *were*. ¹⁷And the men of the city went out, and fought with Joab: and there fell *some* of the people of the servants of David; and Uriah the Hittite died also. ¹⁸Then Joab sent and told David all the things concerning the war; ¹⁹And charged the messenger, saying, When thou hast made an end of telling the matters of the war unto the king, ²⁰And if so be that the king's wrath arise, and he say unto thee, Wherefore approached ye so nigh unto the city when ye did fight? knew ye not that they would shoot from the wall? ²¹Who smote Abimelech the son of Jerubbesheth^e? did not a woman cast a piece of a millstone upon him from the wall, that he died in Thebez? why went ye nigh the wall? then say thou, Thy servant Uriah the Hittite is dead also. ²²So the messenger went, and came and shewed David all that Joab had sent him for. ²³And the messenger said unto David, Surely the men prevailed against us, and came out unto us into the field, and we were upon them even unto the entering of the gate. ²⁴And the shooters shot from off the wall upon thy servants; and *some* of the king's servants be dead, and thy servant Uriah the Hittite is dead also. ²⁵Then David said unto the messenger, Thus shalt thou say unto Joab, Let not this thing displease^f thee, for the sword devoureth one as well as another: make thy battle more strong against the city, and overthrow it: and encourage thou him. ²⁶And when the wife of Uriah heard that Uriah her husband was dead, she mourned for her husband. ²⁷And when the mourning was past, David sent and fetched her to his house, and she became his wife, and bare him a son. But the thing that David had done displeased^g the LORD.

12

¹And the LORD sent Nathan unto David. And he came unto him, and said unto him, There were two men in one city; the one rich, and the other poor. ²The rich *man* had exceeding many flocks and herds: ³But the poor *man* had nothing, save one little ewe lamb, which he had bought and nourished up: and it grew up together with him, and with his children; it did eat of his own meat^a, and drank of his own cup, and lay in his bosom, and was unto him as a daughter. ⁴And there came a traveller unto the rich man, and

^d hottest: Heb. strong
^e Jerubbesheth: also called, Jerubbaal
^f displease . . . : Heb. be evil in thine eyes
^g displeased: Heb. was evil in the eyes of
^a meat: Heb. morsel

519

he spared to take of his own flock and of his own herd, to dress for the wayfaring man that was come unto him; but took the poor man's lamb, and dressed it for the man that was come to him. ⁵And David's anger was greatly kindled against the man; and he said to Nathan, *As* the LORD liveth, the man that hath done this *thing* shall surely die: ⁶And he shall restore the lamb fourfold, because he did this thing, and because he had no pity. ⁷And Nathan said to David, Thou *art* the man. Thus saith the LORD God of Israel, I anointed thee king over Israel, and I delivered thee out of the hand of Saul; ⁸And I gave thee thy master's house, and thy master's wives into thy bosom, and gave thee the house of Israel and of Judah; and if *that had been* too little, I would moreover have given unto thee such and such things. ⁹Wherefore hast thou despised the commandment of the LORD, to do evil in his sight? thou hast killed Uriah the Hittite with the sword, and hast taken his wife *to be* thy wife, and hast slain him with the sword of the children of Ammon. ¹⁰Now therefore the sword shall never depart from thine house; because thou hast despised me, and hast taken the wife of Uriah the Hittite to be thy wife. ¹¹Thus saith the LORD, Behold, I will raise up evil against thee out of thine own house, and I will take thy wives before thine eyes, and give *them* unto thy neighbour, and he shall lie with thy wives in the sight of this sun. ¹²For thou didst *it* secretly: but I will do this thing before all Israel, and before the sun. ¹³And David said unto Nathan, I have sinned against the LORD. And Nathan said unto David, The LORD also hath

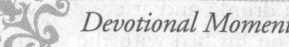

Devotional Moment
•
Consequences

12:10-12 Through the prophet Nathan, David heard these sobering words, "Murder shall be a constant threat in your family from this time on." This prophecy was fulfilled in at least two tragic ways: (1) David's own son Absalom rebelled against him—even stealing his wives! (2) Amnon and Absalom, two of David's sons, met with violent deaths (2 Sam. 13:28-29; 18:14; 1 Kings 2:23-25). If David could have foreseen these terrible consequences, he no doubt would have resisted the urge to pursue Bathsheba. It is easy for us to forget or block from our mind the truth that "whatsoever a man soweth, that shall he also reap" (Gal. 6:7). Are you considering temptation's tantalizing sales pitch? Don't! You may find that what you get is not at all what you bargained for.

put away thy sin; thou shalt not die. ¹⁴Howbeit, because by this deed thou hast given great occasion to the enemies of the LORD to blaspheme, the child also *that is* born unto thee shall surely die.

Devotional Moment
•
Confession

12:13-14 Most adulterers repress their guilt and are blind to God's anger; David sought forgiveness. Most adulterers would prefer that God were dead or asleep or indifferent; David prayed to be renewed in spirit. The king learned a hard lesson that year: Adultery involves hidden and bitter consequences. Yet when he repented and sought God's forgiveness, he was forgiven and his enjoyment of life was restored. If you have sinned, God wants to restore you as he did David. Begin by admitting your sin to God and turning away from any further involvement. Then admit your sin to others and get help. In this life, God graciously gives us second chances as we grow.

¹⁵And Nathan departed unto his house. And the LORD struck the child that Uriah's wife bare unto David, and it was very sick. ¹⁶David therefore besought God for the child; and David fasted[b], and went in, and lay all night upon the earth. ¹⁷And the elders of his house arose, *and went* to him, to raise him up from the earth: but he would not, neither did he eat bread with them. ¹⁸And it came to pass on the seventh day, that the child died. And the servants of David feared to tell him that the child was dead: for they said, Behold, while the child was yet alive, we spake unto him, and he would not hearken unto our voice: how will he then vex[c] himself, if we tell him that the child is dead? ¹⁹But when David saw that his servants whispered, David perceived that the child was dead: therefore David said unto his servants, Is the child dead? And they said, He is dead. ²⁰Then David arose from the earth, and washed, and anointed *himself*, and changed his apparel, and came into the house of the LORD, and worshipped: then he came to his own house; and when he required, they set bread before him, and he did eat. ²¹Then said his servants unto him, What thing *is* this that thou hast done? thou didst fast and weep for the child, *while it was* alive; but when the child was dead, thou didst rise and eat bread. ²²And he said, While the child was yet alive, I fasted and wept: for I said, Who can tell *whether* GOD will be gracious to me, that the child may live? ²³But now he is dead, wherefore should I fast? can I bring him back again? I shall go to him, but he shall not return to me. ²⁴And David comforted Bathsheba his wife, and went in unto her, and lay with her: and she bare a son, and he called his name Solomon: and the LORD loved him. ²⁵And he sent by the hand of Nathan the prophet; and he called his name Jedidiah[d], because of the LORD.

²⁶And Joab fought against Rabbah of the children of Ammon, and took the royal city. ²⁷And Joab sent messengers to David, and said, I have fought against Rabbah, and have taken the city of waters. ²⁸Now therefore gather the rest of the people together, and encamp against the city, and take it: lest I take the city, and it be called[e] after my name. ²⁹And David gathered all the people together, and went to Rabbah, and fought against it, and took it. ³⁰And he took their king's crown from off his head, the weight whereof *was* a talent of gold with the precious stones: and it was *set* on David's head. And he brought forth the spoil of the city in great[f] abundance. ³¹And he brought forth the people that *were* therein, and put *them* under saws, and under harrows of iron, and under axes of iron, and made them pass through the brickkiln: and thus did he unto all the cities of the children of

---

[b] fasted: Heb. fasted a fast
[c] vex: Heb. do hurt
[d] Jedidiah: that is, Beloved of the LORD
[e] it be called . . . : Heb. my name be called upon it
[f] in great . . . : Heb. very great

Ammon. So David and all the people returned unto Jerusalem.

13

¹And it came to pass after this, that Absalom the son of David had a fair sister, whose name *was* Tamar; and Amnon the son of David loved her. ²And Amnon was so vexed, that he fell sick for his sister Tamar; for she *was* a virgin; and Amnon thoughtª it hard for him to do any thing to her. ³But Amnon had a friend, whose name *was* Jonadab, the son of Shimeah David's brother: and Jonadab *was* a very subtil man. ⁴And he said unto him, Why *art* thou, *being* the king's son, leanᵇ from day to day? wilt thou not tell me? And Amnon said unto him, I love Tamar, my brother Absalom's sister. ⁵And Jonadab said unto him, Lay thee down on thy bed, and make thyself sick: and when thy father cometh to see thee, say unto him, I pray thee, let my sister Tamar come, and give me meat, and dress the meat in my sight, that I may see *it*, and eat *it* at her hand. ⁶So Amnon lay down, and made himself sick: and when the king was come to see him, Amnon said unto the king, I pray thee, let Tamar my sister come, and make me a couple of cakes in my sight, that I may eat at her hand. ⁷Then David sent home to Tamar, saying, Go now to thy brother Amnon's house, and dress him meat. ⁸So Tamar went to her brother Amnon's house; and he was laid down. And she took flourᶜ, and kneaded *it*, and made cakes in his sight, and did bake the cakes. ⁹And she took a pan, and poured *them* out before him; but he refused to eat. And Amnon said, Have out all men from me. And they went out every man from him. ¹⁰And Amnon said unto Tamar, Bring the meat into the chamber, that I may eat of thine hand. And Tamar took the cakes which she had made, and brought *them* into the chamber to Amnon her brother. ¹¹And when she had brought *them* unto him to eat, he took hold of her, and said unto her, Come lie with me, my sister. ¹²And she answered him, Nay, my brother, do not forceᵈ me; for no such

---

Devotional Moment

Incest and Rape

13:1-4 A crime more vicious than rape is hard to imagine. Add incest to rape, and the despicableness is multiplied. That which God intended to be joyful and good—sexual intimacy—is made a horror and a shame.

Tamar was right when she predicted that Amnon would be known as a fool (13:13). Not only in his own day, but forever after, Amnon has been remembered for his crime. He gained nothing and lost his life later, through revenge. Rape can never be justified.

If you are a victim of incest or rape, Tamar is your sister. Recovery is a long and difficult process, but God can restore and heal you. Look to him. Lean on others as well—those you can trust and count on. Tell someone who can share your journey toward healing. And perhaps most important of all, tell someone who can bring the offender to account. Amnon had no right to keep his sin secret, and neither does anyone else.

ª Amnon thought . . . : Heb. it was marvellous, or, hidden in the eyes of Amnon

ᵇ lean: Heb. thin

ᶜ flour: or, paste

ᵈ force . . . : Heb. humble me

thing ought to be done in Israel: do not thou this folly. ¹³And I, whither shall I cause my shame to go? and as for thee, thou shalt be as one of the fools in Israel. Now therefore, I pray thee, speak unto the king; for he will not withhold me from thee. ¹⁴Howbeit he would not hearken unto her voice: but, being stronger than she, forced her, and lay with her. ¹⁵Then Amnon hated her exceedingly^e; so that the hatred wherewith he hated her *was* greater than the love wherewith he had loved her. And Amnon said unto her, Arise, be gone. ¹⁶And she said unto him, *There is* no cause: this evil in sending me away *is* greater than the other that thou didst unto me. But he would not hearken unto her. ¹⁷Then he called his servant that ministered unto him, and said, Put now this *woman* out from me, and bolt the door after her. ¹⁸And *she had* a garment of divers colours upon her: for with such robes were the king's daughters *that were* virgins apparelled. Then his servant brought her out, and bolted the door after her. ¹⁹And Tamar put ashes on her head, and rent her garment of divers colours that *was* on her, and laid her hand on her head, and went on crying. ²⁰And Absalom her brother said unto her, Hath Amnon^f thy brother been with thee? but hold now thy peace, my sister: he *is* thy brother; regard not this thing. So Tamar remained desolate in her brother Absalom's house.

²¹But when king David heard of all these things, he was very wroth. ²²And Absalom spake unto his brother Amnon neither good nor bad: for Absalom hated Amnon, because he had forced his sister Tamar. ²³And it came to pass after two full years, that Absalom had sheepshearers in Baalhazor, which *is* beside Ephraim: and Absalom invited all the king's sons. ²⁴And Absalom came to the king, and said, Behold now, thy servant hath sheepshearers; let the king, I beseech thee, and his servants go with thy servant. ²⁵And the king said to Absalom, Nay, my son, let us not all now go, lest we be chargeable unto thee. And he pressed him: howbeit he would not go, but blessed him. ²⁶Then said Absalom, If not, I pray thee, let my brother Amnon go with us. And the king said unto him, Why should he go with thee? ²⁷But Absalom pressed him, that he let Amnon and all the king's sons go with him. ²⁸Now Absalom had commanded his servants, saying, Mark ye now when Amnon's heart is merry with wine, and when I say unto you, Smite Amnon; then kill him, fear not: have not I commanded you? be courageous, and be valiant. ²⁹And the servants of Absalom did unto Amnon as Absalom had commanded. Then all the king's sons arose, and every man gat him up upon his mule, and fled.

³⁰And it came to pass, while they were in the way, that tidings came to David, saying, Absalom hath slain all the king's sons, and there is not one of them left. ³¹Then the king arose, and tare his garments, and lay on the earth; and all his servants stood by with their clothes rent. ³²And Jonadab, the son of Shimeah David's brother, answered and

---

^e exceedingly: Heb. with great hatred greatly
^f Amnon: Heb. Aminon

said, Let not my lord suppose *that* they have slain all the young men the king's sons; for Amnon only is dead: for by the appointment[g] of Absalom this hath been determined from the day that he forced his sister Tamar. ³³Now therefore let not my lord the king take the thing to his heart, to think that all the king's sons are dead: for Amnon only is dead. ³⁴But Absalom fled. And the young man that kept the watch lifted up his eyes, and looked, and, behold, there came much people by the way of the hill side behind him. ³⁵And Jonadab said unto the king, Behold, the king's sons come: as thy servant said, so it is. ³⁶And it came to pass, as soon as he had made an end of speaking, that, behold, the king's sons came, and lifted up their voice and wept: and the king also and all his servants wept very[h] sore. ³⁷But Absalom fled, and went to Talmai, the son of Ammihud[i], king of Geshur. And *David* mourned for his son every day. ³⁸So Absalom fled, and went to Geshur, and was there three years. ³⁹And *the soul of* king David longed[j] to go forth unto Absalom: for he was comforted concerning Amnon, seeing he was dead.

14

¹Now Joab the son of Zeruiah perceived that the king's heart *was* toward Absalom. ²And Joab sent to Tekoah, and fetched thence a wise woman, and said unto her, I pray thee, feign thyself to be a mourner, and put on now mourning apparel, and anoint not thyself with oil, but be as a woman that had a long time mourned for the dead: ³And come to the king, and speak on this manner unto him. So Joab put the words in her mouth. ⁴And when the woman of Tekoah spake to the king, she fell on her face to the ground, and did obeisance, and said, Help[a], O king. ⁵And the king said unto her, What aileth thee? And she answered, I *am* indeed a widow woman, and mine husband is dead. ⁶And thy handmaid had two sons, and they two strove together in the field, and *there was* none to part them, but the one smote the other, and slew him. ⁷And, behold, the whole family is risen against thine handmaid, and they said, Deliver him that smote his brother, that we may kill him, for the life of his brother whom he slew; and we will destroy the heir also: and so they shall quench my coal which is left, and shall not leave to my husband *neither* name nor remainder upon[b] the earth. ⁸And the king said unto the woman, Go to thine house, and I will give charge concerning thee. ⁹And the woman of Tekoah said unto the king, My lord, O king, the iniquity *be* on me, and on my father's house: and the king and his throne *be* guiltless. ¹⁰And the king said, Whosoever saith *ought* unto thee, bring him to me, and he shall not touch thee any more. ¹¹Then said she, I

---

[g] appointment: Heb. mouth
[h] very . . . : Heb. with a great weeping greatly
[i] Ammihud: or, Ammihur
[j] longed: or, was consumed
[a] Help: Heb. Save
[b] upon . . . : Heb. upon the face of the earth

524

pray thee, let the king remember the LORD thy God, that thou wouldest not suffer the revengers of blood to destroy any more, lest they destroy my son. And he said, *As* the LORD liveth, there shall not one hair of thy son fall to the earth. [12]Then the woman said, Let thine handmaid, I pray thee, speak *one* word unto my lord the king. And he said, Say on. [13]And the woman said, Wherefore then hast thou thought such a thing against the people of God? for the king doth speak this thing as one which is faulty, in that the king doth not fetch home again his banished. [14]For we must needs die, and *are* as water spilt on the ground, which cannot be gathered up again; neither doth God respect *any* person: yet doth he devise means, that his banished be not expelled from him. [15]Now therefore that I am come to speak of this thing unto my lord the king, *it is* because the people have made me afraid: and thy handmaid said, I will now speak unto the king; it may be that the king will perform the request of his handmaid. [16]For the king will hear, to deliver his handmaid out of the hand of the man *that would* destroy me and my son together out of the inheritance of God. [17]Then thine handmaid said, The word of my lord the king shall now be comfortable[c]: for as an angel of God, so *is* my lord the king to discern good and bad: therefore the LORD thy God will be with thee. [18]Then the king answered and said unto the woman, Hide not from me, I pray thee, the thing that I shall ask thee. And the woman said, Let my lord the king

now speak. [19]And the king said, *Is not* the hand of Joab with thee in all this? And the woman answered and said, *As* thy soul liveth, my lord the king, none can turn to the right hand or to the left from ought that my lord the king hath spoken: for thy servant Joab, he bade me, and he put all these words in the mouth of thine handmaid: [20]To fetch about this form of speech hath thy servant Joab done this thing: and my lord *is* wise, according to the wisdom of an angel of God, to know all *things* that *are* in the earth.

[21]And the king said unto Joab, Behold now, I have done this thing: go therefore, bring the young man Absalom again. [22]And Joab fell to the ground on his face, and bowed himself, and thanked[d] the king: and Joab said, To day thy servant knoweth that I have found grace in thy sight, my lord, O king, in that the king hath fulfilled the request of his servant. [23]So Joab arose and went to Geshur, and brought Absalom to Jerusalem. [24]And the king said, Let him turn to his own house, and let him not see my face. So Absalom returned to his own house, and saw not the king's face. [25]But in all Israel there was none to be so much praised as Absalom for his beauty: from the sole of his foot even to the crown of his head there was no blemish in him. [26]And when he polled his head, (for it was at every year's end that he polled *it*: because *the hair* was heavy on him, therefore he polled it:) he weighed the hair of his head at two hundred shekels after the king's weight. [27]And unto Absalom

[c] comfortable: Heb. for rest
[d] thanked: Heb. blessed

there were born three sons, and one daughter, whose name *was* Tamar: she was a woman of a fair countenance. ²⁸So Absalom dwelt two full years in Jerusalem, and saw not the king's face. ²⁹Therefore Absalom sent for Joab, to have sent him to the king; but he would not come to him: and when he sent again the second time, he would not come. ³⁰Therefore he said unto his servants, See, Joab's field is near ͤ mine, and he hath barley there; go and set it on fire. And Absalom's servants set the field on fire. ³¹Then Joab arose, and came to Absalom unto *his* house, and said unto him, Wherefore have thy servants set my field on fire? ³²And Absalom answered Joab, Behold, I sent unto thee, saying, Come hither, that I may send thee to the king, to say, Wherefore am I come from Geshur? *it had been* good for me *to have been* there still: now

---

Devotional Moment

Fathers and Forgiveness

14:33 David and Absalom both had choices: They could have been obstinate forever, rude in public, and lonesome in private. They could have put off a meeting until each felt better—until tomorrow (which would never come). They each could have adjusted to the easy but false idea that the other hated him. But note that David the king was not so full of ego that he could not forgive, nor Absalom so haughty that he could not bow in respect. When David kissed his son, he meant it as a complete pardon, as if to say, "Let's start over from here."
Fathers today should heed this example, in word and deed. God forgives grievous wrong; so should we. Fathers, seek out that child, forgive, and embrace him.

---

therefore let me see the king's face; and if there be *any* iniquity in me, let him kill me. ³³So Joab came to the king, and told him: and when he had called for Absalom, he came to the king, and bowed himself on his face to the ground before the king: and the king kissed Absalom.

15

¹And it came to pass after this, that Absalom prepared him chariots and horses, and fifty men to run before him. ²And Absalom rose up early, and stood beside the way of the gate: and it was *so,* that when any man that had a controversy came ͣ to the king for judgment, then Absalom called unto him, and said, Of what city *art* thou? And he said, Thy servant *is* of one of the tribes of Israel. ³And Absalom said unto him, See, thy matters *are* good and right; but *there is* no man *deputed* of the king to hear thee. ⁴Absalom said moreover, Oh that I were made judge in the land, that every man which hath any suit or cause might come unto me, and I would do him justice! ⁵And it was *so,* that when any man came nigh *to him* to do him obeisance, he put forth his hand, and took him, and kissed him. ⁶And on this manner did Absalom to all Israel that came to the king for judgment: so Absalom stole the hearts of the men of Israel.

⁷And it came to pass after forty years, that Absalom said unto the king, I pray thee, let me go and pay my vow, which I have vowed unto the LORD, in Hebron. ⁸For thy servant vowed a

---

ͤ near . . . : Heb. near my place
ͣ came: Heb. to come

vow while I abode at Geshur in Syria, saying, If the LORD shall bring me again indeed to Jerusalem, then I will serve the LORD. ⁹And the king said unto him, Go in peace. So he arose, and went to Hebron. ¹⁰But Absalom sent spies throughout all the tribes of Israel, saying, As soon as ye hear the sound of the trumpet, then ye shall say, Absalom reigneth in Hebron. ¹¹And with Absalom went two hundred men out of Jerusalem, *that were* called; and they went in their simplicity, and they knew not any thing. ¹²And Absalom sent for Ahithophel the Gilonite, David's counsellor, from his city, *even* from Giloh, while he offered sacrifices. And the conspiracy was strong; for the people increased continually with Absalom.

¹³And there came a messenger to David, saying, The hearts of the men of Israel are after Absalom. ¹⁴And David said unto all his servants that *were* with him at Jerusalem, Arise, and let us flee; for we shall not *else* escape from Absalom: make speed to depart, lest he overtake us suddenly, and bringᵇ evil upon us, and smite the city with the edge of the sword. ¹⁵And the king's servants said unto the king, Behold, thy servants *are ready to do* whatsoever my lord the king shall appointᶜ. ¹⁶And the king went forth, and all his household afterᵈ him. And the king left ten women, *which were* concubines, to keep the house. ¹⁷And the king went forth, and all the people after him, and tarried in a place

that was far off. ¹⁸And all his servants passed on beside him; and all the Cherethites, and all the Pelethites, and all the Gittites, six hundred men which came after him from Gath, passed on before the king. ¹⁹Then said the king to Ittai the Gittite, Wherefore goest thou also with us? return to thy place, and abide with the king: for thou *art* a stranger, and also an exile. ²⁰Whereas thou camest *but* yesterday, should I this day make thee go up and down with us? seeing I go whither I may, return thou, and take back thy brethren: mercy and truth *be* with thee. ²¹And Ittai answered the king, and said, *As* the LORD liveth, and *as* my lord the king liveth, surely in what place my lord the king shall be, whether in death or life, even there also will thy servant be. ²²And David said to Ittai, Go and pass over. And Ittai the Gittite passed over, and all his men, and all the little ones that *were* with him. ²³And all the country wept with a loud voice, and all the people passed over: the king also himself passed over the brook Kidronᵉ, and all the people passed over, toward the way of the wilderness.

²⁴And lo Zadok also, and all the Levites *were* with him, bearing the ark of the covenant of God: and they set down the ark of God; and Abiathar went up, until all the people had done passing out of the city. ²⁵And the king said unto Zadok, Carry back the ark of God into the city: if I shall find favour in the eyes of the LORD, he will bring

---

ᵇ bring: Heb. thrust
ᶜ appoint: Heb. choose
ᵈ after . . . : Heb. at his feet
ᵉ Kidron: Gr. Cedron

me again, and shew me *both* it, and his habitation: ²⁶But if he thus say, I have no delight in thee; behold, *here am* I, let him do to me as seemeth good unto him. ²⁷The king said also unto Zadok the priest, *Art not* thou a seer? return into the city in peace, and your two sons with you, Ahimaaz thy son, and Jonathan the son of Abiathar. ²⁸See, I will tarry in the plain of the wilderness, until there come word from you to certify me. ²⁹Zadok therefore and Abiathar carried the ark of God again to Jerusalem: and they tarried there. ³⁰And David went up by the ascent of mount Olivet, and wept^f as he went up, and had his head covered, and he went barefoot: and all the people that *was* with him covered every man his head, and they went up, weeping as they went up.

³¹And *one* told David, saying, Ahithophel *is* among the conspirators with Absalom. And David said, O LORD, I pray thee, turn the counsel of Ahithophel into foolishness. ³²And it came to pass, that *when* David was come to the top *of the mount*, where he worshipped God, behold, Hushai the Archite came to meet him with his coat rent, and earth upon his head: ³³Unto whom David said, If thou passest on with me, then thou shalt be a burden unto me: ³⁴But if thou return to the city, and say unto Absalom, I will be thy servant, O king; *as I have been* thy father's servant hitherto, so *will* I now also *be* thy servant: then mayest thou for me defeat the counsel of Ahithophel. ³⁵And *hast thou* not there with thee Zadok and

Abiathar the priests? therefore it shall be, *that* what thing soever thou shalt hear out of the king's house, thou shalt tell *it* to Zadok and Abiathar the priests. ³⁶Behold, *they have* there with them their two sons, Ahimaaz Zadok's *son*, and Jonathan Abiathar's *son*; and by them ye shall send unto me every thing that ye can hear. ³⁷So Hushai David's friend came into the city, and Absalom came into Jerusalem.

16

¹And when David was a little past the top *of the hill*, behold, Ziba the servant of Mephibosheth met him, with a couple of asses saddled, and upon them two hundred *loaves* of bread, and an hundred bunches of raisins, and an hundred of summer fruits, and a bottle of wine. ²And the king said unto Ziba, What meanest thou by these? And Ziba said, The asses *be* for the king's household to ride on; and the bread and summer fruit for the young men to eat; and the wine, that such as be faint in the wilderness may drink. ³And the king said, And where *is* thy master's son? And Ziba said unto the king, Behold, he abideth at Jerusalem: for he said, To day shall the house of Israel restore me the kingdom of my father. ⁴Then said the king to Ziba, Behold, thine *are* all that *pertained* unto Mephibosheth. And Ziba said, I humbly^a beseech thee *that* I may find grace in thy sight, my lord, O king.

⁵And when king David came to Bahurim, behold, thence came out a man of the family of the house of Saul,

---

^{f} and wept . . . : Heb. going up and weeping
^{a} I humbly . . . : Heb. I do obeisance

whose name *was* Shimei, the son of Gera: he came forth[b], and cursed still as he came. [6]And he cast stones at David, and at all the servants of king David: and all the people and all the mighty men *were* on his right hand and on his left. [7]And thus said Shimei when he cursed, Come out, come out, thou bloody[c] man, and thou man of Belial: [8]The LORD hath returned upon thee all the blood of the house of Saul, in whose stead thou hast reigned; and the LORD hath delivered the kingdom into the hand of Absalom thy son: and, behold, thou *art taken* in thy mischief [d], because thou *art* a bloody man. [9]Then said Abishai the son of Zeruiah unto the king, Why should this dead dog curse my lord the king? let me go over, I pray thee, and take off his head. [10]And the king said, What have I to do with you, ye sons of Zeruiah? so let him curse, because the LORD hath said unto him, Curse David. Who shall then say, Wherefore hast thou done so? [11]And David said to Abishai, and to all his servants, Behold, my son, which came forth of my bowels, seeketh my life: how much more now *may this* Benjamite *do it?* let him alone, and let him curse; for the LORD hath bidden him. [12]It may be that the LORD will look on mine affliction[e], and that the LORD will requite me good for his cursing this day. [13]And as David and his men went by the way, Shimei went along on the hill's side over against him, and cursed

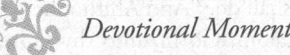

Devotional Moment

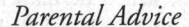

Parental Advice

16:21-23 The advice that Ahithophel gave Absalom was sure to lead to conflict. First David's counselor, then Absalom's, Ahithophel was an opportunist whose advice was self-serving and short-term. In seeking parental advice, choose your advisors carefully. Look for friends, teachers, and counselors who love God, who base their counsel on Bible truths, who know their own limitations, and who believe mightily in the power of prayer.

as he went, and threw stones at him, and cast[f] dust. [14]And the king, and all the people that *were* with him, came weary, and refreshed themselves there.

[15]And Absalom, and all the people the men of Israel, came to Jerusalem, and Ahithophel with him. [16]And it came to pass, when Hushai the Archite, David's friend, was come unto Absalom, that Hushai said unto Absalom, God save the king, God save the king. [17]And Absalom said to Hushai, *Is* this thy kindness to thy friend? why wentest thou not with thy friend? [18]And Hushai said unto Absalom, Nay; but whom the LORD, and this people, and all the men of Israel, choose, his will I be, and with him will I abide. [19]And again, whom should I serve? *should I* not *serve* in the presence of his son? as I have served in thy father's presence, so will I be in thy presence. [20]Then said Absalom to Ahithophel, Give counsel among you

---

[b] he came forth . . . : or, he still came forth and cursed
[c] bloody . . . : Heb. man of blood
[d] behold . . . : Heb. behold thee in thy evil
[e] affliction: or, tears: Heb. eye
[f] cast . . . : Heb. dusted him with dust

what we shall do. ²¹And Ahithophel said unto Absalom, Go in unto thy father's concubines, which he hath left to keep the house; and all Israel shall hear that thou art abhorred of thy father: then shall the hands of all that *are* with thee be strong. ²²So they spread Absalom a tent upon the top of the house; and Absalom went in unto his father's concubines in the sight of all Israel. ²³And the counsel of Ahithophel, which he counselled in those days, *was* as if a man had enquired at the oracle^g of God: so *was* all the counsel of Ahithophel both with David and with Absalom.

17

¹Moreover Ahithophel said unto Absalom, Let me now choose out twelve thousand men, and I will arise and pursue after David this night: ²And I will come upon him while he *is* weary and weak handed, and will make him afraid: and all the people that *are* with him shall flee; and I will smite the king only: ³And I will bring back all the people unto thee: the man whom thou seekest *is* as if all returned: *so* all the people shall be in peace. ⁴And the saying pleased^a Absalom well, and all the elders of Israel. ⁵Then said Absalom, Call now Hushai the Archite also, and let us hear likewise what he saith. ⁶And when Hushai was come to Absalom, Absalom spake unto him, saying, Ahithophel hath spoken after this manner: shall we do *after* his saying^b? if not; speak thou. ⁷And Hushai said unto Absalom, The counsel that Ahithophel hath given^c *is* not good at this time. ⁸For, said Hushai, thou knowest thy father and his men, that they *be* mighty men, and they *be* chafed^d in their minds, as a bear robbed of her whelps in the field: and thy father *is* a man of war, and will not lodge with the people. ⁹Behold, he is hid now in some pit, or in some *other* place: and it will come to pass, when some of them be overthrown^e at the first, that whosoever heareth it will say, There is a slaughter among the people that follow Absalom. ¹⁰And he also *that is* valiant, whose heart *is* as the heart of a lion, shall utterly melt: for all Israel knoweth that thy father *is* a mighty man, and *they* which *be* with him *are* valiant men. ¹¹Therefore I counsel that all Israel be generally gathered unto thee, from Dan even to Beersheba, as the sand that *is* by the sea for multitude; and that thou go to battle in thine own person. ¹²So shall we come upon him in some place where he shall be found, and we will light upon him as the dew falleth on the ground: and of him and of all the men that *are* with him there shall not be left so much as one. ¹³Moreover, if he be gotten into a city, then shall all Israel bring ropes to that city, and we will draw it into the river, until there be not one small stone found there. ¹⁴And Absalom and all the

---

^g oracle: Heb. word

^a pleased . . . : Heb. was right in the eyes of, etc

^b his saying: Heb. his word?

^c given: Heb. counselled

^d chafed . . . : Heb. bitter of soul

^e overthrown: Heb. fallen

men of Israel said, The counsel of Hushai the Archite *is* better than the counsel of Ahithophel. For the LORD had appointed[f] to defeat the good counsel of Ahithophel, to the intent that the LORD might bring evil upon Absalom.

¹⁵Then said Hushai unto Zadok and to Abiathar the priests, Thus and thus did Ahithophel counsel Absalom and the elders of Israel; and thus and thus have I counselled. ¹⁶Now therefore send quickly, and tell David, saying, Lodge not this night in the plains of the wilderness, but speedily pass over; lest the king be swallowed up, and all the people that *are* with him. ¹⁷Now Jonathan and Ahimaaz stayed by Enrogel; for they might not be seen to come into the city: and a wench went and told them; and they went and told king David. ¹⁸Nevertheless a lad saw them, and told Absalom: but they went both of them away quickly, and came to a man's house in Bahurim, which had a well in his court; whither they went down. ¹⁹And the woman took and spread a covering over the well's mouth, and spread ground corn thereon; and the thing was not known. ²⁰And when Absalom's servants came to the woman to the house, they said, Where *is* Ahimaaz and Jonathan? And the woman said unto them, They be gone over the brook of water. And when they had sought and could not find *them*, they returned to Jerusalem. ²¹And it came to pass, after they were departed, that they came up out of the well, and went and

told king David, and said unto David, Arise, and pass quickly over the water: for thus hath Ahithophel counselled against you.

²²Then David arose, and all the people that *were* with him, and they passed over Jordan: by the morning light there lacked not one of them that was not gone over Jordan. ²³And when Ahithophel saw that his counsel was not followed[g], he saddled *his* ass, and arose, and gat him home to his house, to his city, and put his household in order, and hanged himself, and died, and was buried in the sepulchre of his father. ²⁴Then David came to Mahanaim. And Absalom passed over Jordan, he and all the men of Israel with him. ²⁵And Absalom made Amasa captain of the host instead of Joab: which Amasa *was* a man's son, whose name *was* Ithra an Israelite, that went in to Abigail the daughter of Nahash, sister to Zeruiah Joab's mother. ²⁶So Israel and Absalom pitched in the land of Gilead. ²⁷And it came to pass, when David was come to Mahanaim, that Shobi the son of Nahash of Rabbah of the children of Ammon, and Machir the son of Ammiel of Lodebar, and Barzillai the Gileadite of Rogelim, ²⁸Brought beds, and basons[h], and earthen vessels, and wheat, and barley, and flour, and parched *corn*, and beans, and lentiles, and parched *pulse*, ²⁹And honey, and butter, and sheep, and cheese of kine, for David, and for the people that *were* with him, to eat: for they said,

---

[f] appointed: Heb. commanded
[g] followed: Heb. done
[h] basons: or, cups

The people *is* hungry, and weary, and thirsty, in the wilderness.

18

¹And David numbered the people that *were* with him, and set captains of thousands and captains of hundreds over them. ²And David sent forth a third part of the people under the hand of Joab, and a third part under the hand of Abishai the son of Zeruiah, Joab's brother, and a third part under the hand of Ittai the Gittite. And the king said unto the people, I will surely go forth with you myself also. ³But the people answered, Thou shalt not go forth: for if we flee away, they will not care[a] for us; neither if half of us die, will they care for us: but now *thou art* worth

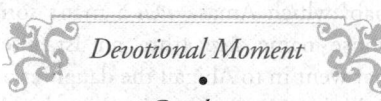

Devotional Moment
•
Gentleness

18:5 David knew firsthand how much damage swords and spears could do. This day his troops would be hunting Absalom, and David urged them to behave unlike soldiers—to deal gently with him. To be gentle with friends is a challenge—with enemies, entirely unnatural. In our world, gentleness can be mistaken for weakness. No company president is hired because of an impressive ability to be gentle. In many lines of work—such as advertising, journalism, politics, sales, and law—gentleness is a ticket to nowhere. Christian parents stand out when they live and breathe the gentle spirit of Christ with children. Children who receive such care pass it around—on the playground and at the lunch table—and become a source of God's comfort in a knock-down world.

ten thousand of us: therefore now *it is* better that thou succour us out of the city. ⁴And the king said unto them, What seemeth you best I will do. And the king stood by the gate side, and all the people came out by hundreds and by thousands. ⁵And the king commanded Joab and Abishai and Ittai, saying, *Deal* gently for my sake with the young man, *even* with Absalom. And all the people heard when the king gave all the captains charge concerning Absalom. ⁶So the people went out into the field against Israel: and the battle was in the wood of Ephraim; ⁷Where the people of Israel were slain before the servants of David, and there was there a great slaughter that day of twenty thousand *men.* ⁸For the battle was there scattered over the face of all the country: and the wood devoured[b] more people that day than the sword devoured.

⁹And Absalom met the servants of David. And Absalom rode upon a mule, and the mule went under the thick boughs of a great oak, and his head caught hold of the oak, and he was taken up between the heaven and the earth; and the mule that *was* under him went away. ¹⁰And a certain man saw *it*, and told Joab, and said, Behold, I saw Absalom hanged in an oak. ¹¹And Joab said unto the man that told him, And, behold, thou sawest *him*, and why didst thou not smite him there to the ground? and I would have given thee ten *shekels* of silver, and a girdle. ¹²And the man said unto Joab, Though I should receive[c] a thousand *shekels* of sil-

---

[a] care . . . : Heb. set their heart on us
[b] devoured: Heb. multiplied to devour
[c] receive: Heb. weigh upon mine hand

ver in mine hand, *yet* would I not put forth mine hand against the king's son: for in our hearing the king charged thee and Abishai and Ittai, saying, Beware that none *touch* the young man Absalom. ¹³Otherwise I should have wrought falsehood against mine own life: for there is no matter hid from the king, and thou thyself wouldest have set thyself against *me*. ¹⁴Then said Joab, I may not tarry thus with thee. And he took three darts in his hand, and thrust them through the heart of Absalom, while he *was* yet alive in the midst of the oak. ¹⁵And ten young men that bare Joab's armour compassed about and smote Absalom, and slew him. ¹⁶And Joab blew the trumpet, and the people returned from pursuing after Israel: for Joab held back the people. ¹⁷And they took Absalom, and cast him into a great pit in the wood, and laid a very great heap of stones upon him: and all Israel fled every one to his tent. ¹⁸Now Absalom in his lifetime had taken and reared up for himself a pillar, which *is* in the king's dale: for he said, I have no son to keep my name in remembrance: and he called the pillar after his own name: and it is called unto this day, Absalom's place.

¹⁹Then said Ahimaaz the son of Zadok, Let me now run, and bear the king tidings, how that the LORD hath avenged[d] him of his enemies. ²⁰And Joab said unto him, Thou shalt not bear tidings this day, but thou shalt bear tidings another day: but this day thou shalt bear no tidings, because the king's son is dead. ²¹Then

said Joab to Cushi, Go tell the king what thou hast seen. And Cushi bowed himself unto Joab, and ran. ²²Then said Ahimaaz the son of Zadok yet again to Joab, But howsoever[e], let me, I pray thee, also run after Cushi. And Joab said, Wherefore wilt thou run, my son, seeing that thou hast no tidings ready? ²³But howsoever, *said he,* let me run. And he said unto him, Run. Then Ahimaaz ran by the way of the plain, and overran Cushi. ²⁴And David sat between the two gates: and the watchman went up to the roof over the gate unto the wall, and lifted up his eyes, and looked, and behold a man running alone. ²⁵And the watchman cried, and told the king. And the king said, If he *be* alone, *there is* tidings in his mouth. And he came apace, and drew near. ²⁶And the watchman saw another man running: and the watchman called unto the porter, and said, Behold *another* man running alone. And the king said, He also bringeth tidings. ²⁷And the watchman said, Me thinketh the running of the foremost is like the running of Ahimaaz the son of Zadok. And the king said, He *is* a good man, and cometh with good tidings. ²⁸And Ahimaaz called, and said unto the king, All is well. And he fell down to the earth upon his face before the king, and said, Blessed *be* the LORD thy God, which hath delivered up the men that lifted up their hand against my lord the king. ²⁹And the king said, Is the young man Absalom safe? And Ahimaaz answered, When Joab sent

---

[d] avenged . . . : Heb. judged him from the hand, etc
[e] howsoever: Heb. be what may

the king's servant, and *me* thy servant, I saw a great tumult, but I knew not what *it was.* ³⁰And the king said *unto him,* Turn aside, *and* stand here. And he turned aside, and stood still. ³¹And, behold, Cushi came; and Cushi said, Tidings[f], my lord the king: for the LORD hath avenged thee this day of all them that rose up against thee. ³²And the king said unto Cushi, Is the young man Absalom safe? And Cushi answered, The enemies of my lord the king, and all that rise against thee to do *thee* hurt, be as *that* young man *is.* ³³And the king was much moved, and went up to the chamber over the gate, and wept: and as he went, thus he said, O my son Absalom, my son, my

---

Devotional Moment

Disappointment

18:33 Perhaps David had hoped his son would be a great king once he settled down and matured—once he accepted the reality that the stars in the sky did not dance at the sound of his name. Absalom needed time, grooming, and perspective. And then . . . but "then" never came. Absalom was killed. David was deeply grieved.

Not all children graduate at the top of the class, play first string, or get into law school. Sometimes the family business must be sold for lack of capable heirs. Sometimes the womb is empty when the heart is full. Disappointment. Life should have been better. When your sky turns gray and your zest for tomorrow vanishes, and when disappointment saps your strength, remember that God promises rest to the weary and joy to all the sorrowing (Jer. 31:25). You can trust him with your tears.

---

son Absalom! would God I had died for thee, O Absalom, my son, my son!

19

¹And it was told Joab, Behold, the king weepeth and mourneth for Absalom. ²And the victory[a] that day was *turned* into mourning unto all the people: for the people heard say that day how the king was grieved for his son. ³And the people gat them by stealth that day into the city, as people being ashamed steal away when they flee in battle. ⁴But the king covered his face, and the king cried with a loud voice, O my son Absalom, O Absalom, my son, my son! ⁵And Joab came into the house to the king, and said, Thou hast shamed this day the faces of all thy servants, which this day have saved thy life, and the lives of thy sons and of thy daughters, and the lives of thy wives, and the lives of thy concubines; ⁶In that thou lovest thine enemies, and hatest thy friends. For thou hast declared this day, that thou regardest neither princes nor servants: for this day I perceive, that if Absalom had lived, and all we had died this day, then it had pleased thee well. ⁷Now therefore arise, go forth, and speak comfortably[b] unto thy servants: for I swear by the LORD, if thou go not forth, there will not tarry one with thee this night: and that will be worse unto thee than all the evil that befell thee from thy youth until now. ⁸Then the king arose, and sat in the gate. And they told unto all the people, saying, Behold, the king doth sit in the gate.

---

[f] Tidings: Heb. Tidings is brought
[a] victory: Heb. salvation, or, deliverance
[b] comfortably . . . : Heb. to the heart of thy servants

And all the people came before the king: for Israel had fled every man to his tent.

⁹And all the people were at strife throughout all the tribes of Israel, saying, The king saved us out of the hand of our enemies, and he delivered us out of the hand of the Philistines; and now he is fled out of the land for Absalom. ¹⁰And Absalom, whom we anointed over us, is dead in battle. Now therefore why speakᶜ ye not a word of bringing the king back? ¹¹And king David sent to Zadok and to Abiathar the priests, saying, Speak unto the elders of Judah, saying, Why are ye the last to bring the king back to his house? seeing the speech of all Israel is come to the king, *even* to his house. ¹²Ye *are* my brethren, ye *are* my bones and my flesh: wherefore then are ye the last to bring back the king? ¹³And say ye to Amasa, *Art* thou not of my bone, and of my flesh? God do so to me, and more also, if thou be not captain of the host before me continually in the room of Joab. ¹⁴And he bowed the heart of all the men of Judah, even as *the heart of* one man; so that they sent *this word* unto the king, Return thou, and all thy servants. ¹⁵So the king returned, and came to Jordan. And Judah came to Gilgal, to go to meet the king, to conduct the king over Jordan.

¹⁶And Shimei the son of Gera, a Benjamite, which *was* of Bahurim, hasted and came down with the men of Judah to meet king David. ¹⁷And *there were* a thousand men of Benjamin with him, and Ziba the servant of the house of Saul, and his fifteen sons and his twenty servants with him; and they went over Jordan before the king. ¹⁸And there went over a ferry boat to carry over the king's household, and to do what he thought good. And Shimei the son of Gera fell down before the king, as he was come over Jordan; ¹⁹And said unto the king, Let not my lord impute iniquity unto me, neither do thou remember that which thy servant did perversely the day that my lord the king went out of Jerusalem, that the king should take it to his heart. ²⁰For thy servant doth know that I have sinned: therefore, behold, I am come the first this day of all the house of Joseph to go down to meet my lord the king. ²¹But Abishai the son of Zeruiah answered and said, Shall not Shimei be put to death for this, because he cursed the LORD'S anointed? ²²And David said, What have I to do with you, ye sons of Zeruiah, that ye should this day be adversaries unto me? shall there any man be put to death this day in Israel? for do not I know that I *am* this day king over Israel? ²³Therefore the king said unto Shimei, Thou shalt not die. And the king sware unto him.

²⁴And Mephibosheth the son of Saul came down to meet the king, and had neither dressed his feet, nor trimmed his beard, nor washed his clothes, from the day the king departed until the day he came *again* in peace. ²⁵And it came to pass, when he was come to Jerusalem to meet the king, that the king said unto him, Wherefore wentest not thou with me, Mephibosheth? ²⁶And he answered, My lord, O king, my servant deceived me: for thy

---

ᶜ speak . . . : Heb. are ye silent?

servant said, I will saddle me an ass, that I may ride thereon, and go to the king; because thy servant *is* lame. ²⁷And he hath slandered thy servant unto my lord the king; but my lord the king *is* as an angel of God: do therefore *what is* good in thine eyes. ²⁸For all *of* my father's house were but dead^d men before my lord the king: yet didst thou set thy servant among them that did eat at thine own table. What right therefore have I yet to cry any more unto the king? ²⁹And the king said unto him, Why speakest thou any more of thy matters? I have said, Thou and Ziba divide the land. ³⁰And Mephibosheth said unto the king, Yea, let him take all, forasmuch as my lord the king is come again in peace unto his own house.

³¹And Barzillai the Gileadite came down from Rogelim, and went over Jordan with the king, to conduct him over Jordan. ³²Now Barzillai was a very aged man, *even* fourscore years old: and he had provided the king of sustenance while he lay at Mahanaim; for he *was* a very great man. ³³And the king said unto Barzillai, Come thou over with me, and I will feed thee with me in Jerusalem. ³⁴And Barzillai said unto the king, How long have I to live, that I should go up with the king unto Jerusalem? ³⁵I *am* this day fourscore years old: *and* can I discern between good and evil? can thy servant taste what I eat or what I drink? can I hear any more the voice of singing men and singing women? wherefore then should thy servant be yet a burden unto my lord the king? ³⁶Thy servant will go a little way over Jordan with the king: and why should the king recompense it me with such a reward? ³⁷Let thy servant, I pray thee, turn back again, that I may die in mine own city, *and be buried* by the grave of my father and of my mother. But behold thy servant Chimham; let him go over with my lord the king; and do to him what shall seem good unto thee. ³⁸And the king answered, Chimham shall go over with me, and I will do to him that which shall seem good unto thee: and whatsoever thou shalt require^e of me, *that* will I do for thee. ³⁹And all the people went over Jordan. And when the king was come over, the king kissed Barzillai, and blessed him; and he returned unto his own place.

⁴⁰Then the king went on to Gilgal, and Chimham^f went on with him: and all the people of Judah conducted the king, and also half the people of Israel. ⁴¹And, behold, all the men of Israel came to the king, and said unto the king, Why have our brethren the men of Judah stolen thee away, and have brought the king, and his household, and all David's men with him, over Jordan? ⁴²And all the men of Judah answered the men of Israel, Because the king *is* near of kin to us: wherefore then be ye angry for this matter? have we eaten at all of the king's *cost?* or hath he given us any gift? ⁴³And the men of Israel answered the men of Judah, and said, We have ten parts in the king, and we have also more *right* in David than

---

^d dead . . . : Heb. men of death
^e require: Heb. choose
^f Chimham: Heb. Chimhan

ye: why then did ye despise[g] us, that our advice should not be first had in bringing back our king? And the words of the men of Judah were fiercer than the words of the men of Israel.

20

¹And there happened to be there a man of Belial, whose name *was* Sheba, the son of Bichri, a Benjamite: and he blew a trumpet, and said, We have no part in David, neither have we inheritance in the son of Jesse: every man to his tents, O Israel. ²So every man of Israel went up from after David, *and* followed Sheba the son of Bichri: but the men of Judah clave unto their king, from Jordan even to Jerusalem. ³And David came to his house at Jerusalem; and the king took the ten women *his* concu-

---

Devotional Moment

•

Sensitivity

20:3 Perhaps these ten women had become Absalom's wives; perhaps they had been disloyal to David in some other way. We don't really know. If we assume they were loyal to David and not part of Sheba's treachery, David's action seems insensitive. For his pleasure they had given up marriage and family in the normal way. Yet David treated them as if they were unworthy of his company. To cut someone off without explanation or appeal is a terrible thing. For the victim, it's like the amputation of a healthy limb. In every bond, consider the others' feelings before taking the "right" course of action. Treat them tenderly.

---

bines, whom he had left to keep the house, and put them in ward[a], and fed them, but went not in unto them. So they were shut up unto the day of their death, living in widowhood.

⁴Then said the king to Amasa, Assemble[b] me the men of Judah within three days, and be thou here present. ⁵So Amasa went to assemble *the men of Judah*: but he tarried longer than the set time which he had appointed him. ⁶And David said to Abishai, Now shall Sheba the son of Bichri do us more harm than *did* Absalom: take thou thy lord's servants, and pursue after him, lest he get him fenced cities, and escape[c] us. ⁷And there went out after him Joab's men, and the Cherethites, and the Pelethites, and all the mighty men: and they went out of Jerusalem, to pursue after Sheba the son of Bichri. ⁸When they *were* at the great stone which *is* in Gibeon, Amasa went before them. And Joab's garment that he had put on was girded unto him, and upon it a girdle *with* a sword fastened upon his loins in the sheath thereof; and as he went forth it fell out. ⁹And Joab said to Amasa, *Art* thou in health, my brother? And Joab took Amasa by the beard with the right hand to kiss him. ¹⁰But Amasa took no heed to the sword that *was* in Joab's hand: so he smote him therewith in the fifth *rib*, and shed out his bowels to the ground, and struck[d] him not again; and he died. So Joab and Abishai his brother pursued after Sheba the son of

---

[g] despise . . . : Heb. set us at light
[a] ward: Heb. an house of ward
[b] Assemble: Heb. Call
[c] escape . . . : Heb. deliver himself from our eyes
[d] struck . . . : Heb. doubled not his stroke

Bichri. ¹¹And one of Joab's men stood by him, and said, He that favoureth Joab, and he that *is* for David, *let him go* after Joab. ¹²And Amasa wallowed in blood in the midst of the highway. And when the man saw that all the people stood still, he removed Amasa out of the highway into the field, and cast a cloth upon him, when he saw that every one that came by him stood still. ¹³When he was removed out of the highway, all the people went on after Joab, to pursue after Sheba the son of Bichri.

¹⁴And he went through all the tribes of Israel unto Abel, and to Beth-maachah, and all the Berites: and they were gathered together, and went also after him. ¹⁵And they came and besieged him in Abel of Bethmaachah, and they cast up a bank against the city, and it stood in the trench°: and all the people that *were* with Joab battered the wall, to throw it down. ¹⁶Then cried a wise woman out of the city, Hear, hear; say, I pray you, unto Joab, Come near hither, that I may speak with thee. ¹⁷And when he was come near unto her, the woman said, *Art* thou Joab? And he answered, I *am he.* Then she said unto him, Hear the words of thine handmaid. And he answered, I do hear. ¹⁸Then she spake, saying, They were wont to speak in old time, saying, They shall surely ask *counsel* at Abel: and so they ended *the matter.* ¹⁹I *am one of them that are* peaceable *and* faithful in

Israel: thou seekest to destroy a city and a mother in Israel: why wilt thou swallow up the inheritance of the LORD? ²⁰And Joab answered and said, Far be it, far be it from me, that I should swallow up or destroy. ²¹The matter *is* not so: but a man of mount Ephraim, Sheba the son of Bichri by nameᶠ, hath lifted up his hand against the king, *even* against David: deliver him only, and I will depart from the city. And the woman said unto Joab, Behold, his head shall be thrown to thee over the wall. ²²Then the woman went unto all the people in her wisdom. And they cut off the head of Sheba the son of Bichri, and cast *it* out to Joab. And he blew a trumpet, and they retiredᵍ from the city, every man to his tent. And Joab returned to Jerusalem unto the king.

²³Now Joab *was* over all the host of Israel: and Benaiah the son of Jehoiada *was* over the Cherethites and over the Pelethites: ²⁴And Adoram *was* over the tribute: and Jehoshaphat the son of Ahilud *was* recorderʰ: ²⁵And Sheva *was* scribe: and Zadok and Abiathar *were* the priests: ²⁶And Ira also the Jairite was a chief ruler about David.

21

¹Then there was a famine in the days of David three years, year after year; and David enquiredᵃ of the LORD. And the LORD answered, It *is* for Saul, and for *his* bloody house, because he slew the Gibeonites. ²And the king called the

---

° in the trench: or, against the outmost wall
ᶠ by name: Heb. by his name
ᵍ retired: Heb. were scattered
ʰ recorder: or, remembrancer
ᵃ enquired . . . : Heb. sought the face, etc

Gibeonites, and said unto them; (now the Gibeonites *were* not of the children of Israel, but of the remnant of the Amorites; and the children of Israel had sworn unto them: and Saul sought to slay them in his zeal to the children of Israel and Judah.) ³Wherefore David said unto the Gibeonites, What shall I do for you? and wherewith shall I make the atonement, that ye may bless the inheritance of the LORD? ⁴And the Gibeonites said unto him, We will have no silver nor gold of Saul, nor of his house; neither for us shalt thou kill any man in Israel. And he said, What ye shall say, *that* will I do for you. ⁵And they answered the king, The man that consumed us, and that devisedᵇ against us *that* we should be destroyed from remaining in any of the coasts of Israel, ⁶Let seven men of his sons be delivered unto us, and we will hang them up unto the LORD in Gibeah of Saul, *whom* the LORD did choose. And the king said, I will give *them.* ⁷But the king spared Mephibosheth, the son of Jonathan the son of Saul, because of the LORD'S oath that *was* between them, between David and Jonathan the son of Saul. ⁸But the king took the two sons of Rizpah the daughter of Aiah, whom she bare unto Saul, Armoni and Mephibosheth; and the five sons of Michalᶜ the daughter of Saul, whom she brought up for Adriel the son of Barzillai the Meholathite: ⁹And he delivered them into the hands of the Gibeonites, and they hanged them in the hill before the LORD: and they fell *all* seven together,

and were put to death in the days of harvest, in the first *days*, in the beginning of barley harvest. ¹⁰And Rizpah the daughter of Aiah took sackcloth, and spread it for her upon the rock, from the beginning of harvest until water dropped upon them out of heaven, and suffered neither the birds of the air to rest on them by day, nor the beasts of the field by night. ¹¹And it was told David what Rizpah the daughter of Aiah, the concubine of Saul, had done. ¹²And David went and took the bones of Saul and the bones of Jonathan his son from the men of Jabeshgilead, which had stolen them from the street of Bethshan, where the Philistines had hanged them, when the Philistines had slain Saul in Gilboa: ¹³And he brought up from thence the bones of Saul and the bones of Jonathan his son; and they gathered the bones of them that were hanged. ¹⁴And the bones of Saul and Jonathan his son buried they in the country of Benjamin in Zelah, in the sepulchre of Kish his father: and they performed all that the king commanded. And after that God was intreated for the land.

¹⁵Moreover the Philistines had yet war again with Israel; and David went down, and his servants with him, and fought against the Philistines: and David waxed faint. ¹⁶And Ishbibenob, which *was* of the sons of the giantᵈ, the weight of whose spear *weighed* three hundred *shekels* of brass in weight, he

---

ᵇ devised . . . : or, cut us off
ᶜ Michal: or, the sister of Michal
ᵈ the giant: or, Rapha

being girded with a new *sword*, thought to have slain David. [17]But Abishai the son of Zeruiah succoured him, and smote the Philistine, and killed him. Then the men of David sware unto him, saying, Thou shalt go no more out with us to battle, that thou quench not the light[e] of Israel. [18]And it came to pass after this, that there was again a battle with the Philistines at Gob: then Sibbechai the Hushathite slew Saph, which *was* of the sons of the giant[f]. [19]And there was again a battle in Gob with the Philistines, where Elhanan the son of Jaareoregim[g], a Bethlehemite, slew *the brother of* Goliath the Gittite, the staff of whose spear *was* like a weaver's beam. [20]And there was yet a battle in Gath, where was a man of *great* stature, that had on every hand six fingers, and on every foot six toes, four and twenty in number; and he also was born to the giant[h]. [21]And when he defied[i] Israel, Jonathan the son of Shimea the brother of David slew him. [22]These four were born to the giant in Gath, and fell by the hand of David, and by the hand of his servants.

22

[1]And David spake unto the LORD the words of this song in the day *that* the LORD had delivered him out of the hand of all his enemies, and out of the hand of Saul:

[2]And he said, The LORD *is* my rock, and my fortress, and my deliverer; [3]The God of my rock; in him will I trust: *he is* my shield, and the horn of my salvation, my high tower, and my refuge, my saviour; thou savest me from violence. [4]I will call on the LORD, *who is* worthy to be praised: so shall I be saved from mine enemies. [5]When the waves[a] of death compassed me, the floods of ungodly men made me afraid; [6]The sorrows[b] of hell compassed me about; the snares of death prevented me; [7]In my distress I called upon the LORD, and cried to my God: and he did hear my voice out of his temple, and my cry *did enter* into his ears. [8]Then the earth shook and trembled; the foundations of heaven moved and shook, because he was wroth. [9]There went up a smoke out of his nostrils[c], and fire out of his mouth devoured: coals were kindled by it. [10]He bowed the heavens also, and came down; and darkness *was* under his feet. [11]And he rode upon a cherub, and did fly: and he was seen upon the wings of the wind. [12]And he made darkness pavilions round about him, dark[d] waters, *and* thick clouds of the skies. [13]Through the brightness before him were coals of fire

---

[e] light: Heb. candle, or, lamp
[f] the giant: or, Rapha
[g] Jaareoregim: or, Jair
[h] the giant: or, Rapha
[i] defied: or, reproached
[a] waves: or, pangs
[b] sorrows: or, cords
[c] out of his nostrils: Heb. by, etc
[d] dark . . . : Heb. binding of waters

kindled. [14]The LORD thundered from heaven, and the most High uttered his voice. [15]And he sent out arrows, and scattered them; lightning, and discomfited them. [16]And the channels of the sea appeared, the foundations of the world were discovered, at the rebuking of the LORD, at the blast of the breath of his nostrils. [17]He sent from above, he took me; he drew me out of many[e] waters; [18]He delivered me from my strong enemy, *and* from them that hated me: for they were too strong for me. [19]They prevented me in the day of my calamity: but the LORD was my stay. [20]He brought me forth also into a large place: he delivered me, because he delighted in me. [21]The LORD rewarded me according to my righteousness: according to the cleanness of my hands hath he recompensed me. [22]For I have kept the ways of the LORD, and have not wickedly departed from my God. [23]For all his judgments *were* before me: and *as for* his statutes, I did not depart from them. [24]I was also upright before him, and have kept myself from mine iniquity. [25]Therefore the LORD hath recompensed me according to my righteousness; according to my cleanness in his eye sight. [26]With the merciful thou wilt shew thyself merciful, *and* with the upright man thou wilt shew thyself upright. [27]With the pure thou wilt shew thyself pure; and with the froward thou wilt shew thyself unsavoury[f]. [28]And the afflicted people thou wilt save: but thine eyes *are* upon the haughty, *that* thou mayest bring *them* down. [29]For thou *art* my lamp[g], O LORD: and the LORD will lighten my darkness. [30]For by thee I have run[h] through a troop: by my God have I leaped over a wall. [31]*As for* God, his way *is* perfect; the word of the LORD *is* tried[i]: he *is* a buckler to all them that trust in him. [32]For who *is* God, save the LORD? and who *is* a rock, save our God? [33]God *is* my strength *and* power: and he maketh[j] my way perfect. [34]He maketh[k] my feet like hinds' *feet*: and setteth me upon my high places. [35]He teacheth my hands to war[l]; so that a bow of steel is broken by mine arms. [36]Thou hast also given me the shield of thy salvation: and thy gentleness hath made me great. [37]Thou hast enlarged my steps under me; so that my feet[m] did not slip. [38]I have pursued mine enemies, and destroyed them; and turned not again until I had consumed them. [39]And I have consumed them, and wounded them, that they could not arise: yea, they are fallen under my feet. [40]For thou hast girded me with strength to battle: them that rose up against me

---

[e] many: or, great
[f] shew thyself unsavoury: or, wrestle
[g] lamp: or, candle
[h] run: or, broken
[i] tried: or, refined
[j] maketh: Heb. riddeth, or, looseth
[k] maketh: Heb. equalleth
[l] to war: Heb. for the war
[m] feet: Heb. ankles

hast thou subdued[n] under me. [41]Thou hast also given me the necks of mine enemies, that I might destroy them that hate me. [42]They looked, but *there was* none to save; *even* unto the LORD, but he answered them not. [43]Then did I beat them as small as the dust of the earth, I did stamp them as the mire of the street, *and* did spread them abroad. [44]Thou also hast delivered me from the strivings of my people, thou hast kept me *to be* head of the heathen: a people *which* I knew not shall serve me. [45]Strangers[o] shall submit themselves unto me: as soon as they hear, they shall be obedient unto me. [46]Strangers shall fade away, and they shall be afraid out of their close places. [47]The LORD liveth; and blessed *be* my rock; and exalted be the God of the rock of my salvation. [48]It *is* God that avengeth[p] me, and that bringeth down the people under me, [49]And that bringeth me forth from mine enemies: thou also hast lifted me up on high above them that rose up against me: thou hast delivered me from the violent man. [50]Therefore I will give thanks unto thee, O LORD, among the heathen, and I will sing praises unto thy name. [51]*He is* the tower of salvation for his king: and sheweth mercy to his anointed, unto David, and to his seed for evermore.

23

[1]Now these *be* the last words of David. David the son of Jesse said, and the man *who was* raised up on high, the anointed of the God of Jacob, and the sweet psalmist of Israel, said, [2]The Spirit of the LORD spake by me, and his word *was* in my tongue. [3]The God of Israel said, the Rock of Israel spake to me, He that ruleth over men *must be* just, ruling in the fear of God. [4]And *he shall be* as the light of the morning, *when* the sun riseth, *even* a morning without clouds; *as* the tender grass *springing* out of the earth by clear shining after rain. [5]Although my house *be* not so with God; yet he hath made with me an everlasting covenant, ordered in all *things*, and sure: for *this is* all my salvation, and all *my* desire, although he make *it* not to grow. [6]But *the sons* of Belial *shall be* all of them as thorns thrust away, because they cannot be taken with hands: [7]But the man *that* shall touch them must be fenced[a] with iron and the staff of a spear; and they shall be utterly burned with fire in the *same* place.

[8]These *be* the names of the mighty men whom David had: The Tachmonite[b] that sat in the seat, chief among the captains; the same *was* Adino the Eznite: *he lift up his spear* against eight hundred, whom he slew at one time. [9]And after him *was* Eleazar the son of Dodo the Ahohite, *one* of the three mighty men with David, when they defied the Philistines *that* were there gathered together to battle, and the men of Israel were gone away: [10]He

---

[n] subdued: Heb. caused to bow
[o] Strangers: Heb. Sons of the stranger
[p] avengeth: Heb. giveth avengement for
[a] fenced: Heb. filled
[b] The Tachmonite . . . : or, Joshebbassebet the Tachmonite, head of the three

arose, and smote the Philistines until his hand was weary, and his hand clave unto the sword: and the LORD wrought a great victory that day; and the people returned after him only to spoil. ¹¹And after him *was* Shammah the son of Agee the Hararite. And the Philistines were gathered together into a troop, where was a piece of ground full of lentiles: and the people fled from the Philistines. ¹²But he stood in the midst of the ground, and defended it, and slew the Philistines: and the LORD wrought a great victory. ¹³And three^c of the thirty chief went down, and came to David in the harvest time unto the cave of Adullam: and the troop of the Philistines pitched in the valley of Rephaim. ¹⁴And David *was* then in an hold, and the garrison of the Philistines *was* then *in* Bethlehem. ¹⁵And David longed, and said, Oh that one would give me drink of the water of the well of Bethlehem, which *is* by the gate! ¹⁶And the three mighty men brake through the host of the Philistines, and drew water out of the well of Bethlehem, that *was* by the gate, and took *it,* and brought *it* to David: nevertheless he would not drink thereof, but poured it out unto the LORD. ¹⁷And he said, Be it far from me, O LORD, that I should do this: *is not this* the blood of the men that went in jeopardy of their lives? therefore he would not drink it. These things did these three mighty men. ¹⁸And Abishai, the brother of Joab, the son of Zeruiah, was chief among three. And he lifted up his spear against three

hundred, *and* slew *them,* and had the name among three. ¹⁹Was he not most honourable of three? therefore he was their captain: howbeit he attained not unto the *first* three. ²⁰And Benaiah the son of Jehoiada, the son of a valiant man, of Kabzeel, who had done many acts, he slew two lionlike men of Moab: he went down also and slew a lion in the midst of a pit in time of snow: ²¹And he slew an Egyptian, a goodly^d man: and the Egyptian had a spear in his hand; but he went down to him with a staff, and plucked the spear out of the Egyptian's hand, and slew him with his own spear. ²²These *things* did Benaiah the son of Jehoiada, and had the name among three mighty men. ²³He was more honourable than the thirty, but he attained not to the *first* three. And David set him over his guard. ²⁴Asahel the brother of Joab *was* one of the thirty; Elhanan the son of Dodo of Bethlehem, ²⁵Shammah the Harodite, Elika the Harodite, ²⁶Helez the Paltite, Ira the son of Ikkesh the Tekoite, ²⁷Abiezer the Anethothite, Mebunnai the Hushathite, ²⁸Zalmon the Ahohite, Maharai the Netophathite, ²⁹Heleb the son of Baanah, a Netophathite, Ittai the son of Ribai out of Gibeah of the children of Benjamin, ³⁰Benaiah the Pirathonite, Hiddai of the brooks^e of Gaash, ³¹Abialbon the Arbathite, Azmaveth the Barhumite, ³²Eliahba the Shaalbonite, of the sons of Jashen, Jonathan, ³³Shammah the Hararite, Ahiam the son of Sharar the Hararite, ³⁴Eliphelet the son of Ahasbai,

---

^c three . . . : or, the three captains over the thirty
^d a goodly . . . : Heb. a man of countenance, or, sight: also called, a man of great stature
^e brooks: or, valleys

the son of the Maachathite, Eliam the son of Ahithophel the Gilonite, ³⁵Hezrai the Carmelite, Paarai the Arbite, ³⁶Igal the son of Nathan of Zobah, Bani the Gadite, ³⁷Zelek the Ammonite, Naharai the Beerothite, armourbearer to Joab the son of Zeruiah, ³⁸Ira an Ithrite, Gareb an Ithrite, ³⁹Uriah the Hittite: thirty and seven in all.

24

¹And again the anger of the LORD was kindled against Israel, and he moved David against them to say, Go, number Israel and Judah. ²For the king said to Joab the captain of the host, which *was* with him, Go now through all the tribes of Israel, from Dan even to Beersheba, and number ye the people, that I may know the number of the people. ³And Joab said unto the king, Now the LORD thy God add unto the people, how many soever they be, an hundred-

Devotional Moment

•

Status

24:2-4 What would you count when trying to measure your prestige? David counted soldiers. If you're hungry for status, chances are good that numbers have become an important measure by which you take stock of yourself: your salary, your grade-point average, your brokerage account, your square footage, your gold-card ceiling, your children's tuition. These are games that obscure God's claim on our lives. Make an effort to look beyond the status symbols that you feel tempted to count and compare. Then dedicate those things to God and to his service—and avoid comparisons with others.

fold, and that the eyes of my lord the king may see *it:* but why doth my lord the king delight in this thing? ⁴Notwithstanding the king's word prevailed against Joab, and against the captains of the host. And Joab and the captains of the host went out from the presence of the king, to number the people of Israel. ⁵And they passed over Jordan, and pitched in Aroer, on the right side of the city that *lieth* in the midst of the riverᵃ of Gad, and toward Jazer: ⁶Then they came to Gilead, and to the land of Tahtimhodshiᵇ; and they came to Danjaan, and about to Zidon, ⁷And came to the strong hold of Tyre, and to all the cities of the Hivites, and of the Canaanites: and they went out to the south of Judah, *even* to Beersheba. ⁸So when they had gone through all the land, they came to Jerusalem at the end of nine months and twenty days. ⁹And Joab gave up the sum of the number of the people unto the king: and there were in Israel eight hundred thousand valiant men that drew the sword; and the men of Judah *were* five hundred thousand men.

¹⁰And David's heart smote him after that he had numbered the people. And David said unto the LORD, I have sinned greatly in that I have done: and now, I beseech thee, O LORD, take away the iniquity of thy servant; for I have done very foolishly. ¹¹For when David was up in the morning, the word of the LORD came unto the prophet Gad, David's seer, saying, ¹²Go and say unto David, Thus saith the LORD, I offer thee three *things;* choose thee one

---

ᵃ river: or, valley
ᵇ land of Tahtimhodshi: or, nether land newly inhabited

of them, that I may *do it* unto thee. [13]So Gad came to David, and told him, and said unto him, Shall seven years of famine come unto thee in thy land? or wilt thou flee three months before thine enemies, while they pursue thee? or that there be three days' pestilence in thy land? now advise, and see what answer I shall return to him that sent me. [14]And David said unto Gad, I am in a great strait: let us fall now into the hand of the LORD; for his mercies *are* great: and let me not fall into the hand of man. [15]So the LORD sent a pestilence upon Israel from the morning even to the time appointed: and there died of the people from Dan even to Beersheba seventy thousand men. [16]And when the angel stretched out his hand upon Jerusalem to destroy it, the LORD repented him of the evil, and said to the angel that destroyed the people, It is enough: stay now thine hand. And the angel of the LORD was by the threshingplace of Araunah[c] the Jebusite. [17]And David spake unto the LORD when he saw the angel that smote the people, and said, Lo, I have sinned, and I have done wickedly: but these sheep, what have they done? let thine hand, I pray thee, be against me, and against my father's house.

[18]And Gad came that day to David, and said unto him, Go up, rear an altar unto the LORD in the threshingfloor of Araunah[d] the Jebusite. [19]And David, according to the saying of Gad, went up as the LORD commanded. [20]And Araunah looked, and saw the king and his servants coming on toward him: and Araunah went out, and bowed himself before the king on his face upon the ground. [21]And Araunah said, Wherefore is my lord the king come to his servant? And David said, To buy the threshingfloor of thee, to build an altar unto the LORD, that the plague may be stayed from the people. [22]And Araunah said unto David, Let my lord the king take and offer up what *seemeth* good unto him: behold, *here be* oxen for burnt sacrifice, and threshing instruments and *other* instruments of the oxen for wood. [23]All these *things* did Araunah, *as* a king, give unto the king. And Araunah said unto the king, The LORD thy God accept thee. [24]And the king said unto Araunah, Nay; but I will surely buy *it* of thee at a price: neither will I offer burnt offerings unto the LORD my God of that which doth cost me nothing. So David bought the threshingfloor and the oxen for fifty shekels of silver. [25]And David built there an altar unto the LORD, and offered burnt offerings and peace offerings. So the LORD was intreated for the land, and the plague was stayed from Israel.

---

[c] Araunah: also called, Ornan
[d] Araunah: Heb. Araniah

FIRST KINGS

Purpose
To contrast the lives of those who live for God and those who refuse to do so through the history of the kings of Israel and Judah

Author
Unknown

Setting
The once-great nation of Israel turns into a land divided, not only physically, but also spiritually.

Key Verses
"And if thou wilt walk before me, as David thy father walked, in integrity of heart, and in uprightness, to do according to all that I have commanded thee . . . then I will establish the throne of thy kingdom upon Israel for ever, as I promised to David thy father, saying 'There shall not fail thee a man upon the throne of Israel.'" (9:4-5)

Key People
David, Solomon, Rehoboam, Jeroboam, Elijah, Ahab, Jezebel

Special Feature
The books of 1 and 2 Kings were originally one book.

How hard it is to give up control. Parents of sixteen-year-old drivers know the feeling. Even walking a five-year-old to kindergarten creates a mix of emotions. Turning over a family business to the next generation is the topic of several books. All such transitions carry considerable risk.

If you happen to be a king, the most successful ever in the history of your nation, and your kids have been squabbling viciously over your kingdom, then you *really* have a problem!

Most parents don't worry about passing kingdoms to heirs or sorting out the rights and privileges of hundreds of children, as David did. On the other hand, the control that Christian parents pass to children does have much to do with the maintenance of the Kingdom of God. Will your children use new resources faithfully? Will the church prosper under their leadership?

The transitions from David to Solomon, then Solomon to his children, were hard times for Israel. As you read, ask: What decisions could have made things easier? What did new leaders do right? wrong? What principles does God reveal during these transitions?

When Israel took its worst turns, God sent prophets. There is comfort in knowing that God cares about all of us—that our mistakes (and our children's) are not the final word. Read on—with heightened hope for a great future!

1

¹Now king David was old *and* stricken[a] in years; and they covered him with clothes, but he gat no heat. ²Wherefore his servants said unto him, Let there be sought for my lord the king a young virgin: and let her stand before the king, and let her cherish him, and let her lie in thy bosom, that my lord the king may get heat. ³So they sought for a fair damsel throughout all the coasts of Israel, and found Abishag a Shunammite, and brought her to the king. ⁴And the damsel *was* very fair, and cherished the king, and ministered to him: but the king knew her not.

⁵Then Adonijah the son of Haggith exalted himself, saying, I will be king[b]: and he prepared him chariots and horsemen, and fifty men to run before him. ⁶And his father had not displeased him at any time in saying, Why hast thou done so? and he also *was a* very goodly *man*; and *his mother* bare him after Absalom. ⁷And he conferred with Joab the son of Zeruiah, and with Abiathar the priest: and they following Adonijah helped *him*. ⁸But Zadok the priest, and Benaiah the son of Jehoiada, and Nathan the prophet, and Shimei, and Rei, and the mighty men which *belonged* to David, were not with Adonijah. ⁹And Adonijah slew sheep and oxen and fat cattle by the stone of Zoheleth, which *is* by Enrogel[c], and called all his brethren the king's sons, and all the men of Judah the king's servants: ¹⁰But Nathan the prophet, and Benaiah, and the mighty men, and Solomon his brother, he called not.

¹¹Wherefore Nathan spake unto Bathsheba the mother of Solomon, saying, Hast thou not heard that Adonijah the son of Haggith doth reign, and David our lord knoweth *it* not? ¹²Now therefore come, let me, I pray thee, give thee counsel, that thou mayest save thine own life, and the life of thy son Solomon. ¹³Go and get thee in unto king David, and say unto him, Didst not thou, my lord, O king, swear unto thine handmaid, saying, Assuredly Solomon thy son shall reign after me, and he shall sit upon my throne? why then doth Adonijah reign? ¹⁴Behold, while thou yet talkest there with the king, I also will come in after thee, and confirm[d] thy words. ¹⁵And Bathsheba

Devotional Moment

Discipline

1:6 Pity the child whose father never gives him any attention or loving discipline. A daughter or son who is given such freedom from fatherly influence will have a hard time learning to deal with the real world of expectations, accountability, and cooperative effort. Adonijah was a prime example. It's a double pity in his case because David had such potential for fatherly greatness. David had courage and faith. He enjoyed celebration. He loved God. But Adonijah apparently never had the chance to soak up his father's passion. Interaction with children not only involves discipline but also guidance and affirmation. Parents who practice these become God's agents for building character and self-discipline in a child's heart.

---

[a] stricken . . . : Heb. entered into days
[b] be king: Heb. reign
[c] Enrogel: or, the well Rogel
[d] confirm: Heb. fill up

went in unto the king into the chamber: and the king was very old; and Abishag the Shunammite ministered unto the king. ¹⁶And Bathsheba bowed, and did obeisance unto the king. And the king said, What wouldest thou? ¹⁷And she said unto him, My lord, thou swarest by the LORD thy God unto thine handmaid, *saying*, Assuredly Solomon thy son shall reign after me, and he shall sit upon my throne. ¹⁸And now, behold, Adonijah reigneth; and now, my lord the king, thou knowest *it* not: ¹⁹And he hath slain oxen and fat cattle and sheep in abundance, and hath called all the sons of the king, and Abiathar the priest, and Joab the captain of the host: but Solomon thy servant hath he not called. ²⁰And thou, my lord, O king, the eyes of all Israel *are* upon thee, that thou shouldest tell them who shall sit on the throne of my lord the king after him. ²¹Otherwise it shall come to pass, when my lord the king shall sleep with his fathers, that I and my son Solomon shall be counted offenders^ᵉ. ²²And, lo, while she yet talked with the king, Nathan the prophet also came in. ²³And they told the king, saying, Behold Nathan the prophet. And when he was come in before the king, he bowed himself before the king with his face to the ground. ²⁴And Nathan said, My lord, O king, hast thou said, Adonijah shall reign after me, and he shall sit upon my throne? ²⁵For he is gone down this day, and hath slain oxen and fat cattle and sheep in abundance, and hath called all the king's sons, and the captains of the host, and Abiathar the priest; and, be-

hold, they eat and drink before him, and say, God save king Adonijah. ²⁶But me, *even* me thy servant, and Zadok the priest, and Benaiah the son of Jehoiada, and thy servant Solomon, hath he not called. ²⁷Is this thing done by my lord the king, and thou hast not shewed *it* unto thy servant, who should sit on the throne of my lord the king after him? ²⁸Then king David answered and said, Call me Bathsheba. And she came into the king's presence, and stood before the king. ²⁹And the king sware, and said, *As* the LORD liveth, that hath redeemed my soul out of all distress, ³⁰Even as I sware unto thee by the LORD God of Israel, saying, Assuredly Solomon thy son shall reign after me, and he shall sit upon my throne in my stead; even so will I certainly do this day. ³¹Then Bathsheba bowed with *her* face to the earth, and did reverence to the king, and said, Let my lord king David live for ever.

³²And king David said, Call me Zadok the priest, and Nathan the prophet, and Benaiah the son of Jehoiada. And they came before the king. ³³The king also said unto them, Take with you the servants of your lord, and cause Solomon my son to ride upon mine own mule, and bring him down to Gihon: ³⁴And let Zadok the priest and Nathan the prophet anoint him there king over Israel: and blow ye with the trumpet, and say, God save king Solomon. ³⁵Then ye shall come up after him, that he may come and sit upon my throne; for he shall be king in my stead: and I have appointed him to be ruler over Israel and over Judah. ³⁶And

---

^ᵉ offenders: Heb. sinners

Benaiah the son of Jehoiada answered the king, and said, Amen: the LORD God of my lord the king say so *too*. ³⁷As the LORD hath been with my lord the king, even so be he with Solomon, and make his throne greater than the throne of my lord king David. ³⁸So Zadok the priest, and Nathan the prophet, and Benaiah the son of Jehoiada, and the Cherethites, and the Pelethites, went down, and caused Solomon to ride upon king David's mule, and brought him to Gihon. ³⁹And Zadok the priest took an horn of oil out of the tabernacle, and anointed Solomon. And they blew the trumpet; and all the people said, God save king Solomon. ⁴⁰And all the people came up after him, and the people piped with pipes*f*, and rejoiced with great joy, so that the earth rent with the sound of them.

⁴¹And Adonijah and all the guests that *were* with him heard *it* as they had made an end of eating. And when Joab heard the sound of the trumpet, he said, Wherefore *is this* noise of the city being in an uproar? ⁴²And while he yet spake, behold, Jonathan the son of Abiathar the priest came: and Adonijah said unto him, Come in; for thou *art* a valiant man, and bringest good tidings. ⁴³And Jonathan answered and said to Adonijah, Verily our lord king David hath made Solomon king. ⁴⁴And the king hath sent with him Zadok the priest, and Nathan the prophet, and Benaiah the son of Jehoiada, and the Cherethites, and the Pelethites, and they have caused him to ride upon the king's mule: ⁴⁵And Zadok the priest and Nathan the prophet have anointed him

king in Gihon: and they are come up from thence rejoicing, so that the city rang again. This *is* the noise that ye have heard. ⁴⁶And also Solomon sitteth on the throne of the kingdom. ⁴⁷And moreover the king's servants came to bless our lord king David, saying, God make the name of Solomon better than thy name, and make his throne greater than thy throne. And the king bowed himself upon the bed. ⁴⁸And also thus said the king, Blessed *be* the LORD God of Israel, which hath given *one* to sit on my throne this day, mine eyes even seeing *it.* ⁴⁹And all the guests that *were* with Adonijah were afraid, and rose up, and went every man his way. ⁵⁰And Adonijah feared because of Solomon, and arose, and went, and caught hold on the horns of the altar. ⁵¹And it was told Solomon, saying, Behold, Adonijah feareth king Solomon: for, lo, he hath caught hold on the horns of the altar, saying, Let king Solomon swear unto me to day that he will not slay his servant with the sword. ⁵²And Solomon said, If he will shew himself a worthy man, there shall not an hair of him fall to the earth: but if wickedness shall be found in him, he shall die. ⁵³So king Solomon sent, and they brought him down from the altar. And he came and bowed himself to king Solomon: and Solomon said unto him, Go to thine house.

2

¹Now the days of David drew nigh that he should die; and he charged Solomon his son, saying, ²I go the way of all the earth: be thou strong therefore, and

---

f pipes: or, flutes

shew thyself a man; [3]And keep the charge of the LORD thy God, to walk in his ways, to keep his statutes, and his commandments, and his judgments, and his testimonies, as it is written in the law of Moses, that thou mayest prosper[a] in all that thou doest, and whithersoever thou turnest thyself: [4]That the LORD may continue his word which he spake concerning me, saying, If thy children take heed to their way, to walk before me in truth with all their heart and with all their soul, there shall not fail[b] thee (said he) a man on the throne of Israel. [5]Moreover thou knowest also what Joab the son of Zeruiah did to me, *and* what he did to the two captains of the hosts of Israel, unto Abner the son of Ner, and unto Amasa the son of Jether, whom he slew, and shed[c] the blood of war in peace, and put the blood of war upon his girdle that *was* about his loins, and in his shoes that *were* on his feet. [6]Do therefore according to thy wisdom, and let not his hoar head go down to the grave in peace. [7]But shew kindness unto the sons of Barzillai the Gileadite, and let them be of those that eat at thy table: for so they came to me when I fled because of Absalom thy brother. [8]And, behold, *thou hast* with thee Shimei the son of Gera, a Benjamite of Bahurim, which cursed me with a grievous[d] curse in the day when I went to Mahanaim: but he came down to meet me at Jordan, and I sware to him by the LORD,

saying, I will not put thee to death with the sword. [9]Now therefore hold him not guiltless: for thou *art* a wise man, and knowest what thou oughtest to do unto him; but his hoar head bring thou down to the grave with blood. [10]So David slept with his fathers, and was buried in the city of David. [11]And the days that David reigned over Israel *were* forty years: seven years reigned he in Hebron, and thirty and three years reigned he in Jerusalem.

[12]Then sat Solomon upon the throne of David his father; and his kingdom was established greatly. [13]And Adonijah the son of Haggith came to Bathsheba the mother of Solomon. And she said, Comest thou peaceably? And he said, Peaceably. [14]He said moreover, I have somewhat to say unto thee. And she said, Say on. [15]And he said, Thou knowest that the kingdom was mine, and *that* all Israel set their faces on me, that I should reign: howbeit the kingdom is turned about, and is become my brother's: for it was his from the LORD. [16]And now I ask one petition of thee, deny[e] me not. And she said unto him, Say on. [17]And he said, Speak, I pray thee, unto Solomon the king, (for he will not say thee nay,) that he give me Abishag the Shunammite to wife. [18]And Bathsheba said, Well; I will speak for thee unto the king. [19]Bathsheba therefore went unto king Solomon, to speak unto him for Adonijah. And the king rose up to meet her,

---

[a] prosper: or, do wisely
[b] fail . . . : Heb. be cut off from thee from the throne
[c] shed: Heb. put
[d] grievous: Heb. strong
[e] deny . . . : Heb. turn not away my face

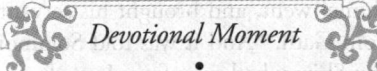

Devotional Moment

Respecting Parents

2:19 When Bathsheba entered Solomon's throne room, he not only stood up, he bowed down. This was an incredible display of respect. A ruler of Solomon's stature held the power of life and death over his subjects, including his family members. In some lands even entering the king's presence improperly could result in the death penalty, as shown in the books of Esther and Nehemiah.

Parents deserve the respect and honor of their children, even when children have reached adulthood. Respect is due because at the very least, parents have given life to their offspring. At best, they will have introduced their children to the Lord and given them a living example of how to follow God. Respect can be shown for parents by giving them places of honor, not only in the home but in the heart as well.

and bowed himself unto her, and sat down on his throne, and caused a seat to be set for the king's mother; and she sat on his right hand. ²⁰Then she said, I desire one small petition of thee; *I pray thee*, say me not nay. And the king said unto her, Ask on, my mother: for I will not say thee nay. ²¹And she said, Let Abishag the Shunammite be given to Adonijah thy brother to wife. ²²And king Solomon answered and said unto his mother, And why dost thou ask Abishag the Shunammite for Adonijah? ask for him the kingdom also; for he *is* mine elder brother; even for him, and for Abiathar the priest, and for Joab the son of Zeruiah. ²³Then king Solomon sware by the LORD, saying, God do so to me, and more also, if Adonijah have not spoken this word against his own life. ²⁴Now therefore, *as* the LORD liveth, which hath established me, and set me on the throne of David my father, and who hath made me an house, as he promised, Adonijah shall be put to death this day. ²⁵And king Solomon sent by the hand of Benaiah the son of Jehoiada; and he fell upon him that he died.

²⁶And unto Abiathar the priest said the king, Get thee to Anathoth, unto thine own fields; for thou *art* worthy ᶠ of death: but I will not at this time put thee to death, because thou barest the ark of the Lord GOD before David my father, and because thou hast been afflicted in all wherein my father was afflicted. ²⁷So Solomon thrust out Abiathar from being priest unto the LORD; that he might fulfil the word of the LORD, which he spake concerning the house of Eli in Shiloh. ²⁸Then tidings came to Joab: for Joab had turned after Adonijah, though he turned not after Absalom. And Joab fled unto the tabernacle of the LORD, and caught hold on the horns of the altar. ²⁹And it was told king Solomon that Joab was fled unto the tabernacle of the LORD; and, behold, *he is* by the altar. Then Solomon sent Benaiah the son of Jehoiada, saying, Go, fall upon him. ³⁰And Benaiah came to the tabernacle of the LORD, and said unto him, Thus saith the king, Come forth. And he said, Nay; but I will die here. And Benaiah brought the king word again, saying, Thus said Joab, and thus he answered me. ³¹And the king said unto him, Do as he hath said, and fall upon him, and bury him; that thou mayest take away the innocent blood, which

ᶠ worthy . . . : Heb. a man of death

Joab shed, from me, and from the house of my father. ³²And the LORD shall return his blood upon his own head, who fell upon two men more righteous and better than he, and slew them with the sword, my father David not knowing *thereof, to wit,* Abner the son of Ner, captain of the host of Israel, and Amasa the son of Jether, captain of the host of Judah. ³³Their blood shall therefore return upon the head of Joab, and upon the head of his seed for ever: but upon David, and upon his seed, and upon his house, and upon his throne, shall there be peace for ever from the LORD. ³⁴So Benaiah the son of Jehoiada went up, and fell upon him, and slew him: and he was buried in his own house in the wilderness.

³⁵And the king put Benaiah the son of Jehoiada in his room over the host: and Zadok the priest did the king put in the room of Abiathar. ³⁶And the king sent and called for Shimei, and said unto him, Build thee an house in Jerusalem, and dwell there, and go not forth thence any whither. ³⁷For it shall be, *that* on the day thou goest out, and passest over the brook Kidron, thou shalt know for certain that thou shalt surely die: thy blood shall be upon thine own head. ³⁸And Shimei said unto the king, The saying *is* good: as my lord the king hath said, so will thy servant do. And Shimei dwelt in Jerusalem many days. ³⁹And it came to pass at the end of three years, that two of the servants of Shimei ran away unto Achish son of Maachah king of Gath. And they told Shimei, saying, Behold, thy servants *be* in Gath. ⁴⁰And Shimei arose, and saddled his ass, and went to Gath to Achish to seek his servants: and

Shimei went, and brought his servants from Gath. ⁴¹And it was told Solomon that Shimei had gone from Jerusalem to Gath, and was come again. ⁴²And the king sent and called for Shimei, and said unto him, Did I not make thee to swear by the LORD, and protested unto thee, saying, Know for a certain, on the day thou goest out, and walkest abroad any whither, that thou shalt surely die? and thou saidst unto me, The word *that* I have heard *is* good. ⁴³Why then hast thou not kept the oath of the LORD, and the commandment that I have charged thee with? ⁴⁴The king said moreover to Shimei, Thou knowest all the wickedness which thine heart is privy to, that thou didst to David my father: therefore the LORD shall return thy wickedness upon thine own head; ⁴⁵And king Solomon *shall be* blessed, and the throne of David shall be established before the LORD for ever. ⁴⁶So the king commanded Benaiah the son of Jehoiada; which went out, and fell upon him, that he died. And the kingdom was established in the hand of Solomon.

3

¹And Solomon made affinity with Pharaoh king of Egypt, and took Pharaoh's daughter, and brought her into the city of David, until he had made an end of building his own house, and the house of the LORD, and the wall of Jerusalem round about. ²Only the people sacrificed in high places, because there was no house built unto the name of the LORD, until those days. ³And Solomon loved the LORD, walking in the statutes of David his father: only he sacrificed and

burnt incense in high places. ⁴And the king went to Gibeon to sacrifice there; for that *was* the great high place: a thousand burnt offerings did Solomon offer upon that altar.

⁵In Gibeon the LORD appeared to Solomon in a dream by night: and God said, Ask what I shall give thee. ⁶And Solomon said, Thou hast shewed unto thy servant David my father great mercy ᵃ, according as he walked before thee in truth, and in righteousness, and in uprightness of heart with thee; and thou hast kept for him this great kindness, that thou hast given him a son to sit on his throne, as *it is* this day. ⁷And now, O LORD my God, thou hast made thy servant king instead of David my father: and I *am but* a little child: I know not *how* to go out or come in. ⁸And thy servant *is* in the midst of thy people which thou hast chosen, a great people, that cannot be numbered nor counted for multitude. ⁹Give therefore thy servant an understanding ᵇ heart to judge thy people, that I may discern between good and bad: for who is able to judge this thy so great a people? ¹⁰And the speech pleased the Lord, that Solomon had asked this thing. ¹¹And God said unto him, Because thou hast asked this thing, and hast not asked for thyself long life ᶜ; neither hast asked riches for thyself, nor hast asked the life of thine enemies; but hast asked for thyself understanding to discern judgment; ¹²Behold, I have done according to thy words: lo, I have given thee a wise and an understanding heart; so

that there was none like thee before thee, neither after thee shall any arise like unto thee. ¹³And I have also given thee that which thou hast not asked, both riches, and honour: so that there shall not be any among the kings like unto thee all thy days. ¹⁴And if thou wilt walk in my ways, to keep my statutes and my commandments, as thy father David did walk, then I will lengthen thy days. ¹⁵And Solomon awoke; and, behold, *it was* a dream. And he came to Jerusalem, and stood before the ark of the covenant of the LORD, and offered up burnt offerings, and offered peace offerings, and made a feast to all his servants.

¹⁶Then came there two women, *that were* harlots, unto the king, and stood before him. ¹⁷And the one woman said, O my lord, I and this woman dwell in one house; and I was delivered of a child with her in the house. ¹⁸And it came to pass the third day after that I was delivered, that this woman was delivered also: and we *were* together; *there was* no stranger with us in the house, save we two in the house. ¹⁹And this woman's child died in the night; because she overlaid it. ²⁰And she arose at midnight, and took my son from beside me, while thine handmaid slept, and laid it in her bosom, and laid her dead child in my bosom. ²¹And when I rose in the morning to give my child suck, behold, it was dead: but when I had considered it in the morning, behold, it was not my son, which I did bear. ²²And the other woman said,

---

ᵃ mercy: or, bounty
ᵇ understanding: Heb. hearing
ᶜ long life: Heb. many days

Nay; but the living *is* my son, and the dead *is* thy son. And this said, No; but the dead *is* thy son, and the living *is* my son. Thus they spake before the king. ²³Then said the king, The one saith, This *is* my son that liveth, and thy son *is* the dead: and the other saith, Nay; but thy son *is* the dead, and my son *is* the living. ²⁴And the king said, Bring me a sword. And they brought a sword before the king. ²⁵And the king said, Divide the living child in two, and give half to the one, and half to the other. ²⁶Then spake the woman whose the living child *was* unto the king, for her bowels yearned^d upon her son, and she said, O my lord, give her the living child, and in no wise slay it. But the other said, Let it be neither mine nor thine, *but* divide *it*. ²⁷Then the king answered and said, Give her the living child, and in no wise slay it: she *is* the mother thereof. ²⁸And all Israel heard of the judgment which the king had judged; and they feared the king: for they saw that the wisdom of God *was* in him^e, to do judgment.

4

¹So king Solomon was king over all Israel. ²And these *were* the princes which he had; Azariah the son of Zadok the priest^a, ³Elihoreph and Ahiah, the sons of Shisha, scribes^b; Jehoshaphat the son of Ahilud, the recorder. ⁴And Benaiah the son of Jehoiada *was* over the host: and Zadok and Abiathar *were* the priests: ⁵And Azariah the son of Nathan *was* over the officers: and Zabud the son of Nathan *was* principal officer, *and* the king's friend: ⁶And Ahishar *was* over the household: and Adoniram the son of Abda *was* over the tribute^c. ⁷And Solomon had twelve officers over all Israel, which provided victuals for the king and his household: each man his month in a year made provision. ⁸And these *are* their names: The son of Hur, in mount Ephraim: ⁹The son of Dekar, in Makaz, and in Shaalbim, and Bethshemesh, and Elonbethhanan: ¹⁰The son of Hesed, in Aruboth; to him *pertained* Sochoh, and all the land of Hepher: ¹¹The son of Abinadab, in all the region of Dor; which had Taphath the daughter of Solomon to wife: ¹²Baana the son of Ahilud; *to him pertained* Taanach

---

Devotional Moment
•
Parenting

3:26 When two women both claimed to be the mother of this baby boy, Solomon devised a clever test. Solomon knew that the real mother would never stand by while her child was sacrificed to resolve a disagreement. Loving parents put the welfare of their children first. When our children's lives are at stake, this is easy to do. But in everyday life, it can be easy to consider our own needs more important. The next time you plan to visit friends late into the evening, consider the needs of your tired young children; the next time you go on vacation, consider your teenagers' preferences. It isn't always possible to please everybody, but by placing your children's welfare ahead of your own, you place yourself in good company.

---

^d yearned: Heb. were hot
^e in him: Heb. in the midst of him
^a priest: or, chief officer
^b scribes: or, secretaries
^c tribute: or, levy

A Mother's Love

by Grace Ketterman, M.D.

Jeanne finally held in her arms the tiny infant she had awaited for nine months. She gazed with wonder into his brand-new eyes, cuddled him, nursed him, comforted and played with him. Jeanne portrayed *tender* love, so vital to healthy personality development.

During a particularly intense temper tantrum, Carol firmly picked up her two-year-old, James. In a stern but calm voice, she spoke to him as she restrained his kicking feet and flailing arms. "I will not let you hurt yourself or break your toys when you are angry," she said. "I love you and will help you learn to behave properly." In a few minutes, James calmed down and soon returned to his toys. Carol showed *tough* love.

Jan, fifteen, casually informed her mother she was going out with Judy in her friend's car. Judy was also fifteen, and Mom knew she had only a learner's permit, requiring a fully qualified driver to be present in the car. Jan's mother refused to allow her to go, explaining that she was concerned about her safety as well as her obeying the law. Jan's mother practiced *protective* love.

Wise King Solomon understood the protective love of a mother. Called upon to decide which of two women was an infant's true mother, he laid a trap by suggesting they divide the baby in two. He knew the real mother would protect her child at all costs.

A mother's love will make her go to great lengths to protect her child. Moses almost became one of thousands of babies killed by the pharaoh in Egypt. But his mother, Jochebed, risked her life to save him. Carefully she made a tiny boat and placed the baby in the river where the king's daughter would find him. With the help of her daughter (and Moses' sister), Miriam, she cleverly maneuvered to become his nursemaid (Exod. 2:1-10).

The principles of a mother's love in that brief story are profound. Jochebed dared to disobey the law that killed all boy babies. She devoted her mind and creative energy to save him. She sacrificed her own legal position as his mother by giving him, at the age of weaning, to the king's daughter.

In another example, Hannah desperately yearned for a child. She wept and prayed earnestly that she would have one. In fact, she vowed to God that if he gave her a son, she would give him back to God to serve in the Temple (1 Sam. 1:9-28).

Both Jochebed and Hannah teach us about the extreme importance of the early years. Each had her son for only a very short time. But in the time they had, each imparted love, discipline, and faith. And God blessed.

Today, motherhood is sadly belittled; it comes far down on the list of what many women value. Yet the healthy heart of an individual as well as the heart of our civilization itself depends on good mothering. Without a deep commitment to having and raising children, our world will not survive.

What, then, is a good mother? Here are some concrete guidelines:

1. Good mothers sacrifice. They give up their own wishes gladly to provide for the needs of their children. Missing sleep, going without possessions and pleasures, calmly accepting the displeasure of a corrected child—all these are marks of mature mothering.

2. Good mothers teach their children. Children need to learn how, in turn, they must give up some pleasures in order to mature. They must achieve self-control and learn respect and consideration for others. They will have to master a sense of duty and responsibility if God is to use them.

3. Good mothers nurture. They provide food for their children's bodies, minds, and

spirits. They foster loving social interaction and teach their children how to be kind and happy with others while maintaining their Godgiven uniqueness.

4. Good mothers are protectors. They look after their children's physical safety but balance that with challenges to their growth and physical prowess. They also protect their children from evil and agnosticism but teach them to face the truth with courage and to discern good from bad.

5. Good mothers are there. Correct prioritizing allows a mother to show her children that they have a special place in her heart. Even if she must be physically separated from her children, they know they can count on her. And in time, she will be able to (and will *have* to) count on them.

All this may sound complex, but the mother who appealed to King Solomon knew the simple essence of motherhood: to be willing to give up all for the benefit of the son or daughter she loves.

DIGGING DEEPER

1. What are some other characteristics of a good mother? See Proverbs 31:10-31 for a description of a godly wife.

2. How can a mother avoid being shamed by her children's behavior? Read Proverbs 29:15.

3. What is the source of joyful mothering? See Psalm 113:9.

---

and Megiddo, and all Bethshean, which *is* by Zartanah beneath Jezreel, from Bethshean to Abelmeholah, *even* unto *the place that is* beyond Jokneam: ¹³The son of Geber, in Ramothgilead; to him *pertained* the towns of Jair the son of Manasseh, which *are* in Gilead; to him *also pertained* the region of Argob, which *is* in Bashan, threescore great cities with walls and brasen bars: ¹⁴Ahinadab the son of Iddo *had* Mahanaim[d]: ¹⁵Ahimaaz *was* in Naphtali; he also took Basmath the daughter of Solomon to wife: ¹⁶Baanah the son of Hushai *was* in Asher and in Aloth: ¹⁷Jehoshaphat the son of Paruah, in Issachar: ¹⁸Shimei the son of Elah, in Benjamin: ¹⁹Geber the son of Uri *was* in the country of Gilead, *in* the country of Sihon king of the

Amorites, and of Og king of Bashan; and *he was* the only officer which *was* in the land.

²⁰Judah and Israel *were* many, as the sand which *is* by the sea in multitude, eating and drinking, and making merry. ²¹And Solomon reigned over all kingdoms from the river unto the land of the Philistines, and unto the border of Egypt: they brought presents, and served Solomon all the days of his life. ²²And Solomon's provision[e] for one day was thirty measures of fine flour, and threescore measures of meal, ²³Ten fat oxen, and twenty oxen out of the pastures, and an hundred sheep, beside harts, and roebucks, and fallowdeer, and fatted fowl. ²⁴For he had dominion over all *the region* on this side the river, from Tiphsah even to

---

ᵈ Mahanaim: or, to Mahanaim
ᵉ provision: Heb. bread

Devotional Moment
•
Home Sweet Home

4:25 Under King Solomon's reign, every family in Judah and Israel lived in peace and safety. Each family even had its own home and garden. As leaders in their homes and families, parents have a responsibility to provide a safe, stable place everyone can call home. Don't allow over-scheduling, personal concerns, or problems to take over. Keep an eye on everyone's stress level, and when it is getting too high, take the lead in reducing it. Being a good parent sometimes involves canceling a planned outing, insisting on a curfew, or turning off the TV.

Azzah, over all the kings on this side the river: and he had peace on all sides round about him. ²⁵And Judah and Israel dwelt safely[f], every man under his vine and under his fig tree, from Dan even to Beersheba, all the days of Solomon. ²⁶And Solomon had forty thousand stalls of horses for his chariots, and twelve thousand horsemen. ²⁷And those officers provided victual for king Solomon, and for all that came unto king Solomon's table, every man in his month: they lacked nothing. ²⁸Barley also and straw for the horses and dromedaries[g] brought they unto the place where *the officers* were, every man according to his charge.

²⁹And God gave Solomon wisdom and understanding exceeding much, and largeness of heart, even as the sand that *is* on the sea shore. ³⁰And Solomon's wisdom excelled the wisdom of all the children of the east country, and all the wisdom of Egypt. ³¹For he was wiser than all men; than Ethan the Ezrahite, and Heman, and Chalcol, and Darda, the sons of Mahol: and his fame was in all nations round about. ³²And he spake three thousand proverbs: and his songs were a thousand and five. ³³And he spake of trees, from the cedar tree that *is* in Lebanon even unto the hyssop that springeth out of the wall: he spake also of beasts, and of fowl, and of creeping things, and of fishes. ³⁴And there came of all people to hear the wisdom of Solomon, from all kings of the earth, which had heard of his wisdom.

5

¹And Hiram[a] king of Tyre sent his servants unto Solomon; for he had heard that they had anointed him king in the room of his father: for Hiram was ever a lover of David. ²And Solomon sent to Hiram, saying, ³Thou knowest how that David my father could not build an house unto the name of the LORD his God for the wars which were about him on every side, until the LORD put them under the soles of his feet. ⁴But now the LORD my God hath given me rest on every side, *so that there is* neither adversary nor evil occurrent. ⁵And, behold, I purpose[b] to build an house unto the name of the LORD my God, as the LORD spake unto David my father, saying, Thy son, whom I will set upon thy throne in thy room, he shall build an house unto my name. ⁶Now there-

---

[f] safely: Heb. confidently
[g] dromedaries: or, mules, or, swift beasts
[a] Hiram: also called, Huram
[b] purpose: Heb. say

fore command thou that they hew me cedar trees out of Lebanon; and my servants shall be with thy servants: and unto thee will I give hire for thy servants according to all that thou shalt appoint ᶜ: for thou knowest that *there is* not among us any that can skill to hew timber like unto the Sidonians. ⁷And it came to pass, when Hiram heard the words of Solomon, that he rejoiced greatly, and said, Blessed *be* the LORD this day, which hath given unto David a wise son over this great people. ⁸And Hiram sent to Solomon, saying, I have considered ᵈ the things which thou sentest to me for: *and* I will do all thy desire concerning timber of cedar, and concerning timber of fir. ⁹My servants shall bring *them* down from Lebanon unto the sea: and I will convey them by sea in floats unto the place that thou shalt appoint ᵉ me, and will cause them to be discharged there, and thou shalt receive *them*: and thou shalt accomplish my desire, in giving food for my household. ¹⁰So Hiram gave Solomon cedar trees and fir trees *according to* all his desire. ¹¹And Solomon gave Hiram twenty thousand measures ᶠ of wheat *for* food to his household, and twenty measures of pure oil: thus gave Solomon to Hiram year by year. ¹²And the LORD gave Solomon wisdom, as he promised him: and there was peace between Hiram and Solomon; and they two made a league together. ¹³And king Solomon raised a levy ᵍ out of all Israel; and the levy was thirty thousand men. ¹⁴And he sent them to Lebanon, ten thousand a month by courses: a month they were in Lebanon, *and* two months at home: and Adoniram *was* over the levy. ¹⁵And Solomon had threescore and ten thousand that bare burdens, and fourscore thousand hewers in the mountains; ¹⁶Beside the chief of Solomon's officers which *were* over the work, three thousand and three hundred, which ruled over the people that wrought in the work. ¹⁷And the king commanded, and they brought great stones, costly stones, *and* hewed stones, to lay the foundation of the house. ¹⁸And Solomon's builders and Hiram's builders did hew *them*, and the stonesquarers: so they prepared timber and stones to build the house.

6

¹And it came to pass in the four hundred and eightieth year after the children of Israel were come out of the land of Egypt, in the fourth year of Solomon's reign over Israel, in the month Zif, which *is* the second month, that he began to build the house of the LORD. ²And the house which king Solomon built for the LORD, the length thereof *was* threescore cubits, and the breadth thereof twenty *cubits*, and the height thereof thirty cubits. ³And the porch before the temple of the house, twenty cubits *was* the length thereof, according to the breadth of the house; *and* ten cu-

---

ᶜ appoint: Heb. say
ᵈ considered: Heb. heard
ᵉ appoint: Heb. send
ᶠ measures: Heb. cors
ᵍ levy: Heb. tribute of men

bits *was* the breadth thereof before the house. ⁴And for the house he made windows of narrow lights. ⁵And against the wallᵃ of the house he built chambers round about, *against* the walls of the house round about, *both* of the temple and of the oracle: and he made chambers round about: ⁶The nethermost chamber *was* five cubits broad, and the middle *was* six cubits broad, and the third *was* seven cubits broad: for without *in the wall* of the house he made narrowed rests round about, that *the beams* should not be fastened in the walls of the house. ⁷And the house, when it was in building, was built of stone made ready before it was brought thither: so that there was neither hammer nor axe *nor* any tool of iron heard in the house, while it was in building. ⁸The door for the middle chamber *was* in the right sideᵇ of the house: and they went up with winding stairs into the middle *chamber*, and out of the middle into the third. ⁹So he built the house, and finished it; and covered the house with beams and boards of cedar. ¹⁰And *then* he built chambers against all the house, five cubits high: and they rested on the house *with* timber of cedar.

¹¹And the word of the LORD came to Solomon, saying, ¹²*Concerning* this house which thou art in building, if thou wilt walk in my statutes, and execute my judgments, and keep all my commandments to walk in them; then will I perform my word with thee, which I spake

unto David thy father: ¹³And I will dwell among the children of Israel, and will not forsake my people Israel. ¹⁴So Solomon built the house, and finished it.

¹⁵And he built the walls of the house within with boards of cedar, both the floor of the house, and the walls of the ceiling: *and* he covered *them* on the inside with wood, and covered the floor of the house with planks of fir. ¹⁶And he built twenty cubits on the sides of the house, both the floor and the walls with boards of cedar: he even built *them* for it within, *even* for the oracle, *even* for the most holy *place*. ¹⁷And the house, that *is*, the temple before it, was forty cubits *long*. ¹⁸And the cedar of the house within *was* carved with knopsᶜ and open flowers: all *was* cedar; there was no stone seen. ¹⁹And the oracle he prepared in the house within, to set there the ark of the covenant of the LORD. ²⁰And the oracle in the forepart *was* twenty cubits in length, and twenty cubits in breadth, and twenty cubits in the height thereof: and he overlaid it with pureᵈ gold; and *so* covered the altar *which was of* cedar. ²¹So Solomon overlaid the house within with pure gold: and he made a partition by the chains of gold before the oracle; and he overlaid it with gold. ²²And the whole house he overlaid with gold, until he had finished all the house: also the whole altar that *was* by the oracle he overlaid with gold. ²³And within the oracle he made two cherubims *of* oliveᵉ tree, *each* ten cubits high. ²⁴And five cu-

---

ᵃ against the wall: or, upon, or, joining to the wall
ᵇ side: Heb. shoulder
ᶜ knops: or, gourds
ᵈ pure: Heb. shut up
ᵉ olive: or, oily: Heb. trees of oil

bits *was* the one wing of the cherub, and five cubits the other wing of the cherub: from the uttermost part of the one wing unto the uttermost part of the other *were* ten cubits. ²⁵And the other cherub *was* ten cubits: both the cherubims *were* of one measure and one size. ²⁶The height of the one cherub *was* ten cubits, and so *was it* of the other cherub. ²⁷And he set the cherubims within the inner house: and they stretched forth the wings of the cherubims, so that the wing of the one touched the *one* wall, and the wing of the other cherub touched the other wall; and their wings touched one another in the midst of the house. ²⁸And he overlaid the cherubims with gold. ²⁹And he carved all the walls of the house round about with carved figures of cherubims and palm trees and open flowers^f, within and without. ³⁰And the floor of the house he overlaid with gold, within and without. ³¹And for the entering of the oracle he made doors *of* olive tree: the lintel *and* side posts *were* a fifth part *of the wall.* ³²The two^g doors also *were of* olive tree; and he carved upon them carvings of cherubims and palm trees and open flowers, and overlaid *them* with gold, and spread gold upon the cherubims, and upon the palm trees. ³³So also made he for the door of the temple posts *of* olive tree, a fourth part *of the wall.* ³⁴And the two doors *were of* fir tree: the two leaves of the one door *were* folding, and the two leaves of the other door *were* folding.

³⁵And he carved *thereon* cherubims and palm trees and open flowers: and covered *them* with gold fitted upon the carved work. ³⁶And he built the inner court with three rows of hewed stone, and a row of cedar beams. ³⁷In the fourth year was the foundation of the house of the LORD laid, in the month Zif: ³⁸And in the eleventh year, in the month Bul, which *is* the eighth month, was the house finished throughout all the parts thereof, and according to all the fashion of it. So was he seven years in building it.

7

¹But Solomon was building his own house thirteen years, and he finished all his house. ²He built also the house of the forest of Lebanon; the length thereof *was* an hundred cubits, and the breadth thereof fifty cubits, and the height thereof thirty cubits, upon four rows of cedar pillars, with cedar beams upon the pillars. ³And *it was* covered with cedar above upon the beams^a, that *lay* on forty five pillars, fifteen *in* a row. ⁴And *there were* windows *in* three rows, and light *was* against light *in* three ranks. ⁵And all the doors^b and posts *were* square, with the windows: and light *was* against light *in* three ranks. ⁶And he made a porch of pillars; the length thereof *was* fifty cubits, and the breadth thereof thirty cubits: and the porch *was* before them^c: and the *other* pillars and the thick beam *were* before

---

^f open flowers: Heb. openings of flowers
^g two . . . : or, leaves of the doors
^a beams: Heb. ribs
^b doors . . . : or, spaces and pillars were square in prospect
^c before them: or, according to them

them.[d] [7]Then he made a porch for the throne where he might judge, *even* the porch of judgment: and *it was* covered with cedar from one side of the floor to the other. [8]And his house where he dwelt *had* another court within the porch, *which* was of the like work. Solomon made also an house for Pharaoh's daughter, whom he had taken *to wife*, like unto this porch. [9]All these *were of* costly stones, according to the measures of hewed stones, sawed with saws, within and without, even from the foundation unto the coping, and *so* on the outside toward the great court. [10]And the foundation *was of* costly stones, even great stones, stones of ten cubits, and stones of eight cubits. [11]And above *were* costly stones, after the measures of hewed stones, and cedars. [12]And the great court round about *was* with three rows of hewed stones, and a row of cedar beams, both for the inner court of the house of the LORD, and for the porch of the house.

[13]And king Solomon sent and fetched Hiram[e] out of Tyre. [14]He *was* a widow's[f] son of the tribe of Naphtali, and his father *was* a man of Tyre, a worker in brass: and he was filled with wisdom, and understanding, and cunning to work all works in brass. And he came to king Solomon, and wrought all his work. [15]For he cast[g] two pillars of brass, of eighteen cubits high apiece: and a line of twelve cubits did compass either of them about. [16]And he made two chapiters *of* molten brass, to set upon the tops of the pillars: the height of the one chapiter *was* five cubits, and the height of the other chapiter *was* five cubits: [17]*And* nets of checker work, and wreaths of chain work, for the chapiters which *were* upon the top of the pillars; seven for the one chapiter, and seven for the other chapiter. [18]And he made the pillars, and two rows round about upon the one network, to cover the chapiters that *were* upon the top, with pomegranates: and so did he for the other chapiter. [19]And the chapiters that *were* upon the top of the pillars *were* of lily work in the porch, four cubits. [20]And the chapiters upon the two pillars *had* *pomegranates* also above, over against the belly which *was* by the network: and the pomegranates *were* two hundred in rows round about upon the other chapiter. [21]And he set up the pillars in the porch of the temple: and he set up the right pillar, and called the name thereof Jachin[h]: and he set up the left pillar, and called the name thereof Boaz. [22]And upon the top of the pillars *was* lily work: so was the work of the pillars finished. [23]And he made a molten sea, ten cubits from the one brim to the other: *it was* round all about, and his height *was* five cubits: and a line of thirty cubits did compass it round about. [24]And under the brim of it round about *there were* knops compassing it, ten in a cubit, compassing the sea round about: the knops *were* cast in two rows, when it was cast. [25]It stood upon twelve oxen, three looking toward the

---

[d] 2before them: or, according to them
[e] Hiram: also called, Huram
[f] a widow's . . . : Heb. the son of a widow woman
[g] cast: Heb. fashioned
[h] Jachin: that is, He shall establish

north, and three looking toward the west, and three looking toward the south, and three looking toward the east: and the sea *was set* above upon them, and all their hinder parts *were* inward. ²⁶And it *was* an hand breadth thick, and the brim thereof was wrought like the brim of a cup, with flowers of lilies: it contained two thousand baths. ²⁷And he made ten bases of brass; four cubits *was* the length of one base, and four cubits the breadth thereof, and three cubits the height of it. ²⁸And the work of the bases *was* on this *manner*: they had borders, and the borders *were* between the ledges: ²⁹And on the borders that *were* between the ledges *were* lions, oxen, and cherubims: and upon the ledges *there was* a base above: and beneath the lions and oxen *were* certain additions made of thin work. ³⁰And every base had four brasen wheels, and plates of brass: and the four corners thereof had undersetters: under the laver *were* undersetters molten, at the side of every addition. ³¹And the mouth of it within the chapiter and above *was* a cubit: but the mouth thereof *was* round *after* the work of the base, a cubit and an half: and also upon the mouth of it *were* gravings with their borders, foursquare, not round. ³²And under the borders *were* four wheels; and the axletrees of the wheels *were joined* to the base: and the height of a wheel *was* a cubit and half a cubit. ³³And the work of the wheels *was* like the work of a chariot wheel: their axletrees, and their naves, and their fel-

loes, and their spokes, *were* all molten. ³⁴And *there were* four undersetters to the four corners of one base: *and* the undersetters *were* of the very base itself. ³⁵And in the top of the base *was there* a round compass of half a cubit high: and on the top of the base the ledges thereof and the borders thereof *were* of the same. ³⁶For on the plates of the ledges thereof, and on the borders thereof, he graved cherubims, lions, and palm trees, according to the proportion[i] of every one, and additions round about. ³⁷After this *manner* he made the ten bases: all of them had one casting, one measure, *and* one size. ³⁸Then made he ten lavers of brass: one laver contained forty baths: *and* every laver was four cubits: *and* upon every one of the ten bases one laver. ³⁹And he put five bases on the right side[j] of the house, and five on the left side of the house: and he set the sea on the right side[k] of the house eastward over against the south. ⁴⁰And Hiram[l] made the lavers, and the shovels, and the basons. So Hiram made an end of doing all the work that he made king Solomon for the house of the LORD: ⁴¹The two pillars, and the *two* bowls of the chapiters that *were* on the top of the two pillars; and the two networks, to cover the two bowls of the chapiters which *were* upon the top of the pillars; ⁴²And four hundred pomegranates for the two networks, *even* two rows of pomegranates for one network, to cover the two bowls of the chapiters that *were* upon[m] the pillars; ⁴³And the ten

---

[i] proportion: Heb. nakedness
[j] side: Heb. shoulder
[k] 2side: Heb. shoulder
[l] And Hiram: Heb. And Hirom
[m] upon . . . : Heb. upon the face of the pillars

bases, and ten lavers on the bases; ⁴⁴And one sea, and twelve oxen under the sea; ⁴⁵And the pots, and the shovels, and the basons: and all these vessels, which Hiram made to king Solomon for the house of the LORD, *were of* brightⁿ brass. ⁴⁶In the plain of Jordan did the king cast them, in the clay ground between Succoth and Zarthan. ⁴⁷And Solomon left all the vessels *unweighed,* because they were exceeding many: neither was the weight of the brass found out.

⁴⁸And Solomon made all the vessels that *pertained* unto the house of the LORD: the altar of gold, and the table of gold, whereupon the shewbread *was,* ⁴⁹And the candlesticks of pure gold, five on the right *side,* and five on the left, before the oracle, with the flowers, and the lamps, and the tongs *of* gold, ⁵⁰And the bowls, and the snuffers, and the basons, and the spoons, and the censers^o *of* pure gold; and the hinges *of* gold, *both* for the doors of the inner house, the most holy *place, and* for the doors of the house, *to wit,* of the temple. ⁵¹So was ended all the work that king Solomon made for the house of the LORD. And Solomon brought in the things which David his father had dedicated; *even* the silver, and the gold, and the vessels, did he put among the treasures of the house of the LORD.

8

¹Then Solomon assembled the elders of Israel, and all the heads of the tribes, the chief^a of the fathers of the children of Israel, unto king Solomon in Jerusalem, that they might bring up the ark of the covenant of the LORD out of the city of David, which *is* Zion. ²And all the men of Israel assembled themselves unto king Solomon at the feast in the month Ethanim, which *is* the seventh month. ³And all the elders of Israel came, and the priests took up the ark. ⁴And they brought up the ark of the LORD, and the tabernacle of the congregation, and all the holy vessels that *were* in the tabernacle, even those did the priests and the Levites bring up. ⁵And king Solomon, and all the congregation of Israel, that were assembled unto him, *were* with him before the ark, sacrificing sheep and oxen, that could not be told nor numbered for multitude. ⁶And the priests brought in the ark of the covenant of the LORD unto his place, into the oracle of the house, to the most holy *place, even* under the wings of the cherubims. ⁷For the cherubims spread forth *their* two wings over the place of the ark, and the cherubims covered the ark and the staves thereof above. ⁸And they drew out the staves, that the ends^b of the staves were seen out in the holy *place* before the oracle, and they were not seen without: and there they are unto this day. ⁹*There was* nothing in the ark save the two tables of stone, which Moses put there at Horeb, when the LORD made *a covenant* with the children of Israel, when they came out^c of the land of Egypt. ¹⁰And it came

---

ⁿ bright: Heb. made bright or, scoured
^o censers: Heb. ash pans
^a chief: Heb. princes
^b ends: Heb. heads
^c when the: or, where the

to pass, when the priests were come out of the holy *place*, that the cloud filled the house of the LORD, ¹¹So that the priests could not stand to minister because of the cloud: for the glory of the LORD had filled the house of the LORD.

¹²Then spake Solomon, The LORD said that he would dwell in the thick darkness. ¹³I have surely built thee an house to dwell in, a settled place for thee to abide in for ever. ¹⁴And the king turned his face about, and blessed all the congregation of Israel: (and all the congregation of Israel stood;) ¹⁵And he said, Blessed *be* the LORD God of Israel, which spake with his mouth unto David my father, and hath with his hand fulfilled *it*, saying, ¹⁶Since the day that I brought forth my people Israel out of Egypt, I chose no city out of all the tribes of Israel to build an house, that my name might be therein; but I chose David to be over my people Israel. ¹⁷And it was in the heart of David my father to build an house for the name of the LORD God of Israel. ¹⁸And the LORD said unto David my father, Whereas it was in thine heart to build an house unto my name, thou didst well that it was in thine heart. ¹⁹Nevertheless thou shalt not build the house; but thy son that shall come forth out of thy loins, he shall build the house unto my name. ²⁰And the LORD hath performed his word that he spake, and I am risen up in the room of David my father, and sit on the throne of Israel, as the LORD promised, and have built an house for the name of the LORD God of Israel. ²¹And I have set there a place for the ark, wherein *is* the covenant of the LORD, which he made with our fathers, when he brought them out of the land of Egypt.

²²And Solomon stood before the altar of the LORD in the presence of all the congregation of Israel, and spread forth his hands toward heaven: ²³And he said, LORD God of Israel, *there is* no God like thee, in heaven above, or on earth beneath, who keepest covenant and mercy with thy servants that walk before thee with all their heart: ²⁴Who hast kept with thy servant David my father that thou promisedst him: thou spakest also with thy mouth, and hast fulfilled *it* with thine hand, as *it is* this day. ²⁵Therefore now, LORD God of Israel, keep with thy servant David my father that thou promisedst him, saying, There shall not fail[d] thee a man in my sight to sit on the throne of Israel; so that thy children take heed to their way, that they walk before me as thou hast walked before me. ²⁶And now, O God of Israel, let thy word, I pray thee, be verified, which thou spakest unto thy servant David my father. ²⁷But will God indeed dwell on the earth? behold, the heaven and heaven of heavens cannot contain thee; how much less this house that I have builded? ²⁸Yet have thou respect unto the prayer of thy servant, and to his supplication, O LORD my God, to hearken unto the cry and to the prayer, which thy servant prayeth before thee to day: ²⁹That thine eyes may be open toward this house night and day, *even* toward the place of which thou hast said, My name shall be there: that thou mayest hearken unto the prayer which thy servant shall make toward this place[e]. ³⁰And hearken thou to the supplication

---

[d] fail . . . : Heb. be cut off unto thee a man from my sight
[e] toward this place: or, in this place

of thy servant, and of thy people Israel, when they shall pray toward this place[f]: and hear thou in heaven thy dwelling place: and when thou hearest, forgive. [31]If any man trespass against his neighbour, and an oath[g] be laid upon him to cause him to swear, and the oath come before thine altar in this house: [32]Then hear thou in heaven, and do, and judge thy servants, condemning the wicked, to bring his way upon his head; and justifying the righteous, to give him according to his righteousness. [33]When thy people Israel be smitten down before the enemy, because they have sinned against thee, and shall turn again to thee, and confess thy name, and pray, and make supplication unto thee in this house: [34]Then hear thou in heaven, and forgive the sin of thy people Israel, and bring them again unto the land which thou gavest unto their fathers. [35]When heaven is shut up, and there is no rain, because they have sinned against thee; if they pray toward this place, and confess thy name, and turn from their sin, when thou afflictest them: [36]Then hear thou in heaven, and forgive the sin of thy servants, and of thy people Israel, that thou teach them the good way wherein they should walk, and give rain upon thy land, which thou hast given to thy people for an inheritance. [37]If there be in the land famine, if there be pestilence, blasting, mildew, locust, or if there be caterpiller; if their enemy besiege them in the land of their cities[h]; whatsoever plague, whatsoever sickness there be;

[38]What prayer and supplication soever be made by any man, or by all thy people Israel, which shall know every man the plague of his own heart, and spread forth his hands toward this house: [39]Then hear thou in heaven thy dwelling place, and forgive, and do, and give to every man according to his ways, whose heart thou knowest; (for thou, even thou only, knowest the hearts of all the children of men;) [40]That they may fear thee all the days that they live in the land which thou gavest unto our fathers. [41]Moreover concerning a stranger, that is not of thy people Israel, but cometh out of a far country for thy name's sake; [42](For they shall hear of thy great name, and of thy strong hand, and of thy stretched out arm;) when he shall come and pray toward this house; [43]Hear thou in heaven thy dwelling place, and do according to all that the stranger calleth to thee for: that all people of the earth may know thy name, to fear thee, as do thy people Israel; and that they may know that this house, which I have builded, is called by thy name. [44]If thy people go out to battle against their enemy, whithersoever thou shalt send them, and shall pray unto the LORD toward the city[i] which thou hast chosen, and toward the house that I have built for thy name: [45]Then hear thou in heaven their prayer and their supplication, and maintain their cause[j]. [46]If they sin against thee, (for there is no man that sinneth not,) and thou be angry with them, and deliver them to the enemy, so

[f] toward this place: or, in this place
[g] and an oath . . . : Heb. and he require an oath of him
[h] cities: or, jurisdiction
[i] toward the city: Heb. the way of the city
[j] cause: or, right

that they carry them away captives unto the land of the enemy, far or near; [47] *Yet* if they shall bethink[k] themselves in the land whither they were carried captives, and repent, and make supplication unto thee in the land of them that carried them captives, saying, We have sinned, and have done perversely, we have committed wickedness; [48]And *so* return unto thee with all their heart, and with all their soul, in the land of their enemies, which led them away captive, and pray unto thee toward their land, which thou gavest unto their fathers, the city which thou hast chosen, and the house which I have built for thy name: [49]Then hear thou their prayer and their supplication in heaven thy dwelling place, and maintain their cause[l], [50]And forgive thy people that have sinned against thee, and all their transgressions wherein they have transgressed against thee, and give them compassion before them who carried them captive, that they may have compassion on them: [51]For they *be* thy people, and thine inheritance, which thou broughtest forth out of Egypt, from the midst of the furnace of iron: [52]That thine eyes may be open unto the supplication of thy servant, and unto the supplication of thy people Israel, to hearken unto them in all that they call for unto thee. [53]For thou didst separate them from among all the people of the earth, *to be* thine inheritance, as thou spakest by the hand of Moses thy servant, when thou broughtest our fathers out of Egypt, O Lord GOD.

[54]And it was *so*, that when Solomon had made an end of praying all this prayer and supplication unto the LORD, he arose from before the altar of the LORD, from kneeling on his knees with his hands spread up to heaven. [55]And he stood, and blessed all the congregation of Israel with a loud voice, saying, [56]Blessed *be* the LORD, that hath given rest unto his people Israel, according to all that he promised: there hath not failed[m] one word of all his good promise, which he promised by the hand of Moses his servant. [57]The LORD our God be with us, as he was with our fathers: let him not leave us, nor forsake us: [58]That he may incline our hearts unto him, to walk in all his ways, and to keep his commandments, and his statutes, and his judgments, which he commanded our fathers. [59]And let these my words, wherewith I have made supplication before the LORD, be nigh unto the LORD our God day and night, that he maintain the cause of his servant, and the cause of his people Israel at all times, as the matter shall require: [60]That all the people of the earth may know that the LORD *is* God, *and that there is* none else. [61]Let your heart therefore be perfect with the LORD our God, to walk in his statutes, and to keep his commandments, as at this day.

[62]And the king, and all Israel with him, offered sacrifice before the LORD. [63]And Solomon offered a sacrifice of peace offerings, which he offered unto the LORD, two and twenty thousand oxen, and an hundred and twenty thousand sheep. So the king and all the

---

[k] bethink . . . : Heb. bring back to their heart
[l] cause: or, right
[m] failed: Heb. fallen

children of Israel dedicated the house of the LORD. [64]The same day did the king hallow the middle of the court that *was* before the house of the LORD: for there he offered burnt offerings, and meat offerings, and the fat of the peace offerings: because the brasen altar that *was* before the LORD *was* too little to receive the burnt offerings, and meat offerings, and the fat of the peace offerings. [65]And at that time Solomon held a feast, and all Israel with him, a great congregation, from the entering in of Hamath unto the river of Egypt, before the LORD our God, seven days and seven days, *even* fourteen days. [66]On the eighth day he sent the people away: and they blessed[n] the king, and went unto their tents joyful and glad of heart for all the goodness that the LORD had done for David his servant, and for Israel his people.

9

[1]And it came to pass, when Solomon had finished the building of the house of the LORD, and the king's house, and all Solomon's desire which he was pleased to do, [2]That the LORD appeared to Solomon the second time, as he had appeared unto him at Gibeon. [3]And the LORD said unto him, I have heard thy prayer and thy supplication, that thou hast made before me: I have hallowed this house, which thou hast built, to put my name there for ever; and mine eyes and mine heart shall be there perpetually. [4]And if thou wilt walk before me, as David thy father walked, in integrity of heart, and in uprightness, to do according to all that I have commanded thee, *and* wilt keep my statutes and my judgments: [5]Then I will establish the throne of thy kingdom upon Israel for ever, as I promised to David thy father, saying, There shall not fail thee a man upon the throne of Israel. [6]*But* if ye shall at all turn from following me, ye or your children, and will not keep my commandments *and* my statutes which I have set before you, but go and serve other gods, and worship them: [7]Then will I cut off Israel out of the land which I have given them; and this house, which I have hallowed for my name, will I cast out of my sight; and Israel shall be a proverb and a byword among all people: [8]And at this house, *which* is high, every one that passeth by it shall be astonished, and shall hiss; and they shall say, Why hath the LORD done thus unto this land, and to this house? [9]And they shall answer, Because they forsook the LORD their God, who brought forth their fathers out of the land of Egypt, and have taken hold upon other gods, and have worshipped them, and served them: therefore hath the LORD brought upon them all this evil.

[10]And it came to pass at the end of twenty years, when Solomon had built the two houses, the house of the LORD, and the king's house, [11](*Now* Hiram the king of Tyre had furnished Solomon with cedar trees and fir trees, and with gold, according to all his desire,) that then king Solomon gave Hiram twenty cities in the land of Galilee. [12]And Hiram came out from Tyre to see the cities which Solomon had given him; and they pleased[a] him not. [13]And he said, What

---

[n] blessed: or, thanked
[a] pleased . . . : Heb. were not right in his eyes

cities *are* these which thou hast given me, my brother? And he called them the land of Cabul[b] unto this day. [14]And Hiram sent to the king sixscore talents of gold.

[15]And this *is* the reason of the levy which king Solomon raised; for to build the house of the LORD, and his own house, and Millo, and the wall of Jerusalem, and Hazor, and Megiddo, and Gezer. [16]*For* Pharaoh king of Egypt had gone up, and taken Gezer, and burnt it with fire, and slain the Canaanites that dwelt in the city, and given it *for* a present unto his daughter, Solomon's wife. [17]And Solomon built Gezer, and Bethhoron the nether, [18]And Baalath, and Tadmor in the wilderness, in the land, [19]And all the cities of store that Solomon had, and cities for his chariots, and cities for his horsemen, and that which Solomon desired to build in Jerusalem, and in Lebanon, and in all the land of his dominion. [20]*And* all the people *that were* left of the Amorites, Hittites, Perizzites, Hivites, and Jebusites, which *were* not of the children of Israel, [21]Their children that were left after them in the land, whom the children of Israel also were not able utterly to destroy, upon those did Solomon levy a tribute of bondservice unto this day. [22]But of the children of Israel did Solomon make no bondmen: but they *were* men of war, and his servants, and his princes, and his captains, and rulers of his chariots, and his horsemen. [23]These *were* the chief of the officers that *were* over Solomon's work, five hundred and fifty, which bare rule over the people that wrought in the work. [24]But Pharaoh's daughter came up out of the city of David unto her house which *Solomon* had built for her: then did he build Millo. [25]And three times in a year did Solomon offer burnt offerings and peace offerings upon the altar which he built unto the LORD, and he burnt incense upon the altar that *was* before the LORD. So he finished the house. [26]And king Solomon made a navy of ships in Eziongeber, which *is* beside Eloth, on the shore[c] of the Red sea, in the land of Edom. [27]And Hiram sent in the navy his servants, shipmen that had knowledge of the sea, with the servants of Solomon. [28]And they came to Ophir, and fetched from thence gold, four hundred and twenty talents, and brought *it* to king Solomon.

10

[1]And when the queen of Sheba heard of the fame of Solomon concerning the name of the LORD, she came to prove him with hard questions. [2]And she came to Jerusalem with a very great train, with camels that bare spices, and very much gold, and precious stones: and when she was come to Solomon, she communed with him of all that was in her heart. [3]And Solomon told her all her questions[a]: there was not *any* thing hid from the king, which he told her not. [4]And when the queen of Sheba had seen all Solomon's wisdom, and the house that he had built, [5]And the meat of his table, and the sitting of his servants, and the attendance[b] of his minis-

---

[b] Cabul: that is, displeasing, or, dirty
[c] shore: Heb. lip
[a] questions: Heb. words
[b] attendance: Heb. standing

ters, and their apparel, and his cupbearers, and his ascent by which he went up unto the house of the LORD; there was no more spirit in her. [6]And she said to the king, It was a true report[c] that I heard in mine own land of thy acts and of thy wisdom. [7]Howbeit I believed not the words, until I came, and mine eyes had seen it: and, behold, the half was not told me: thy wisdom and prosperity exceedeth the fame which I heard. [8]Happy *are* thy men, happy *are* these thy servants, which stand continually before thee, *and* that hear thy wisdom. [9]Blessed be the LORD thy God, which delighted in thee, to set thee on the throne of Israel: because the LORD loved Israel for ever, therefore made he thee king, to do judgment and justice. [10]And she gave the king an hundred and twenty talents of gold, and of spices very great store, and precious stones: there came no more such abundance of spices as these which the queen of Sheba gave to king Solomon. [11]And the navy also of Hiram, that brought gold from Ophir, brought in from Ophir great plenty of almug[d] trees, and precious stones. [12]And the king made of the almug trees pillars[e] for the house of the LORD, and for the king's house, harps also and psalteries for singers: there came no such almug trees, nor were seen unto this day. [13]And king Solomon gave unto the queen of Sheba

all her desire, whatsoever she asked, beside *that* which Solomon gave her of his royal bounty. So she turned and went to her own country, she and her servants.

[14]Now the weight of gold that came to Solomon in one year was six hundred threescore and six talents of gold, [15]Beside *that he had* of the merchantmen, and of the traffick of the spice merchants, and of all the kings of Arabia, and of the governors[f] of the country. [16]And king Solomon made two hundred targets *of* beaten gold: six hundred *shekels* of gold went to one target. [17]And *he made* three hundred shields *of* beaten gold; three pound of gold went to one shield: and the king put them in the house of the forest of Lebanon. [18]Moreover the king made a great throne of ivory, and overlaid it with the best gold. [19]The throne had six steps, and the top of the throne *was* round behind[g]: and *there were* stays on either side on the place of the seat, and two lions stood beside the stays. [20]And twelve lions stood there on the one side and on the other upon the six steps: there was not the like[h] made in any kingdom. [21]And all king Solomon's drinking vessels *were of* gold, and all the vessels of the house of the forest of Lebanon *were of* pure gold; none *were of* silver[i]: it was nothing accounted of in the days of Solomon. [22]For the king had at sea a navy of Tharshish with the navy

---

[c] report: Heb. word
[d] almug . . . : also called, algum trees
[e] pillars: or, rails: Heb. a prop
[f] governors: or, captains
[g] behind: Heb. on the hinder part thereof
[h] the like: Heb. so
[i] none . . . : or, there was no silver in them

of Hiram: once in three years came the navy of Tharshish, bringing gold, and silver, ivory[j], and apes, and peacocks. [23]So king Solomon exceeded all the kings of the earth for riches and for wisdom. [24]And all the earth sought to[k] Solomon, to hear his wisdom, which God had put in his heart. [25]And they brought every man his present, vessels of silver, and vessels of gold, and garments, and armour, and spices, horses, and mules, a rate year by year. [26]And Solomon gathered together chariots and horsemen: and he had a thousand and four hundred chariots, and twelve thousand horsemen, whom he bestowed in the cities for chariots, and with the king at Jerusalem. [27]And the king made[l] silver *to be* in Jerusalem as stones, and cedars made he *to be* as the sycamore trees that *are* in the vale, for abundance. [28]And Solomon[m] had horses brought out of Egypt, and linen yarn: the king's merchants received the linen yarn at a price. [29]And a chariot came up and went out of Egypt for six hundred *shekels* of silver, and an horse for an hundred and fifty: and so for all the kings of the Hittites, and for the kings of Syria, did they bring *them* out by their means.

11

[1]But king Solomon loved many strange women, together with the daughter of Pharaoh, women of the Moabites, Ammonites, Edomites, Zidonians, *and* Hittites; [2]Of the nations *concerning* which

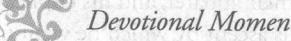

Devotional Moment
•
Idolatry

11:2-4 Solomon's greatness as a ruler was ultimately destroyed by the divided loyalties his foreign wives brought into the kingdom. The problem was a spiritual one: Solomon adopted the gods they brought with them. The same trap awaits anyone who allows other loyalties to compete with his or her devotion to God. Work responsibilities, hobbies, habits, career pursuits, personal indulgences, even friends or church activities can claim too much time or attention. Avoid any outside entanglements that might turn your heart away from the Lord.

the LORD said unto the children of Israel, Ye shall not go in to them, neither shall they come in unto you: *for* surely they will turn away your heart after their gods: Solomon clave unto these in love. [3]And he had seven hundred wives, princesses, and three hundred concubines: and his wives turned away his heart. [4]For it came to pass, when Solomon was old, *that* his wives turned away his heart after other gods: and his heart was not perfect with the LORD his God, as *was* the heart of David his father. [5]For Solomon went after Ashtoreth the goddess of the Zidonians, and after Milcom[a] the abomination of the Ammonites. [6]And Solomon did evil in the sight of the LORD, and went not fully after the LORD, as *did* David his father. [7]Then did Solomon build an high place for Chemosh, the abomination of Moab, in the hill that *is* before Jerusalem, and

---

[j] ivory: or, elephants' teeth
[k] sought to: Heb. sought the face of
[l] made: Heb. gave
[m] And Solomon . . . : Heb. And the going forth of the horses which was Solomon's
[a] Milcom: also called, Molech

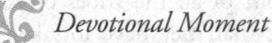

Devotional Moment

Spouses

11:8 Rather than leading his wives to follow the true and living God, Solomon became corrupted by their pagan practices. He even built temples for their hideous gods. These weren't harmless cultural practices either. Practicing these religions involved sacrifice to and worship of false gods. This shows how far Solomon strayed from following the Lord. The pressure to compromise essential values in order to preserve a relationship can be strong. Do family relationships put pressure on your commitment to Christ? Whether the pressure comes from a rebellious child, an unbelieving spouse, or other relatives who do not follow Christ, remember that no relationship should be allowed to drag you away from obedience to God. And if your spouse does not support your faith, make sure you have a church and friends who do.

for Molech, the abomination of the children of Ammon. ⁸And likewise did he for all his strange wives, which burnt incense and sacrificed unto their gods.

⁹And the LORD was angry with Solomon, because his heart was turned from the LORD God of Israel, which had appeared unto him twice, ¹⁰And had commanded him concerning this thing, that he should not go after other gods: but he kept not that which the LORD commanded. ¹¹Wherefore the LORD said unto Solomon, Forasmuch as this is done of thee, and thou hast not kept my covenant and my statutes, which I have commanded thee, I will surely rend the kingdom from thee, and will give it to thy servant. ¹²Notwithstanding in thy days I will not do it for David thy father's sake: but I will rend it out of the hand of thy son. ¹³Howbeit I will not rend away all the kingdom; *but* will give one tribe to thy son for David my servant's sake, and for Jerusalem's sake which I have chosen.

¹⁴And the LORD stirred up an adversary unto Solomon, Hadad the Edomite: he *was* of the king's seed in Edom. ¹⁵For it came to pass, when David was in Edom, and Joab the captain of the host was gone up to bury the slain, after he had smitten every male in Edom; ¹⁶(For six months did Joab remain there with all Israel, until he had cut off every male in Edom:) ¹⁷That Hadad fled, he and certain Edomites of his father's servants with him, to go into Egypt; Hadad *being* yet a little child. ¹⁸And they arose out of Midian, and came to Paran: and they took men with them out of Paran, and they came to Egypt, unto Pharaoh king of Egypt; which gave him an house, and appointed him victuals, and gave him land. ¹⁹And Hadad found great favour in the sight of Pharaoh, so that he gave him to wife the sister of his own wife, the sister of Tahpenes the queen. ²⁰And the sister of Tahpenes bare him Genubath his son, whom Tahpenes weaned in Pharaoh's house: and Genubath was in Pharaoh's household among the sons of Pharaoh. ²¹And when Hadad heard in Egypt that David slept with his fathers, and that Joab the captain of the host was dead, Hadad said to Pharaoh, Let me depart, that I may go to mine own country. ²²Then Pharaoh said unto him, But what hast thou lacked with me, that, behold, thou seekest to go to thine own country? And he answered, Nothing: howbeit let me go[b] in any wise. ²³And God stirred him up *another* adversary, Rezon the son

[b] Nothing: Heb. Not

of Eliadah, which fled from his lord Hadadezer king of Zobah: ²⁴And he gathered men unto him, and became captain over a band, when David slew them *of Zobah*: and they went to Damascus, and dwelt therein, and reigned in Damascus. ²⁵And he was an adversary to Israel all the days of Solomon, beside the mischief that Hadad *did*: and he abhorred Israel, and reigned over Syria.

²⁶And Jeroboam the son of Nebat, an Ephrathite of Zereda, Solomon's servant, whose mother's name *was* Zeruah, a widow woman, even he lifted up *his* hand against the king. ²⁷And this *was* the cause that he lifted up *his* hand against the king: Solomon built Millo, *and* repaired° the breaches of the city of David his father. ²⁸And the man Jeroboam *was* a mighty man of valour: and Solomon seeing the young man that he was industrious°, he made him ruler over all the charge of the house of Joseph. ²⁹And it came to pass at that time when Jeroboam went out of Jerusalem, that the prophet Ahijah the Shilonite found him in the way; and he had clad himself with a new garment; and they two *were* alone in the field: ³⁰And Ahijah caught the new garment that *was* on him, and rent it *in* twelve pieces: ³¹And he said to Jeroboam, Take thee ten pieces: for thus saith the LORD, the God of Israel, Behold, I will rend the kingdom out of the hand of Solomon, and will give ten tribes to thee: ³²(But he shall have one tribe for my servant David's sake, and for Jerusalem's sake, the city which I have

chosen out of all the tribes of Israel:) ³³Because that they have forsaken me, and have worshipped Ashtoreth the goddess of the Zidonians, Chemosh the god of the Moabites, and Milcom the god of the children of Ammon, and have not walked in my ways, to do *that which is* right in mine eyes, and *to keep* my statutes and my judgments, as *did* David his father. ³⁴Howbeit I will not take the whole kingdom out of his hand: but I will make him prince all the days of his life for David my servant's sake, whom I chose, because he kept my commandments and my statutes: ³⁵But I will take the kingdom out of his son's hand, and will give it unto thee, *even* ten tribes. ³⁶And unto his son will I give one tribe, that David my servant may have a light° alway before me in Jerusalem, the city which I have chosen me to put my name there. ³⁷And I will take thee, and thou shalt reign according to all that thy soul desireth, and shalt be king over Israel. ³⁸And it shall be, if thou wilt hearken unto all that I command thee, and wilt walk in my ways, and do *that is* right in my sight, to keep my statutes and my commandments, as David my servant did; that I will be with thee, and build thee a sure house, as I built for David, and will give Israel unto thee. ³⁹And I will for this afflict the seed of David, but not for ever. ⁴⁰Solomon sought therefore to kill Jeroboam. And Jeroboam arose, and fled into Egypt, unto Shishak king of Egypt, and was in Egypt until the death of Solomon.

° repaired: Heb. closed
° was industrious: Heb. did work
° light: Heb. lamp, or, candle

⁴¹And the rest of the acts[f] of Solomon, and all that he did, and his wisdom, *are* they not written in the book of the acts of Solomon? ⁴²And the time[g] that Solomon reigned in Jerusalem over all Israel *was* forty years. ⁴³And Solomon slept with his fathers, and was buried in the city of David his father: and Rehoboam[h] his son reigned in his stead.

12

¹And Rehoboam went to Shechem: for all Israel were come to Shechem to make him king. ²And it came to pass, when Jeroboam the son of Nebat, who was yet in Egypt, heard *of it,* (for he was fled from the presence of king Solomon, and Jeroboam dwelt in Egypt;) ³That they sent and called him. And Jeroboam and all the congregation of Israel came, and spake unto Rehoboam, saying, ⁴Thy father made our yoke grievous: now therefore make thou the grievous service of thy father, and his heavy yoke which he put upon us, lighter, and we will serve thee. ⁵And he said unto them, Depart yet *for* three days, then come again to me. And the people departed. ⁶And king Rehoboam consulted with the old men, that stood before Solomon his father while he yet lived, and said, How do ye advise that I may answer this people? ⁷And they spake unto him, saying, If thou wilt be a servant unto this people this day, and wilt serve them, and answer them, and speak good words to them, then they will be thy servants for ever. ⁸But he forsook the counsel of the old men, which

they had given him, and consulted with the young men that were grown up with him, *and* which stood before him: ⁹And he said unto them, What counsel give ye that we may answer this people, who have spoken to me, saying, Make the yoke which thy father did put upon us lighter? ¹⁰And the young men that were grown up with him spake unto him, saying, Thus shalt thou speak unto this people that spake unto thee, saying, Thy father made our yoke heavy, but make thou *it* lighter unto us; thus shalt thou say unto them, My little *finger* shall be thicker than my father's loins. ¹¹And now whereas my father did lade you with a heavy yoke, I will add to your yoke: my father hath chastised you with whips, but I will chastise you with scorpions. ¹²So Jeroboam and all the people came to Rehoboam the third day, as the king had appointed, saying, Come to me again

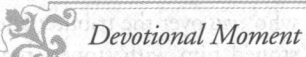

Devotional Moment
•
Advice

12:13-14 Rehoboam refused to listen to the guidance of his elders, preferring instead the advice of his peers. In doing this, Rehoboam cut himself off from the vast experience that his elders had gained over the years. As a result of Rehoboam's placing this foolish confidence in his peers, the people of Israel rebelled against his rule. Always seek the counsel of those who are older and more mature—parents, teachers, pastors, grandparents, older siblings, mentors, more mature friends. Don't rely only on peers for advice and guidance.

---

[f] acts: or, words, or, things
[g] time: Heb. days
[h] Rehoboam: Gr. Roboam

the third day. [13]And the king answered the people roughly[a], and forsook the old men's counsel that they gave him; [14]And spake to them after the counsel of the young men, saying, My father made your yoke heavy, and I will add to your yoke: my father *also* chastised you with whips, but I will chastise you with scorpions. [15]Wherefore the king hearkened not unto the people; for the cause was from the LORD, that he might perform his saying, which the LORD spake by Ahijah the Shilonite unto Jeroboam the son of Nebat.

[16]So when all Israel saw that the king hearkened not unto them, the people answered the king, saying, What portion have we in David? neither *have we* inheritance in the son of Jesse: to your tents, O Israel: now see to thine own house, David. So Israel departed unto their tents. [17]But *as for* the children of Israel which dwelt in the cities of Judah, Rehoboam reigned over them. [18]Then king Rehoboam sent Adoram, who *was* over the tribute; and all Israel stoned him with stones, that he died. Therefore king Rehoboam made speed to get him up to his chariot, to flee to Jerusalem. [19]So Israel rebelled[b] against the house of David unto this day. [20]And it came to pass, when all Israel heard that Jeroboam was come again, that they sent and called him unto the congregation, and made him king over all Israel: there was none that followed the house of David, but the tribe of Judah only. [21]And when Rehoboam was come to Jerusalem, he assembled all the house of Judah, with the tribe of Benjamin, an hundred and fourscore thousand chosen men, which were warriors, to fight against the house of Israel, to bring the kingdom again to Rehoboam the son of Solomon. [22]But the word of God came unto Shemaiah the man of God, saying, [23]Speak unto Rehoboam, the son of Solomon, king of Judah, and unto all the house of Judah and Benjamin, and to the remnant of the people, saying, [24]Thus saith the LORD, Ye shall not go up, nor fight against your brethren the children of Israel: return every man to his house; for this thing is from me. They hearkened therefore to the word of the LORD, and returned to depart, according to the word of the LORD.

[25]Then Jeroboam built Shechem in mount Ephraim, and dwelt therein; and went out from thence, and built Penuel. [26]And Jeroboam said in his heart, Now shall the kingdom return to the house of David: [27]If this people go up to do sacrifice in the house of the LORD at Jerusalem, then shall the heart of this people turn again unto their lord, *even* unto Rehoboam king of Judah, and they shall kill me, and go again to Rehoboam king of Judah. [28]Whereupon the king took counsel, and made two calves *of* gold, and said unto them, It is too much for you to go up to Jerusalem: behold thy gods, O Israel, which brought thee up out of the land of Egypt. [29]And he set the one in Bethel, and the other put he in Dan. [30]And this thing became a sin: for the people went *to worship* before the one, *even* unto Dan. [31]And he made an

---

[a] roughly: Heb. hardly
[b] rebelled: or, fell away

house of high places, and made priests of the lowest of the people, which were not of the sons of Levi. ³²And Jeroboam ordained a feast in the eighth month, on the fifteenth day of the month, like unto the feast that *is* in Judah, and he offered^c upon the altar. So did he in Bethel, sacrificing unto the calves that he had made: and he placed in Bethel the priests of the high places which he had made. ³³So he offered^d upon the altar which he had made in Bethel the fifteenth day of the eighth month, *even* in the month which he had devised of his own heart; and ordained a feast unto the children of Israel: and he offered upon the altar, and burnt incense.

13

¹And, behold, there came a man of God out of Judah by the word of the LORD unto Bethel: and Jeroboam stood by the altar to burn incense. ²And he cried against the altar in the word of the LORD, and said, O altar, altar, thus saith the LORD; Behold, a child shall be born unto the house of David, Josiah by name; and upon thee shall he offer the priests of the high places that burn incense upon thee, and men's bones shall be burnt upon thee. ³And he gave a sign the same day, saying, This *is* the sign which the LORD hath spoken; Behold, the altar shall be rent, and the ashes that *are* upon it shall be poured out. ⁴And it came to pass, when king Jeroboam heard the saying of the man of God, which had cried against the altar in Bethel, that he put forth his hand from the altar, saying, Lay hold

on him. And his hand, which he put forth against him, dried up, so that he could not pull it in again to him. ⁵The altar also was rent, and the ashes poured out from the altar, according to the sign which the man of God had given by the word of the LORD. ⁶And the king answered and said unto the man of God, Intreat now the face of the LORD thy God, and pray for me, that my hand may be restored me again. And the man of God besought the LORD, and the king's hand was restored him again, and became as *it was* before. ⁷And the king said unto the man of God, Come home with me, and refresh thyself, and I will give thee a reward. ⁸And the man of God said unto the king, If thou wilt give me half thine house, I will not go in with thee, neither will I eat bread nor drink water in this place: ⁹For so was it charged me by the word of the LORD, saying, Eat no bread, nor drink water, nor turn again by the same way that thou camest. ¹⁰So he went another way, and returned not by the way that he came to Bethel.

¹¹Now there dwelt an old prophet in Bethel; and his sons came and told him all the works that the man of God had done that day in Bethel: the words which he had spoken unto the king, them they told also to their father. ¹²And their father said unto them, What way went he? For his sons had seen what way the man of God went, which came from Judah. ¹³And he said unto his sons, Saddle me the ass. So they saddled him the ass: and he rode thereon, ¹⁴And went after the man of God, and found him sitting un-

---

^c offered . . . : or, went up to the altar, etc
^d offered . . . : or, went up to the altar, etc

der an oak: and he said unto him, *Art thou the man of God that camest from Judah?* And he said, I *am.* ¹⁵Then he said unto him, Come home with me, and eat bread. ¹⁶And he said, I may not return with thee, nor go in with thee: neither will I eat bread nor drink water with thee in this place: ¹⁷For it was said to me by the word of the LORD, Thou shalt eat no bread nor drink water there, nor turn again to go by the way that thou camest. ¹⁸He said unto him, I *am* a prophet also as thou *art*; and an angel spake unto me by the word of the LORD, saying, Bring him back with thee into thine house, that he may eat bread and drink water. *But* he lied unto him. ¹⁹So he went back with him, and did eat bread in his house, and drank water. ²⁰And it came to pass, as they sat at the table, that the word of the LORD came unto the prophet that brought him back: ²¹And he cried unto the man of God that came from Judah, saying, Thus saith the LORD, Forasmuch as thou hast disobeyed the mouth of the LORD, and hast not kept the commandment which the LORD thy God commanded thee, ²²But camest back, and hast eaten bread and drunk water in the place, of the which *the LORD* did say to thee, Eat no bread, and drink no water; thy carcase shall not come unto the sepulchre of thy fathers.

²³And it came to pass, after he had eaten bread, and after he had drunk, that he saddled for him the ass, *to wit,* for the prophet whom he had brought back. ²⁴And when he was gone, a lion met him by the way, and slew him: and his carcase was cast in the way, and the ass stood by it, the lion also stood by the carcase. ²⁵And, behold, men passed by, and saw the carcase cast in the way, and the lion standing by the carcase: and they came and told *it* in the city where the old prophet dwelt. ²⁶And when the prophet that brought him back from the way heard *thereof,* he said, It *is* the man of God, who was disobedient unto the word of the LORD: therefore the LORD hath delivered him unto the lion, which hath torn[a] him, and slain him, according to the word of the LORD, which he spake unto him. ²⁷And he spake to his sons, saying, Saddle me the ass. And they saddled *him.* ²⁸And he went and found his carcase cast in the way, and the ass and the lion standing by the carcase: the lion had not eaten the carcase, nor torn[b] the ass. ²⁹And the prophet took up the carcase of the man of God, and laid it upon the ass, and brought it back: and the old prophet came to the city, to mourn and to bury him. ³⁰And he laid his carcase in his own grave; and they mourned over him, *saying,* Alas, my brother! ³¹And it came to pass, after he had buried him, that he spake to his sons, saying, When I am dead, then bury me in the sepulchre wherein the man of God *is* buried; lay my bones beside his bones: ³²For the saying which he cried by the word of the LORD against the altar in Bethel, and against all the houses of the high places which *are* in the cities of Samaria, shall surely come to pass. ³³After this thing Jeroboam returned not from his evil way, but made[c] again of the low-

---

[a] torn: Heb. broken
[b] torn: Heb. broken
[c] made . . . : Heb. returned and made

est of the people priests of the high places: whosoever would, he consecrated him, and he became *one* of the priests of the high places. ³⁴And this thing became sin unto the house of Jeroboam, even to cut *it* off, and to destroy *it* from off the face of the earth.

14

¹At that time Abijah the son of Jeroboam fell sick. ²And Jeroboam said to his wife, Arise, I pray thee, and disguise thyself, that thou be not known to be the wife of Jeroboam; and get thee to Shiloh: behold, there *is* Ahijah the prophet, which told me that *I should be* king over this people. ³And take with thee ten loaves, and cracknels, and a cruse of honey, and go to him: he shall tell thee what shall become of the child. ⁴And Jeroboam's wife did so, and arose, and went to Shiloh, and came to the house of Ahijah. But Ahijah could not see; for his eyes were set by reason of his age. ⁵And the LORD said unto Ahijah, Behold, the wife of Jeroboam cometh to ask a thing of thee for her son; for he *is* sick: thus and thus shalt thou say unto her: for it shall be, when she cometh in, that she shall feign herself *to be* another *woman*. ⁶And it was *so*, when Ahijah heard the sound of her feet, as she came in at the door, that he said, Come in, thou wife of Jeroboam; why feignest thou thyself *to be* another? for I *am* sent to thee *with* heavy ᵃ *tidings*.

⁷Go, tell Jeroboam, Thus saith the LORD God of Israel, Forasmuch as I exalted thee from among the people, and made thee prince over my people Israel, ⁸And rent the kingdom away

from the house of David, and gave it thee: and *yet* thou hast not been as my servant David, who kept my commandments, and who followed me with all his heart, to do *that* only *which was* right in mine eyes; ⁹But hast done evil above all that were before thee: for thou hast gone and made thee other gods, and molten images, to provoke me to anger, and hast cast me behind thy back: ¹⁰Therefore, behold, I will bring evil upon the house of Jeroboam, and will cut off from Jeroboam him that pisseth against the wall, *and* him that is shut up and left in Israel, and will take away the remnant of the house of Jeroboam, as a man taketh away dung, till it be all gone. ¹¹Him that dieth of Jeroboam in the city shall the dogs eat; and him that dieth in the field shall the fowls of the air eat: for the LORD hath spoken *it*. ¹²Arise thou therefore, get thee to thine own house: *and* when thy feet enter into the city, the child shall die. ¹³And all Israel shall mourn for him, and bury him: for he only of Jeroboam shall come to the grave, because in him there is found *some* good thing toward the LORD God of Israel in the house of Jeroboam. ¹⁴Moreover the LORD shall raise him up a king over Israel, who shall cut off the house of Jeroboam that day: but what? even now. ¹⁵For the LORD shall smite Israel, as a reed is shaken in the water, and he shall root up Israel out of this good land, which he gave to their fathers, and shall scatter them beyond the river, because they have made their groves, provoking the LORD to anger. ¹⁶And he shall give Israel up because of

---

ᵃ heavy: Heb. hard

the sins of Jeroboam, who did sin, and who made Israel to sin. ¹⁷And Jeroboam's wife arose, and departed, and came to Tirzah: *and* when she came to the threshold of the door, the child died; ¹⁸And they buried him; and all Israel mourned for him, according to the word of the LORD, which he spake by the hand of his servant Ahijah the prophet. ¹⁹And the rest of the acts of Jeroboam, how he warred, and how he reigned, behold, they *are* written in the book of the chronicles of the kings of Israel. ²⁰And the days which Jeroboam reigned *were* two and twenty years: and he slept[b] with his fathers, and Nadab his son reigned in his stead.

²¹And Rehoboam the son of Solomon reigned in Judah. Rehoboam *was* forty and one years old when he began to reign, and he reigned seventeen years in Jerusalem, the city which the LORD did choose out of all the tribes of Israel, to put his name there. And his mother's name *was* Naamah an Ammonitess. ²²And Judah did evil in the sight of the LORD, and they provoked him to jealousy with their sins which they had committed, above all that their fathers had done. ²³For they also built them high places, and images[c], and groves, on every high hill, and under every green tree. ²⁴And there were also sodomites in the land: *and* they did according to all the abominations of the nations which the LORD cast out before the children of Israel. ²⁵And it came to pass in the fifth year of king Rehoboam, *that* Shishak king of Egypt came up against Jerusalem: ²⁶And he took away the treasures of the house of the LORD, and the treasures of the king's house; he even took away all: and he took away all the shields of gold which Solomon had made. ²⁷And king Rehoboam made in their stead brasen shields, and committed *them* unto the hands of the chief of the guard[d], which kept the door of the king's house. ²⁸And it was *so*, when the king went into the house of the LORD, that the guard bare them, and brought them back into the guard chamber. ²⁹Now the rest of the acts of Rehoboam, and all that he did, *are* they not written in the book of the chronicles of the kings of Judah? ³⁰And there was war between Rehoboam and Jeroboam all *their* days. ³¹And Rehoboam slept with his fathers, and was buried with his fathers in the city of David. And his mother's name *was* Naamah an Ammonitess. And Abijam[e] his son reigned in his stead.

15

¹Now in the eighteenth year of king Jeroboam the son of Nebat reigned Abijam over Judah. ²Three years reigned he in Jerusalem. And his mother's name *was* Maachah[a], the daughter of Abishalom. ³And he walked in all the sins of his father, which he had done before him: and his heart was not perfect with the LORD his God, as the heart of David

---

[b] slept: Heb. lay down
[c] images: or, standing images, or, statues
[d] guard: Heb. runners
[e] Abijam: also called, Abijah: Gr. Abia
[a] Maachah . . . : also called, Michaiah the daughter of Uriel

his father. ⁴Nevertheless for David's sake did the LORD his God give him a lamp[b] in Jerusalem, to set up his son after him, and to establish Jerusalem: ⁵Because David did *that which was* right in the eyes of the LORD, and turned not aside from any *thing* that he commanded him all the days of his life, save only in the matter of Uriah the Hittite. ⁶And there was war between Rehoboam and Jeroboam all the days of his life. ⁷Now the rest of the acts of Abijam, and all that he did, *are* they not written in the book of the chronicles of the kings of Judah? And there was war between Abijam and Jeroboam. ⁸And Abijam slept with his fathers; and they buried him in the city of David: and Asa his son reigned in his stead.

⁹And in the twentieth year of Jeroboam king of Israel reigned Asa over Judah. ¹⁰And forty and one years reigned he in Jerusalem. And his mother's[c] name *was* Maachah, the daughter of Abishalom. ¹¹And Asa did *that which was* right in the eyes of the LORD, as *did* David his father. ¹²And he took away the sodomites out of the land, and removed all the idols that his fathers had made. ¹³And also Maachah his mother, even her he removed from *being* queen, because she had made an idol in a grove; and Asa destroyed[d] her idol, and burnt *it* by the brook Kidron. ¹⁴But the high places were not removed: nevertheless Asa's heart was perfect with the LORD all his days. ¹⁵And he brought in the things[e] which his father

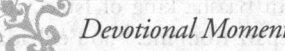

Devotional Moment
•
Parents

15:11-13 Asa pleased the Lord by executing temple prostitutes, removing idols, and deposing Maacah, his idolatrous grandmother, as queen mother. How could Asa's actions please God when God had ordained that parents be shown great honor and respect? The answer is that Maacah had participated in idol worship, which had placed the government stamp of approval on the worship of false gods. Asa had his priorities right. While he was responsible to honor his grandmother, his greater responsibility was to God. When honoring elders would lead a person away from God, the believer must yield to a higher allegiance and honor God instead.

had dedicated, and the things which himself had dedicated, into the house of the LORD, silver, and gold, and vessels. ¹⁶And there was war between Asa and Baasha king of Israel all their days. ¹⁷And Baasha king of Israel went up against Judah, and built Ramah, that he might not suffer any to go out or come in to Asa king of Judah. ¹⁸Then Asa took all the silver and the gold *that were* left in the treasures of the house of the LORD, and the treasures of the king's house, and delivered them into the hand of his servants: and king Asa sent them to Benhadad, the son of Tabrimon, the son of Hezion, king of Syria, that dwelt at Damascus, saying, ¹⁹*There is* a league between me and thee, *and* between my father and thy father: behold, I have sent unto thee a present of silver and gold; come and break thy

---

[b] lamp: or, candle
[c] mother's: that is, grandmother's
[d] destroyed: Heb. cut off
[e] things: Heb. holy

league with Baasha king of Israel, that he may depart[f] from me. ²⁰So Benhadad hearkened unto king Asa, and sent the captains of the hosts which he had against the cities of Israel, and smote Ijon, and Dan, and Abelbethmaachah, and all Cinneroth, with all the land of Naphtali. ²¹And it came to pass, when Baasha heard *thereof,* that he left off building of Ramah, and dwelt in Tirzah. ²²Then king Asa made a proclamation throughout all Judah; none *was* exempted[g]: and they took away the stones of Ramah, and the timber thereof, wherewith Baasha had builded; and king Asa built with them Geba of Benjamin, and Mizpah. ²³The rest of all the acts of Asa, and all his might, and all that he did, and the cities which he built, *are* they not written in the book of the chronicles of the kings of Judah? Nevertheless in the time of his old age he was diseased in his feet. ²⁴And Asa slept with his fathers, and was buried with his fathers in the city of David his father: and Jehoshaphat[h] his son reigned in his stead.

²⁵And Nadab the son of Jeroboam began to reign over Israel in the second year of Asa king of Judah, and reigned over Israel two years. ²⁶And he did evil in the sight of the LORD, and walked in the way of his father, and in his sin wherewith he made Israel to sin. ²⁷And Baasha the son of Ahijah, of the house of Issachar, conspired against him; and Baasha smote him at Gibbethon, which *belonged* to the Philistines; for Nadab and all Israel laid siege to Gibbethon.

²⁸Even in the third year of Asa king of Judah did Baasha slay him, and reigned in his stead. ²⁹And it came to pass, when he reigned, *that* he smote all the house of Jeroboam; he left not to Jeroboam any that breathed, until he had destroyed him, according unto the saying of the LORD, which he spake by his servant Ahijah the Shilonite: ³⁰Because of the sins of Jeroboam which he sinned, and which he made Israel sin, by his provocation wherewith he provoked the LORD God of Israel to anger. ³¹Now the rest of the acts of Nadab, and all that he did, *are* they not written in the book of the chronicles of the kings of Israel? ³²And there was war between Asa and Baasha king of Israel all their days. ³³In the third year of Asa king of Judah began Baasha the son of Ahijah to reign over all Israel in Tirzah, twenty and four years. ³⁴And he did evil in the sight of the LORD, and walked in the way of Jeroboam, and in his sin wherewith he made Israel to sin.

16

¹Then the word of the LORD came to Jehu the son of Hanani against Baasha, saying, ²Forasmuch as I exalted thee out of the dust, and made thee prince over my people Israel; and thou hast walked in the way of Jeroboam, and hast made my people Israel to sin, to provoke me to anger with their sins; ³Behold, I will take away the posterity of Baasha, and the posterity of his house; and will make thy house like the house of Jeroboam the son of Nebat. ⁴Him that

---

[f] depart: Heb. go up
[g] exempted: Heb. free
[h] Jehoshaphat: Gr. Josaphat

16:2-7 Baasha knew about the judgment against the evil of Jeroboam, yet Baasha committed the same sins Jeroboam did. Baasha ignored the warnings in Jeroboam's experiences—and paid for it with his life and the lives of his family members. We, too, often resist learning from the mistakes of others, preferring instead the harsh lessons of our own personal mistakes. We would suffer much less (and be much wiser) if we paid attention to how others lived and learned from them. Consider the examples God has placed before you.

dieth of Baasha in the city shall the dogs eat; and him that dieth of his in the fields shall the fowls of the air eat. ⁵Now the rest of the acts of Baasha, and what he did, and his might, *are* they not written in the book of the chronicles of the kings of Israel? ⁶So Baasha slept with his fathers, and was buried in Tirzah: and Elah his son reigned in his stead. ⁷And also by the hand of the prophet Jehu the son of Hanani came the word of the LORD against Baasha, and against his house, even for all the evil that he did in the sight of the LORD, in provoking him to anger with the work of his hands, in being like the house of Jeroboam; and because he killed him. ⁸In the twenty and sixth year of Asa king of Judah began Elah the son of Baasha to reign over Israel in Tirzah, two years. ⁹And his servant Zimri, captain of half *his* chariots, conspired against him, as he was in Tirzah, drinking himself drunk in the house of Arza steward of *his* house in Tirzah. ¹⁰And Zimri went in and smote

him, and killed him, in the twenty and seventh year of Asa king of Judah, and reigned in his stead. ¹¹And it came to pass, when he began to reign, as soon as he sat on his throne, *that* he slew all the house of Baasha: he left him not one that pisseth against a wall, neither of his kinsfolks, nor of his friends. ¹²Thus did Zimri destroy all the house of Baasha, according to the word of the LORD, which he spake against Baasha byᵃ Jehu the prophet, ¹³For all the sins of Baasha, and the sins of Elah his son, by which they sinned, and by which they made Israel to sin, in provoking the LORD God of Israel to anger with their vanities. ¹⁴Now the rest of the acts of Elah, and all that he did, *are* they not written in the book of the chronicles of the kings of Israel?

¹⁵In the twenty and seventh year of Asa king of Judah did Zimri reign seven days in Tirzah. And the people *were* encamped against Gibbethon, which *belonged* to the Philistines. ¹⁶And

16:13 While Baasha's individual sin was an abomination to God and worthy of punishment, the greater tragedy is that he dragged the people of Israel down with him. Family leaders have a great responsibility before God that extends beyond their individual responsibility to follow and honor the Lord; they are also responsible to guide those who are younger in God's way. Parents, grandparents, uncles, aunts: Realize that younger members of the family take many cues from you. What in your life do you want them to imitate?

ᵃ by: Heb. by the hand of

the people *that were* encamped heard say, Zimri hath conspired, and hath also slain the king: wherefore all Israel made Omri, the captain of the host, king over Israel that day in the camp. [17]And Omri went up from Gibbethon, and all Israel with him, and they besieged Tirzah. [18]And it came to pass, when Zimri saw that the city was taken, that he went into the palace of the king's house, and burnt the king's house over him with fire, and died, [19]For his sins which he sinned in doing evil in the sight of the LORD, in walking in the way of Jeroboam, and in his sin which he did, to make Israel to sin. [20]Now the rest of the acts of Zimri, and his treason that he wrought, *are* they not written in the book of the chronicles of the kings of Israel? [21]Then were the people of Israel divided into two parts: half of the people followed Tibni the son of Ginath, to make him king; and half followed Omri. [22]But the people that followed Omri prevailed against the people that followed Tibni the son of Ginath: so Tibni died, and Omri reigned. [23]In the thirty and first year of Asa king of Judah began Omri to reign over Israel, twelve years: six years reigned he in Tirzah. [24]And he bought the hill Samaria[b] of Shemer for two talents of silver, and built on the hill, and called the name of the city which he built, after the name of Shemer, owner of the hill, Samaria. [25]But Omri wrought evil in the eyes of the LORD, and did worse than all that *were* before him. [26]For he walked in all the way of Jeroboam the son of Nebat,

and in his sin wherewith he made Israel to sin, to provoke the LORD God of Israel to anger with their vanities. [27]Now the rest of the acts of Omri which he did, and his might that he shewed, *are* they not written in the book of the chronicles of the kings of Israel? [28]So Omri slept with his fathers, and was buried in Samaria: and Ahab his son reigned in his stead.

[29]And in the thirty and eighth year of Asa king of Judah began Ahab the son of Omri to reign over Israel: and Ahab the son of Omri reigned over Israel in Samaria twenty and two years. [30]And Ahab the son of Omri did evil in the sight of the LORD above all that *were* before him. [31]And it came to pass, as if it had been a light thing for him to walk in the sins of Jeroboam the son of Nebat, that he took to wife Jezebel the daughter of Ethbaal king of the Zidonians, and went and served Baal, and worshipped him. [32]And he reared up an altar for Baal in the house of Baal, which he had built in Samaria. [33]And Ahab made a grove; and Ahab did more to provoke the LORD God of Israel to anger than all the kings of Israel that were before him. [34]In his days did Hiel the Bethelite build Jericho: he laid the foundation thereof in Abiram his firstborn, and set up the gates thereof in his youngest *son* Segub, according to the word of the LORD, which he spake by Joshua the son of Nun.

17

[1]And Elijah[a] the Tishbite, *who was* of the inhabitants of Gilead, said unto

---

[b] Samaria: Heb. Shomeron
[a] Elijah: Heb. Elijahu: Gr. Elias

Ahab, *As* the LORD God of Israel liveth, before whom I stand, there shall not be dew nor rain these years, but according to my word. ²And the word of the LORD came unto him, saying, ³Get thee hence, and turn thee eastward, and hide thyself by the brook Cherith, that *is* before Jordan. ⁴And it shall be, *that* thou shalt drink of the brook; and I have commanded the ravens to feed thee there. ⁵So he went and did according unto the word of the LORD: for he went and dwelt by the brook Cherith, that *is* before Jordan. ⁶And the ravens brought him bread and flesh in the morning, and bread and flesh in the evening; and he drank of the brook. ⁷And it came to pass after^b a while, that the brook dried up, because there had been no rain in the land.

⁸And the word of the LORD came unto him, saying, ⁹Arise, get thee to Zarephath^c, which *belongeth* to Zidon, and dwell there: behold, I have commanded a widow woman there to sustain thee. ¹⁰So he arose and went to Zarephath. And when he came to the gate of the city, behold, the widow woman *was* there gathering of sticks: and he called to her, and said, Fetch me, I pray thee, a little water in a vessel, that I may drink. ¹¹And as she was going to fetch *it*, he called to her, and said, Bring me, I pray thee, a morsel of bread in thine hand. ¹²And she said, *As* the LORD thy God liveth, I have not a cake, but an handful of meal in a barrel,

and a little oil in a cruse: and, behold, I *am* gathering two sticks, that I may go in and dress it for me and my son, that we may eat it, and die. ¹³And Elijah said unto her, Fear not; go *and* do as thou hast said: but make me thereof a little cake first, and bring *it* unto me, and after make for thee and for thy son. ¹⁴For thus saith the LORD God of Israel, The barrel of meal shall not waste, neither shall the cruse of oil fail, until the day *that* the LORD sendeth^d rain upon the earth. ¹⁵And she went and did according to the saying of Elijah: and she, and he, and her house, did eat *many* days. ¹⁶*And* the barrel of meal wasted not, neither did the cruse of oil fail, according to the word of the LORD, which he spake by^e Elijah.

¹⁷And it came to pass after these things, *that* the son of the woman, the mistress of the house, fell sick; and his sickness was so sore, that there was no breath left in him. ¹⁸And she said unto Elijah, What have I to do with thee, O thou man of God? art thou come unto me to call my sin to remembrance, and to slay my son? ¹⁹And he said unto her, Give me thy son. And he took him out of her bosom, and carried him up into a loft, where he abode, and laid him upon his own bed. ²⁰And he cried unto the LORD, and said, O LORD my God, hast thou also brought evil upon the widow with whom I sojourn, by slaying her son? ²¹And he stretched^f himself upon the child three times, and

---

^b after . . . : Heb. at the end of days
^c Zarephath: Gr. Sarepta
^d sendeth: Heb. giveth
^e by: Heb. by the hand of
^f stretched: Heb. measured

cried unto the LORD, and said, O LORD my God, I pray thee, let this child's soul come into him again. ²²And the LORD heard the voice of Elijah; and the soul of the child came into him again, and he revived. ²³And Elijah took the child, and brought him down out of the chamber into the house, and delivered him unto his mother: and Elijah said, See, thy son liveth. ²⁴And the woman said to Elijah, Now by this I know that thou *art* a man of God, *and* that the word of the LORD in thy mouth *is* truth.

18

¹And it came to pass *after* many days, that the word of the LORD came to Elijah in the third year, saying, Go, shew thyself unto Ahab; and I will send rain upon the earth. ²And Elijah went to shew himself unto Ahab. And *there was* a sore famine in Samaria. ³And Ahab called Obadiahᵃ, which *was* the governor of *his* house. (Now Obadiah feared the LORD greatly: ⁴For it was *so*, when Jezebelᵇ cut off the prophets of the LORD, that Obadiah took an hundred prophets, and hid them by fifty in a cave, and fed them with bread and water.) ⁵And Ahab said unto Obadiah, Go into the land, unto all fountains of water, and unto all brooks: peradventure we may find grass to save the horses and mules alive, that we lose not all the beasts. ⁶So they divided the land between them to pass throughout it: Ahab went one way by himself, and Obadiah went another way by himself. ⁷And as Obadiah was in the way, behold, Elijah

met him: and he knew him, and fell on his face, and said, *Art* thou that my lord Elijah? ⁸And he answered him, I *am*: go, tell thy lord, Behold, Elijah *is here*. ⁹And he said, What have I sinned, that thou wouldest deliver thy servant into the hand of Ahab, to slay me? ¹⁰*As* the LORD thy God liveth, there is no nation or kingdom, whither my lord hath not sent to seek thee: and when they said, *He is* not *there*; he took an oath of the kingdom and nation, that they found thee not. ¹¹And now thou sayest, Go, tell thy lord, Behold, Elijah *is here*. ¹²And it shall come to pass, *as soon as* I am gone from thee, that the Spirit of the LORD shall carry thee whither I know not; and *so* when I come and tell Ahab, and he cannot find thee, he shall slay me: but I thy servant fear the LORD from my youth. ¹³Was it not told my lord what I did when Jezebel slew the prophets of the LORD, how I hid an hundred men of the LORD'S prophets by fifty in a cave, and fed them with bread and water? ¹⁴And now thou sayest, Go, tell thy lord, Behold, Elijah *is here*: and he shall slay me. ¹⁵And Elijah said, *As* the LORD of hosts liveth, before whom I stand, I will surely shew myself unto him to day. ¹⁶So Obadiah went to meet Ahab, and told him: and Ahab went to meet Elijah.

¹⁷And it came to pass, when Ahab saw Elijah, that Ahab said unto him, *Art* thou he that troubleth Israel? ¹⁸And he answered, I have not troubled Israel; but thou, and thy father's house, in that ye have forsaken the commandments of the LORD, and thou hast followed

---

ᵃ Obadiah: Heb. Obadiahu
ᵇ Jezebel: Heb. Izebel

Baalim. [19]Now therefore send, *and* gather to me all Israel unto mount Carmel, and the prophets of Baal four hundred and fifty, and the prophets of the groves four hundred, which eat at Jezebel's table. [20]So Ahab sent unto all the children of Israel, and gathered the prophets together unto mount Carmel.

[21]And Elijah came unto all the people, and said, How long halt ye between two opinions[c]? if the LORD *be* God, follow him: but if Baal, *then* follow him. And the people answered him not a word. [22]Then said Elijah unto the people, I, *even* I only, remain a prophet of the LORD; but Baal's prophets *are* four hundred and fifty men. [23]Let them therefore give us two bullocks; and let them choose one bullock for themselves, and cut it in pieces, and lay *it* on wood, and put no fire *under*: and I will dress the other bullock, and lay *it* on wood, and put no fire *under*: [24]And call ye on the name of your gods, and I will call on the name of the LORD: and the God that answereth by fire, let him be God. And all the people answered and said, It is well spoken. [25]And Elijah said unto the prophets of Baal, Choose you one bullock for yourselves, and dress *it* first; for ye *are* many; and call on the name of your gods, but put no fire *under*. [26]And they took the bullock which was given them, and they dressed *it*, and called on the name of Baal from morning even until noon, saying, O Baal, hear[d] us. But *there was* no voice, nor any that answered. And they leaped upon the altar which was made. [27]And it came to pass at noon, that Elijah mocked them, and said, Cry aloud[e]: for he *is* a god; either he is talking, or he is pursuing, or he is in a journey, *or* peradventure he sleepeth, and must be awaked. [28]And they cried aloud, and cut themselves after their manner with knives and lancets, till the blood[f] gushed out upon them. [29]And it came to pass, when midday was past, and they prophesied until the *time* of the offering[g] of the *evening* sacrifice, that *there was* neither voice, nor any to answer, nor any that regarded. [30]And Elijah said unto all the people, Come near unto me. And all the people came near unto him. And he repaired the altar of the LORD *that was* broken down. [31]And Elijah took twelve stones, according to the number of the tribes of the sons of Jacob, unto whom the word of the LORD came, saying, Israel shall be thy name: [32]And with the stones he built an altar in the name of the LORD: and he made a trench about the altar, as great as would contain two measures of seed. [33]And he put the wood in order, and cut the bullock in pieces, and laid *him* on the wood, and said, Fill four barrels with water, and pour *it* on the burnt sacrifice, and on the wood. [34]And he said, Do *it* the second time. And they did *it* the second time. And he said, Do *it* the third time. And they did *it* the third time. [35]And the water ran[h] round about the altar; and he

---

[c] opinions: or, thoughts?
[d] hear: or, answer
[e] aloud: Heb. with a great voice
[f] the blood . . . : Heb. poured out blood upon them
[g] offering: Heb. ascending
[h] ran: Heb. went

filled the trench also with water. ³⁶And it came to pass at *the time of* the offering of the *evening* sacrifice, that Elijah the prophet came near, and said, LORD God of Abraham, Isaac, and of Israel, let it be known this day that thou *art* God in Israel, and *that* I *am* thy servant, and *that* I have done all these things at thy word. ³⁷Hear me, O LORD, hear me, that this people may know that thou *art* the LORD God, and *that* thou hast turned their heart back again. ³⁸Then the fire of the LORD fell, and consumed the burnt sacrifice, and the wood, and the stones, and the dust, and licked up the water that *was* in the trench. ³⁹And when all the people saw *it*, they fell on their faces: and they said, The LORD, he *is* the God; the LORD, he *is* the God. ⁴⁰And Elijah said unto them, Take ⁱ the prophets of Baal; let not one of them escape. And they took them: and Elijah brought them down to the brook Kishon, and slew them there.

⁴¹And Elijah said unto Ahab, Get thee up, eat and drink; for *there is* a sound ʲ of abundance of rain. ⁴²So Ahab went up to eat and to drink. And Elijah went up to the top of Carmel; and he cast himself down upon the earth, and put his face between his knees, ⁴³And said to his servant, Go up now, look toward the sea. And he went up, and looked, and said, *There is* nothing. And he said, Go again seven times. ⁴⁴And it came to pass at the seventh time, that he said, Behold, there ariseth a little cloud out of the sea, like a man's hand.

And he said, Go up, say unto Ahab, Prepare ᵏ *thy chariot*, and get thee down, that the rain stop thee not. ⁴⁵And it came to pass in the mean while, that the heaven was black with clouds and wind, and there was a great rain. And Ahab rode, and went to Jezreel. ⁴⁶And the hand of the LORD was on Elijah; and he girded up his loins, and ran before Ahab to the entrance of Jezreel.

19

¹And Ahab told Jezebel all that Elijah had done, and withal how he had slain all the prophets with the sword. ²Then Jezebel sent a messenger unto Elijah, saying, So let the gods do *to me*, and more also, if I make not thy life as the life of one of them by to morrow about this time. ³And when he saw *that*, he arose, and went for his life, and came to Beersheba, which *belongeth* to Judah, and left his servant there. ⁴But he himself went a day's journey into the wilderness, and came and sat down under a juniper tree: and he requested for himself ᵃ that he might die; and said, It is enough; now, O LORD, take away my life; for I *am* not better than my fathers. ⁵And as he lay and slept under a juniper tree, behold, then an angel touched him, and said unto him, Arise *and* eat. ⁶And he looked, and, behold, *there was* a cake baken on the coals, and a cruse of water at his head ᵇ. And he did eat and drink, and laid him down again. ⁷And the angel of the LORD came again the second time,

---

ⁱ Take: or, Apprehend
ʲ a sound . . . : or, a sound of a noise of rain
ᵏ Prepare: Heb. Tie, or, Bind
ᵃ for himself: Heb. for his life
ᵇ head: Heb. bolster

and touched him, and said, Arise *and* eat; because the journey *is* too great for thee. ⁸And he arose, and did eat and drink, and went in the strength of that meat forty days and forty nights unto Horeb the mount of God.

⁹And he came thither unto a cave, and lodged there; and, behold, the word of the LORD *came* to him, and he said unto him, What doest thou here, Elijah? ¹⁰And he said, I have been very jealous for the LORD God of hosts: for the children of Israel have forsaken thy covenant, thrown down thine altars, and slain thy prophets with the sword; and I, *even* I only, am left; and they seek my life, to take it away. ¹¹And he said, Go forth, and stand upon the mount before the LORD. And, behold, the LORD passed by, and a great and strong wind rent the mountains, and brake in pieces the rocks before the LORD; *but* the LORD *was* not in the wind: and after the wind an earthquake; *but* the LORD *was* not in the earthquake: ¹²And after the earthquake a fire; *but* the LORD *was* not in the fire: and after the fire a still small voice. ¹³And it was *so,* when Elijah heard *it,* that he wrapped his face in his mantle, and went out, and stood in the entering in of the cave. And, behold, *there came* a voice unto him, and said, What doest thou here, Elijah? ¹⁴And he said, I have been very jealous for the LORD God of hosts: because the children of Israel have forsaken thy covenant, thrown down thine altars, and slain thy prophets with the sword; and I, *even* I only, am left; and they seek my life, to take it away. ¹⁵And the LORD said unto him, Go, return on thy way to the wilderness of Damascus: and when thou comest, anoint Hazael *to be* king over Syria: ¹⁶And Jehu the son of Nimshi shalt thou anoint *to be* king over Israel: and Elisha[c] the son of Shaphat of Abelmeholah shalt thou anoint *to be* prophet in thy room. ¹⁷And it shall come to pass, *that* him that escapeth the sword of Hazael shall Jehu slay: and him that escapeth from the sword of Jehu shall Elisha slay. ¹⁸Yet I have left *me* seven thousand in Israel, all the knees which have not bowed unto Baal, and every mouth which hath not kissed him.

¹⁹So he departed thence, and found Elisha the son of Shaphat, who *was* plowing *with* twelve yoke *of oxen* before him, and he with the twelfth: and Elijah passed by him, and cast his mantle upon him. ²⁰And he left the oxen, and ran after Elijah, and said, Let me, I pray thee, kiss my father and my mother, and *then* I will follow thee. And he said unto him, Go back again: for what have I done to thee? ²¹And he returned back from him, and took a yoke of oxen, and slew them, and boiled their flesh with the instruments of the oxen, and gave unto the people, and they did eat. Then he arose, and went after Elijah, and ministered unto him.

20

¹And Benhadad the king of Syria gathered all his host together: and *there were* thirty and two kings with him, and horses, and chariots: and he went up and besieged Samaria, and warred against it. ²And he sent messengers to Ahab king of Israel into the city, and said unto him, Thus saith Benhadad,

---

[c] Elisha: Gr. Eliseus

³Thy silver and thy gold *is* mine; thy wives also and thy children, *even* the goodliest, *are* mine. ⁴And the king of Israel answered and said, My lord, O king, according to thy saying, I *am* thine, and all that I have. ⁵And the messengers came again, and said, Thus speaketh Benhadad, saying, Although I have sent unto thee, saying, Thou shalt deliver me thy silver, and thy gold, and thy wives, and thy children; ⁶Yet I will send my servants unto thee to morrow about this time, and they shall search thine house, and the houses of thy servants; and it shall be, *that* whatsoever is pleasant ᵃ in thine eyes, they shall put *it* in their hand, and take *it* away. ⁷Then the king of Israel called all the elders of the land, and said, Mark, I pray you, and see how this *man* seeketh mischief: for he sent unto me for my wives, and for my children, and for my silver, and for my gold; and I denied ᵇ him not. ⁸And all the elders and all the people said unto him, Hearken not *unto him*, nor consent. ⁹Wherefore he said unto the messengers of Benhadad, Tell my lord the king, All that thou didst send for to thy servant at the first I will do: but this thing I may not do. And the messengers departed, and brought him word again. ¹⁰And Benhadad sent unto him, and said, The gods do so unto me, and more also, if the dust of Samaria shall suffice for handfuls for all the people that follow ᶜ me. ¹¹And the king of Israel answered and said, Tell *him*, Let not him that girdeth on *his harness* boast himself as he that putteth it off.

¹²And it came to pass, when *Benhadad* heard this message ᵈ, as he *was* drinking, he and the kings in the pavilions, that he said unto his servants, Set *yourselves in array*. And they set *themselves in array* against the city. ¹³And, behold, there came ᵉ a prophet unto Ahab king of Israel, saying, Thus saith the LORD, Hast thou seen all this great multitude? behold, I will deliver it into thine hand this day; and thou shalt know that I *am* the LORD. ¹⁴And Ahab said, By whom? And he said, Thus saith the LORD, *Even* by the young men of the princes of the provinces. Then he said, Who shall order the battle? And he answered, Thou. ¹⁵Then he numbered the young men of the princes of the provinces, and they were two hundred and thirty two: and after them he numbered all the people, *even* all the children of Israel, *being* seven thousand. ¹⁶And they went out at noon. But Benhadad *was* drinking himself drunk in the pavilions, he and the kings, the thirty and two kings that helped him. ¹⁷And the young men of the princes of the provinces went out first; and Benhadad sent out, and they told him, saying, There are men come out of Samaria. ¹⁸And he said, Whether they be come out for peace, take them alive; or whether they be come out for war, take them alive. ¹⁹So these young men of the princes of the provinces came out of the

---

ᵃ pleasant: Heb. desirable
ᵇ I denied . . . : Heb. I kept not back from him
ᶜ follow . . . : Heb. are at my feet
ᵈ message: Heb. word
ᵉ came: Heb. approached

city, and the army which followed them. ²⁰And they slew every one his man: and the Syrians fled; and Israel pursued them: and Benhadad the king of Syria escaped on an horse with the horsemen. ²¹And the king of Israel went out, and smote the horses and chariots, and slew the Syrians with a great slaughter.

²²And the prophet came to the king of Israel, and said unto him, Go, strengthen thyself, and mark, and see what thou doest: for at the return of the year the king of Syria will come up against thee. ²³And the servants of the king of Syria said unto him, Their gods *are* gods of the hills; therefore they were stronger than we; but let us fight against them in the plain, and surely we shall be stronger than they. ²⁴And do this thing, Take the kings away, every man out of his place, and put captains in their rooms: ²⁵And number thee an army, like the army that thou hast lost, horse for horse, and chariot for chariot: and we will fight against them in the plain, *and* surely we shall be stronger than they. And he hearkened unto their voice, and did so. ²⁶And it came to pass at the return of the year, that Benhadad numbered the Syrians, and went up to Aphek, to fight[f] against Israel. ²⁷And the children of Israel were numbered, and were all present, and went against them: and the children of Israel pitched before them like two little flocks of kids; but the Syrians filled the country. ²⁸And there came a man of God, and spake unto the king of Israel, and said, Thus saith the LORD, Because the Syrians have said, The LORD *is* God of the hills, but he *is* not God of the val-

leys, therefore will I deliver all this great multitude into thine hand, and ye shall know that I *am* the LORD. ²⁹And they pitched one over against the other seven days. And *so* it was, that in the seventh day the battle was joined: and the children of Israel slew of the Syrians an hundred thousand footmen in one day. ³⁰But the rest fled to Aphek, into the city; and *there* a wall fell upon twenty and seven thousand of the men *that were* left. And Benhadad fled, and came into the city, into an inner chamber.

³¹And his servants said unto him, Behold now, we have heard that the kings of the house of Israel *are* merciful kings: let us, I pray thee, put sackcloth on our loins, and ropes upon our heads, and go out to the king of Israel: peradventure he will save thy life. ³²So they girded sackcloth on their loins, and *put* ropes on their heads, and came to the king of Israel, and said, Thy servant Benhadad saith, I pray thee, let me live. And he said, *Is* he yet alive? he *is* my brother. ³³Now the men did diligently observe whether *any thing would come* from him, and did hastily catch *it*: and they said, Thy brother Benhadad. Then he said, Go ye, bring him. Then Benhadad came forth to him; and he caused him to come up into the chariot. ³⁴And *Benhadad* said unto him, The cities, which my father took from thy father, I will restore; and thou shalt make streets for thee in Damascus, as my father made in Samaria. Then *said Ahab*, I will send thee away with this covenant. So he made a covenant with him, and sent him away. ³⁵And a certain man of the sons of the prophets said unto his neighbour in the

---

f to fight . . . : Heb. to the war with Israel

word of the LORD, Smite me, I pray thee. And the man refused to smite him. ³⁶Then said he unto him, Because thou hast not obeyed the voice of the LORD, behold, as soon as thou art departed from me, a lion shall slay thee. And as soon as he was departed from him, a lion found him, and slew him. ³⁷Then he found another man, and said, Smite me, I pray thee. And the man smote him, so that in smiting he wounded *him*. ³⁸So the prophet departed, and waited for the king by the way, and disguised himself with ashes upon his face. ³⁹And as the king passed by, he cried unto the king: and he said, Thy servant went out into the midst of the battle; and, behold, a man turned aside, and brought a man unto me, and said, Keep this man: if by any means he be missing, then shall thy life be for his life, or else thou shalt pay ᵍ a talent of silver. ⁴⁰And as thy servant was busy here and there, he was gone. And the king of Israel said unto him, So *shall* thy judgment *be*; thyself hast decided *it*. ⁴¹And he hasted, and took the ashes away from his face; and the king of Israel discerned him that he *was* of the prophets. ⁴²And he said unto him, Thus saith the LORD, Because thou hast let go out of *thy* hand a man whom I appointed to utter destruction, therefore thy life shall go for his life, and thy people for his people. ⁴³And the king of Israel went to his house heavy and displeased, and came to Samaria.

21

¹And it came to pass after these things, *that* Naboth the Jezreelite had a vineyard, which *was* in Jezreel, hard by the palace of Ahab king of Samaria. ²And Ahab spake unto Naboth, saying, Give me thy vineyard, that I may have it for a garden of herbs, because it *is* near unto my house: and I will give thee for it a better vineyard than it; *or*, if it seem good to thee, I will give thee the worth of it in money. ³And Naboth said to Ahab, The LORD forbid it me, that I should give the inheritance of my fathers unto thee. ⁴And Ahab came into his house heavy and displeased because of the word which Naboth the Jezreelite had spoken to him: for he had said, I will not give thee the inheritance of my fathers. And he laid him down upon his bed, and turned away his face, and would eat no bread.

⁵But Jezebel his wife came to him, and said unto him, Why is thy spirit so sad, that thou eatest no bread? ⁶And he said unto her, Because I spake unto Naboth the Jezreelite, and said unto him, Give me thy vineyard for money; or else, if it please thee, I will give thee *another* vineyard for it: and he answered, I will not give thee my vineyard. ⁷And Jezebel his wife said unto him, Dost thou now govern the kingdom of Israel? arise, *and* eat bread, and let thine heart be merry: I will give thee the vineyard of Naboth the Jezreelite. ⁸So she wrote letters in Ahab's name, and sealed *them* with his seal, and sent the letters unto the elders and to the nobles that *were* in his city, dwelling with Naboth. ⁹And she wrote in the letters, saying, Proclaim a fast, and set Naboth on high ᵃ among the people: ¹⁰And set two men, sons of Belial, before him, to bear witness against him, saying, Thou didst

---

ᵍ pay: Heb. weigh
ᵃ on high . . . : Heb. in the top of the people

blaspheme God and the king. And *then* carry him out, and stone him, that he may die. [11]And the men of his city, *even* the elders and the nobles who were the inhabitants in his city, did as Jezebel had sent unto them, *and* as it *was* written in the letters which she had sent unto them. [12]They proclaimed a fast, and set Naboth on high among the people. [13]And there came in two men, children of Belial, and sat before him: and the men of Belial witnessed against him, *even* against Naboth, in the presence of the people, saying, Naboth did blaspheme God and the king. Then they carried him forth out of the city, and stoned him with stones, that he died. [14]Then they sent to Jezebel, saying, Naboth is stoned, and is dead. [15]And it came to pass, when Jezebel heard that Naboth was stoned, and was dead, that Jezebel said to Ahab, Arise, take possession of the vineyard of Naboth the Jezreelite, which he refused to give thee for money: for Naboth is not alive, but dead. [16]And it came to pass, when Ahab heard that Naboth was dead, that Ahab rose up to go down to the vineyard of Naboth the Jezreelite, to take possession of it.

[17]And the word of the LORD came to Elijah the Tishbite, saying, [18]Arise, go down to meet Ahab king of Israel, which *is* in Samaria: behold, *he is* in the vineyard of Naboth, whither he is gone down to possess it. [19]And thou shalt speak unto him, saying, Thus saith the LORD, Hast thou killed, and also taken possession? And thou shalt speak unto him, saying, Thus saith the LORD, In the place where dogs licked the blood of Naboth shall dogs lick thy blood, even thine. [20]And Ahab said to Elijah, Hast

thou found me, O mine enemy? And he answered, I have found *thee*: because thou hast sold thyself to work evil in the sight of the LORD. [21]Behold, I will bring evil upon thee, and will take away thy posterity, and will cut off from Ahab him that pisseth against the wall, and him that is shut up and left in Israel, [22]And will make thine house like the house of Jeroboam the son of Nebat, and like the house of Baasha the son of Ahijah, for the provocation wherewith thou hast provoked *me* to anger, and made Israel to sin. [23]And of Jezebel also spake the LORD, saying, The dogs shall eat Jezebel by the wall[b] of Jezreel. [24]Him that dieth of Ahab in the city the dogs shall eat; and him that dieth in the field shall the fowls of the air eat. [25]But there was none like unto Ahab, which did sell himself to work wickedness in the sight of the LORD, whom Jezebel his wife stirred up. [26]And he did very abominably in following idols, according to all *things* as did the Amorites, whom the LORD cast out before the children of Israel. [27]And it came to pass, when Ahab heard those words, that he rent his clothes, and put sackcloth upon his flesh, and fasted, and lay in sackcloth, and went softly. [28]And the word of the LORD came to Elijah the Tishbite, saying, [29]Seest thou how Ahab humbleth himself before me? because he humbleth himself before me, I will not bring the evil in his days: *but* in his son's days will I bring the evil upon his house.

22

[1]And they continued three years without war between Syria and Israel. [2]And it

---

[b] wall: or, ditch

came to pass in the third year, that Jehoshaphat the king of Judah came down to the king of Israel. [3]And the king of Israel said unto his servants, Know ye that Ramoth in Gilead *is* ours, and we *be* still[a], *and* take it not out of the hand of the king of Syria? [4]And he said unto Jehoshaphat, Wilt thou go with me to battle to Ramothgilead? And Jehoshaphat said to the king of Israel, I *am* as thou *art*, my people as thy people, my horses as thy horses. [5]And Jehoshaphat said unto the king of Israel, Enquire, I pray thee, at the word of the LORD to day. [6]Then the king of Israel gathered the prophets together, about four hundred men, and said unto them, Shall I go against Ramothgilead to battle, or shall I forbear? And they said, Go up; for the Lord shall deliver *it* into the hand of the king. [7]And Jehoshaphat said, *Is there* not here a prophet of the LORD besides, that we might enquire of him? [8]And the king of Israel said unto Jehoshaphat, *There is* yet one man, Micaiah the son of Imlah, by whom we may enquire of the LORD: but I hate him; for he doth not prophesy good concerning me, but evil. And Jehoshaphat said, Let not the king say so. [9]Then the king of Israel called an officer[b], and said, Hasten *hither* Micaiah the son of Imlah. [10]And the king of Israel and Jehoshaphat the king of Judah sat each on his throne, having put on their robes, in a void place in the entrance of the gate of Samaria; and all the prophets prophesied before them. [11]And Zedekiah the son of Chenaanah made him horns of iron: and he said, Thus saith the LORD, With these shalt thou push the Syrians, until thou have consumed them. [12]And all the prophets prophesied so, saying, Go up to Ramothgilead, and prosper: for the LORD shall deliver *it* into the king's hand. [13]And the messenger that was gone to call Micaiah spake unto him, saying, Behold now, the words of the prophets *declare* good unto the king with one mouth: let thy word, I pray thee, be like the word of one of them, and speak *that which is* good. [14]And Micaiah said, *As* the LORD liveth, what the LORD saith unto me, that will I speak.

[15]So he came to the king. And the king said unto him, Micaiah, shall we go against Ramothgilead to battle, or shall we forbear? And he answered him, Go, and prosper: for the LORD shall deliver *it* into the hand of the king. [16]And the king said unto him, How many times shall I adjure thee that thou tell me nothing but *that which is* true in the name of the LORD? [17]And he said, I saw all Israel scattered upon the hills, as sheep that have not a shepherd: and the LORD said, These have no master: let them return every man to his house in peace. [18]And the king of Israel said unto Jehoshaphat, Did I not tell thee that he would prophesy no good concerning me, but evil? [19]And he said, Hear thou therefore the word of the LORD: I saw the LORD sitting on his throne, and all the host of heaven standing by him on his right hand and on his left. [20]And the LORD said, Who shall persuade[c] Ahab, that he may go up and

---

[a] still . . . : Heb. silent from taking it
[b] officer: or, eunuch
[c] persuade: or, deceive

fall at Ramothgilead? And one said on this manner, and another said on that manner. ²¹And there came forth a spirit, and stood before the LORD, and said, I will persuade him. ²²And the LORD said unto him, Wherewith? And he said, I will go forth, and I will be a lying spirit in the mouth of all his prophets. And he said, Thou shalt persuade *him*, and prevail also: go forth, and do so. ²³Now therefore, behold, the LORD hath put a lying spirit in the mouth of all these thy prophets, and the LORD hath spoken evil concerning thee. ²⁴But Zedekiah the son of Chenaanah went near, and smote Micaiah on the cheek, and said, Which way went the Spirit of the LORD from me to speak unto thee? ²⁵And Micaiah said, Behold, thou shalt see in that day, when thou shalt go into an inner chamber to hide thyself. ²⁶And the king of Israel said, Take Micaiah, and carry him back unto Amon the governor of the city, and to Joash the king's son; ²⁷And say, Thus saith the king, Put this *fellow* in the prison, and feed him with bread of affliction and with water of affliction, until I come in peace. ²⁸And Micaiah said, If thou return at all in peace, the LORD hath not spoken by me. And he said, Hearken, O people, every one of you.

²⁹So the king of Israel and Jehoshaphat the king of Judah went up to Ramothgilead. ³⁰And the king of Israel said unto Jehoshaphat, I will disguise myself, and enter into the battle; but put thou on thy robes. And the king of Israel disguised himself, and went into the battle. ³¹But the king of Syria commanded his thirty and two captains that had rule over his chariots, saying, Fight neither with small nor great, save only with the king of Israel. ³²And it came to pass, when the captains of the chariots saw Jehoshaphat, that they said, Surely it *is* the king of Israel. And they turned aside to fight against him: and Jehoshaphat cried out. ³³And it came to pass, when the captains of the chariots perceived that it *was* not the king of Israel, that they turned back from pursuing him. ³⁴And a *certain* man drew a bow at a venture, and smote the king of Israel between the joints of the harness: wherefore he said unto the driver of his chariot, Turn thine hand, and carry me out of the host; for I am wounded. ³⁵And the battle increased^d that day: and the king was stayed up in his chariot against the Syrians, and died at even: and the blood ran out of the wound into the midst of the chariot. ³⁶And there went a proclamation throughout the host about the going down of the sun, saying, Every man to his city, and every man to his own country. ³⁷So the king died, and was brought^e to Samaria; and they buried the king in Samaria. ³⁸And *one* washed the chariot in the pool of Samaria; and the dogs licked up his blood; and they washed his armour; according unto the word of the LORD which he spake. ³⁹Now the rest of the acts of Ahab, and all that he did, and the ivory house which he made, and all the cities that he built, *are* they not written in the book of the chronicles of the kings of Israel? ⁴⁰So Ahab slept with his fathers; and Ahaziah his son reigned in his stead.

---

^d increased: Heb. ascended
^e was brought: Heb. came

⁴¹And Jehoshaphat the son of Asa began to reign over Judah in the fourth year of Ahab king of Israel. ⁴²Jehoshaphat *was* thirty and five years old when he began to reign; and he reigned twenty and five years in Jerusalem. And his mother's name *was* Azubah the daughter of Shilhi. ⁴³And he walked in all the ways of Asa his father; he turned not aside from it, doing *that which was* right in the eyes of the LORD: nevertheless the high places were not taken away; *for* the people offered and burnt incense yet in the high places. ⁴⁴And Jehoshaphat made peace with the king of Israel. ⁴⁵Now the rest of the acts of Jehoshaphat, and his might that he shewed, and how he warred, *are* they not written in the book of the chronicles of the kings of Judah? ⁴⁶And the remnant of the sodomites, which remained in the days of his father Asa, he took out of the land. ⁴⁷*There was* then no king in Edom: a deputy *was* king.

⁴⁸Jehoshaphat made ᶠ ships of Tharshish to go to Ophir for gold: but they went not; for the ships were broken at Eziongeber. ⁴⁹Then said Ahaziah the son of Ahab unto Jehoshaphat, Let my servants go with thy servants in the ships. But Jehoshaphat would not. ⁵⁰And Jehoshaphat slept with his fathers, and was buried with his fathers in the city of David his father: and Jehoram his son reigned in his stead. ⁵¹Ahaziah the son of Ahab began to reign over Israel in Samaria the seventeenth year of Jehoshaphat king of Judah, and reigned two years over Israel. ⁵²And he did evil in the sight of the LORD, and walked in the way of his father, and in the way of his mother, and in the way of Jeroboam the son of Nebat, who made Israel to sin: ⁵³For he served Baal, and worshipped him, and provoked to anger the LORD God of Israel, according to all that his father had done.

ᶠ made . . . : or, had ten ships

SECOND KINGS

We rarely witness flat-out miracles. Nothing like the spectacular events of the Old Testament. But miracles happen, and often they are the sort of events that someone has to remind us about.

"Wasn't Sally's recovery a *miracle?*"

"What a *miracle* that truck missed us!"

"Getting these five tickets—front row upper deck—it's a *miracle!*"

Second Kings is like a series of miracles that nobody recognized (except the prophets). Finally it was too late to save the sinking country, and the book ends on a huge downbeat: The nation of Israel flickers out to the drumbeat of conquering Babylon. All the hopes of the people—present when they left Egypt with Moses and conquered Canaan with Joshua—go dry as a tyrant imprisons the people and takes the land. At the end, the kings of Israel and Judah are mere puppets and the miracles, a distant fading memory.

What would it take for the people to see the miracles of 2 Kings, to recognize God at work, to keep the nation? Why did so many families back then miss the point, blind when God was telling them: "Wake up and see who I am!"?

Do you have a miracle going on today that a keen eye for God would see, that a quiet prayer would acknowledge?

Look around. You could be surprised!

1

¹Then Moab rebelled against Israel after the death of Ahab. ²And Ahaziah fell down through a lattice in his upper chamber that *was* in Samaria, and was sick: and he sent messengers, and said unto them, Go, enquire of Baalzebub the god of Ekron whether I shall recover of this disease. ³But the angel of the LORD said to Elijah the Tishbite, Arise, go up to meet the messengers of the king of Samaria, and say unto them, *Is it* not because *there is* not a God in Israel, *that* ye go to enquire of Baalzebub the god of Ekron? ⁴Now therefore thus saith the LORD, Thou shalt not come down from that bed on which thou art gone up, but shalt surely die. And Elijah departed. ⁵And when the messengers turned back unto him, he said unto them, Why are ye now turned back? ⁶And they said unto him, There came a man up to meet us, and said unto us, Go, turn again unto the king that sent you, and say unto him, Thus saith the LORD, *Is it* not because *there is* not a God in Israel, *that* thou sendest to enquire of Baalzebub the god of Ekron? therefore thou shalt not come down from that bed on which thou art gone up, but shalt surely die. ⁷And he said unto them, What manner of man *was he* which came up to meet you, and told you these words? ⁸And they answered him, *He was* an hairy man, and girt with a girdle of leather about his loins. And he said, It *is* Elijah the Tishbite.

⁹Then the king sent unto him a captain of fifty with his fifty. And he went up to him: and, behold, he sat on the top of an hill. And he spake unto him, Thou man of God, the king hath said, Come down. ¹⁰And Elijah answered and said to the captain of fifty, If I *be* a man of God, then let fire come down from heaven, and consume thee and thy fifty. And there came down fire from heaven, and consumed him and his fifty. ¹¹Again also he sent unto him another captain of fifty with his fifty. And he answered and said unto him, O man of God, thus hath the king said, Come down quickly. ¹²And Elijah answered and said unto them, If I *be* a man of God, let fire come down from heaven, and consume thee and thy fifty. And the fire of God came down from heaven, and consumed him and his fifty. ¹³And he sent again a captain of the third fifty with his fifty. And the third captain of fifty went up, and came and fellᵃ on his knees before Elijah, and besought him, and said unto him, O man of God, I pray thee, let my life, and the life of these fifty thy servants, be precious in thy sight. ¹⁴Behold, there came fire down from heaven, and burnt up the two captains of the former fifties with their fifties: therefore let my life now be precious in thy sight. ¹⁵And the angel of the LORD said unto Elijah, Go down with him: be not afraid of him. And he arose, and went down with him unto the king. ¹⁶And he said unto him, Thus saith the LORD, Forasmuch as thou hast sent messengers to enquire of Baalzebub the god of Ekron, *is it* not because *there is* no God in Israel to enquire of his word? therefore thou shalt not come down off that

---

ᵃ fell: Heb. bowed

bed on which thou art gone up, but shalt surely die. ¹⁷So he died according to the word of the LORD which Elijah had spoken. And Jehoram reigned in his stead in the second year of Jehoram the son of Jehoshaphat king of Judah; because he had no son. ¹⁸Now the rest of the acts of Ahaziah which he did, *are* they not written in the book of the chronicles of the kings of Israel?

2

¹And it came to pass, when the LORD would take up Elijah into heaven by a whirlwind, that Elijah went with Elisha from Gilgal. ²And Elijah said unto Elisha, Tarry here, I pray thee; for the LORD hath sent me to Bethel. And Elisha said *unto him, As* the LORD liveth, and *as* thy soul liveth, I will not leave thee. So they went down to Bethel. ³And the sons of the prophets that *were* at Bethel came forth to Elisha, and said unto him, Knowest thou that the LORD will take away thy master from thy head to day? And he said, Yea, I know *it*; hold ye your peace. ⁴And Elijah said unto him, Elisha, tarry here, I pray thee; for the LORD hath sent me to Jericho. And he said, *As* the LORD liveth, and *as* thy soul liveth, I will not leave thee. So they came to Jericho. ⁵And the sons of the prophets that *were* at Jericho came to Elisha, and said unto him, Knowest thou that the LORD will take away thy master from thy head to day? And he answered, Yea, I know *it*; hold ye your peace. ⁶And Elijah said unto him, Tarry, I pray thee, here; for the LORD hath sent me to Jordan.

And he said, *As* the LORD liveth, and *as* thy soul liveth, I will not leave thee. And they two went on. ⁷And fifty men of the sons of the prophets went, and stood to view ᵃ afar off: and they two stood by Jordan. ⁸And Elijah took his mantle, and wrapped *it* together, and smote the waters, and they were divided hither and thither, so that they two went over on dry ground.

⁹And it came to pass, when they were gone over, that Elijah said unto Elisha, Ask what I shall do for thee, before I be taken away from thee. And Elisha said, I pray thee, let a double portion of thy spirit be upon me. ¹⁰And he said, Thou hast asked a hard thing: *nevertheless*, if thou see me *when I am* taken from thee, it shall be so unto thee; but if not, it shall not be *so*. ¹¹And it came to pass, as they still went on, and talked, that, behold, *there appeared* a chariot of fire, and horses of fire, and parted them both asunder; and Elijah went up by a whirlwind into heaven. ¹²And Elisha saw *it*, and he cried, My father, my father, the chariot of Israel, and the horsemen thereof. And he saw him no more: and he took hold of his own clothes, and rent them in two pieces.

¹³He took up also the mantle of Elijah that fell from him, and went back, and stood by the bankᵇ of Jordan; ¹⁴And he took the mantle of Elijah that fell from him, and smote the waters, and said, Where *is* the LORD God of Elijah? and when he also had smitten the waters, they parted hither and thither: and Elisha went over. ¹⁵And when the sons of the prophets which

---

ᵃ to view: Heb. in sight, or, over against
ᵇ bank: Heb. lip

were to view at Jericho saw him, they said, The spirit of Elijah doth rest on Elisha. And they came to meet him, and bowed themselves to the ground before him. ¹⁶And they said unto him, Behold now, there be with thy servants fifty strong⁣ᶜ men; let them go, we pray thee, and seek thy master: lest peradventure the Spirit of the LORD hath taken him up, and cast him upon some mountain, or into some valley. And he said, Ye shall not send. ¹⁷And when they urged him till he was ashamed, he said, Send. They sent therefore fifty men; and they sought three days, but found him not. ¹⁸And when they came again to him, (for he tarried at Jericho,) he said unto them, Did I not say unto you, Go not?

¹⁹And the men of the city said unto Elisha, Behold, I pray thee, the situation of this city *is* pleasant, as my lord seeth: but the water *is* naught, and the ground barrenᵈ. ²⁰And he said, Bring me a new cruse, and put salt therein. And they brought *it* to him. ²¹And he went forth unto the spring of the waters, and cast the salt in there, and said, Thus saith the LORD, I have healed these waters; there shall not be from thence any more death or barren *land*. ²²So the waters were healed unto this day, according to the saying of Elisha which he spake. ²³And he went up from thence unto Bethel: and as he was going up by the way, there came forth little children out of the city, and mocked him, and said unto him, Go up, thou bald head; go up, thou bald head. ²⁴And

he turned back, and looked on them, and cursed them in the name of the LORD. And there came forth two she bears out of the wood, and tare forty and two children of them. ²⁵And he went from thence to mount Carmel, and from thence he returned to Samaria.

3

¹Now Jehoram the son of Ahab began to reign over Israel in Samaria the eighteenth year of Jehoshaphat king of Judah, and reigned twelve years. ²And he wrought evil in the sight of the LORD; but not like his father, and like his mother: for he put away the imageᵃ of Baal that his father had made. ³Nevertheless he cleaved unto the sins of Jeroboam the son of Nebat, which made Israel to sin; he departed not therefrom. ⁴And Mesha king of Moab was a sheepmaster, and rendered unto the king of Israel an hundred thousand lambs, and an hundred thousand rams, with the wool. ⁵But it came to pass, when Ahab was dead, that the king of Moab rebelled against the king of Israel.

⁶And king Jehoram went out of Samaria the same time, and numbered all Israel. ⁷And he went and sent to Jehoshaphat the king of Judah, saying, The king of Moab hath rebelled against me: wilt thou go with me against Moab to battle? And he said, I will go up: I *am* as thou *art*, my people as thy people, *and* my horses as thy horses. ⁸And he said, Which way shall we go up? And he answered, The way through the

---

ᶜ strong . . . : Heb. sons of strength
ᵈ barren: Heb. causing to miscarry
ᵃ image: Heb. statue

wilderness of Edom. ⁹So the king of Israel went, and the king of Judah, and the king of Edom: and they fetched a compass of seven days' journey: and there was no water for the host, and for the cattle that followed them. ¹⁰And the king of Israel said, Alas! that the LORD hath called these three kings together, to deliver them into the hand of Moab! ¹¹But Jehoshaphat said, *Is there* not here a prophet of the LORD, that we may enquire of the LORD by him? And one of the king of Israel's servants answered and said, Here *is* Elisha the son of Shaphat, which poured water on the hands of Elijah. ¹²And Jehoshaphat said, The word of the LORD is with him. So the king of Israel and Jehoshaphat and the king of Edom went down to him. ¹³And Elisha said unto the king of Israel, What have I to do with thee? get thee to the prophets of thy father, and to the prophets of thy mother. And the king of Israel said unto him, Nay: for the LORD hath called these three kings together, to deliver them into the hand of Moab. ¹⁴And Elisha said, *As* the LORD of hosts liveth, before whom I stand, surely, were it not that I regard the presence of Jehoshaphat the king of Judah, I would not look toward thee, nor see thee. ¹⁵But now bring me a minstrel. And it came to pass, when the minstrel played, that the hand of the LORD came upon him. ¹⁶And he said, Thus saith the LORD, Make this valley full of ditches. ¹⁷For thus saith the LORD, Ye shall not see wind, neither shall ye see rain; yet that valley shall be filled with water, that ye may drink, both ye, and your cattle, and your beasts. ¹⁸And this is *but* a light thing in the sight of the LORD: he will deliver the Moabites also into your hand. ¹⁹And ye shall smite every fenced city, and every choice city, and shall fell every good tree, and stop all wells of water, and mar^b every good piece of land with stones.

²⁰And it came to pass in the morning, when the meat offering was offered, that, behold, there came water by the way of Edom, and the country was filled with water. ²¹And when all the Moabites heard that the kings were come up to fight against them, they gathered^c all that were able to put on armour, and upward, and stood in the border. ²²And they rose up early in the morning, and the sun shone upon the water, and the Moabites saw the water on the other side *as* red as blood: ²³And they said, This *is* blood: the kings are surely slain^d, and they have smitten one another: now therefore, Moab, to the spoil. ²⁴And when they came to the camp of Israel, the Israelites rose up and smote the Moabites, so that they fled before them: but they went forward smiting the Moabites, even in *their* country. ²⁵And they beat down the cities, and on every good piece of land cast every man his stone, and filled it; and they stopped all the wells of water, and felled all the good trees: only in Kirharaseth left they the stones thereof; howbeit the slingers went about *it*, and

---

^b mar: Heb. grieve
^c gathered: Heb. were cried together
^d slain: Heb. destroyed

smote it. ²⁶And when the king of Moab saw that the battle was too sore for him, he took with him seven hundred men that drew swords, to break through *even* unto the king of Edom: but they could not. ²⁷Then he took his eldest son that should have reigned in his stead, and offered him *for* a burnt offering upon the wall. And there was great indignation against Israel: and they departed from him, and returned to *their own* land.

4

¹Now there cried a certain woman of the wives of the sons of the prophets unto Elisha, saying, Thy servant my husband is dead; and thou knowest that thy servant did fear the LORD: and the creditor is come to take unto him my two sons to be bondmen. ²And Elisha said unto her, What shall I do for thee? tell me, what hast thou in the house? And she said, Thine handmaid hath not any thing in the house, save a pot of oil. ³Then he said, Go, borrow thee vessels abroad of all thy neighbours, *even* empty vessels; borrow not a few. ⁴And when thou art come in, thou shalt shut the door upon thee and upon thy sons, and shalt pour out into all those vessels, and thou shalt set aside that which is full. ⁵So she went from him, and shut the door upon her and upon her sons, who brought *the vessels* to her; and she poured out. ⁶And it came to pass, when the vessels were full, that she said unto her son, Bring me yet a vessel. And he said unto her, *There is* not a vessel more. And the oil stayed. ⁷Then she came and told the man of God. And he said, Go, sell the oil, and pay thy debtᵃ, and live thou and thy children of the rest.

⁸And it fell on a dayᵇ, that Elisha passed to Shunem, where *was* a great woman; and she constrained him to eat bread. And *so* it was, *that* as oft as he passed by, he turned in thither to eat bread. ⁹And she said unto her husband,

Devotional Moment
Needs

4:1-7 Because this widow's husband's early death left the family without resources, she felt desperate and helpless. In this woman's ancient culture, her only source of help was the sale of her sons to her creditors. With time running out, she appealed to Elisha. God wants to meet our needs. Like a loving parent who values the relationship, God longs for us to ask him personally for what we need. The widow's story has been multiplied many times since Elisha's day. Go to God with your needs.

Devotional Moment
Hospitality

4:9-10 The woman from Shunem built more than a spare bedroom that day. Her small addition would become a symbol for centuries of the gift of hospitality. The woman was a true giver, a generous soul. Open your home to guests—visitors to church, students, and neighborhood children—and make them feel like prophets and other Very Important Persons. For some families, this may even mean taking in a foster child or two. Your family will discover that an ancient virtue provides a pleasant surprise and a modern blessing.

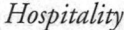

ᵃ debt: or, creditor
ᵇ it fell on a day: Heb. there was a day

Behold now, I perceive that this *is* an holy man of God, which passeth by us continually. ¹⁰Let us make a little chamber, I pray thee, on the wall; and let us set for him there a bed, and a table, and a stool, and a candlestick: and it shall be, when he cometh to us, that he shall turn in thither. ¹¹And it fell on a day, that he came thither, and he turned into the chamber, and lay there. ¹²And he said to Gehazi his servant, Call this Shunammite. And when he had called her, she stood before him. ¹³And he said unto him, Say now unto her, Behold, thou hast been careful for us with all this care; what *is* to be done for thee? wouldest thou be spoken for to the king, or to the captain of the host? And she answered, I dwell among mine own people. ¹⁴And he said, What then *is* to be done for her? And Gehazi answered, Verily she hath no child, and her husband is old. ¹⁵And he said, Call her. And when he had called her, she stood in the door. ¹⁶And he said, About this season^c, according to the time of life, thou shalt embrace a son. And she said, Nay, my lord, *thou* man of God, do not lie unto thine handmaid. ¹⁷And the woman conceived, and bare a son at that season that Elisha had said unto her, according to the time of life.

¹⁸And when the child was grown, it fell on a day, that he went out to his father to the reapers. ¹⁹And he said unto his father, My head, my head. And he said to a lad, Carry him to his mother. ²⁰And when he had taken him, and brought him to his mother, he sat on

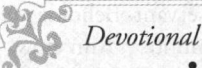

Devotional Moment

Childlessness

4:17 What a gift—a baby boy! The woman from Shunem would never have asked for something so impossible. But God knew her desire and gave her a child. Should childless couples today simply pray for a baby? Certainly. God approves of praying for whatever is good. And today, God has provided medical knowledge that helps some childless couples conceive. God wants us to get that help, too. Utilize all God-given means of realizing your dreams. Some people have considered childlessness as God's penalty for sin. God may work through many means to call us to faith, but it is wrong to interpret childlessness as a curse. Do not add false guilt to your anxiety. Because children are gifts, eagerly come to God and ask. The answer may come in a child of your own, a child to adopt, a foster child, or a group of children in the neighborhood or at church.

her knees till noon, and *then* died. ²¹And she went up, and laid him on the bed of the man of God, and shut *the door* upon him, and went out. ²²And she called unto her husband, and said, Send me, I pray thee, one of the young men, and one of the asses, that I may run to the man of God, and come again. ²³And he said, Wherefore wilt thou go to him to day? *it is* neither new moon, nor sabbath. And she said, *It shall be* well^d. ²⁴Then she saddled an ass, and said to her servant, Drive, and go forward; slack^e not *thy* riding for me, except I bid thee. ²⁵So she went and came unto the man of God to mount Carmel. And it came to pass, when the man of God saw her afar off, that he

---

^c season: Heb. set time
^d well: Heb. peace
^e slack . . . : Heb. restrain not for me to ride

said to Gehazi his servant, Behold, *yonder is* that Shunammite: ²⁶Run now, I pray thee, to meet her, and say unto her, *Is it* well with thee? *is it* well with thy husband? *is it* well with the child? And she answered, *It is* well. ²⁷And when she came to the man of God to the hill, she caught him by the feet: but Gehazi came near to thrust her away. And the man of God said, Let her alone; for her soul *is* vexed within her: and the LORD hath hid *it* from me, and hath not told me. ²⁸Then she said, Did I desire a son of my lord? did I not say, Do not deceive me? ²⁹Then he said to Gehazi, Gird up thy loins, and take my staff in thine hand, and go thy way: if thou meet any man, salute him not; and if any salute thee, answer him not again: and lay my staff upon the face of the child. ³⁰And the mother of the child said, *As* the LORD liveth, and *as* thy soul liveth, I will not leave thee. And he arose, and followed her. ³¹And Gehazi passed on before them, and laid the staff upon the face of the child; but *there was* neither voice, nor hearingᶠ. Wherefore he went again to meet him, and told him, saying, The child is not awaked. ³²And when Elisha was come into the house, behold, the child was dead, *and* laid upon his bed. ³³He went in therefore, and shut the door upon them twain, and prayed unto the LORD. ³⁴And he went up, and lay upon the child, and put his mouth upon his mouth, and his eyes upon his eyes, and his hands upon his hands: and

he stretched himself upon the child; and the flesh of the child waxed warm. ³⁵Then he returned, and walked in the house to and froᵍ; and went up, and stretched himself upon him: and the child sneezed seven times, and the child opened his eyes. ³⁶And he called Gehazi, and said, Call this Shunammite. So he called her. And when she was come in unto him, he said, Take up thy son. ³⁷Then she went in, and fell at his feet, and bowed herself to the ground, and took up her son, and went out.

³⁸And Elisha came again to Gilgal: and *there was* a dearth in the land; and the sons of the prophets *were* sitting before him: and he said unto his servant, Set on the great pot, and seethe pottage for the sons of the prophets. ³⁹And one went out into the field to gather herbs, and found a wild vine, and gathered thereof wild gourds his lap full, and came and shred *them* into the pot of pottage: for they knew *them* not. ⁴⁰So they poured out for the men to eat. And it came to pass, as they were eating of the pottage, that they cried out, and said, O *thou* man of God, *there is* death in the pot. And they could not eat *thereof.* ⁴¹But he said, Then bring meal. And he cast *it* into the pot; and he said, Pour out for the people, that they may eat. And there was no harmʰ in the pot. ⁴²And there came a man from Baalshalisha, and brought the man of God bread of the firstfruits, twenty loaves of barley, and full ears of corn in the huskⁱ thereof. And he said, Give unto the

---

ᶠ hearing: Heb. attention
ᵍ to and fro: Heb. once hither and one thither
ʰ harm: Heb. evil thing
ⁱ the husk . . . : or, his scrip, or, garment

people, that they may eat. ⁴³And his servitor said, What, should I set this before an hundred men? He said again, Give the people, that they may eat: for thus saith the LORD, They shall eat, and shall leave *thereof.* ⁴⁴So he set *it* before them, and they did eat, and left *thereof,* according to the word of the LORD.

5

¹Now Naaman, captain of the host of the king of Syria, was a great man with ͣ his master, and honourable, because by him the LORD had given deliverance unto Syria: he was also a mighty man in valour, *but he was* a leper. ²And the Syrians had gone out by companies, and had brought away captive out of the land of Israel a little maid; and she waited on Naaman's wife. ³And she said unto her mistress, Would God my lord *were* with ᵇ the prophet that *is* in Samaria! for he would recover him of

Devotional Moment
•
Wisdom

5:3 Leprosy was debilitating and contagious. Finding a cure became a consuming passion for early-stage lepers. Where did Naaman find his? Through a young slave girl. Sometimes wisdom comes from unexpected sources. While it's true that we should seek advice from elders, don't be too proud to entertain the suggestion of a little girl or boy with great faith in God. Young people sometimes possess insight that adults lack. Listen to the little children and honor them for the insights God has given them.

his leprosy. ⁴And *one* went in, and told his lord, saying, Thus and thus said the maid that *is* of the land of Israel. ⁵And the king of Syria said, Go to, go, and I will send a letter unto the king of Israel. And he departed, and took with him ten talents of silver, and six thousand *pieces* of gold, and ten changes of raiment. ⁶And he brought the letter to the king of Israel, saying, Now when this letter is come unto thee, behold, I have *therewith* sent Naaman my servant to thee, that thou mayest recover him of his leprosy. ⁷And it came to pass, when the king of Israel had read the letter, that he rent his clothes, and said, *Am* I God, to kill and to make alive, that this man doth send unto me to recover a man of his leprosy? wherefore consider, I pray you, and see how he seeketh a quarrel against me. ⁸And it was *so,* when Elisha the man of God had heard that the king of Israel had rent his clothes, that he sent to the king, saying, Wherefore hast thou rent thy clothes? let him come now to me, and he shall know that there is a prophet in Israel.

⁹So Naaman came with his horses and with his chariot, and stood at the door of the house of Elisha. ¹⁰And Elisha sent a messenger unto him, saying, Go and wash in Jordan seven times, and thy flesh shall come again to thee, and thou shalt be clean. ¹¹But Naaman was wroth, and went away, and said, Behold, I thought ͨ, He will surely come out to me, and stand, and call on the name of the LORD his God, and strike his hand over the

---

ͣ with: Heb. before
ᵇ with: Heb. before
ͨ I thought: Heb. I said

place, and recover the leper. [12]*Are* not Abana[d] and Pharpar, rivers of Damascus, better than all the waters of Israel? may I not wash in them, and be clean? So he turned and went away in a rage. [13]And his servants came near, and spake unto him, and said, My father, *if* the prophet had bid thee *do some* great thing, wouldest thou not have done *it*? how much rather then, when he saith to thee, Wash, and be clean? [14]Then went he down, and dipped himself seven times in Jordan, according to the saying of the man of God: and his flesh came again like unto the flesh of a little child, and he was clean.

[15]And he returned to the man of God, he and all his company, and came, and stood before him: and he said, Behold, now I know that *there is* no God in all the earth, but in Israel: now therefore, I pray thee, take a blessing of thy servant. [16]But he said, *As* the LORD liveth, before whom I stand, I will receive none. And he urged him to take *it*; but he refused. [17]And Naaman said, Shall there not then, I pray thee, be given to thy servant two mules' burden of earth? for thy servant will henceforth offer neither burnt offering nor sacrifice unto other gods, but unto the LORD. [18]In this thing the LORD pardon thy servant, *that* when my master goeth into the house of Rimmon to worship there, and he leaneth on my hand, and I bow myself in the house of Rimmon: when I bow down myself in

the house of Rimmon, the LORD pardon thy servant in this thing. [19]And he said unto him, Go in peace. So he departed from him a little[e] way.

[20]But Gehazi, the servant of Elisha the man of God, said, Behold, my master hath spared Naaman this Syrian, in not receiving at his hands that which he brought: but, *as* the LORD liveth, I will run after him, and take somewhat of him. [21]So Gehazi followed after Naaman. And when Naaman saw *him* running after him, he lighted down from the chariot to meet him, and said, *Is* all well? [22]And he said, All *is* well. My master hath sent me, saying, Behold, even now there be come to me from mount Ephraim two young men of the sons of the prophets: give them, I pray thee, a talent of silver, and two changes of garments. [23]And Naaman said, Be content, take two talents. And he urged him, and bound two talents of silver in two bags, with two changes of garments, and laid *them* upon two of his servants; and they bare *them* before him. [24]And when he came to the tower[f], he took *them* from their hand, and bestowed *them* in the house: and he let the men go, and they departed. [25]But he went in, and stood before his master. And Elisha said unto him, Whence *comest thou*, Gehazi? And he said, Thy servant went no whither[g]. [26]And he said unto him, Went not mine heart *with thee*, when the man turned again from his chariot to meet thee? *Is it* a time to receive money, and to receive garments, and oliveyards, and vineyards,

---

[d] Abana: or, Amana

[e] a little . . . : Heb. a little piece of ground

[f] tower: or, secret place

[g] no whither: Heb. not hither or thither

and sheep, and oxen, and menservants,
and maidservants? ²⁷The leprosy therefore of Naaman shall cleave unto thee,
and unto thy seed for ever. And he went
out from his presence a leper *as white* as
snow.

6

¹And the sons of the prophets said unto
Elisha, Behold now, the place where we
dwell with thee is too strait for us. ²Let
us go, we pray thee, unto Jordan, and
take thence every man a beam, and let
us make us a place there, where we may
dwell. And he answered, Go ye. ³And
one said, Be content, I pray thee, and
go with thy servants. And he answered,
I will go. ⁴So he went with them. And
when they came to Jordan, they cut
down wood. ⁵But as one was felling a
beam, the axe head⁴ fell into the water:
and he cried, and said, Alas, master! for

it was borrowed. ⁶And the man of God
said, Where fell it? And he shewed him
the place. And he cut down a stick, and
cast *it* in thither; and the iron did swim.
⁷Therefore said he, Take *it* up to thee.
And he put out his hand, and took it.

⁸Then the king of Syria warred
against Israel, and took counsel with his
servants, saying, In such and such a
place *shall be* my camp⁵. ⁹And the man
of God sent unto the king of Israel, saying, Beware that thou pass not such a
place; for thither the Syrians are come
down. ¹⁰And the king of Israel sent to
the place which the man of God told
him and warned him of, and saved
himself there, not once nor twice.
¹¹Therefore the heart of the king of
Syria was sore troubled for this thing;
and he called his servants, and said unto
them, Will ye not shew me which of us
is for the king of Israel? ¹²And one of his
servants said, None, my lord⁶, O king:
but Elisha, the prophet that *is* in Israel,
telleth the king of Israel the words that
thou speakest in thy bedchamber.

¹³And he said, Go and spy where
he *is*, that I may send and fetch him.
And it was told him, saying, Behold,
he is in Dothan. ¹⁴Therefore sent he
thither horses, and chariots, and a
great⁴ host: and they came by night,
and compassed the city about. ¹⁵And
when the servant⁶ of the man of God
was risen early, and gone forth, behold,
an host compassed the city both with
horses and chariots. And his servant

ᵃ axe head: Heb. iron
ᵇ camp: or, encamping
ᶜ None: Heb. No
ᵈ great: Heb. heavy
ᵉ the servant: or, the minister

said unto him, Alas, my master! how shall we do? ¹⁶And he answered, Fear not: for they that *be* with us *are* more than they that *be* with them. ¹⁷And Elisha prayed, and said, LORD, I pray thee, open his eyes, that he may see. And the LORD opened the eyes of the young man; and he saw: and, behold, the mountain *was* full of horses and chariots of fire round about Elisha. ¹⁸And when they came down to him, Elisha prayed unto the LORD, and said, Smite this people, I pray thee, with blindness. And he smote them with blindness according to the word of Elisha. ¹⁹And Elisha said unto them, This *is* not the way, neither *is* this the city: follow ᶠ me, and I will bring you to the man whom ye seek. But he led them to Samaria. ²⁰And it came to pass, when they were come into Samaria, that Elisha said, LORD, open the eyes of these *men*, that they may see. And the LORD opened their eyes, and they saw; and, behold, *they were* in the midst of Samaria. ²¹And the king of Israel said unto Elisha, when he saw them, My father, shall I smite *them*? shall I smite *them*? ²²And he answered, Thou shalt not smite *them*: wouldest thou smite those whom thou hast taken captive with thy sword and with thy bow? set bread and water before them, that they may eat and drink, and go to their master. ²³And he prepared great provision for them: and when they had eaten and drunk, he sent them away, and they went to their master. So the bands of Syria came no more into the land of Israel.

²⁴And it came to pass after this, that Benhadad king of Syria gathered all his host, and went up, and besieged Samaria. ²⁵And there was a great famine in Samaria: and, behold, they besieged it, until an ass's head was *sold* for fourscore *pieces* of silver, and the fourth part of a cab of dove's dung for five *pieces* of silver. ²⁶And as the king of Israel was passing by upon the wall, there cried a woman unto him, saying, Help, my lord, O king. ²⁷And he said, If the LORD do not help thee, whence shall I help thee? out of the barnfloor, or out of the winepress? ²⁸And the king said unto her, What aileth thee? And she answered, This woman said unto me, Give thy son, that we may eat him to day, and we will eat my son to morrow. ²⁹So we boiled my son, and did eat him: and I said unto her on the next ᵍ day, Give thy son, that we may eat him: and she hath hid her son. ³⁰And it came to pass, when the king heard the words of the woman, that he rent his clothes; and he passed by upon the wall, and the people looked, and, behold, *he had* sackcloth within upon his flesh. ³¹Then he said, God do so and more also to me, if the head of Elisha the son of Shaphat shall stand on him this day. ³²But Elisha sat in his house, and the elders sat with him; and *the king* sent a man from before him: but ere the messenger came to him, he said to the elders, See ye how this son of a murderer hath sent to take away mine head? look, when the messenger cometh, shut the door, and hold him fast at the door: *is* not the sound of his master's feet be-

---

ᶠ follow . . . : Heb. come ye after me
ᵍ next: Heb. other

hind him? ³³And while he yet talked with them, behold, the messenger came down unto him: and he said, Behold, this evil *is* of the LORD; what should I wait for the LORD any longer?

7

¹Then Elisha said, Hear ye the word of the LORD; Thus saith the LORD, To morrow about this time *shall* a measure of fine flour *be sold* for a shekel, and two measures of barley for a shekel, in the gate of Samaria. ²Then a lordᵃ on whose hand the king leaned answered the man of God, and said, Behold, *if* the LORD would make windows in heaven, might this thing be? And he said, Behold, thou shalt see *it* with thine eyes, but shalt not eat thereof.

³And there were four leprous men at the entering in of the gate: and they said one to another, Why sit we here until we die? ⁴If we say, We will enter into the city, then the famine *is* in the city, and we shall die there: and if we sit still here, we die also. Now therefore come, and let us fall unto the host of the Syrians: if they save us alive, we shall live; and if they kill us, we shall but die. ⁵And they rose up in the twilight, to go unto the camp of the Syrians: and when they were come to the uttermost part of the camp of Syria, behold, *there was* no man there. ⁶For the Lord had made the host of the Syrians to hear a noise of chariots, and a noise of horses, *even* the noise of a great host: and they said one to another, Lo, the king of Israel hath hired against us the kings of the Hittites, and the kings of the Egyptians, to come upon us. ⁷Wherefore they arose and fled in the twilight, and left their tents, and their horses, and their asses, even the camp as it *was*, and fled for their life. ⁸And when these lepers came to the uttermost part of the camp, they went into one tent, and did eat and drink, and carried thence silver, and gold, and raiment, and went and hid *it*; and came again, and entered into another tent, and carried thence *also*, and went and hid *it*. ⁹Then they said one to another, We do not well: this day *is* a day of good tidings, and we hold our peace: if we tarry till the morning light, some mischief will come upon us: now therefore come, that we may go and tell the king's household. ¹⁰So they came and called unto the porter of the city: and they told them, saying, We came to the camp of the Syrians, and, behold, *there was* no man there, neither voice of man, but horses tied, and asses tied, and the tents as they *were*. ¹¹And he called the porters; and they told *it* to the king's house within.

¹²And the king arose in the night, and said unto his servants, I will now shew you what the Syrians have done to us. They know that we *be* hungry; therefore are they gone out of the camp to hide themselves in the field, saying, When they come out of the city, we shall catch them alive, and get into the city. ¹³And one of his servants answered and said, Let *some* take, I pray thee, five of the horses that remain, which are left in the city, (behold, they *are* as all the multitude of Israel that are leftᵇ in it:

ᵃ a lord . . . : Heb. a lord which belonged to the king leaning upon his hand
ᵇ in the city: Heb. in it

behold, *I say*, they *are* even as all the multitude of the Israelites that are consumed:) and let us send and see. ¹⁴They took therefore two chariot horses; and the king sent after the host of the Syrians, saying, Go and see. ¹⁵And they went after them unto Jordan: and, lo, all the way *was* full of garments and vessels, which the Syrians had cast away in their haste. And the messengers returned, and told the king. ¹⁶And the people went out, and spoiled the tents of the Syrians. So a measure of fine flour was *sold* for a shekel, and two measures of barley for a shekel, according to the word of the LORD. ¹⁷And the king appointed the lord on whose hand he leaned to have the charge of the gate: and the people trode upon him in the gate, and he died, as the man of God had said, who spake when the king came down to him. ¹⁸And it came to pass as the man of God had spoken to the king, saying, Two measures of barley for a shekel, and a measure of fine flour for a shekel, shall be to morrow about this time in the gate of Samaria: ¹⁹And that lord answered the man of God, and said, Now, behold, *if* the LORD should make windows in heaven, might such a thing be? And he said, Behold, thou shalt see it with thine eyes, but shalt not eat thereof. ²⁰And so it fell out unto him: for the people trode upon him in the gate, and he died.

8

¹Then spake Elisha unto the woman, whose son he had restored to life, saying, Arise, and go thou and thine household, and sojourn wheresoever thou canst sojourn: for the LORD hath called for a famine; and it shall also come upon the land seven years. ²And the woman arose, and did after the saying of the man of God: and she went with her household, and sojourned in the land of the Philistines seven years. ³And it came to pass at the seven years' end, that the woman returned out of the land of the Philistines: and she went forth to cry unto the king for her house and for her land. ⁴And the king talked with Gehazi the servant of the man of God, saying, Tell me, I pray thee, all the great things that Elisha hath done. ⁵And it came to pass, as he was telling the king how he had restored a dead body to life, that, behold, the woman, whose son he had restored to life, cried to the king for her house and for her land. And Gehazi said, My lord, O king, this *is* the woman, and this *is* her son, whom Elisha restored to life. ⁶And when the king asked the woman, she told him. So the king appointed unto her a certain officer ᵃ, saying, Restore all that *was* hers, and all the fruits of the field since the day that she left the land, even until now.

⁷And Elisha came to Damascus; and Benhadad the king of Syria was sick; and it was told him, saying, The man of God is come hither. ⁸And the king said unto Hazael, Take a present in thine hand, and go, meet the man of God, and enquire of the LORD by him, saying, Shall I recover of this disease? ⁹So Hazael went to meet him, and took a present with him, even of every good thing of Damascus, forty camels'

ᵃ officer: or, eunuch

burden, and came and stood before him, and said, Thy son Benhadad king of Syria hath sent me to thee, saying, Shall I recover of this disease? ¹⁰And Elisha said unto him, Go, say unto him, Thou mayest certainly recover: howbeit the LORD hath shewed me that he shall surely die. ¹¹And he settled his countenance stedfastly ᵇ, until he was ashamed: and the man of God wept. ¹²And Hazael said, Why weepeth my lord? And he answered, Because I know the evil that thou wilt do unto the children of Israel: their strong holds wilt thou set on fire, and their young men wilt thou slay with the sword, and wilt dash their children, and rip up their women with child. ¹³And Hazael said, But what, *is* thy servant a dog, that he should do this great thing? And Elisha answered, The LORD hath shewed me that thou *shalt be* king over Syria. ¹⁴So he departed from Elisha, and came to his master; who said to him, What said Elisha to thee? And he answered, He told me *that* thou shouldest surely recover. ¹⁵And it came to pass on the morrow, that he took a thick cloth, and dipped *it* in water, and spread *it* on his face, so that he died: and Hazael reigned in his stead.

¹⁶And in the fifth year of Joram the son of Ahab king of Israel, Jehoshaphat *being* then king of Judah, Jehoram the son of Jehoshaphat king of Judah began to reign. ¹⁷Thirty and two years old was he when he began to reign; and he reigned eight years in Jerusalem. ¹⁸And

he walked in the way of the kings of Israel, as did the house of Ahab: for the daughter of Ahab was his wife: and he did evil in the sight of the LORD. ¹⁹Yet the LORD would not destroy Judah for David his servant's sake, as he promised him to give him alway a light ᶜ, *and* to his children. ²⁰In his days Edom revolted from under the hand of Judah, and made a king over themselves. ²¹So Joram went over to Zair, and all the chariots with him: and he rose by night, and smote the Edomites which compassed him about, and the captains of the chariots: and the people fled into their tents. ²²Yet Edom revolted from under the hand of Judah unto this day. Then Libnah revolted at the same time. ²³And the rest of the acts of Joram, and all that he did, *are* they not written in the book of the chronicles of the kings of Judah? ²⁴And Joram slept with his fathers, and was buried with his fathers in the city of David: and Ahaziah ᵈ his son reigned in his stead.

²⁵In the twelfth year of Joram the son of Ahab king of Israel did Ahaziah the son of Jehoram king of Judah begin to reign. ²⁶Two and twenty years old *was* Ahaziah when he began to reign; and he reigned one year in Jerusalem. And his mother's name *was* Athaliah, the daughter ᵉ of Omri king of Israel. ²⁷And he walked in the way of the house of Ahab, and did evil in the sight of the LORD, as *did* the house of Ahab: for he *was* the son in law of the house of Ahab. ²⁸And he went with Joram the

son of Ahab to the war against Hazael king of Syria in Ramothgilead; and the Syrians wounded Joram. ²⁹And king Joram went back to be healed in Jezreel of the wounds which the Syrians had given him at Ramah, when he fought against Hazael king of Syria. And Ahaziah the son of Jehoram king of Judah went down to see Joram the son of Ahab in Jezreel, because he was sick.

9

¹And Elisha the prophet called one of the children of the prophets, and said unto him, Gird up thy loins, and take this box of oil in thine hand, and go to Ramothgilead: ²And when thou comest thither, look out there Jehu the son of Jehoshaphat the son of Nimshi, and go in, and make him arise up from among his brethren, and carry him to an inner^a chamber; ³Then take the box of oil, and pour *it* on his head, and say, Thus saith the LORD, I have anointed thee king over Israel. Then open the door, and flee, and tarry not. ⁴So the young man, *even* the young man the prophet, went to Ramothgilead. ⁵And when he came, behold, the captains of the host *were* sitting; and he said, I have an errand to thee, O captain. And Jehu said, Unto which of all us? And he said, To thee, O captain. ⁶And he arose, and went into the house; and he poured the oil on his head, and said unto him, Thus saith the LORD God of Israel, I have anointed thee king over the people of the LORD, *even* over Israel. ⁷And thou shalt smite the house of Ahab thy master, that I may avenge the blood of my servants the prophets, and the blood of all the servants of the LORD, at the hand of Jezebel. ⁸For the whole house of Ahab shall perish: and I will cut off from Ahab him that pisseth against the wall, and him that is shut up and left in Israel: ⁹And I will make the house of Ahab like the house of Jeroboam the son of Nebat, and like the house of Baasha the son of Ahijah: ¹⁰And the dogs shall eat Jezebel in the portion of Jezreel, and *there shall be* none to bury her. And he opened the door, and fled.

¹¹Then Jehu came forth to the servants of his lord: and *one* said unto him, *Is* all well? wherefore came this mad *fellow* to thee? And he said unto them, Ye know the man, and his communication. ¹²And they said, *It is* false; tell us now. And he said, Thus and thus spake he to me, saying, Thus saith the LORD, I have anointed thee king over Israel. ¹³Then they hasted, and took every man his garment, and put *it* under him on the top of the stairs, and blew with trumpets, saying, Jehu is king^b. ¹⁴So Jehu the son of Jehoshaphat the son of Nimshi conspired against Joram. (Now Joram had kept Ramothgilead, he and all Israel, because of Hazael king of Syria. ¹⁵But king Joram^c was returned to be healed in Jezreel of the wounds which the Syrians had given him, when he fought with Hazael king of Syria.) And Jehu said, If it be your minds, *then* let none go forth *nor* escape out of the city to go to tell *it* in Jezreel. ¹⁶So Jehu rode in a chariot, and

---

^a inner . . . : Heb. chamber in a chamber
^b is king: Heb. reigneth
^c Joram: Heb. Jehoram but not in verse sixteen

went to Jezreel; for Joram lay there. And Ahaziah king of Judah was come down to see Joram. ¹⁷And there stood a watchman on the tower in Jezreel, and he spied the company of Jehu as he came, and said, I see a company. And Joram said, Take an horseman, and send to meet them, and let him say, *Is it* peace? ¹⁸So there went one on horseback to meet him, and said, Thus saith the king, *Is it* peace? And Jehu said, What hast thou to do with peace? turn thee behind me. And the watchman told, saying, The messenger came to them, but he cometh not again. ¹⁹Then he sent out a second on horseback, which came to them, and said, Thus saith the king, *Is it* peace? And Jehu answered, What hast thou to do with peace? turn thee behind me. ²⁰And the watchman told, saying, He came even unto them, and cometh not again: and the driving^d *is* like the driving of Jehu the son of Nimshi; for he driveth furiously. ²¹And Joram said, Make ready^e. And his chariot was made ready. And Joram king of Israel and Ahaziah king of Judah went out, each in his chariot, and they went out against Jehu, and met him in the portion of Naboth the Jezreelite. ²²And it came to pass, when Joram saw Jehu, that he said, *Is it* peace, Jehu? And he answered, What peace, so long as the whoredoms of thy mother Jezebel and her witchcrafts *are so* many? ²³And Joram turned his hands, and fled, and said to Ahaziah, *There is* treachery, O Ahaziah. ²⁴And Jehu drew a bow with his full strength, and smote Jehoram between his arms,

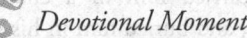

Devotional Moment

Getting Help

9:22-26 Joram had plenty of bad examples for teachers, including his father (the evil king Ahab) and mother (Jezebel, who promoted idolatry and tried to have the prophet Elijah killed). Joram was raised in a very troubled family, from which, unfortunately, he learned quickly. God had sent prophets to correct him, but Joram ignored them. The consequences for his life were grim. If your family isn't working, seek the help of mature Christians in your church, counselors, or older friends whose lives show the fruit of faithfulness to God. Breaking cycles of addiction, family conflict, or bad habits can only start when you— *unlike* Joram—accept help.

and the arrow went out at his heart, and he sunk down in his chariot. ²⁵Then said *Jehu* to Bidkar his captain, Take up, *and* cast him in the portion of the field of Naboth the Jezreelite: for remember how that, when I and thou rode together after Ahab his father, the LORD laid this burden upon him; ²⁶Surely I have seen yesterday the blood^f of Naboth, and the blood of his sons, saith the LORD; and I will requite thee in this plat, saith the LORD. Now therefore take *and* cast him into the plat *of ground*, according to the word of the LORD. ²⁷But when Ahaziah the king of Judah saw *this*, he fled by the way of the garden house. And Jehu followed after him, and said, Smite him also in the chariot. *And they did so* at the going up to Gur, which *is* by Ibleam. And he fled to Megiddo, and died there. ²⁸And his

---

^d driving: or, marching
^e Make ready: Heb. Bind
^f blood: Heb. bloods

servants carried him in a chariot to Jerusalem, and buried him in his sepulchre with his fathers in the city of David. ²⁹And in the eleventh year of Joram the son of Ahab began Ahaziah to reign over Judah.

³⁰And when Jehu was come to Jezreel, Jezebel heard *of it*; and she painted⁸ her face, and tired her head, and looked out at a window. ³¹And as Jehu entered in at the gate, she said, *Had* Zimri peace, who slew his master? ³²And he lifted up his face to the window, and said, Who *is* on my side? who? And there looked out to him two *or* three eunuchsʰ. ³³And he said, Throw her down. So they threw her down: and *some* of her blood was sprinkled on the wall, and on the horses: and he trode her under foot. ³⁴And when he was come in, he did eat and drink, and said, Go, see now this cursed *woman*, and bury her: for she *is* a king's daughter. ³⁵And they went to bury her: but they found no more of her than the skull, and the feet, and the palms of *her* hands. ³⁶Wherefore they came again, and told him. And he said, This *is* the word of the LORD, which he spake by ¹ his servant Elijah the Tishbite, saying, In the portion of Jezreel shall dogs eat the flesh of Jezebel: ³⁷And the carcase of Jezebel shall be as dung upon the face of the field in the portion of Jezreel; *so* that they shall not say, This *is* Jezebel.

10

¹And Ahab had seventy sons in Samaria. And Jehu wrote letters, and sent to Samaria, unto the rulers of Jezreel, to the elders, and to them that brought up Ahab's *children*, saying, ²Now as soon as this letter cometh to you, seeing your master's sons *are* with you, and *there are* with you chariots and horses, a fenced city also, and armour; ³Look even out the best and meetest of your master's sons, and set *him* on his father's throne, and fight for your master's house. ⁴But they were exceedingly afraid, and said, Behold, two kings stood not before him: how then shall we stand? ⁵And he that *was* over the house, and he that *was* over the city, the elders also, and the bringers up *of the children*, sent to Jehu, saying, We *are* thy servants, and will do all that thou shalt bid us; we will not make any king: do thou *that which is* good in thine eyes. ⁶Then he wrote a letter the second time to them, saying, If ye *be* mine, and *if* ye will hearkenᵃ unto my voice, take ye the heads of the men your master's sons, and come to me to Jezreel by to morrow this time. Now the king's sons, *being* seventy persons, *were* with the great men of the city, which brought them up. ⁷And it came to pass, when the letter came to them, that they took the king's sons, and slew seventy persons, and put their heads in baskets, and sent him *them* to Jezreel. ⁸And there came a messenger, and told him, saying, They have brought the heads of the king's sons. And he said, Lay ye them in two heaps at the entering in of the gate until the morning. ⁹And it

---

⁸ painted . . . : Heb. put her eyes in painting
ʰ eunuchs: or, chamberlains
ⁱ by: Heb. by the hand of
ᵃ mine: Heb. for me

came to pass in the morning, that he went out, and stood, and said to all the people, Ye *be* righteous: behold, I conspired against my master, and slew him: but who slew all these? ¹⁰Know now that there shall fall unto the earth nothing of the word of the LORD, which the LORD spake concerning the house of Ahab: for the LORD hath done *that* which he spake by ᵇ his servant Elijah. ¹¹So Jehu slew all that remained of the house of Ahab in Jezreel, and all his great men, and his kinsfolksᶜ, and his priests, until he left him none remaining. ¹²And he arose and departed, and came to Samaria. *And* as he *was* at the shearingᵈ house in the way, ¹³Jehu met with the brethren of Ahaziah king of Judah, and said, Who *are* ye? And they answered, We *are* the brethren of Ahaziah; and we go down to saluteᵉ the children of the king and the children of the queen. ¹⁴And he said, Take them alive. And they took them alive, and slew them at the pit of the shearing house, *even* two and forty men; neither left he any of them.

¹⁵And when he was departed thence, he lighted on Jehonadab the son of Rechab *coming* to meet him: and he saluted him, and said to him, Is thine heart right, as my heart *is* with thy heart? And Jehonadab answered, It is. If it be, give *me* thine hand. And he gave *him* his hand; and he took him up to him into the chariot. ¹⁶And he

said, Come with me, and see my zeal for the LORD. So they made him ride in his chariot. ¹⁷And when he came to Samaria, he slew all that remained unto Ahab in Samaria, till he had destroyed him, according to the saying of the LORD, which he spake to Elijah. ¹⁸And Jehu gathered all the people together, and said unto them, Ahab served Baal a little; *but* Jehu shall serve him much. ¹⁹Now therefore call unto me all the prophets of Baal, all his servants, and all his priests; let none be wanting: for I have a great sacrifice *to do* to Baal; whosoever shall be wanting, he shall not live. But Jehu did *it* in subtilty, to the intent that he might destroy the worshippers of Baal. ²⁰And Jehu said, Proclaimᶠ a solemn assembly for Baal. And they proclaimed *it.* ²¹And Jehu sent through all Israel: and all the worshippers of Baal came, so that there was not a man left that came not. And they came into the house of Baal; and the house of Baal was fullᵍ from one end to another. ²²And he said unto him that *was* over the vestry, Bring forth vestments for all the worshippers of Baal. And he brought them forth vestments. ²³And Jehu went, and Jehonadab the son of Rechab, into the house of Baal, and said unto the worshippers of Baal, Search, and look that there be here with you none of the servants of the LORD, but the worshippers of Baal only. ²⁴And when they went in to offer sacrifices

---

ᵇ by: Heb. by the hand of
ᶜ kinsfolks: or, acquaintance
ᵈ shearing . . . : Heb. house of shepherds binding sheep
ᵉ to salute . . . : Heb. to the peace of, etc
ᶠ Proclaim: Heb. Sanctify
ᵍ full . . . : or, so full that they stood mouth to mouth

and burnt offerings, Jehu appointed fourscore men without, and said, *If* any of the men whom I have brought into your hands escape, *he that letteth him go*, his life *shall be* for the life of him. ²⁵And it came to pass, as soon as he had made an end of offering the burnt offering, that Jehu said to the guard and to the captains, Go in, *and* slay them; let none come forth. And they smote them with the edge[h] of the sword; and the guard and the captains cast *them* out, and went to the city of the house of Baal. ²⁶And they brought forth the images[i] out of the house of Baal, and burned them. ²⁷And they brake down the image of Baal, and brake down the house of Baal, and made it a draught house unto this day. ²⁸Thus Jehu destroyed Baal out of Israel.

²⁹Howbeit *from* the sins of Jeroboam the son of Nebat, who made Israel to sin, Jehu departed not from after them, *to wit*, the golden calves that *were* in Bethel, and that *were* in Dan. ³⁰And the LORD said unto Jehu, Because thou hast done well in executing *that which is* right in mine eyes, *and* hast done unto the house of Ahab according to all that *was* in mine heart, thy children of the fourth *generation* shall sit on the throne of Israel. ³¹But Jehu took no heed to walk in the law of the LORD God of Israel with all his heart: for he departed not from the sins of Jeroboam, which made

Israel to sin. ³²In those days the LORD began to cut[j] Israel short: and Hazael smote them in all the coasts of Israel; ³³From Jordan eastward[k], all the land of Gilead, the Gadites, and the Reubenites, and the Manassites, from Aroer, which *is* by the river Arnon, even Gilead and Bashan. ³⁴Now the rest of the acts of Jehu, and all that he did, and all his might, *are* they not written in the book of the chronicles of the kings of Israel? ³⁵And Jehu slept with his fathers: and they buried him in Samaria. And Jehoahaz his son reigned in his stead. ³⁶And the time[l] that Jehu reigned over Israel in Samaria *was* twenty and eight years.

11

¹And when Athaliah the mother of Ahaziah saw that her son was dead, she arose and destroyed all the seed[a] royal. ²But Jehosheba[b], the daughter of king Joram, sister of Ahaziah, took Joash the son of Ahaziah, and stole him from among the king's sons *which were* slain; and they hid him, *even* him and his nurse, in the bedchamber from Athaliah, so that he was not slain. ³And he was with her hid in the house of the LORD six years. And Athaliah did reign over the land.

⁴And the seventh year Jehoiada sent and fetched the rulers over hundreds, with the captains and the guard, and brought them to him into the house of the LORD, and made a covenant with

---

^h the edge: Heb. the mouth
ⁱ images: Heb. statues
^j to cut: Heb. to cut off the ends
^k eastward: Heb. toward the rising of the sun
^l the time: Heb. the days were
^a seed . . . : Heb. seed of the kingdom
^b Jehosheba: also called, Jehoshabeath

An Unhurried Childhood

by Doug Fields

When he was only seven, a boy named Joash became the king of Judah. This would be a little like making a second-grade student the president of the United States today. Absurd as that sounds, it is symbolic of what is, in fact, happening to many of our children. They are being asked to grow up too quickly—to demonstrate adult behavior while still in a child's body.

Like Joash, our children usually have little to say about the accelerated pace. Their inborn trust causes them to rely on adults and the surrounding society to aid them toward maturity. And the problem is intensified by the fact that we adults are often in a hurry ourselves.

This infatuation with speed can create harmful attitudes that adversely affect our parenting. The following two attitudes may disguise themselves as good intentions, but a closer look brings their dangers to light.

Harmful attitude #1: Bigger is better, and better is best. As our society continues to highlight and emphasize accomplishment, an award-for-performance attitude is communicated loud and clear to our young people. They hear adults boast that bigger is better, richer is more rewarding, power buys prestige, position ensures popularity, possessions bring pleasure. These declarations leave little question in the minds of our children about America's formula: Grow up fast and be better than anyone else, or you will be left behind.

Harmful attitude #2: Normal isn't good enough. Many of today's parents, unlike previous generations, want to raise highly exceptional children. To them, a normal child is not acceptable. If children are going to be free to enjoy their childhood and develop at their God-given pace, we must abandon the notion that they should be pushed to outshine their peers. In some cases, a well-meaning push to succeed can become a subtle form of child abuse that squeezes the precious gift of innocence out of them.

There is nothing wrong with wanting the best for our children. But the best becomes detrimental when we push and pressure our kids excessively.

Don't go another day without letting your child hear words of encouragement. Here are a few ways to do that.

1. Recognize the importance of your children's world. Every child has values, and these values will almost certainly differ from yours. A four-year-old boy, for instance, may consider it very important that you let *him* pour the milk. This importance may not be on *your* priority list, but when you respect his values, you affirm his feelings and show him love.

2. Honor your children's feelings. If your children tell you how they feel about a situation, and their feelings don't agree with yours, don't put their feelings down. Remember, feelings are neither right nor wrong; they're neutral and not subject to judgment.

3. Catch your children doing something right, and be generous praising them for it. You may need to search carefully at times for actions to praise (you can always thank them for flushing the toilet!), but the appreciation they receive from you will be well worth the effort.

4. Encourage your children in front of others. When you praise your children in the presence of others, they receive a double blessing. Children love to be appreciated and to have their friends and others know that someone believes in them and thinks they are special.

5. Weigh your words. Proverbs says it this way: "There is that speaketh like the piercings of a sword; but the tongue of the wise is health" (12:18). Your children may *forgive* the careless words you say, but chances are they won't *forget* them. Negative words cut deeply, and scars may remain.

6. Write it out. If spoken appreciation won't quickly be forgotten, it's likely that written appreciation won't easily be misplaced.

7. Say it now. When you think of something positive about your children, tell it to them right away while it's still fresh in your mind.

It *is* possible to raise children to be decent, moral, godly human beings in a world that seems to value only the fast track to success. But in order for this to happen, we must become good encouragers of our children. This learned love will allow our children to mature at their own rate without having to satisfy outside or parental demands.

DIGGING DEEPER

1. What significance do the familiar words of Proverbs 22:6 have for hurrying or not hurrying your children? How can appropriate parenting help your children now *and* in the future?

2. How important is laughter in a normal childhood? See Proverbs 17:22. How can you bring more fun into your family life?

3. In what ways have you allowed yourself and your children to be driven by the world's standards (Rom. 12:2)?

Devotional Moment

Step In

11:1-3 No argument justifies Athaliah's cruelty. She is universally condemned for the despicable crime of killing innocent children, her own grandchildren. Boldly, Joash's aunt Jehosheba stepped in and gave the child Joash a safe harbor. Like Jehosheba, we must be ready to help those who suffer as a result of domestic violence. The battered women and children of our world, the incest victims and verbally abused, need lots of loving attention to recover their confidence and sense of worth. Jehosheba took the risk. Let the courage of Jehosheba and the love of God help you overcome your fear. Be willing to help those God brings into your life.

the king's son. ⁵And he commanded them, saying, This *is* the thing that ye shall do; A third part of you that enter in on the sabbath shall even be keepers of the watch of the king's house; ⁶And a third part *shall be* at the gate of Sur; and a third part at the gate behind the guard: so shall ye keep the watch of the house, that it be not broken down. ⁷And two parts ᶜ of all you that go forth on the sabbath, even they shall keep the watch of the house of the LORD about the king. ⁸And ye shall compass the king round about, every man with his weapons in his hand: and he that cometh within the ranges, let him be slain: and be ye with the king as he goeth out and as he cometh in. ⁹And the captains over the hundreds did according to all *things* that Jehoiada the priest com-

them, and took an oath of them in the house of the LORD, and shewed them

ᶜ parts: or, companies: Heb. hands

manded: and they took every man his men that were to come in on the sabbath, with them that should go out on the sabbath, and came to Jehoiada the priest. ¹⁰And to the captains over hundreds did the priest give king David's spears and shields, that *were* in the temple of the LORD. ¹¹And the guard stood, every man with his weapons in his hand, round about the king, from the right corner ᵈ of the temple to the left corner of the temple, *along* by the altar and the temple. ¹²And he brought forth the king's son, and put the crown upon him, and *gave him* the testimony; and they made him king, and anointed him; and they clapped their hands, and said, God save the king.

¹³And when Athaliah heard the noise of the guard *and* of the people, she came to the people into the temple of the LORD. ¹⁴And when she looked, behold, the king stood by a pillar, as the manner *was*, and the princes and the trumpeters by the king, and all the people of the land rejoiced, and blew with trumpets: and Athaliah rent her clothes, and cried, Treason, Treason. ¹⁵But Jehoiada the priest commanded the captains of the hundreds, the officers of the host, and said unto them, Have her forth without the ranges: and him that followeth her kill with the sword. For the priest had said, Let her not be slain in the house of the LORD. ¹⁶And they laid hands on her; and she went by the way by the which the horses came into the king's house: and there was she slain.

¹⁷And Jehoiada made a covenant between the LORD and the king and the people, that they should be the LORD'S people; between the king also and the people. ¹⁸And all the people of the land went into the house of Baal, and brake it down; his altars and his images brake they in pieces thoroughly, and slew Mattan the priest of Baal before the altars. And the priest appointed officers ᵉ over the house of the LORD. ¹⁹And he took the rulers over hundreds, and the captains, and the guard, and all the people of the land; and they brought down the king from the house of the LORD, and came by the way of the gate of the guard to the king's house. And he sat on the throne of the kings. ²⁰And all the people of the land rejoiced, and the city was in quiet: and they slew Athaliah with the sword *beside* the king's house. ²¹Seven years old *was* Jehoash when he began to reign.

12

¹In the seventh year of Jehu Jehoash began to reign; and forty years reigned he in Jerusalem. And his mother's name *was* Zibiah of Beersheba. ²And Jehoash did *that which was* right in the sight of the LORD all his days wherein Jehoiada the priest instructed him. ³But the high places were not taken away: the people still sacrificed and burnt incense in the high places.

⁴And Jehoash said to the priests, All the money of the dedicated things ᵃ that is brought into the house of the LORD, *even* the money of every one that passeth *the account*, the money that every man is set at, *and* all the money that cometh

---

ᵈ corner: Heb. shoulder
ᵉ officers: Heb. offices
ᵃ dedicated things: or, holy things: Heb. holinesses

into any man's heart to bring into the house of the LORD, ⁵Let the priests take *it* to them, every man of his acquaintance: and let them repair the breaches of the house, wheresoever any breach shall be found. ⁶But it was so, *that* in the three^b and twentieth year of king Jehoash the priests had not repaired the breaches of the house. ⁷Then king Jehoash called for Jehoiada the priest, and the *other* priests, and said unto them, Why repair ye not the breaches of the house? now therefore receive no *more* money of your acquaintance, but deliver it for the breaches of the house. ⁸And the priests consented to receive no *more* money of the people, neither to repair the breaches of the house. ⁹But Jehoiada the priest took a chest, and bored a hole in the lid of it, and set it beside the altar, on the right side as one cometh into the house of the LORD: and the priests that kept the door^c put therein all the money *that was* brought into the house of the LORD. ¹⁰And it was *so*, when they saw that *there was* much money in the chest, that the king's scribe^d and the high priest came up, and they put up in bags, and told the money that was found in the house of the LORD. ¹¹And they gave the money, being told, into the hands of them that did the work, that had the oversight of the house of the LORD: and they laid it out to the carpenters and builders, that wrought upon the house of the LORD, ¹²And to masons, and hewers of stone, and to buy timber and hewed stone to repair the breaches of the

house of the LORD, and for all that was laid out for the house to repair *it*. ¹³Howbeit there were not made for the house of the LORD bowls of silver, snuffers, basons, trumpets, any vessels of gold, or vessels of silver, of the money *that was* brought into the house of the LORD: ¹⁴But they gave that to the workmen, and repaired therewith the house of the LORD. ¹⁵Moreover they reckoned not with the men, into whose hand they delivered the money to be bestowed on workmen: for they dealt faithfully. ¹⁶The trespass money and sin money was not brought into the house of the LORD: it was the priests'.

¹⁷Then Hazael king of Syria went up, and fought against Gath, and took it: and Hazael set his face to go up to Jerusalem. ¹⁸And Jehoash king of Judah took all the hallowed things that Jehoshaphat, and Jehoram, and Ahaziah, his fathers, kings of Judah, had dedicated, and his own hallowed things, and all the gold *that was* found in the treasures of the house of the LORD, and in the king's house, and sent *it* to Hazael king of Syria: and he went away from Jerusalem. ¹⁹And the rest of the acts of Joash, and all that he did, *are* they not written in the book of the chronicles of the kings of Judah? ²⁰And his servants arose, and made a conspiracy, and slew Joash in the house^e of Millo, which goeth down to Silla. ²¹For Jozachar the son of Shimeath, and Jehozabad the son of Shomer, his servants, smote him, and he died; and

---

^b three . . . : Heb. twentieth year and third year

^c door: Heb. threshold

^d scribe: or, secretary

^e the house . . . : or, Bethmillo

they buried him with his fathers in the city of David: and Amaziah his son reigned in his stead.

13

¹In the three[a] and twentieth year of Joash the son of Ahaziah king of Judah Jehoahaz the son of Jehu began to reign over Israel in Samaria, *and reigned* seventeen years. ²And he did *that which was* evil in the sight of the LORD, and followed[b] the sins of Jeroboam the son of Nebat, which made Israel to sin; he departed not therefrom. ³And the anger of the LORD was kindled against Israel, and he delivered them into the hand of Hazael king of Syria, and into the hand of Benhadad the son of Hazael, all *their* days. ⁴And Jehoahaz besought the LORD, and the LORD hearkened unto him: for he saw the oppression of Israel, because the king of Syria oppressed them. ⁵(And the LORD gave Israel a saviour, so that they went out from under the hand of the Syrians: and the children of Israel dwelt in their tents, as beforetime[c]. ⁶Nevertheless they departed not from the sins of the house of Jeroboam, who made Israel sin, *but* walked[d] therein: and there remained the grove also in Samaria.) ⁷Neither did he leave of the people to Jehoahaz but fifty horsemen, and ten chariots, and ten thousand footmen; for the king of Syria had destroyed them, and had made them like the dust by threshing. ⁸Now the rest of the acts of Jehoahaz, and all that he did, and his might, *are* they not written in the book of the chronicles of the kings of Israel? ⁹And Jehoahaz slept with his fathers; and they buried him in Samaria: and Joash[e] his son reigned in his stead.

¹⁰In the thirty and seventh year of Joash king of Judah began Jehoash the son of Jehoahaz to reign over Israel in Samaria, *and reigned* sixteen years. ¹¹And he did *that which was* evil in the sight of the LORD; he departed not from all the sins of Jeroboam the son of Nebat, who made Israel sin: *but* he walked therein. ¹²And the rest of the acts of Joash, and all that he did, and his might wherewith he fought against Amaziah king of Judah, *are* they not written in the book of the chronicles of the kings of Israel? ¹³And Joash slept with his fathers; and Jeroboam sat upon his throne: and Joash was buried in Samaria with the kings of Israel. ¹⁴Now Elisha was fallen sick of his sickness whereof he died. And Joash the king of Israel came down unto him, and wept over his face, and said, O my father, my father, the chariot of Israel, and the horsemen thereof. ¹⁵And Elisha said unto him, Take bow and arrows. And he took unto him bow and arrows. ¹⁶And he said to the king of Israel, Put thine hand upon the bow. And he put his hand *upon it*: and Elisha put his hands upon the king's hands. ¹⁷And he said, Open the window eastward. And

---

[a] three . . . : Heb. twentieth year and third year
[b] followed: Heb. walked after
[c] as beforetime: Heb. as yesterday, and third day
[d] walked: Heb. he walked
[e] Joash: also called, Jehoash

he opened *it*. Then Elisha said, Shoot. And he shot. And he said, The arrow of the LORD'S deliverance, and the arrow of deliverance from Syria: for thou shalt smite the Syrians in Aphek, till thou have consumed *them*. ¹⁸And he said, Take the arrows. And he took *them*. And he said unto the king of Israel, Smite upon the ground. And he smote thrice, and stayed. ¹⁹And the man of God was wroth with him, and said, Thou shouldest have smitten five or six times; then hadst thou smitten Syria till thou hadst consumed *it*: whereas now thou shalt smite Syria *but* thrice.

²⁰And Elisha died, and they buried him. And the bands of the Moabites invaded the land at the coming in of the year. ²¹And it came to pass, as they were burying a man, that, behold, they spied a band *of men*; and they cast the man into the sepulchre of Elisha: and when the man was let down, and touched the bones of Elisha, he revived, and stood up on his feet. ²²But Hazael king of Syria oppressed Israel all the days of Jehoahaz. ²³And the LORD was gracious unto them, and had compassion on them, and had respect unto them, because of his covenant with Abraham, Isaac, and Jacob, and would not destroy them, neither cast he them from his presence^f as yet. ²⁴So Hazael king of Syria died; and Benhadad his son reigned in his stead. ²⁵And Jehoash the son of Jehoahaz took^g again out of the hand of Benhadad the son of Hazael the cities, which he had taken out of the hand of Jehoahaz his father by war.

Three times did Joash beat him, and recovered the cities of Israel.

14

¹In the second year of Joash son of Jehoahaz king of Israel reigned Amaziah the son of Joash king of Judah. ²He was twenty and five years old when he began to reign, and reigned twenty and nine years in Jerusalem. And his mother's name *was* Jehoaddan of Jerusalem. ³And he did *that which was* right in the sight of the LORD, yet not like David his father: he did according to all things as Joash his father did. ⁴Howbeit the high places were not taken away: as yet the people did sacrifice and burnt incense on the high places. ⁵And it came to pass, as soon as the kingdom was confirmed in his hand, that he slew his servants which had slain the king his father. ⁶But the children of the murderers he slew not: according unto that which is written in the book of the law of Moses, wherein the LORD commanded, saying, The fathers shall not be put to death for the children, nor the children be put to death for the fathers; but every man shall be put to death for his own sin. ⁷He slew of Edom in the valley of salt ten thousand, and took Selah^a by war, and called the name of it Joktheel unto this day.

⁸Then Amaziah sent messengers to Jehoash, the son of Jehoahaz son of Jehu, king of Israel, saying, Come, let us look one another in the face. ⁹And Jehoash the king of Israel sent to Amaziah king of Judah, saying, The thistle that

---

^f presence: Heb. face
^g took . . . : Heb. returned and took
^a Selah: or, the rock

was in Lebanon sent to the cedar that *was* in Lebanon, saying, Give thy daughter to my son to wife: and there passed by a wild beast that *was* in Lebanon, and trode down the thistle. ¹⁰Thou hast indeed smitten Edom, and thine heart hath lifted thee up: glory *of this*, and tarry at home[b]: for why shouldest thou meddle to *thy* hurt, that thou shouldest fall, *even* thou, and Judah with thee? ¹¹But Amaziah would not hear. Therefore Jehoash king of Israel went up; and he and Amaziah king of Judah looked one another in the face at Bethshemesh, which *belongeth* to Judah. ¹²And Judah was put to the worse before Israel; and they fled every man to their tents. ¹³And Jehoash king of Israel took Amaziah king of Judah, the son of Jehoash the son of Ahaziah, at Bethshemesh, and came to Jerusalem, and brake down the wall of Jerusalem from the gate of Ephraim unto the corner gate, four hundred cubits. ¹⁴And he took all the gold and silver, and all the vessels that were found in the house of the LORD, and in the treasures of the king's house, and hostages, and returned to Samaria.

¹⁵Now the rest of the acts of Jehoash which he did, and his might, and how he fought with Amaziah king of Judah, *are* they not written in the book of the chronicles of the kings of Israel? ¹⁶And Jehoash slept with his fathers, and was buried in Samaria with the kings of Israel; and Jeroboam his son reigned in his stead. ¹⁷And Amaziah the son of Joash king of Judah lived after the death of Jehoash son of Jehoahaz king of Israel fifteen years. ¹⁸And the rest of the acts of Amaziah, *are* they not written in the book of the chronicles of the kings of Judah? ¹⁹Now they made a conspiracy against him in Jerusalem: and he fled to Lachish; but they sent after him to Lachish, and slew him there. ²⁰And they brought him on horses: and he was buried at Jerusalem with his fathers in the city of David. ²¹And all the people of Judah took Azariah[c], which *was* sixteen years old, and made him king instead of his father Amaziah. ²²He built Elath, and restored it to Judah, after that the king slept with his fathers.

²³In the fifteenth year of Amaziah the son of Joash king of Judah Jeroboam the son of Joash king of Israel began to reign in Samaria, *and reigned* forty and one years. ²⁴And he did *that which was* evil in the sight of the LORD: he departed not from all the sins of Jeroboam the son of Nebat, who made Israel to sin. ²⁵He restored the coast of Israel from the entering of Hamath unto the sea of the plain, according to the word of the LORD God of Israel, which he spake by the hand of his servant Jonah, the son of Amittai, the prophet, which *was* of Gathhepher. ²⁶For the LORD saw the affliction of Israel, *that it was* very bitter: for *there was* not any shut up, nor any left, nor any helper for Israel. ²⁷And the LORD said not that he would blot out the name of Israel from under heaven: but he saved them by the hand of Jeroboam the son of Joash. ²⁸Now the rest of the acts of Jeroboam, and all that he did, and his

---

b at home: Heb. at thy house
c Azariah: also called, Uzziah

might, how he warred, and how he recovered Damascus, and Hamath, *which belonged* to Judah, for Israel, are they not written in the book of the chronicles of the kings of Israel? [29]And Jeroboam slept with his fathers, *even* with the kings of Israel; and Zachariah his son reigned in his stead.

15

[1]In the twenty and seventh year of Jeroboam king of Israel began Azariah[a] son of Amaziah king of Judah to reign. [2]Sixteen years old was he when he began to reign, and he reigned two and fifty years in Jerusalem. And his mother's name *was* Jecholiah of Jerusalem. [3]And he did *that which was* right in the sight of the LORD, according to all that his father Amaziah had done; [4]Save that the high places were not removed: the people sacrificed and burnt incense still on the high places. [5]And the LORD smote the king, so that he was a leper unto the day of his death, and dwelt in a several

Devotional Moment

Growing Up

15:3-4 Though Azariah accomplished a great deal, he repeated some of the mistakes of his father, Amaziah, and grandfather Joash. To overcome the influence of a broken home or an ineffective parent, seek other examples and role models. You can move beyond the limitations of your upbringing by taking Christ as your example and consciously trying to live as he did. Look to believers in your church for examples of how to live in areas where you lacked a proper upbringing.

house. And Jotham the king's son *was* over the house, judging the people of the land. [6]And the rest of the acts of Azariah, and all that he did, *are* they not written in the book of the chronicles of the kings of Judah? [7]So Azariah slept with his fathers; and they buried him with his fathers in the city of David: and Jotham his son reigned in his stead.

[8]In the thirty and eighth year of Azariah king of Judah did Zachariah the son of Jeroboam reign over Israel in Samaria six months. [9]And he did *that which was* evil in the sight of the LORD, as his fathers had done: he departed not from the sins of Jeroboam the son of Nebat, who made Israel to sin. [10]And Shallum the son of Jabesh conspired against him, and smote him before the people, and slew him, and reigned in his stead. [11]And the rest of the acts of Zachariah, behold, they *are* written in the book of the chronicles of the kings of Israel. [12]This *was* the word of the LORD which he spake unto Jehu, saying, Thy sons shall sit on the throne of Israel unto the fourth *generation*. And so it came to pass. [13]Shallum the son of Jabesh began to reign in the nine and thirtieth year of Uzziah[b] king of Judah; and he reigned a full month in Samaria. [14]For Menahem the son of Gadi went up from Tirzah, and came to Samaria, and smote Shallum the son of Jabesh in Samaria, and slew him, and reigned in his stead. [15]And the rest of the acts of Shallum, and his conspiracy which he made, behold, they *are* written in the book of the chronicles of the kings of Is-

[a] Azariah: also called, Uzziah
[b] Uzziah: Gr. Ozias

rael. ¹⁶Then Menahem smote Tiphsah, and all that *were* therein, and the coasts thereof from Tirzah: because they opened not *to him*, therefore he smote *it; and* all the women therein that were with child he ripped up. ¹⁷In the nine and thirtieth year of Azariah king of Judah began Menahem the son of Gadi to reign over Israel, *and reigned* ten years in Samaria. ¹⁸And he did *that which was* evil in the sight of the LORD: he departed not all his days from the sins of Jeroboam the son of Nebat, who made Israel to sin. ¹⁹*And* Pul the king of Assyria came against the land: and Menahem gave Pul a thousand talents of silver, that his hand might be with him to confirm the kingdom in his hand. ²⁰And Menahem exacted^c the money of Israel, *even* of all the mighty men of wealth, of each man fifty shekels of silver, to give to the king of Assyria. So the king of Assyria turned back, and stayed not there in the land. ²¹And the rest of the acts of Menahem, and all that he did, *are* they not written in the book of the chronicles of the kings of Israel? ²²And Menahem slept with his fathers; and Pekahiah his son reigned in his stead. ²³In the fiftieth year of Azariah king of Judah Pekahiah the son of Menahem began to reign over Israel in Samaria, *and reigned* two years. ²⁴And he did *that which was* evil in the sight of the LORD: he departed not from the sins of Jeroboam the son of Nebat, who made Israel to sin. ²⁵But Pekah the son of Remaliah, a captain of his, conspired against him, and smote him in Samaria, in the palace of the king's house, with Argob and Arieh, and with him fifty men of the Gileadites: and he killed him, and reigned in his room. ²⁶And the rest of the acts of Pekahiah, and all that he did, behold, they *are* written in the book of the chronicles of the kings of Israel. ²⁷In the two and fiftieth year of Azariah king of Judah Pekah the son of Remaliah began to reign over Israel in Samaria, *and reigned* twenty years. ²⁸And he did *that which was* evil in the sight of the LORD: he departed not from the sins of Jeroboam the son of Nebat, who made Israel to sin. ²⁹In the days of Pekah king of Israel came Tiglathpileser king of Assyria, and took Ijon, and Abelbethmaachah, and Janoah, and Kedesh, and Hazor, and Gilead, and Galilee, all the land of Naphtali, and carried them captive to Assyria. ³⁰And Hoshea the son of Elah made a conspiracy against Pekah the son of Remaliah, and smote him, and slew him, and reigned in his stead, in the twentieth year of Jotham the son of Uzziah. ³¹And the rest of the acts of Pekah, and all that he did, behold, they *are* written in the book of the chronicles of the kings of Israel.

³²In the second year of Pekah the son of Remaliah king of Israel began Jotham the son of Uzziah king of Judah to reign. ³³Five and twenty years old was he when he began to reign, and he reigned sixteen years in Jerusalem. And his mother's name *was* Jerusha, the daughter of Zadok. ³⁴And he did *that which was* right in the sight of the LORD: he did according to all that his father Uzziah had done. ³⁵Howbeit the high places were not removed: the people sacrificed and burned incense still in the high places. He built the higher

---

^c exacted: Heb. caused to come forth

gate of the house of the LORD. ³⁶Now the rest of the acts of Jotham, and all that he did, *are* they not written in the book of the chronicles of the kings of Judah? ³⁷In those days the LORD began to send against Judah Rezin the king of Syria, and Pekah the son of Remaliah. ³⁸And Jotham slept with his fathers, and was buried with his fathers in the city of David his father: and Ahaz his son reigned in his stead.

16

¹In the seventeenth year of Pekah the son of Remaliah Ahaz the son of Jotham king of Judah began to reign. ²Twenty years old *was* Ahaz when he began to reign, and reigned sixteen years in Jerusalem, and did not *that which was* right in the sight of the LORD his God, like David his father. ³But he walked in the way of the kings of Israel, yea, and made his son to pass through the fire, according to the abominations of the heathen, whom the LORD cast out from before the children of Israel. ⁴And he sacrificed and burnt incense in the high places, and on the hills, and under every green tree. ⁵Then Rezin king of Syria and Pekah son of Remaliah king of Israel came up to Jerusalem to war: and they besieged Ahaz, but could not overcome *him*. ⁶At that time Rezin king of Syria recovered Elath to Syria, and drave the Jews from Elath^a: and the Syrians came to Elath, and dwelt there unto this day. ⁷So Ahaz sent messengers to Tiglath-

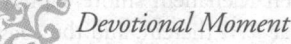

Devotional Moment
•
Worship
16:3; 17:15-17, 31 Truth is stranger than fiction. The Israelite kings who worshiped false gods became so violent and demonic that they even went so far as to sacrifice their own children. Worshiping false gods can lead us down extremely dangerous paths. Perhaps no one you know would dream of throwing his or her child on altars as the Israelites sometimes did. But is golf, boating, your job, sporting events, TV, gambling, or some career pursuit taking a toll on your children? If you fail to honor the Lord God above all other loves and priorities, you are figuratively sacrificing your children on the altar of other gods.

pileser king of Assyria, saying, I *am* thy servant and thy son: come up, and save me out of the hand of the king of Syria, and out of the hand of the king of Israel, which rise up against me. ⁸And Ahaz took the silver and gold that was found in the house of the LORD, and in the treasures of the king's house, and sent *it for* a present to the king of Assyria. ⁹And the king of Assyria hearkened unto him: for the king of Assyria went up against Damascus^b, and took it, and carried *the people of* it captive to Kir, and slew Rezin.

¹⁰And king Ahaz went to Damascus^c to meet Tiglathpileser king of Assyria, and saw an altar that *was* at Damascus: and king Ahaz sent to Urijah the priest the fashion of the altar, and the pattern of it, according to all the workmanship thereof. ¹¹And Urijah the priest built an altar according to all that

---

^a from Elath: Heb. from Eloth
^b Damascus: Heb. Dammesek
^c Damascus: Heb. Dammesek

king Ahaz had sent from Damascus: so Urijah the priest made *it* against king Ahaz came from Damascus. ¹²And when the king was come from Damascus, the king saw the altar: and the king approached to the altar, and offered thereon. ¹³And he burnt his burnt offering and his meat offering, and poured his drink offering, and sprinkled the blood of his peace offerings[d], upon the altar. ¹⁴And he brought also the brasen altar, which *was* before the LORD, from the forefront of the house, from between the altar and the house of the LORD, and put it on the north side of the altar. ¹⁵And king Ahaz commanded Urijah the priest, saying, Upon the great altar burn the morning burnt offering, and the evening meat offering, and the king's burnt sacrifice, and his meat offering, with the burnt offering of all the people of the land, and their meat offering, and their drink offerings; and sprinkle upon it all the blood of the burnt offering, and all the blood of the sacrifice: and the brasen altar shall be for me to enquire *by*. ¹⁶Thus did Urijah the priest, according to all that king Ahaz commanded.

¹⁷And king Ahaz cut off the borders of the bases, and removed the laver from off them; and took down the sea from off the brasen oxen that *were* under it, and put it upon a pavement of stones. ¹⁸And the covert for the sabbath that they had built in the house, and the king's entry without, turned he from the house of the LORD for the king of Assyria. ¹⁹Now the rest of the acts of Ahaz which he did, *are* they not written in the book of the chronicles of the kings of Judah? ²⁰And Ahaz slept with his fathers, and was buried with his fathers in the city of David: and Hezekiah his son reigned in his stead.

17

¹In the twelfth year of Ahaz king of Judah began Hoshea the son of Elah to reign in Samaria over Israel nine years. ²And he did *that which was* evil in the sight of the LORD, but not as the kings of Israel that were before him. ³Against him came up Shalmaneser king of Assyria; and Hoshea became his servant, and gave[a] him presents. ⁴And the king of Assyria found conspiracy in Hoshea: for he had sent messengers to So king of Egypt, and brought no present[b] to the king of Assyria, as *he had done* year by year: therefore the king of Assyria shut him up, and bound him in prison. ⁵Then the king of Assyria came up throughout all the land, and went up to Samaria, and besieged it three years. ⁶In the ninth year of Hoshea the king of Assyria took Samaria, and carried Israel away into Assyria, and placed them in Halah and in Habor *by* the river of Gozan, and in the cities of the Medes.

⁷For *so* it was, that the children of Israel had sinned against the LORD their God, which had brought them up out of the land of Egypt, from under the hand of Pharaoh king of Egypt, and had feared other gods, ⁸And walked in the statutes of the heathen, whom the LORD cast out from before the chil-

---

[d] his peace offerings: Heb. the peace offerings which were his
[a] gave: Heb. rendered
[b] present: or, tribute

dren of Israel, and of the kings of Israel, which they had made. ⁹And the children of Israel did secretly *those* things that *were* not right against the LORD their God, and they built them high places in all their cities, from the tower of the watchmen to the fenced city. ¹⁰And they set them up images^c and groves in every high hill, and under every green tree: ¹¹And there they burnt incense in all the high places, as *did* the heathen whom the LORD carried away before them; and wrought wicked things to provoke the LORD to anger: ¹²For they served idols, whereof the LORD had said unto them, Ye shall not do this thing. ¹³Yet the LORD testified against Israel, and against Judah, by^d all the prophets, *and by* all the seers, saying, Turn ye from your evil ways, and keep my commandments *and* my statutes, according to all the law which I commanded your fathers, and which I sent to you by my servants the prophets. ¹⁴Notwithstanding they would not hear, but hardened their necks, like to the neck of their fathers, that did not believe in the LORD their God. ¹⁵And they rejected his statutes, and his covenant that he made with their fathers, and his testimonies which he testified against them; and they followed vanity, and became vain, and went after the heathen that *were* round about them, *concerning* whom the LORD had charged them, that they should not do like them. ¹⁶And they left all the commandments of the LORD their God, and made them molten images, *even* two calves, and made a grove, and worshipped all the host of heaven,

and served Baal. ¹⁷And they caused their sons and their daughters to pass through the fire, and used divination and enchantments, and sold themselves to do evil in the sight of the LORD, to provoke him to anger. ¹⁸Therefore the LORD was very angry with Israel, and removed them out of his sight: there was none left but the tribe of Judah only. ¹⁹Also Judah kept not the commandments of the LORD their God, but walked in the statutes of Israel which they made. ²⁰And the LORD rejected all the seed of Israel, and afflicted them, and delivered them into the hand of spoilers, until he had cast them out of his sight. ²¹For he rent Israel from the house of David; and they made Jeroboam the son of Nebat king: and Jeroboam drave Israel from following the LORD, and made them sin a great sin. ²²For the children of Israel walked in all the sins of Jeroboam which he did; they departed not from them; ²³Until the LORD removed Israel out of his sight, as he had said by all his servants the prophets. So was Israel carried away out of their own land to Assyria unto this day.

²⁴And the king of Assyria brought *men* from Babylon, and from Cuthah, and from Ava, and from Hamath, and from Sepharvaim, and placed *them* in the cities of Samaria instead of the children of Israel: and they possessed Samaria, and dwelt in the cities thereof. ²⁵And *so* it was at the beginning of their dwelling there, *that* they feared not the LORD: therefore the LORD sent lions among them, which slew *some* of them.

---

^c images: Heb. statues
^d by: Heb. by the hand of

²⁶Wherefore they spake to the king of Assyria, saying, The nations which thou hast removed, and placed in the cities of Samaria, know not the manner of the God of the land: therefore he hath sent lions among them, and, behold, they slay them, because they know not the manner of the God of the land. ²⁷Then the king of Assyria commanded, saying, Carry thither one of the priests whom ye brought from thence; and let them go and dwell there, and let him teach them the manner of the God of the land. ²⁸Then one of the priests whom they had carried away from Samaria came and dwelt in Bethel, and taught them how they should fear the LORD. ²⁹Howbeit every nation made gods of their own, and put *them* in the houses of the high places which the Samaritans had made, every nation in their cities wherein they dwelt. ³⁰And the men of Babylon made Succoth-benoth, and the men of Cuth made Nergal, and the men of Hamath made Ashima, ³¹And the Avites made Nibhaz and Tartak, and the Sepharvites burnt their children in fire to Adrammelech and Anammelech, the gods of Sepharvaim. ³²So they feared the LORD, and made unto themselves of the lowest of them priests of the high places, which sacrificed for them in the houses of the high places. ³³They feared the LORD, and served their own gods, after the manner of the nations whom they carried away from thence. ³⁴Unto this day they do after the former manners: they fear not the LORD, neither do they after their statutes, or after their ordi-

nances, or after the law and commandment which the LORD commanded the children of Jacob, whom he named Israel; ³⁵With whom the LORD had made a covenant, and charged them, saying, Ye shall not fear other gods, nor bow yourselves to them, nor serve them, nor sacrifice to them: ³⁶But the LORD, who brought you up out of the land of Egypt with great power and a stretched out arm, him shall ye fear, and him shall ye worship, and to him shall ye do sacrifice. ³⁷And the statutes, and the ordinances, and the law, and the commandment, which he wrote for you, ye shall observe to do for evermore; and ye shall not fear other gods. ³⁸And the covenant that I have made with you ye shall not forget; neither shall ye fear other gods. ³⁹But the LORD your God ye shall fear; and he shall deliver you out of the hand of all your enemies. ⁴⁰Howbeit they did not hearken, but they did after their former manner. ⁴¹So these nations feared the LORD, and served their graven images, both their children, and their children's children: as did their fathers, so do they unto this day.

18

¹Now it came to pass in the third year of Hoshea son of Elah king of Israel, *that* Hezekiah[a] the son of Ahaz king of Judah began to reign. ²Twenty and five years old was he when he began to reign; and he reigned twenty and nine years in Jerusalem. His mother's name also *was* Abi[b], the daughter of Zachariah. ³And he did *that which was*

---

[a] Hezekiah: he is called Ezekias
[b] Abi: also called, Abijah

right in the sight of the LORD, according to all that David his father did. ⁴He removed the high places, and brake the images^c, and cut down the groves, and brake in pieces the brasen serpent that Moses had made: for unto those days the children of Israel did burn incense to it: and he called it Nehushtan. ⁵He trusted in the LORD God of Israel; so that after him was none like him among all the kings of Judah, nor *any* that were before him. ⁶For he clave to the LORD, *and* departed not from following him, but kept his commandments, which the LORD commanded Moses. ⁷And the LORD was with him; *and* he prospered whithersoever he went forth: and he rebelled against the king of Assyria, and served him not. ⁸He smote the Philistines, *even* unto Gaza^d, and the borders thereof, from the tower of the watchmen to the fenced city.

⁹And it came to pass in the fourth year of king Hezekiah, which *was* the seventh year of Hoshea son of Elah king of Israel, *that* Shalmaneser king of Assyria came up against Samaria, and besieged it. ¹⁰And at the end of three years they took it: *even* in the sixth year of Hezekiah, that *is* the ninth year of Hoshea king of Israel, Samaria was taken. ¹¹And the king of Assyria did carry away Israel unto Assyria, and put them in Halah and in Habor *by* the river of Gozan, and in the cities of the Medes: ¹²Because they obeyed not the voice of the LORD their God, but transgressed his covenant, *and* all that Moses the servant of the LORD commanded, and would not hear *them*, nor do *them*. ¹³Now in the fourteenth year of king Hezekiah did Sennacherib^e king of Assyria come up against all the fenced cities of Judah, and took them. ¹⁴And Hezekiah king of Judah sent to the king of Assyria to Lachish, saying, I have offended; return from me: that which thou puttest on me will I bear. And the king of Assyria appointed unto Hezekiah king of Judah three hundred talents of silver and thirty talents of gold. ¹⁵And Hezekiah gave *him* all the silver that was found in the house of the LORD, and in the treasures of the king's house. ¹⁶At that time did Hezekiah cut off *the gold from* the doors of the temple of the LORD, and *from* the pillars which Hezekiah king of Judah had overlaid, and gave it to the king of Assyria.

¹⁷And the king of Assyria sent Tartan and Rabsaris and Rabshakeh from Lachish to king Hezekiah with a great^f host against Jerusalem. And they went up and came to Jerusalem. And when they were come up, they came and stood by the conduit of the upper pool, which *is* in the highway of the fuller's field. ¹⁸And when they had called to the king, there came out to them Eliakim the son of Hilkiah, which *was* over the household, and Shebna the scribe^g, and Joah the son of Asaph the recorder. ¹⁹And

---

^c images: Heb. statues
^d Gaza: Heb. Azzah
^e Sennacherib: Heb. Sanherib
^f great: Heb. heavy
^g scribe: or, secretary

Rabshakeh said unto them, Speak ye now to Hezekiah, Thus saith the great king, the king of Assyria, What confidence *is* this wherein thou trustest? [20]Thou sayest[h], (but *they are but* vain words,) *I have* counsel and strength for the war. Now on whom dost thou trust, that thou rebellest against me? [21]Now, behold, thou trustest[i] upon the staff of this bruised reed, *even* upon Egypt, on which if a man lean, it will go into his hand, and pierce it: so *is* Pharaoh king of Egypt unto all that trust on him. [22]But if ye say unto me, We trust in the LORD our God: *is* not that he, whose high places and whose altars Hezekiah hath taken away, and hath said to Judah and Jerusalem, Ye shall worship before this altar in Jerusalem? [23]Now therefore, I pray thee, give pledges[j] to my lord the king of Assyria, and I will deliver thee two thousand horses, if thou be able on thy part to set riders upon them. [24]How then wilt thou turn away the face of one captain of the least of my master's servants, and put thy trust on Egypt for chariots and for horsemen? [25]Am I now come up without the LORD against this place to destroy it? The LORD said to me, Go up against this land, and destroy it. [26]Then said Eliakim the son of Hilkiah, and Shebna, and Joah, unto Rabshakeh, Speak, I pray thee, to thy servants in the Syrian language; for we understand *it*: and talk not with us in the Jews' language in the ears of the people that *are* on the wall. [27]But Rabshakeh said unto them, Hath my master sent me to thy master, and to thee, to speak these words? *hath he* not *sent me* to the men which sit on the wall, that they may eat their own dung, and drink their own piss[k] with you? [28]Then Rabshakeh stood and cried with a loud voice in the Jews' language, and spake, saying, Hear the word of the great king, the king of Assyria: [29]Thus saith the king, Let not Hezekiah deceive you: for he shall not be able to deliver you out of his hand: [30]Neither let Hezekiah make you trust in the LORD, saying, The LORD will surely deliver us, and this city shall not be delivered into the hand of the king of Assyria. [31]Hearken not to Hezekiah: for thus saith the king of Assyria, Make[l] *an agreement* with me by a present, and come out to me, and *then* eat ye every man of his own vine, and every one of his fig tree, and drink ye every one the waters of his cistern: [32]Until I come and take you away to a land like your own land, a land of corn and wine, a land of bread and vineyards, a land of oil olive and of honey, that ye may live, and not die: and hearken not unto Hezekiah, when he persuadeth[m] you, saying, The LORD will deliver us. [33]Hath any of the gods of the nations delivered at all his land out of the hand of the king of Assyria? [34]Where *are* the gods of Hamath, and of Arpad? where *are* the gods of Sepharvaim, Hena, and Ivah? have they

---

[h] sayest: or, talkest
[i] trustest: Heb. trustest thee
[j] pledges: or, hostages
[k] their own piss: Heb. the water of their feet
[l] Make . . . : or, Seek my favour: Heb. Make with me a blessing
[m] persuadeth: or, deceiveth

delivered Samaria out of mine hand? [35]Who *are* they among all the gods of the countries, that have delivered their country out of mine hand, that the LORD should deliver Jerusalem out of mine hand? [36]But the people held their peace, and answered him not a word: for the king's commandment was, saying, Answer him not. [37]Then came Eliakim the son of Hilkiah, which *was* over the household, and Shebna the scribe, and Joah the son of Asaph the recorder, to Hezekiah with *their* clothes rent, and told him the words of Rabshakeh.

19

[1]And it came to pass, when king Hezekiah heard *it*, that he rent his clothes, and covered himself with sackcloth, and went into the house of the LORD. [2]And he sent Eliakim, which *was* over the household, and Shebna the scribe, and the elders of the priests, covered with sackcloth, to Isaiah the prophet the son of Amoz. [3]And they said unto him, Thus saith Hezekiah, This day *is* a day of trouble, and of rebuke, and blasphemy[a]: for the children are come to the birth, and *there is* not strength to bring forth. [4]It may be the LORD thy God will hear all the words of Rabshakeh, whom the king of Assyria his master hath sent to reproach the living God; and will reprove the words which the LORD thy God hath heard: wherefore lift up *thy* prayer for the remnant that are left[b]. [5]So the servants of king Hezekiah came to Isaiah. [6]And Isaiah said unto them, Thus shall ye say to your master, Thus saith the LORD, Be

not afraid of the words which thou hast heard, with which the servants of the king of Assyria have blasphemed me. [7]Behold, I will send a blast upon him, and he shall hear a rumour, and shall return to his own land; and I will cause him to fall by the sword in his own land.

[8]So Rabshakeh returned, and found the king of Assyria warring against Libnah: for he had heard that he was departed from Lachish. [9]And when he heard say of Tirhakah king of Ethiopia, Behold, he is come out to fight against thee: he sent messengers again unto Hezekiah, saying, [10]Thus shall ye speak to Hezekiah king of Judah, saying, Let not thy God in whom thou trustest deceive thee, saying, Jerusalem shall not be delivered into the hand of the king of Assyria. [11]Behold, thou hast heard what the kings of Assyria have done to all lands, by destroying them utterly: and shalt thou be delivered? [12]Have the gods of the nations delivered them which my fathers have destroyed; *as* Gozan, and Haran, and Rezeph, and the children of Eden which *were* in Thelasar? [13]Where *is* the king of Hamath, and the king of Arpad, and the king of the city of Sepharvaim, of Hena, and Ivah? [14]And Hezekiah received the letter of the hand of the messengers, and read it: and Hezekiah went up into the house of the LORD, and spread it before the LORD. [15]And Hezekiah prayed before the LORD, and said, O LORD God of Israel, which dwellest *between* the cherubims, thou art the God, *even* thou alone, of all the kingdoms of the earth; thou hast made

---

[a] blasphemy: or, provocation
[b] left: Heb. found

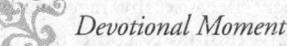

heaven and earth. ¹⁶LORD, bow down thine ear, and hear: open, LORD, thine eyes, and see: and hear the words of Sennacherib, which hath sent him to reproach the living God. ¹⁷Of a truth, LORD, the kings of Assyria have destroyed the nations and their lands, ¹⁸And have cast^c their gods into the fire: for they *were* no gods, but the work of men's hands, wood and stone: therefore they have destroyed them. ¹⁹Now therefore, O LORD our God, I beseech thee, save thou us out of his hand, that all the kingdoms of the earth may know that thou *art* the LORD God, *even* thou only.

²⁰Then Isaiah the son of Amoz sent to Hezekiah, saying, Thus saith the LORD God of Israel, *That* which thou hast prayed to me against Sennacherib king of Assyria I have heard. ²¹This *is* the word that the LORD hath spoken concerning him; The virgin the daughter of Zion hath despised thee, *and* laughed thee to scorn; the daughter of Jerusalem hath shaken her head at thee. ²²Whom hast thou reproached and blasphemed? and against whom hast thou exalted *thy* voice, and lifted up thine eyes on high? *even* against the Holy *One* of Israel. ²³By^d thy messengers thou hast reproached the Lord, and hast said, With the multitude of my chariots I am come up to the height of the mountains, to the sides of Lebanon, and will cut down the tall cedar trees thereof, *and* the choice fir trees thereof: and I will enter into the lodgings of his bor-

Devotional Moment

•

Success

19:25 The king of Assyria had bragged about how great and invincible he was. God had an important message for him: You'd better remember that success comes from God. In the end, Sennacherib's arrogance cost him his life. Every time you watch your child on stage in the orchestra, performing, let a quiet prayer ascend: Success comes from God.

At graduation when your child accepts a diploma or degree, and the nightly struggles to get homework done are but a memory, say it again: Success comes from God.

When the swim team goes to State and your child is numbered among the best, you remember who taught her the dog paddle, but let the world hear: Success comes from God.

When the sun rises on your last dawn and you review the best of life, put fears aside and say with joy: Success comes from God.

ders, *and into* the forest of his Carmel. ²⁴I have digged and drunk strange waters, and with the sole of my feet have I dried up all the rivers of besieged places. ²⁵Hast thou not heard long ago *how* I have done it, *and* of ancient times that I have formed it? now have I brought it to pass, that thou shouldest be to lay waste fenced cities *into* ruinous heaps. ²⁶Therefore their inhabitants were of small^e power, they were dismayed and confounded; they were *as* the grass of the field, and *as* the green herb, *as* the grass on the housetops, and *as corn* blasted before it be grown up. ²⁷But I know thy abode^f, and thy going out, and thy coming in, and thy rage

---

^c cast: Heb. given
^d By: Heb. By the hand of
^e of small . . . : Heb. short of hand
^f abode: or, sitting

against me. ²⁸Because thy rage against me and thy tumult is come up into mine ears, therefore I will put my hook in thy nose, and my bridle in thy lips, and I will turn thee back by the way by which thou camest. ²⁹And this *shall be* a sign unto thee, Ye shall eat this year such things as grow of themselves, and in the second year that which springeth of the same; and in the third year sow ye, and reap, and plant vineyards, and eat the fruits thereof. ³⁰And the remnant^g that is escaped of the house of Judah shall yet again take root downward, and bear fruit upward. ³¹For out of Jerusalem shall go forth a remnant, and they that escape out of mount Zion: the zeal of the LORD *of hosts* shall do this. ³²Therefore thus saith the LORD concerning the king of Assyria, He shall not come into this city, nor shoot an arrow there, nor come before it with shield, nor cast a bank against it. ³³By the way that he came, by the same shall he return, and shall not come into this city, saith the LORD. ³⁴For I will defend this city, to save it, for mine own sake, and for my servant David's sake.

³⁵And it came to pass that night, that the angel of the LORD went out, and smote in the camp of the Assyrians an hundred fourscore and five thousand: and when they arose early in the morning, behold, they *were* all dead corpses. ³⁶So Sennacherib king of Assyria departed, and went and returned, and dwelt at Nineveh. ³⁷And it came to pass, as he was worshipping in the house of Nisroch his god, that Adrammelech and Sharezer his sons smote him with the sword: and they escaped into the land of Armenia^h. And Esarhaddon his son reigned in his stead.

20

¹In those days was Hezekiah sick unto death. And the prophet Isaiah the son of Amoz came to him, and said unto him, Thus saith the LORD, Set thine house in order; for thou shalt die, and not live. ²Then he turned his face to the wall, and prayed unto the LORD, saying, ³I beseech thee, O LORD, remember now how I have walked before thee in truth and with a perfect heart, and have done *that which is* good in thy sight. And Hezekiah wept sore^a. ⁴And it came to pass, afore Isaiah was gone out into the middle court^b, that the word of the LORD came to him, saying, ⁵Turn again, and tell Hezekiah the captain of my people, Thus saith the LORD, the God of David thy father, I have heard thy prayer, I have seen thy tears: behold, I will heal thee: on the third day thou shalt go up unto the house of the LORD. ⁶And I will add unto thy days fifteen years; and I will deliver thee and this city out of the hand of the king of Assyria; and I will defend this city for mine own sake, and for my servant David's sake. ⁷And Isaiah said, Take a lump of figs. And they took and laid *it* on the boil, and he recovered. ⁸And Hezekiah said unto Isaiah, What *shall*

---

^g remnant . . . : Heb. escaping of the house of Judah that remaineth
^h Armenia: Heb. Ararat
^a sore: Heb. with a great weeping
^b court: or, city

be the sign that the LORD will heal me, and that I shall go up into the house of the LORD the third day? ⁹And Isaiah said, This sign shalt thou have of the LORD, that the LORD will do the thing that he hath spoken: shall the shadow go forward ten degrees, or go back ten degrees? ¹⁰And Hezekiah answered, It is a light thing for the shadow to go down ten degrees: nay, but let the shadow return backward ten degrees. ¹¹And Isaiah the prophet cried unto the LORD: and he brought the shadow ten degrees backward, by which it had gone down in the dialᶜ of Ahaz.

¹²At that time Berodachbaladanᵈ, the son of Baladan, king of Babylon, sent letters and a present unto Hezekiah: for he had heard that Hezekiah had been sick. ¹³And Hezekiah hearkened unto them, and shewed them all the house of his precious thingsᵉ, the silver, and the gold, and the spices, and the precious ointment, and *all* the house of his armour, and all that was found in his treasures: there was nothing in his house, nor in all his dominion, that Hezekiah shewed them not. ¹⁴Then came Isaiah the prophet unto king Hezekiah, and said unto him, What said these men? and from whence came they unto thee? And Hezekiah said, They are come from a far country, *even* from Babylon. ¹⁵And he said, What have they seen in thine house? And Hezekiah answered, All *the things* that *are* in mine house have they seen: there is nothing among my treasures that I have not shewed them. ¹⁶And Isaiah said unto Hezekiah, Hear the word of the LORD. ¹⁷Behold, the days come, that all that *is* in thine house, and that which thy fathers have laid up in store unto this day, shall be carried into Babylon: nothing shall be left, saith the LORD. ¹⁸And of thy sons that shall issue from thee, which thou shalt beget, shall they take away; and they shall be eunuchs in the palace of the king of Babylon. ¹⁹Then said Hezekiah unto Isaiah, Good *is* the word of the LORD which thou hast spoken. And he said, *Is it* not *good,* if peace and truth be in my days? ²⁰And the rest of the acts of Hezekiah, and all his might, and how he made a pool, and a conduit, and brought water into the city, *are* they not written in the book of the chronicles of the kings of Judah? ²¹And Hezekiah slept with his fathers: and Manasseh his son reigned in his stead.

21

¹Manasseh *was* twelve years old when he began to reign, and reigned fifty and five years in Jerusalem. And his mother's name *was* Hephzibah. ²And he did *that which was* evil in the sight of the LORD, after the abominations of the heathen, whom the LORD cast out before the children of Israel. ³For he built up again the high places which Hezekiah his father had destroyed; and he reared up altars for Baal, and made a grove, as did Ahab king of Israel; and worshipped all the host of heaven, and served them. ⁴And he built altars in the house of the LORD, of which the LORD said, In Jerusalem will I put my

---

ᶜ dial: Heb. degrees
ᵈ Berodachbaladan: or, Merodachbaladan
ᵉ precious things: or, spicery

name. ⁵And he built altars for all the host of heaven in the two courts of the house of the LORD. ⁶And he made his son pass through the fire, and observed times, and used enchantments, and dealt with familiar spirits and wizards: he wrought much wickedness in the sight of the LORD, to provoke *him* to anger. ⁷And he set a graven image of the grove that he had made in the house, of which the LORD said to David, and to Solomon his son, In this house, and in Jerusalem, which I have chosen out of all tribes of Israel, will I put my name for ever: ⁸Neither will I make the feet of Israel move any more out of the land which I gave their fathers; only if they will observe to do according to all that I have commanded them, and according to all the law that my servant Moses commanded them. ⁹But they hearkened not: and Manasseh seduced them to do more evil than did the nations whom the LORD destroyed before the children of Israel.

¹⁰And the LORD spake by his servants the prophets, saying, ¹¹Because Manasseh king of Judah hath done these abominations, *and* hath done wickedly above all that the Amorites did, which *were* before him, and hath made Judah also to sin with his idols: ¹²Therefore thus saith the LORD God of Israel, Behold, I *am* bringing *such* evil upon Jerusalem and Judah, that whosoever heareth of it, both his ears shall tingle. ¹³And I will stretch over Jerusalem the line of Samaria, and the plummet of the house of Ahab: and I will wipe Jerusalem as *a man* wipeth a dish, wipingᵃ *it*, and turning *it* upside

down. ¹⁴And I will forsake the remnant of mine inheritance, and deliver them into the hand of their enemies; and they shall become a prey and a spoil to all their enemies; ¹⁵Because they have done *that which was* evil in my sight, and have provoked me to anger, since the day their fathers came forth out of Egypt, even unto this day. ¹⁶Moreover Manasseh shed innocent blood very much, till he had filled Jerusalem from one end to another; beside his sin wherewith he made Judah to sin, in doing *that which was* evil in the sight of the LORD. ¹⁷Now the rest of the acts of Manasseh, and all that he did, and his sin that he sinned, *are* they not written in the book of the chronicles of the kings of Judah? ¹⁸And Manasseh slept with his fathers, and was buried in the garden of his own house, in the garden of Uzza: and Amon his son reigned in his stead.

¹⁹Amon *was* twenty and two years old when he began to reign, and he reigned two years in Jerusalem. And his mother's name *was* Meshullemeth, the daughter of Haruz of Jotbah. ²⁰And he did *that which was* evil in the sight of the LORD, as his father Manasseh did. ²¹And he walked in all the way that his father walked in, and served the idols that his father served, and worshipped them: ²²And he forsook the LORD God of his fathers, and walked not in the way of the LORD. ²³And the servants of Amon conspired against him, and slew the king in his own house. ²⁴And the people of the land slew all them that had conspired against king Amon; and the people of the land made

---

ᵃ wiping . . . : Heb. he wipeth and turneth it upon the face thereof

Josiah his son king in his stead. ²⁵Now the rest of the acts of Amon which he did, *are* they not written in the book of the chronicles of the kings of Judah? ²⁶And he was buried in his sepulchre in the garden of Uzza: and Josiah[b] his son reigned in his stead.

22

¹Josiah *was* eight years old when he began to reign, and he reigned thirty and one years in Jerusalem. And his mother's name *was* Jedidah, the daughter of Adaiah of Boscath. ²And he did *that which was* right in the sight of the LORD, and walked in all the way of David his father, and turned not aside to the right hand or to the left. ³And it

---

Devotional Moment

•

Responsibility

22:1-2 Most eight-year-olds are happy if they can decide a dinner menu once a week. Josiah, at that age, could decide a bit more—he was king. From childhood he knew what responsibility was. Parents who are so dominant and so "in control" that kids must ask which socks to wear to school are not likely to teach children how to make decisions. Children need to taste responsibility, to experience failure, to adjust after failing, and to figure out priorities. While it makes sense to limit the amount of responsibility children take on, don't be afraid to give them meaningful tasks, even if you fear they may fail. That's how they grow up. Josiah was certainly an exception, but all children can make a contribution. Use responsibility as a way of introducing your children to the adult world in which they will eventually have to live.

---

came to pass in the eighteenth year of king Josiah, *that* the king sent Shaphan the son of Azaliah, the son of Meshullam, the scribe, to the house of the LORD, saying, ⁴Go up to Hilkiah the high priest, that he may sum the silver which is brought into the house of the LORD, which the keepers of the door[a] have gathered of the people: ⁵And let them deliver it into the hand of the doers of the work, that have the oversight of the house of the LORD: and let them give it to the doers of the work which *is* in the house of the LORD, to repair the breaches of the house, ⁶Unto carpenters, and builders, and masons, and to buy timber and hewn stone to repair the house. ⁷Howbeit there was no reckoning made with them of the money that was delivered into their hand, because they dealt faithfully. ⁸And Hilkiah the high priest said unto Shaphan the scribe, I have found the book of the law in the house of the LORD. And Hilkiah gave the book to Shaphan, and he read it. ⁹And Shaphan the scribe came to the king, and brought the king word again, and said, Thy servants have gathered[b] the money that was found in the house, and have delivered it into the hand of them that do the work, that have the oversight of the house of the LORD. ¹⁰And Shaphan the scribe shewed the king, saying, Hilkiah the priest hath delivered me a book. And Shaphan read it before the king.

¹¹And it came to pass, when the king had heard the words of the book

---

[b] Josiah: Gr. Josias
[a] door: Heb. threshold
[b] gathered: Heb. melted

of the law, that he rent his clothes. [12]And the king commanded Hilkiah the priest, and Ahikam the son of Shaphan, and Achbor[c] the son of Michaiah, and Shaphan the scribe, and Asahiah a servant of the king's, saying, [13]Go ye, enquire of the LORD for me, and for the people, and for all Judah, concerning the words of this book that is found: for great is the wrath of the LORD that is kindled against us, because our fathers have not hearkened unto the words of this book, to do according unto all that which is written concerning us. [14]So Hilkiah the priest, and Ahikam, and Achbor, and Shaphan, and Asahiah, went unto Huldah the prophetess, the wife of Shallum the son of Tikvah, the son of Harhas, keeper of the wardrobe[d]; (now she dwelt in Jerusalem in the college;) and they communed with her. [15]And she said unto them, Thus saith the LORD God of Israel, Tell the man that sent you to me, [16]Thus saith the LORD, Behold, I will bring evil upon this place, and upon the inhabitants thereof, even all the words of the book which the king of Judah hath read: [17]Because they have forsaken me, and have burned incense unto other gods, that they might provoke me to anger with all the works of their hands; therefore my wrath shall be kindled against this place, and shall not be quenched. [18]But to the king of Judah which sent you to enquire of the LORD, thus shall ye say to him, Thus saith the LORD God of Israel, As touching the words which thou hast heard; [19]Because thine heart was tender, and thou hast hum-bled thyself before the LORD, when thou heardest what I spake against this place, and against the inhabitants thereof, that they should become a desolation and a curse, and hast rent thy clothes, and wept before me; I also have heard thee, saith the LORD. [20]Behold therefore, I will gather thee unto thy fathers, and thou shalt be gathered into thy grave in peace; and thine eyes shall not see all the evil which I will bring upon this place. And they brought the king word again.

23

[1]And the king sent, and they gathered unto him all the elders of Judah and of Jerusalem. [2]And the king went up into the house of the LORD, and all the men of Judah and all the inhabitants of Jerusalem with him, and the priests, and the prophets, and all the people, both small and great: and he read in their ears all the words of the book of the covenant which was found in the house of the LORD. [3]And the king stood by a pillar, and made a covenant before the LORD, to walk after the LORD, and to keep his commandments and his testimonies and his statutes with all their heart and all their soul, to perform the words of this covenant that were written in this book. And all the people stood to the covenant.

[4]And the king commanded Hilkiah the high priest, and the priests of the second order, and the keepers of the door, to bring forth out of the temple of the LORD all the vessels

---

[c] Achbor: Abdon
[d] wardrobe: Heb. garments

that were made for Baal, and for the grove, and for all the host of heaven: and he burned them without Jerusalem in the fields of Kidron, and carried the ashes of them unto Bethel. ⁵And he put down the idolatrous priests, whom the kings of Judah had ordained to burn incense in the high places in the cities of Judah, and in the places round about Jerusalem; them also that burned incense unto Baal, to the sun, and to the moon, and to the planets, and to all the host of heaven. ⁶And he brought out the grove from the house of the LORD, without Jerusalem, unto the brook Kidron, and burned it at the brook Kidron, and stamped *it* small to powder, and cast the powder thereof upon the graves of the children of the people. ⁷And he brake down the houses of the sodomites, that *were* by the house of the LORD, where the women wove hangingsᵃ for the grove. ⁸And he brought all the priests out of the cities of Judah, and defiled the high places where the priests had burned incense, from Geba to Beersheba, and brake down the high places of the gates that *were* in the entering in of the gate of Joshua the governor of the city, which *were* on a man's left hand at the gate of the city. ⁹Nevertheless the priests of the high places came not up to the altar of the LORD in Jerusalem, but they did eat of the unleavened bread among their brethren. ¹⁰And he defiled

Topheth, which *is* in the valley of the children of Hinnom, that no man might make his son or his daughter to pass through the fire to Molech. ¹¹And he took away the horses that the kings of Judah had given to the sun, at the entering in of the house of the LORD, by the chamber of Nathanmelech the chamberlainᵇ, which *was* in the suburbs, and burned the chariots of the sun with fire. ¹²And the altars that *were* on the top of the upper chamber of Ahaz, which the kings of Judah had made, and the altars which Manasseh had made in the two courts of the house of the LORD, did the king beat down, and brake *them* downᶜ from thence, and cast the dust of them into the brook Kidron. ¹³And the high places that *were* before Jerusalem, which *were* on the right hand of the mountᵈ of corruption, which Solomon the king of Israel had builded for Ashtoreth the abomination of the Zidonians, and for Chemosh the abomination of the Moabites, and for Milcom the abomination of the children of Ammon, did the king defile. ¹⁴And he brake in pieces the imagesᵉ, and cut down the groves, and filled their places with the bones of men. ¹⁵Moreover the altar that *was* at Bethel, *and* the high place which Jeroboam the son of Nebat, who made Israel to sin, had made, both that altar and the high place he brake down, and burned the high place, *and* stamped *it* small to

---

ᵃ hangings: Heb. houses
ᵇ chamberlain: or, eunuch, or, officer
ᶜ brake . . . : or, ran from thence
ᵈ the mount . . . : that is, the mount of Olives
ᵉ images: Heb. statues

powder, and burned the grove. ¹⁶And as Josiah turned himself, he spied the sepulchres that *were* there in the mount, and sent, and took the bones out of the sepulchres, and burned *them* upon the altar, and polluted it, according to the word of the LORD which the man of God proclaimed, who proclaimed these words. ¹⁷Then he said, What title *is* that that I see? And the men of the city told him, *It is* the sepulchre of the man of God, which came from Judah, and proclaimed these things that thou hast done against the altar of Bethel. ¹⁸And he said, Let him alone; let no man move his bones. So they let his bones alone*, with the bones of the prophet that came out of Samaria. ¹⁹And all the houses also of the high places that *were* in the cities of Samaria, which the kings of Israel had made to provoke *the LORD* to anger, Josiah took away, and did to them according to all the acts that he had done in Bethel. ²⁰And he slew* all the priests of the high places that *were* there upon the altars, and burned men's bones upon them, and returned to Jerusalem. ²¹And the king commanded all the people, saying, Keep the passover unto the LORD your God, as *it is* written in the book of this covenant. ²²Surely there was not holden such a passover from the days of the judges that judged Israel, nor in all the days of the kings of Israel, nor of the kings of Judah; ²³But in the eighteenth year of king Josiah, *wherein* this passover was holden to the LORD in Jerusalem. ²⁴Moreover the *workers with* familiar spirits, and the wizards, and the images*, and the idols, and all the abominations that were spied in the land of Judah and in Jerusalem, did Josiah put away, that he might perform the words of the law which were written in the book that Hilkiah the priest found in the house of the LORD.

²⁵And like unto him was there no king before him, that turned to the LORD with all his heart, and with all his soul, and with all his might, according to all the law of Moses; neither after him arose there *any* like him. ²⁶Notwithstanding the LORD turned not from the fierceness of his great wrath, wherewith his anger was kindled against Judah, because of all the provocations* that Manasseh had provoked him withal. ²⁷And the LORD said, I will remove Judah also out of my sight, as I have removed Israel, and will cast off this city Jerusalem which I have chosen, and the house of which I said, My name shall be there. ²⁸Now the rest of the acts of Josiah, and all that he did, *are* they not written in the book of the chronicles of the kings of Judah? ²⁹In his days Pharaohnechoh king of Egypt went up against the king of Assyria to the river Euphrates: and king Josiah went against him; and he slew him at Megiddo, when he had seen him. ³⁰And his servants carried him in

---

ᶠ bones alone: Heb. bones to escape
ᵍ slew: or, sacrificed
ʰ images: or, teraphim
ⁱ provocations: Heb. angers

a chariot dead from Megiddo, and brought him to Jerusalem, and buried him in his own sepulchre. And the people of the land took Jehoahaz the son of Josiah, and anointed him, and made him king in his father's stead.

³¹Jehoahaz[j] *was* twenty and three years old when he began to reign; and he reigned three months in Jerusalem. And his mother's name *was* Hamutal, the daughter of Jeremiah of Libnah. ³²And he did *that which was* evil in the sight of the LORD, according to all that his fathers had done. ³³And Pharaohnechoh put him in bands at Riblah in the land of Hamath, that he might not reign in Jerusalem; and put the land to a tribute of an hundred talents of silver, and a talent of gold. ³⁴And Pharaohnechoh made Eliakim the son of Josiah king in the room of Josiah his father, and turned his name to Jehoiakim, and took Jehoahaz away: and he came to Egypt, and died there. ³⁵And Jehoiakim gave the silver and the gold to Pharaoh; but he taxed the land to give the money according to the commandment of Pharaoh: he exacted the silver and the gold of the people of the land, of every one according to his taxation, to give *it* unto Pharaohnechoh. ³⁶Jehoiakim *was* twenty and five years old when he began to reign; and he reigned eleven years in Jerusalem. And his mother's name *was* Zebudah, the daughter of Pedaiah of Rumah. ³⁷And he did *that which was* evil in the sight of the LORD, according to all that his fathers had done.

24

¹In his days Nebuchadnezzar king of Babylon came up, and Jehoiakim became his servant three years: then he turned and rebelled against him. ²And the LORD sent against him bands of the Chaldees, and bands of the Syrians, and bands of the Moabites, and bands of the children of Ammon, and sent them against Judah to destroy it, according to the word of the LORD, which he spake by[a] his servants the prophets. ³Surely at the commandment of the LORD came *this* upon Judah, to remove *them* out of his sight, for the sins of Manasseh, according to all that he did; ⁴And also for the innocent blood that he shed: for he filled Jerusalem with innocent blood; which the LORD would not pardon. ⁵Now the rest of the acts of Jehoiakim, and all that he did, *are* they not written in the book of the chronicles of the kings of Judah? ⁶So Jehoiakim slept with his fathers: and Jehoiachin his son reigned in his stead. ⁷And the king of Egypt came not again any more out of his land: for the king of Babylon had taken from the river of Egypt unto the river Euphrates all that pertained to the king of Egypt.

⁸Jehoiachin[b] *was* eighteen years old when he began to reign, and he reigned in Jerusalem three months. And his mother's name *was* Nehushta, the daughter of Elnathan of Jerusalem. ⁹And he did *that which was* evil in the sight of the LORD, according to all that his father had done. ¹⁰At that time the servants of Nebuchadnezzar king of

---

ʲ Jehoahaz: also called, Shallum
ᵃ by: Heb. by the hand of
ᵇ Jehoiachin: also called Jeconiah and Coniah

Babylon came up against Jerusalem, and the city was besieged. ¹¹And Nebuchadnezzar king of Babylon came against the city, and his servants did besiege it. ¹²And Jehoiachin the king of Judah went out to the king of Babylon, he, and his mother, and his servants, and his princes, and his officers²: and the king of Babylon took him in the eighth year of his reign. ¹³And he carried out thence all the treasures of the house of the LORD, and the treasures of the king's house, and cut in pieces all the vessels of gold which Solomon king of Israel had made in the temple of the LORD, as the LORD had said. ¹⁴And he carried away all Jerusalem, and all the princes, and all the mighty men of valour, *even* ten thousand captives, and all the craftsmen and smiths: none remained, save the poorest sort of the people of the land. ¹⁵And he carried away Jehoiachin to Babylon, and the king's mother, and the king's wives, and his officers², and the mighty of the land, *those* carried he into captivity from Jerusalem to Babylon. ¹⁶And all the men of might, *even* seven thousand, and craftsmen and smiths a thousand, all *that were* strong *and* apt for war, even them the king of Babylon brought captive to Babylon. ¹⁷And the king of Babylon made Mattaniah his father's brother king in his stead, and changed his name to Zedekiah. ¹⁸Zedekiah *was* twenty and one years old when he began to reign, and he reigned eleven years in Jerusalem. And his mother's name *was* Hamutal, the daughter of

Jeremiah of Libnah. ¹⁹And he did *that which was* evil in the sight of the LORD, according to all that Jehoiakim had done. ²⁰For through the anger of the LORD it came to pass in Jerusalem and Judah, until he had cast them out from his presence, that Zedekiah rebelled against the king of Babylon.

25

¹And it came to pass in the ninth year of his reign, in the tenth month, in the tenth *day* of the month, *that* Nebuchadnezzar king of Babylon came, he, and all his host, against Jerusalem, and pitched against it; and they built forts against it round about. ²And the city was besieged unto the eleventh year of king Zedekiah. ³And on the ninth *day* of the *fourth* month the famine prevailed in the city, and there was no bread for the people of the land. ⁴And the city was broken up, and all the men of war *fled* by night by the way of the gate between two walls, which *is* by the king's garden: (now the Chaldees *were* against the city round about:) and *the king* went the way toward the plain. ⁵And the army of the Chaldees pursued after the king, and overtook him in the plains of Jericho: and all his army were scattered from him. ⁶So they took the king, and brought him up to the king of Babylon to Riblah; and they gave² judgment upon him. ⁷And they slew the sons of Zedekiah before his eyes, and put out the eyes of Zedekiah, and bound him with fetters of brass, and carried him to Babylon.

ᶜ officers: or, eunuchs
ᵈ officers: or, eunuchs
ᵃ gave . . . : Heb. spake judgment with him

⁸And in the fifth month, on the seventh *day* of the month, which *is* the nineteenth year of king Nebuchadnezzar king of Babylon, came Nebuzaradan, captainᵇ of the guard, a servant of the king of Babylon, unto Jerusalem: ⁹And he burnt the house of the LORD, and the king's house, and all the houses of Jerusalem, and every great *man's* house burnt he with fire. ¹⁰And all the army of the Chaldees, that *were with* the captain of the guard, brake down the walls of Jerusalem round about. ¹¹Now the rest of the people *that were* left in the city, and the fugitivesᶜ that fell away to the king of Babylon, with the remnant of the multitude, did Nebuzaradan the captain of the guard carry away. ¹²But the captain of the guard left of the poor of the land *to be* vinedressers and husbandmen. ¹³And the pillars of brass that *were* in the house of the LORD, and the bases, and the brasen sea that *was* in the house of the LORD, did the Chaldees break in pieces, and carried the brass of them to Babylon. ¹⁴And the pots, and the shovels, and the snuffers, and the spoons, and all the vessels of brass wherewith they ministered, took they away. ¹⁵And the firepans, and the bowls, *and* such things as *were* of gold, *in* gold, and of silver, *in* silver, the captain of the guard took away. ¹⁶The two pillars, oneᵈ sea, and the bases which Solomon had made for the house of the LORD; the brass of all these vessels was without weight. ¹⁷The height of the one pillar *was* eighteen cubits, and the chapiter upon it *was* brass: and the height of the chapiter three cubits; and the wreathen work, and pomegranates upon the chapiter round about, all of brass: and like unto these had the second pillar with wreathen work. ¹⁸And the captain of the guard took Seraiah the chief priest, and Zephaniah the second priest, and the three keepers of the doorᵉ: ¹⁹And out of the city he took an officerᶠ that was set over the men of war, and five men of them that were in the king's presence, which were found in the city, and the principal scribe of the host, which mustered the people of the land, and threescore men of the people of the land *that were* found in the city: ²⁰And Nebuzaradan captain of the guard took these, and brought them to the king of Babylon to Riblah: ²¹And the king of Babylon smote them, and slew them at Riblah in the land of Hamath. So Judah was carried away out of their land.

²²And *as for* the people that remained in the land of Judah, whom Nebuchadnezzar king of Babylon had left, even over them he made Gedaliah the son of Ahikam, the son of Shaphan, ruler. ²³And when all the captains of the armies, they and their men, heard that the king of Babylon had made Gedaliah governor, there came to Gedaliah to Mizpah, even Ishmael the son of Nethaniah, and Johanan the son of

---

ᵇ captain . . . : or, chief marshal
ᶜ fugitives: Heb. fallen away
ᵈ one . . . : Heb. the one sea
ᵉ door: Heb. threshold
ᶠ officer: or, eunuch

Careah, and Seraiah the son of Tan-humeth the Netophathite, and Jaaza-niah the son of a Maachathite, they and their men. ²⁴And Gedaliah sware to them, and to their men, and said unto them, Fear not to be the servants of the Chaldees: dwell in the land, and serve the king of Babylon; and it shall be well with you. ²⁵But it came to pass in the seventh month, that Ishmael the son of Nethaniah, the son of Elishama, of the seed royal^g, came, and ten men with him, and smote Gedaliah, that he died, and the Jews and the Chaldees that were with him at Mizpah. ²⁶And all the people, both small and great, and the captains of the armies, arose, and came to Egypt: for they were afraid of the Chaldees. ²⁷And it came to pass in the seven and thirtieth year of the captivity of Jehoiachin king of Judah, in the twelfth month, on the seven and twen-tieth *day* of the month, *that* Evilmero-dach king of Babylon in the year that he began to reign did lift up the head of Jehoiachin king of Judah out of prison; ²⁸And he spake kindly^h to him, and set his throne above the throne of the kings that *were* with him in Babylon; ²⁹And changed his prison garments: and he did eat bread continually before him all the days of his life. ³⁰And his allowance *was* a continual allowance given him of the king, a daily rate for every day, all the days of his life.

---

^g royal: Heb. of the kingdom
^h kindly . . . : Heb. good things with him

FIRST CHRONICLES

Purpose
To unify God's people, to trace the Davidic line, and to teach that genuine worship ought to be the center of individual and national life

Author
Ezra, according to Jewish tradition

To Whom Written
All Israel

Date Written
Approximately 430 B.C.; recording events that occurred from about 1000–960 B.C.

Setting
First Chronicles parallels 2 Samuel and serves as a commentary on it. Written after the exile from a priestly point of view, 1 Chronicles emphasizes the religious history of Judah and Israel.

Key Verse
"David perceived that the Lord had confirmed him king over Israel, for his kingdom was lifted up on high, because of his people Israel" (14:2).

Key People
David, Solomon

Key Places
Hebron, Jerusalem, the Temple

Anyone who follows organized sports knows how important statistics are. Batting averages tell the story of a baseball season, and first downs indicate which team dominates in football.

Statistics also prove that no one is perfect. A team's best hitter is "out" more than "safe." The puck flies wide of the net more often than into the net. Parents who watch kids play may dispute an umpire's call, but few will insist that every pitch their Jeffrey throws is "down the middle."

The statistics in 1 Chronicles have a message, too. The long lists of names, the people and their jobs, the sons of Elienai and Zillethai and Ishpah, the military rosters—they all have a point: God has made a people for true worship and worldwide witness, and God has not given up on those people yet! Watch our comeback, the chronicler says. Watch what happens when we recognize who we are—where we've been—where we're going. Watch God do a miracle with these people. They are captives now in Babylon, but one day they will be returning to the land of Israel, recovering their heritage, renewing their spirit.

It's as if last season's cellar dwellers suddenly published all their stats, proudly announcing their confidence in the new season. The mother who watched Jeffrey's fastball get clobbered all over the park will be the proudest parent in the bleachers this spring.

The stats and stories of 1 Chronicles—the record of a team God is building for a championship.

1

¹Adam, Sheth, Enosh, ²Kenan, Mahalaleel, Jered, ³Henoch, Methuselah, Lamech, ⁴Noah, Shem, Ham, and Japheth. ⁵The sons of Japheth; Gomer, and Magog, and Madai, and Javan, and Tubal, and Meshech, and Tiras. ⁶And the sons of Gomer; Ashchenaz, and Riphathᵃ, and Togarmah. ⁷And the sons of Javan; Elishah, and Tarshish, Kittim, and Dodanimᵇ. ⁸The sons of Ham; Cush, and Mizraim, Put, and Canaan. ⁹And the sons of Cush; Seba, and Havilah, and Sabta, and Raamah, and Sabtecha. And the sons of Raamah; Sheba, and Dedan. ¹⁰And Cush begat Nimrod: he began to be mighty upon the earth. ¹¹And Mizraim begat Ludim, and Anamim, and Lehabim, and Naphtuhim, ¹²And Pathrusim, and Casluhim, (of whom came the Philistines,) and Caphthorim. ¹³And Canaan begat Zidon his firstborn, and Heth, ¹⁴The Jebusite also, and the Amorite, and the Girgashite, ¹⁵And the Hivite, and the Arkite, and the Sinite, ¹⁶And the Arvadite, and the Zemarite, and the Hamathite. ¹⁷The sons of Shem; Elam, and Asshur, and Arphaxad, and Lud, and Aram, and Uz, and Hul, and Gether, and Meshechᶜ. ¹⁸And Arphaxad begat Shelah, and Shelah begat Eber. ¹⁹And unto Eber were born two sons: the name of the one *was* Pelegᵈ; because in his days the earth was divided: and his brother's name *was* Joktan. ²⁰And Joktan begat Almodad, and Sheleph, and Hazarmaveth, and Jerah, ²¹Hadoram also, and Uzal, and Diklah, ²²And Ebal, and Abimael, and Sheba, ²³And Ophir, and Havilah, and Jobab. All these *were* the sons of Joktan. ²⁴Shem, Arphaxad, Shelah, ²⁵Eber, Peleg, Reu, ²⁶Serug, Nahor, Terah, ²⁷Abram; the same *is* Abraham.

²⁸The sons of Abraham; Isaac, and Ishmael. ²⁹These *are* their generations: The firstborn of Ishmael, Nebaioth; then Kedar, and Adbeel, and Mibsam, ³⁰Mishma, and Dumah, Massa, Hadadᵉ, and Tema, ³¹Jetur, Naphish, and Kedemah. These are the sons of Ishmael. ³²Now the sons of Keturah, Abraham's concubine: she bare Zimran, and Jokshan, and Medan, and Midian, and Ishbak, and Shuah. And the sons of Jokshan; Sheba, and Dedan. ³³And the sons of Midian; Ephah, and Epher, and Henoch, and Abida, and Eldaah. All these *are* the sons of Keturah. ³⁴And Abraham begat Isaac. The sons of Isaac; Esau and Israel. ³⁵The sons of Esau; Eliphaz, Reuel, and Jeush, and Jaalam, and Korah. ³⁶The sons of Eliphaz; Teman, and Omar, Zephiᶠ, and Gatam, Kenaz, and Timna, and Amalek. ³⁷The sons of Reuel; Nahath, Zerah, Shammah, and Mizzah. ³⁸And the sons of Seir; Lotan, and Shobal, and Zibeon, and Anah, and Dishon, and Ezer, and Dishan. ³⁹And the sons of Lotan; Hori, and Homamᵍ: and Timna *was* Lotan's sis-

---

ᵃ Riphath: or, Diphath as it is in some copies
ᵇ Dodanim: or, Rodanim, according to some copies
ᶜ Meshech: or, Mash
ᵈ Peleg: that is, division
ᵉ Hadad: also called, Hadar
ᶠ Zephi: or, Zepho

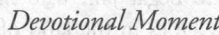
ter. ⁴⁰The sons of Shobal; Alianʰ, and Manahath, and Ebal, Shephi, and Onam. And the sons of Zibeon; Aiah, and Anah. ⁴¹The sons of Anah; Dishon. And the sons of Dishon; Amramⁱ, and Eshban, and Ithran, and Cheran. ⁴²The sons of Ezer; Bilhan, and Zavan, and Jakanʲ. The sons of Dishan; Uz, and Aran. ⁴³Now these are the kings that reigned in the land of Edom before any king reigned over the children of Israel; Bela the son of Beor: and the name of his city was Dinhabah. ⁴⁴And when Bela was dead, Jobab the son of Zerah of Bozrah reigned in his stead. ⁴⁵And when Jobab was dead, Husham of the land of the Temanites reigned in his stead. ⁴⁶And

when Husham was dead, Hadad the son of Bedad, which smote Midian in the field of Moab, reigned in his stead: and the name of his city was Avith. ⁴⁷And when Hadad was dead, Samlah of Masrekah reigned in his stead. ⁴⁸And when Samlah was dead, Shaul of Rehoboth by the river reigned in his stead. ⁴⁹And when Shaul was dead, Baalhanan the son of Achbor reigned in his stead. ⁵⁰And when Baalhanan was dead, Hadadᵏ reigned in his stead: and the name of his city was Pai; and his wife's name was Mehetabel, the daughter of Matred, the daughter of Mezahab. ⁵¹Hadad died also. And the dukes of Edom were; duke Timnah, duke Aliah, duke Jetheth, ⁵²Duke Aholibamah, duke Elah, duke Pinon, ⁵³Duke Kenaz, duke Teman, duke Mibzar, ⁵⁴Duke Magdiel, duke Iram. These are the dukes of Edom.

2

¹These are the sons of Israelᵃ; Reuben, Simeon, Levi, and Judah, Issachar, and Zebulun, ²Dan, Joseph, and Benjamin, Naphtali, Gad, and Asher. ³The sons of Judah; Er, and Onan, and Shelah: which three were born unto him of the daughter of Shua the Canaanitess. And Er, the firstborn of Judah, was evil in the sight of the LORD; and he slew him. ⁴And Tamar his daughter in law bare him Pharez and Zerah. All the sons of Judah were five. ⁵The sons of Pharez;

ᵍ Homam: or, Hemam
ʰ Alian: also called, Alvan
ⁱ Amram: or, Hemdan
ʲ Jakan: or, Akan
ᵏ Hadad: or, Hadar
ᵃ Israel: or, Jacob

Hezron, and Hamul. [6]And the sons of Zerah; Zimri[b], and Ethan, and Heman, and Calcol, and Dara: five of them in all. [7]And the sons of Carmi; Achar[c], the troubler of Israel, who transgressed in the thing accursed. [8]And the sons of Ethan; Azariah. [9]The sons also of Hezron, that were born unto him; Jerahmeel, and Ram[d], and Chelubai. [10]And Ram begat Amminadab; and Amminadab begat Nahshon, prince of the children of Judah; [11]And Nahshon begat Salma[e], and Salma begat Boaz, [12]And Boaz begat Obed, and Obed begat Jesse, [13]And Jesse begat his firstborn Eliab, and Abinadab the second, and Shimma[f] the third, [14]Nethaneel the fourth, Raddai the fifth, [15]Ozem the sixth, David the seventh: [16]Whose sisters *were* Zeruiah, and Abigail. And the sons of Zeruiah; Abishai, and Joab, and Asahel, three. [17]And Abigail bare Amasa: and the father of Amasa *was* Jether[g] the Ishmeelite.

[18]And Caleb the son of Hezron begat *children* of Azubah *his* wife, and of Jerioth: her sons *are* these; Jesher, and Shobab, and Ardon. [19]And when Azubah was dead, Caleb took unto him Ephrath, which bare him Hur. [20]And Hur begat Uri, and Uri begat Bezaleel. [21]And afterward Hezron went in to the daughter of Machir the father of Gilead, whom he married[h] when he *was* threescore years old; and she bare him Segub.

[22]And Segub begat Jair, who had three and twenty cities in the land of Gilead. [23]And he took Geshur, and Aram, with the towns of Jair, from them, with Kenath, and the towns thereof, *even* threescore cities. All these *belonged to* the sons of Machir the father of Gilead. [24]And after that Hezron was dead in Calebephratah, then Abiah Hezron's wife bare him Ashur the father of Tekoa. [25]And the sons of Jerahmeel the firstborn of Hezron were, Ram the firstborn, and Bunah, and Oren, and Ozem, *and* Ahijah. [26]Jerahmeel had also another wife, whose name *was* Atarah; she *was* the mother of Onam. [27]And the sons of Ram the firstborn of Jerahmeel were, Maaz, and Jamin, and Eker. [28]And the sons of Onam were, Shammai, and Jada. And the sons of Shammai; Nadab, and Abishur. [29]And the name of the wife of Abishur *was* Abihail, and she bare him Ahban, and Molid. [30]And the sons of Nadab; Seled, and Appaim: but Seled died without children. [31]And the sons of Appaim; Ishi. And the sons of Ishi; Sheshan. And the children of Sheshan; Ahlai. [32]And the sons of Jada the brother of Shammai; Jether, and Jonathan: and Jether died without children. [33]And the sons of Jonathan; Peleth, and Zaza. These were the sons of Jerahmeel. [34]Now Sheshan had no sons, but daughters. And Sheshan had a servant, an Egyptian, whose name *was* Jarha. [35]And Sheshan

---

[b] Zimri: or, Zabdi
[c] Achar: or, Achan
[d] Ram: Gr. Aram
[e] Salma: also called, Salmon
[f] Shimma: or, Shammah
[g] Jether . . . : also called, Ithra an Israelite
[h] married: Heb. took

gave his daughter to Jarha his servant to wife; and she bare him Attai. ³⁶And Attai begat Nathan, and Nathan begat Zabad, ³⁷And Zabad begat Ephlal, and Ephlal begat Obed, ³⁸And Obed begat Jehu, and Jehu begat Azariah, ³⁹And Azariah begat Helez, and Helez begat Eleasah, ⁴⁰And Eleasah begat Sisamai, and Sisamai begat Shallum, ⁴¹And Shallum begat Jekamiah, and Jekamiah begat Elishama. ⁴²Now the sons of Caleb the brother of Jerahmeel were, Mesha his firstborn, which was the father of Ziph; and the sons of Mareshah the father of Hebron. ⁴³And the sons of Hebron; Korah, and Tappuah, and Rekem, and Shema. ⁴⁴And Shema begat Raham, the father of Jorkoam: and Rekem begat Shammai. ⁴⁵And the son of Shammai was Maon: and Maon was the father of Bethzur. ⁴⁶And Ephah, Caleb's concubine, bare Haran, and Moza, and Gazez: and Haran begat Gazez. ⁴⁷And the sons of Jahdai; Regem, and Jotham, and Geshan, and Pelet, and Ephah, and Shaaph. ⁴⁸Maachah, Caleb's concubine, bare Sheber, and Tirhanah. ⁴⁹She bare also Shaaph the father of Madmannah, Sheva the father of Machbenah, and the father of Gibea: and the daughter of Caleb was Achsah. ⁵⁰These were the sons of Caleb the son of Hur, the firstborn of Ephratahⁱ; Shobal the father of Kirjathjearim, ⁵¹Salma the father of Bethlehem, Hareph the father of Bethgader. ⁵²And Shobal the father of Kirjathjearim had sons; Haroeh^j, and half of the Manahethites. ⁵³And the families of Kirjathjearim; the Ithrites, and the Puhites, and the Shumathites, and the Mishraites; of them came the Zareathites, and the Eshtaulites. ⁵⁴The sons of Salma; Bethlehem, and the Netophathites, Ataroth^k, the house of Joab, and half of the Manahethites, the Zorites. ⁵⁵And the families of the scribes which dwelt at Jabez; the Tirathites, the Shimeathites, and Suchathites. These are the Kenites that came of Hemath, the father of the house of Rechab.

3

¹Now these were the sons of David, which were born unto him in Hebron; the firstborn Amnon, of Ahinoam the Jezreelitess; the second Daniel^a, of Abigail the Carmelitess: ²The third, Absalom the son of Maachah the daughter of Talmai king of Geshur: the fourth, Adonijah the son of Haggith: ³The fifth, Shephatiah of Abital: the sixth, Ithream by Eglah his wife. ⁴These six were born unto him in Hebron; and there he reigned seven years and six months: and in Jerusalem he reigned thirty and three years. ⁵And these were born unto him in Jerusalem; Shimea^b, and Shobab, and Nathan, and Solomon, four, of Bathshua the daughter of Ammiel: ⁶Ibhar also, and Elishama^c, and Eliphelet, ⁷And Nogah, and Nepheg, and Japhia, ⁸And Eli-

---

ⁱ Ephratah: also called, Ephreth
^j Haroeh: or, Reaiah
^k Ataroth . . . : or, Atarites, or, crowns of the house of Joab
^a Daniel: or, Chileab
^b Shimea: or, Shammua
^c Elishama: also called, Elishua

shama, and Eliada[d], and Eliphelet, nine. [9] *These were* all the sons of David, beside the sons of the concubines, and Tamar their sister.

[10]And Solomon's son *was* Rehoboam, Abia[e] his son, Asa his son, Jehoshaphat his son, [11]Joram his son, Ahaziah[f] his son, Joash his son, [12]Amaziah his son, Azariah[g] his son, Jotham his son, [13]Ahaz his son, Hezekiah his son, Manasseh his son, [14]Amon his son, Josiah his son. [15]And the sons of Josiah *were*, the firstborn Johanan[h], the second Jehoiakim, the third Zedekiah, the fourth Shallum. [16]And the sons of Jehoiakim: Jeconiah[i] his son, Zedekiah his son. [17]And the sons of Jeconiah; Assir, Salathiel[j] his son, [18]Malchiram also, and Pedaiah, and Shenazar, Jecamiah, Hoshama, and Nedabiah. [19]And the sons of Pedaiah *were*, Zerubbabel, and Shimei: and the sons of Zerubbabel; Meshullam, and Hananiah, and Shelomith their sister: [20]And Hashubah, and Ohel, and Berechiah, and Hasadiah, Jushabhesed, five. [21]And the sons of Hananiah; Pelatiah, and Jesaiah: the sons of Rephaiah, the sons of Arnan, the sons of Obadiah, the sons of Shechaniah. [22]And the sons of Shechaniah; Shemaiah: and the sons of Shemaiah; Hattush, and Igeal, and Bariah, and Neariah, and Shaphat, six. [23]And the sons of Neariah; Elioenai, and Hezekiah[k], and Azrikam, three. [24]And the sons of Elioenai *were*, Hodaiah, and Eliashib, and Pelaiah, and Akkub, and Johanan, and Dalaiah, and Anani, seven.

4

[1]The sons of Judah; Pharez, Hezron, and Carmi[a], and Hur, and Shobal. [2]And Reaiah[b] the son of Shobal begat Jahath; and Jahath begat Ahumai, and Lahad. These *are* the families of the Zorathites. [3]And these *were of* the father of Etam; Jezreel, and Ishma, and Idbash: and the name of their sister *was* Hazelelponi: [4]And Penuel the father of Gedor, and Ezer the father of Hushah. These *are* the sons of Hur, the firstborn of Ephratah, the father of Bethlehem. [5]And Ashur the father of Tekoa had two wives, Helah and Naarah. [6]And Naarah bare him Ahuzam, and Hepher, and Temeni, and Haahashtari. These *were* the sons of Naarah. [7]And the sons of Helah *were*, Zereth, and Jezoar, and Ethnan. [8]And Coz begat Anub, and Zobebah, and the families of Aharhel the son of Harum. [9]And Jabez[c] was more honourable than his brethren: and his mother called his name Jabez, saying, Because I bare him with sorrow.

---

[d] Eliada: or, Beeliada
[e] Abia: or, Abijam
[f] Ahaziah: or, Azariah
[g] Azariah: or, Uzziah
[h] Johanan: or, Jehoahaz
[i] Jeconiah: also called, Jehoiachin or Coniah
[j] Salathiel: Heb. Shealtiel
[k] Hezekiah: Heb. Hiskijah
[a] Carmi: also called, Chelubai or Caleb
[b] Reaiah: or, Haroeh
[c] Jabez: that is, Sorrowful

¹⁰And Jabez called on the God of Israel, saying, Oh that thou wouldest bless me indeed, and enlarge my coast, and that thine hand might be with me, and that thou wouldest keep *me* from evil, that it may not grieve me! And God granted him that which he requested.

¹¹And Chelub the brother of Shuah begat Mehir, which *was* the father of Eshton. ¹²And Eshton begat Bethrapha, and Paseah, and Tehinnah the father of Irnahash^d. These *are* the men of Rechah. ¹³And the sons of Kenaz; Othniel, and Seraiah: and the sons of Othniel; Hathath^e. ¹⁴And Meonothai begat Ophrah: and Seraiah begat Joab, the father of the valley^f of Charashim; for they were craftsmen. ¹⁵And the sons of Caleb the son of Jephunneh; Iru, Elah, and Naam: and the sons of Elah, even Kenaz^g. ¹⁶And the sons of Jehaleleel; Ziph, and Ziphah, Tiria, and Asareel. ¹⁷And the sons of Ezra *were*, Jether, and Mered, and Epher, and Jalon: and she bare Miriam, and Shammai, and Ishbah the father of Eshtemoa. ¹⁸And his wife Jehudijah^h bare Jered the father of Gedor, and Heber the father of Socho, and Jekuthiel the father of Zanoah. And these *are* the sons of Bithiah the daughter of Pharaoh, which Mered took. ¹⁹And the sons of *his* wife Hodiah^i the sister of Naham, the father of Keilah the Garmite, and Eshtemoa the Maachathite. ²⁰And the sons of Shimon *were*, Amnon, and Rinnah, Benhanan, and Tilon. And the sons of Ishi *were*, Zoheth, and Benzoheth. ²¹The sons of Shelah the son of Judah *were*, Er the father of Lecah, and Laadah the father of Mareshah, and the families of the house of them that wrought fine linen, of the house of Ashbea, ²²And Jokim, and the men of Chozeba, and Joash, and Saraph, who had the dominion in Moab, and Jashubilehem. And *these are* ancient things. ²³These *were* the potters, and those that dwelt among plants and hedges: there they dwelt with the king for his work.

²⁴The sons of Simeon *were*, Nemuel^j, and Jamin, Jarib, Zerah, *and* Shaul: ²⁵Shallum his son, Mibsam his son, Mishma his son. ²⁶And the sons of Mishma; Hamuel his son, Zacchur his son, Shimei his son. ²⁷And Shimei had sixteen sons and six daughters; but his brethren had not many children, neither did all their family multiply, like to the children of Judah. ²⁸And they dwelt at Beersheba, and Moladah, and Hazarshual, ²⁹And at Bilhah^k, and at Ezem, and at Tolad, ³⁰And at Bethuel, and at Hormah, and at Ziklag, ³¹And at Bethmarcaboth, and Hazarsusim^l, and at

---

^d Irnahash: or, the city of Nahash
^e Hathath . . . : or, Hathath, and Meonothai, who begat, etc
^f valley: or, inhabitants of the valley
^g even Kenaz: or, Uknaz
^h Jehudijah: or, the Jewess
^i Hodiah: or, Jehudijah, mentioned before
^j Nemuel: or, Jemuel
^k Bilhah: or, Balah
^l Hazarsusim: or, Hazarsusah

Bethbirei, and at Shaaraim. These *were* their cities unto the reign of David. [32]And their villages *were*, Etam[m], and Ain, Rimmon, and Tochen, and Ashan, five cities: [33]And all their villages that *were* round about the same cities, unto Baal[n]. These *were* their habitations, and their genealogy. [34]And Meshobab, and Jamlech, and Joshah the son of Amaziah, [35]And Joel, and Jehu the son of Josibiah, the son of Seraiah, the son of Asiel, [36]And Elioenai, and Jaakobah, and Jeshohaiah, and Asaiah, and Adiel, and Jesimiel, and Benaiah, [37]And Ziza the son of Shiphi, the son of Allon, the son of Jedaiah, the son of Shimri, the son of Shemaiah; [38]These mentioned[o] by *their* names *were* princes in their families: and the house of their fathers increased greatly. [39]And they went to the entrance of Gedor, *even* unto the east side of the valley, to seek pasture for their flocks. [40]And they found fat pasture and good, and the land *was* wide, and quiet, and peaceable; for *they* of Ham had dwelt there of old. [41]And these written by name came in the days of Hezekiah king of Judah, and smote their tents, and the habitations that were found there, and destroyed them utterly unto this day, and dwelt in their rooms: because *there was* pasture there for their flocks. [42]And *some* of them, *even* of the sons of Simeon, five hundred men, went to mount Seir, having for their captains Pelatiah, and Neariah, and Rephaiah, and Uzziel, the sons of Ishi. [43]And they smote the rest of the Amalekites that were escaped, and dwelt there unto this day.

5

[1]Now the sons of Reuben the firstborn of Israel, (for he *was* the firstborn; but, forasmuch as he defiled his father's bed, his birthright was given unto the sons of Joseph the son of Israel: and the genealogy is not to be reckoned after the birthright. [2]For Judah prevailed above his brethren, and of him *came* the chief ruler; but the birthright *was* Joseph's:) [3]The sons, *I say*, of Reuben the firstborn of Israel *were*, Hanoch, and Pallu, Hezron, and Carmi. [4]The sons of Joel; Shemaiah his son, Gog his son, Shimei his son, [5]Micah his son, Reaia his son, Baal his son, [6]Beerah his son, whom Tilgathpilneser[a] king of Assyria carried away *captive*: he *was* prince of the Reubenites. [7]And his brethren by their families, when the genealogy of their generations was reck-

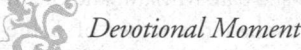

Devotional Moment
•
Honoring Parents

5:1 People don't typically dishonor their parents the way Reuben did, but in many ways our actions or attitudes can slight our parents: We reject them for who they are, disparage their advice, or discount the many experiences that have shaped their lives. Find ways to affirm the good qualities God has given your parents. Overlook their shortcomings to the same extent you overlook your own. Ask God to show you a practical way you can give them respect. Then do it.

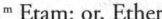

---

[m] Etam: or, Ether

[n] Baal: or, Baalathbeer

[o] mentioned: Heb. coming

[a] Tilgathpilneser: also called, Tiglathpileser

oned, *were* the chief, Jeiel, and Zechariah, ⁸And Bela the son of Azaz, the son of Shema[b], the son of Joel, who dwelt in Aroer, even unto Nebo and Baalmeon: ⁹And eastward he inhabited unto the entering in of the wilderness from the river Euphrates: because their cattle were multiplied in the land of Gilead. ¹⁰And in the days of Saul they made war with the Hagarites, who fell by their hand: and they dwelt in their tents throughout[c] all the east *land* of Gilead. ¹¹And the children of Gad dwelt over against them, in the land of Bashan unto Salchah: ¹²Joel the chief, and Shapham the next, and Jaanai, and Shaphat in Bashan. ¹³And their brethren of the house of their fathers *were*, Michael, and Meshullam, and Sheba, and Jorai, and Jachan, and Zia, and Heber, seven. ¹⁴These *are* the children of Abihail the son of Huri, the son of Jaroah, the son of Gilead, the son of Michael, the son of Jeshishai, the son of Jahdo, the son of Buz; ¹⁵Ahi the son of Abdiel, the son of Guni, chief of the house of their fathers. ¹⁶And they dwelt in Gilead in Bashan, and in her towns, and in all the suburbs of Sharon, upon their borders. ¹⁷All these were reckoned by genealogies in the days of Jotham king of Judah, and in the days of Jeroboam king of Israel.

¹⁸The sons of Reuben, and the Gadites, and half the tribe of Manasseh, of valiant men, men able to bear buckler and sword, and to shoot with bow, and skilful in war, *were* four and forty thousand seven hundred and threescore, that went out to the war. ¹⁹And they made war with the Hagarites, with Jetur, and Nephish, and Nodab. ²⁰And they were helped against them, and the Hagarites were delivered into their hand, and all that *were* with them: for they cried to God in the battle, and he was intreated of them; because they put their trust in him. ²¹And they took away their cattle; of their camels fifty thousand, and of sheep two hundred and fifty thousand, and of asses two thousand, and of men an hundred thousand. ²²For there fell down many slain, because the war *was* of God. And they dwelt in their steads until the captivity. ²³And the children of the half tribe of Manasseh dwelt in the land: they increased from Bashan unto Baalhermon and Senir, and unto mount Hermon. ²⁴And these *were* the heads of the house of their fathers, even Epher, and Ishi, and Eliel, and Azriel, and Jeremiah, and Hodaviah, and Jahdiel,

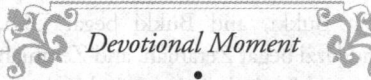

Devotional Moment

•

Priorities

5:24-25 The seven family heads had strong reputations as warriors and leaders but failed in their most important task: living the way God wanted them to live. It's easy for us to become so involved in our work or so influenced by the people around us that we neglect pleasing God. It's easy to think that success in a career or a good reputation means we are doing fine. But we must be careful: What really matters is who or what we worship. Do you live for your house? your career? yourself? some other idol? Success will have little meaning if you drift away from the Lord.

---

[b] Shema: or, Shemaiah
[c] throughout . . . : Heb. upon all the face of the east
[d] famous . . . : Heb. men of names

mighty men of valour, famous[d] men, *and* heads of the house of their fathers. [25]And they transgressed against the God of their fathers, and went a whoring after the gods of the people of the land, whom God destroyed before them. [26]And the God of Israel stirred up the spirit of Pul king of Assyria, and the spirit of Tilgathpilneser king of Assyria, and he carried them away, even the Reubenites, and the Gadites, and the half tribe of Manasseh, and brought them unto Halah, and Habor, and Hara, and to the river Gozan, unto this day.

6

[1]The sons of Levi; Gershon[a], Kohath, and Merari. [2]And the sons of Kohath; Amram, Izhar, and Hebron, and Uzziel. [3]And the children of Amram; Aaron, and Moses, and Miriam. The sons also of Aaron; Nadab, and Abihu, Eleazar, and Ithamar. [4]Eleazar begat Phinehas, Phinehas begat Abishua, [5]And Abishua begat Bukki, and Bukki begat Uzzi, [6]And Uzzi begat Zerahiah, and Zerahiah begat Meraioth, [7]Meraioth begat Amariah, and Amariah begat Ahitub, [8]And Ahitub begat Zadok, and Zadok begat Ahimaaz, [9]And Ahimaaz begat Azariah, and Azariah begat Johanan, [10]And Johanan begat Azariah, (he *it is* that executed the priest's office in the temple[b] that Solomon built in Jeru-

salem:) [11]And Azariah begat Amariah, and Amariah begat Ahitub, [12]And Ahitub begat Zadok, and Zadok begat Shallum[c], [13]And Shallum begat Hilkiah, and Hilkiah begat Azariah, [14]And Azariah begat Seraiah, and Seraiah begat Jehozadak, [15]And Jehozadak went *into captivity*, when the LORD carried away Judah and Jerusalem by the hand of Nebuchadnezzar. [16]The sons of Levi; Gershom[d], Kohath, and Merari. [17]And these *be* the names of the sons of Gershom; Libni, and Shimei. [18]And the sons of Kohath *were*, Amram, and Izhar, and Hebron, and Uzziel. [19]The sons of Merari; Mahli, and Mushi. And these *are* the families of the Levites according to their fathers. [20]Of Gershom; Libni his son, Jahath his son, Zimmah his son, [21]Joah[e] his son, Iddo his son, Zerah his son, Jeaterai his son. [22]The sons of Kohath; Amminadab[f] his son, Korah his son, Assir his son, [23]Elkanah his son, and Ebiasaph his son, and Assir his son, [24]Tahath his son, Uriel his son, Uzziah his son, and Shaul his son. [25]And the sons of Elkanah; Amasai, and Ahimoth. [26]*As for* Elkanah: the sons of Elkanah; Zophai[g] his son, and Nahath his son, [27]Eliab his son, Jeroham his son, Elkanah his son. [28]And the sons of Samuel; the firstborn Vashni[h], and Abiah. [29]The sons of Merari; Mahli, Libni his son, Shimei his son, Uzza his son, [30]Shimea

---

[a] Gershon: or, Gershom
[b] in the temple: Heb. in the house
[c] Shallum: or, Meshullam
[d] Gershom: or, Gershon
[e] Joah: or, Ethan
[f] Amminadab: or, Izhar
[g] Zophai: or, Zuph
[h] Vashni: called also Joel

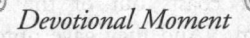

Devotional Moment
•
Music for Praise

6:31 Praising God through music was so important to David that he appointed song leaders and choirs for the Tabernacle. Worshiping God through music and teaching others to sing was their job. Music should have a high priority in the Christian family. Try singing with your family at mealtime, bedtime, or when you ride together in the car. If you are not comfortable singing, play tapes of Scripture songs, hymns, or other music that encourages your children to praise God in song. Your children may learn to play a musical instrument, but don't neglect to train them in the most significant musical skill they can ever learn: singing praises to God.

his son, Haggiah his son, Asaiah his son.

³¹And these *are they* whom David set over the service of song in the house of the LORD, after that the ark had rest. ³²And they ministered before the dwelling place of the tabernacle of the congregation with singing, until Solomon had built the house of the LORD in Jerusalem: and *then* they waited on their office according to their order. ³³And these *are* they that waited ⁱ with their children. Of the sons of the Kohathites: Heman a singer, the son of Joel, the son of Shemuel, ³⁴The son of Elkanah, the son of Jeroham, the son of Eliel, the son of Toah, ³⁵The son of Zuph, the son of Elkanah, the son of Mahath, the son of Amasai, ³⁶The son of Elkanah, the son of Joel, the son of Azariah, the son of Zephaniah, ³⁷The son of Tahath, the son of Assir, the son of Ebiasaph, the son of Korah, ³⁸The son of

Izhar, the son of Kohath, the son of Levi, the son of Israel. ³⁹And his brother Asaph, who stood on his right hand, *even* Asaph the son of Berachiah, the son of Shimea, ⁴⁰The son of Michael, the son of Baaseiah, the son of Malchiah, ⁴¹The son of Ethni, the son of Zerah, the son of Adaiah, ⁴²The son of Ethan, the son of Zimmah, the son of Shimei, ⁴³The son of Jahath, the son of Gershom, the son of Levi. ⁴⁴And their brethren the sons of Merari *stood* on the left hand: Ethan the son of Kishi ʲ, the son of Abdi, the son of Malluch, ⁴⁵The son of Hashabiah, the son of Amaziah, the son of Hilkiah, ⁴⁶The son of Amzi, the son of Bani, the son of Shamer, ⁴⁷The son of Mahli, the son of Mushi, the son of Merari, the son of Levi. ⁴⁸Their brethren also the Levites *were* appointed unto all manner of service of the tabernacle of the house of God. ⁴⁹But Aaron and his sons offered upon the altar of the burnt offering, and on the altar of incense, *and were appointed* for all the work of the *place* most holy, and to make an atonement for Israel, according to all that Moses the servant of God had commanded. ⁵⁰And these *are* the sons of Aaron; Eleazar his son, Phinehas his son, Abishua his son, ⁵¹Bukki his son, Uzzi his son, Zerahiah his son, ⁵²Meraioth his son, Amariah his son, Ahitub his son, ⁵³Zadok his son, Ahimaaz his son.

⁵⁴Now these *are* their dwelling places throughout their castles in their coasts, of the sons of Aaron, of the families of the Kohathites: for theirs was the lot. ⁵⁵And they gave them Hebron in the land of Judah, and the suburbs

---

ⁱ waited: Heb. stood
ʲ Kishi: or, Kushaiah

thereof round about it. ⁵⁶But the fields of the city, and the villages thereof, they gave to Caleb the son of Jephunneh. ⁵⁷And to the sons of Aaron they gave the cities of Judah, *namely*, Hebron, *the city* of refuge, and Libnah with her suburbs, and Jattir, and Eshtemoa, with their suburbs, ⁵⁸And Hilenᵏ with her suburbs, Debir with her suburbs, ⁵⁹And Ashanˡ with her suburbs, and Bethshemesh with her suburbs: ⁶⁰And out of the tribe of Benjamin; Geba with her suburbs, and Alemethᵐ with her suburbs, and Anathoth with her suburbs. All their cities throughout their families *were* thirteen cities. ⁶¹And unto the sons of Kohath, *which were* left of the family of that tribe, *were cities given* out of the half tribe, *namely, out of* the half *tribe* of Manasseh, by lot, ten cities. ⁶²And to the sons of Gershom throughout their families out of the tribe of Issachar, and out of the tribe of Asher, and out of the tribe of Naphtali, and out of the tribe of Manasseh in Bashan, thirteen cities. ⁶³Unto the sons of Merari *were given* by lot, throughout their families, out of the tribe of Reuben, and out of the tribe of Gad, and out of the tribe of Zebulun, twelve cities. ⁶⁴And the children of Israel gave to the Levites *these* cities with their suburbs. ⁶⁵And they gave by lot out of the tribe of the children of Judah, and out of the tribe of the children of Simeon, and out of the tribe of the children of Benjamin, these cities, which are called by *their* names. ⁶⁶And *the residue* of the families of the sons of Kohath had cities of their coasts out of the tribe of Ephraim. ⁶⁷And they gave unto them, *of* the cities of refuge, Shechem in mount Ephraim with her suburbs; *they gave* also Gezer with her suburbs, ⁶⁸And Jokmeam with her suburbs, and Bethhoron with her suburbs, ⁶⁹And Aijalon with her suburbs, and Gathrimmon with her suburbs: ⁷⁰And out of the half tribe of Manasseh; Aner with her suburbs, and Bileam with her suburbs, for the family of the remnant of the sons of Kohath. ⁷¹Unto the sons of Gershom *were given* out of the family of the half tribe of Manasseh, Golan in Bashan with her suburbs, and Ashtaroth with her suburbs: ⁷²And out of the tribe of Issachar; Kedesh with her suburbs, Daberath with her suburbs, ⁷³And Ramoth with her suburbs, and Anem with her suburbs: ⁷⁴And out of the tribe of Asher; Mashal with her suburbs, and Abdon with her suburbs, ⁷⁵And Hukok with her suburbs, and Rehob with her suburbs: ⁷⁶And out of the tribe of Naphtali; Kedesh in Galilee with her suburbs, and Hammon with her suburbs, and Kirjathaim with her suburbs. ⁷⁷Unto the rest of the children of Merari *were given* out of the tribe of Zebulun, Rimmon with her suburbs, Tabor with her suburbs: ⁷⁸And on the other side Jordan by Jericho, on the east side of Jordan, *were given them* out of the tribe of Reuben, Bezer in the wilderness with her suburbs, and Jahzah with her suburbs, ⁷⁹Kedemoth also with her suburbs, and Mephaath with her suburbs: ⁸⁰And out of the tribe of Gad; Ramoth

---

ᵏ Hilen: or, Holon
ˡ Ashan: or, Ain
ᵐ Alemeth: or, Almon

in Gilead with her suburbs, and Mahanaim with her suburbs, [81]And Heshbon with her suburbs, and Jazer with her suburbs.

7

[1]Now the sons of Issachar *were*, Tola, and Puah, Jashub, and Shimron, four. [2]And the sons of Tola; Uzzi, and Rephaiah, and Jeriel, and Jahmai, and Jibsam, and Shemuel, heads of their father's house, *to wit*, of Tola: *they were* valiant men of might in their generations; whose number *was* in the days of David two and twenty thousand and six hundred. [3]And the sons of Uzzi; Izrahiah: and the sons of Izrahiah; Michael, and Obadiah, and Joel, Ishiah, five: all of them chief men. [4]And with them, by their generations, after the house of their fathers, *were* bands of soldiers for war, six and thirty thousand *men*: for they had many wives and sons. [5]And their brethren among all the families of Issachar *were* valiant men of might, reckoned in all by their genealogies fourscore and seven thousand. [6]*The sons* of Benjamin; Bela, and Becher, and Jediael, three. [7]And the sons of Bela; Ezbon, and Uzzi, and Uzziel, and Jerimoth, and Iri, five; heads of the house of *their* fathers, mighty men of valour; and were reckoned by their genealogies twenty and two thousand and thirty and four. [8]And the sons of Becher; Zemira, and Joash, and Eliezer, and Elioenai, and Omri, and Jerimoth, and Abiah, and Anathoth, and Alameth. All these *are* the sons of Becher. [9]And the number of them, after their genealogy by their generations, heads of the house of their fathers, mighty men of valour, *was* twenty thousand and two hundred. [10]The sons also of Jediael; Bilhan: and the sons of Bilhan; Jeush, and Benjamin, and Ehud, and Chenaanah, and Zethan, and Tharshish, and Ahishahar. [11]All these the sons of Jediael, by the heads of their fathers, mighty men of valour, *were* seventeen thousand and two hundred *soldiers*, fit to go out for war *and* battle. [12]Shuppim also, and Huppim, the children of Ir [a], *and* Hushim, the sons of Aher. [13]The sons of Naphtali; Jahziel, and Guni, and Jezer, and Shallum, the sons of Bilhah. [14]The sons of Manasseh; Ashriel, whom she bare: (*but* his concubine the Aramitess bare Machir the father of Gilead: [15]And Machir took to wife *the sister* of Huppim and Shuppim, whose sister's name *was* Maachah;) and the name of the second *was* Zelophehad: and Zelophehad had daughters. [16]And Maachah the wife of Machir bare a son, and she called his name Peresh; and the name of his brother *was* Sheresh; and his sons *were* Ulam and Rakem. [17]And the sons of Ulam; Bedan. These *were* the sons of Gilead, the son of Machir, the son of Manasseh. [18]And his sister Hammoleketh bare Ishod, and Abiezer, and Mahalah. [19]And the sons of Shemida *were*, Ahian, and Shechem, and Likhi, and Aniam.

[20]And the sons of Ephraim; Shuthelah, and Bered his son, and Tahath his son, and Eladah his son, and Tahath his son, [21]And Zabad his son, and Shuthelah his son, and Ezer, and Elead, whom the men of Gath *that were* born in *that* land slew, because they came down to take

[a] Ir: or, Iri

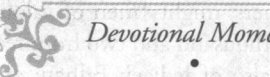

Devotional Moment

•

Grieving

7:21-22 Ephraim faced a double blow: His sons were involved in illegal activity and were killed in the process. What an immense burden for this father to bear! Many parents find that grieving goes along with parenting. If your children have disappointed you, take comfort in knowing that God can redeem mistakes and work through them for good. And if you have lost a child, don't hide your sadness, disappointment, and anger; take time to grieve. Allow others to comfort you. Look to God to heal the deep wounds in your heart and soul.

away their cattle. ²²And Ephraim their father mourned many days, and his brethren came to comfort him. ²³And when he went in to his wife, she conceived, and bare a son, and he called his name Beriah, because it went evil with his house. ²⁴(And his daughter *was*

Devotional Moment

•

Girls Have Gifts, Too

7:24 Most of the people listed in these chapters of genealogies were men. But here the historian mentions Ephraim's daughter, Sheerah, a woman who used her gifts and abilities to build three towns. God gives both men and women extraordinary gifts and abilities. Encourage your daughters, as well as your sons, to pursue whatever gifts God has given them. As they grow up, you can help them discover and develop their gifts and abilities—whatever they may be—through lessons, special programs, or advanced classes as God enables.

Sherah, who built Bethhoron the nether, and the upper, and Uzzensherah.) ²⁵And Rephah *was* his son, also Resheph, and Telah his son, and Tahan his son, ²⁶Laadan his son, Ammihud his son, Elishama his son, ²⁷Nonᵇ his son, Jehoshua his son. ²⁸And their possessions and habitations *were*, Bethel and the towns thereof, and eastward Naaran, and westward Gezer, with the townsᶜ thereof; Shechem also and the towns thereof, unto Gaza and the towns thereof: ²⁹And by the borders of the children of Manasseh, Bethshean and her townsᵈ, Taanach and her towns, Megiddo and her towns, Dor and her towns. In these dwelt the children of Joseph the son of Israel. ³⁰The sons of Asher; Imnah, and Isuah, and Ishuai, and Beriah, and Serah their sister. ³¹And the sons of Beriah; Heber, and Malchiel, who *is* the father of Birzavith. ³²And Heber begat Japhlet, and Shomer, and Hotham, and Shua their sister. ³³And the sons of Japhlet; Pasach, and Bimhal, and Ashvath. These *are* the children of Japhlet. ³⁴And the sons of Shamer; Ahi, and Rohgah, Jehubbah, and Aram. ³⁵And the sons of his brother Helem; Zophah, and Imna, and Shelesh, and Amal. ³⁶The sons of Zophah; Suah, and Harnepher, and Shual, and Beri, and Imrah, ³⁷Bezer, and Hod, and Shamma, and Shilshah, and Ithran, and Beera. ³⁸And the sons of Jether; Jephunneh, and Pispah, and Ara. ³⁹And the sons of Ulla; Arah, and Haniel, and Rezia. ⁴⁰All these *were* the children of Asher, heads of *their* father's house, choice *and* mighty men of valour,

---

ᵇ Non: or, Nun

ᶜ towns: Heb. daughters

ᵈ towns: Heb. daughters

chief of the princes. And the number throughout the genealogy of them that were apt to the war *and* to battle *was* twenty and six thousand men.

8

¹Now Benjamin begat Bela his firstborn, Ashbel the second, and Aharah the third, ²Nohah the fourth, and Rapha the fifth. ³And the sons of Bela were, Addar ᵃ, and Gera, and Abihud, ⁴And Abishua, and Naaman, and Ahoah, ⁵And Gera, and Shephuphan ᵇ, and Huram. ⁶And these *are* the sons of Ehud: these are the heads of the fathers of the inhabitants of Geba, and they removed them to Manahath: ⁷And Naaman, and Ahiah, and Gera, he removed them, and begat Uzza, and Ahihud. ⁸And Shaharaim begat *children* in the country of Moab, after he had sent them away; Hushim and Baara *were* his wives. ⁹And he begat of Hodesh his wife, Jobab, and Zibia, and Mesha, and Malcham, ¹⁰And Jeuz, and Shachia, and Mirma. These *were* his sons, heads of the fathers. ¹¹And of Hushim he begat Abitub, and Elpaal. ¹²The sons of Elpaal; Eber, and Misham, and Shamed, who built Ono, and Lod, with the towns thereof: ¹³Beriah also, and Shema, who *were* heads of the fathers of the inhabitants of Aijalon, who drove away the inhabitants of Gath: ¹⁴And Ahio, Shashak, and Jeremoth, ¹⁵And Zebadiah, and Arad, and Ader, ¹⁶And Michael, and Ispah, and Joha, the sons of Beriah; ¹⁷And Zebadiah, and Meshullam, and Hezeki, and Heber, ¹⁸Ishmerai also, and Jezliah, and Jobab, the sons of Elpaal; ¹⁹And Jakim, and Zichri, and Zabdi, ²⁰And Elienai, and Zilthai, and Eliel, ²¹And Adaiah, and Beraiah, and Shimrath, the sons of Shimhi ᶜ; ²²And Ishpan, and Heber, and Eliel, ²³And Abdon, and Zichri, and Hanan, ²⁴And Hananiah, and Elam, and Antothijah, ²⁵And Iphedeiah, and Penuel, the sons of Shashak; ²⁶And Shamsherai, and Shehariah, and Athaliah, ²⁷And Jaresiah, and Eliah, and Zichri, the sons of Jeroham. ²⁸These *were* heads of the fathers, by their generations, chief *men*. These dwelt in Jerusalem. ²⁹And at Gibeon dwelt the father ᵈ of Gibeon; whose wife's name *was* Maachah: ³⁰And his firstborn son Abdon, and Zur, and Kish, and Baal, and Nadab, ³¹And Gedor, and Ahio, and Zacher ᵉ. ³²And Mikloth begat Shimeah ᶠ. And these

---

Devotional Moment

Lasting Union

8:8-10 Shaharaim divorced two of his wives. Divorce is not new, but it has never been God's ideal. Oneness, unity, love, and faithfulness mark God's design for marriage. And through Christ, he gives us the strength to maintain such a commitment (see Phil. 4:13). In what ways can you strengthen your marriage relationship? Strive to accept one another's differences rather than letting disagreements drive a wedge between you.

ᵃ Addar: or, Ard
ᵇ Shephuphan: or, Shupham
ᶜ Shimhi: or, Shema
ᵈ father . . . : also called Jehiel
ᵉ Zacher: or, Zechariah
ᶠ Shimeah: or, Shimeam

also dwelt with their brethren in Jerusalem, over against them.

³³And Ner begat Kish, and Kish begat Saul, and Saul begat Jonathan, and Malchishua, and Abinadab^g, and Eshbaal. ³⁴And the son of Jonathan *was* Meribbaal^h; and Meribbaal begat Micah. ³⁵And the sons of Micah *were*, Pithon, and Melech, and Tareaⁱ, and Ahaz. ³⁶And Ahaz begat Jehoadah^j; and Jehoadah begat Alemeth, and Azmaveth, and Zimri; and Zimri begat Moza, ³⁷And Moza begat Binea: Rapha^k *was* his son, Eleasah his son, Azel his son: ³⁸And Azel had six sons, whose names *are* these, Azrikam, Bocheru, and Ishmael, and Sheariah, and Obadiah, and Hanan. All these *were* the sons of Azel. ³⁹And the sons of Eshek his brother *were*, Ulam his firstborn, Jehush the second, and Eliphelet the third. ⁴⁰And the sons of Ulam were mighty men of valour, archers, and had many sons, and sons' sons, an hundred and fifty. All these *are* of the sons of Benjamin.

9

¹So all Israel were reckoned by genealogies; and, behold, they *were* written in the book of the kings of Israel and Judah, *who* were carried away to Babylon for their transgression. ²Now the first inhabitants that *dwelt* in their possessions in their cities *were*, the Israelites, the priests, Levites, and the Nethinims. ³And in Jerusalem dwelt of the children of Judah, and of the children of Benjamin, and of

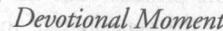

Devotional Moment

Family Tree

9:1 The Israelites took time to record their genealogies. Keeping track of ancestors honors parents and grandparents and the lives they've led. Do your children know about their grandparents and great-grandparents—who they were, what occupations they held, what character qualities made them special, what experiences shaped their lives? Take time to tell your children stories about your parents and how you have seen God's hand in their lives. Record some of these stories on paper or on tape so that your children will be better able to see and remember God's workings in your family's life.

the children of Ephraim, and Manasseh; ⁴Uthai the son of Ammihud, the son of Omri, the son of Imri, the son of Bani, of the children of Pharez the son of Judah. ⁵And of the Shilonites; Asaiah the firstborn, and his sons. ⁶And of the sons of Zerah; Jeuel, and their brethren, six hundred and ninety. ⁷And of the sons of Benjamin; Sallu the son of Meshullam, the son of Hodaviah, the son of Hasenuah, ⁸And Ibneiah the son of Jeroham, and Elah the son of Uzzi, the son of Michri, and Meshullam the son of Shephathiah, the son of Reuel, the son of Ibnijah; ⁹And their brethren, according to their generations, nine hundred and fifty and six. All these men *were* chief of the fathers in the house of their fathers. ¹⁰And of the priests; Jedaiah, and Jehoiarib, and Jachin, ¹¹And Azariah^a the

---

^g Abinadab: also called, Ishui
^h Meribbaal: or, Mephibosheth
ⁱ Tarea: or, Tahrea
^j Jehoadah: also called, Jarah
^k Rapha: also called, Rephaiah
^a Azariah: also called, Seraiah

son of Hilkiah, the son of Meshullam, the son of Zadok, the son of Meraioth, the son of Ahitub, the ruler of the house of God; ¹²And Adaiah the son of Jeroham, the son of Pashur, the son of Malchijah, and Maasiai the son of Adiel, the son of Jahzerah, the son of Meshullam, the son of Meshillemith, the son of Immer; ¹³And their brethren, heads of the house of their fathers, a thousand and seven hundred and threescore; very able men for the work of the service of the house of God.

¹⁴And of the Levites; Shemaiah the son of Hasshub, the son of Azrikam, the son of Hashabiah, of the sons of Merari; ¹⁵And Bakbakkar, Heresh, and Galal, and Mattaniah the son of Micah, the son of Zichri, the son of Asaph; ¹⁶And Obadiah the son of Shemaiah, the son of Galal, the son of Jeduthun, and Berechiah the son of Asa, the son of Elkanah, that dwelt in the villages of the Netophathites. ¹⁷And the porters *were*, Shallum, and Akkub, and Talmon, and Ahiman, and their brethren: Shallum *was* the chief; ¹⁸Who hitherto *waited* in the king's gate eastward: they *were* porters in the companies of the children of Levi. ¹⁹And Shallum the son of Kore, the son of Ebiasaph, the son of Korah, and his brethren, of the house of his father, the Korahites, *were* over the work of the service, keepers of the gates^b of the tabernacle: and their fathers, *being* over the host of the LORD, *were* keepers of the entry. ²⁰And Phinehas the son of Eleazar was the ruler over them in time past, *and* the LORD *was* with him.

²¹*And* Zechariah the son of Meshelemiah *was* porter of the door of the tabernacle of the congregation. ²²All these *which were* chosen to be porters in the gates *were* two hundred and twelve. These were reckoned by their genealogy in their villages, whom David and Samuel the seer did ordain in their set office. ²³So they and their children *had* the oversight of the gates of the house of the LORD, *namely*, the house of the tabernacle, by wards. ²⁴In four quarters were the porters, toward the east, west, north, and south. ²⁵And their brethren, *which were* in their villages, *were* to come after seven days from time to time with them. ²⁶For these Levites, the four chief porters, were in *their* set office, and were over the chambers and treasuries of the house of God. ²⁷And they lodged round about the house of God, because the charge *was* upon them, and the opening thereof every morning *pertained* to them. ²⁸And *certain* of them had the charge of the ministering vessels, that they should bring them in and out by tale. ²⁹*Some* of them also *were* appointed to oversee the vessels, and all the instruments^c of the sanctuary, and the fine flour, and the wine, and the oil, and the frankincense, and the spices. ³⁰And *some* of the sons of the priests made the ointment of the spices. ³¹And Mattithiah, *one* of the Levites, who *was* the firstborn of Shallum the Korahite, had the set office over the things that were made in the pans. ³²And *other* of their brethren, of the sons of the Kohathites, *were* over the shewbread^d, to

---

^b gates: Heb. thresholds
^c instruments: or, vessels
^d shewbread: Heb. bread of ordering

prepare *it* every sabbath. ³³And these *are* the singers, chief of the fathers of the Levites, *who remaining* in the chambers *were* free: for they were employed in *that* work day and night. ³⁴These chief fathers of the Levites *were* chief throughout their generations; these dwelt at Jerusalem.

³⁵And in Gibeon dwelt the father of Gibeon, Jehiel, whose wife's name *was* Maachah: ³⁶And his firstborn son Abdon, then Zur, and Kish, and Baal, and Ner, and Nadab, ³⁷And Gedor, and Ahio, and Zechariah, and Mikloth. ³⁸And Mikloth begat Shimeam. And they also dwelt with their brethren at Jerusalem, over against their brethren. ³⁹And Ner begat Kish; and Kish begat Saul; and Saul begat Jonathan, and Malchishua, and Abinadab, and Eshbaal. ⁴⁰And the son of Jonathan *was* Meribbaal: and Meribbaal begat Micah. ⁴¹And the sons of Micah *were*, Pithon, and Melech, and Tahrea, *and Ahaz*. ⁴²And Ahaz begat Jarah; and Jarah begat Alemeth, and Azmaveth, and Zimri; and Zimri begat Moza; ⁴³And Moza begat Binea; and Rephaiah his son, Eleasah his son, Azel his son. ⁴⁴And Azel had six sons, whose names *are* these, Azrikam, Bocheru, and Ishmael, and Sheariah, and Obadiah, and Hanan: these *were* the sons of Azel.

10

¹Now the Philistines fought against Israel; and the men of Israel fled from before the Philistines, and fell down slainᵃ

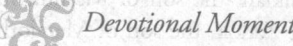

Devotional Moment
Parental Sin

10:2, 13 Saul's disobedience affected his children. When the Philistines came to kill Saul, they killed his sons, too. Today, children are still affected by parents' sins, including sexual sins, bitterness, rage, and the irresponsible use of money, alcohol, and drugs. As adults, some of us still struggle with the consequences of our parents' sins. The good news is that God can heal the scars—if we will let him. Be willing to admit your wounds and invite God and his people to minister to you with the healing power of love and forgiveness.

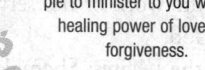

in mount Gilboa. ²And the Philistines followed hard after Saul, and after his sons; and the Philistines slew Jonathan, and Abinadabᵇ, and Malchishua, the sons of Saul. ³And the battle went sore against Saul, and the archersᶜ hit him, and he was wounded of the archers. ⁴Then said Saul to his armourbearer, Draw thy sword, and thrust me through therewith; lest these uncircumcised come and abuse me.ᵈ But his armourbearer would not; for he was sore afraid. So Saul took a sword, and fell upon it. ⁵And when his armourbearer saw that Saul was dead, he fell likewise on the sword, and died. ⁶So Saul died, and his three sons, and all his house died together. ⁷And when all the men of Israel that *were* in the valley saw that they fled, and that Saul and his sons were dead, then they forsook their cities, and fled: and the Philistines came and dwelt in them.

ᵃ slain: or, wounded
ᵇ Abinadab: also called, Ishui
ᶜ and the archers: Heb. and the shooters with bows
ᵈ abuse me: or, mock me

⁸And it came to pass on the morrow, when the Philistines came to strip the slain, that they found Saul and his sons fallen in mount Gilboa. ⁹And when they had stripped him, they took his head, and his armour, and sent into the land of the Philistines round about, to carry tidings unto their idols, and to the people. ¹⁰And they put his armour in the house of their gods, and fastened his head in the temple of Dagon. ¹¹And when all Jabeshgilead heard all that the Philistines had done to Saul, ¹²They arose, all the valiant men, and took away the body of Saul, and the bodies of his sons, and brought them to Jabesh, and buried their bones under the oak in Jabesh, and fasted seven days. ¹³So Saul died for his transgression which he committedᵉ against the LORD, *even* against the word of the LORD, which he kept not, and also for asking *counsel* of *one that had* a familiar spirit, to enquire *of it*; ¹⁴And enquired not of the LORD: therefore he slew him, and turned the kingdom unto David the son of Jesseᶠ.

11

¹Then all Israel gathered themselves to David unto Hebron, saying, Behold, we *are* thy bone and thy flesh. ²And moreover in timeᵃ past, even when Saul was king, thou *wast* he that leddest out and broughtest in Israel: and the LORD thy God said unto thee, Thou shalt feed my people Israel, and thou

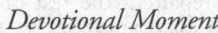

Devotional Moment

Authority

11:1-3 The leaders of Israel came to David to affirm his leadership ability, to recognize his authority over them, and to declare their loyalty. They respected David because, as a military leader, he did the job right and brought the people safely back from battle. Like David, we must earn respect through the responsible exercise of authority. Give your children time to do their tasks in their own way. As much as possible, be reasonable, loving, and sensitive to each child's individual needs in making requests of them. If you respect your children as people, they will learn to respect your authority.

shalt be ruler over my people Israel. ³Therefore came all the elders of Israel to the king to Hebron; and David made a covenant with them in Hebron before the LORD; and they anointed David king over Israel, according to the word of the LORD byᵇ Samuel. ⁴And David and all Israel went to Jerusalem, which *is* Jebus; where the Jebusites *were*, the inhabitants of the land. ⁵And the inhabitants of Jebus said to David, Thou shalt not come hither. Nevertheless David took the castle of Zion, which *is* the city of David. ⁶And David said, Whosoever smiteth the Jebusites first shall be chiefᶜ and captain. So Joab the son of Zeruiah went first up, and was chief. ⁷And David dwelt in the castle; therefore they called it the city of David. ⁸And he built the city round about, even from Millo round about:

ᵉ committed: Heb. transgressed
ᶠ Jesse: Heb. Isai
ᵃ in time . . . : Heb. both yesterday and the third day
ᵇ by: Heb. by the hand of
ᶜ chief: Heb. head

and Joab repaired[d] the rest of the city. [9]So David waxed[e] greater and greater: for the LORD of hosts *was* with him.

[10]These also *are* the chief of the mighty men whom David had, who strengthened[f] themselves with him in his kingdom, *and* with all Israel, to make him king, according to the word of the LORD concerning Israel. [11]And this *is* the number of the mighty men whom David had; Jashobeam, an Hachmonite[g], the chief of the captains: he lifted up his spear against three hundred slain *by him* at one time. [12]And after him *was* Eleazar the son of Dodo, the Ahohite, who *was one* of the three mighties. [13]He was with David at Pasdammim[h], and there the Philistines were gathered together to battle, where was a parcel of ground full of barley; and the people fled from before the Philistines. [14]And they set[i] themselves in the midst of *that* parcel, and delivered it, and slew the Philistines; and the LORD saved *them* by a great deliverance. [15]Now three[j] of the thirty captains went down to the rock to David, into the cave of Adullam; and the host of the Philistines encamped in the valley of Rephaim. [16]And David *was* then in the hold, and the Philistines' garrison *was* then at Bethlehem. [17]And David longed, and said, Oh that one would give me drink of the water of the well of Bethlehem, that *is* at the gate! [18]And the three brake through the host of the Philistines, and drew water out of the well of Bethlehem, that *was* by the gate, and took *it*, and brought *it* to David: but David would not drink *of* it, but poured it out to the LORD, [19]And said, My God forbid it me, that I should do this thing: shall I drink the blood of these men that have put their lives in jeopardy? for with *the jeopardy of* their lives they brought it. Therefore he would not drink it. These things did these three mightiest. [20]And Abishai the brother of Joab, he was chief of the three: for lifting up his spear against three hundred, he slew *them*, and had a name among the three. [21]Of the three, he was more honourable than the two; for he was their captain: howbeit he attained not to the *first* three. [22]Benaiah the son of Jehoiada, the son of a valiant man of Kabzeel, who had done many acts; he slew two lionlike men of Moab: also he went down and slew a lion in a pit in a snowy day. [23]And he slew an Egyptian, a man of *great* stature, five cubits high; and in the Egyptian's hand *was* a spear like a weaver's beam; and he went down to him with a staff, and plucked the spear out of the Egyptian's hand, and slew him with his own spear. [24]These *things* did Benaiah the son of Jehoiada, and had the name among the three mighties. [25]Behold, he was honourable among the thirty, but attained not to the *first* three: and David set him over his guard. [26]Also the valiant men of the armies *were*, Asahel the brother of Joab, Elhanan

---

[d] repaired: Heb. revived

[e] waxed . . . : Heb. went in going and increasing

[f] strengthened . . . : or, held strongly with him

[g] an Hachmonite: or, son of Hachmoni

[h] Pasdammim: also called, Ephesdammim

[i] set . . . : or, stood

[j] three . . . : or, three captains over the thirty

the son of Dodo of Bethlehem, ²⁷Shammoth[k] the Harorite, Helez the Pelonite, ²⁸Ira the son of Ikkesh the Tekoite, Abiezer the Antothite, ²⁹Sibbecai[l] the Hushathite, Ilai the Ahohite, ³⁰Maharai the Netophathite, Heled[m] the son of Baanah the Netophathite, ³¹Ithai the son of Ribai of Gibeah, *that pertained* to the children of Benjamin, Benaiah the Pirathonite, ³²Hurai[n] of the brooks of Gaash, Abiel the Arbathite, ³³Azmaveth the Baharumite, Eliahba the Shaalbonite, ³⁴The sons of Hashem[o] the Gizonite, Jonathan the son of Shage the Hararite, ³⁵Ahiam the son of Sacar[p] the Hararite, Eliphal the son of Ur, ³⁶Hepher the Mecherathite, Ahijah the Pelonite, ³⁷Hezro the Carmelite, Naarai the son of Ezbai, ³⁸Joel the brother of Nathan, Mibhar the son[q] of Haggeri, ³⁹Zelek the Ammonite, Naharai the Berothite, the armourbearer of Joab the son of Zeruiah, ⁴⁰Ira the Ithrite, Gareb the Ithrite, ⁴¹Uriah the Hittite, Zabad the son of Ahlai, ⁴²Adina the son of Shiza the Reubenite, a captain of the Reubenites, and thirty with him, ⁴³Hanan the son of Maachah, and Joshaphat the Mithnite, ⁴⁴Uzzia the Ashterathite, Shama and Jehiel the sons of Hothan the Aroerite, ⁴⁵Jediael the son[r] of Shimri, and Joha his brother, the Tizite, ⁴⁶Eliel the Mahavite, and Jeribai, and Joshaviah, the sons of Elnaam, and Ithmah the Moabite, ⁴⁷Eliel, and Obed, and Jasiel the Mesobaite.

12

¹Now these *are* they that came to David to Ziklag, while he yet kept himself close because of Saul the son of Kish: and they *were* among the mighty men, helpers of the war. ²*They were* armed with bows, and could use both the right hand and the left in *hurling* stones and *shooting* arrows out of a bow, *even* of Saul's brethren of Benjamin. ³The chief *was* Ahiezer, then Joash, the sons of Shemaah[a] the Gibeathite; and Jeziel, and Pelet, the sons of Azmaveth; and Berachah, and Jehu the Antothite, ⁴And Ismaiah the Gibeonite, a mighty man among the thirty, and over the thirty; and Jeremiah, and Jahaziel, and Johanan, and Josabad the Gederathite, ⁵Eluzai, and Jerimoth, and Bealiah, and Shemariah, and Shephatiah the Haruphite, ⁶Elkanah, and Jesiah, and Azareel, and Joezer, and Jashobeam, the Korhites, ⁷And Joelah, and Zebadiah, the sons of Jeroham of Gedor. ⁸And of the Gadites there separated themselves unto David into the hold to the wilderness men of might, *and* men of war[b] *fit* for the battle, that could handle shield

---

[k] Shammoth: or, Shammah
[l] Sibbecai: or, Mebunnai
[m] Heled: or, Heleb
[n] Hurai: or, Hiddai
[o] Hashem: or, Jashen
[p] Sacar: or, Sharar
[q] the son . . . : or, the Haggerite
[r] son . . . : or, Shimrite
[a] Shemaah: or, Hasmaah
[b] of war: Heb. of the host

and buckler, whose faces *were like* the faces of lions, and *were* as swift as the roes upon the mountains; ⁹Ezer the first, Obadiah the second, Eliab the third, ¹⁰Mishmannah the fourth, Jeremiah the fifth, ¹¹Attai the sixth, Eliel the seventh, ¹²Johanan the eighth, Elzabad the ninth, ¹³Jeremiah the tenth, Machbanai the eleventh. ¹⁴These *were* of the sons of Gad, captains of the host: one^c of the least *was* over an hundred, and the greatest over a thousand. ¹⁵These *are* they that went over Jordan in the first month, when it had overflown^d all his banks; and they put to flight all *them* of the valleys, *both* toward the east, and toward the west. ¹⁶And there came of the children of Benjamin and Judah to the hold unto David. ¹⁷And David went out to meet^e them, and answered and said unto them, If ye be come peaceably unto me to help me, mine heart shall be knit unto you: but if *ye be come* to betray me to mine enemies, seeing *there is* no wrong in mine hands, the God of our fathers look *thereon*, and rebuke *it*. ¹⁸Then the spirit came^f upon Amasai, *who was* chief of the captains, *and he said*, Thine *are* we, David, and on thy side, thou son of Jesse: peace, peace *be* unto thee, and peace *be* to thine helpers; for thy God helpeth thee. Then David received them, and made them captains of the band. ¹⁹And there fell *some* of Manasseh to David, when he came with the Philistines against Saul to battle: but they helped them not: for the lords of

the Philistines upon advisement sent him away, saying, He will fall to his master Saul to *the jeopardy of* our heads. ²⁰As he went to Ziklag, there fell to him of Manasseh, Adnah, and Jozabad, and Jediael, and Michael, and Jozabad, and Elihu, and Zilthai, captains of the thousands that *were* of Manasseh. ²¹And they helped David against the band *of the rovers:* for they *were* all mighty men of valour, and were captains in the host. ²²For at *that* time day by day there came to David to help him, until *it was* a great host, like the host of God.

²³And these *are* the numbers of the bands^g *that were* ready armed to the war, *and* came to David to Hebron, to turn the kingdom of Saul to him, according to the word of the LORD. ²⁴The children of Judah that bare shield and spear

Devotional Moment

Know the Times

12:24-37 Among those who joined David at Hebron were the two hundred chiefs of Issachar, "that had understanding of the times" and, just as significantly, knew what Israel should do. They formed a rich resource in the battle against Saul. As parents, we must cultivate both the broad view (keeping up with the events and trends of our society) and a focused view (knowing what is happening in our children's world). Are you aware of current events in the world and in your children's world of school, friends, and other activities? We must understand the times today if we are to be wise parents.

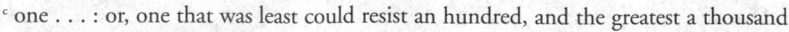

---

^c one . . . : or, one that was least could resist an hundred, and the greatest a thousand
^d overflown: Heb. filled over
^e to meet . . . : Heb. before them
^f came . . . : Heb. clothed
^g bands: or, captains, or, men: Heb. heads

were six thousand and eight hundred, ready armed[h] to the war. [25]Of the children of Simeon, mighty men of valour for the war, seven thousand and one hundred. [26]Of the children of Levi four thousand and six hundred. [27]And Jehoiada *was* the leader of the Aaronites, and with him *were* three thousand and seven hundred; [28]And Zadok, a young man mighty of valour, and of his father's house twenty and two captains. [29]And of the children of Benjamin, the kindred[i] of Saul, three thousand: for hitherto the greatest part of them had kept the ward of the house of Saul. [30]And of the children of Ephraim twenty thousand and eight hundred, mighty men of valour, famous[j] throughout the house of their fathers. [31]And of the half tribe of Manasseh eighteen thousand, which were expressed by name, to come and make David king. [32]And of the children of Issachar, *which were men* that had understanding of the times, to know what Israel ought to do; the heads of them *were* two hundred; and all their brethren *were* at their commandment. [33]Of Zebulun, such as went forth to battle, expert[k] in war, with all instruments of war, fifty thousand, which could keep rank: *they were* not of double heart. [34]And of Naphtali a thousand captains, and with them with shield and spear thirty and seven thousand. [35]And of the Danites expert in war twenty and eight thousand and six hundred. [36]And of Asher, such as went forth to battle, expert[l] in war, forty thousand. [37]And on the other side of Jordan, of the Reubenites, and the Gadites, and of the half tribe of Manasseh, with all manner of instruments of war for the battle, an hundred and twenty thousand. [38]All these men of war, that could keep rank, came with a perfect heart to Hebron, to make David king over all Israel: and all the rest also of Israel *were* of one heart to make David king. [39]And there they were with David three days, eating and drinking: for their brethren had prepared for them. [40]Moreover they that were nigh them, *even* unto Issachar and Zebulun and Naphtali, brought bread on asses, and on camels, and on mules, and on oxen, *and* meat[m], meal, cakes of figs, and bunches of raisins, and wine, and oil, and oxen, and sheep abundantly: for *there was* joy in Israel.

13

[1]And David consulted with the captains of thousands and hundreds, *and* with every leader. [2]And David said unto all the congregation of Israel, If *it seem* good unto you, and *that it be* of the LORD our God, let us send[a] abroad unto our brethren every where, *that are* left in all the land of Israel, and with them *also* to the priests and Levites *which are* in their cities *and* suburbs,

---

[h] armed: or, prepared
[i] kindred: Heb. brethren
[j] famous: Heb. men of names
[k] expert . . . : or, rangers of battle, or, ranged in battle
[l] expert: or, keeping their rank
[m] meat . . . : or, victual of meal
[a] send . . . : Heb. break forth and send

that they may gather themselves unto us: ³And let us bring again the ark of our God to us: for we enquired not at it in the days of Saul. ⁴And all the congregation said that they would do so: for the thing was right in the eyes of all the people. ⁵So David gathered all Israel together, from Shihor of Egypt even unto the entering of Hemath, to bring the ark of God from Kirjathjearim. ⁶And David went up, and all Israel, to Baalah, *that is*, to Kirjathjearim, which *belonged* to Judah, to bring up thence the ark of God the LORD, that dwelleth *between* the cherubims, whose name is called *on it*. ⁷And they carried^b the ark of God in a new cart out of the house of Abinadab: and Uzza and Ahio drave the cart. ⁸And David and all Israel played before God with all *their* might, and with singing^c, and with harps, and with psalteries, and with timbrels, and with cymbals, and with trumpets.

⁹And when they came unto the threshingfloor of Chidon^d, Uzza put forth his hand to hold the ark; for the oxen stumbled. ¹⁰And the anger of the LORD was kindled against Uzza, and he smote him, because he put his hand to the ark: and there he died before God. ¹¹And David was displeased, because the LORD had made a breach upon Uzza: wherefore that place is called Perezuzza^e to this day. ¹²And David was afraid of God that day, saying, How shall I bring the ark of God *home* to me? ¹³So David brought^f not the ark *home* to himself to the city of David, but carried it aside into the house of Obededom the Gittite. ¹⁴And the ark of God remained with the family of Obededom in his house three months. And the LORD blessed the house of Obededom, and all that he had.

14

¹Now Hiram king of Tyre sent messengers to David, and timber of cedars, with masons and carpenters, to build him an house. ²And David perceived that the LORD had confirmed him king over Israel, for his kingdom was lifted up on high, because of his people Israel. ³And David took more wives at Jerusalem: and David begat more sons and daughters. ⁴Now these *are* the names of *his* children which he had in Jerusalem; Shammua, and Shobab,

---

Devotional Moment
•
Everyone's Doing It

14:3 As was common at certain times in history, King David took more than one wife and fathered many children. This was one case of God's people adopting a practice that "everybody" did, but which fell short of God's ideal. Many practices that are common today are equally harmful—whether they fall in gray areas (like watching questionable TV programs) or are outright sin (like cheating on taxes or committing adultery). God wants our behavior and our character to please him; the excuse that "everyone's doing it" carries no weight with him. Don't allow your community's norms to dictate your actions.

---

^b carried . . . : Heb. made the ark to ride
^c singing: Heb. songs
^d Chidon: also called Nachon
^e Perezuzza: that is, The breach of Uzza
^f brought: Heb. removed

Nathan, and Solomon, [5]And Ibhar, and Elishua, and Elpalet, [6]And Nogah, and Nepheg, and Japhia, [7]And Elishama, and Beeliada[a], and Eliphalet.

[8]And when the Philistines heard that David was anointed king over all Israel, all the Philistines went up to seek David. And David heard *of it*, and went out against them. [9]And the Philistines came and spread themselves in the valley of Rephaim. [10]And David enquired of God, saying, Shall I go up against the Philistines? and wilt thou deliver them into mine hand? And the LORD said unto him, Go up; for I will deliver them into thine hand. [11]So they came up to Baalperazim[b]; and David smote them there. Then David said, God hath broken in upon mine enemies by mine hand like the breaking forth of waters: therefore they called the name of that place Baalperazim. [12]And when they had left their gods there, David gave a commandment, and they were burned with fire. [13]And the Philistines yet again spread themselves abroad in the valley. [14]Therefore David enquired again of God; and God said unto him, Go not up after them; turn away from them, and come upon them over against the mulberry trees. [15]And it shall be, when thou shalt hear a sound of going in the tops of the mulberry trees, *that* then thou shalt go out to battle: for God is gone forth before thee to smite the host of the Philistines. [16]David therefore did as God commanded him: and they smote the host of the Philistines from Gibeon[c] even to Gazer. [17]And the fame of David went out into all lands; and the LORD brought the fear of him upon all nations.

15

[1]And *David* made him houses in the city of David, and prepared a place for the ark of God, and pitched for it a tent. [2]Then David said, None ought to carry the ark of God but the Levites: for them hath the LORD chosen to carry the ark of God, and to minister unto him for ever. [3]And David gathered all Israel together to Jerusalem, to bring up the ark of the LORD unto his place, which he had prepared for it. [4]And David assembled the children of Aaron, and the Levites: [5]Of the sons of Kohath; Uriel the chief, and his brethren[a] an hundred and twenty: [6]Of the sons of Merari; Asaiah the chief, and his brethren two hundred and twenty: [7]Of the sons of Gershom; Joel the chief, and his brethren an hundred and thirty: [8]Of the sons of Elizaphan; Shemaiah the chief, and his brethren two hundred: [9]Of the sons of Hebron; Eliel the chief, and his brethren fourscore: [10]Of the sons of Uzziel; Amminadab the chief, and his brethren an hundred and twelve. [11]And David called for Zadok and Abiathar the priests, and for the Levites, for Uriel, Asaiah, and Joel, Shemaiah, and Eliel, and Amminadab, [12]And said unto them, Ye *are* the chief of the fathers of the Levites: sanctify yourselves, *both* ye and your brethren, that ye may bring up the ark

---

[a] Beeliada: also called, Eliada
[b] Baalperazim: that is, A place of breaches
[c] Gibeon: also called, Geba
[a] brethren: or, kinsmen

of the LORD God of Israel unto *the place that* I have prepared for it. [13]For because ye *did it* not at the first, the LORD our God made a breach upon us, for that we sought him not after the due order. [14]So the priests and the Levites sanctified themselves to bring up the ark of the LORD God of Israel. [15]And the children of the Levites bare the ark of God upon their shoulders with the staves thereon, as Moses commanded according to the word of the LORD. [16]And David spake to the chief of the Levites to appoint their brethren *to be* the singers with instruments of musick, psalteries and harps and cymbals, sounding, by lifting up the voice with joy. [17]So the Levites appointed Heman the son of Joel; and of his brethren, Asaph the son of Berechiah; and of the sons of Merari their brethren, Ethan the son of Kushaiah; [18]And with them their brethren of the second *degree*, Zechariah, Ben, and Jaaziel, and Shemiramoth, and Jehiel, and Unni, Eliab, and Benaiah, and Maaseiah, and Mattithiah, and Elipheleh, and Mikneiah, and Obededom, and Jeiel, the porters. [19]So the singers, Heman, Asaph, and Ethan, *were appointed* to sound with cymbals of brass; [20]And Zechariah, and Aziel, and Shemiramoth, and Jehiel, and Unni, and Eliab, and Maaseiah, and Benaiah, with psalteries on Alamoth; [21]And Mattithiah, and Elipheleh, and Mikneiah, and Obededom, and Jeiel, and Azaziah, with harps on the Sheminith to excel. [22]And Chenaniah, chief of the Levites, *was* for song: he instructed about the song, because he *was* skilful. [23]And Berechiah and Elkanah *were* doorkeepers for the ark. [24]And Shebaniah, and Jehoshaphat, and Nethaneel, and Amasai, and Zechariah, and Benaiah, and Eliezer, the priests, did blow with the trumpets before the ark of God: and Obededom and Jehiah *were* doorkeepers for the ark.

[25]So David, and the elders of Israel, and the captains over thousands, went to bring up the ark of the covenant of the LORD out of the house of Obededom with joy. [26]And it came to pass, when God helped the Levites that bare the ark of the covenant of the LORD, that they offered seven bullocks and seven rams. [27]And David *was* clothed with a robe of fine linen, and all the Levites that bare the ark, and the singers, and Chenaniah the master of the song[b] with the singers: David also *had* upon him an ephod of linen. [28]Thus all Israel brought up the ark of the covenant of the LORD with shouting, and with sound of the cornet, and

---

Devotional Moment

Marital Arts

15:29 David danced for joy when the Ark of the Covenant returned to Jerusalem. But his wife Michal watched him from a window and—for her own reasons—began to despise him. Many factors can cause negative thoughts about our spouse to take root—fatigue, financial burdens, and lack of communication, to name a few. Focus on the good in your spouse while working together on problem areas. Do not magnify minor irritations or let them lead to serious conflicts. Pray for God's help to root out seeds of contempt, and thank God for your spouse's good traits.

---

[b] song: or, carriage

with trumpets, and with cymbals, making a noise with psalteries and harps. ²⁹And it came to pass, *as* the ark of the covenant of the LORD came to the city of David, that Michal the daughter of Saul looking out at a window saw king David dancing and playing: and she despised him in her heart.

16

¹So they brought the ark of God, and set it in the midst of the tent that David had pitched for it: and they offered burnt sacrifices and peace offerings before God. ²And when David had made an end of offering the burnt offerings and the peace offerings, he blessed the people in the name of the LORD. ³And he dealt to every one of Israel, both man and woman, to every one a loaf of bread, and a good piece of flesh, and a flagon *of wine.* ⁴And he appointed *certain* of the Levites to minister before the ark of the LORD, and to record, and to thank and praise the LORD God of Israel: ⁵Asaph the chief, and next to him Zechariah, Jeiel, and Shemiramoth, and Jehiel, and Mattithiah, and Eliab, and Benaiah, and Obededom: and Jeiel with psalteries[a] and with harps; but Asaph made a sound with cymbals; ⁶Benaiah also and Jahaziel the priests with trumpets continually before the ark of the covenant of God.

⁷Then on that day David delivered first *this psalm* to thank the LORD into the hand of Asaph and his brethren. ⁸Give thanks unto the LORD, call upon his name, make known his deeds among the people. ⁹Sing unto him, sing

---

Devotional Moment
•
Thanksgiving

16:7 Once David had settled the Ark into its appointed tent and assigned Levites to its care, it was time to thank God. To the director, Asaph, and his associates, he gave the responsibility of singing praises to God. God is at work in our families and churches as well and deserves our thanks. It is honoring to God to have prayers and songs of gratitude in your home, but your grateful attitude is even more important in teaching your children about what God deserves. Consider a family sharing time where each member can express—in words, pictures, or songs—his or her thanks to God.

---

psalms unto him, talk ye of all his wondrous works. ¹⁰Glory ye in his holy name: let the heart of them rejoice that seek the LORD. ¹¹Seek the LORD and his strength, seek his face continually. ¹²Remember his marvellous works that he hath done, his wonders, and the judgments of his mouth; ¹³O ye seed of Israel his servant, ye children of Jacob, his chosen ones. ¹⁴He *is* the LORD our God; his judgments *are* in all the earth. ¹⁵Be ye mindful always of his covenant; the word *which* he commanded to a thousand generations; ¹⁶*Even of the covenant* which he made with Abraham, and of his oath unto Isaac; ¹⁷And hath confirmed the same to Jacob for a law, *and* to Israel *for* an everlasting covenant, ¹⁸Saying, Unto thee will I give the land of Canaan, the lot[b] of your inheritance; ¹⁹When ye were but few, even a few, and strangers in it. ²⁰And *when* they went from nation to nation, and from *one* kingdom to another people;

---

[a] with psalteries . . . : Heb. with instruments of psalteries and harps
[b] the lot: Heb. the cord

²¹He suffered no man to do them wrong: yea, he reproved kings for their sakes, ²²*Saying*, Touch not mine anointed, and do my prophets no harm. ²³Sing unto the LORD, all the earth; shew forth from day to day his salvation. ²⁴Declare his glory among the heathen; his marvellous works among all nations. ²⁵For great *is* the LORD, and greatly to be praised: he also *is* to be feared above all gods. ²⁶For all the gods of the people *are* idols: but the LORD made the heavens. ²⁷Glory and honour *are* in his presence; strength and gladness *are* in his place. ²⁸Give unto the LORD, ye kindreds of the people, give unto the LORD glory and strength. ²⁹Give unto the LORD the glory *due* unto his name: bring an offering, and come before him: worship the LORD in the beauty of holiness. ³⁰Fear before him, all the earth: the world also shall be stable, that it be not moved. ³¹Let the heavens be glad, and let the earth rejoice: and let *men* say among the nations, The LORD reigneth. ³²Let the sea roar, and the fulness thereof: let the fields rejoice, and all that *is* therein. ³³Then shall the trees of the wood sing out at the presence of the LORD, because he cometh to judge the earth. ³⁴O give thanks unto the LORD; for *he is* good; for his mercy *endureth* for ever. ³⁵And say ye, Save us, O God of our salvation, and gather us together, and deliver us from the heathen, that we may give thanks to thy holy name, *and* glory in thy praise. ³⁶Blessed *be* the LORD God of Israel for ever and ever. And all the people said, Amen, and praised the LORD.

³⁷So he left there before the ark of the covenant of the LORD Asaph and his brethren, to minister before the ark continually, as every day's work required: ³⁸And Obededom with their brethren, threescore and eight; Obededom also the son of Jeduthun and Hosah *to be* porters: ³⁹And Zadok the priest, and his brethren the priests, before the tabernacle of the LORD in the high place that *was* at Gibeon, ⁴⁰To offer burnt offerings unto the LORD upon the altar of the burnt offering continually morningᶜ and evening, and *to do* according to all that is written in the law of the LORD, which he commanded Israel; ⁴¹And with them Heman and Jeduthun, and the rest that were chosen, who were expressed by name, to give thanks to the LORD, because his mercy *endureth* for ever; ⁴²And with them Heman and Jeduthun with trumpets and cymbals for those that should make a sound, and with musical instruments of God. And the sons of Jeduthun *were* portersᵈ. ⁴³And all the people departed every man to his house: and David returned to bless his house.

17

¹Now it came to pass, as David sat in his house, that David said to Nathan the prophet, Lo, I dwell in an house of cedars, but the ark of the covenant of the LORD *remaineth* under curtains. ²Then Nathan said unto David, Do all that *is* in thine heart; for God *is* with

---

ᶜ morning . . . : Heb. in the morning, and in the evening
ᵈ porters: Heb. for the gate

thee. ³And it came to pass the same night, that the word of God came to Nathan, saying, ⁴Go and tell David my servant, Thus saith the LORD, Thou shalt not build me an house to dwell in: ⁵For I have not dwelt in an house since the day that I brought up Israel unto this day; but have gone from tent to tent, and from *one* tabernacle *to another.* ⁶Wheresoever I have walked with all Israel, spake I a word to any of the judges of Israel, whom I commanded to feed my people, saying, Why have ye not built me an house of cedars? ⁷Now therefore thus shalt thou say unto my servant David, Thus saith the LORD of hosts, I took thee from the sheepcote, *even* from following[a] the sheep, that thou shouldest be ruler over my people Israel: ⁸And I have been with thee whithersoever thou hast walked, and have cut off all thine enemies from before thee, and have made thee a name like the name of the great men that *are* in the earth. ⁹Also I will ordain a place for my people Israel, and will plant them, and they shall dwell in their place, and shall be moved no more; neither shall the children of wickedness waste them any more, as at the beginning, ¹⁰And since the time that I commanded judges *to be* over my people Israel. Moreover I will subdue all thine enemies. Furthermore I tell thee that the LORD will build thee an house. ¹¹And it shall come to pass, when thy days be expired that thou must go *to be* with thy fathers, that I will raise up thy seed after thee, which shall be of thy sons; and I will establish his kingdom. ¹²He shall build me an house, and I will

---

Devotional Moment
•
The Next Generation

17:11 The prophet Nathan reassured David that God would continue to take care of his people through David's descendants, long after David was dead. Perhaps you worry that you may not accomplish everything you should during your lifetime. Be true to God and do the work that he gives you; trust him to continue his work through your children. Our heavenly Father has as many hopes for them as you do—and they may help fulfill God's purposes. While we should not try to live through our children nor push our dreams on them, we can pray for God to work through their lives and those of future generations.

---

stablish his throne for ever. ¹³I will be his father, and he shall be my son: and I will not take my mercy away from him, as I took *it* from *him* that was before thee: ¹⁴But I will settle him in mine house and in my kingdom for ever: and his throne shall be established for evermore. ¹⁵According to all these words, and according to all this vision, so did Nathan speak unto David.

¹⁶And David the king came and sat before the LORD, and said, Who *am* I, O LORD God, and what *is* mine house, that thou hast brought me hitherto? ¹⁷And *yet* this was a small thing in thine eyes, O God; for thou hast *also* spoken of thy servant's house for a great while to come, and hast regarded me according to the estate of a man of high degree, O LORD God. ¹⁸What can David *speak* more to thee for the honour of thy servant? for thou knowest thy servant. ¹⁹O LORD, for thy servant's sake, and according to thine own heart, hast thou done all this greatness, in making known

---

[a] from following: Heb. from after

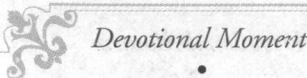

Devotional Moment
•
Gifts from God

17:16 When Nathan told David that Solomon would someday build a great temple, David felt overwhelmed by God's providence and provision. All he could do was wonder, *Who am I to deserve all this?* It is easy to get bogged down in day-to-day concerns and feel discouraged about God's long-range plan for your life. If that's how you feel, take time to reflect on all the benefits God has brought you. Then pray for the future with confidence that God will answer.

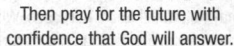

all *these* great things. ²⁰O LORD, *there is* none like thee, neither *is there any* God beside thee, according to all that we have heard with our ears. ²¹And what one nation in the earth *is* like thy people Israel, whom God went to redeem *to be* his own people, to make thee a name of greatness and terribleness, by driving out nations from before thy people, whom thou hast redeemed out of Egypt? ²²For thy people Israel didst thou make thine own people for ever; and thou, LORD, becamest their God. ²³Therefore now, LORD, let the thing that thou hast spoken concerning thy servant and concerning his house be established for ever, and do as thou hast said. ²⁴Let it even be established, that thy name may be magnified for ever, saying, The LORD of hosts *is* the God of Israel, *even* a God to Israel: and *let* the house of David thy servant *be* established before thee. ²⁵For thou, O my God, hast told thy servant that thou wilt build him an house: therefore thy servant hath

found *in his heart* to pray before thee. ²⁶And now, LORD, thou art God, and hast promised this goodness unto thy servant: ²⁷Now therefore let it please thee to bless the house of thy servant, that it may be before thee for ever: for thou blessest, O LORD, and *it shall be* blessed for ever.

18

¹Now after this it came to pass, that David smote the Philistines, and subdued them, and took Gath and her towns out of the hand of the Philistines. ²And he smote Moab; and the Moabites became David's servants, *and* brought gifts. ³And David smote Hadarezerᵃ king of Zobah unto Hamath, as he went to stablish his dominion by the river Euphrates. ⁴And David took from him a thousand chariots, and sevenᵇ thousand horsemen, and twenty thousand footmen: David also houghed all the chariot *horses,* but reserved of them an hundred chariots. ⁵And when the Syrians of Damascusᶜ came to help Hadarezer king of Zobah, David slew of the Syrians two and twenty thousand men. ⁶Then David put *garrisons* in Syriadamascus; and the Syrians became David's servants, *and* brought gifts. Thus the LORD preserved David whithersoever he went. ⁷And David took the shields of gold that were on the servants of Hadarezer, and brought them to Jerusalem. ⁸Likewise from Tibhathᵈ, and from Chun, cities of Hadarezer, brought David very much brass, wherewith Solomon made the

---

ᵃ Hadarezer: or, Hadadezer
ᵇ seven . . . : or, seven hundred
ᶜ Damascus: Heb. Darmesek
ᵈ Tibhath . . . : called in the book of Samuel Betah, and Berothai

brasen sea, and the pillars, and the vessels of brass.

⁹Now when Touᵉ king of Hamath heard how David had smitten all the host of Hadarezer king of Zobah; ¹⁰He sent Hadoramᶠ his son to king David, to enquire of his welfare, and to congratulate him, because he had fought against Hadarezer, and smitten him; (for Hadarezer had war with Tou;) and *with him* all manner of vessels of gold and silver and brass. ¹¹Them also king David dedicated unto the LORD, with the silver and the gold that he brought from all *these* nations; from Edom, and from Moab, and from the children of Ammon, and from the Philistines, and from Amalek. ¹²Moreover Abishaiᵍ the son of Zeruiah slew of the Edomites in the valley of salt eighteen thousand. ¹³And he put garrisons in Edom; and

Devotional Moment
Parenting Fairly
18:14 David was king over all the tribes of Israel, and he had the difficult task of making judgments that affected them all. Yet David had a record of being a just ruler. In your role as a parent, you have the challenge of trying to do what is right for each child while being fair to all. Times will come when you cannot do what each child—or sometimes any child—wants. But trust God to help you do what is best for all of you as a family and that it will prove to be just and right for each of you individually.

Devotional Moment
Counsel from Children
18:17 Among David's chief officials were some of his sons, serving at his side. David had enough humility to listen to his grown sons and to recognize their maturity. Perhaps your children have advice worth heeding, too. Over the years, they may be God's messengers to you in many significant ways. How can you better listen to their ideas and encourage their feedback? Recognize areas in which they have insight, and seek their counsel when you need it.

all the Edomites became David's servants. Thus the LORD preserved David whithersoever he went. ¹⁴So David reigned over all Israel, and executed judgment and justice among all his people. ¹⁵And Joab the son of Zeruiah *was* over the host; and Jehoshaphat the son of Ahilud, recorderʰ. ¹⁶And Zadok the son of Ahitub, and Abimelechⁱ the son of Abiathar, *were* the priests; and Shavsha was scribe; ¹⁷And Benaiah the son of Jehoiada *was* over the Cherethites and the Pelethites; and the sons of David *were* chief aboutʲ the king.

19

¹Now it came to pass after this, that Nahash the king of the children of Ammon died, and his son reigned in his stead. ²And David said, I will shew kindness unto Hanun the son of Na-

ᵉ Tou: also called, Toi
ᶠ Hadoram: also called, Joram
ᵍ Abishai: Heb. Abshai
ʰ recorder: or, remembrancer
ⁱ Abimelech: also called, Ahimelech
ʲ about . . . : Heb. at the hand of the king

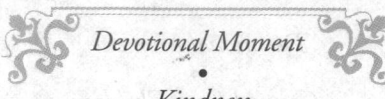

Devotional Moment
•
Kindness

19:2 The Ammonites and the Israelites were enemies, yet David felt compelled to be kind to the Ammonite Hanun when his father, King Nahash, died. The reason: Nahash had been kind to David. So David sent a sympathy delegation to the grieving son. Our dealings with other people often come back to haunt or bless us. The kindness we show to others may someday come around again.

hash, because his father shewed kindness to me. And David sent messengers to comfort him concerning his father. So the servants of David came into the land of the children of Ammon to Hanun, to comfort him. ³But the princes of the children of Ammon said to Hanun, Thinkest[a] thou that David doth honour thy father, that he hath sent comforters unto thee? are not his servants come unto thee for to search, and to overthrow, and to spy out the land? ⁴Wherefore Hanun took David's servants, and shaved them, and cut off their garments in the midst hard by their buttocks, and sent them away. ⁵Then there went *certain*, and told David how the men were served. And he sent to meet them: for the men were greatly ashamed. And the king said, Tarry at Jericho until your beards be grown, and *then* return.

⁶And when the children of Ammon saw that they had made themselves odious[b] to David, Hanun and the children of Ammon sent a thousand talents of silver to hire them chariots and horsemen out of Mesopotamia, and out of Syriamaachah, and out of Zobah. ⁷So they hired thirty and two thousand chariots, and the king of Maachah and his people; who came and pitched before Medeba. And the children of Ammon gathered themselves together from their cities, and came to battle. ⁸And when David heard *of it*, he sent Joab, and all the host of the mighty men. ⁹And the children of Ammon came out, and put the battle in array before the gate of the city: and the kings that were come *were* by themselves in the field. ¹⁰Now when Joab saw that the battle[c] was set against him before and behind, he chose out of all the choice of Israel, and put *them* in array against the Syrians. ¹¹And the rest of the people he delivered unto the hand of Abishai[d] his brother, and they set *themselves* in array against the children of Ammon. ¹²And he said, If the Syrians be too strong for me, then thou shalt help me: but if the children of Ammon be too strong for thee, then I will help thee. ¹³Be of good courage, and let us behave ourselves valiantly for our people, and for the cities of our God: and let the LORD do *that which is* good in his sight. ¹⁴So Joab and the people that *were* with him drew nigh before the Syrians unto the battle; and they fled before him. ¹⁵And when the children of Ammon saw that the Syrians were fled,

---

[a] Thinkest . . . : Heb. In thine eyes doth David, etc
[b] odious: Heb. to stink
[c] the battle . . . : Heb. the face of the battle wars
[d] Abishai: Heb. Abshai

they likewise fled before Abishai his brother, and entered into the city. Then Joab came to Jerusalem. ¹⁶And when the Syrians saw that they were put to the worse before Israel, they sent messengers, and drew forth the Syrians that *were* beyond the river*: and Shophach the captain of the host of Hadarezer *went* before them. ¹⁷And it was told David; and he gathered all Israel, and passed over Jordan, and came upon them, and set *the battle* in array against them. So when David had put the battle in array against the Syrians, they fought with him. ¹⁸But the Syrians fled before Israel; and David slew of the Syrians seven thousand *men which fought in* chariots, and forty thousand footmen, and killed Shophach the captain of the host. ¹⁹And when the servants of Hadarezer saw that they were put to the worse before Israel, they made peace with David, and became his servants: neither would the Syrians help the children of Ammon any more.

20

¹And it came to pass, that after* the year was expired, at the time that kings go out *to battle,* Joab led forth the power of the army, and wasted the country of the children of Ammon, and came and besieged Rabbah. But David tarried at Jerusalem. And Joab smote Rabbah, and destroyed it. ²And David took the crown of their king from off his head,

and found it to weighᵇ a talent of gold, and *there were* precious stones in it; and it was set upon David's head: and he brought also exceeding much spoil out of the city. ³And he brought out the people that *were* in it, and cut *them* with saws, and with harrows of iron, and with axes. Even so dealt David with all the cities of the children of Ammon. And David and all the people returned to Jerusalem.

⁴And it came to pass after this, that there arose* war at Gezer with the Philistines; at which time Sibbechai the Hushathite slew Sippai, *that was* of the children of the giant: and they were subdued. ⁵And there was war again with the Philistines; and Elhanan the son of Jair ᵈ slew Lahmi the brother of Goliath the Gittite, whose spear staff *was* like a weaver's beam. ⁶And yet again there was war at Gath, where was a man of *great* stature, whose fingers and toes *were* four and twenty, six *on each hand,* and six *on each foot:* and he also was the son of the giant. ⁷But when he defiedᵉ Israel, Jonathan the son of Shimea David's brother slew him. ⁸These were born unto the giant in Gath; and they fell by the hand of David, and by the hand of his servants.

21

¹And Satan stood up against Israel, and provoked David to number Israel. ²And David said to Joab and to the

---

ᵃ river: that is, Euphrates
ᵃ after . . . : Heb. at the return of the year
ᵇ to weigh: Heb. the weight of
ᶜ arose: or, continued: Heb. stood
ᵈ Jair: also called, Jaareoregim
ᵉ defied: or, reproached

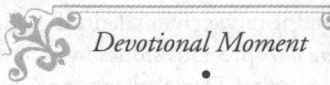

Devotional Moment

Who Gets Hurt?

21:1-14 Although David was a great man of God, even he yielded to Satan's temptations. His purpose in taking the census was to take pride and put his confidence in the size of his army rather than in God. This was clearly against God's will, and David knew it. The consequence was a plague that killed seventy thousand Israelites. We could hardly imagine one of our sins causing that many deaths—yet our disobedience, too, can have far-reaching consequences that we cannot foresee. We risk unseen danger for our children, other relatives, or friends when we callously disobey God, even though Satan may have convinced us it will bring no harm.

rulers of the people, Go, number Israel from Beersheba even to Dan; and bring the number of them to me, that I may know *it*. ³And Joab answered, The LORD make his people an hundred times so many more as they *be*: but, my lord the king, *are* they not all my lord's servants? why then doth my lord require this thing? why will he be a cause of trespass to Israel? ⁴Nevertheless the king's word prevailed against Joab. Wherefore Joab departed, and went throughout all Israel, and came to Jerusalem. ⁵And Joab gave the sum of the number of the people unto David. And all *they of* Israel were a thousand thousand and an hundred thousand men that drew sword: and Judah *was* four hundred threescore and ten thousand men that drew sword. ⁶But Levi and Benjamin counted he not among

them: for the king's word was abominable to Joab.

⁷And God was displeased with this thing; therefore he smote Israel. ⁸And David said unto God, I have sinned greatly, because I have done this thing: but now, I beseech thee, do away the iniquity of thy servant; for I have done very foolishly. ⁹And the LORD spake unto Gad, David's seer, saying, ¹⁰Go and tell David, saying, Thus saith the LORD, I offer ᵃ thee three *things*: choose thee one of them, that I may do *it* unto thee. ¹¹So Gad came to David, and said unto him, Thus saith the LORD, Choose ᵇ thee ¹²Either three years' famine; or three months to be destroyed before thy foes, while that the sword of thine enemies overtaketh *thee*; or else three days the sword of the LORD, even the pestilence, in the land, and the angel of the LORD destroying throughout all the coasts of Israel. Now therefore advise thyself what word I shall bring again to him that sent me. ¹³And David said unto Gad, I am in a great strait: let me fall now into the hand of the LORD; for very great ᶜ *are* his mercies: but let me not fall into the hand of man. ¹⁴So the LORD sent pestilence upon Israel: and there fell of Israel seventy thousand men. ¹⁵And God sent an angel unto Jerusalem to destroy it: and as he was destroying, the LORD beheld, and he repented him of the evil, and said to the angel that destroyed, It is enough, stay now thine hand. And the angel of the LORD stood by the threshingfloor of Ornan ᵈ the

---

ᵃ offer: Heb. stretch out
ᵇ Choose . . . : Heb. Take to thee
ᶜ very great: or, very many
ᵈ Ornan: also called, Araunah

Jebusite. ¹⁶And David lifted up his eyes, and saw the angel of the LORD stand between the earth and the heaven, having a drawn sword in his hand stretched out over Jerusalem. Then David and the elders *of Israel, who were* clothed in sackcloth, fell upon their faces. ¹⁷And David said unto God, *Is it* not I *that* commanded the people to be numbered? even I it is that have sinned and done evil indeed; but *as for* these sheep, what have they done? let thine hand, I pray thee, O LORD my God, be on me, and on my father's house; but not on thy people, that they should be plagued.

¹⁸Then the angel of the LORD commanded Gad to say to David, that David should go up, and set up an altar unto the LORD in the threshingfloor of Ornan the Jebusite. ¹⁹And David went up at the saying of Gad, which he spake in the name of the LORD. ²⁰And Ornanᵉ turned back, and saw the angel; and his four sons with him hid themselves. Now Ornan was threshing wheat. ²¹And as David came to Ornan, Ornan looked and saw David, and went out of the threshingfloor, and bowed himself to David with *his* face to the ground. ²²Then David said to Ornan, Grantᶠ me the place of *this* threshingfloor, that I may build an altar therein unto the LORD: thou shalt grant it me for the full price: that the plague may be stayed from the people. ²³And Ornan said unto David, Take *it* to thee, and let my lord the king do *that which is* good in his eyes: lo, I give *thee* the oxen *also* for burnt offerings, and the threshing instruments for wood, and the wheat for the

meat offering; I give it all. ²⁴And king David said to Ornan, Nay; but I will verily buy it for the full price: for I will not take *that* which *is* thine for the LORD, nor offer burnt offerings without cost. ²⁵So David gave to Ornan for the place six hundred shekels of gold by weight. ²⁶And David built there an altar unto the LORD, and offered burnt offerings and peace offerings, and called upon the LORD; and he answered him from heaven by fire upon the altar of burnt offering. ²⁷And the LORD commanded the angel; and he put up his sword again into the sheath thereof. ²⁸At that time when David saw that the LORD had answered him in the threshingfloor of Ornan the Jebusite, then he sacrificed there. ²⁹For the tabernacle of the LORD, which Moses made in the wilderness, and the altar of the burnt offering, *were* at that season in the high place at Gibeon. ³⁰But David could not go before it to enquire of God: for he was afraid because of the sword of the angel of the LORD.

22

¹Then David said, This *is* the house of the LORD God, and this *is* the altar of the burnt offering for Israel. ²And David commanded to gather together the strangers that *were* in the land of Israel; and he set masons to hew wrought stones to build the house of God. ³And David prepared iron in abundance for the nails for the doors of the gates, and for the joinings; and brass in abundance without weight; ⁴Also cedar trees in abundance: for the Zidonians and they of Tyre

---

ᵉ And Ornan . . . : or, When Ornan turned back and saw the angel, then he and his four sons with him hid themselves
ᶠ Grant: Heb. Give

brought much cedar wood to David. ⁵And David said, Solomon my son *is* young and tender, and the house *that is* to be builded for the LORD *must be* exceeding magnifical, of fame and of glory throughout all countries: I will *therefore* now make preparation for it. So David prepared abundantly before his death.

⁶Then he called for Solomon his son, and charged him to build an house for the LORD God of Israel. ⁷And David said to Solomon, My son, as for me, it was in my mind to build an house unto the name of the LORD my God: ⁸But the word of the LORD came to me, saying, Thou hast shed blood abundantly, and hast made great wars: thou shalt not build an house unto my name, because thou hast shed much blood upon the earth in my sight. ⁹Behold, a son shall be born to thee, who shall be a man of rest; and I will give him rest from all his enemies round about: for his name shall be Solomonª, and I will give peace and quietness unto Israel in his days. ¹⁰He shall build an house for my name; and he shall be my son, and I *will be* his father; and I will establish the throne of his kingdom over Israel for ever. ¹¹Now, my son, the LORD be with thee; and prosper thou, and build the house of the LORD thy God, as he hath said of thee. ¹²Only the LORD give thee wisdom and understanding, and give thee charge concerning Israel, that thou mayest keep the law of the LORD thy God. ¹³Then shalt thou prosper, if thou takest heed to fulfil the statutes and judgments which the LORD charged Moses with concerning Israel: be strong, and of good courage; dread not, nor be dismayed. ¹⁴Now, behold, in my troubleᵇ I have prepared for the house of the LORD an hundred thousand talents of gold, and a thousand thousand talents of silver; and of brass and iron without weight; for it is in abundance: timber also and stone have I prepared; and thou mayest add thereto. ¹⁵Moreover *there are* workmen with thee in abundance, hewers and workersᶜ of stone and timber, and all manner of cunning men for every manner of work. ¹⁶Of the gold, the silver, and the brass, and the iron, *there is* no number. Arise *therefore*, and be doing, and the LORD be with thee.

¹⁷David also commanded all the princes of Israel to help Solomon his son, *saying*, ¹⁸*Is* not the LORD your God with you? and hath he *not* given you rest on every side? for he hath given

---

Devotional Moment

Fatherly Counsel

22:11-12 David had a unique style for passing on wisdom to his son. When they were together, David described how he had prayed for Solomon and what God had told him. David also made it clear to Solomon that even though Solomon would be king, he would still be under God's authority. Solomon would succeed only as far as he remained obedient and responsive to the Lord. Later, when God gave Solomon the opportunity to choose his own divine gift, Solomon echoed his father's prayer and asked for wisdom. Take time to share with your children how you pray for them, and tell them what you ask God to do for them.

ª Solomon: that is, Peaceable
ᵇ trouble: or, poverty
ᶜ workers...: that is, masons and carpenters

Devotional Moment

•

Owned by . . .

22:19 David, like believing parents throughout history, wanted his son to honor God with his whole heart. He gave Solomon a very clear, measurable objective (moving the Ark and the other holy articles into the new Temple) that would show his obedience to God. As our children grow up, they will gradually leave the confines of our authority. Who will they obey once they leave home? As parents, we must point to God as our ultimate authority—the one who created and owns us.

the inhabitants of the land into mine hand; and the land is subdued before the LORD, and before his people. ¹⁹Now set your heart and your soul to seek the LORD your God; arise therefore, and build ye the sanctuary of the LORD God, to bring the ark of the covenant of the LORD, and the holy vessels of God, into the house that is to be built to the name of the LORD.

23

¹So when David was old and full of days, he made Solomon his son king over Israel. ²And he gathered together all the princes of Israel, with the priests and the Levites. ³Now the Levites were numbered from the age of thirty years and upward: and their number by their polls, man by man, was thirty and eight thousand. ⁴Of which, twenty and four thousand *were* to set forward the work of the house of the LORD; and six thousand *were* officers and judges: ⁵Moreover four thousand *were* porters; and four thousand praised the LORD with the instruments which I made, *said David,* to praise *therewith.* ⁶And David divided them into courses^a among the sons of Levi, *namely,* Gershon, Kohath, and Merari. ⁷Of the Gershonites *were,* Laadan^b, and Shimei. ⁸The sons of Laadan; the chief *was* Jehiel, and Zetham, and Joel, three. ⁹The sons of Shimei; Shelomith, and Haziel, and Haran, three. These *were* the chief of the fathers of Laadan. ¹⁰And the sons of Shimei *were,* Jahath, Zina^c, and Jeush, and Beriah. These four *were* the sons of Shimei. ¹¹And Jahath was the chief, and Zizah the second: but Jeush and Beriah had not many sons; therefore they were in one reckoning, according to *their* father's house. ¹²The sons of Kohath; Amram, Izhar, Hebron, and Uzziel, four. ¹³The sons of Amram; Aaron and Moses: and Aaron was separated, that he should sanctify the most holy things, he and his sons for ever, to burn incense before the LORD, to minister unto him, and to bless in his name for ever. ¹⁴Now *concerning* Moses the man of God, his sons were named of the tribe of Levi. ¹⁵The sons of Moses *were,* Gershom, and Eliezer. ¹⁶Of the sons of Gershom, Shebuel^d *was* the chief. ¹⁷And the sons of Eliezer *were,* Rehabiah the chief^e. And Eliezer had none other sons; but the sons of Rehabiah were very many. ¹⁸Of the sons of Izhar; Shelomith^f the chief. ¹⁹Of

---

^a courses: Heb. divisions
^b Laadan: or, Libni
^c Zina: or, Zizah
^d Shebuel: also called, Shubael
^e the chief: or, the first
^f Shelomith: also called, Shelomoth

the sons of Hebron; Jeriah the first, Amariah the second, Jahaziel the third, and Jekameam the fourth. ²⁰Of the sons of Uzziel; Michah the first, and Jesiah the second. ²¹The sons of Merari; Mahli, and Mushi. The sons of Mahli; Eleazar, and Kish. ²²And Eleazar died, and had no sons, but daughters: and their brethren^g the sons of Kish took them. ²³The sons of Mushi; Mahli, and Eder, and Jeremoth, three.

²⁴These *were* the sons of Levi after the house of their fathers; *even* the chief of the fathers, as they were counted by number of names by their polls, that did the work for the service of the house of the LORD, from the age of twenty years and upward. ²⁵For David said, The LORD God of Israel hath given rest unto his people, that they may dwell in Jerusalem for ever: ²⁶And also unto the Levites; they shall no *more* carry the tabernacle, nor any vessels of it for the service thereof. ²⁷For by the last words of David the Levites *were* numbered^h from twenty years old and above: ²⁸Because their office *was* to wait on the sons of Aaron for the service of the house of the LORD, in the courts, and in the chambers, and in the purifying of all holy things, and the work of the service of the house of God; ²⁹Both for the shewbread, and for the fine flour for meat offering, and for the unleavened cakes, and for *that which is baked in* the panⁱ, and for that which is fried, and for all manner of measure and size; ³⁰And to stand every morning to thank and praise the LORD, and likewise at even; ³¹And to offer all burnt sacrifices unto the LORD in the sabbaths, in the new moons, and on the set feasts, by number, according to the order commanded unto them, continually before the LORD: ³²And that they should keep the charge of the tabernacle of the congregation, and the charge of the holy *place*, and the charge of the sons of Aaron their brethren, in the service of the house of the LORD.

24

¹Now *these are* the divisions of the sons of Aaron. The sons of Aaron; Nadab, and Abihu, Eleazar, and Ithamar. ²But Nadab and Abihu died before their father, and had no children: therefore Eleazar and Ithamar executed the priest's office. ³And David distributed them, both Zadok of the sons of Eleazar, and Ahimelech of the sons of Ithamar, according to their offices in their service. ⁴And there were more chief men found of the sons of Eleazar than of the sons of Ithamar; and *thus* were they divided. Among the sons of Eleazar *there were* sixteen chief men of the house of *their* fathers, and eight among the sons of Ithamar according to the house of their fathers. ⁵Thus were they divided by lot, one sort with another; for the governors of the sanctuary, and governors *of the house* of God, were of the sons of Eleazar, and of the sons of Ithamar. ⁶And Shemaiah the son of Nethaneel the scribe, *one* of the Levites, wrote them before the king, and the princes, and Zadok the priest, and

---

^g brethren: or, kinsmen
^h numbered: Heb. number
ⁱ pan: or, flat plate

Ahimelech the son of Abiathar, and *before* the chief of the fathers of the priests and Levites: one principal[a] household being taken for Eleazar, and *one* taken for Ithamar. [7]Now the first lot came forth to Jehoiarib, the second to Jedaiah, [8]The third to Harim, the fourth to Seorim, [9]The fifth to Malchijah, the sixth to Mijamin, [10]The seventh to Hakkoz, the eighth to Abijah, [11]The ninth to Jeshua, the tenth to Shecaniah, [12]The eleventh to Eliashib, the twelfth to Jakim, [13]The thirteenth to Huppah, the fourteenth to Jeshebeab, [14]The fifteenth to Bilgah, the sixteenth to Immer, [15]The seventeenth to Hezir, the eighteenth to Aphses, [16]The nineteenth to Pethahiah, the twentieth to Jehezekel, [17]The one and twentieth to Jachin, the two and twentieth to Gamul, [18]The three and twentieth to Delaiah, the four and twentieth to Maaziah. [19]These *were* the orderings of them in their service to come into the house of the LORD, according to their manner, under Aaron their father, as the LORD God of Israel had commanded him.

[20]And the rest of the sons of Levi *were these*: Of the sons of Amram; Shubael[b]: of the sons of Shubael; Jehdeiah. [21]Concerning Rehabiah: of the sons of Rehabiah, the first *was* Isshiah. [22]Of the Izharites; Shelomoth[c]: of the sons of Shelomoth; Jahath. [23]And the sons *of Hebron*; Jeriah *the first*, Amariah the second, Jahaziel the third, Jekameam the fourth. [24]*Of* the sons of Uzziel; Michah: of the sons of Michah; Shamir. [25]The brother of Michah *was*

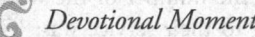

Devotional Moment
•
All Together Now

24:31; 25:8; 26:13 In David's preparation for Temple worship, large groups were trained to perform certain functions: priestly duties, singing, guarding the Temple. But these duties were all delegated without preferential treatment. In smoothly run families, many important duties—some call them chores—have to be done. Teach your children how to do all the family chores. Then everyone in the family can contribute to the best of his or her ability.

Isshiah: of the sons of Isshiah; Zechariah. [26]The sons of Merari *were* Mahli and Mushi: the sons of Jaaziah; Beno. [27]The sons of Merari by Jaaziah; Beno, and Shoham, and Zaccur, and Ibri. [28]Of Mahli *came* Eleazar, who had no sons. [29]Concerning Kish: the son of Kish *was* Jerahmeel. [30]The sons also of Mushi; Mahli, and Eder, and Jerimoth. These *were* the sons of the Levites after the house of their fathers. [31]These likewise cast lots over against their brethren the sons of Aaron in the presence of David the king, and Zadok, and Ahimelech, and the chief of the fathers of the priests and Levites, even the principal fathers over against their younger brethren.

25

[1]Moreover David and the captains of the host separated to the service of the sons of Asaph, and of Heman, and of Jeduthun, who should prophesy with harps, with psalteries, and with cym-

---

[a] principal . . . : Heb. house of the father
[b] Shubael: also called, Shebuel
[c] Shelomoth: also called, Shelomith

bals: and the number of the workmen according to their service was: ²Of the sons of Asaph; Zaccur, and Joseph, and Nethaniah, and Asarelahª, the sons of Asaph under the hands of Asaph, which prophesied according to the order of the king. ³Of Jeduthun: the sons of Jeduthun; Gedaliah, and Zeriᵇ, and Jeshaiah, Hashabiah, and Mattithiah, six, under the hands of their father Jeduthun, who prophesied with a harp, to give thanks and to praise the LORD. ⁴Of Heman: the sons of Heman; Bukkiah, Mattaniah, Uzzielᶜ, Shebuel, and Jerimoth, Hananiah, Hanani, Eliathah, Giddalti, and Romamtiezer, Joshbekashah, Mallothi, Hothir, *and* Mahazioth: ⁵All these *were* the sons of Heman the king's seer in the wordsᵈ of God, to lift up the horn. And God gave to Heman fourteen sons and three daughters. ⁶All these *were* under the hands of their father for song *in* the house of the LORD, with cymbals, psalteries, and harps, for the service of the house of God, according to the king's order to Asaph, Jeduthun, and Heman. ⁷So the number of them, with their brethren that were instructed in the songs of the LORD, *even* all that were cunning, was two hundred fourscore and eight.

⁸And they cast lots, ward against *ward*, as well the small as the great, the teacher as the scholar. ⁹Now the first lot came forth for Asaph to Joseph: the second to Gedaliah, who with his brethren and sons *were* twelve: ¹⁰The third to Zaccur, he, his sons, and his brethren, *were* twelve: ¹¹The fourth to Izri, *he*, his sons, and his brethren, *were* twelve: ¹²The fifth to Nethaniah, *he*, his sons, and his brethren, *were* twelve: ¹³The sixth to Bukkiah, *he*, his sons, and his brethren, *were* twelve: ¹⁴The seventh to Jesharelah, *he*, his sons, and his brethren, *were* twelve: ¹⁵The eighth to Jeshaiah, *he*, his sons, and his brethren, *were* twelve: ¹⁶The ninth to Mattaniah, *he*, his sons, and his brethren, *were* twelve: ¹⁷The tenth to Shimei, *he*, his sons, and his brethren, *were* twelve: ¹⁸The eleventh to Azareel, *he*, his sons, and his brethren, *were* twelve: ¹⁹The twelfth to Hashabiah, *he*, his sons, and his brethren, *were* twelve: ²⁰The thirteenth to Shubael, *he*, his sons, and his brethren, *were* twelve: ²¹The fourteenth to Mattithiah, *he*, his sons, and his brethren, *were* twelve: ²²The fifteenth to Jeremoth, *he*, his sons, and his brethren, *were* twelve: ²³The sixteenth to Hananiah, *he*, his sons, and his brethren, *were* twelve: ²⁴The seventeenth to Joshbekashah, *he*, his sons, and his brethren, *were* twelve: ²⁵The eighteenth to Hanani, *he*, his sons, and his brethren, *were* twelve: ²⁶The nineteenth to Mallothi, *he*, his sons, and his brethren, *were* twelve: ²⁷The twentieth to Eliathah, *he*, his sons, and his brethren, *were* twelve: ²⁸The one and twentieth to Hothir, *he*, his sons, and his brethren, *were* twelve: ²⁹The two and twentieth to Giddalti, *he*, his sons, and his brethren, *were* twelve: ³⁰The three and twentieth

---

ª Asarelah: otherwise called Jesharelah
ᵇ Zeri: or, Izri
ᶜ Uzziel: also called, Azareel
ᵈ words: or, matters

to Mahazioth, *he*, his sons, and his brethren, *were* twelve: [31]The four and twentieth to Romamtiezer, *he*, his sons, and his brethren, *were* twelve.

26

[1]Concerning the divisions of the porters: Of the Korhites *was* Meshelemiah[a] the son of Kore, of the sons of Asaph. [2]And the sons of Meshelemiah *were*, Zechariah the firstborn, Jediael the second, Zebadiah the third, Jathniel the fourth, [3]Elam the fifth, Jehohanan the sixth, Elioenai the seventh. [4]Moreover the sons of Obededom *were*, Shemaiah the firstborn, Jehozabad the second, Joah the third, and Sacar the fourth, and Nethaneel the fifth, [5]Ammiel the sixth, Issachar the seventh, Peulthai the eighth: for God blessed him[b]. [6]Also unto Shemaiah his son were sons born, that ruled throughout the house of their father: for they *were* mighty men of valour. [7]The sons of Shemaiah; Othni, and Rephael, and Obed, Elzabad, whose brethren *were* strong men, Elihu, and Semachiah. [8]All these of the sons of Obededom: they and their sons and their brethren, able men for strength for the service, *were* threescore and two of Obededom. [9]And Meshelemiah had sons and brethren, strong men, eighteen. [10]Also Hosah, of the children of Merari, had sons; Simri the chief, (for *though* he was not the firstborn, yet his father made him the chief;) [11]Hilkiah the second, Tebaliah the third, Zechariah the fourth: all the sons and brethren of Hosah *were* thirteen. [12]Among these *were* the divisions of the porters, *even* among the chief men, *having* wards one against another, to minister in the house of the LORD. [13]And they cast lots, as well the small as the great, according to the house of their fathers, for every gate. [14]And the lot eastward fell to Shelemiah[c]. Then for Zechariah his son, a wise counsellor, they cast lots; and his lot came out northward. [15]To Obededom southward; and to his sons the house of Asuppim[d]. [16]To Shuppim and Hosah *the lot came forth* westward, with the gate Shallecheth, by the causeway of the going up, ward against ward. [17]Eastward *were* six Levites, northward four a day, southward four a day, and toward Asuppim two *and* two. [18]At Parbar westward, four at the causeway, *and* two at Parbar. [19]These *are* the divisions of the porters among the sons of Kore, and among the sons of Merari.

[20]And of the Levites, Ahijah *was* over the treasures of the house of God, and over the treasures of the dedicated things. [21]*As concerning* the sons of Laadan[e]; the sons of the Gershonite Laadan, chief fathers, *even* of Laadan the Gershonite, *were* Jehieli. [22]The sons of Jehieli; Zetham, and Joel his brother, *which were* over the treasures of the house of the LORD. [23]Of the Amramites, *and* the Izharites, the Hebronites, *and* the Uzzielites: [24]And She-

---

[a] Meshelemiah: also called, Shelemiah
[b] him: that is, Obededom
[c] Shelemiah: also called Meshelemiah
[d] Asuppim: Heb. gatherings
[e] Laadan: also called, Libni

buel the son of Gershom, the son of Moses, *was* ruler of the treasures. [25]And his brethren by Eliezer; Rehabiah his son, and Jeshaiah his son, and Joram his son, and Zichri his son, and Shelomith his son. [26]Which Shelomith and his brethren *were* over all the treasures of the dedicated things, which David the king, and the chief fathers, the captains over thousands and hundreds, and the captains of the host, had dedicated. [27]Out of the spoils[f] won in battles did they dedicate to maintain the house of the LORD. [28]And all that Samuel the seer, and Saul the son of Kish, and Abner the son of Ner, and Joab the son of Zeruiah, had dedicated; *and* whosoever had dedicated *any thing, it was* under the hand of Shelomith, and of his brethren.

[29]Of the Izharites, Chenaniah and his sons *were* for the outward business over Israel, for officers and judges. [30]*And* of the Hebronites, Hashabiah and his brethren, men of valour, a thousand and seven hundred, *were* officers[g] among them of Israel on this side Jordan westward in all the business of the LORD, and in the service of the king. [31]Among the Hebronites *was* Jerijah the chief, *even* among the Hebronites, according to the generations of his fathers. In the fortieth year of the reign of David they were sought for, and there were found among them mighty men of valour at Jazer of Gilead. [32]And his brethren, men of valour, *were* two thou-sand and seven hundred chief fathers, whom king David made rulers over the Reubenites, the Gadites, and the half tribe of Manasseh, for every matter pertaining to God, and affairs[h] of the king.

27

[1]Now the children of Israel after their number, *to wit,* the chief fathers and captains of thousands and hundreds, and their officers that served the king in any matter of the courses, which came in and went out month by month throughout all the months of the year, of every course *were* twenty and four thousand. [2]Over the first course for the first month *was* Jashobeam the son of Zabdiel: and in his course *were* twenty and four thousand. [3]Of the children of Perez *was* the chief of all the captains of the host for the first month. [4]And over the course of the second month *was* Dodai[a] an Ahohite, and of his course *was* Mikloth also the ruler: in his course likewise *were* twenty and four thousand. [5]The third captain of the host for the third month *was* Benaiah the son of Jehoiada, a chief[b] priest: and in his course *were* twenty and four thousand. [6]This *is that* Benaiah, *who was* mighty *among* the thirty, and above the thirty: and in his course *was* Ammizabad his son. [7]The fourth *captain* for the fourth month *was* Asahel the brother of Joab, and Zebadiah his son after him: and in his course *were* twenty and four thou-sand. [8]The fifth captain for the fifth

---

[f] spoils . . . : Heb. battles and spoils
[g] officers . . . : Heb. over the charge
[h] affairs: Heb. thing
[a] Dodai: also called, Dodo
[b] chief . . . : or, principal officer

month *was* Shamhuth the Izrahite: and in his course *were* twenty and four thousand. ⁹The sixth *captain* for the sixth month *was* Ira the son of Ikkesh the Tekoite: and in his course *were* twenty and four thousand. ¹⁰The seventh *captain* for the seventh month *was* Helez the Pelonite, of the children of Ephraim: and in his course *were* twenty and four thousand. ¹¹The eighth *captain* for the eighth month *was* Sibbecai the Hushathite, of the Zarhites: and in his course *were* twenty and four thousand. ¹²The ninth *captain* for the ninth month *was* Abiezer the Anetothite, of the Benjamites: and in his course *were* twenty and four thousand. ¹³The tenth *captain* for the tenth month *was* Maharai the Netophathite, of the Zarhites: and in his course *were* twenty and four thousand. ¹⁴The eleventh *captain* for the eleventh month *was* Benaiah the Pirathonite, of the children of Ephraim: and in his course *were* twenty and four thousand. ¹⁵The twelfth *captain* for the twelfth month *was* Heldai ͨ the Netophathite, of Othniel: and in his course *were* twenty and four thousand.

¹⁶Furthermore over the tribes of Israel: the ruler of the Reubenites *was* Eliezer the son of Zichri: of the Simeonites, Shephatiah the son of Maachah: ¹⁷Of the Levites, Hashabiah the son of Kemuel: of the Aaronites, Zadok: ¹⁸Of Judah, Elihu ͩ , *one* of the brethren of David: of Issachar, Omri the son of Michael: ¹⁹Of Zebulun, Ishmaiah the son of Obadiah: of Naphtali, Jerimoth the son of Azriel: ²⁰Of the children of Ephraim, Hoshea the son of Azaziah: of the half tribe of Manasseh, Joel the son of Pedaiah: ²¹Of the half *tribe* of Manasseh in Gilead, Iddo the son of Zechariah: of Benjamin, Jaasiel the son of Abner: ²²Of Dan, Azareel the son of Jeroham. These *were* the princes of the tribes of Israel. ²³But David took not the number of them from twenty years old and under: because the LORD had said he would increase Israel like to the stars of the heavens. ²⁴Joab the son of Zeruiah began to number, but he finished not, because there fell wrath for it against Israel; neither was the number put in the account of the chronicles of king David. ²⁵And over the king's treasures *was* Azmaveth the son of Adiel: and over the storehouses in the fields, in the cities, and in the villages, and in the castles, *was* Jehonathan the son of Uzziah: ²⁶And over them that did the work of the field for tillage of the ground *was* Ezri the son of Chelub: ²⁷And over the vineyards *was* Shimei the Ramathite: over the increase of the vineyards for the wine cellars *was* Zabdi the Shiphmite: ²⁸And over the olive trees and the sycomore trees that *were* in the low plains *was* Baalhanan the Gederite: and over the cellars of oil *was* Joash: ²⁹And over the herds that fed in Sharon *was* Shitrai the Sharonite: and over the herds *that* were in the valleys *was* Shaphat the son of Adlai: ³⁰Over the camels also *was* Obil the Ishmaelite: and over the asses *was* Jehdeiah the Meronothite: ³¹And over the flocks *was* Jaziz the Hagerite. All these *were* the rulers of the substance which *was* king David's. ³²Also Jonathan David's uncle was a counsellor, a wise

---

ͨ Heldai: also called, Heled
ͩ Elihu: also called, Eliab

Devotional Moment

•

Education

27:32 David's sons had two instructors: Jonathan, David's uncle, and a man named Jehiel, their tutor. David's children received the benefits of an older generation's wisdom and the attention of a teacher who was probably closer to their own age. While there is much you can teach your children yourself, wise parents also enlist the help of others. Provide other adult role models for your children, and don't be jealous of the influence they can have in your kids' lives.

man, and a scribe ^e: and Jehiel the son of Hachmoni *was* with the king's sons: ³³And Ahithophel *was* the king's counsellor: and Hushai the Archite *was* the king's companion: ³⁴And after Ahithophel *was* Jehoiada the son of Benaiah, and Abiathar: and the general of the king's army *was* Joab.

28

¹And David assembled all the princes of Israel, the princes of the tribes, and the captains of the companies that ministered to the king by course, and the captains over the thousands, and captains over the hundreds, and the stewards over all the substance and possession^a of the king, and of his sons, with the officers, and with the mighty men, and with all the valiant men, unto Jerusalem. ²Then David the king stood up upon his feet, and said, Hear me, my brethren, and my people: *As for me,* I *had* in mine heart to build an house of

rest for the ark of the covenant of the LORD, and for the footstool of our God, and had made ready for the building: ³But God said unto me, Thou shalt not build an house for my name, because thou *hast been* a man of war, and hast shed blood^b. ⁴Howbeit the LORD God of Israel chose me before all the house of my father to be king over Israel for ever: for he hath chosen Judah *to be* the ruler; and of the house of Judah, the house of my father; and among the sons of my father he liked me to make *me* king over all Israel: ⁵And of all my sons, (for the LORD hath given me many sons,) he hath chosen Solomon my son to sit upon the throne of the kingdom of the LORD over Israel. ⁶And he said unto me, Solomon thy son, he shall build my house and my courts: for I have chosen him *to be* my son, and I will be his father. ⁷Moreover I will establish his kingdom for ever, if he be constant^c to do my commandments and my judg-

Devotional Moment

•

Challenge

28:8-10 As the king, David had the responsibility of choosing the next king. As a father, he challenged his son Solomon to get to know God and serve him always. Of the many lessons we can teach our children in preparation for adulthood, none matters quite as much as the challenge to get to know "the God of thy father" (v. 9). In preparing children for adult life, don't only educate them and acquaint them with the social graces. Challenge them daily to get to know God and to serve him.

---

^e scribe: or, secretary

^a possession: or, cattle

^b blood: Heb. bloods

^c constant: Heb. strong

ments, as at this day. ⁸Now therefore in the sight of all Israel the congregation of the LORD, and in the audience of our God, keep and seek for all the commandments of the LORD your God: that ye may possess this good land, and leave *it* for an inheritance for your children after you for ever. ⁹And thou, Solomon my son, know thou the God of thy father, and serve him with a perfect heart and with a willing mind: for the LORD searcheth all hearts, and understandeth all the imaginations of the thoughts: if thou seek him, he will be found of thee; but if thou forsake him, he will cast thee off for ever. ¹⁰Take heed now; for the LORD hath chosen thee to build an house for the sanctuary: be strong, and do *it*.

¹¹Then David gave to Solomon his son the pattern of the porch, and of the houses thereof, and of the treasuries thereof, and of the upper chambers thereof, and of the inner parlours thereof, and of the place of the mercy seat, ¹²And the pattern of all that he had by the spirit, of the courts of the house of the LORD, and of all the chambers round about, of the treasuries of the house of God, and of the treasuries of the dedicated things: ¹³Also for the courses of the priests and the Levites, and for all the work of the service of the house of the LORD, and for all the vessels of service in the house of the LORD. ¹⁴*He gave* of gold by weight for *things* of gold, for all instruments of all manner of service; *silver also* for all instruments of silver by weight, for all instruments of every kind of service: ¹⁵Even the weight for the candlesticks of gold, and for their lamps of gold, by weight for every candlestick, and for

the lamps thereof: and for the candlesticks of silver by weight, *both* for the candlestick, and *also* for the lamps thereof, according to the use of every candlestick. ¹⁶And by weight *he gave* gold for the tables of shewbread, for every table; and *likewise* silver for the tables of silver: ¹⁷Also pure gold for the fleshhooks, and the bowls, and the cups: and for the golden basons *he gave gold* by weight for every bason; and *likewise silver* by weight for every bason of silver: ¹⁸And for the altar of incense refined gold by weight; and gold for the pattern of the chariot of the cherubims, that spread out *their wings*, and covered the ark of the covenant of the LORD. ¹⁹All *this, said David*, the LORD made me understand in writing by *his* hand upon me, *even* all the works of this pattern. ²⁰And David said to Solomon his son, Be strong and of good courage, and do *it*: fear not, nor be dismayed: for the LORD God, *even* my God, *will be* with thee; he will not fail thee, nor forsake thee, until thou hast finished all the work for the service of the house of the LORD. ²¹And, behold, the courses of the priests and the Levites, *even they shall be with thee* for all the service of the house of God: and *there shall be* with thee for all manner of workmanship every willing skilful man, for any manner of service: also the princes and all the people *will be* wholly at thy commandment.

29

¹Furthermore David the king said unto all the congregation, Solomon my son, whom alone God hath chosen, *is yet* young and tender, and the work *is* great: for the palace *is* not for man, but

for the LORD God. ²Now I have prepared with all my might for the house of my God the gold for *things to be made* of gold, and the silver for *things* of silver, and the brass for *things* of brass, the iron for *things* of iron, and wood for *things* of wood; onyx stones, and *stones* to be set, glistering stones, and of divers colours, and all manner of precious stones, and marble stones in abundance. ³Moreover, because I have set my affection to the house of my God, I have of mine own proper good, of gold and silver, *which* I have given to the house of my God, over and above all that I have prepared for the holy house, ⁴*Even* three thousand talents of gold, of the gold of Ophir, and seven thousand talents of refined silver, to overlay the walls of the houses *withal:* ⁵The gold for *things* of gold, and the silver for *things* of silver, and for all manner of work *to be made* by the hands of artificers. And who *then* is willing to consecrate his serviceᵃ this day unto the LORD? ⁶Then the chief of the fathers and princes of the tribes of Israel, and the captains of thousands and of hundreds, with the rulers of the king's work, offered willingly, ⁷And gave for the service of the house of God of gold five thousand talents and ten thousand drams, and of silver ten thousand talents, and of brass eighteen thousand talents, and one hundred thousand talents of iron. ⁸And they with whom *precious* stones were found gave *them* to the treasure of the house of the LORD, by the hand of Je-

hiel the Gershonite. ⁹Then the people rejoiced, for that they offered willingly, because with perfect heart they offered willingly to the LORD: and David the king also rejoiced with great joy.

¹⁰Wherefore David blessed the LORD before all the congregation: and David said, Blessed *be* thou, LORD God of Israel our father, for ever and ever. ¹¹Thine, O LORD, *is* the greatness, and the power, and the glory, and the victory, and the majesty: for all *that is* in the heaven and in the earth *is thine*; thine *is* the kingdom, O LORD, and thou art exalted as head above all. ¹²Both riches and honour *come* of thee, and thou reignest over all; and in thine hand *is* power and might; and in thine hand *it is* to make great, and to give strength unto all. ¹³Now therefore, our God, we thank thee, and praise thy glorious name. ¹⁴But who *am* I, and what *is* my people, that we should be ableᵇ to offer so willingly after this sort? for all things *come* of thee, and of thine own have we given thee. ¹⁵For we *are* strangers before thee, and sojourners, as *were* all our fathers: our days on the earth *are* as a shadow, and *there is* none abidingᶜ. ¹⁶O LORD our God, all this store that we have prepared to build thee an house for thine holy name *cometh* of thine hand, and *is* all thine own. ¹⁷I know also, my God, that thou triest the heart, and hast pleasure in uprightness. As for me, in the uprightness of mine heart I have willingly offered all these things: and now have I seen with joy thy people, which are presentᵈ here,

---

ᵃ consecrate his service: Heb. fill his hand
ᵇ be able: Heb. retain, or, obtain strength
ᶜ abiding: Heb. expectation
ᵈ present: Heb. found

---

to offer willingly unto thee. ¹⁸O LORD God of Abraham, Isaac, and of Israel, our fathers, keep this for ever in the imagination of the thoughts of the heart of thy people, and prepareᵉ their heart unto thee: ¹⁹And give unto Solomon my son a perfect heart, to keep thy commandments, thy testimonies, and thy statutes, and to do all *these things*, and to build the palace, *for* the which I have made provision. ²⁰And David said to all the congregation, Now bless the LORD your God. And all the congregation blessed the LORD God of their fathers, and bowed down their heads, and worshipped the LORD, and the king. ²¹And they sacrificed sacrifices unto the LORD, and offered burnt offerings unto the LORD, on the morrow after that day, *even* a thousand bullocks, a thousand rams, *and* a thousand lambs, with their drink offer-

ings, and sacrifices in abundance for all Israel: ²²And did eat and drink before the LORD on that day with great gladness. And they made Solomon the son of David king the second time, and anointed *him* unto the LORD *to be* the chief governor, and Zadok *to be* priest.

²³Then Solomon sat on the throne of the LORD as king instead of David his father, and prospered; and all Israel obeyed him. ²⁴And all the princes, and the mighty men, and all the sons likewise of king David, submitted themselves unto Solomon the king. ²⁵And the LORD magnified Solomon exceedingly in the sight of all Israel, and bestowed upon him *such* royal majesty as had not been on any king before him in Israel. ²⁶Thus David the son of Jesse reigned over all Israel. ²⁷And the time that he reigned over Israel *was* forty years; seven years reigned he in Hebron, and thirty and three *years* reigned he in Jerusalem. ²⁸And he died in a good old age, full of days, riches, and honour: and Solomon his son reigned in his stead. ²⁹Now the acts of David the king, first and last, behold, they *are* written in the bookᶠ of Samuel the seer, and in the book of Nathan the prophet, and in the book of Gad the seer, ³⁰With all his reign and his might, and the times that went over him, and over Israel, and over all the kingdoms of the countries.

ᵉ prepare: or, stablish
ᶠ book: or, history: Heb. words

SECOND CHRONICLES

Purpose
To unify the nation around true worship of Jehovah by showing his standard for judging kings

Author
Ezra, according to Jewish tradition

To Whom Written
All Israel

Date Written
Approximately 430 B.C.; recording events from 970 B.C.–586 B.C.

Setting
Second Chronicles parallels 1 and 2 Kings and serves as their commentary. It was written after the exile from a priestly perspective, highlighting the importance of the Temple and religious revivals in Judah.

Key Verse
"If my people . . . shall humble themselves, and pray, and seek my face, and turn from their wicked ways; then will I hear from heaven, and will forgive their sin, and will heal their land" (7:14).

Key People
Solomon, the queen of Sheba, Rehoboam, Asa, Jehoshaphat, Jehoram, Joash, Uzziah, Ahaz, Hezekiah, Manasseh, Josiah

Key Places
Jerusalem, the Temple

If you skip reading 2 Chronicles because it repeats the stories of 2 Kings, ask: How many times have you played your favorite CD or videotape over and over until you know the lines by heart? Most of us know someone between the ages of seven and fourteen (and sometimes older) who can tell you exactly what Spock will do in the next scene, what Biff will say, or what quirky deed of heroism Luke is about to perform. Seeing a good movie again and again is so common that many people have more videos in their library than books—and more knowledge of Hollywood literature than any other genre.

Getting a story twice, from two different angles, can be a very good thing. In the case of 2 Chronicles, a second time through the stories of God's work in Israel—the people's blindness and rebellion, the good kings who recovered true worship, the bad guys who blew it, the struggles and the miracles—helps set the stage for the really good news (God's amazing breakthrough) coming later on.

Good stories twice told can be a way of remembering the past and setting the course for the future. Perhaps the God who led Solomon, Joash, Jotham, Hezekiah, and Josiah will surprise you, too, with prosperity, courage, and happiness. Read with an eye toward action!

1

¹And Solomon the son of David was strengthened in his kingdom, and the LORD his God *was* with him, and magnified him exceedingly. ²Then Solomon spake unto all Israel, to the captains of thousands and of hundreds, and to the judges, and to every governor in all Israel, the chief of the fathers. ³So Solomon, and all the congregation with him, went to the high place that *was* at Gibeon; for there was the tabernacle of the congregation of God, which Moses the servant of the LORD had made in the wilderness. ⁴But the ark of God had David brought up from Kirjathjearim to *the place which* David had prepared for it: for he had pitched a tent for it at Jerusalem. ⁵Moreover the brasen altar, that Bezaleel the son of Uri, the son of Hur, had made, he putᵃ before the tabernacle of the LORD: and Solomon and the congregation sought unto it. ⁶And Solomon went up thither to the brasen altar before the LORD, which *was* at the tabernacle of the congregation, and offered a thousand burnt offerings upon it. ⁷In that night did God appear unto Solomon, and said unto him, Ask what I shall give thee. ⁸And Solomon said unto God, Thou hast shewed great mercy unto David my father, and hast made me to reign in his stead. ⁹Now, O LORD God, let thy promise unto David my father be established: for thou hast made me king over a people like the dust of the earth in multitude. ¹⁰Give me now wisdom and knowledge, that I may go out and come in before this people: for who can judge this thy

---

Devotional Moment
•
Too Hard

1:7-12 Solomon was a young and inexperienced king charged with the responsibility of ruling an entire nation. So when God invited him to ask for anything he wanted, he asked for wisdom. Many of the responsibilities that go with leading a family (a group considerably smaller than a nation) can be intimidating. Solomon was not a perfect king, and none of us can be perfect at leading a family. You will make mistakes. God wants to guide us through the process; all we need to do is ask him to lead the way (see James 1:5).

---

people, *that is so* great? ¹¹And God said to Solomon, Because this was in thine heart, and thou hast not asked riches, wealth, or honour, nor the life of thine enemies, neither yet hast asked long life; but hast asked wisdom and knowledge for thyself, that thou mayest judge my people, over whom I have made thee king: ¹²Wisdom and knowledge *is* granted unto thee; and I will give thee riches, and wealth, and honour, such as none of the kings have had that *have been* before thee, neither shall there any after thee have the like.

¹³Then Solomon came *from his journey* to the high place that *was* at Gibeon to Jerusalem, from before the tabernacle of the congregation, and reigned over Israel. ¹⁴And Solomon gathered chariots and horsemen: and he had a thousand and four hundred chariots, and twelve thousand horsemen, which he placed in the chariot cities, and with the king at Jerusalem. ¹⁵And the king madeᵇ silver and gold at

---

ᵃ he put: or, was there

ᵇ made: Heb. gave

Jerusalem *as plenteous* as stones, and cedar trees made he as the sycamore trees that *are* in the vale for abundance. [16]And Solomon[c] had horses brought out of Egypt, and linen yarn: the king's merchants received the linen yarn at a price. [17]And they fetched up, and brought forth out of Egypt a chariot for six hundred *shekels* of silver, and an horse for an hundred and fifty: and so brought they out *horses* for all the kings of the Hittites, and for the kings of Syria, by their means[d].

2

[1]And Solomon determined to build an house for the name of the LORD, and an house for his kingdom. [2]And Solomon told out threescore and ten thousand men to bear burdens, and fourscore thousand to hew in the mountain, and three thousand and six hundred to oversee them. [3]And Solomon sent to Huram[a] the king of Tyre, saying, As thou didst deal with David my father, and didst send him cedars to build him an house to dwell therein, *even so deal with me.* [4]Behold, I build an house to the name of the LORD my God, to dedicate *it* to him, *and* to burn before him sweet[b] incense, and for the continual shewbread, and for the burnt offerings morning and evening, on the sabbaths, and on the new moons, and on the solemn feasts of the LORD our God. This *is an ordinance* for ever to Israel. [5]And the house which I build *is* great: for great *is* our God above all gods. [6]But who is able[c] to build him an house, seeing the heaven and heaven of heavens cannot contain him? who *am* I then, that I should build him an house, save only to burn sacrifice before him? [7]Send me now therefore a man cunning to work in gold, and in silver, and in brass, and in iron, and in purple, and crimson, and blue, and that can skill to grave[d] with the cunning men that *are* with me in Judah and in Jerusalem, whom David my father did provide. [8]Send me also cedar trees, fir trees, and algum trees, out of Lebanon: for I know that thy servants can skill to cut timber in Lebanon; and, behold, my servants *shall be* with thy servants, [9]Even to prepare me timber in abundance: for the house which I am about to build *shall be* wonderful[c] great. [10]And, behold, I will give to thy servants, the hewers that cut timber, twenty thousand measures of beaten wheat, and twenty thousand measures of barley, and twenty thousand baths of wine, and twenty thousand baths of oil.

[11]Then Huram the king of Tyre answered in writing, which he sent to Solomon, Because the LORD hath loved his people, he hath made thee king over them. [12]Huram said more-

---

[c] Solomon . . . : Heb. the going forth of the horses which was Solomon's
[d] means: Heb. hand
[a] Huram: or, Hiram
[b] sweet . . . : Heb. incense of spices
[c] is able: Heb. hath retained, or, obtained strength
[d] to grave: Heb. to grave gravings
[e] wonderful . . . : Heb. great and wonderful

Devotional Moment

I Need You

2:13-14 Solomon was wise, but that didn't mean he could build a temple by himself. He got the right people to help. God did not create us to do everything on our own—he designed us to rely on each other. Lean on your spouse's strengths; rather than disparaging your differences, see them as God's way of shoring up your weaknesses. If you are single, rely on help from relatives who have skills you don't have. And as a married or single parent, ask your children to help you as their skills and abilities develop.

over, Blessed *be* the LORD God of Israel, that made heaven and earth, who hath given to David the king a wise son, endued[f] with prudence and understanding, that might build an house for the LORD, and an house for his kingdom. [13]And now I have sent a cunning man, endued with understanding, of Huram my father's, [14]The son of a woman of the daughters of Dan, and his father *was* a man of Tyre, skilful to work in gold, and in silver, in brass, in iron, in stone, and in timber, in purple, in blue, and in fine linen, and in crimson; also to grave any manner of graving, and to find out every device which shall be put to him, with thy cunning men, and with the cunning men of my lord David thy father. [15]Now therefore the wheat, and the barley, the oil, and the wine, which my lord hath spoken of, let him send unto his servants: [16]And we will cut wood out of Lebanon, as much as thou shalt need: and we will bring it to thee in floats by sea to Joppa; and thou shalt carry it up to Jerusalem. [17]And Solomon numbered all the strangers[g] that *were* in the land of Israel, after the numbering wherewith David his father had numbered them; and they were found an hundred and fifty thousand and three thousand and six hundred. [18]And he set threescore and ten thousand of them *to be* bearers of burdens, and fourscore thousand *to be* hewers in the mountain, and three thousand and six hundred overseers to set the people a work.

3

[1]Then Solomon began to build the house of the LORD at Jerusalem in mount Moriah, where *the LORD* appeared[a] unto David his father, in the place that David had prepared in the threshingfloor of Ornan the Jebusite. [2]And he began to build in the second *day* of the second month, in the fourth year of his reign. [3]Now these *are the things wherein* Solomon was instructed[b] for the building of the house of God. The length by cubits after the first measure *was* threescore cubits, and the breadth twenty cubits. [4]And the porch that *was* in the front *of the house*, the length *of it was* according to the breadth of the house, twenty cubits, and the height *was* an hundred and twenty: and he overlaid it within with pure gold. [5]And the greater house he cieled with fir tree, which he overlaid

---

[f] endued . . . : Heb. knowing prudence and understanding
[g] the strangers: Heb. the men the strangers
[a] where . . . : or, which was seen of David his father
[b] instructed: Heb. founded

with fine gold, and set thereon palm trees and chains. ⁶And he garnished^c the house with precious stones for beauty: and the gold *was* gold of Parvaim. ⁷He overlaid also the house, the beams, the posts, and the walls thereof, and the doors thereof, with gold; and graved cherubims on the walls. ⁸And he made the most holy house, the length whereof *was* according to the breadth of the house, twenty cubits, and the breadth thereof twenty cubits: and he overlaid it with fine gold, *amounting* to six hundred talents. ⁹And the weight of the nails *was* fifty shekels of gold. And he overlaid the upper chambers with gold.

¹⁰And in the most holy house he made two cherubims of image^d work, and overlaid them with gold. ¹¹And the wings of the cherubims *were* twenty cubits long: one wing *of the one cherub was* five cubits, reaching to the wall of the house: and the other wing *was likewise* five cubits, reaching to the wing of the other cherub. ¹²And *one* wing of the other cherub *was* five cubits, reaching to the wall of the house: and the other wing *was* five cubits *also*, joining to the wing of the other cherub. ¹³The wings of these cherubims spread themselves forth twenty cubits: and they stood on their feet, and their faces *were* inward^e. ¹⁴And he made the vail *of* blue, and purple, and crimson, and fine linen, and wrought^f cherubims thereon. ¹⁵Also

he made before the house two pillars of thirty and five cubits high^g, and the chapiter that *was* on the top of each of them *was* five cubits. ¹⁶And he made chains, *as* in the oracle, and put *them* on the heads of the pillars; and made an hundred pomegranates, and put *them* on the chains. ¹⁷And he reared up the pillars before the temple, one on the right hand, and the other on the left; and called the name of that on the right hand Jachin^h, and the name of that on the left Boaz.

4

¹Moreover he made an altar of brass, twenty cubits the length thereof, and twenty cubits the breadth thereof, and ten cubits the height thereof. ²Also he made a molten sea of ten cubits from brim to brim, round in compass, and five cubits the height thereof; and a line of thirty cubits did compass it round about. ³And under it *was* the similitude of oxen, which did compass it round about: ten in a cubit, compassing the sea round about. Two rows of oxen *were* cast, when it was cast. ⁴It stood upon twelve oxen, three looking toward the north, and three looking toward the west, and three looking toward the south, and three looking toward the east: and the sea *was set* above upon them, and all their hinder parts *were* inward. ⁵And the thickness of it *was* an handbreadth, and the brim of it like the work of the brim of a cup, with flow-

---

^c garnished: Heb. covered
^d image . . . : or, (as some think) of moveable work
^e inward: or, toward the house
^f wrought: Heb. caused to ascend
^g high: Heb. long
^h Jachin: that is, He shall establish

ers[a] of lilies; *and* it received and held three thousand baths. [6]He made also ten lavers, and put five on the right hand, and five on the left, to wash in them: such things as they offered for the burnt offering they washed in them; but the sea *was* for the priests to wash in. [7]And he made ten candlesticks of gold according to their form, and set *them* in the temple, five on the right hand, and five on the left. [8]He made also ten tables, and placed *them* in the temple, five on the right side, and five on the left. And he made an hundred basons[b] of gold. [9]Furthermore he made the court of the priests, and the great court, and doors for the court, and overlaid the doors of them with brass. [10]And he set the sea on the right side of the east end, over against the south.

[11]And Huram made the pots, and the shovels, and the basons[c]. And Huram finished the work that he was to make for king Solomon for the house of God; [12]*To wit*, the two pillars, and the pommels, and the chapiters *which were* on the top of the two pillars, and the two wreaths to cover the two pommels of the chapiters which *were* on the top of the pillars; [13]And four hundred pomegranates on the two wreaths; two rows of pomegranates on each wreath, to cover the two pommels of the chapiters which *were* upon[d] the pillars. [14]He made also bases, and lavers[e] made he upon the bases; [15]One sea, and twelve oxen under it. [16]The pots also, and the shovels, and the fleshhooks, and all their instruments, did Huram his father make to king Solomon for the house of the LORD of bright[f] brass. [17]In the plain of Jordan did the king cast them, in the clay[g] ground between Succoth and Zeredathah. [18]Thus Solomon made all these vessels in great abundance: for the weight of the brass could not be found out. [19]And Solomon made all the vessels that *were for* the house of God, the golden altar also, and the tables whereon the shewbread *was set*; [20]Moreover the candlesticks with their lamps, that they should burn after the manner before the oracle, of pure gold; [21]And the flowers, and the lamps, and the tongs, *made he of* gold, *and* that perfect[h] gold; [22]And the snuffers, and the basons[i], and the spoons, and the censers, *of* pure gold: and the entry of the house, the inner doors thereof for the most holy *place*, and the doors of the house of the temple, *were of* gold.

5

[1]Thus all the work that Solomon made for the house of the LORD was finished: and Solomon brought in *all* the things that David his father had dedicated; and the silver, and the gold, and all the instruments, put he among the treasures of

---

[a] with flowers . . . : or, like a lilyflower
[b] basons: or, bowls
[c] basons: or, bowls
[d] upon: Heb. upon the face of
[e] lavers: or, caldrons
[f] bright: Heb. made bright, or, scoured
[g] clay . . . : Heb. thicknesses of the ground
[h] perfect . . . : Heb. perfections of gold
[i] basons: or, bowls

the house of God. ²Then Solomon assembled the elders of Israel, and all the heads of the tribes, the chief of the fathers of the children of Israel, unto Jerusalem, to bring up the ark of the covenant of the LORD out of the city of David, which *is* Zion. ³Wherefore all the men of Israel assembled themselves unto the king in the feast which *was* in the seventh month. ⁴And all the elders of Israel came; and the Levites took up the ark. ⁵And they brought up the ark, and the tabernacle of the congregation, and all the holy vessels that *were* in the tabernacle, these did the priests *and* the Levites bring up. ⁶Also king Solomon, and all the congregation of Israel that were assembled unto him before the ark, sacrificed sheep and oxen, which could not be told nor numbered for multitude. ⁷And the priests brought in the ark of the covenant of the LORD unto his place, to the oracle of the house, into the most holy *place, even* under the wings of the cherubims: ⁸For the cherubims spread forth *their* wings over the place of the ark, and the cherubims covered the ark and the staves thereof above. ⁹And they drew out the staves *of the ark*, that the ends of the staves were seen from the ark before the oracle; but they were not seen without. And there it is unto this day. ¹⁰*There was* nothing in the ark save the two tables which Moses put *therein* at Horeb, when the LORDª made *a covenant* with the children of Israel, when they came out of Egypt.

¹¹And it came to pass, when the priests were come out of the holy *place:* (for all the priests *that were* present were sanctified, *and* did not *then* wait by course: ¹²Also the Levites *which were* the

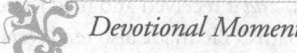

Devotional Moment
•
Worship
5:13 At the dedication of the Temple, hundreds of people blended their voices and instruments, creating worshipful music. Imagine the countless hours of practice and preparation required for that occasion! When God gives us talents to use in worship, it does not mean that we never have to train or practice. We can actually express our gratefulness to God for his gifts by sharpening those skills through their use.

singers, all of them of Asaph, of Heman, of Jeduthun, with their sons and their brethren, *being* arrayed in white linen, having cymbals and psalteries and harps, stood at the east end of the altar, and with them an hundred and twenty priests sounding with trumpets:) ¹³It came even to pass, as the trumpeters and singers *were* as one, to make one sound to be heard in praising and thanking the LORD; and when they lifted up *their* voice with the trumpets and cymbals and instruments of musick, and praised the LORD, *saying,* For *he is* good; for his mercy *endureth* for ever: that *then* the house was filled with a cloud, *even* the house of the LORD; ¹⁴So that the priests could not stand to minister by reason of the cloud: for the glory of the LORD had filled the house of God.

6

¹Then said Solomon, The LORD hath said that he would dwell in the thick darkness. ²But I have built an house of habitation for thee, and a place for thy dwelling for ever. ³And the king turned his face, and blessed the whole congrega-

---

ª when the LORD: or, where, etc

tion of Israel: and all the congregation of Israel stood. ⁴And he said, Blessed *be* the LORD God of Israel, who hath with his hands fulfilled *that* which he spake with his mouth to my father David, saying, ⁵Since the day that I brought forth my people out of the land of Egypt I chose no city among all the tribes of Israel to build an house in, that my name might be there; neither chose I any man to be a ruler over my people Israel: ⁶But I have chosen Jerusalem, that my name might be there; and have chosen David to be over my people Israel. ⁷Now it was in the heart of David my father to build an house for the name of the LORD God of Israel. ⁸But the LORD said to David my father, Forasmuch as it was in thine heart to build an house for my name, thou didst well in that it was in thine heart: ⁹Notwithstanding thou shalt not build the house; but thy son which shall come forth out of thy loins, he shall build the house for my name. ¹⁰The LORD therefore hath performed his word that he hath spoken: for I am risen up in the room of David my father, and am set on the throne of Israel, as the LORD promised, and have built the house for the name of the LORD God of Israel. ¹¹And in it have I put the ark, wherein *is* the covenant of the LORD, that he made with the children of Israel.

¹²And he stood before the altar of the LORD in the presence of all the congregation of Israel, and spread forth his hands: ¹³For Solomon had made a brasen scaffold, of five cubits long[a], and five cubits broad, and three cubits high, and had set it in the midst of the court: and upon it he stood, and kneeled down upon his knees before all the congregation of Israel, and spread forth his hands toward heaven, ¹⁴And said, O LORD God of Israel, *there is* no God like thee in the heaven, nor in the earth; which keepest covenant, and *shewest* mercy unto thy servants, that walk before thee with all their hearts: ¹⁵Thou which hast kept with thy servant David my father that which thou hast promised him; and spakest with thy mouth, and hast fulfilled *it* with thine hand, as *it is* this day. ¹⁶Now therefore, O LORD God of Israel, keep with thy servant David my father that which thou hast promised him, saying, There shall not fail thee a man in my sight to sit upon the throne of Israel; yet so that thy children take heed to their way to walk in my law, as thou hast walked before me. ¹⁷Now then, O LORD God of Israel, let thy word be verified, which thou hast spoken unto thy servant David. ¹⁸But will God in very deed dwell with men on the earth? behold, heaven and the heaven of heavens cannot contain thee; how much less this house which I have built! ¹⁹Have respect therefore to the prayer of thy servant, and to his supplication, O LORD my God, to hearken unto the cry and the prayer which thy servant prayeth before thee: ²⁰That thine eyes may be open upon this house day and night, upon the place whereof thou hast said that thou wouldest put thy name there; to hearken unto the prayer which thy servant prayeth toward this place. ²¹Hearken therefore unto the supplications of thy servant, and of thy people Israel, which they shall make[b] toward this place: hear

---

[a] long . . . : Heb. the length thereof, etc
[b] make: Heb. pray

thou from thy dwelling place, *even* from heaven; and when thou hearest, forgive. ²²If a man sin against his neighbour, and an oathᶜ be laid upon him to make him swear, and the oath come before thine altar in this house; ²³Then hear thou from heaven, and do, and judge thy servants, by requiting the wicked, by recompensing his way upon his own head; and by justifying the righteous, by giving him according to his righteousness. ²⁴And if thy people Israel be put to the worse before the enemy, because they have sinned against thee; and shall return and confess thy name, and pray and make supplication before thee in this house; ²⁵Then hear thou from the heavens, and forgive the sin of thy people Israel, and bring them again unto the land which thou gavest to them and to their fathers. ²⁶When the heaven is shut up, and there is no rain, because they have sinned against thee; *yet* if they pray toward this place, and confess thy name, and turn from their sin, when thou dost afflict them; ²⁷Then hear thou from heaven, and forgive the sin of thy servants, and of thy people Israel, when thou hast taught them the good way, wherein they should walk; and send rain upon thy land, which thou hast given unto thy people for an inheritance. ²⁸If there be dearth in the land, if there be pestilence, if there be blasting, or mildew, locusts, or caterpillers; if their enemies besiege them in the citiesᵈ of their land; whatsoever sore or whatsoever sickness *there be.* ²⁹Then what prayer *or* what supplication soever shall be made of any man, or of all thy people Israel, when every one shall know his own sore and his own grief, and shall spread forth his hands in this house: ³⁰Then hear thou from heaven thy dwelling place, and forgive, and render unto every man according unto all his ways, whose heart thou knowest; (for thou only knowest the hearts of the children of men:) ³¹That they may fear thee, to walk in thy ways, so long as they live in the land which thou gavest unto our fathers. ³²Moreover concerning the stranger, which is not of thy people Israel, but is come from a far country for thy great name's sake, and thy mighty hand, and thy stretched out arm; if they come and pray in this house; ³³Then hear thou from the heavens, *even* from thy dwelling place, and do according to all that the stranger calleth to thee for; that all people of the earth may know thy name, and fear thee, as *doth* thy people Israel, and may know that this house which I have built is called by thy name. ³⁴If thy people go out to war against their enemies by the way that thou shalt send them, and they pray unto thee toward this city which thou hast chosen, and the house which I have built for thy name; ³⁵Then hear thou from the heavens their prayer and their supplication, and maintain their causeᵉ. ³⁶If they sin against thee, (for *there is* no man which sinneth not,) and thou be angry with them, and deliver them over before *their* enemies, and they carry them away captives unto a land far off or near; ³⁷Yet *if* they bethinkᶠ them-

---

ᶜ and an oath . . . : Heb. and he require an oath of him
ᵈ in the cities . . . : Heb. in the land of their gates
ᵉ cause: or, right
ᶠ bethink . . . : Heb. bring back to their heart

selves in the land whither they are carried captive, and turn and pray unto thee in the land of their captivity, saying, We have sinned, we have done amiss, and have dealt wickedly; [38]If they return to thee with all their heart and with all their soul in the land of their captivity, whither they have carried them captives, and pray toward their land, which thou gavest unto their fathers, and *toward* the city which thou hast chosen, and toward the house which I have built for thy name: [39]Then hear thou from the heavens, *even* from thy dwelling place, their prayer and their supplications, and maintain their cause[g], and forgive thy people which have sinned against thee. [40]Now, my God, let, I beseech thee, thine eyes be open, and *let* thine ears *be* attent unto the prayer *that is made* in this place. [41]Now therefore arise, O LORD God, into thy resting place, thou, and the ark of thy strength: let thy priests, O LORD God, be clothed with salvation, and let thy saints rejoice in goodness. [42]O LORD God, turn not away the face of thine anointed: remember the mercies of David thy servant.

7

[1]Now when Solomon had made an end of praying, the fire came down from heaven, and consumed the burnt offering and the sacrifices; and the glory of the LORD filled the house. [2]And the priests could not enter into the house of the LORD, because the glory of the LORD had filled the LORD'S house. [3]And when all the children of Israel saw how the fire came down, and the glory of the LORD upon the house, they bowed themselves with their faces to the ground upon the pavement, and worshipped, and praised the LORD, *saying*, For *he is* good; for his mercy *endureth* for ever. [4]Then the king and all the people offered sacrifices before the LORD. [5]And king Solomon offered a sacrifice of twenty and two thousand oxen, and an hundred and twenty thousand sheep: so the king and all the people dedicated the house of God. [6]And the priests waited on their offices: the Levites also with instruments of musick of the LORD, which David the king had made to praise the LORD, because his mercy *endureth* for ever, when David praised by their ministry; and the priests sounded trumpets before them, and all Israel stood. [7]Moreover Solomon hallowed the middle of the court that *was* before the house of the LORD: for there he offered burnt offerings, and the fat of the peace offerings, because the brasen altar which Solomon had made was not able to receive the burnt offerings, and the meat offerings, and the fat. [8]Also at the same time Solomon kept the feast seven days, and all Israel with him, a very great congregation, from the entering in of Hamath unto the river of Egypt. [9]And in the eighth day they made a solemn assembly: for they kept the dedication of the altar seven days, and the feast seven days. [10]And on the three and twentieth day of the seventh month he sent the people away into their tents, glad and merry in heart for the goodness that the LORD had shewed unto David, and to Solomon, and to Israel his people. [11]Thus Solomon finished the house of the LORD, and the king's

---

[g] cause: or, right

house: and all that came into Solomon's heart to make in the house of the LORD, and in his own house, he prosperously effected.

¹²And the LORD appeared to Solomon by night, and said unto him, I have heard thy prayer, and have chosen this place to myself for an house of sacrifice. ¹³If I shut up heaven that there be no rain, or if I command the locusts to devour the land, or if I send pestilence among my people; ¹⁴If my people, which are called by my name, shall humble themselves, and pray, and seek my face, and turn from their wicked ways; then will I hear from heaven, and will forgive their sin, and will heal their land. ¹⁵Now mine eyes shall be open, and mine ears attent unto the prayer *that is made* in this place. ¹⁶For now have I chosen and sanctified this house, that my name may be there for ever: and mine eyes and mine heart shall be there perpetually. ¹⁷And as for thee, if thou wilt walk before me, as David thy father walked, and to do according to all that I have commanded thee, and shalt observe my statutes and my judgments; ¹⁸Then will I stablish the throne of thy kingdom, according as I have covenanted with David thy father, saying, There shall not fail thee a man *to be* ruler in Israel. ¹⁹But if ye turn away, and forsake my statutes and my commandments, which I have set before you, and shall go and serve other gods, and worship them; ²⁰Then will I pluck them up by the roots out of my land which I have given them; and this house, which I have sanctified for my name, will I cast out of my sight, and will make it *to be* a proverb and a byword among all nations. ²¹And this house, which is

high, shall be an astonishment to every one that passeth by it; so that he shall say, Why hath the LORD done thus unto this land, and unto this house? ²²And it shall be answered, Because they forsook the LORD God of their fathers, which brought them forth out of the land of Egypt, and laid hold on other gods, and worshipped them, and served them: therefore hath he brought all this evil upon them.

8

¹And it came to pass at the end of twenty years, wherein Solomon had built the house of the LORD, and his own house, ²That the cities which Huram had restored to Solomon, Solomon built them, and caused the children of Israel to dwell there. ³And Solomon went to Hamathzobah, and prevailed against it. ⁴And he built Tadmor in the wilderness, and all the store cities, which he built in Hamath. ⁵Also he built Bethhoron the upper, and Bethhoron the nether, fenced cities, with walls, gates, and bars; ⁶And Baalath, and all the store cities that Solomon had, and all the chariot cities, and the cities of the horsemen, and all that Solomon desired to build in Jerusalem, and in Lebanon, and throughout all the land of his dominion. ⁷As *for* all the people *that were* left of the Hittites, and the Amorites, and the Perizzites, and the Hivites, and the Jebusites, which *were* not of Israel, ⁸But of their children, who were left after them in the land, whom the children of Israel consumed not, them did Solomon make to pay tribute until this day. ⁹But of the children of Israel did Solomon make no servants for his work; but they *were*

men of war, and chief of his captains, and captains of his chariots and horsemen. [10]And these *were* the chief of king Solomon's officers, *even* two hundred and fifty, that bare rule over the people. [11]And Solomon brought up the daughter of Pharaoh out of the city of David unto the house that he had built for her: for he said, My wife shall not dwell in the house of David king of Israel, because *the places are* holy[a], whereunto the ark of the LORD hath come.

[12]Then Solomon offered burnt offerings unto the LORD on the altar of the LORD, which he had built before the porch, [13]Even after a certain rate every day, offering according to the commandment of Moses, on the sabbaths, and on the new moons, and on the solemn feasts, three times in the year, *even* in the feast of unleavened bread, and in the feast of weeks, and in the feast of tabernacles. [14]And he appointed, according to the order of David his father, the courses of the priests to their service, and the Levites to their charges, to praise and minister before the priests, as the duty of every day required: the porters also by their courses at every gate: for so had David[b] the man of God commanded. [15]And they departed not from the commandment of the king unto the priests and Levites concerning any matter, or concerning the treasures. [16]Now all the work of Solomon was prepared unto the day of the foundation of the house of the LORD, and until it was finished. *So* the house of the LORD was perfected. [17]Then went Solomon to Eziongeber, and to Eloth[c], at the sea side in the land of Edom. [18]And Huram sent him by the hands of his servants ships, and servants that had knowledge of the sea; and they went with the servants of Solomon to Ophir, and took thence four hundred and fifty talents of gold, and brought *them* to king Solomon.

Devotional Moment

Marriage and Faith

8:11 Solomon's marriage to a pagan princess from Egypt was just one of many he entered into for political purposes. These women had loyalties to other gods, and they corrupted Solomon's faith. God wants his people to marry fellow believers (see 2 Cor. 6:14). If two people disagree about what matters most, their relationship will always have a serious problem at its center—unless someone compromises. If you are single, keep this in mind as you date. If you have teenagers, warn them and encourage them to date guys and girls who love God.

9

[1]And when the queen of Sheba heard of the fame of Solomon, she came to prove Solomon with hard questions at Jerusalem, with a very great company, and camels that bare spices, and gold in abundance, and precious stones: and when she was come to Solomon, she communed with him of all that was in her heart. [2]And Solomon told her all her questions: and there was nothing hid from Solomon which he told her not. [3]And when the queen of Sheba had

---

[a] holy: Heb. holiness
[b] so had David . . . : Heb. so was the commandment of David the man of God
[c] Eloth: also called, Elath

seen the wisdom of Solomon, and the house that he had built, ⁴And the meat of his table, and the sitting of his servants, and the attendance of his ministers, and their apparel; his cupbearersᵃ also, and their apparel; and his ascent by which he went up into the house of the LORD; there was no more spirit in her. ⁵And she said to the king, *It was* a true reportᵇ which I heard in mine own land of thine acts, and of thy wisdom: ⁶Howbeit I believed not their words, until I came, and mine eyes had seen *it*: and, behold, the one half of the greatness of thy wisdom was not told me: *for* thou exceedest the fame that I heard. ⁷Happy *are* thy men, and happy *are* these thy servants, which stand continually before thee, and hear thy wisdom. ⁸Blessed be the LORD thy God, which delighted in thee to set thee on his throne, *to be* king for the LORD thy God: because thy God loved Israel, to establish them for ever, therefore made he thee king over them, to do judgment and justice. ⁹And she gave the king an hundred and twenty talents of gold, and of spices great abundance, and precious stones: neither was there any such spice as the queen of Sheba gave king Solomon. ¹⁰And the servants also of Huram, and the servants of Solomon, which brought gold from Ophir, brought algumᶜ trees and precious stones. ¹¹And the king made *of* the algum trees terracesᵈ to the house of the

LORD, and to the king's palace, and harps and psalteries for singers: and there were none such seen before in the land of Judah. ¹²And king Solomon gave to the queen of Sheba all her desire, whatsoever she asked, beside *that* which she had brought unto the king. So she turned, and went away to her own land, she and her servants.

¹³Now the weight of gold that came to Solomon in one year was six hundred and threescore and six talents of gold; ¹⁴Beside *that which* chapmen and merchants brought. And all the kings of Arabia and governorsᵉ of the country brought gold and silver to Solomon. ¹⁵And king Solomon made two hundred targets *of* beaten gold: six hundred *shekels* of beaten gold went to one target. ¹⁶And three hundred shields *made he of* beaten gold: three hundred *shekels* of gold went to one shield. And the king put them in the house of the forest of Lebanon. ¹⁷Moreover the king made a great throne of ivory, and overlaid it with pure gold. ¹⁸And *there were* six steps to the throne, with a footstool of gold, *which were* fastened to the throne, and staysᶠ on each side of the sitting place, and two lions standing by the stays: ¹⁹And twelve lions stood there on the one side and on the other upon the six steps. There was not the like made in any kingdom. ²⁰And all the drinking vessels of king Solomon *were* of gold, and all the vessels of the house

---

ᵃ cupbearers: or, butlers
ᵇ report: Heb. word
ᶜ algum . . . : also called, almug trees
ᵈ terraces: or, stairs: Heb. highways
ᵉ governors: or, captains
ᶠ stays: Heb. hands

of the forest of Lebanon *were of* pure[g] gold: none *were of* silver; it was *not* any thing accounted of in the days of Solomon. [21]For the king's ships went to Tarshish with the servants of Huram: every three years once came the ships of Tarshish bringing gold, and silver, ivory[h], and apes, and peacocks. [22]And king Solomon passed all the kings of the earth in riches and wisdom. [23]And all the kings of the earth sought the presence of Solomon, to hear his wisdom, that God had put in his heart. [24]And they brought every man his present, vessels of silver, and vessels of gold, and raiment, harness, and spices, horses, and mules, a rate year by year. [25]And Solomon had four thousand stalls for horses and chariots, and twelve thousand horsemen; whom he bestowed in the chariot cities, and with the king at Jerusalem. [26]And he reigned over all the kings from the river[i] even unto the land of the Philistines, and to the border of Egypt. [27]And the king made silver[j] in Jerusalem as stones, and cedar trees made he as the sycomore trees that *are* in the low plains in abundance. [28]And they brought unto Solomon horses out of Egypt, and out of all lands. [29]Now the rest of the acts of Solomon, first and last, *are* they not written in the book[k] of Nathan the prophet, and in the prophecy of Ahijah the Shilonite, and in the visions of Iddo the seer against Jeroboam the son of Nebat? [30]And Solomon reigned in Jerusalem over all Israel forty years. [31]And Solomon slept with his fathers, and he was buried in the city of David his father: and Rehoboam his son reigned in his stead.

10

[1]And Rehoboam went to Shechem: for to Shechem were all Israel come to make him king. [2]And it came to pass, when Jeroboam the son of Nebat, who *was* in Egypt, whither he had fled from the presence of Solomon the king, heard *it,* that Jeroboam returned out of Egypt. [3]And they sent and called him. So Jeroboam and all Israel came and spake to Rehoboam, saying, [4]Thy father made our yoke grievous: now therefore ease thou somewhat the grievous servitude of thy father, and his heavy yoke that he put upon us, and we will serve thee. [5]And he said unto them, Come again unto me after three days. And the people departed. [6]And king Rehoboam took counsel with the old men that had stood before Solomon his father while he yet lived, saying, What counsel give ye *me* to return answer to this people? [7]And they spake unto him, saying, If thou be kind to this people, and please them, and speak good words to them, they will be thy servants for ever. [8]But he forsook the counsel which the old men gave him, and took counsel with the young men that were brought up with him, that stood before him. [9]And he said unto them, What advice give ye

---

[g] pure: Heb. shut up
[h] ivory: or, elephants' teeth
[i] river: that is, Euphrates
[j] made silver: Heb. gave silver
[k] book: Heb. words

that we may return answer to this people, which have spoken to me, saying, Ease somewhat the yoke that thy father did put upon us? ¹⁰And the young men that were brought up with him spake unto him, saying, Thus shalt thou answer the people that spake unto thee, saying, Thy father made our yoke heavy, but make thou *it* somewhat lighter for us; thus shalt thou say unto them, My little *finger* shall be thicker than my father's loins. ¹¹For whereas my father put a heavy yoke upon you, I will put more to your yoke: my father chastised you with whips, but I *will chastise you* with scorpions.

¹²So Jeroboam and all the people came to Rehoboam on the third day, as the king bade, saying, Come again to me on the third day. ¹³And the king answered them roughly; and king Rehoboam forsook the counsel of the old men, ¹⁴And answered them after the advice of the young men, saying, My father made your yoke heavy, but I will add thereto: my father chastised you with whips, but I *will chastise you* with scorpions. ¹⁵So the king hearkened not unto the people: for the cause was of God, that the LORD might perform his word, which he spake by the hand of Ahijah the Shilonite to Jeroboam the son of Nebat. ¹⁶And when all Israel *saw* that the king would not hearken unto them, the people answered the king, saying, What portion have we in David? and *we have* none inheritance in the son of Jesse: every man to your tents, O Israel: *and* now, David, see to thine own house. So all Israel went to their tents. ¹⁷But *as for* the children of Israel that dwelt in the cities of Judah, Rehoboam reigned over them. ¹⁸Then king Rehoboam sent Hadoram that *was* over the tribute; and the children of Israel stoned him with stones, that he died. But king Rehoboam made speed^a to get him up to *his* chariot, to flee to Jerusalem. ¹⁹And Israel rebelled against the house of David unto this day.

11

¹And when Rehoboam was come to Jerusalem, he gathered of the house of Judah and Benjamin an hundred and fourscore thousand chosen *men*, which were warriors, to fight against Israel, that he might bring the kingdom again to Rehoboam. ²But the word of the LORD came to Shemaiah the man of God, saying, ³Speak unto Rehoboam the son of Solomon, king of Judah, and to all Israel in Judah and Benjamin, saying, ⁴Thus saith the LORD, Ye shall not go up, nor fight against your brethren: return every man to his house: for this thing is done of me. And they obeyed the words of the LORD, and returned from going against Jeroboam. ⁵And Rehoboam dwelt in Jerusalem, and built cities for defence in Judah. ⁶He built even Bethlehem, and Etam, and Tekoa, ⁷And Bethzur, and Shoco, and Adullam, ⁸And Gath, and Mareshah, and Ziph, ⁹And Adoraim, and Lachish, and Azekah, ¹⁰And Zorah, and Aijalon, and Hebron, which *are* in Judah and in Benjamin fenced cities. ¹¹And he fortified the strong holds, and put captains in them, and store of victual, and of oil and wine. ¹²And in every several city *he put* shields and spears, and made them

---

ᵃ made speed: Heb. strengthened himself

exceeding strong, having Judah and Benjamin on his side. ¹³And the priests and the Levites that *were* in all Israel resorted[a] to him out of all their coasts. ¹⁴For the Levites left their suburbs and their possession, and came to Judah and Jerusalem: for Jeroboam and his sons had cast them off from executing the priest's office unto the LORD: ¹⁵And he ordained him priests for the high places, and for the devils, and for the calves which he had made. ¹⁶And after them out of all the tribes of Israel such as set their hearts to seek the LORD God of Israel came to Jerusalem, to sacrifice unto the LORD God of their fathers. ¹⁷So they strengthened the kingdom of Judah, and made Rehoboam the son of Solomon strong, three years: for three years they walked in the way of David and Solomon. ¹⁸And Rehoboam took him Mahalath the daughter of Jerimoth the son of David to wife, *and* Abihail the daughter of Eliab the son of Jesse; ¹⁹Which bare him children; Jeush, and Shamariah, and Zaham. ²⁰And after her he took Maachah[b] the daughter of Absalom; which bare him Abijah, and Attai, and Ziza, and Shelomith. ²¹And Rehoboam loved Maachah the daughter of Absalom above all his wives and his concubines: (for he took eighteen wives, and threescore concubines; and begat twenty and eight sons, and threescore daughters.) ²²And Rehoboam made Abijah the son of Maachah the chief, *to be* ruler among his brethren: for *he thought* to make him king. ²³And he dealt wisely,

and dispersed of all his children throughout all the countries of Judah and Benjamin, unto every fenced city: and he gave them victual in abundance. And he desired many wives[c].

12

¹And it came to pass, when Rehoboam had established the kingdom, and had strengthened himself, he forsook the law of the LORD, and all Israel with him. ²And it came to pass, *that* in the fifth year of king Rehoboam Shishak king of Egypt came up against Jerusalem, because they had transgressed against the LORD, ³With twelve hundred chariots, and threescore thousand horsemen: and the people *were* without number that came with him out of Egypt; the Lubims, the Sukkiims, and the Ethiopians. ⁴And he took the fenced cities which *pertained* to Judah, and came to Jerusalem. ⁵Then came Shemaiah the prophet to Rehoboam, and *to* the princes of Judah, that were gathered together to Jerusalem because of Shishak, and said unto them, Thus saith the LORD, Ye have forsaken me, and therefore have I also left you in the hand of Shishak. ⁶Whereupon the princes of Israel and the king humbled themselves; and they said, The LORD *is* righteous. ⁷And when the LORD saw that they humbled themselves, the word of the LORD came to Shemaiah, saying, They have humbled themselves; *therefore* I will not destroy them, but I will grant them some[a] deliverance; and my wrath shall

---

[a] resorted . . . : Heb. presented themselves to him
[b] Maachah: she is also called Michaiah the daughter of Uriel
[c] many wives: Heb. a multitude of wives
[a] some: or, a little while

not be poured out upon Jerusalem by the hand of Shishak. ⁸Nevertheless they shall be his servants; that they may know my service, and the service of the kingdoms of the countries. ⁹So Shishak king of Egypt came up against Jerusalem, and took away the treasures of the house of the LORD, and the treasures of the king's house; he took all: he carried away also the shields of gold which Solomon had made. ¹⁰Instead of which king Rehoboam made shields of brass, and committed *them* to the hands of the chief of the guard, that kept the entrance of the king's house. ¹¹And when the king entered into the house of the LORD, the guard came and fetched them, and brought them again into the guard chamber. ¹²And when he humbled himself, the wrath of the LORD turned from him, that he would not destroy *him* altogether: and also in Judah things went well.

¹³So king Rehoboam strengthened himself in Jerusalem, and reigned: for Rehoboam *was* one and forty years old when he began to reign, and he reigned seventeen years in Jerusalem, the city which the LORD had chosen out of all the tribes of Israel, to put his name there. And his mother's name *was* Naamah an Ammonitess. ¹⁴And he did evil, because he prepared[b] not his heart to seek the LORD. ¹⁵Now the acts of Rehoboam, first and last, *are* they not written in the book[c] of Shemaiah the prophet, and of Iddo the seer concerning genealogies? And *there were* wars between Rehoboam and Jeroboam con-

tinually. ¹⁶And Rehoboam slept with his fathers, and was buried in the city of David: and Abijah[d] his son reigned in his stead.

13

¹Now in the eighteenth year of king Jeroboam began Abijah to reign over Judah. ²He reigned three years in Jerusalem. His mother's name also *was* Michaiah the daughter of Uriel of Gibeah. And there was war between Abijah and Jeroboam. ³And Abijah set the battle in array with an army of valiant men of war, *even* four hundred thousand chosen men: Jeroboam also set the battle in array against him with eight hundred thousand chosen men, *being* mighty men of valour. ⁴And Abijah stood up upon mount Zemaraim, which *is* in mount Ephraim, and said, Hear me, thou Jeroboam, and all Israel; ⁵Ought ye not to know that the LORD God of Israel gave the kingdom over Israel to David for ever, *even* to him and to his sons by a covenant of salt? ⁶Yet Jeroboam the son of Nebat, the servant of Solomon the son of David, is risen up, and hath rebelled against his lord. ⁷And there are gathered unto him vain men, the children of Belial, and have strengthened themselves against Rehoboam the son of Solomon, when Rehoboam was young and tenderhearted, and could not withstand them. ⁸And now ye think to withstand the kingdom of the LORD in the hand of the sons of David; and ye *be* a great multitude, and *there are* with you golden calves, which

---

b prepared: or, fixed
c book: Heb. words
d Abijah: also called, Abijam

Jeroboam made you for gods. ⁹Have ye not cast out the priests of the LORD, the sons of Aaron, and the Levites, and have made you priests after the manner of the nations of *other* lands? so that whosoever cometh to consecrate[a] himself with a young bullock and seven rams, *the same* may be a priest of *them that are* no gods. ¹⁰But as for us, the LORD *is* our God, and we have not forsaken him; and the priests, which minister unto the LORD, *are* the sons of Aaron, and the Levites *wait* upon *their* business: ¹¹And they burn unto the LORD every morning and every evening burnt sacrifices and sweet incense: the shewbread also *set they in order* upon the pure table; and the candlestick of gold with the lamps thereof, to burn every evening: for we keep the charge of the LORD our God; but ye have forsaken him. ¹²And, behold, God himself *is* with us for *our* captain, and his priests with sounding trumpets to cry alarm against you. O children of Israel, fight ye not against the LORD God of your fathers; for ye shall not prosper.

¹³But Jeroboam caused an ambushment to come about behind them: so they were before Judah, and the ambushment *was* behind them. ¹⁴And when Judah looked back, behold, the battle *was* before and behind: and they cried unto the LORD, and the priests sounded with the trumpets. ¹⁵Then the men of Judah gave a shout: and as the men of Judah shouted, it came to pass, that God smote Jeroboam and all Israel before Abijah and Judah. ¹⁶And the children of Israel fled before Judah: and God delivered them into their hand. ¹⁷And Abijah and his people slew them with a great slaughter: so there fell down slain of Israel five hundred thousand chosen men. ¹⁸Thus the children of Israel were brought under at that time, and the children of Judah prevailed, because they relied upon the LORD God of their fathers. ¹⁹And Abijah pursued after Jeroboam, and took cities from him, Bethel with the towns thereof, and Jeshanah with the towns thereof, and Ephrain with the towns thereof. ²⁰Neither did Jeroboam recover strength again in the days of Abijah: and the LORD struck him, and he died. ²¹But Abijah waxed mighty, and married fourteen wives, and begat twenty and two sons, and sixteen daughters. ²²And the rest of the acts of Abijah, and his ways, and his sayings, *are* written in the story of the prophet Iddo.

14

¹So Abijah slept with his fathers, and they buried him in the city of David: and Asa his son reigned in his stead. In his days the land was quiet ten years. ²And Asa did *that which was* good and right in the eyes of the LORD his God: ³For he took away the altars of the strange *gods*, and the high places, and brake down the images[a], and cut down the groves: ⁴And commanded Judah to seek the LORD God of their fathers, and to do the law and the commandment. ⁵Also he took away out of all the cities of Judah the high places and the

---

ᵃ to consecrate . . . : Heb. to fill his hand
ᵃ images: Heb. statues

Asa

No one likes criticism. Some people get better at accepting it graciously as they get older, learning their own limitations and the value of others' advice. But, by and large, we flinch when others tell us we've done something wrong.

Asa, king of Judah, was a good man. He obeyed God and ruled the nation well for thirty-six years. For the most part, his nation was peaceful and secure.

Near the end of his life, Asa's northern rival, King Baasha of Israel, suddenly started fortifying a city near the border with Judah. Asa became alarmed. But rather than turning to God for help, Asa bribed Syria, one of Baasha's allies, to break a peace treaty so Baasha would back off. The plan worked, and Baasha abandoned the base.

Asa's decision to trust in superior military strength was a mistake. He should have turned to God and trusted in him. But when the prophet Hanani confronted Asa with this wrong, Asa lashed out. He threw Hanani in prison and then vented his anger on the nation by imposing harsh rule.

Rather than face his sin, Asa let his anger take over. And his reaction burned all innocent bystanders. Because he couldn't take criticism, everyone else paid.

How do you respond when someone calls attention to a mistake you've made? Does your family pay? Do your coworkers pay? We are a lot like Asa. The next time someone points out a blemish, spare others the temper tantrum.

images[b]: and the kingdom was quiet before him. [6]And he built fenced cities in Judah: for the land had rest, and he had no war in those years; because the LORD had given him rest. [7]Therefore he said unto Judah, Let us build these cities, and make about *them* walls, and towers, gates, and bars, *while* the land *is* yet before us; because we have sought the LORD our God, we have sought *him*, and he hath given us rest on every side. So they built and prospered. [8]And Asa had an army *of men* that bare targets and spears, out of Judah three hundred thousand; and out of Benjamin, that bare shields and drew bows, two hundred and fourscore thousand: all these *were* mighty men of valour.

[9]And there came out against them Zerah the Ethiopian with an host of a thousand thousand, and three hundred chariots; and came unto Mareshah. [10]Then Asa went out against him, and they set the battle in array in the valley of Zephathah at Mareshah. [11]And Asa cried unto the LORD his God, and said, LORD, *it is* nothing with thee to help, whether with many[c], or with them that have no power: help us, O LORD our God; for we rest on thee, and in thy name we go against this multitude. O LORD, thou *art* our God; let not man prevail against thee. [12]So the LORD smote the Ethiopians before Asa, and before Judah; and the Ethiopians fled. [13]And Asa and the people that *were* with him pursued them unto Gerar: and the Ethiopians were overthrown, that they could not recover themselves; for they were destroyed[d] before the LORD, and before his host; and they carried away very much spoil. [14]And they smote all the cities round about Gerar; for the fear of the LORD came upon them: and they spoiled all the cities; for there was exceeding much spoil in them. [15]They smote also the tents of cattle, and carried away sheep and camels in abundance, and returned to Jerusalem.

15

[1]And the Spirit of God came upon Azariah the son of Oded: [2]And he went out to meet[a] Asa, and said unto him, Hear ye me, Asa, and all Judah and Benjamin; The LORD *is* with you, while ye

---

Devotional Moment
Faithfulness to God

15:2-7 As the armies of Judah and Benjamin returned from battle, Azariah had a message for them: "The Lord will stay with you as long as you stay with him!" He wanted them to remember that God was responsible for their success, and that they won because they depended on him. To live with others in a family means you will have problems and conflicts. Relationships can be difficult. The only way to be successful in your relationships is to commit each problem to God. When circumstances go wrong, ask him to lead and guide you. The Lord will stay with you—even at times when you may *not* stay with him: "Even when we are too weak to have any faith left, he remains faithful to us and will help us" (2 Tim. 2:13).

---

[b] images: Heb. sun images
[c] man: or, mortal man
[d] destroyed: Heb. broken
[a] to meet . . . : Heb. before Asa

be with him; and if ye seek him, he will be found of you; but if ye forsake him, he will forsake you. ³Now for a long season Israel *hath been* without the true God, and without a teaching priest, and without law. ⁴But when they in their trouble did turn unto the LORD God of Israel, and sought him, he was found of them. ⁵And in those times *there was* no peace to him that went out, nor to him that came in, but great vexations *were* upon all the inhabitants of the countries. ⁶And nation was destroyed[b] of nation, and city of city: for God did vex them with all adversity. ⁷Be ye strong therefore, and let not your hands be weak: for your work shall be rewarded.

⁸And when Asa heard these words, and the prophecy of Oded the prophet, he took courage, and put away the abominable idols out of all the land of Judah and Benjamin, and out of the cities which he had taken from mount Ephraim, and renewed the altar of the LORD, that *was* before the porch of the LORD. ⁹And he gathered all Judah and Benjamin, and the strangers with them out of Ephraim and Manasseh, and out of Simeon: for they fell to him out of Israel in abundance, when they saw that the LORD his God *was* with him. ¹⁰So they gathered themselves together at Jerusalem in the third month, in the fifteenth year of the reign of Asa. ¹¹And they offered unto the LORD the same time, of the spoil *which* they had brought, seven hundred oxen and seven thousand sheep. ¹²And they entered into a covenant to seek the LORD God of their fathers with all their heart and with all their soul; ¹³That whosoever would not seek the LORD God of Israel should be put to death, whether small or great, whether man or woman. ¹⁴And they sware unto the LORD with a loud voice, and with shouting, and with trumpets, and with cornets. ¹⁵And all Judah rejoiced at the oath: for they had sworn with all their heart, and sought him with their whole desire; and he was found of them: and the LORD gave them rest round about. ¹⁶And also *concerning* Maachah the mother[c] of Asa the king, he removed her from *being* queen, because she had made an idol in a grove: and Asa cut down her idol, and stamped *it,* and burnt *it* at the brook Kidron. ¹⁷But the high places were not taken away out of Israel: nevertheless the heart of Asa was perfect all his days. ¹⁸And he brought into the house of God the things that his father had dedicated, and that he himself had dedicated, silver, and gold, and vessels. ¹⁹And there was no *more* war unto the five and thirtieth year of the reign of Asa.

16

¹In the six and thirtieth year of the reign of Asa Baasha king of Israel came up against Judah, and built Ramah, to the intent that he might let none go out or come in to Asa king of Judah. ²Then Asa brought out silver and gold out of the treasures of the house of the LORD and of the king's house, and sent to Benhadad king of Syria, that dwelt at Damascus[a], saying, ³*There is* a league between me and thee, as *there was* between

---

b destroyed: Heb. beaten in pieces
c mother: that is, grandmother
a Damascus: Heb. Darmesek

my father and thy father: behold, I have sent thee silver and gold; go, break thy league with Baasha king of Israel, that he may depart from me. ⁴And Benhadad hearkened unto king Asa, and sent the captains of his armies against the cities of Israel; and they smote Ijon, and Dan, and Abelmaim, and all the store cities of Naphtali. ⁵And it came to pass, when Baasha heard *it*, that he left off building of Ramah, and let his work cease. ⁶Then Asa the king took all Judah; and they carried away the stones of Ramah, and the timber thereof, wherewith Baasha was building; and he built therewith Geba and Mizpah.

⁷And at that time Hanani the seer came to Asa king of Judah, and said unto him, Because thou hast relied on the king of Syria, and not relied on the LORD thy God, therefore is the host of the king of Syria escaped out of thine hand. ⁸Were not the Ethiopians and the Lubims a huge[b] host, with very many chariots and horsemen? yet, because thou didst rely on the LORD, he delivered them into thine hand. ⁹For the eyes of the LORD run to and fro throughout the whole earth, to shew himself strong in the behalf of *them* whose heart *is* perfect toward him. Herein thou hast done foolishly: therefore from henceforth thou shalt have wars. ¹⁰Then Asa was wroth with the seer, and put him in a prison house; for *he was* in a rage with him because of this *thing*. And Asa oppressed[c] *some* of the people the same time. ¹¹And, behold, the acts of Asa, first and last, lo, they *are* writ-

ten in the book of the kings of Judah and Israel. ¹²And Asa in the thirty and ninth year of his reign was diseased in his feet, until his disease *was* exceeding *great*: yet in his disease he sought not to the LORD, but to the physicians. ¹³And Asa slept with his fathers, and died in the one and fortieth year of his reign. ¹⁴And they buried him in his own sepulchres, which he had made[d] for himself in the city of David, and laid him in the bed which was filled with sweet odours and divers kinds *of spices* prepared by the apothecaries' art: and they made a very great burning for him.

17

¹And Jehoshaphat his son reigned in his stead, and strengthened himself against Israel. ²And he placed forces in all the fenced cities of Judah, and set garrisons in the land of Judah, and in the cities of Ephraim, which Asa his father had taken. ³And the LORD was with Jehoshaphat, because he walked in the first ways of his father David, and sought not unto Baalim; ⁴But sought to the *LORD* God of his father, and walked in his commandments, and not after the doings of Israel. ⁵Therefore the LORD stablished the kingdom in his hand; and all Judah brought[a] to Jehoshaphat presents; and he had riches and honour in abundance. ⁶And his heart was lifted up in the ways of the LORD: moreover he took away the high places and groves out of Judah. ⁷Also in the third year of his reign he sent to his princes, *even* to Ben-

---

[b] a huge: Heb. in abundance
[c] oppressed: Heb. crushed
[d] had made: Heb. had digged
[a] brought: Heb. gave

Devotional Moment
•
Teaching

17:7-10 When the Levites went throughout Judah teaching God's Law, the fear of the Lord fell on all the surrounding nations. These nations saw the strength and unity that Judah had as a result of following God, and this caused them to respect God's work in their lives. Teaching the ways of God to the world at large starts with the way we ourselves behave. If we want the people around us to pay attention to God's Word, we must practice it. Rather than complaining about what's wrong with the world, ask what *you* can do to set the example. Be the kind of neighbor and community member you want others to be.

---

hail, and to Obadiah, and to Zechariah, and to Nethaneel, and to Michaiah, to teach in the cities of Judah. ⁸And with them *he sent* Levites, *even* Shemaiah, and Nethaniah, and Zebadiah, and Asahel, and Shemiramoth, and Jehonathan, and Adonijah, and Tobijah, and Tobadonijah, Levites; and with them Elishama and Jehoram, priests. ⁹And they taught in Judah, and *had* the book of the law of the LORD with them, and went about throughout all the cities of Judah, and taught the people.

¹⁰And the fear of the LORD fell upon all the kingdoms of the lands that *were* round about Judah, so that they made no war against Jehoshaphat. ¹¹Also *some* of the Philistines brought Jehoshaphat presents, and tribute silver; and the Arabians brought him flocks, seven thousand and seven hundred rams, and seven thousand and seven

hundred he goats. ¹²And Jehoshaphat waxed great exceedingly; and he built in Judah castles^b, and cities of store. ¹³And he had much business in the cities of Judah: and the men of war, mighty men of valour, *were* in Jerusalem. ¹⁴And these *are* the numbers of them according to the house of their fathers: Of Judah, the captains of thousands; Adnah the chief, and with him mighty men of valour three hundred thousand. ¹⁵And next^c to him *was* Jehohanan the captain, and with him two hundred and fourscore thousand. ¹⁶And next him *was* Amasiah the son of Zichri, who willingly offered himself unto the LORD; and with him two hundred thousand mighty men of valour. ¹⁷And of Benjamin; Eliada a mighty man of valour, and with him armed men with bow and shield two hundred thousand. ¹⁸And next him *was* Jehozabad, and with him an hundred and fourscore thousand ready prepared for the war. ¹⁹These waited on the king, beside *those* whom the king put in the fenced cities throughout all Judah.

18

¹Now Jehoshaphat had riches and honour in abundance, and joined affinity with Ahab. ²And after^a *certain* years he went down to Ahab to Samaria. And Ahab killed sheep and oxen for him in abundance, and for the people that *he had* with him, and persuaded him to go up *with him* to Ramothgilead. ³And Ahab king of Israel said unto Jehoshaphat king of Judah, Wilt thou go with me to Ramothgilead? And he an-

---

ᵇ castles: or, palaces

ᶜ next . . . : Heb. at his hand

ᵃ after . . . : Heb. at the end of years

swered him, I *am* as thou *art*, and my people as thy people; and *we will be* with thee in the war.

⁴And Jehoshaphat said unto the king of Israel, Enquire, I pray thee, at the word of the LORD to day. ⁵Therefore the king of Israel gathered together of prophets four hundred men, and said unto them, Shall we go to Ramothgilead to battle, or shall I forbear? And they said, Go up; for God will deliver *it* into the king's hand. ⁶But Jehoshaphat said, *Is there* not here a prophet of the LORD besides[b], that we might enquire of him? ⁷And the king of Israel said unto Jehoshaphat, *There is* yet one man, by whom we may enquire of the LORD: but I hate him; for he never prophesied good unto me, but always evil: the same *is* Micaiah the son of Imla. And Jehoshaphat said, Let not the king say so. ⁸And the king of Israel called for one *of his* officers[c], and said, Fetch quickly Micaiah the son of Imla. ⁹And the king of Israel and Jehoshaphat king of Judah sat either of them on his throne, clothed in *their* robes, and they sat in a void place at the entering in of the gate of Samaria; and all the prophets prophesied before them. ¹⁰And Zedekiah the son of Chenaanah had made him horns of iron, and said, Thus saith the LORD, With these thou shalt push Syria until they be consumed. ¹¹And all the prophets prophesied so, saying, Go up to Ramothgilead, and prosper: for the LORD shall deliver *it* into the hand of the king. ¹²And the messenger that went to call Micaiah spake to him, saying, Behold, the words of the prophets *declare* good to the king with one assent; let thy word therefore, I pray thee, be like one of theirs, and speak thou good. ¹³And Micaiah said, *As* the LORD liveth, even what my God saith, that will I speak. ¹⁴And when he was come to the king, the king said unto him, Micaiah, shall we go to Ramothgilead to battle, or shall I forbear? And he said, Go ye up, and prosper, and they shall be delivered into your hand. ¹⁵And the king said to him, How many times shall I adjure thee that thou say nothing but the truth to me in the name of the LORD? ¹⁶Then he said, I did see all Israel scattered upon the mountains, as sheep that have no shepherd: and the LORD said, These have no master; let them return *therefore* every man to his house in peace. ¹⁷And the king of Israel said to Jehoshaphat, Did I not tell thee *that* he would not prophesy good unto me, but evil[d]? ¹⁸Again he said, Therefore hear the word of the LORD; I saw the LORD sitting upon his throne, and all the host of heaven standing on his right hand and *on* his left. ¹⁹And the LORD said, Who shall entice Ahab king of Israel, that he may go up and fall at Ramothgilead? And one spake saying after this manner, and another saying after that manner. ²⁰Then there came out a spirit, and stood before the LORD, and said, I will entice him. And the LORD said unto him, Wherewith? ²¹And he said, I will go out, and be a lying spirit in the mouth of all his prophets. And *the LORD* said, Thou shalt entice *him*, and thou shalt also prevail: go out, and do

---

[b] besides: Heb. yet, or, more
[c] officers: or, eunuchs
[d] but evil: or, but for evil

even so. ²²Now therefore, behold, the LORD hath put a lying spirit in the mouth of these thy prophets, and the LORD hath spoken evil against thee. ²³Then Zedekiah the son of Chenaanah came near, and smote Micaiah upon the cheek, and said, Which way went the Spirit of the LORD from me to speak unto thee? ²⁴And Micaiah said, Behold, thou shalt see on that day when thou shalt go into an inner chamber to hide thyself. ²⁵Then the king of Israel said, Take ye Micaiah, and carry him back to Amon the governor of the city, and to Joash the king's son; ²⁶And say, Thus saith the king, Put this *fellow* in the prison, and feed him with bread of affliction and with water of affliction, until I return in peace. ²⁷And Micaiah said, If thou certainly return in peace, *then* hath not the LORD spoken by me. And he said, Hearken, all ye people.

²⁸So the king of Israel and Jehoshaphat the king of Judah went up to Ramothgilead. ²⁹And the king of Israel said unto Jehoshaphat, I will disguise myself, and will go to the battle; but put thou on thy robes. So the king of Israel disguised himself; and they went to the battle. ³⁰Now the king of Syria had commanded the captains of the chariots that *were* with him, saying, Fight ye not with small or great, save only with the king of Israel. ³¹And it came to pass, when the captains of the chariots saw Jehoshaphat, that they said, It *is* the king of Israel. Therefore they compassed about him to fight: but Jehoshaphat cried out, and the LORD helped him; and God moved them *to depart* from him. ³²For it came to pass,

that, when the captains of the chariots perceived that it was not the king of Israel, they turned back again from pursuing him. ³³And a *certain* man drew a bow at a venture^c, and smote the king of Israel between the joints of the harness: therefore he said to his chariot man, Turn thine hand, that thou mayest carry me out of the host; for I am wounded. ³⁴And the battle increased that day: howbeit the king of Israel stayed *himself* up in *his* chariot against the Syrians until the even: and about the time of the sun going down he died.

19

¹And Jehoshaphat the king of Judah returned to his house in peace to Jerusalem. ²And Jehu the son of Hanani the seer went out to meet him, and said to king Jehoshaphat, Shouldest thou help the ungodly, and love them that hate the LORD? therefore *is* wrath upon thee from before the LORD. ³Nevertheless there are good things found in thee, in that thou hast taken away the groves out of the land, and hast prepared thine heart to seek God. ⁴And Jehoshaphat dwelt at Jerusalem: and he went out again through the people from Beersheba to mount Ephraim, and brought them back unto the LORD God of their fathers.

⁵And he set judges in the land throughout all the fenced cities of Judah, city by city, ⁶And said to the judges, Take heed what ye do: for ye judge not for man, but for the LORD, who *is* with you in the judgment. ⁷Wherefore now let the fear of the LORD be upon you; take heed and do

---

^c at a venture: Heb. in his simplicity

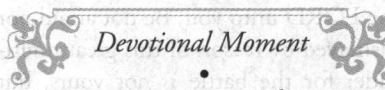

Devotional Moment
•
Parenting Fairly

19:7-11 Those with the job of settling disputes and administering God's Law were charged to be fair. They were to allow absolutely no injustice, partiality, or bribery. Parenting involves a lot of dispute settling. Even the best of parents sometimes play favorites. Make it your goal to be fair and impartial. Listen to every side of the story before passing judgment. When you can't determine who's at fault, don't make only one side suffer the consequences, and have everyone pitch in if restoration is in order.

it. for *there is* no iniquity with the LORD our God, nor respect of persons, nor taking of gifts. ⁸Moreover in Jerusalem did Jehoshaphat set of the Levites, and *of* the priests, and of the chief of the fathers of Israel, for the judgment of the LORD, and for controversies, when they returned to Jerusalem. ⁹And he charged them, saying, Thus shall ye do in the fear of the LORD, faithfully, and with a perfect heart. ¹⁰And what cause soever shall come to you of your brethren that dwell in their cities, between blood and blood, between law and commandment, statutes and judgments, ye shall even warn them that they trespass not against the LORD, and *so* wrath come upon you, and upon your brethren: this do, and ye shall not trespass. ¹¹And, behold, Amariah the chief priest *is* over you in all matters of the LORD; and Zebadiah the son of Ishmael, the ruler of the house of Judah, for all the king's matters: also the Levites *shall be* officers

before you. Deal[a] courageously, and the LORD shall be with the good.

20

¹It came to pass after this also, *that* the children of Moab, and the children of Ammon, and with them *other* beside the Ammonites, came against Jehoshaphat to battle. ²Then there came some that told Jehoshaphat, saying, There cometh a great multitude against thee from beyond the sea on this side Syria; and, behold, they *be* in Hazazontamar, which *is* Engedi. ³And Jehoshaphat feared, and set himself[a] to seek the LORD, and proclaimed a fast throughout all Judah. ⁴And Judah gathered themselves together, to ask *help* of the LORD: even out of all the cities of Judah they came to seek the LORD. ⁵And Jehoshaphat stood in the congregation of Judah and Jerusalem, in the house of the LORD, before the new court, ⁶And said, O LORD God of our fathers, *art* not thou God in heaven? and rulest *not* thou over all the kingdoms of the heathen? and in thine hand *is there not* power and might, so that none is able to withstand thee? ⁷*Art* not thou our God, *who* didst drive out the inhabitants of this land before thy people Israel, and gavest it to the seed of Abraham thy friend for ever? ⁸And they dwelt therein, and have built thee a sanctuary therein for thy name, saying, ⁹If, *when* evil cometh upon us, *as the* sword, judgment, or pestilence, or famine, we stand before this house, and in thy presence, (for thy name *is* in this house,) and cry unto thee in our afflic-

---

ᵃ Deal . . . : Heb. Take courage and do
ᵃ himself: Heb. his face

Devotional Moment
•
Facing Problems
20:13 Threatened by huge attacking armies, the people of Judah brought their wives and children with them and stood before the Lord. This gave the children an example of how to follow the Lord and gave them an opportunity to witness the fulfillment of the Lord's promise of victory. The next time you face problems and difficulties, let your children know what the challenges are, and let them pray with you for counsel and insight. As you do so, they will begin to see God work in your family's life, and their faith will grow.

tion, then thou wilt hear and help. ¹⁰And now, behold, the children of Ammon and Moab and mount Seir, whom thou wouldest not let Israel invade, when they came out of the land of Egypt, but they turned from them, and destroyed them not; ¹¹Behold, *I say, how* they reward us, to come to cast us out of thy possession, which thou hast given us to inherit. ¹²O our God, wilt thou not judge them? for we have no might against this great company that cometh against us; neither know we what to do: but our eyes *are* upon thee. ¹³And all Judah stood before the LORD, with their little ones, their wives, and their children.

¹⁴Then upon Jahaziel the son of Zechariah, the son of Benaiah, the son of Jeiel, the son of Mattaniah, a Levite of the sons of Asaph, came the Spirit of the LORD in the midst of the congregation; ¹⁵And he said, Hearken ye, all Judah, and ye inhabitants of Jerusalem, and thou king Jehoshaphat, Thus saith

the LORD unto you, Be not afraid nor dismayed by reason of this great multitude; for the battle *is* not yours, but God's. ¹⁶To morrow go ye down against them: behold, they come up by the cliff[b] of Ziz; and ye shall find them at the end of the brook, before the wilderness of Jeruel. ¹⁷Ye shall not *need* to fight in this *battle*: set yourselves, stand ye *still,* and see the salvation of the LORD with you, O Judah and Jerusalem: fear not, nor be dismayed; to morrow go out against them: for the LORD *will be* with you. ¹⁸And Jehoshaphat bowed his head with *his* face to the ground: and all Judah and the inhabitants of Jerusalem fell before the LORD, worshipping the LORD. ¹⁹And the Levites, of the children of the Kohathites, and of the children of the Korhites, stood up to praise the LORD God of Israel with a loud voice on high.

²⁰And they rose early in the morning, and went forth into the wilderness of Tekoa: and as they went forth, Jehoshaphat stood and said, Hear me, O Judah, and ye inhabitants of Jerusalem; Believe in the LORD your God, so shall ye be established; believe his prophets, so shall ye prosper. ²¹And when he had consulted with the people, he appointed singers unto the LORD, and that should praise the beauty of holiness, as they went out before the army, and to say, Praise the LORD; for his mercy *endureth* for ever. ²²And when[c] they began to sing and to praise, the LORD set ambushments against the children of Ammon, Moab, and mount Seir, which were come against Judah; and they were

[b] cliff: Heb. ascent
[c] And when . . . : Heb. And in the time that they, etc

smitten. ²³For the children of Ammon and Moab stood up against the inhabitants of mount Seir, utterly to slay and destroy *them*: and when they had made an end of the inhabitants of Seir, every one helped to destroy[d] another. ²⁴And when Judah came toward the watch tower in the wilderness, they looked unto the multitude, and, behold, they *were* dead bodies fallen to the earth, and none escaped. ²⁵And when Jehoshaphat and his people came to take away the spoil of them, they found among them in abundance both riches with the dead bodies, and precious jewels, which they stripped off for themselves, more than they could carry away: and they were three days in gathering of the spoil, it was so much. ²⁶And on the fourth day they assembled themselves in the valley of Berachah[e]; for there they blessed the LORD: therefore the name of the same place was called, The valley of Berachah, unto this day. ²⁷Then they returned, every man of Judah and Jerusalem, and Jehoshaphat in the forefront[f] of them, to go again to Jerusalem with joy; for the LORD had made them to rejoice over their enemies. ²⁸And they came to Jerusalem with psalteries and harps and trumpets unto the house of the LORD. ²⁹And the fear of God was on all the kingdoms of *those* countries, when they had heard that the LORD fought against the enemies of Israel. ³⁰So the realm of Jehoshaphat was quiet: for his God gave him rest round about.

³¹And Jehoshaphat reigned over Judah: *he was* thirty and five years old when he began to reign, and he reigned twenty and five years in Jerusalem. And his mother's name *was* Azubah the daughter of Shilhi. ³²And he walked in the way of Asa his father, and departed not from it, doing *that which was* right in the sight of the LORD. ³³Howbeit the high places were not taken away: for as yet the people had not prepared their hearts unto the God of their fathers. ³⁴Now the rest of the acts of Jehoshaphat, first and last, behold, they *are* written in the book of Jehu[g] the son of Hanani, who *is* mentioned in the book of the kings of Israel. ³⁵And after this did Jehoshaphat king of Judah join himself with Ahaziah king of Israel, who did very wickedly: ³⁶And he joined himself with him to make ships to go to Tarshish: and they made the ships in Eziongeber. ³⁷Then Eliezer the son of Dodavah of Mareshah prophesied against Jehoshaphat, saying, Because thou hast joined thyself with Ahaziah, the LORD hath broken thy works. And the ships were broken, that they were not able to go to Tarshish.

21

¹Now Jehoshaphat slept with his fathers, and was buried with his fathers in the city of David. And Jehoram his son reigned in his stead. ²And he had brethren the sons of Jehoshaphat, Azariah, and Jehiel, and Zechariah, and Azariah, and Michael, and Shephatiah: all these *were* the sons of Jehoshaphat

---

[d] to destroy: Heb. for the destruction
[e] Berachah: that is, blessing
[f] forefront: Heb. head
[g] book of Jehu: Heb. words, etc

king of Israel. ³And their father gave them great gifts of silver, and of gold, and of precious things, with fenced cities in Judah: but the kingdom gave he to Jehoram; because he *was* the firstborn. ⁴Now when Jehoram was risen up to the kingdom of his father, he strengthened himself, and slew all his brethren with the sword, and *divers* also of the princes of Israel. ⁵Jehoram *was* thirty and two years old when he began to reign, and he reigned eight years in Jerusalem. ⁶And he walked in the way of the kings of Israel, like as did the house of Ahab: for he had the daughter of Ahab to wife: and he wrought *that which was* evil in the eyes of the LORD. ⁷Howbeit the LORD would not destroy the house of David, because of the covenant that he had made with David, and as he promised to give a light[a] to him and to his sons for ever. ⁸In his days the Edomites revolted from under the dominion[b] of Judah, and made themselves a king. ⁹Then Jehoram went forth with his princes, and all his chariots with him: and he rose up by night, and smote the Edomites which compassed him in, and the captains of the chariots. ¹⁰So the Edomites revolted from under the hand of Judah unto this day. The same time *also* did Libnah revolt from under his hand; because he had forsaken the LORD God of his fathers. ¹¹Moreover he made high places in the mountains of Judah, and caused the inhabitants of Jerusalem to commit fornication, and compelled Judah *thereto*.

¹²And there came a writing to him from Elijah the prophet, saying, Thus saith the LORD God of David thy father, Because thou hast not walked in the ways of Jehoshaphat thy father, nor in the ways of Asa king of Judah, ¹³But hast walked in the way of the kings of Israel, and hast made Judah and the inhabitants of Jerusalem to go a whoring, like to the whoredoms of the house of Ahab, and also hast slain thy brethren of thy father's house, *which were* better than thyself: ¹⁴Behold, with a great[c] plague will the LORD smite thy people, and thy children, and thy wives, and all thy goods: ¹⁵And thou *shalt have* great sickness by disease of thy bowels, until thy bowels fall out by reason of the sickness day by day. ¹⁶Moreover the LORD stirred up against Jehoram the spirit of the Philistines, and of the Arabians, that *were* near the Ethiopians: ¹⁷And they came up into Judah, and brake into it, and carried away all the substance that was found in the king's house, and his sons also, and his wives; so that there was never a son left him, save Jehoahaz, the youngest of his sons. ¹⁸And after all this the LORD smote him in his bowels with an incurable disease. ¹⁹And it came to pass, that in process of time, after the end of two years, his bowels fell out by reason of his sickness: so he died of sore diseases. And his people made no burning for him, like the burning of his fathers. ²⁰Thirty and two years old was he when he began to reign, and he reigned in Jerusalem eight years, and departed without being desired. Howbeit they

---

[a] light: Heb. lamp, or, candle
[b] dominion: Heb. hand
[c] a great . . . : Heb. a great stroke

buried him in the city of David, but not in the sepulchres of the kings.

22

¹And the inhabitants of Jerusalem made Ahaziah his youngest son king in his stead: for the band of men that came with the Arabians to the camp had slain all the eldest. So Ahaziah the son of Jehoram king of Judah reigned. ²Forty and two years old *was* Ahaziah when he began to reign, and he reigned one year in Jerusalem. His mother's name also *was* Athaliah the daughter of Omri. ³He also walked in the ways of the house of Ahab: for his mother was his counsellor to do wickedly. ⁴Wherefore he did evil in the sight of the LORD like the house of Ahab: for they were his counsellors after the death of his father to his destruction. ⁵He walked also after their counsel, and went with Jehoram the son of Ahab king of Israel to war against Hazael king of Syria at Ramoth-

---

Devotional Moment

Big Responsibility

22:3-4 Ahaziah's downfall is explained very simply. "His mother encouraged him in doing wrong." It is easy to read this and think, *I would never do that.* Yet we must not be self-righteous nor too self-assured. Have you ever encouraged a child to lie about the true motive for not playing with a friend in order to avoid a messy explanation? Have you ever rationalized your kids' bad behavior rather than take the painful step of correcting them? Make a commitment to steer your kids in the right direction, no matter how unpleasant or inconvenient it may be.

---

gilead: and the Syrians smote Joram. ⁶And he returned to be healed in Jezreel because of the wounds which were given him at Ramah, when he fought with Hazael king of Syria. And Azariah the son of Jehoram king of Judah went down to see Jehoram the son of Ahab at Jezreel, because he was sick. ⁷And the destruction[a] of Ahaziah was of God by coming to Joram: for when he was come, he went out with Jehoram against Jehu the son of Nimshi, whom the LORD had anointed to cut off the house of Ahab. ⁸And it came to pass, that, when Jehu was executing judgment upon the house of Ahab, and found the princes of Judah, and the sons of the brethren of Ahaziah, that ministered to Ahaziah, he slew them. ⁹And he sought Ahaziah: and they caught him, (for he was hid in Samaria,) and brought him to Jehu: and when they had slain him, they buried him: Because, said they, he *is* the son of Jehoshaphat, who sought the LORD with all his heart. So the house of Ahaziah had no power to keep still the kingdom.

¹⁰But when Athaliah the mother of Ahaziah saw that her son was dead, she arose and destroyed all the seed royal of the house of Judah. ¹¹But Jehoshabeath[b], the daughter of the king, took Joash the son of Ahaziah, and stole him from among the king's sons that were slain, and put him and his nurse in a bedchamber. So Jehoshabeath, the daughter of king Jehoram, the wife of Jehoiada the priest, (for she was the sister of Ahaziah,) hid him from Athaliah,

---

[a] destruction: Heb. treading down
[b] Jehoshabeath: also called, Jehosheba

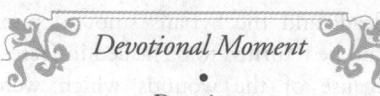

Devotional Moment
Dominoes

22:10-12 When her son Ahaziah died, Athaliah, daughter of wicked King Ahab and architect of Ahaziah's godless regime, murdered her grandsons and took the throne for herself. This conflict started with Jehoshaphat's foolish decision to have his son marry Athaliah. Perhaps if we could see the end result of our choices at the time we make them, we would choose to follow God's way more often. But we can't see the future as God can. That's why obeying him takes trust—we must take him at his word and believe that he knows best. Study God's Word and let it guide your decisions.

so that she slew him not. ¹²And he was with them hid in the house of God six years: and Athaliah reigned over the land.

23

¹And in the seventh year Jehoiada strengthened himself, and took the captains of hundreds, Azariah the son of Jeroham, and Ishmael the son of Jehohanan, and Azariah the son of Obed, and Maaseiah the son of Adaiah, and Elishaphat the son of Zichri, into covenant with him. ²And they went about in Judah, and gathered the Levites out of all the cities of Judah, and the chief of the fathers of Israel, and they came to Jerusalem. ³And all the congregation made a covenant with the king in the house of God. And he said unto them, Behold, the king's son shall reign, as the LORD hath said of the sons of David. ⁴This *is* the thing that ye shall do; A third part of you entering on

the sabbath, of the priests and of the Levites, *shall be* porters of the doors[a]; ⁵And a third part *shall be* at the king's house; and a third part at the gate of the foundation: and all the people *shall be* in the courts of the house of the LORD. ⁶But let none come into the house of the LORD, save the priests, and they that minister of the Levites; they shall go in, for they *are* holy: but all the people shall keep the watch of the LORD. ⁷And the Levites shall compass the king round about, every man with his weapons in his hand; and whosoever *else* cometh into the house, he shall be put to death: but be ye with the king when he cometh in, and when he goeth out. ⁸So the Levites and all Judah did according to all things that Jehoiada the priest had commanded, and took every man his men that were to come in on the sabbath, with them that were to go *out* on the sabbath: for Jehoiada the priest dismissed not the courses. ⁹Moreover Jehoiada the priest delivered to the captains of hundreds spears, and bucklers, and shields, that *had been* king David's, which *were* in the house of God. ¹⁰And he set all the people, every man having his weapon in his hand, from the right side[b] of the temple to the left side of the temple, along by the altar and the temple, by the king round about. ¹¹Then they brought out the king's son, and put upon him the crown, and *gave him* the testimony, and made him king. And Jehoiada and his sons anointed him, and said, God save the king.

¹²Now when Athaliah heard the

ᵃ doors: Heb. thresholds
ᵇ side: Heb. shoulder

noise of the people running and praising the king, she came to the people into the house of the LORD: ¹³And she looked, and, behold, the king stood at his pillar at the entering in, and the princes and the trumpets by the king: and all the people of the land rejoiced, and sounded with trumpets, also the singers with instruments of musick, and such as taught to sing praise. Then Athaliah rent her clothes, and said, Treason᷄, Treason. ¹⁴Then Jehoiada the priest brought out the captains of hundreds that were set over the host, and said unto them, Have her forth of the ranges: and whoso followeth her, let him be slain with the sword. For the priest said, Slay her not in the house of the LORD. ¹⁵So they laid hands on her; and when she was come to the entering of the horse gate by the king's house, they slew her there. ¹⁶And Jehoiada made a covenant between him, and between all the people, and between the king, that they should be the LORD'S people. ¹⁷Then all the people went to the house of Baal, and brake it down, and brake his altars and his images in pieces, and slew Mattan the priest of Baal before the altars. ¹⁸Also Jehoiada appointed the offices of the house of the LORD by the hand of the priests the Levites, whom David had distributed in the house of the LORD, to offer the burnt offerings of the LORD, as it is written in the law of Moses, with rejoicing and with singing, as it was ordained by David. ¹⁹And he set the porters at the gates of the house of the LORD, that none which was unclean in any thing should enter in. ²⁰And he

took the captains of hundreds, and the nobles, and the governors of the people, and all the people of the land, and brought down the king from the house of the LORD: and they came through the high gate into the king's house, and set the king upon the throne of the kingdom. ²¹And all the people of the land rejoiced: and the city was quiet, after that they had slain Athaliah with the sword.

24

¹Joash was seven years old when he began to reign, and he reigned forty years in Jerusalem. His mother's name also was Zibiah of Beersheba. ²And Joash did that which was right in the sight of the LORD all the days of Jehoiada the priest. ³And Jehoiada took for him two wives; and he begat sons and daughters. ⁴And it came to pass after this, that

---

Devotional Moment

•

Surrogate Parents

24:1-2 Joash came from a very dysfunctional home. His father, King Ahaziah, was a wicked man. The life of his grandfather, King Jehoram, was "evil in the eyes of the Lord" (21:6). And his grandmother was one of the most ruthless rulers Judah ever had. Yet the effect his surrogate parents (his aunt and uncle, Jehoshabeath and Jehoiada) had on him was profound. Their positive influence lasted many years and touched many people. The adults whom children see on a day-to-day basis can be more influential than those in their own bloodline. Your influence on an adopted child, a foster child, or a troubled child in your extended family or church fellowship can make the difference of a lifetime.

᷄ Treason: Heb. Conspiracy

Jehoiada and Jehoshabeath

Jehoiada and Jehoshabeath had the unfortunate distinction of being related to Queen Athaliah, one of the most evil rulers Israel ever had.

When Athaliah's son, King Ahaziah, died, she moved quickly to take over. Her grandsons, all princes, threatened her position of power, so she set out immediately to have them executed. Jehoiada and his wife, Jehoshabeath, were horrified at what Athaliah planned to do.

They managed to save one of the children—one-year-old Joash. Jehoshabeath snatched up the baby and hid him in a secret room in the Temple, where Jehoiada served as priest.

Jehoiada and Jehoshabeath raised young Joash in secret for six years. When Joash was seven, Jehoiada finally got up enough courage to confide in others. With support from the Levites and clan leaders, they brought Joash out of hiding, crowned him king, and had Athaliah executed.

Joash ruled Judah for forty years. Throughout Joash's life, Jehoiada and Jehoshabeath served him as protectors, surrogate parents, and, at least in Jehoiada's case, adviser. They had an important impact on his entire life.

It all started, though, when Joash was one—they chose not to look the other way when a troubling family problem surfaced. They decided it was better to risk their own lives for the sake of their nephew than to pretend everything was OK.

Family conflicts and problems can get ugly. If yours ever do—if someone is being abused physically or sexually—risk the relationship and intervene. Now is the best time to stop it.

Joash was minded to repair[a] the house of the LORD. [5]And he gathered together the priests and the Levites, and said to them, Go out unto the cities of Judah, and gather of all Israel money to repair the house of your God from year to year, and see that ye hasten the matter. Howbeit the Levites hastened *it* not. [6]And the king called for Jehoiada the chief, and said unto him, Why hast thou not required of the Levites to bring in out of Judah and out of Jerusalem the collection, *according to the commandment* of Moses the servant of the LORD, and of the congregation of Israel, for the tabernacle of witness? [7]For the sons of Athaliah, that wicked woman, had broken up the house of God; and also all the dedicated things of the house of the LORD did they bestow upon Baalim. [8]And at the king's commandment they made a chest, and set it without at the gate of the house of the LORD. [9]And they made a proclamation[b] through Judah and Jerusalem, to bring in to the LORD the collection *that* Moses the servant of God *laid* upon Israel in the wilderness. [10]And all the princes and all the people rejoiced, and brought in, and cast into the chest, until they had made an end. [11]Now it came to pass, that at what time the chest was brought unto the king's office by the hand of the Levites, and when they saw that *there was* much money, the king's scribe and the high priest's officer came and emptied the chest, and took it, and carried it to his place again.

Thus they did day by day, and gathered money in abundance. [12]And the king and Jehoiada gave it to such as did the work of the service of the house of the LORD, and hired masons and carpenters to repair the house of the LORD, and also such as wrought iron and brass to mend the house of the LORD. [13]So the workmen wrought, and the work[c] was perfected by them, and they set the house of God in his state, and strengthened it. [14]And when they had finished *it*, they brought the rest of the money before the king and Jehoiada, whereof were made vessels for the house of the LORD, *even* vessels to minister, and to offer[d] *withal*, and spoons, and vessels of gold and silver. And they offered burnt offerings in the house of the LORD continually all the days of Jehoiada.

[15]But Jehoiada waxed old, and was full of days when he died; an hundred and thirty years old *was he* when he died. [16]And they buried him in the city of David among the kings, because he had done good in Israel, both toward God, and toward his house. [17]Now after the death of Jehoiada came the princes of Judah, and made obeisance to the king. Then the king hearkened unto them. [18]And they left the house of the LORD God of their fathers, and served groves and idols: and wrath came upon Judah and Jerusalem for this their trespass. [19]Yet he sent prophets to them, to bring them again unto the LORD; and they testified against them: but they would not give ear. [20]And the Spirit of

---

[a] to repair: Heb. to renew
[b] a proclamation: Heb. a voice
[c] the work . . . : Heb. the healing went up upon the work
[d] to offer . . . : or, pestils

Devotional Moment

•

Parenting

24:17-18 After Jehoiada's death, Judah's leaders persuaded Joash to turn away from the Lord. During the preceding years of Joash's reign only one man stood between Judah and the idolatrous sins of the surrounding nations—Jehoiada. Jehoiada's standing for God made a huge difference. Through his influence on Joash, the entire nation followed God during his lifetime. You may not be in a position of power, but you can teach others the importance of being true to God no matter what problems or temptations they face. It may make all the difference in the world.

God came[e] upon Zechariah the son of Jehoiada the priest, which stood above the people, and said unto them, Thus saith God, Why transgress ye the commandments of the LORD, that ye cannot prosper? because ye have forsaken the LORD, he hath also forsaken you. ²¹And they conspired against him, and stoned him with stones at the commandment of the king in the court of the house of the LORD. ²²Thus Joash the king remembered not the kindness which Jehoiada his father had done to him, but slew his son. And when he died, he said, The LORD look upon *it*, and require *it*. ²³And it came to pass at the end of the year, *that* the host of Syria came up against him: and they came to Judah and Jerusalem, and destroyed all the princes of the people from among the people, and sent all the spoil of them unto the king of Damas-cus. ²⁴For the army of the Syrians came with a small company of men, and the LORD delivered a very great host into their hand, because they had forsaken the LORD God of their fathers. So they executed judgment against Joash. ²⁵And when they were departed from him, (for they left him in great diseases,) his own servants conspired against him for the blood of the sons of Jehoiada the priest, and slew him on his bed, and he died: and they buried him in the city of David, but they buried him not in the sepulchres of the kings. ²⁶And these are they that conspired against him; Zabad[f] the son of Shimeath an Ammonitess, and Jehozabad the son of Shimrith a Moabitess. ²⁷Now *concerning* his sons, and the greatness of the burdens *laid* upon him, and the repairing[g] of the house of God, behold, they *are* written in the story of the book of the kings. And Amaziah his son reigned in his stead.

25

¹Amaziah *was* twenty and five years old *when* he began to reign, and he reigned twenty and nine years in Jerusalem. And his mother's name *was* Jehoaddan of Jerusalem. ²And he did *that which was* right in the sight of the LORD, but not with a perfect heart. ³Now it came to pass, when the kingdom was established[a] to him, that he slew his servants that had killed the king his father. ⁴But he slew not their children, but *did* as *it is* written in the law in the book of

---

[e] came . . . : Heb. clothed
[f] Zabad: or, Jozacher
[g] repairing: Heb. founding
[a] established . . . : Heb. confirmed upon him

Moses, where the LORD commanded, saying, The fathers shall not die for the children, neither shall the children die for the fathers, but every man shall die for his own sin. ⁵Moreover Amaziah gathered Judah together, and made them captains over thousands, and captains over hundreds, according to the houses of *their* fathers, throughout all Judah and Benjamin: and he numbered them from twenty years old and above, and found them three hundred thousand choice *men, able* to go forth to war, that could handle spear and shield. ⁶He hired also an hundred thousand mighty men of valour out of Israel for an hundred talents of silver. ⁷But there came a man of God to him, saying, O king, let not the army of Israel go with thee; for the LORD *is* not with Israel, *to wit, with* all the children of Ephraim. ⁸But if thou wilt go, do *it*, be strong for the battle: God shall make thee fall before the enemy: for God hath power to help, and to cast down. ⁹And Amaziah said to the man of God, But what shall we do for the hundred talents which I have given to the armyᵇ of Israel? And the man of God answered, The LORD is able to give thee much more than this. ¹⁰Then Amaziah separated them, *to wit*, the army that was come to him out of Ephraim, to go home againᶜ: wherefore their anger was greatly kindled against Judah, and they returned home in great anger. ¹¹And Amaziah strengthened himself, and led forth his people, and went to the valley of salt,

and smote of the children of Seir ten thousand. ¹²And *other* ten thousand *left* alive did the children of Judah carry away captive, and brought them unto the top of the rock, and cast them down from the top of the rock, that they all were broken in pieces. ¹³But the soldiersᵈ of the army which Amaziah sent back, that they should not go with him to battle, fell upon the cities of Judah, from Samaria even unto Bethhoron, and smote three thousand of them, and took much spoil.

¹⁴Now it came to pass, after that Amaziah was come from the slaughter of the Edomites, that he brought the gods of the children of Seir, and set them up *to be* his gods, and bowed down himself before them, and burned incense unto them. ¹⁵Wherefore the anger of the LORD was kindled against Amaziah, and he sent unto him a prophet, which said unto him, Why hast thou sought after the gods of the people, which could not deliver their own people out of thine hand? ¹⁶And it came to pass, as he talked with him, that *the king* said unto him, Art thou made of the king's counsel? forbear; why shouldest thou be smitten? Then the prophet forbare, and said, I know that God hath determinedᵉ to destroy thee, because thou hast done this, and hast not hearkened unto my counsel.

¹⁷Then Amaziah king of Judah took advice, and sent to Joash, the son of Jehoahaz, the son of Jehu, king of Israel, saying, Come, let us see one an-

---

ᵇ army: Heb. band
ᶜ home again: Heb. to their place
ᵈ the soldiers . . . : Heb. the sons of the band
ᵉ determined: Heb. counselled

other in the face. [18]And Joash king of Israel sent to Amaziah king of Judah, saying, The thistle[f] that *was* in Lebanon sent to the cedar that *was* in Lebanon, saying, Give thy daughter to my son to wife: and there passed by a wild beast that *was* in Lebanon, and trode down the thistle. [19]Thou sayest, Lo, thou hast smitten the Edomites; and thine heart lifteth thee up to boast: abide now at home; why shouldest thou meddle to *thine* hurt, that thou shouldest fall, *even* thou, and Judah with thee? [20]But Amaziah would not hear; for it *came* of God, that he might deliver them into the hand *of their enemies,* because they sought after the gods of Edom. [21]So Joash the king of Israel went up; and they saw one another in the face, *both* he and Amaziah king of Judah, at Bethshemesh, which *belongeth* to Judah. [22]And Judah was put to the worse before Israel, and they fled every man to his tent. [23]And Joash the king of Israel took Amaziah king of Judah, the son of Joash, the son of Jehoahaz, at Bethshemesh, and brought him to Jerusalem, and brake down the wall of Jerusalem from the gate of Ephraim to the corner[g] gate, four hundred cubits. [24]And *he took* all the gold and the silver, and all the vessels that were found in the house of God with Obededom, and the treasures of the king's house, the hostages also, and returned to Samaria. [25]And Amaziah the son of Joash king of Judah lived after the death of Joash son of Jehoahaz king of Israel fifteen years. [26]Now the rest of the acts of Amaziah, first and last, behold, *are* they not written in the book of the kings of Judah and Israel? [27]Now after the time that Amaziah did turn away from following the LORD they made a conspiracy against him in Jerusalem; and he fled to Lachish: but they sent to Lachish after him, and slew him there. [28]And they brought him upon horses, and buried him with his fathers in the city of Judah[h].

26

[1]Then all the people of Judah took Uzziah[a], who *was* sixteen years old, and made him king in the room of his father Amaziah. [2]He built Eloth, and restored it to Judah, after that the king slept with his fathers. [3]Sixteen years old *was* Uzziah when he began to reign, and he reigned fifty and two years in Jerusalem. His mother's name also *was* Jecoliah of Jerusalem. [4]And he did *that which was* right in the sight of the LORD, according to all that his father Amaziah did. [5]And he sought God in the days of Zechariah, who had understanding in the visions[b] of God: and as long as he sought the LORD, God made him to prosper. [6]And he went forth and warred against the Philistines, and brake down the wall of Gath, and the wall of Jabneh, and the wall of Ashdod, and built cities about Ashdod, and among the Philistines. [7]And God

---

[f] thistle: or, furze bush, or, thorn
[g] the corner . . . : Heb. the gate of it that looketh
[h] Judah: that is, the city of David
[a] Uzziah: or, Azariah
[b] in the visions . . . : Heb. in the seeing of God

helped him against the Philistines, and against the Arabians that dwelt in Gurbaal, and the Mehunims. ⁸And the Ammonites gave gifts to Uzziah: and his name spread abroad *even* to the entering in of Egypt; for he strengthened *himself* exceedingly. ⁹Moreover Uzziah built towers in Jerusalem at the corner gate, and at the valley gate, and at the turning *of the wall*, and fortified᷄ them. ¹⁰Also he built towers in the desert, and digged⁴ many wells: for he had much cattle, both in the low country, and in the plains: husbandmen *also*, and vine dressers in the mountains, and in Carmel: for he loved husbandry. ¹¹Moreover Uzziah had an host of fighting men, that went out to war by bands, according to the number of their account by the hand of Jeiel the scribe and Maaseiah the ruler, under the hand of Hananiah, *one* of the king's captains. ¹²The whole number of the chief of the fathers of the mighty men of valour *were* two thousand and six hundred. ¹³And under their hand *was* an army᷄, three hundred thousand and seven thousand and five hundred, that made war with mighty power, to help the king against the enemy. ¹⁴And Uzziah prepared for them throughout all the host shields, and spears, and helmets, and habergeons, and bows, and slings⁴ *to cast* stones. ¹⁵And he made in Jerusalem engines, invented by cunning men, to be on the towers and upon the bulwarks, to shoot arrows and great stones withal. And his name spread᷄ far abroad; for he was marvellously helped, till he was strong.

¹⁶But when he was strong, his heart was lifted up to *his* destruction: for he transgressed against the LORD his God, and went into the temple of the LORD to burn incense upon the altar of incense. ¹⁷And Azariah the priest went in after him, and with him fourscore priests of the LORD, *that were* valiant men: ¹⁸And they withstood Uzziah the king, and said unto him, *It appertaineth* not unto thee, Uzziah, to burn incense unto the LORD, but to the priests the sons of Aaron, that are consecrated to burn incense: go out of the sanctuary; for thou hast trespassed; neither *shall it be* for thine honour from the LORD God. ¹⁹Then Uzziah was wroth, and *had* a censer in his hand to burn incense: and while he was wroth with the priests, the leprosy even rose up in his forehead before the priests in the house of the LORD, from beside the incense altar. ²⁰And Azariah the chief priest, and all the priests, looked upon him, and, behold, he *was* leprous in his forehead, and they thrust him out from thence; yea, himself hasted also to go out, because the LORD had smitten him. ²¹And Uzziah the king was a leper unto the day of his death, and dwelt in a several᷄ house, *being* a leper; for he was cut off from the house of the

---

᷄ fortified: or, repaired
⁴ digged . . . : or, cut out many cisterns
᷄ an army: Heb. the power of an army
⁴ slings . . . : Heb. stones of slings
᷄ spread: Heb. went forth
᷄ several: Heb. free

LORD: and Jotham his son *was* over the king's house, judging the people of the land. ²²Now the rest of the acts of Uzziah, first and last, did Isaiah the prophet, the son of Amoz, write. ²³So Uzziah slept with his fathers, and they buried him with his fathers in the field of the burial which *belonged* to the kings; for they said, He *is* a leper: and Jotham his son reigned in his stead.

27

¹Jotham *was* twenty and five years old when he began to reign, and he reigned sixteen years in Jerusalem. His mother's name also *was* Jerushah, the daughter of Zadok. ²And he did *that which was* right in the sight of the LORD, according to all that his father Uzziah did: howbeit he entered not into the temple of the LORD. And the people did yet corruptly. ³He built the high gate of the house of the LORD, and on the wall of Ophel[a] he built much. ⁴Moreover he built cities in the mountains of Judah, and in the forests he built castles and towers. ⁵He fought also with the king of the Ammonites, and prevailed against them. And the children of Ammon gave him the same year an hundred talents of silver, and ten thousand measures of wheat, and ten thousand of barley. So much did the children of Ammon pay unto him, both the second year, and the third. ⁶So Jotham became mighty, because he prepared[b] his ways before the LORD his God. ⁷Now the rest of the acts of Jotham, and all his wars, and his ways, lo, they *are* written in the book of the kings of Israel and Judah. ⁸He was five and twenty years old when he began to reign, and reigned sixteen years in Jerusalem. ⁹And Jotham slept with his fathers, and they buried him in the city of David: and Ahaz his son reigned in his stead.

28

¹Ahaz *was* twenty years old when he began to reign, and he reigned sixteen years in Jerusalem: but he did not *that which was* right in the sight of the LORD, like David his father: ²For he walked in the ways of the kings of Israel, and made also molten images for Baalim. ³Moreover he burnt incense in the valley of the son of Hinnom, and burnt[a] his children in the fire, after the abominations of the heathen whom the LORD had cast out before the children of Israel. ⁴He sacrificed also and burnt incense in the high places, and on the hills, and under every green tree. ⁵Wherefore the LORD his God delivered him into the hand of the king of Syria; and they smote him, and carried away a great multitude of them captives, and brought *them* to Damascus[b]. And he was also delivered into the hand of the king of Israel, who smote him with a great slaughter.

⁶For Pekah the son of Remaliah slew in Judah an hundred and twenty thousand in one day, *which were* all valiant[c] men; because they had forsaken

---

[a] Ophel: or, the tower
[b] prepared: or, established
[a] burnt . . . : or, offered sacrifice
[b] Damascus: Heb. Darmesek
[c] valiant . . . : Heb. sons of valour

the LORD God of their fathers. [7]And Zichri, a mighty man of Ephraim, slew Maaseiah the king's son, and Azrikam the governor of the house, and Elkanah *that was* next[d] to the king. [8]And the children of Israel carried away captive of their brethren two hundred thousand, women, sons, and daughters, and took also away much spoil from them, and brought the spoil to Samaria. [9]But a prophet of the LORD was there, whose name *was* Oded: and he went out before the host that came to Samaria, and said unto them, Behold, because the LORD God of your fathers was wroth with Judah, he hath delivered them into your hand, and ye have slain them in a rage *that* reacheth up unto heaven. [10]And now ye purpose to keep under the children of Judah and Jerusalem for bondmen and bondwomen unto you: *but are there* not with you, even with you, sins against the LORD your God? [11]Now hear me therefore, and deliver the captives again, which ye have taken captive of your brethren: for the fierce wrath of the LORD *is* upon you. [12]Then certain of the heads of the children of Ephraim, Azariah the son of Johanan, Berechiah the son of Meshillemoth, and Jehizkiah the son of Shallum, and Amasa the son of Hadlai, stood up against them that came from the war, [13]And said unto them, Ye shall not bring in the captives hither: for whereas we have offended against the LORD *already*, ye intend to add *more* to our sins and to our trespass: for our trespass is great, and *there is* fierce wrath against Israel. [14]So the armed men left the captives and the spoil before the princes and all the congregation. [15]And the men which were expressed by name rose up, and took the captives, and with the spoil clothed all that were naked among them, and arrayed them, and shod them, and gave them to eat and to drink, and anointed them, and carried all the feeble of them upon asses, and brought them to Jericho, the city of palm trees, to their brethren: then they returned to Samaria.

[16]At that time did king Ahaz send unto the kings of Assyria to help him. [17]For again the Edomites had come and smitten Judah, and carried away captives[e]. [18]The Philistines also had invaded the cities of the low country, and of the south of Judah, and had taken Bethshemesh, and Ajalon, and Gederoth, and Shocho with the villages thereof, and Timnah with the villages thereof, Gimzo also and the villages thereof: and they dwelt there. [19]For the LORD brought Judah low because of Ahaz king of Israel; for he made Judah naked, and transgressed sore against the LORD. [20]And Tilgathpilneser king of Assyria came unto him, and distressed him, but strengthened him not. [21]For Ahaz took away a portion *out* of the house of the LORD, and *out* of the house of the king, and of the princes, and gave *it* unto the king of Assyria: but he helped him not. [22]And in the time of his distress did he trespass yet more against the LORD: this *is that* king Ahaz. [23]For he sacrificed unto the gods of Damascus[f], which smote him: and he

---

[d] next . . . : Heb. the second to the king
[e] captives: Heb. a captivity
[f] Damascus: Heb. Darmesek

said, Because the gods of the kings of Syria help them, *therefore* will I sacrifice to them, that they may help me. But they were the ruin of him, and of all Israel. ²⁴And Ahaz gathered together the vessels of the house of God, and cut in pieces the vessels of the house of God, and shut up the doors of the house of the LORD, and he made him altars in every corner of Jerusalem. ²⁵And in every several city of Judah he made high places to burn incense unto other gods, and provoked to anger the LORD God of his fathers. ²⁶Now the rest of his acts and of all his ways, first and last, behold, they *are* written in the book of the kings of Judah and Israel. ²⁷And Ahaz slept with his fathers, and they buried him in the city, *even* in Jerusalem: but they brought him not into the sepulchres of the kings of Israel: and Hezekiah his son reigned in his stead.

29

¹Hezekiah began to reign *when he was* five and twenty years old, and he reigned nine and twenty years in Jerusalem. And his mother's name *was* Abijah, the daughter of Zechariah. ²And he did *that which was* right in the sight of the LORD, according to all that David his father had done. ³He in the first year of his reign, in the first month, opened the doors of the house of the LORD, and repaired them. ⁴And he brought in the priests and the Levites, and gathered them together into the east street, ⁵And said unto them, Hear me, ye Levites, sanctify now yourselves, and sanctify the house of the LORD God of your fa-

thers, and carry forth the filthiness out of the holy *place*. ⁶For our fathers have trespassed, and done *that which was* evil in the eyes of the LORD our God, and have forsaken him, and have turned away their faces from the habitation of the LORD, and turned *their* backs. ⁷Also they have shut up the doors of the porch, and put out the lamps, and have not burned incense nor offered burnt offerings in the holy *place* unto the God of Israel. ⁸Wherefore the wrath of the LORD was upon Judah and Jerusalem, and he hath delivered them to trouble[a], to astonishment, and to hissing, as ye see with your eyes. ⁹For, lo, our fathers have fallen by the sword, and our sons and our daughters and our wives *are* in captivity for this. ¹⁰Now *it is* in mine heart to make a covenant with the LORD God of Israel, that his fierce wrath may turn away from us. ¹¹My sons, be not now negligent: for the LORD hath chosen you to stand before him, to serve him, and that ye should minister unto him, and burn incense.

¹²Then the Levites arose, Mahath the son of Amasai, and Joel the son of Azariah, of the sons of the Kohathites: and of the sons of Merari, Kish the son of Abdi, and Azariah the son of Jehalelel: and of the Gershonites; Joah the son of Zimmah, and Eden the son of Joah: ¹³And of the sons of Elizaphan; Shimri, and Jeiel: and of the sons of Asaph; Zechariah, and Mattaniah: ¹⁴And of the sons of Heman; Jehiel, and Shimei: and of the sons of Jeduthun; Shemaiah, and Uzziel. ¹⁵And they gathered their brethren, and sanctified themselves, and came, according to the commandment

---

[a] trouble: Heb. commotion

of the king, by the words[b] of the LORD, to cleanse the house of the LORD. [16]And the priests went into the inner part of the house of the LORD, to cleanse *it*, and brought out all the uncleanness that they found in the temple of the LORD into the court of the house of the LORD. And the Levites took *it*, to carry *it* out abroad into the brook Kidron. [17]Now they began on the first *day* of the first month to sanctify, and on the eighth day of the month came they to the porch of the LORD: so they sanctified the house of the LORD in eight days; and in the sixteenth day of the first month they made an end. [18]Then they went in to Hezekiah the king, and said, We have cleansed all the house of the LORD, and the altar of burnt offering, with all the vessels thereof, and the shewbread table, with all the vessels thereof. [19]Moreover all the vessels, which king Ahaz in his reign did cast away in his transgression, have we prepared and sanctified, and, behold, they *are* before the altar of the LORD.

[20]Then Hezekiah the king rose early, and gathered the rulers of the city, and went up to the house of the LORD. [21]And they brought seven bullocks, and seven rams, and seven lambs, and seven he goats, for a sin offering for the kingdom, and for the sanctuary, and for Judah. And he commanded the priests the sons of Aaron to offer *them* on the altar of the LORD. [22]So they killed the bullocks, and the priests received the blood, and sprinkled *it* on the altar: likewise, when they had killed the rams, they sprinkled the blood upon the altar: they killed also the lambs, and they sprinkled the blood upon the altar. [23]And they brought forth[c] the he goats *for* the sin offering before the king and the congregation; and they laid their hands upon them: [24]And the priests killed them, and they made reconciliation with their blood upon the altar, to make an atonement for all Israel: for the king commanded *that* the burnt offering and the sin offering *should be made* for all Israel. [25]And he set the Levites in the house of the LORD with cymbals, with psalteries, and with harps, according to the commandment of David, and of Gad the king's seer, and Nathan the prophet: for *so was* the commandment of the LORD by his prophets. [26]And the Levites stood with the instruments of David, and the priests with the trumpets. [27]And Hezekiah commanded to offer the burnt offering upon the altar. And when[d] the burnt offering began, the song of the LORD began *also* with the trumpets, and with the instruments *ordained* by David king of Israel. [28]And all the congregation worshipped, and the singers[e] sang, and the trumpeters sounded: *and* all *this continued* until the burnt offering was finished. [29]And when they had made an end of offering, the king and all that were present[f] with him bowed themselves, and worshipped. [30]Moreover Hezekiah the king and the princes com-

---

[b] by the words . . . : or, in the business of the LORD
[c] forth: Heb. near
[d] when: Heb. in the time
[e] singers: Heb. song
[f] present: Heb. found

manded the Levites to sing praise unto the LORD with the words of David, and of Asaph the seer. And they sang praises with gladness, and they bowed their heads and worshipped. [31]Then Hezekiah answered and said, Now ye have consecrated[g] yourselves unto the LORD, come near and bring sacrifices and thank offerings into the house of the LORD. And the congregation brought in sacrifices and thank offerings; and as many as were of a free heart burnt offerings. [32]And the number of the burnt offerings, which the congregation brought, was threescore and ten bullocks, an hundred rams, *and* two hundred lambs: all these *were* for a burnt offering to the LORD. [33]And the consecrated things *were* six hundred oxen and three thousand sheep. [34]But the priests were too few, so that they could not flay all the burnt offerings: wherefore their brethren the Levites did help[h] them, till the work was ended, and until the *other* priests had sanctified themselves: for the Levites *were* more upright in heart to sanctify themselves than the priests. [35]And also the burnt offerings *were* in abundance, with the fat of the peace offerings, and the drink offerings for *every* burnt offering. So the service of the house of the LORD was set in order. [36]And Hezekiah rejoiced, and all the people, that God had prepared the people: for the thing was *done* suddenly.

30

[1]And Hezekiah sent to all Israel and Judah, and wrote letters also to Ephraim and Manasseh, that they should come to the house of the LORD at Jerusalem, to keep the passover unto the LORD God of Israel. [2]For the king had taken counsel, and his princes, and all the congregation in Jerusalem, to keep the passover in the second month. [3]For they could not keep it at that time, because the priests had not sanctified themselves sufficiently, neither had the people gathered themselves together to Jerusalem. [4]And the thing pleased[a] the king and all the congregation. [5]So they established a decree to make proclamation throughout all Israel, from Beersheba even to Dan, that they should come to keep the passover unto the LORD God of Israel at Jerusalem: for they had not done *it* of a long *time in such sort* as it was written. [6]So the posts went with the letters from[b] the king and his princes throughout all Israel and Judah, and according to the commandment of the king, saying, Ye children of Israel, turn again unto the LORD God of Abraham, Isaac, and Israel, and he will return to the remnant of you, that are escaped out of the hand of the kings of Assyria. [7]And be not ye like your fathers, and like your brethren, which trespassed against the LORD God of their fathers, *who* therefore gave them up to desolation, as ye see. [8]Now be ye not stiffnecked, as your fathers *were,* but yield yourselves unto the LORD, and enter into his sanctuary, which he hath sanctified for ever: and serve the LORD your God, that the fierceness of his wrath may turn away from you. [9]For if ye turn again

---

[g] consecrated . . . : or, filled your hand
[h] did help . . . : Heb. strengthened them
[a] pleased . . . : Heb. was right in the eyes of the king
[b] from: Heb. from the hand

Devotional Moment

•

Family Excuses

30:7-14 When the king invited all Israel to come to the Temple and observe the Passover, only the people of Judah and a few others came. Most of the people apparently ignored the king's warning not to be like their fathers and brothers who sinned against the Lord (v. 7). Sometimes it is tempting to use the irresponsible behavior of another family member to justify or excuse our own sins. "Everyone else in the family is this way; I can't help it." "Don't be so hard on me. Like father like son, you know." If you are aware of a negative family tendency, use that knowledge to work against that tendency, not to excuse the wrong behavior.

unto the LORD, your brethren and your children *shall find* compassion before them that lead them captive, so that they shall come again into this land: for the LORD your God *is* gracious and merciful, and will not turn away *his* face from you, if ye return unto him. ¹⁰So the posts passed from city to city through the country of Ephraim and Manasseh even unto Zebulun: but they laughed them to scorn, and mocked them. ¹¹Nevertheless divers of Asher and Manasseh and of Zebulun humbled themselves, and came to Jerusalem. ¹²Also in Judah the hand of God was to give them one heart to do the commandment of the king and of the princes, by the word of the LORD.

¹³And there assembled at Jerusalem much people to keep the feast of unleavened bread in the second month, a very great congregation. ¹⁴And they arose and

took away the altars that *were* in Jerusalem, and all the altars for incense took they away, and cast *them* into the brook Kidron. ¹⁵Then they killed the passover on the fourteenth *day* of the second month: and the priests and the Levites were ashamed, and sanctified themselves, and brought in the burnt offerings into the house of the LORD. ¹⁶And they stood in their place^c after their manner, according to the law of Moses the man of God: the priests sprinkled the blood, *which they received* of the hand of the Levites. ¹⁷For *there were* many in the congregation that were not sanctified: therefore the Levites had the charge of the killing of the passovers for every one *that was* not clean, to sanctify *them* unto the LORD. ¹⁸For a multitude of the people, *even* many of Ephraim, and Manasseh, Issachar, and Zebulun, had not cleansed themselves, yet did they eat the passover otherwise than it was written. But Hezekiah prayed for them, saying, The good LORD pardon every one ¹⁹ *That* prepareth his heart to seek God, the LORD God of his fathers, though *he be* not *cleansed* according to the purification of the sanctuary. ²⁰And the LORD hearkened to Hezekiah, and healed the people.

²¹And the children of Israel that were present^d at Jerusalem kept the feast of unleavened bread seven days with great gladness: and the Levites and the priests praised the LORD day by day, *singing* with loud instruments unto the LORD. ²²And Hezekiah spake comfortably^e unto all the Levites that taught the

---

^c their place: Heb. their standing

^d present: Heb. found

^e comfortably . . . : Heb. to the heart of all

Manasseh

A good home. Good parents. A good education. Privilege. It's all a formula for raising great kids, right?

Manasseh had a good father—Hezekiah, one of Israel's most exemplary kings. He had a good education and many privileges, but he grew up to be a thoroughly evil man. Among his vilest offenses: sacrifice of his own children.

Manasseh's life changed drastically when the invading Assyrians captured him and carried him off to Babylon. The once-proud man was handcuffed and hauled away. The tragedy caused Manasseh to cry out humbly to God for help. God forgave him and returned him to his people.

We don't know exactly how long it took Manasseh to realize his mistakes. We know only that his change of heart was a true conversion. He stopped worshiping idols, restored God's Temple, and started obeying God.

Manasseh's life teaches us that sometimes children go their own way. God in his mercy may use drastic means to get their attention. We know from both the Bible and our own experience that not all of them get the message. But if they listen and desire a change, God will bless them with forgiveness and the power to change.

We can't know what our children will become. We can only pray that, in the end, God will get their attention.

LESSONS FROM MANASSEH AS AN ADULT CONVERT

Sometimes children go their own way. Despite a "privileged" upbringing and a godly father, Manasseh chose to live an evil lifestyle.

Sometimes God in his mercy uses tragedy to get our attention. That's what it took to shake Manasseh out of his spiritual coma.

We are not bound by our past. Even though Manasseh chose evil early on, God enabled him to change. It is never too late to turn from sin and follow God.

good knowledge of the LORD: and they did eat throughout the feast seven days, offering peace offerings, and making confession to the LORD God of their fathers. ²³And the whole assembly took counsel to keep other seven days: and they kept *other* seven days with gladness. ²⁴For Hezekiah king of Judah did give[f] to the congregation a thousand bullocks and seven thousand sheep; and the princes gave to the congregation a thousand bullocks and ten thousand sheep: and a great number of priests sanctified themselves. ²⁵And all the congregation of Judah, with the priests and the Levites, and all the congregation that came out of Israel, and the strangers that came out of the land of Israel, and that dwelt in Judah, rejoiced. ²⁶So there was great joy in Jerusalem: for since the time of Solomon the son of David king of Israel *there was* not the like in Jerusalem. ²⁷Then the priests the Levites arose and blessed the people: and their voice was heard, and their prayer came *up* to his holy[g] dwelling place, *even* unto heaven.

31

¹Now when all this was finished, all Israel that were present[a] went out to the cities of Judah, and brake the images in pieces, and cut down the groves, and threw down the high places and the altars out of all Judah and Benjamin, in Ephraim also and Manasseh, until they had utterly destroyed them all. Then all the children of Israel returned, every man to his possession, into their own cities. ²And Hezekiah appointed the courses of the priests and the Levites after their courses, every man according to his service, the priests and Levites for burnt offerings and for peace offerings, to minister, and to give thanks, and to praise in the gates of the tents of the LORD. ³*He appointed* also the king's portion of his substance for the burnt offerings, *to wit*, for the morning and evening burnt offerings, and the burnt offerings for the sabbaths, and for the new moons, and for the set feasts, as *it is* written in the law of the LORD. ⁴Moreover he commanded the people that dwelt in Jerusalem to give the portion of the priests and the Levites, that they might be encouraged in the law of the LORD. ⁵And as soon as the commandment came abroad, the children of Israel brought in abundance the firstfruits of corn, wine, and oil, and honey, and of all the increase of the field; and the tithe of all *things* brought they in abundantly. ⁶And *concerning* the children of Israel and Judah, that dwelt in the cities of Judah, they also brought in the tithe of oxen and sheep, and the tithe of holy things which were consecrated unto the LORD their God, and laid *them* by heaps[b]. ⁷In the third month they began to lay the foundation of the heaps, and finished *them* in the seventh month. ⁸And when Hezekiah and the princes came and saw the heaps, they blessed the LORD, and his people Israel. ⁹Then Hezekiah questioned with

---

[f] did give: Heb. lifted up, or, offered
[g] his holy . . . : Heb. the habitation of his holiness
[a] present: Heb. found
[b] by heaps: Heb. heaps, heaps

the priests and the Levites concerning the heaps. [10]And Azariah the chief priest of the house of Zadok answered him, and said, Since *the people* began to bring the offerings into the house of the LORD, we have had enough to eat, and have left plenty: for the LORD hath blessed his people; and that which is left *is* this great store.

[11]Then Hezekiah commanded to prepare chambers[c] in the house of the LORD; and they prepared *them*, [12]And brought in the offerings and the tithes and the dedicated *things* faithfully: over which Cononiah the Levite *was* ruler, and Shimei his brother *was* the next. [13]And Jehiel, and Azaziah, and Nahath, and Asahel, and Jerimoth, and Jozabad, and Eliel, and Ismachiah, and Mahath, and Benaiah, *were* overseers under the hand of Cononiah and Shimei his brother, at the commandment of Hezekiah the king, and Azariah the ruler of the house of God. [14]And Kore the son of Imnah the Levite, the porter toward the east, *was* over the freewill offerings of God, to distribute the oblations of the LORD, and the most holy things. [15]And next him *were* Eden, and Miniamin, and Jeshua, and Shemaiah, Amariah, and Shecaniah, in the cities of the priests, in *their* set office, to give to their brethren by courses, as well to the great as to the small: [16]Beside their genealogy of males, from three years old and upward, *even* unto every one that entereth into the house of the LORD, his daily portion for their service in their charges according to their courses; [17]Both to the ge-nealogy of the priests by the house of their fathers, and the Levites from twenty years old and upward, in their charges by their courses; [18]And to the genealogy of all their little ones, their wives, and their sons, and their daughters, through all the congregation: for in their set office they sanctified themselves in holiness: [19]Also of the sons of Aaron the priests, *which were* in the fields of the suburbs of their cities, in every several city, the men that were expressed by name, to give portions to all the males among the priests, and to all that were reckoned by genealogies among the Levites. [20]And thus did Hezekiah throughout all Judah, and wrought *that which was* good and right and truth before the LORD his God. [21]And in every work that he began in the service of the house of God, and in the law, and in the commandments, to seek his God, he did *it* with all his heart, and prospered.

32

[1]After these things, and the establishment thereof, Sennacherib king of Assyria came, and entered into Judah, and encamped against the fenced cities, and thought to win[a] them for himself. [2]And when Hezekiah saw that Sennacherib was come, and that he was purposed to fight against Jerusalem, [3]He took counsel with his princes and his mighty men to stop the waters of the fountains which *were* without the city: and they did help him. [4]So there was gathered much people together, who stopped all the fountains, and the brook that ran[b] through the

---

[c] chambers: or, storehouses
[a] to win . . . : Heb. to break them up
[b] ran: Heb. overflowed

midst of the land, saying, Why should the kings of Assyria come, and find much water? ⁵Also he strengthened himself, and built up all the wall that was broken, and raised *it* up to the towers, and another wall without, and repaired Millo *in* the city of David, and made darts^c and shields in abundance. ⁶And he set captains of war over the people, and gathered them together to him in the street of the gate of the city, and spake^d comfortably to them, saying, ⁷Be strong and courageous, be not afraid nor dismayed for the king of Assyria, nor for all the multitude that *is* with him: for *there be* more with us than with him: ⁸With him *is* an arm of flesh; but with us *is* the LORD our God to help us, and to fight our battles. And the people rested^e themselves upon the words of Hezekiah king of Judah.

⁹After this did Sennacherib king of Assyria send his servants to Jerusalem, (but he *himself laid siege* against Lachish, and all his power with him,) unto Hezekiah king of Judah, and unto all Judah that *were* at Jerusalem, saying, ¹⁰Thus saith Sennacherib king of Assyria, Whereon do ye trust, that ye abide in the siege^f in Jerusalem? ¹¹Doth not Hezekiah persuade you to give over yourselves to die by famine and by thirst, saying, The LORD our God shall deliver us out of the hand of the king of Assyria? ¹²Hath not the same Hezekiah taken away his high places and his altars, and commanded Judah and Jerusalem, saying, Ye shall worship before one altar, and burn incense upon it? ¹³Know ye not what I and my fathers have done unto all the people of *other* lands? were the gods of the nations of those lands any ways able to deliver their lands out of mine hand? ¹⁴Who *was there* among all the gods of those nations that my fathers utterly destroyed, that could deliver his people out of mine hand, that your God should be able to deliver you out of mine hand? ¹⁵Now therefore let not Hezekiah deceive you, nor persuade you on this manner, neither yet believe him: for no god of any nation or kingdom was able to deliver his people out of mine hand, and out of the hand of my fathers: how much less shall your God deliver you out of mine hand? ¹⁶And his servants spake yet *more* against the LORD God, and against his servant Hezekiah. ¹⁷He wrote also letters to rail on the LORD God of Israel, and to speak against him, saying, As the gods of the nations of *other* lands have not delivered their people out of mine hand, so shall not the God of Hezekiah deliver his people out of mine hand. ¹⁸Then they cried with a loud voice in the Jews' speech unto the people of Jerusalem that *were* on the wall, to affright them, and to trouble them; that they might take the city. ¹⁹And they spake against the God of Jerusalem, as against the gods of the people of the earth, *which were* the work of the hands of man. ²⁰And for this *cause* Hezekiah the king, and the prophet Isaiah the son

---

^c darts: or, swords, or, weapons
^d spake . . . : Heb. he spoke to their heart
^e rested . . . : Heb. leaned
^f siege: or, strong hold

of Amoz, prayed and cried to heaven. [21]And the LORD sent an angel, which cut off all the mighty men of valour, and the leaders and captains in the camp of the king of Assyria. So he returned with shame of face to his own land. And when he was come into the house of his god, they that came forth of his own bowels slew[g] him there with the sword. [22]Thus the LORD saved Hezekiah and the inhabitants of Jerusalem from the hand of Sennacherib the king of Assyria, and from the hand of all *other*, and guided them on every side. [23]And many brought gifts unto the LORD to Jerusalem, and presents[h] to Hezekiah king of Judah: so that he was magnified in the sight of all nations from thenceforth.

[24]In those days Hezekiah was sick to the death, and prayed unto the LORD: and he spake unto him, and he gave[i] him a sign. [25]But Hezekiah rendered not again according to the benefit *done* unto him; for his heart was lifted up: therefore there was wrath upon him, and upon Judah and Jerusalem. [26]Notwithstanding Hezekiah humbled himself for the pride[j] of his heart, *both* he and the inhabitants of Jerusalem, so that the wrath of the LORD came not upon them in the days of Hezekiah. [27]And Hezekiah had exceeding much riches and honour: and he made himself treasuries for silver, and for gold, and for precious stones, and for spices, and for shields, and for all manner of pleasant[k] jewels; [28]Storehouses also for the increase of corn, and wine, and oil; and stalls for all manner of beasts, and cotes for flocks. [29]Moreover he provided him cities, and possessions of flocks and herds in abundance: for God had given him substance very much. [30]This same Hezekiah also stopped the upper watercourse of Gihon, and brought it straight down to the west side of the city of David. And Hezekiah prospered in all his works. [31]Howbeit in *the business of* the ambassadors[l] of the princes of Babylon, who sent unto him to enquire of the wonder that was *done* in the land, God left him, to try him, that he might know all *that was* in his heart. [32]Now the rest of the acts of Hezekiah, and his goodness[m], behold, they *are* written in the vision of Isaiah the prophet, the son of Amoz, *and* in the book of the kings of Judah and Israel. [33]And Hezekiah slept with his fathers, and they buried him in the chiefest[n] of the sepulchres of the sons of David: and all Judah and the inhabitants of Jerusalem did him honour at his death. And Manasseh his son reigned in his stead.

33

[1]Manasseh *was* twelve years old when he began to reign, and he reigned fifty

---

[g] slew . . . : Heb. made him fall
[h] presents: Heb. precious things
[i] gave . . . : or, wrought a miracle for him
[j] pride: Heb. lifting up
[k] pleasant . . . : Heb. instruments of desire
[l] ambassadors: Heb. interpreters
[m] goodness: Heb. kindnesses
[n] chiefest: or, highest

and five years in Jerusalem: ²But did *that which was* evil in the sight of the LORD, like unto the abominations of the heathen, whom the LORD had cast out before the children of Israel. ³For he built* again the high places which Hezekiah his father had broken down, and he reared up altars for Baalim, and made groves, and worshipped all the host of heaven, and served them. ⁴Also he built altars in the house of the LORD, whereof the LORD had said, In Jerusalem shall my name be for ever. ⁵And he built altars for all the host of heaven in the two courts of the house of the LORD. ⁶And he caused his children to pass through the fire in the valley of the son of Hinnom: also he observed times, and used enchantments, and used witchcraft, and dealt with a familiar spirit, and with wizards: he wrought much evil in the sight of the LORD, to provoke him to anger. ⁷And he set a carved image, the idol which he had made, in the house of God, of which God had said to David and to Solomon his son, In this house, and in Jerusalem, which I have chosen before all the tribes of Israel, will I put my name for ever: ⁸Neither will I any more remove the foot of Israel from out of the land which I have appointed for your fathers; so that they will take heed to do all that I have commanded them, according to the whole law and the statutes and the ordinances by the hand of Moses. ⁹So Manasseh made Judah and the inhabitants of Jerusalem to err, *and* to do worse than the heathen,

whom the LORD had destroyed before the children of Israel. ¹⁰And the LORD spake to Manasseh, and to his people: but they would not hearken.

¹¹Wherefore the LORD brought upon them the captains of the host of the king* of Assyria, which took Manasseh among the thorns, and bound him with fetters, and carried him to Babylon. ¹²And when he was in affliction, he besought the LORD his God, and humbled himself greatly before the God of his fathers, ¹³And prayed unto him: and he was intreated of him, and heard his supplication, and brought him again to Jerusalem into his kingdom. Then Manasseh knew that the LORD he *was* God. ¹⁴Now after this he built a wall without the city of David, on the west side of Gihon, in the valley, even to the entering in at the fish gate, and compassed about Ophel*, and raised it up a very great height, and put captains of war in all the fenced cities of Judah. ¹⁵And he took away the strange gods, and the idol out of the house of the LORD, and all the altars that he had built in the mount of the house of the LORD, and in Jerusalem, and cast *them* out of the city. ¹⁶And he repaired the altar of the LORD, and sacrificed thereon peace offerings and thank offerings, and commanded Judah to serve the LORD God of Israel. ¹⁷Nevertheless the people did sacrifice still in the high places, *yet* unto the LORD their God only. ¹⁸Now the rest of the acts of Manasseh, and his prayer unto his God, and the words of the seers that spake to

---

ª he built . . . : Heb. he returned and built
ᵇ of the king: Heb. which were the king's
ᶜ Ophel: or, the tower

him in the name of the LORD God of Israel, behold, they *are written* in the book of the kings of Israel. ¹⁹His prayer also, and *how God* was intreated of him, and all his sin, and his trespass, and the places wherein he built high places, and set up groves and graven images, before he was humbled: behold, they *are* written among the sayings of the seers[d]. ²⁰So Manasseh slept with his fathers, and they buried him in his own house: and Amon his son reigned in his stead.

²¹Amon *was* two and twenty years old when he began to reign, and reigned two years in Jerusalem. ²²But he did *that which was* evil in the sight of the LORD, as did Manasseh his father: for Amon sacrificed unto all the carved images which Manasseh his father had made, and served them; ²³And humbled not himself before the LORD, as Manasseh his father had humbled himself; but Amon trespassed more and more. ²⁴And his servants conspired against him, and slew him in his own house. ²⁵But the people of the land slew all them that had conspired against king Amon; and the people of the land made Josiah his son king in his stead.

34

¹Josiah *was* eight years old when he began to reign, and he reigned in Jerusalem one and thirty years. ²And he did *that which was* right in the sight of the LORD, and walked in the ways of David his father, and declined *neither* to the right hand, nor to the left. ³For in the eighth year of his reign, while he was yet young, he be-gan to seek after the God of David his father: and in the twelfth year he began to purge Judah and Jerusalem from the high places, and the groves, and the carved images, and the molten images. ⁴And they brake down the altars of Baalim in his presence; and the images[a], that *were* on high above them, he cut down; and the groves, and the carved images, and the molten images, he brake in pieces, and made dust *of them*, and strowed *it* upon the graves of them that had sacrificed unto them. ⁵And he burnt the bones of the priests upon their altars, and cleansed Judah and Jerusalem. ⁶And *so did he* in the cities of Manasseh, and Ephraim, and Simeon, even unto Naphtali, with their mattocks[b] round about. ⁷And when he had broken down the altars and the groves, and had beaten the graven images into powder, and cut down all the idols throughout all the land of Israel, he returned to Jerusalem.

⁸Now in the eighteenth year of his reign, when he had purged the land, and the house, he sent Shaphan the son of Azaliah, and Maaseiah the governor of the city, and Joah the son of Joahaz the recorder, to repair the house of the LORD his God. ⁹And when they came to Hilkiah the high priest, they delivered the money that was brought into the house of God, which the Levites that kept the doors had gathered of the hand of Manasseh and Ephraim, and of all the remnant of Israel, and of all Judah and Benjamin; and they returned to Jerusalem. ¹⁰And they put *it* in the hand of the workmen that had the oversight of the house

---

[d] the seers: or, Hosai
[a] the images: or, the sun images
[b] mattocks: or, mauls

of the LORD, and they gave it to the workmen that wrought in the house of the LORD, to repair and amend the house: ¹¹Even to the artificers and builders gave they *it*, to buy hewn stone, and timber for couplings, and to floor^c the houses which the kings of Judah had destroyed. ¹²And the men did the work faithfully: and the overseers of them *were* Jahath and Obadiah, the Levites, of the sons of Merari; and Zechariah and Meshullam, of the sons of the Kohathites, to set *it* forward; and *other of* the Levites, all that could skill of instruments of musick. ¹³Also *they were* over the bearers of burdens, and *were* overseers of all that wrought the work in any manner of service: and of the Levites *there were* scribes, and officers, and porters.

¹⁴And when they brought out the money that was brought into the house of the LORD, Hilkiah the priest found a book of the law of the LORD *given* by^d Moses. ¹⁵And Hilkiah answered and said to Shaphan the scribe, I have found the book of the law in the house of the LORD. And Hilkiah delivered the book to Shaphan. ¹⁶And Shaphan carried the book to the king, and brought the king word back again, saying, All that was committed to thy servants, they do *it*. ¹⁷And they have gathered together^e the money that was found in the house of the LORD, and have delivered it into the hand of the overseers, and to the hand of the workmen. ¹⁸Then Shaphan the scribe told the king, saying, Hilkiah

the priest hath given me a book. And Shaphan read it before the king. ¹⁹And it came to pass, when the king had heard the words of the law, that he rent his clothes. ²⁰And the king commanded Hilkiah, and Ahikam the son of Shaphan, and Abdon^f the son of Micah, and Shaphan the scribe, and Asaiah a servant of the king's, saying, ²¹Go, enquire of the LORD for me, and for them that are left in Israel and in Judah, concerning the words of the book that is found: for great *is* the wrath of the LORD that is poured out upon us, because our fathers have not kept the word of the LORD, to do after all that is written in this book. ²²And Hilkiah, and *they* that the king *had appointed*, went to Huldah the prophetess, the wife of Shallum the son of Tikvath, the son of Hasrah^g, keeper of the wardrobe; (now she dwelt in Jerusalem in the college:) and they spake to her to that *effect*. ²³And she answered them, Thus saith the LORD God of Israel, Tell ye the man that sent you to me, ²⁴Thus saith the LORD, Behold, I will bring evil upon this place, and upon the inhabitants thereof, *even* all the curses that are written in the book which they have read before the king of Judah: ²⁵Because they have forsaken me, and have burned incense unto other gods, that they might provoke me to anger with all the works of their hands; therefore my wrath shall be poured out upon this place, and shall not be quenched. ²⁶And as for the king of Ju-

---

^c to floor: or, to rafter
^d by: Heb. by the hand of
^e gathered together: Heb. poured out, or, melted
^f Abdon: or, Achbor
^g Hasrah: also called, Harhas

dah, who sent you to enquire of the LORD, so shall ye say unto him, Thus saith the LORD God of Israel *concerning* the words which thou hast heard; [27]Because thine heart was tender, and thou didst humble thyself before God, when thou heardest his words against this place, and against the inhabitants thereof, and humbledst thyself before me, and didst rend thy clothes, and weep before me; I have even heard *thee* also, saith the LORD. [28]Behold, I will gather thee to thy fathers, and thou shalt be gathered to thy grave in peace, neither shall thine eyes see all the evil that I will bring upon this place, and upon the inhabitants of the same. So they brought the king word again.

[29]Then the king sent and gathered together all the elders of Judah and Jerusalem. [30]And the king went up into the house of the LORD, and all the men of Judah, and the inhabitants of Jerusalem, and the priests, and the Levites, and all the people, great[h] and small: and he read in their ears all the words of the book of the covenant that was found in the house of the LORD. [31]And the king stood in his place, and made a covenant before the LORD, to walk after the LORD, and to keep his commandments, and his testimonies, and his statutes, with all his heart, and with all his soul, to perform the words of the covenant which are written in this book. [32]And he caused all that were present[i] in Jerusalem and Benjamin to stand *to it*. And the inhabitants of Jerusalem did according to the covenant of God, the God of their fathers.

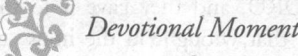

Devotional Moment

•

The Bible

34:29-32 King Josiah called everyone together and read to them the laws of God found in the Temple. Then he led the people in renewing their commitment to follow the Lord. Josiah serves as an example of what every spiritual leader should do: lead others in reading God's Word. If you are a church or family leader, follow Josiah's example by reading and teaching from the Bible and urging others to apply God's Word in their lives. You don't need to speak profound commentary; it is enough that you read to them and lead them in acknowledging the importance of the Bible as God's words to us.

[33]And Josiah took away all the abominations out of all the countries that *pertained* to the children of Israel, and made all that were present[j] in Israel to serve, *even* to serve the LORD their God. *And* all his days they departed not from following the LORD, the God of their fathers.

35

[1]Moreover Josiah kept a passover unto the LORD in Jerusalem: and they killed the passover on the fourteenth *day* of the first month. [2]And he set the priests in their charges, and encouraged them to the service of the house of the LORD, [3]And said unto the Levites that taught all Israel, which were holy unto the LORD, Put the holy ark in the house which Solomon the son of David king of Israel did build; *it shall* not *be* a burden upon *your* shoulders: serve now the LORD your God, and his people Israel, [4]And prepare *yourselves* by

---

[h] great . . . : Heb. from great even to small
[i] present: Heb. found
[j] present: Heb. found

the houses of your fathers, after your courses, according to the writing of David king of Israel, and according to the writing of Solomon his son. ⁵And stand in the holy *place* according to the divisions of the families of the fathers of your brethren the people, and *after* the division of the families of the Levites. ⁶So kill the passover, and sanctify yourselves, and prepare your brethren, that *they* may do according to the word of the LORD by the hand of Moses. ⁷And Josiah gave^a to the people, of the flock, lambs and kids, all for the passover offerings, for all that were present, to the number of thirty thousand, and three thousand bullocks: these *were* of the king's substance. ⁸And his princes gave willingly^b unto the people, to the priests, and to the Levites: Hilkiah and Zechariah and Jehiel, rulers of the house of God, gave unto the priests for the passover offerings two thousand and six hundred *small cattle*, and three hundred oxen. ⁹Conaniah also, and Shemaiah and Nethaneel, his brethren, and Hashabiah and Jeiel and Jozabad, chief of the Levites, gave^c unto the Levites for passover offerings five thousand *small cattle, and five hundred oxen*. ¹⁰So the service was prepared, and the priests stood in their place, and the Levites in their courses, according to the king's commandment. ¹¹And they killed the passover, and the priests sprinkled *the blood* from their hands, and the Levites flayed *them*. ¹²And they removed the burnt offerings, that they might give according to the divisions of the families of the people, to offer unto the LORD, as *it is* written in the book of Moses. And so *did they* with the oxen. ¹³And they roasted the passover with fire according to the ordinance: but the *other* holy *offerings* sod they in pots, and in caldrons, and in pans, and divided *them* speedily^d among all the people. ¹⁴And afterward they made ready for themselves, and for the priests: because the priests the sons of Aaron *were busied* in offering of burnt offerings and the fat until night; therefore the Levites prepared for themselves, and for the priests the sons of Aaron. ¹⁵And the singers the sons of Asaph *were* in their place^e, according to the commandment of David, and Asaph, and Heman, and Jeduthun the king's seer; and the porters *waited* at every gate; they might not depart from their service; for their brethren the Levites prepared for them. ¹⁶So all the service of the LORD was prepared the same day, to keep the passover, and to offer burnt offerings upon the altar of the LORD, according to the commandment of king Josiah. ¹⁷And the children of Israel that were present^f kept the passover at that time, and the feast of unleavened bread seven days. ¹⁸And there was no passover like to that kept in Israel from the days of Samuel the prophet; neither did all the kings of Israel keep such a passover as Josiah kept, and the priests, and the Levites, and all Judah and Israel that were

---

^a gave: Heb. offered
^b gave willingly: Heb. offered, etc
^c gave: Heb. offered
^d divided . . . : Heb. made them run
^e place: Heb. station
^f present: Heb. found

present[g], and the inhabitants of Jerusalem. [19]In the eighteenth year of the reign of Josiah was this passover kept.

[20]After all this, when Josiah had prepared the temple[h], Necho king of Egypt came up to fight against Carchemish by Euphrates: and Josiah went out against him. [21]But he sent ambassadors to him, saying, What have I to do with thee, thou king of Judah? *I come* not against thee this day, but against the house[i] wherewith I have war: for God commanded me to make haste: forbear thee from *meddling with* God, who *is* with me, that he destroy thee not. [22]Nevertheless Josiah would not turn his face from him, but disguised himself, that he might fight with him, and hearkened not unto the words of Necho from the mouth of God, and came to fight in the valley of Megiddo. [23]And the archers shot at king Josiah; and the king said to his servants, Have me away; for I am sore wounded[j]. [24]His servants therefore took him out of that chariot, and put him in the second chariot that he had; and they brought him to Jerusalem, and he died, and was buried in *one of* the sepulchres of his fathers. And all Judah and Jerusalem mourned for Josiah. [25]And Jeremiah lamented for Josiah: and all the singing men and the singing women spake of Josiah in their lamentations to this day, and made them an ordinance in Israel: and, behold, they *are* written in the lamentations. [26]Now the rest of the acts of Josiah, and his goodness[k], according to *that which was* written in the law of the LORD, [27]And his deeds, first and last, behold, they *are* written in the book of the kings of Israel and Judah.

36

[1]Then the people of the land took Jehoahaz the son of Josiah, and made him king in his father's stead in Jerusalem. [2]Jehoahaz *was* twenty and three years old when he began to reign, and he reigned three months in Jerusalem. [3]And the king of Egypt put him down at Jerusalem, and condemned the land in an hundred talents of silver and a talent of gold. [4]And the king of Egypt made Eliakim his brother king over Judah and Jerusalem, and turned his name to Jehoiakim. And Necho took Jehoahaz his brother, and carried him to Egypt. [5]Jehoiakim *was* twenty and five years old when he began to reign, and he reigned eleven years in Jerusalem: and he did *that which was* evil in the sight of the LORD his God. [6]Against him came up Nebuchadnezzar king of Babylon, and bound him in fetters[a], to carry him to Babylon. [7]Nebuchadnezzar also carried of the vessels of the house of the LORD to Babylon, and put them in his temple at Babylon. [8]Now the rest of the acts of Jehoiakim, and his abominations which he did, and that which was found in him, behold, they *are* written in the book of the kings of Israel and Judah: and Jehoiachin[b]

---

[g] present: Heb. found
[h] temple: Heb. house
[i] the house . . . : Heb. the house of my war
[j] wounded: Heb. made sick
[k] goodness: Heb. kindnesses
[a] fetters: or, chains
[b] Jehoiachin: also called, Jeconiah, or, Coniah

his son reigned in his stead. ⁹Jehoiachin *was* eight years old when he began to reign, and he reigned three months and ten days in Jerusalem: and he did *that which was* evil in the sight of the LORD. ¹⁰And when the year was expired, king Nebuchadnezzar sent, and brought him to Babylon, with the goodly vessels of the house of the LORD, and made Zedekiah his brother king over Judah and Jerusalem.

¹¹Zedekiah *was* one and twenty years old when he began to reign, and reigned eleven years in Jerusalem. ¹²And he did *that which was* evil in the sight of the LORD his God, *and* humbled not himself before Jeremiah the prophet *speaking* from the mouth of the LORD. ¹³And he also rebelled against king Nebuchadnezzar, who had made him swear by God: but he stiffened his neck, and hardened his heart from turning unto the LORD God of Israel. ¹⁴Moreover all the chief of the priests, and the people, transgressed very much after all the abominations of the heathen; and polluted the house of the LORD which he had hallowed in Jerusalem. ¹⁵And the LORD God of their fathers sent to them by[c] his messengers, rising up betimes, and sending; because he had compassion on his people, and on his dwelling place: ¹⁶But they mocked the messengers of God, and despised his words, and misused his prophets, until the wrath of the LORD arose against his people, till *there was* no remedy[d]. ¹⁷Therefore he brought upon them the king of the Chaldees, who slew their young men with the sword in the house of their sanctuary, and had no compassion upon young man or maiden, old man, or him that stooped for age: he gave *them* all into his hand. ¹⁸And all the vessels of the house of God, great and small, and the treasures of the house of the LORD, and the treasures of the king, and of his princes; all *these* he brought to Babylon. ¹⁹And they burnt the house of God, and brake down the wall of Jerusalem, and burnt all the palaces thereof with fire, and destroyed all the goodly vessels thereof. ²⁰And them that had escaped from the sword carried he away to Babylon; where they were servants to him and his sons until the reign of the kingdom of Persia: ²¹To fulfil the word of the LORD by the mouth of Jeremiah, until the land had enjoyed her sabbaths: *for* as long as she lay desolate she kept sabbath, to fulfil threescore and ten years.

²²Now in the first year of Cyrus king of Persia, that the word of the LORD *spoken* by the mouth of Jeremiah might be accomplished, the LORD stirred up the spirit of Cyrus king of Persia, that he made a proclamation throughout all his kingdom, and *put it* also in writing, saying, ²³Thus saith Cyrus king of Persia, All the kingdoms of the earth hath the LORD God of heaven given me; and he hath charged me to build him an house in Jerusalem, which *is* in Judah. Who *is there* among you of all his people? The LORD his God *be* with him, and let him go up.

---

[c] by: Heb. by the hand of
[d] remedy: Heb. healing

EZRA

Purpose
To show God's faithfulness and the way he kept his promise to restore his people to their land

Author
Not stated, but probably Ezra

Date Written
Approximately 450 B.C., recording events from about 538–450 B.C.

Setting
Ezra follows 2 Chronicles as a history of the Jewish people, recording their return to Israel after the captivity.

Key Verse
The children of Israel "kept the feast of unleavened bread seven days with joy: for the Lord had made them joyful, and turned the heart of the king of Assyria unto them, to strengthen their hands in the work of the house of God" (6:22).

Key People
Cyrus, Zerubbabel, Haggai, Zechariah, Darius, Artaxerxes I, Ezra

Key Places
Babylon, Jerusalem

Special Features
The books of Haggai and Zechariah should be studied with Ezra since their prophesies were given during the period of the reconstruction.

All of us know the hassle of picking up messes. Socks pile up with heaping regularity in many homes, as do dirty dishes and unopened junk mail. The congressional question is: Whose job is it to sort and distribute the piles, to clean up the mess? Smart parents put these dull duties on kids' chore lists at a ripe young age and never take them off. Perhaps that explains why Cyrus let the Israelites return to Jerusalem. Why should mighty Persians clean up a Babylonian mess? Let the Hebrews do it.

But Ezra offers better reasons for this amazing fix-it mission. Something about the witness of the Hebrew captives compelled the pagan emperor of the East to waste no time authorizing this journey. Cyrus even gave witness to God in his cleanup decree. The Israelites were better missionaries in captivity than when they lived in the Promised Land. Now they were going back to rebuild their Temple and recover their identity.

What a thrilling but treacherous journey! The politically savvy Israelites had no power, no clout—only a chore list. They would clean up the mess. Yet God was with them; the westward caravan was a divine mission. Hope ran high; excitement was contagious. The Israelites had every reason to whistle while they worked—a nifty way for us, too, to get through the daily chores.

1

¹Now in the first year of Cyrus king of Persia, that the word of the LORD by the mouth of Jeremiah might be fulfilled, the LORD stirred up the spirit of Cyrus king of Persia, that he made a proclamation throughout all his kingdom, and *put it* also in writing, saying, ²Thus saith Cyrus king of Persia, The LORD God of heaven hath given me all the kingdoms of the earth; and he hath charged me to build him an house at Jerusalem, which *is* in Judah. ³Who *is there* among you of all his people? his God be with him, and let him go up to Jerusalem, which *is* in Judah, and build the house of the LORD God of Israel, (he *is* the God,) which *is* in Jerusalem. ⁴And whosoever remaineth in any place where he sojourneth, let the men of his place help[a] him with silver, and with gold, and with goods, and with beasts, beside the freewill offering for the house of God that *is* in Jerusalem.

⁵Then rose up the chief of the fa-

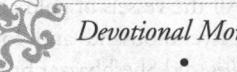

Devotional Moment
•
Family Protection

1:2 A man whose word was law decreed that the powerless Hebrews could return to their religious center, Jerusalem. Imagine the profound delight of Hebrew parents who could now plan to raise children in the nurture and admonition of the Lord. It was a miracle! If you have hopes and dreams for your children that seem unattainable, remember Cyrus's change of heart. Pray often, then sleep well at night. God can change the hearts and minds of people who affect your family.

Devotional Moment
•
Teamwork

1:4-6 Ezra, Jeshua, Zerubbabel, and Nehemiah looked ahead to a monumental job. Without teamwork, Cyrus's decree would be just words on parchment. But the united effort of all the generations in all the Hebrew families would make the difference. What a challenge! When your family faces a challenge—recovery from illness, a move, or remodeling—rely on teamwork. Harness the vision you have to restore order and schedule. Assign key duties to each person, track the daily progress made, and do whatever else it takes to keep everyone motivated. Do it together.

thers of Judah and Benjamin, and the priests, and the Levites, with all *them* whose spirit God had raised, to go up to build the house of the LORD which *is* in Jerusalem. ⁶And all they that *were* about them strengthened[b] their hands with vessels of silver, with gold, with goods, and with beasts, and with precious things, beside all *that* was willingly offered. ⁷Also Cyrus the king brought forth the vessels of the house of the LORD, which Nebuchadnezzar had brought forth out of Jerusalem, and had put them in the house of his gods; ⁸Even those did Cyrus king of Persia bring forth by the hand of Mithredath the treasurer, and numbered them unto Sheshbazzar, the prince of Judah. ⁹And this *is* the number of them: thirty chargers of gold, a thousand chargers of silver, nine and twenty knives, ¹⁰Thirty basons of gold, silver basons of a second *sort* four hundred and ten, *and* other vessels

---

[a] help . . . : Heb. lift him up
[b] strengthened . . . : that is, helped them

a thousand. ¹¹All the vessels of gold and of silver *were* five thousand and four hundred. All *these* did Sheshbazzar bring up with *them of* the captivity[c] that were brought up from Babylon unto Jerusalem.

2

¹Now these *are* the children of the province that went up out of the captivity, of those which had been carried away, whom Nebuchadnezzar the king of Babylon had carried away unto Babylon, and came again unto Jerusalem and Judah, every one unto his city; ²Which came with Zerubbabel: Jeshua, Nehemiah, Seraiah[a], Reelaiah, Mordecai, Bilshan, Mispar, Bigvai, Rehum, Baanah. The number of the men of the people of Israel: ³The children of Parosh, two thousand an hundred seventy and two. ⁴The children of Shephatiah, three hundred seventy and two. ⁵The children of Arah, seven hundred seventy and five. ⁶The children of Pahathmoab, of the children of Jeshua *and* Joab, two thousand eight hundred and twelve. ⁷The children of Elam, a thousand two hundred fifty and four. ⁸The children of Zattu, nine hundred forty and five. ⁹The children of Zaccai, seven hundred and threescore. ¹⁰The children of Bani[b], six hundred forty and two. ¹¹The children of Bebai, six hundred twenty and three. ¹²The children of Azgad, a thousand two hundred twenty and two. ¹³The children of Adonikam, six hundred sixty and six. ¹⁴The children of Bigvai, two thousand fifty and six. ¹⁵The children of Adin, four hundred fifty and four. ¹⁶The children of Ater of Hezekiah, ninety and eight. ¹⁷The children of Bezai, three hundred twenty and three. ¹⁸The children of Jorah[c], an hundred and twelve. ¹⁹The children of Hashum, two hundred twenty and three. ²⁰The children of Gibbar[d], ninety and five. ²¹The children of Bethlehem, an hundred twenty and three. ²²The men of Netophah, fifty and six. ²³The men of Anathoth, an hundred twenty and eight. ²⁴The children of Azmaveth[e], forty and two. ²⁵The children of Kirjatharim, Chephirah, and Beeroth, seven hundred and forty and three. ²⁶The children of Ramah and Gaba, six hundred twenty and one. ²⁷The men of Michmas, an hundred twenty and two. ²⁸The men of Bethel and Ai, two hundred twenty and three. ²⁹The children of Nebo, fifty and two. ³⁰The children of Magbish, an hundred fifty and six. ³¹The children of the other Elam, a thousand two hundred fifty and four. ³²The children of Harim, three hundred and twenty. ³³The children of Lod, Hadid[f], and Ono, seven hundred twenty and five. ³⁴The children of Jericho, three hundred forty and five. ³⁵The children of Senaah, three thousand and six hundred and thirty.

---

[c] the captivity: Heb. the transportation
[a] Seraiah: also called, Azariah
[b] Bani: also called, Binnui
[c] Jorah: also called, Hariph
[d] Gibbar: also called, Gibeon
[e] Azmaveth: also called, Bethazmaveth
[f] Hadid: or, Harid, as it is in some copies

³⁶The priests: the children of Jedaiah, of the house of Jeshua, nine hundred seventy and three. ³⁷The children of Immer, a thousand fifty and two. ³⁸The children of Pashur, a thousand two hundred forty and seven. ³⁹The children of Harim, a thousand and seventeen. ⁴⁰The Levites: the children of Jeshua and Kadmiel, of the children of Hodaviah^g, seventy and four. ⁴¹The singers: the children of Asaph, an hundred twenty and eight. ⁴²The children of the porters: the children of Shallum, the children of Ater, the children of Talmon, the children of Akkub, the children of Hatita, the children of Shobai, *in* all an hundred thirty and nine. ⁴³The Nethinims: the children of Ziha, the children of Hasupha, the children of Tabbaoth, ⁴⁴The children of Keros, the children of Siaha^h, the children of Padon, ⁴⁵The children of Lebanah, the children of Hagabah, the children of Akkub, ⁴⁶The children of Hagab, the children of Shalmai^i, the children of Hanan, ⁴⁷The children of Giddel, the children of Gahar, the children of Reaiah, ⁴⁸The children of Rezin, the children of Nekoda, the children of Gazzam, ⁴⁹The children of Uzza, the children of Paseah, the children of Besai, ⁵⁰The children of Asnah, the children of Mehunim, the children of Nephusim^j, ⁵¹The children of Bakbuk, the children of Hakupha, the children of Harhur, ⁵²The children of Bazluth^k, the children of Mehida, the children of Harsha, ⁵³The children of Barkos, the children of Sisera, the children of Thamah, ⁵⁴The children of Neziah, the children of Hatipha. ⁵⁵The children of Solomon's servants: the children of Sotai, the children of Sophereth, the children of Peruda^l, ⁵⁶The children of Jaalah, the children of Darkon, the children of Giddel, ⁵⁷The children of Shephatiah, the children of Hattil, the children of Pochereth of Zebaim, the children of Ami^m. ⁵⁸All the Nethinims, and the children of Solomon's servants, *were* three hundred ninety and two. ⁵⁹And these *were* they which went up from Telmelah, Telharsa, Cherub, Addan^n, *and* Immer: but they could not shew their father's house, and their seed, whether they *were* of Israel: ⁶⁰The children of Delaiah, the children of Tobiah, the children of Nekoda, six hundred fifty and two. ⁶¹And of the children of the priests: the children of Habaiah, the children of Koz, the children of Barzillai; which took a wife of the daughters of Barzillai the Gileadite, and was called after their name: ⁶²These sought their register *among* those that were reckoned by genealogy, but they were not found: therefore were they, as polluted^o, put from the

---

^{g} Hodaviah: also called, Judah or Hodevah
^{h} Siaha: also called, Sia
^{i} Shalmai: also called, Shamlai
^{j} Nephusim: also called, Nephisheim
^{k} Bazluth: also called, Bazlith
^{l} Peruda: also called, Perida
^{m} Ami: also called, Amon
^{n} Addan: also called, Addon
^{o} were they . . . : Heb. they were polluted from the priesthood

priesthood. [63]And the Tirshatha[p] said unto them, that they should not eat of the most holy things, till there stood up a priest with Urim and with Thummim.

[64]The whole congregation together *was* forty and two thousand three hundred *and* threescore, [65]Beside their servants and their maids, of whom *there were* seven thousand three hundred thirty and seven: and *there were* among them two hundred singing men and singing women. [66]Their horses *were* seven hundred thirty and six; their mules, two hundred forty and five; [67]Their camels, four hundred thirty and five; *their* asses, six thousand seven hundred and twenty. [68]And *some* of the chief of the fathers, when they came to the house of the LORD which *is* at Jerusalem, offered freely for the house of God to set it up in his place: [69]They gave after their ability unto the treasure of the work threescore and one thousand drams of gold, and five thousand pound of silver, and one hundred priests' garments. [70]So the priests, and the Levites, and *some* of the people, and the singers, and the porters, and the Nethinims, dwelt in their cities, and all Israel in their cities.

3

[1]And when the seventh month was come, and the children of Israel *were* in the cities, the people gathered themselves together as one man to Jerusalem. [2]Then stood up Jeshua[a] the son of Jozadak, and his brethren the priests, and Zerubbabel the son of Shealtiel, and his brethren, and builded the altar of the God of Israel, to offer burnt offerings thereon, as *it is* written in the law of Moses the man of God. [3]And they set the altar upon his bases; for fear *was* upon them because of the people of those countries: and they offered burnt offerings thereon unto the LORD, *even* burnt offerings morning and evening. [4]They kept also the feast of tabernacles, as *it is* written, and *offered* the daily burnt offerings by number, according to the custom, as the duty[b] of every day required; [5]And afterward *offered* the continual burnt offering, both of the new moons, and of all the set feasts of the LORD that were consecrated, and of every one that willingly offered a freewill offering unto the LORD. [6]From the first day of the seventh month began they to offer burnt offerings unto the LORD. But the foundation[c] of the temple of the LORD was not *yet* laid. [7]They gave money also unto the masons, and to the carpenters[d]; and meat, and drink, and oil, unto them of Zidon, and to them of Tyre, to bring cedar trees from Lebanon to the sea of Joppa, according to the grant that they had of Cyrus king of Persia.

[8]Now in the second year of their coming unto the house of God at Jerusalem, in the second month, began Zerubbabel the son of Shealtiel, and Jeshua the son of Jozadak, and the rem-

---

[p] Tirshatha: or, governor
[a] Jeshua: also called, Joshua
[b] as the duty . . . : Heb. the matter of the day in his day
[c] the foundation . . . : Heb. the temple of the LORD was not yet founded
[d] carpenters: or, workmen

nant of their brethren the priests and the Levites, and all they that were come out of the captivity unto Jerusalem; and appointed the Levites, from twenty years old and upward, to set forward the work of the house of the LORD. ⁹Then stood Jeshua *with* his sons and his brethren, Kadmiel and his sons, the sons of Judahᶜ, together, to set forward the workmen in the house of God: the sons of Henadad, *with* their sons and their brethren the Levites. ¹⁰And when the builders laid the foundation of the temple of the LORD, they set the priests in their apparel with trumpets, and the Levites the sons of Asaph with cymbals, to praise the LORD, after the ordinance of David king of Israel. ¹¹And they sang together by course in praising and giving thanks unto the LORD; because *he is* good, for his mercy *endureth* for ever toward Israel. And all the people shouted with a great shout, when they praised the LORD, because the foundation of the house of the LORD was laid. ¹²But many of the priests and Levites and chief of the fathers, *who were* ancient men, that had seen the first house, when the foundation of this house was laid before their eyes, wept with a loud voice; and many shouted aloud for joy: ¹³So that the people could not discern the noise of the shout of joy from the noise of the weeping of the people: for the people shouted with a loud shout, and the noise was heard afar off.

4

¹Now when the adversaries of Judah and Benjamin heard that the childrenᵃ

Devotional Moment
•
Persistence

4:1-6 Jeshua and Zerubbabel did God's work despite opposition, a good example for all of us. Make a little progress today; move a mountain tomorrow. People who keep working, through all the opposition, to promote excellence, to develop physical vigor, and to seek God each day will be rewarded.

---

of the captivity builded the temple unto the LORD God of Israel; ²Then they came to Zerubbabel, and to the chief of the fathers, and said unto them, Let us build with you: for we seek your God, as ye *do*; and we do sacrifice unto him since the days of Esarhaddon king of Assur, which brought us up hither. ³But Zerubbabel, and Jeshua, and the rest of the chief of the fathers of Israel, said unto them, Ye have nothing to do with us to build an house unto our God; but we ourselves together will build unto the LORD God of Israel, as king Cyrus

---

Devotional Moment
•
Lying

4:2 The words of Zerubbabel's enemies sounded nice, but they were lies. Words can be deceptive—either intentionally, as in this case, or unintentionally, as when people make glib promises that later prove hard to keep. But without basic honesty, we cannot trust each other. Do everything you can to promote truth telling in your home. If a child confesses a wrongdoing, be sure to affirm the child's honesty along with disciplining appropriately. And, above all, be truthful yourself.

ᶜ Judah: also called, Hodaviah
ᵃ the children . . . : Heb. the sons of the transportation

the king of Persia hath commanded us. [4]Then the people of the land weakened the hands of the people of Judah, and troubled them in building, [5]And hired counsellors against them, to frustrate their purpose, all the days of Cyrus king of Persia, even until the reign of Darius king of Persia.

[6]And in the reign of Ahasuerus[b], in the beginning of his reign, wrote they *unto him* an accusation against the inhabitants of Judah and Jerusalem. [7]And in the days of Artaxerxes wrote Bishlam[c], Mithredath, Tabeel, and the rest of their companions, unto Artaxerxes king of Persia; and the writing of the letter *was* written in the Syrian tongue, and interpreted in the Syrian tongue. [8]Rehum the chancellor and Shimshai the scribe[d] wrote a letter against Jerusalem to Artaxerxes the king in this sort: [9]Then *wrote* Rehum the chancellor, and Shimshai the scribe, and the rest of their companions[e]; the Dinaites, the Apharsathchites, the Tarpelites, the Apharsites, the Archevites, the Babylonians, the Susanchites, the Dehavites, *and* the Elamites, [10]And the rest of the nations whom the great and noble Asnappar brought over, and set in the cities of Samaria, and the rest *that are* on this side the river, and at such a time. [11]This *is* the copy of the letter that they sent unto him, *even* unto Artaxerxes the king; Thy servants the men on this side the river, and at such a time. [12]Be it known unto the king, that the Jews which came up from thee to us are come unto Jerusalem, building the rebellious and the bad city, and have set up[f] the walls *thereof,* and joined the foundations. [13]Be it known now unto the king, that, if this city be builded, and the walls set up *again, then* will they not pay[g] toll, tribute, and custom, and *so* thou shalt endamage the revenue of the kings. [14]Now because we have[h] maintenance from *the king's* palace, and it was not meet for us to see the king's dishonour, therefore have we sent and certified the king; [15]That search may be made in the book of the records of thy fathers: so shalt thou find in the book of the records, and know that this city *is* a rebellious city, and hurtful unto kings and provinces, and that they have moved[i] sedition within the same of old time: for which cause was this city destroyed. [16]We certify the king that, if this city be builded *again,* and the walls thereof set up, by this means thou shalt have no portion on this side the river.

[17]*Then* sent the king an answer unto Rehum the chancellor, and *to* Shimshai the scribe, and *to* the rest of their companions[j] that dwell in Samaria, and *unto* the rest beyond the river, Peace, and at

---

[b] Ahasuerus: Heb. Ahashverosh
[c] Bishlam: or, in peace
[d] scribe: or, secretary
[e] companions: Chaldee, societies
[f] set up: or, finished
[g] pay: Chaldee, give
[h] we have . . . : Chaldee, we are salted with the salt of the palace
[i] moved: Chaldee, made
[j] companions: Chaldee, societies

such a time. [18]The letter which ye sent unto us hath been plainly read before me. [19]And I commanded[k], and search hath been made, and it is found that this city of old time hath made insurrection against kings, and *that* rebellion and sedition have been made therein. [20]There have been mighty kings also over Jerusalem, which have ruled over all *countries* beyond the river; and toll, tribute, and custom, was paid unto them. [21]Give[l] ye now commandment to cause these men to cease, and that this city be not builded, until *another* commandment shall be given from me. [22]Take heed now that ye fail not to do this: why should damage grow to the hurt of the kings? [23]Now when the copy of king Artaxerxes' letter *was* read before Rehum, and Shimshai the scribe, and their companions, they went up in haste to Jerusalem unto the Jews, and made them to cease by force[m] and power. [24]Then ceased the work of the house of God which *is* at Jerusalem. So it ceased unto the second year of the reign of Darius king of Persia.

5

[1]Then the prophets, Haggai the prophet, and Zechariah the son of Iddo, prophesied unto the Jews that *were* in Judah and Jerusalem in the name of the God of Israel, *even* unto them. [2]Then rose up Zerubbabel the son of Shealtiel, and Jeshua the son of Jozadak, and began to build the house of God which *is* at

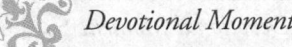

Devotional Moment
•
Encouragement

5:1-2 Encouragement builds confidence. We can well imagine how great the leaders and workers in Jerusalem felt when reminded that God was pleased by their efforts. The prophets who spoke words of God to them were like spark plugs to an engine. Hammers pounded faster and truer; chisels etched cleaner sides of stone. Words of encouragement between co-workers, siblings, or from a parent to a child, can energize love for many a day.

Jerusalem: and with them *were* the prophets of God helping them.

[3]At the same time came to them Tatnai, governor on this side the river, and Shetharboznai, and their companions, and said thus unto them, Who hath commanded you to build this house, and to make up this wall? [4]Then said we unto them after this manner, What are the names of the men that make[a] this building? [5]But the eye of their God was upon the elders of the Jews, that they could not cause them to cease, till the matter came to Darius: and then they returned answer by letter concerning this *matter*. [6]The copy of the letter that Tatnai, governor on this side the river, and Shetharboznai, and his companions the Apharsachites, which *were* on this side the river, sent unto Darius the king: [7]They sent a letter unto him, wherein[b] was written thus; Unto Darius

---

[k] I commanded: Chaldee, by me a decree is set
[l] Give . . . : Chaldee, Make a decree
[m] by force . . . : Chaldee, by arm and power
[a] make: Chaldee, build
[b] wherein: Chaldee, in the midst whereof

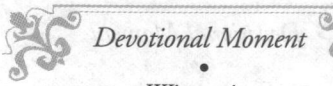

Devotional Moment
•
Witnessing

5:11 God's people had the courage and faithfulness to speak boldly about God to the representatives of King Darius—one of the most powerful men of their time. Christians today have every reason to testify for God. We live on the other side of A.D. 33 and know God's resurrection power. If we live close to God and know the joy of the Holy Spirit, our witness will be as fresh and natural as this letter to Darius—in all likelihood the most important letter that king ever received. If you are a believer in Christ, tell your neighbors.

the king, all peace. ⁸Be it known unto the king, that we went into the province of Judea, to the house of the great God, which is builded with great*ᶜ* stones, and timber is laid in the walls, and this work goeth fast on, and prospereth in their hands. ⁹Then asked we those elders, *and* said unto them thus, Who commanded you to build this house, and to make up these walls? ¹⁰We asked their names also, to certify thee, that we might write the names of the men that *were* the chief of them. ¹¹And thus they returned us answer, saying, We are the servants of the God of heaven and earth, and build the house that was builded these many years ago, which a great king of Israel builded and set up. ¹²But after that our fathers had provoked the God of heaven unto wrath, he gave them into the hand of Nebuchadnezzar the king of Babylon, the Chaldean, who destroyed this house,

and carried the people away into Babylon. ¹³But in the first year of Cyrus the king of Babylon *the same* king Cyrus made a decree to build this house of God. ¹⁴And the vessels also of gold and silver of the house of God, which Nebuchadnezzar took out of the temple that *was* in Jerusalem, and brought them into the temple of Babylon, those did Cyrus the king take out of the temple of Babylon, and they were delivered unto *one*, whose name *was* Sheshbazzar, whom he had made governor*ᵈ*; ¹⁵And said unto him, Take these vessels, go, carry them into the temple that *is* in Jerusalem, and let the house of God be builded in his place. ¹⁶Then came the same Sheshbazzar, *and* laid the foundation of the house of God which *is* in Jerusalem: and since that time even until now hath it been in building, and *yet* it is not finished. ¹⁷Now therefore, if *it seem* good to the king, let there be search made in the king's treasure house, which *is* there at Babylon, whether it be *so*, that a decree was made of Cyrus the king to build this house of God at Jerusalem, and let the king send his pleasure to us concerning this matter.

6

¹Then Darius the king made a decree, and search was made in the house of the rolls*ᵃ*, where the treasures were laid up in Babylon. ²And there was found at Achmetha*ᵇ*, in the palace that *is* in the province of the Medes, a roll, and therein *was* a record thus written: ³In the first year of Cyrus the king *the same*

ᶜ great . . . : Chaldee, stones of rolling
ᵈ governor: or, deputy
ᵃ rolls: Chaldee, books
ᵇ Achmetha: or, Ecbatana, or, in a coffer

Cyrus the king made a decree *concerning* the house of God at Jerusalem, Let the house be builded, the place where they offered sacrifices, and let the foundations thereof be strongly laid; the height thereof threescore cubits, *and* the breadth thereof threescore cubits; ⁴*With* three rows of great stones, and a row of new timber: and let the expenses be given out of the king's house: ⁵And also let the golden and silver vessels of the house of God, which Nebuchadnezzar took forth out of the temple which *is* at Jerusalem, and brought unto Babylon, be restored, and brought again^c unto the temple which *is* at Jerusalem, *every one* to his place, and place *them* in the house of God. ⁶Now *therefore,* Tatnai, governor beyond the river, Shetharboznai, and your companions the Apharsachites, which *are* beyond the river, be ye far from thence: ⁷Let the work of this house of God alone; let the governor of the Jews and the elders of the Jews build this house of God in his place. ⁸Moreover I make^d a decree what ye shall do to the elders of these Jews for the building of this house of God: that of the king's goods, *even* of the tribute beyond the river, forthwith expenses be given unto these men, that they be not hindered. ⁹And that which they have need of, both young bullocks, and rams, and lambs, for the burnt offerings of the God of heaven, wheat, salt, wine, and oil, according to the appointment of the priests which *are* at Jerusalem, let it be given them day by day without fail: ¹⁰That they may offer sacrifices of sweet savours unto the God of heaven, and pray for the life of the king, and of his sons. ¹¹Also I have made a decree, that whosoever shall alter this word, let timber be pulled down from his house, and being set up, let him be hanged thereon; and let his house be made a dunghill for this. ¹²And the God that hath caused his name to dwell there destroy all kings and people, that shall put to their hand to alter *and* to destroy this house of God which *is* at Jerusalem. I Darius have made a decree; let it be done with speed.

¹³Then Tatnai, governor on this side the river, Shetharboznai, and their companions, according to that which Darius the king had sent, so they did speedily. ¹⁴And the elders of the Jews builded, and they prospered through the prophesying of Haggai the prophet and Zechariah the son of Iddo. And they builded, and finished *it*, according to the commandment of the God of Israel, and according to the commandment^e of Cyrus, and Darius, and Artaxerxes king of Persia. ¹⁵And this house was finished on the third day of the month Adar, which was in the sixth year of the reign of Darius the king. ¹⁶And the children of Israel, the priests, and the Levites, and the rest of the children of the captivity, kept the dedication of this house of God with joy, ¹⁷And offered at the dedication of this house of God an hundred bullocks, two hundred rams, four hundred lambs; and for a sin offering for all Israel, twelve he goats,

---

^c brought again: Chaldee, go
^d I make . . . : Chaldee, by me a decree is made
^e commandment: Chaldee, decree

according to the number of the tribes of Israel. ¹⁸And they set the priests in their divisions, and the Levites in their courses, for the service of God, which *is* at Jerusalem; as it is written in the book of Moses. ¹⁹And the children of the captivity kept the passover upon the fourteenth *day* of the first month. ²⁰For the priests and the Levites were purified together, all of them *were* pure, and killed the passover for all the children of the captivity, and for their brethren the priests, and for themselves. ²¹And the children of Israel, which were come again out of captivity, and all such as had separated themselves unto them from the filthiness of the heathen of the land, to seek the LORD God of Israel, did eat, ²²And kept the feast of unleavened bread seven days with joy: for the LORD had made them joyful, and turned the heart of the king of Assyria unto them, to strengthen their hands in the work of the house of God, the God of Israel.

7

¹Now after these things, in the reign of Artaxerxes king of Persia, Ezra the son of Seraiah, the son of Azariah, the son of Hilkiah, ²The son of Shallum, the son of Zadok, the son of Ahitub, ³The son of Amariah, the son of Azariah, the son of Meraioth, ⁴The son of Zerahiah, the son of Uzzi, the son of Bukki, ⁵The son of Abishua, the son of Phinehas, the son of Eleazar, the son of Aaron the chief priest: ⁶This Ezra went up from Babylon; and he *was* a ready scribe in the law of Moses, which the LORD God of Israel had given: and the king

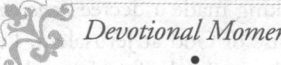

Devotional Moment
Teaching

7:6-10 Teacher Ezra knew his subject well and taught by word and example. Like him, parents need to know the Scriptures, to test life skills before they start giving lessons, to live their words, to make a strong effort to give teaching a pop of humor and a pinch of discipline. As a parent, you teach something nearly every waking hour. Listen to student feedback; consult often with fellow parent-teachers; pray a lot. Give those vital lessons your best shot.

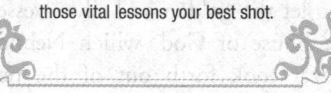

granted him all his request, according to the hand of the LORD his God upon him. ⁷And there went up *some* of the children of Israel, and of the priests, and the Levites, and the singers, and the porters, and the Nethinims, unto Jerusalem, in the seventh year of Artaxerxes the king. ⁸And he came to Jerusalem in the fifth month, which *was* in the seventh year of the king. ⁹For upon the first *day* of the first month beganᵃ he to go up from Babylon, and on the first *day* of the fifth month came he to Jerusalem, according to the good hand of his God upon him. ¹⁰For Ezra had prepared his heart to seek the law of the LORD, and to do *it*, and to teach in Israel statutes and judgments.

¹¹Now this *is* the copy of the letter that the king Artaxerxes gave unto Ezra the priest, the scribe, *even* a scribe of the words of the commandments of the LORD, and of his statutes to Israel. ¹²Artaxerxes, king of kings, unto Ezra the priest, a scribe of the law of the God of heaven, perfect *peace*, and at such a

---

ᵃ began . . . : Heb. was the foundation of the going up

time. ¹³I make a decree, that all they of the people of Israel, and *of* his priests and Levites, in my realm, which are minded of their own freewill to go up to Jerusalem, go with thee. ¹⁴Forasmuch as thou art sent of the king[b], and of his seven counsellors, to enquire concerning Judah and Jerusalem, according to the law of thy God which *is* in thine hand; ¹⁵And to carry the silver and gold, which the king and his counsellors have freely offered unto the God of Israel, whose habitation *is* in Jerusalem, ¹⁶And all the silver and gold that thou canst find in all the province of Babylon, with the freewill offering of the people, and of the priests, offering willingly for the house of their God which *is* in Jerusalem: ¹⁷That thou mayest buy speedily with this money bullocks, rams, lambs, with their meat offerings and their drink offerings, and offer them upon the altar of the house of your God which *is* in Jerusalem. ¹⁸And whatsoever shall seem good to thee, and to thy brethren, to do with the rest of the silver and the gold, that do after the will of your God. ¹⁹The vessels also that are given thee for the service of the house of thy God, *those* deliver thou before the God of Jerusalem. ²⁰And whatsoever more shall be needful for the house of thy God, which thou shalt have occasion to bestow, bestow *it* out of the king's treasure house. ²¹And I, *even* I Artaxerxes the king, do make a decree to all the treasurers which *are* beyond the river, that whatsoever Ezra the priest, the scribe of the law of the God of heaven, shall require of you, it be done speedily, ²²Unto an hundred talents of silver, and to an hundred measures[c] of wheat, and to an hundred baths of wine, and to an hundred baths of oil, and salt without prescribing *how much.* ²³Whatsoever[d] is commanded by the God of heaven, let it be diligently done for the house of the God of heaven: for why should there be wrath against the realm of the king and his sons? ²⁴Also we certify you, that touching any of the priests and Levites, singers, porters, Nethinims, or ministers of this house of God, it shall not be lawful to impose toll, tribute, or custom, upon them. ²⁵And thou, Ezra, after the wisdom of thy God, that *is* in thine hand, set magistrates and judges, which may judge all the people that *are* beyond the river, all such as know the laws of thy God; and teach ye them that know *them* not. ²⁶And whosoever will not do the law of thy God, and the law of the king, let judgment be executed speedily upon him, whether *it be* unto death, or to banishment[e], or to confiscation of goods, or to imprisonment.

²⁷Blessed *be* the LORD God of our fathers, which hath put *such a thing* as this in the king's heart, to beautify the house of the LORD which *is* in Jerusalem: ²⁸And hath extended mercy unto me before the king, and his counsellors, and before all the king's mighty princes. And I was strengthened as the hand of the LORD my God *was* upon

---

[b] of the king: Chaldee, from before the king
[c] measures: Chaldee, cors
[d] Whatsoever . . . : Chaldee, Whatsoever is of the decree
[e] to banishment: Chaldee, to rooting out

me, and I gathered together out of Israel chief men to go up with me.

8

¹These *are* now the chief of their fathers, and *this is* the genealogy of them that went up with me from Babylon, in the reign of Artaxerxes the king. ²Of the sons of Phinehas; Gershom: of the sons of Ithamar; Daniel: of the sons of David; Hattush. ³Of the sons of Shechaniah, of the sons of Pharosh; Zechariah: and with him were reckoned by genealogy of the males an hundred and fifty. ⁴Of the sons of Pahathmoab; Elihoenai the son of Zerahiah, and with him two hundred males. ⁵Of the sons of Shechaniah; the son of Jahaziel, and with him three hundred males. ⁶Of the sons also of Adin; Ebed the son of Jonathan, and with him fifty males. ⁷And of the sons of Elam; Jeshaiah the son of Athaliah, and with him seventy males. ⁸And of the sons of Shephatiah; Zebadiah the son of Michael, and with him fourscore males. ⁹Of the sons of Joab; Obadiah the son of Jehiel, and with him two hundred and eighteen males. ¹⁰And of the sons of Shelomith; the son of Josiphiah, and with him an hundred and threescore males. ¹¹And of the sons of Bebai; Zechariah the son[a] of Bebai, and with him twenty and eight males. ¹²And of the sons of Azgad; Johanan the son of Hakkatan, and with him an hundred and ten males. ¹³And of the last sons of Adonikam, whose names *are* these, Eliphelet, Jeiel, and Shemaiah, and with them threescore males. ¹⁴Of the sons also of Bigvai; Uthai, and Zabbud[b],

and with them seventy males. ¹⁵And I gathered them together to the river that runneth to Ahava; and there abode we in tents three days: and I viewed the people, and the priests, and found there none of the sons of Levi. ¹⁶Then sent I for Eliezer, for Ariel, for Shemaiah, and for Elnathan, and for Jarib, and for Elnathan, and for Nathan, and for Zechariah, and for Meshullam, chief men; also for Joiarib, and for Elnathan, men of understanding. ¹⁷And I sent them with commandment unto Iddo the chief at the place Casiphia, and I told[c] them what they should say unto Iddo, *and* to his brethren the Nethinims, at the place Casiphia, that they should bring unto us ministers for the house of our God. ¹⁸And by the good hand of our God upon us they brought us a man of understanding, of the sons of Mahli, the son of Levi, the son of Israel; and Sherebiah, with his sons and his brethren, eighteen; ¹⁹And Hashabiah, and with him Jeshaiah of the sons of Merari, his brethren and their sons, twenty; ²⁰Also of the Nethinims, whom David and the princes had appointed for the service of the Levites, two hundred and twenty Nethinims: all of them were expressed by name.

²¹Then I proclaimed a fast there, at the river of Ahava, that we might afflict ourselves before our God, to seek of him a right way for us, and for our little ones, and for all our substance. ²²For I was ashamed to require of the king a band of soldiers and horsemen to help us against the enemy in the way: be-

---

[a] the son . . . : or, the youngest son
[b] Zabbud: or, Zaccur, as some read
[c] I told . . . : Heb. I put words in their mouth

cause we had spoken unto the king, saying, The hand of our God *is* upon all them for good that seek him; but his power and his wrath *is* against all them that forsake him. ²³So we fasted and besought our God for this: and he was intreated of us.

²⁴Then I separated twelve of the chief of the priests, Sherebiah, Hashabiah, and ten of their brethren with them, ²⁵And weighed unto them the silver, and the gold, and the vessels, *even* the offering of the house of our God, which the king, and his counsellors, and his lords, and all Israel *there* present, had offered: ²⁶I even weighed unto their hand six hundred and fifty talents of silver, and silver vessels an hundred talents, *and* of gold an hundred talents; ²⁷Also twenty basons of gold, of a thousand drams; and two vessels of fine^d copper, precious as gold. ²⁸And I said unto them, Ye *are* holy unto the LORD; the vessels *are* holy also; and the silver and the gold *are* a freewill offering unto the LORD God of your fathers. ²⁹Watch ye, and keep *them*, until ye weigh *them* before the chief of the priests and the Levites, and chief of the fathers of Israel, at Jerusalem, in the chambers of the house of the LORD. ³⁰So took the priests and the Levites the weight of the silver, and the gold, and the vessels, to bring *them* to Jerusalem unto the house of our God.

³¹Then we departed from the river of Ahava on the twelfth *day* of the first month, to go unto Jerusalem: and the hand of our God was upon us, and he delivered us from the hand of the en-

emy, and of such as lay in wait by the way. ³²And we came to Jerusalem, and abode there three days. ³³Now on the fourth day was the silver and the gold and the vessels weighed in the house of our God by the hand of Meremoth the son of Uriah the priest; and with him *was* Eleazar the son of Phinehas; and with them *was* Jozabad the son of Jeshua, and Noadiah the son of Binnui, Levites; ³⁴By number *and* by weight of every one: and all the weight was written at that time. ³⁵*Also* the children of those that had been carried away, which were come out of the captivity, offered burnt offerings unto the God of Israel, twelve bullocks for all Israel, ninety and six rams, seventy and seven lambs, twelve he goats *for* a sin offering: all *this was* a burnt offering unto the LORD. ³⁶And they delivered the king's commissions unto the king's lieutenants, and to the governors on this side the river: and they furthered the people, and the house of God.

9

¹Now when these things were done, the princes came to me, saying, The people of Israel, and the priests, and the Levites, have not separated themselves from the people of the lands, *doing* according to their abominations, *even* of the Canaanites, the Hittites, the Perizzites, the Jebusites, the Ammonites, the Moabites, the Egyptians, and the Amorites. ²For they have taken of their daughters for themselves, and for their sons: so that the holy seed have mingled themselves with the people of *those* lands: yea, the hand of the princes and

---

^d fine . . . : Heb. yellow, or, shining brass

•
Sensitivity

9:5-15 It is terribly difficult to be sensitive to
sin when our culture treats it as little more than
a joke. Ezra experienced this struggle. His
prayer is an excellent model of the appropriate
response to widespread unfaithfulness and
disobedience: First he confessed his sins and
the sins of his people; then he cried out for
God's mercy. That is exactly where we must
start as we strive to remain sensitive to sin—
and to God—in a world that doesn't
take God or sin seriously.

rulers hath been chief in this trespass.
³And when I heard this thing, I rent my
garment and my mantle, and plucked
off the hair of my head and of my
beard, and sat down astonied. ⁴Then
were assembled unto me every one that
trembled at the words of the God of
Israel, because of the transgression of
those that had been carried away; and
I sat astonied until the evening sacrifice.

⁵And at the evening sacrifice I arose
up from my heaviness[a]; and having rent
my garment and my mantle, I fell upon
my knees, and spread out my hands
unto the LORD my God, ⁶And said, O
my God, I am ashamed and blush to lift
up my face to thee, my God: for our iniquities are increased over *our* head, and
our trespass[b] is grown up unto the heavens. ⁷Since the days of our fathers *have*
we *been* in a great trespass unto this day;
and for our iniquities have we, our kings,

and our priests, been delivered into the
hand of the kings of the lands, to the
sword, to captivity, and to a spoil, and to
confusion of face, as *it is* this day. ⁸And
now for a little space[c] grace hath been
shewed from the LORD our God, to
leave us a remnant to escape, and to give
us a nail in his holy place, that our God
may lighten our eyes, and give us a little
reviving in our bondage. ⁹For we *were*
bondmen; yet our God hath not forsaken us in our bondage, but hath extended mercy unto us in the sight of the
kings of Persia, to give us a reviving, to
set up the house of our God, and to repair[d] the desolations thereof, and to give
us a wall in Judah and in Jerusalem.
¹⁰And now, O our God, what shall we
say after this? for we have forsaken thy
commandments, ¹¹Which thou hast
commanded by[e] thy servants the
prophets, saying, The land, unto which
ye go to possess it, is an unclean land
with the filthiness of the people of the
lands, with their abominations, which
have filled it from one end to another
with their uncleanness. ¹²Now therefore
give not your daughters unto their sons,
neither take their daughters unto your
sons, nor seek their peace or their wealth
for ever: that ye may be strong, and eat
the good of the land, and leave *it* for an
inheritance to your children for ever.
¹³And after all that is come upon us for
our evil deeds, and for our great trespass,
seeing that thou our God hast punished[f]

---

[a] heaviness: or, affliction
[b] trespass: or, guiltiness
[c] space: Heb. moment
[d] to repair: Heb. to set up
[e] by: Heb. by the hand of
[f] hast punished . . . : Heb. hast withheld beneath our iniquities

us less than our iniquities *deserve*, and hast given us *such* deliverance as this; ¹⁴Should we again break thy commandments, and join in affinity with the people of these abominations? wouldest not thou be angry with us till thou hadst consumed *us*, so that *there should be* no remnant nor escaping? ¹⁵O LORD God of Israel, thou *art* righteous: for we remain yet escaped, as *it is* this day: behold, we *are* before thee in our trespasses: for we cannot stand before thee because of this.

10

¹Now when Ezra had prayed, and when he had confessed, weeping and casting himself down before the house of God, there assembled unto him out of Israel a very great congregation of men and women and children: for the people wept^a very sore. ²And Shechaniah the son of Jehiel, *one* of the sons of Elam, answered and said unto Ezra, We have trespassed against our God, and have taken strange wives of the people of the land: yet now there is hope in Israel concerning this thing. ³Now therefore let us make a covenant with our God to put away all the wives, and such as are born of them, according to the counsel of my lord, and of those that tremble at the commandment of our God; and let it be done according to the law. ⁴Arise; for *this* matter *belongeth* unto thee: we also *will be* with thee: be of good courage, and do *it.* ⁵Then arose Ezra, and made the chief priests, the Levites, and all Israel, to swear that they should do according to this word. And they sware.

> ### Devotional Moment
> •
> ### Marriage
> 10:3 God told his people to divorce their pagan spouses and send them away. This harsh measure was necessary because the Israelites had disobeyed God's previous instructions to remain separate from the surrounding pagan nations. The New Testament makes it clear that nobody should divorce a husband or wife for not being a believer (see 1 Cor. 7:12-15), so we must be careful not to misapply this example from Ezra 10. Yet it does serve as another reminder that God wants his people to marry within the faith. If you are single, avoid dating relationships with unbelievers; if you have children approaching marriageable age, keep tabs on whom they date. A bond with an unbeliever will put great strain on anyone's relationship with God.

⁶Then Ezra rose up from before the house of God, and went into the chamber of Johanan the son of Eliashib: and *when* he came thither, he did eat no bread, nor drink water: for he mourned because of the transgression of them that had been carried away. ⁷And they made proclamation throughout Judah and Jerusalem unto all the children of the captivity, that they should gather themselves together unto Jerusalem; ⁸And that whosoever would not come within three days, according to the counsel of the princes and the elders, all his substance should be forfeited^b, and himself separated from the congregation of those that had been carried away. ⁹Then all the men of Judah and Benjamin gathered themselves together unto Jerusalem within three days. It *was* the ninth month, on the twentieth

---

^a wept . . . : Heb. wept a great weeping
^b forfeited: Heb. devoted

day of the month; and all the people sat in the street of the house of God, trembling because of *this* matter, and for the great rain. [10]And Ezra the priest stood up, and said unto them, Ye have transgressed, and have taken[c] strange wives, to increase the trespass of Israel. [11]Now therefore make confession unto the LORD God of your fathers, and do his pleasure: and separate yourselves from the people of the land, and from the strange wives. [12]Then all the congregation answered and said with a loud voice, As thou hast said, so must we do. [13]But the people *are* many, and *it is* a time of much rain, and we are not able to stand without, neither *is this* a work of one day or two: for we are many[d] that have transgressed in this thing. [14]Let now our rulers of all the congregation stand, and let all them which have taken strange wives in our cities come at appointed times, and with them the elders of every city, and the judges thereof, until the fierce wrath of our God for this matter be turned from us. [15]Only Jonathan the son of Asahel and Jahaziah the son of Tikvah were employed about this *matter*: and Meshullam and Shabbethai the Levite helped them. [16]And the children of the captivity did so. And Ezra the priest, *with* certain chief of the fathers, after the house of their fathers, and all of them by *their* names, were separated, and sat down in the first day of the tenth month to examine the matter. [17]And they made an end with all the men that had taken strange wives by the first day of the first month. [18]And among the sons of the priests there were found that had taken strange wives: *namely,* of the sons of Jeshua the son of Jozadak, and his brethren; Maaseiah, and Eliezer, and Jarib, and Gedaliah. [19]And they gave their hands that they would put away their wives; and *being* guilty, *they offered* a ram of the flock for their trespass. [20]And of the sons of Immer; Hanani, and Zebadiah. [21]And of the sons of Harim; Maaseiah, and Elijah, and Shemaiah, and Jehiel, and Uzziah. [22]And of the sons of Pashur; Elioenai, Maaseiah, Ishmael, Nethaneel, Jozabad, and Elasah. [23]Also of the Levites; Jozabad, and Shimei, and Kelaiah, (the same *is* Kelita,) Pethahiah, Judah, and Eliezer. [24]Of the singers also; Eliashib: and of the porters; Shallum, and Telem, and Uri. [25]Moreover of Israel: of the sons of Parosh; Ramiah, and Jeziah, and Malchiah, and Miamin, and Eleazar, and Malchijah, and Benaiah. [26]And of the sons of Elam; Mattaniah, Zechariah, and Jehiel, and Abdi, and Jeremoth, and Eliah. [27]And of the sons of Zattu; Elioenai, Eliashib, Mattaniah, and Jeremoth, and Zabad, and Aziza. [28]Of the sons also of Bebai; Jehohanan, Hananiah, Zabbai, *and* Athlai. [29]And of the sons of Bani; Meshullam, Malluch, and Adaiah, Jashub, and Sheal, and Ramoth. [30]And of the sons of Pahathmoab; Adna, and Chelal, Benaiah, Maaseiah, Mattaniah, Bezaleel, and Binnui, and Manasseh. [31]And *of* the sons of Harim; Eliezer, Ishijah, Malchiah, Shemaiah, Shimeon, [32]Benjamin, Malluch, *and* Shemariah. [33]Of the sons of Hashum; Mattenai, Mat-

---

[c] have taken: Heb. have caused to dwell, or, have brought back
[d] we are many . . . : or, we have greatly offended in this thing

tathah, Zabad, Eliphelet, Jeremai, Manasseh, *and* Shimei. ³⁴Of the sons of Bani; Maadai, Amram, and Uel, ³⁵Benaiah, Bedeiah, Chelluh, ³⁶Vaniah, Meremoth, Eliashib, ³⁷Mattaniah, Mattenai, and Jaasau, ³⁸And Bani, and Binnui, Shimei, ³⁹And Shelemiah, and Nathan, and Adaiah, ⁴⁰Machnadebaiᵉ,

Shashai, Sharai, ⁴¹Azareel, and Shelemiah, Shemariah, ⁴²Shallum, Amariah, *and* Joseph. ⁴³Of the sons of Nebo; Jeiel, Mattithiah, Zabad, Zebina, Jadau, and Joel, Benaiah. ⁴⁴All these had taken strange wives: and *some* of them had wives by whom they had children.

ᵉ Machnadebai: or, Mabnadebai, according to some copies

NEHEMIAH

Purpose
Nehemiah records the history of the third return to Jerusalem after captivity.

Author
Nehemiah probably wrote the book, with Ezra serving as editor.

Date Written
Approximately 445–432 B.C.

Setting
Zerubbabel led the first return to Jerusalem in 537 B.C. In 458 B.C. Ezra led the second return. Finally, in 445 B.C., Nehemiah returned with the third group of exiles to rebuild the city walls.

Key Verses
"The wall was finished . . . in fifty and two days. When all our enemies heard thereof, and all the heathen . . . saw these things, they were much cast down in their own eyes: for they perceived that this work was wrought of our God" (6:15-16).

Key People
Nehemiah, Ezra, Sanballat, Tobiah

Key Place
Jerusalem

Special Features
The book shows the fulfillment of the prophecies of Zechariah and Daniel concerning the rebuilding of Jerusalem's walls.

Car problems during a family vacation can bring out the worst in a parent: anger, depression, the "why me, why now?" syndrome. The worst is a broken water pump on a hot day in the middle of North Dakota, where roadside weeds can blossom and wilt before two cars pass by. Children who want to believe in the absolute virtue of a parent should pray for their city's car mechanics every night.

Nehemiah is a name synonymous with problems. His life had more difficulties than Murphy (of Murphy's Law) ever dreamed of. People ganged up on him, supplies were short, workers grew tired, and on top of all that, authorities sat on paperwork. Most people in Nehemiah's fix would take early retirement, no incentives required.

Facing and solving problems is a skill every child needs to learn. Whether a problem becomes an aggravation or a challenge, whether it draws the anger of a kick to the hubcap or the confidence of a look to the toolbox is largely a parent's decision. How Mom and Dad face difficulty explains a lot about Junior's reactions.

How did Nehemiah leap his hurdles? How did he—eager to finish the work—react to delay and opposition? With lots of people counting on him, how did he explain setbacks and cost overruns? Was this a hood-slamming man?

When problems come, the last thing most people want to do is pray. But there's wisdom in taking a breath and pausing to collect your judgment, even in asking the Maker of all to look over your shoulder while you work.

Teach children Nehemiah's way of facing problems, and you'll give them a gift they'll never outgrow.

1

¹The words of Nehemiah the son of Hachaliah. And it came to pass in the month Chisleu, in the twentieth year, as I was in Shushan the palace, ²That Hanani, one of my brethren, came, he and *certain* men of Judah; and I asked them concerning the Jews that had escaped, which were left of the captivity, and concerning Jerusalem. ³And they said unto me, The remnant that are left of the captivity there in the province *are* in great affliction and reproach: the wall of Jerusalem also *is* broken down, and the gates thereof are burned with fire. ⁴And it came to pass, when I heard these words, that I sat down and wept, and mourned *certain* days, and fasted, and prayed before the God of heaven,

⁵And said, I beseech thee, O LORD God of heaven, the great and terrible God, that keepeth covenant and mercy for them that love him and observe his commandments: ⁶Let thine ear now be attentive, and thine eyes open, that thou mayest hear the prayer of thy servant, which I pray before thee now, day and night, for the children of Israel thy servants, and confess the sins of the children of Israel, which we have sinned against thee: both I and my father's house have sinned. ⁷We have dealt very corruptly against thee, and have not kept the commandments, nor the statutes, nor the judgments, which thou commandedst thy servant Moses. ⁸Remember, I beseech thee, the word that thou commandedst thy servant Moses, saying, *If* ye transgress, I will scatter you abroad among the nations: ⁹But *if* ye turn unto me, and keep my commandments, and do them; though there were of you cast out unto the uttermost part of the heaven, *yet* will I gather them from thence, and will bring them unto the place that I have chosen to set my name there. ¹⁰Now these *are* thy servants and thy people, whom thou hast redeemed by thy great power, and by thy strong hand. ¹¹O Lord, I beseech thee, let now thine ear be attentive to the prayer of thy servant, and to the prayer of thy servants, who desire to fear thy name: and prosper, I pray thee, thy servant this day, and grant him mercy in the sight of this man. For I was the king's cupbearer.

2

¹And it came to pass in the month Nisan, in the twentieth year of Artaxerxes the king, *that* wine *was* before him: and I took up the wine, and gave *it* unto the king. Now I had not been *beforetime* sad in his presence. ²Wherefore the king said unto me, Why *is* thy countenance sad, seeing thou *art* not sick?

Devotional Moment
•
Godly Sorrow

1.9-11 What would have been your response to the negative report Nehemiah received? Anger? Depression? Resignation? Nehemiah obviously felt discouraged upon hearing the bad news, but, good leader that he was, he didn't stop there. He took his pain and disappointment to God, asking for wisdom and consolation. A young couple wonders if they'll *ever* get out of debt; a parent of a preschooler wonders if the little tike will *ever* be potty-trained; a teenage daughter wonders if her father will *ever* talk to her. The question is not *if* nor *when* we will face discouragement; the question is *how* we will deal with it. Nehemiah's response is our model. When you face tough times, bring your struggles to God.

Family Traditions

Restoration of Broken Family Walls

NEHEMIAH

When Nehemiah rebuilt the walls of Jerusalem, he did not rush into the job. His passion to restore the fortification was tempered by patience and four months of prayer and planning. During this period he counted the cost, calculating the materials, manpower, and protection that would be needed.

Rebuilding broken family walls cannot be hurried, either. The broken wall may be a difficult relationship with a teenager, loss of trust in a spouse, or an ongoing struggle with a high-needs child. Perhaps it is simple exhaustion from the demands of parenting. Or maybe, like Nehemiah, you face the near-total ruin of what was once beautiful—a family devastated by years of abuse or neglect. But Christian families can affirm as Nehemiah did thousands of years ago: "The God of heaven, he will prosper us" (Neh. 2:20).

Before he began to rebuild, Nehemiah met with God. There is no substitute for personal prayer. First seek God alone. Then, if possible, seek him together with your spouse and children. Realize you are under God's protection and mercy.

Nehemiah did not expect to restore the ruins by himself; he knew that many others would have to be involved—men and women of like vision who could be trusted. Similarly, every family needs a support system. Select one or more prayer partners in whom you can confide and who will name your family members in prayer. Keep these people aware of specific needs. Get involved with believers who have faced or are going through the same kinds of problems you face. Knowing you are not alone and that yours are not isolated problems is essential.

Write out a mission statement for your family. Statistics show that businesses and ministries that have a written purpose kept in public view reach goals and solve problems more effectively than organizations that don't. What do you want to achieve? What is your purpose? What do you want your family to be, and how will you carry it out?

Be aware that the enemy is Satan, not other people (see Eph. 6:12). Seek promises in the Word of God that deflate each of his tactics. Post them where you will be reminded that God is working with you and for you. Assure each of your family members that you do not live in a vacuum—that your lives influence others and can be influenced by others.

God specializes in repairing broken hearts and broken walls.

this *is* nothing *else* but sorrow of heart. Then I was very sore afraid, ³And said unto the king, Let the king live for ever: why should not my countenance be sad, when the city, the place of my fathers' sepulchres, *lieth* waste, and the gates thereof are consumed with fire? ⁴Then the king said unto me, For what dost thou make request? So I prayed to the God of heaven. ⁵And I said unto the king, If it please the king, and if thy servant have found favour in thy sight, that thou wouldest send me unto Judah, unto the city of my fathers' sepulchres, that I may build it. ⁶And the king said unto me, (the queen also sitting by him,) For how long shall thy journey be? and when wilt thou return? So it pleased the king to send me; and I set him a time. ⁷Moreover I said unto the king, If it please the king, let letters be given me to the governors beyond the river, that they may convey me over till I come into Judah; ⁸And a letter unto Asaph the keeper of the king's forest, that he may give me timber to make beams for the gates of the palace which *appertained* to the house, and for the wall of the city, and for the house that I shall enter into. And the king granted me, according to the good hand of my God upon me.

⁹Then I came to the governors beyond the river, and gave them the king's letters. Now the king had sent captains of the army and horsemen with me. ¹⁰When Sanballat the Horonite, and Tobiah the servant, the Ammonite, heard *of it*, it grieved them exceedingly that there was come a man to seek the welfare of the children of Israel. ¹¹So I came to Jerusalem, and was there three days. ¹²And I arose in the night, I and some few men with me; neither told I *any* man what my God had put in my heart to do at Jerusalem: neither *was there any* beast with me, save the beast that I rode upon. ¹³And I went out by night by the gate of the valley, even before the dragon well, and to the dung port, and viewed the walls of Jerusalem, which were broken down, and the gates thereof were consumed with fire. ¹⁴Then I went on to the gate of the fountain, and to the king's pool: but *there was* no place for the beast *that was* under me to pass. ¹⁵Then went I up in the night by the brook, and viewed the wall, and turned back, and entered by the gate of the valley, and *so* returned. ¹⁶And the rulers knew not whither I went, or what I did; neither had I as yet told *it* to the Jews, nor to the priests, nor to the nobles, nor to the rulers, nor to the rest that did the work. ¹⁷Then said I unto them, Ye see the distress that we *are* in, how Jerusalem *lieth* waste, and the gates thereof are burned with fire: come, and let us build up the wall of Jerusalem, that we be no more a reproach. ¹⁸Then I told them of the hand of my God which was good upon me;

Devotional Moment

Prayer

2:4 This brief, silent prayer of Nehemiah's reveals a great deal about him. Nehemiah was in the middle of a conversation with King Artaxerxes, the most powerful man in Persia, and he was frightened. In spite of his fear, he remembered to pray, asking God to guide his words and the king's heart. Throughout the book of Nehemiah, you will notice that this leader consistently looked to God in prayer when the heat was on. When you experience fear, anxiety, or stress, do you respond in prayer and faith?

as also the king's words that he had spoken unto me. And they said, Let us rise up and build. So they strengthened their hands for *this* good *work*. ¹⁹But when Sanballat the Horonite, and Tobiah the servant, the Ammonite, and Geshem the Arabian, heard *it*, they laughed us to scorn, and despised us, and said, What *is* this thing that ye do? will ye rebel against the king? ²⁰Then answered I them, and said unto them, The God of heaven, he will prosper us; therefore we his servants will arise and build: but ye have no portion, nor right, nor memorial, in Jerusalem.

3

¹Then Eliashib the high priest rose up with his brethren the priests, and they builded the sheep gate; they sanctified it, and set up the doors of it; even unto the tower of Meah they sanctified it, unto the tower of Hananeel. ²And next unto him builded the men of Jericho. And next to them builded Zaccur the son of Imri. ³But the fish gate did the sons of Hassenaah build, who *also* laid the beams thereof, and set up the doors thereof, the locks thereof, and the bars thereof. ⁴And next unto them repaired Meremoth the son of Urijah, the son of Koz. And next unto them repaired Meshullam the son of Berechiah, the son of Meshezabeel. And next unto them repaired Zadok the son of Baana. ⁵And next unto them the Tekoites repaired; but their nobles put not their necks to the work of their Lord. ⁶Moreover the old gate repaired Jehoiada the son of Paseah, and Meshullam the son of Besodeiah; they laid the beams

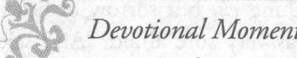

Devotional Moment
Serving

3:1-32 The world's definition of greatness stands in stark contrast to God's. Jesus himself said as much: "Ye know that they which are accounted to rule over the Gentiles exercise lordship over them . . . But so shall it not be among you: but whosoever will be great among you, shall be your minister" (Mark 10:42-43). Nehemiah and the leaders of the people provide a vivid example of ministry. Did it make an impact? Take note that among all those listed in thirty-two verses, only the leaders from Tekoa are singled out as being lazy and unwilling to help (v. 5)! God's work requires strong, bold, hands-on servant leadership. Would your family describe you as that kind of leader or more like the men of Tekoa? Don't let your kids set the pace; you show them the way.

thereof, and set up the doors thereof, and the locks thereof, and the bars thereof. ⁷And next unto them repaired Melatiah the Gibeonite, and Jadon the Meronothite, the men of Gibeon, and of Mizpah, unto the throne of the governor on this side the river. ⁸Next unto him repaired Uzziel the son of Harhaiah, of the goldsmiths. Next unto him also repaired Hananiah the son of *one of* the apothecaries, and they fortified[a] Jerusalem unto the broad wall. ⁹And next unto them repaired Rephaiah the son of Hur, the ruler of the half part of Jerusalem. ¹⁰And next unto them repaired Jedaiah the son of Harumaph, even over against his house. And next unto him repaired Hattush the son of Hashabniah. ¹¹Malchijah the son of Harim, and Hashub the son of Pahathmoab, repaired the other[b] piece, and

[a] fortified . . . : or, left Jerusalem unto the broad wall
[b] other . . . : Heb. second measure

the tower of the furnaces. ¹²And next unto him repaired Shallum the son of Halohesh, the ruler of the half part of Jerusalem, he and his daughters. ¹³The valley gate repaired Hanun, and the inhabitants of Zanoah; they built it, and set up the doors thereof, the locks thereof, and the bars thereof, and a thousand cubits on the wall unto the dung gate. ¹⁴But the dung gate repaired Malchiah the son of Rechab, the ruler of part of Bethhaccerem; he built it, and set up the doors thereof, the locks thereof, and the bars thereof. ¹⁵But the gate of the fountain repaired Shallun the son of Colhozeh, the ruler of part of Mizpah; he built it, and covered it, and set up the doors thereof, the locks thereof, and the bars thereof, and the wall of the pool of Siloah by the king's garden, and unto the stairs that go down from the city of David. ¹⁶After him repaired Nehemiah the son of Azbuk, the ruler of the half part of Bethzur, unto *the place* over against the sepulchres of David, and to the pool that was made, and unto the house of the mighty. ¹⁷After him repaired the Levites, Rehum the son of Bani. Next unto him repaired Hashabiah, the ruler of the half part of Keilah, in his part. ¹⁸After him repaired their brethren, Bavai the son of Henadad, the ruler of the half part of Keilah. ¹⁹And next to him repaired Ezer the son of Jeshua, the ruler of Mizpah, another piece over against the going up to the armoury at the turning *of the wall.* ²⁰After him Baruch the son of Zabbai[c] earnestly repaired the other piece, from the turning *of the wall* unto the door of the house of Eliashib the high priest. ²¹Af-

ter him repaired Meremoth the son of Urijah the son of Koz another piece, from the door of the house of Eliashib even to the end of the house of Eliashib. ²²And after him repaired the priests, the men of the plain. ²³After him repaired Benjamin and Hashub over against their house. After him repaired Azariah the son of Maaseiah the son of Ananiah by his house. ²⁴After him repaired Binnui the son of Henadad another piece, from the house of Azariah unto the turning *of the wall,* even unto the corner. ²⁵Palal the son of Uzai, over against the turning *of the wall,* and the tower which lieth out from the king's high house, that *was* by the court of the prison. After him Pedaiah the son of Parosh. ²⁶Moreover the Nethinims dwelt[d] in Ophel, unto *the place* over against the water gate toward the east, and the tower that lieth out. ²⁷After them the Tekoites repaired another piece, over against the great tower that lieth out, even unto the wall of Ophel. ²⁸From above the horse gate repaired the priests, every one over against his house. ²⁹After them repaired Zadok the son of Immer over against his house. After him repaired also Shemaiah the son of Shechaniah, the keeper of the east gate. ³⁰After him repaired Hananiah the son of Shelemiah, and Hanun the sixth son of Zalaph, another piece. After him repaired Meshullam the son of Berechiah over against his chamber. ³¹After him repaired Malchiah the goldsmith's son unto the place of the Nethinims, and of the merchants, over against the gate Miphkad, and to the going up of the corner. ³²And between the going up of the

---

[c] Zabbai: also called, Zaccai
[d] dwelt . . . : or, which dwelt in Ophel, repaired unto

Do You Honor Your Children?

by Gary Smalley

"Sticks and stones may break my bones, but names will never hurt me!" Every child believes this old adage. But in reality, insults can hurt more than physical attacks.

The Jews learned this lesson when they returned from exile and started rebuilding the walls of Jerusalem. Their enemies assaulted them mercilessly: "What do these feeble Jews?" Sanballat scoffed. "If a fox go up, he shall even break down their stone wall," added Tobiah (see Neh. 4:2-3). The Jews were hurt and shaken by these verbal attacks.

Verbal assaults are a harsh reality of growing up. Most children hear them every day. Honoring children is one powerful way every parent can counterattack. Here are some steps you can take:

Show them how to honor Mom and Dad. "Honour thy father and thy mother: that thy days may be long upon the land which the Lord thy God giveth thee," God commanded (Exod. 20:12). You can't get away from the effects of this one—either your life will be lengthened as you honor your parents, or you risk shortening your days. But it does no good to insist that your child's tone of voice and actions reflect honor toward you if you don't show them how it's done. Are you teaching your children to honor you by showing respect for your own parents?

Help them find value in their troubles. Many parents go to extreme lengths to protect their children from emotional hurt. Yet troubles can teach us patience (James 1:2-4). When we go through embarrassment or defeat, "God giveth grace unto the humble" (James 4:6). Trials can also make us more sensitive to others' suffering (2 Cor. 1:4). One way we can honor our children is to help them see the gain that can come from their troubles. Don't refuse to cry with your children or minimize their hurt with a "buck up" dismissal, but do remind them that when they feel defeated, God gives strength. When they feel lonely, God is with them.

Provide clear boundaries for them. One study of grade-school children looked at the behavior of two groups during recess. Both groups were the same age and had the same play equipment, but one playground had a fence around it and the other had none. Which group showed less aggressive behavior and used more of the playground area? Which group played more cooperatively and showed less tension in the classroom after recess? The group whose playground had a fence. Consistently enforcing realistic limits and talking about the rules with your children will give them a feeling of security.

Treat them with tenderness. Children remember acts of tenderness. They also remember angry words and insensitive actions. Fathers, in particular, need to understand this, for children are especially sensitive to a father's actions. A parent's gentle hugs and soft, loving tone of voice make children feel special. Be tender toward your children. Use your tone of voice to communicate that they are valuable. Touch them and tell them how special they are to you. Respond in gentleness when they're hurting.

Place more value on people than on things. What do your children see you playing, polishing, mowing, or pruning with gusto? Do they ever get that much time and attention from you? For the roots of honor to sink deeply, your children must feel that they are at least as valuable as your work, hobbies, leisure pursuits, and possessions.

No parent is perfect. But if you honor them on a consistent basis, their sense of value will overshadow your mistakes.

- Gently admit to your children when you know you've wronged them. This goes a long way toward building self-worth in them.
- Take time to squeeze their arm or give them a hug *every day.*
- Control or soften your tone of voice when they make a mistake.
- Listen carefully; don't lecture.
- Cry with them when they hurt.
- Write them a letter that expresses your love and commitment.
- Pray with them about upcoming events that concern them.

Treating children with honor doesn't mean wrapping them in cotton; neither does it mean permissiveness. It means treating them consistently with tender care, attention, and respect. If you do that, then all the Sanballats in the world will not be able to stop them from building the part of the wall God has reserved for them.

DIGGING DEEPER
1. In what ways can you treat your children as fellow human beings? See Romans 12:10.
2. Why do children deserve high honor? See Psalm 127:3.
3. What sort of limits should you place on how you scold your children? See Colossians 3:21.

corner unto the sheep gate repaired the goldsmiths and the merchants.

4

¹But it came to pass, that when Sanballat heard that we builded the wall, he was wroth, and took great indignation, and mocked the Jews. ²And he spake before his brethren and the army of Samaria, and said, What do these feeble Jews? will they fortify[a] themselves? will they sacrifice? will they make an end in a day? will they revive the stones out of the heaps of the rubbish which are burned? ³Now Tobiah the Ammonite *was* by him, and he said, Even that which they build, if a fox go up, he shall even break down their stone wall. ⁴Hear, O our God; for we are despised[b]: and turn their reproach upon their own head, and give them for a prey

Devotional Moment

Pray or Work?

4:1-9 Have you ever faced a situation in which you didn't know whether to pray and wait for God to act, or to work like crazy to make something happen and hope you were doing his will? This is exactly the kind of dilemma Nehemiah and friends faced. Instead of doing one or the other, however, they did *both:* They called upon the Lord for deliverance and then took responsible measures to protect themselves. Numerous forces will threaten you and your family— external and internal, subtle and obvious, natural and spiritual. When they do, take a lesson from Nehemiah: Pray often, *and* do all you can to protect and care for your loved ones.

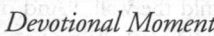

in the land of captivity: ⁵And cover not their iniquity, and let not their sin be blot-

---

[a] fortify . . . : Heb. leave to themselves
[b] despised: Heb. despite

ted out from before thee: for they have provoked *thee* to anger before the builders. ⁶So built we the wall; and all the wall was joined together unto the half thereof: for the people had a mind to work.

⁷But it came to pass, *that* when Sanballat, and Tobiah, and the Arabians, and the Ammonites, and the Ashdodites, heard that the walls of Jerusalem were made up^c, *and* that the breaches began to be stopped, then they were very wroth, ⁸And conspired all of them together to come *and* to fight against Jerusalem, and to hinder^d it. ⁹Nevertheless we made our prayer unto our God, and set a watch against them day and night, because of them. ¹⁰And Judah said, The strength of the bearers of burdens is decayed, and *there is* much rubbish; so that we are not able to build the wall. ¹¹And our adversaries said, They shall not know, neither see, till we come in the midst among them, and slay them, and cause the work to cease. ¹²And it came to pass, that when the Jews which dwelt by them came, they said unto us ten times, From all places whence ye shall return unto us *they will be upon you.* ¹³Therefore set I in the lower places behind the wall, *and* on the higher places, I even set the people after their families with their swords, their spears, and their bows. ¹⁴And I looked, and rose up, and said unto the nobles, and to the rulers, and to the rest of the people, Be not ye afraid of them: remember the Lord, *which is* great and terrible, and fight for your brethren, your sons, and your daughters, your wives,

and your houses. ¹⁵And it came to pass, when our enemies heard that it was known unto us, and God had brought their counsel to nought, that we returned all of us to the wall, every one unto his work.

¹⁶And it came to pass from that time forth, *that* the half of my servants wrought in the work, and the other half of them held both the spears, the shields, and the bows, and the habergeons; and the rulers *were* behind all the house of Judah. ¹⁷They which builded on the wall, and they that bare burdens, with those that laded, *every one* with one of his hands wrought in the work, and with the other *hand* held a weapon. ¹⁸For the builders, every one had his sword girded by his side^e, and *so* builded. And he that sounded the trumpet *was*

Devotional Moment
•
Family Purpose

4:16 The actual execution of Nehemiah's plan was simple: Half the men would work while the other half stood guard. This plan demonstrates the importance of teamwork. Every family member has an important role to fulfill and equally important gifts to bring to the life of the household. Some are more visible and prestigious, but all are crucial. You may be the head of the house or the breadwinner, but somebody has to walk the dog and take out the trash. Make sure every family member has an important share of the chores and family responsibilities. And from time to time ask them if they feel that their contribution is important—and make adjustments where necessary.

---

^c were made up: Heb. ascended
^d to hinder . . . : Heb. to make an error to it
^e by his side: Heb. on his loins

by me. ¹⁹And I said unto the nobles, and to the rulers, and to the rest of the people, The work *is* great and large, and we are separated upon the wall, one far from another. ²⁰In what place *therefore* ye hear the sound of the trumpet, resort ye thither unto us: our God shall fight for us. ²¹So we laboured in the work: and half of them held the spears from the rising of the morning till the stars appeared. ²²Likewise at the same time said I unto the people, Let every one with his servant lodge within Jerusalem, that in the night they may be a guard to us, and labour on the day. ²³So neither I, nor my brethren, nor my servants, nor the men of the guard which followed me, none of us put off our clothes, *saving that* every one put them off for washing.

5

¹And there was a great cry of the people and of their wives against their brethren the Jews. ²For there were that said, We, our sons, and our daughters, *are* many: therefore we take up corn *for them*, that we may eat, and live. ³*Some* also there were that said, We have mortgaged our lands, vineyards, and houses, that we might buy corn, because of the dearth. ⁴There were also that said, We have borrowed money for the king's tribute, *and that upon* our lands and vineyards. ⁵Yet now our flesh *is* as the flesh of our brethren, our children as their children: and, lo, we bring into bondage our sons and our daughters to be servants, and *some* of our daughters are brought unto bondage *already*: neither *is it* in our

power *to redeem them*; for other men have our lands and vineyards.

⁶And I was very angry when I heard their cry and these words. ⁷Then I consulteda with myself, and I rebuked the nobles, and the rulers, and said unto them, Ye exact usury, every one of his brother. And I set a great assembly against them. ⁸And I said unto them, We after our ability have redeemed our brethren the Jews, which were sold unto the heathen; and will ye even sell your brethren? or shall they be sold unto us? Then held they their peace, and found nothing *to answer*. ⁹Also I said, It *is* not good that ye do: ought ye not to walk in the fear of our God because of the reproach of the heathen our enemies? ¹⁰I likewise, *and* my brethren, and my servants, might exact of them money and corn: I pray you, let us leave off this usury. ¹¹Restore, I pray you, to them, even this day, their lands, their vineyards, their oliveyards, and their houses, also the hundredth *part* of the money, and of the corn, the wine,

---

Devotional Moment

The Poor

5:9-11 Nehemiah became angry when he learned that some of his Jewish brethren were taking advantage of others. Those with financial resources were loaning money at high interest rates. Then they were seizing the assets of those who failed to make timely payments. Some needy families even resorted to selling their children into slavery to pay the bills! Nehemiah rebuked this practice and urged more compassionate behavior. Those who love and follow God should *help* those in trouble, not exploit them.

---

a I consulted . . . : Heb. my heart consulted in me

and the oil, that ye exact of them. [12]Then said they, We will restore *them*, and will require nothing of them; so will we do as thou sayest. Then I called the priests, and took an oath of them, that they should do according to this promise. [13]Also I shook my lap, and said, So God shake out every man from his house, and from his labour, that performeth not this promise, even thus be he shaken out, and emptied[b]. And all the congregation said, Amen, and praised the LORD. And the people did according to this promise.

[14]Moreover from the time that I was appointed to be their governor in the land of Judah, from the twentieth year even unto the two and thirtieth year of Artaxerxes the king, *that is,* twelve years, I and my brethren have not eaten the bread of the governor. [15]But the former governors that *had been* before me were chargeable unto the people, and had taken of them bread and wine, beside forty shekels of silver; yea, even their servants bare rule over the people: but so did not I, because of the fear of God. [16]Yea, also I continued in the work of this wall, neither bought we any land: and all my servants *were* gathered thither unto the work. [17]Moreover *there were* at my table an hundred and fifty of the Jews and rulers, beside those that came unto us from among the heathen that *are* about us. [18]Now *that* which was prepared *for me* daily *was* one ox *and* six choice sheep; also fowls were prepared for me, and once in ten days store of all sorts of wine: yet for all this required not I the bread of the governor, because the bondage was heavy upon this people. [19]Think upon me, my God, for good, *according* to all that I have done for this people.

6

[1]Now it came to pass, when Sanballat, and Tobiah, and Geshem the Arabian, and the rest of our enemies, heard that I had builded the wall, and *that* there was no breach left therein; (though at that time I had not set up the doors upon the gates;) [2]That Sanballat and Geshem sent unto me, saying, Come, let us meet together in *some one of* the villages in the plain of Ono. But they thought to do me mischief. [3]And I sent messengers unto them, saying, I *am* doing a great work, so that I cannot come down: why should the work cease, whilst I leave it, and come down to you? [4]Yet they sent unto me four times after this sort; and I answered them after the same manner. [5]Then sent Sanballat his servant unto me in like manner the fifth time with an open letter in his hand; [6]Wherein *was* written, It is reported among the heathen, and Gashmu[a] saith *it, that* thou and the Jews think to rebel: for which cause thou buildest the wall, that thou mayest be their king, according to these words. [7]And thou hast also appointed prophets to preach of thee at Jerusalem, saying, *There is* a king in Judah: and now shall it be reported to the king according to these words. Come now therefore, and let us take counsel together. [8]Then I sent unto him, saying, There are no such things done as thou sayest, but thou

---

[b] emptied: Heb. empty, or, void
[a] Gashmu: also called, Geshem

feignest them out of thine own heart. [9]For they all made us afraid, saying, Their hands shall be weakened from the work, that it be not done. Now therefore, *O God*, strengthen my hands.

[10]Afterward I came unto the house of Shemaiah the son of Delaiah the son of Mehetabeel, who *was* shut up; and he said, Let us meet together in the house of God, within the temple, and let us shut the doors of the temple: for they will come to slay thee; yea, in the night will they come to slay thee. [11]And I said, Should such a man as I flee? and who *is there*, that, *being* as I *am*, would go into the temple to save his life? I will not go in. [12]And, lo, I perceived that God had not sent him; but that he pronounced this prophecy against me: for Tobiah and Sanballat had hired him. [13]Therefore *was* he hired, that I should be afraid, and do so, and sin, and *that* they might have

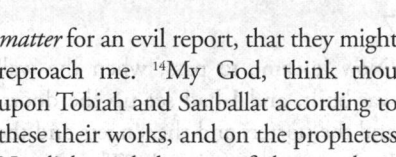

Devotional Moment
•
Prayer for Leaders
6:10-13 Nehemiah's enemies tried to frighten him into hiding out in the Temple. This ploy, if successful, would have been disastrous for two reasons: (1) Nehemiah wasn't a priest, and only priests were allowed in the Temple (Num. 18:22); and (2) Nehemiah's fear would have been evident—and likely contagious—to his countrymen. Like Nehemiah, our church and community leaders must frequently make difficult decisions in the face of complicated situations. No wonder the Bible instructs us to pray for them (1 Tim. 2:2)! Ask God to give those in authority over you the wisdom to know what is best and the courage to do what is right.

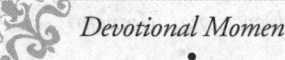

Devotional Moment
•
Perseverance
6:15 Rebuilding the wall of Jerusalem had seemed like a monumental task. But Nehemiah and the Jews kept plugging away despite overwhelming obstacles and fierce opposition, and in less than two months the task was complete. What a great lesson for us! With God's help we can accomplish seemingly impossible goals when we persevere one day at a time. When each person takes a part, the work goes quickly. Remember this the next time you face a monumental task.

matter for an evil report, that they might reproach me. [14]My God, think thou upon Tobiah and Sanballat according to these their works, and on the prophetess Noadiah, and the rest of the prophets, that would have put me in fear.

[15]So the wall was finished in the twenty and fifth *day* of *the month* Elul, in fifty and two days. [16]And it came to pass, that when all our enemies heard *thereof*, and all the heathen that *were* about us saw *these things*, they were much cast down in their own eyes: for they perceived that this work was wrought of our God. [17]Moreover in those days the nobles of Judah sent[b] many letters unto Tobiah, and *the letters* of Tobiah came unto them. [18]For *there were* many in Judah sworn unto him, because he *was* the son in law of Shechaniah the son of Arah; and his son Johanan had taken the daughter of Meshullam the son of Berechiah. [19]Also they reported his good deeds before me, and uttered my words[c] to him. *And* Tobiah sent letters to put me in fear.

[b] sent . . . : Heb. multiplied their letters passing to Tobiah
[c] words: or, matters

775

Devotional Moment
•
Leadership

7:2 When it came time for Nehemiah to select people to govern Jerusalem, he looked for those with integrity and reverence for God. A person of integrity can be trusted and will be respected. A person who reveres God is better equipped to resist pride and all the other intoxicating temptations that come to those in power. As a guide of others, be sure to maintain your integrity and reverence for God. And whenever you must delegate leadership tasks, consider these qualities in making your choice.

7

¹Now it came to pass, when the wall was built, and I had set up the doors, and the porters and the singers and the Levites were appointed, ²That I gave my brother Hanani, and Hananiah the ruler of the palace, charge over Jerusalem: for he *was* a faithful man, and feared God above many. ³And I said unto them, Let not the gates of Jerusalem be opened until the sun be hot; and while they stand by, let them shut the doors, and bar *them*: and appoint watches of the inhabitants of Jerusalem, every one in his watch, and every one *to be* over against his house. ⁴Now the city *was* largeᵃ and great: but the people *were* few therein, and the houses *were* not builded.

⁵And my God put into mine heart to gather together the nobles, and the rulers, and the people, that they might be reckoned by genealogy. And I found a register of the genealogy of them which came up at the first, and found written therein, ⁶These *are* the children of the province, that went up out of the captivity, of those that had been carried away, whom Nebuchadnezzar the king of Babylon had carried away, and came again to Jerusalem and to Judah, every one unto his city; ⁷Who came with Zerubbabel, Jeshua, Nehemiah, Azariahᵇ, Raamiah, Nahamani, Mordecai, Bilshan, Mispereth, Bigvai, Nehum, Baanah. The number, *I say*, of the men of the people of Israel *was this*; ⁸The children of Parosh, two thousand an hundred seventy and two. ⁹The children of Shephatiah, three hundred seventy and two. ¹⁰The children of Arah, six hundred fifty and two. ¹¹The children of Pahathmoab, of the children of Jeshua and Joab, two thousand and eight hundred *and* eighteen. ¹²The children of Elam, a thousand two hundred fifty and four. ¹³The children of Zattu, eight hundred forty and five. ¹⁴The children of Zaccai, seven hundred and threescore. ¹⁵The children of Binnuiᶜ, six hundred forty and eight. ¹⁶The children of Bebai, six hundred twenty and eight. ¹⁷The children of Azgad, two thousand three hundred twenty and two. ¹⁸The children of Adonikam, six hundred threescore and seven. ¹⁹The children of Bigvai, two thousand threescore and seven. ²⁰The children of Adin, six hundred fifty and five. ²¹The children of Ater of Hezekiah, ninety and eight. ²²The children of Hashum, three hundred twenty and eight. ²³The children of Bezai, three hundred twenty and four. ²⁴The chil-

---

ᵃ large: Heb. broad in spaces
ᵇ Azariah: also called, Seraiah
ᶜ Binnui: also called, Bani

dren of Hariph[d], an hundred and twelve. [25]The children of Gibeon[e], ninety and five. [26]The men of Bethlehem and Netophah, an hundred fourscore and eight. [27]The men of Anathoth, an hundred twenty and eight. [28]The men of Bethazmaveth[f], forty and two. [29]The men of Kirjathjearim[g], Chephirah, and Beeroth, seven hundred forty and three. [30]The men of Ramah and Geba, six hundred twenty and one. [31]The men of Michmas, an hundred and twenty and two. [32]The men of Bethel and Ai, an hundred twenty and three. [33]The men of the other Nebo, fifty and two. [34]The children of the other Elam, a thousand two hundred fifty and four. [35]The children of Harim, three hundred and twenty. [36]The children of Jericho, three hundred forty and five. [37]The children of Lod, Hadid, and Ono, seven hundred twenty and one. [38]The children of Senaah, three thousand nine hundred and thirty. [39]The priests: the children of Jedaiah, of the house of Jeshua, nine hundred seventy and three. [40]The children of Immer, a thousand fifty and two. [41]The children of Pashur, a thousand two hundred forty and seven. [42]The children of Harim, a thousand and seventeen. [43]The Levites: the children of Jeshua, of Kadmiel, *and* of the children of Hodevah[h], seventy and four. [44]The singers: the children of Asaph, an hundred forty and eight. [45]The porters: the children of

Shallum, the children of Ater, the children of Talmon, the children of Akkub, the children of Hatita, the children of Shobai, an hundred thirty and eight. [46]The Nethinims: the children of Ziha, the children of Hashupha, the children of Tabbaoth, [47]The children of Keros, the children of Sia, the children of Padon, [48]The children of Lebana, the children of Hagaba, the children of Shalmai, [49]The children of Hanan, the children of Giddel, the children of Gahar, [50]The children of Reaiah, the children of Rezin, the children of Nekoda, [51]The children of Gazzam, the children of Uzza, the children of Phaseah, [52]The children of Besai, the children of Meunim, the children of Nephishesim, [53]The children of Bakbuk, the children of Hakupha, the children of Harhur, [54]The children of Bazlith, the children of Mehida, the children of Harsha, [55]The children of Barkos, the children of Sisera, the children of Tamah, [56]The children of Neziah, the children of Hatipha. [57]The children of Solomon's servants: the children of Sotai, the children of Sophereth, the children of Perida, [58]The children of Jaala, the children of Darkon, the children of Giddel, [59]The children of Shephatiah, the children of Hattil, the children of Pochereth of Zebaim, the children of Amon[i]. [60]All the Nethinims, and the children of Solomon's servants, *were* three hundred ninety and two. [61]And these *were* they

---

[d] Hariph: also called, Jora
[e] Gibeon: also called, Gibbar
[f] Bethazmaveth: also called, Azmaveth
[g] Kirjathjearim: also called, Kirjatharim
[h] Hodevah: also called, Hodaviah or Judah
[i] Amon: also called, Ami

which went up *also* from Telmelah, Telharesha, Cherub, Addon, and Immer: but they could not shew their father's house, nor their seed[j], whether they *were* of Israel. [62]The children of Delaiah, the children of Tobiah, the children of Nekoda, six hundred forty and two. [63]And of the priests: the children of Habaiah, the children of Koz, the children of Barzillai, which took *one* of the daughters of Barzillai the Gileadite to wife, and was called after their name. [64]These sought their register *among* those that were reckoned by genealogy, but it was not found: therefore were they, as polluted, put from the priesthood. [65]And the Tirshatha[k] said unto them, that they should not eat of the most holy things, till there stood *up* a priest with Urim and Thummim. [66]The whole congregation together *was* forty and two thousand three hundred and threescore, [67]Beside their manservants and their maidservants, of whom *there were* seven thousand three hundred thirty and seven: and they had two hundred forty and five singing men and singing women. [68]Their horses, seven hundred thirty and six: their mules, two hundred forty and five: [69] *Their* camels, four hundred thirty and five: six thousand seven hundred and twenty asses. [70]And some of the chief of the fathers gave unto the work. The Tirshatha gave to the treasure a thousand drams of gold, fifty basons, five hundred and thirty priests' garments. [71]And *some* of the chief of the fathers gave to the treasure of the work twenty thousand drams of gold, and two thousand and two hundred pound of silver. [72]And *that* which the rest of the people gave *was* twenty thousand drams of gold, and two thousand pound of silver, and threescore and seven priests' garments. [73]So the priests, and the Levites, and the porters, and the singers, and *some* of the people, and the Nethinims, and all Israel, dwelt in their cities; and when the seventh month came, the children of Israel *were* in their cities.

8

[1]And all the people gathered themselves together as one man into the street that *was* before the water gate; and they spake unto Ezra the scribe to bring the book of the law of Moses, which the LORD had commanded to Israel. [2]And Ezra the priest brought the law before the congregation both of men and women, and all that could hear with understanding, upon the first day of the seventh month. [3]And he read therein before the street that *was* before the water gate from the morning until midday, before the men and the women,

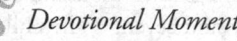

Devotional Moment
•
Devotions
8:1-18 This "national Bible study" deeply affected the Jews, commanding their attention, stirring their emotions, and changing their behavior. We must be careful not to let our own study of the Scriptures, including devotions, get bumped off our overlong to-do list. God's Word is living and active! It can convict us, comfort us, challenge us, and change us— but only if we read it.

---

[j] seed: or, pedigree
[k] the Tirshatha: also called, the governor

and those that could understand; and the ears of all the people *were attentive* unto the book of the law. ⁴And Ezra the scribe stood upon a pulpit[a] of wood, which they had made for the purpose; and beside him stood Mattithiah, and Shema, and Anaiah, and Urijah, and Hilkiah, and Maaseiah, on his right hand; and on his left hand, Pedaiah, and Mishael, and Malchiah, and Hashum, and Hashbadana, Zechariah, *and* Meshullam. ⁵And Ezra opened the book in the sight[b] of all the people; (for he was above all the people;) and when he opened it, all the people stood up: ⁶And Ezra blessed the LORD, the great God. And all the people answered, Amen, Amen, with lifting up their hands: and they bowed their heads, and worshipped the LORD with *their* faces to the ground. ⁷Also Jeshua, and Bani, and Sherebiah, Jamin, Akkub, Shabbethai, Hodijah, Maaseiah, Kelita, Azariah, Jozabad, Hanan, Pelaiah, and the Levites, caused the people to understand the law: and the people *stood* in their place. ⁸So they read in the book in the law of God distinctly, and gave the sense, and caused *them* to understand the reading.

⁹And Nehemiah, which *is* the Tirshatha[c], and Ezra the priest the scribe, and the Levites that taught the people, said unto all the people, This day *is* holy unto the LORD your God; mourn not, nor weep. For all the people wept, when they heard the words of the law.

¹⁰Then he said unto them, Go your way, eat the fat, and drink the sweet, and send portions unto them for whom nothing is prepared: for *this* day *is* holy unto our Lord: neither be ye sorry; for the joy of the LORD is your strength. ¹¹So the Levites stilled all the people, saying, Hold your peace, for the day *is* holy; neither be ye grieved. ¹²And all the people went their way to eat, and to drink, and to send portions, and to make great mirth, because they had understood the words that were declared unto them.

¹³And on the second day were gathered together the chief of the fathers of all the people, the priests, and the Levites, unto Ezra the scribe, even to understand[d] the words of the law. ¹⁴And they found written in the law which the LORD had commanded by[e] Moses, that the children of Israel should dwell in booths in the feast of the seventh month: ¹⁵And that they should publish and proclaim in all their cities, and in Jerusalem, saying, Go forth unto the mount, and fetch olive branches, and pine branches, and myrtle branches, and palm branches, and branches of thick trees, to make booths, as *it is* written. ¹⁶So the people went forth, and brought *them,* and made themselves booths, every one upon the roof of his house, and in their courts, and in the courts of the house of God, and in the street of the water gate, and in the street of the gate of Ephraim.

ᵃ pulpit . . . : Heb. tower of wood
ᵇ sight: Heb. eyes
ᶜ the Tirshatha: or, the governor
ᵈ to understand . . . : or, that they might instruct in the words of the law
ᵉ by: Heb. by the hand of

¹⁷And all the congregation of them that were come again out of the captivity made booths, and sat under the booths: for since the days of Jeshua the son of Nun unto that day had not the children of Israel done so. And there was very great gladness. ¹⁸Also day by day, from the first day unto the last day, he read in the book of the law of God. And they kept the feast seven days; and on the eighth day *was* a solemn assembly, according unto the manner.

9

¹Now in the twenty and fourth day of this month the children of Israel were assembled with fasting, and with sackclothes, and earth upon them. ²And the seed of Israel separated themselves from all strangersª, and stood and confessed their sins, and the iniquities of their fathers. ³And they stood up in their place, and read in the book of the law of the LORD their God *one* fourth part of the day; and *another* fourth part they confessed, and worshipped the LORD their God.

⁴Then stood up upon the stairsᵇ, of the Levites, Jeshua, and Bani, Kadmiel, Shebaniah, Bunni, Sherebiah, Bani, *and* Chenani, and cried with a loud voice unto the LORD their God. ⁵Then the Levites, Jeshua, and Kadmiel, Bani, Hashabniah, Sherebiah, Hodijah, Shebaniah, *and* Pethahiah, said, Stand up *and* bless the LORD your God for ever and ever: and blessed be thy glorious name, which is exalted above all blessing and praise. ⁶Thou, *even* thou, *art* LORD alone; thou hast

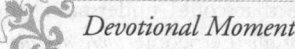

Devotional Moment

Confession

9:3 What a worship service! The Israelites spent two or three hours listening to the Scriptures being read and several more hours confessing their sins. The significance of this event, however, is not its length but its intent. The Israelites wanted to be right with God *no matter what the cost.* Like King David before them, they understood that a refusal to deal with sin blocks intimacy with God (Ps. 66:18). How can you imitate their behavior in your role as a family leader? Ask the Spirit of God to search your life and point out to you wrong attitudes and actions (Ps. 139:23-24). Confess those sins (1 John 1:9) and then worship the Lord. Include these steps in your family prayers, too.

made heaven, the heaven of heavens, with all their host, the earth, and all *things* that *are* therein, the seas, and all that *is* therein, and thou preservest them all; and the host of heaven worshippeth thee. ⁷Thou *art* the LORD the God, who didst choose Abram, and broughtest him forth out of Ur of the Chaldees, and gavest him the name of Abraham; ⁸And foundest his heart faithful before thee, and madest a covenant with him to give the land of the Canaanites, the Hittites, the Amorites, and the Perizzites, and the Jebusites, and the Girgashites, to give *it, I say,* to his seed, and hast performed thy words; for thou *art* righteous: ⁹And didst see the affliction of our fathers in Egypt, and heardest their cry by the Red sea; ¹⁰And shewedst signs and wonders upon Pharaoh, and on all his servants, and on all the people of his land:

ª strangers: Heb. strange children
ᵇ stairs: or, scaffold

for thou knewest that they dealt proudly against them. So didst thou get thee a name, as *it is* this day. ¹¹And thou didst divide the sea before them, so that they went through the midst of the sea on the dry land; and their persecutors thou threwest into the deeps, as a stone into the mighty waters. ¹²Moreover thou leddest them in the day by a cloudy pillar; and in the night by a pillar of fire, to give them light in the way wherein they should go. ¹³Thou camest down also upon mount Sinai, and spakest with them from heaven, and gavest them right judgments, and true° laws, good statutes and commandments: ¹⁴And madest known unto them thy holy sabbath, and commandedst them precepts, statutes, and laws, by the hand of Moses thy servant: ¹⁵And gavest them bread from heaven for their hunger, and broughtest forth water for them out of the rock for their thirst,

---

Devotional Moment

•

Remembering

9:6-38 This prayer summarizes Israel's history. It traces God's faithfulness and power from the first moment of creation until the return of the exiles from Babylonian captivity. Looking back can be a profitable exercise. We can be encouraged by God's goodness. We can be warned by the failures of the past. We can be motivated and challenged by the successes of those before us. We can be thrilled to see how much we personally have grown. Begin preserving your own family's spiritual history in a notebook or journal. Over the years, this record will serve as a wonderful reminder of God's work in your family.

---

and promisedst them that they should go in to possess the land which thou hadst sworn to give them. ¹⁶But they and our fathers dealt proudly, and hardened their necks, and hearkened not to thy commandments, ¹⁷And refused to obey, neither were mindful of thy wonders that thou didst among them; but hardened their necks, and in their rebellion appointed a captain to return to their bondage: but thou *art* a God° ready to pardon, gracious and merciful, slow to anger, and of great kindness, and forsookest them not. ¹⁸Yea, when they had made them a molten calf, and said, This *is* thy God that brought thee up out of Egypt, and had wrought great provocations; ¹⁹Yet thou in thy manifold mercies forsookest them not in the wilderness: the pillar of the cloud departed not from them by day, to lead them in the way; neither the pillar of fire by night, to shew them light, and the way wherein they should go. ²⁰Thou gavest also thy good spirit to instruct them, and withheldest not thy manna from their mouth, and gavest them water for their thirst. ²¹Yea, forty years didst thou sustain them in the wilderness, *so that* they lacked nothing; their clothes waxed not old, and their feet swelled not. ²²Moreover thou gavest them kingdoms and nations, and didst divide them into corners: so they possessed the land of Sihon, and the land of the king of Heshbon, and the land of Og king of Bashan. ²³Their children also multipliedst thou as the stars of heaven, and broughtest them into the land, concerning which thou hadst

---

° true . . . : Heb. laws of truth
ᵈ a God . . . : Heb. a God of pardons

promised to their fathers, that they should go in to possess *it*. ²⁴So the children went in and possessed the land, and thou subduedst before them the inhabitants of the land, the Canaanites, and gavest them into their hands, with their kings, and the people of the land, that they might do with them as they would. ²⁵And they took strong cities, and a fat land, and possessed houses full of all goods, wells^e digged, vineyards, and oliveyards, and fruit trees in abundance: so they did eat, and were filled, and became fat, and delighted themselves in thy great goodness. ²⁶Nevertheless they were disobedient, and rebelled against thee, and cast thy law behind their backs, and slew thy prophets which testified against them to turn them to thee, and they wrought great provocations. ²⁷Therefore thou deliveredst them into the hand of their enemies, who vexed them: and in the time of their trouble, when they cried unto thee, thou heardest *them* from heaven; and according to thy manifold mercies thou gavest them saviours, who saved them out of the hand of their enemies. ²⁸But after they had rest, they did^f evil again before thee: therefore leftest thou them in the hand of their enemies, so that they had the dominion over them: yet when they returned, and cried unto thee, thou heardest *them* from heaven; and many times didst thou deliver them according to thy mercies; ²⁹And testifiedst against them, that thou

mightest bring them again unto thy law: yet they dealt proudly, and hearkened not unto thy commandments, but sinned against thy judgments, (which if a man do, he shall live in them;) and withdrew^g the shoulder, and hardened their neck, and would not hear. ³⁰Yet many years didst thou forbear^h them, and testifiedst against them by thy spirit in thy prophets: yet would they not give ear: therefore gavest thou them into the hand of the people of the lands. ³¹Nevertheless for thy great mercies' sake thou didst not utterly consume them, nor forsake them; for thou *art* a gracious and merciful God. ³²Now therefore, our God, the great, the mighty, and the terrible God, who keepest covenant and mercy, let not all the trouble^i seem little before thee, that hath come upon us, on our kings, on our princes, and on our priests, and on our prophets, and on our fathers, and on all thy people, since the time of the kings of Assyria unto this day. ³³Howbeit thou *art* just in all that is brought upon us; for thou hast done right, but we have done wickedly: ³⁴Neither have our kings, our princes, our priests, nor our fathers, kept thy law, nor hearkened unto thy commandments and thy testimonies, wherewith thou didst testify against them. ³⁵For they have not served thee in their kingdom, and in thy great goodness that thou gavest them, and in the large and fat land which thou gavest before them, neither turned they from

---

^e wells: or, cisterns

^f they did . . . : Heb. they returned to do evil

^g withdrew . . . : Heb. they gave a withdrawing shoulder

^h forbear . . . : Heb. protract over them

^i trouble: Heb. weariness

Devotional Moment
•
Wealth

Devotional Moment
•
Wealth

9:35-36 Despite the fact that the Israelites enjoyed tremendous blessings *from* God, they refused to live *for* God. Their prosperity had become a problem. No wonder the Scriptures repeatedly warn about the dangers of wealth (Prov. 30:8; Matt. 19:16-26; 1 Tim. 6:6-10). Those with much may be tempted to trust in their own resources rather than in God, to become worried about losing what they have, or to become greedy and want to acquire even more things. God gives us resources and families so that we may be a help to others. Develop a humble and thankful heart regarding what you "own"; you'll become more content as well as closer to God.

their wicked works. ³⁶Behold, we *are* servants this day, and *for* the land that thou gavest unto our fathers to eat the fruit thereof and the good thereof, behold, we *are* servants in it: ³⁷And it yieldeth much increase unto the kings whom thou hast set over us because of our sins: also they have dominion over our bodies, and over our cattle, at their pleasure, and we *are* in great distress. ³⁸And because of all this we make a sure *covenant*, and write *it*; and our princes, Levites, *and* priests, seal[ʲ] unto it.

10

¹Now those that sealed *were*, Nehemiah, the Tirshatha, the son of Hachaliah, and Zidkijah, ²Seraiah, Azariah, Jeremiah, ³Pashur, Amariah, Malchijah, ⁴Hattush, Shebaniah, Malluch, ⁵Harim, Meremoth, Obadiah, ⁶Daniel, Ginnethon, Baruch, ⁷Meshullam, Abijah, Mijamin, ⁸Maaziah, Bilgai, Shemaiah: these *were* the priests. ⁹And

the Levites: both Jeshua the son of Azaniah, Binnui of the sons of Henadad, Kadmiel; ¹⁰And their brethren, Shebaniah, Hodijah, Kelita, Pelaiah, Hanan, ¹¹Micha, Rehob, Hashabiah, ¹²Zaccur, Sherebiah, Shebaniah, ¹³Hodijah, Bani, Beninu. ¹⁴The chief of the people; Parosh, Pahathmoab, Elam, Zatthu, Bani, ¹⁵Bunni, Azgad, Bebai, ¹⁶Adonijah, Bigvai, Adin, ¹⁷Ater, Hizkijah, Azzur, ¹⁸Hodijah, Hashum, Bezai, ¹⁹Hariph, Anathoth, Nebai, ²⁰Magpiash, Meshullam, Hezir, ²¹Meshezabeel, Zadok, Jaddua, ²²Pelatiah, Hanan, Anaiah, ²³Hoshea, Hananiah, Hashub, ²⁴Hallohesh, Pileha, Shobek, ²⁵Rehum, Hashabnah, Maaseiah, ²⁶And Ahijah, Hanan, Anan, ²⁷Malluch, Harim, Baanah. ²⁸And the rest of the people, the priests, the Levites, the porters, the singers, the Nethinims, and all they that had separated themselves from the people of the lands unto the law of God, their wives, their sons, and their daughters, every one having knowledge, and having understanding; ²⁹They clave to their brethren, their no-

Devotional Moment
•
Commitment

10:28-40 The people of Israel expressed their commitment to God in the form of a written covenant. In this contract, they pledged to honor God in their relationships (v. 30), in the use of their time (v. 31), and with their money (vv. 32-40). Here is a question for families to consider: If an impartial jury watched a video of your family interaction, examined your daily schedule, and studied your expenditures for the last month, who or what would they conclude you are committed to?

ʲ seal: Heb. are at the sealing, or, sealed

bles, and entered into a curse, and into an oath, to walk in God's law, which was given by[a] Moses the servant of God, and to observe and do all the commandments of the LORD our Lord, and his judgments and his statutes; ³⁰And that we would not give our daughters unto the people of the land, nor take their daughters for our sons: ³¹And *if* the people of the land bring ware or any victuals on the sabbath day to sell, *that* we would not buy it of them on the sabbath, or on the holy day: and *that* we would leave the seventh year, and the exaction of every debt.

³²Also we made ordinances for us, to charge ourselves yearly with the third part of a shekel for the service of the house of our God; ³³For the shewbread, and for the continual meat offering, and for the continual burnt offering, of the sabbaths, of the new moons, for the set feasts, and for the holy *things*, and for the sin offerings to make an atonement for Israel, and *for* all the work of the house of our God. ³⁴And we cast the lots among the priests, the Levites, and the people, for the wood offering, to bring *it* into the house of our God, after the houses of our fathers, at times appointed year by year, to burn upon the altar of the LORD our God, as *it is* written in the law: ³⁵And to bring the firstfruits of our ground, and the firstfruits of all fruit of all trees, year by year, unto the house of the LORD: ³⁶Also the firstborn of our sons, and of our cattle, as *it is* written in the law, and the firstlings of our herds and of our flocks, to bring to the house of our

God, unto the priests that minister in the house of our God: ³⁷And *that* we should bring the firstfruits of our dough, and our offerings, and the fruit of all manner of trees, of wine and of oil, unto the priests, to the chambers of the house of our God; and the tithes of our ground unto the Levites, that the same Levites might have the tithes in all the cities of our tillage. ³⁸And the priest the son of Aaron shall be with the Levites, when the Levites take tithes: and the Levites shall bring up the tithe of the tithes unto the house of our God, to the chambers, into the treasure house. ³⁹For the children of Israel and the children of Levi shall bring the offering of the corn, of the new wine, and the oil, unto the chambers, where *are* the vessels of the sanctuary, and the priests that minister, and the porters, and the singers: and we will not forsake the house of our God.

11

¹And the rulers of the people dwelt at Jerusalem: the rest of the people also cast lots, to bring one of ten to dwell in Jerusalem the holy city, and nine parts *to* dwell in *other* cities. ²And the people blessed all the men, that willingly offered themselves to dwell at Jerusalem. ³Now these *are* the chief of the province that dwelt in Jerusalem: but in the cities of Judah dwelt every one in his possession in their cities, *to wit*, Israel, the priests, and the Levites, and the Nethinims, and the children of Solomon's servants. ⁴And at Jerusalem dwelt *certain* of the children of Judah, and of the children of Benjamin. Of the children of Judah; Athaiah

---

a by: Heb. by the hand of

the son of Uzziah, the son of Zechariah, the son of Amariah, the son of Shephatiah, the son of Mahalaleel, of the children of Perez[a]; ⁵And Maaseiah the son of Baruch, the son of Colhozeh, the son of Hazaiah, the son of Adaiah, the son of Joiarib, the son of Zechariah, the son of Shiloni. ⁶All the sons of Perez that dwelt at Jerusalem *were* four hundred threescore and eight valiant men. ⁷And these *are* the sons of Benjamin; Sallu the son of Meshullam, the son of Joed, the son of Pedaiah, the son of Kolaiah, the son of Maaseiah, the son of Ithiel, the son of Jesaiah. ⁸And after him Gabbai, Sallai, nine hundred twenty and eight. ⁹And Joel the son of Zichri *was* their overseer: and Judah the son of Senuah *was* second over the city. ¹⁰Of the priests: Jedaiah the son of Joiarib, Jachin. ¹¹Seraiah the son of Hilkiah, the son of Meshullam, the son of Zadok, the son of Meraioth, the son of Ahitub, *was* the ruler of the house of God. ¹²And their brethren that did the work of the house *were* eight hundred twenty and two: and Adaiah the son of Jeroham, the son of Pelaliah, the son of Amzi, the son of Zechariah, the son of Pashur, the son of Malchiah, ¹³And his brethren, chief of the fathers, two hundred forty and two: and Amashai the son of Azareel, the son of Ahasai, the son of Meshillemoth, the son of Immer, ¹⁴And their brethren, mighty men of valour, an hundred twenty and eight: and their overseer *was* Zabdiel, the son[b] of *one of* the great men.

¹⁵Also of the Levites: Shemaiah the son of Hashub, the son of Azrikam, the son of Hashabiah, the son of Bunni; ¹⁶And Shabbethai and Jozabad, of the chief of the Levites, *had* the oversight of the outward business of the house of God. ¹⁷And Mattaniah the son of Micha, the son of Zabdi, the son of Asaph, *was* the principal to begin the thanksgiving in prayer: and Bakbukiah the second among his brethren, and Abda the son of Shammua, the son of Galal, the son of Jeduthun. ¹⁸All the Levites in the holy city *were* two hundred fourscore and four. ¹⁹Moreover the porters, Akkub, Talmon, and their brethren that kept the gates[c], *were* an hundred seventy and two.

²⁰And the residue of Israel, of the priests, *and* the Levites, *were* in all the cities of Judah, every one in his inheritance. ²¹But the Nethinims dwelt in Ophel[d]: and Ziha and Gispa *were* over the Nethinims. ²²The overseer also of the Levites at Jerusalem *was* Uzzi the son of Bani, the son of Hashabiah, the son of Mattaniah, the son of Micha. Of the sons of Asaph, the singers *were* over the business of the house of God. ²³For *it was* the king's commandment concerning them, that a certain portion should be for the singers, due for every day. ²⁴And Pethahiah the son of Meshezabeel, of the children of Zerah[e] the son of Judah, *was* at the king's hand in all matters concerning the people. ²⁵And for the villages, with their fields, *some* of the children of Judah dwelt at

---

[a] Perez: also called, Pharez
[b] the son . . . : or, the son of Haggedolim
[c] the gates: Heb. at the gates
[d] Ophel: or, the tower
[e] Zerah: also called, Zarah

Kirjatharba, and *in* the villages thereof, and at Dibon, and *in* the villages thereof, and at Jekabzeel, and *in* the villages thereof, ²⁶And at Jeshua, and at Moladah, and at Bethphelet, ²⁷And at Hazarshual, and at Beersheba, and *in* the villages thereof, ²⁸And at Ziklag, and at Mekonah, and in the villages thereof, ²⁹And at Enrimmon, and at Zareah, and at Jarmuth, ³⁰Zanoah, Adullam, and *in* their villages, at Lachish, and the fields thereof, at Azekah, and *in* the villages thereof. And they dwelt from Beersheba unto the valley of Hinnom. ³¹The children also of Benjamin from Geba *dwelt* at Michmash, and Aija, and Bethel, and *in* their villages, ³²*And* at Anathoth, Nob, Ananiah, ³³Hazor, Ramah, Gittaim, ³⁴Hadid, Zeboim, Neballat, ³⁵Lod, and Ono, the valley of craftsmen. ³⁶And of the Levites *were* divisions *in* Judah, *and* in Benjamin.

12

¹Now these *are* the priests and the Levites that went up with Zerubbabel the son of Shealtiel, and Jeshua: Seraiah, Jeremiah, Ezra, ²Amariah, Malluch[a], Hattush, ³Shechaniah[b], Rehum, Meremoth, ⁴Iddo, Ginnetho[c], Abijah, ⁵Miamin[d], Maadiah, Bilgah, ⁶Shemaiah, and Joiarib, Jedaiah, ⁷Sallu[e], Amok, Hilkiah, Jedaiah. These *were* the chief of the priests and of their brethren in the days of Jeshua. ⁸Moreover the

Levites: Jeshua, Binnui, Kadmiel, Sherebiah, Judah, *and* Mattaniah, *which was* over the thanksgiving[f], he and his brethren. ⁹Also Bakbukiah and Unni, their brethren, *were* over against them in the watches. ¹⁰And Jeshua begat Joiakim, Joiakim also begat Eliashib, and Eliashib begat Joiada, ¹¹And Joiada begat Jonathan, and Jonathan begat Jaddua. ¹²And in the days of Joiakim were priests, the chief of the fathers: of Seraiah, Meraiah; of Jeremiah, Hananiah; ¹³Of Ezra, Meshullam; of Amariah, Jehohanan; ¹⁴Of Melicu, Jonathan; of Shebaniah, Joseph; ¹⁵Of Harim, Adna; of Meraioth, Helkai; ¹⁶Of Iddo, Zechariah; of Ginnethon, Meshullam; ¹⁷Of Abijah, Zichri; of Miniamin, of Moadiah, Piltai; ¹⁸Of Bilgah, Shammua; of Shemaiah, Jehonathan; ¹⁹And of Joiarib, Mattenai; of Jedaiah, Uzzi; ²⁰Of Sallai, Kallai; of Amok, Eber; ²¹Of Hilkiah, Hashabiah; of Jedaiah, Nethaneel. ²²The Levites in the days of Eliashib, Joiada, and Johanan, and Jaddua, *were* recorded chief of the fathers: also the priests, to the reign of Darius the Persian. ²³The sons of Levi, the chief of the fathers, *were* written in the book of the chronicles, even until the days of Johanan the son of Eliashib. ²⁴And the chief of the Levites: Hashabiah, Sherebiah, and Jeshua the son of Kadmiel, with their brethren over against them, to praise *and* to give thanks, according

---

[a] Malluch: also called, Melicu
[b] Shechaniah: also called, Shebaniah
[c] Ginnetho: also called, Ginnethon
[d] Miamin: also called, Miniamin
[e] Sallu: also called, Sallai
[f] the thanksgiving: that is, the psalms of thanksgiving

to the commandment of David the man of God, ward over against ward. [25]Mattaniah, and Bakbukiah, Obadiah, Meshullam, Talmon, Akkub, *were* porters keeping the ward at the thresholds[g] of the gates. [26]These *were* in the days of Joiakim the son of Jeshua, the son of Jozadak, and in the days of Nehemiah the governor, and of Ezra the priest, the scribe.

[27]And at the dedication of the wall of Jerusalem they sought the Levites out of all their places, to bring them to Jerusalem, to keep the dedication with gladness, both with thanksgivings, and with singing, *with* cymbals, psalteries, and with harps. [28]And the sons of the singers gathered themselves together, both out of the plain country round about Jerusalem, and from the villages of Netophathi; [29]Also from the house of Gilgal, and out of the fields of Geba and Azmaveth: for the singers had builded them villages round about Jerusalem. [30]And the priests and the Levites purified themselves, and purified the people, and the gates, and the wall. [31]Then I brought up the princes of Judah upon the wall, and appointed two great *companies of them that gave* thanks, *whereof one* went on the right hand upon the wall toward the dung gate: [32]And after them went Hoshaiah, and half of the princes of Judah, [33]And Azariah, Ezra, and Meshullam, [34]Judah, and Benjamin, and Shemaiah, and Jeremiah, [35]And *certain* of the priests' sons with trumpets; *namely,* Zechariah the son of Jonathan, the son of Shemaiah, the son of Mattaniah, the son of Michaiah, the son of Zaccur, the son of

Asaph: [36]And his brethren, Shemaiah, and Azarael, Milalai, Gilalai, Maai, Nethaneel, and Judah, Hanani, with the musical instruments of David the man of God, and Ezra the scribe before them. [37]And at the fountain gate, which was over against them, they went up by the stairs of the city of David, at the going up of the wall, above the house of David, even unto the water gate eastward. [38]And the other *company of them that gave* thanks went over against *them,* and I after them, and the half of the people upon the wall, from beyond the tower of the furnaces even unto the broad wall; [39]And from above the gate of Ephraim, and above the old gate, and above the fish gate, and the tower of Hananeel, and the tower of Meah, even unto the sheep gate: and they stood still in the prison gate. [40]So stood the two *companies of them that gave* thanks in the house of God, and I, and the half of the rulers with me: [41]And the priests; Eliakim, Maaseiah, Miniamin, Michaiah, Elioenai, Zechariah, *and* Hananiah, with trumpets; [42]And Maaseiah, and Shemaiah, and Eleazar, and Uzzi, and Jehohanan, and Malchijah, and Elam, and Ezer. And the singers sang loud, with Jezrahiah *their* overseer. [43]Also that day they offered great sacrifices, and rejoiced: for God had made them rejoice with great joy: the wives also and the children rejoiced: so that the joy of Jerusalem was heard even afar off.

[44]And at that time were some appointed over the chambers for the treasures, for the offerings, for the firstfruits, and for the tithes, to gather into

---

[g] thresholds: or, treasuries, or, assemblies

them out of the fields of the cities the portions of the law[h] for the priests and Levites: for Judah rejoiced for the priests and for the Levites that waited. [45]And both the singers and the porters kept the ward of their God, and the ward of the purification, according to the commandment of David, *and* of Solomon his son. [46]For in the days of David and Asaph of old *there were* chief of the singers, and songs of praise and thanksgiving unto God. [47]And all Israel in the days of Zerubbabel, and in the days of Nehemiah, gave the portions of the singers and the porters, every day his portion: and they sanctified[i] *holy things* unto the Levites; and the Levites sanctified *them* unto the children of Aaron.

13

[1]On that day they read in the book of Moses in the audience of the people; and therein was found written, that the Ammonite and the Moabite should not come into the congregation of God for ever; [2]Because they met not the children of Israel with bread and with water, but hired Balaam against them, that he should curse them: howbeit our God turned the curse into a blessing. [3]Now it came to pass, when they had heard the law, that they separated from Israel all the mixed multitude. [4]And before this, Eliashib the priest, having the oversight of the chamber of the house of our God, *was* allied unto Tobiah: [5]And he had prepared for him a great chamber, where aforetime they laid the meat offerings, the frankincense, and the vessels, and the tithes of the corn, the new wine, and the oil, which was commanded *to be given* to the Levites, and the singers, and the porters; and the offerings of the priests. [6]But in all this *time* was not I at Jerusalem: for in the two and thirtieth year of Artaxerxes king of Babylon came I unto the king, and after[a] certain days obtained I leave of the king: [7]And I came to Jerusalem, and understood of the evil that Eliashib did for Tobiah, in preparing him a chamber in the courts of the house of God. [8]And it grieved me sore: therefore I cast forth all the household stuff of Tobiah out of the chamber. [9]Then I commanded, and they cleansed the chambers: and thither brought I again the vessels of the house of God, with the meat offering and the frankincense.

[10]And I perceived that the portions of the Levites had not been given *them*: for the Levites and the singers, that did the work, were fled every one to his field. [11]Then contended I with the rulers, and said, Why is the house of God forsaken? And I gathered them together, and set them in their place[b]. [12]Then brought all Judah the tithe of the corn and the new wine and the oil unto the treasuries[c]. [13]And I made treasurers over the treasuries[d], Shelemiah

---

[h] of the law: that is, appointed by the law
[i] sanctified: that is, set apart
[a] after . . . : Heb. at the end of days
[b] place: Heb. standing
[c] treasuries: or, storehouses
[d] treasuries: or, storehouses

the priest, and Zadok the scribe, and of the Levites, Pedaiah: and next to them *was* Hanan the son of Zaccur, the son of Mattaniah: for they were counted faithful, and their office *was* to distribute unto their brethren. ¹⁴Remember me, O my God, concerning this, and wipe not out my good^e deeds that I have done for the house of my God, and for the offices thereof.

¹⁵In those days saw I in Judah *some* treading wine presses on the sabbath, and bringing in sheaves, and lading asses; as also wine, grapes, and figs, and all *manner of* burdens, which they brought into Jerusalem on the sabbath day: and I testified *against them* in the day wherein they sold victuals. ¹⁶There dwelt men of Tyre also therein, which brought fish, and all manner of ware, and sold on the sabbath unto the children of Judah, and in Jerusalem. ¹⁷Then I contended with the nobles of Judah, and said unto them, What evil thing *is* this that ye do, and profane the sabbath day? ¹⁸Did not your fathers thus, and did not our God bring all this evil upon us, and upon this city? yet ye bring more wrath upon Israel by profaning the sabbath. ¹⁹And it came to pass, that when the gates of Jerusalem began to be dark before the sabbath, I commanded that the gates should be shut, and charged that they should not be opened till after the sabbath: and *some* of my servants set I at the gates, *that* there should no burden be brought in on the

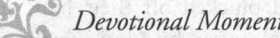

Devotional Moment

Example

13:26 In chastising the men of Judah for marrying unbelieving foreign women, Nehemiah used King Solomon as an example of what *not* to do. Every Israelite knew the sad story of Solomon—the brilliant, talented king who fell into spiritual decline because of his multiple marriages to pagan wives. These women led him away from God and into the sin of idolatry. What a sad legacy! Our lives will serve as either good examples or bad examples for the generations after us.

sabbath day. ²⁰So the merchants and sellers of all kind of ware lodged without Jerusalem once or twice. ²¹Then I testified against them, and said unto them, Why lodge ye about^f the wall? if ye do *so* again, I will lay hands on you. From that time forth came they no *more* on the sabbath. ²²And I commanded the Levites that they should cleanse themselves, and *that* they should come *and* keep the gates, to sanctify the sabbath day. Remember me, O my God, *concerning* this also, and spare me according to the greatness^g of thy mercy.

²³In those days also saw I Jews *that* had married wives of Ashdod, of Ammon, *and* of Moab: ²⁴And their children spake half in the speech of Ashdod, and could^h not speak in the Jews' language, but according to the language of each people. ²⁵And I contended with them, and cursed^i them, and smote certain of

---

^e good . . . : Heb. kindnesses
^f about: Heb. before
^g greatness: or, multitude
^h could . . . : Heb. they discerned not to speak
^i cursed: or, reviled

them, and plucked off their hair, and made them swear by God, *saying*, Ye shall not give your daughters unto their sons, nor take their daughters unto your sons, or for yourselves. ²⁶Did not Solomon king of Israel sin by these things? yet among many nations was there no king like him, who was beloved of his God, and God made him king over all Israel: nevertheless even him did outlandish women cause to sin. ²⁷Shall we then hearken unto you to do all this great evil, to transgress against our God in marrying strange

wives? ²⁸And *one* of the sons of Joiada, the son of Eliashib the high priest, *was* son in law to Sanballat the Horonite: therefore I chased him from me. ²⁹Remember them, O my God, because they have defiled the priesthood, and the covenant of the priesthood, and of the Levites. ³⁰Thus cleansed I them from all strangers, and appointed the wards of the priests and the Levites, every one in his business; ³¹And for the wood offering, at times appointed, and for the firstfruits. Remember me, O my God, for good.

ESTHER

Purpose
To demonstrate God's sovereignty and his loving care for his people

Author
Unknown

Date Written
Approximately 483–471 B.C. (Esther became queen in 479.)

Setting
The Persian Empire, with most of the action taking place in the king's palace at Shushan (Susa), the Persian capital

Key Verse
"If thou altogether holdest thy peace at this time, then shall there enlargement and deliverance arise to the Jews from another place; but thou and thy father's house shall be destroyed: and who knoweth whether thou art come to the kingdom for such a time as this?" (4:14).

Key People
Esther, Mordecai, King Ahasuerus (Xerxes I), Haman

Key Place
The king's palace in Susa, Persia

Special Features
Esther is one of only two books named for a woman (Ruth is the other). The book is unusual in that, in the original language, no name, title, or pronoun for God appears in it.

Our happiest events are often parties, and Esther is full of them. Esther has more parties per chapter than any other Bible book: ten chapters, ten parties. This should be one of the merriest books in the Bible. It isn't.

Instead, the story of Esther is fraught with tension, suspense, danger, deceit, and romance. The ten parties are occasions for ruthless jealousies and vicious plotting. Haman would wipe out the Jews. Mordecai learns of the plot. Esther intervenes. Before the story ends, tables are turned and—no, no, you'll have to read it yourself.

As you read, ponder the role of people in high places. With power comes responsibility, and there is a price. Those who dream about "reaching the top" should know early that the top is a precarious perch with tough demands and hard choices.

Ponder the role of outcast. Persons without power—the homeless, those of a different color, those who speak a strange language—have a life, too. When you're a "reject" (the school nerd), in what ways are you stronger than anyone?

Ponder the role of God, who is not mentioned in Esther (in the original Hebrew). How does God make a difference? If you're afraid, how does God calm the jitters?

If you like celebrating everything that moves, this is your book! But be forewarned—there's more to a party than punch and pretzels. At the kind of parties you'll discover here, your life could change forever!

1

¹Now it came to pass in the days of Ahasuerus, (this *is* Ahasuerus which reigned, from India even unto Ethiopia, *over* an hundred and seven and twenty provinces:) ² *That* in those days, when the king Ahasuerus sat on the throne of his kingdom, which *was* in Shushan the palace, ³In the third year of his reign, he made a feast unto all his princes and his servants; the power of Persia and Media, the nobles and princes of the provinces, *being* before him: ⁴When he shewed the riches of his glorious kingdom and the honour of his excellent majesty many days, *even* an hundred and fourscore days. ⁵And when these days were expired, the king made a feast unto all the people that were presentᵃ in Shushan the palace, both unto great and small, seven days, in the court of the garden of the king's palace; ⁶*Where were* white, green, and blue, *hangings*, fastened with cords of fine linen and purple to silver rings and pillars of marble: the beds *were of* gold and silver, upon a pavement of red, and blue, and white, and black, marble. ⁷And they gave *them* drink in vessels of gold, (the vessels being diverse one from another,) and royalᵇ wine in abundance, according to the state of the king. ⁸And the drinking *was* according to the law; none did compel: for so the king had appointed to all the officers of his house, that they should do according to every man's pleasure. ⁹Also Vashti the queen made a feast for the women

in the royal house which *belonged* to king Ahasuerus.

¹⁰On the seventh day, when the heart of the king was merry with wine, he commanded Mehuman, Biztha, Harbona, Bigtha, and Abagtha, Zethar, and Carcas, the seven chamberlainsᶜ that served in the presence of Ahasuerus the king, ¹¹To bring Vashti the queen before the king with the crown royal, to shew the people and the princes her beauty: for she *was* fairᵈ to look on. ¹²But the queen Vashti refused to come at the king's commandment by *his* chamberlains: therefore was the king very wroth, and his anger burned in him. ¹³Then the king said to the wise men, which knew the times, (for so *was* the king's manner toward all that knew law and judgment: ¹⁴And the next unto him *was* Carshena, Shethar, Admatha, Tarshish, Meres, Marsena, *and* Memucan, the seven princes of Persia and Media, which saw the king's face, *and* which sat the first in the kingdom;) ¹⁵What shall we do unto the queen Vashti according to law, because she hath not performed the commandment of the king Ahasuerus by the chamberlains? ¹⁶And Memucan answered before the king and the princes, Vashti the queen hath not done wrong to the king only, but also to all the princes, and to all the people that *are* in all the provinces of the king Ahasuerus. ¹⁷For *this* deed of the queen shall come abroad unto all women, so that they shall despise their husbands in their

---

ᵃ present: Heb. found
ᵇ royal . . . : Heb. wine of the kingdom
ᶜ chamberlains: or, eunuchs
ᵈ fair . . . : Heb. good of countenance

eyes, when it shall be reported, The king Ahasuerus commanded Vashti the queen to be brought in before him, but she came not. ¹⁸*Likewise* shall the ladies of Persia and Media say this day unto all the king's princes, which have heard of the deed of the queen. Thus *shall there arise* too much contempt and wrath. ¹⁹If it please the king, let there go a royal commandment from him, and let it be written among the laws of the Persians and the Medes, that it be not altered, That Vashti come no more before king Ahasuerus; and let the king give her royal estate unto another that is better than she. ²⁰And when the king's decree which he shall make shall be published throughout all his empire, (for it is great,) all the wives shall give to their husbands honour, both to great and small. ²¹And the saying pleased[c] the king and the princes; and the king did

according to the word of Memucan: ²²For he sent letters into all the king's provinces, into every province according to the writing thereof, and to every people after their language, that every man should bear rule in his own house, and that *it* should be published according to the language of every people.

2

¹After these things, when the wrath of king Ahasuerus was appeased, he remembered Vashti, and what she had done, and what was decreed against her. ²Then said the king's servants that ministered unto him, Let there be fair young virgins sought for the king: ³And let the king appoint officers in all the provinces of his kingdom, that they may gather together all the fair young virgins unto Shushan the palace, to the house of the women, unto the custody of Hege the king's chamberlain, keeper of the women; and let their things for purification be given *them*. ⁴And let the maiden which pleaseth the king be queen instead of Vashti. And the thing pleased the king; and he did so. ⁵*Now* in Shushan the palace there was a certain Jew, whose name *was* Mordecai, the son of Jair, the son of Shimei, the son of Kish, a Benjamite; ⁶Who had been carried away from Jerusalem with the captivity which had been carried away with Jeconiah[a] king of Judah, whom Nebuchadnezzar the king of Babylon had carried away. ⁷And he brought up Hadassah, that *is*, Esther, his uncle's daughter: for she had neither father nor mother, and the maid *was* fair and beautiful; whom Mordecai, when her father and

---

[c] pleased . . . : Heb. was good in the eyes of the king
[a] Jeconiah: also called, Jehoiachin

Family Traditions

The Blessing of Extended Family

ESTHER

When Esther's parents died, she was adopted by her cousin Mordecai. Mordecai had a tremendous influence on Esther's life. The book of Esther tells us that he stayed involved in her life even from outside the palace walls (Esther 2:11).

Extended family members can have a significant impact on the lives of children. There is a natural bond with aunts, uncles, cousins, and grandparents that can impact the spiritual and emotional destiny of kids even when those people don't live under the same roof. Here's how you can minister to the children in your extended family:

Get involved in their lives. Always look for opportunities to learn something about your nieces, nephews, and younger cousins. Find out what each one's gift is. Listen for clues to what they like. Whenever you have opportunity, give verbal affirmation.

Be a mentor. Pray for the children in your extended family. Notice the little things. Inspire them. In the hard times, encourage them with your faith and courage.

Help them appreciate their parents. Bring out old photos, clippings, or toys when they come to visit. Share details of family history—you'll shed light on the stories from a new perspective. Interview elderly members of your extended family about their recollections. Record these interviews on tape or in writing.

Teach them to love and value themselves. Offer to take the children places—not just as a diversion, but to show them they're important to you. Play with them. Choose gifts for them that underscore their strengths and personal interests.

Be there in times of trouble. And when their parents are tired or confused by their behavior, you can point out the positive side to the kids' "negative" traits. Keep fanning the flame of belief and love for your own heritage and traditions in every creative way you can.

Family is like a big puzzle. Every single piece is important, even those on the edge. If just one is missing, the gap detracts from the beauty of the picture. Do everything you can to complete your family portrait.

mother were dead, took for his own daughter. ⁸So it came to pass, when the king's commandment and his decree was heard, and when many maidens were gathered together unto Shushan the palace, to the custody of Hegai, that Esther was brought also unto the king's house, to the custody of Hegai, keeper of the women. ⁹And the maiden pleased him, and she obtained kindness of him; and he speedily gave her her things for purification, with such things as belonged to her, and seven maidens, *which were* meet to be given her, out of the king's house: and he preferred her and her maids unto the best *place* of the house of the women. ¹⁰Esther had not shewed her people nor her kindred: for Mordecai had charged her that she should not shew *it*. ¹¹And Mordecai walked every day before the court of the women's house, to know[b] how Esther did, and what should become of her. ¹²Now when every maid's turn was come to go in to king Ahasuerus, after that she had been twelve months, according to the manner of the women, (for so were the days of their purifications accomplished, *to wit*, six months with oil of myrrh, and six months with sweet odours, and with *other* things for the purifying of the women;) ¹³Then thus came *every* maiden unto the king; whatsoever she desired was given her to go with her out of the house of the women unto the king's house. ¹⁴In the evening she went, and on the morrow she returned into the second house of the women, to the custody of Shaashgaz, the king's chamber-

---

Devotional Moment

Moving

2:17 As the result of one decree, Esther's life changed forever. She moved from her familiar surroundings into the bizarre world of the king's harem. But even there God had a plan for her life. Perhaps you, too, have recently gone through a move that took you from comfortable surroundings into a strange new place. Maybe you have wondered how God could ever use you where you are. Esther's example shows us that we can trust God's plan for our lives, even when that plan takes us into unexpected places.

---

lain, which kept the concubines: she came in unto the king no more, except the king delighted in her, and that she were called by name. ¹⁵Now when the turn of Esther, the daughter of Abihail the uncle of Mordecai, who had taken her for his daughter, was come to go in unto the king, she required nothing but what Hegai the king's chamberlain, the keeper of the women, appointed. And Esther obtained favour in the sight of all them that looked upon her. ¹⁶So Esther was taken unto king Ahasuerus into his house royal in the tenth month, which *is* the month Tebeth, in the seventh year of his reign. ¹⁷And the king loved Esther above all the women, and she obtained grace and favour[c] in his sight more than all the virgins; so that he set the royal crown upon her head, and made her queen instead of Vashti. ¹⁸Then the king made a great feast unto all his princes and his servants, *even* Esther's feast; and he made a release[d] to the provinces, and gave

---

[b] to know . . . : Heb. to know the peace
[c] favour: or, kindness
[d] release: Heb. rest

Mordecai and Esther

Mordecai and Esther were cousins. When Esther was
young, her parents died, and Mordecai adopted her. Esther 2:7 says that he raised her as his own daughter.

By the time we meet them in Esther 2, Mordecai and
Esther had gone through a lot of hardship together. They
had grieved the death of Esther's parents. They had lived
on their own. And they had been taken captive to Babylon.

The most important crisis they faced took place after Esther grew up. A powerful man named Haman felt in-
sulted by Mordecai and hatched a plot to destroy the entire Jewish race. Mordecai urged Esther to intervene at
the risk of her own life, and she did, thus saving the Jews
and bringing justice against Haman.

What we often overlook in this exciting story is the
maturity of Mordecai and Esther's relationship. Before
the crisis began, Esther had kept her Jewish identity secret because she "did the commandment of Mordecai"
(Esther 2:20). Yet when the time came for her to approach the king, she gave Mordecai instructions too, and
he did "all that Esther had commanded him" (Esther
4:17). They respected each other as adults. Esther didn't
assert her independence, nor did Mordecai assert his position.

Mutual respect is an important part of all adult family relationships. Work at developing it with your parents.
And if you have young children, make it a goal for the
time when they become adults. It will take work and
time, but it's certainly possible. Mordecai and Esther did
it. So can you.

gifts, according to the state of the king. ¹⁹And when the virgins were gathered together the second time, then Mordecai sat in the king's gate. ²⁰Esther had not *yet* shewed her kindred nor her people; as Mordecai had charged her: for Esther did the commandment of Mordecai, like as when she was brought up with him.

²¹In those days, while Mordecai sat in the king's gate, two of the king's chamberlains, Bigthanᵉ and Teresh, of those which kept the door, were wroth, and sought to lay hand on the king Ahasuerus. ²²And the thing was known to Mordecai, who told *it* unto Esther the queen; and Esther certified the king *thereof* in Mordecai's name. ²³And when inquisition was made of the matter, it was found out; therefore they were both hanged on a tree: and it was written in the book of the chronicles before the king.

3

¹After these things did king Ahasuerus promote Haman the son of Hammedatha the Agagite, and advanced him, and set his seat above all the princes that *were* with him. ²And all the king's servants, that *were* in the king's gate, bowed, and reverenced Haman: for the king had so commanded concerning him. But Mordecai bowed not, nor did *him* reverence. ³Then the king's servants, which *were* in the king's gate, said unto Mordecai, Why transgressest thou the king's commandment? ⁴Now it came to pass, when they spake daily unto him, and he hearkened not unto them, that they told Haman, to see whether Mordecai's matters would

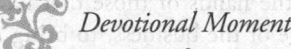

Devotional Moment
•
Obedience to God

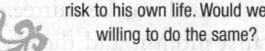

3:2 In refusing to bow when the king passed by, Mordecai disobeyed the king's law. Mordecai chose to obey God's law instead. We, too, may be placed in compromising situations that will force us to choose between a boss's command and God's command, between a family member's request and God's request, between a neighbor's demands and God's demands. Mordecai obeyed God's law at great risk to his own life. Would we be willing to do the same?

stand: for he had told them that he *was* a Jew. ⁵And when Haman saw that Mordecai bowed not, nor did him reverence, then was Haman full of wrath. ⁶And he thought scorn to lay hands on Mordecai alone; for they had shewed him the people of Mordecai: wherefore Haman sought to destroy all the Jews that *were* throughout the whole kingdom of Ahasuerus, *even* the people of Mordecai.

⁷In the first month, that *is*, the month Nisan, in the twelfth year of king Ahasuerus, they cast Pur, that *is*, the lot, before Haman from day to day, and from month to month, *to* the twelfth *month*, that *is*, the month Adar. ⁸And Haman said unto king Ahasuerus, There is a certain people scattered abroad and dispersed among the people in all the provinces of thy kingdom; and their laws *are* diverse from all people; neither keep they the king's laws: therefore it *is* not for the king's profit to suffer them. ⁹If it please the king, let it be written that they may be destroyed: and I will pay ten thousand talents of

---

ᵉ Bigthan: also called, Bigthana

silver to the hands of those that have the charge of the business, to bring *it* into the king's treasuries. ¹⁰And the king took his ring from his hand, and gave it unto Haman the son of Hammedatha the Agagite, the Jews' enemyª. ¹¹And the king said unto Haman, The silver *is* given to thee, the people also, to do with them as it seemeth good to thee. ¹²Then were the king's scribesᵇ called on the thirteenth day of the first month, and there was written according to all that Haman had commanded unto the king's lieutenants, and to the governors that *were* over every province, and to the rulers of every people of every province according to the writing thereof, and *to* every people after their language; in the name of king Ahasuerus was it written, and sealed with the king's ring. ¹³And the letters were sent by posts into all the king's provinces, to destroy, to kill, and to cause to perish, all Jews, both young and old, little children and women, in one day, *even* upon the thirteenth *day* of the twelfth month, which is the month Adar, and *to take* the spoil of them for a prey. ¹⁴The copy of the writing for a commandment to be given in every province was published unto all people, that they should be ready against that day. ¹⁵The posts went out, being hastened by the king's commandment, and the decree was given in Shushan the palace. And the king and Haman sat down to drink; but the city Shushan was perplexed.

4

¹When Mordecai perceived all that was done, Mordecai rent his clothes, and put on sackcloth with ashes, and went out into the midst of the city, and cried with a loud and a bitter cry; ²And came even before the king's gate: for none *might* enter into the king's gate clothed with sackcloth. ³And in every province, whithersoever the king's commandment and his decree came, *there was* great mourning among the Jews, and fasting, and weeping, and wailing; and manyª lay in sackcloth and ashes. ⁴So Esther's maids and her chamberlainsᵇ came and told *it* her. Then was the queen exceedingly grieved; and she sent raiment to clothe Mordecai, and to take away his sackcloth from him: but he received *it* not.

⁵Then called Esther for Hatach, *one* of the king's chamberlains, whom he had appointedᶜ to attend upon her, and gave him a commandment to Mordecai, to know what it *was*, and why it *was*. ⁶So Hatach went forth to Mordecai unto the street of the city, which *was* before the king's gate. ⁷And Mordecai told him of all that had happened unto him, and of the sum of the money that Haman had promised to pay to the king's treasuries for the Jews, to destroy them. ⁸Also he gave him the copy of the writing of the decree that

---

ª enemy: or, oppressor
ᵇ scribes: or,-secretaries
ª many . . . : Heb. sackcloth and ashes were laid under many
ᵇ chamberlains: Heb. eunuchs
ᶜ appointed . . . : Heb. set before her

was given at Shushan to destroy them, to shew *it* unto Esther, and to declare *it* unto her, and to charge her that she should go in unto the king, to make supplication unto him, and to make request before him for her people. ⁹And Hatach came and told Esther the words of Mordecai. ¹⁰Again Esther spake unto Hatach, and gave him commandment unto Mordecai; ¹¹All the king's servants, and the people of the king's provinces, do know, that whosoever, whether man or woman, shall come unto the king into the inner court, who is not called, *there is* one law of his to put *him* to death, except such to whom the king shall hold out the golden sceptre, that he may live: but I have not been called to come in unto the king these thirty days. ¹²And they told to Mordecai Esther's words. ¹³Then Mordecai commanded to answer Esther, Think not with thyself that thou shalt escape in the king's house, more than all the Jews. ¹⁴For if thou altogether holdest thy peace at this time, *then* shall there enlargementᵈ and deliverance arise to the Jews from another place; but thou and thy father's house shall be destroyed: and who knoweth whether thou art come to the kingdom for *such* a time as this? ¹⁵Then Esther bade *them* return Mordecai *this answer,* ¹⁶Go, gather together all the Jews that are presentᵉ in Shushan, and fast ye for me, and neither eat nor drink three days, night or day: I also and my maidens will fast likewise; and so will I go in unto the king, which *is* not according to the law: and if I perish, I perish. ¹⁷So Mordecai

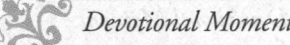
went his way, and did according to all that Esther had commanded him.

5

¹Now it came to pass on the third day, that Esther put on *her* royal *apparel,* and stood in the inner court of the king's house, over against the king's house: and the king sat upon his royal throne in the royal house, over against the gate of the house. ²And it was so, when the king saw Esther the queen standing in the court, *that* she obtained favour in his sight: and the king held out to Esther the golden sceptre that *was* in his hand. So Esther drew near, and touched the top of the sceptre. ³Then said the king unto her, What wilt thou, queen Esther? and what *is* thy request? it shall be even given thee to the half of the kingdom. ⁴And Esther answered, If *it seem* good unto the king,

---

ᵈ enlargement: Heb. respiration
ᵉ present: Heb. found

Devotional Moment
•
Bitterness

5:9 Haman was overcome by his bitterness and hatred. His happiness after an elegant banquet was destroyed when he saw Mordecai. Sometimes bitterness and hatred take over our hearts, too. Someone has wronged us or our children, and the bitterness eats away at our stability. God beseeches us "Let all bitterness, and wrath, and anger . . . be put away from you" (Eph. 4:31). When you feel bitter, examine your bitterness and try to identify the specific injustice that gnaws at you. Separate the *act* from the *person* who did it. Then pray for God's help to set the bitterness aside and replace it with kindness and forgiveness.

let the king and Haman come this day unto the banquet that I have prepared for him. ⁵Then the king said, Cause Haman to make haste, that he may do as Esther hath said. So the king and Haman came to the banquet that Esther had prepared. ⁶And the king said unto Esther at the banquet of wine, What *is* thy petition? and it shall be granted thee: and what *is* thy request? even to the half of the kingdom it shall be performed. ⁷Then answered Esther, and said, My petition and my request *is*; ⁸If I have found favour in the sight of the king, and if it please the king to grant my petition, and to performᵃ my request, let the king and Haman come to the banquet that I shall prepare for them, and I will do to morrow as the king hath said.

⁹Then went Haman forth that day joyful and with a glad heart: but when Haman saw Mordecai in the king's gate, that he stood not up, nor moved for him, he was full of indignation against Mordecai. ¹⁰Nevertheless Haman refrained himself: and when he came home, he sent and calledᵇ for his friends, and Zeresh his wife. ¹¹And Haman told them of the glory of his riches, and the multitude of his children, and all *the things* wherein the king had promoted him, and how he had advanced him above the princes and servants of the king. ¹²Haman said moreover, Yea, Esther the queen did let no man come in with the king unto the banquet that she had prepared but myself; and to morrow am I invited unto her also with the king. ¹³Yet all this availeth me nothing, so long as I see Mordecai the Jew sitting at the king's gate. ¹⁴Then said Zeresh his wife and all his friends unto him, Let a gallowsᶜ be made of fifty cubits high, and to morrow speak thou unto the king that Mordecai may be hanged thereon: then go thou in merrily with the king unto the banquet. And the thing pleased Haman; and he caused the gallows to be made.

6

¹On that night could not the king sleep, and he commanded to bring the book of records of the chronicles; and they were read before the king. ²And it was found written, that Mordecai had told of Bigthanaᵃ and Teresh, two of the king's chamberlains, the keepers of the door, who sought to lay hand on the king Ahasuerus. ³And the king said, What honour and dignity hath been

---

ᵃ perform: Heb. do
ᵇ called . . . : Heb. caused to come
ᶜ gallows: Heb. tree
ᵃ Bigthana: also called, Bigthan

done to Mordecai for this? Then said the king's servants that ministered unto him, There is nothing done for him.

⁴And the king said, Who *is* in the court? Now Haman was come into the outward court of the king's house, to speak unto the king to hang Mordecai on the gallows that he had prepared for him. ⁵And the king's servants said unto him, Behold, Haman standeth in the court. And the king said, Let him come in. ⁶So Haman came in. And the king said unto him, What shall be done unto the man whom the kingᵇ delighteth to honour? Now Haman thought in his heart, To whom would the king delight to do honour more than to myself? ⁷And Haman answered the king, For the man whom the kingᶜ delighteth to honour, ⁸Let the royal apparel be brought which the king *useth* to wear, and the horse that the king rideth upon, and the crown royal which is set upon his head: ⁹And let this apparel and horse be delivered to the hand of one of the king's most noble princes, that they may array the man *withal* whom the king delighteth to honour, and bringᵈ him on horseback through the street of the city, and proclaim before him, Thus shall it be done to the man whom the king delighteth to honour. ¹⁰Then the king said to Haman, Make haste, *and* take the apparel and the horse, as thou hast said, and do even so to Mordecai the Jew, that sitteth at the king's gate: let nothing fail of all that thou hast spoken. ¹¹Then took Haman the apparel and the horse, and arrayed Mordecai, and

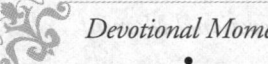

Devotional Moment
•
Patience
6:10-13 While everything appeared bleak to Mordecai and Esther, God was working out a plan, not only to exalt his faithful servants but also to punish the evil conspirator, Haman. Often, like Mordecai and Esther, we don't see God working and are tempted to become discouraged and to doubt that he's there at all. Have patience. Allow God to work out his will in his own time and in his own way. Trust in God's goodness and faithfulness as you wait for his answers to your prayers.

brought him on horseback through the street of the city, and proclaimed before him, Thus shall it be done unto the man whom the king delighteth to honour.

¹²And Mordecai came again to the king's gate. But Haman hasted to his house mourning, and having his head covered. ¹³And Haman told Zeresh his wife and all his friends every *thing* that had befallen him. Then said his wise men and Zeresh his wife unto him, If Mordecai *be* of the seed of the Jews, before whom thou hast begun to fall, thou shalt not prevail against him, but shalt surely fall before him. ¹⁴And while they *were* yet talking with him, came the king's chamberlains, and hasted to bring Haman unto the banquet that Esther had prepared.

7

¹So the king and Haman came to banquetᵃ with Esther the queen. ²And the king said again unto Esther on the second

---

ᵇ whom the king . . . : Heb. in whose honour the king delighteth
ᶜ whom the king . . . : Heb. in whose honour the king delighteth
ᵈ bring . . . : Heb. cause him to ride
ᵃ to banquet: Heb. to drink

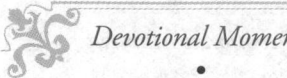

day at the banquet of wine, What *is* thy petition, queen Esther? and it shall be granted thee: and what *is* thy request? and it shall be performed, *even* to the half of the kingdom. ³Then Esther the queen answered and said, If I have found favour in thy sight, O king, and if it please the king, let my life be given me at my petition, and my people at my request: ⁴For we are sold, I and my people, to be destroyed[b], to be slain, and to perish. But if we had been sold for bondmen and bondwomen, I had held my tongue, although the enemy could not countervail the king's damage. ⁵Then the king Ahasuerus answered and said unto Esther the queen, Who is he, and where is he, that durst presume in his heart to do so? ⁶And Esther said, The adversary[c] and enemy *is* this wicked Haman. Then Haman was afraid before the king and the queen.

⁷And the king arising from the banquet of wine in his wrath *went* into the palace garden: and Haman stood up to make request for his life to Esther the queen; for he saw that there was evil determined against him by the king. ⁸Then the king returned out of the palace garden into the place of the banquet of wine; and Haman was fallen upon the bed whereon Esther *was*. Then said the king, Will he force the queen also before me in the house? As the word went out of the king's mouth, they covered Haman's face. ⁹And Harbonah, one of the chamberlains, said before the king, Behold also, the gallows[d] fifty cubits high, which Haman had made for Mordecai, who had spoken good for the king, standeth in the house of Haman. Then the king said, Hang him thereon. ¹⁰So they hanged Haman on the gallows that he had prepared for Mordecai. Then was the king's wrath pacified.

8

¹On that day did the king Ahasuerus give the house of Haman the Jews' enemy unto Esther the queen. And Mordecai came before the king; for Esther had told what he *was* unto her. ²And the king took off his ring, which he had taken from Haman, and gave it unto Mordecai. And Esther set Mordecai over the house of Haman.

³And Esther spake yet again before the king, and fell down at his feet, and besought[a] him with tears to put away the mischief of Haman the Agagite, and his device that he had devised

---

[b] to be destroyed . . . : Heb. that they should destroy, and kill, and cause to perish

[c] The adversary: Heb. The man adversary

[d] gallows: Heb. tree

[a] and besought . . . : Heb. and she wept, and besought him

against the Jews. ⁴Then the king held out the golden sceptre toward Esther. So Esther arose, and stood before the king, ⁵And said, If it please the king, and if I have found favour in his sight, and the thing *seem* right before the king, and I *be* pleasing in his eyes, let it be written to reverse the letters devised[b] by Haman the son of Hammedatha the Agagite, which he wrote to destroy the Jews which *are* in all the king's provinces: ⁶For how can I endure[c] to see the evil that shall come unto my people? or how can I endure to see the destruction of my kindred? ⁷Then the king Ahasuerus said unto Esther the queen and to Mordecai the Jew, Behold, I have given Esther the house of Haman, and him they have hanged upon the gallows, because he laid his hand upon the Jews. ⁸Write ye also for the Jews, as it liketh you, in the king's name, and seal *it* with the king's ring: for the writing which is written in the king's name, and sealed with the king's ring, may no man reverse. ⁹Then were the king's scribes called at that time in the third month, that *is*, the month Sivan, on the three and twentieth *day* thereof; and it was written according to all that Mordecai commanded unto the Jews, and to the lieutenants, and the deputies and rulers of the provinces which *are* from India unto Ethiopia, an hundred twenty and seven provinces, unto every province according to the writing thereof, and unto every people after their language, and to the Jews according to their writ-

ing, and according to their language. ¹⁰And he wrote in the king Ahasuerus' name, and sealed *it* with the king's ring, and sent letters by posts on horseback, *and* riders on mules, camels, *and* young dromedaries: ¹¹Wherein the king granted the Jews which *were* in every city to gather themselves together, and to stand for their life, to destroy, to slay, and to cause to perish, all the power of the people and province that would assault them, *both* little ones and women, and *to take* the spoil of them for a prey, ¹²Upon one day in all the provinces of king Ahasuerus, *namely*, upon the thirteenth *day* of the twelfth month, which *is* the month Adar. ¹³The copy of the writing for a commandment to be given in every province *was* published[d] unto all people, and that the Jews should be ready against that day to avenge themselves on their enemies. ¹⁴So the posts that rode upon mules *and* camels went out, being hastened and pressed on by the king's commandment. And the decree was given at Shushan the palace.

¹⁵And Mordecai went out from the presence of the king in royal apparel of blue[e] and white, and with a great crown of gold, and with a garment of fine linen and purple: and the city of Shushan rejoiced and was glad. ¹⁶The Jews had light, and gladness, and joy, and honour. ¹⁷And in every province, and in every city, whithersoever the king's commandment and his decree came, the Jews had joy and gladness,

---

[b] devised: Heb. the device
[c] endure . . . : Heb. be able that I may see
[d] published: Heb. revealed
[e] blue: or, violet

a feast and a good day. And many of the people of the land became Jews; for the fear of the Jews fell upon them.

9

¹Now in the twelfth month, that *is*, the month Adar, on the thirteenth day of the same, when the king's commandment and his decree drew near to be put in execution, in the day that the enemies of the Jews hoped to have power over them, (though it was turned to the contrary, that the Jews had rule over them that hated them;) ²The Jews gathered themselves together in their cities throughout all the provinces of the king Ahasuerus, to lay hand on such as sought their hurt: and no man could withstand them; for the fear of them fell upon all people. ³And all the rulers of the provinces, and the lieutenants, and the deputies, and officers[a] of the king, helped the Jews; because the fear of Mordecai fell upon them. ⁴For Mordecai *was* great in the king's house, and his fame went out throughout all the provinces: for this man Mordecai waxed greater and greater. ⁵Thus the Jews smote all their enemies with the stroke of the sword, and slaughter, and destruction, and did what they would unto those that hated them. ⁶And in Shushan the palace the Jews slew and destroyed five hundred men. ⁷And Parshandatha, and Dalphon, and Aspatha, ⁸And Poratha, and Adalia, and Aridatha, ⁹And Parmashta, and Arisai, and Aridai, and Vajezatha, ¹⁰The ten sons of Haman the son of Hammedatha, the enemy of the Jews, slew they; but on the spoil laid they not their hand. ¹¹On that day the number of those that were slain in Shushan the palace was brought before the king. ¹²And the king said unto Esther the queen, The Jews have slain and destroyed five hundred men in Shushan the palace, and the ten sons of Haman; what have they done in the rest of the king's provinces? now what *is* thy petition? and it shall be granted thee: or what *is* thy request further? and it shall be done. ¹³Then said Esther, If it please the king, let it be granted to the Jews which *are* in Shushan to do to morrow also according unto this day's decree, and let Haman's[b] ten sons be hanged upon the gallows. ¹⁴And the king commanded it so to be done: and the decree was given at Shushan; and they hanged Haman's ten sons. ¹⁵For the Jews that *were* in Shushan gathered themselves together on the fourteenth day also of the month Adar, and slew three hundred men at Shushan; but on the prey they laid not their hand. ¹⁶But the other Jews that *were* in the king's provinces gathered themselves together, and stood for their lives, and had rest from their enemies, and slew of their foes seventy and five thousand, but they laid not their hands on the prey, ¹⁷On the thirteenth day of the month Adar; and on the fourteenth day of the same rested they, and made it a day of feasting and gladness. ¹⁸But the Jews that *were* at Shushan assembled together on the thirteenth *day* thereof, and on the fourteenth thereof; and on the fifteenth *day* of the same they rested, and made it a day of feast-

---

[a] officers . . . : Heb. those which did the business that belonged to the king
[b] let Haman's . . . : Heb. let men hang, etc

ing and gladness. [19]Therefore the Jews of the villages, that dwelt in the unwalled towns, made the fourteenth day of the month Adar *a day of* gladness and feasting, and a good day, and of sending portions one to another.

[20]And Mordecai wrote these things, and sent letters unto all the Jews that *were* in all the provinces of the king Ahasuerus, *both* nigh and far, [21]To stablish *this* among them, that they should keep the fourteenth day of the month Adar, and the fifteenth day of the same, yearly, [22]As the days wherein the Jews rested from their enemies, and the month which was turned unto them from sorrow to joy, and from mourning into a good day: that they should make them days of feasting and joy, and of

---

Devotional Moment

•

Generational Traditions

9:27-28 The Jews adopted Mordecai's suggestions and made the Feast of Purim an annual celebration. What events in your family's history can you commemorate by an annual celebration? Think of ways God has miraculously delivered your family members (include parents and grandparents) from war, prison camps, a threatening storm, a life-threatening illness, an accident, or some other occurrence. Choose a meaningful way to commemorate those deliverances so that your children and their children will remember God's goodness in specific family crises. Make the celebration a time of praise and blessing.

---

sending portions one to another, and gifts to the poor. [23]And the Jews undertook to do as they had begun, and as Mordecai had written unto them; [24]Because Haman the son of Hammedatha, the Agagite, the enemy of all the Jews, had devised against the Jews to destroy them, and had cast Pur, that *is*, the lot, to consume[c] them, and to destroy them; [25]But when *Esther* came[d] before the king, he commanded by letters that his wicked device, which he devised against the Jews, should return upon his own head, and that he and his sons should be hanged on the gallows. [26]Wherefore they called these days Purim after the name of Pur[e]. Therefore for all the words of this letter, and *of that* which they had seen concerning this matter, and which had come unto them, [27]The Jews ordained, and took upon them, and upon their seed, and upon all such as joined themselves unto them, so as it should not fail[f], that they would keep these two days according to their writing, and according to their *appointed* time every year; [28]And *that* these days *should be* remembered and kept throughout every generation, every family, every province, and every city; and *that* these days of Purim should not fail[g] from among the Jews, nor the memorial of them perish from their seed. [29]Then Esther the queen, the daughter of Abihail, and Mordecai the Jew, wrote with all authority[h], to con-

---

[c] consume: Heb. crush
[d] when . . . : Heb. when she came
[e] Pur: that is, Lot
[f] fail: Heb. pass
[g] fail: Heb. pass
[h] authority: Heb. strength

firm this second letter of Purim. ³⁰And he sent the letters unto all the Jews, to the hundred twenty and seven provinces of the kingdom of Ahasuerus, *with* words of peace and truth, ³¹To confirm these days of Purim in their times *appointed,* according as Mordecai the Jew and Esther the queen had enjoined them, and as they had decreed for themselves^i and for their seed, the matters of the fastings and their cry. ³²And the decree of Esther confirmed these matters of Purim; and it was written in the book.

10

¹And the king Ahasuerus laid a tribute upon the land, and *upon* the isles of the sea. ²And all the acts of his power and of his might, and the declaration of the greatness of Mordecai, whereunto the king advanced^a him, *are* they not written in the book of the chronicles of the kings of Media and Persia? ³For Mordecai the Jew *was* next unto king Ahasuerus, and great among the Jews, and accepted of the multitude of his brethren, seeking the wealth of his people, and speaking peace to all his seed.

> **Devotional Moment**
> •
> ### Leadership
> 10:3 Mordecai won the respect of the king, the people of Media and Persia, and the Jews because he did what was right in his position of power. He did his best for the people of the country and worked toward justice. We need to look at the leadership responsibilities that God has given us and ask ourselves how we are fulfilling them. Do we use our parental authority just to control our children or to serve their best interests by training and teaching them? Use whatever authority you may have to do what is right, to insure justice, and to serve others.

---

^i themselves: Heb. their souls
^a advanced . . . : Heb. made him great

JOB

Purpose
To demonstrate God's sovereignty and the meaning of true faith. It addresses the question, Why do the righteous suffer?

Author
Possibly Job. Some have suggested Moses, Solomon, or Elihu.

Date Written
Unknown. Records events that probably occurred during the time of the patriarchs, approximately 2000–1800 B.C.

Setting
The land of Uz, probably located northeast of Palestine, near desert land between Damascus and the Euphrates River

Key Verse
"Hast thou considered my servant Job, that there is none like him in the earth, a perfect and an upright man, one that feareth God, and escheweth evil? and still he holdeth fast his integrity, although thou movedst me against him, to destroy him without cause" (2:3).

Key People
Job, Eliphaz the Temanite, Bildad the Shuhite, Zophar the Naamathite, Elihu the Buzite

Special Features
Job is the first of the poetic books in the Hebrew Bible. Many believe this to be the oldest book in the Bible.

Children hear about guardian angels but rarely about hideous demons. Adults often disparage both, though experience makes the latter the more credible of the two. Still, most adults dismiss angels and demons, Satan included, along with goblins and genies. It is better to rely on one's own pluck than winged cherubs, adult wisdom tells us.

The story of Job challenges conventional wisdom. Contrary to our notion that hard work pays off, Job loses everything. Destroying the theory that God helps those who help themselves, God seems to bow out while the devil takes over. The book of Job is full of twists that spoil our ideas and frustrate our independence. Is the devil so real? Isn't there a policy to protect against such loss?

Adults who have endured intense grief will identify with Job's pain. Children will wonder why such bad things happen to good people, including innocent children. Parents, prepare for tough questions.

At any age, old or young, Satan may try to strike, sometimes subtly, sometimes with conspicuous aggression. Yet Job is no fatalist. He resists giving up, even in confusion and sadness. As long as God is alive, hope lives.

Job's story will scare you and comfort you. It will draw gray chalk marks in your watercolor world. It will give the child a heavy dose of pain to ponder and the adult a more simple, childlike faith to embrace.

1

¹There was a man in the land of Uz, whose name *was* Job; and that man was perfect and upright, and one that feared God, and eschewed evil. ²And there were born unto him seven sons and three daughters. ³His substance^a also was seven thousand sheep, and three thousand camels, and five hundred yoke of oxen, and five hundred she asses, and a very great household; so that this man was the greatest of all the men of the east.

⁴And his sons went and feasted *in their* houses, every one his day; and sent and called for their three sisters to eat and to drink with them. ⁵And it was so, when the days of *their* feasting were gone about, that Job sent and sanctified

---

Devotional Moment

•

Prayer

1:5 Job had seven sons and three daughters, each a unique person with a unique set of characteristics and tendencies. Yet it was their father's regular custom to have each of them purified after a period of feasting and to sacrifice a burnt offering for each of them. Job knew that his children were only human and feared they might have sinned and turned away from God in their hearts. Our children are only human, too. They need and deserve our prayers. Do you regularly pray for your children? Find a time to pray for each of them, each day—in the morning or at bedtime, after Bible study, or while commuting to work.

---

them, and rose up early in the morning, and offered burnt offerings *according* to the number of them all: for Job said, It may be that my sons have sinned, and cursed God in their hearts. Thus did Job continually^b.

⁶Now there was a day when the sons of God came to present themselves before the LORD, and Satan^c came also among them. ⁷And the LORD said unto Satan, Whence comest thou? Then Satan answered the LORD, and said, From going to and fro in the earth, and from walking up and down in it. ⁸And the LORD said unto Satan, Hast thou considered^d my servant Job, that *there is* none like him in the earth, a perfect and an upright man, one that feareth God, and escheweth evil? ⁹Then Satan answered the LORD, and said, Doth Job fear God for nought? ¹⁰Hast not thou made an hedge about him, and about his house, and about all that he hath on every side? thou hast blessed the work of his hands, and his substance^e is increased in the land. ¹¹But put forth thine hand now, and touch all that he hath, and he will curse thee to thy face. ¹²And the LORD said unto Satan, Behold, all that he hath *is* in thy power^f; only upon himself put not forth thine hand. So Satan went forth from the presence of the LORD.

¹³And there was a day when his sons and his daughters *were* eating and drinking wine in their eldest brother's

---

^a substance: or, cattle
^b continually: Heb. all the days
^c Satan: Heb. the adversary
^d considered: Heb. set thy heart on
^e substance: or, cattle
^f power: Heb. hand

house: ¹⁴And there came a messenger unto Job, and said, The oxen were plowing, and the asses feeding beside them: ¹⁵And the Sabeans fell *upon them*, and took them away; yea, they have slain the servants with the edge of the sword; and I only am escaped alone to tell thee. ¹⁶While he *was* yet speaking, there came also another, and said, The fireᵍ of God is fallen from heaven, and hath burned up the sheep, and the servants, and consumed them; and I only am escaped alone to tell thee. ¹⁷While he *was* yet speaking, there came also another, and said, The Chaldeans made out three bands, and fellʰ upon the camels, and have carried them away, yea, and slain the servants with the edge of the sword; and I only am escaped alone to tell thee. ¹⁸While he *was* yet speaking, there came also another, and said, Thy sons and thy daughters *were* eating and drinking wine in their eldest brother's house: ¹⁹And, behold, there came a great wind fromⁱ the wilderness, and smote the four corners of the house, and it fell upon the young men, and they are dead; and I only am escaped alone to tell thee.

²⁰Then Job arose, and rent his mantleʲ, and shaved his head, and fell down upon the ground, and worshipped, ²¹And said, Naked came I out of my mother's womb, and naked shall I return thither: the LORD gave, and the LORD hath taken away; blessed be the name of the LORD. ²²In all this Job sinned not, nor chargedᵏ God foolishly.

2

¹Again there was a day when the sons of God came to present themselves before the LORD, and Satan came also among them to present himself before the LORD. ²And the LORD said unto Satan, From whence comest thou? And Satan answered the LORD, and said, From going to and fro in the earth, and from walking up and down in it. ³And the LORD said unto Satan, Hast thou considered my servant Job, that *there is* none like him in the earth, a perfect and an upright man, one that feareth God, and escheweth evil? and still he holdeth fast his integrity, although thou movedst me against him, to destroyᵃ him without cause. ⁴And Satan answered the LORD, and said, Skin for

---

ᵍ The fire . . . : or, A great fire
ʰ fell: Heb. rushed
ⁱ from . . . : Heb. from aside, etc
ʲ mantle: or, robe
ᵏ charged . . . : or, attributed folly to God
ᵃ to destroy . . . : Heb. to swallow him up

skin, yea, all that a man hath will he give for his life. ⁵But put forth thine hand now, and touch his bone and his flesh, and he will curse thee to thy face. ⁶And the LORD said unto Satan, Behold, he *is* in thine hand; but save his life.

⁷So went Satan forth from the presence of the LORD, and smote Job with sore boils from the sole of his foot unto his crown. ⁸And he took him a potsherd to scrape himself withal; and he sat down among the ashes. ⁹Then said his wife unto him, Dost thou still retain thine integrity? curse God, and die. ¹⁰But he said unto her, Thou speakest as one of the foolish women speaketh. What? shall we receive good at the hand of God, and shall we not receive evil? In all this did not Job sin with his lips.

¹¹Now when Job's three friends heard of all this evil that was come upon him, they came every one from his own place; Eliphaz the Temanite, and Bildad the Shuhite, and Zophar the Naamathite: for they had made an appointment together to come to mourn with him and to comfort him. ¹²And when they lifted up their eyes afar off, and knew him not, they lifted up their voice, and wept; and they rent every one his mantle, and sprinkled dust upon their heads toward heaven. ¹³So they sat down with him upon the ground seven days and seven nights, and none spake a word unto him: for they saw that *his* grief was very great.

3

¹After this opened Job his mouth, and cursed his day. ²And Job spake*, and said, ³Let the day perish wherein I was born, and the night *in which* it was said, There is a man child conceived. ⁴Let that day be darkness; let not God regard it from above, neither let the light shine upon it. ⁵Let darkness and the shadow of death stain* it; let a cloud dwell upon it; let the blackness of the day terrify it. ⁶As *for* that night, let darkness seize upon it; let it not be joined unto the days of the year, let it not come into the number of the months. ⁷Lo, let that night be solitary, let no joyful voice come therein. ⁸Let them curse it that curse the day, who are ready to raise up their mourning. ⁹Let the stars of the twilight thereof be dark; let it look for light, but *have* none; neither let it see the dawning* of the day: ¹⁰Because it shut not up the doors of my *mother's* womb, nor hid sorrow from mine eyes.

¹¹Why died I not from the womb?

Devotional Moment

•

Silent Comfort

2:13 Eliphaz, Bildad, and Zophar were friends of Job. When they heard of his troubles, they came to comfort and sympathize with him. But so terrible was Job's skin disease that they could hardly recognize him. They wept, tore their clothes, and then sat silently with him for seven days and nights. Have you ever seen someone suffer so much that you couldn't think of anything to say? Your silence was probably a gift from God to the sufferer, for what people need at such times is not words but a comforting presence. Do not underestimate what merely being there and listening can provide.

ᵃ spake: Heb. answered
ᵇ stain: or, challenge
ᶜ the dawning . . . : Heb. the eyelids of the morning

why did I *not* give up the ghost when I came out of the belly? ¹²Why did the knees prevent me? or why the breasts that I should suck? ¹³For now should I have lain still and been quiet, I should have slept: then had I been at rest, ¹⁴With kings and counsellors of the earth, which built desolate places for themselves; ¹⁵Or with princes that had gold, who filled their houses with silver: ¹⁶Or as an hidden untimely birth I had not been; as infants *which* never saw light. ¹⁷There the wicked cease *from* troubling; and there the weary[d] be at rest. ¹⁸*There* the prisoners rest together; they hear not the voice of the oppressor. ¹⁹The small and great are there; and the servant *is* free from his master.

²⁰Wherefore is light given to him that is in misery, and life unto the bitter *in* soul; ²¹Which long[e] for death, but it *cometh* not; and dig for it more than for hid treasures; ²²Which rejoice exceedingly, *and* are glad, when they can find the grave? ²³*Why is light given* to a man whose way is hid, and whom God hath hedged in? ²⁴For my sighing cometh before I eat[f], and my roarings are poured out like the waters. ²⁵For the thing which I greatly feared is come upon me, and that which I was afraid of is come unto me. ²⁶I was not in safety, neither had I rest, neither was I quiet; yet trouble came.

4

¹Then Eliphaz the Temanite answered and said, ²*If* we assay to commune with

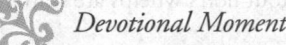

Devotional Moment

Suffering

4:1–5:27 Job was lamenting his situation, cursing the day he was born. His friend Eliphaz was the first to reply. In so many words, he blamed Job, implying that the suffering must be a form of punishment from God for sin. We often think we are being helpful by explaining suffering, especially when the sufferer demands to know why it's happening. But usually our answers are far from comforting and can actually compound the person's anguish with false guilt. When someone you care about is suffering, be there to comfort rather than convict or explain.

thee, wilt thou be grieved? but who can withhold himself from speaking? ³Behold, thou hast instructed many, and thou hast strengthened the weak hands. ⁴Thy words have upholden him that was falling, and thou hast strengthened the feeble knees. ⁵But now it is come upon thee, and thou faintest; it toucheth thee, and thou art troubled. ⁶*Is* not *this* thy fear, thy confidence, thy hope, and the uprightness of thy ways?

⁷Remember, I pray thee, who *ever* perished, being innocent? or where were the righteous cut off? ⁸Even as I have seen, they that plow iniquity, and sow wickedness, reap the same. ⁹By the blast of God they perish, and by the breath[a] of his nostrils are they consumed. ¹⁰The roaring of the lion, and the voice of the fierce lion, and the teeth of the young lions, are broken. ¹¹The old lion perisheth for lack of prey,

---

[d] weary: Heb. wearied in strength
[e] long: Heb. wait
[f] I eat: Heb. my meat
[a] by the breath . . . : that is, by his anger

and the stout lion's whelps are scattered abroad.

¹²Now a thing was secretly brought to me, and mine ear received a little thereof. ¹³In thoughts from the visions of the night, when deep sleep falleth on men, ¹⁴Fear came[b] upon me, and trembling, which made all my bones to shake. ¹⁵Then a spirit passed before my face; the hair of my flesh stood up: ¹⁶It stood still, but I could not discern the form thereof: an image *was* before mine eyes, *there was* silence, and I heard a voice, *saying,* ¹⁷Shall mortal man be more just than God? shall a man be more pure than his maker? ¹⁸Behold, he put no trust in his servants; and his angels he charged with folly: ¹⁹How much less *in* them that dwell in houses of clay, whose foundation *is* in the dust, *which* are crushed before the moth? ²⁰They are destroyed[c] from morning to evening: they perish for ever without any regarding *it.* ²¹Doth not their excellency *which is* in them go away? they die, even without wisdom.

5

¹Call now, if there be any that will answer thee; and to which of the saints wilt thou turn[a]? ²For wrath killeth the foolish man, and envy[b] slayeth the silly one. ³I have seen the foolish taking root: but suddenly I cursed his habitation. ⁴His children are far from safety, and they are crushed in the gate, neither *is there* any to deliver *them.* ⁵Whose harvest the hungry eateth up, and taketh it even out of the thorns, and the robber swalloweth up their substance.

⁶Although affliction[c] cometh not forth of the dust, neither doth trouble spring out of the ground; ⁷Yet man is born unto trouble[d], as the sparks fly upward. ⁸I would seek unto God, and unto God would I commit my cause: ⁹Which doeth great things and unsearchable[e]; marvellous things without number: ¹⁰Who giveth rain upon the earth, and sendeth waters upon the fields[f]: ¹¹To set up on high those that be low; that those which mourn may be exalted to safety. ¹²He disappointeth the devices of the crafty, so that their hands cannot perform *their* enterprise. ¹³He taketh the wise in their own craftiness: and the counsel of the froward is carried headlong. ¹⁴They meet[g] with darkness in the daytime, and grope in the noonday as in the night. ¹⁵But he saveth the poor from the sword, from their mouth, and from the hand of the mighty. ¹⁶So the poor hath hope, and iniquity stoppeth her mouth.

¹⁷Behold, happy *is* the man whom God correcteth: therefore despise not

---

[b] came . . . : Heb. met
[c] destroyed: Heb. beaten in pieces
[a] turn: or, look?
[b] envy: or, indignation
[c] affliction: or, iniquity
[d] trouble: or, labour
[e] unsearchable: Heb. there is no search
[f] fields: Heb. outplaces
[g] meet . . . : or, run into

thou the chastening of the Almighty: [18]For he maketh sore, and bindeth up: he woundeth, and his hands make whole. [19]He shall deliver thee in six troubles: yea, in seven there shall no evil touch thee. [20]In famine he shall redeem thee from death: and in war from the power[h] of the sword. [21]Thou shalt be hid from the scourge of the tongue: neither shalt thou be afraid of destruction when it cometh. [22]At destruction and famine thou shalt laugh: neither shalt thou be afraid of the beasts of the earth. [23]For thou shalt be in league with the stones of the field: and the beasts of the field shall be at peace with thee. [24]And thou shalt know that thy tabernacle[i] *shall be* in peace; and thou shalt visit thy habitation, and shalt not sin. [25]Thou shalt know also that thy seed *shall be* great[j], and thine offspring as the grass of the earth. [26]Thou shalt come to *thy* grave in a full age, like as a shock of corn cometh in[k] in his season. [27]Lo this, we have searched it, so it *is*; hear it, and know thou *it* for thy good.

6

[1]But Job answered and said, [2]Oh that my grief were throughly weighed, and my calamity laid[a] in the balances together! [3]For now it would be heavier than the sand of the sea: therefore my words are[b] swallowed up. [4]For the arrows of the Almighty *are* within me, the poison whereof drinketh up my spirit: the terrors of God do set themselves in array against me. [5]Doth the wild ass bray when he hath grass? or loweth the ox over his fodder? [6]Can that which is unsavoury be eaten without salt? or is there *any* taste in the white of an egg? [7]The things *that* my soul refused to touch *are* as my sorrowful meat.

[8]Oh that I might have my request; and that God would grant *me* the thing that I long for! [9]Even that it would please God to destroy me; that he would let loose his hand, and cut me off! [10]Then should I yet have comfort; yea, I would harden myself in sorrow: let him not spare; for I have not concealed the words of the Holy One. [11]What *is* my strength, that I should hope? and what *is* mine end, that I should prolong my life? [12]*Is* my strength

Devotional Moment

Suicide

6:8-10 In the face of all his suffering, Job wanted to die. After enduring the pious preaching of his friend Eliphaz, he felt that God and the universe were against him and that death would be a relief. Have you ever felt such despair? Your various roles—spouse, parent, child, employee, friend—can lead to great pain. It's easy to feel abandoned by God, yet we must trust that God is with us. Seek out people in your life who have endured and grown despite great suffering. Tell them how you feel and talk with them about how they learned to weather the storms. Job did. So can you.

---

[h] power: Heb. hands
[i] thy tabernacle . . . : or, peace is thy tabernacle
[j] great: or, much
[k] cometh in: Heb. ascendeth
[a] laid: Heb. lifted up
[b] my words . . . : that is, I want words to express my grief

the strength of stones? or *is* my flesh of brass^c? ¹³*Is* not my help in me? and is wisdom driven quite from me?

¹⁴To him that is afflicted^d pity *should be shewed* from his friend; but he forsaketh the fear of the Almighty. ¹⁵My brethren have dealt deceitfully as a brook, *and* as the stream of brooks they pass away; ¹⁶Which are blackish by reason of the ice, *and* wherein the snow is hid: ¹⁷What time they wax warm, they vanish^e: when it is hot, they are consumed out of their place. ¹⁸The paths of their way are turned aside; they go to nothing, and perish. ¹⁹The troops of Tema looked, the companies of Sheba waited for them. ²⁰They were confounded because they had hoped; they came thither, and were ashamed. ²¹For now ye are nothing; ye see *my* casting down, and are afraid.

²²Did I say, Bring unto me? or, Give a reward for me of your substance? ²³Or, Deliver me from the enemy's hand? or, Redeem me from the hand of the mighty? ²⁴Teach me, and I will hold my tongue: and cause me to understand wherein I have erred. ²⁵How forcible are right words! but what doth your arguing reprove? ²⁶Do ye imagine to reprove words, and the speeches of one that is desperate, *which are* as wind? ²⁷Yea, ye overwhelm^f the fatherless, and ye dig *a pit* for your friend. ²⁸Now therefore be content, look upon me; for

it is evident unto you if I lie. ²⁹Return, I pray you, let it not be iniquity; yea, return again, my righteousness *is* in it^g. ³⁰Is there iniquity in my tongue? cannot my taste^h discern perverse things?

7

¹*Is there* not an appointed time to man upon earth? *are not* his days also like the days of an hireling? ²As a servant earnestly desireth the shadow, and as an hireling looketh for *the reward of* his work: ³So am I made to possess months of vanity, and wearisome nights are appointed to me. ⁴When I lie down, I say, When shall I arise, and the night^a be gone? and I am full of tossings to and fro unto the dawning of the day. ⁵My flesh is clothed with worms and clods of dust; my skin is broken, and become loathsome. ⁶My days are swifter than a weaver's shuttle, and are spent without hope.

⁷O remember that my life *is* wind: mine eye shall no more see good. ⁸The eye of him that hath seen me shall see me no *more*: thine eyes *are* upon me, and I *am* not. ⁹*As* the cloud is consumed and vanisheth away: so he that goeth down to the grave shall come up no *more*. ¹⁰He shall return no more to his house, neither shall his place know him any more. ¹¹Therefore I will not refrain my mouth; I will speak in the anguish of my spirit; I will complain in

---

^c of brass: Heb. brasen?
^d is afflicted: Heb. melteth
^e vanish: Heb. are cut off
^f ye overwhelm: Heb. ye cause to fall upon
^g in it: that is, in this matter
^h my taste: Heb. my palate
^a the night . . . : Heb. the evening be measured?

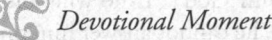

Devotional Moment
•
Crying Out

7:11 The God of the universe has big shoulders, and Job knew that. Job cried out and complained about his loss and physical suffering. He used words like *bitterness* and *anguish*. And God honored his honesty. Besides, could we fool the God who made us by pretending to be happy when feeling great pain? The next time painful feelings build up inside you, find a private place and tell God how you feel. He won't mind.

the bitterness of my soul. ¹²*Am* I a sea, or a whale, that thou settest a watch over me? ¹³When I say, My bed shall comfort me, my couch shall ease my complaint; ¹⁴Then thou scarest me with dreams, and terrifiest me through visions: ¹⁵So that my soul chooseth strangling, *and* death rather than my life[b]. ¹⁶I loathe *it*; I would not live alway: let me alone; for my days *are* vanity.

¹⁷What *is* man, that thou shouldest magnify him? and that thou shouldest set thine heart upon him? ¹⁸And *that* thou shouldest visit him every morning, *and* try him every moment? ¹⁹How long wilt thou not depart from me, nor let me alone till I swallow down my spittle? ²⁰I have sinned; what shall I do unto thee, O thou preserver of men? why hast thou set me as a mark against thee, so that I am a burden to myself? ²¹And why dost thou not pardon my transgression, and take away mine iniq-

uity? for now shall I sleep in the dust; and thou shalt seek me in the morning, but I *shall* not *be*.

8

¹Then answered Bildad the Shuhite, and said, ²How long wilt thou speak these *things*? and *how long shall* the words of thy mouth *be like* a strong wind? ³Doth God pervert judgment? or doth the Almighty pervert justice? ⁴If thy children have sinned against him, and he have cast them away for[a] their transgression; ⁵If thou wouldest seek unto God betimes, and make thy supplication to the Almighty; ⁶If thou *wert* pure and upright; surely now he would awake for thee, and make the habitation of thy righteousness prosperous. ⁷Though thy beginning was small, yet thy latter end should greatly increase.

⁸For enquire, I pray thee, of the former age, and prepare thyself to the search of their fathers: ⁹(For we *are but of* yesterday, and know nothing[b], because our days upon earth *are* a shadow:) ¹⁰Shall not they teach thee, *and* tell thee, and utter words out of their heart? ¹¹Can the rush grow up without mire? can the flag grow without water? ¹²Whilst it *is* yet in his greenness, *and* not cut down, it withereth before any *other* herb. ¹³So *are* the paths of all that forget God; and the hypocrite's hope shall perish: ¹⁴Whose hope shall be cut off, and whose trust *shall be* a spider's web[c]. ¹⁵He shall lean upon his house, but it shall not stand: he shall

---

ᵇ life: Heb. bones
ᵃ for . . . : Heb. in the hand of their transgression
ᵇ nothing: Heb. not
ᶜ web: Heb. house

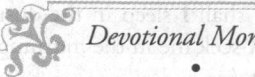

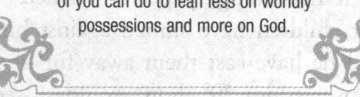

hold it fast, but it shall not endure. ¹⁶He *is* green before the sun, and his branch shooteth forth in his garden. ¹⁷His roots are wrapped about the heap, *and* seeth the place of stones. ¹⁸If he destroy him from his place, then *it* shall deny him, *saying*, I have not seen thee. ¹⁹Behold, this *is* the joy of his way, and out of the earth shall others grow.

²⁰Behold, God will not cast away a perfect *man*, neither will he help[d] the evil doers: ²¹Till he fill thy mouth with laughing, and thy lips with rejoicing[e]. ²²They that hate thee shall be clothed with shame; and the dwelling place of the wicked shall come to nought.

9

¹Then Job answered and said, ²I know *it is* so of a truth: but how should man be just with God[a]? ³If he will contend with him, he cannot answer him one of a thousand. ⁴*He is* wise in heart, and mighty in strength: who hath hardened *himself* against him, and hath prospered? ⁵Which removeth the mountains, and they know not: which overturneth them in his anger. ⁶Which shaketh the earth out of her place, and the pillars thereof tremble. ⁷Which commandeth the sun, and it riseth not; and sealeth up the stars. ⁸Which alone spreadeth out the heavens, and treadeth upon the waves[b] of the sea. ⁹Which maketh Arcturus[c], Orion, and Pleiades, and the chambers of the south. ¹⁰Which doeth great things past finding out; yea, and wonders without number. ¹¹Lo, he goeth by me, and I see *him* not: he passeth on also, but I perceive him not. ¹²Behold, he taketh away, who can hinder[d] him? who will say unto him, What doest thou? ¹³*If* God will not withdraw his anger, the proud[e] helpers do stoop under him.

¹⁴How much less shall I answer him, *and* choose out my words *to reason* with him? ¹⁵Whom, though I were righteous, *yet* would I not answer, *but* I would make supplication to my judge. ¹⁶If I had called, and he had answered me; *yet* would I not believe that he had hearkened unto my voice. ¹⁷For he breaketh me with a tempest, and multiplieth my wounds without cause. ¹⁸He

---

[d] help . . . : Heb. take the ungodly by the hand
[e] rejoicing: Heb. shouting for joy
[a] with God: or, before God?
[b] waves: Heb. heights
[c] Arcturus . . . : Heb. Ash, Cesil, and Cimah
[d] hinder . . . : Heb. turn him away?
[e] proud . . . : Heb. helpers of pride, or, strength

will not suffer me to take my breath, but filleth me with bitterness. ¹⁹If *I speak* of strength, lo, *he is* strong: and if of judgment, who shall set me a time *to plead?* ²⁰If I justify myself, mine own mouth shall condemn me: *if I say*, I *am* perfect, it shall also prove me perverse. ²¹ *Though* I *were* perfect, *yet* would I not know my soul: I would despise my life.

²²This *is* one *thing*, therefore I said *it*, He destroyeth the perfect and the wicked. ²³If the scourge slay suddenly, he will laugh at the trial of the innocent. ²⁴The earth is given into the hand of the wicked: he covereth the faces of the judges thereof; if not, where, *and* who *is* he?

²⁵Now my days are swifter than a post: they flee away, they see no good. ²⁶They are passed away as the swift* ships: as the eagle *that* hasteth to the prey. ²⁷If I say, I will forget my complaint, I will leave off my heaviness, and comfort *myself.* ²⁸I am afraid of all my sorrows, I know that thou wilt not hold me innocent. ²⁹*If* I be wicked, why then labour I in vain? ³⁰If I wash myself with snow water, and make my hands never so clean; ³¹Yet shalt thou plunge me in the ditch, and mine own clothes shall abhor⁸ me. ³²For *he is* not a man, as I *am, that* I should answer him, *and* we should come together in judgment. ³³Neither is there any daysman betwixt us, *that* might lay his hand upon us both. ³⁴Let him take his rod away from me, and let not his fear terrify me:

³⁵*Then* would I speak, and not fear him; but *it is* not so with me.

10

¹My soul is weary* of my life; I will leave my complaint upon myself; I will speak in the bitterness of my soul. ²I will say unto God, Do not condemn me; shew me wherefore thou contendest with me. ³*Is it* good unto thee that thou shouldest oppress, that thou shouldest despise the work⁰ of thine hands, and shine upon the counsel of the wicked? ⁴Hast thou eyes of flesh? or seest thou as man seeth? ⁵*Are* thy days as the days of man? *are* thy years as man's days, ⁶That thou enquirest after mine iniquity, and searchest after my sin? ⁷Thou knowest that I am not wicked; and *there is* none that can deliver out of thine hand.

⁸Thine hands have made me and fashioned me together round about; yet thou dost destroy me. ⁹Remember, I beseech thee, that thou hast made me as the clay; and wilt thou bring me into dust again? ¹⁰Hast thou not poured me out as milk, and curdled me like cheese? ¹¹Thou hast clothed me with skin and flesh, and hast fenced⁰ me with bones and sinews. ¹²Thou hast granted me life and favour, and thy visitation hath preserved my spirit. ¹³And these *things* hast thou hid in thine heart: I know that this *is* with thee.

¹⁴If I sin, then thou markest me, and thou wilt not acquit me from mine

---

ᶠ swift . . . : or, ships of Ebeh: Heb. ships of desire
ᵍ abhor . . . : or, make me to be abhorred
ᵃ weary . . . : or, cut off while I live
ᵇ work: Heb. labour
ᶜ fenced: Heb. hedged

iniquity. ¹⁵If I be wicked, woe unto me; and *if* I be righteous, *yet* will I not lift up my head. *I am* full of confusion; therefore see thou mine affliction; ¹⁶For it increaseth. Thou huntest me as a fierce lion: and again thou shewest thyself marvellous upon me. ¹⁷Thou renewest thy witnessesᵈ against me, and increasest thine indignation upon me; changes and war *are* against me. ¹⁸Wherefore then hast thou brought me forth out of the womb? Oh that I had given up the ghost, and no eye had seen me! ¹⁹I should have been as though I had not been; I should have been carried from the womb to the grave. ²⁰*Are* not my days few? cease *then, and* let me alone, that I may take comfort a little, ²¹Before I go *whence* I shall not return, *even* to the land of darkness and the shadow of death; ²²A land of darkness, as darkness *itself; and* of the shadow of death, without any order, and *where* the light *is* as darkness.

11

¹Then answered Zophar the Naamathite, and said, ²Should not the multitude of words be answered? and should a man full of talk be justified? ³Should thy liesᵃ make men hold their peace? and when thou mockest, shall no man make thee ashamed? ⁴For thou hast said, My doctrine *is* pure, and I am clean in thine eyes. ⁵But oh that God would speak, and open his lips against thee; ⁶And that he would shew thee the secrets of wisdom, that *they are* double

to that which is! Know therefore that God exacteth of thee *less* than thine iniquity *deserveth.*

⁷Canst thou by searching find out God? canst thou find out the Almighty unto perfection? ⁸*It is* as highᵇ as heaven; what canst thou do? deeper than hell; what canst thou know? ⁹The measure thereof *is* longer than the earth, and broader than the sea. ¹⁰If he cut off, and shut up, or gather together, then who can hinder him? ¹¹For he knoweth vain men: he seeth wickedness also; will he not then consider *it*? ¹²For vainᶜ man would be wise, though man be born *like* a wild ass's colt.

¹³If thou prepare thine heart, and stretch out thine hands toward him; ¹⁴If iniquity *be* in thine hand, put it far away, and let not wickedness dwell in thy tabernacles. ¹⁵For then shalt thou lift up thy face without spot; yea, thou shalt be stedfast, and shalt not fear: ¹⁶Because thou shalt forget *thy* misery, *and* remember *it* as waters *that* pass away: ¹⁷And *thine* age shall be clearer

---

Devotional Moment

Hidden from God?

11:11 Nothing is hidden from God, be it good or evil. Do you know people who live as if they could hide their behavior or thoughts from God? Children can be naturally secretive. Discuss with your children how God views them and pray with them about this issue. Help them to welcome Jesus as a constant companion and friend, not as a critical lawgiver.

ᵈ witnesses: that is, plagues
ᵃ lies: or, devices
ᵇ as high . . . : Heb. the heights of heaven
ᶜ vain: Heb. empty

than the noonday; thou shalt shine forth, thou shalt be as the morning. ¹⁸And thou shalt be secure, because there is hope; yea, thou shalt dig *about thee, and* thou shalt take thy rest in safety. ¹⁹Also thou shalt lie down, and none shall make *thee* afraid; yea, many shall make suit^d unto thee. ²⁰But the eyes of the wicked shall fail, and they shall not escape, and their hope *shall be as* the giving up of the ghost.

12

¹And Job answered and said, ²No doubt but ye *are* the people, and wisdom shall die with you. ³But I have understanding^a as well as you; I *am* not inferior to you: yea, who knoweth not such things as these? ⁴I am *as* one mocked of his neighbour, who calleth upon God, and he answereth him: the just upright *man is* laughed to scorn. ⁵He that is ready to slip with *his* feet *is as* a lamp despised in the thought of him that is at ease.

⁶The tabernacles of robbers prosper, and they that provoke God are secure; into whose hand God bringeth *abundantly.* ⁷But ask now the beasts, and they shall teach thee; and the fowls of the air, and they shall tell thee: ⁸Or speak to the earth, and it shall teach thee: and the fishes of the sea shall declare unto thee. ⁹Who knoweth not in

all these that the hand of the LORD hath wrought this? ¹⁰In whose hand *is* the soul^b of every living thing, and the breath of all mankind. ¹¹Doth not the ear try words? and the mouth^c taste his meat?

¹²With the ancient *is* wisdom; and in length of days understanding. ¹³With him *is* wisdom and strength, he hath counsel and understanding. ¹⁴Behold, he breaketh down, and it cannot be built again: he shutteth up^d a man, and there can be no opening. ¹⁵Behold, he withholdeth the waters, and they dry up: also he sendeth them out, and they overturn the earth. ¹⁶With him *is* strength and wisdom: the deceived and the deceiver *are* his. ¹⁷He leadeth counsellors away spoiled, and maketh the judges fools. ¹⁸He looseth the bond of kings, and girdeth their loins with a girdle. ¹⁹He leadeth princes away spoiled, and overthroweth the mighty. ²⁰He removeth away the speech^e of the trusty, and taketh away the understanding of the aged. ²¹He poureth contempt upon princes, and weakeneth^f the strength of the mighty. ²²He discovereth deep things out of darkness, and bringeth out to light the shadow of death. ²³He increaseth the nations, and destroyeth them: he enlargeth the nations, and straiteneth^g them *again.* ²⁴He taketh away the heart of the chief of the peo-

---

^d make suit . . . : Heb. intreat thy face
^a understanding: Heb. an heart
^b soul: or, life
^c mouth: Heb. palate
^d up: Heb. upon
^e speech . . . : Heb. lip of the faithful
^f weakeneth . . . : or, looseth the girdle of the strong
^g straiteneth: Heb. leadeth in

ple of the earth, and causeth them to wander in a wilderness *where there is* no way. ²⁵They grope in the dark without light, and he maketh them to stagger^h like *a drunken man.*

13

¹Lo, mine eye hath seen all *this*, mine ear hath heard and understood it. ²What ye know, *the same* do I know also: I *am* not inferior unto you. ³Surely I would speak to the Almighty, and I desire to reason with God. ⁴But ye *are* forgers of lies, ye *are* all physicians of no value. ⁵O that ye would altogether hold your peace! and it should be your wisdom. ⁶Hear now my reasoning, and hearken to the pleadings of my lips. ⁷Will ye speak wickedly for God? and talk deceitfully for him? ⁸Will ye accept his person? will ye contend for God? ⁹Is it good that he should search you out? or as one man mocketh another, do ye *so* mock him? ¹⁰He will surely reprove you, if ye do secretly accept persons. ¹¹Shall not his excellency make you afraid? and his dread fall upon you? ¹²Your remembrances *are* like unto ashes, your bodies to bodies of clay. ¹³Hold your peace, let me alone, that I may speak, and let come on me what *will.* ¹⁴Wherefore do I take my flesh in my teeth, and put my life in mine hand? ¹⁵Though he slay me, yet will I trust in him: but I will maintain^a mine own ways before him. ¹⁶He also *shall be* my salvation: for an hypocrite shall not come before him. ¹⁷Hear diligently my speech, and my declaration

with your ears. ¹⁸Behold now, I have ordered *my* cause; I know that I shall be justified. ¹⁹Who *is* he *that* will plead with me? for now, if I hold my tongue, I shall give up the ghost. ²⁰Only do not two *things* unto me: then will I not hide myself from thee. ²¹Withdraw thine hand far from me: and let not thy dread make me afraid. ²²Then call thou, and I will answer: or let me speak, and answer thou me.

²³How many *are* mine iniquities and sins? make me to know my transgression and my sin. ²⁴Wherefore hidest thou thy face, and holdest me for thine enemy? ²⁵Wilt thou break a leaf driven to and fro? and wilt thou pursue the dry stubble? ²⁶For thou writest bitter things against me, and makest me to possess the iniquities of my youth. ²⁷Thou puttest my feet also in the stocks, and lookest narrowly unto all my paths; thou settest a print upon the heels of my feet. ²⁸And he, as a rotten thing, consumeth, as a garment that is moth eaten.

14

¹Man *that is* born of a woman *is* of few^a days, and full of trouble. ²He cometh forth like a flower, and is cut down: he fleeth also as a shadow, and continueth not. ³And dost thou open thine eyes upon such an one, and bringest me into judgment with thee? ⁴Who can bring a clean *thing* out of an unclean? not one. ⁵Seeing his days *are* determined, the number of his months *are* with thee, thou hast appointed his bounds that he

---

^h stagger: Heb. wander

^a maintain: Heb. prove, or, argue

^a few . . . : Heb. short of days

cannot pass; ⁶Turn from him, that he may rest⁶, till he shall accomplish, as an hireling, his day.

⁷For there is hope of a tree, if it be cut down, that it will sprout again, and that the tender branch thereof will not cease. ⁸Though the root thereof wax old in the earth, and the stock thereof die in the ground; ⁹Yet through the scent of water it will bud, and bring forth boughs like a plant. ¹⁰But man dieth, and wasteth away: yea, man giveth up the ghost, and where is he? ¹¹As the waters fail from the sea, and the flood decayeth and drieth up: ¹²So man lieth down, and riseth not: till the heavens be no more, they shall not awake, nor be raised out of their sleep. ¹³O that thou wouldest hide me in the grave, that thou wouldest keep me secret, until thy wrath be past, that thou wouldest appoint me a set time, and remember me! ¹⁴If a man die, shall he live again? all the days of my appointed time will I wait, till my change come. ¹⁵Thou shalt call, and I will answer thee: thou wilt have a desire to the work of thine hands.

¹⁶For now thou numberest my steps: dost thou not watch over my sin? ¹⁷My transgression is sealed up in a bag, and thou sewest up mine iniquity. ¹⁸And surely the mountain falling cometh to nought, and the rock is removed out of his place. ¹⁹The waters wear the stones: thou washest away the things which grow out of the dust of the earth; and thou destroyest the hope of man. ²⁰Thou prevailest for ever against him, and he passeth: thou changest his countenance, and sendest him away. ²¹His sons come to honour, and he knoweth it not; and they are brought low, but he perceiveth it not of them. ²²But his flesh upon him shall have pain, and his soul within him shall mourn.

15

¹Then answered Eliphaz the Temanite, and said, ²Should a wise man utter vain* knowledge, and fill his belly with the east wind? ³Should he reason with unprofitable talk? or with speeches wherewith he can do no good? ⁴Yea, thou castest off fear, and restrainest prayer before God. ⁵For thy mouth uttereth⁶ thine iniquity, and thou choosest the tongue of the crafty. ⁶Thine own mouth condemneth thee, and not I: yea, thine own lips testify against thee. ⁷Art thou the first man that was born? or wast thou made before the hills? ⁸Hast thou

---

ᵇ rest: Heb. cease
ᵃ vain . . . : Heb. knowledge of wind
ᵇ uttereth: Heb. teacheth

heard the secret of God? and dost thou restrain wisdom to thyself? ⁹What knowest thou, that we know not? *what* understandest thou, which *is* not in us? ¹⁰With us *are* both the grayheaded and very aged men, much elder than thy father. ¹¹*Are* the consolations of God small with thee? is there any secret thing with thee? ¹²Why doth thine heart carry thee away? and what do thy eyes wink at, ¹³That thou turnest thy spirit against God, and lettest *such* words go out of thy mouth? ¹⁴What *is* man, that he should be clean? and *he which is* born of a woman, that he should be righteous? ¹⁵Behold, he putteth no trust in his saints; yea, the heavens are not clean in his sight. ¹⁶How much more abominable and filthy *is* man, which drinketh iniquity like water?

¹⁷I will shew thee, hear me; and that *which* I have seen I will declare; ¹⁸Which wise men have told from their fathers, and have not hid *it*: ¹⁹Unto whom alone the earth was given, and no stranger passed among them. ²⁰The wicked man travaileth with pain all *his* days, and the number of years is hidden to the oppressor. ²¹A dreadfulᶜ sound *is* in his ears: in prosperity the destroyer shall come upon him. ²²He believeth not that he shall return out of darkness, and he is waited for of the sword. ²³He wandereth abroad for bread, *saying*, Where *is it?* he knoweth that the day of darkness is ready at his hand. ²⁴Trouble and anguish shall make him afraid; they shall prevail against him, as a king ready to the battle. ²⁵For he stretcheth out his hand against God, and strengtheneth himself against the Almighty. ²⁶He runneth upon him, *even* on *his* neck, upon the thick bosses of his bucklers: ²⁷Because he covereth his face with his fatness, and maketh collops of fat on *his* flanks. ²⁸And he dwelleth in desolate cities, *and* in houses which no man inhabiteth, which are ready to become heaps. ²⁹He shall not be rich, neither shall his substance continue, neither shall he prolong the perfection thereof upon the earth. ³⁰He shall not depart out of darkness; the flame shall dry up his branches, and by the breath of his mouth shall he go away. ³¹Let not him that is deceived trust in vanity: for vanity shall be his recompence. ³²It shall be accomplishedᵈ before his time, and his branch shall not be green. ³³He shall shake off his unripe grape as the vine, and shall cast off his flower as the olive. ³⁴For the congregation of hypocrites *shall be* desolate, and fire shall consume the tabernacles of bribery. ³⁵They conceive mischief, and bring forth vanityᵉ, and their belly prepareth deceit.

16

¹Then Job answered and said, ²I have heard many such things: miserableᵃ comforters *are* ye all. ³Shall vainᵇ words have an end? or what emboldeneth thee that thou answerest? ⁴I also could speak

---

ᶜ A dreadful . . . : Heb. A sound of fears
ᵈ accomplished: or, cut off
ᵉ vanity: or, iniquity
ᵃ miserable: or, troublesome
ᵇ vain . . . : Heb. words of wind

Devotional Moment

Giving Comfort

16:2-5 Explanations may seem like the appropriate reply when someone asks, "Why, Lord?" But here Job tells his well-intentioned friends what he really thought of all their long-winded speeches. What a suffering person really needs is a comforting presence and words that bring relief. Who of your friends or family is hurting right now? What words of comfort can you offer? Send a card, a care package, a gift, or make a quick phone call—simply offer your presence and love.

---

as ye *do*: if your soul were in my soul's stead, I could heap up words against you, and shake mine head at you. ⁵*But* I would strengthen you with my mouth, and the moving of my lips should assuage *your grief.*

⁶Though I speak, my grief is not assuaged: and *though* I forbear, what am I eased? ⁷But now he hath made me weary: thou hast made desolate all my company. ⁸And thou hast filled me with wrinkles, *which* is a witness *against me*: and my leanness rising up in me beareth witness to my face. ⁹He teareth *me* in his wrath, who hateth me: he gnasheth upon me with his teeth; mine enemy sharpeneth his eyes upon me. ¹⁰They have gaped upon me with their mouth; they have smitten me upon the cheek reproachfully; they have gathered themselves together against me. ¹¹God hath delivered me to the ungodly, and turned

me over into the hands of the wicked. ¹²I was at ease, but he hath broken me asunder: he hath also taken *me* by my neck, and shaken me to pieces, and set me up for his mark. ¹³His archers compass me round about, he cleaveth my reins asunder, and doth not spare; he poureth out my gall upon the ground. ¹⁴He breaketh me with breach upon breach, he runneth upon me like a giant. ¹⁵I have sewed sackcloth upon my skin, and defiled my horn in the dust. ¹⁶My face is foul with weeping, and on my eyelids *is* the shadow of death;

¹⁷Not for *any* injustice in mine hands: also my prayer *is* pure. ¹⁸O earth, cover not thou my blood, and let my cry have no place. ¹⁹Also now, behold, my witness *is* in heaven, and my record *is* on high*. ²⁰My friends scorn me*: *but* mine eye poureth out *tears* unto God. ²¹O that one might plead for a man with God, as a man *pleadeth* for his neighbour*! ²²When a few* years are come, then I shall go the way *whence* I shall not return.

17

¹My breath* is corrupt, my days are extinct, the graves *are ready* for me. ²*Are there* not mockers with me? and doth not mine eye continue* in their provocation? ³Lay down now, put me in a surety with thee; who *is* he *that* will strike hands with me? ⁴For thou hast hid their heart from understanding: therefore shalt thou not exalt *them*. ⁵He

---

ᶜ on high: Heb. in the high places
ᵈ scorn me: Heb. are my scorners
ᵉ neighbour: or, friend
ᶠ a few . . . : Heb. years of number
ᵃ breath . . . : or, spirit is spent
ᵇ continue: Heb. lodge

Devotional Moment

Whose Wisdom?

17:10-12 The "wisdom" of Job's friends amounted to foolishness because it had only elements of the truth, and what *was* true didn't necessarily apply to Job. The world has plenty of advice for young people, couples, parents, and others concerned about family. Judge the counsel you hear, keeping God's Word close by as a guide. Pray for wisdom (for God promises to give it if we ask—see James 1:5). Read the Proverbs. Seek the counsel of older believers whom you respect. As Job's friends discovered, not all that *seems* true *is* true. Be wise about the wisdom you follow.

that speaketh flattery to *his* friends, even the eyes of his children shall fail. ⁶He hath made me also a byword of the people; and aforetimeᶜ I was as a tabret. ⁷Mine eye also is dim by reason of sorrow, and all my membersᵈ *are* as a shadow. ⁸Upright *men* shall be astonied at this, and the innocent shall stir up himself against the hypocrite. ⁹The righteous also shall hold on his way, and he that hath clean hands shall beᵉ stronger and stronger.

¹⁰But as for you all, do ye return, and come now: for I cannot find *one* wise *man* among you. ¹¹My days are past, my purposes are broken off, *even* the thoughtsᶠ of my heart. ¹²They change the night into day: the light *is* shortᵍ because of darkness. ¹³If I wait, the grave *is* mine house: I have made my bed in the darkness. ¹⁴I have saidʰ to corruption, Thou *art* my father: to the worm, *Thou art* my mother, and my sister. ¹⁵And where *is* now my hope? as for my hope, who shall see it? ¹⁶They shall go down to the bars of the pit, when *our* rest together *is* in the dust.

18

¹Then answered Bildad the Shuhite, and said, ²How long *will it be ere* ye make an end of words? mark, and afterwards we will speak. ³Wherefore are we counted as beasts, *and* reputed vile in your sight? ⁴He teareth himselfᵃ in his anger: shall the earth be forsaken for thee? and shall the rock be removed out of his place?

⁵Yea, the light of the wicked shall be put out, and the spark of his fire shall not shine. ⁶The light shall be dark in his tabernacle, and his candleᵇ shall be put out with him. ⁷The steps of his strength shall be straitened, and his own counsel shall cast him down. ⁸For he is cast into a net by his own feet, and he walketh upon a snare. ⁹The gin shall take *him* by the heel, *and* the robber shall prevail against him. ¹⁰The snare *is* laidᶜ for him in the ground, and a trap for him in the way.

¹¹Terrors shall make him afraid on

ᶜ aforetime: or, before them

ᵈ my members: or, my thoughts

ᵉ be . . . : Heb. add strength

ᶠ the thoughts: Heb. the possessions

ᵍ short: Heb. near

ʰ said: Heb. cried, or, called

ᵃ himself: Heb. his soul

ᵇ candle: or, lamp

ᶜ laid: Heb. hidden

every side, and shall drive[d] him to his feet. [12]His strength shall be hungerbitten, and destruction *shall be* ready at his side. [13]It shall devour the strength[e] of his skin: *even* the firstborn of death shall devour his strength. [14]His confidence shall be rooted out of his tabernacle, and it shall bring him to the king of terrors. [15]It shall dwell in his tabernacle, because *it is* none of his: brimstone shall be scattered upon his habitation. [16]His roots shall be dried up beneath, and above shall his branch be cut off. [17]His remembrance shall perish from the earth, and he shall have no name in the street. [18]He shall be driven from light into darkness, and chased out of the world. [19]He shall neither have son nor nephew among his people, nor any remaining in his dwellings. [20]They that come after *him* shall be astonied at his day, as they that went before were affrighted. [21]Surely such *are* the dwellings of the wicked, and this *is* the place *of him that* knoweth not God.

19

[1]Then Job answered and said, [2]How long will ye vex my soul, and break me in pieces with words? [3]These ten times have ye reproached me: ye are not ashamed *that* ye make yourselves strange to me. [4]And be it indeed *that* I have erred, mine error remaineth with myself. [5]If indeed ye will magnify *yourselves* against me, and plead against me my reproach: [6]Know now that God hath overthrown me, and hath compassed me with his net. [7]Behold, I cry

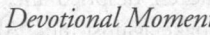

Devotional Moment

•

Sensitivity

19:3-5 Accusing a sufferer of sin because of our own unexamined assumptions, stereotypes, or generalizations doesn't help anybody. Sensitivity toward others in pain requires us to suspend judgment on who is at fault and to give our love and support instead. Remember this the next time someone you love faces the loss of a job, a serious illness, the death of a child, or another unexplainable tragedy.

out of wrong[a], but I am not heard: I cry aloud, but *there is* no judgment.

[8]He hath fenced up my way that I cannot pass, and he hath set darkness in my paths. [9]He hath stripped me of my glory, and taken the crown *from* my head. [10]He hath destroyed me on every side, and I am gone: and mine hope hath he removed like a tree. [11]He hath also kindled his wrath against me, and he counteth me unto him as *one of* his enemies. [12]His troops come together, and raise up their way against me, and encamp round about my tabernacle. [13]He hath put my brethren far from me, and mine acquaintance are verily estranged from me. [14]My kinsfolk have failed, and my familiar friends have forgotten me. [15]They that dwell in mine house, and my maids, count me for a stranger: I am an alien in their sight. [16]I called my servant, and he gave *me* no answer; I intreated him with my mouth. [17]My breath is strange to my wife, though I intreated for the children's *sake* of mine own body. [18]Yea,

---

[d] drive: Heb. scatter

[e] strength: Heb. bars

[a] wrong: or, violence

young children despised me; I arose, and they spake against me. ¹⁹All my inward friends abhorred me: and they whom I loved are turned against me. ²⁰My bone cleaveth to my skin and to my flesh, and I am escaped with the skin of my teeth. ²¹Have pity upon me, have pity upon me, O ye my friends; for the hand of God hath touched me. ²²Why do ye persecute me as God, and are not satisfied with my flesh?

²³Oh that my words were now written! oh that they were printed in a book! ²⁴That they were graven with an iron pen and lead in the rock for ever! ²⁵For I know *that* my redeemer liveth, and *that* he shall stand at the latter *day* upon the earth: ²⁶And *though* after[b] my skin *worms* destroy this *body*, yet in my flesh shall I see God: ²⁷Whom I shall see for myself, and mine eyes shall behold, and not another[c]; *though* my reins be consumed within me. ²⁸But ye should say, Why persecute we him, seeing the root of the matter is found in me? ²⁹Be ye afraid of the sword: for wrath *bringeth* the punishments of the sword, that ye may know *there is* a judgment.

20

¹Then answered Zophar the Naamathite, and said, ²Therefore do my thoughts cause me to answer, and for *this* I make haste. ³I have heard the check of my reproach, and the spirit of my understanding causeth me to answer. ⁴Knowest thou *not* this of old, since man was placed upon earth, ⁵That the triumphing of the wicked *is* short[a], and the joy of the hypocrite *but* for a moment? ⁶Though his excellency mount up to the heavens, and his head reach unto the clouds[b]; ⁷Yet he shall perish for ever like his own dung: they which have seen him shall say, Where *is* he? ⁸He shall fly away as a dream, and shall not be found: yea, he shall be chased away as a vision of the night. ⁹The eye also *which* saw him shall *see him* no more; neither shall his place any more behold him.

¹⁰His children[c] shall seek to please the poor, and his hands shall restore their goods. ¹¹His bones are full *of the sin* of his youth, which shall lie down with him in the dust. ¹²Though wickedness be sweet in his mouth, *though* he hide it under his tongue; ¹³ *Though* he spare it, and forsake it not; but keep it still within[d] his mouth: ¹⁴ *Yet* his meat in his bowels is turned, *it is* the gall of asps within him. ¹⁵He hath swallowed down riches, and he shall vomit them up again: God shall cast them out of his belly. ¹⁶He shall suck the poison of asps: the viper's tongue shall slay him. ¹⁷He shall not see the rivers, the floods[e], the brooks of honey and butter. ¹⁸That which he laboured for shall he restore, and shall not swallow *it* down: according to *his* substance *shall* the restitu-

---

[b] And . . . : or, After I shall awake, though this body be destroyed, yet out of my flesh
[c] another: Heb. a stranger
[a] short: Heb. from near
[b] clouds: Heb. cloud
[c] His children . . . : or, The poor shall oppress his children
[d] within . . . : Heb. in the midst of his palate
[e] the floods . . . : or, streaming brooks

tion *be*, and he shall not rejoice *therein.*
[19]Because he hath oppressed[f] *and* hath
forsaken the poor; *because* he hath violently taken away an house which he
builded not; [20]Surely he shall not feel[g]
quietness in his belly, he shall not save of
that which he desired. [21]There shall none
of his meat be left; therefore shall no
man look for his goods. [22]In the fulness
of his sufficiency he shall be in straits:
every hand of the wicked[h] shall come
upon him.

[23] *When* he is about to fill his belly,
God shall cast the fury of his wrath
upon him, and shall rain *it* upon him
while he is eating. [24]He shall flee from
the iron weapon, *and* the bow of steel
shall strike him through. [25]It is drawn,
and cometh out of the body; yea, the
glittering sword cometh out of his gall:
terrors *are* upon him. [26]All darkness
shall be hid in his secret places: a fire not
blown shall consume him; it shall go ill
with him that is left in his tabernacle.
[27]The heaven shall reveal his iniquity;
and the earth shall rise up against him.
[28]The increase of his house shall depart,
and his goods shall flow away in the day
of his wrath. [29]This *is* the portion of a
wicked man from God, and the heritage appointed[i] unto him by God.

21

[1]But Job answered and said, [2]Hear diligently my speech, and let this be your
consolations. [3]Suffer me that I may
speak; and after that I have spoken,
mock on. [4]As for me, *is* my complaint
to man? and if *it were so*, why should
not my spirit be troubled[a]? [5]Mark[b] me,
and be astonished, and lay *your* hand
upon *your* mouth. [6]Even when I remember I am afraid, and trembling
taketh hold on my flesh.

[7]Wherefore do the wicked live, become old, yea, are mighty in power?
[8]Their seed is established in their sight
with them, and their offspring before
their eyes. [9]Their houses *are* safe[c] from
fear, neither *is* the rod of God upon
them. [10]Their bull gendereth, and
faileth not; their cow calveth, and

Devotional Moment
•
Success

21:1-34 The wicked seem to prosper right up
to the day they die. Long life, secure livelihood,
prosperous children, a nice home, material
wealth—they have it all, or so it seems. The
wicked ascribe success to their own
achievements, independent of God and his ways
(vv. 14-16). The wicked give no thought to the
legacy of sin and its consequences, which pass
from one generation to the next (vv. 19-21). Job
rightly rejected that view of success. No matter
how others seem to prosper, we must follow
God with our whole heart and show
our children that faithfulness
pleases God even if we don't have the
same prosperity as other families.

---

[f] oppressed: Heb. crushed
[g] feel: Heb. know
[h] wicked: or, troublesome
[i] appointed . . . : Heb. of his decree from God
[a] troubled: Heb. shortened?
[b] Mark . . . : Heb. Look unto me
[c] safe . . . : Heb. peace from

casteth not her calf. [11]They send forth their little ones like a flock, and their children dance. [12]They take the timbrel and harp, and rejoice at the sound of the organ. [13]They spend their days in wealth[d], and in a moment go down to the grave. [14]Therefore they say unto God, Depart from us; for we desire not the knowledge of thy ways. [15]What *is* the Almighty, that we should serve him? and what profit should we have, if we pray unto him? [16]Lo, their good *is* not in their hand: the counsel of the wicked is far from me.

[17]How oft is the candle[e] of the wicked put out! and *how oft* cometh their destruction upon them! *God* distributeth sorrows in his anger. [18]They are as stubble before the wind, and as chaff that the storm carrieth away. [19]God layeth up his iniquity[f] for his children: he rewardeth him, and he shall know *it.* [20]His eyes shall see his destruction, and he shall drink of the wrath of the Almighty. [21]For what pleasure *hath* he in his house after him, when the number of his months is cut off in the midst? [22]Shall *any* teach God knowledge? seeing he judgeth those that are high. [23]One dieth in his full strength, being wholly at ease and quiet. [24]His breasts[g] are full of milk, and his bones are moistened with marrow. [25]And another dieth in the bitterness of his soul, and never eateth with pleasure. [26]They shall lie down alike in the dust, and the worms shall cover them.

[27]Behold, I know your thoughts, and the devices *which* ye wrongfully imagine against me. [28]For ye say, Where *is* the house of the prince? and where *are* the dwelling[h] places of the wicked? [29]Have ye not asked them that go by the way? and do ye not know their tokens, [30]That the wicked is reserved to the day of destruction? they shall be brought forth to the day of wrath[i]. [31]Who shall declare his way to his face? and who shall repay him *what* he hath done? [32]Yet shall he be brought to the grave[j], and shall remain in the tomb. [33]The clods of the valley shall be sweet unto him, and every man shall draw after him, as *there are* innumerable before him. [34]How then comfort ye me in vain, seeing in your answers there remaineth falsehood[k]?

22

[1]Then Eliphaz the Temanite answered and said, [2]Can a man be profitable unto God, as he that is wise may be profitable unto himself? [3]*Is it* any pleasure to the Almighty, that thou art righteous? or *is it* gain *to him,* that thou makest thy ways perfect? [4]Will he reprove thee for fear of thee? will he enter with thee into judgment?

---

[d] in wealth: or, in mirth
[e] candle: or, lamp
[f] his iniquity: that is, the punishment of his iniquity
[g] breasts: or, milk pails
[h] the dwelling . . . : Heb. the tent of the tabernacles
[i] wrath: Heb. wraths
[j] grave: Heb. graves
[k] falsehood: Heb. transgression?

⁵*Is* not thy wickedness great? and thine iniquities infinite? ⁶For thou hast taken a pledge from thy brother for nought, and stripped the naked^a of their clothing. ⁷Thou hast not given water to the weary to drink, and thou hast withholden bread from the hungry. ⁸But *as for* the mighty^b man, he had the earth; and the honourable man dwelt in it. ⁹Thou hast sent widows away empty, and the arms of the fatherless have been broken. ¹⁰Therefore snares *are* round about thee, and sudden fear troubleth thee; ¹¹Or darkness, *that* thou canst not see; and abundance of waters cover thee. ¹²*Is* not God in the height of heaven? and behold the height of the stars^c, how high they are! ¹³And thou sayest, How doth God know? can he judge through the dark cloud? ¹⁴Thick clouds *are* a covering to him, that he seeth not; and he walketh in the circuit of heaven.

¹⁵Hast thou marked the old way which wicked men have trodden? ¹⁶Which were cut down out of time, whose foundation was overflown with a flood: ¹⁷Which said unto God, Depart from us: and what can the Almighty do for them? ¹⁸Yet he filled their houses with good *things*: but the counsel of the wicked is far from me. ¹⁹The righteous see *it,* and are glad: and the innocent laugh them to scorn. ²⁰Whereas our substance^d is not cut down, but the remnant of them the fire consumeth.

²¹Acquaint now thyself with him^e, and be at peace: thereby good shall come unto thee. ²²Receive, I pray thee, the law from his mouth, and lay up his words in thine heart. ²³If thou return to the Almighty, thou shalt be built up, thou shalt put away iniquity far from thy tabernacles. ²⁴Then shalt thou lay up gold as dust^f, and the *gold* of Ophir as the stones of the brooks. ²⁵Yea, the Almighty shall be thy defence^g, and thou shalt have plenty of silver. ²⁶For then shalt thou have thy delight in the Almighty, and shalt lift up thy face unto God. ²⁷Thou shalt make thy prayer unto him, and he shall hear thee, and thou shalt pay thy vows. ²⁸Thou shalt also decree a thing, and it shall be established unto thee: and the light shall shine upon thy ways. ²⁹When *men* are cast down, then thou shalt say, *There is* lifting up; and he shall save the humble^h person. ³⁰He shall deliver the island of the innocent: and it is delivered by the pureness of thine hands.

23

¹Then Job answered and said, ²Even to day *is* my complaint bitter: my stroke^a is

---

^a the naked . . . : Heb. the clothes of the naked
^b mighty . . . : Heb. man of arm
^c height of the stars: Heb. head of the stars
^d substance: or, estate
^e him: that is, God
^f as dust: or, on the dust
^g defence: or, gold
^h the humble . . . : Heb. him that hath low eyes
^a stroke: Heb. hand

heavier than my groaning. ³Oh that I knew where I might find him! *that* I might come *even* to his seat! ⁴I would order *my* cause before him, and fill my mouth with arguments. ⁵I would know the words *which* he would answer me, and understand what he would say unto me. ⁶Will he plead against me with *his* great power? No; but he would put *strength* in me. ⁷There the righteous might dispute with him; so should I be delivered for ever from my judge.

⁸Behold, I go forward, but he *is* not *there*; and backward, but I cannot perceive him: ⁹On the left hand, where he doth work, but I cannot behold *him*: he hideth himself on the right hand, that I cannot see *him*: ¹⁰But he knoweth the way that I take: *when* he hath tried me, I shall come forth as gold. ¹¹My foot hath held his steps, his way have I kept, and not declined. ¹²Neither have I gone back from the commandment of his lips; I have es-

teemed[b] the words of his mouth more than my necessary *food*.

¹³But he *is* in one *mind*, and who can turn him? and *what* his soul desireth, even *that* he doeth. ¹⁴For he performeth *the thing that is* appointed for me: and many such *things are* with him. ¹⁵Therefore am I troubled at his presence: when I consider, I am afraid of him. ¹⁶For God maketh my heart soft, and the Almighty troubleth me: ¹⁷Because I was not cut off before the darkness, *neither* hath he covered the darkness from my face.

24

¹Why, seeing times are not hidden from the Almighty, do they that know him not see his days? ²*Some* remove the landmarks; they violently take away flocks, and feed[a] *thereof*. ³They drive away the ass of the fatherless, they take the widow's ox for a pledge. ⁴They turn the needy out of the way: the poor of the earth hide themselves together. ⁵Behold, *as* wild asses in the desert, go they forth to their work; rising betimes for a prey: the wilderness *yieldeth* food for them *and* for *their* children. ⁶They reap *every one* his corn[b] in the field: and they gather the vintage of the wicked. ⁷They cause the naked to lodge without clothing, that *they have* no covering in the cold. ⁸They are wet with the showers of the mountains, and embrace the rock for want of a shelter. ⁹They pluck the fatherless from the breast, and take a pledge of the poor. ¹⁰They cause *him*

ᵇ esteemed: Heb. hid, or, laid up
ᵃ feed . . . : or, feed them
ᵇ corn: Heb. mingled corn, or, dredge

to go naked without clothing, and they take away the sheaf *from* the hungry; ¹¹*Which* make oil within their walls, *and* tread *their* winepresses, and suffer thirst. ¹²Men groan from out of the city, and the soul of the wounded crieth out: yet God layeth not folly *to* them.

¹³They are of those that rebel against the light; they know not the ways thereof, nor abide in the paths thereof. ¹⁴The murderer rising with the light killeth the poor and needy, and in the night is as a thief. ¹⁵The eye also of the adulterer waiteth for the twilight, saying, No eye shall see me: and disguiseth^c *his* face. ¹⁶In the dark they dig through houses, *which* they had marked for themselves in the daytime: they know not the light. ¹⁷For the morning *is* to them even as the shadow of death: if *one* know *them, they are in* the terrors of the shadow of death.

¹⁸He *is* swift as the waters; their portion is cursed in the earth: he beholdeth not the way of the vineyards. ¹⁹Drought and heat consume^d the snow waters: *so doth* the grave *those which* have sinned. ²⁰The womb shall forget him; the worm shall feed sweetly on him; he shall be no more remembered; and wickedness shall be broken as a tree. ²¹He evil entreateth the barren *that* beareth not: and doeth not good to the widow. ²²He draweth also the mighty with his power: he riseth up, and no *man is* sure^e of life. ²³*Though* it be given him *to be* in safety, whereon he resteth; yet

his eyes *are* upon their ways. ²⁴They are exalted for a little while, but are gone and brought low; they are taken out of the way as all *other*, and cut off as the tops of the ears of corn. ²⁵And if *it be* not *so* now, who will make me a liar, and make my speech nothing worth?

25

¹Then answered Bildad the Shuhite, and said, ²Dominion and fear *are* with him, he maketh peace in his high places. ³Is there any number of his armies? and upon whom doth not his light arise? ⁴How then can man be justified with God? or how can he be clean *that is* born of a woman? ⁵Behold even to the moon, and it shineth not; yea, the stars are not pure in his sight. ⁶How much less man, *that is* a worm? and the son of man, *which is* a worm?

26

¹But Job answered and said, ²How hast thou helped *him that is* without power? *how* savest thou the arm *that hath* no strength? ³How hast thou counselled *him that hath* no wisdom? and *how* hast thou plentifully declared the thing as it is? ⁴To whom hast thou uttered words? and whose spirit came from thee?

⁵Dead *things* are formed from under the waters, and the inhabitants thereof. ⁶Hell *is* naked before him, and destruction hath no covering. ⁷He stretcheth out the north over the empty place, *and* hangeth the earth upon nothing. ⁸He bindeth up the waters in

^c disguiseth . . . : Heb. setteth his face in secret
^d consume: Heb. violently take
^e no . . . : or, he trusteth not his own life

his thick clouds; and the cloud is not rent under them. ⁹He holdeth back the face of his throne, *and* spreadeth his cloud upon it. ¹⁰He hath compassed the waters with bounds, until the day and night come to an end. ¹¹The pillars of heaven tremble and are astonished at his reproof. ¹²He divideth the sea with his power, and by his understanding he smiteth through the proudᵃ. ¹³By his spirit he hath garnished the heavens; his hand hath formed the crooked serpent. ¹⁴Lo, these *are* parts of his ways: but how little a portion is heard of him? but the thunder of his power who can understand?

27

¹Moreover Job continuedᵃ his parable, and said, ²*As* God liveth, *who* hath taken away my judgment; and the Almighty, *who* hath vexedᵇ my soul; ³All the while my breath *is* in me, and the spiritᶜ of God *is* in my nostrils; ⁴My lips shall not speak wickedness, nor my tongue utter deceit. ⁵God forbid that I should justify you: till I die I will not remove mine integrity from me. ⁶My righteousness I hold fast, and will not let it go: my heart shall not reproach *me* so long as I live.

⁷Let mine enemy be as the wicked, and he that riseth up against me as the unrighteous. ⁸For what *is* the hope of the hypocrite, though he hath gained, when God taketh away his soul? ⁹Will God hear his cry when trouble cometh upon him? ¹⁰Will he delight himself in the Almighty? will he always call upon God?

¹¹I will teach you by the hand of God: *that* which *is* with the Almighty will I not conceal. ¹²Behold, all ye yourselves have seen *it*; why then are ye thus altogether vain? ¹³This *is* the portion of a wicked man with God, and the heritage of oppressors, *which* they shall receive of the Almighty. ¹⁴If his children be multiplied, *it is* for the sword: and his offspring shall not be satisfied with bread. ¹⁵Those that remain of him shall be buried in death: and his widows shall not weep. ¹⁶Though he heap up silver as the dust, and prepare raiment as the clay; ¹⁷He may prepare *it*, but the just shall put *it* on, and the innocent shall divide the silver. ¹⁸He buildeth his house as a moth, and as a booth *that* the keeper maketh. ¹⁹The rich man shall lie down, but he shall not be gathered: he openeth his eyes, and he *is* not. ²⁰Terrors take hold on him as waters, a tempest stealeth him away in the night. ²¹The east wind carrieth him away, and he departeth: and as a storm hurleth him out of his place. ²²For *God* shall cast upon him, and not spare: he would fain flee out of his hand. ²³*Men* shall clap their hands at him, and shall hiss him out of his place.

28

¹Surely there is a veinᵃ for the silver, and a place for gold *where* they fine *it*. ²Iron

---

ᵃ the proud: Heb. pride
ᵃ continued: Heb. added to take up
ᵇ vexed . . . : Heb. made my soul bitter
ᶜ the spirit . . . : that is, the breath which God gave him
ᵃ vein: or, mine

is taken out of the earth[b], and brass *is* molten *out of* the stone. ³He setteth an end to darkness, and searcheth out all perfection: the stones of darkness, and the shadow of death. ⁴The flood breaketh out from the inhabitant; *even the waters* forgotten of the foot: they are dried up, they are gone away from men. ⁵*As for* the earth, out of it cometh bread: and under it is turned up as it were fire. ⁶The stones of it *are* the place of sapphires: and it hath dust[c] of gold. ⁷*There is* a path which no fowl knoweth, and which the vulture's eye hath not seen: ⁸The lion's whelps have not trodden it, nor the fierce lion passed by it. ⁹He putteth forth his hand upon the rock[d]; he overturneth the mountains by the roots. ¹⁰He cutteth out rivers among the rocks; and his eye seeth every precious thing. ¹¹He bindeth the floods from overflowing[e]; and *the thing that is* hid bringeth he forth to light. ¹²But where shall wisdom be found? and where *is* the place of understanding? ¹³Man knoweth not the price thereof; neither is it found in the land of the living.

¹⁴The depth saith, It *is* not in me: and the sea saith, *It is* not with me. ¹⁵It cannot be gotten for gold, neither shall silver be weighed *for* the price thereof. ¹⁶It cannot be valued with the gold of Ophir, with the precious onyx, or the sapphire. ¹⁷The gold and the crystal cannot equal it: and the exchange of it

---

Devotional Moment

•

Education

28:1-28 In this speech of Job's, he made an important distinction between brains and wisdom. Poking fun at the high technology of the day, he said that it is one thing to know how to mine silver and gold, or to have the tools to bore holes in the ground, but quite another to know how to use that technology responsibly. "The fear of the Lord, that is wisdom; and to depart from evil is understanding" (v. 28). Encourage your children to excel in school; help them with their homework; cheer them on at each game they play. But don't let them miss the distinction between being *smart* and being *wise*. Teach them to fear the Lord and forsake evil. That is how they will know what to *do* with their skills and knowledge.

---

shall not be for jewels[f] of fine gold. ¹⁸No mention shall be made of coral[g], or of pearls: for the price of wisdom *is* above rubies. ¹⁹The topaz of Ethiopia shall not equal it, neither shall it be valued with pure gold.

²⁰Whence then cometh wisdom? and where *is* the place of understanding? ²¹Seeing it is hid from the eyes of all living, and kept close from the fowls of the air[h]. ²²Destruction and death say, We have heard the fame thereof with our ears. ²³God understandeth the way thereof, and he knoweth the place thereof. ²⁴For he looketh to the ends of the earth, *and* seeth under the whole

---

[b] earth: or, dust
[c] dust . . . : or, gold ore
[d] rock: or, flint
[e] overflowing: Heb. weeping
[f] jewels . . . : or, vessels of
[g] coral: or, Ramoth
[h] air: or, heaven

heaven; ²⁵To make the weight for the winds; and he weigheth the waters by measure. ²⁶When he made a decree for the rain, and a way for the lightning of the thunder: ²⁷Then did he see it, and declareⁱ it; he prepared it, yea, and searched it out. ²⁸And unto man he said, Behold, the fear of the Lord, that *is* wisdom; and to depart from evil *is* understanding.

29

¹Moreover Job continued^a his parable, and said, ²Oh that I were as *in* months past, as *in* the days *when* God preserved me; ³When his candle^b shined upon my head, *and when* by his light I walked *through* darkness; ⁴As I was in the days of my youth, when the secret of God *was* upon my tabernacle; ⁵When the Almighty *was* yet with me, *when* my children *were* about me; ⁶When I washed my steps with butter, and the rock poured me out rivers of oil;

⁷When I went out to the gate through the city, *when* I prepared my seat in the street! ⁸The young men saw me, and hid themselves: and the aged arose, *and* stood up. ⁹The princes refrained talking, and laid *their* hand on their mouth. ¹⁰The nobles^c held their peace, and their tongue cleaved to the roof of their mouth. ¹¹When the ear heard *me*, then it blessed me; and when the eye saw *me*, it gave witness to me:

¹²Because I delivered the poor that cried, and the fatherless, and *him that had* none to help him. ¹³The blessing of him that was ready to perish came upon me: and I caused the widow's heart to sing for joy. ¹⁴I put on righteousness, and it clothed me: my judgment *was* as a robe and a diadem. ¹⁵I was eyes to the blind, and feet *was* I to the lame. ¹⁶I *was* a father to the poor: and the cause *which* I knew not I searched out. ¹⁷And I brake the jaws^d of the wicked, and plucked the spoil out of his teeth.

¹⁸Then I said, I shall die in my nest, and I shall multiply *my* days as the sand. ¹⁹My root *was* spread out by the waters, and the dew lay all night upon my branch. ²⁰My glory *was* fresh^e in me, and my bow was renewed in my hand. ²¹Unto me *men* gave ear, and waited, and kept silence at my counsel. ²²After my words they spake not again; and my speech dropped upon them. ²³And they waited for me as for the rain; and they opened their mouth wide *as* for the latter rain. ²⁴*If* I laughed on them, they believed *it* not; and the light of my countenance they cast not down. ²⁵I chose out their way, and sat chief, and dwelt as a king in the army, as one *that* comforteth the mourners.

30

¹But now *they that are* younger^a than I have me in derision, whose fathers I

ⁱ declare . . . : or, number it
^a continued: Heb. added to take up
^b candle: or, lamp
^c The nobles . . . : Heb. The voice of the nobles was hid
^d the jaws: Heb. the jawteeth, or, the grinders
^e fresh: Heb. new
^a younger . . . : Heb. of fewer days than I

Encouraging Sexual Abstinence

by Josh McDowell

Job said, "I made a covenant with mine eyes; why then should I think upon a maid?" (Job 31:1). Because Job had made a covenant with the Lord, the values and convictions he upheld went deeper than the pressures of the moment.

Making and keeping a covenant to remain sexually pure is rare. But isn't that what you, as a parent, want for your teenager?

Your sense that it's an uphill battle is well founded. The American Academy of Pediatrics has urged parents to stop their children from watching MTV because of its preoccupation with sex and violence. According to the Barna Research Group and *Fortune* magazine, in the next twenty-four hours 2,750 children will see their parents divorce or separate and 925 unmarried teenage girls will become pregnant.

Most teens are living in a moral vacuum, with no absolutes and no biblical worldview.

How can you encourage sexual abstinence? You begin by becoming a hero to your children. The more you become a hero to your kids, the more they will listen to you and live by your values.

Parents who want to be heroes to their kids must realize that *rules without relationships lead to rebellion*. Knowing the odds against your teenager staying sexually pure, it would be easy to clamp down with a list of rules. But rules alone won't work. When you are close to them, it is easier for them to internalize a Christian perspective instead of accepting the world's presuppositions.

Research shows that adolescents want their parents to talk to them about sex and be their primary information source. One seventeen-year-old boy wrote: "Mom and Dad . . . it was your responsibility to tell me about sex before I discovered it the wrong way. You may not know it, but I learned sex from the street. Believe me, that is not a very good place to learn it." A survey of fourteen hundred parents found that less than 15 percent of mothers and 8 percent of fathers had ever talked to their children about premarital sex or sexual intercourse. Our kids need us to teach them about their sexual development.

Here are several biblical convictions you can help your teenager develop in the sexual area.

Each person is special and of great worth because each is made in the image of God. This means every individual deserves dignity, respect, and consideration. In practical terms, a boy who sees his mom and dad treating each other as persons of great worth will, in turn, offer respect and consideration to his girlfriend.

No one should use another in order to meet his or her own needs. To use people cheapens them. Teaching your kids how valuable individuals are can have a lasting effect. If, for example, your daughter ever heard her boyfriend say, "If you really loved me, you would have sex with me," she would recognize that not only does he not love her but he doesn't think much of her, either.

We should treat others with the same love and respect God shows to us. First Corinthians 13:4-8 explains what true love (charity) is. Among the most important parts for today's teens is, Love is very patient (13:4). In God's plan, there is a proper time and place for everything, including, as Ecclesiastes 3:5 says, "a time to embrace, and a time to refrain from embracing."

Our world says, "Are you lonely? Do you feel a need for intimacy? Go for it—there is no need to wait until marriage." Our kids need to see us model patience and learn the value of waiting.

Your role as a Christian parent is vital. Your actions, attitudes, and speech have a tremendous impact on your children. Ask yourself: Am I really living out the values I hope to see in my children? Am I deliberately teaching them the Christian values of sexual purity, or am I leaving it up to others? Start when your children are young (or start now, no matter what their age).

Job stood firm in the face of his day's pressures. So can your teenagers. Taking time to explain and model the Christian values by which you live is what will enable them to do it.

DIGGING DEEPER

1. How can you become a more relational parent? See Ephesians 6:4.

2. How, as a parent, can you help build your child's self-esteem and instill the belief that individuals are important? See Genesis 1:26-27, Psalm 8:5, John 1:12-13, 1 Corinthians 6:20, and 1 Peter 1:18-19.

3. What are your own convictions about sexual purity, and how can you communicate those biblical standards to your children? See Romans 12:1-2 and 1 Corinthians 6:12-20.

---

would have disdained to have set with the dogs of my flock. ²Yea, whereto *might* the strength of their hands *profit* me, in whom old age was perished? ³For want and famine *they were* solitary[b]; fleeing into the wilderness in former time desolate and waste. ⁴Who cut up mallows by the bushes, and juniper roots *for* their meat. ⁵They were driven forth from among *men*, (they cried after them as *after* a thief;) ⁶To dwell in the clifts of the valleys, *in* caves[c] of the earth, and *in* the rocks. ⁷Among the bushes they brayed; under the nettles they were gathered together. ⁸*They were* children of fools, yea, children of base men: they were viler than the earth. ⁹And now am I their song, yea, I am their byword. ¹⁰They abhor me, they flee far from me, and spare not to spit in my face. ¹¹Because he hath loosed my

Devotional Moment

Wisdom

30:1-15 Job mocked his accusers for lacking the wisdom he had gained from his years. As a rule, older people have the luxury of hindsight. But God's wisdom is higher than all, as Job would soon learn (38:2). We must remember not to boast of our wisdom or to mock those who are younger for being more foolish than we. No matter how old or wise you are, don't brag about how you compare to others. Let your wisdom speak for itself in actions and wise counsel.

cord, and afflicted me, they have also let loose the bridle before me. ¹²Upon *my* right *hand* rise the youth; they push away my feet, and they raise up against me the ways of their destruction. ¹³They mar my path, they set forward my calamity, they have no helper.

ᵇ solitary: or, dark as the night
ᶜ caves: Heb. holes

¹⁴They came *upon me* as a wide breaking in *of waters*: in the desolation they rolled themselves *upon me*.

¹⁵Terrors are turned upon me: they pursue my soul[d] as the wind: and my welfare passeth away as a cloud. ¹⁶And now my soul is poured out upon me; the days of affliction have taken hold upon me. ¹⁷My bones are pierced in me in the night season: and my sinews take no rest. ¹⁸By the great force *of my disease* is my garment changed: it bindeth me about as the collar of my coat. ¹⁹He hath cast me into the mire, and I am become like dust and ashes. ²⁰I cry unto thee, and thou dost not hear me: I stand up, and thou regardest me *not*. ²¹Thou art become[e] cruel to me: with thy strong hand thou opposest thyself against me. ²²Thou liftest me up to the wind; thou causest me to ride *upon it*, and dissolvest my substance[f]. ²³For I know *that* thou wilt bring me *to* death, and *to* the house appointed for all living. ²⁴Howbeit he will not stretch out *his* hand to the grave[g], though they cry in his destruction. ²⁵Did not I weep for him that was in trouble[h]? was *not* my soul grieved for the poor? ²⁶When I looked for good, then evil came *unto me*: and when I waited for light, there came darkness. ²⁷My bowels boiled, and rested not: the days of affliction prevented me. ²⁸I went mourning without the sun: I stood up, *and* I cried in the congregation. ²⁹I am a brother to dragons, and a companion to owls[i]. ³⁰My skin is black upon me, and my bones are burned with heat. ³¹My harp also is *turned* to mourning, and my organ into the voice of them that weep.

31

¹I made a covenant with mine eyes; why then should I think upon a maid? ²For what portion of God *is there* from above? and *what* inheritance of the Almighty from on high? ³*Is* not destruction to the wicked? and a strange *punishment* to the workers of iniquity? ⁴Doth not he see my ways, and count all my steps? ⁵If I have walked with vanity, or if my foot hath hasted to deceit; ⁶Let me be weighed in an even balance, that God may know mine integrity. ⁷If my step hath turned out of the way, and mine heart walked after mine eyes, and if any blot hath cleaved to mine hands; ⁸*Then* let me sow, and let another eat; yea, let my offspring be rooted out.

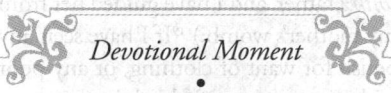

Devotional Moment

•

Adultery

31:1, 9-12 Job made a conscious decision to avoid looking lustfully at women. He knew what we too easily forget: Immorality does not start with sex; it starts with lust. Staying pure in singleness and faithful in marriage means keeping control over what you look at. Out of loyalty to your Lord and your spouse, keep a tight rein on your eyes. And "rejoice with the wife [or husband] of thy youth" (Prov. 5:18).

---

[d] my soul: Heb. my principal one
[e] become . . . : Heb. turned to be cruel
[f] substance: or, wisdom
[g] grave: Heb. heap
[h] in trouble: Heb. hard of day?
[i] owls: or, ostriches

⁹If mine heart have been deceived by a woman, or *if* I have laid wait at my neighbour's door; ¹⁰*Then* let my wife grind unto another, and let others bow down upon her. ¹¹For this *is* an heinous crime; yea, it *is* an iniquity *to be punished by* the judges. ¹²For it *is* a fire *that* consumeth to destruction, and would root out all mine increase. ¹³If I did despise the cause of my manservant or of my maidservant, when they contended with me; ¹⁴What then shall I do when God riseth up? and when he visiteth, what shall I answer him? ¹⁵Did not he that made me in the womb make him? and did not one[a] fashion us in the womb?

¹⁶If I have withheld the poor from *their* desire, or have caused the eyes of the widow to fail; ¹⁷Or have eaten my morsel myself alone, and the fatherless hath not eaten thereof; ¹⁸(For from my youth he was brought up with me, as *with* a father, and I have guided her from my mother's womb;) ¹⁹If I have seen any perish for want of clothing, or any poor without covering; ²⁰If his loins have not blessed me, and *if* he were *not* warmed with the fleece of my sheep; ²¹If I have lifted up my hand against the fatherless, when I saw my help in the gate: ²²*Then* let mine arm fall from my shoulder blade, and mine arm be broken from the bone[b]. ²³For destruction *from* God *was* a terror to me, and by reason of his highness I could not endure.

²⁴If I have made gold my hope, or have said to the fine gold, *Thou art* my confidence; ²⁵If I rejoiced because my wealth *was* great, and because mine hand had gotten[c] much; ²⁶If I beheld the sun[d] when it shined, or the moon walking *in* brightness; ²⁷And my heart hath been secretly enticed, or my mouth[e] hath kissed my hand: ²⁸This also *were* an iniquity *to be punished by* the judge: for I should have denied the God *that is* above. ²⁹If I rejoiced at the destruction of him that hated me, or lifted up myself when evil found him: ³⁰Neither have I suffered my mouth[f] to sin by wishing a curse to his soul. ³¹If the men of my tabernacle said not, Oh that we had of his flesh! we cannot be satisfied. ³²The stranger did not lodge in the street: *but* I opened my doors to the traveller[g].

³³If I covered my transgressions as Adam[h], by hiding mine iniquity in my bosom: ³⁴Did I fear a great multitude, or did the contempt of families terrify me, that I kept silence, *and* went not out of the door? ³⁵Oh that one would hear me! behold, my desire *is, that* the Almighty would answer me, and *that* mine adversary had written a book. ³⁶Surely I would take it upon my shoulder, *and* bind it *as* a crown to me. ³⁷I would declare unto him the number of my steps; as a prince

---

[a] did not one . . . : or, did he not fashion us in one womb?
[b] bone: or, chanelbone
[c] gotten . . . : Heb. found much
[d] sun: Heb. light
[e] my mouth . . . : Heb. my hand hath kissed my mouth
[f] mouth: Heb. palate
[g] traveller: or, way
[h] as Adam: or, after the manner of men

would I go near unto him. ³⁸If my land cry against me, or that the furrows likewise thereof complainⁱ; ³⁹If I have eaten the fruitsʲ thereof without money, or have caused the owners thereof to lose their life: ⁴⁰Let thistles grow instead of wheat, and cockleᵏ instead of barley. The words of Job are ended.

32

¹So these three men ceased to answer Job, because he *was* righteous in his own eyes. ²Then was kindled the wrath of Elihu the son of Barachel the Buzite, of the kindred of Ram: against Job was his wrath kindled, because he justified himselfᵃ rather than God. ³Also against his three friends was his wrath kindled, because they had found no answer, and *yet* had condemned Job. ⁴Now Elihu had waitedᵇ till Job had spoken, because they *were* elder than he. ⁵When Elihu saw that *there was* no answer in the mouth of *these* three men, then his wrath was kindled.

⁶And Elihu the son of Barachel the Buzite answered and said, I *am* youngᶜ, and ye *are* very old; wherefore I was afraid, and durst not shew you mine opinion. ⁷I said, Days should speak, and multitude of years should teach wisdom. ⁸But *there is* a spirit in man: and the inspiration of the Almighty giveth them understanding. ⁹Great men are not *al-*

ways wise: neither do the aged understand judgment. ¹⁰Therefore I said, Hearken to me; I also will shew mine opinion. ¹¹Behold, I waited for your words; I gave ear to your reasonsᵈ, whilst ye searched out what to say. ¹²Yea, I attended unto you, and, behold, *there was* none of you that convinced Job, *or* that answered his words: ¹³Lest ye should say, We have found out wisdom: God thrusteth him down, not man. ¹⁴Now he hath not directedᵉ *his* words against me: neither will I answer him with your speeches.

¹⁵They were amazed, they answered no more: they left off speaking. ¹⁶When I had waited, (for they spake not, but stood still, *and* answered no more;) ¹⁷*I said*, I will answer also my part, I also will shew mine opinion. ¹⁸For I am full of matterᶠ, the spirit within me constraineth me. ¹⁹Behold, my belly *is* as wine *which* hath no vent; it is ready to burst like new bottles. ²⁰I will speak, that I may be refreshed: I will open my lips and answer. ²¹Let me not, I pray you, accept any man's person, neither let me give flattering titles unto man. ²²For I know not to give flattering titles; *in so doing* my maker would soon take me away.

33

¹Wherefore, Job, I pray thee, hear my speeches, and hearken to all my words.

ⁱ complain: Heb. weep
ʲ fruits: Heb. strength
ᵏ cockle: or, noisome weeds
ᵃ himself: Heb. his soul
ᵇ waited . . . : Heb. expected Job in words
ᶜ young: Heb. few of days
ᵈ reasons: Heb. understandings
ᵉ directed: or, ordered
ᶠ matter: Heb. words

²Behold, now I have opened my mouth, my tongue hath spoken in my mouthᵃ. ³My words *shall be of* the uprightness of my heart: and my lips shall utter knowledge clearly. ⁴The Spirit of God hath made me, and the breath of the Almighty hath given me life. ⁵If thou canst answer me, set *thy words* in order before me, stand up. ⁶Behold, I *am* according to thy wishᵇ in God's stead: I also am formed out of the clay. ⁷Behold, my terror shall not make thee afraid, neither shall my hand be heavy upon thee.

⁸Surely thou hast spoken in mine hearingᶜ, and I have heard the voice of *thy* words, *saying,* ⁹I am clean without transgression, I *am* innocent; neither *is there* iniquity in me. ¹⁰Behold, he findeth occasions against me, he counteth me for his enemy, ¹¹He putteth my feet in the stocks, he marketh all my paths. ¹²Behold, *in* this thou art not just: I will answer thee, that God is greater than man. ¹³Why dost thou strive against him? for he giveth not account of any of his matters.

¹⁴For God speaketh once, yea twice, *yet man* perceiveth it not. ¹⁵In a dream, in a vision of the night, when deep sleep falleth upon men, in slumberings upon the bed; ¹⁶Then he openeth the ears of men, and sealeth their instruction, ¹⁷That he may withdraw man *from his* purposeᵈ, and hide pride from man. ¹⁸He keepeth back his soul from the pit, and his life from perishingᵉ by the sword.

¹⁹He is chastened also with pain upon his bed, and the multitude of his bones with strong *pain*. ²⁰So that his life abhorreth bread, and his soul daintyᶠ meat. ²¹His flesh is consumed away, that it cannot be seen; and his bones *that* were not seen stick out. ²²Yea, his soul draweth near unto the grave, and his life to the destroyers. ²³If there be a messenger with him, an interpreter, one among a thousand, to shew unto man his uprightness: ²⁴Then he is gracious unto him, and saith, Deliver him from going down to the pit: I have found a ransomᵍ. ²⁵His flesh shall be fresher than a child'sʰ: he shall return to the days of his youth: ²⁶He shall pray unto God, and he will be favourable unto him: and he shall see his face with joy: for he will render unto man his righteousness. ²⁷He looketh upon men, and *if any* say, I have sinned, and perverted *that which was* right, and it profited me not; ²⁸He will deliver his soul from going into the pit, and his life shall see the light.

²⁹Lo, all these *things* worketh God oftentimesⁱ with man, ³⁰To bring back his soul from the pit, to be enlightened

---

ᵃ in my mouth: Heb. in my palate
ᵇ wish: Heb. mouth
ᶜ hearing: Heb. ears
ᵈ purpose: Heb. work
ᵉ from perishing: Heb. from passing
ᶠ dainty . . . : Heb. meat of desire
ᵍ a ransom: or, an atonement
ʰ a child's: Heb. childhood
ⁱ oftentimes: Heb. twice and thrice

with the light of the living. [31]Mark well, O Job, hearken unto me: hold thy peace, and I will speak. [32]If thou hast any thing to say, answer me: speak, for I desire to justify thee. [33]If not, hearken unto me: hold thy peace, and I shall teach thee wisdom.

34

[1]Furthermore Elihu answered and said, [2]Hear my words, O ye wise *men*; and give ear unto me, ye that have knowledge. [3]For the ear trieth words, as the mouth[a] tasteth meat. [4]Let us choose to us judgment: let us know among ourselves what *is* good. [5]For Job hath said, I am righteous: and God hath taken away my judgment. [6]Should I lie against my right? my wound[b] *is* incurable without transgression. [7]What man *is* like Job, *who* drinketh up scorning like water? [8]Which goeth in company with the workers of iniquity, and walketh with wicked men. [9]For he hath said, It profiteth a man nothing that he should delight himself with God.

[10]Therefore hearken unto me, ye men[c] of understanding: far be it from God, *that he should do* wickedness; and *from* the Almighty, *that he should commit* iniquity. [11]For the work of a man shall he render unto him, and cause every man to find according to *his* ways. [12]Yea, surely God will not do wickedly, neither will the Almighty pervert judgment. [13]Who hath given him a charge over the earth? or who hath disposed the whole world? [14]If he set his heart upon man[d], *if* he gather unto himself his spirit and his breath; [15]All flesh shall perish together, and man shall turn again unto dust.

[16]If now *thou hast* understanding, hear this: hearken to the voice of my words. [17]Shall even he that hateth right govern[e]? and wilt thou condemn him that is most just? [18]*Is it fit* to say to a king, *Thou art* wicked? *and* to princes, *Ye are* ungodly? [19]*How much less to him* that accepteth not the persons of princes, nor regardeth the rich more than the poor? for they all *are* the work of his hands. [20]In a moment shall they die, and the people shall be troubled at midnight, and pass away: and the mighty[f] shall be taken away without

---

Devotional Moment

•

Perseverance

34:17-28 As Elihu pointed out, God is not the author of evil but good and can be trusted to hear the cries of the oppressed. Life is full of disappointment, and we need to teach our children how to persevere in faith during times of difficulty. They will learn this, not by hearing us explain the reason for every instance of suffering, or by our protecting them from every form of trouble, but by seeing *us* persevere with faith in God. When they see your confidence that God knows what he's doing, they will learn that doing what's right without any reward is its own reward.

---

[a] mouth: Heb. palate
[b] my wound: Heb. mine arrow
[c] men . . . : Heb. men of heart
[d] man: Heb. him
[e] govern: Heb. bind?
[f] the mighty . . . : Heb. they shall take away the mighty

hand. ²¹For his eyes *are* upon the ways of man, and he seeth all his goings. ²² *There is* no darkness, nor shadow of death, where the workers of iniquity may hide themselves. ²³For he will not lay upon man more *than right*; that he should enter⁸ into judgment with God. ²⁴He shall break in pieces mighty men without number^h, and set others in their stead. ²⁵Therefore he knoweth their works, and he overturneth *them* in the night, so that they are destroyed^i. ²⁶He striketh them as wicked men in the open^j sight of others; ²⁷Because they turned back from him^k, and would not consider any of his ways: ²⁸So that they cause the cry of the poor to come unto him, and he heareth the cry of the afflicted. ²⁹When he giveth quietness, who then can make trouble? and when he hideth *his* face, who then can behold him? whether *it be done* against a nation, or against a man only: ³⁰That the hypocrite reign not, lest the people be ensnared.

³¹Surely it is meet to be said unto God, I have borne *chastisement*, I will not offend *any more*. ³² *That which* I see not teach thou me: if I have done iniquity, I will do no more. ³³ *Should it be* according to thy mind? he will recompense it, whether thou refuse, or whether thou choose; and not I: therefore speak what thou knowest. ³⁴Let men of understanding tell me, and let a wise man hearken unto me. ³⁵Job hath spoken without knowledge, and his words *were* without wisdom. ³⁶My desire *is that* Job may be tried unto the end because of *his* answers for wicked men. ³⁷For he addeth rebellion unto his sin, he clappeth *his hands* among us, and multiplieth his words against God.

35

¹Elihu spake moreover, and said, ²Thinkest thou this to be right, *that* thou saidst, My righteousness *is* more than God's? ³For thou saidst, What advantage will it be unto thee? *and*, What profit shall I have, *if I be cleansed* from my sin? ⁴I will answer^a thee, and thy companions with thee. ⁵Look unto the heavens, and see; and behold the clouds *which* are higher than thou. ⁶If thou sinnest, what doest thou against him? or *if* thy transgressions be multiplied, what doest thou unto him? ⁷If thou be righteous, what givest thou him? or what receiveth he of thine hand? ⁸Thy wickedness *may hurt* a man as thou *art*; and thy righteousness *may profit* the son of man.

⁹By reason of the multitude of oppressions they make *the oppressed* to cry: they cry out by reason of the arm of the mighty. ¹⁰But none saith, Where *is* God my maker, who giveth songs in the night; ¹¹Who teacheth us more than the beasts of the earth, and maketh us wiser than the fowls of heaven? ¹²There they cry, but none giveth answer, because

---

⁸ enter: Heb. go
^h number: Heb. searching out
^i destroyed: Heb. crushed
^j open . . . : Heb. place of beholders
^k him: Heb. after him
^a answer . . . : Heb. return to thee words

of the pride of evil men. ¹³Surely God will not hear vanity, neither will the Almighty regard it.

¹⁴Although thou sayest thou shalt not see him, *yet* judgment *is* before him; therefore trust thou in him. ¹⁵But now, because *it is* not *so*, he hath visited in his anger; yet he knoweth *it* not in great extremity: ¹⁶Therefore doth Job open his mouth in vain; he multiplieth words without knowledge.

36

¹Elihu also proceeded, and said, ²Suffer me a little, and I will shew thee that *I have* yet to speak on God's behalf. ³I will fetch my knowledge from afar, and will ascribe righteousness to my Maker. ⁴For truly my words *shall* not *be* false: he that is perfect in knowledge *is* with thee.

⁵Behold, God *is* mighty, and despiseth not *any: he is* mighty in strength *and* wisdom[a]. ⁶He preserveth not the life of the wicked: but giveth right to the poor[b]. ⁷He withdraweth not his eyes from the righteous: but with kings *are* they on the throne; yea, he doth establish them for ever, and they are exalted. ⁸And if *they be* bound in fetters, *and* be holden in cords of affliction; ⁹Then he sheweth them their work, and their transgressions that they have exceeded. ¹⁰He openeth also their ear to discipline, and commandeth that they return from iniquity. ¹¹If they obey and serve *him*, they shall spend their days in prosperity, and their years in pleasures. ¹²But if they obey not, they shall perish[c] by the sword, and they shall die without knowledge. ¹³But the hypocrites in heart heap up wrath: they cry not when he bindeth them. ¹⁴They[d] die in youth, and their life *is* among the unclean.

¹⁵He delivereth the poor[e] in his affliction, and openeth their ears in oppression. ¹⁶Even so would he have removed thee out of the strait *into* a broad place, where *there is* no straitness; and that which should be set on thy table *should be* full of fatness. ¹⁷But thou hast fulfilled the judgment of the wicked: judgment and justice take hold *on thee*. ¹⁸Because *there is* wrath, *beware* lest he take thee away with *his* stroke: then a great ransom cannot deliver[f] thee. ¹⁹Will he esteem thy riches? *no*, not gold, nor all the forces of strength. ²⁰Desire not the night, when people are cut off in their place. ²¹Take heed, regard not iniquity: for this hast thou chosen rather than affliction. ²²Behold, God exalteth by his power: who teacheth like him? ²³Who hath enjoined him his way? or who can say, Thou hast wrought iniquity?

²⁴Remember that thou magnify his work, which men behold. ²⁵Every man may see it; man may behold *it* afar off. ²⁶Behold, God *is* great, and we know *him* not, neither can the number of his years be searched out. ²⁷For he maketh

---

[a] wisdom: Heb. heart
[b] poor: or, afflicted
[c] perish: Heb. pass away
[d] They . . . : Heb. Their soul dieth
[e] poor: or, afflicted
[f] deliver . . . : Heb. turn thee aside

small the drops of water: they pour down rain according to the vapour thereof: ²⁸Which the clouds do drop *and* distil upon man abundantly. ²⁹Also can *any* understand the spreadings of the clouds, *or* the noise of his tabernacle? ³⁰Behold, he spreadeth his light upon it, and covereth the bottomᵍ of the sea. ³¹For by them judgeth he the people; he giveth meat in abundance. ³²With clouds he covereth the light; and commandeth it *not to shine* by *the cloud* that cometh betwixt. ³³The noise thereof sheweth concerning it, the cattle also concerning the vapourʰ.

37

¹At this also my heart trembleth, and is moved out of his place. ²Hearᵃ attentively the noise of his voice, and the sound *that* goeth out of his mouth. ³He directeth it under the whole heaven, and his lightningᵇ unto the ends of the earth. ⁴After it a voice roareth: he thundereth with the voice of his excellency; and he will not stay them when his voice is heard. ⁵God thundereth marvellously with his voice; great things doeth he, which we cannot comprehend.

⁶For he saith to the snow, Be thou *on* the earth; likewise to the small rain, and to the great rain of his strength. ⁷He sealeth up the hand of every man; that all men may know his work. ⁸Then the beasts go into dens, and remain in their places. ⁹Out of the southᶜ cometh the whirlwind: and cold out of the north. ¹⁰By the breath of God frost is given: and the breadth of the waters is straitened. ¹¹Also by watering he wearieth the thick cloud: he scattereth his bright cloud: ¹²And it is turned round about by his counsels: that they may do whatsoever he commandeth them upon the face of the world in the earth. ¹³He causeth it to come, whether for correctionᵈ, or for his land, or for mercy.

¹⁴Hearken unto this, O Job: stand still, and consider the wondrous works of God. ¹⁵Dost thou know when God disposed them, and caused the light of his cloud to shine? ¹⁶Dost thou know the balancings of the clouds, the wondrous works of him which is perfect in knowledge? ¹⁷How thy garments *are* warm, when he quieteth the earth by the south *wind?* ¹⁸Hast thou with him spread out the sky, *which is* strong, *and* as a molten looking glass? ¹⁹Teach us what we shall say unto him; *for* we cannot order *our speech* by reason of darkness. ²⁰Shall it be told him that I speak? if a man speak, surely he shall be swallowed up.

²¹And now *men* see not the bright light which *is* in the clouds: but the wind passeth, and cleanseth them. ²²Fair weather cometh out of the north: with God *is* terrible majesty. ²³*Touching* the Almighty, we cannot find him out: *he is* excellent in power, and in judg-

---

ᵍ bottom: Heb. roots
ʰ the vapour: Heb. that which goeth up
ᵃ Hear . . . : Heb. Hear in hearing
ᵇ lightning: Heb. light
ᶜ south: Heb. chamber
ᵈ correction: Heb. a rod

ment, and in plenty of justice: he will not afflict. ²⁴Men do therefore fear him: he respecteth not any *that are* wise of heart.

38

¹Then the LORD answered Job out of the whirlwind, and said, ²Who *is* this that darkeneth counsel by words without knowledge? ³Gird up now thy loins like a man; for I will demand of thee, and answer^a thou me.

⁴Where wast thou when I laid the foundations of the earth? declare, if thou hast^b understanding. ⁵Who hath laid the measures thereof, if thou knowest? or who hath stretched the line upon it? ⁶Whereupon are the foundations^c thereof fastened? or who laid the corner stone thereof; ⁷When the morning stars sang together, and all the sons of God shouted for joy? ⁸Or *who* shut up the sea with doors, when it brake forth, *as if* it had issued out of the womb? ⁹When I made the cloud the garment thereof, and thick darkness a swaddlingband for it, ¹⁰And brake up for it my decreed *place*, and set bars and doors, ¹¹And said, Hitherto shalt thou come, but no further: and here shall thy proud waves be stayed?

¹²Hast thou commanded the morning since thy days; *and* caused the dayspring to know his place; ¹³That it might take hold of the ends^d of the earth, that the wicked might be shaken out of it? ¹⁴It is turned as clay *to* the seal;

Devotional Moment
•
God's Word
38:1ff. God's questions were rhetorical ones. Job had been complaining to God; Job was silenced when he realized what he was doing. Our natural tendency is to complain when something bad happens. Yet God knows all. He created us. He created you and your family, and he knows all about your circumstances. Your painful trouble with the kids, with your spouse, or with family finances are no mystery to him. It makes sense to turn to him for strength, for wisdom, and for guidance. Be content with what he allows. Each time you open the Bible, ask God what he is challenging you to do in your family. Then obey his will as far as you understand it.

and they stand as a garment. ¹⁵And from the wicked their light is withholden, and the high arm shall be broken. ¹⁶Hast thou entered into the springs of the sea? or hast thou walked in the search of the depth? ¹⁷Have the gates of death been opened unto thee? or hast thou seen the doors of the shadow of death? ¹⁸Hast thou perceived the breadth of the earth? declare if thou knowest it all. ¹⁹Where *is* the way *where* light dwelleth? and *as for* darkness, where *is* the place thereof, ²⁰That thou shouldest take it to the bound^e thereof, and that thou shouldest know the paths *to* the house thereof? ²¹Knowest thou *it*, because thou wast then born? or *because* the number of thy days *is* great? ²²Hast thou entered into the treasures of the snow? or hast thou seen the trea-

---

^a answer . . . : Heb. make me know
^b hast . . . : Heb. knowest understanding
^c foundations: Heb. sockets
^d ends: Heb. wings
^e to the bound: or, at, etc

sures of the hail, ²³Which I have reserved against the time of trouble, against the day of battle and war? ²⁴By what way is the light parted, *which* scattereth the east wind upon the earth?

²⁵Who hath divided a watercourse for the overflowing of waters, or a way for the lightning of thunder; ²⁶To cause it to rain on the earth, *where* no man *is; on* the wilderness, wherein *there is* no man; ²⁷To satisfy the desolate and waste *ground;* and to cause the bud of the tender herb to spring forth? ²⁸Hath the rain a father? or who hath begotten the drops of dew? ²⁹Out of whose womb came the ice? and the hoary frost of heaven, who hath gendered it? ³⁰The waters are hid as *with* a stone, and the face of the deep is frozen. ³¹Canst thou bind the sweet influences of Pleiades[f], or loose the bands of Orion? ³²Canst thou bring forth Mazzaroth[g] in his season? or canst thou guide Arcturus with his sons? ³³Knowest thou the ordinances of heaven? canst thou set the dominion thereof in the earth? ³⁴Canst thou lift up thy voice to the clouds, that abundance of waters may cover thee? ³⁵Canst thou send lightnings, that they may go, and say unto thee, Here we *are?* ³⁶Who hath put wisdom in the inward parts? or who hath given understanding to the heart? ³⁷Who can number the clouds in wisdom? or who can stay[h] the bottles of heaven, ³⁸When the dust groweth[i] into

hardness, and the clods cleave fast together? ³⁹Wilt thou hunt the prey for the lion? or fill the appetite[j] of the young lions, ⁴⁰When they couch in *their* dens, *and* abide in the covert to lie in wait? ⁴¹Who provideth for the raven his food? when his young ones cry unto God, they wander for lack of meat.

39

¹Knowest thou the time when the wild goats of the rock bring forth? *or* canst thou mark when the hinds do calve? ²Canst thou number the months *that* they fulfil? or knowest thou the time when they bring forth? ³They bow themselves, they bring forth their young ones, they cast out their sorrows. ⁴Their young ones are in good liking, they grow up with corn; they go forth, and return not unto them. ⁵Who hath sent out the wild ass free? or who hath loosed the bands of the wild ass? ⁶Whose house I have made the wilderness, and the barren[a] land his dwellings. ⁷He scorneth the multitude of the city, neither regardeth he the crying of the driver[b]. ⁸The range of the mountains *is* his pasture, and he searcheth after every green thing. ⁹Will the unicorn be willing to serve thee, or abide by thy crib? ¹⁰Canst thou bind the unicorn with his band in the furrow? or will he harrow the valleys after thee? ¹¹Wilt thou trust him, because his strength *is* great? or

---

[f] Pleiades: or, the seven stars: Heb. Cimah
[g] Mazzaroth: or, the twelve signs
[h] stay: Heb. cause to lie down
[i] groweth . . . : or, is turned into mire: Heb. is poured
[j] the appetite: Heb. the life
[a] barren . . . : Heb. salt places
[b] of the driver: Heb. of the exactor

wilt thou leave thy labour to him? ¹²Wilt thou believe him, that he will bring home thy seed, and gather *it into* thy barn?

¹³*Gavest thou* the goodly wings unto the peacocks? or wings and feathers unto the ostrich? ¹⁴Which leaveth her eggs in the earth, and warmeth them in dust, ¹⁵And forgetteth that the foot may crush them, or that the wild beast may break them. ¹⁶She is hardened against her young ones, as though *they were* not hers: her labour is in vain without fear; ¹⁷Because God hath deprived her of wisdom, neither hath he imparted to her understanding. ¹⁸What time she lifteth up herself on high, she scorneth the horse and his rider.

¹⁹Hast thou given the horse strength? hast thou clothed his neck with thunder? ²⁰Canst thou make him afraid as a grasshopper? the glory of his nostrils *is* terrible[c]. ²¹He paweth[d] in the valley, and rejoiceth in *his* strength: he goeth on to meet the armed men. ²²He mocketh at fear, and is not affrighted; neither turneth he back from the sword. ²³The quiver rattleth against him, the glittering spear and the shield. ²⁴He swalloweth the ground with fierceness and rage: neither believeth he that *it is* the sound of the trumpet. ²⁵He saith among the trumpets, Ha, ha; and he smelleth the battle afar off, the thunder of the captains, and the shouting.

²⁶Doth the hawk fly by thy wisdom, *and* stretch her wings toward the south? ²⁷Doth the eagle mount up at thy command, and make her nest on high? ²⁸She dwelleth and abideth on the rock, upon the crag of the rock, and the strong place. ²⁹From thence she seeketh the prey, *and* her eyes behold afar off. ³⁰Her young ones also suck up blood: and where the slain *are*, there *is* she.

40

¹Moreover the LORD answered Job, and said, ²Shall he that contendeth with the Almighty instruct *him*? he that reproveth God, let him answer it. ³Then Job answered the LORD, and said, ⁴Behold, I am vile; what shall I answer thee? I will lay mine hand upon my mouth. ⁵Once have I spoken; but I will not answer: yea, twice; but I will proceed no further.

⁶Then answered the LORD unto Job out of the whirlwind, and said, ⁷Gird up thy loins now like a man: I will demand of thee, and declare thou unto me. ⁸Wilt thou also disannul my judgment? wilt thou condemn me, that thou mayest be righteous? ⁹Hast thou an arm like God? or canst thou thunder with a voice like him? ¹⁰Deck thyself now *with* majesty and excellency; and array thyself with glory and beauty. ¹¹Cast abroad the rage of thy wrath: and behold every one *that is* proud, and abase him. ¹²Look on every one *that is* proud, *and* bring him low; and tread down the wicked in their place. ¹³Hide them in the dust together; *and* bind their faces in secret. ¹⁴Then will I also confess unto thee that thine own right hand can save thee.

¹⁵Behold now behemoth[a], which I

---

[c] terrible: Heb. terror
[d] He paweth: or, His feet dig
[a] behemoth: an extinct animal of some kind

made with thee; he eateth grass as an ox. [16]Lo now, his strength *is* in his loins, and his force *is* in the navel of his belly. [17]He moveth his tail like a cedar: the sinews of his stones are wrapped together. [18]His bones *are as* strong pieces of brass; his bones *are* like bars of iron. [19]He *is* the chief of the ways of God: he that made him can make his sword to approach *unto him.* [20]Surely the mountains bring him forth food, where all the beasts of the field play. [21]He lieth under the shady trees, in the covert of the reed, and fens. [22]The shady trees cover him *with* their shadow; the willows of the brook compass him about. [23]Behold, he drinketh up a river, *and* hasteth not: he trusteth that he can draw up Jordan into his mouth. [24]He taketh it with his eyes: *his* nose pierceth through snares.

41

[1]Canst thou draw out leviathan[a] with an hook? or his tongue with a cord *which* thou lettest down? [2]Canst thou put an hook into his nose? or bore his jaw through with a thorn? [3]Will he make many supplications unto thee? will he speak soft *words* unto thee? [4]Will he make a covenant with thee? wilt thou take him for a servant for ever? [5]Wilt thou play with him as *with* a bird? or wilt thou bind him for thy maidens? [6]Shall the companions make a banquet of him? shall they part him among the merchants? [7]Canst thou fill his skin with barbed irons? or his head with fish spears? [8]Lay thine hand upon him, re-member the battle, do no more. [9]Behold, the hope of him is in vain: shall not *one* be cast down even at the sight of him? [10]None *is so* fierce that dare stir him up: who then is able to stand before me? [11]Who hath prevented me, that I should repay *him? whatsoever is* under the whole heaven is mine. [12]I will not conceal his parts, nor his power, nor his comely proportion. [13]Who can discover the face of his garment? *or* who can come *to him* with his double bridle? [14]Who can open the doors of his face? his teeth *are* terrible round about. [15]*His* scales[b] *are his* pride, shut up together *as* with a close seal. [16]One is so near to another, that no air can come between them. [17]They are joined one to another, they stick together, that they cannot be sundered. [18]By his neesings a light doth shine, and his eyes *are* like the eyelids of the morning. [19]Out of his mouth go burning lamps, *and* sparks of fire leap out. [20]Out of his nostrils goeth smoke, as *out* of a seething pot or caldron. [21]His breath kindleth coals, and a flame goeth out of his mouth. [22]In his neck re-maineth strength, and sorrow is turned into joy[c] before him. [23]The flakes[d] of his flesh are joined together: they are firm in themselves; they cannot be moved. [24]His heart is as firm as a stone; yea, as hard as a piece of the nether *millstone.* [25]When he raiseth up himself, the mighty are afraid: by reason of break-ings they purify themselves. [26]The sword of him that layeth at him cannot hold: the spear, the dart, nor the haber-

---

[a] leviathan: an extinct animal of some kind
[b] scales: Heb. strong pieces of shields
[c] is turned into joy: Heb. rejoiceth
[d] flakes: Heb. fallings

geon[e]. [27]He esteemeth iron as straw, *and* brass as rotten wood. [28]The arrow cannot make him flee: slingstones are turned with him into stubble. [29]Darts are counted as stubble: he laugheth at the shaking of a spear. [30]Sharp stones[f] *are* under him: he spreadeth sharp pointed things upon the mire. [31]He maketh the deep to boil like a pot: he maketh the sea like a pot of ointment. [32]He maketh a path to shine after him; *one* would think the deep *to be* hoary. [33]Upon earth there is not his like, who is made without fear[g]. [34]He beholdeth all high *things*: he *is* a king over all the children of pride.

42

[1]Then Job answered the LORD, and said, [2]I know that thou canst do every *thing*, and *that* no thought can be withholden from thee. [3]Who *is* he that hideth counsel without knowledge? therefore have I uttered that I understood not; things too wonderful for me, which I knew not. [4]Hear, I beseech thee, and I will speak: I will demand of thee, and declare thou unto me. [5]I have heard of thee by the hearing of the ear: but now mine eye seeth thee. [6]Wherefore I abhor *myself*, and repent in dust and ashes.

[7]And it was *so*, that after the LORD had spoken these words unto Job, the LORD said to Eliphaz the Temanite, My wrath is kindled against thee, and against thy two friends: for ye have not spoken of me *the thing that is* right, as my servant Job *hath*. [8]Therefore take unto you now seven bullocks and seven rams, and go to my servant Job, and offer up for yourselves a burnt offering; and my servant Job shall pray for you: for him[a] will I accept: lest I deal with you *after your* folly, in that ye have not spoken of me *the thing which is* right, like my servant Job. [9]So Eliphaz the Temanite and Bildad the Shuhite *and* Zophar the Naamathite went, and did according as the LORD commanded them: the LORD also accepted Job[b].

[10]And the LORD turned the captivity of Job, when he prayed for his friends: also the LORD gave[c] Job twice as much as he had before. [11]Then came there unto him all his brethren, and all his sisters, and all they that had been of

Devotional Moment

Healing

42:8-10 Because he had suffered, Job could easily have gloated over God's critique of his accusers. Instead, he prayed for them. Ultimately, one of our goals should be to pray for those who have hurt us. Hurts can come in a wide range of forms—from the smallest left-handed compliment to physical or sexual abuse. If you have painful memories that need healing, remember Job. You don't have to like those who hurt you or condone what they did, but as you forgive them and pray for them, God can heal you.

---

[e] habergeon: or, breastplate
[f] Sharp stones: Heb. Sharp pieces of potsherd
[g] is made without fear: or, behave themselves without fear
[a] him: Heb. his face, or, person
[b] Job: Heb. the face of Job
[c] gave . . . : Heb. added all that had been to Job unto the double

his acquaintance before, and did eat bread with him in his house: and they bemoaned him, and comforted him over all the evil that the LORD had brought upon him: every man also gave him a piece of money, and every one an earring of gold. ¹²So the LORD blessed the latter end of Job more than his beginning: for he had fourteen thousand sheep, and six thousand camels, and a thousand yoke of oxen, and a thousand she asses. ¹³He had also seven sons and three daughters. ¹⁴And he called the name of the first, Jemima; and the name of the second, Kezia; and the name of the third, Kerenhappuch. ¹⁵And in all the land were no women found *so* fair as the daughters of Job: and their father gave them inheritance among their brethren. ¹⁶After this lived Job an hundred and forty years, and saw his sons, and his sons' sons, *even* four generations. ¹⁷So Job died, *being* old and full of days.

When God Doesn't Make Sense

by Dr. James Dobson

The eleventh chapter of Hebrews bears relevance to believers who have gone through great sorrow and suffering. Described in that chapter are the men and women who persevered in hardship and danger for the sake of the Cross.

Some were tortured, imprisoned, flogged, stoned, sawed in two, and put to death by the sword. They were destitute, mistreated, persecuted, and inadequately clothed. They wandered in deserts, in mountains, in caves, and in holes in the ground. It is most important to understand that "all, having obtained a good report through faith, received not the promise." In other words, they held onto their faith to the point of death, even though God had not explained what he was doing (Heb. 11:35–40).

Without detracting from the sacredness of that Scripture, I would like to submit for your inspiration my own modern-day "Heroes' Hall of Fame." Listed among these giants of the faith are two incredible human beings who must hold a special place in the great heart of God.

During my fourteen years on the attending staff at Children's Hospital in Los Angeles, many of the kids I saw suffered from terminal illnesses. Others endured chronic disorders that disrupted and warped their childhoods.

Some of them were less than ten years of age, and yet their faith in Jesus Christ was unshakable. They died with a testimony on their lips, witnessing to the goodness of God while their little bodies withered away. What a reception they must have received when they met him who said, "Suffer the little children to come unto me" (Mark 10:14).

Bells Were Ringing In my first film series, *Focus on the Family,* I shared a story about a five-year-old African-American boy who will never be forgotten by those who knew him. A nurse with whom I worked, Gracie Schaeffler, took care of this lad during the latter days of his life. He was dying of lung cancer, which is a terrifying disease in its final stages. The lungs fill with fluid, and the patient is unable to breathe. It is terribly claustrophobic, especially for a small child.

This little boy had a Christian mother who loved him and stayed by his side through the long ordeal. She cradled him on her lap and talked softly about the Lord. Instinctively, the woman was preparing her son for the final hours to come. Gracie told me that she entered his room one day as death approached, and she heard this lad talking about hearing bells.

"The bells are ringing, Mommie," he said, "I can hear them."

Gracie thought he was hallucinating because he was already slipping away. She left and returned a few minutes later and again heard him talking about hearing bells ringing.

The nurse said to his mother, "I'm sure you know your baby is hearing things that aren't there. He is hallucinating because of the sickness."

The mother pulled her son closer to her chest, smiled, and said, "No, Miss Schaeffler. He is not hallucinating, I told him when he was frightened, when he couldn't breathe, if he would listen carefully, he could hear the bells of heaven ringing for him. That is what he's been talking about all day."

That precious child died on his mother's lap later that evening, and he was still talking about the bells of heaven when the angels came to take him. What a brave little trooper he was. His courage was not reported in the newspapers the next day. Neither Tom Brokaw

nor Dan Rather told his story on the evening news. Yet he and his mother belong forever in our "Heroes' Hall of Fame."

My next candidate for faithful immortality is a man I never met, although he touched my life while he was losing his. I learned about him from a television docudrama that I saw many years ago. The producer had obtained permission from a cancer specialist to place cameras in his clinic.

Then with approval from three patients, two men and a woman, he captured on film the moment each of them learned they were afflicted with a malignancy in its later stages. Their initial shock, disbelief, fear, and anger were recorded in graphic detail.

Afterwards, the documentary team followed these three families through the treatment process with its ups and downs, hopes and disappointments, pain and terror. I sat riveted as the drama of life and death unfolded on the screen. Eventually, all three patients died, and the program ended without comment or editorial.

There was so much that should have been said. What struck me were the different ways these people dealt with their frightening circumstances. The two who apparently had no faith reacted with anger and bitterness. They not only fought their disease, but they seemed to be at war with everyone else. Their personal relationships and even their marriages were shaken, especially as the end drew near.

I'm not being critical, mind you. Most of us would respond in much the same manner if faced with imminent death. But that's what made the third individual so inspiring to me.

He was a humble, black pastor of a small inner-city Baptist church. He was in his late sixties and had been a minister throughout his adult life. His love for the Lord was so profound that it was reflected in everything he said.

When he and his wife were told he had only a few months to live, they revealed no panic. They quietly asked the doctor what it all meant. When he had explained the treatment program and what they could anticipate, they politely thanked him for his concern and departed. The cameras followed this little couple to their old car and eavesdropped as they bowed their heads and recommitted themselves to the Lord.

In the months that followed, the pastor never lost his poise. Nor was he glib about his illness. He was not in denial. He simply had come to terms with the cancer and its probable outcome. He knew the Lord was in control, and he refused to be shaken in his faith.

The cameras were present on his final Sunday in his church. He preached the sermon that morning and talked openly about his impending death. To the best of my recollection, this is what he said:

"Some of you have asked me if I'm mad at God for this disease that has taken over my body. I'll tell you honestly that I have nothing but love in my heart for my Lord. He didn't do this to me. We live in a sinful world where sickness and death are the curse man has brought upon himself. And I'm going to a better place where there will be no more tears, no suffering, and no heartache. So don't feel bad for me.

"Besides," he continued, "our Lord suffered and died for our sins. Why should I not share in his suffering?" Then he began to sing, without accompaniment, in an old, broken voice:

> *Must Jesus bear the cross alone,*
> *And all the world go free?*
> *No, there's a cross for everyone,*
> *And there's a cross for me.*
>
> *How happy are the saints above,*
> *Who once went sorr'wing here;*

But now they taste unmingled love,
And joy without a tear.

The consecrated cross I'll bear,
Till death shall set me free,
And then go home, my crown to wear,
For there's a crown for me.

I wept as this gentle man sang of his love for Jesus. He sounded very weak, and his face was drawn from the ravages of the disease. But his comments were as powerful as any I've ever heard. His words that morning were his last from the pulpit, as far as I know. He slipped into eternity a few days later, where he met the Lord he had served for a lifetime. This unnamed pastor and his wife have a prominent place among my list of spiritual giants.

Pieces to Life's Puzzle. There are more heroes in my catalog than I could describe, but I will resist the inclination to name them. My concern at this point, however, is to help those who are not so well grounded in their beliefs. If everyone was gifted with the tenacity of a bulldog and the faith of Father Abraham, there would be no need for a discussion of this nature. But most of us are not spiritual superstars.

That's why these thoughts are addressed affectionately to individuals who have been wounded in spirit by experiences they could not understand. The pieces of life's puzzle simply have not fit together, leaving them confused, angry, and disillusioned.

Perhaps you are among those who have struggled to comprehend a particular heartache and God's reason for allowing it. A thousand unanswered questions have been recycling in your mind—most of them beginning with the word *why.*

You want desperately to trust the Father and believe in his grace and goodness. But deep inside, you're held captive by a sense of betrayal and abandonment. The Lord obviously permitted your difficulties to occur. Why didn't he prevent them—and why has he not attempted to explain or apologize for them? The inability to answer those fundamental questions has become a spiritual barrier a mile high, and you can't seem to find a way around or over it.

For some of my readers, your sorrow can be traced directly to the death of a precious son or daughter. Your pain from that loss has been so intense that you've wondered if you could even carry on. What a joy he (or she) was to your heart. He ran and jumped and giggled and hugged. You loved him far more than you valued your own life.

But then there was that horrible morning at the pool, or the ominous medical report, or the accident on the bicycle. Now your beloved child is gone, and God's purpose in his death has remained a mystery.

For someone else, there will never be anything as painful as the rejection you were dealt by an ex-husband or wife. The day you discovered the infidelity, or when the divorce papers arrived at the door, or that unforgettable night of violence—those were indescribable moments of heartache.

In some ways, it would have been easier to have buried the spouse than to see him or her in the arms of another. How could that person to whom you gave everything be so cruel? Many tears were shed as God was begged to intervene. When the marriage continued to fail, disillusionment and bitterness rolled over you like a tidal wave. You've said you would never trust anyone again—not even the Almighty.

I'm thinking also of widows and widowers trying to survive on their own. If you're one of them, you know what very few of your friends fully comprehend. They want you to get over this loss and return to the business of living. But you just can't do it. For so many years, your

marriage was the centerpiece of your existence. Two separate human beings truly became "one flesh" as God intended. It was such a sweet love affair that could have gone on forever.

In fact, when you were young, you honestly thought it would. But suddenly, it was over. And now for the first time in many years, you're truly alone. Is this what it all comes down to?

To those whom I have been describing—those who have struggled to understand God's providence—I bring hope to you today. No, I can't provide tidy little solutions to all of life's annoying inconsistencies. That will not occur until we see the Lord face-to-face.

But his heart is especially tender toward the downtrodden and the defeated. He knows your name, and he has seen every tear you have shed. He was there on each occasion when life took a wrong turn. And what appears to be divine disinterest or cruelty is a misunderstanding at best and a satanic lie at worst.

How do I know this to be true? Because the Scriptures emphatically tell us so. For starters, David wrote, "The Lord is nigh unto them that are of a broken heart; and saveth such as be of a contrite spirit" (Ps. 34:18). Isn't that a beautiful verse?

How encouraging to know that the very presence of the King, the Creator of all heaven and earth, hovers near those who are wounded and discouraged. If you could fully comprehend how deeply you are loved, you would never feel alone again.

David returned to that thought in Psalm 103:8: "The Lord is merciful and gracious, slow to anger, and plenteous in mercy."

Another favorite passage of mine is Romans 8:26, in which we're told that the Holy Spirit actually prays for you and me with such passion that human language is inadequate to describe it. That verse says, "Likewise the Spirit also helpeth our infirmities: for we know not what we should pray for as we ought: but the Spirit itself maketh intercession for us with groanings which cannot be uttered."

What comfort we should draw from that understanding! He is calling your name to the Father today, pleading your case, and describing your need. How wrong it is, therefore, to place the blame for your troubles on the best Friend mankind ever had! Regardless of other conclusions you draw, please believe this: He is not the source of your pain!

Explanations. If you were sitting before me at this moment, you might be inclined to ask, "Then how do you explain the tragedies and hardships that have come into my life? Why did God do this to me?" My reply is not profound. But I know it is right! God rarely chooses to answer those questions in this life!

That's what I've been trying to say. He will not parade his plans and purposes for our approval. We must never forget that he is God. As such, he wants us to believe and trust in him despite the things we don't understand. It's that straightforward.

Jehovah never did answer Job's intelligent inquiries, and he will not respond to all of yours. Every person who ever lived, I submit, has had to deal with seeming contradictions and enigmas. You will not be the exception.

If that explanation is unsatisfactory and you can't accept it, then you are destined to go through life with a weak, ineffectual faith—or no faith at all. You'll just have to construct your castles on some other foundation. That will be your greatest challenge, however—because there is no other foundation. It is written, "Except the Lord build the house, they labour in vain that build it" (Ps. 127:1).

My strongest advice is that each of us acknowledge *before* the crisis occurs, if possible, that our trust in him must be independent of our understanding. There's nothing wrong with trying to understand, but we must not lean on our ability to comprehend!

Sooner or later, our intellect will pose questions we cannot possibly answer. At that point, we would be wise to remember his words, "As the heavens are higher than the earth,

so are my ways higher than your ways, and my thoughts than your thoughts" (Isa. 55:9). And our reply should be, "Not my will, but thine, be done" (Luke 22:42).

For those who are hurting and discouraged, I think it would be comforting to look forward to the time when the present trials will be a distant memory. A day of celebration is coming like nothing that has ever occurred in the history of mankind.

The Guest of Honor on that morning will be one wearing a seamless robe, with eyes like flames of fire and feet like fine brass. As we bow humbly before him, a great voice will thunder from the heavens saying:

Behold, the tabernacle of God is with men, and he will dwell with them, and they shall be his people, and God himself shall be with them, and be their God. And God shall wipe away all tears from their eyes: and there shall be no more death, neither sorrow, nor crying, neither shall there be any more pain: for the former things are passed away. (Rev. 21:3-4)

And, again the mighty voice will echo through the corridors of time:

They shall hunger no more, neither thirst any more; neither shall the sun light on them, nor any heat. For the Lamb which is in the midst of the throne shall feed them, and shall lead them unto living fountains of waters: and God shall wipe away all tears from their eyes. (Rev. 7:16-17)

This is the hope of the ages that burns within my breast. It is the ultimate answer to those who suffer and struggle today. It is the only solace for those who have said good-bye to a loved one. Though the pain is indescribable now, we must never forget that our separation is temporary. We will be reunited forever on that glad resurrection morning. As the Scripture promises, our tears will be banished forever!

My father and mother will also be in the crowd on that day, standing expectantly beside my little grandmother, who prayed for me before I was born. They will be straining to catch a glimpse of our arrival, just like they did so many Christmas seasons when we flew into the Kansas City airport. Dad will have so much to tell me that he will be bursting with excitement. He'll want to take me to some distant planet he's discovered.

Your loved ones who died in Christ will also be in that great throng, singing and shouting the praises for the Redeemer. What a celebration it will be!

This is the reward for the faithful—for those who overcome their sense of betrayal in tough times and persevere to the end. This is the crown of righteousness prepared for those who have "fought a good fight [and] kept the faith" (2 Tim. 4:7).

Final Thoughts. Throughout our remaining days in this life therefore, let me urge you not to be discouraged by temporal cares. Accept the circumstances as they are presented to you. Expect periods of hardship to occur, and don't' be dismayed when they arrive. "Lean into the pain" when your time to suffer comes around, knowing that God will use the difficulty for his purposes—and, indeed, for your own good. The Lord is very near, and he has promised that your temptation will not be greater than you can bear (1 Cor. 10:13).

I'll leave you with these wonderful words from Psalm 34:

The righteous cry, and the Lord heareth, and delivereth them out of all their troubles. The Lord is nigh unto them that are of a broken heart: and saveth such as be of a contrite spirit. Many are the afflictions of the righteous: but the Lord delivereth him out of them all. (vv. 17-19)

Adapted from *When God Doesn't Make Sense* (Tyndale House, 1993).

PSALMS

PSALMS

Purpose
To provide poetry for the expression of praise, worship, and confession to God

Authors
David wrote 73 psalms; Asaph wrote 12; the sons of Korah wrote 9; Solomon wrote 2; Heman (with the sons of Korah), Ethan, and Moses each wrote one; and 51 psalms are anonymous. The New Testament ascribes two of the anonymous psalms (2 and 95) to David (see Acts 4:25; Heb. 4:7).

Date Written
Between the time of Moses (around 1440 B.C.) and the Babylonian captivity (586 B.C.)

Setting
For the most part, the Psalms were not intended to be narrations of historical events. However, they often parallel events in history, such as David's flight from Saul and his sin with Bathsheba.

Key Verse
"Let every thing that hath breath praise the Lord. Praise ye the Lord" (150:6).

Key Person
David

Key Place
God's holy Temple

How can a person be like a tree? or a bird? or a sheep? or a dog? How are nations like pottery? How is God like a mother?

The Psalms are full of these pictures. Living can be like walking through a valley or climbing a mountain. Happiness is like a good piece of bread.

Perhaps you'll discover that children understand the Psalms sometimes better than adults. A child's imagination can soar with these pictures and images. An adult who wants "only the facts" is frustrated here. Can stars speak? Does God have wings? As far as we know, these words are not literal descriptions but pictures of greater truths. Children are often ready to find them.

But there's every reason for adults to press ahead. If you've been too long on the treadmill of job, cleaning, cooking, and then facing the bills—take a break with the Psalms. Let God's presence come alive for you again, in the clouds, in the sunshine, and in a hundred other ways pictured for you in the Psalms.

Before you're through, even those nasty cleaning chores will be a symbol of God's mighty power running through your life.

856

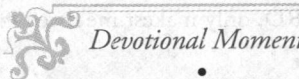

Devotional Moment
•
Friends

1:1 The book of Psalms begins with counsel on choosing friends. Friends can bring us into a deeper relationship with God, causing us to rely on him further and to gain perspective on life. Conversely, they can influence us to turn from God and to seek other sources for our answers. Choose close friends who revere God.

1

¹Blessed *is* the man that walketh not in the counsel of the ungodly[a], nor standeth in the way of sinners, nor sitteth in the seat of the scornful. ²But his delight *is* in the law of the LORD; and in his law doth he meditate day and night. ³And he shall be like a tree planted by the rivers of water, that bringeth forth his fruit in his season; his leaf also shall not wither[b]; and whatsoever he doeth shall prosper.

⁴The ungodly *are* not so: but *are* like the chaff which the wind driveth away. ⁵Therefore the ungodly shall not stand in the judgment, nor sinners in the congregation of the righteous. ⁶For the LORD knoweth the way of the righteous: but the way of the ungodly shall perish.

2

¹Why do the heathen rage[a], and the people imagine a vain thing? ²The kings of the earth set themselves, and the rulers take counsel together, against the LORD, and against his anointed, *saying*, ³Let us break their bands asunder, and cast away their cords from us. ⁴He that sitteth in the heavens shall laugh: the Lord shall have them in derision. ⁵Then shall he speak unto them in his wrath, and vex[b] them in his sore displeasure. ⁶Yet have I set[c] my king upon my holy hill of Zion.

⁷I will declare the decree[d]: the LORD hath said unto me, Thou *art* my Son; this day have I begotten thee. ⁸Ask of me, and I shall give *thee* the heathen *for* thine inheritance, and the uttermost parts of the earth *for* thy possession. ⁹Thou shalt break them with a rod of iron; thou shalt dash them in pieces like a potter's vessel.

¹⁰Be wise now therefore, O ye kings: be instructed, ye judges of the earth. ¹¹Serve the LORD with fear, and rejoice with trembling. ¹²Kiss the Son, lest he be angry, and ye perish *from* the way, when his wrath is kindled but a little. Blessed *are* all they that put their trust in him.

3

A Psalm of David, when he fled from Absalom his son.

¹LORD, how are they increased that trouble me! many *are* they that rise up against me. ²Many *there be* which say of my soul, *There is* no help for him

---

[a] ungodly: or, wicked
[b] wither: Heb. fade
[a] rage: or, tumultuously assemble
[b] vex: or, trouble
[c] set: Heb. anointed
[d] the decree: or, for a decree

in God. Selah. ³But thou, O LORD, *art* a shield for me; my glory, and the lifter up of mine head.

⁴I cried unto the LORD with my voice, and he heard me out of his holy hill. Selah. ⁵I laid me down and slept; I awaked; for the LORD sustained me. ⁶I will not be afraid of ten thousands of people, that have set *themselves* against me round about. ⁷Arise, O LORD; save me, O my God: for thou hast smitten all mine enemies *upon* the cheek bone; thou hast broken the teeth of the ungodly. ⁸Salvation *belongeth* unto the LORD: thy blessing *is* upon thy people. Selah.

4

To the chief Musician on Neginoth, A Psalm of David.

¹Hear me when I call, O God of my righteousness: thou hast enlarged me *when I was* in distress; have mercy upon me, and hear my prayer. ²O ye sons of men, how long *will ye turn* my glory into shame? *how long* will ye love vanity, *and* seek after leasing? Selah. ³But know that the LORD hath set apart him that is godly for himself: the LORD will hear when I call unto him. ⁴Stand in awe, and sin not: commune with your own heart upon your bed, and be still. Selah. ⁵Offer the sacrifices of righteousness, and put your trust in the LORD.

⁶*There be* many that say, Who will shew us *any* good? LORD, lift thou up the light of thy countenance upon us. ⁷Thou hast put gladness in my heart, more than in the time *that* their corn and their wine increased. ⁸I will both lay me down in peace, and sleep: for thou, LORD, only makest me dwell in safety.

5

To the chief Musician upon Nehiloth, A Psalm of David.

¹Give ear to my words, O LORD, consider my meditation. ²Hearken unto the voice of my cry, my King, and my God: for unto thee will I pray. ³My voice shalt thou hear in the morning, O LORD; in the morning will I direct *my prayer* unto thee, and will look up. ⁴For thou *art* not a God that hath pleasure in wickedness: neither shall evil dwell with thee. ⁵The foolish shall not stand in thy sight: thou hatest all workers of iniquity. ⁶Thou shalt destroy them that speak leasing: the LORD will abhor the bloodyª and deceitful man.

⁷But as for me, I will come *into* thy house in the multitude of thy mercy: *and* in thy fear will I worship toward thy holyᵇ temple. ⁸Lead me, O LORD, in thy righteousness because of mine

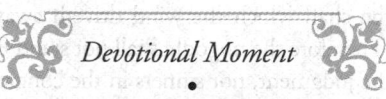

Devotional Moment

Tolerance

5:4 God made it clear through the psalmist that he cannot tolerate sin. It is one thing to show tolerance and mercy toward others; it is quite another to endorse wrong behavior. If you have teenagers, let them be unique individuals, but draw the line where obvious right and wrong are concerned. If you have toddlers or preschoolers, let them express their curiosity, let them explore their world; but don't let them get away with misbehavior. Show tolerance for *people*, not wrong behavior.

ª bloody . . . : Heb. man of bloods and deceit
ᵇ thy holy . . . : Heb. the temple of thy holiness

enemies; make thy way straight before my face. ⁹For *there is* no faithfulness^c in their mouth; their inward part *is* very wickedness; their throat *is* an open sepulchre; they flatter with their tongue. ¹⁰Destroy^d thou them, O God; let them fall by their own counsels; cast them out in the multitude of their transgressions; for they have rebelled against thee. ¹¹But let all those that put their trust in thee rejoice: let them ever shout for joy, because thou defendest^e them: let them also that love thy name be joyful in thee. ¹²For thou, LORD, wilt bless the righteous; with favour wilt thou compass^f him as *with* a shield.

6

To the chief Musician on Neginoth upon Sheminith^a, A Psalm of David.

¹O LORD, rebuke me not in thine anger, neither chasten me in thy hot displeasure. ²Have mercy upon me, O LORD; for I *am* weak: O LORD, heal me; for my bones are vexed. ³My soul is also sore vexed: but thou, O LORD, how long? ⁴Return, O LORD, deliver my soul: oh save me for thy mercies' sake. ⁵For in death *there is* no remembrance of thee: in the grave who shall give thee thanks? ⁶I am weary with my groaning; all the night make I my bed to swim; I water my couch with my tears. ⁷Mine eye is consumed because of grief; it waxeth old because of all mine enemies.

⁸Depart from me, all ye workers of iniquity; for the LORD hath heard the voice of my weeping. ⁹The LORD hath heard my supplication; the LORD will receive my prayer. ¹⁰Let all mine enemies be ashamed and sore vexed: let them return *and* be ashamed suddenly.

7

Shiggaion of David, which he sang unto the LORD, concerning the words^a of Cush the Benjamite.

¹O LORD my God, in thee do I put my trust: save me from all them that persecute me, and deliver me: ²Lest he tear my soul like a lion, rending *it* in pieces, while *there is* none to deliver. ³O LORD my God, if I have done this; if there be iniquity in my hands; ⁴If I have rewarded evil unto him that was at peace with me; (yea, I have delivered him that without cause is mine enemy:) ⁵Let the enemy persecute my soul, and take *it*; yea, let him tread down my life upon the earth, and lay mine honour in the dust. Selah. ⁶Arise, O LORD, in thine anger, lift up thyself because of the rage of mine enemies: and awake for me *to* the judgment *that* thou hast commanded. ⁷So shall the congregation of the people compass thee about: for their sakes therefore return thou on high. ⁸The LORD shall judge the people: judge me, O LORD, according to my righteousness, and according to mine integrity *that is* in me. ⁹Oh let the

---

^c faithfulness: or, stedfastness

^d Destroy . . . : or, Make them guilty

^e defendest . . . : Heb. coverest over, or, protectest them

^f compass: Heb. crown

^a Sheminith: or, the eighth

^a words: or, business

wickedness of the wicked come to an end; but establish the just: for the righteous God trieth the hearts and reins.

[10]My defence *is* of God, which saveth the upright in heart. [11]God judgeth[b] the righteous, and God is angry *with the wicked* every day. [12]If he turn not, he will whet his sword; he hath bent his bow, and made it ready. [13]He hath also prepared for him the instruments of death; he ordaineth his arrows against the persecutors. [14]Behold, he travaileth with iniquity, and hath conceived mischief, and brought forth falsehood. [15]He made a pit[c], and digged it, and is fallen into the ditch *which* he made. [16]His mischief shall return upon his own head, and his violent dealing shall come down upon his own pate. [17]I will praise the LORD according to his righteousness: and will sing praise to the name of the LORD most high.

8

To the chief Musician upon Gittith, A Psalm of David.

[1]O LORD our Lord, how excellent *is* thy name in all the earth! who hast set thy glory above the heavens. [2]Out of the mouth of babes and sucklings hast thou ordained[a] strength because of thine enemies, that thou mightest still the enemy and the avenger.

[3]When I consider thy heavens, the work of thy fingers, the moon and the stars, which thou hast ordained; [4]What is man, that thou art mindful of him? and the son of man, that thou visitest him?

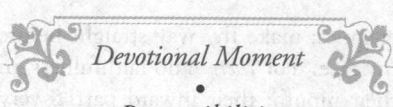

Devotional Moment

Responsibilities

8:6 The psalmist marveled that God had given people the responsibility to care for everything on earth. Our responsibilities at times cause us stress instead of giving us pause to marvel. We may feel inadequate to meet the requirements of being a spouse, parent, employee, homeowner, or friend. When was the last time you thanked God for your responsibilities? Instead of being overwhelmed by the care of people and possessions, give thanks to God for entrusting you with these gifts.

[5]For thou hast made him a little lower than the angels, and hast crowned him with glory and honour. [6]Thou madest him to have dominion over the works of thy hands; thou hast put all *things* under his feet: [7]All sheep and oxen, yea, and the beasts of the field; [8]The fowl of the air, and the fish of the sea, *and whatsoever* passeth through the paths of the seas. [9]O LORD our Lord, how excellent *is* thy name in all the earth!

9

To the chief Musician upon Muthlabben, A Psalm of David.

[1]I will praise *thee*, O LORD, with my whole heart; I will shew forth all thy marvellous works. [2]I will be glad and rejoice in thee: I will sing praise to thy name, O thou most High. [3]When mine enemies are turned back, they shall fall and perish at thy presence. [4]For thou hast maintained[a] my right and my

---

[b] judgeth . . . : or, is a righteous judge
[c] He made a pit: Heb. He hath digged a pit
[a] ordained: Heb. founded
[a] maintained . . . : Heb. made my judgment

cause; thou satest in the throne judging right. ⁵Thou hast rebuked the heathen, thou hast destroyed the wicked, thou hast put out their name for ever and ever. ⁶O thou enemy, destructions are come to a perpetual end: and thou hast destroyed cities; their memorial is perished with them. ⁷But the LORD shall endure for ever: he hath prepared his throne for judgment. ⁸And he shall judge the world in righteousness, he shall minister judgment to the people in uprightness. ⁹The LORD also will be a refugeᵇ for the oppressed, a refuge in times of trouble. ¹⁰And they that know thy name will put their trust in thee: for thou, LORD, hast not forsaken them that seek thee.

¹¹Sing praises to the LORD, which dwelleth in Zion: declare among the people his doings. ¹²When he maketh inquisition for blood, he remembereth

---

Devotional Moment

Needs

9:18 God promised that the needy and poor would not always be ignored. But we may feel forgotten as time passes and our afflictions remain. Over many years, discouragement and bitterness become our "default mode." Remember that God may or may not choose to meet our needs in this life, but he promises to heal us and bring us fulfillment in heaven (see Rev. 21:4). In your meditation time this week, close your eyes and picture God wiping away each of your tears.

---

them: he forgetteth not the cry of the humbleᶜ. ¹³Have mercy upon me, O LORD; consider my trouble *which I suffer* of them that hate me, thou that liftest me up from the gates of death: ¹⁴That I may shew forth all thy praise in the gates of the daughter of Zion: I will rejoice in thy salvation. ¹⁵The heathen are sunk down in the pit *that* they made: in the net which they hid is their own foot taken. ¹⁶The LORD is known *by* the judgment *which* he executeth: the wicked is snared in the work of his own hands. Higgaionᵈ, Selah. ¹⁷The wicked shall be turned into hell, *and* all the nations that forget God. ¹⁸For the needy shall not alway be forgotten: the expectation of the poor shall *not* perish for ever. ¹⁹Arise, O LORD; let not man prevail: let the heathen be judged in thy sight. ²⁰Put them in fear, O LORD: *that* the nations may know themselves *to be but* men. Selah.

10

¹Why standest thou afar off, O LORD? *why* hidest thou *thyself* in times of trouble? ²The wickedᵃ in *his* pride doth persecute the poor: let them be taken in the devices that they have imagined. ³For the wicked boasteth of his heart'sᵇ desire, and blesseth the covetous, *whom* the LORD abhorreth. ⁴The wicked, through the pride of his countenance, will not seek *after God*: God *is* not in all his thoughts. ⁵His ways are always grievous; thy judgments *are* far above

---

ᵇ a refuge: Heb. an high place
ᶜ humble: or, afflicted
ᵈ Higgaion: that is, Meditation
ᵃ The wicked . . . : Heb. In the pride of the wicked he doth persecute
ᵇ heart's: Heb. soul's

out of his sight: *as for* all his enemies, he puffeth at them. [6]He hath said in his heart, I shall not be moved: for *I shall never[c] be* in adversity. [7]His mouth is full of cursing and deceit[d] and fraud: under his tongue *is* mischief and vanity. [8]He sitteth in the lurking places of the villages: in the secret places doth he murder the innocent: his eyes are privily set against the poor. [9]He lieth in wait secretly[e] as a lion in his den: he lieth in wait to catch the poor: he doth catch the poor, when he draweth him into his net. [10]He croucheth, *and* humbleth himself, that the poor may fall by his strong ones. [11]He hath said in his heart, God hath forgotten: he hideth his face; he will never see *it.*

[12]Arise, O LORD; O God, lift up thine hand: forget not the humble[f]. [13]Wherefore doth the wicked contemn God? he hath said in his heart, Thou wilt not require *it.* [14]Thou hast seen *it*; for thou beholdest mischief and spite, to requite *it* with thy hand: the poor committeth[g] himself unto thee; thou art the helper of the fatherless. [15]Break thou the arm of the wicked and the evil *man*: seek out his wickedness *till* thou find none. [16]The LORD *is* King for ever and ever: the heathen are perished out of his land. [17]LORD, thou hast heard the desire of the humble: thou wilt prepare[h] their heart, thou wilt cause thine ear to hear: [18]To judge the fatherless and the oppressed, that the man of the earth may no more oppress[i].

11

To the chief Musician, *A Psalm* of David.

[1]In the LORD put I my trust: how say ye to my soul, Flee *as* a bird to your mountain? [2]For, lo, the wicked bend *their* bow, they make ready their arrow upon the string, that they may privily[a] shoot at the upright in heart. [3]If the foundations be destroyed, what can the righteous do?

[4]The LORD *is* in his holy temple, the LORD'S throne *is* in heaven: his eyes behold, his eyelids try, the children of men. [5]The LORD trieth the righteous: but the wicked and him that loveth violence his soul hateth. [6]Upon the wicked he shall rain snares, fire and brimstone, and an horrible[b] tempest: *this shall be* the portion of their cup. [7]For the righteous LORD loveth righteousness; his countenance doth behold the upright.

12

To the chief Musician upon Sheminith, A Psalm of David.

[1]Help, LORD; for the godly man

---

[c] never: Heb. unto generation and generation
[d] deceit: Heb. deceits
[e] secretly: Heb. in the secret places
[f] humble: or, afflicted
[g] committeth: Heb. leaveth
[h] prepare: or, establish
[i] oppress: or, terrify
[a] privily: Heb. in darkness
[b] an horrible . . . : or, a burning tempest

ceaseth; for the faithful fail from among the children of men. ²They speak vanity every one with his neighbour: *with* flattering lips *and* with a double[a] heart do they speak. ³The LORD shall cut off all flattering lips, *and* the tongue that speaketh proud[b] things: ⁴Who have said, With our tongue will we prevail; our lips *are* our own: who *is* lord over us? ⁵For the oppression of the poor, for the sighing of the needy, now will I arise, saith the LORD; I will set *him* in safety *from him that* puffeth[c] at him. ⁶The words of the LORD *are* pure words: *as* silver tried in a furnace of earth, purified seven times. ⁷Thou shalt keep them, O LORD, thou shalt preserve them from this generation for ever. ⁸The wicked walk on every side, when the vilest men[d] are exalted.

13

To the chief Musician, A Psalm of David.

¹How long wilt thou forget me, O LORD? for ever? how long wilt thou hide thy face from me? ²How long shall I take counsel in my soul, *having* sorrow in my heart daily? how long shall mine enemy be exalted over me? ³Consider *and* hear me, O LORD my God: lighten mine eyes, lest I sleep the *sleep of* death; ⁴Lest mine enemy say, I have prevailed against him; *and* those that trouble me rejoice when I am moved. ⁵But I have trusted in thy mercy; my heart shall rejoice in thy salvation. ⁶I

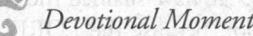

Devotional Moment
Feelings

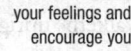

13:1, 5 The psalmist *felt* that God was far away, uncaring. Yet he still *believed* that God's love was unfailing. At times we too can feel that God remains far away, that perhaps he doesn't care or has forgotten about us. Maybe we've prayed for a child to be healed, for a new job, or for the return of a spouse, but God hasn't answered our prayers as we had hoped. Don't let your feelings override the truth—that God still loves you. In the next few days, call a trusted friend who understands your feelings and can also encourage your faith.

will sing unto the LORD, because he hath dealt bountifully with me.

14

To the chief Musician, *A Psalm* of David.

¹The fool hath said in his heart, *There is* no God. They are corrupt, they have done abominable works, *there is* none that doeth good. ²The LORD looked down from heaven upon the children of men, to see if there were any that did understand, *and* seek God. ³They are all gone aside, they are *all* together become filthy[a]: *there is* none that doeth good, no, not one.

⁴Have all the workers of iniquity no knowledge? who eat up my people *as* they eat bread, and call not upon the LORD. ⁵There were they in great fear: for God *is* in the generation of the

---

[a] a double . . . : Heb. an heart and an heart
[b] proud: Heb. great
[c] puffeth . . . : or, would ensnare him
[d] men: Heb. of the sons of the men
[a] filthy: Heb. stinking

righteous. ⁶Ye have shamed the counsel of the poor, because the LORD *is* his refuge. ⁷Oh that the salvation of Israel *were come* out of Zion! when the LORD bringeth back the captivity of his people, Jacob shall rejoice, *and* Israel shall be glad.

15

A Psalm of David.

¹LORD, who shall abideᵃ in thy tabernacle? who shall dwell in thy holy hill? ²He that walketh uprightly, and worketh righteousness, and speaketh the truth in his heart. ³*He that* backbiteth not with his tongue, nor doeth evil to his neighbour, nor taketh up a reproach against his neighbour. ⁴In whose eyes a vile person is contemned; but he honoureth them that fear the LORD. *He that* sweareth to *his own* hurt, and changeth not. ⁵*He that* putteth not out his money to usury, nor taketh reward against the innocent. He that doeth these *things* shall never be moved.

16

Michtam of David.

¹Preserve me, O God: for in thee do I put my trust. ²*O my soul,* thou hast said unto the LORD, Thou *art* my Lord: my goodness *extendeth* not to thee; ³*But* to the saints that *are* in the earth, and *to* the excellent, in whom *is* all my delight. ⁴Their sorrows shall be multiplied *that* hastenᵃ *after* another *god*: their drink offerings of blood will I not offer, nor take up their names into my lips. ⁵The LORD *is* the portion of mine inheritance and of my cup: thou maintainest my lot. ⁶The lines are fallen unto me in pleasant *places*; yea, I have a goodly heritage. ⁷I will bless the LORD, who hath given me counsel: my reins also instruct me in the night seasons.

⁸I have set the LORD always before me: because *he is* at my right hand, I shall not be moved. ⁹Therefore my heart is glad, and my glory rejoiceth: my flesh also shall restᵇ in hope. ¹⁰For thou wilt not leave my soul in hell; neither wilt thou suffer thine Holy One to see corruption. ¹¹Thou wilt shew me the path of life: in thy presence *is* fulness of joy; at thy right hand *there are* pleasures for evermore.

17

A Prayer of David.

¹Hear the rightᵃ, O LORD, attend unto my cry, give ear unto my prayer, *that goeth* not out of feigned lips. ²Let my sentence come forth from thy presence; let thine eyes behold the things that are equal. ³Thou hast proved mine heart; thou hast visited *me* in the night; thou hast tried me, *and* shalt find nothing; I am purposed *that* my mouth shall not transgress. ⁴Concerning the works of men, by the word of thy lips I have kept *me from* the paths of the destroyer. ⁵Hold up my goings in thy paths, *that* my footsteps slipᵇ not. ⁶I have called

---

ᵃ abide: Heb. sojourn
ᵃ hasten . . . : or, give gifts to another
ᵇ rest . . . : Heb. dwell confidently
ᵃ the right: Heb. justice
ᵇ slip . . . : Heb. be not moved

upon thee, for thou wilt hear me, O God: incline thine ear unto me, *and hear* my speech. [7]Shew thy marvellous lovingkindness, O thou that savest by thy right hand them which put their trust *in thee* from those that rise up *against them.*

[8]Keep me as the apple of the eye, hide me under the shadow of thy wings, [9]From the wicked that oppress[c] me, *from* my deadly enemies, *who* compass me about. [10]They are inclosed in their own fat: with their mouth they speak proudly. [11]They have now compassed us in our steps: they have set their eyes bowing down to the earth; [12]Like[d] as a lion *that* is greedy of his prey, and as it were a young lion lurking in secret places. [13]Arise, O LORD, dis-

---

Devotional Moment

•

Is Enough Enough?

17:15 It is easy to compare our family's house, car, or clothes to those of our relatives or friends and come away feeling discontented. Satisfaction with God's presence is the cure. Do you and your spouse grumble to each other about what you don't have or what the neighbors do have? Look around and remind each other that God has given you what you need. Talk about budget and life-style choices and map out both long-term and short-term plans that respect the limits of your material resources.

---

appoint[e] him, cast him down: deliver my soul from the wicked, *which is* thy sword: [14]From men *which are* thy hand, O LORD, from men of the world, *which have* their portion in *this* life, and whose belly thou fillest with thy hid *treasure:* they are full of children, and leave the rest of their *substance* to their babes. [15]As for me, I will behold thy face in righteousness: I shall be satisfied, when I awake, with thy likeness.

18

To the chief Musician, *A Psalm* of David, the servant of the LORD, who spake unto the LORD the words of this song in the day *that* the LORD delivered him from the hand of all his enemies, and from the hand of Saul: And he said,

[1]I will love thee, O LORD, my strength. [2]The LORD *is* my rock, and my fortress, and my deliverer; my God, my strength[a], in whom I will trust; my buckler, and the horn of my salvation, *and* my high tower. [3]I will call upon the LORD, *who is worthy* to be praised: so shall I be saved from mine enemies. [4]The sorrows of death compassed me, and the floods of ungodly men[b] made me afraid. [5]The sorrows[c] of hell compassed me about: the snares of death prevented me. [6]In my distress I called upon the LORD, and cried unto my God: he heard my voice out of his tem-

---

[c] oppress: Heb. waste

[d] Like . . . : Heb. The likeness of him (that is, of every one of them) is as a lion that desireth to ravin

[e] disappoint . . . : Heb. prevent his face

[a] my strength: Heb. my rock

[b] ungodly men: Heb. Belial

[c] sorrows: or, cords

ple, and my cry came before him, *even* into his ears. ⁷Then the earth shook and trembled; the foundations also of the hills moved and were shaken, because he was wroth. ⁸There went up a smoke out of his nostrilsᵈ, and fire out of his mouth devoured: coals were kindled by it. ⁹He bowed the heavens also, and came down: and darkness *was* under his feet. ¹⁰And he rode upon a cherub, and did fly: yea, he did fly upon the wings of the wind. ¹¹He made darkness his secret place; his pavilion round about him *were* dark waters *and* thick clouds of the skies. ¹²At the brightness *that was* before him his thick clouds passed, hail *stones* and coals of fire. ¹³The LORD also thundered in the heavens, and the Highest gave his voice; hail *stones* and coals of fire. ¹⁴Yea, he sent out his arrows, and scattered them; and he shot out lightnings, and discomfited them. ¹⁵Then the channels of waters were seen, and the foundations of the world were discovered at thy rebuke, O LORD, at the blast of the breath of thy nostrils. ¹⁶He sent from above, he took me, he drew me out of manyᵉ waters. ¹⁷He delivered me from my strong enemy, and from them which hated me: for they were too strong for me. ¹⁸They prevented me in the day of my calamity: but the LORD was my stay. ¹⁹He brought me forth also into a large place; he delivered me, because he delighted in me.

²⁰The LORD rewarded me according to my righteousness; according to the

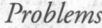

Devotional Moment

•

Problems

18:16, 18 When problems overwhelm us, we usually wish that God would simply rescue us. Sometimes he does that, and other times he throws us a life preserver. Family life can be a source of daily problems. Rather than letting these waters drown you, reach out for the help God offers—whether advice from Scripture or a magazine article, a timely phone call from a friend, or even the encouraging words of young children. Take encouragement from whatever help God offers. Don't concentrate on the waves.

cleanness of my hands hath he recompensed me. ²¹For I have kept the ways of the LORD, and have not wickedly departed from my God. ²²For all his judgments *were* before me, and I did not put away his statutes from me. ²³I was also upright before him, and I kept myself from mine iniquity. ²⁴Therefore hath the LORD recompensed me according to my righteousness, according to the cleanness of my hands in his eyesight. ²⁵With the merciful thou wilt shew thyself merciful; with an upright man thou wilt shew thyself upright; ²⁶With the pure thou wilt shew thyself pure; and with the froward thou wilt shew thyself frowardᶠ. ²⁷For thou wilt save the afflicted people; but wilt bring down high looks. ²⁸For thou wilt light my candleᵍ: the LORD my God will enlighten my darkness.

²⁹For by thee I have run through a troop; and by my God have I leaped over

---

ᵈ out of his nostrils: Heb. by his, etc

ᵉ many: or, great

ᶠ shew thyself froward: or, wrestle

ᵍ candle: or, lamp

a wall. ³⁰*As for* God, his way *is* perfect: the word of the LORD is tried[h]: he *is* a buckler to all those that trust in him. ³¹For who *is* God save the LORD? or who *is* a rock save our God? ³²*It is* God that girdeth me with strength, and maketh my way perfect. ³³He maketh my feet like hinds' *feet*, and setteth me upon my high places. ³⁴He teacheth my hands to war, so that a bow of steel is broken by mine arms. ³⁵Thou hast also given me the shield of thy salvation: and thy right hand hath holden me up, and thy gentleness[i] hath made me great. ³⁶Thou hast enlarged my steps under me, that my feet[j] did not slip. ³⁷I have pursued mine enemies, and overtaken them: neither did I turn again till they were consumed. ³⁸I have wounded them that they were not able to rise: they are fallen under my feet. ³⁹For thou hast girded me with strength

Devotional Moment

Challenges All Around

18:32-34 David could have viewed his problems, be they battles or dizzying heights, as overwhelming onslaughts. Instead he looked at what he faced as challenges and saw that God had equipped him for each one. In the next few days, listen to how you describe your difficulties. You will help yourself and others if you speak positively about the challenges you face, rather than bemoan the problems.

unto the battle: thou hast subdued[k] under me those that rose up against me. ⁴⁰Thou hast also given me the necks of mine enemies; that I might destroy them that hate me. ⁴¹They cried, but *there was* none to save *them: even* unto the LORD, but he answered them not. ⁴²Then did I beat them small as the dust before the wind: I did cast them out as the dirt in the streets. ⁴³Thou hast delivered me from the strivings of the people; *and* thou hast made me the head of the heathen: a people *whom* I have not known shall serve me. ⁴⁴As soon as they hear of me, they shall obey me: the strangers shall submit themselves unto me. ⁴⁵The strangers[l] shall fade away, and be afraid out of their close places. ⁴⁶The LORD liveth; and blessed *be* my rock; and let the God of my salvation be exalted. ⁴⁷*It is* God that avengeth[m] me, and subdueth the people under me. ⁴⁸He delivereth me from mine enemies: yea, thou liftest me up above those that rise up against me: thou hast delivered me from the violent[n] man. ⁴⁹Therefore will I give thanks unto thee, O LORD, among the heathen, and sing praises unto thy name. ⁵⁰Great deliverance giveth he to his king; and sheweth mercy to his anointed, to David, and to his seed for evermore.

19

To the chief Musician, A Psalm of David.

---

[h] tried: or, refined

[i] thy gentleness . . . : or, with thy meekness thou hast multiplied me

[j] my feet: Heb. mine ankles

[k] subdued: Heb. caused to bow

[l] strangers: Heb. sons of the stranger

[m] avengeth: Heb. giveth avengements for

[n] violent . . . : Heb. man of violence

¹The heavens declare the glory of God; and the firmament sheweth his handywork. ²Day unto day uttereth speech, and night unto night sheweth knowledge. ³*There is* no speech nor language, *where* their voice is not heard. ⁴Their line^a is gone out through all the earth, and their words to the end of the world. In them hath he set a tabernacle for the sun, ⁵Which *is* as a bridegroom coming out of his chamber, *and* rejoiceth as a strong man to run a race. ⁶His going forth *is* from the end of the heaven, and his circuit unto the ends of it: and there is nothing hid from the heat thereof.

⁷The law^b of the LORD *is* perfect, converting the soul: the testimony of the LORD *is* sure, making wise the simple. ⁸The statutes of the LORD *are* right, rejoicing the heart: the commandment of the LORD *is* pure, enlightening the eyes. ⁹The fear of the LORD *is* clean, enduring for ever: the judgments of the LORD *are* true^c *and* righteous altogether. ¹⁰More to be desired *are they* than gold, yea, than much fine gold: sweeter also than honey and the honeycomb^d. ¹¹Moreover by them is thy servant warned: *and* in keeping of them *there is* great reward. ¹²Who can understand *his* errors? cleanse thou me from secret *faults*. ¹³Keep back thy servant also from presumptuous *sins*; let them not have dominion over me: then shall I be upright, and I shall be innocent from the great^e transgression. ¹⁴Let the words of my mouth, and the meditation of my heart, be acceptable in thy sight, O LORD, my strength^f, and my redeemer.

20

To the chief Musician, A Psalm of David.

¹The LORD hear thee in the day of trouble; the name of the God of Jacob defend^a thee; ²Send thee help^b from the sanctuary, and strengthen thee out of Zion; ³Remember all thy offerings, and accept^c thy burnt sacrifice; Selah. ⁴Grant thee according to thine own heart, and fulfil all thy counsel. ⁵We will rejoice in thy salvation, and in the name of our God we will set up *our* banners: the LORD fulfil all thy petitions.

⁶Now know I that the LORD saveth his anointed; he will hear him from his holy^d heaven with the saving strength of his right hand. ⁷Some *trust* in chariots, and some in horses: but we will remember the name of the LORD our God. ⁸They are brought down and fallen: but we are risen, and stand upright. ⁹Save, LORD: let the king hear us when we call.

21

To the chief Musician, A Psalm of David.

---

^a line: or, rule, or, direction
^b law: or, doctrine
^c true: Heb. truth
^d the honeycomb: Heb. the dropping of honeycomb
^e the great: or, much
^f strength: Heb. rock
^a defend . . . : Heb. set thee on an high place
^b thee help: Heb. thy help
^c accept: Heb. turn to ashes: or, make fat
^d his holy . . . : Heb. the heaven of his holiness

¹The king shall joy in thy strength, O LORD; and in thy salvation how greatly shall he rejoice! ²Thou hast given him his heart's desire, and hast not withholden the request of his lips. Selah. ³For thou preventest him with the blessings of goodness: thou settest a crown of pure gold on his head. ⁴He asked life of thee, *and* thou gavest *it* him, *even* length of days for ever and ever. ⁵His glory *is* great in thy salvation: honour and majesty hast thou laid upon him. ⁶For thou hast made him most blessed for ever: thou hast made him exceeding glad with thy countenance.

⁷For the king trusteth in the LORD, and through the mercy of the most High he shall not be moved. ⁸Thine hand shall find out all thine enemies: thy right hand shall find out those that hate thee. ⁹Thou shalt make them as a fiery oven in the time of thine anger: the LORD shall swallow them up in his wrath, and the fire shall devour them. ¹⁰Their fruit shalt thou destroy from the earth, and their seed from among the children of men. ¹¹For they intended evil against thee: they imagined a mischievous device, *which* they are not able *to* perform. ¹²Therefore shalt thou make them turn their back, *when* thou shalt make ready *thine arrows* upon thy strings against the face of them. ¹³Be thou exalted, LORD, in thine own strength: *so* will we sing and praise thy power.

22

To the chief Musician upon Aijeleth[a] Shahar, A Psalm of David.

¹My God, my God, why hast thou forsaken me? *why art thou so* far from helping me, *and from* the words of my roaring? ²O my God, I cry in the daytime, but thou hearest not; and in the night season, and am not silent. ³But thou *art* holy, *O thou* that inhabitest the praises of Israel. ⁴Our fathers trusted in thee: they trusted, and thou didst deliver them. ⁵They cried unto thee, and were delivered: they trusted in thee, and were not confounded. ⁶But I *am* a worm, and no man; a reproach of men, and despised of the people. ⁷All they that see me laugh me to scorn: they shoot out the lip, they shake the head, *saying,* ⁸He trusted[b] on the LORD *that* he would deliver him: let him deliver him, seeing he delighted in him. ⁹But thou *art* he that took me out of the womb: thou didst make me hope *when I was* upon my mother's breasts. ¹⁰I was cast upon thee from the womb: thou *art* my God from my mother's belly.

¹¹Be not far from me; for trouble *is* near; for *there is* none to help. ¹²Many bulls have compassed me: strong *bulls* of Bashan have beset me round. ¹³They gaped[c] upon me *with* their mouths, *as* a ravening and a roaring lion. ¹⁴I am poured out like water, and all my bones are out of joint: my heart is like wax; it is melted in the midst of my bowels. ¹⁵My strength is dried up like a potsherd; and my tongue cleaveth to my jaws; and thou hast brought me into the dust of death. ¹⁶For dogs have compassed me: the assembly of the wicked have inclosed me: they pierced my hands and my feet.

---

[a] Aijeleth . . . : or, the hind of the morning
[b] He trusted . . . : Heb. He rolled himself on
[c] gaped . . . : Heb. opened their mouths against me

¹⁷I may tell all my bones: they look *and* stare upon me. ¹⁸They part my garments among them, and cast lots upon my vesture. ¹⁹But be not thou far from me, O LORD: O my strength, haste thee to help me. ²⁰Deliver my soul from the sword; my darling^d from the power of the dog. ²¹Save me from the lion's mouth: for thou hast heard me from the horns of the unicorns.

²²I will declare thy name unto my brethren: in the midst of the congregation will I praise thee. ²³Ye that fear the LORD, praise him; all ye the seed of Jacob, glorify him; and fear him, all ye the seed of Israel. ²⁴For he hath not despised nor abhorred the affliction of the afflicted; neither hath he hid his face from him; but when he cried unto him, he heard. ²⁵My praise *shall be* of thee in the great congregation: I will pay my vows before them that fear him. ²⁶The meek shall eat and be satisfied: they shall praise the LORD that seek him: your heart shall live for ever. ²⁷All the ends of the world shall remember and turn unto the LORD: and all the kindreds of the nations shall worship before thee. ²⁸For the kingdom *is* the LORD'S: and he *is* the governor among the nations. ²⁹All *they that be* fat upon earth shall eat and worship: all they that go down to the dust shall bow before him: and none can keep alive his own soul. ³⁰A seed shall serve him; it shall be accounted to the Lord for a generation. ³¹They shall come, and shall declare his righteousness unto a people that shall be born, that he hath done *this*.

23

A Psalm of David.

¹The LORD *is* my shepherd; I shall not want. ²He maketh me to lie down in green^a pastures: he leadeth me beside the still waters. ³He restoreth my soul: he leadeth me in the paths of righteousness for his name's sake. ⁴Yea, though I walk through the valley of the shadow of death, I will fear no evil: for thou *art* with me; thy rod and thy staff they comfort me. ⁵Thou preparest a table before me in the presence of mine enemies: thou anointest^b

---

Devotional Moment

Training Children

22:30-31 David was delighted because future generations would praise the Lord. That's the kind of joy parents can have when they make the effort to train their children in God's ways rather than leaving it to chance. Children have a natural love for God that can be channeled into listening to music, learning Bible stories, and appreciating your church's traditions. Take seriously your role as spiritual coach. Do not leave it all up to Sunday school teachers.

Devotional Moment

Contentment

23:1 David was a contented man because he had the Lord. Our material world, with advertising designed expressly to make us *discontented*, makes it very easy to forget this. We must consciously remember that God gives us everything we need. Contentment goes a long way toward harmony.

---

^d my darling: Heb. my only one
^a green . . . : Heb. pastures of tender grass
^b anointest: Heb. makest fat

my head with oil; my cup runneth over. [6]Surely goodness and mercy shall follow me all the days of my life: and I will dwell in the house of the LORD for ever[c].

24

A Psalm of David.

[1]The earth *is* the LORD'S, and the fulness thereof; the world, and they that dwell therein. [2]For he hath founded it upon the seas, and established it upon the floods.

[3]Who shall ascend into the hill of the LORD? or who shall stand in his holy place? [4]He that hath clean hands, and a pure heart; who hath not lifted up his soul unto vanity, nor sworn deceitfully. [5]He shall receive the blessing from the LORD, and righteousness from the God of his salvation. [6]This *is* the generation of them that seek him, that seek thy face, O Jacob[a]. Selah.

[7]Lift up your heads, O ye gates; and be ye lift up, ye everlasting doors; and the King of glory shall come in. [8]Who *is* this King of glory? The LORD strong and mighty, the LORD mighty in battle. [9]Lift up your heads, O ye gates; even lift *them* up, ye everlasting doors; and the King of glory shall come in. [10]Who is this King of glory? The LORD of hosts, he *is* the King of glory. Selah.

25

A Psalm of David.

[1]Unto thee, O LORD, do I lift up my soul. [2]O my God, I trust in thee: let me not be ashamed, let not mine enemies triumph over me. [3]Yea, let

---

[c] for ever: Heb. to length of days
[a] O Jacob: or, O God of Jacob

Worship
in Your Home

DEVOTIONS—QUALITY TIME VS. QUANTITY TIME

One thing have I desired . . . that I may dwell in the house of the Lord all the days of my life.
Psalm 27:4

Imagine that God said to you, "I have one minute for you today. But it will be *quality time*."

Frustrating? Of course. We expect God to listen for as long as we need to talk.

We need to give God the same priority. We simply cannot build a relationship with anyone, including God, in short bursts. An occasional minute here and there isn't enough. Just as we value quantity of time from God, we need to give him quantity.

But sixty minutes of nonquality time doesn't build a strong relationship either. Boring, pressured, or guilt-induced devotions will not create a closeness with God, no matter how long the torture lasts. Quite the opposite, in fact. Five minutes of person-to-person, heart-to-heart devotions will profit far more.

And what are quality-time devotions? Readings, prayers, and talks together that are personally meaningful to your children; time in which your children know that they are the most important people in the world—both to you and to God—right now. Quit while your children are hungry rather than feeding them until they're sick, even if your devotional time lasts only five minutes.

Quality time or quantity time—which is more important? Neither and both. Most families can achieve a good balance in ten to fifteen minutes each day. The right mix of quantity and quality is what makes family devotions a delight rather than a chore.

none that wait on thee be ashamed: let them be ashamed which transgress without cause. ⁴Shew me thy ways, O LORD; teach me thy paths. ⁵Lead me in thy truth, and teach me: for thou *art* the God of my salvation; on thee do I wait all the day. ⁶Remember, O LORD, thy tender mercies and thy lovingkindnesses; for they *have been* ever of old. ⁷Remember not the sins of my youth, nor my transgressions: according to thy mercy remember thou me for thy goodness' sake, O LORD.

⁸Good and upright *is* the LORD: therefore will he teach sinners in the way. ⁹The meek will he guide in judgment: and the meek will he teach his way. ¹⁰All the paths of the LORD *are* mercy and truth unto such as keep his covenant and his testimonies. ¹¹For thy name's sake, O LORD, pardon mine iniquity; for it *is* great. ¹²What man *is* he that feareth the LORD? him shall he teach in the way *that* he shall choose. ¹³His soul shall dwellᵃ at ease; and his seed shall inherit the earth. ¹⁴The secret of the LORD *is* with them that fear him; and he will shew them his covenant.

¹⁵Mine eyes *are* ever toward the LORD; for he shall pluckᵇ my feet out of the net. ¹⁶Turn thee unto me, and have mercy upon me; for I *am* desolate and afflicted. ¹⁷The troubles of my heart are enlarged: *O* bring thou me out of my distresses. ¹⁸Look upon mine affliction and my pain; and forgive all my sins. ¹⁹Consider mine enemies; for they are many; and they hate me with cruelᶜ hatred. ²⁰O keep my soul, and deliver me: let me not be ashamed; for I put my trust in thee. ²¹Let integrity and uprightness preserve me; for I wait on thee. ²²Redeem Israel, O God, out of all his troubles.

26

A Psalm of David.

¹Judge me, O LORD; for I have walked in mine integrity: I have trusted also in the LORD; *therefore* I shall not slide. ²Examine me, O LORD, and prove me; try my reins and my heart. ³For thy lovingkindness *is* before mine eyes: and I have walked in thy truth. ⁴I have not sat with vain persons, neither will I go in with dissemblers. ⁵I have hated the congregation of evil doers; and will not sit with the wicked.

⁶I will wash mine hands in innocency: so will I compass thine altar, O LORD: ⁷That I may publish with the voice of thanksgiving, and tell of all thy wondrous works. ⁸LORD, I have loved the habitation of thy house, and the place where thine honour dwelleth. ⁹Gatherᵃ not my soul with sinners, nor my life with bloody men: ¹⁰In whose hands *is* mischief, and their right hand is fullᵇ of bribes. ¹¹But as for me, I will walk in mine integrity: redeem me, and be merciful unto me. ¹²My foot standeth in an even place: in the congregations will I bless the LORD.

ᵃ dwell . . . : Heb. lodge in goodness
ᵇ pluck: Heb. bring forth
ᶜ cruel . . . : Heb. hatred of violence
ᵃ Gather . . . : or, Take not away
ᵇ full . . . : Heb. filled with

27

A Psalm of David.

¹The LORD *is* my light and my salvation; whom shall I fear? the LORD *is* the strength of my life; of whom shall I be afraid? ²When the wicked, *even* mine enemies and my foes, came[a] upon me to eat up my flesh, they stumbled and fell. ³Though an host should encamp against me, my heart shall not fear: though war should rise against me, in this *will* I *be* confident. ⁴One *thing* have I desired of the LORD, that will I seek after; that I may dwell in the house of the LORD all the days of my life, to behold the beauty[b] of the LORD, and to enquire in his temple. ⁵For in the time of trouble he shall hide me in his pavilion: in the secret of his tabernacle shall he hide me; he shall set me up upon a rock. ⁶And now shall mine head

---

Devotional Moment
•
Waiting

27:14 David knew that impatience can lead to dangerous and sinful choices. When life is not going the way we want it to, especially over several months or years, our faith in God's timing is tested. Perhaps home is the most difficult place to be patient—we want a spouse to change, a son or daughter to grow up, or a financial difficulty to vanish. Remember that God has not forgotten you. Wait for the Lord to act. Though his intervention may seem overdue, patience will help you avoid making a hasty choice you will later regret.

---

be lifted up above mine enemies round about me: therefore will I offer in his tabernacle sacrifices of joy[c]; I will sing, yea, I will sing praises unto the LORD.

⁷Hear, O LORD, *when* I cry with my voice: have mercy also upon me, and answer me. ⁸*When thou saidst*, Seek ye my face; my heart said unto thee, Thy face, LORD, will I seek. ⁹Hide not thy face *far* from me; put not thy servant away in anger: thou hast been my help; leave me not, neither forsake me, O God of my salvation. ¹⁰When my father and my mother forsake me, then the LORD will take me up. ¹¹Teach me thy way, O LORD, and lead me in a plain[d] path, because of mine enemies. ¹²Deliver me not over unto the will of mine enemies: for false witnesses are risen up against me, and such as breathe out cruelty. ¹³*I had fainted*, unless I had believed to see the goodness of the LORD in the land of the living. ¹⁴Wait on the LORD: be of good courage, and he shall strengthen thine heart: wait, I say, on the LORD.

28

A Psalm of David.

¹Unto thee will I cry, O LORD my rock; be not silent to me: lest, *if* thou be silent to me[a], I become like them that go down into the pit. ²Hear the voice of my supplications, when I cry unto thee, when I lift up my hands toward thy holy oracle. ³Draw me not away with the wicked, and

---

[a] came . . . : Heb. approached against me
[b] the beauty: or, the delight
[c] joy: Heb. shouting
[d] a plain . . . : Heb. a way of plainness
[a] to me: Heb. from me

with the workers of iniquity, which speak peace to their neighbours, but mischief *is* in their hearts. ⁴Give them according to their deeds, and according to the wickedness of their endeavours: give them after the work of their hands; render to them their desert. ⁵Because they regard not the works of the LORD, nor the operation of his hands, he shall destroy them, and not build them up.

⁶Blessed *be* the LORD, because he hath heard the voice of my supplications. ⁷The LORD *is* my strength and my shield; my heart trusted in him, and I am helped: therefore my heart greatly rejoiceth; and with my song will I praise him. ⁸The LORD *is* their strength, and he *is* the saving strength of his anointed. ⁹Save thy people, and bless thine inheritance: feedᵇ them also, and lift them up for ever.

29

A Psalm of David.

¹Give unto the LORD, O ye mightyᵃ, give unto the LORD glory and strength. ²Give unto the LORD the gloryᵇ due unto his name; worship the LORD in the beauty of holiness. ³The voice of the LORD *is* upon the waters: the God of glory thundereth: the LORD *is* upon manyᶜ waters. ⁴The voice of the LORD *is* powerfulᵈ; the

voice of the LORD *is* full of majesty. ⁵The voice of the LORD breaketh the cedars; yea, the LORD breaketh the cedars of Lebanon. ⁶He maketh them also to skip like a calf; Lebanon and Sirion like a young unicorn. ⁷The voice of the LORD dividethᵉ the flames of fire. ⁸The voice of the LORD shaketh the wilderness; the LORD shaketh the wilderness of Kadesh. ⁹The voice of the LORD maketh the hinds to calveᶠ, and discovereth the forests: and in his temple doth every one speak of *his* glory. ¹⁰The LORD sitteth upon the flood; yea, the LORD sitteth King for ever. ¹¹The LORD will give strength unto his people; the LORD will bless his people with peace.

30

A Psalm *and* Song *at* the dedication of the house of David.

¹I will extol thee, O LORD; for thou hast lifted me up, and hast not made my foes to rejoice over me. ²O LORD my God, I cried unto thee, and thou hast healed me. ³O LORD, thou hast brought up my soul from the grave: thou hast kept me alive, that I should not go down to the pit. ⁴Sing unto the LORD, O ye saints of his, and give thanks at the remembrance of his holiness. ⁵For his angerᵃ *endureth but* a moment; in his favour *is* life: weeping

---

ᵇ feed: or, rule
ᵃ ye mighty: Heb. ye sons of the mighty
ᵇ the glory . . . : Heb. the honour of his name
ᶜ many: or, great
ᵈ powerful: Heb. in power
ᵉ divideth: Heb. cutteth out
ᶠ to calve: or, to be in pain
ᵃ his anger . . . : Heb. there is but a moment in his anger

may endure for a night, but joy *cometh* in the morning.

⁶And in my prosperity I said, I shall never be moved. ⁷LORD, by thy favour thou hast made my mountain to stand strong: thou didst hide thy face, *and* I was troubled. ⁸I cried to thee, O LORD; and unto the LORD I made supplication. ⁹What profit *is there* in my blood, when I go down to the pit? Shall the dust praise thee? shall it declare thy truth? ¹⁰Hear, O LORD, and have mercy upon me: LORD, be thou my helper. ¹¹Thou hast turned for me my mourning into dancing: thou hast put off my sackcloth, and girded me with gladness; ¹²To the end that *my* glory may sing praise to thee, and not be silent. O LORD my God, I will give thanks unto thee for ever.

31

To the chief Musician, A Psalm of David.

¹In thee, O LORD, do I put my trust; let me never be ashamed: deliver me in thy righteousness. ²Bow down thine ear to me; deliver me speedily: be thou my strong rock, for an house of defence to save me. ³For thou *art* my rock and my fortress; therefore for thy name's sake lead me, and guide me. ⁴Pull me out of the net that they have laid privily for me: for thou *art* my strength. ⁵Into thine hand I commit my spirit: thou hast redeemed me, O LORD God of truth. ⁶I have hated them that regard lying vanities: but I trust in the LORD. ⁷I will be glad and rejoice in thy mercy: for thou hast considered my trouble; thou hast known my soul in adversities; ⁸And hast not shut me up into the hand of the enemy: thou hast set my feet in a large room.

⁹Have mercy upon me, O LORD, for I am in trouble: mine eye is consumed with grief, *yea*, my soul and my belly. ¹⁰For my life is spent with grief, and my years with sighing: my strength faileth because of mine iniquity, and my bones are consumed. ¹¹I was a reproach among all mine enemies, but especially among my neighbours, and a fear to mine acquaintance: they that did see me without fled from me. ¹²I am forgotten as a dead man out of mind: I am like a broken^a vessel. ¹³For I have heard the slander of many: fear *was* on every side: while they took counsel together against me, they devised to take away my life. ¹⁴But I trusted in thee, O LORD: I said, Thou *art* my God. ¹⁵My times *are* in thy hand: deliver me from the hand of mine enemies, and from them that persecute me. ¹⁶Make thy face to shine upon thy servant: save me for thy mercies' sake. ¹⁷Let me not be ashamed, O LORD; for I have called upon thee: let the wicked be ashamed, *and* let them be silent^b in the grave. ¹⁸Let the lying lips be put to silence; which speak grievous^c things proudly and contemptuously against the righteous.

¹⁹*Oh* how great *is* thy goodness, which thou hast laid up for them that fear thee; *which* thou hast wrought for them that trust in thee before the sons

---

^a a broken . . . : Heb. a vessel that perisheth
^b silent . . . : or, cut off for
^c grievous . . . : Heb. a hard thing

of men! [20]Thou shalt hide them in the secret of thy presence from the pride of man: thou shalt keep them secretly in a pavilion from the strife of tongues. [21]Blessed *be* the LORD: for he hath shewed me his marvellous kindness in a strong[d] city. [22]For I said in my haste, I am cut off from before thine eyes: nevertheless thou heardest the voice of my supplications when I cried unto thee. [23]O love the LORD, all ye his saints: *for* the LORD preserveth the faithful, and plentifully rewardeth the proud doer. [24]Be of good courage, and he shall strengthen your heart, all ye that hope in the LORD.

32

A Psalm of David, Maschil.

[1]Blessed *is he whose* transgression *is* forgiven, *whose* sin *is* covered. [2]Blessed *is* the man unto whom the LORD imputeth not iniquity, and in whose spirit *there is* no guile. [3]When I kept silence, my bones waxed old through my roaring all the day long. [4]For day and night thy hand was heavy upon me: my moisture is turned into the drought of summer. Selah. [5]I acknowledged my sin unto thee, and mine iniquity have I not hid. I said, I will confess my transgressions unto the LORD; and thou forgavest the iniquity of my sin. Selah. [6]For this shall every one that is godly pray unto thee in a time when thou mayest be found: surely in the floods of great waters they shall not come nigh unto him. [7]Thou *art* my hiding place; thou

shalt preserve me from trouble; thou shalt compass me about with songs of deliverance. Selah. [8]I will instruct thee and teach thee in the way which thou shalt go: I will guide[a] thee with mine eye. [9]Be ye not as the horse, *or* as the mule, *which* have no understanding: whose mouth must be held in with bit and bridle, lest they come near unto thee. [10]Many sorrows *shall be* to the wicked: but he that trusteth in the LORD, mercy shall compass him about. [11]Be glad in the LORD, and rejoice, ye righteous: and shout for joy, all *ye that are* upright in heart.

33

[1]Rejoice in the LORD, O ye righteous: *for* praise is comely for the upright. [2]Praise the LORD with harp: sing unto him with the psaltery *and* an instrument of ten strings. [3]Sing unto him a new song; play skilfully with a loud noise. [4]For the word of the LORD *is* right; and all his works *are done* in truth. [5]He loveth righteousness and judgment: the earth is full of the goodness[a] of the LORD. [6]By the word of the LORD were the heavens made; and all the host of them by the breath of his mouth. [7]He gathereth the waters of the sea together as an heap: he layeth up the depth in storehouses. [8]Let all the earth fear the LORD: let all the inhabitants of the world stand in awe of him. [9]For he spake, and it was *done*; he commanded, and it stood fast. [10]The LORD bringeth[b] the coun-

---

[d] strong: or, fenced
[a] guide . . . : Heb. counsel thee, mine eye shall be upon thee
[a] goodness: or, mercy
[b] bringeth: Heb. maketh frustrate

sel of the heathen to nought: he maketh the devices of the people of none effect. [11]The counsel of the LORD standeth for ever, the thoughts of his heart to all[c] generations.

[12]Blessed *is* the nation whose God *is* the LORD; *and* the people *whom* he hath chosen for his own inheritance. [13]The LORD looketh from heaven; he beholdeth all the sons of men. [14]From the place of his habitation he looketh upon all the inhabitants of the earth. [15]He fashioneth their hearts alike; he considereth all their works. [16]There is no king saved by the multitude of an host: a mighty man is not delivered by much strength. [17]An horse *is* a vain thing for safety: neither shall he deliver *any* by his great strength. [18]Behold, the eye of the LORD *is* upon them that fear him, upon them that hope in his mercy; [19]To deliver their soul from death, and to keep them alive in famine. [20]Our soul waiteth for the LORD: he *is* our help and our shield. [21]For our heart shall rejoice in him, because we have trusted in his holy name. [22]Let thy mercy, O LORD, be upon us, according as we hope in thee.

34

A Psalm of David, when he changed his behaviour before Abimelech[a]; who drove him away, and he departed.

[1]I will bless the LORD at all times: his praise *shall* continually *be* in my mouth. [2]My soul shall make her boast in the LORD: the humble shall hear

thereof, and be glad. [3]O magnify the LORD with me, and let us exalt his name together. [4]I sought the LORD, and he heard me, and delivered me from all my fears. [5]They looked unto him, and were lightened[b]: and their faces were not ashamed. [6]This poor man cried, and the LORD heard *him,* and saved him out of all his troubles. [7]The angel of the LORD encampeth round about them that fear him, and delivereth them. [8]O taste and see that the LORD *is* good: blessed *is* the man *that* trusteth in him. [9]O fear the LORD, ye his saints: for *there is* no want to them that fear him. [10]The young lions do lack, and suffer hunger: but they that seek the LORD shall not want any good *thing.*

[11]Come, ye children, hearken unto me: I will teach you the fear of the LORD. [12]What man *is he that* desireth life, *and* loveth *many* days, that he may

Devotional Moment

•

Commitment

34:9-10 We can reverence the Lord in at least two ways. First, we can hold him in such high honor that we always try to follow his ways. Second, we can worship him and study his Word for guidance. Take great pains to study, learn, and follow every directive God has given you in the Bible, no matter how busy life becomes. Even if it's only three minutes a day, spend time reading and thinking about God's Word. That is where you will get the strength and character to be the person God wants you to be.

---

[c] to all . . . : Heb. to generation and generation
[a] Abimelech: or, Achish
[b] were lightened: or, they flowed unto him

see good? ¹³Keep thy tongue from evil, and thy lips from speaking guile. ¹⁴Depart from evil, and do good; seek peace, and pursue it. ¹⁵The eyes of the LORD *are* upon the righteous, and his ears *are open* unto their cry. ¹⁶The face of the LORD *is* against them that do evil, to cut off the remembrance of them from the earth. ¹⁷*The righteous* cry, and the LORD heareth, and delivereth them out of all their troubles. ¹⁸The LORD *is* nigh unto them that are of a broken heart; and saveth such as be of a contrite spirit. ¹⁹Many *are* the afflictions of the righteous: but the LORD delivereth him out of them all. ²⁰He keepeth all his bones: not one of them is broken. ²¹Evil shall slay the wicked: and they that hate the righteous shall be desolate^c. ²²The LORD redeemeth the soul of his servants: and none of them that trust in him shall be desolate^d.

35

A Psalm of David.

¹Plead *my cause*, O LORD, with them that strive with me: fight against them that fight against me. ²Take hold of shield and buckler, and stand up for mine help. ³Draw out also the spear, and stop *the way* against them that persecute me: say unto my soul, I *am* thy salvation. ⁴Let them be confounded and put to shame that seek after my soul: let them be turned back and brought to confusion that devise my hurt. ⁵Let them be as chaff before the wind: and let the angel of the LORD chase *them*. ⁶Let their way be dark^a and slippery: and let the angel of the LORD persecute them. ⁷For without cause have they hid for me their net *in* a pit, *which* without cause they have digged for my soul. ⁸Let destruction come upon him at unawares; and let his net that he hath hid catch himself: into that very destruction let him fall. ⁹And my soul shall be joyful in the LORD: it shall rejoice in his salvation. ¹⁰All my bones shall say, LORD, who *is* like unto thee, which deliverest the poor from him that is too strong for him, yea, the poor and the needy from him that spoileth him?

¹¹False^b witnesses did rise up; they laid to my charge *things* that I knew not. ¹²They rewarded me evil for good *to* the spoiling^c of my soul. ¹³But as for me, when they were sick, my clothing *was* sackcloth: I humbled^d my soul with fasting; and my prayer returned into mine own bosom. ¹⁴I behaved myself as though *he had been* my friend *or* brother: I bowed down heavily, as one that mourneth *for his* mother. ¹⁵But in mine adversity^e they rejoiced, and gathered themselves together: *yea*, the abjects gathered themselves together against me, and I knew *it* not; they did tear *me*, and ceased not: ¹⁶With hypo-

---

^c desolate: or, guilty
^d desolate: or, guilty
^a dark . . . : Heb. darkness and slipperiness
^b False . . . : Heb. Witnesses of wrong
^c spoiling: Heb. depriving
^d humbled: or, afflicted
^e adversity: Heb. halting

critical mockers in feasts, they gnashed upon me with their teeth.

¹⁷Lord, how long wilt thou look on? rescue my soul from their destructions, my darling^f from the lions. ¹⁸I will give thee thanks in the great congregation: I will praise thee among much^g people. ¹⁹Let not them that are mine enemies wrongfully^h rejoice over me: *neither* let them wink with the eye that hate me without a cause. ²⁰For they speak not peace: but they devise deceitful matters against *them that are* quiet in the land. ²¹Yea, they opened their mouth wide against me, *and* said, Aha, aha, our eye hath seen *it.* ²² *This* thou hast seen, O LORD: keep not silence: O Lord, be not far from me. ²³Stir up thyself, and awake to my judgment, *even* unto my cause, my God and my Lord. ²⁴Judge me, O LORD my God, according to thy righteousness; and let them not rejoice over me. ²⁵Let them not say in their hearts, Ahⁱ, so would we have it: let them not say, We have swallowed him up. ²⁶Let them be ashamed and brought to confusion together that rejoice at mine hurt: let them be clothed with shame and dishonour that magnify *themselves* against me. ²⁷Let them shout for joy, and be glad, that favour my righteous cause: yea, let them say continually, Let the LORD be magnified, which hath pleasure in the prosperity of his servant. ²⁸And my tongue shall speak of thy righteousness *and* of thy praise all the day long.

36

To the chief Musician, *A Psalm* of David the servant of the LORD.

¹The transgression of the wicked saith within my heart, *that there is* no fear of God before his eyes. ²For he flattereth himself in his own eyes, until his iniquity be found to be hateful. ³The words of his mouth *are* iniquity and deceit: he hath left off to be wise, *and* to do good. ⁴He deviseth mischief^a upon his bed; he setteth himself in a way *that is* not good; he abhorreth not evil.

⁵Thy mercy, O LORD, *is* in the heavens; *and* thy faithfulness *reacheth* unto the clouds. ⁶Thy righteousness *is* like the great mountains; thy judgments *are* a great deep: O LORD, thou preservest man and beast. ⁷How excellent^b *is* thy lovingkindness, O God! therefore the children of men put their trust under the shadow of thy wings. ⁸They shall be abundantly satisfied with the fatness of thy house; and thou shalt make them drink of the river of thy pleasures. ⁹For with thee *is* the fountain of life: in thy light shall we see light. ¹⁰O continue^c thy lovingkindness unto them that know thee; and thy righteousness to the upright in heart. ¹¹Let not the foot of pride come against me,

---

^f darling: Heb. only one
^g much: Heb. strong
^h wrongfully: Heb. falsely
ⁱ Ah . . . : Heb. Ah, ah, our soul
^a mischief: or, vanity
^b excellent: Heb. precious
^c continue: Heb. draw out at length

and let not the hand of the wicked remove me. [12]There are the workers of iniquity fallen: they are cast down, and shall not be able to rise.

37

A Psalm of David.

[1]Fret not thyself because of evildoers, neither be thou envious against the workers of iniquity. [2]For they shall soon be cut down like the grass, and wither as the green herb. [3]Trust in the LORD, and do good; *so* shalt thou dwell in the land, and verily[a] thou shalt be fed. [4]Delight thyself also in the LORD; and he shall give thee the desires of thine heart. [5]Commit[b] thy way unto the LORD; trust also in him; and he shall bring *it* to pass. [6]And he shall bring forth thy righteousness as the light, and thy judgment as the noonday.

[7]Rest in the LORD, and wait patiently for him: fret not thyself because

---

Devotional Moment

No Justice?

37:8-9 In the end, there *will* be justice, for God is watching and will right all wrongs. Families who remember this will spare themselves a lot of grief. Fighting is as much a part of family life and growing up as living together, yet God does not want us to live in a state of anger but to trust him to bring about the justice we seek. For those times when anger tempts you to fret, you may want to memorize this psalm. Then the next time you feel anger swelling up inside you, you can remember to trust in God.

---

of him who prospereth in his way, because of the man who bringeth wicked devices to pass. [8]Cease from anger, and forsake wrath: fret not thyself in any wise to do evil. [9]For evildoers shall be cut off: but those that wait upon the LORD, they shall inherit the earth. [10]For yet a little while, and the wicked *shall* not *be*: yea, thou shalt diligently consider his place, and it *shall* not *be*. [11]But the meek shall inherit the earth; and shall delight themselves in the abundance of peace. [12]The wicked plotteth[c] against the just, and gnasheth upon him with his teeth. [13]The Lord shall laugh at him: for he seeth that his day is coming. [14]The wicked have drawn out the sword, and have bent their bow, to cast down the poor and needy, *and* to slay such as be of upright conversation. [15]Their sword shall enter into their own heart, and their bows shall be broken. [16]A little that a righteous man hath *is* better than the riches of many wicked. [17]For the arms of the wicked shall be broken: but the LORD upholdeth the righteous. [18]The LORD knoweth the days of the upright: and their inheritance shall be for ever. [19]They shall not be ashamed in the evil time: and in the days of famine they shall be satisfied. [20]But the wicked shall perish, and the enemies of the LORD *shall be* as the fat[d] of lambs: they shall consume; into smoke shall they consume away.

[21]The wicked borroweth, and payeth not again: but the righteous

---

[a] verily: Heb. in truth, or, stableness
[b] Commit . . . : Heb. Roll thy way upon
[c] plotteth: or, practiseth
[d] the fat: Heb. the preciousness

sheweth mercy, and giveth. ²²For *such as be* blessed of him shall inherit the earth; and *they that be* cursed of him shall be cut off. ²³The steps of a *good* man are ordered^c by the LORD: and he delighteth in his way. ²⁴Though he fall, he shall not be utterly cast down: for the LORD upholdeth *him with* his hand. ²⁵I have been young, and *now* am old; yet have I not seen the righteous forsaken, nor his seed begging bread. ²⁶*He is* ever^f merciful, and lendeth; and his seed *is* blessed. ²⁷Depart from evil, and do good; and dwell for evermore. ²⁸For the LORD loveth judgment, and forsaketh not his saints; they are preserved for ever: but the seed of the wicked shall be cut off. ²⁹The righteous shall inherit the land, and dwell therein for ever. ³⁰The mouth of the righteous speaketh wisdom, and his tongue talketh of judgment. ³¹The law of his God *is* in his heart; none of his steps^g shall slide. ³²The wicked watcheth the righteous, and seeketh to slay him. ³³The LORD will not leave him in his hand, nor condemn him when he is judged.

³⁴Wait on the LORD, and keep his way, and he shall exalt thee to inherit the land: when the wicked are cut off, thou shalt see *it.* ³⁵I have seen the wicked in great power, and spreading himself like a green^h bay tree. ³⁶Yet he passed away, and, lo, he *was* not: yea, I sought him, but he could not be found.

³⁷Mark the perfect *man,* and behold the upright: for the end of *that* man *is* peace. ³⁸But the transgressors shall be destroyed together: the end of the wicked shall be cut off. ³⁹But the salvation of the righteous *is* of the LORD: *he is* their strength in the time of trouble. ⁴⁰And the LORD shall help them, and deliver them: he shall deliver them from the wicked, and save them, because they trust in him.

38

A Psalm of David, to bring to remembrance.

¹O LORD, rebuke me not in thy wrath: neither chasten me in thy hot displeasure. ²For thine arrows stick fast in me, and thy hand presseth me sore. ³*There is* no soundness in my flesh because of thine anger; neither *is there any* rest^a in my bones because of my sin. ⁴For mine iniquities are gone over mine head: as an heavy burden they are too heavy for me. ⁵My wounds stink *and* are corrupt because of my foolishness. ⁶I am troubled^b; I am bowed down greatly; I go mourning all the day long. ⁷For my loins are filled with a loathsome *disease;* and *there is* no soundness in my flesh. ⁸I am feeble and sore broken: I have roared by reason of the disquietness of my heart. ⁹Lord, all my desire *is* before thee; and my groaning is not hid from thee. ¹⁰My heart panteth, my strength faileth me: as for the light

---

^c ordered: or, established
^f ever: Heb. all the day
^g steps: or, goings
^h a green . . . : or, a green tree that groweth in his own soil
^a rest: Heb. peace, or, health
^b troubled: Heb. wried

881

of mine eyes, it also is gone^c from me. ^11My lovers and my friends stand aloof from my sore^d; and my kinsmen stand afar off.

^12They also that seek after my life lay snares *for me*: and they that seek my hurt speak mischievous things, and imagine deceits all the day long. ^13But I, as a deaf *man*, heard not; and *I was* as a dumb man *that* openeth not his mouth. ^14Thus I was as a man that heareth not, and in whose mouth *are* no reproofs. ^15For in thee, O LORD, do I hope: thou wilt hear, O Lord my God. ^16For I said, *Hear me*, lest *otherwise* they should rejoice over me: when my foot slippeth, they magnify *themselves* against me. ^17For I *am* ready to halt^e, and my sorrow *is* continually before me. ^18For I will declare mine iniquity; I will be sorry for my sin. ^19But mine enemies *are* lively, *and* they are strong: and they that hate me wrongfully are multiplied. ^20They also that render evil for good are mine adversaries; because I follow *the thing that good is*. ^21Forsake me not, O LORD: O my God, be not far from me. ^22Make haste to help me, O Lord my salvation.

39

To the chief Musician, *even* to Jeduthun, A Psalm of David.

^1I said, I will take heed to my ways, that I sin not with my tongue: I will keep my mouth^a with a bridle, while the wicked is before me. ^2I was dumb with silence, I held my peace, *even* from good; and my sorrow was stirred^b. ^3My heart was hot within me, while I was musing the fire burned: *then* spake I with my tongue, ^4LORD, make me to know mine end, and the measure of my days, what it *is; that* I may know how frail I *am*. ^5Behold, thou hast made my days *as* an handbreadth; and mine age *is* as nothing before thee: verily every man at his best state *is* altogether vanity. Selah. ^6Surely every man walketh in a vain shew: surely they are disquieted in vain: he heapeth up *riches*, and knoweth not who shall gather them.

^7And now, Lord, what wait I for? my hope *is* in thee. ^8Deliver me from all my transgressions: make me not the reproach of the foolish. ^9I was dumb, I opened not my mouth; because thou didst *it*. ^10Remove thy stroke away from

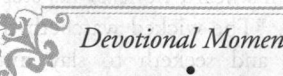

Devotional Moment

Complaining

39:1-3 David said to himself, "I'm going to quit complaining," but the more he thought about the source of his complaint, the more it bothered him. David kept mulling it over, looking at it from every angle. As a result, he became increasingly angry. Then he took it to the Lord. He soon realized that this life is brief; it wasn't worth spending day after day in misery merely because circumstances didn't conform to his wishes. What aspect of your life do you tend to complain about? Stop waiting for perfection and have hope in God. Keep your frustrations in perspective.

^c is gone . . . : Heb. is not with me
^d sore: Heb. stroke
^e to halt: Heb. for halting
^a my mouth . . . : Heb. a bridle, or, muzzle for my mouth
^b stirred: Heb. troubled

me: I am consumed by the blow[c] of thine hand. [11]When thou with rebukes dost correct man for iniquity, thou makest his beauty to consume away like a moth: surely every man *is* vanity. Selah. [12]Hear my prayer, O LORD, and give ear unto my cry; hold not thy peace at my tears: for I *am* a stranger with thee, *and* a sojourner, as all my fathers *were*. [13]O spare me, that I may recover strength, before I go hence, and be no more.

40

To the chief Musician, A Psalm of David.

[1]I waited[a] patiently for the LORD; and he inclined unto me, and heard my cry. [2]He brought me up also out of an horrible[b] pit, out of the miry clay, and set my feet upon a rock, *and* established my goings. [3]And he hath put a new song in my mouth, *even* praise unto our God: many shall see *it*, and fear, and shall trust in the LORD. [4]Blessed *is* that man that maketh the LORD his trust, and respecteth not the proud, nor such as turn aside to lies. [5]Many, O LORD my God, *are* thy wonderful works *which* thou hast done, and thy thoughts *which are* to us-ward: they cannot be reckoned up in order unto thee: *if* I would declare and speak of *them*, they are more than can be numbered.

[6]Sacrifice and offering thou didst not desire; mine ears hast thou opened[c]: burnt offering and sin offering hast thou not required. [7]Then said I, Lo, I come: in the volume of the book *it is* written of me, [8]I delight to do thy will, O my God: yea, thy law *is* within[d] my heart. [9]I have preached righteousness in the great congregation: lo, I have not refrained my lips, O LORD, thou knowest. [10]I have not hid thy righteousness within my heart; I have declared thy faithfulness and thy salvation: I have not concealed thy lovingkindness and thy truth from the great congregation.

[11]Withhold not thou thy tender mercies from me, O LORD: let thy lovingkindness and thy truth continually preserve me. [12]For innumerable evils have compassed me about: mine iniquities have taken hold upon me, so that I am not able to look up; they are more than the hairs of mine head: therefore my heart faileth me. [13]Be pleased, O LORD, to deliver me: O LORD, make haste to help me. [14]Let them be ashamed and confounded together that seek after my soul to destroy it; let them be driven backward and put to shame that wish me evil. [15]Let them be desolate for a reward of their shame that say unto me, Aha, aha. [16]Let all those that seek thee rejoice and be glad in thee: let such as love thy salvation say continually, The LORD be magnified. [17]But I *am* poor and needy; *yet* the Lord thinketh upon me: thou *art* my help and my deliverer; make no tarrying, O my God.

41

To the chief Musician, A Psalm of David.

---

[c] blow: Heb. conflict
[a] I waited . . . : Heb. In waiting I waited
[b] an horrible . . . : Heb. a pit of noise
[c] opened: Heb. digged
[d] within . . . : Heb. in the midst of my bowels

¹Blessed *is* he that considereth the poor[a]: the LORD will deliver him in time of trouble. ²The LORD will preserve him, and keep him alive; *and* he shall be blessed upon the earth: and thou wilt not deliver him unto the will of his enemies. ³The LORD will strengthen him upon the bed of languishing: thou wilt make[b] all his bed in his sickness. ⁴I said, LORD, be merciful unto me: heal my soul; for I have sinned against thee.

⁵Mine enemies speak evil of me, When shall he die, and his name perish? ⁶And if he come to see *me*, he speaketh vanity: his heart gathereth iniquity to itself; *when* he goeth abroad, he telleth *it*. ⁷All that hate me whisper together against me: against me do they devise my hurt. ⁸An evil disease, *say they*, cleaveth fast unto him: and *now* that he lieth he shall rise up no more. ⁹Yea, mine own familiar friend, in whom I trusted, which did eat of my bread, hath lifted up *his* heel against me. ¹⁰But thou, O LORD, be merciful unto me, and raise me up, that I may requite them. ¹¹By this I know that thou favourest me, because mine enemy doth not triumph over me. ¹²And as for me, thou upholdest me in mine integrity, and settest me before thy face for ever. ¹³Blessed *be* the LORD God of Israel from everlasting, and to everlasting. Amen, and Amen.

42

To the chief Musician, Maschil[a], for the sons of Korah.

¹As the hart panteth after the water

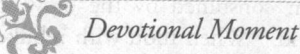

Devotional Moment

•

Depression

42:6-7 This psalm is about depression—those times when we feel as though oceans of misery have swept over us. Thinking about the goodness of the Lord and his kindness to us is not a cure-all for depression; it's difficult to control how we feel, and merely knowing the facts won't necessarily make us feel better. But as we remind ourselves that God loves and cares for us, it will help us through the dark times. Keep a bookmark in your Bible at this psalm for those times when you need such encouragement.

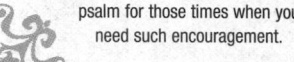

brooks, so panteth my soul after thee, O God. ²My soul thirsteth for God, for the living God: when shall I come and appear before God? ³My tears have been my meat day and night, while they continually say unto me, Where *is* thy God? ⁴When I remember these *things*, I pour out my soul in me: for I had gone with the multitude, I went with them to the house of God, with the voice of joy and praise, with a multitude that kept holyday. ⁵Why art thou cast down, O my soul? and *why* art thou disquieted in me? hope thou in God: for I shall yet praise him *for* the help of his countenance.

⁶O my God, my soul is cast down within me: therefore will I remember thee from the land of Jordan, and of the Hermonites, from the hill[b] Mizar. ⁷Deep calleth unto deep at the noise of thy waterspouts: all thy waves and thy billows are gone over me. ⁸*Yet* the LORD will com-

---

[a] the poor: or, the weak, or, sick

[b] make: Heb. turn

[a] Maschil . . . : or, A Psalm giving instruction of the sons, etc

[b] the hill . . . : or, the little hill

mand his lovingkindness in the daytime, and in the night his song *shall be* with me, *and* my prayer unto the God of my life. ⁹I will say unto God my rock, Why hast thou forgotten me? why go I mourning because of the oppression of the enemy? ¹⁰*As* with a sword^c in my bones, mine enemies reproach me; while they say daily unto me, Where *is* thy God? ¹¹Why art thou cast down, O my soul? and why art thou disquieted within me? hope thou in God: for I shall yet praise him, *who is* the health of my countenance, and my God.

43

¹Judge me, O God, and plead my cause against an ungodly^a nation: O deliver me from the deceitful and unjust man. ²For thou *art* the God of my strength: why dost thou cast me off? why go I mourning because of the oppression of the enemy? ³O send out thy light and thy truth: let them lead me; let them bring me unto thy holy hill, and to thy tabernacles. ⁴Then will I go unto the altar of God, unto God my exceeding^b joy: yea, upon the harp will I praise thee, O God my God. ⁵Why art thou cast down, O my soul? and why art thou disquieted within me? hope in God: for I shall yet praise him, *who is* the health of my countenance, and my God.

44

To the chief Musician for the sons of Korah, Maschil.

¹We have heard with our ears, O God, our fathers have told us, *what* work thou didst in their days, in the

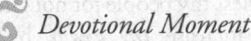

Devotional Moment
•
Share Your Stories

44:1 The psalm writer praised God by saying, "We have heard . . . O God, our fathers have told us, what work thou didst in their days." Because his parents had told him about what God had done, he was able to thank and praise God. Similarly, our children can learn more about God by hearing what he has done for us. Our children can be encouraged by the testimonies of older Christians. Let them hear yours.

times of old. ²*How* thou didst drive out the heathen with thy hand, and plantedst them; *how* thou didst afflict the people, and cast them out. ³For they got not the land in possession by their own sword, neither did their own arm save them: but thy right hand, and thine arm, and the light of thy countenance, because thou hadst a favour unto them. ⁴Thou art my King, O God: command deliverances for Jacob. ⁵Through thee will we push down our enemies: through thy name will we tread them under that rise up against us. ⁶For I will not trust in my bow, neither shall my sword save me. ⁷But thou hast saved us from our enemies, and hast put them to shame that hated us. ⁸In God we boast all the day long, and praise thy name for ever. Selah.

⁹But thou hast cast off, and put us to shame; and goest not forth with our armies. ¹⁰Thou makest us to turn back from the enemy: and they which hate us spoil for themselves. ¹¹Thou hast given us like sheep *appointed* for meat; and hast scattered us among the heathen.

---

^c sword: or, killing
^a ungodly: or, unmerciful
^b my exceeding . . . : Heb. the gladness of my joy

¹²Thou sellest thy people for nought, and dost not increase *thy wealth* by their price. ¹³Thou makest us a reproach to our neighbours, a scorn and a derision to them that are round about us. ¹⁴Thou makest us a byword among the heathen, a shaking of the head among the people. ¹⁵My confusion *is* continually before me, and the shame of my face hath covered me, ¹⁶For the voice of him that reproacheth and blasphemeth; by reason of the enemy and avenger.

¹⁷All this is come upon us; yet have we not forgotten thee, neither have we dealt falsely in thy covenant. ¹⁸Our heart is not turned back, neither have our steps^a declined from thy way; ¹⁹Though thou hast sore broken us in the place of dragons, and covered us with the shadow of death. ²⁰If we have forgotten the name of our God, or stretched out our hands to a strange god; ²¹Shall not God search this out? for he knoweth the secrets of the heart. ²²Yea, for thy sake are we killed all the day long; we are counted as sheep for the slaughter. ²³Awake, why sleepest thou, O Lord? arise, cast *us* not off for ever. ²⁴Wherefore hidest thou thy face, *and* forgettest our affliction and our oppression? ²⁵For our soul is bowed down to the dust: our belly cleaveth unto the earth. ²⁶Arise for our help, and redeem us for thy mercies' sake.

45

To the chief Musician upon Shoshannim, for the sons of Korah, Maschil^a, A Song of loves.

¹My heart is inditing a good matter: I speak of the things which I have made touching the king: my tongue *is* the pen of a ready writer. ²Thou art fairer than the children of men: grace is poured into thy lips: therefore God hath blessed thee for ever. ³Gird thy sword upon *thy* thigh, O *most* mighty, with thy glory and thy majesty. ⁴And in thy majesty ride^b prosperously because of truth and meekness *and* righteousness; and thy right hand shall teach thee terrible things. ⁵Thine arrows *are* sharp in the heart of the king's enemies; *whereby* the people fall under thee.

⁶Thy throne, O God, *is* for ever and ever: the sceptre of thy kingdom *is* a right sceptre. ⁷Thou lovest righteousness, and hatest wickedness: therefore God, thy God, hath anointed thee with the oil of gladness above thy fellows. ⁸All thy garments *smell* of myrrh, and aloes, *and* cassia, out of the ivory palaces, whereby they have made thee glad. ⁹Kings' daughters *were* among thy honourable women: upon thy right hand did stand the queen in gold of Ophir.

¹⁰Hearken, O daughter, and consider, and incline thine ear; forget also thine own people, and thy father's house; ¹¹So shall the king greatly desire thy beauty: for he *is* thy Lord; and worship thou him. ¹²And the daughter of Tyre *shall be there* with a gift; *even* the rich among the people shall intreat thy favour^c. ¹³The king's daughter *is* all glorious within: her clothing *is* of wrought

---

^a steps: or, goings
^a Maschil: or, of instruction
^b ride . . . : Heb. prosper thou, ride thou
^c favour: Heb. face

gold. ¹⁴She shall be brought unto the king in raiment of needlework: the virgins her companions that follow her shall be brought unto thee. ¹⁵With gladness and rejoicing shall they be brought: they shall enter into the king's palace. ¹⁶Instead of thy fathers shall be thy children, whom thou mayest make princes in all the earth. ¹⁷I will make thy name to be remembered in all generations: therefore shall the people praise thee for ever and ever.

46

To the chief Musician for the sons of Korah, A Song upon Alamoth.

¹God *is* our refuge and strength, a very present help in trouble. ²Therefore will not we fear, though the earth be removed, and though the mountains be carried into the midst^a of the sea; ³*Though* the waters thereof roar *and* be troubled, *though* the mountains shake with the swelling thereof. Selah. ⁴*There is* a river, the streams whereof shall make glad the city of God, the holy *place* of the tabernacles of the most High. ⁵God *is* in the midst of her; she shall not be moved: God shall help her, *and that* right early. ⁶The heathen raged, the kingdoms were moved: he uttered his voice, the earth melted. ⁷The LORD of hosts *is* with us; the God of Jacob *is* our refuge. Selah. ⁸Come, behold the works of the LORD, what desolations he hath made in the earth. ⁹He maketh wars to cease unto the end of the earth; he breaketh the bow, and cutteth the spear in sunder; he burneth the chariot in the fire. ¹⁰Be still, and know that I *am* God: I will be exalted among the heathen, I will be exalted in the earth. ¹¹The LORD of hosts *is* with us; the God of Jacob *is* our refuge. Selah.

47

To the chief Musician, A Psalm for the sons of Korah.

¹O clap your hands, all ye people; shout unto God with the voice of triumph. ²For the LORD most high *is* terrible; *he is* a great King over all the earth. ³He shall subdue the people under us, and the nations under our feet. ⁴He shall choose our inheritance for us, the excellency of Jacob whom he loved. Selah.

⁵God is gone up with a shout, the LORD with the sound of a trumpet. ⁶Sing praises to God, sing praises: sing praises unto our King, sing praises. ⁷For God *is* the King of all the earth: sing ye praises with understanding. ⁸God reigneth over the heathen: God sitteth upon the throne of his holiness. ⁹The princes^a of the people are gathered together, *even* the people of the God of Abraham: for the shields of the earth *belong* unto God: he is greatly exalted.

48

A Song *and* Psalm for the sons of Korah.

¹Great *is* the LORD, and greatly to be praised in the city of our God, *in* the mountain of his holiness. ²Beautiful for situation, the joy of the whole earth, *is* mount Zion, *on* the sides of the north, the city of the great King. ³God is known in her palaces for a refuge. ⁴For, lo, the kings were assembled, they

---

^a midst . . . : Heb. heart of the seas
^a princes . . . : or, voluntary of the people are gathered unto the people of the God of Abraham

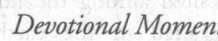

Devotional Moment

Defender and Guide

48:3, 14 When Jerusalem was besieged and successfully resisted its enemies, the Jews thanked God for being their ultimate Defender. He was with them; that was why their city was safe. So it is with you. When you are under siege or suffering a particular crisis, God is your Defender and Guide. Let him lead—whatever direction your life goes.

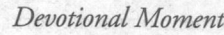

Devotional Moment

Wealth

49:1-20 Death is still the great equalizer that comes to rich and poor alike. And the riches of this world will mean nothing after death. The great temptation for us today is to chase after more and more—bigger houses, nicer home furnishings, newer cars, early retirements. We forget that none of that lasts. Don't give all your attention to pursuits that leave little time or energy for God.

passed by together. ⁵They saw *it, and* so they marvelled; they were troubled, *and* hasted away. ⁶Fear took hold upon them there, *and* pain, as of a woman in travail. ⁷Thou breakest the ships of Tarshish with an east wind.

⁸As we have heard, so have we seen in the city of the LORD of hosts, in the city of our God: God will establish it for ever. Selah. ⁹We have thought of thy lovingkindness, O God, in the midst of thy temple. ¹⁰According to thy name, O God, so *is* thy praise unto the ends of the earth: thy right hand is full of righteousness. ¹¹Let mount Zion rejoice, let the daughters of Judah be glad, because of thy judgments. ¹²Walk about Zion, and go round about her: tell the towers thereof. ¹³Markᵃ ye well her bulwarks, consider her palaces; that ye may tell *it* to the generation following. ¹⁴For this God *is* our God for ever and ever: he will be our guide *even* unto death.

49

To the chief Musician, A Psalm for the sons of Korah.

¹Hear this, all *ye* people; give ear, all *ye* inhabitants of the world: ²Both low and high, rich and poor, together. ³My mouth shall speak of wisdom; and the meditation of my heart *shall be* of understanding. ⁴I will incline mine ear to a parable: I will open my dark saying upon the harp. ⁵Wherefore should I fear in the days of evil, *when* the iniquity of my heels shall compass me about?

⁶They that trust in their wealth, and boast themselves in the multitude of their riches; ⁷None *of them* can by any means redeem his brother, nor give to God a ransom for him: ⁸(For the redemption of their soul *is* precious, and it ceaseth for ever:) ⁹That he should still live for ever, *and* not see corruption. ¹⁰For he seeth *that* wise men die, likewise the fool and the brutish person perish, and leave their wealth to others. ¹¹Their inward thought *is, that* their houses *shall continue* for ever, *and* their dwelling places to allᵃ generations; they call *their* lands after their own names. ¹²Nevertheless man *being* in honour

---

ᵃ Mark . . . : Heb. Set your heart to
ᵃ all . . . : Heb. generation and generation

abideth not: he is like the beasts *that* perish. [13]This their way *is* their folly: yet their posterity approve[b] their sayings. Selah. [14]Like sheep they are laid in the grave; death shall feed on them; and the upright shall have dominion over them in the morning; and their beauty[c] shall consume in the grave from their dwelling.

[15]But God will redeem my soul from the power[d] of the grave: for he shall receive me. Selah. [16]Be not thou afraid when one is made rich, when the glory of his house is increased; [17]For when he dieth he shall carry nothing away: his glory shall not descend after him. [18]Though while he lived he blessed his soul: and *men* will praise thee, when thou doest well to thyself. [19]He shall go to the generation of his fathers; they shall never see light. [20]Man *that is* in honour, and understandeth not, is like the beasts *that* perish.

50

A Psalm of Asaph.

[1]The mighty God, *even* the LORD, hath spoken, and called the earth from the rising of the sun unto the going down thereof. [2]Out of Zion, the perfection of beauty, God hath shined. [3]Our God shall come, and shall not keep silence: a fire shall devour before him, and it shall be very tempestuous round about him. [4]He shall call to the heavens from above, and to the earth, that he may judge his people. [5]Gather my saints together unto me; those that have made a covenant with me by sacrifice. [6]And the heavens shall declare his righteousness: for God *is* judge himself. Selah.

[7]Hear, O my people, and I will speak; O Israel, and I will testify against thee: I *am* God, *even* thy God. [8]I will not reprove thee for thy sacrifices or thy burnt offerings, *to have been* continually before me. [9]I will take no bullock out of thy house, *nor* he goats out of thy folds. [10]For every beast of the forest *is* mine, *and* the cattle upon a thousand hills. [11]I know all the fowls of the mountains: and the wild beasts of the field *are* mine[a]. [12]If I were hungry, I would not tell thee: for the world *is* mine, and the fulness thereof. [13]Will I eat the flesh of bulls, or drink the blood of goats? [14]Offer unto God thanksgiving; and pay thy vows unto the most High: [15]And call upon me in the day of trouble: I will deliver thee, and thou shalt glorify me.

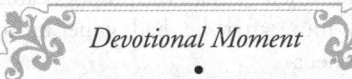

Devotional Moment
•
Faithfulness

50:8-15 God wants more than just our "sacrifices"—what we sing or pledge during a Sunday morning worship service or what we may put in the offering plate. He wants us to show our devotion to him by faithfully keeping the promises we make. How faithful are you in keeping your vows and promises? How faithful are your children in keeping their promises? Make "a promise is a promise" a family policy.

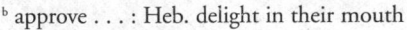

[b] approve . . . : Heb. delight in their mouth
[c] beauty: or, strength
[d] power: Heb. hand
[a] mine: Heb. with me

¹⁶But unto the wicked God saith, What hast thou to do to declare my statutes, or *that* thou shouldest take my covenant in thy mouth? ¹⁷Seeing thou hatest instruction, and castest my words behind thee. ¹⁸When thou sawest a thief, then thou consentedst with him, and hast been partaker with adulterers. ¹⁹Thou givest[b] thy mouth to evil, and thy tongue frameth deceit. ²⁰Thou sittest *and* speakest against thy brother; thou slanderest thine own mother's son. ²¹These *things* hast thou done, and I kept silence; thou thoughtest that I was altogether *such an one* as thyself: *but* I will reprove thee, and set *them* in order before thine eyes. ²²Now consider this, ye that forget God, lest I tear *you* in pieces, and *there be* none to deliver. ²³Whoso offereth praise glorifieth me: and to him that ordereth *his* conversation *aright* will I shew the salvation of God.

51

To the chief Musician, A Psalm of David, when Nathan the prophet came unto him, after he had gone in to Bathsheba.

¹Have mercy upon me, O God, according to thy lovingkindness: according unto the multitude of thy tender mercies blot out my transgressions. ²Wash me throughly from mine iniquity, and cleanse me from my sin. ³For I acknowledge my transgressions: and my sin *is* ever before me. ⁴Against thee, thee only, have I sinned, and done *this* evil in thy sight: that thou mightest be justified

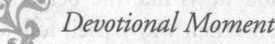

Devotional Moment
·
Forgiveness
51:1-7 David did not rationalize away his sin but called it evil and blameworthy. God will forgive any confessed sin, even the sin of adultery, not because of anything inherently deserving in us, but wholly because he is merciful. Confess your sins to God and let his forgiveness motivate you toward change.

when thou speakest, *and* be clear when thou judgest. ⁵Behold, I was shapen in iniquity; and in sin did my mother conceive[a] me. ⁶Behold, thou desirest truth in the inward parts: and in the hidden *part* thou shalt make me to know wisdom.

⁷Purge me with hyssop, and I shall be clean: wash me, and I shall be whiter than snow. ⁸Make me to hear joy and gladness; *that* the bones *which* thou hast broken may rejoice. ⁹Hide thy face from my sins, and blot out all mine iniquities. ¹⁰Create in me a clean heart, O God; and renew a right[b] spirit within me. ¹¹Cast me not away from thy presence; and take not thy holy spirit from me. ¹²Restore unto me the joy of thy salvation; and uphold me *with thy* free spirit. ¹³*Then* will I teach transgressors thy ways; and sinners shall be converted unto thee.

¹⁴Deliver me from bloodguiltiness[c], O God, thou God of my salvation: *and* my tongue shall sing aloud of thy righteousness. ¹⁵O Lord, open thou my lips; and my mouth shall shew forth thy

---

ᵇ givest: Heb. sendest
ᵃ conceive . . . : Heb. warm me
ᵇ right: or, constant
ᶜ bloodguiltiness: Heb. bloods

praise. ¹⁶For thou desirest not sacrifice; else would I give it: thou delightest not in burnt offering. ¹⁷The sacrifices of God are a broken spirit: a broken and a contrite heart, O God, thou wilt not despise. ¹⁸Do good in thy good pleasure unto Zion: build thou the walls of Jerusalem. ¹⁹Then shalt thou be pleased with the sacrifices of righteousness, with burnt offering and whole burnt offering: then shall they offer bullocks upon thine altar.

52

To the chief Musician, Maschil, *A Psalm* of David, when Doeg the Edomite came and told Saul, and said unto him, David is come to the house of Ahimelech.

¹Why boastest thou thyself in mischief, O mighty man? the goodness of God *endureth* continually. ²Thy tongue deviseth mischiefs; like a sharp razor, working deceitfully. ³Thou lovest evil more than good; *and* lying rather than to speak righteousness. Selah. ⁴Thou lovest all devouring words, O *thou* deceitful tongue. ⁵God shall likewise destroyª thee for ever, he shall take thee away, and pluck thee out of *thy* dwelling place, and root thee out of the land of the living. Selah.

⁶The righteous also shall see, and fear, and shall laugh at him: ⁷Lo, *this is* the man *that* made not God his strength; but trusted in the abundance of his riches, *and* strengthened himself in his wickednessᵇ. ⁸But I *am* like a green olive tree in the house of God: I

trust in the mercy of God for ever and ever. ⁹I will praise thee for ever, because thou hast done it: and I will wait on thy name; for *it is* good before thy saints.

53

To the chief Musician upon Mahalath, Maschil, *A Psalm* of David.

¹The fool hath said in his heart, *There is* no God. Corrupt are they, and have done abominable iniquity: *there is* none that doeth good. ²God looked down from heaven upon the children of men, to see if there were *any* that did understand, that did seek God. ³Every one of them is gone back: they are altogether become filthy; *there is* none that doeth good, no, not one. ⁴Have the workers of iniquity no knowledge? who eat up my people *as* they eat bread: they have not called upon God. ⁵There were they in great fear, *where* no fear was: for God hath scattered the bones of him that encampeth *against* thee: thou hast put *them* to shame, because God hath despised them. ⁶Oh thatª the salvation of Israel *were come* out of Zion! When God bringeth back the captivity of his people, Jacob shall rejoice, *and* Israel shall be glad.

54

To the chief Musician on Neginoth, Maschil, *A Psalm* of David, when the Ziphims came and said to Saul, Doth not David hide himself with us?

¹Save me, O God, by thy name, and judge me by thy strength. ²Hear my prayer, O God; give ear to the

---

ª destroy . . . : Heb. beat thee down
ᵇ wickedness: or, substance
ª Oh that . . . : Heb. Who will give salvation, etc

words of my mouth. ³For strangers are risen up against me, and oppressors seek after my soul: they have not set God before them. Selah.

⁴Behold, God *is* mine helper: the Lord *is* with them that uphold my soul. ⁵He shall reward evil unto mine enemies: cut them off in thy truth. ⁶I will freely sacrifice unto thee: I will praise thy name, O LORD; for *it is* good. ⁷For he hath delivered me out of all trouble: and mine eye hath seen *his desire* upon mine enemies.

55

To the chief Musician on Neginoth, Maschil, *A Psalm* of David.

¹Give ear to my prayer, O God; and hide not thyself from my supplication. ²Attend unto me, and hear me: I mourn in my complaint, and make a noise; ³Because of the voice of the enemy, because of the oppression of the wicked: for they cast iniquity upon me, and in wrath they hate me. ⁴My heart is sore pained within me: and the terrors of death are fallen upon me. ⁵Fearfulness and trembling are come upon me, and horror hath overwhelmed[a] me. ⁶And I said, Oh that I had wings like a dove! *for then* would I fly away, and be at rest. ⁷Lo, *then* would I wander far off, *and* remain in the wilderness. Selah. ⁸I would hasten my escape from the windy storm *and* tempest.

⁹Destroy, O Lord, *and* divide their tongues: for I have seen violence and strife in the city. ¹⁰Day and night they go about it upon the walls thereof: mischief

> ### Devotional Moment
> •
> ### Friendship and Trust
> **55:12-14** David experienced the pain and anguish of betrayed friendship and broken trust. When our life partner, a nurturing parent, or a favorite friend suddenly abandons us, the pain can be too great to bear alone. That's when we need God's love most, as reflected in the support of a caring community or family. Will you be there when someone else is abandoned? And if you have a close friendship or family relationship that has suffered from betrayal or abandonment, begin to pray about how you can take steps to mend the rift.

also and sorrow *are* in the midst of it. ¹¹Wickedness *is* in the midst thereof: deceit and guile depart not from her streets. ¹²For *it was* not an enemy *that* reproached me; then I could have borne *it*: neither *was it* he that hated me *that* did magnify *himself* against me; then I would have hid myself from him: ¹³But *it was* thou, a man mine equal[b], my guide, and mine acquaintance. ¹⁴We took sweet counsel together, *and* walked unto the house of God in company. ¹⁵Let death seize upon them, *and* let them go down quick into hell[c]: for wickedness *is* in their dwellings, *and* among them.

¹⁶As for me, I will call upon God; and the LORD shall save me. ¹⁷Evening, and morning, and at noon, will I pray, and cry aloud: and he shall hear my voice. ¹⁸He hath delivered my soul in peace from the battle *that was* against me: for there were many with me. ¹⁹God

---

[a] overwhelmed: Heb. covered
[b] mine equal: Heb. according to my rank
[c] hell: or, the grave

shall hear, and afflict them, even he that abideth of old. Selah. Because they have no changes, therefore they fear not God. [20]He hath put forth his hands against such as be at peace with him: he hath broken[d] his covenant. [21] *The words* of his mouth were smoother than butter, but war *was* in his heart: his words were softer than oil, yet *were* they drawn swords. [22]Cast thy burden[e] upon the LORD, and he shall sustain thee: he shall never suffer the righteous to be moved. [23]But thou, O God, shalt bring them down into the pit of destruction: bloody[f] and deceitful men shall not live out half their days; but I will trust in thee.

56

To the chief Musician upon Jonath-elemrechokim, Michtam[a] of David, when the Philistines took him in Gath.

[1]Be merciful unto me, O God: for man would swallow me up; he fighting daily oppresseth me. [2]Mine enemies[b] would daily swallow *me* up: for *they be* many that fight against me, O thou most High. [3]What time I am afraid, I will trust in thee. [4]In God I will praise his word, in God I have put my trust; I will not fear what flesh can do unto me. [5]Every day they wrest my words: all their thoughts *are* against me for evil. [6]They gather themselves together, they hide themselves, they mark my steps, when they wait for my soul. [7]Shall they

escape by iniquity? in *thine* anger cast down the people, O God.

[8]Thou tellest my wanderings: put thou my tears into thy bottle: *are they* not in thy book? [9]When I cry *unto thee,* then shall mine enemies turn back: this I know; for God *is* for me. [10]In God will I praise *his* word: in the LORD will I praise *his* word. [11]In God have I put my trust: I will not be afraid what man can do unto me. [12]Thy vows *are* upon me, O God: I will render praises unto thee. [13]For thou hast delivered my soul from death: *wilt* not *thou deliver* my feet from falling, that I may walk before God in the light of the living?

57

To the chief Musician, Altaschith[a], Michtam of David, when he fled from Saul in the cave.

[1]Be merciful unto me, O God, be merciful unto me: for my soul trusteth in thee: yea, in the shadow of thy wings will I make my refuge, until *these* calamities be overpast. [2]I will cry unto God most high; unto God that performeth *all things* for me. [3]He shall send from heaven, and save me *from* the reproach of him that would swallow me up. Selah God shall send forth his mercy and his truth. [4]My soul *is* among lions: *and* I lie *even among* them that are set on fire, *even* the sons of men, whose teeth *are* spears and arrows, and their tongue a sharp sword. [5]Be thou exalted, O God, above the heavens; *let* thy glory *be* above all the

---

[d] broken: Heb. profaned
[e] burden: or, gift
[f] bloody . . . : Heb. men of bloods and deceit
[a] Michtam . . . : or, A golden Psalm of David
[b] enemies: Heb. observers
[a] Altaschith: or, Destroy not

Devotional Moment

•

Protection

57:1-4 The "lions" that were seeking to destroy David's life were likely Saul and his men tracking down the fleeing David, who was hiding in a cave. Despite this terrifying situation, David's heart was quiet and confident (57:7) because he knew God's love is steadfast. Trials, such as gossip, character assassinations, and physical attacks, may hurt us, but God can heal those wounds when we turn our problems over to him rather than responding in kind or seeking revenge. When you are being attacked or are feeling vulnerable, yes, flee like David did. But do not underestimate the importance of praying, too. Through prayer, you can hide under God's protecting wings.

earth. ⁶They have prepared a net for my steps; my soul is bowed down: they have digged a pit before me, into the midst whereof they are fallen *themselves.* Selah.

⁷My heart is fixed[b], O God, my heart is fixed: I will sing and give praise. ⁸Awake up, my glory; awake, psaltery and harp: I *myself* will awake early. ⁹I will praise thee, O Lord, among the people: I will sing unto thee among the nations. ¹⁰For thy mercy *is* great unto the heavens, and thy truth unto the clouds. ¹¹Be thou exalted, O God, above the heavens: *let* thy glory *be* above all the earth.

58

To the chief Musician, Altaschith[a], Michtam of David.

¹Do ye indeed speak righteousness, O congregation? do ye judge uprightly, O ye sons of men? ²Yea, in heart ye work wickedness; ye weigh the violence of your hands in the earth. ³The wicked are estranged from the womb: they go astray as soon as they be born, speaking lies. ⁴Their poison *is* like the poison[b] of a serpent: *they are* like the deaf adder *that* stoppeth her ear; ⁵Which will not hearken to the voice of charmers, charming[c] never so wisely.

⁶Break their teeth, O God, in their mouth: break out the great teeth of the young lions, O LORD. ⁷Let them melt away as waters *which* run continually: *when* he bendeth *his bow to shoot* his arrows, let them be as cut in pieces. ⁸As a snail *which* melteth, let *every one of them* pass away: *like* the untimely birth of a woman, *that* they may not see the sun. ⁹Before your pots can feel the thorns, he shall take them away as with a whirlwind, both living, and in *his* wrath. ¹⁰The righteous shall rejoice when he seeth the vengeance: he shall wash his feet in the blood of the wicked. ¹¹So that a man shall say, Verily *there is* a reward[d] for the righteous: verily he is a God that judgeth in the earth.

59

To the chief Musician, Altaschith[a], Michtam of David; when Saul sent, and they watched the house to kill him.

¹Deliver me from mine enemies, O

ᵇ fixed: or, prepared

ᵃ Altaschith . . . : or, Destroy not, A golden Psalm of David

ᵇ like the poison: Heb. according to the likeness, etc

ᶜ charming . . . : or, be the charmer never so cunning

ᵈ a reward . . . : Heb. fruit of the, etc

ᵃ Altaschith . . . : or, Destroy not, A golden Psalm of David

my God: defend me from them that rise up against me. ²Deliver me from the workers of iniquity, and save me from bloody men. ³For, lo, they lie in wait for my soul: the mighty are gathered against me; not *for* my transgression, nor *for* my sin, O LORD. ⁴They run and prepare themselves without *my* fault: awake to help[b] me, and behold. ⁵Thou therefore, O LORD God of hosts, the God of Israel, awake to visit all the heathen: be not merciful to any wicked transgressors. Selah. ⁶They return at evening: they make a noise like a dog, and go round about the city. ⁷Behold, they belch out with their mouth: swords *are* in their lips: for who, *say they*, doth hear?

⁸But thou, O LORD, shalt laugh at them; thou shalt have all the heathen in derision. ⁹*Because of* his strength will I wait upon thee: for God *is* my defence[c]. ¹⁰The God of my mercy shall prevent me: God shall let me see *my desire* upon mine enemies[d]. ¹¹Slay them not, lest my people forget: scatter them by thy power; and bring them down, O Lord our shield. ¹²*For* the sin of their mouth *and* the words of their lips let them even be taken in their pride: and for cursing and lying *which* they speak. ¹³Consume *them* in wrath, consume *them*, that they *may* not *be*: and let them know that God ruleth in Jacob unto the ends of the earth. Selah. ¹⁴And at evening let them return; *and* let them make a noise like a dog, and go

round about the city. ¹⁵Let them wander up and down for meat[e], and grudge if they be not satisfied. ¹⁶But I will sing of thy power; yea, I will sing aloud of thy mercy in the morning: for thou hast been my defence and refuge in the day of my trouble. ¹⁷Unto thee, O my strength, will I sing: for God *is* my defence, *and* the God of my mercy.

60

To the chief Musician upon Shushaneduth, Michtam[a] of David, to teach; when he strove with Aramnaharaim and with Aramzobah, when Joab returned, and smote of Edom in the valley of salt twelve thousand.

¹O God, thou hast cast us off, thou hast scattered us, thou hast been displeased; O turn thyself to us again. ²Thou hast made the earth to tremble; thou hast broken it: heal the breaches thereof; for it shaketh. ³Thou hast shewed thy people hard things: thou hast made us to drink the wine of astonishment. ⁴Thou hast given a banner to them that fear thee, that it may be displayed because of the truth. Selah. ⁵That thy beloved may be delivered; save *with* thy right hand, and hear me. ⁶God hath spoken in his holiness; I will rejoice, I will divide Shechem, and mete out the valley of Succoth. ⁷Gilead *is* mine, and Manasseh *is* mine; Ephraim also *is* the strength of mine head; Judah *is* my lawgiver; ⁸Moab *is* my washpot; over Edom will

---

ᵇ help: Heb. meet
ᶜ defence: Heb. high place
ᵈ enemies: Heb. observers
ᵉ for meat: Heb. to eat
ᵃ Michtam: or, A golden Psalm

I cast out my shoe: Philistia, triumph[b] thou because of me. ⁹Who will bring me *into* the strong[c] city? who will lead me into Edom? ¹⁰*Wilt* not thou, O God, *which* hadst cast us off? and *thou*, O God, *which* didst not go out with our armies? ¹¹Give us help from trouble: for vain *is* the help of man[d]. ¹²Through God we shall do valiantly: for he *it is that* shall tread down our enemies.

61

To the chief Musician upon Neginah, *A Psalm* of David.

¹Hear my cry, O God; attend unto my prayer. ²From the end of the earth will I cry unto thee, when my heart is overwhelmed: lead me to the rock *that* is higher than I. ³For thou hast been a shelter for me, *and* a strong tower from the enemy. ⁴I will abide in thy taberna-

---

Devotional Moment

•

Leaving Home

61:1-8 Whatever tent site David called home, God was with him there. When strange surroundings left David feeling insecure, his God provided rock-like eternal security. Leaving home—for college, military service, marriage, a job transfer, or whatever—can be a scary experience. Remember to call on God your Father, an ever-present help, and praise God with his people in your home away from home.

---

cle for ever: I will trust[a] in the covert of thy wings. Selah.

⁵For thou, O God, hast heard my vows: thou hast given *me* the heritage of those that fear thy name. ⁶Thou wilt prolong the king's life: *and* his years as many generations. ⁷He shall abide before God for ever: O prepare mercy and truth, *which* may preserve him. ⁸So will I sing praise unto thy name for ever, that I may daily perform my vows.

62

To the chief Musician, to Jeduthun, A Psalm of David.

¹Truly my soul waiteth upon God: from him *cometh* my salvation. ²He only *is* my rock and my salvation; *he is* my defence[a]; I shall not be greatly moved. ³How long will ye imagine mischief against a man? ye shall be slain all of you: as a bowing wall *shall ye be, and as* a tottering fence. ⁴They only consult to cast *him* down from his excellency: they delight in lies: they bless with their mouth, but they curse inwardly[b]. Selah. ⁵My soul, wait thou only upon God; for my expectation *is* from him. ⁶He only *is* my rock and my salvation: *he is* my defence; I shall not be moved. ⁷In God *is* my salvation and my glory: the rock of my strength, *and* my refuge, *is* in God.

⁸Trust in him at all times; *ye* people, pour out your heart before him: God *is* a refuge for us. Selah. ⁹Surely men of low degree *are* vanity, *and* men

---

of high degree *are* a lie: to be laid in the balance, they *are* altogether[c] *lighter* than vanity. [10]Trust not in oppression, and become not vain in robbery: if riches increase, set not your heart *upon them.* [11]God hath spoken once; twice have I heard this; that power[d] *belongeth* unto God. [12]Also unto thee, O Lord, *belongeth* mercy: for thou renderest to every man according to his work.

63

A Psalm of David, when he was in the wilderness of Judah.

[1]O God, thou *art* my God; early will I seek thee: my soul thirsteth for thee, my flesh longeth for thee in a dry and thirsty[a] land, where no water is; [2]To see thy power and thy glory, so *as* I have seen thee in the sanctuary.

[3]Because thy lovingkindness *is* better than life, my lips shall praise thee.

Devotional Moment

Singleness

63:1-8 David, surrounded by assistants and admirers, knew that his best friend was God. Even if colleagues left him, God would fill his heart. Single people can show and feel as much love as anyone else. And they can often identify with what David felt about God. If you are single, whether never married or single again, this is a useful psalm to pray. God can minister to you in your loneliness and yearning for intimacy. Ask him to do it.

[4]Thus will I bless thee while I live: I will lift up my hands in thy name. [5]My soul shall be satisfied as *with* marrow[b] and fatness; and my mouth shall praise *thee* with joyful lips: [6]When I remember thee upon my bed, *and* meditate on thee in the *night* watches.

[7]Because thou hast been my help, therefore in the shadow of thy wings will I rejoice. [8]My soul followeth hard after thee: thy right hand upholdeth me. [9]But those *that* seek my soul, to destroy *it,* shall go into the lower parts of the earth. [10]They shall fall[c] by the sword: they shall be a portion for foxes. [11]But the king shall rejoice in God; every one that sweareth by him shall glory: but the mouth of them that speak lies shall be stopped.

64

To the chief Musician, A Psalm of David.

[1]Hear my voice, O God, in my prayer: preserve my life from fear of the enemy. [2]Hide me from the secret counsel of the wicked; from the insurrection of the workers of iniquity: [3]Who whet their tongue like a sword, *and* bend *their bows to shoot* their arrows, *even* bitter words: [4]That they may shoot in secret at the perfect: suddenly do they shoot at him, and fear not. [5]They encourage themselves *in* an evil matter[a]: they commune of laying snares privily; they say, Who shall see them? [6]They

[c] altogether: or, alike

[d] power: or, strength

[a] thirsty: Heb. weary

[b] marrow: Heb. fatness

[c] They shall fall . . . : Heb. They shall make him run out like water by the hands of

[a] matter: or, speech

search out iniquities; they accomplish a diligent search: both the inward *thought* of every one *of them,* and the heart, *is* deep.

⁷But God shall shoot at them *with* an arrow; suddenly shall they be wounded. ⁸So they shall make their own tongue to fall upon themselves: all that see them shall flee away. ⁹And all men shall fear, and shall declare the work of God; for they shall wisely consider of his doing. ¹⁰The righteous shall be glad in the LORD, and shall trust in him; and all the upright in heart shall glory.

65

To the chief Musician, A Psalm *and* Song of David.

¹Praise waitethª for thee, O God, in Sion: and unto thee shall the vow be performed. ²O thou that hearest prayer, unto thee shall all flesh come. ³Iniquities prevail against me: *as for* our transgressions, thou shalt purge them away. ⁴Blessed *is the man whom* thou choosest, and causest to approach *unto thee, that* he may dwell in thy courts: we shall be satisfied with the goodness of thy house, *even* of thy holy temple. ⁵*By* terrible things in righteousness wilt thou answer us, O God of our salvation; *who art* the confidence of all the ends of the earth, and of them that are afar off *upon* the sea:

⁶Which by his strength setteth fast the mountains; *being* girded with power: ⁷Which stilleth the noise of the seas, the noise of their waves, and the

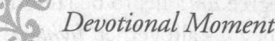

Devotional Moment
•
Land

65:9-13 God shows his care by giving us his creation to enjoy. In times past the homestead was a place where kids, parents, and grandparents could all come together to share time and build family foundations. Whether you own land or not, enjoy the gift of God's creation with your family. Pick a spot to which you can return often—a park for picnics, a lake for fishing, a place for vacations. Let nature point your family back to God.

tumult of the people. ⁸They also that dwell in the uttermost parts are afraid at thy tokens: thou makest the outgoings of the morning and evening to rejoiceᵇ. ⁹Thou visitest the earth, and waterest it: thou greatly enrichest it with the river of God, *which* is full of water: thou preparest them corn, when thou hast so provided for it. ¹⁰Thou waterest the ridges thereof abundantly: thou settlestᶜ the furrows thereof: thou makest it soft with showers: thou blessest the springing thereof. ¹¹Thou crownest the year with thy goodness; and thy paths drop fatness. ¹²They drop *upon* the pastures of the wilderness: and the little hills rejoiceᵈ on every side. ¹³The pastures are clothed with flocks; the valleys also are covered over with corn; they shout for joy, they also sing.

66

To the chief Musician, A Song *or* Psalm.

ª waiteth: Heb. is silent
ᵇ rejoice: or, sing
ᶜ settlest: or, causest rain to descend into
ᵈ rejoice . . . : Heb. are girded with joy

¹Make a joyful noise unto God, all ye lands: ²Sing forth the honour of his name: make his praise glorious. ³Say unto God, How terrible *art thou in* thy works! through the greatness of thy power shall thine enemies submit[a] themselves unto thee. ⁴All the earth shall worship thee, and shall sing unto thee; they shall sing *to* thy name. Selah. ⁵Come and see the works of God: *he is* terrible *in his* doing toward the children of men. ⁶He turned the sea into dry *land*: they went through the flood on foot: there did we rejoice in him. ⁷He ruleth by his power for ever; his eyes behold the nations: let not the rebellious exalt themselves. Selah.

⁸O bless our God, ye people, and make the voice of his praise to be heard: ⁹Which holdeth[b] our soul in life, and suffereth not our feet to be moved. ¹⁰For thou, O God, hast proved us: thou hast tried us, as silver is tried. ¹¹Thou broughtest us into the net; thou laidst affliction upon our loins. ¹²Thou hast caused men to ride over our heads; we went through fire and through water: but thou broughtest us out into a wealthy[c] *place*

¹³I will go into thy house with burnt offerings: I will pay thee my vows, ¹⁴Which my lips have uttered[d], and my mouth hath spoken, when I was in trouble. ¹⁵I will offer unto thee burnt sacrifices of fatlings[e], with the incense of rams; I will offer bullocks with

goats. Selah. ¹⁶Come *and* hear, all ye that fear God, and I will declare what he hath done for my soul. ¹⁷I cried unto him with my mouth, and he was extolled with my tongue. ¹⁸If I regard iniquity in my heart, the Lord will not hear *me*. ¹⁹*But* verily God hath heard *me*; he hath attended to the voice of my prayer. ²⁰Blessed *be* God, which hath not turned away my prayer, nor his mercy from me.

67

To the chief Musician on Neginoth, A Psalm *or* Song.

¹God be merciful unto us, and bless us; *and* cause his face to shine upon us; Selah. ²That thy way may be known upon earth, thy saving health among all nations. ³Let the people praise thee, O God; let all the people praise thee. ⁴O let the nations be glad and sing for joy: for thou shalt judge the people righteously, and govern[a] the nations upon earth. Selah. ⁵Let the people praise thee, O God; let all the people praise thee. ⁶*Then* shall the earth yield her increase; *and* God, *even* our own God, shall bless us. ⁷God shall bless us; and all the ends of the earth shall fear him.

68

To the chief Musician, A Psalm *or* Song of David.

¹Let God arise, let his enemies be

---

[a] submit . . . : or, yield feigned obedience: Heb. lie
[b] holdeth: Heb. putteth
[c] wealthy: Heb. moist
[d] uttered: Heb. opened
[e] fatlings: Heb. marrow
[a] govern: Heb. lead

scattered: let them also that hate him flee before[a] him. [2]As smoke is driven away, *so* drive *them* away: as wax melteth before the fire, *so* let the wicked perish at the presence of God. [3]But let the righteous be glad; let them rejoice before God: yea, let them exceedingly[b] rejoice. [4]Sing unto God, sing praises to his name: extol him that rideth upon the heavens by his name JAH, and rejoice before him. [5]A father of the fatherless, and a judge of the widows, *is* God in his holy habitation. [6]God setteth the solitary in families[c]: he bringeth out those which are bound with chains: but the rebellious dwell in a dry *land*.

[7]O God, when thou wentest forth before thy people, when thou didst march through the wilderness; Selah: [8]The earth shook, the heavens also dropped at the presence of God: *even* Sinai itself *was moved* at the presence of God, the God of Israel. [9]Thou, O God, didst send[d] a plentiful rain, whereby thou didst confirm thine inheritance, when it was weary. [10]Thy congregation hath dwelt therein: thou, O God, hast prepared of thy goodness for the poor. [11]The Lord gave the word: great *was* the company[e] of those that published *it*. [12]Kings of armies did flee apace: and she that tarried at home divided the spoil. [13]Though ye have lien among the pots, *yet shall ye be as* the wings of a dove cov-

ered with silver, and her feathers with yellow gold. [14]When the Almighty scattered kings in it[f], it was *white* as snow in Salmon.

[15]The hill of God *is as* the hill of Bashan; an high hill *as* the hill of Bashan. [16]Why leap ye, ye high hills? *this is* the hill *which* God desireth to dwell in; yea, the LORD will dwell *in it* for ever. [17]The chariots of God *are* twenty thousand, *even* thousands of angels: the Lord *is* among them, *as in* Sinai, in the holy place. [18]Thou hast ascended on high, thou hast led captivity captive: thou hast received gifts for men[g]; yea, *for* the rebellious also, that the LORD God might dwell *among them*. [19]Blessed *be* the Lord, *who* daily loadeth us *with benefits, even* the God of our salvation. Selah. [20]*He that is* our God *is* the God of salvation; and unto GOD the Lord *belong* the issues from death. [21]But God shall wound the head of his enemies, *and* the hairy scalp of such an one as goeth on still in his trespasses.

[22]The Lord said, I will bring again from Bashan, I will bring *my people* again from the depths of the sea: [23]That thy foot may be dipped[h] in the blood of *thine* enemies, *and* the tongue of thy dogs in the same. [24]They have seen thy goings, O God; *even* the goings of my God, my King, in the sanctuary. [25]The singers went before, the players on in-

---

[a] before . . . : Heb. from his face
[b] exceedingly . . . : Heb. rejoice with gladness
[c] in families: Heb. in a house
[d] send: Heb. shake out
[e] company: Heb. army
[f] in it . . . : or, for her, she
[g] for men: Heb. in the man
[h] dipped: or, red

struments *followed* after; among *them were* the damsels playing with timbrels. [26]Bless ye God in the congregations, *even* the Lord, from the fountain of Israel. [27]There *is* little Benjamin *with* their ruler, the princes of Judah *and* their council, the princes of Zebulun, *and* the princes of Naphtali. [28]Thy God hath commanded thy strength: strengthen, O God, that which thou hast wrought for us. [29]Because of thy temple at Jerusalem shall kings bring presents unto thee. [30]Rebuke the company[i] of spearmen, the multitude of the bulls, with the calves of the people, *till every one* submit himself with pieces of silver: scatter thou the people *that* delight in war. [31]Princes shall come out of Egypt; Ethiopia shall soon stretch out her hands unto God.

[32]Sing unto God, ye kingdoms of the earth; O sing praises unto the Lord; Selah: [33]To him that rideth upon the heavens of heavens, *which were* of old; lo, he doth send out his voice, *and that* a mighty voice. [34]Ascribe ye strength unto God: his excellency *is* over Israel, and his strength *is* in the clouds[j]. [35]O God, *thou art* terrible out of thy holy places: the God of Israel *is* he that giveth strength and power unto *his* people. Blessed *be* God.

69

To the chief Musician upon Shoshannim, *A Psalm* of David.

[1]Save me, O God; for the waters are come in unto *my* soul. [2]I sink in

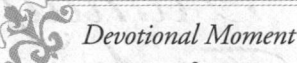

Devotional Moment
•
Mourning
69:3 David's full range of emotions included grief. And David knew that the best thing to do with grief is to cry on God's shoulder. It is good to mourn. When a parent dies, children should mourn. When a child dies, parents should mourn. Bring your grief to God as a child brings tears to a parent's sure shoulder. When you need to cry, cry. And don't be afraid to tell God how you feel.

deep mire[a], where *there is* no standing: I am come into deep waters, where the floods overflow me. [3]I am weary of my crying: my throat is dried: mine eyes fail while I wait for my God. [4]They that hate me without a cause are more than the hairs of mine head: they that would destroy me, *being* mine enemies wrongfully, are mighty: then I restored *that* which I took not away. [5]O God, thou knowest my foolishness; and my sins[b] are not hid from thee. [6]Let not them that wait on thee, O Lord GOD of hosts, be ashamed for my sake: let not those that seek thee be confounded for my sake, O God of Israel. [7]Because for thy sake I have borne reproach; shame hath covered my face. [8]I am become a stranger unto my brethren, and an alien unto my mother's children. [9]For the zeal of thine house hath eaten me up; and the reproaches of them that reproached thee are fallen upon me. [10]When I wept, *and chastened* my soul

---

[i] the company . . . : or, the beasts of the reeds
[j] clouds: or, heavens
[a] deep mire: Heb. the mire of depth
[b] sins: Heb. guiltiness

Family Traditions

There Is Always Time for Worship

PSALMS 66, 98, 100

The Bible tells us the rivers clap, the mountains sing, and people shout and make music. What do your kids see and hear from you—does it include worship?

Music lessons set a fine foundation for family worship. But for those whose talents lie elsewhere, or for whom music lessons are an unaffordable luxury, there are alternatives. The Wilsons were never able to have a piano, but there has always been a tambourine, an old guitar, and a recorder to make music with.

And don't imagine an official sit-down worship hour is the only way to do it.

"I pray with our kids the very first thing each day," says Sally Keehan. "We used to tuck them in at night and do the singing, prayer, and Scripture time then. But now as teenagers, they sometimes stay up later than we do. So I wake them up every morning by sitting beside them, singing and reading the Bible aloud. Then we pray together before they get out of bed."

The McNamarra family says camping trips are their most meaningful times for worship. "There's nothing like sitting around a fire under stars to shut down inhibitions and inspire us to praise God. We pack hymnbooks and chorus sheets right along with the lantern and folding chairs."

"With three little boys close in age, we had a noisy house," says Krista Watney. "One day it hit me—I can tap into this! After all, the Bible says, 'Shout to the Lord!' So whenever I felt it was getting out of hand, I'd sit down at our keyboard and start to play a rousing praise song. Without exception, the boys would gather around and join in. We'd end up taking turns singing their favorites."

Jack Churchill talks about rainbows, ocean waves, rain showers, and blossoming trees as worship opportunities. "We always stop when we see them. We listen. We sniff. We sing a one-liner or repeat a Bible passage. One warm night we were sacked out on our deck when a thunder storm rolled in from the west. We huddled under the eaves and watched it—felt it—pass by. There, without a word, was the most powerful worship our family ever did."

Other families encourage children to put Bible passages to tunes, write their own hymns, or compile books of prayer to be read aloud. However your family lifts their voices, it is music to God's ears. Come into his courts with songs of praise; there is always time for worship!

with fasting, that was to my reproach. ¹¹I made sackcloth also my garment; and I became a proverb to them. ¹²They that sit in the gate speak against me; and I *was* the song of the drunkards*ᶜ*.

¹³But as for me, my prayer *is* unto thee, O LORD, *in* an acceptable time: O God, in the multitude of thy mercy hear me, in the truth of thy salvation. ¹⁴Deliver me out of the mire, and let me not sink: let me be delivered from them that hate me, and out of the deep waters. ¹⁵Let not the waterflood overflow me, neither let the deep swallow me up, and let not the pit shut her mouth upon me. ¹⁶Hear me, O LORD; for thy lovingkindness *is* good: turn unto me according to the multitude of thy tender mercies. ¹⁷And hide not thy face from thy servant; for I am in trouble: hear*ᵈ* me speedily. ¹⁸Draw nigh unto my soul, *and* redeem it: deliver me because of mine enemies. ¹⁹Thou hast known my reproach, and my shame, and my dishonour: mine adversaries *are* all before thee. ²⁰Reproach hath broken my heart; and I am full of heaviness: and I looked *for some* to take pity, but *there was* none; and for comforters, but I found none. ²¹They gave me also gall for my meat; and in my thirst they gave me vinegar to drink.

²²Let their table become a snare before them: and *that which should have been* for *their* welfare, *let it become* a trap. ²³Let their eyes be darkened, that they see not; and make their loins con-

tinually to shake. ²⁴Pour out thine indignation upon them, and let thy wrathful anger take hold of them. ²⁵Let their habitation*ᵉ* be desolate; *and* let none dwell in their tents. ²⁶For they persecute *him* whom thou hast smitten; and they talk to the grief of those whom thou hast wounded. ²⁷Add iniquity unto their iniquity: and let them not come into thy righteousness. ²⁸Let them be blotted out of the book of the living, and not be written with the righteous. ²⁹But I *am* poor and sorrowful: let thy salvation, O God, set me up on high.

³⁰I will praise the name of God with a song, and will magnify him with thanksgiving. ³¹*This* also shall please the LORD better than an ox *or* bullock that hath horns and hoofs. ³²The humble*ᶠ* shall see *this, and* be glad: and your heart shall live that seek God. ³³For the LORD heareth the poor, and despiseth not his prisoners. ³⁴Let the heaven and earth praise him, the seas, and every thing that moveth*ᵍ* therein. ³⁵For God will save Zion, and will build the cities of Judah: that they may dwell there, and have it in possession. ³⁶The seed also of his servants shall inherit it: and they that love his name shall dwell therein.

70

To the chief Musician, *A Psalm* of David, to bring to remembrance.

¹*Make haste*, O God, to deliver me;

ᶜ drunkards: Heb. drinkers of strong drink
ᵈ hear . . . : Heb. make haste to hear me
ᵉ their habitation: Heb. their palace
ᶠ humble: or, meek
ᵍ moveth: Heb. creepeth

make haste to help[a] me, O LORD. [2]Let them be ashamed and confounded that seek after my soul: let them be turned backward, and put to confusion, that desire my hurt. [3]Let them be turned back for a reward of their shame that say, Aha, aha. [4]Let all those that seek thee rejoice and be glad in thee: and let such as love thy salvation say continually, Let God be magnified. [5]But I *am* poor and needy: make haste unto me, O God: thou *art* my help and my deliverer; O LORD, make no tarrying.

71

[1]In thee, O LORD, do I put my trust: let me never be put to confusion. [2]Deliver me in thy righteousness, and cause me to escape: incline thine ear unto me, and save me. [3]Be thou my strong habitation, whereunto I may continually resort: thou hast given commandment to save me; for thou *art* my rock and my fortress. [4]Deliver me, O my God, out of the hand of the wicked, out of the hand of the unrighteous and cruel man. [5]For thou *art* my hope, O Lord GOD: *thou art* my trust from my youth. [6]By thee have I been holden up from the womb: thou art he that took me out of my mother's bowels: my praise *shall be* continually of thee. [7]I am as a wonder unto many; but thou *art* my strong refuge. [8]Let my mouth be filled *with* thy praise *and with* thy honour all the day. [9]Cast me not off in the time of old age; forsake me not when my strength faileth. [10]For mine enemies speak against me; and they that lay wait for my soul take counsel together, [11]Say-

ing, God hath forsaken him: persecute and take him; for *there is* none to deliver *him*. [12]O God, be not far from me: O my God, make haste for my help. [13]Let them be confounded *and* consumed that are adversaries to my soul; let them be covered *with* reproach and dishonour that seek my hurt.

[14]But I will hope continually, and will yet praise thee more and more. [15]My mouth shall shew forth thy righteousness *and* thy salvation all the day; for I know not the numbers *thereof*. [16]I will go in the strength of the Lord GOD: I will make mention of thy righteousness, *even* of thine only. [17]O God, thou hast taught me from my youth: and hitherto have I declared thy wondrous works. [18]Now also when[a] I am old and grayheaded, O God, forsake me not; until I have shewed thy strength unto *this* generation, *and* thy power to every one *that* is to come. [19]Thy righteousness also, O God, *is* very high, who hast done great things: O

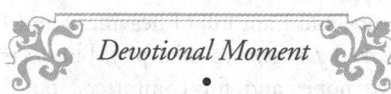

Devotional Moment

•

Aging Gracefully

71:18 Aging brings changes, not always enjoyable. The writer of this psalm recommended that as youthful energies recede, one important life-goal should take over: telling of God's love and care—passing on the faith. For that to happen, a person must shift attention from aches, pains, and pillboxes to God, grace, and promise—from self and its weakness to the gospel and its hope. One way to age gracefully is to tell others of God's goodness. See if you can do that in some way today.

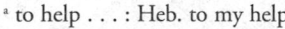

[a] to help . . . : Heb. to my help
[a] when . . . : Heb. unto old age and gray hairs

God, who *is* like unto thee! ²⁰*Thou,* which hast shewed me great and sore troubles, shalt quicken me again, and shalt bring me up again from the depths of the earth. ²¹Thou shalt increase my greatness, and comfort me on every side. ²²I will also praise thee with the psaltery[b], *even* thy truth, O my God: unto thee will I sing with the harp, O thou Holy One of Israel. ²³My lips shall greatly rejoice when I sing unto thee; and my soul, which thou hast redeemed. ²⁴My tongue also shall talk of thy righteousness all the day long: for they are confounded, for they are brought unto shame, that seek my hurt.

72

A Psalm for Solomon.

¹Give the king thy judgments, O God, and thy righteousness unto the king's son. ²He shall judge thy people with righteousness, and thy poor with judgment. ³The mountains shall bring peace to the people, and the little hills, by righteousness. ⁴He shall judge the poor of the people, he shall save the children of the needy, and shall break in pieces the oppressor. ⁵They shall fear thee as long as the sun and moon endure, throughout all generations. ⁶He shall come down like rain upon the mown grass: as showers *that* water the earth. ⁷In his days shall the righteous flourish; and abundance of peace so long as the moon endureth. ⁸He shall have dominion also from sea to sea, and from the river unto the ends of the earth. ⁹They

that dwell in the wilderness shall bow before him; and his enemies shall lick the dust. ¹⁰The kings of Tarshish and of the isles shall bring presents: the kings of Sheba and Seba shall offer gifts. ¹¹Yea, all kings shall fall down before him: all nations shall serve him. ¹²For he shall deliver the needy when he crieth; the poor also, and *him* that hath no helper. ¹³He shall spare the poor and needy, and shall save the souls of the needy. ¹⁴He shall redeem their soul from deceit and violence: and precious shall their blood be in his sight. ¹⁵And he shall live, and to him shall be given[a] of the gold of Sheba: prayer also shall be made for him continually; *and* daily shall he be praised. ¹⁶There shall be an handful of corn in the earth upon the top of the mountains; the fruit thereof shall shake like Lebanon: and *they* of the city shall flourish like grass of the earth. ¹⁷His name shall endure for ever: his name shall be continued as long as the sun: and *men* shall be blessed in him: all nations shall call him blessed.

¹⁸Blessed *be* the LORD God, the God of Israel, who only doeth wondrous things. ¹⁹And blessed *be* his glorious name for ever: and let the whole earth be filled *with* his glory; Amen, and Amen. ²⁰The prayers of David the son of Jesse are ended.

73

A Psalm of Asaph.

¹Truly God *is* good to Israel, *even* to such as are of a clean heart. ²But as for me, my feet were almost gone; my steps had well nigh slipped. ³For I was envious

---

[b] the psaltery: Heb. the instrument of psaltery
[a] shall be given: Heb. one shall give

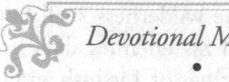

Devotional Moment
•
Envy

73:1-20, 26 It doesn't seem fair that people who live godless lives can prosper while our family struggles. Some families seem to have everything going for them—job security, full health, exciting vacations, kids who get the lead part in the school play, lawns that never have dandelions in them—and we envy them. And envy leads only to unhappiness and discontentment. We can find balance again when we look at ourselves in relation to God rather than in relation to other people.

at the foolish, *when* I saw the prosperity of the wicked. ⁴For *there are* no bands in their death: but their strength *is* firmᵃ. ⁵They *are* not in trouble *as other* men; neither are they plagued like *other* men. ⁶Therefore pride compasseth them about as a chain; violence covereth them *as* a garment. ⁷Their eyes stand out with fatness: they have more than heart could wish. ⁸They are corrupt, and speak wickedly *concerning* oppression: they speak loftily. ⁹They set their mouth against the heavens, and their tongue walketh through the earth. ¹⁰Therefore his people return hither: and waters of a full *cup* are wrung out to them. ¹¹And they say, How doth God know? and is there knowledge in the most High? ¹²Behold, these *are* the ungodly, who prosper in the world; they increase *in* riches. ¹³Verily I have cleansed my heart *in* vain, and washed my hands in innocency.

¹⁴For all the day long have I been plagued, and chastenedᵇ every morning. ¹⁵If I say, I will speak thus; behold, I should offend *against* the generation of thy children. ¹⁶When I thought to know this, it *was* too painful for me; ¹⁷Until I went into the sanctuary of God; *then* understood I their end. ¹⁸Surely thou didst set them in slippery places: thou castedst them down into destruction. ¹⁹How are they *brought* into desolation, as in a moment! they are utterly consumed with terrors. ²⁰As a dream when *one* awaketh; *so,* O Lord, when thou awakest, thou shalt despise their image.

²¹Thus my heart was grieved, and I was pricked in my reins. ²²So foolish *was* I, and ignorantᶜ: I was *as* a beast beforeᵈ thee. ²³Nevertheless I *am* continually with thee: thou hast holden *me* by my right hand. ²⁴Thou shalt guide me with thy counsel, and afterward receive me *to* glory. ²⁵Whom have I in heaven *but thee?* and *there is* none upon earth *that* I desire beside thee. ²⁶My flesh and my heart faileth: *but* God *is* the strengthᵉ of my heart, and my portion for ever. ²⁷For, lo, they that are far from thee shall perish: thou hast destroyed all them that go a whoring from thee. ²⁸But *it is* good for me to draw near to God: I have put my trust in the Lord GOD, that I may declare all thy works.

74

Maschil of Asaph.

¹O God, why hast thou cast *us* off

ᵃ firm: Heb. fat
ᵇ chastened: Heb. my chastisement was
ᶜ ignorant: Heb. I knew not
ᵈ before Heb. with
ᵉ strength: Heb. rock

for ever? *why* doth thine anger smoke against the sheep of thy pasture? [2]Remember thy congregation, *which* thou hast purchased of old; the rod[a] of thine inheritance, *which* thou hast redeemed; this mount Zion, wherein thou hast dwelt. [3]Lift up thy feet unto the perpetual desolations; *even* all *that* the enemy hath done wickedly in the sanctuary. [4]Thine enemies roar in the midst of thy congregations; they set up their ensigns *for* signs. [5]*A man* was famous according as he had lifted up axes upon the thick trees. [6]But now they break down the carved work thereof at once with axes and hammers. [7]They have cast[b] fire into thy sanctuary, they have defiled *by casting down* the dwelling place of thy name to the ground. [8]They said in their hearts, Let us destroy[c] them together: they have burned up all the synagogues of God in the land. [9]We see not our signs: *there is* no more any prophet: neither *is there* among us any that knoweth how long. [10]O God, how long shall the adversary reproach? shall the enemy blaspheme thy name for ever? [11]Why withdrawest thou thy hand, even thy right hand? pluck *it* out of thy bosom. [12]For God *is* my King of old, working salvation in the midst of the earth. [13]Thou didst divide[d] the sea by thy strength: thou brakest the heads of the dragons in the waters. [14]Thou brakest the heads of leviathan in pieces, *and* gavest him *to be* meat to the people inhabiting the wilderness.

---

[a] rod: or, tribe

[b] They have cast . . . : Heb. They have sent thy sanctuary unto the fire

[c] destroy: Heb. break

[d] divide: Heb. break

Worship
in Your Home

BUILDING MEMORIES THROUGH FAMILY DEVOTIONS

I will remember the works of the Lord: surely I will remember thy wonders of old.
Psalm 77:11

Memories weave today and tomorrow with yesterday. We draw upon our best memories and try to avoid our worst ones. What we forget is as important as what we remember.

Good memories encourage us to build upon them. Bad memories tell us, "Don't do that again."

That's why it's important to avoid guilt trips, pressure, and angry exchanges at the devotional "altar"; that's why we must strive to make it a time of joy and delight. It's more important to build a positive memory than to "make them learn." Devotions should be positive experiences as well as times of learning and worship.

Was your last family devotional time a delight or a frustration? If a delight, your children are probably ready to repeat it. If a frustration, they're probably not ready to repeat it.

Here are four suggestions to help you make every devotional time a positive memory-builder: (1) Take joy in the Lord. (2) Take delight in God's Word and show your dependence on it. (3) Appreciate your child as God's growing person. (4) Come into God's presence with thanksgiving and celebration—never grudgingly, sparingly, or hurriedly.

Make devotions a positive memory-building experience. Then your child will catch the glow, and devotions will become rich memories of great joy.

Devotional Moment
•
Waiting

74:11-18 Many times we ask God, "Why do you delay? Why hold back your power?" Waiting for God to answer is hard. Will our son recover from his illness? Will we ever be able to have children? When will our rebellious daughter return to God? God knows you are waiting. Rather than growing bitter, remember what God has done in the past, and know that he hasn't abandoned you. Remind yourself and others who are about to give up, "God is my King of old."

¹⁵Thou didst cleave the fountain and the flood: thou driedst up mighty^e rivers. ¹⁶The day *is* thine, the night also *is* thine: thou hast prepared the light and the sun. ¹⁷Thou hast set all the borders of the earth: thou hast made^f summer and winter.

¹⁸Remember this, *that* the enemy hath reproached, O LORD, and *that* the foolish people have blasphemed thy name. ¹⁹O deliver not the soul of thy turtledove unto the multitude *of the wicked*: forget not the congregation of thy poor for ever. ²⁰Have respect unto the covenant: for the dark places of the earth are full of the habitations of cruelty. ²¹O let not the oppressed return ashamed: let the poor and needy praise thy name. ²²Arise, O God, plead thine own cause: remember how the foolish man reproacheth thee daily. ²³Forget

not the voice of thine enemies: the tumult of those that rise up against thee increaseth^g continually.

75

To the chief Musician, Altaschith^a, A Psalm *or* Song of Asaph.

¹Unto thee, O God, do we give thanks, *unto thee* do we give thanks: for *that* thy name is near thy wondrous works declare. ²When I shall receive^b the congregation I will judge uprightly. ³The earth and all the inhabitants thereof are dissolved: I bear up the pillars of it. Selah. ⁴I said unto the fools, Deal not foolishly: and to the wicked, Lift not up the horn: ⁵Lift not up your horn on high: speak *not with* a stiff neck.

⁶For promotion *cometh* neither from the east, nor from the west, nor from the south^c. ⁷But God *is* the judge: he putteth down one, and setteth up another. ⁸For in the hand of the LORD *there is* a cup, and the wine is red; it is full of mixture; and he poureth out of the same: but the dregs thereof, all the wicked of the earth shall wring *them* out, *and* drink *them*. ⁹But I will declare for ever; I will sing praises to the God of Jacob. ¹⁰All the horns of the wicked also will I cut off; *but* the horns of the righteous shall be exalted.

76

To the chief Musician on Neginoth, A Psalm *or* Song of Asaph.

¹In Judah *is* God known: his name *is*

---

^e mighty . . . : Heb. rivers of strength
^f made: Heb. made them
^g increaseth: Heb. ascendeth
^a Altaschith: or, Destroy not
^b receive . . . : or, take a set time
^c south: Heb. desert

great in Israel. ²In Salem also is his tabernacle, and his dwelling place in Zion. ³There brake he the arrows of the bow, the shield, and the sword, and the battle. Selah. ⁴Thou *art* more glorious *and* excellent than the mountains of prey. ⁵The stouthearted are spoiled, they have slept their sleep: and none of the men of might have found their hands. ⁶At thy rebuke, O God of Jacob, both the chariot and horse are cast into a dead sleep.

⁷Thou, *even* thou, *art* to be feared: and who may stand in thy sight when once thou art angry? ⁸Thou didst cause judgment to be heard from heaven; the earth feared, and was still, ⁹When God arose to judgment, to save all the meek of the earth. Selah. ¹⁰Surely the wrath of man shall praise thee: the remainder of wrath shalt thou restrain. ¹¹Vow, and pay unto the LORD your God: let all that be round about him bring presents unto him that ought to be feared. ¹²He shall cut off the spirit of princes: *he is* terrible to the kings of the earth.

77

To the chief Musician, to Jeduthun, A Psalm of Asaph.

¹I cried unto God with my voice, *even* unto God with my voice; and he gave ear unto me. ²In the day of my trouble I sought the Lord: my sore[a] ran in the night, and ceased not: my soul refused to be comforted. ³I remembered God, and was troubled: I complained, and my spirit was overwhelmed. Selah. ⁴Thou holdest mine eyes waking: I am so troubled that I cannot speak. ⁵I have considered the days of old, the years of ancient times. ⁶I call to remembrance my song in the night: I commune with mine own heart: and my spirit made diligent search. ⁷Will the Lord cast off for ever? and will he be favourable no more? ⁸Is his mercy clean gone for ever? doth *his* promise fail for evermore[b]? ⁹Hath God forgotten to be gracious? hath he in anger shut up his tender mercies? Selah. ¹⁰And I said, This *is* my infirmity: *but I will remember* the years of the right hand of the most High.

¹¹I will remember the works of the LORD: surely I will remember thy wonders of old. ¹²I will meditate also of all thy work, and talk of thy doings. ¹³Thy way, O God, *is* in the sanctuary: who *is so* great a God as *our* God? ¹⁴Thou *art* the God that doest wonders: thou hast declared thy strength among the people. ¹⁵Thou hast with *thine* arm redeemed thy people, the sons of Jacob and Joseph. Selah. ¹⁶The waters saw thee, O God, the waters saw thee; they were afraid: the depths also were trou-

Devotional Moment
•
Family Stress

77:1-4, 11-12 Being human, we often find ourselves in deep trouble, desperately needing God's help. Our troubles overwhelm us, and we find ourselves unable to sleep or even to pray. What can we do when our job is in jeopardy, someone we love has deserted us, our finances are a mess, or our children are uncooperative or rebellious? Whether your life is crippled by stress, discouragement, or depression, remember what God has done for you in the past as did the writer of this psalm. Trust God to hold you in his hands as you go through stressful times.

ᵃ sore: Heb. hand
ᵇ for evermore: Heb. to generation and generation?

bled. ¹⁷The clouds poured out water: the skies sent out a sound: thine arrows also went abroad. ¹⁸The voice of thy thunder *was* in the heaven: the lightnings lightened the world: the earth trembled and shook. ¹⁹Thy way *is* in the sea, and thy path in the great waters, and thy footsteps are not known. ²⁰Thou leddest thy people like a flock by the hand of Moses and Aaron.

78

Maschil of Asaph.

¹Give ear, O my people, *to* my law: incline your ears to the words of my mouth. ²I will open my mouth in a parable: I will utter dark sayings of old: ³Which we have heard and known, and our fathers have told us. ⁴We will not hide *them* from their children, shewing to the generation to come the praises of

---

Devotional Moment

Teaching Children

78:2-5, 8 God gives parents the job of teaching children about his deeds and miracles. Parents in ancient Israel didn't always do this. Successive generations forgot about God's miracles and his power and love. As a result, they rebelled and got themselves into deep trouble. Take the time and energy to talk about God's goodness with your children during mealtimes or before tucking them into bed. Reflect on how you have seen God working in your life today or in the past week. Help your children express their insights about how God works in the world. And read stories of God's acts in the Bible to help your family remember the most important parts of the past.

---

the LORD, and his strength, and his wonderful works that he hath done. ⁵For he established a testimony in Jacob, and appointed a law in Israel, which he commanded our fathers, that they should make them known to their children: ⁶That the generation to come might know *them, even* the children *which* should be born; *who* should arise and declare *them* to their children: ⁷That they might set their hope in God, and not forget the works of God, but keep his commandments: ⁸And might not be as their fathers, a stubborn and rebellious generation; a generation *that* set not their heart aright, and whose spirit was not stedfast with God.

⁹The children of Ephraim, *being* armed, *and* carrying[a] bows, turned back in the day of battle. ¹⁰They kept not the covenant of God, and refused to walk in his law; ¹¹And forgat his works, and his wonders that he had shewed them. ¹²Marvellous things did he in the sight of their fathers, in the land of Egypt, *in* the field of Zoan. ¹³He divided the sea, and caused them to pass through; and he made the waters to stand as an heap. ¹⁴In the daytime also he led them with a cloud, and all the night with a light of fire. ¹⁵He clave the rocks in the wilderness, and gave *them* drink as *out of* the great depths. ¹⁶He brought streams also out of the rock, and caused waters to run down like rivers. ¹⁷And they sinned yet more against him by provoking the most High in the wilderness. ¹⁸And they tempted God in their heart by asking meat for their lust. ¹⁹Yea, they spake against God; they said, Can God furnish[b] a table in the wilder-

---

[a] carrying: Heb. throwing forth
[b] furnish: Heb. order

ness? [20]Behold, he smote the rock, that the waters gushed out, and the streams overflowed; can he give bread also? can he provide flesh for his people? [21]Therefore the LORD heard *this*, and was wroth: so a fire was kindled against Jacob, and anger also came up against Israel; [22]Because they believed not in God, and trusted not in his salvation: [23]Though he had commanded the clouds from above, and opened the doors of heaven, [24]And had rained down manna upon them to eat, and had given them of the corn of heaven. [25]Man[c] did eat angels' food: he sent them meat to the full. [26]He caused an east wind to blow[d] in the heaven: and by his power he brought in the south wind. [27]He rained flesh also upon them as dust, and feathered[e] fowls like as the sand of the sea: [28]And he let *it* fall in the midst of their camp, round about their habitations. [29]So they did eat, and were well filled: for he gave them their own desire; [30]They were not estranged from their lust. But while their meat *was* yet in their mouths, [31]The wrath of God came upon them, and slew the fattest of them, and smote down the chosen *men* of Israel. [32]For all this they sinned still, and believed not for his wondrous works. [33]Therefore their days did he consume in vanity, and their years in trouble. [34]When he slew them, then they sought him: and they returned and enquired early after God. [35]And they remembered that God *was* their rock, and the high God their redeemer. [36]Nevertheless they did flatter him with their mouth, and they lied unto him with their tongues. [37]For their heart was not right with him, neither were they stedfast in his covenant. [38]But he, *being* full of compassion, forgave *their* iniquity, and destroyed *them* not: yea, many a time turned he his anger away, and did not stir up all his wrath. [39]For he remembered that they *were but* flesh; a wind that passeth away, and cometh not again.

[40]How oft did they provoke[f] him in the wilderness, *and* grieve him in the desert! [41]Yea, they turned back and tempted God, and limited the Holy One of Israel. [42]They remembered not his hand, *nor* the day when he delivered them from the enemy. [43]How he had wrought[g] his signs in Egypt, and his wonders in the field of Zoan: [44]And had turned their rivers into blood; and their floods, that they could not drink. [45]He sent divers sorts of flies among them, which devoured them; and frogs, which destroyed them. [46]He gave also their increase unto the caterpiller, and their labour unto the locust. [47]He destroyed[h] their vines with hail, and their sycamore trees with frost. [48]He gave up their cattle also to the hail, and their flocks to hot thunderbolts. [49]He cast upon them the fierceness of his anger, wrath, and indignation, and trouble, by sending evil angels *among them.* [50]He made[i] a way to his

---

[c] Man . . . : or, Every one did eat the bread of the mighty
[d] to blow: Heb. to go
[e] feathered . . . : Heb. fowl of wing
[f] provoke: or, rebel against
[g] wrought: Heb. set
[h] destroyed: Heb. killed
[i] He made . . . : Heb. He weighed a path

anger; he spared not their soul from death, but gave their life over to the pestilence; ⁵¹And smote all the firstborn in Egypt; the chief of *their* strength in the tabernacles of Ham: ⁵²But made his own people to go forth like sheep, and guided them in the wilderness like a flock. ⁵³And he led them on safely, so that they feared not: but the sea overwhelmed ʲ their enemies. ⁵⁴And he brought them to the border of his sanctuary, *even to* this mountain, *which* his right hand had purchased. ⁵⁵He cast out the heathen also before them, and divided them an inheritance by line, and made the tribes of Israel to dwell in their tents. ⁵⁶Yet they tempted and provoked the most high God, and kept not his testimonies: ⁵⁷But turned back, and dealt unfaithfully like their fathers: they were turned aside like a deceitful bow. ⁵⁸For they provoked him to anger with their high places, and moved him to jealousy with their graven images. ⁵⁹When God heard *this*, he was wroth, and greatly abhorred Israel: ⁶⁰So that he forsook the tabernacle of Shiloh, the tent *which* he placed among men; ⁶¹And delivered his strength into captivity, and his glory into the enemy's hand. ⁶²He gave his people over also unto the sword; and was wroth with his inheritance. ⁶³The fire consumed their young men; and their maidens were not given to marriage. ⁶⁴Their priests fell by the sword; and their widows made no lamentation. ⁶⁵Then the Lord awaked as one out of sleep, *and* like a mighty man that shouteth by reason of wine. ⁶⁶And he smote his enemies

in the hinder parts: he put them to a perpetual reproach. ⁶⁷Moreover he refused the tabernacle of Joseph, and chose not the tribe of Ephraim: ⁶⁸But chose the tribe of Judah, the mount Zion which he loved. ⁶⁹And he built his sanctuary like high *palaces*, like the earth which he hath established ᵏ for ever. ⁷⁰He chose David also his servant, and took him from the sheepfolds: ⁷¹From following ˡ the ewes great with young he brought him to feed Jacob his people, and Israel his inheritance. ⁷²So he fed them according to the integrity of his heart; and guided them by the skilfulness of his hands.

79

A Psalm of Asaph.

¹O God, the heathen are come into thine inheritance; thy holy temple have they defiled; they have laid Jerusalem on heaps. ²The dead bodies of thy servants have they given *to be* meat unto the fowls of the heaven, the flesh of thy saints unto the beasts of the earth. ³Their blood have they shed like water round about Jerusalem; and *there was* none to bury *them*. ⁴We are become a reproach to our neighbours, a scorn and derision to them that are round about us. ⁵How long, LORD? wilt thou be angry for ever? shall thy jealousy burn like fire?

⁶Pour out thy wrath upon the heathen that have not known thee, and upon the kingdoms that have not called upon thy name. ⁷For they have devoured Jacob, and laid waste his dwelling place. ⁸O remember not against us former ᵃ iniquities:

ʲ overwhelmed: Heb. covered
ᵏ established: Heb. founded
ˡ following: Heb. after
ᵃ former . . . : or, the iniquities of them that were before us

let thy tender mercies speedily prevent us: for we are brought very low. ⁹Help us, O God of our salvation, for the glory of thy name: and deliver us, and purge away our sins, for thy name's sake. ¹⁰Wherefore should the heathen say, Where *is* their God? let him be known among the heathen in our sight *by* the revenging^b of the blood of thy servants *which is* shed. ¹¹Let the sighing of the prisoner come before thee; according to the greatness of thy power preserve thou those that are appointed to die; ¹²And render unto our neighbours sevenfold into their bosom their reproach, wherewith they have reproached thee, O Lord. ¹³So we thy people and sheep of thy pasture will give thee thanks for ever: we will shew forth thy praise to all^c generations.

80

To the chief Musician upon Shoshannimeduth, A Psalm of Asaph.

¹Give ear, O Shepherd of Israel, thou that leadest Joseph like a flock; thou that dwellest *between* the cherubims, shine forth. ²Before Ephraim and Benjamin and Manasseh stir up thy strength, and come^a *and* save us. ³Turn us again, O God, and cause thy face to shine; and we shall be saved. ⁴O LORD God of hosts, how long wilt thou be angry against the prayer of thy people? ⁵Thou feedest them with the bread of tears; and givest them tears to drink in great measure. ⁶Thou makest us a strife unto our neighbours: and our enemies laugh among themselves. ⁷Turn us

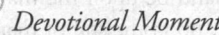

Devotional Moment
•
Failure
80:3, 7, 19 Even good Christian people sometimes turn away from God. Not that we always mean to. We get caught up in the events of life and slowly drift away from him. At other times we consciously turn our backs on him and end up in a mess. Will God forgive us and take us back? Yes, we can count on his grace. When we come to him, he receives us with joy and love. If you have drifted away, pray that God will turn your heart back to himself.

again, O God of hosts, and cause thy face to shine; and we shall be saved.

⁸Thou hast brought a vine out of Egypt: thou hast cast out the heathen, and planted it. ⁹Thou preparedst *room* before it, and didst cause it to take deep root, and it filled the land. ¹⁰The hills were covered with the shadow of it, and the boughs thereof *were like* the goodly^b cedars. ¹¹She sent out her boughs unto the sea, and her branches unto the river. ¹²Why hast thou *then* broken down her hedges, so that all they which pass by the way do pluck her? ¹³The boar out of the wood doth waste it, and the wild beast of the field doth devour it. ¹⁴Return, we beseech thee, O God of hosts: look down from heaven, and behold, and visit this vine; ¹⁵And the vineyard which thy right hand hath planted, and the branch *that* thou madest strong for thyself. ¹⁶*It is* burned with fire, *it is* cut down: they perish at the rebuke of thy countenance.

---

^b revenging: Heb. vengeance
^c to all . . . : Heb. to generation and generation
^a come . . . : Heb. come for salvation to us
^b goodly . . . : Heb. cedars of God

¹⁷Let thy hand be upon the man of thy right hand, upon the son of man *whom* thou madest strong for thyself. ¹⁸So will not we go back from thee: quicken us, and we will call upon thy name. ¹⁹Turn us again, O LORD God of hosts, cause thy face to shine; and we shall be saved.

81

To the chief Musician upon Gittith, *A Psalm* of Asaph[a].

¹Sing aloud unto God our strength: make a joyful noise unto the God of Jacob. ²Take a psalm, and bring hither the timbrel, the pleasant harp with the psaltery. ³Blow up the trumpet in the new moon, in the time appointed, on our solemn feast day. ⁴For this *was* a statute for Israel, *and* a law of the God of Jacob. ⁵This he ordained in Joseph *for* a testimony, when he went out through the land of Egypt: *where* I heard a language *that* I understood not. ⁶I removed his shoulder from the burden: his hands were delivered from the pots. ⁷Thou calledst in trouble, and I delivered thee; I answered thee in the secret place of thunder: I proved thee at the waters of Meribah[b]. Selah.

⁸Hear, O my people, and I will testify unto thee: O Israel, if thou wilt hearken unto me; ⁹There shall no strange god be in thee; neither shalt thou worship any strange god. ¹⁰I *am* the LORD thy God, which brought thee out of the land of Egypt: open thy mouth wide, and I will fill it. ¹¹But my people would not hearken

to my voice; and Israel would none of me. ¹²So I gave them up unto their own hearts' lust: *and* they walked in their own counsels. ¹³Oh that my people had hearkened unto me, *and* Israel had walked in my ways! ¹⁴I should soon have subdued their enemies, and turned my hand against their adversaries. ¹⁵The haters of the LORD should have submitted[c] themselves unto him: but their time should have endured for ever. ¹⁶He should have fed them also with the finest[d] of the wheat: and with honey out of the rock should I have satisfied thee.

82

A Psalm of Asaph[a].

¹God standeth in the congregation

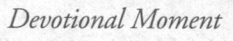

Devotional Moment

•

The Poor

82:3-4 How aware is your family of injustices done to the poor, the afflicted, the fatherless, and the destitute? This psalm calls us to act on behalf of poor families in our community and in the world; on behalf of families afflicted with illness, broken relationships, alcoholism, or other family pain; on behalf of children whose fathers have in some way left them, whether through death, divorce, separation, or lack of love; on behalf of people who are destitute—at the end of their ability to hang on. In what way can you share your resources with families who lack money, food, love, or hope? Consider ways that can involve everyone—Mom, Dad, the kids, anyone else living with you. Talk with children about it to help them learn compassion for the poor.

---

[a] of Asaph: or, for Asaph
[b] Meribah: or, Strife
[c] submitted . . . : or, yielded feigned obedience: Heb. lied
[d] finest . . . : Heb. fat of wheat
[a] of Asaph: or, for Asaph

of the mighty; he judgeth among the gods. ²How long will ye judge unjustly, and accept the persons of the wicked? Selah. ³Defend[b] the poor and fatherless: do justice to the afflicted and needy. ⁴Deliver the poor and needy: rid *them* out of the hand of the wicked. ⁵They know not, neither will they understand; they walk on in darkness: all the foundations of the earth are out of course.

⁶I have said, Ye *are* gods; and all of you *are* children of the most High. ⁷But ye shall die like men, and fall like one of the princes. ⁸Arise, O God, judge the earth: for thou shalt inherit all nations.

83

A Song *or* Psalm of Asaph[a].

¹Keep not thou silence, O God: hold not thy peace, and be not still, O God. ²For, lo, thine enemies make a tumult: and they that hate thee have lifted up the head. ³They have taken crafty counsel against thy people, and consulted against thy hidden ones. ⁴They have said, Come, and let us cut them off from *being* a nation; that the name of Israel may be no more in remembrance. ⁵For they have consulted together with one consent[b]: they are confederate against thee: ⁶The tabernacles of Edom, and the Ishmaelites; of Moab, and the Hagarenes; ⁷Gebal, and Ammon, and Amalek; the Philistines with the inhabitants of Tyre; ⁸Assur also is joined with them: they have holpen[c] the children of Lot. Selah.

⁹Do unto them as *unto* the Midianites; as *to* Sisera, as *to* Jabin, at the brook of Kison: ¹⁰*Which* perished at Endor: they became *as* dung for the earth. ¹¹Make their nobles like Oreb, and like Zeeb: yea, all their princes as Zebah, and as Zalmunna: ¹²Who said, Let us take to ourselves the houses of God in possession. ¹³O my God, make them like a wheel; as the stubble before the wind. ¹⁴As the fire burneth a wood, and as the flame setteth the mountains on fire; ¹⁵So persecute them with thy tempest, and make them afraid with thy storm. ¹⁶Fill their faces with shame; that they may seek thy name, O LORD. ¹⁷Let them be confounded and troubled for ever; yea, let them be put to shame, and perish: ¹⁸That *men* may know that thou, whose name alone *is* JEHOVAH, *art* the most high over all the earth.

84

To the chief Musician upon Gittith, A Psalm for the sons[a] of Korah.

¹How amiable *are* thy tabernacles, O LORD of hosts! ²My soul longeth, yea, even fainteth for the courts of the LORD: my heart and my flesh crieth out for the living God. ³Yea, the sparrow hath found an house, and the swallow a nest for herself, where she may lay her young, *even* thine altars, O LORD of hosts, my King, and my God. ⁴Blessed *are* they that dwell in thy house: they will be still praising thee. Selah. ⁵Blessed *is* the man whose

---

ᵇ Defend: Heb. Judge
ᵃ of Asaph: or, for Asaph
ᵇ consent: Heb. heart
ᶜ holpen: Heb. been an arm to
ᵃ for the sons: or, of the sons

strength *is* in thee; in whose heart *are* the ways *of them.* [6] *Who* passing through the valley of Baca[b] make it a well; the rain also filleth the pools. [7]They go from strength to strength, *every one of them* in Zion appeareth before God.

[8]O LORD God of hosts, hear my prayer: give ear, O God of Jacob. Selah. [9]Behold, O God our shield, and look upon the face of thine anointed. [10]For a day in thy courts *is* better than a thousand. I had rather be a doorkeeper in the house of my God, than to dwell in the tents of wickedness. [11]For the LORD God *is* a sun and shield: the LORD will give grace and glory: no good *thing* will he withhold from them that walk uprightly. [12]O LORD of hosts, blessed *is* the man that trusteth in thee.

85

To the chief Musician, A Psalm for the sons[a] of Korah.

[1]LORD, thou hast been favourable unto thy land: thou hast brought back the captivity of Jacob. [2]Thou hast forgiven the iniquity of thy people, thou hast covered all their sin. Selah. [3]Thou hast taken away all thy wrath: thou hast turned *thyself* from the fierceness of thine anger. [4]Turn us, O God of our salvation, and cause thine anger toward us to cease. [5]Wilt thou be angry with us for ever? wilt thou draw out thine anger to all generations? [6]Wilt thou not revive us again: that thy people may rejoice in thee? [7]Shew us thy mercy, O LORD, and grant us thy salvation.

[8]I will hear what God the LORD will speak: for he will speak peace unto his people, and to his saints: but let them not turn again to folly. [9]Surely his salvation *is* nigh them that fear him; that glory may dwell in our land. [10]Mercy and truth are met together; righteousness and peace have kissed *each other.* [11]Truth shall spring out of the earth; and righteousness shall look down from heaven. [12]Yea, the LORD shall give *that which is* good; and our land shall yield her increase. [13]Righteousness shall go before him; and shall set *us* in the way of his steps.

86

A Prayer of David.

[1]Bow down thine ear, O LORD, hear me: for I *am* poor and needy. [2]Preserve my soul; for I *am* holy[a]: O thou my God, save thy servant that trusteth

---

Devotional Moment
Family Revival

85:1-7 As the writer of this psalm reflected on his nation's history, he realized that while God had kept every promise, the people had no appreciation for what God had done. The writer prayed, "Revive us!" Sometimes our families, too, need revival. Conversations around the table at meals, the way we encourage each other, and how we treat each other show God's role in our family. If we are not careful, God becomes just a visitor or maybe even a stranger in our home. If God seems like a visitor in your family, ask him to help you begin to rejoice in him again. Start today by including him in your family conversations.

---

[b] Baca . . . : or, mulberry trees make him a well, etc
[a] for the sons: or, of the sons
[a] holy: or, one whom thou favourest

in thee. [3]Be merciful unto me, O Lord: for I cry unto thee daily[b]. [4]Rejoice the soul of thy servant: for unto thee, O Lord, do I lift up my soul. [5]For thou, Lord, *art* good, and ready to forgive; and plenteous in mercy unto all them that call upon thee. [6]Give ear, O LORD, unto my prayer; and attend to the voice of my supplications. [7]In the day of my trouble I will call upon thee: for thou wilt answer me.

[8]Among the gods *there is* none like unto thee, O Lord; neither *are there any works* like unto thy works. [9]All nations whom thou hast made shall come and worship before thee, O Lord; and shall glorify thy name. [10]For thou *art* great, and doest wondrous things: thou *art* God alone. [11]Teach me thy way, O LORD; I will walk in thy truth: unite my heart to fear thy name. [12]I will praise thee, O Lord my God, with all my heart: and I will glorify thy name for evermore. [13]For great *is* thy mercy toward me: and thou hast delivered my soul from the lowest hell[c]. [14]O God, the proud are risen against me, and the assemblies of violent[d] *men* have sought after my soul; and have not set thee before them. [15]But thou, O Lord, *art* a God full of compassion, and gracious, longsuffering, and plenteous in mercy and truth. [16]O turn unto me, and have mercy upon me; give thy strength unto thy servant, and save the son of thine handmaid. [17]Shew me a token for good; that they which hate me may see *it*, and be ashamed: because

thou, LORD, hast holpen me, and comforted me.

87

A Psalm *or* Song for the sons[a] of Korah.

[1]His foundation *is* in the holy mountains. [2]The LORD loveth the gates of Zion more than all the dwellings of Jacob. [3]Glorious things are spoken of thee, O city of God. Selah.

[4]I will make mention of Rahab and Babylon to them that know me: behold Philistia, and Tyre, with Ethiopia; this *man* was born there. [5]And of Zion it shall be said, This and that man was born in her: and the highest himself shall establish her. [6]The LORD shall count, when he writeth up the people, *that* this *man* was born there. Selah. [7]As well the singers as the players on instruments *shall be there:* all my springs *are* in thee.

88

A Song *or* Psalm for the sons[a] of Korah, to the chief Musician upon Mahalath Leannoth, Maschil of Heman the Ezrahite.

[1]O LORD God of my salvation, I have cried day *and* night before thee: [2]Let my prayer come before thee: incline thine ear unto my cry; [3]For my soul is full of troubles: and my life draweth nigh unto the grave. [4]I am counted with them that go down into the pit: I am as a man *that hath* no strength: [5]Free among the dead, like the

---

[b] daily: or, all the day
[c] hell: or, grave
[d] violent: Heb. terrible
[a] for the sons: or, of the sons
[a] for the sons: or, of the sons

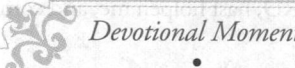

Devotional Moment

•

Dark Days

88:1-18 The author of this psalm openly spoke his feelings to God. Even though not *everything* had turned out wrong, it felt that way. That's life, isn't it? Some days don't go well. Family plans fail. Circumstances take a wrong turn and then get worse. Life can become a nightmare through sickness, divorce, or death. When that happens, the best action is prayer. When we gather to tell God how bad life seems, we help each other recognize that God's still in charge. God never promises to make everything work out the way we want it, but he does promise never to leave us alone. He will always listen to our complaints, give us the strength to endure our problems, and intervene according to his wisdom.

slain that lie in the grave, whom thou rememberest no more: and they are cut off from thy hand. ⁶Thou hast laid me in the lowest pit, in darkness, in the deeps. ⁷Thy wrath lieth hard upon me, and thou hast afflicted *me* with all thy waves. Selah. ⁸Thou hast put away mine acquaintance far from me; thou hast made me an abomination unto them: *I am* shut up, and I cannot come forth. ⁹Mine eye mourneth by reason of affliction: LORD, I have called daily upon thee, I have stretched out my hands unto thee.

¹⁰Wilt thou shew wonders to the dead? shall the dead arise *and* praise thee? Selah. ¹¹Shall thy lovingkindness be declared in the grave? *or* thy faithfulness in destruction? ¹²Shall thy wonders be known in the dark? and thy righteousness in the land of forgetfulness? ¹³But unto thee have I cried, O LORD;

and in the morning shall my prayer prevent thee. ¹⁴LORD, why castest thou off my soul? *why* hidest thou thy face from me? ¹⁵I *am* afflicted and ready to die from *my* youth up: *while* I suffer thy terrors I am distracted. ¹⁶Thy fierce wrath goeth over me; thy terrors have cut me off. ¹⁷They came round about me daily[b] like water; they compassed me about together. ¹⁸Lover and friend hast thou put far from me, *and* mine acquaintance into darkness.

89

Maschil of Ethan the Ezrahite.

¹I will sing of the mercies of the LORD for ever: with my mouth will I make known thy faithfulness to all generations. ²For I have said, Mercy shall be built up for ever: thy faithfulness shalt thou establish in the very heavens. ³I have made a covenant with my chosen, I have sworn unto David my servant, ⁴Thy seed will I establish for ever, and build up thy throne to all generations. Selah.

⁵And the heavens shall praise thy wonders, O LORD: thy faithfulness also in the congregation of the saints. ⁶For who in the heaven can be compared unto the LORD? *who* among the sons of the mighty can be likened unto the LORD? ⁷God is greatly to be feared in the assembly of the saints, and to be had in reverence of all *them that are* about him. ⁸O LORD God of hosts, who *is* a strong LORD like unto thee? or to thy faithfulness round about thee? ⁹Thou rulest the raging of the sea: when the waves thereof arise, thou stillest them. ¹⁰Thou hast broken Ra-

---

[b] daily: or, all the day

hab^a in pieces, as one that is slain; thou hast scattered thine enemies with thy strong arm. ¹¹The heavens *are* thine, the earth also *is* thine: *as for* the world and the fulness^b thereof, thou hast founded them. ¹²The north and the south thou hast created them: Tabor and Hermon shall rejoice in thy name. ¹³Thou hast a mighty arm: strong is thy hand, *and* high is thy right hand. ¹⁴Justice and judgment *are* the habitation^c of thy throne: mercy and truth shall go before thy face.

¹⁵Blessed *is* the people that know the joyful sound: they shall walk, O LORD, in the light of thy countenance. ¹⁶In thy name shall they rejoice all the day: and in thy righteousness shall they be exalted. ¹⁷For thou *art* the glory of their strength: and in thy favour our horn shall be exalted. ¹⁸For the LORD^d *is* our defence; and the Holy One of Israel *is* our king.

¹⁹Then thou spakest in vision to thy holy one, and saidst, I have laid help upon *one that is* mighty; I have exalted *one* chosen out of the people. ²⁰I have found David my servant; with my holy oil have I anointed him: ²¹With whom my hand shall be established: mine arm also shall strengthen him. ²²The enemy shall not exact upon him; nor the son of wickedness afflict him. ²³And I will beat down his foes before his face, and plague them that hate him. ²⁴But my faithfulness and my mercy *shall be* with him: and in my name shall his horn be

exalted. ²⁵I will set his hand also in the sea, and his right hand in the rivers. ²⁶He shall cry unto me, Thou *art* my father, my God, and the rock of my salvation. ²⁷Also I will make him *my* firstborn, higher than the kings of the earth. ²⁸My mercy will I keep for him for evermore, and my covenant shall stand fast with him. ²⁹His seed also will I make *to endure* for ever, and his throne as the days of heaven. ³⁰If his children forsake my law, and walk not in my judgments; ³¹If they break^e my statutes, and keep not my commandments; ³²Then will I visit their transgression with the rod, and their iniquity with stripes. ³³Nevertheless my lovingkindness will I not utterly take from him, nor suffer my faithfulness to fail. ³⁴My covenant will I not break, nor alter the thing that is gone out of my lips. ³⁵Once have I sworn by my holiness that I will not lie unto David. ³⁶His seed shall endure for ever, and his throne as the sun before me. ³⁷It shall be established for ever as the moon, and *as* a faithful witness in heaven. Selah.

³⁸But thou hast cast off and abhorred, thou hast been wroth with thine anointed. ³⁹Thou hast made void the covenant of thy servant: thou hast profaned his crown *by casting it* to the ground. ⁴⁰Thou hast broken down all his hedges; thou hast brought his strong holds to ruin. ⁴¹All that pass by the way spoil him: he is a reproach to his neighbours. ⁴²Thou hast set up the right hand

^a Rahab: or, Egypt
^b the fulness . . . : or, all it containeth
^c habitation: or, establishment
^d the LORD . . . : or, our shield is of the LORD, and our king is of the Holy One of Israel
^e break: Heb. profane

of his adversaries; thou hast made all his enemies to rejoice. ⁴³Thou hast also turned the edge of his sword, and hast not made him to stand in the battle. ⁴⁴Thou hast made his glory[f] to cease, and cast his throne down to the ground. ⁴⁵The days of his youth hast thou shortened: thou hast covered him with shame. Selah. ⁴⁶How long, LORD? wilt thou hide thyself for ever? shall thy wrath burn like fire? ⁴⁷Remember how short my time is: wherefore hast thou made all men in vain? ⁴⁸What man *is he that* liveth, and shall not see death? shall he deliver his soul from the hand of the grave? Selah. ⁴⁹Lord, where *are* thy former lovingkindnesses, *which* thou swarest unto David in thy truth? ⁵⁰Remember, Lord, the reproach of thy servants; *how* I do bear in my bosom *the reproach of* all the mighty people; ⁵¹Wherewith thine enemies have reproached, O LORD; wherewith they have reproached the footsteps of thine anointed. ⁵²Blessed *be* the LORD for evermore. Amen, and Amen.

90

A Prayer of Moses the man of God.

¹Lord, thou hast been our dwelling place in all generations. ²Before the mountains were brought forth, or ever thou hadst formed the earth and the world, even from everlasting to everlasting, thou *art* God. ³Thou turnest man to destruction; and sayest, Return, ye children of men. ⁴For a thousand years in thy sight *are but* as yesterday when it is past, and *as* a watch in the night. ⁵Thou carri-

est them away as with a flood; they are *as* a sleep: in the morning *they are* like grass *which* groweth up. ⁶In the morning it flourisheth, and groweth up; in the evening it is cut down, and withereth.

⁷For we are consumed by thine anger, and by thy wrath are we troubled. ⁸Thou hast set our iniquities before thee, our secret *sins* in the light of thy countenance. ⁹For all our days are passed away in thy wrath: we spend our years as a tale *that is told.* ¹⁰The days[a] of our years *are* threescore years and ten; and if by reason of strength *they be* fourscore years, yet *is* their strength labour and sorrow; for it is soon cut off, and we fly away. ¹¹Who knoweth the power of thine anger? even according to thy fear, *so is* thy wrath.

¹²So teach *us* to number our days, that we may apply[b] *our* hearts unto wisdom. ¹³Return, O LORD, how long? and let it repent thee concerning thy servants. ¹⁴O satisfy us early with thy mercy; that we may rejoice and be glad all our days. ¹⁵Make us glad according to the days *wherein* thou hast afflicted us, *and* the years *wherein* we have seen evil. ¹⁶Let thy work appear unto thy servants, and thy glory unto their children. ¹⁷And let the beauty of the LORD our God be upon us: and establish thou the work of our hands upon us; yea, the work of our hands establish thou it.

91

¹He that dwelleth in the secret place of the most High shall abide[a] under the shadow of the Almighty. ²I will say of the

---

[f] glory: Heb. brightness
[a] The days . . . : Heb. As for the days of our years, in them are seventy years
[b] apply: Heb. cause to come
[a] abide: Heb. lodge

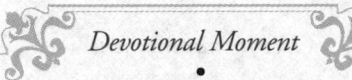

LORD, *He is* my refuge and my fortress: my God; in him will I trust. ³Surely he shall deliver thee from the snare of the fowler, *and* from the noisome pestilence. ⁴He shall cover thee with his feathers, and under his wings shalt thou trust: his truth *shall be thy* shield and buckler. ⁵Thou shalt not be afraid for the terror by night; *nor* for the arrow *that* flieth by day; ⁶*Nor* for the pestilence *that* walketh in darkness; *nor* for the destruction *that* wasteth at noonday. ⁷A thousand shall fall at thy side, and ten thousand at thy right hand; *but* it shall not come nigh thee. ⁸Only with thine eyes shalt thou behold and see the reward of the wicked.

⁹Because thou hast made the LORD, *which is* my refuge, *even* the most High, thy habitation; ¹⁰There shall no evil befall thee, neither shall any plague come nigh thy dwelling. ¹¹For he shall give his angels charge over thee, to keep thee in all thy ways. ¹²They shall bear thee up in *their* hands, lest thou dash thy foot against a stone. ¹³Thou shalt tread upon the lion and adder[b]: the young lion and the dragon shalt thou trample under feet. ¹⁴Because he hath set his love upon me, therefore will I deliver him: I will set him on high, because he hath known my name. ¹⁵He shall call upon me, and I will answer him: I *will be* with him in trouble; I will deliver him, and honour him. ¹⁶With long[c] life will I satisfy him, and shew him my salvation.

92

A Psalm *or* Song for the sabbath day.

¹*It is a* good *thing* to give thanks

Devotional Moment
•
The Thank-You Habit
92:1-2 We don't get into the habit of expressing appreciation without conscious effort. Parents need to teach their children to say thank you to other people and to God. When parents get tired of reminding kids to say thank you, and when kids get tired of being reminded, both need to remember that everyone benefits from expressing gratitude to God. Instead of having one person pray for your next family meal, have each person mention a blessing for which he or she is thankful to God.

unto the LORD, and to sing praises unto thy name, O most High: ²To shew forth thy lovingkindness in the morning, and thy faithfulness every night, ³Upon an instrument of ten strings, and upon the psaltery; upon the harp[a] with a solemn sound. ⁴For thou, LORD, hast made me glad through thy work: I will triumph in the works of thy hands. ⁵O LORD, how great are thy works! *and* thy thoughts are very deep. ⁶A brutish man knoweth not; neither doth a fool understand this.

⁷When the wicked spring as the grass, and when all the workers of iniquity do flourish; *it is* that they shall be destroyed for ever: ⁸But thou, LORD, *art most* high for evermore. ⁹For, lo, thine enemies, O LORD, for, lo, thine enemies shall perish; all the workers of iniquity shall be scattered. ¹⁰But my horn shalt thou exalt like *the horn of* an unicorn: I shall be anointed with fresh oil. ¹¹Mine eye also shall see *my desire* on

---

ᵇ adder: or, asp

ᶜ long . . . : Heb. length of days

ᵃ the harp . . . : or, the solemn sound with the harp

Devotional Moment

Aged toward Perfection

92:14 Far from being a burden, older people who have followed God for many years can enrich our life in many ways. We all need models of Christians who have followed Jesus a long time. Invite older Christians into your home. Give special honor to grandparents who are believers. Ask them for advice, in front of your children. Listen carefully to their counsel and take it to heart. Older people have *much* to contribute to younger families. Tap into this vital resource!

mine enemies, *and* mine ears shall hear *my desire* of the wicked that rise up against me. ¹²The righteous shall flourish like the palm tree: he shall grow like a cedar in Lebanon. ¹³Those that be planted in the house of the LORD shall flourish in the courts of our God. ¹⁴They shall still bring forth fruit in old age; they shall be fat and flourishing[b]; ¹⁵To shew that the LORD *is* upright: *he is* my rock, and *there is* no unrighteousness in him.

93

¹The LORD reigneth, he is clothed with majesty; the LORD is clothed with strength, *wherewith* he hath girded himself: the world also is stablished, that it cannot be moved. ²Thy throne *is* established of old[a]: thou *art* from everlasting. ³The floods have lifted up, O LORD, the floods have lifted up their voice; the floods lift up their waves. ⁴The LORD on high *is* mightier than the noise of many waters, *yea, than* the mighty waves of the sea. ⁵Thy testimonies are very sure: holiness becometh thine house, O LORD, for ever[b].

94

¹O LORD God[a], to whom vengeance belongeth; O God, to whom vengeance belongeth, shew thyself. ²Lift up thyself, thou judge of the earth: render a reward to the proud. ³LORD, how long shall the wicked, how long shall the wicked triumph? ⁴*How long* shall they utter *and* speak hard things? *and* all the workers of iniquity boast themselves? ⁵They break in pieces thy people, O LORD, and afflict thine heritage. ⁶They slay the widow and the stranger, and murder the fatherless. ⁷Yet they say, The LORD shall not see, neither shall the God of Jacob regard *it.* ⁸Understand, ye brutish among the people: and *ye* fools, when will ye be wise? ⁹He that planted the ear, shall he not hear? he that formed the eye, shall he not see? ¹⁰He that chastiseth the heathen, shall not he correct? he that teacheth man knowledge, *shall not he know?* ¹¹The LORD knoweth the thoughts of man, that they *are* vanity.

¹²Blessed *is* the man whom thou chastenest, O LORD, and teachest him out of thy law; ¹³That thou mayest give him rest from the days of adversity, until the pit be digged for the wicked. ¹⁴For the LORD will not cast off his people, neither will he forsake his inheritance. ¹⁵But judgment shall return unto righteousness: and all the upright

[b] flourishing: Heb. green
[a] of old: Heb. from then
[b] for ever: Heb. to length of days
[a] God . . . : Heb. God of revenges

in heart shall follow[b] it. [16]Who will rise up for me against the evildoers? *or* who will stand up for me against the workers of iniquity? [17]Unless the LORD *had been* my help, my soul had almost[c] dwelt in silence. [18]When I said, My foot slippeth; thy mercy, O LORD, held me up. [19]In the multitude of my thoughts within me thy comforts delight my soul. [20]Shall the throne of iniquity have fellowship with thee, which frameth mischief by a law? [21]They gather themselves together against the soul of the righteous, and condemn the innocent blood. [22]But the LORD is my defence; and my God *is* the rock of my refuge. [23]And he shall bring upon them their own iniquity, and shall cut them off in their own wickedness; *yea*, the LORD our God shall cut them off.

95

[1]O come, let us sing unto the LORD: let us make a joyful noise to the rock of our salvation. [2]Let us come[a] before his presence with thanksgiving, and make a joyful noise unto him with psalms. [3]For the LORD *is* a great God, and a great King above all gods. [4]In his hand *are* the deep places of the earth: the strength of the hills *is* his also. [5]The sea[b] *is* his, and he made it: and his hands formed the dry *land.* [6]O come, let us worship and bow down: let us kneel before the LORD our maker.

[7]For he *is* our God; and we *are* the people of his pasture, and the sheep of his hand. To day if ye will hear his voice, [8]Harden not your heart, as in the provocation[c], *and* as *in* the day of temptation in the wilderness: [9]When your fathers tempted me, proved me, and saw my work. [10]Forty years long was I grieved with *this* generation, and said, It *is* a people that do err in their heart, and they have not known my ways: [11]Unto whom I sware in my wrath that they should not enter into my rest.

96

[1]O sing unto the LORD a new song: sing unto the LORD, all the earth. [2]Sing unto the LORD, bless his name; shew forth his salvation from day to day. [3]Declare his glory among the heathen, his wonders among all people. [4]For the LORD *is* great, and greatly to be praised: he *is* to be feared above all gods. [5]For all the gods of the nations *are* idols: but the LORD made the heavens. [6]Honour and majesty *are* before him: strength and beauty *are* in his sanctuary. [7]Give unto the LORD, O ye kindreds of the people, give unto the LORD glory and strength. [8]Give unto the LORD the glory *due unto* his name: bring an offering, and come into his courts. [9]O worship the LORD in the beauty of holiness: fear before him, all the earth.

[10]Say among the heathen *that* the LORD reigneth: the world also shall be established that it shall not be moved: he shall judge the people righteously. [11]Let

---

[b] shall follow . . . : Heb. shall be after it
[c] almost: or, quickly
[a] come . . . : Heb. prevent his face
[b] The sea . . . : Heb. Whose the sea is
[c] provocation: Heb. contention

the heavens rejoice, and let the earth be glad; let the sea roar, and the fulness[a] thereof. [12]Let the field be joyful, and all that *is* therein: then shall all the trees of the wood rejoice [13]Before the LORD: for he cometh, for he cometh to judge the earth: he shall judge the world with righteousness, and the people with his truth.

97

[1]The LORD reigneth; let the earth rejoice; let the multitude[a] of isles be glad *thereof.* [2]Clouds and darkness *are* round about him: righteousness and judgment *are* the habitation[b] of his throne. [3]A fire goeth before him, and burneth up his enemies round about. [4]His lightnings enlightened the world: the earth saw, and trembled. [5]The hills melted like wax at the presence of the LORD, at the presence of the Lord of the whole earth. [6]The heavens declare his righteousness, and all the people see his glory. [7]Confounded be all they that serve graven images, that boast themselves of idols: worship him, all *ye* gods.

[8]Zion heard, and was glad; and the daughters of Judah rejoiced because of thy judgments, O LORD. [9]For thou, LORD, *art* high above all the earth: thou art exalted far above all gods. [10]Ye that love the LORD, hate evil: he preserveth the souls of his saints; he delivereth them out of the hand of the wicked. [11]Light is sown for the righteous, and gladness for the upright in heart. [12]Rejoice in the LORD, ye righ-

teous; and give thanks at the remembrance of his holiness.

98

A Psalm.

[1]O sing unto the LORD a new song; for he hath done marvellous things: his right hand, and his holy arm, hath gotten him the victory. [2]The LORD hath made known his salvation: his righteousness hath he openly shewed in the sight of the heathen. [3]He hath remembered his mercy and his truth toward the house of Israel: all the ends of the earth have seen the salvation of our God.

[4]Make a joyful noise unto the LORD, all the earth: make a loud noise, and rejoice, and sing praise. [5]Sing unto the LORD with the harp; with the harp, and the voice of a psalm. [6]With trumpets and sound of cornet make a joyful noise before the LORD, the King. [7]Let the sea roar, and the fulness[a] thereof; the world, and they that dwell therein. [8]Let the floods clap *their* hands: let the hills be joyful together [9]Before the LORD; for he cometh to judge the earth: with righteousness shall he judge the world, and the people with equity.

99

[1]The LORD reigneth; let the people tremble: he sitteth *between* the cherubims; let the earth be moved[a]. [2]The LORD *is* great in Zion; and he *is* high above all the people. [3]Let them praise thy great and terrible name; *for* it *is* holy. [4]The king's

---

[a] the fulness . . . : or, all it containeth
[a] multitude . . . : Heb. many, or, great isles
[b] habitation: or, establishment
[a] the fulness . . . : or, all it containeth
[a] be moved: Heb. stagger

strength also loveth judgment; thou dost establish equity, thou executest judgment and righteousness in Jacob. [5]Exalt ye the LORD our God, and worship at his footstool; *for* he *is* holy.

[6]Moses and Aaron among his priests, and Samuel among them that call upon his name; they called upon the LORD, and he answered them. [7]He spake unto them in the cloudy pillar: they kept his testimonies, and the ordinance *that* he gave them. [8]Thou answeredst them, O LORD our God: thou wast a God that forgavest them, though thou tookest vengeance of their inventions. [9]Exalt the LORD our God, and worship at his holy hill; for the LORD our God *is* holy.

100

A Psalm of praise[a].

[1]Make a joyful noise unto the LORD, all ye lands. [2]Serve the LORD with gladness: come before his presence with singing. [3]Know ye that the

---

Devotional Moment

Make Sundays Special

100:4 No doubt about it—the writer of this short psalm was enthusiastic about going to the Temple. And he didn't hesitate to encourage others to prepare for worship: to go, enter, give thanks, and bless. Meaningful worship often requires preparation. If we don't *plan* to go, enter, give thanks, and bless God's name, we probably won't do it. This points out an especially important opportunity for young families. Children who anticipate worship will better enjoy participating in it. Talk about church on Saturday evening, and make sure everyone gets to bed in time to wake up for it.

Worship
in Your Home

THE ULTIMATE PURPOSE OF DEVOTIONS
Know ye that the Lord he is God: it is he that hath made us, and not we ourselves; we are his people, and the sheep of his pasture.
Psalm 100:3

Surprise! The ultimate purpose of devotions is not to know your Bible better, but to know God better.

God is Lord over all, and we are privileged to be his people. We can know him. We can love him. We can live with him, talk with him, and enjoy his presence. The delight of being a Christian is not in what God can do for us or give us, but in knowing him as a person.

Preparing for heaven starts with turning from sin and seeking God's forgiveness through Christ. The next step is to get to know God better each day.

Bible study is the best way to know God better. Prayer and meditation is another way, of course, but the study of the Word is most basic. Through the Word, we understand who God is and what he has said to us. Through prayer, we cultivate a personal relationship—an intimacy with our Creator and Lord.

Devotions, then, help us get to know God. The life-changing truths of the Word and prayer work together to bring us closer to him.

---

[a] praise: or, thanksgiving

Refocusing at Mid-Life

by Jim and Sally Conway

Troublesome emotions can assault us at any age, but they strike with unique force at mid-life. Wives may want more fulfillment, mothers feel hassled by their children's demands or sadly see their job coming to an end, and working women wish they had more family time. Husbands may be disappointed with their occupation, feel unhappy in their marriage, and regretfully realize their kids are growing up with a shortage of their input and camaraderie.

The writer of Psalm 102 was overwhelmed by negative emotions. In brief but painfully graphic words, he spelled out the causes of his depression and anxiety—causes reminiscent of mid-life.

Shortness of life. "My days are consumed like smoke. . . . My days are like a shadow that declineth; and I am withered like grass. . . . [God] weakened my strength . . . he shortened my days" (vv. 3, 11, 23). We try to resist the aging process and death, yet the sun rises and sets—and we are another day older.

Poor health. By mid-life, physical health becomes an increasing concern. These are the years of heart attacks, diabetes, breast tumors, and prostate cancer. In short, the body is beginning to fall apart.

Loss of appetite. It's a vicious cycle—loss of appetite causes depression and compounds problems that tend to increase anxiety and depression. "I forget to eat my bread" (v. 4). The writer was preoccupied with his problems. Weight loss is common during great anxiety. The result is that "my bones cleave to my skin" (v. 5).

Loneliness. "I am like a pelican of the wilderness: I am like an owl of the desert. I watch, and am as a sparrow alone upon the house top" (vv. 6-7). Each of these birds describes a special kind of loneliness. The vulture reminds us of detachment as death approaches. We can easily picture the owl, alone and hooting from an isolated branch in the darkness of night. The third bird is a "sparrow alone" on the roof.

Mocked by enemies. "Mine enemies reproach me all the day" (v. 8). Success brings a feeling of having arrived, but also an unmentioned fear that other people are waiting for you to fail. The higher you move up the ladder, the fewer people there are ahead of you, and the more people beneath you ready to take your place.

Loss of poise, control, and stability. Picture the writer, sitting and weeping in mourning and utter humiliation. He lifts a cup of water to his lips, and his tears drop into his cup. He's a broken man with a life out of control. That's what mid-life feels like.

Loss of opportunity. The psalmist contrasted his own fame with God's: "My days are like a shadow that declineth; and I am withered like grass. But thou, O Lord, shalt endure for ever; and thy remembrance unto all generations" (vv. 11-12). The person in mid-life depression sees that life is coming to an end and feels that he or she has done nothing of significance: *I am a passing, finite, frail, dying human who has accomplished nothing.*

Impending death. "He weakened my strength . . . he shortened my days" (v. 23). By mid-life we begin to see death as an imminent reality. Days are numbered, and the focus switches from counting the years since birth to counting the years before death.

We naturally tend to reach out for solutions to depression and anxiety. The difficulty is that some solutions are not effective. Our problems do not have human answers. We cannot lengthen our life, avoid death, in our own strength become famous, change the mind of an enemy, or eliminate a physical health problem.

But we can recognize, as did the psalmist, that God is concerned for us and with us. "He will regard the prayer of the destitute, and not despise their prayer" (v. 17). We can find real help for depression by looking to God and laying the causes of our depression at his feet. God knows our needs and he loves us.

DIGGING DEEPER

1. Aside from the fact that God is all-knowing, how can we be sure that he understands our mid-life struggles? What should we do in response? See Hebrews 4:14-16.

2. The answer for mid-life depression and anxiety is to allow God to define who we should be and what we should be doing with our life. Read how the prophet Elijah went through this process (1 Kings 19).

3. The vulnerability and deep anguish of Psalm 102 immediately precedes Psalm 103, which shows the concern of God for struggling people. How many reasons for encouragement can you find in Psalm 103?

LORD he *is* God: *it is* he *that* hath made us, and not we ourselves; *we are* his people, and the sheep of his pasture. ⁴Enter into his gates with thanksgiving, *and* into his courts with praise: be thankful unto him, *and* bless his name. ⁵For the LORD *is* good; his mercy *is* everlasting; and his truth *endureth* to all^b generations.

101

A Psalm of David.

¹I will sing of mercy and judgment: unto thee, O LORD, will I sing. ²I will behave myself wisely in a perfect way. O when wilt thou come unto me? I will walk within my house with a perfect heart. ³I will set no wicked^a thing before

mine eyes: I hate the work of them that turn aside; *it* shall not cleave to me. ⁴A froward heart shall depart from me: I will not know a wicked *person.* ⁵Whoso priv-

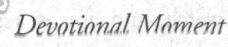

Devotional Moment
•
Home Front

101:2 Our families know us all too well. David knew his failures would be clearer to his family than to anyone else. He also knew that his lifestyle mattered most at home. Sometimes we think it's OK to be a little less disciplined, kind, or patient at home. Don't fool yourself into thinking that home is a place for compromise. Make an extra effort to treat every member of your family with respect, to pray for them, and to live at peace with them.

ᵇ to all . . . : Heb. to generation and generation
ᵃ wicked . . . : Heb. thing of Belial

ily slandereth his neighbour, him will I cut off: him that hath an high look and a proud heart will not I suffer. ⁶Mine eyes *shall be* upon the faithful of the land, that they may dwell with me: he that walketh in a perfect way, he shall serve me. ⁷He that worketh deceit shall not dwell within my house: he that telleth lies shall not tarry*ᵇ* in my sight. ⁸I will early destroy all the wicked of the land; that I may cut off all wicked doers from the city of the LORD.

102

A Prayer of the afflicted, when he is overwhelmed, and poureth out his complaint before the LORD.

¹Hear my prayer, O LORD, and let my cry come unto thee. ²Hide not thy face from me in the day *when* I am in trouble; incline thine ear unto me: in the day *when* I call answer me speedily. ³For my days are consumed like smoke, and my bones are burned as an hearth. ⁴My heart is smitten, and withered like grass; so that I forget to eat my bread. ⁵By reason of the voice of my groaning my bones cleave to my skinᵃ. ⁶I am like a pelican of the wilderness: I am like an owl of the desert. ⁷I watch, and am as a sparrow alone upon the house top. ⁸Mine enemies reproach me all the day; *and* they that are mad against me are sworn against me. ⁹For I have eaten ashes like bread, and mingled my drink with weeping, ¹⁰Because of thine indignation and thy wrath: for thou hast lifted me up, and cast me down. ¹¹My days *are* like a shadow that declineth; and I am withered like grass.

¹²But thou, O LORD, shalt endure for ever; and thy remembrance unto all generations. ¹³Thou shalt arise, *and* have mercy upon Zion: for the time to favour her, yea, the set time, is come. ¹⁴For thy servants take pleasure in her stones, and favour the dust thereof. ¹⁵So the heathen shall fear the name of the LORD, and all the kings of the earth thy glory. ¹⁶When the LORD shall build up Zion, he shall appear in his glory. ¹⁷He will regard the prayer of the destitute, and not despise their prayer. ¹⁸This shall be written for the generation to come: and the people which shall be created shall praise the LORD. ¹⁹For he hath looked down from the height of his sanctuary; from heaven did the LORD behold the earth; ²⁰To hear the groaning of the prisoner; to loose those that are appointed to death; ²¹To declare the name of the LORD in Zion, and his praise in Jerusalem; ²²When the people are gathered together, and the kingdoms, to serve the LORD.

²³He weakenedᵇ my strength in the way; he shortened my days. ²⁴I said, O my God, take me not away in the midst of my days: thy years *are* throughout all generations. ²⁵Of old hast thou laid the foundation of the earth: and the heavens *are* the work of thy hands. ²⁶They shall perish, but thou shalt endureᶜ: yea, all of them shall wax old like a garment; as a vesture shalt thou change them, and they shall be changed: ²⁷But thou *art* the same, and thy years shall have no end. ²⁸The children of thy servants

---

ᵇ shall not tarry: Heb. shall not be established
ᵃ skin: or, flesh
ᵇ weakened: Heb. afflicted
ᶜ endure: Heb. stand

shall continue, and their seed shall be established before thee.

103

A Psalm of David.

¹Bless the LORD, O my soul: and all that is within me, *bless* his holy name. ²Bless the LORD, O my soul, and forget not all his benefits: ³Who forgiveth all thine iniquities; who healeth all thy diseases; ⁴Who redeemeth thy life from destruction; who crowneth thee with lovingkindness and tender mercies; ⁵Who satisfieth thy mouth with good *things; so that* thy youth is renewed like the eagle's.

⁶The LORD executeth righteousness and judgment for all that are oppressed. ⁷He made known his ways unto Moses, his acts unto the children of Israel. ⁸The LORD *is* merciful and gracious, slow to anger, and plenteous in mercy. ⁹He will not always chide: neither will he keep *his anger* for ever. ¹⁰He hath not dealt with us after our sins; nor re-

Devotional Moment

Cure for Complaining

103:1-22 David knew how to praise God. In this psalm he went on and on remembering good and wonderful ways in which God had treated him. Sometimes our motto is, "If you can't think of something good to say, complain!" A better attitude is to look for reasons to praise God. Take note of the good he has done for you. During a day of travel or on an outing when you will be together for many hours, challenge your family to avoid complaints and point out the good. The exercise may be difficult, but it'll be worth it. You can make it easier by turning it into a game.

Devotional Moment

Forgiveness

103:8-12 God wants to remove our sins—not just excuse them, but *remove* them, "as far as the east is from the west." God loves us deeply and wants more than anything to bring us back into a relationship with him. Many people today believe that we can't break free from bad habits, weaknesses, or personality flaws. They think that a little positive mental attitude is all we need—that we should just focus on the good and try to overlook the bad. But no amount of looking on the bright side can do what God can do. We need to have our sins *removed*, and only God can do it. Jesus died to make it possible. All we have to do is believe in him and receive the gift (see Rom. 3:23; 5:8; 6:23).

warded us according to our iniquities. ¹¹For as the heaven is high above the earth, *so* great is his mercy toward them that fear him. ¹²As far as the east is from the west, *so* far hath he removed our transgressions from us. ¹³Like as a father pitieth *his* children, *so* the LORD pitieth them that fear him. ¹⁴For he knoweth our frame; he remembereth that we *are* dust. ¹⁵*As for* man, his days *are* as grass: as a flower of the field, so he flourisheth. ¹⁶For the wind passeth over it, and it is gone; and the place thereof shall know it no more. ¹⁷But the mercy of the LORD *is* from everlasting to everlasting upon them that fear him, and his righteousness unto children's children; ¹⁸To such as keep his covenant, and to those that remember his commandments to do them.

¹⁹The LORD hath prepared his throne in the heavens; and his kingdom ruleth over all. ²⁰Bless the LORD, ye his angels, that excel[a] in strength, that do his

---

[a] that excel . . . : Heb. mighty in strength

commandments, hearkening unto the voice of his word. ²¹Bless ye the LORD, all *ye* his hosts; *ye* ministers of his, that do his pleasure. ²²Bless the LORD, all his works in all places of his dominion: bless the LORD, O my soul.

104

¹Bless the LORD, O my soul. O LORD my God, thou art very great; thou art clothed with honour and majesty. ²Who coverest *thyself* with light as *with* a garment: who stretchest out the heavens like a curtain: ³Who layeth the beams of his chambers in the waters: who maketh the clouds his chariot: who walketh upon the wings of the wind: ⁴Who maketh his angels spirits; his ministers a flaming fire: ⁵*Who* laid the foundations of the earth, *that* it should not be removed for ever. ⁶Thou coveredst it with the deep as *with* a garment: the waters stood above the mountains. ⁷At thy rebuke they fled; at the voice of thy thunder they hasted away. ⁸They go up[a] by the mountains; they go down by the valleys unto the place which thou hast founded for them. ⁹Thou hast set a bound that they may not pass over; that they turn not again to cover the earth.

¹⁰He sendeth the springs into the valleys, *which* run among the hills. ¹¹They give drink to every beast of the field: the wild asses quench[b] their thirst. ¹²By them shall the fowls of the heaven have their habitation, *which* sing[c] among the branches. ¹³He watereth the hills from his chambers: the earth is satisfied with the fruit of thy works. ¹⁴He causeth the grass to grow for the cattle, and herb for the service of man: that he may bring forth food out of the earth; ¹⁵And wine *that* maketh glad the heart of man, *and* oil[d] to make *his* face to shine, and bread *which* strengtheneth man's heart. ¹⁶The trees of the LORD are full *of sap*; the cedars of Lebanon, which he hath planted; ¹⁷Where the birds make their nests: *as for* the stork, the fir trees *are* her house. ¹⁸The high hills *are* a refuge for the wild goats; *and* the rocks for the conies.

¹⁹He appointed the moon for seasons: the sun knoweth his going down. ²⁰Thou makest darkness, and it is night: wherein all the beasts[e] of the forest do creep *forth*. ²¹The young lions roar after their prey, and seek their meat from God. ²²The sun ariseth, they gather themselves together, and lay them down in their dens. ²³Man goeth forth unto his work and to his labour until the evening. ²⁴O LORD, how manifold are thy works! in wisdom hast thou made them all: the earth is full of thy riches. ²⁵*So is* this great and wide sea, wherein *are* things creeping innumerable, both small and great beasts. ²⁶There go the ships: *there is* that leviathan, *whom* thou hast made[f] to play therein. ²⁷These wait all upon thee; that thou mayest give *them* their meat in due season. ²⁸*That* thou givest them they gather: thou openest thine hand, they are filled with

---

[a] They go up . . . : or, The mountains ascend, the valleys descend
[b] quench: Heb. break
[c] sing: Heb. give a voice
[d] oil . . . : Heb. to make his face shine with oil, or, more than oil
[e] beasts . . . : Heb. beasts thereof do trample on the forest
[f] made: Heb. formed

Breaking Free
from Fatherlessness

*Like as a father pitieth his children, so the Lord pitieth them
that fear him.* Psalm 103:13

Psalm 103 is a powerful section of Scripture that can help those who have suffered the loss of a father's love. As you look closely at this description of your heavenly Father, you'll gain insight and encouragement to break negative patterns and replace them with a heart filled with God's love.

Those with a physically or emotionally distant father often have two "holes in the heart": a feeling of insignificance, and a lack of security.

Feelings of insignificance. Brian's father told him that he'd go with him on his scouting camp-out. Brian waited for weeks for the morning they'd pack the van and join his friends in roughing it. But his father came home late from work, and after sleeping in the next morning, the only thing he packed was his golf clubs so he could spend the day with his friends.

"I can see now," Brian said, "that my father never intended to go on that camp-out—he just didn't have the guts to tell me. I grew up knowing that his golf was important to him—more important than his son."

Children lose a much-needed sense of significance when they don't receive a father's love. As a result, they can feel that they are insignificant even to God.

Feelings of insecurity. Diane's father left the family when she was eight and her sister was five. After months of never hearing from him, he finally called and said that he would be coming over on Easter Sunday to see his girls.

Diane helped her little sister get into her finest dress, and together they sat on the back of the couch looking out the window, waiting for their father. He never showed up.

The sad reality of that hurtful day left a deep sense of insecurity in Diane's life. She felt she couldn't trust her father or his words. And, more deeply, she felt she couldn't trust any man (or even God) to keep from hurting her.

God's healing love. A child who grows up without a father's consistent, affirming, touching love is often robbed of significance and security. Yet those twin holes can be healed. And that's because we've got a heavenly Father who loves us better and more deeply than any earthly father ever could.

But to accept that reality, we've got to look at what our heavenly Father is really like and not view him through the defective lenses of an absent or distant earthly father. That's where Psalm 103 can help us.

Read through that psalm right now. Get out a piece of paper and divide it into three columns. In the left column, write every characteristic of God presented in this psalm. For example, "He forgives all my sins."

In the middle column, write a practical application. For example, "My heavenly Father completely forgives me for . . ."

Once you've gone through the entire psalm filling in the left and middle columns, write your own father's name at the top of the right column. Then go back down your list and mark every trait that your own father had or has. For example, put a check mark by "He forgives all my sins" if your own father forgave you when you did wrong. If your list contains only one or two check marks for your own father, you're a strong candidate for the cycle of hurt from fatherlessness.

In addition to letting God's love and acceptance help you break free of hurt in your own life, if you're a father yourself you can break the cycle by making sure your children don't have to suffer this hurt. Even the best of fathers can't match our heavenly Father's perfection. But the best way to give your children a clear picture of a loving God is to love them with Christlike love.

Devotional Moment

•

Chores

104:27-28 While God supplies food for the animals, they are responsible to gather it. The chores and duties we do at home may seem like drudgery, but in actuality we are in a partnership with God. Even children's chores can help us reflect on God's care and provision. When we help around the house, we are using and organizing the many resources God has provided for us.

---

good. ²⁹Thou hidest thy face, they are troubled: thou takest away their breath, they die, and return to their dust. ³⁰Thou sendest forth thy spirit, they are created: and thou renewest the face of the earth.

³¹The glory of the LORD shall endure for ever: the LORD shall rejoice in his works. ³²He looketh on the earth, and it trembleth: he toucheth the hills, and they smoke. ³³I will sing unto the LORD as long as I live: I will sing praise to my God while I have my being. ³⁴My meditation of him shall be sweet: I will be glad in the LORD. ³⁵Let the sinners be consumed out of the earth, and let the wicked be no more. Bless thou the LORD, O my soul. Praise ye the LORD.

105

¹O give thanks unto the LORD; call upon his name: make known his deeds among the people. ²Sing unto him, sing psalms unto him: talk ye of all his wondrous works. ³Glory ye in his holy name: let the heart of them rejoice that seek the LORD. ⁴Seek the LORD, and his strength: seek his face evermore. ⁵Remember his marvellous works that he hath done; his wonders, and the judgments of his mouth; ⁶O ye seed of Abraham his servant, ye children of Jacob his chosen. ⁷He *is* the LORD our God: his judgments *are* in all the earth.

⁸He hath remembered his covenant for ever, the word *which* he commanded

to a thousand generations. ⁹Which *covenant* he made with Abraham, and his oath unto Isaac; ¹⁰And confirmed the same unto Jacob for a law, *and* to Israel *for* an everlasting covenant: ¹¹Saying, Unto thee will I give the land of Canaan, the lotᵃ of your inheritance: ¹²When they were *but* a few men in number; yea, very few, and strangers in it. ¹³When they went from one nation to another, from *one* kingdom to another people; ¹⁴He suffered no man to do them wrong: yea, he reproved kings for their sakes; ¹⁵*Saying,* Touch not mine anointed, and do my prophets no harm. ¹⁶Moreover he called for a famine upon the land: he brake the whole staff of bread. ¹⁷He sent a man before them, *even* Joseph, *who* was sold for a servant: ¹⁸Whose feet they hurt with fetters: heᵇ was laid in iron: ¹⁹Until the time that his word came: the word of the LORD tried him. ²⁰The king sent and loosed him; *even* the ruler of the people, and let him go free. ²¹He made him lord of his house, and ruler of all his substanceᶜ: ²²To bind his princes at his pleasure; and teach his senators wisdom. ²³Israel also came into Egypt; and Jacob sojourned in the land of Ham. ²⁴And he increased his people greatly; and made them stronger than their enemies.

²⁵He turned their heart to hate his people, to deal subtilly with his servants. ²⁶He sent Moses his servant; *and* Aaron whom he had chosen. ²⁷They shewed his signs among them, and wonders in the land of Ham. ²⁸He sent darkness, and made it dark; and they rebelled not against his word. ²⁹He turned their waters into blood, and slew their fish. ³⁰Their land brought forth frogs in abundance, in the chambers of their kings. ³¹He spake, and there came divers sorts of flies, *and* lice in all their coasts. ³²He gave them hail for rain, *and* flaming fire in their land. ³³He smote their vines also and their fig trees; and brake the trees of their coasts. ³⁴He spake, and the locusts came, and caterpillers, and that without number, ³⁵And did eat up all the herbs in their land, and devoured the fruit of their ground. ³⁶He smote also all the firstborn in their land, the chief of all their strength. ³⁷He brought them forth also with silver and gold: and *there was* not one feeble *person* among their tribes. ³⁸Egypt was glad when they departed: for the fear of them fell upon them. ³⁹He spread a cloud for a covering; and fire to give light in the night. ⁴⁰*The people* asked, and he brought quails, and satisfied them with the bread of heaven. ⁴¹He opened the rock, and the waters gushed out; they ran in the dry places *like* a river. ⁴²For he remembered his holy promise, *and* Abraham his servant. ⁴³And he brought forth his people with joy, *and* his chosen with gladnessᵈ: ⁴⁴And gave them the lands of the heathen: and they inherited the labour of the people; ⁴⁵That they might observe his statutes, and keep his laws. Praiseᵉ ye the LORD.

ᵃ lot: Heb. cord
ᵇ he . . . : Heb. his soul came into iron
ᶜ substance: Heb. possession
ᵈ gladness: Heb. singing
ᵉ Praise . . . : Heb. Hallelujah

106

¹Praise[a] ye the LORD. O give thanks unto the LORD; for *he is* good: for his mercy *endureth* for ever. ²Who can utter the mighty acts of the LORD? *who* can shew forth all his praise? ³Blessed *are* they that keep judgment, *and* he that doeth righteousness at all times. ⁴Remember me, O LORD, with the favour *that thou bearest unto* thy people: O visit me with thy salvation; ⁵That I may see the good of thy chosen, that I may rejoice in the gladness of thy nation, that I may glory with thine inheritance.

⁶We have sinned with our fathers, we have committed iniquity, we have done wickedly. ⁷Our fathers understood not thy wonders in Egypt; they remembered not the multitude of thy mercies; but provoked *him* at the sea, *even* at the Red sea. ⁸Nevertheless he saved them for his name's sake, that he might make his mighty power to be known. ⁹He rebuked the Red sea also, and it was dried up: so he led them through the depths, as through the wilderness. ¹⁰And he saved them from the hand of him that hated *them*, and redeemed them from the hand of the enemy. ¹¹And the waters covered their enemies: there was not one of them left. ¹²Then believed they his words; they sang his praise.

¹³They soon[b] forgat his works; they waited not for his counsel: ¹⁴But lusted[c] exceedingly in the wilderness, and tempted God in the desert. ¹⁵And he gave them their request; but sent leanness into their soul. ¹⁶They envied Moses also in the camp, *and* Aaron the saint of the LORD. ¹⁷The earth opened and swallowed up Dathan, and covered the company of Abiram. ¹⁸And a fire was kindled in their company; the flame burned up the wicked. ¹⁹They made a calf in Horeb, and worshipped the molten image. ²⁰Thus they changed their glory into the similitude of an ox that eateth grass. ²¹They forgat God their saviour, which had done great things in Egypt; ²²Wondrous works in the land of Ham, *and* terrible things by the Red sea. ²³Therefore he said that he would destroy them, had not Moses his chosen stood before him in the breach, to turn away his wrath, lest he should destroy *them*. ²⁴Yea, they despised the pleasant[d] land, they believed not his word: ²⁵But murmured in their tents, *and* hearkened not unto the voice of the LORD. ²⁶Therefore he lifted up his hand against them, to overthrow[e] them in the wilderness: ²⁷To overthrow their seed also among the nations, and to scatter them in the lands. ²⁸They joined themselves also unto Baalpeor, and ate the sacrifices of the dead. ²⁹Thus they provoked *him* to anger with their inventions: and the plague brake in upon them. ³⁰Then stood up Phinehas, and executed judgment: and *so* the plague was stayed. ³¹And that was counted unto him for righteousness unto all generations for evermore. ³²They angered *him* also at the waters of strife, so that it went ill with Moses for their sakes:

---

[a] Praise . . . : Heb. Hallelujah
[b] They soon . . . : Heb. They made haste, they forgat
[c] lusted . . . : Heb. lusted a lust
[d] the pleasant . . . : Heb. a land of desire
[e] to overthrow: Heb. to make them fall

³³Because they provoked his spirit, so that he spake unadvisedly with his lips.

³⁴They did not destroy the nations, concerning whom the LORD commanded them: ³⁵But were mingled among the heathen, and learned their works. ³⁶And they served their idols: which were a snare unto them. ³⁷Yea, they sacrificed their sons and their daughters unto devils, ³⁸And shed innocent blood, *even* the blood of their sons and of their daughters, whom they sacrificed unto the idols of Canaan: and the land was polluted with blood. ³⁹Thus were they defiled with their own works, and went a whoring with their own inventions. ⁴⁰Therefore was the wrath of the LORD kindled against his people, insomuch that he abhorred his own inheritance. ⁴¹And he gave them into the hand of the heathen; and they that hated them ruled over them. ⁴²Their enemies also oppressed them, and they were brought into subjection under their hand. ⁴³Many times did he deliver them; but they provoked *him* with their counsel, and were brought low for their iniquity. ⁴⁴Nevertheless he regarded their affliction, when he heard their cry: ⁴⁵And he remembered for them his covenant, and repented according to the multitude of his mercies. ⁴⁶He made them also to be pitied of all those that carried them captives. ⁴⁷Save us, O LORD our God, and gather us from among the heathen, to give thanks unto thy holy name, *and* to triumph in thy praise. ⁴⁸Blessed *be* the LORD God of Israel from everlasting to everlasting: and let all the people say, Amen. Praiseᶠ ye the LORD.

107

¹O give thanks unto the LORD, for *he is* good: for his mercy *endureth* for ever. ²Let the redeemed of the LORD say *so*, whom he hath redeemed from the hand of the enemy; ³And gathered them out of the lands, from the east, and from the west, from the north, and from the southᵃ. ⁴They wandered in the wilderness in a solitary way; they found no city to dwell in. ⁵Hungry and thirsty, their soul fainted in them. ⁶Then they cried unto the LORD in their trouble, *and* he delivered them out of their distresses. ⁷And he led them forth by the right way, that they might go to a city of habitation. ⁸Oh that *men* would praise the LORD *for* his goodness, and *for* his wonderful works to the children of men! ⁹For he satisfieth the longing soul, and filleth the hungry soul with goodness.

Devotional Moment

•

Big Troubles!

106:34-42 Israel's problems may have belonged to the nation, but they showed up in families. Instead of living the way God wanted them to live, they decided to live just like everybody else. Their actions were evil, and they forgot God. Parents even sacrificed their children to idols (v. 37). Consequences are real and painful. This psalm makes the point that rebellion against God will sooner or later create big troubles for us. We ought to remind one another constantly: "Let's live the way God wants us to live!"

ᶠ Praise . . . : Heb. Hallelujah
ᵃ south: Heb. sea

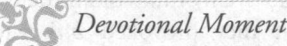

Devotional Moment

•

Hope

107:3-16 Darkness, death, misery, and slavery come upon us today from many sources, including alcohol and other drugs, sexual addiction, and abuse. Families, friends, and loved ones are all affected by even one person's entrapment. But God is able to free people from every kind of slavery, to open any kind of prison gates. He is able to restore us. He is able to heal husbands and wives and children. He is able to rebuild relationships. Have you invited God to use his power and wisdom to help you face the problems and difficulties in your life? He longs to satisfy your thirsty soul.

¹⁰Such as sit in darkness and in the shadow of death, *being* bound in affliction and iron; ¹¹Because they rebelled against the words of God, and contemned the counsel of the most High: ¹²Therefore he brought down their heart with labour; they fell down, and *there was* none to help. ¹³Then they cried unto the LORD in their trouble, *and* he saved them out of their distresses. ¹⁴He brought them out of darkness and the shadow of death, and brake their bands in sunder. ¹⁵Oh that *men* would praise the LORD *for* his goodness, and *for* his wonderful works to the children of men! ¹⁶For he hath broken the gates of brass, and cut the bars of iron in sunder.

¹⁷Fools because of their transgression, and because of their iniquities, are afflicted. ¹⁸Their soul abhorreth all manner of meat; and they draw near unto the gates of death. ¹⁹Then they cry unto the LORD in their trouble, *and* he saveth them out of their distresses. ²⁰He sent his word, and healed them, and delivered *them* from their destructions. ²¹Oh that *men* would praise the LORD *for* his goodness, and *for* his wonderful works to the children of men! ²²And let them sacrifice the sacrifices of thanksgiving, and declare his works with rejoicing^b.

²³They that go down to the sea in ships, that do business in great waters; ²⁴These see the works of the LORD, and his wonders in the deep. ²⁵For he commandeth, and raiseth^c the stormy wind, which lifteth up the waves thereof. ²⁶They mount up to the heaven, they go down again to the depths: their soul is melted because of trouble. ²⁷They reel to and fro, and stagger like a drunken man, and are at their wits' end. ²⁸Then they cry unto the LORD in their trouble, and he bringeth them out of their distresses. ²⁹He maketh the storm a calm, so that the waves thereof are still. ³⁰Then are they glad because they be quiet; so he bringeth them unto their desired haven. ³¹Oh that *men* would praise the LORD *for* his goodness, and *for* his wonderful works to the children of men! ³²Let them exalt him also in the congregation of the people, and praise him in the assembly of the elders.

³³He turneth rivers into a wilderness, and the watersprings into dry ground; ³⁴A fruitful land into barrenness^d, for the wickedness of them that dwell therein. ³⁵He turneth the wilderness into a stand-

---

^b rejoicing: Heb. singing
^c raiseth: Heb. maketh to stand
^d barrenness: Heb. saltiness

ing water, and dry ground into water-springs. ³⁶And there he maketh the hungry to dwell, that they may prepare a city for habitation; ³⁷And sow the fields, and plant vineyards, which may yield fruits of increase. ³⁸He blesseth them also, so that they are multiplied greatly; and suffereth not their cattle to decrease. ³⁹Again, they are minished and brought low through oppression, affliction, and sorrow. ⁴⁰He poureth contempt upon princes, and causeth them to wander in the wilderness*, *where there is* no way. ⁴¹Yet setteth he the poor on high from affliction, and maketh *him* families like a flock. ⁴²The righteous shall see *it*, and rejoice: and all iniquity shall stop her mouth. ⁴³Whoso *is* wise, and will observe these *things*, even they shall understand the lovingkindness of the LORD.

108

A Song *or* Psalm of David.

¹O God, my heart is fixed; I will sing and give praise, even with my glory. ²Awake, psaltery and harp: I *myself* will awake early. ³I will praise thee, O LORD, among the people: and I will sing praises unto thee among the nations. ⁴For thy mercy *is* great above the heavens: and thy truth *reacheth* unto the clouds*. ⁵Be thou exalted, O God, above the heavens: and thy glory above all the earth;

⁶That thy beloved may be delivered: save *with* thy right hand, and answer me.

⁷God hath spoken in his holiness; I will rejoice, I will divide Shechem, and mete out the valley of Succoth. ⁸Gilead *is* mine; Manasseh *is* mine; Ephraim also *is* the strength of mine head; Judah *is* my lawgiver; ⁹Moab *is* my washpot; over Edom will I cast out my shoe; over Philistia will I triumph. ¹⁰Who will bring me into the strong city? who will lead me into Edom? ¹¹*Wilt* not *thou*, O God, *who* hast cast us off? and wilt not thou, O God, go forth with our hosts? ¹²Give us help from trouble: for vain *is* the help of man. ¹³Through God we shall do valiantly: for he *it is that* shall tread down our enemies.

109

To the chief Musician, A Psalm of David.

¹Hold not thy peace, O God of my praise; ²For the mouth of the wicked and the mouth of the deceitfulᵃ are opened against me: they have spoken against me with a lying tongue. ³They compassed me about also with words of hatred; and fought against me without a cause. ⁴For my love they are my adversaries: but I *give myself unto* prayer. ⁵And they have rewarded me evil for good, and hatred for my love.

⁶Set thou a wicked man over him: and let Satanᵇ stand at his right hand. ⁷When he shall be judged, let him be condemnedᶜ: and let his prayer become sin. ⁸Let his days be few; *and* let another take his officeᵈ. ⁹Let his children be fa-

---

ᵉ wilderness: or, void place
ᵃ clouds: or, skies
ᵃ of the deceitful: Heb. of deceit
ᵇ Satan: or, an adversary
ᶜ be condemned: Heb. go out guilty, or, wicked
ᵈ office: or, charge

therless, and his wife a widow. ¹⁰Let his children be continually vagabonds, and beg: let them seek *their bread* also out of their desolate places. ¹¹Let the extortioner catch all that he hath; and let the strangers spoil his labour. ¹²Let there be none to extend mercy unto him: neither let there be any to favour his fatherless children. ¹³Let his posterity be cut off; *and* in the generation following let their name be blotted out. ¹⁴Let the iniquity of his fathers be remembered with the LORD; and let not the sin of his mother be blotted out. ¹⁵Let them be before the LORD continually, that he may cut off the memory of them from the earth. ¹⁶Because that he remembered not to shew mercy, but persecuted the poor and needy man, that he might even slay the broken in heart. ¹⁷As he loved cursing, so let it come unto him: as he delighted not in blessing, so let it be far from him. ¹⁸As he clothed himself with cursing like as with his garment, so let it come into his bowelsᶜ like water, and like oil into his bones. ¹⁹Let it be unto him as the garment *which* covereth him, and for a girdle wherewith he is girded continually. ²⁰*Let* this *be* the reward of mine adversaries from the LORD, and of them that speak evil against my soul.

²¹But do thou for me, O GOD the Lord, for thy name's sake: because thy mercy *is* good, deliver thou me. ²²For I *am* poor and needy, and my heart is wounded within me. ²³I am gone like the shadow when it declineth: I am tossed up and down as the locust. ²⁴My knees are weak through fasting; and my flesh faileth of fatness. ²⁵I became also a reproach unto them: *when* they looked upon me they shaked their heads. ²⁶Help me, O LORD my God: O save me according to thy mercy: ²⁷That they may know that this *is* thy hand; *that* thou, LORD, hast done it. ²⁸Let them curse, but bless thou: when they arise, let them be ashamed; but let thy servant rejoice. ²⁹Let mine adversaries be clothed with shame, and let them cover themselves with their own confusion, as with a mantle. ³⁰I will greatly praise the LORD with my mouth; yea, I will praise him among the multitude. ³¹For he shall stand at the right hand of the poor, to save *him* from those that condemn his soul.

110

A Psalm of David.

¹The LORD said unto my Lord, Sit thou at my right hand, until I make thine enemies thy footstool. ²The LORD shall send the rod of thy strength out of Zion: rule thou in the midst of thine enemies. ³Thy people *shall be* willing in the day of thy power, in the beauties of holiness from the womb of the morning: thou hast the dew of thy youth. ⁴The LORD hath sworn, and will not repent, Thou *art* a priest for ever after the order of Melchizedek.

⁵The Lord at thy right hand shall strike through kings in the day of his wrath. ⁶He shall judge among the heathen, he shall fill *the places* with the dead bodies; he shall wound the heads over manyᵃ countries. ⁷He shall drink of

---

ᶜ into his bowels: Heb. within him
ᵃ many: or, great

the brook in the way: therefore shall he lift up the head.

111

¹Praise ye the LORD. I will praise the LORD with *my* whole heart, in the assembly of the upright, and *in* the congregation. ²The works of the LORD *are* great, sought out of all them that have pleasure therein. ³His work *is* honourable and glorious: and his righteousness endureth for ever. ⁴He hath made his wonderful works to be remembered: the LORD *is* gracious and full of compassion. ⁵He hath given meat* unto them that fear him: he will ever be mindful of his covenant.

⁶He hath shewed his people the power of his works, that he may give them the heritage of the heathen. ⁷The works of his hands *are* verity and judgment; all his commandments *are* sure. ⁸They stand fast for ever and ever, *and are* done in truth and uprightness. ⁹He sent redemption unto his people: he hath commanded his covenant for ever:

holy and reverend *is* his name. ¹⁰The fear of the LORD *is* the beginning of wisdom: a good° understanding have all they that do *his commandments*: his praise endureth for ever.

112

¹Praise° ye the LORD. Blessed *is* the man *that* feareth the LORD, *that* delighteth greatly in his commandments. ²His seed shall be mighty upon earth: the generation of the upright shall be blessed. ³Wealth and riches *shall be* in his house: and his righteousness endureth for ever. ⁴Unto the upright there ariseth light in the darkness: *he is* gracious, and full of compassion, and righteous. ⁵A good man sheweth favour, and lendeth: he will guide his affairs with discretion°.

⁶Surely he shall not be moved for ever: the righteous shall be in everlasting remembrance. ⁷He shall not be afraid of evil tidings: his heart is fixed, trusting in the LORD. ⁸His heart *is* es-

---

Devotional Moment
•
Wisdom

111:10 This verse states that wisdom has a starting point. Wisdom begins through reverence for God. What does *reverence for God* mean? Some Bible translations render it "fear God." It means total respect and reverential awe for God. He is so holy that the only proper attitude toward him is humble worship (see James 4:7-10). *That's* the beginning of wisdom.

Devotional Moment
•
Confidence

112:7 This psalm is about the security that comes from confidence in God. The person who trusts in God really has nothing to fear. Problems will still come, and bad news will still tempt us to fear, but if we continue to count on God, we will survive. Our future rests in the best hands—God's. As Jesus said, "Take therefore no thought for the morrow: for the morrow shall take thought for the things of itself" (Matt. 6:34).

ᵃ meat: Heb. prey
ᵇ a good . . . : or, good success
ᵃ Praise . . . : Heb. Hallelujah
ᵇ discretion: Heb. judgment

tablished, he shall not be afraid, until he see *his desire* upon his enemies. ⁹He hath dispersed, he hath given to the poor; his righteousness endureth for ever; his horn shall be exalted with honour. ¹⁰The wicked shall see *it*, and be grieved; he shall gnash with his teeth, and melt away: the desire of the wicked shall perish.

113

¹Praise ye the LORD. Praise, O ye servants of the LORD, praise the name of the LORD. ²Blessed be the name of the LORD from this time forth and for evermore. ³From the rising of the sun unto the going down of the same the LORD'S name *is* to be praised. ⁴The LORD *is* high above all nations, *and* his glory above the heavens. ⁵Who *is* like unto the LORD our God, who dwelleth\u1d43 on high, ⁶Who humbleth *himself* to behold *the things that are* in heaven, and in the earth! ⁷He raiseth up the poor out of the dust, *and* lifteth the needy out of the dunghill; ⁸That he may set *him* with princes, *even* with the princes of his people. ⁹He maketh the barren woman to keep\u1d47 house, *and to be* a joyful mother of children. Praise ye the LORD.

114

¹When Israel went out of Egypt, the house of Jacob from a people of strange language; ²Judah was his sanctuary, *and* Israel his dominion. ³The sea saw *it*, and fled: Jordan was driven back. ⁴The mountains skipped like rams, *and* the little hills like lambs. ⁵What *ailed* thee,

O thou sea, that thou fleddest? thou Jordan, *that* thou wast driven back? ⁶Ye mountains, *that* ye skipped like rams; *and* ye little hills, like lambs? ⁷Tremble, thou earth, at the presence of the Lord, at the presence of the God of Jacob; ⁸Which turned the rock *into* a standing water, the flint into a fountain of waters.

115

¹Not unto us, O LORD, not unto us, but unto thy name give glory, for thy mercy, *and* for thy truth's sake. ²Wherefore should the heathen say, Where *is* now their God? ³But our God *is* in the heavens: he hath done whatsoever he hath pleased. ⁴Their idols *are* silver and gold, the work of men's hands. ⁵They have mouths, but they speak not: eyes have they, but they see not: ⁶They have ears, but they hear not: noses have they, but they smell not: ⁷They have hands, but they handle not: feet have they, but they walk not: neither speak they through their throat. ⁸They that make them are like unto them; *so is* every one that trusteth in them.

⁹O Israel, trust thou in the LORD: he *is* their help and their shield. ¹⁰O house of Aaron, trust in the LORD: he *is* their help and their shield. ¹¹Ye that fear the LORD, trust in the LORD: he *is* their help and their shield. ¹²The LORD hath been mindful of us: he will bless *us;* he will bless the house of Israel; he will bless the house of Aaron. ¹³He will bless them that fear the LORD, *both* small and great. ¹⁴The LORD shall increase you more and more, you and

---

\u1d43 dwelleth . . . : Heb. exalteth himself to dwell
\u1d47 to keep . . . : Heb. to dwell in an house

your children. [15]Ye *are* blessed of the LORD which made heaven and earth. [16]The heaven, *even* the heavens, *are* the LORD'S: but the earth hath he given to the children of men. [17]The dead praise not the LORD, neither any that go down into silence. [18]But we will bless the LORD from this time forth and for evermore. Praise the LORD.

116

[1]I love the LORD, because he hath heard my voice *and* my supplications. [2]Because he hath inclined his ear unto me, therefore will I call upon *him* as long as I live. [3]The sorrows of death compassed me, and the pains of hell gat hold upon me: I found trouble and sorrow. [4]Then called I upon the name of the LORD; O LORD, I beseech thee, deliver my soul. [5]Gracious *is* the LORD, and righteous; yea, our God *is* merciful. [6]The LORD preserveth the simple: I was brought low, and he helped me. [7]Return unto thy rest, O my soul; for the LORD hath dealt bountifully with thee. [8]For thou hast delivered my soul from death, mine eyes from tears, *and* my feet from falling. [9]I will walk before the LORD in the land of the living.

[10]I believed, therefore have I spoken: I was greatly afflicted: [11]I said in my haste, All men *are* liars. [12]What shall I render unto the LORD *for* all his benefits toward me? [13]I will take the cup of salvation, and call upon the name of the LORD. [14]I will pay my vows unto the LORD now in the presence of all his people. [15]Precious in the sight of the LORD *is* the death of his saints. [16]O LORD, truly I *am* thy servant; I *am* thy servant, *and* the son of thine handmaid:

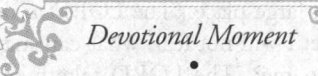

Devotional Moment
•
Death

116:15 Most of us will see loved ones step into eternity. Death affects families deeply. But if we are believers, we know that we are part of an eternal family—God's "loved ones." We may not understand why someone had to die, but we can remember that even death fits into God's loving plans for us. And when we are part of God's family, our good-byes are not permanent—we will see each other again (see 1 Thess. 4:13-18). In gentle ways, comfort one another with this truth.

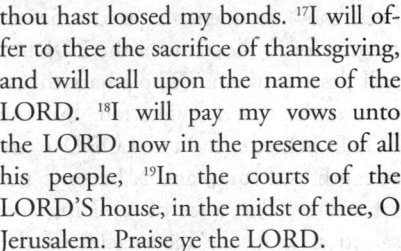

thou hast loosed my bonds. [17]I will offer to thee the sacrifice of thanksgiving, and will call upon the name of the LORD. [18]I will pay my vows unto the LORD now in the presence of all his people, [19]In the courts of the LORD'S house, in the midst of thee, O Jerusalem. Praise ye the LORD.

117

[1]O praise the LORD, all ye nations: praise him, all ye people. [2]For his merciful kindness is great toward us: and the truth of the LORD *endureth* for ever. Praise ye the LORD.

118

[1]O give thanks unto the LORD; for *he is* good: because his mercy *endureth* for ever. [2]Let Israel now say, that his mercy *endureth* for ever. [3]Let the house of Aaron now say, that his mercy *endureth* for ever. [4]Let them now that fear the LORD say, that his mercy *endureth* for ever. [5]I called upon the LORD in distress[a]: the LORD answered me, *and set*

---

[a] in distress: Heb. out of distress

me in a large place. ⁶The LORD *is* on my side; I will not fear: what can man do unto me? ⁷The LORD taketh my part with them that help me: therefore shall I see *my desire* upon them that hate me. ⁸*It is* better to trust in the LORD than to put confidence in man. ⁹*It is* better to trust in the LORD than to put confidence in princes. ¹⁰All nations compassed me about: but in the name of the LORD will I destroy^b them. ¹¹They compassed me about; yea, they compassed me about: but in the name of the LORD I will destroy them. ¹²They compassed me about like bees; they are quenched as the fire of thorns: for in the name of the LORD I will destroy^c them. ¹³Thou hast thrust sore at me that I might fall: but the LORD helped me. ¹⁴The LORD *is* my strength and song, and is become my salvation. ¹⁵The voice of rejoicing and salvation *is* in the tabernacles of the righteous: the right hand of the LORD doeth valiantly. ¹⁶The right hand of the LORD is exalted: the right hand of the LORD doeth valiantly. ¹⁷I shall not die, but live, and declare the works of the LORD. ¹⁸The LORD hath chastened me sore: but he hath not given me over unto death.

¹⁹Open to me the gates of righteousness: I will go into them, *and* I will praise the LORD: ²⁰This gate of the LORD, into which the righteous shall enter. ²¹I will praise thee: for thou hast heard me, and art become my salvation. ²²The stone *which* the builders refused is become the head *stone* of the corner.

²³This is the LORD'S doing; it *is* marvellous in our eyes. ²⁴This *is* the day *which* the LORD hath made; we will rejoice and be glad in it. ²⁵Save now, I beseech thee, O LORD: O LORD, I beseech thee, send now prosperity. ²⁶Blessed *be* he that cometh in the name of the LORD: we have blessed you out of the house of the LORD. ²⁷God *is* the LORD, which hath shewed us light: bind the sacrifice with cords, *even* unto the horns of the altar. ²⁸Thou *art* my God, and I will praise thee: *thou art* my God, I will exalt thee. ²⁹O give thanks unto the LORD; for *he is* good: for his mercy *endureth* for ever.

119

¹ALEPH. Blessed *are* the undefiled^a in the way, who walk in the law of the LORD. ²Blessed *are* they that keep his testimonies, *and that* seek him with the whole heart. ³They also do no iniquity: they walk in his ways.

⁴Thou hast commanded *us* to keep thy precepts diligently. ⁵O that my ways were directed to keep thy statutes! ⁶Then shall I not be ashamed, when I have respect unto all thy commandments.

⁷I will praise thee with uprightness of heart, when I shall have learned thy righteous judgments. ⁸I will keep thy statutes: O forsake me not utterly.

⁹BETH. Wherewithal shall a young man cleanse his way? by taking heed *thereto* according to thy word. ¹⁰With my whole heart have I sought thee: O let me not wander from thy commandments.

---

^b destroy . . . : Heb. cut them off
^c destroy: Heb. cut down
^a undefiled: or, perfect, or, sincere

that are cursed, which do err from thy commandments.

²²Remove from me reproach and contempt; for I have kept thy testimonies.

²³Princes also did sit *and* speak against me: *but* thy servant did meditate in thy statutes.

²⁴Thy testimonies also *are* my delight *and* my counsellors[c].

²⁵DALETH. My soul cleaveth unto the dust: quicken thou me according to thy word.

²⁶I have declared my ways, and thou heardest me: teach me thy statutes. ²⁷Make me to understand the way of thy precepts: so shall I talk of thy wondrous works.

²⁸My soul melteth[d] for heaviness: strengthen thou me according unto thy word. ²⁹Remove from me the way of lying: and grant me thy law graciously.

Devotional Moment

Purity

119:9 In a society where people mock virginity, where integrity is a vanishing commodity, and where the "experts" give confusing and conflicting advice, this is a particularly relevant question: How can young people live pure lives? The psalmist unashamedly points to the unchanging Word of God as the ultimate source of wisdom. However, it isn't enough just to know what God has said; we must also obey his Word in order to avoid the lure—and subsequent consequences—of impurity. Help your children fill their hearts with God's Word to protect them from the impurities of the world, and work together as a family to learn how to follow God's principles for living.

---

¹¹Thy word have I hid in mine heart, that I might not sin against thee.

¹²Blessed *art* thou, O LORD: teach me thy statutes.

¹³With my lips have I declared all the judgments of thy mouth. ¹⁴I have rejoiced in the way of thy testimonies, as *much as* in all riches. ¹⁵I will meditate in thy precepts, and have respect unto thy ways. ¹⁶I will delight myself in thy statutes: I will not forget thy word.

¹⁷GIMEL. Deal bountifully with thy servant, *that* I may live, and keep thy word.

¹⁸Open[b] thou mine eyes, that I may behold wondrous things out of thy law.

¹⁹I *am* a stranger in the earth: hide not thy commandments from me.

²⁰My soul breaketh for the longing *that it hath* unto thy judgments at all times.

²¹Thou hast rebuked the proud

Devotional Moment

Family Rules

119:12-18 The psalmist praised God for his decrees and knew God's law to be full of "wondrous things" (v. 18). He even said that he felt about God's rules as most people feel about riches (v. 14)! In our freedom-loving culture, many people consider *rules* confining and repressive. But our heavenly Father puts limits on our behavior because he wants to protect us from harm and bring good things into our life. Set and enforce rules in your family that achieve these purposes. If a rule only aggravates everyone or sets up barriers, consider whether it is serving any useful purpose. Use rules to guide and protect, not to oppress and control.

ᵇ Open: Heb. Reveal
ᶜ my counsellors: Heb. men of my counsel
ᵈ melteth: Heb. droppeth

³⁰I have chosen the way of truth: thy judgments have I laid *before me.* ³¹I have stuck unto thy testimonies: O LORD, put me not to shame. ³²I will run the way of thy commandments, when thou shalt enlarge my heart.

³³HE. Teach me, O LORD, the way of thy statutes; and I shall keep it *unto* the end. ³⁴Give me understanding, and I shall keep thy law; yea, I shall observe it with *my* whole heart.

³⁵Make me to go in the path of thy commandments; for therein do I delight. ³⁶Incline my heart unto thy testimonies, and not to covetousness.

³⁷Turn away mine eyes from beholding vanity; *and* quicken thou me in thy way.

³⁸Stablish thy word unto thy servant, who *is devoted* to thy fear.

³⁹Turn away my reproach which I fear: for thy judgments *are* good.

⁴⁰Behold, I have longed after thy precepts: quicken me in thy righteousness.

⁴¹VAU. Let thy mercies come also unto me, O LORD, *even* thy salvation, according to thy word. ⁴²So shall I have wherewith to answer him that reproacheth me: for I trust in thy word.

⁴³And take not the word of truth utterly out of my mouth; for I have hoped in thy judgments. ⁴⁴So shall I keep thy law continually for ever and ever.

⁴⁵And I will walk at liberty^e: for I seek thy precepts. ⁴⁶I will speak of thy testimonies also before kings, and will not be ashamed. ⁴⁷And I will delight myself in thy commandments, which I have loved. ⁴⁸My hands also will I lift up unto thy commandments, which I have loved; and I will meditate in thy statutes.

⁴⁹ZAIN. Remember the word unto thy servant, upon which thou hast caused me to hope.

⁵⁰This *is* my comfort in my affliction: for thy word hath quickened me.

⁵¹The proud have had me greatly in derision: *yet* have I not declined from thy law.

⁵²I remembered thy judgments of old, O LORD; and have comforted myself.

⁵³Horror hath taken hold upon me because of the wicked that forsake thy law.

⁵⁴Thy statutes have been my songs in the house of my pilgrimage.

⁵⁵I have remembered thy name, O LORD, in the night, and have kept thy law. ⁵⁶This I had, because I kept thy precepts.

⁵⁷CHETH. *Thou art* my portion, O LORD: I have said that I would keep thy words.

⁵⁸I intreated thy favour^f with *my*

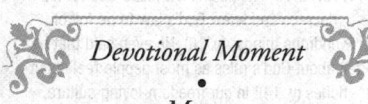

Devotional Moment

Money

119:36 Many people are obsessed with money. They look to cash—not Christ—for security, self-worth, and satisfaction. Such an approach is unwise for at least two reasons: (1) Riches are able to solve only our economic problems; and (2) when we are consumed with thoughts of material gain we become prime candidates for compromise. Like the psalm writer, pray that you will be more concerned with obeying God than with making money.

---

^e at liberty: Heb. at large
^f favour: Heb. face

whole heart: be merciful unto me according to thy word.

⁵⁹I thought on my ways, and turned my feet unto thy testimonies. ⁶⁰I made haste, and delayed not to keep thy commandments.

⁶¹The bandsᵍ of the wicked have robbed me: *but* I have not forgotten thy law.

⁶²At midnight I will rise to give thanks unto thee because of thy righteous judgments.

⁶³I *am* a companion of all *them* that fear thee, and of them that keep thy precepts.

⁶⁴The earth, O LORD, is full of thy mercy: teach me thy statutes.

⁶⁵TETH. Thou hast dealt well with thy servant, O LORD, according unto thy word. ⁶⁶Teach me good judgment and knowledge: for I have believed thy commandments.

⁶⁷Before I was afflicted I went astray: but now have I kept thy word.

⁶⁸Thou *art* good, and doest good; teach me thy statutes.

⁶⁹The proud have forged a lie against me: *but* I will keep thy precepts with *my* whole heart. ⁷⁰Their heart is as fat as grease; *but* I delight in thy law.

⁷¹*It is* good for me that I have been afflicted; that I might learn thy statutes.

⁷²The law of thy mouth *is* better unto me than thousands of gold and silver.

⁷³JOD. Thy hands have made me and fashioned me: give me understanding, that I may learn thy commandments.

⁷⁴They that fear thee will be glad when they see me; because I have hoped in thy word.

⁷⁵I know, O LORD, that thy judgments *are* rightʰ, and *that* thou in faithfulness hast afflicted me.

⁷⁶Let, I pray thee, thy merciful kindness be for my comfort, according to thy word unto thy servant. ⁷⁷Let thy tender mercies come unto me, that I may live: for thy law *is* my delight.

⁷⁸Let the proud be ashamed; for they dealt perversely with me without a cause: *but* I will meditate in thy precepts. ⁷⁹Let those that fear thee turn unto me, and those that have known thy testimonies.

⁸⁰Let my heart be sound in thy statutes; that I be not ashamed.

⁸¹CAPH. My soul fainteth for thy salvation: *but* I hope in thy word. ⁸²Mine eyes fail for thy word, saying, When wilt thou comfort me?

⁸³For I am become like a bottle in the smoke; *yet* do I not forget thy statutes.

⁸⁴How many *are* the days of thy servant? when wilt thou execute judgment on them that persecute me?

⁸⁵The proud have digged pits for me, which *are* not after thy law. ⁸⁶All thy commandments *are* faithful ⁱ: they persecute me wrongfully; help thou me. ⁸⁷They had almost consumed me upon earth; but I forsook not thy precepts.

⁸⁸Quicken me after thy lovingkindness; so shall I keep the testimony of thy mouth.

⁸⁹LAMED. For ever, O LORD,

ᵍ bands: or, companies
ʰ right: Heb. righteousness
ⁱ faithful: Heb. faithfulness

thy word is settled in heaven. ⁹⁰Thy faithfulness *is* unto all generations: thou hast established the earth, and it abideth. ⁹¹They continue this day according to thine ordinances: for all *are* thy servants.

⁹²Unless thy law *had been* my delights, I should then have perished in mine affliction.

⁹³I will never forget thy precepts: for with them thou hast quickened me.

⁹⁴I *am* thine, save me; for I have sought thy precepts.

⁹⁵The wicked have waited for me to destroy me: *but* I will consider thy testimonies.

⁹⁶I have seen an end of all perfection: *but* thy commandment *is* exceeding broad.

⁹⁷MEM. O how love I thy law! it *is* my meditation all the day.

⁹⁸Thou through thy commandments hast made me wiser than mine enemies: for they *are* ever^j with me. ⁹⁹I have more understanding than all my teachers: for thy testimonies *are* my meditation. ¹⁰⁰I understand more than the ancients, because I keep thy precepts.

¹⁰¹I have refrained my feet from every evil way, that I might keep thy word.

¹⁰²I have not departed from thy judgments: for thou hast taught me.

¹⁰³How sweet are thy words unto my taste^k! *yea, sweeter* than honey to my mouth! ¹⁰⁴Through thy precepts I get understanding: therefore I hate every false way.

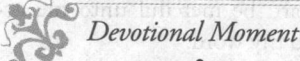

Devotional Moment

•

Bible Reading

119:105 Those who have had to grope their way through a dark house during a power failure can appreciate the imagery of this verse. Without a flashlight or candle, we face the prospect of bruised shins, stubbed toes, or worse. In a similar way, the Bible is a light that, when understood and used properly, can help us avoid stumbling as we make choices and relate to others. Each time you read the Bible, ask yourself, "How does this passage guide me? What does it keep me from stumbling over?"

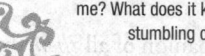

¹⁰⁵NUN. Thy word *is* a lamp^l unto my feet, and a light unto my path.

¹⁰⁶I have sworn, and I will perform *it,* that I will keep thy righteous judgments.

¹⁰⁷I am afflicted very much: quicken me, O LORD, according unto thy word.

¹⁰⁸Accept, I beseech thee, the freewill offerings of my mouth, O LORD, and teach me thy judgments.

¹⁰⁹My soul *is* continually in my hand: yet do I not forget thy law. ¹¹⁰The wicked have laid a snare for me: yet I erred not from thy precepts.

¹¹¹Thy testimonies have I taken as an heritage for ever: for they *are* the rejoicing of my heart. ¹¹²I have inclined mine heart to perform^m thy statutes alway, *even unto* the end.

¹¹³SAMECH. I hate *vain* thoughts: but thy law do I love.

¹¹⁴Thou *art* my hiding place and my shield: I hope in thy word.

---

^j they . . . : Heb. it is ever with me
^k taste: Heb. palate
^l lamp: or, candle
^m to perform: Heb. to do

¹¹⁵Depart from me, ye evildoers: for I will keep the commandments of my God.

¹¹⁶Uphold me according unto thy word, that I may live: and let me not be ashamed of my hope. ¹¹⁷Hold thou me up, and I shall be safe: and I will have respect unto thy statutes continually.

¹¹⁸Thou hast trodden down all them that err from thy statutes: for their deceit *is* falsehood. ¹¹⁹Thou puttest away all the wicked of the earth *like* dross: therefore I love thy testimonies. ¹²⁰My flesh trembleth for fear of thee; and I am afraid of thy judgments.

¹²¹AIN. I have done judgment and justice: leave me not to mine oppressors. ¹²²Be surety for thy servant for good: let not the proud oppress me.

¹²³Mine eyes fail for thy salvation, and for the word of thy righteousness.

¹²⁴Deal with thy servant according unto thy mercy, and teach me thy statutes. ¹²⁵I *am* thy servant; give me understanding, that I may know thy testimonies.

¹²⁶*It is* time for *thee*, LORD, to work: *for* they have made void thy law.

¹²⁷Therefore I love thy commandments above gold; yea, above fine gold. ¹²⁸Therefore I esteem all *thy* precepts *concerning* all *things to be* right; *and* I hate every false way.

¹²⁹PE. Thy testimonies *are* wonderful: therefore doth my soul keep them.

¹³⁰The entrance of thy words giveth light; it giveth understanding unto the simple.

¹³¹I opened my mouth, and panted: for I longed for thy commandments.

¹³²Look thou upon me, and be merciful unto me, as thou usest to do unto those that love thy name.

¹³³Order my steps in thy word: and let not any iniquity have dominion over me.

¹³⁴Deliver me from the oppression of man: so will I keep thy precepts.

¹³⁵Make thy face to shine upon thy servant; and teach me thy statutes.

¹³⁶Rivers of waters run down mine eyes, because they keep not thy law.

¹³⁷TZADDI. Righteous *art* thou, O LORD, and upright *are* thy judgments. ¹³⁸Thy testimonies *that* thou hast commanded *are* righteous[n] and very faithful.

¹³⁹My zeal hath consumed[o] me, because mine enemies have forgotten thy words.

¹⁴⁰Thy word *is* very pure[p]: therefore thy servant loveth it.

¹⁴¹I *am* small and despised: *yet* do not I forget thy precepts.

¹⁴²Thy righteousness *is* an everlasting righteousness, and thy law *is* the truth.

¹⁴³Trouble and anguish have taken hold on me: *yet* thy commandments *are* my delights. ¹⁴⁴The righteousness of thy testimonies *is* everlasting: give me understanding, and I shall live.

¹⁴⁵KOPH. I cried with *my* whole heart; hear me, O LORD: I will keep thy statutes. ¹⁴⁶I cried unto thee; save me, and I shall keep thy testimonies.

¹⁴⁷I prevented the dawning of the

---

[n] righteous: Heb. righteousness

[o] consumed . . . : Heb. cut me off

[p] pure: Heb. tried, or, refined

morning, and cried: I hoped in thy word. [148]Mine eyes prevent the *night* watches, that I might meditate in thy word.

[149]Hear my voice according unto thy lovingkindness: O LORD, quicken me according to thy judgment.

[150]They draw nigh that follow after mischief: they are far from thy law. [151]Thou *art* near, O LORD; and all thy commandments *are* truth.

[152]Concerning thy testimonies, I have known of old that thou hast founded them for ever.

[153]RESH. Consider mine affliction, and deliver me: for I do not forget thy law. [154]Plead my cause, and deliver me: quicken me according to thy word.

[155]Salvation *is* far from the wicked: for they seek not thy statutes.

[156]Great[q] *are* thy tender mercies, O LORD: quicken me according to thy judgments.

[157]Many *are* my persecutors and mine enemies; *yet* do I not decline from thy testimonies.

[158]I beheld the transgressors, and was grieved; because they kept not thy word.

[159]Consider how I love thy precepts: quicken me, O LORD, according to thy lovingkindness.

[160]Thy word[r] *is* true *from* the beginning: and every one of thy righteous judgments *endureth* for ever.

[161]SCHIN. Princes have persecuted me without a cause: but my heart standeth in awe of thy word.

[162]I rejoice at thy word, as one that findeth great spoil.

[163]I hate and abhor lying: *but* thy law do I love.

[164]Seven times a day do I praise thee because of thy righteous judgments.

[165]Great peace have they which love thy law: and nothing shall offend them.

[166]LORD, I have hoped for thy salvation, and done thy commandments.

[167]My soul hath kept thy testimonies; and I love them exceedingly. [168]I have kept thy precepts and thy testimonies: for all my ways *are* before thee.

[169]TAU. Let my cry come near before thee, O LORD: give me understanding according to thy word. [170]Let my supplication come before thee: deliver me according to thy word.

[171]My lips shall utter praise, when thou hast taught me thy statutes.

[172]My tongue shall speak of thy word: for all thy commandments *are* righteousness.

[173]Let thine hand help me; for I have chosen thy precepts. [174]I have longed for thy salvation, O LORD; and thy law *is* my delight.

[175]Let my soul live, and it shall praise thee; and let thy judgments help me.

[176]I have gone astray like a lost sheep; seek thy servant; for I do not forget thy commandments.

120

A Song of degrees.

[1]In my distress I cried unto the LORD, and he heard me. [2]Deliver my soul, O LORD, from lying lips, *and* from a deceitful tongue. [3]What shall be given[a] unto thee? or what shall be done

---

[q] Great: or, Many

[r] Thy word . . . : Heb. The beginning of thy word is true

[a] What shall be given . . . : or, What shall the deceitful tongue give unto thee? or, what shall is profit thee?

unto thee, thou false tongue? ⁴Sharp⁵ arrows of the mighty, with coals of juniper.

⁵Woe is me, that I sojourn in Mesech, *that* I dwell in the tents of Kedar! ⁶My soul hath long dwelt with him that hateth peace. ⁷I *am for* peace: but when I speak, they *are* for war.

121

A Song of degrees.

¹I will lift up mine eyes unto the hills, from whence cometh my help. ²My help *cometh* from the LORD, which made heaven and earth. ³He will not suffer thy foot to be moved: he that keepeth thee will not slumber. ⁴Behold, he that keepeth Israel shall neither slumber nor sleep. ⁵The LORD *is* thy keeper: the LORD *is* thy shade upon thy right hand. ⁶The sun shall not smite thee by day, nor the moon by night. ⁷The LORD shall preserve thee from all evil: he shall preserve thy soul. ⁸The LORD shall preserve thy going

---

Devotional Moment

Security

121:1-8 This psalm reminds of God's constant care and concern. It assures us that he is with us in every situation. Today many people are afraid, as evidenced by the huge number of law-abiding citizens who purchase handguns, carry mace, install burglar alarms, and sign up for self-defense classes. Amidst all these protective measures, the child of God can rely on an even greater security system—our all-powerful Maker who never sleeps. Do what you can to protect your family; then commit them to God, knowing that he has them in the palm of his hand.

---

out and thy coming in from this time forth, and even for evermore.

122

A Song of degrees of David.

¹I was glad when they said unto me, Let us go into the house of the LORD. ²Our feet shall stand within thy gates, O Jerusalem. ³Jerusalem is builded as a city that is compact together: ⁴Whither the tribes go up, the tribes of the LORD, unto the testimony of Israel, to give thanks unto the name of the LORD. ⁵For there are set thrones of judgment, the thrones of the house of David.

⁶Pray for the peace of Jerusalem: they shall prosper that love thee. ⁷Peace be within thy walls, *and* prosperity within thy palaces. ⁸For my brethren and companions' sakes, I will now say, Peace *be* within thee. ⁹Because of the house of the LORD our God I will seek thy good.

123

A Song of degrees.

¹Unto thee lift I up mine eyes, O thou that dwellest in the heavens. ²Behold, as the eyes of servants *look* unto the hand of their masters, *and* as the eyes of a maiden unto the hand of her mistress; so our eyes *wait* upon the LORD our God, until that he have mercy upon us. ³Have mercy upon us, O LORD, have mercy upon us: for we are exceedingly filled with contempt. ⁴Our soul is exceedingly filled with the scorning of those that are at ease, *and* with the contempt of the proud.

124

A Song of degrees of David.

¹If *it had not been* the LORD who

ᵇ Sharp . . . : or, It is as the sharp arrows of the mighty man, with coals of juniper

Children in the Blended Family

by Jim Smoke

Not every family consists of a mom, a dad, and the children that were born to them. When broken families find each other and decide to blend, it's the moms and dads who usually make the decision. The children come along as "part of the package."

Many adults enter into this experience with false expectations. Some of the more unrealistic ones are:

1. Blending two families is easy and just needs sound organization.

2. We will all be one big, happy, contented group.

3. The kids will all love one another at first sight.

4. The kids will understand new parents, new rules, and new living quarters immediately.

5. The kids will simply adore (and perhaps even idolize) their new stepparent.

6. With a little discipline, the kids will all act, live, and think like the children in "The Brady Bunch" or *The Sound of Music*—cheerful, well behaved, and always playing together happily.

If you have been living in a blended family for any length of time, you already know that the above is pure fiction! What really happens when families are blended is this:

1. You spend a great deal of time patching broken family relationships.

2. You come to dread that part of the holidays when the children pass each other in airports.

3. On some days you wonder which children belong to which parent on what planet.

4. You quickly tire of being the "bad guy" stepparent and hearing children say, "My *real* father/mother said I could do . . ."

5. You wish for an easy way out when it comes to dispensing discipline.

6. On some days, you are loved and hated in the very same moment.

Anyone from a blended family could probably add another hundred rude awakenings to the list.

Blending two families successfully depends on two attitudes: realism-inspired patience and love for God. Realism says, "This is how things are, and this is the structure I have to work and grow in. I accept it and will learn how to do it, with God's help." Love for God says, "All these children are gifts of God. God has brought us together. Above all else, God wants us to love each other."

Children often enter this new family structure feeling resentful because what they really want is for their mother and father to get back together and restore their original home. The remarriage tells them that it will not happen, and this may bring all their anger and frustration to the surface in the new family.

Early in the second marriage, children in a blended family often alternately hate and love each other. The remarriage is an unwanted change foisted onto them by someone else. Kids may decide in the first week that they are outsiders while the other children are insiders. As a parent, you may have to work at bringing them inside the new family structure. Allow everyone time. Feelings don't change overnight.

Children need to feel the same sense of security and belonging that adults do. But if the new family blending is not good from their perspective, they may hope it will end. And if it *does* seem good to them, they may fear that it will end.

There are no simple answers or magic formulas to helping children adjust to a blended family. In a first marriage, the parents are both on the scene before the children arrive. In a second marriage with children attached, the children are there before the stepparent arrives. You don't have years for everyone to bond slowly and naturally. It is a spot-welding job at best, and you sincerely hope the weld holds.

In a second marriage, almost everything that preexisted goes into the blender to create a new union. Past, present, and future all become quickly intermixed. We must strive in that process to create a new beginning for both parents and children alike.

But we must remember that the Lord is part of the process. If any of the blending is to work, it will come from God-given grace, understanding, forgiveness, and love. Children are a gift from God. He knows them and what they need. He knows what makes life work.

DIGGING DEEPER

1. What can single parents do to ensure that children are not overlooked in a decision to remarry? See Romans 12:9-10; Philippians 2:3-4.

2. What are some keys to harmony in a blended family? See Psalm 127.

3. How realistic is it to expect members of a blended family to *like* one another? See Ephesians 4:2; Colossians 3:13.

---

was on our side, now may Israel say; ²If *it had not been* the LORD who was on our side, when men rose up against us: ³Then they had swallowed us up quick, when their wrath was kindled against us: ⁴Then the waters had overwhelmed us, the stream had gone over our soul: ⁵Then the proud waters had gone over our soul.

⁶Blessed *be* the LORD, who hath not given us *as* a prey to their teeth. ⁷Our soul is escaped as a bird out of the snare of the fowlers: the snare is broken, and we are escaped. ⁸Our help *is* in the name of the LORD, who made heaven and earth.

125

A Song of degrees.

¹They that trust in the LORD *shall be* as mount Zion, *which* cannot be removed, *but* abideth for ever. ²As the mountains *are* round about Jerusalem, so the LORD *is* round about his people

from henceforth even for ever. ³For the rod of the wickedª shall not rest upon the lot of the righteous; lest the righteous put forth their hands unto iniquity.

⁴Do good, O LORD, unto *those that be* good, and *to them that are* upright in their hearts. ⁵As for such as turn aside unto their crooked ways, the LORD shall lead them forth with the workers of iniquity: *but* peace *shall be* upon Israel.

126

A Song of degrees.

¹When the LORD turned again the captivity of Zion, we were like them that dream. ²Then was our mouth filled with laughter, and our tongue with singing: then said they among the heathen, The LORD hath done great things for them. ³The LORD hath done great things for us; *whereof* we are glad.

⁴Turn again our captivity, O LORD,

ª the wicked: Heb. wickedness

as the streams in the south. ⁵They that sow in tears shall reap in joyᵃ. ⁶He that goeth forth and weepeth, bearing preciousᵇ seed, shall doubtless come again with rejoicing, bringing his sheaves *with him.*

127

A Song of degrees for Solomon.

¹Except the LORD build the house, they labour in vain that build it: except the LORD keep the city, the watchman waketh *but* in vain. ²*It is* vain for you to rise up early, to sit up late, to eat the bread of sorrows: *for* so he giveth his beloved sleep. ³Lo, children *are* an heritage of the LORD: *and* the fruit of the womb *is his* reward. ⁴As arrows *are* in the hand of a mighty man; so *are* children of the youth. ⁵Happy *is* the man that hath his quiver full of them: they shall not be ashamed, but they shall speak with the enemies in the gate.

128

A Song of degrees.

¹Blessed *is* every one that feareth

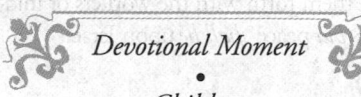

Devotional Moment
•
Children

127:3-5 From time to time most parents complain about the financial, physical, and emotional strains of parenthood. They use words like *responsibility, sacrifice,* and *burden.* But notice the terms used by the inspired psalmist: *gift, reward,* and *help.* He depicted children as cherished gifts. In countless ways God uses our children to mold us into the people he wants us to be. Have you thanked God for your kids today?

the LORD; that walketh in his ways. ²For thou shalt eat the labour of thine hands: happy *shalt* thou *be,* and *it shall be* well with thee. ³Thy wife *shall be* as a fruitful vine by the sides of thine house: thy children like olive plants round about thy table. ⁴Behold, that thus shall the man be blessed that feareth the LORD. ⁵The LORD shall bless thee out of Zion: and thou shalt see the good of Jerusalem all the days of thy life. ⁶Yea, thou shalt see thy children's children, *and* peace upon Israel.

129

A Song of degrees.

¹Many a time have they afflicted me from my youth, may Israel now say: ²Many a time have they afflicted me from my youth: yet they have not prevailed against me. ³The plowers plowed upon my back: they made long their furrows. ⁴The LORD *is* righteous: he hath cut asunder the cords of the wicked.

⁵Let them all be confounded and turned back that hate Zion. ⁶Let them be as the grass *upon* the housetops, which withereth afore it groweth up: ⁷Wherewith the mower filleth not his hand; nor he that bindeth sheaves his bosom. ⁸Neither do they which go by say, The blessing of the LORD *be* upon you: we bless you in the name of the LORD.

130

A Song of degrees.

¹Out of the depths have I cried unto thee, O LORD. ²Lord, hear my voice: let thine ears be attentive to the voice

---

ᵃ joy: or, singing
ᵇ precious . . . : or, seed basket

of my supplications. ³If thou, LORD, shouldest mark iniquities, O Lord, who shall stand? ⁴But *there is* forgiveness with thee, that thou mayest be feared.

⁵I wait for the LORD, my soul doth wait, and in his word do I hope. ⁶My soul *waiteth* for the Lord more than they that watch for the morning: *I say, more than* they that watch[a] for the morning. ⁷Let Israel hope in the LORD: for with the LORD *there is* mercy, and with him *is* plenteous redemption. ⁸And he shall redeem Israel from all his iniquities.

131

A Song of degrees of David.

¹LORD, my heart is not haughty, nor mine eyes lofty: neither do I exercise[a] myself in great matters, or in things too high for me. ²Surely I have behaved and quieted myself[b], as a child

---

Devotional Moment

•

Humility

131:1-2 Parents don't know it all. Children don't know it all. Grandparents don't know it all. But God does. He wants us to be quiet before him, humbly waiting to hear his wisdom, to learn his guidelines, to understand his desires for our life. We should not be afraid to admit that we don't know it all and that we can learn from God's instructions in the Bible. We learn and grow when we admit our limitations and look to God and one another for direction.

---

that is weaned of his mother: my soul *is* even as a weaned child. ³Let Israel hope in the LORD from henceforth and for ever.

132

A Song of degrees.

¹LORD, remember David, *and* all his afflictions: ²How he sware unto the LORD, *and* vowed unto the mighty *God* of Jacob; ³Surely I will not come into the tabernacle of my house, nor go up into my bed; ⁴I will not give sleep to mine eyes, *or* slumber to mine eyelids, ⁵Until I find out a place for the LORD, an habitation[a] for the mighty *God* of Jacob. ⁶Lo, we heard of it at Ephratah: we found it in the fields of the wood. ⁷We will go into his tabernacles: we will worship at his footstool. ⁸Arise, O LORD, into thy rest; thou, and the ark of thy strength. ⁹Let thy priests be clothed with righteousness; and let thy saints shout for joy. ¹⁰For thy servant David's sake turn not away the face of thine anointed.

¹¹The LORD hath sworn *in* truth unto David; he will not turn from it; Of the fruit of thy body[b] will I set upon thy throne. ¹²If thy children will keep my covenant and my testimony that I shall teach them, their children shall also sit upon thy throne for evermore. ¹³For the LORD hath chosen Zion; he hath desired *it* for his habitation. ¹⁴This *is* my rest for ever: here will I dwell; for I have desired it. ¹⁵I will abundantly[c]

---

[a] I say . . . : or, which watch unto
[a] exercise . . . : Heb. walk
[b] myself: Heb. my soul
[a] an habitation: Heb. habitations
[b] body: Heb. belly
[c] abundantly: or, surely

bless her provision: I will satisfy her poor with bread. [16]I will also clothe her priests with salvation: and her saints shall shout aloud for joy. [17]There will I make the horn of David to bud: I have ordained a lamp[d] for mine anointed. [18]His enemies will I clothe with shame: but upon himself shall his crown flourish.

133

A Song of degrees of David.

[1]Behold, how good and how pleasant it is for brethren to dwell together[a] in unity! [2]It is like the precious ointment upon the head, that ran down upon the beard, even Aaron's beard: that went down to the skirts of his garments; [3]As the dew of Hermon, and as the dew that descended upon the mountains of Zion: for there the LORD commanded the blessing, even life for evermore.

134

A Song of degrees.

[1]Behold, bless ye the LORD, all ye servants of the LORD, which by night stand in the house of the LORD. [2]Lift up your hands in the sanctuary[a], and bless the LORD. [3]The LORD that made heaven and earth bless thee out of Zion.

135

[1]Praise ye the LORD. Praise ye the name of the LORD; praise him, O ye servants of the LORD. [2]Ye that stand in the house of the LORD, in the courts of the house of our God, [3]Praise the LORD; for the LORD is good: sing praises unto his name; for it is pleasant. [4]For the LORD hath chosen Jacob unto himself, and Israel for his peculiar treasure.

[5]For I know that the LORD is great, and that our Lord is above all gods. [6]Whatsoever the LORD pleased, that did he in heaven, and in earth, in the seas, and all deep places. [7]He causeth the vapours to ascend from the ends of the earth; he maketh lightnings for the rain; he bringeth the wind out of his treasuries. [8]Who smote the firstborn of Egypt, both of man and beast. [9]Who sent tokens and wonders into the midst of thee, O Egypt, upon Pharaoh, and upon all his servants. [10]Who smote great nations, and slew mighty kings; [11]Sihon king of the Amorites, and Og king of Bashan, and all the kingdoms of Canaan: [12]And gave their land for an heritage, an heritage unto Israel his people. [13]Thy name, O LORD, endureth for ever; and thy memorial, O LORD, throughout all generations. [14]For the LORD will judge his people, and he will repent himself concerning his servants.

[15]The idols of the heathen are silver and gold, the work of men's hands. [16]They have mouths, but they speak not; eyes have they, but they see not; [17]They have ears, but they hear not; neither is there any breath in their mouths. [18]They that make them are like unto them: so is every one that trusteth in them. [19]Bless the LORD, O house of Is-

---

[d] lamp: or, candle
[a] together . . . : Heb. even together
[a] the sanctuary: or, holiness

Family Traditions

Celebrate His Plan
PSALM 139

O Lord, thou hast searched me, and known me. . . . Thine eyes did see my substance, yet being unperfect; and in thy book all my members were written . . . when as yet there was none of them" (Ps. 139:1, 16). Out of these simple truths grows respect for human life—a precious tradition to teach to children.

There are many ways to weave respect for life into your family traditions.

You can start by affirming the sanctity of life before birth. Show your little ones what they looked like when they were still in the womb. Tell them how much you loved them from the beginning.

You can make each birthday a celebration of life. Make ornaments or souvenirs of your child's mementos, baby pictures, and school photos. Each year attach the birthday child's wish or prayer to a special card; keep it in a separate box and bring it out annually to recall the answers.

Affirm life outside your home as well. You can contribute baby clothes and equipment to a crisis pregnancy center. Or you can volunteer to counsel women who have chosen the path of motherhood rather than abortion. You can make quilts or soft animal dolls for a children's home or hospital. You can get to know the kids who live in your neighborhood. Many of them may be hurting. Affirm them, give them some attention, talk to them.

You can take your children to different neighborhoods to see how people live in your city or town. Use the experience to tell them that all people were created in God's image, are known by him, and are in need of Christ's forgiveness. Challenge your kids to bring his love to others who may come from different backgrounds.

You can volunteer as a family in a soup kitchen or a community meal project for the homeless. You can help families who are raising foster children or participate in local programs that provide gifts for children of prisoners and hospitalized parents. You can turn Thanksgiving and Christmas holidays into opportunities to reach out.

You can invite foreign students into your home for a meal—if not for a stay—or invite them to make an ethnic meal from their home country in your kitchen for your family. You can teach your kids to ask questions about the students' homeland and customs. Find out how Christians there worship our God.

Psalm 139 spells out God's intimate involvement with individuals from the point of conception through each day of their earthly lives to everlasting life. We need to share God's perspective and develop a love and respect for humanity. And we need to teach our children to do the same.

rael: bless the LORD, O house of Aaron: ²⁰Bless the LORD, O house of Levi: ye that fear the LORD, bless the LORD. ²¹Blessed be the LORD out of Zion, which dwelleth at Jerusalem. Praise ye the LORD.

136

¹O give thanks unto the LORD; for *he is* good: for his mercy *endureth* for ever. ²O give thanks unto the God of gods: for his mercy *endureth* for ever. ³O give thanks to the Lord of lords: for his mercy *endureth* for ever. ⁴To him who alone doeth great wonders: for his mercy *endureth* for ever. ⁵To him that by wisdom made the heavens: for his mercy *endureth* for ever. ⁶To him that stretched out the earth above the waters: for his mercy *endureth* for ever. ⁷To him that made great lights: for his mercy *endureth* for ever: ⁸The sun to ruleª by day: for his mercy *endureth* for ever: ⁹The moon and stars to rule by night: for his mercy *endureth* for ever.

¹⁰To him that smote Egypt in their

firstborn: for his mercy *endureth* for ever: ¹¹And brought out Israel from among them: for his mercy *endureth* for ever: ¹²With a strong hand, and with a stretched out arm: for his mercy *endureth* for ever. ¹³To him which divided the Red sea into parts: for his mercy *endureth* for ever: ¹⁴And made Israel to pass through the midst of it: for his mercy *endureth* for ever: ¹⁵But overthrewᵇ Pharaoh and his host in the Red sea: for his mercy *endureth* for ever. ¹⁶To him which led his people through the wilderness: for his mercy *endureth* for ever. ¹⁷To him which smote great kings: for his mercy *endureth* for ever: ¹⁸And slew famous kings: for his mercy *endureth* for ever: ¹⁹Sihon king of the Amorites: for his mercy *endureth* for ever: ²⁰And Og the king of Bashan: for his mercy *endureth* for ever: ²¹And gave their land for an heritage: for his mercy *endureth* for ever: ²²*Even* an heritage unto Israel his servant: for his mercy *endureth* for ever.

²³Who remembered us in our low estate: for his mercy *endureth* for ever: ²⁴And hath redeemed us from our enemies: for his mercy *endureth* for ever. ²⁵Who giveth food to all flesh: for his mercy *endureth* for ever. ²⁶O give thanks unto the God of heaven: for his mercy *endureth* for ever.

137

¹By the rivers of Babylon, there we sat down, yea, we wept, when we remembered Zion. ²We hanged our harps upon the willows in the midst thereof. ³For there they that carried us away cap-

---

Devotional Moment

Thankfulness

136:1-26 God has been good to us. We have a long list of reasons to praise God if we only will take the time to recall his power and involvement. If you were to write a psalm like this, what would you praise him for? Family and friends, abilities he has given, and cherished memories are all gifts from God. Take time to answer these questions: For what can we praise God? In what ways has he shown his power, love, and protection to us?

ª to rule . . . : Heb. for the rulings by day
ᵇ overthrew: Heb. shaked off

tive required of us a song[a]; and they that wasted us *required of us* mirth, *saying,* Sing us *one* of the songs of Zion. ⁴How shall we sing the LORD'S song in a strange[b] land? ⁵If I forget thee, O Jerusalem, let my right hand forget *her cunning.* ⁶If I do not remember thee, let my tongue cleave to the roof of my mouth; if I prefer not Jerusalem above my chief[c] joy.

⁷Remember, O LORD, the children of Edom in the day of Jerusalem; who said, Rase *it,* rase *it, even* to the foundation thereof. ⁸O daughter of Babylon, who art to be destroyed[d]; happy *shall he be,* that rewardeth thee as thou hast served us. ⁹Happy *shall he be,* that taketh and dasheth thy little ones against the stones[e].

138

A Psalm of David.

¹I will praise thee with my whole heart: before the gods will I sing praise unto thee. ²I will worship toward thy holy temple, and praise thy name for thy lovingkindness and for thy truth: for thou hast magnified thy word above all thy name. ³In the day when I cried thou answeredst me, *and* strengthenedst me *with* strength in my soul. ⁴All the kings of the earth shall praise thee, O LORD, when they hear the words of thy mouth. ⁵Yea, they shall sing in the ways of the LORD: for great *is* the glory of the LORD.

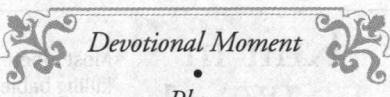

Devotional Moment
•
Plans

138:7-8 Many of us find our plans for the future derailed by unemployment, family illness, financial trouble, or relational conflict. When life-shattering events happen, we are tempted to doubt whether God knows what he's doing. This psalm reminds us that even though we are surrounded by troubles, God can bring us safely through them. He has not abandoned us. We can choose to trust that he will work out his plans for our life despite—or sometimes through—our difficulties.

⁶Though the LORD *be* high, yet hath he respect unto the lowly: but the proud he knoweth afar off. ⁷Though I walk in the midst of trouble, thou wilt revive me: thou shalt stretch forth thine hand against the wrath of mine enemies, and thy right hand shall save me. ⁸The LORD will perfect *that which* concerneth me: thy mercy, O LORD, *endureth* for ever: forsake not the works of thine own hands.

139

To the chief Musician, A Psalm of David.

¹O LORD, thou hast searched me, and known *me.* ²Thou knowest my downsitting and mine uprising, thou understandest my thought afar off. ³Thou compassest[a] my path and my lying down, and art acquainted *with* all my ways. ⁴For

---

[a] a song: Heb. the words of a song
[b] strange . . . : Heb. land of a stranger?
[c] my chief . . . : Heb. the head of my joy
[d] destroyed: Heb. wasted
[e] the stones: Heb. the rock
[a] compassest: or, winnowest

Knit in the Womb

by Joe S. McIlhaney, M.D.

Most doctors who perform abortions realize that they are killing babies. They have enough scientific orientation to know that the signs of the humanity of the fetus cannot be ignored.

As conclusive as this scientific data is, I am even more impressed by the evidence found in the Bible. Psalm 139, for example, leaves no doubt that life begins at the moment of conception.

Some would argue that a woman has total rights to her own body; that argument is not correct. Our rights end where "another person's nose begins," and a baby inside a mother's uterus is another person. It has a totally different chromosomal makeup from its mother, and there's a 50 percent chance that the baby is of a different sex than the mother.

When a woman's right to her body is discussed, the euphemistic term *choice* is often used. I agree that reproductive choice is important, but I believe the choice should be made earlier—before the pregnancy begins. A woman can choose abstinence until marriage, or she can use contraceptive techniques very carefully and usually not get pregnant.

I believe the only reason we tolerate abortions at all is that they take place "out of sight," in the darkness of a woman's uterus. If the babies were taken out of the uterus, for instance, and their little heads crushed in public, our society would immediately put a stop to such killing.

Physicians who care for pregnant mothers know they are caring for two patients—the mother and her unborn child. The only time people rationalize that the unborn child is not a person is when they want to kill it.

The advice I offer to women considering abortion is this:

Don't take the easy way out. The easiest way is not necessarily the best way. Though an abortion may seem to offer the easiest way out of a difficult situation, it may be the worst choice.

A patient came to me in early pregnancy, planning to have an abortion. After we talked for a while, she decided not to have the abortion and later wrote me the following letter:

"Dear Dr. McIlhaney: If a woman comes to you and wants to abort, or her husband wants her to, as mine did . . . please show her this picture and tell her I almost made the biggest mistake of my life and had it done to this beautiful boy. Maybe it might save a life . . . it is a life . . . anything that can make you that sick (when pregnant) has got to be a life.

"Thank you for bringing my two precious children into the world and into my life."

Be realistic. A woman should not be naive when she considers an abortion. Abortionists often picture it as a simple, straightforward procedure. But most women who have had abortions report that it was a traumatic experience. Many complain of being handled "like cattle" in abortion clinics and compare an abortion to rape—something that leaves a woman feeling violated.

Be prepared for guilt. For many women, guilt following abortion is inescapable. The procedure is one that a woman will never forget, and one that she may regret for the rest of her life.

Expect possible infertility. Physicians who treat women with infertility problems often find that these patients have had abortions. Their difficulties conceiving may be related.

Don't base an abortion on finances. Don't let your worries about money cause you to make a bad situation worse. Almost no woman feels she can really afford adding a baby to her family. However, just like millions of other parents, you will, somehow, be able to provide for your child. The baby primarily needs your love, not material things. Besides, the baby would prefer life to death.

Whether for yourself or a friend, this advice is critical whenever someone is considering ending a life that God so "wonderfully made" (Ps. 139:14). At such a moment, there's no better prayer than the one recorded here: "Search me, O God, and know my heart; try me, and know my thoughts; and see if there be any wicked way in me, and lead me in the way everlasting" (139:23-24).

DIGGING DEEPER

1. What else does the Bible say about life at conception? See Genesis 25:22; Psalm 51:5; Jeremiah 1:5; Luke 1:41.

2. Why should we avoid aborting when so many people say it is not wrong? See Romans 12:2.

3. What responsibility do we have toward other people, even when their lives inconvenience ours? See Philippians 2:3-4.

4. Unborn children are the most defenseless people in the world. What is a Christian's responsibility toward those who are unprotected and vulnerable? See James 1:27.

5. How can we help women who are pregnant but don't want to be? See James 2:14-17.

---

there is not a word in my tongue, *but,* lo, O LORD, thou knowest it altogether. ⁵Thou hast beset me behind and before, and laid thine hand upon me. ⁶*Such* knowledge *is* too wonderful for me; it is high, I cannot *attain* unto it.

⁷Whither shall I go from thy spirit? or whither shall I flee from thy presence? ⁸If I ascend up into heaven, thou *art* there: if I make my bed in hell, behold, thou *art there.* ⁹*If* I take the wings of the morning, *and* dwell in the uttermost parts of the sea; ¹⁰Even there shall thy hand lead me, and thy right hand shall hold me. ¹¹If I say, Surely the darkness shall cover me; even the night shall be light about me. ¹²Yea, the darkness hid-

eth[b] not from thee; but the night shineth as the day: the darkness and the light *are* both alike *to thee.* ¹³For thou hast possessed my reins: thou hast covered me in my mother's womb. ¹⁴I will praise thee; for I am fearfully *and* wonderfully made: marvellous *are* thy works; and *that* my soul knoweth right well. ¹⁵My substance[c] was not hid from thee, when I was made in secret, *and* curiously wrought in the lowest parts of the earth. ¹⁶Thine eyes did see my substance, yet being unperfect; and in thy book all *my members* were written[d], *which* in continuance were fashioned, when *as yet there was* none of them.

¹⁷How precious also are thy thoughts

---

[b] hideth . . . : Heb. darkeneth not
[c] substance: or, strength, or, body
[d] all . . . : Heb. all of them

959

unto me, O God! how great is the sum of them! [18]*If* I should count them, they are more in number than the sand: when I awake, I am still with thee. [19]Surely thou wilt slay the wicked, O God: depart from me therefore, ye bloody men. [20]For they speak against thee wickedly, *and* thine enemies take *thy name* in vain. [21]Do not I hate them, O LORD, that hate thee? and am not I grieved with those that rise up against thee? [22]I hate them with perfect hatred: I count them mine enemies. [23]Search me, O God, and know my heart: try me, and know my thoughts: [24]And see if *there be any* wicked[c] way in me, and lead me in the way everlasting.

140

To the chief Musician, A Psalm of David.

[1]Deliver me, O LORD, from the evil man: preserve me from the violent[a] man; [2]Which imagine mischiefs in *their* heart; continually are they gathered together *for* war. [3]They have sharpened their tongues like a serpent; adders' poison *is* under their lips. Selah. [4]Keep me, O LORD, from the hands of the wicked; preserve me from the violent man; who have purposed to overthrow my goings. [5]The proud have hid a snare for me, and cords; they have spread a net by the wayside; they have set gins for me. Selah. [6]I said unto the LORD, Thou *art* my God: hear the voice of my supplications, O LORD. [7]O GOD the Lord, the strength of my salvation, thou hast covered my head in the day of battle.

[8]Grant not, O LORD, the desires of the wicked: further not his wicked

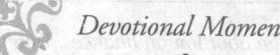

 Devotional Moment

•

The Poor

140:12 In his compassion and mercy, God protects the helpless and hopeless. As his children, we, too, should work to help the poor find food, clothing, shelter, and a means of earning money to support their families. Learn how churches in your area are working with refugees of war-torn countries. Find ways to get involved in projects that supply housing to the homeless, safety for the abused, and hope for the hopeless. Work to reflect God's compassion and mercy.

device; *lest* they exalt themselves. Selah. [9]*As for* the head of those that compass me about, let the mischief of their own lips cover them. [10]Let burning coals fall upon them: let them be cast into the fire; into deep pits, that they rise not up again. [11]Let not an evil speaker be established in the earth: evil shall hunt the violent man to overthrow *him*. [12]I know that the LORD will maintain the cause of the afflicted, *and* the right of the poor. [13]Surely the righteous shall give thanks unto thy name: the upright shall dwell in thy presence.

141

A Psalm of David.

[1]LORD, I cry unto thee: make haste unto me; give ear unto my voice, when I cry unto thee. [2]Let my prayer be set forth before thee *as* incense; *and* the lifting up of my hands *as* the evening sacrifice. [3]Set a watch, O LORD, before my mouth; keep the door of my lips. [4]Incline not my heart to *any* evil thing, to practise wicked

---

[c] wicked . . . : Heb. way of pain, or, grief
[a] violent . . . : Heb. man of violences

works with men that work iniquity: and let me not eat of their dainties.

⁵Let the righteous smite me; *it shall be* a kindness*: and let him reprove me; *it shall be* an excellent oil, *which* shall not break my head: for yet my prayer also *shall be* in their calamities. ⁶When their judges are overthrown in stony places, they shall hear my words; for they are sweet. ⁷Our bones are scattered at the grave's mouth, as when one cutteth and cleaveth *wood* upon the earth. ⁸But mine eyes *are* unto thee, O GOD the Lord: in thee is my trust; leave*ᵇ* not my soul destitute. ⁹Keep me from the snares *which* they have laid for me, and the gins of the workers of iniquity. ¹⁰Let the wicked fall into their own nets, whilst that I withal escape*ᶜ*.

142

Maschil of David; A Prayer when he was in the cave.

¹I cried unto the LORD with my voice; with my voice unto the LORD did I make my supplication. ²I poured out my complaint before him; I shewed before him my trouble. ³When my spirit was overwhelmed within me, then thou knewest my path. In the way wherein I walked have they privily laid a snare for me.

⁴I looked*ᵃ* on *my* right hand, and beheld, but *there was* no man that would know me: refuge failed me; no man cared for my soul. ⁵I cried unto thee, O LORD: I said, Thou *art* my refuge *and* my portion in the land of the living. ⁶Attend unto my cry; for I am brought very low: deliver me from my persecutors; for they are stronger than I. ⁷Bring my soul out of prison, that I may praise thy name: the righteous shall compass me about; for thou shalt deal bountifully with me.

143

A Psalm of David.

¹Hear my prayer, O LORD, give ear to my supplications: in thy faithfulness answer me, *and* in thy righteousness. ²And enter not into judgment with thy servant: for in thy sight shall no man living be justified. ³For the enemy hath persecuted my soul; he hath smitten my life down to the ground; he hath made me to dwell in darkness, as those that have been long dead. ⁴Therefore is my spirit overwhelmed within me; my heart within me is desolate. ⁵I remember the days of old; I meditate on all thy works; I muse on the work of thy hands. ⁶I stretch forth my hands unto thee: my soul *thirsteth* after thee, as a thirsty land. Selah.

⁷Hear me speedily, O LORD: my spirit faileth: hide not thy face from me, lest I be like unto them that go down into the pit. ⁸Cause me to hear thy lovingkindness in the morning; for in thee do I trust: cause me to know the way wherein I should walk; for I lift up my soul unto thee. ⁹Deliver me, O LORD, from mine enemies: I flee unto thee to hide me. ¹⁰Teach me to do thy will; for thou *art* my God: thy spirit *is* good;

ᵃ me: it shall be a . . . : or, me kindly, and reprove me; let not their precious oil break, etc
ᵇ leave . . . : Heb. make not my soul bare
ᶜ escape: Heb. pass over
ᵃ I looked . . . : or, Look on the right hand, and see

lead me into the land of uprightness. [11]Quicken me, O LORD, for thy name's sake: for thy righteousness' sake bring my soul out of trouble. [12]And of thy mercy cut off mine enemies, and destroy all them that afflict my soul: for I *am* thy servant.

144

A Psalm of David.

[1]Blessed *be* the LORD my strength[a], which teacheth my hands to war, *and* my fingers to fight: [2]My goodness[b], and my fortress; my high tower, and my deliverer; my shield, and *he* in whom I trust; who subdueth my people under me. [3]LORD, what *is* man, that thou takest knowledge of him! *or* the son of man, that thou makest account of him! [4]Man is like to vanity: his days *are* as a shadow that passeth away. [5]Bow thy heavens, O LORD, and come down: touch the mountains, and they shall smoke. [6]Cast forth lightning, and scatter them: shoot out thine arrows, and destroy them. [7]Send thine hand from above; rid me, and deliver me out of great waters, from the hand of strange children; [8]Whose mouth speaketh vanity, and their right hand *is* a right hand of falsehood.

[9]I will sing a new song unto thee, O God: upon a psaltery *and* an instrument of ten strings will I sing praises unto thee. [10]*It is he* that giveth salvation[c] unto kings: who delivereth David his servant from the hurtful sword. [11]Rid me, and deliver me from the hand of strange children, whose mouth speaketh vanity, and their right hand *is* a right hand of falsehood: [12]That our sons *may be* as plants grown up in their youth; *that* our daughters *may be* as corner stones, polished[d] *after* the similitude of a palace: [13]*That* our garners *may be* full, affording all manner of store: *that* our sheep may bring forth thousands and ten thousands in our streets: [14]*That* our oxen *may be* strong to labour; *that there be* no breaking in, nor going out; that *there be* no complaining in our streets. [15]Happy *is that* people, that is in such a case: *yea*, happy *is that* people, whose God *is* the LORD.

145

David's *Psalm* of praise.

[1]I will extol thee, my God, O king; and I will bless thy name for ever and ever. [2]Every day will I bless thee; and I will praise thy name for ever and ever. [3]Great *is* the LORD, and greatly to be praised; and his greatness *is* unsearchable. [4]One generation shall praise thy works to another, and shall declare thy mighty acts. [5]I will speak of the glorious honour of thy majesty, and of thy wondrous works[a]. [6]And *men* shall speak of the might of thy terrible acts: and I will declare[b] thy greatness. [7]They shall abundantly utter the memory of thy great goodness, and shall sing of thy righteousness. [8]The LORD *is* gracious, and

---

[a] strength: Heb. rock
[b] My goodness: or, My mercy
[c] salvation: or, victory
[d] polished: Heb. cut
[a] works: Heb. things, or, words
[b] declare: Heb. declare it

Devotional Moment

•

Tell Your Children

145:4-7 People who love God pass their faith on to younger generations—parents to children, grandparents to grandchildren. When you gather with your family, and especially with your extended family, spend time reflecting on God's work in your life. Encourage each other with stories of God's greatness and miracles. Children will always remember their grandparents' stories of how God brought them through difficult circumstances or protected them from danger. Uncles and aunts will benefit from hearing children share how they see God's activity. You can even sing together, praising God for his love. As you celebrate God's goodness together, your family will grow in its ability to trust and glorify God.

Devotional Moment

•

Heavy Loads

145:14 Who are the overburdened people you know of? If they are your children, talk with them about their burdens, pray together, and discuss ways you might be able to help lighten their load. If they are people in your community or church, think of practical ways you can help—by listening, praying together, taking over a meal, helping with a household project, or referring them to a counselor. Others bent beneath heavy loads are famine or war victims. Perhaps you can support a Christian organization that has programs to help such people. As a family, with each making a contribution, be the hands of the Lord as he "raiseth up all those that be bowed down."

full of compassion; slow to anger, and of great^c mercy. ⁹The LORD *is* good to all: and his tender mercies *are* over all his works.

¹⁰All thy works shall praise thee, O LORD; and thy saints shall bless thee. ¹¹They shall speak of the glory of thy kingdom, and talk of thy power; ¹²To make known to the sons of men his mighty acts, and the glorious majesty of his kingdom. ¹³Thy kingdom *is* an everlasting kingdom^d, and thy dominion *endureth* throughout all generations. ¹⁴The LORD upholdeth all that fall, and raiseth up all *those that be* bowed down. ¹⁵The eyes of all wait^e upon thee; and thou givest them their meat in due season. ¹⁶Thou openest thine hand, and satisfiest the desire of every living thing.

¹⁷The LORD *is* righteous in all his ways, and holy^f in all his works. ¹⁸The LORD *is* nigh unto all them that call upon him, to all that call upon him in truth. ¹⁹He will fulfil the desire of them that fear him: he also will hear their cry, and will save them. ²⁰The LORD preserveth all them that love him: but all the wicked will he destroy. ²¹My mouth shall speak the praise of the LORD: and let all flesh bless his holy name for ever and ever.

146

¹Praise ye the LORD. Praise the LORD, O my soul. ²While I live will I praise the LORD: I will sing praises unto my God while I have any being. ³Put not your trust in princes, *nor* in the son of man, in whom *there is* no help^a.

---

^c of great . . . : Heb. great in mercy
^d an . . . : Heb. a kingdom of all ages
^e wait . . . : or, look unto
^f holy: or, merciful, or, bountiful
^a help: or, salvation

[4]His breath goeth forth, he returneth to his earth; in that very day his thoughts perish.

[5]Happy *is he* that *hath* the God of Jacob for his help, whose hope *is* in the LORD his God: [6]Which made heaven, and earth, the sea, and all that therein *is*: which keepeth truth for ever: [7]Which executeth judgment for the oppressed: which giveth food to the hungry. The LORD looseth the prisoners: [8]The LORD openeth *the eyes of* the blind: the LORD raiseth them that are bowed down: the LORD loveth the righteous: [9]The LORD preserveth the strangers; he relieveth the fatherless and widow: but the way of the wicked he turneth upside down. [10]The LORD shall reign for ever, *even* thy God, O Zion, unto all generations. Praise ye the LORD.

147

[1]Praise ye the LORD: for *it is* good to sing praises unto our God; for *it is* pleasant; *and* praise is comely. [2]The LORD doth build up Jerusalem: he gathereth together the outcasts of Israel. [3]He healeth the broken in heart, and bindeth up their wounds[a]. [4]He telleth the number of the stars; he calleth them all by *their* names. [5]Great *is* our Lord, and of great power: his understanding *is* infinite. [6]The LORD lifteth up the meek: he casteth the wicked down to the ground. [7]Sing unto the LORD with thanksgiving; sing praise upon the harp unto our God: [8]Who covereth the heaven with clouds, who prepareth rain for the earth, who maketh grass to grow

upon the mountains. [9]He giveth to the beast his food, *and* to the young ravens which cry. [10]He delighteth not in the strength of the horse: he taketh not pleasure in the legs of a man. [11]The LORD taketh pleasure in them that fear him, in those that hope in his mercy.

[12]Praise the LORD, O Jerusalem; praise thy God, O Zion. [13]For he hath strengthened the bars of thy gates; he hath blessed thy children within thee. [14]He maketh peace *in* thy borders, *and* filleth thee with the finest of the wheat. [15]He sendeth forth his commandment *upon* earth: his word runneth very swiftly. [16]He giveth snow like wool: he scattereth the hoarfrost like ashes. [17]He casteth forth his ice like morsels: who can stand before his cold? [18]He sendeth out his word, and melteth them: he causeth his wind to blow, *and* the waters flow. [19]He sheweth his word[b] unto Jacob, his statutes and his judgments unto Israel. [20]He hath not dealt so with any nation: and *as for his* judgments, they have not known them. Praise ye the LORD.

148

[1]Praise ye the LORD. Praise ye the LORD from the heavens: praise him in the heights. [2]Praise ye him, all his angels: praise ye him, all his hosts. [3]Praise ye him, sun and moon: praise him, all ye stars of light. [4]Praise him, ye heavens of heavens, and ye waters that *be* above the heavens. [5]Let them praise the name of the LORD: for he commanded, and they were created. [6]He hath also stab-

---

[a] wounds: Heb. griefs
[b] his word: Heb. his words

lished them for ever and ever: he hath made a decree which shall not pass.

⁷Praise the LORD from the earth, ye dragons, and all deeps: ⁸Fire, and hail; snow, and vapour; stormy wind fulfilling his word: ⁹Mountains, and all hills; fruitful trees, and all cedars: ¹⁰Beasts, and all cattle; creeping things, and flying^a fowl: ¹¹Kings of the earth, and all people; princes, and all judges of the earth: ¹²Both young men, and maidens; old men, and children: ¹³Let them praise the name of the LORD: for his name alone is excellent^b; his glory *is* above the earth and heaven. ¹⁴He also exalteth the horn of his people, the praise of all his saints; *even* of the children of Israel, a people near unto him. Praise ye the LORD.

149

¹Praise^a ye the LORD. Sing unto the LORD a new song, *and* his praise in the congregation of saints. ²Let Israel rejoice in him that made him: let the children of Zion be joyful in their King. ³Let them praise his name in the dance: let them sing praises unto him with the timbrel and harp. ⁴For the LORD taketh pleasure in his people: he will beautify the meek with salvation. ⁵Let the saints be joyful in glory: let them sing aloud upon their beds.

⁶*Let* the high *praises* of God *be* in their mouth^b, and a twoedged sword in their hand; ⁷To execute vengeance upon the heathen, *and* punishments upon the people; ⁸To bind their kings with chains, and their nobles with fetters of iron; ⁹To execute upon them the judgment written: this honour have all his saints. Praise ye the LORD.

150

¹Praise ye the LORD. Praise God in his sanctuary: praise him in the firmament of his power. ²Praise him for his mighty acts: praise him according to his excellent greatness. ³Praise him with the sound of the trumpet^a: praise him with the psaltery and harp. ⁴Praise him with the timbrel and dance^b: praise him with stringed instruments and organs. ⁵Praise him upon the loud cymbals: praise him upon the high sounding cymbals. ⁶Let every thing that hath breath praise the LORD. Praise ye the LORD.

---

^a flying . . . : Heb. birds of wing
^b excellent: Heb. exalted
^a Praise . . . : Heb. Hallelujah
^b mouth: Heb. throat
^a trumpet: or, cornet
^b dance: or, pipe

PROVERBS

Purpose
To teach people how to be understanding, just, and fair in everything they do, to make the simpleminded wise, to warn young men about some problems they will face, and to help the wise become good leaders (see 1:2-6)—in short, to apply divine wisdom to daily life and to provide moral instruction

Author
Solomon, who wrote most of this book, with Agur and Lemuel contributing some of the later sections

Date Written
Solomon wrote and compiled most of these proverbs early in his reign.

Key Verse
"The fear of the Lord is the beginning of knowledge: but fools despise wisdom and instruction" (1:7).

Special Features
The book uses varied *literary forms:* poems, brief parables, pointed questions, and couplets. Other *literary devices* include antithesis, comparison, and personification.

The wise shall inherit glory: but shame shall be the promotion of fools" (3:35).

"Say unto wisdom, Thou art my sister; and call understanding thy kinswoman" (7:4).

"For wisdom is better than rubies; and all the things that may be desired are not to be compared to it" (8:11).

For everything we do, there's a wise and good way to do it, and there's a foolish one.

Proverbs is not a complicated set of rules that govern every move we make. It is a collection of wise sayings to help us make right decisions and lead happy lives.

Proverbs must be talked about. Reading Proverbs together should make your home full of talk. After dinner when Mom or Dad opens up the book of Proverbs, everyone ought to be asking lots of questions. For example:

"Mom, how has the Lord's correction [3:12] made a difference in your life?"

"Dad, how has wisdom been more valuable than jewels [8:11] in your life?"

"Kids, how has our advice been helpful to you [6:20-22]?"

Don't let Proverbs be just another ho-hum experience—get each other talking!

1

¹The proverbs of Solomon the son of David, king of Israel; ²To know wisdom and instruction; to perceive the words of understanding; ³To receive the instruction of wisdom, justice, and judgment, and equity[a]; ⁴To give subtilty to the simple, to the young man knowledge and discretion[b]. ⁵A wise *man* will hear, and will increase learning; and a man of understanding shall attain unto wise counsels: ⁶To understand a proverb, and the interpretation[c]; the words of the wise, and their dark sayings.

⁷The fear of the LORD *is* the beginning[d] of knowledge: *but* fools despise wisdom and instruction. ⁸My son, hear the instruction of thy father, and forsake not the law of thy mother: ⁹For

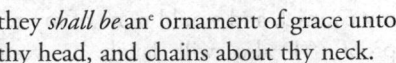

Devotional Moment

Wisdom

1:2-3, 5, 7 The writer of Proverbs spoke of the value of wisdom, that moral insight to discern between good and evil. Wisdom is available to everyone, but at a price. Wisdom is demonstrated in upright character, a disciplined tongue, a teachable spirit, and a devotion to truth and justice. The attainment of it begins with worshiping and submitting to the Lord. Will you pay the price for wisdom by holding your tongue, upholding truth, and doing good? You will be the better for it. See James 3:13-18 for more on wisdom.

they *shall be* an[e] ornament of grace unto thy head, and chains about thy neck.

¹⁰My son, if sinners entice thee, consent thou not. ¹¹If they say, Come with us, let us lay wait for blood, let us lurk privily for the innocent without cause: ¹²Let us swallow them up alive as the grave; and whole, as those that go down into the pit: ¹³We shall find all precious substance, we shall fill our houses with spoil: ¹⁴Cast in thy lot among us; let us all have one purse: ¹⁵My son, walk not thou in the way with them; refrain thy foot from their path: ¹⁶For their feet run to evil, and make haste to shed blood. ¹⁷Surely in vain the net is spread in the sight of any bird. ¹⁸And they lay wait for their *own* blood; they lurk privily for their *own* lives. ¹⁹So *are* the ways of every one that is greedy of gain; *which* taketh away the life of the owners thereof.

²⁰Wisdom[f] crieth without; she uttereth her voice in the streets: ²¹She crieth in the chief place of concourse, in the openings of the gates: in the city she uttereth her words, *saying*, ²²How long, ye simple ones, will ye love simplicity? and the scorners delight in their scorning, and fools hate knowledge? ²³Turn you at my reproof: behold, I will pour out my spirit unto you, I will make known my words unto you. ²⁴Because I have called, and ye refused; I have stretched out my hand, and no man regarded; ²⁵But ye have set at nought all

---

[a] equity: Heb. equities
[b] discretion: or, advisement
[c] the interpretation: or, an eloquent speech
[d] the beginning: or, the principal part
[e] an . . . : Heb. an adding
[f] Wisdom: Heb. Wisdoms, that is, Excellent wisdom

my counsel, and would none of my reproof: [26]I also will laugh at your calamity; I will mock when your fear cometh; [27]When your fear cometh as desolation, and your destruction cometh as a whirlwind; when distress and anguish cometh upon you. [28]Then shall they call upon me, but I will not answer; they shall seek me early, but they shall not find me: [29]For that they hated knowledge, and did not choose the fear of the LORD: [30]They would none of my counsel: they despised all my reproof. [31]Therefore shall they eat of the fruit of their own way, and be filled with their own devices. [32]For the turning away of the simple shall slay them, and the prosperity of fools shall destroy them. [33]But whoso hearkeneth unto me shall dwell safely, and shall be quiet from fear of evil.

2

[1]My son, if thou wilt receive my words, and hide my commandments with thee; [2]So that thou incline thine ear unto wisdom, *and* apply thine heart to understanding; [3]Yea, if thou criest after knowledge, *and* liftest up thy voice for understanding; [4]If thou seekest her as silver, and searchest for her as *for* hid treasures; [5]Then shalt thou understand the fear of the LORD, and find the knowledge of God. [6]For the LORD giveth wisdom: out of his mouth *cometh* knowledge and understanding. [7]He layeth up sound wisdom for the righteous: *he is* a buckler to them that walk uprightly. [8]He keepeth the paths of judgment, and preserveth the way of his saints. [9]Then shalt thou understand righteousness, and judgment, and equity; *yea*, every good path.

[10]When wisdom entereth into thine heart, and knowledge is pleasant unto thy soul; [11]Discretion shall preserve thee, understanding shall keep thee: [12]To deliver thee from the way of the evil *man*, from the man that speaketh froward things; [13]Who leave the paths of uprightness, to walk in the ways of darkness; [14]Who rejoice to do evil, *and* delight in the frowardness of the wicked; [15]Whose ways *are* crooked, and *they* froward in their paths: [16]To deliver thee from the strange woman, *even* from the stranger *which* flattereth with her words; [17]Which forsaketh the guide of her youth, and forgetteth the covenant of her God. [18]For her house inclineth unto death, and her paths unto the dead. [19]None that go unto her return again, neither take they hold of the paths of life. [20]That thou mayest walk in the way of good *men*, and keep the paths of the righteous. [21]For the upright shall dwell in the land, and the perfect shall remain in it. [22]But the wicked shall be cut off from the earth, and the transgressors shall be rooted out of it.

3

[1]My son, forget not my law; but let thine heart keep my commandments: [2]For length of days, and long[a] life, and peace, shall they add to thee. [3]Let not mercy and truth forsake thee: bind them about thy neck; write them upon the table of thine heart: [4]So shalt thou find favour and good[b] understanding in

---

[a] long . . . : Heb. years of life
[b] good . . . : or, good success

Your Child's Lifelong Learning
by Cheri Fuller

Proverbs 1:7 says, "The fear of the Lord is the beginning of knowledge." Leading your child to know and trust God provides a foundation for education and a direction for life. In addition to this crucial first step, there are several other ways you can help your child become a lifelong learner.

How can you be a teacher to your children? I offer four suggestions.

Be an example. Children learn the most from what their parents do.

Let your children see you live life. Let them see you reading your Bible and praying. Be an avid reader of other books, too, and read together. Work together, play board games together, and eat meals together. These experiences let your children see an important part of your life—the values that spring from your knowledge of God.

Watch for teachable moments. Just as we should teach our children about God wherever we go (Deut. 6:6-8), we can share with them the wonders of science, the myriad uses of math, and the power of the written word as we work in the kitchen, ride in the car, or snuggle up with a book before bed. Build kids' math skills by having them weigh apples and estimate the cost at the grocery store, or build writing skills by keeping a travel journal or creating a family newsletter.

Observe your child. In order to bring out your child's best, you need to know his or her unique talents, strengths, weaknesses, and learning style. While some kids have above-average abilities, God has given *every child* unique and significant talents. Whether your child's uniqueness is in painting, music, mechanical dexterity, sports, or some other area, know what it is and give him or her plenty of opportunity to explore it.

Knowing your child also means understanding how he or she learns best. Some children learn best by *hearing* information (auditory learners). Others need to *see* it in pictures, graphs, and words (visual learners). And still others need to *move* and take a hands-on approach (kinesthetic learners).

Teach your child according to his or her learning style:

Auditory learners. Tape-recorded addition, subtraction, and multiplication facts can help the auditory learner gain speed in doing math. The child can use flash cards with the tape recorder or summarize a chapter on tape and play it back for review. When studying spelling at home, have your child say a word aloud and write it several times.

Visual learners. Since visual children learn best by seeing, they can make their own study cards for vocabulary, math, and foreign language (with the word on one side and an illustration on the other side, for example). Post maps, diagrams, or formulas that your child must memorize in his or her room.

Kinesthetic learners. These children learn most effectively by doing experiments, demonstrations, and just *moving* in general. Have the younger kinesthetic learner clap to learn number facts or bounce a ball to practice counting. Make up a cheer to practice spelling, or write words on a big chalkboard at home. Practice putting together a puzzle to learn the fifty states. Count with pennies, beans, or toothpicks. To prepare for a test, the older student can teach *you* the information.

Know your child's teachers. Getting to know faculty and administrators at the school your child attends paves the way for a positive educational experience. Volunteer some time to help in the classroom, serve on the textbook committee, or send notes of thanks and encouragement to the teacher. Then, if a problem over textbook content or policy occurs, you have already built bridges of communication with school personnel and can tackle the problem as partners instead of adversaries.

As your child learns to trust and reverence the Lord *and* becomes a lifelong learner, you will be helping prepare him or her for the special purpose God has in store for one of his precious children.

DIGGING DEEPER

1. Read Deuteronomy 6:6-8 and Proverbs 9:9. How can these instructions to parents be carried out today—particularly in your family situation?

2. Research has shown that most parents criticize their children ten times more often than they affirm or praise them, and that it takes four positive statements to offset each negative one. How can you support your child with positive, uplifting words? See Ephesians 4:29; 6:4.

3. Encouraging your child's *efforts* instead of just focusing on the results (such as A's on a report card or games won in baseball) will go a long way toward helping him or her want to learn. How can you help your child focus on maximum effort? See Colossians 3:23; Proverbs 12:24.

the sight of God and man. ⁵Trust in the LORD with all thine heart; and lean not unto thine own understanding. ⁶In all thy ways acknowledge him, and he shall direct thy paths.

⁷Be not wise in thine own eyes: fear the LORD, and depart from evil. ⁸It shall be health^c to thy navel, and marrow to thy bones. ⁹Honour the LORD with thy substance, and with the firstfruits of all thine increase: ¹⁰So shall thy barns be filled with plenty, and thy presses shall burst out with new wine. ¹¹My son, despise not the chastening of the LORD; neither be weary of his correction: ¹²For whom the LORD loveth he correcteth; even as a father the son *in whom* he delighteth.

¹³Happy *is* the man *that* findeth wisdom, and the man *that* getteth understanding. ¹⁴For the merchandise of it *is* better than the merchandise of silver, and the gain thereof than fine gold.

Devotional Moment
•
Family Loyalty

3:3 The image is powerful: Loyalty and kindness are qualities to hold on to, to write on your heart. The writer of this proverb knew that relationships must not be taken for granted. They must be renewed each day, with a constant barrage of kindness and loyalty poured out on those we cherish. Spend time each day doing loving acts for your spouse, whether that means doing a chore to relieve the other from having to do it, giving a back rub, writing a "love note," staying home to play with the family instead of going out with friends, or whatever. Find a way to be loyal and kind, loving and faithful to your spouse and family each day.

---

^c health: Heb. medicine

Family Traditions

Make Education a Tradition

PROVERBS 1

Learning starts in the family. Studies have shown that students whose parents promote reading at home, supervise study habits, and help with school planning are high achievers and more productive than those whose parents remain uninvolved with the educational process.

A love for reading is a fundamental step of learning. You can find literature at libraries, garage sales, drugstores, doctors' offices, schoolrooms, airports, and churches. Books can be friends, mentors, coaches, true loves. Get them wherever and whenever you can. If you make books as much a part of your family life as dinner, your kids will never go hungry for knowledge.

"But," you say, "be careful! There are so many bad books out there." Ahhh, but there are so many good books. Look for them, read reviews, ask around, get recommendations, search high and low. You'll find them.

The next step is to celebrate school. Get out the crepe paper and balloons and have a "Hooray for School!" party. For favors, use new pencils, erasers, and rulers. For treats, use granola cookies, fruit, string cheese, and popcorn balls. Emphasize new friendships, new skills, new journeys.

Stage a mathematics bash. Decorate by hanging brightly colored numbers around the room. Have the kids guess the number of jelly beans in a large pickle jar, with the prize a crazy mind-teaser book. Play number games.

You can continue the school experience during holidays and vacations. At the beginning of summer, celebrate with creative supplies, and emphasize artistic over academic masteries. Put the kids to "work" daily learning new ways to express their ideas and feelings.

Use mealtimes to teach each other unusual facts and new ways of looking at things. Hide science or history questions under every plate. Hide the answers under the glasses. Go around the table, trying to figure out the right answers before looking.

Have a social studies meal once a month. Use a large map as a tablecloth or centerpiece. Decorate ethnic food with paper flags made with toothpicks and paper. Hide cultural facts under seats. Keep an almanac nearby to look up answers to questions that come up. Listen to the native language on a tape checked out from the library. During the year try to learn the same phrase in at least ten languages.

Value perplexing questions. Come up with questions no one can answer. Make it a family project to research the topic.

In other words, love learning and show that it can be fun—all the time.

Worship
in Your Home

DEVOTIONS: CHARACTER-BUILDING TIMES
Take fast hold of instruction; let her not go: keep her; for she is thy life.
Proverbs 4:13

What we are shapes what we do. In other words, our *character* determines our *conduct*. Honest deeds (conduct) come from an honest person (character). Truthfulness (conduct) is a mark of a truthful person (character).

Devotions should be times of character development. The fruit of Bible study is much more than biblical knowledge. It is applying the life-changing truths of the Word of God to our life. Good character traits—honesty, truthfulness, gratitude—grow out of these life-changing truths.

Bible stories give us role models, both negative and positive. Ruth was a role model of faithfulness; David, fighting Goliath, of trust in God; Daniel, of persistence in prayer.

Memory verses summarize the principles. John 3:16 speaks of God's love without limit; Romans 3:23, of our sinfulness; Romans 6:23, of eternal punishment and eternal life.

From Bible verses, stories, and readings, God's truths emerge. These truths form our beliefs, which influence our character. We become different people.

What we do is merely an extension of what we are.

¹⁵She *is* more precious than rubies: and all the things thou canst desire are not to be compared unto her. ¹⁶Length of days *is* in her right hand; *and* in her left hand riches and honour. ¹⁷Her ways *are* ways of pleasantness, and all her paths *are* peace. ¹⁸She *is* a tree of life to them that lay hold upon her: and happy *is every one* that retaineth her. ¹⁹The LORD by wisdom hath founded the earth; by understanding hath he established^d the heavens. ²⁰By his knowledge the depths are broken up, and the clouds drop down the dew.

²¹My son, let not them depart from thine eyes: keep sound wisdom and discretion: ²²So shall they be life unto thy soul, and grace to thy neck. ²³Then shalt thou walk in thy way safely, and thy foot shall not stumble. ²⁴When thou liest down, thou shalt not be afraid: yea, thou shalt lie down, and thy sleep shall be sweet. ²⁵Be not afraid of sudden fear, neither of the desolation of the wicked, when it cometh. ²⁶For the LORD shall be thy confidence, and shall keep thy foot from being taken.

²⁷Withhold not good from them to whom it is due, when it is in the power of thine hand to do *it*. ²⁸Say not unto thy neighbour, Go, and come again, and to morrow I will give; when thou hast it by thee. ²⁹Devise^e not evil against thy neighbour, seeing he dwelleth securely by thee. ³⁰Strive not with a man without cause, if he have done thee no harm. ³¹Envy thou not the oppressor^f, and choose none of his

---

^d established: or, prepared
^e Devise . . . : or, Practise no evil
^f the oppressor: Heb. a man of violence

Devotional Moment

Decisions

3:5-6 The writer of this proverb wrote forcefully: In *everything* we do we should trust God and put him first. At times we might feel swayed or trust only halfheartedly, but the message is clear. We must trust the Lord completely. And as we do, we can count on God's direction for our decisions.

Are you facing a decision for which you've asked God's guidance, yet you feel shaky in completely trusting him to direct you? Read the passage again, then meditate on complete trust and complete guidance.

ways. ³²For the froward *is* abomination to the LORD: but his secret *is* with the righteous. ³³The curse of the LORD *is* in the house of the wicked: but he blesseth the habitation of the just. ³⁴Surely he scorneth the scorners: but he giveth grace unto the lowly. ³⁵The wise shall inherit glory: but shame shall be the promotion of fools.

4

¹Hear, ye children, the instruction of a father, and attend to know understanding. ²For I give you good doctrine, forsake ye not my law. ³For I was my father's son, tender and only *beloved* in the sight of my mother. ⁴He taught me also, and said unto me, Let thine heart retain my words: keep my commandments, and live. ⁵Get wisdom, get understanding: forget *it* not; neither decline from the words of my mouth. ⁶Forsake her not, and she shall preserve thee: love her, and she shall keep thee. ⁷Wisdom *is* the

principal thing; *therefore* get wisdom: and with all thy getting get understanding. ⁸Exalt her, and she shall promote thee: she shall bring thee to honour, when thou dost embrace her. ⁹She shall give to thine head an ornament of grace: a crownª of glory shall she deliver to thee. ¹⁰Hear, O my son, and receive my sayings; and the years of thy life shall be many. ¹¹I have taught thee in the way of wisdom; I have led thee in right paths. ¹²When thou goest, thy steps shall not be straitened; and when thou runnest, thou shalt not stumble. ¹³Take fast hold of instruction; let *her* not go: keep her; for she *is* thy life.

¹⁴Enter not into the path of the wicked, and go not in the way of evil *men.* ¹⁵Avoid it, pass not by it, turn from it, and pass away. ¹⁶For they sleep not, except they have done mischief; and their sleep is taken away, unless they cause *some* to fall. ¹⁷For they eat the bread of wickedness, and drink the wine of violence. ¹⁸But the path of the just *is* as the shining light, that shineth more and more unto the perfect day. ¹⁹The way of the wicked *is* as darkness: they know not at what they stumble.

²⁰My son, attend to my words; incline thine ear unto my sayings. ²¹Let them not depart from thine eyes; keep them in the midst of thine heart. ²²For they *are* life unto those that find them, and healthᵇ to all their flesh. ²³Keep thy heart with all diligence; for out of it *are* the issues of life. ²⁴Put away from thee a frowardᶜ mouth, and perverse lips put far from thee. ²⁵Let

ª a crown . . . : or, she shall compass thee with a crown of glory
ᵇ health: Heb. medicine
ᶜ a froward . . . : Heb. frowardness of mouth and perverseness of lips

thine eyes look right on, and let thine eyelids look straight before thee. ²⁶Ponder the path of thy feet, and let all thy ways be established. ²⁷Turn not to the right hand nor to the left: remove thy foot from evil.

5

¹My son, attend unto my wisdom, *and* bow thine ear to my understanding: ²That thou mayest regard discretion, and *that* thy lips may keep knowledge. ³For the lips of a strange woman drop *as* an honeycomb, and her mouthᵃ *is* smoother than oil: ⁴But her end is bitter as wormwood, sharp as a twoedged sword. ⁵Her feet go down to death; her steps take hold on hell. ⁶Lest thou shouldest ponder the path of life, her ways are moveable, *that* thou canst not know *them*. ⁷Hear me now therefore, O ye children, and depart not from the words of my mouth. ⁸Remove thy way far from her, and come not nigh the door of her house: ⁹Lest thou give thine honour unto others, and thy years unto the cruel: ¹⁰Lest strangers be filled with thy wealthᵇ; and thy labours *be* in the house of a stranger; ¹¹And thou mourn at the last, when thy flesh and thy body are consumed, ¹²And say, How have I hated instruction, and my heart despised reproof; ¹³And have not obeyed the voice of my teachers, nor inclined mine ear to them that instructed me! ¹⁴I was almost in all evil in the midst of the congregation and assembly.

¹⁵Drink waters out of thine own cistern, and running waters out of thine own well. ¹⁶Let thy fountains be dispersed

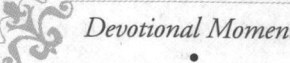

Devotional Moment
• Sex

5:15-20 God himself gave the power and beauty of sex to married couples. With God's blessing—indeed, by his design—husbands and wives have each other to enjoy, exclusively and without shame. Yet two mistakes threaten to tarnish this beautiful design in every couple's experience: (1) rejecting sex as bad or disgusting, and (2) seeking its pleasure without restraint. If you are married, remember that your spouse is a gift from God and a person to serve in giving pleasure. Let your spouse be someone to celebrate—not neglect, abuse, or take for granted. Take the time and energy to nurture this special gift with loving words and touch each day.

abroad, *and* rivers of waters in the streets. ¹⁷Let them be only thine own, and not strangers' with thee. ¹⁸Let thy fountain be blessed: and rejoice with the wife of thy youth. ¹⁹*Let her be as* the loving hind and pleasant roe; let her breasts satisfyᶜ thee at all times; and be thou ravished always with her love. ²⁰And why wilt thou, my son, be ravished with a strange woman, and embrace the bosom of a stranger? ²¹For the ways of man *are* before the eyes of the LORD, and he pondereth all his goings. ²²His own iniquities shall take the wicked himself, and he shall be holden with the cords of his sinsᵈ. ²³He shall die without instruction; and in the greatness of his folly he shall go astray.

6

¹My son, if thou be surety for thy friend, *if* thou hast stricken thy hand

---

ᵃ mouth: Heb. palate

ᵇ thy wealth: Heb. thy strength

ᶜ satisfy . . . : Heb. water thee

ᵈ sins: Heb. sin

with a stranger, ²Thou art snared with the words of thy mouth, thou art taken with the words of thy mouth. ³Do this now, my son, and deliver thyself, when thou art come into the hand of thy friend; go, humble thyself, and make sure thy friend. ⁴Give not sleep to thine eyes, nor slumber to thine eyelids. ⁵Deliver thyself as a roe from the hand *of the hunter*, and as a bird from the hand of the fowler.

⁶Go to the ant, thou sluggard; consider her ways, and be wise: ⁷Which having no guide, overseer, or ruler, ⁸Provideth her meat in the summer, *and* gathereth her food in the harvest. ⁹How long wilt thou sleep, O sluggard? when wilt thou arise out of thy sleep? ¹⁰*Yet* a little sleep, a little slumber, a little folding of the hands to sleep: ¹¹So shall thy poverty come as one that travelleth, and thy want as an armed man.

¹²A naughty person, a wicked man, walketh with a froward mouth. ¹³He winketh with his eyes, he speaketh with his feet, he teacheth with his fingers; ¹⁴Frowardness *is* in his heart, he deviseth mischief continually; he soweth^a discord. ¹⁵Therefore shall his calamity come suddenly; suddenly shall he be broken without remedy. ¹⁶These six *things* doth the LORD hate: yea, seven *are* an abomination unto him: ¹⁷A proud^b look, a lying tongue, and hands that shed innocent blood, ¹⁸An heart that deviseth wicked imaginations, feet that be swift in running to mischief, ¹⁹A false witness *that* speaketh lies, and he that soweth discord among brethren.

²⁰My son, keep thy father's commandment, and forsake not the law of thy mother: ²¹Bind them continually upon thine heart, *and* tie them about thy neck. ²²When thou goest, it shall lead thee; when thou sleepest, it shall keep thee; and *when* thou awakest, it shall talk with thee. ²³For the commandment *is* a lamp^c; and the law *is* light; and reproofs of instruction *are* the way of life: ²⁴To keep thee from the evil woman, from the flattery of the tongue of a strange woman. ²⁵Lust not after her beauty in thine heart; neither let her take thee with her eyelids. ²⁶For by means of a whorish woman *a man is brought* to a piece of bread: and the adulteress^d will hunt for the precious life. ²⁷Can a man take fire in his bosom, and his clothes not be burned? ²⁸Can one go upon hot coals, and his feet not be burned? ²⁹So he that goeth in to his neighbour's wife; whosoever toucheth her shall not be innocent. ³⁰*Men* do not despise a thief, if he steal to satisfy his soul when he is hungry; ³¹But *if* he be found, he shall restore sevenfold; he shall give all the substance of his house. ³²*But* whoso committeth adultery with a woman lacketh understanding^e: he *that* doeth it destroyeth his own soul. ³³A wound and dishonour shall he get; and his reproach shall not be wiped away. ³⁴For jealousy *is* the rage of a man: therefore he will not spare in the day of

---

^a soweth: Heb. casteth forth
^b A proud . . . : Heb. Haughty eyes
^c lamp: or, candle
^d the adulteress: Heb. the woman of a man, or, a man's wife
^e understanding: Heb. heart

vengeance. [35]He will not regard any ransom; neither will he rest content, though thou givest many gifts.

7

[1]My son, keep my words, and lay up my commandments with thee. [2]Keep my commandments, and live; and my law as the apple of thine eye. [3]Bind them upon thy fingers, write them upon the table of thine heart. [4]Say unto wisdom, Thou *art* my sister; and call understanding *thy* kinswoman: [5]That they may keep thee from the strange woman, from the stranger *which* flattereth with her words.

[6]For at the window of my house I looked through my casement, [7]And beheld among the simple ones, I discerned among the youths[a], a young man void of understanding, [8]Passing through the street near her corner; and he went the way to her house, [9]In the twilight, in the evening[b], in the black and dark night: [10]And, behold, there met him a woman *with* the attire of an harlot, and subtil of heart. [11](She *is* loud and stubborn; her feet abide not in her house: [12]Now *is she* without, now in the streets, and lieth in wait at every corner.) [13]So she caught him, and kissed him, *and* with an impudent face said unto him, [14]*I have* peace offerings with me; this day have I payed my vows. [15]Therefore came I forth to meet thee, diligently to seek thy face, and I have found thee. [16]I have decked my bed with coverings of tapestry, with carved *works*, with fine linen of Egypt. [17]I have

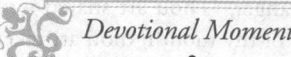

Devotional Moment

Seduced

7:6-27 This married woman had a plan to captivate and seduce the young man into committing adultery. Her words were clever and calculated. Once he took the first step down her street and started listening to her flattering words, she had him. Our culture, the media, and even people you know will try to draw you into sexual sin. Don't let them! Have a healthy distrust of your ability to withstand sexual temptation. Have a *plan* to avoid sexual sin, just as the woman in this story had a plan for seduction. Avoid situations that even *might* be a temptation for you. Decide ahead of time how you will respond if someone does start to entice you. Consider this week what positive steps you can take to bolster your faithfulness to God.

perfumed my bed with myrrh, aloes, and cinnamon. [18]Come, let us take our fill of love until the morning: let us solace ourselves with loves. [19]For the goodman *is* not at home, he is gone a long journey: [20]He hath taken a bag of money with him, *and* will come home at the day appointed. [21]With her much fair speech she caused him to yield, with the flattering of her lips she forced him. [22]He goeth after her straightway[c], as an ox goeth to the slaughter, or as a fool to the correction of the stocks; [23]Till a dart strike through his liver; as a bird hasteth to the snare, and knoweth not that it *is* for his life.

[24]Hearken unto me now therefore, O ye children, and attend to the words of my mouth. [25]Let not thine heart decline to her ways, go not astray in her

---

[a] the youths: Heb. the sons
[b] in the evening of days
[c] straightway: Heb. suddenly

paths. ²⁶For she hath cast down many wounded: yea, many strong *men* have been slain by her. ²⁷Her house *is* the way to hell, going down to the chambers of death.

8

¹Doth not wisdom cry? and understanding put forth her voice? ²She standeth in the top of high places, by the way in the places of the paths. ³She crieth at the gates, at the entry of the city, at the coming in at the doors. ⁴Unto you, O men, I call; and my voice *is* to the sons of man. ⁵O ye simple, understand wisdom: and, ye fools, be ye of an understanding heart. ⁶Hear; for I will speak of excellent things; and the opening of my lips *shall be* right things. ⁷For my mouth shall speak truth; and wickedness *is* an abomination to my lips[a]. ⁸All the words of my mouth *are* in righteousness; *there is* nothing froward[b] or perverse in them. ⁹They *are* all plain to him that understandeth, and right to them that find knowledge. ¹⁰Receive my instruction, and not silver; and knowledge rather than choice gold. ¹¹For wisdom *is* better than rubies; and all the things that may be desired are not to be compared to it.

¹²I wisdom dwell with prudence[c], and find out knowledge of witty inventions. ¹³The fear of the LORD *is* to hate evil: pride, and arrogancy, and the evil way, and the froward mouth, do I hate.

¹⁴Counsel *is* mine, and sound wisdom: I *am* understanding; I have strength. ¹⁵By me kings reign, and princes decree justice. ¹⁶By me princes rule, and nobles, *even* all the judges of the earth. ¹⁷I love them that love me; and those that seek me early shall find me. ¹⁸Riches and honour *are* with me; *yea*, durable riches and righteousness. ¹⁹My fruit *is* better than gold, yea, than fine gold; and my revenue than choice silver. ²⁰I lead[d] in the way of righteousness, in the midst of the paths of judgment: ²¹That I may cause those that love me to inherit substance; and I will fill their treasures.

²²The LORD possessed me in the beginning of his way, before his works of old. ²³I was set up from everlasting, from the beginning, or ever the earth was. ²⁴When *there were* no depths, I was brought forth; when *there were* no fountains abounding with water. ²⁵Before the mountains were settled, before the hills was I brought forth: ²⁶While as yet he had not made the earth, nor the fields[e], nor the highest part of the dust of the world. ²⁷When he prepared the heavens, I *was* there: when he set a compass[f] upon the face of the depth· ²⁸When he established the clouds above: when he strengthened the fountains of the deep: ²⁹When he gave to the sea his decree, that the waters should not pass his commandment: when he appointed the foundations of the earth: ³⁰Then I was by him, *as* one brought up *with*

---

[a] an . . . : Heb. the abomination of my lips
[b] froward: Heb. wreathed
[c] prudence: or, subtilty
[d] lead: or, walk
[e] fields: or, open places
[f] a compass: or, a circle

him: and I was daily *his* delight, rejoicing always before him; ³¹Rejoicing in the habitable part of his earth; and my delights *were* with the sons of men.

³²Now therefore hearken unto me, O ye children: for blessed *are they that* keep my ways. ³³Hear instruction, and be wise, and refuse it not. ³⁴Blessed *is* the man that heareth me, watching daily at my gates, waiting at the posts of my doors. ³⁵For whoso findeth me findeth life, and shall obtain⁸ favour of the LORD. ³⁶But he that sinneth against me wrongeth his own soul: all they that hate me love death.

9

¹Wisdom hath builded her house, she hath hewn out her seven pillars: ²She hath killed her beastsᵃ; she hath mingled her wine; she hath also furnished her table. ³She hath sent forth her maidens: she crieth upon the highest places of the city, ⁴Whoso *is* simple, let him turn in hither: *as for* him that wanteth understanding, she saith to him, ⁵Come, eat of my bread, and drink of the wine *which* I have mingled. ⁶Forsake the foolish, and live; and go in the way of understanding. ⁷He that reproveth a scorner getteth to himself shame: and he that rebuketh a wicked *man getteth* himself a blot. ⁸Reprove not a scorner, lest he hate thee: rebuke a wise man, and he will love thee. ⁹Give *instruction* to a wise *man*, and he will be yet wiser: teach a just *man*, and he will increase in learning. ¹⁰The fear of the LORD *is* the beginning of wisdom: and the knowledge of the holy *is* under-

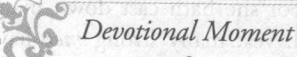

Devotional Moment

Criticism

9:7-10 The writer of Proverbs knew that those who most need correction often are deaf to any outside advice; whereas wise people consider constructive criticism. The passage goes so far as to say that you should not bother trying to help those who will only give a smart retort. Consider this the next time you feel an urge to give unsolicited advice. Don't be surprised if your counsel goes unheeded. Listen first; then speak the truth to those who are wise enough to hear it.

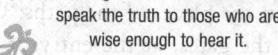

standing. ¹¹For by me thy days shall be multiplied, and the years of thy life shall be increased. ¹²If thou be wise, thou shalt be wise for thyself: but *if* thou scornest, thou alone shalt bear *it*.

¹³A foolish woman *is* clamorous: *she is* simple, and knoweth nothing. ¹⁴For she sitteth at the door of her house, on a seat in the high places of the city, ¹⁵To call passengers who go right on their ways: ¹⁶Whoso *is* simple, let him turn in hither: and *as for* him that wanteth understanding, she saith to him, ¹⁷Stolen waters are sweet, and bread *eaten* in secret is pleasant. ¹⁸But he knoweth not that the dead *are* there; *and that* her guests *are* in the depths of hell.

10

¹The proverbs of Solomon. A wise son maketh a glad father: but a foolish son *is* the heaviness of his mother.

²Treasures of wickedness profit nothing: but righteousness delivereth from death. ³The LORD will not suffer the

---

⁸ obtain: Heb. bring forth
ᵃ her beasts: Heb. her killing

Devotional Moment

Letting Children Go

10:1 The ultimate joy for a Christian parent is to see a child living to please God. Perhaps the greatest grief comes when a son or daughter rejects God. In the end, each child must choose whether to fear the Lord and submit to him. For some parents, letting their children make their own choices is very difficult. They want to control their children's lives. Such children never really grow up and never really have a chance to choose God for themselves, which is what their desperate parents want so badly. If you are a parent, pray for your children, guide them, talk with them, and entrust them to God's care. But don't try to force your kids into living for God. You can't do it.

soul of the righteous to famish: but he casteth away the substance[a] of the wicked.

⁴He becometh poor that dealeth *with* a slack hand: but the hand of the diligent maketh rich.

⁵He that gathereth in summer *is* a wise son: *but* he that sleepeth in harvest *is* a son that causeth shame.

⁶Blessings *are* upon the head of the just: but violence covereth the mouth of the wicked.

⁷The memory of the just *is* blessed: but the name of the wicked shall rot.

⁸The wise in heart will receive commandments: but a prating[b] fool shall fall.

⁹He that walketh uprightly walketh surely: but he that perverteth his ways shall be known.

¹⁰He that winketh with the eye causeth sorrow: but a prating fool shall fall[c].

¹¹The mouth of a righteous *man is* a well of life: but violence covereth the mouth of the wicked.

¹²Hatred stirreth up strifes: but love covereth all sins.

¹³In the lips of him that hath understanding wisdom is found: but a rod *is* for the back of him that is void of understanding[d].

¹⁴Wise *men* lay up knowledge: but the mouth of the foolish *is* near destruction.

¹⁵The rich man's wealth *is* his strong city: the destruction of the poor *is* their poverty.

¹⁶The labour of the righteous *tendeth* to life: the fruit of the wicked to sin.

¹⁷He *is in* the way of life that keepeth instruction: but he that refuseth reproof erreth[e].

¹⁸He that hideth hatred *with* lying

Devotional Moment

Family Conflict

10:12 Children fight. Spouses have disagreements. Families have quarrels and arguments. Kids and parents know how hard it is to overlook insults. We want to fight back! But love for one another means that we learn to overlook insults instead of returning them. Ask for God's help to forgive and settle the hurts. Take the initiative in overlooking offenses.

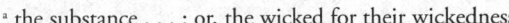

[a] the substance . . . : or, the wicked for their wickedness
[b] a prating . . . : Heb. a fool of lips
[c] fall: Heb. be beaten
[d] of understanding: Heb. of heart
[e] erreth: or, causeth to err

lips, and he that uttereth a slander, *is* a fool.

¹⁹In the multitude of words there wanteth not sin: but he that refraineth his lips *is* wise.

²⁰The tongue of the just *is as* choice silver: the heart of the wicked *is* little worth. ²¹The lips of the righteous feed many: but fools die for want of wisdom[f].

²²The blessing of the LORD, it maketh rich, and he addeth no sorrow with it.

²³*It is* as sport to a fool to do mischief: but a man of understanding hath wisdom.

²⁴The fear of the wicked, it shall come upon him: but the desire of the righteous shall be granted. ²⁵As the whirlwind passeth, so *is* the wicked no *more*: but the righteous *is* an everlasting foundation.

²⁶As vinegar to the teeth, and as smoke to the eyes, so *is* the sluggard to them that send him.

²⁷The fear of the LORD prolongeth[g] days: but the years of the wicked shall be shortened. ²⁸The hope of the righteous *shall be* gladness: but the expectation of the wicked shall perish.

²⁹The way of the LORD *is* strength to the upright: but destruction *shall be* to the workers of iniquity. ³⁰The righteous shall never be removed: but the wicked shall not inhabit the earth.

³¹The mouth of the just bringeth forth wisdom: but the froward tongue shall be cut out. ³²The lips of the righteous know what is acceptable: but the mouth of the wicked *speaketh* frowardness[h].

11

¹A false[a] balance *is* abomination to the LORD: but a just weight *is* his delight.

²*When* pride cometh, then cometh shame: but with the lowly *is* wisdom.

³The integrity of the upright shall guide them: but the perverseness of transgressors shall destroy them.

⁴Riches profit not in the day of wrath: but righteousness delivereth from death.

⁵The righteousness of the perfect shall direct[b] his way: but the wicked shall fall by his own wickedness. ⁶The righteousness of the upright shall de-

---

Devotional Moment

Honesty

11:1, 3 The message could be no clearer—the Lord hates cheating. Even though we know that, both adults and children are often tempted to cheat. When the checkout person at the grocery store gives us back a dollar more than we should receive, we are tempted to say nothing and pocket the money. When other students offer us answers to an upcoming test, we are tempted to take the easy way out and cheat. When we fill out our income-tax forms, we are tempted not to declare the extra money we earned on that small side job. The Bible reminds us that dishonesty destroys. Pray for strength to choose honesty.

---

[f] of wisdom: Heb. of heart

[g] prolongeth: Heb. addeth

[h] frowardness: Heb. frowardnesses

[a] A false . . . : Heb. Balances of deceit

[b] direct: Heb. rectify

liver them: but transgressors shall be taken in *their own* naughtiness.

⁷When a wicked man dieth, *his* expectation shall perish: and the hope of unjust *men* perisheth.

⁸The righteous is delivered out of trouble, and the wicked cometh in his stead.

⁹An hypocrite with *his* mouth destroyeth his neighbour: but through knowledge shall the just be delivered.

¹⁰When it goeth well with the righteous, the city rejoiceth: and when the wicked perish, *there is* shouting. ¹¹By the blessing of the upright the city is exalted: but it is overthrown by the mouth of the wicked.

¹²He that is void of wisdom despiseth his neighbour: but a man of understanding holdeth his peace. ¹³A talebearer revealeth secrets: but he that is of a faithful spirit concealeth the matter.

¹⁴Where no counsel *is*, the people fall: but in the multitude of counsellors *there is* safety.

¹⁵He that is surety for a stranger shall smart *for it*: and he that hateth suretiship is sure.

¹⁶A gracious woman retaineth honour: and strong *men* retain riches.

¹⁷The merciful man doeth good to his own soul: but *he that is* cruel troubleth his own flesh.

¹⁸The wicked worketh a deceitful work: but to him that soweth righteousness *shall be* a sure reward.

¹⁹As righteousness *tendeth* to life: so he that pursueth evil *pursueth it* to his own death.

²⁰They that are of a froward heart *are* abomination to the LORD: but *such as are* upright in *their* way *are* his delight.

²¹*Though* hand *join* in hand, the wicked shall not be unpunished: but the seed of the righteous shall be delivered.

²²*As* a jewel of gold in a swine's snout, *so is* a fair woman which is without discretion.

²³The desire of the righteous *is* only good: *but* the expectation of the wicked *is* wrath.

²⁴There is that scattereth, and yet increaseth; and *there is* that withholdeth more than is meet, but *it tendeth* to poverty.

²⁵The liberal soul shall be made fat: and he that watereth shall be watered also himself.

²⁶He that withholdeth corn, the people shall curse him: but blessing *shall be* upon the head of him that selleth *it*.

²⁷He that diligently seeketh good procureth favour: but he that seeketh mischief, it shall come unto him.

²⁸He that trusteth in his riches shall fall: but the righteous shall flourish as a branch.

²⁹He that troubleth his own house shall inherit the wind: and the fool *shall be* servant to the wise of heart.

³⁰The fruit of the righteous *is* a tree

ᶜ void . . . : Heb. destitute of heart
ᵈ A talebearer: Heb. He that walketh, being a talebearer
ᵉ smart: Heb. be sore broken
ᶠ is without: Heb. departeth from
ᵍ liberal . . . : Heb. soul of blessing

of life; and he that winneth[h] souls *is* wise.

[31]Behold, the righteous shall be recompensed in the earth: much more the wicked and the sinner.

12

[1]Whoso loveth instruction loveth knowledge: but he that hateth reproof *is* brutish.

[2]A good *man* obtaineth favour of the LORD: but a man of wicked devices will he condemn.

[3]A man shall not be established by wickedness: but the root of the righteous shall not be moved.

[4]A virtuous woman *is* a crown to her husband: but she that maketh ashamed *is* as rottenness in his bones.

[5]The thoughts of the righteous *are* right: *but* the counsels of the wicked *are* deceit.

[6]The words of the wicked *are* to lie

Devotional Moment

•

Teamwork

12:4 A husband and wife are a team. The character of one affects the other. When one is noble, it reflects on the other; when one is foolish, the other ducks. Identify in your marriage behaviors and attitudes that could hurt your stability. Start with yourself—don't try to change the other person. Then take time this week to talk together about how you can work as a team to change these destructive patterns. Also take time to enjoy each other, encourage each other, and build each other up.

---

in wait for blood: but the mouth of the upright shall deliver them.

[7]The wicked are overthrown, and *are* not: but the house of the righteous shall stand.

[8]A man shall be commended according to his wisdom: but he that is of a perverse heart shall be despised.

[9]*He that is* despised, and hath a servant, *is* better than he that honoureth himself, and lacketh bread.

[10]A righteous *man* regardeth the life of his beast: but the tender mercies of the wicked *are* cruel.

[11]He that tilleth his land shall be satisfied with bread: but he that followeth vain *persons is* void of understanding.

[12]The wicked desireth the net[a] of evil *men*: but the root of the righteous yieldeth *fruit*.

[13]The wicked[b] is snared by the transgression of *his* lips: but the just shall come out of trouble.

[14]A man shall be satisfied with good by the fruit of *his* mouth: and the recompence of a man's hands shall be rendered unto him.

[15]The way of a fool *is* right in his own eyes: but he that hearkeneth unto counsel *is* wise.

[16]A fool's wrath is presently[c] known: but a prudent *man* covereth shame.

[17]*He that* speaketh truth sheweth forth righteousness: but a false witness deceit.

[18]There is that speaketh like the piercings of a sword: but the tongue of the wise *is* health.

---

[h] winneth: Heb. taketh
[a] the net: or, the fortress
[b] The wicked . . . : Heb. The snare of the wicked is in the transgression of lips
[c] presently: Heb. in that day

¹⁹The lip of truth shall be established for ever: but a lying tongue *is* but for a moment.

²⁰Deceit *is* in the heart of them that imagine evil: but to the counsellors of peace *is* joy.

²¹There shall no evil happen to the just: but the wicked shall be filled with mischief.

²²Lying lips *are* abomination to the LORD: but they that deal truly *are* his delight.

²³A prudent man concealeth knowledge: but the heart of fools proclaimeth foolishness.

²⁴The hand of the diligent shall bear rule: but the slothful[d] shall be under tribute.

²⁵Heaviness in the heart of man maketh it stoop: but a good word maketh it glad.

²⁶The righteous *is* more excellent[e] than his neighbour: but the way of the wicked seduceth them.

Devotional Moment

•

Hang In There!

12:25 This proverb creates a beautiful picture of the importance of encouragement. Many words can be substituted for *heaviness: tired, frightened, lonely, sad, hurting.* No matter how old we are, or what the situation is, we all need encouragement. Remind others that you love and respect them, that you think they're doing well, and that you really want them to succeed. Do it today, and do it often. You can't speak too many words of encouragement.

---

²⁷The slothful *man* roasteth not that which he took in hunting: but the substance of a diligent man *is* precious.

²⁸In the way of righteousness *is* life; and *in* the pathway *thereof there is* no death.

13

¹A wise son *heareth* his father's instruction: but a scorner heareth not rebuke.

²A man shall eat good by the fruit of *his* mouth: but the soul of the transgressors *shall eat* violence.

³He that keepeth his mouth keepeth his life: *but* he that openeth wide his lips shall have destruction.

⁴The soul of the sluggard desireth, and *hath* nothing: but the soul of the diligent shall be made fat.

⁵A righteous *man* hateth lying: but a wicked *man* is loathsome, and cometh to shame.

⁶Righteousness keepeth *him that is* upright in the way: but wickedness overthroweth the sinner[a].

⁷There is that maketh himself rich, yet *hath* nothing: *there is* that maketh himself poor, yet *hath* great riches.

⁸The ransom of a man's life *are* his riches: but the poor heareth not rebuke.

⁹The light of the righteous rejoiceth: but the lamp[b] of the wicked shall be put out.

¹⁰Only by pride cometh contention: but with the well advised *is* wisdom.

¹¹Wealth *gotten* by vanity shall be

---

[d] slothful: or, deceitful
[e] excellent: or, abundant
[a] the sinner: Heb. sin
[b] lamp: or, candle

diminished: but he that gathereth by labour² shall increase.

¹²Hope deferred maketh the heart sick: but *when* the desire cometh, *it is* a tree of life.

¹³Whoso despiseth the word shall be destroyed: but he that feareth the commandment shall be rewarded^d.

¹⁴The law of the wise *is* a fountain of life, to depart from the snares of death.

¹⁵Good understanding giveth favour: but the way of transgressors *is* hard.

¹⁶Every prudent *man* dealeth with knowledge: but a fool layeth open *his* folly.

¹⁷A wicked messenger falleth into mischief: but a faithful² ambassador *is* health.

¹⁸Poverty and shame *shall be to* him that refuseth instruction: but he that regardeth reproof shall be honoured.

¹⁹The desire accomplished is sweet to the soul: but *it is* abomination to fools to depart from evil.

²⁰He that walketh with wise *men* shall be wise: but a companion of fools shall be destroyed^f.

²¹Evil pursueth sinners: but to the righteous good shall be repayed.

²²A good *man* leaveth an inheritance to his children's children: and the wealth of the sinner *is* laid up for the just.

²³Much food *is in* the tillage of the poor: but there is *that is* destroyed for want of judgment.

²⁴He that spareth his rod hateth his son: but he that loveth him chasteneth him betimes.

²⁵The righteous eateth to the satisfying of his soul: but the belly of the wicked shall want.

14

¹Every wise woman buildeth her house: but the foolish plucketh it down with her hands.

²He that walketh in his uprightness feareth the LORD: but *he that is* perverse in his ways despiseth him.

³In the mouth of the foolish *is* a rod of pride: but the lips of the wise shall preserve them.

⁴Where no oxen *are*, the crib *is* clean: but much increase *is* by the strength of the ox.

⁵A faithful witness will not lie: but a false witness will utter lies.

⁶A scorner seeketh wisdom, and *findeth it* not: but knowledge *is* easy unto him that understandeth.

⁷Go from the presence of a foolish man, when thou perceivest not *in him* the lips of knowledge.

⁸The wisdom of the prudent *is* to understand his way: but the folly of fools *is* deceit.

⁹Fools make a mock at sin: but among the righteous *there is* favour.

¹⁰The heart knoweth his own^a bitterness; and a stranger doth not intermeddle with his joy.

¹¹The house of the wicked shall be

---

^c by labour: Heb. with the hand
^d shall be rewarded: or, shall be in peace
^e a faithful . . . : Heb. an ambassador of faithfulness
^f destroyed: Heb. broken
^a his own . . . : Heb. the bitterness of his soul

Your Kids' Grandparents
by Stephen A. Bly

Sometimes I'm not Steve, Mr. Bly, or Russell's dad. I'm three-year-old Zachary's grandpa.

Proverbs 13:22 says that a good man "leaveth an inheritance to his children's children." How can you allow your parents the freedom to leave an inheritance to your kids—a cultural, social, historical, spiritual, and material inheritance—without losing control?

I have seven suggestions:

1. Allow grandparents an important role in your kids' lives. Grandma and Grandpa are not just neighbors, friends, relatives—or old people who live fourteen hundred miles away. They are a blanket of security in a big, lonely world.

Six-year-old Ashley got lost at the mall. She couldn't find her mother, so she called Grandma Johnson. Grandma kept talking to Ashley until her frantic mom found her.

Ashley lives in Arizona. Grandma Johnson lives in Ohio.

To Ashley it seemed like the right thing to do. After all, Grandma's picture sits on her dresser, and it was Grandma Johnson who taught her how to call Ohio collect.

2. Stake out your territory—nicely. You are the parent. Parenting is your responsibility. Grandma and Grandpa need to follow your rules. So make sure they know the rules and the reasons behind them.

While visiting her parents in Florida, Mindy looked forward to a day in the Keys with her husband while the grandparents babysat. On the way out the door, Mindy's mother said, "We're going to take the kids to that new adventure movie. You don't mind, do you?"

Mindy could just shrug and flee to the retreat with her husband. Or she could storm, "Not *that* movie!" But she *should* say something like, "Mom, I'd really prefer that the kids not see such an adult film. Why not take them to that new animated feature that's playing?"

3. Allow them to spoil the kids—a little. If spoiling means to give them better than they deserve, then let Grandma and Grandpa spoil them from time to time. God continually graces us in that fashion.

The pink dress your daughter liked was too expensive, so you told her no. But before the week was out, she had sweet-talked her grandmother into buying it.

"Mother, how could you?" you said despairingly.

It was quite simple, actually.

4. Keep them up-to-date. No matter how far away your kids' grandparents live, you can make sure they're in tune with what's happening. Lynda buys an inexpensive calendar every year and fills in the kids' doctor appointments, piano recitals, basketball games, spelling bees, Sunday school programs, and the like. Each month she rips out the current page and sends it to her mother.

"Grandma always knows what we're doing," Lynda's daughter reported. "It's almost like she lives next door!"

5. Allow your kids some one-on-one time with grandparents. Spending time with grandparents is very important. Some parents insist on twice-a-year dental checkups for their children but think that once every few years is sufficient to visit their kids' grandparents. You've got to show the kids that Grandma and Grandpa are at least as important as tooth decay.

6. *Ask your parents the questions your kids will want to ask after it's too late.* My granddad died in 1959, but it wasn't until 1974 that I realized what I wanted to know from him. Your kids won't know what to ask, so it's up to you to get them together with their grandparents and then pose the questions you wished you'd asked your own grandparents.

7. *Teach your children to pray for their grandparents.* Your kids need to pray for their grandparents. And your parents need their grandchildren's prayers. Pray for Grandma's loneliness, Grandpa's bad back, Grandma's doctor appointment, and Grandpa's salvation.

If your kids' grandparents called and said, "We're dividing up the inheritance for the grandchildren, and we'd like to stop by and give each of the kids a sack of gold," you'd make sure they could come right over. But there are a lot of things much more important to your child's well-being than gold. It's up to moms and dads to help make sure their children's grandparents have an opportunity to leave an inheritance to their grandchildren.

DIGGING DEEPER

1. How important can a grandparent's spiritual commitment be to a grandchild? See 2 Timothy 1:5.

2. What kinds of things should grandparents make sure they communicate to their grandchildren? See Deuteronomy 4:9.

3. How important are your kids to their grandparents? See Proverbs 17:6.

overthrown: but the tabernacle of the upright shall flourish.

¹²There is a way which seemeth right unto a man, but the end thereof *are* the ways of death.

¹³Even in laughter the heart is sorrowful; and the end of that mirth *is* heaviness.

¹⁴The backslider in heart shall be filled with his own ways: and a good man *shall be satisfied* from himself.

¹⁵The simple believeth every word: but the prudent *man* looketh well to his going.

¹⁶A wise *man* feareth, and departeth from evil: but the fool rageth, and is confident.

¹⁷*He that is* soon angry dealeth foolishly: and a man of wicked devices is hated.

¹⁸The simple inherit folly: but the prudent are crowned with knowledge.

¹⁹The evil bow before the good; and the wicked at the gates of the righteous.

²⁰The poor is hated even of his own neighbour: but the rich[b] *hath* many friends.

²¹He that despiseth his neighbour sinneth: but he that hath mercy on the poor, happy *is* he.

²²Do they not err that devise evil? but mercy and truth *shall be* to them that devise good.

²³In all labour there is profit: but the talk of the lips *tendeth* only to penury.

²⁴The crown of the wise *is* their riches: *but* the foolishness of fools *is* folly.

²⁵A true witness delivereth souls: but a deceitful *witness* speaketh lies.

²⁶In the fear of the LORD *is* strong confidence: and his children shall have

---

ᵇ the rich . . . : Heb. many are the lovers of the rich

a place of refuge. ²⁷The fear of the LORD *is* a fountain of life, to depart from the snares of death.

²⁸In the multitude of people *is* the king's honour: but in the want of people *is* the destruction of the prince.

²⁹ *He that is* slow to wrath *is* of great understanding: but *he that is* hasty^c of spirit exalteth folly.

³⁰A sound heart *is* the life of the flesh: but envy the rottenness of the bones.

³¹He that oppresseth the poor reproacheth his Maker: but he that honoureth him hath mercy on the poor.

³²The wicked is driven away in his wickedness: but the righteous hath hope in his death.

³³Wisdom resteth in the heart of him that hath understanding: but *that which is* in the midst of fools is made known.

³⁴Righteousness exalteth a nation: but sin *is* a reproach to any people.

³⁵The king's favour *is* toward a wise servant: but his wrath is *against* him that causeth shame.

15

¹A soft answer turneth away wrath: but grievous words stir up anger.

²The tongue of the wise useth knowledge aright: but the mouth of fools poureth out foolishness.

³The eyes of the LORD *are* in every place, beholding the evil and the good.

⁴A wholesome^a tongue *is* a tree of life: but perverseness therein *is* a breach in the spirit.

⁵A fool despiseth his father's in-

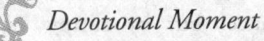

Devotional Moment
•
A Gentle Answer

15:1 This proverb tells us to answer angry attacks with patient and kind responses. Sometimes, anger is necessary. Angry feelings tell you that something important to you is being threatened or challenged. Getting angry doesn't mean you are right, only that what has happened matters to you. The way we handle anger shows a lot about our love for each other. Don't take anger as a personal attack. Rather, view it as an opportunity to help the angry person solve whatever's so important to him or her. Be willing to admit a mistake instead of getting defensive or retaliating. Use gentle words with one another.

struction: but he that regardeth reproof is prudent.

⁶In the house of the righteous *is* much treasure: but in the revenues of the wicked is trouble.

⁷The lips of the wise disperse knowledge: but the heart of the foolish *doeth* not so.

⁸The sacrifice of the wicked *is* an abomination to the LORD: but the prayer of the upright *is* his delight.

⁹The way of the wicked *is* an abomination unto the LORD: but he loveth him that followeth after righteousness.

¹⁰Correction^b *is* grievous unto him that forsaketh the way: *and* he that hateth reproof shall die.

¹¹Hell and destruction *are* before the LORD: how much more then the hearts of the children of men?

¹²A scorner loveth not one that reproveth him: neither will he go unto the wise.

---

^c hasty . . . : Heb. short of spirit
^a A wholesome . . . : Heb. The healing of the tongue
^b Correction: or, Instruction

¹³A merry heart maketh a cheerful countenance: but by sorrow of the heart the spirit is broken.

¹⁴The heart of him that hath understanding seeketh knowledge: but the mouth of fools feedeth on foolishness.

¹⁵All the days of the afflicted *are* evil: but he that is of a merry heart *hath* a continual feast.

¹⁶Better *is* little with the fear of the LORD than great treasure and trouble therewith. ¹⁷Better *is* a dinner of herbs where love is, than a stalled ox and hatred therewith.

¹⁸A wrathful man stirreth up strife: but *he that is* slow to anger appeaseth strife.

¹⁹The way of the slothful *man is* as an hedge of thorns: but the way of the righteous *is* made plain.

²⁰A wise son maketh a glad father: but a foolish man despiseth his mother.

²¹Folly *is* joy to *him that is* destitute^c of wisdom: but a man of understanding walketh uprightly.

²²Without counsel purposes are disappointed: but in the multitude of counsellors they are established.

²³A man hath joy by the answer of his mouth: and a word *spoken* in due season, how good *is it*!

²⁴The way of life *is* above to the wise, that he may depart from hell beneath.

²⁵The LORD will destroy the house of the proud: but he will establish the border of the widow.

²⁶The thoughts of the wicked *are* an abomination to the LORD: but *the words* of the pure *are* pleasant^d words.

²⁷He that is greedy of gain troubleth his own house; but he that hateth gifts shall live.

²⁸The heart of the righteous studieth to answer: but the mouth of the wicked poureth out evil things.

²⁹The LORD *is* far from the wicked: but he heareth the prayer of the righteous.

³⁰The light of the eyes rejoiceth the heart: *and* a good report maketh the bones fat.

³¹The ear that heareth the reproof of life abideth among the wise.

³²He that refuseth instruction^e despiseth his own soul: but he that heareth reproof getteth understanding.

³³The fear of the LORD *is* the instruction of wisdom; and before honour *is* humility.

16

¹The preparations^a of the heart in man, and the answer of the tongue, *is* from the LORD.

²All the ways of a man *are* clean in his own eyes; but the LORD weigheth the spirits.

³Commit^b thy works unto the LORD, and thy thoughts shall be established.

⁴The LORD hath made all *things* for himself: yea, even the wicked for the day of evil.

---

^c destitute . . . : Heb. void of heart
^d pleasant . . . : Heb. words of pleasantness
^e instruction: or, correction
^a preparations: or, disposings
^b Commit: Heb. Roll

Breaking Free from Fear of Aging

The hoary head is a crown of glory, if it be found in the way of righteousness. Proverbs 16:31

Recently nearly four hundred high school seniors were given a questionnaire that listed thirty fears. What were their greatest concerns about the future as they stepped into college or the work force? Was it nuclear war? global population? economic uncertainty?

Surprisingly, the third-ranking fear was the *fear of getting old.*

In our culture today, marketing agents have successfully sold the idea of perpetual youth. From cosmetic surgery to hair coloring and transplants, we spend billions each year trying to stop one of the few certainties in life—aging.

While Madison Avenue may disparage senior citizens, God does not. Listen to his words about those who have grown older: "The hoary head is a crown of glory" (Prov. 16:31). "Thou shalt rise up before the hoary head, and honour the face of the old man, and fear thy God: I am the Lord" (Lev. 19:32). "Honour thy father and thy mother: that thy days may be long upon the land which the Lord thy God giveth thee" (Exod. 20:12).

Breaking loose from the fear of aging can begin with gaining a biblical view of aging—and applying the three antidotes to aging that actually do work.

The challenge of a superordinate goal. Caleb is a tremendous example of someone who didn't fear aging. Listen to his own words: "The Lord hath kept me alive . . . these forty and five years . . . while the children of Israel wandered in the wilderness: and now, lo, I am this day fourscore and five years old. I am as strong this day as I was in the day that Moses sent me" (Josh. 14:10-11).

Why did Caleb have such confidence? He had a superordinate goal: conquering the Promised Land. A superordinate goal—a challenge large enough to keep us pushing forward and looking to the Lord for help—can lift the years off our shoulders and keep us marching forward.

Eighty-five-year-old Caleb's "superordinate goal" was no cakewalk. "Give me this mountain, whereof the Lord spake in that day" (Josh. 14:12). Any military officer will tell you how difficult it is to take a mountain. Yet in this huge challenge, Caleb found himself invigorated to go for the top!

If you're afraid of aging, ask yourself, What challenge have I set for my life that can get me up in the morning and keep me moving forward through the years?

One woman whose children were all grown became a temporary foster parent to a young boy who was disabled. In that relationship, she suddenly found a challenge that rolled back the years. Today, she has added on to her house to make room for the *eleven* disabled foster children she cares for on a daily basis. It's a challenge that requires her to take the mountain, but it also has given her tremendous energy and passion for life.

A source of unquenchable strength. Those who age most healthily maintain close commitments. Evidence of this fact is provided by the profile of the most suicide-prone person in our society: the divorced man, living alone, with rooms full of heartache, and no one to share with.

Caleb rolled back the years by maintaining his commitments. In his eighties, he took on the great challenge of invading Hebron because he "followed the Lord" fully (Josh. 14:8). Maintaining our commitments to our family, our church, and our God can keep our focus on helping, loving, and serving others—not aging.

The promise of eternal life. Confidence in facing old age comes from confidence in what lies behind the veil of death. For the Christian, we have someone we love and serve who's been there—and back.

Gaining a clear, challenging goal, maintaining our commitments to God and others, and resting in the promise of eternal life can help us break free from fear of aging—and begin to celebrate it instead!

---

⁵Every one *that is* proud in heart *is* an abomination to the LORD: *though* hand *join* in hand, he shall not be unpunished[c].

⁶By mercy and truth iniquity is purged: and by the fear of the LORD *men* depart from evil.

⁷When a man's ways please the LORD, he maketh even his enemies to be at peace with him.

⁸Better *is* a little with righteousness than great revenues without right.

⁹A man's heart deviseth his way: but the LORD directeth his steps.

¹⁰A divine sentence *is* in the lips of the king: his mouth transgresseth not in judgment.

¹¹A just weight and balance *are* the LORD'S: all the weights[d] of the bag *are* his work.

¹²*It is* an abomination to kings to commit wickedness: for the throne is established by righteousness.

¹³Righteous lips *are* the delight of kings; and they love him that speaketh right.

¹⁴The wrath of a king *is as* messengers of death: but a wise man will pacify it. ¹⁵In the light of the king's countenance *is* life; and his favour *is* as a cloud of the latter rain.

¹⁶How much better *is it* to get wisdom than gold! and to get understanding rather to be chosen than silver!

---

¹⁷The highway of the upright *is* to depart from evil: he that keepeth his way preserveth his soul.

¹⁸Pride *goeth* before destruction, and an haughty spirit before a fall.

¹⁹Better *it is to be* of an humble spirit with the lowly, than to divide the spoil with the proud.

²⁰He that handleth a matter wisely shall find good: and whoso trusteth in the LORD, happy *is* he.

²¹The wise in heart shall be called prudent: and the sweetness of the lips increaseth learning.

²²Understanding *is* a wellspring of life unto him that hath it: but the instruction of fools *is* folly.

²³The heart of the wise teacheth^e his mouth, and addeth learning to his lips.

²⁴Pleasant words *are as* an honeycomb, sweet to the soul, and health to the bones.

²⁵There is a way that seemeth right unto a man, but the end thereof *are* the ways of death.

²⁶He^f that laboureth laboureth for himself; for his mouth craveth it of him.

²⁷An ungodly man diggeth up evil: and in his lips *there is* as a burning fire. ²⁸A froward man soweth^g strife: and a whisperer separateth chief friends.

²⁹A violent man enticeth his neighbour, and leadeth him into the way *that is* not good. ³⁰He shutteth his eyes to devise froward things: moving his lips he bringeth evil to pass.

---

^e teacheth: Heb. maketh wise
^f He . . . : Heb. The soul of him that
^g soweth: Heb. sendeth forth

Worship
in Your Home

DEVOTIONS: FRIEND-BUILDING TIMES
A friend loveth at all times, and a brother is born for adversity.
Proverbs 17:17

The joys and sorrows of life are often tied to relationships. Broken marriages and friendships and sibling rivalry bring sorrow; good marriages and friendships and sibling relationships bring joy.

Devotional times are friend-building times. Through them we try to help ourselves cultivate a friendship with the Lord. If we are at peace with God through Jesus Christ we will walk with God in a loving relationship. We will cultivate, through Bible reading and prayer, a joyous personal relationship with him—and that is the stuff from which other friendships are made.

We seek also to cultivate best-friend relationships among family members—husband-wife, parent-child, child-child. Friendship is key. In happy marriages, husbands and wives are good friends. Siblings grow up as buddies. A wonderful by-product of our visits with God (building our friendship with him) are those visits with each other as family members during devotions (building our friendship with each other). As we cultivate our family friendship with God, we cultivate our family friendship with each other.

³¹The hoary head *is* a crown of glory, *if* it be found in the way of righteousness.

³²*He that is* slow to anger *is* better than the mighty; and he that ruleth his spirit than he that taketh a city.

³³The lot is cast into the lap; but the whole disposing thereof *is* of the LORD.

17

¹Better *is* a dry morsel, and quietness therewith, than an house full of sacrifices* *with* strife.

²A wise servant shall have rule over a son that causeth shame, and shall have part of the inheritance among the brethren.

³The fining pot *is* for silver, and the furnace for gold: but the LORD trieth the hearts.

⁴A wicked doer giveth heed to false lips; *and* a liar giveth ear to a naughty tongue.

⁵Whoso mocketh the poor reproacheth his Maker: *and* he that is glad at calamities shall not be unpunished*.

⁶Children's children *are* the crown of old men; and the glory of children *are* their fathers.

⁷Excellent* speech becometh not a fool: much less do lying lips a prince.

⁸A gift *is as* a precious* stone in the eyes of him that hath it: whithersoever it turneth, it prospereth.

⁹He that covereth a transgression seeketh* love; but he that repeateth a matter separateth *very* friends.

¹⁰A reproof entereth* more into a wise man than an hundred stripes into a fool.

¹¹An evil *man* seeketh only rebellion: therefore a cruel messenger shall be sent against him.

¹²Let a bear robbed of her whelps meet a man, rather than a fool in his folly.

¹³Whoso rewardeth evil for good, evil shall not depart from his house.

¹⁴The beginning of strife *is as* when one letteth out water: therefore leave off contention, before it be meddled with.

¹⁵He that justifieth the wicked, and he that condemneth the just, even they both *are* abomination to the LORD.

¹⁶Wherefore *is there* a price in the hand of a fool to get wisdom, seeing *he hath* no heart *to it?*

¹⁷A friend loveth at all times, and a brother is born for adversity.

¹⁸A man void of understanding* striketh hands, *and* becometh surety in the presence of his friend.

¹⁹He loveth transgression that loveth strife: *and* he that exalteth his gate seeketh destruction.

²⁰He that hath a froward* heart findeth no good: and he that hath a perverse tongue falleth into mischief.

ᵃ sacrifices: or, good cheer
ᵇ unpunished: Heb. held innocent
ᶜ Excellent . . . : Heb. A lip of excellency
ᵈ a precious . . . : Heb. a stone of grace
ᵉ seeketh: or, procureth
ᶠ entereth . . . : or, aweth more a wise man, than to strike a fool an hundred times
ᵍ understanding: Heb. heart
ʰ He that hath a froward . . . : Heb. The froward of heart

²¹He that begetteth a fool *doeth it* to his sorrow: and the father of a fool hath no joy.

²²A merry heart doeth good *like* a medicine: but a broken spirit drieth the bones.

²³A wicked *man* taketh a gift out of the bosom to pervert the ways of judgment.

²⁴Wisdom *is* before him that hath understanding; but the eyes of a fool *are* in the ends of the earth.

²⁵A foolish son *is* a grief to his father, and bitterness to her that bare him.

²⁶Also to punish the just *is* not good, *nor* to strike princes for equity.

²⁷He that hath knowledge spareth his words: *and* a man of understanding is of an excellent spirit[i]. ²⁸Even a fool, when he holdeth his peace, is counted wise: *and* he that shutteth his lips *is esteemed* a man of understanding.

18

¹Through desire a man, having separated himself, seeketh *and* intermeddleth with all wisdom.

²A fool hath no delight in understanding, but that his heart may discover itself.

³When the wicked cometh, *then* cometh also contempt, and with ignominy reproach.

⁴The words of a man's mouth *are* as deep waters, *and* the wellspring of wisdom as a flowing brook.

⁵*It is* not good to accept the person of the wicked, to overthrow the righteous in judgment.

⁶A fool's lips enter into contention, and his mouth calleth for strokes. ⁷A fool's mouth *is* his destruction, and his lips *are* the snare of his soul.

⁸The words of a talebearer[a] *are* as wounds, and they go down into the innermost parts of the belly.

⁹He also that is slothful in his work is brother to him that is a great waster.

¹⁰The name of the LORD *is* a strong tower: the righteous runneth into it, and is safe[b].

¹¹The rich man's wealth *is* his strong city, and as an high wall in his own conceit.

¹²Before destruction the heart of man is haughty, and before honour *is* humility.

¹³He that answereth[c] a matter before he heareth *it*, it *is* folly and shame unto him.

Devotional Moment
•
Conflict between Kids

18:13, 17 When children play together, conflicts erupt over territory and rights. Parents, be careful to listen to *all* sides before deciding who is right and who is wrong, who did what to whom, and whether there should be any corrective action. And as you listen, consider each child's temperament and past behavior. The account from a child who exaggerates should be considered differently from the account of a child who blames himself or herself. Unjust discipline fosters resentment. Take time to listen to all sides when you help children resolve disputes.

---

[i] an . . . : or, a cool
[a] talebearer: or, whisperer
[b] safe: Heb. set aloft
[c] answereth . . . : Heb. returneth a word

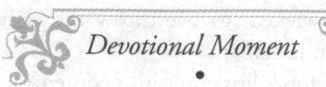

Devotional Moment

•

Companionship

18:22 A stable, healthy marriage is a priceless treasure. Christians recognize that the companionship, friendship, support, and encouragement that one spouse brings to the other are truly blessings from God. Remember to thank him for the gift he has given you in your spouse. Then find ways to communicate how much you appreciate what he or she brings to your marriage and family. A good husband or wife is not only a blessing to a marriage but also a blessing to the whole family because parents who love each other give the children stability.

¹⁴The spirit of a man will sustain his infirmity; but a wounded spirit who can bear?

¹⁵The heart of the prudent getteth knowledge; and the ear of the wise seeketh knowledge.

¹⁶A man's gift maketh room for him, and bringeth him before great men.

¹⁷*He that is* first in his own cause *seemeth* just; but his neighbour cometh and searcheth him.

¹⁸The lot causeth contentions to cease, and parteth between the mighty.

¹⁹A brother offended *is harder to be won* than a strong city: and *their* contentions *are* like the bars of a castle.

²⁰A man's belly shall be satisfied with the fruit of his mouth; *and* with the increase of his lips shall he be filled.

²¹Death and life *are* in the power of the tongue: and they that love it shall eat the fruit thereof.

²²*Whoso* findeth a wife findeth a good *thing,* and obtaineth favour of the LORD.

²³The poor useth intreaties; but the rich answereth roughly.

²⁴A man *that hath* friends must shew himself friendly: and there is a friend *that* sticketh closer than a brother.

19

¹Better *is* the poor that walketh in his integrity, than *he that is* perverse in his lips, and is a fool.

²Also, *that* the soul *be* without knowledge, *it is* not good; and he that hasteth with *his* feet sinneth.

³The foolishness of man perverteth his way: and his heart fretteth against the LORD.

⁴Wealth maketh many friends; but the poor is separated from his neighbour.

⁵A false witness shall not be unpunished[a], and *he that* speaketh lies shall not escape.

⁶Many will intreat the favour of the prince: and every man *is* a friend to him[b] that giveth gifts. ⁷All the brethren of the poor do hate him: how much more do his friends go far from him? he pursueth *them with* words, *yet* they *are* wanting *to him.*

⁸He that getteth wisdom[c] loveth his own soul: he that keepeth understanding shall find good.

⁹A false witness shall not be unpunished, and *he that* speaketh lies shall perish.

---

[a] unpunished: Heb. held innocent
[b] him . . . : Heb. a man of gifts
[c] wisdom: Heb. an heart

¹⁰Delight is not seemly for a fool; much less for a servant to have rule over princes.

¹¹The discretion^d of a man deferreth his anger; and *it is* his glory to pass over a transgression.

¹²The king's wrath *is* as the roaring of a lion; but his favour *is* as dew upon the grass.

¹³A foolish son *is* the calamity of his father: and the contentions of a wife *are* a continual dropping.

¹⁴House and riches *are* the inheritance of fathers: and a prudent wife *is* from the LORD.

¹⁵Slothfulness casteth into a deep sleep; and an idle soul shall suffer hunger.

¹⁶He that keepeth the commandment keepeth his own soul; *but* he that despiseth his ways shall die.

¹⁷He that hath pity upon the poor lendeth unto the LORD; and that which he hath given will he pay him again.

Devotional Moment
•
The Poor

19:17 Here are a few ways we can help the poor: Contribute food to food pantries or homeless shelters; invite a poor family to join you for an outing to a park; send a grocery-store gift certificate to a family struggling with unemployment. Think of something that you could do without for the sake of the poor, such as two restaurant meals a month, a new article of clothing, cable TV service, or whatever—and contribute the money you save to a Christian organization that cares for the poor around the world. And when you give, give joyfully, remembering that "he that hath pity upon the poor lendeth unto the Lord."

Devotional Moment
•
Honoring Parents

19:26; 20:20 An Israelite reading these proverbs might have recalled the Fifth Commandment: "Honour thy father and thy mother" (Exod. 20:12). Under the law, the penalty for cursing one's parents was *death* (Exod. 21:17; Lev. 20:9). When we read these verses, we ought to be challenged to treat our parents with respect. Do you value and show concern for your father and mother, or do you treat them with contempt? If we resist the limited authority of our earthly parents, we will surely have problems with the absolute authority of our heavenly Father!

---

¹⁸Chasten thy son while there is hope, and let not thy soul spare for his crying.

¹⁹A man of great wrath shall suffer punishment: for if thou deliver *him*, yet thou must do it again.

²⁰Hear counsel, and receive instruction, that thou mayest be wise in thy latter end.

²¹ *There are* many devices in a man's heart; nevertheless the counsel of the LORD, that shall stand.

²²The desire of a man *is* his kindness: and a poor man *is* better than a liar.

²³The fear of the LORD *tendeth* to life: and *he that hath it* shall abide satisfied; he shall not be visited with evil.

²⁴A slothful *man* hideth his hand in *his* bosom, and will not so much as bring it to his mouth again.

²⁵Smite a scorner, and the simple will beware^e: and reprove one that hath understanding, *and* he will understand knowledge.

---

^d discretion: or, prudence
^e will beware: Heb. will be cunning

²⁶He that wasteth *his* father, *and* chaseth away *his* mother, *is* a son that causeth shame, and bringeth reproach.

²⁷Cease, my son, to hear the instruction *that causeth* to err from the words of knowledge.

²⁸An ungodly witness scorneth judgment: and the mouth of the wicked devoureth iniquity.

²⁹Judgments are prepared for scorners, and stripes for the back of fools.

20

¹Wine *is* a mocker, strong drink *is* raging: and whosoever is deceived thereby is not wise.

²The fear of a king *is* as the roaring of a lion: *whoso* provoketh him to anger sinneth *against* his own soul.

³*It is* an honour for a man to cease from strife: but every fool will be meddling.

⁴The sluggard will not plow by reason of the cold^a; *therefore* shall he beg in harvest, and *have* nothing.

⁵Counsel in the heart of man *is like* deep water; but a man of understanding will draw it out.

⁶Most men will proclaim every one his own goodness^b: but a faithful man who can find?

⁷The just *man* walketh in his integrity: his children *are* blessed after him.

⁸A king that sitteth in the throne of judgment scattereth away all evil with his eyes.

⁹Who can say, I have made my heart clean, I am pure from my sin?

¹⁰Divers weights^c, *and* divers measures, both of them *are* alike abomination to the LORD.

¹¹Even a child is known by his doings, whether his work *be* pure, and whether *it be* right.

¹²The hearing ear, and the seeing eye, the LORD hath made even both of them.

¹³Love not sleep, lest thou come to poverty; open thine eyes, *and* thou shalt be satisfied with bread.

¹⁴It is naught, *it is* naught, saith the buyer: but when he is gone his way, then he boasteth.

¹⁵There is gold, and a multitude of rubies: but the lips of knowledge *are* a precious jewel.

¹⁶Take his garment that is surety *for* a stranger: and take a pledge of him for a strange woman.

¹⁷Bread of deceit^d *is* sweet to a man; but afterwards his mouth shall be filled with gravel.

¹⁸*Every* purpose is established by counsel: and with good advice make war.

¹⁹He that goeth about *as* a talebearer revealeth secrets: therefore meddle not with him that flattereth^e with his lips.

²⁰Whoso curseth his father or his mother, his lamp^f shall be put out in obscure darkness.

²¹An inheritance *may be* gotten

---

^a cold: or, winter
^b goodness: or, bounty
^c Divers weights: Heb. A stone and a stone
^d deceit: Heb. lying, or, falsehood
^e flattereth: or, enticeth
^f lamp: or, candle

hastily at the beginning; but the end thereof shall not be blessed.

²²Say not thou, I will recompense evil; *but* wait on the LORD, and he shall save thee.

²³Divers weights *are* an abomination unto the LORD; and a false[g] balance *is* not good.

²⁴Man's goings *are* of the LORD; how can a man then understand his own way?

²⁵*It is* a snare to the man *who* devoureth *that which is* holy, and after vows to make enquiry.

²⁶A wise king scattereth the wicked, and bringeth the wheel over them.

²⁷The spirit of man *is* the candle[h] of the LORD, searching all the inward parts of the belly.

²⁸Mercy and truth preserve the king: and his throne is upholden by mercy.

²⁹The glory of young men *is* their strength: and the beauty of old men *is* the gray head.

³⁰The blueness of a wound cleanseth[i] away evil: so *do* stripes the inward parts of the belly.

21

¹The king's heart *is* in the hand of the LORD, *as* the rivers of water: he turneth it whithersoever he will.

²Every way of a man *is* right in his own eyes: but the LORD pondereth the hearts.

³To do justice and judgment *is* more acceptable to the LORD than sacrifice.

⁴An high look, and a proud heart, *and* the plowing of the wicked, *is* sin.

⁵The thoughts of the diligent *tend* only to plenteousness; but of every one *that is* hasty only to want.

⁶The getting of treasures by a lying tongue *is* a vanity tossed to and fro of them that seek death.

⁷The robbery of the wicked shall destroy[a] them; because they refuse to do judgment.

⁸The way of man *is* froward and strange: but *as for* the pure, his work *is* right.

⁹*It is* better to dwell in a corner of the housetop, than with a brawling[b] woman in a wide house.

¹⁰The soul of the wicked desireth evil: his neighbour findeth no favour in his eyes.

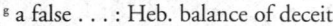

Devotional Moment
•
Friendly Fences

21:10 How we treat our neighbors says a lot about us, particularly if we are unkind to them. What kind of neighbor are you? Make a practice of being kind to those who live near you. Smile at them, say hello when you can, help them when they need a hand, let their kids play at your house, feed their cats when they go on vacation, and never gossip about them to other neighbors. After all, isn't that the kind of neighbors *you'd* like to have?

---

[g] a false . . . : Heb. balance of deceit
[h] candle: or, lamp
[i] cleanseth . . . : Heb. is a purging medicine against
[a] destroy . . . : Heb. saw them, or, dwell with them
[b] a brawling . . . : Heb. a woman of contentions

[11]When the scorner is punished, the simple is made wise: and when the wise is instructed, he receiveth knowledge.

[12]The righteous *man* wisely considereth the house of the wicked: *but God* overthroweth the wicked for *their* wickedness.

[13]Whoso stoppeth his ears at the cry of the poor, he also shall cry himself, but shall not be heard.

[14]A gift in secret pacifieth anger: and a reward in the bosom strong wrath.

[15]*It is* joy to the just to do judgment: but destruction *shall be* to the workers of iniquity.

[16]The man that wandereth out of the way of understanding shall remain in the congregation of the dead.

[17]He that loveth pleasure[c] *shall be* a poor man: he that loveth wine and oil shall not be rich.

[18]The wicked *shall be* a ransom for the righteous, and the transgressor for the upright.

[19]*It is* better to dwell in the wilderness, than with a contentious and an angry woman.

[20]*There is* treasure to be desired and oil in the dwelling of the wise; but a foolish man spendeth it up.

[21]He that followeth after righteousness and mercy findeth life, righteousness, and honour.

[22]A wise *man* scaleth the city of the mighty, and casteth down the strength of the confidence thereof.

[23]Whoso keepeth his mouth and his tongue keepeth his soul from troubles.

[24]Proud *and* haughty scorner *is* his name, who dealeth in proud[d] wrath.

[25]The desire of the slothful killeth him; for his hands refuse to labour. [26]He coveteth greedily all the day long: but the righteous giveth and spareth not.

[27]The sacrifice of the wicked *is* abomination: how much more, *when* he bringeth it with a wicked mind?

[28]A false witness shall perish: but the man that heareth speaketh constantly.

[29]A wicked man hardeneth his face: but *as for* the upright, he directeth[e] his way.

[30]*There is* no wisdom nor understanding nor counsel against the LORD. [31]The horse *is* prepared against the day of battle: but safety[f] *is* of the LORD.

22

[1]A *good* name *is* rather to be chosen than great riches, *and* loving[a] favour rather than silver and gold.

[2]The rich and poor meet together: the LORD *is* the maker of them all.

[3]A prudent *man* foreseeth the evil, and hideth himself: but the simple pass on, and are punished.

[4]By[b] humility *and* the fear of the LORD *are* riches, and honour, and life.

---

[c] pleasure: or, sport
[d] in proud . . . : Heb. in the wrath of pride
[e] directeth: or, considereth
[f] safety: or, victory
[a] loving . . . : or, favour is better than, etc
[b] By . . . : or, The reward of humility, etc

Building Character in Your Children

by Nadine M. Brown

"Even a child is known by his doings, whether his work be pure, and whether it be right" (Prov. 20:11). This important truth lets us know that the task of character building must begin in childhood—a time when it would be easy to excuse our children's faults and weaknesses.

In Deuteronomy 6:6-7 God tells us his two-step plan for character building. It begins with you as a parent.

First, think constantly on God's Word and guide your life by it. If you are convinced that God wants only the very best for your life, this won't be hard to do.

Second, talk about it. Godliness requires an explanation; otherwise kids don't get it. As parents we can talk to our children about God when we get them out of bed in the morning (perhaps with hymns playing on the tape player); while they are eating breakfast (sharing a verse of Scripture); while we drive them to school (quiet the car with prayer for God's protection); when we sit down to supper at night (by each sharing prayers God answered that day); and when we put them to bed (with a Bible story).

Building character, like any construction project, needs a blueprint. Sit down soon with your spouse, or a godly family member or friend, and write out a list of character qualities you want to instill in your children. Then plan to work on just one character quality at a time, perhaps a different one each month. Help your children learn appropriate Scripture verses to reinforce the character quality. And they can be involved in the project by writing a short definition of the quality along with slogans to put on the family bulletin board.

For example, say you wanted to help your children develop the quality of *obedience to parents*. Your kids might define it as "doing what I should, when I should, with the right attitude." Memory verses could include Ephesians 6:1 and 1 Samuel 15:22-23. Simple slogans that would go with this character quality are "Obedience brings happiness" and "Obedience is better than presents."

Scripture can also be a valuable help to you by giving examples of parents who succeeded or failed in teaching children to obey. Eli is probably one of the saddest examples in Scripture of a parent who failed in this respect. He talked to his ungodly sons and scolded them for their immoral behavior, but through the years he had failed to put enough force behind his words (1 Sam. 2:12-36). He is a warning to all parents that talking is the beginning of training, but we dare not forget that punishment that hurts chases evil from the heart (Prov. 20:30).

Another example of a character quality you might work on is *discernment.* You might define it as "knowing how to recognize and choose the best." A good memory verse would be Psalm 119:105, and a good biblical person to study would be Samson (Judg. 13–16). His lack of discernment in choosing friends, especially girlfriends, was fatal! Your children can learn from this that as they work on developing character qualities, they should be looking for these same qualities in their friends, like the little six-year-old who confided, "Mommy, I like Janie, but I'm watching her character!"

Topics for instruction in discernment should include choices in room decorations (art), music, literature, clothing, and even things they purchase. This character quality is taught by repeated contrast of what is pure and good with what is ugly and destructive. Start as early as possible to point out how God has put order and design into his creation, and help your children recognize these qualities. A corner in their room for "A Thing of Beauty" will give them practical experience in this area of discernment. A walk down the aisle of any toy store will provide negative examples, for many grotesque, cruel-looking creatures are being sold as playthings.

Building character in children is a big task. But with a specific plan, daily prayer for God's help, and diligent focus on character building, incorporating biblical principles can become a habit. The benefits are well worth the effort, since even a child is "known by the way he acts," and the character traits your children develop now will help determine the kind of adults they'll become.

DIGGING DEEPER

1. Why did Eli's sons grow up to be such despicable men? See 1 Samuel 2:29.

2. What can you use from Joseph's example to teach your children about moral purity? See Genesis 39:1-12.

3. Read a chapter of Proverbs each day over the next month. Identify the character qualities it discusses, and note the instructions about each one.

---

⁵Thorns *and* snares *are* in the way of the froward: he that doth keep his soul shall be far from them.

⁶Train up a child in the way he should go: and when he is old, he will not depart from it.

⁷The rich ruleth over the poor, and the borrower *is* servant to the lender^c.

⁸He that soweth iniquity shall reap vanity: and the rod^d of his anger shall fail.

⁹He that hath a bountiful eye shall be blessed; for he giveth of his bread to the poor.

¹⁰Cast out the scorner, and contention shall go out; yea, strife and reproach shall cease.

¹¹He that loveth pureness of heart, *for* the grace of his lips the king *shall be* his friend.

¹²The eyes of the LORD preserve knowledge, and he overthroweth the words^e of the transgressor.

¹³The slothful *man* saith, *There is* a lion without, I shall be slain in the streets.

¹⁴The mouth of strange women *is* a deep pit: he that is abhorred of the LORD shall fall therein.

¹⁵Foolishness *is* bound in the heart of a child; *but* the rod of correction shall drive it far from him.

¹⁶He that oppresseth the poor to increase his *riches, and* he that giveth to the rich, *shall* surely *come* to want.

¹⁷Bow down thine ear, and hear the words of the wise, and apply thine heart unto my knowledge. ¹⁸For *it is* a pleasant thing if thou keep them within^f thee; they shall withal be fitted in thy lips. ¹⁹That thy trust may be in the LORD, I have made known to thee this day, even to thee. ²⁰Have not I written to thee excellent things in counsels and knowledge, ²¹That I might make thee know the certainty of the words of truth; that thou mightest an-

---

^c the lender: Heb. the man that lendeth

^d the rod . . . : or, with the rod of his anger he shall be consumed

^e the words: or, the matters

^f within . . . : Heb. in thy belly

Children and Alcohol

by Steve Arterburn

Bloodshot eyes and many wounds, saying foolish, silly things that would embarrass you no end when sober—these phrases from Proverbs 23:29 and 23:33 accurately describe a life given to wine and alcohol. Those who drink vast quantities of alcohol try to convince themselves that they are different, that they will escape the grips of addiction. But they never do. Instead, relationships with God, family, friends, and fellow workers are destroyed, along with life's meaning and purpose.

Most of us agree that we need to teach children about the many dangers of alcohol. But often we don't go any farther than saying, "Don't do it." We need to go deeper than that because we can be assured that in almost every school in every city, our children are being tempted to taste alcohol for the first time—and abuse it for a lifetime. By the age of ten, most children are making the decision whether or not to drink. The peer pressure to drink is so strong that most of them will succumb unless they obtain solid instruction from their parents.

When you ask kids why they drink, most will tell you (if they are honest) that they do it to be part of the group, to feel accepted. Kids need to see that they do not need to do all the things of the world to gain acceptance—that there are other things they can do to feel accepted. We need to help them pick the right group of friends, one that is healthy and allows them to be their best rather than their worst. As part of a positive group of peers, they can develop a reputation as caring and fun people, challenging others to be different—to stand out in the crowd rather than be brought down by it. And we must not rely on someone else, such as school officials, to teach these valuable principles.

If we make an effort, we can teach our children in a way that will make a difference. To begin with, we must examine the example we're setting for them. If we reach for a drink to medicate our wounds, we can be sure our children will learn our method of coping and repeat it as they encounter problems. Incidentally, this principle doesn't only apply to drinking. Some who do not drink might pride themselves on their example, but they need to look at other areas that can be just as harmful. For instance, some parents are overweight because they use food as a drug. Others spend long hours at work or in ministry in an effort to feel good about themselves.

Our children need us to teach them how to cope and how to solve problems without resorting to drinking, drugs, overeating, or any other destructive habit. If they see our stresses managed through prayer, Bible study, open discussion with our spouse or a trusted Christian friend, exercise, and other forms of relaxation, then they'll be more likely to resolve their problems in healthy ways. By teaching children these life skills through example, we instill in them a sense of adequacy that will enable them to deflect the pressures.

It is too late to keep some children from harm. They are already involved in alcohol abuse and alcoholism. Grades have dropped, attitude has plummeted, and signs of rebellion saturate the child's life. Even though the child is young, the parent is witnessing the consequences of addiction.

If that is your child's situation, do not try to convince yourself that it is just a phase or a stage that will soon pass. Your child needs you to act, to stop him or her from continuing toward self-destruction. Although it may be difficult, reach out to someone who can help you help your child. In those hard situations, our children need us to act on their behalf more than they need our words. The sooner we take action, the less time the addiction has to completely dominate a life and destroy it.

Whatever our children's relationship with alcohol, whether they have been drinking for years or have been able to say no until now, they need us to lead them and teach them, so they might be able to avoid the sting of "an adder " (Prov. 23:32). It is never too early to start; it is never too late to intervene.

DIGGING DEEPER

1. Kids try to medicate their wounds in many ways. Look at Jeremiah 6:14, then list three ways you could help your children face the truth about themselves.

2. In James 5:16 we are told to share our faults with each other. How can confessing your faults help motivate your children to open up about themselves?

3. Exodus 20:5 tells about children who inherit a destructive spiritual course from their parents. What is one bad habit you should give up in order to help your children? Make a list of such behaviors and commit them to the Lord. Then make a commitment to your children to continue growing spiritually.

swer the words of truth to them that send unto thee?

²²Rob not the poor, because he *is* poor: neither oppress the afflicted in the gate: ²³For the LORD will plead their cause, and spoil the soul of those that spoiled them.

²⁴Make no friendship with an angry man; and with a furious man thou shalt not go: ²⁵Lest thou learn his ways, and get a snare to thy soul.

²⁶Be not thou *one* of them that strike hands, *or* of them that are sureties for debts. ²⁷If thou hast nothing to pay, why should he take away thy bed from under thee?

²⁸Remove not the ancient landmark[g], which thy fathers have set.

²⁹Seest thou a man diligent in his business? he shall stand before kings; he shall not stand before mean[h] *men*.

23

¹When thou sittest to eat with a ruler, consider diligently what *is* before thee: ²And put a knife to thy throat, if thou *be* a man given to appetite. ³Be not desirous of his dainties: for they *are* deceitful meat.

⁴Labour not to be rich: cease from thine own wisdom. ⁵Wilt thou set[a] thine eyes upon that which is not? for *riches* certainly make themselves wings; they fly away as an eagle toward heaven.

⁶Eat thou not the bread of *him that hath* an evil eye, neither desire thou his dainty meats: ⁷For as he thinketh in his heart, so *is* he: Eat and drink, saith he to thee; but his heart *is* not with thee. ⁸The morsel *which* thou hast eaten shalt thou vomit up, and lose thy sweet words.

⁹Speak not in the ears of a fool: for he will despise the wisdom of thy words.

¹⁰Remove not the old landmark[b];

---

[g] landmark: or, bound

[h] mean . . . : Heb. obscure men

[a] set . . . : Heb. cause thine eyes to fly upon

[b] landmark: or, bound

and enter not into the fields of the fatherless: ¹¹For their redeemer *is* mighty; he shall plead their cause with thee.

¹²Apply thine heart unto instruction, and thine ears to the words of knowledge. ¹³Withhold not correction from the child: for *if* thou beatest him with the rod, he shall not die. ¹⁴Thou shalt beat him with the rod, and shalt deliver his soul from hell. ¹⁵My son, if thine heart be wise, my heart shall rejoice, even mine. ¹⁶Yea, my reins shall rejoice, when thy lips speak right things.

¹⁷Let not thine heart envy sinners: but *be thou* in the fear of the LORD all the day long. ¹⁸For surely there is an end[c]; and thine expectation shall not be cut off.

¹⁹Hear thou, my son, and be wise, and guide thine heart in the way. ²⁰Be not among winebibbers; among riotous eaters of flesh[d]: ²¹For the drunkard and the glutton shall come to poverty: and drowsiness shall clothe *a man* with rags. ²²Hearken unto thy father that begat thee, and despise not thy mother when she is old. ²³Buy the truth, and sell *it* not; *also* wisdom, and instruction, and understanding. ²⁴The father of the righteous shall greatly rejoice: and he that begetteth a wise *child* shall have joy of him. ²⁵Thy father and thy mother shall be glad, and she that bare thee shall rejoice. ²⁶My son, give me thine heart, and let thine eyes observe my ways. ²⁷For a whore *is* a deep ditch; and a strange woman *is* a narrow pit. ²⁸She also lieth in wait as *for* a prey, and increaseth the transgressors among men.

²⁹Who hath woe? who hath sorrow? who hath contentions? who hath babbling? who hath wounds without cause? who hath redness of eyes? ³⁰They that tarry long at the wine; they that go to seek mixed wine. ³¹Look not thou upon the wine when it is red, when it giveth his colour in the cup, *when* it moveth itself aright. ³²At the last it biteth like a serpent, and stingeth like an[e] adder. ³³Thine eyes shall behold strange women, and thine heart shall utter perverse things. ³⁴Yea, thou shalt be as he that lieth down in the midst[f] of the sea, or as he that lieth upon the top of a mast. ³⁵They have stricken me, *shalt thou say, and* I was not sick; they have beaten me, *and* I felt[g] *it* not: when shall I awake? I will seek it yet again.

24

¹Be not thou envious against evil men, neither desire to be with them. ²For their heart studieth destruction, and their lips talk of mischief.

³Through wisdom is an house builded; and by understanding it is established: ⁴And by knowledge shall the chambers be filled with all precious and pleasant riches. ⁵A wise man *is* strong; yea, a man of knowledge increaseth strength. ⁶For by wise counsel thou shalt make thy war: and in multitude of counsellors *there is* safety.

⁷Wisdom *is* too high for a fool: he

---

[c] end: or, reward
[d] of flesh: Heb. of their flesh
[e] an . . . : or, a cockatrice
[f] the midst . . . : Heb. the heart of the sea
[g] I felt . . . : Heb. I knew it not

openeth not his mouth in the gate. ⁸He that deviseth to do evil shall be called a mischievous person. ⁹The thought of foolishness *is* sin: and the scorner *is* an abomination to men.

¹⁰*If* thou faint in the day of adversity, thy strength *is* small ͣ.

¹¹If thou forbear to deliver *them that are* drawn unto death, and *those that are* ready to be slain; ¹²If thou sayest, Behold, we knew it not; doth not he that pondereth the heart consider *it?* and he that keepeth thy soul, doth *not* he know *it?* and shall *not* he render to *every* man according to his works?

¹³My son, eat thou honey, because *it is* good; and the honeycomb, *which is* sweet to thy taste: ¹⁴So *shall* the knowledge of wisdom *be* unto thy soul: when thou hast found *it,* then there shall be a reward, and thy expectation shall not be cut off.

¹⁵Lay not wait, O wicked *man,* against the dwelling of the righteous; spoil not his resting place: ¹⁶For a just *man* falleth seven times, and riseth up again: but the wicked shall fall into mischief.

¹⁷Rejoice not when thine enemy falleth, and let not thine heart be glad when he stumbleth: ¹⁸Lest the LORD see *it,* and it displease him, and he turn away his wrath from him.

¹⁹Fret ͣ not thyself because of evil *men,* neither be thou envious at the wicked; ²⁰For there shall be no reward

to the evil *man;* the candle ͨ of the wicked shall be put out.

²¹My son, fear thou the LORD and the king: *and* meddle not with them that are given to change: ²²For their calamity shall rise suddenly; and who knoweth the ruin of them both?

²³These *things* also *belong* to the wise. *It is* not good to have respect of persons in judgment. ²⁴He that saith unto the wicked, Thou *art* righteous; him shall the people curse, nations shall abhor him: ²⁵But to them that rebuke *him* shall be delight, and a good ͩ blessing shall come upon them. ²⁶*Every man* shall kiss *his* lips that giveth a right answer.

²⁷Prepare thy work without, and make it fit for thyself in the field; and afterwards build thine house.

²⁸Be not a witness against thy neighbour without cause; and deceive *not* with thy lips. ²⁹Say not, I will do so to him as he hath done to me: I will render to the man according to his work.

³⁰I went by the field of the slothful, and by the vineyard of the man void of understanding; ³¹And, lo, it was all grown over with thorns, *and* nettles had covered the face thereof, and the stone wall thereof was broken down. ³²Then I saw, *and* considered *it* well ͤ: I looked upon *it, and* received instruction. ³³*Yet* a little sleep, a little slumber, a little folding of the hands to sleep: ³⁴So shall thy poverty come *as*

ͣ small: Heb. narrow
ͣ Fret . . . : or, Keep not company with the wicked
ͨ candle: or, lamp
ͩ a good . . . : Heb. a blessing of good
ͤ considered . . . : Heb. set my heart

A Oneness Marriage
by Dennis Rainey

We were not created to live in isolation. We yearn for intimacy. And God often provides it by sending a mate, as he did for Adam when he declared, "It is not good that the man should be alone; I will make him an help meet for him" (Gen. 2:18). The real tragedy is that so many people remain lonely even in marriage. Sometimes we fall prey to the lies of the enemy, who wants us to feel that no one cares about us, even the one who is supposed to be closest to us—our mate.

Isolation in marriage starts when husband and wife slowly drift apart without even recognizing it. Signs of isolation include:

- a feeling that your spouse isn't hearing you and doesn't want to understand.
- an attitude of "who cares—why try?" "We'll talk about it tomorrow—let's just get some sleep."
- a feeling of being unable to please or meet the expectations of your spouse.
- a sense that your spouse is detached from you, going another direction.
- a refusal to cope with what's really wrong: "That's your problem, not mine."

Too many couples live in a state of loneliness. They live with each other, but there is no intimacy in their relationship.

The great hope God offers, however, is that no matter how far a couple has traveled down the road to isolation, they can still start on a new road—the road that leads to a Oneness Marriage.

A Oneness Marriage involves a husband and wife who are crafting intimacy, trust, and understanding with one another. They work toward a common direction, purpose, and plan for their lives. A Oneness Marriage demands a lifetime of relying on God and forging an enduring relationship according to his design. It's more than mere cohabitation—it's a tender merger of body, soul, and spirit.

King Solomon spoke of this in Proverbs 24:3-4: "Through wisdom is an house builded; and by understanding it is established: And by knowledge shall the chambers be filled with all precious and pleasant riches." This passage lists three parts of a Oneness Marriage:

A Oneness Marriage takes wisdom. Wisdom is skill in everyday living. It means we respond to circumstances according to God's design. A wise home builder recognizes God as the architect and builder of marriages. As we ask God for wisdom and search the Scriptures, he supplies the skills to build our home.

The psalmist warned, "Except the Lord build the house, they labour in vain that build it" (Ps. 127:1). Many marriages fail because their architect and builder is "self." Couples who experience loneliness in marriage often need to take a hard look at whether they are living their lives in humility and submission to God.

A Oneness Marriage takes common sense and understanding. Understanding means responding to life's circumstances with insight—a perspective that looks at life through God's eyes. Understanding your mate from God's perspective results in accepting his or her differences and learning how God made your spouse to complement you.

A young husband recently told me, "My wife is a prosecuting attorney. In the year and half we have been married, I found out she is a strong woman. But I have finally understood that I don't have to compete with her. I can let her be who she is and not feel insecure about who I am."

What that husband found was an understanding of how he and his wife balanced each other. He realized that he could still lead her. Even though she might challenge him at times, it was good for him.

A Oneness Marriage needs knowledge—"keeping abreast of the facts." Every Sunday morning there are thousands of preachers who present polished gems of outstanding biblical knowledge. But what do we, the parishioners, usually do? At 11:55 the preacher finishes, we sing a song, there's a prayer, and we leave. When do we apply to our life what we've heard?

"Keeping abreast of the facts" is more than merely gathering information. It's having a teachable spirit that applies God's Word in the raw reality of life.

DIGGING DEEPER
    1. What kind of foundation does your marriage need? See Matthew 7:24-27.
    2. Read Philippians 2:1-8. How can you apply this passage in your effort to build a Oneness Marriage?
    3. What is a benefit of unity in marriage according to Ecclesiastes 4:9-12?

one that travelleth; and thy want as an armed man.^f

25

¹These *are* also proverbs of Solomon, which the men of Hezekiah king of Judah copied out.

²*It is* the glory of God to conceal a thing: but the honour of kings *is* to search out a matter. ³The heaven for height, and the earth for depth, and the heart of kings *is* unsearchable.

⁴Take away the dross from the silver, and there shall come forth a vessel for the finer. ⁵Take away the wicked *from* before the king, and his throne shall be established in righteousness.

⁶Put not forth thyself in the presence of the king, and stand not in the place of great *men*: ⁷For better *it is* that it be said unto thee, Come up hither; than that thou shouldest be put lower in the presence of the prince whom thine eyes have seen.

⁸Go not forth hastily to strive, lest *thou know not* what to do in the end thereof, when thy neighbour hath put thee to shame. ⁹Debate thy cause with thy neighbour *himself*, and discover not a secret^a to another: ¹⁰Lest he that heareth *it* put thee to shame, and thine infamy turn not away.

¹¹A word fitly^b spoken *is like* apples of gold in pictures of silver. ¹²*As* an earring of gold, and an ornament of fine gold, *so is* a wise reprover upon an obedient ear.

¹³As the cold of snow in the time of harvest, *so is* a faithful messenger to

---

^f an . . . : Heb. a man of shield
^a a secret . . . : or, the secret of
^b fitly . . . : Heb. spoken upon his wheels

them that send him: for he refresheth the soul of his masters.

¹⁴Whoso boasteth himself of a false gift *is like* clouds and wind without rain.

¹⁵By long forbearing is a prince persuaded, and a soft tongue breaketh the bone.

¹⁶Hast thou found honey? eat so much as is sufficient for thee, lest thou be filled therewith, and vomit it.

¹⁷Withdraw° thy foot from thy neighbour's house; lest he be weary of thee, and *so* hate thee.

¹⁸A man that beareth false witness against his neighbour *is* a maul, and a sword, and a sharp arrow.

¹⁹Confidence in an unfaithful man in time of trouble *is like* a broken tooth, and a foot out of joint.

²⁰*As* he that taketh away a garment in cold weather, *and as* vinegar upon nitre, so *is* he that singeth songs to an heavy heart.

²¹If thine enemy be hungry, give

Devotional Moment
Giving

25:14 The average American receives dozens of requests for money each year. While this verse doesn't specify which churches, missionaries, or organizations are worthy of our support, it does remind us of an important principle: *We must live up to our financial commitments.* Few letdowns are as disheartening to a ministry as waiting for a promised, much-needed gift that never arrives. Churches and other Christian groups depend on the prayers and giving of their supporters. Perhaps this is a good time to review the checkbook to see if you have been giving as you promised.

Devotional Moment
Wearing Out a Welcome

25:17 A home is a special place. Among other things, it is a haven from other people. So be careful how much and how often you venture into others' homes and private lives. Even if they've invited you in, it's possible to show up too often or get too close. Keep this in mind especially if you have children who go over to neighbors' houses to play. Sometimes it's better to say, "We need to let them have some time to themselves." You can also call ahead and ask if it's OK. Then at least they have the opportunity to say no without a face-to-face encounter. Respecting your neighbor's space is one way to keep the peace between friends.

---

him bread to eat; and if he be thirsty, give him water to drink: ²²For thou shalt heap coals of fire upon his head, and the LORD shall reward thee.

²³The north wind driveth away rain: so *doth* an angry countenance a backbiting tongue.

²⁴*It is* better to dwell in the corner of the housetop, than with a brawling woman and in a wide house.

²⁵*As* cold waters to a thirsty soul, so *is* good news from a far country.

²⁶A righteous man falling down before the wicked *is as* a troubled fountain, and a corrupt spring.

²⁷*It is* not good to eat much honey: so *for men* to search their own glory *is not* glory.

²⁸He that *hath* no rule over his own spirit *is like* a city *that is* broken down, *and* without walls.

26

¹As snow in summer, and as rain in harvest, so honour is not seemly for a fool.

ᶜ Withdraw . . . : or, Let thy foot be seldom in

²As the bird by wandering, as the swallow by flying, so the curse causeless shall not come.

³A whip for the horse, a bridle for the ass, and a rod for the fool's back.

⁴Answer not a fool according to his folly, lest thou also be like unto him. ⁵Answer a fool according to his folly, lest he be wise in his own conceit^a.

⁶He that sendeth a message by the hand of a fool cutteth off the feet, *and* drinketh damage^b. ⁷The legs of the lame are not equal: so *is* a parable in the mouth of fools. ⁸As he that bindeth^c a stone in a sling, so *is* he that giveth honour to a fool. ⁹*As* a thorn goeth up into the hand of a drunkard, so *is* a parable in the mouth of fools.

¹⁰The great^d *God* that formed all *things* both rewardeth the fool, and rewardeth transgressors.

¹¹As a dog returneth to his vomit, *so* a fool returneth to his folly^e.

¹²Seest thou a man wise in his own conceit? *there is* more hope of a fool than of him.

¹³The slothful *man* saith, *There is* a lion in the way; a lion *is* in the streets.

¹⁴As the door turneth upon his hinges, so *doth* the slothful upon his bed.

¹⁵The slothful hideth his hand in *his* bosom; it grieveth^f him to bring it again to his mouth.

¹⁶The sluggard *is* wiser in his own conceit than seven men that can render a reason.

¹⁷He that passeth by, *and* meddleth^g with strife *belonging* not to him, *is like* one that taketh a dog by the ears.

¹⁸As a mad *man* who casteth firebrands^h, arrows, and death, ¹⁹So *is* the man *that* deceiveth his neighbour, and saith, Am not I in sport?

²⁰Where noⁱ wood is, *there* the fire goeth out: so where *there is* no talebearer, the strife ceaseth. ²¹*As* coals *are* to burning coals, and wood to fire; so *is* a contentious man to kindle strife. ²²The words of a talebearer *are* as wounds, and they go down into the innermost parts of the belly.

²³Burning lips and a wicked heart *are like* a potsherd covered with silver dross.

²⁴He that hateth dissembleth^j with his lips, and layeth up deceit within him; ²⁵When he speaketh^k fair, believe him not: for *there are* seven abominations in his heart. ²⁶*Whose* hatred is covered by deceit, his wickedness shall be shewed before the *whole* congregation.

²⁷Whoso diggeth a pit shall fall therein: and he that rolleth a stone, it will return upon him.

---

^a conceit: Heb. eyes
^b damage: or, violence
^c bindeth . . . : or, putteth a precious stone in an heap of stones
^d The great . . . : or, A great man grieveth all, and he hireth the fool, he hireth also transgressors
^e returneth to his folly: Heb. iterateth his folly
^f it grieveth . . . : or, he is weary
^g meddleth: or, is enraged
^h firebrands: Heb. flames, or, sparks
ⁱ Where no . . . : Heb. Without wood
^j dissembleth: or, is known
^k speaketh . . . : Heb. maketh his voice gracious

²⁸A lying tongue hateth *those that are* afflicted by it; and a flattering mouth worketh ruin.

27

¹Boast not thyself of to morrow; for thou knowest not what a day may bring forth.

²Let another man praise thee, and not thine own mouth; a stranger, and not thine own lips.

³A stone *is* heavy[a], and the sand weighty; but a fool's wrath *is* heavier than them both. ⁴Wrath[b] *is* cruel, and anger *is* outrageous; but who *is* able to stand before envy?

⁵Open rebuke *is* better than secret love. ⁶Faithful *are* the wounds of a friend; but the kisses of an enemy *are* deceitful[c].

⁷The full soul loatheth[d] an honeycomb; but to the hungry soul every bitter thing is sweet.

⁸As a bird that wandereth from her nest, so *is* a man that wandereth from his place.

Devotional Moment

•

Absentee Parent

27:8 Some parents have jobs that require a lot of out-of-town travel. Others put in lots of overtime. Add to these heavy work responsibilities the fact that many parents also are involved in time-consuming hobbies, and it's no wonder that many families lack intimacy. Neither is it surprising that so many marriages are torn apart by infidelity. Think about your own work and leisure habits. Are you spending enough time at home with your spouse and kids?

Devotional Moment

•

Complaining

27:15-16 Cranky, complaining people are no fun to live with. Their whining mars everything and everyone. If you are that kind of person, determine to change your behavior with God's help. If you live with a chronic complainer, talk about the behavior together to determine whether the constant whining is merely a bad habit that needs to be broken or is a symptom of a deeper discontent that needs to be addressed.

⁹Ointment and perfume rejoice the heart: so *doth* the sweetness of a man's friend by hearty counsel. ¹⁰Thine own friend, and thy father's friend, forsake not; neither go into thy brother's house in the day of thy calamity: *for* better *is* a neighbour *that is* near than a brother far off.

¹¹My son, be wise, and make my heart glad, that I may answer him that reproacheth me.

¹²A prudent *man* foreseeth the evil, *and* hideth himself; *but* the simple pass on, *and* are punished.

¹³Take his garment that is surety for a stranger, and take a pledge of him for a strange woman.

¹⁴He that blesseth his friend with a loud voice, rising early in the morning, it shall be counted a curse to him.

¹⁵A continual dropping in a very rainy day and a contentious woman are alike. ¹⁶Whosoever hideth her hideth the wind, and the ointment of his right hand, *which* bewrayeth *itself*.

---

[a] heavy: Heb. heaviness
[b] Wrath . . . : Heb. Wrath is cruelty, and anger an overflowing
[c] deceitful: or, earnest, or, frequent
[d] loatheth: Heb. treadeth under foot

Worship
in Your Home

THE DISCIPLINE OF DEVOTIONS

He that tilleth his land shall have plenty of bread; but he that followeth after vain persons shall have poverty enough.
Proverbs 28:19

We discipline our children so that they will learn to behave. We discipline ourselves because we recognize the payoff in some unpleasant tasks. Sometimes getting good things accomplished takes discipline.

All good things cost something. Skills are developed through hard work. Christian living comes from disciplined Bible study, prayer, and worship.

Having family devotions takes discipline, too.

It is much easier not to bother with family devotions. It takes conscious effort, planning, and work. Sometimes you have to get it going when no one feels like it.

Yet devotions are worth it. To get to know God and to worship him together is in a sense costly—but there are rich rewards.

A word of caution. Sometimes we parents push too hard. ("It's good for you.") That is not the proper use of discipline in family devotions. Pushing does not help children become followers of Christ.

Devotions should be times of delight, but don't wait for everyone to feel like it before getting started. As much as possible, make family devotions fun and enjoyable. Hopefully your child will learn each time that good things are worth the effort. Being a better Christian, a better follower of Christ, certainly is.

¹⁷Iron sharpeneth iron; so a man sharpeneth the countenance of his friend.

¹⁸Whoso keepeth the fig tree shall eat the fruit thereof: so he that waiteth on his master shall be honoured.

¹⁹As in water face *answereth* to face, so the heart of man to man.

²⁰Hell and destruction are never⁴ full; so the eyes of man are never satisfied.

²¹*As* the fining pot for silver, and the furnace for gold; so *is* a man to his praise.

²²Though thou shouldest bray a fool in a mortar among wheat with a pestle, *yet* will not his foolishness depart from him.

²³Be thou diligent to know the state of thy flocks, *and* look⁴ well to thy herds. ²⁴For riches⁸ *are* not for ever: and doth the crown *endure* to every generation? ²⁵The hay appeareth, and the tender grass sheweth itself, and herbs of the mountains are gathered. ²⁶The lambs *are* for thy clothing, and the goats *are* the price of the field. ²⁷And *thou shalt have* goats' milk enough for thy food, for the food of thy household, and *for* the maintenance⁴ for thy maidens.

28

¹The wicked flee when no man pursueth: but the righteous are bold as a lion.

²For the transgression of a land many *are* the princes thereof: but by a

---

⁴ never: Heb. not
⁴ look . . . : Heb. set thy heart
⁸ riches: Heb. strength
⁴ maintenance: Heb. life

man of understanding *and* knowledge the state *thereof* shall be prolonged.

³A poor man that oppresseth the poor *is like* a sweeping rain which leaveth no food.

⁴They that forsake the law praise the wicked: but such as keep the law contend with them.

⁵Evil men understand not judgment: but they that seek the LORD understand all *things*.

⁶Better *is* the poor that walketh in his uprightness, than *he that is* perverse *in his* ways, though he *be* rich.

⁷Whoso keepeth the law *is* a wise son: but he that is a companionª of riotous *men* shameth his father.

⁸He that by usury and unjust gain increaseth his substance, he shall gather it for him that will pity the poor.

⁹He that turneth away his ear from hearing the law, even his prayer *shall be* abomination.

¹⁰Whoso causeth the righteous to go astray in an evil way, he shall fall himself into his own pit: but the upright shall have good *things* in possession.

¹¹The rich man *is* wise in his own conceit; but the poor that hath understanding searcheth him out.

¹²When righteous *men* do rejoice, *there is* great glory: but when the wicked rise, a man is hiddenᵇ.

¹³He that covereth his sins shall not prosper: but whoso confesseth and forsaketh *them* shall have mercy.

¹⁴Happy *is* the man that feareth alway: but he that hardeneth his heart shall fall into mischief.

¹⁵*As* a roaring lion, and a ranging bear; *so is* a wicked ruler over the poor people.

¹⁶The prince that wanteth understanding *is* also a great oppressor: *but* he that hateth covetousness shall prolong *his* days.

¹⁷A man that doeth violence to the blood of *any* person shall flee to the pit; let no man stay him.

¹⁸Whoso walketh uprightly shall be saved: but *he that is* perverse *in his* ways shall fall at once.

¹⁹He that tilleth his land shall have plenty of bread: but he that followeth after vain *persons* shall have poverty enough.

²⁰A faithful man shall abound with blessings: but he that maketh haste to be rich shall not be innocentᶜ.

²¹To have respect of persons *is* not good: for for a piece of bread *that* man will transgress.

²²He that hastethᵈ to be rich *hath* an evil eye, and considereth not that poverty shall come upon him.

²³He that rebuketh a man afterwards shall find more favour than he that flattereth with the tongue.

²⁴Whoso robbeth his father or his mother, and saith, *It is* no transgression; the same *is* the companion of a destroyerᵉ.

²⁵He that is of a proud heart stirreth up strife: but he that putteth his trust in the LORD shall be made fat.

ª is a companion . . . : or, feedeth gluttons
ᵇ hidden: or, sought for
ᶜ innocent: or, unpunished
ᵈ hasteth . . . : or, hath and evil eye hasteth to be rich
ᵉ a destroyer: Heb. a man destroying

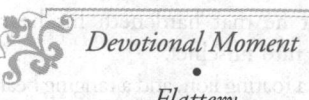

Devotional Moment
•
Flattery

28:23 Here we are counseled against using flattery when frankness, even though it may hurt, is more appropriate. Sometimes we flatter people because we want something from them. Other times we use flattery because we are afraid of how they might react to the truth. But in the long run, people learn to trust those who will be lovingly frank with them. Whenever there is an ugly truth that needs to come to the surface, don't gloss over it with flattery. You don't have to be cruel or rough—just honest.

²⁶He that trusteth in his own heart is a fool: but whoso walketh wisely, he shall be delivered.

²⁷He that giveth unto the poor shall not lack: but he that hideth his eyes shall have many a curse.

²⁸When the wicked rise, men hide themselves: but when they perish, the righteous increase.

29

¹He[a], that being often reproved hardeneth *his* neck, shall suddenly be destroyed, and that without remedy.

²When the righteous are in authority, the people rejoice: but when the wicked beareth rule, the people mourn.

³Whoso loveth wisdom rejoiceth his father: but he that keepeth company with harlots spendeth *his* substance.

⁴The king by judgment establisheth the land: but he[b] that receiveth gifts overthroweth it.

⁵A man that flattereth his neighbour spreadeth a net for his feet.

⁶In the transgression of an evil man *there is* a snare: but the righteous doth sing and rejoice.

⁷The righteous considereth the cause of the poor: *but* the wicked regardeth not to know *it.*

⁸Scornful men bring[c] a city into a snare: but wise *men* turn away wrath.

⁹If a wise man contendeth with a foolish man, whether he rage or laugh, *there is* no rest.

¹⁰The bloodthirsty[d] hate the upright: but the just seek his soul.

¹¹A fool uttereth all his mind: but a wise *man* keepeth it in till afterwards.

¹²If a ruler hearken to lies, all his servants *are* wicked.

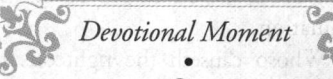

Devotional Moment
•
Sex

29:3 When it comes to sex, the world says that anything goes as long as you are careful. Thanks to that advice, we are faced with unprecedented numbers of teenage pregnancies, record numbers of abortions, powerful new strains of sexually transmitted diseases, and the horrible specter of AIDS. And let's not forget that behind all the cold, impersonal statistics are individual lives that have been shattered by guilt, regret, and physical suffering. We parents need to redouble our efforts to teach our children the value of sexual purity. If we can help our kids understand that God puts limits on sex for our own good, they will be more likely to live wisely and have no cause for regret.

[a] He . . . : Heb. A man of reproofs
[b] he . . . : Heb. a man of oblations
[c] bring . . . : or, set a city on fire
[d] The bloodthirsty: Heb. Men of blood

¹³The poor and the deceitfulᵉ man meet together: the LORD lighteneth both their eyes.

¹⁴The king that faithfully judgeth the poor, his throne shall be established for ever.

¹⁵The rod and reproof give wisdom: but a child left *to himself* bringeth his mother to shame.

¹⁶When the wicked are multiplied, transgression increaseth: but the righteous shall see their fall.

¹⁷Correct thy son, and he shall give thee rest; yea, he shall give delight unto thy soul.

¹⁸Where *there is* no vision, the people perishᶠ: but he that keepeth the law, happy *is* he.

¹⁹A servant will not be corrected by words: for though he understand he will not answer.

²⁰Seest thou a man *that is* hasty in his wordsᵍ? *there is* more hope of a fool than of him.

²¹He that delicately bringeth up his servant from a child shall have him become *his* son at the length.

²²An angry man stirreth up strife, and a furious man aboundeth in transgression.

²³A man's pride shall bring him low: but honour shall uphold the humble in spirit.

²⁴Whoso is partner with a thief hateth his own soul: he heareth cursing, and bewrayeth *it* not.

²⁵The fear of man bringeth a snare: but whoso putteth his trust in the LORD shall be safeʰ.

²⁶Many seek the ruler'sⁱ favour; but *every* man's judgment *cometh* from the LORD.

²⁷An unjust man *is* an abomination to the just: and *he that is* upright in the way *is* abomination to the wicked.

30

¹The words of Agur the son of Jakeh, *even* the prophecy: the man spake unto Ithiel, even unto Ithiel and Ucal, ²Surely I *am* more brutish than *any* man, and have not the understanding of a man. ³I neither learned wisdom, nor haveᵃ the knowledge of the holy. ⁴Who hath ascended up into heaven, or descended? who hath gathered the wind in his fists? who hath bound the waters in a garment? who hath established all the ends of the earth? what *is* his name, and what *is* his son's name, if thou canst tell? ⁵Every word of God *is* pureᵇ: he *is* a shield unto them that put their trust in him. ⁶Add thou not unto his words, lest he reprove thee, and thou be found a liar.

⁷Two *things* have I required of thee; denyᶜ me *them* not before I die: ⁸Remove far from me vanity and lies: give me neither poverty nor riches; feed me

---

ᵉ the deceitful . . . : or, the usurer
ᶠ perish: or, is made naked
ᵍ words: or, matters?
ʰ safe: Heb. set on high
ⁱ the ruler's . . . : Heb. the face of a ruler
ᵃ have: Heb. know
ᵇ pure: Heb. purified
ᶜ deny . . . : Heb. withhold not from me

Family Traditions

No Time to Waste

PROVERBS 31

The Proverbs 31 woman has left a challenging example to do all and be all. She watches over her family and never wastes her time. What ordinary woman today wouldn't feel at least a bit intimidated by her? Many moms today have little time for one-on-one interaction with their children after all the practical necessities are done.

How can you maximize the time you do have? Even brushing your teeth at the same time at the same sink counts! Here are some other suggestions:

- Pick up your kids for lunch and go someplace where you can buy something to drink and eat your sack lunch.
- Grocery shop together, talking about what you need, what you don't need, and how advertisers try to sell.
- Use driving time to talk; turn the radio off.
- Do ironing or sewing in a room where the children have toys or tables for homework.
- Make the kitchen a place to hang out. Reserve a corner where kids, neighbors, and pets can be out of the way yet still part of the action.
- Celebrate weekends. Make a big deal of Friday nights by doing things that the kids love. Have a game night, candy night, shopping night, pizza night, skating night—whatever makes them look forward to being with you.
- Make a lush and bountiful brunch on sleep-in Saturday mornings. Make something exotic, such as strawberry waffles with cream, poppy-seed muffins, bacon and shrimp omelets, or slushy fruit drinks. Create centerpieces and light the candles. Do whatever says, "This is our morning to be together, and we're going to enjoy it!"
- Clean house together. Set limited periods of time to pick up, dust and vacuum, sort and scrub. Set an alarm and take breaks together with rewards, such as having a cup of cocoa or sitting in the sunshine.
- Affirm, affirm between everything. There will be plenty of "opportunities" for correcting, so use every chance you get to give a hug, say yes, and compliment your special kid.
- Go to church together. As much as you can, worship and pray together.
- Keep a playful attitude. You can teach a child anything at all if you make a game of it. Laugh at little things, tickle often (if your child enjoys it), make games of drudgery. Be a fun person and make your home a fun place to bring friends.

Not a single moment can be lived over again. Each one counts for eternity, for we are growing the most precious resource on earth: families. Make family time a tradition.

with food convenient[d] for me: [9]Lest I be full, and deny[e] thee, and say, Who *is* the LORD? or lest I be poor, and steal, and take the name of my God *in vain.*

[10]Accuse[f] not a servant unto his master, lest he curse thee, and thou be found guilty. [11]*There is* a generation *that* curseth their father, and doth not bless their mother. [12]*There is* a generation *that are* pure in their own eyes, and *yet* is not washed from their filthiness. [13]*There is* a generation, O how lofty are their eyes! and their eyelids are lifted up. [14]*There is* a generation, whose teeth *are as* swords, and their jaw teeth *as* knives, to devour the poor from off the earth, and the needy from *among* men.

[15]The horseleach hath two daughters, *crying,* Give, give. There are three *things that* are never satisfied, *yea,* four *things* say not, *It is* enough: [16]The grave; and the barren womb; the earth *that* is not filled with water; and the fire *that* saith not, *It is* enough. [17]The eye *that* mocketh at *his* father, and despiseth to obey *his* mother, the ravens of the valley[g] shall pick it out, and the young eagles shall eat it.

[18]There be three *things which* are too wonderful for me, yea, four which I know not: [19]The way of an eagle in the air; the way of a serpent upon a rock; the way of a ship in the midst[h] of the sea; and the way of a man with a maid. [20]Such *is* the way of an adulterous woman; she eateth, and wipeth her mouth, and saith,

I have done no wickedness. [21]For three *things* the earth is disquieted, and for four *which* it cannot bear: [22]For a servant when he reigneth; and a fool when he is filled with meat; [23]For an odious *woman* when she is married; and an handmaid that is heir to her mistress.

[24]There be four *things which are* little upon the earth, but they *are* exceeding[i] wise: [25]The ants *are* a people not strong, yet they prepare their meat in the summer; [26]The conies *are but* a feeble folk, yet make they their houses in the rocks; [27]The locusts have no king, yet go they forth all of them by bands; [28]The spider taketh hold with her hands, and is in kings' palaces.

[29]There be three *things* which go well, yea, four are comely in going: [30]A lion *which is* strongest among beasts, and turneth not away for any; [31]A greyhound[j]; an he goat also; and a king, against whom *there is* no rising up. [32]If thou hast done foolishly in lifting up thyself, or if thou hast thought evil, *lay* thine hand upon thy mouth. [33]Surely the churning of milk bringeth forth butter, and the wringing of the nose bringeth forth blood: so the forcing of wrath bringeth forth strife.

31

[1]The words of king Lemuel, the prophecy that his mother taught him. [2]What, my son? and what, the son of my womb? and

---

[d] convenient . . . : Heb. of my allowance
[e] deny . . . : Heb. belie thee
[f] Accuse . . . : Heb. Hurt not with thy tongue
[g] the valley: or, the brook
[h] midst: Heb. heart
[i] exceeding . . . : Heb. wise, made wise
[j] greyhound: or, horse: Heb. girt in the loins

what, the son of my vows? ³Give not thy strength unto women, nor thy ways to that which destroyeth kings. ⁴*It is* not for kings, O Lemuel, *it is* not for kings to drink wine; nor for princes strong drink: ⁵Lest they drink, and forget the law, and pervert the judgment of any of the afflicted. ⁶Give strong drink unto him that is ready to perish, and wine unto those that be of heavy hearts. ⁷Let him drink, and forget his poverty, and remember his misery no more. ⁸Open thy mouth for the dumb in the cause of all such as are appointed to destruction. ⁹Open thy mouth, judge righteously, and plead the cause of the poor and needy.

¹⁰Who can find a virtuous woman? for her price *is* far above rubies. ¹¹The heart of her husband doth safely trust in her, so that he shall have no need of spoil. ¹²She will do him good and not evil all the days of her life. ¹³She seeketh wool, and flax, and worketh willingly with her hands. ¹⁴She is like the merchants' ships; she bringeth her food from afar. ¹⁵She riseth also while it is yet night, and giveth meat to her household, and a portion to her maidens. ¹⁶She considereth a field, and buyethª it: with the fruit of her hands she planteth a vineyard. ¹⁷She girdeth her loins with strength, and strengtheneth her arms. ¹⁸She perceiveth that her merchandise *is* good: her candle goeth not out by night. ¹⁹She layeth her hands to the spindle, and her hands hold the distaff. ²⁰She stretcheth out her hand to the poor; yea, she reacheth forth her hands to the needy. ²¹She is not afraid of the snow for her household: for all her household *are* clothed with scarletᵇ. ²²She maketh herself coverings of tapestry; her clothing *is* silk and purple. ²³Her husband is known in the gates, when he sitteth among the elders of the land. ²⁴She maketh fine linen, and selleth *it*; and delivereth girdles unto the merchant. ²⁵Strength and honour *are* her clothing; and she shall rejoice in time to come. ²⁶She openeth her mouth with wisdom; and in her tongue *is* the law of kindness. ²⁷She looketh well to the ways of her household, and eateth not the bread of idleness. ²⁸Her children arise up, and call her blessed; her husband *also*, and he praiseth her. ²⁹Many daughters have done virtuously, but thou excellest them all. ³⁰Favour *is* deceitful, and beauty *is* vain: *but* a woman *that* feareth the LORD, she shall be praised. ³¹Give her of the fruit of her hands; and let her own works praise her in the gates.

ª buyeth: Heb. taketh
ᵇ scarlet: or, double garments

ECCLESIASTES

Purpose
To spare future generations the bitterness of learning through their own experience that life is meaningless apart from God

Author
Solomon, although no passages mention him by name

To Whom Written
Solomon's subjects in particular, and all people in general

Date Written
Probably around 935 B.C., late in Solomon's life

Setting
Solomon looks back on his life, much of which was lived apart from God

Key Verse
"Let us hear the conclusion of the whole matter: Fear God, and keep his commandments: for this is the whole duty of man" (12:13).

Reading Ecclesiastes too early, too soon in life, is like viewing the Sistine Chapel as an infant. Genuine appreciation requires maturity.

The writer of this Bible book was an older man, perhaps a grandfather, who wonders why his time has gone so fast and what it all means. He's looking for the bottom line.

We all want the answers he seeks, but we're not all ready to ask his questions. Children are too busy collecting experiences and defining themselves. Adults are too busy keeping up with a schedule of demands they never imagined. But we all need to acknowledge the bottom line that Ecclesiastes describes. The key to what's real is here.

Reading Ecclesiastes may remind you of listening to Grandpa's advice. There's a tone of solemn sadness here, of youth spent and often wasted, of little ahead but the grave.

As you read this book, imagine that you're sitting at Grandma's knee again, like a child, hearing the quiet reflections of one who has lived long and whose vision has turned, through the years, from cradles and diapers, career and home, to . . . the Center.

1

¹The words of the Preacher, the son of David, king in Jerusalem. ²Vanity of vanities, saith the Preacher, vanity of vanities; all *is* vanity. ³What profit hath a man of all his labour which he taketh under the sun?

⁴*One* generation passeth away, and *another* generation cometh: but the earth abideth for ever. ⁵The sun also ariseth, and the sun goeth down, and hasteth^a to his place where he arose. ⁶The wind goeth toward the south, and turneth about unto the north; it whirleth about continually, and the wind returneth again according to his circuits. ⁷All the rivers run into the sea; yet the sea *is* not full; unto the place from whence the rivers come, thither they return^b again. ⁸All things *are* full of labour; man cannot utter *it*: the eye is not satisfied with seeing, nor the ear filled with hearing.

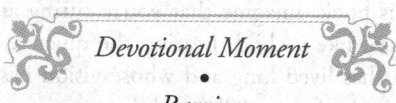

Devotional Moment

Barriers

1:12-15 Solomon lamented his frustration that, even as king, he could not accomplish everything, correct all the problems, and meet all the needs he saw. Similarly, we cannot fix everything in our lives. At times we lack knowledge, we lack energy, we lack resources. And many of the problems we encounter are the result of other people's choices over which we have no control. Acknowledge the barriers in your situation, and ask God for strength to persevere as you fulfill your role and responsibilities.

⁹The thing that hath been, it *is* that which shall be; and that which is done *is* that which shall be done: and there *is* no new *thing* under the sun. ¹⁰Is there *any* thing whereof it may be said, See, this *is* new? it hath been already of old time, which was before us. ¹¹*There is* no remembrance of former *things*; neither shall there be *any* remembrance of *things* that are to come with *those* that shall come after.

¹²I the Preacher was king over Israel in Jerusalem. ¹³And I gave my heart to seek and search out by wisdom concerning all *things* that are done under heaven: this sore travail hath God given to the sons of man to be exercised therewith. ¹⁴I have seen all the works that are done under the sun; and, behold, all *is* vanity and vexation of spirit. ¹⁵*That which is* crooked cannot be made straight: and that which is wanting^c cannot be numbered. ¹⁶I communed with mine own heart, saying, Lo, I am come to great estate, and have gotten more wisdom than all *they* that have been before me in Jerusalem: yea, my heart had great experience of wisdom and knowledge. ¹⁷And I gave my heart to know wisdom, and to know madness and folly: I perceived that this also is vexation of spirit. ¹⁸For in much wisdom *is* much grief: and he that increaseth knowledge increaseth sorrow.

2

¹I said in mine heart, Go to now, I will prove thee with mirth, therefore enjoy pleasure: and, behold, this also *is* vanity.

---

^a hasteth: Heb. panteth
^b return . . . : Heb. return to go
^c that which is wanting: Heb. defect

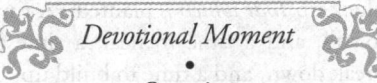

Devotional Moment

Overtime

2:4-11 Solomon had many great accomplishments. He built houses, vineyards, reservoirs, herds; he acquired great treasures. "I looked on all the works that my hands had wrought . . . and, behold, all was vanity," he said (v. 11). While we must work hard as we start a home, begin a career, or build a business, remember Solomon's experience. Don't work sixty hours a week (or more) just to make a name for yourself. You may accomplish a lot, as Solomon did. But will it matter as much in your old age or will you just have been "chasing the wind"?

²I said of laughter, It is mad: and of mirth, What doeth it? ³I sought in mine heart to giveᵃ myself unto wine, yet acquainting mine heart with wisdom; and to lay hold on folly, till I might see what was that good for the sons of men, which they should do under the heaven all the days of their life. ⁴I made me great works; I builded me houses; I planted me vineyards: ⁵I made me gardens and orchards, and I planted trees in them of all kind of fruits: ⁶I made me pools of water, to water therewith the wood that bringeth forth trees: ⁷I got me servants and maidens, and had servants bornᵇ in my house; also I had great possessions of great and small cattle above all that were in Jerusalem before me: ⁸I gathered me also silver and gold, and the peculiar treasure of kings and of the provinces: I gat me men singers and women singers, and the de-

lights of the sons of men, as musical instruments, and that of all sorts. ⁹So I was great, and increased more than all that were before me in Jerusalem: also my wisdom remained with me. ¹⁰And whatsoever mine eyes desired I kept not from them, I withheld not my heart from any joy; for my heart rejoiced in all my labour: and this was my portion of all my labour. ¹¹Then I looked on all the works that my hands had wrought, and on the labour that I had laboured to do: and, behold, all was vanity and vexation of spirit, and there was no profit under the sun.

¹²And I turned myself to behold wisdom, and madness, and folly: for what can the man do that cometh after the king? even that which hath been already done. ¹³Then I saw thatᶜ wisdom excelleth folly, as far as light excelleth darkness. ¹⁴The wise man's eyes are in his head; but the fool walketh in darkness: and I myself perceived also that one event happeneth to them all. ¹⁵Then said I in my heart, As it happeneth to the fool, so it happeneth even to me; and why was I then more wise? Then I said in my heart, that this also is vanity. ¹⁶For there is no remembrance of the wise more than of the fool for ever; seeing that which now is in the days to come shall all be forgotten. And how dieth the wise man? as the fool.

¹⁷Therefore I hated life; because the work that is wrought under the sun is grievous unto me: for all is vanity and vexation of spirit. ¹⁸Yea, I hated all my labour which I had takenᵈ under the

---

ᵃ to give . . . : Heb. to draw my flesh with wine
ᵇ servants born . . . : Heb. sons of my house
ᶜ that . . . : Heb. that there is an excellency in wisdom more than in folly, etc
ᵈ taken: Heb. laboured

sun: because I should leave it unto the man that shall be after me. [19]And who knoweth whether he shall be a wise *man* or a fool? yet shall he have rule over all my labour wherein I have laboured, and wherein I have shewed myself wise under the sun. This *is* also vanity. [20]Therefore I went about to cause my heart to despair of all the labour which I took under the sun. [21]For there is a man whose labour *is* in wisdom, and in knowledge, and in equity; yet to a man that hath not laboured therein shall he leave[e] it *for* his portion. This also *is* vanity and a great evil. [22]For what hath man of all his labour, and of the vexation of his heart, wherein he hath laboured under the sun? [23]For all his days *are* sorrows, and his travail grief; yea, his heart taketh not rest in the night. This is also vanity. [24]*There is* nothing better for a man, *than* that he should eat and drink, and *that* he should make his soul enjoy good in his labour. This also I saw, that it *was* from the hand of God. [25]For who can eat, or who else can hasten *hereunto*, more than I? [26]For *God* giveth to a man that *is* good in his sight wisdom, and knowledge, and joy: but to the sinner he giveth travail, to gather and to heap up, that he may give to *him that is* good before God. This also *is* vanity and vexation of spirit.

3

[1]To every *thing there is* a season, and a time to every purpose under the heaven: [2]A time to be born, and a time to die; a time to plant, and a time to pluck up *that which is* planted; [3]A time to kill, and a time to heal; a time to break down, and a time to build up; [4]A time to weep, and a time to laugh; a time to mourn, and a time to dance; [5]A time to cast away stones, and a time to gather stones together; a time to embrace, and a time to refrain from embracing; [6]A time to get[a], and a time to lose; a time to keep, and a time to cast away; [7]A time to rend, and a time to sew; a time to keep silence, and a time to speak; [8]A time to love, and a time to hate; a time of war, and a time of peace. [9]What profit hath he that worketh in that wherein he laboureth? [10]I have seen the travail, which God hath given to the sons of men to be exercised in it.

[11]He hath made every *thing* beautiful in his time: also he hath set the world in their heart, so that no man can find out the work that God maketh from the beginning to the end. [12]I know that *there is* no good in them,

Devotional Moment

Consistency

3:1-8 Sometimes we feel strong and ready to praise God, and sometimes we feel down and need his help. In Solomon's words, "To every thing there is a season . . ." Quite naturally, we want just the good times—births, dancing, and healing. But in this world affected by sin, joy is interspersed with heartache. Loving God and praising him for his matchless worth is the only way for us to find peace and consistency in the inconsistent ups and downs of life.

---

[e] leave: Heb. give
[a] get: or, seek

but for *a man* to rejoice, and to do good in his life. [13]And also that every man should eat and drink, and enjoy the good of all his labour, it *is* the gift of God. [14]I know that, whatsoever God doeth, it shall be for ever: nothing can be put to it, nor any thing taken from it: and God doeth *it,* that *men* should fear before him. [15]That which hath been is now; and that which is to be hath already been; and God requireth that which is past[b].

[16]And moreover I saw under the sun the place of judgment, *that* wickedness *was* there; and the place of righteousness, *that* iniquity *was* there. [17]I said in mine heart, God shall judge the righteous and the wicked: for *there is* a time there for every purpose and for every work. [18]I said in mine heart concerning the estate of the sons of men, that God[c] might manifest them, and that they might see that they themselves are beasts. [19]For that which befalleth the sons of men befalleth beasts; even one thing befalleth them: as the one dieth, so dieth the other; yea, they have all one breath; so that a man hath no preeminence above a beast: for all *is* vanity. [20]All go unto one place; all are of the dust, and all turn to dust again. [21]Who knoweth the spirit of man[d] that goeth upward, and the spirit of the beast that goeth downward to the earth? [22]Wherefore I perceive that *there is* nothing better, than that a man should rejoice in his own

---

[b] that which is past: Heb. that which is driven away

[c] that God . . . : or, that they might clear God, and see, etc

[d] of man: Heb. of the sons of man

Worship
in Your Home

HUMOR AND DEVOTIONS—IS THERE A TIME TO LAUGH?

To every thing there is a season: . . . a time to weep, and a time to laugh; a time to mourn, and a time to dance.
Ecclesiastes 3:1, 4

Does God have a sense of humor? Is humor appropriate in devotions? If so, what kind?

The guidelines for humor in devotions should be much the same as in any other facet of life. After all, devotions are not merely brief times for talking in a more pious tone. They are an extension of how we live—or how we should live—all the time.

Here are some general guidelines: (1) Never laugh at someone, belittling that person. Making fun of a person is never funny. (2) Go ahead and laugh when others say something funny or point out a funny circumstance or a strange event in nature. Most people enjoy making others laugh. (3) If it's inappropriate outside of devotional time, it's inappropriate during devotional time.

Learning to laugh is part of the joy and delight of life, especially that of a Christian. It certainly is part of the delight that is so essential in devotions. The Bible says that "a merry heart doeth good like a medicine: but a broken spirit drieth the bones" (Prov. 17:22). Laughter is good—even in devotions.

works; for that *is* his portion: for who shall bring him to see what shall be after him?

4

¹So I returned, and considered all the oppressions that are done under the sun: and behold the tears of *such as were* oppressed, and they had no comforter; and on the side[a] of their oppressors *there was* power; but they had no comforter. ²Wherefore I praised the dead which are already dead more than the living which are yet alive. ³Yea, better *is* he than both they, which hath not yet been, who hath not seen the evil work that is done under the sun.

⁴Again, I considered all travail, and every right work, that for this a man is envied of his neighbour. This *is* also vanity and vexation of spirit. ⁵The fool foldeth his hands together, and eateth his own flesh. ⁶Better *is* an handful *with* quietness, than both the hands full *with* travail and vexation of spirit.

⁷Then I returned, and I saw vanity under the sun. ⁸There is one *alone*, and *there is* not a second; yea, he hath neither child nor brother: yet *is there* no end of all his labour; neither is his eye satisfied with riches; neither *saith he*, For whom do I labour, and bereave my soul of good? This *is* also vanity, yea, it *is* a sore travail. ⁹Two *are* better than one; because they have a good reward for their labour. ¹⁰For if they fall, the one will lift up his fellow: but woe to him *that is* alone when he falleth; for *he hath* not another to help him up. ¹¹Again, if two lie together, then they

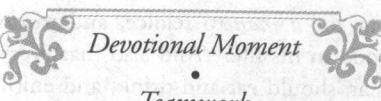

Devotional Moment
•
Teamwork

4:9-12 In our independent society we tend to think we can make it on our own. Not so. God designed us to need each other. Without teamwork, life can be unbearably difficult. If you are married, find ways to build on each other's strengths. If you are single, find ways to fulfill needs in your family and friendships. Stick together. Help each other out. Respect each other's strengths, and protect each other's weaknesses.

have heat: but how can one be warm *alone*? ¹²And if one prevail against him, two shall withstand him; and a threefold cord is not quickly broken.

¹³Better *is* a poor and a wise child than an old and foolish king, who will no more be admonished. ¹⁴For out of prison he cometh to reign; whereas also *he that is* born in his kingdom becometh poor. ¹⁵I considered all the living which walk under the sun, with the second child that shall stand up in his stead. ¹⁶*There is* no end of all the people, *even* of all that have been before them: they also that come after shall not rejoice in him. Surely this also *is* vanity and vexation of spirit.

5

¹Keep thy foot when thou goest to the house of God, and be more ready to hear, than to give the sacrifice of fools: for they consider not that they do evil. ²Be not rash with thy mouth, and let not thine heart be hasty to utter *any* thing[a] before God: for God *is* in heaven, and thou

---

ᵃ side: Heb. hand
ᵃ thing: or, word

Working Parents Need Help

by John and Carol Dettoni

Ecclesiastes 4:9-12 tells us that two are better than one—that all of us need help. Verse 12 also reminds us that the two need a third person—God. Raising children these days is difficult. Parents need help nurturing their children. They need each other and they need the Lord.

But life is often even more complicated and demanding for parents who have jobs in addition to child rearing. The stresses of life are multiplied because these parents simply don't have the time and energy that full-time parents have for their children.

Who has time? Most frustrations of working parents focus on one factor—*time.* There is little time for one's spouse, special friends, or children, and even less time to be alone. *Fatigue* enters in when the already busy, stretched parent is pushed for time that he or she does not have. Even mundane chores and the details of daily living become stresses.

Which of the following should the stressed parent put first: housework, child care, time for family and leisure, time for oneself, time for spouse or a special friend, or spiritual life? Some parents have learned how to prioritize. Like Mary in Luke 10:41-42, these parents choose what is better rather than being worried and upset about many things. But a number of parents are so overwhelmed that even thinking about their lives is out of the question.

There are no easy answers. Some parents work so their children may have the benefits that two incomes bring. The stresses and time commitment of working must be weighed against those benefits. But in many cases, there is no alternative to both parents working. Of course, most single parents have no choice: They must work to support themselves and their children.

Take heart. If you are a working parent, take heart. You are not alone, and you can do something to change your circumstances.

As Ecclesiastes says, "Two are better than one." Take advantage of the relationships God has placed in your life. If you are married, take time to talk to each other about your stresses. What causes the stress? Do your priorities reflect what they should? Do you place enough importance on nurturing your children and your marriage? If necessary, set new priorities.

Single parents need to find other single parents or close friends on whom they can depend. Seek out these people at church. They can become a crucial source of support in times of need.

And all parents need to find their spiritual strength in their relationship with the Lord.

Take inventory. Consider how much time you spend with your children each work day. How many minutes do you talk to, play with, and work alongside your children? Do your children get enough of your attention for them to learn from you? Think of two or three priorities you might set to help make more time for them each day.

When was the last time you went on a date with your spouse? If it was not in the last two weeks, what can you do together in the next seven days?

In what other ways can you juggle the household chores? For example, how can your children be involved in the shopping? Consider taking an hour or two over the next few weeks to teach older children how to help more.

Sundays look a lot like Saturdays for many people—a day to get work done. In what ways can you make Sunday a true day of rest? What can you shift to another day or put off indefinitely so you can have a more relaxed, family-renewing Sunday?

How can you reprioritize your time and activities? Determine what is important and cannot be left undone—for instance, the grocery shopping. Determine what can be left for another time, such as washing the car.

The task of parenting today is indeed difficult. But with God's guidance and thoughtful effort, you can overcome these modern challenges.

DIGGING DEEPER

1. Children are a gift from God that we should receive gratefully and joyfully (Gen. 1:28; 4:1, 25; 17:16; 28:3; 33:5; Ruth 4:12-14; 1 Sam. 1:17, 19-20; Job 1:21; Pss. 113:9; 127:3-5). What are some tangible ways dual-working and single parents can show that they value their children?

2. One of the roles parents must fill involves teaching their children to love and obey God (Deut. 6:1-9). What special challenges does this pose for dual-working and single parents? How can working parents meet the challenges?

3. What is a parent's job? See 1 Thessalonians 2:11-12.

upon earth: therefore let thy words be few. ³For a dream cometh through the multitude of business; and a fool's voice *is known* by multitude of words.

⁴When thou vowest a vow unto God, defer not to pay it; for *he hath* no pleasure in fools: pay that which thou hast vowed. ⁵Better *is it* that thou shouldest not vow, than that thou shouldest vow and not pay. ⁶Suffer not thy mouth to cause thy flesh to sin; neither say thou before the angel, that it *was* an error: wherefore should God be angry at thy voice, and destroy the work of thine hands? ⁷For in the multitude of dreams and many words *there are* also *divers* vanities: but fear thou God. ⁸If thou seest the oppression of the poor, and violent perverting of judgment and justice in a province, marvel not at the matter: for *he that is* higher than the highest regardeth; and *there be* higher than they.

⁹Moreover the profit of the earth is for all: the king *himself* is served by the field. ¹⁰He that loveth silver shall not be satisfied with silver; nor he that loveth abundance with increase: this *is* also vanity. ¹¹When goods increase, they are increased that eat them: and what good *is there* to the owners thereof, saving the beholding *of them* with their eyes? ¹²The sleep of a labouring man *is* sweet, whether he eat little or much: but the abundance of the rich will not suffer him to sleep. ¹³There is a sore evil *which* I have seen under the sun, *namely,*

Devotional Moment
•
Contentment

5:10-11 Loving wealth carries a price tag we seldom consider: a life void of contentment. God offers a better way. As we focus on what we *have* instead of what we *want,* we can learn to thank God for our possessions, enjoy them, and trust God to meet our future needs. Devote your time to a balance of pursuits, not to getting rich. Your health will be the better for it.

riches kept for the owners thereof to their hurt. ¹⁴But those riches perish by evil travail: and he begetteth a son, and *there is* nothing in his hand. ¹⁵As he came forth of his mother's womb, naked shall he return to go as he came, and shall take nothing of his labour, which he may carry away in his hand. ¹⁶And this also *is* a sore evil, *that* in all points as he came, so shall he go: and what profit hath he that hath laboured for the wind? ¹⁷All his days also he eateth in darkness, and *he hath* much sorrow and wrath with his sickness.

¹⁸Behold *that* which I have seen: *it is* good and comely *for one* to eat and to drink, and to enjoy the good of all his labour that he taketh under the sun all the days of his life, which God giveth him: for it *is* his portion. ¹⁹Every man also to whom God hath given riches and wealth, and hath given him power to eat thereof, and to take his portion, and to rejoice in his labour; this *is* the gift of God. ²⁰For he shall not much remember the days of his life; because God answereth *him* in the joy of his heart.

6

¹There is an evil which I have seen under the sun, and it *is* common among men: ²A man to whom God hath given riches, wealth, and honour, so that he wanteth nothing for his soul of all that he desireth, yet God giveth him not power to eat thereof, but a stranger eateth it: this *is* vanity, and it *is* an evil disease. ³If a man beget an hundred *children,* and live many years, so that the days of his years

be many, and his soul be not filled with good, and also *that* he have no burial; I say, *that* an untimely birth *is* better than he. ⁴For he cometh in with vanity, and departeth in darkness, and his name shall be covered with darkness. ⁵Moreover he hath not seen the sun, nor known *any thing:* this hath more rest than the other. ⁶Yea, though he live a thousand years twice *told,* yet hath he seen no good: do not all go to one place?

⁷All the labour of man *is* for his mouth, and yet the appetiteª is not filled. ⁸For what hath the wise more than the fool? what hath the poor, that knoweth to walk before the living? ⁹Better *is* the sight of the eyes than the wandering of the desire: this *is* also vanity and vexation of spirit. ¹⁰That which hath been is named already, and it is known that it *is* man: neither may he contend with him that is mightier than he.

¹¹Seeing there be many things that increase vanity, what *is* man the better? ¹²For who knoweth what *is* good for man in *this* life, allᵇ the days of his vain life which he spendeth as a shadow? for who can tell a man what shall be after him under the sun?

7

¹A good name *is* better than precious ointment; and the day of death than the day of one's birth. ²*It is* better to go to the house of mourning, than to go to the house of feasting: for that *is* the end of all men; and the living will lay *it* to his heart. ³Sorrowª *is* better than laughter: for by the sadness of the countenance

---

ª appetite: Heb. soul
ᵇ all . . . : Heb. the number of the days of the life of his vanity
ª Sorrow: or, Anger

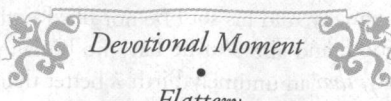

Devotional Moment
•
Flattery

7:5-6 Flattery—excessive or insincere praise—gives people an inaccurate view of themselves. How much better to follow God's way of speaking the truth in loving ways and with loving intentions (Eph. 4:15-16). Although it sometimes hurts to speak the truth, building strong relationships requires that we not gloss over problems that need to be addressed. Don't flatter; instead, speak the truth, using tact and kindness.

the heart is made better. ⁴The heart of the wise *is* in the house of mourning; but the heart of fools *is* in the house of mirth. ⁵*It is* better to hear the rebuke of the wise, than for a man to hear the song of fools. ⁶For as the cracklingᵇ of thorns under a pot, so *is* the laughter of the fool: this also *is* vanity.

⁷Surely oppression maketh a wise man mad; and a gift destroyeth the heart. ⁸Better *is* the end of a thing than the beginning thereof: *and* the patient in spirit *is* better than the proud in spirit. ⁹Be not hasty in thy spirit to be angry: for anger resteth in the bosom of fools. ¹⁰Say not thou, What is *the cause* that the former days were better than these? for thou dost not enquire wiselyᶜ concerning this.

¹¹Wisdom *is* goodᵈ with an inheritance: and *by it there is* profit to them that see the sun. ¹²For wisdom *is* a defenceᵉ, *and* money *is* a defence: but the excellency of knowledge *is, that* wisdom giveth life to them that have it. ¹³Consider the work of God: for who can make *that* straight, which he hath made crooked? ¹⁴In the day of prosperity be joyful, but in the day of adversity consider: God also hath setᶠ the one over against the other, to the end that man should find nothing after him. ¹⁵All *things* have I seen in the days of my vanity: there is a just *man* that perisheth in his righteousness, and there is a wicked *man* that prolongeth *his life* in his wickedness. ¹⁶Be not righteous over much; neither make thyself over wise: why shouldest thou destroyᵍ thyself? ¹⁷Be not over much wicked, neither be thou foolish: why shouldest thou die before thy time? ¹⁸*It is* good that thou shouldest take hold of this; yea, also from this withdraw not thine hand: for he that feareth God shall come forth of them all. ¹⁹Wisdom strengtheneth the wise more than ten mighty *men* which are in the city. ²⁰For *there is* not a just man upon earth, that doeth good, and sinneth not. ²¹Also takeʰ no heed unto all words that are spoken; lest thou hear thy servant curse thee: ²²For oftentimes also thine own heart knoweth that thou thyself likewise hast cursed others.

²³All this have I proved by wisdom: I said, I will be wise; but it *was* far from

---

ᵇ crackling: Heb. sound
ᶜ wisely: Heb. out of wisdom
ᵈ good . . . : or, as good as an inheritance, yea, better too
ᵉ defence: Heb. shadow
ᶠ set: Heb. made
ᵍ destroy . . . : Heb. be desolate?
ʰ take . . . : Heb. give not thine heart

me. ²⁴That which is far off, and exceeding deep, who can find it out? ²⁵I applied[i] mine heart to know, and to search, and to seek out wisdom, and the reason *of things*, and to know the wickedness of folly, even of foolishness *and* madness: ²⁶And I find more bitter than death the woman, whose heart *is* snares and nets, *and* her hands *as* bands: whoso pleaseth God shall escape from her; but the sinner shall be taken by her. ²⁷Behold, this have I found, saith the preacher, *counting* one by one, to find out the account: ²⁸Which yet my soul seeketh, but I find not: one man among a thousand have I found; but a woman among all those have I not found. ²⁹Lo, this only have I found, that God hath made man upright; but they have sought out many inventions.

8

¹Who *is* as the wise *man*? and who knoweth the interpretation of a thing? a man's wisdom maketh his face to shine, and the boldness[a] of his face shall be changed. ²I *counsel thee* to keep the king's commandment, and *that* in regard of the oath of God. ³Be not hasty to go out of his sight: stand not in an evil thing; for he doeth whatsoever pleaseth him. ⁴Where the word of a king *is, there is* power: and who may say unto him, What doest thou? ⁵Whoso keepeth the commandment shall feel no evil thing: and a wise man's heart discerneth both time and judgment.

⁶Because to every purpose there is time and judgment, therefore the misery of man *is* great upon him. ⁷For he knoweth not that which shall be: for who can tell him when it shall be? ⁸*There is* no man that hath power over the spirit to retain the spirit; neither *hath he* power in the day of death: and *there is* no discharge[b] in *that* war; neither shall wickedness deliver those that are given to it.

⁹All this have I seen, and applied my heart unto every work that is done under the sun: *there is* a time wherein one man ruleth over another to his own hurt. ¹⁰And so I saw the wicked buried, who had come and gone from the place of the holy, and they were forgotten in the city where they had so done: this *is* also vanity. ¹¹Because sentence against an evil work is not executed speedily, therefore the heart of the sons of men is fully set in them to do evil. ¹²Though a sinner do evil an hundred times, and his *days* be prolonged, yet surely I know that it shall be well with them that fear God, which fear before him: ¹³But it shall not be well with the wicked, neither shall he prolong *his* days, *which are* as a shadow; because he feareth not before God.

¹⁴There is a vanity which is done upon the earth; that there be just *men*, unto whom it happeneth according to the work of the wicked; again, there be wicked *men*, to whom it happeneth according to the work of the righteous: I said that this also *is* vanity. ¹⁵Then I commended mirth, because a man hath no better thing under the sun, than to eat, and to drink, and to be merry: for that

---

ⁱ I applied . . . : Heb. I and mine heart compassed
ᵃ the boldness: Heb. the strength
ᵇ discharge: or, casting off weapons

shall abide with him of his labour the days of his life, which God giveth him under the sun. ¹⁶When I applied mine heart to know wisdom, and to see the business that is done upon the earth: (for also *there is that* neither day nor night seeth sleep with his eyes:) ¹⁷Then I beheld all the work of God, that a man cannot find out the work that is done under the sun: because though a man labour to seek *it* out, yet he shall not find *it*; yea further; though a wise *man* think to know *it*, yet shall he not be able to find *it*.

9

¹For all this I considered[a] in my heart even to declare all this, that the righteous, and the wise, and their works, *are* in the hand of God: no man knoweth either love or hatred *by* all *that is* before them. ²All *things come* alike to all: *there is* one event to the righteous, and to the wicked; to the good and to the clean, and to the unclean; to him that sacrificeth, and to him that sacrificeth not: as *is* the good, so *is* the sinner; *and* he that sweareth, as *he* that feareth an oath. ³This *is* an evil among all *things* that are done under the sun, that *there is* one event unto all: yea, also the heart of the sons of men is full of evil, and madness *is* in their heart while they live, and after that *they go* to the dead.

⁴For to him that is joined to all the living there is hope: for a living dog is better than a dead lion. ⁵For the living know that they shall die: but the dead know not any thing, neither have they any more a reward; for the memory of

them is forgotten. ⁶Also their love, and their hatred, and their envy, is now perished; neither have they any more a portion for ever in any *thing* that is done under the sun. ⁷Go thy way, eat thy bread with joy, and drink thy wine with a merry heart; for God now accepteth thy works. ⁸Let thy garments be always white; and let thy head lack no ointment. ⁹Live[b] joyfully with the wife whom thou lovest all the days of the life of thy vanity, which he hath given thee under the sun, all the days of thy vanity: for that *is* thy portion in *this* life, and in thy labour which thou takest under the sun. ¹⁰Whatsoever thy hand findeth to do, do *it* with thy might; for *there is* no work, nor device, nor knowledge, nor wisdom, in the grave, whither thou goest.

¹¹I returned, and saw under the sun, that the race *is* not to the swift, nor the battle to the strong, neither yet bread to the wise, nor yet riches to men of understanding, nor yet favour to men of skill; but time and chance hap-

---

[a] I considered . . . : Heb. I gave, or, set to my heart
[b] Live . . . : Heb. See, or, Enjoy life

Caring for Aging Parents

by Barbara Deane

The book of Ecclesiastes is full of hard truths about the experience of life. One of the most unpleasant realities we read about is death. No one likes to think about the aging process and particularly the eventual death of parents. "I know," the head affirms, "that every person will grow old and die." But emotionally the heart says, "Not *my* parents."

Reality has a way of intruding on our denial, as Ecclesiastes 12:2-7 points out. As parents age and die, the family that we knew in the past changes forever.

The signs creep up on you. Your mother says she can no longer prepare the big holiday meals for the family, and it falls on you to have *them* over for Thanksgiving or Christmas dinner. Your father, who always used to tell you what to do, calls and asks *your* advice on whether he should travel in bad weather. Your mother, who was a math whiz, suddenly can't seem to balance her checkbook. You realize that your father's eyesight is failing, and he really shouldn't be driving.

Incidents like these are the first inklings of the inevitable role reversal, the day when you become the protector of those who protected you. And you won't like it. (Neither, in all probability, will they.) We all want life to go on as usual. All change is uncomfortable, and this change really threatens us. Yet, as this passage of Ecclesiastes reminds us, youth and strength do not last for anyone.

Ecclesiastes comforts us, not with soothing clichés, but with the reassurance that what we are going through is both natural and normal. Troubles will come with advancing age; darkness and cloudiness are as much a part of life as light and sunshine.

Why is it so hard for us to accept this?

Unfortunately, we live in a death-denying culture that demands we suppress our awareness of life's shadows. Nobody wants to talk about sickness and death—it's too depressing—and as for mourning, forget it! Nobody wants to see us mourn. Yet, because people live so much longer today, the old sometimes suffer poor health for a long time. As a result, adult children are often forced to begin the mourning process long before their parents' actual death.

When your parents are no longer the strong, active people you used to depend on, you mourn the loss. When you have to help them do things they can no longer do for themselves, you mourn—and so do they.

Whom can we talk to about this gradual grieving process? Fortunately, we can talk to God. As our Creator, he understands our needs. We can also share our feelings with our siblings who, you may be sure, struggle with negative emotions of their own. Finally, we should be able to share these thoughts with fellow Christians who can accept our grief without judging or condemning us.

Of course, there is no substitute for experience. Those who have helped their own elderly parents are often the best source for practical advice and empathy. Caring for an aging parent is not an impossible burden when it is shared, as God intended it to be.

What we must *not* do is condemn ourselves for what the Bible says is only to be expected. We cannot fix old age or make those who are preparing to leave this world young and whole again. It does no good for family members to "be strong" for one another and never express what they feel. Talk to your parents about the aging process that is robbing them of their vitality. This may be difficult, but you must prepare each other for the eventual and inevitable separation. Neither should we be putting on a happy face and pretending all is well for the benefit of other believers who think there's something wrong with our Christian walk if we're not joyful all the time.

When we are honest before God, he will draw us closer to himself and give us his strength and joy.

DIGGING DEEPER

1. The world gives us many negative ideas about aging. What positive statements does Scripture make about aging? See Psalm 92:12-14 and Proverbs 16:31.

2. Some degree of wisdom, which the Bible says is very desirable, cannot be attained without aging. Read Proverbs 1–4 and 8. How does the aging process make us wise? How can wisdom help us accept some of the negatives of life?

3. Empathizing with your parents' feelings as they age will help you help them. Psalm 71 expresses an aging person's fear of abandonment. How can you reassure your parents with your own love and from God's Word?

peneth to them all. ¹²For man also knoweth not his time: as the fishes that are taken in an evil net, and as the birds that are caught in the snare; so *are* the sons of men snared in an evil time, when it falleth suddenly upon them.

¹³This wisdom have I seen also under the sun, and it *seemed* great unto me: ¹⁴*There was* a little city, and few men within it; and there came a great king against it, and besieged it, and built great bulwarks against it: ¹⁵Now there was found in it a poor wise man, and he by his wisdom delivered the city; yet no man remembered that same poor man. ¹⁶Then said I, Wisdom *is* better than strength: nevertheless the poor man's wisdom *is* despised, and his words are not heard. ¹⁷The words of wise *men are* heard in quiet more than the cry of him that ruleth among fools. ¹⁸Wisdom *is* better than weapons of war: but one sinner destroyeth much good.

10

¹Dead[a] flies cause the ointment of the apothecary to send forth a stinking savour: *so doth* a little folly him that is in reputation for wisdom *and* honour. ²A wise man's heart *is* at his right hand; but a fool's heart at his left. ³Yea also, when he that is a fool walketh by the way, his wisdom faileth *him*, and he saith to every one *that* he *is* a fool.

⁴If the spirit of the ruler rise up against thee, leave not thy place; for yielding pacifieth great offences. ⁵There is an evil *which* I have seen under the sun, as an error *which* proceedeth from[b] the ruler: ⁶Folly is set in great[c] dignity, and the rich sit in low place. ⁷I have seen servants upon horses, and princes walking as servants upon the earth. ⁸He that diggeth a pit shall fall into it; and

---

ᵃ Dead . . . : Heb. Flies of death
ᵇ from: Heb. from before
ᶜ in great . . . : Heb. in great heights

whoso breaketh an hedge, a serpent shall bite him. [9]Whoso removeth stones shall be hurt therewith; *and* he that cleaveth wood shall be endangered thereby. [10]If the iron be blunt, and he do not whet the edge, then must he put to more strength: but wisdom *is* profitable to direct. [11]Surely the serpent will bite without enchantment; and a babbler[d] is no better.

[12]The words of a wise man's mouth *are* gracious[e]; but the lips of a fool will swallow up himself. [13]The beginning of the words of his mouth *is* foolishness: and the end of his talk[f] *is* mischievous madness. [14]A fool also is full[g] of words: a man cannot tell what shall be; and what shall be after him, who can tell him? [15]The labour of the foolish wearieth every one of them, because he knoweth not how to go to the city.

[16]Woe to thee, O land, when thy king *is* a child, and thy princes eat in the morning! [17]Blessed *art* thou, O land, when thy king *is* the son of nobles, and thy princes eat in due season, for strength, and not for drunkenness! [18]By much slothfulness the building decayeth; and through idleness of the hands the house droppeth through. [19]A feast is made for laughter, and wine maketh merry: but money answereth all *things.* [20]Curse not the king, no not in thy thought[h]; and curse not the rich in thy bedchamber: for a bird of the air shall carry the voice, and that which hath wings shall tell the matter.

11

[1]Cast thy bread upon[a] the waters: for thou shalt find it after many days. [2]Give a portion to seven, and also to eight; for thou knowest not what evil shall be upon the earth. [3]If the clouds be full of rain, they empty *themselves* upon the earth: and if the tree fall toward the south, or toward the north, in the place where the tree falleth, there it shall be. [4]He that observeth the wind shall not sow; and he that regardeth the clouds shall not reap. [5]As thou knowest not what *is* the way of the spirit, *nor* how the bones *do grow* in the womb of her that is with child: even so thou knowest not the works of God who maketh all. [6]In the morning sow thy seed, and in the evening withhold not thine hand: for thou knowest not whether shall prosper[b], either this or that, or whether they both *shall be* alike good.

[7]Truly the light *is* sweet, and a pleasant *thing it is* for the eyes to behold the sun: [8]But if a man live many years, *and* rejoice in them all; yet let him remember the days of darkness; for they shall be many. All that cometh *is* vanity. [9]Rejoice, O young man, in thy youth; and let thy heart cheer thee in the days of thy youth, and walk in the ways of thine heart, and in the sight of thine eyes: but know thou, that for

---

[d] a babbler: Heb. the master of the tongue
[e] gracious: Heb. grace
[f] his talk: Heb. his mouth
[g] is full . . . : Heb. multiplieth words
[h] thought: or, conscience
[a] upon . . . : Heb. upon the face of the waters
[b] shall prosper: Heb. shall be right

all these *things* God will bring thee into judgment. [10]Therefore remove sorrow[c] from thy heart, and put away evil from thy flesh: for childhood and youth *are* vanity.

12

[1]Remember now thy Creator in the days of thy youth, while the evil days come not, nor the years draw nigh, when thou shalt say, I have no pleasure in them; [2]While the sun, or the light, or the moon, or the stars, be not darkened, nor the clouds return after the rain: [3]In the day when the keepers of the house shall tremble, and the strong men shall bow themselves, and the grinders[a] cease because they are few, and those that look out of the windows be darkened, [4]And the doors shall be shut in the streets, when the sound of the grinding is low, and he shall rise up at the voice of the bird, and all the daughters of musick shall be brought low; [5]Also *when* they shall be afraid of *that which is* high, and fears *shall be* in the way, and the almond tree shall flourish, and the grasshopper shall be a burden, and desire shall fail: because man goeth to his long home, and the mourners go about the streets: [6]Or ever the silver cord be loosed, or the golden bowl be broken, or the pitcher be broken at the fountain, or the wheel broken at the cistern. [7]Then shall the dust return to the earth as it was: and the spirit shall return unto God who gave it.

[8]Vanity of vanities, saith the

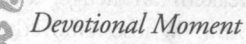

Devotional Moment

•

Aging

12:1-7 In the book of Ecclesiastes we sense Solomon's bitterness and disappointment in this world. Old age approaches, this brief life ends, and we die. Thankfully, the story does not end there for those who know God personally. The New Testament tells us that all who believe in Jesus as their Savior will be given new bodies that will never be sick and never die, and we will spend eternity with him (see Rom. 8:18-23 and 1 Thess. 4:13-18). Let that hope take the edge off of growing old and its aches and pains.

preacher; all *is* vanity. [9]And moreover[b], because the preacher was wise, he still taught the people knowledge; yea, he gave good heed, and sought out, *and* set in order many proverbs. [10]The preacher sought to find out acceptable[c] words: and *that which was* written *was* upright, *even* words of truth. [11]The words of the wise *are* as goads, and as nails fastened *by* the masters of assemblies, *which* are given from one shepherd. [12]And further, by these, my son, be admonished: of making many books *there is* no end; and much study[d] *is* a weariness of the flesh.

[13]Let us hear the conclusion of the whole matter: Fear God, and keep his commandments: for this *is* the whole *duty* of man. [14]For God shall bring every work into judgment, with every secret thing, whether *it be* good, or whether *it be* evil.

---

[c] sorrow: or, anger
[a] the grinders . . . : or, the grinders fail, because they grind little
[b] moreover . . . : or, the more wise the preacher was, etc
[c] acceptable . . . : Heb. words of delight
[d] study: or, reading

SONG OF SOLOMON

Purpose
To tell of the love be-
tween a bridegroom
(King Solomon) and his
bride, to affirm the
sanctity of marriage,
and to picture God's
love for his people

Author
Solomon

Date Written
Probably early in
Solomon's reign

Setting
Israel—the Shulamite
woman's garden and
the king's palace

Key Verse
"I am my beloved's and
my beloved is mine. He
feedeth among the
lilies." (6:3).

Key People
King Solomon, the Shu-
lamite woman, and the
young women of
Jerusalem

What does the world need more of? Give anyone three guesses, and only the first one counts.

Here is a book that deserves more hype than any romance novel, more glitz than a blockbuster movie. In the Song of Solomon we celebrate the wonder and mystery of what the world needs more of. Its very title means "greatest of all songs." And those who know its truth would quickly agree. By comparison, alternatives appear cheap—quick sellouts to what the world needs less of.

Why should we be surprised that a book so sensuous as this appears almost in the middle of the Bible? Isn't the Bible a real book about real people who knew full well what the world needs more of? And doesn't God also know, since it was God who created male and female?

True lovers will enjoy this book. They will see reflected in the love they share an image of another love greater still—love more constant, more committed, more complete.

So when the daily grind is getting you down, the cat has ruined your curtains, and the kids are passing around their second winter virus, pick up Song of Solomon. Let it lift your day and perfume your night. What God has brought together, let no one put asunder.

1

¹The song of songs, which *is* Solomon's.

²Let him kiss me with the kisses of his mouth: for thy love *is* better than wine. ³Because of the savour of thy good ointments thy name *is as* ointment poured forth, therefore do the virgins love thee. ⁴Draw me, we will run after thee: the king hath brought me into his chambers: we will be glad and rejoice in thee, we will remember thy love more than wine: the upright^a love thee. ⁵I *am* black, but comely, O ye daughters of Jerusalem, as the tents of Kedar, as the curtains of Solomon. ⁶Look not upon me, because I *am* black, because the sun hath looked upon me: my mother's children were angry with me; they made me the keeper of the vineyards; *but* mine own vineyard have I not kept.

⁷Tell me, O thou whom my soul loveth, where thou feedest, where thou makest *thy flock* to rest at noon: for why should I be as one that turneth aside by the flocks of thy companions? ⁸If thou know not, O thou fairest among women, go thy way forth by the footsteps of the flock, and feed thy kids beside the shepherds' tents. ⁹I have compared thee, O my love, to a company of horses in Pharaoh's chariots. ¹⁰Thy cheeks are comely with rows *of jewels*, thy neck with chains *of gold*. ¹¹We will make thee borders of gold with studs of silver.

¹²While the king *sitteth* at his table, my spikenard sendeth forth the smell thereof. ¹³A bundle of myrrh *is* my well-beloved unto me; he shall lie all night betwixt my breasts. ¹⁴My beloved *is* unto me *as* a cluster of camphire^b in the vineyards of Engedi. ¹⁵Behold, thou *art* fair, my love^c; behold, thou *art* fair; thou *hast* doves' eyes. ¹⁶Behold, thou *art* fair, my beloved, yea, pleasant: also our bed *is* green. ¹⁷The beams of our house *are* cedar, *and* our rafters^d of fir.

2

¹I *am* the rose of Sharon, *and* the lily of the valleys. ²As the lily among thorns, so *is* my love among the daughters.

³As the apple tree among the trees of the wood, so *is* my beloved among the sons. I sat^a down under his shadow with great delight, and his fruit *was* sweet to my taste. ⁴He brought me to the banqueting^b house, and his banner over me *was* love. ⁵Stay me with flagons, comfort^c me with apples: for I *am* sick of love. ⁶His left hand *is* under my head, and his right hand doth embrace me. ⁷I charge^d you, O ye daughters of Jerusalem, by the roes, and by the hinds of the field, that ye stir not up, nor awake *my* love, till he please.

⁸The voice of my beloved! behold,

ᵃ the upright . . . : or, they love thee uprightly
ᵇ camphire: or, cypress
ᶜ my love: or, my companion
ᵈ rafters: or, galleries
ᵃ I sat . . . : Heb. I delighted and sat down, etc
ᵇ banqueting . . . : Heb. house of wine
ᶜ comfort . . . : Heb. straw me with apples
ᵈ I charge . . . : Heb. I adjure you

he cometh leaping upon the mountains, skipping upon the hills. ⁹My beloved is like a roe or a young hart: behold, he standeth behind our wall, he looketh forth at the windows, shewingᵉ himself through the lattice. ¹⁰My beloved spake, and said unto me, Rise up, my love, my fair one, and come away. ¹¹For, lo, the winter is past, the rain is over *and* gone; ¹²The flowers appear on the earth; the time of the singing *of birds* is come, and the voice of the turtle is heard in our land; ¹³The fig tree putteth forth her green figs, and the vines *with* the tender grape give a *good* smell. Arise, my love, my fair one, and come away.

¹⁴O my dove, *that art* in the clefts of the rock, in the secret *places* of the stairs, let me see thy countenance, let me hear thy voice; for sweet *is* thy voice, and thy countenance *is* comely. ¹⁵Take us the foxes, the little foxes, that spoil the vines: for our vines *have* tender grapes. ¹⁶My beloved *is* mine, and I *am*

Devotional Moment
•
Partners at Work
2:15 Those who tend vineyards or gardens have more than the sun and the rain to consider. Insects can invade, as can other animals. Small foxes might seem harmless, but they can quickly ruin a vineyard in bloom. Just like the little foxes, small annoyances or bickering may seem insignificant, but over time they can ruin the best of relationships. With your spouse, identify one or two small problem areas that have invaded your marriage. Then think of one way you can work together to solve them.

Devotional Moment
•
Independence
2:16 The lover was deeply in love with his beloved, yet he had other interests. He browsed among the lilies, evidently by himself. We need not feel threatened or abandoned when our spouses pursue projects or interests independent of us. Two people in love do not have to share every waking moment. Respect one another as individuals. The next time your spouse wants to do something that does not interest you, encourage him or her to pursue the interest alone or with other friends. Grudgingly going along may not be the most loving response.

---

his: he feedeth among the lilies. ¹⁷Until the day break, and the shadows flee away, turn, my beloved, and be thou like a roe or a young hart upon the mountains of Betherᶠ.

3

¹By night on my bed I sought him whom my soul loveth: I sought him, but I found him not. ²I will rise now, and go about the city in the streets, and in the broad ways I will seek him whom my soul loveth: I sought him, but I found him not. ³The watchmen that go about the city found me: *to whom I said*, Saw ye him whom my soul loveth? ⁴*It was* but a little that I passed from them, but I found him whom my soul loveth: I held him, and would not let him go, until I had brought him into my mother's house, and into the chamber of her that conceived me. ⁵I charge you, O ye daughters of Jerusalem, by the roes, and by the hinds of the field,

---

ᵉ shewing . . . : Heb. flourishing
ᶠ of Bether: or, of division

that ye stir not up, nor awake *my* love, till he please.

⁶Who *is* this that cometh out of the wilderness like pillars of smoke, perfumed with myrrh and frankincense, with all powders of the merchant?

⁷Behold his bed, which *is* Solomon's; threescore valiant men *are* about it, of the valiant of Israel. ⁸They all hold swords, *being* expert in war: every man *hath* his sword upon his thigh because of fear in the night. ⁹King Solomon made himself a chariotᵃ of the wood of Lebanon. ¹⁰He made the pillars thereof *of* silver, the bottom thereof *of* gold, the covering of it *of* purple, the midst thereof being paved *with* love, for the daughters of Jerusalem. ¹¹Go forth, O ye daughters of Zion, and behold king Solomon with the crown wherewith his mother crowned him in the day of his espousals, and in the day of the gladness of his heart.

4

¹Behold, thou *art* fair, my love; behold, thou *art* fair; thou *hast* doves' eyes within thy locks: thy hair *is* as a flock of goats, that appear from mount Gilead. ²Thy teeth *are* like a flock *of sheep that are even* shorn, which came up from the washing; whereof every one bear twins, and none *is* barren among them. ³Thy lips *are* like a thread of scarlet, and thy speech *is* comely: thy temples *are* like a piece of a pomegranate within thy locks. ⁴Thy neck *is* like the tower of David builded for an armoury, whereon there hang a thousand bucklers, all shields of mighty

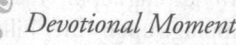

Devotional Moment

•

Sex

4:1-16 The intense feelings and vivid images communicated by the lover describing the beloved one's body may surprise us. Yet this passage shows us what we already know—that physical attraction is part of an intimate relationship. Married couples are invited by God to enjoy sexual pleasure. Do whatever is necessary so that you and your spouse have the time, energy, and privacy to enjoy each other sexually. Delight in the wife (or husband) of your youth!

men. ⁵Thy two breasts *are* like two young roes that are twins, which feed among the lilies. ⁶Until the day breakᵃ, and the shadows flee away, I will get me to the mountain of myrrh, and to the hill of frankincense. ⁷Thou *art* all fair, my love; *there is* no spot in thee.

⁸Come with me from Lebanon, *my* spouse, with me from Lebanon: look from the top of Amana, from the top of Shenir and Hermon, from the lions' dens, from the mountains of the leopards. ⁹Thou hast ravished my heart, my sister, *my* spouse; thou hast ravished my heart with one of thine eyes, with one chain of thy neck. ¹⁰How fair is thy love, my sister, *my* spouse! how much better is thy love than wine! and the smell of thine ointments than all spices! ¹¹Thy lips, O *my* spouse, drop *as* the honeycomb: honey and milk *are* under thy tongue; and the smell of thy garments *is* like the smell of Lebanon. ¹²A garden inclosedᵇ *is* my sister, *my* spouse;

ᵃ a chariot: or, a bed
ᵃ break: Heb. breathe
ᵇ inclosed: Heb. barred

Solomon

Romantic love. Is it a blessing or a curse?

Some people get tied in knots just thinking about it. The idea of dimming the lights and putting on soft music makes them feel uncomfortable, ill at ease, and dumb. Married or not, makes no difference.

And then there's 1 Corinthians 13—which says nothing at all about romance. If it's not there, is it a part of love at all?

Solomon knew the answer.

Of course, Solomon was not a perfect husband. Official records put his total number of wives at seven hundred and concubines at three hundred. He married these women mainly to seal alliances with surrounding nations. Many of them turned his heart against God.

But Solomon didn't have a heart of stone. He also wrote the Song of Solomon. This unconventional passage is the Bible's boldest endorsement of romantic and sexual love.

Of course, we should not casually assume that because Solomon wrote about sex, any and all sex is right and good. From the very beginning, God designed sexual union to be a bonding experience for husbands and wives together in marriage (see Gen. 2:24).

But as Solomon shows us, romance and sexual enjoyment is a critical part of marriage. God invented it, and it doesn't have to end on your wedding day—marriage is where it is free to grow.

So go on a date with your spouse. Light some candles. Turn out the lights. Put on some soft music. Enjoy each other.

LESSONS FROM SOLOMON AS A HUSBAND

Marriage is good. The Song of Solomon is a celebration of married love.

Romance is an important part of marriage. In poetic eloquence, Solomon told his bride of her beauty (1:10; 2:2; 7:1-7). He took delight in her body and spoke of how he would touch her (7:8-9). She in turn told him how much she adored him and imagined him (8:1-3). Anyone who wants to find validation for romantic love between spouses can find plenty of it right here. Just try quoting Song of Solomon 4:1-15 or 5:2-8 to your spouse at a good place and time and see if it doesn't have an effect.

Be careful whom you marry. Many of the women Solomon married simply destroyed his faith. Marry someone who shares your love for God!

a spring shut up, a fountain sealed. [13]Thy plants *are* an orchard of pomegranates, with pleasant fruits; camphire[c], with spikenard, [14]Spikenard and saffron; calamus and cinnamon, with all trees of frankincense; myrrh and aloes, with all the chief spices:

[15]A fountain of gardens, a well of living waters, and streams from Lebanon. [16]Awake, O north wind; and come, thou south; blow upon my garden, *that* the spices thereof may flow out. Let my beloved come into his garden, and eat his pleasant fruits.

5

[1]I am come into my garden, my sister, *my* spouse: I have gathered my myrrh with my spice; I have eaten my honeycomb with my honey; I have drunk my wine with my milk: eat, O friends; drink, yea[a], drink abundantly, O beloved.

[2]I sleep, but my heart waketh: *it is* the voice of my beloved that knocketh, *saying*, Open to me, my sister, my love, my dove, my undefiled: for my head is filled with dew, *and* my locks with the drops of the night. [3]I have put off my coat; how shall I put it on? I have washed my feet; how shall I defile them? [4]My beloved put in his hand by the hole *of the door*, and my bowels were moved for him[b]. [5]I rose up to open to my beloved; and my hands dropped *with* myrrh, and my fingers *with* sweet smelling myrrh, upon the handles of the lock. [6]I opened

to my beloved; but my beloved had withdrawn himself, *and* was gone: my soul failed when he spake: I sought him, but I could not find him; I called him, but he gave me no answer. [7]The watchmen that went about the city found me, they smote me, they wounded me; the keepers of the walls took away my veil from me. [8]I charge you, O daughters of Jerusalem, if ye find my beloved, that ye tell him, that I *am* sick of love.

[9]What *is* thy beloved more than *another* beloved, O thou fairest among women? what *is* thy beloved more than *another* beloved, that thou dost so charge us? [10]My beloved *is* white and ruddy, the chiefest[c] among ten thousand. [11]His head *is as* the most fine gold, his locks *are* bushy[d], *and* black as a raven. [12]His eyes *are as the eyes* of doves by the rivers of waters, washed with milk, *and* fitly set. [13]His cheeks *are as* a bed of spices, *as* sweet flowers[e]: his lips

---

Devotional Moment

•

Friendship in Marriage

5:16 We are called in marriage to be friends as well as lovers. Is your life so filled with the duties of your other roles—parent, lover, financial partner, professional, homemaker—that the joy and companionship of your friendship has gotten pushed aside? Talk together about what activities or outings would give your friendship a boost. A concert, volunteering together, a project you both would enjoy, or taking walks are only a few possibilities.

---

[c] camphire: or, cypress
[a] yea . . . : or, and be drunken with loves
[b] for him: or, (as some read) in me
[c] the chiefest: Heb. a standard bearer
[d] bushy: or, curled
[e] sweet flowers: or, towers of perfumes

like lilies, dropping sweet smelling myrrh. ¹⁴His hands *are as* gold rings set with the beryl: his belly *is as* bright ivory overlaid *with* sapphires. ¹⁵His legs *are as* pillars of marble, set upon sockets of fine gold: his countenance *is as* Lebanon, excellent as the cedars. ¹⁶His mouth^f *is* most sweet: yea, he *is* altogether lovely. This *is* my beloved, and this *is* my friend, O daughters of Jerusalem.

6

¹Whither is thy beloved gone, O thou fairest among women? whither is thy beloved turned aside? that we may seek him with thee. ²My beloved is gone down into his garden, to the beds of spices, to feed in the gardens, and to gather lilies. ³I *am* my beloved's, and my beloved *is* mine: he feedeth among the lilies.

⁴Thou *art* beautiful, O my love, as Tirzah, comely as Jerusalem, terrible as *an army* with banners. ⁵Turn away thine eyes from me, for they have overcome^a me: thy hair *is* as a flock of goats that appear from Gilead. ⁶Thy teeth *are* as a flock of sheep which go up from the washing, whereof every one beareth twins, and *there is* not one barren among them. ⁷As a piece of a pomegranate *are* thy temples within thy locks. ⁸There are threescore queens, and fourscore concubines, and virgins without number. ⁹My dove, my undefiled is *but* one; she *is* the *only* one of her mother, she *is* the choice *one* of her that bare her. The daughters saw her, and blessed her; *yea*, the queens and the concubines, and they praised her. ¹⁰Who *is*

Devotional Moment
•
Words

6:4-9 King Solomon freely expressed his thoughts and feelings about his beloved. He was uninhibited in his praise and delight, which no doubt delighted her. Relationships need communication, constant care, and frequent updates. Express your love in a way that your spouse can hear and understand, be it a return to the love letters of your courtship, a musical expression, or a heart-to-heart talk. Share with your spouse what you are feeling, thinking, and needing. Try not to fall into the trap of waiting for your spouse to initiate communication. Take the initiative yourself. It works.

she *that* looketh forth as the morning, fair as the moon, clear as the sun, *and* terrible as *an army* with banners?

¹¹I went down into the garden of nuts to see the fruits of the valley, *and* to see whether the vine flourished, *and* the pomegranates budded. ¹²Or ever I was aware, my soul made me *like* the chariots of Amminadib. ¹³Return, return, O Shulamite; return, return, that we may look upon thee. What will ye see in the Shulamite? As it were the company of two armies.

7

¹How beautiful are thy feet with shoes, O prince's daughter! the joints of thy thighs *are* like jewels, the work of the hands of a cunning workman. ²Thy navel *is like* a round goblet, *which* wanteth not liquor^a: thy belly *is like* an heap of wheat set about with lilies. ³Thy two breasts *are* like two young

---

^f mouth: Heb. palate
^a overcome . . . : or, puffed me up
^a liquor: Heb. mixture

Family Traditions

A Tradition of Intimacy

SONG OF SOLOMON

"When did you first love Dad with a real love?" my teenage daughter asked.

"I'm still learning to," I said.

"But how do you know that you've found the right one?"

"When you set your heart and mind to making him the right one," I replied.

Marrying is not a once-done thing. Getting married is something you add to every day. When you set your heart and mind to it, marrying can be like building a great cathedral to the glory of God. In the great cathedrals of old, passion, skill, and effort were equally valued. Combined, they created a place that was spacious, safe, and inspirational. Similarly, a marriage needs to be:

Spacious. Love does not smother. It allows for diversity of interests and preference. Never stop discovering new things about yourself. Never stop your spouse from discovering new things about himself or herself. Encourage each other to grow, to change, and (occasionally) to be alone.

Safe. Learn what makes the other person feel cherished. Find out how your spouse loves to be touched, conversed with, celebrated. Find three things you are both wild about: Sushi? Chamber music? Roller skating? Do them together, often. When conflicts arise, journal about your feelings privately before confronting your spouse with the problem. This will help you release pent-up feelings in a neutral zone and may bring new insights.

Inspirational. Create a place of prayer in your lives, the same place every day or week. Pray together consistently. When alone, make every thought of your spouse a prayer. Look for quiet moments to talk about your relationship—strolling through the garden, walking around the block, or driving in the dark. Find new ways to say, "I love you. I'm committed to you." And say them often.

Getting married is something you do every day.

roes *that are* twins. ⁴Thy neck *is* as a tower of ivory; thine eyes *like* the fishpools in Heshbon, by the gate of Bathrabbim: thy nose *is* as the tower of Lebanon which looketh toward Damascus. ⁵Thine head upon thee *is* like Carmel[b], and the hair of thine head like purple; the king *is* held in the galleries. ⁶How fair and how pleasant art thou, O love, for delights! ⁷This thy stature is like to a palm tree, and thy breasts to clusters *of grapes.* ⁸I said, I will go up to the palm tree, I will take hold of the boughs thereof: now also thy breasts shall be as clusters of the vine, and the smell of thy nose like apples; ⁹And the roof of thy mouth like the best wine for my beloved, that goeth *down* sweetly[c], causing the lips of those that are asleep to speak.

¹⁰I *am* my beloved's, and his desire *is* toward me. ¹¹Come, my beloved, let us go forth into the field; let us lodge in the villages. ¹²Let us get up early to the vineyards; let us see if the vine flourish, *whether* the tender grape appear[d], *and* the pomegranates bud forth: there will I give thee my loves. ¹³The mandrakes give a smell, and at our gates *are* all manner of pleasant *fruits,* new and old, *which* I have laid up for thee, O my beloved.

8

¹O that thou *wert* as my brother, that sucked the breasts of my mother! *when* I should find thee without, I would kiss thee; yea, I should not be despised. ²I would lead thee, *and* bring thee into my mother's house, *who* would instruct me: I would cause thee to drink of spiced wine of the juice of my pomegranate. ³His left hand *should be* under my head, and his right hand should embrace me. ⁴I charge you, O daughters of Jerusalem, that ye stir not up, nor awake *my* love, until he please.

⁵Who *is* this that cometh up from the wilderness, leaning upon her beloved? I raised thee up under the apple tree: there thy mother brought thee forth: there she brought thee forth *that* bare thee. ⁶Set me as a seal upon thine heart, as a seal upon thine arm: for love *is* strong as death; jealousy *is* cruel[a] as the grave: the coals thereof *are* coals of fire, *which hath a* most vehement flame. ⁷Many waters cannot quench love, neither can the floods drown it: if *a* man would give all the substance of his house for love, it would utterly be contemned.

⁸We have a little sister, and she hath no breasts: what shall we do for our sister in the day when she shall be spoken for? ⁹If she *be* a wall, we will build upon her a palace of silver: and if she *be* a door, we will inclose her with boards of cedar. ¹⁰I *am* a wall, and my breasts like towers: then was I in his eyes as one that found favour[b]. ¹¹Solomon had a vineyard at Baalhamon; he let out the vineyard unto keep-

---

ᵇ Carmel: or, crimson
ᶜ sweetly: Heb. straightly
ᵈ appear: Heb. open
ᵃ cruel: Heb. hard
ᵇ favour: Heb. peace

ers; every one for the fruit thereof was to bring a thousand *pieces* of silver. ¹²My vineyard, which *is* mine, *is* before me: thou, O Solomon, *must have* a thousand, and those that keep the fruit thereof two hundred.

¹³Thou that dwellest in the gardens, the companions hearken to thy voice: cause me to hear *it*. ¹⁴Make haste, my beloved, and be thou like to a roe or to a young hart upon the mountains of spices.

ISAIAH

Purpose
To call the nation of Judah back to God and to tell of God's salvation through the Messiah

Author
The prophet Isaiah, son of Amoz

Date Written
The events of chapters 1–39 occurred during Isaiah's ministry, so they were probably written about 700 B.C. Chapters 40–66, however, may have been written near the end of his life, about 681 B.C.

Setting
Isaiah is speaking and writing mainly in Jerusalem.

Key Verse
"But he was wounded for our transgressions, he was bruised for our iniquities: the chastisement of our peace was upon him; and with his stripes we are healed" (53:5).

Key People
Isaiah

Special Features
The book of Isaiah contains both prose and poetry and uses personification (attributing personal qualities to divine beings or inanimate objects). Also, many of the prophecies in Isaiah contain predictions that foretell a soon-to-occur event and a distant future event at the same time.

Over a generation ago warnings began to appear on cigarette packs. The nation's chief medical officer wanted tar and nicotine users to know the dangers of their habit. Now similar warnings are posted, by law, at nearly every point of purchase for tobacco products.

Do people still buy cigarettes? Indeed they do, from teens to seniors, proving that warnings are easily disregarded.

Isaiah was a constant, articulate warning sign to God's people. Come back to God, he would say. Trust in God. Follow his ways. Our deliverer is God, not pagan emperors, he would say.

Like children warned about hot stoves, the Israelites seemed unable to resist the urge to touch. And they got burned. The hard lesson was Babylonian captivity, but the hope Isaiah offered was a savior who would appear as a servant. What an odd disguise for the Messiah!

The average parent issues a hundred warnings a day to young children and thinks, but dares not voice, twice that many to teenagers. That same parent is probably warned a hundred times daily, too, of dangers from cholesterol to foam packaging. So many warnings—so little time to understand them all.

But some warnings need our eyes-open attention, for the sake of our future and our children's future. Some warnings are too costly to disregard. Some can't be given too often.

Let Isaiah lead your heart to safe haven.

1

¹The vision of Isaiah the son of Amoz, which he saw concerning Judah and Jerusalem in the days of Uzziah, Jotham, Ahaz, *and* Hezekiah, kings of Judah.

²Hear, O heavens, and give ear, O earth: for the LORD hath spoken, I have nourished and brought up children, and they have rebelled against me. ³The ox knoweth his owner, and the ass his master's crib: *but* Israel doth not know, my people doth not consider. ⁴Ah sinful nation, a people ladenᵃ with iniquity, a seed of evildoers, children that are corrupters: they have forsaken the LORD, they have provoked the Holy One of Israel unto anger, they are gone away backward. ⁵Why should ye be stricken any more? ye will revoltᵇ more and more: the whole head is sick, and the whole heart faint. ⁶From the sole of the foot even unto the head *there is* no soundness in it; *but* wounds, and bruises, and putrifying sores: they have not been closed, neither bound up, neither mollified with ointmentᶜ. ⁷Your country *is* desolate, your cities *are* burned with fire: your land, strangers devour it in your presence, and *it is* desolate, as overthrownᵈ by strangers. ⁸And the daughter of Zion is left as a cottage in a vineyard, as a lodge in a garden of cucumbers, as a besieged city. ⁹Except the LORD of hosts had left unto us a very small remnant, we should have been as Sodom, *and* we should have been like unto Gomorrah.

¹⁰Hear the word of the LORD, ye rulers of Sodom; give ear unto the law of our God, ye people of Gomorrah. ¹¹To what purpose *is* the multitude of your sacrifices unto me? saith the LORD: I am full of the burnt offerings of rams, and the fat of fed beasts; and I delight not in the blood of bullocks, or of lambs, or of he goatsᵉ. ¹²When ye come to appearᶠ before me, who hath required this at your hand, to tread my courts? ¹³Bring no more vain oblations; incense is an abomination unto me; the new moons and sabbaths, the calling of assemblies, I cannot away with; *it is* iniquityᵍ, even the solemn meeting. ¹⁴Your new moons and your appointed feasts my soul hateth: they are a trouble unto me; I am weary to bear *them*. ¹⁵And when ye spread forth your hands, I will hide mine eyes from you: yea, when ye make many prayers, I will not hear: your hands are full of blood.

¹⁶Wash you, make you clean; put away the evil of your doings from before mine eyes; cease to do evil; ¹⁷Learn to do well; seek judgment, relieveʰ the oppressed, judge the fatherless, plead for the widow. ¹⁸Come now, and let us reason together, saith the LORD:

ᵃ laden: Heb. of heaviness
ᵇ revolt . . . : Heb. increase revolt
ᶜ ointment: or, oil
ᵈ overthrown . . . : Heb. the overthrow of
ᵉ he goats: Heb. great he goats
ᶠ to appear: Heb. to be seen
ᵍ iniquity: or, grief
ʰ relieve: or, righten

though your sins be as scarlet, they shall be as white as snow; though they be red like crimson, they shall be as wool. ¹⁹If ye be willing and obedient, ye shall eat the good of the land: ²⁰But if ye refuse and rebel, ye shall be devoured with the sword: for the mouth of the LORD hath spoken *it.*

²¹How is the faithful city become an harlot! it was full of judgment; righteousness lodged in it; but now murderers. ²²Thy silver is become dross, thy wine mixed with water: ²³Thy princes *are* rebellious, and companions of thieves: every one loveth gifts, and followeth after rewards: they judge not the fatherless, neither doth the cause of the widow come unto them. ²⁴Therefore saith the Lord, the LORD of hosts, the mighty One of Israel, Ah, I will ease me of mine adversaries, and avenge me of mine enemies: ²⁵And I will turn my hand upon thee, and purely[i] purge away thy dross, and take away all thy tin: ²⁶And I will restore thy judges as at the first, and thy counsellors as at the beginning: afterward thou shalt be called, The city of righteousness, the faithful city. ²⁷Zion shall be redeemed with judgment, and her converts with righteousness. ²⁸And the destruction[j] of the transgressors and of the sinners *shall be* together, and they that forsake the LORD shall be consumed. ²⁹For they shall be ashamed of the oaks which ye have desired, and ye shall be confounded for the gardens that ye have chosen. ³⁰For ye shall be as an oak whose leaf fadeth, and as a garden that hath no water. ³¹And the strong shall be as tow, and the maker[k] of it as a spark, and they shall both burn together, and none shall quench *them.*

2

¹The word that Isaiah the son of Amoz saw concerning Judah and Jerusalem. ²And it shall come to pass in the last days, *that* the mountain of the LORD'S house shall be established[a] in the top of the mountains, and shall be exalted above the hills; and all nations shall flow unto it. ³And many people shall go and say, Come ye, and let us go up to the mountain of the LORD, to the house of the God of Jacob; and he will teach us of his ways, and we will walk in his paths: for out of Zion shall go forth the law, and the word of the LORD from Jerusalem. ⁴And he shall judge among the nations, and shall rebuke many people: and they shall beat their swords into plowshares, and their

---

Devotional Moment

•

A Challenge

2:5 The prophet's words to God's people were plain and direct, challenging them to walk in God's light. A simple challenge parents and children can all issue to each other: Adore God's holiness and try to do what pleases him. Over dinner conversations and in between homework assignments, encourage one another to please God.

---

[i] purely: Heb. according to pureness
[j] destruction: Heb. breaking
[k] maker . . . : or, and his work
[a] established: or, prepared

spears into pruninghooks[b]: nation shall not lift up sword against nation, neither shall they learn war any more. [5]O house of Jacob, come ye, and let us walk in the light of the LORD.

[6]Therefore thou hast forsaken thy people the house of Jacob, because they be replenished from the east, and *are* soothsayers like the Philistines, and they please themselves in the children of strangers. [7]Their land also is full of silver and gold, neither *is there any* end of their treasures; their land is also full of horses, neither *is there any* end of their chariots: [8]Their land also is full of idols; they worship the work of their own hands, that which their own fingers have made: [9]And the mean man boweth down, and the great man humbleth himself: therefore forgive them not.

[10]Enter into the rock, and hide thee in the dust, for fear of the LORD, and for the glory of his majesty. [11]The lofty looks of man shall be humbled, and the haughtiness of men shall be bowed down, and the LORD alone shall be exalted in that day. [12]For the day of the LORD of hosts *shall be* upon every *one that is* proud and lofty, and upon every *one that is* lifted up; and he shall be brought low: [13]And upon all the cedars of Lebanon, *that are* high and lifted up, and upon all the oaks of Bashan, [14]And upon all the high mountains, and upon all the hills *that are* lifted up, [15]And upon every high tower, and upon every fenced wall, [16]And

upon all the ships of Tarshish, and upon all pleasant[c] pictures. [17]And the loftiness of man shall be bowed down, and the haughtiness of men shall be made low: and the LORD alone shall be exalted in that day. [18]And the idols he shall utterly abolish. [19]And they shall go into the holes of the rocks, and into the caves of the earth[d], for fear of the LORD, and for the glory of his majesty, when he ariseth to shake terribly the earth. [20]In that day a man shall cast his idols of silver, and his idols of gold, which they made *each one* for himself to worship, to the moles and to the bats; [21]To go into the clefts of the rocks, and into the tops of the ragged rocks, for fear of the LORD, and for the glory of his majesty, when he ariseth to shake terribly the earth. [22]Cease ye from man, whose breath *is* in his nostrils: for wherein is he to be accounted of?

3

[1]For, behold, the Lord, the LORD of hosts, doth take away from Jerusalem and from Judah the stay and the staff, the whole stay of bread, and the whole stay of water, [2]The mighty man, and the man of war, the judge, and the prophet, and the prudent, and the ancient, [3]The captain of fifty, and the honourable[a] man, and the counsellor, and the cunning artificer, and the eloquent orator. [4]And I will give children *to be* their princes, and babes shall rule over them. [5]And the people shall be oppressed, every one by another, and every one by his

---

[b] pruninghooks: or, scythes
[c] pleasant . . . : Heb. pictures of desire
[d] of the earth: Heb. of the dust
[a] the honourable . . . : Heb. a man eminent in countenance

neighbour: the child shall behave himself proudly against the ancient, and the base against the honourable. ⁶When a man shall take hold of his brother of the house of his father, *saying*, Thou hast clothing, be thou our ruler, and *let* this ruin *be* under thy hand: ⁷In that day shall he swearᵇ, saying, I will not be an healer; for in my house *is* neither bread nor clothing: make me not a ruler of the people. ⁸For Jerusalem is ruined, and Judah is fallen: because their tongue and their doings *are* against the LORD, to provoke the eyes of his glory.

⁹The shew of their countenance doth witness against them; and they declare their sin as Sodom, they hide *it* not. Woe unto their soul! for they have rewarded evil unto themselves. ¹⁰Say ye to the righteous, that *it shall be* well *with him*: for they shall eat the fruit of their doings. ¹¹Woe unto the wicked! *it shall be* ill *with him*: for the reward of his hands shall be givenᶜ him. ¹²*As for* my people, children *are* their oppressors, and women rule over them. O my people, they which leadᵈ thee cause *thee* to err, and destroy the way of thy paths. ¹³The LORD standeth up to plead, and standeth to judge the people. ¹⁴The LORD will enter into judgment with the ancients of his people, and the princes thereof: for ye have eaten up the vineyard; the spoil of the poor *is* in your

Devotional Moment

•

Fleeting Beauty

3:16 The Lord was disgusted with the women of Zion because they were so taken with their own beauty and clothing. Sometimes the pull of the mirror seems irresistible. The problem is, concentration on beauty and possessions can easily make us blind to others' needs. What importance do you place on physical beauty? How is this balanced with response to others' needs?

houses. ¹⁵What mean ye *that* ye beat my people to pieces, and grind the faces of the poor? saith the Lord GOD of hosts.

¹⁶Moreover the LORD saith, Because the daughters of Zion are haughty, and walk with stretched forth necks and wantonᵉ eyes, walking and mincing *as* they go, and making a tinkling with their feet: ¹⁷Therefore the Lord will smite with a scab the crown of the head of the daughters of Zion, and the LORD will discoverᶠ their secret parts. ¹⁸In that day the Lord will take away the bravery of *their* tinkling ornaments *about their feet*, and *their* caulsᵍ, and *their* round tires like the moon, ¹⁹The chainsʰ, and the bracelets, and the mufflers, ²⁰The bonnets, and the ornaments of the legs, and the headbands, and the tabletsⁱ, and the earrings, ²¹The rings, and nose jewels, ²²The changeable

---

ᵇ swear: Heb. lift up the hand
ᶜ given . . . : Heb. done to him
ᵈ lead . . . : or, call thee blessed
ᵉ wanton . . . : Heb. deceiving with their eyes
ᶠ discover: Heb. make naked
ᵍ cauls: or, networks
ʰ chains: or, sweet balls
ⁱ tablets: Heb. houses of the soul

suits of apparel, and the mantles, and the wimples, and the crisping pins, ²³The glasses, and the fine linen, and the hoods, and the vails. ²⁴And it shall come to pass, *that* instead of sweet smell there shall be stink; and instead of a girdle a rent; and instead of well set hair baldness; and instead of a stomacher a girding of sackcloth; *and* burning instead of beauty. ²⁵Thy men shall fall by the sword, and thy mighty^j in the war. ²⁶And her gates shall lament and mourn; and she *being* desolate^k shall sit upon the ground.

4

¹And in that day seven women shall take hold of one man, saying, We will eat our own bread, and wear our own apparel: only let us be called by thy name, to take away our reproach.

²In that day shall the branch of the LORD be beautiful^a and glorious, and the fruit of the earth *shall be* excellent and comely for them that are escaped of Israel. ³And it shall come to pass, *that* he that is left in Zion, and he that remaineth in Jerusalem, shall be called holy, *even* every one that is written among the living in Jerusalem: ⁴When the Lord shall have washed away the filth of the daughters of Zion, and shall have purged the blood of Jerusalem from the midst thereof by the spirit of judgment, and by the spirit of burning. ⁵And the LORD will create upon every dwelling place of mount Zion, and upon her assemblies, a cloud and smoke by day, and the shining of a flaming fire by night: for upon all the glory *shall be* a defence. ⁶And there shall be a tabernacle for a shadow in the daytime from the heat, and for a place of refuge, and for a covert from storm and from rain.

5

¹Now will I sing to my wellbeloved a song of my beloved touching his vineyard. My wellbeloved hath a vineyard in a very fruitful hill: ²And he fenced^a it, and gathered out the stones thereof, and planted it with the choicest vine, and built a tower in the midst of it, and also made a winepress therein: and he looked that it should bring forth grapes, and it brought forth wild grapes. ³And now, O inhabitants of Jerusalem, and men of Judah, judge, I pray you, betwixt me and my vineyard. ⁴What could have been done more to my vineyard, that I have not done in it? wherefore, when I looked that it should bring forth grapes, brought it forth wild grapes? ⁵And now go to; I will tell you what I will do to my vineyard: I will take away the hedge thereof, and it shall be eaten up; *and* break down the wall thereof, and it shall be trodden down: ⁶And I will lay it waste: it shall not be pruned, nor digged; but there shall come up briers and thorns: I will also command the clouds that they rain no rain upon it. ⁷For the vineyard of the LORD of hosts *is* the house of Israel, and the men of Judah his pleasant plant: and he looked for judg-

---

^j mighty: Heb. might
^k desolate: or, emptied: Heb. cleansed
^a beautiful . . . : Heb. beauty and glory
^a fenced: or, made a wall about

Devotional Moment
•
Drinking

5:11-12 It's hard to do what God wants when you're drinking all day and partying all night. That's just one reason the Bible tells about the dangers of drinking and the ruin that alcohol can bring (for example, see Prov. 23:19-21, 29-30). If you have someone in the family who drinks too much, get help. Contact someone (your pastor, a family counselor, someone locally associated with Alcoholics Anonymous) who can help you address the problem with your loved one before it's too late.

ment, but behold oppression; for righteousness, but behold a cry.

⁸Woe unto them that join house to house, *that* lay field to field, till *there be* no place, that they may be placed alone in the midst of the earth! ⁹In mine ears *said* the LORD of hosts, Of a truth many houses shall be desolate, *even* great and fair, without inhabitant. ¹⁰Yea, ten acres of vineyard shall yield one bath, and the seed of an homer shall yield an ephah. ¹¹Woe unto them that rise up early in the morning, *that* they may follow strong drink; that continue until night, *till* wine inflameᵇ them! ¹²And the harp, and the viol, the tabret, and pipe, and wine, are in their feasts: but they regard not the work of the LORD, neither consider the operation of his hands. ¹³Therefore my people are gone into captivity, because *they have* no knowledge:

and their honourableᶜ men *are* famished, and their multitude dried up with thirst. ¹⁴Therefore hell hath enlarged herself, and opened her mouth without measure: and their glory, and their multitude, and their pomp, and he that rejoiceth, shall descend into it. ¹⁵And the mean man shall be brought down, and the mighty man shall be humbled, and the eyes of the lofty shall be humbled: ¹⁶But the LORD of hosts shall be exalted in judgment, and Godᵈ that is holy shall be sanctified in righteousness. ¹⁷Then shall the lambs feed after their manner, and the waste places of the fat ones shall strangers eat.

¹⁸Woe unto them that draw iniquity with cords of vanity, and sin as it were with a cart rope: ¹⁹That say, Let him make speed, *and* hasten his work, that we may see *it*: and let the counsel of the Holy One of Israel draw nigh and come, that we may know *it!* ²⁰Woe unto them that callᵉ evil good, and good evil; that put darkness for light, and light for darkness; that put bitter for sweet, and sweet for bitter! ²¹Woe unto *them that are* wise in their own eyes, and prudent in their own sightᶠ! ²²Woe unto *them that are* mighty to drink wine, and men of strength to mingle strong drink: ²³Which justify the wicked for reward, and take away the righteousness of the righteous from him! ²⁴Therefore as the fireᵍ devoureth the stubble, and the flame consumeth the chaff, *so* their root shall be as

---

ᵇ inflame: of, pursue
ᶜ honourable . . . : Heb. glory are men of famine
ᵈ God . . . : or, the holy God: Heb. the God the holy
ᵉ call . . . : Heb. say concerning evil, It is good, etc
ᶠ in their own sight: Heb. before their face
ᵍ fire: Heb. tongue of fire

rottenness, and their blossom shall go up as dust: because they have cast away the law of the LORD of hosts, and despised the word of the Holy One of Israel. 25Therefore is the anger of the LORD kindled against his people, and he hath stretched forth his hand against them, and hath smitten them: and the hills did tremble, and their carcases *were* torn[h] in the midst of the streets. For all this his anger is not turned away, but his hand *is* stretched out still. 26And he will lift up an ensign to the nations from far, and will hiss unto them from the end of the earth: and, behold, they shall come with speed swiftly: 27None shall be weary nor stumble among them; none shall slumber nor sleep; neither shall the girdle of their loins be loosed, nor the latchet of their shoes be broken: 28Whose arrows *are* sharp, and all their bows bent, their horses' hoofs shall be counted like flint, and their wheels like a whirlwind: 29Their roaring *shall be* like a lion, they shall roar like young lions: yea, they shall roar, and lay hold of the prey, and shall carry *it* away safe, and none shall deliver it. 30And in that day they shall roar against them like the roaring of the sea: and if *one* look unto the land, behold darkness *and* sorrow[i], and the light is darkened in the heavens thereof.

6

1In the year that king Uzziah died I saw also the Lord sitting upon a throne, high and lifted up, and his train filled the temple. 2Above it stood the seraphims: each one had six wings; with twain he covered his face, and with twain he covered his feet, and with twain he did fly. 3And one cried unto another, and said, Holy, holy, holy, *is* the LORD of hosts: the whole earth *is* full of his glory. 4And the posts of the door[a] moved at the voice of him that cried, and the house was filled with smoke.

5Then said I, Woe *is* me! for I am undone[b]; because I *am* a man of unclean lips, and I dwell in the midst of a people of unclean lips: for mine eyes have seen the King, the LORD of hosts. 6Then flew one of the seraphims unto me, having a live coal in his hand, *which* he had taken with the tongs from off the altar: 7And he laid *it* upon my mouth, and said, Lo, this hath touched thy lips; and thine iniquity is taken away, and thy sin purged. 8Also I heard the voice of the Lord, saying, Whom shall I send, and who will go for us? Then said I, Here *am* I; send[c] me.

9And he said, Go, and tell this people, Hear ye indeed, but understand[d] not; and see ye indeed, but perceive not. 10Make the heart of this people fat, and make their ears heavy, and shut their eyes; lest they see with their eyes, and hear with their ears, and understand with their heart, and convert, and be healed. 11Then said I, Lord, how

---

[h] torn: or, as dung
[i] sorrow: or, distress
[a] door: Heb. thresholds
[b] undone: Heb. cut off
[c] Here . . . : Heb. behold me
[d] indeed, but understand: or, without ceasing, etc: Heb. in hearing, etc

long? And he answered, Until the cities be wasted without inhabitant, and the houses without man, and the land be utterly^c desolate, ¹²And the LORD have removed men far away, and *there be* a great forsaking in the midst of the land. ¹³But yet in it *shall be* a tenth, and *it* shall return, and shall be eaten: as a teil tree, and as an oak, whose substance *is* in them, when they cast *their leaves: so* the holy seed *shall be* the substance thereof.

7

¹And it came to pass in the days of Ahaz the son of Jotham, the son of Uzziah, king of Judah, *that* Rezin the king of Syria, and Pekah the son of Remaliah, king of Israel, went up toward Jerusalem to war against it, but could not prevail against it. ²And it was told the house of David, saying, Syria is confederate^a with Ephraim. And his heart was moved, and the heart of his people, as the trees of the wood are moved with the wind. ³Then said the LORD unto Isaiah, Go forth now to meet Ahaz, thou, and Shearjashub^b thy son, at the end of the conduit of the upper pool in the highway of the fuller's field; ⁴And say unto him, Take heed, and be quiet; fear not, neither be fainthearted for the two tails of these smoking firebrands, for the fierce anger of Rezin with Syria, and of the son of Remaliah. ⁵Because Syria, Ephraim, and the son of Remaliah, have taken evil counsel against thee, saying,

⁶Let us go up against Judah, and vex^c it, and let us make a breach therein for us, and set a king in the midst of it, *even* the son of Tabeal: ⁷Thus saith the Lord GOD, It shall not stand, neither shall it come to pass. ⁸For the head of Syria *is* Damascus, and the head of Damascus *is* Rezin; and within threescore and five years shall Ephraim be broken, that it be not a people. ⁹And the head of Ephraim *is* Samaria, and the head of Samaria *is* Remaliah's son. If ye will not believe, surely ye shall not be established.

¹⁰Moreover the LORD spake again unto Ahaz, saying, ¹¹Ask thee a sign of the LORD thy God; ask it either in the depth, or in the height above. ¹²But Ahaz said, I will not ask, neither will I tempt the LORD. ¹³And he said, Hear ye now, O house of David; *Is it* a small thing for you to weary men, but will ye weary my God also? ¹⁴Therefore the Lord himself shall give you a sign; Behold, a virgin shall conceive, and bear a son, and shall call^d his name Immanuel. ¹⁵Butter and honey shall he eat, that he may know to refuse the evil, and choose the good. ¹⁶For before the child shall know to refuse the evil, and choose the good, the land that thou abhorrest shall be forsaken of both her kings.

¹⁷The LORD shall bring upon thee, and upon thy people, and upon thy father's house, days that have not come, from the day that Ephraim departed from Judah; *even* the king of Assyria. ¹⁸And it shall come to pass in that

---

^c utterly . . . : Heb. desolate with desolation
^a is confederate . . . : Heb. resteth on
^b Shearjashub: that is, The remnant shall return
^c vex: or, waken
^d shall call: or, thou, O virgin, shalt call

day, *that* the LORD shall hiss for the fly that *is* in the uttermost part of the rivers of Egypt, and for the bee that *is* in the land of Assyria. ¹⁹And they shall come, and shall rest all of them in the desolate valleys, and in the holes of the rocks, and upon all thorns, and upon all bushesᵉ. ²⁰In the same day shall the Lord shave with a razor that is hired, *namely*, by them beyond the river, by the king of Assyria, the head, and the hair of the feet: and it shall also consume the beard. ²¹And it shall come to pass in that day, *that* a man shall nourish a young cow, and two sheep; ²²And it shall come to pass, for the abundance of milk *that* they shall give he shall eat butter: for butter and honey shall every one eat that is left in the landᶠ. ²³And it shall come to pass in that day, *that* every place shall be, where there were a thousand vines at a thousand silverlings, it shall *even* be for briers and thorns. ²⁴With arrows and with bows shall *men* come thither; because all the land shall become briers and thorns. ²⁵And *on* all hills that shall be digged with the mattock, there shall not come thither the fear of briers and thorns: but it shall be for the sending forth of oxen, and for the treading of lesser cattle.

8

¹Moreover the LORD said unto me, Take thee a great roll, and write in it with a man's pen concerning Mahershal-alhashbazᵃ. ²And I took unto me faithful witnesses to record, Uriah the priest, and Zechariah the son of Jeberechiah. ³And I wentᵇ unto the prophetess; and she conceived, and bare a son. Then said the LORD to me, Call his name Mahershalalhashbaz. ⁴For before the child shall have knowledge to cry, My father, and my mother, the richesᶜ of Damascus and the spoil of Samaria shall be taken away before the king of Assyria. ⁵The LORD spake also unto me again, saying, ⁶Forasmuch as this people refuseth the waters of Shiloah that go softly, and rejoice in Rezin and Remaliah's son; ⁷Now therefore, behold, the Lord bringeth up upon them the waters of the river, strong and many, *even* the king of Assyria, and all his glory: and he shall come up over all his channels, and go over all his banks: ⁸And he shall pass through Judah; he shall overflow and go over, he shall reach *even* to the neck; and the stretching out of his wings shall fill the breadth of thy land, O Immanuel.

⁹Associate yourselves, O ye people, and ye shall be broken in pieces; and give ear, all ye of far countries: gird yourselves, and ye shall be broken in pieces; gird yourselves, and ye shall be broken in pieces. ¹⁰Take counsel together, and it shall come to nought; speak the word, and it shall not stand: for God *is* with us. ¹¹For the LORD spake thus to me with a strong hand, and instructed me that I should not walk in the way of this people, saying, ¹²Say ye not, A confederacy,

---

ᵉ bushes: or, commendable trees
ᶠ the land: Heb. the midst of the land
ᵃ Mahershalalhashbaz: Heb. In making speed to the spoil he hasteneth the prey, or, Make speed, etc
ᵇ went: Heb. approached
ᶜ the riches . . . : or, he that is before the king of Assyria shall take away the riches, etc

to all *them to* whom this people shall say, A confederacy; neither fear ye their fear, nor be afraid. ¹³Sanctify the LORD of hosts himself; and *let* him *be* your fear, and *let* him *be* your dread. ¹⁴And he shall be for a sanctuary; but for a stone of stumbling and for a rock of offence to both the houses of Israel, for a gin and for a snare to the inhabitants of Jerusalem. ¹⁵And many among them shall stumble, and fall, and be broken, and be snared, and be taken.

¹⁶Bind up the testimony, seal the law among my disciples. ¹⁷And I will wait upon the LORD, that hideth his face from the house of Jacob, and I will look for him. ¹⁸Behold, I and the children whom the LORD hath given me *are* for signs and for wonders in Israel from the LORD of hosts, which dwelleth in mount Zion. ¹⁹And when they shall say unto you, Seek unto them that have familiar spirits, and unto wizards that peep, and that mutter: should not a people seek unto their God? for the living to the dead? ²⁰To the law and to the testimony: if they speak not according to this word, *it is* because *there is* no light in them^d. ²¹And they shall pass through it, hardly bestead and hungry: and it shall come to pass, that when they shall be hungry, they shall fret themselves, and curse their king and their God, and look upward. ²²And they shall look unto the earth; and behold trouble and darkness, dimness of anguish; and *they shall be* driven to darkness.

9

¹Nevertheless the dimness *shall* not *be* such as *was* in her vexation, when at the first he lightly afflicted the land of Zebulun and the land of Naphtali, and afterward did more grievously afflict *her by* the way of the sea, beyond Jordan, in Galilee of the nations^a. ²The people that walked in darkness have seen a great light: they that dwell in the land of the shadow of death, upon them hath the light shined. ³Thou hast multiplied the nation, *and* not increased the joy: they joy before thee according to the joy in harvest, *and* as *men* rejoice when they divide the spoil. ⁴For thou hast broken the yoke of his burden, and the staff of his shoulder, the rod of his oppressor, as in the day of Midian. ⁵For every battle of the warrior *is* with confused noise, and garments rolled in blood; but *this* shall be with burning *and* fuel of fire. ⁶For unto us a child is born, unto us a son is given: and the government shall be upon his shoulder: and his name shall be called Wonderful, Counsellor, The mighty God, The everlasting Father, The Prince of Peace. ⁷Of the increase of *his* government and peace *there shall be* no end, upon the throne of David, and upon his kingdom, to order it, and to establish

---

Devotional Moment

•

Help!

9:8-10 In their foolish pride, Israel thought they did not need God. They bragged that they would be able to correct their problems all by themselves. Don't think you can solve all your problems on your own. The first step in conquering a bad habit is to admit your powerlessness and dependence on God. Place your problem in God's capable hands, and ask him for help.

---

^d no . . . : Heb. no morning
^a of the nations: or, populous

it with judgment and with justice from henceforth even for ever. The zeal of the LORD of hosts will perform this.

[8]The Lord sent a word into Jacob, and it hath lighted upon Israel. [9]And all the people shall know, *even* Ephraim and the inhabitant of Samaria, that say in the pride and stoutness of heart, [10]The bricks are fallen down, but we will build with hewn stones: the sycomores are cut down, but we will change *them into* cedars. [11]Therefore the LORD shall set up the adversaries of Rezin against him, and join[b] his enemies together; [12]The Syrians before, and the Philistines behind; and they shall devour Israel with open mouth. For all this his anger is not turned away, but his hand *is* stretched out still. [13]For the people turneth not unto him that smiteth them, neither do they seek the LORD of hosts. [14]Therefore the LORD will cut off from Israel head and tail, branch and rush, in one day. [15]The ancient and honourable, he *is* the head; and the prophet that teacheth lies, he *is* the tail. [16]For the leaders[c] of this people cause *them* to err; and *they that are* led of them *are* destroyed. [17]Therefore the Lord shall have no joy in their young men, neither shall have mercy on their fatherless and widows: for every one *is* an hypocrite and an evildoer, and every mouth speaketh folly[d]. For all this his anger is not turned away, but his hand *is* stretched out still. [18]For wickedness burneth as the fire: it shall devour the briers and thorns, and shall kindle in the thickets of the forest, and they shall mount up *like* the lifting up of smoke. [19]Through the wrath of the LORD of hosts is the land darkened, and the people shall be as the fuel[e] of the fire: no man shall spare his brother. [20]And he shall snatch[f] on the right hand, and be hungry; and he shall eat on the left hand, and they shall not be satisfied: they shall eat every man the flesh of his own arm: [21]Manasseh, Ephraim; and Ephraim, Manasseh: *and* they together *shall be* against Judah. For all this his anger is not turned away, but his hand *is* stretched out still.

10

[1]Woe unto them that decree unrighteous decrees, and that write[a] grievousness *which* they have prescribed; [2]To turn aside the needy from judgment, and to take away the right from the poor of my people, that widows may be their prey, and *that* they may rob the fatherless! [3]And what will ye do in the day of visitation, and in the desolation *which* shall come from far? to whom will ye flee for help? and where will ye leave your glory? [4]Without me they shall bow down under the prisoners, and they shall fall under the slain. For all this his anger is not turned away, but his hand *is* stretched out still.

[5]O[b] Assyrian, the rod of mine anger, and the staff in their hand is mine indignation. [6]I will send him against an hyp-

---

[b] join: Heb. mingle
[c] the leaders: or, they that call them blessed
[d] folly: or, villany
[e] fuel: Heb. meat
[f] snatch: Heb cut
[a] that write . . . : or, to the writers that write grievousness
[b] O . . . : or, Woe to the Assyrian: Heb. Asshur

ocritical nation, and against the people of my wrath will I give him a charge, to take the spoil, and to take the prey, and to tread them down like the mire of the streets. [7]Howbeit he meaneth not so, neither doth his heart think so; but *it is* in his heart to destroy and cut off nations not a few. [8]For he saith, *Are* not my princes altogether kings? [9]*Is* not Calno as Carchemish? *is* not Hamath as Arpad? *is* not Samaria as Damascus? [10]As my hand hath found the kingdoms of the idols, and whose graven images did excel them of Jerusalem and of Samaria; [11]Shall I not, as I have done unto Samaria and her idols, so do to Jerusalem and her idols? [12]Wherefore it shall come to pass, *that* when the Lord hath performed his whole work upon mount Zion and on Jerusalem, I will punish[c] the fruit of the stout heart of the king of Assyria, and the glory of his high looks. [13]For he saith, By the strength of my hand I have done *it*, and by my wisdom; for I am prudent: and I have removed the bounds of the people, and have robbed their treasures, and I have put down the inhabitants like a valiant[d] *man*. [14]And my hand hath found as a nest the riches of the people: and as one gathereth eggs *that are* left, have I gathered all the earth; and there was none that moved the wing, or opened the mouth, or peeped. [15]Shall the axe boast itself against him that heweth therewith? *or* shall the saw magnify itself against him that shaketh it? as if the rod[e] should shake *itself* against them that lift it up, *or* as if the staff should lift up *itself,*

as if it were no wood. [16]Therefore shall the Lord, the Lord of hosts, send among his fat ones leanness; and under his glory he shall kindle a burning like the burning of a fire. [17]And the light of Israel shall be for a fire, and his Holy One for a flame: and it shall burn and devour his thorns and his briers in one day; [18]And shall consume the glory of his forest, and of his fruitful field, both soul and body: and they shall be as when a standard-bearer fainteth. [19]And the rest of the trees of his forest shall be few[f], that a child may write them.

[20]And it shall come to pass in that day, *that* the remnant of Israel, and such as are escaped of the house of Jacob, shall no more again stay upon him that smote them; but shall stay upon the LORD, the Holy One of Israel, in truth. [21]The remnant shall return, *even* the remnant of Jacob, unto the mighty God. [22]For though thy people Israel be

---

Devotional Moment

•

Family Faith Traditions

10:20-21 Those left in Judah and Israel feared and served the conquering Assyrians. But a time would come, God said, when a new generation would return to serving the Lord. That remnant would choose to go against the traditions and ways of their parents. If you find your faith rubbing against the grain of family tradition, you must, like the remnant in Judah and Israel, find your own faith in the true and living God. If your parents are followers of the Lord, praise God. If not, stand firmly and graciously in your commitment to follow him.

---

[c] punish: Heb. visit upon
[d] a valiant . . . : or, many people
[e] the rod . . . : or, a rod should shake them that lift it up
[f] few: Heb. number

as the sand of the sea, *yet* a remnant of them shall return: the consumption decreed shall overflow with righteousness. ²³For the Lord GOD of hosts shall make a consumption, even determined, in the midst of all the land.

²⁴Therefore thus saith the Lord GOD of hosts, O my people that dwellest in Zion, be not afraid of the Assyrian: he shall smite thee with a rod, and shall lift up his staff against thee, after the manner of Egypt. ²⁵For yet a very little while, and the indignation shall cease, and mine anger in their destruction. ²⁶And the LORD of hosts shall stir up a scourge for him according to the slaughter of Midian at the rock of Oreb: and *as* his rod *was* upon the sea, so shall he lift it up after the manner of Egypt. ²⁷And it shall come to pass in that day, *that* his burden shall be taken away from off thy shoulder, and his yoke from off thy neck, and the yoke shall be destroyed because of the anointing. ²⁸He is come to Aiath, he is passed to Migron; at Michmash he hath laid up his carriages: ²⁹They are gone over the passage: they have taken up their lodging at Geba; Ramah is afraid; Gibeah of Saul is fled. ³⁰Lift up thy voice, O daughter of Gallim: cause it to be heard unto Laish, O poor Anathoth. ³¹Madmenah is removed; the inhabitants of Gebim gather themselves to flee. ³²As yet shall he remain at Nob that day: he shall shake his hand *against* the mount of the daughter of Zion, the hill of Jerusalem. ³³Behold, the Lord, the LORD of hosts, shall lop the bough with terror: and the high ones of stature *shall be* hewn down, and the haughty shall be humbled. ³⁴And he

shall cut down the thickets of the forest with iron, and Lebanon shall fall by a mighty one.

11

¹And there shall come forth a rod out of the stem of Jesse, and a Branch shall grow out of his roots: ²And the spirit of the LORD shall rest upon him, the spirit of wisdom and understanding, the spirit of counsel and might, the spirit of knowledge and of the fear of the LORD; ³And shall make him of quick understanding in the fear of the LORD: and he shall not judge after the sight of his eyes, neither reprove after the hearing of his ears: ⁴But with righteousness shall he judge the poor, and reprove[a] with equity for the meek of the earth: and he shall smite the earth with the rod of his mouth, and with the breath of his lips shall he slay the wicked. ⁵And righteousness shall be the girdle of his loins, and faithfulness the girdle of his reins. ⁶The wolf also shall dwell with the lamb, and the leopard shall lie down with the kid; and the calf and the young lion and the fatling together; and a little child shall lead them. ⁷And the cow and the bear shall feed; their young ones shall lie down together: and the lion shall eat straw like the ox. ⁸And the sucking child shall play on the hole of the asp, and the weaned child shall put his hand on the cockatrice' den. ⁹They shall not hurt nor destroy in all my holy mountain: for the earth shall be full of the knowledge of the LORD, as the waters cover the sea.

¹⁰And in that day there shall be a root of Jesse, which shall stand for an en-

---

[a] reprove: or, argue

sign of the people; to it shall the Gentiles seek: and his rest shall be glorious[b]. [11]And it shall come to pass in that day, *that* the Lord shall set his hand again the second time to recover the remnant of his people, which shall be left, from Assyria, and from Egypt, and from Pathros, and from Cush, and from Elam, and from Shinar, and from Hamath, and from the islands of the sea. [12]And he shall set up an ensign for the nations, and shall assemble the outcasts of Israel, and gather together the dispersed of Judah from the four corners[c] of the earth. [13]The envy also of Ephraim shall depart, and the adversaries of Judah shall be cut off: Ephraim shall not envy Judah, and Judah shall not vex Ephraim. [14]But they shall fly upon the shoulders of the Philistines toward the west; they shall spoil them of the east together: they shall lay their hand upon Edom and Moab; and the children of Ammon shall obey them. [15]And the LORD shall utterly destroy the tongue of the Egyptian sea; and with his mighty wind shall he shake his hand over the river, and shall smite it in the seven streams, and make *men* go over dryshod[d]. [16]And there shall be an highway for the remnant of his people, which shall be left, from Assyria; like as it was to Israel in the day that he came up out of the land of Egypt.

12

[1]And in that day thou shalt say, O LORD, I will praise thee: though thou wast angry with me, thine anger is

---

[b] glorious: Heb. glory
[c] corners: Heb. wings
[d] dryshod: Heb. in shoes

Worship
in Your Home

HELP YOUR CHILDREN LEAD DEVOTIONS
A little child shall lead them.
Isaiah 11:6

One of a leader's main jobs is to train followers how to lead. Helping children learn to lead devotions gives them a sense of responsibility and cultivates in them a feeling that they share in the family ownership.

What can children do to lead devotions? For teens, agree on a certain time and let them do it. Or talk together about what your teens could do. Talk about topics and how your teens could handle them.

Preteens and younger children need more help. You may want to ask your child, "What would you like to do if you led devotions next time?" Help your child fine-tune any ideas he or she has. Ask your child for topical suggestions for a devotion ("What would you like for us to talk about next time?"). Or you can start a story about a topic and let your child complete it. Other ideas include asking your child to bring nature objects, such as colored leaves, as the basis for a devotional, or letting your child ask questions, which you answer.

Don't pressure. If your child does not want to lead, don't push. But you may be surprised at how ready your child is to lead—and at the results.

turned away, and thou comfortedst me. [2]Behold, God *is* my salvation; I will trust, and not be afraid: for the LORD JEHOVAH *is* my strength and *my* song; he also is become my salvation. [3]Therefore with joy shall ye draw water out of the wells of salvation.

[4]And in that day shall ye say, Praise the LORD, call[a] upon his name, declare his doings among the people, make mention that his name is exalted. [5]Sing unto the LORD; for he hath done excellent things: this *is* known in all the earth. [6]Cry out and shout, thou inhabitant[b] of Zion: for great *is* the Holy One of Israel in the midst of thee.

13

[1]The burden of Babylon, which Isaiah the son of Amoz did see. [2]Lift ye up a banner upon the high mountain, exalt the voice unto them, shake the hand, that they may go into the gates of the nobles. [3]I have commanded my sanctified ones, I have also called my mighty ones for mine anger, *even* them that rejoice in my highness. [4]The noise of a multitude in the mountains, like[a] as of a great people; a tumultuous noise of the kingdoms of nations gathered together: the LORD of hosts mustereth the host of the battle. [5]They come from a far country, from the end of heaven, *even* the LORD, and the weapons of his indignation, to destroy the whole land.

[6]Howl ye; for the day of the LORD *is* at hand; it shall come as a destruction from the Almighty. [7]Therefore shall all hands be faint[b], and every man's heart shall melt: [8]And they shall be afraid: pangs and sorrows shall take hold of them; they shall be in pain as a woman that travaileth: they shall be amazed[c] one at another; their faces *shall be as* flames. [9]Behold, the day of the LORD cometh, cruel both with wrath and fierce anger, to lay the land desolate: and he shall destroy the sinners thereof out of it. [10]For the stars of heaven and the constellations thereof shall not give their light: the sun shall be darkened in his going forth, and the moon shall not cause her light to shine. [11]And I will punish the world for *their* evil, and the wicked for their iniquity; and I will cause the arrogancy of the proud to cease, and will lay low the haughtiness of the terrible. [12]I will make a man more precious than fine gold; even a man than the golden wedge of Ophir. [13]Therefore I will shake the heavens, and the earth shall remove out of her place, in the wrath of the LORD of hosts, and in the day of his fierce anger. [14]And it shall be as the chased roe, and as a sheep that no man taketh up: they shall every man turn to his own people, and flee every one into his own land. [15]Every one that is found shall be thrust through; and every one that is joined *unto them* shall fall by the sword. [16]Their children also shall be dashed to pieces before their eyes; their houses shall be spoiled, and their wives

---

[a] call . . . : or, proclaim
[b] inhabitant: Heb. inhabitress
[a] like . . . : Heb. the likeness of
[b] be faint: or, fall down
[c] be amazed: Heb. wonder

ravished. ¹⁷Behold, I will stir up the Medes against them, which shall not regard silver; and *as for* gold, they shall not delight in it. ¹⁸ *Their* bows also shall dash the young men to pieces; and they shall have no pity on the fruit of the womb; their eye shall not spare children.

¹⁹And Babylon, the glory of kingdoms, the beauty of the Chaldees' excellency, shall be as when God overthrew Sodom and Gomorrah. ²⁰It shall never be inhabited, neither shall it be dwelt in from generation to generation: neither shall the Arabian pitch tent there; neither shall the shepherds make their fold there. ²¹But wild beasts of the desert shall lie there; and their houses shall be full of doleful creatures; and owls shall dwell there, and satyrs shall dance there. ²²And the wild beasts of the islands shall cry in their desolate houses, and dragons in *their* pleasant palaces: and her time *is* near to come, and her days shall not be prolonged.

14

¹For the LORD will have mercy on Jacob, and will yet choose Israel, and set them in their own land: and the strangers shall be joined with them, and they shall cleave to the house of Jacob. ²And the people shall take them, and bring them to their place: and the house of Israel shall possess them in the land of the LORD for servants and handmaids: and they shall take them captives, whose captives they were; and

they shall rule over their oppressors. ³And it shall come to pass in the day that the LORD shall give thee rest from thy sorrow, and from thy fear, and from the hard bondage wherein thou wast made to serve,

⁴That thou shalt take up this proverb[a] against the king of Babylon, and say, How hath the oppressor ceased! the golden city ceased! ⁵The LORD hath broken the staff of the wicked, *and* the sceptre of the rulers. ⁶He who smote the people in wrath with a continual[b] stroke, he that ruled the nations in anger, is persecuted, *and* none hindereth. ⁷The whole earth is at rest, *and* is quiet: they break forth into singing. ⁸Yea, the fir trees rejoice at thee, *and* the cedars of Lebanon, *saying*, Since thou art laid down, no feller is come up against us. ⁹Hell[c] from beneath is moved for thee to meet *thee* at thy coming: it stirreth up the dead for thee, *even* all the chief ones of the earth; it hath raised up from their thrones all the kings of the nations. ¹⁰All they shall speak and say unto thee, Art thou also become weak as we? art thou become like unto us? ¹¹Thy pomp is brought down to the grave, *and* the noise of thy viols: the worm is spread under thee, and the worms cover thee. ¹²How art thou fallen from heaven, O Lucifer[d], son of the morning! *how* art thou cut down to the ground, which didst weaken the nations! ¹³For thou hast said in thine heart, I will ascend into heaven, I will exalt my throne above the stars of God: I will sit also upon the

---

[a] proverb: or, taunting speech
[b] a continual . . . : Heb. a stroke without removing
[c] Hell: or, The grave
[d] O Lucifer: or, O day star

mount of the congregation, in the sides of the north: [14]I will ascend above the heights of the clouds; I will be like the most High. [15]Yet thou shalt be brought down to hell, to the sides of the pit. [16]They that see thee shall narrowly look upon thee, *and* consider thee, *saying, Is* this the man that made the earth to tremble, that did shake kingdoms; [17]*That* made the world as a wilderness, and destroyed the cities thereof; *that* opened[e] not the house of his prisoners? [18]All the kings of the nations, *even* all of them, lie in glory, every one in his own house. [19]But thou art cast out of thy grave like an abominable branch, *and as* the raiment of those that are slain, thrust through with a sword, that go down to the stones of the pit; as a carcase trodden under feet. [20]Thou shalt not be joined with them in burial, because thou hast destroyed thy land, *and* slain thy people: the seed of evildoers shall never be renowned. [21]Prepare slaughter for his children for the iniquity of their fathers; that they do not rise, nor possess the land, nor fill the face of the world with cities. [22]For I will rise up against them, saith the LORD of hosts, and cut off from Babylon the name, and remnant, and son, and nephew, saith the LORD. [23]I will also make it a possession for the bittern, and pools of water: and I will sweep it with the besom of destruction, saith the LORD of hosts.

[24]The LORD of hosts hath sworn, saying, Surely as I have thought, so shall it come to pass; and as I have purposed, so shall it stand: [25]That I will break the Assyrian in my land, and upon my mountains tread him under foot: then shall his yoke depart from off them, and his burden depart from off their shoulders. [26]This *is* the purpose that is purposed upon the whole earth: and this *is* the hand that is stretched out upon all the nations. [27]For the LORD of hosts hath purposed, and who shall disannul *it?* and his hand *is* stretched out, and who shall turn it back? [28]In the year that king Ahaz died was this burden. [29]Rejoice not thou, whole Palestina, because the rod of him that smote thee is broken: for out of the serpent's root shall come forth a cockatrice[f], and his fruit *shall be* a fiery flying serpent. [30]And the firstborn of the poor shall feed, and the needy shall lie down in safety: and I will kill thy root with famine, and he shall slay thy remnant. [31]Howl, O gate; cry, O city; thou, whole Palestina, *art* dissolved: for there shall come from the north a smoke, and none *shall be* alone[g] in his appointed times. [32]What shall *one* then answer the messengers of the nation? That the LORD hath founded Zion, and the poor of his people shall trust[h] in it.

15

[1]The burden of Moab. Because in the night Ar of Moab is laid waste, *and* brought to silence; because in the night Kir of Moab is laid waste, *and* brought to silence; [2]He is gone up to Bajith, and to Dibon, the high places, to weep: Moab shall howl over Nebo, and over Medeba:

---

[e] opened . . . : or, did not let his prisoners loose homeward?
[f] cockatrice: or, adder
[g] none . . . : or, he shall not be alone
[h] trust . . . : or, betake themselves unto it

on all their heads *shall be* baldness, *and* every beard cut off. ³In their streets they shall gird themselves with sackcloth: on the tops of their houses, and in their streets, every one shall howl, weeping[a] abundantly. ⁴And Heshbon shall cry, and Elealeh: their voice shall be heard *even* unto Jahaz: therefore the armed soldiers of Moab shall cry out; his life shall be grievous unto him. ⁵My heart shall cry out for Moab; his fugitives *shall flee* unto Zoar, an heifer of three years old: for by the mounting up of Luhith with weeping shall they go it up; for in the way of Horonaim they shall raise up a cry of destruction.

⁶For the waters of Nimrim shall be desolate[b]: for the hay is withered away, the grass faileth, there is no green thing. ⁷Therefore the abundance they have gotten, and that which they have laid up, shall they carry away to the brook[c] of the willows. ⁸For the cry is gone round about the borders of Moab; the howling thereof unto Eglaim, and the howling thereof unto Beerelim. ⁹For the waters of Dimon shall be full of blood: for I will bring more[d] upon Dimon, lions upon him that escapeth of Moab, and upon the remnant of the land.

16

¹Send ye the lamb to the ruler of the land from Sela[a] to the wilderness, unto the mount of the daughter of Zion. ²For it shall be, *that*, as a wandering bird cast out of the nest, *so* the daughters of Moab shall be at the fords of Arnon. ³Take[b] counsel, execute judgment; make thy shadow as the night in the midst of the noonday; hide the outcasts; bewray not him that wandereth. ⁴Let mine outcasts dwell with thee, Moab; be thou a covert to them from the face of the spoiler: for the extortioner[c] is at an end, the spoiler ceaseth, the oppressors are consumed out of the land. ⁵And in mercy shall the throne be established[d]: and he shall sit upon it in truth in the tabernacle of David, judging, and seeking judgment, and hasting righteousness.

⁶We have heard of the pride of Moab; *he is* very proud: *even* of his haughtiness, and his pride, and his wrath: *but* his lies *shall* not *be* so. ⁷Therefore shall Moab howl for Moab, every one shall howl: for the foundations of Kirhareseth shall ye mourn[e]; surely *they are* stricken. ⁸For the fields of Heshbon languish, *and* the vine of Sibmah: the lords of the heathen have broken down the principal plants thereof, they are come *even* unto Jazer, they wandered *through* the wilderness: her branches are stretched out, they are gone over the sea. ⁹Therefore I will bewail with the weeping of Jazer the vine

---

[a] weeping . . . : Heb. descending into weeping, or, coming down with weeping
[b] desolate: Heb. desolations
[c] brook . . . : or, valley of the Arabians
[d] more: Heb. additions
[a] Sela: or, Petra: Heb. A rock
[b] Take: Heb. Bring
[c] extortioner: Heb. wringer
[d] established: or, prepared
[e] mourn: or, mutter

of Sibmah: I will water thee with my tears, O Heshbon, and Elealeh: for the shouting[f] for thy summer fruits and for thy harvest is fallen. ¹⁰And gladness is taken away, and joy out of the plentiful field; and in the vineyards there shall be no singing, neither shall there be shouting: the treaders shall tread out no wine in *their* presses; I have made *their vintage* shouting to cease. ¹¹Wherefore my bowels shall sound like an harp for Moab, and mine inward parts for Kirharesh. ¹²And it shall come to pass, when it is seen that Moab is weary on the high place, that he shall come to his sanctuary to pray; but he shall not prevail. ¹³This *is* the word that the LORD hath spoken concerning Moab since that time. ¹⁴But now the LORD hath spoken, saying, Within three years, as the years of an hireling, and the glory of Moab shall be contemned, with all that great multitude; and the remnant *shall be* very small *and* feeble[g].

17

¹The burden of Damascus. Behold, Damascus is taken away from *being* a city, and it shall be a ruinous heap. ²The cities of Aroer *are* forsaken: they shall be for flocks, which shall lie down, and none shall make *them* afraid. ³The fortress also shall cease from Ephraim, and the kingdom from Damascus, and the remnant of Syria: they shall be as the glory of the children of Israel, saith the LORD of hosts. ⁴And in that day it shall come to pass, *that* the glory of Jacob shall be made thin, and the fatness of his flesh shall wax lean. ⁵And it shall be as when the harvestman gathereth the corn, and reapeth the ears with his arm; and it shall be as he that gathereth ears in the valley of Rephaim.

⁶Yet gleaning grapes shall be left in it, as the shaking of an olive tree, two *or* three berries in the top of the uppermost bough, four *or* five in the outmost fruitful branches thereof, saith the LORD God of Israel. ⁷At that day shall a man look to his Maker, and his eyes shall have respect to the Holy One of Israel. ⁸And he shall not look to the altars, the work of his hands, neither shall respect *that* which his fingers have made, either the groves, or the images[a].

⁹In that day shall his strong cities be as a forsaken bough, and an uppermost branch, which they left because of the children of Israel: and there shall be desolation. ¹⁰Because thou hast forgotten the God of thy salvation, and hast not been mindful of the rock of thy strength, therefore shalt thou plant pleasant plants, and shalt set it with strange slips: ¹¹In the day shalt thou make thy plant to grow, and in the morning shalt thou make thy seed to flourish: *but* the harvest *shall be* a heap[b] in the day of grief and of desperate sorrow.

¹²Woe to the multitude[c] of many people, *which* make a noise like the noise of the seas; and to the rushing of

---

[f] the shouting . . . : or, the alarm is fallen upon, etc
[g] feeble: or, not many
[a] images: or, sun images
[b] a heap . . . : or, removed in the day of inheritance, and there shall be deadly sorrow
[c] multitude: or, noise

nations, *that* make a rushing like the rushing of mighty waters! ¹³The nations shall rush like the rushing of many waters: but *God* shall rebuke them, and they shall flee far off, and shall be chased as the chaff of the mountains before the wind, and like a rolling thing before the whirlwind. ¹⁴And behold at eveningtide trouble; *and* before the morning he *is* not. This *is* the portion of them that spoil us, and the lot of them that rob us.

18

¹Woe to the land shadowing with wings, which *is* beyond the rivers of Ethiopia: ²That sendeth ambassadors by the sea, even in vessels of bulrushes upon the waters, *saying,* Go, ye swift messengers, to a nation scattered[a] and peeled, to a people terrible from their beginning hitherto; a nation meted out and trodden down, whose land the rivers have spoiled! ³All ye inhabitants of the world, and dwellers on the earth, see ye, when he lifteth up an ensign on the mountains; and when he bloweth a trumpet, hear ye. ⁴For so the LORD said unto me, I will take my rest, and I will consider[b] in my dwelling place like a clear heat upon herbs, *and* like a cloud of dew in the heat of harvest. ⁵For afore the harvest, when the bud is perfect, and the sour grape is ripening in the flower, he shall both cut off the sprigs with pruning hooks, and take away *and* cut down the branches. ⁶They

shall be left together unto the fowls of the mountains, and to the beasts of the earth: and the fowls shall summer upon them, and all the beasts of the earth shall winter upon them. ⁷In that time shall the present be brought unto the LORD of hosts of a people scattered[c] and peeled, and from a people terrible from their beginning hitherto; a nation meted out and trodden under foot, whose land the rivers have spoiled, to the place of the name of the LORD of hosts, the mount Zion.

19

¹The burden of Egypt. Behold, the LORD rideth upon a swift cloud, and shall come into Egypt: and the idols of Egypt shall be moved at his presence, and the heart of Egypt shall melt in the midst of it. ²And I will set[a] the Egyptians against the Egyptians: and they shall fight every one against his brother, and every one against his neighbour; city against city, *and* kingdom against kingdom. ³And the spirit of Egypt shall fail[b] in the midst thereof; and I will destroy the counsel thereof: and they shall seek to the idols, and to the charmers, and to them that have familiar spirits, and to the wizards. ⁴And the Egyptians will I give over into the hand of a cruel lord; and a fierce king shall rule over them, saith the Lord, the LORD of hosts. ⁵And the waters shall fail from the sea, and the river shall be wasted and dried up. ⁶And they shall turn the

---

ᵃ scattered . . . : or, outspread and polished
ᵇ consider . . . : or, regard my set dwelling
ᶜ scattered . . . : or, outspread and polished
ᵃ set: Heb. mingle
ᵇ fail: Heb. be emptied

rivers far away; *and* the brooks of defence shall be emptied and dried up: the reeds and flags shall wither. [7]The paper reeds by the brooks, by the mouth of the brooks, and every thing sown by the brooks, shall wither, be driven away, and be no *more*. [8]The fishers also shall mourn, and all they that cast angle into the brooks shall lament, and they that spread nets upon the waters shall languish. [9]Moreover they that work in fine flax, and they that weave networks[c], shall be confounded. [10]And they shall be broken in the purposes[d] thereof, all that make sluices *and* ponds for fish. [11]Surely the princes of Zoan *are* fools, the counsel of the wise counsellors of Pharaoh is become brutish: how say ye unto Pharaoh, I *am* the son of the wise, the son of ancient kings? [12]Where *are* they? where *are* thy wise *men*? and let them tell thee now, and let

Devotional Moment

•

Advice

19:11-15 Pharaoh sought counsel from the wise men of Egypt, but the counsel Pharaoh got ruined the country! He and his counselors had no regard for God, and reverence for the Lord is the beginning of wisdom (see Prov. 1:7). Troubles of all kinds can lead to the need for formal counseling. As God's people, we must look for counselors who know God or at least respect his Word. If you need help, by all means seek counsel, but don't go to just anybody. Ask your pastor for help or for a referral to another Christian counselor. Counselors who know God and respect his wisdom can offer true help.

them know what the LORD of hosts hath purposed upon Egypt. [13]The princes of Zoan are become fools, the princes of Noph are deceived; they have also seduced Egypt, *even they that are* the stay of the tribes thereof. [14]The LORD hath mingled a perverse[e] spirit in the midst thereof: and they have caused Egypt to err in every work thereof, as a drunken *man* staggereth in his vomit. [15]Neither shall there be *any* work for Egypt, which the head or tail, branch or rush, may do. [16]In that day shall Egypt be like unto women: and it shall be afraid and fear because of the shaking of the hand of the LORD of hosts, which he shaketh over it. [17]And the land of Judah shall be a terror unto Egypt, every one that maketh mention thereof shall be afraid in himself, because of the counsel of the LORD of hosts, which he hath determined against it.

[18]In that day shall five cities in the land of Egypt speak the language[f] of Canaan, and swear to the LORD of hosts; one shall be called, The city of destruction. [19]In that day shall there be an altar to the LORD in the midst of the land of Egypt, and a pillar at the border thereof to the LORD. [20]And it shall be for a sign and for a witness unto the LORD of hosts in the land of Egypt: for they shall cry unto the LORD because of the oppressors, and he shall send them a saviour, and a great one, and he shall deliver them. [21]And the LORD shall be known to Egypt,

---

[c] networks: or, white works
[d] purposes: Heb. foundations
[e] a perverse . . . : Heb. a spirit of perversities
[f] the language: Heb. the lip

and the Egyptians shall know the LORD in that day, and shall do sacrifice and oblation; yea, they shall vow a vow unto the LORD, and perform *it*. [22]And the LORD shall smite Egypt: he shall smite and heal *it*: and they shall return *even* to the LORD, and he shall be intreated of them, and shall heal them. [23]In that day shall there be a highway out of Egypt to Assyria, and the Assyrian shall come into Egypt, and the Egyptian into Assyria, and the Egyptians shall serve with the Assyrians. [24]In that day shall Israel be the third with Egypt and with Assyria, *even* a blessing in the midst of the land: [25]Whom the LORD of hosts shall bless, saying, Blessed *be* Egypt my people, and Assyria the work of my hands, and Israel mine inheritance.

20

[1]In the year that Tartan came unto Ashdod, (when Sargon the king of Assyria sent him,) and fought against Ashdod, and took it; [2]At the same time spake the LORD by[a] Isaiah the son of Amoz, saying, Go and loose the sackcloth from off thy loins, and put off thy shoe from thy foot. And he did so, walking naked and barefoot. [3]And the LORD said, Like as my servant Isaiah hath walked naked and barefoot three years *for* a sign and wonder upon Egypt and upon Ethiopia; [4]So shall the king of Assyria lead away the Egyptians[b] prisoners, and the Ethiopians captives, young and old,

naked and barefoot, even with *their* buttocks uncovered, to the shame of Egypt. [5]And they shall be afraid and ashamed of Ethiopia their expectation, and of Egypt their glory. [6]And the inhabitant of this isle[c] shall say in that day, Behold, such *is* our expectation, whither we flee for help to be delivered from the king of Assyria: and how shall we escape?

21

[1]The burden of the desert of the sea. As whirlwinds in the south pass through; *so* it cometh from the desert, from a terrible land. [2]A grievous[a] vision is declared unto me; the treacherous dealer dealeth treacherously, and the spoiler spoileth. Go up, O Elam: besiege, O Media; all the sighing thereof have I made to cease. [3]Therefore are my loins filled with pain: pangs have taken hold upon me, as the pangs of a woman that travaileth: I was bowed down at the hearing *of it*; I was dismayed at the seeing *of it*. [4]My heart[b] panted, fearfulness affrighted me: the night of my pleasure hath he turned into fear unto me. [5]Prepare the table, watch in the watchtower, eat, drink: arise, ye princes, *and* anoint the shield. [6]For thus hath the Lord said unto me, Go, set a watchman, let him declare what he seeth. [7]And he saw a chariot *with* a couple of horsemen, a chariot of asses, *and* a chariot of camels; and he hearkened diligently with much heed: [8]And he cried, A lion: My lord, I stand continually upon the watchtower

---

[a] by: Heb. by the hand of
[b] the Egyptians . . . : Heb. the captivity of Egypt
[c] isle: or, country
[a] grievous: Heb. hard
[b] heart . . . : or, mind wandered

in the daytime, and I am set in my ward whole nights: ⁹And, behold, here cometh a chariot of men, *with* a couple of horsemen. And he answered and said, Babylon is fallen, is fallen; and all the graven images of her gods he hath broken unto the ground. ¹⁰O my threshing, and the corn^c of my floor: that which I have heard of the LORD of hosts, the God of Israel, have I declared unto you.

¹¹The burden of Dumah. He calleth to me out of Seir, Watchman, what of the night? Watchman, what of the night? ¹²The watchman said, The morning cometh, and also the night: if ye will enquire, enquire ye: return, come.

¹³The burden upon Arabia. In the forest in Arabia shall ye lodge, O ye travelling companies of Dedanim. ¹⁴The inhabitants of the land of Tema brought^d water to him that was thirsty, they prevented with their bread him that fled. ¹⁵For they fled from the swords^e, from the drawn sword, and from the bent bow, and from the grievousness of war. ¹⁶For thus hath the Lord said unto me, Within a year, according to the years of an hireling, and all the glory of Kedar shall fail: ¹⁷And the residue of the number of archers^f, the mighty men of the children of Kedar, shall be diminished: for the LORD God of Israel hath spoken *it*.

22

¹The burden of the valley of vision. What aileth thee now, that thou art wholly gone up to the housetops? ²Thou that art full of stirs, a tumultuous city, a joyous city: thy slain *men are* not slain with the sword, nor dead in battle. ³All thy rulers are fled together, they are bound by the archers: all that are found in thee are bound together, *which* have fled from far. ⁴Therefore said I, Look away from me; I will weep^a bitterly, labour not to comfort me, because of the spoiling of the daughter of my people. ⁵For *it is* a day of trouble, and of treading down, and of perplexity by the Lord GOD of hosts in the valley of vision, breaking down the walls, and of crying to the mountains. ⁶And Elam bare the quiver with chariots of men *and* horsemen, and Kir uncovered^b the shield. ⁷And it shall come to pass, *that* thy choicest valleys shall be full of chariots, and the horsemen shall set themselves in array at the gate.

⁸And he discovered the covering of Judah, and thou didst look in that day to the armour of the house of the forest. ⁹Ye have seen also the breaches of the city of David, that they are many: and ye gathered together the waters of the lower pool. ¹⁰And ye have numbered the houses of Jerusalem, and the houses have ye broken down to fortify the wall. ¹¹Ye made also a ditch between the two walls for the water of the old pool: but ye have not looked unto the maker thereof, neither had respect unto him

---

^c corn: Heb. son

^d brought: or, bring ye

^e from the swords: or, for fear, etc: Heb. from the face, etc

^f archers: Heb. bows

^a weep . . . : Heb. be bitter in weeping

^b uncovered: Heb. made naked

that fashioned it long ago. [12]And in that day did the Lord GOD of hosts call to weeping, and to mourning, and to baldness, and to girding with sackcloth: [13]And behold joy and gladness, slaying oxen, and killing sheep, eating flesh, and drinking wine: let us eat and drink; for to morrow we shall die. [14]And it was revealed in mine ears by the LORD of hosts, Surely this iniquity shall not be purged from you till ye die, saith the Lord GOD of hosts.

[15]Thus saith the Lord GOD of hosts, Go, get thee unto this treasurer, *even* unto Shebna, which *is* over the house, *and say,* [16]What hast thou here? and whom hast thou here, that thou hast hewed thee out a sepulchre here, *as* he that heweth him out a sepulchre on high, *and* that graveth an habitation for himself in a rock? [17]Behold, the LORD will carry thee away with a mighty captivity, and will surely cover thee. [18]He will surely violently turn and toss thee *like* a ball into a large[c] country: there shalt thou die, and there the chariots of thy glory *shall be* the shame of thy lord's house. [19]And I will drive thee from thy station, and from thy state shall he pull thee down. [20]And it shall come to pass in that day, that I will call my servant Eliakim the son of Hilkiah: [21]And I will clothe him with thy robe, and strengthen him with thy girdle, and I will commit thy government into his hand: and he shall be a father to the inhabitants of Jerusalem, and to the house of Judah. [22]And the key of the house of David will I lay upon his shoulder; so he shall open, and none shall shut; and he shall shut, and none shall open. [23]And I will fasten him *as* a nail in a sure place; and he shall be for a glorious throne to his father's house. [24]And they shall hang upon him all the glory of his father's house, the offspring and the issue, all vessels of small quantity, from the vessels of cups, even to all the vessels of flagons[d]. [25]In that day, saith the LORD of hosts, shall the nail that is fastened in the sure place be removed, and be cut down, and fall; and the burden that *was* upon it shall be cut off: for the LORD hath spoken *it.*

23

[1]The burden of Tyre. Howl, ye ships of Tarshish; for it is laid waste, so that there is no house, no entering in: from the land of Chittim it is revealed to them. [2]Be still[a], ye inhabitants of the isle; thou whom the merchants of Zidon, that pass over the sea, have replenished. [3]And by great waters the seed of Sihor, the harvest of the river, *is* her revenue; and she is a mart of nations. [4]Be thou ashamed, O Zidon: for the sea hath spoken, *even* the strength of the sea, saying, I travail not, nor bring forth children, neither do I nourish up young men, *nor* bring up virgins. [5]As at the report concerning Egypt, *so* shall they be sorely pained at the report of Tyre. [6]Pass ye over to Tarshish; howl, ye inhabitants of the isle. [7]*Is* this your joyous *city,* whose antiquity *is* of ancient days? her own feet shall carry her afar off to sojourn. [8]Who hath taken this counsel

---

[c] large: Heb. large of spaces
[d] vessels of flagons: or, instruments of viols
[a] still: Heb. silent

against Tyre, the crowning *city*, whose merchants *are* princes, whose traffickers *are* the honourable of the earth? ⁹The LORD of hosts hath purposed it, to stainᵇ the pride of all glory, *and* to bring into contempt all the honourable of the earth. ¹⁰Pass through thy land as a river, O daughter of Tarshish: *there is* no more strengthᶜ. ¹¹He stretched out his hand over the sea, he shook the kingdoms: the LORD hath given a commandment against the merchant *city*, to destroy the strong holds thereof. ¹²And he said, Thou shalt no more rejoice, O thou oppressed virgin, daughter of Zidon: arise, pass over to Chittim; there also shalt thou have no rest. ¹³Behold the land of the Chaldeans; this people was not, *till* the Assyrian founded it for them that dwell in the wilderness: they set up the towers thereof, they raised up the palaces thereof; *and* he brought it to ruin. ¹⁴Howl, ye ships of Tarshish: for your strength is laid waste.

¹⁵And it shall come to pass in that day, that Tyre shall be forgotten seventy years, according to the days of one king: after the end of seventy years shall Tyreᵈ sing as an harlot. ¹⁶Take an harp, go about the city, thou harlot that hast been forgotten; make sweet melody, sing many songs, that thou mayest be remembered. ¹⁷And it shall come to pass after the end of seventy years, that the LORD will visit Tyre, and she shall turn to her hire, and shall commit fornication with all the kingdoms of the world upon the face of the earth. ¹⁸And her merchandise and her hire shall be holiness to the LORD: it shall not be treasured nor laid up; for her merchandise shall be for them that dwell before the LORD, to eat sufficiently, and for durableᵉ clothing.

24

¹Behold, the LORD maketh the earth empty, and maketh it waste, and turnethᵃ it upside down, and scattereth abroad the inhabitants thereof. ²And it shall be, as with the people, so with the priestᵇ; as with the servant, so with his master; as with the maid, so with her mistress; as with the buyer, so with the seller; as with the lender, so with the borrower; as with the taker of usury, so with the giver of usury to him. ³The land shall be utterly emptied, and utterly spoiled: for the LORD hath spoken this word. ⁴The earth mourneth *and* fadeth away, the world languisheth *and* fadeth away, the haughtyᶜ people of the earth do languish. ⁵The earth also is defiled under the inhabitants thereof; because they have transgressed the laws, changed the ordinance, broken the everlasting covenant. ⁶Therefore hath the curse devoured the earth, and they that dwell therein are desolate: therefore the inhabitants of the earth are

---

ᵇ to stain: Heb. to pollute
ᶜ strength: Heb. girdle
ᵈ shall Tyre . . . : Heb. it shall be unto Tyre as the song of an harlot
ᵉ durable: Heb. old
ᵃ turneth . . . : Heb. perverteth the face thereof
ᵇ priest: or, prince
ᶜ the haughty . . . : Heb. the height of the people

burned, and few men left. ⁷The new wine mourneth, the vine languisheth, all the merryhearted do sigh. ⁸The mirth of tabrets ceaseth, the noise of them that rejoice endeth, the joy of the harp ceaseth. ⁹They shall not drink wine with a song; strong drink shall be bitter to them that drink it. ¹⁰The city of confusion is broken down: every house is shut up, that no man may come in. ¹¹ *There is* a crying for wine in the streets; all joy is darkened, the mirth of the land is gone. ¹²In the city is left desolation, and the gate is smitten with destruction.

¹³When thus it shall be in the midst of the land among the people, *there shall be* as the shaking of an olive tree, *and* as the gleaning grapes when the vintage is done. ¹⁴They shall lift up their voice, they shall sing for the majesty of the LORD, they shall cry aloud from the sea. ¹⁵Wherefore glorify ye the LORD in the fires^d, *even* the name of the LORD God of Israel in the isles of the sea.

¹⁶From the uttermost part of the earth have we heard songs, *even* glory to the righteous. But I said, My leanness, my leanness, woe unto me! the treacherous dealers have dealt treacherously; yea, the treacherous dealers have dealt very treacherously. ¹⁷Fear, and the pit, and the snare, *are* upon thee, O inhabitant of the earth. ¹⁸And it shall come to pass, *that* he who fleeth from the noise of the fear shall fall into the pit; and he that cometh up out of the midst of the pit shall be taken in the snare: for the windows from on high are open, and the foundations of the earth do shake.

¹⁹The earth is utterly broken down, the earth is clean dissolved, the earth is moved exceedingly. ²⁰The earth shall reel to and fro like a drunkard, and shall be removed like a cottage; and the transgression thereof shall be heavy upon it; and it shall fall, and not rise again. ²¹And it shall come to pass in that day, *that* the LORD shall punish^e the host of the high ones *that are* on high, and the kings of the earth upon the earth. ²²And they shall be gathered together, *as* prisoners are gathered in the pit, and shall be shut up in the prison, and after many days shall they be visited. ²³Then the moon shall be confounded, and the sun ashamed, when the LORD of hosts shall reign in mount Zion, and in Jerusalem, and before his ancients gloriously.

25

¹O LORD, thou *art* my God; I will exalt thee, I will praise thy name; for thou hast done wonderful *things; thy* counsels of old *are* faithfulness *and* truth. ²For thou hast made of a city an heap; *of* a defenced city a ruin: a palace of strangers to be no city; it shall never be built. ³Therefore shall the strong people glorify thee, the city of the terrible nations shall fear thee. ⁴For thou hast been a strength to the poor, a strength to the needy in his distress, a refuge from the storm, a shadow from the heat, when the blast of the terrible ones *is* as a storm *against* the wall. ⁵Thou shalt bring down the noise of strangers, as the heat in a dry place; *even* the heat with the shadow of a cloud: the branch

---

^d fires: or, valleys
^e punish: Heb. visit upon

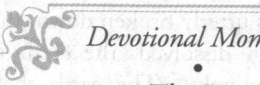

Devotional Moment
•
The Poor

25:4 The poor have a special place of compassion in God's heart, and they should find similar compassion and caring in the hearts of God's people. Poor families often have an especially difficult time since they cannot afford the food, clothing, housing, and other necessities that most people have. This can create hardship for the children and depression for the parents. You can help. Is there a poor family in your church or neighborhood? Perhaps you could provide child care for a single working parent, give yard work to the children so they can help contribute to the family income, do home maintenance or auto repairs that they can't afford to do, or leave an anonymous gift. Your ministry to a poor family may involve no more than providing a listening ear and some loving advice, but even that will be helpful.

of the terrible ones shall be brought low.

⁶And in this mountain shall the LORD of hosts make unto all people a feast of fat things, a feast of wines on the lees, of fat things full of marrow, of wines on the lees well refined. ⁷And he will destroyᵃ in this mountain the face of the covering cast over all people, and the vail that is spread over all nations. ⁸He will swallow up death in victory; and the Lord GOD will wipe away tears from off all faces; and the rebuke of his people shall he take away from off all the earth: for the LORD hath spoken *it*.

⁹And it shall be said in that day, Lo, this *is* our God; we have waited for him, and he will save us: this *is* the LORD; we have waited for him, we will be glad and rejoice in his salvation. ¹⁰For in this mountain shall the hand of the LORD rest, and Moab shall be trodden down under him, even as straw is trodden down for the dunghill. ¹¹And he shall spread forth his hands in the midst of them, as he that swimmeth spreadeth forth *his hands* to swim: and he shall bring down their pride together with the spoils of their hands. ¹²And the fortress of the high fort of thy walls shall he bring down, lay low, *and* bring to the ground, *even* to the dust.

26

¹In that day shall this song be sung in the land of Judah; We have a strong city; salvation will *God* appoint *for* walls and bulwarks. ²Open ye the gates, that the righteous nation which keepeth the truthᵃ may enter in. ³Thou wilt keep *him* in perfectᵇ peace, *whose* mind *is* stayed *on thee*: because he trusteth in thee. ⁴Trust ye in the LORD for ever: for in the LORD JEHOVAH *is* everlastingᶜ strength:

⁵For he bringeth down them that dwell on high; the lofty city, he layeth it low; he layeth it low, *even* to the ground; he bringeth it *even* to the dust. ⁶The foot shall tread it down, *even* the feet of the poor, *and* the steps of the needy. ⁷The way of the just *is* uprightness: thou, most upright, dost weigh the path of the just. ⁸Yea, in the way of thy judgments, O LORD, have we

---

ᵃ destroy: Heb. swallow up

ᵃ truth: Heb. truths

ᵇ perfect . . . : Heb. peace, peace

ᶜ everlasting . . . : Heb. the rock of ages

waited for thee; the desire of *our* soul *is* to thy name, and to the remembrance of thee. ⁹With my soul have I desired thee in the night; yea, with my spirit within me will I seek thee early: for when thy judgments *are* in the earth, the inhabitants of the world will learn righteousness. ¹⁰Let favour be shewed to the wicked, *yet* will he not learn righteousness: in the land of uprightness will he deal unjustly, and will not behold the majesty of the LORD. ¹¹LORD, *when* thy hand is lifted up, they will not see: *but* they shall see, and be ashamed for *their* envy at the people; yea, the fire of thine enemies shall devour them.

¹²LORD, thou wilt ordain peace for us: for thou also hast wrought all our works in us^d. ¹³O LORD our God, *other* lords beside thee have had dominion over us: *but* by thee only will we make mention of thy name. ¹⁴*They are* dead, they shall not live; *they are* deceased, they shall not rise: therefore hast thou visited and destroyed them, and made all their memory to perish. ¹⁵Thou hast increased the nation, O LORD, thou hast increased the nation: thou art glorified: thou hadst removed *it* far *unto* all the ends of the earth. ¹⁶LORD, in trouble have they visited thee, they poured out a prayer^e *when* thy chastening *was* upon them. ¹⁷Like as a woman with child, *that* draweth near the time of her delivery, is in pain, *and* crieth out in her pangs; so have we

been in thy sight, O LORD. ¹⁸We have been with child, we have been in pain, we have as it were brought forth wind; we have not wrought any deliverance in the earth; neither have the inhabitants of the world fallen. ¹⁹Thy dead *men* shall live, *together with* my dead body shall they arise. Awake and sing, ye that dwell in dust: for thy dew *is as* the dew of herbs, and the earth shall cast out the dead.

²⁰Come, my people, enter thou into thy chambers, and shut thy doors about thee: hide thyself as it were for a little moment, until the indignation be overpast. ²¹For, behold, the LORD cometh out of his place to punish the inhabitants of the earth for their iniquity: the earth also shall disclose her blood^f, and shall no more cover her slain.

27

¹In that day the LORD with his sore and great and strong sword shall punish leviathan the piercing^a serpent, even leviathan that crooked serpent; and he shall slay the dragon that *is* in the sea. ²In that day sing ye unto her, A vineyard of red wine. ³I the LORD do keep it; I will water it every moment: lest *any* hurt it, I will keep it night and day. ⁴Fury *is* not in me: who would set the briers *and* thorns against me in battle? I would go^b through them, I would burn them together. ⁵Or let him take hold of my strength, *that* he may make peace with me; *and* he shall

---

^d in us: or, for us
^e prayer: Heb. secret speech
^f blood: Heb. bloods
^a piercing: or, crossing like a bar
^b go . . . : or, march against

make peace with me. [6]He shall cause them that come of Jacob to take root: Israel shall blossom and bud, and fill the face of the world with fruit.

[7]Hath he smitten him, as he smote those that smote him? or is he slain according to the slaughter of them that are slain by him? [8]In measure, when it shooteth forth, thou wilt debate with it: he stayeth his rough wind in the day of the east wind. [9]By this therefore shall the iniquity of Jacob be purged; and this *is* all the fruit to take away his sin; when he maketh all the stones of the altar as chalkstones that are beaten in sunder, the groves and images[c] shall not stand up. [10]Yet the defenced city *shall be* desolate, *and* the habitation forsaken, and left like a wilderness: there shall the calf feed, and there shall he lie down, and consume the branches thereof. [11]When the boughs thereof are withered, they shall be broken off: the women come, *and* set them on fire: for it *is* a people of no understanding: therefore he that made them will not have mercy on them, and he that formed them will shew them no favour. [12]And it shall come to pass in that day, *that* the LORD shall beat off from the channel of the river unto the stream of Egypt, and ye shall be gathered one by one, O ye children of Israel. [13]And it shall come to pass in that day, *that* the great trumpet shall be blown, and they shall come which were ready to perish in the land of Assyria, and the outcasts in the land of Egypt, and shall worship the LORD in the holy mount at Jerusalem.

28

[1]Woe to the crown of pride, to the drunkards of Ephraim, whose glorious beauty *is* a fading flower, which *are* on the head of the fat valleys of them that are overcome[a] with wine! [2]Behold, the Lord hath a mighty and strong one, *which* as a tempest of hail *and* a destroying storm, as a flood of mighty waters overflowing, shall cast down to the earth with the hand. [3]The crown of pride, the drunkards of Ephraim, shall be trodden under feet: [4]And the glorious beauty, which *is* on the head of the fat valley, shall be a fading flower, *and* as the hasty fruit before the summer; which *when* he that looketh upon it seeth, while it is yet in his hand he eateth it up. [5]In that day shall the LORD of hosts be for a crown of glory, and for a diadem of beauty, unto the residue of his people, [6]And for a spirit of judgment to him that sitteth in judgment, and for strength to them that turn the battle to the gate. [7]But they also have erred through wine, and through strong drink are out of the way; the priest and the prophet have erred through strong drink, they are swallowed up of wine, they are out of the way through strong drink; they err in vision, they stumble *in* judgment. [8]For all tables are full of vomit *and* filthiness, *so that there is* no place *clean*.

[9]Whom shall he teach knowledge? and whom shall he make to understand doctrine[b]? *them that are* weaned from

---

[c] images: or, sun images
[a] overcome: Heb. broken
[b] doctrine: Heb. the hearing?

the milk, *and* drawn from the breasts. ¹⁰For precept *must be* upon precept, precept upon precept; line upon line, line upon line; here a little, *and* there a little: ¹¹For with stammering[c] lips and another tongue will he speak to this people. ¹²To whom he said, This *is* the rest *wherewith* ye may cause the weary to rest; and this *is* the refreshing: yet they would not hear. ¹³But the word of the LORD was unto them precept upon precept, precept upon precept; line upon line, line upon line; here a little, *and* there a little; that they might go, and fall backward, and be broken, and snared, and taken.

¹⁴Wherefore hear the word of the LORD, ye scornful men, that rule this people which *is* in Jerusalem. ¹⁵Because ye have said, We have made a covenant with death, and with hell are we at agreement; when the overflowing scourge shall pass through, it shall not come unto us: for we have made lies our refuge, and under falsehood have we hid ourselves: ¹⁶Therefore thus saith the Lord GOD, Behold, I lay in Zion for a foundation a stone, a tried stone, a precious corner *stone*, a sure foundation: he that believeth shall not make haste. ¹⁷Judgment also will I lay to the line, and righteousness to the plummet: and the hail shall sweep away the refuge of lies, and the waters shall overflow the hiding place. ¹⁸And your covenant with death shall be disannulled, and your agreement with hell shall not stand; when the overflowing scourge shall pass through, then ye shall be trodden down by it. ¹⁹From the time that it goeth forth

Devotional Moment
Sensitivity

28:23-28 Isaiah used a farming illustration to picture the skillful way God leads and disciplines his people. It is also a good illustration of the need to tailor the ways we treat other people. One friend may need structured guidance. Another may be capable of handling more responsibility and need higher expectations in order to achieve his or her potential. The key is sensitivity to the needs of the individual.

it shall take you: for morning by morning shall it pass over, by day and by night: and it shall be a vexation only *to* understand the report. ²⁰For the bed is shorter than that *a man* can stretch himself *on it*: and the covering narrower than that he can wrap himself *in it*. ²¹For the LORD shall rise up as *in* mount Perazim, he shall be wroth as *in* the valley of Gibeon, that he may do his work, his strange work; and bring to pass his act, his strange act. ²²Now therefore be ye not mockers, lest your bands be made strong: for I have heard from the Lord GOD of hosts a consumption, even determined upon the whole earth.

²³Give ye ear, and hear my voice; hearken, and hear my speech. ²⁴Doth the plowman plow all day to sow? doth he open and break the clods of his ground? ²⁵When he hath made plain the face thereof, doth he not cast abroad the fitches, and scatter the cummin, and cast in the principal[d] wheat and the appointed barley and the rie in

---

[c] stammering . . . : Heb. stammerings of lip
[d] the principal . . . : or, the wheat in the principal place, and barley in the appointed place

their place? ²⁶For his God doth instruct him to discretion, *and* doth teach him. ²⁷For the fitches are not threshed with a threshing instrument, neither is a cart wheel turned about upon the cummin; but the fitches are beaten out with a staff, and the cummin with a rod. ²⁸Bread *corn* is bruised; because he will not ever be threshing it, nor break *it with* the wheel of his cart, nor bruise it *with* his horsemen. ²⁹This also cometh forth from the LORD of hosts, *which* is wonderful in counsel, *and* excellent in working.

29

¹Woe[a] to Ariel, to Ariel, the city *where* David dwelt! add ye year to year; let them kill sacrifices. ²Yet I will distress Ariel, and there shall be heaviness and sorrow: and it shall be unto me as Ariel. ³And I will camp against thee round about, and will lay siege against thee with a mount, and I will raise forts against thee. ⁴And thou shalt be brought down, *and* shalt speak out of the ground, and thy speech shall be low out of the dust, and thy voice shall be, as of one that hath a familiar spirit, out of the ground, and thy speech shall whisper[b] out of the dust. ⁵Moreover the multitude of thy strangers shall be like small dust, and the multitude of the terrible ones *shall be* as chaff that passeth away: yea, it shall be at an instant suddenly. ⁶Thou shalt be visited of the LORD of hosts with thunder, and with earthquake, and great noise, with storm and tempest, and the flame of devouring fire. ⁷And the multitude of all the nations that fight against Ariel, even all that fight against her and her munition, and that distress her, shall be as a dream of a night vision. ⁸It shall even be as when an hungry *man* dreameth, and, behold, he eateth; but he awaketh, and his soul is empty: or as when a thirsty man dreameth, and, behold, he drinketh; but he awaketh, and, behold, *he is* faint, and his soul hath appetite: so shall the multitude of all the nations be, that fight against mount Zion.

⁹Stay yourselves, and wonder; cry ye out, and cry: they are drunken, but not with wine; they stagger, but not with strong drink. ¹⁰For the LORD hath poured out upon you the spirit of deep sleep, and hath closed your eyes: the prophets and your rulers[c], the seers hath he covered. ¹¹And the vision of all is become unto you as the words of a book[d] that is sealed, which *men* deliver to one that is learned, saying, Read this, I pray thee: and he saith, I cannot; for it *is* sealed: ¹²And the book is delivered to him that is not learned, saying, Read this, I pray thee: and he saith, I am not learned. ¹³Wherefore the Lord said, Forasmuch as this people draw near *me* with their mouth, and with their lips do honour me, but have removed their heart far from me, and their fear toward me is taught by the precept of men: ¹⁴Therefore, behold, I will proceed[e] to

---

[a] Woe . . . : or, O Ariel, that is, the lion of God
[b] whisper: Heb. peep, or, chirp
[c] rulers: Heb. heads
[d] book: or, letter
[e] proceed: Heb. add

do a marvellous work among this people, *even* a marvellous work and a wonder: for the wisdom of their wise *men* shall perish, and the understanding of their prudent *men* shall be hid. ¹⁵Woe unto them that seek deep to hide their counsel from the LORD, and their works are in the dark, and they say, Who seeth us? and who knoweth us? ¹⁶Surely your turning of things upside down shall be esteemed as the potter's clay: for shall the work say of him that made it, He made me not? or shall the thing framed say of him that framed it, He had no understanding?

¹⁷*Is* it not yet a very little while, and Lebanon shall be turned into a fruitful field, and the fruitful field shall be esteemed as a forest? ¹⁸And in that day shall the deaf hear the words of the book, and the eyes of the blind shall see out of obscurity, and out of darkness. ¹⁹The meek also shall increase[f] *their* joy in the LORD, and the poor among men shall rejoice in the Holy One of Israel. ²⁰For the terrible one is brought to nought, and the scorner is consumed, and all that watch for iniquity are cut off: ²¹That make a man an offender for a word, and lay a snare for him that reproveth in the gate, and turn aside the just for a thing of nought. ²²Therefore thus saith the LORD, who redeemed Abraham, concerning the house of Jacob, Jacob shall not now be ashamed, neither shall his face now wax pale. ²³But when he seeth his children, the work of mine hands, in the midst of him, they shall sanctify my name, and sanctify the Holy One of Jacob, and shall fear the God of Israel. ²⁴They also that erred in spirit shall come[g] to understanding, and they that murmured shall learn doctrine.

30

¹Woe to the rebellious children, saith the LORD, that take counsel, but not of me; and that cover with a covering, but not of my spirit, that they may add sin to sin: ²That walk to go down into Egypt, and have not asked at my mouth; to strengthen themselves in the strength of Pharaoh, and to trust in the shadow of Egypt! ³Therefore shall the strength of Pharaoh be your shame, and the trust in the shadow of Egypt *your* confusion. ⁴For his princes were at Zoan, and his ambassadors came to Hanes. ⁵They were all ashamed of a people *that* could not profit them, nor be an help nor profit, but a shame, and also a reproach. ⁶The burden of the beasts of the south: into the land of trouble and anguish, from whence *come* the young and old lion, the viper and fiery flying serpent, they will carry their riches upon the shoulders of young asses, and their treasures upon the bunches of camels, to a people *that* shall not profit *them*. ⁷For the Egyptians shall help in vain, and to no purpose: therefore have I cried concerning this, Their strength *is* to sit still.

⁸Now go, write it before them in a table, and note it in a book, that it may be for the[a] time to come for ever and ever: ⁹That this *is* a rebellious people,

---

[f] increase: Heb. add
[g] come . . . : Heb. know understanding
[a] the . . . : Heb. the latter day

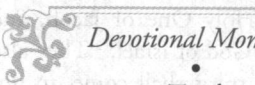

Devotional Moment
•
Truth

30:10-11 The people of Israel wanted to hear nothing but good news and positive feedback. "Forget all this gloom," they said. "Tell us nice things." But the truth about their actions and the outcome of their choices was *not* good news, and they did *not* want to hear it. It would have been far better for them to face the truth, however unpleasant, and deal with it. The truth may be hard to speak and hard to take, but it is always preferable to lies or cover-up schemes. Commerce, government, and families are all designed by God to function best in a climate of honesty. Is truthfulness valued in your family? Consider having house rules against lying, glossing over problems, promise breaking, and exaggerating.

lying children, children *that* will not hear the law of the LORD: ¹⁰Which say to the seers, See not; and to the prophets, Prophesy not unto us right things, speak unto us smooth things, prophesy deceits: ¹¹Get you out of the way, turn aside out of the path, cause the Holy One of Israel to cease from before us. ¹²Wherefore thus saith the Holy One of Israel, Because ye despise this word, and trust in oppression[b] and perverseness, and stay thereon: ¹³Therefore this iniquity shall be to you as a breach ready to fall, swelling out in a high wall, whose breaking cometh suddenly at an instant. ¹⁴And he shall break it as the breaking of the potters' vessel that is broken in pieces; he shall not spare: so that there shall not be found in the bursting of it a sherd to take fire

from the hearth, or to take water *withal* out of the pit. ¹⁵For thus saith the Lord GOD, the Holy One of Israel; In returning and rest shall ye be saved; in quietness and in confidence shall be your strength: and ye would not. ¹⁶But ye said, No; for we will flee upon horses; therefore shall ye flee: and, We will ride upon the swift; therefore shall they that pursue you be swift. ¹⁷One thousand *shall flee* at the rebuke of one; at the rebuke of five shall ye flee: till ye be left as a beacon[c] upon the top of a mountain, and as an ensign on an hill.

¹⁸And therefore will the LORD wait, that he may be gracious unto you, and therefore will he be exalted, that he may have mercy upon you: for the LORD *is* a God of judgment: blessed *are* all they that wait for him. ¹⁹For the people shall dwell in Zion at Jerusalem: thou shalt weep no more: he will be very gracious unto thee at the voice of thy cry; when he shall hear it, he will answer thee. ²⁰And *though* the Lord give you the bread of adversity, and the water of affliction[d], yet shall not thy teachers be removed into a corner any more, but thine eyes shall see thy teachers: ²¹And thine ears shall hear a word behind thee, saying, This *is* the way, walk ye in it, when ye turn to the right hand, and when ye turn to the left. ²²Ye shall defile also the covering of thy graven images of silver, and the ornament of thy molten images of gold: thou shalt cast them away as a menstruous cloth; thou shalt say unto it, Get thee hence. ²³Then shall he give the rain of thy seed,

---

[b] oppression: or, fraud
[c] a beacon: or, a tree bereft of branches, or, boughs: or, a mast
[d] affliction: or, oppression

that thou shalt sow the ground withal; and bread of the increase of the earth, and it shall be fat and plenteous: in that day shall thy cattle feed in large pastures. ²⁴The oxen likewise and the young asses that ear the ground shall eat clean^e provender, which hath been winnowed with the shovel and with the fan. ²⁵And there shall be upon every high mountain, and upon every high hill^f, rivers *and* streams of waters in the day of the great slaughter, when the towers fall. ²⁶Moreover the light of the moon shall be as the light of the sun, and the light of the sun shall be sevenfold, as the light of seven days, in the day that the LORD bindeth up the breach of his people, and healeth the stroke of their wound.

²⁷Behold, the name of the LORD cometh from far, burning *with* his anger, and the burden^g *thereof is* heavy: his lips are full of indignation, and his tongue as a devouring fire: ²⁸And his breath, as an overflowing stream, shall reach to the midst of the neck, to sift the nations with the sieve of vanity: and *there shall be* a bridle in the jaws of the people, causing *them* to err. ²⁹Ye shall have a song, as in the night *when* a holy solemnity is kept; and gladness of heart, as when one goeth with a pipe to come into the mountain of the LORD, to the mighty One of Israel. ³⁰And the LORD shall cause his glorious^h voice to be heard, and shall shew the lighting down of his arm, with the indignation of *his*

anger, and *with* the flame of a devouring fire, *with* scattering, and tempest, and hailstones. ³¹For through the voice of the LORD shall the Assyrian be beaten down, *which* smote with a rod. ³²And *in* every place where the grounded staff shall pass, which the LORD shall lay upon him, *it* shall be with tabrets and harps: and in battles of shaking will he fight with it. ³³For Tophet *is* ordained of oldⁱ; yea, for the king it is prepared; he hath made *it* deep *and* large: the pile thereof *is* fire and much wood; the breath of the LORD, like a stream of brimstone, doth kindle it.

31

¹Woe to them that go down to Egypt for help; and stay on horses, and trust in chariots, because *they are* many; and in horsemen, because they are very strong; but they look not unto the Holy One of Israel, neither seek the LORD! ²Yet he also *is* wise, and will bring evil, and will not call back his words: but will arise against the house of the evildoers, and against the help of them that work iniquity. ³Now the Egyptians *are* men, and not God; and their horses flesh, and not spirit. When the LORD shall stretch out his hand, both he that helpeth shall fall, and he that is holpen shall fall down, and they all shall fail together. ⁴For thus hath the LORD spoken unto me, Like as the lion and the young lion roaring on his prey, when a

---

^e clean: or, savoury: Heb. leavened
^f high hill: Heb. lifted up, etc
^g burden . . . : or, grievousness of flame
^h his glorious . . . : Heb. the glory of his voice
ⁱ of old: Heb. from yesterday

multitude of shepherds is called forth against him, *he* will not be afraid of their voice, nor abase himself for the noise[a] of them: so shall the LORD of hosts come down to fight for mount Zion, and for the hill thereof. ⁵As birds flying, so will the LORD of hosts defend Jerusalem; defending also he will deliver *it; and* passing over he will preserve it.

⁶Turn ye unto *him from* whom the children of Israel have deeply revolted. ⁷For in that day every man shall cast away his idols of silver, and his idols of gold, which your own hands have made unto you *for* a sin. ⁸Then shall the Assyrian fall with the sword, not of a mighty man; and the sword, not of a mean man, shall devour him: but he shall flee from[b] the sword, and his young men shall be discomfited. ⁹And he shall pass over to his strong hold for fear, and his princes shall be afraid of the ensign, saith the LORD, whose fire *is* in Zion, and his furnace in Jerusalem.

32

¹Behold, a king shall reign in righteousness, and princes shall rule in judgment. ²And a man shall be as an hiding place from the wind, and a covert from the tempest; as rivers of water in a dry place, as the shadow of a great[a] rock in a weary land. ³And the eyes of them that see shall not be dim, and the ears of them that hear shall hearken. ⁴The heart also of the rash[b] shall understand knowledge, and the tongue of the stammerers shall be ready to speak plainly. ⁵The vile person shall be no more called liberal, nor the churl said *to be* bountiful. ⁶For the vile person will speak villany, and his heart will work iniquity, to practise hypocrisy, and to utter error against the LORD, to make empty the soul of the hungry, and he will cause the drink of the thirsty to fail. ⁷The instruments also of the churl *are* evil: he deviseth wicked devices to destroy the poor with lying words, even when the needy[c] speaketh right. ⁸But the liberal deviseth liberal things; and by liberal things shall he stand[d].

⁹Rise up, ye women that are at ease; hear my voice, ye careless daughters; give ear unto my speech. ¹⁰Many days and years shall ye be troubled, ye careless women: for the vintage shall fail, the gathering shall not come. ¹¹Tremble, ye women that are at ease; be troubled, ye careless ones: strip you, and make you bare, and gird *sackcloth* upon *your* loins. ¹²They shall lament for the teats, for the pleasant[e] fields, for the fruitful vine. ¹³Upon the land of my people shall come up thorns *and* briers; yea,[f] upon all the houses of joy *in* the joyous city: ¹⁴Because the palaces shall

---

[a] noise: or, multitude
[b] from: or, for fear of
[a] great: Heb. heavy
[b] rash: Heb. hasty
[c] the needy . . . : or, he speaketh against the poor in judgment
[d] stand: or, be established
[e] pleasant . . . : Heb. fields of desire
[f] yea . . . : or, burning upon

be forsaken; the multitude of the city shall be left; the forts[g] and towers shall be for dens for ever, a joy of wild asses, a pasture of flocks; ¹⁵Until the spirit be poured upon us from on high, and the wilderness be a fruitful field, and the fruitful field be counted for a forest. ¹⁶Then judgment shall dwell in the wilderness, and righteousness remain in the fruitful field. ¹⁷And the work of righteousness shall be peace; and the effect of righteousness quietness and assurance for ever. ¹⁸And my people shall dwell in a peaceable habitation, and in sure dwellings, and in quiet resting places; ¹⁹When it shall hail, coming down on the forest; and the city shall be low in a low place. ²⁰Blessed *are* ye that sow beside all waters, that send forth *thither* the feet of the ox and the ass.

33

¹Woe to thee that spoilest, and thou *wast* not spoiled; and dealest treacherously, and they dealt not treacherously with thee! when thou shalt cease to spoil, thou shalt be spoiled; *and* when thou shalt make an end to deal treacherously, they shall deal treacherously with thee. ²O LORD, be gracious unto us; we have waited for thee: be thou their arm every morning, our salvation also in the time of trouble. ³At the noise of the tumult the people fled; at the lifting up of thyself the nations were scattered. ⁴And your spoil shall be gathered *like* the gathering of the caterpiller: as the running to and fro of locusts shall he run upon them. ⁵The LORD is exalted; for he dwelleth on high: he hath

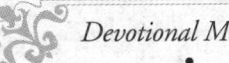

Devotional Moment
•
Play Fair

33:1 The Assyrians were like schoolyard bullies, expecting others to cooperate with them while they refused to live up to their promises. We know people should play fair, keep their promises, and not keep changing the rules. All relationships work best when everyone keeps their promises. When we don't do what we say we will do, then we can't be trusted.

filled Zion with judgment and righteousness. ⁶And wisdom and knowledge shall be the stability of thy times, *and* strength of salvation[a]: the fear of the LORD *is* his treasure. ⁷Behold, their valiant ones shall cry without: the ambassadors of peace shall weep bitterly. ⁸The highways lie waste, the wayfaring man ceaseth: he hath broken the covenant, he hath despised the cities, he regardeth no man. ⁹The earth mourneth *and* languisheth: Lebanon is ashamed *and* hewn down: Sharon is like a wilderness; and Bashan and Carmel shake off *their fruits.* ¹⁰Now will I rise, saith the LORD; now will I be exalted; now will I lift up myself. ¹¹Ye shall conceive chaff, ye shall bring forth stubble: your breath, *as* fire, shall devour you. ¹²And the people shall be *as* the burnings of lime: *as* thorns cut up shall they be burned in the fire.

¹³Hear, ye *that are* far off, what I have done; and, ye *that are* near, acknowledge my might. ¹⁴The sinners in Zion are afraid; fearfulness hath surprised the hypocrites. Who among us

---

[g] forts . . . : or, clifts and watchtowers
[a] salvation: Heb. salvations

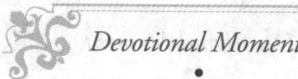

Devotional Moment
•
Honesty

33:14-16 Our first lessons in honesty and fairness take place within family life. Your children will grow to both value and demonstrate honesty and fairness if they can experience it at home. Make sure your family doesn't cheat (by not paying bills, not returning extra change), avoids favoritism, and doesn't let older kids gang up on younger ones. Some children are naturally fair-minded, but most have to learn it. And Mom or Dad is the best teacher.

shall dwell with the devouring fire? who among us shall dwell with everlasting burnings? [15]He that walketh righteously[b], and speaketh uprightly; he that despiseth the gain of oppressions, that shaketh his hands from holding of bribes, that stoppeth his ears from hearing of blood, and shutteth his eyes from seeing evil; [16]He shall dwell on high[c]: his place of defence *shall be* the munitions of rocks: bread shall be given him; his waters *shall be* sure. [17]Thine eyes shall see the king in his beauty: they shall behold the land that is very far off. [18]Thine heart shall meditate terror. Where *is* the scribe? where *is* the receiver[d]? where *is* he that counted the towers? [19]Thou shalt not see a fierce people, a people of a deeper speech than thou canst perceive; of a stammering[e] tongue, *that thou canst* not understand. [20]Look upon Zion, the city of our solemnities: thine eyes shall see Jerusalem a quiet habitation, a tabernacle *that* shall not be taken down; not one of the stakes thereof shall ever be removed, neither shall any of the cords thereof be broken. [21]But there the glorious LORD *will be* unto us a place of broad rivers *and* streams; wherein shall go no galley with oars, neither shall gallant ship pass thereby. [22]For the LORD *is* our judge, the LORD *is* our lawgiver[f], the LORD *is* our king; he will save us. [23]Thy tacklings are loosed; they could not well strengthen their mast, they could not spread the sail: then is the prey of a great spoil divided; the lame take the prey. [24]And the inhabitant shall not say, I am sick: the people that dwell therein *shall be* forgiven *their* iniquity.

34

[1]Come near, ye nations, to hear; and hearken, ye people: let the earth hear, and all that is therein; the world, and all things that come forth of it. [2]For the indignation of the LORD *is* upon all nations, and *his* fury upon all their armies: he hath utterly destroyed them, he hath delivered them to the slaughter. [3]Their slain also shall be cast out, and their stink shall come up out of their carcases, and the mountains shall be melted with their blood. [4]And all the host of heaven shall be dissolved, and the heavens shall be rolled together as a scroll: and all their host shall fall down, as the leaf falleth off from the vine, and as a falling *fig* from the fig tree. [5]For my

[b] righteously: Heb. in righteousnesses
[c] high: Heb. heights, or, high places
[d] receiver: Heb. weigher?
[e] stammering: or, ridiculous
[f] lawgiver: Heb. statutemaker

sword shall be bathed in heaven: behold, it shall come down upon Idumea, and upon the people of my curse, to judgment. ⁶The sword of the LORD is filled with blood, it is made fat with fatness, *and* with the blood of lambs and goats, with the fat of the kidneys of rams: for the LORD hath a sacrifice in Bozrah, and a great slaughter in the land of Idumea. ⁷And the unicorns^a shall come down with them, and the bullocks with the bulls; and their land shall be soaked with blood, and their dust made fat with fatness. ⁸For *it is* the day of the LORD'S vengeance, *and* the year of recompences for the controversy of Zion.

⁹And the streams thereof shall be turned into pitch, and the dust thereof into brimstone, and the land thereof shall become burning pitch. ¹⁰It shall not be quenched night nor day; the smoke thereof shall go up for ever: from generation to generation it shall lie waste; none shall pass through it for ever and ever. ¹¹But the cormorant^b and the bittern shall possess it; the owl also and the raven shall dwell in it: and he shall stretch out upon it the line of confusion, and the stones of emptiness. ¹²They shall call the nobles thereof to the kingdom, but none *shall be* there, and all her princes shall be nothing. ¹³And thorns shall come up in her palaces, nettles and brambles in the fortresses thereof: and it shall be an habitation of dragons, *and* a court for owls^c. ¹⁴The wild beasts of the desert shall also meet with the wild beasts of the island, and the satyr shall cry to his fellow; the screech owl also shall rest there, and find for herself a place of rest. ¹⁵There shall the great owl make her nest, and lay, and hatch, and gather under her shadow: there shall the vultures also be gathered, every one with her mate. ¹⁶Seek ye out of the book of the LORD, and read: no one of these shall fail, none shall want her mate: for my mouth it hath commanded, and his spirit it hath gathered them. ¹⁷And he hath cast the lot for them, and his hand hath divided it unto them by line: they shall possess it for ever, from generation to generation shall they dwell therein.

35

¹The wilderness and the solitary place shall be glad for them; and the desert shall rejoice, and blossom as the rose. ²It shall blossom abundantly, and rejoice even with joy and singing: the glory of Lebanon shall be given unto it, the excellency of Carmel and Sharon, they shall see the glory of the LORD, *and* the excellency of our God. ³Strengthen ye the weak hands, and confirm the feeble knees. ⁴Say to them *that are* of a fearful^a heart, Be strong, fear not: behold, your God will come *with* vengeance, *even* God *with* a recompence; he will come and save you.

⁵Then the eyes of the blind shall be opened, and the ears of the deaf shall be unstopped. ⁶Then shall the lame *man*

---

^a unicorns: or, rhinocerots

^b cormorant: or, pelican

^c owls: or, ostriches: Heb. daughters of the owl

^a fearful: Heb. hasty

leap as an hart, and the tongue of the dumb sing: for in the wilderness shall waters break out, and streams in the desert. [7]And the parched ground shall become a pool, and the thirsty land springs of water: in the habitation of dragons, where each lay, *shall be* grass[b] with reeds and rushes. [8]And an highway shall be there, and a way, and it shall be called The way of holiness; the unclean shall not pass over it; but it *shall be* for those: the wayfaring men, though fools, shall not err *therein*. [9]No lion shall be there, nor *any* ravenous beast shall go up thereon, it shall not be found there; but the redeemed shall walk *there*. [10]And the ransomed of the LORD shall return, and come to Zion with songs and everlasting joy upon their heads: they shall obtain joy and gladness, and sorrow and sighing shall flee away.

36

[1]Now it came to pass in the fourteenth year of king Hezekiah, *that* Sennacherib king of Assyria came up against all the defenced cities of Judah, and took them. [2]And the king of Assyria sent Rabshakeh from Lachish to Jerusalem unto king Hezekiah with a great army. And he stood by the conduit of the upper pool in the highway of the fuller's field. [3]Then came forth unto him Eliakim, Hilkiah's son, which was over the house, and Shebna the scribe[a], and Joah, Asaph's son, the recorder. [4]And Rabshakeh said unto them, Say ye now to Hezekiah, Thus saith the great king, the king of Assyria, What confidence *is* this wherein thou

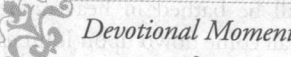

Devotional Moment

Bullies

36:5 Children often feel they will be safe if they make friends with the biggest kids in school. Adults also act that way. Israel, with a relatively small army, was tempted to rely on Egypt for protection. But God reminded his people that no nation could ever replace the protection that he could give them. The same is true for us: Our friends and connections cannot substitute for God. Friends do stick up for each other, but we can't depend on them as we can depend on God.

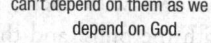

trustest? [5]I say, *sayest thou*, (but *they are but* vain words) *I have* counsel and strength for war: now on whom dost thou trust, that thou rebellest against me? [6]Lo, thou trustest in the staff of this broken reed, on Egypt; whereon if a man lean, it will go into his hand, and pierce it: so *is* Pharaoh king of Egypt to all that trust in him. [7]But if thou say to me, We trust in the LORD our God: *is it* not he, whose high places and whose altars Hezekiah hath taken away, and said to Judah and to Jerusalem, Ye shall worship before this altar? [8]Now therefore give pledges[b], I pray thee, to my master the king of Assyria, and I will give thee two thousand horses, if thou be able on thy part to set riders upon them. [9]How then wilt thou turn away the face of one captain of the least of my master's servants, and put thy trust on Egypt for chariots and for horsemen? [10]And am I now come up without the LORD against this land to destroy it? the LORD said unto me, Go up against this land, and destroy it.

---

[b] grass . . . : or, a court for reeds, etc
[a] scribe: or, secretary
[b] pledges: or, hostages

¹¹Then said Eliakim and Shebna and Joah unto Rabshakeh, Speak, I pray thee, unto thy servants in the Syrian language; for we understand *it*: and speak not to us in the Jews' language, in the ears of the people that *are* on the wall. ¹²But Rabshakeh said, Hath my master sent me to thy master and to thee to speak these words? *hath he* not *sent me* to the men that sit upon the wall, that they may eat their own dung, and drink their own piss with you? ¹³Then Rabshakeh stood, and cried with a loud voice in the Jews' language, and said, Hear ye the words of the great king, the king of Assyria. ¹⁴Thus saith the king, Let not Hezekiah deceive you: for he shall not be able to deliver you. ¹⁵Neither let Hezekiah make you trust in the LORD, saying, The LORD will surely deliver us: this city shall not be delivered into the hand of the king of Assyria. ¹⁶Hearken not to Hezekiah: for thus saith the king of Assyria, Make^c an *agreement* with me *by* a present, and come out to me: and eat ye every one of his vine, and every one of his fig tree, and drink ye every one the waters of his own cistern; ¹⁷Until I come and take you away to a land like your own land, a land of corn and wine, a land of bread and vineyards. ¹⁸*Beware* lest Hezekiah persuade you, saying, The LORD will deliver us. Hath any of the gods of the nations delivered his land out of the hand of the king of Assyria? ¹⁹Where *are* the gods of Hamath and Arphad? where *are* the gods of Sepharvaim? and have they delivered Samaria out of my hand? ²⁰Who *are they* among all the gods of these lands, that have delivered their land out of my hand, that the LORD should deliver Jerusalem out of my hand? ²¹But they held their peace, and answered him not a word: for the king's commandment was, saying, Answer him not. ²²Then came Eliakim, the son of Hilkiah, that *was* over the household, and Shebna the scribe, and Joah, the son of Asaph, the recorder, to Hezekiah with *their* clothes rent, and told him the words of Rabshakeh.

37

¹And it came to pass, when king Hezekiah heard *it*, that he rent his clothes, and covered himself with sackcloth, and went into the house of the LORD. ²And he sent Eliakim, who *was* over the household, and Shebna the scribe, and the elders of the priests covered with sackcloth, unto Isaiah the prophet the son of Amoz. ³And they said unto him, Thus saith Hezekiah, This day *is* a day of trouble, and of rebuke, and of blasphemy^a: for the children are come to the birth, and *there is* not strength to bring forth. ⁴It may be the LORD thy God will hear the words of Rabshakeh, whom the king of Assyria his master hath sent to reproach the living God, and will reprove the words which the LORD thy God hath heard: wherefore lift up *thy* prayer for the remnant that is left^b. ⁵So the servants of king Hezekiah came to Isaiah. ⁶And Isaiah said unto them, Thus shall ye say unto your master, Thus saith the

---

^c Make . . . : or, Seek my favour by a present: Heb. Make with me a blessing
^a blasphemy: or, provocation
^b left: Heb. found

LORD, Be not afraid of the words that thou hast heard, wherewith the servants of the king of Assyria have blasphemed me. [7]Behold, I will send[c] a blast upon him, and he shall hear a rumour, and return to his own land; and I will cause him to fall by the sword in his own land.

[8]So Rabshakeh returned, and found the king of Assyria warring against Libnah: for he had heard that he was departed from Lachish. [9]And he heard say concerning Tirhakah king of Ethiopia, He is come forth to make war with thee. And when he heard *it*, he sent messengers to Hezekiah, saying, [10]Thus shall ye speak to Hezekiah king of Judah, saying, Let not thy God, in whom thou trustest, deceive thee, saying, Jerusalem shall not be given into the hand of the king of Assyria. [11]Behold, thou hast heard what the kings of Assyria have done to all lands by destroying them utterly; and shalt thou be delivered? [12]Have the gods of the nations delivered them which my fathers have destroyed, *as* Gozan, and Haran, and Rezeph, and the children of Eden which *were* in Telassar? [13]Where *is* the king of Hamath, and the king of Arphad, and the king of the city of Sepharvaim, Hena, and Ivah? [14]And Hezekiah received the letter from the hand of the messengers, and read it: and Hezekiah went up unto the house of the LORD, and spread it before the LORD. [15]And Hezekiah prayed unto the LORD, saying, [16]O LORD of hosts, God of Israel, that dwellest be-

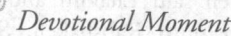

Devotional Moment

Prayer

37:14-20 King Hezekiah was under tremendous pressure: A huge army was preparing to crush his people. But that army's leader, King Sennacherib, made a big mistake: He claimed he was more powerful than God. Hezekiah spread the letter out before God and prayed, in effect, "Lord, this is your problem too." God responded (see vv. 21-38). Whether our problems are as great as Hezekiah's or just day-to-day struggles, we need to remember that God cares about us. Take your needs to God—even spreading out before him any tangible evidence of them if you want to—and trust him to work in your situation.

tween the cherubims, thou *art* the God, *even* thou alone, of all the kingdoms of the earth: thou hast made heaven and earth. [17]Incline thine ear, O LORD, and hear; open thine eyes, O LORD, and see: and hear all the words of Sennacherib, which hath sent to reproach the living God. [18]Of a truth, LORD, the kings of Assyria have laid waste all the nations[d], and their countries, [19]And have cast[e] their gods into the fire: for they *were* no gods, but the work of men's hands, wood and stone: therefore they have destroyed them. [20]Now therefore, O LORD our God, save us from his hand, that all the kingdoms of the earth may know that thou *art* the LORD, *even* thou only.

[21]Then Isaiah the son of Amoz sent unto Hezekiah, saying, Thus saith the LORD God of Israel, Whereas thou hast prayed to me against Sennacherib

---

[c] send . . . : or, put a spirit into him
[d] nations: Heb. lands
[e] cast: Heb. given

king of Assyria: ²²This *is* the word which the LORD hath spoken concerning him; The virgin, the daughter of Zion, hath despised thee, *and* laughed thee to scorn; the daughter of Jerusalem hath shaken her head at thee. ²³Whom hast thou reproached and blasphemed? and against whom hast thou exalted *thy* voice, and lifted up thine eyes on high? *even* against the Holy One of Israel. ²⁴By thy servants hast thou reproached the Lord, and hast said, By the multitude of my chariots am I come up to the height of the mountains, to the sides of Lebanon; and I will cut down the tall cedars thereof, *and* the choice fir trees thereof: and I will enter into the height of his border, *and* the forest of his Carmel. ²⁵I have digged, and drunk water; and with the sole of my feet have I dried up all the rivers of the besieged places. ²⁶Hast thou not heard long ago, *how* I have done it; *and* of ancient times, that I have formed it? now have I brought it to pass, that thou shouldest be to lay waste defenced cities *into* ruinous heaps. ²⁷Therefore their inhabitants *were* of small[f] power, they were dismayed and confounded: they were *as* the grass of the field, and *as* the green herb, *as* the grass on the housetops, and *as corn* blasted before it be grown up. ²⁸But I know thy abode[g], and thy going out, and thy coming in, and thy rage against me. ²⁹Because thy rage against me, and thy tumult, is come up into mine ears, therefore will I put my hook

in thy nose, and my bridle in thy lips, and I will turn thee back by the way by which thou camest. ³⁰And this *shall be* a sign unto thee, Ye shall eat *this* year such as groweth of itself; and the second year that which springeth of the same: and in the third year sow ye, and reap, and plant vineyards, and eat the fruit thereof. ³¹And the remnant[h] that is escaped of the house of Judah shall again take root downward, and bear fruit upward: ³²For out of Jerusalem shall go forth a remnant, and they that escape out of mount Zion: the zeal of the LORD of hosts shall do this. ³³Therefore thus saith the LORD concerning the king of Assyria, He shall not come into this city, nor shoot an arrow there, nor come before it with shields, nor cast a bank against it. ³⁴By the way that he came, by the same shall he return, and shall not come into this city, saith the LORD. ³⁵For I will defend this city to save it for mine own sake, and for my servant David's sake. ³⁶Then the angel of the LORD went forth, and smote in the camp of the Assyrians a hundred and fourscore and five thousand: and when they arose early in the morning, behold, they *were* all dead corpses. ³⁷So Sennacherib king of Assyria departed, and went and returned, and dwelt at Nineveh. ³⁸And it came to pass, as he was worshipping in the house of Nisroch his god, that Adrammelech and Sharezer his sons smote him with the sword; and they escaped into the land of Armenia[i]: and

---

[f] of small . . . : Heb. short of hand

[g] abode: or, sitting

[h] the remnant . . . : Heb. the escaping of the house of Judah that remaineth

[i] Armenia: Heb. Ararat

Esarhaddon his son reigned in his stead.

38

¹In those days was Hezekiah sick unto death. And Isaiah the prophet the son of Amoz came unto him, and said unto him, Thus saith the LORD, Set thine house in order: for thou shalt die, and not live. ²Then Hezekiah turned his face toward the wall, and prayed unto the LORD, ³And said, Remember now, O LORD, I beseech thee, how I have walked before thee in truth and with a perfect heart, and have done *that which is* good in thy sight. And Hezekiah wept sore³. ⁴Then came the word of the LORD to Isaiah, saying, ⁵Go, and say to Hezekiah, Thus saith the LORD, the God of David thy father, I have heard thy prayer, I have seen thy tears: behold, I will add unto thy days fifteen years. ⁶And I will deliver thee and this city out of the hand of the king of As-

---

Devotional Moment

Hope

38:1-6 Hezekiah had already learned that when everything seemed hopeless, he could still pray. So when Isaiah told him that he was about to die, he cried and prayed, and God prolonged his life by fifteen years. God has not promised to give us everything we want, but he does encourage us to talk to him about all our concerns. You will also face situations that seem hopeless. Keep depending on God. Pray and welcome God into your home (and crises) every day.

---

syria: and I will defend this city. ⁷And this *shall be* a sign unto thee from the LORD, that the LORD will do this thing that he hath spoken; ⁸Behold, I will bring again the shadow of the degrees, which is gone down in the sun dialᵇ of Ahaz, ten degrees backward. So the sun returned ten degrees, by which degrees it was gone down.

⁹The writing of Hezekiah king of Judah, when he had been sick, and was recovered of his sickness: ¹⁰I said in the cutting off of my days, I shall go to the gates of the grave: I am deprived of the residue of my years. ¹¹I said, I shall not see the LORD, *even* the LORD, in the land of the living: I shall behold man no more with the inhabitants of the world. ¹²Mine age is departed, and is removed from me as a shepherd's tent: I have cut off like a weaver my life: he will cut me off with pining sickness: from day *even* to night wilt thou make an end of me. ¹³I reckoned till morning, *that*, as a lion, so will he break all my bones: from day *even* to night wilt thou make an end of me. ¹⁴Like a crane *or* a swallow, so did I chatter: I did mourn as a dove: mine eyes fail *with looking* upward: O LORD, I am oppressed; undertakeᶜ for me. ¹⁵What shall I say? he hath both spoken unto me, and himself hath done *it*: I shall go softly all my years in the bitterness of my soul. ¹⁶O Lord, by these *things men* live, and in all these *things is* the life of my spirit: so wilt thou recover me, and make me to live. ¹⁷Behold, for peaceᵈ I

---

³ sore: Heb. with great weeping
ᵇ sun dial: Heb. degrees by, or, with the sun
ᶜ undertake . . . : or, ease me
ᵈ for peace . . . : or, on my peace came great bitterness

Devotional Moment

Inheritance

38:19-20 Hezekiah reminds us that children really do learn about God from their parents. When the Bible says, "The father to the children shall make known thy truth," it certainly doesn't mean that parents need only send their children to church. Most of the lessons children learn about God come from their parents, not Sunday school teachers. We must tell our children what they need to know and demonstrate it for them, too. In what ways are your children learning about God's faithfulness from you?

had great bitterness: but thou hast in love to my soul *delivered it* from the pit of corruption: for thou hast cast all my sins behind thy back. ¹⁸For the grave cannot praise thee, death can *not* celebrate thee: they that go down into the pit cannot hope for thy truth. ¹⁹The living, the living, he shall praise thee, as I *do* this day: the father to the children shall make known thy truth. ²⁰The LORD *was ready* to save me: therefore we will sing my songs to the stringed instruments all the days of our life in the house of the LORD. ²¹For Isaiah had said, Let them take a lump of figs, and lay *it* for a plaister upon the boil, and he shall recover. ²²Hezekiah also had said, What *is* the sign that I shall go up to the house of the LORD?

39

¹At that time Merodachbaladan, the son of Baladan, king of Babylon, sent letters and a present to Hezekiah: for he had heard that he had been sick, and was recovered. ²And Hezekiah was glad of them, and shewed them the house of his precious things^a, the silver, and the gold, and the spices, and the precious ointment, and all the house of his armour, and all that was found in his treasures: there was nothing in his house, nor in all his dominion, that Hezekiah shewed them not. ³Then came Isaiah the prophet unto king Hezekiah, and said unto him, What said these men? and from whence came they unto thee? And Hezekiah said, They are come from a far country unto me, *even* from Babylon. ⁴Then said he, What have they seen in thine house? And Hezekiah answered, All that *is* in mine house have they seen: there is nothing among my treasures that I have not shewed them.

⁵Then said Isaiah to Hezekiah, Hear the word of the LORD of hosts: ⁶Behold, the days come, that all that *is* in thine house, and *that* which thy fathers have laid up in store until this day, shall be carried to Babylon: nothing shall be left, saith the LORD. ⁷And of thy sons that shall issue from thee, which thou shalt beget, shall they take away; and they shall be eunuchs in the palace of the king of Babylon. ⁸Then said Hezekiah to Isaiah, Good *is* the word of the LORD which thou hast spoken. He said moreover, For there shall be peace and truth in my days.

40

¹Comfort ye, comfort ye my people, saith your God. ²Speak ye comfortably^a to Jerusalem, and cry unto her, that her

---

ª precious things: or, spicery
ª comfortably: Heb. to the heart

Breaking Free from Doubt

Why sayest thou, O Jacob, and speakest, O Israel, My way is hid from the Lord? . . . Hast thou not known? hast thou not heard, that the everlasting God . . . fainteth not, neither is weary? Isaiah 40:27-28

It's common for people from an unstable or unsafe background to struggle with doubts. They doubt themselves, others, and even God. In fact, most people who struggle with long-term problems (such as a relationship with a parent that has never been mended, a lingering health problem, or a child who has gone astray) eventually come to doubt God in one of two ways: They doubt that he is there, or they doubt that he is willing to help them.

In Isaiah's day God's people were in the middle of a serious long-term trial—threats from their enemy Babylon and the prophetic assurance of nearly seventy years in captivity ahead. Even though they'd brought this trouble on themselves, they grumbled, complained, and doubted God. By looking at Israel's complaints—and God's answers—we can find the key to breaking free from doubt in our own life.

"Why sayest thou, O Jacob . . . O Israel, My way is hid from the Lord?" (v. 27). The people felt convinced that God could not help them because he was not there; he was absent. That's how many people feel when their circumstances don't change—that something has blocked God out. It is as though God has lost sight of us.

The second doubt that besieges us questions God's *willingness* to come to our aid. Sometimes we don't doubt God's presence and ability so much as his desire to help. We think that he *can* help but just doesn't want to. To us, our rights have been violated, and we think that he has refused to intervene, like an unjust, uncaring, unloving judge.

Doubting God's presence or willingness to help can lead to major bouts with discouragement, heartache, and even depression. Unchecked doubt can cause us to feel helpless and hopeless. While this cycle can be difficult to break, it's not impossible. Isaiah gives us specific tools to help lead us back to hope and faith.

During times of trial when you doubt God, take a few moments to remember just who God is. "Hast thou not known? hast thou not heard, that the everlasting God, the Creator of the ends of the earth, fainteth not, neither is weary? there is no searching of his understanding" (v. 28). He is the everlasting God who will outlast any problem and stay with us when even the most faithful friend turns aside. He is the "Lord," Elohim, the God of Genesis 1 who not only created the ends of the earth but also can give us fresh perspective and new options when we have run up against a dead end. He doesn't become weary as we do when we've shouldered too many heavy problems; nor does he become faint as we do when our stomach has been tied up in knots.

God is quite capable of helping us. He hasn't disappeared.

But is he really willing to help us? Absolutely.

The New Testament encourages us, "by prayer and supplication with thanksgiving let your requests be made known unto God. And the peace of God, which passeth all understanding, shall keep your hearts and minds through Christ Jesus" (Phil. 4:6-7).

Those who wait on the Lord, in faith, can draw strength though each new season of life. They "shall renew their strength; they shall mount up with wings as eagles; they shall run, and not be weary; and they shall walk, and not faint" (Isa. 40:31).

Doubt doesn't have to crush you. Failure doesn't have to be final. Hope comes when you break the cycle by considering God's character and waiting on the Lord in faith.

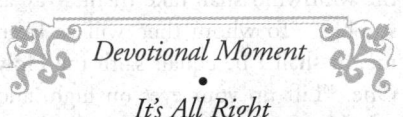

Devotional Moment

It's All Right

40:1-2 What Israel would need during their captivity in Babylon was *comfort.* They could comfort one another by reminding each other of God's love; that even though their own sinful choices had caused their troubles, God had not given up on them and would help them recover. The world is a harsh place; a comforting word, gesture, or smile can make it all bearable. When someone you know is sad or discouraged, perhaps because of a mistake or wrong, remind him or her that sadness has an end and that God forgives. Help others not to be crushed by discouragement or despair.

warfare is accomplished, that her iniquity is pardoned: for she hath received of the LORD'S hand double for all her sins.

³The voice of him that crieth in the wilderness, Prepare ye the way of the LORD, make straight in the desert a highway for our God. ⁴Every valley shall be exalted, and every mountain and hill shall be made low: and the crooked shall be made straight[b], and the rough places plain: ⁵And the glory of the LORD shall be revealed, and all flesh shall see *it* together: for the mouth of the LORD hath spoken *it.* ⁶The voice said, Cry. And he said, What shall I cry? All flesh *is* grass, and all the goodliness thereof *is* as the flower of the field: ⁷The grass withereth, the flower fadeth: because the spirit of the LORD bloweth upon it: surely the people *is* grass. ⁸The grass withereth, the flower fadeth: but the word of our God shall stand for ever.

⁹O Zion[c], that bringest good tidings, get thee up into the high mountain; O Jerusalem, that bringest good tidings, lift up thy voice with strength; lift *it* up, be not afraid; say unto the cities of Judah, Behold your God! ¹⁰Be-

---

b straight: or, a straight place
c O Zion . . . : or, O thou that tellest good tidings to Zion

hold, the Lord GOD will come with strong[d] *hand*, and his arm shall rule for him: behold, his reward *is* with him, and his work before him. [11]He shall feed his flock like a shepherd: he shall gather the lambs with his arm, and carry *them* in his bosom, *and* shall gently lead those that are with young.

[12]Who hath measured the waters in the hollow of his hand, and meted out heaven with the span, and comprehended the dust of the earth in a measure[e], and weighed the mountains in scales, and the hills in a balance? [13]Who hath directed the Spirit of the LORD, or *being* his counsellor hath taught him? [14]With whom took he counsel, and *who* instructed[f] him, and taught him in the path of judgment, and taught him knowledge, and shewed to him the way of understanding? [15]Behold, the nations *are* as a drop of a bucket, and are counted as the small dust of the balance: behold, he taketh up the isles as a very little thing. [16]And Lebanon *is* not sufficient to burn, nor the beasts thereof sufficient for a burnt offering. [17]All nations before him *are* as nothing; and they are counted to him less than nothing, and vanity.

[18]To whom then will ye liken God? or what likeness will ye compare unto him? [19]The workman melteth a graven image, and the goldsmith spreadeth it over with gold, and casteth silver chains. [20]He that *is* so impoverished that he hath no oblation chooseth a tree *that* will not rot; he seeketh unto him a cunning workman to prepare a graven image, *that* shall not be moved. [21]Have ye not known? have ye not heard? hath it not been told you from the beginning? have ye not understood from the foundations of the earth? [22]*It is* he that sitteth upon the circle of the earth, and the inhabitants thereof *are* as grasshoppers; that stretcheth out the heavens as a curtain, and spreadeth them out as a tent to dwell in: [23]That bringeth the princes to nothing; he maketh the judges of the earth as vanity. [24]Yea, they shall not be planted; yea, they shall not be sown: yea, their stock shall not take root in the earth: and he shall also blow upon them, and they shall wither, and the whirlwind shall take them away as stubble. [25]To whom then will ye liken me, or shall I be equal? saith the Holy One. [26]Lift up your eyes on high, and behold who hath created these *things*, that bringeth out their host by number: he calleth them all by names by the greatness of his might, for that *he is* strong in power; not one faileth.

[27]Why sayest thou, O Jacob, and speakest, O Israel, My way is hid from the LORD, and my judgment is passed over from my God? [28]Hast thou not known? hast thou not heard, *that* the everlasting God, the LORD, the Creator of the ends of the earth, fainteth not, neither is weary? *there is* no searching of his understanding. [29]He giveth power to the faint; and to *them that have* no might he increaseth strength. [30]Even the youths shall faint and be weary, and the young men shall utterly fall: [31]But they that wait upon the

---

[d] with strong . . . : or, against the strong
[e] a measure: Heb. a tierce
[f] instructed . . . : Heb. made him understand

LORD shall renew[g] *their* strength; they shall mount up with wings as eagles; they shall run, and not be weary; *and* they shall walk, and not faint.

41

[1]Keep silence before me, O islands; and let the people renew *their* strength: let them come near; then let them speak: let us come near together to judgment. [2]Who raised up the righteous[a] *man* from the east, called him to his foot, gave the nations before him, and made *him* rule over kings? he gave *them* as the dust to his sword, *and* as driven stubble to his bow. [3]He pursued them, *and* passed safely[b]; *even* by the way *that* he had not gone with his feet. [4]Who hath wrought and done *it*, calling the generations from the beginning? I the LORD, the first, and with the last; I *am* he. [5]The isles saw *it*, and feared; the ends of the earth were afraid, drew near, and came. [6]They helped every one his neighbour; and *every one* said to his brother, Be of good courage. [7]So the carpenter encouraged the goldsmith[c], *and* he that smootheth *with* the hammer him that smote the anvil, saying, It *is* ready for the sodering: and he fastened it with nails, *that* it should not be moved. [8]But thou, Israel, *art* my servant, Jacob whom I have chosen, the seed of Abraham my friend. [9]*Thou* whom I have taken from the ends of the earth, and called thee from the chief

men thereof, and said unto thee, Thou *art* my servant; I have chosen thee, and not cast thee away.

[10]Fear thou not; for I *am* with thee: be not dismayed; for I *am* thy God: I will strengthen thee; yea, I will help thee; yea, I will uphold thee with the right hand of my righteousness. [11]Behold, all they that were incensed against thee shall be ashamed and confounded: they shall be as nothing; and they that strive[d] with thee shall perish. [12]Thou shalt seek them, and shalt not find them, *even* them that contended with thee: they that war against thee shall be as nothing, and as a thing of nought. [13]For I the LORD thy God will hold thy right hand, saying unto thee, Fear not; I will help thee. [14]Fear not, thou worm Jacob, *and* ye men[e] of Israel; I

---

[g] renew: Heb. change
[a] the righteous . . . : Heb. righteousness
[b] safely: Heb. in peace
[c] goldsmith: or, founder
[d] they that strive . . . : Heb. the men of thy strife
[e] men: or, few men

will help thee, saith the LORD, and thy redeemer, the Holy One of Israel. [15]Behold, I will make thee a new sharp threshing instrument having teeth[f]: thou shalt thresh the mountains, and beat *them* small, and shalt make the hills as chaff. [16]Thou shalt fan them, and the wind shall carry them away, and the whirlwind shall scatter them: and thou shalt rejoice in the LORD, *and* shalt glory in the Holy One of Israel. [17]*When* the poor and needy seek water, and *there is* none, *and* their tongue faileth for thirst, I the LORD will hear them, I the God of Israel will not forsake them. [18]I will open rivers in high places, and fountains in the midst of the valleys: I will make the wilderness a pool of water, and the dry land springs of water. [19]I will plant in the wilderness the cedar, the shittah tree, and the myrtle, and the oil tree; I will set in the desert the fir tree, *and* the pine, and the box tree together: [20]That they may see, and know, and consider, and understand together, that the hand of the LORD hath done this, and the Holy One of Israel hath created it.

[21]Produce[g] your cause, saith the LORD; bring forth your strong *reasons*, saith the King of Jacob. [22]Let them bring *them* forth, and shew us what shall happen: let them shew the former things, what they *be*, that we may consider[h] them, and know the latter end of them; or declare us things for to come. [23]Shew the things that are to come hereafter, that we may know that ye *are* gods: yea, do good, or do evil, that we may be dismayed, and behold *it* together. [24]Behold, ye *are* of nothing[i], and your work of nought: an abomination *is he that* chooseth you. [25]I have raised up *one* from the north, and he shall come: from the rising of the sun shall he call upon my name: and he shall come upon princes as *upon* morter, and as the potter treadeth clay. [26]Who hath declared from the beginning, that we may know? and beforetime, that we may say, *He is* righteous? yea, *there is* none that sheweth, yea, *there is* none that declareth, yea, *there is* none that heareth your words. [27]The first *shall say* to Zion, Behold, behold them: and I will give to Jerusalem one that bringeth good tidings. [28]For I beheld, and *there was* no man; even among them, and *there was* no counsellor, that, when I asked of them, could answer[j] a word. [29]Behold, they *are* all vanity; their works *are* nothing: their molten images *are* wind and confusion.

42

[1]Behold my servant, whom I uphold; mine elect, *in whom* my soul delighteth; I have put my spirit upon him: he shall bring forth judgment to the Gentiles. [2]He shall not cry, nor lift up, nor cause his voice to be heard in the street. [3]A bruised reed shall he not break, and the smoking[a] flax shall he

---

[f] teeth: Heb. mouths
[g] Produce: Heb. Cause to come near
[h] consider . . . : Heb. set our heart upon them
[i] of nothing: or, worse than nothing
[j] answer: Heb. return
[a] smoking: or, dimly burning

Devotional Moment

•

Tender Mercy

42:1-4 Hundreds of years before Jesus was born, the Bible was already telling what he would be like. Here in Isaiah he was described as servant, revealer of justice, gentle, merciful, encouraging, enforcer of justice, proclaimer of truth and righteousness, and trustworthy enough for the whole world. Those who trust in Christ, young and old, have the challenge to become like him. What better way than by acting the way he acted? What a difference it makes when we are gentle, encouraging, and merciful toward one another.

---

not quench: he shall bring forth judgment unto truth. ⁴He shall not fail nor be discouraged[b], till he have set judgment in the earth: and the isles shall wait for his law.

⁵Thus saith God the LORD, he that created the heavens, and stretched them out; he that spread forth the earth, and that which cometh out of it; he that giveth breath unto the people upon it, and spirit to them that walk therein: ⁶I the LORD have called thee in righteousness, and will hold thine hand, and will keep thee, and give thee for a covenant of the people, for a light of the Gentiles; ⁷To open the blind eyes, to bring out the prisoners from the prison, *and* them that sit in darkness out of the prison house. ⁸I *am* the LORD: that *is* my name: and my glory will I not give to another, neither my praise to graven images. ⁹Behold, the former things are come to pass, and

new things do I declare: before they spring forth I tell you of them. ¹⁰Sing unto the LORD a new song, *and* his praise from the end of the earth, ye that go down to the sea, and all that is therein; the isles, and the inhabitants thereof. ¹¹Let the wilderness and the cities thereof lift up *their voice*, the villages *that* Kedar doth inhabit: let the inhabitants of the rock sing, let them shout from the top of the mountains. ¹²Let them give glory unto the LORD, and declare his praise in the islands.

¹³The LORD shall go forth as a mighty man, he shall stir up jealousy like a man of war: he shall cry, yea, roar; he shall prevail[c] against his enemies. ¹⁴I have long time holden my peace; I been still, *and* refrained myself: *now* will I cry like a travailing woman; I will destroy and devour[d] at once. ¹⁵I will make waste mountains and hills, and dry up all their herbs; and I will make the rivers islands, and I will dry up the pools. ¹⁶And I will bring the blind by a way *that* they knew not; I will lead them in paths *that* they have not known: I will make darkness light before them, and crooked things straight[e]. These things will I do unto them, and not forsake them. ¹⁷They shall be turned back, they shall be greatly ashamed, that trust in graven images, that say to the molten images, Ye *are* our gods.

¹⁸Hear, ye deaf; and look, ye blind, that ye may see. ¹⁹Who *is* blind, but my servant? or deaf, as my messenger *that* I sent? who *is* blind as *he that is* perfect, and blind as the LORD'S servant? ²⁰See-

---

[b] discouraged: Heb. broken
[c] prevail: or, behave himself mightily
[d] devour: Heb. swallow, or, sup up
[e] straight: Heb. into straightness

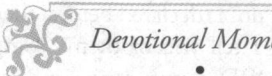

Devotional Moment

•

Hint, Hint

42:20, 23, 25 Israel knew what was right; they just wouldn't do it. Any parent knows full well that it's part of human nature to avoid doing what we're told—all children do it. But many parents who wish their children were more obedient have set a bad example more times than they realize. They disobey traffic laws, skirt regulations here, avoid rules there, put off doing what they're supposed to around the house. Is it any wonder children learn to do the same? Parents should consider what kind of example they set. Do your kids see you respecting the rules or avoiding them?

ing many things, but thou observest not; opening the ears, but he heareth not. ²¹The LORD is well pleased for his righteousness' sake; he will magnify the law, and make *it* honourable. ²²But this *is* a people robbed and spoiled; *they are* all of them snared in holes, and they are hid in prison houses: they are for a prey, and none delivereth; for a spoil, and none saith, Restore. ²³Who among you will give ear to this? *who* will hearken and hear for the time to come? ²⁴Who gave Jacob for a spoil, and Israel to the robbers? did not the LORD, he against whom we have sinned? for they would not walk in his ways, neither were they obedient unto his law. ²⁵Therefore he hath poured upon him the fury of his anger, and the strength of battle: and it hath set him on fire round about, yet he knew not; and it burned him, yet he laid *it* not to heart.

43

¹But now thus saith the LORD that created thee, O Jacob, and he that formed thee, O Israel, Fear not: for I have redeemed thee, I have called *thee* by thy name; thou *art* mine. ²When thou passest through the waters, I *will be* with thee; and through the rivers, they shall not overflow thee: when thou walkest through the fire, thou shalt not be burned; neither shall the flame kindle upon thee. ³For I *am* the LORD thy God, the Holy One of Israel, thy Saviour: I gave Egypt *for* thy ransom, Ethiopia and Seba for thee. ⁴Since thou wast precious in my sight, thou hast been honourable, and I have loved thee: therefore will I give men for thee, and people for thy life[a]. ⁵Fear not: for I *am* with thee: I will bring thy seed from the east, and gather thee from the west; ⁶I will say to the north, Give up; and to the south, Keep not back: bring my sons from far, and my daughters from the ends of the earth; ⁷*Even* every one that is called by my name: for I have created him for my glory, I have formed him; yea, I have made him.

⁸Bring forth the blind people that have eyes, and the deaf that have ears. ⁹Let all the nations be gathered together, and let the people be assembled: who among them can declare this, and shew us former things? let them bring forth their witnesses, that they may be justified: or let them hear, and say, *It is* truth. ¹⁰Ye *are* my witnesses, saith the LORD, and my servant whom I have chosen: that ye may know and believe me, and understand that I *am* he: before me there was no God formed, neither shall there be after me. ¹¹I, *even* I, *am* the LORD; and beside me *there is* no saviour. ¹²I have declared, and have

---

[a] life: or, person

saved, and I have shewed, when *there was* no strange *god* among you: therefore ye *are* my witnesses, saith the LORD, that I *am* God. [13]Yea, before the day *was* I *am* he; and *there is* none that can deliver out of my hand: I will work, and who shall let it[b]?

[14]Thus saith the LORD, your redeemer, the Holy One of Israel; For your sake I have sent to Babylon, and have brought down all their nobles[c], and the Chaldeans, whose cry *is* in the ships. [15]I *am* the LORD, your Holy One, the creator of Israel, your King. [16]Thus saith the LORD, which maketh a way in the sea, and a path in the mighty waters; [17]Which bringeth forth the chariot and horse, the army and the power; they shall lie down together, they shall not rise: they are extinct, they are quenched as tow. [18]Remember ye not the former things, neither consider the things of old. [19]Behold, I will do a new thing; now it shall spring forth; shall ye not know it? I will even make a way in the wilderness, *and* rivers in the desert. [20]The beast of the field shall honour me, the dragons and the owls[d]: because I give waters in the wilderness, *and* rivers in the desert, to give drink to my people, my chosen. [21]This people have I formed for myself; they shall shew forth my praise.

[22]But thou hast not called upon me, O Jacob; but thou hast been weary of me, O Israel. [23]Thou hast not

---

Devotional Moment

•

Forgiveness

43:25 We have a hard time forgiving the way God forgives. When someone hurts us, we may hold on to the anger and hurt, even when we know we should forgive. God doesn't do that. He forgives and forgets. One of the ways we can imitate God is to practice this kind of forgiveness. That doesn't mean we should ignore problems, like abusive behavior, and it certainly doesn't imply that it's easy to do. It simply means that letting go of daily hurts and misunderstandings can go a long way in keeping relationships healthy and strong. Work? Yes. Costly? Indeed. Worth it? Many times over.

---

brought me the small cattle of thy burnt offerings; neither hast thou honoured me with thy sacrifices. I have not caused thee to serve with an offering, nor wearied thee with incense. [24]Thou hast bought me no sweet cane with money, neither hast thou filled[e] me with the fat of thy sacrifices: but thou hast made me to serve with thy sins, thou hast wearied me with thine iniquities. [25]I, *even* I, *am* he that blotteth out thy transgressions for mine own sake, and will not remember thy sins. [26]Put me in remembrance: let us plead together: declare thou, that thou mayest be justified. [27]Thy first father hath sinned, and thy teachers[f] have transgressed against me. [28]Therefore I have profaned the princes[g] of the sanc-

---

[b] let it: Heb. turn it back?

[c] nobles: Heb. bars

[d] owls: or, ostriches: Heb. daughters of the owl

[e] filled . . . : Heb. made me drunk, or, abundantly moistened

[f] teachers: Heb. interpreters

[g] princes . . . : or, holy princes

tuary, and have given Jacob to the curse, and Israel to reproaches.

44

¹Yet now hear, O Jacob my servant; and Israel, whom I have chosen: ²Thus saith the LORD that made thee, and formed thee from the womb, *which* will help thee; Fear not, O Jacob, my servant; and thou, Jesurun, whom I have chosen. ³For I will pour water upon him that is thirsty, and floods upon the dry ground: I will pour my spirit upon thy seed, and my blessing upon thine offspring: ⁴And they shall spring up *as* among the grass, as willows by the water courses. ⁵One shall say, I *am* the LORD'S; and another shall call *himself* by the name of Jacob; and another shall subscribe *with* his hand unto the LORD, and surname *himself* by the name of Israel. ⁶Thus saith the LORD the King of Israel, and his redeemer the LORD of hosts; I *am* the first, and I *am* the last; and beside me *there is* no God. ⁷And who, as I, shall call, and shall declare it, and set it in order for me, since I appointed the ancient people? and the things that are coming, and shall come, let them shew unto them. ⁸Fear ye not, neither be afraid: have not I told thee from that time, and have declared *it?* ye *are* even my witnesses. Is there a God beside me? yea, *there is* no God[a]; I know not *any.*

⁹They that make a graven image *are* all of them vanity; and their delectable things shall not profit; and they *are* their own witnesses; they see not, nor know; that they may be ashamed. ¹⁰Who hath formed a god, or molten a graven image *that* is profitable for nothing? ¹¹Behold, all his fellows shall be ashamed: and the workmen, they *are* of men: let them all be gathered together, let them stand up; *yet* they shall fear, *and* they shall be ashamed together. ¹²The smith with the tongs[b] both worketh in the coals, and fashioneth it with hammers, and worketh it with the strength of his arms: yea, he is hungry, and his strength faileth: he drinketh no water, and is faint. ¹³The carpenter stretcheth out *his* rule; he marketh it out with a line; he fitteth it with planes, and he marketh it out with the compass, and maketh it after the figure of a man, according to the beauty of a man; that it may remain in the house. ¹⁴He heweth him down cedars, and taketh the cypress and the oak, which he strengtheneth[c] for himself among the trees of the forest: he planteth an ash, and the rain doth nourish *it.* ¹⁵Then shall it be for a man to burn: for he will take thereof, and warm himself; yea, he kindleth *it,* and baketh bread; yea, he maketh a god, and worshippeth *it;* he maketh it a graven image, and falleth down thereto. ¹⁶He burneth part thereof in the fire; with part thereof he eateth flesh; he roasteth roast, and is satisfied: yea, he warmeth *himself,* and saith, Aha, I am warm, I have seen the fire: ¹⁷And the residue thereof he maketh a god, *even* his graven image: he falleth down unto it, and worshippeth *it,* and prayeth unto it, and saith, De-

---

ᵃ God; I: Heb. rock, etc

ᵇ with the tongs: or, with an axe

ᶜ strengtheneth: or, taketh courage

liver me; for thou *art* my god. ¹⁸They have not known nor understood: for he hath shut[d] their eyes, that they cannot see; *and* their hearts, that they cannot understand. ¹⁹And none considereth[e] in his heart, neither *is there* knowledge nor understanding to say, I have burned part of it in the fire; yea, also I have baked bread upon the coals thereof; I have roasted flesh, and eaten *it*: and shall I make the residue thereof an abomination? shall I fall down to the stock of a tree? ²⁰He feedeth on ashes: a deceived heart hath turned him aside, that he cannot deliver his soul, nor say, *Is there* not a lie in my right hand?

²¹Remember these, O Jacob and Israel; for thou *art* my servant: I have formed thee; thou *art* my servant: O Israel, thou shalt not be forgotten of me. ²²I have blotted out, as a thick cloud, thy transgressions, and, as a cloud, thy sins: return unto me; for I have redeemed thee. ²³Sing, O ye heavens; for the LORD hath done *it*: shout, ye lower parts of the earth: break forth into singing, ye mountains, O forest, and every tree therein: for the LORD hath redeemed Jacob, and glorified himself in Israel. ²⁴Thus saith the LORD, thy redeemer, and he that formed thee from the womb, I *am* the LORD that maketh all *things*; that stretcheth forth the heavens alone; that spreadeth abroad the earth by myself; ²⁵That frustrateth the tokens of the liars, and maketh diviners mad; that turneth wise *men* backward, and maketh their knowledge foolish; ²⁶That confirmeth the word of his servant, and

performeth the counsel of his messengers; that saith to Jerusalem, Thou shalt be inhabited; and to the cities of Judah, Ye shall be built, and I will raise up the decayed places thereof: ²⁷That saith to the deep, Be dry, and I will dry up thy rivers: ²⁸That saith of Cyrus, *He is* my shepherd, and shall perform all my pleasure: even saying to Jerusalem, Thou shalt be built; and to the temple, Thy foundation shall be laid.

45

¹Thus saith the LORD to his anointed, to Cyrus, whose right hand I have holden, to subdue nations before him; and I will loose the loins of kings, to open before him the two leaved gates; and the gates shall not be shut; ²I will go before thee, and make the crooked places straight: I will break in pieces the gates of brass, and cut in sunder the bars of iron: ³And I will give thee the treasures of darkness, and hidden riches of secret places, that thou mayest know that I, the LORD, which call *thee* by thy name, *am* the God of Israel. ⁴For Jacob my servant's sake, and Israel mine elect, I have even called thee by thy name: I have surnamed thee, though thou hast not known me.

⁵I *am* the LORD, and *there is* none else, *there is* no God beside me: I girded thee, though thou hast not known me: ⁶That they may know from the rising of the sun, and from the west, that *there is* none beside me. I *am* the LORD, and *there is* none else. ⁷I form the light, and create darkness: I make peace, and create evil: I

---

[d] shut: Heb. daubed
[e] considereth . . . : Heb. setteth to his heart

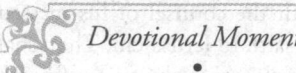

Devotional Moment
·
Tough Times

45:7 God sends both "light and darkness." Though we can never know the reason for every problem, tough times can teach us things like nothing else can. Hardships can lead us to God, teach us not to trust in our own strength, and build our patience, humility, and character. For similar reasons, good parents allow their children to make mistakes. Let children suffer the consequences of some of their poor choices and bad decisions. Resist the temptation to spare your children from every unpleasant experience.

the LORD do all these *things*. ⁸Drop down, ye heavens, from above, and let the skies pour down righteousness: let the earth open, and let them bring forth salvation, and let righteousness spring up together; I the LORD have created it. ⁹Woe unto him that striveth with his Maker! *Let* the potsherd *strive* with the potsherds of the earth. Shall the clay say to him that fashioneth it, What makest thou? or thy work, He hath no hands? ¹⁰Woe unto him that saith unto *his* father, What begettest thou? or to the woman, What hast thou brought forth?

¹¹Thus saith the LORD, the Holy One of Israel, and his Maker, Ask me of things to come concerning my sons, and concerning the work of my hands command ye me. ¹²I have made the earth, and created man upon it: I, *even* my hands, have stretched out the heavens, and all their host have I commanded. ¹³I have raised him up in righteousness, and I will directᵃ all his ways: he shall build my city, and he

shall let go my captives, not for price nor reward, saith the LORD of hosts. ¹⁴Thus saith the LORD, The labour of Egypt, and merchandise of Ethiopia and of the Sabeans, men of stature, shall come over unto thee, and they shall be thine: they shall come after thee; in chains they shall come over, and they shall fall down unto thee, they shall make supplication unto thee, *saying*, Surely God *is* in thee; and *there is* none else, *there is* no God. ¹⁵Verily thou *art* a God that hidest thyself, O God of Israel, the Saviour. ¹⁶They shall be ashamed, and also confounded, all of them: they shall go to confusion together *that are* makers of idols. ¹⁷*But* Israel shall be saved in the LORD with an everlasting salvation: ye shall not be ashamed nor confounded world without end. ¹⁸For thus saith the LORD that created the heavens; God himself that formed the earth and made it; he hath established it, he created it not in vain, he formed it to be inhabited: I *am* the LORD; and *there is* none else. ¹⁹I have not spoken in secret, in a dark place of the earth: I said not unto the seed of Jacob, Seek ye me in vain: I the LORD speak righteousness, I declare things that are right.

²⁰Assemble yourselves and come; draw near together, ye *that are* escaped of the nations: they have no knowledge that set up the wood of their graven image, and pray unto a god *that* cannot save. ²¹Tell ye, and bring *them* near; yea, let them take counsel together: who hath declared this from ancient time? *who* hath told it from

---

ᵃ direct: or, make straight

that time? *have* not I the LORD? and *there is* no God else beside me; a just God and a Saviour; *there is* none beside me. ²²Look unto me, and be ye saved, all the ends of the earth: for I *am* God, and *there is* none else. ²³I have sworn by myself, the word is gone out of my mouth *in* righteousness, and shall not return, That unto me every knee shall bow, every tongue shall swear. ²⁴Surely, shall *one* say[b], in the LORD have I righteousness and strength: *even* to him shall *men* come; and all that are incensed against him shall be ashamed. ²⁵In the LORD shall all the seed of Israel be justified, and shall glory.

46

¹Bel boweth down, Nebo stoopeth, their idols were upon the beasts, and upon the cattle: your carriages *were* heavy loaden; *they are* a burden to the weary *beast.* ²They stoop, they bow down together; they could not deliver the burden, but themselves[a] are gone into captivity. ³Hearken unto me, O house of Jacob, and all the remnant of the house of Israel, which are borne *by me* from the belly, which are carried from the womb: ⁴And *even* to *your* old age I *am* he; and *even* to hoar hairs will I carry *you:* I have made, and I will bear; even I will carry, and will deliver *you.*

⁵To whom will ye liken me, and make *me* equal, and compare me, that we may be like? ⁶They lavish gold out of the bag, and weigh silver in the balance, *and* hire a goldsmith; and he maketh it a god: they fall down, yea, they worship. ⁷They bear him upon the shoulder, they carry him, and set him in his place, and he standeth; from his place shall he not remove: yea, *one* shall cry unto him, yet can he not answer, nor save him out of his trouble. ⁸Remember this, and shew yourselves men: bring *it* again to mind, O ye transgressors. ⁹Remember the former things of old: for I *am* God, and *there is* none else; *I am* God, and *there is* none like me, ¹⁰Declaring the end from the beginning, and from ancient times *the things* that are not *yet* done, saying, My counsel shall stand, and I will do all my pleasure: ¹¹Calling a ravenous bird from the east, the man that executeth my counsel from a far country: yea, I have spoken *it,* I will also bring it to pass; I have purposed *it,* I will also do it. ¹²Hearken unto me, ye stouthearted, that *are* far from righteousness: ¹³I bring near my righteousness; it shall not be far off, and my salvation shall not tarry: and I will place salvation in Zion for Israel my glory.

47

¹Come down, and sit in the dust, O virgin daughter of Babylon, sit on the ground: *there is* no throne, O daughter of the Chaldeans: for thou shalt no more be called tender and delicate. ²Take the millstones, and grind meal: uncover thy locks, make bare the leg, uncover the thigh, pass over the rivers. ³Thy nakedness shall be uncovered, yea, thy shame shall be seen: I will take vengeance, and I will not meet *thee as* a man. ⁴*As for* our redeemer, the LORD

---

b Surely . . . : or, Surely he shall say of me, In the LORD is all righteousness and strength

a themselves: Heb. their soul

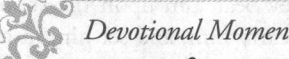

Devotional Moment
•
Pride's Outcome

47:8-9 Babylon, a powerful and prosperous nation, became proud, boastful, and arrogant toward God. When we think we have become the greatest, we are close to losing everything. Instead of boasting, we should thank God for giving us what we have. We can help family and friends celebrate achievements, such as good grades, promotions, awards, and special recognition, by complimenting each other and taking time to thank God for his part in each success.

of hosts *is* his name, the Holy One of Israel. ⁵Sit thou silent, and get thee into darkness, O daughter of the Chaldeans: for thou shalt no more be called, The lady of kingdoms. ⁶I was wroth with my people, I have polluted mine inheritance, and given them into thine hand: thou didst shew them no mercy; upon the ancient hast thou very heavily laid thy yoke.

⁷And thou saidst, I shall be a lady for ever: *so* that thou didst not lay these *things* to thy heart, neither didst remember the latter end of it. ⁸Therefore hear now this, *thou that art* given to pleasures, that dwellest carelessly, that sayest in thine heart, I *am*, and none else beside me; I shall not sit *as* a widow, neither shall I know the loss of children: ⁹But these two *things* shall come to thee in a moment in one day, the loss of children, and widowhood: they shall come upon thee in their perfection for the multitude of thy sorceries, *and* for the great abundance of thine enchant-

ments. ¹⁰For thou hast trusted in thy wickedness: thou hast said, None seeth me. Thy wisdom and thy knowledge, it hath perverted[a] thee; and thou hast said in thine heart, I *am*, and none else beside me. ¹¹Therefore shall evil come upon thee; thou shalt not know from whence it riseth: and mischief shall fall upon thee; thou shalt not be able to put it off: and desolation shall come upon thee suddenly, *which* thou shalt not know. ¹²Stand now with thine enchantments, and with the multitude of thy sorceries, wherein thou hast laboured from thy youth; if so be thou shalt be able to profit, if so be thou mayest prevail. ¹³Thou art wearied in the multitude of thy counsels. Let now the astrologers[b], the stargazers, the monthly prognosticators, stand up, and save thee from *these things* that shall come upon thee. ¹⁴Behold, they shall be as stubble; the fire shall burn them; they shall not deliver themselves[c] from the power of the flame: *there shall* not *be* a coal to warm at, *nor* fire to sit before it. ¹⁵Thus shall they be unto thee with whom thou hast laboured, *even* thy merchants, from thy youth: they shall wander every one to his quarter; none shall save thee.

48

¹Hear ye this, O house of Jacob, which are called by the name of Israel, and are come forth out of the waters of Judah, which swear by the name of the LORD, and make mention of the God of Israel, *but* not in truth, nor in righteousness. ²For they call themselves of

---

[a] perverted . . . : or, caused thee to turn away
[b] astrologers: Heb. viewers of the heavens
[c] themselves: Heb. their souls

the holy city, and stay themselves upon the God of Israel; The LORD of hosts *is* his name. ³I have declared the former things from the beginning; and they went forth out of my mouth, and I shewed them; I did *them* suddenly, and they came to pass. ⁴Because I knew that thou *art* obstinate[a], and thy neck *is* an iron sinew, and thy brow brass; ⁵I have even from the beginning declared *it* to thee; before it came to pass I shewed *it* thee: lest thou shouldest say, Mine idol hath done them, and my graven image, and my molten image, hath commanded them. ⁶Thou hast heard, see all this; and will not ye declare *it?* I have shewed thee new things from this time, even hidden things, and thou didst not know them. ⁷They are created now, and not from the beginning; even before the day when thou heardest them not; lest thou shouldest say, Behold, I knew them. ⁸Yea, thou heardest not; yea, thou knewest not; yea, from that time *that* thine ear was not opened: for I knew that thou wouldest deal very treacherously, and wast called a transgressor from the womb.

⁹For my name's sake will I defer mine anger, and for my praise will I refrain for thee, that I cut thee not off. ¹⁰Behold, I have refined thee, but not with silver; I have chosen thee in the furnace of affliction. ¹¹For mine own sake, *even* for mine own sake, will I do *it*: for how should *my name* be polluted? and I will not give my glory unto another. ¹²Hearken unto me, O Jacob and Israel, my called; I *am* he; I *am* the first, I also *am* the last. ¹³Mine hand also hath laid the foundation of the earth, and my right hand hath spanned the heavens: *when* I call unto them, they stand up together. ¹⁴All ye, assemble yourselves, and hear; which among them hath declared these *things?* The LORD hath loved him: he will do his pleasure on Babylon, and his arm *shall be on* the Chaldeans. ¹⁵I, *even* I, have spoken; yea, I have called him: I have brought him, and he shall make his way prosperous.

¹⁶Come ye near unto me, hear ye this; I have not spoken in secret from the beginning; from the time that it was, there *am* I: and now the Lord GOD, and his Spirit, hath sent me. ¹⁷Thus saith the LORD, thy Redeemer, the Holy One of Israel; I *am* the LORD thy God which teacheth thee to profit, which leadeth thee by the way *that* thou shouldest go. ¹⁸O that thou hadst hearkened to my commandments! then had thy peace been as a river, and thy righteousness as the waves of the sea: ¹⁹Thy seed also had been as the sand, and the offspring of thy bowels like the gravel thereof; his name should not have been cut off nor destroyed from before me. ²⁰Go ye forth of Babylon, flee ye from the Chaldeans, with a voice of singing declare ye, tell this, utter it *even* to the end of the earth; say ye, The LORD hath redeemed his servant Jacob. ²¹And they thirsted not *when* he led them through the deserts: he caused the waters to flow out of the rock for them: he clave the rock also, and the waters gushed out. ²²*There is* no peace, saith the LORD, unto the wicked.

49

¹Listen, O isles, unto me; and hearken, ye people, from far; The LORD hath

---

[a] obstinate: Heb. hard

called me from the womb; from the bowels of my mother hath he made mention of my name. ²And he hath made my mouth like a sharp sword; in the shadow of his hand hath he hid me, and made me a polished shaft; in his quiver hath he hid me; ³And said unto me, Thou *art* my servant, O Israel, in whom I will be glorified. ⁴Then I said, I have laboured in vain, I have spent my strength for nought, and in vain: *yet* surely my judgment *is* with the LORD, and my work* with my God. ⁵And now, saith the LORD that formed me from the womb *to be* his servant, to bring Jacob again to him, Though Israel be not gathered, yet shall I be glorious in the eyes of the LORD, and my God shall be my strength. ⁶And he said, It is a light thing that thou shouldest be my servant to raise up the tribes of Jacob, and to restore the preserved of Israel: I will also give thee for a light to the Gentiles, that thou mayest be my salvation unto the end of the earth.

⁷Thus saith the LORD, the Redeemer of Israel, *and* his Holy One, to him whom man^b despiseth, to him whom the nation abhorreth, to a servant of rulers, Kings shall see and arise, princes also shall worship, because of the LORD that is faithful, *and* the Holy One of Israel, and he shall choose thee. ⁸Thus saith the LORD, In an acceptable time have I heard thee, and in a day of salvation have I helped thee: and I will preserve thee, and give thee for a covenant of the people, to establish^c the earth, to cause to inherit the desolate heritages; ⁹That thou mayest say to the prisoners, Go forth; to them that *are* in darkness, Shew yourselves. They shall feed in the ways, and their pastures *shall be* in all high places. ¹⁰They shall not hunger nor thirst; neither shall the heat nor sun smite them: for he that hath mercy on them shall lead them, even by the springs of water shall he guide them. ¹¹And I will make all my mountains a way, and my highways shall be exalted. ¹²Behold, these shall come from far: and, lo, these from the north and from the west; and these from the land of Sinim.

¹³Sing, O heavens; and be joyful, O earth; and break forth into singing, O mountains: for the LORD hath comforted his people, and will have mercy upon his afflicted. ¹⁴But Zion said, The LORD hath forsaken me, and my Lord hath forgotten me. ¹⁵Can a woman forget her sucking child, that she should not have compassion on the son of her womb? yea, they may forget, yet will I not forget thee. ¹⁶Behold, I have graven thee upon the palms of *my* hands; thy walls *are* continually before me. ¹⁷Thy children shall make haste; thy destroyers and they that made thee waste shall go forth of thee.

¹⁸Lift up thine eyes round about, and behold: all these gather themselves together, *and* come to thee. *As* I live, saith the LORD, thou shalt surely clothe thee with them all, as with an ornament, and bind them *on thee*, as a bride *doeth*. ¹⁹For thy waste and thy desolate places, and the land of thy de-

---

^a my work: or, my reward
^b whom man . . . : or, that is despised in soul
^c establish: or, raise up

struction, shall even now be too narrow by reason of the inhabitants, and they that swallowed thee up shall be far away. ²⁰The children which thou shalt have, after thou hast lost the other, shall say again in thine ears, The place *is* too strait for me: give place to me that I may dwell. ²¹Then shalt thou say in thine heart, Who hath begotten me these, seeing I have lost my children, and am desolate, a captive, and removing to and fro? and who hath brought up these? Behold, I was left alone; these, where *had* they *been*? ²²Thus saith the Lord GOD, Behold, I will lift up mine hand to the Gentiles, and set up my standard to the people: and they shall bring thy sons in *their* arms^d, and thy daughters shall be carried upon *their* shoulders. ²³And kings shall be thy nursing fathers^e, and their queens thy nursing mothers: they shall bow down to thee with *their* face toward the earth, and lick up the dust of thy feet; and thou shalt know that I *am* the LORD: for they shall not be ashamed that wait for me.

²⁴Shall the prey be taken from the mighty, or the lawful^f captive delivered? ²⁵But thus saith the LORD, Even the captives^g of the mighty shall be taken away, and the prey of the terrible shall be delivered: for I will contend with him that contendeth with thee, and I will save thy children. ²⁶And I will feed them that oppress thee with their own flesh; and they shall be drunken with their own blood, as with sweet wine:

and all flesh shall know that I the LORD *am* thy Saviour and thy Redeemer, the mighty One of Jacob.

50

¹Thus saith the LORD, Where *is* the bill of your mother's divorcement, whom I have put away? or which of my creditors *is it* to whom I have sold you? Behold, for your iniquities have ye sold yourselves, and for your transgressions is your mother put away. ²Wherefore, when I came, *was there* no man? when I called, *was there* none to answer? Is my hand shortened at all, that it cannot redeem? or have I no power to deliver? behold, at my rebuke I dry up the sea, I make the rivers a wilderness: their fish stinketh, because *there is* no water, and dieth for thirst. ³I clothe the heavens with blackness, and I make sackcloth their covering.

⁴The Lord GOD hath given me the tongue of the learned, that I should know how to speak a word in season to *him that is* weary: he wakeneth morning by morning, he wakeneth mine ear to hear as the learned. ⁵The Lord GOD hath opened mine ear, and I was not rebellious, neither turned away back. ⁶I gave my back to the smiters, and my cheeks to them that plucked off the hair: I hid not my face from shame and spitting. ⁷For the Lord GOD will help me; therefore shall I not be confounded: therefore have I set my face like a flint, and I know that I shall not be ashamed. ⁸*He is* near that justifieth me; who will

---

^d arms: Heb. bosom
^e nursing fathers: Heb. nourishers
^f lawful . . . : Heb. captivity of the just
^g captives: Heb. captivity

contend with me? let us stand together: who *is* mine adversary? let him come near to me. ⁹Behold, the Lord GOD will help me; who *is* he *that* shall condemn me? lo, they all shall wax old as a garment; the moth shall eat them up.

¹⁰Who *is* among you that feareth the LORD, that obeyeth the voice of his servant, that walketh *in* darkness, and hath no light? let him trust in the name of the LORD, and stay upon his God. ¹¹Behold, all ye that kindle a fire, that compass *yourselves* about with sparks: walk in the light of your fire, and in the sparks *that* ye have kindled. This shall ye have of mine hand; ye shall lie down in sorrow.

51

¹Hearken to me, ye that follow after righteousness, ye that seek the LORD: look unto the rock *whence* ye are hewn, and to the hole of the pit *whence* ye are digged. ²Look unto Abraham your father, and unto Sarah *that* bare you: for I called him alone, and blessed him, and increased him. ³For the LORD shall comfort Zion: he will comfort all her waste places; and he will make her wilderness like Eden, and her desert

Devotional Moment
•
Marble

51:1-2 We are like rough stones, and our God is like a master sculptor. As God told the Israelites to do, we need to remember that we came from his quarry—we are God's creation. He designed us, made us, and knows what is best for us. You may feel like only a rough stone, one being chiseled randomly, but God has the finished work in mind. Trust him to carve a masterpiece.

Devotional Moment
•
Backlash

51:7 God told those who cherished his laws to not be afraid when they were rejected or mistreated by others. If you have faith in Christ, it is inevitable that you will clash with some of your peers. Know that (1) it's inevitable that some people will dislike your life-style and values, and (2) it's OK—you don't have to change just to please others. The opinions of people don't determine right and wrong.

like the garden of the LORD; joy and gladness shall be found therein, thanksgiving, and the voice of melody.

⁴Hearken unto me, my people; and give ear unto me, O my nation: for a law shall proceed from me, and I will make my judgment to rest for a light of the people. ⁵My righteousness *is* near; my salvation is gone forth, and mine arms shall judge the people; the isles shall wait upon me, and on mine arm shall they trust. ⁶Lift up your eyes to the heavens, and look upon the earth beneath: for the heavens shall vanish away like smoke, and the earth shall wax old like a garment, and they that dwell therein shall die in like manner: but my salvation shall be for ever, and my righteousness shall not be abolished. ⁷Hearken unto me, ye that know righteousness, the people in whose heart *is* my law; fear ye not the reproach of men, neither be ye afraid of their revilings. ⁸For the moth shall eat them up like a garment, and the worm shall eat them like wool: but my righteousness shall be for ever, and my salvation from generation to generation.

⁹Awake, awake, put on strength, O

arm of the LORD; awake, as in the ancient days, in the generations of old. *Art* thou not it that hath cut Rahab, *and* wounded the dragon? ¹⁰*Art* thou not it which hath dried the sea, the waters of the great deep; that hath made the depths of the sea a way for the ransomed to pass over? ¹¹Therefore the redeemed of the LORD shall return, and come with singing unto Zion; and everlasting joy *shall be* upon their head: they shall obtain gladness and joy; *and* sorrow and mourning shall flee away. ¹²I, *even* I, *am* he that comforteth you: who *art* thou, that thou shouldest be afraid of a man *that* shall die, and of the son of man *which* shall be made *as* grass; ¹³And forgettest the LORD thy maker, that hath stretched forth the heavens, and laid the foundations of the earth; and hast feared continually every day because of the fury of the oppressor, as if he were ready to destroy? and where *is* the fury of the oppressor? ¹⁴The captive exile hasteneth that he may be loosed, and that he should not die in the pit, nor that his bread should fail. ¹⁵But I *am* the LORD thy God, that divided the sea, whose waves roared: The LORD of hosts *is* his name. ¹⁶And I have put my words in thy mouth, and I have covered thee in the shadow of mine hand, that I may plant the heavens, and lay the foundations of the earth, and say unto Zion, Thou *art* my people.

¹⁷Awake, awake, stand up, O Jerusalem, which hast drunk at the hand of the LORD the cup of his fury; thou hast drunken the dregs of the cup of trembling, *and* wrung *them* out. ¹⁸*There is* none to guide her among all the sons *whom* she hath brought forth; neither *is*

there any that taketh her by the hand of all the sons *that* she hath brought up. ¹⁹These two *things* are come unto thee; who shall be sorry for thee? desolation, and destruction, and the famine, and the sword: by whom shall I comfort thee? ²⁰Thy sons have fainted, they lie at the head of all the streets, as a wild bull in a net: they are full of the fury of the LORD, the rebuke of thy God. ²¹Therefore hear now this, thou afflicted, and drunken, but not with wine: ²²Thus saith thy Lord the LORD, and thy God *that* pleadeth the cause of his people, Behold, I have taken out of thine hand the cup of trembling, *even* the dregs of the cup of my fury; thou shalt no more drink it again: ²³But I will put it into the hand of them that afflict thee; which have said to thy soul, Bow down, that we may go over: and thou hast laid thy body as the ground, and as the street, to them that went over.

52

¹Awake, awake; put on thy strength, O Zion; put on thy beautiful garments, O Jerusalem, the holy city: for henceforth there shall no more come into thee the uncircumcised and the unclean. ²Shake thyself from the dust; arise, *and* sit down, O Jerusalem: loose thyself from the bands of thy neck, O captive daughter of Zion. ³For thus saith the LORD, Ye have sold yourselves for nought; and ye shall be redeemed without money. ⁴For thus saith the Lord GOD, My people went down aforetime into Egypt to sojourn there; and the Assyrian oppressed them without cause. ⁵Now therefore, what have I here, saith the LORD, that my people is taken away for nought? they that rule

over them make them to howl, saith the LORD; and my name continually every day *is* blasphemed. ⁶Therefore my people shall know my name: therefore *they shall know* in that day that I *am* he that doth speak: behold, *it is* I.

⁷How beautiful upon the mountains are the feet of him that bringeth good tidings, that publisheth peace; that bringeth good tidings of good, that publisheth salvation; that saith unto Zion, Thy God reigneth! ⁸Thy watchmen shall lift up the voice; with the voice together shall they sing: for they shall see eye to eye, when the LORD shall bring again Zion. ⁹Break forth into joy, sing together, ye waste places of Jerusalem: for the LORD hath comforted his people, he hath redeemed Jerusalem. ¹⁰The LORD hath made bare his holy arm in the eyes of all the nations; and all the ends of the earth shall see the salvation of our God. ¹¹Depart ye, depart ye, go ye out from thence, touch no unclean *thing*, go ye out of the midst of her; be ye clean, that bear the vessels of the LORD. ¹²For ye shall not go out with haste, nor go by flight: for the LORD will go before you; and the God of Israel *will be* your rereward.

¹³Behold, my servant shall deal prudently, he shall be exalted and extolled, and be very high. ¹⁴As many were astonied at thee; his visage was so marred more than any man, and his form more than the sons of men: ¹⁵So shall he sprinkle many nations; the kings shall shut their mouths at him: for *that* which had not been told them shall they see; and *that* which they had not heard shall they consider.

53

¹Who hath believed our report[a]? and to whom is the arm of the LORD revealed? ²For he shall grow up before him as a tender plant, and as a root out of a dry ground: he hath no form nor comeliness; and when we shall see him, *there is* no beauty that we should desire him. ³He is despised and rejected of men; a man of sorrows, and acquainted with grief: and we hid as it were *our* faces from him; he was despised, and we esteemed him not.

⁴Surely he hath borne our griefs, and carried our sorrows: yet we did esteem him stricken, smitten of God, and afflicted. ⁵But he *was* wounded[b] for our transgressions, *he was* bruised for our iniquities: the chastisement of our peace *was* upon him; and with his stripes we are healed. ⁶All we like sheep have gone astray; we have turned every one to his own way; and the LORD hath laid[c] on him the iniquity of us all. ⁷He was oppressed, and he was afflicted, yet he opened not his mouth: he is brought as a lamb to the slaughter, and as a sheep before her shearers is dumb, so he openeth not his mouth. ⁸He was taken from prison[d] and from judgment: and who shall declare his generation? for he was cut off out of the land of the living: for the transgression of my people was he

---

[a] report: or, doctrine?: Heb. hearing?
[b] wounded: or, tormented
[c] laid . . . : Heb. made the iniquity of us all to meet on him
[d] from prison . . . : or, away my distress and judgment: but, etc

stricken. ⁹And he made his grave with the wicked, and with the rich in his death; because he had done no violence, neither *was any* deceit in his mouth.

¹⁰Yet it pleased the LORD to bruise him; he hath put *him* to grief: when thou shalt make his soul an offering for sin, he shall see *his* seed, he shall prolong *his* days, and the pleasure of the LORD shall prosper in his hand. ¹¹He shall see of the travail of his soul, *and* shall be satisfied: by his knowledge shall my righteous servant justify many; for he shall bear their iniquities. ¹²Therefore will I divide him *a portion* with the great, and he shall divide the spoil with the strong; because he hath poured out his soul unto death: and he was numbered with the transgressors; and he bare the sin of many, and made intercession for the transgressors.

54

¹Sing, O barren, thou *that* didst not bear; break forth into singing, and cry aloud, thou *that* didst not travail with child: for more *are* the children of the desolate than the children of the married wife, saith the LORD. ²Enlarge the place of thy tent, and let them stretch forth the curtains of thine habitations: spare not, lengthen thy cords, and strengthen thy stakes; ³For thou shalt break forth on the right hand and on the left; and thy seed shall inherit the Gentiles, and make the desolate cities to be inhabited. ⁴Fear not; for thou shalt not be ashamed: neither be thou confounded; for thou shalt not be put to shame: for thou shalt forget the shame of thy youth, and shalt not remember the reproach of thy widowhood any more.

⁵For thy Maker *is* thine husband; the LORD of hosts *is* his name; and thy Redeemer the Holy One of Israel; The God of the whole earth shall he be called. ⁶For the LORD hath called thee as a woman forsaken and grieved in spirit, and a wife of youth, when thou wast refused, saith thy God. ⁷For a small moment have I forsaken thee; but with great mercies will I gather thee. ⁸In a little wrath I hid my face from thee for a moment; but with everlasting kindness will I have mercy on thee, saith the LORD thy Redeemer. ⁹For this *is as* the waters of Noah unto me: for *as* I have sworn that the waters of Noah should no more go over the earth; so have I sworn that I would not be wroth with thee, nor rebuke thee. ¹⁰For the mountains shall depart, and the hills be removed; but my kindness shall not depart from thee, neither shall the covenant of my peace be removed, saith the LORD that hath mercy on thee.

¹¹O thou afflicted, tossed with tempest, *and* not comforted, behold, I will lay thy stones with fair colours, and lay thy foundations with sapphires. ¹²And I will make thy windows of agates, and thy gates of carbuncles, and all thy borders of pleasant stones. ¹³And all thy children *shall be* taught of the LORD; and great *shall be* the peace of thy children. ¹⁴In righteousness shalt thou be established: thou shalt be far from oppression; for thou shalt not fear: and from terror; for it shall not come near thee. ¹⁵Behold, they shall surely gather together, *but* not by me: whosoever shall gather together against thee shall fall for thy sake. ¹⁶Behold, I

ᵉ death: Heb. deaths

have created the smith that bloweth the coals in the fire, and that bringeth forth an instrument for his work; and I have created the waster to destroy. [17]No weapon that is formed against thee shall prosper; and every tongue *that* shall rise against thee in judgment thou shalt condemn. This *is* the heritage of the servants of the LORD, and their righteousness *is* of me, saith the LORD.

55

[1]Ho, every one that thirsteth, come ye to the waters, and he that hath no money; come ye, buy, and eat; yea, come, buy wine and milk without money and without price. [2]Wherefore do ye spend[a] money for *that which is* not bread? and your labour for *that which* satisfieth not? hearken diligently unto me, and eat ye *that which is* good, and let your soul delight itself in fatness. [3]Incline your ear, and come unto me: hear, and your soul shall live; and I will make an everlasting covenant with you, *even* the sure mercies of David. [4]Behold, I have given him *for* a witness to the people, a leader and commander to the people. [5]Behold, thou shalt call a nation *that* thou knowest not, and nations *that* knew not thee shall run unto thee because of the LORD thy God, and for the Holy One of Israel; for he hath glorified thee.

[6]Seek ye the LORD while he may be found, call ye upon him while he is near: [7]Let the wicked forsake his way, and the unrighteous[b] man his thoughts: and let him return unto the LORD, and he will have mercy upon him; and

to our God, for he will abundantly pardon. [8]For my thoughts *are* not your thoughts, neither *are* your ways my ways, saith the LORD. [9]For *as* the heavens are higher than the earth, so are my ways higher than your ways, and my thoughts than your thoughts. [10]For as the rain cometh down, and the snow from heaven, and returneth not thither, but watereth the earth, and maketh it bring forth and bud, that it may give seed to the sower, and bread to the eater: [11]So shall my word be that goeth forth out of my mouth: it shall not return unto me void, but it shall accomplish that which I please, and it shall prosper *in the thing* whereto I sent it. [12]For ye shall go out with joy, and be led forth with peace: the mountains and the hills shall break forth before you into singing, and all the trees of the field shall clap *their* hands. [13]Instead of the thorn shall come up the fir tree, and instead of the brier shall come up the myrtle tree: and it shall be to the LORD for a name, for an everlasting sign *that* shall not be cut off.

56

[1]Thus saith the LORD, Keep ye judgment[a], and do justice: for my salvation *is* near to come, and my righteousness to be revealed. [2]Blessed *is* the man *that* doeth this, and the son of man *that* layeth hold on it; that keepeth the sabbath from polluting it, and keepeth his hand from doing any evil.

[3]Neither let the son of the stranger, that hath joined himself to

---

[a] spend: Heb. weigh
[b] the unrighteous . . . : Heb. the man of iniquity
[a] judgment: or, equity

The "Widow's Verse"—It's for All Single Moms

by Sandra Picklesimer Aldrich

In December 1982 my husband, Don, lost a difficult sixteen-month battle with brain cancer. As the Scottish piper played "Amazing Grace," the funeral director closed the casket. In that moment I felt as though my life closed, too.

Fear overwhelmed me. How could I go on without Don's loving authority? How could I take over the many decisions that had been his? How could I raise two children alone? What was I going to do? I felt paralyzed.

I had never balanced a checkbook, read the tax papers I signed, or made major financial decisions. Not only did I miss my husband, I *needed* him.

Classroom teaching and caring for my children filled my days. But the evenings were too quiet. So after I tucked my youngsters into bed, I'd wrap a quilt around my shoulders and open God's Word. I was especially comforted by Isaiah 54:5: "For thy Maker is thine husband; the Lord of hosts is his name."

I read that portion over and over. God himself had promised to be my husband!

So I prayed about everything—large and small—and talked as naturally to God as I had to Don. As I struggled with replacing the vacuum cleaner belt and changing the oil in my car, I'd mutter, "OK, you're my husband now, and I need help figuring this out."

Amazingly, each time I asked for God's help, a creative idea would come or a helpful neighbor would show up. One afternoon the family room ceiling lightbulb burned out. I tried to unscrew the bulb, but it refused to budge. "You know, Lord, husbands are supposed to take care of things like this," I grumbled. "So please help me get this out."

In the quiet moment that followed, the clear thought came: *Try turning it the other way.*

I did. Immediately the lightbulb fell into my hands!

I also tried to concentrate on what I had—my children—instead of on what I had lost. I forced myself to remember that I still had choices in life, even if they were nothing more than how I would react to my circumstances.

Three years after Don's death, I was offered a position with a Christian publication in New York. The only problem was that the housing market was beyond my reach. Where would we live? And where would the kids attend school?

I was unable to sleep that night. I worried, fretted, and prayed, begging for direction. Finally, I said aloud, "OK, Lord. Husbands take care of houses and schools. You figure it out; I'm going to sleep."

Immediately I relaxed, confident God would lead us to the right neighborhood and the right school. He did exactly that, and we settled into our new life fairly quickly.

I have met many women who suddenly, unexpectedly faced a future alone. I've found these principles helpful, no matter what the specific reasons:

Pray—a lot! Talking with your heavenly Father about everything reminds you that you aren't alone, strengthens you for the task at hand, and provides creative ways for you to handle your challenges.

Trust God's promises. On my first visit to southern California, I was disappointed that the smog was obscuring the mountains. When I asked the location of majestic Mount Baldy, my friend gestured over her left shoulder. "But I can't see it," I complained. "It's still there," she replied. And that's how it is with God: He's promised to be with us even when we can't see him.

Read the Word. The women in the Bible often dealt with impossible situations. As I read about their struggles, I am strengthened. I'm especially drawn to the courage of Deborah, the humility of Ruth, the wisdom of Abigail, and the faith of Anna.

Stay in the church. With a busy schedule, it's tempting to turn Sunday into another errand day. Don't do it; you need Christian fellowship—and your children need the example of godly men.

Help others. As you reach out to others, you are the one who benefits.

Even though you didn't choose singlehood, you can thrive in it! Remember Isaiah 54:5 in every challenge: "For thy Maker is thine husband; the Lord of hosts is his name."

DIGGING DEEPER

1. What does God ask his people to do for widows and orphans? See Exodus 22:22 and Deuteronomy 10:18.

2. See 2 Kings 4:1-7, Luke 7:11-17, and Luke 18:1-8 for the accounts of three widows whose problems were solved in unusual ways. How does this give you hope?

3. Read Mark 12:41-44 and Luke 2:36-38. Where did these widows hang out?

the LORD, speak, saying, The LORD hath utterly separated me from his people: neither let the eunuch say, Behold, I *am* a dry tree. ⁴For thus saith the LORD unto the eunuchs that keep my sabbaths, and choose *the things* that please me, and take hold of my covenant; ⁵Even unto them will I give in mine house and within my walls a place and a name better than of sons and of daughters: I will give them an everlasting name, that shall not be cut off. ⁶Also the sons of the stranger, that join themselves to the LORD, to serve him, and to love the name of the LORD, to be his servants, every one that keepeth the sabbath from polluting it, and taketh hold of my covenant; ⁷Even them will I bring to my holy mountain, and make them joyful in my house of prayer: their burnt offerings and their sacrifices *shall be* accepted upon mine altar; for mine house shall be called an house of prayer for all people. ⁸The Lord GOD which gathereth the outcasts of Israel saith, Yet will I gather *others* to him, beside those that are gathered unto him.

⁹All ye beasts of the field, come to devour, *yea,* all ye beasts in the forest. ¹⁰His watchmen *are* blind: they are all ignorant, they *are* all dumb dogs, they cannot bark; sleeping[b], lying down, loving to slumber. ¹¹Yea, *they are* greedy[c] dogs *which* can never have enough, and they *are* shepherds *that* cannot understand: they all look to their own way, every one for his gain, from his quarter. ¹²Come ye, *say they,* I will fetch wine, and we will fill ourselves with strong

---

[b] sleeping: or, dreaming, or, talking in their sleep
[c] greedy: Heb. strong of appetite

drink; and to morrow shall be as this day, *and* much more abundant.

57

[1]The righteous perisheth, and no man layeth *it* to heart: and merciful[a] men *are* taken away, none considering that the righteous is taken away from the evil *to come*. [2]He shall enter into peace: they shall rest in their beds, *each one* walking *in* his uprightness.

[3]But draw near hither, ye sons of the sorceress, the seed of the adulterer and the whore. [4]Against whom do ye sport yourselves? against whom make ye a wide mouth, *and* draw out the tongue? *are* ye not children of transgression, a seed of falsehood, [5]Enflaming yourselves with idols under every green tree, slaying the children in the valleys under the clifts of the rocks? [6]Among the smooth *stones* of the stream *is* thy portion; they, they *are* thy lot: even to them hast thou poured a drink offering, thou hast offered a meat offering. Should I receive comfort in these? [7]Upon a lofty and high mountain hast thou set thy bed: even thither wentest thou up to offer sacrifice. [8]Behind the doors also and the posts hast thou set up thy remembrance: for thou hast discovered *thyself to another* than me, and art gone up; thou hast enlarged thy bed, and made[b] thee *a covenant* with them; thou lovedst their bed where thou sawest *it*. [9]And thou wentest to the king with ointment, and didst increase thy perfumes, and didst send thy messengers far off, and didst debase *thyself even* unto hell. [10]Thou art wearied in the greatness of thy way; *yet* saidst thou not, There is no hope: thou hast found the life[c] of thine hand; therefore thou wast not grieved. [11]And of whom hast thou been afraid or feared, that thou hast lied, and hast not remembered me, nor laid *it* to thy heart? have not I held my peace even of old, and thou fearest me not? [12]I will declare thy righteousness, and thy works; for they shall not profit thee.

[13]When thou criest, let thy companies deliver thee; but the wind shall carry them all away; vanity shall take *them*: but he that putteth his trust in me shall possess the land, and shall inherit my holy mountain; [14]And shall say, Cast ye up, cast ye up, prepare the way, take up the stumblingblock out of the way of my people. [15]For thus saith the high and lofty One that inhabiteth eternity, whose name *is* Holy; I dwell in the high and holy *place*, with him also *that is* of a contrite and humble spirit, to revive the spirit of the humble, and to revive the heart of the contrite ones. [16]For I will not contend for ever, neither will I be always wroth: for the spirit should fail before me, and the souls *which* I have made.

[17]For the iniquity of his covetousness was I wroth, and smote him: I hid me, and was wroth, and he went on frowardly[d] in the way of his heart. [18]I have seen his ways, and will heal him: I will lead him also, and restore comforts

---

[a] merciful . . . : Heb. men of kindness, or, godliness
[b] made . . . : or, hewed it for thyself larger than theirs
[c] life: or, living
[d] frowardly: Heb. turning away

Family Traditions

A Rich Family Life Without Cost

ISAIAH 55

Studies show most Americans believe that if they earned just 20 to 30 percent more money they would be happy. The prophet Isaiah sang God's challenge to that kind of thinking: "Wherefore do ye spend money for that which is not bread? . . . hearken diligently unto me, and eat ye that which is good, and let your soul delight itself in fatness" (55:2). Jesus repeated that theme when he said, "Blessed be ye poor: for yours is the kingdom of God" (Luke 6:20).

When we have the mind of Christ, we will crave spiritual riches rather than material ones, and our families will become a source of blessing for others who have less.

The Hansen family decided to limit their standard of living to a responsible level, regardless of how their income might rise. "The things we thought we wanted became pretty unimportant when we saw how people lived in poverty just over the U.S. border," said Ray Hansen.

His wife, Susan, agreed. "After our mission trip to Mexico, we couldn't accumulate luxuries once we had seen small children going without food."

In grooming family consumer habits, think in terms of God's priorities. Is there any connection between a product you want to buy and exploitation of other people or places? Will this product become more valuable with use? Can you pass it on or recycle it? For the luxuries you buy, can you match the amount of purchase and donate it to a missionary family overseas or to a relief agency?

Cultivate simple living in your family. One couple chose elegant bike-trek picnics as a regular event with their kids in place of fast-food outings. They took fresh rolls, cheeses, fruit, and sparkling water to a nearby park. It was easy, economical, and helped them preserve the traditions of their European background.

Keep a running list of the simple things your family enjoys. Consciously be content with what you have, rather than always looking to get new things. Take what you have and "use it up, wear it out, make it do, or do without."

Be lavishly generous with your attention and time. Splurge on affection—it's free and everybody wants it. You can always give away compliments, courage, and confidence. Instilling these qualities in others at every occasion is an inexpensive way to make your environment a better place.

Make it a family tradition to replace waste and extravagance with an abundant and functional life-style that glorifies God.

unto him and to his mourners. [19]I create the fruit of the lips; Peace, peace to *him that is* far off, and to *him that is* near, saith the LORD; and I will heal him. [20]But the wicked *are* like the troubled sea, when it cannot rest, whose waters cast up mire and dirt. [21]*There is* no peace, saith my God, to the wicked.

58

[1]Cry aloud[a], spare not, lift up thy voice like a trumpet, and shew my people their transgression, and the house of Jacob their sins. [2]Yet they seek me daily, and delight to know my ways, as a nation that did righteousness, and forsook not the ordinance of their God: they ask of me the ordinances of justice; they take delight in approaching to God.

[3]Wherefore have we fasted, *say they*, and thou seest not? *wherefore* have we afflicted our soul, and thou takest no knowledge? Behold, in the day of your fast ye find pleasure, and exact all your labours[b]. [4]Behold, ye fast for strife and debate, and to smite with the fist of wickedness: ye shall not fast as *ye do this* day, to make your voice to be heard on high. [5]Is it such a fast that I have chosen? a day[c] for a man to afflict his soul? *is it* to bow down his head as a bulrush, and to spread sackcloth and ashes *under him*? wilt thou call this a fast, and an acceptable day to the LORD? [6]*Is* not this the fast that I have chosen? to loose the bands of wickedness, to undo the heavy[d] burdens, and to let

---

Devotional Moment
•
Golden Rule

58:7, 10 Each of us probably knows someone in the neighborhood, at school, at work, or at church who needs help. These verses remind us that when we know what other people need, we have a God-given responsibility to do what we can to help them. Brainstorm together about what your family can do for a friend. Encourage your children to share the needs they have noticed in other people's lives. Then help meet the need together. Sometimes a good deed must be done alone, but doing good things as a family can be great fun!

---

the oppressed go free, and that ye break every yoke? [7]*Is it* not to deal thy bread to the hungry, and that thou bring the poor that are cast out to thy house? when thou seest the naked, that thou cover him; and that thou hide not thyself from thine own flesh?

[8]Then shall thy light break forth as the morning, and thine health shall spring forth speedily: and thy righteousness shall go before thee; the glory of the LORD shall be thy rereward. [9]Then shalt thou call, and the LORD shall answer; thou shalt cry, and he shall say, Here I *am*. If thou take away from the midst of thee the yoke, the putting forth of the finger, and speaking vanity; [10]And *if* thou draw out thy soul to the hungry, and satisfy the afflicted soul; then shall thy light rise in obscurity, and thy darkness *be* as the noonday: [11]And the LORD shall guide thee continually, and satisfy thy soul in

---

[a] aloud: Heb. with the throat
[b] labours: or, things wherewith ye grieve others: Heb. griefs
[c] a day . . . : or, to afflict his soul for a day?
[d] the heavy . . . : Heb. the bundles of the yoke

drought^c, and make fat thy bones: and thou shalt be like a watered garden, and like a spring of water, whose waters fail not. ¹²And *they that shall be* of thee shall build the old waste places: thou shalt raise up the foundations of many generations; and thou shalt be called, The repairer of the breach, The restorer of paths to dwell in.

¹³If thou turn away thy foot from the sabbath, *from* doing thy pleasure on my holy day; and call the sabbath a delight, the holy of the LORD, honourable; and shalt honour him, not doing thine own ways, nor finding thine own pleasure, nor speaking *thine own* words: ¹⁴Then shalt thou delight thyself in the LORD; and I will cause thee to ride upon the high places of the earth, and feed thee with the heritage of Jacob thy father: for the mouth of the LORD hath spoken *it*.

59

¹Behold, the LORD'S hand is not shortened, that it cannot save; neither his ear heavy, that it cannot hear: ²But your iniquities have separated between you and your God, and your sins have hid^a *his* face from you, that he will not hear. ³For your hands are defiled with blood, and your fingers with iniquity; your lips have spoken lies, your tongue hath muttered perverseness. ⁴None calleth for justice, nor *any* pleadeth for truth: they trust in vanity, and speak lies; they conceive mischief, and bring forth iniquity.

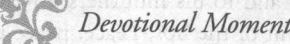

Devotional Moment

Honesty

59:4 One of God's chief complaints about his people in Isaiah's day was that fairness and honesty were almost nonexistent. Do you know that God feels this strongly about dishonesty? Our discipline should reflect God's stance. We do ourselves no favor when we overlook dishonesty or dismiss cheating as harmless. Too much of our society winks at lying, cheating, and dishonesty. We must reflect God's perspective about such behavior.

⁵They hatch cockatrice' eggs, and weave the spider's web: he that eateth of their eggs dieth, and that which is crushed breaketh out into a viper. ⁶Their webs shall not become garments, neither shall they cover themselves with their works: their works *are* works of iniquity, and the act of violence *is* in their hands. ⁷Their feet run to evil, and they make haste to shed innocent blood: their thoughts *are* thoughts of iniquity; wasting and destruction^b *are* in their paths. ⁸The way of peace they know not; and *there is* no judgment^c in their goings: they have made them crooked paths: whosoever goeth therein shall not know peace.

⁹Therefore is judgment far from us, neither doth justice overtake us: we wait for light, but behold obscurity; for brightness, *but* we walk in darkness. ¹⁰We grope for the wall like the blind, and we grope as if *we had* no eyes: we

---

^c drought: Heb. droughts
^a have hid: or, have made him hide
^b destruction: Heb. breaking
^c judgment: or, right

stumble at noonday as in the night; *we are* in desolate places as dead *men.* [11]We roar all like bears, and mourn sore like doves: we look for judgment, but *there is* none; for salvation, *but* it is far off from us. [12]For our transgressions are multiplied before thee, and our sins testify against us: for our transgressions *are* with us; and *as for* our iniquities, we know them; [13]In transgressing and lying against the LORD, and departing away from our God, speaking oppression and revolt, conceiving and uttering from the heart words of falsehood. [14]And judgment is turned away backward, and justice standeth afar off: for truth is fallen in the street, and equity cannot enter. [15]Yea, truth faileth; and he *that* departeth from evil maketh himself a prey: and the LORD saw *it,* and it displeased him that *there was* no judgment.

[16]And he saw that *there was* no man, and wondered that *there was* no intercessor: therefore his arm brought salvation unto him; and his righteousness, it sustained him. [17]For he put on righteousness as a breastplate, and an helmet of salvation upon his head; and he put on the garments of vengeance *for* clothing, and was clad with zeal as a cloke. [18]According to *their* deeds[d], accordingly he will repay, fury to his adversaries, recompence to his enemies; to the islands he will repay recompence. [19]So shall they fear the name of the LORD from the west, and his glory from the rising of the sun. When the enemy shall come in like a flood, the Spirit of the LORD shall lift up a standard against him. [20]And the Redeemer shall come to Zion, and unto them that turn from transgression in Jacob, saith the LORD. [21]As for me, this *is* my covenant with them, saith the LORD; My spirit that *is* upon thee, and my words which I have put in thy mouth, shall not depart out of thy mouth, nor out of the mouth of thy seed, nor out of the mouth of thy seed's seed, saith the LORD, from henceforth and for ever.

60

[1]Arise, shine[a]; for thy light is come, and the glory of the LORD is risen upon thee. [2]For, behold, the darkness shall cover the earth, and gross darkness the people: but the LORD shall arise upon thee, and his glory shall be seen upon thee. [3]And the Gentiles shall come to thy light, and kings to the brightness of thy rising. [4]Lift up thine eyes round about, and see: all they gather themselves together, they come to thee: thy sons shall come from far, and thy daughters shall be nursed at *thy* side. [5]Then thou shalt see, and flow together, and thine heart shall fear, and be enlarged; because the abundance[b] of the sea shall be converted unto thee, the forces of the Gentiles shall come unto thee. [6]The multitude of camels shall cover thee, the dromedaries of Midian and Ephah; all they from Sheba shall come: they shall bring gold and in-

---

[d] deeds: Heb. recompences
[a] shine . . . : or, be enlightened; for thy light cometh
[b] abundance . . . : or, noise of the sea shall be turned toward thee

cense; and they shall shew forth the praises of the LORD. ⁷All the flocks of Kedar shall be gathered together unto thee, the rams of Nebaioth shall minister unto thee: they shall come up with acceptance on mine altar, and I will glorify the house of my glory. ⁸Who *are* these *that* fly as a cloud, and as the doves to their windows?

⁹Surely the isles shall wait for me, and the ships of Tarshish first, to bring thy sons from far, their silver and their gold with them, unto the name of the LORD thy God, and to the Holy One of Israel, because he hath glorified thee. ¹⁰And the sons of strangers shall build up thy walls, and their kings shall minister unto thee: for in my wrath I smote thee, but in my favour have I had mercy on thee. ¹¹Therefore thy gates shall be open continually; they shall not be shut day nor night; that *men* may bring unto thee the forcesᶜ of the Gentiles, and *that* their kings *may be* brought. ¹²For the nation and kingdom that will not serve thee shall perish; yea, *those* nations shall be utterly wasted. ¹³The glory of Lebanon shall come unto thee, the fir tree, the pine tree, and the box together, to beautify the place of my sanctuary; and I will make the place of my feet glorious. ¹⁴The sons also of them that afflicted thee shall come bending unto thee; and all they that despised thee shall bow themselves down at the soles of thy feet; and they shall call thee, The city of the LORD, The Zion of the Holy One of Israel.

¹⁵Whereas thou hast been forsaken and hated, so that no man went through *thee*, I will make thee an eternal excel-

lency, a joy of many generations. ¹⁶Thou shalt also suck the milk of the Gentiles, and shalt suck the breast of kings: and thou shalt know that I the LORD *am* thy Saviour and thy Redeemer, the mighty One of Jacob. ¹⁷For brass I will bring gold, and for iron I will bring silver, and for wood brass, and for stones iron: I will also make thy officers peace, and thine exactors righteousness. ¹⁸Violence shall no more be heard in thy land, wasting nor destruction within thy borders; but thou shalt call thy walls Salvation, and thy gates Praise. ¹⁹The sun shall be no more thy light by day; neither for brightness shall the moon give light unto thee: but the LORD shall be unto thee an everlasting light, and thy God thy glory. ²⁰Thy sun shall no more go down; neither shall thy moon withdraw itself: for the LORD shall be thine everlasting light, and the days of thy mourning shall be ended. ²¹Thy people also *shall be* all righteous: they shall inherit the land for ever, the branch of my planting, the work of my hands, that I may be glorified. ²²A little one shall become a thousand, and a small one a strong nation: I the LORD will hasten it in his time.

61

¹The Spirit of the Lord GOD *is* upon me; because the LORD hath anointed me to preach good tidings unto the meek; he hath sent me to bind up the brokenhearted, to proclaim liberty to the captives, and the opening of the prison to *them that are* bound; ²To proclaim the acceptable year of the LORD, and the day of vengeance of our God; to comfort all that mourn; ³To appoint unto them that

---

ᶜ forces: or, wealth

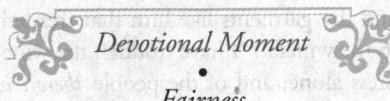

Devotional Moment
•
Fairness

61:8 Injustice occurs whenever a powerful person or group uses a superior position to mistreat another person or group. Anyone who has felt the sting of injustice despises such behavior. God hates it too. On the other hand, God is delighted when people treat each other with kindness and fairness. We must make a special effort to ensure that we are islands of justice in an unfair world. Ask yourself these tough questions: Am I fair? Do I keep my word? Do I hold others to an equivalent standard?

mourn in Zion, to give unto them beauty for ashes, the oil of joy for mourning, the garment of praise for the spirit of heaviness; that they might be called trees of righteousness, the planting of the LORD, that he might be glorified.

⁴And they shall build the old wastes, they shall raise up the former desolations, and they shall repair the waste cities, the desolations of many generations. ⁵And strangers shall stand and feed your flocks, and the sons of the alien *shall be* your plowmen and your vinedressers. ⁶But ye shall be named the Priests of the LORD: *men* shall call you the Ministers of our God: ye shall eat the riches of the Gentiles, and in their glory shall ye boast yourselves. ⁷For your shame *ye shall have* double; and *for* confusion they shall rejoice in their portion: therefore in their land they shall possess the double: everlasting joy shall be unto them. ⁸For I the LORD love judgment, I hate robbery for burnt offering; and I will direct their work in truth, and I will make an everlasting covenant with them. ⁹And their seed shall be known among the Gentiles, and their offspring among the people: all that see them shall acknowledge them, that they *are* the seed *which* the LORD hath blessed.

¹⁰I will greatly rejoice in the LORD, my soul shall be joyful in my God; for he hath clothed me with the garments of salvation, he hath covered me with the robe of righteousness, as a bridegroom deckethᵃ *himself* with ornaments, and as a bride adorneth *herself* with her jewels. ¹¹For as the earth bringeth forth her bud, and as the garden causeth the things that are sown in it to spring forth; so the Lord GOD will cause righteousness and praise to spring forth before all the nations.

62

¹For Zion's sake will I not hold my peace, and for Jerusalem's sake I will not rest, until the righteousness thereof go forth as brightness, and the salvation thereof as a lamp *that* burneth. ²And the Gentiles shall see thy righteousness, and all kings thy glory: and thou shalt be called by a new name, which the mouth of the LORD shall name. ³Thou shalt also be a crown of glory in the hand of the LORD, and a royal diadem in the hand of thy God. ⁴Thou shalt no more be termed Forsaken; neither shall thy land any more be termed Desolate: but thou shalt be called Hephzibahᵃ, and thy land Beulah: for the LORD delighteth in thee, and thy land shall be married. ⁵For *as* a young man marrieth a virgin, *so* shall thy sons marry thee: and *as* the bridegroom rejoiceth over the

---

ᵃ decketh: Heb. decketh as a priest
ᵃ Hephzibah: that is, My delight is in her

bride, *so* shall thy God rejoice over thee.

⁶I have set watchmen upon thy walls, O Jerusalem, *which* shall never hold their peace day nor night: ye that make mention of the LORD, keep not silence, ⁷And give him no rest[b], till he establish, and till he make Jerusalem a praise in the earth. ⁸The LORD hath sworn by his right hand, and by the arm of his strength, Surely I will no more give thy corn *to be* meat for thine enemies; and the sons of the stranger shall not drink thy wine, for the which thou hast laboured: ⁹But they that have gathered it shall eat it, and praise the LORD; and they that have brought it together shall drink it in the courts of my holiness.

¹⁰Go through, go through the gates; prepare ye the way of the people; cast up, cast up the highway; gather out the stones; lift up a standard for the people. ¹¹Behold, the LORD hath proclaimed unto the end of the world, Say ye to the daughter of Zion, Behold, thy salvation cometh; behold, his reward *is* with him, and his work[c] before him. ¹²And they shall call them, The holy people, The redeemed of the LORD: and thou shalt be called, Sought out, A city not forsaken.

63

¹Who *is* this that cometh from Edom, with dyed garments from Bozrah? this *that is* glorious[a] in his apparel, travelling in the greatness of his strength? I that speak in righteousness, mighty to save. ²Wherefore *art thou* red in thine apparel,

and thy garments like him that treadeth in the winefat? ³I have trodden the winepress alone; and of the people *there was* none with me: for I will tread them in mine anger, and trample them in my fury; and their blood shall be sprinkled upon my garments, and I will stain all my raiment. ⁴For the day of vengeance *is* in mine heart, and the year of my redeemed is come. ⁵And I looked, and *there was* none to help; and I wondered that *there was* none to uphold: therefore mine own arm brought salvation unto me; and my fury, it upheld me. ⁶And I will tread down the people in mine anger, and make them drunk in my fury, and I will bring down their strength to the earth.

⁷I will mention the lovingkindnesses of the LORD, *and* the praises of the LORD, according to all that the LORD hath bestowed on us, and the great goodness toward the house of Israel, which he hath bestowed on them according to his mercies, and according to the multitude of his lovingkindnesses. ⁸For he said, Surely they *are* my people, children *that* will not lie: so he was their Saviour. ⁹In all their affliction he was afflicted, and the angel of his presence saved them: in his love and in his pity he redeemed them; and he bare them, and carried them all the days of old. ¹⁰But they rebelled, and vexed his holy Spirit: therefore he was turned to be their enemy, *and* he fought against them. ¹¹Then he remembered the days of old, Moses, *and* his people, *saying*, Where *is* he that brought them up out of the sea with the shepherd[b] of his flock?

---

[b] rest: Heb. silence
[c] work: or, recompense
[a] glorious: Heb. decked
[b] shepherd: or, shepherds

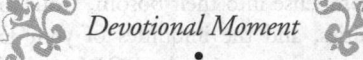

Devotional Moment
•
Fathering

63:16 For some, the word *father* evokes unpleasant images—coldness, aloofness, lack of concern, anger, sternness, harshness. Unlike earthly fathers, who inevitably fail, God consistently deals with us in a loving fashion. He is tender, compassionate, generous, sensitive, merciful, trustworthy, and kind. Every earthly dad should make it his goal to relate to his children in such a way that they are eager to meet and know their heavenly Father.

where *is* he that put his holy Spirit within him? ¹²That led *them* by the right hand of Moses with his glorious arm, dividing the water before them, to make himself an everlasting name? ¹³That led them through the deep, as an horse in the wilderness, *that* they should not stumble? ¹⁴As a beast goeth down into the valley, the Spirit of the LORD caused him to rest: so didst thou lead thy people, to make thyself a glorious name.

¹⁵Look down from heaven, and behold from the habitation of thy holiness and of thy glory: where *is* thy zeal and thy strength, the sounding^c of thy bowels and of thy mercies toward me? are they restrained? ¹⁶Doubtless thou *art* our father, though Abraham be ignorant of us, and Israel acknowledge us not: thou, O LORD, *art* our father, our redeemer^d; thy name *is* from everlasting. ¹⁷O LORD, why hast thou made us to err from thy ways, *and* hardened our heart

from thy fear? Return for thy servants' sake, the tribes of thine inheritance. ¹⁸The people of thy holiness have possessed *it* but a little while: our adversaries have trodden down thy sanctuary. ¹⁹We are *thine*: thou never barest rule over them; they were not called by thy name.

64

¹Oh that thou wouldest rend the heavens, that thou wouldest come down, that the mountains might flow down at thy presence, ²As *when* the melting^a fire burneth, the fire causeth the waters to boil, to make thy name known to thine adversaries, *that* the nations may tremble at thy presence! ³When thou didst terrible things *which* we looked not for, thou camest down, the mountains flowed down at thy presence. ⁴For since the beginning of the world *men* have not heard, nor perceived by the ear, neither hath the eye seen^b, O God, beside thee, *what* he hath prepared for him that waiteth for him. ⁵Thou meetest him that rejoiceth and worketh righteousness, *those that* remember thee in thy ways: behold, thou art wroth; for we have sinned: in those is continuance, and we shall be saved.

⁶But we are all as an unclean *thing*, and all our righteousnesses *are* as filthy rags; and we all do fade as a leaf; and our iniquities, like the wind, have taken us away. ⁷And *there is* none that calleth upon thy name, that stirreth up himself to take hold of thee: for thou hast hid thy face from us, and hast consumed^c us, be-

---

^c the sounding: or, the multitude
^d our redeemer . . . : or, our redeemer from everlasting is thy name
^a the melting . . . : Heb. the fire of meltings
^b seen . . . : or, seen a God beside thee, which doeth so for him, etc
^c consumed: Heb. melted

cause of our iniquities. ⁸But now, O LORD, thou *art* our father; we *are* the clay, and thou our potter; and we all *are* the work of thy hand. ⁹Be not wroth very sore, O LORD, neither remember iniquity for ever: behold, see, we beseech thee, we *are* all thy people. ¹⁰Thy holy cities are a wilderness, Zion is a wilderness, Jerusalem a desolation. ¹¹Our holy and our beautiful house, where our fathers praised thee, is burned up with fire: and all our pleasant things are laid waste. ¹²Wilt thou refrain thyself for these *things*, O LORD? wilt thou hold thy peace, and afflict us very sore?

65

¹I am sought of *them that* asked not *for me*; I am found of *them that* sought me not: I said, Behold me, behold me, unto a nation *that* was not called by my name. ²I have spread out my hands all the day unto a rebellious people, which walketh in a way *that was* not good, after their own thoughts; ³A people that provoketh me to anger continually to my face; that sacrificeth in gardens, and burneth incense upon altars of brick; ⁴Which remain among the graves, and lodge in the monuments, which eat swine's flesh, and broth ͣ of abominable *things is in* their vessels; ⁵Which say, Stand by thyself, come not near to me; for I am holier than thou. These *are* a smoke in my nose ᵇ, a fire that burneth all the day. ⁶Behold, *it is* written before me: I will not keep silence, but will recompense, even

recompense into their bosom, ⁷Your iniquities, and the iniquities of your fathers together, saith the LORD, which have burned incense upon the mountains, and blasphemed me upon the hills: therefore will I measure their former work into their bosom.

⁸Thus saith the LORD, As the new wine is found in the cluster, and *one* saith, Destroy it not; for a blessing *is* in it: so will I do for my servants' sakes, that I may not destroy them all. ⁹And I will bring forth a seed out of Jacob, and out of Judah an inheritor of my mountains: and mine elect shall inherit it, and my servants shall dwell there. ¹⁰And Sharon shall be a fold of flocks, and the valley of Achor a place for the herds to lie down in, for my people that have sought me.

¹¹But ye *are* they that forsake the LORD, that forget my holy mountain, that prepare a table for that troop ᶜ, and that furnish the drink offering unto that number. ¹²Therefore will I number you to the sword, and ye shall all bow down to the slaughter: because when I called, ye did not answer; when I spake, ye did not hear; but did evil before mine eyes, and did choose *that* wherein I delighted not. ¹³Therefore thus saith the Lord GOD, Behold, my servants shall eat, but ye shall be hungry: behold, my servants shall drink, but ye shall be thirsty: behold, my servants shall rejoice, but ye shall be ashamed: ¹⁴Behold, my servants shall sing for joy of heart, but ye shall cry for sorrow of heart, and shall howl for vexation ᵈ of

---

ͣ broth: or, pieces

ᵇ nose: or, anger

ᶜ troop: or, Gad

ᵈ vexation: Heb. breaking

spirit. ¹⁵And ye shall leave your name for a curse unto my chosen: for the Lord GOD shall slay thee, and call his servants by another name: ¹⁶That he who blesseth himself in the earth shall bless himself in the God of truth; and he that sweareth in the earth shall swear by the God of truth; because the former troubles are forgotten, and because they are hid from mine eyes.

¹⁷For, behold, I create new heavens and a new earth: and the former shall not be remembered, nor come[c] into mind. ¹⁸But be ye glad and rejoice for ever *in that* which I create: for, behold, I create Jerusalem a rejoicing, and her people a joy. ¹⁹And I will rejoice in Jerusalem, and joy in my people: and the voice of weeping shall be no more heard in her, nor the voice of crying. ²⁰There shall be no more thence an infant of days, nor an old man that hath not filled his days: for the child shall die an hundred years old; but the sinner *being* an hundred years old shall be accursed.

Devotional Moment

Hope

65:17-25 The promise of "new heavens and a new earth" provides hope in a sinful world. The day is surely coming when tragedy will give way to triumph and pressures will be replaced by peace. We have a choice: We can either focus on our problems and succumb to worry and fear, or we can focus on God, who controls the affairs of the world and is making all things new. Let others see you as one with an attitude of hopefulness— not hopelessness!

---

²¹And they shall build houses, and inhabit *them*; and they shall plant vineyards, and eat the fruit of them. ²²They shall not build, and another inhabit; they shall not plant, and another eat: for as the days of a tree *are* the days of my people, and mine elect shall long enjoy the work of their hands. ²³They shall not labour in vain, nor bring forth for trouble; for they *are* the seed of the blessed of the LORD, and their offspring with them. ²⁴And it shall come to pass, that before they call, I will answer; and while they are yet speaking, I will hear. ²⁵The wolf and the lamb shall feed together, and the lion shall eat straw like the bullock: and dust *shall be* the serpent's meat. They shall not hurt nor destroy in all my holy mountain, saith the LORD.

66

¹Thus saith the LORD, The heaven *is* my throne, and the earth *is* my footstool: where *is* the house that ye build unto me? and where *is* the place of my rest? ²For all those *things* hath mine hand made, and all those *things* have been, saith the LORD: but to this *man* will I look, *even* to *him that is* poor and of a contrite spirit, and trembleth at my word. ³He that killeth an ox *is as if* he slew a man; he that sacrificeth a lamb[a], *as if* he cut off a dog's neck; he that offereth an oblation, *as if he offered* swine's blood; he that burneth incense, *as if* he blessed an idol. Yea, they have chosen their own ways, and their soul delighteth in their abominations. ⁴I also will choose their delusions[b], and will

---

ᶜ come . . . : Heb. come upon the heart
ª lamb: or, kid
ᵇ delusions: or, devices

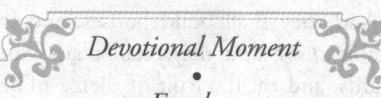

Devotional Moment
•
Freedom

66:2-4 God grants each person the freedom to decide how he or she will live. We can either submit to him and respond to his commands with reverence and obedience, or we can reject the Lord's instructions and pridefully go our own way. Pray earnestly for those close to you—that each will choose to live as God commands.

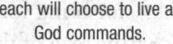

bring their fears upon them; because when I called, none did answer; when I spake, they did not hear: but they did evil before mine eyes, and chose *that* in which I delighted not.

⁵Hear the word of the LORD, ye that tremble at his word; Your brethren that hated you, that cast you out for my name's sake, said, Let the LORD be glorified: but he shall appear to your joy, and they shall be ashamed. ⁶A voice of noise from the city, a voice from the temple, a voice of the LORD that rendereth recompence to his enemies. ⁷Before she travailed, she brought forth; before her pain came, she was delivered of a man child. ⁸Who hath heard such a thing? who hath seen such things? Shall the earth be made to bring forth in one day? *or* shall a nation be born at once? for as soon as Zion travailed, she brought forth her children. ⁹Shall I bring to the birth, and not cause to bring forth? saith the LORD: shall I cause to bring forth, and shut *the womb*? saith thy God. ¹⁰Rejoice ye with Jerusalem, and be glad with her, all ye

that love her: rejoice for joy with her, all ye that mourn for her: ¹¹That ye may suck, and be satisfied with the breasts of her consolations; that ye may milk out, and be delighted with the abundance^c of her glory. ¹²For thus saith the LORD, Behold, I will extend peace to her like a river, and the glory of the Gentiles like a flowing stream: then shall ye suck, ye shall be borne upon *her* sides, and be dandled upon *her* knees. ¹³As one whom his mother comforteth, so will I comfort you; and ye shall be comforted in Jerusalem. ¹⁴And when ye see *this*, your heart shall rejoice, and your bones shall flourish like an herb: and the hand of the LORD shall be known toward his servants, and *his* indignation toward his enemies.

¹⁵For, behold, the LORD will come with fire, and with his chariots like a whirlwind, to render his anger with fury, and his rebuke with flames of fire. ¹⁶For by fire and by his sword will the LORD plead with all flesh: and the slain of the LORD shall be many. ¹⁷They that sanctify themselves, and purify themselves in the gardens behind^d one *tree* in the midst, eating swine's flesh, and the abomination, and the mouse, shall be consumed together, saith the LORD. ¹⁸For I *know* their works and their thoughts: it shall come, that I will gather all nations and tongues; and they shall come, and see my glory. ¹⁹And I will set a sign among them, and I will send those that escape of them unto the nations, *to* Tarshish, Pul, and Lud, that draw the bow, *to* Tubal, and Javan, *to* the isles afar off,

^c abundance: or, brightness
^d behind . . . : or, one after another

that have not heard my fame, neither have seen my glory; and they shall declare my glory among the Gentiles. ²⁰And they shall bring all your brethren *for* an offering unto the LORD out of all nations upon horses, and in chariots, and in litters^e, and upon mules, and upon swift beasts, to my holy mountain Jerusalem, saith the LORD, as the children of Israel bring an offering in a clean vessel into the house of the LORD. ²¹And I will also take of them for priests *and* for Levites, saith the LORD. ²²For as the new heavens and the new earth, which I will make, shall remain before me, saith the LORD, so shall your seed and your name remain. ²³And it shall come to pass, *that* from one new moon to another, and from one sabbath to another, shall all flesh come to worship before me, saith the LORD. ²⁴And they shall go forth, and look upon the carcases of the men that have transgressed against me: for their worm shall not die, neither shall their fire be quenched; and they shall be an abhorring unto all flesh.

---

^e litters: or, coaches

JEREMIAH

Purpose
To urge God's people to turn from
their sin and to turn back to God

Author
Jeremiah

To Whom Written
Judah (the Southern Kingdom)
and its capital city, Jerusalem

Date Written
During Jeremiah's ministry, approximately 627–586 B.C.

Setting
Jeremiah ministered during the
reigns of Judah's last five
kings—Josiah, Jehoahaz, Jehoiakim, Jehoiachin, and
Zedekiah. The nation was sliding
quickly toward destruction and
was eventually conquered by
Babylon in 586 B.C. (see 2 Kings
21–25). The prophet Zephaniah
preceded Jeremiah, and
Habakkuk was his contemporary.

Key Verse
"Thine own wickedness shall
correct thee . . . know therefore
and see that it is an evil thing
and bitter, that thou hast forsaken the Lord thy God, and that
my fear is not in thee, saith the
Lord God of hosts" (2:19).

Key People
Jeremiah, Judah's kings (listed
above), Baruch, Ebed-melech,
King Nebuchadnezzar

Key Places
Anathoth, Jerusalem, Ramah, Egypt

Children can say the funniest things. A five-year-old playing with a turtle or a four-year-old picking at her toes can come up with some of the most hilarious remarks, usually catching us completely off guard.

Sometimes an adult will say something memorable, too. We still quote Winston Churchill, John Kennedy, and Yogi Berra. Two of the most famous speeches in U.S. history were delivered by adults: the first in Gettysburg, Pennsylvania, in 1863; the second to a crowd gathered at the Washington, D.C., memorial of the first speech-giver a hundred years later. Most everyone can quote at least a line or two from both of those speeches, because they were so historically significant.

Jeremiah was probably the type of kid who could sting an audience with a well-timed one-liner. If not, then he surely developed the gift as an adult. His is the longest book in all of the Bible and contains some of the most memorable and oft-quoted words: "Before I formed thee in the belly I knew thee" (1:5). "Oh that . . . mine eyes [were] a fountain of tears, that I might weep day and night" (9:1). "For I know the thoughts that I think toward you, saith the Lord, thoughts of peace, and not of evil, to give you an expected end" (29:11).

Reading Jeremiah will be like finding treasures hidden for years in dusty closets, but still fresh and powerful. Jeremiah's book is a quotable classic.

1

¹The words of Jeremiah the son of Hilkiah, of the priests that *were* in Anathoth in the land of Benjamin: ²To whom the word of the LORD came in the days of Josiah the son of Amon king of Judah, in the thirteenth year of his reign. ³It came also in the days of Jehoiakim the son of Josiah king of Judah, unto the end of the eleventh year of Zedekiah the son of Josiah king of Judah, unto the carrying away of Jerusalem captive in the fifth month.

⁴Then the word of the LORD came unto me, saying, ⁵Before I formed thee in the belly I knew thee; and before thou camest forth out of the womb I sanctified thee, *and* I ordained[a] thee a prophet unto the nations. ⁶Then said I, Ah, Lord GOD! behold, I cannot speak: for I *am* a child. ⁷But the LORD said unto me, Say not, I *am* a child: for thou shalt go to all that I shall send thee, and whatsoever I command thee thou shalt speak. ⁸Be not afraid of their faces: for I *am* with thee to deliver thee, saith the LORD. ⁹Then the LORD put forth his hand, and touched my mouth. And the LORD said unto me, Behold, I have put my words in thy mouth. ¹⁰See, I have this day set thee over the nations and over the kingdoms, to root out, and to pull down, and to destroy, and to throw down, to build, and to plant.

¹¹Moreover the word of the LORD came unto me, saying, Jeremiah, what seest thou? And I said, I see a rod of an almond tree. ¹²Then said the LORD unto me, Thou hast well seen: for I will hasten my word to perform it. ¹³And the word of the LORD came unto me the second time, saying, What seest thou? And I said, I see a seething pot; and the face thereof *is* toward[b] the north. ¹⁴Then the LORD said unto me, Out of the north an evil shall break forth upon all the inhabitants of the land. ¹⁵For, lo, I will call all the families of the kingdoms of the north, saith the LORD; and they shall come, and they shall set every one his throne at the entering of the gates of Jerusalem, and against all the walls thereof round about, and against all the cities of Judah. ¹⁶And I will utter my judgments against them touching all their wickedness, who have forsaken me, and have burned incense unto other gods, and worshipped the works of their own hands. ¹⁷Thou therefore gird up thy loins, and arise, and speak unto them all that I command thee: be not dis-

---

Devotional Moment
•
Idolatry

1:16 Many people tend to think of idolatry as a curious phenomenon of primitive peoples. Not so. Idolatry is simply the act of worshiping a false god. Almost anything can be an idol because almost anything can take God's place in our life. If we are obsessed with our possessions, consumed with thoughts of making money, or desperate for the approval of others, we are guilty of idolatry. Even the pursuit of something good—personal hopes and dreams, relationships, career, church activities—can tend toward idolatry if it becomes the central focus of our life. What idol is strongly tempting you? Make sure nothing takes God's place.

---

[a] ordained: Heb. gave
[b] toward . . . : Heb. from the face of the north

mayed at their faces, lest I confound[c] thee before them. [18]For, behold, I have made thee this day a defenced city, and an iron pillar, and brasen walls against the whole land, against the kings of Judah, against the princes thereof, against the priests thereof, and against the people of the land. [19]And they shall fight against thee; but they shall not prevail against thee; for I *am* with thee, saith the LORD, to deliver thee.

2

[1]Moreover the word of the LORD came to me, saying, [2]Go and cry in the ears of Jerusalem, saying, Thus saith the LORD; I remember thee, the kindness[a] of thy youth, the love of thine espousals, when thou wentest after me in the wilderness, in a land *that was* not sown. [3]Israel *was* holiness unto the LORD, *and* the firstfruits of his increase: all that devour him shall offend; evil shall come upon them, saith the LORD. [4]Hear ye the word of the LORD, O house of Jacob, and all the families of the house of Israel: [5]Thus saith the LORD, What iniquity have your fathers found in me, that they are gone far from me, and have walked after vanity, and are become vain? [6]Neither said they, Where *is* the LORD that brought us up out of the land of Egypt, that led us through the wilderness, through a land of deserts and of pits, through a land of drought, and of the shadow of death, through a land that no man passed through, and where no man dwelt? [7]And I brought you into a plentiful[b] country, to eat the fruit thereof and the goodness thereof; but when ye entered, ye defiled my land, and made mine heritage an abomination. [8]The priests said not, Where *is* the LORD? and they that handle the law knew me not: the pastors also transgressed against me, and the prophets prophesied by Baal, and walked after *things that* do not profit.

[9]Wherefore I will yet plead with you, saith the LORD, and with your children's children will I plead. [10]For pass over[c] the isles of Chittim, and see; and send unto Kedar, and consider diligently, and see if there be such a thing. [11]Hath a nation changed *their* gods, which *are* yet no gods? but my people have changed their glory for *that which* doth not profit. [12]Be astonished, O ye heavens, at this, and be horribly afraid, be ye very desolate, saith the LORD. [13]For my people have committed two evils; they have forsaken me the fountain of living waters, *and* hewed them out cisterns, broken cisterns, that can hold no water.

[14]*Is* Israel a servant? *is* he a homeborn *slave?* why is he spoiled[d]? [15]The young lions roared upon him, *and* yelled[e], and they made his land waste: his cities are burned without inhabitant. [16]Also the children of Noph and

---

[c] confound: or, break to pieces
[a] thee: or, for thy sake
[b] a plentiful . . . : or, the land of Carmel
[c] over: or, over to
[d] spoiled: Heb. become a spoil?
[e] yelled: Heb. gave out their voice

Tahapanes have broken the crown of thy head. ¹⁷Hast thou not procured this unto thyself, in that thou hast forsaken the LORD thy God, when he led thee by the way? ¹⁸And now what hast thou to do in the way of Egypt, to drink the waters of Sihor? or what hast thou to do in the way of Assyria, to drink the waters of the river? ¹⁹Thine own wickedness shall correct thee, and thy backslidings shall reprove thee: know therefore and see that *it is* an evil *thing* and bitter, that thou hast forsaken the LORD thy God, and that my fear *is* not in thee, saith the Lord GOD of hosts.

²⁰For of old time I have broken thy yoke, *and* burst thy bands; and thou saidst, I will not transgress[f]; when upon every high hill and under every green tree thou wanderest, playing the harlot. ²¹Yet I had planted thee a noble vine, wholly a right seed: how then art thou turned into the degenerate plant of a strange vine unto me? ²²For though thou wash thee with nitre, and take thee much soap, *yet* thine iniquity is marked before me, saith the Lord GOD. ²³How canst thou say, I am not polluted, I have not gone after Baalim? see thy way in the valley, know what thou hast done: *thou art* a swift dromedary traversing her ways; ²⁴A wild ass used to the wilderness, *that* snuffeth up the wind at her pleasure; in her occasion who can turn her away? all they that seek her will not weary themselves; in her month they shall find her. ²⁵Withhold thy foot from being unshod, and thy throat from thirst: but thou saidst, There is no hope: no; for I have loved strangers, and after them will I go. ²⁶As the thief is ashamed when he is found, so is the house of Israel ashamed; they, their kings, their princes, and their priests, and their prophets, ²⁷Saying to a stock, Thou *art* my father; and to a stone, Thou hast brought me forth: for they have turned *their* back unto me, and not *their* face: but in the time of their trouble they will say, Arise, and save us. ²⁸But where *are* thy gods that thou hast made thee? let them arise, if they can save thee in the time of thy trouble[g]: for *according to* the number of thy cities are thy gods, O Judah.

²⁹Wherefore will ye plead with me? ye all have transgressed against me, saith the LORD. ³⁰In vain have I smitten your children; they received no correction: your own sword hath devoured your prophets, like a destroying lion. ³¹O generation, see ye the word of the LORD. Have I been a wilderness unto Israel? a land of darkness? wherefore say my people, We are lords; we will come no more unto thee? ³²Can a maid forget her orna-

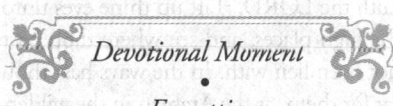

Devotional Moment

Forgetting

2:31-32 Though it seems incredible, God's own people have often been guilty of forgetting God. You can help avoid this trap by (1) setting aside regular times to remember all that God has done for you; (2) devoting some time, energy, and attention to prayer and Bible reading each day; and (3) making a conscious effort to "set your affection on things above," instead of "things on the earth" (Col. 3:2).

---

[f] transgress: or, serve
[g] trouble: Heb. evil

ments, *or* a bride her attire? yet my people have forgotten me days without number. ³³Why trimmest thou thy way to seek love? therefore hast thou also taught the wicked ones thy ways. ³⁴Also in thy skirts is found the blood of the souls of the poor innocents: I have not found it by secret search, but upon all these. ³⁵Yet thou sayest, Because I am innocent, surely his anger shall turn from me. Behold, I will plead with thee, because thou sayest, I have not sinned. ³⁶Why gaddest thou about so much to change thy way? thou also shalt be ashamed of Egypt, as thou wast ashamed of Assyria. ³⁷Yea, thou shalt go forth from him, and thine hands upon thine head: for the LORD hath rejected thy confidences, and thou shalt not prosper in them.

3

¹They say*, If a man put away his wife, and she go from him, and become another man's, shall he return unto her again? shall not that land be greatly polluted? but thou hast played the harlot with many lovers; yet return again to me, saith the LORD. ²Lift up thine eyes unto the high places, and see where thou hast not been lien with. In the ways hast thou sat for them, as the Arabian in the wilderness; and thou hast polluted the land with thy whoredoms and with thy wickedness. ³Therefore the showers have been withholden, and there hath been no latter rain; and thou hadst a whore's forehead, thou refusedst to be ashamed. ⁴Wilt thou not from this time cry unto me, My father, thou *art* the guide of my youth?

Devotional Moment
•
Confession
3:4-5, 11-13 God longs for his people to acknowledge their guilt and "return" to him. That involves confession to him and to others. Confession makes a person vulnerable, so make it a policy to respect and protect anyone who confesses a wrong. Confession heals our relationship with God and with other people, but it won't happen if anyone feels unsafe about it.

---

⁵Will he reserve *his anger* for ever? will he keep *it* to the end? Behold, thou hast spoken and done evil things as thou couldest. ⁶The LORD said also unto me in the days of Josiah the king, Hast thou seen *that* which backsliding Israel hath done? she is gone up upon every high mountain and under every green tree, and there hath played the harlot. ⁷And I said after she had done all these *things*, Turn thou unto me. But she returned not. And her treacherous sister Judah saw *it*. ⁸And I saw, when for all the causes whereby backsliding Israel committed adultery I had put her away, and given her a bill of divorce; yet her treacherous sister Judah feared not, but went and played the harlot also. ⁹And it came to pass through the lightnessᵇ of her whoredom, that she defiled the land, and committed adultery with stones and with stocks. ¹⁰And yet for all this her treacherous sister Judah hath not turned unto me with her whole heart, but feignedlyᶜ, saith the LORD.

ᵃ They say: Heb. Saying
ᵇ lightness: or, fame
ᶜ feignedly: Heb. in falsehood

¹¹And the LORD said unto me, The backsliding Israel hath justified herself more than treacherous Judah.

¹²Go and proclaim these words toward the north, and say, Return, thou backsliding Israel, saith the LORD; *and* I will not cause mine anger to fall upon you: for I *am* merciful, saith the LORD, *and* I will not keep *anger* for ever. ¹³Only acknowledge thine iniquity, that thou hast transgressed against the LORD thy God, and hast scattered thy ways to the strangers under every green tree, and ye have not obeyed my voice, saith the LORD. ¹⁴Turn, O backsliding children, saith the LORD; for I am married unto you: and I will take you one of a city, and two of a family, and I will bring you to Zion: ¹⁵And I will give you pastors according to mine heart, which shall feed you with knowledge and understanding. ¹⁶And it shall come to pass, when ye be multiplied and increased in the land, in those days, saith the LORD, they shall say no more, The ark of the covenant of the LORD: neither shall it come to mind^d: neither shall they remember it; neither shall they visit *it*; neither shall *that* be done any more. ¹⁷At that time they shall call Jerusalem the throne of the LORD; and all the nations shall be gathered unto it, to the name of the LORD, to Jerusalem: neither shall they walk any more after the imagination^e of their evil heart. ¹⁸In those days the house of Judah shall walk with the house of Israel, and they shall come together out of the land of the north to the land that I have given for an inheritance unto your fathers. ¹⁹But I said, How shall I put thee among the children, and give thee a pleasant^f land, a goodly heritage of the hosts of nations? and I said, Thou shalt call me, My father; and shalt not turn away from me.

²⁰Surely *as* a wife treacherously departeth from her husband^g, so have ye dealt treacherously with me, O house of Israel, saith the LORD. ²¹A voice was heard upon the high places, weeping *and* supplications of the children of Israel: for they have perverted their way, *and* they have forgotten the LORD their God. ²²Return, ye backsliding children, *and* I will heal your backslidings. Behold, we come unto thee; for thou *art* the LORD our God. ²³Truly in vain *is salvation hoped for* from the hills, *and from* the multitude of mountains: truly in the LORD our God *is* the salvation of Israel. ²⁴For shame hath devoured the labour of our fathers from our youth; their flocks and their herds, their sons and their daughters. ²⁵We lie down in our shame, and our confusion covereth us: for we have sinned against the LORD our God, we and our fathers, from our youth even unto this day, and have not obeyed the voice of the LORD our God.

4

¹If thou wilt return, O Israel, saith the LORD, return unto me: and if thou wilt put away thine abominations out of my sight, then shalt thou not remove. ²And thou shalt swear, The

---

^{d} come to mind: Heb. come upon the heart
^{e} imagination: or, stubbornness
^{f} pleasant . . . : Heb. land of desire
^{g} husband: Heb. friend

LORD liveth, in truth, in judgment, and in righteousness; and the nations shall bless themselves in him, and in him shall they glory.

³For thus saith the LORD to the men of Judah and Jerusalem, Break up your fallow ground, and sow not among thorns. ⁴Circumcise yourselves to the LORD, and take away the foreskins of your heart, ye men of Judah and inhabitants of Jerusalem: lest my fury come forth like fire, and burn that none can quench *it*, because of the evil of your doings.

⁵Declare ye in Judah, and publish in Jerusalem; and say, Blow ye the trumpet in the land: cry, gather together, and say, Assemble yourselves, and let us go into the defenced cities. ⁶Set up the standard toward Zion: retireª, stay not: for I will bring evil from the north, and a great destruction. ⁷The lion is come up from his thicket, and the destroyer of the Gentiles is on his way; he is gone forth from his place to make thy land desolate; *and* thy cities shall be laid waste, without an inhabitant. ⁸For this gird you with sackcloth, lament and howl: for the fierce anger of the LORD is not turned back from us. ⁹And it shall come to pass at that day, saith the LORD, *that* the heart of the king shall perish, and the heart of the princes; and the priests shall be astonished, and the prophets shall wonder. ¹⁰Then said I, Ah, Lord GOD! surely thou hast greatly deceived this people and Jerusalem, saying, Ye shall have peace; whereas the sword reacheth unto the soul. ¹¹At that time shall it be said to this people and to Jerusalem, A dry wind of the high places in the wilderness toward the daughter of my people, not to fan, nor to cleanse, ¹²*Even* a full ᵇ wind from those *places* shall come unto me: now also will I give sentence against them. ¹³Behold, he shall come up as clouds, and his chariots *shall be* as a whirlwind: his horses are swifter than eagles. Woe unto us! for we are spoiled. ¹⁴O Jerusalem, wash thine heart from wickedness, that thou mayest be saved. How long shall thy vain thoughts lodge within thee? ¹⁵For a voice declareth from Dan, and publisheth affliction from mount Ephraim. ¹⁶Make ye mention to the nations; behold, publish against Jerusalem, *that* watchers come from a far country, and give out their voice against the cities of Judah. ¹⁷As keepers of a field, are they against her round about; because she hath been rebellious against me, saith the LORD. ¹⁸Thy way and thy doings have procured these *things* unto thee; this *is* thy wickedness, because it is bitter, because it reacheth unto thine heart.

¹⁹My bowels, my bowels! I am pained at my veryᶜ heart; my heart maketh a noise in me; I cannot hold my peace, because thou hast heard, O my soul, the sound of the trumpet, the alarm of war. ²⁰Destruction upon destruction is cried; for the whole land is spoiled: suddenly are my tents spoiled, *and* my curtains in a moment. ²¹How long shall I see the standard, *and* hear the sound of the trumpet? ²²For my

---

ª retire: or, strengthen
ᵇ a full . . . : or, a fuller wind than those
ᶜ my very . . . : Heb. the walls of my heart

people *is* foolish, they have not known me; they *are* sottish children, and they have none understanding: they *are* wise to do evil, but to do good they have no knowledge. ²³I beheld the earth, and, lo, *it was* without form, and void; and the heavens, and they *had* no light. ²⁴I beheld the mountains, and, lo, they trembled, and all the hills moved lightly. ²⁵I beheld, and, lo, *there was* no man, and all the birds of the heavens were fled. ²⁶I beheld, and, lo, the fruitful place *was* a wilderness, and all the cities thereof were broken down at the presence of the LORD, *and* by his fierce anger. ²⁷For thus hath the LORD said, The whole land shall be desolate; yet will I not make a full end. ²⁸For this shall the earth mourn, and the heavens above be black: because I have spoken *it*, I have purposed *it*, and will not repent, neither will I turn back from it. ²⁹The whole city shall flee for the noise of the horsemen and bowmen; they shall go into thickets, and climb up upon the rocks: every city *shall be* forsaken, and not a man dwell therein. ³⁰And *when* thou *art* spoiled, what wilt thou do? Though thou clothest thyself with crimson, though thou deckest thee with ornaments of gold, though thou rentest thy face*ᵈ* with painting, in vain shalt thou make thyself fair; *thy* lovers will despise thee, they will seek thy life. ³¹For I have heard a voice as of a woman in travail, *and* the anguish as of her that bringeth forth her first child, the voice of the daughter of Zion, *that* bewaileth herself, *that* spreadeth her hands, *saying*, Woe *is* me now! for my soul is wearied because of murderers.

5

¹Run ye to and fro through the streets of Jerusalem, and see now, and know, and seek in the broad places thereof, if ye can find a man, if there be *any* that executeth judgment, that seeketh the truth; and I will pardon it. ²And though they say, The LORD liveth; surely they swear falsely. ³O LORD, *are* not thine eyes upon the truth? thou hast stricken them, but they have not grieved; thou hast consumed them, *but* they have refused to receive correction: they have made their faces harder than a rock; they have refused to return. ⁴Therefore I said, Surely these *are* poor; they are foolish: for they know not the way of the LORD, *nor* the judgment of their God. ⁵I will get me unto the great men, and will speak unto them; for they have known the way of the LORD, *and* the judgment of their God: but these have altogether broken the yoke, *and* burst the bonds. ⁶Wherefore a lion out of the forest shall slay them, *and* a wolf of the evenings*ᵃ* shall spoil them, a leopard shall watch over their cities: every one that goeth out thence shall be torn in pieces: because their transgressions are many, *and* their backslidings are increased. ⁷How shall I pardon thee for this? thy children have forsaken me, and sworn by *them that are* no gods: when I had fed them to the full, they then committed adultery, and assembled themselves by troops in the harlots' houses. ⁸They were *as* fed horses in

---

ᵈ face: Heb. eyes
ᵃ evenings: or, deserts

the morning: every one neighed after his neighbour's wife. ⁹Shall I not visit for these *things*? saith the LORD: and shall not my soul be avenged on such a nation as this?

¹⁰Go ye up upon her walls, and destroy; but make not a full end: take away her battlements; for they *are* not the LORD'S. ¹¹For the house of Israel and the house of Judah have dealt very treacherously against me, saith the LORD. ¹²They have belied the LORD, and said, *It is* not he; neither shall evil come upon us; neither shall we see sword nor famine: ¹³And the prophets shall become wind, and the word *is* not in them: thus shall it be done unto them. ¹⁴Wherefore thus saith the LORD God of hosts, Because ye speak this word, behold, I will make my words in thy mouth fire, and this people wood, and it shall devour them. ¹⁵Lo, I will bring a nation upon you from far, O house of Israel, saith the LORD: it *is* a mighty nation, it *is* an ancient nation, a nation whose language thou knowest not, neither understandest what they say. ¹⁶Their quiver *is* as an open sepulchre, they *are* all mighty men. ¹⁷And they shall eat up thine harvest, and thy bread, *which* thy sons and thy daughters should eat: they shall eat up thy flocks and thine herds: they shall eat up thy vines and thy fig trees: they shall impoverish thy fenced cities, wherein thou trustedst, with the sword. ¹⁸Nevertheless in those days, saith the LORD, I will not make a full end with you. ¹⁹And it shall come to pass, when ye shall say, Wherefore doeth the LORD our God all these *things* unto us? then shalt thou answer them, Like as ye have forsaken me, and served strange gods in your land, so shall ye serve strangers in a land *that is* not yours.

²⁰Declare this in the house of Jacob, and publish it in Judah, saying, ²¹Hear now this, O foolish people, and without understandingᵇ; which have eyes, and see not; which have ears, and hear not: ²²Fear ye not me? saith the LORD: will ye not tremble at my presence, which have placed the sand *for* the bound of the sea by a perpetual decree, that it cannot pass it: and though the waves thereof toss themselves, yet can they not prevail; though they roar, yet can they not pass over it? ²³But this people hath a revolting and a rebellious heart; they are revolted and gone. ²⁴Neither say they in their heart, Let us now fear the LORD our God, that giveth rain, both the former and the latter, in his season: he reserveth unto us the appointed weeks of the harvest.

²⁵Your iniquities have turned away these *things*, and your sins have withholden good *things* from you. ²⁶For among my people are found wicked *men*: they lay wait, as he that setteth snares; they set a trap, they catch men. ²⁷As a cageᶜ is full of birds, so *are* their houses full of deceit: therefore they are become great, and waxen rich. ²⁸They are waxen fat, they shine: yea, they overpass the deeds of the wicked: they judge not the cause, the cause of the fatherless, yet they prosper; and the right of the needy do they not judge. ²⁹Shall I

ᵇ understanding: Heb. heart
ᶜ cage: or, coop

not visit for these *things?* saith the LORD: shall not my soul be avenged on such a nation as this? ³⁰A wonderfulᵈ and horrible thing is committed in the land; ³¹The prophets prophesy falsely, and the priests bear rule by their means; and my people love *to have it* so: and what will ye do in the end thereof?

6

¹O ye children of Benjamin, gather yourselves to flee out of the midst of Jerusalem, and blow the trumpet in Tekoa, and set up a sign of fire in Beth-haccerem: for evil appeareth out of the north, and great destruction. ²I have likened the daughter of Zion to a comelyᵃ and delicate *woman.* ³The shepherds with their flocks shall come unto her; they shall pitch *their* tents against her round about; they shall feed every one in his place. ⁴Prepare ye war against her; arise, and let us go up at noon. Woe unto us! for the day goeth away, for the shadows of the evening are stretched out. ⁵Arise, and let us go by night, and let us destroy her palaces. ⁶For thus hath the LORD of hosts said, Hew ye down trees, and castᵇ a mount against Jerusalem: this *is* the city to be visited; she *is* wholly oppression in the midst of her. ⁷As a fountain casteth out her waters, so she casteth out her wickedness: violence and spoil is heard in her; before me continually *is* grief and wounds. ⁸Be thou instructed, O Jerusalem, lest my soul departᶜ from thee; lest I make thee desolate, a land not inhabited.

⁹Thus saith the LORD of hosts, They shall throughly glean the remnant of Israel as a vine: turn back thine hand as a grapegatherer into the baskets. ¹⁰To whom shall I speak, and give warning,

ᵈ A wonderful . . . : or, Astonishment and filthiness
ᵃ comely: or, dwelling at home
ᵇ cast . . . : or, pour out the engine of shot
ᶜ depart: Heb. be loosed, or, disjointed

that they may hear? behold, their ear *is* uncircumcised, and they cannot hearken: behold, the word of the LORD is unto them a reproach; they have no delight in it. ¹¹Therefore I am full of the fury of the LORD; I am weary with holding in: I will pour it out upon the children abroad, and upon the assembly of young men together: for even the husband with the wife shall be taken, the aged with *him that is* full of days. ¹²And their houses shall be turned unto others, *with their* fields and wives together: for I will stretch out my hand upon the inhabitants of the land, saith the LORD. ¹³For from the least of them even unto the greatest of them every one *is* given to covetousness; and from the prophet even unto the priest every one dealeth falsely. ¹⁴They have healed also the hurt^d *of the daughter* of my people slightly, saying, Peace, peace; when *there is* no peace. ¹⁵Were they ashamed when they had committed abomination? nay, they were not at all ashamed, neither could they blush: therefore they shall fall among them that fall: at the time *that* I visit them they shall be cast down, saith the LORD. ¹⁶Thus saith the LORD, Stand ye in the ways, and see, and ask for the old paths, where *is* the good way, and walk therein, and ye shall find rest for your souls. But they said, We will not walk *therein.* ¹⁷Also I set watchmen over you, *saying,* Hearken to the sound of the trumpet. But they said, We will not hearken.

¹⁸Therefore hear, ye nations, and know, O congregation, what *is* among them. ¹⁹Hear, O earth: behold, I will bring evil upon this people, *even* the fruit of their thoughts, because they have not hearkened unto my words, nor to my law, but rejected it. ²⁰To what purpose cometh there to me incense from Sheba, and the sweet cane from a far country? your burnt offerings *are* not acceptable, nor your sacrifices sweet unto me. ²¹Therefore thus saith the LORD, Behold, I will lay stumblingblocks before this people, and the fathers and the sons together shall fall upon them; the neighbour and his friend shall perish. ²²Thus saith the LORD, Behold, a people cometh from the north country, and a great nation shall be raised from the sides of the earth. ²³They shall lay hold on bow and spear; they *are* cruel, and have no mercy; their voice roareth like the sea; and they ride upon horses, set in array as men for war against thee, O daughter of Zion. ²⁴We have heard the fame thereof: our hands wax feeble: anguish hath taken hold of us, *and* pain, as of a woman in travail. ²⁵Go not forth into the field, nor walk by the way; for the sword of the enemy *and* fear *is* on every side. ²⁶O daughter of my people, gird *thee* with sackcloth, and wallow thyself in ashes: make thee mourning, *as for* an only son, most bitter lamentation: for the spoiler shall suddenly come upon us. ²⁷I have set thee *for* a tower *and* a fortress among my people, that thou mayest know and try their way. ²⁸They *are* all grievous revolters, walking with slanders: *they are* brass and iron; they *are* all corrupters. ²⁹The bellows are burned, the lead is consumed of the fire; the founder melteth in vain: for the wicked are not plucked away. ³⁰Reprobate^e silver shall

---

^d hurt: Heb. bruise, or, breach

^e Reprobate . . . : or, Refuse silver

men call them, because the LORD hath rejected them.

7

¹The word that came to Jeremiah from the LORD, saying, ²Stand in the gate of the LORD'S house, and proclaim there this word, and say, Hear the word of the LORD, all *ye of* Judah, that enter in at these gates to worship the LORD. ³Thus saith the LORD of hosts, the God of Israel, Amend your ways and your doings, and I will cause you to dwell in this place. ⁴Trust ye not in lying words, saying, The temple of the LORD, The temple of the LORD, The temple of the LORD, *are* these. ⁵For if ye throughly amend your ways and your doings; if ye throughly execute judgment between a man and his neighbour; ⁶*If* ye oppress not the stranger, the fatherless, and the widow, and shed not innocent blood in this place, neither walk after other gods to your hurt: ⁷Then will I cause you to dwell in this place, in the land that I gave to your fathers, for ever and ever. ⁸Behold, ye trust in lying words, that cannot profit. ⁹Will ye steal, murder, and commit adultery, and swear falsely, and burn incense unto Baal, and walk after other gods whom ye know not; ¹⁰And come and stand before me in this house, which is called by my name, and say, We are delivered to do all these abominations? ¹¹Is this house, which is called by my name, become a den of robbers in your eyes? Behold, even I have seen *it*, saith the LORD. ¹²But go ye now unto my place which *was* in Shiloh, where I set my name at the first, and see what I did to it for the wickedness of my people Israel. ¹³And now, because ye have done all these works, saith the LORD, and I spake unto you, rising up early and speaking, but ye heard not; and I called you, but ye answered not; ¹⁴Therefore will I do unto *this* house, which is called by my name, wherein ye trust, and unto the place which I gave to you and to your fathers, as I have done to Shiloh. ¹⁵And I will cast you out of my sight, as I have cast out all your brethren, *even* the whole seed of Ephraim.

¹⁶Therefore pray not thou for this people, neither lift up cry nor prayer for them, neither make intercession to me: for I will not hear thee. ¹⁷Seest thou not what they do in the cities of Judah and in the streets of Jerusalem? ¹⁸The children gather wood, and the fathers kindle the fire, and the women knead *their* dough, to make cakes to the queenᵃ of heaven, and to pour out drink offerings unto other gods, that they may provoke me to anger. ¹⁹Do they provoke me to anger? saith the LORD: *do they* not *provoke* themselves to the confusion of their own faces? ²⁰Therefore thus saith the Lord GOD; Behold, mine anger and my fury shall be poured out upon this place, upon man, and upon beast, and upon the trees of the field, and upon the fruit of the ground; and it shall burn, and shall not be quenched.

²¹Thus saith the LORD of hosts, the God of Israel; Put your burnt offerings unto your sacrifices, and eat flesh. ²²For I spake not unto your fathers, nor commanded them in the day that I brought them out of the land of Egypt,

---

ᵃ queen . . . : or, frame, or, workmanship of heaven

concerning[b] burnt offerings or sacrifices: [23]But this thing commanded I them, saying, Obey my voice, and I will be your God, and ye shall be my people: and walk ye in all the ways that I have commanded you, that it may be well unto you. [24]But they hearkened not, nor inclined their ear, but walked in the counsels *and* in the imagination[c] of their evil heart, and went backward, and not forward. [25]Since the day that your fathers came forth out of the land of Egypt unto this day I have even sent unto you all my servants the prophets, daily rising up early and sending *them*: [26]Yet they hearkened not unto me, nor inclined their ear, but hardened their neck: they did worse than their fathers. [27]Therefore thou shalt speak all these words unto them; but they will not hearken to thee: thou shalt also call unto them; but they will not answer thee. [28]But thou shalt say unto them, This *is* a nation that obeyeth not the voice of the LORD their God, nor receiveth correction[d]: truth is perished, and is cut off from their mouth.

[29]Cut off thine hair, *O Jerusalem*, and cast *it* away, and take up a lamentation on high places; for the LORD hath rejected and forsaken the generation of his wrath. [30]For the children of Judah have done evil in my sight, saith the LORD: they have set their abominations in the house which is called by my name, to pollute it. [31]And they have built the high places of Tophet, which *is* in the valley of the son of Hinnom, to burn their sons and their daughters in the fire; which I commanded *them* not, neither came[e] it into my heart. [32]Therefore, behold, the days come, saith the LORD, that it shall no more be called Tophet, nor the valley of the son of Hinnom, but the valley of slaughter: for they shall bury in Tophet, till there be no place. [33]And the carcases of this people shall be meat for the fowls of the heaven, and for the beasts of the earth; and none shall fray *them* away. [34]Then will I cause to cease from the cities of Judah, and from the streets of Jerusalem, the voice of mirth, and the voice of gladness, the voice of the bridegroom, and the voice of the bride: for the land shall be desolate.

8

[1]At that time, saith the LORD, they shall bring out the bones of the kings of Judah, and the bones of his princes, and the bones of the priests, and the bones of the prophets, and the bones of the inhabitants of Jerusalem, out of their graves: [2]And they shall spread them before the sun, and the moon, and all the host of heaven, whom they have loved, and whom they have served, and after whom they have walked, and whom they have sought, and whom they have worshipped: they shall not be gathered, nor be buried; they shall be for dung upon the face of the earth. [3]And death shall be chosen rather than life by all the residue of them that remain of this evil family, which remain in all the

---

[b] concerning: Heb. concerning the matter of
[c] imagination: or, stubbornness
[d] correction: or, instruction
[e] came . . . : Heb. came it upon my heart

places whither I have driven them, saith the LORD of hosts.

⁴Moreover thou shalt say unto them, Thus saith the LORD; Shall they fall, and not arise? shall he turn away, and not return? ⁵Why *then* is this people of Jerusalem slidden back by a perpetual backsliding? they hold fast deceit, they refuse to return. ⁶I hearkened and heard, *but* they spake not aright: no man repented him of his wickedness, saying, What have I done? every one turned to his course, as the horse rusheth into the battle. ⁷Yea, the stork in the heaven knoweth her appointed times; and the turtle and the crane and the swallow observe the time of their coming; but my people know not the judgment of the LORD. ⁸How do ye say, We *are* wise, and the law of the LORD *is* with us? Lo, certainly in vain made[a] he *it*; the pen of the scribes *is* in vain. ⁹The wise[b] men are ashamed, they are dismayed and taken: lo, they have rejected the word of the LORD; and what wisdom *is* in them? ¹⁰Therefore will I give their wives unto others, *and* their fields to them that shall inherit *them*: for every one from the least even unto the greatest is given to covetousness, from the prophet even unto the priest every one dealeth falsely. ¹¹For they have healed the hurt of the daughter of my people slightly, saying, Peace, peace; when *there is* no peace. ¹²Were they ashamed when they had committed abomination? nay, they were not at all ashamed, neither could they blush: therefore shall they fall among them that fall: in the time of their visitation they shall be cast down, saith the LORD.

¹³I will surely consume them, saith the LORD: *there shall be* no grapes on the vine, nor figs on the fig tree, and the leaf shall fade; and *the things that* I have given them shall pass away from them. ¹⁴Why do we sit still? assemble yourselves, and let us enter into the defenced cities, and let us be silent there: for the LORD our God hath put us to silence, and given us water of gall[c] to drink, because we have sinned against the LORD. ¹⁵We looked for peace, but no good *came; and* for a time of health, and behold trouble! ¹⁶The snorting of his horses was heard from Dan: the whole land trembled at the sound of the neighing of his strong ones; for they are come, and have devoured the land, and all[d] that is in it; the city, and those that dwell therein. ¹⁷For, behold, I will

---

Devotional Moment

Compassion for the Lost

8:18–9:2 Despite their thick heads and hard hearts, Jeremiah felt compassion for his countrymen. Although their sinful actions frustrated him (9:2), he pleaded with God to bring healing to their anguished souls. This is a wonderful example for us to follow. Consider those you know who don't know Christ or who have strayed from him. Instead of pointing the finger and saying, "That's just what they deserve," try to feel their pain. Let the full weight of their lost condition overwhelm you. If you find it difficult to feel sorrow, ask God to break your heart for those he so deeply loves.

---

[a] in vain made . . . : or, the false pen of the scribes worketh for falsehood
[b] The wise . . . : or, Have they been ashamed, etc
[c] gall: or, poison
[d] all . . . : Heb. the fulness thereof

send serpents, cockatrices, among you, which *will* not *be* charmed, and they shall bite you, saith the LORD. ¹⁸*When* I would comfort myself against sorrow, my heart *is* faint in me. ¹⁹Behold the voice of the cry of the daughter of my people because of them that dwell in a far country: *Is* not the LORD in Zion? *is* not her king in her? Why have they provoked me to anger with their graven images, *and* with strange vanities? ²⁰The harvest is past, the summer is ended, and we are not saved. ²¹For the hurt of the daughter of my people am I hurt; I am black; astonishment hath taken hold on me. ²²*Is there* no balm in Gilead; *is there* no physician there? why then is not the health of the daughter of my people recovered°?

9

¹Oh that my head were waters, and mine eyes a fountain of tears, that I might weep day and night for the slain of the daughter of my people! ²Oh that I had in the wilderness a lodging place of wayfaring men; that I might leave my people, and go from them! for they *be* all adulterers, an assembly of treacherous men. ³And they bend their tongues *like* their bow *for* lies: but they are not valiant for the truth upon the earth; for they proceed from evil to evil, and they know not me, saith the LORD. ⁴Take ye heed every one of his neighbour°, and trust ye not in any

brother: for every brother will utterly supplant, and every neighbour will walk with slanders. ⁵And they will deceive° every one his neighbour, and will not speak the truth: they have taught their tongue to speak lies, *and* weary themselves to commit iniquity. ⁶Thine habitation *is* in the midst of deceit; through deceit they refuse to know me, saith the LORD. ⁷Therefore thus saith the LORD of hosts, Behold, I will melt them, and try them; for how shall I do for the daughter of my people? ⁸Their tongue *is as* an arrow shot out; it speaketh deceit: *one* speaketh peaceably to his neighbour with his mouth, but in heart° he layeth his wait. ⁹Shall I not visit them for these *things*? saith the LORD: shall not my soul be avenged on such a nation as this? ¹⁰For the mountains will I take up a weeping and wailing, and for the habitations° of the wilderness a lamentation, because they are burned up, so that none can pass through *them*; neither can *men* hear the voice of the cattle; both the fowl of the heavens and the beast are fled; they are gone. ¹¹And I will make Jerusalem heaps, *and* a den of dragons; and I will make the cities of Judah desolate°, without an inhabitant.

¹²Who *is* the wise man, that may understand this? and *who is he* to whom the mouth of the LORD hath spoken, that he may declare it, for what the land perisheth *and* is burned up like a

---

° recovered: Heb. gone up?

° neighbour: or, friend

° deceive: or, mock

° in heart: Heb. in the midst of him

° habitations: or, pastures

° desolate: Heb. desolation

wilderness, that none passeth through? ¹³And the LORD saith, Because they have forsaken my law which I set before them, and have not obeyed my voice, neither walked therein; ¹⁴But have walked after the imagination[f] of their own heart, and after Baalim, which their fathers taught them: ¹⁵Therefore thus saith the LORD of hosts, the God of Israel; Behold, I will feed them, *even* this people, with wormwood, and give them water of gall to drink. ¹⁶I will scatter them also among the heathen, whom neither they nor their fathers have known: and I will send a sword after them, till I have consumed them. ¹⁷Thus saith the LORD of hosts, Consider ye, and call for the mourning women, that they may come; and send for cunning *women*, that they may come: ¹⁸And let them make haste, and take up a wailing for us, that our eyes may run down with tears, and our eyelids gush out with waters. ¹⁹For a voice of wailing is heard out of Zion, How are we spoiled! we are greatly confounded, because we have forsaken the land, because our dwellings have cast *us* out. ²⁰Yet hear the word of the LORD, O ye women, and let your ear receive the word of his mouth, and teach your daughters wailing, and every one her neighbour lamentation. ²¹For death is come up into our windows, *and* is entered into our palaces, to cut off the children from without, *and* the young men from the streets. ²²Speak, Thus saith the LORD, Even the carcases of men shall fall as dung upon the open

> ## Devotional Moment
> •
> ### Goals
> 9:23-24 While it is certainly not wrong to be wise, powerful, or wealthy, God says here that the most important thing in life is a close relationship with him. Perhaps it is time to readjust your goals. This is important not only for finding personal fulfillment, but also for setting a good example.

field, and as the handful after the harvestman, and none shall gather *them*.

²³Thus saith the LORD, Let not the wise *man* glory in his wisdom, neither let the mighty *man* glory in his might, let not the rich *man* glory in his riches: ²⁴But let him that glorieth glory in this, that he understandeth and knoweth me, that I *am* the LORD which exercise lovingkindness, judgment, and righteousness, in the earth: for in these *things* I delight, saith the LORD. ²⁵Behold, the days come, saith the LORD, that I will punish[g] all *them which are* circumcised with the uncircumcised; ²⁶Egypt, and Judah, and Edom, and the children of Ammon, and Moab, and all *that are* in the utmost[h] corners, that dwell in the wilderness: for all *these* nations *are* uncircumcised, and all the house of Israel *are* uncircumcised in the heart.

10

¹Hear ye the word which the LORD speaketh unto you, O house of Israel: ²Thus saith the LORD, Learn not the way of the heathen, and be not dis-

---

[f] imagination: or, stubbornness

[g] punish: Heb. visit upon

[h] in the utmost . . . : Heb. cut off into corners, or, having the corners of their hair polled

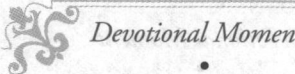

Devotional Moment

•

Occult

10:2-3, 6-7 Many people believe that horoscopes, Ouija boards, tarot cards, psychic readings, and other occult practices are harmless, but the Bible says otherwise. Don't get involved with them. Not only are they "a pack of lies," but God expressly forbids his people to engage in them (Deut. 18:9-13). Don't buy these kinds of games for your kids or give them as gifts to others. Instead, recognize that among the wise people of the earth and in all the kingdoms of the world, there isn't anyone like the Lord God. He alone is our guide and source of wisdom.

mayed at the signs of heaven; for the heathen are dismayed at them. ³For the customsª of the people *are* vain: for *one* cutteth a tree out of the forest, the work of the hands of the workman, with the axe. ⁴They deck it with silver and with gold; they fasten it with nails and with hammers, that it move not. ⁵They *are* upright as the palm tree, but speak not: they must needs be borne, because they cannot go. Be not afraid of them; for they cannot do evil, neither also *is it* in them to do good. ⁶Forasmuch as *there is* none like unto thee, O LORD; thou *art* great, and thy name *is* great in might. ⁷Who would not fear thee, O King of nations? for to thee doth it appertain: forasmuch as among all the wise *men* of the nations, and in all their kingdoms, *there is* none like unto thee. ⁸But they are altogetherᵇ brutish and

foolish: the stock *is* a doctrine of vanities. ⁹Silver spread into plates is brought from Tarshish, and gold from Uphaz, the work of the workman, and of the hands of the founder: blue and purple *is* their clothing: they *are* all the work of cunning *men*. ¹⁰But the LORD *is* the trueᶜ God, he *is* the living God, and an everlasting king: at his wrath the earth shall tremble, and the nations shall not be able to abide his indignation. ¹¹Thus shall ye say unto them, The gods that have not made the heavens and the earth, *even* they shall perish from the earth, and from under these heavens. ¹²He hath made the earth by his power, he hath established the world by his wisdom, and hath stretched out the heavens by his discretion. ¹³When he uttereth his voice, *there is* a multitudeᵈ of waters in the heavens, and he causeth the vapours to ascend from the ends of the earth; he maketh lightnings with rain, and bringeth forth the wind out of his treasures. ¹⁴Every man is brutish in *his* knowledge: every founder is confounded by the graven image: for his molten image *is* falsehood, and *there is* no breath in them. ¹⁵They *are* vanity, *and* the work of errors: in the time of their visitation they shall perish. ¹⁶The portion of Jacob *is* not like them: for he *is* the former of all *things*; and Israel *is* the rod of his inheritance: The LORD of hosts *is* his name.

¹⁷Gather up thy wares out of the land, O inhabitantᵉ of the fortress. ¹⁸For

---

ª customs . . . : Heb. statutes, or, ordinances are vanity

ᵇ altogether: Heb. in one, or, at once

ᶜ true . . . : Heb. God of truth

ᵈ multitude: or, noise

ᵉ inhabitant: Heb. inhabitress

thus saith the LORD, Behold, I will sling out the inhabitants of the land at this once, and will distress them, that they may find *it so.* ¹⁹Woe is me for my hurt! my wound is grievous: but I said, Truly this *is* a grief, and I must bear it. ²⁰My tabernacle is spoiled, and all my cords are broken: my children are gone forth of me, and they *are* not: *there is* none to stretch forth my tent any more, and to set up my curtains. ²¹For the pastors are become brutish, and have not sought the LORD: therefore they shall not prosper, and all their flocks shall be scattered. ²²Behold, the noise of the bruit is come, and a great commotion out of the north country, to make the cities of Judah desolate, *and* a den of dragons. ²³O LORD, I know that the way of man *is* not in himself: *it is* not in man that walketh to direct his steps. ²⁴O LORD, correct me, but with judgment; not in thine anger, lest thou bring me to nothing. ²⁵Pour out thy fury upon the heathen that know thee not, and upon the families that call not on thy name: for they have eaten up Jacob, and devoured him, and consumed him, and have made his habitation desolate.

11

¹The word that came to Jeremiah from the LORD, saying, ²Hear ye the words of this covenant, and speak unto the men of Judah, and to the inhabitants of Jerusalem; ³And say thou unto them, Thus saith the LORD God of Israel; Cursed *be* the man that obeyeth not the words of this covenant, ⁴Which I commanded your fathers in the day *that* I

Devotional Moment
•
Consistency

11:1-8 God made a clear agreement with Israel. God's people knew what he expected and what the consequences of their actions would be. That's a good model for discipline within the family. If we clearly tell our children what we expect from them, that we will reward obedience and punish disobedience, then we must be sure to follow through on our word. We can err in three ways: (1) Sometimes we fail to clearly tell our children what we expect. (2) We fail to reward them for obeying. (3) We fail to follow through with promised consequences when they disobey. Consistency is the key. When we become dependable, we help our children understand the dependability of God's Word—both the promises and the warnings.

---

brought them forth out of the land of Egypt, from the iron furnace, saying, Obey my voice, and do them, according to all which I command you: so shall ye be my people, and I will be your God: ⁵That I may perform the oath which I have sworn unto your fathers, to give them a land flowing with milk and honey, as *it is* this day. Then answered I, and said, So be it, O LORD. ⁶Then the LORD said unto me, Proclaim all these words in the cities of Judah, and in the streets of Jerusalem, saying, Hear ye the words of this covenant, and do them. ⁷For I earnestly protested unto your fathers in the day *that* I brought them up out of the land of Egypt, *even* unto this day, rising early and protesting, saying, Obey my voice. ⁸Yet they obeyed not, nor inclined their ear, but walked every one in the imaginationª of their evil heart: therefore I will bring upon them all the words of

---

ª imagination: or, stubbornness

this covenant, which I commanded *them* to do; but they did *them* not. ⁹And the LORD said unto me, A conspiracy is found among the men of Judah, and among the inhabitants of Jerusalem. ¹⁰They are turned back to the iniquities of their forefathers, which refused to hear my words; and they went after other gods to serve them: the house of Israel and the house of Judah have broken my covenant which I made with their fathers.

¹¹Therefore thus saith the LORD, Behold, I will bring evil upon them, which they shall not be able to escape[b]; and though they shall cry unto me, I will not hearken unto them. ¹²Then shall the cities of Judah and inhabitants of Jerusalem go, and cry unto the gods unto whom they offer incense: but they shall not save them at all in the time of their trouble[c]. ¹³For *according to* the number of thy cities were thy gods, O Judah; and *according to* the number of the streets of Jerusalem have ye set up altars to *that* shameful thing, *even* altars to burn incense unto Baal. ¹⁴Therefore pray not thou for this people, neither lift up a cry or prayer for them: for I will not hear *them* in the time that they cry unto me for their trouble[d]. ¹⁵What hath my beloved to do in mine house, *seeing* she hath wrought lewdness with many, and the holy flesh is passed from thee? when thou doest evil, then thou rejoicest. ¹⁶The LORD called thy name, A green olive tree, fair, *and* of goodly fruit: with the noise of a great tumult he hath kindled fire upon it, and the branches of it are broken. ¹⁷For the LORD of hosts, that planted thee, hath pronounced evil against thee, for the evil of the house of Israel and of the house of Judah, which they have done against themselves to provoke me to anger in offering incense unto Baal.

¹⁸And the LORD hath given me knowledge *of it*, and I know *it*: then thou shewedst me their doings. ¹⁹But I *was* like a lamb *or* an ox *that* is brought to the slaughter; and I knew not that they had devised devices against me, *saying*, Let us destroy the tree[e] with the fruit thereof, and let us cut him off from the land of the living, that his name may be no more remembered. ²⁰But, O LORD of hosts, that judgest righteously, that triest the reins and the heart, let me see thy vengeance on them: for unto thee have I revealed my cause. ²¹Therefore thus saith the LORD of the men of Anathoth, that seek thy life, saying, Prophesy not in the name of the LORD, that thou die not by our hand: ²²Therefore thus saith the LORD of hosts, Behold, I will punish[f] them: the young men shall die by the sword; their sons and their daughters shall die by famine: ²³And there shall be no remnant of them: for I will bring evil upon the men of Anathoth, *even* the year of their visitation.

12

¹Righteous *art* thou, O LORD, when I plead with thee: yet let me talk[a] with thee

---

[b] to escape: Heb. to go forth of
[c] trouble: Heb. evil
[d] trouble: Heb. evil
[e] the tree . . . : Heb. the stalk with his bread
[f] punish: Heb. visit upon
[a] talk . . . : or, reason the case with thee

of *thy* judgments: Wherefore doth the way of the wicked prosper? *wherefore* are all they happy that deal very treacherously? ²Thou hast planted them, yea, they have taken root: they grow^b, yea, they bring forth fruit: thou *art* near in their mouth, and far from their reins. ³But thou, O LORD, knowest me: thou hast seen me, and tried mine heart toward thee: pull them out like sheep for the slaughter, and prepare them for the day of slaughter. ⁴How long shall the land mourn, and the herbs of every field wither, for the wickedness of them that dwell therein? the beasts are consumed, and the birds; because they said, He shall not see our last end. ⁵If thou hast run with the footmen, and they have wearied thee, then how canst thou contend with horses? and *if* in the land of peace, *wherein* thou trustedst, *they wearied thee*, then how wilt thou do in the swelling of Jordan? ⁶For even thy brethren, and the house of thy father, even they have dealt treacherously with thee; yea, they have called^c a multitude after thee: believe them not, though they speak fair words unto thee.

⁷I have forsaken mine house, I have left mine heritage; I have given the dearly beloved of my soul into the hand of her enemies. ⁸Mine heritage is unto me as a lion in the forest; it crieth out against me: therefore have I hated it. ⁹Mine heritage *is* unto me *as* a speckled^d bird, the birds round about *are* against her; come ye, assemble all the beasts of the field, come to devour. ¹⁰Many pastors have destroyed my vineyard, they have trodden my portion under foot, they have made my pleasant^e portion a desolate wilderness. ¹¹They have made it desolate, *and being* desolate it mourneth unto me; the whole land is made desolate, because no man layeth *it* to heart. ¹²The spoilers are come upon all high places through the wilderness: for the sword of the LORD shall devour from the *one* end of the land even to the *other* end of the land: no flesh shall have peace. ¹³They have sown wheat, but shall reap thorns: they have put themselves to pain, *but* shall not profit: and they shall be ashamed of your revenues because of the fierce anger of the LORD.

¹⁴Thus saith the LORD against all mine evil neighbours, that touch the inheritance which I have caused my people Israel to inherit; Behold, I will pluck them out of their land, and pluck out the house of Judah from among them. ¹⁵And it shall come to pass, after that I have plucked them out I will return, and have compassion on them, and will bring them again, every man to his heritage, and every man to his land. ¹⁶And it shall come to pass, if they will diligently learn the ways of my people, to swear by my name, The LORD liveth; as they taught my people to swear by Baal; then shall they be built in the midst of my people. ¹⁷But if they will not obey, I will utterly pluck up and destroy that nation, saith the LORD.

13

¹Thus saith the LORD unto me, Go and get thee a linen girdle, and put it upon

---

^b they grow: Heb. they go on
^c they have called . . . : or, they cried after thee fully
^d speckled: or, taloned
^e pleasant . . . : Heb. portion of desire

thy loins, and put it not in water. ²So I got a girdle according to the word of the LORD, and put *it* on my loins. ³And the word of the LORD came unto me the second time, saying, ⁴Take the girdle that thou hast got, which *is* upon thy loins, and arise, go to Euphrates, and hide it there in a hole of the rock. ⁵So I went, and hid it by Euphrates, as the LORD commanded me. ⁶And it came to pass after many days, that the LORD said unto me, Arise, go to Euphrates, and take the girdle from thence, which I commanded thee to hide there. ⁷Then I went to Euphrates, and digged, and took the girdle from the place where I had hid it: and, behold, the girdle was marred, it was profitable for nothing. ⁸Then the word of the LORD came unto me, saying, ⁹Thus saith the LORD, After this manner will I mar the pride of Judah, and the great pride of Jerusalem. ¹⁰This evil people, which refuse to hear my words, which walk in the imaginationᵃ of their heart, and walk after other gods, to serve them, and to worship them, shall even be as this girdle, which is good for nothing. ¹¹For as the girdle cleaveth to the loins of a man, so have I caused to cleave unto me the whole house of Israel and the whole house of Judah, saith the LORD; that they might be unto me for a people, and for a name, and for a praise, and for a glory: but they would not hear.

¹²Therefore thou shalt speak unto them this word; Thus saith the LORD God of Israel, Every bottle shall be filled with wine: and they shall say unto thee, Do we not certainly know that every bottle shall be filled with wine? ¹³Then shalt thou say unto them, Thus saith the LORD, Behold, I will fill all the inhabitants of this land, even the kings that sit upon David's throne, and the priests, and the prophets, and all the inhabitants of Jerusalem, with drunkenness. ¹⁴And I will dash them oneᵇ against another, even the fathers and the sons together, saith the LORD: I will not pity, nor spare, nor have mercy, but destroy them. ¹⁵Hear ye, and give ear; be not proud: for the LORD hath spoken. ¹⁶Give glory to the LORD your God, before he cause darkness, and before your feet stumble upon the dark mountains, and, while ye look for light, he turn it into the shadow of death, *and* make *it* gross darkness. ¹⁷But if ye will not hear it, my soul shall weep in secret places for *your* pride; and mine eye shall weep sore, and run down with tears, because the LORD'S flock is carried away captive. ¹⁸Say unto the king and to the queen, Humble yourselves, sit down: for your principalitiesᶜ shall come down, *even* the crown of your glory. ¹⁹The cities of the south shall be shut up, and none shall open *them*: Judah shall be carried away captive all of it, it shall be wholly carried away captive. ²⁰Lift up your eyes, and behold them that come from the north: where *is* the flock *that* was given thee, thy beautiful flock? ²¹What wilt thou say when he shall punishᵈ thee? for thou

---

ᵃ imagination: or, stubbornness
ᵇ one . . . : Heb. a man against his brother
ᶜ principalities: or, head tires
ᵈ punish: Heb visit upon

hast taught them *to be* captains, *and* as chief over thee: shall not sorrows take thee, as a woman in travail? ²²And if thou say in thine heart, Wherefore come these things upon me? For the greatness of thine iniquity are thy skirts discovered, *and* thy heels made bare. ²³Can the Ethiopian change his skin, or the leopard his spots? *then* may ye also do good, that are accustomed^e to do evil. ²⁴Therefore will I scatter them as the stubble that passeth away by the wind of the wilderness. ²⁵This *is* thy lot, the portion of thy measures from me, saith the LORD; because thou hast forgotten me, and trusted in falsehood. ²⁶Therefore will I discover thy skirts upon thy face, that thy shame may appear. ²⁷I have seen thine adulteries, and thy neighings, the lewdness of thy whoredom, *and* thine abominations on the hills in the fields. Woe unto thee, O Jerusalem! wilt thou not be made clean? when *shall it* once^f *be*?

14

¹The word of the LORD that came to Jeremiah concerning the dearth^a. ²Judah mourneth, and the gates thereof languish; they are black unto the ground; and the cry of Jerusalem is gone up. ³And their nobles have sent their little ones to the waters: they came to the pits, *and* found no water; they returned with their vessels empty; they were ashamed and confounded, and covered their heads. ⁴Because the ground is

chapt, for there was no rain in the earth, the plowmen were ashamed, they covered their heads. ⁵Yea, the hind also calved in the field, and forsook *it*, because there was no grass. ⁶And the wild asses did stand in the high places, they snuffed up the wind like dragons; their eyes did fail, because *there was* no grass. ⁷O LORD, though our iniquities testify against us, do thou *it* for thy name's sake: for our backslidings are many; we have sinned against thee. ⁸O the hope of Israel, the saviour thereof in time of trouble, why shouldest thou be as a stranger in the land, and as a wayfaring man *that* turneth aside to tarry for a night? ⁹Why shouldest thou be as a man astonied, as a mighty man *that* cannot save? yet thou, O LORD, *art* in the midst of us, and we are called by thy name; leave us not.

¹⁰Thus saith the LORD unto this people, Thus have they loved to wander, they have not refrained their feet, therefore the LORD doth not accept them; he will now remember their iniquity, and visit their sins. ¹¹Then said the LORD unto me, Pray not for this people for *their* good. ¹²When they fast, I will not hear their cry; and when they offer burnt offering and an oblation, I will not accept them: but I will consume them by the sword, and by the famine, and by the pestilence. ¹³Then said I, Ah, Lord GOD! behold, the prophets say unto them, Ye shall not see the sword, neither shall ye have famine; but I will give you assured^b peace in this place. ¹⁴Then the LORD

---

^e accustomed: Heb. taught
^f when . . . : Heb. after when yet?
^a the dearth: Heb. the words of the dearths, or, restraints
^b assured . . . : Heb. peace of truth

said unto me, The prophets prophesy lies in my name: I sent them not, neither have I commanded them, neither spake unto them: they prophesy unto you a false vision and divination, and a thing of nought, and the deceit of their heart. ¹⁵Therefore thus saith the LORD concerning the prophets that prophesy in my name, and I sent them not, yet they say, Sword and famine shall not be in this land; By sword and famine shall those prophets be consumed. ¹⁶And the people to whom they prophesy shall be cast out in the streets of Jerusalem because of the famine and the sword; and they shall have none to bury them, them, their wives, nor their sons, nor their daughters: for I will pour their wickedness upon them.

¹⁷Therefore thou shalt say this word unto them; Let mine eyes run down with tears night and day, and let them not cease: for the virgin daughter of my people is broken with a great breach, with a very grievous blow. ¹⁸If I go forth into the field, then behold the slain with the sword! and if I enter into the city, then behold them that are sick with famine! yea, both the prophet and the priest go about^c into a land that they know not. ¹⁹Hast thou utterly rejected Judah? hath thy soul lothed Zion? why hast thou smitten us, and *there is* no healing for us? we looked for peace, and *there is* no good; and for the time of healing, and behold trouble! ²⁰We acknowledge, O LORD, our wickedness, *and* the iniquity of our fathers: for we have sinned against thee. ²¹Do not abhor *us*, for thy name's sake, do not disgrace the throne of thy glory: remember, break not thy covenant with us. ²²Are there *any* among the vanities of the Gentiles that can cause rain? or can the heavens give showers? *art* not thou he, O LORD our God? therefore we will wait upon thee: for thou hast made all these *things*.

15

¹Then said the LORD unto me, Though Moses and Samuel stood before me, *yet* my mind *could* not *be* toward this people: cast *them* out of my sight, and let them go forth. ²And it shall come to pass, if they say unto thee, Whither shall we go forth? then thou shalt tell them, Thus saith the LORD; Such as *are* for death, to death; and such as *are* for the sword, to the sword; and such as *are* for the famine, to the famine; and such as *are* for the captivity, to the captivity. ³And I will appoint over them four kinds^a, saith the LORD:

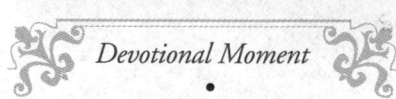

Devotional Moment

Second Chances

15:6 God had decided to stop giving his people "another chance." This may seem harsh, but God had warned his people again and again and *again* before he made this declaration. They had stubbornly refused to listen.

There are times when the best way for parents to teach their children is to stop bailing them out. Mercy can be abused. Don't be too easy on your children by never disciplining them. There comes a time when you need to allow them to suffer the consequences of their actions. It takes wisdom to know when that point has come, of course, but it's a skill every parent can learn with practice and prayer for wisdom.

---

^c go about . . . : or, make merchandise against a land, and men acknowledge it not
^a kinds: Heb. families

the sword to slay, and the dogs to tear, and the fowls of the heaven, and the beasts of the earth, to devour and destroy. [4]And I will cause[b] them to be removed into all kingdoms of the earth, because of Manasseh the son of Hezekiah king of Judah, for *that* which he did in Jerusalem. [5]For who shall have pity upon thee, O Jerusalem? or who shall bemoan thee? or who shall go aside to ask how thou doest? [6]Thou hast forsaken me, saith the LORD, thou art gone backward: therefore will I stretch out my hand against thee, and destroy thee; I am weary with repenting. [7]And I will fan them with a fan in the gates of the land; I will bereave *them* of children, I will destroy[c] my people, *since* they return not from their ways. [8]Their widows are increased to me above the sand of the seas: I have brought upon them against the mother[d] of the young men a spoiler at noonday: I have caused *him* to fall upon it suddenly, and terrors upon the city. [9]She that hath borne seven languisheth: she hath given up the ghost; her sun is gone down while *it was* yet day: she hath been ashamed and confounded: and the residue of them will I deliver to the sword before their enemies, saith the LORD.

[10]Woe is me, my mother, that thou hast borne me a man of strife and a man of contention to the whole earth! I have neither lent on usury, nor men have lent to me on usury; *yet* every one of them doth curse me. [11]The LORD said, Verily it shall be well with thy remnant; verily I will cause the enemy to entreat thee *well* in the time of evil and in the time of affliction. [12]Shall iron break the northern iron and the steel? [13]Thy substance and thy treasures will I give to the spoil without price, and *that* for all thy sins, even in all thy borders. [14]And I will make *thee* to pass with thine enemies into a land *which* thou knowest not: for a fire is kindled in mine anger, *which* shall burn upon you.

[15]O LORD, thou knowest: remember me, and visit me, and revenge me of my persecutors; take me not away in thy longsuffering: know that for thy sake I have suffered rebuke. [16]Thy words were found, and I did eat them; and thy word was unto me the joy and rejoicing of mine heart: for I am called by thy name, O LORD God of hosts. [17]I sat not in the assembly of the mockers, nor rejoiced; I sat alone because of thy hand: for thou

---

Devotional Moment
•
Community

15:19 Jeremiah was so discouraged by the opposition to his message that he accused God of abandoning him. God reprimanded him by saying, "You are to influence *them,* not let them influence *you!*" We are often like Jeremiah. We let people and circumstances influence us when we ought to be influencing them. No matter what the apparent obstacles, strive to have a good influence on your neighborhood and community, whether through attending city council meetings, supporting a local crisis pregnancy center, being an active evangelist, or some other way. The needs of your community are unique. Believe that God is with you, and take an active role in meeting those needs.

---

[b] cause . . . : Heb. give them for a removing
[c] children: or, whatsoever is dear
[d] the mother . . . : or, the mother city a young man spoiling, etc, or, the mother and the young men

hast filled me with indignation. ¹⁸Why is my pain perpetual, and my wound incurable, *which* refuseth to be healed? wilt thou be altogether unto me as a liar, *and as* waters *that* fail^c? ¹⁹Therefore thus saith the LORD, If thou return, then will I bring thee again, *and* thou shalt stand before me: and if thou take forth the precious from the vile, thou shalt be as my mouth: let them return unto thee; but return not thou unto them. ²⁰And I will make thee unto this people a fenced brasen wall: and they shall fight against thee, but they shall not prevail against thee: for I *am* with thee to save thee and to deliver thee, saith the LORD. ²¹And I will deliver thee out of the hand of the wicked, and I will redeem thee out of the hand of the terrible.

16

¹The word of the LORD came also unto me, saying, ²Thou shalt not take thee a wife, neither shalt thou have sons or daughters in this place. ³For thus saith the LORD concerning the sons and concerning the daughters that are born in this place, and concerning their mothers that bare them, and concerning their fathers that begat them in this land; ⁴They shall die of grievous deaths; they shall not be lamented; neither shall they be buried; *but* they shall be as dung upon the face of the earth: and they shall be consumed by the sword, and by famine; and their carcases shall be meat for the fowls of heaven, and for the beasts of the earth. ⁵For thus saith the LORD, Enter not

into the house of mourning^a, neither go to lament nor bemoan them: for I have taken away my peace from this people, saith the LORD, *even* lovingkindness and mercies. ⁶Both the great and the small shall die in this land: they shall not be buried, neither shall *men* lament for them, nor cut themselves, nor make themselves bald for them: ⁷Neither shall *men* tear^b *themselves* for them in mourning, to comfort them for the dead; neither shall *men* give them the cup of consolation to drink for their father or for their mother. ⁸Thou shalt not also go into the house of feasting, to sit with them to eat and to drink. ⁹For thus saith the LORD of hosts, the God of Israel; Behold, I will cause to cease out of this place in your eyes, and in your days, the voice of mirth, and the voice of gladness, the voice of the bridegroom, and the voice of the bride.

¹⁰And it shall come to pass, when thou shalt shew this people all these words, and they shall say unto thee, Wherefore hath the LORD pronounced all this great evil against us? or what *is* our iniquity? or what *is* our sin that we have committed against the LORD our God? ¹¹Then shalt thou say unto them, Because your fathers have forsaken me, saith the LORD, and have walked after other gods, and have served them, and have worshipped them, and have forsaken me, and have not kept my law; ¹²And ye have done worse than your fathers; for, behold, ye walk every one after the imagination^c of his evil heart, that

---

^c fail: Heb. be not sure?
^a mourning: or, mourning feast
^b tear . . . : or, break bread for them
^c imagination: or, stubbornness

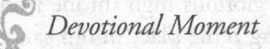

Devotional Moment

Hiding

16:17 We cannot hide our sins and weaknesses from God. Nor can we hide them from others. Parents and children, friends and neighbors and co-workers see each other in the best of times and the worst of times. If you're bold enough, ask a friend to show you your areas of inconsistency. Then take the first step toward being more consistent.

they may not hearken unto me: ¹³Therefore will I cast you out of this land into a land that ye know not, *neither* ye nor your fathers; and there shall ye serve other gods day and night; where I will not shew you favour.

¹⁴Therefore, behold, the days come, saith the LORD, that it shall no more be said, The LORD liveth, that brought up the children of Israel out of the land of Egypt; ¹⁵But, The LORD liveth, that brought up the children of Israel from the land of the north, and from all the lands whither he had driven them: and I will bring them again into their land that I gave unto their fathers. ¹⁶Behold, I will send for many fishers, saith the LORD, and they shall fish them; and after will I send for many hunters, and they shall hunt them from every mountain, and from every hill, and out of the holes of the rocks. ¹⁷For mine eyes *are* upon all their ways: they are not hid from my face, neither is their iniquity hid from mine eyes. ¹⁸And first I will recompense their iniquity and their sin double; because

they have defiled my land, they have filled mine inheritance with the carcases of their detestable and abominable things. ¹⁹O LORD, my strength, and my fortress, and my refuge in the day of affliction, the Gentiles shall come unto thee from the ends of the earth, and shall say, Surely our fathers have inherited lies, vanity, and *things* wherein *there is* no profit. ²⁰Shall a man make gods unto himself, and they *are* no gods? ²¹Therefore, behold, I will this once cause them to know, I will cause them to know mine hand and my might; and they shall know that my name *is* The LORD^d.

17

¹The sin of Judah *is* written with a pen of iron, *and* with the point^a of a diamond: *it is* graven upon the table of their heart, and upon the horns of your altars; ²Whilst their children remember their altars and their groves by the green trees upon the high hills. ³O my mountain in the field, I will give thy substance *and* all thy treasures to the spoil, *and* thy high places for sin, throughout all thy borders. ⁴And thou, even thyself, shalt discontinue^b from thine heritage that I gave thee; and I will cause thee to serve thine enemies in the land which thou knowest not: for ye have kindled a fire in mine anger, *which* shall burn for ever.

⁵Thus saith the LORD; Cursed *be* the man that trusteth in man, and maketh flesh his arm, and whose heart departeth from the LORD. ⁶For he shall be like the heath in the desert, and shall

---

^d The LORD: or, JEHOVAH
^a point: Heb. nail
^b thyself: Heb. in thyself

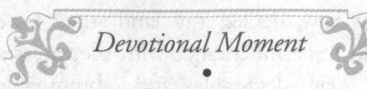

Devotional Moment
•
Expectations

17:9 Well-meaning parents sometimes demand too much of their children, expecting perfection from them. These parents express shock every time their kids do something bad. But Jeremiah reminds us that the human heart is "desperately wicked." Even good children have faults. What they need from us is forgiveness, acceptance, and encouragement to live above their shortcomings in the strength of Christ. While we can and should set high standards, we must also allow for human imperfection. If we are shocked and overly harsh with them every time they exhibit a negative behavior, they will learn to hide from us and deceive us, not trust us and confide in us. Allow your children to be as human as you are.

not see when good cometh; but shall inhabit the parched places in the wilderness, *in* a salt land and not inhabited. ⁷Blessed *is* the man that trusteth in the LORD, and whose hope the LORD is. ⁸For he shall be as a tree planted by the waters, and *that* spreadeth out her roots by the river, and shall not see when heat cometh, but her leaf shall be green; and shall not be careful in the year of drought^c, neither shall cease from yielding fruit. ⁹The heart *is* deceitful above all *things*, and desperately wicked: who can know it? ¹⁰I the LORD search the heart, *I* try the reins, even to give every man according to his ways, *and* according to the fruit of his doings. ¹¹*As* the partridge sitteth^d *on eggs*, and hatcheth *them* not; *so* he that getteth riches, and not by right, shall leave them in the midst of his days, and at his end shall be a fool.

¹²A glorious high throne from the beginning *is* the place of our sanctuary. ¹³O LORD, the hope of Israel, all that forsake thee shall be ashamed, *and* they that depart from me shall be written in the earth, because they have forsaken the LORD, the fountain of living waters. ¹⁴Heal me, O LORD, and I shall be healed; save me, and I shall be saved: for thou *art* my praise. ¹⁵Behold, they say unto me, Where *is* the word of the LORD? let it come now. ¹⁶As for me, I have not hastened from *being* a pastor to follow thee: neither have I desired the woeful day; thou knowest: that which came out of my lips was *right* before thee. ¹⁷Be not a terror unto me: thou *art* my hope in the day of evil. ¹⁸Let them be confounded that persecute me, but let not me be confounded: let them be dismayed, but let not me be dismayed: bring upon them the day of evil, and destroy^e them with double destruction.

¹⁹Thus said the LORD unto me; Go and stand in the gate of the children of the people, whereby the kings of Judah come in, and by the which they go out, and in all the gates of Jerusalem; ²⁰And say unto them, Hear ye the word of the LORD, ye kings of Judah, and all Judah, and all the inhabitants of Jerusalem, that enter in by these gates: ²¹Thus saith the LORD; Take heed to yourselves, and bear no burden on the sabbath day, nor bring *it* in by the gates of Jerusalem; ²²Neither carry forth a burden out of your houses on the sabbath day, neither do ye any work, but hallow ye the sabbath day, as I

---

^c drought: or, restraint
^d sitteth . . . : or, gathereth young which she hath not brought forth
^e destroy . . . : Heb. break them with a double breach

commanded your fathers. [23]But they obeyed not, neither inclined their ear, but made their neck stiff, that they might not hear, nor receive instruction. [24]And it shall come to pass, if ye diligently hearken unto me, saith the LORD, to bring in no burden through the gates of this city on the sabbath day, but hallow the sabbath day, to do no work therein; [25]Then shall there enter into the gates of this city kings and princes sitting upon the throne of David, riding in chariots and on horses, they, and their princes, the men of Judah, and the inhabitants of Jerusalem: and this city shall remain for ever. [26]And they shall come from the cities of Judah, and from the places about Jerusalem, and from the land of Benjamin, and from the plain, and from the mountains, and from the south, bringing burnt offerings, and sacrifices, and meat offerings, and incense, and bringing sacrifices of praise, unto the house of the LORD. [27]But if ye will not hearken unto me to hallow the sabbath day, and not to bear a burden, even entering in at the gates of Jerusalem on the sabbath day; then will I kindle a fire in the gates thereof, and it shall devour the palaces of Jerusalem, and it shall not be quenched.

18

[1]The word which came to Jeremiah from the LORD, saying, [2]Arise, and go down to the potter's house, and there I will cause thee to hear my words. [3]Then I went down to the potter's house, and, behold, he wrought a work on the wheels[a]. [4]And the vessel that he made of clay[b] was marred in the hand of the potter: so he made it again another vessel, as seemed good to the potter to make *it*. [5]Then the word of the LORD came to me, saying, [6]O house of Israel, cannot I do with you as this potter? saith the LORD. Behold, as the clay *is* in the potter's hand, so *are* ye in mine hand, O house of Israel. [7]*At what* instant I shall speak concerning a nation, and concerning a kingdom, to pluck up, and to pull down, and to destroy *it*; [8]If that nation, against whom I have pronounced, turn from their evil, I will repent of the evil that I thought to do unto them. [9]And *at what* instant I shall speak concerning a nation, and concerning a kingdom, to build and to plant *it*; [10]If it do evil in my sight, that it obey not my voice, then I will repent of the good, wherewith I said I would benefit them.

[11]Now therefore go to, speak to the men of Judah, and to the inhabitants of Jerusalem, saying, Thus saith the LORD; Behold, I frame evil against you, and devise a device against you: return ye now every one from his evil way, and make your ways and your doings good. [12]And they said, There is no hope: but we will walk after our own devices, and we will every one do the imagination of his evil heart. [13]Therefore thus saith the LORD; Ask ye now among the heathen, who hath heard such things: the virgin of Israel hath done a very horrible thing. [14]Will *a man* leave the snow[c] of Lebanon *which*

---

[a] wheels: or, frames, or, seats

[b] of clay . . . : or, was marred, as clay in the hand of the potter

[c] the snow . . . : or, my fields for a rock, or for the snow of Lebanon? shall the running waters be forsaken for the strange cold waters?

cometh from the rock of the field? *or* shall the cold flowing waters that come from another place be forsaken? ¹⁵Because my people hath forgotten me, they have burned incense to vanity, and they have caused them to stumble in their ways *from* the ancient paths, to walk in paths, *in* a way not cast up; ¹⁶To make their land desolate, *and* a perpetual hissing; every one that passeth thereby shall be astonished, and wag his head. ¹⁷I will scatter them as with an east wind before the enemy; I will shew them the back, and not the face, in the day of their calamity.

¹⁸Then said they, Come, and let us devise devices against Jeremiah; for the law shall not perish from the priest, nor counsel from the wise, nor the word from the prophet. Come, and let us smite him with the tongue, and let us not give heed to any of his words. ¹⁹Give heed to me, O LORD, and hearken to the voice of them that contend with me. ²⁰Shall evil be recompensed for good? for they have digged a pit for my soul. Remember that I stood before thee to speak good for them, *and* to turn away thy wrath from them. ²¹Therefore deliver up their children to the famine, and pour out their *blood* by the force of the sword; and let their wives be bereaved of their children, and *be* widows; and let their men be put to death; *let* their young men *be* slain by the sword in battle. ²²Let a cry be heard from their houses, when thou shalt bring a troop suddenly upon them: for they have digged a pit to take me, and hid snares for my feet. ²³Yet, LORD,

thou knowest all their counsel against me to slay[d] *me*: forgive not their iniquity, neither blot out their sin from thy sight, but let them be overthrown before thee; deal *thus* with them in the time of thine anger.

19

¹Thus saith the LORD, Go and get a potter's earthen bottle, and *take* of the ancients of the people, and of the ancients of the priests; ²And go forth unto the valley of the son of Hinnom, which *is* by the entry of the east[a] gate, and proclaim there the words that I shall tell thee, ³And say, Hear ye the word of the LORD, O kings of Judah, and inhabitants of Jerusalem; Thus saith the LORD of hosts, the God of Israel; Behold, I will bring evil upon this place, the which whosoever heareth, his ears shall tingle. ⁴Because they have forsaken me, and have estranged this place, and have burned incense in it unto other gods, whom neither they nor their fathers have known, nor the kings of Judah, and have filled this place with the blood of innocents; ⁵They have built also the high places of Baal, to burn their sons with fire *for* burnt offerings unto Baal, which I commanded not, nor spake *it*, neither came *it* into my mind: ⁶Therefore, behold, the days come, saith the LORD, that this place shall no more be called Tophet, nor The valley of the son of Hinnom, but The valley of slaughter. ⁷And I will make void the counsel of Judah and Jerusalem in this place; and I will cause them to fall by the sword before their

---

[d] to slay . . . : Heb. for death

[a] the east . . . : Heb. the sun gate

enemies, and by the hands of them that seek their lives: and their carcases will I give to be meat for the fowls of the heaven, and for the beasts of the earth. ⁸And I will make this city desolate, and an hissing; every one that passeth thereby shall be astonished and hiss because of all the plagues thereof. ⁹And I will cause them to eat the flesh of their sons and the flesh of their daughters, and they shall eat every one the flesh of his friend in the siege and straitness, wherewith their enemies, and they that seek their lives, shall straiten them.

¹⁰Then shalt thou break the bottle in the sight of the men that go with thee, ¹¹And shalt say unto them, Thus saith the LORD of hosts; Even so will I break this people and this city, as *one* breaketh a potter's vessel, that cannot be made whole again: and they shall bury *them* in Tophet, till *there be* no place to bury. ¹²Thus will I do unto this place, saith the LORD, and to the inhabitants thereof, and *even* make this city as Tophet: ¹³And the houses of Jerusalem, and the houses of the kings of Judah, shall be defiled as the place of Tophet, because of all the houses upon whose roofs they have burned incense unto all the host of heaven, and have poured out drink offerings unto other gods. ¹⁴Then came Jeremiah from Tophet, whither the LORD had sent him to prophesy; and he stood in the court of the LORD'S house; and said to all the people, ¹⁵Thus saith the LORD of hosts, the God of Israel; Behold, I will bring upon this city and upon all her towns all the evil that I have pronounced

against it, because they have hardened their necks, that they might not hear my words.

20

¹Now Pashur the son of Immer the priest, who *was* also chief governor in the house of the LORD, heard that Jeremiah prophesied these things. ²Then Pashur smote Jeremiah the prophet, and put him in the stocks that *were* in the high gate of Benjamin, which *was* by the house of the LORD. ³And it came to pass on the morrow, that Pashur brought forth Jeremiah out of the stocks. Then said Jeremiah unto him, The LORD hath not called thy name Pashur, but Magormissabibᵃ. ⁴For thus saith the LORD, Behold, I will make thee a terror to thyself, and to all thy friends: and they shall fall by the sword of their enemies, and thine eyes shall behold *it*: and I will give all Judah into the hand of the king of Babylon, and he shall carry them captive into Babylon, and shall slay them with the sword. ⁵Moreover I will deliver all the

---

Devotional Moment

Accepting Criticism

20:1-3 When Jeremiah told the people what the Lord had commanded him to say, the priest reacted by arresting him, having him whipped, and putting him in stocks. The priest didn't like the message, so he punished the messenger. Are we like the priest who jailed Jeremiah? Do we accept constructive criticism—or retaliate against those who give it? If you're wrong and someone points it out, have the humility to admit it and accept it.

ᵃ Magormissabib: that is, Fear round about

strength of this city, and all the labours thereof, and all the precious things thereof, and all the treasures of the kings of Judah will I give into the hand of their enemies, which shall spoil them, and take them, and carry them to Babylon. ⁶And thou, Pashur, and all that dwell in thine house shall go into captivity: and thou shalt come to Babylon, and there thou shalt die, and shalt be buried there, thou, and all thy friends, to whom thou hast prophesied lies.

⁷O LORD, thou hast deceived me, and I was deceivedᵇ: thou art stronger than I, and hast prevailed: I am in derision daily, every one mocketh me. ⁸For since I spake, I cried out, I cried violence and spoil; because the word of the LORD was made a reproach unto me, and a derision, daily. ⁹Then I said, I will not make mention of him, nor speak any more in his name. But *his word* was in mine heart as a burning fire shut up in my bones, and I was weary with forbearing, and I could not *stay*. ¹⁰For I heard the defaming of many, fear on every side. Report, *say they*, and we will report it. All my familiars watched for my halting, *saying*, Peradventure he will be enticed, and we shall prevail against him, and we shall take our revenge on him. ¹¹But the LORD *is* with me as a mighty terrible one: therefore my persecutors shall stumble, and they shall not prevail: they shall be greatly ashamed; for they shall not prosper: *their* everlasting confusion shall never be forgotten. ¹²But, O LORD of hosts, that triest the righteous, *and* seest the reins and the heart, let me see thy vengeance on them: for unto thee have I opened my cause. ¹³Sing unto the LORD, praise ye the LORD: for he hath delivered the soul of the poor from the hand of evildoers.

¹⁴Cursed *be* the day wherein I was born: let not the day wherein my mother bare me be blessed. ¹⁵Cursed *be* the man who brought tidings to my father, saying, A man child is born unto thee; making him very glad. ¹⁶And let that man be as the cities which the LORD overthrew, and repented not: and let him hear the cry in the morning, and the shouting at noontide; ¹⁷Because he slew me not from the womb; or that my mother might have been my grave, and her womb *to be* always great *with me*. ¹⁸Wherefore came I forth out of the womb to see labour and sorrow, that my days should be consumed with shame?

21

¹The word which came unto Jeremiah from the LORD, when king Zedekiah sent unto him Pashur the son of Melchiah, and Zephaniah the son of Maaseiah the priest, saying, ²Enquire, I pray thee, of the LORD for us; for Nebuchadrezzar king of Babylon maketh war against us; if so be that the LORD will deal with us according to all his wondrous works, that he may go up from us. ³Then said Jeremiah unto them, Thus shall ye say to Zedekiah: ⁴Thus saith the LORD God of Israel; Behold, I will turn back the weapons of war that *are* in your hands, wherewith ye fight against the king of Babylon, and *against* the Chaldeans, which be-

---

ᵇ was deceived: or, was enticed

siege you without the walls, and I will assemble them into the midst of this city. ⁵And I myself will fight against you with an outstretched hand and with a strong arm, even in anger, and in fury, and in great wrath. ⁶And I will smite the inhabitants of this city, both man and beast: they shall die of a great pestilence. ⁷And afterward, saith the LORD, I will deliver Zedekiah king of Judah, and his servants, and the people, and such as are left in this city from the pestilence, from the sword, and from the famine, into the hand of Nebuchadrezzar king of Babylon, and into the hand of their enemies, and into the hand of those that seek their life: and he shall smite them with the edge of the sword; he shall not spare them, neither have pity, nor have mercy.

⁸And unto this people thou shalt

Devotional Moment
•
Crisis

21:1-14 When Nebuchadnezzar decided to attack Israel, King Zedekiah begged Jeremiah to pray for him. Jeremiah did, but it was too late. Zedekiah and the people of Israel did not really want to obey God; they merely wanted to escape their crisis.
Don't ignore God until a time of crisis. While God can and does mercifully rescue people who may not have a relationship with him, he wants to give us so much more than sporadic crisis intervention. Make it a priority to seek God regularly, by reading the Bible and praying at mealtimes or later in the evening. Then when crises arise, asking God to help will be a natural extension of the relationship you have with him.

---

say, Thus saith the LORD; Behold, I set before you the way of life, and the way of death. ⁹He that abideth in this city shall die by the sword, and by the famine, and by the pestilence: but he that goeth out, and falleth to the Chaldeans that besiege you, he shall live, and his life shall be unto him for a prey. ¹⁰For I have set my face against this city for evil, and not for good, saith the LORD: it shall be given into the hand of the king of Babylon, and he shall burn it with fire. ¹¹And touching the house of the king of Judah, *say,* Hear ye the word of the LORD; ¹²O house of David, thus saith the LORD; Executeᵃ judgment in the morning, and deliver *him that is* spoiled out of the hand of the oppressor, lest my fury go out like fire, and burn that none can quench *it,* because of the evil of your doings. ¹³Behold, I *am* against thee, O inhabitantᵇ of the valley, *and* rock of the plain, saith the LORD; which say, Who shall come down against us? or who shall enter into our habitations? ¹⁴But I will punishᶜ you according to the fruit of your doings, saith the LORD: and I will kindle a fire in the forest thereof, and it shall devour all things round about it.

22

¹Thus saith the LORD; Go down to the house of the king of Judah, and speak there this word, ²And say, Hear the word of the LORD, O king of Judah, that sittest upon the throne of David, thou, and thy servants, and thy people that en-

---

ᵃ Execute: Heb. Judge
ᵇ inhabitant: Heb. inhabitress
ᶜ punish: Heb. visit upon

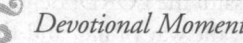

Devotional Moment
•
Abortion and Adoption

22:3, 16-17 God reprimanded his people for murdering the innocent. One group of innocents in our society is unborn children. Find ways to celebrate the sanctity of life. You can support crisis pregnancy centers. You can discuss the legislative changes that affect the rights of unborn children. You can pray, asking God to lead you as to your involvement.

You can also help friends or relatives facing unwanted pregnancies. If you know someone in this situation, help her cope with the difficulties of carrying a child she didn't plan for. You can suggest ways to help her care for the child or steer her to a Christian adoption agency. Show mercy and kindness, not judgment.

ter in by these gates: ³Thus saith the LORD; Execute ye judgment and righteousness, and deliver the spoiled out of the hand of the oppressor: and do no wrong, do no violence to the stranger, the fatherless, nor the widow, neither shed innocent blood in this place. ⁴For if ye do this thing indeed, then shall there enter in by the gates of this house kings sitting upon the throne of David, riding in chariots and on horses, he, and his servants, and his people. ⁵But if ye will not hear these words, I swear by myself, saith the LORD, that this house shall become a desolation. ⁶For thus saith the LORD unto the king's house of Judah; Thou *art* Gilead unto me, *and* the head of Lebanon: *yet* surely I will make thee a wilderness, *and* cities *which* are not inhabited. ⁷And I will prepare destroyers against thee, every one with his weapons: and they shall cut down thy choice cedars, and cast *them* into the fire. ⁸And many nations shall pass by this city, and they shall say every man to his neighbour, Wherefore hath the LORD done thus unto this great city? ⁹Then they shall answer, Because they have forsaken the covenant of the LORD their God, and worshipped other gods, and served them.

¹⁰Weep ye not for the dead, neither bemoan him: *but* weep sore for him that goeth away: for he shall return no more, nor see his native country. ¹¹For thus saith the LORD touching Shallum the son of Josiah king of Judah, which reigned instead of Josiah his father, which went forth out of this place; He shall not return thither any more: ¹²But he shall die in the place whither they have led him captive, and shall see this land no more. ¹³Woe unto him that buildeth his house by unrighteousness, and his chambers by wrong; *that* useth his neighbour's service without wages, and giveth him not for his work; ¹⁴That saith, I will build me a wide house and large[a] chambers, and cutteth him out windows; and *it is* cieled with cedar, and painted with vermilion. ¹⁵Shalt thou reign, because thou closest *thyself* in cedar? did not thy father eat and drink, and do judgment and justice, *and* then *it was* well with him? ¹⁶He judged the cause of the poor and needy; then *it was* well *with him: was* not this to know me? saith the LORD. ¹⁷But thine eyes and thine heart *are* not but for thy covetousness, and for to shed innocent blood, and for oppression, and for violence[b], to do

---

[a] large: Heb. through-aired
[b] violence: or, incursion

it. ¹⁸Therefore thus saith the LORD concerning Jehoiakim the son of Josiah king of Judah; They shall not lament for him, *saying,* Ah my brother! or, Ah sister! they shall not lament for him, *saying,* Ah lord! or, Ah his glory! ¹⁹He shall be buried with the burial of an ass, drawn and cast forth beyond the gates of Jerusalem.

²⁰Go up to Lebanon, and cry; and lift up thy voice in Bashan, and cry from the passages: for all thy lovers are destroyed. ²¹I spake unto thee in thy prosperity^c; *but* thou saidst, I will not hear. This *hath been* thy manner from thy youth, that thou obeyedst not my voice. ²²The wind shall eat up all thy pastors, and thy lovers shall go into captivity: surely then shalt thou be ashamed and confounded for all thy wickedness. ²³O inhabitant^d of Lebanon, that makest thy nest in the cedars, how gracious shalt

---

Devotional Moment

The Terrible Twos

22:21 Jehoiakim had refused to listen to warnings since childhood. Patterns of behavior are set very early. Child psychologists say that much of a child's personality is determined by age *five.*
Parents of young children, take heart. Guide your children to do what is right, from the moment they can hold up their heads! Correct wrong behavior and reward good. Praise them for being kind, good, and fair, and don't let them pick on smaller kids. Ignore temper tantrums rather than responding to them. These matters may seem small now, but they will bear fruit for a lifetime.

---

thou be when pangs come upon thee, the pain as of a woman in travail! ²⁴*As* I live, saith the LORD, though Coniah the son of Jehoiakim king of Judah were the signet upon my right hand, yet would I pluck thee thence; ²⁵And I will give thee into the hand of them that seek thy life, and into the hand *of them* whose face thou fearest, even into the hand of Nebuchadrezzar king of Babylon, and into the hand of the Chaldeans. ²⁶And I will cast thee out, and thy mother that bare thee, into another country, where ye were not born; and there shall ye die. ²⁷But to the land whereunto they desire^e to return, thither shall they not return. ²⁸*Is* this man Coniah a despised broken idol? *is he* a vessel wherein *is* no pleasure? wherefore are they cast out, he and his seed, and are cast into a land which they know not? ²⁹O earth, earth, earth, hear the word of the LORD. ³⁰Thus saith the LORD, Write ye this man childless, a man *that* shall not prosper in his days: for no man of his seed shall prosper, sitting upon the throne of David, and ruling any more in Judah.

23

¹Woe be unto the pastors that destroy and scatter the sheep of my pasture! saith the LORD. ²Therefore thus saith the LORD God of Israel against the pastors that feed my people; Ye have scattered my flock, and have driven them away, and have not visited them: behold, I will visit upon you the evil of your doings, saith the LORD. ³And I

---

^c prosperity: Heb. prosperities
^d inhabitant: Heb. inhabitress
^e desire: Heb. lift up their mind

will gather the remnant of my flock out of all countries whither I have driven them, and will bring them again to their folds; and they shall be fruitful and increase. ⁴And I will set up shepherds over them which shall feed them: and they shall fear no more, nor be dismayed, neither shall they be lacking, saith the LORD. ⁵Behold, the days come, saith the LORD, that I will raise unto David a righteous Branch, and a King shall reign and prosper, and shall execute judgment and justice in the earth. ⁶In his days Judah shall be saved, and Israel shall dwell safely: and this *is* his name whereby he shall be called, THE LORD OUR RIGHTEOUSNESS. ⁷Therefore, behold, the days come, saith the LORD, that they shall no more say, The LORD liveth, which brought up the children of Israel out of the land of Egypt; ⁸But, The LORD liveth, which brought up and which led the seed of the house of Israel out of the north country, and from all countries whither I had driven them; and they shall dwell in their own land.

⁹Mine heart within me is broken because of the prophets; all my bones shake; I am like a drunken man, and like a man whom wine hath overcome, because of the LORD, and because of the words of his holiness. ¹⁰For the land is full of adulterers; for because of swearingᵃ the land mourneth; the pleasant places of the wilderness are dried up, and their course is evil, and their force *is* not right. ¹¹For both prophet and priest are profane; yea, in my house have I found their wickedness, saith the LORD. ¹²Wherefore their way shall be unto them as slippery *ways* in the darkness: they shall be driven on, and fall therein: for I will bring evil upon them, *even* the year of their visitation, saith the LORD. ¹³And I have seen follyᵇ in the prophets of Samaria; they prophesied in Baal, and caused my people Israel to err. ¹⁴I have seen also in the prophets of Jerusalem an horrible thing: they commit adultery, and walk in lies: they strengthen also the hands of evildoers, that none doth return from his wickedness: they are all of them unto me as Sodom, and the inhabitants thereof as Gomorrah. ¹⁵Therefore thus saith the LORD of hosts concerning the prophets; Behold, I will feed them with wormwood, and make them drink the water of gall: for from the prophets of Jerusalem is profanenessᶜ gone forth into all the land. ¹⁶Thus saith the LORD of hosts, Hearken not unto the words of the prophets that prophesy unto you: they make you vain: they speak a vision of their own heart, *and* not out of the mouth of the LORD. ¹⁷They say still unto them that despise me, The LORD hath said, Ye shall have peace; and they say unto every one that walketh after the imaginationᵈ of his own heart, No evil shall come upon you. ¹⁸For who hath stood in the counselᵉ of the LORD, and hath perceived

---

ᵃ swearing: or, cursing
ᵇ folly: or, an absurd thing: Heb. unsavoury
ᶜ profaneness: or, hypocrisy
ᵈ imagination: or, stubbornness
ᵉ counsel: or, secret

and heard his word? who hath marked his word, and heard *it*? ¹⁹Behold, a whirlwind of the LORD is gone forth in fury, even a grievous whirlwind: it shall fall grievously upon the head of the wicked. ²⁰The anger of the LORD shall not return, until he have executed, and till he have performed the thoughts of his heart: in the latter days ye shall consider it perfectly. ²¹I have not sent these prophets, yet they ran: I have not spoken to them, yet they prophesied. ²²But if they had stood in my counsel, and had caused my people to hear my words, then they should have turned them from their evil way, and from the evil of their doings. ²³*Am* I a God at hand, saith the LORD, and not a God afar off? ²⁴Can any hide himself in secret places that I shall not see him? saith the LORD. Do not I fill heaven and earth? saith the LORD. ²⁵I have heard what the prophets said, that prophesy lies in my name, saying, I have dreamed, I have dreamed. ²⁶How long shall *this* be in the heart of the prophets that prophesy lies? yea, *they are* prophets of the deceit of their own heart; ²⁷Which think to cause my people to forget my name by their dreams which they tell every man to his neighbour, as their fathers have forgotten my name for Baal. ²⁸The prophet that hath a dream,ᶠ let him tell a dream; and he that hath my word, let him speak my word faithfully. What *is* the chaff to the wheat? saith the LORD. ²⁹*Is* not my word like as a fire? saith the LORD; and like a hammer *that* breaketh the rock in pieces? ³⁰Therefore, behold, I

am against the prophets, saith the LORD, that steal my words every one from his neighbour. ³¹Behold, I *am* against the prophets, saith the LORD, that use their tongues, and say, He saith. ³²Behold, I *am* against them that prophesy false dreams, saith the LORD, and do tell them, and cause my people to err by their lies, and by their lightness; yet I sent them not, nor commanded them: therefore they shall not profit this people at all, saith the LORD.

³³And when this people, or the prophet, or a priest, shall ask thee, saying, What *is* the burden of the LORD? thou shalt then say unto them, What burden? I will even forsake you, saith the LORD. ³⁴And *as for* the prophet, and the priest, and the people, that shall say, The burden of the LORD, I will even punishᵍ that man and his house. ³⁵Thus shall ye say every one to his neighbour, and every one to his brother, What hath the LORD answered? and, What hath the LORD spoken? ³⁶And the burden of the LORD shall ye mention no more: for every man's word shall be his burden; for ye have perverted the words of the living God, of the LORD of hosts our God. ³⁷Thus shalt thou say to the prophet, What hath the LORD answered thee? and, What hath the LORD spoken? ³⁸But since ye say, The burden of the LORD; therefore thus saith the LORD; Because ye say this word, The burden of the LORD, and I have sent unto you, saying, Ye shall not say, The burden of the LORD; ³⁹There-

---

ᶠ that hath a dream: Heb. with whom is, etc
ᵍ punish: Heb. visit upon

fore, behold, I, even I, will utterly forget you, and I will forsake you, and the city that I gave you and your fathers, *and cast you* out of my presence: ⁴⁰And I will bring an everlasting reproach upon you, and a perpetual shame, which shall not be forgotten.

24

¹The LORD shewed me, and, behold, two baskets of figs *were* set before the temple of the LORD, after that Nebuchadrezzar king of Babylon had carried away captive Jeconiah the son of Jehoiakim king of Judah, and the princes of Judah, with the carpenters and smiths, from Jerusalem, and had brought them to Babylon. ²One basket *had* very good figs, *even* like the figs *that are* first ripe: and the other basket *had* very naughty figs, which could not be eaten, they were so bad. ³Then said the LORD unto me, What seest thou, Jeremiah? And I said, Figs; the good figs, very good; and the evil, very evil, that cannot be eaten, they are so evil. ⁴Again the word of the LORD came unto me, saying, ⁵Thus saith the LORD, the God of Israel; Like these good figs, so will I acknowledge them that are carried away captive of Judah, whom I have sent out of this place into the land of the Chaldeans for *their* good. ⁶For I will set mine eyes upon them for good, and I will bring them again to this land: and I will build them, and not pull *them* down; and I will plant them, and not pluck *them* up. ⁷And I will give them an heart to know me, that I *am* the LORD: and they shall be my people, and I will be their

God: for they shall return unto me with their whole heart. ⁸And as the evil figs, which cannot be eaten, they are so evil; surely thus saith the LORD, So will I give Zedekiah the king of Judah, and his princes, and the residue of Jerusalem, that remain in this land, and them that dwell in the land of Egypt: ⁹And I will deliver them to be removed^a into all the kingdoms of the earth for *their* hurt, *to be* a reproach and a proverb, a taunt and a curse, in all places whither I shall drive them. ¹⁰And I will send the sword, the famine, and the pestilence, among them, till they be consumed from off the land that I gave unto them and to their fathers.

25

¹The word that came to Jeremiah concerning all the people of Judah in the fourth year of Jehoiakim the son of Josiah king of Judah, that *was* the first year of Nebuchadrezzar king of Baby-

---

Devotional Moment

•

Perseverance in Parenting

25:2-3 For twenty-three years Jeremiah had delivered God's messages of warning. For twenty-three years he had given the people opportunity to listen to God and turn from their evil ways—to no avail. Many parents can identify with Jeremiah. They have repeated the same warnings and guidelines day after day, only to realize that their children haven't listened to anything they've said. We need Jeremiah's perseverance. Training children takes effort, endurance, and faithfulness. One day our children will grow up, and they will be responsible for what they do. Our job is simply to be faithful to the task of teaching them, loving them, and guiding them.

ᵃ to be removed: Heb. for removing, or, vexation

lon; ²The which Jeremiah the prophet spake unto all the people of Judah, and to all the inhabitants of Jerusalem, saying, ³From the thirteenth year of Josiah the son of Amon king of Judah, even unto this day, that *is* the three and twentieth year, the word of the LORD hath come unto me, and I have spoken unto you, rising early and speaking; but ye have not hearkened. ⁴And the LORD hath sent unto you all his servants the prophets, rising early and sending *them*; but ye have not hearkened, nor inclined your ear to hear. ⁵They said, Turn ye again now every one from his evil way, and from the evil of your doings, and dwell in the land that the LORD hath given unto you and to your fathers for ever and ever: ⁶And go not after other gods to serve them, and to worship them, and provoke me not to anger with the works of your hands; and I will do you no hurt. ⁷Yet ye have not hearkened unto me, saith the LORD; that ye might provoke me to anger with the works of your hands to your own hurt.

⁸Therefore thus saith the LORD of hosts; Because ye have not heard my words, ⁹Behold, I will send and take all the families of the north, saith the LORD, and Nebuchadrezzar the king of Babylon, my servant, and will bring them against this land, and against the inhabitants thereof, and against all these nations round about, and will utterly destroy them, and make them an astonishment, and an hissing, and perpetual desolations. ¹⁰Moreover I will take from them the voice of mirth, and the voice of gladness, the voice of the bridegroom, and the voice of the bride, the sound of the millstones, and the light of the candle. ¹¹And this whole land shall be a desolation, *and* an astonishment; and these nations shall serve the king of Babylon seventy years. ¹²And it shall come to pass, when seventy years are accomplished, *that* I will punishᵃ the king of Babylon, and that nation, saith the LORD, for their iniquity, and the land of the Chaldeans, and will make it perpetual desolations. ¹³And I will bring upon that land all my words which I have pronounced against it, *even* all that is written in this book, which Jeremiah hath prophesied against all the nations. ¹⁴For many nations and great kings shall serve themselves of them also: and I will recompense them according to their deeds, and according to the works of their own hands.

¹⁵For thus saith the LORD God of Israel unto me; Take the wine cup of this fury at my hand, and cause all the nations, to whom I send thee, to drink it. ¹⁶And they shall drink, and be moved, and be mad, because of the sword that I will send among them. ¹⁷Then took I the cup at the LORD'S hand, and made all the nations to drink, unto whom the LORD had sent me: ¹⁸ *To wit,* Jerusalem, and the cities of Judah, and the kings thereof, and the princes thereof, to make them a desolation, an astonishment, an hissing, and a curse; as *it is* this day; ¹⁹Pharaoh king of Egypt, and his servants, and his princes, and all his people; ²⁰And all the mingled people, and all the kings of the land of Uz, and all the kings of the land of the

---

ᵃ punish: Heb. visit upon

Philistines, and Ashkelon, and Azzah, and Ekron, and the remnant of Ashdod, ²¹Edom, and Moab, and the children of Ammon, ²²And all the kings of Tyrus, and all the kings of Zidon, and the kings of the islesᵇ which *are* beyond the sea, ²³Dedan, and Tema, and Buz, and all *that are* in the utmost corners, ²⁴And all the kings of Arabia, and all the kings of the mingled people that dwell in the desert, ²⁵And all the kings of Zimri, and all the kings of Elam, and all the kings of the Medes, ²⁶And all the kings of the north, far and near, one with another, and all the kingdoms of the world, which *are* upon the face of the earth: and the king of Sheshach shall drink after them. ²⁷Therefore thou shalt say unto them, Thus saith the LORD of hosts, the God of Israel; Drink ye, and be drunken, and spue, and fall, and rise no more, because of the sword which I will send among you. ²⁸And it shall be, if they refuse to take the cup at thine hand to drink, then shalt thou say unto them, Thus saith the LORD of hosts; Ye shall certainly drink. ²⁹For, lo, I begin to bring evil on the city which is called by my name, and should ye be utterly unpunished? Ye shall not be unpunished: for I will call for a sword upon all the inhabitants of the earth, saith the LORD of hosts.

³⁰Therefore prophesy thou against them all these words, and say unto them, The LORD shall roar from on high, and utter his voice from his holy habitation; he shall mightily roar upon his habitation; he shall give a shout, as they that tread *the grapes*, against all the inhabitants of the earth. ³¹A noise shall come *even* to the ends of the earth; for the LORD hath a controversy with the nations, he will plead with all flesh; he will give them *that are* wicked to the sword, saith the LORD. ³²Thus saith the LORD of hosts, Behold, evil shall go forth from nation to nation, and a great whirlwind shall be raised up from the coasts of the earth. ³³And the slain of the LORD shall be at that day from *one* end of the earth even unto the *other* end of the earth: they shall not be lamented, neither gathered, nor buried; they shall be dung upon the ground. ³⁴Howl, ye shepherds, and cry; and wallow yourselves *in the ashes*, ye principal of the flock: for the daysᶜ of your slaughter and of your dispersions are accomplished; and ye shall fall like a pleasant vessel. ³⁵And the shepherdsᵈ shall have no way to flee, nor the principal of the flock to escape. ³⁶A voice of the cry of the shepherds, and an howling of the principal of the flock, *shall be heard*: for the LORD hath spoiled their pasture. ³⁷And the peaceable habitations are cut down because of the fierce anger of the LORD. ³⁸He hath forsaken his covert, as the lion: for their land is desolateᵉ because of the fierceness of the oppressor, and because of his fierce anger.

26

¹In the beginning of the reign of Jehoiakim the son of Josiah king of Judah came this word from the LORD, saying,

---

ᵇ isles: or, region by the sea side
ᶜ the days . . . : Heb. your days for slaughter
ᵈ the shepherds . . . : Heb. flight shall perish from the shepherds, and escaping from, etc
ᵉ desolate: Heb. a desolation

²Thus saith the LORD; Stand in the court of the LORD'S house, and speak unto all the cities of Judah, which come to worship in the LORD'S house, all the words that I command thee to speak unto them; diminish not a word: ³If so be they will hearken, and turn every man from his evil way, that I may repent me of the evil, which I purpose to do unto them because of the evil of their doings. ⁴And thou shalt say unto them, Thus saith the LORD; If ye will not hearken to me, to walk in my law, which I have set before you, ⁵To hearken to the words of my servants the prophets, whom I sent unto you, both rising up early, and sending *them*, but ye have not hearkened; ⁶Then will I make this house like Shiloh, and will make this city a curse to all the nations of the earth.

⁷So the priests and the prophets and all the people heard Jeremiah speaking these words in the house of the LORD. ⁸Now it came to pass, when Jeremiah had made an end of speaking all that the LORD had commanded *him* to speak unto all the people, that the priests and the prophets and all the people took him, saying, Thou shalt surely die. ⁹Why hast thou prophesied in the name of the LORD, saying, This house shall be like Shiloh, and this city shall be desolate without an inhabitant? And all the people were gathered against Jeremiah in the house of the LORD. ¹⁰When the princes of Judah heard these things, then they came up from the king's house unto the house of the LORD, and sat down in the entry of the new gate of the LORD'S *house*. ¹¹Then spake the priests and the prophets unto the princes and to all the people, saying, This man* *is* worthy to die; for he hath prophesied against this city, as ye have heard with your ears. ¹²Then spake Jeremiah unto all the princes and to all the people, saying, The LORD sent me to prophesy against this house and against this city all the words that ye have heard. ¹³Therefore now amend your ways and your doings, and obey the voice of the LORD your God; and the LORD will repent him of the evil that he hath pronounced against you. ¹⁴As for me, behold, I *am* in your hand: do with me as seemeth good and meet unto you. ¹⁵But know ye for certain, that if ye put me to death, ye shall surely bring innocent blood upon yourselves, and upon this city, and upon the inhabitants thereof: for of a truth the LORD hath sent me unto you to speak all these words in your ears.

¹⁶Then said the princes and all the people unto the priests and to the prophets; This man *is* not worthy to die: for he hath spoken to us in the name of the LORD our God. ¹⁷Then rose up certain of the elders of the land, and spake to all the assembly of the people, saying, ¹⁸Micah the Morasthite prophesied in the days of Hezekiah king of Judah, and spake to all the people of Judah, saying, Thus saith the LORD of hosts; Zion shall be plowed *like* a field, and Jerusalem shall become heaps, and the mountain of the house as the high places of a forest. ¹⁹Did Hezekiah king of Judah and all Judah put him at all to death? did he not fear

---

ᵃ This man . . . : Heb. The judgment of death is for this man

the LORD, and besought the LORD, and the LORD repented him of the evil which he had pronounced against them? Thus might we procure great evil against our souls. ²⁰And there was also a man that prophesied in the name of the LORD, Urijah the son of Shemaiah of Kirjathjearim, who prophesied against this city and against this land according to all the words of Jeremiah: ²¹And when Jehoiakim the king, with all his mighty men, and all the princes, heard his words, the king sought to put him to death: but when Urijah heard it, he was afraid, and fled, and went into Egypt; ²²And Jehoiakim the king sent men into Egypt, *namely*, Elnathan the son of Achbor, and *certain* men with him into Egypt. ²³And they fetched forth Urijah out of Egypt, and brought him unto Jehoiakim the king; who slew him with the sword, and cast his dead body into the graves of the common[b] people. ²⁴Nevertheless the hand of Ahikam the son of Shaphan was with Jeremiah, that they should not give him into the hand of the people to put him to death.

27

¹In the beginning of the reign of Jehoiakim the son of Josiah king of Judah came this word unto Jeremiah from the LORD, saying, ²Thus saith[a] the LORD to me; Make thee bonds and yokes, and put them upon thy neck, ³And send them to the king of Edom, and to the king of Moab, and to the king of the Ammonites, and to the king of Tyrus,

and to the king of Zidon, by the hand of the messengers which come to Jerusalem unto Zedekiah king of Judah; ⁴And command them to say[b] unto their masters, Thus saith the LORD of hosts, the God of Israel; Thus shall ye say unto your masters; ⁵I have made the earth, the man and the beast that *are* upon the ground, by my great power and by my outstretched arm, and have given it unto whom it seemed meet unto me. ⁶And now have I given all these lands into the hand of Nebuchadnezzar the king of Babylon, my servant; and the beasts of the field have I given him also to serve him. ⁷And all nations shall serve him, and his son, and his son's son, until the very time of his land come: and then many nations and great kings shall serve themselves of him. ⁸And it shall come to pass, *that* the nation and kingdom which will not serve the same Nebuchadnezzar the king of Babylon, and that will not put their neck under the yoke of the king of Babylon, that nation will I punish, saith

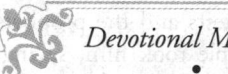

Devotional Moment

Friends

27:9-11 Listen to the wrong people and your life will be a disaster, Jeremiah warned. Our task is to discern which voices are true and good. Not an easy task! Our choice of friends is crucial. When we face grief, trouble at home, emergencies, and big decisions, godly friends are more important than prestige, money, or power. Godly friends steer us away from modern "false prophets," who offer sugarcoated lies about life.

---

[b] common . . . : Heb. sons of the people
[a] saith . . . : or, hath the LORD said
[b] to say . . . : or, concerning their masters, saying

the LORD, with the sword, and with the famine, and with the pestilence, until I have consumed them by his hand. ⁹Therefore hearken not ye to your prophets, nor to your diviners, nor to your dreamersᶜ, nor to your enchanters, nor to your sorcerers, which speak unto you, saying, Ye shall not serve the king of Babylon: ¹⁰For they prophesy a lie unto you, to remove you far from your land; and that I should drive you out, and ye should perish. ¹¹But the nations that bring their neck under the yoke of the king of Babylon, and serve him, those will I let remain still in their own land, saith the LORD; and they shall till it, and dwell therein.

¹²I spake also to Zedekiah king of Judah according to all these words, saying, Bring your necks under the yoke of the king of Babylon, and serve him and his people, and live. ¹³Why will ye die, thou and thy people, by the sword, by the famine, and by the pestilence, as the LORD hath spoken against the nation that will not serve the king of Babylon? ¹⁴Therefore hearken not unto the words of the prophets that speak unto you, saying, Ye shall not serve the king of Babylon: for they prophesy a lie unto you. ¹⁵For I have not sent them, saith the LORD, yet they prophesy a lieᵈ in my name; that I might drive you out, and that ye might perish, ye, and the prophets that prophesy unto you. ¹⁶Also I spake to the priests and to all this people, saying, Thus saith the LORD; Hearken not to the words of your prophets that prophesy unto you, saying, Behold, the vessels of the LORD'S

house shall now shortly be brought again from Babylon: for they prophesy a lie unto you. ¹⁷Hearken not unto them; serve the king of Babylon, and live: wherefore should this city be laid waste? ¹⁸But if they *be* prophets, and if the word of the LORD be with them, let them now make intercession to the LORD of hosts, that the vessels which are left in the house of the LORD, and *in* the house of the king of Judah, and at Jerusalem, go not to Babylon. ¹⁹For thus saith the LORD of hosts concerning the pillars, and concerning the sea, and concerning the bases, and concerning the residue of the vessels that remain in this city, ²⁰Which Nebuchadnezzar king of Babylon took not, when he carried away captive Jeconiah the son of Jehoiakim king of Judah from Jerusalem to Babylon, and all the nobles of Judah and Jerusalem; ²¹Yea, thus saith the LORD of hosts, the God of Israel, concerning the vessels that remain *in* the house of the LORD, and *in* the house of the king of Judah and of Jerusalem; ²²They shall be carried to Babylon, and there shall they be until the day that I visit them, saith the LORD; then will I bring them up, and restore them to this place.

28

¹And it came to pass the same year, in the beginning of the reign of Zedekiah king of Judah, in the fourth year, *and in* the fifth month, *that* Hananiah the son of Azur the prophet, which *was* of Gibeon, spake unto me in the house of the LORD, in the presence of the

---

ᶜ dreamers: Heb. dreams
ᵈ a lie: Heb. in a lie, or, lyingly

priests and of all the people, saying, [2]Thus speaketh the LORD of hosts, the God of Israel, saying, I have broken the yoke of the king of Babylon. [3]Within two full years will I bring again into this place all the vessels of the LORD'S house, that Nebuchadnezzar king of Babylon took away from this place, and carried them to Babylon: [4]And I will bring again to this place Jeconiah the son of Jehoiakim king of Judah, with all the captives[a] of Judah, that went into Babylon, saith the LORD: for I will break the yoke of the king of Babylon. [5]Then the prophet Jeremiah said unto the prophet Hananiah in the presence of the priests, and in the presence of all the people that stood in the house of the LORD, [6]Even the prophet Jeremiah said, Amen: the LORD do so: the LORD perform thy words which thou hast prophesied, to bring again the vessels of the LORD'S house, and all that is carried away captive, from Babylon into this place. [7]Nevertheless hear thou now this word that I speak in thine ears, and in the ears of all the people; [8]The prophets that have been before me and before thee of old prophesied both against many countries, and against great kingdoms, of war, and of evil, and of pestilence. [9]The prophet which prophesieth of peace, when the word of the prophet shall come to pass, *then* shall the prophet be known, that the LORD hath truly sent him.

[10]Then Hananiah the prophet took the yoke from off the prophet Jeremiah's neck, and brake it. [11]And Hananiah spake in the presence of all the people, saying, Thus saith the LORD; Even so will I break the yoke of Nebuchadnezzar king of Babylon from the neck of all nations within the space of two full years. And the prophet Jeremiah went his way. [12]Then the word of the LORD came unto Jeremiah *the prophet*, after that Hananiah the prophet had broken the yoke from off the neck of the prophet Jeremiah, saying, [13]Go and tell Hananiah, saying, Thus saith the LORD; Thou hast broken the yokes of wood; but thou shalt make for them yokes of iron. [14]For thus saith the LORD of hosts, the God of Israel; I have put a yoke of iron upon the neck of all these nations, that they may serve Nebuchadnezzar king of Babylon; and they shall serve him: and I have given him the beasts of the field also. [15]Then said the prophet Jeremiah unto Hananiah the prophet, Hear now, Hananiah; The LORD hath not sent thee; but thou makest this people to trust in a lie. [16]Therefore thus saith the LORD; Behold, I will cast thee from off the face of the earth: this year thou shalt die, because thou hast taught rebellion[b] against the LORD. [17]So Hananiah the prophet died the same year in the seventh month.

29

[1]Now these *are* the words of the letter that Jeremiah the prophet sent from Jerusalem unto the residue of the elders which were carried away captives, and to the priests, and to the prophets, and to all the people whom Nebuchadnezzar had carried away captive from

---

[a] captives: Heb. captivity
[b] rebellion: Heb. revolt

Jerusalem to Babylon; ²(After that Jeconiah the king, and the queen, and the eunuchs, the princes of Judah and Jerusalem, and the carpenters, and the smiths, were departed from Jerusalem;) ³By the hand of Elasah the son of Shaphan, and Gemariah the son of Hilkiah, (whom Zedekiah king of Judah sent unto Babylon to Nebuchadnezzar king of Babylon) saying, ⁴Thus saith the LORD of hosts, the God of Israel, unto all that are carried away captives, whom I have caused to be carried away from Jerusalem unto Babylon; ⁵Build ye houses, and dwell *in them*; and plant gardens, and eat the fruit of them; ⁶Take ye wives, and beget sons and daughters; and take wives for your sons, and give your daughters to husbands, that they may bear sons and daughters; that ye may be increased there, and not diminished. ⁷And seek the peace of the city whither I have caused you to be carried away captives, and pray unto the LORD for it: for in the peace thereof shall ye have peace.

⁸For thus saith the LORD of hosts, the God of Israel; Let not your prophets and your diviners, that *be* in the midst of you, deceive you, neither hearken to your dreams which ye cause to be dreamed. ⁹For they prophesy falsely[a] unto you in my name: I have not sent them, saith the LORD. ¹⁰For thus saith the LORD, That after seventy years be accomplished at Babylon I will visit you, and perform my good word toward you, in causing you to return to this place. ¹¹For I know the thoughts that I think toward you, saith the LORD, thoughts of peace, and not of evil, to give you an expected[b] end. ¹²Then shall ye call upon me, and ye shall go and pray unto me, and I will hearken unto you. ¹³And ye shall seek me, and find *me*, when ye shall search for me with all your heart. ¹⁴And I will be found of you, saith the LORD: and I will turn away your captivity, and I will gather you from all the nations, and from all the places whither I have driven you, saith the LORD; and I will bring you again into the place whence I caused you to be carried away captive.

¹⁵Because ye have said, The LORD hath raised us up prophets in Babylon; ¹⁶*Know* that thus saith the LORD of the king that sitteth upon the throne of David, and of all the people that dwelleth in this city, *and* of your brethren that are not gone forth with you into captivity; ¹⁷Thus saith the LORD of hosts; Behold, I will send

---

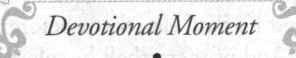

Devotional Moment

•

Abandonment

29:12-14 The Israelites were heading into captivity. Babylon would destroy everything: the Temple, vestiges of David's golden era, residual splendors of Solomon, and worse, the promise of God's nation flowing "with milk and honey." Yet, without trivializing the pain, Jeremiah assured the people of God's constant care, listening ear, and plans for restoration—the promise that would make their feeling of isolation bearable.

We often feel isolated, too, when we face overwhelming challenges and friends or family seem indifferent. Yet this passage reminds us that God never abandons us.

---

[a] falsely: Heb. in a lie
[b] expected . . . : Heb. end and expectation

upon them the sword, the famine, and the pestilence, and will make them like vile figs, that cannot be eaten, they are so evil. ¹⁸And I will persecute them with the sword, with the famine, and with the pestilence, and will deliver them to be removed to all the kingdoms of the earth, to be a curse^c, and an astonishment, and an hissing, and a reproach, among all the nations whither I have driven them: ¹⁹Because they have not hearkened to my words, saith the LORD, which I sent unto them by my servants the prophets, rising up early and sending *them*; but ye would not hear, saith the LORD. ²⁰Hear ye therefore the word of the LORD, all ye of the captivity, whom I have sent from Jerusalem to Babylon: ²¹Thus saith the LORD of hosts, the God of Israel, of Ahab the son of Kolaiah, and of Zedekiah the son of Maaseiah, which prophesy a lie unto you in my name; Behold, I will deliver them into the hand of Nebuchadrezzar king of Babylon; and he shall slay them before your eyes; ²²And of them shall be taken up a curse by all the captivity of Judah which *are* in Babylon, saying, The LORD make thee like Zedekiah and like Ahab, whom the king of Babylon roasted in the fire; ²³Because they have committed villany in Israel, and have committed adultery with their neighbours' wives, and have spoken lying words in my name, which I have not commanded them; even I know, and *am* a witness, saith the LORD.

²⁴ *Thus* shalt thou also speak to Shemaiah the Nehelamite^d, saying, ²⁵Thus speaketh the LORD of hosts, the God of Israel, saying, Because thou hast sent letters in thy name unto all the people that *are* at Jerusalem, and to Zephaniah the son of Maaseiah the priest, and to all the priests, saying, ²⁶The LORD hath made thee priest in the stead of Jehoiada the priest, that ye should be officers in the house of the LORD, for every man *that is* mad, and maketh himself a prophet, that thou shouldest put him in prison, and in the stocks. ²⁷Now therefore why hast thou not reproved Jeremiah of Anathoth, which maketh himself a prophet to you? ²⁸For therefore he sent unto us *in* Babylon, saying, This *captivity is* long: build ye houses, and dwell *in them*; and plant gardens, and eat the fruit of them. ²⁹And Zephaniah the priest read this letter in the ears of Jeremiah the prophet. ³⁰Then came the word of the LORD unto Jeremiah, saying, ³¹Send to all them of the captivity, saying, Thus saith the LORD concerning Shemaiah the Nehelamite; Because that Shemaiah hath prophesied unto you, and I sent him not, and he caused you to trust in a lie: ³²Therefore thus saith the LORD; Behold, I will punish Shemaiah the Nehelamite, and his seed: he shall not have a man to dwell among this people; neither shall he behold the good that I will do for my people, saith the LORD; because he hath taught rebellion^e against the LORD.

30

¹The word that came to Jeremiah from the LORD, saying, ²Thus speaketh the

---

^c to be a curse: Heb. for a curse
^d Nehelamite: or, dreamer
^e rebellion: Heb. revolt

LORD God of Israel, saying, Write thee all the words that I have spoken unto thee in a book. ³For, lo, the days come, saith the LORD, that I will bring again the captivity of my people Israel and Judah, saith the LORD: and I will cause them to return to the land that I gave to their fathers, and they shall possess it. ⁴And these *are* the words that the LORD spake concerning Israel and concerning Judah. ⁵For thus saith the LORD; We have heard a voice of trembling, of fearª, and not of peace. ⁶Ask ye now, and see whether a manᵇ doth travail with child? wherefore do I see every man with his hands on his loins, as a woman in travail, and all faces are turned into paleness? ⁷Alas! for that day *is* great, so that none *is* like it: it *is* even the time of Jacob's trouble; but he shall be saved out of it. ⁸For it shall come to pass in that day, saith the LORD of hosts, *that* I will break his yoke from off thy neck, and will burst thy bonds, and strangers shall no more serve themselves of him: ⁹But they shall serve the LORD their God, and David their king, whom I will raise up unto them.

¹⁰Therefore fear thou not, O my servant Jacob, saith the LORD; neither be dismayed, O Israel: for, lo, I will save thee from afar, and thy seed from the land of their captivity; and Jacob shall return, and shall be in rest, and be quiet, and none shall make *him* afraid. ¹¹For I *am* with thee, saith the LORD, to save thee: though I make a full end of all nations whither I have scattered thee, yet will I not make a full end of thee: but I will

correct thee in measure, and will not leave thee altogether unpunished. ¹²For thus saith the LORD, Thy bruise *is* incurable, *and* thy wound *is* grievous. ¹³ *There is* none to plead thy cause, that thou mayest be bound up: thou hast no healing medicines. ¹⁴All thy lovers have forgotten thee; they seek thee not; for I have wounded thee with the wound of an enemy, with the chastisement of a cruel one, for the multitude of thine iniquity; *because* thy sins were increased. ¹⁵Why criest thou for thine affliction? thy sorrow *is* incurable for the multitude of thine iniquity: *because* thy sins were increased, I have done these things unto thee. ¹⁶Therefore all they that devour thee shall be devoured; and all thine adversaries, every one of them, shall go into captivity; and they that spoil thee shall be a spoil, and all that prey upon thee will I give for a prey. ¹⁷For I will restore health unto thee, and I will heal thee of thy wounds, saith the LORD; because they called thee an Outcast, *saying*, This *is* Zion, whom no man seeketh after.

¹⁸Thus saith the LORD; Behold, I will bring again the captivity of Jacob's tents, and have mercy on his dwellingplaces; and the city shall be builded upon her own heapᶜ, and the palace shall remain after the manner thereof. ¹⁹And out of them shall proceed thanksgiving and the voice of them that make merry: and I will multiply them, and they shall not be few; I will also glorify them, and they shall not be small. ²⁰Their children also shall be as aforetime, and their congregation shall be established before me, and I will pun-

---

ª of fear . . . : or, there is fear, and not peace
ᵇ a man: Heb. a male
ᶜ heap: or, little hill

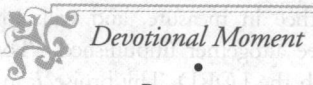

Devotional Moment
•
Restoration

30:15-22 Jeremiah wanted us all to know that God disciplines the guilty. If we sin, we're going to suffer the consequences. God will not spoil us by pretending we are perfect. God loves us too much for that.

But note Jeremiah's good news—after discipline comes reconciliation. God's discipline is tempered by compassion. God is eager to hug us afterward. The lesson for parents? In disciplining children, parents need to be firm about the rules, precise about the consequences, and careful to emphasize restoration. The discipline will be unpleasant— for parents as well as kids—but it is necessary if our children are to experience the joy of forgiveness and restoration.

ish all that oppress them. ²¹And their nobles shall be of themselves, and their governor shall proceed from the midst of them; and I will cause him to draw near, and he shall approach unto me: for who *is* this that engaged his heart to approach unto me? saith the LORD. ²²And ye shall be my people, and I will be your God. ²³Behold, the whirlwind of the LORD goeth forth with fury, a continuing[d] whirlwind: it shall fall with pain upon the head of the wicked. ²⁴The fierce anger of the LORD shall not return, until he have done *it*, and until he have performed the intents of his heart: in the latter days ye shall consider it.

31

¹At the same time, saith the LORD, will I be the God of all the families of Israel, and they shall be my people. ²Thus saith the LORD, The people *which were* left of the sword found grace in the wilderness; *even* Israel, when I went to cause him to rest. ³The LORD hath appeared of old unto me, *saying*, Yea, I have loved thee with an everlasting love: therefore with lovingkindness have I drawn thee. ⁴Again I will build thee, and thou shalt be built, O virgin of Israel: thou shalt again be adorned with thy tabrets[a], and shalt go forth in the dances of them that make merry. ⁵Thou shalt yet plant vines upon the mountains of Samaria: the planters shall plant, and shall eat *them* as common things[b]. ⁶For there shall be a day, *that* the watchmen upon the mount Ephraim shall cry, Arise ye, and let us go up to Zion unto the LORD our God. ⁷For thus saith the LORD; Sing with gladness for Jacob, and shout among the chief of the nations: publish ye, praise ye, and say, O LORD, save thy people, the remnant of Israel. ⁸Behold, I will bring them from the north country, and gather them from the coasts of the earth, *and* with them the blind and the lame, the woman with child and her that travaileth with child together: a great company shall return thither. ⁹They shall come with weeping, and with supplications[c] will I lead them: I will cause them to walk by the rivers of waters in a straight way, wherein they shall not stumble: for I am a father to Israel, and Ephraim *is* my firstborn.

ᵈ continuing: Heb. cutting
ᵃ tabrets: or, timbrels
ᵇ eat . . . : Heb. profane them
ᶜ supplications: or, favours

¹⁰Hear the word of the LORD, O ye nations, and declare *it* in the isles afar off, and say, He that scattered Israel will gather him, and keep him, as a shepherd *doth* his flock. ¹¹For the LORD hath redeemed Jacob, and ransomed him from the hand of *him that was* stronger than he. ¹²Therefore they shall come and sing in the height of Zion, and shall flow together to the goodness of the LORD, for wheat, and for wine, and for oil, and for the young of the flock and of the herd: and their soul shall be as a watered garden; and they shall not sorrow any more at all. ¹³Then shall the virgin rejoice in the dance, both young men and old together: for I will turn their mourning into joy, and will comfort them, and make them rejoice from their sorrow. ¹⁴And I will satiate the soul of the priests with fatness, and my people shall be satisfied with my goodness, saith the LORD. ¹⁵Thus saith the LORD; A voice was heard in Ramah, lamentation, *and* bitter weeping; Rahel weeping for her children refused to be comforted for her children, because they *were* not. ¹⁶Thus saith the LORD; Refrain thy voice from weeping, and thine eyes from tears: for thy work shall be rewarded, saith the LORD; and they shall come again from the land of the enemy. ¹⁷And there is hope in thine end, saith the LORD, that thy children shall come again to their own border.

¹⁸I have surely heard Ephraim bemoaning himself *thus*; Thou hast chastised me, and I was chastised, as a bullock unaccustomed *to the yoke*: turn thou me, and I shall be turned; for thou *art* the LORD my God. ¹⁹Surely after that I was turned, I repented; and after that I was instructed, I smote upon *my* thigh: I was ashamed, yea, even confounded, because I did bear the reproach of my youth. ²⁰*Is* Ephraim my dear son? *is he* a pleasant child? for since I spake against him, I do earnestly remember him still: therefore my bowels are troubled for him; I will surely have mercy upon him, saith the LORD. ²¹Set thee up waymarks, make thee high heaps: set thine heart toward the highway, *even* the way *which* thou wentest: turn again, O virgin of Israel, turn again to these thy cities. ²²How long wilt thou go about, O thou backsliding daughter? for the LORD hath created a new thing in the earth, A woman shall compass a man. ²³Thus saith the LORD of hosts, the God of Israel; As yet they shall use this speech in the land of Judah and in the cities thereof, when I shall bring again their captivity; The LORD bless thee, O habitation of justice, *and* mountain of holiness. ²⁴And there shall dwell in Judah itself, and in all the cities thereof together, husbandmen, and they *that* go forth with flocks. ²⁵For I have satiated the weary soul, and I have replenished every sorrowful soul. ²⁶Upon this I awaked, and beheld; and my sleep was sweet unto me.

²⁷Behold, the days come, saith the LORD, that I will sow the house of Israel and the house of Judah with the seed of man, and with the seed of beast. ²⁸And it shall come to pass, *that* like as I have watched over them, to pluck up, and to break down, and to throw down, and to destroy, and to afflict; so will I watch over them, to build, and to plant, saith the LORD. ²⁹In those days they shall say no more, The fathers have eaten a sour grape, and the children's

teeth are set on edge. ³⁰But every one shall die for his own iniquity: every man that eateth the sour grape, his teeth shall be set on edge. ³¹Behold, the days come, saith the LORD, that I will make a new covenant with the house of Israel, and with the house of Judah: ³²Not according to the covenant that I made with their fathers in the day *that* I took them by the hand to bring them out of the land of Egypt; which my covenant they brake, although I was an husband unto them, saith the LORD: ³³But this *shall be* the covenant that I will make with the house of Israel; After those days, saith the LORD, I will put my law in their inward parts, and write it in their hearts; and will be their God, and they shall be my people. ³⁴And they shall teach no more every man his neighbour, and every man his brother, saying, Know the LORD: for they shall all know me, from the least of them unto the greatest of them, saith the LORD: for I will forgive their iniquity, and I will remember their sin no more.

³⁵Thus saith the LORD, which giveth the sun for a light by day, *and* the ordinances of the moon and of the stars for a light by night, which divideth the sea when the waves thereof roar; The LORD of hosts *is* his name: ³⁶If those ordinances depart from before me, saith the LORD, *then* the seed of Israel also shall cease from being a nation before me for ever. ³⁷Thus saith the LORD; If heaven above can be measured, and the foundations of the earth searched out beneath, I will also cast off all the seed of Israel for all that they have done, saith the LORD. ³⁸Behold, the days come, saith the LORD, that the city

shall be built to the LORD from the tower of Hananeel unto the gate of the corner. ³⁹And the measuring line shall yet go forth over against it upon the hill Gareb, and shall compass about to Goath. ⁴⁰And the whole valley of the dead bodies, and of the ashes, and all the fields unto the brook of Kidron, unto the corner of the horse gate toward the east, *shall be* holy unto the LORD; it shall not be plucked up, nor thrown down any more for ever.

32

¹The word that came to Jeremiah from the LORD in the tenth year of Zedekiah king of Judah, which *was* the eighteenth year of Nebuchadrezzar. ²For then the king of Babylon's army besieged Jerusalem: and Jeremiah the prophet was shut up in the court of the prison, which *was* in the king of Judah's house. ³For Zedekiah king of Judah had shut him up, saying, Wherefore dost thou prophesy, and say, Thus saith the LORD, Behold, I will give this city into the hand of the king of Babylon, and he shall take it; ⁴And Zedekiah king of Judah shall not escape out of the hand of the Chaldeans, but shall surely be delivered into the hand of the king of Babylon, and shall speak with him mouth to mouth, and his eyes shall behold his eyes; ⁵And he shall lead Zedekiah to Babylon, and there shall he be until I visit him, saith the LORD: though ye fight with the Chaldeans, ye shall not prosper. ⁶And Jeremiah said, The word of the LORD came unto me, saying, ⁷Behold, Hanameel the son of Shallum thine uncle shall come unto thee, saying, Buy thee my field that *is* in Anathoth: for the right of redemption

is thine to buy *it.* ⁸So Hanameel mine uncle's son came to me in the court of the prison according to the word of the LORD, and said unto me, Buy my field, I pray thee, that *is* in Anathoth, which *is* in the country of Benjamin: for the right of inheritance *is* thine, and the redemption *is* thine; buy *it* for thyself. Then I knew that this *was* the word of the LORD. ⁹And I bought the field of Hanameel my uncle's son, that *was* in Anathoth, and weighed him the money, *even* seventeenᵃ shekels of silver. ¹⁰And I subscribedᵇ the evidence, and sealed *it,* and took witnesses, and weighed *him* the money in the balances. ¹¹So I took the evidence of the purchase, *both* that which was sealed *according* to the law and custom, and that which was open: ¹²And I gave the evidence of the purchase unto Baruch the son of Neriah, the son of Maaseiah, in the sight of Hanameel mine uncle's *son,* and in the presence of the witnesses that subscribed the book of the purchase, before all the Jews that sat in the court of the prison. ¹³And I charged Baruch before them, saying, ¹⁴Thus saith the LORD of hosts, the God of Israel; Take these evidences, this evidence of the purchase, both which is sealed, and this evidence which is open; and put them in an earthen vessel, that they may continue many days. ¹⁵For thus saith the LORD of hosts, the God of Israel; Houses and fields and vineyards shall be possessed again in this land.

¹⁶Now when I had delivered the evidence of the purchase unto Baruch the

---

Devotional Moment
•
Trust

32:6-15 It made no sense to buy land when the Babylonian army was set to pillage the country. But God told Jeremiah to do just that, and Jeremiah obeyed. The land he bought would be a symbol that God would restore the people after exile. Jeremiah was buying land in preparation for a return from captivity that no one could humanly foresee.

Do we trust God? We often say we do. Preachers say we should. Sometimes our prayers attest to it. But do we? When crisis breaks, when reality checks our dreams, whom do you trust? Where's that pottery jar with a promise in it that tells you of a hope and a future you cannot see?

---

son of Neriah, I prayed unto the LORD, saying, ¹⁷Ah Lord GOD! behold, thou hast made the heaven and the earth by thy great power and stretched out arm, *and* there is nothing too hard for thee: ¹⁸Thou shewest lovingkindness unto thousands, and recompensest the iniquity of the fathers into the bosom of their children after them: the Great, the Mighty God, the LORD of hosts, *is* his name, ¹⁹Great in counsel, and mighty in workᶜ: for thine eyes *are* open upon all the ways of the sons of men: to give every one according to his ways, and according to the fruit of his doings: ²⁰Which hast set signs and wonders in the land of Egypt, *even* unto this day, and in Israel, and among *other* men; and hast made thee a name, as at this day; ²¹And hast brought forth thy people Israel out of the land

---

ᵃ seventeen . . . : or, seven shekels and ten pieces of silver
ᵇ subscribed . . . : Heb. wrote in the book
ᶜ work: Heb. doing

of Egypt with signs, and with wonders, and with a strong hand, and with a stretched out arm, and with great terror; ²²And hast given them this land, which thou didst swear to their fathers to give them, a land flowing with milk and honey; ²³And they came in, and possessed it; but they obeyed not thy voice, neither walked in thy law; they have done nothing of all that thou commandedst them to do: therefore thou hast caused all this evil to come upon them: ²⁴Behold the mounts^d, they are come unto the city to take it; and the city is given into the hand of the Chaldeans, that fight against it, because of the sword, and of the famine, and of the pestilence: and what thou hast spoken is come to pass; and, behold, thou seest *it.* ²⁵And thou hast said unto me, O Lord GOD, Buy thee the field for money, and take witnesses; for the city is given into the hand of the Chaldeans.

²⁶Then came the word of the LORD unto Jeremiah, saying, ²⁷Behold, I *am* the LORD, the God of all flesh: is there any thing too hard for me? ²⁸Therefore thus saith the LORD; Behold, I will give this city into the hand of the Chaldeans, and into the hand of Nebuchadrezzar king of Babylon, and he shall take it: ²⁹And the Chaldeans, that fight against this city, shall come and set fire on this city, and burn it with the houses, upon whose roofs they have offered incense unto Baal, and poured out drink offerings unto other gods, to provoke me to anger. ³⁰For the children of Israel and the children of Judah have only done

evil before me from their youth: for the children of Israel have only provoked me to anger with the work of their hands, saith the LORD. ³¹For this city hath been to me *as* a provocation of mine anger and of my fury from the day that they built it even unto this day; that I should remove it from before my face, ³²Because of all the evil of the children of Israel and of the children of Judah, which they have done to provoke me to anger, they, their kings, their princes, their priests, and their prophets, and the men of Judah, and the inhabitants of Jerusalem. ³³And they have turned unto me the back^e, and not the face: though I taught them, rising up early and teaching *them,* yet they have not hearkened to receive instruction. ³⁴But they set their abominations in the house, which is called by my name, to defile it. ³⁵And they built the high places of Baal, which *are* in the valley of the son of Hinnom, to cause their sons and their daughters to pass through *the fire* unto Molech; which I commanded them not, neither came it into my mind, that they should do this abomination, to cause Judah to sin. ³⁶And now therefore thus saith the LORD, the God of Israel, concerning this city, whereof ye say, It shall be delivered into the hand of the king of Babylon by the sword, and by the famine, and by the pestilence; ³⁷Behold, I will gather them out of all countries, whither I have driven them in mine anger, and in my fury, and in great wrath; and I will bring them again unto this place, and I will cause them to

---

^d mounts: or, engines of shot
^e back: Heb. neck

dwell safely: ³⁸And they shall be my people, and I will be their God: ³⁹And I will give them one heart, and one way, that they may fear me for ever^f, for the good of them, and of their children after them: ⁴⁰And I will make an everlasting covenant with them, that I will not turn away from them^g, to do them good; but I will put my fear in their hearts, that they shall not depart from me. ⁴¹Yea, I will rejoice over them to do them good, and I will plant them in this land assuredly^h with my whole heart and with my whole soul. ⁴²For thus saith the LORD; Like as I have brought all this great evil upon this people, so will I bring upon them all the good that I have promised them. ⁴³And fields shall be bought in this land, whereof ye say, *It is* desolate without man or beast; it is given into the hand of the Chaldeans. ⁴⁴Men shall buy fields for money, and subscribe evidences, and seal *them*, and take witnesses in the land of Benjamin, and in the places about Jerusalem, and in the cities of Judah, and in the cities of the mountains, and in the cities of the valley, and in the cities of the south: for I will cause their captivity to return, saith the LORD.

33

¹Moreover the word of the LORD came unto Jeremiah the second time, while he was yet shut up in the court of the prison, saying, ²Thus saith the LORD the maker thereof, the LORD that formed it, to establish it; the LORD *is* his name; ³Call unto me, and I will answer thee, and shew thee great and mighty things, which thou knowest not. ⁴For thus saith the LORD, the God of Israel, concerning the houses of this city, and concerning the houses of the kings of Judah, which are thrown down by the mounts, and by the sword; ⁵They come to fight with the Chaldeans, but *it is* to fill them with the dead bodies of men, whom I have slain in mine anger and in my fury, and for all whose wickedness I have hid my face from this city. ⁶Behold, I will bring it health and cure, and I will cure them, and will reveal unto them the abundance of peace and truth. ⁷And I will cause the captivity of Judah and the captivity of Israel to return, and will build them, as at the first. ⁸And I will cleanse them from all their iniquity, whereby they have sinned against me; and I will pardon all their iniquities, whereby they have sinned, and whereby they have transgressed against me. ⁹And it shall be to me a name of joy, a praise and an honour before all the nations of the earth, which shall hear all the good that I do unto them: and they shall fear and tremble for all the goodness and for all the prosperity that I procure unto it.

¹⁰Thus saith the LORD; Again there shall be heard in this place, which ye say *shall be* desolate without man and without beast, *even* in the cities of Judah, and in the streets of Jerusalem, that are desolate, without man, and without inhabitant, and without beast, ¹¹The voice of joy, and the voice of gladness, the voice of the bridegroom,

---

^f for ever: Heb. all days
^g from them: Heb. from after them
^h assuredly: Heb. in truth, or, stability

and the voice of the bride, the voice of them that shall say, Praise the LORD of hosts: for the LORD *is* good; for his mercy *endureth* for ever: *and* of them that shall bring the sacrifice of praise into the house of the LORD. For I will cause to return the captivity of the land, as at the first, saith the LORD. ¹²Thus saith the LORD of hosts; Again in this place, which is desolate without man and without beast, and in all the cities thereof, shall be an habitation of shepherds causing *their* flocks to lie down. ¹³In the cities of the mountains, in the cities of the vale, and in the cities of the south, and in the land of Benjamin, and in the places about Jerusalem, and in the cities of Judah, shall the flocks pass again under the hands of him that telleth *them*, saith the LORD. ¹⁴Behold, the days come, saith the LORD, that I will perform that good thing which I have promised unto the house of Israel and to the house of Judah. ¹⁵In those days, and at that time, will I cause the Branch of righteousness to grow up unto David; and he shall execute judgment and righteousness in the land. ¹⁶In those days shall Judah be saved, and Jerusalem shall dwell safely: and this *is the name* wherewith she shall be called, The LORD our righteousness.

¹⁷For thus saith the LORD; David[a] shall never want a man to sit upon the throne of the house of Israel; ¹⁸Neither shall the priests the Levites want a man before me to offer burnt offerings, and to kindle meat offerings, and to do sacrifice continually. ¹⁹And the word of the LORD came unto Jeremiah, saying, ²⁰Thus saith the LORD; If ye can break my covenant of the day, and my covenant of the night, and that there should not be day and night in their season; ²¹*Then* may also my covenant be broken with David my servant, that he should not have a son to reign upon his throne; and with the Levites the priests, my ministers. ²²As the host of heaven cannot be numbered, neither the sand of the sea measured: so will I multiply the seed of David my servant, and the Levites that minister unto me. ²³Moreover the word of the LORD came to Jeremiah, saying, ²⁴Considerest thou not what this people have spoken, saying, The two families which the LORD hath chosen, he hath even cast them off? thus they have despised my people, that they should be no more a nation before them. ²⁵Thus saith the LORD; If my covenant *be* not with day and night, *and if* I have not appointed the ordinances of heaven and earth; ²⁶Then will I cast away the seed of Jacob, and David my servant, *so* that I will not take *any* of his seed *to be* rulers over the seed of Abraham, Isaac, and Jacob: for I will cause their captivity to return, and have mercy on them.

34

¹The word which came unto Jeremiah from the LORD, when Nebuchadnezzar king of Babylon, and all his army, and all the kingdoms of the earth of his dominion, and all the people, fought against Jerusalem, and against all the cities thereof, saying, ²Thus saith the LORD, the God of Israel; Go and speak to Zedekiah king of Judah, and tell him, Thus saith the LORD; Be-

---

[a] David . . . : Heb. There shall not be cut off from David

hold, I will give this city into the hand of the king of Babylon, and he shall burn it with fire: ³And thou shalt not escape out of his hand, but shalt surely be taken, and delivered into his hand; and thine eyes shall behold the eyes of the king of Babylon, and he shall speak with thee mouth to mouth, and thou shalt go to Babylon. ⁴Yet hear the word of the LORD, O Zedekiah king of Judah; Thus saith the LORD of thee, Thou shalt not die by the sword: ⁵*But* thou shalt die in peace: and with the burnings of thy fathers, the former kings which were before thee, so shall they burn *odours* for thee; and they will lament thee, *saying*, Ah lord! for I have pronounced the word, saith the LORD. ⁶Then Jeremiah the prophet spake all these words unto Zedekiah king of Judah in Jerusalem, ⁷When the king of Babylon's army fought against Jerusalem, and against all the cities of Judah that were left, against Lachish, and against Azekah: for these defenced cities remained of the cities of Judah.

⁸*This is* the word that came unto Jeremiah from the LORD, after that the king Zedekiah had made a covenant with all the people which *were* at Jerusalem, to proclaim liberty unto them; ⁹That every man should let his manservant, and every man his maidservant, *being* an Hebrew or an Hebrewess, go free; that none should serve himself of them, *to wit*, of a Jew his brother. ¹⁰Now when all the princes, and all the people, which had entered into the covenant, heard that every one should let his manservant, and every one his maidservant, go free, that none should serve themselves of them any more, then they

> ### Devotional Moment
> •
> #### Promises
> 34:15-16 Zedekiah would promise anything to keep his throne another day. His word was only as good as his whim. Surely, anyone who trusted Zedekiah was a fool. Parents who keep promises build confident, secure children. Children who keep promises ("I'll be home by nine" or "I'll call for a ride if there's any drinking" or "I'll follow Jesus") are to a parent like cold mountain water on a hot dusty day. God is delighted, too—reason enough to keep our word.

obeyed, and let *them* go. ¹¹But afterward they turned, and caused the servants and the handmaids, whom they had let go free, to return, and brought them into subjection for servants and for handmaids. ¹²Therefore the word of the LORD came to Jeremiah from the LORD, saying, ¹³Thus saith the LORD, the God of Israel; I made a covenant with your fathers in the day that I brought them forth out of the land of Egypt, out of the house of bondmen, saying, ¹⁴At the end of seven years let ye go every man his brother an Hebrew, which hath been sold unto thee; and when he hath served thee six years, thou shalt let him go free from thee: but your fathers hearkened not unto me, neither inclined their ear. ¹⁵And ye were nowª turned, and had done right in my sight, in proclaiming liberty every man to his neighbour; and ye had made a covenant before me in the house which is called by my name: ¹⁶But ye turned and polluted my name, and caused every man his servant, and every man his handmaid, whom ye had set at liberty at their plea-

ª now: Heb. to day

sure, to return, and brought them into subjection, to be unto you for servants and for handmaids. [17]Therefore thus saith the LORD; Ye have not hearkened unto me, in proclaiming liberty, every one to his brother, and every man to his neighbour: behold, I proclaim a liberty for you, saith the LORD, to the sword, to the pestilence, and to the famine; and I will make you to be removed into all the kingdoms of the earth. [18]And I will give the men that have transgressed my covenant, which have not performed the words of the covenant which they had made before me, when they cut the calf in twain, and passed between the parts thereof, [19]The princes of Judah, and the princes of Jerusalem, the eunuchs, and the priests, and all the people of the land, which passed between the parts of the calf; [20]I will even give them into the hand of their enemies, and into the hand of them that seek their life: and their dead bodies shall be for meat unto the fowls of the heaven, and to the beasts of the earth. [21]And Zedekiah king of Judah and his princes will I give into the hand of their enemies, and into the hand of them that seek their life, and into the hand of the king of Babylon's army, which are gone up from you. [22]Behold, I will command, saith the LORD, and cause them to return to this city; and they shall fight against it, and take it, and burn it with fire: and I will make the cities of Judah a desolation without an inhabitant.

35

[1]The word which came unto Jeremiah from the LORD in the days of Jehoiakim the son of Josiah king of Judah,

saying, [2]Go unto the house of the Rechabites, and speak unto them, and bring them into the house of the LORD, into one of the chambers, and give them wine to drink. [3]Then I took Jaazaniah the son of Jeremiah, the son of Habaziniah, and his brethren, and all his sons, and the whole house of the Rechabites; [4]And I brought them into the house of the LORD, into the chamber of the sons of Hanan, the son of Igdaliah, a man of God, which *was* by the chamber of the princes, which *was* above the chamber of Maaseiah the son of Shallum, the keeper of the door[a]: [5]And I set before the sons of the house of the Rechabites pots full of wine, and cups, and I said unto them, Drink ye wine. [6]But they said, We will drink no wine: for Jonadab the son of Rechab our father commanded us, saying, Ye shall drink no wine, *neither ye*, nor your sons for ever: [7]Neither shall ye build house, nor sow seed, nor plant vineyard, nor have *any*: but all your days ye shall dwell in tents; that ye may live many days in the land where ye *be* strangers. [8]Thus have we obeyed the voice of Jonadab the son of Rechab our father in all that he hath charged us, to drink no wine all our days, we, our wives, our sons, nor our daughters; [9]Nor to build houses for us to dwell in: neither have we vineyard, nor field, nor seed: [10]But we have dwelt in tents, and have obeyed, and done according to all that Jonadab our father commanded us. [11]But it came to pass, when Nebuchadrezzar king of Babylon came up into the land, that we said, Come, and let us go to Jerusalem for fear of the army of the Chaldeans, and

---

[a] door: Heb. threshold, or, vessel

A Father to Follow

by Greg Johnson

The dad spoke, the kids listened and obeyed. If it worked for Jonadab and his family, the Rechabite descendants (Jer. 35), it should work for you, right?

You know that it rarely does. In most homes we find (1) no commitment to family traditions, (2) no teamwork between the husband and wife, and (3) no respect for Dad's authority, let alone God's. Here are a few ideas for building commitment to family tradition, teamwork between spouses, and respect for Dad in your family.

Valuing family traditions. Establishing traditions that your children will want to carry on must be intentional. Your keys to success are creativity and consistency.

Religious holidays should get top priority. Christmas traditions, for example, must go beyond opening one present on Christmas Eve and the rest in the morning. Have Dad read the Christmas story from the same well-worn Bible every year. Go to church and then to a live nativity scene. Watch a reenactment of Christ's birth on a film that dramatizes it well. Make a big deal out of an Advent wreath. Have everyone color pictures of their favorite part of the Christmas story. Sing Christmas songs around the piano.

Easter, Pentecost, and even Thanksgiving are other opportunities to build family unity. Don't let the busyness of the holidays rob you of the energy to try new activities.

Birthdays, spiritual birthdays, and other big-ticket days should be something each member of the family looks forward to. Get the kids involved and be creative. If you can't be creative, there are wonderful books at your local Christian bookstore that can give you ideas.

A solid parent team. It inevitably happens to new parents. Mom makes the children her number one priority. But while she spends years trying to be the "mom who's everything," the marriage gets left in the dust. Dad makes work his main priority. Building a future through an upwardly mobile career becomes the goal instead of the means to a higher end. Both forget that their main priority should be their marriage (see Gen. 2:24).

Generations of marital success are founded upon a husband and wife being committed to each other as friends, partners, and lovers—for the long haul, as a team. To do that, couples need to set aside time alone to talk with and romance each other. That priority should never be allowed to waver.

A father worth listening to. If TV sitcom characterizations of the "dad out of touch" are allowed to prevail at your home, respect will decrease with each episode.

Sadly, some fathers welcome the opportunity to run from earning the family's respect. It's easier to be a buffoon than to stay in charge. They have abdicated that leadership role, and their wives, by necessity, have taken over. They won't help lead the family spiritually or even help with discipline. Their minds are on their work, hobbies, or recreation. When this occurs, the family is out of order and headed for trouble.

Other fathers would *like* to have some respect but don't get any from their wives. Naturally, the kids follow Mom's lead. At every opportunity, the wife should affirm the fatherly role and authority of her husband. With all her heart, she needs to buy into the concept that God has asked the father to lead the home. It's an attitude as well as an action.

When life gets busy, it's OK for a wife to encourage her husband to exercise more leadership, but then the husband must take those reminders as words from God. *Press forward. Move the family up one more notch. Don't give in to fatigue. Examine the poor habits you've allowed to form. Try again. Play your role with enthusiasm, and try not to let Satan get a foothold in your family.*

As the father is followed, so must he follow the Father. A dad not pressing ahead in his own spiritual life cannot lead his family where it needs to go. The example of an obedient and vital Christian life is the greatest legacy a father can pass on to his children.

DIGGING DEEPER

1. Read Ephesians 5:31. What things are you tempted to become "one" with instead of your spouse? How did they get there, and how can they be put back in their proper place?

2. Read Acts 2:46-47. The early Christians had traditions that kept them unified. What three steps can you take in your family to begin building stronger traditions?

3. Though Jesus wasn't a parent or a husband, no one could say he wasn't respected. What are five character qualities he had that you think commanded such respect? As a husband, what small steps can you take to help build these qualities into your own life?

for fear of the army of the Syrians: so we dwell at Jerusalem.

¹²Then came the word of the LORD unto Jeremiah, saying, ¹³Thus saith the LORD of hosts, the God of Israel; Go and tell the men of Judah and the inhabitants of Jerusalem, Will ye not receive instruction to hearken to my words? saith the LORD. ¹⁴The words of Jonadab the son of Rechab, that he commanded his sons not to drink wine, are performed; for unto this day they drink none, but obey their father's commandment: notwithstanding I have spoken unto you, rising early and speaking; but ye hearkened not unto me. ¹⁵I have sent also unto you all my servants the prophets, rising up early and sending *them*, saying, Return ye now every man from his evil way, and amend your doings, and go not after other gods to serve them, and ye shall dwell in the land which I have given to you and to your fathers:

but ye have not inclined your ear, nor hearkened unto me. ¹⁶Because the sons of Jonadab the son of Rechab have performed the commandment of their father, which he commanded them; but this people hath not hearkened unto me: ¹⁷Therefore thus saith the LORD God of hosts, the God of Israel; Behold, I will bring upon Judah and upon all the inhabitants of Jerusalem all the evil that I have pronounced against them: because I have spoken unto them, but they have not heard; and I have called unto them, but they have not answered. ¹⁸And Jeremiah said unto the house of the Rechabites, Thus saith the LORD of hosts, the God of Israel; Because ye have obeyed the commandment of Jonadab your father, and kept all his precepts, and done according unto all that he hath commanded you: ¹⁹Therefore thus saith the LORD of hosts, the God of Israel; Jonadab[b] the son of Rechab shall

---

[b] Jonadab . . . : Heb. There shall not a man be cut off from Jonadab the son of Rechab to stand, etc

not want a man to stand before me for ever.

36

¹And it came to pass in the fourth year of Jehoiakim the son of Josiah king of Judah, *that* this word came unto Jeremiah from the LORD, saying, ²Take thee a roll of a book, and write therein all the words that I have spoken unto thee against Israel, and against Judah, and against all the nations, from the day I spake unto thee, from the days of Josiah, even unto this day. ³It may be that the house of Judah will hear all the evil which I purpose to do unto them; that they may return every man from his evil way; that I may forgive their iniquity and their sin. ⁴Then Jeremiah called Baruch the son of Neriah: and Baruch wrote from the mouth of Jeremiah all the words of the LORD, which he had spoken unto him, upon a roll of a book. ⁵And Jeremiah commanded Baruch, saying, I *am* shut up; I cannot go into the house of the LORD: ⁶Therefore go thou, and read in the roll, which thou hast written from my mouth, the words of the LORD in the ears of the people in the LORD'S house upon the fasting day: and also thou shalt read them in the ears of all Judah that come out of their cities. ⁷It may be they will present their supplication before the LORD, and will return every one from his evil way: for great *is* the anger and the fury that the LORD hath pronounced against this people. ⁸And Baruch the son of Neriah did according to all that Jeremiah the prophet commanded him, reading in the book

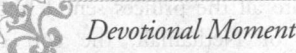

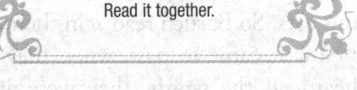

Devotional Moment

God's Word

36:10-32 Jehoiakim had Jeremiah's scroll burned to show how little he thought of God's Word. Thousands after him have similarly tried to eradicate God's Word, but it is not so easily destroyed. The Bible is a treasure—God's gift to us. We all need the nourishment this book supplies. Read it. Read it together.

the words of the LORD in the LORD'S house.

⁹And it came to pass in the fifth year of Jehoiakim the son of Josiah king of Judah, in the ninth month, *that* they proclaimed a fast before the LORD to all the people in Jerusalem, and to all the people that came from the cities of Judah unto Jerusalem. ¹⁰Then read Baruch in the book the words of Jeremiah in the house of the LORD, in the chamber of Gemariah the son of Shaphan the scribe, in the higher court, at the entry[a] of the new gate of the LORD'S house, in the ears of all the people. ¹¹When Michaiah the son of Gemariah, the son of Shaphan, had heard out of the book all the words of the LORD, ¹²Then he went down into the king's house, into the scribe's chamber: and, lo, all the princes sat there, *even* Elishama the scribe, and Delaiah the son of Shemaiah, and Elnathan the son of Achbor, and Gemariah the son of Shaphan, and Zedekiah the son of Hananiah, and all the princes. ¹³Then Michaiah declared unto them all the words that he had heard, when Baruch read the book in the ears of the people.

[a] entry: or, door

¹⁴Therefore all the princes sent Jehudi the son of Nethaniah, the son of Shelemiah, the son of Cushi, unto Baruch, saying, Take in thine hand the roll wherein thou hast read in the ears of the people, and come. So Baruch the son of Neriah took the roll in his hand, and came unto them. ¹⁵And they said unto him, Sit down now, and read it in our ears. So Baruch read *it* in their ears. ¹⁶Now it came to pass, when they had heard all the words, they were afraid both one and other, and said unto Baruch, We will surely tell the king of all these words. ¹⁷And they asked Baruch, saying, Tell us now, How didst thou write all these words at his mouth? ¹⁸Then Baruch answered them, He pronounced all these words unto me with his mouth, and I wrote *them* with ink in the book. ¹⁹Then said the princes unto Baruch, Go, hide thee, thou and Jeremiah; and let no man know where ye be.

²⁰And they went in to the king into the court, but they laid up the roll in the chamber of Elishama the scribe, and told all the words in the ears of the king. ²¹So the king sent Jehudi to fetch the roll: and he took it out of Elishama the scribe's chamber. And Jehudi read it in the ears of the king, and in the ears of all the princes which stood beside the king. ²²Now the king sat in the winterhouse in the ninth month: and *there was a fire* on the hearth burning before him. ²³And it came to pass, *that* when Jehudi had read three or four leaves, he cut it with the penknife, and cast *it* into the fire that *was* on the hearth, until all the roll was consumed in the fire that *was* on the hearth. ²⁴Yet they were not afraid, nor rent their garments, *neither* the king, nor any of his servants that heard all these words. ²⁵Nevertheless Elnathan and Delaiah and Gemariah had made intercession to the king that he would not burn the roll: but he would not hear them. ²⁶But the king commanded Jerahmeel the son of Hammelech[b], and Seraiah the son of Azriel, and Shelemiah the son of Abdeel, to take Baruch the scribe and Jeremiah the prophet: but the LORD hid them. ²⁷Then the word of the LORD came to Jeremiah, after that the king had burned the roll, and the words which Baruch wrote at the mouth of Jeremiah, saying, ²⁸Take thee again another roll, and write in it all the former words that were in the first roll, which Jehoiakim the king of Judah hath burned. ²⁹And thou shalt say to Jehoiakim king of Judah, Thus saith the LORD; Thou hast burned this roll, saying, Why hast thou written therein, saying, The king of Babylon shall certainly come and destroy this land, and shall cause to cease from thence man and beast? ³⁰Therefore thus saith the LORD of Jehoiakim king of Judah; He shall have none to sit upon the throne of David: and his dead body shall be cast out in the day to the heat, and in the night to the frost. ³¹And I will punish[c] him and his seed and his servants for their iniquity; and I will bring upon them, and upon the inhabitants of Jerusalem, and upon the men of Judah, all the evil that I have pronounced against them; but they

---

ᵇ of Hammelech: or, of the king
ᶜ punish: Heb. visit upon

hearkened not. ³²Then took Jeremiah another roll, and gave it to Baruch the scribe, the son of Neriah; who wrote therein from the mouth of Jeremiah all the words of the book which Jehoiakim king of Judah had burned in the fire: and there were added besides unto them many like^d words.

37

¹And king Zedekiah the son of Josiah reigned instead of Coniah the son of Jehoiakim, whom Nebuchadrezzar king of Babylon made king in the land of Judah. ²But neither he, nor his servants, nor the people of the land, did hearken unto the words of the LORD, which he spake by^a the prophet Jeremiah. ³And Zedekiah the king sent Jehucal the son of Shelemiah and Zephaniah the son of Maaseiah the priest to the prophet Jeremiah, saying, Pray now unto the LORD our God for us. ⁴Now Jeremiah came in and went out among the people: for they had not put him into prison. ⁵Then Pharaoh's army was come forth out of Egypt: and when the Chaldeans that besieged Jerusalem heard tidings of them, they departed from Jerusalem. ⁶Then came the word of the LORD unto the prophet Jeremiah, saying, ⁷Thus saith the LORD, the God of Israel; Thus shall ye say to the king of Judah, that sent you unto me to enquire of me; Behold, Pharaoh's army, which is come forth to help you, shall return to Egypt into their own land. ⁸And the Chaldeans shall come again, and fight against this city, and take it, and burn it with fire. ⁹Thus saith the LORD; Deceive not yourselves^b, saying, The Chaldeans shall surely depart from us: for they shall not depart. ¹⁰For though ye had smitten the whole army of the Chaldeans that fight against you, and there remained *but* wounded^c men among them, *yet* should they rise up every man in his tent, and burn this city with fire.

¹¹And it came to pass, that when the army of the Chaldeans was broken up from Jerusalem for fear of Pharaoh's army, ¹²Then Jeremiah went forth out of Jerusalem to go into the land of Benjamin, to separate^d himself thence in the midst of the people. ¹³And when he was in the gate of Benjamin, a captain of the ward *was* there, whose name *was* Irijah, the son of Shelemiah, the son of Hananiah; and he took Jeremiah the prophet, saying, Thou fallest away to the Chaldeans. ¹⁴Then said Jeremiah, *It is* false^e; I fall not away to the Chaldeans. But he hearkened not to him: so Irijah took Jeremiah, and brought him to the princes. ¹⁵Wherefore the princes were wroth with Jeremiah, and smote him, and put him in prison in the house of Jonathan the scribe: for they had made that the prison. ¹⁶When Jeremiah was entered into the dungeon, and into the cabins^f,

---

^d like: Heb. as they

^a by . . . : Heb. by the hand of the prophet

^b yourselves: Heb. your souls

^c wounded: Heb. thrust through

^d separate . . . : or, to slip away from thence in the midst of the people

^e false: Heb. falsehood, or, a lie

^f cabins: or, cells

and Jeremiah had remained there many days; ¹⁷Then Zedekiah the king sent, and took him out: and the king asked him secretly in his house, and said, Is there *any* word from the LORD? And Jeremiah said, There is: for, said he, thou shalt be delivered into the hand of the king of Babylon. ¹⁸Moreover Jeremiah said unto king Zedekiah, What have I offended against thee, or against thy servants, or against this people, that ye have put me in prison? ¹⁹Where *are* now your prophets which prophesied unto you, saying, The king of Babylon shall not come against you, nor against this land? ²⁰Therefore hear now, I pray thee, O my lord the king: let my supplication, I pray thee, be accepted before thee; that thou cause me not to return to the house of Jonathan the scribe, lest I die there. ²¹Then Zedekiah the king commanded that they should commit Jeremiah into the court of the prison, and that they should give him daily a piece of bread out of the bakers' street, until all the bread in the city were spent. Thus Jeremiah remained in the court of the prison.

38

¹Then Shephatiah the son of Mattan, and Gedaliah the son of Pashur, and Jucal the son of Shelemiah, and Pashur the son of Malchiah, heard the words that Jeremiah had spoken unto all the people, saying, ²Thus saith the LORD, He that remaineth in this city shall die by the sword, by the famine, and by the pestilence: but he that goeth forth to the Chaldeans shall live; for he shall have his life for a prey, and shall live. ³Thus saith the LORD, This city shall surely be given into the hand of the king of Babylon's army, which shall take it. ⁴Therefore the princes said unto the king, We beseech thee, let this man be put to death: for thus he weakeneth the hands of the men of war that remain in this city, and the hands of all the people, in speaking such words unto them: for this man seeketh not the welfareᵃ of this people, but the hurt. ⁵Then Zedekiah the king said, Behold, he *is* in your hand: for the king *is* not *he that* can do *any* thing against you. ⁶Then took they Jeremiah, and cast him into the dungeon of Malchiah the son of Hammelechᵇ, that *was* in the court of the prison: and they let down Jeremiah with cords. And in the dungeon *there was* no water, but mire: so Jeremiah sunk in the mire. ⁷Now when Ebedmelech the Ethiopian, one of the eunuchs which was in the king's house, heard that they had put Jeremiah in the dungeon; the king then sitting in the gate of Benjamin; ⁸Ebedmelech went forth out of the king's house, and spake to the king, saying, ⁹My lord the king, these men have done evil in all that they have done to Jeremiah the prophet, whom they have cast into the dungeon; and he is like to die for hunger in the place where he is: for *there is* no more bread in the city. ¹⁰Then the king commanded Ebedmelech the Ethiopian, saying, Take from hence thirty men with theeᶜ, and take up Jeremiah the

---

ᵃ welfare: Heb. peace
ᵇ of Hammelech: or, of the king
ᶜ with thee: Heb. in thine hand

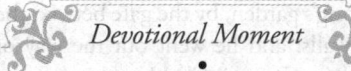

Devotional Moment

Kindness

38:7-13 Ebed-melech the Ethiopian leaves one enduring lesson: When you have the means to make a difference, do it. To have the means and lack the will is laziness. To have the means and lack the love is selfishness. God is pleased when we go out of our way to help someone else.

prophet out of the dungeon, before he die. ¹¹So Ebedmelech took the men with him, and went into the house of the king under the treasury, and took thence old cast clouts and old rotten rags, and let them down by cords into the dungeon to Jeremiah. ¹²And Ebed-melech the Ethiopian said unto Jeremiah, Put now *these* old cast clouts and rotten rags under thine armholes under the cords. And Jeremiah did so. ¹³So they drew up Jeremiah with cords, and took him up out of the dungeon: and Jeremiah remained in the court of the prison.

¹⁴Then Zedekiah the king sent, and took Jeremiah the prophet unto him into the third[d] entry that *is* in the house of the LORD: and the king said unto Jeremiah, I will ask thee a thing; hide nothing from me. ¹⁵Then Jeremiah said unto Zedekiah, If I declare *it* unto thee, wilt thou not surely put me to death? and if I give thee counsel, wilt thou not hearken unto me? ¹⁶So Zedekiah the king sware secretly unto Jeremiah, saying, *As* the LORD liveth, that made us this soul, I will not put thee to death, neither will I give thee into the hand of these men that seek thy life. ¹⁷Then said Jeremiah unto Zedekiah, Thus saith the LORD, the God of hosts, the God of Israel; If thou wilt assuredly go forth unto the king of Babylon's princes, then thy soul shall live, and this city shall not be burned with fire; and thou shalt live, and thine house: ¹⁸But if thou wilt not go forth to the king of Babylon's princes, then shall this city be given into the hand of the Chaldeans, and they shall burn it with fire, and thou shalt not escape out of their hand. ¹⁹And Zedekiah the king said unto Jeremiah, I am afraid of the Jews that are fallen to the Chaldeans, lest they deliver me into their hand, and they mock me. ²⁰But Jeremiah said, They shall not deliver *thee*. Obey, I beseech thee, the voice of the LORD, which I speak unto thee: so it shall be well unto thee, and thy soul shall live. ²¹But if thou refuse to go forth, this *is* the word that the LORD hath shewed me: ²²And, behold, all the women that are left in the king of Judah's house *shall be* brought forth to the king of Babylon's princes, and those *women* shall say, Thy friends[e] have set thee on, and have prevailed against thee: thy feet are sunk in the mire, *and* they are turned away back. ²³So they shall bring out all thy wives and thy children to the Chaldeans: and thou shalt not escape out of their hand, but shalt be taken by the hand of the king of Babylon: and thou shalt cause this city to be burned with fire. ²⁴Then said Zedekiah unto Jeremiah, Let no man know of these

---

ᵈ third: or, principal
ᵉ Thy friends: Heb. Men of thy peace

words, and thou shalt not die. ²⁵But if the princes hear that I have talked with thee, and they come unto thee, and say unto thee, Declare unto us now what thou hast said unto the king, hide it not from us, and we will not put thee to death; also what the king said unto thee: ²⁶Then thou shalt say unto them, I presented my supplication before the king, that he would not cause me to return to Jonathan's house, to die there. ²⁷Then came all the princes unto Jeremiah, and asked him: and he told them according to all these words that the king had commanded. So they left off speaking with him; for the matter was not perceived. ²⁸So Jeremiah abode in the court of the prison until the day that Jerusalem was taken: and he was *there* when Jerusalem was taken.

39

¹In the ninth year of Zedekiah king of Judah, in the tenth month, came Nebuchadrezzar king of Babylon and all his army against Jerusalem, and they besieged it. ²*And* in the eleventh year of Zedekiah, in the fourth month, the ninth *day* of the month, the city was broken up. ³And all the princes of the king of Babylon came in, and sat in the middle gate, *even* Nergalsharezer, Samgarnebo, Sarsechim, Rabsaris, Nergalsharezer, Rabmag, with all the residue of the princes of the king of Babylon. ⁴And it came to pass, *that* when Zedekiah the king of Judah saw them, and all the men of war, then they fled, and went forth out of the city by night, by the way of the king's garden, by the gate betwixt the two walls: and he went out the way of the plain. ⁵But the Chaldeans' army pursued after them, and overtook Zedekiah in the plains of Jericho: and when they had taken him, they brought him up to Nebuchadnezzar king of Babylon to Riblah in the land of Hamath, where he gave^a judgment upon him. ⁶Then the king of Babylon slew the sons of Zedekiah in Riblah before his eyes: also the king of Babylon slew all the nobles of Judah. ⁷Moreover he put out Zedekiah's eyes, and bound him with chains, to carry him to Babylon. ⁸And the Chaldeans burned the king's house, and the houses of the people, with fire, and brake down the walls of Jerusalem. ⁹Then Nebuzaradan the captain^b of the guard carried away captive into Babylon the remnant of the people that remained in the city, and those that fell away, that fell to him, with the rest of the people that remained. ¹⁰But Nebuzaradan the captain of the guard left of the poor of the people, which had nothing, in the land of Judah, and gave them vineyards and fields at the same time.

¹¹Now Nebuchadrezzar king of Babylon gave charge concerning Jeremiah to^c Nebuzaradan the captain of the guard, saying, ¹²Take him, and look well to him, and do him no harm; but do unto him even as he shall say unto thee. ¹³So Nebuzaradan the captain of the guard sent, and Nebushasban, Rabsaris, and Nergalsharezer, Rabmag, and all the king of Babylon's princes; ¹⁴Even they sent,

---

^a gave . . . : Heb. spake with him judgments
^b captain . . . : or, chief marshal: Heb. chief of the executioners, or, slaughtermen
^c to: Heb. by the hand of

and took Jeremiah out of the court of the prison, and committed him unto Gedaliah the son of Ahikam the son of Shaphan, that he should carry him home: so he dwelt among the people. ¹⁵Now the word of the LORD came unto Jeremiah, while he was shut up in the court of the prison, saying, ¹⁶Go and speak to Ebedmelech the Ethiopian, saying, Thus saith the LORD of hosts, the God of Israel; Behold, I will bring my words upon this city for evil, and not for good; and they shall be *accomplished* in that day before thee. ¹⁷But I will deliver thee in that day, saith the LORD: and thou shalt not be given into the hand of the men of whom thou *art* afraid. ¹⁸For I will surely deliver thee, and thou shalt not fall by the sword, but thy life shall be for a prey unto thee: because thou hast put thy trust in me, saith the LORD.

40

¹The word that came to Jeremiah from the LORD, after that Nebuzaradan the captain of the guard had let him go from Ramah, when he had taken him being bound in chains^a among all that were carried away captive of Jerusalem and Judah, which were carried away captive unto Babylon. ²And the captain of the guard took Jeremiah, and said unto him, The LORD thy God hath pronounced this evil upon this place. ³Now the LORD hath brought *it*, and done according as he hath said: because ye have sinned against the LORD, and have not obeyed his voice, therefore this thing is come upon you. ⁴And now, behold, I loose thee this day from the chains

which *were* upon thine hand. If it seem good unto thee to come with me into Babylon, come; and I will look well unto thee: but if it seem ill unto thee to come with me into Babylon, forbear: behold, all the land *is* before thee: whither it seemeth good and convenient for thee to go, thither go. ⁵Now while he was not yet gone back, *he said*, Go back also to Gedaliah the son of Ahikam the son of Shaphan, whom the king of Babylon hath made governor over the cities of Judah, and dwell with him among the people: or go wheresoever it seemeth convenient unto thee to go. So the captain of the guard gave him victuals and a reward, and let him go. ⁶Then went Jeremiah unto Gedaliah the son of Ahikam to Mizpah; and dwelt with him among the people that were left in the land.

⁷Now when all the captains of the forces which *were* in the fields, *even* they and their men, heard that the king of Babylon had made Gedaliah the son of Ahikam governor in the land, and had committed unto him men, and women, and children, and of the poor of the land, of them that were not carried away captive to Babylon; ⁸Then they came to Gedaliah to Mizpah, even Ishmael the son of Nethaniah, and Johanan and Jonathan the sons of Kareah, and Seraiah the son of Tanhumeth, and the sons of Ephai the Netophathite, and Jezaniah the son of a Maachathite, they and their men. ⁹And Gedaliah the son of Ahikam the son of Shaphan sware unto them and to their men, saying, Fear not to serve the Chaldeans: dwell in the land, and serve the king of Babylon, and it shall be well with you. ¹⁰As for me, behold, I will dwell

---

^a chains: or, manicles

at Mizpah to serve[b] the Chaldeans, which will come unto us: but ye, gather ye wine, and summer fruits, and oil, and put *them* in your vessels, and dwell in your cities that ye have taken. ¹¹Likewise when all the Jews that *were* in Moab, and among the Ammonites, and in Edom, and that *were* in all the countries, heard that the king of Babylon had left a remnant of Judah, and that he had set over them Gedaliah the son of Ahikam the son of Shaphan; ¹²Even all the Jews returned out of all places whither they were driven, and came to the land of Judah, to Gedaliah, unto Mizpah, and gathered wine and summer fruits very much. ¹³Moreover Johanan the son of Kareah, and all the captains of the forces that *were* in the fields, came to Gedaliah to Mizpah, ¹⁴And said unto him, Dost thou certainly know that Baalis the king of the Ammonites hath sent Ishmael the son of Nethaniah to slay[c] thee? But Gedaliah the son of Ahikam believed them not. ¹⁵Then Johanan the son of Kareah spake to Gedaliah in Mizpah secretly, saying, Let me go, I pray thee, and I will slay Ishmael the son of Nethaniah, and no man shall know *it*: wherefore should he slay thee, that all the Jews which are gathered unto thee should be scattered, and the remnant in Judah perish? ¹⁶But Gedaliah the son of Ahikam said unto Johanan the son of Kareah, Thou shalt not do this thing: for thou speakest falsely of Ishmael.

41

¹Now it came to pass in the seventh month, *that* Ishmael the son of Netha-niah the son of Elishama, of the seed royal, and the princes of the king, even ten men with him, came unto Gedaliah the son of Ahikam to Mizpah; and there they did eat bread together in Mizpah. ²Then arose Ishmael the son of Nethaniah, and the ten men that were with him, and smote Gedaliah the son of Ahikam the son of Shaphan with the sword, and slew him, whom the king of Babylon had made governor over the land. ³Ishmael also slew all the Jews that were with him, *even* with Gedaliah, at Mizpah, and the Chaldeans that were found there, *and* the men of war. ⁴And it came to pass the second day after he had slain Gedaliah, and no man knew *it*, ⁵That there came certain from Shechem, from Shiloh, and from Samaria, *even* fourscore men, having their beards shaven, and their clothes rent, and having cut themselves, with offerings and incense in their hand, to bring *them* to the house of the LORD. ⁶And Ishmael the son of Nethaniah went forth from Mizpah to meet them, weeping[a] all along as he went: and it came to pass, as he met them, he said unto them, Come to Gedaliah the son of Ahikam. ⁷And it was *so*, when they came into the midst of the city, that Ishmael the son of Nethaniah slew them, *and cast them* into the midst of the pit, he, and the men that *were* with him. ⁸But ten men were found among them that said unto Ishmael, Slay us not: for we have treasures in the field, of wheat, and of barley, and of oil, and of honey. So he forbare, and slew them not among their brethren. ⁹Now the pit wherein Ishmael

---

[b] to serve: Heb. to stand before
[c] to slay . . . : Heb. to strike thee in soul?
[a] weeping . . . : Heb. in going and weeping

had cast all the dead bodies of the men, whom he had slain because[b] of Gedaliah, *was* it which Asa the king had made for fear of Baasha king of Israel: *and* Ishmael the son of Nethaniah filled it with *them that were* slain. ¹⁰Then Ishmael carried away captive all the residue of the people that *were* in Mizpah, *even* the king's daughters, and all the people that remained in Mizpah, whom Nebuzaradan the captain of the guard had committed to Gedaliah the son of Ahikam: and Ishmael the son of Nethaniah carried them away captive, and departed to go over to the Ammonites.

¹¹But when Johanan the son of Kareah, and all the captains of the forces that *were* with him, heard of all the evil that Ishmael the son of Nethaniah had done, ¹²Then they took all the men, and went to fight with Ishmael the son of Nethaniah, and found him by the great waters that *are* in Gibeon. ¹³Now it came to pass, *that* when all the people which *were* with Ishmael saw Johanan the son of Kareah, and all the captains of the forces that *were* with him, then they were glad. ¹⁴So all the people that Ishmael had carried away captive from Mizpah cast about and returned, and went unto Johanan the son of Kareah. ¹⁵But Ishmael the son of Nethaniah escaped from Johanan with eight men, and went to the Ammonites. ¹⁶Then took Johanan the son of Kareah, and all the captains of the forces that *were* with him, all the remnant of the people whom he had recovered from Ishmael the son of Nethaniah, from Mizpah, after *that* he had slain Gedaliah the son of Ahikam, *even* mighty men of war, and the women, and the children, and the eunuchs, whom he had brought again from Gibeon: ¹⁷And they departed, and dwelt in the habitation of Chimham, which is by Bethlehem, to go to enter into Egypt, ¹⁸Because of the Chaldeans: for they were afraid of them, because Ishmael the son of Nethaniah had slain Gedaliah the son of Ahikam, whom the king of Babylon made governor in the land.

42

¹Then all the captains of the forces, and Johanan the son of Kareah, and Jezaniah the son of Hoshaiah, and all the people from the least even unto the greatest, came near, ²And said unto Jeremiah the prophet, Let, we beseech thee, our supplication[a] be accepted before thee, and pray for us unto the LORD thy God, *even* for all this remnant; (for we are left *but* a few of many, as thine eyes do behold us:) ³That the LORD thy God may shew us the way wherein we may walk, and the thing that we may do. ⁴Then Jeremiah the prophet said unto them, I have heard *you*; behold, I will pray unto the LORD your God according to your words; and it shall come to pass, *that* whatsoever thing the LORD shall answer you, I will declare *it* unto you; I will keep nothing back from you. ⁵Then they said to Jeremiah, The LORD be a true and faithful witness between us, if we do not even according to all things for the which the LORD thy God shall send thee to us. ⁶Whether *it be* good, or whether *it be* evil, we will obey the voice of the LORD our God, to whom we

---

[b] because . . . : or, near Gedaliah: Heb. by the hand, or, by the side of Gedaliah
[a] Let . . . : or, Let our supplication fall before thee

send thee; that it may be well with us, when we obey the voice of the LORD our God.

⁷And it came to pass after ten days, that the word of the LORD came unto Jeremiah. ⁸Then called he Johanan the son of Kareah, and all the captains of the forces which *were* with him, and all the people from the least even to the greatest, ⁹And said unto them, Thus saith the LORD, the God of Israel, unto whom ye sent me to present your supplication before him; ¹⁰If ye will still abide in this land, then will I build you, and not pull *you* down, and I will plant you, and not pluck *you* up: for I repent me of the evil that I have done unto you. ¹¹Be not afraid of the king of Babylon, of whom ye are afraid; be not afraid of him, saith the LORD: for I *am* with you to save you, and to deliver you from his hand. ¹²And I will shew mercies unto you, that he may have mercy upon you, and cause you to return to your own land. ¹³But if ye say, We will not dwell in this land, neither obey the voice of the LORD your God, ¹⁴Saying, No; but we will go into the land of Egypt, where we shall see no war, nor hear the sound of the trumpet, nor have hunger of bread; and there will we dwell: ¹⁵And now therefore hear the word of the LORD, ye remnant of Judah; Thus saith the LORD of hosts, the God of Israel; If ye wholly set your faces to enter into Egypt, and go to sojourn there; ¹⁶Then it shall come to pass, *that* the sword, which ye feared, shall overtake you there in the land of Egypt, and the famine, whereof ye were afraid, shall fol-low close after you there in Egypt; and there ye shall die. ¹⁷So shall it be with all the men that set their faces to go into Egypt to sojourn there; they shall die by the sword, by the famine, and by the pestilence: and none of them shall remain or escape from the evil that I will bring upon them. ¹⁸For thus saith the LORD of hosts, the God of Israel; As mine anger and my fury hath been poured forth upon the inhabitants of Jerusalem; so shall my fury be poured forth upon you, when ye shall enter into Egypt: and ye shall be an execration, and an astonishment, and a curse, and a reproach; and ye shall see this place no more. ¹⁹The LORD hath said concerning you, O ye remnant of Judah; Go ye not into Egypt: know certainly that I have admonished[b] you this day. ²⁰For ye dissembled[c] in your hearts, when ye sent me unto the LORD your God, saying, Pray for us unto the LORD our God; and according unto all that the LORD our God shall say, so declare unto us, and we will do *it.* ²¹And *now* I have this day declared *it* to you; but ye have not obeyed the voice of the LORD your God, nor any *thing* for the which he hath sent me unto you. ²²Now therefore know certainly that ye shall die by the sword, by the famine, and by the pestilence, in the place whither ye desire to go[d] *and* to sojourn.

43

¹And it came to pass, *that* when Jeremiah had made an end of speaking unto all the people all the words of the LORD their God, for which the

---

[b] admonished . . . : Heb. testified against you

[c] ye dissembled . . . : or, ye have used deceit against your souls

[d] to go . . . : or, to go to sojourn

LORD their God had sent him to them, *even* all these words, ²Then spake Azariah the son of Hoshaiah, and Johanan the son of Kareah, and all the proud men, saying unto Jeremiah, Thou speakest falsely: the LORD our God hath not sent thee to say, Go not into Egypt to sojourn there: ³But Baruch the son of Neriah setteth thee on against us, for to deliver us into the hand of the Chaldeans, that they might put us to death, and carry us away captives into Babylon. ⁴So Johanan the son of Kareah, and all the captains of the forces, and all the people, obeyed not the voice of the LORD, to dwell in the land of Judah. ⁵But Johanan the son of Kareah, and all the captains of the forces, took all the remnant of Judah, that were returned from all nations, whither they had been driven, to dwell in the land of Judah; ⁶*Even* men, and women, and children, and the king's daughters, and every person that Nebuzaradan the captain of the guard had left with Gedaliah the son of Ahikam the son of Shaphan, and Jeremiah the prophet, and Baruch the son of Neriah. ⁷So they came into the land of Egypt: for they obeyed not the voice of the LORD: thus came they *even* to Tahpanhes.

⁸Then came the word of the LORD unto Jeremiah in Tahpanhes, saying, ⁹Take great stones in thine hand, and hide them in the clay in the brickkiln, which *is* at the entry of Pharaoh's house in Tahpanhes, in the sight of the men of Judah; ¹⁰And say unto them, Thus saith the LORD of hosts, the God of Israel; Behold, I will send and take Nebuchadrezzar the king of Babylon, my servant, and will set his throne upon these stones that I have hid; and he shall spread his royal pavilion over them. ¹¹And when he cometh, he shall smite the land of Egypt, *and deliver* such *as are* for death to death; and such *as are* for captivity to captivity; and such *as are* for the sword to the sword. ¹²And I will kindle a fire in the houses of the gods of Egypt; and he shall burn them, and carry them away captives: and he shall array himself with the land of Egypt, as a shepherd putteth on his garment; and he shall go forth from thence in peace. ¹³He shall break also the images[a] of Bethshemesh, that *is* in the land of Egypt; and the houses of the gods of the Egyptians shall he burn with fire.

44

¹The word that came to Jeremiah concerning all the Jews which dwell in the land of Egypt, which dwell at Migdol, and at Tahpanhes, and at Noph, and in

---

[a] images: Heb. statues, or, standing images

the country of Pathros, saying, [2]Thus saith the LORD of hosts, the God of Israel; Ye have seen all the evil that I have brought upon Jerusalem, and upon all the cities of Judah; and, behold, this day they *are* a desolation, and no man dwelleth therein, [3]Because of their wickedness which they have committed to provoke me to anger, in that they went to burn incense, *and* to serve other gods, whom they knew not, *neither* they, ye, nor your fathers. [4]Howbeit I sent unto you all my servants the prophets, rising early and sending *them*, saying, Oh, do not this abominable thing that I hate. [5]But they hearkened not, nor inclined their ear to turn from their wickedness, to burn no incense unto other gods. [6]Wherefore my fury and mine anger was poured forth, and was kindled in the cities of Judah and in the streets of Jerusalem; and they are wasted *and* desolate, as at this day. [7]Therefore now thus saith the LORD, the God of hosts, the God of Israel; Wherefore commit ye *this* great evil against your souls, to cut off from you man and woman, child and suckling, out[a] of Judah, to leave you none to remain; [8]In that ye provoke me unto wrath with the works of your hands, burning incense unto other gods in the land of Egypt, whither ye be gone to dwell, that ye might cut yourselves off, and that ye might be a curse and a reproach among all the nations of the earth? [9]Have ye forgotten the wickedness[b] of your fathers, and the wickedness of the kings of Judah, and the

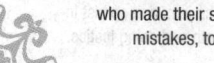

Devotional Moment

Learning from the Past

44:9-10 God was calling the Israelites to learn from past mistakes so they wouldn't repeat them. In one sense every generation moves through its own cycle of mistakes, regrets, and wisdom. But no generation can afford to be oblivious to lessons from the past. Kids, want a good conversation with Mom and Dad? Ask them what lessons they'd like you to learn from your extended family or from the lives of loved ones now deceased, who made their share of mistakes, too.

wickedness of their wives, and your own wickedness, and the wickedness of your wives, which they have committed in the land of Judah, and in the streets of Jerusalem? [10]They are not humbled[c] *even* unto this day, neither have they feared, nor walked in my law, nor in my statutes, that I set before you and before your fathers. [11]Therefore thus saith the LORD of hosts, the God of Israel; Behold, I will set my face against you for evil, and to cut off all Judah. [12]And I will take the remnant of Judah, that have set their faces to go into the land of Egypt to sojourn there, and they shall all be consumed, *and* fall in the land of Egypt; they shall *even* be consumed by the sword *and* by the famine: they shall die, from the least even unto the greatest, by the sword and by the famine: and they shall be an execration, *and* an astonishment, and a curse, and a reproach. [13]For I will punish them that dwell in the land of Egypt, as I

---

[a] out . . . : Heb. out of the midst of Judah
[b] wickedness . . . : Heb. wickednesses, or, punishments, etc
[c] humbled: Heb. contrite

have punished Jerusalem, by the sword, by the famine, and by the pestilence: ¹⁴So that none of the remnant of Judah, which are gone into the land of Egypt to sojourn there, shall escape or remain, that they should return into the land of Judah, to the which they have^d a desire to return to dwell there: for none shall return but such as shall escape.

¹⁵Then all the men which knew that their wives had burned incense unto other gods, and all the women that stood by, a great multitude, even all the people that dwelt in the land of Egypt, in Pathros, answered Jeremiah, saying, ¹⁶*As for* the word that thou hast spoken unto us in the name of the LORD, we will not hearken unto thee. ¹⁷But we will certainly do whatsoever thing goeth forth out of our own mouth, to burn incense unto the queen^e of heaven, and to pour out drink offerings unto her, as we have done, we, and our fathers, our kings, and our princes, in the cities of Judah, and in the streets of Jerusalem: for *then* had we plenty of victuals, and were well, and saw no evil. ¹⁸But since we left off to burn incense to the queen of heaven, and to pour out drink offerings unto her, we have wanted all *things*, and have been consumed by the sword and by the famine. ¹⁹And when we burned incense to the queen of heaven, and poured out drink offerings unto her, did we make her cakes to worship her, and pour out drink offerings unto her, without our men^f?

²⁰Then Jeremiah said unto all the people, to the men, and to the women, and to all the people which had given him *that* answer, saying, ²¹The incense that ye burned in the cities of Judah, and in the streets of Jerusalem, ye, and your fathers, your kings, and your princes, and the people of the land, did not the LORD remember them, and came it *not* into his mind? ²²So that the LORD could no longer bear, because of the evil of your doings, *and* because of the abominations which ye have committed; therefore is your land a desolation, and an astonishment, and a curse, without an inhabitant, as at this day. ²³Because ye have burned incense, and because ye have sinned against the LORD, and have not obeyed the voice of the LORD, nor walked in his law, nor in his statutes, nor in his testimonies; therefore this evil is happened unto you, as at this day. ²⁴Moreover Jeremiah said unto all the people, and to all the women, Hear the word of the LORD, all Judah that *are* in the land of Egypt: ²⁵Thus saith the LORD of hosts, the God of Israel, saying; Ye and your wives have both spoken with your mouths, and fulfilled with your hand, saying, We will surely perform our vows that we have vowed, to burn incense to the queen of heaven, and to pour out drink offerings unto her: ye will surely accomplish your vows, and surely perform your vows. ²⁶Therefore hear ye the word of the LORD, all Judah that dwell in the land of Egypt; Behold, I have sworn by my great name, saith the LORD, that my name shall no more be

---

^d have . . . : Heb. lift up their soul
^e queen . . . : or, frame of heaven
^f men: or, husbands?

named in the mouth of any man of Judah in all the land of Egypt, saying, The Lord GOD liveth. ²⁷Behold, I will watch over them for evil, and not for good: and all the men of Judah that *are* in the land of Egypt shall be consumed by the sword and by the famine, until there be an end of them. ²⁸Yet a small number that escape the sword shall return out of the land of Egypt into the land of Judah, and all the remnant of Judah, that are gone into the land of Egypt to sojourn there, shall know whose words shall stand, mine*, or theirs. ²⁹And this *shall be* a sign unto you, saith the LORD, that I will punish you in this place, that ye may know that my words shall surely stand against you for evil: ³⁰Thus saith the LORD; Behold, I will give Pharaohhophra king of Egypt into the hand of his enemies, and into the hand of them that seek his life; as I gave Zedekiah king of Judah into the hand of Nebuchadrezzar king of Babylon, his enemy, and that sought his life.

45

¹The word that Jeremiah the prophet spake unto Baruch the son of Neriah, when he had written these words in a book at the mouth of Jeremiah, in the fourth year of Jehoiakim the son of Josiah king of Judah, saying, ²Thus saith the LORD, the God of Israel, unto thee, O Baruch; ³Thou didst say, Woe is me now! for the LORD hath added grief to my sorrow; I fainted in my sighing, and I find no rest. ⁴Thus shalt thou say unto him, The LORD saith thus; Behold, *that* which I have

---

Devotional Moment

Attitude of Gratitude

45:2-5 Baruch had put his own career in jeopardy by serving a very unpopular prophet. He had recorded Jeremiah's words and helped him become a success (as prophets measure success). Now he was feeling unappreciated and thinking he deserved "great things" as his reward.

We, too, can feel unappreciated. We often wonder if anyone recognizes our hard work and many sacrifices. The more a person gives, the more he or she wonders. The answer is to look upward, taking the focus off self. Fix your eyes on God and continue serving him wholeheartedly.

---

built will I break down, and that which I have planted I will pluck up, even this whole land. ⁵And seekest thou great things for thyself? seek *them* not: for, behold, I will bring evil upon all flesh, saith the LORD: but thy life will I give unto thee for a prey in all places whither thou goest.

46

¹The word of the LORD which came to Jeremiah the prophet against the Gentiles; ²Against Egypt, against the army of Pharaohnecho king of Egypt, which was by the river Euphrates in Carchemish, which Nebuchadrezzar king of Babylon smote in the fourth year of Jehoiakim the son of Josiah king of Judah. ³Order ye the buckler and shield, and draw near to battle. ⁴Harness the horses; and get up, ye horsemen, and stand forth with *your* helmets; furbish the spears, *and* put on the brigandines. ⁵Wherefore have I seen them dismayed

---

ᵍ mine . . . : Heb. from me, or, from them

and turned away back? and their mighty ones are beaten down, and are fled apace, and look not back: *for* fear *was* round about, saith the LORD. ⁶Let not the swift flee away, nor the mighty man escape; they shall stumble, and fall toward the north by the river Euphrates. ⁷Who *is* this *that* cometh up as a flood, whose waters are moved as the rivers? ⁸Egypt riseth up like a flood, and *his* waters are moved like the rivers; and he saith, I will go up, *and* will cover the earth; I will destroy the city and the inhabitants thereof. ⁹Come up, ye horses; and rage, ye chariots; and let the mighty men come forth; the Ethiopiansᵃ and the Libyans, that handle the shield; and the Lydians, that handle *and* bend the bow. ¹⁰For this *is* the day of the Lord GOD of hosts, a day of vengeance, that he may avenge him of his adversaries: and the sword shall devour, and it shall be satiate and made drunk with their blood: for the Lord GOD of hosts hath a sacrifice in the north country by the river Euphrates. ¹¹Go up into Gilead, and take balm, O virgin, the daughter of Egypt: in vain shalt thou use many medicines; *for* thou shalt not be cured.

¹²The nations have heard of thy shame, and thy cry hath filled the land: for the mighty man hath stumbled against the mighty, *and* they are fallen both together. ¹³The word that the LORD spake to Jeremiah the prophet, how Nebuchadrezzar king of Babylon should come *and* smite the land of Egypt. ¹⁴Declare ye in Egypt, and publish in Migdol, and publish in Noph and in Tahpanhes: say ye, Stand fast, and prepare thee; for the sword shall devour round about thee. ¹⁵Why are thy valiant *men* swept away? they stood not, because the LORD did drive them. ¹⁶He made many to fall, yea, one fell upon another: and they said, Arise, and let us go again to our own people, and to the land of our nativity, from the oppressing sword. ¹⁷They did cry there, Pharaoh king of Egypt *is but* a noise; he hath passed the time appointed. ¹⁸*As* I live, saith the King, whose name *is* the LORD of hosts, Surely as Tabor *is* among the mountains, and as Carmel by the sea, *so* shall he come. ¹⁹O thou daughter dwelling in Egypt, furnishᵇ thyself to go into captivity: for Noph shall be waste and desolate without an inhabitant. ²⁰Egypt *is like* a very fair heifer, *but* destruction cometh; it cometh out of the north. ²¹Also her hired men *are* in the midst of her like fattedᶜ bullocks; for they also are turned back, *and* are fled away together: they did not stand, because the day of their calamity was come upon them, *and* the time of their visitation. ²²The voice thereof shall go like a serpent; for they shall march with an army, and come against her with axes, as hewers of wood. ²³They shall cut down her forest, saith the LORD, though it cannot be searched; because they are more than the grasshoppers, and *are* innumerable. ²⁴The daughter of Egypt shall be confounded; she shall be delivered

---

ᵃ the Ethiopians: Heb. Cush
ᵇ furnish . . . : Heb. make thee instruments of captivity
ᶜ fatted . . . : Heb. bullocks of the stall

Devotional Moment

•

Comfort

46:27-28 The most reassuring words a young child ever hears from a parent are, "Don't be afraid, I'm here." From that point on, facing the world's scariest monster is easy. Babylon was certainly a monster, and Israel was facing it. Yet with the confidence that God was with them, the people could move ahead. Adults sometimes shun such comfort, but anyone who is discouraged or overwhelmed needs it. Aging grandparents need it; parents moving through mid-life need it; children, teens, and young adults need it, too. No matter what our age, God promises to stay with us and lead us home.

into the hand of the people of the north. ²⁵The LORD of hosts, the God of Israel, saith; Behold, I will punish the multitude^d of No, and Pharaoh, and Egypt, with their gods, and their kings; even Pharaoh, and *all* them that trust in him: ²⁶And I will deliver them into the hand of those that seek their lives, and into the hand of Nebuchadrezzar king of Babylon, and into the hand of his servants: and afterward it shall be inhabited, as in the days of old, saith the LORD. ²⁷But fear not thou, O my servant Jacob, and be not dismayed, O Israel: for, behold, I will save thee from afar off, and thy seed from the land of their captivity; and Jacob shall return, and be in rest and at ease, and none shall make *him* afraid. ²⁸Fear thou not, O Jacob my servant, saith the LORD: for I *am* with thee; for I will make a full end of all the na-

tions whither I have driven thee: but I will not make a full end of thee, but correct thee in measure; yet will I not leave thee wholly unpunished.

47

¹The word of the LORD that came to Jeremiah the prophet against the Philistines, before that Pharaoh smote Gaza^a. ²Thus saith the LORD; Behold, waters rise up out of the north, and shall be an overflowing flood, and shall overflow the land, and all that is therein; the city, and them that dwell therein: then the men shall cry, and all the inhabitants of the land shall howl. ³At the noise of the stamping of the hoofs of his strong *horses,* at the rushing of his chariots, *and at* the rumbling of his wheels, the fathers shall not look back to *their* children for feebleness of hands; ⁴Because of the day that cometh to spoil all the Philistines, *and* to cut off from Tyrus and Zidon every helper that remaineth: for the LORD will spoil the Philistines, the remnant of the country^b of Caphtor. ⁵Baldness is come upon Gaza; Ashkelon is cut off *with* the remnant of their valley: how long wilt thou cut thyself? ⁶O thou sword of the LORD, how long *will it be* ere thou be quiet? put up thyself into thy scabbard, rest, and be still. ⁷How can it be quiet, seeing the LORD hath given it a charge against Ashkelon, and against the sea shore? there hath he appointed it.

48

¹Against Moab thus saith the LORD of hosts, the God of Israel; Woe unto

---

^d multitude: or, nourisher: Heb. Amon
^a Gaza: Heb. Azzah
^b the country: Heb. the isle

Nebo! for it is spoiled: Kiriathaim is confounded *and* taken: Misgab[a] is confounded and dismayed. ²*There shall be* no more praise of Moab: in Heshbon they have devised evil against it; come, and let us cut it off from *being* a nation. Also thou shalt be cut down, O Madmen; the sword shall pursue thee. ³A voice of crying *shall be* from Horonaim, spoiling and great destruction. ⁴Moab is destroyed; her little ones have caused a cry to be heard. ⁵For in the going up of Luhith continual[b] weeping shall go up; for in the going down of Horonaim the enemies have heard a cry of destruction. ⁶Flee, save your lives, and be like the heath[c] in the wilderness. ⁷For because thou hast trusted in thy works and in thy treasures, thou shalt also be taken: and Chemosh shall go forth into captivity *with* his priests and his princes together. ⁸And the spoiler shall come upon every city, and no city shall escape: the valley also shall perish, and the plain shall be destroyed, as the LORD hath spoken. ⁹Give wings unto Moab, that it may flee and get away: for the cities thereof shall be desolate, without any to dwell therein. ¹⁰Cursed *be* he that doeth the work of the LORD deceitfully[d], and cursed *be* he that keepeth back his sword from blood. ¹¹Moab hath been at ease from his youth, and he hath settled on his lees, and hath not been emptied from vessel to vessel, neither hath he gone into captivity: there-

fore his taste remained[e] in him, and his scent is not changed. ¹²Therefore, behold, the days come, saith the LORD, that I will send unto him wanderers, that shall cause him to wander, and shall empty his vessels, and break their bottles. ¹³And Moab shall be ashamed of Chemosh, as the house of Israel was ashamed of Bethel their confidence.

¹⁴How say ye, We *are* mighty and strong men for the war? ¹⁵Moab is spoiled, and gone up *out of* her cities, and his chosen young men are gone down to the slaughter, saith the King, whose name *is* the LORD of hosts. ¹⁶The calamity of Moab *is* near to come, and his affliction hasteth fast. ¹⁷All ye that are about him, bemoan him; and all ye that know his name, say, How is the strong staff broken, *and* the beautiful rod! ¹⁸Thou daughter that dost inhabit Dibon, come down from *thy* glory, and sit in thirst; for the spoiler of Moab shall come upon thee, *and* he shall destroy thy strong holds. ¹⁹O inhabitant[f] of Aroer, stand by the way, and espy; ask him that fleeth, and her that escapeth, *and* say, What is done? ²⁰Moab is confounded; for it is broken down: howl and cry; tell ye it in Arnon, that Moab is spoiled, ²¹And judgment is come upon the plain country; upon Holon, and upon Jahazah, and upon Mephaath, ²²And upon Dibon, and upon Nebo, and upon Bethdiblathaim, ²³And upon Kiriathaim, and upon Bethgamul, and upon Beth-

---

[a] Misgab: or, the high place
[b] continual . . . : Heb. weeping with weeping
[c] the heath: or, a naked tree
[d] deceitfully: or, negligently
[e] remained: Heb. stood
[f] inhabitant: Heb. inhabitress

meon, ²⁴And upon Kerioth, and upon Bozrah, and upon all the cities of the land of Moab, far or near. ²⁵The horn of Moab is cut off, and his arm is broken, saith the LORD. ²⁶Make ye him drunken: for he magnified *himself* against the LORD: Moab also shall wallow in his vomit, and he also shall be in derision. ²⁷For was not Israel a derision unto thee? was he found among thieves? for since thou spakest of him, thou skippedst^g for joy. ²⁸O ye that dwell in Moab, leave the cities, and dwell in the rock, and be like the dove *that* maketh her nest in the sides of the hole's mouth. ²⁹We have heard the pride of Moab, (he is exceeding proud) his loftiness, and his arrogancy, and his pride, and the haughtiness of his heart. ³⁰I know his wrath, saith the LORD; but *it shall* not *be* so; his lies^h shall not so effect *it.* ³¹Therefore will I howl for Moab, and I will cry out for all Moab; *mine heart* shall mourn for the men of Kirheres. ³²O vine of Sibmah, I will weep for thee with the weeping of Jazer: thy plants are gone over the sea, they reach *even* to the sea of Jazer: the spoiler is fallen upon thy summer fruits and upon thy vintage. ³³And joy and gladness is taken from the plentiful field, and from the land of Moab; and I have caused wine to fail from the winepresses: none shall tread with shouting; *their* shouting *shall be* no shouting. ³⁴From the cry of Heshbon *even* unto Elealeh, *and even* unto Jahaz, have they uttered their voice, from Zoar *even* unto Horonaim, *as* an heifer of three years old: for the waters also of Nimrim shall be desolate^i. ³⁵Moreover I will cause to cease in Moab, saith the LORD, him that offereth in the high places, and him that burneth incense to his gods. ³⁶Therefore mine heart shall sound for Moab like pipes, and mine heart shall sound like pipes for the men of Kirheres: because the riches *that* he hath gotten are perished. ³⁷For every head *shall be* bald, and every beard clipped^j: upon all the hands *shall be* cuttings, and upon the loins sackcloth. ³⁸*There shall be* lamentation generally upon all the housetops of Moab, and in the streets thereof: for I have broken Moab like a vessel wherein *is* no pleasure, saith the LORD. ³⁹They shall howl, *saying,* How is it broken down! how hath Moab turned the back^k with shame! so shall Moab be a derision and a dismaying to all them about him. ⁴⁰For thus saith the LORD; Behold, he shall fly as an eagle, and shall spread his wings over Moab. ⁴¹Kerioth^l is taken, and the strong holds are surprised, and the mighty men's hearts in Moab at that day shall be as the heart of a woman in her pangs. ⁴²And Moab shall be destroyed from *being* a people, because he hath magnified *himself* against the LORD. ⁴³Fear, and the pit, and the snare, *shall be* upon thee, O inhabitant of Moab, saith the LORD. ⁴⁴He that fleeth from the fear shall fall into the pit; and he that getteth up out

---

^g skippedst . . . : or, movedst thyself
^h his lies . . . : or, those on whom he stayeth (Heb. his bars) do not right
^i desolate: Heb. desolations
^j clipped: Heb. diminished
^k back: Heb. neck
^l Kerioth: or, The cities

of the pit shall be taken in the snare: for I will bring upon it, *even* upon Moab, the year of their visitation, saith the LORD. ⁴⁵They that fled stood under the shadow of Heshbon because of the force: but a fire shall come forth out of Heshbon, and a flame from the midst of Sihon, and shall devour the corner of Moab, and the crown of the head of the tumultuous^m ones. ⁴⁶Woe be unto thee, O Moab! the people of Chemosh perisheth: for thy sons are taken captives, and thy daughters captives. ⁴⁷Yet will I bring again the captivity of Moab in the latter days, saith the LORD. Thus far *is* the judgment of Moab.

49

¹Concerning the Ammonites, thus saith the LORD; Hath Israel no sons? hath he no heir? why *then* doth their king inherit Gad, and his people dwell in his cities? ²Therefore, behold, the days come, saith the LORD, that I will cause an alarm of war to be heard in Rabbah of the Ammonites; and it shall be a desolate heap, and her daughters shall be burned with fire: then shall Israel be heir unto them that were his heirs, saith the LORD. ³Howl, O Heshbon, for Ai is spoiled: cry, ye daughters of Rabbah, gird you with sackcloth; lament, and run to and fro by the hedges; for their king^a shall go into captivity, *and* his priests and his princes together. ⁴Wherefore gloriest thou in the valleys, thy flowing valley, O backsliding daughter? that trusted in her treasures, *saying,* Who shall come unto me? ⁵Behold, I will bring a fear upon thee, saith the Lord GOD of hosts, from all those that be about thee; and ye shall be driven out every man right forth; and none shall gather up him that wandereth. ⁶And afterward I will bring again the captivity of the children of Ammon, saith the LORD.

⁷Concerning Edom, thus saith the LORD of hosts; *Is* wisdom no more in Teman? is counsel perished from the prudent? is their wisdom vanished? ⁸Flee ye, turn back, dwell deep, O inhabitants of Dedan; for I will bring the calamity of Esau upon him, the time *that* I will visit him. ⁹If grapegatherers come to thee, would they not leave *some* gleaning grapes? if thieves by night, they will destroy till they have enough. ¹⁰But I have made Esau bare, I have uncovered his secret places, and he shall not be able to hide himself: his seed is spoiled, and his brethren, and his neighbours, and he *is* not. ¹¹Leave thy fatherless children, I will preserve *them* alive; and let thy widows trust in me. ¹²For thus saith the LORD; Behold, they whose judgment *was* not to drink of the cup have assuredly drunken; and *art* thou he *that* shall altogether go unpunished? thou shalt not go unpunished, but thou shalt surely drink *of it.* ¹³For I have sworn by myself, saith the LORD, that Bozrah shall become a desolation, a reproach, a waste, and a curse; and all the cities thereof shall be perpetual wastes. ¹⁴I have heard a rumour from the LORD, and an ambassador is sent unto the heathen, *saying,* Gather ye together, and come against her, and rise up to the battle. ¹⁵For, lo, I will make thee small among the heathen, *and* despised

---

^m tumultuous . . . : Heb. children of noise
^a their king: or, Melcom

among men. [16]Thy terribleness hath deceived thee, *and* the pride of thine heart, O thou that dwellest in the clefts of the rock, that holdest the height of the hill: though thou shouldest make thy nest as high as the eagle, I will bring thee down from thence, saith the LORD. [17]Also Edom shall be a desolation: every one that goeth by it shall be astonished, and shall hiss at all the plagues thereof. [18]As in the overthrow of Sodom and Gomorrah and the neighbour *cities* thereof, saith the LORD, no man shall abide there, neither shall a son of man dwell in it. [19]Behold, he shall come up like a lion from the swelling of Jordan against the habitation of the strong: but I will suddenly make him run away from her: and who *is* a chosen *man, that* I may appoint over her? for who *is* like me? and who will appoint me the time? and who *is* that shepherd that will stand before me? [20]Therefore hear the counsel of the LORD, that he hath taken against Edom; and his purposes, that he hath purposed against the inhabitants of Teman: Surely the least of the flock shall draw them out: surely he shall make their habitations desolate with them. [21]The earth is moved at the noise of their fall, at the cry the noise thereof was heard in the Red sea[b]. [22]Behold, he shall come up and fly as the eagle, and spread his wings over Bozrah: and at that day shall the heart of the mighty men of Edom be as the heart of a woman in her pangs.

[23]Concerning Damascus. Hamath is confounded, and Arpad: for they have heard evil tidings: they are fainthearted[c]; *there is* sorrow on the sea; it cannot be quiet. [24]Damascus is waxed feeble, *and* turneth herself to flee, and fear hath seized on *her*: anguish and sorrows have taken her, as a woman in travail. [25]How is the city of praise not left, the city of my joy! [26]Therefore her young men shall fall in her streets, and all the men of war shall be cut off in that day, saith the LORD of hosts. [27]And I will kindle a fire in the wall of Damascus, and it shall consume the palaces of Benhadad.

[28]Concerning Kedar, and concerning the kingdoms of Hazor, which Nebuchadrezzar king of Babylon shall smite, thus saith the LORD; Arise ye, go up to Kedar, and spoil the men of the east. [29]Their tents and their flocks shall they take away: they shall take to themselves their curtains, and all their vessels, and their camels; and they shall cry unto them, Fear *is* on every side. [30]Flee, get[d] you far off, dwell deep, O ye inhabitants of Hazor, saith the LORD; for Nebuchadrezzar king of Babylon hath taken counsel against you, and hath conceived a purpose against you. [31]Arise, get you up unto the wealthy[e] nation, that dwelleth without care, saith the LORD, which have neither gates nor bars, *which* dwell alone. [32]And their camels shall be a booty, and the multitude of their cattle a spoil: and I will scatter into all winds them *that are* in the utmost corners; and I will bring

---

[b] Red sea: Heb. Weedy sea
[c] fainthearted: Heb. melted
[d] get . . . : Heb. flit greatly
[e] wealthy: or, that is at ease

their calamity from all sides thereof, saith the LORD. ³³And Hazor shall be a dwelling for dragons, *and* a desolation for ever: there shall no man abide there, nor *any* son of man dwell in it.

³⁴The word of the LORD that came to Jeremiah the prophet against Elam in the beginning of the reign of Zedekiah king of Judah, saying, ³⁵Thus saith the LORD of hosts; Behold, I will break the bow of Elam, the chief of their might. ³⁶And upon Elam will I bring the four winds from the four quarters of heaven, and will scatter them toward all those winds; and there shall be no nation whither the outcasts of Elam shall not come. ³⁷For I will cause Elam to be dismayed before their enemies, and before them that seek their life: and I will bring evil upon them, *even* my fierce anger, saith the LORD; and I will send the sword after them, till I have consumed them: ³⁸And I will set my throne in Elam, and will destroy from thence the king and the princes, saith the LORD. ³⁹But it shall come to pass in the latter days, *that* I will bring again the captivity of Elam, saith the LORD.

50

¹The word that the LORD spake against Babylon *and* against the land of the Chaldeans byᵃ Jeremiah the prophet. ²Declare ye among the nations, and publish, and set upᵇ a standard; publish, *and* conceal not: say, Babylon is taken, Bel is confounded, Merodach is broken in pieces; her idols are confounded, her images are broken in pieces. ³For out of the north there cometh up a nation against her, which shall make her land desolate, and none shall dwell therein: they shall remove, they shall depart, both man and beast. ⁴In those days, and in that time, saith the LORD, the children of Israel shall come, they and the children of Judah together, going and weeping: they shall go, and seek the LORD their God. ⁵They shall ask the way to Zion with their faces thitherward, *saying*, Come, and let us join ourselves to the LORD in a perpetual covenant *that* shall not be forgotten. ⁶My people hath been lost sheep: their shepherds have caused them to go astray, they have turned them away *on* the mountains: they have gone from mountain to hill, they have forgotten their restingplaceᶜ. ⁷All that found them have devoured them: and their adversaries said, We offend not, because they have sinned against the LORD, the habitation of justice, even the LORD, the hope of their fathers. ⁸Remove out of the midst of Babylon, and go forth out of the land of the Chaldeans, and be as the he goats before the flocks.

⁹For, lo, I will raise and cause to come up against Babylon an assembly of great nations from the north country: and they shall set themselves in array against her; from thence she shall be taken: their arrows *shall be* as of a mighty expert man; none shall return in vain. ¹⁰And Chaldea shall be a spoil: all that spoil her shall be satisfied, saith

---

ᵃ by . . . : Heb. by the hand of Jeremiah
ᵇ set up: Heb. lift up
ᶜ restingplace: Heb. place to lie down in

the LORD. [11]Because ye were glad, because ye rejoiced, O ye destroyers of mine heritage, because ye are grown fat[d] as the heifer at grass, and bellow as bulls; [12]Your mother shall be sore confounded; she that bare you shall be ashamed: behold, the hindermost of the nations *shall be* a wilderness, a dry land, and a desert. [13]Because of the wrath of the LORD it shall not be inhabited, but it shall be wholly desolate: every one that goeth by Babylon shall be astonished, and hiss at all her plagues. [14]Put yourselves in array against Babylon round about: all ye that bend the bow, shoot at her, spare no arrows: for she hath sinned against the LORD. [15]Shout against her round about: she hath given her hand: her foundations are fallen, her walls are thrown down: for it *is* the vengeance of the LORD: take vengeance upon her; as she hath done, do unto her. [16]Cut off the sower from Babylon, and him that handleth the sickle[e] in the time of harvest: for fear of the oppressing sword they shall turn every one to his people, and they shall flee every one to his own land. [17]Israel *is* a scattered sheep; the lions have driven *him* away: first the king of Assyria hath devoured him; and last this Nebuchadrezzar king of Babylon hath broken his bones. [18]Therefore thus saith the LORD of hosts, the God of Israel; Behold, I will punish the king of Babylon and his land, as I have punished the king of Assyria. [19]And I will bring Israel again to his habitation, and he shall feed on Carmel and Bashan,

and his soul shall be satisfied upon mount Ephraim and Gilead. [20]In those days, and in that time, saith the LORD, the iniquity of Israel shall be sought for, and *there shall be* none; and the sins of Judah, and they shall not be found: for I will pardon them whom I reserve.

[21]Go up against the land of Merathaim[f], *even* against it, and against the inhabitants of Pekod: waste and utterly destroy after them, saith the LORD, and do according to all that I have commanded thee. [22]A sound of battle *is* in the land, and of great destruction. [23]How is the hammer of the whole earth cut asunder and broken! how is Babylon become a desolation among the nations! [24]I have laid a snare for thee, and thou art also taken, O Babylon, and thou wast not aware: thou art found, and also caught, because thou hast striven against the LORD. [25]The LORD hath opened his armoury, and hath brought forth the weapons of his indignation: for this *is* the work of the Lord GOD of hosts in the land of the Chaldeans. [26]Come against her from the utmost border, open her storehouses: cast her up as heaps, and destroy her utterly: let nothing of her be left. [27]Slay all her bullocks; let them go down to the slaughter: woe unto them! for their day is come, the time of their visitation. [28]The voice of them that flee and escape out of the land of Babylon, to declare in Zion the vengeance of the LORD our God, the vengeance of his temple. [29]Call together

---

[d] fat: Heb. big, or, corpulent
[e] sickle; or, scythe
[f] of Merathaim: or, of the rebels

the archers against Babylon: all ye that bend the bow, camp against it round about; let none thereof escape: recompense her according to her work; according to all that she hath done, do unto her: for she hath been proud against the LORD, against the Holy One of Israel. ³⁰Therefore shall her young men fall in the streets, and all her men of war shall be cut off in that day, saith the LORD. ³¹Behold, I *am* against thee, *O thou* most proud, saith the Lord GOD of hosts: for thy day is come, the time *that* I will visit thee. ³²And the most proud shall stumble and fall, and none shall raise him up: and I will kindle a fire in his cities, and it shall devour all round about him.

³³Thus saith the LORD of hosts; The children of Israel and the children of Judah *were* oppressed together: and all that took them captives held them fast; they refused to let them go. ³⁴Their Redeemer *is* strong; the LORD of hosts

is his name: he shall throughly plead their cause, that he may give rest to the land, and disquiet the inhabitants of Babylon. ³⁵A sword *is* upon the Chaldeans, saith the LORD, and upon the inhabitants of Babylon, and upon her princes, and upon her wise *men*. ³⁶A sword *is* upon the liars⁸; and they shall dote: a sword *is* upon her mighty men; and they shall be dismayed. ³⁷A sword *is* upon their horses, and upon their chariots, and upon all the mingled people that *are* in the midst of her; and they shall become as women: a sword *is* upon her treasures; and they shall be robbed. ³⁸A drought *is* upon her waters; and they shall be dried up: for it *is* the land of graven images, and they are mad upon *their* idols. ³⁹Therefore the wild beasts of the desert with the wild beasts of the islands shall dwell *there*, and the owls shall dwell therein: and it shall be no more inhabited for ever; neither shall it be dwelt in from generation to generation. ⁴⁰As God overthrew Sodom and Gomorrah and the neighbour *cities* thereof, saith the LORD; *so* shall no man abide there, neither shall any son of man dwell therein. ⁴¹Behold, a people shall come from the north, and a great nation, and many kings shall be raised up from the coasts of the earth. ⁴²They shall hold the bow and the lance: they *are* cruel, and will not shew mercy: their voice shall roar like the sea, and they shall ride upon horses, *every one* put in array, like a man to the battle, against thee, O daughter of Babylon. ⁴³The king of Babylon hath heard the report of them, and his hands waxed feeble: anguish took hold of

---

⁸ liars: or, chief stays: Heb. bars

him, *and* pangs as of a woman in travail. ⁴⁴Behold, he shall come up like a lion from the swelling of Jordan unto the habitation of the strong: but I will make them suddenly run away from her: and who *is* a chosen *man, that* I may appoint over her? for who *is* like me? and who will appoint me the time? and who *is* that shepherd that will stand before me? ⁴⁵Therefore hear ye the counsel of the LORD, that he hath taken against Babylon; and his purposes, that he hath purposed against the land of the Chaldeans: Surely the least of the flock shall draw them out: surely he shall make *their* habitation desolate with them. ⁴⁶At the noise of the taking of Babylon the earth is moved, and the cry is heard among the nations.

51

¹Thus saith the LORD; Behold, I will raise up against Babylon, and against them that dwell in the midstª of them that rise up against me, a destroying wind; ²And will send unto Babylon fanners, that shall fan her, and shall empty her land: for in the day of trouble they shall be against her round about. ³Against *him that* bendeth let the archer bend his bow, and against *him that* lifteth himself up in his brigandine: and spare ye not her young men; destroy ye utterly all her host. ⁴Thus the slain shall fall in the land of the Chaldeans, and *they that are* thrust through in her streets. ⁵For Israel *hath* not *been* forsaken, nor Judah of his God, of the

LORD of hosts; though their land was filled with sin against the Holy One of Israel. ⁶Flee out of the midst of Babylon, and deliver every man his soul: be not cut off in her iniquity; for this *is* the time of the LORD'S vengeance; he will render unto her a recompence. ⁷Babylon *hath been* a golden cup in the LORD'S hand, that made all the earth drunken: the nations have drunken of her wine; therefore the nations are mad. ⁸Babylon is suddenly fallen and destroyed: howl for her; take balm for her pain, if so be she may be healed. ⁹We would have healed Babylon, but she is not healed: forsake her, and let us go every one into his own country: for her judgment reacheth unto heaven, and is lifted up *even* to the skies. ¹⁰The LORD hath brought forth our righteousness: come, and let us declare in Zion the work of the LORD our God. ¹¹Make brightᵇ the arrows; gather the shields: the LORD hath raised up the spirit of the kings of the Medes: for his device *is* against Babylon, to destroy it; because it *is* the vengeance of the LORD, the vengeance of his temple. ¹²Set up the standard upon the walls of Babylon, make the watch strong, set up the watchmen, prepare the ambushesᶜ: for the LORD hath both devised and done that which he spake against the inhabitants of Babylon. ¹³O thou that dwellest upon many waters, abundant in treasures, thine end is come, *and* the measure of thy covetousness. ¹⁴The LORD of hosts hath sworn by himselfᵈ, *saying,*

ª midst: Heb. heart
ᵇ bright: Heb. pure
ᶜ ambushes: Heb. liers in wait
ᵈ by himself: Heb. by his soul

Surely I will fill thee with men, as with caterpillers; and they shall lift up a shout against thee. [15]He hath made the earth by his power, he hath established the world by his wisdom, and hath stretched out the heaven by his understanding. [16]When he uttereth *his* voice, *there is* a multitude[e] of waters in the heavens; and he causeth the vapours to ascend from the ends of the earth: he maketh lightnings with rain, and bringeth forth the wind out of his treasures. [17]Every man is brutish[f] by *his* knowledge; every founder is confounded by the graven image: for his molten image *is* falsehood, and *there is* no breath in them. [18]They *are* vanity, the work of errors: in the time of their visitation they shall perish. [19]The portion of Jacob *is* not like them; for he *is* the former of all things: and *Israel is* the rod of his inheritance: the LORD of hosts *is* his name. [20]Thou *art* my battle axe *and* weapons of war: for with thee will I break in pieces the nations, and with thee will I destroy kingdoms; [21]And with thee will I break in pieces the horse and his rider; and with thee will I break in pieces the chariot and his rider; [22]With thee also will I break in pieces man and woman; and with thee will I break in pieces old and young; and with thee will I break in pieces the young man and the maid; [23]I will also break in pieces with thee the shepherd and his flock; and with thee will I break in pieces the husbandman and his yoke of oxen; and with thee will I break in pieces captains and rulers. [24]And I will

render unto Babylon and to all the inhabitants of Chaldea all their evil that they have done in Zion in your sight, saith the LORD. [25]Behold, I *am* against thee, O destroying mountain, saith the LORD, which destroyest all the earth: and I will stretch out mine hand upon thee, and roll thee down from the rocks, and will make thee a burnt mountain. [26]And they shall not take of thee a stone for a corner, nor a stone for foundations; but thou shalt be desolate[g] for ever, saith the LORD. [27]Set ye up a standard in the land, blow the trumpet among the nations, prepare the nations against her, call together against her the kingdoms of Ararat, Minni, and Ashchenaz; appoint a captain against her; cause the horses to come up as the rough caterpillers. [28]Prepare against her the nations with the kings of the Medes, the captains thereof, and all the rulers thereof, and all the land of his dominion. [29]And the land shall tremble and sorrow: for every purpose of the LORD shall be performed against Babylon, to make the land of Babylon a desolation without an inhabitant. [30]The mighty men of Babylon have forborn to fight, they have remained in *their* holds: their might hath failed; they became as women: they have burned her dwellingplaces; her bars are broken. [31]One post shall run to meet another, and one messenger to meet another, to shew the king of Babylon that his city is taken at *one* end, [32]And that the passages are stopped, and the reeds they have burned with fire, and the men of war

---

[e] multitude: or, noise
[f] is brutish . . . : or, is more brutish than to know
[g] desolate . . . : Heb. everlasting desolations

are affrighted. ³³For thus saith the LORD of hosts, the God of Israel; The daughter of Babylon *is* like a threshingfloor, *it is* time to thresh her: yet a little while, and the time of her harvest shall come. ³⁴Nebuchadrezzar the king of Babylon hath devoured me, he hath crushed me, he hath made me an empty vessel, he hath swallowed me up like a dragon, he hath filled his belly with my delicates, he hath cast me out. ³⁵The violence[h] done to me and to my flesh *be* upon Babylon, shall the inhabitant of Zion say; and my blood upon the inhabitants of Chaldea, shall Jerusalem say. ³⁶Therefore thus saith the LORD; Behold, I will plead thy cause, and take vengeance for thee; and I will dry up her sea, and make her springs dry. ³⁷And Babylon shall become heaps, a dwellingplace for dragons, an astonishment, and an hissing, without an inhabitant. ³⁸They shall roar together like lions: they shall yell[i] as lions' whelps. ³⁹In their heat I will make their feasts, and I will make them drunken, that they may rejoice, and sleep a perpetual sleep, and not wake, saith the LORD. ⁴⁰I will bring them down like lambs to the slaughter, like rams with he goats. ⁴¹How is Sheshach taken! and how is the praise of the whole earth surprised! how is Babylon become an astonishment among the nations! ⁴²The sea is come up upon Babylon: she is covered with the multitude of the waves thereof. ⁴³Her cities are a desolation, a dry land, and a wilderness, a land wherein no man dwelleth, neither doth

any son of man pass thereby. ⁴⁴And I will punish Bel in Babylon, and I will bring forth out of his mouth that which he hath swallowed up: and the nations shall not flow together any more unto him: yea, the wall of Babylon shall fall. ⁴⁵My people, go ye out of the midst of her, and deliver ye every man his soul from the fierce anger of the LORD. ⁴⁶And lest your heart faint, and ye fear for the rumour that shall be heard in the land; a rumour shall both come *one* year, and after that in *another* year *shall come* a rumour, and violence in the land, ruler against ruler. ⁴⁷Therefore, behold, the days come, that I will do judgment upon the graven images of Babylon: and her whole land shall be confounded, and all her slain shall fall in the midst of her. ⁴⁸Then the heaven and the earth, and all that *is* therein, shall sing for Babylon: for the spoilers shall come unto her from the north, saith the LORD. ⁴⁹As[j] Babylon *hath caused* the slain of Israel to fall, so at Babylon shall fall the slain of all the earth. ⁵⁰Ye that have escaped the sword, go away, stand not still: remember the LORD afar off, and let Jerusalem come into your mind. ⁵¹We are confounded, because we have heard reproach: shame hath covered our faces: for strangers are come into the sanctuaries of the LORD'S house. ⁵²Wherefore, behold, the days come, saith the LORD, that I will do judgment upon her graven images: and through all her land the wounded shall groan. ⁵³Though Babylon should mount up to heaven, and

---

[h] The violence . . . : Heb. My violence
[i] yell: or, shake themselves
[j] As . . . : or, Both Babylon is to fall, O ye slain of Israel, and with Babylon, etc

though she should fortify the height of her strength, *yet* from me shall spoilers come unto her, saith the LORD. ⁵⁴A sound of a cry *cometh* from Babylon, and great destruction from the land of the Chaldeans: ⁵⁵Because the LORD hath spoiled Babylon, and destroyed out of her the great voice; when her waves do roar like great waters, a noise of their voice is uttered: ⁵⁶Because the spoiler is come upon her, *even* upon Babylon, and her mighty men are taken, every one of their bows is broken: for the LORD God of recompences shall surely requite. ⁵⁷And I will make drunk her princes, and her wise *men*, her captains, and her rulers, and her mighty men: and they shall sleep a perpetual sleep, and not wake, saith the King, whose name *is* the LORD of hosts. ⁵⁸Thus saith the LORD of hosts; The broad^k walls of Babylon shall be utterly broken, and her high gates shall be burned with fire; and the people shall labour in vain, and the folk in the fire, and they shall be weary.

⁵⁹The word which Jeremiah the prophet commanded Seraiah the son of Neriah, the son of Maaseiah, when he went with Zedekiah the king of Judah into Babylon in the fourth year of his reign. And *this* Seraiah *was* a quiet prince. ⁶⁰So Jeremiah wrote in a book all the evil that should come upon Babylon, *even* all these words that are written against Babylon. ⁶¹And Jeremiah said to Seraiah, When thou comest to Babylon, and shalt see, and shalt read all these words; ⁶²Then shalt thou say, O LORD, thou hast spoken against this place, to cut it off, that none shall remain in it, neither man nor beast, but that it shall be desolate^l for ever. ⁶³And it shall be, when thou hast made an end of reading this book, *that* thou shalt bind a stone to it, and cast it into the midst of Euphrates: ⁶⁴And thou shalt say, Thus shall Babylon sink, and shall not rise from the evil that I will bring upon her: and they shall be weary. Thus far *are* the words of Jeremiah.

52

¹Zedekiah *was* one and twenty years old when he began to reign, and he reigned eleven years in Jerusalem. And his mother's name *was* Hamutal the daughter of Jeremiah of Libnah. ²And he did *that which was* evil in the eyes of the LORD, according to all that Jehoiakim had done. ³For through the anger of the LORD it came to pass in Jerusalem and Judah, till he had cast them out from his presence, that Zedekiah rebelled against the king of Babylon. ⁴And it came to pass in the ninth year of his reign, in the tenth month, in the tenth *day* of the month, *that* Nebuchadrezzar king of Babylon came, he and all his army, against Jerusalem, and pitched against it, and built forts against it round about. ⁵So the city was besieged unto the eleventh year of king Zedekiah. ⁶And in the fourth month, in the ninth *day* of the month, the famine was sore in the city, so that there was no bread for the people of the land. ⁷Then the city was broken up, and all the men of war fled, and

---

^k The broad . . . : or, The walls of broad Babylon
^l desolate: Heb. desolations

went forth out of the city by night by the way of the gate between the two walls, which *was* by the king's garden; (now the Chaldeans *were* by the city round about:) and they went by the way of the plain. ⁸But the army of the Chaldeans pursued after the king, and overtook Zedekiah in the plains of Jericho; and all his army was scattered from him. ⁹Then they took the king, and carried him up unto the king of Babylon to Riblah in the land of Hamath; where he gave judgment upon him. ¹⁰And the king of Babylon slew the sons of Zedekiah before his eyes: he slew also all the princes of Judah in Riblah. ¹¹Then he put out* the eyes of Zedekiah; and the king of Babylon bound him in chains, and carried him to Babylon, and put him in prison till the day of his death.

¹²Now in the fifth month, in the tenth *day* of the month, which *was* the nineteenth year of Nebuchadrezzar king of Babylon, came Nebuzaradan, captainᵇ of the guard, *which* served the king of Babylon, into Jerusalem, ¹³And burned the house of the LORD, and the king's house; and all the houses of Jerusalem, and all the houses of the great *men*, burned he with fire: ¹⁴And all the army of the Chaldeans, that *were* with the captain of the guard, brake down all the walls of Jerusalem round about. ¹⁵Then Nebuzaradan the captain of the guard carried away captive *cer-*

tain of the poor of the people, and the residue of the people that remained in the city, and those that fell away, that fell to the king of Babylon, and the rest of the multitude. ¹⁶But Nebuzaradan the captain of the guard left *certain* of the poor of the land for vinedressers and for husbandmen. ¹⁷Also the pillars of brass that *were* in the house of the LORD, and the bases, and the brasen sea that *was* in the house of the LORD, the Chaldeans brake, and carried all the brass of them to Babylon. ¹⁸The caldrons also, and the shovelsᶜ, and the snuffers, and the bowls, and the spoons, and all the vessels of brass wherewith they ministered, took they away. ¹⁹And the basons, and the firepansᵈ, and the bowls, and the caldrons, and the candlesticks, and the spoons, and the cups; *that* which *was* of gold *in* gold, and *that* which *was* of silver *in* silver, took the captain of the guard away. ²⁰The two pillars, one sea, and twelve brasen bulls that *were* under the bases, which king Solomon had made in the house of the LORD: the brassᵉ of all these vessels was without weight. ²¹And *concerning* the pillars, the height of one pillar *was* eighteen cubits; and a filletᶠ of twelve cubits did compass it; and the thickness thereof *was* four fingers: *it was* hollow. ²²And a chapiter of brass *was* upon it; and the height of one chapiter *was* five cubits, with network and pomegranates upon the chapiters round about, all *of*

ᵃ put out: Heb. blinded
ᵇ captain . . . : or, chief marshal: Heb. chief of the executioners, or, slaughtermen
ᶜ shovels: or, instruments to remove the ashes
ᵈ firepans: or, censers
ᵉ the brass: Heb. their brass
ᶠ fillet: Heb. thread

brass. The second pillar also and the pomegranates *were* like unto these. ²³And there were ninety and six pomegranates on a side; *and* all the pomegranates upon the network *were* an hundred round about.

²⁴And the captain of the guard took Seraiah the chief priest, and Zephaniah the second priest, and the three keepers of the door^g: ²⁵He took also out of the city an eunuch, which had the charge of the men of war; and seven men of them that were near^h the king's person, which were found in the city; and the principal scribe of the host, who mustered the people of the land; and threescore men of the people of the land, that were found in the midst of the city. ²⁶So Nebuzaradan the captain of the guard took them, and brought them to the king of Babylon to Riblah. ²⁷And the king of Babylon smote them, and put them to death in Riblah in the land of Hamath. Thus Judah was carried away captive out of his own land. ²⁸This *is* the people whom Nebuchadrezzar carried away captive: in the seventh year three thousand Jews and three and twenty: ²⁹In the eighteenth year of Nebuchadrezzar he carried away captive from Jerusalem eight hundred thirty and two personsⁱ: ³⁰In the three and twentieth year of Nebuchadrezzar Nebuzaradan the captain of the guard carried away captive of the Jews seven hundred forty and five persons: all the persons *were* four thousand and six hundred.

³¹And it came to pass in the seven and thirtieth year of the captivity of Jehoiachin king of Judah, in the twelfth month, in the five and twentieth *day* of the month, *that* Evilmerodach king of Babylon in the *first* year of his reign lifted up the head of Jehoiachin king of Judah, and brought him forth out of prison, ³²And spake kindly^j unto him, and set his throne above the throne of the kings that *were* with him in Babylon, ³³And changed his prison garments: and he did continually eat bread before him all the days of his life. ³⁴And *for* his diet, there was a continual diet given him of the king of Babylon, every^k day a portion until the day of his death, all the days of his life.

---

^g door: Heb. threshold
^h were near . . . : Heb. saw the face of the king
ⁱ persons: Heb. souls
^j kindly . . . : Heb. good things with him
^k every . . . : Heb. the matter of the day in his day

LAMENTATIONS

Purpose
To teach people that to disobey God is to invite disaster and to show that God suffers when his people suffer

Author
Jeremiah

Date Written
Soon after the fall of Jerusalem in 586 B.C.

Setting
Jerusalem had been destroyed by Babylon and her people killed, tortured, or taken captive.

Key Verse
"Mine eyes do fail with tears . . . for the destruction of the daughter of my people; because the children and the sucklings swoon in the streets of the city" (2:11).

Key People
Jeremiah, the people of Jerusalem

Key Place
Jerusalem

Special Features
Three strands of Hebrew thought meet in Lamentations—prophesy, ritual, and wisdom. Lamentations is written in the rhythm and style of ancient Jewish funeral songs or chants. It contains five poems corresponding to the five chapters.

Famous primers of the past taught letters of the alphabet and the Bible at the same time with such statements as:

A is for Adam, who sinned against God.
Z is for Zion, the city of hope.

Lamentations makes its points similarly. The book contains five lament poems, each twenty-two verses long (except the third, which is sixty-six verses long). Poems 1–4, in Hebrew, are similar to the lines from those early primers—three verses begin with the first letter of the alphabet, then three with the second, and so on. These poems express the writer's sadness at the destruction of Solomon's Temple in 586 B.C. Many people think the writer was Jeremiah, and indeed, like the book of his name, Lamentations contains many memorable and oft-quoted sayings.

Children may find it difficult to empathize with all the distress in these poems. God's judgment has fallen on Judah, and the situation here is bleak indeed. Ask the children: What has made you really sad? What helped you smile again? What can help sad people feel happy?

Adults should not skip over the opportunity here, either. Failures, disappointments, accidents—all have left a residue of sadness that needs to be dealt with. What hope does Lamentations point to? How can that hope be effective in your life?

Let Lamentations be the first-aid cream on your cuts and bruises. Let its hope heal your wounds. Let your healing spread to others, like turning back a plague.

1

¹How doth the city sit solitary, *that was* full of people! *how* is she become as a widow! she *that was* great among the nations, *and* princess among the provinces, *how* is she become tributary! ²She weepeth sore in the night, and her tears *are* on her cheeks: among all her lovers she hath none to comfort *her*: all her friends have dealt treacherously with her, they are become her enemies. ³Judah is gone into captivity because of affliction, and because of greatª servitude: she dwelleth among the heathen, she findeth no rest: all her persecutors overtook her between the straits. ⁴The ways of Zion do mourn, because none come to the solemn feasts: all her gates are desolate: her priests sigh, her virgins are afflicted, and she *is* in bitterness. ⁵Her adversaries are the chief, her enemies prosper; for the LORD hath afflicted her for the multitude of her transgressions: her children are gone into captivity before the enemy. ⁶And from the daughter of Zion all her beauty is departed: her princes are become like harts *that* find no pasture, and they are gone without strength before the pursuer. ⁷Jerusalem remembered in the days of her affliction and of her miseries all her pleasant things that she had in the days of old, when her people fell into the hand of the enemy, and none did help her: the adversaries saw her, *and* did mock at her sabbaths. ⁸Jerusalem hath grievously sinned; therefore she is removed: all that honoured her despise her, because they have seen her nakedness: yea, she sigheth, and turneth back-

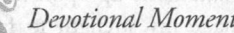
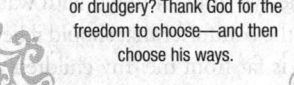
ward. ⁹Her filthiness *is* in her skirts; she remembereth not her last end; therefore she came down wonderfully: she had no comforter. O LORD, behold my affliction: for the enemy hath magnified *himself.* ¹⁰The adversary hath spread out his hand upon all her pleasant things: for she hath seen *that* the heathen entered into her sanctuary, whom thou didst command *that* they should not enter into thy congregation. ¹¹All her people sigh, they seek bread; they have given their pleasant things for meat to relieve the soul: see, O LORD, and consider; for I am become vile.

¹²*Is it* nothing to you, all ye that pass by? behold, and see if there be any sorrow like unto my sorrow, which is done unto me, wherewith the LORD hath afflicted *me* in the day of his fierce anger. ¹³From above hath he sent fire into my bones, and it prevaileth against them: he hath spread a net for my feet, he hath turned me back: he hath made me desolate *and* faint all the day. ¹⁴The yoke of my transgressions is bound by his hand: they are

---

ª because of great . . . : Heb. for the greatness of servitude

1211

wreathed, *and* come up upon my neck: he hath made my strength to fall, the Lord hath delivered me into *their* hands, *from whom* I am not able to rise up. ¹⁵The Lord hath trodden under foot all my mighty *men* in the midst of me: he hath called an assembly against me to crush my young men: the Lord hath trodden the virgin^b, the daughter of Judah, *as* in a winepress. ¹⁶For these *things* I weep; mine eye, mine eye runneth down with water, because the comforter that should relieve^c my soul is far from me: my children are desolate, because the enemy prevailed. ¹⁷Zion spreadeth forth her hands, *and there is* none to comfort her: the LORD hath commanded concerning Jacob, *that* his adversaries *should be* round about him: Jerusalem is as a menstruous woman among them. ¹⁸The LORD is righteous; for I have rebelled against his commandment^d: hear, I pray you, all people, and behold my sorrow: my virgins and my young men are gone into captivity. ¹⁹I called for my lovers, *but* they deceived me: my priests and mine elders gave up the ghost in the city, while they sought their meat to relieve their souls. ²⁰Behold, O LORD; for I *am* in distress: my bowels are troubled; mine heart is turned within me; for I have grievously rebelled: abroad the sword bereaveth, at home *there is* as death. ²¹They have heard that I sigh: *there is* none to comfort me: all mine enemies have heard of my trouble; they are glad that thou hast done *it*:

thou wilt bring the day *that* thou hast called^e, and they shall be like unto me. ²²Let all their wickedness come before thee; and do unto them, as thou hast done unto me for all my transgressions: for my sighs *are* many, and my heart *is* faint.

2

¹How hath the Lord covered the daughter of Zion with a cloud in his anger, *and* cast down from heaven unto the earth the beauty of Israel, and remembered not his footstool in the day of his anger! ²The Lord hath swallowed up all the habitations of Jacob, and hath not pitied: he hath thrown down in his wrath the strong holds of the daughter of Judah; he hath brought *them* down^a to the ground: he hath polluted the kingdom and the princes thereof. ³He hath cut off in *his* fierce anger all the horn of Israel: he hath drawn back his right hand from before the enemy, and he burned against Jacob like a flaming fire, *which* devoureth round about. ⁴He hath bent his bow like an enemy: he stood with his right hand as an adversary, and slew all *that were* pleasant^b to the eye in the tabernacle of the daughter of Zion: he poured out his fury like fire. ⁵The Lord was as an enemy: he hath swallowed up Israel, he hath swallowed up all her palaces: he hath destroyed his strong holds, and hath increased in the daughter of Judah

---

^b the virgin . . . : or, the winepress of the virgin, etc
^c relieve: Heb. bring back
^d commandment: Heb. mouth
^e called: or, proclaimed
^a brought . . . : Heb. made to touch
^b all . . . : Heb. all the desirable of the eye

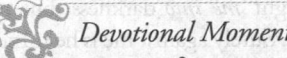

Devotional Moment
•
Worship
2:7 The people of Judah had a beautiful Temple, yet they did not worship God in their day-to-day lives. Their worship services had become a lie and a mockery of God. God requires that people worship in their hearts, irrespective of the outer trappings or rituals. The most organized and spiritually correct devotions cannot make up for a lack of love for God the rest of the day. At home, work, school, or wherever, make your activities an act of worship. Pray for a fresh vision and renewed zeal for God.

mourning and lamentation. ⁶And he hath violently taken away his tabernacleᶜ, as *if it were of* a garden: he hath destroyed his places of the assembly: the LORD hath caused the solemn feasts and sabbaths to be forgotten in Zion, and hath despised in the indignation of his anger the king and the priest. ⁷The Lord hath cast off his altar, he hath abhorred his sanctuary, he hath given upᵈ into the hand of the enemy the walls of her palaces; they have made a noise in the house of the LORD, as in the day of a solemn feast. ⁸The LORD hath purposed to destroy the wall of the daughter of Zion: he hath stretched out a line, he hath not withdrawn his hand from destroyingᵉ: therefore he made the rampart and the wall to lament; they languished together. ⁹Her gates are sunk into the ground; he hath destroyed and broken her bars: her king and her princes *are* among the Gentiles: the law

is no *more*; her prophets also find no vision from the LORD.

¹⁰The elders of the daughter of Zion sit upon the ground, *and* keep silence: they have cast up dust upon their heads; they have girded themselves with sackcloth: the virgins of Jerusalem hang down their heads to the ground. ¹¹Mine eyes do fail with tears, my bowels are troubled, my liver is poured upon the earth, for the destruction of the daughter of my people; because the children and the sucklings swoonᶠ in the streets of the city. ¹²They say to their mothers, Where *is* corn and wine? when they swooned as the wounded in the streets of the city, when their soul was poured out into their mothers' bosom. ¹³What thing shall I take to witness for thee? what thing shall I liken to thee, O daughter of Jerusalem? what shall I equal to thee, that I may comfort thee, O virgin daughter of Zion? for thy breach *is* great like the sea: who can heal thee? ¹⁴Thy prophets have seen vain and foolish things for thee: and they have not discovered thine iniquity, to turn away thy captivity; but have seen for thee false burdens and causes of banishment. ¹⁵All that pass by clap *their* hands at thee; they hiss and wag their head at the daughter of Jerusalem, *saying, Is* this the city that *men* call The perfection of beauty, The joy of the whole earth? ¹⁶All thine enemies have opened their mouth against thee: they hiss and gnash the teeth: they say, We have swallowed *her* up: certainly this *is* the day that we looked for; we have found, we have seen *it*. ¹⁷The LORD hath done

---

ᶜ tabernacle: or, hedge
ᵈ given up: Heb. shut up
ᵉ destroying: Heb. swallowing up
ᶠ swoon: or, faint

that which he had devised; he hath fulfilled his word that he had commanded in the days of old: he hath thrown down, and hath not pitied: and he hath caused *thine* enemy to rejoice over thee, he hath set up the horn of thine adversaries. ¹⁸Their heart cried unto the Lord, O wall of the daughter of Zion, let tears run down like a river day and night: give thyself no rest; let not the apple of thine eye cease. ¹⁹Arise, cry out in the night: in the beginning of the watches pour out thine heart like water before the face of the Lord: lift up thy hands toward him for the life of thy young children, that faint for hunger in the top of every street. ²⁰Behold, O LORD, and consider to whom thou hast done this. Shall the women eat their fruit, *and* children of a span long? shall the priest and the prophet be slain in the sanctuary of the Lord? ²¹The young and the old lie on the ground in the streets: my virgins and my young men are fallen by the sword; thou hast slain *them* in the day of thine anger; thou hast killed, *and* not pitied. ²²Thou hast called as in a solemn day my terrors round about, so that in the day of the LORD'S anger none escaped nor remained: those that I have swaddled and brought up hath mine enemy consumed.

3

¹I *am* the man *that* hath seen affliction by the rod of his wrath. ²He hath led me,

and brought *me into* darkness, but not *into* light. ³Surely against me is he turned; he turneth his hand *against me* all the day. ⁴My flesh and my skin hath he made old; he hath broken my bones. ⁵He hath builded against me, and compassed *me* with gall and travail. ⁶He hath set me in dark places, as *they that be* dead of old. ⁷He hath hedged me about, that I cannot get out: he hath made my chain heavy. ⁸Also when I cry and shout, he shutteth out my prayer. ⁹He hath inclosed my ways with hewn stone, he hath made my paths crooked. ¹⁰He *was* unto me *as* a bear lying in wait, *and as* a lion in secret places. ¹¹He hath turned aside my ways, and pulled me in pieces: he hath made me desolate. ¹²He hath bent his bow, and set me as a mark for the arrow. ¹³He hath caused the arrowsª of his quiver to enter into my reins. ¹⁴I was a derision to all my people; *and* their song all the day. ¹⁵He hath filled me with bitternessᵇ, he hath made me drunken with wormwood. ¹⁶He hath also broken my teeth with gravel stones, he hath coveredᶜ me with ashes. ¹⁷And thou hast removed my soul far off from peace: I forgat prosperityᵈ. ¹⁸And I said, My strength and my hope is perished from the LORD: ¹⁹Rememberingᵉ mine affliction and my misery, the wormwood and the gall. ²⁰My soul hath *them* still in remembrance, and is humbledᶠ in me.

²¹This I recallᵍ to my mind, therefore

ª arrows: Heb. sons
ᵇ bitterness: Heb. bitternesses
ᶜ covered . . . : or, rolled me in the ashes
ᵈ prosperity: Heb. good
ᵉ Remembering: or, Remember
ᶠ humbled: Heb. bowed
ᵍ recall . . . : Heb. make to return to my heart

have I hope. ²²*It is of* the LORD'S mercies that we are not consumed, because his compassions fail not. ²³*They are* new every morning: great *is* thy faithfulness. ²⁴The LORD *is* my portion, saith my soul; therefore will I hope in him. ²⁵The LORD *is* good unto them that wait for him, to the soul *that* seeketh him. ²⁶*It is* good that *a man* should both hope and quietly wait for the salvation of the LORD. ²⁷*It is* good for a man that he bear the yoke in his youth. ²⁸He sitteth alone and keepeth silence, because he hath borne *it* upon him. ²⁹He putteth his mouth in the dust; if so be there may be hope. ³⁰He giveth *his* cheek to him that smiteth him: he is filled full with reproach. ³¹For the Lord will not cast off for ever: ³²But though he cause grief, yet will he have compassion according to the multitude of his mercies. ³³For he doth not afflict willingly[h] nor grieve the children of men. ³⁴To crush under his feet all the prisoners of the earth, ³⁵To turn aside the right of a man before the face of the most High[i], ³⁶To subvert a man in his cause, the Lord approveth not[j].

³⁷Who *is* he *that* saith, and it cometh to pass, *when* the Lord commandeth *it* not? ³⁸Out of the mouth of the most High proceedeth not evil and good? ³⁹Wherefore doth a living man complain[k], a man for the punishment of his sins? ⁴⁰Let us search and try our ways, and turn again to the LORD. ⁴¹Let us lift up our heart with *our* hands unto God in the heavens.

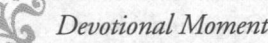

Devotional Moment

Hope

3:21-26 No matter how dark our circumstances, one ray of hope shines through—God's faithfulness and endless mercy. Like Jeremiah, we need to open our eyes in order to see it. Perhaps someone you love is headed down the wrong path, and you feel as though your prayers are going unanswered. God's steadfast love and mercy are meant for you, not just Jerusalem of long ago. If a situation seems hopeless, call a friend. Together, pray that God's ray of hope will reach you.

⁴²We have transgressed and have rebelled: thou hast not pardoned. ⁴³Thou hast covered with anger, and persecuted us: thou hast slain, thou hast not pitied. ⁴⁴Thou hast covered thyself with a cloud, that *our* prayer should not pass through. ⁴⁵Thou hast made us *as* the offscouring and refuse in the midst of the people. ⁴⁶All our enemies have opened their mouths against us. ⁴⁷Fear and a snare is come upon us, desolation and destruction. ⁴⁸Mine eye runneth down with rivers of water for the destruction of the daughter of my people. ⁴⁹Mine eye trickleth down, and ceaseth not, without any intermission, ⁵⁰Till the LORD look down, and behold from heaven. ⁵¹Mine eye affecteth mine heart[l] because of all the daughters of my city. ⁵²Mine enemies chased me sore, like a bird, without cause. ⁵³They have cut off my life in the dungeon, and cast a stone

---

[h] willingly: Heb. from his heart
[i] the most High: or, a superior
[j] approveth not: or, seeth not
[k] complain: or, murmur
[l] mine heart: Heb. my soul

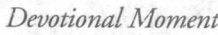

Devotional Moment

Reality Discipline

3:39-42 God's people brought this punishment on themselves, so they had no reason to complain. God did nothing more than make them face the natural consequences of their choices. Sometimes parents want to *protect* their children from all unpleasantness, even if it's an experience the children have brought on themselves. There's a better option. As a general rule, children need to face the natural outcome of their choices if they are ever going to learn to take responsibility for their actions. Don't protect your children from all harsh reality; help them learn to face it.

upon me. [54]Waters flowed over mine head; *then* I said, I am cut off.

[55]I called upon thy name, O LORD, out of the low dungeon. [56]Thou hast heard my voice: hide not thine ear at my breathing, at my cry. [57]Thou drewest near in the day *that* I called upon thee: thou saidst, Fear not. [58]O Lord, thou hast pleaded the causes of my soul; thou hast redeemed my life. [59]O LORD, thou hast seen my wrong: judge thou my cause. [60]Thou hast seen all their vengeance *and* all their imaginations against me. [61]Thou hast heard their reproach, O LORD, *and* all their imaginations against me; [62]The lips of those that rose up against me, and their device against me all the day. [63]Behold their sitting down, and their rising up; I *am* their musick. [64]Render unto them a recompence, O LORD, according to the work of their hands. [65]Give them sorrow[m] of heart, thy curse unto them.

[66]Persecute and destroy them in anger from under the heavens of the LORD.

4

[1]How is the gold become dim! *how* is the most fine gold changed! the stones of the sanctuary are poured out in the top of every street. [2]The precious sons of Zion, comparable to fine gold, how are they esteemed as earthen pitchers, the work of the hands of the potter! [3]Even the sea monsters draw out the breast, they give suck to their young ones: the daughter of my people *is become* cruel, like the ostriches in the wilderness. [4]The tongue of the sucking child cleaveth to the roof of his mouth for thirst: the young children ask bread, *and* no man breaketh *it* unto them. [5]They that did feed delicately are desolate in the streets: they that were brought up in scarlet embrace dunghills. [6]For the punishment of the iniquity[a] of the daughter of my people is greater than the punishment of the sin of Sodom, that was overthrown as in a moment, and no hands stayed on her. [7]Her Nazarites were purer than snow, they were whiter than milk, they were more ruddy in body than rubies, their polishing *was* of sapphire: [8]Their visage is blacker[b] than a coal; they are not known in the streets: their skin cleaveth to their bones; it is withered, it is become like a stick. [9]*They that be* slain with the sword are better than *they that be* slain with hunger: for these pine away, stricken through for *want of* the fruits of the field. [10]The hands of the

---

[m] sorrow . . . : or, obstinacy of heart
[a] punishment of the iniquity: or, iniquity
[b] blacker . . . : Heb. darker than blackness

pitiful women have sodden their own children: they were their meat in the destruction of the daughter of my people. [11]The LORD hath accomplished his fury; he hath poured out his fierce anger, and hath kindled a fire in Zion, and it hath devoured the foundations thereof. [12]The kings of the earth, and all the inhabitants of the world, would not have believed that the adversary and the enemy should have entered into the gates of Jerusalem.

[13]For the sins of her prophets, *and* the iniquities of her priests, that have shed the blood of the just in the midst of her, [14]They have wandered *as* blind *men* in the streets, they have polluted themselves with blood, so that men could not touch their garments. [15]They cried unto them, Depart ye; *it is* unclean; depart, depart, touch not: when they fled away and wandered, they said among the heathen, They shall no more sojourn *there*. [16]The anger[c] of the LORD hath divided them; he will no more regard them: they respected not the persons of the priests, they favoured not the elders. [17]As for us, our eyes as yet failed for our vain help: in our watching we have watched for a nation *that* could not save *us*. [18]They hunt our steps, that we cannot go in our streets: our end is near, our days are fulfilled; for our end is come. [19]Our persecutors are swifter than the eagles of the heaven: they pursued us upon the mountains, they laid wait for us in the wilderness. [20]The breath of our nostrils, the anointed of the LORD, was taken in their pits, of whom we said, Under

his shadow we shall live among the heathen. [21]Rejoice and be glad, O daughter of Edom, that dwellest in the land of Uz; the cup also shall pass through unto thee: thou shalt be drunken, and shalt make thyself naked. [22]The punishment of thine iniquity is accomplished, O daughter of Zion; he will no more carry thee away into captivity: he will visit thine iniquity, O daughter of Edom; he will discover thy sins.

5

[1]Remember, O LORD, what is come upon us: consider, and behold our reproach. [2]Our inheritance is turned to strangers, our houses to aliens. [3]We are orphans and fatherless, our mothers *are* as widows. [4]We have drunken our water for money; our wood is sold unto us. [5]Our necks *are* under persecution: we labour, *and* have no rest. [6]We have given the hand *to* the Egyptians, *and to* the Assyrians, to be satisfied with bread. [7]Our fathers have sinned, *and are* not; and we have borne their iniquities. [8]Servants have ruled over us: *there is* none that doth deliver *us* out of their hand. [9]We gat our bread with *the peril of* our lives because of the sword of the wilderness. [10]Our skin was black like an oven because of the terrible[a] famine. [11]They ravished the women in Zion, *and* the maids in the cities of Judah. [12]Princes are hanged up by their hand: the faces of elders were not honoured. [13]They took the young men to grind, and the children fell under the wood. [14]The elders have ceased from the gate, the

---

[c] anger: or, face
[a] terrible: or, terrors, or, storms

Devotional Moment
•
Hoping for Hope

5:19-21 Jeremiah concluded his lament over
Jerusalem's hopeless condition with a direct
plea to God. Your challenges—emotions,
finances, relationships, problems at school,
health crises—may seem hopeless. But many
times feelings of despair are based on faulty
thinking. Reach out to God, as Jeremiah did. Ask
him to help you see distortions in your thinking,
such as *overgeneralization* ("because things are
bad now, they will always be this way"), *all-or-
nothing thinking* ("God must save me now or he
never will"), and *emotional reasoning* ("because
I *feel* hopeless, the situation *is* hopeless").
What are the problems that seem
hopeless to you? Ask God to
restore your hope.

young men from their musick. ¹⁵The
joy of our heart is ceased; our dance is
turned into mourning. ¹⁶The crown is
fallen *from* our head: woe unto us, that
we have sinned!

¹⁷For this our heart is faint; for these
things our eyes are dim. ¹⁸Because of the
mountain of Zion, which is desolate, the
foxes walk upon it. ¹⁹Thou, O LORD, remainest for ever; thy throne from generation to generation. ²⁰Wherefore dost thou
forget us for ever, *and* forsake us so long
time? ²¹Turn thou us unto thee, O
LORD, and we shall be turned; renew
our days as of old. ²²But thou hast utterly
rejected us; thou art very wroth against us.

EZEKIEL

Purpose
To announce God's judgment
on Israel and other nations
and to foretell the eventual
salvation of God's people

Author
Ezekiel—the son of Buzi, a
Zadokite priest

To Whom Written
The Jews in captivity in
Babylon and God's people
everywhere

Date Written
Approximately 571 B.C.

Setting
Ezekiel was a younger contemporary of Jeremiah.
While Jeremiah ministered
to the people still in Judah,
Ezekiel prophesied to those
already exiled in Babylon after the defeat of Jehoiachin.
He was among the captives
taken there in 597 B.C.

Key Verses
"A new heart also will I give
you, and a new spirit will I
put within you: and I will take
away the stony heart out of
your flesh, and I will give you
an heart of flesh" (36:26).

Key People
Ezekiel, Israel's leaders,
Ezekiel's wife, Nebuchad-
nezzar, the "Prince"

Key Places
Jerusalem, Babylon, and Egypt

If you think it's hard to focus on God when the water heater and the carburetor both give up on the same day, when three children each need birthday presents for three friends, or when relatives visit by surprise, consider Ezekiel.

This prophet saw his nation plundered, went as a captive to Babylon, and later watched the Persians waste Babylon. He became a priest at Israel's darkest hour. God was judging the nation in their desperate defeat, and recovery was a long way off. No quick fixes to this mess-up.

Even Ezekiel's family felt the pain of holy anger. Not far into the book, you'll notice that Ezekiel's wife became a symbol of the nation. She died. Ezekiel, mourning, was instructed to show no grief in public. His ordeal was to teach the people of Israel the burden of their sin.

Like other prophets, Ezekiel reminds us that life carries penalties for wrongdoing. In Israel's case, penalties had a divine link. Too often we fail to see that our hardship may be God's way of breaking into our comfortable lives to get us moving upward.

Like other prophets, Ezekiel knew that despair was not the end of the story. His charge to Israel to hope in God is our invitation also.

Hope in God, Ezekiel would say, when children get in trouble. Hope in God when aging parents take ill. Hope in God when the layoff comes. Hope, for God will deliver us.

1

¹Now it came to pass in the thirtieth year, in the fourth *month*, in the fifth *day* of the month, as I *was* among the captivesᵃ by the river of Chebar, *that* the heavens were opened, and I saw visions of God. ²In the fifth *day* of the month, which *was* the fifth year of king Jehoiachin's captivity, ³The word of the LORD came expressly unto Ezekielᵇ the priest, the son of Buzi, in the land of the Chaldeans by the river Chebar; and the hand of the LORD was there upon him.

⁴And I looked, and, behold, a whirlwind came out of the north, a great cloud, and a fire infoldingᶜ itself, and a brightness *was* about it, and out of the midst thereof as the colour of amber, out of the midst of the fire. ⁵Also out of the midst thereof *came* the likeness of four living creatures. And this *was* their appearance; they had the likeness of a man. ⁶And every one had four faces, and every one had four wings. ⁷And their feet *were* straightᵈ feet; and the sole of their feet *was* like the sole of a calf's foot: and they sparkled like the colour of burnished brass. ⁸And *they had* the hands of a man under their wings on their four sides; and they four had their faces and their wings. ⁹Their wings *were* joined one to another; they turned not when they went; they went every one straight forward. ¹⁰As for the likeness of their faces, they four had the face of a man, and the face of a lion, on the right side: and they four had the face of an ox on the left side; they four also had the face of an eagle. ¹¹Thus *were* their faces: and their wings *were* stretchedᵉ upward; two *wings* of every one *were* joined one to another, and two covered their bodies. ¹²And they went every one straight forward: whither the spirit was to go, they went; *and* they turned not when they went. ¹³As for the likeness of the living creatures, their appearance *was* like burning coals of fire, *and* like the appearance of lamps: it went up and down among the living creatures; and the fire was bright, and out of the fire went forth lightning. ¹⁴And the living creatures ran and returned as the appearance of a flash of lightning.

¹⁵Now as I beheld the living creatures, behold one wheel upon the earth by the living creatures, with his four faces. ¹⁶The appearance of the wheels and their work *was* like unto the colour of a beryl: and they four had one likeness: and their appearance and their work *was* as it were a wheel in the middle of a wheel. ¹⁷When they went, they went upon their four sides: *and* they turned not when they went. ¹⁸As for their rings, they were so high that they were dreadful; and their ringsᶠ *were* full of eyes round about them four. ¹⁹And when the living creatures went, the wheels went by them: and when the liv-

---

ᵃ captives: Heb. captivity
ᵇ Ezekiel: Heb. Jehezkel
ᶜ infolding . . . : Heb. catching itself
ᵈ straight . . . : Heb. a straight foot
ᵉ stretched . . . : or, divided above
ᶠ and their rings: or, and their strakes

ing creatures were lifted up from the earth, the wheels were lifted up. ²⁰Whithersoever the spirit was to go, they went, thither *was their* spirit to go; and the wheels were lifted up over against them: for the spirit of the living creature *was* in the wheels. ²¹When those went, *these* went; and when those stood, *these* stood; and when those were lifted up from the earth, the wheels were lifted up over against them: for the spirit of the living creatures *was* in the wheels. ²²And the likeness of the firmament upon the heads of the living creature *was* as the colour of the terrible crystal, stretched forth over their heads above. ²³And under the firmament *were* their wings straight, the one toward the other: every one had two, which covered on this side, and every one had two, which covered on that side, their bodies. ²⁴And when they went, I heard the noise of their wings, like the noise of great waters, as the voice of the Almighty, the voice of speech, as the noise of an host: when they stood, they let down their wings. ²⁵And there was a voice from the firmament that *was* over their heads, when they stood, *and* had let down their wings.

²⁶And above the firmament that *was* over their heads *was* the likeness of a throne, as the appearance of a sapphire stone: and upon the likeness of the throne *was* the likeness as the appearance of a man above upon it. ²⁷And I saw as the colour of amber, as the appearance of fire round about within it, from the appearance of his loins even upward, and from the appearance of his loins even downward, I saw as it were the appearance of fire, and it had brightness round about. ²⁸As the appearance of the bow that is in the cloud in the day of rain, so *was* the appearance of the brightness round about. This *was* the appearance of the likeness of the glory of the LORD. And when I saw *it,* I fell upon my face, and I heard a voice of one that spake.

2

¹And he said unto me, Son of man, stand upon thy feet, and I will speak unto thee. ²And the spirit entered into me when he spake unto me, and set me upon my feet, that I heard him that spake unto me. ³And he said unto me, Son of man, I send thee to the children of Israel, to a rebellious nation[a] that hath rebelled against me: they and their fathers have transgressed against me, *even* unto this very day. ⁴For *they are* impudent[b] children and stiffhearted. I do

---

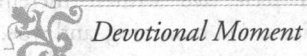

Devotional Moment

True Success

2:3-5 God called Ezekiel to prophesy to a very stubborn people. The measure of his success was his obedience to the Lord, not the response of the exiled Jews. Like Ezekiel, we are called to obey God regardless of how successful we seem to be to others. Much of what we do both in and out of the home is repetitive and exhausting and would not make an impressive entry on a résumé. Yet we can claim "success" in God's eyes if we are obedient to his call to love. Do you feel like a failure if you can't check off a staggering list of tangible accomplishments? Ask God for strength and wisdom to be a success for him.

---

[a] nation: Heb. nations
[b] impudent: Heb. hard of face

send thee unto them; and thou shalt say unto them, Thus saith the Lord GOD. ⁵And they, whether they will hear, or whether they will forbear, (for they *are* a rebellious house,) yet shall know that there hath been a prophet among them.

⁶And thou, son of man, be not afraid of them, neither be afraid of their words, though briersᶜ and thorns *be* with thee, and thou dost dwell among scorpions: be not afraid of their words, nor be dismayed at their looks, though they *be* a rebellious house. ⁷And thou shalt speak my words unto them, whether they will hear, or whether they will forbear: for they *are* most rebellious. ⁸But thou, son of man, hear what I say unto thee; Be not thou rebellious like that rebellious house: open thy mouth, and eat that I give thee. ⁹And when I looked, behold, an hand *was* sent unto me; and, lo, a roll of a book *was* therein; ¹⁰And he spread it before me; and it *was* written within and without: and *there was* written therein lamentations, and mourning, and woe.

3

¹Moreover he said unto me, Son of man, eat that thou findest; eat this roll, and go speak unto the house of Israel. ²So I opened my mouth, and he caused me to eat that roll. ³And he said unto me, Son of man, cause thy belly to eat, and fill thy bowels with this roll that I give thee. Then did I eat *it*; and it was in my mouth as honey for sweetness. ⁴And he said unto me, Son of man, go,

---

Devotional Moment

•

Devotion to Devotions

3:1-3 The scroll that God commanded Ezekiel to eat—God's Word—tasted like honey. God wants the Bible to be our "food." Just as meals are a regular and desirable part of each day, devotions sustain your spiritual health. Hold devotions, even if it's only occasionally and informally. Read the Bible and pray with others. Share with friends and family ideas and suggestions. Try different approaches, including acting out Bible stories, taking turns leading the devotions. Be creative and make it fun!

---

get thee unto the house of Israel, and speak with my words unto them. ⁵For thou *art* not sent to a people of a strange speech and of an hardᵃ language, *but* to the house of Israel; ⁶Not to many people of a strange speech and of an hardᵇ language, whose words thou canst not understand. Surely, had I sent thee to them, they would have hearkened unto thee. ⁷But the house of Israel will not hearken unto thee; for they will not hearken unto me: for all the house of Israel *are* impudentᶜ and hardhearted. ⁸Behold, I have made thy face strong against their faces, and thy forehead strong against their foreheads. ⁹As an adamant harder than flint have I made thy forehead: fear them not, neither be dismayed at their looks, though they *be* a rebellious house. ¹⁰Moreover he said unto me, Son of man, all my words that I shall speak unto thee receive in thine heart, and hear with thine

---

ᶜ briers . . . : or, rebels
ᵃ of a . . . : Heb. deep of lip, and heavy of tongue
ᵇ of a . . . : Heb. deep of lip, and heavy of language
ᶜ impudent . . . : Heb. stiff of forehead, and hard of heart

ears. ¹¹And go, get thee to them of the captivity, unto the children of thy people, and speak unto them, and tell them, Thus saith the Lord GOD; whether they will hear, or whether they will forbear. ¹²Then the spirit took me up, and I heard behind me a voice of a great rushing, *saying*, Blessed *be* the glory of the LORD from his place. ¹³*I heard* also the noise of the wings of the living creatures that touched*ᵈ one another, and the noise of the wheels over against them, and a noise of a great rushing. ¹⁴So the spirit lifted me up, and took me away, and I went in bitternessᵉ, in the heat of my spirit; but the hand of the LORD was strong upon me. ¹⁵Then I came to them of the captivity at Telabib, that dwelt by the river of Chebar, and I sat where they sat, and remained there astonished among them seven days.

¹⁶And it came to pass at the end of seven days, that the word of the LORD came unto me, saying, ¹⁷Son of man, I

Devotional Moment

Feelings

3:14-15 Ezekiel had just received a powerful vision from God. Suddenly, he was whisked away to the unenviable job of speaking God's truth to stubborn and belligerent people. Despite feeling stunned for seven days, Ezekiel still had to do his job. Your roles as a parent, spouse, in-law, or employee can put you on an emotional roller coaster; yet at some point you must fulfill your responsibilities. While feelings are an important part of who we are, we must not be driven by them. Take time in each day to relax and refresh yourself from the pressures; then do what you must do.

---

have made thee a watchman unto the house of Israel: therefore hear the word at my mouth, and give them warning from me. ¹⁸When I say unto the wicked, Thou shalt surely die; and thou givest him not warning, nor speakest to warn the wicked from his wicked way, to save his life; the same wicked *man* shall die in his iniquity; but his blood will I require at thine hand. ¹⁹Yet if thou warn the wicked, and he turn not from his wickedness, nor from his wicked way, he shall die in his iniquity; but thou hast delivered thy soul. ²⁰Again, When a righteous *man* doth turn from his righteousness, and commit iniquity, and I lay a stumblingblock before him, he shall die: because thou hast not given him warning, he shall die in his sin, and his righteousness which he hath done shall not be remembered; but his blood will I require at thine hand. ²¹Nevertheless if thou warn the righteous *man*, that the righteous sin not, and he doth not sin, he shall surely live, because he is warned; also thou hast delivered thy soul.

²²And the hand of the LORD was there upon me; and he said unto me, Arise, go forth into the plain, and I will there talk with thee. ²³Then I arose, and went forth into the plain: and, behold, the glory of the LORD stood there, as the glory which I saw by the river of Chebar: and I fell on my face. ²⁴Then the spirit entered into me, and set me upon my feet, and spake with me, and said unto me, Go, shut thyself within thine house. ²⁵But thou, O son of man, behold, they shall put bands upon thee,

---

ᵈ touched: Heb. kissed
ᵉ in bitterness: Heb. bitter

and shall bind thee with them, and thou shalt not go out among them: ²⁶And I will make thy tongue cleave to the roof of thy mouth, that thou shalt be dumb, and shalt not be to them a reproverᶠ: for they *are* a rebellious house. ²⁷But when I speak with thee, I will open thy mouth, and thou shalt say unto them, Thus saith the Lord GOD; He that heareth, let him hear; and he that forbeareth, let him forbear: for they *are* a rebellious house.

4

¹Thou also, son of man, take thee a tile, and lay it before thee, and pourtray upon it the city, *even* Jerusalem: ²And lay siege against it, and build a fort against it, and cast a mount against it; set the camp also against it, and set *battering* rams against it round about. ³Moreover take thou unto thee an ironᵃ pan, and set it *for* a wall of iron between thee and the city: and set thy face against it, and it shall be besieged, and thou shalt lay siege against it. This *shall be* a sign to the house of Israel. ⁴Lie thou also upon thy left side, and lay the iniquity of the house of Israel upon it: *according* to the number of the days that thou shalt lie upon it thou shalt bear their iniquity. ⁵For I have laid upon thee the years of their iniquity, according to the number of the days, three hundred and ninety days: so shalt thou bear the iniquity of the house of Israel. ⁶And when thou hast accomplished them, lie again on thy right side, and thou shalt bear the iniquity of

the house of Judah forty days: I have appointed thee each day for a year. ⁷Therefore thou shalt set thy face toward the siege of Jerusalem, and thine arm *shall be* uncovered, and thou shalt prophesy against it. ⁸And, behold, I will lay bands upon thee, and thou shalt not turn thee from one side to another, till thou hast ended the days of thy siege.

⁹Take thou also unto thee wheat, and barley, and beans, and lentiles, and millet, and fitchesᵇ, and put them in one vessel, and make thee bread thereof, *according* to the number of the days that thou shalt lie upon thy side, three hundred and ninety days shalt thou eat thereof. ¹⁰And thy meat which thou shalt eat *shall be* by weight, twenty shekels a day: from time to time shalt thou eat it. ¹¹Thou shalt drink also water by measure, the sixth part of an hin: from time to time shalt thou drink. ¹²And thou shalt eat it *as* barley cakes, and thou shalt bake it with dung that cometh out of man, in their sight. ¹³And the LORD said, Even thus shall the children of Israel eat their defiled bread among the Gentiles, whither I will drive them. ¹⁴Then said I, Ah Lord GOD! behold, my soul hath not been polluted: for from my youth up even till now have I not eaten of that which dieth of itself, or is torn in pieces; neither came there abominable flesh into my mouth. ¹⁵Then he said unto me, Lo, I have given thee cow's dung for man's dung, and thou shalt prepare thy bread therewith. ¹⁶Moreover he said unto me, Son of man, behold, I will break the

---

ᶠ a reprover: Heb. a man reproving
ᵃ an iron . . . : or, a flat plate, or, slice
ᵇ fitches: or, spelt

staff of bread in Jerusalem: and they shall eat bread by weight, and with care; and they shall drink water by measure, and with astonishment: ¹⁷That they may want bread and water, and be astonied one with another, and consume away for their iniquity.

5

¹And thou, son of man, take thee a sharp knife, take thee a barber's razor, and cause it to pass upon thine head and upon thy beard: then take thee balances to weigh, and divide the hair. ²Thou shalt burn with fire a third part in the midst of the city, when the days of the siege are fulfilled: and thou shalt take a third part, and smite about it with a knife: and a third part thou shalt scatter in the wind; and I will draw out a sword after them. ³Thou shalt also take thereof a few in number, and bind them in thy skirtsᵃ. ⁴Then take of them again, and cast them into the midst of the fire, and burn them in the fire; for thereof shall a fire come forth into all the house of Israel.

⁵Thus saith the Lord GOD; This is Jerusalem: I have set it in the midst of the nations and countries that are round about her. ⁶And she hath changed my judgments into wickedness more than the nations, and my statutes more than the countries that are round about her: for they have refused my judgments and my statutes, they have not walked in them. ⁷Therefore thus saith the Lord GOD; Because ye multiplied more than the nations that are round about you, and have not walked in my statutes, nei-

ther have kept my judgments, neither have done according to the judgments of the nations that are round about you; ⁸Therefore thus saith the Lord GOD; Behold, I, even I, am against thee, and will execute judgments in the midst of thee in the sight of the nations. ⁹And I will do in thee that which I have not done, and whereunto I will not do any more the like, because of all thine abominations. ¹⁰Therefore the fathers shall eat the sons in the midst of thee, and the sons shall eat their fathers; and I will execute judgments in thee, and the whole remnant of thee will I scatter into all the winds. ¹¹Wherefore, as I live, saith the Lord GOD; Surely, because thou hast defiled my sanctuary with all thy detestable things, and with all thine abominations, therefore will I also diminish thee; neither shall mine eye spare, neither will I have any pity. ¹²A third part of thee shall die with the pestilence, and with famine shall they be consumed in the midst of thee: and

---

Devotional Moment

Consistent Discipline

5:13 God was angry and jealous. He said that he would punish the Israelites for their sins. And they could be sure he would keep his word. Many parents, by contrast, give warning after warning and never follow through. They say, "I'm not going to tell you again"—but then they do. Do you follow through on your warnings? Take note of your inconsistencies, and resolve to improve. Make a pact with your spouse to hold each other accountable to be true to your word.

ᵃ skirts: Heb. wings

Taking Time to Be Alone with God

by Roger C. Palms

Ezekiel's heart must have been beating fast when God told him, "Arise, go forth into the plain, and I will there talk with thee." God wanted to talk with Ezekiel alone, away from everyone else. What was he going to say? What would God ask Ezekiel to do?

Ezekiel obeyed, and the glory of the Lord met him there. That time was like no other for Ezekiel. He experienced the very presence of God. It was a time with the Holy God in his glory.

It is not easy to find time to be alone with God. Certainly it isn't always convenient. We tend to say, "God can speak to me while I'm working or commuting or shopping or playing golf." But God said then and says now, "We need to get away from the interruptions. We need focused time with each other." Ezekiel had to make the conscious decision to go out into the plain—then he had to do it.

Learning to meet with God alone was not easy for me at first. It was a struggle to keep the appointment I knew he wanted. But I couldn't ignore the invitation. I knew, too, that if I tried to ignore it, I would never really know what God wanted for me. My days would only be my own, incomplete and confusing. I had lived like that before; I didn't want to live like that anymore.

But I found that I couldn't do it. The desire for sleep kept winning.

Finally, after a lot of struggle, I asked a friend to help me. He would call me to get up early, and we would meet to pray together. For the first few days we only walked together to become accustomed to the new schedule. Then we began to pray. Slowly I adjusted to the new experience. I realized I had to go to bed earlier and change my whole life around in order to have that morning time with God.

God has honored that commitment. Now it is ingrained in me—a habit, perhaps, but a necessary one. No matter where I am in the world, and no matter what time I'm obliged to get up in the morning, I know that the first part of the day is meant for God. Now I have a wonderful sense of freedom in that morning worship, a desire for God's presence. I am full of anticipation.

Not everyone can have time with God in the morning, of course. I have a friend who takes the last half hour of his day to be quiet with God, reading the Word and praying. And one young mom told me that the only place she can get alone for a quiet time with God is in the bath. So that's what she does. It is her time, and no one disturbs her.

Susanna Wesley (the mother of John and Charles) had nineteen children. She had neither a lot of time nor a quiet place to go for devotions. She got around that by putting her apron over her head. The children knew that when her apron was up, Mother was talking to God, and they left her alone.

The way of meeting God varies with each one of us, but the need for that time with God is the same. We all need the renewal, blessing, strength, and encouragement that comes from confession and from filling our mind with God's Word. As we do that, we gain a sense of wonder and anticipation as he walks into the day with us. We know that whatever the day ahead holds, God is there.

God's compassion is there for me, new, every morning. I need that, and that's what gets me up early each morning. To be alone with God, to soak up his Word so that it becomes a part of me, has become an absolute need. That's why when God says, "Arise, go forth into the plain," I'm eager to go. Ezekiel has recorded that call of God. It has become a call to me.

DIGGING DEEPER
    1. Jesus took quiet time alone after hearing about the death of John the Baptist (Matt. 14:13); yet notice his busy day and how he finally got his time alone. See Matthew 14:23-24.
    2. At least one of the psalm writers went to be alone with God. Notice his pleas and discoveries in Psalms 139–143.

a third part shall fall by the sword round about thee; and I will scatter a third part into all the winds, and I will draw out a sword after them. [13]Thus shall mine anger be accomplished, and I will cause my fury to rest upon them, and I will be comforted: and they shall know that I the LORD have spoken *it* in my zeal, when I have accomplished my fury in them. [14]Moreover I will make thee waste, and a reproach among the nations that *are* round about thee, in the sight of all that pass by. [15]So it shall be a reproach and a taunt, an instruction and an astonishment unto the nations that *are* round about thee, when I shall execute judgments in thee in anger and in fury and in furious rebukes. I the LORD have spoken *it*. [16]When I shall send upon them the evil arrows of famine, which shall be for *their* destruction, *and* which I will send to destroy you: and I will increase the famine upon you, and will break your staff of bread: [17]So will I send upon you famine and evil beasts, and they shall bereave thee; and pestilence and blood shall pass through thee; and I will bring the sword upon thee. I the LORD have spoken *it.*

6

[1]And the word of the LORD came unto me, saying, [2]Son of man, set thy face toward the mountains of Israel, and prophesy against them, [3]And say, Ye mountains of Israel, hear the word of the Lord GOD; Thus saith the Lord GOD to the mountains, and to the hills, to the rivers, and to the valleys; Behold, I, *even* I, will bring a sword upon you, and I will destroy your high places. [4]And your altars shall be desolate, and your images[a] shall be broken: and I will cast down your slain *men* before your idols. [5]And I will lay[b] the dead carcases of the children of Israel before their idols; and I will scatter your bones round about your altars. [6]In all your dwellingplaces the cities shall be laid waste, and the high places shall be desolate; that your altars may be laid waste and made desolate, and your idols may be broken and cease, and your images may be

---

[a] images: or, sun images
[b] lay: Heb. give

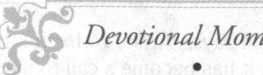

cut down, and your works may be abolished. ⁷And the slain shall fall in the midst of you, and ye shall know that I *am* the LORD.

⁸Yet will I leave a remnant, that ye may have *some* that shall escape the sword among the nations, when ye shall be scattered through the countries. ⁹And they that escape of you shall remember me among the nations whither they shall be carried captives, because I am broken with their whorish heart, which hath departed from me, and with their eyes, which go a whoring after their idols: and they shall lothe themselves for the evils which they have committed in all their abominations. ¹⁰And they shall know that I *am* the LORD, *and that* I have not said in vain that I would do this evil unto them.

¹¹Thus saith the Lord GOD; Smite with thine hand, and stamp with thy foot, and say, Alas for all the evil abominations of the house of Israel! for they shall fall by the sword, by the famine, and by the pestilence. ¹²He that is far off shall die of the pestilence; and

he that is near shall fall by the sword; and he that remaineth and is besieged shall die by the famine: thus will I accomplish my fury upon them. ¹³Then shall ye know that I *am* the LORD, when their slain *men* shall be among their idols round about their altars, upon every high hill, in all the tops of the mountains, and under every green tree, and under every thick oak, the place where they did offer sweet savour to all their idols. ¹⁴So will I stretch out my hand upon them, and make the land desolate, yea, more desolate than the wilderness toward Diblath, in all their habitations: and they shall know that I *am* the LORD.

7

¹Moreover the word of the LORD came unto me, saying, ²Also, thou son of man, thus saith the Lord GOD unto the land of Israel; An end, the end is come upon the four corners of the land. ³Now *is* the end *come* upon thee, and I will send mine anger upon thee, and will judge thee according to thy ways, and will recompense[a] upon thee all thine abominations. ⁴And mine eye shall not spare thee, neither will I have pity: but I will recompense thy ways upon thee, and thine abominations shall be in the midst of thee: and ye shall know that I *am* the LORD. ⁵Thus saith the Lord GOD; An evil, an only evil, behold, is come. ⁶An end is come, the end is come: it watcheth for thee; behold, it is come. ⁷The morning is come unto thee, O thou that dwellest in the land: the time is come, the day of trouble *is* near, and not the sounding again of the mountains. ⁸Now will I shortly pour out my fury

---

ᵃ recompense: Heb. give

upon thee, and accomplish mine anger upon thee: and I will judge thee according to thy ways, and will recompense thee for all thine abominations. ⁹And mine eye shall not spare, neither will I have pity: I will recompense thee according to thy ways and thine abominations *that* are in the midst of thee; and ye shall know that I *am* the LORD that smiteth. ¹⁰Behold the day, behold, it is come: the morning is gone forth; the rod hath blossomed, pride hath budded. ¹¹Violence is risen up into a rod of wickedness: none of them *shall remain*, nor of their multitude, nor of any of theirs: neither *shall there be* wailing[b] for them. ¹²The time is come, the day draweth near: let not the buyer rejoice, nor the seller mourn: for wrath *is* upon all the multitude thereof. ¹³For the seller shall not return to that which is sold, although they were yet alive: for the vision *is* touching the whole multitude thereof, *which* shall not return; neither shall any strengthen himself in the iniquity of his life. ¹⁴They have blown the trumpet, even to make all ready; but none goeth to the battle: for my wrath *is* upon all the multitude thereof. ¹⁵The sword *is* without, and the pestilence and the famine within: he that *is* in the field shall die with the sword; and he that *is* in the city, famine and pestilence shall devour him.

¹⁶But they that escape of them shall escape, and shall be on the mountains like doves of the valleys, all of them mourning, every one for his iniquity. ¹⁷All hands shall be feeble, and all knees shall be weak[c]

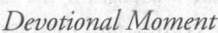

Devotional Moment
•
Money
7:19-20 God's people had let their love for money lead them into sin, even to the point of making idols out of gold that had been reserved for decorating the Temple. God gives resources to accomplish his will and his work. But individual or family desires can subtly, usually over time, draw money away from God's work. Has your giving increased or decreased in recent years? How do you and your spouse make stewardship decisions? Over what issues do you have the most disagreement?

as water. ¹⁸They shall also gird *themselves* with sackcloth, and horror shall cover them; and shame *shall be* upon all faces, and baldness upon all their heads. ¹⁹They shall cast their silver in the streets, and their gold shall be removed[d]: their silver and their gold shall not be able to deliver them in the day of the wrath of the LORD: they shall not satisfy their souls, neither fill their bowels: because it is the stumblingblock of their iniquity. ²⁰As for the beauty of his ornament, he set it in majesty: but they made the images of their abominations *and* of their detestable things therein: therefore have I set it far[e] from them. ²¹And I will give it into the hands of the strangers for a prey, and to the wicked of the earth for a spoil; and they shall pollute it. ²²My face will I turn also from them, and they shall pollute my secret *place*: for the robbers[f] shall enter into it, and defile it.

---

[b] theirs: or, their tumultuous persons: Heb. tumult
[c] be weak . . . : Heb. go into water
[d] removed: Heb. for a separation, or, uncleanness
[e] set it far . . . : or, made it unto them an unclean thing
[f] robbers: or, buglers

²³Make a chain: for the land is full of bloody crimes, and the city is full of violence. ²⁴Wherefore I will bring the worst of the heathen, and they shall possess their houses: I will also make the pomp of the strong to cease; and their holy places shall be defiled. ²⁵Destruction^g cometh; and they shall seek peace, and *there shall be* none. ²⁶Mischief shall come upon mischief, and rumour shall be upon rumour; then shall they seek a vision of the prophet; but the law shall perish from the priest, and counsel from the ancients. ²⁷The king shall mourn, and the prince shall be clothed with desolation, and the hands of the people of the land shall be troubled: I will do unto them after their way, and according to their deserts will I judge them; and they shall know that I *am* the LORD.

8

¹And it came to pass in the sixth year, in the sixth *month*, in the fifth *day* of the month, *as* I sat in mine house, and the elders of Judah sat before me, that the hand of the Lord GOD fell there upon me. ²Then I beheld, and lo a likeness as the appearance of fire: from the appearance of his loins even downward, fire; and from his loins even upward, as the appearance of brightness, as the colour of amber. ³And he put forth the form of an hand, and took me by a lock of mine head; and the spirit lifted me up between the earth and the heaven, and brought me in the visions of God to Jerusalem, to the door of the inner gate that looketh toward the north; where *was* the seat of the image of jealousy, which provoketh to jealousy. ⁴And, behold, the glory of the God of Israel *was* there, according to the vision that I saw in the plain. ⁵Then said he unto me, Son of man, lift up thine eyes now the way toward the north. So I lifted up mine eyes the way toward the north, and behold northward at the gate of the altar this image of jealousy in the entry. ⁶He said furthermore unto me, Son of man, seest thou what they do? *even* the great abominations that the house of Israel committeth here, that I should go far off from my sanctuary? but turn thee yet again, *and* thou shalt see greater abominations.

⁷And he brought me to the door of the court; and when I looked, behold a hole in the wall. ⁸Then said he unto me, Son of man, dig now in the wall: and when I had digged in the wall, behold a door. ⁹And he said unto me, Go in, and behold the wicked abominations that they do here. ¹⁰So I went in and saw; and behold every form of creeping things, and abominable beasts, and all the idols of the house of Israel, pourtrayed upon the wall round about. ¹¹And there stood before them seventy men of the ancients of the house of Israel, and in the midst of them stood Jaazaniah the son of Shaphan, with every man his censer in his hand; and a thick cloud of incense went up. ¹²Then said he unto me, Son of man, hast thou seen what the ancients of the house of Israel do in the dark, every man in the chambers of his imagery? for they say, The LORD seeth us not; the LORD hath forsaken the earth.

¹³He said also unto me, Turn thee yet again, *and* thou shalt see greater

---

^g Destruction: Heb. Cutting off

abominations that they do. ¹⁴Then he brought me to the door of the gate of the LORD'S house which *was* toward the north; and, behold, there sat women weeping for Tammuz. ¹⁵Then said he unto me, Hast thou seen *this*, O son of man? turn thee yet again, *and* thou shalt see greater abominations than these. ¹⁶And he brought me into the inner court of the LORD'S house, and, behold, at the door of the temple of the LORD, between the porch and the altar, *were* about five and twenty men, with their backs toward the temple of the LORD, and their faces toward the east; and they worshipped the sun toward the east. ¹⁷Then he said unto me, Hast thou seen *this*, O son of man? Is it a light thing to the house of Judah that they commit the abominations which they commit here? for they have filled the land with violence, and have returned to provoke me to anger: and, lo, they put the branch to their nose. ¹⁸Therefore will I also deal in fury: mine eye shall not spare, neither will I have pity: and though they cry in mine ears with a loud voice, *yet* will I not hear them.

9

¹He cried also in mine ears with a loud voice, saying, Cause them that have charge over the city to draw near, even every man *with* his destroying weapon in his hand. ²And, behold, six men came from the way of the higher gate,

which lieth^a toward the north, and every man a slaughter weapon in his hand; and one man among them *was* clothed with linen, with a writer's inkhorn by his side: and they went in, and stood beside the brasen altar. ³And the glory of the God of Israel was gone up from the cherub, whereupon he was, to the threshold of the house. And he called to the man clothed with linen, which *had* the writer's inkhorn by his side; ⁴And the LORD said unto him, Go through the midst of the city, through the midst of Jerusalem, and set a mark^b upon the foreheads of the men that sigh and that cry for all the abominations that be done in the midst thereof.

⁵And to the others he said in mine hearing^c, Go ye after him through the city, and smite: let not your eye spare, neither have ye pity: ⁶Slay utterly^d old *and* young, both maids, and little children, and women: but come not near any man upon whom *is* the mark; and begin at my sanctuary. Then they began at the ancient men which *were* before the house. ⁷And he said unto them, Defile the house, and fill the courts with the slain: go ye forth. And they went forth, and slew in the city. ⁸And it came to pass, while they were slaying them, and I was left, that I fell upon my face, and cried, and said, Ah Lord GOD! wilt thou destroy all the residue of Israel in thy pouring out of thy fury upon Jerusalem? ⁹Then said he unto me, The iniquity of the house of Israel and Ju-

---

^{a} which lieth: Heb. which is turned
^{b} set a mark: Heb. mark a mark
^{c} mine hearing: Heb. mine ears
^{d} utterly: Heb. to destruction

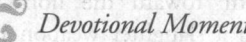

Devotional Moment
·
Rationalizing

9:9-10 The people said that God had gone away and didn't see their sin. People still have convenient excuses for sin: "It's not hurting anybody," "Everybody's doing it," or "Don't I deserve it?" Have you heard rationalizations like these in your household? What standards do your children observe in you and your spouse? What standards are they adopting for themselves? Have a family discussion about wrong being wrong, even if nobody finds out about it. And remind each other that God knows our heart, even when other people don't.

dah *is* exceeding great, and the land is full of blood[e], and the city full of perverseness: for they say, The LORD hath forsaken the earth, and the LORD seeth not. [10]And as for me also, mine eye shall not spare, neither will I have pity, *but* I will recompense their way upon their head. [11]And, behold, the man clothed with linen, which *had* the inkhorn by his side, reported[f] the matter, saying, I have done as thou hast commanded me.

10

[1]Then I looked, and, behold, in the firmament that was above the head of the cherubims there appeared over them as it were a sapphire stone, as the appearance of the likeness of a throne. [2]And he spake unto the man clothed with linen, and said, Go in between the wheels, *even* under the cherub, and fill thine hand[a] with coals of fire from between the cherubims, and scatter *them* over the city. And he went in in my sight. [3]Now the cherubims stood on the right side of the house, when the man went in; and the cloud filled the inner court. [4]Then the glory of the LORD went up[b] from the cherub, *and stood* over the threshold of the house; and the house was filled with the cloud, and the court was full of the brightness of the LORD'S glory. [5]And the sound of the cherubims' wings was heard *even* to the outer court, as the voice of the Almighty God when he speaketh. [6]And it came to pass, *that* when he had commanded the man clothed with linen, saying, Take fire from between the wheels, from between the cherubims; then he went in, and stood beside the wheels. [7]And *one* cherub stretched forth[c] his hand from between the cherubims unto the fire that *was* between the cherubims, and took *thereof,* and put *it* into the hands of *him that was* clothed with linen: who took *it,* and went out.

[8]And there appeared in the cherubims the form of a man's hand under their wings. [9]And when I looked, behold the four wheels by the cherubims, one wheel by one cherub, and another wheel by another cherub: and the appearance of the wheels *was* as the colour of a beryl stone. [10]And *as for* their appearances, they four had one likeness, as if a wheel

---

[e] full of blood: Heb. filled with, etc

[f] reported . . . : Heb. returned the word

[a] thine hand: Heb. the hollow of thine hand

[b] went up: Heb. was lifted up

[c] stretched forth: Heb. sent forth

had been in the midst of a wheel.
¹¹When they went, they went upon their
four sides; they turned not as they went,
but to the place whither the head looked
they followed it; they turned not as they
went. ¹²And their whole body^d, and their
backs, and their hands, and their wings,
and the wheels, *were* full of eyes round
about, *even* the wheels that they four
had. ¹³As for the wheels, it was cried unto
them in my hearing, O wheel. ¹⁴And
every one had four faces: the first face
was the face of a cherub, and the second
face *was* the face of a man, and the third
the face of a lion, and the fourth the face
of an eagle. ¹⁵And the cherubims were
lifted up. This *is* the living creature that
I saw by the river of Chebar. ¹⁶And when
the cherubims went, the wheels went by
them: and when the cherubims lifted up
their wings to mount up from the earth,
the same wheels also turned not from
beside them. ¹⁷When they stood, *these*
stood; and when they were lifted up,
these lifted up themselves *also*: for the
spirit of the living creature *was* in them.
¹⁸Then the glory of the LORD departed
from off the threshold of the house, and
stood over the cherubims. ¹⁹And the
cherubims lifted up their wings, and
mounted up from the earth in my sight:
when they went out, the wheels also
were beside them, and *every one* stood at
the door of the east gate of the LORD'S
house; and the glory of the God of Israel
was over them above. ²⁰This *is* the living
creature that I saw under the God of Israel by the river of Chebar; and I knew
that they *were* the cherubims. ²¹Every
one had four faces apiece, and every one
four wings; and the likeness of the hands

of a man *was* under their wings. ²²And
the likeness of their faces *was* the same
faces which I saw by the river of Chebar,
their appearances and themselves: they
went every one straight forward.

11

¹Moreover the spirit lifted me up, and
brought me unto the east gate of the
LORD'S house, which looketh eastward: and behold at the door of the
gate five and twenty men; among
whom I saw Jaazaniah the son of Azur,
and Pelatiah the son of Benaiah, princes
of the people. ²Then said he unto me,
Son of man, these *are* the men that devise mischief, and give wicked counsel
in this city: ³Which say, *It is* not near;
let us build houses: this *city is* the caldron, and we *be* the flesh. ⁴Therefore
prophesy against them, prophesy, O
son of man. ⁵And the Spirit of the
LORD fell upon me, and said unto me,
Speak; Thus saith the LORD; Thus
have ye said, O house of Israel: for I
know the things that come into your
mind, *every one of* them. ⁶Ye have multiplied your slain in this city, and ye
have filled the streets thereof with the
slain. ⁷Therefore thus saith the Lord
GOD; Your slain whom ye have laid in
the midst of it, they *are* the flesh, and
this *city is* the caldron: but I will bring
you forth out of the midst of it. ⁸Ye
have feared the sword; and I will bring
a sword upon you, saith the Lord
GOD. ⁹And I will bring you out of the
midst thereof, and deliver you into the
hands of strangers, and will execute
judgments among you. ¹⁰Ye shall fall by
the sword; I will judge you in the bor-

---

^d body: Heb. flesh

Devotional Moment
•
In God We Trust

11:3-7, 16 The disobedient people in Jerusalem wanted to rebuild their city, thinking it would protect them. But God told them it wouldn't. Then God went on to promise his protection to the righteous remnant, far from Jerusalem.

It's easy to think we've got it made when the kids (and our bank accounts) are healthy, our job is secure, and we have a nice home and possessions. This passage cautions us against trusting in circumstances or material things for security. Only God can ultimately protect us, and his ability to do so is totally unrelated to our outward circumstances. Where are you placing your trust today?

der of Israel; and ye shall know that I *am* the LORD. [11]This *city* shall not be your caldron, neither shall ye be the flesh in the midst thereof; *but* I will judge you in the border of Israel: [12]And ye shall know that I *am* the LORD: for ye have not walked in my statutes, neither executed my judgments, but have done after the manners of the heathen that *are* round about you. [13]And it came to pass, when I prophesied, that Pelatiah the son of Benaiah died. Then fell I down upon my face, and cried with a loud voice, and said, Ah Lord GOD! wilt thou make a full end of the remnant of Israel?

[14]Again the word of the LORD came unto me, saying, [15]Son of man, thy brethren, *even* thy brethren, the men of thy kindred, and all the house of Israel wholly, *are* they unto whom the inhabitants of Jerusalem have said, Get you far from the LORD: unto us is this land given in possession. [16]Therefore say, Thus saith the Lord GOD; Although I have cast them far off among the heathen, and although I have scattered them among the countries, yet will I be to them as a little sanctuary in the countries where they shall come. [17]Therefore say, Thus saith the Lord GOD; I will even gather you from the people, and assemble you out of the countries where ye have been scattered, and I will give you the land of Israel. [18]And they shall come thither, and they shall take away all the detestable things thereof and all the abominations thereof from thence. [19]And I will give them one heart, and I will put a new spirit within you; and I will take the stony heart out of their flesh, and will give them an heart of flesh: [20]That they may walk in my statutes, and keep mine ordinances, and do them: and they shall be my people, and I will be their God. [21]But *as for them* whose heart walketh after the heart of their detestable things and their abominations, I will recompense their way upon their own heads, saith the Lord GOD.

[22]Then did the cherubims lift up

Devotional Moment
•
Family Unity

11:19-20 The Israelites were disobedient to God and had no sense of unity. God's answer? One heart and a new spirit to replace their old heart of stone. Having "one heart" does not imply that people will be identical, unthinking clones who all feel the same about everything. But the Lord does long for families to be united together through him. In what ways is your family not pulling together? Are there telltale signs of disunity and disobedience to God? Ask God to give your family "one heart" for him.

their wings, and the wheels beside them; and the glory of the God of Israel *was* over them above. ²³And the glory of the LORD went up from the midst of the city, and stood upon the mountain which *is* on the east side of the city. ²⁴Afterwards the spirit took me up, and brought me in a vision by the Spirit of God into Chaldea, to them of the captivity. So the vision that I had seen went up from me. ²⁵Then I spake unto them of the captivity all the things that the LORD had shewed me.

12

¹The word of the LORD also came unto me, saying, ²Son of man, thou dwellest in the midst of a rebellious house, which have eyes to see, and see not; they have ears to hear, and hear not: for they *are* a rebellious house. ³Therefore, thou son of man, prepare thee stuff ᵃ for removing, and remove by day in their sight; and thou shalt remove from thy place to another place in their sight: it may be they will consider, though they *be* a rebellious house. ⁴Then shalt thou bring forth thy stuff by day in their sight, as stuff for removing: and thou shalt go forth at even in their sight, as they that go forth into captivity. ⁵Digᵇ thou through the wall in their sight, and carry out thereby. ⁶In their sight shalt thou bear *it* upon *thy* shoulders, *and* carry *it* forth in the twilight: thou shalt cover thy face, that thou see not the ground: for I have set thee *for* a sign unto the house of Israel.

⁷And I did so as I was commanded: I brought forth my stuff by day, as stuff for captivity, and in the even I diggedᶜ through the wall with mine hand; I brought *it* forth in the twilight, *and* I bare *it* upon *my* shoulder in their sight. ⁸And in the morning came the word of the LORD unto me, saying, ⁹Son of man, hath not the house of Israel, the rebellious house, said unto thee, What doest thou? ¹⁰Say thou unto them, Thus saith the Lord GOD; This burden *concerneth* the prince in Jerusalem, and all the house of Israel that *are* among them. ¹¹Say, I *am* your sign: like as I have done, so shall it be done unto them: they shall remove *and* go into captivity. ¹²And the prince that *is* among them shall bear upon *his* shoulder in the twilight, and shall go forth: they shall dig through the wall to carry out thereby: he shall cover his face, that he see not the ground with *his* eyes. ¹³My net also will I spread upon him, and he shall be taken in my snare: and I will bring him to Babylon *to* the land of the Chaldeans; yet shall he not see it, though he shall die there. ¹⁴And I will scatter toward every wind all that *are* about him to help him, and all his bands; and I will draw out the sword after them. ¹⁵And they shall know that I *am* the LORD, when I shall scatter them among the nations, and disperse them in the countries. ¹⁶But I will leave a fewᵈ men of them from the sword, from the famine, and from the pestilence; that they may declare all their

---

ᵃ stuff: or, instruments
ᵇ Dig . . . : Heb. Dig for thee
ᶜ digged: Heb. digged for me
ᵈ a few . . . : Heb. men of number

abominations among the heathen whither they come; and they shall know that I *am* the LORD.

¹⁷Moreover the word of the LORD came to me, saying, ¹⁸Son of man, eat thy bread with quaking, and drink thy water with trembling and with carefulness; ¹⁹And say unto the people of the land, Thus saith the Lord GOD of the inhabitants of Jerusalem, *and* of the land of Israel; They shall eat their bread with carefulness, and drink their water with astonishment, that her land may be desolate from all that is therein, because of the violence of all them that dwell therein. ²⁰And the cities that are inhabited shall be laid waste, and the land shall be desolate; and ye shall know that I *am* the LORD.

²¹And the word of the LORD came unto me, saying, ²²Son of man, what *is* that proverb *that* ye have in the land of Israel, saying, The days are prolonged, and every vision faileth? ²³Tell them therefore, Thus saith the Lord GOD; I will make this proverb to cease, and they shall no more use it as a proverb in Israel; but say unto them, The days are at hand, and the effect of every vision. ²⁴For there shall be no more any vain vision nor flattering divination within the house of Israel. ²⁵For I *am* the LORD: I will speak, and the word that I shall speak shall come to pass; it shall be no more prolonged: for in your days, O rebellious house, will I say the word, and will perform it, saith the Lord GOD. ²⁶Again the word of the LORD came to me, saying, ²⁷Son of man, behold, *they of* the

house of Israel say, The vision that he seeth *is* for many days *to come*, and he prophesieth of the times *that are* far off. ²⁸Therefore say unto them, Thus saith the Lord GOD; There shall none of my words be prolonged any more, but the word which I have spoken shall be done, saith the Lord GOD.

13

¹And the word of the LORD came unto me, saying, ²Son of man, prophesy against the prophets of Israel that prophesy, and say thou unto them that prophesy out of their own hearts, Hear ye the word of the LORD; ³Thus saith the Lord GOD; Woe unto the foolish prophets, that follow^a their own spirit, and have seen nothing! ⁴O Israel, thy prophets are like the foxes in the deserts. ⁵Ye have not gone up into the gaps^b, neither made up the hedge for the house of Israel to stand in the battle in the day of the LORD. ⁶They have seen vanity and lying divination, saying, The LORD saith: and the LORD hath not sent them: and they have made *others* to hope that they would confirm the word. ⁷Have ye not seen a vain vision, and have ye not spoken a lying divination, whereas ye say, The LORD saith *it*; albeit I have not spoken? ⁸Therefore thus saith the Lord GOD; Because ye have spoken vanity, and seen lies, therefore, behold, I *am* against you, saith the Lord GOD. ⁹And mine hand shall be upon the prophets that see vanity, and that divine lies: they shall not be in the assembly^c of my peo-

---

^a follow: Heb. walk after
^b gaps: or, breaches
^c assembly: or, secret, or, counsel

ple, neither shall they be written in the writing of the house of Israel, neither shall they enter into the land of Israel; and ye shall know that I *am* the Lord GOD.

¹⁰Because, even because they have seduced my people, saying, Peace; and *there was* no peace; and one built up a wall[d], and, lo, others daubed it with untempered *morter*: ¹¹Say unto them which daub *it* with untempered *morter*, that it shall fall: there shall be an overflowing shower; and ye, O great hailstones, shall fall; and a stormy wind shall rend *it*. ¹²Lo, when the wall is fallen, shall it not be said unto you, Where *is* the daubing wherewith ye have daubed *it*? ¹³Therefore thus saith the Lord GOD; I will even rend *it* with a stormy wind in my fury; and there shall be an overflowing shower in mine anger, and great hailstones in *my* fury to consume *it*. ¹⁴So will I break down the wall that ye have daubed with untempered *morter*, and bring it down to the ground, so that the foundation thereof shall be discovered, and it shall fall, and ye shall be consumed in the midst thereof: and ye shall know that I *am* the LORD. ¹⁵Thus will I accomplish my wrath upon the wall, and upon them that have daubed it with untempered *morter*, and will say unto you, The wall *is* no *more*, neither they that daubed it; ¹⁶*To wit*, the prophets of Israel which prophesy concerning Jerusalem, and which see visions of peace for her, and *there is* no peace, saith the Lord GOD.

¹⁷Likewise, thou son of man, set thy face against the daughters of thy people, which prophesy out of their own heart; and prophesy thou against them, ¹⁸And say, Thus saith the Lord GOD; Woe to the *women* that sew pillows to all armholes[e], and make kerchiefs upon the head of every stature to hunt souls! Will ye hunt the souls of my people, and will ye save the souls alive *that come* unto you? ¹⁹And will ye pollute me among my people for handfuls of barley and for pieces of bread, to slay the souls that should not die, and to save the souls alive that should not live, by your lying to my people that hear *your* lies? ²⁰Wherefore thus saith the Lord GOD; Behold, I *am* against your pillows, wherewith ye there hunt the souls to make *them* fly[f], and I will tear them from your arms, and will let the souls go, *even* the souls that ye hunt to make *them* fly. ²¹Your kerchiefs also will I tear, and deliver my people out of your hand, and they shall be no more in your hand to be hunted; and ye shall know that I *am* the LORD. ²²Because with lies ye have made the heart of the righteous sad, whom I have not made sad; and strengthened the hands of the wicked, that he should not return from his wicked way, by promising him life: ²³Therefore ye shall see no more vanity, nor divine divinations: for I will deliver my people out of your hand: and ye shall know that I *am* the LORD.

14

¹Then came certain of the elders of Israel unto me, and sat before me. ²And the

---

[d] a wall: or, a slight wall
[e] armholes: or, elbows
[f] to make . . . : or, into gardens

word of the LORD came unto me, saying, [3]Son of man, these men have set up their idols in their heart, and put the stumblingblock of their iniquity before their face: should I be enquired of at all by them? [4]Therefore speak unto them, and say unto them, Thus saith the Lord GOD; Every man of the house of Israel that setteth up his idols in his heart, and putteth the stumblingblock of his iniquity before his face, and cometh to the prophet; I the LORD will answer him that cometh according to the multitude of his idols; [5]That I may take the house of Israel in their own heart, because they are all estranged from me through their idols. [6]Therefore say unto the house of Israel, Thus saith the Lord GOD; Repent, and turn *yourselves* from your idols; and turn away your faces from all your abominations. [7]For every one of the house of Israel, or of the stranger that sojourneth in Israel, which separateth himself from me, and setteth up his idols in his heart, and putteth the stumblingblock of his iniquity before his face, and cometh to a prophet to enquire of him concerning me; I the LORD will answer him by myself: [8]And I will set my face against that man, and will make him a sign and a proverb, and I will cut him off from the midst of my people; and ye shall know that I *am* the LORD. [9]And if the prophet be deceived when he hath spoken a thing, I the LORD have deceived that prophet, and I will stretch out my hand upon him, and will destroy him from the midst of my people Israel. [10]And they shall bear the punishment of their iniquity: the punishment of the prophet shall be even as the punishment of him that seeketh *unto him*; [11]That the house of Israel may go no more astray from me, neither be polluted any more with all their transgressions; but that they may be my people, and I may be their God, saith the Lord GOD.

[12]The word of the LORD came again to me, saying, [13]Son of man, when the land sinneth against me by trespassing grievously, then will I stretch out mine hand upon it, and will break the staff of the bread thereof, and will send famine upon it, and will cut off man and beast from it: [14]Though these three men, Noah, Daniel, and Job, were in it, they should deliver *but* their own souls by their righteousness, saith the Lord GOD. [15]If I cause noisome beasts to pass through the land, and they spoil[a] it, so that it be desolate, that no man may pass through because of the beasts: [16]*Though* these three men *were* in it[b], *as* I live, saith the Lord GOD, they shall deliver neither sons nor daughters; they only shall be delivered, but the land shall be desolate. [17]Or *if* I bring a sword upon that land, and say, Sword, go through the land; so that I cut off man and beast from it: [18]Though these three men *were* in it, *as* I live, saith the Lord GOD, they shall deliver neither sons nor daughters, but they only shall be delivered themselves. [19]Or *if* I send a pestilence into that land, and pour out my fury upon it in blood, to cut off from it man and beast: [20]Though Noah, Daniel, and Job, *were* in it, *as* I live, saith the Lord GOD, they shall deliver neither son nor daughter; they shall *but* deliver their own souls by their righ-

---

[a] spoil: or, bereave
[b] in it: Heb. in the midst of it

teousness. ²¹For thus saith the Lord GOD; How much more when I send my four sore judgments upon Jerusalem, the sword, and the famine, and the noisome beast, and the pestilence, to cut off from it man and beast? ²²Yet, behold, therein shall be left a remnant that shall be brought forth, *both* sons and daughters: behold, they shall come forth unto you, and ye shall see their way and their doings: and ye shall be comforted concerning the evil that I have brought upon Jerusalem, *even* concerning all that I have brought upon it. ²³And they shall comfort you, when ye see their ways and their doings: and ye shall know that I have not done without cause all that I have done in it, saith the Lord GOD.

15

¹And the word of the LORD came unto me, saying, ²Son of man, What is the vine tree more than any tree, *or than* a branch which is among the trees of the forest? ³Shall wood be taken thereof to do any work? or will *men* take a pin of it to hang any vessel thereon? ⁴Behold, it is cast into the fire for fuel; the fire devoureth both the ends of it, and the midst of it is burned. Is it meet for *any* work? ⁵Behold, when it was whole, it was meetª for no work: how much less shall it be meet yet for *any* work, when the fire hath devoured it, and it is burned? ⁶Therefore thus saith the Lord GOD; As the vine tree among the trees of the forest, which I have given to the fire for fuel, so will I give the inhabitants of Jerusalem. ⁷And I will set my face against them; they shall go out from *one* fire, and *another* fire shall devour them; and ye shall know that I *am* the LORD, when I set my face against them. ⁸And I will make the land desolate, because they have committedᵇ a trespass, saith the Lord GOD.

16

¹Again the word of the LORD came unto me, saying, ²Son of man, cause Jerusalem to know her abominations, ³And say, Thus saith the Lord GOD unto Jerusalem; Thy birthª and thy nativity *is* of the land of Canaan; thy father *was* an Amorite, and thy mother an Hittite. ⁴And *as for* thy nativity, in the day thou wast born thy navel was not cut, neither wast thou washed in water to suppleᵇ *thee*; thou wast not salted at all, nor swaddled at all. ⁵None

---

ª meet: Heb. made fit
ᵇ committed . . . : Heb. trespassed a trespass
ª birth: Heb. cutting out, or, habitation
ᵇ to supple . . . : or, when I looked upon thee

eye pitied thee, to do any of these unto thee, to have compassion upon thee; but thou wast cast out in the open field, to the lothing of thy person, in the day that thou wast born.

⁶And when I passed by thee, and saw thee polluted^c in thine own blood, I said unto thee *when thou wast* in thy blood, Live; yea, I said unto thee *when thou wast* in thy blood, Live. ⁷I have caused^d thee to multiply as the bud of the field, and thou hast increased and waxen great, and thou art come to excellent ornaments: *thy* breasts are fashioned, and thine hair is grown, whereas thou *wast* naked and bare. ⁸Now when I passed by thee, and looked upon thee, behold, thy time *was* the time of love; and I spread my skirt over thee, and covered thy nakedness: yea, I sware unto thee, and entered into a covenant with thee, saith the Lord GOD, and thou becamest mine. ⁹Then washed I thee with water; yea, I throughly washed away thy blood^e from thee, and I anointed thee with oil. ¹⁰I clothed thee also with broidered work, and shod thee with badgers' skin, and I girded thee about with fine linen, and I covered thee with silk. ¹¹I decked thee also with ornaments, and I put bracelets upon thy hands, and a chain on thy neck. ¹²And I put a jewel on thy forehead^f, and earrings in thine ears, and a beautiful crown upon thine head. ¹³Thus wast thou decked with gold and silver; and thy raiment *was of* fine linen, and silk, and broidered work; thou didst eat fine flour, and honey, and oil: and thou wast exceeding beautiful, and thou didst prosper into a kingdom. ¹⁴And thy renown went forth among the heathen for thy beauty: for it *was* perfect through my comeliness, which I had put upon thee, saith the Lord GOD.

¹⁵But thou didst trust in thine own beauty, and playedst the harlot because of thy renown, and pouredst out thy fornications on every one that passed by; his it was. ¹⁶And of thy garments thou didst take, and deckedst thy high places with divers colours, and playedst the harlot thereupon: *the like things* shall not come, neither shall it be *so*. ¹⁷Thou hast also taken thy fair jewels of my gold and of my silver, which I had given thee, and madest to thyself images of men^g, and didst commit whoredom with them, ¹⁸And tookest thy broidered garments, and coveredst them: and thou hast set mine oil and mine incense before them. ¹⁹My meat also which I gave thee, fine flour, and oil, and honey, *wherewith* I fed thee, thou hast even set it before them for a sweet^h savour: and *thus* it was, saith the Lord GOD. ²⁰Moreover thou hast taken thy sons and thy daughters, whom thou hast borne unto me, and these hast thou sacrificed unto them to be devoured. *Is this* of thy whoredoms a

---

^c polluted: or, trodden under foot
^d caused . . . : Heb. made thee a million
^e blood: Heb. bloods
^f forehead: Heb. nose
^g of men: Heb. of a male
^h a sweet . . . : Heb. a savour of rest

small matter, ²¹That thou hast slain my children, and delivered them to cause them to pass through *the fire* for them? ²²And in all thine abominations and thy whoredoms thou hast not remembered the days of thy youth, when thou wast naked and bare, *and* wast polluted in thy blood. ²³And it came to pass after all thy wickedness, (woe, woe unto thee! saith the Lord GOD;) ²⁴*That* thou hast also built unto thee an eminent place, and hast made thee an high place in every street. ²⁵Thou hast built thy high place at every head of the way, and hast made thy beauty to be abhorred, and hast opened thy feet to every one that passed by, and multiplied thy whoredoms. ²⁶Thou hast also committed fornication with the Egyptians thy neighbours, great of flesh; and hast increased thy whoredoms, to provoke me to anger. ²⁷Behold, therefore I have stretched out my hand over thee, and have diminished thine ordinary *food*, and delivered thee unto the will of them that hate thee, the daughtersⁱ of the Philistines, which are ashamed of thy lewd way. ²⁸Thou hast played the whore also with the Assyrians, because thou wast unsatiable; yea, thou hast played the harlot with them, and yet couldest not be satisfied. ²⁹Thou hast moreover multiplied thy fornication in the land of Canaan unto Chaldea; and yet thou wast not satisfied herewith. ³⁰How weak is thine heart, saith the Lord GOD, seeing thou doest all these *things*, the work of an imperious whorish woman; ³¹In that thou buildest^j

thine eminent place in the head of every way, and makest thine high place in every street; and hast not been as an harlot, in that thou scornest hire; ³²*But as* a wife that committeth adultery, *which* taketh strangers instead of her husband! ³³They give gifts to all whores: but thou givest thy gifts to all thy lovers, and hirest^k them, that they may come unto thee on every side for thy whoredom. ³⁴And the contrary is in thee from *other* women in thy whoredoms, whereas none followeth thee to commit whoredoms: and in that thou givest a reward, and no reward is given unto thee, therefore thou art contrary.

³⁵Wherefore, O harlot, hear the word of the LORD: ³⁶Thus saith the Lord GOD; Because thy filthiness was poured out, and thy nakedness discovered through thy whoredoms with thy lovers, and with all the idols of thy abominations, and by the blood of thy children, which thou didst give unto them; ³⁷Behold, therefore I will gather all thy lovers, with whom thou hast taken pleasure, and all *them* that thou hast loved, with all *them* that thou hast hated; I will even gather them round about against thee, and will discover thy nakedness unto them, that they may see all thy nakedness. ³⁸And I will judge thee, as women that break wedlock and shed blood are judged; and I will give thee blood in fury and jealousy. ³⁹And I will also give thee into their hand, and they shall throw down thine eminent place, and shall break down thy high places: they shall strip

---

ⁱ daughters: or, cities
^j In that thou buildest . . . : or, In thy daughters is thine, etc
^k hirest: Heb. bribest

thee also of thy clothes, and shall take thy fair[1] jewels, and leave thee naked and bare. [40]They shall also bring up a company against thee, and they shall stone thee with stones, and thrust thee through with their swords. [41]And they shall burn thine houses with fire, and execute judgments upon thee in the sight of many women: and I will cause thee to cease from playing the harlot, and thou also shalt give no hire any more. [42]So will I make my fury toward thee to rest, and my jealousy shall depart from thee, and I will be quiet, and will be no more angry. [43]Because thou hast not remembered the days of thy youth, but hast fretted me in all these *things*; behold, therefore I also will recompense thy way upon *thine* head, saith the Lord GOD: and thou shalt not commit this lewdness above all thine abominations.

[44]Behold, every one that useth proverbs shall use *this* proverb against thee, saying, As *is* the mother, *so is* her daughter. [45]Thou *art* thy mother's daughter, that lotheth her husband and her children; and thou *art* the sister of thy sisters, which lothed their husbands and their children: your mother *was* an Hittite, and your father an Amorite. [46]And thine elder sister *is* Samaria, she and her daughters that dwell at thy left hand: and thy younger[m] sister, that dwelleth at thy right hand, *is* Sodom and her daughters. [47]Yet hast thou not walked after their ways, nor done after their abominations: but, as *if that were* a very little *thing*, thou wast corrupted more

than they in all thy ways. [48]*As* I live, saith the Lord GOD, Sodom thy sister hath not done, she nor her daughters, as thou hast done, thou and thy daughters. [49]Behold, this was the iniquity of thy sister Sodom, pride, fulness of bread, and abundance of idleness was in her and in her daughters, neither did she strengthen the hand of the poor and needy. [50]And they were haughty, and committed abomination before me: therefore I took them away as I saw *good*. [51]Neither hath Samaria committed half of thy sins; but thou hast multiplied thine abominations more than they, and hast justified thy sisters in all thine abominations which thou hast done. [52]Thou also, which hast judged thy sisters, bear thine own shame for thy sins that thou hast committed more abominable than they: they are more righteous than thou: yea, be thou confounded also, and bear thy shame, in that thou hast justified thy sisters. [53]When I shall bring again their captivity, the captivity of Sodom and her daughters, and the captivity of Samaria and her daughters, then *will I bring again* the captivity of thy captives in the midst of them: [54]That thou mayest bear thine own shame, and mayest be confounded in all that thou hast done, in that thou art a comfort unto them. [55]When thy sisters, Sodom and her daughters, shall return to their former estate, and Samaria and her daughters shall return to their former estate, then thou and thy daughters shall return to your former estate. [56]For thy sister Sodom was not mentioned[n] by thy

---

[1] thy fair . . . : Heb. instruments of thine ornament
[m] thy younger: Heb. lesser than thou
[n] mentioned: Heb. for a report, or, hearing

mouth in the day of thy pride, [57]Before thy wickedness was discovered, as at the time of *thy* reproach of the daughters of Syria°, and all *that are* round about her, the daughters of the Philistines, which despise thee round about. [58]Thou hast borne[p] thy lewdness and thine abominations, saith the LORD. [59]For thus saith the Lord GOD; I will even deal with thee as thou hast done, which hast despised the oath in breaking the covenant.

[60]Nevertheless I will remember my covenant with thee in the days of thy youth, and I will establish unto thee an everlasting covenant. [61]Then thou shalt remember thy ways, and be ashamed, when thou shalt receive thy sisters, thine elder and thy younger: and I will give them unto thee for daughters, but not by thy covenant. [62]And I will establish my covenant with thee; and thou shalt know that I *am* the LORD: [63]That

---

Devotional Moment

God's Forgiveness

16:59-63 The Israelites' sins were great, but God's forgiveness was greater. Although they had broken his commandments and his heart, his promise to be their Lord remained. God's forgiveness is offered to everyone. Do you feel shame over something you have done or failed to do? Do you feel that your mistakes are too great for God to forgive? Reach out to God, acknowledging your weakness and errors. Receive his forgiveness, turn from your sin, and begin a new chapter.

---

thou mayest remember, and be confounded, and never open thy mouth any more because of thy shame, when I am pacified toward thee for all that thou hast done, saith the Lord GOD.

17

[1]And the word of the LORD came unto me, saying, [2]Son of man, put forth a riddle, and speak a parable unto the house of Israel; [3]And say, Thus saith the Lord GOD; A great eagle with great wings, longwinged, full of feathers, which had divers colours, came unto Lebanon, and took the highest branch of the cedar: [4]He cropped off the top of his young twigs, and carried it into a land of traffick; he set it in a city of merchants. [5]He took also of the seed of the land, and planted[a] it in a fruitful field; he placed *it* by great waters, *and* set it *as* a willow tree. [6]And it grew, and became a spreading vine of low stature, whose branches turned toward him, and the roots thereof were under him: so it became a vine, and brought forth branches, and shot forth sprigs. [7]There was also another great eagle with great wings and many feathers: and, behold, this vine did bend her roots toward him, and shot forth her branches toward him, that he might water it by the furrows of her plantation. [8]It was planted in a good soil[b] by great waters, that it might bring forth branches, and that it might bear fruit, that it might be a goodly vine. [9]Say thou, Thus saith the Lord GOD; Shall it prosper? shall he

---

° Syria: Heb. Aram
[p] borne: Heb. borne them
[a] planted . . . : Heb. put it in a field of seed
[b] soil: Heb. field

not pull up the roots thereof, and cut off the fruit thereof, that it wither? it shall wither in all the leaves of her spring, even without great power or many people to pluck it up by the roots thereof. [10]Yea, behold, *being* planted, shall it prosper? shall it not utterly wither, when the east wind toucheth it? it shall wither in the furrows where it grew. [11]Moreover the word of the LORD came unto me, saying, [12]Say now to the rebellious house, Know ye not what these *things mean?* tell *them,* Behold, the king of Babylon is come to Jerusalem, and hath taken the king thereof, and the princes thereof, and led them with him to Babylon; [13]And hath taken of the king's seed, and made a covenant with him, and hath taken an oath of him: he hath also taken the mighty of the land: [14]That the kingdom might be base, that it might not lift itself up, *but* that by keeping of his covenant it might stand. [15]But he rebelled against him in sending his ambassadors into Egypt, that they might give him horses and much people. Shall he prosper? shall he escape that doeth such *things?* or shall he break the covenant, and be delivered? [16]*As* I live, saith the Lord GOD, surely in the place *where* the king *dwelleth* that made him king, whose oath he despised, and whose covenant he brake, *even* with him in the midst of Babylon he shall die. [17]Neither shall Pharaoh with *his* mighty army and great company make for him in the war, by casting up mounts, and building forts, to cut off many persons: [18]Seeing he despised the oath by breaking the covenant, when, lo, he had given his hand, and hath done all these *things,* he shall not escape. [19]Therefore thus saith the Lord GOD; *As* I live, surely mine oath that he hath despised, and my covenant that he hath broken, even it will I recompense upon his own head. [20]And I will spread my net upon him, and he shall be taken in my snare, and I will bring him to Babylon, and will plead with him there for his trespass that he hath trespassed against me. [21]And all his fugitives with all his bands shall fall by the sword, and they that remain shall be scattered toward all winds: and ye shall know that I the LORD have spoken *it.*

[22]Thus saith the Lord GOD; I will also take of the highest branch of the high cedar, and will set *it;* I will crop off from the top of his young twigs a tender one, and will plant *it* upon an high mountain and eminent: [23]In the mountain of the height of Israel will I plant it: and it shall bring forth boughs, and bear fruit, and be a goodly cedar: and under it shall dwell all fowl of every wing; in the shadow of the branches thereof shall they dwell. [24]And all the trees of the field shall know that I the LORD have brought down the high tree, have exalted the low tree, have dried up the green tree, and have made the dry tree to flourish: I the LORD have spoken and have done *it.*

18

[1]The word of the LORD came unto me again, saying, [2]What mean ye, that ye use this proverb concerning the land of Israel, saying, The fathers have eaten sour grapes, and the children's teeth are set on edge? [3]*As* I live, saith the Lord GOD, ye shall not have *occasion* any more to use this proverb in Israel. [4]Behold, all souls are mine; as the soul of

the father, so also the soul of the son is mine: the soul that sinneth, it shall die. [5]But if a man be just, and do that which is lawful and right, [6]*And* hath not eaten upon the mountains, neither hath lifted up his eyes to the idols of the house of Israel, neither hath defiled his neighbour's wife, neither hath come near to a menstruous woman, [7]And hath not oppressed any, *but* hath restored to the debtor his pledge, hath spoiled none by violence, hath given his bread to the hungry, and hath covered the naked with a garment; [8]He *that* hath not given forth upon usury, neither hath taken any increase, *that* hath withdrawn his hand from iniquity, hath executed true judgment between man and man, [9]Hath walked in my statutes, and hath kept my judgments, to deal truly; he *is* just, he shall surely live, saith the Lord GOD.

[10]If he beget a son *that is* a robber[a], a shedder of blood, and *that* doeth the like to *any* one of these *things*, [11]And that doeth not any of those *duties*, but even hath eaten upon the mountains, and defiled his neighbour's wife, [12]Hath oppressed the poor and needy, hath spoiled by violence, hath not restored the pledge, and hath lifted up his eyes to the idols, hath committed abomination, [13]Hath given forth upon usury, and hath taken increase: shall he then live? he shall not live: he hath done all these abominations; he shall surely die; his blood[b] shall be upon him. [14]Now, lo, *if* he beget a son, that seeth all his father's sins which he hath done, and considereth, and doeth not such like,

[15]*That* hath not eaten upon the mountains, neither hath lifted up his eyes to the idols of the house of Israel, hath not defiled his neighbour's wife, [16]Neither hath oppressed any, hath not withholden the pledge, neither hath spoiled by violence, *but* hath given his bread to the hungry, and hath covered the naked with a garment, [17]*That* hath taken off his hand from the poor, *that* hath not received usury nor increase, hath executed my judgments, hath walked in my statutes; he shall not die for the iniquity of his father, he shall surely live. [18]*As for* his father, because he cruelly oppressed, spoiled his brother by violence, and did *that* which *is* not good among his people, lo, even he shall die in his iniquity. [19]Yet say ye, Why? doth not the son bear the iniquity of the father? When the son hath done that which is lawful and right, *and* hath kept all my statutes, and hath done them, he shall surely live. [20]The soul that sinneth, it

---

Devotional Moment

Family Traditions

18:14-18 Although passing along a rich heritage to the next generation was very important to the Israelites, God made it clear that traditions of sin were to end. Did you grow up with traditions or beliefs that you now recognize to be wrong? Be the generation to break sin's grip, whether the sin is denial, unhealthy communication, or something as serious as immorality. Talk and pray with a trusted friend or counselor about patterns in your family that you do not want to pass on to your children.

---

[a] robber: or, breaker up of an house
[b] blood: Heb. bloods

shall die. The son shall not bear the iniquity of the father, neither shall the father bear the iniquity of the son: the righteousness of the righteous shall be upon him, and the wickedness of the wicked shall be upon him.

²¹But if the wicked will turn from all his sins that he hath committed, and keep all my statutes, and do that which is lawful and right, he shall surely live, he shall not die. ²²All his transgressions that he hath committed, they shall not be mentioned unto him: in his righteousness that he hath done he shall live. ²³Have I any pleasure at all that the wicked should die? saith the Lord GOD: *and* not that he should return from his ways, and live? ²⁴But when the righteous turneth away from his righteousness, and committeth iniquity, *and* doeth according to all the abominations that the wicked *man* doeth, shall he live? All his righteousness that he hath done shall not be mentioned: in his trespass that he hath trespassed, and in his sin that he hath sinned, in them shall he die. ²⁵Yet ye say, The way of the Lord is not equal. Hear now, O house of Israel; Is not my way equal? are not your ways unequal? ²⁶When a righteous *man* turneth away from his righteousness, and committeth iniquity, and dieth in them; for his iniquity that he hath done shall he die. ²⁷Again, when the wicked *man* turneth away from his wickedness that he hath committed, and doeth that which is lawful and right, he shall save his soul alive. ²⁸Because he considereth, and turneth away from all his transgressions that he hath committed, he shall surely live, he shall not die. ²⁹Yet saith the house of Israel, The way of the Lord is not equal. O

house of Israel, are not my ways equal? are not your ways unequal?

³⁰Therefore I will judge you, O house of Israel, every one according to his ways, saith the Lord GOD. Repent, and turn *yourselves* from all your transgressions; so iniquity shall not be your ruin. ³¹Cast away from you all your transgressions, whereby ye have transgressed; and make you a new heart and a new spirit: for why will ye die, O house of Israel? ³²For I have no pleasure in the death of him that dieth, saith the Lord GOD: wherefore turn *yourselves*, and live ye.

19

¹Moreover take thou up a lamentation for the princes of Israel, ²And say, What *is* thy mother? A lioness: she lay down among lions, she nourished her whelps among young lions. ³And she brought up one of her whelps: it became a young lion, and it learned to catch the prey; it devoured men. ⁴The nations also heard of him; he was taken in their pit, and they brought him with chains unto the land of Egypt. ⁵Now when she saw that she had waited, *and* her hope was lost, then she took another of her whelps, *and* made him a young lion. ⁶And he went up and down among the lions, he became a young lion, and learned to catch the prey, *and* devoured men. ⁷And he knew their desolate palaces, and he laid waste their cities; and the land was desolate, and the fulness thereof, by the noise of his roaring. ⁸Then the nations set against him on every side from the provinces, and spread their net over him: he was taken in their pit. ⁹And they put him in ward in chainsᵃ, and brought him to the king of Babylon:

ᵃ in chains: or, in hooks

they brought him into holds, that his voice should no more be heard upon the mountains of Israel. [10]Thy mother *is* like a vine in thy blood, planted by the waters: she was fruitful and full of branches by reason of many waters. [11]And she had strong rods for the sceptres of them that bare rule, and her stature was exalted among the thick branches, and she appeared in her height with the multitude of her branches. [12]But she was plucked up in fury, she was cast down to the ground, and the east wind dried up her fruit: her strong rods were broken and withered; the fire consumed them. [13]And now she *is* planted in the wilderness, in a dry and thirsty ground. [14]And fire is gone out of a rod of her branches, *which* hath devoured her fruit, so that she hath no strong rod *to be* a sceptre to rule. This *is* a lamentation, and shall be for a lamentation.

20

[1]And it came to pass in the seventh year, in the fifth *month*, the tenth *day* of the month, *that* certain of the elders of Israel came to enquire of the LORD, and sat before me. [2]Then came the word of the LORD unto me, saying, [3]Son of man, speak unto the elders of Israel, and say unto them, Thus saith the Lord GOD; Are ye come to enquire of me? *As* I live, saith the Lord GOD, I will not be enquired of by you. [4]Wilt thou judge them, son of man, wilt thou judge *them*? cause them to know the abominations of their fathers: [5]And say unto them, Thus saith

the Lord GOD; In the day when I chose Israel, and lifted up mine hand unto the seed of the house of Jacob, and made myself known unto them in the land of Egypt, when I lifted[a] up mine hand unto them, saying, I *am* the LORD your God; [6]In the day *that* I lifted up mine hand unto them, to bring them forth of the land of Egypt into a land that I had espied for them, flowing with milk and honey, which *is* the glory of all lands: [7]Then said I unto them, Cast ye away every man the abominations of his eyes, and defile not yourselves with the idols of Egypt: I *am* the LORD your God. [8]But they rebelled against me, and would not hearken unto me: they did not every man cast away the abominations of their eyes, neither did they forsake the idols of Egypt: then I said, I will pour out my fury upon them, to accomplish my anger against them in the midst of the land of Egypt. [9]But I wrought for my name's sake, that it should not be polluted before the heathen, among whom they *were*, in whose sight I made myself known unto them, in bringing them forth out of the land of Egypt.

[10]Wherefore I caused them to go forth out of the land of Egypt, and brought them into the wilderness. [11]And I gave them my statutes, and shewed[b] them my judgments, which *if* a man do, he shall even live in them. [12]Moreover also I gave them my sabbaths, to be a sign between me and them, that they might know that I *am* the LORD that sanctify them. [13]But the house of Israel rebelled against me in

---

[a] lifted . . . : or, sware
[b] shewed . . . : Heb. made them to know

the wilderness: they walked not in my statutes, and they despised my judgments, which *if* a man do, he shall even live in them; and my sabbaths they greatly polluted: then I said, I would pour out my fury upon them in the wilderness, to consume them. ¹⁴But I wrought for my name's sake, that it should not be polluted before the heathen, in whose sight I brought them out. ¹⁵Yet also I lifted up my hand unto them in the wilderness, that I would not bring them into the land which I had given *them*, flowing with milk and honey, which *is* the glory of all lands; ¹⁶Because they despised my judgments, and walked not in my statutes, but polluted my sabbaths: for their heart went after their idols. ¹⁷Nevertheless mine eye spared them from destroying them, neither did I make an end of them in the wilderness. ¹⁸But I said unto their children in the wilderness, Walk ye not in the statutes of your fathers, neither observe their judgments, nor defile yourselves with their idols: ¹⁹I *am* the LORD your God; walk in my statutes, and keep my judgments, and do them; ²⁰And hallow my sabbaths; and they shall be a sign between me and you, that ye may know that I *am* the LORD your God. ²¹Notwithstanding the children rebelled against me: they walked not in my statutes, neither kept my judgments to do them, which *if* a man do, he shall even live in them; they polluted my sabbaths: then I said, I would pour out my fury upon them, to accomplish my anger against them in the wilderness. ²²Nevertheless I withdrew

mine hand, and wrought for my name's sake, that it should not be polluted in the sight of the heathen, in whose sight I brought them forth. ²³I lifted up mine hand unto them also in the wilderness, that I would scatter them among the heathen, and disperse them through the countries; ²⁴Because they had not executed my judgments, but had despised my statutes, and had polluted my sabbaths, and their eyes were after their fathers' idols. ²⁵Wherefore I gave them also statutes *that were* not good, and judgments whereby they should not live; ²⁶And I polluted them in their own gifts, in that they caused to pass through *the fire* all that openeth the womb, that I might make them desolate, to the end that they might know that I *am* the LORD.

²⁷Therefore, son of man, speak unto the house of Israel, and say unto them, Thus saith the Lord GOD; Yet in this your fathers have blasphemed me, in that they have committed^c a trespass against me. ²⁸*For* when I had brought them into the land, *for* the which I lifted up mine hand to give it to them, then they saw every high hill, and all the thick trees, and they offered there their sacrifices, and there they presented the provocation of their offering: there also they made their sweet savour, and poured out there their drink offerings. ²⁹Then I said^d unto them, What *is* the high place whereunto ye go? And the name thereof is called Bamah unto this day. ³⁰Wherefore say unto the house of Israel, Thus saith the Lord GOD; Are ye polluted after the manner

---

^c committed . . . : Heb. trespassed a trespass
^d I said . . . : or, I told them what the high place was, or, Bamah

of your fathers? and commit ye whoredom after their abominations? ³¹For when ye offer your gifts, when ye make your sons to pass through the fire, ye pollute yourselves with all your idols, even unto this day: and shall I be enquired of by you, O house of Israel? *As I live*, saith the Lord GOD, I will not be enquired of by you. ³²And that which cometh into your mind shall not be at all, that ye say, We will be as the heathen, as the families of the countries, to serve wood and stone.

³³*As* I live, saith the Lord GOD, surely with a mighty hand, and with a stretched out arm, and with fury poured out, will I rule over you: ³⁴And I will bring you out from the people, and will gather you out of the countries wherein ye are scattered, with a mighty hand, and with a stretched out arm, and with fury poured out. ³⁵And I will bring you into the wilderness of the people, and there will I plead with you face to face. ³⁶Like as I pleaded with your fathers in the wilderness of the land of Egypt, so will I plead with you, saith the Lord GOD. ³⁷And I will cause you to pass under the rod, and I will bring you into the bondᵉ of the covenant: ³⁸And I will purge out from among you the rebels, and them that transgress against me: I will bring them forth out of the country where they sojourn, and they shall not enter into the land of Israel: and ye shall know that I *am* the LORD. ³⁹As for you, O house of Israel, thus saith the Lord GOD; Go ye, serve ye every one

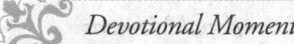

Devotional Moment
•
Consistency

20:39 God was angry at the Israelites for pretending to be a faithful people. They were worshiping the true God while sacrificing to idols. God demands and deserves our single-minded devotion. Is your involvement at church representative of your weekday life, the public expression of a life spent worshiping God in all ways? Or does your attendance at church stand in contrast to your activities the rest of the week? Strive for consistent worship and service to God each day—not just two hours on Sunday morning.

his idols, and hereafter *also*, if ye will not hearken unto me: but pollute ye my holy name no more with your gifts, and with your idols. ⁴⁰For in mine holy mountain, in the mountain of the height of Israel, saith the Lord GOD, there shall all the house of Israel, all of them in the land, serve me: there will I accept them, and there will I require your offerings, and the firstfruitsᶠ of your oblations, with all your holy things. ⁴¹I will accept you with your sweetᵍ savour, when I bring you out from the people, and gather you out of the countries wherein ye have been scattered; and I will be sanctified in you before the heathen. ⁴²And ye shall know that I *am* the LORD, when I shall bring you into the land of Israel, into the country *for* the which I lifted up mine hand to give it to your fathers. ⁴³And there shall ye remember your ways, and all your doings,

ᵉ bond: or, delivering
ᶠ firstfruits: or, chief
ᵍ sweet . . . : Heb. savour of rest

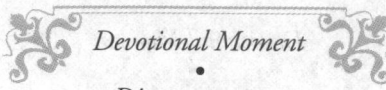

Devotional Moment

Discouragement

20:49 The prophet was understandably discouraged. His audience refused to listen, complaining that he only spoke in riddles. Yet God had still more messages for Ezekiel to deliver. We all experience moments or even seasons of discouragement. What has been discouraging you lately? God still values the work you are doing for him. Share your thoughts with someone who has endured similar discouragement. Together, ask God for renewal and strength.

wherein ye have been defiled; and ye shall lothe yourselves in your own sight for all your evils that ye have committed. ⁴⁴And ye shall know that I *am* the LORD, when I have wrought with you for my name's sake, not according to your wicked ways, nor according to your corrupt doings, O ye house of Israel, saith the Lord GOD.

⁴⁵Moreover the word of the LORD came unto me, saying, ⁴⁶Son of man, set thy face toward the south, and drop *thy word* toward the south, and prophesy against the forest of the south field; ⁴⁷And say to the forest of the south, Hear the word of the LORD; Thus saith the Lord GOD; Behold, I will kindle a fire in thee, and it shall devour every green tree in thee, and every dry tree: the flaming flame shall not be quenched, and all faces from the south to the north shall be burned therein. ⁴⁸And all flesh shall see that I the LORD have kindled it: it shall not be quenched. ⁴⁹Then said I, Ah Lord GOD! they say of me, Doth he not speak parables?

21

¹And the word of the LORD came unto me, saying, ²Son of man, set thy face toward Jerusalem, and drop *thy word* toward the holy places, and prophesy against the land of Israel, ³And say to the land of Israel, Thus saith the LORD; Behold, I *am* against thee, and will draw forth my sword out of his sheath, and will cut off from thee the righteous and the wicked. ⁴Seeing then that I will cut off from thee the righteous and the wicked, therefore shall my sword go forth out of his sheath against all flesh from the south to the north: ⁵That all flesh may know that I the LORD have drawn forth my sword out of his sheath: it shall not return any more. ⁶Sigh therefore, thou son of man, with the breaking of *thy* loins; and with bitterness sigh before their eyes. ⁷And it shall be, when they say unto thee, Wherefore sighest thou? that thou shalt answer, For the tidings; because it cometh: and every heart shall melt, and all hands shall be feeble, and every spirit shall faint, and all knees shall be weakᵃ *as* water: behold, it cometh, and shall be brought to pass, saith the Lord GOD.

⁸Again the word of the LORD came unto me, saying, ⁹Son of man, prophesy, and say, Thus saith the LORD; Say, A sword, a sword is sharpened, and also furbished: ¹⁰It is sharpened to make a sore slaughter; it is furbished that it may glitter: should we then make mirth? it contemnethᵇ the

---

ᵃ shall be weak . . . : Heb. shall go into water
ᵇ it contemneth . . . : or, it is the rod of my son, it despiseth every tree

rod of my son, *as* every tree. ¹¹And he hath given it to be furbished, that it may be handled: this sword is sharpened, and it is furbished, to give it into the hand of the slayer. ¹²Cry and howl, son of man: for it shall be upon my people, it *shall be* upon all the princes of Israel: terrors^c by reason of the sword shall be upon my people: smite therefore upon *thy* thigh. ¹³Because *it is* a trial^d, and what if *the sword* contemn even the rod? it shall be no *more*, saith the Lord GOD. ¹⁴Thou therefore, son of man, prophesy, and smite *thine* hands^e together, and let the sword be doubled the third time, the sword of the slain: it *is* the sword of the great *men that are* slain, which entereth into their privy chambers. ¹⁵I have set the point^f of the sword against all their gates, that *their* heart may faint, and *their* ruins be multiplied: ah! *it is* made bright, *it is* wrapped up for the slaughter. ¹⁶Go thee one way or other, *either* on the right hand, *or* on the left, whithersoever thy face *is* set. ¹⁷I will also smite mine hands together, and I will cause my fury to rest: I the LORD have said *it*.

¹⁸The word of the LORD came unto me again, saying, ¹⁹Also, thou son of man, appoint thee two ways, that the sword of the king of Babylon may come: both twain shall come forth out of one land: and choose thou a place, choose *it* at the head of the way to the city. ²⁰Appoint a way, that the sword may come to Rabbath of the Ammonites, and to Judah in Jerusalem the defenced. ²¹For the king of Babylon stood at the parting of the way, at the head of the two ways, to use divination: he made *his* arrows bright, he consulted with images, he looked in the liver. ²²At his right hand was the divination for Jerusalem, to appoint captains^g, to open the mouth in the slaughter, to lift up the voice with shouting, to appoint *battering* rams against the gates, to cast a mount, *and* to build a fort. ²³And it shall be unto them as a false divination in their sight, to them that have sworn oaths: but he will call to remembrance the iniquity, that they may be taken. ²⁴Therefore thus saith the Lord GOD; Because ye have made your iniquity to be remembered, in that your transgressions are discovered, so that in all your doings your sins do appear; because, *I say*, that ye are come to remembrance, ye shall be taken with the hand. ²⁵And thou, profane wicked prince of Israel, whose day is come, when iniquity *shall have* an end, ²⁶Thus saith the Lord GOD; Remove the diadem, and take off the crown: this *shall* not *be* the same: exalt *him that is* low, and abase *him that is* high. ²⁷I will overturn^h, overturn, overturn, it: and it shall be no *more*, un-

---

^c terrors . . . : or, they are thrust down to the sword with my people
^d Because . . . : or, When the trial hath been, what then? shall they not also belong to the despising rod?
^e hands . . . : Heb. hand to hand
^f point: or, glittering, or, fear
^g captains: or, battering rams: Heb. rams
^h I will overturn . . . : Heb. Perverted, perverted, perverted, will I make it

til he come whose right it is; and I will give it *him.*

²⁸And thou, son of man, prophesy and say, Thus saith the Lord GOD concerning the Ammonites, and concerning their reproach; even say thou, The sword, the sword *is* drawn: for the slaughter *it is* furbished, to consume because of the glittering: ²⁹Whiles they see vanity unto thee, whiles they divine a lie unto thee, to bring thee upon the necks of *them that are* slain, of the wicked, whose day is come, when their iniquity *shall have* an end. ³⁰Shall I cause *it* to return into his sheath? I will judge thee in the place where thou wast created, in the land of thy nativity. ³¹And I will pour out mine indignation upon thee, I will blow against thee in the fire of my wrath, and deliver thee into the hand of brutishⁱ men, *and* skilful to destroy. ³²Thou shalt be for fuel to the fire; thy blood shall be in the midst of the land; thou shalt be no *more* remembered: for I the LORD have spoken *it.*

22

¹Moreover the word of the LORD came unto me, saying, ²Now, thou son of man, wilt thou judgeᵃ, wilt thou judge the bloody city? yea, thou shalt shew her all her abominations. ³Then say thou, Thus saith the Lord GOD, The city sheddeth blood in the midst of it, that her time may come, and maketh idols against herself to defile herself. ⁴Thou art

become guilty in thy blood that thou hast shed; and hast defiled thyself in thine idols which thou hast made; and thou hast caused thy days to draw near, and art come *even* unto thy years: therefore have I made thee a reproach unto the heathen, and a mocking to all countries. ⁵ *Those that be* near, and *those that be* far from thee, shall mock thee, *which art* infamousᵇ *and* much vexed. ⁶Behold, the princes of Israel, every one were in thee to their powerᶜ to shed blood. ⁷In thee have they set light by father and mother: in the midst of thee have they dealt by oppressionᵈ with the stranger: in thee have they vexed the fatherless and the widow. ⁸Thou hast despised mine holy things, and hast profaned my sabbaths. ⁹In thee are men that carry tales to shed blood: and in thee they eat upon the mountains: in the midst of thee they commit lewdness. ¹⁰In thee have they

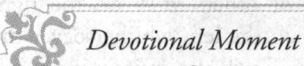

Devotional Moment
•
Prayer
22:6-13 Satan had had a field day attacking the leaders of Israel, leading them into sin that made them forget their allegiance to God. Satan is still on the offensive today. The family is one of his chief targets, and his ways are often subtle. Fight back with prayer for your marriage, your spouse, yourself, and your children. Consider making a prayer covenant with one or two other families, upholding each other in your struggle to love and serve the Lord.

ⁱ brutish: or, burning

ᵃ judge: or, plead for

ᵇ infamous . . . : Heb. polluted of name, much in vexation

ᶜ power: Heb. arm

ᵈ oppression: or, deceit

discovered their fathers' nakedness: in thee have they humbled her that was set apart for pollution. [11]And one[e] hath committed abomination with his neighbour's wife; and another hath lewdly defiled his daughter in law; and another in thee hath humbled his sister, his father's daughter. [12]In thee have they taken gifts to shed blood; thou hast taken usury and increase, and thou hast greedily gained of thy neighbours by extortion, and hast forgotten me, saith the Lord GOD. [13]Behold, therefore I have smitten mine hand at thy dishonest gain which thou hast made, and at thy blood which hath been in the midst of thee. [14]Can thine heart endure, or can thine hands be strong, in the days that I shall deal with thee? I the LORD have spoken it, and will do it. [15]And I will scatter thee among the heathen, and disperse thee in the countries, and will consume thy filthiness out of thee. [16]And thou shalt take thine inheritance in thyself in the sight of the heathen, and thou shalt know that I am the LORD.

[17]And the word of the LORD came unto me, saying, [18]Son of man, the house of Israel is to me become dross: all they are brass, and tin, and iron, and lead, in the midst of the furnace; they are even the dross of silver[f]. [19]Therefore thus saith the Lord GOD; Because ye are all become dross, behold, therefore I will gather you into the midst of Jerusalem. [20]As they gather silver, and brass, and iron, and lead, and tin, into the midst of the furnace, to blow the fire upon it, to melt it; so will

I gather you in mine anger and in my fury, and I will leave you there, and melt you. [21]Yea, I will gather you, and blow upon you in the fire of my wrath, and ye shall be melted in the midst thereof. [22]As silver is melted in the midst of the furnace, so shall ye be melted in the midst thereof; and ye shall know that I the LORD have poured out my fury upon you.

[23]And the word of the LORD came unto me, saying, [24]Son of man, say unto her, Thou art the land that is not cleansed, nor rained upon in the day of indignation. [25]There is a conspiracy of her prophets in the midst thereof, like a roaring lion ravening the prey; they have devoured souls; they have taken the treasure and precious things; they have made her many widows in the midst thereof. [26]Her priests have violated[g] my law, and have profaned mine holy things: they have put

---

Devotional Moment

Character

22:30 God used the picture of a wall in disrepair to communicate the need for strong leadership. There was no one to "stand in the gap" to lead the people back to faithful obedience. True spiritual leaders remain in short supply. Does the wall of your faith need reconstruction? Resist the temptation simply to "whitewash," and initiate real repairs instead. What might you do to apply the principles of God's Word to your financial discussions with your spouse, your commitment to church activities, or your relationships at work?

---

[e] one: or, every one
[f] dross of silver: Heb. drosses, etc
[g] violated: Heb. offered violence to

no difference between the holy and profane, neither have they shewed *difference* between the unclean and the clean, and have hid their eyes from my sabbaths, and I am profaned among them. [27]Her princes in the midst thereof *are* like wolves ravening the prey, to shed blood, *and* to destroy souls, to get dishonest gain. [28]And her prophets have daubed them with untempered *morter*, seeing vanity, and divining lies unto them, saying, Thus saith the Lord GOD, when the LORD hath not spoken. [29]The people of the land have used oppression[h], and exercised robbery, and have vexed the poor and needy: yea, they have oppressed the stranger wrongfully. [30]And I sought for a man among them, that should make up the hedge, and stand in the gap before me for the land, that I should not destroy it: but I found none. [31]Therefore have I poured out mine indignation upon them; I have consumed them with the fire of my wrath: their own way have I recompensed upon their heads, saith the Lord GOD.

23

[1]The word of the LORD came again unto me, saying, [2]Son of man, there were two women, the daughters of one mother: [3]And they committed whoredoms in Egypt; they committed whoredoms in their youth: there were their breasts pressed, and there they bruised the teats of their virginity. [4]And the names of them *were* Aholah[a] the elder,

and Aholibah her sister: and they were mine, and they bare sons and daughters. Thus *were* their names; Samaria *is* Aholah, and Jerusalem Aholibah. [5]And Aholah played the harlot when she was mine; and she doted on her lovers, on the Assyrians *her* neighbours, [6]*Which were* clothed with blue, captains and rulers, all of them desirable young men, horsemen riding upon horses. [7]Thus she committed[b] her whoredoms with them, with all them *that were* the chosen men of Assyria, and with all on whom she doted: with all their idols she defiled herself. [8]Neither left she her whoredoms *brought* from Egypt: for in her youth they lay with her, and they bruised the breasts of her virginity, and poured their whoredom upon her. [9]Wherefore I have delivered her into the hand of her lovers, into the hand of the Assyrians, upon whom she doted. [10]These discovered her nakedness: they took her sons and her daughters, and slew her with the sword: and she became famous[c] among women; for they had executed judgment upon her.

[11]And when her sister Aholibah saw *this*, she was more corrupt in her inordinate love than she, and in her whoredoms more than her sister in *her* whoredoms. [12]She doted upon the Assyrians *her* neighbours, captains and rulers clothed most gorgeously, horsemen riding upon horses, all of them desirable young men. [13]Then I saw that she was defiled, *that* they *took* both one way, [14]And *that* she increased her

---

[h] oppression: or, deceit
[a] Aholah: that is, His tent, or, tabernacle
[b] committed . . . : Heb. bestowed her whoredoms upon them
[c] famous: Heb. a name

whoredoms: for when she saw men pourtrayed upon the wall, the images of the Chaldeans pourtrayed with vermilion, ¹⁵Girded with girdles upon their loins, exceeding in dyed attire upon their heads, all of them princes to look to, after the manner of the Babylonians of Chaldea, the land of their nativity: ¹⁶And as soon as she saw them with her eyes, she doted upon them, and sent messengers unto them into Chaldea. ¹⁷And the Babyloniansᵈ came to her into the bed of love, and they defiled her with their whoredom, and she was polluted with them, and her mind was alienated from them. ¹⁸So she discovered her whoredoms, and discovered her nakedness: then my mind was alienated from her, like as my mind was alienated from her sister. ¹⁹Yet she multiplied her whoredoms, in calling to remembrance the days of her youth, wherein she had played the harlot in the land of Egypt. ²⁰For she doted upon their paramours, whose flesh *is as* the flesh of asses, and whose issue *is like* the issue of horses. ²¹Thus thou calledst to remembrance the lewdness of thy youth, in bruising thy teats by the Egyptians for the paps of thy youth.

²²Therefore, O Aholibah, thus saith the Lord GOD; Behold, I will raise up thy lovers against thee, from whom thy mind is alienated, and I will bring them against thee on every side; ²³The Babylonians, and all the Chaldeans, Pekod, and Shoa, and Koa, *and* all the Assyrians with them: all of them desirable young men, captains and rulers, great lords and renowned, all of them riding upon horses. ²⁴And they shall come against thee with chariots, wagons, and wheels, and with an assembly of people, *which* shall set against thee buckler and shield and helmet round about: and I will set judgment before them, and they shall judge thee according to their judgments. ²⁵And I will set my jealousy against thee, and they shall deal furiously with thee: they shall take away thy nose and thine ears; and thy remnant shall fall by the sword: they shall take thy sons and thy daughters; and thy residue shall be devoured by the fire. ²⁶They shall also strip thee out of thy clothes, and take away thy fairᵉ jewels. ²⁷Thus will I make thy lewdness to cease from thee, and thy whoredom *brought* from the land of Egypt: so that thou shalt not lift up thine eyes unto them, nor remember Egypt any more. ²⁸For thus saith the Lord GOD; Behold, I will deliver thee into the hand *of them* whom thou hatest, into the hand *of them* from whom thy mind is alienated: ²⁹And they shall deal with thee hatefully, and shall take away all thy labour, and shall leave thee naked and bare: and the nakedness of thy whoredoms shall be discovered, both thy lewdness and thy whoredoms. ³⁰I will do these *things* unto thee, because thou hast gone a whoring after the heathen, *and* because thou art polluted with their idols. ³¹Thou hast walked in the way of thy sister; therefore will I give her cup into thine hand. ³²Thus saith the Lord GOD; Thou shalt drink of thy sister's cup deep and large: thou shalt be laughed to scorn and had in

---

ᵈ Babylonians: Heb. children of Babel
ᵉ fair . . . : Heb. instruments of thy decking

derision; it containeth much. ³³Thou shalt be filled with drunkenness and sorrow, with the cup of astonishment and desolation, with the cup of thy sister Samaria. ³⁴Thou shalt even drink it and suck *it* out, and thou shalt break the sherds thereof, and pluck off thine own breasts: for I have spoken *it*, saith the Lord GOD. ³⁵Therefore thus saith the Lord GOD; Because thou hast forgotten me, and cast me behind thy back, therefore bear thou also thy lewdness and thy whoredoms.

³⁶The LORD said moreover unto me; Son of man, wilt thou judge[f] Aholah and Aholibah? yea, declare unto them their abominations; ³⁷That they have committed adultery, and blood *is* in their hands, and with their idols have they committed adultery, and have also caused their sons, whom they bare unto me, to pass for them through *the fire*, to devour *them*. ³⁸Moreover this they have done unto me: they have defiled my sanctuary in the same day, and have profaned my sabbaths. ³⁹For when they had slain their children to their idols, then they came the same day into my sanctuary to profane it; and, lo, thus have they done in the midst of mine house. ⁴⁰And furthermore, that ye have sent for men to come[g] from far, unto whom a messenger *was* sent; and, lo, they came: for whom thou didst wash thyself, paintedst thy eyes, and deckedst thyself with ornaments, ⁴¹And satest upon a stately[h] bed, and a table prepared before it, where-

upon thou hast set mine incense and mine oil. ⁴²And a voice of a multitude being at ease *was* with her: and with the men of the common sort *were* brought Sabeans from the wilderness, which put bracelets upon their hands, and beautiful crowns upon their heads. ⁴³Then said I unto *her that was* old in adulteries, Will they now commit whoredoms[i] with her, and she *with them*? ⁴⁴Yet they went in unto her, as they go in unto a woman that playeth the harlot: so went they in unto Aholah and unto Aholibah, the lewd women. ⁴⁵And the righteous men, they shall judge them after the manner of adulteresses, and after the manner of women that shed blood; because they *are* adulteresses, and blood *is* in their hands. ⁴⁶For thus saith the Lord GOD; I will bring up a company upon them, and will give them to be removed and spoiled. ⁴⁷And the company shall stone them with stones, and dispatch[j] them with their swords; they shall slay their sons and their daughters, and burn up their houses with fire. ⁴⁸Thus will I cause lewdness to cease out of the land, that all women may be taught not to do after your lewdness. ⁴⁹And they shall recompense your lewdness upon you, and ye shall bear the sins of your idols: and ye shall know that I *am* the Lord GOD.

24

¹Again in the ninth year, in the tenth month, in the tenth *day* of the month, the word of the LORD came unto me,

---

[f] judge: or, plead for
[g] to come: Heb. coming
[h] stately: Heb. honourable
[i] whoredoms . . . : Heb. her whoredoms
[j] dispatch . . . : or, single them out

saying, ²Son of man, write thee the name of the day, *even* of this same day: the king of Babylon set himself against Jerusalem this same day. ³And utter a parable unto the rebellious house, and say unto them, Thus saith the Lord GOD; Set on a pot, set *it* on, and also pour water into it: ⁴Gather the pieces thereof into it, *even* every good piece, the thigh, and the shoulder; fill *it* with the choice bones. ⁵Take the choice of the flock, and burnª also the bones under it, *and* make it boil well, and let them seethe the bones of it therein. ⁶Wherefore thus saith the Lord GOD; Woe to the bloody city, to the pot whose scum *is* therein, and whose scum is not gone out of it! bring it out piece by piece; let no lot fall upon it. ⁷For her blood is in the midst of her; she set it upon the top of a rock; she poured it not upon the ground, to cover it with dust; ⁸That it might cause fury to come up to take vengeance; I have set her blood upon the top of a rock, that it should not be covered. ⁹Therefore thus saith the Lord GOD; Woe to the bloody city! I will even make the pile for fire great. ¹⁰Heap on wood, kindle the fire, consume the flesh, and spice it well, and let the bones be burned. ¹¹Then set it empty upon the coals thereof, that the brass of it may be hot, and may burn, and *that* the filthiness of it may be molten in it, *that* the scum of it may be consumed. ¹²She hath wearied *herself* with lies, and her great scum went not forth out of her: her scum *shall be* in the fire. ¹³In thy filthiness *is*

lewdness: because I have purged thee, and thou wast not purged, thou shalt not be purged from thy filthiness any more, till I have caused my fury to rest upon thee. ¹⁴I the LORD have spoken *it*: it shall come to pass, and I will do *it*; I will not go back, neither will I spare, neither will I repent; according to thy ways, and according to thy doings, shall they judge thee, saith the Lord GOD.

¹⁵Also the word of the LORD came unto me, saying, ¹⁶Son of man, behold, I take away from thee the desire of thine eyes with a stroke: yet neither shalt thou mourn nor weep, neither shall thy tears run downᵇ. ¹⁷Forbearᶜ to cry, make no mourning for the dead, bind the tire of thine head upon thee, and put on thy shoes upon thy feet, and cover not *thy* lips, and eat not the bread of men. ¹⁸So I spake unto the people in the morning: and at even my wife died; and I did in the morning as I was commanded. ¹⁹And the people said unto

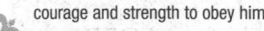

Devotional Moment

Costly Obedience

24:15-18 God asked Ezekiel not to grieve in public when his wife died, and the prophet obeyed. Her death and Ezekiel's response were meant to be symbols of God's relationship with his people, but what Ezekiel had to do was very tangible—and painful. God never asks us to do what we cannot do, but often our obedience will be difficult and painful. What have been some of the costs of your obedience to God in your role as a spouse or as a parent? Ask God for courage and strength to obey him.

ª burn: or, heap
ᵇ run down: Heb. go
ᶜ Forbear: Heb. Be silent

me, Wilt thou not tell us what these *things are* to us, that thou doest *so*? [20]Then I answered them, The word of the LORD came unto me, saying, [21]Speak unto the house of Israel, Thus saith the Lord GOD; Behold, I will profane my sanctuary, the excellency of your strength, the desire of your eyes, and that which your soul pitieth; and your sons and your daughters whom ye have left shall fall by the sword. [22]And ye shall do as I have done: ye shall not cover *your* lips, nor eat the bread of men. [23]And your tires *shall be* upon your heads, and your shoes upon your feet: ye shall not mourn nor weep; but ye shall pine away for your iniquities, and mourn one toward another. [24]Thus Ezekiel is unto you a sign: according to all that he hath done shall ye do: and when this cometh, ye shall know that I *am* the Lord GOD. [25]Also, thou son of man, *shall it* not *be* in the day when I take from them their strength, the joy of their glory, the desire of their eyes, and that whereupon they set their minds, their sons and their daughters, [26]*That* he that escapeth in that day shall come unto thee, to cause *thee* to hear *it* with *thine* ears? [27]In that day shall thy mouth be opened to him which is escaped, and thou shalt speak, and be no more dumb: and thou shalt be a sign unto them; and they shall know that I *am* the LORD.

25

[1]The word of the LORD came again unto me, saying, [2]Son of man, set thy face against the Ammonites, and

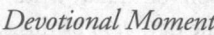

Devotional Moment
•
Sensitivity

25:2-7 In his message for the Ammonites, God communicated his concern for the Israelites by judging the Ammonites for their malice. His punishment was severe. God's distaste for insensitivity should get our attention. In most families, so many emotions, interests, and abilities are represented that insensitivity can creep in undetected. How readily do you consider the opinions and feelings of your spouse and children? Do you give greater weight to the interests of friends, relatives, or even strangers than to those of your household? Think of new ways that you can listen and respond to even the quietest member of your family.

prophesy against them; [3]And say unto the Ammonites, Hear the word of the Lord GOD; Thus saith the Lord GOD; Because thou saidst, Aha, against my sanctuary, when it was profaned; and against the land of Israel, when it was desolate; and against the house of Judah, when they went into captivity; [4]Behold, therefore I will deliver thee to the men[a] of the east for a possession, and they shall set their palaces in thee, and make their dwellings in thee: they shall eat thy fruit, and they shall drink thy milk. [5]And I will make Rabbah a stable for camels, and the Ammonites a couchingplace for flocks: and ye shall know that I *am* the LORD. [6]For thus saith the Lord GOD; Because thou hast clapped *thine* hands[b], and stamped with the feet, and rejoiced in heart with all thy despite against the land of Israel; [7]Behold, therefore I will stretch out

---

[a] men: Heb. children
[b] hands: Heb. hand

mine hand upon thee, and will deliver thee for a spoilᶜ to the heathen; and I will cut thee off from the people, and I will cause thee to perish out of the countries: I will destroy thee; and thou shalt know that I *am* the LORD.

⁸Thus saith the Lord GOD; Because that Moab and Seir do say, Behold, the house of Judah *is* like unto all the heathen; ⁹Therefore, behold, I will open the sideᵈ of Moab from the cities, from his cities *which are* on his frontiers, the glory of the country, Bethjeshimoth, Baalmeon, and Kiriathaim, ¹⁰Unto the men of the east with the Ammonites, and will give them in possession, that the Ammonites may not be remembered among the nations. ¹¹And I will execute judgments upon Moab; and they shall know that I *am* the LORD. ¹²Thus saith the Lord GOD; Because that Edom hath dealt against the house of Judah by taking vengeance, and hath greatly offended, and revenged himself upon them; ¹³Therefore thus saith the Lord GOD; I will also stretch out mine hand upon Edom, and will cut off man and beast from it; and I will make it desolate from Teman; and they of Dedan shall fall by the sword. ¹⁴And I will lay my vengeance upon Edom by the hand of my people Israel: and they shall do in Edom according to mine anger and according to my fury; and they shall know my vengeance, saith the Lord GOD. ¹⁵Thus saith the Lord GOD; Because the Philistines have dealt by re-

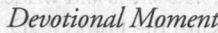

Devotional Moment
Don't Get Mad

25:15-17 The Philistines were known by their neighbors for their destructive vengeance. This prophecy expressed God's judgment on such revenge—that eventually they would know *his* vengeance. Revenge angers the Lord, even when it is cloaked in rationalizations like "She had it coming to her," "Somebody had to put them in their place," or "I did it for the children." When others wrong you in any way, do what you feel is necessary to protect or bring healing to yourself or your family, but let God punish the offender. If such restraint seems impossible, ask God for strength to obey him. You might even ask a friend to join you in prayer.

venge, and have taken vengeance with a despiteful heart, to destroy *it* for the old hatred; ¹⁶Therefore thus saith the Lord GOD; Behold, I will stretch out mine hand upon the Philistines, and I will cut off the Cherethims, and destroy the remnant of the sea coastᵉ. ¹⁷And I will execute great vengeanceᶠ upon them with furious rebukes; and they shall know that I *am* the LORD, when I shall lay my vengeance upon them.

26

¹And it came to pass in the eleventh year, in the first *day* of the month, *that* the word of the LORD came unto me, saying, ²Son of man, because that Tyrus hath said against Jerusalem, Aha, she is broken *that was* the gates of the people: she is turned unto me: I shall be re-

---

ᶜ a spoil: or, meat
ᵈ side . . . : Heb. shoulder of Moab
ᵉ sea coast: or, haven of the sea
ᶠ great vengeance: Heb. great vengeances

plenished, *now* she is laid waste: ³Therefore thus saith the Lord GOD; Behold, I *am* against thee, O Tyrus, and will cause many nations to come up against thee, as the sea causeth his waves to come up. ⁴And they shall destroy the walls of Tyrus, and break down her towers: I will also scrape her dust from her, and make her like the top of a rock. ⁵It shall be *a place for* the spreading of nets in the midst of the sea: for I have spoken *it*, saith the Lord GOD: and it shall become a spoil to the nations. ⁶And her daughters which *are* in the field shall be slain by the sword; and they shall know that I *am* the LORD. ⁷For thus saith the Lord GOD; Behold, I will bring upon Tyrus Nebuchadrezzar king of Babylon, a king of kings, from the north, with horses, and with chariots, and with horsemen, and companies, and much people. ⁸He shall slay with the sword thy daughters in the field: and he shall make a fort against thee, and cast^a a mount against thee, and lift up the buckler against thee. ⁹And he shall set engines of war against thy walls, and with his axes he shall break down thy towers. ¹⁰By reason of the abundance of his horses their dust shall cover thee: thy walls shall shake at the noise of the horsemen, and of the wheels, and of the chariots, when he shall enter into thy gates, as men enter into a city wherein is made a breach. ¹¹With the hoofs of his horses shall he tread down all thy streets: he shall slay thy people by the sword, and thy strong garrisons shall go down to the ground.

¹²And they shall make a spoil of thy riches, and make a prey of thy merchandise: and they shall break down thy walls, and destroy thy pleasant^b houses: and they shall lay thy stones and thy timber and thy dust in the midst of the water. ¹³And I will cause the noise of thy songs to cease; and the sound of thy harps shall be no more heard. ¹⁴And I will make thee like the top of a rock: thou shalt be *a place* to spread nets upon; thou shalt be built no more: for I the LORD have spoken *it*, saith the Lord GOD.

¹⁵Thus saith the Lord GOD to Tyrus; Shall not the isles shake at the sound of thy fall, when the wounded cry, when the slaughter is made in the midst of thee? ¹⁶Then all the princes of the sea shall come down from their thrones, and lay away their robes, and put off their broidered garments: they shall clothe themselves with trembling^c; they shall sit upon the ground, and shall tremble at *every* moment, and be astonished at thee. ¹⁷And they shall take up a lamentation for thee, and say to thee, How art thou destroyed, *that wast* inhabited of seafaring men, the renowned city, which wast strong in the sea, she and her inhabitants, which cause their terror *to be* on all that haunt it! ¹⁸Now shall the isles tremble in the day of thy fall; yea, the isles that *are* in the sea shall be troubled at thy departure. ¹⁹For thus saith the Lord GOD; When I shall make thee a desolate city, like the cities that are not inhabited; when I shall bring up the deep upon

---

^a cast . . . : or, pour out the engine of shot
^b thy pleasant . . . : Heb. houses of thy desire
^c trembling: Heb. tremblings

thee, and great waters shall cover thee; [20]When I shall bring thee down with them that descend into the pit, with the people of old time, and shall set thee in the low parts of the earth, in places desolate of old, with them that go down to the pit, that thou be not inhabited; and I shall set glory in the land of the living; [21]I will make thee a terror[d], and thou *shalt be* no *more*: though thou be sought for, yet shalt thou never be found again, saith the Lord GOD.

27

[1]The word of the LORD came again unto me, saying, [2]Now, thou son of man, take up a lamentation for Tyrus; [3]And say unto Tyrus, O thou that art situate at the entry of the sea, *which art* a merchant of the people for many isles, Thus saith the Lord GOD; O Tyrus, thou hast said, I *am* of perfect[a] beauty. [4]Thy borders *are* in the midst[b] of the seas, thy builders have perfected thy beauty. [5]They have made[c] all thy *ship* boards of fir trees of Senir: they have taken cedars from Lebanon to make masts for thee. [6]*Of* the oaks of Bashan have they made thine oars; the company[d] of the Ashurites have made thy benches *of* ivory, *brought* out of the isles of Chittim. [7]Fine linen with broidered work from Egypt was that which thou spreadest forth to be thy sail; blue[e]

and purple from the isles of Elishah was that which covered thee. [8]The inhabitants of Zidon and Arvad were thy mariners: thy wise *men*, O Tyrus, *that* were in thee, were thy pilots. [9]The ancients of Gebal and the wise *men* thereof were in thee thy calkers[f]: all the ships of the sea with their mariners were in thee to occupy thy merchandise. [10]They of Persia and of Lud and of Phut were in thine army, thy men of war: they hanged the shield and helmet in thee; they set forth thy comeliness. [11]The men of Arvad with thine army *were* upon thy walls round about, and the Gammadims were in thy towers: they hanged their shields upon thy walls round about; they have made thy beauty perfect. [12]Tarshish *was* thy merchant by reason of the multitude of all *kind of* riches; with silver, iron, tin, and lead, they traded in thy fairs. [13]Javan, Tubal, and Meshech, they *were* thy merchants: they traded the persons of men and vessels of brass in thy market[g]. [14]They of the house of Togarmah traded in thy fairs with horses and horsemen and mules. [15]The men of Dedan *were* thy merchants; many isles *were* the merchandise of thine hand: they brought thee *for* a present horns of ivory and ebony. [16]Syria *was* thy merchant by reason of the multitude of the wares of thy making: they occupied in thy fairs with

---

[d] a terror: Heb. terrors
[a] of perfect . . . : Heb. perfect of beauty
[b] midst: Heb. heart
[c] made: Heb. built
[d] the company . . . : or, they have made thy hatches of ivory well trodden
[e] blue . . . : or, purple and scarlet
[f] calkers: or, stoppers of chinks: Heb. strengtheners, etc
[g] market: or, merchandise

emeralds, purple, and broidered work, and fine linen, and coral, and agate. [17]Judah, and the land of Israel, they *were* thy merchants: they traded in thy market wheat of Minnith, and Pannag, and honey, and oil, and balm[h]. [18]Damascus *was* thy merchant in the multitude of the wares of thy making, for the multitude of all riches; in the wine of Helbon, and white wool. [19]Dan also and Javan going to and fro occupied in thy fairs: bright iron, cassia, and calamus, were in thy market. [20]Dedan *was* thy merchant in precious[i] clothes for chariots. [21]Arabia, and all the princes of Kedar, they occupied[j] with thee in lambs, and rams, and goats: in these *were they* thy merchants. [22]The merchants of Sheba and Raamah, they *were* thy merchants: they occupied in thy fairs with chief of all spices, and with all precious stones, and gold. [23]Haran, and Canneh, and Eden, the merchants of Sheba, Asshur, *and* Chilmad, *were* thy merchants. [24]These *were* thy merchants in all sorts *of things*, in blue clothes, and broidered work, and in chests of rich apparel, bound with cords, and made of cedar, among thy merchandise. [25]The ships of Tarshish did sing of thee in thy market: and thou wast replenished, and made very glorious in the midst of the seas.

[26]Thy rowers have brought thee into great waters: the east wind hath broken thee in the midst[k] of the seas. [27]Thy riches, and thy fairs, thy merchandise, thy mariners, and thy pilots, thy calkers, and the occupiers of thy merchandise, and all thy men of war, that *are* in thee, and in all thy company which *is* in the midst of thee, shall fall into the midst of the seas in the day of thy ruin. [28]The suburbs[l] shall shake at the sound of the cry of thy pilots. [29]And all that handle the oar, the mariners, *and* all the pilots of the sea, shall come down from their ships, they shall stand upon the land; [30]And shall cause their voice to be heard against thee, and shall cry bitterly, and shall cast up dust upon their heads, they shall wallow themselves in the ashes: [31]And they shall make themselves utterly bald for thee, and gird them with sackcloth, and they shall weep for thee with bitterness of heart *and* bitter wailing. [32]And in their wailing they shall take up a lamentation for thee, and lament over thee, *saying*, What *city is* like Tyrus, like the destroyed in the midst of the sea? [33]When thy wares went forth out of the seas, thou filledst many people; thou didst enrich the kings of the earth with the multitude of thy riches and of thy merchandise. [34]In the time *when* thou shalt be broken by the seas in the depths of the waters thy merchandise and all thy company in the midst of thee shall fall. [35]All the inhabitants of the isles shall be astonished at thee, and their kings shall be sore afraid, they shall be troubled in *their* countenance. [36]The merchants among the people shall hiss at thee;

---

[h] balm: or, rosin
[i] precious . . . : Heb. clothes of freedom
[j] they occupied . . . : Heb. they were the merchants of thy hand
[k] midst: Heb. heart
[l] suburbs: or, waves

thou shalt be a terror[m], and never *shalt be* any more.

28

[1]The word of the LORD came again unto me, saying, [2]Son of man, say unto the prince of Tyrus, Thus saith the Lord GOD; Because thine heart *is* lifted up, and thou hast said, I *am* a God, I sit *in* the seat of God, in the midst[a] of the seas; yet thou *art* a man, and not God, though thou set thine heart as the heart of God: [3]Behold, thou *art* wiser than Daniel; there is no secret that they can hide from thee: [4]With thy wisdom and with thine understanding thou hast gotten thee riches, and hast gotten gold and silver into thy treasures: [5]By thy great[b] wisdom *and* by thy traffick hast thou increased thy riches, and thine heart is lifted up because of thy riches: [6]Therefore thus saith the Lord GOD; Because thou hast set thine heart as the heart of God; [7]Behold, therefore I will bring strangers upon thee, the terrible of the nations: and they shall draw their swords against the beauty of thy wisdom, and they shall defile thy brightness. [8]They shall bring thee down to the pit, and thou shalt die the deaths of *them that are* slain in the midst of the seas. [9]Wilt thou yet say before him that slayeth thee, I *am* God? but thou *shalt be* a man, and no God, in the hand of him that slayeth[c] thee. [10]Thou shalt die the deaths of the uncircumcised by the hand of strangers: for I have spoken *it*, saith the Lord GOD.

[11]Moreover the word of the LORD came unto me, saying, [12]Son of man, take up a lamentation upon the king of Tyrus, and say unto him, Thus saith the Lord GOD; Thou sealest up the sum, full of wisdom, and perfect in beauty. [13]Thou hast been in Eden the garden of God; every precious stone *was* thy covering, the sardius[d], topaz, and the diamond, the beryl, the onyx, and the jasper, the sapphire, the emerald, and the carbuncle, and gold: the workmanship of thy tabrets and of thy pipes was prepared in thee in the day that thou wast created. [14]Thou *art* the anointed cherub that covereth; and I have set thee *so*: thou wast upon the holy mountain of God; thou hast walked up and down in the midst of the stones of fire. [15]Thou *wast* perfect in thy ways from the day that thou wast created, till iniquity was found in thee. [16]By the multitude of thy merchandise they have filled the midst of thee with violence, and thou hast sinned: therefore I will cast thee as profane out of the mountain of God: and I will destroy thee, O covering cherub, from the midst of the stones of fire. [17]Thine heart was lifted up because of thy beauty, thou hast corrupted thy wisdom by reason of thy brightness: I will cast thee to the ground, I will lay thee before kings, that they may behold thee. [18]Thou hast defiled thy sanctuaries by the multitude of thine iniquities, by the iniquity of thy traffick; therefore will I bring forth a

---

[m] a terror: Heb. terrors
[a] midst: Heb. heart
[b] thy great . . . : Heb. the greatness of thy wisdom
[c] of him that slayeth: or, of him that woundeth
[d] sardius: or, ruby

fire from the midst of thee, it shall devour thee, and I will bring thee to ashes upon the earth in the sight of all them that behold thee. ¹⁹All they that know thee among the people shall be astonished at thee: thou shalt be a terror^e, and never *shalt* thou *be* any more.

²⁰Again the word of the LORD came unto me, saying, ²¹Son of man, set thy face against Zidon, and prophesy against it, ²²And say, Thus saith the Lord GOD; Behold, I *am* against thee, O Zidon; and I will be glorified in the midst of thee: and they shall know that I *am* the LORD, when I shall have executed judgments in her, and shall be sanctified in her. ²³For I will send into her pestilence, and blood into her streets; and the wounded shall be judged in the midst of her by the sword upon her on every side; and they shall know that I *am* the LORD. ²⁴And there shall be no more a pricking brier unto the house of Israel, nor *any* grieving thorn of all *that are* round about them, that despised them; and they shall know that I *am* the Lord GOD. ²⁵Thus saith the Lord GOD; When I shall have gathered the house of Israel from the people among whom they are scattered, and shall be sanctified in them in the sight of the heathen, then shall they dwell in their land that I have given to my servant Jacob. ²⁶And they shall dwell safely^f therein, and shall build houses, and plant vineyards; yea, they shall dwell with confidence, when I have executed judgments upon all those that despise them round about them; and

they shall know that I *am* the LORD their God.

29

¹In the tenth year, in the tenth *month*, in the twelfth *day* of the month, the word of the LORD came unto me, saying, ²Son of man, set thy face against Pharaoh king of Egypt, and prophesy against him, and against all Egypt: ³Speak, and say, Thus saith the Lord GOD; Behold, I *am* against thee, Pharaoh king of Egypt, the great dragon that lieth in the midst of his rivers, which hath said, My river *is* mine own, and I have made *it* for myself. ⁴But I will put hooks in thy jaws, and I will cause the fish of thy rivers to stick unto thy scales, and I will bring thee up out of the midst of thy rivers, and all the fish of thy rivers shall stick unto thy scales. ⁵And I will leave thee *thrown* into the wilderness, thee and all the fish of thy rivers: thou shalt fall upon the open^a fields; thou shalt not be brought together, nor gathered: I have given thee for meat to the beasts of the field and to the fowls of the heaven. ⁶And all the inhabitants of Egypt shall know that I *am* the LORD, because they have been a staff of reed to the house of Israel. ⁷When they took hold of thee by thy hand, thou didst break, and rend all their shoulder: and when they leaned upon thee, thou brakest, and madest all their loins to be at a stand.

⁸Therefore thus saith the Lord GOD; Behold, I will bring a sword upon thee, and cut off man and beast

---

^e a terror: Heb. terrors
^f safely: or, with confidence
^a open . . . : Heb. face of the field

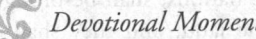

Devotional Moment

•

Pride

29:9-10 Prophesying against Egypt, Ezekiel portrayed God's anger at the people's pride in the Nile River. He promised that desolation would come to the land. We are guilty of pride when we boast of our accomplishments or our possessions. For which of your qualities or accomplishments do you find it most tempting to take full credit? How does this hurt both you and the Lord?

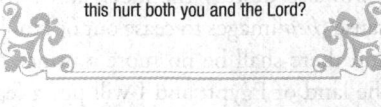

out of thee. ⁹And the land of Egypt shall be desolate and waste; and they shall know that I *am* the LORD: because he hath said, The river *is* mine, and I have made *it*. ¹⁰Behold, therefore I *am* against thee, and against thy rivers, and I will make the land of Egypt utterly^b waste *and* desolate, from the tower of Syene even unto the border of Ethiopia. ¹¹No foot of man shall pass through it, nor foot of beast shall pass through it, neither shall it be inhabited forty years. ¹²And I will make the land of Egypt desolate in the midst of the countries *that are* desolate, and her cities among the cities *that are* laid waste shall be desolate forty years: and I will scatter the Egyptians among the nations, and will disperse them through the countries. ¹³Yet thus saith the Lord GOD; At the end of forty years will I gather the Egyptians from the people whither they were scattered: ¹⁴And I will bring again the captivity of Egypt, and will cause them to return *into* the land of Pathros, into the land of their habitation^c; and they shall

be there a base kingdom. ¹⁵It shall be the basest of the kingdoms; neither shall it exalt itself any more above the nations: for I will diminish them, that they shall no more rule over the nations. ¹⁶And it shall be no more the confidence of the house of Israel, which bringeth *their* iniquity to remembrance, when they shall look after them: but they shall know that I *am* the Lord GOD.

¹⁷And it came to pass in the seven and twentieth year, in the first *month*, in the first *day* of the month, the word of the LORD came unto me, saying, ¹⁸Son of man, Nebuchadrezzar king of Babylon caused his army to serve a great service against Tyrus: every head *was* made bald, and every shoulder *was* peeled: yet had he no wages, nor his army, for Tyrus, for the service that he had served against it: ¹⁹Therefore thus saith the Lord GOD; Behold, I will give the land of Egypt unto Nebuchadrezzar king of Babylon; and he shall take her multitude, and take her spoil^d, and take her prey; and it shall be the wages for his army. ²⁰I have given him the land of Egypt *for* his labour wherewith he served against it, because they wrought for me, saith the Lord GOD. ²¹In that day will I cause the horn of the house of Israel to bud forth, and I will give thee the opening of the mouth in the midst of them; and they shall know that I *am* the LORD.

30

¹The word of the LORD came again unto me, saying, ²Son of man, prophesy

---

^b utterly . . . : Heb. wastes of waste
^c habitation: or, birth
^d take her spoil . . . : Heb. spoil her spoil, and prey her prey

and say, Thus saith the Lord GOD; Howl ye, Woe worth the day! ³For the day *is* near, even the day of the LORD *is* near, a cloudy day; it shall be the time of the heathen. ⁴And the sword shall come upon Egypt, and great pain^a shall be in Ethiopia, when the slain shall fall in Egypt, and they shall take away her multitude, and her foundations shall be broken down. ⁵Ethiopia, and Libya^b, and Lydia, and all the mingled people, and Chub, and the men of the land that is in league, shall fall with them by the sword. ⁶Thus saith the LORD; They also that uphold Egypt shall fall; and the pride of her power shall come down: from the tower of Syene shall they fall in it by the sword, saith the Lord GOD. ⁷And they shall be desolate in the midst of the countries *that are* desolate, and her cities shall be in the midst of the cities *that are* wasted. ⁸And they shall know that I *am* the LORD, when I have set a fire in Egypt, and *when* all her helpers shall be destroyed^c. ⁹In that day shall messengers go forth from me in ships to make the careless Ethiopians afraid, and great pain shall come upon them, as in the day of Egypt: for, lo, it cometh. ¹⁰Thus saith the Lord GOD; I will also make the multitude of Egypt to cease by the hand of Nebuchadrezzar king of Babylon. ¹¹He and his people with him, the terri-

ble of the nations, shall be brought to destroy the land: and they shall draw their swords against Egypt, and fill the land with the slain. ¹²And I will make the rivers dry^d, and sell the land into the hand of the wicked: and I will make the land waste, and all that is therein, by the hand of strangers: I the LORD have spoken *it.* ¹³Thus saith the Lord GOD; I will also destroy the idols, and I will cause *their* images to cease out of Noph; and there shall be no more a prince of the land of Egypt: and I will put a fear in the land of Egypt. ¹⁴And I will make Pathros desolate, and will set fire in Zoan^e and will execute judgments in No. ¹⁵And I will pour my fury upon Sin^f, the strength of Egypt; and I will cut off the multitude of No. ¹⁶And I will set fire in Egypt: Sin shall have great pain, and No shall be rent asunder, and Noph *shall have* distresses daily. ¹⁷The young men of Aven^g and of Pibeseth shall fall by the sword: and these *cities* shall go into captivity. ¹⁸At Tehaphnehes also the day shall be darkened^h, when I shall break there the yokes of Egypt: and the pomp of her strength shall cease in her: as for her, a cloud shall cover her, and her daughters shall go into captivity. ¹⁹Thus will I execute judgments in Egypt: and they shall know that I *am* the LORD.

²⁰And it came to pass in the

---

^a pain: or, fear
^b Libya: Heb. Phut
^c destroyed: Heb. broken
^d dry: Heb. drought
^e Zoan: or, Tanis
^f Sin: or, Pelusium
^g Aven: or, Heliopolis
^h darkened: or, restrained

eleventh year, in the first *month*, in the seventh *day* of the month, *that* the word of the LORD came unto me, saying, ²¹Son of man, I have broken the arm of Pharaoh king of Egypt; and, lo, it shall not be bound up to be healed, to put a roller to bind it, to make it strong to hold the sword. ²²Therefore thus saith the Lord GOD; Behold, I *am* against Pharaoh king of Egypt, and will break his arms, the strong, and that which was broken; and I will cause the sword to fall out of his hand. ²³And I will scatter the Egyptians among the nations, and will disperse them through the countries. ²⁴And I will strengthen the arms of the king of Babylon, and put my sword in his hand: but I will break Pharaoh's arms, and he shall groan before him with the groanings of a deadly wounded *man*. ²⁵But I will strengthen the arms of the king of Babylon, and the arms of Pharaoh shall fall down; and they shall know that I *am* the LORD, when I shall put my sword into the hand of the king of Babylon, and he shall stretch it out upon the land of Egypt. ²⁶And I will scatter the Egyptians among the nations, and disperse them among the countries; and they shall know that I *am* the LORD.

31

¹And it came to pass in the eleventh year, in the third *month*, in the first *day* of the month, *that* the word of the LORD came unto me, saying, ²Son of man, speak unto Pharaoh king of Egypt, and to his multitude; Whom art thou like in thy greatness? ³Behold, the Assyrian *was* a cedar in Lebanon with fair branches, and with a shadowing shroud, and of an high stature; and his top was among the thick boughs. ⁴The waters made him great, the deep set him up on high with her rivers running round about his plants, and sent out her little rivers unto all the trees of the field. ⁵Therefore his height was exalted above all the trees of the field, and his boughs were multiplied, and his branches became long because of the multitude of waters, when he shot forth. ⁶All the fowls of heaven made their nests in his boughs, and under his branches did all the beasts of the field bring forth their young, and under his shadow dwelt all great nations. ⁷Thus was he fair in his greatness, in the length of his branches: for his root was by great waters. ⁸The cedars in the garden of God could not hide him: the fir trees were not like his boughs, and the chesnut trees were not like his branches; nor any tree in the garden of God was like unto him in his beauty. ⁹I have made him fair by the multitude of his branches: so that all the trees of Eden, that *were* in the garden of God, envied him.

¹⁰Therefore thus saith the Lord GOD; Because thou hast lifted up thyself in height, and he hath shot up his top among the thick boughs, and his heart is lifted up in his height; ¹¹I have therefore delivered him into the hand of the mighty one of the heathen; he shall surely deal with him: I have driven him out for his wickedness. ¹²And strangers, the terrible of the nations, have cut him off, and have left him: upon the mountains and in all the valleys his branches are fallen, and his boughs are broken by all the rivers of the land; and all the people of the earth are gone down from his shadow, and have left him. ¹³Upon his

ruin shall all the fowls of the heaven remain, and all the beasts of the field shall be upon his branches: ¹⁴To the end that none of all the trees by the waters exalt themselves for their height, neither shoot up their top among the thick boughs, neither their trees^a stand up in their height, all that drink water: for they are all delivered unto death, to the nether parts of the earth, in the midst of the children of men, with them that go down to the pit. ¹⁵Thus saith the Lord GOD; In the day when he went down to the grave I caused a mourning: I covered the deep for him, and I restrained the floods thereof, and the great waters were stayed: and I caused Lebanon to mourn^b for him, and all the trees of the field fainted for him. ¹⁶I made the nations to shake at the sound of his fall, when I cast him down to hell with them that descend into the pit: and all the trees of Eden, the choice and best of Lebanon, all that drink water, shall be comforted in the nether parts of the earth. ¹⁷They also went down into hell with him unto *them that be* slain with the sword; and *they that were* his arm, *that* dwelt under his shadow in the midst of the heathen. ¹⁸To whom art thou thus like in glory and in greatness among the trees of Eden? yet shalt thou be brought down with the trees of Eden unto the nether parts of the earth: thou shalt lie in the midst of the uncircumcised with *them that be* slain

by the sword. This *is* Pharaoh and all his multitude, saith the Lord GOD.

32

¹And it came to pass in the twelfth year, in the twelfth month, in the first *day* of the month, *that* the word of the LORD came unto me, saying, ²Son of man, take up a lamentation for Pharaoh king of Egypt, and say unto him, Thou art like a young lion of the nations, and thou *art* as a whale^a in the seas: and thou camest forth with thy rivers, and troubledst the waters with thy feet, and fouledst their rivers. ³Thus saith the Lord GOD; I will therefore spread out my net over thee with a company of many people; and they shall bring thee up in my net. ⁴Then will I leave thee upon the land, I will cast thee forth upon the open field, and will cause all the fowls of the heaven to remain upon thee, and I will fill the beasts of the whole earth with thee. ⁵And I will lay thy flesh upon the mountains, and fill the valleys with thy height. ⁶I will also water with thy blood the land wherein thou swimmest, *even* to the mountains; and the rivers shall be full of thee. ⁷And when I shall put thee out, I will cover the heaven, and make the stars thereof dark; I will cover the sun with a cloud, and the moon shall not give her light. ⁸All the bright^b lights of heaven will I make dark over thee, and set darkness upon thy land, saith the Lord GOD. ⁹I will also vex^c the hearts of many people,

---

^a their trees . . . : or, stand upon themselves for their height
^b to mourn: Heb. to be black
^a whale: or, dragon
^b bright . . . : Heb. lights of the light in heaven
^c vex: Heb. provoke to anger, or, grief

when I shall bring thy destruction among the nations, into the countries which thou hast not known. [10]Yea, I will make many people amazed at thee, and their kings shall be horribly afraid for thee, when I shall brandish my sword before them; and they shall tremble at *every* moment, every man for his own life, in the day of thy fall. [11]For thus saith the Lord GOD; The sword of the king of Babylon shall come upon thee. [12]By the swords of the mighty will I cause thy multitude to fall, the terrible of the nations, all of them: and they shall spoil the pomp of Egypt, and all the multitude thereof shall be destroyed. [13]I will destroy also all the beasts thereof from beside the great waters; neither shall the foot of man trouble them any more, nor the hoofs of beasts trouble them. [14]Then will I make their waters deep, and cause their rivers to run like oil, saith the Lord GOD. [15]When I shall make the land of Egypt desolate, and the country shall be destitute[d] of that whereof it was full, when I shall smite all them that dwell therein, then shall they know that I *am* the LORD. [16]This *is* the lamentation wherewith they shall lament her: the daughters of the nations shall lament her: they shall lament for her, *even* for Egypt, and for all her multitude, saith the Lord GOD.

[17]It came to pass also in the twelfth year, in the fifteenth *day* of the month, *that* the word of the LORD came unto me, saying, [18]Son of man, wail for the multitude of Egypt, and cast them down, *even* her, and the daughters of the famous nations, unto the nether parts of the earth, with them that go down into the pit. [19]Whom dost thou pass in beauty? go down, and be thou laid with the uncircumcised. [20]They shall fall in the midst of *them that are* slain by the sword: she is delivered to the sword: draw her and all her multitudes. [21]The strong among the mighty shall speak to him out of the midst of hell with them that help him: they are gone down, they lie uncircumcised, slain by the sword. [22]Asshur *is* there and all her company: his graves *are* about him: all of them slain, fallen by the sword: [23]Whose graves are set in the sides of the pit, and her company is round about her grave: all of them slain, fallen by the sword, which caused terror[e] in the land of the living. [24]There *is* Elam and all her multitude round about her grave, all of them slain, fallen by the sword, which are gone down uncircumcised into the nether parts of the earth, which caused their terror in the land of the living; yet have they borne their shame with them that go down to the pit. [25]They have set her a bed in the midst of the slain with all her multitude: her graves *are* round about him: all of them uncircumcised, slain by the sword: though their terror was caused in the land of the living, yet have they borne their shame with them that go down to the pit: he is put in the midst of *them that be* slain. [26]There *is* Meshech, Tubal, and all her multitude: her graves *are* round about him: all of them uncircumcised, slain by the sword, though they caused their terror in the

---

[d] destitute . . . : Heb. desolate from the fulness thereof
[e] terror: or, dismaying

land of the living. ²⁷And they shall not lie with the mighty *that are* fallen of the uncircumcised, which are gone down to hell with their weapons of war: and they have laid their swords under their heads, but their iniquities shall be upon their bones, though *they were* the terror of the mighty in the land of the living. ²⁸Yea, thou shalt be broken in the midst of the uncircumcised, and shalt lie with *them that are* slain with the sword. ²⁹There *is* Edom, her kings, and all her princes, which with their might are laid^f by *them that were* slain by the sword: they shall lie with the uncircumcised, and with them that go down to the pit. ³⁰There *be* the princes of the north, all of them, and all the Zidonians, which are gone down with the slain; with their terror they are ashamed of their might; and they lie uncircumcised with *them that be* slain by the sword, and bear their shame with them that go down to the pit. ³¹Pharaoh shall see them, and shall be comforted over all his multitude, *even* Pharaoh and all his army slain by the sword, saith the Lord GOD. ³²For I have caused my terror in the land of the living: and he shall be laid in the midst of the uncircumcised with *them that are* slain with the sword, *even* Pharaoh and all his multitude, saith the Lord GOD.

33

¹Again the word of the LORD came unto me, saying, ²Son of man, speak to the children of thy people, and say unto them, When I bring the sword upon a land, if the people of the land take a man

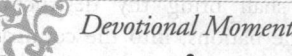

Devotional Moment

Watch Out!

33:1-6 Watchmen had to be constantly alert because the entire city depended on their ability to see the enemy in time to sound the alarm. People in the city could sleep securely because they knew the watchmen would stay awake all night, peering into the darkness, listening for any sound that indicated enemy presence. God designates parents to be watchmen for the family. Parents must be alert and perceptive, detecting any enemy that threatens their children's well-being. Parents can't fight their children's battles for them, but they can and should warn their children of ideas, activities, people, and situations that could harm them.

of their coasts, and set him for their watchman: ³If when he seeth the sword come upon the land, he blow the trumpet, and warn the people; ⁴Then whosoever^a heareth the sound of the trumpet, and taketh not warning; if the sword come, and take him away, his blood shall be upon his own head. ⁵He heard the sound of the trumpet, and took not warning; his blood shall be upon him. But he that taketh warning shall deliver his soul. ⁶But if the watchman see the sword come, and blow not the trumpet, and the people be not warned; if the sword come, and take *any* person from among them, he is taken away in his iniquity; but his blood will I require at the watchman's hand. ⁷So thou, O son of man, I have set thee a watchman unto the house of Israel; therefore thou shalt hear the word at my mouth, and warn them from me. ⁸When I say unto the wicked, O wicked *man*, thou shalt surely

---

^f laid: Heb. given, or, put
^a whosoever . . . : Heb. he that hearing heareth

die; if thou dost not speak to warn the wicked from his way, that wicked *man* shall die in his iniquity; but his blood will I require at thine hand. ⁹Nevertheless, if thou warn the wicked of his way to turn from it; if he do not turn from his way, he shall die in his iniquity; but thou hast delivered thy soul.

¹⁰Therefore, O thou son of man, speak unto the house of Israel; Thus ye speak, saying, If our transgressions and our sins *be* upon us, and we pine away in them, how should we then live? ¹¹Say unto them, *As* I live, saith the Lord GOD, I have no pleasure in the death of the wicked; but that the wicked turn from his way and live: turn ye, turn ye from your evil ways; for why will ye die, O house of Israel? ¹²Therefore, thou son of man, say unto the children of thy people, The righteousness of the righteous shall not deliver him in the day of his transgression: as for the wickedness of the wicked, he shall not fall thereby in the day that he turneth from his wickedness; neither shall the righteous be able to live for his *righteousness* in the

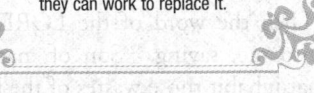

Devotional Moment

Restoration

33:10-12 God commands us to turn from evil so that we can live fruitful lives. When we feel burdened by sin and guilt, we may feel as if life is over—that we can't possibly recover. But God draws us back to himself and promises: "The wicked . . . shall not fall in the day that he turneth from his wickedness." In the New Testament, we read, "If we confess our sins, he is faithful and just to forgive us our sins, and to cleanse us from all unrighteousness" (1 John 1:9). No matter how serious our sin, God invites us to turn to him for forgiveness and restoration.

Devotional Moment

Restitution

33:14-16 God repeated what he had said before: When you have wronged someone, you must do what you can to make amends. This principle of restitution has many applications in your life. If you break something you have borrowed from a neighbor, buy your neighbor a replacement for the broken item. When children break something in the house, they can work to replace it.

day that he sinneth. ¹³When I shall say to the righteous, *that* he shall surely live; if he trust to his own righteousness, and commit iniquity, all his righteousnesses shall not be remembered; but for his iniquity that he hath committed, he shall die for it. ¹⁴Again, when I say unto the wicked, Thou shalt surely die; if he turn from his sin, and do that which is lawful and right; ¹⁵*If* the wicked restore the pledge, give again that he had robbed, walk in the statutes of life, without committing iniquity; he shall surely live, he shall not die. ¹⁶None of his sins that he hath committed shall be mentioned unto him: he hath done that which is lawful and right; he shall surely live. ¹⁷Yet the children of thy people say, The way of the Lord is not equal: but as for them, their way is not equal. ¹⁸When the righteous turneth from his righteousness, and committeth iniquity, he shall even die thereby. ¹⁹But if the wicked turn from his wickedness, and do that which is lawful and right, he shall live thereby. ²⁰Yet ye say, The way of the Lord is not equal. O ye house of Israel, I will judge you every one after his ways.

²¹And it came to pass in the twelfth

year of our captivity, in the tenth *month*, in the fifth *day* of the month, *that* one that had escaped out of Jerusalem came unto me, saying, The city is smitten. ²²Now the hand of the LORD was upon me in the evening, afore he that was escaped came; and had opened my mouth, until he came to me in the morning; and my mouth was opened, and I was no more dumb. ²³Then the word of the LORD came unto me, saying, ²⁴Son of man, they that inhabit those wastes of the land of Israel speak, saying, Abraham was one, and he inherited the land: but we *are* many; the land is given us for inheritance. ²⁵Wherefore say unto them, Thus saith the Lord GOD; Ye eat with the blood, and lift up your eyes toward your idols, and shed blood: and shall ye possess the land? ²⁶Ye stand upon your sword, ye work abomination, and ye defile every one his neighbour's wife: and shall ye possess the land? ²⁷Say thou thus unto them, Thus saith the Lord GOD; *As* I live, surely they that *are* in the wastes shall fall by the sword, and him that *is* in the open field will I give to the beasts to be devoured, and they that *be* in the forts and in the caves shall die of the pestilence. ²⁸For I will lay the land most^b desolate, and the pomp of her strength shall cease; and the mountains of Israel shall be desolate, that none shall pass through. ²⁹Then shall they know that I *am* the LORD, when I have laid the land most desolate because of all their abominations which they have committed.

³⁰Also, thou son of man, the children of thy people still are talking

---

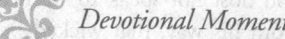
against thee by the walls and in the doors of the houses, and speak one to another, every one to his brother, saying, Come, I pray you, and hear what is the word that cometh forth from the LORD. ³¹And they come unto thee as the people cometh, and they sit before thee *as* my people, and they hear thy words, but they will not do them: for with their mouth they shew much love, *but* their heart goeth after their covetousness. ³²And, lo, thou *art* unto them as a very lovely song of one that hath a pleasant voice, and can play well on an instrument: for they hear thy words, but they do them not. ³³And when this cometh to pass, (lo, it will come,) then shall they know that a prophet hath been among them.

34

¹And the word of the LORD came unto me, saying, ²Son of man, prophesy against the shepherds of Israel, prophesy, and say unto them, Thus saith the Lord GOD unto the shepherds; Woe *be* to the shepherds of Israel that do feed themselves! should not the shep-

---

^b most . . . : Heb. desolation and desolation

herds feed the flocks? ³Ye eat the fat, and ye clothe you with the wool, ye kill them that are fed: *but* ye feed not the flock. ⁴The diseased have ye not strengthened, neither have ye healed that which was sick, neither have ye bound up *that which was* broken, neither have ye brought again that which was driven away, neither have ye sought that which was lost; but with force and with cruelty have ye ruled them. ⁵And they were scattered, because *there is* no shepherdᵃ: and they became meat to all the beasts of the field, when they were scattered. ⁶My sheep wandered through all the mountains, and upon every high hill: yea, my flock was scattered upon all the face of the earth, and none did search or seek *after them.*

⁷Therefore, ye shepherds, hear the word of the LORD; ⁸*As* I live, saith the Lord GOD, surely because my flock became a prey, and my flock became meat to every beast of the field, because *there was* no shepherd, neither did my

---

Devotional Moment

Job One

34:7-23 The leaders of Israel had responsibility over the people God had entrusted to them. Yet many of these leaders failed to take their responsibility seriously and cared only for themselves. That left the people vulnerable, and they suffered as a result of this neglect. Parents are God-appointed leaders, too, and having charge of children is a serious responsibility. Children have many needs that only parents can fill. If you have children, don't view caring for them as a distraction from life but as your main responsibility. Give them the first and best of your time and energy.

---

shepherds search for my flock, but the shepherds fed themselves, and fed not my flock; ⁹Therefore, O ye shepherds, hear the word of the LORD; ¹⁰Thus saith the Lord GOD; Behold, I *am* against the shepherds; and I will require my flock at their hand, and cause them to cease from feeding the flock; neither shall the shepherds feed themselves any more; for I will deliver my flock from their mouth, that they may not be meat for them. ¹¹For thus saith the Lord GOD; Behold, I, *even* I, will both search my sheep, and seek them out. ¹²As a shepherd seeketh out his flock in the day that he is among his sheep *that are* scattered; so will I seek out my sheep, and will deliver them out of all places where they have been scattered in the cloudy and dark day. ¹³And I will bring them out from the people, and gather them from the countries, and will bring them to their own land, and feed them upon the mountains of Israel by the rivers, and in all the inhabited places of the country. ¹⁴I will feed them in a good pasture, and upon the high mountains of Israel shall their fold be: there shall they lie in a good fold, and *in* a fat pasture shall they feed upon the mountains of Israel. ¹⁵I will feed my flock, and I will cause them to lie down, saith the Lord GOD. ¹⁶I will seek that which was lost, and bring again that which was driven away, and will bind up *that which was* broken, and will strengthen that which was sick: but I will destroy the fat and the strong; I will feed them with judgment.

¹⁷And *as for* you, O my flock, thus saith the Lord GOD; Behold, I judge

---

ᵃ because . . . : or, without a shepherd

between cattle[b] and cattle, between the rams and the he goats. [18]*Seemeth it* a small thing unto you to have eaten up the good pasture, but ye must tread down with your feet the residue of your pastures? and to have drunk of the deep waters, but ye must foul the residue with your feet? [19]And *as for* my flock, they eat that which ye have trodden with your feet; and they drink that which ye have fouled with your feet. [20]Therefore thus saith the Lord GOD unto them; Behold, I, *even* I, will judge between the fat cattle and between the lean cattle. [21]Because ye have thrust with side and with shoulder, and pushed all the diseased with your horns, till ye have scattered them abroad; [22]Therefore will I save my flock, and they shall no more be a prey; and I will judge between cattle and cattle. [23]And I will set up one shepherd over them, and he shall feed them, *even* my servant David; he shall feed them, and he shall be their shepherd. [24]And I the LORD will be their God, and my servant David a prince among them; I the LORD have spoken *it.* [25]And I will make with them a covenant of peace, and will cause the evil beasts to cease out of the land: and they shall dwell safely in the wilderness, and sleep in the woods. [26]And I will make them and the places round about my hill a blessing; and I will cause the shower to come down in his season; there shall be showers of blessing. [27]And the tree of the field shall yield her fruit, and the earth shall yield her increase, and they shall be safe in their land, and shall know

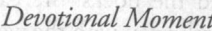

Devotional Moment

•

Restoration

34:25-27 God gives fresh starts to those who trust in him. Here, God told the people that he would restore peace, safety, blessing, and fruitfulness to their lives. Similarly, when relationships are devastated by disagreements, resentments, hurt, and separation, God can bring new life, blessing, and peace. Identify the relationships in your life that need the Lord's restoring grace. First, ask God to show you what you can do to heal any of these broken relationships: You may need to confess a wrong, say you're sorry, ask forgiveness, or let go of a grudge. Then, ask God for his healing and restoration.

that I *am* the LORD, when I have broken the bands of their yoke, and delivered them out of the hand of those that served themselves of them. [28]And they shall no more be a prey to the heathen, neither shall the beast of the land devour them; but they shall dwell safely, and none shall make *them* afraid. [29]And I will raise up for them a plant of renown[c], and they shall be no more consumed with hunger in the land, neither bear the shame of the heathen any more. [30]Thus shall they know that I the LORD their God *am* with them, and *that* they, *even* the house of Israel, *are* my people, saith the Lord GOD. [31]And ye my flock, the flock of my pasture, *are* men, *and* I *am* your God, saith the Lord GOD.

35

[1]Moreover the word of the LORD came unto me, saying, [2]Son of man, set thy face against mount Seir, and proph-

---

[b] cattle: Heb. small cattle of lambs and kids
[c] of renown: or, for renown

esy against it, ³And say unto it, Thus saith the Lord GOD; Behold, O mount Seir, I *am* against thee, and I will stretch out mine hand against thee, and I will make thee most ͣ desolate. ⁴I will lay thy cities waste, and thou shalt be desolate, and thou shalt know that I *am* the LORD. ⁵Because thou hast had a perpetual ᵇ hatred, and hast shed *the blood of* the children of Israel by the force of the sword in the time of their calamity, in the time *that their* iniquity *had* an end: ⁶Therefore, *as* I live, saith the Lord GOD, I will prepare thee unto blood, and blood shall pursue thee: sith thou hast not hated blood, even blood shall pursue thee. ⁷Thus will I make mount Seir most ͨ desolate, and cut off from it him that passeth out and him that returneth. ⁸And I will fill his mountains with his slain *men*: in thy hills, and in thy valleys, and in all thy rivers, shall they fall that are slain with the sword. ⁹I will make thee perpetual desolations, and thy cities shall not return: and ye shall know that I *am* the LORD.

¹⁰Because thou hast said, These two nations and these two countries shall be mine, and we will possess it; whereas the LORD was there: ¹¹Therefore, *as* I live, saith the Lord GOD, I will even do according to thine anger, and according to thine envy which thou hast used out of thy hatred against them; and I will make myself known among them, when I have judged thee. ¹²And thou shalt know that

I *am* the LORD, *and that* I have heard all thy blasphemies which thou hast spoken against the mountains of Israel, saying, They are laid desolate, they are given us to consume ͩ. ¹³Thus with your mouth ye have boasted ͤ against me, and have multiplied your words against me: I have heard *them*. ¹⁴Thus saith the Lord GOD; When the whole earth rejoiceth, I will make thee desolate. ¹⁵As thou didst rejoice at the inheritance of the house of Israel, because it was desolate, so will I do unto thee: thou shalt be desolate, O mount Seir, and all Idumea, *even* all of it: and they shall know that I *am* the LORD.

36

¹Also, thou son of man, prophesy unto the mountains of Israel, and say, Ye mountains of Israel, hear the word of the LORD: ²Thus saith the Lord GOD; Because the enemy hath said against you, Aha, even the ancient high places are ours in possession: ³Therefore prophesy and say, Thus saith the Lord GOD; Because they have made *you* desolate, and swallowed you up on every side, that ye might be a possession unto the residue of the heathen, and ye are taken up in the lips of talkers, and *are* an infamy of the people: ⁴Therefore, ye mountains of Israel, hear the word of the Lord GOD; Thus saith the Lord GOD to the mountains, and to the hills, to the rivers ͣ, and to the valleys, to

---

ͣ most . . . : Heb. desolation and desolation
ᵇ perpetual . . . : or, hatred of old
ͨ most . . . : Heb. desolation and desolation
ͩ to consume: Heb. to devour
ͤ boasted: Heb. magnified
ͣ rivers: or, bottoms, or, dales

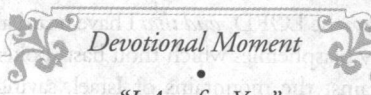

Devotional Moment

"I Am for You"

36:9 When difficulties come to us, we sometimes feel as if the world is against us, that maybe even God is against us. But his word to us is reassuring: "I am for you, and I will turn unto you." He is our advocate and our friend. We can trust him to be for us when we face unemployment, hard times in school, misunderstanding from friends, incurable illnesses, or painful relationships. Ask God to help you with whatever difficult circumstance you are facing. Trust that he is for you; he will come and help you!

the desolate wastes, and to the cities that are forsaken, which became a prey and derision to the residue of the heathen that *are* round about; ⁵Therefore thus saith the Lord GOD; Surely in the fire of my jealousy have I spoken against the residue of the heathen, and against all Idumea, which have appointed my land into their possession with the joy of all *their* heart, with despiteful minds, to cast it out for a prey. ⁶Prophesy therefore concerning the land of Israel, and say unto the mountains, and to the hills, to the rivers, and to the valleys, Thus saith the Lord GOD; Behold, I have spoken in my jealousy and in my fury, because ye have borne the shame of the heathen: ⁷Therefore thus saith the Lord GOD; I have lifted up mine hand, Surely the heathen that *are* about you, they shall bear their shame. ⁸But ye, O mountains of Israel, ye shall shoot forth your branches, and yield your fruit to my people of Israel; for they are at hand to come. ⁹For, behold, I *am* for you, and I will turn unto you, and ye shall be tilled and sown: ¹⁰And I will multiply men upon you, all the house of Israel, *even* all of it: and the cities shall be inhabited, and the wastes shall be builded: ¹¹And I will multiply upon you man and beast; and they shall increase and bring fruit: and I will settle you after your old estates, and will do better *unto you* than at your beginnings: and ye shall know that I *am* the LORD. ¹²Yea, I will cause men to walk upon you, *even* my people Israel; and they shall possess thee, and thou shalt be their inheritance, and thou shalt no more henceforth bereave them *of men.* ¹³Thus saith the Lord GOD; Because they say unto you, Thou *land* devourest up men, and hast bereaved thy nations; ¹⁴Therefore thou shalt devour men no more, neither bereaveᵇ thy nations any more, saith the Lord GOD. ¹⁵Neither will I cause *men* to hear in thee the shame of the heathen any more, neither shalt thou bear the reproach of the people any more, neither shalt thou cause thy nations to fall any more, saith the Lord GOD.

¹⁶Moreover the word of the LORD came unto me, saying, ¹⁷Son of man, when the house of Israel dwelt in their own land, they defiled it by their own way and by their doings: their way was before me as the uncleanness of a removed woman. ¹⁸Wherefore I poured my fury upon them for the blood that they had shed upon the land, and for their idols *wherewith* they had polluted it: ¹⁹And I scattered them among the heathen, and they were dispersed through the countries: according to

---

ᵇ bereave: or, cause to fall

their way and according to their doings I judged them. ²⁰And when they entered unto the heathen, whither they went, they profaned my holy name, when they said to them, These *are* the people of the LORD, and are gone forth out of his land. ²¹But I had pity for mine holy name, which the house of Israel had profaned among the heathen, whither they went. ²²Therefore say unto the house of Israel, Thus saith the Lord GOD; I do not *this* for your sakes, O house of Israel, but for mine holy name's sake, which ye have profaned among the heathen, whither ye went. ²³And I will sanctify my great name, which was profaned among the heathen, which ye have profaned in the midst of them; and the heathen shall know that I *am* the LORD, saith the Lord GOD, when I shall be sanctified in you before their eyes. ²⁴For I will take you from among the heathen, and gather you out of all countries, and will bring you into your own land.

²⁵Then will I sprinkle clean water upon you, and ye shall be clean: from all your filthiness, and from all your idols, will I cleanse you. ²⁶A new heart also will I give you, and a new spirit will I put within you: and I will take away the stony heart out of your flesh, and I will give you an heart of flesh. ²⁷And I will put my spirit within you, and cause you to walk in my statutes, and ye shall keep my judgments, and do *them*. ²⁸And ye shall dwell in the land that I gave to your fathers; and ye shall be my people, and I will be your God. ²⁹I will also save you from all your uncleannesses: and I will call for the corn, and will increase it, and lay no famine upon you. ³⁰And I will multiply the fruit of the tree, and the increase of the field, that ye shall receive no more reproach of famine among the heathen. ³¹Then shall ye remember your own evil ways, and your doings that *were* not good, and shall lothe yourselves in your own sight for your iniquities and for your abominations. ³²Not for your sakes do I *this*, saith the Lord GOD, be it known unto you: be ashamed and confounded for your own ways, O house of Israel. ³³Thus saith the Lord GOD; In the day that I shall have cleansed you from all your iniquities I will also cause *you* to dwell in the cities, and the wastes shall be builded. ³⁴And the desolate land shall be tilled, whereas it lay desolate in the sight of all that passed by. ³⁵And they shall say, This land that was desolate is become like the garden of Eden; and the waste and desolate and ruined cities *are become* fenced, *and* are inhabited. ³⁶Then the heathen that are left round about you shall know that I the LORD build the ruined *places, and* plant that that was desolate: I the LORD have spoken *it*, and I will do *it*.

Devotional Moment

Healing

36:25-27 These hopeful verses remind us that no matter how far from God we may be, we can receive new hearts with new and right desires. This promise brings hope not only to us as individuals but also on behalf of our loved ones who seem beyond help. God is willing and able to wash away any greed, infidelity, self-centeredness, dishonesty, abuse, addiction, rebelliousness, resentment, or disrespect that plagues our family. What an exciting promise! Thank God for his healing love, and ask him to fill your life and the lives of your loved ones with his Spirit.

³⁷Thus saith the Lord GOD; I will yet *for* this be enquired of by the house of Israel, to do *it* for them; I will increase them with men like a flock. ³⁸As the holyᶜ flock, as the flock of Jerusalem in her solemn feasts; so shall the waste cities be filled with flocks of men: and they shall know that I *am* the LORD.

37

¹The hand of the LORD was upon me, and carried me out in the spirit of the LORD, and set me down in the midst of the valley which *was* full of bones, ²And caused me to pass by them round about: and, behold, *there were* very many in the open valleyᵃ; and, lo, *they were* very dry. ³And he said unto me, Son of man, can these bones live? And I answered, O Lord GOD, thou knowest. ⁴Again he said unto me, Prophesy upon these bones, and say unto them, O ye dry bones, hear the word of the LORD. ⁵Thus saith the Lord GOD unto these bones; Behold, I will cause breath to enter into you, and ye shall live: ⁶And I will lay sinews upon you, and will bring up flesh upon you, and cover you with skin, and put breath in you, and ye shall live; and ye shall know that I *am* the LORD. ⁷So I prophesied as I was commanded: and as I prophesied, there was a noise, and behold a shaking, and the bones came together, bone to his bone. ⁸And when I beheld, lo, the sinews and the flesh came up upon them, and the skin covered them above: but *there was* no breath in them. ⁹Then said he unto me, Prophesy unto

the windᵇ, prophesy, son of man, and say to the wind, Thus saith the Lord GOD; Come from the four winds, O breath, and breathe upon these slain, that they may live. ¹⁰So I prophesied as he commanded me, and the breath came into them, and they lived, and stood up upon their feet, an exceeding great army. ¹¹Then he said unto me, Son of man, these bones are the whole house of Israel: behold, they say, Our bones are dried, and our hope is lost: we are cut off for our parts. ¹²Therefore prophesy and say unto them, Thus saith the Lord GOD; Behold, O my people, I will open your graves, and cause you to come up out of your graves, and bring you into the land of Israel. ¹³And ye shall know that I *am* the LORD, when I have opened your graves, O my people, and brought you up out of your graves, ¹⁴And shall put my spirit in you, and ye shall live, and I shall place you in your own land: then shall ye know that I the LORD have

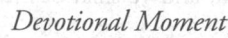

Devotional Moment
•
New Life
37:11-14 Ezekiel had a message of hope for Israel: God would miraculously restore them, despite their past sins. He would return them to their land and renew their spiritual lives. Sometimes feelings and relationships seem beyond all hope. Yet through the power of his Spirit, God can bring new life—to a marriage, to relatives recovering from illness or addictions, to those set against the Lord. God can do miracles. Ask him to revive your hope.

ᶜ holy . . . : Heb. flock of holy things
ᵃ valley: or, champaign
ᵇ wind: or, breath

spoken *it*, and performed *it*, saith the LORD.

[15]The word of the LORD came again unto me, saying, [16]Moreover, thou son of man, take thee one stick, and write upon it, For Judah, and for the children of Israel his companions: then take another stick, and write upon it, For Joseph, the stick of Ephraim, and *for* all the house of Israel his companions: [17]And join them one to another into one stick; and they shall become one in thine hand. [18]And when the children of thy people shall speak unto thee, saying, Wilt thou not shew us what thou *meanest* by these? [19]Say unto them, Thus saith the Lord GOD; Behold, I will take the stick of Joseph, which *is* in the hand of Ephraim, and the tribes of Israel his fellows, and will put them with him, *even* with the stick of Judah, and make them one stick, and they shall be one in mine hand. [20]And the sticks whereon thou writest shall be in thine hand before their eyes. [21]And say unto them, Thus saith the Lord GOD; Behold, I will take the children of Israel from among the heathen, whither they be gone, and will gather them on every side, and bring them into their own land: [22]And I will make them one nation in the land upon the mountains of Israel; and one king shall be king to them all: and they shall be no more two nations, neither shall they be divided into two kingdoms any more at all: [23]Neither shall they defile themselves any more with their idols, nor with their detestable things, nor with any of their transgressions: but I will save them out of all their dwellingplaces, wherein they have sinned, and will cleanse them: so shall they be my people,

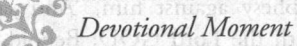

Devotional Moment

God's Home

37:27 This verse speaks of God's deep desire to make his home among his people. God wants to be close to us, personally. He wants to belong to us and have us belong to him. He wants to be a part of all we do and think and say. What more significant part of our life can that involve than our family? Let God be a part of your family's life.

and I will be their God. [24]And David my servant *shall be* king over them; and they all shall have one shepherd: they shall also walk in my judgments, and observe my statutes, and do them. [25]And they shall dwell in the land that I have given unto Jacob my servant, wherein your fathers have dwelt; and they shall dwell therein, *even* they, and their children, and their children's children for ever: and my servant David *shall be* their prince for ever. [26]Moreover I will make a covenant of peace with them; it shall be an everlasting covenant with them: and I will place them, and multiply them, and will set my sanctuary in the midst of them for evermore. [27]My tabernacle also shall be with them: yea, I will be their God, and they shall be my people. [28]And the heathen shall know that I the LORD do sanctify Israel, when my sanctuary shall be in the midst of them for evermore.

38

[1]And the word of the LORD came unto me, saying, [2]Son of man, set thy face against Gog, the land of Magog, the chief[a] prince of Meshech and Tubal,

---

[a] the chief . . . : or, prince of the chief

and prophesy against him, ³And say, Thus saith the Lord GOD; Behold, I *am* against thee, O Gog, the chief prince of Meshech and Tubal: ⁴And I will turn thee back, and put hooks into thy jaws, and I will bring thee forth, and all thine army, horses and horsemen, all of them clothed with all sorts *of armour, even* a great company *with* bucklers and shields, all of them handling swords: ⁵Persia, Ethiopia, and Libyaᵇ with them; all of them with shield and helmet: ⁶Gomer, and all his bands; the house of Togarmah of the north quarters, and all his bands: *and* many people with thee. ⁷Be thou prepared, and prepare for thyself, thou, and all thy company that are assembled unto thee, and be thou a guard unto them. ⁸After many days thou shalt be visited: in the latter years thou shalt come into the land *that is* brought back from the sword, *and is* gathered out of many people, against the mountains of Israel, which have been always waste: but it is brought forth out of the nations, and they shall dwell safely all of them. ⁹Thou shalt ascend and come like a storm, thou shalt be like a cloud to cover the land, thou, and all thy bands, and many people with thee. ¹⁰Thus saith the Lord GOD; It shall also come to pass, *that* at the same time shall things come into thy mind, and thou shalt thinkᶜ an evil thought: ¹¹And thou shalt say, I will go up to the land of unwalled villages; I will go to them

that are at rest, that dwell safelyᵈ, all of them dwelling without walls, and having neither bars nor gates, ¹²To takeᵉ a spoil, and to take a prey; to turn thine hand upon the desolate places *that are now* inhabited, and upon the people *that are* gathered out of the nations, which have gotten cattle and goods, that dwell in the midst of the land. ¹³Sheba, and Dedan, and the merchants of Tarshish, with all the young lions thereof, shall say unto thee, Art thou come to take a spoil? hast thou gathered thy company to take a prey? to carry away silver and gold, to take away cattle and goods, to take a great spoil?

¹⁴Therefore, son of man, prophesy and say unto Gog, Thus saith the Lord GOD; In that day when my people of Israel dwelleth safely, shalt thou not know *it?* ¹⁵And thou shalt come from thy place out of the north parts, thou, and many people with thee, all of them riding upon horses, a great company, and a mighty army: ¹⁶And thou shalt come up against my people of Israel, as a cloud to cover the land; it shall be in the latter days, and I will bring thee against my land, that the heathen may know me, when I shall be sanctified in thee, O Gog, before their eyes. ¹⁷Thus saith the Lord GOD; *Art* thou he of whom I have spoken in old time byᶠ my servants the prophets of Israel, which prophesied in those days *many* years that I would bring thee against them? ¹⁸And it shall come to pass at the same

---

ᵇ Libya: or, Phut
ᶜ think . . . : or, conceive a mischievous purpose
ᵈ safely: or, confidently
ᵉ To take . . . : Heb. To spoil the spoil, and to prey the prey
ᶠ by: Heb. by the hand of

time when Gog shall come against the land of Israel, saith the Lord GOD, *that* my fury shall come up in my face. ¹⁹For in my jealousy *and* in the fire of my wrath have I spoken, Surely in that day there shall be a great shaking in the land of Israel; ²⁰So that the fishes of the sea, and the fowls of the heaven, and the beasts of the field, and all creeping things that creep upon the earth, and all the men that *are* upon the face of the earth, shall shake at my presence, and the mountains shall be thrown down, and the steep places shall fall, and every wall shall fall to the ground. ²¹And I will call for a sword against him throughout all my mountains, saith the Lord GOD: every man's sword shall be against his brother. ²²And I will plead against him with pestilence and with blood; and I will rain upon him, and upon his bands, and upon the many people that *are* with him, an overflowing rain, and great hailstones, fire, and brimstone. ²³Thus will I magnify myself, and sanctify myself; and I will be known in the eyes of many nations, and they shall know that I *am* the LORD.

39

¹Therefore, thou son of man, prophesy against Gog, and say, Thus saith the Lord GOD; Behold, I *am* against thee, O Gog, the chief prince of Meshech and Tubal: ²And I will turn thee back, and leave but the sixth part of thee, and will cause thee to come up from the north parts, and will bring thee upon the mountains of Israel: ³And I will smite thy bow out of thy left hand, and will cause thine arrows to fall out of thy right hand. ⁴Thou shalt fall upon the mountains of Israel, thou, and all thy bands, and the people that *is* with thee: I will give thee unto the ravenous birds of every sortª, and *to* the beasts of the field to be devoured. ⁵Thou shalt fall upon the openᵇ field: for I have spoken *it*, saith the Lord GOD. ⁶And I will send a fire on Magog, and among them that dwell carelesslyᶜ in the isles: and they shall know that I *am* the LORD. ⁷So will I make my holy name known in the midst of my people Israel; and I will not *let them* pollute my holy name any more: and the heathen shall know that I *am* the LORD, the Holy One in Israel.

⁸Behold, it is come, and it is done, saith the Lord GOD; this *is* the day whereof I have spoken. ⁹And they that dwell in the cities of Israel shall go forth, and shall set on fire and burn the weapons, both the shields and the bucklers, the bows and the arrows, and the handstavesᵈ, and the spears, and they shall burn them with fire seven years: ¹⁰So that they shall take no wood out of the field, neither cut down *any* out of the forests; for they shall burn the weapons with fire: and they shall spoil those that spoiled them, and rob those that robbed them, saith the Lord GOD. ¹¹And it shall come to pass in that day, *that* I will give unto Gog a place there of graves in Israel, the valley

---

ª sort: Heb. wing
ᵇ the open . . . : Heb. the face of the field
ᶜ carelessly: or, confidently
ᵈ handstaves: or, javelins

of the passengers on the east of the sea: and it shall stop the *noses* of the passengers: and there shall they bury Gog and all his multitude: and they shall call *it* The valley of Hamongog. ¹²And seven months shall the house of Israel be burying of them, that they may cleanse the land. ¹³Yea, all the people of the land shall bury *them*; and it shall be to them a renown the day that I shall be glorified, saith the Lord GOD. ¹⁴And they shall sever out men^e of continual employment, passing through the land to bury with the passengers those that remain upon the face of the earth, to cleanse it: after the end of seven months shall they search. ¹⁵And the passengers *that* pass through the land, when *any* seeth a man's bone, then shall he set up^f a sign by it, till the buriers have buried it in the valley of Hamongog. ¹⁶And also the name of the city *shall be* Hamonah^g. Thus shall they cleanse the land. ¹⁷And, thou son of man, thus saith the Lord GOD; Speak unto every feathered fowl, and to every beast of the field, Assemble yourselves, and come; gather yourselves on every side to my sacrifice that I do sacrifice for you, *even* a great sacrifice upon the mountains of Israel, that ye may eat flesh, and drink blood. ¹⁸Ye shall eat the flesh of the mighty, and drink the blood of the princes of the earth, of rams, of lambs, and of goats^h, of bullocks, all of them fatlings of Bashan. ¹⁹And ye shall eat fat till ye be full, and drink blood till ye be drunken, of my sacrifice which I have

sacrificed for you. ²⁰Thus ye shall be filled at my table with horses and chariots, with mighty men, and with all men of war, saith the Lord GOD. ²¹And I will set my glory among the heathen, and all the heathen shall see my judgment that I have executed, and my hand that I have laid upon them. ²²So the house of Israel shall know that I *am* the LORD their God from that day and forward.

²³And the heathen shall know that the house of Israel went into captivity for their iniquity: because they trespassed against me, therefore hid I my face from them, and gave them into the hand of their enemies: so fell they all by the sword. ²⁴According to their uncleanness and according to their transgressions have I done unto them, and hid my face from them. ²⁵Therefore thus saith the Lord GOD; Now will I bring again the captivity of Jacob, and have mercy upon the whole house of Israel, and will be jealous for my holy name; ²⁶After that they have borne their shame, and all their trespasses whereby they have trespassed against me, when they dwelt safely in their land, and none made *them* afraid. ²⁷When I have brought them again from the people, and gathered them out of their enemies' lands, and am sanctified in them in the sight of many nations; ²⁸Then shall they know that I *am* the LORD their God, which caused them to be led into captivity among the heathen: but I have gathered them unto their own land,

---

^e men . . . : Heb. men of continuance
^f set up: Heb. build
^g Hamonah: that is, The multitude
^h goats: Heb. great goats

and have left none of them any more there. [29]Neither will I hide my face any more from them: for I have poured out my spirit upon the house of Israel, saith the Lord GOD.

40

[1]In the five and twentieth year of our captivity, in the beginning of the year, in the tenth *day* of the month, in the fourteenth year after that the city was smitten, in the selfsame day the hand of the LORD was upon me, and brought me thither. [2]In the visions of God brought he me into the land of Israel, and set me upon a very high mountain, by which *was* as the frame[a] of a city on the south. [3]And he brought me thither, and, behold, *there was* a man, whose appearance *was* like the appearance of brass, with a line of flax in his hand, and a measuring reed; and he stood in the gate. [4]And the man said unto me, Son of man, behold with thine eyes, and hear with thine ears, and set thine heart upon all that I shall shew thee; for to the intent that I might shew *them* unto thee *art* thou brought hither: declare all that thou seest to the house of Israel. [5]And behold a wall on the outside of the house round about, and in the man's hand a measuring reed of six cubits *long* by the cubit and an hand breadth: so he measured the breadth of the building, one reed; and the height, one reed. [6]Then came he unto the gate which looketh[b] toward the east, and went up the stairs thereof, and measured the threshold of the gate, *which was* one reed broad; and the other threshold *of the gate, which was* one reed broad. [7]And *every* little chamber *was* one reed long, and one reed broad; and between the little chambers *were* five cubits; and the threshold of the gate by the porch of the gate within *was* one reed. [8]He measured also the porch of the gate within, one reed. [9]Then measured he the porch of the gate, eight cubits; and the posts thereof, two cubits; and the porch of the gate *was* inward. [10]And the little chambers of the gate eastward *were* three on this side, and three on that side; they three *were* of one measure: and the posts had one measure on this side and on that side. [11]And he measured the breadth of the entry of the gate, ten cubits; *and* the length of the gate, thirteen cubits. [12]The space[c] also before the little chambers *was* one cubit *on this side,* and the space *was* one cubit on that side: and the little chambers *were* six cubits on this side, and six cubits on that side. [13]He measured then the gate from the roof of *one* little chamber to the roof of another: the breadth *was* five and twenty cubits, door against door. [14]He made also posts of threescore cubits, even unto the post of the court round about the gate. [15]And from the face of the gate of the entrance unto the face of the porch of the inner gate *were* fifty cubits. [16]And *there were* narrow[d] windows to the little chambers, and to their posts

---

[a] by which: or, upon which
[b] which looketh . . . : Heb. whose face was the way toward the east
[c] space: Heb. limit, or, bound
[d] narrow: Heb. closed

within the gate round about, and likewise to the arches: and windows *were* round about inward: and upon *each* post *were* palm trees. [17]Then brought he me into the outward court, and, lo, *there were* chambers, and a pavement made for the court round about: thirty chambers *were* upon the pavement. [18]And the pavement by the side of the gates over against the length of the gates *was* the lower pavement. [19]Then he measured the breadth from the forefront of the lower gate unto the forefront of the inner court without[e], an hundred cubits eastward and northward. [20]And the gate of the outward court that looked[f] toward the north, he measured the length thereof, and the breadth thereof. [21]And the little chambers thereof *were* three on this side and three on that side; and the posts thereof and the arches[g] thereof were after the measure of the first gate: the length thereof *was* fifty cubits, and the breadth five and twenty cubits. [22]And their windows, and their arches, and their palm trees, *were* after the measure of the gate that looketh toward the east; and they went up unto it by seven steps; and the arches thereof *were* before them. [23]And the gate of the inner court *was* over against the gate toward the north, and toward the east; and he measured from gate to gate an hundred cubits. [24]After that he brought me toward the south, and behold a gate toward the south: and he measured the posts thereof and the arches thereof according to these measures. [25]And *there were* windows in it and in the arches thereof round about, like those windows: the length *was* fifty cubits, and the breadth five and twenty cubits. [26]And *there were* seven steps to go up to it, and the arches thereof *were* before them: and it had palm trees, one on this side, and another on that side, upon the posts thereof.

[27]And *there was* a gate in the inner court toward the south: and he measured from gate to gate toward the south an hundred cubits. [28]And he brought me to the inner court by the south gate: and he measured the south gate according to these measures; [29]And the little chambers thereof, and the posts thereof, and the arches thereof, according to these measures: and *there were* windows in it and in the arches thereof round about: *it was* fifty cubits long, and five and twenty cubits broad. [30]And the arches round about *were* five and twenty cubits long, and five cubits broad[h]. [31]And the arches thereof *were* toward the utter court; and palm trees *were* upon the posts thereof: and the going up to it *had* eight steps. [32]And he brought me into the inner court toward the east: and he measured the gate according to these measures. [33]And the little chambers thereof, and the posts thereof, and the arches thereof, *were* according to these measures: and *there were* windows therein and in the arches thereof round about: *it was* fifty cubits long, and five and twenty cubits broad.

---

[e] without: or, from without
[f] that looked: Heb. whose face was
[g] arches: or, galleries, or, porches
[h] broad: Heb. breadth

³⁴And the arches thereof *were* toward the outward court; and palm trees *were* upon the posts thereof, on this side, and on that side: and the going up to it *had* eight steps. ³⁵And he brought me to the north gate, and measured *it* according to these measures; ³⁶The little chambers thereof, the posts thereof, and the arches thereof, and the windows to it round about: the length *was* fifty cubits, and the breadth five and twenty cubits. ³⁷And the posts thereof *were* toward the utter court; and palm trees *were* upon the posts thereof, on this side, and on that side: and the going up to it *had* eight steps. ³⁸And the chambers and the entries thereof *were* by the posts of the gates, where they washed the burnt offering.

³⁹And in the porch of the gate *were* two tables on this side, and two tables on that side, to slay thereon the burnt offering and the sin offering and the trespass offering. ⁴⁰And at the side without, as one goeth up to the entry of the north gate, *were* two tables; and on the other side, which *was* at the porch of the gate, *were* two tables. ⁴¹Four tables *were* on this side, and four tables on that side, by the side of the gate; eight tables, whereupon they slew *their sacrifices.* ⁴²And the four tables *were* of hewn stone for the burnt offering, of a cubit and an half long, and a cubit and an half broad, and one cubit high: whereupon also they laid the instruments wherewith they slew the burnt offering and the sacrifice. ⁴³And within *were* hooksⁱ, an hand broad, fastened round about: and upon the tables

was the flesh of the offering. ⁴⁴And without the inner gate *were* the chambers of the singers in the inner court, which *was* at the side of the north gate; and their prospect *was* toward the south: one at the side of the east gate *having* the prospect toward the north. ⁴⁵And he said unto me, This chamber, whose prospect *is* toward the south, *is* for the priests, the keepers of the chargeʲ of the house. ⁴⁶And the chamber whose prospect *is* toward the north *is* for the priests, the keepers of the charge of the altar: these *are* the sons of Zadok among the sons of Levi, which come near to the LORD to minister unto him. ⁴⁷So he measured the court, an hundred cubits long, and an hundred cubits broad, foursquare; and the altar *that was* before the house. ⁴⁸And he brought me to the porch of the house, and measured *each* post of the porch, five cubits on this side, and five cubits on that side: and the breadth of the gate *was* three cubits on this side, and three cubits on that side. ⁴⁹The length of the porch *was* twenty cubits, and the breadth eleven cubits; and *he brought me* by the steps whereby they went up to it: and *there were* pillars by the posts, one on this side, and another on that side.

41

¹Afterward he brought me to the temple, and measured the posts, six cubits broad on the one side, and six cubits broad on the other side, *which was* the breadth of the tabernacle. ²And the breadth of the doorᵃ *was* ten cubits; and the sides of the door *were* five cubits on

---

ⁱ hooks: or, and irons, or, the two hearthstones
ʲ charge: or, ward, or, ordinance
ᵃ door: or, entrance

the one side, and five cubits on the other side: and he measured the length thereof, forty cubits: and the breadth, twenty cubits. ³Then went he inward, and measured the post of the door, two cubits; and the door, six cubits; and the breadth of the door, seven cubits. ⁴So he measured the length thereof, twenty cubits; and the breadth, twenty cubits, before the temple: and he said unto me, This *is* the most holy *place.* ⁵After he measured the wall of the house, six cubits; and the breadth of *every* side chamber, four cubits, round about the house on every side. ⁶And the side chambers *were* three, one over another, and thirty in order; and they entered into the wall which *was* of the house for the side chambers round about, that they might have hold, but they had not hold in the wall of the house. ⁷And *there was* an enlarging, and a winding about still upward to the side chambers: for the winding about of the house went still upward round about the house: therefore the breadth of the house *was still* upward, and so increased *from* the lowest *chamber* to the highest by the midst. ⁸I saw also the height of the house round about: the foundations of the side chambers *were* a full reed of six great cubits. ⁹The thickness of the wall, which *was* for the side chamber without, *was* five cubits: and *that* which *was* left *was* the place of the side chambers that *were* within. ¹⁰And between the chambers *was* the wideness of twenty cubits round about the house on every side. ¹¹And the doors of the

side chambers *were* toward *the place that was* left, one door toward the north, and another door toward the south: and the breadth of the place that was left *was* five cubits round about.

¹²Now the building that *was* before the separate place at the end toward the west *was* seventy cubits broad; and the wall of the building *was* five cubits thick round about, and the length thereof ninety cubits. ¹³So he measured the house, an hundred cubits long; and the separate place, and the building, with the walls thereof, an hundred cubits long; ¹⁴Also the breadth of the face of the house, and of the separate place toward the east, an hundred cubits. ¹⁵And he measured the length of the building over against the separate place which *was* behind it, and the galleries[b] thereof on the one side and on the other side, an hundred cubits, with the inner temple, and the porches of the court; ¹⁶The door posts, and the narrow windows, and the galleries round about on their three stories, over against the door, cieled[c] with wood round about, and from the ground up to the windows, and the windows *were* covered; ¹⁷To that above the door, even unto the inner house, and without, and by all the wall round about within and without, by measure[d]. ¹⁸And *it was* made with cherubims and palm trees, so that a palm tree *was* between a cherub and a cherub; and *every* cherub had two faces; ¹⁹So that the face of a man *was* toward the palm tree on the one side, and the face of a young lion toward the palm

---

b galleries: or, several walks, or, walks with pillars
c cieled . . . : Heb. cieling of wood
d measure: Heb. measures

tree on the other side: *it was* made through all the house round about. ²⁰From the ground unto above the door *were* cherubims and palm trees made, and *on* the wall of the temple. ²¹The posts^c of the temple *were* squared, *and* the face of the sanctuary; the appearance *of the one* as the appearance *of the other.* ²²The altar of wood *was* three cubits high, and the length thereof two cubits; and the corners thereof, and the length thereof, and the walls thereof, *were* of wood: and he said unto me, This *is* the table that *is* before the LORD. ²³And the temple and the sanctuary had two doors. ²⁴And the doors had two leaves *apiece,* two turning leaves; two *leaves* for the one door, and two leaves for the other *door.* ²⁵And *there were* made on them, on the doors of the temple, cherubims and palm trees, like as *were* made upon the walls; and *there were* thick planks upon the face of the porch without. ²⁶And *there were* narrow windows and palm trees on the one side and on the other side, on the sides of the porch, and *upon* the side chambers of the house, and thick planks.

42

¹Then he brought me forth into the utter court, the way toward the north: and he brought me into the chamber that *was* over against the separate place, and which *was* before the building toward the north. ²Before the length of an hundred cubits *was* the north door, and the breadth *was* fifty cubits. ³Over against the twenty *cubits* which *were* for the inner court, and over against the pavement which *was* for the utter court, *was* gallery against gallery in three *stories.* ⁴And before the chambers *was* a walk of ten cubits breadth inward, a way of one cubit; and their doors toward the north. ⁵Now the upper chambers *were* shorter: for the galleries were higher^a than these, than the lower, and than the middlemost of the building. ⁶For they *were* in three *stories,* but had not pillars as the pillars of the courts: therefore *the building* was straitened more than the lowest and the middlemost from the ground. ⁷And the wall that *was* without over against the chambers, toward the utter court on the forepart of the chambers, the length thereof *was* fifty cubits. ⁸For the length of the chambers that *were* in the utter court *was* fifty cubits: and, lo, before the temple *were* an hundred cubits. ⁹And from under these chambers *was* the entry on the east side, as one goeth into them from the utter court. ¹⁰The chambers *were* in the thickness of the wall of the court toward the east, over against the separate place, and over against the building. ¹¹And the way before them *was* like the appearance of the chambers which *were* toward the north, as long as they, *and* as broad as they: and all their goings out *were* both according to their fashions, and according to their doors. ¹²And according to the doors of the chambers that *were* toward the south *was* a door in the head of the way, *even* the way directly before the wall toward the east, as one entereth into them. ¹³Then said he unto me, The

---

^c posts: Heb. post
^a were higher . . . : or, did eat of these

north chambers *and* the south chambers, which *are* before the separate place, they *be* holy chambers, where the priests that approach unto the LORD shall eat the most holy things: there shall they lay the most holy things, and the meat offering, and the sin offering, and the trespass offering; for the place *is* holy. ¹⁴When the priests enter therein, then shall they not go out of the holy *place* into the utter court, but there they shall lay their garments wherein they minister; for they *are* holy; and shall put on other garments, and shall approach to *those things* which *are* for the people.

¹⁵Now when he had made an end of measuring the inner house, he brought me forth toward the gate whose prospect *is* toward the east, and measured it round about. ¹⁶He measured the east side[b] with the measuring reed, five hundred reeds, with the measuring reed round about. ¹⁷He measured the north side, five hundred reeds, with the measuring reed round about. ¹⁸He measured the south side, five hundred reeds, with the measuring reed. ¹⁹He turned about to the west side, *and* measured five hundred reeds with the measuring reed. ²⁰He measured it by the four sides: it had a wall round about, five hundred *reeds* long, and five hundred broad, to make a separation between the sanctuary and the profane place.

43

¹Afterward he brought me to the gate, *even* the gate that looketh toward the east: ²And, behold, the glory of the God of Israel came from the way of the east: and his voice *was* like a noise of many waters: and the earth shined with his glory. ³And *it was* according to the appearance of the vision which I saw, *even* according to the vision that I saw when I came to destroy the city: and the visions *were* like the vision that I saw by the river Chebar; and I fell upon my face. ⁴And the glory of the LORD came into the house by the way of the gate whose prospect *is* toward the east. ⁵So the spirit took me up, and brought me into the inner court; and, behold, the glory of the LORD filled the house. ⁶And I heard *him* speaking unto me out of the house; and the man stood by me.

⁷And he said unto me, Son of man, the place of my throne, and the place of the soles of my feet, where I will dwell in the midst of the children of Israel for ever, and my holy name, shall the house of Israel no more defile, *neither* they, nor their kings, by their whoredom, nor by the carcases of their kings in their high places. ⁸In their setting of their threshold by my thresholds, and their post by my posts, and the wall between me and them, they have even defiled[a] my holy name by their abominations that they have committed: wherefore I have consumed them in mine anger. ⁹Now let them put away their whoredom, and the carcases of their kings, far from me, and I will dwell in the midst of them for ever. ¹⁰Thou son of man, shew the house to the house of Israel, that they may be ashamed of their iniquities: and let

---

b side: Heb. wind
a and the . . . : or, for there was but a wall between me and them

them measure the pattern[b]. ¹¹And if they be ashamed of all that they have done, shew them the form of the house, and the fashion thereof, and the goings out thereof, and the comings in thereof, and all the forms thereof, and all the ordinances thereof, and all the forms thereof, and all the laws thereof: and write *it* in their sight, that they may keep the whole form thereof, and all the ordinances thereof, and do them. ¹²This *is* the law of the house; Upon the top of the mountain the whole limit thereof round about *shall be* most holy. Behold, this *is* the law of the house.

¹³And these *are* the measures of the altar after the cubits: The cubit *is* a cubit and an hand breadth; even the bottom[c] *shall be* a cubit, and the breadth a cubit, and the border thereof by the edge thereof round about *shall be* a span: and this *shall be* the higher place of the altar. ¹⁴And from the bottom upon the ground *even* to the lower settle *shall be* two cubits, and the breadth one cubit; and from the lesser settle *even* to the greater settle *shall be* four cubits, and the breadth *one* cubit. ¹⁵So the altar *shall be* four cubits; and from the altar and upward *shall be* four horns. ¹⁶And the altar *shall be* twelve *cubits* long, twelve broad, square in the four squares thereof. ¹⁷And the settle *shall be* fourteen *cubits* long and fourteen broad in the four squares thereof; and the border about it *shall be* half a cubit; and the bottom thereof *shall be* a cubit about; and his stairs shall look toward the east.

¹⁸And he said unto me, Son of man, thus saith the Lord GOD; These *are* the ordinances of the altar in the day when they shall make it, to offer burnt offerings thereon, and to sprinkle blood thereon. ¹⁹And thou shalt give to the priests the Levites that be of the seed of Zadok, which approach unto me, to minister unto me, saith the Lord GOD, a young bullock for a sin offering. ²⁰And thou shalt take of the blood thereof, and put *it* on the four horns of it, and on the four corners of the settle, and upon the border round about: thus shalt thou cleanse and purge it. ²¹Thou shalt take the bullock also of the sin offering, and he shall burn it in the appointed place of the house, without the sanctuary. ²²And on the second day thou shalt offer a kid of the goats without blemish for a sin offering; and they shall cleanse the altar, as they did cleanse *it* with the bullock. ²³When thou hast made an end of cleansing *it*, thou shalt offer a young bullock with-

---

Devotional Moment
•
Holiness

43:12 God told Ezekiel that the basic law of the Temple was holiness: God is holy; his Temple is holy; the place where his Temple sits is holy. What does this mean? When God lives among us, he sets us apart for his service. Are you—your activities, goals, relationships—set aside for God to use? Maybe he will use you to welcome neighborhood children around your table, where they can get a glimpse of God in your life. Maybe he will use you to demonstrate his grace in dealing with conflict. Maybe he will use you to reach out to needy people. Ask God how he wants to express his holiness through you.

---

[b] pattern: or, sum, or, number
[c] bottom: Heb. bosom

out blemish, and a ram out of the flock without blemish. ²⁴And thou shalt offer them before the LORD, and the priests shall cast salt upon them, and they shall offer them up *for* a burnt offering unto the LORD. ²⁵Seven days shalt thou prepare every day a goat *for* a sin offering: they shall also prepare a young bullock, and a ram out of the flock, without blemish. ²⁶Seven days shall they purge the altar and purify it; and they shall consecrate themselves. ²⁷And when these days are expired, it shall be, *that* upon the eighth day, and *so* forward, the priests shall make your burnt offerings upon the altar, and your peace offerings; and I will accept you, saith the Lord GOD.

44

¹Then he brought me back the way of the gate of the outward sanctuary which looketh toward the east; and it *was* shut. ²Then said the LORD unto me; This gate shall be shut, it shall not be opened, and no man shall enter in by it; because the LORD, the God of Israel, hath entered in by it, therefore it shall be shut. ³*It is* for the prince; the prince, he shall sit in it to eat bread before the LORD; he shall enter by the way of the porch of *that* gate, and shall go out by the way of the same.

⁴Then brought he me the way of the north gate before the house: and I looked, and, behold, the glory of the LORD filled the house of the LORD: and I fell upon my face. ⁵And the LORD said unto me, Son of man,

mark well[a], and behold with thine eyes, and hear with thine ears all that I say unto thee concerning all the ordinances of the house of the LORD, and all the laws thereof; and mark well the entering in of the house, with every going forth of the sanctuary. ⁶And thou shalt say to the rebellious, *even* to the house of Israel, Thus saith the Lord GOD; O ye house of Israel, let it suffice you of all your abominations, ⁷In that ye have brought *into my sanctuary* strangers[b], uncircumcised in heart, and uncircumcised in flesh, to be in my sanctuary, to pollute it, *even* my house, when ye offer my bread, the fat and the blood, and they have broken my covenant because of all your abominations. ⁸And ye have not kept the charge of mine holy things: but ye have set keepers of my charge[c] in my sanctuary for yourselves. ⁹Thus saith the Lord GOD; No stranger, uncircumcised in heart, nor uncircumcised in flesh, shall enter into my sanctuary, of any stranger that *is* among the children of Israel.

¹⁰And the Levites that are gone away far from me, when Israel went astray, which went astray away from me after their idols; they shall even bear their iniquity. ¹¹Yet they shall be ministers in my sanctuary, *having* charge at the gates of the house, and ministering to the house: they shall slay the burnt offering and the sacrifice for the people, and they shall stand before them to minister unto them. ¹²Because they ministered unto them before their idols, and caused the house of Israel to

---

[a] mark well: Heb. set thine heart
[b] strangers: Heb. children of a stranger
[c] my charge: or, my ward, or, ordinance

fall into iniquity; therefore have I lifted up mine hand against them, saith the Lord GOD, and they shall bear their iniquity. ¹³And they shall not come near unto me, to do the office of a priest unto me, nor to come near to any of my holy things, in the most holy *place*: but they shall bear their shame, and their abominations which they have committed. ¹⁴But I will make them keepers of the charge of the house, for all the service thereof, and for all that shall be done therein. ¹⁵But the priests the Levites, the sons of Zadok, that kept the charge of my sanctuary when the children of Israel went astray from me, they shall come near to me to minister unto me, and they shall stand before me to offer unto me the fat and the blood, saith the Lord GOD: ¹⁶They shall enter into my sanctuary, and they shall come near to my table, to minister unto me, and they shall keep my charge.

¹⁷And it shall come to pass, *that* when they enter in at the gates of the inner court, they shall be clothed with linen garments; and no wool shall come upon them, whiles they minister in the gates of the inner court, and within. ¹⁸They shall have linen bonnets upon their heads, and shall have linen breeches upon their loins; they shall not gird *themselves* with any thing that causeth sweat. ¹⁹And when they go forth into the utter court, *even* into the utter court to the people, they shall put off their garments wherein they ministered, and lay them in the holy chambers, and they shall put on other garments; and they shall not sanctify the people with their garments. ²⁰Neither shall they shave their heads, nor suffer their locks to grow long; they shall only poll their heads. ²¹Neither shall any priest drink wine, when they enter into the inner court. ²²Neither shall they take for their wives a widow, nor her that is put away: but they shall take maidens of the seed of the house of Israel, or a widow that had a priest before. ²³And they shall teach my people *the difference* between the holy and profane, and cause them to discern between the unclean and the clean. ²⁴And in controversy they shall stand in judgment; *and* they shall judge it according to my judgments: and they shall keep my laws and my statutes in all mine assemblies; and they shall hallow my sabbaths. ²⁵And they shall come at no dead person to defile themselves: but for father, or for mother, or for son, or for daughter, for brother, or for sister that hath had no husband, they may defile themselves. ²⁶And after he is cleansed, they shall reckon unto him seven days. ²⁷And in the day that he goeth into the sanctuary, unto the inner court, to minister in the sanctuary, he shall offer his sin offering, saith the Lord GOD. ²⁸And it shall be unto them for an inheritance: I *am* their inheritance: and ye shall give them no possession in Israel: I *am* their possession. ²⁹They shall eat the meat offering, and the sin offering, and the trespass offering; and every dedicated thing in Israel shall be theirs. ³⁰And the first⁴ of all the firstfruits of all *things*, and every oblation of all, of every *sort* of your oblations, shall be the priest's: ye shall also give unto the priest

---

⁴ And the first: or, And the chief

the first of your dough, that he may cause the blessing to rest in thine house. [31]The priests shall not eat of any thing that is dead of itself, or torn, whether it be fowl or beast.

45

[1]Moreover, when ye shall divide by lot the land for inheritance, ye shall offer an oblation unto the LORD, an holy portion of the land: the length *shall be* the length of five and twenty thousand *reeds*, and the breadth *shall be* ten thousand. This *shall be* holy in all the borders thereof round about. [2]Of this there shall be for the sanctuary five hundred *in length*, with five hundred *in breadth*, square round about; and fifty cubits round about for the suburbs[a] thereof. [3]And of this measure shalt thou measure the length of five and twenty thousand, and the breadth of ten thousand: and in it shall be the sanctuary *and* the most holy *place*. [4]The holy *portion* of the land shall be for the priests the ministers of the sanctuary, which shall come near to minister unto the LORD: and it shall be a place for their houses, and an holy place for the sanctuary. [5]And the five and twenty thousand of length, and the ten thousand of breadth, shall also the Levites, the ministers of the house, have for themselves, for a possession for twenty chambers. [6]And ye shall appoint the possession of the city five thousand broad, and five and twenty thousand long, over against the oblation of the holy *portion*: it shall be for the whole house of Israel. [7]And a *portion shall be* for the prince on the one side and on the other side of the oblation of the holy *portion*, and of the possession of the city, before the oblation of the holy *portion*, and before the possession of the city, from the west side westward, and from the east side eastward: and the length *shall be* over against one of the portions, from the west border unto the east border. [8]In the land shall be his possession in Israel: and my princes shall no more oppress my people; and *the rest of* the land shall they give to the house of Israel according to their tribes.

Devotional Moment
•
Tithing

45:1-7 When it was time to divide the land, Ezekiel told the people first to give a section of it to the Lord as his "holy portion." The Old Testament repeatedly teaches this principle of tithing—of giving back to the Lord a portion of what he has given us. It is our privilege to give back to God, not only a tithe of our income, but also a portion of our time, possessions, abilities—whatever we have (and not from the leftovers, but from the best). In paying your bills and making your schedule, remember to set aside a portion for the Lord.

Devotional Moment
•
Honesty

45:9-11 Honesty and integrity were so important to the Lord that he specifically told the people how to measure goods and calculate the value of their currency. God's people were to be honest. For you, what is the greatest temptation to dishonesty? Glossing over conflicts? Managing money? Be fair and honest in all you do, both in your family and in dealings with others.

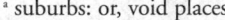

[a] suburbs: or, void places

⁹Thus saith the Lord GOD; Let it suffice you, O princes of Israel: remove violence and spoil, and execute judgment and justice, take away your exactionsᵇ from my people, saith the Lord GOD. ¹⁰Ye shall have just balances, and a just ephah, and a just bath. ¹¹The ephah and the bath shall be of one measure, that the bath may contain the tenth part of an homer, and the ephah the tenth part of an homer: the measure thereof shall be after the homer. ¹²And the shekel *shall be* twenty gerahs: twenty shekels, five and twenty shekels, fifteen shekels, shall be your maneh.

¹³This *is* the oblation that ye shall offer; the sixth part of an ephah of an homer of wheat, and ye shall give the sixth part of an ephah of an homer of barley: ¹⁴Concerning the ordinance of oil, the bath of oil, *ye shall offer* the tenth part of a bath out of the cor, *which is* an homer of ten baths; for ten baths *are* an homer: ¹⁵And one lambᶜ out of the flock, out of two hundred, out of the fat pastures of Israel; for a meat offering, and for a burnt offering, and for peace offerings, to make reconciliation for them, saith the Lord GOD. ¹⁶All the people of the land shall give this oblation for the prince in Israel. ¹⁷And it shall be the prince's part *to give* burnt offerings, and meat offerings, and drink offerings, in the feasts, and in the new moons, and in the sabbaths, in all solemnities of the house of Israel: he shall prepare the sin offering, and the meat offering, and the burnt offering, and the peace offerings, to make reconciliation for the house of Israel. ¹⁸Thus saith the Lord GOD; In the first *month*, in the first *day* of the month, thou shalt take a young bullock without blemish, and cleanse the sanctuary: ¹⁹And the priest shall take of the blood of the sin offering, and put *it* upon the posts of the house, and upon the four corners of the settle of the altar, and upon the posts of the gate of the inner court. ²⁰And so thou shalt do the seventh *day* of the month for every one that erreth, and for *him that is* simple: so shall ye reconcile the house. ²¹In the first *month*, in the fourteenth day of the month, ye shall have the passover, a feast of seven days; unleavened bread shall be eaten. ²²And upon that day shall the prince prepare for himself and for all the people of the land a bullock *for* a sin offering. ²³And seven days of the feast he shall prepare a burnt offering to the LORD, seven bullocks and seven rams without blemish daily the seven days; and a kid of the goats daily *for* a sin offering. ²⁴And he shall prepare a meat offering of an ephah for a bullock, and an ephah for a ram, and an hin of oil for an ephah. ²⁵In the seventh *month*, in the fifteenth day of the month, shall he do the like in the feast of the seven days, according to the sin offering, according to the burnt offering, and according to the meat offering, and according to the oil.

46

¹Thus saith the Lord GOD; The gate of the inner court that looketh toward the east shall be shut the six working days; but on the sabbath it shall be opened,

---

ᵇ exactions: Heb. expulsions
ᶜ lamb: or, kid

and in the day of the new moon it shall be opened. ²And the prince shall enter by the way of the porch of *that* gate without, and shall stand by the post of the gate, and the priests shall prepare his burnt offering and his peace offerings, and he shall worship at the threshold of the gate: then he shall go forth; but the gate shall not be shut until the evening. ³Likewise the people of the land shall worship at the door of this gate before the LORD in the sabbaths and in the new moons. ⁴And the burnt offering that the prince shall offer unto the LORD in the sabbath day *shall be* six lambs without blemish, and a ram without blemish. ⁵And the meat offering *shall be* an ephah for a ram, and the meat offering for the lambs as he shall be able to give, and an hin of oil to an ephah. ⁶And in the day of the new moon *it shall be* a young bullock without blemish, and six lambs, and a ram: they shall be without blemish. ⁷And he shall prepare a meat offering, an ephah for a bullock, and an ephah for a ram, and for the lambs according as his hand shall attain unto, and an hin of oil to an ephah. ⁸And when the prince shall enter, he shall go in by the way of the porch of *that* gate, and he shall go forth by the way thereof. ⁹But when the people of the land shall come before the LORD in the solemn feasts, he that entereth in by the way of the north gate to worship shall go out by the way of the south gate; and he that entereth by the way of the south gate shall go forth by the way of the north gate: he shall not return by the way of the gate whereby he came in, but shall go forth over against it. ¹⁰And the prince in the midst of them, when they go in, shall go in; and when they go forth, shall go forth. ¹¹And in the feasts and in the solemnities the meat offering shall be an ephah to a bullock, and an ephah to a ram, and to the lambs as he is able to give, and an hin of oil to an ephah. ¹²Now when the prince shall prepare a voluntary burnt offering or peace offerings voluntarily unto the LORD, *one* shall then open him the gate that looketh toward the east, and he shall prepare his burnt offering and his peace offerings, as he did on the sabbath day: then he shall go forth; and after his going forth *one* shall shut the gate. ¹³Thou shalt daily prepare a burnt offering unto the LORD *of* a lamb of the first year without blemish: thou shalt prepare it every morning. ¹⁴And thou shalt prepare a meat offering for it every morning, the sixth part of an ephah, and the third part of an hin of oil, to temper with the fine flour; a meat offering continually by a perpetual ordinance unto the LORD. ¹⁵Thus shall they prepare the lamb, and the meat offering, and the oil, every morning *for* a continual burnt offering.

¹⁶Thus saith the Lord GOD; If the prince give a gift unto any of his sons, the inheritance thereof shall be his sons'; it *shall be* their possession by inheritance. ¹⁷But if he give a gift of his inheritance to one of his servants, then it shall be his to the year of liberty; after it shall return to the prince: but his inheritance shall be his sons' for them. ¹⁸Moreover the prince shall not take of the people's inheritance by oppression, to thrust them out of their possession; *but* he shall give his sons inheritance out of his own possession: that my people be not scattered every man from his possession.

¹⁹After he brought me through the

entry, which *was* at the side of the gate, into the holy chambers of the priests, which looked toward the north: and, behold, there *was* a place on the two sides westward. ²⁰Then said he unto me, This *is* the place where the priests shall boil the trespass offering and the sin offering, where they shall bake the meat offering; that they bear *them* not out into the utter court, to sanctify the people. ²¹Then he brought me forth into the utter court, and caused me to pass by the four corners of the court; and, behold, in every* corner of the court *there was* a court. ²²In the four corners of the court *there were* courts joined* of forty *cubits* long and thirty broad: these four corners *were* of one measure. ²³And *there was* a row *of building* round about in them, round about them four, and *it was* made with boiling places under the rows round about. ²⁴Then said he unto me, These *are* the places of them that boil, where the ministers of the house shall boil the sacrifice of the people.

47

¹Afterward he brought me again unto the door of the house; and, behold, waters issued out from under the threshold of the house eastward: for the forefront of the house *stood toward* the east, and the waters came down from under from the right side of the house, at the south *side* of the altar. ²Then brought he me out of the way of the gate northward, and led me about the way without unto the utter gate by the way that looketh eastward; and, behold, there ran out waters on the right side. ³And when the man that had the line in his hand went forth eastward, he measured a thousand cubits, and he brought me through the waters; the waters *were* to the ankles. ⁴Again he measured a thousand, and brought me through the waters; the waters *were* to the knees. Again he measured a thousand, and brought me through; the waters *were* to the loins. ⁵Afterward he measured a thousand; *and it was* a river that I could not pass over: for the waters were risen, waters to swim in, a river that could not be passed over. ⁶And he said unto me, Son of man, hast thou seen *this?* Then he brought me, and caused me to return to the brink of the river. ⁷Now when I had returned, behold, at the bank* of the river *were* very many trees on the one side and on the other. ⁸Then said he unto me, These waters issue out toward the east country, and go down into the desert*, and go into the sea: *which being* brought forth into the sea, the waters shall be healed. ⁹And it shall come to pass, *that* every thing that liveth, which moveth, whithersoever the rivers* shall come, shall live: and there shall be a very great multitude of fish, because these waters shall come thither: for they shall be healed; and every thing shall live whither the river cometh. ¹⁰And it shall come to pass, *that* the fishers shall stand upon it from Engedi even unto Eneglaim; they shall be a *place* to spread forth nets; their fish shall

---

* in every . . . : Heb. a court in a corner of a court, and a court in a corner of a court
* joined: or, made with chimneys
* bank: Heb. lip
* desert: or, plain
* rivers: Heb. two rivers

be according to their kinds, as the fish of the great sea, exceeding many. ¹¹But the miry places thereof and the marishes thereof shall not be healed; they shall be given to salt. ¹²And by the river upon the bank thereof, on this side and on that side, shall grow^d all trees for meat, whose leaf shall not fade, neither shall the fruit thereof be consumed: it shall bring forth new fruit according to his months, because their waters they issued out of the sanctuary: and the fruit thereof shall be for meat, and the leaf thereof for medicine.

¹³Thus saith the Lord GOD; This *shall be* the border, whereby ye shall inherit the land according to the twelve tribes of Israel: Joseph *shall have two* portions. ¹⁴And ye shall inherit it, one as well as another: *concerning* the which I lifted up mine hand to give it unto your fathers: and this land shall fall unto you for inheritance. ¹⁵And this *shall be* the border of the land toward the north side, from the great sea, the way of Hethlon, as men go to Zedad; ¹⁶Hamath, Berothah, Sibraim, which *is* between the border of Damascus and the border of Hamath; Hazarhatticon^e, which *is* by the coast of Hauran. ¹⁷And the border from the sea shall be Hazarenan, the border of Damascus, and the north northward, and the border of Hamath. And *this is* the north side. ¹⁸And the east side ye shall measure from Hauran, and from Damascus, and from Gilead, and from the land of Israel *by* Jordan, from the border unto the east sea. And *this is* the east side. ¹⁹And the south side southward, from Tamar *even* to the waters of strife^f *in* Kadesh, the river to the great sea. And *this is* the south side southward. ²⁰The west side also *shall be* the great sea from the border, till a man come over against Hamath. This *is* the west side. ²¹So shall ye divide this land unto you according to the tribes of Israel. ²²And it shall come to pass, *that* ye shall divide it by lot for an inheritance unto you, and to the strangers that sojourn among you, which shall beget children among you: and they shall be unto you as born in the country among the children of Israel; they shall have inheritance with you among the tribes of Israel. ²³And it shall come to pass, *that* in what tribe the stranger sojourneth, there shall ye give *him* his inheritance, saith the Lord GOD.

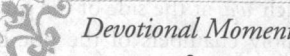

Devotional Moment
•
Foreigners

47:21-23 God told his people to give foreigners the same rights and privileges as the native-born citizens. God did not want his people to discriminate along ethnic or national lines, as people tend to do. If immigrants, refugees, or foreign visitors come to your church or school, help them adjust to their new life in a strange culture. Extend to them the same love and acceptance you would extend to your own family—the open-arms welcome that God has shown to you.

48

¹Now these *are* the names of the tribes. From the north end to the coast of the

---

^d shall grow: Heb. shall come up
^e Hazarhatticon: or, the middle village
^f strife: or, Meribah

way of Hethlon, as one goeth to Hamath, Hazarenan, the border of Damascus northward, to the coast of Hamath; for these are his sides east *and* west; a *portion for* Dan. [2]And by the border of Dan, from the east side unto the west side, a *portion for* Asher. [3]And by the border of Asher, from the east side even unto the west side, a *portion for* Naphtali. [4]And by the border of Naphtali, from the east side unto the west side, a *portion for* Manasseh. [5]And by the border of Manasseh, from the east side unto the west side, a *portion for* Ephraim. [6]And by the border of Ephraim, from the east side even unto the west side, a *portion for* Reuben. [7]And by the border of Reuben, from the east side unto the west side, a *portion for* Judah. [8]And by the border of Judah, from the east side unto the west side, shall be the offering which ye shall offer of five and twenty thousand *reeds in* breadth, and *in* length as one of the *other* parts, from the east side unto the west side: and the sanctuary shall be in the midst of it. [9]The oblation that ye shall offer unto the LORD *shall be* of five and twenty thousand in length, and of ten thousand in breadth. [10]And for them, *even* for the priests, shall be *this* holy oblation; toward the north five and twenty thousand *in length*, and toward the west ten thousand in breadth, and toward the east ten thousand in breadth, and toward the south five and twenty thousand in length: and the sanctuary of the LORD shall be in the midst thereof. [11]*It shall be* for the priests that are sanctified of the sons of Zadok; which have kept my charge, which went not astray when the children of Israel went astray, as the Levites went astray. [12]And *this* oblation of the land that is offered shall

be unto them a thing most holy by the border of the Levites. [13]And over against the border of the priests the Levites *shall have* five and twenty thousand in length, and ten thousand in breadth: all the length *shall be* five and twenty thousand, and the breadth ten thousand. [14]And they shall not sell of it, neither exchange, nor alienate the firstfruits of the land: for *it is* holy unto the LORD. [15]And the five thousand, that are left in the breadth over against the five and twenty thousand, shall be a profane *place* for the city, for dwelling, and for suburbs: and the city shall be in the midst thereof. [16]And these *shall be* the measures thereof; the north side four thousand and five hundred, and the south side four thousand and five hundred, and on the east side four thousand and five hundred, and the west side four thousand and five hundred. [17]And the suburbs of the city shall be toward the north two hundred and fifty, and toward the south two hundred and fifty, and toward the east two hundred and fifty, and toward the west two hundred and fifty. [18]And the residue in length over against the oblation of the holy *portion shall be* ten thousand eastward, and ten thousand westward: and it shall be over against the oblation of the holy *portion*; and the increase thereof shall be for food unto them that serve the city. [19]And they that serve the city shall serve it out of all the tribes of Israel. [20]All the oblation *shall be* five and twenty thousand by five and twenty thousand: ye shall offer the holy oblation foursquare, with the possession of the city. [21]And the residue *shall be* for the prince, on the one side and on the other of the holy oblation, and of the possession of the city, over against the five and twenty thousand of the oblation toward the east border, and westward over against the five and twenty thousand toward the west border, over against the portions for the prince: and it shall be the holy oblation; and the sanctuary of the house *shall be* in the midst thereof. ²²Moreover from the possession of the Levites, and from the possession of the city, *being* in the midst *of that* which is the prince's, between the border of Judah and the border of Benjamin, shall be for the prince. ²³As for the rest of the tribes, from the east side unto the west side, Benjamin *shall have* a *portion.* ²⁴And by the border of Benjamin, from the east side unto the west side, Simeon *shall have* a *portion.* ²⁵And by the border of Simeon, from the east side unto the west side, Issachar a *portion.* ²⁶And by the border of Issachar, from the east side unto the west side, Zebulun a *portion.* ²⁷And by the border of Zebulun, from the east side unto the west side, Gad a *portion.* ²⁸And by the border of Gad, at the south side southward, the border shall be even from Tamar *unto* the waters of strife^a *in* Kadesh, *and* to the river toward the great sea. ²⁹This *is* the land which ye shall divide by lot unto the tribes of Israel for inheritance, and these *are* their portions, saith the Lord GOD. ³⁰And these *are* the goings out of the city on the north side, four thousand and five hundred measures.

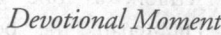

Devotional Moment
•
God's Presence

48:35 God named this new city "The City of God." While Ezekiel's vision of God's future perfect Kingdom is yet to be fulfilled, God lives among us even now. He lives in our homes, always present with us. If you could *see* the Lord in your home, sitting at the dinner table with you, working alongside you as you go about your routines, sitting with you ready to talk about anything that troubles you, would you act any differently? God truly wants to live in our homes. Does he live in yours?

³¹And the gates of the city *shall be* after the names of the tribes of Israel: three gates northward; one gate of Reuben, one gate of Judah, one gate of Levi. ³²And at the east side four thousand and five hundred: and three gates; and one gate of Joseph, one gate of Benjamin, one gate of Dan. ³³And at the south side four thousand and five hundred measures: and three gates; one gate of Simeon, one gate of Issachar, one gate of Zebulun. ³⁴At the west side four thousand and five hundred, *with* their three gates; one gate of Gad, one gate of Asher, one gate of Naphtali. ³⁵*It was* round about eighteen thousand *measures*: and the name of the city from *that* day *shall be,* The LORD *is* there^b.

---

^a strife . . . : or, Meribahkadesh
^b The LORD . . . . : Heb. Jehovahshammah

DANIEL

Purpose
To give a historical account of the faithful Jews who lived in captivity and to show how God is in control of heaven and earth, directing the forces of nature, the destiny of nations, and the care of his people

Author
Daniel

To Whom Written
The other captives in Babylon and God's people everywhere

Date Written
Approximately 535 B.C., recording events that occurred from about 605–535 B.C.

Setting
Daniel had been taken captive and deported to Babylon by Nebuchadnezzar in 605 B.C. There he served in the government for about sixty years during the reigns of four kings.

Key People
Daniel, Nebuchadnezzar, Shadrach, Meshach, Abednego, Belshazzar, Darius

Special Features
Daniel's apocalyptic visions (chapters 8–12) give a glimpse of God's plan for the ages, including a direct prediction of the Messiah.

What would happen if all the dangers of the world became like sleepy lions? if all parents were cheerful around the clock? if no one got sick and died?

Kids like Daniel because his story is filled with opposites. He's a captive in a pagan city; he prays more than he eats. He is punished for praying, but the penalty doesn't hurt. He is used as lion food, but the big cats just yawn at him. His enemies try to get rid of him, but the king honors him instead.

Kids like Daniel because he is brave. He walks into places that would give most people the scare of their lives. He witnesses about the true God while people laugh at him. He follows God's rules instead of the king's rules. Daniel just isn't afraid.

Maybe that's the key to facing life's dangers: trusting in God and telling fear to take a hike. Kids can do that better than many adults, who must calculate risks and analyze cost-benefit ratios.

Maybe it's time for children to read the book of Daniel to adults and for all of us to agree that living up front for God is better than worrying about money, jobs, relatives, grades, or germs. Let those in the world know that God is in charge. Let God make your home the "home of the brave."

1

¹In the third year of the reign of Jehoiakim king of Judah came Nebuchadnezzar king of Babylon unto
Jerusalem, and besieged it. ²And the
Lord gave Jehoiakim king of Judah into
his hand, with part of the vessels of the
house of God: which he carried into the
land of Shinar to the house of his god;
and he brought the vessels into the treasure house of his god. ³And the king
spake unto Ashpenaz the master of his
eunuchs, that he should bring *certain* of
the children of Israel, and of the king's
seed, and of the princes; ⁴Children in
whom *was* no blemish, but well
favoured, and skilful in all wisdom, and
cunning in knowledge, and understanding science, and such as *had* ability in them to stand in the king's palace,
and whom they might teach the learning and the tongue of the Chaldeans.

Devotional Moment
•
Teenagers

1:3-5 Nebuchadnezzar knew the importance of
investing in young people. He invested three
years in training and grooming them to be his
counselors, a fairly responsible position. Too
often adults see teenagers as inconveniences or
irritations. We can learn from Nebuchadnezzar. If
we are willing to help teenagers develop, we
can help shape their lives and also the lives of
the people *they* will touch: future spouses and
children, the church, the workplace, the
community. Be patient with teenagers; ask how
you can help them. And listen to them as they
discuss their world. They have a lot
to teach moms and dads.

---

⁵And the king appointed them a daily
provision of the king's meat, and of the
wineª which he drank: so nourishing
them three years, that at the end thereof
they might stand before the king. ⁶Now
among these were of the children of Judah, Daniel, Hananiah, Mishael, and
Azariah: ⁷Unto whom the prince of the
eunuchs gave names: for he gave unto
Daniel *the name* of Belteshazzar; and to
Hananiah, of Shadrach; and to
Mishael, of Meshach; and to Azariah,
of Abednego.

⁸But Daniel purposed in his heart
that he would not defile himself with
the portion of the king's meat, nor with
the wine which he drank: therefore he
requested of the prince of the eunuchs
that he might not defile himself. ⁹Now
God had brought Daniel into favour
and tender love with the prince of the
eunuchs. ¹⁰And the prince of the eunuchs said unto Daniel, I fear my lord
the king, who hath appointed your
meat and your drink: for why should he
see your faces worse liking than the
children which *are* of your sort? then
shall ye make *me* endanger my head to
the king. ¹¹Then said Daniel to Melzarᵇ,
whom the prince of the eunuchs had set
over Daniel, Hananiah, Mishael, and
Azariah, ¹²Prove thy servants, I beseech
thee, ten days; and let them give us
pulseᶜ to eat, and water to drink. ¹³Then
let our countenances be looked upon
before thee, and the countenance of the
children that eat of the portion of the
king's meat: and as thou seest, deal with
thy servants. ¹⁴So he consented to them

ª the wine . . . : Heb. the wine of his drink
ᵇ Melzar: or, the steward
ᶜ pulse: Heb. of pulse

in this matter, and proved them ten days. ¹⁵And at the end of ten days their countenances appeared fairer and fatter in flesh than all the children which did eat the portion of the king's meat. ¹⁶Thus Melzar took away the portion of their meat, and the wine that they should drink; and gave them pulse.

¹⁷As for these four children, God gave them knowledge and skill in all learning and wisdom: and Daniel^d had understanding in all visions and dreams. ¹⁸Now at the end of the days that the king had said he should bring them in, then the prince of the eunuchs brought them in before Nebuchadnezzar. ¹⁹And the king communed with them; and among them all was found none like Daniel, Hananiah, Mishael, and Azariah: therefore stood they before the king. ²⁰And in all matters of wisdom^e *and* understanding, that the king enquired of them, he found them ten times better than all the magicians *and* astrologers that *were* in all his realm. ²¹And Daniel continued *even* unto the first year of king Cyrus.

2

¹And in the second year of the reign of Nebuchadnezzar Nebuchadnezzar dreamed dreams, wherewith his spirit was troubled, and his sleep brake from him. ²Then the king commanded to call the magicians, and the astrologers, and the sorcerers, and the Chaldeans, for to shew the king his dreams. So they came and stood before the king. ³And the king said unto them, I have dreamed a dream, and my spirit was troubled to know the dream. ⁴Then spake the Chaldeans to the king in Syriack, O king, live for ever: tell thy servants the dream, and we will shew the interpretation. ⁵The king answered and said to the Chaldeans, The thing is gone from me: if ye will not make known unto me the dream, with the interpretation thereof, ye shall be cut^a in pieces, and your houses shall be made a dunghill. ⁶But if ye shew the dream, and the interpretation thereof, ye shall receive of me gifts and rewards^b and great honour: therefore shew me the dream, and the interpretation thereof. ⁷They answered again and said, Let the king tell his servants the dream, and we will shew the interpretation of it. ⁸The king answered and said, I know of certainty that ye would gain^c the time, because ye see the thing is gone from me. ⁹But if ye will not make known unto me the dream, *there is but* one decree for you: for ye have prepared lying and corrupt words to speak before me, till the time be changed: therefore tell me the dream, and I shall know that ye can shew me the interpretation thereof. ¹⁰The Chaldeans answered before the king, and said, There is not a man upon the earth that can shew the king's matter: therefore *there is* no king, lord, nor ruler, *that* asked such things at any magician, or astrologer, or Chaldean.

---

^d Daniel . . . : or, he made Daniel understand
^e wisdom . . . : Heb. wisdom of understanding
^a cut . . . : Chaldee made pieces
^b rewards: or, fee
^c gain: Chaldee buy

¹¹And *it is* a rare thing that the king requireth, and there is none other that can shew it before the king, except the gods, whose dwelling is not with flesh. ¹²For this cause the king was angry and very furious, and commanded to destroy all the wise *men* of Babylon. ¹³And the decree went forth that the wise *men* should be slain; and they sought Daniel and his fellows to be slain.

¹⁴Then Daniel answered[d] with counsel and wisdom to Arioch the captain of the king's guard, which was gone forth to slay the wise *men* of Babylon: ¹⁵He answered and said to Arioch the king's captain, Why *is* the decree *so* hasty from the king? Then Arioch made the thing known to Daniel. ¹⁶Then Daniel went in, and desired of the king that he would give him time, and that he would shew the king the interpretation. ¹⁷Then Daniel went to his house, and made the thing known to Hananiah, Mishael, and Azariah, his companions: ¹⁸That they would desire mercies of the God[e] of heaven concerning this secret; that Daniel and his fellows should not perish with the rest of the wise *men* of Babylon. ¹⁹Then was the secret revealed unto Daniel in a night vision. Then Daniel blessed the God of heaven. ²⁰Daniel answered and said, Blessed be the name of God for ever and ever: for wisdom and might are his: ²¹And he changeth the times and the seasons: he removeth kings, and setteth up kings: he giveth wisdom unto the wise, and knowledge to them that know understanding: ²²He revealeth the deep and secret things: he knoweth

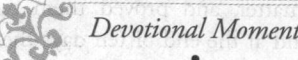

Devotional Moment
•
Problem Solving

2:16-18 Daniel had a huge problem: He and his three friends were scheduled for execution because the king wanted to know the meaning of a dream he couldn't remember. Daniel took three important steps: (1) He asked for more time. (2) He told three believing friends about it. (3) He prayed. That's a great model. We can face many overwhelming problems—huge financial burdens, the threat of death, rebellious children, betrayal by people who were trusted, and unfair teachers, just to name a few. Don't allow them to overpower or panic you. Place your confidence in God's ability, talk about the problem with a few trustworthy friends, and pray together, asking God to help and to give you wisdom.

what *is* in the darkness, and the light dwelleth with him. ²³I thank thee, and praise thee, O thou God of my fathers, who hast given me wisdom and might, and hast made known unto me now

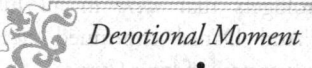

Devotional Moment
•
Thankfulness

2:20-23 When God revealed the king's dream to Daniel, the young man's first response was to praise God, thanking him for his mercy and wisdom. Daniel didn't immediately rush to the king and announce that he had solved the problem; he didn't gloat to his friends, saying, "Whew, we're in luck. I know the king's dream!" He *prayed*. He stopped to thank the Giver of the wisdom that would save his life. When God gives us wisdom to solve a problem, is our first response to sigh with relief that the problem is solved, or do we stop to thank the Giver of wisdom?

---

[d] answered . . . : Chaldee returned
[e] of the God: Chaldee from before God

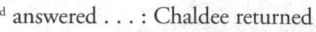

what we desired of thee: for thou hast *now* made known unto us the king's matter.

²⁴Therefore Daniel went in unto Arioch, whom the king had ordained to destroy the wise *men* of Babylon: he went and said thus unto him; Destroy not the wise *men* of Babylon: bring me in before the king, and I will shew unto the king the interpretation. ²⁵Then Arioch brought in Daniel before the king in haste, and said thus unto him, I have found a man of the captives of Judah, that will make known unto the king the interpretation. ²⁶The king answered and said to Daniel, whose name *was* Belteshazzar, Art thou able to make known unto me the dream which I have seen, and the interpretation thereof? ²⁷Daniel answered in the presence of the king, and said, The secret which the king hath demanded cannot the wise *men*, the astrologers, the magicians, the soothsayers, shew unto the king; ²⁸But there is a God in heaven that revealeth secrets, and maketh known to the king Nebuchadnezzar what shall be in the latter days. Thy dream, and the visions of thy head upon thy bed, are these; ²⁹As for thee, O king, thy thoughts came[f] *into thy mind* upon thy bed, what should come to pass hereafter: and he that revealeth secrets maketh known to thee what shall come to pass. ³⁰But as for me, this secret is not revealed to me for *any* wisdom that I have more than any living, but for *their* sakes[g] that shall

make known the interpretation to the king, and that thou mightest know the thoughts of thy heart.

³¹Thou, O king, sawest[h], and behold a great image. This great image, whose brightness *was* excellent, stood before thee; and the form thereof *was* terrible. ³²This image's head *was* of fine gold, his breast and his arms of silver, his belly and his thighs[i] of brass, ³³His legs of iron, his feet part of iron and part of clay. ³⁴Thou sawest till that a stone was cut out without[j] hands, which smote the image upon his feet *that were* of iron and clay, and brake them to pieces. ³⁵Then was the iron, the clay, the brass, the silver, and the gold, broken to pieces together, and became like the chaff of the summer threshingfloors; and the wind carried them away, that no place was found for them: and the stone that smote the image became a great mountain, and filled the whole earth. ³⁶This *is* the dream; and we will tell the interpretation thereof before the king. ³⁷Thou, O king, *art* a king of kings: for the God of heaven hath given thee a kingdom, power, and strength, and glory. ³⁸And wheresoever the children of men dwell, the beasts of the field and the fowls of the heaven hath he given into thine hand, and hath made thee ruler over them all. Thou *art* this head of gold. ³⁹And after thee shall arise another kingdom inferior to thee, and another third kingdom of brass, which shall bear rule over all the earth. ⁴⁰And the fourth king-

---

[f] came: Chaldee came up
[g] but for . . . : or, but for the intent that the interpretation may be made known to the king
[h] sawest: Chaldee wast seeing
[i] thighs: or, sides
[j] without . . . : or, which was not in hands

dom shall be strong as iron: forasmuch as iron breaketh in pieces and subdueth all *things*: and as iron that breaketh all these, shall it break in pieces and bruise. [41]And whereas thou sawest the feet and toes, part of potters' clay, and part of iron, the kingdom shall be divided; but there shall be in it of the strength of the iron, forasmuch as thou sawest the iron mixed with miry clay. [42]And *as* the toes of the feet *were* part of iron, and part of clay, *so* the kingdom shall be partly strong, and partly broken[k]. [43]And whereas thou sawest iron mixed with miry clay, they shall mingle themselves with the seed of men: but they shall not cleave one[l] to another, even as iron is not mixed with clay. [44]And in the days[m] of these kings shall the God of heaven set up a kingdom, which shall never be destroyed: and the kingdom shall not be left to other people, *but* it shall break in pieces and consume all these kingdoms, and it shall stand for ever. [45]Forasmuch as thou sawest that the stone was cut out of the mountain without[n] hands, and that it brake in pieces the iron, the brass, the clay, the silver, and the gold; the great God hath made known to the king what shall come to pass hereafter: and the dream *is* certain, and the interpretation thereof sure.

[46]Then the king Nebuchadnezzar fell upon his face, and worshipped Daniel, and commanded that they should offer an oblation and sweet odours unto him. [47]The king answered unto Daniel, and said, Of a truth *it is*, that your God *is* a God of gods, and a Lord of kings, and a revealer of secrets, seeing thou couldest reveal this secret. [48]Then the king made Daniel a great man, and gave him many great gifts, and made him ruler over the whole province of Babylon, and chief of the governors over all the wise *men* of Babylon. [49]Then Daniel requested of the king, and he set Shadrach, Meshach, and Abednego, over the affairs of the province of Babylon: but Daniel *sat* in the gate of the king.

3

[1]Nebuchadnezzar the king made an image of gold, whose height *was* threescore cubits, *and* the breadth thereof six cubits: he set it up in the plain of Dura, in the province of Babylon. [2]Then Nebuchadnezzar the king sent to gather together the princes, the governors, and the captains, the judges, the treasurers, the counsellors, the sheriffs, and all the rulers of the provinces, to come to the dedication of the image which Nebuchadnezzar the king had set up. [3]Then the princes, the governors, and captains, the judges, the treasurers, the counsellors, the sheriffs, and all the rulers of the provinces, were gathered together unto the dedication of the image that Nebuchadnezzar the king had set up; and they stood before the image that Nebuchadnezzar had set up. [4]Then an herald cried aloud[a], To you it is commanded, O

---

[k] broken: or, brittle
[l] one . . . : Chaldee this with this
[m] the days: Chaldee their days
[n] without . . . : or, which was not in hands
[a] aloud: Chaldee with might

people, nations, and languages, ⁵*That* at what time ye hear the sound of the cornet, flute, harp, sackbut, psaltery, dulcimer*ᵇ*, and all kinds of musick, ye fall down and worship the golden image that Nebuchadnezzar the king hath set up: ⁶And whoso falleth not down and worshippeth shall the same hour be cast into the midst of a burning fiery furnace. ⁷Therefore at that time, when all the people heard the sound of the cornet, flute, harp, sackbut, psaltery, and all kinds of musick, all the people, the nations, and the languages, fell down *and* worshipped the golden image that Nebuchadnezzar the king had set up.

⁸Wherefore at that time certain Chaldeans came near, and accused the Jews. ⁹They spake and said to the king Nebuchadnezzar, O king, live for ever. ¹⁰Thou, O king, hast made a decree, that every man that shall hear the

Devotional Moment
•
Convictions

3:12 Shadrach, Meshach, and Abednego refused to worship the king's golden statue. They were fully aware of the king's rage and irrational behavior, so they knew there was risk involved in disobeying him. But they believed that it was more important to obey God than to compromise their beliefs to please a man, even the powerful king. These courageous young men held to their convictions in the face of tremendous pressure. Young or old, we can all learn from Shadrach, Meshach, and Abednego to take a stand for God and hold to it, no matter what the personal cost.

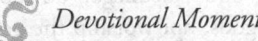

Devotional Moment
•
Courage

3:15-18 Even when the king threatened to throw these men into the furnace, they courageously stood up to him. They explained that they believed their God would keep them safe. "But if he doesn't," they went on, "we will never under any circumstance serve your gods or worship the gold statue you have erected." Where does that kind of courage come from? Faith. Everyone occasionally questions God's goodness. The only way to have courage in a crisis is to ask God to give pure faith. "Even if my son does not recover from his terminal illness, I will believe in God's goodness." "Even if my unemployment goes on another year, I will not doubt God's care for me." "Even if I do not get into the college I want, I will not give up on God." In what area can you express this kind of faith today?

sound of the cornet, flute, harp, sackbut, psaltery, and dulcimer, and all kinds of musick, shall fall down and worship the golden image: ¹¹And whoso falleth not down and worshippeth, *that* he should be cast into the midst of a burning fiery furnace. ¹²There are certain Jews whom thou hast set over the affairs of the province of Babylon, Shadrach, Meshach, and Abednego; these men, O king, have*ᶜ* not regarded thee: they serve not thy gods, nor worship the golden image which thou hast set up. ¹³Then Nebuchadnezzar in *his* rage and fury commanded to bring Shadrach, Meshach, and Abednego. Then they brought these men before the king. ¹⁴Nebuchadnezzar spake and said unto them, *Is it* true*ᵈ*, O Shadrach,

---

ᵇ dulcimer: or, singing: Chaldee symphony
ᶜ have . . . : Chaldee have set no regard upon thee
ᵈ true: or, of purpose

Meshach, and Abednego, do not ye serve my gods, nor worship the golden image which I have set up? ¹⁵Now if ye be ready that at what time ye hear the sound of the cornet, flute, harp, sackbut, psaltery, and dulcimer, and all kinds of musick, ye fall down and worship the image which I have made; *well:* but if ye worship not, ye shall be cast the same hour into the midst of a burning fiery furnace; and who *is* that God that shall deliver you out of my hands? ¹⁶Shadrach, Meshach, and Abednego, answered and said to the king, O Nebuchadnezzar, we *are* not careful to answer thee in this matter. ¹⁷If it be *so,* our God whom we serve is able to deliver us from the burning fiery furnace, and he will deliver *us* out of thine hand, O king. ¹⁸But if not, be it known unto thee, O king, that we will not serve thy gods, nor worship the golden image which thou hast set up.

¹⁹Then was Nebuchadnezzar full[e] of fury, and the form of his visage was changed against Shadrach, Meshach, and Abednego: *therefore* he spake, and commanded that they should heat the furnace one seven times more than it was wont to be heated. ²⁰And he commanded the most[f] mighty men that *were* in his army to bind Shadrach, Meshach, and Abednego, *and* to cast *them* into the burning fiery furnace. ²¹Then these men were bound in their coats[g], their hosen, and their hats, and their *other* garments, and were cast into the midst of the burning fiery furnace. ²²Therefore because the king's commandment[h] was urgent, and the furnace exceeding hot, the flame of the fire slew those men that took up Shadrach, Meshach, and Abednego. ²³And these three men, Shadrach, Meshach, and Abednego, fell down bound into the midst of the burning fiery furnace. ²⁴Then Nebuchadnezzar the king was astonied, and rose up in haste, *and* spake, and said unto his counsellors[i], Did not we cast three men bound into the midst of the fire? They answered and said unto the king, True, O king. ²⁵He answered and said, Lo, I see four men loose, walking in the midst of the fire, and they have no hurt; and the form of the fourth is like the Son of God. ²⁶Then Nebuchadnezzar came near to the mouth[j] of the burning fiery furnace, *and* spake, and said, Shadrach, Meshach, and Abednego, ye servants of the most high God, come forth, and come *hither.* Then Shadrach, Meshach, and Abednego, came forth of the midst of the fire. ²⁷And the princes, governors, and captains, and the king's counsellors, being gathered together, saw these men, upon whose bodies the fire had no power, nor was an hair of their head singed, neither were their coats changed, nor the smell of fire had passed on them.

²⁸ *Then* Nebuchadnezzar spake, and

---

e full: Chaldee filled
f most . . . : Chaldee mighty of strength
g coats: or, mantles
h commandment: Chaldee word
i counsellors: or, governors
j mouth: Chaldee door

said, Blessed *be* the God of Shadrach, Meshach, and Abednego, who hath sent his angel, and delivered his servants that trusted in him, and have changed the king's word, and yielded their bodies, that they might not serve nor worship any god, except their own God. ²⁹Therefore I make[k] a decree, That every people, nation, and language, which speak any thing amiss against the God of Shadrach, Meshach, and Abednego, shall be cut in pieces, and their houses shall be made a dunghill: because there is no other God that can deliver after this sort. ³⁰Then the king promoted[l] Shadrach, Meshach, and Abednego, in the province of Babylon.

4

¹Nebuchadnezzar the king, unto all people, nations, and languages, that dwell in all the earth; Peace be multi-

---

Devotional Moment

•

Humility

4:1-3, 37 After Nebuchadnezzar came to his senses, he not only realized that God was the source of all power and strength but also proclaimed it to people of every nation in every language. He openly told them of how God had reduced him to an animal existence. In humility he acknowledged the true God and the true source of power. He called them to join him in praising the Most High God. When God transforms our life, we, too, can tell others of his power even if he uses humiliating circumstances to bring us to our senses.

---

plied unto you. ²I thought[a] it good to shew the signs and wonders that the high God hath wrought toward me. ³How great *are* his signs! and how mighty *are* his wonders! his kingdom *is* an everlasting kingdom, and his dominion *is* from generation to generation.

⁴I Nebuchadnezzar was at rest in mine house, and flourishing in my palace: ⁵I saw a dream which made me afraid, and the thoughts upon my bed and the visions of my head troubled me. ⁶Therefore made I a decree to bring in all the wise *men* of Babylon before me, that they might make known unto me the interpretation of the dream. ⁷Then came in the magicians, the astrologers, the Chaldeans, and the soothsayers: and I told the dream before them; but they did not make known unto me the interpretation thereof. ⁸But at the last Daniel came in before me, whose name *was* Belteshazzar, according to the name of my god, and in whom *is* the spirit of the holy gods: and before him I told the dream, *saying*, ⁹O Belteshazzar, master of the magicians, because I know that the spirit of the holy gods *is* in thee, and no secret troubleth thee, tell me the visions of my dream that I have seen, and the interpretation thereof. ¹⁰Thus *were* the visions of mine head in my bed; I saw[b], and behold a tree in the midst of the earth, and the height thereof *was* great. ¹¹The tree grew, and was strong, and the height thereof reached unto heaven,

---

[k] I make . . . : Chaldee a decree is made by me
[l] promoted: Chaldee made to prosper
[a] I thought . . . : Chaldee It was seemly before me
[b] I saw: Chaldee I was seeing

and the sight thereof to the end of all the earth: ¹²The leaves thereof *were* fair, and the fruit thereof much, and in it *was* meat for all: the beasts of the field had shadow under it, and the fowls of the heaven dwelt in the boughs thereof, and all flesh was fed of it. ¹³I saw in the visions of my head upon my bed, and, behold, a watcher and an holy one came down from heaven; ¹⁴He cried aloudᶜ, and said thus, Hew down the tree, and cut off his branches, shake off his leaves, and scatter his fruit: let the beasts get away from under it, and the fowls from his branches: ¹⁵Nevertheless leave the stump of his roots in the earth, even with a band of iron and brass, in the tender grass of the field; and let it be wet with the dew of heaven, and *let* his portion *be* with the beasts in the grass of the earth: ¹⁶Let his heart be changed from man's, and let a beast's heart be given unto him; and let seven times pass over him. ¹⁷This matter *is* by the decree of the watchers, and the demand by the word of the holy ones: to the intent that the living may know that the most High ruleth in the kingdom of men, and giveth it to whomsoever he will, and setteth up over it the basest of men. ¹⁸This dream I king Nebuchadnezzar have seen. Now thou, O Belteshazzar, declare the interpretation thereof, forasmuch as all the wise *men* of my kingdom are not able to make known unto me the interpretation: but thou *art* able; for the spirit of the holy gods *is* in thee.

¹⁹Then Daniel, whose name *was* Belteshazzar, was astonied for one hour, and his thoughts troubled him. The king spake, and said, Belteshazzar, let not the dream, or the interpretation thereof, trouble thee. Belteshazzar answered and said, My lord, the dream *be* to them that hate thee, and the interpretation thereof to thine enemies. ²⁰The tree that thou sawest, which grew, and was strong, whose height reached unto the heaven, and the sight thereof to all the earth; ²¹Whose leaves *were* fair, and the fruit thereof much, and in it *was* meat for all; under which the beasts of the field dwelt, and upon whose branches the fowls of the heaven had their habitation: ²²It *is* thou, O king, that art grown and become strong: for thy greatness is grown, and reacheth unto heaven, and thy dominion to the end of the earth. ²³And whereas the king saw a watcher and an holy one coming down from heaven, and saying, Hew the tree down, and destroy it; yet leave the stump of the roots thereof in the earth, even with a band of iron and brass, in the tender grass of the field; and let it be wet with the dew of heaven, and *let* his portion *be* with the beasts of the field, till seven times pass over him; ²⁴This *is* the interpretation, O king, and this *is* the decree of the most High, which is come upon my lord the king: ²⁵That they shall drive thee from men, and thy dwelling shall be with the beasts of the field, and they shall make thee to eat grass as oxen, and they shall wet thee with the dew of heaven, and seven times shall pass over thee, till thou know that the most High ruleth in the kingdom of men, and giveth it to whomsoever he will. ²⁶And whereas they commanded to leave the stump of

---

ᶜ aloud: Chaldee with might

the tree roots; thy kingdom shall be sure unto thee, after that thou shalt have known that the heavens do rule. [27]Wherefore, O king, let my counsel be acceptable unto thee, and break off thy sins by righteousness, and thine iniquities by shewing mercy to the poor; if it may be a lengthening[d] of thy tranquillity.

[28]All this came upon the king Nebuchadnezzar. [29]At the end of twelve months he walked in[e] the palace of the kingdom of Babylon. [30]The king spake, and said, Is not this great Babylon, that I have built for the house of the kingdom by the might of my power, and for the honour of my majesty? [31]While the word *was* in the king's mouth, there fell a voice from heaven, *saying*, O king Nebuchadnezzar, to thee it is spoken; The kingdom is departed from thee. [32]And they shall drive thee from men, and thy dwelling *shall be* with the beasts of the field: they

---

Devotional Moment

•

Pride

4:29-33 After all Nebuchadnezzar had seen God do and after all he had learned from Daniel and his three friends, the king took pride in himself, not in God. God punished him by making him live like an animal for seven years. It's easy for us to shake our heads at Nebuchadnezzar and wonder how he could be so blind. But watch out! If God has blessed you, don't take full credit for it. If God has given you a good job, don't pat yourself on the back for your accomplishments. If God has given you cooperative children, give him the credit! May we learn from Nebuchadnezzar that all the credit, all the glory, all the honor belongs to God.

---

shall make thee to eat grass as oxen, and seven times shall pass over thee, until thou know that the most High ruleth in the kingdom of men, and giveth it to whomsoever he will. [33]The same hour was the thing fulfilled upon Nebuchadnezzar: and he was driven from men, and did eat grass as oxen, and his body was wet with the dew of heaven, till his hairs were grown like eagles' *feathers*, and his nails like birds' *claws*.

[34]And at the end of the days I Nebuchadnezzar lifted up mine eyes unto heaven, and mine understanding returned unto me, and I blessed the most High, and I praised and honoured him that liveth for ever, whose dominion *is* an everlasting dominion, and his kingdom *is* from generation to generation: [35]And all the inhabitants of the earth *are* reputed as nothing: and he doeth according to his will in the army of heaven, and *among* the inhabitants of the earth: and none can stay his hand, or say unto him, What doest thou? [36]At the same time my reason returned unto me; and for the glory of my kingdom, mine honour and brightness returned unto me; and my counsellors and my lords sought unto me; and I was established in my kingdom, and excellent majesty was added unto me. [37]Now I Nebuchadnezzar praise and extol and honour the King of heaven, all whose works *are* truth, and his ways judgment: and those that walk in pride he is able to abase.

5

[1]Belshazzar the king made a great feast to a thousand of his lords, and drank

---

[d] a lengthening . . . : or, an healing of thine error
[e] in: or, upon

wine before the thousand. ²Belshazzar, whiles he tasted the wine, commanded to bring the golden and silver vessels which his father[a] Nebuchadnezzar had taken out of the temple which *was* in Jerusalem; that the king, and his princes, his wives, and his concubines, might drink therein. ³Then they brought the golden vessels that were taken out of the temple of the house of God which *was* at Jerusalem; and the king, and his princes, his wives, and his concubines, drank in them. ⁴They drank wine, and praised the gods of gold, and of silver, of brass, of iron, of wood, and of stone. ⁵In the same hour came forth fingers of a man's hand, and wrote over against the candlestick upon the plaister of the wall of the king's palace: and the king saw the part of the hand that wrote. ⁶Then the king's countenance[b] was changed, and his thoughts troubled him, so that the joints of his loins were loosed, and his knees smote one against another. ⁷The king cried aloud[c] to bring in the astrologers, the Chaldeans, and the soothsayers. *And* the king spake, and said to the wise *men* of Babylon, Whosoever shall read this writing, and shew me the interpretation thereof, shall be clothed with scarlet, and *have* a chain of gold about his neck, and shall be the third ruler in the kingdom. ⁸Then came in all the king's wise *men*: but they could not read the writing, nor make known to the king the interpretation thereof. ⁹Then was king Belshazzar greatly troubled, and his countenance[d] was changed in him, and his lords were astonied.

¹⁰*Now* the queen, by reason of the words of the king and his lords, came into the banquet house: *and* the queen spake and said, O king, live for ever: let not thy thoughts trouble thee, nor let thy countenance be changed: ¹¹There is a man in thy kingdom, in whom *is* the spirit of the holy gods; and in the days of thy father[e] light and understanding and wisdom, like the wisdom of the gods, was found in him; whom the king Nebuchadnezzar thy father, the king, *I say*, thy father, made master of the magicians, astrologers, Chaldeans, *and* soothsayers; ¹²Forasmuch as an excellent spirit, and knowledge, and understanding, interpreting[f] of dreams, and shewing of hard sentences, and dissolving of doubts, were found in the same Daniel, whom the king named Belteshazzar: now let Daniel be called, and he will shew the interpretation. ¹³Then was Daniel brought in before the king. *And* the king spake and said unto Daniel, *Art* thou that Daniel, which *art* of the children of the captivity of Judah, whom the king my father[g] brought out of Jewry? ¹⁴I have even heard of thee, that the spirit of the gods *is* in thee, and *that* light and understanding and excel-

---

[a] father: or, grandfather
[b] countenance: Chaldee brightnesses
[c] aloud: Chaldee with might
[d] countenance: Chaldee brightnesses
[e] father: or, grandfather
[f] interpreting: or, of an interpreter
[g] father: or, grandfather

lent wisdom is found in thee. ¹⁵And now the wise *men*, the astrologers, have been brought in before me, that they should read this writing, and make known unto me the interpretation thereof: but they could not shew the interpretation of the thing: ¹⁶And I have heard of thee, that thou canst make interpretations[h], and dissolve doubts: now if thou canst read the writing, and make known to me the interpretation thereof, thou shalt be clothed with scarlet, and *have* a chain of gold about thy neck, and shalt be the third ruler in the kingdom. ¹⁷Then Daniel answered and said before the king, Let thy gifts be to thyself, and give thy rewards[i] to another; yet I will read the writing unto the king, and make known to him the interpretation. ¹⁸O thou king, the most high God gave Nebuchadnezzar thy father a kingdom, and majesty, and glory, and honour: ¹⁹And for the majesty that he gave him, all people, nations, and languages, trembled and feared before him: whom he would he slew; and whom he would he kept alive; and whom he would he set up; and whom he would he put down. ²⁰But when his heart was lifted up, and his mind hardened in pride[j], he was deposed from his kingly throne, and they took his glory from him: ²¹And he was driven from the sons of men; and his heart[k] was made like the beasts, and his dwelling *was* with the wild asses: they fed him with grass like oxen, and his body was wet with the dew of heaven; till he knew that the most high God ruled in the kingdom of men, and *that* he appointeth over it whomsoever he will. ²²And thou his son, O Belshazzar, hast not humbled thine heart, though thou knewest all this; ²³But hast lifted up thyself against the Lord of heaven; and they have brought the vessels of his house before thee, and thou, and thy lords, thy wives, and thy concubines, have drunk wine in them; and thou hast praised the gods of silver, and gold, of brass, iron, wood, and stone, which see not, nor hear, nor know: and the God in whose hand thy breath *is*, and whose *are* all thy ways, hast thou not glorified: ²⁴Then was the part of the hand sent from him; and this writing was written. ²⁵And this *is* the writing that was written, MENE, MENE, TEKEL, UPHARSIN. ²⁶This *is* the in-

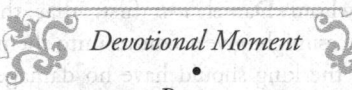

Devotional Moment

Parents

5:18-23 Belshazzar could have saved himself a lot of trouble if only he had learned from his predecessor's mistakes. Belshazzar had seen Nebuchadnezzar changed from a powerful man to an animal and then, by God's grace, changed back again to a man of power and honor. Belshazzar had heard about the Most High God, but he had stubbornly refused to listen. In many ways we are like Belshazzar, repeating our forebears' mistakes because we refuse to learn and insisting on going our own way. May God make us open to learning from the experience of our parents and other adults who have gained valuable lessons from life.

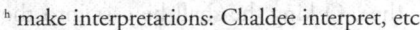

h make interpretations: Chaldee interpret, etc
i rewards: or, fee
j in pride: or, to deal proudly
k his heart . . . : or, he made his heart equal, etc

terpretation of the thing: MENE; God hath numbered thy kingdom, and finished it. ²⁷TEKEL; Thou art weighed in the balances, and art found wanting. ²⁸PERES; Thy kingdom is divided, and given to the Medes and Persians. ²⁹Then commanded Belshazzar, and they clothed Daniel with scarlet, and *put* a chain of gold about his neck, and made a proclamation concerning him, that he should be the third ruler in the kingdom.

³⁰In that night was Belshazzar the king of the Chaldeans slain. ³¹And Darius the Median took the kingdom, *being* about threescore and two years old.

6

¹It pleased Darius to set over the kingdom an hundred and twenty princes, which should be over the whole kingdom; ²And over these three presidents; of whom Daniel *was* first: that the princes might give accounts unto them, and the king should have no damage. ³Then this Daniel was preferred above

---

Devotional Moment

•

Reputation

6:4-5 In their jealousy over Daniel's success, the other government officials plotted to discredit him. And though they searched for a flaw in his character, they could find none. Daniel was capable, faithful, honest, wise, and meticulous. The surest way to build a sterling reputation is not to "avoid getting caught," but to consistently obey God and his Word—to faithfully fulfill the responsibilities he has given you, even if they seem menial. Live in such a way that if other people looked for ways to discredit you, they could find nothing.

Devotional Moment

•

Disciplined Prayer

6:10 Daniel's enemies knew that the king's decree against prayer would get Daniel into trouble because they knew Daniel would pray. It was his usual routine. Can your spouse, children, and friends count on that kind of consistency in prayer from you? Disciplined prayer takes work, but it shows where your faith is. And it puts you in the best possible position to hear from God and to speak to him of your gratitude and longings. Schedule time for prayer every day, and don't be afraid of getting caught!

---

the presidents and princes, because an excellent spirit *was* in him; and the king thought to set him over the whole realm. ⁴Then the presidents and princes sought to find occasion against Daniel concerning the kingdom; but they could find none occasion nor fault; forasmuch as he *was* faithful, neither was there any error or fault found in him. ⁵Then said these men, We shall not find any occasion against this Daniel, except we find *it* against him concerning the law of his God.

⁶Then these presidents and princes assembled together to the king, and said thus unto him, King Darius, live for ever. ⁷All the presidents of the kingdom, the governors, and the princes, the counsellors, and the captains, have consulted together to establish a royal statute, and to make a firm decreeᵃ, that whosoever shall ask a petition of any God or man for thirty days, save of thee, O king, he shall be cast into the den of lions. ⁸Now, O king, establish

---

ᵃ decree: or, interdict

the decree, and sign the writing, that it be not changed, according to the law of the Medes and Persians, which altereth not[b]. [9]Wherefore king Darius signed the writing and the decree. [10]Now when Daniel knew that the writing was signed, he went into his house; and his windows being open in his chamber toward Jerusalem, he kneeled upon his knees three times a day, and prayed, and gave thanks before his God, as he did aforetime.

[11]Then these men assembled, and found Daniel praying and making supplication before his God. [12]Then they came near, and spake before the king concerning the king's decree; Hast thou not signed a decree, that every man that shall ask *a petition* of any God or man within thirty days, save of thee, O king, shall be cast into the den of lions? The king answered and said, The thing *is* true, according to the law of the Medes and Persians, which altereth not. [13]Then answered they and said before the king, That Daniel, which *is* of the children of the captivity of Judah, regardeth not thee, O king, nor the decree that thou hast signed, but maketh his petition three times a day. [14]Then the king, when he heard *these* words, was sore displeased with himself, and set *his* heart on Daniel to deliver him: and he laboured till the going down of the sun to deliver him. [15]Then these men assembled unto the king, and said unto the king, Know, O king, that the law of the Medes and Persians *is*, That no decree nor statute which the king establisheth may be changed. [16]Then the

king commanded, and they brought Daniel, and cast *him* into the den of lions. *Now* the king spake and said unto Daniel, Thy God whom thou servest continually, he will deliver thee. [17]And a stone was brought, and laid upon the mouth of the den; and the king sealed it with his own signet, and with the signet of his lords; that the purpose might not be changed concerning Daniel.

[18]Then the king went to his palace, and passed the night fasting: neither were instruments[c] of musick brought before him: and his sleep went from him. [19]Then the king arose very early in the morning, and went in haste unto the den of lions. [20]And when he came to the den, he cried with a lamentable voice unto Daniel: *and* the king spake and said to Daniel, O Daniel, servant of the living God, is thy God, whom thou servest continually, able to deliver thee from the lions? [21]Then said Daniel unto the king, O king, live for ever. [22]My God hath sent his angel, and hath shut the lions' mouths, that they have not hurt me: forasmuch as before him innocency was found in me; and also before thee, O king, have I done no hurt. [23]Then was the king exceeding glad for him, and commanded that they should take Daniel up out of the den. So Daniel was taken up out of the den, and no manner of hurt was found upon him, because he believed in his God. [24]And the king commanded, and they brought those men which had accused Daniel, and they cast *them* into the den of lions, them, their children,

---

[b] altereth not: Chaldee passeth not
[c] instruments . . . : or, table

and their wives; and the lions had the mastery of them, and brake all their bones in pieces or ever they came at the bottom of the den.

²⁵Then king Darius wrote unto all people, nations, and languages, that dwell in all the earth; Peace be multiplied unto you. ²⁶I make a decree, That in every dominion of my kingdom men tremble and fear before the God of Daniel: for he *is* the living God, and stedfast for ever, and his kingdom *that* which shall not be destroyed, and his dominion *shall be even* unto the end. ²⁷He delivereth and rescueth, and he worketh signs and wonders in heaven and in earth, who hath delivered Daniel from the power[d] of the lions. ²⁸So this Daniel prospered in the reign of Darius, and in the reign of Cyrus the Persian.

7

¹In the first year of Belshazzar king of Babylon Daniel had[a] a dream and visions of his head upon his bed: then he wrote the dream, *and* told the sum of the matters. ²Daniel spake and said, I saw in my vision by night, and, behold, the four winds of the heaven strove upon the great sea. ³And four great beasts came up from the sea, diverse one from another. ⁴The first *was* like a lion, and had eagle's wings: I beheld till the wings thereof were plucked, and it was lifted up from the earth, and made stand upon the feet as a man, and a man's heart was given to it. ⁵And behold another beast, a second, like to a bear, and it raised up itself on one side, and

it had three ribs in the mouth of it between the teeth of it: and they said thus unto it, Arise, devour much flesh. ⁶After this I beheld, and lo another, like a leopard, which had upon the back of it four wings of a fowl; the beast had also four heads; and dominion was given to it. ⁷After this I saw in the night visions, and behold a fourth beast, dreadful and terrible, and strong exceedingly; and it had great iron teeth: it devoured and brake in pieces, and stamped the residue with the feet of it: and it *was* diverse from all the beasts that *were* before it; and it had ten horns. ⁸I considered the horns, and, behold, there came up among them another little horn, before whom there were three of the first horns plucked up by the roots: and, behold, in this horn *were* eyes like the eyes of man, and a mouth speaking great things.

⁹I beheld till the thrones were cast down, and the Ancient of days did sit,

Devotional Moment
•
Accountability
7:9-10 Daniel had a vision of God's final judgment, when every person will have to give account for his or her actions. In a sense, life is as simple as loving God with all our heart and loving our neighbor as ourself; in another sense, this is life's biggest challenge. Progressing toward spiritual maturity means encountering difficult choices and facing subtle temptations every day. It's easy to forget that though we may hide our faults from others, we can't hide them from God.

[d] power: Chaldee hand
[a] had: Chaldee saw

whose garment *was* white as snow, and the hair of his head like the pure wool: his throne *was like* the fiery flame, *and* his wheels *as* burning fire. ¹⁰A fiery stream issued and came forth from before him: thousand thousands ministered unto him, and ten thousand times ten thousand stood before him: the judgment was set, and the books were opened. ¹¹I beheld then because of the voice of the great words which the horn spake: I beheld *even* till the beast was slain, and his body destroyed, and given to the burning flame. ¹²As concerning the rest of the beasts, they had their dominion taken away: yet their lives^b were prolonged for a season and time. ¹³I saw in the night visions, and, behold, *one* like the Son of man came with the clouds of heaven, and came to the Ancient of days, and they brought him near before him. ¹⁴And there was given him dominion, and glory, and a kingdom, that all people, nations, and languages, should serve him: his dominion *is* an everlasting dominion, which shall not pass away, and his kingdom *that* which shall not be destroyed.

¹⁵I Daniel was grieved in my spirit in the midst of *my* body^c, and the visions of my head troubled me. ¹⁶I came near unto one of them that stood by, and asked him the truth of all this. So he told me, and made me know the interpretation of the things. ¹⁷These great beasts, which are four, *are* four kings, *which* shall arise out of the earth. ¹⁸But the saints of the most High shall take the kingdom, and possess the kingdom

for ever, even for ever and ever. ¹⁹Then I would know the truth of the fourth beast, which was diverse from^d all the others, exceeding dreadful, whose teeth *were of* iron, and his nails *of* brass; *which* devoured, brake in pieces, and stamped the residue with his feet; ²⁰And of the ten horns that *were* in his head, and *of* the other which came up, and before whom three fell; even *of* that horn that had eyes, and a mouth that spake very great things, whose look *was* more stout than his fellows. ²¹I beheld, and the same horn made war with the saints, and prevailed against them; ²²Until the Ancient of days came, and judgment was given to the saints of the most High; and the time came that the saints possessed the kingdom. ²³Thus he said, The fourth beast shall be the fourth kingdom upon earth, which shall be diverse from all kingdoms, and shall devour the whole earth, and shall tread it down, and break it in pieces. ²⁴And the ten horns out of this kingdom *are* ten kings *that* shall arise: and another shall rise after them; and he shall be diverse from the first, and he shall subdue three kings. ²⁵And he shall speak *great* words against the most High, and shall wear out the saints of the most High, and think to change times and laws: and they shall be given into his hand until a time and times and the dividing of time. ²⁶But the judgment shall sit, and they shall take away his dominion, to consume and to destroy *it* unto the end. ²⁷And the kingdom and dominion, and the greatness

---

^b their lives . . . : Chaldee a prolonging in life was given them
^c body: Chaldee sheath
^d from . . . : Chaldee from all those

of the kingdom under the whole heaven, shall be given to the people of the saints of the most High, whose kingdom *is* an everlasting kingdom, and all dominions^e shall serve and obey him. ²⁸Hitherto *is* the end of the matter. As for me Daniel, my cogitations much troubled me, and my countenance changed in me: but I kept the matter in my heart.

8

¹In the third year of the reign of king Belshazzar a vision appeared unto me, *even unto* me Daniel, after that which appeared unto me at the first. ²And I saw in a vision; and it came to pass, when I saw, that I *was* at Shushan *in* the palace, which *is* in the province of Elam; and I saw in a vision, and I was by the river of Ulai. ³Then I lifted up mine eyes, and saw, and, behold, there stood before the river a ram which had *two* horns: and the *two* horns *were* high; but one *was* higher than the other^a, and the higher came up last. ⁴I saw the ram pushing westward, and northward, and southward; so that no beasts might stand before him, neither *was there any* that could deliver out of his hand; but he did according to his will, and became great. ⁵And as I was considering, behold, an he goat came from the west on the face of the whole earth, and touched^b not the ground: and the goat *had* a notable horn between his eyes. ⁶And he came to the ram that had *two*

horns, which I had seen standing before the river, and ran unto him in the fury of his power. ⁷And I saw him come close unto the ram, and he was moved with choler against him, and smote the ram, and brake his two horns: and there was no power in the ram to stand before him, but he cast him down to the ground, and stamped upon him: and there was none that could deliver the ram out of his hand. ⁸Therefore the he goat waxed very great: and when he was strong, the great horn was broken; and for it came up four notable ones toward the four winds of heaven. ⁹And out of one of them came forth a little horn, which waxed exceeding great, toward the south, and toward the east, and toward the pleasant *land.* ¹⁰And it waxed great, *even* to the host^c of heaven; and it cast down *some* of the host and of the stars to the ground, and stamped upon them. ¹¹Yea, he magnified *himself* even to the prince of the host, and by him the daily *sacrifice* was taken away, and the place of his sanctuary was cast down. ¹²And an host^d was given *him* against the daily *sacrifice* by reason of transgression, and it cast down the truth to the ground; and it practised, and prospered. ¹³Then I heard one saint speaking, and another saint said unto that certain *saint* which spake, How long *shall be* the vision *concerning* the daily *sacrifice,* and the transgression of desolation, to give both the sanctuary and the host to be trodden under foot?

---

^e dominions: or, rulers
^a the other: Heb. the second
^b touched . . . : or, none touched him in the earth
^c to the host: or, against the host
^d an host . . . : or, the host was given over for the transgression against the daily sacrifice

¹⁴And he said unto me, Unto two thousand and three hundred days^e; then shall the sanctuary be cleansed.

¹⁵And it came to pass, when I, *even* I Daniel, had seen the vision, and sought for the meaning, then, behold, there stood before me as the appearance of a man. ¹⁶And I heard a man's voice between *the banks of* Ulai, which called, and said, Gabriel, make this *man* to understand the vision. ¹⁷So he came near where I stood: and when he came, I was afraid, and fell upon my face: but he said unto me, Understand, O son of man: for at the time of the end *shall be* the vision. ¹⁸Now as he was speaking with me, I was in a deep sleep on my face toward the ground: but he touched me, and set^f me upright. ¹⁹And he said, Behold, I will make thee know what shall be in the last end of the indignation: for at the time appointed the end *shall be.* ²⁰The ram which thou sawest having *two* horns *are* the kings of Media and Persia. ²¹And the rough goat *is* the king of Grecia: and the great horn that *is* between his eyes *is* the first king. ²²Now that being broken, whereas four stood up for it, four kingdoms shall stand up out of the nation, but not in his power. ²³And in the latter time of their kingdom, when the transgressors are come to the full, a king of fierce countenance, and understanding dark sentences, shall stand up. ²⁴And his power shall be mighty, but not by his own power: and he shall destroy wonderfully, and shall prosper, and practise,

and shall destroy the mighty and the holy^g people. ²⁵And through his policy also he shall cause craft to prosper in his hand; and he shall magnify *himself* in his heart, and by peace^h shall destroy many: he shall also stand up against the Prince of princes; but he shall be broken without hand. ²⁶And the vision of the evening and the morning which was told *is* true: wherefore shut thou up the vision; for it *shall be* for many days. ²⁷And I Daniel fainted, and was sick *certain* days; afterward I rose up, and did the king's business; and I was astonished at the vision, but none understood *it.*

9

¹In the first year of Darius the son of Ahasuerus, of the seed of the Medes, which was made king over the realm of the Chaldeans; ²In the first year of his reign I Daniel understood by books the number of the years, whereof the word of the LORD came to Jeremiah the prophet, that he would accomplish seventy years in the desolations of Jerusalem. ³And I set my face unto the Lord God, to seek by prayer and supplications, with fasting, and sackcloth, and ashes:

⁴And I prayed unto the LORD my God, and made my confession, and said, O Lord, the great and dreadful God, keeping the covenant and mercy to them that love him, and to them that keep his commandments; ⁵We have sinned, and have committed iniq-

---

^e days: Heb. evening morning
^f set . . . : Heb. made me stand upon my standing
^g holy . . . : Heb. people of the holy ones
^h peace: or, prosperity

uity, and have done wickedly, and have rebelled, even by departing from thy precepts and from thy judgments: ⁶Neither have we hearkened unto thy servants the prophets, which spake in thy name to our kings, our princes, and our fathers, and to all the people of the land. ⁷O Lord, righteousness *belongeth* unto thee, but unto us confusion of faces, as at this day; to the men of Judah, and to the inhabitants of Jerusalem, and unto all Israel, *that are* near, and *that are* far off, through all the countries whither thou hast driven them, because of their trespass that they have trespassed against thee. ⁸O Lord, to us *belongeth* confusion of face, to our kings, to our princes, and to our fathers, because we have sinned against thee. ⁹To the Lord our God *belong* mercies and forgivenesses, though we have rebelled against him; ¹⁰Neither have we obeyed the voice of the LORD our God, to walk in his laws, which he set before us by his servants the prophets. ¹¹Yea, all Israel have transgressed thy law, even by departing, that they might not obey thy voice; therefore the curse is poured upon us, and the oath that *is* written in the law of Moses the servant of God, because we have sinned against him. ¹²And he hath confirmed his words, which he spake against us, and against our judges that judged us, by bringing upon us a great evil: for under the whole heaven hath not been done as hath been done upon Jerusalem. ¹³As *it is* written in the law of Moses, all this evil is come upon us: yet made we not our prayer before the LORD our God, that we might turn from our iniquities,

and understand thy truth. ¹⁴Therefore hath the LORD watched upon the evil, and brought it upon us: for the LORD our God *is* righteous in all his works which he doeth: for we obeyed not his voice. ¹⁵And now, O Lord our God, that hast brought thy people forth out of the land of Egypt with a mighty hand, and hast gottenª thee renown, as at this day; we have sinned, we have done wickedly. ¹⁶O Lord, according to all thy righteousness, I beseech thee, let thine anger and thy fury be turned away from thy city Jerusalem, thy holy mountain: because for our sins, and for the iniquities of our fathers, Jerusalem and thy people *are become* a reproach to all *that are* about us. ¹⁷Now therefore, O our God, hear the prayer of thy servant, and his supplications, and cause thy face to shine upon thy sanctuary that is desolate, for the Lord's sake. ¹⁸O my God, incline thine ear, and hear; open thine eyes, and behold our desolations, and the city which is called by thy name: for we do not present our supplications before thee for our righteousnesses, but for thy great mercies. ¹⁹O Lord, hear; O Lord, forgive; O Lord, hearken and do; defer not, for thine own sake, O my God: for thy city and thy people are called by thy name.

²⁰And whiles I *was* speaking, and praying, and confessing my sin and the sin of my people Israel, and presenting my supplication before the LORD my God for the holy mountain of my God; ²¹Yea, whiles I *was* speaking in prayer, even the man Gabriel, whom I had seen in the vision at the beginning, being

---

ª gotten . . . : Heb. made thee a name

caused to fly swiftly[b], touched me about the time of the evening oblation. [22]And he informed *me*, and talked with me, and said, O Daniel, I am now come forth to give thee skill and understanding. [23]At the beginning of thy supplications the commandment[c] came forth, and I am come to shew *thee*; for thou *art* greatly beloved: therefore understand the matter, and consider the vision. [24]Seventy weeks are determined upon thy people and upon thy holy city, to finish[d] the transgression, and to make an end of sins, and to make reconciliation for iniquity, and to bring in everlasting righteousness, and to seal up the vision and prophecy, and to anoint the most Holy. [25]Know therefore and understand, *that* from the going forth of the commandment to restore and to build Jerusalem unto the Messiah the Prince *shall be* seven weeks, and threescore and two weeks: the street shall be built[e] again, and the wall, even in troublous times. [26]And after threescore and two weeks shall Messiah be cut off, but not for himself: and the people of the prince that shall come shall destroy the city and the sanctuary; and the end thereof *shall be* with a flood, and unto the end of the war desolations are determined. [27]And he shall confirm the covenant[f] with many for one week: and in the midst of the week he shall cause the sacrifice and the oblation to cease, and for the overspreading of abominations he shall make *it* desolate, even until the consummation, and that determined shall be poured upon the desolate.

10

[1]In the third year of Cyrus king of Persia a thing was revealed unto Daniel, whose name was called Belteshazzar; and the thing *was* true, but the time appointed *was* long[a]: and he understood the thing, and had understanding of the vision. [2]In those days I Daniel was mourning three full[b] weeks. [3]I ate no pleasant[c] bread, neither came flesh nor wine in my mouth, neither did I anoint myself at all, till three whole weeks were fulfilled. [4]And in the four and twentieth day of the first month, as I was by the side of the great river, which *is* Hiddekel; [5]Then I lifted up mine eyes, and looked, and behold a certain man clothed in linen, whose loins *were* girded with fine gold of Uphaz: [6]His body also *was* like the beryl, and his face as the appearance of lightning, and his eyes as lamps of fire, and his arms and his feet like in colour to polished brass, and the voice of his words like the voice of a multitude. [7]And I Daniel alone saw the vision: for the men that were with me saw not the vision; but a

---

[b] swiftly: Heb. with weariness, or, flight
[c] commandment: Heb. word
[d] finish: or, restrain
[e] be built . . . : Heb. return and be built
[f] the covenant: or, a covenant
[a] long: great
[b] full . . . : Heb. weeks of days
[c] pleasant . . . : Heb. bread of desires

great quaking fell upon them, so that they fled to hide themselves. ⁸Therefore I was left alone, and saw this great vision, and there remained no strength in me: for my comeliness^d was turned in me into corruption, and I retained no strength. ⁹Yet heard I the voice of his words: and when I heard the voice of his words, then was I in a deep sleep on my face, and my face toward the ground.

¹⁰And, behold, an hand touched me, which set^e me upon my knees and *upon* the palms of my hands. ¹¹And he said unto me, O Daniel, a man greatly beloved, understand the words that I speak unto thee, and stand upright: for unto thee am I now sent. And when he had spoken this word unto me, I stood trembling. ¹²Then said he unto me, Fear not, Daniel: for from the first day that thou didst set thine heart to understand, and to chasten thyself before thy God, thy words were heard, and I am come for thy words. ¹³But the prince of the kingdom of Persia withstood me one and twenty days: but, lo, Michael, one of the chief^f princes, came to help me; and I remained there with the kings of Persia. ¹⁴Now I am come to make thee understand what shall befall thy people in the latter days: for yet the vision *is* for *many* days. ¹⁵And when he had spoken such words unto me, I set my face toward the ground, and I became dumb. ¹⁶And, behold, *one* like the similitude of the sons of men touched my lips: then I opened my mouth, and

spake, and said unto him that stood before me, O my lord, by the vision my sorrows are turned upon me, and I have retained no strength. ¹⁷For how can the servant of this my lord talk with this my lord? for as for me, straightway there remained no strength in me, neither is there breath left in me. ¹⁸Then there came again and touched me *one* like the appearance of a man, and he strengthened me, ¹⁹And said, O man greatly beloved, fear not: peace *be* unto thee, be strong, yea, be strong. And when he had spoken unto me, I was strengthened, and said, Let my lord speak; for thou hast strengthened me. ²⁰Then said he, Knowest thou wherefore I come unto thee? and now will I return to fight with the prince of Persia: and when I am gone forth, lo, the prince of Grecia shall come. ²¹But I will shew thee that which is noted in the scripture of truth: and *there is* none that holdeth^g with me in these things, but Michael your prince.

11

¹Also I in the first year of Darius the Mede, *even* I, stood to confirm and to strengthen him. ²And now will I shew thee the truth. Behold, there shall stand up yet three kings in Persia; and the fourth shall be far richer than *they* all: and by his strength through his riches he shall stir up all against the realm of Grecia. ³And a mighty king shall stand up, that shall rule with great dominion, and do according to his will. ⁴And

---

^d comeliness: or, vigour
^e set: Heb. moved
^f chief: or, first
^g holdeth: Heb. strengtheneth himself

when he shall stand up, his kingdom shall be broken, and shall be divided toward the four winds of heaven; and not to his posterity, nor according to his dominion which he ruled: for his kingdom shall be plucked up, even for others beside those.

⁵And the king of the south shall be strong, and *one* of his princes; and he shall be strong above him, and have dominion; his dominion *shall be* a great dominion. ⁶And in the end of years they shall join themselves together; for the king's daughter of the south shall come to the king of the north to make an agreement: but she shall not retain the power of the arm; neither shall he stand, nor his arm: but she shall be given up, and they that brought her, and he that begat her, and he that strengthened her in *these* times. ⁷But out of a branch of her roots shall *one* stand up in his estate, which shall come with an army, and shall enter into the fortress of the king of the north, and shall deal against them, and shall prevail: ⁸And shall also carry captives into Egypt their gods, with their princes, *and* with their precious* vessels of silver and of gold; and he shall continue *more* years than the king of the north. ⁹So the king of the south shall come into *his* kingdom, and shall return into his own land. ¹⁰But his sons shall be stirred up, and shall assemble a multitude of great forces: and *one* shall certainly come, and overflow, and pass through: then shall he return, and be stirred up, *even*

to his fortress. ¹¹And the king of the south shall be moved with choler, and shall come forth and fight with him, *even* with the king of the north: and he shall set forth a great multitude; but the multitude shall be given into his hand. ¹²*And* when he hath taken away the multitude, his heart shall be lifted up; and he shall cast down *many* ten thousands: but he shall not be strengthened *by it.* ¹³For the king of the north shall return, and shall set forth a multitude greater than the former, and shall certainly come after* certain years with a great army and with much riches. ¹⁴And in those times there shall many stand up against the king of the south: also the robbers* of thy people shall exalt themselves to establish the vision; but they shall fall. ¹⁵So the king of the north shall come, and cast up a mount, and take the most fenced cities: and the arms of the south shall not withstand, neither his chosen people, neither *shall there be any* strength to withstand. ¹⁶But he that cometh against him shall do according to his own will, and none shall stand before him: and he shall stand in the glorious* land, which by his hand shall be consumed. ¹⁷He shall also set his face to enter with the strength of his whole kingdom, and upright ones with him; thus shall he do: and he shall give him the daughter of women, corrupting her: but she shall not stand *on his side*, neither be for him. ¹⁸After this shall he turn his face unto the isles, and shall take many: but a prince for his

---

ᵃ their precious . . . : Heb. vessels of their desire
ᵇ after . . . : Heb. at the end of times, even years
ᶜ the robbers: Heb. the children of robbers
ᵈ glorious . . . : or, goodly, etc.: Heb. land of ornament

1321

own behalf shall cause the reproach offered by him to cease; without his own reproach he shall cause *it* to turn upon him. ¹⁹Then he shall turn his face toward the fort of his own land: but he shall stumble and fall, and not be found. ²⁰Then shall stand up in his estate^e a raiser of taxes *in* the glory of the kingdom: but within few days he shall be destroyed, neither in anger, nor in battle.

²¹And in his estate^f shall stand up a vile person, to whom they shall not give the honour of the kingdom: but he shall come in peaceably, and obtain the kingdom by flatteries. ²²And with the arms of a flood shall they be overflown from before him, and shall be broken; yea, also the prince of the covenant. ²³And after the league *made* with him he shall work deceitfully: for he shall come up, and shall become strong with a small people. ²⁴He shall enter peaceably^g even upon the fattest places of the province; and he shall do *that* which his fathers have not done, nor his fathers' fathers; he shall scatter among them the prey, and spoil, and riches: *yea*, and he shall forecast his devices against the strong holds, even for a time. ²⁵And he shall stir up his power and his courage against the king of the south with a great army; and the king of the south shall be stirred up to battle with a very great and mighty army; but he shall not stand: for they shall forecast

devices against him. ²⁶Yea, they that feed of the portion of his meat shall destroy him, and his army shall overflow: and many shall fall down slain. ²⁷And both these kings' hearts^h *shall be* to do mischief, and they shall speak lies at one table; but it shall not prosper: for yet the end *shall be* at the time appointed. ²⁸Then shall he return into his land with great riches; and his heart *shall be* against the holy covenant; and he shall do *exploits*, and return to his own land. ²⁹At the time appointed he shall return, and come toward the south; but it shall not be as the former, or as the latter. ³⁰For the ships of Chittim shall come against him: therefore he shall be grieved, and return, and have indignation against the holy covenant: so shall he do; he shall even return, and have intelligence with them that forsake the holy covenant. ³¹And arms shall stand on his part, and they shall pollute the sanctuary of strength, and shall take away the daily *sacrifice*, and they shall place the abomination that maketh desolate. ³²And such as do wickedly against the covenant shall he corruptⁱ by flatteries: but the people that do know their God shall be strong, and do *exploits*. ³³And they that understand among the people shall instruct many: yet they shall fall by the sword, and by flame, by captivity, and by spoil, *many* days. ³⁴Now when they shall fall, they shall be

---

^e estate: or, place
^f estate: or, place
^g peaceably . . . : or, into the peaceable and fat, etc
^h hearts: Heb. their hearts
ⁱ corrupt: or, cause to dissemble

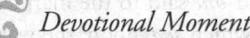

Devotional Moment
•
Suffering

11:33 Suffering presents us with a big problem: Why does a loving God allow it? Especially when a child suffers, or when an elderly person lingers in pain, the question begs for a satisfactory answer. The Bible does not completely explain suffering, but it does tell us this: We are never cut off from God's love. Romans 8:39 assures us that nothing "shall be able to separate us from the love of God, which is in Jesus Christ our Lord." Be comforted by this promise, and comfort those who suffer.

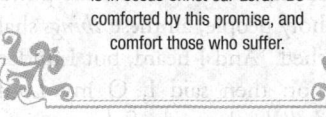

holpen with a little help: but many shall cleave to them with flatteries. ³⁵And *some* of them of understanding shall fall, to try them, and to purge^j, and to make *them* white, *even* to the time of the end: because *it is* yet for a time appointed. ³⁶And the king shall do according to his will; and he shall exalt himself, and magnify himself

Devotional Moment
•
Problems with Life

11:35 The messenger told Daniel that even wise believers may stumble, but it will serve to refine and purify them. Sometimes God's lesson plans include setbacks, difficulties, and knockdowns. If you or someone you love has stumbled, remember that God wants to use the experience to strengthen you. Ask for the help and prayers of other Christians in whom you can confide. Look at every setback as an opportunity for understanding, growth, and learning.

above every god, and shall speak marvellous things against the God of gods, and shall prosper till the indignation be accomplished: for that that is determined shall be done. ³⁷Neither shall he regard the God of his fathers, nor the desire of women, nor regard any god: for he shall magnify himself above all. ³⁸But in his estate shall he honour the God of forces: and a god whom his fathers knew not shall he honour with gold, and silver, and with precious stones, and pleasant things. ³⁹Thus shall he do in the most strong holds with a strange god, whom he shall acknowledge *and* increase with glory: and he shall cause them to rule over many, and shall divide the land for gain. ⁴⁰And at the time of the end shall the king of the south push at him: and the king of the north shall come against him like a whirlwind, with chariots, and with horsemen, and with many ships; and he shall enter into the countries, and shall overflow and pass over. ⁴¹He shall enter also into the glorious^k land, and many *countries* shall be overthrown: but these shall escape out of his hand, *even* Edom, and Moab, and the chief of the children of Ammon. ⁴²He shall stretch forth his hand also upon the countries: and the land of Egypt shall not escape. ⁴³But he shall have power over the treasures of gold and of silver, and over all the precious things of Egypt: and the Libyans and the Ethiopians *shall be* at his steps. ⁴⁴But tidings out of the east and out of the north shall

---

^j try them: or, try by them
^k glorious . . . : or, goodly, etc.: Heb. land of delight, or, ornament

trouble him: therefore he shall go forth with great fury to destroy, and utterly to make away many. ⁴⁵And he shall plant the tabernacles of his palace between the seas in the glorious¹ holy mountain; yet he shall come to his end, and none shall help him.

12

¹And at that time shall Michael stand up, the great prince which standeth for the children of thy people: and there shall be a time of trouble, such as never was since there was a nation *even* to that same time: and at that time thy people shall be delivered, every one that shall be found written in the book. ²And many of them that sleep in the dust of the earth shall awake, some to everlasting life, and some to shame *and* everlasting contempt. ³And they that be wiseᵃ shall shine as the brightness of the firmament; and they that turn many to righteousness as the stars for ever and ever. ⁴But thou, O Daniel, shut up the words, and seal the book, *even* to the time of the end: many shall run to and fro, and knowledge shall be increased.

⁵Then I Daniel looked, and, behold, there stood other two, the one on this side of the bankᵇ of the river, and the other on that side of the bank of the river. ⁶And *one* said to the man clothed in linen, which *was* uponᶜ the waters of the river, How long *shall it be to* the end of these wonders? ⁷And I heard the man clothed in linen, which *was* upon the waters of the river, when he held up his right hand and his left hand unto heaven, and sware by him that liveth for ever that *it shall be* for a timeᵈ, times, and an half; and when he shall have accomplished to scatter the power of the holy people, all these *things* shall be finished. ⁸And I heard, but I understood not: then said I, O my Lord, what *shall be* the end of these *things*? ⁹And he said, Go thy way, Daniel: for the words *are* closed up and sealed till the time of the end. ¹⁰Many shall be purified, and made white, and tried; but the wicked shall do wickedly: and none of the wicked shall understand; but the wise shall understand. ¹¹And from the time *that* the daily *sacrifice* shall be taken away, and the abominationᵉ that maketh desolate set up, *there shall be* a thousand two hundred and ninety days. ¹²Blessed *is* he that waiteth, and cometh to the thousand three hundred and five and thirty days. ¹³But go thou thy way till the end *be*: for thou shalt rest, and stand in thy lot at the end of the days.

---

¹ glorious . . . : or, goodly, etc.: Heb. mountain of delight of holiness
ᵃ wise: or, teachers
ᵇ bank: Heb. lip
ᶜ upon . . . : or, from above
ᵈ a time . . . : or, part
ᵉ the abomination: Heb. to set up the abomination

HOSEA

Purpose
To illustrate God's love for
his sinful people

Author
Hosea, son of Beeri. (*Hosea* is
derived from the verb *to save*.)

To Whom Written
Israel (the Northern Kingdom)
and God's people everywhere

Date Written
Approximately 715 B.C.,
recording events from
753–715 B.C.

Setting
Hosea began his ministry
during the end of the prosperous but morally declining
reign of Jeroboam II of Israel
(the upper classes were doing well, but they were oppressing the poor). He prophesied until shortly after the
fall of Samaria in 722 B.C.

Key Verse
"Then said the Lord unto
me, Go yet, love a woman
beloved of her friend, yet an
adulteress, according to the
love of the Lord toward the
children of Israel, who took
to other gods, and love
flagons of wine" (3:1).

Key People
Hosea, Gomer, their children

Key Places
The Northern Kingdom (Is-
rael), Samaria, Ephraim

Dysfunctional best describes the family at the center of this Bible book. The wife-mother, Gomer, was a prostitute. We can only imagine what the unrecorded family discussions were like.

Hosea's family troubles were a picture of Israel's sin. The people were prostitutes in a spiritual sense. The nation, especially its corrupt leaders, had abandoned true faith in the same way that Gomer abandoned her husband and children. Just as Hosea desired to reconcile with Gomer, God desired to reconcile with his people. He begged them to come back to him and "Keep mercy and judgment, and wait on thy God continually" (12:6).

In this book, Hosea employs many images from daily life—God is depicted as husband, father, lion, leopard, she-bear, dew, rain, moth, and others; Israel is pictured as wife, sick person, grapevine, grapes, early fig, olive tree, woman in labor, oven, morning mist, chaff, and smoke, to name a few.

Worried about family? Marriage turning dull? Toying with an affair? Job going nowhere? Your own *esprit* running low? Can't get much worse?

God has a big surprise for you. There's a vanload of love at God's warehouse, and the sale is on now. Customer service has never been better, and delivery is guaranteed. Read about it in Hosea. Product satisfaction is off the charts.

1

¹The word of the LORD that came unto Hosea, the son of Beeri, in the days of Uzziah, Jotham, Ahaz, *and* Hezekiah, kings of Judah, and in the days of Jeroboam the son of Joash, king of Israel.

²The beginning of the word of the LORD by Hosea. And the LORD said to Hosea, Go, take unto thee a wife of whoredoms and children of whoredoms: for the land hath committed great whoredom, *departing* from the LORD. ³So he went and took Gomer the daughter of Diblaim; which conceived, and bare him a son. ⁴And the LORD said unto him, Call his name Jezreel; for yet a little *while*, and I will avengeª the blood of Jezreel upon the house of Jehu, and will cause to cease the kingdom of the house of Israel. ⁵And it shall come to pass at that day, that I will break the bow of Israel in the valley of Jezreel. ⁶And she conceived again, and bare a daughter. And *God* said unto him, Call her name Loruhamahᵇ: for I will no more have mercy upon the house of Israel; but I will utterly take them away. ⁷But I will have mercy upon the house of Judah, and will save them by the LORD their God, and will not save them by bow, nor by sword, nor by battle, by horses, nor by horsemen.

⁸Now when she had weaned Loruhamah, she conceived, and bare a son. ⁹Then said *God*, Call his name Loammiᶜ: for ye *are* not my people, and I will not be your *God*. ¹⁰Yet the number of the children of Israel shall be as the sand of the sea, which cannot be measured nor numbered; and it shall come to pass, *that* in the place where it was said unto them, Ye *are* not my people, *there* it shall be said unto them, *Ye are* the sons of the living God. ¹¹Then shall the children of Judah and the children of Israel be gathered together, and appoint themselves one head, and they shall come up out of the land: for great *shall be* the day of Jezreel.

2

¹Say ye unto your brethren, Ammiª; and to your sisters, Ruhamah. ²Plead with your mother, plead: for she *is* not my wife, neither *am* I her husband: let her therefore put away her whoredoms out of her sight, and her adulteries from between her breasts; ³Lest I strip her naked, and set her as in the day that she was born, and make her as a wilderness,

---

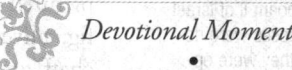

Devotional Moment
•
Whose Gift?

2:8 Gomer did not appreciate the fact that Hosea had provided her with money, food, and drink. Israel had a similar attitude: They had forgotten that God was their source of strength. Most of us, like Gomer, tend to overlook God's goodness to us. We take for granted the many little gifts that fill our day and sometimes the big ones too—the ones that come in fancy boxes, with bows and bells and special gift wrap. Take time today to thank God for the gifts you enjoy—all of them.

ª avenge: Heb. visit
ᵇ Loruhamah: that is, Not having obtained mercy
ᶜ Loammi: that is, Not my people
ª Ammi: that is, My people

and set her like a dry land, and slay her with thirst. ⁴And I will not have mercy upon her children; for they *be* the children of whoredoms. ⁵For their mother hath played the harlot: she that conceived them hath done shamefully: for she said, I will go after my lovers, that give *me* my bread and my water, my wool and my flax, mine oil and my drink^b.

⁶Therefore, behold, I will hedge up thy way with thorns, and make^c a wall, that she shall not find her paths. ⁷And she shall follow after her lovers, but she shall not overtake them; and she shall seek them, but shall not find *them*: then shall she say, I will go and return to my first husband; for then *was it* better with me than now. ⁸For she did not know that I gave her corn, and wine^d, and oil, and multiplied her silver and gold, *which* they prepared for Baal. ⁹Therefore will I return, and take away my corn in the time thereof, and my wine in the season thereof, and will recover^e my wool and my flax *given* to cover her nakedness. ¹⁰And now will I discover her lewdness^f in the sight of her lovers, and none shall deliver her out of mine hand. ¹¹I will also cause all her mirth to cease, her feast days, her new moons, and her sabbaths, and all her solemn feasts. ¹²And I will destroy^g her vines and her fig trees, whereof she

hath said, These *are* my rewards that my lovers have given me: and I will make them a forest, and the beasts of the field shall eat them. ¹³And I will visit upon her the days of Baalim, wherein she burned incense to them, and she decked herself with her earrings and her jewels, and she went after her lovers, and forgat me, saith the LORD.

¹⁴Therefore, behold, I will allure her, and bring her into the wilderness, and speak comfortably^h unto her. ¹⁵And I will give her her vineyards from thence, and the valley of Achor for a door of hope: and she shall sing there, as in the days of her youth, and as in the day when she came up out of the land of Egypt. ¹⁶And it shall be at that day, saith the LORD, *that* thou shalt call me Ishiⁱ; and shalt call me no more Baali. ¹⁷For I will take away the names of Baalim out of her mouth, and they shall no more be remembered by their name. ¹⁸And in that day will I make a covenant for them with the beasts of the field, and with the fowls of heaven, and *with* the creeping things of the ground: and I will break the bow and the sword and the battle out of the earth, and will make them to lie down safely. ¹⁹And I will betroth thee unto me for ever; yea, I will betroth thee unto me in righteousness, and in judgment, and in lovingkindness, and in mercies. ²⁰I will even betroth thee unto me in faithfulness: and

---

^b drink: Heb. drinks
^c make . . . : Heb. wall a wall
^d wine: Heb. new wine
^e recover: or, take away
^f lewdness: Heb. folly, or, villany
^g destroy: Heb. make desolate
^h comfortably: or, friendly: Heb. to her heart
ⁱ Ishi: that is, My husband

thou shalt know the LORD. ²¹And it shall come to pass in that day, I will hear, saith the LORD, I will hear the heavens, and they shall hear the earth; ²²And the earth shall hear the corn, and the wine, and the oil; and they shall hear Jezreel. ²³And I will sow her unto me in the earth; and I will have mercy upon her that had not obtained mercy; and I will say to *them which were* not my people, Thou *art* my people; and they shall say, *Thou art* my God.

3

¹Then said the LORD unto me, Go yet, love a woman beloved of *her* friend, yet an adulteress, according to the love of the LORD toward the children of Israel, who look to other gods, and love flagons of wineᵃ. ²So I bought her to me for fifteen *pieces* of silver, and *for* an homer of barley, and an half homer of barley: ³And I said unto her, Thou shalt abide for me many days; thou shalt not play the harlot, and thou shalt not be for *another* man: so *will* I also *be* for thee. ⁴For the children of Israel shall abide many days without a king, and without a prince, and without a sacrifice, and without an imageᵇ, and without an ephod, and *without* teraphim: ⁵Afterward shall the children of Israel return, and seek the LORD their God, and David their king; and shall fear the LORD and his goodness in the latter days.

4

¹Hear the word of the LORD, ye children of Israel: for the LORD hath a

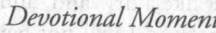

Devotional Moment
•
Healthy Environment
4:1-3 Some people believe that private sins between consenting adults behind closed doors are "victimless crimes," but the Bible strikes a different chord. When people scorn God's claim on their lives, the spreading effects of sin eat away at social harmony, and eventually all of creation—the land, the water, the animals, the birds—become infected.
God calls us to be stewards of creation, caretakers of the plains and mountains and rivers. We do well to follow God's way in these matters as a first line of defense against environmental decay.

controversy with the inhabitants of the land, because *there is* no truth, nor mercy, nor knowledge of God in the land. ²By swearing, and lying, and killing, and stealing, and committing adultery, they break out, and bloodᵃ toucheth blood. ³Therefore shall the land mourn, and every one that dwelleth therein shall languish, with the beasts of the field, and with the fowls of heaven; yea, the fishes of the sea also shall be taken away. ⁴Yet let no man strive, nor reprove another: for thy people *are* as they that strive with the priest. ⁵Therefore shalt thou fall in the day, and the prophet also shall fall with thee in the night, and I will destroyᵇ thy mother.

⁶My people are destroyedᶜ for lack of knowledge: because thou hast rejected knowledge, I will also reject

---

ᵃ of wine: Heb. of grapes
ᵇ image: Heb. a standing, or, statue, or, pillar
ᵃ blood: Heb. bloods
ᵇ destroy: Heb. cut off
ᶜ destroyed: Heb. cut off

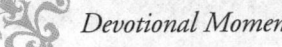

Devotional Moment
•
He Did It!

4:4 Just like children, the religious leaders were shifting the blame to others. There's no picture more classic than a young child pointing to his brother and saying, "He did it!" But adults do the same thing. We look for scapegoats, for social causes, for extenuating circumstances— anything to divert judgment and escape guilt. In reality, accepting blame and admitting a mistake is the first step toward healing. We relieve others' tensions when we shoulder responsibility, and we take a step toward our own maturity. Have you lost contact with a friend? hurt your spouse? offended a parent? Take responsibility, and you'll take a step toward finding each other again.

Devotional Moment
•
Staying Faithful

4:10-14 These verses speak about two kinds of prostitution: physical and spiritual. We destroy our bodies and emotions with both. If we worship anything but the true God, we are spiritual whores who mock God by choosing a pitiful substitute. We must stay faithful at all costs to God and his plans, including his plan for sexuality. As God planned it, sex is pure delight. Greed and abuse cheapen the gift of sex and spoil the real fun.

thee, that thou shalt be no priest to me: seeing thou hast forgotten the law of thy God, I will also forget thy children. [7]As they were increased, so they sinned against me: *therefore* will I change their glory into shame. [8]They eat up the sin of my people, and they set[d] their heart on their iniquity. [9]And there shall be, like people, like priest: and I will punish[e] them for their ways, and reward them their doings. [10]For they shall eat, and not have enough: they shall commit whoredom, and shall not increase: because they have left off to take heed to the LORD. [11]Whoredom and wine and new wine take away the heart.

[12]My people ask counsel at their stocks, and their staff declareth unto them: for the spirit of whoredoms hath caused *them* to err, and they have gone a whoring from under their God. [13]They sacrifice upon the tops of the mountains, and burn incense upon the hills, under oaks and poplars and elms, because the shadow thereof *is* good: therefore your daughters shall commit whoredom, and your spouses shall commit adultery. [14]I will not punish your daughters when they commit whoredom, nor your spouses when they commit adultery: for themselves are separated with whores, and they sacrifice with harlots: therefore the people *that* doth not understand shall fall. [15]Though thou, Israel, play the harlot, *yet* let not Judah offend; and come not ye unto Gilgal, neither go ye up to Bethaven, nor swear, The LORD liveth. [16]For Israel slideth back as a backsliding heifer: now the LORD will feed them as a lamb in a large place. [17]Ephraim *is* joined to idols: let him alone. [18]Their drink is sour[f]: they have committed whoredom continually: her rulers *with* shame do love, Give ye. [19]The wind hath bound her up in her

---

[d] set . . . : Heb. lift up their soul to
[e] punish: Heb. visit upon
[f] sour: Heb. gone

Hosea and Gomer

Immorality always hurts: It hurts the offender; it
hurts the violated spouse; it hurts the offender's
relationship with God; it hurts the children and
other relatives close by; it hurts God. No one wins
and everybody loses. It hurts even more when the
offender has spurned true love.

That is exactly what happened to Hosea. A
prophet of God to the Northern Kingdom of Israel,
Hosea was very good to his wife, Gomer, but she
became an adulteress anyway.

What did Hosea do about this? He stayed
faithful to her. He loved her. He forgave her. He
brought her back home.

Hosea married because God told him to. His
miserable experience was an exact parallel of how
God's people treated God—unfaithful to him even
though he stayed faithful to them.

The fact that God commanded Hosea to marry
and stay faithful to Gomer does not discount the
applicability of the story to your marriage. Because
Hosea's relationship with Gomer is a picture of
God's perfect love, it is also a picture of the kind of
love that all spouses need to have for each other.
Hosea had characteristics that all spouses should
have toward one another: faithfulness, persistence,
and forgiveness.

What should you do when a spouse deliberately hurts you? There are no step-by-step instructions, but there are some guidelines. Hosea gives
us one example.

wings, and they shall be ashamed because of their sacrifices.

5

¹Hear ye this, O priests; and hearken, ye house of Israel; and give ye ear, O house of the king; for judgment is toward you, because ye have been a snare on Mizpah, and a net spread upon Tabor. ²And the revolters are profound to make slaughter, though I *have been* a rebuker of them all. ³I know Ephraim, and Israel is not hid from me: for now, O Ephraim, thou committest whoredom, *and* Israel is defiled. ⁴They will not frame their doings to turn unto their God: for the spirit of whoredoms is in the midst of them, and they have not known the LORD. ⁵And the pride of Israel doth testify to his face: therefore shall Israel and Ephraim fall in their iniquity; Judah also shall fall with them. ⁶They shall go with their flocks and with their herds to seek the LORD; but they shall not find *him*; he hath withdrawn himself from them. ⁷They have dealt treacherously against the LORD: for they have begotten strange children: now shall a month devour them with their portions.

⁸Blow ye the cornet in Gibeah, *and* the trumpet in Ramah: cry aloud *at* Bethaven, after thee, O Benjamin. ⁹Ephraim shall be desolate in the day of rebuke: among the tribes of Israel have I made known that which shall surely be. ¹⁰The princes of Judah were like them that remove the bound: *therefore* I will pour out my wrath upon them like water. ¹¹Ephraim *is* oppressed *and* broken in judgment, because he willingly walked after the commandment. ¹²Therefore *will* I *be* unto Ephraim as a moth, and to the house of Judah as rottennessᵃ. ¹³When Ephraim saw his sickness, and Judah *saw* his wound, then went Ephraim to the Assyrian, and sent to king Jarebᵇ: yet could he not heal you, nor cure you of your wound. ¹⁴For I *will be* unto Ephraim as a lion, and as a young lion to the house of Judah: I, *even* I, will tear and go away; I will take away, and none shall rescue *him*. ¹⁵I will go *and* return to my place, till they acknowledge their offence, and seek my face: in their affliction they will seek me early.

6

¹Come, and let us return unto the LORD: for he hath torn, and he will heal us; he hath smitten, and he will bind us up. ²After two days will he revive us: in the third day he will raise us up, and we shall live in his sight. ³Then shall we know, *if* we follow on to know the LORD: his going forth is prepared as the morning; and he shall come unto us as the rain, as the latter *and* former rain unto the earth.

⁴O Ephraim, what shall I do unto thee? O Judah, what shall I do unto thee? for your goodnessᵃ *is* as a morning cloud, and as the early dew it goeth away. ⁵Therefore have I hewed *them* by the prophets; I have slain them by the words of my mouth: and thy judgments *are as* the light *that* goeth forth.

ᵃ rottenness: or, a worm
ᵇ king Jareb: or, the king of Jareb: or, the king that should plead
ᵃ goodness: or, mercy, or, kindness

⁶For I desired mercy, and not sacrifice; and the knowledge of God more than burnt offerings. ⁷But they like men[b] have transgressed the covenant: there have they dealt treacherously against me. ⁸Gilead *is* a city of them that work iniquity, *and is* polluted[c] with blood. ⁹And as troops of robbers wait for a man, *so* the company of priests murder in the way by consent: for they commit lewdness. ¹⁰I have seen an horrible thing in the house of Israel: there *is* the whoredom of Ephraim, Israel is defiled. ¹¹Also, O Judah, he hath set an harvest for thee, when I returned the captivity of my people.

7

¹When I would have healed Israel, then the iniquity of Ephraim was discovered, and the wickedness[a] of Samaria: for they commit falsehood; and the thief cometh in, *and* the troop of robbers

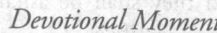

Devotional Moment
•
Hiding Sins

7:1-2 God uncovers hidden things. He exposes the truth about us. There is never any good to be gained from presuming that we can hide our sins from God. Hiding sin from God is like burying a tire—you might seem to succeed at first, but it won't stay buried. Yet people still try, even when God himself tells us it cannot be done. Take the better way—admit your mistakes and ask for forgiveness. Then God will blot out your sins so that even he cannot find them.

Devotional Moment
•
Lust

7:4 The Israelites burned like a hot oven with two kinds of lust: lust for sex and lust for power. Once ablaze, these flames are impossible to douse. Lust is like an open fire hydrant, like an eighteen-wheeler without brakes on a downhill grade. What had enflamed the Israelites? The evil ways of the people around them. It is natural to pick up attitudes, language, preferences, and styles from the people we live and work with. Check to see if your desires stem from the influence of those around you rather than from God. Make a habit of reading the Bible often as a reminder—to keep the flames under control.

spoileth without. ²And they consider[b] not in their hearts *that* I remember all their wickedness: now their own doings have beset them about; they are before my face. ³They make the king glad with their wickedness, and the princes with their lies. ⁴They *are* all adulterers, as an oven heated by the baker, *who* ceaseth from raising after he hath kneaded the dough, until it be leavened. ⁵In the day of our king the princes have made *him* sick with bottles[c] of wine; he stretched out his hand with scorners. ⁶For they have made ready their heart like an oven, whiles they lie in wait: their baker sleepeth all the night; in the morning it burneth as a flaming fire. ⁷They are all hot as an oven, and have devoured their judges; all their kings are fallen: *there is* none among them that calleth unto me.

[b] men: or, Adam
[c] polluted: or, cunning for
[a] wickedness: Heb. evils
[b] consider . . . : Heb. say not to
[c] bottles . . . : or, heat through wine

⁸Ephraim, he hath mixed himself among the people; Ephraim is a cake not turned. ⁹Strangers have devoured his strength, and he knoweth *it* not: yea, gray hairs are here and there upon him, yet he knoweth not. ¹⁰And the pride of Israel testifieth to his face: and they do not return to the LORD their God, nor seek him for all this. ¹¹Ephraim also is like a silly dove without heart: they call to Egypt, they go to Assyria. ¹²When they shall go, I will spread my net upon them; I will bring them down as the fowls of the heaven; I will chastise them, as their congregation hath heard. ¹³Woe unto them! for they have fled from me: destruction[d] unto them! because they have transgressed against me: though I have redeemed them, yet they have spoken lies against me. ¹⁴And they have not cried unto me with their heart, when they howled upon their beds: they assemble themselves for corn and wine, *and* they rebel against me. ¹⁵Though I have bound *and* strengthened their arms, yet do they imagine mischief against me. ¹⁶They return, *but* not to the most High: they are like a deceitful bow: their princes shall fall by the sword for the rage of their tongue: this *shall be* their derision in the land of Egypt.

8

¹ *Set* the trumpet to thy mouth. *He shall come* as an eagle against the house of the LORD, because they have transgressed

my covenant, and trespassed against my law. ²Israel shall cry unto me, My God, we know thee. ³Israel hath cast off *the thing that is* good: the enemy shall pursue him. ⁴They have set up kings, but not by me: they have made princes, and I knew *it* not: of their silver and their gold have they made them idols, that they may be cut off. ⁵Thy calf, O Samaria, hath cast *thee* off; mine anger is kindled against them: how long *will it be* ere they attain to innocency? ⁶For from Israel *was* it also: the workman made it; therefore it *is* not God: but the calf of Samaria shall be broken in pieces. ⁷For they have sown the wind, and they shall reap the whirlwind: it hath no stalk[a]: the bud shall yield no meal: if so be it yield, the strangers shall swallow it up.

⁸Israel is swallowed up: now shall they be among the Gentiles as a vessel wherein *is* no pleasure. ⁹For they are gone up to Assyria, a wild ass alone by himself: Ephraim hath hired lovers[b]. ¹⁰Yea, though they have hired among the nations, now will I gather them, and they shall sorrow[c] a little for the burden of the king of princes. ¹¹Because Ephraim hath made many altars to sin, altars shall be unto him to sin. ¹²I have written to him the great things of my law, *but* they were counted as a strange thing. ¹³They sacrifice[d] flesh *for* the sacrifices of mine offerings, and eat *it; but* the LORD accepteth them not; now will he remember their iniquity, and

---

[d] destruction: Heb. spoil
[a] stalk: or, standing corn
[b] lovers: Heb. loves
[c] sorrow: or, begin
[d] They sacrifice . . . : or, In the sacrifices of mine offerings they, etc

visit their sins: they shall return to Egypt. ¹⁴For Israel hath forgotten his Maker, and buildeth temples; and Judah hath multiplied fenced cities: but I will send a fire upon his cities, and it shall devour the palaces thereof.

9

¹Rejoice not, O Israel, for joy, as *other* people: for thou hast gone a whoring from thy God, thou hast loved a reward upon every cornfloor. ²The floor and the winepressᵃ shall not feed them, and the new wine shall fail in her. ³They shall not dwell in the LORD'S land; but Ephraim shall return to Egypt, and they shall eat unclean *things* in Assyria. ⁴They shall not offer wine *offerings* to the LORD, neither shall they be pleasing unto him: their sacrifices *shall be* unto them as the bread of mourners; all that eat thereof shall be polluted: for their bread for their soul shall not come into the house of the LORD. ⁵What will ye do in the solemn day, and in the day of the feast of the LORD? ⁶For, lo, they are gone because of destructionᵇ: Egypt shall gather them up, Memphis shall bury them: the pleasant *places* for their silver, nettles shall possess them: thorns *shall be* in their tabernacles.

⁷The days of visitation are come, the days of recompence are come; Israel shall know *it*: the prophet *is* a fool, the spiritualᶜ man *is* mad, for the multitude of thine iniquity, and the great hatred. ⁸The watchman of Ephraim *was* with my God: *but* the prophet *is* a snare of a fowler in all his ways, *and* hatred in the house of his God. ⁹They have deeply corrupted *themselves*, as in the days of Gibeah: *therefore* he will remember their iniquity, he will visit their sins. ¹⁰I found Israel like grapes in the wilderness; I saw your fathers as the firstripe in the fig tree at her first time: *but* they went to Baalpeor, and separated themselves unto *that* shame; and *their* abominations were according as they loved.

¹¹*As for* Ephraim, their glory shall fly away like a bird, from the birth, and from the womb, and from the conception. ¹²Though they bring up their children, yet will I bereave them, *that there shall* not *be* a man *left*: yea, woe also to them when I depart from them! ¹³Ephraim, as I saw Tyrus, *is* planted in a pleasant place: but Ephraim shall bring forth his children to the murderer. ¹⁴Give them, O LORD: what wilt thou give? give them a miscarryingᵈ womb and dry breasts. ¹⁵All their wickedness *is* in Gilgal: for there I hated them: for the wickedness of their doings I will drive them out of mine house, I will love them no more: all their princes *are* revolters. ¹⁶Ephraim is smitten, their root is dried up, they shall bearᵉ no fruit: yea, though they bring forth, yet will I slay *even* the beloved *fruit* of their womb. ¹⁷My God will cast them away, because they did

---

ᵃ winepress: or, winefat
ᵇ destruction: Heb. spoil
ᶜ spiritual . . . : Heb. man of the spirit
ᵈ miscarrying: Heb. that casteth the fruit
ᵉ the . . . : Heb. the desires

not hearken unto him: and they shall be wanderers among the nations.

10

¹Israel *is* an empty vine, he bringeth forth fruit unto himself: according to the multitude of his fruit he hath increased the altars; according to the goodness of his land they have made goodly images. ²Their heart[a] is divided; now shall they be found faulty: he shall break down their altars, he shall spoil their images. ³For now they shall say, We have no king, because we feared not the LORD; what then should a king do to us? ⁴They have spoken words, swearing falsely in making a covenant: thus judgment springeth up as hemlock in the furrows of the field. ⁵The inhabitants of Samaria shall fear because of the calves of Bethaven: for the people thereof shall mourn over it, and the priests[b] thereof *that* rejoiced on it, for the glory thereof, because it is departed from it. ⁶It shall be also carried unto Assyria *for* a present to king Jareb: Ephraim shall receive shame, and Israel shall be ashamed of his own counsel. ⁷*As for* Samaria, her king is cut off as the foam upon the water[c]. ⁸The high places also of Aven, the sin of Israel, shall be destroyed: the thorn and the thistle shall come up on their altars; and they shall say to the mountains, Cover us; and to the hills, Fall on us.

⁹O Israel, thou hast sinned from the days of Gibeah: there they stood: the battle in Gibeah against the children of iniquity did not overtake them. ¹⁰*It is* in my desire that I should chastise them; and the people shall be gathered against them, when they shall bind themselves in their two furrows. ¹¹And Ephraim *is as* an heifer *that is* taught, *and* loveth to tread out *the corn*; but I passed over upon her fair neck: I will make Ephraim to ride; Judah shall plow, *and* Jacob shall break his clods. ¹²Sow to yourselves in righteousness, reap in mercy; break up your fallow ground: for *it is* time to seek the LORD, till he come and rain righteousness upon you. ¹³Ye have plowed wickedness, ye have reaped iniquity; ye have eaten the fruit of lies: because thou didst trust in thy way, in the multitude of thy mighty men. ¹⁴Therefore shall a tumult arise among thy people, and all thy fortresses shall be spoiled, as Shalman spoiled Betharbel in the day of battle: the mother was dashed in pieces upon *her* children. ¹⁵So shall Bethel do unto you because of your great wickedness: in a morning shall the king of Israel utterly be cut off.

11

¹When Israel *was* a child, then I loved him, and called my son out of Egypt.

> ### Devotional Moment
> •
> #### Promises
> 10:4 In Hosea's time, people were not keeping their word. Their oaths and promises had become jokes. We should not be so foolish. We promise lots of things flippantly: "Sure, I'll write," or "No problem. I'll be there," or "Yes, dear, it's tops on my list." Almost as soon as the words are out, we forget about them. God's promises are sure, and ours should be, too.

---

[a] Their heart . . . : or, He hath divided their heart
[b] the priests . . . : or, Chemarim
[c] the water: Heb. the face of the water

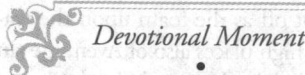

Devotional Moment

•

Giving Thanks

11:1-3 The people of Israel had received God's loving-kindness without a word of thanks. In fact, they rebelled. Did they think God was obliged to care for them? Was this relationship all one-way? We show the same attitude when we soak up others' love and care and never whisper a thank-you. Eventually the giver wonders, *Why? What's wrong? Why can't this relationship be mutual?* We need to thank God for his care rather than take his kindness for granted. People who care for us want to be connected to us. Our thanks helps contribute to that. Start the "thanks" habit.

²*As* they called them, so they went from them: they sacrificed unto Baalim, and burned incense to graven images. ³I taught Ephraim also to go, taking them by their arms; but they knew not that I healed them. ⁴I drew them with cords of a man, with bands of love: and I was to them as they that take off ᵃ the yoke on their jaws, and I laid meat unto them. ⁵He shall not return into the land of Egypt, but the Assyrian shall be his king, because they refused to return. ⁶And the sword shall abide on his cities, and shall consume his branches, and devour *them*, because of their own counsels. ⁷And my people are bent to backsliding from me: though they called them to the most High, none at all would exalt *him*.

⁸How shall I give thee up, Ephraim? *how* shall I deliver thee, Israel? how shall I make thee as Admah? *how* shall I set thee as Zeboim? mine heart is turned within me, my repentings are kindled together. ⁹I will not execute the fierceness of mine anger, I will not return to destroy Ephraim: for I *am* God, and not man; the Holy One in the midst of thee: and I will not enter into the city. ¹⁰They shall walk after the LORD: he shall roar like a lion: when he shall roar, then the children shall tremble from the west. ¹¹They shall tremble as a bird out of Egypt, and as a dove out of the land of Assyria: and I will place them in their houses, saith the LORD. ¹²Ephraim compasseth me about with lies, and the house of Israel with deceit: but Judah yet ruleth with God, and is faithful with the saintsᵇ.

12

¹Ephraim feedeth on wind, and followeth after the east wind: he daily increaseth lies and desolation; and they do make a covenant with the Assyrians, and oil is carried into Egypt. ²The LORD hath also a controversy with Judah, and will punishᵃ Jacob according to his ways; according to his doings will he recompense him. ³He took his brother by the heel in the womb, and by his strength he had power with God: ⁴Yea, he had power over the angel, and prevailed: he wept, and made supplication unto him: he found him *in* Bethel, and there he spake with us; ⁵Even the LORD God of hosts; the LORD *is* his memorial. ⁶Therefore turn thou to thy God: keep mercy and judgment, and wait on thy God continually.

ᵃ take off: Heb. lift up
ᵇ saints: or, most holy
ᵃ punish: Heb. visit upon

⁷*He is* a merchant[b], the balances of deceit *are* in his hand: he loveth to oppress. ⁸And Ephraim said, Yet I am become rich, I have found me out substance: *in* all my labours they shall find none iniquity in me that *were* sin. ⁹And I *that am* the LORD thy God from the land of Egypt will yet make thee to dwell in tabernacles, as in the days of the solemn feast. ¹⁰I have also spoken by the prophets, and I have multiplied visions, and used similitudes, by the ministry[c] of the prophets. ¹¹*Is there* iniquity *in* Gilead? surely they are vanity: they sacrifice bullocks in Gilgal; yea, their altars *are* as heaps in the furrows of the fields. ¹²And Jacob fled into the country of Syria, and Israel served for a wife, and for a wife he kept *sheep*. ¹³And by a prophet the LORD brought Israel out of Egypt, and by a prophet was he preserved.

¹⁴Ephraim provoked *him* to anger most bitterly: therefore shall he leave his blood upon him, and his reproach shall his Lord return unto him.

13

¹When Ephraim spake trembling, he exalted himself in Israel; but when he offended in Baal, he died. ²And now they sin[a] more and more, and have made them molten images of their silver, *and* idols according to their own understanding, all of it the work of the craftsmen: they say of them, Let the men that sacrifice kiss the calves. ³Therefore they shall be as the morning cloud, and as the early dew that passeth away, as the chaff *that* is driven with the whirlwind out of the floor, and as the smoke out of the chimney. ⁴Yet I *am* the LORD thy God from the land of Egypt, and thou shalt know no god but me: for *there is* no saviour beside me. ⁵I did know thee in the wilderness, in the land of great drought. ⁶According to their pasture, so were they filled; they were filled, and their heart was exalted; therefore have they forgotten me. ⁷Therefore I will be unto them as a lion: as a leopard by the way will I observe *them*: ⁸I will meet them as a bear *that is* bereaved *of her whelps*, and will rend the caul of their heart, and there will I devour them like a lion: the wild[b] beast shall tear them.

⁹O Israel, thou hast destroyed thyself; but in me *is* thine help. ¹⁰I will[c] be

---

[b] a merchant: or, Canaan
[c] ministry: Heb. hand
[a] they sin . . . : Heb. they add to sin
[b] wild . . . : Heb. beast of the field
[c] I will . . . : rather, Where is thy king?

thy king: where *is any other* that may save thee in all thy cities? and thy judges of whom thou saidst, Give me a king and princes? [11]I gave thee a king in mine anger, and took *him* away in my wrath. [12]The iniquity of Ephraim *is* bound up; his sin *is* hid. [13]The sorrows of a travailing woman shall come upon him: he *is* an unwise son; for he should not stay long[d] in *the place of* the breaking forth of children. [14]I will ransom them from the power[e] of the grave; I will redeem them from death: O death, I will be thy plagues; O grave, I will be thy destruction: repentance shall be hid from mine eyes. [15]Though he be fruitful among *his* brethren, an east wind shall come, the wind of the LORD shall come up from the wilderness, and his spring shall become dry, and his fountain shall be dried up: he shall spoil the treasure of all pleasant[f] vessels. [16]Samaria shall become desolate; for she hath rebelled against her God: they shall fall by the sword: their infants shall be dashed in pieces, and their women with child shall be ripped up.

14

[1]O Israel, return unto the LORD thy God; for thou hast fallen by thine iniquity. [2]Take with you words, and turn to the LORD: say unto him, Take away all iniquity, and receive[a] *us* graciously: so will we render the calves of our lips. [3]Asshur shall not save us; we will not ride upon horses: neither will we say any more to the work of our hands, *Ye are* our gods: for in thee the fatherless findeth mercy.

[4]I will heal their backsliding, I will love them freely: for mine anger is turned away from him. [5]I will be as the dew unto Israel: he shall grow[b] as the lily, and cast forth his roots as Lebanon. [6]His branches shall spread[c], and his beauty shall be as the olive tree, and his smell as Lebanon. [7]They that dwell under his shadow shall return; they shall revive *as* the corn, and grow[d] as the vine: the scent thereof *shall be* as the wine of Lebanon.

[8]Ephraim *shall say*, What have I to do any more with idols? I have heard *him*, and observed him: I *am* like a green fir tree. From me is thy fruit found. [9]Who *is* wise, and he shall understand these *things*? prudent, and he shall know them? for the ways of the LORD *are* right, and the just shall walk in them: but the transgressors shall fall therein.

---

[d] long: Heb. a time
[e] power: Heb. hand
[f] pleasant . . . : Heb. vessels of desire
[a] receive . . . : or, give good
[b] grow: or, blossom
[c] spread: Heb. go
[d] grow: or, blossom

JOEL

Purpose
To warn Judah of God's impending judgment because of their sins and to urge them to turn back to God

Author
Joel, son of Pethuel

To Whom Written
The people of Judah, the Southern Kingdom, and God's people everywhere

Date Written
Probably during the time Joel prophesied, from approximately 835 to 796 B.C.

Key Verses
"Therefore also now, saith the Lord, turn ye even to me with all your heart, and with fasting, and with weeping, and with mourning: And rend your heart, and not your garments, and turn unto the Lord your God: for he is gracious and merciful, slow to anger, and of great kindness, and repenteth him of the evil" (2:12-13).

Key People
Joel, the people of Judah

Key Place
Jerusalem

Everyone has a personal reaction to bugs. We collect them or poison them, tolerate them or stomp on them.

Single bugs crawling in a house are no great problem. Multiple bugs crawling around walls and under sinks are a declaration of war. An army of bugs is reason for people to pack up and run.

Joel is about bugs. Lots of bugs. Far too many in one place at one time. Joel was concerned about grasshopper plagues that could do real damage.

The people of Judah had become prosperous and complacent. Taking God for granted, they had turned to self-centeredness, idolatry, and sin. Joel warns them that this kind of life-style will inevitably bring God's judgment.

Joel helps us understand the meaning of bugs of all kinds in our life. We've got more bugs to deal with than the crawling kind, and we need the help Joel describes. We also need the assurance that a God mightier than all our bugs has a plan and purpose for life. Here God's plan reaches to a new dimension—something quite surprising, like nothing we've seen before.

1

¹The word of the LORD that came to Joel the son of Pethuel. ²Hear this, ye old men, and give ear, all ye inhabitants of the land. Hath this been in your days, or even in the days of your fathers? ³Tell ye your children of it, and *let* your children *tell* their children, and their children another generation. ⁴That which the palmerworm^a hath left hath the locust eaten; and that which the locust hath left hath the cankerworm eaten; and that which the cankerworm hath left hath the caterpiller eaten. ⁵Awake, ye drunkards, and weep; and howl, all ye drinkers of wine, because of the new wine; for it is cut off from your mouth. ⁶For a nation is come up upon my land, strong, and without number, whose teeth *are* the teeth of a lion, and he hath the cheek teeth of a great lion. ⁷He hath laid my vine waste,

---

Devotional Moment
•
Natural Hazards

1:4 What a negative picture—locusts eating everything. Natural disasters come without much warning. These disasters hurt because they take away what we've worked hard for, and there's usually no way to recover the losses. Yet this tale of devastation has a lesson for us. Natural disasters can teach us to keep a loose grip on material things. At the heart of life is our relationship with God and with each other, treasures that wind, fire, or water cannot touch. We all collect a lot of stuff—closets and attics are usually filled with the overflow. If "locusts" were to come some night and destroy it all, would you fall apart? Make God your center and be free of the rest.

---

and barked^b my fig tree: he hath made it clean bare, and cast *it* away; the branches thereof are made white.

⁸Lament like a virgin girded with sackcloth for the husband of her youth. ⁹The meat offering and the drink offering is cut off from the house of the LORD; the priests, the LORD'S ministers, mourn. ¹⁰The field is wasted, the land mourneth; for the corn is wasted: the new wine is dried up, the oil languisheth. ¹¹Be ye ashamed, O ye husbandmen; howl, O ye vinedressers, for the wheat and for the barley; because the harvest of the field is perished. ¹²The vine is dried up, and the fig tree languisheth; the pomegranate tree, the palm tree also, and the apple tree, *even* all the trees of the field, are withered: because joy is withered away from the sons of men. ¹³Gird yourselves, and lament, ye priests: howl, ye ministers of the altar: come, lie all night in sackcloth, ye ministers of my God: for the meat offering and the drink offering is withholden from the house of your God. ¹⁴Sanctify ye a fast, call a solemn assembly, gather the elders *and* all the inhabitants of the land *into* the house of the LORD your God, and cry unto the LORD, ¹⁵Alas for the day! for the day of the LORD *is* at hand, and as a destruction from the Almighty shall it come. ¹⁶Is not the meat cut off before our eyes, *yea*, joy and gladness from the house of our God? ¹⁷The seed^c is rotten under their clods, the garners are laid desolate, the barns are broken down; for the corn

---

^a That which the palmerworm . . . : Heb. The residue of the palmerworm
^b barked . . . : Heb. laid my fig tree for a barking
^c seed: Heb. grains

is withered. ¹⁸How do the beasts groan! the herds of cattle are perplexed, because they have no pasture; yea, the flocks of sheep are made desolate. ¹⁹O LORD, to thee will I cry: for the fire hath devoured the pastures^d of the wilderness, and the flame hath burned all the trees of the field. ²⁰The beasts of the field cry also unto thee: for the rivers of waters are dried up, and the fire hath devoured the pastures of the wilderness.

2

¹Blow ye the trumpet^a in Zion, and sound an alarm in my holy mountain: let all the inhabitants of the land tremble: for the day of the LORD cometh, for *it is* nigh at hand; ²A day of darkness and of gloominess, a day of clouds and of thick darkness, as the morning spread upon the mountains: a great people and a strong; there hath not been ever the like, neither shall be any more after it, *even* to the years of many^b generations. ³A fire devoureth before them; and behind them a flame burneth: the land *is* as the garden of Eden before them, and behind them a desolate wilderness; yea, and nothing shall escape them. ⁴The appearance of them *is* as the appearance of horses; and as horsemen, so shall they run. ⁵Like the noise of chariots on the tops of mountains shall they leap, like the noise of a flame of fire that devoureth the stubble, as a strong people set in battle array.

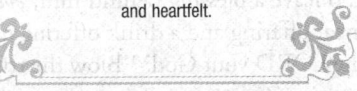

Devotional Moment
•
Being Sorry
2:13 In Old Testament days it was considered a sign of deep sorrow to tear one's clothes. But God was not satisfied with an outward show if there was no inner change of heart. God knew his people just as loving parents know their children. We may convince other people of our sincerity, but we must remember that God sees our heart. Repentance must be genuine and heartfelt.

⁶Before their face the people shall be much pained: all faces shall gather blackness^c. ⁷They shall run like mighty men; they shall climb the wall like men of war; and they shall march every one on his ways, and they shall not break their ranks: ⁸Neither shall one thrust another; they shall walk every one in his path: and *when* they fall upon the sword^d, they shall not be wounded. ⁹They shall run to and fro in the city; they shall run upon the wall, they shall climb up upon the houses; they shall enter in at the windows like a thief. ¹⁰The earth shall quake before them; the heavens shall tremble: the sun and the moon shall be dark, and the stars shall withdraw their shining: ¹¹And the LORD shall utter his voice before his army: for his camp *is* very great: for *he is* strong that executeth his word: for the day of the LORD *is* great and very terrible; and who can abide it?

¹²Therefore also now, saith the

---

^d pastures: or, habitations
^a trumpet: or, cornet
^b of many . . . : Heb. of generation and generation
^c blackness: Heb. pot
^d sword: or, dart

LORD, turn ye *even* to me with all your heart, and with fasting, and with weeping, and with mourning: ¹³And rend your heart, and not your garments, and turn unto the LORD your God: for he *is* gracious and merciful, slow to anger, and of great kindness, and repenteth him of the evil. ¹⁴Who knoweth *if* he will return and repent, and leave a blessing behind him; *even* a meat offering and a drink offering unto the LORD your God? ¹⁵Blow the trumpet in Zion, sanctify a fast, call a solemn assembly: ¹⁶Gather the people, sanctify the congregation, assemble the elders, gather the children, and those that suck the breasts: let the bridegroom go forth of his chamber, and the bride out of her closet. ¹⁷Let the priests, the ministers of the LORD, weep between the porch and the altar, and let them say, Spare thy people, O LORD, and give not thine heritage to reproach, that the heathen should rule over[e] them: wherefore should they say among the people, Where *is* their God?

¹⁸Then will the LORD be jealous for his land, and pity his people. ¹⁹Yea, the LORD will answer and say unto his people, Behold, I will send you corn, and wine, and oil, and ye shall be satisfied therewith: and I will no more make you a reproach among the heathen: ²⁰But I will remove far off from you the northern *army*, and will drive him into a land barren and desolate, with his face toward the east sea, and his hinder part toward the utmost sea, and his stink shall come up, and his ill savour shall come up, because he hath done great things. ²¹Fear not, O land; be glad and

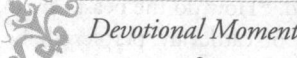

Devotional Moment

•

Reasons

2:21 The people of Israel were encouraged to remember God's faithfulness. Families can approach difficult times with the same hope. Take time to notice and point out to each other those "amazing things" that God has done for your family: an accident in which all were kept safe, the providential finding or selling of a home, a job provided, or some other unexpected help from God. Use family history to teach your children that they can trust God.

rejoice: for the LORD will do great things. ²²Be not afraid, ye beasts of the field: for the pastures of the wilderness do spring, for the tree beareth her fruit, the fig tree and the vine do yield their strength. ²³Be glad then, ye children of Zion, and rejoice in the LORD your God: for he hath given you the former rain moderately, and he will cause to come down for you the rain, the former rain, and the latter rain in the first *month.* ²⁴And the floors shall be full of wheat, and the fats shall overflow with wine and oil. ²⁵And I will restore to you the years that the locust hath eaten, the cankerworm, and the caterpiller, and the palmerworm, my great army which I sent among you. ²⁶And ye shall eat in plenty, and be satisfied, and praise the name of the LORD your God, that hath dealt wondrously with you: and my people shall never be ashamed. ²⁷And ye shall know that I *am* in the midst of Israel, and *that* I *am* the LORD your God, and none else: and my people shall never be ashamed.

²⁸And it shall come to pass afterward, *that* I will pour out my spirit

[e] rule over: or, use a byword against

upon all flesh; and your sons and your daughters shall prophesy, your old men shall dream dreams, your young men shall see visions: ²⁹And also upon the servants and upon the handmaids in those days will I pour out my spirit. ³⁰And I will shew wonders in the heavens and in the earth, blood, and fire, and pillars of smoke. ³¹The sun shall be turned into darkness, and the moon into blood, before the great and the terrible day of the LORD come. ³²And it shall come to pass, *that* whosoever shall call on the name of the LORD shall be delivered: for in mount Zion and in Jerusalem shall be deliverance, as the LORD hath said, and in the remnant whom the LORD shall call.

3

¹For, behold, in those days, and in that time, when I shall bring again the captivity of Judah and Jerusalem, ²I will also gather all nations, and will bring them down into the valley of Jehoshaphat, and will plead with them there for my people and *for* my heritage Israel, whom they have scattered among the nations, and parted my land. ³And they have cast lots for my people; and have given a boy for an harlot, and sold a girl for wine, that they might drink. ⁴Yea, and what have ye to do with me, O Tyre, and Zidon, and all the coasts of Palestine? will ye render me a recompence? and if ye recompense me, swiftly *and* speedily will I return your recompence upon your own head;

⁵Because ye have taken my silver and my gold, and have carried into your temples my goodly pleasant things: ⁶The children also of Judah and the children of Jerusalem have ye sold unto the Grecians^a, that ye might remove them far from their border. ⁷Behold, I will raise them out of the place whither ye have sold them, and will return your recompence upon your own head: ⁸And I will sell your sons and your daughters into the hand of the children of Judah, and they shall sell them to the Sabeans, to a people far off: for the LORD hath spoken *it.*

⁹Proclaim ye this among the Gentiles; Prepare^b war, wake up the mighty men, let all the men of war draw near; let them come up: ¹⁰Beat your plowshares into swords, and your pruninghooks^c into spears: let the weak say, I *am* strong. ¹¹Assemble yourselves, and come, all ye heathen, and gather yourselves together round about: thither cause thy mighty ones to come down, O LORD. ¹²Let the heathen be wakened, and come up to the valley of Jehoshaphat: for there will I sit to judge all the heathen round about. ¹³Put ye in the sickle, for the harvest is ripe: come, get you down; for the press is full, the fats overflow; for their wickedness *is* great. ¹⁴Multitudes, multitudes in the valley of decision^d: for the day of the LORD *is* near in the valley of decision. ¹⁵The sun and the moon shall be darkened, and the stars shall withdraw their shining. ¹⁶The LORD also shall roar

---

^a the Grecians: Heb. the sons of the Grecians
^b Prepare: Heb. Sanctify
^c pruninghooks: or, scythes
^d decision: or, concision, or, threshing

out of Zion, and utter his voice from Jerusalem; and the heavens and the earth shall shake: but the LORD *will be* the hope^e of his people, and the strength of the children of Israel. ^{17}So shall ye know that I *am* the LORD your God dwelling in Zion, my holy mountain: then shall Jerusalem be holy^f, and there shall no strangers pass through her any more.

^{18}And it shall come to pass in that day, *that* the mountains shall drop down new wine, and the hills shall flow with milk, and all the rivers of Judah shall flow^g with waters, and a fountain shall come forth of the house of the LORD, and shall water the valley of Shittim. ^{19}Egypt shall be a desolation, and Edom shall be a desolate wilderness, for the violence *against* the children of Judah, because they have shed innocent blood in their land. ^{20}But Judah shall dwell^h for ever, and Jerusalem from generation to generation. ^{21}For I will cleanse their blood *that* I have not cleansed: for the LORD dwelleth in Zion.

---

^{e} hope: Heb. place of repair, or, harbour
^{f} holy: Heb. holiness
^{g} flow: Heb. go
^{h} dwell: or, abide

AMOS

Purpose
To pronounce God's judgment on Israel, the Northern Kingdom, for their complacency, idolatry, and oppression of the poor

Author
Amos

To Whom Written
Israel, the Northern Kingdom, and God's people everywhere

Date Written
Probably during the reigns of Jeroboam II of Israel and Uzziah of Judah (approximately 760–750 B.C.)

Setting
The wealthy people of Israel were enjoying peace and prosperity. They were quite complacent and were oppressing the poor, even selling them into slavery. Soon, however, Israel would be conquered by Assyria, and the rich would themselves be made slaves.

Key Verse
"But let judgment run down as waters, and righteousness as a mighty stream" (5:24).

Key People
Amos, Amaziah, Jeroboam II

Key Places
Bethel, Samaria

City people idealize life on the farm. Space, land, animals, chores—they all seem idyllic from the point of view of someone for whom tomatoes come shrink-wrapped.

Parents of city kids sometimes threaten to send their children "to the farm" for behavior modification. Any farm will do, as long as chores start at 5:00 a.m.! On the farm, city softies soon learn that toil, not TV, is normal, that getting up with the sun is better than sleeping in till noon.

Amos was a herdsman as well as a prophet. He knew life well, firsthand, raw, and beautiful. He knew that nothing comes from nothing, that simple can be wonderful but never easy. Amos had a sense of justice born of nature and inspired by God.

City folk in Amos's time needed a day in his line of work. They would learn the importance of streambeds filled with rushing water and how life suffered when streams dried up. For them, Amos connected flooding streams and justice (5:24). If they were slow to get the point, as some city folk can be, Amos would use other farmland illustrations. Amos uses striking metaphors from his shepherding and farming experience—an overloaded cart (2:13), a roaring lion (3:8), a torn lamb (3:12), fat cows (4:1), and a basket of fruit (8:1-2). Everywhere Amos could see pictures of life lived right and true, with God at the center.

Spend time learning from this prophet-herdsman, and you'll see the world with a different set of eyes.

1

¹The words of Amos, who was among the herdmen of Tekoa, which he saw concerning Israel in the days of Uzziah king of Judah, and in the days of Jeroboam the son of Joash king of Israel, two years before the earthquake. ²And he said, The LORD will roar from Zion, and utter his voice from Jerusalem; and the habitations of the shepherds shall mourn, and the top of Carmel shall wither.

³Thus saith the LORD; For three transgressions of Damascus, and for four, I will not turn away *the punishment* thereof; because they have threshed Gilead with threshing instruments of iron: ⁴But I will send a fire into the house of Hazael, which shall devour the palaces of Benhadad. ⁵I will break also the bar of Damascus, and cut off the inhabitant from the plainª of Aven, and him that holdeth the sceptre from the house of Eden: and the people of Syria shall go into captivity unto Kir, saith the LORD. ⁶Thus saith the LORD; For three transgressions of Gaza, and for four, I will not turn away *the punishment* thereof; because they carried away captiveᵇ the whole captivity, to deliver *them* up to Edom: ⁷But I will send a fire on the wall of Gaza, which shall devour the palaces thereof: ⁸And I will cut off the inhabitant from Ashdod, and him that holdeth the sceptre from Ashkelon, and I will turn mine hand against Ekron: and the remnant of the Philistines shall perish, saith the Lord GOD. ⁹Thus saith the LORD; For three transgressions of Tyrus, and for four, I will not turn away *the punishment* thereof; because they delivered up the whole captivity to Edom, and remembered not the brotherlyᶜ covenant: ¹⁰But I will send a fire on the wall of Tyrus, which shall devour the palaces thereof. ¹¹Thus saith the LORD; For three transgressions of Edom, and for four, I will not turn away *the punishment* thereof; because he did pursue his brother with the sword, and did cast off all pity, and his anger did tear perpetually, and he kept his wrath for ever: ¹²But I will send a fire upon Teman, which shall devour the palaces of Bozrah. ¹³Thus saith the LORD; For three transgressions of the children of Ammon, and for four, I will not turn away *the punishment* thereof; because they have ripped up the women with child of Gilead, that they might enlarge their border: ¹⁴But I will kindle a fire in the wall of Rabbah, and it shall devour the palaces thereof, with shouting in the day of battle, with a tempest in the day of

---

Devotional Moment
•
On the Job
1:1 Some jobs sound as though they would be exciting every moment, while others sound boring. Amos's job as a herdsman would probably be filed in the less-than-thrilling folder. Yet God chose him to be a prophet (spokesman) for him. Our usefulness to God does not depend on the nature of our work. Whatever you do for a living, realize that it's only a part of God's plan for your life. Be open to all the special ways in which God might want to touch others through you and what you do, whether on the job or off.

ª the plain . . . : or, Bikathaven
ᵇ away captive . . . : or, them away with an entire
ᶜ the brotherly . . . : Heb. the covenant of brethren

the whirlwind: ¹⁵And their king shall go into captivity, he and his princes together, saith the LORD.

2

¹Thus saith the LORD; For three transgressions of Moab, and for four, I will not turn away *the punishment* thereof; because he burned the bones of the king of Edom into lime: ²But I will send a fire upon Moab, and it shall devour the palaces of Kerioth: and Moab shall die with tumult, with shouting, *and* with the sound of the trumpet: ³And I will cut off the judge from the midst thereof, and will slay all the princes thereof with him, saith the LORD. ⁴Thus saith the LORD; For three transgressions of Judah, and for four, I will not turn away *the punishment* thereof; because they have despised the law of the LORD, and have not kept his commandments, and their lies caused them to err, after the which their fathers have walked: ⁵But I will send a fire upon Judah, and it shall devour the palaces of Jerusalem. ⁶Thus saith the LORD; For three transgressions of Israel, and for four, I will not turn away *the punishment* thereof; because they sold the righteous for silver, and the poor for a pair of shoes; ⁷That pant after the dust of the earth on the head of the poor, and turn aside the way of the meek: and a man and his father will go in unto the *same* maidᵃ, to profane my holy name: ⁸And they lay *themselves* down upon clothes laid to pledge by every altar, and they drink

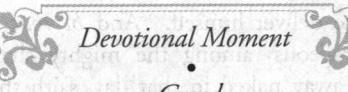

Devotional Moment
•
Greed

2:6-7 The people of Israel were selling the poor into slavery, accepting bribes, and engaging in sex with prostitutes as part of pagan temple worship. The root of their problems was simple greed. It is not easy to admit that greed could be a part of our life, but at times we let it creep in and we need to face it as the sin that it is. Do you have any greedy attitudes or motives?

the wine of the condemnedᵇ *in* the house of their god.

⁹Yet destroyed I the Amorite before them, whose height *was* like the height of the cedars, and he *was* strong as the oaks; yet I destroyed his fruit from above, and his roots from beneath. ¹⁰Also I brought you up from the land of Egypt, and led you forty years through the wilderness, to possess the land of the Amorite. ¹¹And I raised up of your sons for prophets, and of your young men for Nazarites. *Is it* not even thus, O ye children of Israel? saith the LORD. ¹²But ye gave the Nazarites wine to drink; and commanded the prophets, saying, Prophesy not. ¹³Behold, I am pressed under you, as a cart is pressed *that is* full of sheaves. ¹⁴Therefore the flight shall perish from the swift, and the strong shall not strengthen his force, neither shall the mighty deliver himselfᶜ: ¹⁵Neither shall he stand that handleth the bow; and *he that is* swift of foot shall not deliver *himself*: neither shall he that rideth the

---

ᵃ maid: or, young woman
ᵇ the condemned: or, such as have fined, or, mulcted
ᶜ himself: Heb. his soul, or, life

horse deliver himself. ¹⁶And *he that is* courageousᵈ among the mighty shall flee away naked in that day, saith the LORD.

3

¹Hear this word that the LORD hath spoken against you, O children of Israel, against the whole family which I brought up from the land of Egypt, saying, ²You only have I known of all the families of the earth: therefore I will punishª you for all your iniquities. ³Can two walk together, except they be agreed? ⁴Will a lion roar in the forest, when he hath no prey? will a young lion cry out of his den, if he have taken nothing? ⁵Can a bird fall in a snare upon the earth, where no gin *is* for him? shall *one* take up a snare from the earth, and have taken nothing at all? ⁶Shall a trumpet be blown in the city, and the people not be afraidᵇ? shall there be evil in a city, and the LORD hath not done *it*? ⁷Surely the Lord GOD will do nothing, but he revealeth his secret unto his servants the prophets. ⁸The lion hath roared, who will not fear? the Lord GOD hath spoken, who can but prophesy?

⁹Publish in the palaces at Ashdod, and in the palaces in the land of Egypt, and say, Assemble yourselves upon the mountains of Samaria, and behold the great tumults in the midst thereof, and

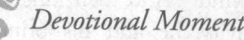

Devotional Moment
•
Walls

3:3 When God seems far away, sometimes that distance has been created by our sin. We need to ask God for forgiveness. This same process also happens in families and friendships. If we get angry, or say something hurtful, it can create a wall. We need to admit our mistakes and ask for forgiveness from others we have wronged just as we do with God.

the oppressedᶜ in the midst thereof. ¹⁰For they know not to do right, saith the LORD, who store up violence and robberyᵈ in their palaces. ¹¹Therefore thus saith the Lord GOD; An adversary *there shall be* even round about the land; and he shall bring down thy strength from thee, and thy palaces shall be spoiled. ¹²Thus saith the LORD; As the shepherd taketh out of the mouth of the lion two legs, or a piece of an ear; so shall the children of Israel be taken out that dwell in Samaria in the corner of a bed, and in Damascus *in* a couch. ¹³Hear ye, and testify in the house of Jacob, saith the Lord GOD, the God of hosts, ¹⁴That in the day that I shall visitᵉ the transgressions of Israel upon him I will also visit the altars of Bethel: and the horns of the altar shall be cut off, and fall to the ground. ¹⁵And I will smite the winter house with the summer house; and the houses of ivory shall perish, and the

---

ᵈ courageous: Heb. strong of his heart
ª punish: Heb. visit upon
ᵇ be afraid: or, run together? the LORD . . . : or, shall not the LORD do somewhat?
ᶜ oppressed: or, oppressions
ᵈ robbery: or, spoil
ᵉ visit: or, punish Israel for

great houses shall have an end, saith the LORD.

4

¹Hear this word, ye kine of Bashan, that *are* in the mountain of Samaria, which oppress the poor, which crush the needy, which say to their masters, Bring, and let us drink. ²The Lord GOD hath sworn by his holiness, that, lo, the days shall come upon you, that he will take you away with hooks, and your posterity with fishhooks. ³And ye shall go out at the breaches, every *cow at that which is* before her; and ye shall cast² *them* into the palace, saith the LORD. ⁴Come to Bethel, and transgress; at Gilgal multiply transgression; and bring your sacrifices every morning, *and* your tithes after three⁶ years: ⁵And offerᶜ a sacrifice of thanksgiving with leaven, and proclaim *and* publish the free offerings: for this liketh you, O ye children of Israel, saith the Lord GOD.

⁶And I also have given you cleanness of teeth in all your cities, and want of bread in all your places: yet have ye not returned unto me, saith the LORD. ⁷And also I have withholden the rain from you, when *there were* yet three months to the harvest: and I caused it to rain upon one city, and caused it not to rain upon another city: one piece was rained upon, and the piece whereupon it rained not withered. ⁸So two *or* three cities wandered unto one city, to drink water; but they were not satisfied: yet have ye not returned unto me, saith the LORD. ⁹I have smitten you with blasting and mildew: when your gardens and your vineyards and your fig trees and your olive trees increased, the palmerworm devoured *them:* yet have ye not returned unto me, saith the LORD. ¹⁰I have sent among you the pestilence after the manner of Egypt: your young men have I slain with the sword, and have taken away your horses; and I have made the stink of your camps to come up unto your nostrils: yet have ye not returned unto me, saith the LORD. ¹¹I have overthrown *some* of you, as God overthrew Sodom and Gomorrah, and ye were as a firebrand plucked out of the burning: yet have ye not returned unto me, saith the LORD. ¹²Therefore thus will I do unto thee, O Israel: *and* because I will do this unto thee, prepare to meet thy God, O Israel. ¹³For, lo, he that formeth the mountains, and createth the windᵈ, and declareth unto man what *is* his thought, that maketh the morning darkness, and treadeth upon the high places of the earth, The LORD, The God of hosts, *is* his name.

5

¹Hear ye this word which I take up against you, *even* a lamentation, O house of Israel. ²The virgin of Israel is fallen; she shall no more rise: she is forsaken upon her land; *there is* none to raise her up. ³For thus saith the Lord GOD; The city that went out *by* a

---

ᵃ cast . . . : or, cast away the things of the palace
ᵇ three . . . : Heb. three years of days
ᶜ offer: Heb. offer by burning
ᵈ wind: or, spirit

thousand shall leave an hundred, and that which went forth *by* an hundred shall leave ten, to the house of Israel.

⁴For thus saith the LORD unto the house of Israel, Seek ye me, and ye shall live: ⁵But seek not Bethel, nor enter into Gilgal, and pass not to Beersheba: for Gilgal shall surely go into captivity, and Bethel shall come to nought. ⁶Seek the LORD, and ye shall live; lest he break out like fire in the house of Joseph, and devour *it*, and *there be* none to quench *it* in Bethel. ⁷Ye who turn judgment to wormwood, and leave off righteousness in the earth, ⁸*Seek him* that maketh the seven stars and Orion, and turneth the shadow of death into the morning, and maketh the day dark with night: that calleth for the waters of the sea, and poureth them out upon the face of the earth: The LORD *is* his name: ⁹That strengtheneth the spoiled*ᵃ* against the strong, so that the spoiled shall come against the fortress. ¹⁰They hate him that rebuketh in the gate, and

---

Devotional Moment

•

Cats and Dogs

5:11-12, 24 God said that he wanted a mighty flood of justice, not just people doing good once in a while. When homes are steadily supplying good, they become shelters from disaster. When people go out of their way to help each other, those homes become joyful places. Is fair treatment "flowing" in your home? Is there a drought, a few scattered showers, a steady rain, or a real downpour of love for each other?

---

they abhor him that speaketh uprightly. ¹¹Forasmuch therefore as your treading *is* upon the poor, and ye take from him burdens of wheat: ye have built houses of hewn stone, but ye shall not dwell in them; ye have planted pleasant*ᵇ* vineyards, but ye shall not drink wine of them. ¹²For I know your manifold transgressions and your mighty sins: they afflict the just, they take a bribe*ᶜ*, and they turn aside the poor in the gate *from their right.* ¹³Therefore the prudent shall keep silence in that time; for it *is* an evil time. ¹⁴Seek good, and not evil, that ye may live: and so the LORD, the God of hosts, shall be with you, as ye have spoken. ¹⁵Hate the evil, and love the good, and establish judgment in the gate: it may be that the LORD God of hosts will be gracious unto the remnant of Joseph.

¹⁶Therefore the LORD, the God of hosts, the Lord, saith thus; Wailing *shall be* in all streets; and they shall say in all the highways, Alas! alas! and they shall call the husbandman to mourning, and such as are skilful of lamentation to wailing. ¹⁷And in all vineyards *shall be* wailing: for I will pass through thee, saith the LORD. ¹⁸Woe unto you that desire the day of the LORD! to what end *is* it for you? the day of the LORD *is* darkness, and not light. ¹⁹As if a man did flee from a lion, and a bear met him; or went into the house, and leaned his hand on the wall, and a serpent bit him. ²⁰*Shall* not the day of the LORD *be* darkness, and not light? even very dark, and no brightness in it?

ᵃ spoiled: Heb. spoil
ᵇ pleasant . . . : Heb. vineyards of desire
ᶜ a bribe: or, a ransom

²¹I hate, I despise your feast days, and I will not smell in your solemn assemblies. ²²Though ye offer me burnt offerings and your meat offerings, I will not accept *them*: neither will I regard the peace offerings of your fat beasts. ²³Take thou away from me the noise of thy songs; for I will not hear the melody of thy viols. ²⁴But let judgment run down as waters, and righteousness as a mighty stream. ²⁵Have ye offered unto me sacrifices and offerings in the wilderness forty years, O house of Israel? ²⁶But ye have borne the tabernacle[d] of your Moloch and Chiun your images, the star of your god, which ye made to yourselves. ²⁷Therefore will I cause you to go into captivity beyond Damascus, saith the LORD, whose name *is* The God of hosts.

6

¹Woe to them *that are* at ease in Zion, and trust in the mountain of Samaria, *which are* named chief of the nations, to whom the house of Israel came! ²Pass ye unto Calneh, and see; and from thence go ye to Hamath the great: then go down to Gath of the Philistines: *be they* better than these kingdoms? or their border greater than your border? ³Ye that put far away the evil day, and cause the seat[a] of violence to come near; ⁴That lie upon beds of ivory, and stretch[b] themselves upon their couches, and eat the lambs out of the flock, and the calves out of the midst of the stall;

⁵That chant[c] to the sound of the viol, *and* invent to themselves instruments of musick, like David; ⁶That drink wine[d] in bowls, and anoint themselves with the chief ointments: but they are not grieved for the affliction of Joseph. ⁷Therefore now shall they go captive with the first that go captive, and the banquet of them that stretched themselves shall be removed.

⁸The Lord GOD hath sworn by himself, saith the LORD the God of hosts, I abhor the excellency of Jacob, and hate his palaces: therefore will I deliver up the city with all that is therein. ⁹And it shall come to pass, if there remain ten men in one house, that they shall die. ¹⁰And a man's uncle shall take him up, and he that burneth him, to bring out the bones out of the house, and shall say unto him that *is* by the

---

[d] the tabernacle . . . : or, Siccuth your king
[a] seat: or, habitation
[b] stretch . . . : or, abound with superfluities
[c] chant: or, quaver
[d] wine . . . : or, in bowls of wine

sides of the house, *Is there* yet *any* with thee? and he shall say, No. Then shall he say, Hold thy tongue: for we may not make mention of the name of the LORD. ¹¹For, behold, the LORD commandeth, and he will smite the great house with breachesᵉ, and the little house with clefts. ¹²Shall horses run upon the rock? will *one* plow *there* with oxen? for ye have turned judgment into gall, and the fruit of righteousness into hemlock: ¹³Ye which rejoice in a thing of nought, which say, Have we not taken to us horns by our own strength? ¹⁴But, behold, I will raise up against you a nation, O house of Israel, saith the LORD the God of hosts; and they shall afflict you from the entering in of Hemath unto the riverᶠ of the wilderness.

7

¹Thus hath the Lord GOD shewed unto me; and, behold, he formed grasshoppersᵃ in the beginning of the shooting up of the latter growth; and,

---

Devotional Moment

•

Prayer

7:1-3 Just when Amos thought life couldn't get any worse, it did. God gave him a frightening vision of impending judgment: nationwide famine. Amos began to pray frantically. And God answered by relenting and not fulfilling the vision. God encourages us to talk to him about everything (see Phil. 4:6), even scary possibilities, because he hears and answers. When we stay in touch with God, we see results.

---

lo, *it was* the latter growth after the king's mowings. ²And it came to pass, *that* when they had made an end of eating the grass of the land, then I said, O Lord GOD, forgive, I beseech thee: by whom shall Jacob arise? for he *is* small. ³The LORD repented for this: It shall not be, saith the LORD. ⁴Thus hath the Lord GOD shewed unto me: and, behold, the Lord GOD called to contend by fire, and it devoured the great deep, and did eat up a part. ⁵Then said I, O Lord GOD, cease, I beseech thee: by whom shall Jacob arise? for he *is* small. ⁶The LORD repented for this: This also shall not be, saith the Lord GOD. ⁷Thus he shewed me: and, behold, the Lord stood upon a wall *made* by a plumbline, with a plumbline in his hand. ⁸And the LORD said unto me, Amos, what seest thou? And I said, A plumbline. Then said the Lord, Behold, I will set a plumbline in the midst of my people Israel: I will not again pass by them any more: ⁹And the high places of Isaac shall be desolate, and the sanctuaries of Israel shall be laid waste; and I will rise against the house of Jeroboam with the sword.

¹⁰Then Amaziah the priest of Bethel sent to Jeroboam king of Israel, saying, Amos hath conspired against thee in the midst of the house of Israel: the land is not able to bear all his words. ¹¹For thus Amos saith, Jeroboam shall die by the sword, and Israel shall surely be led away captive out of their own land. ¹²Also Amaziah said unto Amos, O thou seer, go, flee thee away into the land of Judah,

---

ᵉ breaches: or, droppings
ᶠ river: or, valley
ᵃ grasshoppers: or, green worms

and there eat bread, and prophesy there: [13]But prophesy not again any more at Bethel: for it *is* the king's chapel[b], and it *is* the king's court. [14]Then answered Amos, and said to Amaziah, I *was* no prophet, neither *was* I a prophet's son; but I *was* an herdman, and a gatherer of sycomore fruit: [15]And the LORD took me as I followed the flock, and the LORD said unto me, Go, prophesy unto my people Israel. [16]Now therefore hear thou the word of the LORD: Thou sayest, Prophesy not against Israel, and drop not *thy word* against the house of Isaac. [17]Therefore thus saith the LORD; Thy wife shall be an harlot in the city, and thy sons and thy daughters shall fall by the sword, and thy land shall be divided by line; and thou shalt die in a polluted land: and Israel shall surely go into captivity forth of his land.

8

[1]Thus hath the Lord GOD shewed unto me: and behold a basket of summer fruit. [2]And he said, Amos, what seest thou? And I said, A basket of summer fruit. Then said the LORD unto me, The end is come upon my people of Israel; I will not again pass by them any more. [3]And the songs of the temple shall be howlings[a] in that day, saith the Lord GOD: *there shall be* many dead bodies in every place; they shall cast *them* forth with silence.

[4]Hear this, O ye that swallow up the needy, even to make the poor of the land to fail, [5]Saying, When will the new moon be gone, that we may sell corn? and the sabbath, that we may set forth wheat, making the ephah small, and the shekel great, and falsifying the balances by deceit? [6]That we may buy the poor for silver, and the needy for a pair of shoes; *yea*, and sell the refuse of the wheat? [7]The LORD hath sworn by the excellency of Jacob, Surely I will never forget any of their works. [8]Shall not the land tremble for this, and every one mourn that dwelleth therein? and it shall rise up wholly as a flood; and it shall be cast out and drowned, as *by* the flood of Egypt. [9]And it shall come to pass in that day, saith the Lord GOD, that I will cause the sun to go down at noon, and I will darken the earth in the clear day: [10]And I will turn your feasts into mourning, and all your songs into lamentation; and I will bring up sackcloth upon all loins, and baldness upon every head; and I will make it as the mourning of an only *son*, and the end thereof as a bitter day.

[11]Behold, the days come, saith the Lord GOD, that I will send a famine in the land, not a famine of bread, nor a thirst for water, but of hearing the

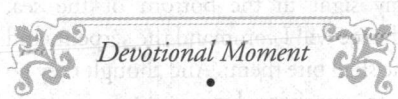

Devotional Moment

•

Feast or Famine?

8:11-13 God told Amos of a time when he would send a famine of hearing God's words, and the people would search in vain to hear from God. Today we have God's written Word readily available, but do we take advantage of the opportunity to hear from God? We can easily take God's Word for granted. Do your best to make Bible reading a consistent part of your life.

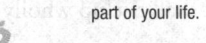

---

b chapel: or, sanctuary
a shall be howlings: Heb. shall howl

words of the LORD: [12]And they shall wander from sea to sea, and from the north even to the east, they shall run to and fro to seek the word of the LORD, and shall not find *it*. [13]In that day shall the fair virgins and young men faint for thirst. [14]They that swear by the sin of Samaria, and say, Thy god, O Dan, liveth; and, The manner[b] of Beersheba liveth; even they shall fall, and never rise up again.

9

[1]I saw the Lord standing upon the altar: and he said, Smite the lintel of the door, that the posts may shake: and cut them in the head, all of them; and I will slay the last of them with the sword: he that fleeth of them shall not flee away, and he that escapeth of them shall not be delivered. [2]Though they dig into hell, thence shall mine hand take them; though they climb up to heaven, thence will I bring them down: [3]And though they hide themselves in the top of Carmel, I will search and take them out thence; and though they be hid from my sight in the bottom of the sea, thence will I command the serpent, and he shall bite them: [4]And though they go into captivity before their enemies, thence will I command the sword, and it shall slay them: and I will set mine eyes upon them for evil, and not for good. [5]And the Lord GOD of hosts *is* he that toucheth the land, and it shall melt, and all that dwell therein shall mourn: and it shall rise up wholly like a

flood; and shall be drowned, as *by* the flood of Egypt. [6]*It is* he that buildeth his stories[a] in the heaven, and hath founded his troop in the earth; he that calleth for the waters of the sea, and poureth them out upon the face of the earth: The LORD *is* his name. [7]*Are* ye not as children of the Ethiopians unto me, O children of Israel? saith the LORD. Have not I brought up Israel out of the land of Egypt? and the Philistines from Caphtor, and the Syrians from Kir? [8]Behold, the eyes of the Lord GOD *are* upon the sinful kingdom, and I will destroy it from off the face of the earth; saving that I will not utterly destroy the house of Jacob, saith the LORD. [9]For, lo, I will command, and I will sift[b] the house of Israel among all nations, like as *corn* is sifted in a sieve, yet shall not the least grain fall upon the earth. [10]All the sinners of my people shall die by the sword, which say, The evil shall not overtake nor prevent us.

[11]In that day will I raise up the tabernacle of David that is fallen, and close up the breaches thereof; and I will raise up his ruins, and I will build it as in the days of old: [12]That they may possess the remnant of Edom, and of all the heathen, which are called by my name, saith the LORD that doeth this. [13]Behold, the days come, saith the LORD, that the plowman shall overtake the reaper, and the treader of grapes him that soweth[c] seed; and the mountains shall drop sweet wine, and

---

[b] manner: Heb. way
[a] stories: or, spheres: Heb. ascensions
[b] sift: Heb. cause to move
[c] soweth: Heb. draweth forth

all the hills shall melt. ¹⁴And I will bring again the captivity of my people of Israel, and they shall build the waste cities, and inhabit *them*; and they shall plant vineyards, and drink the wine thereof; they shall also make gardens,

and eat the fruit of them. ¹⁵And I will plant them upon their land, and they shall no more be pulled up out of their land which I have given them, saith the LORD thy God.

OBADIAH

Purpose
To show that God judges those who have harmed his people

Author
Obadiah. Very little is known about this man whose name means "servant."

To Whom Written
The Edomites, the Jews in Judah, and God's people everywhere

Date Written
Possibly during the reign of Jehoram in Judah, 853–841 B.C.

Setting
Historically, Edom had constantly harassed the Jews. Prior to the time this book was written, the Edomites had participated in attacks against Judah.

Key Verse
"For the day of the Lord is near upon all the heathen: as thou hast done, it shall be done unto thee: thy reward shall return upon thine own head" (1:15).

Key People
The Edomites

Key Places
Edom, Jerusalem

Special Features
The book of Obadiah uses vigorous poetic language and is written in the form of a dirge of doom.

Obadiah knew what all children know by the time they're knee high: Brothers stick together. At home, brothers pick on each other, sometimes mercilessly. But out in the world, where bullies roam, a different rule takes over: Brothers stick together.

This rule is so universal that if you *don't* help a brother in trouble, you're worse than an enemy—you're a traitor.

Once you're a traitor, the only way back into the fold is to have a resurgence of loyalty. You have to defend your brother against a bully. A long-term traitor will probably have to fight two bullies to make sure the first one wasn't a fluke.

During Obadiah's life, Israel was up against a bully. To the southeast, below the Salt Sea, sat Edom, the ancient home of Esau. Because Jacob and Esau were brothers, Edom and Israel were brother nations. But Edom had betrayed Israel. Edom watched whenever the bullies came and beat up on Israel. Edom even plundered their Israelite brothers along with the bullies.

Obadiah warned Edom of the consequences of being traitors. You can read about them. It's not a pretty scene.

Is the opposite of betrayal to fight all your brother's battles for him? Probably not. The proper approach is called loyalty.

Trusting in the living God, we should not hesitate to help weaker brothers against bullies in ways that reflect God's justice and love. That's not easy, but it's what God wants of us.

1

¹The vision of Obadiah. Thus saith the Lord GOD concerning Edom; We have heard a rumour from the LORD, and an ambassador is sent among the heathen, Arise ye, and let us rise up against her in battle. ²Behold, I have made thee small among the heathen: thou art greatly despised. ³The pride of thine heart hath deceived thee, thou that dwellest in the clefts of the rock, whose habitation *is* high; that saith in his heart, Who shall bring me down to the ground? ⁴Though thou exalt *thyself* as the eagle, and though thou set thy nest among the stars, thence will I bring thee down, saith the LORD. ⁵If thieves came to thee, if robbers by night, (how art thou cut off!) would they not have stolen till they had enough? if the grapegatherers came to thee, would they not leave *some* grapes? ⁶How are *the things* of Esau searched out! how are his hidden things sought up! ⁷All the

---

Devotional Moment

•

Without God

1:3 The Edomites had everything: safe homes, plenty of food, lots of friends, and proud independence. If they lived on our block, we might be jealous of them. But they also had a fatal flaw: They were so proud of their success that they assumed they didn't need God. God eventually showed them that they owed everything to him. No matter how much a person achieves, without God he or she eventually comes to nothing. We see many people who accomplish a lot, trying to prove they can do it without God. A person will accomplish much more of lasting value living for Christ.

Devotional Moment

•

Family Ties

1:10-12 Edom and Israel were not just neighbors, they were distant relatives. The two nations had descended from brothers—Jacob and Esau. But when Israel was in trouble, the people of Edom did nothing to help. In fact, they gloated. God said that this was sin. Family members don't always agree or get along well, but when real problems come, families need to stick together. If we don't care for others in our family when they are in need, we may suddenly find ourselves all alone and in trouble, like Edom. Who in your family could be helped by your encouragement? And even if someone is suffering under self-inflicted trouble, don't gloat.

---

men of thy confederacy have brought thee *even* to the border: the men that were at peace with thee have deceived thee, *and* prevailed against thee; *they that eat* thy bread have laid a wound under thee: *there is* none understanding in him. ⁸Shall I not in that day, saith the LORD, even destroy the wise *men* out of Edom, and understanding out of the mount of Esau? ⁹And thy mighty *men*, O Teman, shall be dismayed, to the end that every one of the mount of Esau may be cut off by slaughter.

¹⁰For *thy* violence against thy brother Jacob shame shall cover thee, and thou shalt be cut off for ever. ¹¹In the day that thou stoodest on the other side, in the day that the strangers carried away captive ᵃ his forces, and foreigners entered into his gates, and cast lots upon Jerusalem, even thou *wast* as one of them. ¹²But thou shouldest not have looked on the day of thy brother in the day that he became a stranger;

ᵃ captive . . . : or, his substance

neither shouldest thou have rejoiced over the children of Judah in the day of their destruction; neither shouldest thou have spoken[b] proudly in the day of distress. [13]Thou shouldest not have entered into the gate of my people in the day of their calamity; yea, thou shouldest not have looked on their affliction in the day of their calamity, nor have laid *hands* on their substance[c] in the day of their calamity; [14]Neither shouldest thou have stood in the crossway, to cut off those of his that did escape; neither shouldest thou have delivered up[d] those of his that did remain in the day of distress. [15]For the day of the LORD *is* near upon all the heathen: as thou hast done, it shall be done unto thee: thy reward shall return upon thine own head. [16]For as ye have drunk upon my holy mountain, *so* shall all the heathen drink continually, yea, they shall drink, and they shall swallow down, and they shall be as though they had not been.

[17]But upon mount Zion shall be deliverance[e], and there shall be holiness; and the house of Jacob shall possess their possessions. [18]And the house of Jacob shall be a fire, and the house of Joseph a flame, and the house of Esau for stubble, and they shall kindle in them, and devour them; and there shall not be *any* remaining of the house of Esau; for the LORD hath spoken *it*. [19]And *they of* the south shall possess the mount of Esau; and *they of* the plain the Philistines: and they shall possess the fields of Ephraim, and the fields of Samaria: and Benjamin *shall possess* Gilead. [20]And the captivity of this host of the children of Israel *shall possess* that of the Canaanites, *even* unto Zarephath; and the captivity of Jerusalem, which *is* in Sepharad[f], shall possess the cities of the south. [21]And saviours shall come up on mount Zion to judge the mount of Esau; and the kingdom shall be the LORD'S.

---

[b] spoken . . . : Heb. magnified thy mouth
[c] substance: or, forces
[d] delivered up: or, shut up
[e] deliverance: or, they that escape
[f] which . . . : or, shall possess that which is in

JONAH

Purpose
To show the extent of God's grace—the message of salvation is for all people

Setting
Jonah preceded Amos and ministered under Jeroboam II, Israel's most powerful king (793–753 B.C.; see 2 Kings 14:23-25). Assyria was Israel's great enemy, and Israel was conquered by them in 722 B.C. Nineveh's repentance must have been short-lived, for it was destroyed in 612 B.C.

Key Verse
"And should not I spare Nineveh, that great city, wherein are more than sixscore thousand persons that cannot discern between their right hand and their left hand; and also much cattle?" (4:11).

Key People
Jonah, the ship's captain and crew

Key Places
Joppa, Nineveh

Special Features
This book is different from the other prophetic books because it tells the story of the prophet and does not center on his prophecies. In fact, only one verse summarizes his message to the people of Nineveh (3:4). Jonah's experience is also mentioned by Jesus as a picture of his death and resurrection (Matt. 12:38-41).

No carnival thrill-ride could begin to compare with Jonah's adventure. Roller-coasters can't match it—they just go up and down and take curves fast. Tilt-A-Whirls merely spin around. Ferris wheels are made for hugging children and kissing boyfriends. Jonah would laugh at them all.

The closest most kids come to Jonah's ride from the whale's mouth into his belly is when they take off at the top of a water slide. They weave and bob down the wet passageway, holding their noses and closing their eyes, and slosh into a pool at the bottom. If you can imagine a water slide that smells like a fish and feels slimy and mushy—and pitch dark besides—then you know what Jonah's ride was like. Pretty scary, huh?

God has important work for each person to do. God wants people everywhere to know the truth and enjoy his love. Even in Nineveh, the capital of evil Assyria, God wanted people to know him. It was Jonah's job to tell them.

So what's more scary, sliding into a whale's belly after a storm at sea, or walking into the center of an evil city and preaching about God's love and forgiveness? Pick the worst city you can imagine—Gotham City—and imagine preaching there. You're all alone. People are laughing. Someone threatens to break your arms. Then you see the Joker walking toward you, smiling ugly. Talk about scary!

God has a mission for you—for every adult and every child. The whole world needs to know about God's love, and God wants you to tell people wherever you are and wherever you go.

Wherever your mission, God will be there with you. It's OK to be a little scared, but don't let fear stop you. Even Jonah knew that prayer would make him bolder. Jonah came through for God, and so will you!

1

¹Now the word of the LORD came unto Jonah[a] the son of Amittai, saying, ²Arise, go to Nineveh, that great city, and cry against it; for their wickedness is come up before me. ³But Jonah rose up to flee unto Tarshish from the presence of the LORD, and went down to Joppa; and he found a ship going to Tarshish: so he paid the fare thereof, and went down into it, to go with them unto Tarshish from the presence of the LORD.

⁴But the LORD sent out[b] a great wind into the sea, and there was a mighty tempest in the sea, so that the ship was like to be broken. ⁵Then the mariners were afraid, and cried every man unto his god, and cast forth the wares that *were* in the ship into the sea, to lighten *it* of them. But Jonah was gone down into the sides of the ship; and he lay, and was fast asleep. ⁶So the shipmaster came to him, and said unto him, What meanest thou, O sleeper? arise, call upon thy God, if so be that God will think upon us, that we perish not. ⁷And they said every one to his fellow, Come, and let us cast lots, that we may know for whose cause this evil *is* upon us. So they cast lots, and the lot fell upon Jonah. ⁸Then said they unto him, Tell us, we pray thee, for whose cause this evil *is* upon us; What *is* thine occupation? and whence comest thou? what *is* thy country? and of what people *art* thou? ⁹And he said unto them, I *am* an Hebrew; and I fear the LORD[c], the God of heaven, which hath made the sea and the dry *land*. ¹⁰Then were the men exceedingly[d] afraid, and said unto him, Why hast thou done this? For the men knew that he fled from the presence of the LORD, because he had told them.

¹¹Then said they unto him, What shall we do unto thee, that the sea may be calm unto us? for the sea wrought, and was tempestuous. ¹²And he said unto them, Take me up, and cast me forth into the sea; so shall the sea be calm unto you: for I know that for my sake this great tempest *is* upon you. ¹³Nevertheless the men rowed hard to bring *it* to the land; but they could not: for the sea wrought, and was tempestuous against them. ¹⁴Wherefore they cried unto the LORD, and said, We beseech thee, O LORD, we beseech thee, let us not perish for this man's life, and lay not upon us innocent blood: for thou, O LORD, hast done as it pleased

---

Devotional Moment
Forgiveness

1:3 When Jonah thought of Nineveh, he only saw people who needed to be wiped out by God. But when God looked at Nineveh, he saw people who needed a chance to repent. When we refuse to forgive someone, we are saying that our right to hold a grudge overrules God's command to forgive. Forgiving others is a step we must take, even when it's difficult. Who in your life is a Nineveh? Ask God to help you care for that person the way he does.

---

[a] Jonah: Gr. Jonas
[b] sent out: Heb. cast forth
[c] the LORD: or, JEHOVAH
[d] exceedingly . . . . : Heb. with great fear

thee. ¹⁵So they took up Jonah, and cast him forth into the sea: and the sea ceased⁰ from her raging. ¹⁶Then the men feared the LORD exceedingly, and offeredᶠ a sacrifice unto the LORD, and made vows. ¹⁷Now the LORD had prepared a great fish to swallow up Jonah. And Jonah was in the bellyᵍ of the fish three days and three nights.

2

¹Then Jonah prayed unto the LORD his God out of the fish's belly, ²And said, I cried by reason of mine affliction unto the LORD, and he heard me; out of the belly of hell cried I, *and* thou heardest my voice. ³For thou hadst cast me into the deep, in the midstᵃ of the seas; and the floods compassed me about: all thy billows and thy waves passed over me. ⁴Then I said, I am cast out of thy sight; yet I will look again toward thy holy temple. ⁵The waters compassed me about, *even* to the soul: the depth closed me round about, the weeds were wrapped about my head. ⁶I went down to the bottomsᵇ of the mountains; the earth with her bars *was* about me for ever: yet hast thou brought up my life from corruption, O LORD my God. ⁷When my soul fainted within me I remembered the LORD: and my prayer came in unto thee, into thine holy temple. ⁸They that observe lying vanities forsake their own

mercy. ⁹But I will sacrifice unto thee with the voice of thanksgiving; I will pay *that* that I have vowed. Salvation *is* of the LORD.

¹⁰And the LORD spake unto the fish, and it vomited out Jonah upon the dry *land.*

3

¹And the word of the LORD came unto Jonah the second time, saying, ²Arise, go unto Nineveh, that great city, and preach unto it the preaching that I bid thee. ³So Jonah arose, and went unto Nineveh, according to the word of the LORD. Now Nineveh was an exceedingᵃ great city of three days' journey. ⁴And Jonah began to enter into the city a day's journey, and he cried, and said, Yet forty days, and Nineveh shall be overthrown.

⁵So the people of Nineveh believed God, and proclaimed a fast, and put on sackcloth, from the greatest of them even to the least of them. ⁶For word came unto the king of Nineveh, and he arose from his throne, and he laid his robe from him, and covered *him* with sackcloth, and sat in ashes. ⁷And he caused *it* to be proclaimed and publishedᵇ through Nineveh by the decree of the king and his nobles, saying, Let neither man nor beast, herd nor flock, taste any thing: let them not feed, nor drink water: ⁸But let man and beast be

---

ᵉ ceased: Heb. stood
ᶠ offered . . . : Heb. sacrifice unto the LORD, and vowed vows
ᵍ belly: Heb. bowels
ᵃ midst: Heb. heart
ᵇ bottoms: Heb. cuttings off
ᵃ exceeding: Heb. of God
ᵇ published: Heb. said

Devotional Moment
•
Repent!

3:4-5 Jonah had a unique message to preach: "Forty days from now Nineveh will be destroyed!" It was short and to the point. From Jonah's reaction to the Ninevites' repentance (4:1) it seems as though Jonah hoped this message would offend the people rather than cause them to change. He made it sound as though there was no escape. Hopefully, we will never share our faith with our family and friends out of contempt for them. Telling others about our relationship with God should be an expression of love. Here's a recipe for what to include: (1) What you have learned; (2) how you have responded to the gospel; (3) how knowing God has made a difference in your life; and (4) how they, too, can know him.

covered with sackcloth, and cry mightily unto God: yea, let them turn every one from his evil way, and from the violence that *is* in their hands. ⁹Who can tell *if* God will turn and repent, and turn away from his fierce anger, that we perish not? ¹⁰And God saw their works, that they turned from their evil way; and God repented of the evil, that he had said that he would do unto them; and he did *it* not.

4

¹But it displeased Jonah exceedingly, and he was very angry. ²And he prayed unto the LORD, and said, I pray thee, O LORD, *was* not this my saying, when I was yet in my country? Therefore I fled before unto Tarshish: for I knew that thou *art* a gracious God, and merciful, slow to anger, and of great kindness, and repentest thee of the evil.

³Therefore now, O LORD, take, I beseech thee, my life from me; for *it is* better for me to die than to live. ⁴Then said the LORD, Doest thou well to be angry?

⁵So Jonah went out of the city, and sat on the east side of the city, and there made him a booth, and sat under it in the shadow, till he might see what would become of the city. ⁶And the LORD God prepared a gourdᵃ, and made *it* to come up over Jonah, that it might be a shadow over his head, to deliver him from his grief. So Jonah was exceeding glad of the gourd. ⁷But God prepared a worm when the morning rose the next day, and it smote the gourd that it withered. ⁸And it came to pass, when the sun did arise, that God prepared a vehementᵇ east wind; and the sun beat upon the head of Jonah, that he fainted, and wished in himself to die, and said, *It is* better for me to die

Devotional Moment
•
Anger

4:9-11 Jonah's anger made it impossible for him to think straight. He lost his shade plant, and that was it—he wanted to die. Jonah had it all backwards because of his feelings. What *should* have mattered to him (the lives of 120,000 Ninevites) didn't, and what should not have been important (having some shade) mattered very much. God patiently reasoned with him; we can only assume that Jonah got the point. The next time you feel the anger building, ask yourself: Does this matter to God? And remember: "A fool uttereth all his mind: but a wise man keepeth it in till afterwards" (Prov. 29:11).

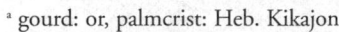

ᵃ gourd: or, palmcrist: Heb. Kikajon
ᵇ vehement: or, silent

than to live. ⁹And God said to Jonah, Doest thou well to be angry for the gourd? And he said, I do well to be angry, *even* unto death. ¹⁰Then said the LORD, Thou hast had pity^c on the gourd, for the which thou hast not laboured, neither madest it grow; which came up in a night, and perished in a night: ¹¹And should not I spare Nineveh, that great city, wherein are more than sixscore thousand persons that cannot discern between their right hand and their left hand; and *also* much cattle?

---

^c had pity: or, spared

MICAH

Purpose
To warn God's people that judgment is coming and to offer pardon to all who repent

Author
Micah, a native of Moresheth, near Gath, about twenty miles southeast of Jerusalem

Date Written
Possibly during the reigns of Jotham, Ahaz, and Hezekiah (742–687 B.C.)

Setting
The political situation is described in 2 Kings 15-20 and 2 Chronicles 26-30. Micah was a contemporary of Isaiah and Hosea.

Key Verse
"He hath shewed thee . . . what is good; and what doth the Lord require of thee, but to do justly, and to love mercy, and to walk humbly with thy God" (6:8).

Key People
The people of Samaria and Jerusalem

Key Places
Samaria, Jerusalem, Bethlehem

Special Features
This is a beautiful example of classical Hebrew poetry. There are three parts, each beginning with a call for the reader's attention (1:2; 3:1; 6:1) and closing with a promise.

Note how frequently Micah uses family words to refer to Israel's trouble. He knows that a breakdown in family intimacy is part and parcel of the larger Assyrian threat, the impending judgment of God, the fickleness of the people's faith. Strong, sensitive mothers and caring, disciplined fathers are assets that no strong nation can do without.

So, what help does Micah provide?

The advice the Bible gives isn't like the advice you get from a secular counselor. Bible writers must have skipped the course in Positive Mental Attitude! But they knew something about how people tick that escapes the secular psychologists whose theories have no room for the living God.

Reading Micah you'll find that answers to health and happiness don't pop out of each chapter, one-two-three. To discover the wisdom God gave us in Micah, you may have to read it twice, think about it thrice, and work at the connections four times. But the wisdom is there, and when you find it, change begins. Old sight gives way to new; tattered attitudes to fresh energy; beat-up relationships to upbeat expectations.

Who's to say your neighborhood might not also change in the wake of your discoveries? Or your city? Or—watch out, world!

1

¹The word of the LORD that came to Micah the Morasthite in the days of Jotham, Ahaz, *and* Hezekiah, kings of Judah, which he saw concerning Samaria and Jerusalem. ²Hear, all ye people; hearken, O earth, and all that therein is: and let the Lord GOD be witness against you, the Lord from his holy temple. ³For, behold, the LORD cometh forth out of his place, and will come down, and tread upon the high places of the earth. ⁴And the mountains shall be molten under him, and the valleys shall be cleft, as wax before the fire, *and* as the waters *that are* poured down a steep place. ⁵For the transgression of Jacob *is* all this, and for the sins of the house of Israel. What *is* the transgression of Jacob? *is it* not Samaria? and what *are* the high places of Judah? *are they* not Jerusalem? ⁶Therefore I will make Samaria as an heap of the field, *and* as plantings of a vineyard: and I will pour down the stones thereof into the valley, and I will discover the foundations thereof. ⁷And all the graven images thereof shall be beaten to pieces, and all the hires thereof shall be burned with the fire, and all the idols thereof will I lay desolate: for she gathered *it* of the hire of an harlot, and they shall return to the hire of an harlot.

⁸Therefore I will wail and howl, I will go stripped and naked: I will make a wailing like the dragons, and mourning as the owlsᵃ. ⁹For her wound *is* incurable; for it is come unto Judah; he is come unto

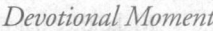

Devotional Moment

Trendsetters

1:13 The city of Lachish was the first city in the Southern Kingdom (Judah) to follow the Northern Kingdom (Israel) in the practice of idolatry. When it came to sin, they were trendsetters. As an individual or as a family, are you setting a standard of righteousness or simply following the trends around you? Following trends may seem harmless in matters of clothing style and popular games, but children sometimes don't know where to draw the line between the harmless and the sinful. Those who follow the trends make two mistakes: (1) They damage their own relationship with God by not placing him first, and (2) they may be a bad example to others. How we live does matter to God and to others.

the gate of my people, *even* to Jerusalem. ¹⁰Declare ye *it* not at Gath, weep ye not at all: in the house of Aphrahᵇ roll thyself in the dust. ¹¹Pass ye away, thou inhabitant of Saphir, having thy shame naked: the inhabitant of Zaanan came not forth in the mourning of Bethezel; he shall receive of you his standing. ¹²For the inhabitantᶜ of Maroth waited carefully for good: but evil came down from the LORD unto the gate of Jerusalem. ¹³O thou inhabitantᵈ of Lachish, bind the chariot to the swift beast: she *is* the beginning of the sin to the daughter of Zion: for the transgressions of Israel were found in thee. ¹⁴Therefore shalt thou give presents to Moreshethgath: the houses of Achzib *shall be* a lie to the kings of Israel. ¹⁵Yet will I bring an heir unto thee, O inhabitantᵉ of Mare-

ᵃ owls: Heb. daughters of the owl
ᵇ Aphrah: that is, Dust
ᶜ inhabitant: Heb. inhabitress
ᵈ inhabitant: Heb. inhabitress
ᵉ inhabitant: Heb. inhabitress

shah: he shall come unto Adullam the glory of Israel. [16]Make thee bald, and poll thee for thy delicate children; enlarge thy baldness as the eagle; for they are gone into captivity from thee.

2

[1]Woe to them that devise iniquity, and work evil upon their beds! when the morning is light, they practise it, because it is in the power of their hand. [2]And they covet fields, and take *them* by violence; and houses, and take *them* away: so they oppress[a] a man and his house, even a man and his heritage. [3]Therefore thus saith the LORD; Behold, against this family do I devise an evil, from which ye shall not remove your necks; neither shall ye go haughtily: for this time *is* evil. [4]In that day shall *one* take up a parable against you,

---

Devotional Moment
•
Offended!

2:6-7 When Micah told the people God's message, they were offended. They didn't argue with God's accusations; they just told Micah to stop. They didn't want to hear negative talk, even though it was true. Sometimes the truth hurts. If you've got bad news to deliver, it will take discernment to know the right time to speak. Don't hold back from telling it merely to placate people who have entrenched themselves in bad or destructive habits. Tell it like it is if it will help someone make a necessary correction.

---

and lament with a doleful[b] lamentation, *and* say, We be utterly spoiled: he hath changed the portion of my people: how hath he removed *it* from me! turning away he hath divided our fields. [5]Therefore thou shalt have none that shall cast a cord by lot in the congregation of the LORD.

[6]Prophesy ye not, *say they to them that* prophesy: they shall not prophesy to them, *that* they shall not take shame. [7]O *thou that art* named the house of Jacob, is the spirit of the LORD straitened[c]? *are* these his doings? do not my words do good to him that walketh uprightly? [8]Even of late[d] my people is risen up as an enemy: ye pull off the robe with the garment from them that pass by securely as men averse from war. [9]The women[e] of my people have ye cast out from their pleasant houses; from their children have ye taken away my glory for ever. [10]Arise ye, and depart; for this *is* not *your* rest: because it is polluted, it shall destroy *you*, even with a sore destruction. [11]If a man walking[f] in the spirit and falsehood do lie, *saying*, I will prophesy unto thee of wine and of strong drink; he shall even be the prophet of this people.

[12]I will surely assemble, O Jacob, all of thee; I will surely gather the remnant of Israel; I will put them together as the sheep of Bozrah, as the flock in the midst of their fold: they shall make great noise by reason of *the multitude of*

---

[a] oppress: or, defraud
[b] a doleful . . . : Heb. a lamentation of lamentations
[c] straitened: or, shortened?
[d] of late: Heb. yesterday
[e] women: or, wives
[f] walking . . . : or, walk with the wind, and lie falsely

men. ¹³The breaker is come up before them: they have broken up, and have passed through the gate, and are gone out by it: and their king shall pass before them, and the LORD on the head of them.

3

¹And I said, Hear, I pray you, O heads of Jacob, and ye princes of the house of Israel; *Is it* not for you to know judgment? ²Who hate the good, and love the evil; who pluck off their skin from off them, and their flesh from off their bones; ³Who also eat the flesh of my people, and flay their skin from off them; and they break their bones, and chop them in pieces, as for the pot, and as flesh within the caldron. ⁴Then shall they cry unto the LORD, but he will not hear them: he will even hide his face from them at that time, as they have behaved themselves ill in their doings. ⁵Thus saith the LORD concerning the prophets that make my people err, that bite with their teeth, and cry, Peace; and he that putteth not into their mouths, they even prepare war against him. ⁶Therefore night *shall be* unto you, that ye shall not have a vision; and it shall be dark unto you, that ye shall not divine; and the sun shall go down over the prophets, and the day shall be dark over them. ⁷Then shall the seers be ashamed, and the diviners confounded: yea, they shall all cover their lips^a; for *there is* no answer of God.

⁸But truly I am full of power by the spirit of the LORD, and of judg-

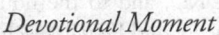
ment, and of might, to declare unto Jacob his transgression, and to Israel his sin. ⁹Hear this, I pray you, ye heads of the house of Jacob, and princes of the house of Israel, that abhor judgment, and pervert all equity. ¹⁰They build up Zion with blood^b, and Jerusalem with iniquity. ¹¹The heads thereof judge for reward, and the priests thereof teach for hire, and the prophets thereof divine for money: yet will they lean upon the LORD, and say^c, *Is* not the LORD among us? none evil can come upon us. ¹²Therefore shall Zion for your sake be plowed *as* a field, and Jerusalem shall become heaps, and the mountain of the house as the high places of the forest.

4

¹But in the last days it shall come to pass, *that* the mountain of the house of the LORD shall be established in the top of the mountains, and it shall be exalted above the hills; and people shall flow unto it. ²And many nations shall come, and say, Come, and let us go up to the mountain

---

^a lips: Heb. upper lip
^b blood: Heb. bloods
^c and say: Heb. saying

of the LORD, and to the house of the God of Jacob; and he will teach us of his ways, and we will walk in his paths: for the law shall go forth of Zion, and the word of the LORD from Jerusalem. ³And he shall judge among many people, and rebuke strong nations afar off; and they shall beat their swords into plowshares, and their spears into pruninghooks^a: nation shall not lift up a sword against nation, neither shall they learn war any more. ⁴But they shall sit every man under his vine and under his fig tree; and none shall make *them* afraid: for the mouth of the LORD of hosts hath spoken *it*. ⁵For all people will walk every one in the name of his god, and we will walk in the name of the LORD our God for ever and ever. ⁶In that day, saith the LORD, will I assemble her that halteth, and I will gather her that is driven out, and her that I have afflicted; ⁷And I will make her that halted a remnant, and her that was cast far off a strong nation: and the LORD shall reign over them in mount Zion from henceforth, even for ever.

⁸And thou, O tower of the flock, the strong hold of the daughter of Zion, unto thee shall it come, even the first dominion; the kingdom shall come to the daughter of Jerusalem. ⁹Now why dost thou cry out aloud? *is there* no king in thee? is thy counsellor perished? for pangs have taken thee as a woman in travail. ¹⁰Be in pain, and labour to bring forth, O daughter of Zion, like a woman in travail: for now shalt thou go forth out of the city, and thou shalt dwell in the field, and thou shalt go

even to Babylon; there shalt thou be delivered; there the LORD shall redeem thee from the hand of thine enemies. ¹¹Now also many nations are gathered against thee, that say, Let her be defiled, and let our eye look upon Zion. ¹²But they know not the thoughts of the LORD, neither understand they his counsel: for he shall gather them as the sheaves into the floor. ¹³Arise and thresh, O daughter of Zion: for I will make thine horn iron, and I will make thy hoofs brass: and thou shalt beat in pieces many people: and I will consecrate their gain unto the LORD, and their substance unto the Lord of the whole earth.

5

¹Now gather thyself in troops, O daughter of troops: he hath laid siege against us: they shall smite the judge of Israel with a rod upon the cheek. ²But thou, Bethlehem Ephratah, *though* thou be little among the thousands of Judah, *yet* out of thee shall he come forth unto me *that is* to be ruler in Israel; whose goings forth *have been* from of old, from everlasting^a. ³Therefore will he give them up, until the time *that* she which travaileth hath brought forth: then the remnant of his brethren shall return unto the children of Israel. ⁴And he shall stand and feed^b in the strength of the LORD, in the majesty of the name of the LORD his God; and they shall abide: for now shall he be great unto the ends of the earth. ⁵And this *man* shall be the peace, when the Assyr-

---

^a pruninghooks: or, scythes
^a everlasting: Heb. the days of eternity
^b feed or, rule

ian shall come into our land: and when he shall tread in our palaces, then shall we raise against him seven shepherds, and eight principal[c] men. [6]And they shall waste[d] the land of Assyria with the sword, and the land of Nimrod in the entrances thereof: thus shall he deliver *us* from the Assyrian, when he cometh into our land, and when he treadeth within our borders.

[7]And the remnant of Jacob shall be in the midst of many people as a dew from the LORD, as the showers upon the grass, that tarrieth not for man, nor waiteth for the sons of men. [8]And the remnant of Jacob shall be among the Gentiles in the midst of many people as a lion among the beasts of the forest, as a young lion among the flocks of sheep[e]: who, if he go through, both treadeth down, and teareth in pieces, and none can deliver. [9]Thine hand shall be lifted up upon thine adversaries, and all thine enemies shall be cut off. [10]And it shall come to pass in that day, saith the LORD, that I will cut off thy horses out of the midst of thee, and I will destroy thy chariots: [11]And I will cut off the cities of thy land, and throw down all thy strong holds: [12]And I will cut off witchcrafts out of thine hand; and thou shalt have no *more* soothsayers: [13]Thy graven images also will I cut off, and thy standing images out of the midst of thee; and thou shalt no more worship the work of thine hands. [14]And I will pluck up thy groves out of the midst of thee: so will I destroy thy cities[f]. [15]And I will execute

vengeance in anger and fury upon the heathen, such as they have not heard.

6

[1]Hear ye now what the LORD saith; Arise, contend thou before the mountains, and let the hills hear thy voice. [2]Hear ye, O mountains, the LORD'S controversy, and ye strong foundations of the earth: for the LORD hath a controversy with his people, and he will plead with Israel. [3]O my people, what have I done unto thee? and wherein have I wearied thee? testify against me. [4]For I brought thee up out of the land of Egypt, and redeemed thee out of the house of servants; and I sent before thee Moses, Aaron, and Miriam. [5]O my people, remember now what Balak king of Moab consulted, and what Balaam the son of Beor answered him from Shittim unto Gilgal; that ye may know the righteousness of the LORD.

[6]Wherewith shall I come before the LORD, *and* bow myself before the high

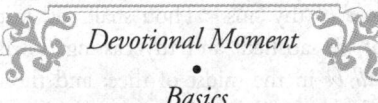

Devotional Moment

•

Basics

6:8 This verse is one of several places in the Bible where God summarizes how he wants us to live (see also Jer. 9:23-24; Hos. 6:6; Mark 12:28-34). Micah presents the ABCs of our relationship with God: (1) **A**cting justly and fairly; (2) **B**eing merciful; and (3) **C**ontinually walking humbly with God. We show how much God means to us by the way we treat other people. How well do you do at acting fairly, practicing mercy, and showing humility toward others?

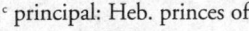

[c] principal: Heb. princes of
[d] waste: Heb. eat up
[e] sheep: or, goats
[f] cities: or, enemies

God? shall I come before him with burnt offerings, with calves of a year old? [7]Will the LORD be pleased with thousands of rams, *or* with ten thousands of rivers of oil? shall I give my firstborn *for* my transgression, the fruit of my body[a] *for* the sin of my soul? [8]He hath shewed thee, O man, what *is* good; and what doth the LORD require of thee, but to do justly, and to love mercy, and to walk[b] humbly with thy God?

[9]The LORD'S voice crieth unto the city, and *the man of* wisdom shall see thy name: hear ye the rod, and who hath appointed it. [10]Are there yet the treasures of wickedness in the house of the wicked, and the scant measure *that is* abominable? [11]Shall I count *them* pure[c] with the wicked balances, and with the bag of deceitful weights? [12]For the rich men thereof are full of violence, and the inhabitants thereof have spoken lies, and their tongue *is* deceitful in their mouth. [13]Therefore also will I make *thee* sick in smiting thee, in making *thee* desolate because of thy sins. [14]Thou shalt eat, but not be satisfied; and thy casting down *shall be* in the midst of thee; and thou shalt take hold, but shalt not deliver; and *that* which thou deliverest will I give up to the sword. [15]Thou shalt sow, but thou shalt not reap; thou shalt tread the olives, but thou shalt not anoint thee with oil; and sweet wine, but shalt not drink wine. [16]For the statutes of Omri are kept, and all the works of the house of Ahab, and ye walk in their counsels; that I should make thee a desolation, and the inhabitants thereof an hissing: therefore ye shall bear the reproach of my people.

7

[1]Woe is me! for I am as when they have gathered the summer fruits, as the grapegleanings of the vintage: *there is* no cluster to eat: my soul desired the firstripe fruit. [2]The good[a] *man* is perished out of the earth: and *there is* none upright among men: they all lie in wait for blood; they hunt every man his brother with a net. [3]That they may do evil with both hands earnestly, the prince asketh, and the judge *asketh* for a reward; and the great *man*, he uttereth his mischievous desire: so they wrap it up. [4]The best of them *is* as a brier: the most upright *is sharper* than a thorn hedge: the day of thy watchmen *and* thy visitation cometh; now shall be their perplexity. [5]Trust ye not in a friend, put ye not confidence in a guide: keep the doors of thy mouth from her that lieth in thy bosom. [6]For the son dishonoureth the father, the daughter riseth up against her mother, the daughter in law against her mother in law; a man's enemies *are* the men of his own house.

[7]Therefore I will look unto the LORD; I will wait for the God of my salvation: my God will hear me. [8]Rejoice not against me, O mine enemy: when I fall, I shall arise; when I sit in darkness, the LORD *shall be* a light unto me. [9]I will bear the indignation of the LORD, because I have sinned against him, until he plead my cause,

---

[a] body: Heb. belly
[b] walk . . . : Heb. humble thyself to walk
[c] count . . . : or, be pure with, etc
[a] good: or, godly, or, merciful

and execute judgment for me: he will bring me forth to the light, *and* I shall behold his righteousness. [10]Then *she that is* mine enemy[b] shall see *it*, and shame shall cover her which said unto me, Where is the LORD thy God? mine eyes shall behold her: now shall she be trodden down as the mire of the streets. [11]*In* the day that thy walls are to be built, *in* that day shall the decree be far removed. [12]*In* that day *also* he shall come even to thee from Assyria, and *from* the fortified cities, and from the fortress even to the river, and from sea to sea, and *from* mountain to mountain. [13]Notwithstanding the land shall be desolate because of them that dwell therein, for the fruit of their doings.

[14]Feed[c] thy people with thy rod, the flock of thine heritage, which dwell solitarily *in* the wood, in the midst of Carmel: let them feed *in* Bashan and Gilead, as in the days of old. [15]According to the days of thy coming out of the land of Egypt will I shew unto him marvellous *things*. [16]The nations shall see and be confounded at all their might: they shall lay *their* hand upon *their* mouth, their ears shall be deaf. [17]They shall lick the dust like a serpent, they shall move out of their holes like worms[d] of the earth: they shall be afraid of the LORD our God, and shall fear because of thee. [18]Who *is* a God like unto thee, that pardoneth iniquity, and passeth by the transgression of the remnant of his heritage? he retaineth not his anger for ever, because he delighteth *in* mercy. [19]He will turn again, he will have compassion upon us; he will subdue our iniquities; and thou wilt cast all their sins into the depths of the sea. [20]Thou wilt perform the truth to Jacob, *and* the mercy to Abraham, which thou hast sworn unto our fathers from the days of old.

Devotional Moment
•
Have Mercy!

7:18-20 The closing thoughts of Micah's prophecy are filled with hope, reminding us that even in judgment, God is merciful. God gets angry, but he never *stays* angry. And in his mercy he holds back the punishment we deserve.

As parents we can give our children an understanding of God's character by being merciful. Do you sometimes hold back on deserved punishment because of circumstances? Have you demonstrated mercy in giving them what they didn't deserve? Don't be cold and calculating in how you discipline. Even God grants pardons.

---

[b] Then . . . : or, And thou wilt see her that is mine enemy, and cover her with shame
[c] Feed: or, Rule
[d] worms: or, creeping things

NAHUM

Purpose
To pronounce God's judgment on Assyria and to comfort Judah with this truth

Author
Nahum

To Whom Written
The people of Nineveh and Judah

Date Written
Sometime during Nahum's prophetic ministry (probably 663–612 B.C.)

Setting
This particular prophecy took place after the fall of Thebes in 663 B.C. (see 3:8-10).

Key Verses
"The Lord is good, a strong hold in the day of trouble; and he knoweth them that trust in him. But with an overrunning flood he will make an utter end of the place thereof, and darkness shall pursue his enemies. What do ye imagine against the Lord? he will make an utter end: affliction shall not rise up the second time" (1:7-9).

Key Place
Nineveh

The Northern Kingdom, Israel, finally succumbed to Assyrian forces in 722 B.C. when Samaria fell. The Assyrians were notoriously cruel. Did the victory of savages over Israel mean the end of God and God's people?

Nahum answers that question.

Nahum's audience, the Southern Kingdom of Judah, hears the surprising news that Nineveh, Assyria's capital city, is as good as gone—kaput, finis, final act; fourth quarter, ninth inning, tenth frame. And 110 years after Assyria beat up on Samaria, it was indeed conquered, just as Nahum said. Nahum is all about the most feared power of his day turning into jelly.

Nahum offers us lots of food for thought. What makes your hometown different from the city Nahum describes? What would your life be like in a place like Nineveh? How is God pictured here? How does God make a difference in your decisions, in how your family operates, in how you spend leisure time?

Nineveh was perhaps the last place to find a close-knit, caring community. Yet all places—from Arkansas farm towns to sweltering Los Angeles to the fresh-air villages of Minnesota—all have the potential to move in Nineveh's direction. What are you and your family doing today to help your city or town move instead toward opportunity, peace, beauty, and God?

1

¹The burden of Nineveh. The book of the vision of Nahum the Elkoshite.

²Godᵃ *is* jealous, and the LORD revengeth; the LORD revengeth, and *is* furious; the LORD will take vengeance on his adversaries, and he reserveth *wrath* for his enemies. ³The LORD *is* slow to anger, and great in power, and will not at all acquit *the wicked*: the LORD hath his way in the whirlwind and in the storm, and the clouds *are* the dust of his feet. ⁴He rebuketh the sea, and maketh it dry, and drieth up all the rivers: Bashan languisheth, and Carmel, and the flower of Lebanon languisheth. ⁵The mountains quake at him, and the hills melt, and the earth is burned at his presence, yea, the world, and all that dwell therein. ⁶Who can stand before his indignation? and who can abideᵇ in the fierceness of his anger? his fury is poured out like fire, and the rocks are thrown down by him. ⁷The LORD *is* good, a strong holdᶜ in the day of trouble; and he knoweth them that

---

Devotional Moment

Choosing God

1:6-8 Nahum described God as being angry, taking vengeance on sinners. But Nahum reminds us that the Lord is good to those who trust him. Can others see that you trust in God?

---

trust in him. ⁸But with an overrunning flood he will make an utter end of the place thereof, and darkness shall pursue his enemies.

⁹What do ye imagine against the LORD? he will make an utter end: affliction shall not rise up the second time. ¹⁰For while *they be* folden together *as* thorns, and while they are drunken *as* drunkards, they shall be devoured as stubble fully dry. ¹¹There is *one* come out of thee, that imagineth evil against the LORD, a wickedᵈ counsellor. ¹²Thus saith the LORD; Though *they be* quietᵉ, and likewise many, yet thus shall they be cut down, when he shall pass through. Though I have afflicted thee, I will afflict thee no more. ¹³For now will I break his yoke from off thee, and will burst thy bonds in sunder. ¹⁴And the LORD hath given a commandment concerning thee, *that* no more of thy name be sown: out of the house of thy gods will I cut off the graven image and the molten image: I will make thy grave; for thou art vile. ¹⁵Behold upon the mountains the feet of him that bringeth good tidings, that publisheth peace! O Judah, keepᶠ thy solemn feasts, perform thy vows: for the wicked shall no more pass through thee; he is utterly cut off.

2

¹He that dasheth in pieces is come up before thy face: keep the munition,

---

ᵃ God . . . : or, The LORD is a jealous God, and a revenger, etc
ᵇ abide: Heb. stand up
ᶜ strong hold: or, strength
ᵈ a wicked . . . : Heb. a counsellor of Belial
ᵉ Though . . . : or, If they would have been at peace, so should they have been many, and so should they have been shorn, and he should have passed away
ᶠ keep . . . : Heb. feast

watch the way, make *thy* loins strong, fortify *thy* power mightily. ²For the LORD hath turned away the excellency of Jacob, as the excellency of Israel: for the emptiers have emptied them out, and marred their vine branches. ³The shield of his mighty men is made red, the valiant men *are* in scarlet[a]: the chariots *shall be* with flaming torches in the day of his preparation, and the fir trees shall be terribly shaken. ⁴The chariots shall rage in the streets, they shall justle one against another in the broad ways: they shall seem like torches, they shall run like the lightnings. ⁵He shall recount his worthies[b]: they shall stumble in their walk; they shall make haste to the wall thereof, and the defence shall be prepared. ⁶The gates of the rivers shall be opened, and the palace shall be dissolved[c]. ⁷And Huzzab[d] shall be led away captive, she shall be brought up, and her maids shall lead *her* as with the voice of doves, tabering upon their breasts. ⁸But Nineveh *is* of old[e] like a pool of water: yet they shall flee away. Stand, stand, *shall they cry*; but none shall look back. ⁹Take ye the spoil of silver, take the spoil of gold: for *there is* none end[f] of the store *and* glory out of all the pleasant furniture. ¹⁰She is empty, and void, and waste: and the heart melteth, and the knees smite together, and much pain *is* in all loins,

and the faces of them all gather blackness.

¹¹Where *is* the dwelling of the lions, and the feedingplace of the young lions, where the lion, *even* the old lion, walked, *and* the lion's whelp, and none made *them* afraid? ¹²The lion did tear in pieces enough for his whelps, and strangled for his lionesses, and filled his holes with prey, and his dens with ravin. ¹³Behold, I *am* against thee, saith the LORD of hosts, and I will burn her chariots in the smoke, and the sword shall devour thy young lions: and I will cut off thy prey from the earth, and the voice of thy messengers shall no more be heard.

3

¹Woe to the bloody[a] city! it *is* all full of lies *and* robbery; the prey departeth not; ²The noise of a whip, and the noise of the rattling of the wheels, and of the pransing horses, and of the jumping chariots. ³The horseman lifteth up both the bright[b] sword and the glittering spear: and *there is* a multitude of slain, and a great number of carcases; and *there is* none end of *their* corpses; they stumble upon their corpses: ⁴Because of the multitude of the whoredoms of the wellfavoured harlot, the mistress of witchcrafts, that selleth nations through her whoredoms, and families through her witchcrafts. ⁵Behold, I *am* against thee, saith the LORD of hosts;

---

[a] in scarlet: or, dyed scarlet
[b] worthies: or, gallants
[c] dissolved: or, molten
[d] Huzzab: or, that which was established, or, there was a stand made
[e] of old: or, from the days that she hath been
[f] for . . . : or, and their infinite store, etc
[a] bloody . . . : Heb. city of bloods
[b] the bright . . . : Heb. the flame of the sword, and the lightning of the spear

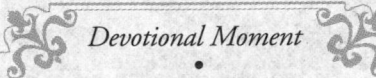

Devotional Moment
•
Beauty

3:4 When God looked at Nineveh, he saw that its beauty was only paint-deep. The outside loveliness of the city covered an inner wickedness. Though she looked like a delicious fruit, Nineveh was rotten on the inside. God is never fooled by appearances (see 1 Sam. 16:7); he always knows what's inside. There is nothing wrong with a positive outward appearance as long as it matches our inside motivation. We need God's help to make sure that our outward appearance matches our inner life.

and I will discover thy skirts upon thy face, and I will shew the nations thy nakedness, and the kingdoms thy shame. ⁶And I will cast abominable filth upon thee, and make thee vile, and will set thee as a gazingstock. ⁷And it shall come to pass, *that* all they that look upon thee shall flee from thee, and say, Nineveh is laid waste: who will bemoan her? whence shall I seek comforters for thee?

⁸Art thou better than populousᶜ No, that was situate among the rivers, *that had* the waters round about it, whose rampart *was* the sea, *and* her wall *was* from the sea? ⁹Ethiopia and Egypt *were* her strength, and *it was* infinite; Put and Lubim were thy helpersᵈ. ¹⁰Yet *was* she carried away, she went into captivity: her young children also were dashed in pieces at the top of all the streets: and they cast lots for her honourable men, and all her great men

were bound in chains. ¹¹Thou also shalt be drunken: thou shalt be hid, thou also shalt seek strength because of the enemy. ¹²All thy strong holds *shall be like* fig trees with the firstripe figs: if they be shaken, they shall even fall into the mouth of the eater. ¹³Behold, thy people in the midst of thee *are* women: the gates of thy land shall be set wide open unto thine enemies: the fire shall devour thy bars. ¹⁴Draw thee waters for the siege, fortify thy strong holds: go into clay, and tread the morter, make strong the brickkiln. ¹⁵There shall the fire devour thee; the sword shall cut thee off, it shall eat thee up like the cankerworm: make thyself many as the cankerworm, make thyself many as the locusts. ¹⁶Thou hast multiplied thy merchants above the stars of heaven: the cankerworm spoilethᵉ, and flieth away. ¹⁷Thy crowned *are* as the locusts, and thy captains as the great grasshoppers, which camp in the hedges in the cold day, *but* when the sun ariseth they flee away, and their place is not known where they *are*. ¹⁸Thy shepherds slumber, O king of Assyria: thy noblesᶠ shall dwell *in the dust*: thy people is scattered upon the mountains, and no man gathereth *them*. ¹⁹*There is* no healingᵍ of thy bruise; thy wound is grievous: all that hear the bruit of thee shall clap the hands over thee: for upon whom hath not thy wickedness passed continually?

ᶜ populous . . . : or, nourishing, etc: Heb. No Amon
ᵈ thy helpers: Heb. in thy help
ᵉ spoileth: or, spreadeth himself
ᶠ nobles: or, valiant ones
ᵍ healing: Heb. wrinkling

HABAKKUK

Purpose
To show that God is still in control of the world despite the apparent triumph of evil

Author
Habakkuk

To Whom Written
Judah (the Southern Kingdom) and God's people everywhere

Date Written
612–588 B.C.

Setting
Babylon was becoming the dominant world power, and Judah would soon feel Babylon's destructive force.

Key Verse
"O Lord, I have heard thy speech, and was afraid: O Lord, revive thy work in the midst of the years . . . in wrath remember mercy" (3:2).

Key People
Habakkuk, the Babylonians

Key Place
Judah

What shows your family's mettle? Some parents quiet squabbling children with sweet food—candy or ice cream—and consider the food-truce a major victory. Some coax children into piano lessons with bribes—a new bike or bedroom TV—and take the deal to be a sign of the child's growing cultural maturity.

What happens to your family when there are no deals because there is nothing to deal with—no money for ice cream or extra TVs? What happens to family spirit when your van hits a deer on the first day of your summer vacation? when having to attend a sick grandparent cancels vacation plans? when Dad is less than perfectly patient, and Mom tires of playing limousine driver?

Does your family's attitude go sour without the steady props of excitement, privilege, and consumerism?

Habakkuk's life looks like a storm front approaching—greenish-black the sky, grim the attitude of people around him. And there's precious little sunshine behind the coming front. Will right behavior break the clouds? Is there anything Habakkuk can say or do to cut a deal with God?

This Bible book comes to a stunning conclusion. We're shocked by it because the deal at the end doesn't square with our best insights into people motivation and family-attitude management. Habakkuk's surprise ending could change the way your family does business.

1

¹The burden which Habakkuk the prophet did see. ²O LORD, how long shall I cry, and thou wilt not hear! *even* cry out unto thee *of* violence, and thou wilt not save! ³Why dost thou shew me iniquity, and cause *me* to behold grievance? for spoiling and violence *are* before me: and there are *that* raise up strife and contention. ⁴Therefore the law is slacked, and judgment doth never go forth: for the wicked doth compass about the righteous; therefore wrongᵃ judgment proceedeth.

⁵Behold ye among the heathen, and regard, and wonder marvellously: for *I* will work a work in your days, *which* ye will not believe, though it be told *you.* ⁶For, lo, I raise up the Chaldeans, *that* bitter and hasty nation, which shall march through

the breadthᵇ of the land, to possess the dwellingplaces *that are* not theirs. ⁷They *are* terrible and dreadful: their judgmentᶜ and their dignity shall proceed of themselves. ⁸Their horses also are swifter than the leopards, and are more fierceᵈ than the evening wolves: and their horsemen shall spread themselves, and their horsemen shall come from far; they shall fly as the eagle *that* hasteth to eat. ⁹They shall come all for violence: their faces shall sup up *as* the east wind, and they shall gather the captivity as the sand. ¹⁰And they shall scoff at the kings, and the princes shall be a scorn unto them: they shall deride every strong hold; for they shall heap dust, and take it. ¹¹Then shall *his* mind change, and he shall pass over, and offend, *imputing* this his power unto his god.

¹²*Art* thou not from everlasting, O LORD my God, mine Holy One? we shall not die. O LORD, thou hast ordained them for judgment; and, O mighty God, thou hast established them for correction. ¹³*Thou art* of purer eyes than to behold evil, and canst not look on iniquityᵉ: wherefore lookest thou upon them that deal treacherously, *and* holdest thy tongue when the wicked devoureth *the man that is* more righteous than he? ¹⁴And makest men as the fishes of the sea, as the creeping things, *that* have no ruler over them? ¹⁵They take up all of them with the angle, they catch them in their net, and gather them in their drag: therefore they rejoice and are

---

Devotional Moment
•
Outlook/Inlook

1:2-17 Habakkuk's world was much like ours— sin was considered normal, and even the leaders were dishonest. What's more, God seemed not to care.
Life sometimes seems unfair. At school, mean classmates are replaced by meaner classmates. At work, a difficult job is replaced by a layoff notice. Selfish people get breaks, while honest people get hurt. But like Habakkuk, Christians know that God is still in control. He wants us to trust him. When difficulties confront you, put your trust in the Lord.

ᵃ wrong: or, wrested
ᵇ breadth: Heb. breadths
ᶜ their judgment . . . : or, from them shall proceed the judgment of these, and the captivity of these
ᵈ fierce: Heb. sharp
ᵉ iniquity: or, grievance

Family Traditions

Discover Treasure Buried in Tragedy

HABAKKUK

Celebrations tell about families; so does pain. Learning to live and love through disappointment, disillusionment, and tragedy is an art. We can learn from those who have survived the worst and still sing with joy.

The prophet Habakkuk knew tragedy. He poured out his complaint to the Lord and waited for a personal response. His book, a song written for stringed instruments, concludes with the prophet's assurance that God would give him the speed of a hind and bring him safely over the mountains (3:19).

With God we trek *through* tragedy, not necessarily *around* it. One woman watched her little boy die slowly of AIDS. "On the good days, we lived every moment fully," she said. "On the bad days, we waited for the good days." When walking through the final moments of her son's life, she encouraged him to go on to the Lord he'd learned to trust. Family tragedies are dealt with one moment at a time.

Joyce Feazel, whose husband became terminally ill with cancer shortly after they were married, says, "It was the little things that brought me light. A friend picked me up at my small apartment and took me to her house for a candlelight soak in a real tub. The next day another friend arrived with an embroidered pillow she'd made for Bruce. It was simple acts of kindness when I felt that God was remote that made his love real."

You cannot take away the pain, but you can do something, no matter how small, to alleviate it.

Little comforts for hurting people: Fresh, crisp sheets soothe the skin. Classical poetry and music quiet the mind. A warm, nourishing beverage steadies nerves. A back rub with perfumed lotion or the scent of fresh roses brings sweetness when it's dark. A foot massage or long talk about simple things brings a kind of distracting grace. Color brightens a day for people whose world is mostly dark: a pretty throw for the bed, a comfortable and patterned robe, a bright manicure, a painting, a colorful whimsical toy.

There is always hope—in sickness, in financial devastation, in broken dreams, even in death. No power in this world can completely dash hope or expel it from the human spirit. Give hope room to grow. Fan its flame. Read about people who've overcome what you're facing. Believe when God whispers, "It'll be OK." And pray hope into your life and the lives of those you love.

glad. [16]Therefore they sacrifice unto their net, and burn incense unto their drag; because by them their portion *is* fat, and their meat plenteous[g]. [17]Shall they therefore empty their net, and not spare continually to slay the nations?

2

[1]I will stand upon my watch, and set me upon the tower[a], and will watch to see what he will say unto me, and what I shall answer when I am reproved. [2]And the LORD answered me, and said, Write the vision, and make *it* plain upon tables, that he may run that readeth it. [3]For the vision *is* yet for an appointed time, but at the end it shall speak, and not lie: though it tarry, wait for it; because it will surely come, it will not tarry. [4]Behold, his soul *which* is

---

Devotional Moment
•
Idolatry

2:18-20 Habakkuk's people were making idols out of wood and then worshiping them as gods. God pointed out that their idols had no life; they could not act or speak; they were their own creations. This mistake may seem obvious, even foolish, yet we do it, too. Any time we ascribe great importance to something other than the living God, we have made an idol. We may not call it a god, but we are worshiping it. What's most important to you? Who decides how you live? Things, ambitions, people—all can become idols. Make sure your life-style grows out of a devotion to God and not something else.

---

lifted up is not upright in him: but the just shall live by his faith.

[5]Yea also, because he transgresseth by wine, *he is* a proud man, neither keepeth at home, who enlargeth his desire as hell, and *is* as death, and cannot be satisfied, but gathereth unto him all nations, and heapeth unto him all people: [6]Shall not all these take up a parable against him, and a taunting proverb against him, and say, Woe[b] to him that increaseth *that which is* not his! how long? and to him that ladeth himself with thick clay! [7]Shall they not rise up suddenly that shall bite thee, and awake that shall vex thee, and thou shalt be for booties unto them? [8]Because thou hast spoiled many nations, all the remnant of the people shall spoil thee; because of men's blood[c], and *for* the violence of the land, of the city, and of all that dwell therein. [9]Woe to him that coveteth[d] an evil covetousness to his house, that he may set his nest on high, that he may be delivered from the power of evil! [10]Thou hast consulted shame to thy house by cutting off many people, and hast sinned *against* thy soul. [11]For the stone shall cry out of the wall, and the beam out of the timber shall answer it. [12]Woe to him that buildeth a town with blood[e], and stablisheth a city by iniquity! [13]Behold, *is it* not of the LORD of hosts that the people shall labour in the very fire, and the people shall weary themselves for very vanity? [14]For the earth shall be filled with

---

[g] plenteous: or, dainty: Heb. fat
[a] tower: Heb. fenced place
[b] Woe . . . : or, Ho, he
[c] blood: Heb. bloods
[d] coveteth . . . : or, gaineth and evil gain
[e] blood: Heb. bloods

the knowledge of the glory of the LORD, as the waters cover the sea.

¹⁵Woe unto him that giveth his neighbour drink, that puttest thy bottle to *him*, and makest *him* drunken also, that thou mayest look on their nakedness! ¹⁶Thou art filled with shame for glory: drink thou also, and let thy foreskin be uncovered: the cup of the LORD'S right hand shall be turned unto thee, and shameful spewing *shall be* on thy glory. ¹⁷For the violence of Lebanon shall cover thee, and the spoil of beasts, *which* made them afraid, because of men's blood, and for the violence of the land, of the city, and of all that dwell therein. ¹⁸What profiteth the graven image that the maker thereof hath graven it; the molten image, and a teacher of lies, that the maker of his work trusteth therein, to make dumb idols? ¹⁹Woe unto him that saith to the wood, Awake; to the dumb stone, Arise, it shall teach! Behold, it *is* laid over with gold and silver, and *there is* no breath at all in the midst of it. ²⁰But the LORD *is* in his holy temple: let all the earth keep silence before him.

3

¹A prayer of Habakkuk the prophet upon Shigionoth. ²O LORD, I have heard thy speechᵃ, *and* was afraid: O LORD, revive thy work in the midst of the years, in the midst of the years make known; in wrath remember mercy.

³God came from Temanᵇ, and the

Devotional Moment

•

God's Mercy

3:2 In spite of the terrible reality of God's judgment on his own people, Habakkuk knew God was right. Instead of arguing that God was unfair or pouting because God was being too harsh, Habakkuk simply asked God to help. In essence he was saying, "I realize we got ourselves into this mess, and we deserve what will happen. But please help us survive it, Lord." If we deserve our troubles, we need to accept them and move on to obedience. We can gain hope and offer it to others by remembering that God is merciful as well as just.

Holy One from mount Paran. Selah. His glory covered the heavens, and the earth was full of his praise. ⁴And *his* brightness was as the light; he had hornsᶜ *coming* out of his hand: and there *was* the hiding of his power. ⁵Before him went the pestilence, and burning coalsᵈ went forth at his feet. ⁶He stood, and measured the earth: he beheld, and drove asunder the nations; and the everlasting mountains were scattered, the perpetual hills did bow: his ways *are* everlasting. ⁷I saw the tents of Cushanᵉ in affliction: *and* the curtains of the land of Midian did tremble. ⁸Was the LORD displeased against the rivers? *was* thine anger against the rivers? *was* thy wrath against the sea, that thou didst ride upon thine horses *and* thy chariots of salvation? ⁹Thy bow was made quite naked, *according* to the oaths of the

---

ᵃ speech: Heb. report, or, hearing
ᵇ Teman: or, the south
ᶜ horns . . . : or, bright beams out of his side
ᵈ coals: or, diseases
ᵉ Cushan: or, Ethiopia

tribes, *even thy* word. Selah. Thou didst cleave the earth[f] with rivers. [10]The mountains saw thee, *and* they trembled: the overflowing of the water passed by: the deep uttered his voice, *and* lifted up his hands on high. [11]The sun *and* moon stood still in their habitation: at the light[g] of thine arrows they went, *and* at the shining of thy glittering spear. [12]Thou didst march through the land in indignation, thou didst thresh the heathen in anger. [13]Thou wentest forth for the salvation of thy people, *even* for salvation with thine anointed; thou woundedst the head out of the house of the wicked, by discovering the foundation unto the neck. Selah. [14]Thou didst strike through with his staves the head of his villages: they came out as a whirlwind to scatter me: their rejoicing *was* as to devour the poor secretly. [15]Thou didst walk through the sea with thine horses, *through* the heap[h] of great waters.

[16]When I heard, my belly trembled; my lips quivered at the voice: rottenness entered into my bones, and I trembled in myself, that I might rest in the day of trouble: when he cometh up unto the people, he will invade them with his troops. [17]Although the fig tree shall not blossom, neither *shall* fruit *be* in the vines; the labour of the olive shall fail, and the fields shall yield no meat; the flock shall be cut off from the fold, and *there shall be* no herd in the stalls: [18]Yet I will rejoice in the LORD, I will joy in the God of my salvation. [19]The LORD God *is* my strength, and he will make my feet like hinds' *feet*, and he will make me to walk upon mine high places. To the chief singer on my stringed instruments.

---

[f] earth . . . : or, rivers of the earth
[g] at the light . . . : or, thine arrows walked in the light
[h] heap: or, mud

ZEPHANIAH

Purpose
To shake the people of Judah out of their complacency and urge them to return to God

Date Written
Probably near the end of Zephaniah's ministry (640–621 B.C.), when King Josiah's great reforms began

Setting
King Josiah of Judah was attempting to reverse the evil trends set by the two previous kings of Judah—Manasseh and Amon. Josiah was able to extend his influence because there wasn't a strong superpower dominating the world at that time (Assyria was declining rapidly). Zephaniah's prophecy may have been the motivating factor in Josiah's reform. Zephaniah was a contemporary of Jeremiah.

Key Verse
"Seek ye the Lord, all ye meek of the earth, which have wrought his judgment; seek righteousness, seek meekness: it may be ye shall be hid in the day of the Lord's anger" (2:3).

Punishment hurts. If it didn't, it wouldn't be punishment. There's no punishment in saying, "Teddy, you've done wrong. Here, eat this chocolate cake."

There are many different ways to discipline children: confinement to room, elimination of TV, confiscation of allowance, spanking. Each one can also have varying degrees of duration and intensity. The bottom line is that discipline has got to hurt. Only then can it help.

But parents also need to learn that pain is only a partial solution to behavior problems. In the long run, a kid needs more hugs than spankings.

Zephaniah captures the gist of these everyday family truths in his amazing Bible prophecies. Count the punishments Zephaniah announces. Then count the hugs. The former seeks to correct bad behavior, the latter to reassure of God's continued love.

This book is short and to the point, as all good punishment is. There's no long-winded sermonizing on all the people's sins—they know when they're naughty. On the contrary, Zephaniah calls sin *sin*, prophesies punishment, and announces God's eagerness to hug them warmly again and again. Zephaniah is short, tough, and sweet.

Punished by such a God as this, who wouldn't change? Raised in this kind of home, who wouldn't be strong and wise? Nurtured by this discipline, we as God's children come to see our place in the family of God.

1

¹The word of the LORD which came unto Zephaniah the son of Cushi, the son of Gedaliah, the son of Amariah, the son of Hizkiah, in the days of Josiah the son of Amon, king of Judah. ²I will utterly consume all *things* from off the land, saith the LORD. ³I will consume man and beast; I will consume the fowls of the heaven, and the fishes of the sea, and the stumblingblocks[a] with the wicked; and I will cut off man from off the land, saith the LORD. ⁴I will also stretch out mine hand upon Judah, and upon all the inhabitants of Jerusalem; and I will cut off the remnant of Baal from this place, *and* the name of the Chemarims with the priests; ⁵And them that worship the host of heaven upon the housetops; and them that worship *and* that swear by the LORD, and that swear by Malcham; ⁶And them that are turned back from the LORD; and *those* that have not sought the LORD, nor enquired for him.

⁷Hold thy peace at the presence of the Lord GOD: for the day of the LORD *is* at hand: for the LORD hath prepared a sacrifice, he hath bid[b] his guests. ⁸And it shall come to pass in the day of the LORD'S sacrifice, that I will punish[c] the princes, and the king's children, and all such as are clothed with strange apparel. ⁹In the same day also will I punish all those that leap on the threshold, which fill their masters' houses with violence and deceit. ¹⁰And it shall come to pass in that day, saith the LORD, *that there shall be* the noise of a cry from the fish gate, and an howling from the second, and a great crashing from the hills. ¹¹Howl, ye inhabitants of Maktesh, for all the merchant people are cut down; all they that bear silver are cut off. ¹²And it shall come to pass at that time, *that* I will search Jerusalem with candles, and punish the men that are settled[d] on their lees: that say in their heart, The LORD will not do good, neither will he do evil. ¹³Therefore their goods shall become a booty, and their houses a desolation: they shall also build houses, but not inhabit *them*; and they shall plant vineyards, but not drink the wine thereof.

¹⁴The great day of the LORD *is* near, *it is* near, and hasteth greatly, *even* the voice of the day of the LORD: the mighty man shall cry there bitterly. ¹⁵That day *is* a day of wrath, a day of trouble and distress, a day of wasteness and desolation, a day of darkness and gloominess, a day of clouds and thick darkness, ¹⁶A day of the trumpet and alarm against the fenced cities, and against the high towers. ¹⁷And I will bring distress upon men, that they shall walk like blind men, because they have sinned against the LORD: and their blood shall be poured out as dust, and their flesh as the dung. ¹⁸Neither their silver nor their gold shall be able to deliver them in the day of the LORD'S wrath; but the whole land shall be devoured by the fire of his jealousy: for he

---

[a] stumblingblocks: or, idols
[b] bid: Heb. sanctified, or, prepared
[c] punish: Heb. visit upon
[d] settled: Heb. curded, or, thickened

shall make even a speedy riddance of all them that dwell in the land.

2

¹Gather yourselves together, yea, gather together, O nation not desired; ²Before the decree bring forth, *before* the day pass as the chaff, before the fierce anger of the LORD come upon you, before the day of the LORD'S anger come upon you. ³Seek ye the LORD, all ye meek of the earth, which have wrought his judgment; seek righteousness, seek meekness: it may be ye shall be hid in the day of the LORD'S anger.

⁴For Gaza shall be forsaken, and Ashkelon a desolation: they shall drive out Ashdod at the noon day, and Ekron shall be rooted up. ⁵Woe unto the inhabitants of the sea coast, the nation of the Cherethites! the word of the LORD *is* against you; O Canaan, the land of the Philistines, I will even destroy thee, that there shall be no inhabitant. ⁶And the sea coast shall be dwellings *and* cottages for shepherds, and folds for flocks. ⁷And the coast shall be for the remnant of the house of Judah; they shall feed thereupon: in the houses of Ashkelon shall they lie down in the evening: for the LORDᵃ their God shall visit them, and turn away their captivity.

⁸I have heard the reproach of Moab, and the revilings of the children of Ammon, whereby they have reproached my people, and magnified *themselves* against their border. ⁹Therefore *as* I live, saith the LORD of hosts, the God of Israel, Surely Moab shall be as Sodom, and the children of Ammon as Gomorrah, *even* the breeding of nettles, and saltpits, and a perpetual desolation: the residue of my people shall spoil them, and the remnant of my people shall possess them. ¹⁰This shall they have for their pride, because they have reproached and magnified *themselves* against the people of the LORD of hosts. ¹¹The LORD *will be* terrible unto them: for he will famishᵇ all the gods of the earth; and *men* shall worship him, every one from his place, *even* all the isles of the heathen.

¹²Ye Ethiopians also, ye *shall be* slain by my sword. ¹³And he will stretch out his hand against the north, and destroy Assyria; and will make Nineveh a desolation, *and* dry like a wilderness. ¹⁴And flocks shall lie down in the midst of her, all the beasts of the nations: both the cormorantᶜ and the bittern shall lodge in the upper lintels of it; *their* voice shall sing in the windows; desolation *shall be* in the thresholds: for he shall uncover the cedar work. ¹⁵This *is* the rejoicing city that dwelt carelessly, that said in her heart, I *am*, and *there is* none beside me: how is she become a desolation, a place for beasts to lie down in! every one that passeth by her shall hiss, *and* wag his hand.

3

¹Woe to her that is filthy and polluted, to the oppressing city! ²She obeyed not the voice; she received not correctionᵃ; she trusted not in the LORD; she drew

---

ᵃ for the LORD: or, when, etc
ᵇ famish: Heb. make lean
ᶜ cormorant: or, pelican
ᵃ correction: or, instruction

Devotional Moment
•
Correction

3:2 The only thing worse than disobeying God is blatantly *continuing* to disobey after you have been shown the error of your ways. This was Jerusalem's prideful state. They ignored the warnings of the prophets and, in fact, turned farther away from God. How do you respond when a minister, friend, or family member offers constructive criticism? Do you listen to such counsel? As the book of Proverbs points out (9:8-9; 12:1; 15:12) and as this passage so vividly illustrates, a humble response to such correction is the difference between wise and foolish behavior.

not near to her God. ³Her princes within her *are* roaring lions; her judges *are* evening wolves; they gnaw not the bones till the morrow. ⁴Her prophets *are* light *and* treacherous persons: her priests have polluted the sanctuary, they have done violence to the law. ⁵The just LORD *is* in the midst thereof; he will not do iniquity: every morning doth he bring his judgment to light, he faileth not; but the unjust knoweth no shame. ⁶I have cut off the nations: their towersᵇ are desolate; I made their streets waste, that none passeth by: their cities are destroyed, so that there is no man, that there is none inhabitant. ⁷I said, Surely thou wilt fear me, thou wilt receive instruction; so their dwelling should not be cut off, howsoever I punished them: but they rose early, *and* corrupted all their doings.

⁸Therefore wait ye upon me, saith the LORD, until the day that I rise up to the prey: for my determination *is* to gather the nations, that I may assemble the kingdoms, to pour upon them mine indignation, *even* all my fierce anger: for all the earth shall be devoured with the fire of my jealousy. ⁹For then will I turn to the people a pure languageᶜ, that they may all call upon the name of the LORD, to serve him with one consent. ¹⁰From beyond the rivers of Ethiopia my suppliants, *even* the daughter of my dispersed, shall bring mine offering. ¹¹In that day shalt thou not be ashamed for all thy doings, wherein thou hast transgressed against me: for then I will take away out of the midst of thee them that rejoice in thy pride, and thou shalt no more be haughty because of my holy mountain. ¹²I will also leave in the midst of thee an afflicted and poor people, and they shall trust in the name of the LORD. ¹³The remnant of Israel shall not do iniquity, nor speak lies; neither shall a deceitful tongue be found in their mouth: for they shall feed and lie down, and none shall make *them* afraid.

¹⁴Sing, O daughter of Zion; shout, O Israel; be glad and rejoice with all the heart, O daughter of Jerusalem. ¹⁵The LORD hath taken away thy judgments, he hath cast out thine enemy: the king of Israel, *even* the LORD, *is* in the midst of thee: thou shalt not see evil any more. ¹⁶In that day it shall be said to Jerusalem, Fear thou not: *and to* Zion, Let not thine hands be slackᵈ. ¹⁷The LORD thy God in the midst of thee *is* mighty; he will save, he will re-

---

ᵇ towers: or, corners
ᶜ language: Heb. lip
ᵈ slack: or, faint

joice over thee with joy; he will rest[e] in his love, he will joy over thee with singing. [18]I will gather *them that are* sorrowful for the solemn assembly, *who* are of thee, *to whom* the reproach[f] of it *was* a burden. [19]Behold, at that time I will undo all that afflict thee: and I will save her that halteth, and gather her that was driven out; and I will get[g] them

praise and fame in every land where they have been put to shame. [20]At that time will I bring you *again*, even in the time that I gather you: for I will make you a name and a praise among all people of the earth, when I turn back your captivity before your eyes, saith the LORD.

---

[e] rest: Heb. be silent
[f] reproach . . . : Heb. the burden upon it was reproach
[g] get . . . : Heb. set them for a praise

HAGGAI

Purpose
To call the people to complete the rebuilding of the Temple

Author
Haggai

To Whom Written
The people living in Jerusalem and those who had returned from exile

Date Written
520 B.C.

Setting
The Temple in Jerusalem had been destroyed in 586 B.C. Cyrus allowed the Jews to return to their homeland and rebuild their Temple in 538 B.C. They began the work but were unable to complete it. Through the ministry of Haggai and Zechariah, the Temple was completed (520–515 B.C.).

Key Verse
"Is it time for you, O ye, to dwell in your ceiled houses, and this house lie waste?" (1:4).

Key People
Haggai, Zerubbabel, Joshua

Key Place
Jerusalem

Special Features
Haggai was the first of the post-exilic prophets. The other two were Zechariah and Malachi. The literary style of this book is simple and direct.

When Cyrus, king of Persia, authorized the Jews to return to Jerusalem and rebuild their Temple, there was a burst of enormous energy and progress, then a sputter, then a halt. The half-finished Temple lay dormant while leaders hassled with local demonstrators. With the Temple building project at a standstill, people turned their attention to their own creature comforts.

At this point Haggai stepped in. Almost tactlessly, he asked, "Why are luxury homes taking priority over Temple construction? Why are saunas and Jacuzzis popping up around Jerusalem, while God's house is little more than rusted scaffolding?"

These are tough questions for today's families, too. The push to upgrade one's standard of living is justified by reasonable arguments such as: It's for the children . . . it's for my wife . . . it's for aging parents . . . it's an investment. Honest souls may admit it's for themselves, too. Meanwhile, the church's needs are endless, and around the world mission agencies beg for resources.

Haggai has hard words for families who check out of the church's worldwide mission. The self-absorbed family, spending every discretionary dollar on musical, athletic, or home improvements, will need to have a sit-down talk about the family budget after Haggai has finished with them.

None of us should trade our house for a hovel in order to finance the church's educational wing. Neither should we spoil ourselves when others, often not so far away, have so few of life's needs. Haggai urges compassion for God's work.

Everybody needs to share. Even little children can learn important lessons from this book. Their nickels in the Sunday school offering are as dear to God as the largest charitable trust. Sharing shows we care.

1

¹In the second year of Darius the king, in the sixth month, in the first day of the month, came the word of the LORD by^a Haggai the prophet unto Zerubbabel the son of Shealtiel, governor of Judah, and to Joshua the son of Josedech, the high priest, saying, ²Thus speaketh the LORD of hosts, saying, This people say, The time is not come, the time that the LORD'S house should be built. ³Then came the word of the LORD by Haggai the prophet, saying, ⁴*Is it* time for you, O ye, to dwell in your ceiled houses, and this house *lie* waste? ⁵Now therefore thus saith the LORD of hosts; Consider^b your ways. ⁶Ye have sown much, and bring in little; ye eat, but ye have not enough; ye

---

Devotional Moment

Priorities

1:3-9 Our values and priorities are most clearly demonstrated in how we spend our time and what we do with our money. This was certainly the case in Haggai's day. Upon returning to their homeland in 538 B.C., the Jews immediately began rebuilding the Temple in Jerusalem. Before long, however, the people stopped serving God and became selfserving. Their top priority became their own wishes rather than God's will. As a result, God removed his hand of blessing from their lives. This incident reminds us of our need to check our priorities on a regular basis. If someone examined your check register and/or personal schedule for the last month, what would he or she conclude about your values?

---

drink, but ye are not filled with drink; ye clothe you, but there is none warm; and he that earneth wages earneth wages *to put it* into a bag with holes^c. ⁷Thus saith the LORD of hosts; Consider^d your ways. ⁸Go up to the mountain, and bring wood, and build the house; and I will take pleasure in it, and I will be glorified, saith the LORD. ⁹Ye looked for much, and, lo, *it came* to little; and when ye brought *it* home, I did blow^e upon it. Why? saith the LORD of hosts. Because of mine house that *is* waste, and ye run every man unto his own house. ¹⁰Therefore the heaven over you is stayed from dew, and the earth is stayed *from* her fruit. ¹¹And I called for a drought upon the land, and upon the mountains, and upon the corn, and upon the new wine, and upon the oil, and upon *that* which the ground bringeth forth, and upon men, and upon cattle, and upon all the labour of the hands.

¹²Then Zerubbabel the son of Shealtiel, and Joshua the son of Josedech, the high priest, with all the remnant of the people, obeyed the voice of the LORD their God, and the words of Haggai the prophet, as the LORD their God had sent him, and the people did fear before the LORD. ¹³Then spake Haggai the LORD'S messenger in the LORD'S message unto the people, saying, I *am* with you, saith the LORD. ¹⁴And the LORD stirred up the spirit of Zerubbabel the son of Shealtiel, governor

---

^a by: Heb. by the hand of
^b Consider . . . : Heb. Set your heart on your ways
^c with holes: Heb. pierced through
^d Consider . . . : Heb. Set your heart on your ways
^e blow . . . : or, blow it away

Devotional Moment
•
Family Obligations

1:14-15 Success can be defined as knowing and doing the will of God (see Josh. 1:8). This passage illustrates that truth. Through the prophet Haggai, God revealed his will for the Jewish remnant: "Build the house" (1:8). Bolstered by the assurance of God's presence (1:13), the people began the work. Through the written Scriptures God has revealed his will for our life. The big decision we face on a daily basis is: Am I going to fulfill my God-given obligations, or am I going to ignore what God says and do what I want? Our response to that question determines whether we find success or end in failure.

of Judah, and the spirit of Joshua the son of Josedech, the high priest, and the spirit of all the remnant of the people; and they came and did work in the house of the LORD of hosts, their God, ¹⁵In the four and twentieth day of the sixth month, in the second year of Darius the king.

2

¹In the seventh *month*, in the one and twentieth *day* of the month, came the word of the LORD by^a the prophet Haggai, saying, ²Speak now to Zerubbabel the son of Shealtiel, governor of Judah, and to Joshua the son of Josedech, the high priest, and to the residue of the people, saying, ³Who *is* left among you that saw this house in her first glory? and how do ye see it now? *is it* not in your eyes in comparison of it as nothing? ⁴Yet now be strong, O Zerubbabel, saith the LORD; and be strong, O Joshua, son of Josedech, the high priest; and be strong, all ye people of the land, saith the LORD, and work:

for I *am* with you, saith the LORD of hosts: ⁵*According to* the word that I covenanted with you when ye came out of Egypt, so my spirit remaineth among you: fear ye not. ⁶For thus saith the LORD of hosts; Yet once, it *is* a little while, and I will shake the heavens, and the earth, and the sea, and the dry *land*; ⁷And I will shake all nations, and the desire of all nations shall come: and I will fill this house with glory, saith the LORD of hosts. ⁸The silver *is* mine, and the gold *is* mine, saith the LORD of hosts. ⁹The glory of this latter house shall be greater than of the former, saith the LORD of hosts: and in this place will I give peace, saith the LORD of hosts.

¹⁰In the four and twentieth *day* of the ninth *month*, in the second year of Darius, came the word of the LORD by Haggai the prophet, saying, ¹¹Thus saith the LORD of hosts; Ask now the priests *concerning* the law, saying, ¹²If one bear holy flesh in the skirt of his garment, and with his skirt do touch bread, or pottage, or wine, or oil, or any meat, shall it be holy? And the priests answered and said, No. ¹³Then said Haggai, If *one that is* unclean by a dead body touch any of these, shall it be unclean? And the priests answered and said, It shall be unclean. ¹⁴Then answered Haggai, and said, So *is* this people, and so *is* this nation before me, saith the LORD; and so *is* every work of their hands; and that which they offer there *is* unclean. ¹⁵And now, I pray you, consider from this day and upward, from before a stone was laid upon a stone in the temple of the LORD:

---

^a by: Heb. by the hand of

¹⁶Since those *days* were, when *one* came to an heap of twenty *measures*, there were *but* ten: when *one* came to the pressfat for to draw out fifty *vessels* out of the press, there were *but* twenty. ¹⁷I smote you with blasting and with mildew and with hail in all the labours of your hands; yet ye *turned* not to me, saith the LORD. ¹⁸Consider now from this day and upward, from the four and twentieth day of the ninth *month, even* from the day that the foundation of the LORD'S temple was laid, consider *it.* ¹⁹Is the seed yet in the barn? yea, as yet the vine, and the fig tree, and the pomegranate, and the olive tree, hath not brought forth: from this day will I bless *you.*

²⁰And again the word of the LORD came unto Haggai in the four and twentieth *day* of the month, saying, ²¹Speak to Zerubbabel, governor of Judah, saying, I will shake the heavens and the earth; ²²And I will overthrow the throne of kingdoms, and I will destroy the strength of the kingdoms of the heathen; and I will overthrow the chariots, and those that ride in them; and the horses and their riders shall come down, every one by the sword of his brother. ²³In that day, saith the LORD of hosts, will I take thee, O Zerubbabel, my servant, the son of Shealtiel, saith the LORD, and will make thee as a signet: for I have chosen thee, saith the LORD of hosts.

ZECHARIAH

Purpose
To give hope to God's people by revealing God's future deliverance through the Messiah

Author
Zechariah

To Whom Written
The Jews in Jerusalem who had returned from their captivity in Babylon and to God's people everywhere

Date Written
Chapters 1–8 were written about 520–518 B.C. Chapters 9–14 were written around 480 B.C.

Setting
The exiles had returned from Babylon to rebuild the Temple. Haggai and Zechariah confronted the people with their task and encouraged them to complete it.

Key Verses
"Rejoice greatly, O daughter of Zion; shout, O daughter of Jerusalem: behold, thy King cometh unto thee: he is just, and having salvation; lowly, and riding upon an ass . . . he shall speak peace unto the heathen: and his dominion shall be from sea even to sea, and from the river even to the ends of the earth" (9:9-10).

Key People
Zerubbabel, Joshua

Moving is hard work. Someone has to pack the dishes one by one. Someone has to sort those items to pack from those to be sold at the garage sale. Someone has to wipe the tears from a child's eyes while holding back their own. New doctors and car mechanics must be found, routes to schools and supermarkets mapped out—the list goes on.

Zechariah was born to move. His birthplace was Babylon, and his father was a priest. Zechariah was to become a great prophet. There was no way he could sit still while the Jews were returning from captivity to rebuild the Temple. He had to go. To stay behind would have denied his identity and surrendered his calling. Whatever hard work or emotional upset he might have faced, he had to go.

The result for us is a Bible book rich in images of Jesus and pictures of God's great future. Much of that material was obscure to Zechariah's readers, but for us, on the other side of Christmas, it's a treasure of symbols and promises. We owe Zechariah a big thank-you for taking the trouble to move, to write, and to do his faithful work for God.

When you move or think about moving, remember that lots of people in your new location may be grateful to God for bringing you into their lives. Zechariah got a clearer vision of Jesus as part of his move, and if you submit to what God wants to do in your life, so can you. Knowing that makes the salty stuff running down those cheeks a bit easier to wipe away.

1

¹In the eighth month, in the second year of Darius, came the word of the LORD unto Zechariah, the son of Berechiah, the son of Iddo the prophet, saying, ²The LORD hath been sore*a* displeased with your fathers. ³Therefore say thou unto them, Thus saith the LORD of hosts; Turn ye unto me, saith the LORD of hosts, and I will turn unto you, saith the LORD of hosts. ⁴Be ye not as your fathers, unto whom the former prophets have cried, saying, Thus saith the LORD of hosts; Turn ye now from your evil ways, and *from* your evil doings: but they did not hear, nor hearken unto me, saith the LORD. ⁵Your fathers, where *are* they? and the prophets, do they live for ever? ⁶But my words and my statutes, which I commanded my servants the prophets, did they not take hold of your fathers? and they returned and said, Like as the LORD of hosts thought to do unto us,

---

Devotional Moment
•
Family Mistakes

1:5-6 Through the prophet Zechariah, God urged his people to come back to him. If they refused, they would suffer the harsh consequences of disobedience just as their ancestors had. In short, God was saying, "Don't be foolish! Learn from the mistakes of your forefathers." How valuable it is for us to have the biblical record. We are *encouraged* by the stories of those who have walked with God. We are *warned* by the examples of those who have walked away from God. As parents we are wise to use such biblical accounts (as well as our own failures and successes) to help point our children in the right direction.

---

according to our ways, and according to our doings, so hath he dealt with us.

⁷Upon the four and twentieth day of the eleventh month, which *is* the month Sebat, in the second year of Darius, came the word of the LORD unto Zechariah, the son of Berechiah, the son of Iddo the prophet, saying, ⁸I saw by night, and behold a man riding upon a red horse, and he stood among the myrtle trees that *were* in the bottom; and behind him *were there* red horses, speckled*b*, and white. ⁹Then said I, O my lord, what *are* these? And the angel that talked with me said unto me, I will shew thee what these *be*. ¹⁰And the man that stood among the myrtle trees answered and said, These *are they* whom the LORD hath sent to walk to and fro through the earth. ¹¹And they answered the angel of the LORD that stood among the myrtle trees, and said, We have walked to and fro through the earth, and, behold, all the earth sitteth still, and is at rest. ¹²Then the angel of the LORD answered and said, O LORD of hosts, how long wilt thou not have mercy on Jerusalem and on the cities of Judah, against which thou hast had indignation these threescore and ten years? ¹³And the LORD answered the angel that talked with me *with* good words *and* comfortable words. ¹⁴So the angel that communed with me said unto me, Cry thou, saying, Thus saith the LORD of hosts; I am jealous for Jerusalem and for Zion with a great jealousy. ¹⁵And I am very sore displeased with the heathen *that are* at ease: for I was but a little displeased, and they helped forward the affliction. ¹⁶Therefore thus saith the LORD; I am

---

a sore . . . : Heb. with displeasure
b speckled: or, bay

returned to Jerusalem with mercies: my house shall be built in it, saith the LORD of hosts, and a line shall be stretched forth upon Jerusalem. ¹⁷Cry yet, saying, Thus saith the LORD of hosts; My cities through prosperity^c shall yet be spread abroad; and the LORD shall yet comfort Zion, and shall yet choose Jerusalem.

¹⁸Then lifted I up mine eyes, and saw, and behold four horns. ¹⁹And I said unto the angel that talked with me, What *be* these? And he answered me, These *are* the horns which have scattered Judah, Israel, and Jerusalem. ²⁰And the LORD shewed me four carpenters. ²¹Then said I, What come these to do? And he spake, saying, These *are* the horns which have scattered Judah, so that no man did lift up his head: but these are come to fray them, to cast out the horns of the Gentiles, which lifted up *their* horn over the land of Judah to scatter it.

2

¹I lifted up mine eyes again, and looked, and behold a man with a measuring line in his hand. ²Then said I, Whither goest thou? And he said unto me, To measure Jerusalem, to see what *is* the breadth thereof, and what *is* the length thereof. ³And, behold, the angel that talked with me went forth, and another angel went out to meet him, ⁴And said unto him, Run, speak to this young man, saying, Jerusalem shall be inhabited *as* towns without walls for the multitude of men and cattle therein: ⁵For I, saith the LORD, will be unto her a wall of fire round about, and will be the glory in the midst of her.

⁶Ho, ho, *come forth*, and flee from the land of the north, saith the LORD: for I have spread you abroad as the four winds of the heaven, saith the LORD. ⁷Deliver thyself, O Zion, that dwellest *with* the daughter of Babylon. ⁸For thus saith the LORD of hosts; After the glory hath he sent me unto the nations which spoiled you: for he that toucheth you toucheth the apple of his eye. ⁹For, behold, I will shake mine hand upon them, and they shall be a spoil to their servants: and ye shall know that the LORD of hosts hath sent me.

¹⁰Sing and rejoice, O daughter of Zion: for, lo, I come, and I will dwell in the midst of thee, saith the LORD. ¹¹And many nations shall be joined to the LORD in that day, and shall be my people: and I will dwell in the midst of thee, and thou shalt know that the LORD of hosts hath sent me unto thee. ¹²And the LORD shall inherit Judah his portion in the holy land, and shall choose Jerusalem again. ¹³Be silent, O all flesh, before the LORD: for he is raised up out of his holy habitation.

3

¹And he shewed me Joshua the high priest standing before the angel of the LORD, and Satan^a standing at his right hand to resist him. ²And the LORD said unto Satan, The LORD rebuke thee, O Satan; even the LORD that hath chosen Jerusalem rebuke thee: *is* not this a brand plucked out of the fire? ³Now Joshua was clothed with filthy garments, and stood before the angel. ⁴And he answered and spake unto those

---

^c prosperity: Heb. good
^a Satan: that is, an adversary

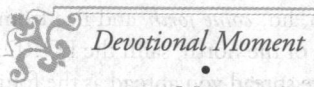

Devotional Moment

Mercy

3:2-4 In this vision Zechariah saw the Lord step in and defend his High Priest Joshua from the attacks of Satan. Zechariah saw the filthy clothes of the High Priest (representing sin) removed. He watched as the Lord ordered Joshua to be fitted in clean clothes (representing righteousness). The point? God is merciful! He transforms guilty sinners into forgiven saints. When we feel defeated by our own sinfulness and discouraged by the accusations of the devil, it is important to remember that God wants to forgive, restore, and renew us. Genuine change begins with changing our view of God. We need to return to God and repent of our wrong attitudes and actions (see 1:3-6). God promises to respond.

that stood before him, saying, Take away the filthy garments from him. And unto him he said, Behold, I have caused thine iniquity to pass from thee, and I will clothe thee with change of raiment. ⁵And I said, Let them set a fair mitre upon his head. So they set a fair mitre upon his head, and clothed him with garments. And the angel of the LORD stood by. ⁶And the angel of the LORD protested unto Joshua, saying, ⁷Thus saith the LORD of hosts; If thou wilt walk in my ways, and if thou wilt keep my charge[b], then thou shalt also judge my house, and shalt also keep my courts, and I will give thee places to walk among these that stand by.

⁸Hear now, O Joshua the high priest, thou, and thy fellows that sit before thee: for they *are* men wondered at: for, behold, I will bring forth my servant the BRANCH. ⁹For behold the stone that I have laid before Joshua;

upon one stone *shall be* seven eyes: behold, I will engrave the graving thereof, saith the LORD of hosts, and I will remove the iniquity of that land in one day. ¹⁰In that day, saith the LORD of hosts, shall ye call every man his neighbour under the vine and under the fig tree.

4

¹And the angel that talked with me came again, and waked me, as a man that is wakened out of his sleep, ²And said unto me, What seest thou? And I said, I have looked, and behold a candlestick all *of* gold, with a bowl[a] upon the top of it, and his seven lamps thereon, and seven pipes to the seven lamps, which *are* upon the top thereof: ³And two olive trees by it, one upon the right *side* of the bowl, and the other upon the left *side* thereof. ⁴So I answered and spake to the angel that talked with me, saying, What *are* these,

Devotional Moment

Discouragement

4:6 As the governor charged with leading the people and rebuilding the Temple, Zerubbabel faced a daunting task. Resources were few. Motivation was low. Apathy and discouragement were rampant. How would the people complete the task before them? By relying on the awesome, unlimited power of the Spirit of God! Our circumstances are vastly different, but we have access to the same Spirit (Acts 1:8; Gal. 5:22-23). When we rely on the Spirit, we are able to do things that we could *never* do in our own strength. Think of an "impossible" problem. Ask God's Spirit to work in and through you today as you attempt to address it.

---

[b] charge: or, ordinance
[a] a bowl: Heb. her bowl

my lord? ⁵Then the angel that talked with me answered and said unto me, Knowest thou not what these be? And I said, No, my lord. ⁶Then he answered and spake unto me, saying, This *is* the word of the LORD unto Zerubbabel, saying, Not by might*ᵇ*, nor by power, but by my spirit, saith the LORD of hosts. ⁷Who *art* thou, O great mountain? before Zerubbabel *thou shalt become* a plain: and he shall bring forth the headstone *thereof with* shoutings, *crying,* Grace, grace unto it. ⁸Moreover the word of the LORD came unto me, saying, ⁹The hands of Zerubbabel have laid the foundation of this house; his hands shall also finish it; and thou shalt know that the LORD of hosts hath sent me unto you. ¹⁰For who hath despised the day of small things? for they shall rejoice, and shall see the plummet in the hand of Zerubbabel *with* those seven; they *are* the eyes of the LORD, which run to and fro through the whole earth.

¹¹Then answered I, and said unto him, What *are* these two olive trees upon the right *side* of the candlestick and upon the left *side* thereof? ¹²And I answered again, and said unto him, What *be these* two olive branches which throughᶜ the two golden pipes empty the golden *oil* out of themselves? ¹³And he answered me and said, Knowest thou not what these *be*? And I said, No, my lord. ¹⁴Then said

he, These *are* the two anointedᵈ ones, that stand by the Lord of the whole earth.

5

¹Then I turned, and lifted up mine eyes, and looked, and behold a flying roll. ²And he said unto me, What seest thou? And I answered, I see a flying roll; the length thereof *is* twenty cubits, and the breadth thereof ten cubits. ³Then said he unto me, This *is* the curse that goeth forth over the face of the whole earth: for every one that stealethᵃ shall be cut off *as* on this side according to it; and every one that sweareth shall be cut off *as* on that side according to it. ⁴I will bring it forth, saith the LORD of hosts, and it shall enter into the house of the thief, and into the house of him that sweareth falsely by my name: and it shall remain in the midst of his house, and shall consume it with the timber thereof and the stones thereof. ⁵Then the angel that talked with me went forth, and said unto me, Lift up now thine eyes, and see what *is* this that goeth forth. ⁶And I said, What *is* it? And he said, This *is* an ephah that goeth forth. He said moreover, This *is* their resemblance through all the earth. ⁷And, behold, there was lifted up a talentᵇ of lead: and this *is* a woman sitteth in the midst of the ephah. ⁸And he said, This *is* wickedness. And he cast it into the midst of the ephah; and he

---

ᵇ might: or, army
ᶜ through: Heb. by the hand of
ᵈ anointed . . . : Heb. sons of oil
ᵃ every one that stealeth . . . : or, every one of this people that stealeth holdeth himself guiltless, as it doth
ᵇ talent: or, weighty piece

cast the weight of lead upon the mouth thereof. ⁹Then lifted I up mine eyes, and looked, and, behold, there came out two women, and the wind *was* in their wings; for they had wings like the wings of a stork: and they lifted up the ephah between the earth and the heaven. ¹⁰Then said I to the angel that talked with me, Whither do these bear the ephah? ¹¹And he said unto me, To build it an house in the land of Shinar: and it shall be established, and set there upon her own base.

6

¹And I turned, and lifted up mine eyes, and looked, and, behold, there came four chariots out from between two mountains; and the mountains *were* mountains of brass. ²In the first chariot *were* red horses; and in the second chariot black horses; ³And in the third chariot white horses; and in the fourth chariot grisled and bayª horses. ⁴Then I answered and said unto the angel that talked with me, What *are* these, my lord? ⁵And the angel answered and said unto me, These *are* the four spiritsᵇ of the heavens, which go forth from standing before the Lord of all the earth. ⁶The black horses which *are* therein go forth into the north country; and the white go forth after them; and the grisled go forth toward the south country. ⁷And the bay went forth, and sought to go that they might walk to and fro through the earth: and he said, Get you hence, walk to and fro through the earth. So they walked to and fro through the earth. ⁸Then cried he upon me, and

spake unto me, saying, Behold, these that go toward the north country have quieted my spirit in the north country. ⁹And the word of the LORD came unto me, saying, ¹⁰Take of *them of* the captivity, *even* of Heldai, of Tobijah, and of Jedaiah, which are come from Babylon, and come thou the same day, and go into the house of Josiah the son of Zephaniah; ¹¹Then take silver and gold, and make crowns, and set *them* upon the head of Joshua the son of Josedech, the high priest; ¹²And speak unto him, saying, Thus speaketh the LORD of hosts, saying, Behold the man whose name *is* The BRANCH; and he shall grow up out of his place, and he shall build the temple of the LORD: ¹³Even he shall build the temple of the LORD; and he shall bear the glory, and shall sit and rule upon his throne; and he shall be a priest upon his throne: and the counsel of peace shall be between them both. ¹⁴And the crowns shall be to Helem, and to Tobijah, and to Jedaiah, and to Hen the son of Zephaniah, for a memorial in the temple of the LORD. ¹⁵And they *that are* far off shall come and build in the temple of the LORD, and ye shall know that the LORD of hosts hath sent me unto you. And *this* shall come to pass, if ye will diligently obey the voice of the LORD your God.

7

¹And it came to pass in the fourth year of king Darius, *that* the word of the LORD came unto Zechariah in the fourth *day* of the ninth month, *even* in Chisleu; ²When

---

ª bay: or, strong
ᵇ spirits: or, winds

they had sent unto the house of God Sherezer and Regemmelech, and their men, to pray[a] before the LORD, ³*And* to speak unto the priests which *were* in the house of the LORD of hosts, and to the prophets, saying, Should I weep in the fifth month, separating myself, as I have done these so many years? ⁴Then came the word of the LORD of hosts unto me, saying, ⁵Speak unto all the people of the land, and to the priests, saying, When ye fasted and mourned in the fifth and seventh *month*, even those seventy years, did ye at all fast unto me, *even* to me? ⁶And when ye did eat, and when ye did drink, did not ye eat *for yourselves*, and drink *for yourselves?* ⁷Should ye not *hear* the words which the LORD hath cried by the former prophets, when Jerusalem was inhabited and in prosperity, and the cities thereof round about her, when *men* inhabited the south and the plain?

⁸And the word of the LORD came unto Zechariah, saying, ⁹Thus speaketh the LORD of hosts, saying, Execute[b] true judgment, and shew mercy and compassions every man to his brother: ¹⁰And oppress not the widow, nor the fatherless, the stranger, nor the poor; and let none of you imagine evil against his brother in your heart. ¹¹But they refused to hearken, and pulled away the shoulder, and stopped their ears, that they should not hear. ¹²Yea, they made their hearts *as* an adamant stone, lest they should hear the law, and the words which the LORD of hosts hath sent in his spirit by[c] the former prophets: therefore came a great wrath from the LORD of hosts. ¹³Therefore it is come to pass, *that* as he cried, and they would not hear; so they cried, and I would not hear, saith the LORD of hosts: ¹⁴But I scattered them with a whirlwind among all the nations whom they knew not. Thus the land was desolate after them,

---

[a] pray . . . : Heb. intreat the face of
[b] Execute . . . : Heb. Judge judgment of truth
[c] by: Heb. by the hand of

that no man passed through nor returned: for they laid the pleasant[d] land desolate.

8

[1]Again the word of the LORD of hosts came *to me*, saying, [2]Thus saith the LORD of hosts; I was jealous for Zion with great jealousy, and I was jealous for her with great fury. [3]Thus saith the LORD; I am returned unto Zion, and will dwell in the midst of Jerusalem: and Jerusalem shall be called a city of truth; and the mountain of the LORD of hosts the holy mountain. [4]Thus saith the LORD of hosts; There shall yet old men and old women dwell in the streets of Jerusalem, and every man with his staff in his hand for very[a] age. [5]And the streets of the city shall be full of boys and girls playing in the streets thereof. [6]Thus saith the LORD of hosts; If it be marvellous[b] in the eyes of the remnant of this people in these days, should it also be marvellous in mine eyes? saith the LORD of hosts. [7]Thus saith the LORD of hosts; Behold, I will save my people from the east country, and from the west[c] country; [8]And I will bring them, and they shall dwell in the midst of Jerusalem: and they shall be my people, and I will be their God, in truth and in righteousness.

[9]Thus saith the LORD of hosts; Let your hands be strong, ye that hear in these days these words by the mouth of the prophets, which *were* in the day *that* the foundation of the house of the LORD of hosts was laid, that the temple might be built. [10]For before these days there was[d] no hire for man, nor any hire for beast; neither *was there any* peace to him that went out or came in because of the affliction: for I set all men every one against his neighbour. [11]But now I *will* not *be* unto the residue of this people as in the former days, saith the LORD of hosts. [12]For the seed *shall be* prosperous[e]; the vine shall give her fruit, and the ground shall give her increase, and the heavens shall give their dew; and I will cause the remnant of this people to possess all these *things*. [13]And it shall come to pass, *that* as ye were a curse among the heathen, O house of Judah, and house of Israel; so

---

Devotional Moment

•

Problem Solving

8:6 In a cynical world full of doubt and pessimism, we are apt to forget that our heavenly Father routinely does marvelous things. This was the word of comfort given to the remnant in Jerusalem. As gloomy as their situation appeared, God promised them a bright future. In the same way, we need to look at our problems in the light of the Lord's unlimited power and infinite goodness. What problem looms large and seems insurmountable? Ask yourself, "Is any thing too hard for the Lord?" (Gen. 18:14). Then ask God to reveal his power in that situation.

---

[d] pleasant . . . : Heb. land of desire
[a] very . . . : Heb. multitude of days
[b] marvellous: or, hard, or, difficult
[c] the west . . . : Heb. the country of the going down of the sun
[d] there was . . . : or, the hire of man became nothing
[e] prosperous: Heb. of peace

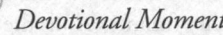

Devotional Moment
•
Honesty

8:16-17 God told his people that they could (and would) enjoy his blessings if they did certain things. Chief among these requirements was being truthful. Why are we so tempted by dishonesty? One reason is that denying or sidestepping the truth often helps us avoid pain—at least in the short run. But notice what God says about dishonesty—he hates it. Do you have a policy of complete truthfulness? Keep your word. Deal honestly with each other. Care enough to speak the truth lovingly, no matter how hard your words may seem. God will honor your efforts.

will I save you, and ye shall be a blessing: fear not, *but* let your hands be strong. ¹⁴For thus saith the LORD of hosts; As I thought to punish you, when your fathers provoked me to wrath, saith the LORD of hosts, and I repented not: ¹⁵So again have I thought in these days to do well unto Jerusalem and to the house of Judah: fear ye not. ¹⁶These *are* the things that ye shall do; Speak ye every man the truth to his neighbour; execute[f] the judgment of truth and peace in your gates: ¹⁷And let none of you imagine evil in your hearts against his neighbour; and love no false oath: for all these *are things* that I hate, saith the LORD.

¹⁸And the word of the LORD of hosts came unto me, saying, ¹⁹Thus saith the LORD of hosts; The fast of the fourth *month*, and the fast of the fifth, and the fast of the seventh, and the fast of the tenth, shall be to the house of Judah joy and gladness, and cheerful feasts[g]; therefore love the truth and peace. ²⁰Thus saith the LORD of hosts; *It shall* yet *come to pass*, that there shall come people, and the inhabitants of many cities: ²¹And the inhabitants of one *city* shall go to another, saying, Let us go speedily[h] to pray before the LORD, and to seek the LORD of hosts: I will go also. ²²Yea, many people and strong nations shall come to seek the LORD of hosts in Jerusalem, and to pray[i] before the LORD. ²³Thus saith the LORD of hosts; In those days *it shall come to pass*, that ten men shall take hold out of all languages of the nations, even shall take hold of the skirt of him that is a Jew, saying, We will go with you: for we have heard *that* God *is* with you.

9

¹The burden of the word of the LORD in the land of Hadrach, and Damascus *shall be* the rest thereof: when the eyes of man, as of all the tribes of Israel, *shall be* toward the LORD. ²And Hamath also shall border thereby; Tyrus, and Zidon, though it be very wise. ³And Tyrus did build herself a strong hold, and heaped up silver as the dust, and fine gold as the mire of the streets. ⁴Behold, the Lord will cast her out, and he will smite her power in the sea; and she shall be devoured with fire. ⁵Ashkelon shall see *it*, and fear; Gaza also *shall see it*, and be very sorrowful,

---

[f] execute . . . : Heb. judge truth, and the judgment of peace
[g] feasts: or, solemn, or, set times
[h] speedily: or, continually: Heb. going
[i] to pray . . . : Heb. to intreat the face of

and Ekron; for her expectation shall be ashamed; and the king shall perish from Gaza, and Ashkelon shall not be inhabited. ⁶And a bastard shall dwell in Ashdod, and I will cut off the pride of the Philistines. ⁷And I will take away his blood[a] out of his mouth, and his abominations from between his teeth: but he that remaineth, even he, *shall be* for our God, and he shall be as a governor in Judah, and Ekron as a Jebusite. ⁸And I will encamp about mine house because of the army, because of him that passeth by, and because of him that returneth: and no oppressor shall pass through them any more: for now have I seen with mine eyes.

⁹Rejoice greatly, O daughter of Zion; shout, O daughter of Jerusalem: behold, thy King cometh unto thee: he *is* just, and having salvation; lowly, and riding upon an ass, and upon a colt the foal of an ass. ¹⁰And I will cut off the chariot from Ephraim, and the horse from Jerusalem, and the battle bow shall be cut off: and he shall speak peace unto the heathen: and his dominion *shall be* from sea *even* to sea, and from the river *even* to the ends of the earth. ¹¹As for thee also, by the blood of thy covenant I have sent forth thy prisoners out of the pit wherein *is* no water.

¹²Turn you to the strong hold, ye prisoners of hope: even to day do I declare *that* I will render double unto thee; ¹³When I have bent Judah for me, filled the bow with Ephraim, and raised up thy sons, O Zion, against thy sons,

O Greece, and made thee as the sword of a mighty man. ¹⁴And the LORD shall be seen over them, and his arrow shall go forth as the lightning: and the Lord GOD shall blow the trumpet, and shall go with whirlwinds of the south. ¹⁵The LORD of hosts shall defend them; and they shall devour, and subdue with sling stones; and they shall drink, *and* make a noise as through wine; and they shall be filled like bowls, *and* as the corners of the altar. ¹⁶And the LORD their God shall save them in that day as the flock of his people: for they *shall be as* the stones of a crown, lifted up as an ensign upon his land. ¹⁷For how great *is* his goodness, and how great *is* his beauty! corn shall make the young men cheerful[b], and new wine the maids.

10

¹Ask ye of the LORD rain in the time of the latter rain; *so* the LORD shall make bright clouds, and give them showers of rain, to every one grass in the field. ²For the idols[a] have spoken vanity, and the diviners have seen a lie, and have told false dreams; they comfort in vain: therefore they went their way as a flock, they were troubled, because *there was* no shepherd. ³Mine anger was kindled against the shepherds, and I punished[b] the goats: for the LORD of hosts hath visited his flock the house of Judah, and hath made them as his goodly horse in the battle. ⁴Out of him came forth the corner, out

---

[a] blood: Heb. bloods
[b] cheerful: or, grow, or, speak
[a] idols: Heb. teraphims
[b] punished: Heb. visited upon

of him the nail, out of him the battle bow, out of him every oppressor together.

⁵And they shall be as mighty *men*, which tread down *their enemies* in the mire of the streets in the battle: and they shall fight, because the LORD *is* with them, and the riders^c on horses shall be confounded. ⁶And I will strengthen the house of Judah, and I will save the house of Joseph, and I will bring them again to place them; for I have mercy upon them: and they shall be as though I had not cast them off: for I *am* the LORD their God, and will hear them. ⁷And *they of* Ephraim shall be like a mighty *man*, and their heart shall rejoice as through wine: yea, their children shall see *it*, and be glad; their heart shall rejoice in the LORD. ⁸I will hiss for them, and gather them; for I have redeemed them: and they shall increase as they have increased. ⁹And I will sow them among the people: and they shall remember me in far countries; and they shall live with their children, and turn again. ¹⁰I will bring them again also out of the land of Egypt, and gather them out of Assyria; and I will bring them into the land of Gilead and Lebanon; and *place* shall not be found for them. ¹¹And he shall pass through the sea with affliction, and shall smite the waves in the sea, and all the deeps of the river shall dry up: and the pride of Assyria shall be brought down, and the sceptre of Egypt shall depart away. ¹²And I will strengthen

them in the LORD; and they shall walk up and down in his name, saith the LORD.

11

¹Open thy doors, O Lebanon, that the fire may devour thy cedars. ²Howl, fir tree; for the cedar is fallen; because the mighty^a are spoiled: howl, O ye oaks of Bashan; for the forest of the vintage is come down. ³*There is* a voice of the howling of the shepherds; for their glory is spoiled: a voice of the roaring of young lions; for the pride of Jordan is spoiled.

⁴Thus saith the LORD my God; Feed the flock of the slaughter; ⁵Whose possessors slay them, and hold themselves not guilty: and they that sell them say, Blessed *be* the LORD; for I am rich: and their own shepherds pity them not. ⁶For I will no more pity the inhabitants of the land, saith the LORD: but, lo, I will deliver^b the men every one into his neighbour's hand, and into the hand of his king: and they shall smite the land, and out of their hand I will not deliver *them*. ⁷And I will feed the flock of slaughter, *even* you, O poor of the flock. And I took unto me two staves; the one I called Beauty, and the other I called Bands; and I fed the flock. ⁸Three shepherds also I cut off in one month; and my soul lothed^c them, and their soul also abhorred me. ⁹Then said I, I will not feed you: that that dieth, let it die; and that that is to be cut off, let it be cut off; and let the rest

---

^c the riders . . . : or, they shall make the riders on horses ashamed
^a mighty: or, gallants
^b deliver: Heb. make to be found
^c lothed . . . : Heb. was straightened for them

Hope for the Hopeless

*Turn you to the strong hold, ye prisoners of hope: even today do
I declare that I will render double unto thee.* Zechariah 9:12

Life experience and clinical studies point out our need for hope—and the destruction that can come when hopelessness becomes chronic.

In the late 1970s there was an animal study done by researchers at the University of Pennsylvania. It was a "pain" study that used laboratory dogs restrained by harnesses. Totally unable to escape or even to move, they were given a series of random, variable length shocks—roughly sixty-four shocks in a sixty-minute period. Muzzled and held fast, these dogs had to endure an unexpected, harsh experience without being able to do anything about it.

After the pain study was concluded, the researchers needed dogs to participate in a maze test. Hungry dogs were put in a maze with food at the end of the twists, turns, and obstacles. An average hungry dog could jump over the barriers and navigate the maze in under a minute. But then the dogs from the pain study were introduced.

What happened? When these otherwise healthy dogs came up to the first barrier, they just lay down. Later, the researchers shocked the dogs in an attempt to motivate them to get up and jump over the barrier, but with little success. In most cases the dogs would just hunker down in resignation, accepting the pain without trying to escape it.

These early studies became the basis of a concept that came to be called "learned helplessness." It names the tendency that many animals—and humans— have to stop and give up whenever obstacles stand in their way after they have experienced inescapable pain.

How can we break free of chronic hopelessness?

1. Looking at the future, not the past. For many people, the past becomes like a broken record, where an event or period of time is replayed over and over. Hope calls us to look forward—to look at the future, a time when there will be no hurt. Numerous studies of those who were prisoners of war during the Korean and Vietnam wars show that those who were best able to handle captivity—even when placed in shocking, inescapable situations—were people who made positive plans for the *future*.

2. Action, not inaction. Some prisoners of the Korean and Vietnam wars literally designed homes they would build when free (in their minds or with available materials); others worked on cell-to-cell communication systems (one cough plus three taps means . . .) that allowed them to break the silence. Even these small, barely discernible steps gave many prisoners hope that one day their release would be granted and their hope rewarded. They *did something*.

3. Service to others, not self. Studies of British prisoners of war in the Pacific show that sacrificial service to others became one of the most inspiring and important parts of many camps. By taking their eyes off themselves and looking after those even worse off, many prisoners built inner reserves to withstand the harsh treatment they received.

Perhaps you've been a "prisoner" of a painful past. Maybe you come from a home where you were repeatedly "shocked" emotionally or physically and couldn't escape because of your age or situation. There is an option besides learned helplessness—it's called "learned hopefulness," and it's found in God. The apostle Paul spoke of it despite repeated imprisonment: "We trust in the living God, who is the Saviour of all men, specially of those that believe" (1 Tim. 4:10). You can have that hope, too.

---

eat every one the flesh of another[d]. [10]And I took my staff, *even* Beauty, and cut it asunder, that I might break my covenant which I had made with all the people. [11]And it was broken in that day: and so the poor of the flock that waited upon me knew that it *was* the word of the LORD. [12]And I said unto them, If ye think good, give *me* my price; and if not, forbear. So they weighed for my price thirty *pieces* of silver. [13]And the LORD said unto me, Cast it unto the potter: a goodly price that I was prised at of them. And I took the thirty *pieces* of silver, and cast them to the potter in the house of the LORD. [14]Then I cut asunder mine other staff, *even* Bands[e], that I might break the brotherhood between Judah and Israel.

[15]And the LORD said unto me, Take unto thee yet the instruments of a foolish shepherd. [16]For, lo, I will raise up a shepherd in the land, *which* shall not visit those that be cut off[f], neither shall seek the young one, nor heal that

that is broken, nor feed that that standeth still: but he shall eat the flesh of the fat, and tear their claws in pieces. [17]Woe to the idol shepherd that leaveth the flock! the sword *shall be* upon his arm, and upon his right eye: his arm shall be clean dried up, and his right eye shall be utterly darkened.

12

[1]The burden of the word of the LORD for Israel, saith the LORD, which stretcheth forth the heavens, and layeth the foundation of the earth, and formeth the spirit of man within him. [2]Behold, I will make Jerusalem a cup of trembling[a] unto all the people round about, when they shall be in the siege both against Judah *and* against Jerusalem. [3]And in that day will I make Jerusalem a burdensome stone for all people: all that burden themselves with it shall be cut in pieces, though all the people of the earth be gathered together against it. [4]In that day, saith the LORD,

---

[d] another: Heb. his fellow, or, neighbour
[e] Bands: or, Binders
[f] cut off: or, hidden
[a] trembling: or, slumber, or, poison

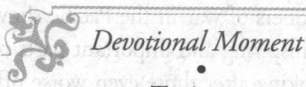

I will smite every horse with astonishment, and his rider with madness: and I will open mine eyes upon the house of Judah, and will smite every horse of the people with blindness. ⁵And the governors of Judah shall say in their heart, The inhabitants^b of Jerusalem *shall be* my strength in the LORD of hosts their God. ⁶In that day will I make the governors of Judah like an hearth of fire among the wood, and like a torch of fire in a sheaf; and they shall devour all the people round about, on the right hand and on the left: and Jerusalem shall be inhabited again in her own place, *even* in Jerusalem. ⁷The LORD also shall save the tents of Judah first, that the glory of the house of David and the glory of the inhabitants of Jerusalem do not magnify *themselves* against Judah. ⁸In that day shall the LORD defend the inhabitants of Jerusalem; and he that is feeble^c among

them at that day shall be as David; and the house of David *shall be* as God, as the angel of the LORD before them.

⁹And it shall come to pass in that day, *that* I will seek to destroy all the nations that come against Jerusalem. ¹⁰And I will pour upon the house of David, and upon the inhabitants of Jerusalem, the spirit of grace and of supplications: and they shall look upon me whom they have pierced, and they shall mourn for him, as one mourneth for *his* only *son*, and shall be in bitterness for him, as one that is in bitterness for *his* firstborn. ¹¹In that day shall there be a great mourning in Jerusalem, as the mourning of Hadadrimmon in the valley of Megiddon. ¹²And the land shall mourn, every family apart; the family of the house of David apart, and their wives apart; the family of the house of Nathan apart, and their wives apart; ¹³The family of the house of Levi apart, and their wives apart; the family of Shimei^d apart, and their wives apart; ¹⁴All the families that remain, every family apart, and their wives apart.

13

¹In that day there shall be a fountain opened to the house of David and to the inhabitants of Jerusalem for sin and for uncleanness^a. ²And it shall come to pass in that day, saith the LORD of hosts, *that* I will cut off the names of the idols out of the land, and they shall no more be remembered: and also I will cause the prophets and the unclean

^b The inhabitants . . . : or, There is strength to me and to the inhabitants, etc
^c feeble: or, abject: Heb. fallen
^d of Shimei: or, of Simeon, as LXX
^a uncleanness: Heb. separation for uncleanness

spirit to pass out of the land. ³And it shall come to pass, *that* when any shall yet prophesy, then his father and his mother that begat him shall say unto him, Thou shalt not live; for thou speakest lies in the name of the LORD: and his father and his mother that begat him shall thrust him through when he prophesieth. ⁴And it shall come to pass in that day, *that* the prophets shall be ashamed every one of his vision, when he hath prophesied; neither shall they wear a rough[b] garment to deceive: ⁵But he shall say, I *am* no prophet, I *am* an husbandman; for man taught me to keep cattle from my youth. ⁶And *one* shall say unto him, What *are* these wounds in thine hands? Then he shall answer, *Those* with which I was wounded *in* the house of my friends.

⁷Awake, O sword, against my shepherd, and against the man *that is* my fellow, saith the LORD of hosts: smite the shepherd, and the sheep shall be scattered: and I will turn mine hand upon the little ones. ⁸And it shall come to pass, *that* in all the land, saith the LORD, two parts therein shall be cut off *and* die; but the third shall be left therein. ⁹And I will bring the third part through the fire, and will refine them as silver is refined, and will try them as gold is tried: they shall call on my name, and I will hear them: I will say, It *is* my people: and they shall say, The LORD *is* my God.

14

¹Behold, the day of the LORD cometh, and thy spoil shall be divided in the midst of thee. ²For I will gather all nations against Jerusalem to battle; and the city shall be taken, and the houses rifled, and the women ravished; and half of the city shall go forth into captivity, and the residue of the people shall not be cut off from the city. ³Then shall the LORD go forth, and fight against those nations, as when he fought in the day of battle. ⁴And his feet shall stand in that day upon the mount of Olives, which *is* before Jerusalem on the east, and the mount of Olives shall cleave in the midst thereof toward the east and toward the west, *and there shall be* a very great valley; and half of the mountain shall remove toward the north, and half of it toward the south. ⁵And ye shall flee *to* the valley of the mountains[a]; for the valley of the mountains shall reach unto Azal: yea, ye shall flee, like as ye fled from before the earthquake in the days of Uzziah king of Judah: and the LORD my God shall come, *and* all the saints with thee. ⁶And it shall come to pass in that day, *that* the light shall not be clear, *nor* dark: ⁷But it shall be one day which shall be known to the LORD, not day, nor night: but it shall come to pass, *that* at evening time it shall be light.

⁸And it shall be in that day, *that* living waters shall go out from Jerusalem; half of them toward the former[b] sea, and half of them toward the hinder sea: in summer and in winter shall it be. ⁹And the LORD shall be king over all the earth: in that day shall there be one LORD, and his name one. ¹⁰All the

---

[b] a rough . . . : Heb. a garment of hair
[a] the mountains: or, my mountains
[b] former: or, eastern

land shall be turned^c as a plain from Geba to Rimmon south of Jerusalem: and it shall be lifted up, and inhabited in her place, from Benjamin's gate unto the place of the first gate, unto the corner gate, and *from* the tower of Hananeel unto the king's winepresses. ¹¹And *men* shall dwell in it, and there shall be no more utter destruction; but Jerusalem shall be safely inhabited. ¹²And this shall be the plague wherewith the LORD will smite all the people that have fought against Jerusalem; Their flesh shall consume away while they stand upon their feet, and their eyes shall consume away in their holes, and their tongue shall consume away in their mouth. ¹³And it shall come to pass in that day, *that* a great tumult from the LORD shall be among them; and they shall lay hold every one on the hand of his neighbour, and his hand shall rise up against the hand of his neighbour. ¹⁴And Judah^d also shall fight at Jerusalem; and the wealth of all the heathen round about shall be gathered together, gold, and silver, and apparel, in great abundance. ¹⁵And so shall be the plague of the horse, of the mule, of the camel, and of the ass, and of all the beasts that shall be in these tents, as this plague.

¹⁶And it shall come to pass, *that* every one that is left of all the nations which came against Jerusalem shall even go up from year to year to worship the King, the LORD of hosts, and to keep the feast of tabernacles. ¹⁷And it shall be, *that* whoso will not come up of *all* the families of the earth unto Jerusalem to worship the King, the LORD of hosts, even upon them shall be no rain. ¹⁸And if the family of Egypt go not up, and come not, that *have* no *rain*; there shall be the plague, wherewith the LORD will smite the heathen that come not up to keep the feast of tabernacles. ¹⁹This shall be the punishment^e of Egypt, and the punishment of all nations that come not up to keep the feast of tabernacles. ²⁰In that day shall there be upon the bells^f of the horses, HOLINESS UNTO THE LORD; and the pots in the LORD'S house shall be like the bowls before the altar. ²¹Yea, every pot in Jerusalem and in Judah shall be holiness unto the LORD of hosts: and all they that sacrifice shall come and take of them, and seethe therein: and in that day there shall be no more the Canaanite in the house of the LORD of hosts.

---

^c turned: or, compassed
^d Judah . . . : or, thou also, O Judah shalt
^e punishment: or, sin
^f bells: or, bridles

MALACHI

Purpose
To confront the people with
their sins and to restore
their relationship with God

Author
Malachi

To Whom Written
The Jews in Jerusalem and
God's people everywhere

Date Written
About 430 B.C.

Setting
Malachi, Haggai, and
Zechariah were prophets
to Judah (the Southern
Kingdom) after they re-
turned from exile in Babylon. Malachi confronted
the people with their ne-
glect of the Temple and
their false and profane
worship.

Key Verses
"For, behold, the day
cometh, that shall burn as
an oven; . . . But unto you
that fear my name shall
the Sun of righteousness
arise with healing in his
wings; and ye shall go
forth, and grow up as
calves of the stall" (4:1-2).

Special Features
Malachi's literary style employs a dramatic use of
questions asked by God
and his people (for exam-
ple, see 3:7-8).

Malachi's readers were tired of waiting. They wanted the glory days of David and Solomon again now that the new Temple was completed. They wanted Israel to be a respected nation again, to watch new queens of Sheba bring their caravans of tribute to the city. But nothing like that was happening, and people were giving up.

Do you blame them? Most kids give up on their Major League team by midsummer, long before the World Series, having seen their stars strike out too often. Lots of teens give up on ambitious career plans because school is too hard, teachers too mean, and parties too frequent. Many adults wave *sayonara* to dreams of a happy marriage when disillusionment cracks romance. Lots of people with lots of dreams end up disappointed. They quit hoping.

To all this, Malachi says: God has a time. It's coming. Take heart. Live expectantly. Be faithful.

Malachi's message to you: God has a loving plan and purpose for you. Your prayers are vital; your hopes are close to God's heart; the time is coming; don't give up. Believe and go forward.

Notice how often Malachi uses family images to make his point. That should give us an extra burst of hope to believe God for our families, to pray for children, to put the future firmly in God's hands and be more grateful for the past. God's plan, at the close of the Old Testament, has a lot to do with making families stronger, connected to something wonderful ahead. Believe it. Watch and see!

1 ¹The burden of the word of the LORD to Israel by[a] Malachi. ²I have loved you, saith the LORD. Yet ye say, Wherein hast thou loved us? *Was* not Esau Jacob's brother? saith the LORD: yet I loved Jacob, ³And I hated Esau, and laid his mountains and his heritage waste for the dragons of the wilderness. ⁴Whereas Edom saith, We are impoverished, but we will return and build the desolate places; thus saith the LORD of hosts, They shall build, but I will throw down; and they shall call them, The border of wickedness, and, The people against whom the LORD hath indignation for ever. ⁵And your eyes shall see, and ye shall say, The LORD will be magnified from the border of Israel.

⁶A son honoureth *his* father, and a servant his master: if then I *be* a father, where *is* mine honour? and if I *be* a master, where *is* my fear? saith the LORD of

---

Devotional Moment
•
Giving

1:6-8 God scolded Israel for offering less-than-excellent animal sacrifices. God wants the very best that we have to offer. We may be tempted to give only *leftover* time, energy, and money. But when it comes to giving, it makes no sense to shortchange God. Do you wait until all the bills are paid each month to see if you can afford to help your church financially? Do you volunteer any of your leisure time? Do you set aside any time to read the Bible and pray? Think about ways to give the first and best of your time, energy, and money to God.

---

hosts unto you, O priests, that despise my name. And ye say, Wherein have we despised thy name? ⁷Ye offer[b] polluted bread upon mine altar; and ye say, Wherein have we polluted thee? In that ye say, The table of the LORD *is* contemptible. ⁸And if ye offer the blind for sacrifice, *is it* not evil? and if ye offer the lame and sick, *is it* not evil? offer it now unto thy governor; will he be pleased with thee, or accept thy person? saith the LORD of hosts. ⁹And now, I pray you, beseech God[c] that he will be gracious unto us: this hath been by your means: will he regard your persons? saith the LORD of hosts. ¹⁰Who *is there* even among you that would shut the doors *for nought*? neither do ye kindle *fire* on mine altar for nought. I have no pleasure in you, saith the LORD of hosts, neither will I accept an offering at your hand. ¹¹For from the rising of the sun even unto the going down of the same my name *shall be* great among the Gentiles; and in every place incense *shall be* offered unto my name, and a pure offering: for my name *shall be* great among the heathen, saith the LORD of hosts. ¹²But ye have profaned it, in that ye say, The table of the LORD *is* polluted; and the fruit thereof, *even* his meat, *is* contemptible. ¹³Ye said also, Behold, what a weariness *is it*! and ye have snuffed at it, saith the LORD of hosts; and ye brought *that which was* torn, and the lame, and the sick; thus ye brought an offering: should I accept this of your hand? saith the LORD. ¹⁴But cursed *be* the deceiver, which[d] hath in his flock a male, and voweth, and sacrificeth

---

[a] by . . . : Heb. by the hand of
[b] offer . . . : or, bring unto, etc
[c] God: Heb. the face of God
[d] which . . . : Heb. in whose flock is

unto the Lord a corrupt thing: for I *am* a great King, saith the LORD of hosts, and my name *is* dreadful among the heathen.

2

[1] And now, O ye priests, this commandment *is* for you. [2] If ye will not hear, and if ye will not lay *it* to heart, to give glory unto my name, saith the LORD of hosts, I will even send a curse upon you, and I will curse your blessings: yea, I have cursed them already, because ye do not lay *it* to heart. [3] Behold, I will corrupt[a] your seed, and spread dung upon your faces, *even* the dung of your solemn feasts; and *one* shall take you away with it. [4] And ye shall know that I have sent this commandment unto you, that my covenant might be with Levi, saith the LORD of hosts. [5] My covenant was with him of life and peace; and I gave them to him *for* the fear wherewith he feared me, and was afraid before my name. [6] The law of truth was in his mouth, and iniquity was not found in his lips: he walked with me in peace and equity, and did turn many away from iniquity. [7] For the priest's lips should keep knowledge, and they should seek the law at his mouth: for he *is* the messenger of the LORD of hosts. [8] But ye are departed out of the way; ye have caused many to stumble at the law; ye have corrupted the covenant of Levi, saith the LORD of hosts. [9] Therefore have I also made you contemptible and base before all the people, according as ye have not kept my ways, but have been partial in the law.

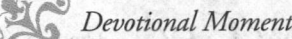

Devotional Moment
•
Faithfulness in Marriage

2:10-16 When the men of Israel began divorcing their wives for any and every reason, God's anger was aroused. He let them know in strong, clear terms that he hates divorce. Christians need to work hard at building strong bonds with their spouses. If our children are to have successful marriages, they need to see us model what commitment really means. Ask God to give you the strength to be faithful to your marriage vows. Take a step toward the continuing development of your marriage each and every day.

[10] Have we not all one father? hath not one God created us? why do we deal treacherously every man against his brother, by profaning the covenant of our fathers? [11] Judah hath dealt treacherously, and an abomination is committed in Israel and in Jerusalem; for Judah hath profaned the holiness of the LORD which he loved[b], and hath married the daughter of a strange god. [12] The LORD will cut off the man that doeth this, the master[c] and the scholar, out of the tabernacles of Jacob, and him that offereth an offering unto the LORD of hosts. [13] And this have ye done again, covering the altar of the LORD with tears, with weeping, and with crying out, insomuch that he regardeth not the offering any more, or receiveth *it* with good will at your hand. [14] Yet ye say, Wherefore? Because the LORD hath been witness between thee and the wife of thy youth, against whom thou hast dealt treacherously:

---

[a] corrupt: or, reprove
[b] loved: or, ought to love
[c] the master . . . : or, him that waketh, and him that answereth

Why God Hates Divorce

by Rolf Zettersten

I know a place created by God as part of his plan for our existence and survival. I know a place where I am loved and accepted. I know a place where I am forgiven when I make a mistake. I know a place where I belong. This place is called the family.

For these reasons and more, God declared his hatred of divorce (Mal. 2:14). It is his plan that a man and a woman come together in lifelong matrimony and create a nurturing environment for their children. That model can lead to generations of happiness and harmony. When a marriage is dissolved by circumstances other than death, the family unit crumbles, and patterns of hostility, insecurity, and even poverty can begin.

Recent studies have demonstrated the long-term effects of divorce on children. Their productivity in school is reduced by conflict at home. They often blame themselves for their parents' disharmony and begin to feel isolated and insecure. These consequences are now known to last into the adult years!

There are some situations (abusive, violent, or adulterous) in which divorce may be justified. But Malachi reminds us that God intends for marriage to be a lifelong relationship, and as a general rule, divorce is to be avoided at all costs.

A commitment to marriage is the first step to building a strong family. Why is a strong family so important? I can think of several reasons.

First, the family is where we receive our *identity*. That identity starts with the surname we are given at birth. One of my friends recalled that as a child he was repeatedly told: "No matter what happens to you in life, always remember that you are a McDonald."

What does this say to a youngster? It says loud and clear that *you belong*. As a result, we know who we are by knowing who we are related to.

Second, family is the place where we can find *shelter and forgiveness*. I once received a letter from a man who wrote about his experience as a modern-day prodigal son. In recalling his own wayward youth, he said: "I gave my parents more reason to give up on me than most. I was from a middle-class family, and I was involved in alcohol, drugs, and wild parties. My dad paid fines and bails for me. I was arrested for dealing drugs and given a two-year sentence in prison. While incarcerated I finally allowed the Holy Spirit to speak to me. My parents' prayers were answered when I accepted Christ in my prison cell. I am so grateful today that my mom and dad's faith never wavered. Never give up on your kids. God is faithful!"

The family should be a safe harbor where we can recover from the tempests and trials of life. The home is God's place for acceptance after we have failed and healing after we have been hurt.

A third virtue of the family relates to *celebration*. Your mom, dad, sisters, and brothers began that process on your first birthday, and it should continue throughout your life.

A colleague of mine has decorated the walls of his family room with photographs and framed copies of newspaper articles about his daughter's victories as a high school track star. While these would seem vain in any other place, they are entirely appropriate at home because there can never be an excess of honor within the family. When one member of the family succeeds, everyone in the home can celebrate because they are all related and share in that triumph.

Finally, the family is the first place for *evangelism*. We teach our children to pray at the dinner table and at bedtime. We reinforce spiritual truths by our conversation and behavior. We read Scripture, share values-oriented stories, and model godly characteristics in our own life. Ultimately, these efforts will do more to contribute to our offsprings' lives than any other investment we may make on their behalf. God gave us the family as a natural spiritual incubator where our children can be birthed and nurtured in the faith.

God designed the family for these and other purposes, and that's why he wants marriage to be a lifelong commitment. May God help you to keep your home intact!

DIGGING DEEPER

1. What other principles has God given us on marriage and on making it last? See Proverbs 3:3; John 16:33; Romans 12:1-21; 1 Corinthians 7:1-40; 10:13; 2 Corinthians 5:15; Ephesians 5:1-33; Titus 3:14.

2. What makes it difficult to stay committed to a marriage in today's world? Read Romans 1:27; 2:14; Ephesians 2:2; 4:19; 6:12; 1 Timothy 6:10; 2 Timothy 3:2-4; Titus 3:3.

3. What can you do to strengthen your relationship with your spouse?

---

yet *is* she thy companion, and the wife of thy covenant. ¹⁵And did not he make one? Yet had he the residue^d of the spirit. And wherefore one? That he might seek a godly seed. Therefore take heed to your spirit, and let none deal treacherously against the wife of his youth. ¹⁶For the LORD, the God of Israel, saith that he hateth putting away: for *one* covereth violence with his garment, saith the LORD of hosts: therefore take heed to your spirit, that ye deal not treacherously. ¹⁷Ye have wearied the LORD with your words. Yet ye say, Wherein have we wearied *him*? When ye say, Every one that doeth evil *is* good in the sight of the LORD, and he delighteth in them; or, Where *is* the God of judgment?

3

¹Behold, I will send my messenger, and he shall prepare the way before me: and the Lord, whom ye seek, shall suddenly come to his temple, even the messenger of the covenant, whom ye delight in: behold, he shall come, saith the LORD of hosts. ²But who may abide the day of his coming? and who shall stand when he appeareth? for he *is* like a refiner's fire, and like fullers' soap: ³And he shall sit *as* a refiner and purifier of silver: and he shall purify the sons of Levi, and

Devotional Moment

•

Consistency

3:6 In a world where everything is constantly in a state of flux, God speaks these reassuring words: "I am the Lord—I change not." What a promise! We do not have to fear that we will catch God in a bad mood. We do not have to wonder if God is going to unexpectedly change the rules on us. He is always the same—a solid Rock in the midst of an unstable world. As children of God called to imitate God (Eph. 5:1), we should work at developing an atmosphere of stability in our own home. Are our responses to situations even-handed and (at least somewhat) predictable? How can you and your spouse increase your home's stability?

---

^{d} residue: or, excellency

purge them as gold and silver, that they may offer unto the LORD an offering in righteousness. ⁴Then shall the offering of Judah and Jerusalem be pleasant unto the LORD, as in the days of old, and as in former^a years. ⁵And I will come near to you to judgment; and I will be a swift witness against the sorcerers, and against the adulterers, and against false swearers, and against those that oppress^b the hireling in *his* wages, the widow, and the fatherless, and that turn aside the stranger *from his right*, and fear not me, saith the LORD of hosts. ⁶For I *am* the LORD, I change not; therefore ye sons of Jacob are not consumed.

⁷Even from the days of your fathers ye are gone away from mine ordinances, and have not kept *them*. Return unto me, and I will return unto you, saith the LORD of hosts. But ye said, Wherein shall we return? ⁸Will a man rob God? Yet ye have robbed me. But ye say, Wherein have we robbed thee? In tithes and offerings. ⁹Ye *are* cursed with a curse: for ye have robbed me, *even* this whole nation. ¹⁰Bring ye all the tithes into the storehouse, that there may be meat in mine house, and prove me now herewith, saith the LORD of hosts, if I will not open you the windows of heaven, and pour you out a blessing, that *there shall* not *be room* enough *to receive it*. ¹¹And I will rebuke the devourer for your sakes, and he

shall not destroy^c the fruits of your ground; neither shall your vine cast her fruit before the time in the field, saith the LORD of hosts. ¹²And all nations shall call you blessed: for ye shall be a delightsome land, saith the LORD of hosts.

¹³Your words have been stout against me, saith the LORD. Yet ye say, What have we spoken *so much* against thee? ¹⁴Ye have said, It *is* vain to serve God: and what profit *is it* that we have kept his ordinance^d, and that we have walked mournfully before the LORD of hosts? ¹⁵And now we call the proud happy; yea, they that work wickedness are set up^e; yea, *they that* tempt God are even delivered. ¹⁶Then they that feared the LORD spake often one to another: and the LORD hearkened, and heard *it*, and a book of remembrance was written before him for them that feared the LORD, and that thought upon his name. ¹⁷And they shall be mine, saith the LORD of hosts, in that day when I make up my jewels^f; and I will spare them, as a man spareth his own son that serveth him. ¹⁸Then shall ye return, and discern between the righteous and the wicked, between him that serveth God and him that serveth him not.

4

¹For, behold, the day cometh, that shall burn as an oven; and all the proud, yea, and all that do wickedly, shall be stub-

---

^a former: or, ancient
^b oppress: or, defraud
^c destroy: Heb. corrupt
^d ordinance: Heb. observation
^e are set up: Heb. are built
^f jewels: or, special treasure

ble: and the day that cometh shall burn them up, saith the LORD of hosts, that it shall leave them neither root nor branch. ²But unto you that fear my name shall the Sun of righteousness arise with healing in his wings; and ye shall go forth, and grow up as calves of the stall. ³And ye shall tread down the wicked; for they shall be ashes under the soles of your feet in the day that I shall do *this*, saith the LORD of hosts.

⁴Remember ye the law of Moses my servant, which I commanded unto him in Horeb for all Israel, *with* the statutes and judgments. ⁵Behold, I will send you Elijah the prophet before the coming of the great and dreadful day of the LORD: ⁶And he shall turn the heart of the fathers to the children, and the heart of the children to their fathers, lest I come and smite the earth with a curse.

The New Testament

MATTHEW

Purpose
To prove that Jesus is the Messiah, the eternal King

Author
Matthew (Levi)

To Whom Written
Matthew wrote especially to the Jews (Jewish Christians).

Date Written
Probably A.D. 60–65

Setting
Matthew was a Jewish tax collector who became one of Jesus' disciples. This Gospel forms the connecting link between the Old and New Testaments because of its emphasis on the fulfillment of prophecy.

Special Features
Matthew is filled with messianic language ("Son of David" is used throughout) and Old Testament references (sixty-one quotes and seventy-six other references). This Gospel is not written as a chronological account; its purpose is to present the clear evidence that Jesus is the Messiah, the Savior.

"Daddy, what does it mean?" A small child wants to know why or what or how come. It's his parents' open door, golden opportunity, auspicious moment. Dad and Mom give it their best shot.

"God, what does it mean?" Same question, from a child now grown. Same need to know, to figure out, to understand. But now the inquirer has life experience, and the question demands an answer complicated enough to cover many of the subquestions. Who but God has the answer?

The book of Matthew is God's answer to all the pain, grief, misfortune, dashed hopes, and gruff impatience building ever since the first hint of a Savior was given in Genesis. Why the Exodus? Why David and not Goliath? Why Solomon's Temple, not Baal's? Why the Babylonian plunder? Why Jeremiah's doldrums? What's it all about? Where's it all leading?

Matthew was one of Jesus' disciples. (He tells how Jesus personally recruited him in 9:9-13.) He watched Jesus firsthand and carefully noted the stories Jesus told. His big question: Is Jesus the Savior we've all been waiting for, the Messiah, the promised one? Matthew's answer: "Come and see. Listen to his teaching. Follow his life and death, and life again. Here he is!"

Matthew is God's response to a toddler's "But why?" and to a senior's "Could it be?" This book, the first of the four Gospels that begin the New Testament, is filled with Jesus' own stories and explanations. It begins with a list of names, reminding us that Jesus is deeply connected to all that happened in the Old Testament. It ends with an appeal to tell the whole world about this wonderful God-given answer.

Here are explanations and instructions for all ages—for anyone young enough to ask and old enough to listen.

1

¹The book of the generation of Jesus Christ, the son of David, the son of Abraham. ²Abraham begat Isaac; and Isaac begat Jacob; and Jacob begat Judas and his brethren; ³And Judas begat Phares and Zara of Thamar; and Phares begat Esrom; and Esrom begat Aram; ⁴And Aram begat Aminadab; and Aminadab begat Naasson; and Naasson begat Salmon; ⁵And Salmon begat Booz of Rachab; and Booz begat Obed of Ruth; and Obed begat Jesse; ⁶And Jesse begat David the king; and David the king begat Solomon of her *that had been the wife* of Urias; ⁷And Solomon begat Roboam; and Roboam begat Abia; and Abia begat Asa; ⁸And Asa begat Josaphat; and Josaphat begat Joram; and Joram begat Ozias; ⁹And Ozias begat Joatham; and Joatham begat Achaz; and Achaz begat Ezekias; ¹⁰And Ezekias begat Manasses; and Manasses begat Amon; and Amon begat Josias; ¹¹And Josias[a] begat Jechonias and his brethren, about the time they were carried away to Babylon: ¹²And after they were brought to Babylon, Jechonias begat Salathiel; and Salathiel begat Zorobabel; ¹³And Zorobabel begat Abiud; and Abiud begat Eliakim; and Eliakim begat Azor; ¹⁴And Azor begat Sadoc; and Sadoc begat Achim; and Achim begat Eliud; ¹⁵And Eliud begat Eleazar; and Eleazar begat Matthan; and Matthan begat Jacob; ¹⁶And Jacob begat Joseph the husband of Mary, of whom was born Jesus, who is called Christ. ¹⁷So all the generations from Abraham to

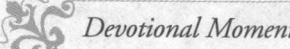

Devotional Moment
•
Character

1:18-24 Joseph's reputation was threatened when he discovered that Mary, his fiancée, was pregnant. How was Joseph going to explain Mary's pregnancy without looking bad in the eyes of family and friends? Remarkably, Joseph didn't concern himself with that. Although some people might never understand, he kept his commitment to Mary when she needed him. When members of your family are in trouble or experience unexpected difficulties that might tarnish your family reputation, don't focus on what other people might think about you. Give your family member the support and love that he or she needs.

David *are* fourteen generations; and from David until the carrying away into Babylon *are* fourteen generations; and from the carrying away into Babylon unto Christ *are* fourteen generations.

¹⁸Now the birth of Jesus Christ was on this wise: When as his mother Mary was espoused to Joseph, before they came together, she was found with child of the Holy Ghost. ¹⁹Then Joseph her husband, being a just *man*, and not willing to make her a publick example, was minded to put her away privily. ²⁰But while he thought on these things, behold, the angel of the Lord appeared unto him in a dream, saying, Joseph, thou son of David, fear not to take unto thee Mary thy wife: for that which is conceived[b] in her is of the Holy Ghost. ²¹And she shall bring forth a son, and thou shalt call his name JESUS[c]: for he shall save his people

---

[a] Josias . . . : some read, Josias begat Jakim, and Jakim begat Jechonias
[b] conceived: Gr. begotten
[c] JESUS: that is, Saviour, Heb

Joseph

Although he was the earthly father to the Son of God, we know remarkably little about Joseph. The bare facts: Joseph was a descendant of King David, was a carpenter by trade. He had at least nine children (Jesus and his six brothers, plus at least two girls), lived in Nazareth, and was a righteous man who obeyed God faithfully. That's about it.

Read the story of Jesus' birth and early years in Matthew 1:18–2:23 and notice every mention of Joseph and what he did: "Joseph being raised from sleep did as the angel of the Lord had bidden him" (1:24). This happened at least four times—an angel appeared to Joseph in a dream, gave him specific instructions, and Joseph immediately got up and did exactly as he was told.

Joseph's obedience to God wasn't limited to "special delivery" messages, either. He treated people with respect, demonstrated in how he treated Mary when he first found out she was pregnant (and didn't yet know that her child was the Son of God). Joseph did not exclude certain areas of his life from his faith.

And Joseph was no slouch. A carpenter by trade, he worked to put food on the table.

They say a good man is hard to find. But just try to find something not to like about Joseph. He simply did what God called him to do. We should do the same.

LESSONS FROM JOSEPH AS A HUSBAND AND FATHER

The kind of person you are matters more than your special abilities. Joseph was unassuming, hard-working, faithful, kind, loyal, skilled, honest, and obedient to God. He did what he was told. He followed God and fulfilled his duties. *That's* what God cares about.

The kind of person you are matters more than the kind of job you have. Joseph was not a rabbi, Pharisee, or scribe. He was a tradesman—a carpenter, a man who worked with his hands. God chose to place his Son in this man's "blue-collar" family.

Every father, in his fathering responsibilities, is God's servant. Being a dad is more than just a role. It's a God-given mission.

Family Traditions

Celebrate Epiphany—the Coming of the Magi

MATTHEW 2:1-12

W e revisit Christmas on January 6," says Claudette Wilson of Des Moines, Iowa. "In traditional church history, this is the day the wise men from the East visited Jesus in Bethlehem, the first manifestation of Christ to the Gentiles."

"At breakfast we read the Scripture from Matthew," adds Jake. "And though we're off to work or school afterward, everyone looks forward to afternoon."

The Wilsons' oldest child, Cherie, arrives home first and makes sure the star in the front window (a five-pointed star made of wood strips strung with tiny Christmas lights) is glowing.

A choral tape blasts praise from the stereo, and a gift for each family member—it must be something that will help the recipient grow spiritually—is hidden somewhere in the house. Gift exchange is by secret name drawing among the five children, Claudette, Jake, and Jake's parents, who live nearby.

"We try to outdo each other in wrapping them," Claudette says. "This is the one time, unlike Christmas or birthdays, when we go all out to make the packaging beautiful and fancy—like the magi would have done."

"We use a lot of stars as the symbol of this day," their daughter Kristine adds. "I like to see how many star things I can find in stores during the year: glitter, stickers, garlands, paper, and toys that can be made into ornaments or package toppers. I save them, always, for January 6."

At dusk the family gathers for hors d'oeuvres and conversation about New Year's goals and plans. Then, one at a time, they search for the gifts hidden earlier. Afterward, they lay them before the Lord in prayer, asking him to use them to glorify himself. Dinner is simple, but the table is elegantly decorated with white tulle and gold ribbon, the theme colors of the Wilsons' Epiphany.

"This celebration has become more and more important to me," says Claudette. "It's the time we recapture the spiritual significance of Christ's coming in the flesh, his being accepted by a people who weren't his own. It seems to give us a spiritual start on the new year, apart from crazy December with all its activities outside the family circle."

As many families within the Christian community focus more clearly on unifying visions and goals, Epiphany serves to bring the family home again. It is a way to make a big deal of encouraging each other's growth in the Lord and to remember: Wise men—and women—still seek him.

from their sins. ²²Now all this was done, that it might be fulfilled which was spoken of the Lord by the prophet, saying, ²³Behold, a virgin shall be with child, and shall bring forth a son, and they shall call his name Emmanuel, which being interpreted is, God with us. ²⁴Then Joseph being raised from sleep did as the angel of the Lord had bidden him, and took unto him his wife: ²⁵And knew her not till she had brought forth her firstborn son: and he called his name JESUS.

2

¹Now when Jesus was born in Bethlehem of Judaea in the days of Herod the king, behold, there came wise men from the east to Jerusalem, ²Saying, Where is he that is born King of the Jews? for we have seen his star in the east, and are come to worship him. ³When Herod the king had heard *these things*, he was troubled, and all Jerusalem with him. ⁴And when he had gathered all the chief priests and scribes of the people together, he demanded of them where Christ should be born. ⁵And they said unto him, In Bethlehem of Judaea: for thus it is written by the prophet, ⁶And thou Bethlehem, *in* the land of Juda, art not the least among the princes of Juda: for out of thee shall come a Governor, that shall rule[a] my people Israel. ⁷Then Herod, when he had privily called the wise men, enquired of them diligently what time the star appeared. ⁸And he sent them to Bethlehem, and said, Go and search diligently for the young child; and when ye have found *him*, bring me word again, that I may come and worship him also.

⁹When they had heard the king, they departed; and, lo, the star, which they saw in the east, went before them, till it came and stood over where the young child was. ¹⁰When they saw the star, they rejoiced with exceeding great joy. ¹¹And when they were come into the house, they saw the young child with Mary his mother, and fell down, and worshipped him: and when they had opened their treasures, they presented[b] unto him gifts; gold, and frankincense, and myrrh. ¹²And being warned of God in a dream that they should not return to Herod, they departed into their own country another way.

¹³And when they were departed, behold, the angel of the Lord appeareth to Joseph in a dream, saying, Arise, and take the young child and his mother, and flee into Egypt, and be thou there until I bring thee word: for Herod will seek the young child to destroy him. ¹⁴When he arose, he took the young child and his mother by

---

[a] rule: or, feed
[b] presented: or, offered

night, and departed into Egypt: ¹⁵And was there until the death of Herod: that it might be fulfilled which was spoken of the Lord by the prophet, saying, Out of Egypt have I called my son.

¹⁶Then Herod, when he saw that he was mocked of the wise men, was exceeding wroth, and sent forth, and slew all the children that were in Bethlehem, and in all the coasts thereof, from two years old and under, according to the time which he had diligently enquired of the wise men. ¹⁷Then was fulfilled that which was spoken by Jeremy the prophet, saying, ¹⁸In Rama was there a voice heard, lamentation, and weeping, and great mourning, Rachel weeping *for* her children, and would not be comforted, because they are not.

¹⁹But when Herod was dead, behold, an angel of the Lord appeareth in a dream to Joseph in Egypt, ²⁰Saying, Arise, and take the young child and his mother, and go into the land of Israel: for they are dead which sought the young child's life. ²¹And he arose, and took the young child and his mother, and came into the land of Israel. ²²But when he heard that Archelaus did reign in Judaea in the room of his father Herod, he was afraid to go thither: notwithstanding, being warned of God in a dream, he turned aside into the parts of Galilee: ²³And he came and dwelt in a city called Nazareth: that it might be fulfilled which was spoken by the prophets, He shall be called a Nazarene.

3

¹In those days came John the Baptist, preaching in the wilderness of Judaea, ²And saying, Repent ye: for the king-

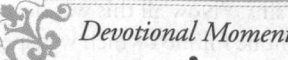

Devotional Moment

Embarrassment

3:4-6 John the Baptist stood out in a crowd. His distinctive dress, unusual diet, and bold preaching polarized the crowd—some loved him, but others rejected him as being crazy or demon-possessed (see Luke 7:33). Living as a Christian family makes you act and talk differently from other families. Would you be ashamed if your family joined hands and prayed together before eating in a public place? Would you feel embarrassed to read the Bible to the whole family after dinner when a guest was eating with you? We are called to reflect the light of Christ to a self-absorbed world. Don't be ashamed of Christ when you are out in public.

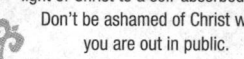

dom of heaven is at hand. ³For this is he that was spoken of by the prophet Esaias, saying, The voice of one crying in the wilderness, Prepare ye the way of the Lord, make his paths straight. ⁴And the same John had his raiment of camel's hair, and a leathern girdle about his loins; and his meat was locusts and wild honey. ⁵Then went out to him Jerusalem, and all Judaea, and all the region round about Jordan, ⁶And were baptized of him in Jordan, confessing their sins.

⁷But when he saw many of the Pharisees and Sadducees come to his baptism, he said unto them, O generation of vipers, who hath warned you to flee from the wrath to come? ⁸Bring forth therefore fruits meet[a] for repentance: ⁹And think not to say within yourselves, We have Abraham to *our* father: for I say unto you, that God is able of these stones to raise up children unto Abraham. ¹⁰And now also the axe

---

ᵃ meet . . . : or, answerable to amendment of life

Zebedee & Salome

Zebedee and Salome were empty nesters when Jesus came to town. But they were fortunate: Their two grown sons, James and John, were working for Dad in the family fishing business.

We don't know how close Zebedee and his sons were, but they must have had a healthy adult relationship. It takes a certain amount of maturity, mutual respect, and family harmony to work for your father. Surely Zebedee was proud.

Jesus tipped the boat, so to speak, when he called the brothers to follow him (Matt. 4:21; Mark 1:19-20). Evidently Jesus didn't ask permission of Zebedee; he just aimed the call squarely at James and John. And they didn't even hesitate: The two brothers dropped their nets and followed.

Anxious to strike out on their own? Who knows. Zebedee let them go, though. When Jesus called them, Zebedee didn't stand in the way. In fact, this following of Jesus became a true family affair. At some point his wife, Salome, became part of the group of women who followed Jesus and supported his ministry (see Matt. 27:56 and Mark 15:40). In a culture of all-male breadwinners, that meant she was supporting Jesus out of Zebedee's earnings. Zebedee gave up quite a bit.

Once the children grow up, the rules change. The playing field becomes much more level. The children are no longer kids; they're *adults*, they have adult responsibilities and choices to make, just like their parents.

LESSONS FROM SALOME AND ZEBEDEE AS PARENTS OF ADULT CHILDREN

Some day, every child must leave home. It's our job as parents to support them in their good pursuits. Sometimes that means pushing them out of the nest. Sometimes it means letting them go. Like Zebedee, we need to give them up to Jesus.

When they leave, we need to entrust them to God. Zebedee's decision to let his sons go turned out to be a very wise choice. Maybe Zebedee didn't have any choice, but that's what letting go means. The hardest thing is to accept it, and then bless the kids as they go. That takes trust in God. That takes faith.

Plans for our children must be tempered with respect for their own choices. Adult children must steer their own course.

is laid unto the root of the trees: therefore every tree which bringeth not forth good fruit is hewn down, and cast into the fire. ¹¹I indeed baptize you with water unto repentance: but he that cometh after me is mightier than I, whose shoes I am not worthy to bear: he shall baptize you with the Holy Ghost, and *with* fire: ¹²Whose fan *is* in his hand, and he will throughly purge his floor, and gather his wheat into the garner; but he will burn up the chaff with unquenchable fire.

¹³Then cometh Jesus from Galilee to Jordan unto John, to be baptized of him. ¹⁴But John forbad him, saying, I have need to be baptized of thee, and comest thou to me? ¹⁵And Jesus answering said unto him, Suffer *it to be so* now: for thus it becometh us to fulfil all righteousness. Then he suffered him. ¹⁶And Jesus, when he was baptized, went up straightway out of the water: and, lo, the heavens were opened unto him, and he saw the Spirit of God descending like a dove, and lighting upon him: ¹⁷And lo a voice from heaven, saying, This is my beloved Son, in whom I am well pleased.

4

¹Then was Jesus led up of the Spirit into the wilderness to be tempted of the devil. ²And when he had fasted forty days and forty nights, he was afterward an hungred. ³And when the tempter came to him, he said, If thou be the Son of God, command that these stones be made bread. ⁴But he answered and said, It is written, Man shall not live by bread alone, but by every word that proceedeth out of the mouth of God. ⁵Then the devil taketh him up into the holy city, and setteth him on a pinnacle of the temple, ⁶And saith unto him, If thou be the Son of God, cast thyself down: for it is written, He shall give his angels charge concerning thee: and in *their* hands they shall bear thee up, lest at any time thou dash thy foot against a stone. ⁷Jesus said unto him, It is written again, Thou shalt not tempt[a] the Lord thy God. ⁸Again, the devil taketh him up into an exceeding high mountain, and sheweth him all the kingdoms of the world, and the glory of them; ⁹And saith unto him, All these things will I give thee, if thou wilt fall down and worship me. ¹⁰Then saith Jesus unto him, Get thee hence, Satan: for it is written, Thou shalt worship the Lord thy God, and him only shalt thou serve. ¹¹Then the devil leaveth him, and, behold, angels came and ministered unto him.

¹²Now when Jesus had heard that John was cast into prison, he departed into Galilee; ¹³And leaving Nazareth, he came and dwelt in Capernaum, which is upon the sea coast, in the borders of Zabulon and Nephthalim: ¹⁴That it might be fulfilled which was spoken by Esaias the prophet, saying, ¹⁵The land of Zabulon, and the land of Nephthalim, *by* the way of the sea, beyond Jordan, Galilee of the Gentiles; ¹⁶The people which sat in darkness saw great light; and to them which sat in the region and shadow of death light is sprung up. ¹⁷From that time Jesus began to preach, and to say, Repent: for the kingdom of heaven is at hand.

---

a tempt: or, try, or, put to trial, or, proof

4:22 James and John were established in their family fishing business when they heard Jesus' call to follow. We don't know how their father, Zebedee, reacted when they left their boats, but he did let them go. Later, even his wife went along (see 27:56).
Allowing and encouraging children to follow God's leading for their lives is difficult for some parents. Even the finest Christian parents may hesitate when their children indicate interest in living and working in a ministry position that lacks comfort, status, safety, or financial security. Consider how you can help your children recognize God's call. And when they do, release them to serve God and exercise their faith.

¹⁸And Jesus, walking by the sea of Galilee, saw two brethren, Simon called Peter, and Andrew his brother, casting a net into the sea: for they were fishers. ¹⁹And he saith unto them, Follow me, and I will make you fishers of men. ²⁰And they straightway left *their* nets, and followed him. ²¹And going on from thence, he saw other two brethren, James *the son* of Zebedee, and John his brother, in a ship with Zebedee their father, mending their nets; and he called them. ²²And they immediately left the ship and their father, and followed him.

²³And Jesus went about all Galilee, teaching in their synagogues, and preaching the gospel of the kingdom, and healing all manner of sickness and all manner of disease among the people. ²⁴And his fame went throughout all Syria: and they brought unto him all sick people that were taken with divers diseases and torments, and those which were possessed with devils, and those which were lunatick, and those that had the palsy; and he healed them. ²⁵And there followed him great multitudes of people from Galilee, and *from* Decapolis, and *from* Jerusalem, and *from* Judaea, and *from* beyond Jordan.

5

¹And seeing the multitudes, he went up into a mountain: and when he was set, his disciples came unto him: ²And he opened his mouth, and taught them, saying,

³Blessed *are* the poor in spirit: for theirs is the kingdom of heaven. ⁴Blessed *are* they that mourn: for they shall be comforted. ⁵Blessed *are* the meek: for they shall inherit the earth. ⁶Blessed *are* they which do hunger and thirst after righteousness: for they shall be filled. ⁷Blessed *are* the merciful: for they shall obtain mercy. ⁸Blessed *are* the pure in heart: for they shall see God. ⁹Blessed *are* the peacemakers: for they shall be called the children of God. ¹⁰Blessed *are* they which are persecuted for righteousness' sake: for theirs is the kingdom of heaven. ¹¹Blessed are ye, when *men* shall revile you, and per-

5:3-12 The character qualities listed by Jesus in these verses bring eternal happiness and God's blessing. The Beatitudes stress eternal rewards—quite different from what society defines as good and necessary for "happiness." Compare these godly attitudes of humility, mourning, meekness, goodness, mercy, purity, peacefulness, and faithfulness with the values beamed at you from TV and the newspaper. What differences do you see? Which set of values are most strongly influencing your life? Talk about practical ways you can practice each one of the Beatitudes.

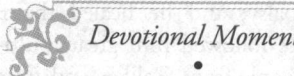

Devotional Moment
•
Mercy

5:7 Jesus taught that those who show mercy to others will receive mercy. Many of the people who seek counsel do so because they are dealing with situations and relationships in which they have been unwilling to forgive. Bitterness and grudges destroy happiness when people are unwilling to forgive. In a family, children learn to forgive by watching their parents forgive others. If they see that their parents' forgiveness is limited or conditional, they will place the same limits on their forgiveness of others. Be careful of the example you set.

secute *you*, and shall say all manner of evil against you falsely[a], for my sake. ¹²Rejoice, and be exceeding glad: for great *is* your reward in heaven: for so persecuted they the prophets which were before you.

¹³Ye are the salt of the earth: but if the salt have lost his savour, wherewith shall it be salted? it is thenceforth good for nothing, but to be cast out, and to be trodden under foot of men. ¹⁴Ye are the light of the world. A city that is set on an hill cannot be hid. ¹⁵Neither do men light a candle, and put it under a bushel[b], but on a candlestick; and it giveth light unto all that are in the house. ¹⁶Let your light so shine before men, that they may see your good works, and glorify your Father which is in heaven.

¹⁷Think not that I am come to destroy the law, or the prophets: I am not come to destroy, but to fulfil. ¹⁸For verily I say unto you, Till heaven and earth pass, one jot or one tittle shall in no wise pass

from the law, till all be fulfilled. ¹⁹Whosoever therefore shall break one of these least commandments, and shall teach men so, he shall be called the least in the kingdom of heaven: but whosoever shall do and teach *them*, the same shall be called great in the kingdom of heaven. ²⁰For I say unto you, That except your righteousness shall exceed *the righteousness* of the scribes and Pharisees, ye shall in no case enter into the kingdom of heaven.

²¹Ye have heard that it was said by them of old time, Thou shalt not kill; and whosoever shall kill shall be in danger of the judgment: ²²But I say unto you, That whosoever is angry with his brother without a cause shall be in danger of the judgment: and whosoever shall say to his brother, Raca[c], shall be in danger of the council: but whosoever shall say, Thou fool, shall be in danger of hell fire. ²³Therefore if thou bring thy gift to the altar, and there rememberest that thy brother hath ought against thee; ²⁴Leave there thy gift before the altar, and go thy way; first be reconciled to thy brother, and then come and offer thy gift. ²⁵Agree with thine adversary quickly, whiles thou art in the way with him; lest at any time the adversary deliver thee to the judge, and the judge deliver thee to the officer, and thou be cast into prison. ²⁶Verily I say unto thee, Thou shalt by no means come out thence, till thou hast paid the uttermost farthing.

²⁷Ye have heard that it was said by them of old time, Thou shalt not commit adultery: ²⁸But I say unto you, That whosoever looketh on a woman to lust

---

[a] falsely: Gr. lying
[b] a bushel: the word in the original signifieth a measure containing about a pint less than a peck
[c] Raca: that is, Vain fellow

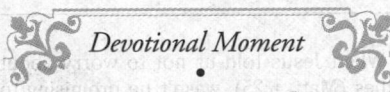

after her hath committed adultery with her already in his heart. ²⁹And if thy right eye offend[d] thee, pluck it out, and cast *it* from thee: for it is profitable for thee that one of thy members should perish, and not *that* thy whole body should be cast into hell. ³⁰And if thy right hand offend thee, cut it off, and cast *it* from thee: for it is profitable for thee that one of thy members should perish, and not *that* thy whole body should be cast into hell. ³¹It hath been said, Whosoever shall put away his wife, let him give her a writing of divorcement: ³²But I say unto you, That whosoever shall put away his wife, saving for the cause of fornication, causeth her to commit adultery: and whosoever shall marry her that is divorced committeth adultery.

³³Again, ye have heard that it hath been said by them of old time, Thou shalt not forswear thyself, but shalt perform unto the Lord thine oaths: ³⁴But I say unto you, Swear not at all; neither by heaven; for it is God's throne: ³⁵Nor by the earth; for it is his footstool: neither by Jerusalem; for it is the city of the great King. ³⁶Neither

shalt thou swear by thy head, because thou canst not make one hair white or black. ³⁷But let your communication be, Yea, yea; Nay, nay: for whatsoever is more than these cometh of evil.

³⁸Ye have heard that it hath been said, An eye for an eye, and a tooth for a tooth: ³⁹But I say unto you, That ye resist not evil: but whosoever shall smite thee on thy right cheek, turn to him the other also. ⁴⁰And if any man will sue thee at the law, and take away thy coat, let him have *thy* cloke also. ⁴¹And whosoever shall compel thee to go a mile, go with him twain. ⁴²Give to him that asketh thee, and from him that would borrow of thee turn not thou away.

⁴³Ye have heard that it hath been said, Thou shalt love thy neighbour, and hate thine enemy. ⁴⁴But I say unto you, Love your enemies, bless them that curse you, do good to them that hate you, and pray for them which despitefully use you, and persecute you; ⁴⁵That ye may be the children of your Father which is in heaven: for he maketh his sun to rise on the evil and on the good, and sendeth rain on the just and on the unjust. ⁴⁶For if ye love them which love you, what reward have ye? do not even the publicans the same? ⁴⁷And if ye salute your brethren only, what do ye more *than others?* do not even the publicans so? ⁴⁸Be ye therefore perfect, even as your Father which is in heaven is perfect.

6

¹Take heed that ye do not your alms[a] before men, to be seen of them: otherwise ye have no reward of your Father

---

[d] offend . . . : or, do cause thee to offend
[a] alms: or, righteousness

Taking Care of Tomorrow

by Ron Blue

Is it wrong to plan? When Jesus told us not to worry about food, drink, and clothes (Matt. 6:25), wasn't he promising to supply all our needs?

Indeed, we can depend on God to meet our needs. But that *doesn't* mean we shouldn't plan.

When Joseph planned for the seven years of famine in Egypt by setting aside resources in the seven years of plenty, he was practicing sound financial planning. When Nehemiah rebuilt the walls of Jerusalem, he spent months in prayer, preparation, and planning before he even arrived at the city. David planned and collected the resources for his son Solomon to build the Temple.

I see three main benefits in doing financial planning.

Benefit: Peace of mind. Probably the most rewarding reason for doing financial planning is the peace of mind that comes with knowing where you're headed and how you're going to get there. A person who fails to plan is like someone who starts out on a trip, yet has no idea how long the trip will last or where he's going. The likely result is that he gets nowhere. The same thing happens when people manage their finances with no discernible plan. They are paralyzed with indecision and accomplish little.

Benefit: Basis of communication. Developing a financial plan also provides a basis for family communication. During the planning process, the family is required to establish and prioritize goals, and everybody knows what they are. Once the family is committed to a plan, the reason for disagreement—which in most cases is uncertainty—has been handled once and for all in a reasonable manner.

Benefit: Guide for decision making. A financial plan serves as a guide for making ongoing decisions. It also eliminates some options, decreasing the number of financial decisions that need to be made on a day-to-day basis. For example, if the plan calls for the establishment of an IRA for a working wife, then $2,000 has been committed for that objective and is not available for any other use, regardless of how attractive an alternative might look. If money has been allocated for home remodeling or college education, the use of those funds has been locked in, and other possible uses don't even need to be considered. In other words, a financial plan brings order.

How to begin. A financial plan is usually drawn up in five steps. The first step is *to assess your present situation.* This means answering such questions as: Do you spend less than you earn? What percentage of your income do you give to the Lord's work? What percentage do you save? Is debt repayment taking a large portion of your cash flow? What percentage is being spent on your life-style? Is your insurance coverage adequate?

The second step of the planning process is *to set financial goals.* A goal is an objective toward which you believe God wants you to move, and it has two characteristics. First, a goal is defined by a specific dollar amount. Second, a definite time frame is set in which the goal is to be accomplished. Because goals are quantified, you can tell whether you're accomplishing them.

The third step is *to make decisions that will move you from where you are to where you want to go.* Those decisions are expressed in a short-term cash-flow plan—a budget. The plan summarizes in dollars how you're going to spend your money. Remember, the most important thing in making this plan is to spend less than you earn.

The fourth step is *to develop a way of ensuring that the budget plan is being followed.* The simplest monitoring system is a set of envelopes. When you receive your monthly income, divide it into envelopes, one for each category, such as food, clothes, entertainment, donations, debt repayment, and savings. Spending stops when the envelope is empty.

If your budget from step 3 and your monitoring system from step 4 are working, you should have at least a little money left over at the end of the month. Step 5 is *to decide how to invest that money.* Jesus told us not to worry about tomorrow, and it is the people without a financial plan who tend to worry the most. Begin now to plan your use of God's resources, then joyfully and freely live one day at a time (Matt. 6:34).

DIGGING DEEPER

1. A financial plan makes possible a careful approach to spending. What is the *primary* reason for taking such care? See Psalms 24:1; 50:9-12.

2. While saving money is biblical, what are the pitfalls to avoid? See Luke 12:13-21; 1 Timothy 6:7-10, 17-19; James 4:13-16.

3. How is financial planning a stepping-stone to greater responsibilities? See Luke 16:10-12.

which is in heaven. ²Therefore when thou doest *thine* alms, do not[b] sound a trumpet before thee, as the hypocrites do in the synagogues and in the streets, that they may have glory of men. Verily I say unto you, They have their reward. ³But when thou doest alms, let not thy left hand know what thy right hand doeth: ⁴That thine alms may be in secret: and thy Father which seeth in secret himself shall reward thee openly.

⁵And when thou prayest, thou shalt not be as the hypocrites *are*: for they love to pray standing in the synagogues and in the corners of the streets, that they may be seen of men. Verily I say unto you, They have their reward. ⁶But thou, when thou prayest, enter into thy closet, and when thou hast shut thy door, pray to thy Father which is in secret; and thy Father which seeth in secret shall reward thee

openly. ⁷But when ye pray, use not vain repetitions, as the heathen *do*: for they think that they shall be heard for their much speaking. ⁸Be not ye therefore like unto them: for your Father knoweth what things ye have need of, before ye ask him.

⁹After this manner therefore pray ye: Our Father which art in heaven, Hallowed be thy name. ¹⁰Thy kingdom

---

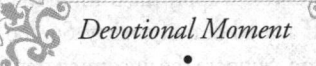

Devotional Moment

•

God's Name

6:9-13 Jesus gave his disciples a model prayer, which he directed to "our Father in heaven." God is both a loving parent and the majestic Lord of the universe, and he desires to be honored as both. Using God's name respectfully is one way to honor him. How is God's name used in your house? Is it taken lightly? Is it an exclamation of anger? Be thoughtful about how you use God's name.

ᵇ do not . . . : or, cause not a trumpet to be sounded

Breaking Free from
Fear of Transition

And the rain descended, and the floods came, and the winds blew, and beat upon that house; and it fell not; for it was founded upon a rock. Matthew 7:25

I f we've come from a difficult background, the uncertainty of the past can make every life transition a fearful event. We're fearful and anxious about how we'll make it and what will happen to us.

Yet in the soothing words of comfort and trust that Christ offered on that mountainside years ago comes hope for us today to break this aspect of an anxious life. For while there is much in our life that doesn't come with advance warning, there are many transitions we can plan for and commit in advance to the Lord.

For example, if you have children, you can see what is likely to come by asking questions like these: What transitions can we see coming in our lives or our children's lives in the next six months? in the next year? in the next five years? What passages of Scripture and what books do I need to read that will give me insight and skills to ease into these transitions? Have we prayed about them, asking God in advance for his strength and wisdom? How can we help each member of the family achieve the maximum benefit and the minimum stress through each of these changes? If you're married, discuss these together with your spouse. If not, perhaps you can work through them with a close friend who has kids the same age as yours. This will help you prepare for the upcoming transitions and turn your anxieties over to Christ.

As we seek to apply the truth in Matthew 7:25, talking about upcoming transitions can head off a good deal of anxiety. So, too, can *letting go, starting fresh,* and *reaching out.*

Let go. Suppose the upcoming transition you fear involves emptying your nest. The last of your kids is about to leave home, and you are filled with anxiety. Talk about your fears with your spouse or friend, cry together, and then throw a "leaving home" party. While there are always deeds left undone and words left unsaid as a parent, do as much as you can to mend every fence . . . and then *let go.*

Start fresh. What changes will this "new era" mean in your life? What new priorities will replace the old ones? When Jesus rose into the sky and disappeared, the disciples stood staring at the cloud until two angels finally said to them, "Men of Galilee, why stand ye gazing up into heaven?" (Acts 1:11). In other words, *Come on you guys! Why are you standing around staring into the sky? Jesus has gone into heaven. That era's over. But get ready! A new era's on the way, and you're an important part of it!*

Starting fresh isn't always easy, but it's an important second step when we face transitions and anxiety.

Reach out. The best way to deal with a major transition is not to sit and sulk, but to reach out to others—to make yourself available rather than to retreat and to seek rather than hide.

Times of transition don't have to become cycles of defeat. The transitions that we can anticipate, we can also pray about and prepare for. The transitions that come unexpectedly and that detour us in life also come with the written promise of almighty God: "Be careful for nothing; but in every thing by prayer and supplication with thanksgiving let your requests be made known unto God" (Phil. 4:6). We need not be anxious because we can trust God to be our source of life and sustenance.

---

come. Thy will be done in earth, as *it is* in heaven. [11]Give us this day our daily bread. [12]And forgive us our debts, as we forgive our debtors. [13]And lead us not into temptation, but deliver us from evil: For thine is the kingdom, and the power, and the glory, for ever. Amen. [14]For if ye forgive men their trespasses, your heavenly Father will also forgive you: [15]But if ye forgive not men their trespasses, neither will your Father forgive your trespasses.

[16]Moreover when ye fast, be not, as the hypocrites, of a sad countenance: for they disfigure their faces, that they may appear unto men to fast. Verily I say unto you, They have their reward. [17]But thou, when thou fastest, anoint thine head, and wash thy face; [18]That thou appear not unto men to fast, but unto thy Father which is in secret: and thy Father, which seeth in secret, shall reward thee openly.

[19]Lay not up for yourselves treasures upon earth, where moth and rust doth corrupt, and where thieves break through and steal: [20]But lay up for yourselves treasures in heaven, where neither moth nor rust doth corrupt, and where thieves do not break through nor steal: [21]For where your treasure is, there will your heart be

also. [22]The light of the body is the eye: if therefore thine eye be single, thy whole body shall be full of light. [23]But if thine eye be evil, thy whole body shall be full of darkness. If therefore the light that is in thee be darkness, how great *is* that darkness! [24]No man can serve two masters: for either he will hate the one, and love the other; or else he will hold to the one, and despise the other. Ye cannot serve God and mammon.

[25]Therefore I say unto you, Take no thought for your life, what ye shall eat, or what ye shall drink; nor yet for your body, what ye shall put on. Is not the life more than meat, and the body than raiment? [26]Behold the fowls of the air: for they sow not, neither do they reap, nor gather into barns; yet your heavenly Father feedeth them. Are ye not much better than they? [27]Which of you by taking thought can add one cubit unto his stature? [28]And why take ye thought for raiment? Consider the lilies of the field, how they grow; they toil not, neither do they spin: [29]And yet I say unto you, That even Solomon in all his glory was not arrayed like one of these. [30]Wherefore, if God so clothe the grass of the field,

Breaking Free from Touch Withheld

When he was come down from the mountain, great multitudes followed him. And, behold, there came a leper and worshipped him, saying, "Lord, if thou wilt, thou canst make me clean." And Jesus put forth his hand, and touched him, saying "I will; be thou clean." And immediately his leprosy was cleansed. Matthew 8:1-3

There is an epidemic afoot that is claiming many victims. While it's seldom seen as a major problem, it can and often does create major problems in relationships. For some, it's a negative cycle that has been carried on for generations. It's the very problem that Jesus addressed when he met both the spiritual, emotional, and *physical* needs of a leper who confronted him—the lack of *meaningful touch*.

For years researchers have pointed to the disastrous effects of touch deprivation, called "mirasmus." Perhaps you have heard of the misguided study in which some caregivers of newborn infants were forbidden to touch the babies under their care (apart from holding a bottle for them and cleaning them). In the absence of touch, these babies failed to thrive, and many died.

With all the fears of abuse and inappropriate touch in our society, many people are actually cutting back on meaningful touch—even though we are already one of the least "touchie" countries in the world. A recent study observed couples in coffee shops in major cities of four nations. On average, Italian couples touched each other sixty times or more in one hour's time; the French, forty times; Americans, eight times; and those in England, zero.

Here in the Gospel of Matthew, a man sick with leprosy humbly asked Jesus to heal him. Christ healed many people, even other lepers, without touching them. But here in particular it is recorded that he touched the man even before speaking to him.

Why the specific act of touch when Jesus could simply have spoken a word? One curse of someone who carried the horrible, communicable disease of leprosy in Christ's day was to be cut off from all social contact. The expression "More than a stone's throw away" came from the requirement that lepers stay away. Any leper coming "within a stone's throw" of a healthy person would get pelted! Christ broke the rules—he reached out and touched a leper. His gesture was an incredible act of compassion that healed more than just the man's disease.

Perhaps you've come from a home where touch was withheld. That past leaves a cycle of hurt that can be difficult to escape—without the Master's touch. Other people fear touching because they have been touched only in anger. And still others fear meaningful touch because of tradition. Yet all of us have the power to touch—right at our fingertips. You do too.

Breaking the cycle of unexpressed physical touch can be a powerful way to encourage and bless *your* loved ones. If you've ever felt like that leper—an untouchable—here are some suggestions on applying this important aspect of healthy relationships.

First, talk with a close friend, pastor, or counselor about the absence of meaningful touch in your past.

Second, look for appropriate ways to encourage others through touch. At home, at church, and in other positive settings, a gentle pat can convey connection and caring. Studies show that the "safest" place to touch a person is on the elbow.

Third, recognize that the lack of meaningful touch can make you vulnerable to negative influences.

And finally, consider getting a pet. Your "touch bank" can be filled *in part* with this aspect of God's creation, a gift that can at times help us deal with hurt.

Is it time for you to begin making meaningful touch a part of your interaction with loved ones? In appropriate ways and doses, it can also provide an antidote to *their* having to break free of touch deprivation.

---

which to day is, and to morrow is cast into the oven, *shall he* not much more *clothe* you, O ye of little faith? [31] Therefore take no thought, saying, What shall we eat? or, What shall we drink? or, Wherewithal shall we be clothed? [32] (For after all these things do the Gentiles seek:) for your heavenly Father knoweth that ye have need of all these things. [33] But seek ye first the kingdom of God, and his righteousness; and all these things shall be added unto you. [34] Take therefore no thought for the morrow: for the morrow shall take thought for the things of itself. Sufficient unto the day *is* the evil thereof.

7

[1] Judge not, that ye be not judged. [2] For with what judgment ye judge, ye shall be judged: and with what measure ye mete, it shall be measured to you again. [3] And why beholdest thou the mote that is in thy brother's eye, but considerest not the beam that is in thine own eye? [4] Or how wilt thou say to thy brother, Let me pull out the mote out of thine eye; and, behold, a beam *is* in thine own eye? [5] Thou hypocrite, first cast out the beam out of thine own eye; and then shalt thou see clearly to cast out the mote out of thy brother's eye. [6] Give not that which is holy unto the dogs, neither cast ye your pearls before swine, lest they trample them under their feet, and turn again and rend you.

[7] Ask, and it shall be given you; seek, and ye shall find; knock, and it shall be opened unto you: [8] For every one that asketh receiveth; and he that seeketh findeth; and to him that knocketh it shall be opened. [9] Or what man is there of you, whom if his son ask bread, will he give him a stone? [10] Or if he ask a fish, will he give him a serpent? [11] If ye

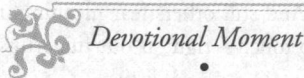

Devotional Moment

•

The Golden Rule

7:12 Jesus told people how they should treat others. To this day his command is repeated and called the Golden Rule. How golden a rule is it in your family? Are all members treated with respect? Your children are watching how you treat other people—the driver in the next car, your brother-in-law, the cashier at the grocery store. What do they see? Ask each member of your family how they like to be treated; what actions make a difference to them? Try to respect their preferences.

then, being evil, know how to give good gifts unto your children, how much more shall your Father which is in heaven give good things to them that ask him? ¹²Therefore all things whatsoever ye would that men should do to you, do ye even so to them: for this is the law and the prophets. ¹³Enter ye in at the strait^a gate: for wide *is* the gate, and broad *is* the way, that leadeth to destruction, and many there be which go in thereat: ¹⁴Because^b strait *is* the gate, and narrow *is* the way, which leadeth unto life, and few there be that find it.

¹⁵Beware of false prophets, which come to you in sheep's clothing, but inwardly they are ravening wolves. ¹⁶Ye shall know them by their fruits. Do men gather grapes of thorns, or figs of thistles? ¹⁷Even so every good tree bringeth forth good fruit; but a corrupt tree bringeth forth evil fruit. ¹⁸A good tree cannot bring forth evil fruit, neither *can* a corrupt tree bring forth good fruit. ¹⁹Every tree that bringeth not forth good fruit is hewn down, and cast into the fire. ²⁰Wherefore by their fruits ye shall know them.

²¹Not every one that saith unto me, Lord, Lord, shall enter into the kingdom of heaven; but he that doeth the will of my Father which is in heaven. ²²Many will say to me in that day, Lord, Lord, have we not prophesied in thy name? and in thy name have cast out devils? and in thy name done many wonderful works? ²³And then will I profess unto them, I never knew you: depart from me, ye that work iniquity. ²⁴Therefore whosoever heareth these sayings of mine, and doeth them, I will liken him unto a wise man, which built his house upon a rock: ²⁵And the rain descended, and the floods came, and the winds blew, and beat upon that house; and it fell not: for it was founded upon a rock. ²⁶And every one that heareth these sayings of mine, and doeth them not, shall be likened unto a foolish man, which built his house upon the sand: ²⁷And the rain descended, and the floods came, and the winds blew, and beat upon that house; and it fell: and great was the fall of it. ²⁸And it came to pass, when Jesus had ended these sayings, the people were astonished at his doctrine: ²⁹For he taught them as *one* having authority, and not as the scribes.

8

¹When he was come down from the mountain, great multitudes followed him. ²And, behold, there came a leper and worshipped him, saying, Lord, if

---

^{a} strait: or, narrow
^{b} Because: or, How

thou wilt, thou canst make me clean. ³And Jesus put forth *his* hand, and touched him, saying, I will; be thou clean. And immediately his leprosy was cleansed. ⁴And Jesus saith unto him, See thou tell no man; but go thy way, shew thyself to the priest, and offer the gift that Moses commanded, for a testimony unto them.

⁵And when Jesus was entered into Capernaum, there came unto him a centurion, beseeching him, ⁶And saying, Lord, my servant lieth at home sick of the palsy, grievously tormented. ⁷And Jesus saith unto him, I will come and heal him. ⁸The centurion answered and said, Lord, I am not worthy that thou shouldest come under my roof: but speak the word only, and my servant shall be healed. ⁹For I am a man under authority, having soldiers under me: and I say to this *man*, Go, and he goeth; and to another, Come, and he cometh; and to my servant, Do this, and he doeth *it*. ¹⁰When Jesus heard *it*, he marvelled, and said to them that followed, Verily I say unto you, I have not found so great faith, no, not in Israel. ¹¹And I say unto you, That many shall come from the east and west, and shall sit down with Abraham, and Isaac, and Jacob, in the kingdom of heaven. ¹²But the children of the kingdom shall be cast out into outer darkness: there shall be weeping and gnashing of teeth. ¹³And Jesus said unto the centurion, Go thy way; and as thou hast believed, *so* be it done unto thee. And his servant was healed in the selfsame hour.

¹⁴And when Jesus was come into Peter's house, he saw his wife's mother laid, and sick of a fever. ¹⁵And he touched her hand, and the fever left her: and she arose, and ministered unto them. ¹⁶When the even was come, they brought unto him many that were possessed with devils: and he cast out the spirits with *his* word, and healed all that were sick: ¹⁷That it might be fulfilled which was spoken by Esaias the prophet, saying, Himself took our infirmities, and bare *our* sicknesses.

¹⁸Now when Jesus saw great multitudes about him, he gave commandment to depart unto the other side. ¹⁹And a certain scribe came, and said unto him, Master, I will follow thee whithersoever thou goest. ²⁰And Jesus saith unto him, The foxes have holes, and the birds of the air *have* nests; but the Son of man hath not where to lay *his* head. ²¹And another of his disciples said unto him, Lord, suffer me first to go and bury my father. ²²But Jesus said unto him, Follow me; and let the dead bury their dead.

²³And when he was entered into a ship, his disciples followed him. ²⁴And, behold, there arose a great tempest in the sea, insomuch that the ship was covered with the waves: but he was asleep. ²⁵And his disciples came to *him,* and awoke him, saying, Lord, save us: we perish. ²⁶And he saith unto them, Why are ye fearful, O ye of little faith? Then he arose, and rebuked the winds and the sea; and there was a great calm. ²⁷But the men marvelled, saying, What manner of man is this, that even the winds and the sea obey him!

²⁸And when he was come to the other side into the country of the Gergesenes, there met him two possessed with devils, coming out of the tombs, exceeding fierce, so that no man might pass by that way. ²⁹And, behold,

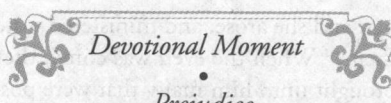

Devotional Moment

•

Prejudice

8:28-34 Jesus came upon two men who were unclean in at least three ways, according to Jewish law: They were Gentiles (non-Jews), they were possessed by demons, and they lived in a graveyard. Yet Jesus did not avoid them; instead, he healed them. We sometimes encounter people who are unpleasant, even repulsive, to us. What do you do when you see a homeless person? How do you react to those whose moral standards, methods of child rearing, or religious beliefs differ from yours? Pray for Jesus' compassion.

they cried out, saying, What have we to do with thee, Jesus, thou Son of God? art thou come hither to torment us before the time? [30]And there was a good way off from them an herd of many swine feeding. [31]So the devils besought him, saying, If thou cast us out, suffer us to go away into the herd of swine. [32]And he said unto them, Go. And when they were come out, they went into the herd of swine: and, behold, the whole herd of swine ran violently down a steep place into the sea, and perished in the waters. [33]And they that kept them fled, and went their ways into the city, and told every thing, and what was befallen to the possessed of the devils. [34]And, behold, the whole city came out to meet Jesus: and when they saw him, they besought *him* that he would depart out of their coasts.

9

[1]And he entered into a ship, and passed over, and came into his own city. [2]And, behold, they brought to him a man sick of the palsy, lying on a bed: and Jesus seeing their faith said unto the sick of the palsy; Son, be of good cheer; thy sins be forgiven thee. [3]And, behold, certain of the scribes said within themselves, This *man* blasphemeth. [4]And Jesus knowing their thoughts said, Wherefore think ye evil in your hearts? [5]For whether is easier, to say, *Thy* sins be forgiven thee; or to say, Arise, and walk? [6]But that ye may know that the Son of man hath power on earth to forgive sins, (then saith he to the sick of the palsy,) Arise, take up thy bed, and go unto thine house. [7]And he arose, and departed to his house. [8]But when the multitudes saw *it*, they marvelled, and glorified God, which had given such power unto men.

[9]And as Jesus passed forth from thence, he saw a man, named Matthew, sitting at the receipt of custom: and he saith unto him, Follow me. And he arose, and followed him. [10]And it came to pass, as Jesus sat at meat in the house, behold, many publicans and sinners came and sat down with him and his disciples. [11]And when the Pharisees saw *it*, they said unto his disciples, Why eateth your Master with publicans and sinners? [12]But when Jesus heard *that*, he

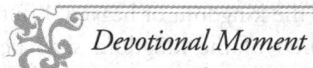

Devotional Moment

•

Hiding

9:4 When Jesus forgave the sins of a paralyzed man, the scribes thought he was blaspheming. But Jesus knew their thoughts, and he let them know it. We can fool many people—even our family and close friends—but God knows our thoughts. Let this truth be comforting as well as convicting. Pray for the faith to go to him as you are. He loves you so much—you need not hide from him.

said unto them, They that be whole need not a physician, but they that are sick. ¹³But go ye and learn what *that* meaneth, I will have mercy, and not sacrifice: for I am not come to call the righteous, but sinners to repentance.

¹⁴Then came to him the disciples of John, saying, Why do we and the Pharisees fast oft, but thy disciples fast not? ¹⁵And Jesus said unto them, Can the children of the bridechamber mourn, as long as the bridegroom is with them? but the days will come, when the bridegroom shall be taken from them, and then shall they fast. ¹⁶No man putteth a piece of newᵃ cloth unto an old garment, for that which is put in to fill it up taketh from the garment, and the rent is made worse. ¹⁷Neither do men put new wine into old bottlesᵇ: else the bottles break, and the wine runneth out, and the bottles perish: but they put new wine into new bottles, and both are preserved.

¹⁸While he spake these things unto them, behold, there came a certain ruler, and worshipped him, saying, My daughter is even now dead: but come and lay thy hand upon her, and she shall live. ¹⁹And Jesus arose, and followed him, and *so did* his disciples. ²⁰And, behold, a woman, which was diseased with an issue of blood twelve years, came behind *him*, and touched the hem of his garment: ²¹For she said within herself, If I may but touch his garment, I shall be whole. ²²But Jesus turned him about, and when he saw her, he said, Daughter, be of good com-

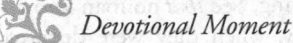

Devotional Moment

Why?

9:27-30 Two blind men followed Jesus, asking for mercy. After he questioned their faith in him, they responded positively and were healed. Like the blind men, perhaps you, too, have been praying for something for a long time. You may wonder why God is waiting so long to heal an illness, restore a relationship, or ease the stress in a work situation. And if your spouse or children are involved, you may also wonder how he could let them suffer. We cannot always understand God's timing or plans; our part is to trust that he does care and is working on our behalf.

fort; thy faith hath made thee whole. And the woman was made whole from that hour. ²³And when Jesus came into the ruler's house, and saw the minstrels and the people making a noise, ²⁴He said unto them, Give place: for the maid is not dead, but sleepeth. And they laughed him to scorn. ²⁵But when the people were put forth, he went in, and took her by the hand, and the maid arose. ²⁶And the fameᶜ hereof went abroad into all that land.

²⁷And when Jesus departed thence, two blind men followed him, crying, and saying, *Thou* Son of David, have mercy on us. ²⁸And when he was come into the house, the blind men came to him: and Jesus saith unto them, Believe ye that I am able to do this? They said unto him, Yea, Lord. ²⁹Then touched he their eyes, saying, According to your faith be it unto you. ³⁰And their eyes were opened; and Jesus straitly charged

---

ᵃ new: or, raw, or, unwrought
ᵇ bottles: or, sacks of skin, or, leather
ᶜ the fame . . . : or, this fame

them, saying, See *that* no man know *it*. [31]But they, when they were departed, spread abroad his fame in all that country. [32]As they went out, behold, they brought to him a dumb man possessed with a devil. [33]And when the devil was cast out, the dumb spake: and the multitudes marvelled, saying, It was never so seen in Israel. [34]But the Pharisees said, He casteth out devils through the prince of the devils.

[35]And Jesus went about all the cities and villages, teaching in their synagogues, and preaching the gospel of the kingdom, and healing every sickness and every disease among the people. [36]But when he saw the multitudes, he was moved with compassion on them, because they fainted[d], and were scattered abroad, as sheep having no shepherd. [37]Then saith he unto his disciples, The harvest truly *is* plenteous, but the labourers *are* few; [38]Pray ye therefore the Lord of the harvest, that he will send forth labourers into his harvest.

10

[1]And when he had called unto *him* his twelve disciples, he gave them power *against* unclean spirits, to cast them out, and to heal all manner of sickness and all manner of disease. [2]Now the names of the twelve apostles are these; The first, Simon, who is called Peter, and Andrew his brother; James *the son* of Zebedee, and John his brother; [3]Philip, and Bartholomew; Thomas, and Matthew the publican; James *the son* of Alphaeus, and Lebbaeus, whose surname was

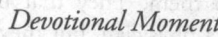

Devotional Moment
•
Self-Esteem

10:2-4 The list of the twelve disciples reads like an impressive roll call of—well, ordinary folks. Jesus did not pick these men for their startling résumés or worldly connections, but in order that they might follow him. The true basis for self-esteem has always been a person's relationship with God. Read the Gospel passages about the call of the disciples, and thank God that he continues to use ordinary folks to do his work.

Thaddaeus; [4]Simon the Canaanite, and Judas Iscariot, who also betrayed him.

[5]These twelve Jesus sent forth, and commanded them, saying, Go not into the way of the Gentiles, and into *any* city of the Samaritans enter ye not: [6]But go rather to the lost sheep of the house of Israel. [7]And as ye go, preach, saying, The kingdom of heaven is at hand. [8]Heal the sick, cleanse the lepers, raise the dead, cast out devils: freely ye have received, freely give. [9]Provide[a] neither gold, nor silver, nor brass in your purses, [10]Nor scrip for *your* journey, neither two coats, neither shoes, nor yet staves[b]: for the workman is worthy of his meat. [11]And into whatsoever city or town ye shall enter, enquire who in it is worthy; and there abide till ye go thence. [12]And when ye come into an house, salute it. [13]And if the house be worthy, let your peace come upon it: but if it be not worthy, let your peace return to you. [14]And whosoever shall not receive you, nor hear your words, when ye depart out of that house or city, shake off the dust of your

---

[d] fainted . . . : or, were tired and lay down
[a] Provide: or, Get
[b] staves: Gr. a staff

feet. ¹⁵Verily I say unto you, It shall be more tolerable for the land of Sodom and Gomorrha in the day of judgment, than for that city.

¹⁶Behold, I send you forth as sheep in the midst of wolves: be ye therefore wise as serpents, and harmless^c as doves. ¹⁷But beware of men: for they will deliver you up to the councils, and they will scourge you in their synagogues; ¹⁸And ye shall be brought before governors and kings for my sake, for a testimony against them and the Gentiles. ¹⁹But when they deliver you up, take no thought how or what ye shall speak: for it shall be given you in that same hour what ye shall speak. ²⁰For it is not ye that speak, but the Spirit of your Father which speaketh in you. ²¹And the brother shall deliver up the brother to death, and the father the child: and the children shall rise up against *their* parents, and cause them to be put to death. ²²And ye shall be hated of all *men* for my name's sake: but he that endureth to the end shall be saved. ²³But when they persecute you in this city, flee ye into another: for verily I say unto you, Ye shall not have gone over the cities of Israel, till the Son of man be come. ²⁴The disciple is not above *his* master, nor the servant above his lord. ²⁵It is enough for the disciple that he be as his master, and the servant as his lord. If they have called the master of the house Beelzebub^d, how much more *shall they call* them of his household? ²⁶Fear them not therefore: for there is nothing covered, that shall not be revealed; and hid, that shall not be

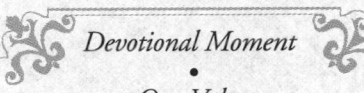

Devotional Moment
•
Our Value

10:29-31 Perhaps the disciples were worried about having enough of life's daily necessities. Jesus reassured them: God deeply loved and valued them, and he would provide for them and protect them. Are you feeling undervalued—even rejected—lately? The same heavenly Father values you more than you realize. He even has your hairs numbered! And that's just the beginning of what he keeps track of. Thank God today for such care.

known. ²⁷What I tell you in darkness, *that* speak ye in light: and what ye hear in the ear, *that* preach ye upon the housetops. ²⁸And fear not them which kill the body, but are not able to kill the soul: but rather fear him which is able to destroy both soul and body in hell. ²⁹Are not two sparrows sold for a farthing^e? and one of them shall not fall on the ground without your Father. ³⁰But the very hairs of your head are all numbered. ³¹Fear ye not therefore, ye are of more value than many sparrows. ³²Whosoever therefore shall confess me before men, him will I confess also before my Father which is in heaven. ³³But whosoever shall deny me before men, him will I also deny before my Father which is in heaven. ³⁴Think not that I am come to send peace on earth: I came not to send peace, but a sword. ³⁵For I am come to set a man at variance against his father, and the daughter against her mother, and the daughter in law against her mother in

---

^c harmless: or, simple
^d Beelzebub: Gr. Beelzebul
^e farthing: it is in value halfpenny farthing in the original, as being the tenth part of the Roman penny

Worship
in Your Home

BUILDING SELF-ESTEEM THROUGH DEVOTIONS

Are not two sparrows sold for a farthing? and one of them shall not fall on the ground without your Father. But the very hairs of your head are all numbered. Fear ye not therefore, ye are of more value than many sparrows. Matthew 10:29-31

What does God really think of us? He tells us that he will never forsake us (Josh. 1:5; Heb. 13:5), that his love for us endures forever (Ps. 118:2-4), and that he crowns us with love and compassion (Ps. 103:4). Most of all, Jesus gave his life for us (John 3:16). No person is worthless; in fact, each person matters a great deal.

Don't skip devotions just because you feel unworthy. Many people have developed a low self-image because they have confused their personal failings with personal worth. They recognize that they have sinned. Thus they conclude that they are worthless. But the keynote of the Bible is how much God loves us and wants us to live with him forever.

Devotions are times for person building—for reminding one another that we each matter a great deal to God.

Devotional Moment
Children

10:42 Jesus gave strong, and at times even stern, advice to the Twelve as he sent them out. Yet he concluded his instructions with the gentle image of giving a cup of cold water to a little child. Jesus wanted his "unimportant disciples" to know that God rewards those who serve "unimportant" or "small" people. In our society, children are still not always valued as real people. Pray for empathy and kindness in your dealings with children.

law. ³⁶And a man's foes *shall be* they of his own household. ³⁷He that loveth father or mother more than me is not worthy of me: and he that loveth son or daughter more than me is not worthy of me. ³⁸And he that taketh not his cross, and followeth after me, is not worthy of me. ³⁹He that findeth his life shall lose it: and he that loseth his life for my sake shall find it. ⁴⁰He that receiveth you receiveth me, and he that receiveth me receiveth him that sent me. ⁴¹He that receiveth a prophet in the name of a prophet shall receive a prophet's reward; and he that receiveth a righteous man in the name of a righteous man shall receive a righteous man's reward. ⁴²And whosoever shall give to drink unto one of these little ones a cup of cold *water* only in the name of a disciple, verily I say unto you, he shall in no wise lose his reward.

11

¹And it came to pass, when Jesus had made an end of commanding his twelve disciples, he departed thence to teach and to preach in their cities. ²Now when John had heard in the prison the works of Christ, he sent two

---
🌿 *Devolional Moment* 🌿
•
Questioning the Lord

11:1-6 From prison, John the Baptist sent his question: Jesus, are you really the Messiah? Instead of reprimanding John for lack of faith, Jesus answered him gently, recognizing how John's trials had led him to question. Sometimes we are embarrassed, even afraid, to question God. But the Lord honors our genuine desire to know and to be reassured. Living by faith can include wrestling with doubts, facing real questions, and talking honestly with God. Don't be afraid to share some of your questions with God.

---

of his disciples, ³And said unto him, Art thou he that should come, or do we look for another? ⁴Jesus answered and said unto them, Go and shew John again those things which ye do hear and see: ⁵The blind receive their sight, and the lame walk, the lepers are cleansed, and the deaf hear, the dead are raised up, and the poor have the gospel preached to them. ⁶And blessed is *he*, whosoever shall not be offended in me.

⁷And as they departed, Jesus began to say unto the multitudes concerning John, What went ye out into the wilderness to see? A reed shaken with the wind? ⁸But what went ye out for to see? A man clothed in soft raiment? behold, they that wear soft *clothing* are in kings' houses. ⁹But what went ye out for to see? A prophet? yea, I say unto you, and more than a prophet. ¹⁰For this is *he*, of whom it is written, Behold, I send my messenger before thy face, which shall prepare thy way before thee. ¹¹Verily I say unto you, Among them that are born of women there hath not risen a greater than John the Baptist: notwithstanding he that is least

in the kingdom of heaven is greater than he. ¹²And from the days of John the Baptist until now the kingdom of heaven suffereth violence, and the violent take it by force. ¹³For all the prophets and the law prophesied until John. ¹⁴And if ye will receive *it*, this is Elias, which was for to come. ¹⁵He that hath ears to hear, let him hear.

¹⁶But whereunto shall I liken this generation? It is like unto children sitting in the markets, and calling unto their fellows, ¹⁷And saying, We have piped unto you, and ye have not danced; we have mourned unto you, and ye have not lamented. ¹⁸For John came neither eating nor drinking, and they say, He hath a devil. ¹⁹The Son of man came eating and drinking, and they say, Behold a man gluttonous, and a winebibber, a friend of publicans and sinners. But wisdom is justified of her children. ²⁰Then began he to upbraid the cities wherein most of his mighty works were done, because they repented not: ²¹Woe unto thee, Chorazin! woe unto thee, Bethsaida! for if the mighty works, which were done in you, had been done in Tyre and Sidon, they would have repented long ago in sackcloth and ashes. ²²But I say unto you, It shall be more tolerable for Tyre and Sidon at the day of judgment, than for you. ²³And thou, Capernaum, which art exalted unto heaven, shalt be brought down to hell: for if the mighty works, which have been done in thee, had been done in Sodom, it would have remained until this day. ²⁴But I say unto you, That it shall be more tolerable for the land of Sodom in the day of judgment, than for thee.

²⁵At that time Jesus answered and

said, I thank thee, O Father, Lord of heaven and earth, because thou hast hid these things from the wise and prudent, and hast revealed them unto babes. [26]Even so, Father: for so it seemed good in thy sight. [27]All things are delivered unto me of my Father: and no man knoweth the Son, but the Father; neither knoweth any man the Father, save the Son, and *he* to whomsoever the Son will reveal *him*. [28]Come unto me, all *ye* that labour and are heavy laden, and I will give you rest. [29]Take my yoke upon you, and learn of me; for I am meek and lowly in heart: and ye shall find rest unto your souls. [30]For my yoke *is* easy, and my burden is light.

12

[1]At that time Jesus went on the sabbath day through the corn; and his disciples were an hungred, and began to pluck the ears of corn, and to eat. [2]But when the Pharisees saw *it*, they said unto him, Behold, thy disciples do that which is not lawful to do upon the sabbath day. [3]But he said unto them, Have ye not read what David did, when he was an hungred, and they that were with him; [4]How he entered into the house of God, and did eat the shewbread, which was not lawful for him to eat, neither for them which were with him, but only for the priests? [5]Or have ye not read in the law, how that on the sabbath days the priests in the temple profane the sabbath, and are blameless? [6]But I say unto you, That in this place is *one* greater than the temple. [7]But if ye had known what *this* meaneth, I will have mercy, and not sacrifice, ye would not

have condemned the guiltless. [8]For the Son of man is Lord even of the sabbath day. [9]And when he was departed thence, he went into their synagogue: [10]And, behold, there was a man which had *his* hand withered. And they asked him, saying, Is it lawful to heal on the sabbath days? that they might accuse him. [11]And he said unto them, What man shall there be among you, that shall have one sheep, and if it fall into a pit on the sabbath day, will he not lay hold on it, and lift *it* out? [12]How much then is a man better than a sheep? Wherefore it is lawful to do well on the sabbath days. [13]Then saith he to the man, Stretch forth thine hand. And he stretched *it* forth; and it was restored whole, like as the other.

[14]Then the Pharisees went out, and held[a] a council against him, how they might destroy him. [15]But when Jesus knew *it*, he withdrew himself from thence: and great multitudes followed him, and he healed them all; [16]And charged them that they should not make him known: [17]That it might be fulfilled which was spoken by Esaias the prophet, saying, [18]Behold my servant, whom I have chosen; my beloved, in whom my soul is well pleased: I will put my spirit upon him, and he shall shew judgment to the Gentiles. [19]He shall not strive, nor cry; neither shall any man hear his voice in the streets. [20]A bruised reed shall he not break, and smoking flax shall he not quench, till he send forth judgment unto victory. [21]And in his name shall the Gentiles trust.

[22]Then was brought unto him one

---

[a] held . . . : or, took counsel

possessed with a devil, blind, and dumb: and he healed him, insomuch that the blind and dumb both spake and saw. ²³And all the people were amazed, and said, Is not this the son of David? ²⁴But when the Pharisees heard *it*, they said, This *fellow* doth not cast out devils, but by Beelzebub[b] the prince of the devils. ²⁵And Jesus knew their thoughts, and said unto them, Every kingdom divided against itself is brought to desolation; and every city or house divided against itself shall not stand: ²⁶And if Satan cast out Satan, he is divided against himself; how shall then his kingdom stand? ²⁷And if I by Beelzebub cast out devils, by whom do your children cast *them* out? therefore they shall be your judges. ²⁸But if I cast out devils by the Spirit of God, then the kingdom of God is come unto you. ²⁹Or else how can one enter into a strong man's house, and spoil his goods, except he first bind the strong man? and then he will spoil his house. ³⁰He that is not with me is against me; and he that gathereth not with me scattereth abroad. ³¹Wherefore I say unto you, All manner of sin and blasphemy shall be forgiven unto men: but the blasphemy *against* the *Holy* Ghost shall not be forgiven unto men. ³²And whosoever speaketh a word against the Son of man, it shall be forgiven him: but whosoever speaketh against the Holy Ghost, it shall not be forgiven him, neither in this world, neither in the *world* to come. ³³Either make the tree good, and his fruit good; or else make the tree corrupt, and his fruit corrupt: for the tree is known by *his* fruit.

³⁴O generation of vipers, how can ye, being evil, speak good things? for out of the abundance of the heart the mouth speaketh. ³⁵A good man out of the good treasure of the heart bringeth forth good things: and an evil man out of the evil treasure bringeth forth evil things. ³⁶But I say unto you, That every idle word that men shall speak, they shall give account thereof in the day of judgment. ³⁷For by thy words thou shalt be justified, and by thy words thou shalt be condemned.

³⁸Then certain of the scribes and of the Pharisees answered, saying, Master, we would see a sign from thee. ³⁹But he answered and said unto them, An evil and adulterous generation seeketh after a sign; and there shall no sign be given to it, but the sign of the prophet Jonas: ⁴⁰For as Jonas was three days and three nights in the whale's belly; so shall the Son of man be three days and three nights in the heart of the earth. ⁴¹The men of Nineveh shall rise in judgment with this generation, and shall condemn it: because they repented at the preaching of Jonas; and, behold, a greater than Jonas *is* here. ⁴²The queen of the south shall rise up in the judgment with this generation, and shall condemn it: for she came from the uttermost parts of the earth to hear the wisdom of Solomon; and, behold, a greater than Solomon *is* here. ⁴³When the unclean spirit is gone out of a man, he walketh through dry places, seeking rest, and findeth none. ⁴⁴Then he saith, I will return into my house from whence I came out; and when he is come, he findeth *it* empty, swept, and

---

[b] Beelzebub: Gr. Beelzebul

garnished. ⁴⁵Then goeth he, and taketh with himself seven other spirits more wicked than himself, and they enter in and dwell there: and the last *state* of that man is worse than the first. Even so shall it be also unto this wicked generation.

⁴⁶While he yet talked to the people, behold, *his* mother and his brethren stood without, desiring to speak with him. ⁴⁷Then one said unto him, Behold, thy mother and thy brethren stand without, desiring to speak with thee. ⁴⁸But he answered and said unto him that told him, Who is my mother? and who are my brethren? ⁴⁹And he stretched forth his hand toward his disciples, and said, Behold my mother and my brethren! ⁵⁰For whosoever shall do the will of my Father which is in heaven, the same is my brother, and sister, and mother.

13

¹The same day went Jesus out of the house, and sat by the sea side. ²And great multitudes were gathered together unto him, so that he went into a ship, and sat; and the whole multitude stood on the shore. ³And he spake many things unto them in parables, saying, Behold, a sower went forth to sow; ⁴And when he sowed, some *seeds* fell by the way side, and the fowls came and devoured them up: ⁵Some fell upon stony places, where they had not much earth: and forthwith they sprung up, because they had no deepness of earth: ⁶And when the sun was up, they were scorched; and because they had no root, they withered away. ⁷And some fell among thorns; and the thorns sprung up, and choked them: ⁸But

Devotional Moment
•
Spiritual Growth

13:1-9 Jesus used the parable of the sower to explain how people differ in their openness to God's Word. Some people are very receptive to God's Word, and others are indifferent or even hostile to it. What have you found helpful in preparing the "soil" of your heart to receive the Word and produce good fruit? Share ideas with friends and family, and encourage each other in your God-given responsibility.

other fell into good ground, and brought forth fruit, some an hundredfold, some sixtyfold, some thirtyfold. ⁹Who hath ears to hear, let him hear. ¹⁰And the disciples came, and said unto him, Why speakest thou unto them in parables? ¹¹He answered and said unto them, Because it is given unto you to know the mysteries of the kingdom of heaven, but to them it is not given. ¹²For whosoever hath, to him shall be given, and he shall have more abundance: but whosoever hath not, from him shall be taken away even that he hath. ¹³Therefore speak I to them in parables: because they seeing see not; and hearing they hear not, neither do they understand. ¹⁴And in them is fulfilled the prophecy of Esaias, which saith, By hearing ye shall hear, and shall not understand; and seeing ye shall see, and shall not perceive: ¹⁵For this people's heart is waxed gross, and *their* ears are dull of hearing, and their eyes they have closed; lest at any time they should see with *their* eyes, and hear with *their* ears, and should understand with *their* heart, and should be converted, and I should heal them. ¹⁶But blessed *are* your eyes, for they see: and your ears, for they hear. ¹⁷For verily I say unto you, That many prophets and righteous *men* have desired to see *those things* which ye see, and have not seen *them*; and to hear *those things* which ye hear, and have not heard *them*. ¹⁸Hear ye therefore the parable of the sower. ¹⁹When any one heareth the word of the kingdom, and understandeth *it* not, then cometh the wicked *one*, and catcheth away that which was sown in his heart. This is he which received seed by the way side. ²⁰But he that received the seed into stony places, the same is he that heareth the word, and anon with joy receiveth it; ²¹Yet hath he not root in himself, but dureth for a while: for when tribulation or persecution ariseth because of the word, by and by he is offended ᵃ. ²²He also that received seed among the thorns is he that heareth the word; and the care of this world, and the deceitfulness of riches, choke the word, and he becometh unfruitful. ²³But he that received seed into the good ground is he that heareth the word, and understandeth *it*; which also beareth fruit, and bringeth forth, some an hundredfold, some sixty, some thirty.

²⁴Another parable put he forth unto them, saying, The kingdom of heaven is likened unto a man which sowed good seed in his field: ²⁵But while men slept, his enemy came and sowed tares among the wheat, and went his way. ²⁶But when the blade was sprung up, and brought forth fruit, then appeared the tares also. ²⁷So the servants of the householder came and said unto him, Sir, didst not thou sow good seed in thy field? from whence then hath it tares? ²⁸He said unto them, An enemy hath done this. The servants said unto him, Wilt thou then that we go and gather them up? ²⁹But he said, Nay; lest while ye gather up the tares, ye root up also the wheat with them. ³⁰Let both grow together until the harvest: and in the time of harvest I will say to the reapers, Gather ye together first the tares, and bind them in bundles to burn them: but gather the wheat into my barn. ³¹Another parable put he forth unto them, saying, The kingdom of heaven is like to a grain of mustard seed, which a man took, and sowed in his field: ³²Which indeed is the least of all seeds: but when it is grown, it is the greatest among herbs, and becometh a tree, so that the birds of the air come and lodge in the branches thereof. ³³Another parable spake he unto them; The kingdom of heaven is like unto leaven, which a woman took, and hid in three measures ᵇ of meal, till the whole was leavened. ³⁴All these things spake Jesus unto the multitude in parables; and without a parable spake he not unto them: ³⁵That it might be fulfilled which was spoken by the prophet, saying, I will open my mouth in parables; I will utter things which have been kept secret from the foundation of the world. ³⁶Then Jesus sent the multitude away, and went into the house: and his disciples came unto him, saying, Declare unto us the parable of the tares of the

---

ᵃ offended: he relapseth, or, falleth into sin
ᵇ measures: the word in the Greek is a measure containing about a peck and a half, wanting a little more than a pint

field. ³⁷He answered and said unto them, He that soweth the good seed is the Son of man; ³⁸The field is the world; the good seed are the children of the kingdom; but the tares are the children of the wicked one; ³⁹The enemy that sowed them is the devil; the harvest is the end of the world; and the reapers are the angels. ⁴⁰As therefore the tares are gathered and burned in the fire; so shall it be in the end of this world. ⁴¹The Son of man shall send forth his angels, and they shall gather out of his kingdom all things⁽ᶜ⁾ that offend, and them which do iniquity; ⁴²And shall cast them into a furnace of fire: there shall be wailing and gnashing of teeth. ⁴³Then shall the righteous shine forth as the sun in the kingdom of their Father. Who hath ears to hear, let him hear.

⁴⁴Again, the kingdom of heaven is like unto treasure hid in a field; the which when a man hath found, he hideth, and for joy thereof goeth and selleth all that he hath, and buyeth that field. ⁴⁵Again, the kingdom of heaven is like unto a merchant man, seeking goodly pearls: ⁴⁶Who, when he had found one pearl of great price, went and sold all that he had, and bought it. ⁴⁷Again, the kingdom of heaven is like unto a net, that was cast into the sea, and gathered of every kind: ⁴⁸Which, when it was full, they drew to shore, and sat down, and gathered the good into vessels, but cast the bad away. ⁴⁹So shall it be at the end of the world: the angels shall come forth, and sever the wicked from among the just, ⁵⁰And

shall cast them into the furnace of fire: there shall be wailing and gnashing of teeth. ⁵¹Jesus saith unto them, Have ye understood all these things? They say unto him, Yea, Lord. ⁵²Then said he unto them, Therefore every scribe which is instructed unto the kingdom of heaven is like unto a man that is an householder, which bringeth forth out of his treasure things new and old.

⁵³And it came to pass, that when Jesus had finished these parables, he departed thence. ⁵⁴And when he was come into his own country, he taught them in their synagogue, insomuch that they were astonished, and said, Whence hath this man this wisdom, and these mighty works? ⁵⁵Is not this the carpenter's son? is not his mother called Mary? and his brethren, James, and Joses, and Simon, and Judas? ⁵⁶And his sisters, are they not all with us? Whence then hath this man all these things? ⁵⁷And they were offended in him. But Jesus said unto them, A prophet is not without honour, save in his own country, and in his own house. ⁵⁸And he did not many mighty works there because of their unbelief.

14

¹At that time Herod the tetrarch⁽ᵃ⁾ heard of the fame of Jesus, ²And said unto his servants, This is John the Baptist; he is risen from the dead; and therefore mighty works do shew forth themselves in him. ³For Herod had laid hold on John, and bound him, and put him in prison for Herodias' sake, his brother Philip's wife. ⁴For John said unto him,

---

ᶜ things . . . : or, scandals
ᵃ tetrarch: or, governor over four provinces

It is not lawful for thee to have her. [5]And when he would have put him to death, he feared the multitude, because they counted him as a prophet. [6]But when Herod's birthday was kept, the daughter of Herodias danced before them, and pleased Herod. [7]Whereupon he promised with an oath to give her whatsoever she would ask. [8]And she, being before instructed of her mother, said, Give me here John Baptist's head in a charger. [9]And the king was sorry: nevertheless for the oath's sake, and them which sat with him at meat, he commanded *it* to be given *her*. [10]And he sent, and beheaded John in the prison. [11]And his head was brought in a charger, and given to the damsel: and she brought *it* to her mother. [12]And his disciples came, and took up the body, and buried it, and went and told Jesus.

[13]When Jesus heard *of it*, he departed thence by ship into a desert place apart: and when the people had heard *thereof*, they followed him on foot out of the cities. [14]And Jesus went forth, and saw a great multitude, and was moved with compassion toward them, and he healed their sick. [15]And when it was evening, his disciples came to him, saying, This is a desert place, and the time is now past; send the multitude away, that they may go into the villages, and buy themselves victuals. [16]But Jesus said unto them, They need not depart; give ye them to eat. [17]And they say unto him, We have here but five loaves, and two fishes. [18]He said, Bring them hither to me. [19]And he commanded the multitude to sit down on the grass, and took the five loaves, and the two fishes, and looking up to heaven, he blessed, and brake, and gave

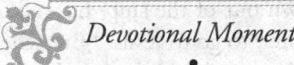

Devotional Moment
•
Solitude
14:23-24 Jesus knew when to withdraw himself, to refresh and restore himself. Do you feel so overwhelmed by constantly giving and providing that you never have time or energy to draw back for quiet times with God? Remember that everyone benefits when you take good care of your spiritual health. As much as possible, make time each day to read the Bible and pray alone. Do what you can to build up your spiritual reserves by praying and meditating on God's Word.

the loaves to *his* disciples, and the disciples to the multitude. [20]And they did all eat, and were filled: and they took up of the fragments that remained twelve baskets full. [21]And they that had eaten were about five thousand men, beside women and children.

[22]And straightway Jesus constrained his disciples to get into a ship, and to go before him unto the other side, while he sent the multitudes away. [23]And when he had sent the multitudes away, he went up into a mountain apart to pray: and when the evening was come, he was there alone. [24]But the ship was now in the midst of the sea, tossed with waves: for the wind was contrary. [25]And in the fourth watch of the night Jesus went unto them, walking on the sea. [26]And when the disciples saw him walking on the sea, they were troubled, saying, It is a spirit; and they cried out for fear. [27]But straightway Jesus spake unto them, saying, Be of good cheer; it is I; be not afraid. [28]And Peter answered him and said, Lord, if it be thou, bid me come unto thee on the water. [29]And he said, Come. And when Peter was

come down out of the ship, he walked on the water, to go to Jesus. ³⁰But when he saw the wind boisterous[b], he was afraid; and beginning to sink, he cried, saying, Lord, save me. ³¹And immediately Jesus stretched forth *his* hand, and caught him, and said unto him, O thou of little faith, wherefore didst thou doubt? ³²And when they were come into the ship, the wind ceased. ³³Then they that were in the ship came and worshipped him, saying, Of a truth thou art the Son of God.

³⁴And when they were gone over, they came into the land of Gennesaret. ³⁵And when the men of that place had knowledge of him, they sent out into all that country round about, and brought unto him all that were diseased; ³⁶And besought him that they might only touch the hem of his garment: and as many as touched were made perfectly whole.

15

¹Then came to Jesus scribes and Pharisees, which were of Jerusalem, saying, ²Why do thy disciples transgress the tradition of the elders? for they wash not their hands when they eat bread. ³But he answered and said unto them, Why do ye also transgress the commandment of God by your tradition? ⁴For God commanded, saying, Honour thy father and mother: and, He that curseth father or mother, let him die the death. ⁵But ye say, Whosoever shall say to *his* father or *his* mother, It is a gift, by whatsoever thou mightest be profited by me; ⁶And honour not his father or his mother, *he shall be free.* Thus have ye

made the commandment of God of none effect by your tradition. ⁷ *Ye* hypocrites, well did Esaias prophesy of you, saying, ⁸This people draweth nigh unto me with their mouth, and honoureth me with *their* lips; but their heart is far from me. ⁹But in vain they do worship me, teaching *for* doctrines the commandments of men.

¹⁰And he called the multitude, and said unto them, Hear, and understand: ¹¹Not that which goeth into the mouth defileth a man; but that which cometh out of the mouth, this defileth a man. ¹²Then came his disciples, and said unto him, Knowest thou that the Pharisees were offended, after they heard this saying? ¹³But he answered and said, Every plant, which my heavenly Father hath not planted, shall be rooted up. ¹⁴Let them alone: they be blind leaders of the blind. And if the blind lead the blind, both shall fall into the ditch. ¹⁵Then answered Peter and said unto him, Declare unto us this parable. ¹⁶And Jesus said, Are ye also yet without understanding? ¹⁷Do not ye yet understand, that whatsoever entereth in at the mouth goeth into the belly, and is cast

---

[b] boisterous: or, strong

Breaking Free from One-Sided Love

When Jesus came into the coasts of Caesarea Philippi, he asked his disciples, saying, "Whom do men say that I the Son of man am?" Matthew 16:13

There are two sides to love, both a hard side and a soft side, and each makes a positive contribution to a healthy relationship.

Picture a beautiful rose. The stem and thorns of a rose represent the hard side. They offer strength, stability, consistency, and protection. But no one would travel to see a garden of stems and thorns. These hard elements provide the environment in which soft petals can bloom and display their beauty. To have a beautiful rose takes both the hardness of stems and thorns and the softness of petals.

Love for others similarly requires a hardness and a softness.

Susan came from a family where she only saw God's hard side. Susan grew up knowing all about judgment and discipline. What she never experienced was God's soft side—his forgiveness, compassion, and unconditional love. Even today, Susan struggles with truly feeling loved and accepted by God or others.

Jana, on the other hand, came from a home in which God's soft side was emphasized too much. In her family, there were no rules—just an unspoken message that God would forgive them for "anything." They felt free to live however they wanted. Because her parents ignored the hard side of God's love, which includes rules and ethical commands, such as to avoid sexual temptation, Jana became pregnant and ran headlong into the hard consequences of sin.

Jesus loved Peter with both sides. In Matthew 16:17-19 he blessed Peter for his great confession of faith—genuine words of warmth and affirmation. But when Peter tried to turn Jesus from his mission, Jesus forcefully confronted Peter because that's what Peter needed (Matt. 16:23).

Is this an isolated example of God's love? Certainly not. The book of Isaiah gives a wonderfully descriptive picture of the two sides of God's love. In Isaiah 40, the prophet is reintroducing the people to God after nearly forty years of captivity in Babylon. How did Isaiah represent God?

"Behold, the Lord God will come with strong hand, and his arm shall rule for him" (Isa. 40:10).

Clearly, that's a picture of God's hard-side traits and love. Our God is like a mighty warrior, confident in battle. But Isaiah goes on:

"He shall feed his flock like a shepherd: he shall gather the lambs with his arm, . . . and shall gently lead those that are with young" (Isa. 40:11).

How much softer can you get than gently leading ewes with their young? Such softness represents God's caring, love, and compassion for us.

Perhaps you've been giving only one side of love. Maybe you can point out someone's mistake in a second but haven't uttered a word of praise in years. Perhaps your natural softness has been exaggerated into an acceptance and "nonconfrontation" of your spouse's drinking problem—and your unwillingness to confront the situation is actually perpetuating it. In either case, your love is out of balance.

Take time for reflection right now. Which side of love—hard side or soft side—do you see yourself expressing more? What are three steps you could take in the next six months that would help you develop the soft side of love (such as volunteering to help at vacation Bible school or working with people with AIDS)? What are three steps that would help you develop a more healthy hard side (such as saying no once a day—even if it's to a second piece of pie—to build discipline and confidence, or setting a date to confront a problem with a friend)? Like a rose, your love won't bloom the way God intended unless you're showing both sides of love.

---

out into the draught? ¹⁸But those things which proceed out of the mouth come forth from the heart; and they defile the man. ¹⁹For out of the heart proceed evil thoughts, murders, adulteries, fornications, thefts, false witness, blasphemies: ²⁰These are *the things* which defile a man: but to eat with unwashen hands defileth not a man.

²¹Then Jesus went thence, and departed into the coasts of Tyre and Sidon. ²²And, behold, a woman of Canaan came out of the same coasts, and cried unto him, saying, Have mercy on me, O Lord, *thou* Son of David; my daughter is grievously vexed with a devil. ²³But he answered her not a word. And his disciples came and besought him, saying, Send her away; for she crieth after us. ²⁴But he answered and said, I am not sent but unto the lost sheep of the house of Israel. ²⁵Then came she and worshipped him, saying, Lord, help me. ²⁶But he answered and said, It is not meet to take the children's

bread, and to cast *it* to dogs. ²⁷And she said, Truth, Lord: yet the dogs eat of the crumbs which fall from their masters' table. ²⁸Then Jesus answered and said unto her, O woman, great *is* thy faith: be it unto thee even as thou wilt. And her daughter was made whole from that very hour.

²⁹And Jesus departed from thence, and came nigh unto the sea of Galilee; and went up into a mountain, and sat down there. ³⁰And great multitudes came unto him, having with them *those that were* lame, blind, dumb, maimed, and many others, and cast them down at Jesus' feet; and he healed them: ³¹Insomuch that the multitude wondered, when they saw the dumb to speak, the maimed to be whole, the lame to walk, and the blind to see: and they glorified the God of Israel. ³²Then Jesus called his disciples *unto him*, and said, I have compassion on the multitude, because they continue with me now three days, and have nothing to eat: and I will not

send them away fasting, lest they faint in the way. ³³And his disciples say unto him, Whence should we have so much bread in the wilderness, as to fill so great a multitude? ³⁴And Jesus saith unto them, How many loaves have ye? And they said, Seven, and a few little fishes. ³⁵And he commanded the multitude to sit down on the ground. ³⁶And he took the seven loaves and the fishes, and gave thanks, and brake *them*, and gave to his disciples, and the disciples to the multitude. ³⁷And they did all eat, and were filled: and they took up of the broken *meat* that was left seven baskets full. ³⁸And they that did eat were four thousand men, beside women and children. ³⁹And he sent away the multitude, and took ship, and came into the coasts of Magdala.

16
¹The Pharisees also with the Sadducees came, and tempting desired him that he would shew them a sign from heaven. ²He answered and said unto them, When it is evening, ye say, *It will be* fair weather: for the sky is red. ³And in the morning, *It will be* foul weather to day: for the sky is red and lowring. O *ye* hypocrites, ye can discern the face of the sky; but can ye not *discern* the signs of the times? ⁴A wicked and adulterous generation seeketh after a sign; and there shall no sign be given unto it, but the sign of the prophet Jonas. And he left them, and departed.

⁵And when his disciples were come to the other side, they had forgotten to take bread. ⁶Then Jesus said unto them, Take heed and beware of the leaven of the Pharisees and of the Sadducees. ⁷And they reasoned among themselves, saying, *It is* because we have taken no bread. ⁸*Which* when Jesus perceived, he said unto them, O ye of little faith, why reason ye among yourselves, because ye have brought no bread? ⁹Do ye not yet understand, neither remember the five loaves of the five thousand, and how many baskets ye took up? ¹⁰Neither the seven loaves of the four thousand, and how many baskets ye took up? ¹¹How is it that ye do not understand that I spake *it* not to you concerning bread, that ye should beware of the leaven of the Pharisees and of the Sadducees? ¹²Then understood they how that he bade *them* not beware of the leaven of bread, but of the doctrine of the Pharisees and of the Sadducees.

¹³When Jesus came into the coasts of Caesarea Philippi, he asked his disciples, saying, Whom do men say that I the Son of man am? ¹⁴And they said, Some *say that thou art* John the Baptist: some, Elias; and others, Jeremias, or one of the prophets. ¹⁵He saith unto them, But whom say ye that I am? ¹⁶And Simon Peter answered and said, Thou art the Christ, the Son of the living God. ¹⁷And Jesus answered and said unto him, Blessed art thou, Simon Barjona: for flesh and blood hath not revealed *it* unto thee, but my Father which is in heaven. ¹⁸And I say also unto thee, That thou art Peterᵃ, and upon this rock I will build my church; and the gates of hell shall not prevail against it. ¹⁹And I will give unto thee the keys of the kingdom of heaven: and whatsoever thou shalt bind on earth

---

ᵃ Peter: this name signifies a rock

shall be bound in heaven: and whatsoever thou shalt loose on earth shall be loosed in heaven. ²⁰Then charged he his disciples that they should tell no man that he was Jesus the Christ.

²¹From that time forth began Jesus to shew unto his disciples, how that he must go unto Jerusalem, and suffer many things of the elders and chief priests and scribes, and be killed, and be raised again the third day. ²²Then Peter took him, and began to rebuke him, saying, Be it far from thee, Lord: this shall not be unto thee. ²³But he turned, and said unto Peter, Get thee behind me, Satan: thou art an offence unto me: for thou savourest not the things that be of God, but those that be of men.

²⁴Then said Jesus unto his disciples, If any *man* will come after me, let him deny himself, and take up his cross, and follow me. ²⁵For whosoever will save his life shall lose it: and whosoever will lose his life for my sake shall find it. ²⁶For what is a man profited, if he shall gain the whole world, and lose his own soul? or what shall a man give in exchange for his soul? ²⁷For the Son of man shall come in the glory of his Father with his angels; and then he shall reward every man according to his works. ²⁸Verily I say unto you, There be some standing here, which shall not taste of death, till they see the Son of man coming in his kingdom.

17

¹And after six days Jesus taketh Peter, James, and John his brother, and bringeth them up into an high mountain apart, ²And was transfigured before them: and his face did shine as the sun, and his raiment was white as the light.

Devotional Moment

A Taxing Question

17:24-27 The collectors of the Temple tax thought they had caught Jesus, but he obeyed the law and paid the money (throwing in a miracle for good measure!). Most people complain about taxes, yet Jesus teaches the importance of obeying the law and supporting the government. Doing our "civic duty" is one way to invest in the future. Make sure you pay the taxes you owe. And follow up your paying of taxes by voting and expressing your opinion about how such taxes are spent.

---

³And, behold, there appeared unto them Moses and Elias talking with him. ⁴Then answered Peter, and said unto Jesus, Lord, it is good for us to be here: if thou wilt, let us make here three tabernacles; one for thee, and one for Moses, and one for Elias. ⁵While he yet spake, behold, a bright cloud overshadowed them: and behold a voice out of the cloud, which said, This is my beloved Son, in whom I am well pleased; hear ye him. ⁶And when the disciples heard *it*, they fell on their face, and were sore afraid. ⁷And Jesus came and touched them, and said, Arise, and be not afraid. ⁸And when they had lifted up their eyes, they saw no man, save Jesus only. ⁹And as they came down from the mountain, Jesus charged them, saying, Tell the vision to no man, until the Son of man be risen again from the dead. ¹⁰And his disciples asked him, saying, Why then say the scribes that Elias must first come? ¹¹And Jesus answered and said unto them, Elias truly shall first come, and restore all things. ¹²But I say unto you, That Elias is come already, and they knew him not, but have

done unto him whatsoever they listed. Likewise shall also the Son of man suffer of them. ¹³Then the disciples understood that he spake unto them of John the Baptist.

¹⁴And when they were come to the multitude, there came to him a *certain* man, kneeling down to him, and saying, ¹⁵Lord, have mercy on my son: for he is lunatick, and sore vexed: for ofttimes he falleth into the fire, and oft into the water. ¹⁶And I brought him to thy disciples, and they could not cure him. ¹⁷Then Jesus answered and said, O faithless and perverse generation, how long shall I be with you? how long shall I suffer you? bring him hither to me. ¹⁸And Jesus rebuked the devil; and he departed out of him: and the child was cured from that very hour. ¹⁹Then came the disciples to Jesus apart, and said, Why could not we cast him out? ²⁰And Jesus said unto them, Because of your unbelief: for verily I say unto you, If ye have faith as a grain of mustard seed, ye shall say unto this mountain, Remove hence to yonder place; and it shall remove; and nothing shall be impossible unto you. ²¹Howbeit this kind goeth not out but by prayer and fasting.

²²And while they abode in Galilee, Jesus said unto them, The Son of man shall be betrayed into the hands of men: ²³And they shall kill him, and the third day he shall be raised again. And they were exceeding sorry.

²⁴And when they were come to Capernaum, they that received tribute[a] *money* came to Peter, and said, Doth not your master pay tribute? ²⁵He saith, Yes. And when he was come into the house, Jesus prevented him, saying, What thinkest thou, Simon? of whom do the kings of the earth take custom or tribute? of their own children, or of strangers? ²⁶Peter saith unto him, Of strangers. Jesus saith unto him, Then are the children free. ²⁷Notwithstanding, lest we should offend them, go thou to the sea, and cast an hook, and take up the fish that first cometh up; and when thou hast opened his mouth, thou shalt find a piece of money: that take, and give unto them for me and thee.

18

¹At the same time came the disciples unto Jesus, saying, Who is the greatest in the kingdom of heaven? ²And Jesus called a little child unto him, and set him in the midst of them, ³And said, Verily I say unto you, Except ye be converted, and become as little children, ye shall not enter into the kingdom of heaven. ⁴Whosoever therefore shall humble himself as this little child, the same is greatest in the kingdom of heaven. ⁵And whoso shall receive one such little child in my name receiveth me. ⁶But whoso shall offend one of these little ones which believe in me, it were better for him that a millstone were hanged about his neck, and *that* he were drowned in the depth of the sea.

⁷Woe unto the world because of offences! for it must needs be that offences come; but woe to that man by whom the offence cometh! ⁸Wherefore

---

[a] tribute: called in the original, didrachma, being in value fifteen pence sterling; about thirty seven cents

if thy hand or thy foot offend thee, cut them off, and cast *them* from thee: it is better for thee to enter into life halt or maimed, rather than having two hands or two feet to be cast into everlasting fire. ⁹And if thine eye offend thee, pluck it out, and cast *it* from thee: it is better for thee to enter into life with one eye, rather than having two eyes to be cast into hell fire. ¹⁰Take heed that ye despise not one of these little ones; for I say unto you, That in heaven their angels do always behold the face of my Father which is in heaven. ¹¹For the Son of man is come to save that which was lost. ¹²How think ye? if a man have an hundred sheep, and one of them be gone astray, doth he not leave the ninety and nine, and goeth into the mountains, and seeketh that which is gone astray? ¹³And if so be that he find it, verily I say unto you, he rejoiceth more of that *sheep*, than of the ninety and nine which went not astray. ¹⁴Even so it is not the will of your Father which is in heaven, that one of these little ones should perish.

¹⁵Moreover if thy brother shall trespass against thee, go and tell him his fault between thee and him alone: if he shall hear thee, thou hast gained thy brother. ¹⁶But if he will not hear *thee*, *then* take with thee one or two more, that in the mouth of two or three witnesses every word may be established. ¹⁷And if he shall neglect to hear them, tell *it* unto the church: but if he neglect to hear the church, let him be unto thee as an heathen man and a publican. ¹⁸Verily I say unto you, Whatsoever ye shall bind on earth shall be bound in heaven: and whatsoever ye shall loose on earth shall be loosed in heaven. ¹⁹Again I say unto you, That if two of you shall agree on earth as touching any thing that they shall ask, it shall be done for them of my Father which is in heaven. ²⁰For where two or three are gathered together in my name, there am I in the midst of them.

²¹Then came Peter to him, and said, Lord, how oft shall my brother sin against me, and I forgive him? till seven times? ²²Jesus saith unto him, I say not unto thee, Until seven times: but, Until seventy times seven. ²³Therefore is the kingdom of heaven likened unto a cer-

Getting Past Your Childhood

by David Stoop

The Bible makes it clear that the only way we can put negative parts of the past behind us is through forgiveness—unlimited forgiveness. Like Peter, we struggle with this. Our problem with forgiving comes mainly from four myths about it.

Myth: Forgiveness is something we do quickly. Sometimes it takes time for us to work through the hurts involved. We can't *easily* forgive because sin does real, lasting damage. Yet God has made forgiveness possible through the completed work of Jesus Christ on the cross. If we are willing to take the necessary *time* to forgive, we can do it.

Myth: Forgiveness is the same as condoning what the person did. Many people withhold forgiveness because they believe that to forgive is to condone the offense that occurred. But true forgiveness never condones the wrong. No one hates sin more than God, yet God forgives. Sin is serious—that is made clear by the high price that Jesus Christ paid on the cross. When we forgive, we acknowledge that wrong has been done, but we don't condone it.

Myth: In order to forgive, we must forget. We often support this mistaken idea with verses such as Psalm 103:12, which says that God removes our sins "as far as the east is from the west"— that is, he "forgets." But when we insist that our forgiving must be just like God's, we lose sight of the fact that God doesn't need to learn from the experience, we do—and to learn, we *must* remember. If we do not, we will repeatedly place ourselves in hurtful situations. To forgive does not necessarily mean to forget.

Myth: Forgiveness and reconciliation are the same. Some believe that in order to forgive we must first be reconciled with the offender. We believe that forgiveness and reconciliation are the same. But what if the person I am seeking to forgive refuses to be reconciled? Then am I unable to forgive? Not at all. Forgiveness and reconciliation are completely separate. When one person refuses reconciliation, the other can still forgive.

The truth about forgiveness. Forgiveness is the canceling of a debt that cannot be paid. When God forgave all our sins, he "took it out of the way, nailing it to his cross" (Col. 2:14). Whatever someone has done to us, we need to acknowledge that he or she can never "pay the debt." When a bank cannot collect payment on a debt, it carefully investigates whether there is any hope of ever collecting payment, and if there isn't, it forgives the loan—cancels the debt. We must learn to forgive others regardless of their ability or willingness to "pay the debt" we feel they owe us for whatever wrong was done. Most often, whatever is owed to us can never be paid back anyway.

In Jesus' day, the rabbis said that a person should forgive three times. Why did Jesus stretch Peter's generous offer to the exorbitant number of 490 times? Because he wants us to realize that forgiveness is at the very heart of God. If we want to be set free from the bondage of the past, we can find that freedom through forgiving.

We are like the servant in the parable of the unforgiving debtor (Matt. 18:23-35), who was forgiven a debt he could never repay. Gratitude for our canceled debt must make us into forgiving people. We have been forgiven, and now we need to go home and forgive. It's not easy, but families who do will thrive.

DIGGING DEEPER

1. What happens if the other person denies the issue or refuses to hear us out? Can we be unreconciled and still forgive? See Matthew 5:23-24 and also Genesis 26:26-29, Matthew 18:15-17, Philippians 4:2-3, and Philemon 1:25.

2. What role does anger play in forgiveness? Often, someone who forgives but holds on to anger ends up simply excusing the other person's behavior. How can we be angry without sinning (Eph. 4:26) in our process of forgiveness?

3. Read through Genesis 42:1–50:26. Joseph had already forgiven his brothers, and he was testing them to see how they felt about the wicked deed they had done to him. He wanted to know if he could be reconciled to them. What tests could you use to see if the person you have forgiven is ready to reconcile?

Devotional Moment
•
Forgiveness, Part 2

18:35 Jesus commanded us to forgive one another as God forgives us. Forgiving someone for words spoken in anger or for matters that only hurt our pride is relatively simple—it's basically a decision we must make. Where there is serious or even permanent damage, however, forgiveness becomes more complicated. While we are still called to *forgive*, we must not confuse forgiving with the excusing of sin. When the offense is habitual, perhaps verbal, physical, or sexual abuse, the offender needs to be confronted, not excused. If you face a situation like this, seek out a trusted Christian friend or counselor to help you discern the appropriate, biblical course of action.

tain king, which would take account of his servants. ²⁴And when he had begun to reckon, one was brought unto him, which owed him ten thousand talents[a]. ²⁵But forasmuch as he had not to pay, his lord commanded him to be sold,

and his wife, and children, and all that he had, and payment to be made. ²⁶The servant therefore fell down, and worshipped him[b], saying, Lord, have patience with me, and I will pay thee all. ²⁷Then the lord of that servant was moved with compassion, and loosed him, and forgave him the debt. ²⁸But the same servant went out, and found one of his fellowservants, which owed him an hundred pence[c]: and he laid hands on him, and took *him* by the throat, saying, Pay me that thou owest. ²⁹And his fellowservant fell down at his feet, and besought him, saying, Have patience with me, and I will pay thee all. ³⁰And he would not: but went and cast him into prison, till he should pay the debt. ³¹So when his fellowservants saw what was done, they were very sorry, and came and told unto their lord all that was done. ³²Then his lord, after that he had called him, said unto him, O thou wicked servant, I forgave thee

---

[a] talents: a talent is an ancient unit of weight

[b] worshipped him: or, besought him

[c] pence: the Roman penny is the eighth part of an ounce, which after five shillings the ounce is seven pence halfpenny; about fourteen cents

all that debt, because thou desiredst me: ³³Shouldest not thou also have had compassion on thy fellowservant, even as I had pity on thee? ³⁴And his lord was wroth, and delivered him to the tormentors, till he should pay all that was due unto him. ³⁵So likewise shall my heavenly Father do also unto you, if ye from your hearts forgive not every one his brother their trespasses.

19

¹And it came to pass, *that* when Jesus had finished these sayings, he departed from Galilee, and came into the coasts of Judaea beyond Jordan; ²And great multitudes followed him; and he healed them there.

³The Pharisees also came unto him, tempting him, and saying unto him, Is it lawful for a man to put away his wife for every cause? ⁴And he answered and said unto them, Have ye not read, that he which made *them* at the beginning made them male and female, ⁵And said, For this cause shall a man leave father and mother, and shall cleave to his wife: and they twain shall be one flesh? ⁶Wherefore they are no more twain, but one flesh. What therefore God hath joined together, let not man put asunder. ⁷They say unto him, Why did Moses then command to give a writing of divorcement, and to put her away? ⁸He saith unto them, Moses because of the hardness of your hearts suffered you to put away your wives: but from the beginning it was not so. ⁹And I say unto you, Whosoever shall put away his wife, except *it be* for fornication, and shall marry another, committeth adultery: and whoso marrieth her which is put away doth commit

---

Devotional Moment
•
Marriage and Divorce
19:7-8 The Pharisees again tried to trick Jesus—this time with a question about divorce. His reply affirmed that marriage was created to be a permanent bond. Many in our day roll their eyes at such a view of marriage. Yet God still sets this ideal before us. Even if divorce has touched your life, do you still revere God's standard?

---

adultery. ¹⁰His disciples say unto him, If the case of the man be so with *his* wife, it is not good to marry. ¹¹But he said unto them, All *men* cannot receive this saying, save *they* to whom it is given. ¹²For there are some eunuchs, which were so born from *their* mother's womb: and there are some eunuchs, which were made eunuchs of men: and there be eunuchs, which have made themselves eunuchs for the kingdom of heaven's sake. He that is able to receive *it*, let him receive *it*.

¹³Then were there brought unto him little children, that he should put

---

Devotional Moment
•
Childlike Faith
19:13-15 Although the disciples wanted to send the children away, Jesus wanted them close and held out their faith as an example to all. We often emphasize how much we need to teach our children. But when it comes to faith, the tables are turned, and the child teaches the adult. How would you describe your children's faith? What can they teach you about trusting God? Write down the childlike qualities you would like to see enhance your faith. Pray confidently before your heavenly Father, asking him to help you learn from your children and grow with them.

---

his hands on them, and pray: and the disciples rebuked them. ¹⁴But Jesus said, Suffer little children, and forbid them not, to come unto me: for of such is the kingdom of heaven. ¹⁵And he laid *his* hands on them, and departed thence.

¹⁶And, behold, one came and said unto him, Good Master, what good thing shall I do, that I may have eternal life? ¹⁷And he said unto him, Why callest thou me good? *there is* none good but one, *that is*, God: but if thou wilt enter into life, keep the commandments. ¹⁸He saith unto him, Which? Jesus said, Thou shalt do no murder, Thou shalt not commit adultery, Thou shalt not steal, Thou shalt not bear false witness, ¹⁹Honour thy father and *thy* mother: and, Thou shalt love thy neighbour as thyself. ²⁰The young man saith unto him, All these things have I kept from my youth up: what lack I yet? ²¹Jesus said unto him, If thou wilt be perfect, go *and* sell that thou hast, and give to the poor, and thou shalt have treasure in heaven: and come *and* follow me. ²²But when the young man heard that saying, he went away sorrowful: for he had great possessions.

²³Then said Jesus unto his disciples, Verily I say unto you, That a rich man shall hardly enter into the kingdom of heaven. ²⁴And again I say unto you, It is easier for a camel to go through the eye of a needle, than for a rich man to enter into the kingdom of God. ²⁵When his disciples heard *it*, they were exceedingly amazed, saying, Who then can be saved? ²⁶But Jesus beheld *them*, and said unto them, With men this is impossible; but with God all things are possible. ²⁷Then answered Peter and said unto him, Behold, we have forsaken all, and followed thee; what shall we have therefore? ²⁸And Jesus said unto them, Verily I say unto you, That ye which have followed me, in the regeneration when the Son of man shall sit in the throne of his glory, ye also shall sit upon twelve thrones, judging the twelve tribes of Israel. ²⁹And every one that hath forsaken houses, or brethren, or sisters, or father, or mother, or wife, or children, or lands, for my name's sake, shall receive an hundredfold, and shall inherit everlasting life. ³⁰But many *that are* first shall be last; and the last *shall be* first.

20

¹For the kingdom of heaven is like unto a man *that is* an householder, which went out early in the morning to hire labourers into his vineyard. ²And when he had agreed with the labourers for a penny[a] a day, he sent them into his vineyard. ³And he went out about the third hour, and saw others standing idle in the marketplace, ⁴And said unto them; Go ye also into the vineyard, and whatsoever is right I will give you. And they went their way. ⁵Again he went out about the sixth and ninth hour, and did likewise. ⁶And about the eleventh hour he went out, and found others standing idle, and saith unto them, Why stand ye here all the day idle? ⁷They say unto him, Because no man hath hired us. He saith unto them, Go ye also into the vineyard; and whatsoever is right, *that*

---

[a] penny: the Roman penny is the eighth part of an ounce, which after five shillings the ounce is seven pence halfpenny; about fourteen cents

shall ye receive. ⁸So when even was come, the lord of the vineyard saith unto his steward, Call the labourers, and give them *their* hire, beginning from the last unto the first. ⁹And when they came that *were hired* about the eleventh hour, they received every man a penny. ¹⁰But when the first came, they supposed that they should have received more; and they likewise received every man a penny. ¹¹And when they had received *it*, they murmured against the goodman of the house, ¹²Saying, These last have wrought[b] *but* one hour, and thou hast made them equal unto us, which have borne the burden and heat of the day. ¹³But he answered one of them, and said, Friend, I do thee no wrong: didst not thou agree with me for a penny? ¹⁴Take *that* thine *is*, and go thy way: I will give unto this last, even as unto thee. ¹⁵Is it not lawful for me to do what I will with mine own? Is thine eye evil, because I am good? ¹⁶So the last shall be first, and the first last: for many be called, but few chosen.

¹⁷And Jesus going up to Jerusalem took the twelve disciples apart in the way, and said unto them, ¹⁸Behold, we go up to Jerusalem; and the Son of man shall be betrayed unto the chief priests and unto the scribes, and they shall condemn him to death, ¹⁹And shall deliver him to the Gentiles to mock, and to scourge, and to crucify *him*: and the third day he shall rise again.

²⁰Then came to him the mother of Zebedee's children with her sons, worshipping *him*, and desiring a certain thing of him. ²¹And he said unto her, What wilt thou? She saith unto him,

---

Devotional Moment
•
Pushy Parents

20:20-23 The mother of James and John had high ambitions for her sons, but Jesus said that she did not know what she was asking. We all have high hopes and dreams for our children. We try to give them a good education and opportunities to shine, hoping that they will be successful. But we can go overboard, pushing our children beyond their interests and abilities. To do so only makes them obsessive and self-centered. Pushing them to excel in an area where they are not naturally gifted can also damage their self-esteem. When you pray for your children, do you envision specific careers and prospective jobs? Ask God to help you guide them while respecting their individual personalities and interests.

Grant that these my two sons may sit, the one on thy right hand, and the other on the left, in thy kingdom. ²²But Jesus answered and said, Ye know not what ye ask. Are ye able to drink of the cup that I shall drink of, and to be baptized with the baptism that I am baptized with? They say unto him, We are able. ²³And he saith unto them, Ye shall drink indeed of my cup, and be baptized with the baptism that I am baptized with: but to sit on my right hand, and on my left, is not mine to give, but *it shall be given to them* for whom it is prepared of my Father. ²⁴And when the ten heard *it*, they were moved with indignation against the two brethren. ²⁵But Jesus called them *unto him*, and said, Ye know that the princes of the Gentiles exercise dominion over them, and they that are great exercise authority upon them. ²⁶But it shall not be so among you: but whosoever will be great

---

b have wrought . . . : or, have continued one hour only

among you, let him be your minister; ²⁷And whosoever will be chief among you, let him be your servant: ²⁸Even as the Son of man came not to be ministered unto, but to minister, and to give his life a ransom for many.

²⁹And as they departed from Jericho, a great multitude followed him. ³⁰And, behold, two blind men sitting by the way side, when they heard that Jesus passed by, cried out, saying, Have mercy on us, O Lord, *thou* Son of David. ³¹And the multitude rebuked them, because they should hold their peace: but they cried the more, saying, Have mercy on us, O Lord, *thou* Son of David. ³²And Jesus stood still, and called them, and said, What will ye that I shall do unto you? ³³They say unto him, Lord, that our eyes may be opened. ³⁴So Jesus had compassion *on them,* and touched their eyes: and immediately their eyes received sight, and they followed him.

21

¹And when they drew nigh unto Jerusalem, and were come to Bethphage, unto the mount of Olives, then sent Jesus two disciples, ²Saying unto them, Go into the village over against you, and straightway ye shall find an ass tied, and a colt with her: loose *them,* and bring *them* unto me. ³And if any *man* say ought unto you, ye shall say, The Lord hath need of them; and straightway he will send them. ⁴All this was done, that it might be fulfilled which was spoken by the prophet, saying, ⁵Tell ye the daughter of Sion, Behold, thy King cometh unto thee, meek, and sitting upon an ass, and a colt the foal of an ass. ⁶And the disciples

went, and did as Jesus commanded them, ⁷And brought the ass, and the colt, and put on them their clothes, and they set *him* thereon. ⁸And a very great multitude spread their garments in the way; others cut down branches from the trees, and strawed *them* in the way. ⁹And the multitudes that went before, and that followed, cried, saying, Hosanna to the Son of David: Blessed *is* he that cometh in the name of the Lord; Hosanna in the highest. ¹⁰And when he was come into Jerusalem, all the city was moved, saying, Who is this? ¹¹And the multitude said, This is Jesus the prophet of Nazareth of Galilee.

¹²And Jesus went into the temple of God, and cast out all them that sold and bought in the temple, and overthrew the tables of the moneychangers, and the seats of them that sold doves, ¹³And said unto them, It is written, My house shall be called the house of prayer; but ye have made it a den of thieves. ¹⁴And the blind and the lame came to him in the temple; and he healed them. ¹⁵And when the chief priests and scribes saw the wonderful things that he did, and the children crying in the temple, and saying, Hosanna to the Son of David; they were sore displeased, ¹⁶And said unto him, Hearest thou what these say? And Jesus saith unto them, Yea; have ye never read, Out of the mouth of babes and sucklings thou hast perfected praise? ¹⁷And he left them, and went out of the city into Bethany; and he lodged there.

¹⁸Now in the morning as he returned into the city, he hungered. ¹⁹And when he saw a fig tree^a in the way, he

---

^a a fig tree: Gr. one fig tree

came to it, and found nothing thereon, but leaves only, and said unto it, Let no fruit grow on thee henceforward for ever. And presently the fig tree withered away. ²⁰And when the disciples saw *it*, they marvelled, saying, How soon is the fig tree withered away! ²¹Jesus answered and said unto them, Verily I say unto you, If ye have faith, and doubt not, ye shall not only do this *which is done* to the fig tree, but also if ye shall say unto this mountain, Be thou removed, and be thou cast into the sea; it shall be done. ²²And all things, whatsoever ye shall ask in prayer, believing, ye shall receive.

²³And when he was come into the temple, the chief priests and the elders of the people came unto him as he was teaching, and said, By what authority doest thou these things? and who gave thee this authority? ²⁴And Jesus answered and said unto them, I also will ask you one thing, which if ye tell me, I in like wise will tell you by what authority I do these things. ²⁵The baptism of John, whence was it? from heaven, or of men? And they reasoned with themselves, saying, If we shall say, From heaven; he will say unto us, Why did ye not then believe him? ²⁶But if we shall say, Of men; we fear the people; for all hold John as a prophet. ²⁷And they answered Jesus, and said, We cannot tell. And he said unto them, Neither tell I you by what authority I do these things.

²⁸But what think ye? A *certain* man had two sons; and he came to the first, and said, Son, go work to day in my vineyard. ²⁹He answered and said, I will not: but afterward he repented, and went. ³⁰And he came to the second, and said likewise. And he answered and said, I *go*, sir: and went not. ³¹Whether of them twain did the will of *his* father? They say unto him, The first. Jesus saith unto them, Verily I say unto you, That the publicans and the harlots go into the kingdom of God before you. ³²For John came unto you in the way of righteousness, and ye believed him not: but the publicans and the harlots believed him: and ye, when ye had seen *it*, repented not afterward, that ye might believe him.

³³Hear another parable: There was a certain householder, which planted a vineyard, and hedged it round about, and digged a winepress in it, and built a tower, and let it out to husbandmen, and went into a far country: ³⁴And when the time of the fruit drew near, he sent his servants to the husbandmen, that they might receive the fruits of it. ³⁵And the husbandmen took his servants, and beat one, and killed another, and stoned another. ³⁶Again, he sent other servants more than the first: and they did unto them likewise. ³⁷But last of all he sent unto them his son, saying, They will reverence my son. ³⁸But when the husbandmen saw the son, they said among them-

---

Devotional Moment

Obedience

21:28-32 In the parable of the two sons, Jesus made it clear that God values obedience more than words of good intention. We like to believe in our own good intentions. We'll even announce them to others to make sure everyone knows how well-intentioned we are. But what matters most is right actions. If you have a habit of saying and not doing, think about the consequences for not following through.

selves, This is the heir; come, let us kill him, and let us seize on his inheritance. ³⁹And they caught him, and cast *him* out of the vineyard, and slew *him.* ⁴⁰When the lord therefore of the vineyard cometh, what will he do unto those husbandmen? ⁴¹They say unto him, He will miserably destroy those wicked men, and will let out *his* vineyard unto other husbandmen, which shall render him the fruits in their seasons. ⁴²Jesus saith unto them, Did ye never read in the scriptures, The stone which the builders rejected, the same is become the head of the corner: this is the Lord's doing, and it is marvellous in our eyes? ⁴³Therefore say I unto you, The kingdom of God shall be taken from you, and given to a nation bringing forth the fruits thereof. ⁴⁴And whosoever shall fall on this stone shall be broken: but on whomsoever it shall fall, it will grind him to powder. ⁴⁵And when the chief priests and Pharisees had heard his parables, they perceived that he spake of them. ⁴⁶But when they sought to lay hands on him, they feared the multitude, because they took him for a prophet.

22

¹And Jesus answered and spake unto them again by parables, and said, ²The kingdom of heaven is like unto a certain king, which made a marriage for his son, ³And sent forth his servants to call them that were bidden to the wedding: and they would not come. ⁴Again, he sent forth other servants, saying, Tell them which are bidden, Behold, I have prepared my dinner: my oxen and *my* fatlings *are* killed, and all things *are* ready: come unto the marriage. ⁵But they

made light of *it,* and went their ways, one to his farm, another to his merchandise: ⁶And the remnant took his servants, and entreated *them* spitefully, and slew *them.* ⁷But when the king heard *thereof,* he was wroth: and he sent forth his armies, and destroyed those murderers, and burned up their city. ⁸Then saith he to his servants, The wedding is ready, but they which were bidden were not worthy. ⁹Go ye therefore into the highways, and as many as ye shall find, bid to the marriage. ¹⁰So those servants went out into the highways, and gathered together all as many as they found, both bad and good: and the wedding was furnished with guests. ¹¹And when the king came in to see the guests, he saw there a man which had not on a wedding garment: ¹²And he saith unto him, Friend, how camest thou in hither not having a wedding garment? And he was speechless. ¹³Then said the king to the servants, Bind him hand and foot, and take him away, and cast *him* into outer darkness; there shall be weeping and gnashing of teeth. ¹⁴For many are called, but few *are* chosen.

¹⁵Then went the Pharisees, and took counsel how they might entangle him in *his* talk. ¹⁶And they sent out unto him their disciples with the Herodians, saying, Master, we know that thou art true, and teachest the way of God in truth, neither carest thou for any *man:* for thou regardest not the person of men. ¹⁷Tell us therefore, What thinkest thou? Is it lawful to give tribute unto Caesar, or not? ¹⁸But Jesus perceived their wickedness, and said, Why tempt ye me, *ye* hypocrites? ¹⁹Shew me the tribute money. And they brought unto him a penny^a.

ª penny: in value seven pence halfpenny

²⁰And he saith unto them, Whose *is* this image and superscription^b? ²¹They say unto him, Caesar's. Then saith he unto them, Render therefore unto Caesar the things which are Caesar's; and unto God the things that are God's. ²²When they had heard *these words*, they marvelled, and left him, and went their way.

²³The same day came to him the Sadducees, which say that there is no resurrection, and asked him, ²⁴Saying, Master, Moses said, If a man die, having no children, his brother shall marry his wife, and raise up seed unto his brother. ²⁵Now there were with us seven brethren: and the first, when he had married a wife, deceased, and, having no issue, left his wife unto his brother: ²⁶Likewise the second also, and the third, unto the seventh^c. ²⁷And last of all the woman died also. ²⁸Therefore in the resurrection whose wife shall she be of the seven? for they all had her. ²⁹Jesus answered and said unto them, Ye do err, not knowing the scriptures, nor the power of God. ³⁰For in the resurrection they neither marry, nor are given in marriage, but are as the angels of God in heaven. ³¹But as touching the resurrection of the dead, have ye not read that which was spoken unto you by God, saying, ³²I am the God of Abraham, and the God of Isaac, and the God of Jacob? God is not the God of the dead, but of the living. ³³And when the multitude heard *this*, they were astonished at his doctrine.

³⁴But when the Pharisees had heard that he had put the Sadducees to silence, they were gathered together.

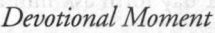

Devotional Moment

Loving God and Neighbor

22:36-40 God commands us to love him with all our heart, soul, and mind, and our neighbor as ourself. We are to love God, our spouse, our children, our neighbors, and we can't forget ourself either. That's a lot of loving! And if your day has been long and the work hard, you may wonder if all that loving is an unattainable ideal. Remember the Source. You will find that the days your heart is close to God are also the days you will have loads of love for the Very Important Persons around you. "Beloved, let us love one another: for love is of God" (1 John 4:7).

³⁵Then one of them, *which was* a lawyer, asked *him a question*, tempting him, and saying, ³⁶Master, which *is* the great commandment in the law? ³⁷Jesus said unto him, Thou shalt love the Lord thy God with all thy heart, and with all thy soul, and with all thy mind. ³⁸This is the first and great commandment. ³⁹And the second *is* like unto it, Thou shalt love thy neighbour as thyself. ⁴⁰On these two commandments hang all the law and the prophets.

⁴¹While the Pharisees were gathered together, Jesus asked them, ⁴²Saying, What think ye of Christ? whose son is he? They say unto him, *The Son* of David. ⁴³He saith unto them, How then doth David in spirit call him Lord, saying, ⁴⁴The LORD said unto my Lord, Sit thou on my right hand, till I make thine enemies thy footstool? ⁴⁵If David then call him Lord, how is he his son? ⁴⁶And no man was able to answer him a word, neither durst any *man*

---

^b superscription: or, inscription
^c seventh: Gr. seven

from that day forth ask him any more *questions.*

23

[1]Then spake Jesus to the multitude, and to his disciples, [2]Saying, The scribes and the Pharisees sit in Moses' seat: [3]All therefore whatsoever they bid you observe, *that* observe and do; but do not ye after their works: for they say, and do not. [4]For they bind heavy burdens and grievous to be borne, and lay *them* on men's shoulders; but they *themselves* will not move them with one of their fingers. [5]But all their works they do for to be seen of men: they make broad their phylacteries[a], and enlarge the borders of their garments, [6]And love the uppermost rooms at feasts, and the chief seats in the synagogues, [7]And greetings in the markets, and to be called of men, Rabbi, Rabbi. [8]But be not ye called Rabbi: for one is your Master, *even* Christ; and all ye are brethren. [9]And call no *man* your father upon the earth: for one is your Father, which is in heaven. [10]Neither be ye called masters: for one is your Master, *even* Christ. [11]But he that is greatest among you shall be your servant. [12]And whosoever shall exalt himself shall be abased; and he that shall humble himself shall be exalted.

[13]But woe unto you, scribes and Pharisees, hypocrites! for ye shut up the kingdom of heaven against men: for ye neither go in *yourselves,* neither suffer ye them that are entering to go in. [14]Woe unto you, scribes and Pharisees, hypocrites! for ye devour widows' houses, and for a pretence make long prayer: therefore ye shall receive the greater damnation. [15]Woe unto you, scribes and Pharisees, hypocrites! for ye compass sea and land to make one proselyte, and when he is made, ye make him twofold more the child of hell than yourselves. [16]Woe unto you, *ye* blind guides, which say, Whosoever shall swear by the temple, it is nothing; but whosoever shall swear by the gold of the temple, he is a debtor! [17]*Ye* fools and blind: for whether is greater, the gold, or the temple that sanctifieth the gold? [18]And, Whosoever shall swear by the altar, it is nothing; but whosoever sweareth by the gift that is upon it, he is guilty[b]. [19]*Ye* fools and blind: for whether *is* greater, the gift, or the altar that sanctifieth the gift? [20]Whoso therefore shall swear by the altar, sweareth by it, and by all things thereon. [21]And whoso shall swear by the temple, sweareth by it, and by him that dwelleth therein. [22]And he that shall swear by heaven, sweareth by the throne of God, and by him that sitteth thereon. [23]Woe unto you, scribes and Pharisees, hypocrites! for ye pay tithe of mint and anise[c] and cummin, and have omitted the weightier *matters* of the law, judgment, mercy, and faith: these ought ye to have done, and not to leave the other undone. [24]*Ye* blind guides, which strain at a gnat, and swallow a camel. [25]Woe unto you, scribes and Pharisees, hypocrites! for ye make clean the outside of the cup and of the platter, but within they are full of extortion

---

[a] phylacteries: pieces of parchment containing sentences of the law
[b] guilty: or, debtor, or, bound
[c] anise: Gr. dill

and excess. ²⁶*Thou* blind Pharisee, cleanse first that *which is* within the cup and platter, that the outside of them may be clean also. ²⁷Woe unto you, scribes and Pharisees, hypocrites! for ye are like unto whited sepulchres, which indeed appear beautiful outward, but are within full of dead *men's* bones, and of all uncleanness. ²⁸Even so ye also outwardly appear righteous unto men, but within ye are full of hypocrisy and iniquity. ²⁹Woe unto you, scribes and Pharisees, hypocrites! because ye build the tombs of the prophets, and garnish the sepulchres of the righteous, ³⁰And say, If we had been in the days of our fathers, we would not have been partakers with them in the blood of the prophets. ³¹Wherefore ye be witnesses unto yourselves, that ye are the children of them which killed the prophets. ³²Fill ye up then the measure of your fathers. ³³*Ye* serpents, *ye* generation of vipers, how can ye escape the damnation of hell?

³⁴Wherefore, behold, I send unto you prophets, and wise men, and scribes: and *some* of them ye shall kill and crucify; and *some* of them shall ye scourge in your synagogues, and persecute *them* from city to city: ³⁵That upon you may come all the righteous blood shed upon the earth, from the blood of righteous Abel unto the blood of Zacharias son of Barachias, whom ye slew between the temple and the altar. ³⁶Verily I say unto you, All these things shall come upon this generation. ³⁷O Jerusalem, Jerusalem, *thou* that killest the prophets, and stonest them which are sent unto thee, how often would I have gathered thy children together, even as a hen gathereth her chickens under *her* wings, and ye would not!

Devotional Moment
•
The Key

23:37 Jesus grieved over the city of Jerusalem because the people who lived there had rejected God's spokesmen. They had heard the words; they had understood the messages; yet they had rejected God's ways because their hearts were hard. God pleads with all of us to stop resisting his love. Soften your heart to God's Word.

---

³⁸Behold, your house is left unto you desolate. ³⁹For I say unto you, Ye shall not see me henceforth, till ye shall say, Blessed *is* he that cometh in the name of the Lord.

24

¹And Jesus went out, and departed from the temple: and his disciples came to *him* for to shew him the buildings of the temple. ²And Jesus said unto them, See ye not all these things? verily I say unto you, There shall not be left here one stone upon another, that shall not be thrown down. ³And as he sat upon the mount of Olives, the disciples came unto him privately, saying, Tell us, when shall these things be? and what *shall be* the sign of thy coming, and of the end of the world?

⁴And Jesus answered and said unto them, Take heed that no man deceive you. ⁵For many shall come in my name, saying, I am Christ; and shall deceive many. ⁶And ye shall hear of wars and rumours of wars: see that ye be not troubled: for all *these things* must come to pass, but the end is not yet. ⁷For nation shall rise against nation, and kingdom against kingdom: and there shall be famines, and pestilences, and earth-

quakes, in divers places. ⁸All these *are* the beginning of sorrows. ⁹Then shall they deliver you up to be afflicted, and shall kill you: and ye shall be hated of all nations for my name's sake. ¹⁰And then shall many be offended, and shall betray one another, and shall hate one another. ¹¹And many false prophets shall rise, and shall deceive many. ¹²And because iniquity shall abound, the love of many shall wax cold. ¹³But he that shall endure unto the end, the same shall be saved. ¹⁴And this gospel of the kingdom shall be preached in all the world for a witness unto all nations; and then shall the end come. ¹⁵When ye therefore shall see the abomination of desolation, spoken of by Daniel the prophet, stand in the holy place, (whoso readeth, let him understand:) ¹⁶Then let them which be in Judaea flee into the mountains: ¹⁷Let him which is on the housetop not come down to take any thing out of his house: ¹⁸ Neither let him which is in the field return back to take his clothes. ¹⁹And woe unto them that are with child, and to them that give suck in those days! ²⁰But pray ye that your flight be not in the winter, neither on the sabbath day: ²¹For then shall be great tribulation, such as was not since the beginning of the world to this time, no, nor ever shall be. ²²And except those days should be shortened, there should no flesh be saved: but for the elect's sake those days shall be shortened. ²³Then if any man shall say unto you, Lo, here *is* Christ, or there; believe *it* not. ²⁴For there shall arise false Christs, and false prophets, and shall shew great signs and wonders;

insomuch that, if *it were* possible, they shall deceive the very elect. ²⁵Behold, I have told you before. ²⁶Wherefore if they shall say unto you, Behold, he is in the desert; go not forth: behold, *he is* in the secret chambers; believe *it* not. ²⁷For as the lightning cometh out of the east, and shineth even unto the west; so shall also the coming of the Son of man be. ²⁸For wheresoever the carcase is, there will the eagles be gathered together. ²⁹Immediately after the tribulation of those days shall the sun be darkened, and the moon shall not give her light, and the stars shall fall from heaven, and the powers of the heavens shall be shaken: ³⁰And then shall appear the sign of the Son of man in heaven: and then shall all the tribes of the earth mourn, and they shall see the Son of man coming in the clouds of heaven with power and great glory. ³¹And he shall send his angels with[a] a great sound of a trumpet, and they shall gather together his elect from the four winds, from one end of heaven to the other.

³²Now learn a parable of the fig tree; When his branch is yet tender, and putteth forth leaves, ye know that summer *is* nigh: ³³So likewise ye, when ye shall see all these things, know that it is near, *even* at the doors. ³⁴Verily I say unto you, This generation shall not pass, till all these things be fulfilled. ³⁵Heaven and earth shall pass away, but my words shall not pass away. ³⁶But of that day and hour knoweth no *man*, no, not the angels of heaven, but my Father only. ³⁷But as the days of Noe *were*, so shall also the coming of the Son of man be. ³⁸For as in the days that were before the flood they were

---

[a] with . . . : or, with a trumpet, and a great voice

eating and drinking, marrying and giving in marriage, until the day that Noe entered into the ark, ³⁹And knew not until the flood came, and took them all away; so shall also the coming of the Son of man be. ⁴⁰Then shall two be in the field; the one shall be taken, and the other left. ⁴¹Two *women shall be* grinding at the mill; the one shall be taken, and the other left. ⁴²Watch therefore: for ye know not what hour your Lord doth come. ⁴³But know this, that if the goodman of the house had known in what watch the thief would come, he would have watched, and would not have suffered his house to be broken up. ⁴⁴Therefore be ye also ready: for in such an hour as ye think not the Son of man cometh. ⁴⁵Who then is a faithful and wise servant, whom his lord hath made ruler over his household, to give them meat in due season? ⁴⁶Blessed *is* that servant, whom his lord when he cometh shall find so doing. ⁴⁷Verily I say unto you, That he shall make him ruler over all his goods. ⁴⁸But and if that evil servant shall say in his heart, My lord delayeth his coming; ⁴⁹And shall begin to smite *his* fellowservants, and to eat and drink with the drunken; ⁵⁰The lord of that servant shall come in a day when he looketh not for *him*, and in an hour that he is not aware of, ⁵¹And shall cutᵇ him asunder, and appoint *him* his portion with the hypocrites: there shall be weeping and gnashing of teeth.

25

¹Then shall the kingdom of heaven be likened unto ten virgins, which took their lamps, and went forth to meet the bridegroom. ²And five of them were wise, and five *were* foolish. ³They that *were* foolish took their lamps, and took no oil with them: ⁴But the wise took oil in their vessels with their lamps. ⁵While the bridegroom tarried, they all slumbered and slept. ⁶And at midnight there was a cry made, Behold, the bridegroom cometh; go ye out to meet him. ⁷Then all those virgins arose, and trimmed their lamps. ⁸And the foolish said unto the wise, Give us of your oil; for our lamps are gone outᵃ. ⁹But the wise answered, saying, *Not so*; lest there be not enough for us and you: but go ye rather to them that sell, and buy for yourselves. ¹⁰And while they went to buy, the bridegroom came; and they that were ready went in with him to the marriage: and the door was shut. ¹¹Afterward came also the other virgins, saying, Lord, Lord, open to us. ¹²But he answered and said, Verily I say unto you, I know you not. ¹³Watch therefore, for ye know neither the day nor the hour wherein the Son of man cometh.

¹⁴For *the kingdom of heaven is* as a man travelling into a far country, *who* called his own servants, and delivered unto them his goods. ¹⁵And unto one he gave five talentsᵇ, to another two, and to another one; to every man according to his several ability; and straightway took his journey. ¹⁶Then he that had received the five talents went and traded with the same, and made *them* other five talents. ¹⁷And likewise he that *had received* two, he also gained

---

ᵇ cut . . . : or, cut him off
ᵃ gone out: or, going out
ᵇ talents: a talent is <187> pounds ten shillings

other two. ¹⁸But he that had received one went and digged in the earth, and hid his lord's money. ¹⁹After a long time the lord of those servants cometh, and reckoneth with them. ²⁰And so he that had received five talents came and brought other five talents, saying, Lord, thou deliveredst unto me five talents: behold, I have gained beside them five talents more. ²¹His lord said unto him, Well done, *thou* good and faithful servant: thou hast been faithful over a few things, I will make thee ruler over many things: enter thou into the joy of thy lord. ²²He also that had received two talents came and said, Lord, thou deliveredst unto me two talents: behold, I have gained two other talents beside them. ²³His lord said unto him, Well done, good and faithful servant; thou hast been faithful over a few things, I will make thee ruler over many things: enter thou into the joy of thy lord. ²⁴Then he which had received the one talent came and said, Lord, I knew thee that thou art an hard man, reaping where thou hast not sown, and gathering where thou hast not strawed: ²⁵And I was afraid, and went and hid thy talent in the earth: lo, *there* thou hast *that is* thine. ²⁶ His lord answered and said unto him, *Thou* wicked and slothful servant, thou knewest that I reap where I sowed not, and gather where I have not strawed: ²⁷Thou oughtest therefore to have put my money to the exchangers, and *then* at my coming I should have received mine own with usury. ²⁸Take therefore the talent from him, and give *it* unto him which hath ten talents. ²⁹For unto every one that hath shall be given, and he shall have abundance: but from him that hath not shall

---

> ### Devotional Moment
> •
> ### Laziness
>
> 25:24-30 God rewards our honest efforts and holds us accountable for how we use our resources and abilities. If your home is a refuge from the demanding and competitive world, it can also become a hideout for couch potatoes who prefer cool comfort and video entertainment to study, chores, and other responsibilities. Don't let your home be a lodge for the lazy.

---

be taken away even that which he hath. ³⁰And cast ye the unprofitable servant into outer darkness: there shall be weeping and gnashing of teeth.

³¹When the Son of man shall come in his glory, and all the holy angels with him, then shall he sit upon the throne of his glory: ³²And before him shall be gathered all nations: and he shall separate them one from another, as a shepherd divideth *his* sheep from the goats: ³³And he shall set the sheep on his right hand, but the goats on the left. ³⁴Then shall the King say unto them on his right hand, Come, ye blessed of my Father, inherit the kingdom prepared for you from the foundation of the world: ³⁵For I was an hungred, and ye gave me meat: I was thirsty, and ye gave me drink: I was a stranger, and ye took me in: ³⁶Naked, and ye clothed me: I was sick, and ye visited me: I was in prison, and ye came unto me. ³⁷Then shall the righteous answer him, saying, Lord, when saw we thee an hungred, and fed *thee?* or thirsty, and gave *thee* drink? ³⁸When saw we thee a stranger, and took *thee* in? or naked, and clothed *thee?* ³⁹Or when saw we thee sick, or in prison, and came unto thee? ⁴⁰And the King shall answer and say unto them,

Verily I say unto you, Inasmuch as ye have done *it* unto one of the least of these my brethren, ye have done *it* unto me. ⁴¹Then shall he say also unto them on the left hand, Depart from me, ye cursed, into everlasting fire, prepared for the devil and his angels: ⁴²For I was an hungred, and ye gave me no meat: I was thirsty, and ye gave me no drink: ⁴³I was a stranger, and ye took me not in: naked, and ye clothed me not: sick, and in prison, and ye visited me not. ⁴⁴Then shall they also answer him, saying, Lord, when saw we thee an hungred, or athirst, or a stranger, or naked, or sick, or in prison, and did not minister unto thee? ⁴⁵Then shall he answer them, saying, Verily I say unto you, Inasmuch as ye did *it* not to one of the least of these, ye did *it* not to me. ⁴⁶And these shall go away into everlasting punishment: but the righteous into life eternal.

26

¹And it came to pass, when Jesus had finished all these sayings, he said unto his disciples, ²Ye know that after two days is *the feast of* the passover, and the Son of man is betrayed to be crucified. ³Then assembled together the chief priests, and the scribes, and the elders of the people, unto the palace of the high priest, who was called Caiaphas, ⁴And consulted that they might take Jesus by subtilty, and kill *him.* ⁵But they said, Not on the feast *day,* lest there be an uproar among the people.

⁶Now when Jesus was in Bethany, in the house of Simon the leper, ⁷There came unto him a woman having an alabaster box of very precious ointment, and poured it on his head, as he sat *at meat.* ⁸But when his disciples saw *it,* they had indignation, saying, To what purpose *is* this waste? ⁹For this ointment might have been sold for much, and given to the poor. ¹⁰When Jesus understood *it,* he said unto them, Why trouble ye the woman? for she hath wrought a good work upon me. ¹¹For ye have the poor always with you; but me ye have not always. ¹²For in that she hath poured this ointment on my body, she did *it* for my burial. ¹³Verily I say unto you, Wheresoever this gospel shall be preached in the whole world, *there* shall also this, that this woman hath done, be told for a memorial of her.

¹⁴Then one of the twelve, called Judas Iscariot, went unto the chief priests, ¹⁵And said *unto them,* What will ye give me, and I will deliver him unto you? And they covenanted with him for thirty pieces of silver. ¹⁶And from that time he sought opportunity to betray him.

¹⁷Now the first *day* of the *feast of* unleavened bread the disciples came to Jesus, saying unto him, Where wilt thou that we prepare for thee to eat the passover? ¹⁸And he said, Go into the city to such a man, and say unto him, The Master saith, My time is at hand; I will keep the passover at thy house with my disciples. ¹⁹And the disciples did as Jesus had appointed them; and they made ready the passover. ²⁰Now when the even was come, he sat down with the twelve. ²¹And as they did eat, he said, Verily I say unto you, that one of you shall betray me. ²²And they were exceeding sorrowful, and began every one of them to say unto him, Lord, is it I? ²³And he answered and said, He that dippeth *his* hand with me in the dish, the same shall betray me. ²⁴The Son of

man goeth as it is written of him: but woe unto that man by whom the Son of man is betrayed! it had been good for that man if he had not been born. ²⁵Then Judas, which betrayed him, answered and said, Master, is it I? He said unto him, Thou hast said.

²⁶And as they were eating, Jesus took bread, and blessed *it*, and brake *it*, and gave *it* to the disciples, and said, Take, eat; this is my body. ²⁷And he took the cup, and gave thanks, and gave *it* to them, saying, Drink ye all of it; ²⁸For this is my blood of the new testament, which is shed for many for the remission of sins. ²⁹But I say unto you, I will not drink henceforth of this fruit of the vine, until that day when I drink it new with you in my Father's kingdom. ³⁰And when they had sung an hymnᵃ, they went out into the mount of Olives.

³¹Then saith Jesus unto them, All ye shall be offended because of me this night: for it is written, I will smite the shepherd, and the sheep of the flock shall be scattered abroad. ³²But after I am risen again, I will go before you into Galilee. ³³Peter answered and said unto him, Though all *men* shall be offendedᵇ because of thee, *yet* will I never be offended. ³⁴Jesus said unto him, Verily I say unto thee, That this night, before the cock crow, thou shalt deny me thrice. ³⁵Peter said unto him, Though I should die with thee, yet will I not deny thee. Likewise also said all the disciples.

³⁶Then cometh Jesus with them unto a place called Gethsemane, and saith unto the disciples, Sit ye here, while I go and pray yonder. ³⁷And he took with him Peter and the two sons of Zebedee, and began to be sorrowful and very heavy. ³⁸Then saith he unto them, My soul is exceeding sorrowful, even unto death: tarry ye here, and watch with me. ³⁹And he went a little further, and fell on his face, and prayed, saying, O my Father, if it be possible, let this cup pass from me: nevertheless not as I will, but as thou *wilt*. ⁴⁰And he cometh unto the disciples, and findeth them asleep, and saith unto Peter, What, could ye not watch with me one hour? ⁴¹Watch and pray, that ye enter not into temptation: the spirit indeed *is* willing, but the flesh *is* weak. ⁴²He went away again the second time, and prayed, saying, O my Father, if this cup may not pass away from me, except I drink it, thy will be done. ⁴³And he came and found them asleep again: for their eyes were heavy. ⁴⁴And he left them, and went away again, and prayed the third time, saying the same words. ⁴⁵Then cometh he to his disciples, and saith unto them, Sleep on now, and

---

Devotional Moment

•

Stay Alert

26:40-41 Peter should have been alert, but instead he dozed off. Jesus needed a friend to pray with him in that hour. People need rest, but not when a crisis calls for alert and focused prayer. Be available when a close friend or family member needs you to pray with him or her.

ᵃ hymn: or, psalm
ᵇ offended: or, though the faith of other men should be shaken and fail, yet mine will be firm and constant

take *your* rest: behold, the hour is at hand, and the Son of man is betrayed into the hands of sinners. ⁴⁶Rise, let us be going: behold, he is at hand that doth betray me.

⁴⁷And while he yet spake, lo, Judas, one of the twelve, came, and with him a great multitude with swords and staves, from the chief priests and elders of the people. ⁴⁸Now he that betrayed him gave them a sign, saying, Whomsoever I shall kiss, that same is he: hold him fast. ⁴⁹And forthwith he came to Jesus, and said, Hail, master; and kissed him. ⁵⁰And Jesus said unto him, Friend, wherefore art thou come? Then came they, and laid hands on Jesus, and took him. ⁵¹And, behold, one of them which were with Jesus stretched out *his* hand, and drew his sword, and struck a servant of the high priest's, and smote off his ear. ⁵²Then said Jesus unto him, Put up again thy sword into his place: for all they that take the sword shall perish with the sword. ⁵³ Thinkest thou that I cannot now pray to my Father, and he shall presently give me more than twelve legions of angels? ⁵⁴But how then shall the scriptures be fulfilled, that thus it must be? ⁵⁵In that same hour said Jesus to the multitudes, Are ye come out as against a thief with swords and staves for to take me? I sat daily with you teaching in the temple, and ye laid no hold on me. ⁵⁶But all this was done, that the scriptures of the prophets might be fulfilled. Then all the disciples forsook him, and fled.

⁵⁷And they that had laid hold on Jesus led *him* away to Caiaphas the high priest, where the scribes and the elders were assembled. ⁵⁸But Peter followed him afar off unto the high priest's palace, and went in, and sat with the servants, to see the end. ⁵⁹Now the chief priests, and elders, and all the council, sought false witness against Jesus, to put him to death; ⁶⁰But found none: yea, though many false witnesses came, *yet* found they none. At the last came two false witnesses, ⁶¹And said, This *fellow* said, I am able to destroy the temple of God, and to build it in three days. ⁶²And the high priest arose, and said unto him, Answerest thou nothing? what *is it which* these witness against thee? ⁶³But Jesus held his peace. And the high priest answered and said unto him, I adjure thee by the living God, that thou tell us whether thou be the Christ, the Son of God. ⁶⁴Jesus saith unto him, Thou hast said: nevertheless I say unto you, Hereafter shall ye see the Son of man sitting on the right hand of power, and coming in the clouds of heaven. ⁶⁵Then the high priest rent his clothes, saying, He hath spoken blasphemy; what further need have we of witnesses? behold, now ye have heard his blasphemy. ⁶⁶What think ye? They answered and said, He is guilty of death. ⁶⁷Then did they spit in his face, and buffeted him; and others smote *him* with the palms of their hands, ⁶⁸Saying, Prophesy unto us, thou Christ, Who is he that smote thee?

⁶⁹Now Peter sat without in the palace: and a damsel came unto him, saying, Thou also wast with Jesus of Galilee. ⁷⁰But he denied before *them* all, saying, I know not what thou sayest. ⁷¹And when he was gone out into the porch, another *maid* saw him, and said unto them that were there, This *fellow* was also with Jesus of Nazareth. ⁷²And again he denied with an oath, I do not

know the man. ⁷³And after a while came unto *him* they that stood by, and said to Peter, Surely thou also art *one* of them; for thy speech betrayeth thee. ⁷⁴Then began he to curse and to swear, *saying,* I know not the man. And immediately the cock crew. ⁷⁵And Peter remembered the word of Jesus, which said unto him, Before the cock crow, thou shalt deny me thrice. And he went out, and wept bitterly.

27

¹When the morning was come, all the chief priests and elders of the people took counsel against Jesus to put him to death: ²And when they had bound him, they led *him* away, and delivered him to Pontius Pilate the governor. ³Then Judas, which had betrayed him, when he saw that he was condemned, repented himself, and brought again the thirty pieces of silver to the chief priests and elders, ⁴Saying, I have sinned in that I have betrayed the innocent blood. And they said, What *is that* to us? see thou *to that.* ⁵And he cast down the pieces of silver in the temple, and departed, and went and hanged himself. ⁶And the chief priests took the silver pieces, and said, It is not lawful for to put them into the treasury, because it is the price of blood. ⁷And they took counsel, and bought with them the potter's field, to bury strangers in. ⁸Wherefore that field was called, The field of blood, unto this day. ⁹Then was fulfilled that which was spoken by Jeremy the prophet, saying, And they took the thirty pieces of silver, the price of him that was valued, whomᵃ they of the children of Israel did

value; ¹⁰And gave them for the potter's field, as the Lord appointed me.

¹¹And Jesus stood before the governor: and the governor asked him, saying, Art thou the King of the Jews? And Jesus said unto him, Thou sayest. ¹²And when he was accused of the chief priests and elders, he answered nothing. ¹³Then said Pilate unto him, Hearest thou not how many things they witness against thee? ¹⁴And he answered him to never a word; insomuch that the governor marvelled greatly. ¹⁵Now at *that* feast the governor was wont to release unto the people a prisoner, whom they would. ¹⁶And they had then a notable prisoner, called Barabbas. ¹⁷Therefore when they were gathered together, Pilate said unto them, Whom will ye that I release unto you? Barabbas, or Jesus which is called Christ? ¹⁸For he knew that for envy they had delivered him. ¹⁹When he was set down on the judgment seat, his wife sent unto him, saying, Have thou nothing to do with that

---

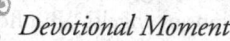

Devotional Moment
•
Listen to Your Spouse
27:19 Powerful influences were forcing Pilate into a narrow corner. Then his wife spoke some of the best common sense ever recorded: "Have thou nothing to do with that just man." He should have listened.
Your spouse can be your best friend and clearest moral barometer. When a big decision looms, your spouse can feel your emotional pulse and sense your deepest conviction. God has given you this person to help you. Listen when your spouse advises, since your own judgment may be clouded by outside pressures and personal interests.

ᵃ whom . . . : or, whom they bought of the children of Israel just man: for I have suffered many things this day in a dream because of him. ²⁰But the chief priests and elders persuaded the multitude that they should ask Barabbas, and destroy Jesus. ²¹The governor answered and said unto them, Whether of the twain will ye that I release unto you? They said, Barabbas. ²²Pilate saith unto them, What shall I do then with Jesus which is called Christ? *They* all say unto him, Let him be crucified. ²³And the governor said, Why, what evil hath he done? But they cried out the more, saying, Let him be crucified. ²⁴When Pilate saw that he could prevail nothing, but *that* rather a tumult was made, he took water, and washed *his* hands before the multitude, saying, I am innocent of the blood of this just person: see ye *to it.* ²⁵Then answered all the people, and said, His blood *be* on us, and on our children.

²⁶Then released he Barabbas unto them: and when he had scourged Jesus,

---

Devotional Moment
•
Name-Calling

27:29 Surely Jesus was hurt by this mockery, but his response was to take it quietly and not answer back. Most families could write a dictionary of insulting words—how to use them and when to say them. Such words are common between siblings and often quickly forgotten, but when harsh words are used between spouses or between parent and child, the hurt goes deeper. If name-calling or mockery is common in your family, take steps to correct it. Set the tone yourself! And when someone slips and you're the target, break the cycle with a response that leads to hugs instead of verbal missiles.

---

he delivered *him* to be crucified. ²⁷Then the soldiers of the governor took Jesus into the common hall[b], and gathered unto him the whole band *of soldiers.* ²⁸And they stripped him, and put on him a scarlet robe. ²⁹And when they had platted a crown of thorns, they put *it* upon his head, and a reed in his right hand: and they bowed the knee before him, and mocked him, saying, Hail, King of the Jews! ³⁰And they spit upon him, and took the reed, and smote him on the head. ³¹And after that they had mocked him, they took the robe off from him, and put his own raiment on him, and led him away to crucify *him.* ³²And as they came out, they found a man of Cyrene, Simon by name: him they compelled to bear his cross.

³³And when they were come unto a place called Golgotha, that is to say, a place of a skull, ³⁴They gave him vinegar to drink mingled with gall: and when he had tasted *thereof,* he would not drink. ³⁵And they crucified him, and parted his garments, casting lots: that it might be fulfilled which was spoken by the prophet, They parted my garments among them, and upon my vesture did they cast lots. ³⁶And sitting down they watched him there; ³⁷And set up over his head his accusation written, THIS IS JESUS THE KING OF THE JEWS. ³⁸Then were there two thieves crucified with him, one on the right hand, and another on the left. ³⁹And they that passed by reviled him, wagging their heads, ⁴⁰And saying, Thou that destroyest the temple, and buildest *it* in three days, save thyself. If thou be the Son of God, come down from the cross. ⁴¹Likewise also the

---

[b] common hall: or, governor's house

chief priests mocking *him*, with the scribes and elders, said, ⁴²He saved others; himself he cannot save. If he be the King of Israel, let him now come down from the cross, and we will believe him. ⁴³He trusted in God; let him deliver him now, if he will have him: for he said, I am the Son of God. ⁴⁴The thieves also, which were crucified with him, cast the same in his teeth. ⁴⁵Now from the sixth hour there was darkness over all the land unto the ninth hour. ⁴⁶And about the ninth hour Jesus cried with a loud voice, saying, Eli, Eli, lama sabachthani? that is to say, My God, my God, why hast thou forsaken me? ⁴⁷Some of them that stood there, when they heard *that*, said, This *man* calleth for Elias. ⁴⁸And straightway one of them ran, and took a spunge, and filled *it* with vinegar, and put *it* on a reed, and gave him to drink. ⁴⁹The rest said, Let be, let us see whether Elias will come to save him.

⁵⁰Jesus, when he had cried again with a loud voice, yielded up the ghost. ⁵¹And, behold, the veil of the temple was rent in twain from the top to the bottom; and the earth did quake, and the rocks rent; ⁵²And the graves were opened; and many bodies of the saints which slept arose, ⁵³And came out of the graves after his resurrection, and went into the holy city, and appeared unto many. ⁵⁴Now when the centurion, and they that were with him, watching Jesus, saw the earthquake, and those things that were done, they feared greatly, saying, Truly this was the Son of God. ⁵⁵And many women were there beholding afar off, which followed Jesus from Galilee, ministering unto him: ⁵⁶Among

which was Mary Magdalene, and Mary the mother of James and Joses, and the mother of Zebedee's children.

⁵⁷When the even was come, there came a rich man of Arimathaea, named Joseph, who also himself was Jesus' disciple: ⁵⁸He went to Pilate, and begged the body of Jesus. Then Pilate commanded the body to be delivered. ⁵⁹And when Joseph had taken the body, he wrapped it in a clean linen cloth, ⁶⁰And laid it in his own new tomb, which he had hewn out in the rock: and he rolled a great stone to the door of the sepulchre, and departed. ⁶¹And there was Mary Magdalene, and the other Mary, sitting over against the sepulchre. ⁶²Now the next day, that followed the day of the preparation, the chief priests and Pharisees came together unto Pilate, ⁶³Saying, Sir, we remember that that deceiver said, while he was yet alive, After three days I will rise again. ⁶⁴Command therefore that the sepulchre be made sure until the third day, lest his disciples come by night, and steal him away, and say unto the people, He is risen from the dead: so the last error shall be worse than the first. ⁶⁵Pilate said unto them, Ye have a watch: go your way, make *it* as sure as ye can. ⁶⁶So they went, and made the sepulchre sure, sealing the stone, and setting a watch.

28

¹In the end of the sabbath, as it began to dawn toward the first *day* of the week, came Mary Magdalene and the other Mary to see the sepulchre. ²And, behold, there was[a] a great earthquake:

---

[a] was: or, had been

for the angel of the Lord descended from heaven, and came and rolled back the stone from the door, and sat upon it. [3]His countenance was like lightning, and his raiment white as snow: [4]And for fear of him the keepers did shake, and became as dead *men*. [5]And the angel answered and said unto the women, Fear not ye: for I know that ye seek Jesus, which was crucified. [6]He is not here: for he is risen, as he said. Come, see the place where the Lord lay. [7]And go quickly, and tell his disciples that he is risen from the dead; and, behold, he goeth before you into Galilee; there shall ye see him: lo, I have told you. [8]And they departed quickly from the sepulchre with fear and great joy; and did run to bring his disciples word. [9]And as they went to tell his disciples, behold, Jesus met them, saying, All hail. And they came and held him by the feet, and worshipped him. [10]Then said Jesus unto them, Be not afraid: go tell my brethren that they go into Galilee, and there shall they see me.

[11]Now when they were going, behold, some of the watch came into the city, and shewed unto the chief priests all the things that were done. [12]And when they were assembled with the elders, and had taken counsel, they gave large money unto the soldiers, [13]Saying, Say ye, His disciples came by night, and stole him *away* while we slept. [14]And if

> ## Devotional Moment
> •
> ### Making Disciples
> 28:18-20 The words *go and make disciples* frequently appear on banners at missionary conventions. Let them be a banner over your home, too. Pray, sing praise songs, work together for God's kingdom, and read often from God's Word. Find a church that cares about children and help it grow. And at the end of life, when your family is grown and your career is past, the time you spent discipling your children may prove to be your greatest satisfaction. Make that time count while you can.

this come to the governor's ears, we will persuade him, and secure you. [15]So they took the money, and did as they were taught: and this saying is commonly reported among the Jews until this day.

[16]Then the eleven disciples went away into Galilee, into a mountain where Jesus had appointed them. [17]And when they saw him, they worshipped him: but some doubted. [18]And Jesus came and spake unto them, saying, All power is given unto me in heaven and in earth. [19]Go ye therefore, and teach[b] all nations, baptizing them in the name of the Father, and of the Son, and of the Holy Ghost: [20]Teaching them to observe all things whatsoever I have commanded you: and, lo, I am with you alway, *even* unto the end of the world. Amen.

[b] teach . . . : or, make disciples, or, Christians of all nations

MARK

Purpose
To present the person, work, and teachings of Jesus

Author
John Mark. He was not one of the twelve disciples, but he accompanied Paul on his first missionary journey (Acts 13:13).

Date Written
Between A.D. 55 and 65

Setting
The Roman Empire under Tiberius Caesar. The Empire, with its common language and excellent transportation and communication systems, was ripe to hear Jesus' message, which spread quickly from nation to nation.

Key Verse
"For even the Son of man came not to be ministered unto, but to minister, and to give his life a ransom for many" (10:45).

Special Features
Mark may have been the first Gospel written. Mark records more miracles than does any other Gospel.

Two men at the front door at 3:00 A.M. They rap hard, demanding entry. Behind them is a carload of thugs, all armed. It's your last night—last moment—last look at loved ones.

You're brought before a judge, who's paid by the prosecution. The trial is short, a sham. Your sentence, a creative mix of humiliation and pain, is intended to entertain the emperor and his guests.

A nightmare, you say?

Put yourself in the situation of those for whom John Mark wrote this book. They were Romans in the generation following Jesus' resurrection. Their government was corrupt, their culture hostile to all that they believed.

In A.D. 64, Christians became the scapegoats for a massive fire that swept through Rome. The emperor himself, the infamous Nero, was likely responsible. Unfairly blamed, Christians were then unfairly punished. Some perished in the celebrated Coliseum. Others lost property and suffered abuse and ridicule. To these people John Mark wrote his Gospel.

Families are vulnerable. Children are open to peer and advertising pressure. Injuries and illness cut lives short, leaving families with a vacuum—father gone, mother gone. Marriages rust; jobs are lost; hungry emotions lust for pleasure; adolescents "check out." Families suffer.

What kind of book do hurting people need? What fortifies against struggles to come? What gives courage to face a grim day?

Mark is the story of a struggle for you, over you, and before you. That struggle, finished and done, is your family's strength—the raincoat in your thunderstorm, the sunshine of your life. This is the book that kept the Roman Christians strong. Let it change your life, too.

1

¹The beginning of the gospel of Jesus Christ, the Son of God; ²As it is written in the prophets, Behold, I send my messenger before thy face, which shall prepare thy way before thee. ³The voice of one crying in the wilderness, Prepare ye the way of the Lord, make his paths straight. ⁴John did baptize in the wilderness, and preach the baptism of repentance for ᵃ the remission of sins. ⁵And there went out unto him all the land of Judaea, and they of Jerusalem, and were all baptized of him in the river of Jordan, confessing their sins. ⁶And John was clothed with camel's hair, and with a girdle of a skin about his loins; and he did eat locusts and wild honey; ⁷And preached, saying, There cometh one mightier than I after me, the latchet of whose shoes I am not worthy to stoop down and unloose. ⁸I indeed have baptized you with water: but he shall baptize you with the Holy Ghost. ⁹And it came to pass in those days,

that Jesus came from Nazareth of Galilee, and was baptized of John in Jordan. ¹⁰And straightway coming up out of the water, he saw the heavens opened ᵇ, and the Spirit like a dove descending upon him: ¹¹And there came a voice from heaven, *saying*, Thou art my beloved Son, in whom I am well pleased. ¹²And immediately the Spirit driveth him into the wilderness. ¹³And he was there in the wilderness forty days, tempted of Satan; and was with the wild beasts; and the angels ministered unto him.

¹⁴Now after that John was put in prison, Jesus came into Galilee, preaching the gospel of the kingdom of God, ¹⁵And saying, The time is fulfilled, and the kingdom of God is at hand: repent ye, and believe the gospel. ¹⁶Now as he walked by the sea of Galilee, he saw Simon and Andrew his brother casting a net into the sea: for they were fishers. ¹⁷And Jesus said unto them, Come ye after me, and I will make you to become fishers of men. ¹⁸And straightway they forsook their nets, and followed him. ¹⁹And when he had gone a little further thence, he saw James the *son* of Zebedee, and John his brother, who also were in the ship mending their nets. ²⁰And straightway he called them: and they left their father Zebedee in the ship with the hired servants, and went after him. ²¹And they went into Capernaum; and straightway on the sabbath day he entered into the synagogue, and taught. ²²And they were astonished at his doctrine: for he taught them as one that had authority, and not as the scribes.

Devotional Moment
•
Repentance

1:5 *Confession of sin.* What an old-fashioned phrase! Many people regard it as an old-fashioned idea, too. But real confession opens the door to the power of God, which is ever fresh and new. When we can say, "I'm sorry" and back those words with changed behavior and new attitudes, the Holy Spirit is free to rebuild trust and renew love. Today we need this message more than new cars, new bikes, or even new clothes from the mall. Don't forget to confess your sins—to God and to others.

ᵃ for: or, unto
ᵇ opened: or, cloven, or, rent

²³And there was in their synagogue a man with an unclean spirit; and he cried out, ²⁴Saying, Let *us* alone; what have we to do with thee, thou Jesus of Nazareth? art thou come to destroy us? I know thee who thou art, the Holy One of God. ²⁵And Jesus rebuked him, saying, Hold thy peace, and come out of him. ²⁶And when the unclean spirit had torn him, and cried with a loud voice, he came out of him. ²⁷And they were all amazed, insomuch that they questioned among themselves, saying, What thing is this? what new doctrine *is* this? for with authority commandeth he even the unclean spirits, and they do obey him. ²⁸And immediately his fame spread abroad throughout all the region round about Galilee.

²⁹And forthwith, when they were come out of the synagogue, they entered into the house of Simon and Andrew, with James and John. ³⁰But Simon's wife's mother lay sick of a fever, and anon they tell him of her. ³¹And he came and took her by the hand, and lifted her up; and immediately the fever left her, and she ministered unto them. ³²And at even, when the sun did set, they brought unto him all that were diseased, and them that were possessed with devils. ³³And all the city was gathered together at the door. ³⁴And he healed many that were sick of divers diseases, and cast out many devils; and suffered not the devils to speakᶜ, because they knew him. ³⁵And in the morning, rising up a great while before day, he went out, and departed into a solitary place, and there prayed. ³⁶And Simon and they that were with him fol-

Devotional Moment

Pray

1:35 If anyone had a busy schedule, it was Jesus. Yet prayer was so central to his life that it came first, always. A family creates demands on our day that squeeze out priorities, such as prayer. Some families need a regimen, others need spontaneity. But all families need to pray together. We need to pray with our children so regularly that it feels odd when we skip it.

lowed after him. ³⁷And when they had found him, they said unto him, All *men* seek for thee. ³⁸And he said unto them, Let us go into the next towns, that I may preach there also: for therefore came I forth. ³⁹And he preached in their synagogues throughout all Galilee, and cast out devils.

⁴⁰And there came a leper to him, beseeching him, and kneeling down to him, and saying unto him, If thou wilt, thou canst make me clean. ⁴¹And Jesus, moved with compassion, put forth *his* hand, and touched him, and saith unto him, I will; be thou clean. ⁴²And as soon as he had spoken, immediately the leprosy departed from him, and he was cleansed. ⁴³And he straitly charged him, and forthwith sent him away; ⁴⁴And saith unto him, See thou say nothing to any man: but go thy way, shew thyself to the priest, and offer for thy cleansing those things which Moses commanded, for a testimony unto them. ⁴⁵But he went out, and began to publish *it* much, and to blaze abroad the matter, insomuch that Jesus could no more openly enter into the city, but was with-

---

ᶜ to speak . . . : or, to say that they knew him

Coping with Family Illnesses

by Paul C. Reisser, M.D.

Although three of the four Gospels tell of Jesus healing Peter's mother-in-law, I've often wished that one of them would have added a few more details. Only Luke, the doctor, mentions that it was a *high fever*—implying that it was probably a serious illness. In ancient times, this would certainly be cause for alarm because so many fevers (for which causes and cures were unknown) could be deadly.

But even in our era of sophisticated diagnostic tools and potent antibiotics, few of us can stare at a thermometer reading 103 degrees for one of our children (or ourself) without experiencing at least a wave of anxiety. Can we learn anything from this brief vignette in Jesus' life that applies to fevers (and cuts, bruises, heart attacks, and strokes) in our own families?

Obviously, we do not have direct physical contact with Jesus as Peter's mother-in-law did. But when someone in our family becomes sick, we would be wise to take our concern to God just as the disciples did: promptly, naturally, virtually as a reflex. Unfortunately, in our technology-driven age it is all too common for us to talk to God as an afterthought—after we have thumbed through the home health advisor, phoned the family doctor, or set out for a high-powered regional medical center.

On the other hand, some people go to the other extreme, insisting that seeking help from anyone but God shows a lack of faith. They are mistaken. God has given us minds to develop tools and skills that can relieve suffering and save lives; thus, answers to prayer don't necessarily require miracles. Those who stubbornly refuse medical care because they regard it as "unspiritual" forget that God *normally* uses people to do his work.

For some of us, a less severe illness may provide an unexpected benefit: a time to reflect and review. Did the problem come about because of an overstressed life? too much food? too little sleep? inadequate exercise? Some health problems may serve as a warning that serious, lifelong course corrections are necessary. Others may signal the need for short-term measures: some extra rest, a time out from an overloaded agenda, or a shift in priorities.

One of the most common questions I hear in my office is, "Why did this happen? Why did I (or my loved one) get sick?" Some believe that a hidden meaning or unconfessed sin lurks behind every sore throat. But Jesus' answer to the disciples' question about the man born blind (John 9:1-12) suggests that not all health problems can be interpreted as messages from God or consequences of wrong. "Was it a result of his own sins," they asked, "or those of his parents?" "Neither," Jesus responded. Blindness, in this case, served a wholly different purpose. How it ultimately glorified God is a remarkable story.

Finally, in addition to prayer and medical treatment, our care for a sick family member or friend should not overlook simple acts that may have a profound impact on recovery. Quietly touching a hand or stroking the head, reading aloud a favorite book or passage of Scripture, or just being there (without having to say anything in particular) may provide more relief than the most sophisticated medical therapy or the most insightful counseling.

DIGGING DEEPER

1. "A sound heart is the life of the flesh: but envy the rottenness of the bones." This proverb of Solomon (Prov. 14:30) is one of several that describe how attitudes affect our health. Look at Proverbs 10:1–30:33 to find others, including a harrowing description of alcoholism in Proverbs 23:29-35.

2. Read 1 Corinthians 7:10-17 for a powerful health advisory that, if implemented worldwide, would end the current AIDS epidemic (and several other serious infections).

3. Does God guarantee perfect physical health in a fallen world? Consider what Paul wrote about the condition of the entire creation in Romans 8:18-23.

out in desert places: and they came to him from every quarter.

2

¹And again he entered into Capernaum after *some* days; and it was noised that he was in the house. ²And straightway many were gathered together, insomuch that there was no room to receive *them*, no, not so much as about the door: and he preached the word unto them. ³And they come unto him, bringing one sick of the palsy, which was borne of four. ⁴And when they could not come nigh unto him for the press, they uncovered the roof where he was: and when they had broken *it* up, they let down the bed wherein the sick of the palsy lay. ⁵When Jesus saw their faith, he said unto the sick of the palsy, Son,

thy sins be forgiven thee. ⁶But there were certain of the scribes sitting there, and reasoning in their hearts, ⁷Why doth this *man* thus speak blasphemies? who can forgive sins but God only? ⁸And immediately when Jesus perceived in his spirit that they so reasoned within themselves, he said unto them, Why reason ye these things in your hearts? ⁹Whether is it easier to say to the sick of the palsy, *Thy* sins be forgiven thee; or to say, Arise, and take up thy bed, and walk? ¹⁰But that ye may know that the Son of man hath power on earth to forgive sins, (he saith to the sick of the palsy,) ¹¹I say unto thee, Arise, and take up thy bed, and go thy way into thine house. ¹²And immediately he arose, took up the bed, and went forth before them all; insomuch that they were all amazed, and glorified God, saying, We never saw it on this fashion.

¹³And he went forth again by the sea side; and all the multitude resorted unto him, and he taught them. ¹⁴And as he passed by, he saw Levi the *son* of Alphaeus sitting at the receipt of custom, and said unto him, Follow me. And he arose and followed him. ¹⁵And it came to pass, that, as Jesus sat at meat in his house, many publicans and sinners sat also together with Jesus and his disciples: for there were many, and they followed him. ¹⁶And when the scribes and

---

Devotional Moment

Sick People

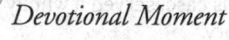

2:3 Transporting disabled people in Jesus' day required old-fashioned technology: several friends or family members and a stretcher. A family or a group of friends of all ages has a great opportunity to show compassion for the sick, disabled, infirm, or aged. People need an extended family today just as much as they did in Jesus' day. At the nursing home in your neighborhood are people who would find lots of joy in the smiles of children, in the sound of their singing, in the touch of their hands. Plan an hour's visit sometime soon.

Pharisees saw him eat with publicans and sinners, they said unto his disciples, How is it that he eateth and drinketh with publicans and sinners? ¹⁷When Jesus heard *it*, he saith unto them, They that are whole have no need of the physician, but they that are sick: I came not to call the righteous, but sinners to repentance.

¹⁸And the disciples of John and of the Pharisees used to fast: and they come and say unto him, Why do the disciples of John and of the Pharisees fast, but thy disciples fast not? ¹⁹And Jesus said unto them, Can the children of the bridechamber fast, while the bridegroom is with them? as long as they have the bridegroom with them, they cannot fast. ²⁰But the days will come, when the bridegroom shall be taken away from them, and then shall they fast in those days. ²¹No man also seweth a piece of new cloth* on an old garment: else the new piece that filled it up taketh away from the old, and the rent is made worse. ²²And no man putteth new wine into old bottles*: else the new wine doth burst the bottles, and the wine is spilled, and the bottles will be marred: but new wine must be put into new bottles. ²³And it came to pass, that he went through the corn fields on the sabbath day; and his disciples began, as they went, to pluck the ears of corn. ²⁴And the Pharisees said unto him, Behold, why do they on the sabbath day that which is not lawful? ²⁵And he said unto them, Have ye never read what David did, when he had need,

and was an hungred, he, and they that were with him? ²⁶How he went into the house of God in the days of Abiathar the high priest, and did eat the shewbread, which is not lawful to eat but for the priests, and gave also to them which were with him? ²⁷And he said unto them, The sabbath was made for man, and not man for the sabbath: ²⁸Therefore the Son of man is Lord also of the sabbath.

3

¹And he entered again into the synagogue; and there was a man there which had a withered hand. ²And they watched him, whether he would heal him on the sabbath day; that they might accuse him. ³And he saith unto the man which had the withered hand, Stand forth*. ⁴And he saith unto them, Is it lawful to do good on the sabbath days, or to do evil? to save life, or to kill? But they held their peace. ⁵And when he had looked round about on them with anger, being grieved for the hardness* of their hearts, he saith unto the man, Stretch forth thine hand. And he stretched *it* out: and his hand was restored whole as the other. ⁶And the Pharisees went forth, and straightway took counsel with the Herodians against him, how they might destroy him. ⁷But Jesus withdrew himself with his disciples to the sea: and a great multitude from Galilee followed him, and from Judaea, ⁸And from Jerusalem, and from Idumaea, and *from* beyond Jordan; and they about Tyre and Sidon, a

---

ª new cloth: or, raw, or, unwrought cloth
ᵇ bottles: or, sacks of skin
ª Stand forth: Gr. Arise, stand forth in the midst
ᵇ hardness: or, blindness

Your True Family

by Max Lucado

It may surprise you to know that Jesus had a difficult family. Mark quoted Jesus' hometown critics as saying, "Is not this the carpenter, the son of Mary, the brother of James, and Joses, and of Juda, and Simon? and are not his sisters here with us?" (Mark 6:3).

If your family doesn't appreciate you, take heart—neither did Jesus' brothers appreciate him. "A prophet is not without honour, but in his own country, and among his own kin, and in his own house" (Mark 6:4).

Jesus had gone to the synagogue, where he was asked to speak. The people were proud that this hometown boy had done well—until they heard what he said. He referred to himself as the Messiah, the one to fulfill prophecy.

Their response? *This is no Messiah! He's the kid from down the street.* He's the accountant on the third floor. He's the construction worker who used to date my sister.

One minute he was a hero, the next a heretic. Then they "led him unto the brow of the hill whereon their city was built, that they might cast him down headlong. But he passing through the midst of them went his way" (Luke 4:29-30).

What an ugly moment! Jesus' neighborhood friends tried to kill him. But even uglier than what we see is what we *don't* see. Notice what is missing. Does the text go on to say, "They planned to push him over the cliff, but Jesus' brothers came and stood up for him"?

We'd like to read that, but that's not what happened. When Jesus was in trouble, his family was nowhere to be found.

Each of us has a fantasy that our family will be close-knit. Jesus didn't have that expectation. Look how he defined his family: "Whosoever shall do the will of God, the same is my brother, and my sister, and mother" (Mark 3:35). He recognized that his spiritual family could provide what his biological family didn't.

If Jesus himself couldn't force his family to share his convictions, what makes you think you can force yours? We have to move beyond the naive expectation that if we do everything right, our family will respond the way we want them to. They may, or they may not. If your father is a jerk, you could be the world's best daughter, but he still wouldn't tell you so. If your mother doesn't like your career, you could change jobs a dozen times and still never satisfy her. If your sister is always complaining about what you got and she didn't, you could give her everything, and she still might not change.

Your family may never give you the blessing you seek, but God will. Let God give you what your family doesn't. If your earthly father doesn't affirm you, then let your heavenly Father take his place.

We don't know if Joseph affirmed his son Jesus in his ministry, but we know God did: "This is my beloved Son, in whom I am well pleased" (Matt. 3:17).

God has proven himself as a faithful Father. Now it falls to us to be trusting children. Let God give you what your family doesn't. Let him fill the void others have left. Rely upon him for your affirmation and encouragement. Ideally, a father is the one in your life who provides and protects. That is exactly what God has done. He has provided for your needs (Matt. 6:25-33). He protects you from harm (Ps. 91). He has adopted you into his own family (Eph. 1:5) and given you his name (1 John 3:1).

Having your family's approval is desirable but not necessary for happiness. Jesus did not let the difficult dynamic of his family overshadow his call from God.

What happened to Jesus' family?

Take a peek at the book of Acts. After Jesus' ascension, the disciples held a prayer meeting. The list of those in attendance includes Jesus' brothers (see Acts 1:12-14).

What a change! The ones who mocked him came to worship him. What if Jesus had disowned them? What if he had suffocated his family with his demand for change?

Thankfully, we'll never know. Jesus gave them space, time, and grace. And in the end, they changed. One brother became an apostle (Gal. 1:19), and others became missionaries (1 Cor. 9:5).

So don't lose heart. God still changes families.

DIGGING DEEPER

1. Whose child are you, and what is the result? See Galatians 4:7.
2. Who are your true brothers and sisters? See Mark 10:29-30 and 1 Timothy 5:1-2.

---

great multitude, when they had heard what great things he did, came unto him. ⁹And he spake to his disciples, that a small ship should wait on him because of the multitude, lest they should throng him. ¹⁰For he had healed many; insomuch that they pressed upon him for to touch him, as many as had plagues. ¹¹And unclean spirits, when they saw him, fell down before him, and cried, saying, Thou art the Son of God. ¹²And he straitly charged them that they should not make him known.

¹³And he goeth up into a mountain, and calleth *unto him* whom he would: and they came unto him. ¹⁴And he ordained twelve, that they should be with him, and that he might send them forth to preach, ¹⁵And to have power to heal sicknesses, and to cast out devils: ¹⁶And Simon he surnamed Peter; ¹⁷And James the *son* of Zebedee, and John the brother of James; and he surnamed them Boanerges, which is, The sons of thunder: ¹⁸And Andrew, and Philip, and Bartholomew, and Matthew, and Thomas, and James the *son* of Alphaeus, and Thaddaeus, and Simon the Canaanite, ¹⁹And Judas Iscariot, which also betrayed him: and they went intoᶜ an house. ²⁰And the multitude cometh together again, so that they could not so much as eat bread. ²¹And when his friendsᵈ heard *of it*, they went out to lay hold on him: for they said, He is beside himself.

²²And the scribes which came down from Jerusalem said, He hath Beelzebub, and by the prince of the devils casteth he out devils. ²³And he called them *unto him*, and said unto them in parables, How can Satan cast out Satan? ²⁴And if a kingdom be divided against itself, that kingdom cannot stand. ²⁵And if a house be divided against itself, that house cannot stand. ²⁶And if Satan rise up against himself, and be divided, he cannot stand, but hath an end. ²⁷No man can enter into a strong man's house, and spoil his goods, except he will first bind the strong man; and then he will spoil his house. ²⁸Verily I say unto you, All sins shall be forgiven

---

ᶜ into . . . : or, home
ᵈ friends: or, kinsmen

unto the sons of men, and blasphemies wherewith soever they shall blaspheme: ²⁹But he that shall blaspheme against the Holy Ghost hath never forgiveness, but is in danger of eternal damnation: ³⁰Because they said, He hath an unclean spirit.

³¹There came then his brethren and his mother, and, standing without, sent unto him, calling him. ³²And the multitude sat about him, and they said unto him, Behold, thy mother and thy brethren without seek for thee. ³³And he answered them, saying, Who is my mother, or my brethren? ³⁴And he looked round about on them which sat about him, and said, Behold my mother and my brethren! ³⁵For whosoever shall do the will of God, the same is my brother, and my sister, and mother.

4

¹And he began again to teach by the sea side: and there was gathered unto him a great multitude, so that he entered into a ship, and sat in the sea; and the whole multitude was by the sea on the land. ²And he taught them many things by parables, and said unto them in his doctrine, ³Hearken; Behold, there went out a sower to sow: ⁴And it came to pass, as he sowed, some fell by the way side, and the fowls of the air came and devoured it up. ⁵And some fell on stony ground, where it had not much earth; and immediately it sprang up, because it had no depth of earth: ⁶But when the sun was up, it was scorched; and because it had no root, it withered away. ⁷And some fell among thorns, and the thorns grew up, and choked it, and it yielded no fruit. ⁸And other fell on good ground, and did yield fruit that sprang up and increased; and brought forth, some thirty, and some sixty, and some an hundred. ⁹And he said unto them, He that hath ears to hear, let him hear. ¹⁰And when he was alone, they that were about him with the twelve asked of him the parable. ¹¹And he said unto them, Unto you it is given to know the mystery of the kingdom of God: but unto them that are without, all *these* things are done in parables: ¹²That seeing they may see, and not perceive; and hearing they may hear, and not understand; lest at any time they should be converted, and *their* sins should be forgiven them. ¹³And he said unto them, Know ye not this parable? and how then will ye know all parables? ¹⁴The sower soweth the word. ¹⁵And these are they by the way side, where the word is sown; but when they have heard, Satan cometh immediately, and taketh away the word that was sown in their hearts. ¹⁶And these are they like-

wise which are sown on stony ground; who, when they have heard the word, immediately receive it with gladness; [17]And have no root in themselves, and so endure but for a time: afterward, when affliction or persecution ariseth for the word's sake, immediately they are offended[a]. [18]And these are they which are sown among thorns; such as hear the word, [19]And the cares of this world, and the deceitfulness of riches, and the lusts[b] of other things entering in, choke the word, and it becometh unfruitful. [20]And these are they which are sown on good ground; such as hear the word, and receive it, and bring forth fruit, some thirtyfold, some sixty, and some an hundred.

[21]And he said unto them, Is a candle brought to be put under a bushel[c], or under a bed? and not to be set on a candlestick? [22]For there is nothing hid, which shall not be manifested; neither was any thing kept secret, but that it should come abroad. [23]If any man have ears to hear, let him hear. [24]And he said unto them, Take heed what ye hear: with what measure ye mete, it shall be measured to you: and unto you that hear shall more be given. [25]For he that hath, to him shall be given: and he that hath not, from him shall be taken even that which he hath. [26]And he said, So is the kingdom of God, as if a man should cast seed into the ground; [27]And should sleep, and rise night and day, and the seed should spring and grow up, he knoweth not how. [28]For the earth bringeth forth fruit of herself; first the blade, then the ear, after that the full corn in the ear. [29]But when the fruit is brought forth, immediately he putteth in the sickle, because the harvest is come. [30]And he said, Whereunto shall we liken the kingdom of God? or with what comparison shall we compare it? [31]It is like a grain of mustard seed, which, when it is sown in the earth, is less than all the seeds that be in the earth: [32]But when it is sown, it groweth up, and becometh greater than all herbs, and shooteth out great branches; so that the fowls of the air may lodge under the shadow of it. [33]And with many such parables spake he the word unto them, as they were able to hear it. [34]But without a parable spake he not unto them: and when they were alone, he expounded all things to his disciples.

[35]And the same day, when the even was come, he saith unto them, Let us pass over unto the other side. [36]And when they had sent away the multitude, they took him even as he was in the ship. And there were also with him other little ships. [37]And there arose a great storm of wind, and the waves beat into the ship, so that it was now full. [38]And he was in the hinder part of the ship, asleep on a pillow: and they awake him, and say unto him, Master, carest thou not that we perish? [39]And he arose, and rebuked the wind, and said unto the sea, Peace, be still. And the wind ceased, and there was a great calm. [40]And he said unto them, Why are ye so fearful? how is it that ye have no faith? [41]And they feared exceedingly, and said

---

[a] offended: or, stumbled, or, caused to fall into sin
[b] lusts: or, inordinate desires
[c] bushel: the word in the original signifieth a less measure

one to another, What manner of man is this, that even the wind and the sea obey him?

5

¹And they came over unto the other side of the sea, into the country of the Gadarenes. ²And when he was come out of the ship, immediately there met him out of the tombs a man with an unclean spirit, ³Who had *his* dwelling among the tombs; and no man could bind him, no, not with chains: ⁴Because that he had been often bound with fetters and chains, and the chains had been plucked asunder by him, and the fetters broken in pieces: neither could any *man* tame him. ⁵And always, night and day, he was in the mountains, and in the tombs, crying, and cutting himself with stones. ⁶But when he saw Jesus afar off, he ran and worshipped him, ⁷And cried with a loud voice, and said, What have I to do with thee, Jesus, *thou* Son of the most high God? I adjure thee by God, that thou torment me not. ⁸For he said unto him, Come out of the man, *thou* unclean spirit. ⁹And he asked him, What *is* thy name? And he answered, saying, My name *is* Legion: for we are many. ¹⁰And he besought him much that he would not send them away out of the country. ¹¹Now there was there nigh unto the mountains a great herd of swine feeding. ¹²And all the devils besought him, saying, Send us into the swine, that we may enter into them. ¹³And forthwith Jesus gave them leave. And the unclean spirits went out, and entered into the swine: and the herd ran violently down a steep place into the sea, (they were about two thousand;) and were choked in the sea. ¹⁴And they that fed the swine fled, and

told *it* in the city, and in the country. And they went out to see what it was that was done. ¹⁵And they come to Jesus, and see him that was possessed with the devil, and had the legion, sitting, and clothed, and in his right mind: and they were afraid. ¹⁶And they that saw *it* told them how it befell to him that was possessed with the devil, and *also* concerning the swine. ¹⁷And they began to pray him to depart out of their coasts. ¹⁸And when he was come into the ship, he that had been possessed with the devil prayed him that he might be with him. ¹⁹Howbeit Jesus suffered him not, but saith unto him, Go home to thy friends, and tell them how great things the Lord hath done for thee, and hath had compassion on thee. ²⁰And he departed, and began to publish in Decapolis how great things Jesus had done for him: and all *men* did marvel.

²¹And when Jesus was passed over again by ship unto the other side, much people gathered unto him: and he was nigh unto the sea. ²²And, behold, there cometh one of the rulers of the synagogue, Jairus by name; and when he saw him, he fell at his feet, ²³And besought him greatly, saying, My little daughter lieth at the point of death: *I pray thee*, come and lay thy hands on her, that she may be healed; and she shall live. ²⁴And *Jesus* went with him; and much people followed him, and thronged him. ²⁵And a certain woman, which had an issue of blood twelve years, ²⁶And had suffered many things of many physicians, and had spent all that she had, and was nothing bettered, but rather grew worse, ²⁷When she had heard of Jesus, came in the press behind, and touched his garment. ²⁸For

she said, If I may touch but his clothes, I shall be whole. ²⁹And straightway the fountain of her blood was dried up; and she felt in *her* body that she was healed of that plague. ³⁰And Jesus, immediately knowing in himself that virtue had gone out of him, turned him about in the press, and said, Who touched my clothes? ³¹And his disciples said unto him, Thou seest the multitude thronging thee, and sayest thou, Who touched me? ³²And he looked round about to see her that had done this thing. ³³But the woman fearing and trembling, knowing what was done in her, came and fell down before him, and told him all the truth. ³⁴And he said unto her, Daughter, thy faith hath made thee whole; go in peace, and be whole of thy plague.

³⁵While he yet spake, there came from the ruler of the synagogue's *house certain* which said, Thy daughter is dead: why troublest thou the Master any further? ³⁶As soon as Jesus heard the word that was spoken, he saith unto the ruler of the synagogue, Be not afraid, only believe. ³⁷And he suffered no man to follow him, save Peter, and James, and John the brother of James. ³⁸And he cometh to the house of the ruler of the synagogue, and seeth the tumult, and them that wept and wailed greatly. ³⁹And when he was come in, he saith unto them, Why make ye this ado, and weep? the damsel is not dead, but sleepeth. ⁴⁰And they laughed him to scorn. But when he had put them all out, he taketh the father and the mother of the damsel, and them that were with him, and entereth in where the damsel was lying. ⁴¹And he took the damsel by the hand, and said unto her,

Devotional Moment

Don't Be Afraid

5:36 A thousand troubles can beset each of us on any given day: A pet is injured; a friend moves away; a curfew is missed without a phone call; a virus invades a body. And Jesus says, "Don't be afraid. Just trust me." Often, God's mercy arrests the tragic plot, sorrow is averted, and life eventually returns to happy normality. But sometimes the tragedy plays out: The virus wins; the kidnapper gets away. In due time, death comes, and we grieve and try to adjust. In every circumstance, we must rely on Jesus' words: "Don't be afraid. Just trust me."

Talitha cumi; which is, being interpreted, Damsel, I say unto thee, arise. ⁴²And straightway the damsel arose, and walked; for she was *of the age* of twelve years. And they were astonished with a great astonishment. ⁴³And he charged them straitly that no man should know it; and commanded that something should be given her to eat.

6

¹And he went out from thence, and came into his own country; and his disciples follow him. ²And when the sabbath day was come, he began to teach in the synagogue: and many hearing *him* were astonished, saying, From whence hath this *man* these things? and what wisdom *is* this which is given unto him, that even such mighty works are wrought by his hands? ³Is not this the carpenter, the son of Mary, the brother of James, and Joses, and of Judah, and Simon? and are not his sisters here with us? And they were offended[a] at him.

ᵃ offended: scandalized in, or, by him

⁴But Jesus said unto them, A prophet is not without honour, but in his own country, and among his own kin, and in his own house. ⁵And he could there do no mighty work, save that he laid his hands upon a few sick folk, and healed *them*. ⁶And he marvelled because of their unbelief. And he went round about the villages, teaching.

⁷And he called *unto him* the twelve, and began to send them forth by two and two; and gave them power over unclean spirits; ⁸And commanded them that they should take nothing for *their* journey, save a staff only; no scrip, no bread, no money[b] in *their* purse: ⁹But *be* shod with sandals; and not put on two coats. ¹⁰And he said unto them, In what place soever ye enter into an house, there abide till ye depart from that place. ¹¹And whosoever shall not receive you, nor hear you, when ye depart thence, shake off the dust under your feet for a testimony against them. Verily I say unto you, It shall be more tolerable for Sodom and[c] Gomorrha in the day of judgment, than for that city. ¹²And they went out, and preached that men should repent. ¹³And they cast out many devils, and anointed with oil many that were sick, and healed *them*.

¹⁴And king Herod heard *of him*; (for his name was spread abroad:) and he said, That John the Baptist was risen from the dead, and therefore mighty works do shew forth themselves in him. ¹⁵Others said, That it is Elias. And oth-

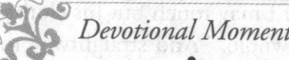

Devotional Moment

Respect

6:14 How odd that Jesus faced such doubt in his own hometown. You'd think his family and friends would see the truth with clearer vision. If even Jesus' relatives had a hard time accepting his calling, how much more difficult it is for us to respect and honor our flawed human family members. Sometimes family life gets so familiar that no matter what the honor, life change, or promotion, we fail to be impressed. We have seen too many faults in each other to believe that spiritual strength could reside *there!* It may be time to wake up and show a little respect for the unique talent of that kid brother, the special gift of that husband or wife, the warm heart and good humor of that aging grandparent.

ers said, That it is a prophet, or as one of the prophets. ¹⁶But when Herod heard *thereof*, he said, It is John, whom I beheaded: he is risen from the dead. ¹⁷For Herod himself had sent forth and laid hold upon John, and bound him in prison for Herodias' sake, his brother Philip's wife: for he had married her. ¹⁸For John had said unto Herod, It is not lawful for thee to have thy brother's wife. ¹⁹Therefore Herodias had a quarrel[d] against him, and would have killed him; but she could not: ²⁰For Herod feared John, knowing that he was a just man and an holy, and observed him[e]; and when he heard him, he did many things, and heard him gladly. ²¹And when a convenient day was come, that Herod on his birthday made a supper to his lords, high captains, and chief es-

---

[b] money: the word signifieth a piece of brass money, in value somewhat less than a farthing
[c] and: Gr. or
[d] a quarrel: or, an inward grudge
[e] observed him: or, kept him, or, saved him

Devotional Moment

Peer Pressure

6:26 Herod's order to execute John was one of the biggest injustices of all time. John was guilty only of offending the pride of Herodias, and the weak-willed Herod could not refuse the evil desires of his wife. Pressure and the fear of embarrassment corner us in similar ways. Teenagers conform to trendsetters; attorneys conform to partners; welders conform to the union. We fear to stand up against the crowd because we want to be liked and need the support of friends. Yet peer pressure needs to bend to God's standards. When we compromise, we play the role of the weakling Herod.

tates of Galilee; ²²And when the daughter of the said Herodias came in, and danced, and pleased Herod and them that sat with him, the king said unto the damsel, Ask of me whatsoever thou wilt, and I will give *it* thee. ²³And he sware unto her, Whatsoever thou shalt ask of me, I will give *it* thee, unto the half of my kingdom. ²⁴And she went forth, and said unto her mother, What shall I ask? And she said, The head of John the Baptist. ²⁵And she came in straightway with haste unto the king, and asked, saying, I will that thou give me by and by in a charger the head of John the Baptist. ²⁶And the king was exceeding sorry; *yet* for his oath's sake, and for their sakes which sat with him, he would not reject her. ²⁷And immediately the king sent an executioner, and commanded[f] his head to be brought: and he went and beheaded him in the prison, ²⁸And brought his head in a charger, and gave it to the damsel: and the damsel gave it to her mother. ²⁹And

when his disciples heard *of it*, they came and took up his corpse, and laid it in a tomb.

³⁰And the apostles gathered themselves together unto Jesus, and told him all things, both what they had done, and what they had taught. ³¹And he said unto them, Come ye yourselves apart into a desert place, and rest a while: for there were many coming and going, and they had no leisure so much as to eat. ³²And they departed into a desert place by ship privately. ³³And the people saw them departing, and many knew him, and ran afoot thither out of all cities, and outwent them, and came together unto him. ³⁴And Jesus, when he came out, saw much people, and was moved with compassion toward them, because they were as sheep not having a shepherd: and he began to teach them many things. ³⁵And when the day was now far spent, his disciples came unto him, and said, This is a desert place, and now the time *is* far passed: ³⁶Send them away, that they may go into the

Devotional Moment

Resting Up

6:31 Some people seem to regard rest as a sin. Not Jesus. Rest for him was a welcome break, a needed reprieve, an opportunity for restoration. Rest helps the weary regain strength and set direction. Rest provides extra time for prayer and meditation—for long-range planning and problem solving. Jesus called his disciples to rest and not to feel guilty for it. You need to take a break and to create an atmosphere in which you can rest and relax as well. Follow the Master even when he calls you to stop and put your feet up.

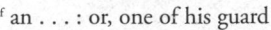

[f] an . . . : or, one of his guard

Jairus

Any parent who has had a very sick child knows the range of emotions that go with it: fear, anxiety, helplessness, confusion, anger, frustration, and sometimes even panic and desperation. If the illness drags on over time, the constant care you have to give can drain the physical energy out of you as well.

Jairus had already experienced a range of emotions as he approached Jesus. " 'My little daughter lieth at the point of death,' he said in desperation. 'I pray thee, come and lay thy hands on her that . . . she shall live' " (Mark 5:23). We know from Luke 8:42 that this was his only child. She was twelve years old.

How long had Jairus's daughter been sick? Was it a slow, gradual decline, or a sudden onset of high fever? We don't know the details. We only know that they knew she was dying. The doctors had done what they could, and it wasn't enough.

When news of his daughter's death threatened to take away Jairus's last hope, Jesus immediately turned to him with words of reassurance: "Be not afraid, only believe." They went straight into Jairus's home, and Jesus brought this precious little girl back to life.

Force yourself—before the inevitable emergency thrusts the question upon you—to think about what life would be like without your child. Then do what you can to make today count.

LESSONS FROM JAIRUS AS A FATHER

Sickness and death are inevitable. Only faith in God can help us accept that truth and deal with it. The challenge for us, as it was for Jairus, is to trust in God's ways and timing. God has not lost control, even in sickness.

God is bigger than any illness. It is human nature to fear germs—to be afraid of getting sick and of dying. But we don't have to live in fear of them. Trust in God.

Our children belong to God. There are no guarantees in life, and none of us knows if we'll have a "tomorrow." Make the most of each day that you have with your kids.

country round about, and into the villages, and buy themselves bread: for they have nothing to eat. [37]He answered and said unto them, Give ye them to eat. And they say unto him, Shall we go and buy two hundred pennyworth[g] of bread, and give them to eat? [38]He saith unto them, How many loaves have ye? go and see. And when they knew, they say, Five, and two fishes. [39]And he commanded them to make all sit down by companies upon the green grass. [40]And they sat down in ranks, by hundreds, and by fifties. [41]And when he had taken the five loaves and the two fishes, he looked up to heaven, and blessed, and brake the loaves, and gave *them* to his disciples to set before them; and the two fishes divided he among them all. [42]And they did all eat, and were filled. [43]And they took up twelve baskets full of the fragments, and of the fishes. [44]And they that did eat of the loaves were about five thousand men.

[45]And straightway he constrained his disciples to get into the ship, and to go to the other side before unto[h] Bethsaida, while he sent away the people. [46]And when he had sent them away, he departed into a mountain to pray. [47]And when even was come, the ship was in the midst of the sea, and he alone on the land. [48]And he saw them toiling in rowing; for the wind was contrary unto them: and about the fourth watch of the night he cometh unto them, walking upon the sea, and would

have passed by them. [49]But when they saw him walking upon the sea, they supposed it had been a spirit, and cried out: [50]For they all saw him, and were troubled. And immediately he talked with them, and saith unto them, Be of good cheer: it is I; be not afraid. [51]And he went up unto them into the ship; and the wind ceased: and they were sore amazed in themselves beyond measure, and wondered. [52]For they considered not *the miracle* of the loaves: for their heart was hardened. [53]And when they had passed over, they came into the land of Gennesaret, and drew to the shore. [54]And when they were come out of the ship, straightway they knew him, [55]And ran through that whole region round about, and began to carry about in beds those that were sick, where they heard he was. [56]And whithersoever he entered, into villages, or cities, or country, they laid the sick in the streets, and besought him that they might touch if it were but the border of his garment: and as many as touched him[i] were made whole.

7

[1]Then came together unto him the Pharisees, and certain of the scribes, which came from Jerusalem. [2]And when they saw some of his disciples eat bread with defiled[a], that is to say, with unwashen, hands, they found fault. [3]For the Pharisees, and all the Jews, except they wash *their* hands oft[b], eat not, holding the tradition of the elders.

---

[g] pennyworth: the Roman penny is sevenpence halfpenny
[h] unto . . . : or, over against Bethsaida
[i] him: or, it
[a] defiled: or, common
[b] oft: or, diligently: in the original, with the fist: Theophylact, up to the elbow

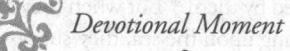

Devotional Moment

•

Traditions of the Elders

7:5-9 How easy it is to let customs and traditions become as important to us as God's laws. At church, we sometimes begin to think our particular style of music, pattern of worship, or choice of hymnal or Bible version is as important as God's commands. But where differences are merely cultural or generational, *vive la différence!* Let variety enrich your worship. When we respect variety, encourage creativity, and seek God wholeheartedly we can provide a home in which all generations feel welcome.

⁴And *when they come* from the market, except they wash, they eat not. And many other things there be, which they have received to hold, *as* the washing of cups, and pots^c, brasen vessels, and of tables. ⁵Then the Pharisees and scribes asked him, Why walk not thy disciples according to the tradition of the elders, but eat bread with unwashen hands? ⁶He answered and said unto them, Well hath Esaias prophesied of you hypocrites, as it is written, This people honoureth me with *their* lips, but their heart is far from me. ⁷Howbeit in vain do they worship me, teaching *for* doctrines the commandments of men. ⁸For laying aside the commandment of God, ye hold the tradition of men, *as* the washing of pots and cups: and many other such like things ye do. ⁹And he said unto them, Full well ye reject^d the commandment of God, that ye may keep your own tradition. ¹⁰For Moses said, Honour thy father and thy mother; and, Whoso curseth father or mother, let him die the death: ¹¹But ye say, If a man shall say to his father or mother, *It is* Corban, that is to say, a gift, by whatsoever thou mightest be profited by me; *he shall be free.* ¹²And ye suffer him no more to do ought for his father or his mother; ¹³Making the word of God of none effect through your tradition, which ye have delivered: and many such like things do ye. ¹⁴And when he had called all the people *unto him,* he said unto them, Hearken unto me every one *of you,* and understand: ¹⁵There is nothing from without a man, that entering into him can defile him: but the things which come out of him, those are they that defile the man. ¹⁶If any man have ears to hear, let him hear. ¹⁷And when he was entered into the house from the people, his disciples asked him concerning the parable. ¹⁸And he saith unto them, Are ye so without understanding also? Do ye not perceive, that whatsoever thing from without entereth into the man, *it* cannot defile him; ¹⁹Because it entereth not into his heart, but into the belly, and goeth out into the draught, purging all meats? ²⁰And he said, That which cometh out of the man, that defileth the man. ²¹For from within, out of the heart of men, proceed evil thoughts, adulteries, fornications, murders, ²²Thefts, covetousness^e, wickedness, deceit, lasciviousness, an evil eye, blasphemy, pride, foolishness: ²³All these evil things come from within, and defile the man.

---

^c pots: sextarius is about a pint and an half

^d reject: or, frustrate

^e covetousness . . . : Gr. covetousnesses, wickednesses

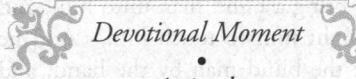

Devotional Moment
•
Attitudes

7:14-20 The Jews stressed dietary regulations to keep themselves from unclean living. Yet Jesus said that inner character mattered more than outward religious acts. While it's important to teach your children to behave properly, it's even more crucial to help them develop godly character qualities, such as resiliency, confidence, generosity, compassion, decisiveness, honesty, persistence. That's a lot to learn, but it can all be modeled at home. Open your own mind and heart to the work of God's Spirit. Then help your children to do the same.

²⁴And from thence he arose, and went into the borders of Tyre and Sidon, and entered into an house, and would have no man know *it*: but he could not be hid. ²⁵For a *certain* woman, whose young daughter had an unclean spirit, heard of him, and came and fell at his feet: ²⁶The woman was a Greek^f, a Syrophenician by nation; and she besought him that he would cast forth the devil out of her daughter. ²⁷But Jesus said unto her, Let the children first be filled: for it is not meet to take the children's bread, and to cast *it* unto the dogs. ²⁸And she answered and said unto him, Yes, Lord: yet the dogs under the table eat of the children's crumbs. ²⁹And he said unto her, For this saying go thy way; the devil is gone out of thy daughter. ³⁰And when she was come to her house, she found the devil gone out, and her daughter laid upon the bed.

³¹And again, departing from the coasts of Tyre and Sidon, he came unto the sea of Galilee, through the midst of the coasts of Decapolis. ³²And they bring unto him one that was deaf, and had an impediment in his speech; and they beseech him to put his hand upon him. ³³And he took him aside from the multitude, and put his fingers into his ears, and he spit, and touched his tongue; ³⁴And looking up to heaven, he sighed, and saith unto him, Ephphatha, that is, Be opened. ³⁵And straightway his ears were opened, and the string of his tongue was loosed, and he spake plain. ³⁶And he charged them that they should tell no man: but the more he charged them, so much the more a great deal they published *it*; ³⁷And were beyond measure astonished, saying, He hath done all things well: he maketh both the deaf to hear, and the dumb to speak.

8

¹In those days the multitude being very great, and having nothing to eat, Jesus called his disciples *unto him*, and saith unto them, ²I have compassion on the multitude, because they have now been with me three days, and have nothing to eat: ³And if I send them away fasting to their own houses, they will faint by the way: for divers of them came from far. ⁴And his disciples answered him, From whence can a man satisfy these *men* with bread here in the wilderness? ⁵And he asked them, How many loaves have ye? And they said, Seven. ⁶And he commanded the people to sit down on the ground: and he took the seven loaves, and gave thanks, and brake, and gave to his disciples to set before *them*; and they did set *them* before the people.

---

^f Greek: or, Gentile

⁷And they had a few small fishes: and he blessed, and commanded to set them also before *them*. ⁸So they did eat, and were filled: and they took up of the broken *meat* that was left seven baskets. ⁹And they that had eaten were about four thousand: and he sent them away.

¹⁰And straightway he entered into a ship with his disciples, and came into the parts of Dalmanutha. ¹¹And the Pharisees came forth, and began to question with him, seeking of him a sign from heaven, tempting him. ¹²And he sighed deeply in his spirit, and saith, Why doth this generation seek after a sign? verily I say unto you, There shall no sign be given unto this generation. ¹³And he left them, and entering into the ship again departed to the other side. ¹⁴Now *the disciples* had forgotten to take bread, neither had they in the ship with them more than one loaf. ¹⁵And he charged them, saying, Take heed, beware of the leaven of the Pharisees, and *of* the leaven of Herod. ¹⁶And they reasoned among themselves, saying, *It is* because we have no bread. ¹⁷And when Jesus knew *it*, he saith unto them, Why reason ye, because ye have no bread? perceive ye not yet, neither understand? have ye your heart yet hardened? ¹⁸Having eyes, see ye not? and having ears, hear ye not? and do ye not remember? ¹⁹When I brake the five loaves among five thousand, how many baskets full of fragments took ye up? They say unto him, Twelve. ²⁰And when the seven among four thousand, how many baskets full of fragments took ye up? And they said, Seven. ²¹And he said unto them, How is it that ye do not understand?

²²And he cometh to Bethsaida; and they bring a blind man unto him, and besought him to touch him. ²³And he took the blind man by the hand, and led him out of the town; and when he had spit on his eyes, and put his hands upon him, he asked him if he saw ought. ²⁴And he looked up, and said, I see men as trees, walking. ²⁵After that he put *his* hands again upon his eyes, and made him look up: and he was restored, and saw every man clearly. ²⁶And he sent him away to his house, saying, Neither go into the town, nor tell *it* to any in the town.

²⁷And Jesus went out, and his disciples, into the towns of Caesarea Philippi: and by the way he asked his disciples, saying unto them, Whom do men say that I am? ²⁸And they answered, John the Baptist: but some *say,* Elias; and others, One of the prophets. ²⁹And he saith unto them, But whom say ye that I am? And Peter answereth and saith unto him, Thou art the Christ. ³⁰And he charged them that they should tell no man of him. ³¹And he began to teach them, that the Son of man must suffer many things, and be rejected of the elders, and *of* the chief priests, and scribes, and be killed, and after three days rise again. ³²And he spake that saying openly. And Peter took him, and began to rebuke him. ³³But when he had turned about and looked on his disciples, he rebuked Peter, saying, Get thee behind me, Satan: for thou savourest not the things that be of God, but the things that be of men. ³⁴And when he had called the people *unto him* with his disciples also, he said unto them, Whosoever will come after me, let him deny himself, and take up his cross, and follow me. ³⁵For whosoever will save his life shall lose it; but whosoever shall lose

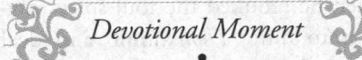

his life for my sake and the gospel's, the same shall save it. ³⁶For what shall it profit a man, if he shall gain the whole world, and lose his own soul? ³⁷Or what shall a man give in exchange for his soul? ³⁸Whosoever therefore shall be ashamed of me and of my words in this adulterous and sinful generation; of him also shall the Son of man be ashamed, when he cometh in the glory of his Father with the holy angels.

9

¹And he said unto them, Verily I say unto you, That there be some of them that stand here, which shall not taste of death, till they have seen the kingdom of God come with power. ²And after six days Jesus taketh *with him* Peter, and James, and John, and leadeth them up into an high mountain apart by themselves: and he was transfigured before them. ³And his raiment became shining, exceeding white as snow; so as no fuller on earth can white them. ⁴And there appeared unto them Elias with Moses: and they were talking with Jesus. ⁵And Peter answered and said to Jesus, Master, it is good for us to be here: and let us make three tabernacles; one for thee, and one for Moses, and one for Elias. ⁶For he wist not what to say; for they were sore afraid. ⁷And there was a cloud that overshadowed them: and a voice came out of the cloud, saying, This is my beloved Son: hear him. ⁸And suddenly, when they had looked round about, they saw no man any more, save Jesus only with themselves. ⁹And as they came down from the mountain, he charged them that they should tell no man what things they had seen, till the Son of man were risen from the dead. ¹⁰And they kept that saying with themselves, questioning one with another what the rising from the dead should mean. ¹¹And they asked him, saying, Why say the scribes that Elias must first come? ¹²And he answered and told them, Elias verily cometh first, and restoreth all things; and how it is written of the Son of man, that he must suffer many things, and be set at nought. ¹³But I say unto you, That Elias is indeed come, and they have done unto him whatsoever they listed, as it is written of him.

¹⁴And when he came to *his* disciples, he saw a great multitude about them, and the scribes questioning with them. ¹⁵And straightway all the people, when they beheld him, were greatly amazed, and running to *him* saluted him. ¹⁶And he asked the scribes, What question ye with them?ᵃ ¹⁷And one of

ᵃ with them: or, among yourselves

the multitude answered and said, Master, I have brought unto thee my son, which hath a dumb spirit; [18]And wheresoever he taketh him, he teareth[b] him: and he foameth, and gnasheth with his teeth, and pineth away: and I spake to thy disciples that they should cast him out; and they could not. [19]He answereth him, and saith, O faithless generation, how long shall I be with you? how long shall I suffer you? bring him unto me. [20]And they brought him unto him: and when he saw him, straightway the spirit tare him; and he fell on the ground, and wallowed foaming. [21]And he asked his father, How long is it ago since this came unto him? And he said, Of a child. [22]And ofttimes it hath cast him into the fire, and into the waters, to destroy him: but if thou canst do any thing, have compassion on us, and help us. [23]Jesus said unto him, If thou canst believe, all things *are* possible to him that believeth. [24]And straightway the father of the child cried out, and said with tears, Lord, I believe; help thou mine unbelief. [25]When Jesus saw that the people came running together, he rebuked the foul spirit, saying unto him, *Thou* dumb and deaf spirit, I charge thee, come out of him, and enter no more into him. [26]And *the spirit* cried, and rent him sore, and came out of him: and he was as one dead; insomuch that many said, He is dead. [27]But Jesus took him by the hand, and lifted him up; and he arose. [28]And when he was come into the house, his disciples asked him privately, Why could not we cast him out? [29]And he said unto them, This kind can come forth by nothing, but by prayer and fasting.

[30]And they departed thence, and passed through Galilee; and he would not that any man should know *it*. [31]For he taught his disciples, and said unto them, The Son of man is delivered into the hands of men, and they shall kill him; and after that he is killed, he shall rise the third day. [32]But they understood not that saying, and were afraid to ask him. [33]And he came to Capernaum: and being in the house he asked them, What was it that ye disputed among yourselves by the way? [34]But they held their peace: for by the way they had disputed among themselves, who *should be* the greatest. [35]And he sat down, and called the twelve, and saith unto them, If any man desire to be first, *the same* shall be last of all, and servant of all. [36]And he took a child, and set him in the midst of them: and when he had taken him in his arms, he said unto them, [37]Whosoever shall receive one of such children in my name, receiveth me: and whosoever shall receive me, receiveth not me, but him that sent me.

Devotional Moment

Evil in the World

9:17-29 Jesus did not elaborate on demons in this situation; he indicated only that this one belonged to a tougher breed. Here's what we know: (1) Demons are real and troublesome; they cause a lot of the evil around us. (2) Faith and prayer are effective in fighting demons and beating back evil where science, technology, medicine, psychology, and a thousand other tools fail. Never underestimate the power of believing prayer.

---

[b] teareth . . . : or, dasheth him

38And John answered him, saying, Master, we saw one casting out devils in thy name, and he followeth not us: and we forbad him, because he followeth not us. 39But Jesus said, Forbid him not: for there is no man which shall do a miracle in my name, that can lightly speak evil of me. 40For he that is not against us is on our part.

41For whosoever shall give you a cup of water to drink in my name, because ye belong to Christ, verily I say unto you, he shall not lose his reward. 42And whosoever shall offend one of *these* little ones that believe in me, it is better for him that a millstone were hanged about his neck, and he were cast into the sea. 43And if thy hand offendᶜ thee, cut it off: it is better for thee to enter into life maimed, than having two hands to go into hell, into the fire that never shall be quenched: 44Where their worm dieth not, and the fire is not quenched. 45And if thy foot offendᵈ thee, cut it off: it is better for thee to enter halt into life, than having two feet to be cast into hell, into the fire that never shall be quenched: 46Where their worm dieth not, and the fire is not quenched. 47And if thine eye offendᵉ thee, pluck it out: it is better for thee to enter into the kingdom of God with one eye, than having two eyes to be cast into hell fire: 48Where their worm dieth not, and the fire is not quenched. 49For every one shall be salted with fire, and every sacrifice shall be salted with salt. 50Salt *is* good: but if the salt have lost his saltness, wherewith will ye season it? Have salt in yourselves, and have peace one with another.

10

1And he arose from thence, and cometh into the coasts of Judaea by the farther side of Jordan: and the people resort unto him again; and, as he was wont, he taught them again. 2And the Pharisees came to him, and asked him, Is it lawful for a man to put away *his* wife? tempting him. 3And he answered and said unto them, What did Moses command you? 4And they said, Moses suffered to write a bill of divorcement, and to put *her* away. 5And Jesus answered and said unto them, For the hardness of your heart he wrote you this precept. 6But from the beginning of the creation God made them male and female. 7For this cause shall a man leave his father and mother, and cleave to his wife; 8And they twain shall be one flesh: so then they are no more twain, but one flesh. 9What therefore God hath joined together, let not man put asunder. 10And in the house his disciples asked him again of the same *matter*. 11And he saith unto them, Whosoever shall put away his wife, and marry another, committeth adultery against her. 12And if a woman shall put away her husband, and be married to another, she committeth adultery.

13And they brought young children to him, that he should touch them: and *his* disciples rebuked those that brought *them*. 14But when Jesus saw *it*, he was much displeased, and said unto them,

---

ᶜ offend . . . : or, cause thee to offend
ᵈ offend . . . : or, cause thee to offend
ᵉ offend . . . : or, cause thee to offend

Recognizing Child Abuse

by Bill Anderson

Jesus placed a high priority on children (see Mark 9:37, 42), and one of the contemporary issues that must sadden his heart is the sexual abuse of children. It is an unpleasant subject, but one that poses a serious threat; statistically, one out of three girls and one out of five boys will suffer some form of sexual abuse by age eighteen. It is dangerous to think it cannot happen in your family or church because it happens to all kinds of people.

Surprisingly, children (because of fear and shame) often do not tell anybody when they have been abused. Therefore, adults must be on the alert for symptoms of abuse in children under their care. Physical symptoms include unexplained redness, swelling, bruises, infections, or bleeding. Other symptoms usually include some form of marked change in behavior that is uncharacteristic of the child, such as reverting to bedwetting or thumbsucking, showing fear of a person or place, or having nightmares or sleep disorders. Any single physical or behavioral symptom can be caused by something other than abuse, but each should still be checked out. When clusters of these symptoms occur, they are definite warning signs.

When you have valid reasons to suspect that your child has been abused, file a police report. Resist the urge to investigate the case privately.

Many Christians cringe at the thought of "causing" someone to go to jail, and this may be especially true if the perpetrator is a friend or family member. (Most abused children are victimized by someone they know or trust.) However, we must remember that God established civil government to punish wrongdoing (see Rom. 13:4). Furthermore, many abusers are habitual offenders, and those who are not prosecuted remain free to abuse other children.

Abused children should be given a medical examination. Children sometimes sustain physical damage or contract diseases through abuse, and early detection and treatment are very important.

Parents will also wonder whether an abused child needs professional counseling or therapy. While needs vary greatly from child to child, it is a good idea to schedule at least one evaluative session with a trained counselor. Some children will need no more than this, while others may need multiple sessions to help them work through fear, anger, and mistrust; those who have suffered repeated abuse, have been victims of incest, exhibit serious behavioral symptoms, or will be participating in a trial fit into this category.

The most important factor in a child's recovery is the response by his or her parents. Tell your child that you are sorry that something bad happened and that you will do all you can to prevent further harm. You should remain calm in the child's presence because hysteria can convey the message that he or she has done something wrong. Excessive anger expressed toward the perpetrator can make a child feel guilty for getting someone else in trouble. Most of all, abused children need to be assured that they have done nothing wrong.

You *can* take steps to prevent sexual abuse from happening. Start teaching your children early about safety issues. At age two or three, instruct them about the private zones of the body ("the parts that a bathing suit covers") and that others should not be allowed to touch these parts. As children get older, warn them that sexual abuse can happen in many settings and that they need to say no, get away, and tell an adult at the first sign of danger.

Parents should realize that no child can fully protect himself or herself. It is the nature of abuse that a more powerful person victimizes those who are helpless. Therefore, parents must take the lead: Make sure you know your baby-sitter, drop in unexpectedly at your day-care center, know where your children are playing in your neighborhood, talk with your children regularly about how their day went, and even make sure that your church has protective policies in its children's ministry. The only sure way of preventing the sexual abuse of children is to deny would-be perpetrators access to our children.

Jesus used harsh language in referring to those who would jeopardize the well-being of children (Mark 9:42). On the other hand, he intimated that when we care for these little lambs of the flock, we are engaged in his work (9:37).

DIGGING DEEPER

1. What is the relationship of civil government to God? What is the God-ordained function of civil government? See Romans 13:1-7.

2. What is the difference between civil suits among believers and criminal trials conducted by the state? See 1 Corinthians 6:1-8.

Suffer the little children to come unto me, and forbid them not: for of such is the kingdom of God. ¹⁵Verily I say unto you, Whosoever shall not receive the kingdom of God as a little child, he shall not enter therein. ¹⁶And he took them up in his arms, put *his* hands upon them, and blessed them.

¹⁷And when he was gone forth into the way, there came one running, and kneeled to him, and asked him, Good Master, what shall I do that I may inherit eternal life? ¹⁸And Jesus said unto him, Why callest thou me good? *there is* none good but one, *that is*, God. ¹⁹Thou knowest the commandments, Do not commit adultery, Do not kill, Do not steal, Do not bear false witness, Defraud not, Honour thy father and mother. ²⁰And he answered and said unto him, Master, all these have I observed from my youth. ²¹Then Jesus beholding him loved him, and said unto him, One thing thou lackest: go thy way, sell whatsoever thou hast, and give to the poor, and thou shalt have treasure in heaven: and come, take up the cross, and follow me. ²²And he was sad

at that saying, and went away grieved: for he had great possessions. ²³And Jesus looked round about, and saith unto his disciples, How hardly shall they that have riches enter into the kingdom of God! ²⁴And the disciples were astonished at his words. But Jesus answereth again, and saith unto them, Children, how hard is it for them that trust in riches to enter into the kingdom of God! ²⁵It is easier for a camel to go through the eye of a needle, than for a

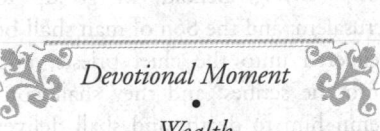

Devotional Moment

Wealth

10:23 Jesus warned: Wealth can be a barrier to entering God's Kingdom. Why? (1) Wealth can bring *self-assurance*, the sense that we have done well by our own efforts (without God). (2) Wealth can bring *worry over losing it*. (3) Wealth can bring *a false sense of security*—the belief that we will never have any need and that we don't need God or other people. Jesus wants us to live a life of service to him and others. Wealthy people can live this way—but many don't. Understand that wealth simply isn't the answer to every problem.

rich man to enter into the kingdom of God. ²⁶And they were astonished out of measure, saying among themselves, Who then can be saved? ²⁷And Jesus looking upon them saith, With men *it is* impossible, but not with God: for with God all things are possible. ²⁸Then Peter began to say unto him, Lo, we have left all, and have followed thee. ²⁹And Jesus answered and said, Verily I say unto you, There is no man that hath left house, or brethren, or sisters, or father, or mother, or wife, or children, or lands, for my sake, and the gospel's, ³⁰But he shall receive an hundredfold now in this time, houses, and brethren, and sisters, and mothers, and children, and lands, with persecutions; and in the world to come eternal life. ³¹But many *that are* first shall be last; and the last first.

³²And they were in the way going up to Jerusalem; and Jesus went before them: and they were amazed; and as they followed, they were afraid. And he took again the twelve, and began to tell them what things should happen unto him, ³³*Saying*, Behold, we go up to Jerusalem; and the Son of man shall be delivered unto the chief priests, and unto the scribes; and they shall condemn him to death, and shall deliver him to the Gentiles: ³⁴And they shall mock him, and shall scourge him, and shall spit upon him, and shall kill him: and the third day he shall rise again. ³⁵And James and John, the sons of Zebedee, come unto him, saying, Master, we would that thou shouldest do for us whatsoever we shall desire. ³⁶And he said unto them, What would ye that I should do for you? ³⁷They said unto him, Grant unto us that we may sit,

one on thy right hand, and the other on thy left hand, in thy glory. ³⁸But Jesus said unto them, Ye know not what ye ask: can ye drink of the cup that I drink of? and be baptized with the baptism that I am baptized with? ³⁹And they said unto him, We can. And Jesus said unto them, Ye shall indeed drink of the cup that I drink of; and with the baptism that I am baptized withal shall ye be baptized: ⁴⁰But to sit on my right hand and on my left hand is not mine to give; but *it shall be given to them* for whom it is prepared. ⁴¹And when the ten heard *it*, they began to be much displeased with James and John. ⁴²But Jesus called them *to him*, and saith unto them, Ye know that they which are accounted to rule over the Gentiles exercise lordship over them; and their great ones exercise authority upon them. ⁴³But so shall it not be among you: but whosoever will be great among you, shall be your minister: ⁴⁴And whosoever of you will be the chiefest, shall be servant of all. ⁴⁵For even the Son of man came not to be ministered unto, but to minister, and to give his life a ransom for many.

⁴⁶And they came to Jericho: and as he went out of Jericho with his disciples and a great number of people, blind Bartimaeus, the son of Timaeus, sat by the highway side begging. ⁴⁷And when he heard that it was Jesus of Nazareth, he began to cry out, and say, Jesus, *thou* Son of David, have mercy on me. ⁴⁸And many charged him that he should hold his peace: but he cried the more a great deal, *Thou* Son of David, have mercy on me. ⁴⁹And Jesus stood still, and commanded him to be called. And they call the blind man, saying unto him, Be of

good comfort, rise; he calleth thee. [50]And he, casting away his garment, rose, and came to Jesus. [51]And Jesus answered and said unto him, What wilt thou that I should do unto thee? The blind man said unto him, Lord, that I might receive my sight. [52]And Jesus said unto him, Go thy way; thy faith hath made[a] thee whole. And immediately he received his sight, and followed Jesus in the way.

11

[1]And when they came nigh to Jerusalem, unto Bethphage and Bethany, at the mount of Olives, he sendeth forth two of his disciples, [2]And saith unto them, Go your way into the village over against you: and as soon as ye be entered into it, ye shall find a colt tied, whereon never man sat; loose him, and bring *him*. [3]And if any man say unto you, Why do ye this? say ye that the Lord hath need of him; and straightway he will send him hither. [4]And they went their way, and found the colt tied by the door without in a place where two ways met; and they loose him. [5]And certain of them that stood there said unto them, What do ye, loosing the colt? [6]And they said unto them even as Jesus had commanded: and they let them go. [7]And they brought the colt to Jesus, and cast their garments on him; and he sat upon him. [8]And many spread their garments in the way: and others cut down branches off the trees, and strawed *them* in the way. [9]And they that went before, and they that followed, cried, saying, Hosanna; Blessed

is he that cometh in the name of the Lord: [10]Blessed *be* the kingdom of our father David, that cometh in the name of the Lord: Hosanna in the highest. [11]And Jesus entered into Jerusalem, and into the temple: and when he had looked round about upon all things, and now the eventide was come, he went out unto Bethany with the twelve.

[12]And on the morrow, when they were come from Bethany, he was hungry: [13]And seeing a fig tree afar off having leaves, he came, if haply he might find any thing thereon: and when he came to it, he found nothing but leaves; for the time of figs was not *yet*. [14]And Jesus answered and said unto it, No man eat fruit of thee hereafter for ever. And his disciples heard *it*. [15]And they come to Jerusalem: and Jesus went into the temple, and began to cast out them that sold and bought in the temple, and overthrew the tables of the money-changers, and the seats of them that sold doves; [16]And would not suffer that any man should carry *any* vessel through the temple. [17]And he taught, saying unto them, Is it not written, My house shall be called of all[a] nations the house of prayer? but ye have made it a den of thieves. [18]And the scribes and chief priests heard *it*, and sought how they might destroy him: for they feared him, because all the people was astonished at his doctrine. [19]And when even was come, he went out of the city. [20]And in the morning, as they passed by, they saw the fig tree dried up from the roots. [21]And Peter calling to remembrance saith unto him, Master, behold,

---

[a] made . . . : or, saved thee
[a] of all . . . : or, an house of prayer for all nations

James and John

There's no rivalry quite like sibling rivalry. Brothers and sisters can't help but clash as they try to occupy the same space and share the same things. But underneath the surface of hostility, at least among siblings, there is usually an undercurrent of devotion. James and John had that kind of bond.

When Jesus came to call them, they had the same job: partners with their father Zebedee in the family fishing business. They left their work together to follow Jesus together. In lists of the disciples, they are often mentioned together. Two of Jesus' three closest friends were the sons of Zebedee.

Even in asking Jesus if they could rule with him, James and John acted as a team: "We would that thou shouldest do for us whatsoever we shall desire," they said (Mark 10:35). We don't have any evidence that they fought over who would get to sit at Jesus' right hand and who would get the left. It seems plain that they had the same ambition.

The Bible (as well as our own experience) is full of stories of sibling rivalry: Cain and Abel; Rachel and Leah; Jacob and Esau; Absalom and Amnon; Solomon and Adonijah. But James and John were different.

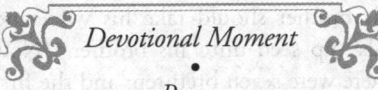

Devotional Moment
•
Prayer

11:22-25 Jesus' promise is incredible: "What things soever ye desire, when ye pray, believe that ye receive them, and ye shall have them." (v. 24). Have you ever prayed to move a mountain? Did it move? Jesus was not endorsing self-serving requests. He was talking about the power of real, sincere faith. Even when it is weak and faltering, like the faith of children, confidence in God works.

the fig tree which thou cursedst is withered away. ²²And Jesus answering saith unto them, Have[b] faith in God. ²³For verily I say unto you, That whosoever shall say unto this mountain, Be thou removed, and be thou cast into the sea; and shall not doubt in his heart, but shall believe that those things which he saith shall come to pass; he shall have whatsoever he saith. ²⁴Therefore I say unto you, What things soever ye desire, when ye pray, believe that ye receive them, and ye shall have them. ²⁵And when ye stand praying, forgive, if ye have ought against any: that your Father also which is in heaven may forgive you your trespasses. ²⁶But if ye do not forgive, neither will your Father which is in heaven forgive your trespasses.

²⁷And they come again to Jerusalem: and as he was walking in the temple, there come to him the chief priests, and the scribes, and the elders, ²⁸And say unto him, By what authority doest thou these things? and who gave thee this authority to do these things? ²⁹And Jesus answered and said unto them, I will also ask of you one question[c], and answer me, and I will tell you by what authority I do these things. ³⁰The baptism of John, was *it* from heaven, or of men? answer me. ³¹And they reasoned with themselves, saying, If we shall say, From heaven; he will say, Why then did ye not believe him? ³²But if we shall say, Of men; they feared the people: for all *men* counted John, that he was a prophet indeed. ³³And they answered and said unto Jesus, We cannot tell. And Jesus answering saith unto them, Neither do I tell you by what authority I do these things.

12

¹And he began to speak unto them by parables. A *certain* man planted a vineyard, and set an hedge about *it*, and digged *a place for* the winefat, and built a tower, and let it out to husbandmen, and went into a far country. ²And at the season he sent to the husbandmen a servant, that he might receive from the husbandmen of the fruit of the vineyard. ³And they caught *him*, and beat him, and sent *him* away empty. ⁴And again he sent unto them another servant; and at him they cast stones, and wounded *him* in the head, and sent *him* away shamefully handled. ⁵And again he sent another; and him they killed, and many others; beating some, and killing some. ⁶Having yet therefore one son, his wellbeloved, he sent him also last unto them, saying, They will reverence my son. ⁷But those husbandmen said among themselves, This is the heir; come, let us kill him, and the inheri-

[b] Have . . . : or, Have the faith of God
[c] question: or, thing

tance shall be ours. [8]And they took him, and killed *him*, and cast *him* out of the vineyard. [9]What shall therefore the lord of the vineyard do? he will come and destroy the husbandmen, and will give the vineyard unto others. [10]And have ye not read this scripture; The stone which the builders rejected is become the head of the corner: [11]This was the Lord's doing, and it is marvellous in our eyes? [12]And they sought to lay hold on him, but feared the people: for they knew that he had spoken the parable against them: and they left him, and went their way.

[13]And they send unto him certain of the Pharisees and of the Herodians, to catch him in *his* words. [14]And when they were come, they say unto him, Master, we know that thou art true, and carest for no man: for thou regardest not the person of men, but teachest the way of God in truth: Is it lawful to give tribute to Caesar, or not? [15]Shall we give, or shall we not give? But he, knowing their hypocrisy, said unto them, Why tempt ye me? bring me a penny[a], that I may see *it*. [16]And they brought *it*. And he saith unto them, Whose *is* this image and superscription? And they said unto him, Caesar's. [17]And Jesus answering said unto them, Render to Caesar the things that are Caesar's, and to God the things that are God's. And they marvelled at him.

[18]Then come unto him the Sadducees, which say there is no resurrection; and they asked him, saying, [19]Master, Moses wrote unto us, If a man's brother die, and leave *his* wife *behind him*, and leave no children, that his brother should take his wife, and raise up seed unto his brother. [20]Now there were seven brethren: and the first took a wife, and dying left no seed. [21]And the second took her, and died, neither left he any seed: and the third likewise. [22]And the seven had her, and left no seed: last of all the woman died also. [23]In the resurrection therefore, when they shall rise, whose wife shall she be of them? for the seven had her to wife. [24]And Jesus answering said unto them, Do ye not therefore err, because ye know not the scriptures, neither the power of God? [25]For when they shall rise from the dead, they neither marry, nor are given in marriage; but are as the angels which are in heaven. [26]And as touching the dead, that they rise: have ye not read in the book of Moses, how in the bush God spake unto him, saying, I *am* the God of Abraham, and the God of Isaac, and the God of Jacob? [27]He is not the God of the dead, but the God of the living: ye therefore do greatly err.

[28]And one of the scribes came, and having heard them reasoning together, and perceiving that he had answered them well, asked him, Which is the first commandment of all? [29]And Jesus answered him, The first of all the commandments *is*, Hear, O Israel; The Lord our God is one Lord: [30]And thou shalt love the Lord thy God with all thy heart, and with all thy soul, and with all thy mind, and with all thy strength: this *is* the first commandment. [31]And the second *is* like, *namely* this, Thou shalt love thy neighbour as thyself. There is none other commandment greater than

---

[a] penny: valuing of our money seven pence halfpenny

these. ³²And the scribe said unto him, Well, Master, thou hast said the truth: for there is one God; and there is none other but he: ³³And to love him with all the heart, and with all the understanding, and with all the soul, and with all the strength, and to love *his* neighbour as himself, is more than all whole burnt offerings and sacrifices. ³⁴And when Jesus saw that he answered discreetly, he said unto him, Thou art not far from the kingdom of God. And no man after that durst ask him *any question.*

³⁵And Jesus answered and said, while he taught in the temple, How say the scribes that Christ is the Son of David? ³⁶For David himself said by the Holy Ghost, The LORD said to my Lord, Sit thou on my right hand, till I make thine enemies thy footstool. ³⁷David therefore himself calleth him Lord; and whence is he *then* his son? And the common people heard him gladly. ³⁸And he said unto them in his doctrine, Beware of the scribes, which love to go in long clothing, and *love* salutations in the marketplaces, ³⁹And the chief seats in the synagogues, and the uppermost rooms at feasts: ⁴⁰Which devour widows' houses, and for a pretence make long prayers: these shall receive greater damnation.

⁴¹And Jesus sat over against the treasury, and beheld how the people cast money[b] into the treasury: and many that were rich cast in much. ⁴²And there came a certain poor widow, and she threw in two mites[c], which make a farthing. ⁴³And he called *unto him* his disciples, and saith unto them,

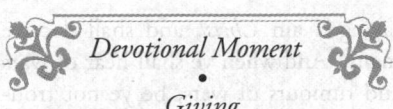

Devotional Moment
·
Giving

12:41-44 The widow gave her two pennies out of a generous heart. In Jesus' economy, the value of a gift is not measured by the exact amount but by how much it means to the giver. Everyone can give from the heart. A child who earns an allowance for chores, a parent who brings home a salary, a grandparent on a pension—all have the means to share something. All should. Giving helps remind us where our true treasure lies. Giving is a tangible way to show gratitude. Giving loosens our ties to money and strengthens our ties to God.

Verily I say unto you, That this poor widow hath cast more in, than all they which have cast into the treasury: ⁴⁴For all *they* did cast in of their abundance; but she of her want did cast in all that she had, *even* all her living.

13

¹And as he went out of the temple, one of his disciples saith unto him, Master, see what manner of stones and what buildings *are here!* ²And Jesus answering said unto him, Seest thou these great buildings? there shall not be left one stone upon another, that shall not be thrown down. ³And as he sat upon the mount of Olives over against the temple, Peter and James and John and Andrew asked him privately, ⁴Tell us, when shall these things be? and what *shall be* the sign when all these things shall be fulfilled?

⁵And Jesus answering them began to say, Take heed lest any *man* deceive you: ⁶For many shall come in my name,

---

[b] money: a piece of brass money
[c] mites: it is the seventh part of one piece of that brass money

saying, I am *Christ*, and shall deceive many. [7]And when ye shall hear of wars and rumours of wars, be ye not troubled: for *such things* must needs be; but the end *shall* not *be* yet. [8]For nation shall rise against nation, and kingdom against kingdom: and there shall be earthquakes in divers places, and there shall be famines and troubles: these *are* the beginnings of sorrows[a]. [9]But take heed to yourselves: for they shall deliver you up to councils; and in the synagogues ye shall be beaten: and ye shall be brought before rulers and kings for my sake, for a testimony against them. [10]And the gospel must first be published among all nations. [11]But when they shall lead *you*, and deliver you up, take no thought beforehand what ye shall speak, neither do ye premeditate: but whatsoever shall be given you in that hour, that speak ye: for it is not ye that speak, but the Holy Ghost. [12]Now the brother shall betray the brother to death, and the father the son; and children shall rise up against *their* parents, and shall cause them to be put to death. [13]And ye shall be hated of all *men* for my name's sake: but he that shall endure unto the end, the same shall be saved.

[14]But when ye shall see the abomination of desolation, spoken of by Daniel the prophet, standing where it ought not, (let him that readeth understand,) then let them that be in Judaea flee to the mountains: [15]And let him that is on the housetop not go down into the house, neither enter *therein*, to take any thing out of his house: [16]And let him that is in the field not turn back again for to take up his garment. [17]But woe to them that are with child, and to them that give suck in those days! [18]And pray ye that your flight be not in the winter. [19]For *in* those days shall be affliction, such as was not from the beginning of the creation which God created unto this time, neither shall be. [20]And except that the Lord had shortened those days, no flesh should be saved: but for the elect's sake, whom he hath chosen, he hath shortened the days. [21]And then if any man shall say to you, Lo, here *is* Christ; or, lo, *he is* there; believe *him* not: [22]For false Christs and false prophets shall rise, and shall shew signs and wonders, to seduce, if *it were* possible, even the elect. [23]But take ye heed: behold, I have foretold you all things.

[24]But in those days, after that tribulation, the sun shall be darkened, and the moon shall not give her light, [25]And the stars of heaven shall fall, and the powers that are in heaven shall be shaken. [26]And then shall they see the Son of man coming in the clouds with great power and glory. [27]And then shall he send his angels, and shall gather together his elect from the four winds, from the uttermost part of the earth to the uttermost part of heaven.

[28]Now learn a parable of the fig tree; When her branch is yet tender, and putteth forth leaves, ye know that summer is near: [29]So ye in like manner, when ye shall see these things come to pass, know that it is nigh, *even* at the doors. [30]Verily I say unto you, that this generation shall not pass, till all these things be done. [31]Heaven and earth shall pass away: but

---

[a] sorrows: the word in the original importeth the pains of a woman in travail

my words shall not pass away. ³²But of that day and *that* hour knoweth no man, no, not the angels which are in heaven, neither the Son, but the Father. ³³Take ye heed, watch and pray: for ye know not when the time is. ³⁴*For the Son of man is* as a man taking a far journey, who left his house, and gave authority to his servants, and to every man his work, and commanded the porter to watch. ³⁵Watch ye therefore: for ye know not when the master of the house cometh, at even, or at midnight, or at the cockcrowing, or in the morning: ³⁶Lest coming suddenly he find you sleeping. ³⁷And what I say unto you I say unto all, Watch.

14

¹After two days was *the feast of* the passover, and of unleavened bread: and the chief priests and the scribes sought how they might take him by craft, and put *him* to death. ²But they said, Not on the feast *day*, lest there be an uproar of the people. ³And being in Bethany in the house of Simon the leper, as he sat at meat, there came a woman having an alabaster box of ointment of spikenardᵃ very precious; and she brake the box, and poured *it* on his head. ⁴And there were some that had indignation within themselves, and said, Why was this waste of the ointment made? ⁵For it might have been sold for more than three hundred pence, and have been given to the poor. And they murmured against her. ⁶And Jesus said, Let her alone; why trouble ye her? she hath wrought a good work on me. ⁷For ye have the poor with you always, and whensoever ye will ye may do them good: but me ye have not always. ⁸She hath done what she could: she is come aforehand to anoint my body to the burying. ⁹Verily I say unto you, Wheresoever this gospel shall be preached throughout the whole world, *this* also that she hath done shall be spoken of for a memorial of her. ¹⁰And Judas Iscariot, one of the twelve, went unto the chief priests, to betray him unto them. ¹¹And when they heard *it*, they were glad, and promised to give him money. And he sought how he might conveniently betray him.

¹²And the first day of unleavened bread, when they killedᵇ the passover, his disciples said unto him, Where wilt thou that we go and prepare that thou mayest eat the passover? ¹³And he sendeth forth two of his disciples, and saith unto them, Go ye into the city, and there shall meet you a man bearing a pitcher of water: fol-

---

Devotional Moment
•
A Grateful Heart

14:3-8 Many times we are guilty of giving God our leftovers. We pay the bills and buy the things we want, and then—if there is anything left—we give to God's work. Or we fill up our schedule with the activities we enjoy doing and then try to squeeze God in somewhere. By contrast, Mary's gift to Jesus was costly, sacrificial, and extravagant. Her offering was pleasing to the Lord, not because of the amount, but because of the unselfish attitude behind it. It came from a heart bursting with love and gratitude. Consider how you might "waste" something valuable—vacation time, extra income, expertise—in order to show gratitude to Christ.

ᵃ spikenard: or, pure nard, or, liquid nard
ᵇ killed: or, sacrificed

low him. ¹⁴And wheresoever he shall go in, say ye to the goodman of the house, The Master saith, Where is the guestchamber, where I shall eat the passover with my disciples? ¹⁵And he will shew you a large upper room furnished *and* prepared: there make ready for us. ¹⁶And his disciples went forth, and came into the city, and found as he had said unto them: and they made ready the passover. ¹⁷And in the evening he cometh with the twelve. ¹⁸And as they sat and did eat, Jesus said, Verily I say unto you, One of you which eateth with me shall betray me. ¹⁹And they began to be sorrowful, and to say unto him one by one, Is it I? and another *said*, Is it I? ²⁰And he answered and said unto them, *It is* one of the twelve, that dippeth with me in the dish. ²¹The Son of man indeed goeth, as it is written of him: but woe to that man by whom the Son of man is betrayed! good were it for that man if he had never been born. ²²And as they did eat, Jesus took bread, and blessed, and brake *it*, and gave to them, and said, Take, eat: this is my body. ²³And he took the cup, and when he had given thanks, he gave *it* to them: and they all drank of it. ²⁴And he said unto them, This is my blood of the new testament, which is shed for many. ²⁵Verily I say unto you, I will drink no more of the fruit of the vine, until that day that I drink it new in the kingdom of God. ²⁶And when they had sung an hymn^c, they went out into the mount of Olives. ²⁷And Jesus saith unto them, All ye shall be offended^d because of me this night: for it is written, I will smite the shepherd, and the sheep shall be scattered. ²⁸But after

that I am risen, I will go before you into Galilee. ²⁹But Peter said unto him, Although all shall be offended, yet *will* not I. ³⁰And Jesus saith unto him, Verily I say unto thee, That this day, *even* in this night, before the cock crow twice, thou shalt deny me thrice. ³¹But he spake the more vehemently, If I should die with thee, I will not deny thee in any wise. Likewise also said they all.

³²And they came to a place which was named Gethsemane: and he saith to his disciples, Sit ye here, while I shall pray. ³³And he taketh with him Peter and James and John, and began to be sore amazed, and to be very heavy; ³⁴And saith unto them, My soul is exceeding sorrowful unto death: tarry ye here, and watch. ³⁵And he went forward a little, and fell on the ground, and prayed that, if it were possible, the hour might pass from him. ³⁶And he said, Abba, Father, all things *are* possible unto thee; take away this cup from me: nevertheless not what I will, but what thou wilt. ³⁷And he cometh, and findeth them sleeping, and saith unto Peter, Simon, sleepest thou? couldest not thou watch one hour? ³⁸Watch ye and pray, lest ye enter into temptation. The spirit truly *is* ready, but the flesh *is* weak. ³⁹And again he went away, and prayed, and spake the same words. ⁴⁰And when he returned, he found them asleep again, (for their eyes were heavy,) neither wist they what to answer him. ⁴¹And he cometh the third time, and saith unto them, Sleep on now, and take *your* rest: it is enough, the hour is come; behold, the Son of man is betrayed into the hands of sinners. ⁴²Rise

---

^c hymn: or, psalm
^d offended: or, scandalized, or, shall stumble

up, let us go; lo, he that betrayeth me is at hand.

⁴³And immediately, while he yet spake, cometh Judas, one of the twelve, and with him a great multitude with swords and staves, from the chief priests and the scribes and the elders. ⁴⁴And he that betrayed him had given them a token, saying, Whomsoever I shall kiss, that same is he; take him, and lead *him* away safely. ⁴⁵And as soon as he was come, he goeth straightway to him, and saith, Master, master; and kissed him. ⁴⁶And they laid their hands on him, and took him. ⁴⁷And one of them that stood by drew a sword, and smote a servant of the high priest, and cut off his ear. ⁴⁸And Jesus answered and said unto them, Are ye come out, as against a thief, with swords and *with* staves to take me? ⁴⁹I was daily with you in the temple teaching, and ye took me not: but the scriptures must be fulfilled. ⁵⁰And they all forsook him, and fled. ⁵¹And there followed him a certain young man, having a linen cloth cast about *his* naked *body*; and the young men laid hold on him: ⁵²And he left the linen cloth, and fled from them naked.

⁵³And they led Jesus away to the high priest: and with him were assembled all the chief priests and the elders and the scribes. ⁵⁴And Peter followed him afar off, even into the palace of the high priest: and he sat with the servants, and warmed himself at the fire. ⁵⁵And the chief priests and all the council sought for witness against Jesus to put him to death; and found none. ⁵⁶For many bare false witness against him, but their witness agreed not together. ⁵⁷And there arose certain, and bare false witness against him, say-ing, ⁵⁸We heard him say, I will destroy this temple that is made with hands, and within three days I will build another made without hands. ⁵⁹But neither so did their witness agree together. ⁶⁰And the high priest stood up in the midst, and asked Jesus, saying, Answerest thou noth-ing? what *is it which* these witness against thee? ⁶¹But he held his peace, and an-swered nothing. Again the high priest asked him, and said unto him, Art thou the Christ, the Son of the Blessed? ⁶²And Jesus said, I am: and ye shall see the Son of man sitting on the right hand of power, and coming in the clouds of heaven. ⁶³Then the high priest rent his clothes, and saith, What need we any fur-ther witnesses? ⁶⁴Ye have heard the blas-phemy: what think ye? And they all con-demned him to be guilty of death. ⁶⁵And some began to spit on him, and to cover his face, and to buffet him, and to say unto him, Prophesy: and the servants did strike him with the palms of their hands.

⁶⁶And as Peter was beneath in the palace, there cometh one of the maids of the high priest: ⁶⁷And when she saw Peter warming himself, she looked upon him, and said, And thou also wast with Jesus of Nazareth. ⁶⁸But he denied, saying, I know not, neither understand I what thou sayest. And he went out into the porch; and the cock crew. ⁶⁹And a maid saw him again, and began to say to them that stood by, This is *one* of them. ⁷⁰And he denied it again. And a little after, they that stood by said again to Peter, Surely thou art *one* of them: for thou art a Galilaean, and thy speech agreeth *thereto*. ⁷¹But he began to curse and to swear, *saying*, I know not this man of whom ye speak. ⁷²And the second time the cock crew. And Peter

Family Traditions

Passover and Easter Celebrations

MARK 14:12-26; 16:1-12

During Passover, the Jewish nation remembers the safe exodus from Egypt bought by a lamb's blood sprinkled on the doorpost of each home. To commemorate the hasty flight, they eat unleavened bread, and they remember the thirst in the desert as they taste the bitter herbs. Wine symbolizes the fulfillment of God's promise in a land flowing with milk and honey and abounding in ripe fruit. When Jesus Christ lived and worked among his people, he lifted the bread and wine of Passover, thanked God for it, and called it his body and blood.

"We never observe Passover without adding the reading from Mark 14–16 to our reading from Exodus," says Anne Freid, a messianic Jew living in Denver, Colorado. "On Passover we invite Jewish friends and neighbors into our home. The meal and decorations all come from our heritage as Hebrews. But as a family, we make no secret about knowing the Messiah. Just as Mary Magdalene went back to the disciples and told them Jesus was alive, the Passover feast is our way to take the gospel outside our home."

For the Westergaards of Milwaukee, the Scandinavian *Paaske,* or Easter celebration, is a time to pull out all stops in celebrating new life because Christ lives. On Saturday they prepare spring decorations using symbols of crocus bulbs, budding flowers, and lambs. A budding branch is decorated with tiny silk blooms, pastel colored ribbons, and little parchment Scriptures from Mark's Gospel. Around the base lie the toy and porcelain lambs Martha collects. A hand-painted ribbon banner proclaims: "Welcome Easter, Jesus Is the Lamb of God."

The Westergaards' weekend is reserved for family activities in the backyard, weather permitting, or games on the living room floor—spread out on the picnic blanket. They make up their own Bible memory and history games that are as wacky and as lively as possible.

"When the children were small, we dramatized the Easter story on Sunday morning before church," Martha tells us, "complete with taking spices to the tomb (our dining table draped with white sheets), an 'angel' bathed in light (using an extra bright bulb in our ceiling lamp), and exclamations of unbelief from the doubting 'disciples.' "

However symbols change or differ from family to family, for those who know the power of his life within, Christ's triumph over death poised on our calendar at the end of winter is prime time to celebrate.

Breaking Free from Denied Grief

[Jesus] taketh with him Peter and James and John, and began to be sore amazed, and to be very heavy; and saith unto them, "My soul is exceeding sorrowful unto death: tarry ye here, and watch." Mark 14:33-34

One of the most destructive patterns that can hold a person back from experiencing warm, fulfilling relationships is an inability to grieve honestly over difficult times or losses. Don't be surprised if you've never thought of grieving as a *good* thing. Alan never did.

He was nine years old, the oldest of seven kids, when his father died suddenly. Alan's uncle pulled him aside the next day, looked him in the eye, and said: "You've got to be strong for your brothers and sisters. Do you understand? *Don't you let me see you cry!*"

Alan didn't disappoint his uncle. He fought back an avalanche of emotions and tears at his father's funeral so that he could be "strong." He did the same thing when he lost comrades in Vietnam and also later when he lost his closest brother died in an automobile accident.

Holding all his hurt and pain inside actually kept Alan from living and relating authentically instead of making him a "real man." Soon after he married, his wife realized that by blocking out his negative emotions, he had also effectively turned off any expression of warmth and affection.

Is it really Christlike to express our hurts and fears—to grieve genuinely and share that hurt with others?

Jesus was with his disciples in the Garden of Gethsemane when he told Peter, James, and John, "My soul is exceeding sorrowful unto death: tarry ye here, and watch." Jesus talked about his feelings in straightforward language.

Then Jesus went on a little farther, fell to the ground, and prayed: " 'Father, all things are possible unto thee; take away this cup from me' " (Mark 14:36). In the most tender form of address that a son could make to his father, Jesus cried out to his Father like a child waiting to face an operation who pleads, "Daddy, don't let them hurt me!" And then, in complete submission to and trust in the Father, he said: "Not what I will, but what thou wilt" (Mark 14:36).

The God of the universe, clothed in humanity, experienced the pain and confusion that we all face in grief. Yet one clear principle stands out: When Jesus faced his greatest time of trial and grief, he sought support from people and prayed. While he still wrestled alone with the decision to go to the cross, he didn't isolate himself from others, nor abandon prayer in the process.

For Jesus, expressing his grief was the storm before the calm. Honestly battling through the pain and anguish and giving it to the Father enabled him to go on. He woke up his sleeping disciples to tell them calmly that he was about to be arrested. He did not shudder at the guards as they came with torches to seize him. He did not whimper during the unjust trials or even break down at the cross. The battle had first been won in a lonely garden as he honestly faced death and dying and laid his life in the Father's hands. Wrestling with his emotions honestly, openly, and in prayer strengthened him to fulfill the Father's plan.

Maybe if Alan had only realized that the strongest man of all time admitted his feelings instead of stuffing them inside, he could have saved himself—and his family—much hurt and pain. Thankfully, today Alan has changed. At times he even cries in front of his wife and family. But it's taken courage to break a negative pattern from the past and model a side of Christlikeness that is often overlooked. Honest, genuine grieving doesn't emasculate us; rather, it empowers us to face even the most difficult challenges and losses.

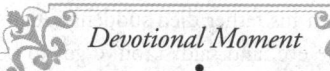

Devotional Moment

Judging

14:66-71 Our tendency may be to read this passage and say: "I can't believe Peter denied Christ. I would *never* do such a thing!" Such statements are unwise for at least three reasons. First, we can't fully appreciate the extreme pressure of the situation that Peter and the disciples were facing. Second, such an arrogant attitude invites trouble (Prov. 16:18). Third, we all have denied Christ in numerous, though perhaps less dramatic, ways. Before you point your finger at someone else, remember the old saying, "There, but for the grace of God, go I." Instead of condemning those who have fallen, pray for them and offer whatever help you can give.

called to mind the word that Jesus said unto him, Before the cock crow twice, thou shalt deny me thrice. And when he thought thereon, he wept.

15

¹And straightway in the morning the chief priests held a consultation with the elders and scribes and the whole council, and bound Jesus, and carried *him* away, and delivered *him* to Pilate. ²And Pilate asked him, Art thou the King of the Jews? And he answering said unto him, Thou sayest *it.* ³And the chief priests accused him of many things: but he answered nothing. ⁴And Pilate asked him again, saying, Answerest thou nothing? behold how many things they witness against thee. ⁵But Jesus yet answered nothing; so that Pilate marvelled. ⁶Now at *that* feast he released unto them one prisoner, whomsoever they desired. ⁷And there was *one* named Barabbas, *which lay* bound with them that had made insurrection with him, who had committed murder in the insurrection. ⁸And the multitude crying aloud began to desire *him to do* as he had ever done unto them. ⁹But Pilate answered them, saying, Will ye that I release unto you the King of the Jews? ¹⁰For he knew that the chief priests had delivered him for envy. ¹¹But the chief priests moved the people, that he should rather release Barabbas unto

them. [12]And Pilate answered and said again unto them, What will ye then that I shall do *unto him* whom ye call the King of the Jews? [13]And they cried out again, Crucify him. [14]Then Pilate said unto them, Why, what evil hath he done? And they cried out the more exceedingly, Crucify him.

[15]And *so* Pilate, willing to content the people, released Barabbas unto them, and delivered Jesus, when he had scourged *him*, to be crucified. [16]And the soldiers led him away into the hall, called Praetorium[a]; and they call together the whole band. [17]And they clothed him with purple, and platted a crown of thorns, and put it about his *head*, [18]And began to salute him, Hail, King of the Jews! [19]And they smote him on the head with a reed, and did spit upon him, and bowing *their* knees worshipped him. [20]And when they had mocked him, they took off the purple from him, and put his own clothes on him, and led him out to crucify him.

Devotional Moment

Compromise

15:15 Pilate knew Jesus was innocent. But he also knew that releasing him would mean civil unrest and political suicide. So the Roman governor opted to do what was expedient rather than what was right. He ordered that Christ be flogged and crucified. The moment we replace God's clear standards of right and wrong with "what the majority says" or "what feels right" or "what will make me popular," we are in trouble. What are the areas of compromise in your life? Ask God to help you eliminate them. By your words and your example do what is right, no matter what the cost.

---

[21]And they compel one Simon a Cyrenian, who passed by, coming out of the country, the father of Alexander and Rufus, to bear his cross.

[22]And they bring him unto the place Golgotha, which is, being interpreted, The place of a skull. [23]And they gave him to drink wine mingled with myrrh: but he received *it* not. [24]And when they had crucified him, they parted his garments, casting lots upon them, what every man should take. [25]And it was the third hour, and they crucified him. [26]And the superscription of his accusation was written over, THE KING OF THE JEWS. [27]And with him they crucify two thieves; the one on his right hand, and the other on his left. [28]And the scripture was fulfilled, which saith, And he was numbered with the transgressors. [29]And they that passed by railed on him, wagging their heads, and saying, Ah, thou that destroyest the temple, and buildest *it* in three days, [30]Save thyself, and come down from the cross. [31]Likewise also the chief priests mocking said among themselves with the scribes, He saved others; himself he cannot save. [32]Let Christ the King of Israel descend now from the cross, that we may see and believe. And they that were crucified with him reviled him.

[33]And when the sixth hour was come, there was darkness over the whole land until the ninth hour. [34]And at the ninth hour Jesus cried with a loud voice, saying, Eloi, Eloi, lama sabachthani? which is, being interpreted, My God, my God, why hast thou forsaken me? [35]And some of them that stood by, when they heard *it*, said, Behold, he calleth Elias.

---

[a] Praetorium: or, the palace, or, hall of audience

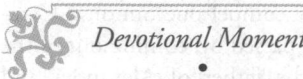

³⁶And one ran and filled a spunge full of vinegar, and put *it* on a reed, and gave him to drink, saying, Let alone; let us see whether Elias will come to take him down. ³⁷And Jesus cried with a loud voice, and gave up the ghost. ³⁸And the veil of the temple was rent in twain from the top to the bottom. ³⁹And when the centurion, which stood over against him, saw that he so cried out, and gave up the ghost, he said, Truly this man was the Son of God. ⁴⁰There were also women looking on afar off: among whom was Mary Magdalene, and Mary the mother of James the less and of Joses, and Salome; ⁴¹(Who also, when he was in Galilee, followed him, and ministered unto him;) and many other women which came up with him unto Jerusalem.

⁴²And now when the even was come, because it was the preparation, that is, the day before the sabbath, ⁴³Joseph of Arimathaea, an honourable counsellor, which also waited for the kingdom of God, came, and went in boldly unto Pilate, and craved the body of Jesus. ⁴⁴And Pilate marvelled if he were already dead: and calling *unto him* the centurion, he asked him whether he had been any while dead. ⁴⁵And when he knew *it* of the centurion, he gave the body to Joseph. ⁴⁶And he bought fine linen, and took him down, and wrapped him in the linen, and laid him in a sepulchre which was hewn out of a rock, and rolled a stone unto the door of the sepulchre. ⁴⁷And Mary Magdalene and Mary *the mother* of Joses beheld where he was laid.

16

¹And when the sabbath was past, Mary Magdalene, and Mary the *mother* of James, and Salome, had bought sweet spices, that they might come and anoint him. ²And very early in the morning the first *day* of the week, they came unto the sepulchre at the rising of the sun. ³And they said among themselves, Who shall roll us away the stone from the door of the sepulchre? ⁴And when they looked, they saw that the stone was rolled away: for it was very great. ⁵And entering into the sepulchre, they saw a young man sitting on the right side, clothed in a long white garment; and they were affrighted. ⁶And he saith unto them, Be not affrighted: Ye seek Jesus of Nazareth, which was crucified: he is risen; he is not here: behold the place where they laid him. ⁷But go your way, tell his disciples and Peter that he goeth before you into Galilee: there shall ye see him, as he said unto you. ⁸And they went out quickly, and fled from the sepulchre; for they trembled and were amazed: neither said they any thing to any *man*; for they were afraid.

⁹Now when *Jesus* was risen early the first *day* of the week, he appeared first to Mary Magdalene, out of whom he had cast seven devils. ¹⁰*And* she went and told them that had been with him,

as they mourned and wept. ¹¹And they, when they had heard that he was alive, and had been seen of her, believed not. ¹²After that he appeared in another form unto two of them, as they walked, and went into the country. ¹³And they went and told *it* unto the residue: neither believed they them.

¹⁴Afterward he appeared unto the eleven as they sat at meatᵃ, and upbraided them with their unbelief and hardness of heart, because they believed not them which had seen him after he was risen. ¹⁵And he said unto them, Go ye into all the world, and preach the gospel to every creature. ¹⁶He that believeth and is bap-

tized shall be saved; but he that believeth not shall be damned. ¹⁷And these signs shall follow them that believe; In my name shall they cast out devils; they shall speak with new tongues; ¹⁸They shall take up serpents; and if they drink any deadly thing, it shall not hurt them; they shall lay hands on the sick, and they shall recover.

¹⁹So then after the Lord had spoken unto them, he was received up into heaven, and sat on the right hand of God. ²⁰And they went forth, and preached every where, the Lord working with *them*, and confirming the word with signs following. Amen.

ᵃ at meat: or, together

LUKE

Author
Luke—a doctor (Col. 4:14), a Greek, and a Gentile Christian. He is the only known Gentile author in the New Testament. He was a close friend and companion of Paul. He also wrote Acts, and the two books go together.

To Whom Written
Theophilus (translated "dear friend who loves God"), Gentiles, and people everywhere

Date Written
About A.D. 60

Setting
Luke wrote from Caesarea or from Rome.

Key Places
Bethlehem, Galilee, Judea, Jerusalem

Special Features
This is the most comprehensive of the four Gospels in the New Testament. The general vocabulary shows that the author was educated. He makes frequent references to illnesses and diagnoses. Luke stresses Jesus' relationships with people; emphasizes prayer, miracles, and angels; records inspired hymns of praise; and gives a prominent place to women. Most of 9:51 to 18:35 is not found in any other Gospel.

G etting a package in the mail is a big event. Email and junk mail arrive every day—packages don't.

When a *package* arrives, something big is afoot. Something important. There's excitement because trivial things rarely come in packages. And if the package comes unannounced, it is wrapped in mystery as well: What's inside? Why did the person send it?

And when the return address is that of someone you know . . .

One day long ago a person named Theophilus received a package as large as his name. It was from his doctor friend, Luke. Theophilus must have opened that package like a kid tearing into a birthday present.

Inside, Theo found volume one in a two-volume book of all that Luke knew about an amazing new thing God was just beginning to do. Luke wanted his friend to know "the truth of all you were taught." This was more than a mere letter. This was Official Documentation. This was Evidence. This was The Truth.

Just what you'd expect to find in a package. Something special.

As you read, watch for all the familiar stories. Some of the world's most famous stories are right here. Watch for all the prayers. Luke wanted Theophilus to know that busy Jesus took lots of time to pray. (Hint for other busy people?)

So sit down with Luke's book as if it arrived in a big brown box, special delivery, hand-addressed from a good friend. When you read with the family together, pray. When a story moves you, talk about the loves that make your life strong. Whenever you read about Jesus doing something terrific for a family in Luke, ask him to make a difference where you live. And he will! And then you'll have lots to write and tell friends about, too.

1516

1

¹Forasmuch as many have taken in hand to set forth in order a declaration of those things which are most surely believed among us, ²Even as they delivered them unto us, which from the beginning were eyewitnesses, and ministers of the word; ³It seemed good to me also, having had perfect understanding of all things from the very first, to write unto thee in order, most excellent Theophilus, ⁴That thou mightest know the certainty of those things, wherein thou hast been instructed.

⁵There was in the days of Herod, the king of Judaea, a certain priest named Zacharias, of the course of Abia: and his wife *was* of the daughters of Aaron, and her name *was* Elisabeth. ⁶And they were both righteous before God, walking in all the commandments and ordinances of the Lord blameless. ⁷And they had no child, because that Elisabeth was barren, and they both were *now* well stricken in years. ⁸And it came to pass, that while he executed the priest's office before God in the order of his course, ⁹According to the custom of the priest's office, his lot was to burn incense when he went into the temple of the Lord. ¹⁰And the whole multitude of the people were praying without at the time of incense. ¹¹And there appeared unto him an angel of the Lord standing on the right side of the altar of incense. ¹²And when Zacharias saw *him*, he was troubled, and fear fell upon him. ¹³But the angel said unto him, Fear not, Zacharias: for thy prayer is heard; and

thy wife Elisabeth shall bear thee a son, and thou shalt call his name John. ¹⁴And thou shalt have joy and gladness; and many shall rejoice at his birth. ¹⁵For he shall be great in the sight of the Lord, and shall drink neither wine nor strong drink; and he shall be filled with the Holy Ghost, even from his mother's womb. ¹⁶And many of the children of Israel shall he turn to the Lord their God. ¹⁷And he shall go before him in the spirit and power of Elias, to turn the hearts of the fathers to the children, and the disobedient to the wisdomᵃ of the just; to make ready a people prepared for the Lord. ¹⁸And Zacharias said unto the angel, Whereby shall I know this? for I am an old man, and my wife well stricken in years. ¹⁹And the angel answering said unto him, I am Gabriel, that stand in the presence of God; and am sent to speak unto thee, and to shew thee these glad tidings. ²⁰And, behold, thou shalt be dumb, and not able to speak, until the day that these things shall be performed, because thou believest not my words, which shall be

Devotional Moment
•
Trust

1:18-20 Like Zacharias, many modern-day believers have profound doubts about God and what he can do. They haven't personally experienced the mighty working power of God, so they may conclude that he *doesn't* work in powerful ways. Or they listen to skeptics or atheists and label certain situations "impossible." What "impossible" situation are you facing that needs the miraculous touch of God? Ask him to move in surprising and powerful ways. And then watch for him to work.

ᵃ to the wisdom: or, by the wisdom

Mary

(the mother of Jesus)

The way people react to the news of a pregnancy is as
unpredictable as conception itself. Just say, "We're expecting a baby!" and see what happens. You will receive
all kinds of responses: excitement, surprise, anticipation,
fear, amazement, dread.

Many factors will influence our own first emotional
response, such as whether we're married, whether we
wanted a baby, whether we've been trying to conceive
for a long time, or whether we have other children. What
we feel first rarely lasts long—other feelings soon take
over.

That's what happened to Mary. The angel Gabriel
went to her and announced that she was favored by God.
At first, she was "troubled" (Luke 1:29). But the angel reassured her that she had no reason to fear—God had
chosen her to give birth to the Messiah!

Mary's response to this news was amazement: "How
shall this be, seeing I know not a man" (Luke 1:34). God
will bring it about by the Holy Ghost, the angel explained. Talk about surprise!

Make no mistake; Mary's plans were disrupted. She
didn't have this in mind when she agreed to marry
Joseph. But that was OK. If God wanted it, she was willing for her plans to change. She accepted the news, not
with resignation, but with joy at being chosen by God to
fulfill this role in God's plans. She said: "Behold the handmaid of the Lord; be it unto me according to thy word."
Mary accepted her pregnancy as a blessing and an
honor.

fulfilled in their season. ²¹And the people waited for Zacharias, and marvelled that he tarried so long in the temple. ²²And when he came out, he could not speak unto them: and they perceived that he had seen a vision in the temple: for he beckoned unto them, and remained speechless. ²³And it came to pass, that, as soon as the days of his ministration were accomplished, he departed to his own house. ²⁴And after those days his wife Elisabeth conceived, and hid herself five months, saying, ²⁵Thus hath the Lord dealt with me in the days wherein he looked on *me*, to take away my reproach among men.

²⁶And in the sixth month the angel Gabriel was sent from God unto a city of Galilee, named Nazareth, ²⁷To a virgin espoused to a man whose name was Joseph, of the house of David; and the virgin's name *was* Mary. ²⁸And the angel came in unto her, and said, Hail, *thou that art* highly favoured, the Lord *is* with thee: blessed *art* thou among women. ²⁹And when she saw *him*, she was troubled at his saying, and cast in her mind what manner of salutation this should be. ³⁰And the angel said unto her, Fear not, Mary: for thou hast found favour with God. ³¹And, behold, thou shalt conceive in thy womb, and bring forth a son, and shalt call his name JESUS. ³²He shall be great, and shall be called the Son of the Highest: and the Lord God shall give unto him the throne of his father David: ³³And he shall reign over the house of Jacob for ever; and of his kingdom there shall be no end. ³⁴Then said Mary unto the angel, How shall this be, seeing I know not a man? ³⁵And the angel answered and said unto her, The Holy Ghost

shall come upon thee, and the power of the Highest shall overshadow thee: therefore also that holy thing which shall be born of thee shall be called the Son of God. ³⁶And, behold, thy cousin Elisabeth, she hath also conceived a son in her old age: and this is the sixth month with her, who was called barren. ³⁷For with God nothing shall be impossible. ³⁸And Mary said, Behold the handmaid of the Lord; be it unto me according to thy word. And the angel departed from her.

³⁹And Mary arose in those days, and went into the hill country with haste, into a city of Juda; ⁴⁰And entered into the house of Zacharias, and saluted Elisabeth. ⁴¹And it came to pass, that, when Elisabeth heard the salutation of Mary, the babe leaped in her womb; and Elisabeth was filled with the Holy Ghost: ⁴²And she spake out with a loud voice, and said, Blessed *art* thou among women, and blessed *is* the fruit of thy womb. ⁴³And whence *is* this to me, that the mother of my Lord should come to me? ⁴⁴For, lo, as soon as the voice of thy

---

Devotional Moment

Comparing Children

1:42-43 Friends and relatives have a tendency to compete with each other by bragging about the accomplishments of their children. Such a practice not only overlooks the unique personality and abilities of each individual child but also can spark feelings of jealousy. Though her son, John, would never be as great as Jesus, Elisabeth was joyful about Mary's news and, in fact, felt privileged to be in Mary's presence. How was this possible? Elisabeth was filled with the Holy Spirit. It is when we want to serve God above all else and are filled with his Spirit that we can dispense with competitions for bragging rights.

Family Traditions

Christmas Eve Traditions

LUKE 2:1-20

Since Bud and Mary Walker were both reared on farms, they're eager to preserve those rich country images for their children, Kevin, three, and Edie, seven.

"The manger, the straw, the animals . . . and a moment of glory when the Son of God was laid in the middle of it all," says Bud, "is what it's all about."

Bud built a tabletop barn and whittled sheep, pigs, and horses out of soft pine. Mary drapes a dressy brocade scarf made from a red Chinese robe (a thrift store find) under it. The kids play with the scene all season. When a wooden donkey shows up in the menagerie, that's a signal Christmas is just a few days away.

"From that evening," Mary says, "we gather nightly around the wood stove for Christmas carols accompanied by guitar. The children shape angels out of modeling compound while we sing."

Bud adds, "Christmas eve, we lay the Jesus figure on the straw in the manger and exchange the presents we've prepared, reminding each other they're given in the spirit of Christ. The evening ends with praise choruses and retelling the old story from Luke."

Another Christian family, neighbors to the Walkers, also highlights togetherness. Celebrating each night of Advent, December 1 to 24, the Henrys string out the joy. Instead of one great gift exchange on the twenty-fifth, they present personal gifts to each other on Advent Sundays, while weeknights they take turns unwrapping family presents: books to read together, games, special foods, tickets to a holiday event, or even practical jokes, bringing the gift of laughter.

On Christmas Eve, candles are lit all around the Henry home, music rings from front door to back, and a table is piled with (mostly) nutritious snacks—a casual affair. Their emphasis on that holy night is on being together, worshiping, and relaxing.

The Ed Dayton family visits a convalescent hospital near their home, bringing glitter-covered homemade Christmas cards to every resident. "It only takes an hour or so," says Ed, "but it gives to the people left there on Christmas Eve something wonderful. It can make their holiday just to see smiling children racing the halls looking for folks to visit. Those kids give away a lot more than glittery cards."

salutation sounded in mine ears, the babe leaped in my womb for joy. [45]And blessed *is* she that believed: for there shall be a performance of those things which were told her from the Lord. [46]And Mary said, My soul doth magnify the Lord, [47]And my spirit hath rejoiced in God my Saviour. [48]For he hath regarded the low estate of his handmaiden: for, behold, from henceforth all generations shall call me blessed. [49]For he that is mighty hath done to me great things; and holy *is* his name. [50]And his mercy *is* on them that fear him from generation to generation. [51]He hath shewed strength with his arm; he hath scattered the proud in the imagination of their hearts. [52]He hath put down the mighty from *their* seats, and exalted them of low degree. [53]He hath filled the hungry with good things; and the rich he hath sent empty away. [54]He hath holpen his servant Israel, in remembrance of *his* mercy; [55]As he spake to our fathers, to Abraham, and to his seed for ever. [56]And Mary abode with her about three months, and returned to her own house.

[57]Now Elisabeth's full time came that she should be delivered; and she brought forth a son. [58]And her neighbours and her cousins heard how the Lord had shewed great mercy upon her; and they rejoiced with her. [59]And it came to pass, that on the eighth day they came to circumcise the child; and they called him Zacharias, after the name of his father. [60]And his mother answered and said, Not *so*; but he shall be called John. [61]And they said unto her, There is none of thy kindred that is called by this name. [62]And they made signs to his father, how he would have him called. [63]And he asked for a writing table, and wrote, saying, His name is John. And they marvelled all. [64]And his mouth was opened immediately, and his tongue *loosed*, and he spake, and praised God. [65]And fear came on all that dwelt round about them: and all these sayings[b] were noised abroad throughout all the hill country of Judaea. [66]And all they that heard *them* laid *them* up in their hearts, saying, What manner of child shall this be! And the hand of the Lord was with him.

[67]And his father Zacharias was filled with the Holy Ghost, and prophesied, saying, [68]Blessed *be* the Lord God of Israel; for he hath visited and redeemed his people, [69]And hath raised up an horn of salvation for us in the house of his servant David; [70]As he spake by the mouth of his holy prophets, which have been since the world began: [71]That we should be saved from our enemies, and from the hand of all that hate us; [72]To perform the mercy *promised* to our fathers, and to remember his holy covenant; [73]The oath which he sware to our father Abraham, [74]That he would grant unto us, that we being delivered out of the hand of our enemies might serve him without fear, [75]In holiness and righteousness before him, all the days of our life. [76]And thou, child, shalt be called the prophet of the Highest: for thou shalt go before the face of the Lord to prepare his ways; [77]To give knowledge of salvation unto his people by[c] the remis-

---

[b] sayings: or, things
[c] by: or, for

sion of their sins, [78]Through the tender[d] mercy of our God; whereby the dayspring from on high hath visited us, [79]To give light to them that sit in darkness and *in* the shadow of death, to guide our feet into the way of peace. [80]And the child grew, and waxed strong in spirit, and was in the deserts till the day of his shewing unto Israel.

2

[1]And it came to pass in those days, that there went out a decree from Caesar Augustus, that all the world should be taxed[a]. [2](*And* this taxing was first made when Cyrenius was governor of Syria.) [3]And all went to be taxed[b], every one into his own city. [4]And Joseph also went up from Galilee, out of the city of Nazareth, into Judaea, unto the city of

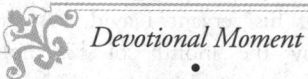

Devotional Moment
•
Problems

2:3-5 Sometimes we assume that obeying God is a surefire ticket to a comfortable and easy life. Such thinking is contradicted by both Scripture and experience. Joseph and Mary, even as they followed the will of God, endured hardships (tough travel, poor accommodations, and the hint of scandal). Many people who have earnestly sought to honor God encounter only hardship and persecution. God has not promised his people the absence of problems, but rather his presence and peace. God can use difficult circumstances to build our character (James 1:2-4) and to bring about greater good (Rom. 8:28).

David, which is called Bethlehem; (because he was of the house and lineage of David:) [5]To be taxed[c] with Mary his espoused wife, being great with child. [6]And so it was, that, while they were there, the days were accomplished that she should be delivered. [7]And she brought forth her firstborn son, and wrapped him in swaddling clothes, and laid him in a manger; because there was no room for them in the inn.

[8]And there were in the same country shepherds abiding in the field, keeping watch[d] over their flock by night. [9]And, lo, the angel of the Lord came upon them, and the glory of the Lord shone round about them: and they were sore afraid. [10]And the angel said unto them, Fear not: for, behold, I bring you good tidings of great joy, which shall be to all people. [11]For unto you is born this day in the city of David a Saviour, which is Christ the Lord. [12]And this *shall be* a sign unto you; Ye shall find the babe wrapped in swaddling clothes, lying in a manger. [13]And suddenly there was with the angel a multitude of the heavenly host praising God, and saying, [14]Glory to God in the highest, and on earth peace, good will toward men. [15]And it came to pass, as the angels were gone away from them into heaven, the shepherds[e] said one to another, Let us now go even unto Bethlehem, and see this thing which is come to pass, which the Lord hath made

[d] tender . . . : or, bowels of the mercy
[a] taxed: or, enrolled
[b] taxed: or, inrolled
[c] taxed: or, inrolled
[d] watch: or, the night watches
[e] the shepherds: Gr. the men the shepherds

Jesus the Teenager

by Jay Kesler

The Bible has very little to say, at least in volume, about Jesus' late adolescence and early childhood. Luke 2:41-52, however, contains some insights into Jesus' life between his twelfth birthday and his emergence into adulthood at thirty years of age.

We often ask questions only in our heart: *What does God expect us to accomplish with our teenagers? What is a job well done? What does an ideal young adult look like?* Luke 2:52 sums it up: "Jesus increased in wisdom and stature, and in favour with God and man."

Jesus grew physically, mentally, spiritually, and socially. His life was in balance. The tendency of parents to care most about "spiritual matters" splits life into two artificial pieces. Actually, spirituality cannot take place in a vacuum. We are not disconnected "souls," but total people. As parents, we are responsible to help our children see that all areas of life are God's concern and that the development of each is important.

Physical development. Teenagers are physically active and very much aware of their bodies. Their lives are full of sports, cosmetics, acne, orthodontists, and diets. The physical in all its aspects—including our sexuality—is God's idea. To develop strong, healthy bodies and to commit them to God's use is spiritual worship. Parents sometimes feel they are compromising to some degree if their teenagers are involved in sports or other physical activities, secretly feeling that Jesus must have spent all his time reading scrolls and praying with fervency. He surely did those things, but this short passage in Luke gives us reason to believe that God was also pleased with Jesus' physical growth.

The apostle Paul was interested in and informed about sports, and he made sure that young Timothy was as well (see 2 Tim. 2:5). The letter to the Hebrews (12:1-3) shows an understanding of the demands of competition. Apparently the author felt his readers could connect with these illustrations because physical activity is important to life and health.

Mental development. Our mind is the creation of God and provides much of the evidence for our being created in his image. We learn to think as God thinks and to build our worldview on God's precepts. All that is in the world was created by God; therefore, the study of subjects other than the Bible, such as math, science, history, philosophy, music, art, or any other topic, helps develop our appreciation of his creative effort. We are as spiritual when we study secular topics as we are when we pray if we do it as children of God.

Encouraging our teenagers to see their academic efforts as worship and obedience is important, not only to their personal development and success, but also to the future of the church.

Social development. No area of adolescence is so prominent as social life. Again we see that Jesus was loved by people. He was discerning of people's character and adept at human relationships. Jesus was a student of people and their behavior. He was not an oddball. He fit in and was sought out by his peers. He was a friend to his associates. They loved him and missed him when he was gone. As our children become more adept at social skills, they become more able to influence others for Christ. As their faith and self-confidence grow, they are able to live in a diverse world with ease and not be swayed by peer pressure.

We as parents can provide the encouragement, guidance, and atmosphere in which our teenagers can grow physically, mentally, and socially with Jesus Christ at the center of their lives. That is the biblical model.

DIGGING DEEPER
1. How can being committed to Christ help us weather the adolescent years of our kids? Read Romans 12:6-12.
2. In what ways did Jesus identify with our lives and humanity? Read Hebrews 4:14-16; 5:8-9; Luke 2:41-42, 51-52.
3. How did Jesus feel about his earthly parents? Read John 19:25-27 to see what was on his mind while he was suffering.

known unto us. ¹⁶And they came with haste, and found Mary, and Joseph, and the babe lying in a manger. ¹⁷And when they had seen *it*, they made known abroad the saying which was told them concerning this child. ¹⁸And all they that heard *it* wondered at those things which were told them by the shepherds. ¹⁹But Mary kept all these things, and pondered *them* in her heart. ²⁰And the shepherds returned, glorifying and praising God for all the things that they had heard and seen, as it was told unto them.

²¹And when eight days were accomplished for the circumcising of the child, his name was called JESUS, which was so named of the angel before he was conceived in the womb. ²²And when the days of her purification according to the law of Moses were accomplished, they brought him to Jerusalem, to present *him* to the Lord; ²³(As it is written in the law of the Lord, Every male that openeth the womb shall be called holy to the Lord;) ²⁴And to offer a sacrifice according to that which is said in the law of the Lord, A pair of turtledoves, or two young pigeons.

²⁵And, behold, there was a man in Jerusalem, whose name *was* Simeon; and the same man *was* just and devout, waiting for the consolation of Israel: and the Holy Ghost was upon him. ²⁶And it was revealed unto him by the Holy Ghost, that he should not see death, before he had seen the Lord's Christ. ²⁷And he came by the Spirit into the temple: and when the parents brought in the child Jesus, to do for him after the custom of the law, ²⁸Then took he him up in his arms, and blessed God, and said, ²⁹Lord, now lettest thou thy servant depart in peace, according to thy word: ³⁰For mine eyes have seen thy salvation, ³¹Which thou hast prepared before the face of all people; ³²A light to lighten the Gentiles, and the glory of thy people Israel. ³³And Joseph and his mother marvelled at those things which were spoken of him. ³⁴And Simeon blessed them, and said unto Mary his mother, Behold, this *child* is set for the fall and rising again of many in Israel; and for a sign which shall be spoken against; ³⁵(Yea, a sword shall pierce through thy own soul also,) that the thoughts of many hearts may be revealed. ³⁶And there was

one Anna, a prophetess, the daughter of Phanuel, of the tribe of Aser: she was of a great age, and had lived with an husband seven years from her virginity; ³⁷And she *was* a widow of about fourscore and four years, which departed not from the temple, but served *God* with fastings and prayers night and day. ³⁸And she coming in that instant gave thanks likewise unto the Lord, and spake of him to all them that looked for redemption in Jerusalem[f]. ³⁹And when they had performed all things according to the law of the Lord, they returned into Galilee, to their own city Nazareth. ⁴⁰And the child grew, and waxed strong in spirit, filled with wisdom: and the grace of God was upon him.

⁴¹Now his parents went to Jerusalem every year at the feast of the passover. ⁴²And when he was twelve

---

Devotional Moment
•
Releasing Children

2:48 Mary and Joseph were upset because they couldn't find Jesus. They were concerned, just as any good parents would be. Our parental instincts tell us to protect our children, to shield them from the harsh realities of a fallen world. But as Mary and Joseph learned, there comes a time when we must step back and let our children become the people God made them to be. We must let them learn responsibility, make decisions, and face consequences. As parents, our goals should be to love, nurture, and equip our children when they are young, and to love, support, and encourage them as they mature. Give your children the emotional support and practical skills they will need to live successfully apart from your care.

---

years old, they went up to Jerusalem after the custom of the feast. ⁴³And when they had fulfilled the days, as they returned, the child Jesus tarried behind in Jerusalem; and Joseph and his mother knew not *of it*. ⁴⁴But they, supposing him to have been in the company, went a day's journey; and they sought him among *their* kinsfolk and acquaintance. ⁴⁵And when they found him not, they turned back again to Jerusalem, seeking him. ⁴⁶And it came to pass, that after three days they found him in the temple, sitting in the midst of the doctors, both hearing them, and asking them questions. ⁴⁷And all that heard him were astonished at his understanding and answers. ⁴⁸And when they saw him, they were amazed: and his mother said unto him, Son, why hast thou thus dealt with us? behold, thy father and I have sought thee sorrowing. ⁴⁹And he said unto them, How is it that ye sought me? wist ye not that I must be about my Father's business? ⁵⁰And they understood not the saying which he spake unto them. ⁵¹And he went down with them, and came to Nazareth, and was subject unto them: but his mother kept all these sayings in her heart. ⁵²And Jesus increased in wisdom and stature[g], and in favour with God and man.

3

¹Now in the fifteenth year of the reign of Tiberius Caesar, Pontius Pilate being governor of Judaea, and Herod being tetrarch[a] of Galilee, and his brother

---

[f] Jerusalem: or, Israel
[g] stature: or, age
[a] tetrarch: or, governor of four provinces

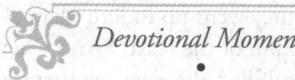

Devotional Moment

•

Salvation

3:8 The people in John's audience counted too much on their religious heritage. We do it too. "My great-grandfather was a preacher." "My mom is *very* religious." "Of course I'm a Christian—I've been going to church all my life." Statements like these reveal a very common but dangerous assumption: that we can count on a strong religious upbringing to make us right with God. Though our religious heritage can have a big impact, it can't save us. We must each personally trust in Christ (and only Christ) for forgiveness. Faith is a personal decision.

Philip tetrarch of Ituraea and of the region of Trachonitis, and Lysanias the tetrarch of Abilene, ²Annas and Caiaphas being the high priests, the word of God came unto John the son of Zacharias in the wilderness. ³And he came into all the country about Jordan, preaching the baptism of repentance for the remission of sins; ⁴As it is written in the book of the words of Esaias the prophet, saying, The voice of one crying in the wilderness, Prepare ye the way of the Lord, make his paths straight. ⁵Every valley shall be filled, and every mountain and hill shall be brought low; and the crooked shall be made straight, and the rough ways *shall be* made smooth; ⁶And all flesh shall see the salvation of God. ⁷Then said he to the multitude that came forth to be baptized of him, O generation of vipers, who hath warned you to flee from the wrath to come? ⁸Bring forth therefore fruits worthy of repentance,

and begin not to say within yourselves, We have Abraham to *our* father: for I say unto you, That God is able of these stones to raise up children unto Abraham. ⁹And now also the axe is laid unto the root of the trees: every tree therefore which bringeth not forth good fruit is hewn down, and cast into the fire. ¹⁰And the people asked him, saying, What shall we do then? ¹¹He answereth and saith unto them, He that hath two coats, let him impart to him that hath none; and he that hath meat, let him do likewise. ¹²Then came also publicans to be baptized, and said unto him, Master, what shall we do? ¹³And he said unto them, Exact no more than that which is appointed you. ¹⁴And the soldiers likewise demanded of him, saying, And what shall we do? And he said unto them, Do violence[b] to no man, neither accuse *any* falsely; and be content with your wages.

¹⁵And as the people were in expectation[c], and all men mused in their hearts of John, whether he were the Christ, or not; ¹⁶John answered, saying unto *them* all, I indeed baptize you with water; but one mightier than I cometh, the latchet of whose shoes I am not worthy to unloose: he shall baptize you with the Holy Ghost and with fire: ¹⁷Whose fan *is* in his hand, and he will throughly purge his floor, and will gather the wheat into his garner; but the chaff he will burn with fire unquenchable. ¹⁸And many other things in his exhortation preached he unto the people. ¹⁹But Herod the tetrarch, being reproved by him for Herodias his

---

[b] Do violence . . . : or, Put no man in fear

[c] in expectation: or, in suspense

Zacharias
(John the Baptist's father)

Most new fathers feel intimidated. To start with, they doubt their own abilities. Even those who aren't afraid to hold their new infant wonder if they can successfully juggle a job, a marriage, *and* a family. Most doubt it.

They may even have doubts about God's power in their lives.

When the angel Gabriel told Zacharias that he and Elisabeth would have a son and that this son would be special, Zacharias simply couldn't believe it. *Impossible!* was his only thought. Elisabeth and Zacharias had lived so long without children that they expected none. They were both very old Luke tells us (1:7). They had been through the hoping, the waiting, and finally the surrender.

Yet God had it all planned. He had it all under control. No need to worry. Just keep on praying because God hears.

Most dads can sympathize with Zacharias, the skeptic. We can wear the same shoes because we have his clay feet: We pray to God, and yet we doubt him. We ask him to guide and to help, while at the same time we worry sick over bills, bruises, and bullies.

Is God as big as our prayers say he is? No. He's bigger.

No doubt as a dad you have hopes and dreams for your children. No doubt God does, too.

Don't be intimidated—keep praying.

LESSONS FROM ZACHARIAS AS A NEW FATHER

God can do anything. Dads have lots to fear and much to worry about. They've seen how the world hurts people. Their kids won't get any breaks. Dads wonder what's in store for their young charges, and if they have the mettle to prepare their kids adequately for the onslaught. All the more reason to pray—and believe. God loves those kids even more than you do, you know.

Even believers may doubt. Zacharias, though a devout and righteous man, doubted God's word. Don't let doubt overwhelm your trust in God.

God works through ordinary people. Perhaps Zacharias's skepticism was heightened by his feelings of insignificance. Yet God cared about his life and used him.

brother Philip's wife, and for all the evils which Herod had done, ²⁰Added yet this above all, that he shut up John in prison.

²¹Now when all the people were baptized, it came to pass, that Jesus also being baptized, and praying, the heaven was opened, ²²And the Holy Ghost descended in a bodily shape like a dove upon him, and a voice came from heaven, which said, Thou art my beloved Son; in thee I am well pleased. ²³And Jesus himself began to be about thirty years of age, being (as was supposed) the son of Joseph, which was *the son* of Heli, ²⁴Which was *the son* of Matthat, which was *the son* of Levi, which was *the son* of Melchi, which was *the son* of Janna, which was *the son* of Joseph, ²⁵Which was *the son* of Mattathias, which was *the son* of Amos, which was *the son* of Naum, which was *the son* of Esli, which was *the son* of Nagge, ²⁶Which was *the son* of Maath, which was *the son* of Mattathias, which was *the son* of Semei, which was *the son* of Joseph, which was *the son* of Juda, ²⁷Which was *the son* of Joanna, which

---

Devotional Moment
•
Patience

3:23 The next time you get impatient with God, remember that Jesus did not begin his public ministry until he was thirty! To some this seems a colossal waste—the Master Teacher, the Great Physician, the Savior of the world cooped up in a carpenter's shop until almost the end of his life. Whether your waiting involves a job promotion or a birthday party, don't race ahead of God or minimize the importance of where you are right now. God wants you to faithfully serve him in the present, not impatiently focus on the future.

---

was *the son* of Rhesa, which was *the son* of Zorobabel, which was *the son* of Salathiel, which was *the son* of Neri, ²⁸Which was *the son* of Melchi, which was *the son* of Addi, which was *the son* of Cosam, which was *the son* of Elmodam, which was *the son* of Er, ²⁹Which was *the son* of Jose, which was *the son* of Eliezer, which was *the son* of Jorim, which was *the son* of Matthat, which was *the son* of Levi, ³⁰Which was *the son* of Simeon, which was *the son* of Juda, which was *the son* of Joseph, which was *the son* of Jonan, which was *the son* of Eliakim, ³¹Which was *the son* of Melea, which was *the son* of Menan, which was *the son* of Mattatha, which was *the son* of Nathan, which was *the son* of David, ³²Which was *the son* of Jesse, which was *the son* of Obed, which was *the son* of Booz, which was *the son* of Salmon, which was *the son* of Naasson, ³³Which was *the son* of Aminadab, which was *the son* of Aram, which was *the son* of Esrom, which was *the son* of Phares, which was *the son* of Juda, ³⁴Which was *the son* of Jacob, which was *the son* of Isaac, which was *the son* of Abraham, which was *the son* of Thara, which was *the son* of Nachor, ³⁵Which was *the son* of Saruch, which was *the son* of Ragau, which was *the son* of Phalec, which was *the son* of Heber, which was *the son* of Sala, ³⁶Which was *the son* of Cainan, which was *the son* of Arphaxad, which was *the son* of Sem, which was *the son* of Noe, which was *the son* of Lamech, ³⁷Which was *the son* of Mathusala, which was *the son* of Enoch, which was *the son* of Jared, which was *the son* of Maleleel, which was *the son* of Cainan, ³⁸Which was *the son* of Enos, which was *the son* of Seth, which was *the son* of Adam, which was *the son* of God.

4

¹And Jesus being full of the Holy Ghost returned from Jordan, and was led by the Spirit into the wilderness, ²Being forty days tempted of the devil. And in those days he did eat nothing: and when they were ended, he afterward hungered. ³And the devil said unto him, If thou be the Son of God, command this stone that it be made bread. ⁴And Jesus answered him, saying, It is written, That man shall not live by bread alone, but by every word of God. ⁵And the devil, taking him up into an high mountain, shewed unto him all the kingdoms of the world in a moment of time. ⁶And the devil said unto him, All this power will I give thee, and the glory of them: for that is delivered unto me; and to whomsoever I will I give it. ⁷If thou therefore wilt worship me[a], all shall be thine. ⁸And Jesus answered and said unto him, Get thee behind me, Satan: for it is written, Thou shalt worship the Lord thy God, and him only shalt thou serve. ⁹And he brought him to Jerusalem, and set him on a pinnacle of the temple, and said unto him, If thou be the Son of God, cast thyself down from hence: ¹⁰For it is written, He shall give his angels charge over thee, to keep thee: ¹¹And in *their* hands they shall bear thee up, lest at any time thou dash thy foot against a stone. ¹²And Jesus answering said unto him, It is said, Thou shalt not tempt the Lord thy God. ¹³And when the devil had ended all the temptation, he departed from him for a season.

¹⁴And Jesus returned in the power of the Spirit into Galilee: and there went out a fame of him through all the region round about. ¹⁵And he taught in their synagogues, being glorified of all. ¹⁶And he came to Nazareth, where he had been brought up: and, as his custom was, he went into the synagogue on the sabbath day, and stood up for to read. ¹⁷And there was delivered unto him the book of the prophet Esaias. And when he had opened the book, he found the place where it was written, ¹⁸The Spirit of the Lord *is* upon me, because he hath anointed me to preach the gospel to the poor; he hath sent me to heal the brokenhearted, to preach deliverance to the captives, and recovering of sight to the blind, to set at liberty them that are bruised, ¹⁹To preach the acceptable year of the Lord. ²⁰And he closed the book, and he gave *it* again to the minister, and sat down. And the eyes of all them that were in the synagogue were fastened on him. ²¹And he began to say unto them, This day is this scripture fulfilled in your ears. ²²And all bare him witness, and wondered at the gracious words which proceeded out of his mouth. And they said, Is not this Joseph's son? ²³And he said unto them, Ye will surely say unto me this proverb, Physician, heal thyself: whatsoever we have heard done in Capernaum, do also here in thy country. ²⁴And he said, Verily I say unto you, No prophet is accepted in his own country. ²⁵But I tell you of a truth, many widows were in Israel in the days of Elias, when the heaven was shut up three years and six months, when great famine was throughout all the land; ²⁶But unto none of them was Elias sent, save unto Sarepta, *a city* of Sidon, unto a woman *that was* a widow.

[a] worship me: or, fall down before me

²⁷And many lepers were in Israel in the time of Eliseus the prophet; and none of them was cleansed, saving Naaman the Syrian. ²⁸And all they in the synagogue, when they heard these things, were filled with wrath, ²⁹And rose up, and thrust him out of the city, and led him unto the brow[b] of the hill whereon their city was built, that they might cast him down headlong. ³⁰But he passing through the midst of them went his way,

³¹And came down to Capernaum, a city of Galilee, and taught them on the sabbath days. ³²And they were astonished at his doctrine: for his word was with power. ³³And in the synagogue there was a man, which had a spirit of an unclean devil, and cried out with a loud voice, ³⁴Saying, Let *us* alone[c]; what have we to do with thee, *thou* Jesus of Nazareth? art thou come to destroy us? I know thee who thou art; the Holy One of God. ³⁵And Jesus rebuked him, saying, Hold thy peace, and come out of him. And when the devil had thrown him in the midst, he came out of him, and hurt him not. ³⁶And they were all amazed, and spake among themselves, saying, What a word *is* this! for with authority and power he commandeth the unclean spirits, and they come out. ³⁷And the fame of him went out into every place of the country round about. ³⁸And he arose out of the synagogue, and entered into Simon's house. And Simon's wife's mother was taken with a great fever; and they besought him for her. ³⁹And he stood over her, and rebuked the fever; and it left her: and immediately she arose and ministered

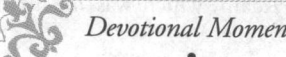

Devotional Moment
•
Occult

4:36 In recent years the media have devoted a great deal of attention to Satan worship and other demonic practices. These shocking stories usually spark terror in our heart. The next time you find yourself trembling at the very mention of the occult, remember that Jesus Christ has all authority. Demons are subject to him, and one day he will crush the devil under our feet (Rom. 16:20). Pray that you and your family will be protected from evil. But more than that, pray that everyone will know the infinite and amazing power of God.

unto them. ⁴⁰Now when the sun was setting, all they that had any sick with divers diseases brought them unto him; and he laid his hands on every one of them, and healed them. ⁴¹And devils also came out of many, crying out, and saying, Thou art Christ the Son of God. And he rebuking *them* suffered them not to speak[d]: for they

Devotional Moment
•
Time with God

4:42 When things are crazy at home or work, our time alone with God is often the first casualty. We ignore our devotions so that we will have more time to accomplish all the other tasks that are clamoring for our attention. Jesus, on the other hand, looked for opportunities to slip away and pray (Mark 1:35; Luke 6:12). Begin the habit of carving a few minutes out of your schedule each day and finding a quiet place where you can be alone with God. After you let him speak to you through his Word, tell him about your needs and concerns. You will then be better prepared to face both your family and work responsibilities.

---

[b] brow: or, edge
[c] Let . . . : or, Away
[d] to speak . . . : or, to say that they knew him to be Christ

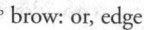

knew that he was Christ. ⁴²And when it was day, he departed and went into a desert place: and the people sought him, and came unto him, and stayed him, that he should not depart from them. ⁴³And he said unto them, I must preach the kingdom of God to other cities also: for therefore am I sent. ⁴⁴And he preached in the synagogues of Galilee.

5

¹And it came to pass, that, as the people pressed upon him to hear the word of God, he stood by the lake of Gennesaret, ²And saw two ships standing by the lake: but the fishermen were gone out of them, and were washing *their* nets. ³And he entered into one of the ships, which was Simon's, and prayed him that he would thrust out a little from the land. And he sat down, and taught the people out of the ship. ⁴Now when he had left speaking, he said unto Simon, Launch out into the deep, and let down your nets for a draught. ⁵And Simon answering said unto him, Master, we have toiled all the night, and have taken nothing: nevertheless at thy word I will let down the net. ⁶And when they had this done, they inclosed a great multitude of fishes: and their net brake. ⁷And they beckoned unto *their* partners, which were in the other ship, that they should come and help them. And they came, and filled both the ships, so that they began to sink. ⁸When Simon Peter saw *it*, he fell down at Jesus' knees, saying, Depart from me; for I am a sinful man, O Lord. ⁹For he was astonished, and all that were with him, at the draught of the fishes which they had taken: ¹⁰And so *was* also James, and John, the sons of Zebedee,

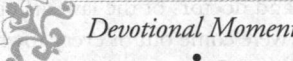

Devotional Moment
•
Obedience

5:5 Put yourself in Peter's place: Jesus (a carpenter) is telling you (a professional fisherman) how to do your job! How would you respond? Peter may have been reluctant, but at least he was willing to comply. And the result? Blessing and a deeper knowledge of the Lord. We may not always understand the reasons for God's commands, but our attitude should be like Peter's: "If you say so, we'll try again." Think of a situation where you have been ignoring God's advice. No matter how difficult, determine to try what he says.

which were partners with Simon. And Jesus said unto Simon, Fear not; from henceforth thou shalt catch men. ¹¹And when they had brought their ships to land, they forsook all, and followed him.

¹²And it came to pass, when he was in a certain city, behold a man full of leprosy: who seeing Jesus fell on *his* face, and besought him, saying, Lord, if thou wilt, thou canst make me clean. ¹³And he put forth *his* hand, and touched him, saying, I will: be thou clean. And immediately the leprosy departed from him. ¹⁴And he charged him to tell no man: but go, and shew thyself to the priest, and offer for thy cleansing, according as Moses commanded, for a testimony unto them. ¹⁵But so much the more went there a fame abroad of him: and great multitudes came together to hear, and to be healed by him of their infirmities. ¹⁶And he withdrew himself into the wilderness, and prayed.

¹⁷And it came to pass on a certain day, as he was teaching, that there were

Pharisees and doctors of the law sitting by, which were come out of every town of Galilee, and Judaea, and Jerusalem: and the power of the Lord was *present* to heal them. ¹⁸And, behold, men brought in a bed a man which was taken with a palsy: and they sought *means* to bring him in, and to lay *him* before him. ¹⁹And when they could not find by what *way* they might bring him in because of the multitude, they went upon the housetop, and let him down through the tiling with *his* couch into the midst before Jesus. ²⁰And when he saw their faith, he said unto him, Man, thy sins are forgiven thee. ²¹And the scribes and the Pharisees began to reason, saying, Who is this which speaketh blasphemies? Who can forgive sins, but God alone? ²²But when Jesus perceived their thoughts, he answering said unto them, What reason ye in your hearts? ²³Whether is easier, to say, Thy sins be forgiven thee; or to say, Rise up and walk? ²⁴But that ye may know that the Son of man hath power upon earth to forgive sins, (he said unto the sick of the palsy,) I say unto thee, Arise, and take up thy couch, and go into thine house. ²⁵And immediately he rose up before them, and took up that whereon he lay, and departed to his own house, glorifying God. ²⁶And they were all amazed, and they glorified God, and were filled with fear, saying, We have seen strange things to day.

²⁷And after these things he went forth, and saw a publican, named Levi, sitting at the receipt of custom: and he said unto him, Follow me. ²⁸And he left all, rose up, and followed him. ²⁹And Levi made him a great feast in his own house: and there was a great company of publicans and of others that sat down with them. ³⁰But their scribes and Pharisees murmured against his disciples, saying, Why do ye eat and drink with publicans and sinners? ³¹And Jesus answering said unto them, They that are whole need not a physician; but they that are sick. ³²I came not to call the righteous, but sinners to repentance. ³³And they said unto him, Why do the disciples of John fast often, and make prayers, and likewise *the disciples* of the Pharisees; but thine eat and drink? ³⁴And he said unto them, Can ye make the children of the bridechamber fast, while the bridegroom is with them? ³⁵But the days will come, when the bridegroom shall be taken away from them, and then shall they fast in those days. ³⁶And he spake also a parable unto them; No man putteth a piece of a new garment upon an old; if otherwise, then both the new maketh a rent, and the piece that was *taken* out of the new agreeth not with the old. ³⁷And no man putteth new wine into old bottles; else the new wine will burst the bottles, and be spilled, and the bottles shall perish. ³⁸But new wine must be put into new bottles; and both are preserved. ³⁹No man also having drunk old *wine* straightway desireth new: for he saith, The old is better.

6

¹And it came to pass on the second sabbath after the first, that he went through the corn fields; and his disciples plucked the ears of corn, and did eat, rubbing *them* in *their* hands. ²And certain of the Pharisees said unto them, Why do ye that which is not lawful to do on the sabbath days? ³And Jesus an-

swering them said, Have ye not read so much as this, what David did, when himself was an hungred, and they which were with him; ⁴How he went into the house of God, and did take and eat the shewbread, and gave also to them that were with him; which it is not lawful to eat but for the priests alone? ⁵And he said unto them, That the Son of man is Lord also of the sabbath. ⁶And it came to pass also on another sabbath, that he entered into the synagogue and taught: and there was a man whose right hand was withered. ⁷And the scribes and Pharisees watched him, whether he would heal on the sabbath day; that they might find an accusation against him. ⁸But he knew their thoughts, and said to the man which had the withered hand, Rise up, and stand forth in the midst. And he arose and stood forth. ⁹Then said Jesus unto them, I will ask you one thing; Is it lawful on the sabbath days to do good, or to do evil? to save life, or to destroy it? ¹⁰And looking round about upon them all, he said unto the man, Stretch forth thy hand. And he did so: and his hand was restored whole as the other. ¹¹And they were filled with madness; and communed one with another what they might do to Jesus.

¹²And it came to pass in those days, that he went out into a mountain to pray, and continued all night in prayer to God. ¹³And when it was day, he called unto him his disciples: and of them he chose twelve, whom also he named apostles; ¹⁴Simon, (whom he also named Peter,) and Andrew his brother, James and John, Philip and Bartholomew, ¹⁵Matthew and Thomas, James the son of Alphaeus, and Simon called Zelotes, ¹⁶And Judas the brother of James, and Judas Iscariot, which also was the traitor. ¹⁷And he came down with them, and stood in the plain, and the company of his disciples, and a great multitude of people out of all Judaea and Jerusalem, and from the sea coast of Tyre and Sidon, which came to hear him, and to be healed of their diseases; ¹⁸And they that were vexed with unclean spirits: and they were healed. ¹⁹And the whole multitude sought to touch him: for there went virtue out of him, and healed them all.

²⁰And he lifted up his eyes on his disciples, and said, Blessed be ye poor: for yours is the kingdom of God. ²¹Blessed are ye that hunger now: for ye shall be filled. Blessed are ye that weep now: for ye shall laugh. ²²Blessed are ye, when men shall hate you, and when they shall separate you from their company, and shall reproach you, and cast out your name as evil, for the Son of man's sake. ²³Rejoice ye in that day, and leap for joy: for, behold, your reward is great in heaven: for in the like manner did their fathers unto the prophets. ²⁴But woe unto you that are rich! for ye have received your consolation. ²⁵Woe unto you that are full! for ye shall hunger. Woe unto you that laugh now! for ye shall mourn and weep. ²⁶Woe unto you, when all men shall speak well of you! for so did their fathers to the false prophets.

²⁷But I say unto you which hear, Love your enemies, do good to them which hate you, ²⁸Bless them that curse you, and pray for them which despitefully use you. ²⁹And unto him that smiteth thee on the one cheek offer also the other; and him that taketh away thy

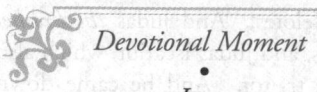

Devotional Moment
·
Love

6:27-28 Christ's instructions go against all our natural instincts. When people hurt us, our instinct is to hurt back. When people misuse us or curse us, we want to even the score. But Christ's way is love. He wants us to pray for people who curse us and do good to people who hate us. Let God enable you to love unlovable people in difficult situations.

cloke forbid not *to take thy* coat also. ³⁰Give to every man that asketh of thee; and of him that taketh away thy goods ask *them* not again. ³¹And as ye would that men should do to you, do ye also to them likewise. ³²For if ye love them which love you, what thank have ye? for sinners also love those that love them. ³³And if ye do good to them which do good to you, what thank have ye? for sinners also do even the same. ³⁴And if ye lend *to them* of whom ye hope to receive, what thank have ye? for sinners also lend to sinners, to receive as much again. ³⁵But love ye your enemies, and

Devotional Moment
·
Giving

6:35 When we give to people who can't possibly repay us or who are ungrateful, we reflect God's character. What could you give to those who cannot repay you or who would never even know you had given? Some possibilities: money, food, or clothing to Christian organizations that help people in countries you consider to be "enemies"; Christmas gifts to families of prisoners; compliments to people who have hurt you.

do good, and lend, hoping for nothing again; and your reward shall be great, and ye shall be the children of the Highest: for he is kind unto the unthankful and *to* the evil. ³⁶Be ye therefore merciful, as your Father also is merciful.

³⁷Judge not, and ye shall not be judged: condemn not, and ye shall not be condemned: forgive, and ye shall be forgiven: ³⁸Give, and it shall be given unto you; good measure, pressed down, and shaken together, and running over, shall men give into your bosom. For with the same measure that ye mete withal it shall be measured to you again. ³⁹And he spake a parable unto them, Can the blind lead the blind? shall they not both fall into the ditch? ⁴⁰The disciple is not above his master: but every one that is perfect shall be as his master. ⁴¹And why beholdest thou the mote that is in thy brother's eye, but perceivest not the beam that is in thine own eye? ⁴²Either how canst thou say to thy brother, Brother, let me pull out the mote that is in thine eye, when thou thyself beholdest not the beam that is in thine own eye? Thou hypocrite, cast out first the beam out of thine own eye, and then shalt thou see clearly to pull out the mote that is in thy brother's eye. ⁴³For a good tree bringeth not forth corrupt fruit; neither doth a corrupt tree bring forth good fruit. ⁴⁴For every tree is known by his own fruit. For of thorns men do not gather figs, nor of a bramble bush gather they grapesª. ⁴⁵A good man out of the good treasure of his heart bringeth forth that which is good; and an evil man out of the evil treasure

ª grapes: Gr. a grape

of his heart bringeth forth that which is evil: for of the abundance of the heart his mouth speaketh. ⁴⁶And why call ye me, Lord, Lord, and do not the things which I say? ⁴⁷Whosoever cometh to me, and heareth my sayings, and doeth them, I will shew you to whom he is like: ⁴⁸He is like a man which built an house, and digged deep, and laid the foundation on a rock: and when the flood arose, the stream beat vehemently upon that house, and could not shake it: for it was founded upon a rock. ⁴⁹But he that heareth, and doeth not, is like a man that without a foundation built an house upon the earth; against which the stream did beat vehemently, and immediately it fell; and the ruin of that house was great.

7

¹Now when he had ended all his sayings in the audience of the people, he entered into Capernaum. ²And a certain centurion's servant, who was dear unto him, was sick, and ready to die. ³And when he heard of Jesus, he sent unto him the elders of the Jews, beseeching him that he would come and heal his servant. ⁴And when they came to Jesus, they besought him instantly, saying, That he was worthy for whom he should do this: ⁵For he loveth our nation, and he hath built us a synagogue. ⁶Then Jesus went with them. And when he was now not far from the house, the centurion sent friends to him, saying unto him, Lord, trouble not thyself: for I am not worthy that thou shouldest enter under my roof: ⁷Wherefore nei-

ther thought I myself worthy to come unto thee: but say in a word, and my servant shall be healed. ⁸For I also am a man set under authority, having under me soldiers, and I say unto oneª, Go, and he goeth; and to another, Come, and he cometh; and to my servant, Do this, and he doeth *it*. ⁹When Jesus heard these things, he marvelled at him, and turned him about, and said unto the people that followed him, I say unto you, I have not found so great faith, no, not in Israel. ¹⁰And they that were sent, returning to the house, found the servant whole that had been sick.

¹¹And it came to pass the day after, that he went into a city called Nain; and many of his disciples went with him, and much people. ¹²Now when he came nigh to the gate of the city, behold, there was a dead man carried out, the only son of his mother, and she was a widow: and much people of the city was with her. ¹³And when the Lord saw her, he had compassion on her, and said unto her, Weep not. ¹⁴And he came and touched the bierᵇ: and they that bare *him* stood still. And he said, Young man, I say unto thee, Arise. ¹⁵And he that was dead sat up, and began to speak. And he delivered him to his mother. ¹⁶And there came a fear on all: and they glorified God, saying, That a great prophet is risen up among us; and, That God hath visited his people. ¹⁷And this rumour of him went forth throughout all Judaea, and throughout all the region round about. ¹⁸And the disciples of John shewed him of all these things.

ª one: Gr. this man
ᵇ bier: or, coffin

¹⁹And John calling *unto him* two of his disciples sent *them* to Jesus, saying, Art thou he that should come? or look we for another? ²⁰When the men were come unto him, they said, John Baptist hath sent us unto thee, saying, Art thou he that should come? or look we for another? ²¹And in that same hour he cured many of *their* infirmities and plagues, and of evil spirits; and unto many *that were* blind he gave sight. ²²Then Jesus answering said unto them, Go your way, and tell John what things ye have seen and heard; how that the blind see, the lame walk, the lepers are cleansed, the deaf hear, the dead are raised, to the poor the gospel is preached. ²³And blessed is *he*, whosoever shall not be offended in me. ²⁴And when the messengers of John were departed, he began to speak unto the people concerning John, What went ye out into the wilderness for to see? A reed shaken with the wind? ²⁵But what went ye out for to see? A man clothed in soft raiment? Behold, they which are gorgeously apparelled, and live delicately, are in kings' courts. ²⁶But what went ye out for to see? A prophet? Yea, I say unto you, and much more than a prophet. ²⁷This is *he*, of whom it is written, Behold, I send my messenger before thy face, which shall prepare thy way before thee. ²⁸For I say unto you, Among those that are born of women there is not a greater prophet than John the Baptist: but he that is least in the kingdom of God is greater than he. ²⁹And all the people that heard *him*, and the publicans, justified God, being baptized with the baptism of John. ³⁰But the Pharisees and lawyers

rejected[c] the counsel of God against themselves, being not baptized of him. ³¹And the Lord said, Whereunto then shall I liken the men of this generation? and to what are they like? ³²They are like unto children sitting in the marketplace, and calling one to another, and saying, We have piped unto you, and ye have not danced; we have mourned to you, and ye have not wept. ³³For John the Baptist came neither eating bread nor drinking wine; and ye say, He hath a devil. ³⁴The Son of man is come eating and drinking; and ye say, Behold a gluttonous man, and a winebibber, a friend of publicans and sinners! ³⁵But wisdom is justified of all her children.

³⁶And one of the Pharisees desired him that he would eat with him. And he went into the Pharisee's house, and sat down to meat. ³⁷And, behold, a woman in the city, which was a sinner, when she knew that *Jesus* sat at meat in the Pharisee's house, brought an alabaster box of ointment, ³⁸And stood at his feet behind *him* weeping, and began to wash his feet with tears, and did wipe *them* with the hairs of her head, and kissed his feet, and anointed *them* with the ointment. ³⁹Now when the Pharisee which had bidden him saw *it*, he spake within himself, saying, This man, if he were a prophet, would have known who and what manner of woman *this is* that toucheth him: for she is a sinner. ⁴⁰And Jesus answering said unto him, Simon, I have somewhat to say unto thee. And he saith, Master, say on. ⁴¹There was a certain creditor which had two debtors: the one owed five hundred pence, and the other fifty. ⁴²And when they had nothing to pay, he

---

[c] rejected: or, frustrated

frankly forgave them both. Tell me therefore, which of them will love him most? ⁴³Simon answered and said, I suppose that *he*, to whom he forgave most. And he said unto him, Thou hast rightly judged. ⁴⁴And he turned to the woman, and said unto Simon, Seest thou this woman? I entered into thine house, thou gavest me no water for my feet: but she hath washed my feet with tears, and wiped *them* with the hairs of her head. ⁴⁵Thou gavest me no kiss: but this woman since the time I came in hath not ceased to kiss my feet. ⁴⁶My head with oil thou didst not anoint: but this woman hath anointed my feet with ointment. ⁴⁷Wherefore I say unto thee, Her sins, which are many, are forgiven; for she loved much: but to whom little is forgiven, *the same* loveth little. ⁴⁸And he said unto her, Thy sins are forgiven. ⁴⁹And they that sat at meat with him began to say within themselves, Who is this that forgiveth sins also? ⁵⁰And he said to the woman, Thy faith hath saved thee; go in peace.

8

¹And it came to pass afterward, that he went throughout every city and village,

---

Devotional Moment

Giving

8:2-3 Several women contributed from their private means to support Jesus and his disciples. All of us have the opportunity to support God's work. You can financially support your church as well as missionaries and other full-time Christian workers. Consider contributing money to support a missionary family; use a picture of that family as a reminder to pray for them.

---

preaching and shewing the glad tidings of the kingdom of God: and the twelve *were* with him, ²And certain women, which had been healed of evil spirits and infirmities, Mary called Magdalene, out of whom went seven devils, ³And Joanna the wife of Chuza Herod's steward, and Susanna, and many others, which ministered unto him of their substance.

⁴And when much people were gathered together, and were come to him out of every city, he spake by a parable: ⁵A sower went out to sow his seed: and as he sowed, some fell by the way side; and it was trodden down, and the fowls of the air devoured it. ⁶And some fell upon a rock; and as soon as it was sprung up, it withered away, because it lacked moisture. ⁷And some fell among thorns; and the thorns sprang up with it, and choked it. ⁸And other fell on good ground, and sprang up, and bare fruit an hundredfold. And when he had said these things, he cried, He that hath ears to hear, let him hear. ⁹And his disciples asked him, saying, What might this parable be? ¹⁰And he said, Unto you it is given to know the mysteries of the kingdom of God: but to others in parables; that seeing they might not see, and hearing they might not understand. ¹¹Now the parable is this: The seed is the word of God. ¹²Those by the way side are they that hear; then cometh the devil, and taketh away the word out of their hearts, lest they should believe and be saved. ¹³They on the rock *are they*, which, when they hear, receive the word with joy; and these have no root, which for a while believe, and in time of temptation fall away. ¹⁴And that which fell

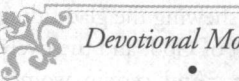

among thorns are they, which, when they have heard, go forth, and are choked with cares and riches and pleasures of *this* life, and bring no fruit to perfection. ¹⁵But that on the good ground are they, which in an honest and good heart, having heard the word, keep *it*, and bring forth fruit with patience. ¹⁶No man, when he hath lighted a candle, covereth it with a vessel, or putteth *it* under a bed; but setteth *it* on a candlestick, that they which enter in may see the light. ¹⁷For nothing is secret, that shall not be made manifest; neither *any thing* hid, that shall not be known and come abroad. ¹⁸Take heed therefore how ye hear: for whosoever hath, to him shall be given; and whosoever hath not, from him shall be taken even that which he seemeth[a] to have. ¹⁹Then came to him *his* mother and his brethren, and could not come at him for the press. ²⁰And it was told him *by certain* which said, Thy mother and thy brethren stand without, desiring to see

thee. ²¹And he answered and said unto them, My mother and my brethren are these which hear the word of God, and do it. ²²Now it came to pass on a certain day, that he went into a ship with his disciples: and he said unto them, Let us go over unto the other side of the lake. And they launched forth. ²³But as they sailed he fell asleep: and there came down a storm of wind on the lake; and they were filled *with water*, and were in jeopardy. ²⁴And they came to him, and awoke him, saying, Master, master, we perish. Then he arose, and rebuked the wind and the raging of the water: and they ceased, and there was a calm. ²⁵And he said unto them, Where is your faith? And they being afraid wondered, saying one to another, What manner of man is this! for he commandeth even the winds and water, and they obey him. ²⁶And they arrived at the country of the Gadarenes, which is over against Galilee. ²⁷And when he went forth to land, there met him out of the city a certain man, which had devils long time, and ware no clothes, neither abode in *any* house, but in the tombs. ²⁸When he saw Jesus, he cried out, and fell down before him, and with a loud voice said, What have I to do with thee, Jesus, *thou* Son of God most high? I beseech thee, torment me not. ²⁹(For he had commanded the unclean spirit to come out of the man. For oftentimes it had caught him: and he was kept bound with chains and in fetters; and he brake the bands, and was driven of the devil into the wilderness.) ³⁰And Jesus asked him, saying, What is thy

---

[a] seemeth . . . : or, thinketh that he hath

name? And he said, Legion: because many devils were entered into him. [31]And they besought him that he would not command them to go out into the deep. [32]And there was there an herd of many swine feeding on the mountain: and they besought him that he would suffer them to enter into them. And he suffered them. [33]Then went the devils out of the man, and entered into the swine: and the herd ran violently down a steep place into the lake, and were choked. [34]When they that fed *them* saw what was done, they fled, and went and told *it* in the city and in the country. [35]Then they went out to see what was done; and came to Jesus, and found the man, out of whom the devils were departed, sitting at the feet of Jesus, clothed, and in his right mind: and they were afraid. [36]They also which saw *it* told them by what means he that was possessed of the devils was healed. [37]Then the whole multitude of the country of the Gadarenes round about besought him to depart from them; for they were taken with great fear: and he went up into the ship, and returned back again. [38]Now the man out of whom the devils were departed besought him that he might be with him: but Jesus sent him away, saying, [39]Return to thine own house, and shew how great things God hath done unto thee. And he went his way, and published throughout the whole city how great things Jesus had done unto him.

[40]And it came to pass, that, when Jesus was returned, the people *gladly* received him: for they were all waiting for him. [41]And, behold, there came a man named Jairus, and he was a ruler of the synagogue: and he fell down at Jesus'

feet, and besought him that he would come into his house: [42]For he had one only daughter, about twelve years of age, and she lay a dying. But as he went the people thronged him. [43]And a woman having an issue of blood twelve years, which had spent all her living upon physicians, neither could be healed of any, [44]Came behind *him*, and touched the border of his garment: and immediately her issue of blood stanched. [45]And Jesus said, Who touched me? When all denied, Peter and they that were with him said, Master, the multitude throng thee and press *thee*, and sayest thou, Who touched me? [46]And Jesus said, Somebody hath touched me: for I perceive that virtue is gone out of me. [47]And when the woman saw that she was not hid, she came trembling, and falling down before him, she declared unto him before all the people for what cause she had touched him, and how she was healed immediately. [48]And he said unto her, Daughter, be of good comfort: thy faith

---

Devotional Moment

Prayer/Advice

8:41-42 Out of his deep love for his daughter and his belief in Jesus' power to help her, this leader of the synagogue came to Jesus and begged for his help. At that moment the leader was not thinking about his position in the community or what the crowds would think about him. He had only one thing in mind: He needed Jesus' help. How often we need help with the care of our children! We look everywhere for advice—books, education, doctors, etc. Those are all legitimate sources of help that can be used by God. But first we need to come to him in prayer, asking for his wisdom and guidance.

hath made thee whole; go in peace. [49]While he yet spake, there cometh one from the ruler of the synagogue's *house*, saying to him, Thy daughter is dead; trouble not the Master. [50]But when Jesus heard *it*, he answered him, saying, Fear not: believe only, and she shall be made whole. [51]And when he came into the house, he suffered no man to go in, save Peter, and James, and John, and the father and the mother of the maiden. [52]And all wept, and bewailed her: but he said, Weep not; she is not dead, but sleepeth. [53]And they laughed him to scorn, knowing that she was dead. [54]And he put them all out, and took her by the hand, and called, saying, Maid, arise. [55]And her spirit came again, and she arose straightway: and he commanded to give her meat. [56]And her parents were astonished: but he charged them that they should tell no man what was done.

9

[1]Then he called his twelve disciples together, and gave them power and authority over all devils, and to cure diseases. [2]And he sent them to preach the kingdom of God, and to heal the sick. [3]And he said unto them, Take nothing for *your* journey, neither staves, nor scrip, neither bread, neither money; neither have two coats apiece. [4]And whatsoever house ye enter into, there abide, and thence depart. [5]And whosoever will not receive you, when ye go out of that city, shake off the very dust from your feet for a testimony against them. [6]And they departed, and went through the towns, preaching the gospel, and healing every where. [7]Now Herod the tetrarch heard of all that was

done by him: and he was perplexed, because that it was said of some, that John was risen from the dead; [8]And of some, that Elias had appeared; and of others, that one of the old prophets was risen again. [9]And Herod said, John have I beheaded: but who is this, of whom I hear such things? And he desired to see him.

[10]And the apostles, when they were returned, told him all that they had done. And he took them, and went aside privately into a desert place belonging to the city called Bethsaida. [11]And the people, when they knew *it*, followed him: and he received them, and spake unto them of the kingdom of God, and healed them that had need of healing. [12]And when the day began to wear away, then came the twelve, and said unto him, Send the multitude away, that they may go into the towns and country round about, and lodge, and get victuals: for we are here in a desert place. [13]But he said unto them, Give ye them to eat. And they said, We have no more but five loaves and two fishes; except we should go and buy

Devotional Moment

Sharing

9:12-17 When the disciples urged Jesus to send the hungry crowd away, Jesus told the *disciples* to feed the people. When God's people come to him today and ask him to feed starving and homeless people, he turns to us and says, *"You feed them."* He can take whatever we give—our lunch—and multiply it. Every community has people in need—the homeless, refugees, unemployed people in your church, unwed mothers, abused children, elderly shut-ins. Thank God for all of the blessings he has given you, and share what you can in time, money, and possessions.

meat for all this people. ¹⁴For they were about five thousand men. And he said to his disciples, Make them sit down by fifties in a company. ¹⁵And they did so, and made them all sit down. ¹⁶Then he took the five loaves and the two fishes, and looking up to heaven, he blessed them, and brake, and gave to the disciples to set before the multitude. ¹⁷And they did eat, and were all filled: and there was taken up of fragments that remained to them twelve baskets.

¹⁸And it came to pass, as he was alone praying, his disciples were with him: and he asked them, saying, Whom say the people that I am? ¹⁹They answering said, John the Baptist; but some *say*, Elias; and others *say*, that one of the old prophets is risen again. ²⁰He said unto them, But whom say ye that I am? Peter answering said, The Christ of God. ²¹And he straitly charged them, and commanded *them* to tell no man that thing; ²²Saying, The Son of man must suffer many things, and be rejected of the elders and chief priests and scribes, and be slain, and be raised the third day. ²³And he said to *them* all, If any *man* will come after me, let him deny himself, and take up his cross daily, and follow me. ²⁴For whosoever will save his life shall lose it: but whosoever will lose his life for my sake, the same shall save it. ²⁵For what is a man advantaged, if he gain the whole world, and lose himself, or be cast away? ²⁶For whosoever shall be ashamed of me and of my words, of him shall the Son of man be ashamed, when he shall come in his own glory, and *in his* Father's, and of the holy angels. ²⁷But I tell you of a

truth, there be some standing here, which shall not taste of death, till they see the kingdom of God.

²⁸And it came to pass about an eight days after these sayings*, he took Peter and John and James, and went up into a mountain to pray. ²⁹And as he prayed, the fashion of his countenance was altered, and his raiment *was* white *and* glistering. ³⁰And, behold, there talked with him two men, which were Moses and Elias: ³¹Who appeared in glory, and spake of his decease which he should accomplish at Jerusalem. ³²But Peter and they that were with him were heavy with sleep: and when they were awake, they saw his glory, and the two men that stood with him. ³³And it came to pass, as they departed from him, Peter said unto Jesus, Master, it is good for us to be here: and let us make three tabernacles; one for thee, and one for Moses, and one for Elias: not knowing what he said. ³⁴While he thus spake, there came a cloud, and overshadowed them: and they feared as they entered into the cloud. ³⁵And there came a voice out of the cloud, saying, This is my beloved Son: hear him. ³⁶And when the voice was past, Jesus was found alone. And they kept *it* close, and told no man in those days any of those things which they had seen.

³⁷And it came to pass, that on the next day, when they were come down from the hill, much people met him. ³⁸And, behold, a man of the company cried out, saying, Master, I beseech thee, look upon my son: for he is mine only child. ³⁹And, lo, a spirit taketh him, and he suddenly crieth out; and it

---

ª sayings: or, things

teareth him that he foameth again, and bruising him hardly departeth from him. ⁴⁰And I besought thy disciples to cast him out; and they could not. ⁴¹And Jesus answering said, O faithless and perverse generation, how long shall I be with you, and suffer you? Bring thy son hither. ⁴²And as he was yet a coming, the devil threw him down, and tare *him.* And Jesus rebuked the unclean spirit, and healed the child, and delivered him again to his father.

⁴³And they were all amazed at the mighty power of God. But while they wondered every one at all things which Jesus did, he said unto his disciples, ⁴⁴Let these sayings sink down into your ears: for the Son of man shall be delivered into the hands of men. ⁴⁵But they understood not this saying, and it was hid from them, that they perceived it not: and they feared to ask him of that saying. ⁴⁶Then there arose a reasoning among them, which of them should be greatest. ⁴⁷And Jesus, perceiving the thought of their heart, took a child, and set him by him, ⁴⁸And said unto them, Whosoever shall receive this child in my name receiveth me: and whosoever shall receive me receiveth him that sent me: for he that is least among you all, the same shall be great. ⁴⁹And John answered and said, Master, we saw one casting out devils in thy name; and we forbad him, because he followeth not with us. ⁵⁰And Jesus said unto him, Forbid *him* not: for he that is not against us is for us.

⁵¹And it came to pass, when the time was come that he should be received up, he stedfastly set his face to go to Jerusalem, ⁵²And sent messengers before his face: and they went, and en-

tered into a village of the Samaritans, to make ready for him. ⁵³And they did not receive him, because his face was as though he would go to Jerusalem. ⁵⁴And when his disciples James and John saw *this,* they said, Lord, wilt thou that we command fire to come down from heaven, and consume them, even as Elias did? ⁵⁵But he turned, and rebuked them, and said, Ye know not what manner of spirit ye are of. ⁵⁶For the Son of man is not come to destroy men's lives, but to save *them.* And they went to another village.

⁵⁷And it came to pass, that, as they went in the way, a certain *man* said unto him, Lord, I will follow thee whithersoever thou goest. ⁵⁸And Jesus said unto him, Foxes have holes, and birds of the air *have* nests; but the Son of man hath not where to lay *his* head. ⁵⁹And he said unto another, Follow me. But he said, Lord, suffer me first to go and bury my father. ⁶⁰Jesus said unto him, Let the dead bury their dead: but go thou and preach the kingdom of God. ⁶¹And another also said, Lord, I will follow thee; but let me first go bid them farewell, which are at

Devotional Moment
•
Commitment

9:59-60 When Jesus invited this man to follow him, the man told Jesus he would like to wait until his father's death. Most likely the man was making an excuse to put Jesus off. Some people skip church during the summer "for the family." Some, even though capable of giving to the Lord's work, give little or no money because they want to spend it "on the family." We need to be sure God always comes first. God commands us to care for our family, but we must not use our family's needs as an excuse to keep from obeying him in other areas.

home at my house. [62]And Jesus said unto him, No man, having put his hand to the plough, and looking back, is fit for the kingdom of God.

10

[1]After these things the Lord appointed other seventy also, and sent them two and two before his face into every city and place, whither he himself would come. [2]Therefore said he unto them, The harvest truly *is* great, but the labourers *are* few: pray ye therefore the Lord of the harvest, that he would send forth labourers into his harvest. [3]Go your ways: behold, I send you forth as lambs among wolves. [4]Carry neither purse, nor scrip, nor shoes: and salute no man by the way. [5]And into whatsoever house ye enter, first say, Peace *be* to this house. [6]And if the son of peace be there, your peace shall rest upon it: if not, it shall turn to you again. [7]And in the same house remain, eating and drinking such things as they give: for the labourer is worthy of his hire. Go not from house to house. [8]And into whatsoever city ye enter, and they receive you, eat such things as are set before you: [9]And heal the sick that are therein, and say unto them, The kingdom of God is come nigh unto you. [10]But into whatsoever city ye enter, and they receive you not, go your ways out into the streets of the same, and say, [11]Even the very dust of your city, which cleaveth on us, we do wipe off against you: notwithstanding be ye sure of this, that the kingdom of God is come nigh unto you. [12]But I say unto you, that it shall be more tolerable in that day for Sodom, than for that city. [13]Woe unto thee, Chorazin! woe unto thee, Bethsaida! for if the mighty works had been done in Tyre and Sidon, which have been done in you, they had a great while ago repented, sitting in sackcloth and ashes. [14]But it shall be more tolerable for Tyre and Sidon at the judgment, than for you. [15]And thou, Capernaum, which art exalted to heaven, shalt be thrust down to hell. [16]He that heareth you heareth me; and he that despiseth you despiseth me; and he that despiseth me despiseth him that sent me.

[17]And the seventy returned again with joy, saying, Lord, even the devils are subject unto us through thy name. [18]And he said unto them, I beheld Satan as lightning fall from heaven. [19]Behold, I give unto you power to tread on serpents and scorpions, and over all the power of the enemy: and nothing shall by any means hurt you. [20]Notwithstanding in this rejoice not, that the spirits are subject unto you; but rather rejoice, because your names are written in heaven. [21]In that hour Jesus rejoiced in spirit, and said, I thank thee, O Father, Lord of heaven and earth, that thou hast hid these things from the wise and prudent, and hast revealed them unto babes: even so, Father; for so it seemed good in thy sight. [22]All things are delivered to me of my Father: and no man knoweth who the Son is, but the Father; and who the Father is, but the Son, and *he* to whom the Son will reveal *him*.[a] [23]And he turned him unto *his* disciples, and said privately, Blessed

---

[a] many ancient copies add these words at the beginning of verse, and <2532> turning <4762> (5651) to <4314> his disciples <3101>, he said <2036> (5627)

are the eyes which see the things that ye see: ²⁴For I tell you, that many prophets and kings have desired to see those things which ye see, and have not seen *them*; and to hear those things which ye hear, and have not heard *them*.

²⁵And, behold, a certain lawyer stood up, and tempted him, saying, Master, what shall I do to inherit eternal life? ²⁶He said unto him, What is written in the law? how readest thou? ²⁷And he answering said, Thou shalt love the Lord thy God with all thy heart, and with all thy soul, and with all thy strength, and with all thy mind; and thy neighbour as thyself. ²⁸And he said unto him, Thou hast answered right: this do, and thou shalt live. ²⁹But he, willing to justify himself, said unto Jesus, And who is my neighbour? ³⁰And Jesus answering said, A certain *man* went down from Jerusalem to Jericho, and fell among thieves, which stripped him of his raiment, and wounded *him*, and departed, leaving *him* half dead. ³¹And by chance there came down a certain priest that way: and when he saw him, he passed by on the other side. ³²And likewise a Levite, when he was at the place, came and looked *on him*, and passed by on the other side. ³³But a certain Samaritan, as he journeyed, came where he was: and when he saw him, he had compassion *on him*, ³⁴And went to *him*, and bound up his wounds, pouring in oil and wine, and set him on his own beast, and brought him to an inn, and took care of him. ³⁵And on the morrow when he departed, he took out two pence, and gave *them* to the host, and said unto him, Take care of him; and whatsoever thou spendest more, when I come again, I will repay thee.

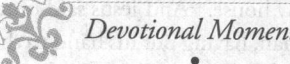

Devotional Moment

Generosity

10:33-35 When the Samaritan saw the wounded man, he felt great compassion. But the Samaritan didn't stop with his pity; he put his compassion into action. He gave what he had—time, transportation, care, sleep, and money. Perhaps you know of a Christian organization—an "innkeeper" that cares for hurting people—that can use your generous giving. Find a way to give to such an organization to help it bring wholeness to broken people in the name of Jesus.

³⁶Which now of these three, thinkest thou, was neighbour unto him that fell among the thieves? ³⁷And he said, He that shewed mercy on him. Then said Jesus unto him, Go, and do thou likewise.

³⁸Now it came to pass, as they went, that he entered into a certain village: and a certain woman named Martha received him into her house. ³⁹And she had a sister called Mary, which also sat at Jesus' feet, and heard

Devotional Moment

Devotions

10:38-42 More than anything else, Martha wanted her house to be ready for the guests who were to stay at her home that night. She wanted that even more than she wanted to hear what Jesus had to say. Jesus gently reminded her that the cares of this life don't matter as much as eternal life. It is easy to be like Martha and forget that our greatest priority is to listen to God. Life is so filled with events—meetings, rehearsals, sports, performances, chores, errands, work—that it's easy to neglect reserving time for reading the Bible, praying, or planning a devotional time. Schedule time each day for these important parts of your spiritual life.

his word. ⁴⁰But Martha was cumbered about much serving, and came to him, and said, Lord, dost thou not care that my sister hath left me to serve alone? bid her therefore that she help me. ⁴¹And Jesus answered and said unto her, Martha, Martha, thou art careful and troubled about many things: ⁴²But one thing is needful: and Mary hath chosen that good part, which shall not be taken away from her.

11

¹And it came to pass, that, as he was praying in a certain place, when he ceased, one of his disciples said unto him, Lord, teach us to pray, as John also taught his disciples. ²And he said unto them, When ye pray, say, Our Father which art in heaven, Hallowed be thy name. Thy kingdom come. Thy will be done, as in heaven, so in earth. ³Give us day by day*ᵃ our daily bread. ⁴And forgive us our sins; for we also forgive every one that is indebted to us. And lead us not into temptation; but deliver us from evil. ⁵And he said unto them, Which of you shall have a friend, and shall go unto him at midnight, and say unto him, Friend, lend me three loaves; ⁶For a friend of mine inᵇ his journey is come to me, and I have nothing to set before him? ⁷And he from within shall answer and say, Trouble me not: the door is now shut, and my children are with me in bed; I cannot rise and give thee. ⁸I say unto you, Though he will not rise and give him, because he is his

> ### Devotional Moment
> •
> ### Persistence in Prayer
> 11:8-10 These verses remind us that prayer needs to be an ongoing discipline in our life—that we must consciously keep on asking, looking, and knocking. Our days provide countless opportunities for prayer. We don't insult God by praying about the same concerns over long periods of time. On the contrary, it shows how concerned we really are. God honors our persistence in looking to him for answers and wisdom. Keep at it.

friend, yet because of his importunity he will rise and give him as many as he needeth. ⁹And I say unto you, Ask, and it shall be given you; seek, and ye shall find; knock, and it shall be opened unto you. ¹⁰For every one that asketh receiveth; and he that seeketh findeth; and to him that knocketh it shall be opened. ¹¹If a son shall ask bread of any of you that is a father, will he give him a stone? or if *he ask* a fish, will he for a fish give him a serpent? ¹²Or if he shall ask an egg, will he offerᶜ him a scorpion? ¹³If ye then, being evil, know how to give good gifts unto your children: how much more shall *your* heavenly Father give the Holy Spirit to them that ask him?

¹⁴And he was casting out a devil, and it was dumb. And it came to pass, when the devil was gone out, the dumb spake; and the people wondered. ¹⁵But some of them said, He casteth out devils through Beelzebubᵈ the chief of the

---

ᵃ day by day: or, for the day
ᵇ in . . . : or, out of his way
ᶜ offer: Gr. give
ᵈ Beelzebub: Gr. Beelzebul

Breaking Free from "Undercover Anger"

Jesus and his disciples "entered into a certain village; and a certain woman named Martha received him into her house." Luke 10:38

Exactly what is "undercover anger"? For a good illustration, recall the Japanese attack on Pearl Harbor in 1941. Admiral Yamamoto was able to bring his task force extremely close to the island of Hawaii undetected, in large part because he followed a tropical storm. The Japanese fleet was *hidden behind the storm.*

Martha's outburst to Jesus similarly took everyone by surprise. She felt stuck with all the responsibility, while Mary was sloughing off and gabbing with the guests. With each preparation she made, her frustration built. Finally, she couldn't take it anymore, and she said to Jesus with exasperation, "Lord, dost thou not care that my sister hath left me to serve alone? bid her therefore that she help me" (Luke 10:40). Her extreme frustration is obvious.

Yet there is also no indication that Martha ever asked Mary to come and help—no hint that she expressed her feelings in an honest, straightforward way.

That's how undercover anger works. Instead of dealing with frustrations directly, we hide our feelings from others and let them build into an internal storm. No one knows what's brewing—until finally we blow up in an outburst of rage that catches everyone by surprise.

Breaking the cycle of undercover anger is important if a marriage or parent-child relationship is to grow. Children who grow up with a mother or father who acts like a rumbling volcano may feel anxious, afraid, and unwilling to trust others. A spouse who harbors undercover anger may feel blindsided and betrayed and may lash out. This can wreak havoc on a family.

How to break the pattern? Two lessons stand out from this passage.

A gentle answer. Jesus met Martha's anger with softness: "Martha, Martha." Softness is one of the strongest ways to defeat the indirect barbs of someone using undercover anger. You might matter-of-factly say something like, "I can sense by your words that you're angry with me. Can we talk about it?" This gently urges the other person to deal with his or her emotions in a direct, honest way.

Realistic—and shared—expectations. Among the reasons for a lot of undercover anger are unfulfilled desires or expectations that we place on ourself or others. Notice Jesus' words: "Martha, thou art careful and troubled about many things. But one thing is needful." Martha's priorities were not the same as those of either Jesus or Mary. Martha expected Mary to be working, while Mary had different expectations for herself.

Almost without exception, those who struggle with indirect anger have high, unspoken expectations for both themselves and others. Think back to the last time you blew up at someone: (1) What were the expectations you had that weren't being fulfilled? (2) What goals seemed blocked by the other person? (3) With what plans did the other person not comply?

Outbursts of anger can be triggered by minor events: A five-year-old has dragged her feet getting ready for school four days in a row; then on the fifth day Mom explodes. The boss has been worried about cash flow for weeks; then one small, unexpected expense pushes him over the edge.

Practice dealing with your frustrations as they come up, rather than letting them build. Make a commitment *this week* to express your frustration honestly *at the time you feel it*. This can help break the cycle and increase the level of healthy communication in your home.

---

devils. [16]And others, tempting *him*, sought of him a sign from heaven. [17]But he, knowing their thoughts, said unto them, Every kingdom divided against itself is brought to desolation; and a house *divided* against a house falleth. [18]If Satan also be divided against himself, how shall his kingdom stand? because ye say that I cast out devils through Beelzebub. [19]And if I by Beelzebub cast out devils, by whom do your sons cast *them* out? therefore shall they be your judges. [20]But if I with the finger of God cast out devils, no doubt the kingdom of God is come upon you. [21]When a strong man armed keepeth his palace, his goods are in peace: [22]But when a stronger than he shall come upon him, and overcome him, he taketh from him all his armour wherein he trusted, and divideth his spoils. [23]He that is not with me is against me: and he that gathereth not with me scattereth. [24]When the unclean spirit is gone out of a man, he walketh through dry places, seeking rest; and finding none, he saith, I will return unto my house whence I came out. [25]And when he cometh, he findeth *it* swept and garnished. [26]Then goeth he, and taketh *to him* seven other spirits more wicked than himself; and they enter in, and dwell there: and the last *state* of that man is worse than the first.

[27]And it came to pass, as he spake these things, a certain woman of the company lifted up her voice, and said unto him, Blessed *is* the womb that bare thee, and the paps which thou hast sucked. [28]But he said, Yea rather, blessed *are* they that hear the word of God, and keep it.

[29]And when the people were gathered thick together, he began to say, This is an evil generation: they seek a sign; and there shall no sign be given it, but the sign of Jonas the prophet. [30]For as Jonas was a sign unto the Ninevites, so shall also the Son of man be to this generation. [31]The queen of the south shall rise up in the judgment with the men of this generation, and condemn

Values for a Lifetime

by Jerry B. Jenkins

Martha had pure motives. Jesus gently informed her that Mary—with her eyes on him—had right priorities.

How we need that counsel today! Too many who work as hard as Martha are chasing a dream, trying to achieve goals that others have told them they should have. Books, tapes, and seminars aimed at the achiever market all have the same message: If you want to get to the top, you have to set goals.

There's nothing wrong with setting goals. Too many people try to accomplish too much without identifying their main mission. But goals that serve only the goal setter are, by definition, selfish—hardly a value that God shares. The formulas all begin and end with goal setting. What do *you* really want? A six-figure salary by age twenty-five? A dream home? Do you want to be company president, own land, companies, a private plane?

In trying to instill values in our children, we have to fight this fake avenue to success.

There is nothing wrong with being an achiever. God may call your child to be a leader or a wealthy, influential person of independent means. But what a responsibility! The key—and the challenge—is to keep our motives and goals pure and God-honoring.

The God-fearing parent should tell his or her children in all sincerity: "If you raise a family on a lower middle-class income because you're a servant of Christ, if you never own a second car, if you wear the same clothes for ten years, if you can't afford to take your family out to dinner, I will still be proud of you. Make it your goal to be the best you can be at whatever task is set before you because it's your God-given work.

"If you are called to a place of visibility, and your work is recognized, imagine the satisfaction of knowing that you are doing what you're doing for the right motives. If your way of earning a living is secular, do it for the purpose of advancing the Kingdom, both in your workplace and by providing enough income so you can support it elsewhere.

"If you make a million dollars a year, it should be because your goal was to be the best you could be at doing whatever made you the million.

"If you become famous and sought after, I hope it's because your goal was to glorify God and serve him and others.

"If you become the best there ever was at your profession, I hope it's because you made the decision to give yourself—all of yourself—to Christ."

Spiritually, we are depraved and worthless, yet God showed his love to us in that Christ died for us. What can we offer in return?

Nothing.

Then why present our life as a sacrifice?

In gratitude.

When I bought my child a bike and he brought me a handful of dandelions, he wasn't repaying me—he was thanking me. And those otherwise worthless weeds were precious to me. Figuratively, they were a sweet fragrance to me because they came from the pure, grateful heart of a child who had no ability to repay.

I didn't want or expect repayment. I wanted to show my love, and I cherished my child's expression of thanks.

That's what we are able to offer God: lives framed by goals that don't serve ourselves but which serve God's higher purposes.

DIGGING DEEPER
1. What value is there in striving to be a "great person"? See Isaiah 64:6.
2. What's ironic about striving to be great for our own sake? See Matthew 5:20.
3. What part do we play in making ourselves great? See Ephesians 2:8-9 and Titus 3:5.

them: for she came from the utmost parts of the earth to hear the wisdom of Solomon; and, behold, a greater than Solomon *is* here. ³²The men of Nineve shall rise up in the judgment with this generation, and shall condemn it: for they repented at the preaching of Jonas; and, behold, a greater than Jonas *is* here. ³³ No man, when he hath lighted a candle, putteth *it* in a secret place, neither under a bushel, but on a candlestick, that they which come in may see the light. ³⁴The light of the body is the eye: therefore when thine eye is single, thy whole body also is full of light; but when *thine eye* is evil, thy body also *is* full of darkness. ³⁵Take heed therefore that the light which is in thee be not darkness. ³⁶If thy whole body therefore *be* full of light, having no part dark, the whole shall be full of light, as when the bright shining of a candle doth give thee light.

³⁷And as he spake, a certain Pharisee besought him to dine with him: and he went in, and sat down to meat. ³⁸And when the Pharisee saw *it*, he marvelled that he had not first washed before dinner. ³⁹And the Lord said unto him, Now do ye Pharisees make clean the outside of the cup and the platter; but your inward part is full of ravening and wickedness. ⁴⁰*Ye* fools, did not he that made that which is without make that which is within also? ⁴¹But rather give alms of such things as ye have; and, behold, all things are clean unto you. ⁴²But woe unto you, Pharisees! for ye tithe mint and rue and all manner of herbs, and pass over judgment and the love of God: these ought ye to have done, and not to leave the other undone. ⁴³Woe unto you, Pharisees! for ye love the uppermost seats in the synagogues, and greetings in the markets. ⁴⁴Woe unto you, scribes and Pharisees, hypocrites! for ye are as graves which appear not, and the men that walk over *them* are not aware *of them*. ⁴⁵Then answered one of the lawyers, and said unto him, Master, thus saying thou re-

Devotional Moment

Purity

11:33-36 Jesus said that our eyes are the window to our soul. If we fill our mind with pure and good sights, our soul will only benefit. And if we fill our mind with impure, sinful, and corrupt sights, our soul will feel the effects. Some people say that viewing violent or pornographic scenes doesn't make a person violent or immoral, but Jesus has cleared the smoke concealing that lie. Never underestimate the power of any visual image, whether good or bad. What books and magazines do you read, and what television programs and movies do you watch? Commit yourself to viewing what is good, pure, and right. Shut out what is pornographic, violent, and disrespectful.

proachest us also. ⁴⁶And he said, Woe unto you also, *ye* lawyers! for ye lade men with burdens grievous to be borne, and ye yourselves touch not the burdens with one of your fingers. ⁴⁷Woe unto you! for ye build the sepulchres of the prophets, and your fathers killed them. ⁴⁸Truly ye bear witness that ye allow the deeds of your fathers: for they indeed killed them, and ye build their sepulchres. ⁴⁹Therefore also said the wisdom of God, I will send them prophets and apostles, and *some* of them they shall slay and persecute: ⁵⁰That the blood of all the prophets, which was shed from the foundation of the world, may be required of this generation; ⁵¹From the blood of Abel unto the blood of Zacharias, which perished between the altar and the temple: verily I say unto you, It shall be required of this generation. ⁵²Woe unto you, lawyers! for ye have taken away the key of knowledge: ye entered not in yourselves, and them that were entering in ye hindered. ⁵³And as he said these

things unto them, the scribes and the Pharisees began to urge *him* vehemently, and to provoke him to speak of many things: ⁵⁴Laying wait for him, and seeking to catch something out of his mouth, that they might accuse him.

12

¹In the mean time, when there were gathered together an innumerable multitude of people, insomuch that they trode one upon another, he began to say unto his disciples first of all, Beware ye of the leaven of the Pharisees, which is hypocrisy. ²For there is nothing covered, that shall not be revealed; neither hid, that shall not be known. ³Therefore whatsoever ye have spoken in darkness shall be heard in the light; and that which ye have spoken in the ear in closets shall be proclaimed upon the housetops. ⁴And I say unto you my friends, Be not afraid of them that kill the body, and after that have no more that they can do. ⁵But I will forewarn you whom ye shall fear: Fear him, which after he hath killed hath power to cast into hell; yea, I say unto you, Fear him. ⁶Are not five spar-

Devotional Moment
• Expectations

11:46-48 Jesus condemned the Pharisees for crushing people with unreasonable demands. Sometimes parents place unrealistic expectations on children or friends, then blame them when they don't measure up. To persist with unrealistic demands crushes people's spirit and kills their confidence. Take a look at the expectations you have of your children and your friends. If you have been unreasonable, apologize and ask for their forgiveness. Help them to see when they have unrealistic expectations of others, too.

Devotional Moment
• Self-esteem

12:6-7 Our culture encourages us to measure our worth by what we accomplish, wear, or own; what grades we get in school; or where we live. But the Bible tells us that the true measure of our worth lies in the fact that God cares about us. God values and cares for every part of his creation—especially each person made in his image. We need to see ourselves as infinitely valuable to God.

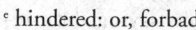

ᵉ hindered: or, forbad

rows sold for two farthings, and not one of them is forgotten before God? ⁷But even the very hairs of your head are all numbered. Fear not therefore: ye are of more value than many sparrows. ⁸Also I say unto you, Whosoever shall confess me before men, him shall the Son of man also confess before the angels of God: ⁹But he that denieth me before men shall be denied before the angels of God. ¹⁰And whosoever shall speak a word against the Son of man, it shall be forgiven him: but unto him that blasphemeth against the Holy Ghost it shall not be forgiven. ¹¹And when they bring you unto the synagogues, and *unto* magistrates, and powers, take ye no thought how or what thing ye shall answer, or what ye shall say: ¹²For the Holy Ghost shall teach you in the same hour what ye ought to say.

¹³And one of the company said unto him, Master, speak to my brother, that he divide the inheritance with me. ¹⁴And he said unto him, Man, who made me a judge or a divider over you? ¹⁵And he said unto them, Take heed, and beware of covetousness: for a man's life consisteth not in the abundance of

Worship
in Your Home

ENOUGH TIME FOR DEVOTIONS
Rather seek ye the kingdom of God; and all these things shall be added unto you.
Luke 12:31

"I don't have time for devotions." "I don't have time to go to church." "I don't have time to read my Bible."

Such statements are value judgments. Everyone has exactly the same amount of time—twenty-four hours each day. You don't have twenty-three hours while I have twenty-five. Yet I find time for devotions. So the statement "I don't have time" really means, "I don't value devotions enough to make time for them."

In a moment of excitement, you may say that you should spend a half hour on devotions each day. Don't trap yourself in unrealistic expectations—if you're just getting started, try ten to fifteen minutes each day and see how it goes.

Do people who have devotions each day really have more time? No, they merely value time with God's Word enough to give it high priority.

If you really want to, you can do it too.

Devotional Moment
•
Contentment
12:15 Jesus warned us to not always be wishing for what we don't have. In our consumer-oriented society, with an effective multibillion-dollar advertising industry constantly trying to convince us we need more, that can be *very* difficult. When your children plead for more stuff, don't spoil them! Otherwise they will think that life *does* consist in the abundance of possessions. Encourage your children to be content by modeling contentment yourself.

the things which he possesseth. ¹⁶And he spake a parable unto them, saying, The ground of a certain rich man brought forth plentifully: ¹⁷And he thought within himself, saying, What shall I do, because I have no room where to bestow my fruits? ¹⁸And he said, This will I do: I will pull down my barns, and build greater; and there will I bestow all my fruits and my goods. ¹⁹And I will say to my soul, Soul, thou hast much goods laid up for many years; take thine ease, eat, drink, *and* be merry. ²⁰But God said unto him, *Thou* fool, this night thy* soul shall be required of thee: then whose shall those things be, which thou hast provided? ²¹So *is* he that layeth up treasure for himself, and is not rich toward God.

²²And he said unto his disciples, Therefore I say unto you, Take no thought for your life, what ye shall eat; neither for the body, what ye shall put on. ²³The life is more than meat, and the body *is more* than raiment. ²⁴Consider the ravens: for they neither sow nor reap; which neither have storehouse nor barn; and God feedeth them: how much more are ye better than the fowls? ²⁵And which of you with taking thought can add to his stature one cubit? ²⁶If ye then be not able to do that thing which is least, why take ye thought for the rest? ²⁷Consider the lilies how they grow: they toil not, they spin not; and yet I say unto you, that Solomon in all his glory was not arrayed like one of these. ²⁸If then God so clothe the grass, which is to day in the field, and to morrow is cast into the oven; how much more *will he clothe* you, O ye of little faith? ²⁹And seek not ye what ye shall eat, or what ye shall drink, neither* be ye of doubtful mind. ³⁰For all these things do the nations of the world seek after: and your Father knoweth that ye have need of these things. ³¹But rather seek ye the kingdom of God; and all these things shall be added unto you. ³²Fear not, little flock; for it is your Father's good pleasure to give you the kingdom. ³³Sell that ye have, and give alms; provide yourselves bags which wax not old, a treasure in the heavens that faileth not, where no thief approacheth, neither moth corrupteth. ³⁴For where your treasure is, there will your heart be also. ³⁵Let your loins be girded about, and *your* lights burning; ³⁶And ye yourselves like unto men that wait for their lord, when he will return from the wedding; that when he cometh and knocketh, they may open unto him immediately. ³⁷Blessed *are* those servants, whom the lord when he cometh shall find watching: verily I say unto you, that he shall gird himself, and make them to sit down to meat, and will come forth and serve them. ³⁸And if he shall come in the second watch, or come in the third watch, and find *them* so, blessed are those servants. ³⁹And this know, that if the goodman of the house had known what hour the thief would come, he would have watched, and not have suffered his house to be broken through. ⁴⁰Be ye therefore ready also: for the Son of man cometh at an hour when ye think not.

ª thy . . . : Gr. do they require thy soul
ᵇ neither . . . : or, live not in careful suspense

⁴¹Then Peter said unto him, Lord, speakest thou this parable unto us, or even to all? ⁴²And the Lord said, Who then is that faithful and wise steward, whom *his* lord shall make ruler over his household, to give *them their* portion of meat in due season? ⁴³Blessed *is* that servant, whom his lord when he cometh shall find so doing. ⁴⁴Of a truth I say unto you, that he will make him ruler over all that he hath. ⁴⁵But and if that servant say in his heart, My lord delayeth his coming; and shall begin to beat the menservants and maidens, and to eat and drink, and to be drunken; ⁴⁶The lord of that servant will come in a day when he looketh not for *him*, and at an hour when he is not aware, and will cutᶜ him in sunder, and will appoint him his portion with the unbelievers. ⁴⁷And that servant, which knew his lord's will, and prepared not *himself*, neither did according to his will, shall be beaten with many *stripes*. ⁴⁸But he that knew not, and did commit things worthy of stripes, shall be beaten with few *stripes*. For unto whomsoever much is given, of him shall be much required: and to whom men have committed much, of him they will ask the more. ⁴⁹I am come to send fire on the earth; and what will I, if it be already kindled? ⁵⁰But I have a baptism to be baptized with; and how am I straitenedᵈ till it be accomplished! ⁵¹Suppose ye that I am come to give peace on earth? I tell you, Nay; but rather division: ⁵²For from henceforth there shall be five in one house divided, three against two, and two against three. ⁵³The father shall be divided against the son, and the son against the father; the mother against the daughter, and the daughter against the mother; the mother in law against her daughter in law, and the daughter in law against her mother in law.

⁵⁴And he said also to the people, When ye see a cloud rise out of the west, straightway ye say, There cometh a shower; and so it is. ⁵⁵And when *ye see* the south wind blow, ye say, There will be heat; and it cometh to pass. ⁵⁶*Ye* hypocrites, ye can discern the face of the sky and of the earth; but how is it that ye do not discern this time? ⁵⁷Yea, and why even of yourselves judge ye not what is right? ⁵⁸When thou goest with thine adversary to the magistrate, *as thou art* in the way, give diligence that thou mayest be delivered from him; lest he hale thee to the judge, and the judge deliver thee to the officer, and the officer cast thee into prison. ⁵⁹I tell thee, thou shalt not depart thence, till thou hast paid the very last mite.

13

¹There were present at that season some that told him of the Galilaeans, whose blood Pilate had mingled with their sacrifices. ²And Jesus answering said unto them, Suppose ye that these Galilaeans were sinners above all the Galilaeans, because they suffered such things? ³I tell you, Nay: but, except ye repent, ye shall all likewise perish. ⁴Or those eighteen, upon whom the tower in Siloam fell, and slew them, think ye that they were sinnersᵃ above all men

---

ᶜ cut . . . : or, cut him off
ᵈ straitened: or, pained
ᵃ sinners: or, debtors

that dwelt in Jerusalem? ⁵I tell you, Nay: but, except ye repent, ye shall all likewise perish.

⁶He spake also this parable; A certain *man* had a fig tree planted in his vineyard; and he came and sought fruit thereon, and found none. ⁷Then said he unto the dresser of his vineyard, Behold, these three years I come seeking fruit on this fig tree, and find none: cut it down; why cumbereth it the ground? ⁸And he answering said unto him, Lord, let it alone this year also, till I shall dig about it, and dung *it*: ⁹And if it bear fruit, *well*: and if not, *then* after that thou shalt cut it down.

¹⁰And he was teaching in one of the synagogues on the sabbath. ¹¹And, behold, there was a woman which had a spirit of infirmity eighteen years, and was bowed together, and could in no wise lift up *herself*. ¹²And when Jesus saw her, he called *her to him*, and said unto her, Woman, thou art loosed from thine infirmity. ¹³And he laid *his* hands on her: and immediately she was made straight, and glorified God. ¹⁴And the ruler of the synagogue answered with indignation, because that Jesus had healed on the sabbath day, and said unto the people, There are six days in which men ought to work: in them therefore come and be healed, and not on the sabbath day. ¹⁵The Lord then answered him, and said, *Thou* hypocrite, doth not each one of you on the sabbath loose his ox or *his* ass from the stall, and lead *him* away to watering? ¹⁶And ought not this woman, being a daughter of Abraham, whom Satan hath bound, lo, these eighteen years, be loosed from this bond on the sabbath day? ¹⁷And when he had said these

things, all his adversaries were ashamed: and all the people rejoiced for all the glorious things that were done by him.

¹⁸Then said he, Unto what is the kingdom of God like? and whereunto shall I resemble it? ¹⁹It is like a grain of mustard seed, which a man took, and cast into his garden; and it grew, and waxed a great tree; and the fowls of the air lodged in the branches of it. ²⁰And again he said, Whereunto shall I liken the kingdom of God? ²¹It is like leaven, which a woman took and hid in three measures of meal, till the whole was leavened. ²²And he went through the cities and villages, teaching, and journeying toward Jerusalem.

²³Then said one unto him, Lord, are there few that be saved? And he said unto them, ²⁴Strive to enter in at the strait gate: for many, I say unto you, will seek to enter in, and shall not be able. ²⁵When once the master of the house is risen up, and hath shut to the door, and ye begin to stand without, and to knock at the door, saying, Lord, Lord, open unto us; and he shall answer and say unto you, I know you not

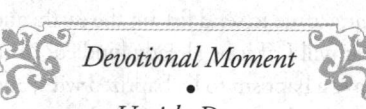

Devotional Moment

Upside Down

13:22-30 In this story Jesus gave us a glimpse of God's priorities. What most people regard as important—social status, wealth, "connections"—actually means little to God. These things may give us a false sense of security, making us think that we have God's favor when in reality we don't. We need to stop worrying about appearance, gaining "the right" friends, accumulating wealth, and striving for position because God is more concerned with our heart. Is your heart right with him?

whence ye are: ²⁶Then shall ye begin to say, We have eaten and drunk in thy presence, and thou hast taught in our streets. ²⁷But he shall say, I tell you, I know you not whence ye are; depart from me, all *ye* workers of iniquity. ²⁸There shall be weeping and gnashing of teeth, when ye shall see Abraham, and Isaac, and Jacob, and all the prophets, in the kingdom of God, and you *yourselves* thrust out. ²⁹And they shall come from the east, and *from* the west, and from the north, and *from* the south, and shall sit down in the kingdom of God. ³⁰And, behold, there are last which shall be first, and there are first which shall be last.

³¹The same day there came certain of the Pharisees, saying unto him, Get thee out, and depart hence: for Herod will kill thee. ³²And he said unto them, Go ye, and tell that fox, Behold, I cast out devils, and I do cures to day and to morrow, and the third *day* I shall be perfected. ³³Nevertheless I must walk to day, and to morrow, and the *day* following: for it cannot be that a prophet perish out of Jerusalem. ³⁴O Jerusalem, Jerusalem, which killest the prophets, and stonest them that are sent unto thee; how often would I have gathered thy children together, as a hen *doth gather* her brood under *her* wings, and ye would not! ³⁵Behold, your house is left unto you desolate: and verily I say unto you, Ye shall not see me, until *the time* come when ye shall say, Blessed *is* he that cometh in the name of the Lord.

14

¹And it came to pass, as he went into the house of one of the chief Pharisees

---

Devotional Moment
Honor

14:7-11 Many people will pull crazy and even dangerous stunts to get attention or a place of prominence. But Jesus encouraged his followers to look for ways to serve others, rather than worry about where they are in line or whether they are getting the recognition they think they deserve.

---

to eat bread on the sabbath day, that they watched him. ²And, behold, there was a certain man before him which had the dropsy. ³And Jesus answering spake unto the lawyers and Pharisees, saying, Is it lawful to heal on the sabbath day? ⁴And they held their peace. And he took *him*, and healed him, and let him go; ⁵And answered them, saying, Which of you shall have an ass or an ox fallen into a pit, and will not straightway pull him out on the sabbath day? ⁶And they could not answer him again to these things.

⁷And he put forth a parable to those which were bidden, when he marked how they chose out the chief rooms; saying unto them, ⁸When thou art bidden of any *man* to a wedding, sit not down in the highest room; lest a more honourable man than thou be bidden of him; ⁹And he that bade thee and him come and say to thee, Give this man place; and thou begin with shame to take the lowest room. ¹⁰But when thou art bidden, go and sit down in the lowest room; that when he that bade thee cometh, he may say unto thee, Friend, go up higher: then shalt thou have worship in the presence of them that sit at meat with thee. ¹¹For whosoever exalteth himself shall be abased; and he that humbleth himself

shall be exalted. ¹²Then said he also to him that bade him, When thou makest a dinner or a supper, call not thy friends, nor thy brethren, neither thy kinsmen, nor *thy* rich neighbours; lest they also bid thee again, and a recompence be made thee. ¹³But when thou makest a feast, call the poor, the maimed, the lame, the blind: ¹⁴And thou shalt be blessed; for they cannot recompense thee: for thou shalt be recompensed at the resurrection of the just.

¹⁵And when one of them that sat at meat with him heard these things, he said unto him, Blessed *is* he that shall eat bread in the kingdom of God. ¹⁶Then said he unto him, A certain man made a great supper, and bade many: ¹⁷And sent his servant at supper time to say to them that were bidden, Come; for all things are now ready. ¹⁸And they all with one *consent* began to make excuse. The first said unto him, I have bought a piece of ground, and I must needs go and see it: I pray thee have me excused. ¹⁹And another said, I have bought five yoke of oxen, and I go to prove them: I pray thee have me excused. ²⁰And another said, I have married a wife, and therefore I cannot come. ²¹So that servant came, and shewed his lord these things. Then the master of the house being angry said to his servant, Go out quickly into the streets and lanes of the city, and bring in hither the poor, and the maimed, and the halt, and the blind. ²²And the servant said, Lord, it is done as thou hast commanded, and yet there is room. ²³And the lord said unto the servant, Go out into the highways and hedges, and compel *them* to come in, that my house may be filled. ²⁴For I say unto you, That none of those men which were bidden shall taste of my supper.

²⁵And there went great multitudes with him: and he turned, and said unto them, ²⁶If any *man* come to me, and hate not his father, and mother, and wife, and children, and brethren, and sisters, yea, and his own life also, he cannot be my disciple. ²⁷And whosoever doth not bear his cross, and come after me, cannot be my disciple. ²⁸For which of you, intending to build a tower, sitteth not down first, and counteth the cost, whether he have *sufficient* to finish *it*? ²⁹Lest haply, after he hath laid the foundation, and is not able to finish *it*, all that behold *it* begin to mock him, ³⁰Saying, This man began to build, and was not able to finish. ³¹Or what king, going to make war against another king, sitteth not down first, and consulteth whether he be able with ten thousand to meet him that cometh against him with twenty thousand? ³²Or else, while the other is yet a great way off, he sendeth an ambassage, and desireth conditions of peace. ³³So likewise, whosoever he be of you that forsaketh not all that he hath, he cannot be my disciple. ³⁴Salt *is* good: but if the salt have lost his savour, wherewith shall it be seasoned? ³⁵It is neither fit for the land, nor yet for the dunghill; *but* men cast it out. He that hath ears to hear, let him hear.

15

¹Then drew near unto him all the publicans and sinners for to hear him. ²And the Pharisees and scribes murmured, saying, This man receiveth sinners, and eateth with them. ³And he spake this parable unto them, saying, ⁴What man of you, having an hundred sheep, if he lose one of them, doth not leave the

ninety and nine in the wilderness, and go after that which is lost, until he find it? ⁵And when he hath found *it*, he layeth *it* on his shoulders, rejoicing. ⁶And when he cometh home, he calleth together *his* friends and neighbours, saying unto them, Rejoice with me; for I have found my sheep which was lost. ⁷I say unto you, that likewise joy shall be in heaven over one sinner that repenteth, more than over ninety and nine just persons, which need no repentance. ⁸Either what woman having ten pieces of silver, if she lose one piece, doth not light a candle, and sweep the house, and seek diligently till she find it? ⁹And when she hath found *it*, she calleth *her* friends and *her* neighbours together, saying, Rejoice with me; for I have found the piece which I had lost. ¹⁰Likewise, I say unto you, there is joy in the presence of the angels of God over one sinner that repenteth.

¹¹**And he said,** A certain man had two sons: ¹²And the younger of them said to *his* father, Father, give me the portion of goods that falleth *to me.* And he divided unto them *his* living. ¹³And not many days after the younger son gathered all together, and took his journey into a far country, and there wasted his substance with riotous living. ¹⁴And when he had spent all, there arose a mighty famine in that land; and he began to be in want. ¹⁵And he went and joined himself to a citizen of that country; and he sent him into his fields to feed swine. ¹⁶And he would fain have filled his belly with the husks that the swine did eat: and no man gave unto him. ¹⁷And when he came to himself, he said, How many hired servants of my father's have bread enough and to

spare, and I perish with hunger! ¹⁸I will arise and go to my father, and will say unto him, Father, I have sinned against heaven, and before thee, ¹⁹And am no more worthy to be called thy son: make me as one of thy hired servants. ²⁰And he arose, and came to his father. But when he was yet a great way off, his father saw him, and had compassion, and ran, and fell on his neck, and kissed him. ²¹And the son said unto him, Father, I have sinned against heaven, and in thy sight, and am no more worthy to be called thy son. ²²But the father said to his servants, Bring forth the best robe, and put *it* on him; and put a ring on his hand, and shoes on *his* feet: ²³And bring hither the fatted calf, and kill *it*; and let us eat, and be merry: ²⁴For this my son was dead, and is alive again; he was lost, and is found. And they began to be merry. ²⁵Now his elder son was in the field: and as he came and drew nigh to the house, he heard musick and dancing. ²⁶And he called one of the servants, and asked what these things meant. ²⁷And he said unto him, Thy brother is come; and thy father hath killed the fatted calf, because he hath received him safe and sound. ²⁸And he was angry, and would not go in: therefore came his father out, and intreated him. ²⁹And he answering said to *his* father, Lo, these many years do I serve thee, neither transgressed I at any time thy commandment: and yet thou never gavest me a kid, that I might make merry with my friends: ³⁰But as soon as this thy son was come, which hath devoured thy living with harlots, thou hast killed for him the fatted calf. ³¹And he said unto him, Son, thou art ever with me, and all that I have is thine. ³²It was meet that we should make merry, and be glad: for this thy brother was dead, and is alive again; and was lost, and is found.

16

¹And he said also unto his disciples, There was a certain rich man, which had a steward; and the same was accused unto him that he had wasted his goods. ²And he called him, and said unto him, How is it that I hear this of thee? give an account of thy stewardship; for thou mayest be no longer steward. ³Then the steward said within himself, What shall I do? for my lord taketh away from me the stewardship: I cannot dig; to beg I am ashamed. ⁴I am resolved what to do, that, when I am put out of the stewardship, they may receive me into their houses. ⁵So he called every one of his lord's debtors *unto him*, and said unto the first,

How much owest thou unto my lord? ⁶And he said, An hundred measuresᵃ of oil. And he said unto him, Take thy bill, and sit down quickly, and write fifty. ⁷Then said he to another, And how much owest thou? And he said, An hundred measuresᵇ of wheat. And he said unto him, Take thy bill, and write fourscore. ⁸And the lord commended the unjust steward, because he had done wisely: for the children of this world are in their generation wiser than the children of light. ⁹And I say unto you, Make to yourselves friends of the mammonᶜ of unrighteousness; that, when ye fail, they may receive you into everlasting habitations. ¹⁰He that is faithful in that which is least is faithful also in much: and he that is unjust in the least is unjust also in much. ¹¹If therefore ye have not been faithful in the unrighteous mammonᵈ, who will commit to your trust the true *riches?* ¹²And if ye have not been faithful in that which is another man's, who shall give you that which is your own? ¹³No servant can serve two masters: for either he will hate the one, and love the other; or else he will hold to the one, and despise the other. Ye cannot serve God and mammon. ¹⁴And the Pharisees also, who were covetous, heard all these things: and they derided him. ¹⁵And he said unto them, Ye are they which justify yourselves before men; but God knoweth your hearts: for that which is highly esteemed among men is abomination in the sight of God. ¹⁶The law and the prophets *were*

ᵃ measures: the word Batus in the original containeth nine gallons three quarts
ᵇ measures: the word here interpreted a measure in the original containeth about fourteen bushels and two quarts
ᶜ mammon: or, riches
ᵈ mammon: or, riches

until John: since that time the kingdom of God is preached, and every man presseth into it. [17]And it is easier for heaven and earth to pass, than one tittle of the law to fail. [18]Whosoever putteth away his wife, and marrieth another, committeth adultery: and whosoever marrieth her that is put away from *her* husband committeth adultery.

[19]There was a certain rich man, which was clothed in purple and fine linen, and fared sumptuously every day: [20]And there was a certain beggar named Lazarus, which was laid at his gate, full of sores, [21]And desiring to be fed with the crumbs which fell from the rich man's table: moreover the dogs came and licked his sores. [22]And it came to pass, that the beggar died, and was carried by the angels into Abraham's bosom: the rich man also died, and was buried; [23]And in hell he lift up his eyes, being in torments, and seeth Abraham afar off, and Lazarus in his bosom. [24]And he cried and said, Father Abraham, have mercy on me, and send Lazarus, that he may dip the tip of his finger in water, and cool my tongue; for I am tormented in this flame. [25]But Abraham said, Son, remember that thou in thy lifetime receivedst thy good things, and likewise Lazarus evil things: but now he is comforted, and thou art tormented. [26]And beside all this, between us and you there is a great gulf fixed: so that they which would pass from hence to you cannot; neither can they pass to us, that *would come* from thence. [27]Then he said, I pray thee therefore, father, that thou wouldest send him to my father's house: [28]For I have five brethren; that he may testify unto them, lest they also come into this place of torment. [29]Abraham saith unto him, They have Moses and the prophets; let them hear them. [30]And he said, Nay, father Abraham: but if one went unto them from the dead, they will repent. [31]And he said unto him, If they hear not Moses and the prophets, neither will they be persuaded, though one rose from the dead.

17

[1]Then said he unto the disciples, It is impossible but that offences will come: but woe *unto him*, through whom they come! [2]It were better for him that a millstone were hanged about his neck, and he cast into the sea, than that he should offend one of these little ones. [3]Take heed to yourselves: If thy brother trespass against thee, rebuke him; and if he repent, forgive him. [4]And if he trespass against thee seven times in a day, and seven times in a day turn again to thee, saying, I repent; thou shalt forgive him. [5]And the apostles said unto the Lord, Increase our faith. [6]And the Lord said, If ye had faith as a grain of mustard seed, ye might say unto this sycamine tree, Be thou plucked up by the root, and be thou planted in the sea; and it should obey you. [7]But which of you, having a servant plowing or feeding cattle, will say unto him by and by, when he is come from the field, Go and sit down to meat? [8]And will not rather say unto him, Make ready wherewith I may sup, and gird thyself, and serve me, till I have eaten and drunken; and afterward thou shalt eat and drink? [9]Doth he thank that servant because he did the things that were commanded him? I trow not. [10]So likewise ye, when ye shall have done all those things which are commanded you, say, We are un-

profitable servants: we have done that which was our duty to do.

¹¹And it came to pass, as he went to Jerusalem, that he passed through the midst of Samaria and Galilee. ¹²And as he entered into a certain village, there met him ten men that were lepers, which stood afar off: ¹³And they lifted up *their* voices, and said, Jesus, Master, have mercy on us. ¹⁴And when he saw *them*, he said unto them, Go shew yourselves unto the priests. And it came to pass, that, as they went, they were cleansed. ¹⁵And one of them, when he saw that he was healed, turned back, and with a loud voice glorified God, ¹⁶And fell down on *his* face at his feet, giving him thanks: and he was a Samaritan. ¹⁷And Jesus answering said, Were there not ten cleansed? but where *are* the nine? ¹⁸There are not found that returned to give glory to God, save this stranger. ¹⁹And he said unto him, Arise, go thy way: thy faith hath made thee whole.

²⁰And when he was demanded of the Pharisees, when the kingdom of God should come, he answered them and said, The kingdom of God cometh not with[a] observation: ²¹Neither shall they say, Lo here! or, lo there! for, behold, the kingdom of God is within you[b]. ²²And he said unto the disciples, The days will come, when ye shall desire to see one of the days of the Son of man, and ye shall not see *it.* ²³And they shall say to you, See here; or, see there: go not after *them*, nor follow *them.* ²⁴For as the lightning, that lighteneth out of the one *part* under heaven, shineth unto the other *part* under heaven; so shall also the Son of man

be in his day. ²⁵But first must he suffer many things, and be rejected of this generation. ²⁶And as it was in the days of Noe, so shall it be also in the days of the Son of man. ²⁷They did eat, they drank, they married wives, they were given in marriage, until the day that Noe entered into the ark, and the flood came, and destroyed them all. ²⁸Likewise also as it was in the days of Lot; they did eat, they drank, they bought, they sold, they planted, they builded; ²⁹But the same day that Lot went out of Sodom it rained fire and brimstone from heaven, and destroyed *them* all. ³⁰Even thus shall it be in the day when the Son of man is revealed. ³¹In that day, he which shall be upon the housetop, and his stuff in the house, let him not come down to take it away: and he that is in the field, let him likewise not return back. ³²Remember Lot's wife. ³³Whosoever shall seek to save his life shall lose it; and whosoever shall lose his life shall preserve it. ³⁴I tell you, in that night there shall be two *men* in one bed; the one shall be taken, and the other shall be left. ³⁵Two *women* shall be grinding together; the one shall be taken, and the other left. ³⁶Two *men* shall be in the field; the one shall be taken, and the other left.[c] ³⁷And they answered and said unto him, Where, Lord? And he said unto them, Wheresoever the body *is*, thither will the eagles be gathered together.

18

¹And he spake a parable unto them *to this end*, that men ought always to pray, and not to faint; ²Saying, There was in

---

ᵃ with . . . : or, with outward shew
ᵇ within you: or, among you
ᶜ this verse is not found in most of the Greek copies

a city[a] a judge, which feared not God, neither regarded man: [3]And there was a widow in that city; and she came unto him, saying, Avenge me of mine adversary. [4]And he would not for a while: but afterward he said within himself, Though I fear not God, nor regard man; [5]Yet because this widow troubleth me, I will avenge her, lest by her continual coming she weary me. [6]And the Lord said, Hear what the unjust judge saith. [7]And shall not God avenge his own elect, which cry day and night unto him, though he bear long with them? [8]I tell you that he will avenge them speedily. Nevertheless when the Son of man cometh, shall he find faith on the earth?

[9]And he spake this parable unto certain which trusted in themselves that[b] they were righteous, and despised others: [10]Two men went up into the temple to pray; the one a Pharisee, and the other a publican. [11]The Pharisee stood and prayed thus with himself, God, I thank thee, that I am not as other men are, extortioners, unjust, adulterers, or even as this publican. [12]I fast twice in the week, I give tithes of all that I possess. [13]And the publican, standing afar off, would not lift up so much as his eyes unto heaven, but smote upon his breast, saying, God be merciful to me a sinner. [14]I tell you, this man went down to his house justified rather than the other: for every one that exalteth himself shall be abased; and he that humbleth himself shall be exalted.

[15]And they brought unto him also infants, that he would touch them: but when his disciples saw it, they rebuked them. [16]But Jesus called them unto him, and said, Suffer little children to come unto me, and forbid them not: for of such is the kingdom of God. [17]Verily I say unto you, Whosoever shall not receive the kingdom of God as a little child shall in no wise enter therein.

[18]And a certain ruler asked him, saying, Good Master, what shall I do to inherit eternal life? [19]And Jesus said unto him, Why callest thou me good? none is good, save one, that is, God. [20]Thou knowest the commandments, Do not commit adultery, Do not kill, Do not steal, Do not bear false witness, Honour thy father and thy mother. [21]And he said, All these have I kept from my youth up. [22]Now when Jesus heard these things, he said unto him, Yet lackest thou one thing: sell all that thou hast, and distribute unto the poor, and thou shalt have treasure in heaven: and come, follow me. [23]And when he heard this, he was very sorrowful: for he was very rich. [24]And when Jesus saw that he was very sorrowful, he said,

---

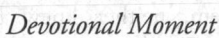

Devotional Moment
•
Children—Blessing or Bother?

18:15-17 Jesus welcomed children. Children are important to God. Unfortunately, many people see children as a bother. Children are too inconvenient, too expensive, too annoying, and too difficult. Jesus shares none of those views. Pay attention to the children around you. Give them time, respect, and love. It's one of the most Christlike things you can do.

---

[a] in a city: Gr. in a certain city
[b] that . . . : or, as being righteous

How hardly shall they that have riches enter into the kingdom of God! ²⁵For it is easier for a camel to go through a needle's eye, than for a rich man to enter into the kingdom of God. ²⁶And they that heard *it* said, Who then can be saved? ²⁷And he said, The things which are impossible with men are possible with God. ²⁸Then Peter said, Lo, we have left all, and followed thee. ²⁹And he said unto them, Verily I say unto you, There is no man that hath left house, or parents, or brethren, or wife, or children, for the kingdom of God's sake, ³⁰Who shall not receive manifold more in this present time, and in the world to come life everlasting.

³¹Then he took *unto him* the twelve, and said unto them, Behold, we go up to Jerusalem, and all things that are written by the prophets concerning the Son of man shall be accomplished. ³²For he shall be delivered unto the Gentiles, and shall be mocked, and spitefully entreated, and spitted on: ³³And they shall scourge *him*, and put him to death: and the third day he shall rise again. ³⁴And they understood none of these things: and this saying was hid from them, neither knew they the things which were spoken.

³⁵And it came to pass, that as he was come nigh unto Jericho, a certain blind man sat by the way side begging: ³⁶And hearing the multitude pass by, he asked what it meant. ³⁷And they told him, that Jesus of Nazareth passeth by. ³⁸And he cried, saying, Jesus, *thou* Son of David, have mercy on me. ³⁹And they which went before rebuked him, that he should hold his peace: but he cried so much the more, *Thou* Son of David, have mercy on me. ⁴⁰And Jesus stood, and commanded him to be brought unto him: and when he was come near, he asked him, ⁴¹Saying, What wilt thou that I shall do unto thee? And he said, Lord, that I may receive my sight. ⁴²And Jesus said unto him, Receive thy sight: thy faith hath saved thee. ⁴³And immediately he received his sight, and followed him, glorifying God: and all the people, when they saw *it*, gave praise unto God.

19

¹And *Jesus* entered and passed through Jericho. ²And, behold, *there was* a man named Zacchaeus, which was the chief among the publicans, and he was rich. ³And he sought to see Jesus who he was; and could not for the press, because he was little of stature. ⁴And he ran before, and climbed up into a sycomore tree to see him: for he was to pass that *way*. ⁵And when Jesus came to the place, he looked up, and saw him, and said unto him, Zacchaeus, make haste, and come down; for to day I must abide at thy house. ⁶And he made haste, and came down, and received him joyfully. ⁷And when they saw *it*, they all murmured, saying, That he was gone to be guest with a man that is a sinner. ⁸And Zacchaeus stood, and said unto the Lord; Behold, Lord, the half of my goods I give to the poor; and if I have taken any thing from any man by false accusation, I restore *him* fourfold. ⁹And Jesus said unto him, This day is salvation come to this house, forsomuch as he also is a son of Abraham. ¹⁰For the Son of man is come to seek and to save that which was lost.

¹¹And as they heard these things, he added and spake a parable, because he

Leading Your Child in Faith

by John and Carol Dettoni

How does a young child receive the faith that Christ offers? Simply, with full trust. But as the child grows and matures, he or she needs increasingly to understand just what that faith and acceptance means. How can parents help a child do this?

Understand the child. Until a child is 4 to 7 years old, his faith is virtually the same as his parents'. The child imitates the family's beliefs and practices; many children from Christian families "play church" at home. Some young children will even respond to Christ as early as age three.

It doesn't happen by accident. From early days their parents have sung and read to them and told them about God's love. They have explained in simple words and concepts the gospel story: "Jesus loves you and wants to be your friend and Savior." The young child's response to that simple message is the work of the Holy Spirit. Parents should encourage their children to give their lives to Christ in this way.

Of course, most children under the ages of twelve or fourteen cannot think abstractly and will not really understand much about God, sin, redemption, salvation, justification, or eternity. But they *can* make a significant commitment to God.

Between the ages of six and eleven, children begin to see their faith in a broader context, realizing they are recipients of the teachings not only of their parents but of the local church. Children at this age still do not critically examine their faith but accept what is taught them. Their commitments are largely defined by direct input from others.

In the early teen years, they notice there are many other churches, denominations, and organizations that believe as they do. They begin to identify with this larger group and receive from this network the teachings and practices that help make them more committed to Christ.

When the child matures (ages fifteen and up), he or she thinks more abstractly and is able to examine the teaching received. In one sense, this is the biggest milestone: The child examines his or her faith and decides whether it is true.

Take inventory. Here are some specific ways to help your children grow in their faith.

Surround preschoolers and early elementary-age children with experiences that stress who God is. Books, tapes, and church contacts are especially helpful for children.

Look for teachable moments. Wise parents will talk *about* God throughout the day and talk *with* him in the presence of their children. Children will soon learn that God is constantly with us and that he cares for us day and night.

Read a Bible story or Scripture to children at one of the daily meals or at bedtime. Make sure the length, vocabulary, and concepts fit their age. Keep the Scripture short for younger children, and choose Bible story books with good pictures.

Pray at meals, at bedtime, and when daily crises or happy times make prayer appropriate. Encourage the child to pray. Lead by example, letting children see you ask God for guidance and also praise and thank him.

Expose children to church ministries for children. Prepare children for an adult service by explaining simply, on their level of understanding, what happens in the adult service and what each part means.

Own your own faith. Parents need to be ready to talk with their teenagers and answer their questions. Talk with your older children about their faith in relation to your faith, the local church's faith, and a broader group's (denomination's) faith. Know what and why you believe so you can discuss it with them.

Don't be afraid if your older child questions his or her faith. This is a normal part of taking ownership of one's faith, and how you react is important. Be a good listener when the child asks questions. Help the child find answers from Scripture. Pat answers or emotional reactions won't help them. They need thoughtful, biblical answers.

Trust the work of the Holy Spirit in your child's life.

DIGGING DEEPER
1. Why is it important for children to own their faith instead of simply imitating their parents' faith? See 1 Peter 1:23 and 2 Timothy 1:5-6.
2. What Scriptures can you read to your children that tell about God's plan of salvation? See John 1:12; 3:16; Acts 16:31.
3. What is the role of parents in teaching children about God? See Deuteronomy 6:6-9; 11:18-21; Exodus 13:8-10.

Adapted from *Parenting Before and After Work* (Victor Books, 1992).

Devotional Moment
•
Faith

19:8-10 When Zacchaeus believed, Jesus said, "Salvation has come to this home." Zacchaeus's faith in Jesus affected his whole family. We don't know who or how many people this involved, but it reminds us that every person's faith affects the members of his or her family. If you're newly converted to Christ, be gentle, patient, and careful how you present your new life to your loved ones.

was nigh to Jerusalem, and because they thought that the kingdom of God should immediately appear. ¹²He said therefore, A certain nobleman went into a far country to receive for himself a kingdom, and to return. ¹³And he called his ten servants, and delivered them ten pounds[a], and said unto them, Occupy till I come. ¹⁴But his citizens hated him, and sent a message after him, saying, We will not have this *man* to reign over us. ¹⁵And it came to pass, that when he was returned, having received the kingdom, then he commanded these servants to be called unto him, to whom he had given the money[b], that he might know how much every man had gained by trading. ¹⁶Then came the first, saying, Lord, thy pound hath gained ten pounds. ¹⁷And he said unto him, Well, thou good servant: because thou hast been faithful in a very little, have thou authority over ten cities. ¹⁸And the second came, saying, Lord, thy pound hath gained five pounds. ¹⁹And he said likewise to him, Be thou also over five cities. ²⁰And another came, saying, Lord, behold, *here is* thy pound, which I have kept laid up in a napkin: ²¹For I feared thee, because thou art an austere

[a] pounds: mina, here translated a pound, is twelve ounces and an half: which according to five shillings the ounce is three pounds two shillings and sixpence
[b] money: Gr. silver

man: thou takest up that thou layedst not down, and reapest that thou didst not sow. ²²And he saith unto him, Out of thine own mouth will I judge thee, *thou* wicked servant. Thou knewest that I was an austere man, taking up that I laid not down, and reaping that I did not sow: ²³Wherefore then gavest not thou my money into the bank, that at my coming I might have required mine own with usury? ²⁴And he said unto them that stood by, Take from him the pound, and give *it* to him that hath ten pounds. ²⁵(And they said unto him, Lord, he hath ten pounds.) ²⁶For I say unto you, That unto every one which hath shall be given; and from him that hath not, even that he hath shall be taken away from him. ²⁷But those mine enemies, which would not that I should reign over them, bring hither, and slay *them* before me.

²⁸And when he had thus spoken, he went before, ascending up to Jerusalem. ²⁹And it came to pass, when he was come nigh to Bethphage and Bethany, at the mount called *the mount* of Olives, he sent two of his disciples, ³⁰Saying, Go ye into the village over against *you*; in the which at your entering ye shall find a colt tied, whereon yet never man sat: loose him, and bring *him hither*. ³¹And if any man ask you, Why do ye loose *him?* thus shall ye say unto him, Because the Lord hath need of him. ³²And they that were sent went their way, and found even as he had said unto them. ³³And as they were loosing the colt, the owners thereof said unto them, Why loose ye the colt? ³⁴And they said, The Lord hath need of him. ³⁵And they brought him to Jesus: and they cast their garments upon the colt, and they set Jesus thereon. ³⁶And as he went, they spread their clothes in the way. ³⁷And

when he was come nigh, even now at the descent of the mount of Olives, the whole multitude of the disciples began to rejoice and praise God with a loud voice for all the mighty works that they had seen; ³⁸Saying, Blessed *be* the King that cometh in the name of the Lord: peace in heaven, and glory in the highest. ³⁹And some of the Pharisees from among the multitude said unto him, Master, rebuke thy disciples. ⁴⁰And he answered and said unto them, I tell you that, if these should hold their peace, the stones would immediately cry out.

⁴¹And when he was come near, he beheld the city, and wept over it, ⁴²Saying, If thou hadst known, even thou, at least in this thy day, the things *which belong* unto thy peace! but now they are hid from thine eyes. ⁴³For the days shall come upon thee, that thine enemies shall cast a trench about thee, and compass thee round, and keep thee in on every side, ⁴⁴And shall lay thee even with the ground, and thy children within thee; and they shall not leave in thee one stone upon another; because thou knewest not the time of thy visitation. ⁴⁵And he went into the temple, and began to cast out them that sold therein, and them that bought; ⁴⁶Saying unto them, It is written, My house is the house of prayer: but ye have made it a den of thieves. ⁴⁷And he taught daily in the temple. But the chief priests and the scribes and the chief of the people sought to destroy him, ⁴⁸And could not find what they might do: for all the people were very attentive to hear him.

20

¹And it came to pass, *that* on one of those days, as he taught the people in

the temple, and preached the gospel, the chief priests and the scribes came upon *him* with the elders, ²And spake unto him, saying, Tell us, by what authority doest thou these things? or who is he that gave thee this authority? ³And he answered and said unto them, I will also ask you one thing; and answer me: ⁴The baptism of John, was it from heaven, or of men? ⁵And they reasoned with themselves, saying, If we shall say, From heaven; he will say, Why then believed ye him not? ⁶But and if we say, Of men; all the people will stone us: for they be persuaded that John was a prophet. ⁷And they answered, that they could not tell whence *it was*. ⁸And Jesus said unto them, Neither tell I you by what authority I do these things.

⁹Then began he to speak to the people this parable; A certain man planted a vineyard, and let it forth to husbandmen, and went into a far country for a long time. ¹⁰And at the season he sent a servant to the husbandmen, that they should give him of the fruit of the vineyard: but the husbandmen beat him, and sent *him* away empty. ¹¹And again he sent another servant: and they beat him also, and entreated *him* shamefully, and sent *him* away empty. ¹²And again he sent a third: and they wounded him also, and cast *him* out. ¹³Then said the lord of the vineyard, What shall I do? I will send my beloved son: it may be they will reverence *him* when they see him. ¹⁴But when the husbandmen saw him, they reasoned among themselves, saying, This is the heir: come, let us kill him, that the inheritance may be ours. ¹⁵So they cast him out of the vineyard, and killed *him*. What therefore shall the lord of the vineyard do unto them? ¹⁶He shall come and destroy these husbandmen, and shall give the vineyard to others. And when they heard *it*, they said, God forbid. ¹⁷And he beheld them, and said, What is this then that is written, The stone which the builders rejected, the same is become the head of the corner? ¹⁸Whosoever shall fall upon that stone shall be broken; but on whomsoever it shall fall, it will grind him to powder. ¹⁹And the chief priests and the scribes the same hour sought to lay hands on him; and they feared the people: for they perceived that he had spoken this parable against them.

²⁰And they watched *him*, and sent forth spies, which should feign themselves just men, that they might take hold of his words, that so they might deliver him unto the power and authority of the governor. ²¹And they asked him, saying, Master, we know that thou sayest and teachest rightly, neither acceptest thou the person *of any*, but teachest the way of God truly*: ²²Is it lawful for us to give tribute unto Caesar, or no? ²³But he perceived their craftiness, and said unto them, Why tempt ye me? ²⁴Shew me a penny. Whose image and superscription hath it? They answered and said, Caesar's. ²⁵And he said unto them, Render therefore unto Caesar the things which be Caesar's, and unto God the things which be God's. ²⁶And they could not take hold of his words before the people: and they marvelled at his answer, and held their peace.

---

* truly: or, of a truth

²⁷Then came to *him* certain of the Sadducees, which deny that there is any resurrection; and they asked him, ²⁸Saying, Master, Moses wrote unto us, If any man's brother die, having a wife, and he die without children, that his brother should take his wife, and raise up seed unto his brother. ²⁹There were therefore seven brethren: and the first took a wife, and died without children. ³⁰And the second took her to wife, and he died childless. ³¹And the third took her; and in like manner the seven also: and they left no children, and died. ³²Last of all the woman died also. ³³Therefore in the resurrection whose wife of them is she? for seven had her to wife. ³⁴And Jesus answering said unto them, The children of this world marry, and are given in marriage: ³⁵But they which shall be accounted worthy to obtain that world, and the resurrection from the dead, neither marry, nor are given in marriage: ³⁶Neither can they die any more: for they are equal unto the angels; and are the children of God, being the children of the resurrection. ³⁷Now that the dead are raised, even Moses shewed at the bush, when he calleth the Lord the God of Abraham, and the God of Isaac, and the God of Jacob. ³⁸For he is not a God of the dead, but of the living: for all live unto him.

³⁹Then certain of the scribes answering said, Master, thou hast well said. ⁴⁰And after that they durst not ask him any *question at all.* ⁴¹And he said unto them, How say they that Christ is David's son? ⁴²And David himself saith in the book of Psalms, The LORD said unto my Lord, Sit thou on my right hand, ⁴³Till I make thine enemies thy footstool. ⁴⁴David therefore calleth him Lord, how is he then his son? ⁴⁵Then in the audience of all the people he said unto his disciples, ⁴⁶Beware of the scribes, which desire to walk in long robes, and love greetings in the markets, and the highest seats in the synagogues, and the chief rooms at feasts; ⁴⁷Which devour widows' houses, and for a shew make long prayers: the same shall receive greater damnation.

21

¹And he looked up, and saw the rich men casting their gifts into the treasury. ²And he saw also a certain poor widow casting in thither two mites. ³And he said, Of a truth I say unto you, that this poor widow hath cast in more than they all: ⁴For all these have of their abundance cast in unto the offerings of God: but she of her penury hath cast in all the living that she had.

⁵And as some spake of the temple, how it was adorned with goodly stones and gifts, he said, ⁶*As for* these things which ye behold, the days will come, in the which there shall not be left one stone upon another, that shall not be thrown down. ⁷And they asked him, saying, Master, but when shall these things be? and what sign *will there be* when these things shall come to pass? ⁸And he said, Take heed that ye be not deceived: for many shall come in my name, saying, I am *Christ*; and the timeᵃ draweth near: go ye not therefore after them. ⁹But when ye shall hear of wars and commotions, be not terrified: for these things must first come to pass;

ᵃ and the time: or, and, The time

but the end *is* not by and by. ¹⁰Then said he unto them, Nation shall rise against nation, and kingdom against kingdom: ¹¹And great earthquakes shall be in divers places, and famines, and pestilences; and fearful sights and great signs shall there be from heaven. ¹²But before all these, they shall lay their hands on you, and persecute *you,* delivering *you* up to the synagogues, and into prisons, being brought before kings and rulers for my name's sake. ¹³And it shall turn to you for a testimony. ¹⁴Settle *it* therefore in your hearts, not to meditate before what ye shall answer: ¹⁵For I will give you a mouth and wisdom, which all your adversaries shall not be able to gainsay nor resist. ¹⁶And ye shall be betrayed both by parents, and brethren, and kinsfolks, and friends; and *some* of you shall they cause to be put to death. ¹⁷And ye shall be hated of all *men* for my name's sake. ¹⁸But there shall not an hair of your head perish. ¹⁹In your patience possess ye your souls.

²⁰And when ye shall see Jerusalem compassed with armies, then know that the desolation thereof is nigh. ²¹Then let them which are in Judaea flee to the mountains; and let them which are in the midst of it depart out; and let not them that are in the countries enter thereinto. ²²For these be the days of vengeance, that all things which are written may be fulfilled. ²³But woe unto them that are with child, and to them that give suck, in those days! for there shall be great distress in the land, and wrath upon this people. ²⁴And they shall fall by the edge of the sword, and shall be led away captive into all nations: and Jerusalem shall be trodden down of the Gentiles, until the times of the Gentiles be fulfilled. ²⁵And there shall be signs in the sun, and in the moon, and in the stars; and upon the earth distress of nations, with perplexity; the sea and the waves roaring; ²⁶Men's hearts failing them for fear, and for looking after those things which are coming on the earth: for the powers of heaven shall be shaken. ²⁷And then shall they see the Son of man coming in a cloud with power and great glory. ²⁸And when these things begin to come to pass, then look up, and lift up your heads; for your redemption draweth nigh.

²⁹And he spake to them a parable; Behold the fig tree, and all the trees; ³⁰When they now shoot forth, ye see and know of your own selves that summer is now nigh at hand. ³¹So likewise ye, when ye see these things come to pass, know ye that the kingdom of God is nigh at hand. ³²Verily I say unto you, This generation shall not pass away, till all be fulfilled. ³³Heaven and earth shall pass away: but my words shall not pass away. ³⁴And take heed to yourselves, lest at any time your hearts be overcharged

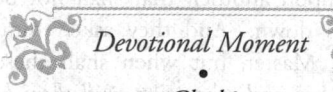

Devotional Moment

•

Clash!

21:16 Jesus warned his disciples that faith in him would get strong reactions from some family members and friends. For many people, following Christ strains close relationships. Jesus told us that such discord is inevitable. That doesn't give us license to be obnoxious; it just means that being a Christian rarely makes everyone we know happy, and at some point we must choose following Christ over appeasing others. Maintain your faith even if it's under fire.

with surfeiting, and drunkenness, and cares of this life, and *so* that day come upon you unawares. ³⁵For as a snare shall it come on all them that dwell on the face of the whole earth. ³⁶Watch ye therefore, and pray always, that ye may be accounted worthy to escape all these things that shall come to pass, and to stand before the Son of man. ³⁷And in the day time he was teaching in the temple; and at night he went out, and abode in the mount that is called *the mount* of Olives. ³⁸And all the people came early in the morning to him in the temple, for to hear him.

22

¹Now the feast of unleavened bread drew nigh, which is called the Passover. ²And the chief priests and scribes sought how they might kill him; for they feared the people. ³Then entered Satan into Judas surnamed Iscariot, being of the number of the twelve. ⁴And he went his way, and communed with the chief priests and captains, how he might betray him unto them. ⁵And they were glad, and covenanted to give him money. ⁶And he promised, and sought opportunity to betray him unto them in the absence of the multitude.

⁷Then came the day of unleavened bread, when the passover must be killed. ⁸And he sent Peter and John, saying, Go and prepare us the passover, that we may eat. ⁹And they said unto him, Where wilt thou that we prepare? ¹⁰And he said unto them, Behold, when ye are entered into the city, there shall a man meet you, bearing a pitcher of water; follow him into the house where he entereth in. ¹¹And ye shall say unto the goodman of the house, The Master saith unto thee, Where is the guest chamber, where I shall eat the passover with my disciples? ¹²And he shall shew you a large upper room furnished: there make ready. ¹³And they went, and found as he had said unto them: and they made ready the passover. ¹⁴And when the hour was come, he sat down, and the twelve apostles with him. ¹⁵And he said unto them, With desire[a] I have desired to eat this passover with you before I suffer: ¹⁶For I say unto you, I will not any more eat thereof, until it be fulfilled in the kingdom of God. ¹⁷And he took the cup, and gave thanks, and said, Take this, and divide *it* among yourselves: ¹⁸For I say unto you, I will not drink of the fruit of the vine, until the kingdom of God shall come. ¹⁹And he took bread, and gave thanks, and brake *it,* and gave unto them, saying, This is my body which is given for you: this do in remembrance of me. ²⁰Likewise also the cup after supper, saying, This cup *is* the new testament in my blood, which is shed for you.

²¹But, behold, the hand of him that betrayeth me *is* with me on the table. ²²And truly the Son of man goeth, as it was determined: but woe unto that man by whom he is betrayed! ²³And they began to enquire among themselves, which of them it was that should do this thing. ²⁴And there was also a strife among them, which of them should be accounted the greatest. ²⁵And he said unto them, The kings of the Gentiles exercise lordship over them; and they that exercise authority upon

---

[a] With desire . . . : or, I have heartily desired

them are called benefactors. ²⁶But ye *shall* not *be* so: but he that is greatest among you, let him be as the younger; and he that is chief, as he that doth serve. ²⁷For whether *is* greater, he that sitteth at meat, or he that serveth? *is* not he that sitteth at meat? but I am among you as he that serveth. ²⁸Ye are they which have continued with me in my temptations. ²⁹And I appoint unto you a kingdom, as my Father hath appointed unto me; ³⁰That ye may eat and drink at my table in my kingdom, and sit on thrones judging the twelve tribes of Israel. ³¹And the Lord said, Simon, Simon, behold, Satan hath desired *to have* you, that he may sift *you* as wheat: ³²But I have prayed for thee, that thy faith fail not: and when thou art converted, strengthen thy brethren. ³³And he said unto him, Lord, I am ready to go with thee, both into prison, and to death. ³⁴And he said, I tell thee, Peter, the cock shall not crow this day, before that thou shalt thrice deny that thou knowest me. ³⁵And he said unto them, When I sent you without purse, and scrip, and shoes, lacked ye any thing? And they said, Nothing. ³⁶Then said he unto them, But now, he that hath a purse, let him take *it*, and likewise *his* scrip: and he that hath no sword, let him sell his garment, and buy one. ³⁷For I say unto you, that this that is written must yet be accomplished in me, And he was reckoned among the transgressors: for the things concerning me have an end. ³⁸And they said, Lord, behold, here *are* two swords. And he said unto them, It is enough.

³⁹And he came out, and went, as he was wont, to the mount of Olives; and his disciples also followed him. ⁴⁰And when he was at the place, he said unto them, Pray that ye enter not into temptation. ⁴¹And he was withdrawn from them about a stone's cast, and kneeled down, and prayed, ⁴²Saying, Father, if thou be willing, remove[b] this cup from me: nevertheless not my will, but thine, be done. ⁴³And there appeared an angel unto him from heaven, strengthening him. ⁴⁴And being in an agony he prayed more earnestly: and his sweat was as it were great drops of blood falling down to the ground. ⁴⁵And when he rose up from prayer, and was come to his disciples, he found them sleeping for sorrow, ⁴⁶And said unto them, Why sleep ye? rise and pray, lest ye enter into temptation.

⁴⁷And while he yet spake, behold a multitude, and he that was called Judas, one of the twelve, went before them, and drew near unto Jesus to kiss him. ⁴⁸But Jesus said unto him, Judas, betrayest thou the Son of man with a kiss? ⁴⁹When they which were about him saw what would follow, they said unto him, Lord, shall we smite with the sword? ⁵⁰And one of them smote the servant of the high priest, and cut off his right ear. ⁵¹And Jesus answered and said, Suffer ye thus far. And he touched his ear, and healed him. ⁵²Then Jesus said unto the chief priests, and captains of the temple, and the elders, which were come to him, Be ye come out, as against a thief, with swords and staves? ⁵³When I was daily with you in the temple, ye stretched forth no hands against me: but this is your hour, and the power of darkness.

ᵇ willing, remove: Gr. willing to remove

⁵⁴Then took they him, and led *him*, and brought him into the high priest's house. And Peter followed afar off. ⁵⁵And when they had kindled a fire in the midst of the hall, and were set down together, Peter sat down among them. ⁵⁶But a certain maid beheld him as he sat by the fire, and earnestly looked upon him, and said, This man was also with him. ⁵⁷And he denied him, saying, Woman, I know him not. ⁵⁸And after a little while another saw him, and said, Thou art also of them. And Peter said, Man, I am not. ⁵⁹And about the space of one hour after another confidently affirmed, saying, Of a truth this *fellow* also was with him: for he is a Galilaean. ⁶⁰And Peter said, Man, I know not what thou sayest. And immediately, while he yet spake, the cock crew. ⁶¹And the Lord turned, and looked upon Peter. And Peter remembered the word of the Lord, how he had said unto him, Before the cock crow, thou shalt deny me thrice. ⁶²And Peter went out, and wept bitterly.

⁶³And the men that held Jesus mocked him, and smote *him*. ⁶⁴And when they had blindfolded him, they struck him on the face, and asked him, saying, Prophesy, who is it that smote thee? ⁶⁵And many other things blasphemously spake they against him. ⁶⁶And as soon as it was day, the elders of the people and the chief priests and the scribes came together, and led him into their council, saying, ⁶⁷Art thou the Christ? tell us. And he said unto them, If I tell you, ye will not believe: ⁶⁸And if I also ask *you*, ye will not answer me, nor let *me* go. ⁶⁹Hereafter shall the Son of man sit on the right hand of the power of God. ⁷⁰Then said they all, Art

---

Devotional Moment
•
Big Boys Cry

22:62 When Peter realized his failure, he cried bitterly. Later, after Jesus had risen from the dead, Jesus forgave Peter. He also reiterated his invitation to Peter to follow him and carry on with his work (see John 21:15-19). Jesus knew that Peter's remorse was genuine.

Most of us are profoundly aware of our failures. After you have made a mistake, be aware of how your conscience has worked on your heart. If the mistake has already produced repentance, forgive yourself.

---

thou then the Son of God? And he said unto them, Ye say that I am. ⁷¹And they said, What need we any further witness? for we ourselves have heard of his own mouth.

23

¹And the whole multitude of them arose, and led him unto Pilate. ²And they began to accuse him, saying, We found this *fellow* perverting the nation, and forbidding to give tribute to Caesar, saying that he himself is Christ a King. ³And Pilate asked him, saying, Art thou the King of the Jews? And he answered him and said, Thou sayest *it*. ⁴Then said Pilate to the chief priests and *to* the people, I find no fault in this man. ⁵And they were the more fierce, saying, He stirreth up the people, teaching throughout all Jewry, beginning from Galilee to this place. ⁶When Pilate heard of Galilee, he asked whether the man were a Galilaean. ⁷And as soon as he knew that he belonged unto Herod's jurisdiction, he sent him to Herod, who himself also was at Jerusalem at that time. ⁸And when Herod saw Jesus, he was exceeding glad: for he was desirous to see

him of a long *season*, because he had heard many things of him; and he hoped to have seen some miracle done by him. ⁹Then he questioned with him in many words; but he answered him nothing. ¹⁰And the chief priests and scribes stood and vehemently accused him. ¹¹And Herod with his men of war set him at nought, and mocked *him*, and arrayed him in a gorgeous robe, and sent him again to Pilate. ¹²And the same day Pilate and Herod were made friends together: for before they were at enmity between themselves.

¹³And Pilate, when he had called together the chief priests and the rulers and the people, ¹⁴Said unto them, Ye have brought this man unto me, as one that perverteth the people: and, behold, I, having examined *him* before you, have found no fault in this man touching those things whereof ye accuse him: ¹⁵No, nor yet Herod: for I sent you to him; and, lo, nothing worthy of death is done unto him. ¹⁶I will therefore chastise him, and release *him*. ¹⁷(For of necessity he must release one unto them at the feast.) ¹⁸And they cried out all at once, saying, Away with this *man*, and release unto us Barabbas: ¹⁹(Who for a certain sedition made in the city, and for murder, was cast into prison.) ²⁰Pilate therefore, willing to release Jesus, spake again to them. ²¹But they cried, saying, Crucify *him*, crucify him. ²²And he said unto them the third time, Why, what evil hath he done? I have found no cause of death in him: I will therefore chastise him, and let *him* go. ²³And they were instant with loud voices, requiring that he might be crucified. And the voices of them and of the chief priests

prevailed. ²⁴And Pilate gave sentence that it should be as they required. ²⁵And he released unto them him that for sedition and murder was cast into prison, whom they had desired; but he delivered Jesus to their will.

²⁶And as they led him away, they laid hold upon one Simon, a Cyrenian, coming out of the country, and on him they laid the cross, that he might bear *it* after Jesus. ²⁷And there followed him a great company of people, and of women, which also bewailed and lamented him. ²⁸But Jesus turning unto them said, Daughters of Jerusalem, weep not for me, but weep for yourselves, and for your children. ²⁹For, behold, the days are coming, in the which they shall say, Blessed *are* the barren, and the wombs that never bare, and the paps which never gave suck. ³⁰Then shall they begin to say to the mountains, Fall on us; and to the hills, Cover us. ³¹For if they do these things in a green tree, what shall be done in the dry?

³²And there were also two other, malefactors, led with him to be put to death. ³³And when they were come to the place, which is called Calvaryª, there they crucified him, and the malefactors, one on the right hand, and the other on the left. ³⁴Then said Jesus, Father, forgive them; for they know not what they do. And they parted his raiment, and cast lots. ³⁵And the people stood beholding. And the rulers also with them derided *him*, saying, He saved others; let him save himself, if he be Christ, the chosen of God. ³⁶And the soldiers also mocked him, coming to him, and offering him vinegar, ³⁷And saying, If

---

ª Calvary: or, The place of a skull

thou be the king of the Jews, save thyself. ³⁸And a superscription also was written over him in letters of Greek, and Latin, and Hebrew, THIS IS THE KING OF THE JEWS. ³⁹And one of the malefactors which were hanged railed on him, saying, If thou be Christ, save thyself and us. ⁴⁰But the other answering rebuked him, saying, Dost not thou fear God, seeing thou art in the same condemnation? ⁴¹And we indeed justly; for we receive the due reward of our deeds: but this man hath done nothing amiss. ⁴²And he said unto Jesus, Lord, remember me when thou comest into thy kingdom. ⁴³And Jesus said unto him, Verily I say unto thee, Today shalt thou be with me in paradise.

⁴⁴And it was about the sixth hour, and there was a darkness over all the earth[b] until the ninth hour. ⁴⁵And the sun was darkened, and the veil of the temple was rent in the midst. ⁴⁶And when Jesus had cried with a loud voice, he said, Father, into thy hands I commend my spirit: and having said thus, he gave up the ghost. ⁴⁷Now when the centurion saw what was done, he glorified God, saying, Certainly this was a righteous man. ⁴⁸And all the people that came together to that sight, beholding the things which were done, smote their breasts, and returned. ⁴⁹And all his acquaintance, and the women that followed him from Galilee, stood afar off, beholding these things.

⁵⁰And, behold, *there was* a man named Joseph, a counsellor; *and he was* a good man, and a just: ⁵¹(The same had not consented to the counsel and deed of them;) *he was* of Arimathaea, a city of the Jews: who also himself waited for the kingdom of God. ⁵²This *man* went unto Pilate, and begged the body of Jesus. ⁵³And he took it down, and wrapped it in linen, and laid it in a sepulchre that was hewn in stone, wherein never man before was laid. ⁵⁴And that day was the preparation, and the sabbath drew on. ⁵⁵And the women also, which came with him from Galilee, followed after, and beheld the sepulchre, and how his body was laid. ⁵⁶And they returned, and prepared spices and ointments; and rested the sabbath day according to the commandment.

24

¹Now upon the first *day* of the week, very early in the morning, they came unto the sepulchre, bringing the spices which they had prepared, and certain *others* with them. ²And they found the stone rolled away from the sepulchre. ³And they entered in, and found not the body of the Lord Jesus. ⁴And it came to pass, as they were much perplexed thereabout, behold, two men stood by them in shining garments: ⁵And as they were afraid, and bowed down *their* faces to the earth, they said unto them, Why seek ye the living[a] among the dead? ⁶He is not here, but is risen: remember how he spake unto you when he was yet in Galilee, ⁷Saying, The Son of man must be delivered into the hands of sinful men, and be crucified, and the third day rise again. ⁸And they remembered his words, ⁹And returned from the sepulchre, and told all these things unto the eleven, and to all the rest.

ᵇ earth: or, land
ᵃ the living: or, him that liveth

¹⁰It was Mary Magdalene, and Joanna, and Mary *the mother* of James, and other *women that were* with them, which told these things unto the apostles. ¹¹And their words seemed to them as idle tales, and they believed them not. ¹²Then arose Peter, and ran unto the sepulchre; and stooping down, he beheld the linen clothes laid by themselves, and departed, wondering in himself at that which was come to pass.

¹³And, behold, two of them went that same day to a village called Emmaus, which was from Jerusalem *about* threescore furlongs. ¹⁴And they talked together of all these things which had happened. ¹⁵And it came to pass, that, while they communed *together* and reasoned, Jesus himself drew near, and went with them. ¹⁶But their eyes were holden that they should not know him. ¹⁷And he said unto them, What manner of communications *are* these that ye have one to another, as ye walk, and are sad? ¹⁸And the one of them, whose name was Cleopas, answering said unto him, Art thou only a stranger in Jerusalem, and hast not known the things which are come to pass there in these days? ¹⁹And he said unto them, What things? And they said unto him, Concerning Jesus of Nazareth, which was a prophet mighty in deed and word before God and all the people: ²⁰And how the chief priests and our rulers delivered him to be condemned to death, and have crucified him. ²¹But we trusted that it had been he which should have redeemed Israel: and beside all this, to day is the third day since these things were done. ²²Yea, and certain women also of our company made us astonished, which were early at the sepulchre; ²³And when they found not his body, they came, saying, that they had also seen a vision of angels, which said that he was alive. ²⁴And certain of them which were with us went to the sepulchre, and found *it* even so as the women had said: but him they saw not. ²⁵Then he said unto them, O fools, and slow of heart to believe all that the prophets have spoken: ²⁶Ought not Christ to have suffered these things, and to enter into his glory? ²⁷And beginning at Moses and all the prophets, he expounded unto them in all the scriptures the things concerning himself. ²⁸And they drew nigh unto the village, whither they went: and he made as though he would have gone further. ²⁹But they constrained him, saying, Abide with us: for it is toward evening, and the day is far spent. And he went in to tarry with them. ³⁰And it came to pass, as he sat at meat with them, he took bread, and blessed *it*, and brake, and gave to them. ³¹And their eyes were opened, and they knew him; and he vanished^b out of their sight. ³²And they said one to another, Did not our heart burn within us, while he talked with us by the way, and while he opened to us the scriptures? ³³And they rose up the same hour, and returned to Jerusalem, and found the eleven gathered together, and them that were with them, ³⁴Saying, The Lord is risen indeed, and hath appeared to Simon. ³⁵And they told what things *were done* in the way, and how he was known of them in breaking of bread.

³⁶And as they thus spake, Jesus himself stood in the midst of them, and saith unto them, Peace *be* unto you. ³⁷But they were terrified and affrighted,

---

^b vanished . . . : or, ceased to be seen of them

and supposed that they had seen a spirit. [38]And he said unto them, Why are ye troubled? and why do thoughts arise in your hearts? [39]Behold my hands and my feet, that it is I myself: handle me, and see; for a spirit hath not flesh and bones, as ye see me have. [40]And when he had thus spoken, he shewed them *his* hands and *his* feet. [41]And while they yet believed not for joy, and wondered, he said unto them, Have ye here any meat? [42]And they gave him a piece of a broiled fish, and of an honeycomb. [43]And he took *it*, and did eat before them. [44]And he said unto them, These *are* the words which I spake unto you, while I was yet with you, that all things must be fulfilled, which were written in the law of Moses, and *in* the prophets, and *in* the psalms, concerning me. [45]Then opened he their understanding,

that they might understand the scriptures, [46]And said unto them, Thus it is written, and thus it behoved Christ to suffer, and to rise from the dead the third day: [47]And that repentance and remission of sins should be preached in his name among all nations, beginning at Jerusalem. [48]And ye are witnesses of these things. [49]And, behold, I send the promise of my Father upon you: but tarry ye in the city of Jerusalem, until ye be endued with power from on high.

[50]And he led them out as far as to Bethany, and he lifted up his hands, and blessed them. [51]And it came to pass, while he blessed them, he was parted from them, and carried up into heaven. [52]And they worshipped him, and returned to Jerusalem with great joy: [53]And were continually in the temple, praising and blessing God. Amen.

JOHN

Purpose
To prove conclusively that
Jesus is the Son of God
and that all who believe in
him will have eternal life

Author
John, the apostle, son of
Zebedee, brother of
James, called a "Son of
Thunder"

To Whom Written
New Christians and
searching non-Christians

Date Written
Between A.D. 85 and 90

Setting
Written after the destruction of Jerusalem in A.D.
70 and before John's exile
to the island of Patmos

Key Verses
"And many other signs
truly did Jesus in the
presence of his disciples,
which are not written in
this book: but these are
written, that ye might believe that Jesus is the
Christ, the Son of God;
and that believing ye
might have life through
his name" (20:30-31).

Key Places
Judean countryside,
Samaria, Galilee, Bethany,
Jerusalem

John has a different approach to the story of Jesus. Instead of Bethlehem, John writes about light and life.
Instead of angels and wise men, it's *logos,* the elusive
Greek term that can be translated only roughly as "word,"
a term whose meaning has taken shelves of books to explain.

Of the eight miracles recorded, six appear only in the
Gospel of John, as does the Upper Room Discourse
(chapters 14–17). Over 90 percent of John is unique to
his Gospel—John does not contain a genealogy or any
record of Jesus' birth. It has no reference to his childhood,
temptation, transfiguration, appointment of the disciples, parables, ascension, or great commission.

John's version of Jesus' story provides a unique perspective. He was the disciple emotionally closest to Jesus,
the one who understood Jesus and loved him as a personal friend. His Gospel reflects this intimacy.

John's Gospel celebrates a new and different way of
living.

1

¹In the beginning was the Word, and the Word was with God, and the Word was God. ²The same was in the beginning with God. ³All things were made by him; and without him was not any thing made that was made. ⁴In him was life; and the life was the light of men. ⁵And the light shineth in darkness; and the darkness comprehended[a] it not. ⁶There was a man sent from God, whose name *was* John. ⁷The same came for a witness, to bear witness of the Light, that all *men* through him might believe. ⁸He was not that Light, but *was sent* to bear witness of that Light. ⁹*That* was the true Light, which lighteth every man that cometh into the world. ¹⁰He was in the world, and the world was made by him, and the world knew him not. ¹¹He came unto his own, and his own received him not. ¹²But as many as received him, to them gave he power[b] to become the sons of God, *even* to them that believe on his name: ¹³Which were born, not of blood, nor of the will of the flesh, nor of the will of man, but of God. ¹⁴And the Word was made flesh, and dwelt among us, (and we beheld his glory, the glory as of the only begotten of the Father,) full of grace and truth. ¹⁵John bare witness of him, and cried, saying, This was he of whom I spake, He that cometh after me is preferred before me: for he was before me. ¹⁶And of his fulness have all we received, and grace for grace. ¹⁷For the law was given by Moses, *but* grace and truth came by Jesus Christ. ¹⁸No man hath seen God at any time; the only begotten Son, which is in the bosom of the Father, he hath declared *him*.

¹⁹And this is the record of John, when the Jews sent priests and Levites from Jerusalem to ask him, Who art thou? ²⁰And he confessed, and denied not; but confessed, I am not the Christ. ²¹And they asked him, What then? Art thou Elias? And he saith, I am not. Art thou that prophet[c]? And he answered, No. ²²Then said they unto him, Who art thou? that we may give an answer to them that sent us. What sayest thou of thyself? ²³He said, I *am* the voice of one crying in the wilderness, Make straight the way of the Lord, as said the prophet Esaias. ²⁴And they which were sent were of the Pharisees. ²⁵And they asked him, and said unto him, Why baptizest thou then, if thou be not that Christ, nor Elias, neither that prophet? ²⁶John answered them, saying, I baptize with water: but there standeth one among you, whom ye know not; ²⁷He it is, who coming after me is preferred before me, whose shoe's latchet I am not worthy to unloose. ²⁸These things were done in Bethabara beyond Jordan, where John was baptizing.

²⁹The next day John seeth Jesus coming unto him, and saith, Behold the Lamb of God, which taketh away[d] the sin of the world. ³⁰This is he of whom I said, After me cometh a man which is preferred before me: for he was

---

[a] comprehended: or, did not admit, or, receive
[b] power: or, the right, or, privilege
[c] that prophet: or, a prophet?
[d] taketh away: or, beareth

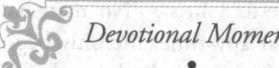

Devotional Moment
•
Contentment

1:30 Much of our happiness in life comes from finding a job we can do, then doing it well without regard to whether it puts us on someone's list of Very Important Persons. John the Baptist was the one who introduced the person everybody wanted to hear. He was content to let Jesus surpass him. To be content at work is to accept the giftedness God has given us and to use the skills we have learned in God's service. Contentment does not mean laziness, ceasing to learn, or being indifferent about quality. Contentment is the cordial acceptance of the role God has given us.

before me. ³¹And I knew him not: but that he should be made manifest to Israel, therefore am I come baptizing with water. ³²And John bare record, saying, I saw the Spirit descending from heaven like a dove, and it abode upon him. ³³And I knew him not: but he that sent me to baptize with water, the same said unto me, Upon whom thou shalt see the Spirit descending, and remaining on him, the same is he which baptizeth with the Holy Ghost. ³⁴And I saw, and bare record that this is the Son of God. ³⁵Again the next day after John stood, and two of his disciples; ³⁶And looking upon Jesus as he walked, he saith, Behold the Lamb of God!

³⁷And the two disciples heard him speak, and they followed Jesus. ³⁸Then Jesus turned, and saw them following, and saith unto them, What seek ye? They said unto him, Rabbi, (which is to say, being interpreted, Master,) where dwellest thou? ³⁹He saith unto them, Come and see. They came and saw where he dwelt,

and abode with him that day: for it was about ͤ the tenth hour. ⁴⁰One of the two which heard John *speak*, and followed him, was Andrew, Simon Peter's brother. ⁴¹He first findeth his own brother Simon, and saith unto him, We have found the Messias, which is, being interpreted, the Christᶠ. ⁴²And he brought him to Jesus. And when Jesus beheld him, he said, Thou art Simon the son of Jona: thou shalt be called Cephas, which is by interpretation, A stone.

⁴³The day following Jesus would go forth into Galilee, and findeth Philip, and saith unto him, Follow me. ⁴⁴Now Philip was of Bethsaida, the city of Andrew and Peter. ⁴⁵Philip findeth Nathanael, and saith unto him, We have found him, of whom Moses in the law, and the prophets, did write, Jesus of Nazareth, the son of Joseph. ⁴⁶And Nathanael said unto him, Can there any good thing come out of Nazareth? Philip saith unto him, Come and see. ⁴⁷Jesus saw Nathanael coming to him, and saith of him, Behold an Israelite indeed, in whom is no guile! ⁴⁸Nathanael saith unto him, Whence knowest thou me? Jesus answered and said unto him, Before that Philip called thee, when thou wast under the fig tree, I saw thee. ⁴⁹Nathanael answered and saith unto him, Rabbi, thou art the Son of God; thou art the King of Israel. ⁵⁰Jesus answered and said unto him, Because I said unto thee, I saw thee under the fig tree, believest thou? thou shalt see greater things than these. ⁵¹And he saith unto him, Verily, verily, I say unto you, Hereafter ye shall see heaven open, and

---

ͤ about . . . : that was two hours before night
ᶠ the Christ: or, the Anointed

Family Traditions

Baptism Traditions

John 1:1-34

Baptism by water, the symbolic acting out of burial, cleansing, and resurrection in Christ, may be the most joyful and meaningful event on your calendar!

"My wife and I wanted to make sure our son knew the importance we placed on his decision to be baptized," explains Wayne Conklin of Tarrytown, New York. "So we invited his four closest school friends (two of them weren't Christians). It was a great testimony when we followed the church ceremony with a party at home."

An urban couple, the Watnes from Atlanta, Georgia, celebrated both their baptisms not long after they committed their lives to Christ at a Billy Graham meeting. They held a formal dinner in their apartment. The table was decorated with white flowers, paper doves, and white helium balloons.

"Our families, who don't yet know the Lord, were pretty amazed by our sense of joy that day," says Jane Watne. "They were kind of quiet, but it opened doors for us to share the plan of salvation with them in a natural way."

There are many ways you can celebrate a baptism in your family. For a child who is being baptized, start a fund for summer missionary service. Create a spiritual journal out of a blank book with headings to denote prayers, answers to prayer, struggles, surprises, feelings, decisions. Take photographs of the baptism and party, then arrange them in a small scrapbook with captions, Bible verses, and poems to remember the day. Splurge on fresh flowers, with satin ribbons for a girl to wear the day of baptism, or for a boy, a new pair of his favorite kind of shoes to denote he's now walking a new way of life. Bring in a wheelbarrow full of flowers for an adult. Take a group of kids to fly a kite, and talk about how the Holy Spirit leads us in our new life. Go swimming or water sliding to capitalize on God's picture of cleansing. Take a walk along a deserted beach, or arrange a one-day spiritual retreat.

Look around; you'll find dozens of personal ways to say, "It's a brand-new start."

the angels of God ascending and descending upon the Son of man.

2

¹And the third day there was a marriage in Cana of Galilee; and the mother of Jesus was there: ²And both Jesus was called, and his disciples, to the marriage. ³And when they wanted wine, the mother of Jesus saith unto him, They have no wine. ⁴Jesus saith unto her, Woman, what have I to do with thee? mine hour is not yet come. ⁵His mother saith unto the servants, Whatsoever he saith unto you, do *it*. ⁶And there were set there six waterpots of stone, after the manner of the purifying of the Jews, containing two or three firkins apiece. ⁷Jesus saith unto them, Fill the waterpots with water. And they filled them up to the brim. ⁸And he saith unto them, Draw out now, and bear unto the governor of the feast. And they bare *it*. ⁹When the ruler of the feast had tasted the water that was made wine, and knew not whence it was: (but the servants which drew the water knew;) the governor of the feast called the bridegroom, ¹⁰And saith unto him, Every man at the beginning doth set forth good wine; and when men have well drunk, then that which is worse: *but* thou hast kept the good wine until now. ¹¹This beginning of miracles did Jesus in Cana of Galilee, and manifested forth his glory; and his disciples believed on him.

¹²After this he went down to Capernaum, he, and his mother, and his brethren, and his disciples: and they continued there not many days. ¹³And the Jews' passover was at hand, and Jesus went up to Jerusalem, ¹⁴And found in the temple those that sold oxen and sheep and doves, and the changers of money sitting: ¹⁵And when he had made a scourge of small cords, he drove them all out of the temple, and the sheep, and the oxen; and poured out the changers' money, and overthrew the tables; ¹⁶And said unto them that sold doves, Take these things hence; make not my Father's house an house of merchandise. ¹⁷And his disciples remembered that it was written, The zeal of thine house hath eaten me up. ¹⁸Then answered the Jews and said unto him, What sign shewest thou unto us, seeing that thou doest these things? ¹⁹Jesus answered and said unto them, Destroy this temple, and in three days I will raise it up. ²⁰Then said the Jews, Forty and six years was this temple in building, and wilt thou rear it up in three days? ²¹But he spake of the temple of his body. ²²When therefore he was risen from the dead, his disciples remembered that he had said this unto them; and they believed the scripture, and the word which Jesus had said.

Devotional Moment

•

Weddings

2:1-2 Jesus' first miracle took place at a wedding. Weddings are among a family's purest pleasures and happiest memories. They are celebrations where everyone can feel renewed by joy and love.

But weddings can also open ugly wounds. A couple that intentionally excludes family from important traditional roles may create painful and bitter memories. Relatives who refuse to attend send messages that years of anniversary cards cannot undo. If your family has a wedding coming up, help make it a generous, joyous, affirming, happy celebration with memories to last a lifetime.

²³Now when he was in Jerusalem at the passover, in the feast *day*, many believed in his name, when they saw the miracles which he did. ²⁴But Jesus did not commit himself unto them, because he knew all *men*, ²⁵And needed not that any should testify of man: for he knew what was in man.

3

¹There was a man of the Pharisees, named Nicodemus, a ruler of the Jews: ²The same came to Jesus by night, and said unto him, Rabbi, we know that thou art a teacher come from God: for no man can do these miracles that thou doest, except God be with him. ³Jesus answered and said unto him, Verily, verily, I say unto thee, Except a man be born again[a], he cannot see the kingdom of God. ⁴Nicodemus saith unto him, How can a man be born when he is old? can he enter the second time into his mother's womb, and be born? ⁵Jesus answered, Verily, verily, I say unto thee, Except a man be born of water and *of* the Spirit, he cannot enter into the kingdom of God. ⁶That which is born of the flesh is flesh; and that which is born of the Spirit is spirit. ⁷Marvel not that I said unto thee, Ye must be born again[b]. ⁸The wind bloweth where it listeth, and thou hearest the sound thereof, but canst not tell whence it cometh, and whither it goeth: so is every one that is born of the Spirit. ⁹Nicodemus answered and said unto him, How can these things be? ¹⁰Jesus answered and said unto him, Art thou a master of Is-

rael, and knowest not these things? ¹¹Verily, verily, I say unto thee, We speak that we do know, and testify that we have seen; and ye receive not our witness. ¹²If I have told you earthly things, and ye believe not, how shall ye believe, if I tell you *of* heavenly things? ¹³And no man hath ascended up to heaven, but he that came down from heaven, *even* the Son of man which is in heaven. ¹⁴And as Moses lifted up the serpent in the wilderness, even so must the Son of man be lifted up: ¹⁵That whosoever believeth in him should not perish, but have eternal life. ¹⁶For God so loved the world, that he gave his only begotten Son, that whosoever believeth in him should not perish, but have everlasting life. ¹⁷For God sent not his Son into the world to condemn the world; but that the world through him might be saved. ¹⁸He that believeth on him is not condemned: but he that believeth not is condemned already, because he hath not believed in the name of the only begotten Son of God. ¹⁹And this is the condemnation, that light is come into the world, and men loved darkness rather than light, because their deeds were evil. ²⁰For every one that doeth evil hateth the light, neither cometh to the light, lest his deeds should be reproved[c]. ²¹But he that doeth truth cometh to the light, that his deeds may be made manifest, that they are wrought in God.

²²After these things came Jesus and his disciples into the land of Judaea; and there he tarried with them, and

---

ª again: or, from above
ᵇ again: or, from above
ᶜ reproved: or, discovered

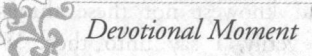

Devotional Moment

•

Trusting Christ

3:36 "He that believeth on the Son hath everlasting life." Words don't get much plainer than this. This news is for every person, and God desires everyone to believe it. What does it mean to trust Christ? Jesus is inviting us to place our entire life in his hands and to accept that all that he says is true—to admit our sinfulness before God and our total dependence on him to forgive our sin. The way to heaven is open, through faith in Jesus Christ.

baptized. ²³And John also was baptizing in Aenon near to Salim, because there was much water there: and they came, and were baptized. ²⁴For John was not yet cast into prison. ²⁵Then there arose a question between *some* of John's disciples and the Jews about purifying. ²⁶And they came unto John, and said unto him, Rabbi, he that was with thee beyond Jordan, to whom thou barest witness, behold, the same baptizeth, and all *men* come to him. ²⁷John answered and said, A man can receiveᵈ nothing, except it be given him from heaven. ²⁸Ye yourselves bear me witness, that I said, I am not the Christ, but that I am sent before him. ²⁹He that hath the bride is the bridegroom: but the friend of the bridegroom, which standeth and heareth him, rejoiceth greatly because of the bridegroom's voice: this my joy therefore is fulfilled. ³⁰He must increase, but I *must* decrease. ³¹He that cometh from above is above all: he that is of the earth is earthly, and speaketh of the earth: he that cometh from heaven is above all.

³²And what he hath seen and heard, that he testifieth; and no man receiveth his testimony. ³³He that hath received his testimony hath set to his seal that God is true. ³⁴For he whom God hath sent speaketh the words of God: for God giveth not the Spirit by measure *unto him.* ³⁵The Father loveth the Son, and hath given all things into his hand. ³⁶He that believeth on the Son hath everlasting life: and he that believeth not the Son shall not see life; but the wrath of God abideth on him.

4

¹When therefore the Lord knew how the Pharisees had heard that Jesus made and baptized more disciples than John, ²(Though Jesus himself baptized not, but his disciples,) ³He left Judaea, and departed again into Galilee.

⁴And he must needs go through Samaria. ⁵Then cometh he to a city of Samaria, which is called Sychar, near to the parcel of ground that Jacob gave to his son Joseph. ⁶Now Jacob's well was there. Jesus therefore, being wearied with *his* journey, sat thus on the well: *and* it was about the sixth hour. ⁷There cometh a woman of Samaria to draw water: Jesus saith unto her, Give me to drink. ⁸(For his disciples were gone away unto the city to buy meat.) ⁹Then saith the woman of Samaria unto him, How is it that thou, being a Jew, askest drink of me, which am a woman of Samaria? for the Jews have no dealings with the Samaritans. ¹⁰Jesus answered and said unto her, If thou knewest the gift of God, and who it is that saith to thee, Give me to drink; thou wouldest

ᵈ receive: or, take unto himself

have asked of him, and he would have given thee living water. ¹¹The woman saith unto him, Sir, thou hast nothing to draw with, and the well is deep: from whence then hast thou that living water? ¹²Art thou greater than our father Jacob, which gave us the well, and drank thereof himself, and his children, and his cattle? ¹³Jesus answered and said unto her, Whosoever drinketh of this water shall thirst again: ¹⁴But whosoever drinketh of the water that I shall give him shall never thirst; but the water that I shall give him shall be in him a well of water springing up into everlasting life. ¹⁵The woman saith unto him, Sir, give me this water, that I thirst not, neither come hither to draw. ¹⁶Jesus saith unto her, Go, call thy husband, and come hither. ¹⁷The woman answered and said, I have no husband. Jesus said unto her, Thou hast well said, I have no husband: ¹⁸For thou hast had five husbands; and he whom thou now hast is not thy husband: in that saidst thou truly. ¹⁹The woman saith unto him, Sir, I perceive that thou art a prophet. ²⁰Our fathers worshipped in this mountain; and ye say, that in

Jerusalem is the place where men ought to worship. ²¹Jesus saith unto her, Woman, believe me, the hour cometh, when ye shall neither in this mountain, nor yet at Jerusalem, worship the Father. ²²Ye worship ye know not what: we know what we worship: for salvation is of the Jews. ²³But the hour cometh, and now is, when the true worshippers shall worship the Father in spirit and in truth: for the Father seeketh such to worship him. ²⁴God *is* a Spirit: and they that worship him must worship *him* in spirit and in truth. ²⁵The woman saith unto him, I know that Messias cometh, which is called Christ: when he is come, he will tell us all things. ²⁶Jesus saith unto her, I that speak unto thee am *he.*

²⁷And upon this came his disciples, and marvelled that he talked with the woman: yet no man said, What seekest thou? or, Why talkest thou with her? ²⁸The woman then left her waterpot, and went her way into the city, and saith to the men, ²⁹Come, see a man, which told me all things that ever I did: is not this the Christ? ³⁰Then they went out of the city, and

came unto him. ³¹In the mean while his disciples prayed him, saying, Master, eat. ³²But he said unto them, I have meat to eat that ye know not of. ³³Therefore said the disciples one to another, Hath any man brought him *ought* to eat? ³⁴Jesus saith unto them, My meat is to do the will of him that sent me, and to finish his work. ³⁵Say not ye, There are yet four months, and *then* cometh harvest? behold, I say unto you, Lift up your eyes, and look on the fields; for they are white already to harvest. ³⁶And he that reapeth receiveth wages, and gathereth fruit unto life eternal: that both he that soweth and he that reapeth may rejoice together. ³⁷And herein is that saying true, One soweth, and another reapeth. ³⁸I sent you to reap that whereon ye bestowed no labour: other men laboured, and ye are entered into their labours. ³⁹And many of the Samaritans of that city believed on him for the saying of the woman, which testified, He told me all that ever I did. ⁴⁰So when the Samaritans were come unto him, they besought him that he would tarry with them: and he abode there two days. ⁴¹And many more believed because of his own word; ⁴²And said unto the woman, Now we believe, not because of thy saying: for we have heard *him* ourselves, and know that this is indeed the Christ, the Saviour of the world.

⁴³Now after two days he departed thence, and went into Galilee. ⁴⁴For Jesus himself testified, that a prophet hath no honour in his own country. ⁴⁵Then when he was come into Galilee, the Galilaeans received him, having seen all the things that he did at Jerusalem at the feast: for they also went unto the feast. ⁴⁶So Jesus came again into Cana of Galilee, where he made the water wine. And there was a certain nobleman^a, whose son was sick at Capernaum. ⁴⁷When he heard that Jesus was come out of Judaea into Galilee, he went unto him, and besought him that he would come down, and heal his son: for he was at the point of death. ⁴⁸Then said Jesus unto him, Except ye see signs and wonders, ye will not believe. ⁴⁹The nobleman saith unto him, Sir, come down ere my child die. ⁵⁰Jesus saith unto him, Go thy way; thy son liveth. And the man believed the word that Jesus had spoken unto him, and he went his way. ⁵¹And as he was now going down, his servants met him, and told *him*, saying, Thy son liveth. ⁵²Then enquired he of them the hour when he began to amend. And they said unto him, Yesterday at the seventh hour the fever left him. ⁵³So the father knew that *it was* at the same hour, in the which Jesus said unto him, Thy son liveth: and himself believed, and his whole house. ⁵⁴This *is* again the second miracle *that* Jesus did, when he was come out of Judaea into Galilee.

5

¹After this there was a feast of the Jews; and Jesus went up to Jerusalem. ²Now there is at Jerusalem by the sheep *market* a pool, which is called in the Hebrew tongue Bethesda, having five porches. ³In these lay a great multitude of impotent folk, of blind, halt, withered, waiting for the moving of the wa-

---

^a nobleman: or, courtier, or, ruler

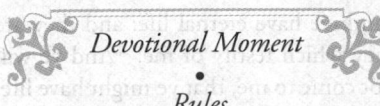

Devotional Moment

•

Rules

5:10 Rules need to be wisely applied and regularly reviewed. Here, a good rule had become repressive: It hurt people, overlooked the work God was doing, and no longer served its purpose (to glorify God). A good rule had fallen into the hands of people who loved rules for their own sake. Rules at home set boundaries and help us learn discipline. But rules must serve a purpose. If a rule doesn't improve our life or lead us to God, then it is time to revise or discard it.

ter. ⁴For an angel went down at a certain season into the pool, and troubled the water: whosoever then first after the troubling of the water stepped in was made whole of whatsoever disease he had. ⁵And a certain man was there, which had an infirmity thirty and eight years. ⁶When Jesus saw him lie, and knew that he had been now a long time *in that case,* he saith unto him, Wilt thou be made whole? ⁷The impotent man answered him, Sir, I have no man, when the water is troubled, to put me into the pool: but while I am coming, another steppeth down before me. ⁸Jesus saith unto him, Rise, take up thy bed, and walk. ⁹And immediately the man was made whole, and took up his bed, and walked: and on the same day was the sabbath. ¹⁰The Jews therefore said unto him that was cured, It is the sabbath day: it is not lawful for thee to carry *thy* bed. ¹¹He answered them, He that made me whole, the same said unto me, Take up thy bed, and walk. ¹²Then asked they him, What man is that which said unto thee, Take up thy

bed, and walk? ¹³And he that was healed wist not who it was: for Jesus had conveyed himself away, a multitude[a] being in *that* place. ¹⁴Afterward Jesus findeth him in the temple, and said unto him, Behold, thou art made whole: sin no more, lest a worse thing come unto thee. ¹⁵The man departed, and told the Jews that it was Jesus, which had made him whole. ¹⁶And therefore did the Jews persecute Jesus, and sought to slay him, because he had done these things on the sabbath day.

¹⁷But Jesus answered them, My Father worketh hitherto, and I work. ¹⁸Therefore the Jews sought the more to kill him, because he not only had broken the sabbath, but said also that God was his Father, making himself equal with God. ¹⁹Then answered Jesus and said unto them, Verily, verily, I say unto you, The Son can do nothing of himself, but what he seeth the Father do: for what things soever he doeth, these also doeth the Son likewise. ²⁰For the Father loveth the Son, and sheweth him all things that himself doeth: and he will shew him greater works than these, that ye may marvel. ²¹For as the Father raiseth up the dead, and quickeneth *them;* even so the Son quickeneth whom he will. ²²For the Father judgeth no man, but hath committed all judgment unto the Son: ²³That all *men* should honour the Son, even as they honour the Father. He that honoureth not the Son honoureth not the Father which hath sent him. ²⁴Verily, verily, I say unto you, He that heareth my word, and believeth on him that sent me, hath everlasting life, and shall not come into

[a] a multitude . . . : or, from the multitude that was

condemnation; but is passed from death unto life. 25Verily, verily, I say unto you, The hour is coming, and now is, when the dead shall hear the voice of the Son of God: and they that hear shall live. 26For as the Father hath life in himself; so hath he given to the Son to have life in himself; 27And hath given him authority to execute judgment also, because he is the Son of man. 28Marvel not at this: for the hour is coming, in the which all that are in the graves shall hear his voice, 29And shall come forth; they that have done good, unto the resurrection of life; and they that have done evil, unto the resurrection of damnation. 30I can of mine own self do nothing: as I hear, I judge: and my judgment is just; because I seek not mine own will, but the will of the Father which hath sent me.

31If I bear witness of myself, my witness is not true. 32There is another that beareth witness of me; and I know that the witness which he witnesseth of me is true. 33Ye sent unto John, and he bare witness unto the truth. 34But I receive not testimony from man: but these things I say, that ye might be saved. 35He was a burning and a shining light: and ye were willing for a season to rejoice in his light. 36But I have greater witness than that of John: for the works which the Father hath given me to finish, the same works that I do, bear witness of me, that the Father hath sent me. 37And the Father himself, which hath sent me, hath borne witness of me. Ye have neither heard his voice at any time, nor seen his shape. 38And ye have not his word abiding in you: for whom he hath sent, him ye believe not. 39Search the scriptures; for in them ye

think ye have eternal life: and they are they which testify of me. 40And ye will not come to me, that ye might have life. 41I receive not honour from men. 42But I know you, that ye have not the love of God in you. 43I am come in my Father's name, and ye receive me not: if another shall come in his own name, him ye will receive. 44How can ye believe, which receive honour one of another, and seek not the honour that cometh from God only? 45Do not think that I will accuse you to the Father: there is one that accuseth you, even Moses, in whom ye trust. 46For had ye believed Moses, ye would have believed me: for he wrote of me. 47But if ye believe not his writings, how shall ye believe my words?

6

1After these things Jesus went over the sea of Galilee, which is the sea of Tiberias. 2And a great multitude followed him, because they saw his miracles which he did on them that were diseased. 3And Jesus went up into a mountain, and there he sat with his disciples. 4And the passover, a feast of the Jews, was nigh. 5When Jesus then lifted up his eyes, and saw a great company come unto him, he saith unto Philip, Whence shall we buy bread, that these may eat? 6And this he said to prove him: for he himself knew what he would do. 7Philip answered him, Two hundred pennyworth of bread is not sufficient for them, that every one of them may take a little. 8One of his disciples, Andrew, Simon Peter's brother, saith unto him, 9There is a lad here, which hath five barley loaves, and two small fishes: but what are they among

Devotional Moment

Children Serving God

6:8-9 A boy shared his food with Jesus, who used it miraculously to feed an entire crowd. This boy teaches us all a good lesson. He gave what he had to see how it could be used. Too often we bemoan what we don't have, escalate the problem, and blame the unfairness of it all on somebody (God?). But this boy spontaneously acted without regard for his own hunger or needs. Don't stifle the spontaneity of your kids. Let them serve. God loves their loaves and fishes.

so many? ¹⁰And Jesus said, Make the men sit down. Now there was much grass in the place. So the men sat down, in number about five thousand. ¹¹And Jesus took the loaves; and when he had given thanks, he distributed to the disciples, and the disciples to them that were set down; and likewise of the fishes as much as they would. ¹²When they were filled, he said unto his disciples, Gather up the fragments that remain, that nothing be lost. ¹³Therefore they gathered *them* together, and filled twelve baskets with the fragments of the five barley loaves, which remained over and above unto them that had eaten. ¹⁴Then those men, when they had seen

Devotional Moment

Grace at Meals

6:11-12 Jesus thanked God for the food before serving it. Start your meals with prayer: Say it, sing it, hold hands. As much as possible, make each meal a warm family time. Yes, it's difficult to restrain a hungry stomach while pausing to pray. That's the point of doing it— it's that important.

the miracle that Jesus did, said, This is of a truth that prophet that should come into the world.

¹⁵When Jesus therefore perceived that they would come and take him by force, to make him a king, he departed again into a mountain himself alone. ¹⁶And when even was *now* come, his disciples went down unto the sea, ¹⁷And entered into a ship, and went over the sea toward Capernaum. And it was now dark, and Jesus was not come to them. ¹⁸And the sea arose by reason of a great wind that blew. ¹⁹So when they had rowed about five and twenty or thirty furlongs, they see Jesus walking on the sea, and drawing nigh unto the ship: and they were afraid. ²⁰But he saith unto them, It is I; be not afraid. ²¹Then they willingly received him into the ship: and immediately the ship was at the land whither they went.

²²The day following, when the people which stood on the other side of the sea saw that there was none other boat there, save that one whereinto his disciples were entered, and that Jesus went not with his disciples into the boat, but *that* his disciples were gone away alone; ²³(Howbeit there came other boats from Tiberias nigh unto the place where they did eat bread, after that the Lord had given thanks:) ²⁴When the people therefore saw that Jesus was not there, neither his disciples, they also took shipping, and came to Capernaum, seeking for Jesus. ²⁵And when they had found him on the other side of the sea, they said unto him, Rabbi, when camest thou hither? ²⁶Jesus answered them and said, Verily, verily, I say unto you, Ye seek me, not because ye saw the miracles, but because ye did

eat of the loaves, and were filled. ²⁷Labour not[a] for the meat which perisheth, but for that meat which endureth unto everlasting life, which the Son of man shall give unto you: for him hath God the Father sealed.

²⁸Then said they unto him, What shall we do, that we might work the works of God? ²⁹Jesus answered and said unto them, This is the work of God, that ye believe on him whom he hath sent. ³⁰They said therefore unto him, What sign shewest thou then, that we may see, and believe thee? what dost thou work? ³¹Our fathers did eat manna in the desert; as it is written, He gave them bread from heaven to eat. ³²Then Jesus said unto them, Verily, verily, I say unto you, Moses gave you not that bread from heaven; but my Father giveth you the true bread from heaven. ³³For the bread of God is he which cometh down from heaven, and giveth life unto the world. ³⁴Then said they unto him, Lord, evermore give us this bread. ³⁵And Jesus said unto them, I am the bread of life: he that cometh to me shall never hunger; and he that believeth on me shall never thirst. ³⁶But I said unto you, That ye also have seen me, and believe not. ³⁷All that the Father giveth me shall come to me; and him that cometh to me I will in no wise cast out. ³⁸For I came down from heaven, not to do mine own will, but the will of him that sent me. ³⁹And this is the Father's will which hath sent me, that of all which he hath given me I should lose nothing, but should raise it up again at the last day. ⁴⁰And this is the will of him that sent me, that every one

which seeth the Son, and believeth on him, may have everlasting life: and I will raise him up at the last day. ⁴¹The Jews then murmured at him, because he said, I am the bread which came down from heaven. ⁴²And they said, Is not this Jesus, the son of Joseph, whose father and mother we know? how is it then that he saith, I came down from heaven? ⁴³Jesus therefore answered and said unto them, Murmur not among yourselves. ⁴⁴No man can come to me, except the Father which hath sent me draw him: and I will raise him up at the last day. ⁴⁵It is written in the prophets, And they shall be all taught of God. Every man therefore that hath heard, and hath learned of the Father, cometh unto me. ⁴⁶Not that any man hath seen the Father, save he which is of God, he hath seen the Father. ⁴⁷Verily, verily, I say unto you, He that believeth on me hath everlasting life. ⁴⁸I am that bread of life. ⁴⁹Your fathers did eat manna in the wilderness, and are dead. ⁵⁰This is the bread which cometh down from heaven, that a man may eat thereof, and not die. ⁵¹I am the living bread which came down from heaven: if any man eat of this bread, he shall live for ever: and the bread that I will give is my flesh, which I will give for the life of the world. ⁵²The Jews therefore strove among themselves, saying, How can this man give us *his* flesh to eat? ⁵³Then Jesus said unto them, Verily, verily, I say unto you, Except ye eat the flesh of the Son of man, and drink his blood, ye have no life in you. ⁵⁴Whoso eateth my flesh, and drinketh my blood, hath eternal life; and I will raise him up at

---

^a Labour not: or, Work not

the last day. ⁵⁵For my flesh is meat indeed, and my blood is drink indeed. ⁵⁶He that eateth my flesh, and drinketh my blood, dwelleth in me, and I in him. ⁵⁷As the living Father hath sent me, and I live by the Father: so he that eateth me, even he shall live by me. ⁵⁸This is that bread which came down from heaven: not as your fathers did eat manna, and are dead: he that eateth of this bread shall live for ever. ⁵⁹These things said he in the synagogue, as he taught in Capernaum.

⁶⁰Many therefore of his disciples, when they had heard *this*, said, This is an hard saying; who can hear it? ⁶¹When Jesus knew in himself that his disciples murmured at it, he said unto them, Doth this offend[b] you? ⁶²*What* and if ye shall see the Son of man ascend up where he was before? ⁶³It is the spirit that quickeneth; the flesh profiteth nothing: the words that I speak unto you, *they* are spirit, and *they* are life. ⁶⁴But there are some of you that believe not. For Jesus knew from the beginning who they were that believed not, and who should betray him. ⁶⁵And he said, Therefore said I unto you, that no man can come unto me, except it were given unto him of my Father. ⁶⁶From that *time* many of his disciples went back, and walked no more with him. ⁶⁷Then said Jesus unto the twelve, Will ye also go away? ⁶⁸Then Simon Peter answered him, Lord, to whom shall we go? thou hast the words of eternal life. ⁶⁹And we believe and are sure that thou art that Christ, the Son of the living God. ⁷⁰Jesus answered them, Have not I chosen you twelve, and one of you is a devil?

⁷¹He spake of Judas Iscariot *the son* of Simon: for he it was that should betray him, being one of the twelve.

7

¹After these things Jesus walked in Galilee: for he would not walk in Jewry, because the Jews sought to kill him. ²Now the Jews' feast of tabernacles was at hand. ³His brethren therefore said unto him, Depart hence, and go into Judaea, that thy disciples also may see the works that thou doest. ⁴For *there is* no man *that* doeth any thing in secret, and he himself seeketh to be known openly. If thou do these things, shew thyself to the world. ⁵For neither did his brethren believe in him. ⁶Then Jesus said unto them, My time is not yet come: but your time is alway ready. ⁷The world cannot hate you; but me it hateth, because I testify of it, that the works thereof are evil. ⁸Go ye up unto this feast: I go not up yet unto this feast; for my time is not yet full come. ⁹When he had said these words unto them, he abode *still* in Galilee. ¹⁰But when his brethren were gone up, then went he also up unto the feast, not openly, but as it were in secret. ¹¹Then the Jews sought him at the feast, and said, Where is he? ¹²And there was much murmuring among the people concerning him: for some said, He is a good man: others said, Nay; but he deceiveth the people. ¹³Howbeit no man spake openly of him for fear of the Jews.

¹⁴Now about the midst of the feast Jesus went up into the temple, and taught. ¹⁵And the Jews marvelled, saying, How knoweth this man letters[a],

---

[b] offend: or, scandalize, or, cause you to stumble
[a] letters: or, learning

having never learned? [16]Jesus answered them, and said, My doctrine is not mine, but his that sent me. [17]If any man will do his will, he shall know of the doctrine, whether it be of God, or *whether* I speak of myself. [18]He that speaketh of himself seeketh his own glory: but he that seeketh his glory that sent him, the same is true, and no unrighteousness is in him. [19]Did not Moses give you the law, and *yet* none of you keepeth the law? Why go ye about to kill me? [20]The people answered and said, Thou hast a devil: who goeth about to kill thee? [21]Jesus answered and said unto them, I have done one work, and ye all marvel. [22]Moses therefore gave unto you circumcision; (not because it is of Moses, but of the fathers;) and ye on the sabbath day circumcise a man. [23]If a man on the sabbath day receive circumcision, that[b] the law of Moses should not be broken; are ye angry at me, because I have made a man every whit whole on the sabbath day? [24]Judge not according to the appearance, but judge righteous judgment. [25]Then said some of them of Jerusalem, Is not this he, whom they seek to kill? [26]But, lo, he speaketh boldly, and they say nothing unto him. Do the rulers know indeed that this is the very Christ? [27]Howbeit we know this man whence he is: but when Christ cometh, no man knoweth whence he is. [28]Then cried Jesus in the temple as he taught, saying, Ye both know me, and ye know whence I am: and I am not come of myself, but he that sent me is true, whom ye know not. [29]But I know him:

for I am from him, and he hath sent me. [30]Then they sought to take him: but no man laid hands on him, because his hour was not yet come. [31]And many of the people believed on him, and said, When Christ cometh, will he do more miracles than these which this *man* hath done? [32]The Pharisees heard that the people murmured such things concerning him; and the Pharisees and the chief priests sent officers to take him. [33]Then said Jesus unto them, Yet a little while am I with you, and *then* I go unto him that sent me. [34]Ye shall seek me, and shall not find *me*: and where I am, *thither* ye cannot come. [35]Then said the Jews among themselves, Whither will he go, that we shall not find him? will he go unto the dispersed among the Gentiles[c], and teach the Gentiles? [36]What *manner of* saying is this that he said, Ye shall seek me, and shall not find *me*: and where I am, *thither* ye cannot come?

[37]In the last day, that great *day* of the feast, Jesus stood and cried, saying, If any man thirst, let him come unto me, and drink. [38]He that believeth on me, as the scripture hath said, out of his belly shall flow rivers of living water. [39](But this spake he of the Spirit, which they that believe on him should receive: for the Holy Ghost was not yet *given*; because that Jesus was not yet glorified.) [40]Many of the people therefore, when they heard this saying, said, Of a truth this is the Prophet. [41]Others said, This is the Christ. But some said, Shall Christ come out of Galilee? [42]Hath not the scripture said, That Christ cometh of the seed of David,

---

[b] that . . . : or, without breaking the law of Moses
[c] Gentiles: or, Greeks

and out of the town of Bethlehem, where David was? ⁴³So there was a division among the people because of him. ⁴⁴And some of them would have taken him; but no man laid hands on him.

⁴⁵Then came the officers to the chief priests and Pharisees; and they said unto them, Why have ye not brought him? ⁴⁶The officers answered, Never man spake like this man. ⁴⁷Then answered them the Pharisees, Are ye also deceived? ⁴⁸Have any of the rulers or of the Pharisees believed on him? ⁴⁹But this people who knoweth not the law are cursed. ⁵⁰Nicodemus saith unto them, (he that came to Jesusᵈ by night, being one of them,) ⁵¹Doth our law judge *any* man, before it hear him, and know what he doeth? ⁵²They answered and said unto him, Art thou also of Galilee? Search, and look: for out of Galilee ariseth no prophet. ⁵³And every man went unto his own house.

8

¹Jesus went unto the mount of Olives. ²And early in the morning he came again into the temple, and all the people came unto him; and he sat down, and taught them. ³And the scribes and Pharisees brought unto him a woman taken in adultery; and when they had set her in the midst, ⁴They say unto him, Master, this woman was taken in adultery, in the very act. ⁵Now Moses in the law commanded us, that such should be stoned: but what sayest thou? ⁶This they said, tempting him, that they might have to accuse him. But Jesus stooped down, and with *his* finger wrote on the ground, *as though he heard them not.* ⁷So when they continued asking him, he lifted up himself, and said unto them, He that is without sin among you, let him first cast a stone at her. ⁸And again he stooped down, and wrote on the ground. ⁹And they which heard *it,* being convicted by *their own* conscience, went out one by one, beginning at the eldest, *even* unto the last: and Jesus was left alone, and the woman standing in the midst. ¹⁰When Jesus had lifted up himself, and saw none but the woman, he said unto her, Woman, where are those thine accusers? hath no man condemned thee? ¹¹She said, No man, Lord. And Jesus said unto her, Neither do I condemn thee: go, and sin no more.

¹²Then spake Jesus again unto them, saying, I am the light of the world: he that followeth me shall not walk in darkness, but shall have the light of life. ¹³The Pharisees therefore said unto him, Thou bearest record of thyself; thy record is not true. ¹⁴Jesus answered and said unto them, Though I bear record of myself, *yet* my record is true: for I know whence I came, and

ᵈ to Jesus: Gr. to him

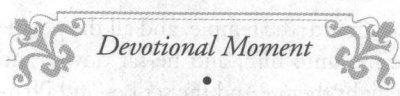

whither I go; but ye cannot tell whence I come, and whither I go. ¹⁵Ye judge after the flesh; I judge no man. ¹⁶And yet if I judge, my judgment is true: for I am not alone, but I and the Father that sent me. ¹⁷It is also written in your law, that the testimony of two men is true. ¹⁸I am one that bear witness of myself, and the Father that sent me beareth witness of me. ¹⁹Then said they unto him, Where is thy Father? Jesus answered, Ye neither know me, nor my Father: if ye had known me, ye should have known my Father also. ²⁰These words spake Jesus in the treasury, as he taught in the temple: and no man laid hands on him; for his hour was not yet come.

²¹Then said Jesus again unto them, I go my way, and ye shall seek me, and shall die in your sins: whither I go, ye cannot come. ²²Then said the Jews, Will he kill himself? because he saith, Whither I go, ye cannot come. ²³And he said unto them, Ye are from beneath; I am from above: ye are of this world; I am not of this world. ²⁴I said therefore unto you, that ye shall die in your sins:

for if ye believe not that I am *he*, ye shall die in your sins. ²⁵Then said they unto him, Who art thou? And Jesus saith unto them, Even *the same* that I said unto you from the beginning. ²⁶I have many things to say and to judge of you: but he that sent me is true; and I speak to the world those things which I have heard of him. ²⁷They understood not that he spake to them of the Father. ²⁸Then said Jesus unto them, When ye have lifted up the Son of man, then shall ye know that I am *he*, and *that* I do nothing of myself; but as my Father hath taught me, I speak these things. ²⁹And he that sent me is with me: the Father hath not left me alone; for I do always those things that please him. ³⁰As he spake these words, many believed on him.

³¹Then said Jesus to those Jews which believed on him, If ye continue in my word, *then* are ye my disciples indeed; ³²And ye shall know the truth, and the truth shall make you free. ³³They answered him, We be Abraham's seed, and were never in bondage to any man: how sayest thou, Ye shall be made free? ³⁴Jesus answered them, Verily, verily, I say unto you, Whosoever committeth sin is the servant of sin. ³⁵And the servant abideth not in the house for ever: *but* the Son abideth ever. ³⁶If the Son therefore shall make you free, ye shall be free indeed. ³⁷I know that ye are Abraham's seed; but ye seek to kill me, because my word hath no place in you.

³⁸I speak that which I have seen with my Father: and ye do that which ye have seen with your father. ³⁹They answered and said unto him, Abraham is our father. Jesus saith unto them, If ye were Abraham's children, ye would

do the works of Abraham. ⁴⁰But now ye seek to kill me, a man that hath told you the truth, which I have heard of God: this did not Abraham. ⁴¹Ye do the deeds of your father. Then said they to him, We be not born of fornication; we have one Father, *even* God. ⁴²Jesus said unto them, If God were your Father, ye would love me: for I proceeded forth and came from God; neither came I of myself, but he sent me. ⁴³Why do ye not understand my speech? *even* because ye cannot hear my word. ⁴⁴Ye are of *your* father the devil, and the lusts of your father ye will do. He was a murderer from the beginning, and abode not in the truth, because there is no truth in him. When he speaketh a lie, he speaketh of his own[a]: for he is a liar, and the father of it. ⁴⁵And because I tell *you* the truth, ye believe me not.

⁴⁶Which of you convinceth me of sin? And if I say the truth, why do ye not believe me? ⁴⁷He that is of God heareth God's words: ye therefore hear *them* not, because ye are not of God. ⁴⁸Then answered the Jews, and said unto him, Say we not well that thou art a Samaritan, and hast a devil? ⁴⁹Jesus answered, I have not a devil; but I honour my Father, and ye do dishonour me. ⁵⁰And I seek not mine own glory: there is one that seeketh and judgeth.

⁵¹Verily, verily, I say unto you, If a man keep my saying, he shall never see death. ⁵²Then said the Jews unto him, Now we know that thou hast a devil. Abraham is dead, and the prophets; and thou sayest, If a man keep my saying, he shall never taste of death. ⁵³Art thou greater than our father Abraham, which is dead? and the prophets are dead: whom makest thou thyself? ⁵⁴Jesus answered, If I honour myself, my honour is nothing: it is my Father that honoureth me; of whom ye say, that he is your God: ⁵⁵Yet ye have not known him; but I know him: and if I should say, I know him not, I shall be a liar like unto you: but I know him, and keep his saying. ⁵⁶Your father Abraham rejoiced to see my day: and he saw *it*, and was glad. ⁵⁷Then said the Jews unto him, Thou art not yet fifty years old, and hast thou seen Abraham? ⁵⁸Jesus said unto them, Verily, verily, I say unto you, Before Abraham was, I am. ⁵⁹Then took they up stones to cast at him: but Jesus hid himself, and went out of the temple, going through the midst of them, and so passed by.

9

¹And as *Jesus* passed by, he saw a man which was blind from *his* birth. ²And his disciples asked him, saying, Master, who did sin, this man, or his parents, that he was born blind? ³Jesus answered, Neither hath this man sinned, nor his parents: but that the works of God should be made manifest in him. ⁴I must work the works of him that sent me, while it is day: the night cometh, when no man can work. ⁵As long as I am in the world, I am the light of the world. ⁶When he had thus spoken, he spat on the ground, and made clay of the spittle, and he anointed[a] the eyes of the blind man with the clay, ⁷And said unto him, Go, wash in the pool of

---

[a] of his own: or, from his own will or disposition
[a] anointed . . . : or, spread the clay upon the eyes of the blind man

Breaking Free from
Emotional Freezing Points

And ye shall know the truth, and the truth shall make you free.
John 8:32

These words from our Lord are often memorized and quoted. Yet the preceding verse sets the context: "If ye continue in my word," Jesus said to those Jews who had believed in him. That's the standard of truth that frees his disciples.

As we seek to understand and apply Jesus' teaching and other truths from God's Word, one way its penetrating truth can free us is to force us to face a powerful, negative cycle—*emotional freezing points.*

An emotional freeze point is an event or period of time that becomes a roadblock to later growth and change. Note how it negatively affected one woman's life and all her later relationships. Notice also how the searchlight of God's Word and truth broke through this wall of pain to bring her freedom in Christ.

Jan was a successful saleswoman in a competitive field. Yet after eight tumultuous years, she was a failure at her marriage. Why?

As she traced her story, she recalls a day when her emotional life seemed to freeze up. It was the night of her parents' twenty-fifth wedding anniversary—the night her father chose to call home and tell his wife that he wouldn't be coming home. Rather, he was leaving her, "now that the kids are grown," and starting life with another woman he'd already picked out.

As Jan saw the devastation on her mother's face, it was like a light switch turned off in her emotional life. In fact, she decided then and there that no matter what, she would *never* be hurt by a man. She would be just as competitive, just as tough, and just as rough as any male—and in so doing, she sacrificed the God-given side of her femininity.

While men and women can do numerous things equally well, God did not make two identical people when he created Adam and Eve. The differences between men and women are pronounced, both physically and emotionally, and can wonderfully complement each other. Jan concentrated so hard on being strong that she sacrificed the softness that had once been a part of her life—and courtship. She took competition and anger from the salesroom to the living room of her home. And after eight years of running battles, her husband served her with divorce papers.

For this woman, it had been a single night, years before, that became an emotional freezing point. For others, it could be a season of time that leads us to block off the free flow of emotions. In either case, recognizing and coming to grips with major times or events of trauma is an important way of "thawing out" from them.

What did Jan do to regain her softness—and win her husband back? In the midst of her pain, she opened the Bible in a lonely hotel room and found God's Word speaking to her. She read in Psalm 139 of God's love in creating her and in 1 Corinthians 13 of a love that outlasts all. She finally stumbled across this passage in Hebrews 3:7-8: "The Holy Ghost saith, Today if ye will hear his voice, harden not your hearts." It was as if God had touched her on the shoulder and said, "It's time. Enough is enough. You've got to deal with your past."

Reading God's Word broke through the emotional freezing point that had chilled Jan's emotions. She saw her own selfishness, how wrong she had been in piling up hate for her father, and how far she had yet to go. Yet over the next six months she changed. Today, she and her husband are together and much closer than ever.

If you've experienced an emotional freezing point in your life—from learning at twenty-one that you were adopted, to going through the horrors of war, to recovering from the broken trust of a spouse—God's Word can warm your life and guide your path to freedom. It wasn't simply "personal insight" that changed Jan; it was God's truth. For "ye shall know the truth, and the truth shall make you free."

Devotional Moment

Disabilities

9:2-3 The disciples wondered who was at fault for the man's disability. We often feel compelled to assign moral causes for misfortune. Yet not every human pain can be linked to a specific sin. If you or a loved one suffers from a disability, a genetic flaw, or a long-term illness, remember that God can use disabilities to show us his power. Don't waste time looking for someone to blame or—perhaps worse—blaming yourself.

Siloam, (which is by interpretation, Sent.) He went his way therefore, and washed, and came seeing.

⁸The neighbours therefore, and they which before had seen him that he was blind, said, Is not this he that sat and begged? ⁹Some said, This is he: others said, He is like him: but he said, I am he. ¹⁰Therefore said they unto him, How were thine eyes opened? ¹¹He an-swered and said, A man that is called Jesus made clay, and anointed mine eyes, and said unto me, Go to the pool of Siloam, and wash: and I went and washed, and I received sight. ¹²Then said they unto him, Where is he? He said, I know not.

¹³They brought to the Pharisees him that aforetime was blind. ¹⁴And it was the sabbath day when Jesus made the clay, and opened his eyes. ¹⁵Then again the Pharisees also asked him how he had received his sight. He said unto them, He put clay upon mine eyes, and I washed, and do see. ¹⁶Therefore said some of the Pharisees, This man is not of God, because he keepeth not the sabbath day. Others said, How can a man that is a sinner do such miracles? And there was a division among them. ¹⁷They say unto the blind man again, What sayest thou of him, that he hath opened thine eyes? He said, He is a

prophet. [18]But the Jews did not believe concerning him, that he had been blind, and received his sight, until they called the parents of him that had received his sight. [19]And they asked them, saying, Is this your son, who ye say was born blind? how then doth he now see? [20]His parents answered them and said, We know that this is our son, and that he was born blind: [21]But by what means he now seeth, we know not; or who hath opened his eyes, we know not: he is of age; ask him: he shall speak for himself. [22]These *words* spake his parents, because they feared the Jews: for the Jews had agreed already, that if any man did confess that he was Christ, he should be put out of the synagogue. [23]Therefore said his parents, He is of age; ask him. [24]Then again called they the man that was blind, and said unto him, Give God the praise: we know that this man is a sinner. [25]He answered and said, Whether he be a sinner *or no*, I know not: one thing I know, that, whereas I was blind, now I see. [26]Then said they to him again, What did he to thee? how opened he thine eyes? [27]He answered them, I have told you already, and ye did not hear: wherefore would ye hear *it* again? will ye also be his disciples? [28]Then they reviled him, and said, Thou art his disciple; but we are Moses' disciples. [29]We know that God spake unto Moses: *as for* this *fellow*, we know not from whence he is. [30]The man answered and said unto them, Why herein is a marvellous thing, that ye know not from whence he is, and *yet* he hath opened mine eyes. [31]Now we know that God heareth not sinners: but if any man be a worshipper of God, and doeth his will, him he heareth. [32]Since the world began was it not heard that any man opened the eyes of one that was born blind. [33]If this man were not of God, he could do nothing. [34]They answered and said unto him, Thou wast altogether born in sins, and dost thou teach us? And they cast[b] him out.

[35]Jesus heard that they had cast him out; and when he had found him, he said unto him, Dost thou believe on the Son of God? [36]He answered and said, Who is he, Lord, that I might believe on him? [37]And Jesus said unto him, Thou hast both seen him, and it is he that talketh with thee. [38]And he said, Lord, I believe. And he worshipped him.

[39]And Jesus said, For judgment I am come into this world, that they which see not might see; and that they which see might be made blind. [40]And *some* of the Pharisees which were with him heard these words, and said unto him, Are we blind also? [41]Jesus said unto them, If ye were blind, ye should have no sin: but now ye say, We see; therefore your sin remaineth.

10

[1]Verily, verily, I say unto you, He that entereth not by the door into the sheepfold, but climbeth up some other way, the same is a thief and a robber. [2]But he that entereth in by the door is the shepherd of the sheep. [3]To him the porter openeth; and the sheep hear his voice: and he calleth his own sheep by name, and leadeth them out. [4]And when he putteth forth his own sheep, he goeth

[b] cast . . . : or, excommunicated him

before them, and the sheep follow him: for they know his voice. 5 And a stranger will they not follow, but will flee from him: for they know not the voice of strangers. 6 This parable spake Jesus unto them: but they understood not what things they were which he spake unto them. 7 Then said Jesus unto them again, Verily, verily, I say unto you, I am the door of the sheep. 8 All that ever came before me are thieves and robbers: but the sheep did not hear them. 9 I am the door: by me if any man enter in, he shall be saved, and shall go in and out, and find pasture. 10 The thief cometh not, but for to steal, and to kill, and to destroy: I am come that they might have life, and that they might have *it* more abundantly. 11 I am the good shepherd: the good shepherd giveth his life for the sheep. 12 But he that is an hireling, and not the shepherd, whose own the sheep are not, seeth the wolf coming, and leaveth the sheep, and fleeth: and the wolf catcheth them, and scattereth the sheep. 13 The hireling fleeth, because he is an hireling, and careth not for the sheep. 14 I am the good shepherd, and know my *sheep*, and am known of mine. 15 As the Father knoweth me, even so know I the Father: and I lay down my life for the sheep. 16 And other sheep I have, which are not of this fold: them also I must bring, and they shall hear my voice; and there shall be one fold, *and* one shepherd. 17 Therefore doth my Father love me, because I lay down my life, that I might take it again. 18 No man taketh it from me, but I lay it down of myself. I have power to lay it down, and I have

power to take it again. This commandment have I received of my Father.

19 There was a division therefore again among the Jews for these sayings. 20 And many of them said, He hath a devil, and is mad; why hear ye him? 21 Others said, These are not the words of him that hath a devil. Can a devil open the eyes of the blind?

22 And it was at Jerusalem the feast of the dedication, and it was winter. 23 And Jesus walked in the temple in Solomon's porch. 24 Then came the Jews round about him, and said unto him, How long dost thou make[a] us to doubt? If thou be the Christ, tell us plainly. 25 Jesus answered them, I told you, and ye believed not: the works that I do in my Father's name, they bear witness of me. 26 But ye believe not, because ye are not of my sheep, as I said unto you. 27 My sheep hear my voice, and I know them, and they follow me: 28 And I give unto them eternal life; and they shall never perish, neither shall any *man* pluck them out of my hand. 29 My Father, which gave *them* me, is greater than all; and no *man* is able to pluck *them* out of my Father's hand. 30 I and *my* Father are one. 31 Then the Jews took up stones again to stone him. 32 Jesus answered them, Many good works have I shewed you from my Father; for which of those works do ye stone me? 33 The Jews answered him, saying, For a good work we stone thee not; but for blasphemy; and because that thou, being a man, makest thyself God. 34 Jesus answered them, Is it not written in your law, I said, Ye are gods? 35 If he called them gods, unto whom the word of

a make . . . : or, hold us in suspense

God came, and the scripture cannot be broken; ³⁶Say ye of him, whom the Father hath sanctified, and sent into the world, Thou blasphemest; because I said, I am the Son of God? ³⁷If I do not the works of my Father, believe me not. ³⁸But if I do, though ye believe not me, believe the works: that ye may know, and believe, that the Father *is* in me, and I in him.

³⁹Therefore they sought again to take him: but he escaped out of their hand, ⁴⁰And went away again beyond Jordan into the place where John at first baptized; and there he abode. ⁴¹And many resorted unto him, and said, John did no miracle: but all things that John spake of this man were true. ⁴²And many believed on him there.

11

¹Now a certain *man* was sick, *named* Lazarus, of Bethany, the town of Mary and her sister Martha. ²(It was *that* Mary which anointed the Lord with ointment, and wiped his feet with her hair, whose brother Lazarus was sick.) ³Therefore his sisters sent unto him, saying, Lord, behold, he whom thou lovest is sick. ⁴When Jesus heard *that*, he said, This sickness is not unto death, but for the glory of God, that the Son of God might be glorified thereby. ⁵Now Jesus loved Martha, and her sister, and Lazarus. ⁶When he had heard therefore that he was sick, he abode two days still in the same place where he was. ⁷Then after that saith he to *his* disciples, Let us go into Judaea again. ⁸*His* disciples say unto him, Master, the Jews of late sought to stone thee; and goest thou thither again? ⁹Jesus answered, Are there not twelve hours in the day? If any man walk in the day, he stumbleth not, because he seeth the light of this world. ¹⁰But if a man walk in the night, he stumbleth, because there is no light in him. ¹¹These things said he: and after that he saith unto them, Our friend Lazarus sleepeth; but I go, that I may awake him out of sleep. ¹²Then said his disciples, Lord, if he sleep, he shall do well. ¹³Howbeit Jesus spake of his death: but they thought that he had spoken of taking of rest in sleep. ¹⁴Then said Jesus unto them plainly, Lazarus is dead. ¹⁵And I am glad for your sakes that I was not there, to the intent ye may believe; nevertheless let us go unto him. ¹⁶Then said Thomas, which is called Didymus, unto his fellowdisciples, Let us also go, that we may die with him.

¹⁷Then when Jesus came, he found that he had *lain* in the grave four days already. ¹⁸Now Bethany was nigh unto Jerusalem, about[a] fifteen furlongs off: ¹⁹And many of the Jews came to Martha and Mary, to comfort them concerning their brother. ²⁰Then Martha, as soon as she heard that Jesus was coming, went and met him: but Mary sat *still* in the house. ²¹Then said Martha unto Jesus, Lord, if thou hadst been here, my brother had not died. ²²But I know, that even now, whatsoever thou wilt ask of God, God will give *it* thee. ²³Jesus saith unto her, Thy brother shall rise again. ²⁴Martha saith unto him, I know that he shall rise again in the resurrection at the last day. ²⁵Jesus said unto her, I am the resurrection, and the life: he that believeth in me, though he were dead,

---

[a] about . . . : that is, about two miles

yet shall he live: ²⁶And whosoever liveth and believeth in me shall never die. Believest thou this? ²⁷She saith unto him, Yea, Lord: I believe that thou art the Christ, the Son of God, which should come into the world. ²⁸And when she had so said, she went her way, and called Mary her sister secretly, saying, The Master is come, and calleth for thee. ²⁹As soon as she heard *that*, she arose quickly, and came unto him. ³⁰Now Jesus was not yet come into the town, but was in that place where Martha met him. ³¹The Jews then which were with her in the house, and comforted her, when they saw Mary, that she rose up hastily and went out, followed her, saying, She goeth unto the grave to weep there. ³²Then when Mary was come where Jesus was, and saw him, she fell down at his feet, saying unto him, Lord, if thou hadst been here, my brother had not died.

³³When Jesus therefore saw her weeping, and the Jews also weeping which came with her, he groaned in the spirit, and was troubled^b, ³⁴And said, Where have ye laid him? They said unto him, Lord, come and see. ³⁵Jesus wept. ³⁶Then said the Jews, Behold how he loved him! ³⁷And some of them said, Could not this man, which opened the eyes of the blind, have caused that even this man should not have died? ³⁸Jesus therefore again groaning in himself cometh to the grave. It was a cave, and a stone lay upon it. ³⁹Jesus said, Take ye away the stone. Martha, the sister of him that was dead, saith unto him, Lord, by this time he stinketh: for he hath been *dead* four days. ⁴⁰Jesus saith unto her, Said I not unto thee, that, if thou wouldest believe, thou shouldest see the glory of God? ⁴¹Then they took away the stone *from the place* where the dead was laid. And Jesus lifted up *his* eyes, and said, Father, I thank thee that thou hast heard me. ⁴²And I knew that thou hearest me always: but because of the people which stand by I said *it*, that they may believe that thou hast sent me. ⁴³And when he thus had spoken, he cried with a loud voice, Lazarus, come forth. ⁴⁴And he that was dead came forth, bound hand and foot with graveclothes: and his face was bound about with a napkin. Jesus saith unto them, Loose him, and let him go.

⁴⁵Then many of the Jews which came to Mary, and had seen the things which Jesus did, believed on him. ⁴⁶But some of them went their ways to the Pharisees, and told them what things Jesus had done. ⁴⁷Then gathered the chief priests and the Pharisees a council, and said, What do we? for this man doeth many miracles. ⁴⁸If we let him

---

Devotional Moment
•
Mourning

11:33-38 Jesus let his feelings show. In many churches, mourning over the death of a loved one is regarded as a sign that one's faith is faulty. Stoic reserve—accepting "God's will"—shows greater faith, so it seems. But Jesus wept when Lazarus died.
Not everyone will show great emotion in mourning, but we need at least to allow the option. When you attend a wake, reach out and hug the grieving, hold their hands, and speak words of comfort to show that you share their feelings of loss.

---

^b was troubled: Gr. he troubled himself

thus alone, all *men* will believe on him: and the Romans shall come and take away both our place and nation. ⁴⁹And one of them, *named* Caiaphas, being the high priest that same year, said unto them, Ye know nothing at all, ⁵⁰Nor consider that it is expedient for us, that one man should die for the people, and that the whole nation perish not. ⁵¹And this spake he not of himself: but being high priest that year, he prophesied that Jesus should die for that nation; ⁵²And not for that nation only, but that also he should gather together in one the children of God that were scattered abroad. ⁵³Then from that day forth they took counsel together for to put him to death. ⁵⁴Jesus therefore walked no more openly among the Jews; but went thence unto a country near to the wilderness, into a city called Ephraim, and there continued with his disciples. ⁵⁵And the Jews' passover was nigh at hand: and many went out of the country up to Jerusalem before the passover, to purify themselves. ⁵⁶Then sought they for Jesus, and spake among themselves, as they stood in the temple, What think ye, that he will not come to the feast? ⁵⁷Now both the chief priests and the Pharisees had given a commandment, that, if any man knew where he were, he should shew *it*, that they might take him.

12

¹Then Jesus six days before the passover came to Bethany, where Lazarus was which had been dead, whom he raised from the dead. ²There they made him a supper; and Martha served: but Lazarus was one of them that sat at the table with him. ³Then took Mary a pound of ointment of spikenard, very costly, and anointed the feet of Jesus, and wiped his feet with her hair: and the house was filled with the odour of the ointment. ⁴Then saith one of his disciples, Judas Iscariot, Simon's *son*, which should betray him, ⁵Why was not this ointment sold for three hundred pence, and given to the poor? ⁶This he said, not that he cared for the poor; but because he was a thief, and had the bag, and bare what was put therein. ⁷Then said Jesus, Let her alone: against the day of my burying hath she kept this. ⁸For the poor always ye have with you; but me ye have not always. ⁹Much people of the Jews therefore knew that he was there: and they came not for Jesus' sake only, but that they might see Lazarus also, whom he had raised from the dead. ¹⁰But the chief priests consulted that they might put Lazarus also to death; ¹¹Because that by reason of him many of the Jews went away, and believed on Jesus.

¹²On the next day much people that were come to the feast, when they

Devotional Moment

•

Money

12:4-8 Most families think of money a lot. There's never enough, and we always seek more. That can make it hard to be willing to support the Lord's work.

Judas seemed to have a good reason for not wanting to honor Jesus with something of value: He claimed he wanted to give the money to the poor. In reality, it was just an excuse to try to hold on to the money for his own use.

When we set limits on our giving, we need to carefully examine our reasons for doing so. Are they legitimate (such as responsible savings plans for education or retirement), or are they simply excuses for having more money to spend on ourselves now?

heard that Jesus was coming to Jerusalem, ¹³Took branches of palm trees, and went forth to meet him, and cried, Hosanna: Blessed *is* the King of Israel that cometh in the name of the Lord. ¹⁴And Jesus, when he had found a young ass, sat thereon; as it is written, ¹⁵Fear not, daughter of Sion: behold, thy King cometh, sitting on an ass's colt. ¹⁶These things understood not his disciples at the first: but when Jesus was glorified, then remembered they that these things were written of him, and *that* they had done these things unto him. ¹⁷The people therefore that was with him when he called Lazarus out of his grave, and raised him from the dead, bare record. ¹⁸For this cause the people also met him, for that they heard that he had done this miracle. ¹⁹The Pharisees therefore said among themselves, Perceive ye how ye prevail nothing? behold, the world is gone after him.

²⁰And there were certain Greeks among them that came up to worship at the feast: ²¹The same came therefore to Philip, which was of Bethsaida of Galilee, and desired him, saying, Sir, we would see Jesus. ²²Philip cometh and telleth Andrew: and again Andrew and Philip tell Jesus. ²³And Jesus answered them, saying, The hour is come, that the Son of man should be glorified. ²⁴Verily, verily, I say unto you, Except a corn of wheat fall into the ground and die, it abideth alone: but if it die, it bringeth forth much fruit. ²⁵He that loveth his life shall lose it; and he that hateth his life in this world shall keep it unto life eternal. ²⁶If any man serve me, let him follow me; and where I am, there shall also my servant be: if any

man serve me, him will *my* Father honour.

²⁷Now is my soul troubled; and what shall I say? Father, save me from this hour: but for this cause came I unto this hour. ²⁸Father, glorify thy name. Then came there a voice from heaven, *saying*, I have both glorified *it*, and will glorify *it* again. ²⁹The people therefore, that stood by, and heard *it*, said that it thundered: others said, An angel spake to him. ³⁰Jesus answered and said, This voice came not because of me, but for your sakes. ³¹Now is the judgment of this world: now shall the prince of this world be cast out. ³²And I, if I be lifted up from the earth, will draw all *men* unto me. ³³This he said, signifying what death he should die. ³⁴The people answered him, We have heard out of the law that Christ abideth for ever: and how sayest thou, The Son of man must be lifted up? who is this Son of man? ³⁵Then Jesus said unto them, Yet a little while is the light with you. Walk while ye have the light, lest darkness come upon you: for he that walketh in darkness knoweth not whither he goeth. ³⁶While ye have light, believe in the light, that ye may be the children of light. These things spake Jesus, and departed, and did hide himself from them.

³⁷But though he had done so many miracles before them, yet they believed not on him: ³⁸That the saying of Esaias the prophet might be fulfilled, which he spake, Lord, who hath believed our report? and to whom hath the arm of the Lord been revealed? ³⁹Therefore they could not believe, because that Esaias said again, ⁴⁰He hath blinded their eyes, and hardened their heart;

that they should not see with *their* eyes, nor understand with *their* heart, and be converted, and I should heal them. ⁴¹These things said Esaias, when he saw his glory, and spake of him.

⁴²Nevertheless among the chief rulers also many believed on him; but because of the Pharisees they did not confess *him*, lest they should be put out of the synagogue: ⁴³For they loved the praise of men more than the praise of God.

⁴⁴Jesus cried and said, He that believeth on me, believeth not on me, but on him that sent me. ⁴⁵And he that seeth me seeth him that sent me. ⁴⁶I am come a light into the world, that whosoever believeth on me should not abide in darkness. ⁴⁷And if any man hear my words, and believe not, I judge him not: for I came not to judge the world, but to save the world. ⁴⁸He that rejecteth me, and receiveth not my words, hath one that judgeth him: the word that I have spoken, the same shall judge him in the last day. ⁴⁹For I have not spoken of myself; but the Father which sent me, he gave me a commandment, what I should say, and what I should speak. ⁵⁰And I know that his commandment is life everlasting: whatsoever I speak therefore, even as the Father said unto me, so I speak.

13

¹Now before the feast of the passover, when Jesus knew that his hour was come that he should depart out of this world unto the Father, having loved his own which were in the world, he loved them unto the end. ²And supper being ended,

the devil having now put into the heart of Judas Iscariot, Simon's *son*, to betray him; ³Jesus knowing that the Father had given all things into his hands, and that he was come from God, and went to God; ⁴He riseth from supper, and laid aside his garments; and took a towel, and girded himself. ⁵After that he poureth water into a bason, and began to wash the disciples' feet, and to wipe *them* with the towel wherewith he was girded. ⁶Then cometh he to Simon Peter: and Peter saithᵃ unto him, Lord, dost thou wash my feet? ⁷Jesus answered and said unto him, What I do thou knowest not now; but thou shalt know hereafter. ⁸Peter saith unto him, Thou shalt never wash my feet. Jesus answered him, If I wash thee not, thou hast no part with me. ⁹Simon Peter saith unto him, Lord, not my feet only, but also *my* hands and *my* head. ¹⁰Jesus saith to him, He that is washed needeth not save to wash *his* feet, but is clean every whit: and ye are clean, but not all. ¹¹For he knew who should betray him; therefore said he, Ye are not all clean. ¹²So after he had washed their feet, and had taken his garments, and was set down again, he said unto them, Know ye what I have done to you? ¹³Ye call me Master and Lord: and ye say well; for *so* I am. ¹⁴If I then, *your* Lord and Master, have washed your feet; ye also ought to wash one another's feet. ¹⁵For I have given you an example, that ye should do as I have done to you. ¹⁶Verily, verily, I say unto you, The servant is not greater than his lord; neither he that is sent greater than he that sent him. ¹⁷If ye know these things, happy are ye if ye do them.

ᵃ Peter saith: Gr. he saith

Jesus Understands Our Grief

by Dale Hanson Bourke

"It's hopeless." When I heard the doctor use these words about my father, I was angry. I wanted to hold on to the last shred of hope, even when human reasoning told me it would be foolish to believe in my dad's recovery.

Mary and Martha could see that their situation was hopeless. They had hoped and prayed for Jesus to come and save their brother, Lazarus, but by the time Jesus arrived, Lazarus had been dead four days. They had hoped the man who could heal the blind would save his beloved friend. But it was too late.

Both Mary and Martha expressed sorrow that Jesus had arrived too late. And yet Martha, despite the evidence, was willing to acknowledge that Jesus was capable of performing any miracle. She didn't understand how it could happen, but she did know that somehow, in some way, anything was possible.

As I saw the evidence of disease and the toll it had taken on my father's body, I knew the doctor was right. My once-healthy, vibrant father lay in a coma, the brain tumor robbing him of consciousness, the medications creating side effects that were as lethal as the cancer itself. The physical facts were there for anyone to see.

The nurses who lovingly tended my father encouraged me to talk to him, to touch him, and to believe that he was aware of my presence. And so, feeling foolish at first, I began to talk to my father and remind him of the many happy memories we had as a family. I told him of all the wisdom I had learned from him, and I thanked him for being such a good father.

I touched his cheek and gently hugged him, telling him I knew he wanted to tell us once more that he loved us all, and that we all knew he did. I told him I understood that he wanted to be there to take care of us, just as he always had. I told him he had done a good job. He had given us all we needed, and it was all right for him to rest now.

I knew that Jesus cared about my father, and he cared about me. I somehow knew he would honor my father's faithfulness. I didn't know if that meant he would perform a miracle and raise my father up or simply let him go peacefully, releasing him from the body that was wracked with disease. Like Martha, I struggled to believe that the reality I saw was not all there was.

As my father's breathing grew more labored, I began to see the signs of death that the doctor had described. Remembering the advice of the nurses, I tried to comfort my father and ease his passage for him. I reminded him that we would see him again in heaven, and I tried desperately to gain comfort from that belief. I wondered if my father could hear my words or feel my touch.

And then a remarkable thing happened: My father wept.

It was remarkable because he was in a coma and dehydrated. Even before the coma, his tear glands had been blocked, causing his eyes to become dry and irritated. And yet, as he drew his last breath, my father wept. Somehow I knew it was out of both sorrow from leaving us and joy in the reality of heaven. To me, it was a miracle and a great comfort.

As I read John 11:35, I am reminded that Jesus understood my grief and pain at that point—and he still understands now, years later. Part of his earthly experience was to feel that pain of loss. God the Son went through the human pain of grief before he raised Lazarus.

And when Jesus prays to the Father, it is a reminder to all of us that God always hears us, even at our points of deepest grief and desolation.

There are no easy ways to grieve. It is a process that wrenches us out of life as we know it. But it is a comfort to know that Jesus feels our pain. He does not promise to heal our loved ones, but he does promise always to hear us. For me, the confirmation that my father knew I was there was a great blessing. And it was a reminder that my heavenly Father hears me, too, even when I don't immediately see the evidence of his response.

DIGGING DEEPER

1. How can Christians grieve differently from non-Christians? See 1 Thessalonians 4:13-17.

2. In what ways is grieving like childbirth? See John 16:19-24.

3. What promise do we have about death and resurrection? See 1 Corinthians 15.

¹⁸I speak not of you all: I know whom I have chosen: but that the scripture may be fulfilled, He that eateth bread with me hath lifted up his heel against me. ¹⁹Now[b] I tell you before it come, that, when it is come to pass, ye may believe that I am *he*. ²⁰Verily, verily, I say unto you, He that receiveth whomsoever I send receiveth me; and he that receiveth me receiveth him that sent me. ²¹When Jesus had thus said, he was troubled in spirit, and testified, and said, Verily, verily, I say unto you, that one of you shall betray me. ²²Then the disciples looked one on another, doubting of whom he spake. ²³Now there was leaning on Jesus' bosom one of his disciples, whom Jesus loved. ²⁴Simon Peter therefore beckoned to him, that he should ask who it should be of whom he spake. ²⁵He then lying on Jesus' breast saith unto him, Lord, who is it? ²⁶Jesus answered, He it is, to whom I shall give a sop[c], when I have dipped *it*. And when he had dipped the sop, he gave *it* to Judas Iscariot, *the son* of Simon. ²⁷And after the sop Satan entered into him. Then said Jesus unto him,

That thou doest, do quickly. ²⁸Now no man at the table knew for what intent he spake this unto him. ²⁹For some *of them* thought, because Judas had the bag, that Jesus had said unto him, Buy *those things* that we have need of against the feast; or, that he should give something to the poor. ³⁰He then having received the sop went immediately out: and it was night.

³¹Therefore, when he was gone out, Jesus said, Now is the Son of man glorified, and God is glorified in him.

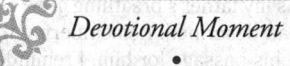

Devotional Moment
•
Let Love Prevail

13:34-35 Such a simple command Jesus gave: Love each other. Yet it can be so difficult to keep. Every family member has occasional trouble loving people: Preschoolers holler, "I hate you!"; adolescents are sure that the world is filled with fools; and many adults believe that most other people are enemies of some kind. Yet Jesus commands that love prevail. Let love thrive in you. Say kind words to others, pray for your "enemies," forgive liberally. Let love prevail.

ᵇ Now: or, From henceforth

ᶜ sop: or, morsel

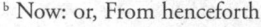

³²If God be glorified in him, God shall also glorify him in himself, and shall straightway glorify him. ³³Little children, yet a little while I am with you. Ye shall seek me: and as I said unto the Jews, Whither I go, ye cannot come; so now I say to you. ³⁴A new commandment I give unto you, That ye love one another; as I have loved you, that ye also love one another. ³⁵By this shall all *men* know that ye are my disciples, if ye have love one to another.

³⁶Simon Peter said unto him, Lord, whither goest thou? Jesus answered him, Whither I go, thou canst not follow me now; but thou shalt follow me afterwards. ³⁷Peter said unto him, Lord, why cannot I follow thee now? I will lay down my life for thy sake. ³⁸Jesus answered him, Wilt thou lay down thy life for my sake? Verily, verily, I say unto thee, The cock shall not crow, till thou hast denied me thrice.

14

¹Let not your heart be troubled: ye believe in God, believe also in me. ²In my Father's house are many mansions: if *it were* not *so*, I would have told you. I go to prepare a place for you. ³And if I go and prepare a place for you, I will come again, and receive you unto myself; that where I am, *there* ye may be also. ⁴And whither I go ye know, and the way ye know. ⁵Thomas saith unto him, Lord, we know not whither thou goest; and how can we know the way? ⁶Jesus saith unto him, I am the way, the truth, and the life: no man cometh unto the Father, but by me. ⁷If ye had known me, ye should have known my Father also: and from henceforth ye know him, and have seen him. ⁸Philip saith unto him, Lord, shew us the Father, and it sufficeth us. ⁹Jesus saith unto him, Have I been so long time with you, and yet hast thou not known me, Philip? he that hath seen me hath seen the Father; and how sayest thou *then*, Shew us the Father? ¹⁰Believest thou not that I am in the Father, and the Father in me? the words that I speak unto you I speak not of myself: but the Father that dwelleth in me, he doeth the works. ¹¹Believe me that I *am* in the Father, and the Father in me: or else believe me for the very works' sake.

¹²Verily, verily, I say unto you, He that believeth on me, the works that I do shall he do also; and greater *works* than these shall he do; because I go unto my Father. ¹³And whatsoever ye shall ask in my name, that will I do, that the Father may be glorified in the Son. ¹⁴If ye shall ask any thing in my name, I will do *it*.

¹⁵If ye love me, keep my commandments. ¹⁶And I will pray the Father, and he shall give you another Comforter, that he may abide with you for ever; ¹⁷*Even* the Spirit of truth; whom the world cannot receive, because it seeth him not, neither knoweth him: but ye know him; for he dwelleth with you, and shall be in you.

¹⁸I will not leave you comfortlessᵃ: I will come to you. ¹⁹Yet a little while, and the world seeth me no more; but ye see me: because I live, ye shall live also. ²⁰At that day ye shall know that I *am* in my Father, and ye in me, and I in you. ²¹He that hath my commandments,

---

ᵃ comfortless: or, orphans

Devotional Moment

•

Never Abandoned

14:18 Jesus promised to keep us company: "I will not abandon you or leave you as orphans." *Family* often means love and companionship, loyalty and support—but not always. For some people, *family* means abuse, hurt, bitter disappointment, abandonment, and loneliness. Many wives wish their husbands would say, "I will not leave you." Many children want to hear this promise from parents. Today both men and women abandon marriage and family and leave hearts longing for faithful love. Jesus promises comfort with the perfect faithfulness only he can offer: He will not leave.

and keepeth them, he it is that loveth me: and he that loveth me shall be loved of my Father, and I will love him, and will manifest myself to him. ²²Judas saith unto him, not Iscariot, Lord, how is it that thou wilt manifest thyself unto us, and not unto the world? ²³Jesus answered and said unto him, If a man love me, he will keep my words: and my Father will love him, and we will come unto him, and make our abode with him. ²⁴He that loveth me not keepeth not my sayings: and the word which ye hear is not mine, but the Father's which sent me.

²⁵These things have I spoken unto you, being *yet* present with you. ²⁶But the Comforter, *which is* the Holy Ghost, whom the Father will send in my name, he shall teach you all things, and bring all things to your remembrance, whatsoever I have said unto you. ²⁷Peace I leave with you, my peace I give unto you: not as the world giveth, give I unto you. Let not your heart be troubled, neither let it be afraid. ²⁸Ye have heard how I said unto you, I go away, and come *again* unto

you. If ye loved me, ye would rejoice, because I said, I go unto the Father: for my Father is greater than I. ²⁹And now I have told you before it come to pass, that, when it is come to pass, ye might believe. ³⁰Hereafter I will not talk much with you: for the prince of this world cometh, and hath nothing in me. ³¹But that the world may know that I love the Father; and as the Father gave me commandment, even so I do. Arise, let us go hence.

15

¹I am the true vine, and my Father is the husbandman. ²Every branch in me that beareth not fruit he taketh away: and every *branch* that beareth fruit, he purgeth it, that it may bring forth more fruit. ³Now ye are clean through the word which I have spoken unto you. ⁴Abide in me, and I in you. As the branch cannot bear fruit of itself, except it abide in the vine; no more can ye, except ye abide in me. ⁵I am the vine, ye *are* the branches: He that abideth in me, and I in him, the same bringeth forth much fruit: for without me ye can do nothing. ⁶If a man abide not in me, he is cast forth as a branch, and is withered; and men gather them, and cast *them* into the fire, and they are burned. ⁷If ye abide in me, and my words abide in you, ye shall ask what ye will, and it shall be done unto you. ⁸Herein is my Father glorified, that ye bear much fruit; so shall ye be my disciples.

⁹As the Father hath loved me, so have I loved you: continue ye in my love. ¹⁰If ye keep my commandments, ye shall abide in my love; even as I have kept my Father's commandments, and abide in his love. ¹¹These things have I

spoken unto you, that my joy might remain in you, and *that* your joy might be full. ¹²This is my commandment, That ye love one another, as I have loved you. ¹³Greater love hath no man than this, that a man lay down his life for his friends. ¹⁴Ye are my friends, if ye do whatsoever I command you. ¹⁵Henceforth I call you not servants; for the servant knoweth not what his lord doeth: but I have called you friends; for all things that I have heard of my Father I have made known unto you. ¹⁶Ye have not chosen me, but I have chosen you, and ordained you, that ye should go and bring forth fruit, and *that* your fruit should remain: that whatsoever ye shall ask of the Father in my name, he may give it you. ¹⁷These things I command you, that ye love one another.

¹⁸If the world hate you, ye know

Devotional Moment

Love

15:12 Jesus' command that we love one another went beyond the mere statement, "Love each other." He commanded us to copy his example—to love as he loved. The so-called *love* touted in popular music, movies, and romance novels comes and goes, a fluke of the emotions, something you can fall into and out of. The world's kind of love can't be commanded because it can't be controlled! It involves no commitment, only hopes.

Jesus says, "Love as I have loved you." Even a surface familiarity with Jesus tells us that his kind of love is unconditional, sacrificial, selfless, committed, and indestructible. That kind of love makes all the difference. It is God's way—a commitment to keep loving whether it feels good or not.

that it hated me before *it hated* you. ¹⁹If ye were of the world, the world would love his own: but because ye are not of the world, but I have chosen you out of the world, therefore the world hateth you. ²⁰Remember the word that I said unto you, The servant is not greater than his lord. If they have persecuted me, they will also persecute you; if they have kept my saying, they will keep yours also. ²¹But all these things will they do unto you for my name's sake, because they know not him that sent me. ²²If I had not come and spoken unto them, they had not had sin: but now they have no cloke[a] for their sin. ²³He that hateth me hateth my Father also. ²⁴If I had not done among them the works which none other man did, they had not had sin: but now have they both seen and hated both me and my Father. ²⁵But *this cometh to pass*, that the word might be fulfilled that is written in their law, They hated me without a cause.

²⁶But when the Comforter is come, whom I will send unto you from the Father, *even* the Spirit of truth, which proceedeth from the Father, he shall testify of me: ²⁷And ye also shall bear witness, because ye have been with me from the beginning.

16

¹These things have I spoken unto you, that ye should not be offended[a]. ²They shall put you out of the synagogues: yea, the time cometh, that whosoever killeth you will think that he doeth God service. ³And these things will they

---

[a] cloke: or, excuse
[a] offended: scandalized or, made to stumble

do unto you, because they have not known the Father, nor me. 4But these things have I told you, that when the time shall come, ye may remember that I told you of them. And these things I said not unto you at the beginning, because I was with you. 5But now I go my way to him that sent me; and none of you asketh me, Whither goest thou? 6But because I have said these things unto you, sorrow hath filled your heart.

7Nevertheless I tell you the truth; It is expedient for you that I go away: for if I go not away, the Comforter will not come unto you; but if I depart, I will send him unto you. 8And when he is come, he will reprove[b] the world of sin, and of righteousness, and of judgment: 9Of sin, because they believe not on me; 10Of righteousness, because I go to my Father, and ye see me no more; 11Of judgment, because the prince of this world is judged. 12I have yet many things to say unto you, but ye cannot bear them now. 13Howbeit when he, the Spirit of truth, is come, he will guide you into all truth: for he shall not speak of himself; but whatsoever he shall hear, *that* shall he speak: and he will shew you things to come. 14He shall glorify me: for he shall receive of mine, and shall shew *it* unto you. 15All things that the Father hath are mine: therefore said I, that he shall take of mine, and shall shew *it* unto you.

16A little while, and ye shall not see me: and again, a little while, and ye shall see me, because I go to the Father. 17Then said *some* of his disciples among themselves, What is this that he saith unto us, A little while, and ye shall not see me: and again, a little while, and ye shall see me: and, Because I go to the Father? 18They said therefore, What is this that he saith, A little while? we cannot tell what he saith. 19Now Jesus knew that they were desirous to ask him, and said unto them, Do ye enquire among yourselves of that I said, A little while, and ye shall not see me: and again, a little while, and ye shall see me? 20Verily, verily, I say unto you, That ye shall weep and lament, but the world shall rejoice: and ye shall be sorrowful, but your sorrow shall be turned into joy. 21A woman when she is in travail hath sorrow, because her hour is come: but as soon as she is delivered of the child, she remembereth no more the anguish, for joy that a man is born into the world. 22And ye now therefore have sorrow: but I will see you again, and your heart shall rejoice, and your joy no man taketh from you.

23And in that day ye shall ask me nothing. Verily, verily, I say unto you, Whatsoever ye shall ask the Father in my name, he will give *it* you. 24Hitherto have ye asked nothing in my name: ask, and ye shall receive, that your joy may be full. 25These things have I spoken unto you in proverbs[c]: but the time cometh, when I shall no more speak unto you in proverbs, but I shall shew you plainly of the Father. 26At that day ye shall ask in my name: and I say not unto you, that I will pray the Father for you: 27For the Father himself loveth you, because ye have loved me, and have believed that I came out from God.

---

b reprove: or, convince
c proverbs: or, parables

²⁸I came forth from the Father, and am come into the world: again, I leave the world, and go to the Father. ²⁹His disciples said unto him, Lo, now speakest thou plainly, and speakest no proverb[d]. ³⁰Now are we sure that thou knowest all things, and needest not that any man should ask thee: by this we believe that thou camest forth from God. ³¹Jesus answered them, Do ye now believe? ³²Behold, the hour cometh, yea, is now come, that ye shall be scattered, every man to his own[e], and shall leave me alone: and yet I am not alone, because the Father is with me. ³³These things I have spoken unto you, that in me ye might have peace. In the world ye shall have tribulation: but be of good cheer; I have overcome the world.

17

¹These words spake Jesus, and lifted up his eyes to heaven, and said, Father, the hour is come; glorify thy Son, that thy Son also may glorify thee: ²As thou hast given him power over all flesh, that he should give eternal life to as many as thou hast given him. ³And this is life eternal, that they might know thee the only true God, and Jesus Christ, whom thou hast sent. ⁴I have glorified thee on the earth: I have finished the work which thou gavest me to do. ⁵And now, O Father, glorify thou me with thine own self with the glory which I had with thee before the world was.

⁶I have manifested thy name unto the men which thou gavest me out of the world: thine they were, and thou gavest them me; and they have kept thy word. ⁷Now they have known that all things whatsoever thou hast given me are of thee. ⁸For I have given unto them the words which thou gavest me; and they have received *them*, and have known surely that I came out from thee, and they have believed that thou didst send me. ⁹I pray for them: I pray not for the world, but for them which thou hast given me; for they are thine. ¹⁰And all mine are thine, and thine are mine; and I am glorified in them.

¹¹And now I am no more in the world, but these are in the world, and I come to thee. Holy Father, keep through thine own name those whom thou hast given me, that they may be one, as we *are*. ¹²While I was with them in the world, I kept them in thy name: those that thou gavest me I have kept, and none of them is lost, but the son of perdition; that the scripture might be fulfilled. ¹³And now come I to thee; and these things I speak in the world, that they might have my joy fulfilled in themselves. ¹⁴I have given them thy word; and the world hath hated them, because they are not of the world, even as I am not of the world. ¹⁵I pray not that thou shouldest take them out of the world, but that thou shouldest keep them from the evil. ¹⁶They are not of the world, even as I am not of the world. ¹⁷Sanctify them through thy truth: thy word is truth. ¹⁸As thou hast sent me into the world, even so have I also sent them into the world. ¹⁹And for their sakes I sanctify myself, that they also might be sanctified[a] through the truth.

²⁰Neither pray I for these alone, but

---

[d] proverb: or, parable
[e] his own: or, his own home
[a] sanctified . . . : or, truly sanctified

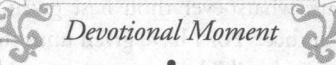

Devotional Moment
•
Purity

17:17 "Make them pure and holy," Jesus prayed. How can we possibly be holy in a world like ours? Is it even possible? Yes. Regular input from the Bible, Christian teaching, and music that honors God will lead us in quite an opposite direction than will repeated doses of the corruption that much of today's media has to offer. Examine your diet of TV, radio, music, concerts, movies, books, and magazines. Is there a change you need to make?

for them also which shall believe on me through their word; ²¹That they all may be one; as thou, Father, *art* in me, and I in thee, that they also may be one in us: that the world may believe that thou hast sent me. ²²And the glory which thou gavest me I have given them; that they may be one, even as we are one: ²³I in them, and thou in me, that they may be made perfect in one; and that the world may know that thou hast sent me, and hast loved them, as thou hast loved me. ²⁴Father, I will that they also, whom thou hast given me, be with me where I am; that they may behold my glory, which thou hast given me: for thou lovedst me before the foundation of the world. ²⁵O righteous Father, the world hath not known thee: but I have known thee, and these have known that thou hast sent me. ²⁶And I have declared unto them thy name, and will declare *it*: that the love wherewith thou hast loved me may be in them, and I in them.

18

¹When Jesus had spoken these words, he went forth with his disciples over the brook Cedron, where was a garden, into the which he entered, and his disciples. ²And Judas also, which betrayed him, knew the place: for Jesus ofttimes resorted thither with his disciples. ³Judas then, having received a band *of men* and officers from the chief priests and Pharisees, cometh thither with lanterns and torches and weapons. ⁴Jesus therefore, knowing all things that should come upon him, went forth, and said unto them, Whom seek ye? ⁵They answered him, Jesus of Nazareth. Jesus saith unto them, I am *he.* And Judas also, which betrayed him, stood with them. ⁶As soon then as he had said unto them, I am *he,* they went backward, and fell to the ground. ⁷Then asked he them again, Whom seek ye? And they said, Jesus of Nazareth. ⁸Jesus answered, I have told you that I am *he*: if therefore ye seek me, let these go their way: ⁹That the saying might be fulfilled, which he spake, Of them which thou gavest me have I lost none. ¹⁰Then Simon Peter having a sword drew it, and smote the high priest's servant, and cut off his right ear. The servant's name was Malchus. ¹¹Then said Jesus unto Peter, Put up thy sword into the sheath: the cup which my Father hath given me, shall I not drink it? ¹²Then the band and the captain and officers of the Jews took Jesus, and bound him, ¹³And led him away to Annas first; for he was father in law to Caiaphas, which was the high priest that same yearᵃ. ¹⁴Now Caiaphas was he, which gave counsel to the Jews, that it was expedient that one man should die for the people. ¹⁵And Simon Peter followed Je-

---

ᵃ year: year. And Annas sent Christ bound unto Caiaphas the high priest

sus, and *so did* another disciple: that disciple was known unto the high priest, and went in with Jesus into the palace of the high priest. ¹⁶But Peter stood at the door without. Then went out that other disciple, which was known unto the high priest, and spake unto her that kept the door, and brought in Peter. ¹⁷Then saith the damsel that kept the door unto Peter, Art not thou also *one* of this man's disciples? He saith, I am not. ¹⁸And the servants and officers stood there, who had made a fire of coals; for it was cold: and they warmed themselves: and Peter stood with them, and warmed himself. ¹⁹The high priest then asked Jesus of his disciples, and of his doctrine. ²⁰Jesus answered him, I spake openly to the world; I ever taught in the synagogue, and in the temple, whither the Jews always resort; and in secret have I said nothing. ²¹Why askest thou me? ask them which heard me, what I have said unto them: behold, they know what I said. ²²And when he had thus spoken, one of the officers which stood by struck Jesus with the palm of his hand, saying, Answerest thou the high priest so? ²³Jesus answered him, If I have spoken evil, bear witness of the evil: but if well, why smitest thou me? ²⁴Now Annas had sent him bound unto Caiaphas the high priest. ²⁵And Simon Peter stood and warmed himself. They said therefore unto him, Art not thou also *one* of his disciples? He denied *it*, and said, I am not. ²⁶One of the servants of the high priest, being *his* kinsman whose ear Peter cut off, saith, Did not I see thee in the garden with him? ²⁷Peter then denied again: and immediately the cock crew.

²⁸Then led they Jesus from Caiaphas unto the hall of judgment: and it was early; and they themselves went not into the judgment hall, lest they should be defiled; but that they might eat the passover. ²⁹Pilate then went out unto them, and said, What accusation bring ye against this man? ³⁰They answered and said unto him, If he were not a malefactor, we would not have delivered him up unto thee. ³¹Then said Pilate unto them, Take ye him, and judge him according to your law. The Jews therefore said unto him, It is not lawful for us to put any man to death: ³²That the saying of Jesus might be fulfilled, which he spake, signifying what death he should die. ³³Then Pilate entered into the judgment hall again, and called Jesus, and said unto him, Art thou the King of the Jews? ³⁴Jesus answered him, Sayest thou this thing of thyself, or did others tell it thee of me? ³⁵Pilate answered, Am I a Jew? Thine own nation and the chief priests have delivered thee unto me: what hast thou done? ³⁶Jesus answered, My kingdom is not of this world: if my kingdom were of this world, then would my servants fight, that I should not be delivered to the Jews: but now is my kingdom not from hence. ³⁷Pilate therefore said unto him, Art thou a king then? Jesus answered, Thou sayest that I am a king. To this end was I born, and for this cause came I into the world, that I should bear witness unto the truth. Every one that is of the truth heareth my voice. ³⁸Pilate saith unto him, What is truth? And when he had said this, he went out again unto the Jews, and saith unto them, I find in him no fault *at all*. ³⁹But ye have a custom, that I should release

unto you one at the passover: will ye therefore that I release unto you the King of the Jews? ⁴⁰Then cried they all again, saying, Not this man, but Barabbas. Now Barabbas was a robber.

19

¹Then Pilate therefore took Jesus, and scourged *him*. ²And the soldiers platted a crown of thorns, and put *it* on his head, and they put on him a purple robe, ³And said, Hail, King of the Jews! and they smote him with their hands. ⁴Pilate therefore went forth again, and saith unto them, Behold, I bring him forth to you, that ye may know that I find no fault in him. ⁵Then came Jesus forth, wearing the crown of thorns, and the purple robe. And *Pilate* saith unto them, Behold the man! ⁶When the chief priests therefore and officers saw him, they cried out, saying, Crucify *him*, crucify *him*. Pilate saith unto them, Take ye him, and crucify *him*: for I find no fault in him. ⁷The Jews answered him, We have a law, and by our law he ought to die, because he made himself the Son of God. ⁸When Pilate therefore heard that saying, he was the more afraid; ⁹And went again into the judgment hall, and saith unto Jesus, Whence art thou? But Jesus gave him no answer. ¹⁰Then saith Pilate unto him, Speakest thou not unto me? knowest thou not that I have power to crucify thee, and have power to release thee? ¹¹Jesus answered, Thou couldest have no power *at all* against me, except it were given thee from above: therefore he that delivered me unto thee hath the greater sin. ¹²And from thenceforth Pilate sought to release him: but the Jews

cried out, saying, If thou let this man go, thou art not Caesar's friend: whosoever maketh himself a king speaketh against Caesar. ¹³When Pilate therefore heard that saying, he brought Jesus forth, and sat down in the judgment seat in a place that is called the Pavement, but in the Hebrew, Gabbatha. ¹⁴And it was the preparation of the passover, and about the sixth hour: and he saith unto the Jews, Behold your King! ¹⁵But they cried out, Away with *him*, away with *him*, crucify him. Pilate saith unto them, Shall I crucify your King? The chief priests answered, We have no king but Caesar.

¹⁶Then delivered he him therefore unto them to be crucified. And they took Jesus, and led *him* away. ¹⁷And he bearing his cross went forth into a place called *the place* of a skull, which is called in the Hebrew Golgotha: ¹⁸Where they crucified him, and two other with him, on either side one, and Jesus in the midst.

¹⁹And Pilate wrote a title, and put *it* on the cross. And the writing was, JESUS OF NAZARETH THE KING OF THE JEWS. ²⁰This title then read many of the Jews: for the place where Jesus was crucified was nigh to the city: and it was written in Hebrew, *and* Greek, *and* Latin. ²¹Then said the chief priests of the Jews to Pilate, Write not, The King of the Jews; but that he said, I am King of the Jews. ²²Pilate answered, What I have written I have written. ²³Then the soldiers, when they had crucified Jesus, took his garments, and made four parts, to every soldier a part; and also *his* coat: now the coat was without seam, woven* from the top throughout. ²⁴They said therefore among

---

ᵃ woven: or, wrought

themselves, Let us not rend it, but cast lots for it, whose it shall be: that the scripture might be fulfilled, which saith, They parted my raiment among them, and for my vesture they did cast lots. These things therefore the soldiers did. ²⁵Now there stood by the cross of Jesus his mother, and his mother's sister, Mary the *wife* of Cleophas*ᵇ*, and Mary Magdalene. ²⁶When Jesus therefore saw his mother, and the disciple standing by, whom he loved, he saith unto his mother, Woman, behold thy son! ²⁷Then saith he to the disciple, Behold thy mother! And from that hour that disciple took her unto his own *home*. ²⁸After this, Jesus knowing that all things were now accomplished, that the scripture might be fulfilled, saith, I thirst. ²⁹Now there was set a vessel full of vinegar: and they filled a spunge with vinegar, and put *it* upon hyssop, and put *it* to his mouth. ³⁰When Jesus therefore had received the vinegar, he said, It is finished: and he bowed his head, and gave up the ghost.

³¹The Jews therefore, because it was the preparation, that the bodies should not remain upon the cross on the sabbath day, (for that sabbath day was an high day,) besought Pilate that their legs might be broken, and *that* they might be taken away. ³²Then came the soldiers, and brake the legs of the first, and of the other which was crucified with him. ³³But when they came to Jesus, and saw that he was dead already, they brake not his legs: ³⁴But one of the soldiers with a spear pierced his side, and forthwith came there out blood and water. ³⁵And he that saw *it* bare record, and his record is true: and he knoweth that he saith true, that ye might believe. ³⁶For these things were done, that the scripture should be fulfilled, A bone of him shall not be broken. ³⁷And again another scripture saith, They shall look on him whom they pierced.

³⁸And after this Joseph of Arimathaea, being a disciple of Jesus, but secretly for fear of the Jews, besought Pilate that he might take away the body of Jesus: and Pilate gave *him* leave. He came therefore, and took the body of Jesus. ³⁹And there came also Nicodemus, which at the first came to Jesus by night, and brought a mixture of myrrh and aloes, about an hundred pound *weight*. ⁴⁰Then took they the body of Jesus, and wound it in linen clothes with the spices, as the manner of the Jews is to bury. ⁴¹Now in the place where he was crucified there was a garden; and in the garden a new sepulchre, wherein was never man yet laid. ⁴²There laid they Jesus therefore because of the Jews' preparation *day*; for the sepulchre was nigh at hand.

20

¹The first *day* of the week cometh Mary Magdalene early, when it was yet dark,

---

Devotional Moment
•
Priority One

19:25-27 Even as he was dying on the cross, Jesus was concerned about his mother's welfare. He entrusted her into the care of John, his friend and disciple. John became an adopted son, trustee, helper, and caretaker. The Bible teaches that Christians have a wide and serious responsibility to their families (see 1 Tim. 5:8). Treat your family with tender, loving care. Spend time with them. Make sure you provide for their needs, through your work, life insurance, and a will.

ᵇ Cleophas: or, Clopas

unto the sepulchre, and seeth the stone taken away from the sepulchre. ²Then she runneth, and cometh to Simon Peter, and to the other disciple, whom Jesus loved, and saith unto them, They have taken away the Lord out of the sepulchre, and we know not where they have laid him. ³Peter therefore went forth, and that other disciple, and came to the sepulchre. ⁴So they ran both together: and the other disciple did outrun Peter, and came first to the sepulchre. ⁵And he stooping down, *and looking in,* saw the linen clothes lying; yet went he not in. ⁶Then cometh Simon Peter following him, and went into the sepulchre, and seeth the linen clothes lie, ⁷And the napkin, that was about his head, not lying with the linen clothes, but wrapped together in a place by itself. ⁸Then went in also that other disciple, which came first to the sepulchre, and he saw, and believed. ⁹For as yet they knew not the scripture, that he must rise again from the dead. ¹⁰Then the disciples went away again unto their own home.

¹¹But Mary stood without at the sepulchre weeping: and as she wept, she stooped down, *and looked* into the sepulchre, ¹²And seeth two angels in white sitting, the one at the head, and the other at the feet, where the body of Jesus had lain. ¹³And they say unto her, Woman, why weepest thou? She saith unto them, Because they have taken away my Lord, and I know not where they have laid him. ¹⁴And when she had thus said, she turned herself back, and saw Jesus standing, and knew not that it was Jesus. ¹⁵Jesus saith unto her, Woman, why weepest thou? whom seekest thou? She, supposing him to be the gardener, saith unto him, Sir, if thou have borne him hence, tell me where thou hast laid him, and I will take him away. ¹⁶Jesus saith unto her, Mary. She turned herself, and saith unto him, Rabboni; which is to say, Master. ¹⁷Jesus saith unto her, Touch me not; for I am not yet ascended to my Father: but go to my brethren, and say unto them, I ascend unto my Father, and your Father; and *to* my God, and your God. ¹⁸Mary Magdalene came and told the disciples that she had seen the Lord, and *that* he had spoken these things unto her.

¹⁹Then the same day at evening, being the first *day* of the week, when the doors were shut where the disciples were assembled for fear of the Jews, came Jesus and stood in the midst, and saith unto them, Peace *be* unto you. ²⁰And when he had so said, he shewed unto them *his* hands and his side. Then were the disciples glad, when they saw the Lord. ²¹Then said Jesus to them again, Peace *be* unto you: as *my* Father hath sent me, even so send I you. ²²And

---

Devotional Moment

•

Forgiving

20:23 Jesus granted power to his disciples on a grander scale and with far greater consequences than the kind of power any government official is familiar with. Acting on his behalf and guided by the Spirit, these disciples had the authority to forgive sin.

If we do not practice forgiveness we may store up an attic full of anger, and cleaning out is hard work. If we keep short accounts—dealing with hurts and wrongs as they come up—we can bring the awesome power of forgiveness into the very heart of our homes.

when he had said this, he breathed on *them*, and saith unto them, Receive ye the Holy Ghost: ²³Whosesoever sins ye remit, they are remitted unto them; *and* whosesoever *sins* ye retain, they are retained. ²⁴But Thomas, one of the twelve, called Didymus, was not with them when Jesus came. ²⁵The other disciples therefore said unto him, We have seen the Lord. But he said unto them, Except I shall see in his hands the print of the nails, and put my finger into the print of the nails, and thrust my hand into his side, I will not believe.

²⁶And after eight days again his disciples were within, and Thomas with them: *then* came Jesus, the doors being shut, and stood in the midst, and said, Peace *be* unto you. ²⁷Then saith he to Thomas, Reach hither thy finger, and behold my hands; and reach hither thy hand, and thrust *it* into my side: and be not faithless, but believing. ²⁸And Thomas answered and said unto him, My Lord and my God. ²⁹Jesus saith unto him, Thomas, because thou hast seen me, thou hast believed: blessed *are* they that have not seen, and *yet* have believed. ³⁰And many other signs truly did Jesus in the presence of his disciples, which are not written in this book: ³¹But these are written, that ye might believe that Jesus is the Christ, the Son of God; and that believing ye might have life through his name.

21

¹After these things Jesus shewed himself again to the disciples at the sea of Tiberias; and on this wise shewed he *himself*. ²There were together Simon Peter, and Thomas called Didymus, and Nathanael of Cana in Galilee, and the *sons* of Zebedee, and two other of his disciples. ³Simon Peter saith unto them, I go a fishing. They say unto him, We also go with thee. They went forth, and entered into a ship immediately; and that night they caught nothing. ⁴But when the morning was now come, Jesus stood on the shore: but the disciples knew not that it was Jesus. ⁵Then Jesus saith unto them, Children^a, have ye any meat? They answered him, No. ⁶And he said unto them, Cast the net on the right side of the ship, and ye shall find. They cast therefore, and now they were not able to draw it for the multitude of fishes. ⁷Therefore that disciple whom Jesus loved saith unto Peter, It is the Lord. Now when Simon Peter heard that it was the Lord, he girt *his* fisher's coat *unto him*, (for he was naked,) and did cast himself into the sea. ⁸And the other disciples came in a little ship; (for they were not far from land, but as it were two hundred cubits,) dragging the net with fishes. ⁹As soon then as they were come to land, they saw a fire of coals there, and fish laid thereon, and bread. ¹⁰Jesus saith unto them, Bring of the fish which ye have now caught. ¹¹Simon Peter went up, and drew the net to land full of great fishes, an hundred and fifty and three: and for all there were so many, yet was not the net broken. ¹²Jesus saith unto them, Come *and* dine. And none of the disciples durst ask him, Who art thou? knowing that it was the Lord. ¹³Jesus then cometh, and taketh bread, and giveth them, and fish likewise. ¹⁴This is now the third time

---

^a Children: or, Sirs

Jesus

Besides Jesus, Mary and Joseph had at least eight children: six boys and two girls. Plenty to care for them in their old age, right?

Actually, it appears as if Mary and Joseph's kids reneged on this important obligation. Joseph probably died before Jesus began his ministry, but Mary was still around. And probably because Mary believed in Jesus and followed and supported him, Jesus' brothers left all the care of Mary to him. They thought that Jesus was crazy and stayed away from him (and their mother) all during his public ministry.

That's why, when Jesus was dying on the cross, he had a brief conversation with John. "Behold thy mother," Jesus said to him. John knew what he meant: *I can no longer take care of Mary, John. Will you do it for me?*

It's no coincidence that Jesus asked John to do this. John was one of Jesus' closest friends. Jesus knew he could count on him. He didn't give the job to just anybody.

There were no nursing homes, government agencies, or special programs for the needy in Jesus' day. When Jesus said to John, "She is your mother," he was giving the job to someone who would not let him down.

The issue is the same for us: What will we do when our parents can no longer take care of themselves?

LESSONS FROM JESUS AS A CHILD OF AGING PARENTS

Adult children have a responsibility to care for their aging parents. If aging parents need someone to care for them, we need to answer the call. Take good care of your parents if they cannot take good care of themselves.

Parents need their children. In the beginning, parents take care of children. But eventually the roles reverse. Plan for it. As a child, Jesus obeyed his mother. As an adult, he cared for her. As a dying man, he arranged for her to be well cared for after he was gone. That's how it should be.

that Jesus shewed himself to his disciples, after that he was risen from the dead.

¹⁵So when they had dined, Jesus saith to Simon Peter, Simon, *son* of Jonas, lovest thou me more than these? He saith unto him, Yea, Lord; thou knowest that I love thee. He saith unto him, Feed my lambs. ¹⁶He saith to him again the second time, Simon, *son* of Jonas, lovest thou me? He saith unto him, Yea, Lord; thou knowest that I love thee. He saith unto him, Feed my sheep. ¹⁷He saith unto him the third time, Simon, *son* of Jonas, lovest thou me? Peter was grieved because he said unto him the third time, Lovest thou me? And he said unto him, Lord, thou knowest all things; thou knowest that I love thee. Jesus saith unto him, Feed my sheep. ¹⁸Verily, verily, I say unto thee, When thou wast young, thou girdedst thyself, and walkedst whither thou wouldest: but when thou shalt be old, thou shalt stretch forth thy hands, and another shall gird thee, and carry *thee* whither thou wouldest not. ¹⁹This

spake he, signifying by what death he should glorify God. And when he had spoken this, he saith unto him, Follow me.

²⁰Then Peter, turning about, seeth the disciple whom Jesus loved following; which also leaned on his breast at supper, and said, Lord, which is he that betrayeth thee? ²¹Peter seeing him saith to Jesus, Lord, and what *shall* this man *do*? ²²Jesus saith unto him, If I will that he tarry till I come, what *is that* to thee? follow thou me. ²³Then went this saying abroad among the brethren, that that disciple should not die: yet Jesus said not unto him, He shall not die; but, If I will that he tarry till I come, what *is that* to thee? ²⁴This is the disciple which testifieth of these things, and wrote these things: and we know that his testimony is true. ²⁵And there are also many other things which Jesus did, the which, if they should be written every one, I suppose that even the world itself could not contain the books that should be written. Amen.

ACTS

Purpose
To give an accurate account
of the birth and growth of the
Christian church

Author
Luke

To Whom Written
Theophilus

Date Written
Between A.D. 63 and 70

Setting
Acts is the connecting link between Christ's life and the life
of the church, between the
Gospels and the Epistles

Key Verse
"But ye shall receive power, after that the Holy Ghost is come
upon you: and ye shall be witnesses unto me both in
Jerusalem, and in all Judaea,
and in Samaria, and unto the uttermost part of the earth" (1:8).

Key People
Peter, John, James, Stephen,
Philip, Paul, Barnabas, Cor-
nelius, James (Jesus'
brother), Timothy, Lydia,
Silas, Titus, Apollos, Agabus,
Ananias, Felix, Festus,
Agrippa, Luke

Special Features
Acts is a sequel to the
Gospel of Luke. Because it
ends so abruptly, scholars
believe Luke may have
planned to write a third book
continuing the story.

If a book called *Acts of the Parents* were ever written, it would be filled with energy-depleting adventures, drama, conflict, tenderness, pain, regret, and frustration. However, the connecting theme throughout the story would be love. Without love, the story would end as a tragedy, with many small tragedies building to the climax. With love—steady, weather-beaten, and passionate—the story becomes a kind of romance: Characters grow closer, relationships deepen, challenges are overcome, griefs are endured, and through it all, a ring of happiness—life well lived.

The Acts of the Apostles has a central theme, too. It shows how the Holy Spirit empowered people to take the gospel to all the known world. Without the Holy Spirit, men and women merely go through their paces. But with the Holy Spirit, these everyday people change the world.

Notice the similarities between the hypothetical *Acts of the Parents* and the book you are about to read. You could write the former yourself, and probably have several chapters already in mind. Does your story work without love? Not really. Does love come from nowhere? Not really.

The apostles have the Spirit; they learn a lot about love in this book. You want love and need the Spirit to find it. Your family needs the Holy Spirit, and Acts is the place to learn about him.

You can't go far into Acts without realizing these people have a rare inner strength. Your children, spouse, neighbors, and colleagues at work should see that same strength in you, as the Spirit makes his love shine through.

1

¹The former treatise have I made, O Theophilus, of all that Jesus began both to do and teach, ²Until the day in which he was taken up, after that he through the Holy Ghost had given commandments unto the apostles whom he had chosen: ³To whom also he shewed himself alive after his passion by many infallible proofs, being seen of them forty days, and speaking of the things pertaining to the kingdom of God: ⁴And, being assembled together with *them*, commanded them that they should not depart from Jerusalem, but wait for the promise of the Father, which, *saith he*, ye have heard of me. ⁵For John truly baptized with water; but ye shall be baptized with the Holy Ghost not many days hence.

⁶When they therefore were come together, they asked of him, saying, Lord, wilt thou at this time restore again the kingdom to Israel? ⁷And he said unto them, It is not for you to know the times or the seasons, which the Father hath put in his own power. ⁸But ye shall receive powerᵃ, after that the Holy Ghost is come upon you: and ye shall be witnesses unto me both in Jerusalem, and in all Judaea, and in Samaria, and unto the uttermost part of the earth. ⁹And when he had spoken these things, while they beheld, he was taken up; and a cloud received him out of their sight. ¹⁰And while they looked stedfastly toward heaven as he went up, behold, two men stood by them in white apparel; ¹¹Which also said, Ye men of Galilee, why stand ye gazing up into heaven? this same Jesus, which is taken up from you into heaven, shall so come in like manner as ye have seen him go into heaven.

¹²Then returned they unto Jerusalem from the mount called Olivet, which is from Jerusalem a sabbath day's journey. ¹³And when they were come in, they went up into an upper room, where abode both Peter, and James, and John, and Andrew, Philip, and Thomas, Bartholomew, and Matthew, James *the son* of Alphaeus, and Simon Zelotes, and Judas *the brother* of James. ¹⁴These all continued with one accord in prayer and supplication, with the women, and Mary the mother of Jesus, and with his brethren.

¹⁵And in those days Peter stood up in the midst of the disciples, and said, (the number of names together were about an hundred and twenty,) ¹⁶Men *and* brethren, this scripture must needs have been fulfilled, which the Holy Ghost by the mouth of David spake before concerning Judas, which was guide to them that took Jesus. ¹⁷For he was

---

Devotional Moment

Prayer/Choices

1:12-13 Surely a formidable future faced the eleven disciples here. Commissioned to take God's message about Christ to all the world, they began the task with a prayer meeting. What does your future hold: Job change? Schooling? Marriage? Special care for problem children? for aging parents? Each major decision involves a string of smaller decisions as you evaluate and adjust your course. God is with you all the way. Pray often during the day, seeking God's heart and mind.

ᵃ power . . . : or, the power of the Holy Ghost coming upon you

numbered with us, and had obtained part of this ministry. ¹⁸Now this man purchased a field with the reward of iniquity; and falling headlong, he burst asunder in the midst, and all his bowels gushed out. ¹⁹And it was known unto all the dwellers at Jerusalem; insomuch as that field is called in their proper tongue, Aceldama, that is to say, The field of blood. ²⁰For it is written in the book of Psalms, Let his habitation be desolate, and let no man dwell therein: and his bishoprick[b] let another take. ²¹Wherefore of these men which have companied with us all the time that the Lord Jesus went in and out among us, ²²Beginning from the baptism of John, unto that same day that he was taken up from us, must one be ordained to be a witness with us of his resurrection. ²³And they appointed two, Joseph called Barsabas, who was surnamed Justus, and Matthias. ²⁴And they prayed, and said, Thou, Lord, which knowest the hearts of all *men*, shew whether of these two thou hast chosen, ²⁵That he may take part of this ministry and apostleship, from which Judas by transgression fell, that he might go to his own place. ²⁶And they gave forth their lots; and the lot fell upon Matthias; and he was numbered with the eleven apostles.

2

¹And when the day of Pentecost was fully come, they were all with one accord in one place. ²And suddenly there came a sound from heaven as of a rushing mighty wind, and it filled all the house where they were sitting. ³And there appeared unto them cloven tongues like as of fire, and it sat upon each of them. ⁴And they were all filled with the Holy Ghost, and began to speak with other tongues, as the Spirit gave them utterance.

⁵And there were dwelling at Jerusalem Jews, devout men, out of every nation under heaven. ⁶Now when this was[a] noised abroad, the multitude came together, and were confounded, because that every man heard them speak in his own language. ⁷And they were all amazed and marvelled, saying one to another, Behold, are not all these which speak Galilaeans? ⁸And how hear we every man in our own tongue, wherein we were born? ⁹Parthians, and Medes, and Elamites, and the dwellers in Mesopotamia, and in Judaea, and Cappadocia, in Pontus, and Asia, ¹⁰Phrygia, and Pamphylia, in Egypt, and in the parts of Libya about Cyrene, and strangers of Rome, Jews and proselytes, ¹¹Cretes and Arabians, we do hear them speak in our tongues the wonderful works of God. ¹²And they were all amazed, and were in doubt, saying one to another, What meaneth this? ¹³Others mocking said, These men are full of new wine.

¹⁴But Peter, standing up with the eleven, lifted up his voice, and said unto them, Ye men of Judaea, and all *ye* that dwell at Jerusalem, be this known unto you, and hearken to my words: ¹⁵For these are not drunken, as ye suppose, seeing it is *but* the third hour of the day. ¹⁶But this is that which was spoken by the prophet Joel; ¹⁷And it

---

[b] bishoprick: or, office, or, charge

[a] was . . . : Gr. voice was made confounded: or, troubled in mind

Breaking Free
Through Community

They continued stedfastly in the apostles' doctrine and fellowship, and in breaking of bread, and in prayers. Acts 2:42

In Acts 2:42 we read that the founding members of Christ's church did four things: "They continued stedfastly in the apostles' doctrine and fellowship, and in breaking of bread, and in prayers." While all four aspects of worship (fellowship, teaching, Communion, and prayer) are crucial in a believer's life, the element of *fellowship* can be especially important in breaking negative patterns.

How so?

Take the example of two couples. One shows clearly the life-changing difference biblical fellowship can make, and the other shows the price that can be paid if it's absent.

Debbie and Joe and Tom and Christy were roughly the same age. They lived in the same neighborhood, and each couple had two children in identical grades. Yet they differed in one crucial way: Debbie and Joe were part of a small group of friends at their church, while Tom and Christy were not.

During a two-month period of time, both couples fell on hard times. For Debbie and Joe it centered around his losing his job in the aerospace industry, and for Tom and Christy it centered around the death of Tom's mother. Both couples began to get stressed out and emotionally distanced from one another and (unknown to each other at the time) both men walked out of the house "for good" during this period. Yet what happened shows the difference between these two couples—and why a small group is so important in breaking negative cycles.

Joe's father had been married twice, and his mother once, before they met. Joe was a Christian and felt he loved Debbie, but he walked out one Saturday in a rage over their family finances. Debbie immediately went to the phone and contacted two friends from their small group. Within ten minutes, two men had arrived at the house. While Joe was throwing clothes into his car, they persuaded him to stop and think about the consequences of his actions. After his emotions subsided, they prayed with him and told him that they were committed to him and Debbie. Finally, Joe came back into the house and agreed before his two friends to seek a counselor—not a divorce lawyer.

Today, over two years later, Debbie and Joe are doing better than ever, even making it through the nine months that he was un- and under-employed. Why? They credit their small group of friends as being the source of fellowship, prayer, instruction, and worship that helped them get through their darkest moments.

What about Tom and Christy? The day Tom walked out, there was no one for Christy to call except her mother. No fellowship group to come and help them. No prayers from a committed group of believers to stand with them. And no stopping a divorce that was final in near-record time.

Couples that are part of small groups don't always survive the bumps and bruises of life. Yet far more often, it is the isolated couple that breaks apart. There is truth in the old adage The wolf loves lone sheep.

With that in mind, ask yourself this question: Do I have a group of supportive Christian friends who are close enough to know me and caring enough to confront me if I need it? If you do, then you're well on your way toward breaking any negative cycle. They may have to support you through tears, counseling, or anger, but like the early church, they will be examples of Christ's sacrificial love on earth.

If you've got a negative cycle to break from your past, don't be a lone sheep. There is too much at stake and too much to be gained by committing yourself to part of the body of Christ in a small group.

---

shall come to pass in the last days, saith God, I will pour out of my Spirit upon all flesh: and your sons and your daughters shall prophesy, and your young men shall see visions, and your old men shall dream dreams: [18]And on my servants and on my handmaidens I will pour out in those days of my Spirit; and they shall prophesy: [19]And I will shew wonders in heaven above, and signs in the earth beneath; blood, and fire, and vapour of smoke: [20]The sun shall be turned into darkness, and the moon into blood, before that great and notable day of the Lord come: [21]And it shall come to pass, *that* whosoever shall call on the name of the Lord shall be saved. [22]Ye men of Israel, hear these words; Jesus of Nazareth, a man approved of God among you by miracles and wonders and signs, which God did by him in the midst of you, as ye yourselves also know: [23]Him, being delivered by the determinate counsel and foreknowledge of God, ye have taken, and by wicked hands have crucified and slain: [24]Whom God hath raised up, having loosed the pains of death: because it was not possible that he should be holden of it. [25]For David speaketh concerning him, I foresaw the Lord always before my face, for he is on my right hand, that I should not be moved: [26]Therefore did my heart rejoice, and my tongue was glad; moreover also my flesh shall rest in hope: [27]Because thou wilt not leave my soul in hell, neither wilt thou suffer thine Holy One to see corruption. [28]Thou hast made known to me the ways of life; thou shalt make me full of joy with thy countenance. [29]Men *and* brethren, let me[b] freely speak unto you of the patriarch David, that he is both dead and buried, and his sepulchre is with us unto this day. [30]Therefore being a prophet, and knowing that God had sworn with an oath to him, that of the fruit of his loins, according to the flesh, he would raise up Christ to sit on his throne; ³¹He seeing this before spake of the resurrection of Christ, that his soul was not left in hell, neither his flesh did see corruption. ³²This Jesus hath God raised up, whereof we all are witnesses. ³³Therefore being by the right hand of God exalted, and having received of the Father the promise of the Holy Ghost, he hath shed forth this, which ye now see and hear. ³⁴For David is not ascended into the heavens: but he saith himself, The LORD said unto my Lord, Sit thou on my right hand, ³⁵Until I make thy foes thy footstool. ³⁶Therefore let all the house of Israel know assuredly, that God hath made that same Jesus, whom ye have crucified, both Lord and Christ.

³⁷Now when they heard *this*, they were pricked in their heart, and said unto Peter and to the rest of the apostles, Men *and* brethren, what shall we do? ³⁸Then Peter said unto them, Repent, and be baptized every one of you in the name of Jesus Christ for the remission of sins, and ye shall receive the gift of the Holy Ghost. ³⁹For the promise is unto you, and to your children, and to all that are afar off, *even* as many as the Lord our God shall call. ⁴⁰And with many other words did he testify and exhort, saying, Save yourselves from this untoward generation. ⁴¹Then they that gladly received his word were baptized: and the same day there were added *unto them* about three thousand souls.

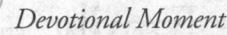

Devotional Moment

God's Family

2:44-47 These verses describe a family, of course: God's family called the church. Today churches have the same Spirit, the same risen Lord, the same God as did early believers—and the same reasons to carry on this happy sound. Help raise the rafters with God's family this week. Do it with smiles, heartfelt greetings, affirmations, and songs. Go to church with the goal of being a part of the fellowship.

⁴²And they continued stedfastly in the apostles' doctrine and fellowship, and in breaking of bread, and in prayers. ⁴³And fear came upon every soul: and many wonders and signs were done by the apostles. ⁴⁴And all that believed were together, and had all things common; ⁴⁵And sold their possessions and goods, and parted them to all *men*, as every man had need. ⁴⁶And they, continuing daily with one accord in the temple, and breaking bread from^c house to house, did eat their meat with gladness and singleness of heart, ⁴⁷Praising God, and having favour with all the people. And the Lord added to the church daily such as should be saved.

3

¹Now Peter and John went up together into the temple at the hour of prayer, *being* the ninth *hour*. ²And a certain man lame from his mother's womb was carried, whom they laid daily at the gate of the temple which is called Beautiful, to ask alms of them that entered into the temple; ³Who seeing Peter and John about to go into the temple asked an

---

ᶜ from . . . : or, at home

The Family of Families

by Ray Seldomridge

The church has always been a big family. When Christianity began in Jerusalem, the very first believers gathered daily to learn the fundamentals of the faith, to share Communion, to pray, to praise God, and to share—together. The apostles' teaching probably took place in the Temple precincts (Acts 2:46), where large crowds could assemble, while Communion, prayer, and praising God often took place in each other's homes. These meetings were not just rallies, but close, big-family experiences. So attractive was their warm, familylike behavior that the whole city took notice (v. 47).

This made sense. Jesus' followers had been adopted by God as his children. The church was, in fact, the very household of God (Eph. 2:19), and as such, they had been called to know each other and care for each other as if they were members of the same family (see Gal. 6:10). That is why the New Testament places such a strong emphasis on believers meeting *together*—a direct result of Jesus' command, "Love one another; as I have loved you" (John 13:34).

But this presents us with a dilemma because most Americans prefer to lead very independent lives.

Dick Wulf, a Christian psychotherapist and author, has compiled a list of activities that God calls believers to do together. Here is just a sample:

Worship God together. (Heb. 13:15-16)
Serve one another. (Gal. 5:13)
Live together in unity. (John 17:22-23)
Comfort each other. (2 Cor. 1:3-5)
Confess sins to one another. (James 5:16)
Counsel each other. (Prov. 27:9)
Contend for the faith together. (Phil. 1:27-29)
Look out for each other's good. (Titus 3:14)

Many in the early church had that kind of commitment to each other. Who needs such an "extended family" today?

Everyone in broken homes. The church family may be the only place that many children from single-parent homes will ever know the love of a substitute "father" or "mother."

Every elderly person and every single person who lives far away from children, grandchildren, and other family. There is no need for elderly and single people to be lonely in the Christian church today!

All children. Children cannot possibly grow in their faith unless they have a chance to see it at work in the lives of more mature believers who openly share, confess, weep, laugh, bear witness, and praise God together in a setting of meaningful relationships.

The rest of us. Being squeezed between busy lives and a hostile society will either drive us together for mutual support or isolate us from each other. Only *together* can we fight and win the battle we fight against Satan (Eph. 6:10-20).

Can't Christian families get all the love and support they need from each other? No! Any family that is isolated from God's household lacks a crucial source of support. Among other things, a close connection to other believers gives families a place to go *before* divorce becomes a serious temptation or parent-teen conflict gets out of control. Husbands and wives need others who know them well and can counsel them lovingly when they need help. Parents need the help of other adults who get to know their kids and provide an "aunt's" or "uncle's" sage advice during the turbulent teen years. Young people need other young people and older mentors who can encourage and bolster them in their convictions.

Whatever your situation, work hard at making friends among the people of your church, and stay committed to those relationships. For some Christians, the best way to do this is to join a small group of eight to twelve people; for others, it is to form friendships one at a time with people who share common experiences. The mechanism for every person and every family will be different. But every family needs more than itself—a group of believers who don't just study the Bible but also share needs, pray together, confess weaknesses, counsel one another, and enjoy each other's company. A church family.

DIGGING DEEPER

1. Jesus said, "Love one another; as I have loved you" (John 13:34). In what ways did Jesus love his disciples? How does he love us? What would you have to do to love other Christians as Christ has loved you?

2. What does it mean to be a Christian friend? See Philippians 2:4. Read all of Philippians, keeping in mind that almost every *you* is plural (referring to the whole group of Christians at Philippi).

3. What are the benefits of meeting with other Christians? Why is it important to do so? See Hebrews 10:24-25.

---

alms. ⁴And Peter, fastening his eyes upon him with John, said, Look on us. ⁵And he gave heed unto them, expecting to receive something of them. ⁶Then Peter said, Silver and gold have I none; but such as I have give I thee: In the name of Jesus Christ of Nazareth rise up and walk. ⁷And he took him by the right hand, and lifted *him* up: and immediately his feet and ankle bones received strength. ⁸And he leaping up stood, and walked, and entered with them into the temple, walking, and leaping, and praising God. ⁹And all the people saw him walking and praising God: ¹⁰And they knew that it was he which sat for alms at the Beautiful gate of the temple: and they were filled with wonder and amazement at that which had happened unto him. ¹¹And as the lame man which was healed held Peter and John, all the people ran together unto them in the porch that is called Solomon's, greatly wondering.

¹²And when Peter saw *it*, he answered unto the people, Ye men of Israel, why marvel ye at this? or why look ye so earnestly on us, as though by our own power or holiness we had made this man to walk? ¹³The God of Abraham, and of Isaac, and of Jacob, the God of our fathers, hath glorified his Son Jesus; whom ye delivered up, and denied him in the presence of Pilate, when he was determined to let *him* go. ¹⁴But ye denied the Holy One and the Just, and desired a murderer to be granted unto you; ¹⁵And killed the Prince[a] of life, whom God hath raised from the dead; whereof we are witnesses. ¹⁶And his name through faith in his name hath made this man strong,

---

[a] Prince: or, Author

whom ye see and know: yea, the faith which is by him hath given him this perfect soundness in the presence of you all. ¹⁷And now, brethren, I wot that through ignorance ye did *it*, as *did* also your rulers. ¹⁸But those things, which God before had shewed by the mouth of all his prophets, that Christ should suffer, he hath so fulfilled. ¹⁹Repent ye therefore, and be converted, that your sins may be blotted out, when the times of refreshing shall come from the presence of the Lord; ²⁰And he shall send Jesus Christ, which before was preached unto you: ²¹Whom the heaven must receive until the times of restitution of all things, which God hath spoken by the mouth of all his holy prophets since the world began. ²²For Moses truly said unto the fathers, A prophet shall the Lord your God raise up unto you of your brethren, like unto me; him shall ye hear in all things whatsoever he shall say unto you. ²³And it shall come to pass, *that* every soul, which will not hear that prophet, shall be destroyed from among the people. ²⁴Yea, and all the prophets from Samuel and those that follow after, as many as have spoken, have likewise foretold of these days. ²⁵Ye are the children of the prophets, and of the covenant which God made with our fathers, saying unto Abraham, And in thy seed shall all the kindreds of the earth be blessed. ²⁶Unto you first God, having raised up his Son Jesus, sent him to bless you, in turning away every one of you from his iniquities.

4

¹And as they spake unto the people, the priests, and the captain[a] of the temple, and the Sadducees, came upon them, ²Being grieved that they taught the people, and preached through Jesus the resurrection from the dead. ³And they laid hands on them, and put *them* in hold unto the next day: for it was now eventide. ⁴Howbeit many of them which heard the word believed; and the number of the men was about five thousand.

⁵And it came to pass on the morrow, that their rulers, and elders, and scribes, ⁶And Annas the high priest, and Caiaphas, and John, and Alexander, and as many as were of the kindred of the high priest, were gathered together at Jerusalem. ⁷And when they had set them in the midst, they asked, By what power, or by what name, have ye done this? ⁸Then Peter, filled with the Holy Ghost, said unto them, Ye rulers of the people, and elders of Israel, ⁹If we this day be examined of the good deed done to the impotent man, by what means he is made whole; ¹⁰Be it known unto you all, and to all the people of Israel, that by the name of Jesus Christ of Nazareth, whom ye crucified, whom God raised from the dead, *even* by him doth this man stand here before you whole. ¹¹This is the stone which was set at nought of you builders, which is become the head of the corner. ¹²Neither is there salvation in any other: for there is none other name under heaven given among men, whereby we must be saved. ¹³Now when they saw the boldness of Peter and John, and perceived that they were unlearned and ignorant men, they marvelled; and they took knowledge of them, that they had been with Jesus. ¹⁴And beholding the man which was healed standing with them, they could say nothing against it.

---

a captain: or, ruler

Family Traditions

A Tradition of Outreach

ACTS 4:12-31

Like Peter and John, when we know Jesus we can't stop telling about the wonderful things we have seen and heard. Establish a family tradition of sharing Jesus with those around you.

Get the family involved in Bible studies, after-game parties, and youth group meetings in your home. Every time you invite unbelievers to fellowship with you, even when teaching is not involved, you are exposing them to the love of Christ evident in your family's life. Initiate fun events at your house around holidays and school events.

Invite missionaries and preachers into your home. Encourage your children to ask them questions about their work—why they do it, how they do it, and ways in which they've seen God at work. Help your children to develop a healthy curiosity about other cultures and beliefs that keep people from God. This will help them to be comfortable sharing Christ with those who don't know him.

Make an effort to get outside your Christian circles and, as a family, discover that unsaved people can be neat, wonderful people, with special gifts and personalities. Help your children realize that the main difference is that those people haven't yet met Jesus, the Savior.

Avoid a "them-us" mentality in your conversations. Mix and mingle with unchurched families. This alone might be the greatest lesson to your kids about the difference Christ can make. And it will open opportunities for you to witness as an entire family to others. Speak kindly about cult missionaries that ring your doorbell; teach your children to respect them as people and to know what to say and courteously respond to them.

Create your own family mission statement. Have it printed and framed. A mission statement details the purpose and direction your family wants to go spiritually along with what kind of difference you want to make in the world. Encourage each of your children to do the same as individuals and to write their personal mission statement in their Bibles.

¹⁵But when they had commanded them to go aside out of the council, they conferred among themselves, ¹⁶Saying, What shall we do to these men? for that indeed a notable miracle hath been done by them is manifest to all them that dwell in Jerusalem; and we cannot deny it. ¹⁷But that it spread no further among the people, let us straitly threaten them, that they speak henceforth to no man in this name. ¹⁸And they called them, and commanded them not to speak at all nor teach in the name of Jesus. ¹⁹But Peter and John answered and said unto them, Whether it be right in the sight of God to hearken unto you more than unto God, judge ye. ²⁰For we cannot but speak the things which we have seen and heard. ²¹So when they had further threatened them, they let them go, finding nothing how they might punish them, because of the people: for all men glorified God for that which was done. ²²For the man was above forty years old, on whom this miracle of healing was shewed.

²³And being let go, they went to their own company, and reported all that the chief priests and elders had said unto them. ²⁴And when they heard that, they lifted up their voice to God with one accord, and said, Lord, thou art God, which hast made heaven, and earth, and the sea, and all that in them is: ²⁵Who by the mouth of thy servant David hast said, Why did the heathen rage, and the people imagine vain things? ²⁶The kings of the earth stood up, and the rulers were gathered together against the Lord, and against his Christ. ²⁷For of a truth against thy holy child Jesus, whom thou hast anointed, both Herod, and Pontius Pilate, with the Gentiles, and the people of Israel, were gathered together, ²⁸For to do whatsoever thy hand and thy counsel determined before to be done. ²⁹And now, Lord, behold their threatenings: and grant unto thy servants, that with all boldness they may speak thy word, ³⁰By stretching forth thine hand to heal; and that signs and wonders may be done by the name of thy holy child Jesus. ³¹And when they had prayed, the place was shaken where they were assembled together; and they were all filled with the Holy Ghost, and they spake the word of God with boldness.

³²And the multitude of them that believed were of one heart and of one soul: neither said any of them that ought of the things which he possessed was his own; but they had all things common. ³³And with great power gave the apostles witness of the resurrection of the Lord Jesus: and great grace was upon them all. ³⁴Neither was there any among them that lacked: for as many as were possessors of lands or houses sold them, and brought the prices of the things that were sold, ³⁵And laid them down at the apostles' feet: and distribution was made unto every man according as he had need. ³⁶And Joses, who by the apostles was surnamed Barnabas, (which is, being interpreted, The son of consolation,) a Levite, and of the country of Cyprus, ³⁷Having land, sold it, and brought the money, and laid it at the apostles' feet.

5

¹But a certain man named Ananias, with Sapphira his wife, sold a possession, ²And kept back part of the price, his wife also being privy to it, and brought a certain part, and laid it at the apostles' feet. ³But Peter said, Ananias, why hath Satan filled

Breaking Free from
Destructive Family Secrets

A certain man named Ananias, with Sapphira his wife, sold a possession. And kept back part of the price, his wife also being privy to it. Acts 5:1-2

The early church lived in a time when political and personal corruption was rampant—much like our own. And the death of Ananias and Sapphira was a gripping testimony to a fledgling church that God would not tolerate lies and deception.

But today judgment over lying or secret sins isn't always immediate or forceful. As a result, some people fall into a negative cycle of hiding things—of carrying secrets. That cycle needs to be broken. Why? Because keeping secrets can threaten the emotional, spiritual, and even *physical* lives of our loved ones.

A modern example of that is a couple named Barry and Lori. Barry had a good job, a wonderful family, and a supportive, elderly father who came to live with them when Barry's mother died.

Then the day came when in a previously secure industry, cuts came down, and Barry lost his job. Barry told Lori what had happened, but not his father. They thought that the news would be too much for him to take.

So they decided to go on as if nothing had changed. Every morning, Barry would get up, shower and shave, and then "go off to work." Actually, he'd go to a library or friend's office to make calls and job-hunt, thinking he was actually helping his father by sheltering him from the truth.

As the weeks went by with them living this lie, the tension began to mount between Barry and Lori, and the lie became harder to maintain. In the middle of all their efforts to maintain this charade, his father's health began to deteriorate.

Concerned over his failing condition, Barry "got off work" and took his father to the doctor.

Upon being questioned by the doctor about any stressful situations he was facing, Barry's father broke down. "Doc, there's something wrong with Barry and his wife that I don't understand. I can see the tension, and I know there's something wrong, but I can't find out what it is. It's just killing me not being able to help, or at least know how to pray for them." Indeed, the tension he was feeling was killing him.

The doctor called Barry into the room and confronted him about what was going on at home. Finally, Barry himself broke down and, in tears, told how he had lost his job and had been living a lie.

His father was incredulous. "Son, why didn't you tell me? I lost my job when I was your age, and I had to struggle through what you're experiencing now. I could have helped you through this if you had just told me!" All the support Barry could have received from his father had been suppressed by an unhealthy family secret.

While Barry's sin of covering up the truth didn't lead to immediate judgment, over the weeks it almost had a killing effect on his father's life. And that's just one reason why the cycle of untruth can be so damaging.

If you've come from a background of abuse or alcohol addiction, are you carrying that secret inside? Are there *any* secrets that you try to keep from your family?

What people often don't realize is that family secrets *increase* internal pressure rather than decrease it. In fact, the stress in a relationship where there is concealed sin often *triples* as the lies become more complicated and the fear of being found out becomes more pronounced.

It's important that we take to heart the words of the apostle Peter: "Thou hast not lied unto men, but unto God" (Acts 5:4). We don't escape from family problems by turning them into secrets; instead, we only magnify them.

---

thine heart to lie to the Holy Ghost, and to keep back *part* of the price of the land? ⁴Whiles it remained, was it not thine own? and after it was sold, was it not in thine own power? why hast thou conceived this thing in thine heart? thou hast not lied unto men, but unto God. ⁵And Ananias hearing these words fell down, and gave up the ghost: and great fear came on all them that heard these things. ⁶And the young men arose, wound him up, and carried *him* out, and buried *him*. ⁷And it was about the space of three hours after, when his wife, not knowing what was done, came in. ⁸And Peter answered unto her, Tell me whether ye sold the land for so much? And she said, Yea, for so much. ⁹Then Peter said unto her, How is it that ye have agreed together to tempt the Spirit of the Lord? behold, the feet of them which have buried thy husband *are* at the door, and shall carry thee

out. ¹⁰Then fell she down straightway at his feet, and yielded up the ghost: and the young men came in, and found her dead, and, carrying *her* forth, buried *her* by her husband. ¹¹And great fear came upon all the church, and upon as many as heard these things.

¹²And by the hands of the apostles were many signs and wonders wrought among the people; (and they were all with one accord in Solomon's porch. ¹³And of the rest durst no man join himself to them: but the people magnified them. ¹⁴And believers were the more added to the Lord, multitudes both of men and women.) ¹⁵Insomuch that they brought forth the sick intoª the streets, and laid *them* on beds and couches, that at the least the shadow of Peter passing by might overshadow some of them. ¹⁶There came also a multitude *out* of the cities round about

---

ª into . . . : or, in every street

unto Jerusalem, bringing sick folks, and them which were vexed with unclean spirits: and they were healed every one. ¹⁷Then the high priest rose up, and all they that were with him, (which is the sect of the Sadducees,) and were filled with indignation^b, ¹⁸And laid their hands on the apostles, and put them in the common prison. ¹⁹But the angel of the Lord by night opened the prison doors, and brought them forth, and said, ²⁰Go, stand and speak in the temple to the people all the words of this life. ²¹And when they heard *that*, they entered into the temple early in the morning, and taught. But the high priest came, and they that were with him, and called the council together, and all the senate of the children of Israel, and sent to the prison to have them brought. ²²But when the officers came, and found them not in the prison, they returned, and told, ²³Saying, The prison truly found we shut with all safety, and the keepers standing without before the doors: but when we had opened, we found no man within. ²⁴Now when the high priest and the captain of the temple and the chief priests heard these things, they doubted of them whereunto this would grow. ²⁵Then came one and told them, saying, Behold, the men whom ye put in prison are standing in the temple, and teaching the people. ²⁶Then went the captain with the officers, and brought them without violence: for they feared the people, lest they should have been stoned. ²⁷And when they had brought them, they set *them* before the council: and the high

priest asked them, ²⁸Saying, Did not we straitly command you that ye should not teach in this name? and, behold, ye have filled Jerusalem with your doctrine, and intend to bring this man's blood upon us. ²⁹Then Peter and the *other* apostles answered and said, We ought to obey God rather than men. ³⁰The God of our fathers raised up Jesus, whom ye slew and hanged on a tree. ³¹Him hath God exalted with his right hand *to be* a Prince and a Saviour, for to give repentance to Israel, and forgiveness of sins. ³²And we are his witnesses of these things; and *so is* also the Holy Ghost, whom God hath given to them that obey him. ³³When they heard *that*, they were cut *to the heart*, and took counsel to slay them. ³⁴Then stood there up one in the council, a Pharisee, named Gamaliel, a doctor of the law, had in reputation among all the people, and commanded to put the apostles forth a little space; ³⁵And said unto

---

Devotional Moment
•
Home

5:42 Much of the early church's ministry took place in homes. Believers and seekers would gather to discuss the teachings of the written Scriptures and of the resurrected Christ. As a result, lives were touched, and the world was changed! This kind of impact is still possible. Throw open your doors to neighbors and friends and give a simple meal, a cup of coffee, a listening ear, a barbecue, a youth group meeting, a backyard Bible club, an invitation to come watch the big game, a small-group Bible study, an evangelistic dinner party. Amazing things can (and do) happen when we ask God to make our homes lighthouses for the kingdom!

---

^b indignation: or, envy

them, Ye men of Israel, take heed to yourselves what ye intend to do as touching these men. [36]For before these days rose up Theudas, boasting himself to be somebody; to whom a number of men, about four hundred, joined themselves: who was slain; and all, as many as obeyed[c] him, were scattered, and brought to nought. [37]After this man rose up Judas of Galilee in the days of the taxing, and drew away much people after him: he also perished; and all, *even* as many as obeyed[d] him, were dispersed. [38]And now I say unto you, Refrain from these men, and let them alone: for if this counsel or this work be of men, it will come to nought: [39]But if it be of God, ye cannot overthrow it; lest haply ye be found even to fight against God. [40]And to him they agreed: and when they had called the apostles, and beaten *them*, they commanded that they should not speak in the name of Jesus, and let them go. [41]And they departed from the presence of the council, rejoicing that they were counted worthy to suffer shame for his name. [42]And daily in the temple, and in every house, they ceased not to teach and preach Jesus Christ.

6

[1]And in those days, when the number of the disciples was multiplied, there arose a murmuring of the Grecians against the Hebrews, because their widows were neglected in the daily ministration. [2]Then the twelve called the multitude of the disciples *unto them*, and said, It is not reason that we should leave the word of God, and serve tables. [3]Wherefore, brethren, look ye out among you seven men of honest report, full of the Holy Ghost and wisdom, whom we may appoint over this business. [4]But we will give ourselves continually to prayer, and to the ministry of the word. [5]And the saying pleased the whole multitude: and they chose Stephen, a man full of faith and of the Holy Ghost, and Philip, and Prochorus, and Nicanor, and Timon, and Parmenas, and Nicolas a proselyte of Antioch: [6]Whom they set before the apostles: and when they had prayed, they laid *their* hands on them. [7]And the word of God increased; and the number of the disciples multiplied in Jerusalem greatly; and a great company of the priests were obedient to the faith.

[8]And Stephen, full of faith and power, did great wonders and miracles

---

Devotional Moment

•

Abilities

6:2-4 When they decided to delegate administration of the feeding program, the apostles were not implying that they were too important to do menial tasks. They simply recognized that an organization is healthiest (and happiest) when each member is freed up to do what he or she does best. This principle is also true for families. Parents should help each family member discover his or her God-given strengths and then find opportunities to develop them. Whether it's dividing household chores, choosing a personal hobby, or pursuing extra-curricular activities, be sensitive to each one's abilities. Don't force family members into roles they can't fill. Help them excel in areas where they have special talent.

---

[c] obeyed: or, believed
[d] obeyed: or, believed

among the people. ⁹Then there arose certain of the synagogue, which is called *the synagogue* of the Libertines, and Cyrenians, and Alexandrians, and of them of Cilicia and of Asia, disputing with Stephen. ¹⁰And they were not able to resist the wisdom and the spirit by which he spake. ¹¹Then they suborned men, which said, We have heard him speak blasphemous words against Moses, and *against* God. ¹²And they stirred up the people, and the elders, and the scribes, and came upon *him*, and caught him, and brought *him* to the council, ¹³And set up false witnesses, which said, This man ceaseth not to speak blasphemous words against this holy place, and the law: ¹⁴For we have heard him say, that this Jesus of Nazareth shall destroy this place, and shall change the customs[a] which Moses delivered us. ¹⁵And all that sat in the council, looking stedfastly on him, saw his face as it had been the face of an angel.

7

¹Then said the high priest, Are these things so? ²And he said, Men, brethren, and fathers, hearken; The God of glory appeared unto our father Abraham, when he was in Mesopotamia, before he dwelt in Charran, ³And said unto him, Get thee out of thy country, and from thy kindred, and come into the land which I shall shew thee. ⁴Then came he out of the land of the Chaldaeans, and dwelt in Charran: and from thence, when his father was dead, he removed him into this land, wherein ye now dwell. ⁵And he gave him none inheritance in it, no, not *so much as* to set his foot on: yet he promised that he would give it to him for a possession, and to his seed after him, when *as yet* he had no child. ⁶And God spake on this wise, That his seed should sojourn in a strange land; and that they should bring them into bondage, and entreat *them* evil four hundred years. ⁷And the nation to whom they shall be in bondage will I judge, said God: and after that shall they come forth, and serve me in this place. ⁸And he gave him the covenant of circumcision: and so *Abraham* begat Isaac, and circumcised him the eighth day; and Isaac *begat* Jacob; and Jacob *begat* the twelve patriarchs. ⁹And the patriarchs, moved with envy, sold Joseph into Egypt: but God was with him, ¹⁰And delivered him out of all his afflictions, and gave him favour and wisdom in the sight of Pharaoh king of Egypt; and he made him governor over Egypt and all his house. ¹¹Now there came a dearth over all the land of Egypt and Chanaan, and great affliction: and our fathers found no sustenance. ¹²But when Jacob heard that there was corn in Egypt, he sent out our fathers first. ¹³And at the second *time* Joseph was made known to his brethren; and Joseph's kindred was made known unto Pharaoh. ¹⁴Then sent Joseph, and called his father Jacob to *him*, and all his kindred, threescore and fifteen souls. ¹⁵So Jacob went down into Egypt, and died, he, and our fathers, ¹⁶And were carried over into Sychem, and laid in the sepulchre that Abraham bought for a sum of money of the sons of Emmor *the father* of Sychem.

¹⁷But when the time of the promise

---

[a] customs: or, rites

drew nigh, which God had sworn to Abraham, the people grew and multiplied in Egypt, ¹⁸Till another king arose, which knew not Joseph. ¹⁹The same dealt subtilly with our kindred, and evil entreated our fathers, so that they cast out their young children, to the end they might not live. ²⁰In which time Moses was born, and was exceeding fair, and nourished up in his father's house three months: ²¹And when he was cast out, Pharaoh's daughter took him up, and nourished him for her own son. ²²And Moses was learned in all the wisdom of the Egyptians, and was mighty in words and in deeds. ²³And when he was full forty years old, it came into his heart to visit his brethren the children of Israel. ²⁴And seeing one *of them* suffer wrong, he defended *him*, and avenged him that was oppressed, and smote the Egyptian: ²⁵Forᵃ he supposed his brethren would have understood how that God by his hand would deliver them: but they understood not. ²⁶And the next day he shewed himself unto them as they strove, and would have set them at one again, saying, Sirs, ye are brethren; why do ye wrong one to another? ²⁷But he that did his neighbour wrong thrust him away, saying, Who made thee a ruler and a judge over us? ²⁸Wilt thou kill me, as thou diddest the Egyptian yesterday? ²⁹Then fled Moses at this saying, and was a stranger in the land of Madian, where he begat two sons.

³⁰And when forty years were expired, there appeared to him in the wilderness of mount Sina an angel of the Lord in a flame of fire in a bush. ³¹When Moses saw *it*, he wondered at the sight: and as he drew near to behold *it*, the voice of the Lord came unto him, ³²*Saying*, I *am* the God of thy fathers, the God of Abraham, and the God of Isaac, and the God of Jacob. Then Moses trembled, and durst not behold. ³³Then said the Lord to him, Put off thy shoes from thy feet: for the place where thou standest is holy ground. ³⁴I have seen, I have seen the affliction of my people which is in Egypt, and I have heard their groaning, and am come down to deliver them. And now come, I will send thee into Egypt. ³⁵This Moses whom they refused, saying, Who made thee a ruler and a judge? the same did God send *to be* a ruler and a deliverer by the hand of the angel which appeared to him in the bush. ³⁶He brought them out, after that he had shewed wonders and signs in the land of Egypt, and in the Red sea, and in the wilderness forty years. ³⁷This is that Moses, which said unto the children of Israel, A prophet shall the Lord your God raise up unto you of your brethren, likeᵇ unto me; him shall ye hear. ³⁸This is he, that was in the church in the wilderness with the angel which spake to him in the mount Sina, and *with* our fathers: who received the lively oracles to give unto us: ³⁹To whom our fathers would not obey, but thrust *him* from them, and in their hearts turned back again into Egypt, ⁴⁰Saying unto Aaron, Make us gods to go before us: for *as for* this Moses, which brought us out of the land of Egypt, we wot not

---

ᵃ For: or, Now

ᵇ like . . . : or, as myself

what is become of him. ⁴¹And they made a calf in those days, and offered sacrifice unto the idol, and rejoiced in the works of their own hands.

⁴²Then God turned, and gave them up to worship the host of heaven; as it is written in the book of the prophets, O ye house of Israel, have ye offered to me slain beasts and sacrifices *by the space of* forty years in the wilderness? ⁴³Yea, ye took up the tabernacle of Moloch, and the star of your god Remphan, figures which ye made to worship them: and I will carry you away beyond Babylon. ⁴⁴Our fathers had the tabernacle of witness in the wilderness, as he had appointed, speakingᶜ unto Moses, that he should make it according to the fashion that he had seen. ⁴⁵Which also our fathers that came after brought in with Jesus into the possession of the Gentiles, whom God drave out before the face of our fathers, unto the days of David; ⁴⁶Who found favour before God, and desired to find a tabernacle for the God of Jacob. ⁴⁷But Solomon built him an house. ⁴⁸Howbeit the most High dwelleth not in temples made with hands; as saith the prophet, ⁴⁹Heaven *is* my throne, and earth *is* my footstool: what house will ye build me? saith the Lord: or what *is* the place of my rest? ⁵⁰Hath not my hand made all these things?

⁵¹Ye stiffnecked and uncircumcised in heart and ears, ye do always resist the Holy Ghost: as your fathers *did*, so *do* ye. ⁵²Which of the prophets have not your fathers persecuted? and they have slain them which shewed before of the coming of the Just One; of whom ye have been now the betrayers and murderers: ⁵³Who have received the law by the disposition of angels, and have not kept *it*.

⁵⁴When they heard these things, they were cut to the heart, and they gnashed on him with *their* teeth. ⁵⁵But he, being full of the Holy Ghost, looked up stedfastly into heaven, and saw the glory of God, and Jesus standing on the right hand of God, ⁵⁶And said, Behold, I see the heavens opened, and the Son of man standing on the right hand of God. ⁵⁷Then they cried out with a loud voice, and stopped their ears, and ran upon him with one accord, ⁵⁸And cast *him* out of the city, and stoned *him*: and the witnesses laid down their clothes at a young man's feet, whose name was Saul. ⁵⁹And they stoned Stephen, calling upon *God*, and saying, Lord Jesus, receive my spirit. ⁶⁰And he kneeled down, and cried with a loud voice, Lord, lay not this sin to their charge. And when he had said this, he fell asleep.

8

¹And Saul was consenting unto his death. And at that time there was a great persecution against the church which was at Jerusalem; and they were all scattered abroad throughout the regions of Judaea and Samaria, except the apostles. ²And devout men carried Stephen *to his burial*, and made great lamentation over him. ³As for Saul, he made havock of the church, entering into every house, and haling men and women committed *them* to prison.

⁴Therefore they that were scattered

ᶜ speaking: or, who spake

Ananias & Sapphira

LESSONS FROM ANANIAS AND SAPPHIRA AS A COUPLE

There's more to life than getting along. As unpleasant as it is, we need to be willing to clash when a moral issue is at stake. Be careful not to compromise on matters concerning God's law.

Sometimes to do what is right, you must take a risk. Be willing to confront your spouse. It doesn't have to be a fight—angry, ugly, mean, or accusatory. It can be done kindly, respectfully, calmly. It just has to be done.

Think twice before getting married. If you're not married, consider carefully how a prospective mate may reinforce your weaknesses rather than compensate for them. Help your children keep this in mind, too, as they form close friendships or consider marriage.

Strong marriages impress others with how well the husband and wife function together as a team. Close couples often agree. And when they don't, they come to an agreement about their disagreement so they can go on with life peacefully.

Ananias and Sapphira had a strong marriage. These new believers in the early church were generous—they agreed together to sell some land and give the money to the apostles. Unfortunately, they also agreed together to lie to the church about what they were giving. Tragically, their sin caused them to die together.

In their story, brief as it is, it's clear that Ananias and Sapphira were a team. They acted together. They supported each other, for better or for worse. Ananias and Sapphira were true partners.

They are a sad but clear warning to us that togetherness has a downside. When spouses agree together to sin—in the name of unity—it's a serious problem.

Reinforcing each other's weaknesses is a live possibility in any marriage. United we stand, united we fall.

Be willing to stand for truth, even against the wishes of a family member, for the sake of your family's relationship with God.

abroad went every where preaching the word. ⁵Then Philip went down to the city of Samaria, and preached Christ unto them. ⁶And the people with one accord gave heed unto those things which Philip spake, hearing and seeing the miracles which he did. ⁷For unclean spirits, crying with loud voice, came out of many that were possessed *with them*: and many taken with palsies, and that were lame, were healed. ⁸And there was great joy in that city. ⁹But there was a certain man, called Simon, which beforetime in the same city used sorcery, and bewitched the people of Samaria, giving out that himself was some great one: ¹⁰To whom they all gave heed, from the least to the greatest, saying, This man is the great power of God. ¹¹And to him they had regard, because that of long time he had bewitched them with sorceries. ¹²But when they believed Philip preaching the things concerning the kingdom of God, and the name of Jesus Christ, they were baptized, both men and women. ¹³Then Simon himself believed also: and when he was baptized, he continued with Philip, and wondered, beholding the miraclesª and signs which were done.

¹⁴Now when the apostles which were at Jerusalem heard that Samaria had received the word of God, they sent unto them Peter and John: ¹⁵Who, when they were come down, prayed for them, that they might receive the Holy Ghost: ¹⁶(For as yet he was fallen upon none of them: only they were baptized in the name of the Lord Jesus.) ¹⁷Then laid they *their* hands on them, and they received the Holy Ghost. ¹⁸And when Simon saw that through laying on of the apostles' hands the Holy Ghost was given, he offered them money, ¹⁹Saying, Give me also this power, that on whomsoever I lay hands, he may receive the Holy Ghost. ²⁰But Peter said unto him, Thy money perish with thee, because thou hast thought that the gift of God may be purchased with money. ²¹Thou hast neither part nor lot in this matter: for thy heart is not right in the sight of God. ²²Repent therefore of this thy wickedness, and pray God, if perhaps the thought of thine heart may be forgiven thee. ²³For I perceive that thou art in the gall of bitterness, and *in* the bond of iniquity. ²⁴Then answered Simon, and said, Pray ye to the Lord for me, that none of these things which ye have spoken come upon me. ²⁵And they, when they had testified and preached the word of the Lord, returned to Jerusalem, and preached the gospel in many villages of the Samaritans.

²⁶And the angel of the Lord spake unto Philip, saying, Arise, and go toward the south unto the way that goeth down from Jerusalem unto Gaza, which is desert. ²⁷And he arose and went: and, behold, a man of Ethiopia, an eunuch of great authority under Candace queen of the Ethiopians, who had the charge of all her treasure, and had come to Jerusalem for to worship, ²⁸Was returning, and sitting in his chariot read Esaias the prophet. ²⁹Then the Spirit said unto Philip, Go near, and join thyself to this chariot. ³⁰And Philip ran thither to *him*, and heard him read

---

ª miracles . . . : Gr. signs and great miracles

the prophet Esaias, and said, Understandest thou what thou readest? ³¹And he said, How can I, except some man should guide me? And he desired Philip that he would come up and sit with him. ³²The place of the scripture which he read was this, He was led as a sheep to the slaughter; and like a lamb dumb before his shearer, so opened he not his mouth: ³³In his humiliation his judgment was taken away: and who shall declare his generation? for his life is taken from the earth. ³⁴And the eunuch answered Philip, and said, I pray thee, of whom speaketh the prophet this? of himself, or of some other man? ³⁵Then Philip opened his mouth, and began at the same scripture, and preached unto him Jesus. ³⁶And as they went on *their* way, they came unto a certain water: and the eunuch said, See, *here is* water; what doth hinder me to be baptized? ³⁷And Philip said, If thou believest with

---

Devotional Moment

Help

8:30-31 Because we value independence, the idea of asking someone for help often seems repugnant. We reason that requiring assistance implies that we're weak, inadequate, or deficient in some way. That kind of thinking is prideful— and foolish! The fact is we *can't* do everything. We are *not* self-sufficient. Because the Ethiopian official was willing to admit his need, he found the help he desperately desired. God has designed us to need others (and for them to need us). Don't be ashamed to ask for help. And look for ways to use your gifts and abilities to enrich the lives of those you love. Helping, when it is done in a spirit of humility, strengthens relationships.

---

all thine heart, thou mayest. And he answered and said, I believe that Jesus Christ is the Son of God. ³⁸And he commanded the chariot to stand still: and they went down both into the water, both Philip and the eunuch; and he baptized him. ³⁹And when they were come up out of the water, the Spirit of the Lord caught away Philip, that the eunuch saw him no more: and he went on his way rejoicing. ⁴⁰But Philip was found at Azotus: and passing through he preached in all the cities, till he came to Caesarea.

9

¹And Saul, yet breathing out threatenings and slaughter against the disciples of the Lord, went unto the high priest, ²And desired of him letters to Damascus to the synagogues, that if he found any of this way[a], whether they were men or women, he might bring them bound unto Jerusalem. ³And as he journeyed, he came near Damascus: and suddenly there shined round about him a light from heaven: ⁴And he fell to the earth, and heard a voice saying unto him, Saul, Saul, why persecutest thou me? ⁵And he said, Who art thou, Lord? And the Lord said, I am Jesus whom thou persecutest: *it is* hard for thee to kick against the pricks. ⁶And he trembling and astonished said, Lord, what wilt thou have me to do? And the Lord *said* unto him, Arise, and go into the city, and it shall be told thee what thou must do. ⁷And the men which journeyed with him stood speechless, hearing a voice, but seeing no man. ⁸And Saul arose from the earth; and when his

---

[a] of this way: Gr. of the way

eyes were opened, he saw no man: but they led him by the hand, and brought *him* into Damascus. ⁹And he was three days without sight, and neither did eat nor drink.

¹⁰And there was a certain disciple at Damascus, named Ananias; and to him said the Lord in a vision, Ananias. And he said, Behold, I *am here*, Lord. ¹¹And the Lord *said* unto him, Arise, and go into the street which is called Straight, and enquire in the house of Judas for *one* called Saul, of Tarsus: for, behold, he prayeth, ¹²And hath seen in a vision a man named Ananias coming in, and putting *his* hand on him, that he might receive his sight. ¹³Then Ananias answered, Lord, I have heard by many of this man, how much evil he hath done to thy saints at Jerusalem: ¹⁴And here he hath authority from the chief priests to bind all that call on thy name. ¹⁵But the Lord said unto him, Go thy way: for he is a chosen vessel unto me, to bear my name before the Gentiles, and kings, and the children of Israel: ¹⁶For I will shew him how great things he must suffer for my name's sake. ¹⁷And Ananias went his way, and entered into the house; and putting his hands on him said, Brother Saul, the Lord, *even* Jesus, that appeared unto thee in the way as thou camest, hath sent me, that thou mightest receive thy sight, and be filled with the Holy Ghost. ¹⁸And immediately there fell from his eyes as it had been scales: and he received sight forthwith, and arose, and was baptized. ¹⁹And when he had received meat, he was strengthened. Then was Saul certain days with the disciples which were at Damascus. ²⁰And straightway he preached Christ in the synagogues, that he is the Son of God. ²¹But all that heard *him* were amazed, and said; Is not this he that destroyed them which called on this name in Jerusalem, and came hither for that intent, that he might bring them bound unto the chief priests? ²²But Saul increased the more in strength, and confounded the Jews which dwelt at Damascus, proving that this is very Christ.

²³And after that many days were fulfilled, the Jews took counsel to kill him: ²⁴But their laying await was known of Saul. And they watched the gates day and night to kill him. ²⁵Then the disciples took him by night, and let *him* down by the wall in a basket. ²⁶And when Saul was come to Jerusalem, he assayed to join himself to the disciples: but they were all afraid of him, and believed not that he was a disciple. ²⁷But Barnabas took him, and brought *him* to the apostles, and declared unto them how he had seen the Lord in the way, and that he had spoken to him, and how he had preached boldly at Damascus in the name of Jesus. ²⁸And he was with them coming in and going out at Jerusalem. ²⁹And he spake boldly in the name of the Lord Jesus, and disputed against the Grecians: but they went about to slay him. ³⁰*Which* when the brethren knew, they brought him down to Caesarea, and sent him forth to Tarsus. ³¹Then had the churches rest throughout all Judaea and Galilee and Samaria, and were edified; and walking in the fear of the Lord, and in the comfort of the Holy Ghost, were multiplied.

³²And it came to pass, as Peter passed throughout all *quarters*, he came

Paul

You can get dizzy just reading about the apostle Paul's life-style. He went on three missionary journeys, wrote thirteen New Testament books, took Christianity to much of the non-Jewish world throughout the Roman Empire, and trained many of the early church's key leaders. In his extensive travels, he supported himself with freelance tent-making and often stayed with whoever would take him in.

Paul's work involved more than just busyness, too; it also involved great risk to his life. He got into arguments and got beaten up. He even got arrested. See 2 Corinthians 11:24-29 for a detailed list of the occupational hazards he endured.

Do you think Paul could have lived as he did with a family to think about, protect, and care for? Even if he were *willing*, he would have a moral obligation not to (see 1 Tim. 5:8). Thousands of divorced people can tell you what happens when a spouse is never home, totally consumed by a cause all his or her own, or always at the beck and call of others. Many of Paul's exploits would have been out of the question if he had been a husband and father. Being single has its advantages, and Paul knew it (see 1 Cor. 7:32-33).

God gives some the gift of a husband or wife, and others he gives the gift of being able to stay happily unmarried, Paul wrote (1 Cor. 7:7-8). Be content, and use well the gift you have.

LESSONS FROM PAUL AS A SINGLE PERSON

God calls some people to stay single. It's a gift just as legitimate as marriage. Never pressure kids or siblings to get married. Pray for God's leading.

Being single has its advantages. You can serve a broader range of people. You have more freedom, more choices, more options, fewer obligations, more flexibility, and less laundry.

Contentment is the key. Paul probably struggled at times with loneliness and other challenges that face single adults. But he didn't complain. Perhaps keeping busy with his life mission kept him from dwelling on what he didn't have (see Phil. 4:12). Whether you're single or married, your situation is a gift from God (1 Cor. 7:7). Don't complain about it—make the most of it.

down also to the saints which dwelt at Lydda. [33]And there he found a certain man named Aeneas, which had kept his bed eight years, and was sick of the palsy. [34]And Peter said unto him, Aeneas, Jesus Christ maketh thee whole: arise, and make thy bed. And he arose immediately. [35]And all that dwelt at Lydda and Saron saw him, and turned to the Lord.

[36]Now there was at Joppa a certain disciple named Tabitha, which by interpretation is called Dorcas[b]: this woman was full of good works and almsdeeds which she did. [37]And it came to pass in those days, that she was sick, and died: whom when they had washed, they laid her in an upper chamber. [38]And forasmuch as Lydda was nigh to Joppa, and the disciples had heard that Peter was there, they sent unto him two men, desiring him that he would not delay[c] to come to them. [39]Then Peter arose and went with them. When he was come, they brought him into the upper chamber: and all the widows stood by him

weeping, and shewing the coats and garments which Dorcas made, while she was with them. [40]But Peter put them all forth, and kneeled down, and prayed; and turning him to the body said, Tabitha, arise. And she opened her eyes: and when she saw Peter, she sat up. [41]And he gave her his hand, and lifted her up, and when he had called the saints and widows, presented her alive. [42]And it was known throughout all Joppa; and many believed in the Lord. [43]And it came to pass, that he tarried many days in Joppa with one Simon a tanner.

10

[1]There was a certain man in Caesarea called Cornelius, a centurion of the band called the Italian band, [2]A devout man, and one that feared God with all his house, which gave much alms to the people, and prayed to God alway. [3]He saw in a vision evidently about the ninth hour of the day an angel of God coming in to him, and saying unto him, Cornelius. [4]And when he looked on him, he was afraid, and said, What is it, Lord? And he said unto him, Thy prayers and thine alms are come up for a memorial before God. [5]And now send men to Joppa, and call for one Simon, whose surname is Peter: [6]He lodgeth with one Simon a tanner, whose house is by the sea side: he shall tell thee what thou oughtest to do. [7]And when the angel which spake unto Cornelius was departed, he called two of his household servants, and a devout soldier of them that waited on him continually; [8]And

---

Devotional Moment

Kindness

9:36 Don't think that being a missionary or church worker is the only way to deeply impact the world for Christ. Dorcas had a significant ministry in Joppa just helping others—especially the poor. She wasn't a professional minister, she was just a Christian expressing her love for God by doing kind things for others. An encouraging word, a love note, a spontaneous hug, help with an unpleasant task—any of these small acts can make a big difference.

---

[b] Dorcas: or, Doe, or, Roe
[c] delay: or, be grieved

when he had declared all *these* things unto them, he sent them to Joppa.

⁹On the morrow, as they went on their journey, and drew nigh unto the city, Peter went up upon the housetop to pray about the sixth hour: ¹⁰And he became very hungry, and would have eaten: but while they made ready, he fell into a trance, ¹¹And saw heaven opened, and a certain vessel descending unto him, as it had been a great sheet knit at the four corners, and let down to the earth: ¹²Wherein were all manner of fourfooted beasts of the earth, and wild beasts, and creeping things, and fowls of the air. ¹³And there came a voice to him, Rise, Peter; kill, and eat. ¹⁴But Peter said, Not so, Lord; for I have never eaten any thing that is common or unclean. ¹⁵And the voice *spake* unto him again the second time, What God hath cleansed, *that* call not thou common. ¹⁶This was done thrice: and the vessel was received up again into heaven. ¹⁷Now while Peter doubted in himself what this vision which he had seen should mean, behold, the men which were sent from Cornelius had made enquiry for Simon's house, and stood before the gate, ¹⁸And called, and asked whether Simon, which was surnamed Peter, were lodged there.

¹⁹While Peter thought on the vision, the Spirit said unto him, Behold, three men seek thee. ²⁰Arise therefore, and get thee down, and go with them, doubting nothing: for I have sent them. ²¹Then Peter went down to the men which were sent unto him from Cornelius; and said, Behold, I am he whom ye seek: what *is* the cause wherefore ye are come? ²²And they said, Cornelius the centurion, a just man, and one that

feareth God, and of good report among all the nation of the Jews, was warned from God by an holy angel to send for thee into his house, and to hear words of thee. ²³Then called he them in, and lodged *them*. And on the morrow Peter went away with them, and certain brethren from Joppa accompanied him. ²⁴And the morrow after they entered into Caesarea. And Cornelius waited for them, and had called together his kinsmen and near friends. ²⁵And as Peter was coming in, Cornelius met him, and fell down at his feet, and worshipped *him*. ²⁶But Peter took him up, saying, Stand up; I myself also am a man. ²⁷And as he talked with him, he went in, and found many that were come together. ²⁸And he said unto them, Ye know how that it is an unlawful thing for a man that is a Jew to keep company, or come unto one of another nation; but God hath shewed me that I should not call any man common or unclean. ²⁹Therefore came I *unto you* without gainsaying, as soon as I was sent for: I ask therefore for what intent ye have sent for me? ³⁰And Cornelius said, Four days ago I was fasting until this hour; and at the ninth hour I prayed in my house, and, behold, a man stood before me in bright clothing, ³¹And said, Cornelius, thy prayer is heard, and thine alms are had in remembrance in the sight of God. ³²Send therefore to Joppa, and call hither Simon, whose surname is Peter; he is lodged in the house of *one* Simon a tanner by the sea side: who, when he cometh, shall speak unto thee. ³³Immediately therefore I sent to thee; and thou hast well done that thou art come. Now therefore are we all here present before God, to hear all things that are commanded thee of God.

³⁴Then Peter opened *his* mouth, and said, Of a truth I perceive that God is no respecter of persons: ³⁵But in every nation he that feareth him, and worketh righteousness, is accepted with him. ³⁶The word which *God* sent unto the children of Israel, preaching peace by Jesus Christ: (he is Lord of all:) ³⁷That word, *I say,* ye know, which was published throughout all Judaea, and began from Galilee, after the baptism which John preached; ³⁸How God anointed Jesus of Nazareth with the Holy Ghost and with power: who went about doing good, and healing all that were oppressed of the devil; for God was with him. ³⁹And we are witnesses of all things which he did both in the land of the Jews, and in Jerusalem; whom they slew and hanged on a tree: ⁴⁰Him God raised up the third day, and shewed him openly; ⁴¹Not to all the people, but unto witnesses chosen before of God, *even* to us, who did eat and drink with him after he rose from the dead. ⁴²And he commanded us to preach unto the people, and to testify that it is he which was ordained of God *to be* the Judge of quick and dead. ⁴³To him give all the prophets witness, that through his name whosoever believeth in him shall receive remission of sins.

⁴⁴While Peter yet spake these words, the Holy Ghost fell on all them which heard the word. ⁴⁵And they of the circumcision which believed were astonished, as many as came with Peter, because that on the Gentiles also was poured out the gift of the Holy Ghost. ⁴⁶For they heard them speak with tongues, and magnify God. Then an-

swered Peter, ⁴⁷Can any man forbid water, that these should not be baptized, which have received the Holy Ghost as well as we? ⁴⁸And he commanded them to be baptized in the name of the Lord. Then prayed they him to tarry certain days.

11

¹And the apostles and brethren that were in Judaea heard that the Gentiles had also received the word of God. ²And when Peter was come up to Jerusalem, they that were of the circumcision contended with him, ³Saying, Thou wentest in to men uncircumcised, and didst eat with them. ⁴But Peter rehearsed *the matter* from the beginning, and expounded *it* by order unto them, saying, ⁵I was in the city of Joppa praying: and in a trance I saw a vision, A certain vessel descend, as it had been a great sheet, let down from heaven by four corners; and it came even to me: ⁶Upon the which when I had fastened mine eyes, I considered, and saw fourfooted beasts of the earth, and wild beasts, and creeping things, and fowls of the air. ⁷And I heard a

---

Devotional Moment

•

Judging Others

11:2-18 As soon as the Jewish believers in Jerusalem heard that Peter had shared a meal with some non-Jews, they began to criticize him. It is never wise to judge quickly without first learning the facts. We tend to be harder on others than we are on ourselves; we justify our own actions while often assuming the worst of others. This doesn't mean we have to be naive or gullible but just give others the benefit of the doubt. Gather and weigh all pertinent information before passing judgment.

voice saying unto me, Arise, Peter; slay and eat. [8]But I said, Not so, Lord: for nothing common or unclean hath at any time entered into my mouth. [9]But the voice answered me again from heaven, What God hath cleansed, *that* call not thou common. [10]And this was done three times: and all were drawn up again into heaven. [11]And, behold, immediately there were three men already come unto the house where I was, sent from Caesarea unto me. [12]And the Spirit bade me go with them, nothing doubting. Moreover these six brethren accompanied me, and we entered into the man's house: [13]And he shewed us how he had seen an angel in his house, which stood and said unto him, Send men to Joppa, and call for Simon, whose surname is Peter; [14]Who shall tell thee words, whereby thou and all thy house shall be saved. [15]And as I began to speak, the Holy Ghost fell on them, as on us at the beginning. [16]Then remembered I the word of the Lord, how that he said, John indeed baptized with water; but ye shall be baptized with the Holy Ghost. [17]Forasmuch then as God gave them the like gift as *he did* unto us, who believed on the Lord Jesus Christ; what was I, that I could withstand God? [18]When they heard these things, they held their peace, and glorified God, saying, Then hath God also to the Gentiles granted repentance unto life.

[19]Now they which were scattered abroad upon the persecution that arose about Stephen travelled as far as Phenice, and Cyprus, and Antioch, preaching the word to none but unto the Jews only. [20]And some of them were men of Cyprus and Cyrene, which, when they were come to Antioch, spake unto the Grecians, preaching the Lord Jesus. [21]And the hand of the Lord was with them: and a great number believed, and turned unto the Lord. [22]Then tidings of these things came unto the ears of the church which was in Jerusalem: and they sent forth Barnabas, that he should go as far as Antioch. [23]Who, when he came, and had seen the grace of God, was glad, and exhorted them all, that with purpose of heart they would cleave unto the Lord. [24]For he was a good man, and full of the Holy Ghost and of faith: and much people was added unto the Lord. [25]Then departed Barnabas to Tarsus, for to seek Saul: [26]And when he had found him, he brought him unto Antioch. And it came to pass, that a whole year they assembled themselves with[a] the church, and taught much people. And the disci-

---

Devotional Moment

Encouragement

11:22-26 The name *Barnabas* means "son of encouragement." It was a nickname given to Joseph (see 4:36) because of his lifelong practice of coming alongside others to support and advise them. Barnabas was a kind man who enjoyed helping new believers grow in their faith. He was willing to believe in Saul (9:26-28) and John Mark (15:36-40) when nobody else wanted to give them a chance. If you want to make a major difference in the lives of others, make a practice of encouraging them. Praise them whenever they do something right; tell them that you believe in them; cheer them on; remind them that they can do it. Sincere encouragement will make a big difference.

---

[a] with . . . : or, in the church

ples were called Christians first in Antioch. ²⁷And in these days came prophets from Jerusalem unto Antioch. ²⁸And there stood up one of them named Agabus, and signified by the Spirit that there should be great dearth throughout all the world: which came to pass in the days of Claudius Caesar. ²⁹Then the disciples, every man according to his ability, determined to send relief unto the brethren which dwelt in Judaea: ³⁰Which also they did, and sent it to the elders by the hands of Barnabas and Saul.

12

¹Now about that time Herod the king stretched forth *his* hands to vex certain of the church. ²And he killed James the brother of John with the sword. ³And because he saw it pleased the Jews, he proceeded further to take Peter also. (Then were the days of unleavened bread.) ⁴And when he had apprehended him, he put *him* in prison, and delivered *him* to four quaternions of soldiers to keep him; intending after Easterᵃ to bring him forth to the people. ⁵Peter therefore was kept in prison: but prayerᵇ was made without ceasing of the church unto God for him. ⁶And when Herod would have brought him forth, the same night Peter was sleeping between two soldiers, bound with two chains: and the keepers before the door kept the prison. ⁷And, behold, the angel of the Lord came upon *him*, and a light shined in the prison: and he smote Peter on the side, and raised him up, say-

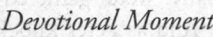

Devotional Moment

•

Prayer

12:5 Burly soldiers, brutal arrests, prison cells, death sentences—what could the struggling church possibly do in the face of such fierce opposition? They could pray, and they did so, earnestly and faithfully. They may not have had great faith (vv. 14-16), but they had a great God who heard their pleas and worked on their behalf. If you sometimes catch yourself saying, "I guess there's nothing left to do but pray," remember this episode. Prayer should not be used merely as a last resort. Prayer should be an immediate response to every challenge you face. (See Phil. 4:6-7 and 1 Thess. 5:17 for more on prayer.)

ing, Arise up quickly. And his chains fell off from *his* hands. ⁸And the angel said unto him, Gird thyself, and bind on thy sandals. And so he did. And he saith unto him, Cast thy garment about thee, and follow me. ⁹And he went out, and followed him; and wist not that it was true which was done by the angel; but thought he saw a vision. ¹⁰When they were past the first and the second ward, they came unto the iron gate that leadeth unto the city; which opened to them of his own accord: and they went out, and passed on through one street; and forthwith the angel departed from him. ¹¹And when Peter was come to himself, he said, Now I know of a surety, that the Lord hath sent his angel, and hath delivered me out of the hand of Herod, and *from* all the expectation of the people of the Jews. ¹²And when he had considered *the thing*, he came to the house of Mary the mother of John, whose surname was Mark;

ᵃ Easter: Gr. Passover

ᵇ prayer . . . : or, instant and earnest prayer was made

where many were gathered together praying. ¹³And as Peter knocked at the door of the gate, a damsel came to hearken^c, named Rhoda. ¹⁴And when she knew Peter's voice, she opened not the gate for gladness, but ran in, and told how Peter stood before the gate. ¹⁵And they said unto her, Thou art mad. But she constantly affirmed that it was even so. Then said they, It is his angel. ¹⁶But Peter continued knocking: and when they had opened *the door*, and saw him, they were astonished. ¹⁷But he, beckoning unto them with the hand to hold their peace, declared unto them how the Lord had brought him out of the prison. And he said, Go shew these things unto James, and to the brethren. And he departed, and went into another place. ¹⁸Now as soon as it was day, there was no small stir among the soldiers, what was become of Peter. ¹⁹And when Herod had sought for him, and found him not, he examined the keepers, and commanded that *they* should be put to death. And he went down from Judaea to Caesarea, and *there* abode.

²⁰And Herod was highly displeased with them of Tyre and Sidon: but they came with one accord to him, and, having made Blastus the king's chamberlain their friend, desired peace; because their country was nourished by the king's *country*. ²¹And upon a set day Herod, arrayed in royal apparel, sat upon his throne, and made an oration unto them. ²²And the people gave a shout, *saying, It is* the voice of a god, and not of a man. ²³And immediately the angel of the Lord smote him, because he gave not God the glory: and he was eaten of worms, and gave up the ghost. ²⁴But the word of God grew and multiplied. ²⁵And Barnabas and Saul returned from Jerusalem, when they had fulfilled *their* ministry^d, and took with them John, whose surname was Mark.

13

¹Now there were in the church that was at Antioch certain prophets and teachers; as Barnabas, and Simeon that was called Niger, and Lucius of Cyrene, and Manaen, which had been brought up with Herod the tetrarch, and Saul. ²As they ministered to the Lord, and fasted, the Holy Ghost said, Separate me Barnabas and Saul for the work whereunto I have called them. ³And when they had fasted and prayed, and laid *their* hands on them, they sent *them* away.

⁴So they, being sent forth by the Holy Ghost, departed unto Seleucia; and from thence they sailed to Cyprus. ⁵And when they were at Salamis, they preached the word of God in the synagogues of the Jews: and they had also John to *their* minister. ⁶And when they had gone through the isle unto Paphos, they found a certain sorcerer, a false prophet, a Jew, whose name *was* Barjesus: ⁷Which was with the deputy of the country, Sergius Paulus, a prudent man; who called for Barnabas and Saul, and desired to hear the word of God. ⁸But Elymas the sorcerer (for so is his name by interpretation) withstood them, seeking to turn away the deputy from the faith. ⁹Then Saul, (who also *is*

---

^c to hearken: or, to ask who was there
^d ministry: or, charge

called Paul,) filled with the Holy Ghost, set his eyes on him, ¹⁰And said, O full of all subtilty and all mischief, *thou* child of the devil, *thou* enemy of all righteousness, wilt thou not cease to pervert the right ways of the Lord? ¹¹And now, behold, the hand of the Lord *is* upon thee, and thou shalt be blind, not seeing the sun for a season. And immediately there fell on him a mist and a darkness; and he went about seeking some to lead him by the hand. ¹²Then the deputy, when he saw what was done, believed, being astonished at the doctrine of the Lord. ¹³Now when Paul and his company loosed from Paphos, they came to Perga in Pamphylia: and John departing from them returned to Jerusalem.

¹⁴But when they departed from Perga, they came to Antioch in Pisidia, and went into the synagogue on the sabbath day, and sat down. ¹⁵And after the reading of the law and the prophets the rulers of the synagogue sent unto them, saying, *Ye* men *and* brethren, if ye have any word of exhortation for the people, say on. ¹⁶Then Paul stood up, and beckoning with *his* hand said, Men of Israel, and ye that fear God, give audience. ¹⁷The God of this people of Israel chose our fathers, and exalted the people when they dwelt as strangers in the land of Egypt, and with an high arm brought he them out of it. ¹⁸And about the time of forty years suffered he their manners in the wilderness. ¹⁹And when he had destroyed seven nations in the land of Chanaan, he divided their land to them by lot. ²⁰And after that he gave *unto them* judges about the space of four hundred and fifty years, until Samuel the prophet. ²¹And afterward they desired a king: and

God gave unto them Saul the son of Cis, a man of the tribe of Benjamin, by the space of forty years. ²²And when he had removed him, he raised up unto them David to be their king; to whom also he gave testimony, and said, I have found David the *son* of Jesse, a man after mine own heart, which shall fulfil all my will. ²³Of this man's seed hath God according to *his* promise raised unto Israel a Saviour, Jesus: ²⁴When John had first preached before his coming the baptism of repentance to all the people of Israel. ²⁵And as John fulfilled his course, he said, Whom think ye that I am? I am not *he.* But, behold, there cometh one after me, whose shoes of *his* feet I am not worthy to loose. ²⁶Men *and* brethren, children of the stock of Abraham, and whosoever among you feareth God, to you is the word of this salvation sent. ²⁷For they that dwell at Jerusalem, and their rulers, because they knew him not, nor yet the voices of the prophets which are read every sabbath day, they have fulfilled *them* in condemning *him.* ²⁸And though they found no cause of death *in him,* yet desired they Pilate that he should be slain. ²⁹And when they had fulfilled all that was written of him, they took *him* down from the tree, and laid *him* in a sepulchre. ³⁰But God raised him from the dead: ³¹And he was seen many days of them which came up with him from Galilee to Jerusalem, who are his witnesses unto the people. ³²And we declare unto you glad tidings, how that the promise which was made unto the fathers, ³³God hath fulfilled the same unto us their children, in that he hath raised up Jesus again; as it is also written in the second psalm, Thou art my Son, this day have I begotten thee. ³⁴And as concerning that he raised him up from the dead, *now* no more to return to corruption, he said on this wise, I will give you the sure mercies[a] of David. [35]Wherefore he saith also in another *psalm*, Thou shalt not suffer thine Holy One to see corruption. [36]For David, after he had served his own generation by the will of God, fell on sleep, and was laid unto his fathers, and saw corruption: [37]But he, whom God raised again, saw no corruption. [38]Be it known unto you therefore, men *and* brethren, that through this man is preached unto you the forgiveness of sins: [39]And by him all that believe are justified from all things, from which ye could not be justified by the law of Moses. [40]Beware therefore, lest that come upon you, which is spoken of in the prophets; [41]Behold, ye despisers, and wonder, and perish: for I work a work in your days, a work which ye shall in no wise believe, though a man declare it unto you.

[42]And when the Jews were gone out of the synagogue, the Gentiles besought that these words might be preached to them the next[b] sabbath. [43]Now when the congregation was broken up, many of the Jews and religious proselytes followed Paul and Barnabas: who, speaking to them, persuaded them to continue in the grace of God. [44]And the next sabbath day came almost the whole city together to hear the word of God. [45]But when the Jews saw the multitudes, they were filled with envy, and spake against those things which were spoken by Paul, contradicting and blaspheming. [46]Then Paul and

Barnabas waxed bold, and said, It was necessary that the word of God should first have been spoken to you: but seeing ye put it from you, and judge yourselves unworthy of everlasting life, lo, we turn to the Gentiles. [47]For so hath the Lord commanded us, *saying*, I have set thee to be a light of the Gentiles, that thou shouldest be for salvation unto the ends of the earth. [48]And when the Gentiles heard this, they were glad, and glorified the word of the Lord: and as many as were ordained to eternal life believed. [49]And the word of the Lord was published throughout all the region. [50]But the Jews stirred up the devout and honourable women, and the chief men of the city, and raised persecution against Paul and Barnabas, and expelled them out of their coasts. [51]But they shook off the dust of their feet against them, and came unto Iconium. [52]And the disciples were filled with joy, and with the Holy Ghost.

14

[1]And it came to pass in Iconium, that they went both together into the synagogue of the Jews, and so spake, that a great multitude both of the Jews and also of the Greeks believed. [2]But the unbelieving Jews stirred up the Gentiles, and made their minds evil affected against the brethren. [3]Long time therefore abode they speaking boldly in the Lord, which gave testimony unto the word of his grace, and granted signs and wonders to be done by their hands. [4]But the multitude of the city was di-

---

[a] mercies: Gr. holy, or just things: which word the Septuagint in many places, uses for that which is in the Hebrew, mercies

[b] the next . . . : Gr. in the week between, or, in the sabbath between

vided: and part held with the Jews, and part with the apostles. ⁵And when there was an assault made both of the Gentiles, and also of the Jews with their rulers, to use *them* despitefully, and to stone them, ⁶They were ware of *it*, and fled unto Lystra and Derbe, cities of Lycaonia, and unto the region that lieth round about: ⁷And there they preached the gospel.

⁸And there sat a certain man at Lystra, impotent in his feet, being a cripple from his mother's womb, who never had walked: ⁹The same heard Paul speak: who stedfastly beholding him, and perceiving that he had faith to be healed, ¹⁰Said with a loud voice, Stand upright on thy feet. And he leaped and walked. ¹¹And when the people saw what Paul had done, they lifted up their voices, saying in the speech of Lycaonia, The gods are come down to us in the likeness of men. ¹²And they called Barnabas, Jupiter; and Paul, Mercurius, because he was the chief speaker. ¹³Then the priest of Jupiter, which was before their city, brought oxen and garlands unto the gates, and would have done sacrifice with the people. ¹⁴*Which* when the apostles, Barnabas and Paul, heard *of*, they rent their clothes, and ran in among the people, crying out, ¹⁵And saying, Sirs, why do ye these things? We also are men of like passions with you, and preach unto you that ye should turn from these vanities unto the living God, which made heaven, and earth, and the sea, and all things that are therein: ¹⁶Who in times past suffered all nations to walk in their own ways. ¹⁷Nevertheless he left not himself without witness, in that he did good, and gave us rain from heaven, and fruitful seasons, filling

Worship
in Your Home

DEVOTIONS ARE FOR THE WHOLE FAMILY
When he had brought them into his house, he set meat before them, and rejoiced, believing in God with all his house. Acts 16:34

There are times when each of us meet God privately in Bible study and prayer. We may call these "devotions" or "quiet times."

But family devotions are a little different. Instead of meeting God individually, our family meets God together. An assortment of ages, needs, problems, and responses is involved.

Let's take a subject such as forgiveness. Suppose we read the Bible story of Joseph forgiving his brothers. Everyone in the family could respond to questions such as: Do you think Joseph did the right thing when he forgave his brothers? What would you have done? Think of some time when you wanted to get even—what did you want to do? Why didn't you (or did you)? How do you want others to act when you do something wrong against them? Why is it hard to forgive someone who has hurt you?

Responses will be very different among family members. The richness of family devotions is the opportunity to help one another with such matters as forgiveness, honesty, truthfulness, and loving others.

our hearts with food and gladness. [18]And with these sayings scarce restrained they the people, that they had not done sacrifice unto them.

[19]And there came thither *certain* Jews from Antioch and Iconium, who persuaded the people, and, having stoned Paul, drew *him* out of the city, supposing he had been dead. [20]Howbeit, as the disciples stood round about him, he rose up, and came into the city: and the next day he departed with Barnabas to Derbe. [21]And when they had preached the gospel to that city, and had taught many[a], they returned again to Lystra, and *to* Iconium, and Antioch, [22]Confirming the souls of the disciples, *and* exhorting them to continue in the faith, and that we must through much tribulation enter into the kingdom of God. [23]And when they had ordained them elders in every church, and had prayed with fasting, they commended them to the Lord, on whom they believed. [24]And after they had passed throughout Pisidia, they came to Pamphylia. [25]And when they had preached the word in Perga, they went down into Attalia: [26]And thence sailed to Antioch, from whence they had been recommended to the grace of God for the work which they fulfilled. [27]And when they were come, and had gathered the church together, they rehearsed all that God had done with them, and how he had opened the door of faith unto the Gentiles. [28]And there they abode long time with the disciples.

15

[1]And certain men which came down from Judaea taught the brethren, *and* *said,* Except ye be circumcised after the manner of Moses, ye cannot be saved. [2]When therefore Paul and Barnabas had no small dissension and disputation with them, they determined that Paul and Barnabas, and certain other of them, should go up to Jerusalem unto the apostles and elders about this question. [3]And being brought on their way by the church, they passed through Phenice and Samaria, declaring the conversion of the Gentiles: and they caused great joy unto all the brethren. [4]And when they were come to Jerusalem, they were received of the church, and *of* the apostles and elders, and they declared all things that God had done with them. [5]But there rose up certain of the sect of the Pharisees which believed, saying, That it was needful to circumcise them, and to command *them* to keep the law of Moses.

[6]And the apostles and elders came together for to consider of this matter. [7]And when there had been much disputing, Peter rose up, and said unto them, Men *and* brethren, ye know how that a good while ago God made choice among us, that the Gentiles by my mouth should hear the word of the gospel, and believe. [8]And God, which knoweth the hearts, bare them witness, giving them the Holy Ghost, even as *he did* unto us; [9]And put no difference between us and them, purifying their hearts by faith. [10]Now therefore why tempt ye God, to put a yoke upon the neck of the disciples, which neither our fathers nor we were able to bear? [11]But we believe that through the grace of the Lord Jesus Christ we shall be saved, even as they. [12]Then all the multitude kept silence, and gave audience to Barnabas

---

[a] had taught many: Gr. had made many disciples

and Paul, declaring what miracles and wonders God had wrought among the Gentiles by them. ¹³And after they had held their peace, James answered, saying, Men *and* brethren, hearken unto me: ¹⁴Simeon hath declared how God at the first did visit the Gentiles, to take out of them a people for his name. ¹⁵And to this agree the words of the prophets; as it is written, ¹⁶After this I will return, and will build again the tabernacle of David, which is fallen down; and I will build again the ruins thereof, and I will set it up: ¹⁷That the residue of men might seek after the Lord, and all the Gentiles, upon whom my name is called, saith the Lord, who doeth all these things. ¹⁸Known unto God are all his works from the beginning of the world. ¹⁹Wherefore my sentence is, that we trouble not them, which from among the Gentiles are turned to God: ²⁰But that we write unto them, that they abstain from pollutions of idols, and *from* fornication, and *from* things strangled, and *from* blood. ²¹For Moses of old time hath in every city them that preach him, being read in the synagogues every sabbath day.

²²Then pleased it the apostles and elders, with the whole church, to send chosen men of their own company to Antioch with Paul and Barnabas; *namely,* Judas surnamed Barsabas, and Silas, chief men among the brethren: ²³And they wrote *letters* by them after this manner; The apostles and elders and brethren *send* greeting unto the brethren which are of the Gentiles in Antioch and Syria and Cilicia: ²⁴Forasmuch as we have heard, that certain which went out from us have

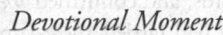

Devotional Moment
•
Disputes
15:23-31 The young, rapidly growing church had a diverse membership composed of both Jews and Gentiles, with legalism on one extreme and excessive freedom on the other. But guided by the Holy Spirit, they were able to agree upon a course of action that was sensitive, sensible, and unifying. They came to this decision *together,* after careful consideration of what mattered to God. When you are called upon to mediate a dispute—whether in your family or elsewhere—this is a good example to follow.

troubled you with words, subverting your souls, saying, Ye *must* be circumcised, and keep the law: to whom we gave no *such* commandment: ²⁵It seemed good unto us, being assembled with one accord, to send chosen men unto you with our beloved Barnabas and Paul, ²⁶Men that have hazarded their lives for the name of our Lord Jesus Christ. ²⁷We have sent therefore Judas and Silas, who shall also tell *you* the same things by mouth[a]. ²⁸For it seemed good to the Holy Ghost, and to us, to lay upon you no greater burden than these necessary things; ²⁹That ye abstain from meats offered to idols, and from blood, and from things strangled, and from fornication: from which if ye keep yourselves, ye shall do well. Fare ye well. ³⁰So when they were dismissed, they came to Antioch: and when they had gathered the multitude together, they delivered the epistle: ³¹*Which* when they had read, they rejoiced for the consolation[b]. ³²And Judas and Silas, being prophets also themselves, exhorted the brethren with

[a] mouth: Gr. word
[b] consolation: or, exhortation

many words, and confirmed *them.* ³³And after they had tarried *there* a space, they were let go in peace from the brethren unto the apostles. ³⁴Notwithstanding it pleased Silas to abide there still. ³⁵Paul also and Barnabas continued in Antioch, teaching and preaching the word of the Lord, with many others also.

³⁶And some days after Paul said unto Barnabas, Let us go again and visit our brethren in every city where we have preached the word of the Lord, *and see* how they do. ³⁷And Barnabas determined to take with them John, whose surname was Mark. ³⁸But Paul thought not good to take him with them, who departed from them from Pamphylia, and went not with them to the work. ³⁹And the contention was so sharp between them, that they departed asunder one from the other: and so Barnabas took Mark, and sailed unto Cyprus; ⁴⁰And Paul chose Silas, and departed, being recommended by the brethren unto the grace of God. ⁴¹And he went through Syria and Cilicia, confirming the churches.

16

¹Then came he to Derbe and Lystra: and, behold, a certain disciple was there, named Timotheus, the son of a certain woman, which was a Jewess, and believed; but his father *was* a Greek: ²Which was well reported of by the brethren that were at Lystra and Iconium. ³Him would Paul have to go forth with him; and took and circumcised him because of the Jews which were in those quarters: for they knew all that his father was a Greek. ⁴And as they went through the cities, they de-

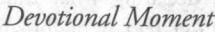

Devotional Moment

Nature vs. Nurture

16:1 Although Timothy's mother was a Christian, his father was not. Despite this mixed marriage, Timothy became an effective leader in the early church. If one of your parents or your spouse is not a believer, remember the example of Timothy. God is bigger than circumstances; he can shape you into an effective servant of Christ, even in a challenging environment.

livered them the decrees for to keep, that were ordained of the apostles and elders which were at Jerusalem. ⁵And so were the churches established in the faith, and increased in number daily.

⁶Now when they had gone throughout Phrygia and the region of Galatia, and were forbidden of the Holy Ghost to preach the word in Asia, ⁷After they were come to Mysia, they assayed to go into Bithynia: but the Spirit suffered them not. ⁸And they passing by Mysia came down to Troas. ⁹And a vision appeared to Paul in the night; There stood a man of Macedonia, and prayed him, saying, Come over into Macedonia, and help us. ¹⁰And after he had seen the vision, immediately we endeavoured to go into Macedonia, assuredly gathering that the Lord had called us for to preach the gospel unto them. ¹¹Therefore loosing from Troas, we came with a straight course to Samothracia, and the next *day* to Neapolis; ¹²And from thence to Philippi, which is the chief ᵃ city of that part of Macedonia, *and* a colony: and we were in that city abiding certain days. ¹³And on the sabbath ᵇ we went out of the

ᵃ the chief: or, the first
ᵇ sabbath: Gr. sabbath day

city by a river side, where prayer was wont to be made; and we sat down, and spake unto the women which resorted *thither.* ¹⁴And a certain woman named Lydia, a seller of purple, of the city of Thyatira, which worshipped God, heard *us:* whose heart the Lord opened, that she attended unto the things which were spoken of Paul. ¹⁵And when she was baptized, and her household, she besought *us,* saying, If ye have judged me to be faithful to the Lord, come into my house, and abide *there.* And she constrained us.

¹⁶And it came to pass, as we went to prayer, a certain damsel possessed with a spirit of divination^c met us, which brought her masters much gain by soothsaying: ¹⁷The same followed Paul and us, and cried, saying, These men are the servants of the most high God, which shew unto us the way of salvation. ¹⁸And this did she many days. But Paul, being grieved, turned and said to the spirit, I command thee in the name of Jesus Christ to come out of her. And he came out the same hour. ¹⁹And when her masters saw that the hope of their gains was gone, they caught Paul and Silas, and drew *them* into the marketplace^d unto the rulers, ²⁰And brought them to the magistrates, saying, These men, being Jews, do exceedingly trouble our city, ²¹And teach customs, which are not lawful for us to receive, neither to observe, being Romans. ²²And the multitude rose up together against them: and the magistrates rent off their clothes, and commanded to beat *them.* ²³And when they had laid many stripes upon them,

they cast *them* into prison, charging the jailor to keep them safely: ²⁴Who, having received such a charge, thrust them into the inner prison, and made their feet fast in the stocks.

²⁵And at midnight Paul and Silas prayed, and sang praises unto God: and the prisoners heard them. ²⁶And suddenly there was a great earthquake, so that the foundations of the prison were shaken: and immediately all the doors were opened, and every one's bands were loosed. ²⁷And the keeper of the prison awaking out of his sleep, and seeing the prison doors open, he drew out his sword, and would have killed himself, supposing that the prisoners had been fled. ²⁸But Paul cried with a loud voice, saying, Do thyself no harm: for we are all here. ²⁹Then he called for a light, and sprang in, and came trembling, and fell down before Paul and Silas, ³⁰And brought them out, and said, Sirs, what must I do to be saved? ³¹And they said, Believe on the Lord Jesus Christ, and thou shalt be saved, and thy house. ³²And they spake unto him the word of the Lord, and to all that were in his house. ³³And he took them the same hour of the night, and washed *their* stripes; and was baptized, he and all his, straightway. ³⁴And when he had brought them into his house, he set meat before them, and rejoiced, believing in God with all his house.

³⁵And when it was day, the magistrates sent the serjeants, saying, Let those men go. ³⁶And the keeper of the prison told this saying to Paul, The magistrates have sent to let you go: now

---

^c of divination: or, of Python
^d marketplace: or, court

therefore depart, and go in peace. [37]But Paul said unto them, They have beaten us openly uncondemned, being Romans, and have cast *us* into prison; and now do they thrust us out privily? nay verily; but let them come themselves and fetch us out. [38]And the serjeants told these words unto the magistrates: and they feared, when they heard that they were Romans. [39]And they came and besought them, and brought *them* out, and desired *them* to depart out of the city. [40]And they went out of the prison, and entered into *the house of* Lydia: and when they had seen the brethren, they comforted them, and departed.

17

[1]Now when they had passed through Amphipolis and Apollonia, they came to Thessalonica, where was a synagogue of the Jews: [2]And Paul, as his manner was, went in unto them, and three sabbath days reasoned with them out of the scriptures, [3]Opening and alleging, that Christ must needs have suffered, and risen again from the dead; and that this Jesus, whom[a] I preach unto you, is Christ. [4]And some of them believed, and consorted with Paul and Silas; and of the devout Greeks a great multitude, and of the chief women not a few. [5]But the Jews which believed not, moved with envy, took unto them certain lewd fellows of the baser sort, and gathered a company, and set all the city on an uproar, and assaulted the house of Jason, and sought to bring them out to the people. [6]And when they found them not, they drew Jason and certain brethren unto the rulers of the city, crying, These that have turned the world upside down are come hither also; [7]Whom Jason hath received: and these all do contrary to the decrees of Caesar, saying that there is another king, *one* Jesus. [8]And they troubled the people and the rulers of the city, when they heard these things. [9]And when they had taken security of Jason, and of the other, they let them go.

[10]And the brethren immediately sent away Paul and Silas by night unto Berea: who coming *thither* went into the synagogue of the Jews. [11]These were more noble than those in Thessalonica, in that they received the word with all readiness of mind, and searched the scriptures daily, whether those things were so. [12]Therefore many of them believed; also of honourable women which were Greeks, and of men, not a few. [13]But when the Jews of Thessalonica had knowledge that the word of God was preached of Paul at Berea, they came thither also, and stirred up the people. [14]And then immediately the brethren sent away Paul to go as it were to the sea: but Silas and Timotheus abode there still. [15]And they that conducted Paul brought him unto Athens: and receiving a commandment unto Silas and Timotheus for to come to him with all speed, they departed.

[16]Now while Paul waited for them at Athens, his spirit was stirred in him, when he saw the city wholly given to idolatry. [17]Therefore disputed he in the synagogue with the Jews, and with the devout persons, and in the market daily with them that met with him. [18]Then

---

[a] whom . . . : or, whom, said he, I preach

certain philosophers of the Epicureans, and of the Stoicks, encountered him. And some said, What will this babbler[b] say? other some, He seemeth to be a setter forth of strange gods: because he preached unto them Jesus, and the resurrection. ¹⁹And they took him, and brought him unto Areopagus, saying, May we know what this new doctrine, whereof thou speakest, *is*? ²⁰For thou bringest certain strange things to our ears: we would know therefore what these things mean. ²¹(For all the Athenians and strangers which were there spent their time in nothing else, but either to tell, or to hear some new thing.)

²²Then Paul stood in the midst of Mars' hill[c], and said, *Ye* men of Athens, I perceive that in all things ye are too superstitious. ²³For as I passed by, and beheld your devotions[d], I found an altar with this inscription, TO THE UNKNOWN GOD. Whom therefore ye ignorantly worship, him declare I unto you. ²⁴God that made the world and all things therein, seeing that he is Lord of heaven and earth, dwelleth not in temples made with hands; ²⁵Neither is worshipped with men's hands, as though he needed any thing, seeing he giveth to all life, and breath, and all things; ²⁶And hath made of one blood all nations of men for to dwell on all the face of the earth, and hath determined the times before appointed, and the bounds of their habitation; ²⁷That they should seek the Lord, if haply they might feel after him, and find him, though he be

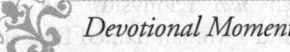

Devotional Moment
·
Respect

17:23 When Paul spoke to the Athenians, who worshiped idols, he spoke to them respectfully. He didn't mock them or call them names. This won him the right to speak to them about the one true God. Respect for people goes a long way toward winning their ear. Everyone can gain a hearing for important views by showing others the same respect that he or she wishes to receive. Treat children as people. Treat spouses as equals. Treat neighbors with deference. Respect breeds respect. Don't wait for someone else to do it first.

not far from every one of us: ²⁸For in him we live, and move, and have our being; as certain also of your own poets have said, For we are also his offspring. ²⁹Forasmuch then as we are the offspring of God, we ought not to think that the Godhead is like unto gold, or silver, or stone, graven by art and man's device. ³⁰And the times of this ignorance God winked at; but now commandeth all men every where to repent: ³¹Because he hath appointed a day, in the which he will judge the world in righteousness by *that* man whom he hath ordained; *whereof* he hath given[e] assurance unto all *men*, in that he hath raised him from the dead.

³²And when they heard of the resurrection of the dead, some mocked: and others said, We will hear thee again of this *matter*. ³³So Paul departed from among them. ³⁴Howbeit certain men clave unto him, and believed: among

---

[b] babbler: or, base fellow
[c] Mars' hill: or, the court of the Areopagites
[d] devotions: or, gods that ye worship
[e] hath given . . . : or, offered faith

the which *was* Dionysius the Areopagite, and a woman named Damaris, and others with them.

18

¹After these things Paul departed from Athens, and came to Corinth; ²And found a certain Jew named Aquila, born in Pontus, lately come from Italy, with his wife Priscilla; (because that Claudius had commanded all Jews to depart from Rome:) and came unto them. ³And because he was of the same craft, he abode with them, and wrought: for by their occupation they were tentmakers. ⁴And he reasoned in the synagogue every sabbath, and persuaded the Jews and the Greeks. ⁵And when Silas and Timotheus were come from Macedonia, Paul was pressed in the spirit, and testified to the Jews *that* Jesus *was* Christ. ⁶And when they opposed themselves, and blasphemed, he shook *his* raiment, and said unto them, Your blood *be* upon your own heads; I *am* clean: from henceforth I will go unto the Gentiles.

⁷And he departed thence, and entered into a certain *man's* house, named Justus, *one* that worshipped God, whose house joined hard to the synagogue. ⁸And Crispus, the chief ruler of the synagogue, believed on the Lord with all his house; and many of the Corinthians hearing believed, and were baptized. ⁹Then spake the Lord to Paul in the night by a vision, Be not afraid, but speak, and hold not thy peace: ¹⁰For I am with thee, and no man shall set on thee to hurt thee: for I have much people in this city. ¹¹And he continued *there* a year and six months, teaching the word of God among them.

¹²And when Gallio was the deputy of Achaia, the Jews made insurrection with one accord against Paul, and brought him to the judgment seat, ¹³Saying, This *fellow* persuadeth men to worship God contrary to the law. ¹⁴And when Paul was now about to open *his* mouth, Gallio said unto the Jews, If it were a matter of wrong or wicked lewdness, O *ye* Jews, reason would that I should bear with you: ¹⁵But if it be a question of words and names, and *of* your law, look ye *to it*; for I will be no judge of such *matters*. ¹⁶And he drave them from the judgment seat. ¹⁷Then all the Greeks took Sosthenes, the chief ruler of the synagogue, and beat *him* before the judgment seat. And Gallio cared for none of those things.

¹⁸And Paul *after this* tarried *there* yet a good while, and then took his leave of the brethren, and sailed thence into Syria, and with him Priscilla and Aquila; having shorn *his* head in Cenchrea: for he had a vow. ¹⁹And he came to Ephesus, and left them there: but he himself entered into the synagogue, and reasoned with the Jews. ²⁰When they desired *him* to tarry longer time with them, he consented not; ²¹But bade them farewell, saying, I must by all means keep this feast that cometh in Jerusalem: but I will return again unto you, if God will. And he sailed from Ephesus. ²²And when he had landed at Caesarea, and gone up, and saluted the church, he went down to Antioch. ²³And after he had spent some time *there*, he departed, and went over *all* the country of Galatia and Phrygia in order, strengthening all the disciples.

²⁴And a certain Jew named Apollos, born at Alexandria, an eloquent

man, *and* mighty in the scriptures, came to Ephesus. ²⁵This man was instructed in the way of the Lord; and being fervent in the spirit, he spake and taught diligently the things of the Lord, knowing only the baptism of John. ²⁶And he began to speak boldly in the synagogue: whom when Aquila and Priscilla had heard, they took him unto *them*, and expounded unto him the way of God more perfectly. ²⁷And when he was disposed to pass into Achaia, the brethren wrote, exhorting the disciples to receive him: who, when he was come, helped them much which had believed through grace: ²⁸For he mightily convinced the Jews, *and that* publickly, shewing by the scriptures that Jesus was Christ[a].

19

¹And it came to pass, that, while Apollos was at Corinth, Paul having passed through the upper coasts came to Ephesus: and finding certain disciples, ²He said unto them, Have ye received the Holy Ghost since ye believed? And they said unto him, We have not so much as heard whether there be any Holy Ghost. ³And he said unto them, Unto what then were ye baptized? And they said, Unto John's baptism. ⁴Then said Paul, John verily baptized with the baptism of repentance, saying unto the people, that they should believe on him which should come after him, that is, on Christ Jesus. ⁵When they heard *this*, they were baptized in the name of the Lord Jesus. ⁶And when Paul had laid *his* hands upon them, the Holy Ghost came on them; and they spake with tongues, and prophesied. ⁷And all the men were about twelve.

⁸And he went into the synagogue, and spake boldly for the space of three months, disputing and persuading the things concerning the kingdom of God. ⁹But when divers were hardened, and believed not, but spake evil of that way before the multitude, he departed from them, and separated the disciples, disputing daily in the school of one Tyrannus. ¹⁰And this continued by the space of two years; so that all they which dwelt in Asia heard the word of the Lord Jesus, both Jews and Greeks. ¹¹And God wrought special miracles by the hands of Paul: ¹²So that from his body were brought unto the sick handkerchiefs or aprons, and the diseases departed from them, and the evil spirits went out of them.

¹³Then certain of the vagabond Jews, exorcists, took upon them to call over them which had evil spirits the name of the Lord Jesus, saying, We adjure you by Jesus whom Paul preacheth. ¹⁴And there were seven sons of *one* Sceva, a Jew, *and* chief of the priests, which did so. ¹⁵And the evil spirit answered and said, Jesus I know, and Paul I know; but who are ye? ¹⁶And the man in whom the evil spirit was leaped on them, and overcame them, and prevailed against them, so that they fled out of that house naked and wounded. ¹⁷And this was known to all the Jews and Greeks also dwelling at Ephesus; and fear fell on them all, and the name of the Lord Jesus was magnified. ¹⁸And many that believed came, and confessed, and shewed their deeds. ¹⁹Many

---

[a] Christ: or, is the Christ

of them also which used curious arts brought their books together, and burned them before all *men*: and they counted the price of them, and found *it* fifty thousand *pieces* of silver. ²⁰So mightily grew the word of God and prevailed.

²¹After these things were ended, Paul purposed in the spirit, when he had passed through Macedonia and Achaia, to go to Jerusalem, saying, After I have been there, I must also see Rome. ²²So he sent into Macedonia two of them that ministered unto him, Timotheus and Erastus; but he himself stayed in Asia for a season. ²³And the same time there arose no small stir about that way. ²⁴For a certain *man* named Demetrius, a silversmith, which made silver shrines for Diana, brought no small gain unto the craftsmen; ²⁵Whom he called together with the workmen of like occupation, and said, Sirs, ye know that by this craft we have our wealth. ²⁶Moreover ye see and hear, that not alone at Ephesus, but almost throughout all Asia, this Paul hath persuaded and turned away much people, saying that they be no gods, which are made with hands: ²⁷So that not only this our craft is in danger to be set at nought*; but also that the temple of the great goddess Diana should be despised, and her magnificence should be destroyed, whom all Asia and the world worshippeth. ²⁸And when they heard *these sayings*, they were full of wrath, and cried out, saying, Great *is* Diana of the Ephesians. ²⁹And the whole city was filled with confusion: and having caught Gaius and Aristarchus, men of Macedonia, Paul's companions in travel, they rushed with one accord into the theatre. ³⁰And when Paul would have entered in unto the people, the disciples suffered him not. ³¹And certain of the chief of Asia, which were his friends, sent unto him, desiring *him* that he would not adventure himself into the theatre. ³²Some therefore cried one thing, and some another: for the assembly was confused; and the more part knew not wherefore they were come together. ³³And they drew Alexander out of the multitude, the Jews putting him forward. And Alexander beckoned with the hand, and would have made his defence unto the people. ³⁴But when they knew that he was a Jew, all with one voice about the space of two hours cried out, Great *is* Diana of the Ephesians. ³⁵And when the townclerk had appeased the people, he said, *Ye* men of Ephesus, what man is there that knoweth not how that the city of the Ephesians is a worshipperᵇ of the great goddess Diana, and of the *image* which fell down from Jupiter? ³⁶Seeing then that these things cannot be spoken against, ye ought to be quiet, and to do nothing rashly. ³⁷For ye have brought hither these men, which are neither robbers of churches, nor yet blasphemers of your goddess. ³⁸Wherefore if Demetrius, and the craftsmen which are with him, have a matter against any man, the lawᶜ is open, and there are deputies: let them implead one another.

ª set at nought: or, brought into disrepute, or, contempt
ᵇ a worshipper: Gr. the temple keeper
ᶜ the law . . . : or, the court days are kept

Priscilla & Aquila

Some people think that married couples can't work together. Priscilla and Aquila show us that it is certainly possible for married couples to work together in serving the Lord. We shouldn't automatically assume that couples make poor coworkers.

Of course, it can't be forced. Priscilla and Aquila both had the same job (tentmaking), evidence that they already worked well together. But even those who must work separately can work toward similar goals or on the same projects while fulfilling different roles.

Priscilla and Aquila were tentmakers living in Corinth when the apostle Paul came to town. They allowed him to stay in their home while he was there.

Their gesture of hospitality turned out to be an apprenticeship. Paul's enthusiasm for Jesus infected them both, and they soaked up what they could. They assisted Paul together in his work.

When the time came for Paul to leave Corinth, Priscilla and Aquila went with him. In the middle of the trip, Paul kept going, and Priscilla and Aquila stayed behind to minister together in Ephesus.

Their marriage was a ministry partnership. Priscilla and Aquila are never mentioned separately in the Bible. They are always a team. While they were in Ephesus, they met Apollos and explained the gospel to him—together. As husband and wife, they were partners, working together to spread the news about Jesus.

LESSONS FROM PRISCILLA AND AQUILA AS PARTNERS IN MINISTRY

A marriage partner can be a ministry partner. It's not a requirement of marriage, but it is possible. Husbands and wives can work together in serving God. And there are benefits: You get to be united in an important task. You have common goals. You have something to talk about together.

Husbands and wives are partners, and that includes ministry. Look for opportunities to serve God together. If you disagree on issues of faith, look for an area of common ground. One possibility available to many is hospitality.

³⁹But if ye enquire any thing concerning other matters, it shall be determined in a lawful[d] assembly. ⁴⁰For we are in danger to be called in question for this day's uproar, there being no cause whereby we may give an account of this concourse. ⁴¹And when he had thus spoken, he dismissed the assembly.

20

¹And after the uproar was ceased, Paul called unto *him* the disciples, and embraced *them*, and departed for to go into Macedonia. ²And when he had gone over those parts, and had given them much exhortation, he came into Greece, ³And *there* abode three months. And when the Jews laid wait for him, as he was about to sail into Syria, he purposed to return through Macedonia. ⁴And there accompanied him into Asia Sopater of Berea; and of the Thessalonians, Aristarchus and Secundus; and Gaius of Derbe, and Timotheus; and of Asia, Tychicus and Trophimus. ⁵These going before tarried for us at Troas. ⁶And we sailed away from Philippi after the days of unleavened bread, and came unto them to Troas in five days; where we abode seven days.

⁷And upon the first *day* of the week, when the disciples came together to break bread, Paul preached unto them, ready to depart on the morrow; and continued his speech until midnight. ⁸And there were many lights in the upper chamber, where they were gathered together. ⁹And there sat in a window a certain young man named Eutychus, being fallen into a deep sleep: and as Paul was long preaching, he sunk down with sleep, and fell down from the third loft, and was taken up dead. ¹⁰And Paul went down, and fell on him, and embracing *him* said, Trouble not yourselves; for his life is in him. ¹¹When he therefore was come up again, and had broken bread, and eaten, and talked a long while, even till break of day, so he departed. ¹²And they brought the young man alive, and were not a little comforted.

¹³And we went before to ship, and sailed unto Assos, there intending to take in Paul: for so had he appointed, minding himself to go afoot. ¹⁴And when he met with us at Assos, we took him in, and came to Mitylene. ¹⁵And we sailed thence, and came the next *day* over against Chios; and the next *day* we arrived at Samos, and tarried at Trogyllium; and the next *day* we came to Miletus. ¹⁶For Paul had determined to sail by Ephesus, because he would not spend the time in Asia: for he hasted, if it were possible for him, to be at Jerusalem the day of Pentecost.

¹⁷And from Miletus he sent to Ephesus, and called the elders of the church. ¹⁸And when they were come to him, he said unto them, Ye know, from the first day that I came into Asia, after what manner I have been with you at all seasons, ¹⁹Serving the Lord with all humility of mind, and with many tears, and temptations, which befell me by the lying in wait of the Jews: ²⁰*And* how I kept back nothing that was profitable *unto you*, but have shewed you, and have taught you publickly, and from house to house, ²¹Testifying both to the Jews, and also to the Greeks, repen-

---

[d] lawful: or, ordinary

tance toward God, and faith toward our Lord Jesus Christ. ²²And now, behold, I go bound in the spirit unto Jerusalem, not knowing the things that shall befall me there: ²³Save that the Holy Ghost witnesseth in every city, saying that bonds and afflictions abide meᵃ. ²⁴But none of these things move me, neither count I my life dear unto myself, so that I might finish my course with joy, and the ministry, which I have received of the Lord Jesus, to testify the gospel of the grace of God. ²⁵And now, behold, I know that ye all, among whom I have gone preaching the kingdom of God, shall see my face no more. ²⁶Wherefore I take you to record this day, that I *am* pure from the blood of all *men*. ²⁷For I have not shunned to declare unto you all the counsel of God. ²⁸Take heed therefore unto yourselves, and to all the flock, over the which the Holy Ghost hath made you overseers, to feed the church of God, which he hath purchased with his own blood. ²⁹For I know this, that after my departing shall grievous wolves enter in among you, not sparing the flock. ³⁰Also of your own selves shall men arise, speaking perverse things, to draw away disciples after them. ³¹Therefore watch, and remember, that by the space of three years I ceased not to warn every one night and day with tears. ³²And now, brethren, I commend you to God, and to the word of his grace, which is able to build you up, and to give you an inheritance among all them which are sanctified. ³³I have coveted no man's silver, or gold, or apparel. ³⁴Yea, ye yourselves know, that these hands have min-

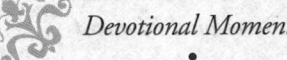

Devotional Moment
•
Chores, Allowance, and Responsibility

20:33-35 Paul was a tentmaker, which means that he made and sold tents for a living. He held this job to pay the bills even though he had a right to expect payment from the churches he served. His work enabled him not only to pay his own way but also to supply the needs of his coworkers and to help the poor. In a family, each person needs to contribute as his or her ability allows. Whether you consider an allowance to be payment for chores or part of the family resources shared with all, always make sure each person carries a fair share of the load. Spread the responsibility— and the rewards—to all.

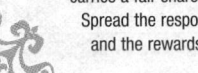

istered unto my necessities, and to them that were with me. ³⁵I have shewed you all things, how that so labouring ye ought to support the weak, and to remember the words of the Lord Jesus, how he said, It is more blessed to give than to receive.

³⁶And when he had thus spoken, he kneeled down, and prayed with them all. ³⁷And they all wept sore, and fell on Paul's neck, and kissed him, ³⁸Sorrowing most of all for the words which he spake, that they should see his face no more. And they accompanied him unto the ship.

21

¹And it came to pass, that after we were gotten from them, and had launched, we came with a straight course unto Coos, and the *day* following unto Rhodes, and from thence unto Patara: ²And finding a ship sailing over unto Phenicia, we went aboard, and set

---

ᵃ abide me: or, wait for me

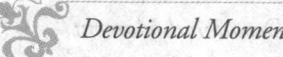

Devotional Moment

•

Family Ministry

21:5 When it was time for Paul to leave Tyre, the entire congregation, including the children, went with him to the ship and prayed together before saying good-bye. We don't know what impact this farewell had on the children, but we do know that they witnessed their parents' spiritual values in action. In your acts of service for God, include your children whenever possible. That way, faith is a part of the family experience. Consider opening your home to missionary families who visit your church. If your kids are old enough, let them accompany you wherever you minister.

forth. ³Now when we had discovered Cyprus, we left it on the left hand, and sailed into Syria, and landed at Tyre: for there the ship was to unlade her burden. ⁴And finding disciples, we tarried there seven days: who said to Paul through the Spirit, that he should not go up to Jerusalem. ⁵And when we had accomplished those days, we departed and went our way; and they all brought us on our way, with wives and children, till *we were* out of the city: and we kneeled down on the shore, and prayed. ⁶And when we had taken our leave one of another, we took ship; and they returned home again. ⁷And when we had finished *our* course from Tyre, we came to Ptolemais, and saluted the brethren, and abode with them one day.

⁸And the next *day* we that were of Paul's company departed, and came unto Caesarea: and we entered into the house of Philip the evangelist, which was *one* of the seven; and abode with him. ⁹And the same man had four daughters, virgins, which did prophesy. ¹⁰And as we tarried *there* many days, there came down from Judaea a certain prophet, named Agabus. ¹¹And when he was come unto us, he took Paul's girdle, and bound his own hands and feet, and said, Thus saith the Holy Ghost, So shall the Jews at Jerusalem bind the man that owneth this girdle, and shall deliver *him* into the hands of the Gentiles. ¹²And when we heard these things, both we, and they of that place, besought him not to go up to Jerusalem. ¹³Then Paul answered, What mean ye to weep and to break mine heart? for I am ready not to be bound only, but also to die at Jerusalem for the name of the Lord Jesus. ¹⁴And when he would not be persuaded, we ceased, saying, The will of the Lord be done.

¹⁵And after those days we took up our carriages, and went up to Jerusalem. ¹⁶There went with us also *certain* of the disciples of Caesarea, and brought with them one Mnason of Cyprus, an old disciple, with whom we should lodge. ¹⁷And when we were come to Jerusalem, the brethren received us gladly. ¹⁸And the *day* following Paul went in with us unto James; and all the elders were present. ¹⁹And when he had saluted them, he declared particularly what things God had wrought among the Gentiles by his ministry. ²⁰And when they heard *it*, they glorified the Lord, and said unto him, Thou seest, brother, how many thousands of Jews there are which believe; and they are all zealous of the law: ²¹And they are informed of thee, that thou teachest all the Jews which are among the Gentiles to forsake Moses, saying that they ought not to circumcise *their* children, neither to walk after the customs. ²²What is it therefore? the

multitude must needs come together: for they will hear that thou art come. ²³Do therefore this that we say to thee: We have four men which have a vow on them; ²⁴Them take, and purify thyself with them, and be at charges with them, that they may shave *their* heads: and all may know that those things, whereof they were informed concerning thee, are nothing; but *that* thou thyself also walkest orderly, and keepest the law. ²⁵As touching the Gentiles which believe, we have written *and* concluded that they observe no such thing, save only that they keep themselves from *things* offered to idols, and from blood, and from strangled, and from fornication. ²⁶Then Paul took the men, and the next day purifying himself with them entered into the temple, to signify the accomplishment of the days of purification, until that an offering should be offered for every one of them.

²⁷And when the seven days were almost ended, the Jews which were of Asia, when they saw him in the temple, stirred up all the people, and laid hands on him, ²⁸Crying out, Men of Israel, help: This is the man, that teacheth all *men* every where against the people, and the law, and this place: and further brought Greeks also into the temple, and hath polluted this holy place. ²⁹(For they had seen before with him in the city Trophimus an Ephesian, whom they supposed that Paul had brought into the temple.) ³⁰And all the city was moved, and the people ran together: and they took Paul, and drew him out of the temple: and forthwith the doors were shut. ³¹And as they went about to kill him, tidings came unto the chief captain of the band, that all Jerusalem was in an uproar. ³²Who immediately took soldiers and centurions, and ran down unto them: and when they saw the chief captain and the soldiers, they left beating of Paul. ³³Then the chief captain came near, and took him, and commanded *him* to be bound with two chains; and demanded who he was, and what he had done. ³⁴And some cried one thing, some another, among the multitude: and when he could not know the certainty for the tumult, he commanded him to be carried into the castle. ³⁵And when he came upon the stairs, so it was, that he was borne of the soldiers for the violence of the people. ³⁶For the multitude of the people followed after, crying, Away with him. ³⁷And as Paul was to be led into the castle, he said unto the chief captain, May I speak unto thee? Who said, Canst thou speak Greek? ³⁸Art not thou that Egyptian, which before these days madest an uproar, and leddest out into the wilderness four thousand men that were murderers? ³⁹But Paul said, I am a man *which am* a Jew of Tarsus, *a city* in Cilicia, a citizen of no mean city: and, I beseech thee, suffer me to speak unto the people. ⁴⁰And when he had given him licence, Paul stood on the stairs, and beckoned with the hand unto the people. And when there was made a great silence, he spake unto *them* in the Hebrew tongue, saying,

22

¹Men, brethren, and fathers, hear ye my defence *which I make* now unto you. ²(And when they heard that he spake in the Hebrew tongue to them, they kept the more silence: and he saith,)

³I am verily a man *which am* a Jew, born in Tarsus, *a city* in Cilicia, yet brought up in this city at the feet of Gamaliel, *and* taught according to the perfect manner of the law of the fathers, and was zealous toward God, as ye all are this day. ⁴And I persecuted this way unto the death, binding and delivering into prisons both men and women. ⁵As also the high priest doth bear me witness, and all the estate of the elders: from whom also I received letters unto the brethren, and went to Damascus, to bring them which were there bound unto Jerusalem, for to be punished. ⁶And it came to pass, that, as I made my journey, and was come nigh unto Damascus about noon, suddenly there shone from heaven a great light round about me. ⁷And I fell unto the ground, and heard a voice saying unto me, Saul, Saul, why persecutest thou me? ⁸And I answered, Who art thou, Lord? And he said unto me, I am Jesus of Nazareth, whom thou persecutest. ⁹And they that were with me saw indeed the light, and were afraid; but they heard not the voice of him that spake to me. ¹⁰And I said, What shall I do, Lord? And the Lord said unto me, Arise, and go into Damascus; and there it shall be told thee of all things which are appointed for thee to do. ¹¹And when I could not see for the glory of that light, being led by the hand of them that were with me, I came into Damascus. ¹²And one Ananias, a devout man according to the law, having a good report of all the Jews which dwelt *there*, ¹³Came unto me, and stood, and said unto me, Brother Saul, receive thy sight. And the same hour I looked up upon him. ¹⁴And he said, The God of our fathers hath chosen thee, that thou shouldest know his will, and see that Just One, and shouldest hear the voice of his mouth. ¹⁵For thou shalt be his witness unto all men of what thou hast seen and heard. ¹⁶And now why tarriest thou? arise, and be baptized, and wash away thy sins, calling on the name of the Lord. ¹⁷And it came to pass, that, when I was come again to Jerusalem, even while I prayed in the temple, I was in a trance; ¹⁸And saw him saying unto me, Make haste, and get thee quickly out of Jerusalem: for they will not receive thy testimony concerning me. ¹⁹And I said, Lord, they know that I imprisoned and beat in every synagogue them that believed on thee: ²⁰And when the blood of thy martyr Stephen was shed, I also was standing by, and consenting unto his death, and kept the raiment of them that slew him. ²¹And he said unto me, Depart: for I will send thee far hence unto the Gentiles.

²²And they gave him audience unto this word, and *then* lifted up their voices, and said, Away with such a *fellow* from the earth: for it is not fit that he should live. ²³And as they cried out, and cast off *their* clothes, and threw dust into the air, ²⁴The chief captain commanded him to be brought into the castle, and bade that he should be examined by scourging; that he might know wherefore they cried so against him. ²⁵And as they bound him with thongs, Paul said unto the centurion that stood by, Is it lawful for you to scourge a man that is a Roman, and uncondemned? ²⁶When the centurion heard *that*, he went and told the chief captain, saying, Take heed what thou doest: for this man is a Roman. ²⁷Then

the chief captain came, and said unto him, Tell me, art thou a Roman? He said, Yea. ²⁸And the chief captain answered, With a great sum obtained I this freedom. And Paul said, But I was *free* born. ²⁹Then straightway they departed from him which should have examined him[a]: and the chief captain also was afraid, after he knew that he was a Roman, and because he had bound him. ³⁰On the morrow, because he would have known the certainty wherefore he was accused of the Jews, he loosed him from *his* bands, and commanded the chief priests and all their council to appear, and brought Paul down, and set him before them.

23

¹And Paul, earnestly beholding the council, said, Men *and* brethren, I have lived in all good conscience before God until this day. ²And the high priest Ananias commanded them that stood by him to smite him on the mouth. ³Then said Paul unto him, God shall smite thee, *thou* whited wall: for sittest thou to judge me after the law, and commandest me to be smitten contrary to the law? ⁴And they that stood by said, Revilest thou God's high priest? ⁵Then said Paul, I wist not, brethren, that he was the high priest: for it is written, Thou shalt not speak evil of the ruler of thy people.

⁶But when Paul perceived that the one part were Sadducees, and the other Pharisees, he cried out in the council, Men *and* brethren, I am a Pharisee, the son of a Pharisee: of the hope and res-urrection of the dead I am called in question. ⁷And when he had so said, there arose a dissension between the Pharisees and the Sadducees: and the multitude was divided. ⁸For the Sadducees say that there is no resurrection, neither angel, nor spirit: but the Pharisees confess both. ⁹And there arose a great cry: and the scribes *that were* of the Pharisees' part arose, and strove, saying, We find no evil in this man: but if a spirit or an angel hath spoken to him, let us not fight against God. ¹⁰And when there arose a great dissension, the chief captain, fearing lest Paul should have been pulled in pieces of them, commanded the soldiers to go down, and to take him by force from among them, and to bring *him* into the castle. ¹¹And the night following the Lord stood by him, and said, Be of good cheer, Paul: for as thou hast testified of me in Jerusalem, so must thou bear witness also at Rome.

¹²And when it was day, certain of the Jews banded together, and bound themselves under a curse[a], saying that they would neither eat nor drink till they had killed Paul. ¹³And they were more than forty which had made this conspiracy. ¹⁴And they came to the chief priests and elders, and said, We have bound ourselves under a great curse, that we will eat nothing until we have slain Paul. ¹⁵Now therefore ye with the council signify to the chief captain that he bring him down unto you to morrow, as though ye would enquire something more perfectly concerning him: and we, or ever he come near, are ready to kill him. ¹⁶And when

---

[a] examined him: or, tortured him
[a] under a curse: or, with an oath of execration

Paul's sister's son heard of their lying in wait, he went and entered into the castle, and told Paul. [17]Then Paul called one of the centurions unto *him,* and said, Bring this young man unto the chief captain: for he hath a certain thing to tell him. [18]So he took him, and brought *him* to the chief captain, and said, Paul the prisoner called me unto *him,* and prayed me to bring this young man unto thee, who hath something to say unto thee. [19]Then the chief captain took him by the hand, and went *with him* aside privately, and asked *him,* What is that thou hast to tell me? [20]And he said, The Jews have agreed to desire thee that thou wouldest bring down Paul to morrow into the council, as though they would enquire somewhat of him more perfectly. [21]But do not thou yield unto them: for there lie in wait for him of them more than forty men, which have bound themselves with an oath, that they will neither eat nor drink till they have killed him: and now are they ready, looking for a promise from thee. [22]So the chief captain *then* let the young man depart, and charged *him,* See thou tell no man that thou hast shewed these things to me. [23]And he called unto *him* two centurions, saying, Make ready two hundred soldiers to go to Caesarea, and horsemen threescore and ten, and spearmen two hundred, at the third hour of the night; [24]And provide *them* beasts, that they may set Paul on, and bring *him* safe unto Felix the governor. [25]And he wrote a letter after this manner: [26]Claudius Lysias unto the most excellent governor Felix *sendeth* greeting. [27]This man was taken of the Jews, and should have been killed of them: then came I with an army, and rescued him, having understood that he was a Roman. [28]And when I would have

known the cause wherefore they accused him, I brought him forth into their council: [29]Whom I perceived to be accused of questions of their law, but to have nothing laid to his charge worthy of death or of bonds. [30]And when it was told me how that the Jews laid wait for the man, I sent straightway to thee, and gave commandment to his accusers also to say before thee what *they had* against him. Farewell. [31]Then the soldiers, as it was commanded them, took Paul, and brought *him* by night to Antipatris. [32]On the morrow they left the horsemen to go with him, and returned to the castle: [33]Who, when they came to Caesarea, and delivered the epistle to the governor, presented Paul also before him. [34]And when the governor had read *the letter,* he asked of what province he was. And when he understood that *he was* of Cilicia; [35]I will hear thee, said he, when thine accusers are also come. And he commanded him to be kept in Herod's judgment hall.

24

[1]And after five days Ananias the high priest descended with the elders, and *with* a certain orator *named* Tertullus, who informed the governor against Paul. [2]And when he was called forth, Tertullus began to accuse *him,* saying, Seeing that by thee we enjoy great quietness, and that very worthy deeds are done unto this nation by thy providence, [3]We accept *it* always, and in all places, most noble Felix, with all thankfulness. [4]Notwithstanding, that I be not further tedious unto thee, I pray thee that thou wouldest hear us of thy clemency a few words. [5]For we have found this man *a* pestilent *fellow,* and a mover of sedition among all the Jews

throughout the world, and a ringleader of the sect of the Nazarenes: ⁶Who also hath gone about to profane the temple: whom we took, and would have judged according to our law. ⁷But the chief captain Lysias came *upon us,* and with great violence took *him* away out of our hands, ⁸Commanding his accusers to come unto thee: by examining of whom thyself mayest take knowledge of all these things, whereof we accuse him. ⁹And the Jews also assented, saying that these things were so.

¹⁰Then Paul, after that the governor had beckoned unto him to speak, answered, Forasmuch as I know that thou hast been of many years a judge unto this nation, I do the more cheerfully answer for myself: ¹¹Because that thou mayest understand, that there are yet but twelve days since I went up to Jerusalem for to worship. ¹²And they neither found me in the temple disputing with any man, neither raising up the people, neither in the synagogues, nor in the city: ¹³Neither can they prove the things whereof they now accuse me. ¹⁴But this I confess unto thee, that after the way which they call heresy, so worship I the God of my fathers, believing all things which are written in the law and in the prophets: ¹⁵And have hope toward God, which they themselves also allow, that there shall be a resurrection of the dead, both of the just and unjust. ¹⁶And herein do I exercise myself, to have always a conscience void of offence toward God, and *toward* men. ¹⁷Now after many years I came to bring alms to my nation, and offerings. ¹⁸Whereupon certain Jews from Asia found me purified in the temple, neither with multitude, nor with tumult.

¹⁹Who ought to have been here before thee, and object, if they had ought against me. ²⁰Or else let these same *here* say, if they have found any evil doing in me, while I stood before the council, ²¹Except it be for this one voice, that I cried standing among them, Touching the resurrection of the dead I am called in question by you this day.

²²And when Felix heard these things, having more perfect knowledge of *that* way, he deferred them, and said, When Lysias the chief captain shall come down, I will know the uttermost of your matter. ²³And he commanded a centurion to keep Paul, and to let *him* have liberty, and that he should forbid none of his acquaintance to minister or come unto him. ²⁴And after certain days, when Felix came with his wife Drusilla, which was a Jewess, he sent for Paul, and heard him concerning the faith in Christ. ²⁵And as he reasoned of righteousness, temperance, and judgment to come, Felix trembled, and answered, Go thy way for this time; when I have a convenient season, I will call for thee. ²⁶He hoped also that money should have been given him of Paul, that he might loose him: wherefore he sent for him the oftener, and communed with him. ²⁷But after two years Porcius Festus came into Felix' room: and Felix, willing to shew the Jews a pleasure, left Paul bound.

25

¹Now when Festus was come into the province, after three days he ascended from Caesarea to Jerusalem. ²Then the high priest and the chief of the Jews informed him against Paul, and besought

him, ³And desired favour against him, that he would send for him to Jerusalem, laying wait in the way to kill him. ⁴But Festus answered, that Paul should be kept at Caesarea, and that he himself would depart shortly *thither*. ⁵Let them therefore, said he, which among you are able, go down with *me*, and accuse this man, if there be any wickedness in him. ⁶And when he had tarried among them moreᵃ than ten days, he went down unto Caesarea; and the next day sitting on the judgment seat commanded Paul to be brought. ⁷And when he was come, the Jews which came down from Jerusalem stood round about, and laid many and grievous complaints against Paul, which they could not prove. ⁸While he answered for himself, Neither against the law of the Jews, neither against the temple, nor yet against Caesar, have I offended any thing at all. ⁹But Festus, willing to do the Jews a pleasure, answered Paul, and said, Wilt thou go up to Jerusalem, and there be judged of these things before me? ¹⁰Then said Paul, I stand at Caesar's judgment seat, where I ought to be judged: to the Jews have I done no wrong, as thou very well knowest. ¹¹For if I be an offender, or have committed any thing worthy of death, I refuse not to die: but if there be none of these things whereof these accuse me, no man may deliver me unto them. I appeal unto Caesar. ¹²Then Festus, when he had conferred with the council, answered, Hast thou appealed unto Caesar? unto Caesar shalt thou go.

¹³And after certain days king Agrippa and Bernice came unto Caesarea to salute Festus. ¹⁴And when they had been there many days, Festus declared Paul's cause unto the king, saying, There is a certain man left in bonds by Felix: ¹⁵About whom, when I was at Jerusalem, the chief priests and the elders of the Jews informed *me*, desiring *to have* judgment against him. ¹⁶To whom I answered, It is not the manner of the Romans to deliver any man to die, before that he which is accused have the accusers face to face, and have licence to answer for himself concerning the crime laid against him. ¹⁷Therefore, when they were come hither, without any delay on the morrow I sat on the judgment seat, and commanded the man to be brought forth. ¹⁸Against whom when the accusers stood up, they brought none accusation of such things as I supposed: ¹⁹But had certain questions against him of their own superstition, and of one Jesus, which was dead, whom Paul affirmed to be alive. ²⁰And because I doubtedᵇ of such manner of questions, I asked *him* whether he would go to Jerusalem, and there be judged of these matters. ²¹But when Paul had appealed to be reserved unto the hearingᶜ of Augustus, I commanded him to be kept till I might send him to Caesar. ²²Then Agrippa said unto Festus, I would also hear the man myself. To morrow, said he, thou shalt hear him. ²³And on the morrow, when Agrippa was come, and Bernice, with great pomp, and was entered into the place of hearing, with the chief captains, and princi-

---

ᵃ more . . . : or, as some copies read, no more than eight or ten days
ᵇ I doubted . . . : or, I was doubtful how to enquire hereof
ᶜ hearing: or, judgment

Breaking Free from Procrastination

As [Paul] reasoned of righteousness, temperance, and judgment to come, Felix trembled, and answered, "Go thy way for this time; when I have a convenient season, I will call for thee." Acts 24:25

Have you ever put off doing something important? Who hasn't? Everyone procrastinates at times, and for most people it causes only minor problems. Yet for some, procrastination becomes a powerful negative pattern that can ruin a family. And it must be broken.

In the book of Acts we find a story that illustrates a great deal about procrastination—what gets us started procrastinating, the primary emotion that fuels procrastination, and how to break its hold on our life. The story concerns Felix, a Roman governor with a Jewish wife, who was familiar with Christianity but was not himself a believer (Acts 24:22). Paul had been summoned to see Felix (24:24). As Paul spoke about faith in Christ, he discussed three topics: righteousness, self-control, and the judgment to come. Felix preferred not to think about any of these, so he sent Paul away.

The topics Paul discussed with Felix are the primary issues God wants us to care about. *Righteousness* means to live in the right, to obey God's commands. *Temperance* means to "pull in the reins," as to restrain a horse. *The judgment to come* simply refers to the fact that eventually every person will give an account to God for his or her actions.

It's those three issues that often bring *conviction* into our life.

Why we procrastinate in the first place: conviction. Conviction alerts us to an unpleasant change that needs to be made. Felix, for example, had much to hide. (Historians have credited him with murdering his own brother!) Paul's talk exposed areas of sin and personal weakness that Felix did not want to change. He felt convicted.

Consider your own life and struggles for a moment. Where does the battle over procrastination begin? Doesn't it usually begin when you realize that a change needs to be made? Conviction is what often puts us on the path to procrastination.

The emotion that fuels procrastination: fear. How does conviction grow into full-fledged procrastination? Fear.

Just look at Felix. As he listened to Paul, the Bible says, "Felix trembled." It is *fear* that feeds procrastination and keeps it going. Commonly, this fear comes in three varieties:

Fear of failure. Some people become convicted about changing, and then their fear of not measuring up blocks real change. When Brian was young, his father would make him work on complicated projects in his workshop—then criticize his every move. Today, many important projects go undone around Brian's house because of his deep fear of failure.

Fear of success. Bob is intelligent, hardworking, and industrious. He also fears success. The last five jobs he has taken are all well below his abilities. Inevitably, he'll start a job with a flourish and often gain a quick promotion. But the added demands make him afraid of success, which would bring higher expectations and more need for personal acceptance. So each time, he begins to procrastinate until he finally loses his job.

Fear of being controlled. For Felix, as for many of us, the problem with responding to conviction is a fear of giving up control over our own life. His problem was *moral, not intellectual.* It isn't that he didn't know enough, it's that he didn't want to stop doing what he was doing—and start going God's way.

How to break the cycle: action. Think about your life today. Is there an area in which God has convicted you recently? If you're putting off changing, ask yourself right now, What am I afraid of? Failure? Success? Being controlled? Face your fear, set it aside, trust God that his way is in your best interest, and make the change.

---

pal men of the city, at Festus' commandment Paul was brought forth. ²⁴And Festus said, King Agrippa, and all men which are here present with us, ye see this man, about whom all the multitude of the Jews have dealt with me, both at Jerusalem, and *also* here, crying that he ought not to live any longer. ²⁵But when I found that he had committed nothing worthy of death, and that he himself hath appealed to Augustus, I have determined to send him. ²⁶Of whom I have no certain thing to write unto my lord. Wherefore I have brought him forth before you, and specially before thee, O king Agrippa, that, after examination had, I might have somewhat to write. ²⁷For it seemeth to me unreasonable to send a prisoner, and not withal to signify the crimes *laid* against him.

26

¹Then Agrippa said unto Paul, Thou art permitted to speak for thyself. Then Paul stretched forth the hand, and answered for himself: ²I think myself happy, king Agrippa, because I shall answer for myself this day before thee touching all the things whereof I am accused of the Jews: ³Especially *because I know* thee to be expert in all customs and questions which are among the Jews: wherefore I beseech thee to hear me patiently. ⁴My manner of life from my youth, which was at the first among mine own nation at Jerusalem, know all the Jews; ⁵Which knew me from the beginning, if they would testify, that after the most straitest sect of our religion I lived a Pharisee. ⁶And now I stand and am judged for the hope of the promise made of God unto our fathers: ⁷Unto which *promise* our twelve tribes, instantly serving *God* day and night, hope to come. For which hope's sake, king Agrippa, I am accused of the Jews. ⁸Why should it be thought a thing incredible with you, that God should raise the dead? ⁹I verily thought with myself, that I ought to do

many things contrary to the name of Jesus of Nazareth. ¹⁰Which thing I also did in Jerusalem: and many of the saints did I shut up in prison, having received authority from the chief priests; and when they were put to death, I gave my voice against *them*. ¹¹And I punished them oft in every synagogue, and compelled *them* to blaspheme; and being exceedingly mad against them, I persecuted *them* even unto strange cities.

¹²Whereupon as I went to Damascus with authority and commission from the chief priests, ¹³At midday, O king, I saw in the way a light from heaven, above the brightness of the sun, shining round about me and them which journeyed with me. ¹⁴And when we were all fallen to the earth, I heard a voice speaking unto me, and saying in the Hebrew tongue, Saul, Saul, why persecutest thou me? *it is* hard for thee to kick against the pricks. ¹⁵And I said, Who art thou, Lord? And he said, I am Jesus whom thou persecutest. ¹⁶But rise, and stand upon thy feet: for I have appeared unto thee for this purpose, to make thee a minister and a witness both of these things which thou hast seen, and of those things in the which I will appear unto thee; ¹⁷Delivering thee from the people, and *from* the Gentiles, unto whom now I send thee, ¹⁸To open their eyes, *and* to turn *them* from darkness to light, and *from* the power of Satan unto God, that they may receive forgiveness of sins, and inheritance among them which are sanctified by faith that is in me. ¹⁹Whereupon, O king Agrippa, I was not disobedient unto the heavenly vision: ²⁰But shewed first unto them of Damascus, and at Jerusalem, and throughout all the coasts of Judaea, and *then* to the Gentiles, that they should repent and turn to

God, and do works meet for repentance. ²¹For these causes the Jews caught me in the temple, and went about to kill *me*. ²²Having therefore obtained help of God, I continue unto this day, witnessing both to small and great, saying none other things than those which the prophets and Moses did say should come: ²³That Christ should suffer, *and* that he should be the first that should rise from the dead, and should shew light unto the people, and to the Gentiles.

²⁴And as he thus spake for himself, Festus said with a loud voice, Paul, thou art beside thyself; much learning doth make thee mad. ²⁵But he said, I am not mad, most noble Festus; but speak forth the words of truth and soberness. ²⁶For the king knoweth of these things, before whom also I speak freely: for I am persuaded that none of these things are hidden from him; for this thing was not done in a corner. ²⁷King Agrippa, believest thou the prophets? I know that thou believest. ²⁸Then Agrippa said unto Paul, Almost thou persuadest me to be a Christian. ²⁹And Paul said, I would to God, that not only thou, but also all that hear me this day, were both almost, and altogether such as I am, except these bonds. ³⁰And when he had thus spoken, the king rose up, and the governor, and Bernice, and they that sat with them: ³¹And when they were gone aside, they talked between themselves, saying, This man doeth nothing worthy of death or of bonds. ³²Then said Agrippa unto Festus, This man might have been set at liberty, if he had not appealed unto Caesar.

27

¹And when it was determined that we should sail into Italy, they delivered Paul

and certain other prisoners unto *one* named Julius, a centurion of Augustus' band. ²And entering into a ship of Adramyttium, we launched, meaning to sail by the coasts of Asia; *one* Aristarchus, a Macedonian of Thessalonica, being with us. ³And the next *day* we touched at Sidon. And Julius courteously entreated Paul, and gave *him* liberty to go unto his friends to refresh himself. ⁴And when we had launched from thence, we sailed under Cyprus, because the winds were contrary. ⁵And when we had sailed over the sea of Cilicia and Pamphylia, we came to Myra, *a city* of Lycia. ⁶And there the centurion found a ship of Alexandria sailing into Italy; and he put us therein. ⁷And when we had sailed slowly many days, and scarce were come over against Cnidus, the wind not suffering us, we sailed under Crete*, over against Salmone; ⁸And, hardly passing it, came unto a place which is called The fair havens; nigh whereunto was the city *of* Lasea. ⁹Now when much time was spent, and when sailing was now dangerous, because the fast* was now already past, Paul admonished *them*, ¹⁰And said unto them, Sirs, I perceive that this voyage will be with hurt* and much damage, not only of the lading and ship, but also of our lives. ¹¹Nevertheless the centurion believed the master and the owner of the ship, more than those things which were spoken by Paul.

¹²And because the haven was not commodious to winter in, the more part advised to depart thence also, if by any means they might attain to Phenice, *and there* to winter; *which is* an haven of Crete, and lieth toward the south west and north west. ¹³And when the south wind blew softly, supposing that they had obtained *their* purpose, loosing *thence*, they sailed close by Crete. ¹⁴But not long after there arose* against it a tempestuous wind, called Euroclydon. ¹⁵And when the ship was caught, and could not bear up into the wind, we let *her* drive. ¹⁶And running under a certain island which is called Clauda, we had much work to come by the boat: ¹⁷Which when they had taken up, they used helps, undergirding the ship; and, fearing lest they should fall into the quicksands, strake sail, and so were driven. ¹⁸And we being exceedingly tossed with a tempest, the next *day* they lightened the ship; ¹⁹And the third *day* we cast out with our own hands the tackling of the ship. ²⁰And when neither sun nor stars in many days appeared, and no small tempest lay on *us*, all hope that we should be saved was then taken away.

²¹But after long abstinence Paul stood forth in the midst of them, and said, Sirs, ye should have hearkened unto me, and not have loosed from Crete, and to have gained this harm and loss. ²²And now I exhort you to be of good cheer: for there shall be no loss of *any man's* life among you, but of the ship. ²³For there stood by me this night the angel of God, whose I am, and whom I serve, ²⁴Saying, Fear not, Paul; thou must be brought before Caesar: and, lo, God hath given thee all them

---

ᵃ Crete: or, Candy
ᵇ the fast: the fast was on the tenth day of the seventh month
ᶜ hurt: or, injury
ᵈ arose: or, beat

that sail with thee. ²⁵Wherefore, sirs, be of good cheer: for I believe God, that it shall be even as it was told me. ²⁶Howbeit we must be cast upon a certain island. ²⁷But when the fourteenth night was come, as we were driven up and down in Adria, about midnight the shipmen deemed that they drew near to some country; ²⁸And sounded, and found *it* twenty fathoms: and when they had gone a little further, they sounded again, and found *it* fifteen fathoms. ²⁹Then fearing lest we should have fallen upon rocks, they cast four anchors out of the stern, and wished for the day. ³⁰And as the shipmen were about to flee out of the ship, when they had let down the boat into the sea, under colour as though they would have cast anchors out of the foreship, ³¹Paul said to the centurion and to the soldiers, Except these abide in the ship, ye cannot be saved. ³²Then the soldiers cut off the ropes of the boat, and let her fall off. ³³And while the day was coming on, Paul besought *them* all to take meat, saying, This day is the fourteenth day that ye have tarried and continued fasting, having taken nothing. ³⁴Wherefore I pray you to take *some* meat: for this is for your health: for there shall not an hair fall from the head of any of you. ³⁵And when he had thus spoken, he took bread, and gave thanks to God in presence of them all: and when he had broken *it*, he began to eat. ³⁶Then were they all of good cheer, and they also took *some* meat. ³⁷And we were in all in the ship two hundred threescore and sixteen souls. ³⁸And when they had eaten enough, they lightened the ship, and cast out the wheat into the sea. ³⁹And when it was day, they knew not

the land: but they discovered a certain creek with a shore, into the which they were minded, if it were possible, to thrust in the ship. ⁴⁰And when they had taken up the anchors, they committed *themselves* unto the sea, and loosed the rudder bands, and hoised up the mainsail to the wind, and made toward shore. ⁴¹And falling into a place where two seas met, they ran the ship aground; and the forepart stuck fast, and remained unmoveable, but the hinder part was broken with the violence of the waves. ⁴²And the soldiers' counsel was to kill the prisoners, lest any of them should swim out, and escape. ⁴³But the centurion, willing to save Paul, kept them from *their* purpose; and commanded that they which could swim should cast *themselves* first *into the sea*, and get to land: ⁴⁴And the rest, some on boards, and some on *broken pieces* of the ship. And so it came to pass, that they escaped all safe to land.

28

¹And when they were escaped, then they knew that the island was called Melita. ²And the barbarous people shewed us no little kindness: for they kindled a fire, and received us every one, because of the present rain, and because of the cold. ³And when Paul had gathered a bundle of sticks, and laid *them* on the fire, there came a viper out of the heat, and fastened on his hand. ⁴And when the barbarians saw the *venomous* beast hang on his hand, they said among themselves, No doubt this man is a murderer, whom, though he hath escaped the sea, yet vengeance suffereth not to live. ⁵And he shook off the beast into the fire, and felt no harm.

⁶Howbeit they looked when he should have swollen, or fallen down dead suddenly: but after they had looked a great while, and saw no harm come to him, they changed their minds, and said that he was a god. ⁷In the same quarters were possessions of the chief man of the island, whose name was Publius; who received us, and lodged us three days courteously. ⁸And it came to pass, that the father of Publius lay sick of a fever and of a bloody flux: to whom Paul entered in, and prayed, and laid his hands on him, and healed him. ⁹So when this was done, others also, which had diseases in the island, came, and were healed: ¹⁰Who also honoured us with many honours; and when we departed, they laded *us* with such things as were necessary.

¹¹And after three months we departed in a ship of Alexandria, which had wintered in the isle, whose sign was Castor and Pollux. ¹²And landing at

---

Devotional Moment

Helping the "Shipwrecked"

28:1ff. When Paul and his companions were shipwrecked on Melita, the people of the island were very kind to them. It doesn't surprise us that the ship-wrecked crowd received such an outpouring of hospitality—they were, after all, victims of disaster. People often reach out generously to such victims.

Many people have been "shipwrecked" by difficult experiences in life: There are mothers who are suddenly single, single women who are mothers, college students who are living on a shoestring, refugees and homeless people, and fathers who feel like failures. You can offer help in many ways: a meal, temporary lodging, time for listening to their thoughts and feelings, prayer together. Open your home and your heart.

Syracuse, we tarried *there* three days. ¹³And from thence we fetched a compass, and came to Rhegium: and after one day the south wind blew, and we came the next day to Puteoli: ¹⁴Where we found brethren, and were desired to tarry with them seven days: and so we went toward Rome. ¹⁵And from thence, when the brethren heard of us, they came to meet us as far as Appii forum, and the three taverns: whom when Paul saw, he thanked God, and took courage. ¹⁶And when we came to Rome, the centurion delivered the prisoners to the captain of the guard: but Paul was suffered to dwell by himself with a soldier that kept him.

¹⁷And it came to pass, that after three days Paul called the chief of the Jews together: and when they were come together, he said unto them, Men *and* brethren, though I have committed nothing against the people, or customs of our fathers, yet was I delivered prisoner from Jerusalem into the hands of the Romans. ¹⁸Who, when they had examined me, would have let *me* go, because there was no cause of death in me. ¹⁹But when the Jews spake against *it*, I was constrained to appeal unto Caesar; not that I had ought to accuse my nation of. ²⁰For this cause therefore have I called for you, to see *you*, and to speak with *you*: because that for the hope of Israel I am bound with this chain. ²¹And they said unto him, We neither received letters out of Judaea concerning thee, neither any of the brethren that came shewed or spake any harm of thee. ²²But we desire to hear of thee what thou thinkest: for as concerning this sect, we know that every where it is spoken against.

²³And when they had appointed him a day, there came many to him into *his* lodging; to whom he expounded and testified the kingdom of God, persuading them concerning Jesus, both out of the law of Moses, and *out of* the prophets, from morning till evening. ²⁴And some believed the things which were spoken, and some believed not. ²⁵And when they agreed not among themselves, they departed, after that Paul had spoken one word, Well spake the Holy Ghost by Esaias the prophet unto our fathers, ²⁶Saying, Go unto this people, and say, Hearing ye shall hear, and shall not understand; and seeing ye shall see, and not perceive: ²⁷For the heart of this people is waxed gross, and their ears are dull of hearing, and their eyes have they closed; lest they should see with *their* eyes, and hear with *their* ears, and understand with *their* heart, and should be converted, and I should heal them. ²⁸Be it known therefore unto you, that the salvation of God is sent unto the Gentiles, and *that* they will hear it. ²⁹And when he had said these words, the Jews departed, and had great reasoning among themselves.

³⁰And Paul dwelt two whole years in his own hired house, and received all that came in unto him, ³¹Preaching the kingdom of God, and teaching those things which concern the Lord Jesus Christ, with all confidence, no man forbidding him.

ROMANS

Purpose
To introduce Paul to the Romans and to give a sample of his message before he arrives in Rome

Author
Paul

To Whom Written
The Christians in Rome and believers everywhere

Date Written
About A.D. 57

Setting
Apparently Paul had finished his work in the east, and he planned to visit Rome on his way to Spain after first bringing a collection to Jerusalem for the poor Christians there (15:22-28). The Roman church was mostly Jewish, but there were also a great number of Gentiles.

Key Verse
"Therefore being justified by faith, we have peace with God through our Lord Jesus Christ" (5:1).

Special Features
Paul writes Romans as an organized and carefully presented statement of his faith. It begins and ends as a letter, but it does not have the content or the length of a typical letter. He does, however, spend considerable time greeting people in Rome at the end.

The best-selling book *How Things Work* explains modern machinery. Another famous book, entitled simply *Breads*, tells in 748 pages everything a person would want to know about this dietary staple. We need such books to keep our appliances running and our appetites appeased.

In the spiritual life department, we need a book to answer all the questions we are too bashful to ask—why Jesus came, why he died, and why faith makes a difference in every part of our life. That's Romans.

Romans is not a simple manual or cookbook. Parts of it may put your head in a spin. But you will take from Romans greater confidence in God and deeper love for Jesus, having seen the grand plan described here.

If the going gets rough, remember the 8-3-5 plan. Of the sixteen chapters in Romans, the first eight explain basic Christian doctrine. This section ends with a stirring declaration of God's commitment to you. The next three chapters fit the Old Testament into the New. And the concluding five chapters describe the practical difference these doctrines make—life with a new plan of action.

Romans is spiritual business. Each verse and chapter explains how we are connected to God, to each other, and to the world. As a guidebook is to a nature trail, as a dictionary is to a language, so Romans helps us know the God we worship and serve.

1

¹Paul, a servant of Jesus Christ, called *to be* an apostle, separated unto the gospel of God, ²(Which he had promised afore by his prophets in the holy scriptures,) ³Concerning his Son Jesus Christ our Lord, which was made of the seed of David according to the flesh; ⁴And declared[a] *to be* the Son of God with power, according to the spirit of holiness, by the resurrection from the dead: ⁵By whom we have received grace and apostleship, for obedience[b] to the faith among all nations, for his name: ⁶Among whom are ye also the called of Jesus Christ: ⁷To all that be in Rome, beloved of God, called *to be* saints: Grace to you and peace from God our Father, and the Lord Jesus Christ.

⁸First, I thank my God through Jesus Christ for you all, that your faith is spoken of throughout the whole world. ⁹For God is my witness, whom I serve with[c] my spirit in the gospel of his Son, that without ceasing I make mention of you always in my prayers; ¹⁰Making request, if by any means now at length I might have a prosperous journey by the will of God to come unto you. ¹¹For I long to see you, that I may impart unto you some spiritual gift, to the end ye may be established; ¹²That is, that I may be comforted together with[d] you by the mutual faith both of you and me. ¹³Now I would not have you ignorant, brethren, that oftentimes I purposed to

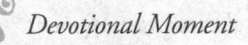

Devotional Moment

Praying

1:9-10 Paul cared so much for the new believers in Rome that he always mentioned them in his prayers. They were at the top of his list. If you care about someone, one way to show that you care is to pray for him or her. Pray every day for your loved ones—each by name. Thank God for them, ask him to guide them and shape them, and ask him to guide you in your dealings with that person. Post a reminder to pray where you can see it every morning.

come unto you, (but was let hitherto,) that I might have some fruit among[e] you also, even as among other Gentiles. ¹⁴I am debtor both to the Greeks, and to the Barbarians; both to the wise, and to the unwise. ¹⁵So, as much as in me is, I am ready to preach the gospel to you that are at Rome also.

¹⁶For I am not ashamed of the gospel of Christ: for it is the power of God unto salvation to every one that believeth; to the Jew first, and also to the Greek. ¹⁷For therein is the righteousness of God revealed from faith to faith: as it is written, The just shall live by faith. ¹⁸For the wrath of God is revealed from heaven against all ungodliness and unrighteousness of men, who hold the truth in unrighteousness; ¹⁹Because that which may be known of God is manifest in them[f]; for God hath shewed *it* unto them. ²⁰For the invisible

---

ᵃ declared: Gr. determined
ᵇ for obedience . . . : or, to the obedience of faith
ᶜ with: or, in
ᵈ with: or, in
ᵉ among: or, in
ᶠ in them: or, to them

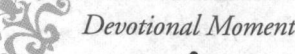

Devotional Moment

If It Feels Right

1:24-27 This passage of Scripture explains the problem with using feelings and desires as moral guides: They may not match God's design for our life. When we indulge our sinful desires in disregard of God's law, we eventually become hardened to the evil that we're doing. We may come to believe, quite sincerely, that bad is good and that wrong is right. Read God's Word, the Bible, every day so you will be reminded of God's high moral standards and become sensitive to his will.

things of him from the creation of the world are clearly seen, being understood by the things that are made, *even* his eternal power and Godhead; so[g] that they are without excuse: [21]Because that, when they knew God, they glorified *him* not as God, neither were thankful; but became vain in their imaginations, and their foolish heart was darkened. [22]Professing themselves to be wise, they became fools, [23]And changed the glory of the uncorruptible God into an image made like to corruptible man, and to birds, and fourfooted beasts, and creeping things. [24]Wherefore God also gave them up to uncleanness through the lusts of their own hearts, to dishonour their own bodies between themselves: [25]Who changed the truth of God into a lie, and worshipped and served the creature more than the Creator, who is blessed for ever. Amen. [26]For this cause God gave them up unto vile affections: for even their women did change the natural use into that which is against nature: [27]And likewise also the men, leaving the natural use of the woman, burned in their lust one toward another; men with men working that which is unseemly, and receiving in themselves that recompence of their error which was meet. [28]And even as they did not like to retain[h] God in *their* knowledge, God gave them over to a reprobate mind, to do those things which are not convenient; [29]Being filled with all unrighteousness, fornication, wickedness, covetousness, maliciousness; full of envy, murder, debate, deceit, malignity; whisperers, [30]Backbiters, haters of God, despiteful, proud, boasters, inventors of evil things, disobedient to parents, [31]Without understanding, covenantbreakers, without natural affection, implacable, unmerciful: [32]Who knowing the judgment of God, that they which commit such things are worthy of death, not only do the same, but have pleasure in them that do them.

2

[1]Therefore thou art inexcusable, O man, whosoever thou art that judgest: for wherein thou judgest another, thou condemnest thyself; for thou that judgest doest the same things. [2]But we are sure that the judgment of God is according to truth against them which commit such things. [3]And thinkest thou this, O man, that judgest them which do such things, and doest the same, that thou shalt escape the judgment of God? [4]Or despisest thou the riches of his goodness and forbearance and longsuffering; not knowing that

[g] so . . . : or, that they may be
[h] to retain: or, to acknowledge

Understanding Homosexuality

by William Consiglio

God's Word is truthful, and we can rely on it. It reveals God's standards about life and human sexuality. In Romans 1:24-27 we can see four moral and spiritual truths about homosexuality.

Homosexuality is a behavior. The Bible never calls homosexuality an identity or an alternative sexuality created by God. The Word says: "Women did change the natural use into that which is against nature. . . . The men, leaving the natural use of the woman, burned in their lust one toward another; men with men working that which is unseemly . . ." (vv. 26-27).

Homosexuality is a sinful behavior. Sinful means that such behavior is displeasing to God. The Word says: "God also gave them up to uncleanness . . . to dishonour their own bodies between themselves" (v. 24).

Homosexuality is a substitute for God's natural plan. God's Word says that "even their women did change the natural use into that which is against nature" (v. 26). God created all people to be heterosexuals. Homosexuality is a spiritual and emotional disorientation, deviation, and disorder of his plan.

As with all sin, the root of homosexual behavior is caused and maintained by those who refuse to honor God. "When they knew God, they glorified him not as God, neither were thankful" (v. 21).

All sin is a turning away from God. All healing comes from a return to God. Spiritually and morally, homosexuality is a sinful behavior that distorts God's natural plan for human sexuality.

Homosexuality is not the unforgivable sin. It is important to understand that homosexual behavior has emotional and psychological roots. While homosexuality is sin, it is not the unforgivable sin. God knows that all of us are sinners, prone to emotional wounding and disordered behavior.

John 8:1-11 contains the story of an adulterous woman who was brought before Jesus. If this had been a homosexual person, what would Jesus have done? Jesus loved the woman just as he loves all sinners, including homosexuals. He forgave her and commanded her to stop sinning. He said, "Neither do I condemn thee. Go, and sin no more" (John 8:11). God loves homosexual people and calls them to repent and be healed. He seeks their conversion, not their shame and ruin.

There is healing for those overcoming homosexuality. How can those who struggle with homosexuality "sin no more"? How can they change their feelings, behavior, and life-style? There are six elements to an effective healing program for Christians who are overcoming homosexuality:

• The overcomer needs a personal relationship with God the Father through Jesus Christ. He or she needs to become a child of God. Only Jesus can give the overcomer this real relationship to God because, as he says, "no man cometh unto the Father, but by me" (John 14:6). "As many as received him [Jesus], to them gave he power to become the sons of God" (John 1:12).

• The overcomer needs a personal devotional life that includes regular study and meditation on God's Word and a vital life of prayer.

• The overcomer needs to be actively involved with a good Bible teaching/preaching church that offers fellowship and nurture in Christian holiness.

• The overcomer needs a good Christian friend or married couple with whom to share burdens and be held accountable. Perhaps you can be such a friend.

• The overcomer needs to be committed to professional Christian counseling to learn about the roots of homosexuality, gain personal insight, and work through emotional healing.

• Finally, the overcomer needs to be involved in a group support ministry with other overcomers. Such a group offers weekly support and education. It provides HOPE—a place of **Honesty, Openness, Prayer,** and **Encouragement.** God loves the overcomer, so there is plenty of hope for those trying to overcome.

DIGGING DEEPER

    1. Can a person who continues to live as a homosexual have fellowship with God? See 1 Corinthians 6:9-11.

    2. Choosing to be an overcomer is choosing the narrow way. What promise does Jesus make to the one who chooses the narrow way? See Matthew 7:13-14.

    3. If you are helping an overcomer, ask him or her to find a Scripture passage on which to base the decision to change. Here are some great ones: Psalm 37:5; Matthew 7:7-8; and (my favorite) Romans 8:28.

the goodness of God leadeth thee to repentance? ⁵But after thy hardness and impenitent heart treasurest up unto thyself wrath against the day of wrath and revelation of the righteous judgment of God; ⁶Who will render to every man according to his deeds: ⁷To them who by patient continuance in well doing seek for glory and honour and immortality, eternal life: ⁸But unto them that are contentious, and do not obey the truth, but obey unrighteousness, indignation and wrath, ⁹Tribulation and anguish, upon every soul of man that doeth evil, of the Jew first, and also of the Gentile[a]; ¹⁰But glory, honour, and peace, to every man that worketh good, to the Jew first, and also to the Gentile[b]: ¹¹For there is no respect of persons with God. ¹²For as many as have sinned without law shall also perish without law: and as many as have sinned in the law shall be judged by the law; ¹³(For not the hearers of the law *are* just before God, but the doers of the law shall be justified. ¹⁴For when the Gentiles, which have not the law, do by nature the things contained in the law, these, having not the law, are a law unto themselves: ¹⁵Which shew the work of the law written in their hearts, their conscience[c] also bearing witness, and

---

[a] Gentile: Gr. Greek
[b] Gentile: Gr. Greek
[c] their conscience . . . : or, the conscience witnessing with them

their thoughts the mean while accusing or else excusing one another;) ¹⁶In the day when God shall judge the secrets of men by Jesus Christ according to my gospel.

¹⁷Behold, thou art called a Jew, and restest in the law, and makest thy boast of God, ¹⁸And knowest *his* will, and approvest[d] the things that are more excellent, being instructed out of the law; ¹⁹And art confident that thou thyself art a guide of the blind, a light of them which are in darkness, ²⁰An instructor of the foolish, a teacher of babes, which hast the form of knowledge and of the truth in the law. ²¹Thou therefore which teachest another, teachest thou not thyself? thou that preachest a man should not steal, dost thou steal? ²²Thou that sayest a man should not commit adultery, dost thou commit adultery? thou that abhorrest idols, dost thou commit sacrilege? ²³Thou that makest thy boast of the law, through breaking the law dishonourest thou God? ²⁴For the name of God is blasphemed among the Gentiles through you, as it is written. ²⁵For circumcision verily profiteth, if thou keep the law: but if thou be a breaker of the law, thy circumcision is made uncircumcision. ²⁶Therefore if the uncircumcision keep the righteousness of the law, shall not his uncircumcision be counted for circumcision? ²⁷And shall not uncircumcision which is by nature, if it fulfil the law, judge thee, who by the letter and circumcision dost transgress the law? ²⁸For he is not a Jew, which is one outwardly; neither *is that* circumcision, which is outward in the flesh: ²⁹But he *is* a Jew, which is one inwardly; and circumcision *is that* of the heart, in the spirit, *and* not in the letter; whose praise *is* not of men, but of God.

3

¹What advantage then hath the Jew? or what profit *is there* of circumcision? ²Much every way: chiefly, because that unto them were committed the oracles of God. ³For what if some did not believe? shall their unbelief make the faith of God without effect? ⁴God forbid: yea, let God be true, but every man a liar; as it is written, That thou mightest be justified in thy sayings, and mightest overcome when thou art judged. ⁵But if our unrighteousness commend the righteousness of God, what shall we say? *Is* God unrighteous who taketh vengeance? (I speak as a man) ⁶God forbid: for then how shall God judge the world? ⁷For if the truth of God hath more abounded through my lie unto his glory; why yet am I also judged as a sinner? ⁸And not *rather*, (as we be slanderously reported, and as some affirm

---

Devotional Moment
•
Faith of . . .

2:28-29 Every Jewish boy was circumcised eight days after birth. This practice symbolized the Jewish covenant relationship with God (see Gen. 17:9-11). Jews valued circumcision as a unique mark of their faith. But Paul reminded them that it is a changed heart and mind God looks for—not outward signs of religiosity. With your kids, be sure you place emphasis on the inner person—thoughts, values, loyalties, and beliefs—rather than on perfect behavior. What matters most is not that they look perfect but that they love God and strive to serve him.

---

[d] approvest . . . : or, triest the things that differ

that we say,) Let us do evil, that good may come? whose damnation is just. ⁹What then? are we better *than they*? No, in no wise: for we have before proved[a] both Jews and Gentiles, that they are all under sin; ¹⁰As it is written, There is none righteous, no, not one: ¹¹There is none that understandeth, there is none that seeketh after God. ¹²They are all gone out of the way, they are together become unprofitable; there is none that doeth good, no, not one. ¹³Their throat *is* an open sepulchre; with their tongues they have used deceit; the poison of asps *is* under their lips: ¹⁴Whose mouth *is* full of cursing and bitterness: ¹⁵Their feet *are* swift to shed blood: ¹⁶Destruction and misery *are* in their ways: ¹⁷And the way of peace have they not known: ¹⁸There is no fear of God before their eyes.

¹⁹Now we know that what things soever the law saith, it saith to them who are under the law: that every mouth may be stopped, and all the world may become guilty[b] before God. ²⁰Therefore by the deeds of the law there shall no flesh be justified in his sight: for by the law *is* the knowledge of sin. ²¹But now the righteousness of God without the law is manifested, being witnessed by the law and the prophets; ²²Even the righteousness of God *which is* by faith of Jesus Christ unto all and upon all them that believe: for there is no difference: ²³For all have sinned, and come short of the glory of God; ²⁴Being justified freely by his grace through the redemption that is in Christ Jesus: ²⁵Whom God hath set forth[c] *to be* a propitiation through faith in his blood, to declare his righteousness for the remission of sins that are past, through the forbearance of God; ²⁶To declare, *I say*, at this time his righteousness: that he might be just, and the justifier of him which believeth in Jesus. ²⁷Where *is* boasting then? It is excluded. By what law? of works? Nay: but by the law of faith. ²⁸Therefore we conclude that a man is justified by faith without the deeds of the law. ²⁹*Is he* the God of the Jews only? *is he* not also of the Gentiles? Yes, of the Gentiles also: ³⁰Seeing *it is* one God, which shall justify the circumcision by faith, and uncircumcision through faith. ³¹Do we then make void the law through faith? God forbid: yea, we establish the law.

4

¹What shall we say then that Abraham our father, as pertaining to the flesh, hath found? ²For if Abraham were justified by

---

Devotional Moment
•
Free Gift

3:27-28 We do not need to earn God's love and forgiveness. He offers it to us as a free gift. And yet how easily we fall into performance-based Christianity, trying to do all the right things so God will love us and approve of us. The good news of the gospel is that it's not necessary! There's a family application here, too. Be sure your kids know that you love and accept them unconditionally, *just because* they're yours—the way God loves and accepts us. It will help your children develop a needed sense of security in the family as well as prepare them to receive God's unconditional love.

---

[a] proved: Gr. charged
[b] guilty . . . : or, subject to the judgment of God
[c] set forth: or, foreordained

works, he hath *whereof* to glory; but not before God. [3]For what saith the scripture? Abraham believed God, and it was counted unto him for righteousness. [4]Now to him that worketh is the reward not reckoned of grace, but of debt. [5]But to him that worketh not, but believeth on him that justifieth the ungodly, his faith is counted for righteousness. [6]Even as David also describeth the blessedness of the man, unto whom God imputeth righteousness without works, [7]*Saying,* Blessed *are* they whose iniquities are forgiven, and whose sins are covered. [8]Blessed *is* the man to whom the Lord will not impute sin.

[9]*Cometh* this blessedness then upon the circumcision *only,* or upon the uncircumcision also? for we say that faith was reckoned to Abraham for righteousness. [10]How was it then reckoned? when he was in circumcision, or in uncircumcision? Not in circumcision, but in uncircumcision. [11]And he received the sign of circumcision, a seal of the righteousness of the faith which *he had yet* being uncircumcised: that he might be the father of all them that believe, though they be not circumcised; that righteousness might be imputed unto them also: [12]And the father of circumcision to them who are not of the circumcision only, but who also walk in the steps of that faith of our father Abraham, which *he had* being *yet* uncircumcised. [13]For the promise, that he should be the heir of the world, *was* not to Abraham, or to his seed, through the law, but through the righteousness of faith. [14]For if they which are of the law *be* heirs, faith is made void, and the promise made of none effect: [15]Because the law worketh wrath: for where no law is, *there is* no transgression. [16]Therefore *it is* of faith, that *it might be* by grace; to the end the promise might be sure to all the seed; not to that only which is of the law, but to that also which is of the faith of Abraham; who is the father of us all,

[17](As it is written, I have made thee a father of many nations,) before him whom he believed, *even* God, who quickeneth the dead, and calleth those things which be not as though they were. [18]Who against hope believed in hope, that he might become the father of many nations, according to that which was spoken, So shall thy seed be. [19]And being not weak in faith, he considered not his own body now dead, when he was about an hundred years old, neither yet the deadness of Sara's womb: [20]He staggered not at the promise of God through unbelief; but was strong in faith, giving glory to God; [21]And being fully persuaded that, what he had promised, he was able also to perform. [22]And therefore it was imputed to him for righteousness.

[23]Now it was not written for his sake alone, that it was imputed to him; [24]But for us also, to whom it shall be imputed, if we believe on him that raised up Jesus our Lord from the dead;

Devotional Moment
•
Forgiveness
4:6-8 Just as we experience great joy in realizing that God has forgiven us, our friends and family will benefit immeasurably when we forgive them. Few choices can destroy a relationship more thoroughly than the decision to hold a grudge. Extend forgiveness to others when they need it.

²⁵Who was delivered for our offences, and was raised again for our justification.

5

¹Therefore being justified by faith, we have peace with God through our Lord Jesus Christ: ²By whom also we have access by faith into this grace wherein we stand, and rejoice in hope of the glory of God. ³And not only *so*, but we glory in tribulations also: knowing that tribulation worketh patience; ⁴And patience, experience; and experience, hope: ⁵And hope maketh not ashamed; because the love of God is shed abroad in our hearts by the Holy Ghost which is given unto us.

⁶For when we were yet without strength, in due timeª Christ died for the ungodly. ⁷For scarcely for a righteous man will one die: yet peradventure for a good man some would even dare to die. ⁸But God commendeth his love toward us, in that, while we were yet sinners, Christ died for us. ⁹Much more then, being now justified by his blood, we shall be saved from wrath through him. ¹⁰For if, when we were enemies, we were reconciled to God by the death of his Son, much more, being reconciled, we shall be saved by his life. ¹¹And not only *so*, but we also joy in God through our Lord Jesus Christ, by whom we have now received the atonementᵇ. ¹²Wherefore, as by one man sin entered into the world, and death by sin; and so death passed upon all men, for thatᶜ all have sinned: ¹³(For until the law sin was in the world: but sin is not imputed when there is no law. ¹⁴Nevertheless death reigned from Adam to Moses, even over them that had not sinned after the similitude of Adam's transgression, who is the figure of him that was to come. ¹⁵But not as the offence, so also *is* the free gift. For if through the offence of one many be dead, much more the grace of God, and the gift by grace, *which is* by one man, Jesus Christ, hath abounded unto many. ¹⁶And not as *it was* by one that sinned, *so is* the gift: for the judgment *was* by one to condemnation, but the free gift *is* of many offences unto justification. ¹⁷For if by one man'sᵈ offence death reigned by one; much more they which receive abundance of grace and of the gift of righteousness shall reign in life by one, Jesus Christ.) ¹⁸Therefore as by the offenceᵉ of one *judgment came* upon all men to condemnation; even so by the righteousness of one *the free gift came* upon all men unto justification of life. ¹⁹For as by one man's disobedience many were made sinners, so by the obedience of one shall

---

Devotional Moment
Love

5:8 God didn't withhold his love until we deserved it. He loved us while we were completely unlovable. That's the kind of love he asks us to have for each other. No one is an ideal parent, child, sibling, spouse, or friend. Love others as God has loved you—exactly as they are. Love them unconditionally.

ª in due time: or, according to the time
ᵇ atonement: or, reconciliation
ᶜ for that: or, in whom
ᵈ by one man's . . . : or, by one offence
ᵉ by the offence . . . : or, by one offence

many be made righteous. ²⁰Moreover the law entered, that the offence might abound. But where sin abounded, grace did much more abound: ²¹That as sin hath reigned unto death, even so might grace reign through righteousness unto eternal life by Jesus Christ our Lord.

6

¹What shall we say then? Shall we continue in sin, that grace may abound? ²God forbid. How shall we, that are dead to sin, live any longer therein? ³Know ye not, that so many of us as were baptized into Jesus Christ were baptized into his death? ⁴Therefore we are buried with him by baptism into death: that like as Christ was raised up from the dead by the glory of the Father, even so we also should walk in newness of life. ⁵For if we have been planted together in the likeness of his death, we shall be also *in the likeness* of *his* resurrection: ⁶Knowing this, that our old man is crucified with *him*, that the body of sin might be destroyed, that henceforth we should not serve sin. ⁷For he that is dead is freed^a from sin. ⁸Now if we be dead with Christ, we believe that we shall also live with him: ⁹Knowing that Christ being raised from the dead dieth no more; death hath no more dominion over him. ¹⁰For in that he died, he died unto sin once: but in that he liveth, he liveth unto God. ¹¹Likewise reckon ye also yourselves to be dead indeed unto sin, but alive unto God through Jesus Christ our Lord. ¹²Let not sin therefore reign in your mortal body, that ye should obey it in the lusts thereof. ¹³Neither yield ye your members *as* instruments^b of unrighteousness unto sin: but yield yourselves unto God, as those that are alive from the dead, and your members *as* instruments of righteousness unto God. ¹⁴For sin shall not have dominion over you: for ye are not under the law, but under grace. ¹⁵What then? shall we sin, because we are not under the law, but under grace? God forbid. ¹⁶Know ye not, that to whom ye yield yourselves servants to obey, his servants ye are to whom ye obey; whether of sin unto death, or of obedience unto righteousness? ¹⁷But God be thanked, that ye were the servants of sin, but ye have obeyed from the heart that form of doctrine which^c was delivered you. ¹⁸Being then made free from sin, ye became the

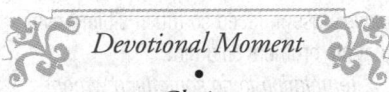

Devotional Moment

Choices

6:16-18 Christ's death and resurrection free us from the power of sin. We are no longer prisoners (slaves) of sinful desires, thoughts, and habits. That doesn't mean a Christian never feels a desire to sin; it means that he has a *choice* about whether to sin or not. A person who has placed his or her trust in Christ can choose to obey God, and the Holy Spirit will help that person to do so. Sometimes the most difficult place to make the right choice is in our home, with our family. We assume that we need an emotional outlet, and that the best place for it is at home. But we do not have to succumb to our sinful tendencies with our family. The place to start submitting ourselves to God is at home.

^a freed: Gr. justified
^b instruments: Gr. arms, or, weapons
^c which . . . : Gr. whereto ye were delivered

Worship
in Your Home

DEVOTIONS AS A PROBLEM-SOLVING TIME
Likewise the Spirit also helpeth our infirmities: for we know not what we should pray for. . . . Romans 8:26

Problem solving is a good approach for devotions.

One idea is to start with a Bible person and read through his or her story. Look for problems he or she experienced, and also look for anything you can find that shows how the person dealt with them. Take Joseph, for example:

Brothers or sisters having trouble getting along: Joseph faced so much sibling rivalry that his brothers sold him.

Temptation to do something wrong: Potiphar's wife tempted Joseph.

Being wrongfully accused: Both Potiphar and his wife accused Joseph wrongfully; Joseph was even thrown into prison for something he didn't do.

Forgiving people who beat you up: Joseph's brothers actually wanted to kill him. When he could have killed or hurt them, he forgave them.

Another approach is to ask each member of the prayer group for a specific problem he or she faces, and then try to find a Bible person who experienced a similar problem. Or find Bible verses that provide Bible responses to that problem.

servants of righteousness. [19]I speak after the manner of men because of the infirmity of your flesh: for as ye have yielded your members servants to uncleanness and to iniquity unto iniquity; even so now yield your members servants to righteousness unto holiness. [20]For when ye were the servants of sin, ye were free from righteousness. [21]What fruit had ye then in those things whereof ye are now ashamed? for the end of those things *is* death. [22]But now being made free from sin, and become servants to God, ye have your fruit unto holiness, and the end everlasting life. [23]For the wages of sin *is* death; but the gift of God *is* eternal life through Jesus Christ our Lord.

7

[1]Know ye not, brethren, (for I speak to them that know the law,) how that the law hath dominion over a man as long as he liveth? [2]For the woman which hath an husband is bound by the law to *her* husband so long as he liveth; but if the husband be dead, she is loosed from the law of *her* husband. [3]So then if, while *her* husband liveth, she be married to another man, she shall be called an adulteress: but if her husband be dead, she is free from that law; so that she is no adulteress, though she be married to another man. [4]Wherefore, my brethren, ye also are become dead to the law by the body of Christ; that ye should be married to another, *even* to him who is raised from the dead, that we should bring forth fruit unto God. [5]For when we were in the flesh, the motions[a] of sins, which were by the

---

[a] motions: Gr. passions

law, did work in our members to bring forth fruit unto death. ⁶But now we are delivered from the law, that being dead wherein we were held; that we should serve in newness of spirit, and not *in* the oldness of the letter.

⁷What shall we say then? *Is* the law sin? God forbid. Nay, I had not known sin, but by the law: for I had not known lust[b], except the law had said, Thou shalt not covet. ⁸But sin, taking occasion by the commandment, wrought in me all manner of concupiscence. For without the law sin *was* dead. ⁹For I was alive without the law once: but when the commandment came, sin revived, and I died. ¹⁰And the commandment, which *was ordained* to life, I found *to be* unto death. ¹¹For sin, taking occasion by the commandment, deceived me, and by it slew *me*. ¹²Wherefore the law *is* holy, and the commandment holy, and just, and good. ¹³Was then that which is good made death unto me? God forbid. But sin, that it might appear sin, working death in me by that which is good; that sin by the commandment might become exceeding sinful.

¹⁴For we know that the law is spiritual: but I am carnal, sold under sin. ¹⁵For that which I do I allow[c] not: for what I would, that do I not; but what I hate, that do I. ¹⁶If then I do that which I would not, I consent unto the law that *it is* good. ¹⁷Now then it is no more I that do it, but sin that dwelleth in me. ¹⁸For I know that in me (that is, in my flesh,) dwelleth no good thing: for to will is present with me; but *how* to perform that which is good I find not. ¹⁹For the good that I would I do

not: but the evil which I would not, that I do. ²⁰Now if I do that I would not, it is no more I that do it, but sin that dwelleth in me. ²¹I find then a law, that, when I would do good, evil is present with me. ²²For I delight in the law of God after the inward man: ²³But I see another law in my members, warring against the law of my mind, and bringing me into captivity to the law of sin which is in my members. ²⁴O wretched man that I am! who shall deliver me from the body[d] of this death? ²⁵I thank God through Jesus Christ our Lord. So then with the mind I myself serve the law of God; but with the flesh the law of sin.

8

¹*There is* therefore now no condemnation to them which are in Christ Jesus, who walk not after the flesh, but after the Spirit. ²For the law of the Spirit of life in Christ Jesus hath made me free

---

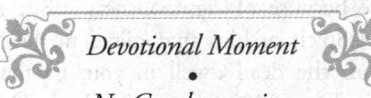

Devotional Moment
•
No Condemnation

8:1 God does not condemn those who belong to Christ, and the great irony is that only God has the right to do so! Only God is perfect. Only he has a claim on our life. We have sinned (see Rom. 3:10-18).

Our tendency is to be hard on family members, rather than gracious, because we can see each flaw close up. Out of gratitude for God's mercy toward you, resist that temptation. Give your kids room to fail. Accept your spouse's weaknesses (we all have them). And when Uncle Tom blows a financial deal, don't point the finger— see if you can help him recover.

---

[b] lust: or, concupiscence
[c] allow: Gr. know
[d] the body . . . : or, this body of death

from the law of sin and death. ³For what the law could not do, in that it was weak through the flesh, God sending his own Son in the likeness of sinful flesh, and for sinᵃ, condemned sin in the flesh: ⁴That the righteousness of the law might be fulfilled in us, who walk not after the flesh, but after the Spirit. ⁵For they that are after the flesh do mind the things of the flesh; but they that are after the Spirit the things of the Spirit. ⁶For to be carnallyᵇ minded *is* death; but to be spiritually minded *is* life and peace. ⁷Because the carnalᶜ mind *is* enmity against God: for it is not subject to the law of God, neither indeed can be. ⁸So then they that are in the flesh cannot please God. ⁹But ye are not in the flesh, but in the Spirit, if so be that the Spirit of God dwell in you. Now if any man have not the Spirit of Christ, he is none of his.

¹⁰And if Christ *be* in you, the body *is* dead because of sin; but the Spirit *is* life because of righteousness. ¹¹But if the Spirit of him that raised up Jesus from the dead dwell in you, he that raised up Christ from the dead shall also quicken your mortal bodies byᵈ his Spirit that dwelleth in you. ¹²Therefore, brethren, we are debtors, not to the flesh, to live after the flesh. ¹³For if ye live after the flesh, ye shall die: but if ye through the Spirit do mortify the deeds of the body, ye shall live. ¹⁴For as many as are led by the Spirit of God, they are the sons of God. ¹⁵For ye have not received the spirit of bondage again to

fear; but ye have received the Spirit of adoption, whereby we cry, Abba, Father. ¹⁶The Spirit itself beareth witness with our spirit, that we are the children of God:

¹⁷And if children, then heirs; heirs of God, and joint-heirs with Christ; if so be that we suffer with *him*, that we may be also glorified together. ¹⁸For I reckon that the sufferings of this present time *are* not worthy *to be compared* with the glory which shall be revealed in us. ¹⁹For the earnest expectation of the creature waiteth for the manifestation of the sons of God. ²⁰For the creature was made subject to vanity, not willingly, but by reason of him who hath subjected *the same* in hope, ²¹Because the creature itself also shall be delivered from the bondage of corruption into the glorious liberty of the children of God. ²²For we know that the whole creation groaneth and travaileth in pain together until now. ²³And not only *they*, but ourselves also, which have the firstfruits of the Spirit, even we ourselves groan within ourselves, waiting for the adoption, *to wit*, the redemption of our body. ²⁴For we are saved by hope: but hope that is seen is not hope: for what a man seeth, why doth he yet hope for? ²⁵But if we hope for that we see not, *then* do we with patience wait for *it.*

²⁶Likewise the Spirit also helpeth our infirmities: for we know not what we should pray for as we ought: but the Spirit itself maketh intercession for us with groanings which cannot be ut-

---

ᵃ for sin: or, by a sacrifice for sin
ᵇ to be carnally . . . : Gr. the minding of the flesh
ᶜ the carnal . . . : Gr. the minding of the flesh
ᵈ by: or, because of

tered. ²⁷And he that searcheth the hearts knoweth what *is* the mind of the Spirit, because^e he maketh intercession for the saints according to *the will of* God. ²⁸And we know that all things work together for good to them that love God, to them who are the called according to *his* purpose.

²⁹For whom he did foreknow, he also did predestinate *to be* conformed to the image of his Son, that he might be the firstborn among many brethren. ³⁰Moreover whom he did predestinate, them he also called: and whom he called, them he also justified: and whom he justified, them he also glorified.

³¹What shall we then say to these things? If God *be* for us, who *can be* against us? ³²He that spared not his own Son, but delivered him up for us all, how shall he not with him also freely give us all things? ³³Who shall lay any thing to the charge of God's elect? *It is* God that

---

Devotional Moment
•
Problems

8:28 When crisis hits, you may feel as if God has abandoned you. You may lose hope or become cynical about life—*expecting* bad to happen (and no good to come of it), doubting God's presence, power, and goodness. The next time a problem or crisis affects you, remember this verse. Then calmly deal with the problem, instead of panicking, and be confident that God has allowed your circumstances for a good reason. Don't cynically grouse and complain; accept the circumstance as the means God is using to bring about something good you cannot see. Thank God for his power and goodness.

---

justifieth. ³⁴Who *is* he that condemneth? *It is* Christ that died, yea rather, that is risen again, who is even at the right hand of God, who also maketh intercession for us. ³⁵Who shall separate us from the love of Christ? *shall* tribulation, or distress, or persecution, or famine, or nakedness, or peril, or sword? ³⁶As it is written, For thy sake we are killed all the day long; we are accounted as sheep for the slaughter. ³⁷Nay, in all these things we are more than conquerors through him that loved us. ³⁸For I am persuaded, that neither death, nor life, nor angels, nor principalities, nor powers, nor things present, nor things to come, ³⁹Nor height, nor depth, nor any other creature, shall be able to separate us from the love of God, which is in Christ Jesus our Lord.

9

¹I say the truth in Christ, I lie not, my conscience also bearing me witness in the Holy Ghost, ²That I have great heaviness and continual sorrow in my heart. ³For I could wish that myself were accursed^a from Christ for my brethren, my kinsmen according to the flesh: ⁴Who are Israelites; to whom *pertaineth* the adoption, and the glory, and the covenants^b, and the giving of the law, and the service *of God*, and the promises; ⁵Whose *are* the fathers, and of whom as concerning the flesh Christ *came*, who is over all, God blessed for ever. Amen.

⁶Not as though the word of God hath taken none effect. For they *are* not

---

^{e} because: or, that
^{a} accursed: or, separated
^{b} covenants: or, testaments

all Israel, which are of Israel: [7]Neither, because they are the seed of Abraham, *are they* all children: but, In Isaac shall thy seed be called. [8]That is, They which are the children of the flesh, these *are* not the children of God: but the children of the promise are counted for the seed. [9]For this *is* the word of promise, At this time will I come, and Sara shall have a son. [10]And not only *this*; but when Rebecca also had conceived by one, *even* by our father Isaac; [11](For *the children* being not yet born, neither having done any good or evil, that the purpose of God according to election might stand, not of works, but of him that calleth;) [12]It was said unto her, The elder[c] shall serve the younger. [13]As it is written, Jacob have I loved, but Esau have I hated.

[14]What shall we say then? *Is there* unrighteousness with God? God forbid. [15]For he saith to Moses, I will have mercy on whom I will have mercy, and I will have compassion on whom I will have compassion. [16]So then *it is* not of him that willeth, nor of him that runneth, but of God that sheweth mercy. [17]For the scripture saith unto Pharaoh, Even for this same purpose have I raised thee up, that I might shew my power in thee, and that my name might be declared throughout all the earth. [18]Therefore hath he mercy on whom he will *have mercy*, and whom he will he hardeneth. [19]Thou wilt say then unto me, Why doth he yet find fault? For who hath resisted his will? [20]Nay but, O man, who art thou that repliest against God? Shall the thing formed say to him that formed *it*, Why hast thou made me thus? [21]Hath not the potter power over the clay, of the same lump to make one vessel unto honour, and another unto dishonour? [22]*What* if God, willing to shew *his* wrath, and to make his power known, endured with much longsuffering the vessels of wrath fitted[d] to destruction: [23]And that he might make known the riches of his glory on the vessels of mercy, which he had afore prepared unto glory, [24]Even us, whom he hath called, not of the Jews only, but also of the Gentiles?

[25]As he saith also in Osee, I will call them my people, which were not my people; and her beloved, which was not beloved. [26]And it shall come to pass, *that* in the place where it was said unto them, Ye *are* not my people; there shall they be called the children of the living God. [27]Esaias also crieth concerning Israel, Though the number of the children of Israel be as the sand of the sea, a remnant shall be saved: [28]For he will finish the work[e], and cut *it* short in righteousness: because a short work will the Lord make upon the earth. [29]And as Esaias said before, Except the Lord of Sabaoth had left us a seed, we had been as Sodoma, and been made like unto Gomorrha.

[30]What shall we say then? That the Gentiles, which followed not after righteousness, have attained to righteousness, even the righteousness which is of faith. [31]But Israel, which followed after the law of righteousness, hath not attained to the law of righteousness. [32]Wherefore? Be-

---

[c] elder: or, greater
[d] fitted: or, made up
[e] the work: or, the account

cause *they sought it* not by faith, but as it were by the works of the law. For they stumbled at that stumblingstone; [33]As it is written, Behold, I lay in Sion a stumblingstone and rock of offence: and whosoever believeth on him shall not be ashamed[f].

10

[1]Brethren, my heart's desire and prayer to God for Israel is, that they might be saved. [2]For I bear them record that they have a zeal of God, but not according to knowledge. [3]For they being ignorant of God's righteousness, and going about to establish their own righteousness, have not submitted themselves unto the righteousness of God. [4]For Christ *is* the end of the law for righteousness to every one that believeth. [5]For Moses describeth the righteousness which is of the law, That the man which doeth those things shall live by them. [6]But the righteousness which is of faith speaketh on this wise, Say not in thine heart, Who shall ascend into heaven? (that is, to bring Christ down *from above*:) [7]Or, Who shall descend into the deep? (that is, to bring up Christ again from the dead.) [8]But what saith it? The word is nigh thee, *even* in thy mouth, and in thy heart: that is, the word of faith, which we preach; [9]That if thou shalt confess with thy mouth the Lord Jesus, and shalt believe in thine heart that God hath raised him from the dead, thou shalt be saved. [10]For with the heart man believeth unto righteousness; and with the mouth confession is made unto salvation. [11]For the scripture saith, Whosoever believeth on him shall not be ashamed.

[12]For there is no difference between the Jew and the Greek: for the same Lord over all is rich unto all that call upon him. [13]For whosoever shall call upon the name of the Lord shall be saved. [14]How then shall they call on him in whom they have not believed? and how shall they believe in him of whom they have not heard? and how shall they hear without a preacher? [15]And how shall they preach, except they be sent? as it is written, How beautiful are the feet of them that preach the gospel of peace, and bring glad tidings of good things! [16]But they have not all obeyed the gospel. For Esaias saith, Lord, who hath believed our report[a]? [17]So then faith *cometh* by hearing, and hearing by the word of God. [18]But I say, Have they not heard? Yes verily, their sound went into all the earth, and their words unto the ends of the world. [19]But I say, Did not Israel know? First Moses saith, I will provoke you to jealousy by *them that are* no people, *and* by a foolish nation I will anger you. [20]But Esaias is very bold, and saith, I was found of them that sought me not; I was made manifest unto them that asked not after me. [21]But to Israel he saith, All day long I have stretched forth my hands unto a disobedient and gainsaying people.

11

[1]I say then, Hath God cast away his people? God forbid. For I also am an Israelite, of the seed of Abraham, *of* the tribe of Benjamin. [2]God hath not cast away his people which he foreknew. Wot ye not what the scripture saith of Elias[a]?

[f] ashamed: or confounded
[a] our report: Gr. the hearing of us?
[a] of Elias: Gr. in Elias?

Your Child's Unique Talents

by Marcia L. Mitchell

The birth of a child sets into motion an intricate plan—a plan for that person's life, custom-made of that person's gifts and abilities. Born with a beautiful purpose, each child fills a special place in God's family. God invites us to give back in service what he gave us at birth. "I beseech you . . . that ye present your bodies a living sacrifice," the apostle Paul wrote (Rom. 12:1-2).

Attitudes to teach. Parents can instill the idea early in a child's life that what we are belongs to God for his use. Our value is not based on the profession we choose but rather on how we allow God to work in us. In God's eyes we are all formed equally. No one is any greater or less than anyone else. All our God-given talents are useful to God.

"Having then gifts differing according to the grace that is given to us" (Rom. 12:6). When we all use our gifts the way God planned, we fit together like pieces of a puzzle. No one has to worry about trying to do someone else's job but can concentrate on doing what God intended for him or her.

Find each child's talents. It would be wonderful if God sent an instruction packet with each new child that explained exactly what he wanted this person to do. But God's intricate plan includes the freedom to discover and choose how we spend our life.

As early as I can remember, I loved to make up stories. Often, using a set of flannel-backed Bible-story figures, I created endless tales for a pretend audience. No one suspected I would grow up to become an author and speaker, but God knew I was exploring how to use the talents he had woven into me before I was born.

Children need the opportunity to express their inner curiosities. Alert parents can watch for signs that signal a child's talents.

For example, an interest in details about bugs or animals could lead to the sciences. Are your children always singing or moving to music? Allow them to explore, without undue pressure, various areas of music, gymnastics, or dance.

Do they like to play with tools, or are they always asking how things work? Get them real tools and something to take apart or build.

Do they like to grow things? Give them seeds and a plot of ground or several flower-pots of soil. Are they interested in cooking, or are they hungry all the time? Supervised cooking with freedom to experiment will allow this talent to develop.

Do they have a sense of color? Let them explore art in a free sense or try flower arranging. Plain paper, crayons, paints, and colored pencils are great basic tools.

Notice whether they are people-oriented or would rather be by themselves. Do they like to have their work judged, or is criticism difficult to accept? Do they prefer to be outdoors or inside?

Provide new opportunities. As sensitive parents become aware of their children's interests, they can look for ways to expose them to new opportunities. Exposure can come in a variety of ways: kids' clubs, summer programs, 4-H, school, home, and church activities. Remember also that children may dislike an activity one day but enjoy it six months later.

Use the library—a lot! This will teach children how to discover. Subscribe to children's magazines in their own names.

The keys are time and freedom to explore, along with loving encouragement. One of the hardest things to provide is time and freedom to explore. Parents often try to fit their children's activities into their own work schedule, but this can create problems if the kids are so busy rushing to events that the child doesn't have time to enjoy them.

How many doctors and scientists have we missed—or mistakenly created—because children weren't given the opportunity to follow their inner yearnings? Children are not duplicates of their parents, nor are they born to fulfill their parents' frustrated dreams. Each child has his or her own special place to fill.

DIGGING DEEPER

1. When did God make the plans for your child's life and talents? See Psalm 139:13-16; Jeremiah 1:5; Acts 17:26.

2. How can parents play a role in developing their child's God-given talents? See 2 Timothy 1:5; 3:15; Luke 2:41-51; Deuteronomy 6:7; Luke 1:5-17; Ephesians 6:4; Psalm 34:11; Proverbs 22:6.

3. What godly values can we teach our children that may be different from the world's values? See 1 Samuel 15:22; 16:7; Matthew 7:21; 25:35-36; 1 Timothy 6:10.

---

how he maketh intercession to God against Israel, saying, ³Lord, they have killed thy prophets, and digged down thine altars; and I am left alone, and they seek my life. ⁴But what saith the answer of God unto him? I have reserved to myself seven thousand men, who have not bowed the knee to *the image of* Baal. ⁵Even so then at this present time also there is a remnant according to the election of grace. ⁶And if by grace, then *is it* no more of works: otherwise grace is no more grace. But if *it be* of works, then is it no more grace: otherwise work is no more work. ⁷What then? Israel hath not obtained that which he seeketh for; but the election hath obtained it, and the rest were blinded[b] ⁸(According as it is written, God hath given them the spirit of slumber[c], eyes that they should not see, and ears that they should not hear;)

unto this day. ⁹And David saith, Let their table be made a snare, and a trap, and a stumblingblock, and a recompence unto them: ¹⁰Let their eyes be darkened, that they may not see, and bow down their back alway. ¹¹I say then, Have they stumbled that they should fall? God forbid: but *rather* through their fall salvation *is come* unto the Gentiles, for to provoke them to jealousy. ¹²Now if the fall of them *be* the riches of the world, and the diminishing[d] of them the riches of the Gentiles; how much more their fulness? ¹³For I speak to you Gentiles, inasmuch as I am the apostle of the Gentiles, I magnify mine office: ¹⁴If by any means I may provoke to emulation *them which are* my flesh, and might save some of them. ¹⁵For if the casting away of them *be* the reconciling of the world, what *shall* the receiving *of them be*, but

---

[b] blinded: or, hardened

[c] slumber: or, remorse

[d] diminishing: or, decay, or, loss

life from the dead? ¹⁶For if the firstfruit *be* holy, the lump *is* also *holy:* and if the root *be* holy, so *are* the branches. ¹⁷And if some of the branches be broken off, and thou, being a wild olive tree, wert graffed in among them,ᵉ and with them partakest of the root and fatness of the olive tree; ¹⁸Boast not against the branches. But if thou boast, thou bearest not the root, but the root thee. ¹⁹Thou wilt say then, The branches were broken off, that I might be graffed in. ²⁰Well; because of unbelief they were broken off, and thou standest by faith. Be not highminded, but fear: ²¹For if God spared not the natural branches, *take heed* lest he also spare not thee. ²²Behold therefore the goodness and severity of God: on them which fell, severity; but toward thee, goodness, if thou continue in *his* goodness: otherwise thou also shalt be cut off. ²³And they also, if they abide not still in unbelief, shall be graffed in: for God is able to graff them in again. ²⁴For if thou wert cut out of the olive tree which is wild by nature, and wert graffed contrary to nature into a good olive tree: how much more shall these, which be the natural *branches,* be graffed into their own olive tree? ²⁵For I would not, brethren, that ye should be ignorant of this mystery, lest ye should be wise in your own conceits; that blindnessᶠ in part is happened to Israel, until the fulness of the Gentiles be come in. ²⁶And so all Israel shall be saved: as it is written, There shall come out of Sion the Deliverer, and shall turn away ungodliness from Jacob: ²⁷For this *is* my covenant unto them, when I shall take away their sins. ²⁸As concerning the gospel, *they are* enemies for your sakes: but as touching the election, *they are* beloved for the fathers' sakes. ²⁹For the gifts and calling of God *are* without repentance. ³⁰For as ye in times past have not believedᵍ God, yet have now obtained mercy through their unbelief: ³¹Even so have these also now not believedʰ, that through your mercy they also may obtain mercy. ³²For God hath concludedⁱ them all in unbelief, that he might have mercy upon all.

³³O the depth of the riches both of the wisdom and knowledge of God! how unsearchable *are* his judgments, and his ways past finding out! ³⁴For who hath known the mind of the Lord? or who hath been his counsellor? ³⁵Or who hath first given to him, and it shall be recompensed unto him again? ³⁶For of him, and through him, and to him, *are* all things: to whomʲ *be* glory for ever. Amen.

12

¹I beseech you therefore, brethren, by the mercies of God, that ye present your bodies a living sacrifice, holy, acceptable unto God, *which is* your reasonable service. ²And be not conformed to this world: but be ye transformed by the renewing of your mind, that ye may

---

ᵉ among them: or, for them
ᶠ blindness: or, hardness
ᵍ believed: or, obeyed
ʰ believed: or, obeyed
ⁱ concluded . . . : or, shut them all up together
ʲ whom: Gr. him

Family Traditions

Traditions that Enhance Family Unity

ROMANS 12:6-21

Romans 12 gives great advice for fostering unity among believers—whether in the body of Christ at large or an individual family. The key is to *emphasize a spirit of community in all you do*—cleaning, building, sewing, taking care of pets, cooking, eating, driving, listening, talking, being.

Do all you can to create family identity: lots of photographs on the walls of your home; scrapbooks full of photos from vacations and outings; lots of talk about memories; lots of questions when one family member experiences something the others didn't; exploration of your family's ethnic background; setting goals together and planning ways to meet them.

Don't be afraid to allow differences to flourish in your family. Unity does not require that everyone must be alike but that everyone agrees to love each other in spite of the differences. And remember, there are cycles of unity; if you're on a downward spiral for a while, wait and pray. It doesn't mean the family climate is always going to be that way.

Unity doesn't have to lessen as children grow. Teenagers who are becoming independent need your spiritual and emotional presence more than ever. At this stage, unity means letting go and loving hard. A strong foundation of family unity set in the earlier years will mean the cord they're straining against is really elastic.

Create your own family memos of commendation for jobs well done. Bestow blue ribbons for prize-winning efforts. Fly the flag for outstanding achievements. Bring a bouquet to recitals and performing arts events. Wave banners at ball games and sports events. Meet traveling family members at airports with streamers and party hats. Throw a party when your family has overcome something difficult, endured a hardship, or made it through a serious problem.

Keep finding what your family does right. Look for original acts of heroism and daring. Praise others' gifts and talents, even the small ones. See the one-of-a-kind qualities each member brings to your family and treasure them.

Sometimes those happy families you envy only *seem* happy. Appearing to have it all together can be a guise for deeper troubles. The most unified families are those who can openly deal with problems, then go on living and learning together. If you are that kind of family, celebrate it. Determine to be each other's biggest fans in spite of individual quirks! Stand behind each other, and cheer on your spouse, child, brother, or sister.

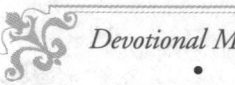

Devotional Moment

•

Peer Pressure

12:1-2 God tells us not to copy the behavior of the world. These words challenge us as families, parents, and children because we find great security in acting just like everyone else. It's easy for us to feel justified in buying, wearing, and watching whatever everyone else is buying, wearing, and watching. In your family, remind each other that you serve Christ. If you see a spouse, child, or sibling considering doing something wrong, take some time to talk it over and help them discern their true motives.

prove what *is* that good, and acceptable, and perfect, will of God. ³For I say, through the grace given unto me, to every man that is among you, not to think *of himself* more highly than he ought to think; but to think soberly[a], according as God hath dealt to every man the measure of faith. ⁴For as we have many members in one body, and all members have not the same office: ⁵So we, *being* many, are one body in Christ, and every one members one of another. ⁶Having then gifts differing according to the grace that is given to us, whether prophecy, *let us prophesy* according to the proportion of faith; ⁷Or ministry, *let us wait* on *our* ministering: or he that teacheth, on teaching; ⁸Or he that exhorteth, on exhortation: he that giveth[b], *let him do it* with simplicity; he that ruleth, with diligence; he that sheweth mercy, with cheerfulness. ⁹*Let*

love be without dissimulation. Abhor that which is evil; cleave to that which is good. ¹⁰*Be* kindly affectioned one to another with brotherly love; in honour preferring one another; ¹¹Not slothful in business; fervent in spirit; serving the Lord; ¹²Rejoicing in hope; patient in tribulation; continuing instant in prayer; ¹³Distributing to the necessity of saints; given to hospitality. ¹⁴Bless them which persecute you: bless, and curse not. ¹⁵Rejoice with them that do rejoice, and weep with them that weep. ¹⁶*Be* of the same mind one toward another. Mind not high things, but condescend[c] to men of low estate. Be not wise in your own conceits. ¹⁷Recompense to no man evil for evil. Provide things honest in the sight of all men. ¹⁸If it be possible, as much as lieth in you, live peaceably with all men. ¹⁹Dearly beloved, avenge not yourselves, but *rather* give place unto wrath: for it is written, Vengeance *is* mine; I will repay, saith the Lord. ²⁰Therefore if thine enemy hunger, feed him; if he thirst, give him drink: for in so doing thou shalt heap coals of fire on his head. ²¹Be not overcome of evil, but overcome evil with good.

13

¹Let every soul be subject unto the higher powers. For there is no power but of God: the powers that be are ordained[a] of God. ²Whosoever therefore resisteth the power, resisteth the ordinance of God: and they that resist shall receive to themselves damnation. ³For

---

[a] soberly: Gr. to sobriety
[b] giveth: or, imparteth
[c] condescend . . . : or, be contented with mean things
[a] ordained: or, ordered

Breaking Free from Hostility

If it be possible . . . live peaceably with all men. Romans 12:18

In Romans 12:18 we find an important concept for those who struggle with breaking past patterns. There we read, "If it be possible . . . live peaceably with all men." And then the following verse: "Dearly beloved, avenge not yourselves. . . . Vengeance is mine, saith the Lord."

What this means in short is a biblical mandate: *The stronger person always initiates the peace.* How does that challenge relate to those from a difficult past? Just ask Karl.

Karl never met his father until he was sixteen years old, and their first meeting was a terrible disappointment. In all honesty, Karl hated his father for having deserted him and his mother.

Finally, the truth captured in these verses in Romans broke through to Karl. His father wasn't losing any sleep over their broken relationship—Karl was! He had waited for years for his father to walk in the door and initiate a conversation that would lead to forgiveness and reconciliation—but that was about as likely to happen as his television set walking over and giving him a hug.

Karl finally realized that if there was to be any reconciliation, he would have to initiate it. He talked his father into meeting him for dinner at a nice, local seafood restaurant, and there at the table he asked his father to forgive him for the anger he had carried and for the negative things he had done and felt in the past.

Karl's father said nothing. Throughout the entire dinner, he said not one word of direct response. He was no different from before—no words of love, no expression of regret, no asking for forgiveness.

But from that day forward, Karl was different. "Just as much as possible," Karl had made peace with his father, and it had set him free from the cycle of hostility.

How powerful this concept could be if applied by the average couple. What if every time they got into an argument, they asked themselves, Who's going to be the stronger one? Who's going to initiate the peace? Do I really want to be the weak one and not walk over, take her (or his) hand, and make things as right as I can?

The alternative is what Carol tried to do. She grew up jaded by her father's verbal cruelty. While he never physically abused anyone, his harsh words had cut through each child's heart.

Then, in a miraculous chain of events, her father was led to Christ by a retired minister in his nursing home. For the first time he felt ashamed and embarrassed for all the cruel and critical words he had spoken to his children. Eventually, he wrote a long letter of apology to each child—Carol included.

All but Carol responded to his offer of peace with incredible appreciation, surprise, and encouragement. Carol sent his letter back—ripped into tiny pieces— with these few lines penned in response: "I will never forgive you. I will spend my whole life overcoming you if that's what it takes."

Carol never did see her father until his funeral, and even today, she is still living out her own negative prophecy and trying to overcome her hatred and bitterness. A famous poet once wrote, "Revenge is the sweetest morsel ever cooked in hell." It may taste sweet to rip a letter of apology in pieces, but it will go down bitter and caustic in the months and years to come.

How about you? As you seek to close the door on past hurts (or present ones), commit yourself to the challenge of this one principle: *The stronger person initiates the peace.*

---

rulers are not a terror to good works, but to the evil. Wilt thou then not be afraid of the power? do that which is good, and thou shalt have praise of the same: ⁴For he is the minister of God to thee for good. But if thou do that which is evil, be afraid; for he beareth not the sword in vain: for he is the minister of God, a revenger to *execute* wrath upon him that doeth evil. ⁵Wherefore ye must needs be subject, not only for wrath, but also for conscience sake. ⁶For

for this cause pay ye tribute also: for they are God's ministers, attending continually upon this very thing.

⁷Render therefore to all their dues: tribute to whom tribute *is due*; custom to whom custom; fear to whom fear; honour to whom honour. ⁸Owe no man any thing, but to love one another: for he that loveth another hath fulfilled the law. ⁹For this, Thou shalt not commit adultery, Thou shalt not kill, Thou shalt not steal, Thou shalt not bear false witness, Thou shalt not covet; and if *there be* any other commandment, it is briefly comprehended in this saying, namely, Thou shalt love thy neighbour as thyself. ¹⁰Love worketh no ill to his neighbour: therefore love *is* the fulfilling of the law.

¹¹And that, knowing the time, that now *it is* high time to awake out of sleep: for now *is* our salvation nearer than when we believed. ¹²The night is far spent, the day is at hand: let us therefore cast off the works of darkness, and let us put on the armour of light. ¹³Let us walk

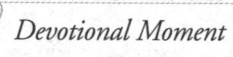

Devotional Moment
•
The Ultimate Rule
13:9-10 God's commandments can be summarized in one rule: "Thou shalt love thy neighbour as thyself." The law of love supersedes all other rules and regulations because it provides a standard of behavior that can be applied in every possible situation. When tension builds, apply the law of love. Don't focus on pleasing yourself but on giving others the same treatment you would give yourself.

honestlyᵇ, as in the day; not in rioting and drunkenness, not in chambering and wantonness, not in strife and envying. ¹⁴But put ye on the Lord Jesus Christ, and make not provision for the flesh, to *fulfil* the lusts *thereof.*

14

¹Him that is weak in the faith receive ye, *but* notª to doubtful disputations. ²For one believeth that he may eat all things: another, who is weak, eateth herbs. ³Let not him that eateth despise him that eateth not; and let not him which eateth not judge him that eateth: for God hath received him. ⁴Who art thou that judgest another man's servant? to his own master he standeth or falleth. Yea,

---

Devotional Moment

Disagreements

14:1-4 Divisions in churches often occur when disagreements over life-style issues grow into major arguments. Paul warned the church not to pass judgment on younger believers whose faith is still young and growing.

Divisions in families can also result from disagreements over issues that really aren't very important (such as how kids wear their hair or how a spouse stacks the dishes). Children can be driven away from a close family relationship and a living faith by a rigid, judgmental approach to superficial, life-style issues.

The church is commanded to accept and love young believers until their faith matures. Families have the same obligation—to be accepting and patient with members who are still growing toward maturity.

---

he shall be holden up: for God is able to make him stand. ⁵One man esteemeth one day above another: another esteemeth every day *alike.* Let every man be fully persuadedᵇ in his own mind. ⁶He that regardethᶜ the day, regardeth *it* unto the Lord; and he that regardeth not the day, to the Lord he doth not regard *it.* He that eateth, eateth to the Lord, for he giveth God thanks; and he that eateth not, to the Lord he eateth not, and giveth God thanks. ⁷For none of us liveth to himself, and no man dieth to himself. ⁸For whether we live, we live unto the Lord; and whether we die, we die unto the Lord: whether we live therefore, or die, we are the Lord's. ⁹For to this end Christ both died, and rose, and revived, that he might be Lord both of the dead and living. ¹⁰But why dost thou judge thy brother? or why dost thou set at nought thy brother? for we shall all stand before the judgment seat of Christ. ¹¹For it is written, *As* I live, saith the Lord, every knee shall bow to me, and every tongue shall confess to God. ¹²So then every one of us shall give account of himself to God. ¹³Let us not therefore judge one another any more: but judge this rather, that no man put a stumblingblock or an occasion to fall in *his* brother's way. ¹⁴I know, and am persuaded by the Lord Jesus, that *there is* nothing uncleanᵈ of itself: but to him that esteemeth any thing to be unclean, to him *it is* unclean. ¹⁵But if thy brother be grieved with *thy* meat, now walkest

---

ᵇ honestly: or, decently
ª not . . . : or, not to judge his doubtful thoughts
ᵇ fully persuaded: or, fully assured
ᶜ regardeth: or, observeth
ᵈ unclean: Gr. common

thou not charitably[e]. Destroy not him with thy meat, for whom Christ died. [16]Let not then your good be evil spoken of: [17]For the kingdom of God is not meat and drink; but righteousness, and peace, and joy in the Holy Ghost. [18]For he that in these things serveth Christ *is* acceptable to God, and approved of men. [19]Let us therefore follow after the things which make for peace, and things wherewith one may edify another. [20]For meat destroy not the work of God. All things indeed *are* pure; but *it is* evil for that man who eateth with offence. [21]*It is* good neither to eat flesh, nor to drink wine, nor *any thing* whereby thy brother stumbleth, or is offended, or is made weak. [22]Hast thou faith? have *it* to thyself before God. Happy *is* he that condemneth not himself in that thing which he alloweth. [23]And he that doubteth[f] is damned if he eat, because *he eateth* not of faith: for whatsoever *is* not of faith is sin.

15

[1]We then that are strong ought to bear the infirmities of the weak, and not to please ourselves. [2]Let every one of us please *his* neighbour for *his* good to edification. [3]For even Christ pleased not himself; but, as it is written, The reproaches of them that reproached thee fell on me. [4]For whatsoever things were written aforetime were written for our learning, that we through patience and comfort of the scriptures might have hope. [5]Now the God of patience and consolation grant you to be likeminded one toward another according to Christ

Jesus: [6]That ye may with one mind *and* one mouth glorify God, even the Father of our Lord Jesus Christ.

[7]Wherefore receive ye one another, as Christ also received us to the glory of God. [8]Now I say that Jesus Christ was a minister of the circumcision for the truth of God, to confirm the promises *made* unto the fathers: [9]And that the Gentiles might glorify God for *his* mercy; as it is written, For this cause I will confess to thee among the Gentiles, and sing unto thy name. [10]And again he saith, Rejoice, ye Gentiles, with his people. [11]And again, Praise the Lord, all ye Gentiles; and laud him, all ye people. [12]And again, Esaias saith, There shall be a root of Jesse, and he that shall rise to reign over the Gentiles; in him shall the Gentiles trust.

[13]Now the God of hope fill you with all joy and peace in believing, that ye may abound in hope, through the power of the Holy Ghost.

[14]And I myself also am persuaded of you, my brethren, that ye also are full of goodness, filled with all knowledge, able also to admonish one another. [15]Nevertheless, brethren, I have written the more boldly unto you in some sort, as putting you in mind, because of the grace that is given to me of God, [16]That I should be the minister of Jesus Christ to the Gentiles, ministering the gospel of God, that the offering up[a] of the Gentiles might be acceptable, being sanctified by the Holy Ghost.

[17]I have therefore whereof I may glory through Jesus Christ in those things which pertain to God. [18]For I

---

[e] charitably: Gr. according to charity
[f] doubteth: or, discerneth and putteth a difference between meats
[a] offering up: or, sacrificing

will not dare to speak of any of those things which Christ hath not wrought by me, to make the Gentiles obedient, by word and deed, [19]Through mighty signs and wonders, by the power of the Spirit of God; so that from Jerusalem, and round about unto Illyricum, I have fully preached the gospel of Christ. [20]Yea, so have I strived to preach the gospel, not where Christ was named, lest I should build upon another man's foundation: [21]But as it is written, To whom he was not spoken of, they shall see: and they that have not heard shall understand.

[22]For which cause also I have been much[b] hindered from coming to you. [23]But now having no more place in these parts, and having a great desire these many years to come unto you; [24]Whensoever I take my journey into Spain, I will come to you: for I trust to see you in my journey, and to be brought on my way thitherward by you, if first I be somewhat filled with[c] your *company*. [25]But now I go unto Jerusalem to minister unto the saints. [26]For it hath pleased them of Macedonia and Achaia to make a certain contribution for the poor saints which are at Jerusalem. [27]It hath pleased them verily; and their debtors they are. For if the Gentiles have been made partakers of their spiritual things, their duty is also to minister unto them in carnal things. [28]When therefore I have performed this, and have sealed to them this fruit, I will come by you into Spain. [29]And I am sure that, when I come unto you, I shall come in the fulness of the blessing of the gospel of Christ.

[30]Now I beseech you, brethren, for the Lord Jesus Christ's sake, and for the love of the Spirit, that ye strive together with me in *your* prayers to God for me; [31]That I may be delivered from them that do not believe in Judaea; and that my service which *I have* for Jerusalem may be accepted of the saints; [32]That I may come unto you with joy by the will of God, and may with you be refreshed. [33]Now the God of peace *be* with you all. Amen.

16

[1]I commend unto you Phebe our sister, which is a servant of the church which is at Cenchrea: [2]That ye receive her in the Lord, as becometh saints, and that ye assist her in whatsoever business she hath need of you: for she hath been a succourer of many, and of myself also. [3]Greet Priscilla and Aquila my helpers in Christ Jesus: [4]Who have for my life laid down their own necks: unto

Devotional Moment
•
Marriage = Teamwork
16:3 Priscilla and Aquila, a married couple who served God together, received a special greeting from Paul. He mentioned their courage in protecting him and explained how their actions benefited many other churches. Sometimes church responsibilities keep husbands and wives busy spending time with everyone but each other. The results can be resentment, anger, even sexual temptation. Husbands and wives should look for opportunities to serve the church where they can work together and complement each other's spiritual gifts. Where could you and your spouse serve the Lord together?

---

[b] much: or, many ways, or oftentimes
[c] with . . . : Gr. with you

whom not only I give thanks, but also all the churches of the Gentiles. ⁵Likewise *greet* the church that is in their house. Salute my wellbeloved Epaenetus, who is the firstfruits of Achaia unto Christ. ⁶Greet Mary, who bestowed much labour on us. ⁷Salute Andronicus and Junia, my kinsmen, and my fellowprisoners, who are of note among the apostles, who also were in Christ before me. ⁸Greet Amplias my beloved in the Lord. ⁹Salute Urbane, our helper in Christ, and Stachys my beloved. ¹⁰Salute Apelles approved in Christ. Salute them which are of Aristobulus' *household.* ¹¹Salute Herodion my kinsman. Greet them that be of the *household* of Narcissus, which are in the Lord. ¹²Salute Tryphena and Tryphosa, who labour in the Lord. Salute the beloved Persis, which laboured much in the Lord. ¹³Salute Rufus chosen in the Lord, and his mother and mine. ¹⁴Salute Asyncritus, Phlegon, Hermas, Patrobas, Hermes, and the brethren which are with them. ¹⁵Salute Philologus, and Julia, Nereus, and his sister, and Olympas, and all the saints which are with them. ¹⁶Salute one another with an holy kiss. The churches of Christ salute you.

¹⁷Now I beseech you, brethren, mark them which cause divisions and offences contrary to the doctrine which ye have learned; and avoid them. ¹⁸For they that are such serve not our Lord Jesus Christ, but their own belly; and by good words and fair speeches deceive the hearts of the simple. ¹⁹For your obedience is come abroad unto all *men.* I am glad therefore on your behalf: but yet I would have you wise unto that which is good, and simpleª concerning evil. ²⁰And the God of peace shall bruiseᵇ Satan under your feet shortly. The grace of our Lord Jesus Christ *be* with you. Amen.

²¹Timotheus my workfellow, and Lucius, and Jason, and Sosipater, my kinsmen, salute you. ²²I Tertius, who wrote *this* epistle, salute you in the Lord. ²³Gaius mine host, and of the whole church, saluteth you. Erastus the chamberlain of the city saluteth you, and Quartus a brother. ²⁴The grace of our Lord Jesus Christ *be* with you all. Amen.

²⁵Now to him that is of power to stablish you according to my gospel, and the preaching of Jesus Christ, according to the revelation of the mystery, which was kept secret since the world began, ²⁶But now is made manifest, and by the scriptures of the prophets, according to the commandment of the everlasting God, made known to all nations for the obedience of faith: ²⁷To God only wise, *be* glory through Jesus Christ for ever. Amen.

[Written to the Romans from Corinthus, *and sent* by Phebe servant of the church at Cenchrea.]

ª simple: or, harmless
ᵇ bruise: or, tread

FIRST CORINTHIANS

Purpose
To identify problems in the Corinthian church, to offer solutions, and to teach the believers how to live for Christ in a corrupt society

Author
Paul

To Whom Written
The church in Corinth

Date Written
About A.D. 55, near the end of Paul's three-year ministry in Ephesus, and during his third missionary journey

Setting
Corinth was a major cosmopolitan city, a seaport, and a major trade center—the most important city in Achaia. It was filled with idolatry and immorality. The church was largely made up of Gentiles. Paul had established this church on his second missionary journey.

Key Verse
"I beseech you, brethren, by the name of our Lord Jesus Christ, that ye all speak the same thing, and that there be no divisions among you; but that ye be perfectly joined together in the same mind and in the same judgment" (1:10).

Key People
Paul, Timothy, members of Chloe's household

What was life like in Corinth in Paul's day? Imagine teenagers cranking up the volume on the dirtiest, most abusive heavy rock available; spending evenings viewing the raunchiest videos from your town's most unscrupulous rental store; browsing the pulp magazines; allowing small kids to watch daytime television soap operas; drinking too much; eating till they groan; and cursing at every driver they pass.

That would be close to life in the city of Corinth. Then add: living out Hollywood-style sexual fantasies; hanging crystals around the house; partying till dawn; and sleeping till noon. You're getting closer.

Add to all that some well-organized pagan religion, and you've pretty well got the picture.

In such a city the story of Jesus fell like a lightning bolt. When a Corinthian became a Christian, everything got zapped. Life-style changes were drastic. A punk rocker arriving at marine boot camp might be something similar.

First Corinthians is about problems people had changing from being ego-driven to Spirit-led—from a hunger for fleshly things to a hunger for God. These changes were not easy, and occasionally Paul advocated severe discipline.

Got a problem child at home? Take a look at Paul's approach. In all of his severity, Paul writes thirteen classic verses on love. No softy, Paul urges tough, eager, steady love as the bedrock of change.

Need help with knotty problems of conduct and life-style? Your Corinthian cousins found it in this letter. You will, too.

1

¹Paul, called *to be* an apostle of Jesus Christ through the will of God, and Sosthenes *our* brother, ²Unto the church of God which is at Corinth, to them that are sanctified in Christ Jesus, called *to be* saints, with all that in every place call upon the name of Jesus Christ our Lord, both theirs and ours: ³Grace *be* unto you, and peace, from God our Father, and *from* the Lord Jesus Christ. ⁴I thank my God always on your behalf, for the grace of God which is given you by Jesus Christ; ⁵That in every thing ye are enriched by him, in all utterance, and *in* all knowledge; ⁶Even as the testimony of Christ was confirmed in you: ⁷So that ye come behind in no gift; waiting for the coming[a] of our Lord Je-sus Christ: ⁸Who shall also confirm you unto the end, *that ye may be* blameless in the day of our Lord Jesus Christ. ⁹God *is* faithful, by whom ye were called unto the fellowship of his Son Jesus Christ our Lord.

¹⁰Now I beseech you, brethren, by the name of our Lord Jesus Christ, that ye all speak the same thing, and *that* there be no divisions[b] among you; but *that* ye be perfectly joined together in the same mind and in the same judgment. ¹¹For it hath been declared unto me of you, my brethren, by them *which are of the house* of Chloe, that there are contentions among you. ¹²Now this I say, that every one of you saith, I am of Paul; and I of Apollos; and I of Cephas; and I of Christ. ¹³Is Christ divided? was Paul crucified for you? or were ye baptized in the name of Paul?

¹⁴I thank God that I baptized none of you, but Crispus and Gaius; ¹⁵Lest any should say that I had baptized in mine own name. ¹⁶And I baptized also the household of Stephanas: besides, I know not whether I baptized any other. ¹⁷For Christ sent me not to baptize, but to preach the gospel: not with wisdom of words[c], lest the cross of Christ should be made of none effect. ¹⁸For the preaching of the cross is to them that perish foolishness; but unto us which are saved it is the power of God. ¹⁹For it is written, I will destroy the wisdom of the wise, and will bring to nothing the understanding of the prudent. ²⁰Where *is* the wise? where *is* the scribe? where *is* the disputer of this world? hath not

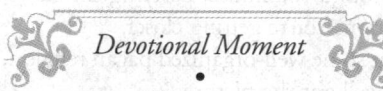

Devotional Moment

Affirmation

1:4-7 Paul started his letter to the Corinthians by affirming them and reminding them of how they fit into God's grand plan of redemption. Though the church had numerous problems, he began with sincerely positive comments about them. People thrive on sincere praise. Workers are happier and more productive in an environment of positive affirmation. Young people remember more about the atmosphere of a youth group than about the lesson. When you see your family after being gone all day, what are the first words to come out of your mouth? Are they words of criticism or words of praise? Do you focus your first thoughts on the negatives of your day or the positive blessings of God? Choose words that build up people. Remind them of what they do well and how they enrich your life.

ª coming: Gr. revelation
ᵇ divisions: Gr. schisms
ᶜ words: or, speech

God made foolish the wisdom of this world? ²¹For after that in the wisdom of God the world by wisdom knew not God, it pleased God by the foolishness of preaching to save them that believe. ²²For the Jews require a sign, and the Greeks seek after wisdom: ²³But we preach Christ crucified, unto the Jews a stumblingblock, and unto the Greeks foolishness; ²⁴But unto them which are called, both Jews and Greeks, Christ the power of God, and the wisdom of God. ²⁵Because the foolishness of God is wiser than men; and the weakness of God is stronger than men. ²⁶For ye see your calling, brethren, how that not many wise men after the flesh, not many mighty, not many noble, *are called*: ²⁷But God hath chosen the foolish things of the world to confound the wise; and God hath chosen the weak things of the world to confound the things which are mighty; ²⁸And base things of the world, and things which are despised, hath God chosen, *yea*, and things which are not, to bring to nought things that are: ²⁹That no flesh should glory in his presence. ³⁰But of him are ye in Christ Jesus, who of God is made unto us wisdom, and righteousness, and sanctification, and redemption: ³¹That, according as it is written, He that glorieth, let him glory in the Lord.

2

¹And I, brethren, when I came to you, came not with excellency of speech or of wisdom, declaring unto you the testimony of God. ²For I determined not to know any thing among you, save Jesus Christ, and him crucified. ³And I was with you in weakness, and in fear,

Worship
in Your Home

WHEN *NOT* TO HAVE FAMILY DEVOTIONS
I thank my God always on your behalf, for the grace of God which is given you by Jesus Christ. That in every thing ye are enriched by him.
1 Corinthians 1:4-5

Through devotions, we want to cultivate a genuine delight in God and his Word. Anything that squelches that delight, no matter how excellent otherwise, gets in the way of our long-term goals.

It is wise *not* to have family devotions whenever (1) one family member's schedule is too pressured, such as an urgent need to get to a scheduled event; (2) they may encourage or enhance a temporarily rebellious spirit; (3) they may undercut or undermine any family member in any way; (4) they become too long or tedious; (5) they are so demanding or rigid that family members lose the joy of having them; or (6) one or more family members is angry with another (reconcile first!).

You can probably add a dozen or more of your own reasons. If tonight is a counterproductive time to have devotions, wait until another night when it can truly be a time of delight. Five minutes of building delight in the Lord is much better than an hour of just going through the motions.

Breaking Free from
Spiritual Immaturity

And I, brethren, could not speak unto you as unto spiritual, but as unto carnal, even as unto babes in Christ. 1 Corinthians 3:1

While Paul went on to talk about the many divisions that were a part of the church, he could have also been talking about the division that exists in many homes. Breaking free from spiritual immaturity—particularly as a couple—can be a challenge. For those who want to move past childhood and grow together spiritually, here are four opportunities for spiritual growth to keep in mind.

1. **If you don't set your schedule, someone else will set it for you.** Keeping this principle in mind is an important part of keeping our spiritual life in proper perspective. We all gravitate to the most urgent, most immediate needs. Those activities that pay off farther down the road (such as studying the Scriptures, going to a class, or even going on a missions trip) often get completely crowded out by everyday urgencies. As a couple ask yourselves, "Where in our week are the times we've aggressively set aside to pray with each other and to study God's Word together?" We may waste hundreds of hours watching television each year, but we're reluctant to spend even five minutes praying with our spouse.

2. **Recognize and talk through different levels of maturity.** David came from a strong Christian background. He was a third-generation seminary graduate, and he strongly felt that God had called him into the ministry. His wife, Janet, came to know Christ in college—the first one in her family to do so. While they both genuinely knew Christ, they were at odds over everyday decisions and actions. She felt he was "spiritualizing" everything, and he accused her of being "secular" in her attitudes and actions. Actually, David failed to recognize that spiritual growth happens over time, not overnight. Patience and gentleness, without compromise or spiritualized lectures, is a key to encouraging the other person to keep moving toward maturity.

3. **You can't live on yesterday's revelation of God's power.** The Old Testament contains a beautiful picture of how quickly spiritual highs can fade. In Exodus 14 one of God's greatest miracles occurred as the waters of the Red Sea separated to allow the Israelites to escape and then descended on the pursuing Egyptians.

Don't you think that experiencing a great miracle like that would leave a lasting spiritual impact on their lives? This spiritual high lasted only until they became thirsty. Then when the people found no water (except the bitter water at Marah), they began to grumble about not having anything to drink.

We often do the same thing. As individuals or couples, we may go to a retreat, listen to an outstanding Bible teacher, or receive a special revelation about some great spiritual truth from a Bible reading. But it's only a matter of time before those spiritual highs fade without consistent, daily contact with God.

4. Remember always that we have an adversary who wants us to remain spiritual infants. Babies need to be taken care of; they're not responsible for the care of others. Babies are good at creating messes but don't have the skills to clean them up.

Our adversary, the devil, would like nothing more than to keep every Christian at a level of spiritual infancy—dependent, irresponsible, simpleminded, and shallow.

There is a battle on for the family today, and it takes warriors and leaders—not babies—to join the fight. If you're stuck in a cycle of immaturity, put spiritual growth in your schedule, share honestly with your spouse about differing maturity levels, stop living on yesterdays, and stay on guard for the devil. And above all, keep reaching for the meat of the Word.

---

and in much trembling. [4]And my speech and my preaching *was* not with enticing[a] words of man's wisdom, but in demonstration of the Spirit and of power: [5]That your faith should not stand[b] in the wisdom of men, but in the power of God.

[6]Howbeit we speak wisdom among them that are perfect: yet not the wisdom of this world, nor of the princes of this world, that come to nought: [7]But we speak the wisdom of God in a mystery, *even* the hidden *wisdom,* which God ordained before the world unto our glory: [8]Which none of the princes of this world knew: for had they known *it,* they would not have crucified the Lord of glory. [9]But as it is written, Eye hath not seen, nor ear heard, neither have entered into the heart of man, the things which God hath prepared for them that love him. [10]But God hath re-vealed *them* unto us by his Spirit: for the Spirit searcheth all things, yea, the deep things of God. [11]For what man knoweth the things of a man, save the spirit of man which is in him? even so the things of God knoweth no man, but the Spirit of God. [12]Now we have received, not the spirit of the world, but the spirit which is of God; that we might know the things that are freely given to us of God. [13]Which things also we speak, not in the words which man's wisdom teacheth, but which the Holy Ghost teacheth; comparing spiritual things with spiritual. [14]But the natural man receiveth not the things of the Spirit of God: for they are foolishness unto him: neither can he know *them,* because they are spiritually discerned. [15]But he that is spiritual judgeth[c] all things, yet he himself is judged of no man. [16]For who hath known the mind

---

[a] enticing: or, persuasible
[b] stand: Gr. be
[c] judgeth: or, discerneth

Worship
in Your Home

KEEP IT SIMPLE

My speech and my preaching was not with enticing words of man's wisdom, but in demonstration of the Spirit and of power.
1 Corinthians 2:4

Devotions need a healthy dose of simplicity, not a truckload of profound insights. Family devotions should be directed to the "littlest lamb" of the family, and trust that the rest can add enough depth to bring it to their own level.

The Wall Street Journal, which is read daily by the most sophisticated business leaders in America, was having trouble until it reduced its reading level to about fifth grade. Reader's Digest, read by millions of adults, is written at a simple, easy-to-read level. Both of these publications present profound matters to sophisticated people. But they do it with simplicity.

Don't be afraid to read and study together the profound truths of the Word in all their simplicity. If you and some other adults or thoughtful teens want to talk about profound matters in a profound manner, OK. But don't turn off the young child with "high speech."

Generally, it is better to keep devotions simple for all ages. That way, everyone can talk about the Word with understanding, the way God intended us to do.

of the Lord, that he may instruct him? But we have the mind of Christ.

3

¹And I, brethren, could not speak unto you as unto spiritual, but as unto carnal, *even* as unto babes in Christ. ²I have fed you with milk, and not with meat: for hitherto ye were not able *to bear it*, neither yet now are ye able. ³For ye are yet carnal: for whereas *there is* among you envying, and strife, and divisionsª, are ye not carnal, and walk as men? ⁴For while one saith, I am of Paul; and another, I *am* of Apollos; are ye not carnal?

⁵Who then is Paul, and who *is* Apollos, but ministers by whom ye believed, even as the Lord gave to every man? ⁶I have planted, Apollos watered; but God gave the increase. ⁷So then neither is he that planteth any thing, neither he that watereth; but God that giveth the increase. ⁸Now he that planteth and he that watereth are one: and every man shall receive his own reward according to his own labour. ⁹For we are labourers together with God: ye are God's husbandryᵇ, *ye are* God's building. ¹⁰According to the grace of God which is given unto me, as a wise masterbuilder, I have laid the foundation, and another buildeth thereon. But let every man take heed how he buildeth thereupon.

¹¹For other foundation can no man lay than that is laid, which is Jesus Christ. ¹²Now if any man build upon this foundation gold, silver, precious stones, wood, hay, stubble;

ª divisions: or, factions
ᵇ husbandry: or, tillage

¹³Every man's work shall be made manifest: for the day shall declare it, because it shall be revealed by fire; and the fire shall try every man's work of what sort it is. ¹⁴If any man's work abide which he hath built thereupon, he shall receive a reward. ¹⁵If any man's work shall be burned, he shall suffer loss: but he himself shall be saved; yet so as by fire.

¹⁶Know ye not that ye are the temple of God, and *that* the Spirit of God dwelleth in you? ¹⁷If any man defile^c the temple of God, him shall God destroy; for the temple of God is holy, which *temple* ye are.

¹⁸Let no man deceive himself. If any man among you seemeth to be wise in this world, let him become a fool, that he may be wise. ¹⁹For the wisdom of this world is foolishness with God. For it is written, He taketh the wise in their own craftiness. ²⁰And again, The Lord knoweth the thoughts of the wise, that they are vain.

²¹Therefore let no man glory in men. For all things are yours; ²²Whether Paul, or Apollos, or Cephas, or the world, or life, or death, or things present, or things to come; all are yours; ²³And ye are Christ's; and Christ *is* God's.

4

¹Let a man so account of us, as of the ministers of Christ, and stewards of the mysteries of God. ²Moreover it is required in stewards, that a man be found faithful. ³But with me it is a very small thing that I should be judged of you, or of man's judgment^a: yea, I judge not mine own self. ⁴For I know^b nothing by myself; yet am I not hereby justified: but he that judgeth me is the Lord. ⁵Therefore judge nothing before the time, until the Lord come, who both will bring to light the hidden things of darkness, and will make manifest the counsels of the hearts: and then shall every man have praise of God. ⁶And these things, brethren, I have in a figure transferred to myself and *to* Apollos for your sakes; that ye might learn in us not to think *of men* above that which is written, that no one of you be puffed up for one against another.

⁷For who maketh^c thee to differ *from another*? and what hast thou that thou didst not receive? now if thou didst receive *it*, why dost thou glory, as if thou hadst not received *it*? ⁸Now ye are full, now ye are rich, ye have reigned as kings without us: and I would to God ye did reign, that we also might reign with you. ⁹For I think that God hath set forth us^d the apostles last, as it were appointed to death: for we are made a spectacle unto the world, and to angels, and to men. ¹⁰We *are* fools for Christ's sake, but ye *are* wise in Christ; we *are* weak, but ye *are* strong; ye *are* honourable, but we *are* despised. ¹¹Even unto this present hour we both hunger, and thirst, and are naked, and are buffeted, and have no certain dwellingplace; ¹²And labour, working with our own hands: being reviled, we bless; being persecuted, we suffer it: ¹³Being defamed, we intreat: we

---

^c defile: or, destroy
^a judgment: Gr. day
^b know: or, I am not conscious of any fault
^c maketh . . . : Gr. distinguisheth thee
^d us . . . : or, us the last apostles

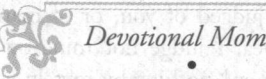

Devotional Moment
•
Fathering

4:16 Paul boldly told the Corinthians to follow his example as their spiritual father. He was so intent on pleasing God that he knew his life would be a positive model for them as growing Christians.

A parent sets a powerful example for his or her children. Knowing that your child is watching provides high motivation to do what is right. Be so intent on pleasing God that you can invite your children to follow your example— and then do so!

are made as the filth of the world, *and are* the offscouring of all things unto this day.

[14]I write not these things to shame you, but as my beloved sons I warn *you*. [15]For though ye have ten thousand instructors in Christ, yet *have ye* not many fathers: for in Christ Jesus I have begotten you through the gospel. [16]Wherefore I beseech you, be ye followers of me.

[17]For this cause have I sent unto you Timotheus, who is my beloved son, and faithful in the Lord, who shall bring you into remembrance of my ways which be in Christ, as I teach every where in every church. [18]Now some are puffed up, as though I would not come to you. [19]But I will come to you shortly, if the Lord will, and will know, not the speech of them which are puffed up, but the power. [20]For the kingdom of God *is* not in word, but in power. [21]What will ye? shall I come unto you with a rod, or in love, and *in* the spirit of meekness?

5

[1]It is reported commonly *that there is* fornication among you, and such fornica-

tion as is not so much as named among the Gentiles, that one should have his father's wife. [2]And ye are puffed up, and have not rather mourned, that he that hath done this deed might be taken away from among you. [3]For I verily, as absent in body, but present in spirit, have judged[a] already, as though I were present, *concerning* him that hath so done this deed, [4]In the name of our Lord Jesus Christ, when ye are gathered together, and my spirit, with the power of our Lord Jesus Christ, [5]To deliver such an one unto Satan for the destruction of the flesh, that the spirit may be saved in the day of the Lord Jesus. [6]Your glorying *is* not good. Know ye not that a little leaven leaveneth the whole lump?

[7]Purge out therefore the old leaven, that ye may be a new lump, as ye are unleavened. For even Christ our passover is sacrificed[b] for us: [8]Therefore

Devotional Moment
•
Confronting Sin

5:1-13 The people in the Corinthian church were overlooking a serious sin in their midst. Paul instructed them to confront the person openly and deal with the sin.

Confronting people can be unpleasant—it can cause disruption and stress. Yet denying the problem or playing along is like allowing an infection to fester and spread. Healing will come only when the infection is treated directly. Talk about your problems. If the problems are serious, talk to your pastor or a professional Christian counselor. Don't try to pretend they aren't there.

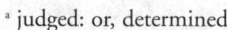

---

[a] judged: or, determined
[b] is sacrificed; or, is slain

let us keep the feast^c, not with old leaven, neither with the leaven of malice and wickedness; but with the unleavened *bread* of sincerity and truth.

⁹I wrote unto you in an epistle not to company with fornicators: ¹⁰Yet not altogether with the fornicators of this world, or with the covetous, or extortioners, or with idolaters; for then must ye needs go out of the world. ¹¹But now I have written unto you not to keep company, if any man that is called a brother be a fornicator, or covetous, or an idolater, or a railer, or a drunkard, or an extortioner; with such an one no not to eat. ¹²For what have I to do to judge them also that are without? do not ye judge them that are within? ¹³But them that are without God judgeth. Therefore put away from among yourselves that wicked person.

6

¹Dare any of you, having a matter against another, go to law before the unjust, and not before the saints? ²Do ye not know that the saints shall judge the world? and if the world shall be judged by you, are ye unworthy to judge the smallest matters? ³Know ye not that we shall judge angels? how much more things that pertain to this life? ⁴If then ye have judgments of things pertaining to this life, set them to judge who are least esteemed in the church. ⁵I speak to your shame. Is it so, that there is not a wise man among you? no, not one that shall be able to judge between his brethren? ⁶But brother goeth to law with brother, and

that before the unbelievers. ⁷Now therefore there is utterly a fault among you, because ye go to law one with another. Why do ye not rather take wrong? why do ye not rather *suffer yourselves to* be defrauded? ⁸Nay, ye do wrong, and defraud, and that *your* brethren.

⁹Know ye not that the unrighteous shall not inherit the kingdom of God? Be not deceived: neither fornicators, nor idolaters, nor adulterers, nor effeminate, nor abusers of themselves with mankind, ¹⁰Nor thieves, nor covetous, nor drunkards, nor revilers, nor extortioners, shall inherit the kingdom of God. ¹¹And such were some of you: but ye are washed, but ye are sanctified, but ye are justified in the name of the Lord Jesus, and by the Spirit of our God.

¹²All things are lawful unto me, but all things are not expedient: all things are lawful for me, but I will not be brought under the power of any. ¹³Meats^a for the belly, and the belly for meats: but God shall destroy both it and them. Now the body *is* not for fornication, but for the Lord; and the Lord for the body. ¹⁴And God hath both raised up the Lord, and will also raise up us by his own power. ¹⁵Know ye not that your bodies are the members of Christ? shall I then take the members of Christ, and make *them* the members of an harlot? God forbid. ¹⁶What? know ye not that he which is joined to an harlot is one body? for two, saith he, shall be one flesh. ¹⁷But he that is joined unto the Lord is one spirit. ¹⁸Flee fornication. Every sin that a man doeth is without the body; but he that committeth fornication sinneth against his own

---

^c the feast: or, holyday
^a Meats: not flesh only, but food of any kind

Fanning the Flames

by Bill and Lynne Hybels

The notion of sex as something important we must give to our spouses comes straight from the Bible. First Corinthians 7 teaches clearly that a wife does not have full rights to her own body; her husband has rights to it, too. Similarly, his body belongs also to her (v. 4). These are not-so-subtle reminders that we each owe our spouse a satisfying sexual relationship. We are, after all, our spouse's only sexual option. The commitment to marital fidelity, which every sincere Christian couple must make, means that if we don't find sexual fulfillment in our marriage, we don't find it at all. It is as simple, and sometimes as tragic, as that. All of us must take our sexual responsibility seriously, and lovingly and enthusiastically do everything in our power to meet and fulfill our spouse's legitimate sexual needs and desires.

Getting started. Fun sex doesn't start in the bedroom. It starts in the kitchen, during a private moment when a nonsexual touch slides over into the realm of the blatantly sexual. It begins with a playful suggestion of sexual intent, a not-so-subtle sexual innuendo, or a well-placed flirtatious remark.

Bill: "Over the years we have developed our own physical love language. When I leave for the evening and Lynne whispers, 'If you make it home on time tonight, I'll make it worth your while,' I don't have to wonder what she means. I know that's an open invitation, and you can bet I get home on time.

"When I'm traveling and I call home and Lynne says, 'You don't know what you're missing tonight,' I know that's her way of telling me I have an interested wife waiting at home."

Another way to encourage sexual enthusiasm is to actively build one another's concept of desirability. Husbands and wives will be much more interested in sex if they feel like desirable sexual partners.

Lynne: "With the unavoidable media onslaught of strikingly beautiful, sexually stimulating, airbrushed female bodies, real live women need a heavy dose of sexual affirmation. We need to know that even though we don't have perfect bodies, we have the power to excite and delight our husbands.

"My sexual confidence, and my ability to enjoy my sexuality, are strongly tied to Bill's enthusiastic, consistent, verbal affirmation of my sexual desirability. Many spouses wish their husbands or wives had greater sexual interest and confidence. They don't realize the power they have to instill that confidence through affirmation and compliments."

How spouses dress can also heighten—or squelch—sexual desire. We know that for some people, dress truly makes little difference. Most spouses admit, however, that what their husband or wife wears—clothes that are overly modest or too casual, for example—affects their sexual interest.

Maintaining good health is yet another way to enhance sexual interest. The general sense of well-being and increased body consciousness that come from regular exercise enhance sexuality. Eating right and getting enough sleep are important, too. Everybody knows that exhaustion is one of the greatest sex-busters.

Talk, talk, talk. Too many people expect their spouses to "just know" what they want sexually, then do a slow burn when their spouses don't come through. A more constructive option is to openly discuss issues directly related to sexuality. You might suggest ways your spouse could help you feel more sexually desirable, and ask for ideas about how you could do the same in return. Another idea is to describe the kinds of circumstances, events, or conversations that are most likely to spark your sexual interest. You could also talk about guaranteed turnoffs, personal sex-busters, and past sexual disappointments. Talk openly, vulnerably, specifically, and regularly about your sexual relationship.

Husbands and wives who have never done this often find it very difficult to get started. Picking one question and discussing it after a day of lighthearted fun may be the best way for such couples to start.

Sensitive, open communication is a hefty challenge, whether you are discussing a backlog of anger or a way to spice up a less-than-sizzling sexual relationship. But it always pays off. So give it a try. You just might be glad you did.

DIGGING DEEPER

Together read the Song of Solomon aloud. Then discuss what you felt and heard. In what ways did the lovers talk about their physical attraction for one another? What else did they do to meet each other's sexual needs?

Taken from the book Fit to Be Tied, © 1991 *by Bill and Lynne Hybels. Used by permission of Zondervan Publishing House.*

Devotional Moment
•
Sex Education

6:18-20 Our bodies were bought by God; they belong to him. What's more, our bodies are God's home, where the Holy Spirit actually lives. There's no doubt about it—God is definitely involved in our sex lives. Many people are concerned about "safe sex," but there's more at stake in sexual morality than just the protection of our physical health. While sexual purity does protect us from emotional, spiritual, and physical harm, it is also a matter of showing respect for the place where God dwells. Sexual purity is important. Don't shy away from discussing it with your kids as they enter adolescence. Take opportunities to share God's design with them.

body. ¹⁹What? know ye not that your body is the temple of the Holy Ghost *which is* in you, which ye have of God, and ye are not your own? ²⁰For ye are bought with a price: therefore glorify God in your body, and in your spirit, which are God's.

7

¹Now concerning the things whereof ye wrote unto me: *It is* good for a man not

to touch a woman. ²Nevertheless, *to avoid* fornication, let every man have his own wife, and let every woman have her own husband. ³Let the husband render unto the wife due benevolence: and likewise also the wife unto the husband. ⁴The wife hath not power of her own body, but the husband: and likewise also the husband hath not power of his own body, but the wife. ⁵Defraud ye not one the other, except *it be* with

---

Devotional Moment
•
Sex

7:3-5 Sexual desire is a normal, natural desire given by God to be fulfilled in marriage, where husbands and wives share their bodies with each other in mutual respect and physical affection. In a world filled with sexual immorality, husbands and wives can help each other fight sexual temptation by mutually satisfying their sexual desires. Sex should not be used by either spouse as a weapon to punish or as a bargaining tool to gain control. Talk openly with your spouse about your sexual relationship. What can you do to satisfy his or her natural desires and build a stronger bond of love between the two of you?

consent for a time, that ye may give yourselves to fasting and prayer; and come together again, that Satan tempt you not for your incontinency. ⁶But I speak this by permission, *and* not of commandment. ⁷For I would that all men were even as I myself. But every man hath his proper gift of God, one after this manner, and another after that. ⁸I say therefore to the unmarried and widows, It is good for them if they abide even as I. ⁹But if they cannot contain, let them marry: for it is better to marry than to burn.

¹⁰And unto the married I command, *yet* not I, but the Lord, Let not the wife depart from *her* husband: ¹¹But and if she depart, let her remain unmarried, or be reconciled to *her* husband: and let not the husband put away *his* wife. ¹²But to the rest speak I, not the Lord: If any brother hath a wife that

Devotional Moment

•

Mixed Marriages

7:12-16 Tension is common in marriages where only one spouse is a Christian. Paul urged believers in such relationships not to get divorced merely because of the mismatch. It's easy in a tense marriage to seek personal happiness above all else—to do what is best for our own immediate desires. But staying in the marriage may give the other an opportunity to change. If your spouse isn't a believer, ask God to give you the strength and love to be a witness for his life-changing power. If you have a friend in a struggling marriage, support that person as you are able.

believeth not, and she be pleased to dwell with him, let him not put her away. ¹³And the woman which hath an husband that believeth not, and if he be pleased to dwell with her, let her not leave him. ¹⁴For the unbelieving husband is sanctified by the wife, and the unbelieving wife is sanctified by the husband: else were your children unclean; but now are they holy. ¹⁵But if the unbelieving depart, let him depart. A brother or a sister is not under bondage in such *cases*: but God hath called us to peace*ᵃ*. ¹⁶For what knowest thou, O wife, whether thou shalt save *thy* husband? or how*ᵇ* knowest thou, O man, whether thou shalt save *thy* wife?

¹⁷But as God hath distributed to every man, as the Lord hath called every one, so let him walk. And so ordain I in all churches. ¹⁸Is any man called being circumcised? let him not become uncircumcised. Is any called in uncircumcision? let him not be circumcised. ¹⁹Circumcision is nothing, and uncircumcision is nothing, but the keeping of the commandments of God. ²⁰Let every man abide in the same calling wherein he was called. ²¹Art thou called *being* a servant? care not for it: but if thou mayest be made free, use *it* rather. ²²For he that is called in the Lord, *being* a servant, is the Lord's freeman*ᶜ*: likewise also he that is called, *being* free, is Christ's servant. ²³Ye are bought with a price; be not ye the servants of men. ²⁴Brethren, let every man, wherein he is called, therein abide with God.

ᵃ to peace: Gr. in peace
ᵇ how: Gr. what
ᶜ freeman: Gr. made free

²⁵Now concerning virgins I have no commandment of the Lord: yet I give my judgment, as one that hath obtained mercy of the Lord to be faithful. ²⁶I suppose therefore that this is good for the present distress*d*, *I say*, that *it is* good for a man so to be. ²⁷Art thou bound unto a wife? seek not to be loosed. Art thou loosed from a wife? seek not a wife. ²⁸But and if thou marry, thou hast not sinned; and if a virgin marry, she hath not sinned. Nevertheless such shall have trouble in the flesh: but I spare you. ²⁹But this I say, brethren, the time *is* short: it remaineth, that both they that have wives be as though they had none; ³⁰And they that weep, as though they wept not; and they that rejoice, as though they rejoiced not; and they that buy, as though they possessed not; ³¹And they that use this world, as not abusing *it*: for the fashion of this world passeth away. ³²But I would have you without carefulness. He that is unmarried careth for the things that belong to the Lord, how he may please the Lord: ³³But he that is married careth for the things that are of the world, how he may please *his* wife. ³⁴There is difference *also* between a wife and a virgin. The unmarried woman careth for the things of the Lord, that she may be holy both in body and in spirit: but she that is married careth for the things of the world, how she may please *her* husband. ³⁵And this I speak for your own profit; not that I may cast a snare upon you, but for that which is comely, and that ye may attend upon the Lord without distraction.

³⁶But if any man think that he behaveth himself uncomely toward his virgin, if she pass the flower of *her* age, and need so require, let him do what he will, he sinneth not: let them marry. ³⁷Nevertheless he that standeth stedfast in his heart, having no necessity, but hath power over his own will, and hath so decreed in his heart that he will keep his virgin, doeth well. ³⁸So then he that giveth *her* in marriage doeth well; but he that giveth *her* not in marriage doeth better.

³⁹The wife is bound by the law as long as her husband liveth; but if her husband be dead, she is at liberty to be married to whom she will; only in the Lord. ⁴⁰But she is happier if she so abide, after my judgment: and I think also that I have the Spirit of God.

8

¹Now as touching things offered unto idols, we know that we all have knowledge. Knowledge puffeth up, but char-

---

Devotional Moment

Singleness

7:26, 32-34, 38 "I have someone for you to meet!" —seven words that a single person hears all too often from well-intentioned friends. Paul declared that being single isn't merely a time of waiting for marriage; it's a unique opportunity to serve God! Single people have an important part in God's plan. They can devote more time and energy to serving God than a person with a family could ever spare. Single people are often more mobile, flexible, and energetic. So honor your single friends. They don't need to be demeaned or bombarded with potential mates. Encourage and support them in God's service.

---

d distress: or, necessity

Breaking Free from Unfulfilled Intimacy

Let the husband render unto the wife due benevolence: and likewise also the wife unto the husband. 1 Corinthians 7:3

A pattern of hurt that is rarely talked about for many couples is the frustration of unfulfilled intimacy.

This passage in 1 Corinthians makes it clear that husbands and wives need regularly to engage in physical intimacy. Yet there are many couples who have endured their sexual relationship and not really enjoyed it. So how can a couple break free from frustrations in this area and begin a positive cycle of physical closeness?

Three suggestions can help a couple grow in this area, and the first is to recognize the part God plays in their sexual relationship.

1. God really does approve of sex. After all, he created it! His desire was that the earth be fruitful and that his creatures enjoy all his good gifts, one of them being the "one flesh" bonding, or the marriage bed. Yet some couples have not only never prayed about their sexual relationship but feel that God rejects or is somehow disgusted with intimacy.

It's true that God rejects sexual perversion. But he created passion. Just look at the Song of Solomon: In chapter 4, Solomon records his wedding in beautiful poetic form. He praises his wife seven times before he begins to touch her (wise advice for any husband). Then in poetic form, he speaks of enjoying the full sexual experience.

God was present on their wedding night and on every night that followed. It is he who can give every married couple the freedom to truly give themselves to each other and seek to meet the other's needs.

2. Couples should seek to please each other, not chase a national average. In the glut of television and newspaper reports on sex, much information has been given out on how often the "average couple" engages in intercourse. What's wrong with these figures is that they don't chart a couple over the life cycle. Most couples vary their involvement due to changing circumstances (such as being newly married, being pregnant, or being separated). The problem comes when we try to match an arbitrary standard rather than try to please our spouse. Following the clear, freeing words of Scripture instead of a national average is a second way to move toward a more fulfilling marriage.

3. Focus on creative caring outside the bedroom. Many women feel that the only time their husband is physically expressive is when he wants intercourse. A husband who is rough and unreachable for days and then suddenly turns tender at bedtime will either make his wife feel exploited or frustrate her into resisting his advances. It's much better to realize that intimacy begins outside the bedroom.

In counseling, many couples are taught to use a chart where they list ten small, specific, positive ways their spouse could demonstrate love. Almost without exception, when couples begin regularly working on those items on their spouse's list, they see a heightened passion for their mate. Why? Because as the days and weeks go by and caring activities build up, love and appreciation for the other person builds, and a natural expression of that love lies in touching.

Couples don't have to stay in a cycle of sexual frustration. There are many good books, counselors, and resources that can give them more knowledge and advice on the subject of intimacy. But always keep in mind the best advice—that of the Scriptures—to lovingly seek to please your spouse and to regularly express your love through physical affection.

---

ity edifieth. ²And if any man think that he knoweth any thing, he knoweth nothing yet as he ought to know. ³But if any man love God, the same is known of him.

⁴As concerning therefore the eating of those things that are offered in sacrifice unto idols, we know that an idol *is* nothing in the world, and that *there is* none other God but one. ⁵For though there be that are called gods, whether in heaven or in earth, (as there be gods many, and lords many,) ⁶But to us *there is but* one God, the Father, of whom *are* all things, and we in[a] him; and one Lord Jesus Christ, by whom *are* all things, and we by him.

⁷Howbeit *there is* not in every man that knowledge: for some with conscience of the idol unto this hour eat *it* as a thing offered unto an idol; and their conscience being weak is defiled. ⁸But meat commendeth us not to God: for neither, if we eat, are we the better[b]; neither, if we eat not, are we the worse. ⁹But take heed lest by any means this liberty[c] of yours become a stumblingblock to them that are weak. ¹⁰For if any man see thee which hast knowledge sit at meat in the idol's temple, shall not the conscience of him which is weak be emboldened[d] to eat those things which are offered to idols; ¹¹And through thy knowledge shall the weak brother perish, for whom Christ died? ¹²But when ye sin so against the brethren, and wound their weak conscience, ye sin against Christ. ¹³Wherefore, if meat make my brother to offend, I will eat no flesh while the world standeth, lest I make my brother to offend.

9

¹Am I not an apostle? am I not free? have I not seen Jesus Christ our Lord? are not ye my work in the Lord? ²If I be not an apostle unto others, yet doubtless I am to you: for the seal of mine apostleship are ye in the Lord.

---

[a] in: or, for
[b] are we the better: or, have we the more
[c] liberty: or, power
[d] emboldened: Gr. edified

Worship
in Your Home

GOOD FOOD AND DEVOTIONS MAKE GOOD COMPANIONS

Whether therefore ye eat, or drink, or whatsoever ye do, do all to the glory of God.
1 Corinthians 10:31

Many of the happy events of life are celebrated with meals. Weddings, birthdays, anniversaries, and church potluck dinners are times of feasting. We celebrate good events with good food.

Food and devotions fit together. Having delighted in good food, it is easier to delight in the food of the Word. The joy of food fosters the joy of devotions. In the afterglow of "having been fed" and therefore comforted, the joy and delight of a devotional time with the Lord is a natural relationship.

Actually, thanking God for our food before we eat is something of a minidevotion. It is acknowledging God as the giver of the feast.

As a family you can spend many meals or parts of meals talking about the Lord and his Word informally. These times—before a meal, during a meal, immediately after a meal—are great times for devotions.

Think of it—feeding our souls as we feed our bodies, or soon after. It makes sense, doesn't it?

³Mine answer to them that do examine me is this, ⁴Have we not power to eat and to drink? ⁵Have we not power to lead about a sister, a wifeᵃ, as well as other apostles, and *as* the brethren of the Lord, and Cephas? ⁶Or I only and Barnabas, have not we power to forbear working? ⁷Who goeth a warfare any time at his own charges? who planteth a vineyard, and eateth not of the fruit thereof? or who feedeth a flock, and eateth not of the milk of the flock? ⁸Say I these things as a man? or saith not the law the same also? ⁹For it is written in the law of Moses, Thou shalt not muzzle the mouth of the ox that treadeth out the corn. Doth God take care for oxen? ¹⁰Or saith he *it* altogether for our sakes? For our sakes, no doubt, *this* is written: that he that ploweth should plow in hope; and that he that thresheth in hope should be partaker of his hope. ¹¹If we have sown unto you spiritual things, *is it* a great thing if we shall reap your carnal things? ¹²If others be partakers of *this* power over you, *are* not we rather? Nevertheless we have not used this power; but suffer all things, lest we should hinder the gospel of Christ. ¹³Do ye not know that they which minister about holy things liveᵇ *of the things* of the temple? and they which wait at the altar are partakers with the altar? ¹⁴Even so hath the Lord ordained that they which preach the gospel should live of the gospel.

¹⁵But I have used none of these things: neither have I written these things, that it should be so done unto

---

ᵃ wife: or, woman
ᵇ live: or, feed

me: for *it were* better for me to die, than that any man should make my glorying void. [16]For though I preach the gospel, I have nothing to glory of: for necessity is laid upon me; yea, woe is unto me, if I preach not the gospel! [17]For if I do this thing willingly, I have a reward: but if against my will, a dispensation *of the gospel* is committed unto me. [18]What is my reward then? *Verily* that, when I preach the gospel, I may make the gospel of Christ without charge, that I abuse not my power in the gospel.

[19]For though I be free from all *men*, yet have I made myself servant unto all, that I might gain the more. [20]And unto the Jews I became as a Jew, that I might gain the Jews; to them that are under the law, as under the law, that I might gain them that are under the law; [21]To them that are without law, as without law, (being not without law to God, but under the law to Christ,) that I might gain them that are without law. [22]To the weak became I as weak, that I might gain the weak: I am made all things to all *men*, that I might by all means save some. [23]And this I do for the gospel's sake, that I might be partaker thereof with *you*.

[24]Know ye not that they which run in a race run all, but one receiveth the prize? So run, that ye may obtain. [25]And every man that striveth for the mastery is temperate in all things. Now they *do it* to obtain a corruptible crown; but we an incorruptible. [26]I therefore so run, not as uncertainly; so fight I, not as one that beateth the air: [27]But I keep under my body, and bring *it* into subjection: lest that by any means, when I have preached to others, I myself should be a castaway.

10

[1]Moreover, brethren, I would not that ye should be ignorant, how that all our fathers were under the cloud, and all passed through the sea; [2]And were all baptized unto Moses in the cloud and in the sea; [3]And did all eat the same spiritual meat; [4]And did all drink the same spiritual drink: for they drank of that spiritual Rock that followed them: and that Rock was Christ. [5]But with many of them God was not well pleased: for they were overthrown in the wilderness.

[6]Now these things were our[a] examples, to the intent we should not lust after evil things, as they also lusted. [7]Neither be ye idolaters, as *were* some of them; as it is written, The people sat

---

Devotional Moment
•
Witness

9:22 Paul continually tried to find areas of common ground with people he met so that he would have a chance to tell them about Christ. He wasn't being deceitful; he understood that getting close to people and winning their trust was more effective than just preaching to strangers. Christian families have many opportunities to build relationships beyond their church friends. Committing time to school activities, sports teams, and special interest groups doesn't diminish work for the church; it takes the message of Christ to those who need to hear it. Where can you build relationships with people outside your church? Pray today about one person you have a burden for, and take the time to share your faith in Christ with him or her.

---

[a] our . . . : Gr. our figures

down to eat and drink, and rose up to play. ⁸Neither let us commit fornication, as some of them committed, and fell in one day three and twenty thousand. ⁹Neither let us tempt Christ, as some of them also tempted, and were destroyed of serpents. ¹⁰Neither murmur ye, as some of them also murmured, and were destroyed of the destroyer. ¹¹Now all these things happened unto them for ensamplesᵇ: and they are written for our admonition, upon whom the ends of the world are come. ¹²Wherefore let him that thinketh he standeth take heed lest he fall. ¹³There hath no temptation taken you but such as is common to man: but God *is* faithful, who will not suffer you to be tempted above that ye are able; but will with the temptation also make a way to escape, that ye may be able to bear *it.* ¹⁴Wherefore, my dearly beloved, flee from idolatry.

¹⁵I speak as to wise men; judge ye

Devotional Moment
Watch Out!

10:12-13 Paul wanted the Corinthians to be careful managers of their human weakness. They had the Scriptures, so they knew how to live and what to avoid. But that didn't make them immune to temptation. Paul told them, in effect, "Don't trust yourselves!"

The same advice rings true for us. Don't put yourself in a situation that could tempt you to be dishonest or sexually immoral. Teach your teens to recognize and avoid situations where they might feel pressured to experiment with drinking or sex. Few people are thoroughly evil, but neither is anyone thoroughly good. Have a healthy respect for the power of temptation in your family's life.

---

what I say. ¹⁶The cup of blessing which we bless, is it not the communion of the blood of Christ? The bread which we break, is it not the communion of the body of Christ? ¹⁷For we *being* many are one bread, *and* one body: for we are all partakers of that one bread. ¹⁸Behold Israel after the flesh: are not they which eat of the sacrifices partakers of the altar? ¹⁹What say I then? that the idol is any thing, or that which is offered in sacrifice to idols is any thing? ²⁰But I *say*, that the things which the Gentiles sacrifice, they sacrifice to devils, and not to God: and I would not that ye should have fellowship with devils. ²¹Ye cannot drink the cup of the Lord, and the cup of devils: ye cannot be partakers of the Lord's table, and of the table of devils. ²²Do we provoke the Lord to jealousy? are we stronger than he?

²³All things are lawful for me, but all things are not expedient: all things are lawful for me, but all things edify not. ²⁴Let no man seek his own, but every man another's *wealth.* ²⁵Whatsoever is sold in the shambles, *that* eat, asking no question for conscience sake: ²⁶For the earth *is* the Lord's, and the fulness thereof. ²⁷If any of them that believe not bid you *to a feast,* and ye be disposed to go; whatsoever is set before you, eat, asking no question for conscience sake. ²⁸But if any man say unto you, This is offered in sacrifice unto idols, eat not for his sake that shewed it, and for conscience sake: for the earth *is* the Lord's, and the fulness thereof: ²⁹Conscience, I say, not thine own, but of the other: for why is my liberty judged of another *man's* conscience?

ᵇ ensamples: or, types

³⁰For if I by grace° be a partaker, why am I evil spoken of for that for which I give thanks? ³¹Whether therefore ye eat, or drink, or whatsoever ye do, do all to the glory of God. ³²Give none offence, neither to the Jews, nor to the Gentiles°, nor to the church of God: ³³Even as I please all *men* in all *things*, not seeking mine own profit, but the *profit* of many, that they may be saved.

11

¹Be ye followers of me, even as I also *am* of Christ. ²Now I praise you, brethren, that ye remember me in all things, and keep the ordinances°, as I delivered *them* to you. ³But I would have you know, that the head of every man is Christ; and the head of the woman *is* the man; and the head of Christ *is* God. ⁴Every man praying or prophesying, having *his* head covered, dishonoureth his head. ⁵But every woman that prayeth or prophesieth with *her* head uncovered dishonoureth her head: for that is even all one as if she were shaven. ⁶For if the woman be not covered, let her also be shorn: but if it be a shame for a woman to be shorn or shaven, let her be covered. ⁷For a man indeed ought not to cover *his* head, forasmuch as he is the image and glory of God: but the woman is the glory of the man. ⁸For the man is not of the woman; but the woman of the man. ⁹Neither was the man created for the woman; but the woman for the man. ¹⁰For this cause

ought the woman to have power° on *her* head because of the angels. ¹¹Nevertheless neither is the man without the woman, neither the woman without the man, in the Lord. ¹²For as the woman *is* of the man, even so *is* the man also by the woman; but all things of God. ¹³Judge in yourselves: is it comely that a woman pray unto God uncovered? ¹⁴Doth not even nature itself teach you, that, if a man have long hair, it is a shame unto him? ¹⁵But if a woman have long hair, it is a glory to her: for *her* hair is given her for a covering°. ¹⁶But if any man seem to be contentious, we have no such custom, neither the churches of God.

¹⁷Now in this that I declare *unto you* I praise *you* not, that ye come together not for the better, but for the

---

Devotional Moment

Teamwork

11:11 God created men and women to complement each other. Women and men are different in many ways, and those differences mean opportunities to help each other, to depend on each other, and to *work together*. In a marriage, neither person is more important because both were created by God with unique strengths. Conflicts and misunderstandings will naturally arise from these differences, but they don't have to drive a wedge between a husband and wife. When your spouse does something you don't understand, try to see the situation from his or her perspective and thus enlarge your own. Value your differences; God created them for a reason.

° grace: or, thanksgiving
° Gentiles: Gr. Greeks
° ordinances: or, traditions
° power: that is a covering in sign that she is under the power of her husband
° covering: or, veil

worse. [18]For first of all, when ye come together in the church, I hear that there be divisions[d] among you; and I partly believe it. [19]For there must be also heresies[e] among you, that they which are approved may be made manifest among you. [20]When ye come together therefore into one place, *this* is not to eat the Lord's supper. [21]For in eating every one taketh before *other* his own supper: and one is hungry, and another is drunken. [22]What? have ye not houses to eat and to drink in? or despise ye the church of God, and shame them that have not[f]? What shall I say to you? shall I praise you in this? I praise *you* not.

[23]For I have received of the Lord that which also I delivered unto you, That the Lord Jesus the *same* night in which he was betrayed took bread: [24]And when he had given thanks, he brake *it*, and said, Take, eat: this is my body, which is broken for you: this do in[g] remembrance of me. [25]After the same manner also *he took* the cup, when he had supped, saying, This cup is the new testament in my blood: this do ye, as oft as ye drink *it*, in remembrance of me. [26]For as often as ye eat this bread, and drink this cup, ye do shew the Lord's death till he come. [27]Wherefore whosoever shall eat this bread, and drink *this* cup of the Lord, unworthily, shall be guilty of the body and blood of the Lord. [28]But let a man examine himself, and so let him eat of *that* bread, and drink of *that* cup. [29]For he that eateth and drinketh unworthily, eateth and drinketh damnation[h] to himself, not discerning the Lord's body. [30]For this cause many *are* weak and sickly among you, and many sleep. [31]For if we would judge ourselves, we should not be judged. [32]But when we are judged, we are chastened of the Lord, that we should not be condemned with the world. [33]Wherefore, my brethren, when ye come together to eat, tarry one for another. [34]And if any man hunger, let him eat at home; that ye come not together unto condemnation[i]. And the rest will I set in order when I come.

12

[1]Now concerning spiritual *gifts*, brethren, I would not have you ignorant. [2]Ye know that ye were Gentiles, carried away unto these dumb idols, even as ye were led. [3]Wherefore I give you to understand, that no man speaking by the Spirit of God calleth Jesus accursed[a]: and *that* no man can say that Jesus is the Lord, but by the Holy Ghost. [4]Now there are diversities of gifts, but the same Spirit. [5]And there are differences of administrations[b], but the same Lord. [6]And there are diversities of operations, but it is the same God

---

[d] divisions: or, schisms
[e] heresies: or, sects
[f] have not: or, are poor?
[g] in . . . : or, for a remembrance
[h] damnation: or, judgment
[i] condemnation: or, judgment
[a] accursed: or, anathema
[b] administrations: or, ministries

which worketh all in all. ⁷But the manifestation of the Spirit is given to every man to profit withal. ⁸For to one is given by the Spirit the word of wisdom; to another the word of knowledge by the same Spirit; ⁹To another faith by the same Spirit; to another the gifts of healing by the same Spirit; ¹⁰To another the working of miracles; to another prophecy; to another discerning of spirits; to another *divers* kinds of tongues; to another the interpretation of tongues: ¹¹But all these worketh that one and the selfsame Spirit, dividing to every man severally as he will.

¹²For as the body is one, and hath many members, and all the members of that one body, being many, are one body: so also *is* Christ. ¹³For by one Spirit are we all baptized into one body, whether *we be* Jews or Gentiles^c, whether *we be* bond or free; and have been all made to drink into one Spirit. ¹⁴For the body is not one member, but many. ¹⁵If the foot shall say, Because I am not the hand, I am not of the body; is it therefore not of the body? ¹⁶And if the ear shall say, Because I am not the eye, I am not of the body; is it therefore not of the body? ¹⁷If the whole body *were* an eye, where *were* the hearing? If the whole *were* hearing, where *were* the smelling? ¹⁸But now hath God set the members every one of them in the body, as it hath pleased him. ¹⁹And if they were all one member, where *were* the body? ²⁰But now *are they* many members, yet but one body. ²¹And the eye cannot say unto the hand, I have no need of thee: nor again the head to the feet, I have no need of you. ²²Nay, much more those members of the body, which seem to be more feeble, are necessary: ²³And those *members* of the body, which we think to be less honourable, upon these we bestow^d more abundant honour; and our uncomely *parts* have more abundant comeliness. ²⁴For our comely *parts* have no need: but God hath tempered the body together, having given more abundant honour to that *part* which lacked: ²⁵That there should be no schism^e in the body; but *that* the members should have the same care one for another. ²⁶And whether one member suffer, all the members suffer with it; or one member be honoured, all the members rejoice with it.

²⁷Now ye are the body of Christ, and members in particular. ²⁸And God hath set some in the church, first apostles, secondarily prophets, thirdly teachers, after that miracles, then gifts of healings, helps, governments, diversities^f of tongues. ²⁹*Are* all apostles? *are* all prophets? *are* all teachers? *are* all workers of miracles? ³⁰Have all the gifts of healing? do all speak with tongues? do all interpret? ³¹But covet earnestly the best gifts: and yet shew I unto you a more excellent way.

13

¹Though I speak with the tongues of men and of angels, and have not charity,

---

^c Gentiles: Gr. Greeks
^d bestow: or, put on
^e schism: or, division
^f diversities: or, kinds

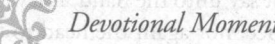

Devotional Moment
•
Love (Charity)
13:4-7 Copy this description of love, and display it where your whole family can see it every day. Make it the "house custom" to honor one another. Make it apply to visitors, too (as much as possible). If this seems too hard, remember that this kind of love doesn't require warm feelings; it's rooted in God's character. Ask him to teach you to love as he loves.
People learn to love at home. How Mom and Dad do it is how the kids will do it. If this is your pattern, everyone will benefit.

I am become *as* sounding brass, or a tinkling cymbal. ²And though I have *the gift of* prophecy, and understand all mysteries, and all knowledge; and though I have all faith, so that I could remove mountains, and have not charity, I am nothing. ³And though I bestow all my goods to feed *the poor*, and though I give my body to be burned, and have not charity, it profiteth me nothing.

⁴Charity suffereth long, *and* is kind; charity envieth not; charity vaunteth[a] not itself, is not puffed up, ⁵Doth not behave itself unseemly, seeketh not her own, is not easily provoked, thinketh no evil; ⁶Rejoiceth not in iniquity, but rejoiceth in the truth[b]; ⁷Beareth all things, believeth all things, hopeth all things, endureth all things.

⁸Charity never faileth: but whether *there be* prophecies, they shall fail[c]; whether *there be* tongues, they shall cease; whether *there be* knowledge, it shall vanish away. ⁹For we know in part, and we prophesy in part. ¹⁰But when that which is perfect is come, then that which is in part shall be done away[d]. ¹¹When I was a child, I spake as a child, I understood as a child, I thought[e] as a child: but when I became a man, I put away childish things. ¹²For now we see through a glass, darkly[f]; but then face to face: now I know in part; but then shall I know even as also I am known. ¹³And now abideth faith, hope, charity, these three; but the greatest of these *is* charity.

14

¹Follow after charity, and desire spiritual *gifts*, but rather that ye may prophesy. ²For he that speaketh in an *unknown* tongue speaketh not unto men, but unto God: for no man understandeth[a] *him*; howbeit in the spirit he speaketh mysteries. ³But he that prophesieth speaketh unto men *to* edification, and exhortation, and comfort. ⁴He that speaketh in an *unknown* tongue edifieth himself; but he that prophesieth edifieth the church. ⁵I would that ye all spake with tongues, but rather that ye prophesied: for greater *is* he that prophesieth than he that speaketh with tongues, except he interpret, that the church may receive edifying.

---

[a] vaunteth . . . : or, is not rash
[b] in the truth: or, with the truth
[c] fail: Gr. vanish away
[d] done away: Gr. vanish away
[e] thought: or, reasoned
[f] darkly: Gr. in a riddle
[a] understandeth: Gr. heareth

⁶Now, brethren, if I come unto you speaking with tongues, what shall I profit you, except I shall speak to you either by revelation, or by knowledge, or by prophesying, or by doctrine? ⁷And even things without life giving sound, whether pipe or harp, except they give a distinction in the sounds[b], how shall it be known what is piped or harped? ⁸For if the trumpet give an uncertain sound, who shall prepare himself to the battle? ⁹So likewise ye, except ye utter by the tongue words easy to be understood, how shall it be known what is spoken? for ye shall speak into the air. ¹⁰There are, it may be, so many kinds of voices in the world, and none of them *is* without signification. ¹¹Therefore if I know not the meaning of the voice, I shall be unto him that speaketh a barbarian, and he that speaketh *shall be* a barbarian unto me. ¹²Even so ye, forasmuch as ye are zealous of spiritual *gifts*, seek that ye may excel to the edifying of the church. ¹³Wherefore let him that speaketh in an *unknown* tongue pray that he may interpret. ¹⁴For if I pray in an *unknown* tongue, my spirit prayeth, but my understanding is unfruitful.

¹⁵What is it then? I will pray with the spirit, and I will pray with the understanding also: I will sing with the spirit, and I will sing with the understanding also. ¹⁶Else when thou shalt bless with the spirit, how shall he that occupieth the room of the unlearned say Amen at thy giving of thanks, seeing he understandeth not what thou sayest? ¹⁷For thou verily givest thanks well, but the other is not edified. ¹⁸I thank my God, I speak with tongues more than ye all: ¹⁹Yet in the church I had rather speak five words with my understanding, that *by my voice* I might teach others also, than ten thousand words in an *unknown* tongue. ²⁰Brethren, be not children in understanding: howbeit in malice be ye children, but in understanding be men[c].

²¹In the law it is written, With *men of* other tongues and other lips will I speak unto this people; and yet for all that will they not hear me, saith the Lord. ²²Wherefore tongues are for a sign, not to them that believe, but to them that believe not: but prophesying *serveth* not for them that believe not, but for them which believe. ²³If therefore the whole church be come together into one place, and all speak with tongues, and there come in *those that are* unlearned, or unbelievers, will they not say that ye are mad? ²⁴But if all prophesy, and there come in one that believeth not, or *one* unlearned, he is convinced of all, he is judged of all: ²⁵And thus are the secrets of his heart made manifest; and so falling down on *his* face he will worship God, and report that God is in you of a truth.

²⁶How is it then, brethren? when ye come together, every one of you hath a psalm, hath a doctrine, hath a tongue, hath a revelation, hath an interpretation. Let all things be done unto edifying. ²⁷If any man speak in an *unknown* tongue, *let it be* by two[d], or at the most by three, and *that* by course; and let one

---

[b] sounds: or, tunes
[c] men: Gr. perfect, or, of a ripe age
[d] two . . . : by two or three sentences separately

interpret. [28]But if there be no interpreter, let him keep silence in the church; and let him speak to himself, and to God. [29]Let the prophets speak two or three, and let the other judge. [30]If *any thing* be revealed to another that sitteth by, let the first hold his peace. [31]For ye may all prophesy one by one, that all may learn, and all may be comforted. [32]And the spirits of the prophets are subject to the prophets. [33]For God is not *the author* of confusion[e], but of peace, as in all churches of the saints.

[34]Let your women keep silence in the churches: for it is not permitted unto them to speak; but *they are commanded* to be under obedience, as also saith the law. [35]And if they will learn any thing, let them ask their husbands at home: for it is a shame for women to speak in the church.

[36]What? came the word of God out from you? or came it unto you only? [37]If any man think himself to be a prophet, or spiritual, let him acknowledge that the things that I write unto you are the commandments of the Lord. [38]But if any man be ignorant, let him be ignorant. [39]Wherefore, brethren, covet to prophesy, and forbid not to speak with tongues. [40]Let all things be done decently and in order.

15

[1]Moreover, brethren, I declare unto you the gospel which I preached unto you, which also ye have received, and wherein ye stand; [2]By which also ye are saved, if ye keep[a] in memory what I preached unto you, unless ye have believed in vain. [3]For I delivered unto you first of all that which I also received, how that Christ died for our sins according to the scriptures; [4]And that he was buried, and that he rose again the third day according to the scriptures: [5]And that he was seen of Cephas, then of the twelve: [6]After that, he was seen of above five hundred brethren at once; of whom the greater part remain unto this present, but some are fallen asleep. [7]After that, he was seen of James; then of all the apostles. [8]And last of all he was seen of me also, as of one born out of due time. [9]For I am the least of the apostles, that am not meet to be called an apostle, because I persecuted the church of God. [10]But by the grace of God I am what I am: and his grace which *was bestowed* upon me was not in vain; but I laboured more abundantly than they all: yet not I, but the grace of God which was with me. [11]Therefore whether *it were* I or they, so we preach, and so ye believed.

[12]Now if Christ be preached that he rose from the dead, how say some among you that there is no resurrection of the dead? [13]But if there be no resurrection of the dead, then is Christ not risen: [14]And if Christ be not risen, then *is* our preaching vain, and your faith *is* also vain. [15]Yea, and we are found false witnesses of God; because we have testified of God that he raised up Christ: whom he raised not up, if so be that the dead rise not. [16]For if the dead rise not, then is not Christ raised: [17]And if Christ be not raised, your faith *is* vain; ye are yet in your sins. [18]Then they also which are

---

[e] confusion: Gr. tumult, or, unquietness
[a] keep . . . : or, hold fast

fallen asleep in Christ are perished. ¹⁹If in this life only we have hope in Christ, we are of all men most miserable.

²⁰But now is Christ risen from the dead, *and* become the firstfruits of them that slept. ²¹For since by man *came* death, by man *came* also the resurrection of the dead. ²²For as in Adam all die, even so in Christ shall all be made alive. ²³But every man in his own order: Christ the firstfruits; afterward they that are Christ's at his coming. ²⁴Then *cometh* the end, when he shall have delivered up the kingdom to God, even the Father; when he shall have put down all rule and all authority and power. ²⁵For he must reign, till he hath put all enemies under his feet. ²⁶The last enemy *that* shall be destroyed *is* death. ²⁷For he hath put all things under his feet. But when he saith all things are put under *him, it is* manifest that he is excepted, which did put all things under him. ²⁸And when all things shall be subdued unto him, then shall the Son also himself be subject unto him that put all things under him, that God may be all in all. ²⁹Else what shall they do which are baptized for the dead, if the dead rise not at all? why are they then baptized for the dead? ³⁰And why stand we in jeopardy every hour? ³¹I protest by your[b] rejoicing which I have in Christ Jesus our Lord, I die daily. ³²If after the manner of men I have fought with beasts at Ephesus, what advantageth it me, if the dead rise not? let us eat and drink; for to morrow we die. ³³Be not deceived: evil communications corrupt good manners. ³⁴Awake to righteousness, and sin not; for some have not the knowledge of God: I speak *this* to your shame.

³⁵But some *man* will say, How are the dead raised up? and with what body do they come? ³⁶*Thou* fool, that which thou sowest is not quickened, except it die: ³⁷And that which thou sowest, thou sowest not that body that shall be, but bare grain, it may chance of wheat, or of some other *grain*: ³⁸But God giveth it a body as it hath pleased him, and to every seed his own body. ³⁹All flesh *is* not the same flesh: but *there is* one *kind of* flesh of men, another flesh of beasts, another of fishes, *and* another of birds. ⁴⁰*There are* also celestial bodies, and bodies terrestrial: but the glory of the celestial *is* one, and the *glory* of the terrestrial *is* another. ⁴¹*There is* one glory of the sun, and another glory of the moon, and another glory of the stars: for *one* star differeth from *another* star in glory. ⁴²So also *is* the resurrection of the dead. It is sown in corruption; it is raised in incorruption: ⁴³It is sown in dishonour; it is raised in glory: it is sown in weakness; it is raised in power: ⁴⁴It is sown a natural body; it is raised a spiritual body. There is a natural body, and there is a spiritual body. ⁴⁵And so it is written, The first man Adam was made a living soul; the last Adam *was made* a quickening spirit. ⁴⁶Howbeit that *was* not first which is spiritual, but that which is natural; and afterward that which is spiritual. ⁴⁷The first man *is* of the earth, earthy: the second man *is* the Lord from heaven. ⁴⁸As *is* the earthy, such *are* they also that are earthy: and as *is* the heavenly, such *are* they also that

---

[b] your: some read our

are heavenly. [49]And as we have borne the image of the earthy, we shall also bear the image of the heavenly. [50]Now this I say, brethren, that flesh and blood cannot inherit the kingdom of God; neither doth corruption inherit incorruption.

[51]Behold, I shew you a mystery; We shall not all sleep, but we shall all be changed, [52]In a moment, in the twinkling of an eye, at the last trump: for the trumpet shall sound, and the dead shall be raised incorruptible, and we shall be changed. [53]For this corruptible must put on incorruption, and this mortal *must* put on immortality. [54]So when this corruptible shall have put on incorruption, and this mortal shall have put on immortality, then shall be brought to pass the saying that is written, Death is swallowed up in victory.

Devotional Moment

This Old Body

15:50-53 In this passage Paul told the Corinthians about the future return of Christ. In a flash God will change our perishable human body with all its limitations and weaknesses into a new, eternal, imperishable form. We will be released from sickness, disabilities, and decay.

It will be a day of great rejoicing for everyone affected by physical disabilities or disease. After a lifetime of watching disease stifle the spirit of the real person inside the decaying body, we who have served them will rejoice to see our loved one set free.

If you have the opportunity to serve a loved one who suffers with a physical disability, give that person your best care, and look forward to the day when he or she will be given a new body.

[55]O death, where *is* thy sting? O grave[c], where *is* thy victory? [56]The sting of death *is* sin; and the strength of sin *is* the law. [57]But thanks *be* to God, which giveth us the victory through our Lord Jesus Christ.

[58]Therefore, my beloved brethren, be ye stedfast, unmoveable, always abounding in the work of the Lord, forasmuch as ye know that your labour is not in vain in the Lord.

16

[1]Now concerning the collection for the saints, as I have given order to the churches of Galatia, even so do ye. [2]Upon the first *day* of the week let every one of you lay by him in store, as *God* hath prospered him, that there be no gatherings when I come. [3]And when I come, whomsoever ye shall approve by *your* letters, them will I send to bring your liberality[a] unto Jerusalem. [4]And if it be meet that I go also, they shall go with me.

[5]Now I will come unto you, when I shall pass through Macedonia: for I do pass through Macedonia. [6]And it may be that I will abide, yea, and winter with you, that ye may bring me on my journey whithersoever I go. [7]For I will not see you now by the way; but I trust to tarry a while with you, if the Lord permit. [8]But I will tarry at Ephesus until Pentecost. [9]For a great door and effectual is opened unto me, and *there are* many adversaries.

[10]Now if Timotheus come, see that he may be with you without fear: for he worketh the work of the Lord, as I also *do*. [11]Let no man therefore despise him:

---

[c] grave: or, hell
[a] liberality: Gr. gift

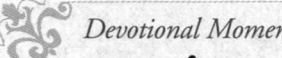

Devotional Moment

Hospitality

16:5-9 Paul didn't need a hotel directory or a toll-free 800 number when he traveled across Asia on his missionary journeys. He stayed with friends and believers in various churches.

Opening your home to assist people who are serving the Lord can result in a double blessing: The visiting worker is assisted and encouraged by your generosity and hospitality, and you will be inspired and blessed by the opportunity to interact with a person who is serving God. What opportunities do you have to host Christian workers who are visiting your area? Youth groups traveling on mission projects are often in need of a meal or a place to sleep. Volunteer at your church for any upcoming hospitality opportunities.

but conduct him forth in peace, that he may come unto me: for I look for him with the brethren. ¹²As touching *our* brother Apollos, I greatly desired him to come unto you with the brethren: but his will was not at all to come at this time; but he will come when he shall have convenient time.

¹³Watch ye, stand fast in the faith, quit you like men, be strong. ¹⁴Let all your things be done with charity. ¹⁵I beseech you, brethren, (ye know the house of Stephanas, that it is the firstfruits of Achaia, and *that* they have addicted themselves to the ministry of the saints,) ¹⁶That ye submit yourselves unto such, and to every one that helpeth with *us*, and laboureth. ¹⁷I am glad of the coming of Stephanas and Fortunatus and Achaicus: for that which was lacking on your part they have supplied. ¹⁸For they have refreshed my spirit and yours: therefore acknowledge ye them that are such.

¹⁹The churches of Asia salute you. Aquila and Priscilla salute you much in the Lord, with the church that is in their house. ²⁰All the brethren greet you. Greet ye one another with an holy kiss. ²¹The salutation of *me* Paul with mine own hand. ²²If any man love not the Lord Jesus Christ, let him be Anathema Maranatha. ²³The grace of our Lord Jesus Christ *be* with you. ²⁴My love *be* with you all in Christ Jesus. Amen.

[The first *epistle* to the Corinthians was written from Philippi by Stephanas and Fortunatus and Achaicus and Timotheus.]

SECOND CORINTHIANS

Purpose
To affirm Paul's own ministry, defend his authority as an apostle, and refute the false teachers in Corinth

Author
Paul

To Whom Written
The church in Corinth and Christians everywhere

Date Written
About A.D. 55–57, from Macedonia

Setting
Paul had already written previous letters to the Corinthians. In 1 Corinthians, he used strong words to correct and teach. Most of the church had responded in the right spirit; however, there were those who were denying Paul's authority and questioning his motives.

Key Verses
"Now then we are ambassadors for Christ, as though God did beseech you by us: we pray you in Christ's stead, be ye reconciled to God" (5:20).

Key People
Paul, Timothy, Titus, false teachers

Key Places
Corinth, Jerusalem

Special Features
This is an intensely personal and autobiographical letter.

"Did she really say that? I *never* would have believed it!"

"I know! I can't believe it either, but I have it on good authority."

Gossip.

It can come between the closest of friends and can divide families. Even an impeccable reputation can't always protect someone from lies and false accusations that hit the rumor mill.

Paul faced a similar problem at the church in Corinth, ancient Greece's sin capital. In addition to other problems, in Corinth there appeared teachers and preachers who bad-mouthed Paul and undercut the work he had done there. It was character assassination with the intention of luring Paul's converts into new "churches" and away from the apostle's influence. And while this intrigue mounted, Paul was many miles away.

Second Corinthians is the plea of a parent to children who question the integrity of their once-beloved teacher and friend. With great compassion, Paul explains himself and urges faithfulness, not to himself, but to Christ.

It's a neat example for anyone facing unfair attacks—whether at work, at school, or even at home. With Christ at the center, we can rise to the test, until we finally hear those immortal words: "I'm sorry I doubted you."

Just like the Christians at Corinth eventually said to Paul.

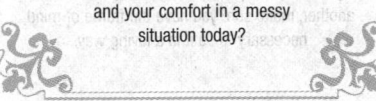

Devotional Moment
Comfort

1:3-5 Many people view all hardships as entirely negative, that nothing good can ever come of them. They may also believe that God will remove all unpleasantness from their lives if they only have enough faith. But according to this passage (and others like James 1 and 1 Pet. 3), God can comfort us in these troubles and can teach us through them to be a comfort to others. Who needs your prayers, your encouragement, and your comfort in a messy situation today?

1

¹Paul, an apostle of Jesus Christ by the will of God, and Timothy *our* brother, unto the church of God which is at Corinth, with all the saints which are in all Achaia: ²Grace *be* to you and peace from God our Father, and *from* the Lord Jesus Christ.

³Blessed *be* God, even the Father of our Lord Jesus Christ, the Father of mercies, and the God of all comfort; ⁴Who comforteth us in all our tribulation, that we may be able to comfort them which are in any trouble, by the comfort wherewith we ourselves are comforted of God. ⁵For as the sufferings of Christ abound in us, so our consolation also aboundeth by Christ. ⁶And whether we be afflicted, *it is* for your consolation and salvation, which is effectual[a] in the enduring of the same sufferings which we also suffer: or whether we be comforted, *it is* for your consolation and salvation. ⁷And our hope of you *is* stedfast,

knowing, that as ye are partakers of the sufferings, so *shall ye be* also of the consolation. ⁸For we would not, brethren, have you ignorant of our trouble which came to us in Asia, that we were pressed out of measure, above strength, insomuch that we despaired even of life: ⁹But we had the sentence[b] of death in ourselves, that we should not trust in ourselves, but in God which raiseth the dead: ¹⁰Who delivered us from so great a death, and doth deliver: in whom we trust that he will yet deliver *us*; ¹¹Ye also helping together by prayer for us, that for the gift *bestowed* upon us by the means of many persons thanks may be given by many on our behalf.

¹²For our rejoicing is this, the testimony of our conscience, that in simplicity and godly sincerity, not with fleshly wisdom, but by the grace of God, we have had our conversation in the world, and more abundantly to

Devotional Moment
Discouragement

1:8-10 What are we to do when our disappointments turn to discouragement and discouragement gives way to despair? The *world* encourages us to "keep a stiff upper lip," to fight harder, to utilize our inner strength. The *Word* reminds us of our need to rely on God alone. He is the ultimate source of wisdom, strength, and deliverance. Until we quit trusting in ourselves and lean on God, we will never know how dependable and infinite his resources are. Think of a problem that is nagging you. What human solutions have failed to fix it? Ask God for the wisdom to see the situation from his perspective and for the courage to depend on him.

---

[a] is effectual: or, is wrought
[b] sentence: or, answer

you-ward. ¹³For we write none other things unto you, than what ye read or acknowledge; and I trust ye shall acknowledge even to the end; ¹⁴As also ye have acknowledged us in part, that we are your rejoicing, even as ye also *are* ours in the day of the Lord Jesus.

¹⁵And in this confidence I was minded to come unto you before, that ye might have a second benefit^c; ¹⁶And to pass by you into Macedonia, and to come again out of Macedonia unto you, and of you to be brought on my way toward Judaea. ¹⁷When I therefore was thus minded, did I use lightness? or the things that I purpose, do I purpose according to the flesh, that with me there should be yea yea, and nay nay? ¹⁸But *as* God *is* true, our word^d toward you was not yea and nay. ¹⁹For the Son of God, Jesus Christ, who was preached among you by us, *even* by me and Silvanus and Timotheus, was not yea and nay, but in him was yea. ²⁰For all the promises of God in him *are* yea, and in him Amen, unto the glory of God by us. ²¹Now he which stablisheth us with you in Christ, and hath anointed us, *is* God; ²²Who hath also sealed us, and given the earnest of the Spirit in our hearts. ²³Moreover I call God for a record upon my soul, that to spare you I came not as yet unto Corinth. ²⁴Not for that we have dominion over your faith, but are helpers of your joy: for by faith ye stand.

2

¹But I determined this with myself, that I would not come again to you in

Devotional Moment

Confronting Sin

2:4 Correcting others is one of life's most unpleasant tasks. Our attempts may elicit misunderstanding, countercharges, or even angry retorts. How can we know that our motives are pure? How can we be sure that we aren't reacting out of anger or merely being judgmental? Notice Paul's attitude. Before he addressed the Corinthians about their wrongdoing, he was in anguish—to the point of tears! Before you correct another, make sure you have the frame of mind necessary to do it in a loving way.

heaviness. ²For if I make you sorry, who is he then that maketh me glad, but the same which is made sorry by me? ³And I wrote this same unto you, lest, when I came, I should have sorrow from them of whom I ought to rejoice; having confidence in you all, that my joy is *the joy* of you all. ⁴For out of much affliction and anguish of heart I wrote unto you with many tears; not that ye should be grieved, but that ye might know the love which I have more abundantly unto you.

⁵But if any have caused grief, he hath not grieved me, but in part: that I may not overcharge you all. ⁶Sufficient to such a man *is* this punishment^a, which *was inflicted* of many. ⁷So that contrariwise ye *ought* rather to forgive *him*, and comfort *him*, lest perhaps such a one should be swallowed up with overmuch sorrow. ⁸Wherefore I beseech you that ye would confirm *your* love toward him. ⁹For to this end also

---

^c benefit: or, grace

^d word: or, preaching

^a punishment: or, censure

did I write, that I might know the proof of you, whether ye be obedient in all things. ¹⁰To whom ye forgive any thing, I *forgive* also: for if I forgave any thing, to whom I forgave *it*, for your sakes *forgave I it* in the person[b] of Christ; ¹¹Lest Satan should get an advantage of us: for we are not ignorant of his devices.

¹²Furthermore, when I came to Troas to *preach* Christ's gospel, and a door was opened unto me of the Lord, ¹³I had no rest in my spirit, because I found not Titus my brother: but taking my leave of them, I went from thence into Macedonia. ¹⁴Now thanks *be* unto God, which always causeth us to triumph in Christ, and maketh manifest the savour of his knowledge by us in every place. ¹⁵For we are unto God a sweet savour of Christ, in them that are saved, and in them that perish: ¹⁶To the one *we are* the savour of death unto death; and to the other the savour of life unto life. And who *is* sufficient for these things? ¹⁷For we are not as many, which corrupt[c] the word of God: but as of sincerity, but as of God, in the sight of God speak we in Christ.

3

¹Do we begin again to commend ourselves? or need we, as some *others*, epistles of commendation to you, or *letters* of commendation from you? ²Ye are our epistle written in our hearts, known and read of all men: ³*Forasmuch as ye are* manifestly declared to be the epistle of Christ ministered by us, written not with ink, but with the Spirit of the liv-

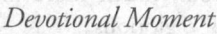

Devotional Moment
•
Success

3:4-5 In contrast to the false teachers who liked to boast about their accomplishments, Paul stated clearly that God was the source of all his success. We do well to remember this same principle. Everything good that we are and have comes from God. If you are prospering, make sure that you do not take the credit. If you feel like a failure, consider that God can give you whatever you need to help you accomplish his will. Let your feelings of weakness cause you to trust God more completely.

ing God; not in tables of stone, but in fleshy tables of the heart. ⁴And such trust have we through Christ to Godward: ⁵Not that we are sufficient of ourselves to think any thing as of ourselves; but our sufficiency *is* of God;

⁶Who also hath made us able ministers of the new testament; not of the letter, but of the spirit: for the letter killeth, but the spirit giveth life[a]. ⁷But if the ministration of death, written *and* engraven in stones, was glorious, so that the children of Israel could not stedfastly behold the face of Moses for the glory of his countenance; which *glory* was to be done away: ⁸How shall not the ministration of the spirit be rather glorious? ⁹For if the ministration of condemnation *be* glory, much more doth the ministration of righteousness exceed in glory. ¹⁰For even that which was made glorious had no glory in this respect, by reason of the glory that excelleth. ¹¹For if that which is done away

---

[b] person: or, sight

[c] corrupt: or, deal deceitfully with

[a] giveth life: or, quickeneth

was glorious, much more that which remaineth *is* glorious.

¹²Seeing then that we have such hope, we use great plainness of speech: ¹³And not as Moses, *which* put a vail over his face, that the children of Israel could not stedfastly look to the end of that which is abolished: ¹⁴But their minds were blinded: for until this day remaineth the same vail untaken away in the reading of the old testament; which *vail* is done away in Christ. ¹⁵But even unto this day, when Moses is read, the vail is upon their heart. ¹⁶Nevertheless when it shall turn to the Lord, the vail shall be taken away. ¹⁷Now the Lord is that Spirit: and where the Spirit of the Lord *is*, there *is* liberty. ¹⁸But we all, with open face beholding as in a glass the glory of the Lord, are changed into the same image from glory to glory, *even* as by the Spirit of the Lord.

4

¹Therefore seeing we have this ministry, as we have received mercy, we faint not; ²But have renounced the hidden things of dishonesty[a], not walking in craftiness, nor handling the word of God deceitfully; but by manifestation of the truth commending ourselves to every man's conscience in the sight of God. ³But if our gospel be hid, it is hid to them that are lost: ⁴In whom the god of this world hath blinded the minds of them which believe not, lest the light of the glorious gospel of Christ, who is the image of God, should shine unto them. ⁵For we preach not ourselves, but Christ Jesus the Lord; and ourselves

your servants for Jesus' sake. ⁶For God, who commanded the light to shine out of darkness, hath shined in our hearts, to *give* the light of the knowledge of the glory of God in the face of Jesus Christ. ⁷But we have this treasure in earthen vessels, that the excellency of the power may be of God, and not of us.

⁸*We are* troubled on every side, yet not distressed; *we are* perplexed, but not in despair[b]; ⁹Persecuted, but not forsaken; cast down, but not destroyed; ¹⁰Always bearing about in the body the dying of the Lord Jesus, that the life also of Jesus might be made manifest in our body. ¹¹For we which live are alway delivered unto death for Jesus' sake, that the life also of Jesus might be made manifest in our mortal flesh. ¹²So then death worketh in us, but life in you. ¹³We having the same spirit of faith, according as it is written, I believed, and therefore have I spoken; we also believe,

---

Devotional Moment

Manipulation

4:2 The false teachers in Corinth twisted the truth for selfish reasons. Paul rejected such deceptive practices. He chose to have a ministry marked by integrity and a clear conscience before God. In a similar fashion, we need to resist the temptation to trick or manipulate other people. Manipulation is a selfish and deceitful way to fulfill your short-term desires that falls short of the honest interaction God wants us to have with others. Ask God to help you recognize deceitful, manipulative patterns in your life. Then seek his help (and, if necessary, the help of a Christian counselor) to begin building new patterns of honest, open communication.

---

[a] dishonesty: Gr. shame
[b] in despair: or, altogether without help, or, means

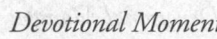

Devotional Moment

•

Problems

4:8-12 Paul's life was filled with hardship, pain, disappointment, and stress. Yet despite constant trials, he was able to maintain a sense of hope. How? By remembering that Christ was with him during his problems, and by viewing each difficulty as a further opportunity to rely on God's power. When trouble comes, let your prayer be: "Lord, please give me the wisdom to see this situation from your perspective. Help me to respond in such a way that others may see Jesus in me. Thank you that you will never abandon me.

and therefore speak; ¹⁴Knowing that he which raised up the Lord Jesus shall raise up us also by Jesus, and shall present *us* with you. ¹⁵For all things *are* for your sakes, that the abundant grace might through the thanksgiving of many redound to the glory of God. ¹⁶For which cause we faint not; but though our outward man perish, yet the inward *man* is renewed day by day. ¹⁷For our light affliction, which is but for a moment, worketh for us a far more exceeding *and* eternal weight of glory; ¹⁸While we look not at the things which are seen, but at the things which are not seen: for the things which are seen *are* temporal; but the things which are not seen *are* eternal.

5

¹For we know that if our earthly house of *this* tabernacle were dissolved, we have a building of God, an house not made with hands, eternal in the heavens. ²For in this we groan, earnestly desiring to be clothed upon with our house which is from heaven: ³If so be that being clothed we shall not be found naked. ⁴For we that are in *this* tabernacle do groan, being burdened: not for that we would be unclothed, but clothed upon, that mortality might be swallowed up of life. ⁵Now he that hath wrought us for the selfsame thing *is* God, who also hath given unto us the earnest of the Spirit. ⁶Therefore *we are* always confident, knowing that, whilst we are at home in the body, we are absent from the Lord: ⁷(For we walk by faith, not by sight:) ⁸We are confident, *I say*, and willing rather to be absent from the body, and to be present with the Lord. ⁹Wherefore we labour[a], that, whether present or absent, we may be accepted of him. ¹⁰For we must all appear before the judgment seat of Christ; that every one may receive the things *done* in *his* body, according to that he hath done, whether *it be* good or bad. ¹¹Knowing therefore the terror of the Lord, we persuade men; but we are made manifest unto God; and I trust also are made manifest in your consciences.

¹²For we commend not ourselves again unto you, but give you occasion to glory on our behalf, that ye may have somewhat to *answer* them which glory in appearance[b], and not in heart. ¹³For whether we be beside ourselves, *it is* to God: or whether we be sober, *it is* for your cause. ¹⁴For the love of Christ constraineth us; because we thus judge, that if one died for all, then were all dead: ¹⁵And *that* he died for all, that

---

[a] labour: or, endeavour
[b] in appearance: Gr. in the face

they which live should not henceforth live unto themselves, but unto him which died for them, and rose again.

[16]Wherefore henceforth know we no man after the flesh: yea, though we have known Christ after the flesh, yet now henceforth know we *him* no more. [17]Therefore if any man *be* in Christ, *he is* a new creature: old things are passed away; behold, all things are become new. [18]And all things *are* of God, who hath reconciled us to himself by Jesus Christ, and hath given to us the ministry of reconciliation; [19]To wit, that God was in Christ, reconciling the world unto himself, not imputing their trespasses unto them; and hath committed[c] unto us the word of reconciliation. [20]Now then we are ambassadors for Christ, as though God did beseech *you* by us: we pray *you* in Christ's stead, be ye reconciled to God. [21]For he hath made him *to be* sin for us, who knew no sin; that we might be made the righteousness of God in him.

6

[1]We then, *as* workers together *with him*, beseech *you* also that ye receive not the grace of God in vain. [2](For he saith, I have heard thee in a time accepted, and in the day of salvation have I succoured thee: behold, now *is* the accepted time; behold, now *is* the day of salvation.) [3]Giving no offence in any thing, that the ministry be not blamed: [4]But in all *things* approving[a] ourselves as the ministers of God, in much patience, in afflictions, in necessities, in distresses, [5]In

Devotional Moment
•
Life-Style

6:3-4 Because he knew that others were watching him closely, Paul was extremely careful about how he lived. He wanted to make sure that he did what he told others to do. He did not want any hypocrisy in his life to keep someone from God. Parents have a similar need for credibility with their children. Children watch their parents even more closely than Paul's hearers (and detractors) watched him. Don't have two sets of rules in your home—one for you and one for the kids. Be what you ask your kids to be.

stripes, in imprisonments, in tumults[b], in labours, in watchings, in fastings; [6]By pureness, by knowledge, by longsuffering, by kindness, by the Holy Ghost, by love unfeigned, [7]By the word of truth, by the power of God, by the armour of righteousness on the right hand and on the left, [8]By honour and dishonour, by evil report and good report: as deceivers, and *yet* true; [9]As unknown, and *yet* well known; as dying, and, behold, we live; as chastened, and not killed; [10]As sorrowful, yet alway rejoicing; as poor, yet making many rich; as having nothing, and *yet* possessing all things.

[11]O *ye* Corinthians, our mouth is open unto you, our heart is enlarged. [12]Ye are not straitened in us, but ye are straitened in your own bowels. [13]Now for a recompence in the same, (I speak as unto *my* children,) be ye also enlarged. [14]Be ye not unequally yoked together with unbelievers: for what fellowship hath righteousness with un-

---

[c] committed . . . : Gr. put in us
[a] approving: Gr. commending
[b] in tumults: or, in tossings to and fro

Devotional Moment

Loyalty

6:14-17 Here God plainly forbids believers to team up with unbelievers—and the partnership of marriage is certainly no exception. Some Christians enter such marriages intending to be strong, positive witnesses. They generally emerge with watered-down convictions and worldly values. While we must befriend unbelievers and try to lead them to Christ, marriage is a special situation. Marrying someone who doesn't share your faith in Christ will pull you away from the Lord. Steer clear of relationships that could lead you down that path, and help your teens to choose wisely their close friends and prospective mates as well.

righteousness? and what communion hath light with darkness? ¹⁵And what concord hath Christ with Belial? or what part hath he that believeth with an infidel? ¹⁶And what agreement hath the temple of God with idols? for ye are the temple of the living God; as God hath said, I will dwell in them, and walk in *them*; and I will be their God, and they shall be my people. ¹⁷Wherefore come out from among them, and be ye separate, saith the Lord, and touch not the unclean *thing*; and I will receive you, ¹⁸And will be a Father unto you, and ye shall be my sons and daughters, saith the Lord Almighty.

7

¹Having therefore these promises, dearly beloved, let us cleanse ourselves from all filthiness of the flesh and spirit, perfecting holiness in the fear of God. ²Receive us; we have wronged no man, we have corrupted no man, we have de-frauded no man. ³I speak not *this* to condemn *you*: for I have said before, that ye are in our hearts to die and live with *you*. ⁴Great *is* my boldness of speech toward you, great *is* my glorying of you: I am filled with comfort, I am exceeding joyful in all our tribulation.

⁵For, when we were come into Macedonia, our flesh had no rest, but we were troubled on every side; without *were* fightings, within *were* fears. ⁶Nevertheless God, that comforteth those that are cast down, comforted us by the coming of Titus; ⁷And not by his coming only, but by the consolation wherewith he was comforted in you, when he told us your earnest desire, your mourning, your fervent mind toward me; so that I rejoiced the more. ⁸For though I made you sorry with a letter, I do not repent, though I did repent: for I perceive that the same epistle hath made you sorry, though *it were* but for a season. ⁹Now I rejoice, not that ye were made sorry, but that ye sorrowed to repentance: for ye were made sorry afterᵃ a

Devotional Moment

Correction

7:8-11 Earlier, Paul had rebuked the Corinthians for sin in their midst. It was painful for them to hear the truth, but they listened, pondered, and acted. And they were better off for this "grief from the Lord."

How do you respond when someone points out a problem in your life? Do you get angry? blame others? make excuses? According to the Old Testament, these are the reactions of a proud fool (Prov. 14:6, 33; 17:10; 23:9; 27:22). Make this your goal: to see correction, not as a personal attack, but as an opportunity to grow and change in positive ways.

ᵃ after . . . : or, according to God

godly manner, that ye might receive damage by us in nothing. ¹⁰For godly sorrow worketh repentance to salvation not to be repented of: but the sorrow of the world worketh death. ¹¹For behold this selfsame thing, that ye sorrowed after a godly sort, what carefulness it wrought in you, yea, *what* clearing of yourselves, yea, *what* indignation, yea, *what* fear, yea, *what* vehement desire, yea, *what* zeal, yea, *what* revenge! In all *things* ye have approved yourselves to be clear in this matter.

¹²Wherefore, though I wrote unto you, *I did it* not for his cause that had done the wrong, nor for his cause that suffered wrong, but that our care for you in the sight of God might appear unto you. ¹³Therefore we were comforted in your comfort: yea, and exceedingly the more joyed we for the joy of Titus, because his spirit was refreshed by you all. ¹⁴For if I have boasted any thing to him of you, I am not ashamed; but as we spake all things to you in truth, even so our boasting, which *I made* before Titus, is found a truth. ¹⁵And his inward affection is more abundant toward you, whilst he remembereth the obedience of you all, how with fear and trembling ye received him. ¹⁶I rejoice therefore that I have confidence in you in all *things*.

8

¹Moreover, brethren, we do you to wit of the grace of God bestowed on the churches of Macedonia; ²How that in a great trial of affliction the abundance of their joy and their deep poverty abounded unto the riches of their liberalityᵃ. ³For to

their power, I bear record, yea, and beyond *their* power *they were* willing of themselves; ⁴Praying us with much intreaty that we would receive the gift, and *take upon us* the fellowship of the ministering to the saints. ⁵And *this they did,* not as we hoped, but first gave their own selves to the Lord, and unto us by the will of God. ⁶Insomuch that we desired Titus, that as he had begun, so he would also finish in you the same graceᵇ also.

⁷Therefore, as ye abound in every *thing, in* faith, and utterance, and knowledge, and *in* all diligence, and *in* your love to us, *see* that ye abound in this grace also. ⁸I speak not by commandment, but by occasion of the forwardness of others, and to prove the sincerity of your love. ⁹For ye know the grace of our Lord Jesus Christ, that, though he was rich, yet for your sakes he became poor, that ye through his poverty might be rich. ¹⁰And herein I give *my* advice: for this is expedient for you,

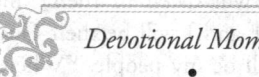

Devotional Moment

•

Giving

8:10-15 Paul listed several principles about giving in this passage. First, because it is easy to rationalize in the area of giving, we need to make sure that we carry out our financial commitments (v. 11). Second, we ought to give willingly as much as we can (v. 12). Third, when we help others, we are more likely to receive help from others (v. 14). Evaluate your own habit of giving. Do you give as much as you can or only what's left over? Have you failed to live up to a commitment? Look for creative ways to give. Perhaps you can even find a source of extra income that you can devote wholly to giving to those in need.

ᵃ liberality: Gr. simplicity
ᵇ grace: or, gift
ᶜ forward: Gr. willing

who have begun before, not only to do, but also to be forward[c] a year ago. [11]Now therefore perform the doing *of it*; that as *there was* a readiness to will, so *there may be* a performance also out of that which ye have. [12]For if there be first a willing mind, *it is* accepted according to that a man hath, *and* not according to that he hath not. [13]For *I mean* not that other men be eased, and ye burdened: [14]But by an equality, *that* now at this time your abundance *may be a supply* for their want, that their abundance also may be *a supply* for your want: that there may be equality: [15]As it is written, He that *had gathered* much had nothing over; and he that *had gathered* little had no lack.

[16]But thanks *be* to God, which put the same earnest care into the heart of Titus for you. [17]For indeed he accepted the exhortation; but being more forward, of his own accord he went unto you. [18]And we have sent with him the brother, whose praise *is* in the gospel throughout all the churches; [19]And not *that* only, but who was also chosen of the churches to travel with us with this grace[d], which is administered by us to the glory of the same Lord, and *declaration of* your ready mind: [20]Avoiding this, that no man should blame us in this abundance which is administered by us: [21]Providing for honest things, not only in the sight of the Lord, but also in the sight of men. [22]And we have sent with them our brother, whom we have oftentimes proved diligent in many things, but now much more diligent, upon the great confidence which *I have* in you. [23]Whether *any do enquire* of Titus, *he is* my partner and fellowhelper concerning you: or our brethren *be enquired of, they are* the messengers of the churches, *and* the glory of Christ. [24]Wherefore shew ye to them, and before the churches, the proof of your love, and of our boasting on your behalf.

9

[1]For as touching the ministering to the saints, it is superfluous for me to write to you: [2]For I know the forwardness of your mind, for which I boast of you to them of Macedonia, that Achaia was ready a year ago; and your zeal hath provoked very many. [3]Yet have I sent the brethren, lest our boasting of you should be in vain in this behalf; that, as I said, ye may be ready: [4]Lest haply if they of Macedonia come with me, and find you unprepared, we (that we say not, ye) should be ashamed in this same confident boasting. [5]Therefore I thought it necessary to exhort the brethren, that they would go before unto you, and make up beforehand your bounty[a], whereof ye had notice before, that the same might be ready, as *a matter of* bounty, and not as *of* covetousness.

[6]But this *I say*, He which soweth sparingly shall reap also sparingly; and he which soweth bountifully shall reap also bountifully. [7]Every man according as he purposeth in his heart, *so let him give*; not grudgingly, or of necessity: for God loveth a cheerful giver. [8]And God *is* able to make all grace abound toward you; that ye, always having all sufficiency in all *things*, may abound to every good work: [9](As it is written, He hath dis-

---

[d] grace: or, gift
[a] bounty: Gr. blessing

persed abroad; he hath given to the poor: his righteousness remaineth for ever. [10]Now he that ministereth seed to the sower both minister bread for *your* food, and multiply your seed sown, and increase the fruits of your righteousness;) [11]Being enriched in every thing to all bountifulness[b], which causeth through us thanksgiving to God. [12]For the administration of this service not only supplieth the want of the saints, but is abundant also by many thanksgivings unto God; [13]Whiles by the experiment of this ministration they glorify God for your professed subjection unto the gospel of Christ, and for *your* liberal distribution unto them, and unto all *men;* [14]And by their prayer for you, which long after you for the exceeding grace of God in you. [15]Thanks *be* unto God for his unspeakable gift.

10

[1]Now I Paul myself beseech you by the meekness and gentleness of Christ, who in presence[a] *am* base among you, but being absent am bold toward you: [2]But I beseech *you,* that I may not be bold when I am present with that confidence, wherewith I think to be bold against some, which think[b] of us as if we walked according to the flesh. [3]For though we walk in the flesh, we do not war after the flesh: [4](For the weapons of our warfare *are* not carnal, but mighty

through God to the pulling down of strong holds;) [5]Casting down imaginations[c], and every high thing that exalteth itself against the knowledge of God, and bringing into captivity every thought to the obedience of Christ; [6]And having in a readiness to revenge all disobedience, when your obedience is fulfilled.

[7]Do ye look on things after the outward appearance? If any man trust to himself that he is Christ's, let him of himself think this again, that, as he *is* Christ's, even so *are* we Christ's. [8]For though I should boast somewhat more of our authority, which the Lord hath given us for edification, and not for your destruction, I should not be ashamed: [9]That I may not seem as if I would terrify you by letters. [10]For *his* letters, say they[d], *are* weighty and powerful; but *his* bodily presence *is* weak, and *his* speech contemptible. [11]Let such an one think this, that, such as we are in word by letters when we are absent, such *will we be* also in deed when we are present.

[12]For we dare not make ourselves of the number, or compare ourselves with some that commend themselves: but they measuring themselves by themselves, and comparing themselves among themselves, are[e] not wise. [13]But we will not boast of things without *our* measure, but according to the measure of the rule[f] which God hath distributed to us, a

---

[b] bountifulness: or, liberality: Gr. simplicity
[a] in presence: or, in outward appearance
[b] think: or, reckon
[c] imaginations: or, reasonings
[d] say they: Gr. saith he
[e] are . . . : or, understand it not
[f] rule: or, line

measure to reach even unto you. ¹⁴For we stretch not ourselves beyond *our measure*, as though we reached not unto you: for we are come as far as to you also in *preaching* the gospel of Christ: ¹⁵Not boasting of things without *our* measure, *that is*, of other men's labours; but having hope, when your faith is increased, that we shall be enlargedᵍ by you according to our rule abundantly, ¹⁶To preach the gospel in the *regions* beyond you, *and* not to boast in another man's lineʰ of things made ready to our hand. ¹⁷But he that glorieth, let him glory in the Lord. ¹⁸For not he that commendeth himself is approved, but whom the Lord commendeth.

11

¹Would to God ye could bear with me a little in *my* folly: and indeed bear with me. ²For I am jealous over you with godly jealousy: for I have espoused you to one husband, that I may present *you as* a chaste virgin to Christ. ³But I fear, lest by any means, as the serpent beguiled Eve through his subtilty, so your minds should be corrupted from the simplicity that is in Christ. ⁴For if he that cometh preacheth another Jesus, whom we have not preached, or *if* ye receive another spirit, which ye have not received, or another gospel, which ye have not accepted, ye might well bear with *him*.

⁵For I suppose I was not a whit behind the very chiefest apostles. ⁶But though *I be* rude in speech, yet not in

knowledge; but we have been throughly made manifest among you in all things. ⁷Have I committed an offence in abasing myself that ye might be exalted, because I have preached to you the gospel of God freely? ⁸I robbed other churches, taking wages *of them*, to do you service. ⁹And when I was present with you, and wanted, I was chargeable to no man: for that which was lacking to me the brethren which came from Macedonia supplied: and in all *things* I have kept myself from being burdensome unto you, and *so* will I keep *myself*. ¹⁰As the truth of Christ is in me, no manᵃ shall stop me of this boasting in the regions of Achaia. ¹¹Wherefore? because I love you not? God knoweth. ¹²But what I do, that I will do, that I may cut off occasion from them which desire occasion; that wherein they glory, they may be found even as we. ¹³For such *are* false apostles, deceitful workers, transforming themselves into the apostles of Christ. ¹⁴And no marvel; for Satan himself is transformed into an angel of light. ¹⁵Therefore *it is* no great thing if his ministers also be transformed as the ministers of righteousness; whose end shall be according to their works.

¹⁶I say again, Let no man think me a fool; if otherwise, yet as a fool receiveᵇ me, that I may boast myself a little. ¹⁷That which I speak, I speak *it* not after the Lord, but as it were foolishly, in this confidence of boasting. ¹⁸Seeing that many glory after the flesh, I will glory also. ¹⁹For ye suffer fools gladly,

---

ᵍ enlarged . . . : or, magnified in you
ʰ line: or, rule
ᵃ no man . . . : Gr. this boasting shall not bo stopped in me
ᵇ receive: or, suffer

seeing ye *yourselves* are wise. [20]For ye suffer, if a man bring you into bondage, if a man devour *you*, if a man take *of you*, if a man exalt himself, if a man smite you on the face. [21]I speak as concerning reproach, as though we had been weak. Howbeit whereinsoever any is bold, (I speak foolishly,) I am bold also.

[22]Are they Hebrews? so *am* I. Are they Israelites? so *am* I. Are they the seed of Abraham? so *am* I. [23]Are they ministers of Christ? (I speak as a fool) I *am* more; in labours more abundant, in stripes above measure, in prisons more frequent, in deaths oft. [24]Of the Jews five times received I forty *stripes* save one. [25]Thrice was I beaten with rods, once was I stoned, thrice I suffered shipwreck, a night and a day I have been in the deep; [26]*In* journeyings of-

---

Devotional Moment
•
Leadership

11:28-29 Even though he was a busy leader with a host of problems (vv. 23-27), Paul felt an enormous personal concern for individuals in the churches he had planted. He balanced his *global mission* (taking the gospel to the uttermost ends of the earth) with an *individual ministry.* Parents need this same perspective. We must be careful not to get so caught up in our "global" plans and agendas that we overlook the individual needs of our children. Are you aware of the struggles and fears your children have? Do you feel what they are feeling and sympathize with them when they hurt? Do you pray for them on a daily basis? Ask each of your children today to tell you of one area in their lives that they'd like you to pray about. Then pray for them daily. God will bless you both.

---

ten, *in* perils of waters, *in* perils of robbers, *in* perils by *mine own* countrymen, *in* perils by the heathen, *in* perils in the city, *in* perils in the wilderness, *in* perils in the sea, *in* perils among false brethren; [27]In weariness and painfulness, in watchings often, in hunger and thirst, in fastings often, in cold and nakedness. [28]Beside those things that are without, that which cometh upon me daily, the care of all the churches. [29]Who is weak, and I am not weak? who is offended, and I burn not? [30]If I must needs glory, I will glory of the things which concern mine infirmities. [31]The God and Father of our Lord Jesus Christ, which is blessed for evermore, knoweth that I lie not. [32]In Damascus the governor under Aretas the king kept the city of the Damascenes with a garrison, desirous to apprehend me: [33]And through a window in a basket was I let down by the wall, and escaped his hands.

12

[1]It is not expedient for me doubtless to glory. I will come[a] to visions and revelations of the Lord. [2]I knew a man in Christ above fourteen years ago, (whether in the body, I cannot tell; or whether out of the body, I cannot tell: God knoweth;) such an one caught up to the third heaven. [3]And I knew such a man, (whether in the body, or out of the body, I cannot tell: God knoweth;) [4]How that he was caught up into paradise, and heard unspeakable words, which it is not lawful[b] for a man to utter. [5]Of such an one will I glory: yet of

---

[a] I will come: Gr. For I will come
[b] lawful: or, possible

myself I will not glory, but in mine infirmities. ⁶For though I would desire to glory, I shall not be a fool; for I will say the truth: but *now* I forbear, lest any man should think of me above that which he seeth me *to be*, or *that* he heareth of me. ⁷And lest I should be exalted above measure through the abundance of the revelations, there was given to me a thorn in the flesh, the messenger of Satan to buffet me, lest I should be exalted above measure. ⁸For this thing I besought the Lord thrice, that it might depart from me. ⁹And he said unto me, *My grace is sufficient for thee: for my strength is made perfect in weakness.* Most gladly therefore will I rather glory in my infirmities, that the power of Christ may rest upon me. ¹⁰Therefore I take pleasure in infirmities, in reproaches, in necessities, in persecutions, in distresses for Christ's sake: for when I am weak, then am I strong.

¹¹I am become a fool in glorying; ye have compelled me: for I ought to have been commended of you: for in nothing am I behind the very chiefest apostles, though I be nothing. ¹²Truly the signs of an apostle were wrought among you in all patience, in signs, and wonders, and mighty deeds. ¹³For what is it wherein ye were inferior to other churches, except *it be* that I myself was not burdensome to you? forgive me this wrong. ¹⁴Behold, the third time I am ready to come to you; and I will not be burdensome to you: for I seek not yours, but you: for the children ought not to lay up for the parents, but the parents for the children. ¹⁵And I will

very gladly spend and be spent for you*ᶜ*; though the more abundantly I love you, the less I be loved. ¹⁶But be it so, I did not burden you: nevertheless, being crafty, I caught you with guile. ¹⁷Did I make a gain of you by any of them whom I sent unto you? ¹⁸I desired Titus, and with *him* I sent a brother. Did Titus make a gain of you? walked we not in the same spirit? *walked we* not in the same steps? ¹⁹Again, think ye that we excuse ourselves unto you? we speak before God in Christ: but *we do* all things, dearly beloved, for your edifying. ²⁰For I fear, lest, when I come, I shall not find you such as I would, and *that* I shall be found unto you such as ye would not: lest *there be* debates, envyings, wraths, strifes, backbitings, whisperings, swellings, tumults: ²¹*And* lest, when I come again, my God will humble me among you, and *that* I shall bewail many which have sinned already, and have not repented of the uncleanness and fornication and lasciviousness which they have committed.

13

¹This *is* the third *time* I am coming to you. In the mouth of two or three witnesses shall every word be established. ²I told you before, and foretell you, as if I were present, the second time; and being absent now I write to them which heretofore have sinned, and to all other, that, if I come again, I will not spare: ³Since ye seek a proof of Christ speaking in me, which to you-ward is not weak, but is mighty in you. ⁴For though he was crucified through weakness, yet he liveth by the power of God. For we

---

ᶜ for you: Gr. for your souls

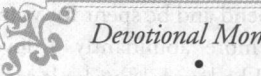

Devotional Moment
•
Parenting

13:7-9 Here is a good (though convicting!) test of our true motives as parents: When our children misbehave publicly, are we concerned that they learn to do right, or are we more worried about what others are thinking of our parenting skills?

As their "spiritual father," Paul wanted the Corinthians to grow and mature. His chief concern was not for *his* reputation, but for *their* well-being. Like Paul, we should pray that our children live good lives, not so that others will say what great parents we are, but so that our kids might enjoy the blessings of righteousness.

also are weak in him[a], but we shall live with him by the power of God toward you. ⁵Examine yourselves, whether ye be in the faith; prove your own selves. Know ye not your own selves, how that Jesus Christ is in you, except ye be reprobates? ⁶But I trust that ye shall know that we are not reprobates.

⁷Now I pray to God that ye do no evil; not that we should appear approved, but that ye should do that which is honest, though we be as reprobates. ⁸For we can do nothing against the truth, but for the truth. ⁹For we are glad, when we are weak, and ye are strong: and this also we wish, *even* your perfection[b]. ¹⁰Therefore I write these things being absent, lest being present I should use sharpness, according to the power which the Lord hath given me to edification, and not to destruction.

¹¹Finally, brethren, farewell. Be perfect, be of good comfort, be of one mind, live in peace; and the God of love and peace shall be with you. ¹²Greet one another with an holy kiss. ¹³All the saints salute you. ¹⁴The grace of the Lord Jesus Christ, and the love of God, and the communion of the Holy Ghost, *be* with you all. Amen.

[The second *epistle* to the Corinthians was written from Philippi, *a city* of Macedonia, by Titus and Lucas.]

[a] in him: or, with him
[b] perfection: or, reformation, or, restoration

GALATIANS

A t the heart of Galatians is a simple theological fact: Faith is the key.

The apostle Paul, who wrote this letter to correct some folks who had earlier missed the point, says it over and over: Good behavior does not save us; salvation is by faith in Christ who gave his life to save us from sin.

Faith, not works. No, not that we should ignore God's law, not at all. But obedience is the response of faith, not the way to secure God's favor.

Seems simple enough. Why, then, the need for so much repetition? So many reminders, explanations, examples, clarifications?

Paul is acting like a parent, for whom the repetition of simple truths is a special calling. Any parent knows that five to fifteen repetitions is a daily average. Over an eighteen-year growing season, some children will actually get the point.

The point—salvation by faith, not works—deserves repetition. It's the heart of the Christian message. Miss it and you've missed everything.

Galatians is like the parent with a habit of hugging children at bedtime and saying, "I love you." Repeated night after night, that point never grows old. It's the heart of a parent's relationship with a child. Miss it, and you've missed everything.

Faith is the key.

What's that again?

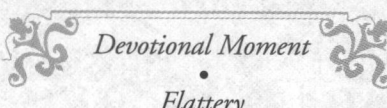

Devotional Moment

•

Flattery

1:10 When confronting others, we must always speak in a firm, straightforward manner and never water down the truth. This was Paul's approach to the Galatian Christians who were embracing a dangerous false teaching. When friends or family members are going astray, we must speak up. We must be loving and tactful and look for opportunities to affirm. But we must not sacrifice the truth in an effort to spare someone's feelings.

1

¹Paul, an apostle, (not of men, neither by man, but by Jesus Christ, and God the Father, who raised him from the dead;) ²And all the brethren which are with me, unto the churches of Galatia: ³Grace *be* to you and peace from God the Father, and *from* our Lord Jesus Christ, ⁴Who gave himself for our sins, that he might deliver us from this present evil world, according to the will of God and our Father: ⁵To whom *be* glory for ever and ever. Amen.

⁶I marvel that ye are so soon removed from him that called you into the grace of Christ unto another gospel: ⁷Which is not another; but there be some that trouble you, and would pervert the gospel of Christ. ⁸But though we, or an angel from heaven, preach any other gospel unto you than that which we have preached unto you, let him be accursed. ⁹As we said before, so say I now again, If any *man* preach any other gospel unto you than that ye have received, let him be accursed.

¹⁰For do I now persuade men, or God? or do I seek to please men? for if I yet pleased men, I should not be the servant of Christ. ¹¹But I certify you, brethren, that the gospel which was preached of me is not after man. ¹²For I neither received it of man, neither was I taught *it,* but by the revelation of Jesus Christ. ¹³For ye have heard of my conversation in time past in the Jews' religion, how that beyond measure I persecuted the church of God, and wasted it: ¹⁴And profited in the Jews' religion above many my equalsᵃ in mine own nation, being more exceedingly zealous of the traditions of my fathers. ¹⁵But when it pleased God, who separated me from my mother's womb, and called *me* by his grace, ¹⁶To reveal his Son in me, that I might preach him among the heathen; immediately I conferred not with flesh and blood: ¹⁷Neither went I up to Jerusalem to them which were apostles before me; but I went into Arabia, and returned again unto Damascus. ¹⁸Then after three years I went upᵇ to Jerusalem to see Peter, and abode with him fifteen days. ¹⁹But other of the apostles saw I none, save James the Lord's brother. ²⁰Now the things which I write unto you, behold, before God, I lie not. ²¹Afterwards I came into the regions of Syria and Cilicia; ²²And was unknown by face unto the churches of Judaea which were in Christ: ²³But they had heard only, That he which persecuted us in times past now preacheth the faith which once he destroyed. ²⁴And they glorified God in me.

2

¹Then fourteen years after I went up again to Jerusalem with Barnabas, and

---

ᵃ equals: Gr. equals in years
ᵇ went up: or, returned

took Titus with *me* also. ²And I went up by revelation, and communicated unto them that gospel which I preach among the Gentiles, but privately[a] to them which were of reputation, lest by any means I should run, or had run, in vain. ³But neither Titus, who was with me, being a Greek, was compelled to be circumcised: ⁴And that because of false brethren unawares brought in, who came in privily to spy out our liberty which we have in Christ Jesus, that they might bring us into bondage: ⁵To whom we gave place by subjection, no, not for an hour; that the truth of the gospel might continue with you. ⁶But of these who seemed to be somewhat, (whatsoever they were, it maketh no matter to me: God accepteth no man's person:) for they who seemed *to be somewhat* in conference added nothing to me: ⁷But contrariwise, when they saw that the gospel of the uncircumcision was committed unto me, as *the gospel* of the circumcision *was* unto Peter; ⁸(For he that wrought effectually in Peter to the apostleship of the circumcision, the same was mighty in me toward the Gentiles:) ⁹And when James, Cephas, and John, who seemed to be pillars, perceived the grace that was given unto me, they gave to me and Barnabas the right hands of fellowship; that we *should go* unto the heathen, and they unto the circumcision. ¹⁰Only *they would* that we should remember the poor; the same which I also was forward to do.

¹¹But when Peter was come to Antioch, I withstood him to the face, because he was to be blamed. ¹²For before

that certain came from James, he did eat with the Gentiles: but when they were come, he withdrew and separated himself, fearing them which were of the circumcision. ¹³And the other Jews dissembled likewise with him; insomuch that Barnabas also was carried away with their dissimulation. ¹⁴But when I saw that they walked not uprightly according to the truth of the gospel, I said unto Peter before *them* all, If thou, being a Jew, livest after the manner of Gentiles, and not as do the Jews, why compellest thou the Gentiles to live as do the Jews? ¹⁵We *who are* Jews by nature, and not sinners of the Gentiles, ¹⁶Knowing that a man is not justified by the works of the law, but by the faith of Jesus Christ, even we have believed in Jesus Christ, that we might be justified by the faith of Christ, and not by the works of the law: for by the works of the law shall no flesh be justified. ¹⁷But if, while we seek to be justified by

---

[a] privately: or, severally

Christ, we ourselves also are found sinners, *is* therefore Christ the minister of sin? God forbid. [18]For if I build again the things which I destroyed, I make myself a transgressor. [19]For I through the law am dead to the law, that I might live unto God. [20]I am crucified with Christ: nevertheless I live; yet not I, but Christ liveth in me: and the life which I now live in the flesh I live by the faith of the Son of God, who loved me, and gave himself for me. [21]I do not frustrate the grace of God: for if righteousness *come* by the law, then Christ is dead in vain.

3

[1]O foolish Galatians, who hath bewitched you, that ye should not obey the truth, before whose eyes Jesus Christ hath been evidently set forth, crucified among you? [2]This only would I learn of you, Received ye the Spirit by the works of the law, or by the hearing of faith? [3]Are ye so foolish? having begun in the Spirit, are ye now made perfect by the flesh? [4]Have ye suffered so many things in vain? if *it be* yet in vain. [5]He therefore that ministereth to you the Spirit, and worketh miracles among you, *doeth he it* by the works of the law, or by the hearing of faith?

[6]Even as Abraham believed God, and it was accounted[a] to him for righteousness. [7]Know ye therefore that they which are of faith, the same are the children of Abraham. [8]And the scripture, foreseeing that God would justify the heathen through faith, preached before the gospel unto Abraham, *saying,*

In thee shall all nations be blessed. [9]So then they which be of faith are blessed with faithful Abraham. [10]For as many as are of the works of the law are under the curse: for it is written, Cursed *is* every one that continueth not in all things which are written in the book of the law to do them. [11]But that no man is justified by the law in the sight of God, *it is* evident: for, The just shall live by faith. [12]And the law is not of faith: but, The man that doeth them shall live in them. [13]Christ hath redeemed us from the curse of the law, being made a curse for us: for it is written, Cursed *is* every one that hangeth on a tree: [14]That the blessing of Abraham might come on the Gentiles through Jesus Christ; that we might receive the promise of the Spirit through faith. [15]Brethren, I speak after the manner of men; Though *it be* but a man's covenant[b], yet *if it be* confirmed, no man disannulleth, or addeth thereto. [16]Now to Abraham and his seed were the promises made. He saith not, And to seeds, as of many; but as of one, And to thy seed, which is Christ. [17]And this I say, *that* the covenant, that was confirmed before of God in Christ, the law, which was four hundred and thirty years after, cannot disannul, that it should make the promise of none effect. [18]For if the inheritance *be* of the law, *it is* no more of promise: but God gave *it* to Abraham by promise.

[19]Wherefore then *serveth* the law? It was added because of transgressions, till the seed should come to whom the promise was made; *and it was* ordained

---

[a] accounted: or, imputed
[b] covenant: or, testament

by angels in the hand of a mediator. [20]Now a mediator is not *a mediator* of one, but God is one. [21]*Is* the law then against the promises of God? God forbid: for if there had been a law given which could have given life, verily righteousness should have been by the law. [22]But the scripture hath concluded all under sin, that the promise by faith of Jesus Christ might be given to them that believe. [23]But before faith came, we were kept under the law, shut up unto the faith which should afterwards be revealed. [24]Wherefore the law was our schoolmaster *to bring us* unto Christ, that we might be justified by faith. [25]But after that faith is come, we are no longer under a schoolmaster. [26]For ye are all the children of God by faith in Christ Jesus. [27]For as many of you as have been baptized into Christ have put on Christ. [28]There is neither Jew nor Greek, there is neither bond nor free, there is neither male nor female: for ye are all one in Christ Jesus. [29]And if ye *be*

Devotional Moment

Equality

3:28 We live in a world torn by division, prejudice, and suspicion. People band together against one another—women versus men, ethnic group versus ethnic group, privileged versus poor. But when God looks at us, he sees us all as equal. And when he brings a person into his family in Christ, he calls that person to leave his or her concern for differences at the door. Our ethnic background, economic status, and gender should have absolutely no bearing on how we treat fellow Christians.

Christ's, then are ye Abraham's seed, and heirs according to the promise.

4

[1]Now I say, *That* the heir, as long as he is a child, differeth nothing from a servant, though he be lord of all; [2]But is under tutors and governors until the time appointed of the father. [3]Even so we, when we were children, were in bondage under the elements[a] of the world: [4]But when the fulness of the time was come, God sent forth his Son, made of a woman, made under the law, [5]To redeem them that were under the law, that we might receive the adoption of sons. [6]And because ye are sons, God hath sent forth the Spirit of his Son into your hearts, crying, Abba, Father. [7]Wherefore thou art no more a servant, but a son; and if a son, then an heir of God through Christ.

[8]Howbeit then, when ye knew not God, ye did service unto them which by nature are no gods. [9]But now, after that ye have known God, or rather are known of God, how turn ye again[b] to the weak and beggarly elements, whereunto ye desire again to be in bondage? [10]Ye observe days, and months, and times, and years. [11]I am afraid of you, lest I have bestowed upon you labour in vain.

[12]Brethren, I beseech you, be as I *am*, for I *am* as ye *are*: ye have not injured me at all. [13]Ye know how through infirmity of the flesh I preached the gospel unto you at the first. [14]And my temptation which was in my flesh ye despised not, nor rejected; but received me as an angel of God, *even* as

---

[a] elements: or, rudiments
[b] turn ye again: or, turn ye back

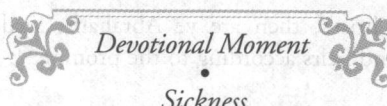

Christ Jesus. ¹⁵Where[c] is then the blessedness ye spake of? for I bear you record, that, if *it had been* possible, ye would have plucked out your own eyes, and have given them to me. ¹⁶Am I therefore become your enemy, because I tell you the truth?

¹⁷They zealously affect you, *but* not well; yea, they would exclude you[d], that ye might affect them. ¹⁸But *it is* good to be zealously affected always in *a* good *thing*, and not only when I am present with you.

¹⁹My little children, of whom I travail in birth again until Christ be formed in you, ²⁰I desire to be present with you now, and to change my voice; for I stand in doubt of you.

²¹Tell me, ye that desire to be under the law, do ye not hear the law? ²²For it is written, that Abraham had two sons, the one by a bondmaid, the other by a freewoman. ²³But he *who was* of the bondwoman was born after the flesh; but he of the freewoman *was* by promise. ²⁴Which things are an allegory: for these are the two covenants[e]; the one from the mount Sinai, which gendereth to bondage, which is Agar. ²⁵For this Agar is mount Sinai in Arabia, and answereth to Jerusalem which now is, and is in bondage with her children. ²⁶But Jerusalem which is above is free, which is the mother of us all. ²⁷For it is written, Rejoice, *thou* barren that bearest not; break forth and cry, thou that travailest not: for the desolate hath many more children than she which hath an husband. ²⁸Now we, brethren, as Isaac was, are the children of promise. ²⁹But as then he that was born after the flesh persecuted him *that was born* after the Spirit, even so *it is* now. ³⁰Nevertheless what saith the scripture? Cast out the bondwoman and her son: for the son of the bondwoman shall not be heir with the son of the freewoman. ³¹So then, brethren, we are not children of the bondwoman, but of the free.

5

¹Stand fast therefore in the liberty wherewith Christ hath made us free, and be not entangled again with the yoke of bondage. ²Behold, I Paul say unto you, that if ye be circumcised, Christ shall profit you nothing. ³For I testify again to every man that is circumcised, that he is a debtor to do the whole law. ⁴Christ is become of no effect unto you, whosoever of you are justified by the law; ye are fallen from grace. ⁵For we through the Spirit wait for the hope of righteousness by faith. ⁶For in Jesus Christ neither circumcision availeth any thing,

---

[c] Where . . . : or, What was then
[d] exclude you: or, exclude us
[e] covenants: or, testaments

nor uncircumcision; but faith which worketh by love. [7]Ye did run well; who did hinder you[a] that ye should not obey the truth? [8]This persuasion *cometh* not of him that calleth you. [9]A little leaven leaveneth the whole lump. [10]I have confidence in you through the Lord, that ye will be none otherwise minded: but he that troubleth you shall bear his judgment, whosoever he be. [11]And I, brethren, if I yet preach circumcision, why do I yet suffer persecution? then is the offence of the cross ceased. [12]I would they were even cut off which trouble you.

[13]For, brethren, ye have been called unto liberty; only *use* not liberty for an occasion to the flesh, but by love serve one another. [14]For all the law is fulfilled in one word, *even* in this; Thou shalt love thy neighbour as thyself. [15]But if ye bite and devour one another, take heed that ye be not consumed one of another. [16]*This* I say then, Walk in the Spirit, and ye shall not fulfil the lust of the flesh. [17]For the flesh lusteth against the Spirit, and the Spirit against the flesh: and these are contrary the one to the other: so that ye cannot do the things that ye would. [18]But if ye be led of the Spirit, ye are not under the law. [19]Now the works of the flesh are manifest, which are *these*; Adultery, fornication, uncleanness, lasciviousness, [20]Idolatry, witchcraft, hatred, variance, emulations, wrath, strife, seditions, heresies, [21]Envyings, murders, drunkenness, revellings, and such like: of the which I tell you before, as I have also told *you* in time past, that they which do such things shall not inherit the kingdom of God. [22]But the fruit of the Spirit is love, joy, peace, longsuffering, gentleness, goodness, faith, [23]Meekness, temperance: against such there is no law. [24]And they that are Christ's have crucified the flesh with the affections[b] and lusts. [25]If we live in the Spirit, let us also walk in the Spirit. [26]Let us not be desirous of vain glory, provoking one another, envying one another.

6

[1]Brethren, if a man be overtaken in a fault, ye which are spiritual, restore such an one in the spirit of meekness; considering thyself, lest thou also be tempted. [2]Bear ye one another's burdens, and so fulfil the law of Christ. [3]For if a man think himself to be something, when he is nothing, he deceiveth himself. [4]But let every man prove his own work, and then shall he have rejoicing in himself alone, and not in another. [5]For every man shall bear his own burden. [6]Let him that is taught in the word communicate unto him that teacheth in all good things. [7]Be not deceived; God is not

---

Devotional Moment

•

Chomp Chomp

5:13-15 Paul told the Galatians that Christ had set them free from sin, but he quickly added: *Don't use your freedom as an excuse to plunge back into it!* He reminded them that the greatest command is to love others as you love yourself. Home is where you're free to relax, to be yourself. But don't let this "freedom" extend to relaxing the restraints you place on name-calling, talking behind each other's back, second-guessing, or grumbling. Nothing destroys family unity faster than being "critical and catty"! Discipline yourself to love the other members of your family.

---

[a] hinder you: or, drive you back
[b] affections: or, passions

Devotional Moment
•
Help

6:1-3 The Bible paints a picture of Christians being honest with each other, confronting each other, and helping each other get through hard times. This kind of deep interaction and involvement is possible only when we first recognize our need for one another. God did not create us to function in solitude. Others desperately need our unique talents and strengths. Likewise we need others to help us overcome our weaknesses. Don't let pride keep you from building close relationships with those around you.

mocked: for whatsoever a man soweth, that shall he also reap. [8]For he that soweth to his flesh shall of the flesh reap corruption; but he that soweth to the Spirit shall of the Spirit reap life everlasting. [9]And let us not be weary in well doing: for in due season we shall reap, if we faint not. [10]As we have therefore opportunity, let us do good unto all *men*, especially unto them who are of the household of faith.

[11]Ye see how large a letter I have writ-ten unto you with mine own hand. [12]As many as desire to make a fair shew in the flesh, they constrain you to be circumcised; only lest they should suffer persecution for the cross of Christ. [13]For neither they themselves who are circumcised keep the law; but desire to have you circumcised, that they may glory in your flesh. [14]But God forbid that I should glory, save in the cross of our Lord Jesus Christ, by whom[a] the world is crucified unto me, and I unto the world. [15]For in Christ Jesus neither circumcision availeth any thing, nor uncircumcision, but a new creature. [16]And as many as walk according to this rule, peace *be* on them, and mercy, and upon the Israel of God. [17]From henceforth let no man trouble me: for I bear in my body the marks of the Lord Jesus. [18]Brethren, the grace of our Lord Jesus Christ *be* with your spirit. Amen.

[To the Galatians written from Rome.]

Devotional Moment
•
Consequences

6:7-8 If you don't want wheat, don't plant wheat. If you want corn, plant corn. That's the principle here—we reap whatever we sow. This is not just a truth for the farm, it is a law of life. Every action in life has consequences. Good, wise, right choices bring about good results. Bad, unwise, wrong choices bring about bad results. Check the crops at your house. What's growing in your life? If you don't like what you're harvesting, perhaps it's time to do some weeding. Uproot (confess and turn away from) wrong behavior. Then replant some "good things of the Spirit" in your life.

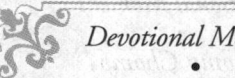

Devotional Moment
•
Tuckered Out

6:9-10 How many times have you felt so tired from responsibilities that you just wanted to quit or escape? Sometimes simply living from day to day can take all our resources: We have to work hard at communicating with our spouse, work hard on the job, work hard at contributing at church—and no one seems to notice or appreciate it. But we have the assurance that the effort *will* make a difference if we don't give up. Don't get discouraged. Keep at it. Some day, it will pay off (if it hasn't already in ways you cannot see).

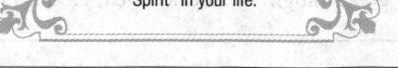

[a] by whom: or, whereby

EPHESIANS

Purpose
To strengthen the believers in
Ephesus in their Christian
faith by explaining the nature
and purpose of the church,
the body of Christ

Author
Paul

To Whom Written
The church at Ephesus

Date Written
About A.D. 60, from Rome, during Paul's imprisonment there

Setting
The letter was written to
strengthen and encourage
the churches in the area,
rather than to confront any
heresy or problem in the
churches. Because there are
no specific references to
people or problems in the
Ephesian church, Paul may
have intended this to be a
circular letter—read to all
the churches in the area.

Key Verse
"There is one body, and one
Spirit, even as ye are called in
one hope of your calling" (4:4).

Key People
Paul, Tychicus

Special Features
Several pictures of the
church are presented: body,
temple, mystery, new man,
bride, and soldier.

What keeps your life from really taking off?
Adults feel pressure from all sides: money,
jobs, kids' need for time, friends' and parents' demands—the list never ends. Wringing the last
drop from limited resources becomes a daily challenge.
Limits begin to define our goals.

Young children dream big, then settle for less. The
child who loved animals and once wanted to be a vet-
erinarian now thinks that school is too hard and loses
sight of his goal. The athlete who dreamed of compet-
ing in the Olympics finds that practice is hard work
and drops out to watch the games on television. Caring parents will help a child reach for the stars. Ephesians is for people who stretch for the gold.

Ephesians challenges everything that holds us
back. This book enlarges our goals, expands our vision,
gets us moving. The point of Ephesians is to show how
big God really is—how the mystery of his plan for our
salvation can motivate us, and how differences can be
reconciled when we are in union with Christ.

If your days are humdrum and predictable, and
you like it that way, bypass Ephesians. If ordinary spiritual life satisfies your hunger for knowing God, read
something else.

Ephesians reveals God as a caring parent who has
more to show us than we can imagine. Ephesians challenges us like a father who might say to a teen, "Turn
off that boom box, and let's go for a run."

1

¹Paul, an apostle of Jesus Christ by the will of God, to the saints which are at Ephesus, and to the faithful in Christ Jesus: ²Grace *be* to you, and peace, from God our Father, and *from* the Lord Jesus Christ.

³Blessed *be* the God and Father of our Lord Jesus Christ, who hath blessed us with all spiritual blessings in heavenly *places* in Christ: ⁴According as he hath chosen us in him before the foundation of the world, that we should be holy and without blame before him in love: ⁵Having predestinated us unto the adoption of children by Jesus Christ to himself, according to the good pleasure of his will, ⁶To the praise of the glory of his grace, wherein he hath made us accepted in the beloved. ⁷In whom we have redemption through his blood, the forgiveness of sins, according to the riches of his grace; ⁸Wherein he hath abounded toward us in all wisdom and prudence; ⁹Having made known unto us the mystery of his will, according to his good pleasure which he hath purposed in himself: ¹⁰That in the dispensation of the fulness of times he might gather together in one

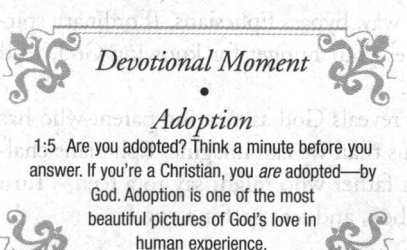

Devotional Moment
•
Adoption

1:5 Are you adopted? Think a minute before you answer. If you're a Christian, you *are* adopted—by God. Adoption is one of the most beautiful pictures of God's love in human experience.

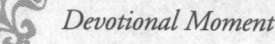

Devotional Moment
•
Spiritual Growth

1:15-17 Paul prayed for the Ephesian believers. He asked God to give them wisdom so they could know God better. What do you want to give your children? Love, security, a happy home, a good education? Every mother and father wants these for their kids. But what about your children's spiritual foundation? Are you also providing what they need for a significant relationship with God? That includes praying for and with them. Thank God for your children, and pray that God will give them "wisdom to see clearly and really understand who Christ is and all that he has done."

all things in Christ, both which are in heaven[a], and which are on earth; *even* in him: ¹¹In whom also we have obtained an inheritance, being predestinated according to the purpose of him who worketh all things after the counsel of his own will: ¹²That we should be to the praise of his glory, who first trusted[b] in Christ. ¹³In whom ye also *trusted,* after that ye heard the word of truth, the gospel of your salvation: in whom also after that ye believed, ye were sealed with that holy Spirit of promise, ¹⁴Which is the earnest of our inheritance until the redemption of the purchased possession, unto the praise of his glory.

¹⁵Wherefore I also, after I heard of your faith in the Lord Jesus, and love unto all the saints, ¹⁶Cease not to give thanks for you, making mention of you in my prayers; ¹⁷That the God of our Lord Jesus Christ, the Father of glory, may give unto you the spirit of wisdom and revelation in[c] the knowledge of

[a] heaven: Gr. the heavens
[b] trusted: or, hoped
[c] in . . . : or, for the acknowledgement

Understanding Adoption

by Beth Spring

Every Christian is adopted. Ephesians 1:5 tells us, [God has] "predestinated us unto the adoption of children by Jesus Christ to himself."

Yet today adoption is often misunderstood. Learning about adoption—both the biblical concept and the contemporary practice—helps us understand how much God loves us and how adopting children may be his very best plan for some families.

God's view of adoption. The Bible first mentions adoption in the book of Exodus. The mother of Moses hid her infant in a basket in an effort to save him from Pharaoh's order that all Hebrew boys be put to death (see Exod. 1:22). As a result, Moses was adopted by Pharaoh's daughter and grew up in Pharaoh's household.

Adoption was practiced widely by the Greeks and Romans of New Testament days. In Paul's writings, the concept is used several times to illustrate the unmerited favor God shows believers. While Jesus is God's only Son, those who believe in him receive the full inheritance of eternal life. Paul wrote, "For ye have not received the spirit of bondage again to fear; but ye have received the Spirit of adoption, whereby we cry, 'Abba, Father'" (Rom. 8:15).

Those who come into a right relationship with God through Christ do so through adoption.

A family's view of adoption. Just as our spiritual selves are transformed when God adopts us, an adopted child's identity is transformed by the decisions of his birth parents and his adoptive parents. An entirely new relationship is created.

Human adoption involves loss, trust, and love, just as our adoption into God's family begins with our brokenness and redemption by God. Birth parents who make the wrenching decision to relinquish a child usually do so out of a realistic awareness of their own inability to raise a child.

Many parents who eventually adopt have had to cope with the heartbreak of infertility. But then they discover that their love for a child can transcend their own bloodlines and even their own race and culture. As attachment grows between adoptive parents and children, they find that the child is truly their own.

Myths about adoption. Many people harbor four misconceptions about adoption:

1. "It's wonderful of you to take in this poor child." Some people view adoption as a sign of the parents' unusual sense of social service or duty. The fact is, most adoptive parents simply want a bigger family. They long to share the joys of child rearing, and adoption is one way to do so.

2. "Too bad you couldn't have one of your own." Even if adoption is a couple's second choice after trying in vain to bear a child, it is not second-best. Reaching a decision to adopt may not be easy, but it generally reflects enthusiasm about the process and the new family member.

3. "Adopted children will bring you nothing but trouble." The "bad seed" theory of adoption has no foundation in fact. The overwhelming majority of adoptions result in securely attached parents and children who experience the same ups and downs as families formed in other ways.

4. "The child will never really be yours." Virtually all adoptees wonder about their ori-

gins and need to integrate the loss of their first family into their self-image, but only a small proportion of them actually search for and find their birth relatives. When they do, it is most often a one-time meeting that satisfies curiosity or provides answers about medical questions. And it reinforces the child's view of his or her adoptive parents as the real parents—the ones who raised, loved, fed, and clothed the child.

By forming a loving, secure relationship where none existed before, adoption mirrors God's love and concern that all may come to a saving knowledge of him. As one Caucasian adoptive father said of his Korean-born son, "He may not look like me, but he sure looks like my son."

DIGGING DEEPER

1. In what ways does human adoption resemble our adoption into God's family of faith? How is it different? See Ephesians 1:5.

2. What rights and responsibilities do we receive when we are adopted by God? See Galatians 4:5 and Romans 8:15.

3. Consider how attitudes about adoption may affect an adopted child and his parents. What could you say to an adoptive family to encourage and affirm them? See Ephesians 4:29–5:2.

him: [18]The eyes of your understanding being enlightened; that ye may know what is the hope of his calling, and what the riches of the glory of his inheritance in the saints, [19]And what *is* the exceeding greatness of his power to us-ward who believe, according to the working of his mighty power, [20]Which he wrought in Christ, when he raised him from the dead, and set *him* at his own right hand in the heavenly *places*, [21]Far above all principality, and power, and might, and dominion, and every name that is named, not only in this world, but also in that which is to come: [22]And hath put all *things* under his feet, and gave him *to be* the head over all *things* to the church, [23]Which is his body, the fulness of him that filleth all in all.

2

[1]And you *hath he quickened*, who were dead in trespasses and sins; [2]Wherein in time past ye walked according to the course of this world, according to the prince of the power of the air, the spirit that now worketh in the children of disobedience: [3]Among whom also we all had our conversation in times past in the lusts of our flesh, fulfilling the de-

Devotional Moment

Children Are Sinners, Too

2:1-3 "We started out bad, being born with evil natures, and were under God's anger just like everyone else." That sounds harsh, doesn't it? After all, who could look at a sweet, innocent infant and say he or she was born with an evil nature? Don't misunderstand—babies are sweet, lovable, and adorable. But they are also born into a sinful race. Don't be surprised when your child is rebellious or disobedient. It is human nature to be that way. You must lovingly, patiently, firmly, and consistently teach your children right from wrong. They won't learn it automatically.

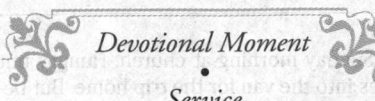

Devotional Moment
Service

2:8-10 Most of us struggle at one time or another with questions of meaning and purpose: Why am I here? What is my purpose in life? This passage won't tell you whether you are to be an entrepreneur or a biophysicist, but it does cut to the heart of the issue of why we are here: to spend our lives in helping others. All our careers, roles, and vocations need to be pursued with a view to serving God.

sires[a] of the flesh and of the mind; and were by nature the children of wrath, even as others.

[4]But God, who is rich in mercy, for his great love wherewith he loved us, [5]Even when we were dead in sins, hath quickened us together with Christ, (by grace ye are saved;) [6]And hath raised *us* up together, and made *us* sit together in heavenly *places* in Christ Jesus: [7]That in the ages to come he might shew the exceeding riches of his grace in *his* kindness toward us through Christ Jesus. [8]For by grace are ye saved through faith; and that not of yourselves: *it is* the gift of God: [9]Not of works, lest any man should boast. [10]For we are his workmanship, created in Christ Jesus unto good works, which God hath before ordained[b] that we should walk in them.

[11]Wherefore remember, that ye *being* in time past Gentiles in the flesh, who are called Uncircumcision by that which is called the Circumcision in the flesh made by hands; [12]That at that time ye were without Christ, being aliens from the commonwealth of Israel, and strangers from the covenants of promise, having no hope, and without God in the world: [13]But now in Christ Jesus ye who sometimes were far off are made nigh by the blood of Christ.

[14]For he is our peace, who hath made both one, and hath broken down the middle wall of partition *between us*; [15]Having abolished in his flesh the enmity, *even* the law of commandments *contained* in ordinances; for to make in himself of twain one new man, *so* making peace; [16]And that he might reconcile both unto God in one body by the cross, having slain the enmity thereby[c]: [17]And came and preached peace to you which were afar off, and to them that were nigh. [18]For through him we both have access by one Spirit unto the Father. [19]Now therefore ye are no more strangers and foreigners, but fellowcitizens with the saints, and of the household of God; [20]And are built upon the foundation of the apostles and prophets, Jesus Christ himself being the chief corner *stone*; [21]In whom all the building fitly framed together groweth unto an holy temple in the Lord: [22]In whom ye also are builded together for an habitation of God through the Spirit.

3

[1]For this cause I Paul, the prisoner of Jesus Christ for you Gentiles, [2]If ye have heard of the dispensation of the grace of God which is given me to you-ward: [3]How that by revelation he made known unto me the mystery; (as I

[a] desires: Gr. wills
[b] ordained: or, prepared
[c] thereby: or, in himself

Imagine This

by Ray Seldomridge

It's been a wonderful Sunday morning at church. Hungry but happy, your family piles into the van for the trip home. But before the first stoplight, your kids are at each other's throats.

"Ben shoved me."

"Well, John was leaning on me."

"That's 'cause he called me a ———."

What does it take? you wonder. *How can we ever get them to see what being a Christian is all about?*

There are many answers to that question, not the least of which is the consistent example of parents and friends who love Christ. But consider this prayer of the apostle Paul's: "The eyes of your understanding being enlightened; that ye may know what is the hope of his calling" (Eph. 1:18). The key is letting God enlighten us to the point where we can "see" what is up ahead—and that involves the imagination.

Only God can truly enable us to see the invisible. But there are steps we can take to exercise and develop our God-given imagination.

Expose yourself and your children to the Bible's stories as accounts of real human experience. The Bible is a collection of stories about real life, not just a textbook of information about God. Jump into those stories with both feet, seeing and hearing and testing and smelling and feeling all that the people themselves did when the events first happened. Make it your goal to relive their experiences as if they were your own.

If something about a story seems strange, consult Bible reference works—atlases, handbooks, dictionaries, and other sources that describe what life was like in those days. Get study tools that will allow you to step into the ancient world and hear God's Word just as they did then. Then when you read about the Israelites fleeing Egypt, you'll be able to picture several million people wandering across the hot desert on foot in sandals (see Num. 1:45-46).

Delve into other stories that convey the truth. A story doesn't have to be factual to tell a truth. In fact, a great storehouse of fiction awaits your discovery— stories that can powerfully awaken the hearts of children, young and old, to the central realities of life.

The first such books that come to my mind are C. S. Lewis's famous *Chronicles of Narnia.* Others include the George Macdonald novels edited for children by Bethany House (*At the Back of the North Wind, Alec Forbes and His Friend Annie, Adventures of Ranald Bannerman*), the newly edited classics series from Multnomah (*A Little Princess, Robinson Crusoe, Sir Gibbie, Little Women*), and the stories of such contemporary Christian writers as Sigmund Brouwer (*Accidental Detective* series, *Winds of Light* books), Denise Williamson (*Forbidden Gates, Chariot to China*), and Lois Walfrid Johnson (*Adventures in the North Woods*).

Many novels offer a Christian (or at least a highly moral) perspective. Examples include the works of Meindert De Jong, E. B. White, Beverly Cleary, Laura Ingalls Wilder, Katherine Paterson, and Robert McCloskey, plus biographies of famous Christians such as J. S. Bach, Florence Nightingale, and St. Augustine. (See Kathryn Lindskoog's *How to Grow a Young Reader* or Elizabeth Wilson's *Books Children Love* for more ideas.)

As you seek the best imaginary stories for your children, look for stories with interesting, believable characters with whom you and your children can identify. Avoid books that merely preach or moralize; they don't capture the imagination.

Wallpaper your children's minds with images from real life. In Sunday school, children learn about the Christian faith, but interacting with other believers of all ages enables them to *see* it in action. Remember the adage Faith is caught, not taught. Our children need to see examples of true Christian service from their own family life and the wider family of believers (including Sunday school teachers). They need to be present when the adults are praying, singing, or celebrating the Lord; when the homeless are served a meal; or even when Grandma goes home to be with the Lord.

Only when the light of God's love floods our heart will we begin to grasp the riches he has given us.

DIGGING DEEPER

1. Turn to any part of Matthew, Mark, Luke, or John. Then study how Jesus taught others. What did he say that you can picture in your mind? How did he use stories to communicate?

2. How does God capture our mind and heart? See 2 Corinthians 4:3-6 and Mark 12:29-30.

3. How do Christian relationships affect our understanding of God's love? See Ephesians 3:14-19, especially verse 17, keeping in mind that Paul was writing to the whole church at Ephesus.

wrote afore in few words, ⁴Whereby, when ye read, ye may understand my knowledge in the mystery of Christ) ⁵Which in other ages was not made known unto the sons of men, as it is now revealed unto his holy apostles and prophets by the Spirit; ⁶That the Gentiles should be fellowheirs, and of the same body, and partakers of his promise in Christ by the gospel: ⁷Whereof I was made a minister, according to the gift of the grace of God given unto me by the effectual working of his power. ⁸Unto me, who am less than the least of all saints, is this grace given, that I should preach among the Gentiles the unsearchable riches of Christ; ⁹And to make all *men* see what *is* the fellowship of the mystery, which from the beginning of the world hath been hid in God, who created all things by Jesus Christ: ¹⁰To the intent that now unto the principalities and powers in heavenly *places* might be known by the church the manifold wisdom of God, ¹¹According to the eternal purpose which he purposed in Christ Jesus our Lord: ¹²In whom we have boldness and access with confidence by the faith of him. ¹³Wherefore I desire that ye faint

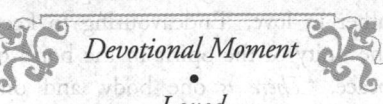

Devotional Moment

Loved

3:18-19 God's love so far surpasses our comprehension that Paul prayed for the Ephesian believers to have the power to grasp it! God has indeed loved us, and yet we easily let the breadth of his love escape our notice. It's all too easy to take love for granted—whether it's from God or from a human being. Sometimes along the way it pays to stop and think about it—and then say thank you, or, "I love you too." Does someone love you? Take a few minutes to let that person know it matters to you.

not at my tribulations for you, which is your glory.

[14]For this cause I bow my knees unto the Father of our Lord Jesus Christ, [15]Of whom the whole family in heaven and earth is named, [16]That he would grant you, according to the riches of his glory, to be strengthened with might by his Spirit in the inner man; [17]That Christ may dwell in your hearts by faith; that ye, being rooted and grounded in love, [18]May be able to comprehend with all saints what *is* the breadth, and length, and depth, and height; [19]And to know the love of Christ, which passeth knowledge, that ye might be filled with all the fulness of God. [20]Now unto him that is able to do exceeding abundantly above all that we ask or think, according to the power that worketh in us, [21]Unto him *be* glory in the church by Christ Jesus throughout all ages, world without end. Amen.

4

[1]I therefore, the prisoner of the Lord[a], beseech you that ye walk worthy of the vocation wherewith ye are called,

[2]With all lowliness and meekness, with longsuffering, forbearing one another in love; [3]Endeavouring to keep the unity of the Spirit in the bond of peace. [4]*There is* one body, and one Spirit, even as ye are called in one hope of your calling; [5]One Lord, one faith, one baptism, [6]One God and Father of all, who *is* above all, and through all, and in you all. [7]But unto every one of us is given grace according to the measure of the gift of Christ. [8]Wherefore he saith, When he ascended up on high, he led captivity[b] captive, and gave gifts unto men. [9](Now that he ascended, what is it but that he also descended first into the lower parts of the earth? [10]He that descended is the same also that ascended up far above all heavens, that he might fill[c] all things.) [11]And he gave some, apostles; and some, prophets; and some, evangelists; and some, pastors and teachers; [12]For the perfecting of the saints, for the work of the ministry, for the edifying of the body of Christ: [13]Till we all come in[d] the unity of the faith, and of the knowledge of the Son of God, unto a perfect man, unto the measure of the stature of the fulness of Christ: [14]That we *henceforth* be no more children, tossed to and fro, and carried about with every wind of doctrine, by the sleight of men, *and*

Devotional Moment

Special Abilities

4:7-13 When we hear the word *gifted,* we usually think of someone who is extremely good in sports, the arts, or math. But all of God's people are given at least one spiritual gift. (For more on these gifts, see Rom. 12:3-8 and 1 Cor. 12:4-11.) God gives us these gifts so that we can serve Christ better and build each other up. What is one way you can serve Christ with your gifts? Your church surely has ways for you to contribute: teaching Sunday school, writing responsive readings, setting up for a missions conference, ushering, helping in the nursery, and so on.

---

[a] of the Lord: or, in the Lord
[b] captivity . . . : or, a multitude of captives
[c] fill: or, fulfil
[d] in: or, into

cunning craftiness, whereby they lie in wait to deceive; [15]But speaking the truth in love, may grow up into him in all things, which is the head, *even* Christ: [16]From whom the whole body fitly joined together and compacted by that which every joint supplieth, according to the effectual working in the measure of every part, maketh increase of the body unto the edifying of itself in love.

[17]This I say therefore, and testify in the Lord, that ye henceforth walk not as other Gentiles walk, in the vanity of their mind, [18]Having the understanding darkened, being alienated from the life of God through the ignorance that is in them, because of the blindness[e] of their heart: [19]Who being past feeling have given themselves over unto lasciviousness, to work all uncleanness with greediness. [20]But ye have not so learned Christ; [21]If so be that ye have heard him, and have been taught by him, as

---

Devotional Moment

•

Anger

4:26-27 If you become angry, you are not to sin by "nursing a grudge." It is important to understand that anger by itself is not sin. If it were, God would never be angry—and the Bible sometimes describes God as exactly that. Whenever we get angry, we need to guard how we express our anger and make sure we don't damage others. If your anger is out of control, seek help from a pastor or a Christian counselor. Whatever you do, don't try to pretend the anger isn't there. You cannot possibly get it under control until you acknowledge that it exists.

---

the truth is in Jesus: [22]That ye put off concerning the former conversation the old man, which is corrupt according to the deceitful lusts; [23]And be renewed in the spirit of your mind; [24]And that ye put on the new man, which after God is created in righteousness and true[f] holiness. [25]Wherefore putting away lying, speak every man truth with his neighbour: for we are members one of another. [26]Be ye angry, and sin not: let not the sun go down upon your wrath: [27]Neither give place to the devil. [28]Let him that stole steal no more: but rather let him labour, working with *his* hands the thing which is good, that he may have to give[g] to him that needeth. [29]Let no corrupt communication proceed out of your mouth, but that which is good to[h] the use of edifying, that it may minister grace unto the hearers. [30]And grieve not the holy Spirit of God, whereby ye are sealed unto the day of redemption. [31]Let all bitterness, and wrath, and anger, and clamour, and evil speaking, be put away from you, with all malice: [32]And be ye kind one to another, tenderhearted, forgiving one another, even as God for Christ's sake hath forgiven you.

5

[1]Be ye therefore followers of God, as dear children; [2]And walk in love, as Christ also hath loved us, and hath given himself for us an offering and a sacrifice to God for a sweetsmelling savour.

---

[e] blindness: or, hardness

[f] true . . . : or, holiness of truth

[g] to give: or, to distribute

[h] to . . . : or, to edify profitably

Family Traditions

Traditions for Two

EPHESIANS 5

Hold hands every day. Pray together every day.

Find a way to make your spouse laugh—clip a cartoon or copy down a joke you've heard and share it; read a funny story out loud.

When you've had a terrible, horrible, no-good, very bad day, ask gently for space and time to unwind.

Leave a bouquet of flowers or a little gift in the bathroom for your spouse if he or she has had to work late.

Sleep under the stars once each year—or at least gaze at them together.

Sit up late and read to each other.

Pamper your mate once a week with a special dinner (in or out), a lavish breakfast in bed, or an evening of a favorite activity.

Sometime tomorrow jot down a note of appreciation to your spouse, and hide it in his or her sock drawer.

Tell your spouse what you dreamed about last night.

When your spouse mentions something he or she really likes, buy it secretly, wrap it, and present it on the next gloomy day.

Keep a pad of paper or small chalkboard in your kitchen for leaving daily notes whenever you come and go without seeing each other. Use it to share your feelings, too.

Little courtesies go a long way: Say good morning, good night, and good-bye no matter how used you are to coming and going.

Bring a cup of tea or coffee to your spouse in bed when he or she is just waking up. Find other little comforts or pleasures that you can provide for each other.

Take care of little problems as soon as they arise. The effect of small irritations accumulates like interest. If something is broken, fix it; if a system doesn't work, find a better way; if there's a kink in the relationship, smooth it.

Read one or two books together each year—books that both of you have always wanted to read.

Surprise your spouse by doing something totally out of character or on a whim.

There are many ways to say, "I'm glad I married you," but the best is still the old-fashioned, sweet-to-the-ear phrase—spoken often and with feeling—"I love you."

³But fornication, and all unclean-ness, or covetousness, let it not be once named among you, as becometh saints; ⁴Neither filthiness, nor foolish talking, nor jesting, which are not con-venient: but rather giving of thanks. ⁵For this ye know, that no whoremon-ger, nor unclean person, nor covetous man, who is an idolater, hath any in-heritance in the kingdom of Christ and of God. ⁶Let no man deceive you with vain words: for because of these things cometh the wrath of God upon the children of disobedienceª. ⁷Be not ye therefore partakers with them. ⁸For ye were sometimes darkness, but now *are ye* light in the Lord: walk as chil-dren of light: ⁹(For the fruit of the Spirit *is* in all goodness and righteous-ness and truth;) ¹⁰Proving what is ac-ceptable unto the Lord. ¹¹And have no fellowship with the unfruitful works of darkness, but rather reprove *them*. ¹²For it is a shame even to speak of those things which are done of them in secret. ¹³But all things that are re-provedᵇ are made manifest by the light: for whatsoever doth make manifest is light. ¹⁴Wherefore he saith, Awake thou that sleepest, and arise from the dead, and Christ shall give thee light. ¹⁵See then that ye walk circumspectly, not as fools, but as wise, ¹⁶Redeeming the time, because the days are evil. ¹⁷Wherefore be ye not unwise, but un-derstanding what the will of the Lord *is*. ¹⁸And be not drunk with wine, wherein is excess; but be filled with the Spirit; ¹⁹Speaking to yourselves in psalms and hymns and spiritual songs,

Worship
in Your Home

COMMUNICATE WITH EACH OTHER DURING DEVOTIONS
Speaking to yourselves in psalms and hymns and spiritual songs, singing and making melody in your heart to the Lord.
Ephesians 5:19

Devotions offer the opportune time to open the communications pipeline—between the Lord and us and among friends and family members.

As we share our concerns with the Lord, we can also share them with one another. As we ask God for his help, we can ask one another for support and help. As we thank God and praise him, we can also express our thanks and appreciation to one another for gifts given, favors done, or for just who they are.

As we ask God for direction, counsel, and answers, we can also ask one another for suggestions, counsel, and advice. And as we seek to know God and his ways, we can through devotional times seek to know each other and delight in one another's ways.

Devotions give natural and meaningful opportunities to communicate with each other as well as with God.

ª disobedience: or, unbelief
ᵇ reproved: or, discovered

singing and making melody in your heart to the Lord; [20]Giving thanks always for all things unto God and the Father in the name of our Lord Jesus Christ;

[21]Submitting yourselves one to another in the fear of God. [22]Wives, submit yourselves unto your own husbands, as unto the Lord. [23]For the husband is the head of the wife, even as Christ is the head of the church: and he is the saviour of the body. [24]Therefore as the church is subject unto Christ, so *let* the wives *be* to their own husbands in every thing. [25]Husbands, love your wives, even as Christ also loved the church, and gave himself for it; [26]That he might sanctify and cleanse it with the washing of water by the word, [27]That he might present it to himself a glorious church, not having spot, or wrinkle, or any such thing; but that it should be holy and without blemish. [28]So ought men to love their wives as their own bodies. He that loveth his wife loveth himself. [29]For no man ever yet hated his own flesh; but nourisheth and cherisheth it, even as the Lord the church: [30]For we are members of his body, of his flesh, and of his bones. [31]For this cause shall a man leave his fa-

Devotional Moment

Submission

5:21 Paul began this passage on submission in specific relationships (5:21–6:9) by stating a principle for Christian living that applies to every believer: "Submitting yourselves one to another in the fear of God." The idea is simple: Show deference to others; respect them. It's an important part of every relationship, especially at home.

Devotional Moment

Husbands and Wives

5:22-33 This section on marriage sets out two broad guidelines for how husbands and wives need to relate to one another: (1) *The wife's responsibility* is to honor her husband and submit to his leadership. (2) *The husband's responsibility* is to honor his wife and love her as Christ loves the church. It is possible to misinterpret and abuse both of these; unfortunately, churches are filled with Christian couples and divorced people who are living proof of that. But if these principles are taken seriously and applied with integrity, they are a tremendous foundation for a Christian marriage. Honor your spouse as God has directed.

ther and mother, and shall be joined unto his wife, and they two shall be one flesh. [32]This is a great mystery: but I speak concerning Christ and the church. [33]Nevertheless let every one of you in particular so love his wife even as himself; and the wife *see* that she reverence *her* husband.

6

[1]Children, obey your parents in the Lord: for this is right. [2]Honour thy father and mother; (which is the first commandment with promise;) [3]That it may be well with thee, and thou mayest live long on the earth. [4]And, ye fathers, provoke not your children to wrath: but bring them up in the nurture and admonition of the Lord. [5]Servants, be obedient to them that are *your* masters according to the flesh, with fear and trembling, in singleness of your heart, as unto Christ; [6]Not with eyeservice, as menpleasers; but as the servants of Christ, doing the will of God from the heart; [7]With good will doing service, as to the Lord, and not to men: [8]Knowing

that whatsoever good thing any man doeth, the same shall he receive of the Lord, whether *he be* bond or free. [9]And, ye masters, do the same things unto them, forbearing[a] threatening: knowing that your Master also is in heaven; neither is there respect of persons with him.

[10]Finally, my brethren, be strong in the Lord, and in the power of his might. [11]Put on the whole armour of God, that ye may be able to stand against the wiles of the devil. [12]For we wrestle not against flesh[b] and blood, but against principalities, against powers, against the rulers of the darkness of this world, against spiritual wickedness in high *places*. [13]Wherefore take unto you the whole armour of God, that ye may be able to withstand in the evil day, and having done all, to stand. [14]Stand therefore, having your loins girt about with truth, and having on the breastplate of righteousness; [15]And your feet shod with the preparation of the gospel of peace; [16]Above all, taking the shield of faith, wherewith ye shall be able to quench all the fiery darts of the wicked. [17]And take the helmet of salvation, and the sword of the Spirit, which is the word of God: [18]Praying always with all prayer and supplication in the Spirit, and watching thereunto with all perseverance and supplication for all saints;

[19]And for me, that utterance may be given unto me, that I may open my mouth boldly, to make known the mystery of the gospel, [20]For which I am an ambassador in bonds[c]: that therein I may speak boldly, as I ought to speak. [21]But that ye also may know my affairs, *and* how I do, Tychicus, a beloved brother and faithful minister in the Lord, shall make known to you all things: [22]Whom I have sent unto you for the same purpose, that ye might know our affairs, and *that* he might comfort your hearts. [23]Peace *be* to the brethren, and love with faith, from God the Father and the Lord Jesus Christ. [24]Grace *be* with all them that love our Lord Jesus Christ in sincerity[d]. Amen.

[To *the* Ephesians written from Rome, by Tychicus.]

---

[a] forbearing: or, moderating
[b] flesh . . . : Gr. blood and flesh
[c] in bonds: or, in a chain
[d] in sincerity: or, with incorruption

PHILIPPIANS

Purpose
To thank the Philippians for the gift they had sent him and to strengthen these believers by showing them that true joy comes from Jesus Christ alone

Author
Paul

To Whom Written
The Christians at Philippi

Date Written
About A.D. 61, from Rome, during Paul's imprisonment there

Setting
Paul and his companions founded the church at Philippi on his second missionary journey (Acts 16:11-40). This was the first church established on the European continent. The Philippian church had sent a gift with Epaphroditus (one of their members) to be delivered to Paul (4:18). Paul was in a Roman prison at the time. He wrote this letter to thank them for their gift and to encourage them in their faith.

Key Verse
"Rejoice in the Lord alway: and again I say, Rejoice" (4:4).

Key People
Paul, Timothy, Epaphroditus, Euodias, Syntyche, and Clement

Key Place
Philippi

". . . and may we never hurt at all. Amen."

What a strange prayer. To ask God to keep all hurts away seems silly since small hurts are common and even healthy, as in muscles that ache after a bike ride or C-minuses that remind us to study harder. Yet often we assume that all hurts are bad. We want to pray them away.

Almost every TV commercial, billboard, political speech, greeting card, and celebrity testimonial encourages this. They picture life as best when hurts have vanished. Ease and pleasure are said to define the good life. And so we pray. . . .

But Philippians cuts closer to real life. Hurts will come, as the apostle Paul knows full well. Stoics stand firm and take the punches as bad luck or fate, in either case unavoidable. Optimists search for a silver lining. Pragmatists figure that the law of averages will turn in their favor eventually. What should Christians think? How should a Christian respond to the hurts of life?

When we struggle to face hurts with confidence in God's care, we will find no better resource than Philippians. Each verse speaks of a loving Savior whose concern for us towers high above all hurts. Children need to know that hurts will come, and when they do, God can be depended on. Come to think of it, adults can use a reminder on that point, too.

1

¹Paul and Timotheus, the servants of Jesus Christ, to all the saints in Christ Jesus which are at Philippi, with the bishops and deacons: ²Grace *be* unto you, and peace, from God our Father, and *from* the Lord Jesus Christ.

³I thank my God upon every remembrance[a] of you, ⁴Always in every prayer of mine for you all making request with joy, ⁵For your fellowship in the gospel from the first day until now; ⁶Being confident of this very thing, that he which hath begun a good work in you will perform[b] *it* until the day of Jesus Christ:

⁷Even as it is meet for me to think this of you all, because I have[c] you in my heart; inasmuch as both in my bonds, and in the defence and confirmation of the gospel, ye all are partakers of my grace. ⁸For God is my record, how greatly I long after you all in the bowels of Jesus Christ.

⁹And this I pray, that your love may abound yet more and more in knowledge and *in* all judgment[d]; ¹⁰That ye may approve[e] things that are excellent; that ye may be sincere and without offence till the day of Christ; ¹¹Being filled with the fruits of righteousness, which are by Jesus Christ, unto the glory and praise of God.

¹²But I would ye should understand, brethren, that the things *which happened* unto me have fallen out rather unto the furtherance of the gospel; ¹³So that my bonds in Christ[f] are manifest in all the palace, and in all other *places*; ¹⁴And many of the brethren in the Lord, waxing confident by my bonds, are much more bold to speak the word without fear. ¹⁵Some indeed preach Christ even of envy and strife; and some also of good will: ¹⁶The one preach Christ of contention, not sincerely, supposing to add affliction to my bonds: ¹⁷But the other of love, knowing that I am set for the defence of the gospel. ¹⁸What then? notwithstanding, every way, whether in pretence, or in truth, Christ is preached; and I therein do rejoice, yea, and will rejoice. ¹⁹For I know that this shall turn to my salvation through your prayer, and the supply of the Spirit of Jesus Christ, ²⁰According to my earnest expectation and *my* hope, that in nothing I shall be ashamed, but *that* with all boldness, as always, *so* now also Christ shall be magnified in my body, whether *it be* by life, or by death.

²¹For to me to live *is* Christ, and to die *is* gain. ²²But if I live in the flesh, this *is* the fruit of my labour: yet what I shall choose I wot not. ²³For I am in a strait betwixt two, having a desire to depart, and to be with Christ; which is far better: ²⁴Nevertheless to abide in the flesh *is* more needful for you. ²⁵And having this confidence, I know that I shall abide and continue with you all for your furtherance and joy of faith;

---

[a] remembrance: or, mention
[b] perform: or, finish
[c] I have . . . : or, ye have me in your heart
[d] judgment: or, sense
[e] approve: or, try
[f] in Christ: or, for Christ

This Is What We Live For

by Rolf Zettersten

It's called March Madness, and to millions of basketball fans it is the sporting event of the year. The National Collegiate Athletic Association selects America's top sixty-four teams and pits them in do-or-die contests. For several weeks the tournament is held in arenas across the country, and roundball fans are glued to their television sets.

The capper to March Madness is appropriately called the Final Four—when the surviving quartet of teams meets to determine the national champion. The site for this three- game play-off becomes a Mecca for basketball enthusiasts. One year I had the opportunity to attend the Final Four tournament at New Orleans, Louisiana, where more than eighty thousand fans gathered to celebrate and witness the sporting contest.

All the main events were held at the Superdome, a massive indoor coliseum that normally hosts professional football games. Even though I had no particular allegiance to any of the teams, it was not hard to get swept up in the excitement inside the enclosed stadium. Bands from each school blared fight songs as their respective supporters sang along. The cheerleaders motivated their fans to participate in chants and yells. People were dressed and painted in their team's colors.

Of course, once the games began, the cheering intensified. I was sitting in front of a large section of University of Michigan alumni. Every time their team scored, they applauded, hooted, and screamed as if their lives depended on it. Many of the fans brought signs with them that conveyed clever slogans.

I'll never forget one such poster because it suddenly brought me back to reality. At one point in the game, after the Michigan team made a comeback, one man got up from his seat and began parading up and down the aisles holding a large cardboard sign above his head with this message: This Is What We Live For.

Although many people in the crowd apparently agreed with his theme, it had an adverse effect on me. I suddenly had a healthy dose of proper perspective. I turned to my friend who was also reading the sign and said, "I'm sure glad this isn't what I live for."

I was reminded of the apostle Paul; if he had held a sign above his head, it would have said, "For to me, to live is Christ, and to die is gain" (Phil. 1:21). In other words, his existence had only one purpose—to serve and glorify God. And Paul viewed his inevitable death as a promotion because it would take him to the Lord's presence.

So what do we live for? "Opportunities for Christ." I believe they can begin at home, where we demonstrate our faith in simple, everyday ways. We live for accepting and loving our spouse. We live for teaching our children the wonderful truths of God's creation. We live for demonstrating God's forgiveness when our family members fail. We live for honoring our parents and grandparents. We live for supporting our relatives when they need help. We live for encouraging our children. We live for teaching them God's Word and leading them to faith in Christ. We live for enjoying quiet moments with loved ones. We live for laughter around the dinner table. We live for achieving the intimacy that God wants us to have. We live for demonstrating the benefits of a disciplined life-style. We live for modeling charity, hospitality, and equality to others outside our family circle.

Sure, I'm crazy about competitive sporting events. The Final Four, the World Series, the Super Bowl, the Stanley Cup, and the NBA Finals are thrilling highlights of every year. But they are nothing compared to the excitement of a family intent on living for God.

1. Scripture has much to say about what is truly important in life. Consult these references: Micah 6:8; John 15:7-12; Galatians 5:22-23; Ephesians 6:10-20.

2. What do you live for? Develop your own list of priorities and set them as goals for your family. Create a family document that begins with this phrase: "This year our family will live for these characteristics. . . ." Make sure they fit with the priorities and goals outlined in the Scriptures. Then have a discussion about how you can put these objectives into practice.

---

²⁶That your rejoicing may be more abundant in Jesus Christ for me by my coming to you again.

²⁷Only let your conversation be as it becometh the gospel of Christ: that whether I come and see you, or else be absent, I may hear of your affairs, that ye stand fast in one spirit, with one mind striving together for the faith of the gospel; ²⁸And in nothing terrified by your adversaries: which is to them an evident token of perdition, but to you of salvation, and that of God. ²⁹For unto you it is given in the behalf of Christ, not only to believe on him, but also to suffer for his sake; ³⁰Having the same conflict which ye saw in me, and now hear *to be* in me.

2

¹If *there be* therefore any consolation in Christ, if any comfort of love, if any fellowship of the Spirit, if any bowels and mercies, ²Fulfil ye my joy, that ye be likeminded, having the same love, *being* of one accord, of one mind. ³*Let* nothing *be done* through strife or vainglory; but in lowliness of mind let each esteem other better than themselves. ⁴Look not every man on his own things, but every man also on the things of others. ⁵Let this mind be in you, which was also in Christ Jesus: ⁶Who, being in the form of God, thought it not robbery to be equal with God: ⁷But made himself of no reputation, and took upon him the form of a servant, and was made in the likeness of men: ⁸And being found in fashionᵃ as a man, he humbled himself, and became obedient unto death, even the death of the cross. ⁹Wherefore God also hath highly exalted him, and given him a name which is above every name: ¹⁰That at the name of Jesus every knee should bow, of *things* in heaven, and *things* in earth, and *things* under the earth; ¹¹And *that* every tongue should confess that Jesus Christ *is* Lord, to the glory of God the Father.

¹²Wherefore, my beloved, as ye have always obeyed, not as in my presence only, but now much more in my absence, work out your own salvation with fear and trembling. ¹³For it is God which worketh in you both to will and to do of *his* good pleasure.

¹⁴Do all things without murmurings and disputings: ¹⁵That ye may be blameless and harmlessᵇ, the sons of God, with-

---

ᵃ fashion: or habit

ᵇ harmless: or, sincere

Learning To Be Content

by Kurt Bruner

Nothing in this life can bring a greater sense of joy and fulfillment than your family. At the same time, however, family life can be filled with the disappointment of unmet expectations. When the flame of romance dies, marriage becomes less than exciting. When the kids rebel, parental pride sours into the pain of rejection. When Dad's office hours increase and Mom's pile of laundry grows, the joys of companionship are overshadowed by the pressures of modern living. Disappointment can quickly replace the sense of satisfaction we desire.

How do we maintain our joy despite unmet expectations? How do we balance the hope of ideal family life with the reality of the daily grind? Is it possible to achieve contentment when our deepest longings are unfulfilled?

The apostle Paul shared some key insights about fulfillment in life regardless of our circumstances. Imprisoned in Rome for the crime of sharing his faith, Paul revealed the secret of contentment. He said that he had learned to be content in every situation. He had experienced poverty and wealth, going hungry and eating well, the praise of people, and the stones of an angry mob. He had endured both good and bad, maintaining a deep sense of satisfaction throughout. What was his secret?

First, Paul did not depend upon other people or circumstances for his satisfaction. The word *contentment* in this passage comes from a compound word that suggests selfsufficiency. In other words, we can find contentment apart from external factors—primarily due to the sense of purpose and identity we experience in our relationship with God. If we depend on a mate to meet our emotional needs, we will be disappointed no matter how hard he or she tries. If we tie our identity to well-behaved and loving children, we will face disillusionment when they rebel. If our standard of living must reach a certain level before we can be happy, we will never arrive. According to Paul, contentment does not come from such external factors.

Second, Paul said that he had learned to be content *in* every situation—not *with* every situation. There is a vast difference between being fulfilled in spite of circumstances and pretending that the bad things in our life are pleasant. If your marriage is falling apart, seek counseling to improve it. If your children misbehave, discipline them. If your job pays too little for a decent life-style, seek a better one. Don't confuse contentment with either complacency or denial. Seek to improve your circumstances while not letting them undermine your sense of peace and contentment.

Finally, Paul had confidence that he could endure anything through his dependence on Christ. In this context, we can understand Paul's intended message: We can cope with any circumstance that comes our way when we are self-sufficient in Christ's sufficiency. We are able to endure anything, not in our own strength, but in the confidence of our relationship to the Lord. No matter who may hurt us, he will be there to comfort us. Regardless of what may go wrong, he will work good out of it. Despite the disappointment of unmet expectations, he offers us the ability to experience contentment in less than ideal circumstances. We can endure anything through his strength and overcome anything through his provision.

Learned contentment is fundamental to long-term family commitment and fulfillment. Once we find contentment apart from relationships, our relationships improve. We no longer look to our mate or children to meet our needs but rather seek to meet the needs of others. When we are content regardless of circumstances, circumstances no longer dictate our level of joy. We can then work to improve the bad things without relying upon improvement for our happiness. Contentment frees us to pursue the best in life with the right motivation and to endure the worst in life with the right attitude.

Don't allow the mundane or the frantic to rob you of a joyful family life. Don't let the hope of "someday" distract you from the blessings of today. Trust in the Lord when circumstances don't cooperate with your plans. Learned contentment is the key to satisfaction and success in family life.

DIGGING DEEPER

1. What lessons do we learn from Christ's teachings about being content with our financial situation? See Matthew 6:19-34.

2. Who is the ultimate source of our happiness? Hebrews 13:5-6 helps us put our desires into proper perspective.

---

out rebuke, in the midst of a crooked and perverse nation, among whom ye shine as lights in the world; [16]Holding forth the word of life; that I may rejoice in the day of Christ, that I have not run in vain, neither laboured in vain. [17]Yea, and if I be offered[c] upon the sacrifice and service of your faith, I joy, and rejoice with you all. [18]For the same cause also do ye joy, and rejoice with me. [19]But[d] I trust in the Lord Jesus to send Timotheus shortly unto you, that I also may be of good comfort, when I know your state. [20]For I have no man likeminded[e], who will naturally care for your state. [21]For all seek their own, not the things which are Jesus Christ's. [22]But ye know the proof of him, that, as a son with the father, he hath served with me in the gospel. [23]Him therefore I hope to send presently, so soon as I shall see how it will go with me. [24]But I trust in the Lord that I also myself shall come shortly. [25]Yet I supposed it necessary to send to you Epaphroditus, my brother, and companion in labour, and fellowsoldier, but your messenger, and he that ministered to my wants. [26]For he longed after you all, and was full of heaviness, because that ye had heard that he had been sick. [27]For indeed he was sick nigh unto death: but God had mercy on him; and not on him only, but on me also, lest I should have sorrow upon sorrow. [28]I sent him therefore the more carefully, that, when ye see him

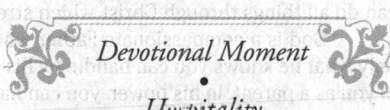

Devotional Moment

Hospitality

2:28-30 Epaphroditus, a faithful worker for God, had been quite ill. Paul urged the church to shelter and support this brother in Christ. Every Christian home can be a haven for God's workers. To be hospitable is to offer a home away from home—to meet needs and offer rest for tired folk. Consider how you could help church workers, missionaries, and others in ministry who need a place to stay. You'll experience the joy of helping, and learn from their ministry.

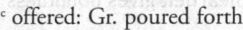

[c] offered: Gr. poured forth

[d] But: or, Moreover

[e] likeminded: or, so dear unto me

You Can Do All Things . . . Even with a Disability

by Joni Eareckson Tada

The rain pattered against the windows of the church meeting room, yet the feeling inside was warm and comfortable. After I finished my short speech and prayed, the small group of young people with disabilities began asking me questions. A teenager with cerebral palsy asked, "Joni, I've been quoting Philippians 4:13 for years, telling people I can do all things through Christ who strengthens me. But lately it's hit me that . . ." She paused, looked down at her paralyzed legs, then continued, "I *can't* do all things. I can't walk, I can't drive, I can't be like my friends. I don't get it."

I grinned and shook my head. I identified. There are plenty of activities in which I can't participate. I can't peel an orange, play a piano, or tie my shoes. The list of "I can'ts" would fill pages.

But Philippians 4:13 isn't an against-all-odds guarantee that you can do everything you want. It is a promise that you can do everything God *asks* you to do. How? With the help of Christ, who gives you strength and power.

That's a big promise, especially if you are the parent of a little boy or girl with spina bifida, cystic fibrosis, cerebral palsy, or muscular dystrophy. Your heart breaks when you see other children race across a field after a soccer ball. You lie awake at night wondering whether your child's friends will stick by them. And then, when you hear your handicapped child cough and cry at 2:00 A.M., you wonder how you will find the strength to stumble out of bed and face another night.

I can't do everything! True, you can't. It's impossible to be a super mom or dad who can successfully juggle every therapy appointment, insurance form, leg brace, need of your spouse, sibling's jealousy, or pitiful remark from well-meaning friends. You can't do everything.

But you *can* tackle the task God has placed squarely in front of you as you wholly depend upon Jesus for all the power. That's really what Paul was saying in Philippians 4:13: "I can do all things through Christ which strengtheneth me."

God is a compassionate Father who understands your limitations; he will ask of you only what he knows you can handle by his grace. In his strength, you can do what's expected of you as a parent. In his power, you can have energy for the responsibilities at hand. You can have wisdom for the daily problems, and your patience can grow into hard-won endurance. In his rest, you can discover deep and abiding peace. In his comfort, you can humble yourself and ask for help, which you may find in a parent support group, caring church, or friendly neighbor.

Through Christ, you can draw upon his limitless resources for every spiritual, emotional, and physical need. You can even let go of the pain you've been carrying on behalf of your disabled child as you trust that your boy or girl will find his or her own strength in Christ.

Perhaps you, like the teenager with cerebral palsy, are asking, "Exactly how do I find this grace? I'm so weak. I still feel overwhelmed by all the things I can't do."

My point exactly. When we realize that we have nowhere else to go, we are often driven to our knees. It is when we take the focus off our "can't do" list and fix our eyes on Jesus that we see him as our power supply. Deep and abiding devotion to the Lord energizes service that is tiring or rigorous. Affection for him that is warm and heartfelt gives boundless joy to every task. You can handle everything God expects you to do when you have a deep and personal union with the Lord.

Some would say it this way: I can see this task as an opportunity to draw closer to the Lord, a chance to draw on his grace. I can handle everything he puts in my path. And I can do it with a smile.

And the miracle? You will be able to smile, not in spite of that wheelchair in your family, but because of it.

DIGGING DEEPER

1. A disability doesn't have to be a minus in a family; it can be a plus. Read 2 Corinthians 12:9-10 and learn why.

2. The good news is that diseases and disabilities will not last forever. Read Isaiah 35:1-6 and be reminded of what's coming in the future.

---

again, ye may rejoice, and that I may be the less sorrowful. ²⁹Receive him therefore in the Lord with all gladness; and hold[f] such in reputation: ³⁰Because for the work of Christ he was nigh unto death, not regarding his life, to supply your lack of service toward me.

3

¹Finally, my brethren, rejoice in the Lord. To write the same things to you, to me indeed *is* not grievous, but for you *it is* safe. ²Beware of dogs, beware of evil workers, beware of the concision. ³For we are the circumcision, which worship God in the spirit, and rejoice in Christ Jesus, and have no confidence in the flesh.

⁴Though I might also have confidence in the flesh. If any other man thinketh that he hath whereof he might trust in the flesh, I more: ⁵Circumcised the eighth day, of the stock of Israel, *of* the tribe of Benjamin, an Hebrew of the Hebrews; as touching the law, a Pharisee; ⁶Concerning zeal, persecuting the church; touching the righteousness which is in the

law, blameless. ⁷But what things were gain to me, those I counted loss for Christ. ⁸Yea doubtless, and I count all things *but* loss for the excellency of the knowledge of Christ Jesus my Lord: for whom I have suffered the loss of all things, and do count them *but* dung, that I may win Christ,

Devotional Moment

•

The Past

3:12-14 If he had dwelled on his past, Paul could have bogged down in guilt and regrets deeper than a desert well. Instead, he chose to live in the present reality of Christ's forgiveness and to work toward new goals. And he encouraged the Philippians to do likewise. Everyone has something to regret, but God urges us to learn from our mistakes, to put them behind us, and to move on in his grace. Even our biggest mistakes—or at least the ones that weigh most heavily on our mind—don't have to hinder us. Once we have confessed them, God has forgiven us, and we do not need to let them hold us back. In what relationships or responsibilities do you feel the weight of the past? Confess them to God and put the matter behind you. Then begin working on a new skill, a new character trait, a new goal.

---

[f] hold . . . : or, honour such

⁹And be found in him, not having mine own righteousness, which is of the law, but that which is through the faith of Christ, the righteousness which is of God by faith: ¹⁰That I may know him, and the power of his resurrection, and the fellowship of his sufferings, being made conformable unto his death; ¹¹If by any means I might attain unto the resurrection of the dead. ¹²Not as though I had already attained, either were already perfect: but I follow after, if that I may apprehend that for which also I am apprehended of Christ Jesus. ¹³Brethren, I count not myself to have apprehended: but *this* one thing *I do*, forgetting those things which are behind, and reaching forth unto those things which are before, ¹⁴I press toward the mark for the prize of the high calling of God in Christ Jesus.

¹⁵Let us therefore, as many as be perfect, be thus minded: and if in any thing ye be otherwise minded, God shall reveal even this unto you. ¹⁶Nevertheless, whereto we have already attained, let us walk by the same rule, let us mind the same thing.

¹⁷Brethren, be followers together of me, and mark them which walk so as ye have us for an ensample. ¹⁸(For many walk, of whom I have told you often, and now tell you even weeping, *that they are* the enemies of the cross of Christ: ¹⁹Whose end *is* destruction, whose God *is their* belly, and *whose* glory *is* in their shame, who mind earthly things.) ²⁰For our conversationᵃ is in heaven; from whence also we look for the Saviour, the Lord Jesus Christ: ²¹Who shall change our vile body, that

it may be fashioned like unto his glorious body, according to the working whereby he is able even to subdue all things unto himself.

4

¹Therefore, my brethren dearly beloved and longed for, my joy and crown, so stand fast in the Lord, *my* dearly beloved. ²I beseech Euodias, and beseech Syntyche, that they be of the same mind in the Lord. ³And I intreat thee also, true yokefellow, help those women which laboured with me in the gospel, with Clement also, and *with* other my fellowlabourers, whose names *are* in the book of life. ⁴Rejoice in the Lord alway: *and* again I say, Rejoice. ⁵Let your moderation be known unto all men. The Lord *is* at hand. ⁶Be careful for nothing; but in every thing by prayer and supplication with thanksgiving let your requests be made known unto God. ⁷And the peace of God, which passeth all understanding, shall keep your hearts and minds through Christ Jesus. ⁸Finally, brethren, whatso-

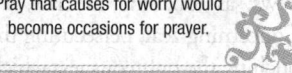

Devotional Moment
•
Don't Worry—Pray

4:6-7 Paul wrote that believers should not worry about *anything* but should pray about their concerns. The promise: that they would experience God's peace. Though most of us know that prayer is basic to the Christian life, we sometimes forget that it remains one of our most potent defenses against the parasites that infect our peace of mind. God promises that we can have peace of mind for the big and small concerns we have. Pray that causes for worry would become occasions for prayer.

ᵃ conversation . . . : or, we live or conduct ourselves as citizens of heaven, or, for obtaining heaven

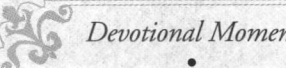

Devotional Moment

•

Think about It

4:8 Paul challenged the Philippians to refine their thinking—to think about the pure ways of Christ. Some people say that our environment doesn't affect us—that what we see and hear really has no impact on us. They are wrong. Countering the bombardment of unholy ideas and images on our mind every day requires conscious effort. If we do nothing to control what we think about, the things we see and hear will have us thinking about sexual immorality, greed, selfishness, vulgarity, and violence on a regular basis. To take back our mind, we need consciously to think about whatever is true and good and right. What fills your mind each day? Focus your thoughts on the pure ways of Christ. Encourage the others to do the same by holding devotions, reading passages from the Bible together, memorizing Scripture, and choosing carefully what you watch and listen to.

ever things are true, whatsoever things *are* honest[a], whatsoever things *are* just, whatsoever things *are* pure, whatsoever things *are* lovely, whatsoever things *are* of good report; if *there be* any virtue, and if *there be* any praise, think on these things. ⁹Those things, which ye have both learned, and received, and heard, and seen in me, do: and the God of peace shall be with you.

¹⁰But I rejoiced in the Lord greatly, that now at the last your care of me hath flourished again; wherein ye were also careful, but ye lacked opportunity. ¹¹Not that I speak in respect of want: for I have learned, in whatsoever state I am, *there-*

with to be content. ¹²I know both how to be abased, and I know how to abound: every where and in all things I am instructed both to be full and to be hungry, both to abound and to suffer need. ¹³I can do all things through Christ which strengtheneth me. ¹⁴Notwithstanding ye have well done, that ye did communicate with my affliction. ¹⁵Now ye Philippians know also, that in the beginning of the gospel, when I departed from Macedonia, no church communicated with me as concerning giving and receiving, but ye only. ¹⁶For even in Thessalonica ye sent once and again unto my necessity. ¹⁷Not because I desire a gift: but I desire fruit that may abound to your account. ¹⁸But I have all[b], and abound: I am full, having received of Epaphroditus the things *which were sent* from you, an odour of a sweet smell, a sacrifice acceptable, well-pleasing to God. ¹⁹But my God shall supply all your need according to his riches in glory by Christ Jesus.

²⁰Now unto God and our Father *be* glory for ever and ever. Amen. ²¹Salute every saint in Christ Jesus. The brethren which are with me greet you. ²²All the saints salute you, chiefly they that are of Caesar's household. ²³The grace of our Lord Jesus Christ *be* with you all. Amen.

[To *the* Philippians written from Rome, by Epaphroditus.]

---

[a] honest: or, venerable
[b] I have all: or, I have received all

COLOSSIANS

Purpose
To combat errors in the church and to show that believers have everything they need in Christ

Author
Paul

To Whom Written
The church at Colosse, a city in Asia Minor

Date Written
About A.D. 60, during Paul's imprisonment in Rome

Key Verses
"For in him dwelleth all the fulness of the Godhead bodily. And ye are complete in him, which is the head of all principality and power" (2:9-10).

Key People
Paul, Timothy, Tychicus, Onesimus, Aristarchus, Mark, Epaphras, Luke, Demas, Nymphas

Key Places
Colosse, Laodicea (4:15-16)

Special Features
Christ is presented as having absolute supremacy and sole sufficiency. Colossians has similarities to Ephesians, probably because it was written at about the same time, but it has a different emphasis.

Suppose you come back from a dinner date, pay the baby-sitter and take her home, and go to bed. The next morning you discover that during your absence the children were converted to a strange new tattoo cult, and that they are now, in fact, covered with tattoos. Hold the phone! Stop the cameras!

In the city of Colosse, something like that happened. One of Paul's coworkers had founded the church there during their missionary travels. After they left, however, some weird people moved in to mess up their work. Rather abruptly, Paul's children in the faith were mixing the gospel with all sorts of strange ideas. Paul drafts a letter to urge these early Christians to recover what they had lost.

Most parents don't lose children overnight, but some do lose children—to values and life-styles, not just generationally different, but false and hurtful, far from God. That loss brings pain and guilt, often a long break in communication, and layers of hard feelings. What's to be done?

Paul's answer for the Colossian Christians was to refocus on Christ. So this letter emphasizes the wonder and power of Jesus, Son of God, Savior.

Families in trouble need a jump start toward recovery. Parents whose hearts are hurting need a power-packed remedy for healing. Children caught in a tattoo cult (of which there are many varieties) need a trustworthy leader who can wash the blues away.

Here he is!

1

¹Paul, an apostle of Jesus Christ by the will of God, and Timotheus *our* brother, ²To the saints and faithful brethren in Christ which are at Colosse: Grace *be* unto you, and peace, from God our Father and the Lord Jesus Christ.

³We give thanks to God and the Father of our Lord Jesus Christ, praying always for you, ⁴Since we heard of your faith in Christ Jesus, and of the love *which ye have* to all the saints, ⁵For the hope which is laid up for you in heaven, whereof ye heard before in the word of the truth of the gospel; ⁶Which is come unto you, as *it is* in all the world; and bringeth forth fruit, as *it doth* also in you, since the day ye heard *of it*, and knew the grace of God in truth: ⁷As ye also learned of Epaphras our dear fellowservant, who is for you a faithful minister of Christ; ⁸Who also declared unto us your love in the Spirit.

⁹For this cause we also, since the day we heard *it*, do not cease to pray for you, and to desire that ye might be filled with the knowledge of his will in all wisdom and spiritual understanding; ¹⁰That ye might walk worthy of the Lord unto all pleasing, being fruitful in every good work, and increasing in the knowledge of God; ¹¹Strengthened with all might, according to his glorious power, unto all patience and longsuffering with joyfulness;

¹²Giving thanks unto the Father, which hath made us meet to be partakers of the inheritance of the saints in light: ¹³Who hath delivered us from the power of darkness, and hath translated *us* into the kingdom of his[a] dear Son: ¹⁴In whom we have redemption through his blood, *even* the forgiveness of sins: ¹⁵Who is the image of the invisible God, the firstborn of every creature: ¹⁶For by him were all things created, that are in heaven, and that are in earth, visible and invisible, whether *they be* thrones, or dominions, or principalities, or powers: all things were created by him, and for him: ¹⁷And he is before all things, and by him all things consist. ¹⁸And he is the head of the body, the church: who is the beginning, the firstborn from the dead; that in[b] all *things* he might have the preeminence. ¹⁹For it pleased *the Father* that in him should all fulness dwell; ²⁰And, having made peace through the blood of his cross, by him to reconcile all things unto himself; by him, *I say*, whether *they be* things in earth, or things in heaven. ²¹And you, that were sometime alienated and enemies in *your* mind[c] by wicked works, yet now hath he reconciled ²²In the body of his flesh through death, to present you holy and unblameable and unreproveable in his sight: ²³If ye continue in the faith grounded and settled, and *be* not moved away from the hope of the gospel, which ye have heard, *and* which was preached to every creature which is under heaven; whereof I Paul am made a minister; ²⁴Who now rejoice in my sufferings for you, and fill up that which is behind of the afflictions of Christ in my flesh for his body's sake,

---

[a] his . . . : Gr. the Son of his love

[b] in . . . : or, among all

[c] in . . . : or, by your mind in

which is the church: ²⁵Whereof I am made a minister, according to the dispensation of God which is given to me for you, to fulfil[d] the word of God; ²⁶*Even* the mystery which hath been hid from ages and from generations, but now is made manifest to his saints: ²⁷To whom God would make known what *is* the riches of the glory of this mystery among the Gentiles; which is Christ in[e] you, the hope of glory: ²⁸Whom we preach, warning every man, and teaching every man in all wisdom; that we may present every man perfect in Christ Jesus: ²⁹Whereunto I also labour, striving according to his working, which worketh in me mightily.

2

¹For I would that ye knew what great conflict[a] I have for you, and *for* them at Laodicea, and *for* as many as have not seen my face in the flesh; ²That their hearts might be comforted, being knit together in love, and unto all riches of the full assurance of understanding, to the acknowledgement of the mystery of God, and of the Father, and of Christ; ³In whom[b] are hid all the treasures of wisdom and knowledge.

⁴And this I say, lest any man should beguile you with enticing words. ⁵For though I be absent in the flesh, yet am I with you in the spirit, joying and beholding your order, and the stedfastness of your faith in Christ. ⁶As ye have therefore received Christ Jesus the Lord, *so* walk ye in him: ⁷Rooted and built up in him, and stablished in

---

[d] to fulfil . . . : or, fully to preach the word

[e] in: or, among

[a] conflict: or, fear, or, care

[b] In whom: or, Wherein

the faith, as ye have been taught, abounding therein with thanksgiving. [8]Beware lest any man spoil you through philosophy and vain deceit, after the tradition of men, after the rudiments[c] of the world, and not after Christ. [9]For in him dwelleth all the fulness of the Godhead bodily. [10]And ye are complete in him, which is the head of all principality and power: [11]In whom also ye are circumcised with the circumcision made without hands, in putting off the body of the sins of the flesh by the circumcision of Christ: [12]Buried with him in baptism, wherein also ye are risen with *him* through the faith of the operation of God, who hath raised him from the dead.

[13]And you, being dead in your sins and the uncircumcision of your flesh, hath he quickened together with him, having forgiven you all trespasses; [14]Blotting out the handwriting of ordinances that was against us, which was contrary to us, and took it out of the way, nailing it to his cross; [15]*And* having spoiled principalities and powers, he made a shew of them openly, triumphing over them in it[d].

[16]Let no man therefore judge you in meat[e], or in drink, or in respect of an holyday, or of the new moon, or of the sabbath *days*: [17]Which are a shadow of things to come; but the body *is* of Christ. [18]Let no man beguile[f] you of your reward in a voluntary humility and worshipping of angels, intruding into those things which he hath not

---

[c] rudiments: or, elements

[d] in it: or, in himself

[e] in meat . . . : or, for eating and drinking

[f] beguile . . . : or, judge against you

Worship
in Your Home

VALUES, CHARACTER, AND DEVOTIONS— GROWING IN CHRIST

Rooted and built up in him, and stablished in the faith, as ye have been taught, abounding therein with thanksgiving.
Colossians 2:7

What would life be without honesty, truthfulness, faithfulness, love, patience, gentleness, and kindness? It would be like a brick building without the bricks. It is impossible to lead a good moral life without such values or character qualities.

When we live a godly life, we reflect strong moral and spiritual values. Where do we get those values? From Bible truths that have taken root in our character. Thus, the best source of value development is through Bible reading and Bible study—exactly what devotional times are.

Bible truths first shape our view of the world—our system of belief. Then we learn from the Bible what our response should be. These beliefs and convictions shape our character. Our values, in turn, become evident in our conduct: kindness, tenderness, faithfulness, truthfulness, and peacefulness.

In devotions, times when we all can reflect on the Word, we help each other form a Christian life view, a Christian character, and ultimately a Christian conduct.

That surely makes it worth having devotions regularly!

seen, vainly puffed up by his fleshly mind, [19]And not holding the Head, from which all the body by joints and bands having nourishment ministered, and knit together, increaseth with the increase of God. [20]Wherefore if ye be dead with Christ from the rudiments[g] of the world, why, as though living in the world, are ye subject to ordinances, [21](Touch not; taste not; handle not; [22]Which all are to perish with the using;) after the commandments and doctrines of men? [23]Which things have indeed a shew of wisdom in will worship, and humility, and neglecting[h] of the body; not in any honour to the satisfying of the flesh.

3

[1]If ye then be risen with Christ, seek those things which are above, where Christ sitteth on the right hand of God. [2]Set your affection[a] on things above, not on things on the earth. [3]For ye are dead, and your life is hid with Christ in God. [4]When Christ, *who is* our life, shall appear, then shall ye also appear with him in glory.

[5]Mortify therefore your members which are upon the earth; fornication, uncleanness, inordinate affection, evil concupiscence, and covetousness, which is idolatry: [6]For which things' sake the wrath of God cometh on the children of disobedience: [7]In the which ye also walked some time, when ye lived in them.

[8]But now ye also put off all these; anger, wrath, malice, blasphemy, filthy

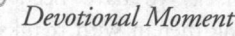

Devotional Moment
•
Family Honesty
3:9 "Don't tell lies to each other." People lie for many reasons: to save face, to cover up mistakes, to look and feel important. As Christians with a new life, we don't need those crutches. To defend or enrich ourselves by lying is to show fear and retreat from faith. The world needs people who love God and hate corruption and cover-up. These convictions are taught in homes that respect and encourage truth-telling. Let your children know that you value honesty. Encourage them to be honest even about disobedience by modifying your discipline in the face of an open confession. And most important, model honesty in your own dealings with family and strangers alike.

communication out of your mouth. [9]Lie not one to another, seeing that ye have put off the old man with his deeds; [10]And have put on the new *man*, which is renewed in knowledge after the image of him that created him: [11]Where there is neither Greek nor Jew, circumcision nor uncircumcision, Barbarian, Scythian, bond *nor* free: but Christ *is* all, and in all.

[12]Put on therefore, as the elect of God, holy and beloved, bowels of mercies, kindness, humbleness of mind, meekness, longsuffering; [13]Forbearing one another, and forgiving one another, if any man have a quarrel[b] against any: even as Christ forgave you, so also *do* ye. [14]And above all these things *put on* charity, which is the bond of perfectness. [15]And let the peace of God rule in your hearts, to the which also ye are called in one body; and be ye thankful. [16]Let the word of Christ dwell in you

---

[g] rudiments: or, elements
[h] neglecting: or, punishing, or, not sparing
[a] affection: or, mind
[b] quarrel: or, complaint

Sing Your Praises—and Blues—to the Lord

by Robert DeMoss, Jr.

There once lived a young, Godfearing teenager. Reared in a good home, this boy had some rather exceptional musical talents. The only problem was his boredom with the music played at his church. He probably wondered why his church seemed to specialize in antiquated styles when the world had such interesting music to offer. Worn out by constant complaining around the house, his father challenged him to write his own hymns. The year was 1690; the boy, Isaac Watts.

Responding to his father's prompting, Watts ultimately penned more than 350 hymns. Among them were "When I Survey the Wondrous Cross," "Joy to the World," and "O God, Our Help in Ages Past." It's amazing what can happen when we encourage the expression of music in our homes!

Granted, few children will respond to their parents' prompting by authoring a library of timeless Christian hymns. Nevertheless, advocating music in the home can produce a wide range of benefits for the entire family.

If we want the Word of God to enrich our life (Col. 3:16), what better way than through a song? I still remember a tune we sang as children, "This Little Light of Mine." Through this simple melody, my parents taught me the importance of being "salt and light" to the world—and of not letting Satan douse God's light within me.

Music in the home can also be an agent of peace. Some of my fondest childhood memories were of Mom and Dad sitting at the piano singing Scripture choruses. This nightly routine filled our home with a peaceful spirit, enabling us children to drift comfortably to sleep.

A third benefit of music in the home might not be apparent at first. Every family faces times of fear, uncertainty, even anger or disappointment. Perhaps these emotions are prompted by the loss of a loved one, extended unemployment, sickness, or even uncertainty about God's leading. Whatever the case, it's healthy to vocalize our blues to God. That's exactly what King David did on many occasions. In Psalm 13, for example, David wrote of his distress at God's apparent lack of response to David's fervent cries for help. We can also see David "singing the blues" in Psalm 42:3-6.

How can you get the entire family singing in chorus? Here are several ideas:

Start when they're young. Soft lullabies noting the assurance of God's love are more than music in a baby's tender ear—they are the starting place for an appreciation of Christian music in the home.

Pray in song. Consider singing a doxology or Scripture chorus as the family gathers around the dinner table.

Encourage musical "instruments." This may start with the youngest keeping time on pots and pans as you add the piano accompaniment.

Pave the way. Facilitate a child's interest in a musical instrument by offering to provide private instruction. And be sure to show up when it's time for the recital.

Set up a Sunday song session. Dedicate a portion of Sunday for a family sing-along. In our home, Dad played guitar and harmonica, my sister and a brother took to the piano, another brother and I played drums, while Mom kept us all on pitch.

Jesus was criticized for the crowds who sang his praise. "Some of the Pharisees from among the multitude said unto him, 'Master, rebuke thy disciples.' And he answered, 'I tell you that, if these should hold their peace, the stones would immediately cry out.' " (Luke 19:39-40).

Who wants to be upstaged by a rock? Using this text as background, contemporary songwriter James Ward penned a song with the declaration, "Ain't no rock gonna cry in my place!"

This passion for a musical expression can begin in your home today. Strike up the band!

DIGGING DEEPER

1. Have you ever heard a tree sing? According to 1 Chronicles 16:33 and Psalm 96:12, one day even trees will break out in song. What will prompt their song? And if trees will one day sing, what might be preventing your family from doing the same today?

2. In Psalm 150, how many different instruments does the psalmist urge us to incorporate into our personal worship? Why might God encourage us to express ourselves through a wide variety of musical instruments?

3. In Psalm 101:2-3, King David asked God to help him refuse "wicked" things. How might his example set the stage for appropriate musical selections in your home?

richly in all wisdom; teaching and admonishing one another in psalms and hymns and spiritual songs, singing with grace in your hearts to the Lord. ¹⁷And whatsoever ye do in word or deed, *do* all in the name of the Lord Jesus, giving thanks to God and the Father by him.

Devotional Moment

For Dads Only

3:21 Excessive scolding and criticizing can take the heart right out of a kid. Many dads sincerely want the best for their children but unintentionally discourage them by being unclear about the rules and inflicting harsh punishments. This makes them feel they can never do enough and are being treated unfairly.

There is a better way. Christian fathers can encourage children to reach for the best, help them stand up after a fall, show them how to live, and then leave them to stand with the help of God. A dad has a great opportunity to help his kids develop self-confidence and perseverance.

¹⁸Wives, submit yourselves unto your own husbands, as it is fit in the Lord. ¹⁹Husbands, love *your* wives, and be not bitter against them. ²⁰Children, obey *your* parents in all things: for this is well pleasing unto the Lord. ²¹Fathers, provoke not your children *to anger*, lest they be discouraged. ²²Servants, obey in all things *your* masters according to the flesh; not with eyeservice, as menpleasers; but in singleness of heart, fearing God: ²³And whatsoever ye do, do *it* heartily, as to the Lord, and not unto men; ²⁴Knowing that of the Lord ye shall receive the reward of the inheritance: for ye serve the Lord Christ. ²⁵But he that doeth wrong shall receive for the wrong which he hath done: and there is no respect of persons.

4

¹Masters, give unto *your* servants that which is just and equal; knowing that ye also have a Master in heaven.

Family Traditions

Traditions That Enhance Sibling Relationships

COLOSSIANS 3:12-17

The family is never static. It is constantly changing, always in process of becoming. Children grow and pass through stages of physical and personality development. Adults grow mentally and go through emotional changes. The relationships between individuals need constant adjusting. How can families facilitate those adjustments, particularly those between siblings?

"By being a consistent, bold example—or trying to," says Dale Rothburn of Dallas, Texas. "When there's any offense, any reason to react, we make a conscious effort to act calmly. And we compliment a lot, hoping the kids will pick up on our pride in each other. The younger the children, the more effective this is. We know—we have five."

It seems that the largest families enhance sibling relationships by finding ways to thrive in a kind of ordered disorder. They embrace the chaos, allowing themselves to mingle with each other in all sorts of ups and downs, crises, and the flow of daily life. "Hang on for the wild ride," they seem to say—and they enjoy it.

"We play a lot of team games and sports with our four sons," says a mom of four boys. "They need the action and competitive challenge. We hope they're picking up on strategies for working together at the same time."

The Griswald family of Tampa, Florida, has four daughters. "Verbal skills are our priority; girls tend to clobber each other with words. We're trying to emphasize listening skills, courtesy, and truth in all their interaction. Our girls are a lot of fun, but they tend to grow up learning to defend themselves rather than others. We keep reminding them of the larger picture."

A family is like a muscle. It grows strong and resilient through exercise. Practicing the skills of cooperation will make for peace at home and enable the family muscle to work for peace and justice in the world.

"We've memorized Colossians 3:12-17 as a family," says Ray Davidson of Los Angeles, father of four. "It's simple, straightforward, and deals with everyday feelings. My wife even wrote it out, framed it, and hung it in our kitchen. If called on, all the kids know it by heart now. I think it sinks into their lives a little deeper each year. Maybe, by the time they become young adults, it'll become second nature. Who knows?"

²Continue in prayer, and watch in the same with thanksgiving; ³Withal praying also for us, that God would open unto us a door of utterance, to speak the mystery of Christ, for which I am also in bonds: ⁴That I may make it manifest, as I ought to speak.

⁵Walk in wisdom toward them that are without, redeeming the time. ⁶Let your speech *be* alway with grace, seasoned with salt, that ye may know how ye ought to answer every man.

⁷All my state shall Tychicus declare unto you, *who is* a beloved brother, and a faithful minister and fellowservant in the Lord: ⁸Whom I have sent unto you for the same purpose, that he might know your estate, and comfort your hearts; ⁹With Onesimus, a faithful and beloved brother, who is *one* of you. They shall make known unto you all things which *are done* here. ¹⁰Aristarchus my fellowprisoner saluteth you, and Marcus, sister's son to Barnabas, (touching whom ye received commandments: if he come unto you, receive him;) ¹¹And Jesus, which is called Justus, who are of the circumcision. These only *are my* fellowworkers unto the kingdom of God, which have been a comfort unto me. ¹²Epaphras, who is *one* of you, a servant of Christ, saluteth you, always labouring fervently for you in prayers, that ye may stand perfect and complete in all the will of God. ¹³For I bear him record, that he hath a great zeal for you, and them *that are* in Laodicea, and them in Hierapolis. ¹⁴Luke, the beloved physician, and Demas, greet you. ¹⁵Salute the brethren which are in Laodicea, and Nymphas, and the church which is in his house. ¹⁶And when this epistle is read among you, cause that it be read also in the church of the Laodiceans; and that ye likewise read the *epistle* from Laodicea. ¹⁷And say to Archippus, Take heed to the ministry which thou hast received in the Lord, that thou fulfil it. ¹⁸The salutation by the hand of me Paul. Remember my bonds. Grace *be* with you. Amen.

[Written from Rome to Colossians by Tychicus and Onesimus.]

Devotional Moment

Words as Witness

4:6 Paul urged the Colossians to watch over their speech as closely as their actions and deeds. It's ironic, but as powerful as our actions are, so also are our words and speech. We will make a big difference today with the words we use to argue a point at work, to challenge a teacher's instruction, or to return a faulty item for refund. If those words are bitter, demeaning, or selfish, who will listen when we try to talk about the goodness of the Lord?

Words can change the world. Choose yours wisely for positive change and for personal integrity so that others—whether parents or children, friends or neighbors—will listen to all you have to say.

FIRST THESSALONIANS

Purpose
To strengthen the Thessalonian Christians in their faith and give them the assurance of Christ's return

Author
Paul

To Whom Written
The church at Thessalonica

Date Written
About A.D. 51 from Corinth; one of Paul's earliest letters

Setting
The church at Thessalonica was very young, having been established only two or three years before this letter was written. The Thessalonian Christians needed to mature in their faith.

Key Verse
"For if we believe that Jesus died and rose again, even so them also which sleep in Jesus will God bring with him" (4:14).

Key People
Paul, Timothy, Silas

Key Place
Thessalonica

Special Features
Paul received from Timothy a favorable report about the Thessalonians. However, he wrote this letter to correct their misconceptions about the resurrection and the second coming of Christ.

What grown child can ever forget that first visit home from college or the army or some other far-off assignment? Oh, how sweet that visit was! How eagerly those hugs were given and those fresh cookies served. How excited the conversation. How warm the feelings!

Paul's letter to the Thessalonian church was written to new Christians already under stress for their faith. They were unpopular and misunderstood; their neighbors were hostile; they needed a sense of home.

Paul writes to encourage them and, incidentally, to remind them of a great reunion yet to come, a hug-time supreme, a joy-time to make all others pale by comparison. This reunion will be orchestrated by God, with angels singing and no shortage of conversation. All the hurts of the journey will be forgotten in that welcome-home embrace. Separation will be ended; people and God will be together at last and always.

Who's serving the coffee at the end of your road? When the work is done, the bills are paid, the kids are raised, the miles are traveled, and the last checkout comes 'round, who's waiting up?

This book offers an awesome destination. Read about it gratefully, and anticipate more than you can ever imagine. Not a bad thing for a traveler to have—a place to call home.

1

¹Paul, and Silvanus, and Timotheus, unto the church of the Thessalonians *which is* in God the Father and *in* the Lord Jesus Christ: Grace *be* unto you, and peace, from God our Father, and the Lord Jesus Christ.

²We give thanks to God always for you all, making mention of you in our prayers; ³Remembering without ceasing your work of faith, and labour of love, and patience of hope in our Lord Jesus Christ, in the sight of God and our Father; ⁴Knowing, brethren belovedᵃ, your election of God. ⁵For our gospel came not unto you in word only, but also in power, and in the Holy Ghost, and in much assurance; as ye know what manner of men we were among you for your sake.

⁶And ye became followers of us, and of the Lord, having received the word in much affliction, with joy of the

Devotional Moment
Family Appreciation

1:2-3 Paul, Silas, and Timothy recognized and appreciated the Thessalonians' work and endurance, and they told them so. "Well done!" they said. They didn't just say vaguely, "You're wonderful" but listed specific traits for which they thanked God. All people need to know what they are doing right. Catch your family—children and parents, brothers and sisters, uncles and aunts—in the act of doing good. Call it to their attention and say, "That's really neat the way you did that." Encourage them when they show extra effort or display patience. Everybody appreciates a pat on the back, especially when they know what it's for.

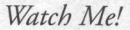

Devotional Moment
Watch Me!

1:5 The Thessalonians did not simply hear sermons or receive motivational letters from Paul. They observed his life and his faith, for he and his fellow missionaries lived among them. Thus, the gospel came alive to the new Christians because they had examples to follow. Just as the most moving sermon cannot compare with the power of a life of faith seen each day, speeches and scoldings communicate far less than your own example. Say little, show much.

Holy Ghost: ⁷So that ye were ensamples to all that believe in Macedonia and Achaia. ⁸For from you sounded out the word of the Lord not only in Macedonia and Achaia, but also in every place your faith to God-ward is spread abroad; so that we need not to speak any thing. ⁹For they themselves shew of us what manner of entering in we had unto you, and how ye turned to God from idols to serve the living and true God; ¹⁰And to wait for his Son from heaven, whom he raised from the dead, *even* Jesus, which delivered us from the wrath to come.

2

¹For yourselves, brethren, know our entrance in unto you, that it was not in vain: ²But even after that we had suffered before, and were shamefully entreated, as ye know, at Philippi, we were bold in our God to speak unto you the gospel of God with much contention. ³For our exhortation *was* not of deceit, nor of uncleanness, nor in guile: ⁴But as we were allowed of God to be put in

---

ᵃ beloved . . . : or, beloved of God, your election

trust with the gospel, even so we speak; not as pleasing men, but God, which trieth our hearts. [5]For neither at any time used we flattering words, as ye know, nor a cloke of covetousness; God *is* witness: [6]Nor of men sought we glory, neither of you, nor *yet* of others, when we might have been[a] burdensome, as the apostles of Christ.

[7]But we were gentle among you, even as a nurse cherisheth her children: [8]So being affectionately desirous of you, we were willing to have imparted unto you, not the gospel of God only, but also our own souls, because ye were dear unto us. [9]For ye remember, brethren, our labour and travail: for labouring night and day, because we would not be chargeable unto any of you, we preached unto you the gospel of God. [10]Ye *are* witnesses, and God *also*, how holily and justly and unblameably we behaved ourselves among you that believe: [11]As ye know how we exhorted and comforted and charged every one of you, as a father *doth* his children, [12]That ye would walk worthy of God, who hath called you unto his kingdom and glory.

[13]For this cause also thank we God without ceasing, because, when ye received the word of God which ye heard of us, ye received *it* not *as* the word of men, but as it is in truth, the word of God, which effectually worketh also in you that believe. [14]For ye, brethren, became followers of the churches of God which in Judaea are in Christ Jesus: for ye also have suffered like things of your own country-men, even as they *have* of the Jews: [15]Who both killed the Lord Jesus, and their own prophets, and have persecuted us[b]; and they please not God, and are contrary to all men: [16]Forbidding us to speak to the Gentiles that they might be saved, to fill up their sins alway: for the wrath is come upon them to the uttermost.

[17]But we, brethren, being taken from you for a short time in presence, not in heart, endeavoured the more abundantly to see your face with great desire. [18]Wherefore we would have come unto you, even I Paul, once and again; but Satan hindered us. [19]For what *is* our hope, or joy, or crown of rejoicing[c]? *Are* not even ye in the presence of our Lord Jesus Christ at his coming? [20]For ye are our glory and joy.

3

[1]Wherefore when we could no longer forbear, we thought it good to be left at Athens alone; [2]And sent Timotheus, our brother, and minister of God, and our fellowlabourer in the gospel of Christ, to establish you, and to comfort you concerning your faith: [3]That no man should be moved by these afflictions: for yourselves know that we are appointed thereunto. [4]For verily, when we were with you, we told you before that we should suffer tribulation; even as it came to pass, and ye know. [5]For this cause, when I could no longer forbear, I sent to know your faith, lest by some means the tempter have tempted you, and our labour be in vain.

[6]But now when Timotheus came

---

[a] been . . . : or, used authority
[b] persecuted us: or, chased us out
[c] rejoicing: or, glorying

from you unto us, and brought us good tidings of your faith and charity, and that ye have good remembrance of us always, desiring greatly to see us, as we also *to see* you: [7]Therefore, brethren, we were comforted over you in all our affliction and distress by your faith: [8]For now we live, if ye stand fast in the Lord. [9]For what thanks can we render to God again for you, for all the joy wherewith we joy for your sakes before our God; [10]Night and day praying exceedingly that we might see your face, and might perfect that which is lacking in your faith?

[11]Now God himself and our Father, and our Lord Jesus Christ, direct[a] our way unto you. [12]And the Lord make you to increase and abound in love one toward another, and toward all *men*, even as we *do* toward you: [13]To the end he may stablish your hearts unblameable in holiness before God, even our Father, at the coming of our Lord Jesus Christ with all his saints[b].

4

[1]Furthermore then we beseech[a] you, brethren, and exhort *you* by the Lord Jesus, that as ye have received of us how ye ought to walk and to please God, *so* ye would abound more and more. [2]For ye know what commandments we gave you by the Lord Jesus. [3]For this is the will of God, *even* your sanctification, that ye should abstain from fornication: [4]That every one of you should know

how to possess his vessel in sanctification and honour; [5]Not in the lust of concupiscence, even as the Gentiles which know not God: [6]That no *man* go beyond and defraud[b] his brother in *any* matter: because that the Lord *is* the avenger of all such, as we also have forewarned you and testified. [7]For God hath not called us unto uncleanness, but unto holiness. [8]He therefore that despiseth[c], despiseth not man, but God, who hath also given unto us his holy Spirit.

[9]But as touching brotherly love ye need not that I write unto you: for ye

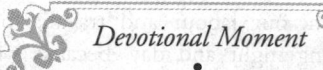

Devotional Moment

•

Purity

4:3-8 The Thessalonians faced temptations and threats to sexual purity just as surely as they were human. Teen pregnancies? Adultery? Rocky marriages? Yes, they had to deal with all of these just as we do. Paul called them to sexual purity— to restrain sexual desires, to reserve sexual expression for marriage, and to respect one another's marriage vows. Paul emphasized that these were God's ideals, not just his. Sexual purity is God's ideal for us.

When we obey God's instructions for its expression, sexual intimacy becomes a powerful force that creates a strong bond between husbands and wives. Don't place yourself in situations that tempt you to compromise God's design for your sexuality. If you are married, make it your goal to please your mate. At the same time, respect your spouse's body and control your own passions, with God's help. Don't use sex as a weapon or a tool for getting what you want. Let us honor God's design for sexual intimacy.

---

[a] direct: or, guide
[b] saints: or, holy ones, or, angels
[a] beseech: or, request
[b] defraud: or, oppress, or, overreach
[c] despiseth: or, rejecteth

Life in the Fast Lane

by Dr. Archibald Hart

Sixty-five million Americans (almost one person in four) have high blood pressure. Fifty million have problems with sleep. Forty million suffer from some form of anxiety disorder. Untold millions are troubled with headaches, ulcers, back pain, and tension. This is an overstressed culture.

What does the Bible have to say about this? "That ye study to be quiet, and to do your own business, and to work with your own hands" (1 Thess. 4:11).

Living a quiet life cuts right to the core of the stress problem because all stress problems have one central cause: *overarousal*. Whenever we are faced with demands or pressures, our body makes adrenaline. That's good because adrenaline gives us energy to respond. But too much adrenaline for too long is destructive. Even if the pressures are good experiences, such as being excited about a project or challenged in competition, the constant release of adrenaline can lead to many distressing consequences, including the most serious of all—heart attacks.

So God tells us that our ambition should be to live a quiet life. First Thessalonians 5:16-18 adds: "Rejoice evermore. Pray without ceasing. In every thing give thanks: for this is the will of God in Christ Jesus concerning you."

These injunctions are the soundest advice I have ever encountered on how to counteract the ravaging effects of stress. The antidote for high stress is simply this: Live a quiet life, be joyful, keep on praying, and be thankful.

What does this say to us as parents? If we are guilty of living in the fast lane, we need to make our home a "haven of rest" where we can find refuge and live at a healthy pace. Fast-track living is contagious. Children catch it from their parents. So if a home is hectic and everyone is rushing hither and thither, everyone in that home will learn to live a highly stressed life.

Parents in the fast lane often pressure their children too much. They scrutinize school performance, criticize poor grades, and punish children for not fulfilling high standards. They push kids into activities too fast and too often. What is the effect of pushing a child too far or too fast? The child becomes overstressed *and so do you*.

You also disrupt the child's development. While stress problems are mainly seen in adults, they always *begin* in childhood. Each child is different and must be allowed to develop at his or her own pace.

What does it mean to live a quiet life? It certainly doesn't mean that you give up all ambition and quit everything. First Thessalonians 5:14 tells us to "warn them that are unruly." Scripture nowhere affirms sloth, idleness, or inactivity as a style of life. But in the midst of life's demands we have to find time to be quiet, to let the systems of our body and mind come down from a high state of arousal and rejuvenate. The body needs time to cool off so it doesn't overheat.

What is interesting to me is how God has linked spiritual disciplines with our need for rejuvenation. Scripture is full of injunctions for stillness and quietness (see 1 Sam. 12:7; Job 37:14; Ps. 4:4; 46:10; Isa. 32:17; 1 Thess. 4:11; 1 Pet. 3:4). Communication with God requires that we quiet ourselves. In other words, being joyful, praying, and maintaining a spirit of thankfulness is a two-way street. We need the spiritual disciplines of prayer and thankfulness to help us live a quiet life, and the act of quieting ourselves enables us to exercise these disciplines.

Parents need to be models of peaceful composure for their children (1 Thess. 5:13).

We need not only to take the pressure off our children when it is unreasonable but to take it off ourselves as well. We need to get rid of obligations that are petty or unimportant and focus on the essentials of life. We need to cultivate an inner peace and be at harmony with God's purposes (4:1). We need to dispose of anger and bitterness (5:15) and to focus on the essentials of our own work. This is what a quiet life is all about.

Make quietness your ambition so you can experience God's peace (5:24). Slow down.

DIGGING DEEPER

1. Read 1 Thessalonians 4:1-2 as a family. Challenge each member of your family to consider whether a fast-paced life has stressed the family. What activities can be abandoned in favor of more leisure time together as a family, and what activities can be encouraged that will help to slow down the pace a little?

2. What is the value to God's kingdom when we give priority to living a quiet and less stressful life? See 1 Thessalonians 4:12.

yourselves are taught of God to love one another. ¹⁰And indeed ye do it toward all the brethren which are in all Macedonia: but we beseech you, brethren, that ye increase more and more; ¹¹And that ye study to be quiet, and to do your own business, and to work with your own hands, as we commanded you; ¹²That ye may walk honestly toward them that are without, and *that* ye may have lack of nothing.

¹³But I would not have you to be ignorant, brethren, concerning them which are asleep, that ye sorrow not, even as others which have no hope. ¹⁴For if we believe that Jesus died and rose again, even so them also which sleep in Jesus will God bring with him. ¹⁵For this we say unto you by the word of the Lord, that we which are alive *and* remain unto the coming of the Lord shall not prevent[d] them which are asleep. ¹⁶For the Lord himself shall de-

scend from heaven with a shout, with the voice of the archangel, and with the trump of God: and the dead in Christ shall rise first: ¹⁷Then we which are alive *and* remain shall be caught up together with them in the clouds, to meet the Lord in the air: and so shall we ever be with the Lord. ¹⁸Wherefore comfort[e] one another with these words.

5

¹But of the times and the seasons, brethren, ye have no need that I write unto you. ²For yourselves know perfectly that the day of the Lord so cometh as a thief in the night. ³For when they shall say, Peace and safety; then sudden destruction cometh upon them, as travail upon a woman with child; and they shall not escape. ⁴But ye, brethren, are not in darkness, that that day should overtake you as a thief. ⁵Ye are all the children of light, and the

---

[d] prevent: or, come before, or, anticipate, or, precede

[e] comfort: or, exhort

children of the day: we are not of the night, nor of darkness.

⁶Therefore let us not sleep, as *do* others; but let us watch and be sober. ⁷For they that sleep sleep in the night; and they that be drunken are drunken in the night. ⁸But let us, who are of the day, be sober, putting on the breastplate of faith and love; and for an helmet, the hope of salvation. ⁹For God hath not appointed us to wrath, but to obtain salvation by our Lord Jesus Christ, ¹⁰Who died for us, that, whether we wake or sleep, we should live together with him.

¹¹Wherefore comfortª yourselves together, and edify one another, even as also ye do. ¹²And we beseech you, brethren, to know them which labour among you, and are over you in the Lord, and admonish you; ¹³And to esteem them very highly in love for their work's sake. *And* be at peace among yourselves. ¹⁴Now we exhortᵇ you, brethren, warn them that are unruly, comfort the feebleminded, support the weak, be patient toward all *men*. ¹⁵See

that none render evil for evil unto any *man*; but ever follow that which is good, both among yourselves, and to all *men*.

¹⁶Rejoice evermore. ¹⁷Pray without ceasing. ¹⁸In every thing give thanks: for this is the will of God in Christ Jesus concerning you. ¹⁹Quench not the Spirit. ²⁰Despise not prophesyings. ²¹Prove all things; hold fast that which is good. ²²Abstain from all appearance of evil.

²³And the very God of peace sanctify you wholly; and *I pray God* your whole spirit and soul and body be preserved blameless unto the coming of our Lord Jesus Christ. ²⁴Faithful *is* he that calleth you, who also will do *it*. ²⁵Brethren, pray for us. ²⁶Greet all the brethren with an holy kiss. ²⁷I chargeᶜ you by the Lord that this epistle be read unto all the holy brethren. ²⁸The grace of our Lord Jesus Christ *be* with you. Amen.

[The first *epistle* to the Thessalonians was written from Athens.]

ª comfort: or, exhort
ᵇ exhort: or, beseech
ᶜ charge: or, adjure

SECOND THESSALONIANS

Purpose
To clear up the confusion about the second coming of Christ

Author
Paul

To Whom Written
The church at Thessalonica

Date Written
About A.D. 51 or 52, a few months after 1 Thessalonians, from Corinth

Setting
Many in the church were confused about the timing of Christ's return. Because of mounting persecution, they thought the day of the Lord must be imminent, and they interpreted Paul's first letter to say that the second coming would be at any moment. In light of this misunderstanding, many persisted in being lazy and disorderly with the excuse of waiting for Christ's return.

Key Verse
"And the Lord direct your hearts into the love of God, and into the patient waiting for Christ" (3:5).

Special Features
This is a follow-up to 1 Thessalonians. In this letter, Paul indicates various events that must happen before the second coming of Christ.

"Valerie, this is your second warning!"

Will any parent fail to recognize the familiarity of a second call to chores, a second whistle for dinner, a second shout for lights-out? Second calling is a parent's second nature.

Paul's second letter to the Christians in Thessalonica reads as if the first envelope were lost in the mail. If not lost, perhaps just lightly read. Here Paul elaborates on themes central to 1 Thessalonians, adding information and new encouragement to the earlier correspondence.

There's practical advice here for everyone. Don't be fooled by fast talkers. Work hard, reject laziness, don't meddle in your neighbor's personal business. Pray more, stand by your friends, and trust God every day.

Such advice is hardly so complicated as to need a second shout, but somehow it does. You may need to read this book twice before you catch all the subtleties, three times before you connect with the message.

1

¹Paul, and Silvanus, and Timotheus, unto the church of the Thessalonians in God our Father and the Lord Jesus Christ: ²Grace unto you, and peace, from God our Father and the Lord Jesus Christ. ³We are bound to thank God always for you, brethren, as it is meet, because that your faith groweth exceedingly, and the charity of every one of you all toward each other aboundeth; ⁴So that we ourselves glory in you in the churches of God for your patience and faith in all your persecutions and tribulations that ye endure:

⁵*Which is* a manifest token of the righteous judgment of God, that ye may be counted worthy of the kingdom of God, for which ye also suffer: ⁶Seeing *it is* a righteous thing with God to recompense tribulation to them that trouble you; ⁷And to you who are troubled rest with us, when the Lord Jesus shall be revealed from heaven with his[a] mighty angels, ⁸In flaming fire taking[b]

Devotional Moment

Way to Go!

1:3-4 The young Thessalonian church faced many hardships, and Paul and his companions were proud of how they responded. Their perseverance and faith were the right response and deserved recognition. The next time someone does something right, don't hesitate to say, "That was great the way you did such and such!" or, "Well done!" You can't go wrong by recognizing a good deed.

---

vengeance on them that know not God, and that obey not the gospel of our Lord Jesus Christ: ⁹Who shall be punished with everlasting destruction from the presence of the Lord, and from the glory of his power; ¹⁰When he shall come to be glorified in his saints, and to be admired in all them that believe (because our testimony among you was believed) in that day.

¹¹Wherefore also we pray always for you, that our God would count[c] you worthy of *this* calling, and fulfil all the good pleasure of *his* goodness, and the work of faith with power: ¹²That the name of our Lord Jesus Christ may be glorified in you, and ye in him, according to the grace of our God and the Lord Jesus Christ.

2

¹Now we beseech you, brethren, by the coming of our Lord Jesus Christ, and *by* our gathering together unto him[a], ²That ye be not soon shaken in mind, or be troubled, neither by spirit, nor by word, nor by letter as from us, as that the day of Christ is at hand.

³Let no man deceive you by any means: for *that day shall not come*, except there come a falling away first, and that man of sin be revealed, the son of perdition; ⁴Who opposeth and exalteth himself above all that is called God, or that is worshipped; so that he as God sitteth in the temple of God, shewing himself that he is God. ⁵Remember ye not, that, when I was yet with you, I

---

[a] his . . . : Gr. the angels of his power
[b] taking: or, yielding
[c] count: or, vouchsafe
[a] unto him: or, around him

told you these things? ⁶And now ye know what withholdethᵇ that he might be revealed in his time. ⁷For the mystery of iniquity doth already work: only he who now letteth *will let*, until he be taken out of the way. ⁸And then shall that Wicked be revealed, whom the Lord shall consume with the spirit of his mouth, and shall destroy with the brightness of his coming: ⁹*Even him*, whose coming is after the working of Satan with all power and signs and lying wonders, ¹⁰And with all deceivableness of unrighteousness in them that perish; because they received not the love of the truth, that they might be saved. ¹¹And for this cause God shall send them strong delusion, that they should believe a lie: ¹²That they all might be damned who believed not the truth, but had pleasure in unrighteousness.

¹³But we are bound to give thanks alway to God for you, brethren beloved of the Lord, because God hath from the beginning chosen you to salvation through sanctification of the Spirit and belief of the truth: ¹⁴Whereunto he called you by our gospel, to the obtaining of the glory of our Lord Jesus Christ. ¹⁵Therefore, brethren, stand fast, and hold the traditions which ye have been taught, whether by word, or our epistle.

¹⁶Now our Lord Jesus Christ himself, and God, even our Father, which hath loved us, and hath given *us* everlasting consolation and good hope through grace, ¹⁷Comfort your hearts,

and stablish you in every good word and work.

3

¹Finally, brethren, pray for us, that the word of the Lord may have *free* courseᵃ, and be glorified, even as *it is* with you: ²And that we may be delivered from unreasableᵇ and wicked men: for all *men* have not faith. ³But the Lord is faithful, who shall stablish you, and keep *you* from evil. ⁴And we have confidence in the Lord touching you, that ye both do and will do the things which we command you. ⁵And the Lord direct your hearts into the love of God, and into the patient waiting for Christ.

⁶Now we command you, brethren, in the name of our Lord Jesus Christ, that ye withdraw yourselves from every brother that walketh disorderly, and

---

Devotional Moment
•
Correction

3:11-13 Paul was not afraid to confront those who were doing wrong—even such "minor" things as being lazy and gossiping. Here he commanded them to quiet down and get to work. Next he affirmed those who were doing right. This is a good example for us. Anyone can get off the path; a true friend guides (or even pushes!) us back on it. How good a friend are you to others? Can you lovingly point out areas in which they are straying from what they know to be right? In the same way, be sure to encourage and affirm those who are doing right— whether it's a new attempt or a well-established pattern.

ᵇ withholdeth: or, holdeth
ᵃ have . . . : Gr. run
ᵇ unreasonable: Gr. absurd

not after the tradition which he received of us. [7]For yourselves know how ye ought to follow us: for we behaved not ourselves disorderly among you; [8]Neither did we eat any man's bread for nought; but wrought with labour and travail night and day, that we might not be chargeable to any of you: [9]Not because we have not power, but to make ourselves an ensample unto you to follow us. [10]For even when we were with you, this we commanded you, that if any would not work, neither should he eat. [11]For we hear that there are some which walk among you disorderly, working not at all, but are busybodies. [12]Now them that are such we command and exhort by our Lord Jesus Christ, that with quietness they work, and eat their own bread. [13]But ye, brethren, be[c] not weary in well doing. [14]And if any man obey not our word by[d] this epistle, note that man, and have no company with him, that he may be ashamed. [15]Yet count *him* not as an enemy, but admonish *him* as a brother.

[16]Now the Lord of peace himself give you peace always by all means. The Lord *be* with you all. [17]The salutation of Paul with mine own hand, which is the token in every epistle: so I write. [18]The grace of our Lord Jesus Christ *be* with you all. Amen.

[The second *epistle* to the Thessalonians was written from Athens.]

---

[c] be . . . : or, faint not
[d] by . . . : or, signify that man by an epistle

FIRST TIMOTHY

Surrogate parents are people we can all admire. It takes a special gift to step in and fill the void left when a child's parents are unable—or unwilling—to fulfill their responsibilities.

In this letter to Timothy, Paul twice calls him a son. We don't know what became of Timothy's natural father, but he isn't mentioned when Paul speaks of Timothy's family (2 Tim. 1:5). Paul didn't take the place of Timothy's father, but he did fill the spiritual vacancy. Quite probably, Timothy had come to faith in Christ under Paul's teaching.

Read this letter as a parent's advice to a young adult, a child still maturing but ready for responsibility. Notice how Paul refuses to coddle ("Let no man despise thy youth," 4:12) but pleads for Timothy to think like an adult. Paul wants to see stronger spiritual muscle on his son and less surrender to the passions of youth. Paul hopes to take a father's pride in this emerging adult, yet he knows better than Timothy that attractive pitfalls glare on the road ahead. Can he spare the boy a great fall? Can he coax the boy to a manhood shaped by faith and given to service?

Parents would do well to follow Paul's example by writing with warmth and concern to older children. Uncles and aunts—all surrogate parents—can do the same, especially when a young person is without a natural parent.

1

¹Paul, an apostle of Jesus Christ by the commandment of God our Saviour, and Lord Jesus Christ, *which is* our hope; ²Unto Timothy, *my* own son in the faith: Grace, mercy, *and* peace, from God our Father and Jesus Christ our Lord. ³As I besought thee to abide still at Ephesus, when I went into Macedonia, that thou mightest charge some that they teach no other doctrine, ⁴Neither give heed to fables and endless genealogies, which minister questions, rather than godly edifying which is in faith: *so do.*

⁵Now the end of the commandment is charity out of a pure heart, and *of* a good conscience, and *of* faith unfeigned: ⁶From which some having swerved have turned aside unto vain jangling; ⁷Desiring to be teachers of the law; understanding neither what they say, nor whereof they affirm. ⁸But we know that the law *is* good, if a man use it lawfully; ⁹Knowing this, that the law is not made for a righteous man, but for the lawless and disobedient, for the ungodly and for sinners, for unholy and profane, for murderers of fathers and murderers of mothers, for manslayers, ¹⁰For whoremongers, for them that defile themselves with mankind, for menstealers, for liars, for perjured persons, and if there be any other thing that is contrary to sound doctrine; ¹¹According to the glorious gospel of the blessed God, which was committed to my trust.

¹²And I thank Christ Jesus our Lord, who hath enabled me, for that he counted me faithful, putting me into the ministry; ¹³Who was before a blasphemer, and a persecutor, and injurious: but I obtained mercy, because I did *it* ignorantly in unbelief. ¹⁴And the grace of our Lord was exceeding abundant with faith and love which is in Christ Jesus. ¹⁵This *is* a faithful saying, and worthy of all acceptation, that Christ Jesus came into the world to save sinners; of whom I am chief. ¹⁶Howbeit for this cause I obtained mercy, that in me first Jesus Christ might shew forth all longsuffering, for a pattern to them which should hereafter believe on him to life everlasting. ¹⁷Now unto the King eternal, immortal, invisible, the only wise God, *be* honour and glory for ever and ever. Amen.

¹⁸This charge I commit unto thee, son Timothy, according to the prophecies which went before on thee, that thou by them mightest war a good warfare; ¹⁹Holding faith, and a good conscience; which some having put away concerning faith have made shipwreck: ²⁰Of whom is Hymenaeus and Alexander; whom I have delivered unto Satan, that they may learn not to blaspheme.

2

¹I exhort[a] therefore, that, first of all, supplications, prayers, intercessions, *and* giving of thanks, be made for all men; ²For kings, and *for* all that are in authority[b]; that we may lead a quiet and peaceable life in all godliness and honesty. ³For this *is* good and acceptable in the sight of God our Saviour; ⁴Who will have all men to be saved, and to come unto the knowledge

---

[a] exhort: or, desire
[b] authority: or, eminent place

Respect Your Elders

by Rolf Zettersten

My friend John Eckhardt operates one of the finest dude ranches in North America. In a beautiful place nestled along the Smith River in Montana, his guests spend their days riding horses over rugged hills and across lush valleys. One of the highlights of this ranch is the tremendous service and attention these guests receive. An army of young people serve as waiters, ranch hands, maids, drivers, and even baby-sitters.

Every winter John travels a circuit of colleges in the southern states where he recruits his summer staff. When I asked why he goes so far to find help, his response startled me: "Because that's the only part of the country where I can find young people who haven't forgotten their 'Yes ma'ams' and 'Yes sirs,'" he said.

When I was young, I was taught never to address adults by their first names. My parents felt it was important for me to show respect by this formality. I realize that our society is more casual today, and I enjoy many aspects of that. But one problem with that approach to life is the declining honor and respect we show for our elders.

When I was a teenager, I picked up odd jobs during high school that also gave me an appreciation for senior citizens. I spent one year driving an elderly woman on her Saturday errands. When I first met her, I was put off by her incessant smoking. But as we drove around town together, worked side by side in her rose garden, and shared afternoon snacks in her kitchen, I began to see her for who she really was. This woman had lived a life of tremendous joys, great accomplishments, and deep sorrow. As I spent time with her, my appreciation for all senior citizens grew tremendously.

I also worked for an elderly man in our neighborhood who needed help around the house. He taught me how to use various tools in his workroom that his frail body no longer permitted him to use. In spite of his weakening physical condition, I grew to love him for the person he was inside.

As a result of these and other interactions with the elderly, I never felt the generation gap or identified with those who talked about being alienated from their elders. Instead, I felt great love and respect for older people. I want my own children to have that same experience.

As parents we can help our children learn to know and love older people, to begin to appreciate their wisdom, and to feel the blessing of giving to others. We can provide them with opportunities to participate in nursing home ministry, to run errands to neighbors, to share with elderly family members and friends. And, best of all, these are things we can do *with* our children. The whole family can benefit.

Indeed, we must recognize the warmth, strength, and depth of character that lie beneath the infirmed and frail shells of old age. Given my own early experiences with elderly people, it is evident that showing respect for the aged, treating them well, and appreciating their contributions has its own rewards. Whatever we give the elderly, we receive back tenfold. We can learn from them, enrich our own life by hearing about their experiences in this world, and deepen our own relationship with God through them.

We live in a society that values youth, almost above all else. Forty is often considered over the hill. Countless people who still have years of service to give are forced to retire at age sixty-five. Untold numbers of older people are warehoused and ignored. While we may not be able to change an entire society's disrespect, we can teach our children to appreciate the elderly—for their benefit and for our kids' sake as well.

1. What do older people have to offer younger people? See Proverbs 3:1; 4:1; 6:20-23.

2. Who are the older people in your life? In what ways can you show them that you value their company? See 1 Timothy 5:1-2; Titus 2:2-7; 1 Peter 5:5.

---

of the truth. ⁵For *there is* one God, and one mediator between God and men, the man Christ Jesus; ⁶Who gave himself a ransom for all, to be testified in due time. ⁷Whereunto I am ordained a preacher, and an apostle, (I speak the truth in Christ, *and* lie not;) a teacher of the Gentiles in faith and verity. ⁸I will therefore that men pray every where, lifting up holy hands, without wrath and doubting.

⁹In like manner also, that women adorn themselves in modest apparel, with shamefacedness and sobriety; not with broided hair, or gold, or pearls, or costly array; ¹⁰But (which becometh women professing godliness) with good works. ¹¹Let the woman learn in silence with all subjection. ¹²But I suffer not a woman to teach, nor to usurp authority over the man, but to be in silence. ¹³For Adam was first formed, then Eve. ¹⁴And Adam was not deceived, but the woman being deceived was in the transgression. ¹⁵Notwithstanding she shall be saved in childbearing, if they continue in faith and charity and holiness with sobriety.

3

¹This *is* a true saying, If a man desire the office of a bishop, he desireth a good work. ²A bishop then must be blameless, the husband of one wife, vigilant, sober, of good behaviour, given to hospitality, apt to teach; ³Not given to wine, no striker, not greedy of filthy lucre; but patient, not a brawler, not covetous; ⁴One that ruleth well his own house, having his children in subjection with all gravity; ⁵(For if a man know not how to rule his own house, how shall he take care of the church of God?) ⁶Not a noviceᵃ, lest being lifted up with pride he fall into the condemnation of the devil. ⁷Moreover he must have a good report of them which are without; lest he fall into reproach and the snare of the devil.

⁸Likewise *must* the deacons *be* grave,

Devotional Moment

Leadership Training

3:4-5 The early church looked for leaders who led well at home. Suitability for serving as a pastor is best gauged by one's leadership at home because firm, loving oversight is needed in both settings. This does not mean that no one should serve in church unless he or she has a perfect family, but in many ways the family is a training ground for other forms of service. Among other things, the family can teach us how to solve people problems. Be a willing trainee. Pay attention to your life at home, and improvements in your public service will most likely follow.

ᵃ a novice: or, one newly come to the faith

not doubletongued, not given to much wine, not greedy of filthy lucre; ⁹Holding the mystery of the faith in a pure conscience. ¹⁰And let these also first be proved; then let them use the office of a deacon, being *found* blameless. ¹¹Even so *must their* wives *be* grave, not slanderers, sober, faithful in all things. ¹²Let the deacons be the husbands of one wife, ruling their children and their own houses well. ¹³For they that have used the office of a deacon well purchase to themselves a good degree, and great boldness in the faith which is in Christ Jesus.

¹⁴These things write I unto thee, hoping to come unto thee shortly: ¹⁵But if I tarry long, that thou mayest know how thou oughtest to behave thyself in the house of God, which is the church of the living God, the pillar and ground[b] of the truth. ¹⁶And without controversy great is the mystery of godliness: God was manifest in the flesh, justified in the Spirit, seen of angels, preached unto the Gentiles, believed on in the world, received up into glory.

4

¹Now the Spirit speaketh expressly, that in the latter times some shall depart from the faith, giving heed to seducing spirits, and doctrines of devils; ²Speaking lies in hypocrisy; having their conscience seared with a hot iron; ³Forbidding to marry, *and commanding* to abstain from meats, which God hath created to be received with thanksgiving of them which believe and know the truth. ⁴For every creature of God *is* good, and nothing to be refused, if it be received with thanksgiving: ⁵For it is sanctified by the word of God and prayer.

Devotional Moment
•
Thankful for Marriage
4:3-5 Some false teachers forbade people from marrying or eating certain foods, judging these things to be evil indulgences. In contrast, Paul told Timothy to receive all good things as gifts from God to be enjoyed and to be thankful for them. Some people like to dictate others' tastes and customs. Yet God has given us all good things to enjoy—including marriage and good food. Receive them with thanks; enjoy them as good.

⁶If thou put the brethren in remembrance of these things, thou shalt be a good minister of Jesus Christ, nourished up in the words of faith and of good doctrine, whereunto thou hast attained. ⁷But refuse profane and old wives' fables, and exercise thyself *rather* unto godliness. ⁸For bodily exercise profiteth little[a]: but godliness is prof-

Devotional Moment
•
Youth
4:12-13 Paul urged Timothy to live in such a way that older people could not find fault with him for being young. While Timothy may have been in his thirties, Paul knew that older members of the church would discount Timothy for being younger than they. Timothy's "youth" could be a barrier for those people. Paul encouraged him to live above their modest expectations.
If you are relatively young, no doubt you have people who expect little from you because of your age, even if you consider yourself mature, grown up, or adult. If so, you have control over whether their judgment is justified. Live above their expectations; prove them wrong; set the example for *them*. How? Read those verses again.

---

[b] ground: or, stay
[a] little: or, for a little time

Timothy

Timothy's mother was a Jew, and his father, a Greek. His mother and grandmother taught him the Old Testament Scriptures. At some point he heard Paul preach and became a Christian.

Timothy grew rapidly as a Christian. He eventually joined Paul and Silas on their second missionary journey. His commitment to Christ was so strong that he was willing to be circumcised so that Jewish audiences would not reject him (and thus his message about Christ) as a non-Jew. Timothy worked tirelessly alongside Paul and Silas for many years, telling people about Jesus, starting new churches, and pastoring. Paul considered him a close personal friend, brother, and son.

These things were all true of Timothy when he was relatively young—young enough to make others discount him because of his age (1 Tim. 4:12).

What made Timothy so wonderful? Quite simply, devotion to Christ.

Timothy wasn't a "gifted child" or even unusually outgoing. He was shy and hesitant, enough so that Paul warned him not to be intimidated by others (2 Tim. 1:7). He had at least one significant professional failure (in the church at Corinth). He wasn't rich or privileged. Yet unlike his peers, Timothy lived above the median level of maturity.

Devotion to Christ makes all the difference. It's the biggest, most significant contribution anyone can make to his or her family—young or old, rich or poor, parent or child, single or married.

LESSONS FROM TIMOTHY AS A YOUNG ADULT

Maturity comes from devotion to Christ. Timothy grew and matured as he did because he *listened.* He respected elders who were wise and who knew the Scriptures. Being an adult doesn't make you mature. Listening to God's wisdom does.

Young people can be mature. Some parents excuse poor behavior in children with the adage Kids will be kids. That is unwise and unnecessary. You *can* teach your children to live right.

Youth is no excuse for sloppy living. Kids *can* be nice to each other (they don't have to fight). Teenagers can restrain their passions. Young adults can make selfless career and family choices.

Worship
in Your Home

DOCTRINES AND DEVOTIONS—LEARNING KEY TRUTHS OF THE BIBLE AT EACH AGE LEVEL
If any man teach otherwise, and consent not to wholesome words, even the words of our Lord Jesus Christ, and to the doctrine which is according to godliness.
1 Timothy 6:3

Aren't doctrines only for theologians and scholars? Not at all. Bible doctrines are merely Bible teachings; some of these are so simple that even a small child can grasp them.

For example, consider these truths about God: God loves me; God takes care of me; God leads me; God gives me food to eat; God gives me a home; God is with me everywhere; and God is good. All are doctrines—on the one hand profound, on the other hand extremely simple.

Most doctrines can be life changing; that is, when appropriated into a person's life, they make that person different.

Devotions are great times to think about Bible doctrines. A doctrine such as "God takes care of me" can touch every generation. At each age level it will be understood and expressed in different ways. But all ages should be able to talk together about this single, simple truth.

itable unto all things, having promise of the life that now is, and of that which is to come. ⁹This *is* a faithful saying and worthy of all acceptation. ¹⁰For therefore we both labour and suffer reproach, because we trust in the living God, who is the Saviour of all men, specially of those that believe. ¹¹These things command and teach. ¹²Let no man despise thy youth; but be thou an example of the believers, in word, in conversation, in charity, in spirit, in faith, in purity. ¹³Till I come, give attendance to reading, to exhortation, to doctrine. ¹⁴Neglect not the gift that is in thee, which was given thee by prophecy, with the laying on of the hands of the presbytery. ¹⁵Meditate upon these things; give thyself wholly to them; that thy profiting may appear to all[b]. ¹⁶Take heed unto thyself, and unto the doctrine; continue in them: for in doing this thou shalt both save thyself, and them that hear thee.

5

¹Rebuke not an elder, but intreat *him* as a father; *and* the younger men as brethren; ²The elder women as mothers; the younger as sisters, with all purity.

³Honour widows that are widows indeed. ⁴But if any widow have children or nephews, let them learn first to shew piety[a] at home, and to requite their parents: for that is good and acceptable before God. ⁵Now she that is a widow indeed, and desolate, trusteth in God, and continueth in supplications and prayers night and day. ⁶But she that liveth in pleasure is dead while she liveth. ⁷And

---

[b] to all: or, in all things
[a] piety: or, kindness

these things give in charge, that they may be blameless. ⁸But if any provide not for his own, and specially for those of his own house[b], he hath denied the faith, and is worse than an infidel. ⁹Let not a widow be taken into the number under threescore years old, having been the wife of one man, ¹⁰Well reported of for good works; if she have brought up children, if she have lodged strangers, if she have washed the saints' feet, if she have relieved the afflicted, if she have diligently followed every good work. ¹¹But the younger widows refuse: for when they have begun to wax wanton against Christ, they will marry; ¹²Having damnation, because they have cast off their first faith. ¹³And withal they learn *to be* idle, wandering about from house to house; and not only idle, but tattlers also and busybodies, speaking things which they ought not. ¹⁴I will therefore that the younger women marry, bear children,

---

Devotional Moment
•
Respect for Elders

5:1-4 The apostle Paul urged his son in the faith to treat older people with respect—older men as fathers, older women as mothers. And he left instructions that those with elderly relatives were to see to it that they were well cared for. Some people undervalue older people; they may even see the elderly as burdens. Yet God calls us to esteem older people *highly.* Your relationship with your parents, grandparents, and other older relatives is important—to you, to them, to your children, and to God. Show them respect. If necessary, take care of them. Encourage your children to respect adults; to greet them politely; to speak up and answer when spoken to.

Devotional Moment
•
Look Out for Your Own

5:8 Being a Christian carries with it many responsibilities, but among the greatest is that of taking care of our immediate families. Paul called anyone who did not take care of his or her family "worse than an infidel." This is one of the most direct commands anywhere in the Bible instructing us to take care of our family. It doesn't give us a license to indulge our family's every material fantasy, but it does call us to a particular set of priorities and involvements: (1) We have limited resources, and we need to use them to provide for our family. (2) If a family member is in need, we are to be their first source of help. Make your family a financial priority because doing so is part of what it means to serve God.

---

guide the house, give none occasion to the adversary to speak reproachfully. ¹⁵For some are already turned aside after Satan. ¹⁶If any man or woman that believeth have widows, let them relieve them, and let not the church be charged; that it may relieve them that are widows indeed.

¹⁷Let the elders that rule well be counted worthy of double honour, especially they who labour in the word and doctrine. ¹⁸For the scripture saith, Thou shalt not muzzle the ox that treadeth out the corn. And, The labourer *is* worthy of his reward. ¹⁹Against an elder receive not an accusation, but before[c] two or three witnesses. ²⁰Them that sin rebuke before all, that others also may fear. ²¹I charge *thee* before God, and the Lord Jesus Christ, and the elect angels, that thou observe these things without preferring one before another, doing

---

[b] house: or, kindred
[c] before: or, under

nothing by partiality. ²²Lay hands suddenly on no man, neither be partaker of other men's sins: keep thyself pure. ²³Drink no longer water, but use a little wine for thy stomach's sake and thine often infirmities. ²⁴Some men's sins are open beforehand, going before to judgment; and some *men* they follow after. ²⁵Likewise also the good works *of some* are manifest beforehand; and they that are otherwise cannot be hid.

6

¹Let as many servants as are under the yoke count their own masters worthy of all honour, that the name of God and *his* doctrine be not blasphemed. ²And they that have believing masters, let them not despise *them*, because they are brethren; but rather do *them* service, because they are faithful[a] and beloved, partakers of the benefit. These things teach and exhort. ³If any man teach otherwise, and consent not to wholesome words, *even* the words of our Lord Jesus Christ, and to the doctrine which is according to godliness; ⁴He is proud[b], knowing nothing, but doting about questions and strifes of words, whereof cometh envy, strife, railings, evil surmisings, ⁵Perverse disputings of men of corrupt minds, and destitute of the truth, supposing that gain is godliness: from such withdraw thyself.

⁶But godliness with contentment is great gain. ⁷For we brought nothing into *this* world, *and it is* certain we can carry nothing out. ⁸And having food and raiment let us be therewith content. ⁹But they that will be rich fall into temptation and a snare, and *into* many foolish and hurtful lusts, which drown men in destruction and perdition. ¹⁰For the love of money is the root of all evil: which while some coveted after, they have erred[c] from the faith, and pierced themselves through with many sorrows. ¹¹But thou, O man of God, flee these things; and follow after righteousness, godliness, faith, love, patience, meekness. ¹²Fight the good fight of faith, lay hold on eternal life, whereunto thou art also called, and hast professed a good profession before many witnesses.

¹³I give thee charge in the sight of God, who quickeneth all things, and *before* Christ Jesus, who before Pontius Pilate witnessed a good confession[d]; ¹⁴That thou keep *this* commandment without spot, unrebukeable, until the appearing of our Lord Jesus Christ: ¹⁵Which in his times he shall shew, *who is* the blessed and only Potentate, the King of kings, and Lord of lords; ¹⁶Who only hath immortality, dwelling in the light which no man can approach unto; whom no man hath seen, nor can see: to whom *be* honour and power everlasting. Amen. ¹⁷Charge them that are rich in this world, that they be not highminded, nor trust in uncertain[e] riches, but in the living God, who giveth us richly all things to enjoy; ¹⁸That they do good, that they be rich

---

[a] faithful: or, believing
[b] proud: or, a fool
[c] erred: or, been seduced
[d] confession: or, profession
[e] uncertain . . . : Gr. uncertainty of riches

in good works, ready to distribute, willing to communicate; [19]Laying up in store for themselves a good foundation against the time to come, that they may lay hold on eternal life. [20]O Timothy, keep that which is committed to thy trust, avoiding profane *and* vain babblings, and oppositions of science[f]

falsely so called: [21]Which some professing have erred concerning the faith. Grace *be* with thee. Amen.

[The first to Timothy was written from Laodicea, which is the chiefest city of Phrygia Pacatiana.]

---

[f] science: Gr. knowledge

"Tomorrow, tomorrow, I love you, tomorrow; you're only a day away" goes the popular theme song expressing the optimism of youth.

The apostle Paul, Timothy's spiritual father, sees trouble down the road. This second letter is a warning about tomorrow. Timothy cannot expect to coast into middle age and retirement. Because Paul's days are numbered, he urges Timothy to endure the hard times and keep the faith strong.

This letter can be read by people of every age. Paul's advice can help everyone to keep going in faith, keep trusting Christ, never coast.

But Paul's letter is not all sermon. Notice the switch from spiritual advice to worry over a coat Paul has left in a house in Troas.

That's how our lives work—in a constant mix of small details and huge cosmic conflicts. It's Timothy against false teachers at one point, with the future of the church in the balance. Then it's Timothy running errands for a forgetful father and friend, picking up a coat to keep Paul warm. Such small favors give Timothy a chance to show his love concretely.

Parents, take hints. Give your children something to do and something to be. Show them a piece of the future, and remind them that fortitude and faith cannot be put on the shelf for even a day. Write them a letter that describes your own heart for God, then write them another. Then read them *these* letters, now almost two thousand years old but still helping us look toward "tomorrow," both bright and treacherous.

1

[1]Paul, an apostle of Jesus Christ by the will of God, according to the promise of life which is in Christ Jesus, [2]To Timothy, *my* dearly beloved son: Grace, mercy, *and* peace, from God the Father and Christ Jesus our Lord. [3]I thank God, whom I serve from *my* forefathers with pure conscience, that without ceasing I have remembrance of thee in my prayers night and day; [4]Greatly desiring to see thee, being mindful of thy tears, that I may be filled with joy; [5]When I call to remembrance the unfeigned faith that is in thee, which dwelt first in thy grandmother Lois, and thy mother Eunice; and I am persuaded that in thee also.

[6]Wherefore I put thee in remembrance that thou stir up the gift of God, which is in thee by the putting on of my hands. [7]For God hath not given us the spirit of fear; but of power, and of love, and of a sound mind. [8]Be not thou therefore ashamed of the testimony of our Lord, nor of me his prisoner: but be thou partaker of the afflictions of the gospel according to the power of God; [9]Who hath saved us, and called *us* with an holy calling, not according to our works, but according to his own purpose and grace, which was given us in Christ Jesus before the world began, [10]But is now made manifest by the appearing of our Saviour Jesus Christ, who hath abolished death, and hath brought life and immortality to light through the gospel: [11]Whereunto I am appointed a preacher, and an apostle, and a teacher of the Gentiles. [12]For the which cause I also suffer these things: nevertheless I am not ashamed: for I know whom I have believed[a], and am persuaded that he is able to keep that which I have committed unto him against that day. [13]Hold fast the form of sound words, which thou hast heard of me, in faith and love which is in Christ Jesus. [14]That good thing which was committed unto thee keep by the Holy Ghost which dwelleth in us.

[15]This thou knowest, that all they which are in Asia be turned away from me; of whom are Phygellus and Hermogenes. [16]The Lord give mercy unto the house of Onesiphorus; for he oft refreshed me, and was not ashamed of my chain: [17]But, when he was in Rome, he sought me out very diligently, and found *me*. [18]The Lord grant unto him that he may find mercy of the Lord in that day: and in how many things he ministered unto me at Ephesus, thou knowest very well.

2

[1]Thou therefore, my son, be strong in the grace that is in Christ Jesus. [2]And the things that thou hast heard of me

---

Devotional Moment
•
Keep in Touch

1:3-4 As he neared the end of his life, Paul expressed a deep desire to see Timothy, his "dear son" in Christ. We don't know how long the two had been separated, but we can easily see that a reunion was overdue. Reunions are great opportunities to relive fond memories, to catch up on personal news, and to carry on old traditions. If, like Paul and Timothy, circumstances or distance prevent you from getting together with your loved ones, consider doing as they did— write a letter expressing your affection. You can also make a long-distance phone call or maybe even videotape a message.

---

[a] believed: or, trusted

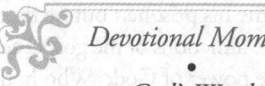

Devotional Moment
•
God's Word

2:15 Timothy was surrounded by false teachers who threatened to harm his congregation with their pleasant-sounding (but deceptive) ideas. For this reason Paul exhorted his young friend to be a diligent student of God's Word. We must know what the Bible says, understand what it means, and see how it applies to our life in order to be ready to reject and refute false teachings. How can you become more competent in handling God's Word? You could start a Scripture memory plan, do a group Bible study, help a family member prepare and teach a Bible lesson, act out a famous Bible scene, or take turns reading aloud your favorite psalms and Bible stories. The possibilities are endless!

among[a] many witnesses, the same commit thou to faithful men, who shall be able to teach others also. ³Thou therefore endure hardness, as a good soldier of Jesus Christ. ⁴No man that warreth entangleth himself with the affairs of *this* life; that he may please him who hath chosen him to be a soldier. ⁵And if a man also strive for masteries, *yet* is he not crowned, except he strive lawfully. ⁶The husbandman that laboureth must be first partaker of the fruits. ⁷Consider what I say; and the Lord give thee understanding in all things.

⁸Remember that Jesus Christ of the seed of David was raised from the dead according to my gospel: ⁹Wherein I suffer trouble, as an evil doer, *even* unto bonds; but the word of God is not bound. ¹⁰Therefore I endure all things for the elect's sakes, that they may also obtain the salvation which is in Christ Jesus with eternal glory. ¹¹*It is* a faithful saying: For if we be dead with *him,* we shall also live with *him:* ¹²If we suffer, we shall also reign with *him:* if we deny *him,* he also will deny us: ¹³If we believe not, *yet* he abideth faithful: he cannot deny himself.

¹⁴Of these things put *them* in remembrance, charging *them* before the Lord that they strive not about words to no profit, *but* to the subverting of the hearers. ¹⁵Study to shew thyself approved unto God, a workman that needeth not to be ashamed, rightly dividing the word of truth. ¹⁶But shun profane *and* vain babblings: for they will increase unto more ungodliness. ¹⁷And their word will eat as doth a canker[b]: of whom is Hymenaeus and Philetus; ¹⁸Who concerning the truth have erred, saying that the resurrection is past already; and overthrow the faith of some.

¹⁹Nevertheless the foundation of God

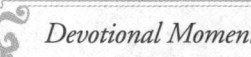

Devotional Moment
•
Temptation

2:22 Theologians have written massive tomes explaining temptation and sin and righteousness. Yet here in a few words Paul summarizes the goal for every Christian: Run away from evil and run toward good. By contrast, most people—even Christians—try to see how close they can get to sin without actually crossing the line. What situations, relationships, places, or activities tend to take your mind off doing good? Ask God to show you how to eliminate or avoid these bad influences. What people and commitments tend to encourage spiritual growth in you? Look for ways to deepen those involvements.

---

[a] among: or, by
[b] canker: or, gangrene

standeth sure[c], having this seal, The Lord knoweth them that are his. And, Let every one that nameth the name of Christ depart from iniquity. [20]But in a great house there are not only vessels of gold and of silver, but also of wood and of earth; and some to honour, and some to dishonour. [21]If a man therefore purge himself from these, he shall be a vessel unto honour, sanctified, and meet for the master's use, *and* prepared unto every good work.

[22]Flee also youthful lusts: but follow righteousness, faith, charity, peace, with them that call on the Lord out of a pure heart. [23]But foolish and unlearned questions avoid, knowing that they do gender strifes. [24]And the servant of the Lord must not strive; but be gentle unto all *men*, apt to teach, patient[d], [25]In meekness instructing those that oppose themselves; if God peradventure will give them repentance to the acknowledging of the truth; [26]And *that* they may recover themselves out of the snare of the devil, who are taken captive by him at his will.

3

[1]This know also, that in the last days perilous times shall come. [2]For men shall be lovers of their own selves, covetous, boasters, proud, blasphemers, disobedient to parents, unthankful, unholy, [3]Without natural affection, trucebreakers, false accusers, incontinent, fierce, despisers of those that are good, [4]Traitors, heady, highminded, lovers of pleasures more than lovers of God; [5]Having a form of godliness, but denying the power thereof: from such turn away. [6]For of this sort are

they which creep into houses, and lead captive silly women laden with sins, led away with divers lusts, [7]Ever learning, and never able to come to the knowledge of the truth. [8]Now as Jannes and Jambres withstood Moses, so do these also resist the truth: men of corrupt minds, reprobate[a] concerning the faith. [9]But they shall proceed no further: for their folly shall be manifest unto all *men*, as theirs also was.

[10]But thou hast fully known my doctrine, manner of life, purpose, faith, longsuffering, charity, patience, [11]Persecutions, afflictions, which came unto me at Antioch, at Iconium, at Lystra; what persecutions I endured: but out of *them* all the Lord delivered me. [12]Yea, and all that will live godly in Christ Jesus shall suffer persecution. [13]But evil men and seducers shall wax worse and worse, deceiving, and being deceived. [14]But continue thou in the things which thou hast learned and hast been assured of, knowing of whom thou hast learned *them*, [15]And that from a child thou hast known the holy scriptures, which are able to make thee wise unto salvation through faith which is in Christ Jesus. [16]All scripture *is* given by inspiration of God, and *is* profitable for doctrine, for reproof, for correction, for instruction in righteousness: [17]That the man of God may be perfect, throughly furnished unto all good works.

4

[1]I charge *thee* therefore before God, and the Lord Jesus Christ, who shall judge the quick and the dead at his appearing and his kingdom; [2]Preach the word; be instant in season, out of season; reprove, rebuke,

---

[c] sure: or, steady
[d] patient: or, forbearing
[a] reprobate: or, of no judgment

exhort with all longsuffering and doctrine. ³For the time will come when they will not endure sound doctrine; but after their own lusts shall they heap to themselves teachers, having itching ears; ⁴And they shall turn away *their* ears from the truth, and shall be turned unto fables. ⁵But watch thou in all things, endure afflictions, do the work of an evangelist, make full proof of thy ministry. ⁶For I am now ready to be offered, and the time of my departure is at hand. ⁷I have fought a good fight, I have finished *my* course, I have kept the faith: ⁸Henceforth there is laid up for me a crown of righteousness, which the Lord, the righteous judge, shall give me at that day: and not to me only, but unto all them also that love his appearing.

⁹Do thy diligence to come shortly unto me: ¹⁰For Demas hath forsaken me, having loved this present world, and is departed unto Thessalonica; Crescens to Galatia, Titus unto Dalmatia. ¹¹Only Luke is with me. Take Mark, and bring him with thee: for he is profitable to me for the ministry. ¹²And Tychicus have I sent to Ephesus. ¹³The cloke that I left at Troas with Carpus, when thou comest, bring *with thee,* and the books, *but* especially the parchments. ¹⁴Alexander the coppersmith did me much evil: the Lord reward him according to his works: ¹⁵Of whom be thou ware also; for he hath greatly withstood our words^a.

¹⁶At my first answer no man stood with me, but all *men* forsook me: *I pray God* that it may not be laid to their charge. ¹⁷Notwithstanding the Lord stood with me, and strengthened me; that by me the preaching might be fully known, and *that* all the Gentiles might hear: and I was deliv-

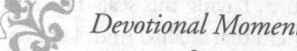

Devotional Moment

Encouragement

4:9-13 Here Paul pleads with Timothy to come and visit him. In some ways the apostle Paul seems larger than life—fearless, never discouraged, always filled with joy, a bona fide hero. The picture here, however, is a much more human one: a weary, possibly discouraged prisoner; cold (see v. 13); very much alone; a man who needed company. Paul's request reminds us of two facts: (1) It is OK to ask for help when we're hurting; and (2) we need to be sensitive to the needs of others—especially those in positions of leadership or authority. Even God-loving, much-admired spiritual leaders need encouragement. Make it a project to do something soon to brighten the life of your pastor, a missionary, or some other "biggie" you know: Send a card, mail a care package, give a little gift, make a phone call, or write a letter of appreciation. Such personal gestures of love and support can be a lifeline to them.

ered out of the mouth of the lion. ¹⁸And the Lord shall deliver me from every evil work, and will preserve *me* unto his heavenly kingdom: to whom *be* glory for ever and ever. Amen. ¹⁹Salute Prisca and Aquila, and the household of Onesiphorus. ²⁰Erastus abode at Corinth: but Trophimus have I left at Miletum sick. ²¹Do thy diligence to come before winter. Eubulus greeteth thee, and Pudens, and Linus, and Claudia, and all the brethren. ²²The Lord Jesus Christ *be* with thy spirit. Grace *be* with you. Amen.

[The second *epistle* unto Timotheus, ordained the first bishop of the church of the Ephesians, was written from Rome, when Paul was brought before Nero the second time.]

---

^a our words: or, our preachings

Family Traditions

Memorize Scripture

2 TIMOTHY 3

If you didn't make a game of memorizing Scripture with your toddlers, it's not too late to start, even with teenagers. Make it nonthreatening by starting with a passage that is simple and practical. Repeat it several times throughout the day; later, repeat only a few words or a phrase and challenge the children to finish it for you. Repeat a sentence, and ask them to start the next sentence. Keep this pattern up throughout the week, a line or two here, a paragraph there. Make sure that each child gets involved in quoting different parts of the passage at different times. And keep going until the whole family learns it by heart. Older children can memorize more than one passage at a time this way. Don't force anything. Just make the game a tradition in your family.

One family I know uses summer vacations to hide large portions of the Word of God in their hearts. Long car trips are an excellent opportunity to memorize the Bible with your kids. You've got a captive audience. Choose short passages, and practice them off and on. Plan an ice cream stop when the whole family has learned the chosen Scripture. Don't overdo it; quit while it's still fun.

Another family selects Bible verses appropriate for each child, copies them in an attractive blank book, and presents the book to a child on his or her birthday, a different book each year. The parents work with the children to learn by heart the verses they were given that year.

Create a Scripture memory calendar at the beginning of each year: Buy a nice wall calendar with a Christian theme and a bunch of stickers (different kinds) from your Bible bookstore. Select a major passage of Scripture each month, and write the reference for it in large print at the top of each month on the calendar. Now put sticky tabs in each child's Bible at the places where a Scripture has been chosen. Write the appropriate date on each note. The child is responsible to learn one verse at intervals throughout the month. Mark these intervals in color on the calendar. When the verse has been learned, allow the child to put a sticker on that day. You can use the same calendar for the whole family, writing the child's name on the sticker, or make a separate calendar for each child.

TITUS

Purpose
To advise Titus in his responsibility of supervising the churches on the island of Crete

Author
Paul

To Whom Written
Titus, a Greek convert, who had become Paul's special representative to the island of Crete

Date Written
About A.D. 64, around the same time 1 Timothy was written; probably from Macedonia when Paul traveled in between his Roman imprisonments

Setting
Paul sent Titus to organize and oversee the churches on Crete. This letter tells him how to do this job.

Key Verse
"For this cause left I thee in Crete, that thou shouldst set in order the things that are wanting, and ordain elders in every city, as I had appointed thee" (1:5).

Special Features
Titus is very similar to 1 Timothy with its instructions to church leaders.

From a very early age, children begin to want something of their very own—something they don't have to share with anybody, even a sibling. Eventually they may come to want a bedroom of their own or at least a private space. At no age in recorded history have children resolutely insisted on sharing anything. Sometimes, depending on gender and age, children find it hard to share a house with other children who rightfully live there.

If Paul has one message for Titus in this compact letter, it's that his dear son in the faith is vitally connected. It's as if Paul were saying, among other things, that Titus is part of a big, growing family and here's what he needs to do about it.

Search it out. What relational connections do you find here? What strength do they give Titus's life? What responsibilities?

What about your life? Is Christian faith just a Sunday thing, or does it bear upon all the activities and responsibilities that comprise your life?

Think about a Titus-sized view of Christian life, one that suggests that connections and sharing make all the difference.

1

¹Paul, a servant of God, and an apostle of Jesus Christ, according to the faith of God's elect, and the acknowledging of the truth which is after godliness; ²In[a] hope of eternal life, which God, that cannot lie, promised before the world began; ³But hath in due times manifested his word through preaching, which is committed unto me according to the commandment of God our Saviour; ⁴To Titus, *mine* own son after the common faith: Grace, mercy, *and* peace, from God the Father and the Lord Jesus Christ our Saviour.

⁵For this cause left I thee in Crete, that thou shouldest set in order the things that are wanting[b], and ordain elders in every city, as I had appointed thee:

⁶If any be blameless, the husband of one wife, having faithful children not accused of riot or unruly. ⁷For a bishop must be blameless, as the steward of God; not selfwilled, not soon angry, not given to wine, no striker, not given to filthy lucre; ⁸But a lover of hospitality, a lover of good men[c], sober, just, holy, temperate; ⁹Holding fast the faithful word as[d] he hath been taught, that he may be able by sound doctrine both to exhort and to convince the gainsayers. ¹⁰For there are many unruly and vain talkers and deceivers, specially they of the circumcision: ¹¹Whose mouths must be stopped, who subvert whole houses, teaching things which they ought not, for filthy lucre's sake. ¹²One of themselves, *even* a prophet of their own, said, The Cretians *are* alway liars, evil beasts, slow bellies. ¹³This witness is true. Wherefore rebuke them sharply, that they may be sound in the faith; ¹⁴Not giving heed to Jewish fables, and commandments of men, that turn from the truth. ¹⁵Unto the pure all things *are* pure: but unto them that are defiled and unbelieving *is* nothing pure; but even their mind and conscience is defiled. ¹⁶They profess that they know God; but in works they deny *him*, being abominable, and disobedient, and unto every good work reprobate[e].

2

¹But speak thou the things which become sound doctrine: ²That the aged men be sober[a], grave, temperate, sound in faith, in charity, in patience. ³The aged women likewise, that *they be* in behaviour as becometh holiness[b], not false accusers, not given to much wine, teachers of good things; ⁴That they may teach the young women to be sober[c], to love their husbands, to love their children, ⁵*To be* discreet, chaste, keepers at home, good, obedient to their own husbands, that the word of God be not

---

[a] In: or, For
[b] wanting: or, left undone
[c] men: or, things
[d] as . . . : or, in teaching
[e] reprobate: or, void of judgment
[a] sober: or, vigilant
[b] holiness: or, holy women
[c] sober: or, wise

Devotional Moment
·
Role Models

2:3-7 Paul mapped out a very commonsense path to growth, discipleship, and healthy homes: The older men were to teach and model what it meant to be a husband and father to the younger men, while the older women in the church were to teach the younger women how to live as wives and mothers. We learn family living best from older, more mature Christians who have the benefit of both experience and faith. If you do not have such a teacher or mentor, look for someone in your church who is older and wiser and from whom you can learn. Ask this person to consider meeting with you either on occasion or consistently to review your growth in Christ. We all need these God-given sources of wisdom.

blasphemed. ⁶Young men likewise exhort to be sober minded. ⁷In all things shewing thyself a pattern of good works: in doctrine *shewing* uncorruptness, gravity, sincerity, ⁸Sound speech, that cannot be condemned; that he that is of the contrary part may be ashamed, having no evil thing to say of you. ⁹*Exhort* servants to be obedient unto their own masters, *and* to please *them* well in all *things*; not answering again; ¹⁰Not purloining, but shewing all good fidelity; that they may adorn the doctrine of God our Saviour in all things.

¹¹For the grace of God that bringeth salvation hath appeared to all men, ¹²Teaching us that, denying ungodliness and worldly lusts, we should live soberly, righteously, and godly, in this present world; ¹³Looking for that blessed hope, and the glorious^d appearing of the great God and our Saviour Jesus Christ; ¹⁴Who gave himself for us, that he might redeem us from all iniquity, and purify unto himself a peculiar people, zealous of good works.

¹⁵These things speak, and exhort, and rebuke with all authority. Let no man despise thee.

3

¹Put them in mind to be subject to principalities and powers, to obey magistrates, to be ready to every good work, ²To speak evil of no man, to be no brawlers, *but* gentle, shewing all meekness unto all men. ³For we ourselves also were sometimes foolish, disobedient, deceived, serving divers lusts and pleasures, living in malice and envy, hateful, *and* hating one another. ⁴But after that the kindness and love^a of God our Saviour toward man appeared, ⁵Not by works of righteousness which we have done, but according to his mercy he saved us, by the washing of regeneration, and renewing of the Holy Ghost; ⁶Which he shed on us abundantly^b through Jesus Christ our Saviour; ⁷That being justified by his grace, we should be made heirs according to the hope of eternal life. ⁸*This is* a faithful saying, and these things I will that thou affirm constantly, that they which have believed in God might be careful to maintain good works. These things are good and profitable unto men.

⁹But avoid foolish questions, and genealogies, and contentions, and striv-

---

^d glorious . . . : Gr. the appearance of the glory of the great God, and of our Saviour Jesus Christ
^a love: or, pity
^b abundantly: Gr. richly

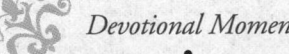

Devotional Moment
•
"Mom, I'm Bored!"

3:14 "Help all who need assistance"—what a simple command, yet how busy it can keep us. Children, teens, and young adults often complain, "I'm bored! There's nothing to do!" Almost as if in answer, the Scriptures say again and again, "Help all those who need assistance." Imagine the difference if we all began curing our boredom with good works and service to others. We need to experience the importance and utility of this command. Turn your next boring evening at home into an adventure in doing good. Your children may catch a vision for ministering to others.

ings about the law; for they are unprofitable and vain. ¹⁰A man that is an heretick after the first and second admonition reject; ¹¹Knowing that he that is such is subverted, and sinneth, being condemned of himself. ¹²When I shall send Artemas unto thee, or Tychicus, be diligent to come unto me to Nicopolis: for I have determined there to winter. ¹³Bring Zenas the lawyer and Apollos on their journey diligently, that nothing be wanting unto them. ¹⁴And let ours also learn to maintainᶜ good works for necessary uses, that they be not unfruitful. ¹⁵All that are with me salute thee. Greet them that love us in the faith. Grace *be* with you all. Amen.

[It was written to Titus, ordained the first bishop of the church of the Cretians, from Nicopolis of Macedonia.]

ᶜ maintain . . . : or, profess honest trades

PHILEMON

Purpose
To convince Philemon to
forgive his runaway
slave, Onesimus, and to
accept him as a brother
in the faith

Author
Paul

To Whom Written
Philemon, who was
probably a wealthy
member of the Colos-
sian church

Date Written
About A.D. 60, during
Paul's first imprison-
ment in Rome, at about
the same time Ephe-
sians and Colossians
were written

Key Verses
"For perhaps he there-
fore departed for a sea-
son, that thou shouldst
receive him for ever; not
now as a servant, but
above a servant, a
brother beloved, spe-
cially to me" (1:15-16).

Key People
Paul, Philemon,
Onesimus

Key Places
Colosse, Rome

Adopting children is hard work. Interviews, paper-work, character checks, and income projections come in a tiring barrage that seems designed to prepare prospective parents for the sleepless nights they may soon face.

For Paul, "adopting" children presented different problems for he is writing about spiritual adoption, not physical adoption. In winning a young man named Ones-imus to the Lord, Paul comes to regard him as a son. Then Paul must deal with the implications of his commitment, for legally his new son belongs to another master.

Slavery was very common in the Roman Empire, and evidently some Christians had slaves. Onesimus, Paul's new convert and "son," was a slave belonging to Philemon. Paul does not condemn the idea of slavery in this letter, but he makes a radical statement by calling this slave Phile-mon's brother in Christ.

When you read this short book, ask, How do you think Onesimus felt about his life after Paul adopted him? What if Paul had merely told Onesimus that they could be good friends? On his way back to Philemon with Paul's let-ter, do you think Onesimus ever thought about escape? Why or why not?

Take note of Paul. His expressions of warm affection and confidence in Onesimus must have been a powerful part of God's work in this young man's life. Everyone needs a parent like the one Onesimus found in Paul.

1

¹Paul, a prisoner of Jesus Christ, and Timothy *our* brother, unto Philemon our dearly beloved, and fellowlabourer, ²And to *our* beloved Apphia, and Archippus our fellowsoldier, and to the church in thy house: ³Grace to you, and peace, from God our Father and the Lord Jesus Christ. ⁴I thank my God, making mention of thee always in my prayers, ⁵Hearing of thy love and faith, which thou hast toward the Lord Jesus, and toward all saints; ⁶That the communication of thy faith may become effectual by the acknowledging of every good thing which is in you in Christ Jesus. ⁷For we have great joy and consolation in thy love, because the bowels of the saints are refreshed by thee, brother.

⁸Wherefore, though I might be much bold in Christ to enjoin thee that which is convenient, ⁹Yet for love's sake I rather beseech *thee*, being such an one as Paul the aged, and now also a prisoner of Jesus Christ. ¹⁰I beseech thee for my son Onesimus, whom I have begotten in my bonds: ¹¹Which in time past was to thee unprofitable, but now profitable to thee and to me: ¹²Whom I have sent again: thou therefore receive him, that is, mine own bowels: ¹³Whom I would have retained with me, that in thy stead he might have ministered unto me in the bonds of the gospel: ¹⁴But without thy mind would I do nothing; that thy benefit should not be as it were of necessity, but willingly. ¹⁵For perhaps he therefore departed for a season, that thou shouldest receive him for ever; ¹⁶Not now as a servant, but above a servant, a brother beloved, specially to me, but how much more unto thee, both in the flesh, and in the Lord? ¹⁷If thou count me therefore a partner, receive him as myself. ¹⁸If he hath wronged thee, or oweth *thee* ought, put that on mine account; ¹⁹I Paul have written *it* with mine own hand, I will repay *it*: albeit I do not say to thee how thou owest unto me even

Philemon

LESSONS FROM PHILEMON AS A HEAD OF HOUSEHOLD

Being in charge means treating others with respect. Legally, Philemon had the right to have Onesimus put to death. But Paul urged him, as a Christian, to forgive Onesimus and restore him to good favor. Similarly, we need to extend grace and forgiveness to those under our care, even when they disobey.

Dealing with rebellion does not require cruelty or harsh measures, only firm action. We don't know how Philemon responded to Paul's letter, but it seems reasonable to guess that he heeded Paul's appeal. Philemon's love for God and for God's people was so well known that Paul was confident he would listen. In your family, strive to resolve disputes without squashing the offenders.

Could a Christian own a slave? Believe it or not, that's exactly what Philemon was—a Christian slave owner. The book in the New Testament known as Philemon is actually a letter that this man received from Paul. It concerned a slave of Philemon's named Onesimus.

Onesimus was not a Christian. One day he broke into the family vault, stole some stuff, and fled. While on the run, he met Paul. Onesimus heard about Jesus and became a Christian.

Paul sent him back to Philemon with this letter in which he pleaded with his friend to take back Onesimus as a Christian brother and forgive him for his offense.

It's tempting to condemn Philemon for having a slave in the first place, but that would be provincial as well as self-righteous. Philemon lived in the Roman Empire. Most work was done by slaves; all sorts of people owned slaves; and many people who were slaves then had little means for supporting themselves if they were free. In that context, a Christian slave owner could provide an important act of social justice by owning slaves and treating them with respect and grace.

Philemon's biggest dilemma was more familiar to us: How should he deal with a repentant rebel? Every head of household faces the same dilemma. As we learn from Paul's letter to Philemon, we need to recognize that *all* people deserve respect and grace. That's the Christian way. Let it be yours, too.

thine own self besides. ²⁰Yea, brother, let me have joy of thee in the Lord: refresh my bowels in the Lord. ²¹Having confidence in thy obedience I wrote unto thee, knowing that thou wilt also do more than I say. ²²But withal prepare me also a lodging: for I trust that through your prayers I shall be given unto you. ²³There salute thee Epaphras, my fellowprisoner in Christ Jesus; ²⁴Marcus, Aristarchus, Demas, Lucas, my fellowlabourers. ²⁵The grace of our Lord Jesus Christ *be* with your spirit. Amen.

[Written from Rome to Philemon, by Onesimus a servant.]

HEBREWS

Purpose
To present the sufficiency and superiority of Christ

Author
The name of the author is not given in the biblical text itself. Paul, Luke, Barnabas, Apollos, Silas, Philip, Priscilla, and others have been suggested.

To Whom Written
Hebrew Christians who may have been considering a return to Judaism

Date Written
Probably before the destruction of the Temple in Jerusalem in A.D. 70

Setting
These Jewish Christians were probably undergoing fierce persecution. The people needed to be reassured that Christianity was true and that Jesus was indeed the Messiah.

Key Verse
(The Son) "being the brightness of (God's) glory, and the express image of his person, and upholding all things by the word of his power" (1:3).

Key People
Old Testament men and women of faith (chapter 11)

Special Features
Although Hebrews is called a "letter" (13:22), it has the form and the content of a sermon.

Big families have a special aura. A big family is usually not a rich one, which means that everybody makes sacrifices and nobody skips chores. A big family means hand-me-downs, used cars, and state park vacations. When someone gets sick, the bug can last a year. Noise levels at dinner are measured in relation to jet aircraft takeoffs. One sibling a night stands duty at the phone, directing calls and taking messages. The basement laundry pile doubles as a trampoline. Don't ask about the toothpaste tube at bedtime.

Hebrews is about a big family, the family of faith. This book stretches back beyond time; it picks up where the Bible begins and looks ahead to the biggest reunion ever planned. Always its focus is on Christ, the Savior, who is both higher than angels and beside us as a brother. Hebrews delights in the joy of a big family.

Maybe your family is two, three, or four. You're not enough for a baseball team, a basketball team, even a bobsled team. Enjoy the family history here; look forward to the big reunion; learn about your wonderful brother-Savior; get involved with the family of Christians around you and around the world.

Hebrews can turn a quiet room into a bustling, booming household.

Devotional Moment

•

Forgiven

1:3 Jesus had many skills, taught great truths, and helped many people, yet his greatest accomplishment was paying for our sins. If you have ever needed a doctor with a specialty in healing souls, or a counselor with a gift for helping people through guilt and remorse, or an attorney with the ability to win acquittals—then you know how important Jesus' work is. There's no sin so big, no guilt so intense, no crime so heinous that Jesus cannot deal with it. He made cleansing us from sin his top priority. He can handle your case.

1

¹God, who at sundry times and in divers manners spake in time past unto the fathers by the prophets, ²Hath in these last days spoken unto us by *his* Son, whom he hath appointed heir of all things, by whom also he made the worlds; ³Who being the brightness of *his* glory, and the express image of his person, and upholding all things by the word of his power, when he had by himself purged our sins, sat down on the right hand of the Majesty on high;

⁴Being made so much better than the angels, as he hath by inheritance obtained a more excellent name than they. ⁵For unto which of the angels said he at any time, Thou art my Son, this day have I begotten thee? And again, I will be to him a Father, and he shall be to me a Son? ⁶And againᵃ, when he bringeth in the firstbegotten into the world, he saith, And let all the angels of God worship him. ⁷And ofᵇ the angels he saith, Who maketh his angels spirits, and his ministers a flame of fire. ⁸But unto the Son *he saith*, Thy throne, O God, *is* for ever and ever: a sceptre of righteousnessᶜ *is* the sceptre of thy kingdom. ⁹Thou hast loved righteousness, and hated iniquity; therefore God, *even* thy God, hath anointed thee with the oil of gladness above thy fellows. ¹⁰And, Thou, Lord, in the beginning hast laid the foundation of the earth; and the heavens are the works of thine hands: ¹¹They shall perish; but thou remainest; and they all shall wax old as doth a garment; ¹²And as a vesture shalt thou fold them up, and they shall be changed: but thou art the same, and thy years shall not fail. ¹³But to which of the angels said he at any time, Sit on my right hand, until I make thine enemies thy footstool? ¹⁴Are they not all ministering spirits, sent forth to minister for them who shall be heirs of salvation?

2

¹Therefore we ought to give the more earnest heed to the things which we have heard, lest at any time we should let *them* slipᵃ. ²For if the word spoken by angels was stedfast, and every transgression and disobedience received a just recompence of reward; ³How shall we escape, if we neglect so great salvation; which at the first began to be spoken by the Lord, and was confirmed unto us by them that heard *him*; ⁴God

---

ᵃ again . . . : or, when he bringeth again
ᵇ And of: Gr. And unto
ᶜ righteousness: Gr. rightness, or, straightness
ᵃ let . . . : Gr. run out as leaking vessels

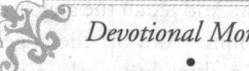

Devotional Moment
•
Paying Attention

2:1-3 Much can happen during the course of a day that would put personal and family devotions on the back burner. These verses remind us of the supreme importance of remembering God and the priority of God's Word and prayer amid the rush of a day and evening. We should pay attention to God's Word because our salvation is more important than anything else. We need to anchor busy lives in hope, love, and faith, and we find that anchor in the Bible and in prayerful communion with God. Treat devotions like a drinking fountain on a hot day. Come to the table to count your blessings, to hear the promise, to sing your thanks.

also bearing *them* witness, both with signs and wonders, and with divers miracles, and gifts[b] of the Holy Ghost, according to his own will?

⁵For unto the angels hath he not put in subjection the world to come, whereof we speak. ⁶But one in a certain place testified, saying, What is man, that thou art mindful of him? or the son of man, that thou visitest him? ⁷Thou madest him a little lower[c] than the angels; thou crownedst him with glory and honour, and didst set him over the works of thy hands: ⁸Thou hast put all things in subjection under his feet. For in that he put all in subjection under him, he left nothing *that is* not put under him. But now we see not yet all things put under him. ⁹But we see Jesus, who was made a little lower than the angels for the suffering of death, crowned with glory and honour; that he by the grace of God should taste death for every man.

¹⁰For it became him, for whom *are* all things, and by whom *are* all things, in bringing many sons unto glory, to make the captain of their salvation perfect through sufferings. ¹¹For both he that sanctifieth and they who are sanctified *are* all of one: for which cause he is not ashamed to call them brethren, ¹²Saying, I will declare thy name unto my brethren, in the midst of the church will I sing praise unto thee. ¹³And again, I will put my trust in him. And again, Behold I and the children which God hath given me.

¹⁴Forasmuch then as the children are partakers of flesh and blood, he also himself likewise took part of the same; that through death he might destroy him that had the power of death, that is, the devil; ¹⁵And deliver them who

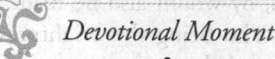

Devotional Moment
•
Family Problems

2:14-18 Jesus became a real, live, human being, with all the aches, pains, hurts, and troubles that go with it. Every family has problems, from bike repair to body repair. Phone numbers taped to kitchen refrigerators speak of our need for mechanics, doctors, dentists, plumbers, hardware stores, and fire departments.

These verses describe the greatest helper families could ever hope for. He can free us, take away fear, and deliver us from death's power. He feels our hurts and shares our frustrations. He stands before Almighty God to build us a heavenly home that lasts forever.

Next to all those other numbers on the refrigerator, tape this one: P-R-A-Y-E-R. Call it often. Every member of the family should know that this number gets an answer on the first ring, always. It's a busy line, but it never gives a busy signal.

---

[b] gifts: or, distributions

[c] lower . . . : or, while inferior to

through fear of death were all their lifetime subject to bondage. ¹⁶For verily he took not[d] on *him the nature of* angels; but he took on *him* the seed of Abraham. ¹⁷Wherefore in all things it behoved him to be made like unto *his* brethren, that he might be a merciful and faithful high priest in things *pertaining* to God, to make reconciliation for the sins of the people. ¹⁸For in that he himself hath suffered being tempted, he is able to succour them that are tempted.

3

¹Wherefore, holy brethren, partakers of the heavenly calling, consider the Apostle and High Priest of our profession, Christ Jesus; ²Who was faithful to him that appointed[a] him, as also Moses *was faithful* in all his house. ³For this *man* was counted worthy of more glory than Moses, inasmuch as he who hath builded the house hath more honour than the house. ⁴For every house is builded by some *man;* but he that built all things *is* God. ⁵And Moses verily *was* faithful in all his house, as a servant, for a testimony of those things which were to be spoken after; ⁶But Christ as a son over his own house; whose house are we, if we hold fast the confidence and the rejoicing of the hope firm unto the end.

⁷Wherefore (as the Holy Ghost saith, To day if ye will hear his voice, ⁸Harden not your hearts, as in the provocation, in the day of temptation in the wilderness: ⁹When your fathers tempted me, proved me, and saw my works forty years. ¹⁰Wherefore I was grieved with that generation, and said, They do alway err in *their* heart; and they have not known my ways. ¹¹So I sware in my wrath, They shall not enter into my rest.) ¹²Take heed, brethren, lest there be in any of you an evil heart of unbelief, in departing from the living God. ¹³But exhort one another daily, while it is called To day; lest any of you be hardened through the deceitfulness of sin. ¹⁴For we are made partakers of Christ, if we hold the beginning of our confidence stedfast unto the end; ¹⁵While it is said, To day if ye will hear his voice, harden not your hearts, as in the provocation. ¹⁶For some, when they had heard, did provoke: howbeit not all that came out of Egypt by Moses. ¹⁷But with whom was he grieved forty years? *was it* not with them that had sinned, whose carcases fell in the wilderness? ¹⁸And to whom sware he that they should not enter into his rest, but to them that believed not? ¹⁹So we see that they could not enter in because of unbelief.

Devotional Moment
•
Old Testament Treasures

3:5 This footnote on Moses reminds us of the treasure we have in Old Testament stories. Courage, sacrifice, romance, gallantry, struggle against great adversaries—it's all there. In many ways, men and women of the Old Testament era lived as we do, and their faithfulness can help us. But the footnote also reminds us that the Old Testament is incomplete. To stop there is never to know the climax of the Bible's big story: Jesus Christ, the Messiah, Son of God, Savior. Everyone caught in wonder at Daniel's faith should know that Jesus is our strength in any lions' den. Everyone drawn to Ruth's happily-ever-after ending should know that Jesus wants to love us and lead us to a home he has prepared.

---

[d] took not . . . : Gr. taketh not hold of angels, but of the seed of Abraham he taketh hold
[a] appointed: Gr. made

4

¹Let us therefore fear, lest, a promise being left *us* of entering into his rest, any of you should seem to come short of it. ²For unto us was the gospel preached, as well as unto them: but the word[a] preached did not profit them, not being mixed with faith in them that heard *it.* ³For we which have believed do enter into rest, as he said, As I have sworn in my wrath, if they shall enter into my rest: although the works were finished from the foundation of the world. ⁴For he spake in a certain place of the seventh *day* on this wise, And God did rest the seventh day from all his works. ⁵And in this *place* again, If they shall enter into my rest. ⁶Seeing therefore it remaineth that some must enter therein, and they to whom it was first preached entered not in because of unbelief: ⁷Again, he limiteth a certain day, saying in David, To day, after so long a time; as it is said, To day if ye will hear his voice, harden not your hearts. ⁸For if Jesus[b] had given them rest, then would he not afterward have spoken of another day. ⁹There remaineth therefore a rest[c] to the people of God. ¹⁰For he that is entered into his rest, he also hath ceased from his own works, as God *did* from his.

¹¹Let us labour therefore to enter into that rest, lest any man fall after the same example of unbelief[d]. ¹²For the word of God *is* quick, and powerful, and sharper than any twoedged sword, piercing even to the dividing asunder of soul and spirit, and of the joints and

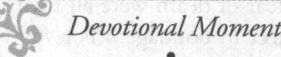

Devotional Moment
•
A Powerful Read

4:12 The Word of God has great power. It helps us uncover, understand, and deal with our thoughts and desires. The Bible is no ordinary book. It's not magic; it is God's Word—living and active, powerful and effective. All of us need to remember that the Bible holds more authority and power than we'll ever have; we need to take advantage of that. That doesn't mean we should use the Bible as a club or a weapon; we should let it speak for itself. But we can make it a daily part of our life through devotions, readings at dinner, or in singing Scripture choruses.

marrow, and *is* a discerner of the thoughts and intents of the heart. ¹³Neither is there any creature that is not manifest in his sight: but all things *are* naked and opened unto the eyes of him with whom we have to do. ¹⁴Seeing then that we have a great high priest, that is passed into the heavens, Jesus the Son of God, let us hold fast *our* profession. ¹⁵For we have not an high priest which cannot be touched with the feeling of our infirmities; but was in all points tempted like as *we are, yet* without sin. ¹⁶Let us therefore come boldly unto the throne of grace, that we may obtain mercy, and find grace to help in time of need.

5

¹For every high priest taken from among men is ordained for men in things *pertaining* to God, that he may

---

[a] the word . . . : Gr. the word of hearing
[b] Jesus: that is, Joshua
[c] rest: or, keeping of a sabbath
[d] unbelief: or, disobedience

offer both gifts and sacrifices for sins: [2]Who can[a] have compassion on the ignorant, and on them that are out of the way; for that he himself also is compassed with infirmity. [3]And by reason hereof he ought, as for the people, so also for himself, to offer for sins. [4]And no man taketh this honour unto himself, but he that is called of God, as *was* Aaron. [5]So also Christ glorified not himself to be made an high priest; but he that said unto him, Thou art my Son, to day have I begotten thee. [6]As he saith also in another *place*, Thou *art* a priest for ever after the order of Melchisedec. [7]Who in the days of his flesh, when he had offered up prayers and supplications with strong crying and tears unto him that was able to save him from death, and was heard in that[b] he feared; [8]Though he were a Son, yet learned he obedience by the things which he suffered; [9]And being made perfect, he became the author of eternal salvation unto all them that obey him;

[10]Called of God an high priest after the order of Melchisedec. [11]Of whom we have many things to say, and hard to be uttered, seeing ye are dull of hearing. [12]For when for the time ye ought to be teachers, ye have need that one teach you again which *be* the first principles of the oracles of God; and are become such as have need of milk, and not of strong meat. [13]For every one that useth milk *is* unskilful in the word of righteousness: for he is a babe. [14]But strong meat belongeth to them that are of full

---

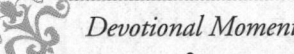

Devotional Moment
•
Growing (Up)

5:12-14 The believers who received this letter had known the basics of their faith long enough; it was time for them to move on, to mature. But these believers who should have been acting like adults were behaving like infants.

To live as a Christian means to grow from basic truth about God to a more muscular faith that can see right from wrong and stand with the right. The people described here were still passively learning when they should have been witnessing boldly and working hard for justice and peace. Let your family be a greenhouse of growing people—strong, faithful, loving—nourished by God's gourmet menu: the Bible at its deepest, the Spirit at his fullest.

---

age[c], *even* those who by reason of use have their senses exercised to discern both good and evil.

6

[1]Therefore leaving the principles[a] of the doctrine of Christ, let us go on unto perfection; not laying again the foundation of repentance from dead works, and of faith toward God, [2]Of the doctrine of baptisms, and of laying on of hands, and of resurrection of the dead, and of eternal judgment. [3]And this will we do, if God permit. [4]For *it is* impossible for those who were once enlightened, and have tasted of the heavenly gift, and were made partakers of the Holy Ghost, [5]And have tasted the good word of God, and the powers of the world to come, [6]If they shall fall away,

---

[a] can . . . : or, can reasonably bear with
[b] in that . . . : or, for his piety
[c] of full age: or, perfect
[a] principles . . . : or, word of the beginning of

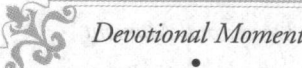

Devotional Moment
•
Never Give Up

6:10-12 The writer did not want the Hebrews to get discouraged. He knew that faithfulness to God, in service to others and helping them, rarely brings instant rewards. In the middle of a tiring day or a seemingly endless battle with a strong will, you may think, *Is this really worth it? Has God forgotten me?* Rest assured: God won't forget your hard work for him. Keep reminding yourself that one day your work in nurturing others will bring a reward greater than any straight-A report card or scholarship to Harvard.

to renew them again unto repentance; seeing they crucify to themselves the Son of God afresh, and put *him* to an open shame. ⁷For the earth which drinketh in the rain that cometh oft upon it, and bringeth forth herbs meet for them byᵇ whom it is dressed, receiveth blessing from God: ⁸But that which beareth thorns and briers *is* rejected, and *is* nigh unto cursing; whose end *is* to be burned.

⁹But, beloved, we are persuaded better things of you, and things that accompany salvation, though we thus speak. ¹⁰For God *is* not unrighteous to forget your work and labour of love, which ye have shewed toward his name, in that ye have ministered to the saints, and do minister. ¹¹And we desire that every one of you do shew the same diligence to the full assurance of hope unto the end: ¹²That ye be not slothful, but followers of them who through faith and patience inherit the promises. ¹³For

when God made promise to Abraham, because he could swear by no greater, he sware by himself, ¹⁴Saying, Surely blessing I will bless thee, and multiplying I will multiply thee. ¹⁵And so, after he had patiently endured, he obtained the promise. ¹⁶For men verily swear by the greater: and an oath for confirmation *is* to them an end of all strife. ¹⁷Wherein God, willing more abundantly to shew unto the heirs of promise the immutability of his counsel, confirmed *it* byᶜ an oath: ¹⁸That by two immutable things, in which *it was* impossible for God to lie, we might have a strong consolation, who have fled for refuge to lay hold upon the hope set before us: ¹⁹Which *hope* we have as an anchor of the soul, both sure and stedfast, and which entereth into that within the veil; ²⁰Whither the forerunner is for us entered, *even* Jesus, made an high priest for ever after the order of Melchisedec.

7

¹For this Melchisedec, king of Salem, priest of the most high God, who met Abraham returning from the slaughter of the kings, and blessed him; ²To whom also Abraham gave a tenth part of all; first being by interpretation King of righteousness, and after that also King of Salem, which is, King of peace; ³Without father, without mother, without descentᵃ, having neither beginning of days, nor end of life; but made like unto the Son of God; abideth a priest continually. ⁴Now consider how great

ᵇ by: or, for
ᶜ confirmed . . . : Gr. interposed himself by
ᵃ without descent: Gr. without pedigree

this man *was*, unto whom even the patriarch Abraham gave the tenth of the spoils. ⁵And verily they that are of the sons of Levi, who receive the office of the priesthood, have a commandment to take tithes of the people according to the law, that is, of their brethren, though they come out of the loins of Abraham: ⁶But he whose descent is not counted from them received tithes of Abraham, and blessed him that had the promises. ⁷And without all contradiction the less is blessed of the better. ⁸And here men that die receive tithes; but there he *receiveth them*, of whom it is witnessed that he liveth. ⁹And as I may so say, Levi also, who receiveth tithes, payed tithes in Abraham. ¹⁰For he was yet in the loins of his father, when Melchisedec met him.

¹¹If therefore perfection were by the Levitical priesthood, (for under it the people received the law,) what further need *was there* that another priest should rise after the order of Melchisedec, and not be called after the order of Aaron? ¹²For the priesthood being changed, there is made of necessity a change also of the law. ¹³For he of whom these things are spoken pertaineth to another tribe, of which no man gave attendance at the altar. ¹⁴For *it is* evident that our Lord sprang out of Juda; of which tribe Moses spake nothing concerning priesthood. ¹⁵And it is yet far more evident: for that after the similitude of Melchisedec there ariseth another priest, ¹⁶Who is made, not after the law of a carnal commandment, but after the power of an endless life. ¹⁷For he testifieth, Thou *art* a priest

for ever after the order of Melchisedec. ¹⁸For there is verily a disannulling of the commandment going before for the weakness and unprofitableness thereof. ¹⁹For the law made nothing perfect, but the bringing in of a better hope *did*; by the which we draw nigh unto God. ²⁰And inasmuch as not without an oath *he was made priest*: ²¹(For those priests were made without[b] an oath; but this with an oath by him that said unto him, The Lord sware and will not repent, Thou *art* a priest for ever after the order of Melchisedec:) ²²By so much was Jesus made a surety of a better testament. ²³And they truly were many priests, because they were not suffered to continue by reason of death: ²⁴But this *man*, because he continueth ever, hath an unchangeable priesthood. ²⁵Wherefore he is able also to save them to the uttermost that come unto God by him, seeing he ever liveth to make intercession for them. ²⁶For such an high priest became us, *who is* holy, harmless, undefiled, separate from sinners, and made higher than the heavens; ²⁷Who needeth not daily, as those high priests, to offer up sacrifice, first for his own sins, and then for the people's: for this he did once, when he offered up himself. ²⁸For the law maketh men high priests which have infirmity; but the word of the oath, which was since the law, *maketh* the Son, who is consecrated[c] for evermore.

8

¹Now of the things which we have spoken *this is* the sum: We have such an high priest, who is set on the right hand

---

[b] without . . . : or, without swearing of an oath
[c] consecrated: Gr. perfected

of the throne of the Majesty in the heavens; ²A minister of the sanctuaryª, and of the true tabernacle, which the Lord pitched, and not man. ³For every high priest is ordained to offer gifts and sacrifices: wherefore *it is* of necessity that this man have somewhat also to offer. ⁴For if he were on earth, he should not be a priest, seeing that there are priests that offer gifts according to the law: ⁵Who serve unto the example and shadow of heavenly things, as Moses was admonished of God when he was about to make the tabernacle: for, See, saith he, *that* thou make all things according to the pattern shewed to thee in the mount.

⁶But now hath he obtained a more excellent ministry, by how much also he is the mediator of a better covenantᵇ, which was established upon better promises. ⁷For if that first *covenant* had been faultless, then should no place have been sought for the second. ⁸For finding fault with them, he saith, Behold, the days come, saith the Lord, when I will make a new covenant with the house of Israel and with the house of Judah: ⁹Not according to the covenant that I made with their fathers in the day when I took them by the hand to lead them out of the land of Egypt; because they continued not in my covenant, and I regarded them not, saith the Lord. ¹⁰For this *is* the covenant that I will make with the house of Israel after those days, saith the Lord; I will putᶜ my laws into their mind, and write them in their hearts: and I will be to them a God, and they shall be to me a people: ¹¹And they shall not teach every man his neighbour, and every man his brother, saying, Know the Lord: for all shall know me, from the least to the greatest. ¹²For I will be merciful to their unrighteousness, and their sins and their iniquities will I remember no more. ¹³In that he saith, A new *covenant,* he hath made the first old. Now that which decayeth and waxeth old *is* ready to vanish away.

9

¹Then verily the first *covenant* had also ordinancesª of divine service, and a worldly sanctuary. ²For there was a tabernacle made; the first, wherein *was* the candlestick, and the table, and the shewbread; which is called the sanctuaryᵇ. ³And after the second veil, the tabernacle which is called the Holiest of all; ⁴Which had the golden censer, and the ark of the covenant overlaid round about with gold, wherein *was* the golden pot that had manna, and Aaron's rod that budded, and the tables of the covenant; ⁵And over it the cherubims of glory shadowing the mercyseat; of which we cannot now speak particularly. ⁶Now when these things were thus ordained, the priests went always into the first tabernacle, accomplishing the service *of God.* ⁷But into the second *went* the high priest alone once every

---

ª of the sanctuary: or, of holy things
ᵇ covenant: or, testament
ᶜ put: Gr. give
ª ordinances: or, ceremonies
ᵇ the sanctuary: or, holy

Family Traditions

Making Faith a Family Tradition
HEBREWS 11–12

What is faith? It is the confident assurance that something we want is going to happen."

As a family, what are your hopes? What are your common and individual aspirations? Here are practices that families across the continent use to keep faith aflame:

• A family journal records the crossroads faced and the decisions made every year. It documents fears and questions and how they are overcome. Keep the family journal with photo albums so everyone can look at it frequently.

• Affirm the joy of life in Christ. Did one of the children lead a friend to Christ? Did one of them make a difficult personal decision to do the right thing? Did any of them finish a Bible study course? Did they return from a mission trip? Find a way to say, "We're proud of you. Our whole family rejoices in what you've done."

• Establish an agenda for reaching family goals. Spiritually, where do you want to be in five years? What steps are necessary to grow? Which of these will you take this year, the next, and the next? What difficulties inherent in your family do you want to overcome? What monuments to faith do you want to build? What kind of family legacy do you want to leave? What do you want people to say about your family? Make these questions part of a discussion around your dinner table at least once a year.

• Climb a mountain as a family—literally! Hiking a steep trail in the foothills may be the best example of what it takes to stay with the program, keep going, and do not give up. One family does this every summer just to illustrate the spiritual pilgrimage.

• Establish a quiet hour each weekend, when everyone is home, to pray specifically for your family. Encourage each family member to get alone with God for at least part of that hour. Some families also set aside a day of prayer once a year. Keep pictures of family members on hand and a small notebook and pencil to jot down prayer requests. Short prayers can also be written in the notebook to encourage the next one who uses it.

year, not without blood, which he offered for himself, and *for* the errors of the people:

⁸The Holy Ghost this signifying, that the way into the holiest of all was not yet made manifest, while as the first tabernacle was yet standing: ⁹Which *was* a figure for the time then present, in which were offered both gifts and sacrifices, that could not make him that did the service perfect, as pertaining to the conscience; ¹⁰*Which stood* only in meats and drinks, and divers washings, and carnal ordinances^c, imposed *on them* until the time of reformation. ¹¹But Christ being come an high priest of good things to come, by a greater and more perfect tabernacle, not made with hands, that is to say, not of this building; ¹²Neither by the blood of goats and calves, but by his own blood he entered in once into the holy place, having obtained eternal redemption *for us.* ¹³For if the blood of bulls and of goats, and the ashes of an heifer sprinkling the unclean, sanctifieth to the purifying of the flesh: ¹⁴How much more shall the blood of Christ, who through the eternal Spirit offered himself without spot^d to God, purge your conscience from dead works to serve the living God?

¹⁵And for this cause he is the mediator of the new testament, that by means of death, for the redemption of the transgressions *that were* under the first testament, they which are called

might receive the promise of eternal inheritance. ¹⁶For where a testament *is,* there must also of necessity be^e the death of the testator. ¹⁷For a testament *is* of force after men are dead: otherwise it is of no strength at all while the testator liveth. ¹⁸Whereupon neither the first *testament* was dedicated^f without blood. ¹⁹For when Moses had spoken every precept to all the people according to the law, he took the blood of calves and of goats, with water, and scarlet^g wool, and hyssop, and sprinkled both the book, and all the people, ²⁰Saying, This *is* the blood of the testament which God hath enjoined unto you. ²¹Moreover he sprinkled with blood both the tabernacle, and all the vessels of the ministry. ²²And almost all things are by the law purged with blood; and without shedding of blood is no remission.

²³*It was* therefore necessary that the patterns of things in the heavens should be purified with these; but the heavenly things themselves with better sacrifices than these. ²⁴For Christ is not entered into the holy places made with hands, *which are* the figures of the true; but into heaven itself, now to appear in the presence of God for us: ²⁵Nor yet that he should offer himself often, as the high priest entereth into the holy place every year with blood of others; ²⁶For then must he often have suffered since the foundation of the world: but now once in the end of the world hath he appeared to put away sin by the sacri-

---

^c ordinances: or, rites, or, ceremonies
^d spot: or, fault
^e be: or, be brought in
^f dedicated: or, purified
^g scarlet: or, purple

fice of himself. [27]And as it is appointed unto men once to die, but after this the judgment: [28]So Christ was once offered to bear the sins of many; and unto them that look for him shall he appear the second time without sin unto salvation.

10

[1]For the law having a shadow of good things to come, *and* not the very image of the things, can never with those sacrifices which they offered year by year continually make the comers thereunto perfect. [2]For then would they not have ceased to be offered? because that the worshippers once purged should have had no more conscience of sins. [3]But in those *sacrifices there is* a remembrance again *made* of sins every year. [4]For *it is* not possible that the blood of bulls and of goats should take away sins. [5]Wherefore when he cometh into the world, he saith, Sacrifice and offering thou wouldest not, but a body hast thou prepared me: [6]In burnt offerings and *sacrifices* for sin thou hast had no pleasure.

[7]Then said I, Lo, I come (in the volume of the book it is written of me,) to do thy will, O God. [8]Above when he said, Sacrifice and offering and burnt offerings and *offering* for sin thou wouldest not, neither hadst pleasure *therein*; which are offered by the law; [9]Then said he, Lo, I come to do thy will, O God. He taketh away the first, that he may establish the second. [10]By the which will we are sanctified through the offering of the body of Jesus Christ once *for all.* [11]And every priest standeth daily ministering and offering oftentimes the same sacrifices, which can never take away sins: [12]But this man, after he had offered one sacrifice for sins for ever, sat down on the right hand of God; [13]From henceforth expecting till his enemies be made his footstool. [14]For by one offering he hath perfected for ever them that are sanctified. [15]*Whereof* the Holy Ghost also is a witness to us: for after that he had said before, [16]This *is* the covenant that I will make with them after those days, saith the Lord, I will put my laws into their hearts, and in their minds will I write them; [17]And their[a] sins and iniquities will I remember no more. [18]Now where remission of these *is, there is* no more offering for sin.

[19]Having therefore, brethren, boldness[b] to enter into the holiest by the blood of Jesus, [20]By a new and living way, which he hath consecrated[c] for us, through the veil, that is to say, his flesh; [21]And *having* an high priest over the house of God; [22]Let us draw near with a true heart in full assurance of faith, having our hearts sprinkled from an evil conscience, and our bodies washed with pure water. [23]Let us hold fast the profession of *our* faith without wavering; (for he *is* faithful that promised;) [24]And let us consider one another to provoke unto love and to good works: [25]Not forsaking the assembling of ourselves together, as the manner of some *is*; but exhorting *one another*: and so much the more, as ye see the day ap-

---

[a] And their: some copies have, Then he said, And their
[b] boldness: or, liberty
[c] consecrated: or, new made

proaching. ²⁶For if we sin wilfully after that we have received the knowledge of the truth, there remaineth no more sacrifice for sins, ²⁷But a certain fearful looking for of judgment and fiery indignation, which shall devour the adversaries. ²⁸He that despised Moses' law died without mercy under two or three witnesses: ²⁹Of how much sorer punishment, suppose ye, shall he be thought worthy, who hath trodden under foot the Son of God, and hath counted the blood of the covenant, wherewith he was sanctified, an unholy thing, and hath done despite unto the Spirit of grace? ³⁰For we know him that hath said, Vengeance *belongeth* unto me, I will recompense, saith the Lord. And again, The Lord shall judge his people. ³¹*It is* a fearful thing to fall into the hands of the living God. ³²But call to remembrance the former days, in which, after ye were illuminated, ye endured a great fight of afflictions; ³³Partly, whilst ye were made a gazingstock both by reproaches and afflictions; and partly, whilst ye became companions of them that were so used. ³⁴For ye had compassion of me in my bonds, and took joyfully the spoiling of your goods, knowing in yourselves^d that ye have in heaven a better and an enduring substance. ³⁵Cast not away therefore your confidence, which hath great recompence of reward. ³⁶For ye have need of patience, that, after ye have done the will of God, ye might receive the promise. ³⁷For yet a little while, and he that shall come will come, and will not tarry. ³⁸Now the

---

Devotional Moment
•
Enduring Struggle

10:32-39 Once again the Hebrews were urged to persevere in the face of opposition. The key to their endurance is mentioned in verse 35—their trust (faith) in God and in his truth. Perseverance is much more than just pressing on. It comes from being convinced that God is with us and will guide us, reward us, and one day return for us. It's a simple idea and absolutely true. Where do you feel opposition to your efforts to fulfill your God-given roles? Don't lose confidence in God's way; remember that he is with you.

---

just shall live by faith: but if *any man* draw back, my soul shall have no pleasure in him. ³⁹But we are not of them who draw back unto perdition; but of them that believe to the saving of the soul.

11

¹Now faith is the substance^a of things hoped for, the evidence of things not seen. ²For by it the elders obtained a good report. ³Through faith we understand that the worlds were framed by the word of God, so that things which are seen were not made of things which do appear.

⁴By faith Abel offered unto God a more excellent sacrifice than Cain, by which he obtained witness that he was righteous, God testifying of his gifts: and by it he being dead yet^b speaketh. ⁵By faith Enoch was translated that he should not see death; and was not found, because God had translated

---

^d in yourselves . . . : or, that ye have in [or, for] yourselves

^a substance: or, ground, or, confidence

^b yet . . . : or, is yet spoken of

Discipline or Punishment?

by Bruce Narramore

There is a world of difference between discipline and vengeful, angry punishment. God's righteousness requires that sin be punished, but Christ took that punishment once and for all when he was crucified two thousand years ago.

While Hebrews 12:5-11 speaks of punishment as "chastisement," the context shows that the meaning is what we would more commonly call *discipline*. Contrast Hebrews 12:5-11, which refers to Christians, with the following passage, which concerns those who have rejected God.

"Behold, the day of the Lord cometh, cruel both with wrath and fierce anger, to lay the land desolate; and he shall destroy the sinners. . . . For the stars of heaven and the constellations thereof shall not give their light: the sun shall be darkened in his going forth, and the moon shall not cause her light to shine. And I will punish the world for their evil, and the wicked for their iniquity; and I will cause the arrogancy of the proud to cease, and will lay low the haughtiness of the terrible" (Isa. 13:9-11).

Notice the differences between God's *punishment* and his *discipline*. First, the purpose of punishment is to inflict pain as a penalty or to balance the scales of justice. Those who do not place their faith in Christ must suffer the penalty of their sin. In contrast, the purpose of discipline is to help God's children mature and grow.

Second, the focus of punishment is different from the focus of discipline. Punishment focuses largely on the past; it says, "You did that back then. Now you have to pay." Discipline focuses largely on the future; it says, "I want you to learn to respond better next time."

Third, the attitude of the parent is different. Punishment is done in anger (in God's case, righteous anger), while discipline is done in purposeful love.

Finally, the child's responses to punishment and discipline are different. The natural reactions to angry punishment are fear, guilt, and resentment. But Hebrews 12:5-12 reminds us that we shouldn't become angry or discouraged by God's correction because it's not punishment—it's discipline, with the purpose of training us. The natural response to loving discipline, even firm discipline, is a sense of security and respect.

Just as God never angrily or vengefully punishes his children, we should never punish ours. We should discipline them, of course, and sometimes our discipline will need to be firm and painful. But that is different from punishing. Punishment is a way to make children pay for their misdeeds. Discipline is the work of a loving mother or father committed to teaching his or her children how to live.

Punishment may bring short-term changes in behavior because it intimidates children. But even when it produces the behavior we want, it makes our children angry, guilty, fearful, or depressed. Many children who are punished in anger later rebel. They silently retort, *I'll show you,* or *Just wait until I'm eighteen!*

If you are like most parents, you react to your children's misbehavior with a mixture of discipline and punishment. You want to help your children change, but you also want them to suffer and pay for their misdeeds. You want to train your children to behave better, but you also focus on how badly they have been behaving all day. You love your children, but at the moment you are angry and want to get even. That's human nature.

You will always get better results with loving discipline. Restrain your first angry impulse, wait until you calm down, and then lovingly but firmly tell your children what you require of them and the consequences they will face if they continue to disobey. This loving discipline, intended to help our children grow, is the kind of discipline God gives to his people.

1. Using the following verses, develop a chart or table showing the differences between discipline and punishment: Proverbs 3:11-12; Isaiah 13:9-11; 2 Thessalonians 1:6-9; Revelation 3:19; Matthew 25:46; 1 John 4:18.

2. Think of a recent time you tried to correct one of your children. Were you disciplining or punishing? What helped you decide whether you were disciplining or punishing?

3. Jesus' training of his disciples is a great example for us as parents. Read Mark 10:35-45. How did Jesus discipline (or teach) James and John to have a less selfish attitude

him: for before his translation he had this testimony, that he pleased God. ⁶But without faith *it is* impossible to please *him*: for he that cometh to God must believe that he is, and *that* he is a rewarder of them that diligently seek him. ⁷By faith Noah, being warned of God of things not seen as yet, moved with fear, prepared an ark to the saving of his house; by the which he condemned the world, and became heir of the righteousness which is by faith. ⁸By faith Abraham, when he was called to go out into a place which he should after receive for an inheritance, obeyed; and he went out, not knowing whither he went. ⁹By faith he sojourned in the land of promise, as *in* a strange country, dwelling in tabernacles with Isaac and Jacob, the heirs with him of the same promise: ¹⁰For he looked for a city which hath foundations, whose builder and maker *is* God. ¹¹Through faith also Sara herself received strength to conceive seed, and was delivered of a child when she was past age, because she judged him faithful who had promised. ¹²Therefore sprang there even of one, and him as good as dead, *so many* as the stars of the sky in multitude, and as the sand which is by the sea shore innumerable. ¹³These all died in faith^c, not having received the promises, but having seen them afar off, and were persuaded of *them*, and embraced *them*, and confessed that they were strangers and pilgrims on the earth. ¹⁴For they that say such things declare plainly that they seek a country. ¹⁵And truly, if they had been mindful of that *country* from whence they came out, they might have

Devotional Moment

Trusting Children to God

11:17-19 Abraham's faith was tested when God called on him to give up his son, the promised one. What an ordeal for Abraham! And yet God did not let him down.

Children are precious. We give them our best, our utmost, our full measure of hope, support, and strength. But finally, like Abraham, we must give them to God. Parents can mold the character of children only so far and protect them only so long before peers, pressures, and the force of individual personality take over. In prayer we need to trust God for our children's future. On days when our children want to do it alone, when they're out with the car past curfew, or when they're leaving home for work or college—we need to trust in God! Those kids are in good hands.

^c in faith: Gr. according to faith

had opportunity to have returned. ¹⁶But now they desire a better *country*, that is, an heavenly: wherefore God is not ashamed to be called their God: for he hath prepared for them a city. ¹⁷By faith Abraham, when he was tried, offered up Isaac: and he that had received the promises offered up his only begotten *son*, ¹⁸Of whom it was said, That in Isaac shall thy seed be called: ¹⁹Accounting that God *was* able to raise *him* up, even from the dead; from whence also he received him in a figure. ²⁰By faith Isaac blessed Jacob and Esau concerning things to come. ²¹By faith Jacob, when he was a dying, blessed both the sons of Joseph; and worshipped, *leaning* upon the top of his staff. ²²By faith Joseph, when he died, made mention of the departing of the children of Israel; and gave commandment concerning his bones. ²³By faith Moses, when he was born, was hid three months of his parents, because they saw *he was* a proper child; and they were not afraid of the king's commandment. ²⁴By faith Moses, when he was come to years, refused to be called the son of Pharaoh's daughter; ²⁵Choosing rather to suffer affliction with the people of God, than to enjoy the pleasures of sin for a season; ²⁶Esteeming the reproach of Christ[d] greater riches than the treasures in Egypt: for he had respect unto the recompence of the reward. ²⁷By faith he forsook Egypt, not fearing the wrath of the king: for he endured, as seeing him who is invisible. ²⁸Through faith he kept the passover, and the sprinkling of blood, lest he that destroyed the firstborn should touch them. ²⁹By faith they passed through the Red sea as by dry *land*: which the Egyptians assaying to do were drowned. ³⁰By faith the walls of Jericho fell down, after they were compassed about seven days. ³¹By faith the harlot Rahab perished not with them that believed not, when she had received the spies with peace.

³²And what shall I more say? for the time would fail me to tell of Gedeon, and *of* Barak, and *of* Samson, and *of* Jephthae; *of* David also, and Samuel, and *of* the prophets: ³³Who through faith subdued kingdoms, wrought righteousness, obtained promises, stopped the mouths of lions, ³⁴Quenched the violence of fire, escaped the edge of the sword, out of weakness were made strong, waxed valiant in fight, turned to flight the armies of the aliens. ³⁵Women received their dead raised to life again:

---

d of Christ: or, for Christ

Breaking Free from Isolation

Let brotherly love continue. Be not forgetful to entertain strangers: for thereby some have entertained angels unawares.
Hebrews 13:1-2

When was the last time you asked an angel home for dinner? Don't laugh—it has happened before. The author of the book of Hebrews mentions what happened to some people in his time.

The admonition "Be not forgetful to entertain strangers" exposes another pattern that some of us need to break. Namely, some families live in *isolation* instead of reaching out to others. And yet in the household of faith, connection— rather than isolation—is the key to outreach, evangelism, fellowship, and deep friendship.

Unquestionably, some people argue that with all the crazy people in society, opening our doors to just anyone wouldn't be a good idea at all. And that's true. But in Christ's time and in our own, the admonition to be kind and hospitable to those around us is still an important part of healthy relationships.

Take the Stewart family, for example. Kevin is an engineer, and Brenda, a loving mom who works full-time with the children. Kevin grew up in a home where there was little love—and no reaching out to others. His parents never gave to any organization and certainly never invited people to come over to their home to befriend them or make them feel welcome. The only guests that came in the door were an occasional relative or salesman who insisted on visiting.

In contrast, Brenda came from a home where visiting pastors or missionaries could always count on a meal. What's more, every year her parents would bundle up all the children, and together they would volunteer to serve the poor at the Salvation Army Thanksgiving dinner. Brenda learned naturally to reach out to those who were hurting, and it made her a loving, attractive person.

Brenda's warmth began to rub off on her husband. At first, it was just the senior pastor who was invited to their home for dinner. Then a few more of the staff were invited. A Sunday school class party was even held at their home, and then school events began to be scheduled around their backyard pool.

What Brenda modeled for Kevin in a loving, nonpushy way was the joy of opening their home to others. It was also a wonderful lesson for the children. They began to see single parents invited over (and the kids kept overnight to give their mom a break); a lonely senior, who had no family of her own, became "Grandma" over Christmastime; and the family befriended a foreign exchange student from India who had never been in a Christian home.

Some people from difficult backgrounds have various insecurities or fears that block them from reaching out in biblical hospitality. They fear that the house isn't clean enough, that the conversation might not be stimulating enough, or that the guests will never leave! Yet being hospitable takes our eyes off ourselves and allows us to function in the role Christ called the greatest—that of servant.

There are great benefits to showing hospitality—besides the fact that we might entertain an angel without realizing it! Don't let a negative cycle of isolation from the past hold you or your family back from experiencing the healthy joy of reaching out to others.

Devotional Moment

Grandparents

11:22 When Joseph was ready to die, he talked about Israel's exodus from Egypt. He told the young of God's care and providence. Today young people get most of their stories from television. It's time to recover Joseph's faith. If old age has dampened your spirits, diminished your joy, or made you bitter, remember God—still with you, still your Savior, still guiding, and now nearer than when you romped and laughed in youth. Make God's love your keynote, the song of your heart that grandchildren will never forget. Grandparents need to write down, tape-record, or verbally share stories of family crisis and God's care so that "precious moments" with grandchildren—rare open doors to their hearts and souls—become opportunities for faith building and family unity.

and others were tortured, not accepting deliverance; that they might obtain a better resurrection: ³⁶And others had trial of *cruel* mockings and scourgings, yea, moreover of bonds and imprisonment: ³⁷They were stoned, they were sawn asunder, were tempted, were slain with the sword: they wandered about in sheepskins and goatskins; being destitute, afflicted, tormented; ³⁸(Of whom the world was not worthy:) they wandered in deserts, and *in* mountains, and *in* dens and caves of the earth. ³⁹And these all, having obtained a good report through faith, received not the promise: ⁴⁰God having provided᷄ some better thing for us, that they without us should not be made perfect.

12

¹Wherefore seeing we also are compassed about with so great a cloud of witnesses, let us lay aside every weight, and the sin which doth so easily beset *us,* and let us run with patience the race that is set before us, ²Looking unto Jesus the author᷄ and finisher of *our* faith; who for the joy that was set before him endured the cross, despising the shame, and is set down at the right hand of the throne of God. ³For consider him that endured such contradiction of sinners against himself, lest ye be wearied and faint in your minds.

⁴Ye have not yet resisted unto blood, striving against sin. ⁵And ye have forgotten the exhortation which speaketh unto you as unto children, My son, despise not thou the chastening of the Lord, nor faint

---

᷄ provided: or, foreseen
᷄ author: or, beginner

Breaking Free by John Trent

Breaking Free from Broken Commitments

. . . (God) hath said, "I will never leave thee, nor forsake thee." Hebrews 13:5

Dan was a new believer who had married a mature Christian woman. This was his third marriage. Things would be different in this relationship, as Dan came to recognize a negative cycle in his family that he knew must stop with him.

Between Dan, his two brothers and two sisters, his parents and their five siblings, and his grandparents, Dan could name *twenty-two divorces in three generations!*

Think of the heartache trapped inside this extended family: children who had to trade fathers or mothers like baseball cards; vows spoken in reverent terms that proved to be only as binding as paper chains; the mixed messages, the broken hearts, the easy excuses for broken commitments.

Clearly, Dan faced a negative generational pattern that gave its members the message "When the going gets tough, get another partner."

Yet broken commitments have never been God's design.

God himself set the example. Here in the book of Hebrews is one of the most comforting, encouraging verses in all the Scriptures, for we read of a love God has for us that is independent of circumstances and unbreakable in its hold on us— something that Dan would have loved to have seen as a child and now wants his own children to experience.

Since 1978, the foremost reason for couples divorcing has been financial stress. There are some spouses who don't provide financially for their families, and in God's eyes they are "worse than an infidel" (1 Tim. 5:8). Yet for many people, what severely challenges their commitment is a love of money that causes them to get over their heads in debt. Continual warring over spending habits and priorities takes place. Soon, all time for a healthy spiritual or marital relationship is choked out—and what is left often leads to divorce.

In contrast, those who strive for contentment in Christ have this promise direct from our Lord: "I will never leave thee, nor forsake thee." Think of the security in that statement! No matter what our circumstances, we have a secure commitment from God.

Dan's first marriage deteriorated because of a wife who spent more than he could bring in. His second marriage caved in when *he* was the one that got them into massive debt. Both times, money played an important role in driving to the surface the insecurity and selfishness— rather than contentment—trapped in Dan's heart.

But now that he is a Christian, God has given him a new heart. He made a commitment to find contentment in Christ and never to leave his wife. And he followed up that commitment by deciding to do whatever it took—from counseling to being in a small accountability group—to back it up.

Perhaps it isn't financial pressures that have stressed your commitments; perhaps it is in-law problems, sexual temptation, a special-needs child, or some other difficulty that has caused the strain. But for all who struggle with a cycle of broken commitments, God's words to us can be an antidote to running away. He offers contentment, security, and a helping hand that can calm our fears and keep our commitments strong.

when thou art rebuked of him: ⁶For whom the Lord loveth he chasteneth, and scourgeth every son whom he receiveth. ⁷If ye endure chastening, God dealeth with you as with sons; for what son is he whom the father chasteneth not? ⁸But if ye be without chastisement, whereof all are partakers, then are ye bastards, and not sons. ⁹Furthermore we have had fathers of our flesh which corrected *us*, and

---

Devotional Moment

Correction

12:7-11 The Hebrew Christians had struggles and hardship. Accept God's training, the writer told them because God's discipline serves a good purpose. All good and proper discipline, come from a desire to train—to make someone more responsible, more mature, stronger. It never strives merely to punish. It is never a "pay back."

Parents know that child rearing can be an emotional roller coaster. Yet for that very reason we need to copy God (as much as possible)—to be self-controlled and *purposeful* in how we correct children.

If you're a child or teen, you know that discipline hurts. Try to see it as a lesson—learn from it. Yes, it's hard! But in the long run, it's the people who heed instruction that really know how to live (see Prov. 4:13).

---

we gave *them* reverence: shall we not much rather be in subjection unto the Father of spirits, and live? ¹⁰For they verily for a few days chastened *us* after[b] their own pleasure; but he for *our* profit, that *we* might be partakers of his holiness. ¹¹Now no chastening for the present seemeth to be joyous, but grievous: nevertheless afterward it yieldeth the peaceable fruit of righteousness unto them which are exercised thereby. ¹²Wherefore lift up the hands which hang down, and the feeble knees; ¹³And make straight[c] paths for your feet, lest that which is lame be turned out of the way; but let it rather be healed. ¹⁴Follow peace with all *men*, and holiness, without which no man shall see the Lord: ¹⁵Looking diligently lest any man fail[d] of the grace of God; lest any root of bitterness springing up trouble *you*, and thereby many be defiled; ¹⁶Lest there *be* any fornicator, or profane person, as Esau, who for one morsel of meat sold his birthright. ¹⁷For ye know how that afterward, when he would have inherited the blessing, he was rejected: for he found no place[e] of repentance, though he sought it carefully with tears.

ᵇ after . . . : or, as seemed good, or, meet to them

ᶜ straight: or, even

ᵈ fail . . . ; or, fall from

ᵉ place . . . : or, way to change his mind

¹⁸For ye are not come unto the mount that might be touched, and that burned with fire, nor unto blackness, and darkness, and tempest, ¹⁹And the sound of a trumpet, and the voice of words; which *voice* they that heard intreated that the word should not be spoken to them any more: ²⁰(For they could not endure that which was commanded, And if so much as a beast touch the mountain, it shall be stoned, or thrust through with a dart: ²¹And so terrible was the sight, *that* Moses said, I exceedingly fear and quake:) ²²But ye are come unto mount Sion, and unto the city of the living God, the heavenly Jerusalem, and to an innumerable company of angels, ²³To the general assembly and church of the firstborn, which are written^f in heaven, and to God the Judge of all, and to the spirits of just men made perfect, ²⁴And to Jesus the mediator of the new covenant^g, and to the blood of sprinkling, that speaketh better things than *that of* Abel. ²⁵See that ye refuse not him that speaketh. For if they escaped not who refused him that spake on earth, much more *shall not* we *escape*, if we turn away from him that *speaketh* from heaven: ²⁶Whose voice then shook the earth: but now he hath promised, saying, Yet once more I shake not the earth only, but also heaven. ²⁷And this *word*, Yet once more, signifieth the removing of those things that are shaken^h, as of things that are made, that those things which cannot be shaken may remain. ²⁸Wherefore we receiving a kingdom which cannot be moved, let us have grace, whereby we may serve God acceptably with reverence and godly fear: ²⁹For our God *is* a consuming fire.

13

¹Let brotherly love continue. ²Be not forgetful to entertain strangers: for thereby some have entertained angels unawares. ³Remember them that are in bonds, as bound with them; *and* them which suffer adversity, as being yourselves also in the body. ⁴Marriage *is* honourable in all, and the bed undefiled: but whoremongers and adulterers God will judge. ⁵*Let your* conversation *be* without covetousness; *and be* content with such things as ye have: for he hath said, I will never leave thee, nor forsake thee. ⁶So that we may boldly say, The Lord *is* my helper, and I will not fear what man shall do unto me. ⁷Remember them which have the rule^a over you, who have spoken

---

Devotional Moment

Empathy

13:2-3 The Hebrews were called to remember suffering people as if they themselves were suffering. That's called *empathy* —imagining what other people are going through so that we can be more sensitive and understanding toward others. As simple as this sounds, most of us don't empathize very well. Make it a goal to empathize with others; imagine yourself in their shoes, as if you yourself were wearing them. Make an effort to be sensitive and understanding. Put your antennae up and tune in to the needs of those around you: parents, spouse, kids, friends, neighbors, church family. We all love to be cared for by others.

---

^{f} written: or, enrolled

^{g} covenant: or, testament

^{h} are shaken: or, may be shaken

^{a} have the rule: or, are the guides

unto you the word of God: whose faith follow, considering the end of *their* conversation. [8]Jesus Christ the same yesterday, and to day, and for ever. [9]Be not carried about with divers and strange doctrines. For *it is* a good thing that the heart be established with grace; not with meats, which have not profited them that have been occupied therein. [10]We have an altar, whereof they have no right to eat which serve the tabernacle. [11]For the bodies of those beasts, whose blood is brought into the sanctuary by the high priest for sin, are burned without the camp. [12]Wherefore Jesus also, that he might sanctify the people with his own blood, suffered without the gate. [13]Let us go forth therefore unto him without the

---

Devotional Moment
•
Marriage: The Family Cornerstone

13:4 The command is simple and direct: Let everyone respect marriage. Our world needs strong families, and strong families are built on strong marriages. Many people think that it's nearly impossible to make marriages last. But marriage is God's idea, and we can all do a little to keep it strong. In addition to working on your own marriage (or even if you're single), here are some ways to respect and honor the institution of marriage: (1) Give couples space by respecting their privacy. (2) Respect other couples' relationships—men, don't get too close to other men's wives, and women, don't get too close to other women's husbands. (3) Help couples find time for each other—church leaders can sponsor classes and seminars that help them, and avoid demanding too much of their time for church involvements; single people can offer to baby-sit for couples with small children so they can get some time together. The strength and stability of the marriages in your church matters a great deal.

Devotional Moment
•
Sharing

13:16 Sharing is a sacrifice. To share is to interrupt a moment of enjoying a thing, to surrender something valuable, and to risk not getting it back. But such sacrifices please God. Let's all share—food that you enjoy for your church's or community's food pantry, a grocery-store gift certificate for an unemployed family, children's outgrown clothing for families in need, time and energy for an elderly neighbor needing yard work done, money for organizations that help victims of disasters, and toys for a brother or sister. With such sacrifices, God is well pleased. It also teaches us to cling less tightly to our things—slovenly gods that they are.

---

camp, bearing his reproach. [14]For here have we no continuing city, but we seek one to come. [15]By him therefore let us offer the sacrifice of praise to God continually, that is, the fruit of *our* lips giving thanks to his name. [16]But to do good and to communicate forget not: for with such sacrifices God is well pleased. [17]Obey them that have the rule over you, and submit yourselves: for they watch for your souls, as they that must give account, that they may do it with joy, and not with grief: for that *is* unprofitable for you.

[18]Pray for us: for we trust we have a good conscience, in all things willing to live honestly. [19]But I beseech *you* the rather to do this, that I may be restored to you the sooner. [20]Now the God of peace, that brought again from the dead our Lord Jesus, that great shepherd of the sheep, through the blood of the everlasting covenant[b], [21]Make you perfect in every good work to do his

---

[b] covenant: or, testament

will, working[c] in you that which is wellpleasing in his sight, through Jesus Christ; to whom *be* glory for ever and ever. Amen. [22]And I beseech you, brethren, suffer the word of exhortation: for I have written a letter unto you in few words. [23]Know ye that *our* brother Timothy is set at liberty; with whom, if he come shortly, I will see you. [24]Salute all them that have the rule over you, and all the saints. They of Italy salute you. [25]Grace *be* with you all. Amen.

[Written to the Hebrews from Italy, by Timothy.]

---

[c] working: or, doing

JAMES

Purpose
To expose unethical practices and to teach right Christian behavior

Author
James, Jesus' half brother, a leader in the Jerusalem church

To Whom Written
First-century Jewish Christians residing in Gentile communities outside Palestine

Date Written
Probably A.D. 49, prior to the Jerusalem Council held in A.D. 50

Setting
This letter expresses James's concern for persecuted Christians who were once part of the Jerusalem church.

Key Verse
"A man may say, Thou hast faith, and I have works: shew me thy faith without thy works, and I will shew thee my faith by my works" (2:18).

Many grandparents are from the hard-life-on-the-farm school. Their chores were equivalent to a full-time job, and they always started before dawn. School was the basic three *Rs,* and music was whatever noise they created.

James writes like a grandfather, a seasoned man who has seen many up and downs, who has tried and failed enough to know what works. His illustrations are farm stories about wind and sun, crops and horses.

James's advice on faithful Christian service is downright basic. With the passing of years, a person begins to come around to basic values and choices if he has had a lifetime of prayer and service.

Grandparents can be irritated by too much commotion. James puts up with no shenanigans from know-it-alls or naysayers. He knows life will bring some losses, but he chooses to focus on the good, the happy, and the true. These come from God, and James is grateful.

Grandparents can be lonely, especially if a spouse has died and the other lives alone. James must know the feeling because he wants Christians to show special care to people who don't have any family.

James doesn't write about the grand theological ideas you find in earlier New Testament books. James writes like a grandpa who has worked hard all his life and has something to say to youngsters.

We're all young enough to learn from him.

1

¹James, a servant of God and of the Lord Jesus Christ, to the twelve tribes which are scattered abroad, greeting.

²My brethren, count it all joy when ye fall into divers temptations[a]; ³Knowing *this*, that the trying of your faith worketh patience. ⁴But let patience have *her* perfect work, that ye may be perfect and entire, wanting nothing. ⁵If any of you lack wisdom, let him ask of God, that giveth to all *men* liberally, and upbraideth not; and it shall be given him. ⁶But let him ask in faith, nothing wavering. For he that wavereth is like a wave of the sea driven with the wind and tossed. ⁷For let not that man think that he shall receive any thing of the Lord. ⁸A double minded man *is* unstable in all his ways. ⁹Let the brother of low degree rejoice[b] in that he is exalted: ¹⁰But the rich, in that he is made low: because as the flower of the grass he shall pass away. ¹¹For the sun is no sooner risen with a burning heat, but it withereth the grass, and the flower thereof falleth, and the grace of the fashion of it perisheth: so also shall the rich man fade away in his ways. ¹²Blessed *is* the man that endureth temptation: for when he is tried, he shall receive the crown of life, which the Lord hath promised to them that love him.

¹³Let no man say when he is tempted, I am tempted of God: for God cannot be tempted with evil[c], neither tempteth he any man: ¹⁴But every man is tempted, when he is drawn away of his own lust, and enticed. ¹⁵Then when lust hath conceived, it bringeth forth sin: and sin, when it is finished, bringeth forth death. ¹⁶Do not err, my beloved brethren. ¹⁷Every good gift and every perfect gift is from above, and cometh down from the Father of lights, with whom is no variableness, neither shadow of turning. ¹⁸Of his own will begat he us with the word of truth, that we should be a kind of firstfruits of his creatures.

¹⁹Wherefore, my beloved brethren, let every man be swift to hear, slow to speak, slow to wrath: ²⁰For the wrath of man worketh not the righteousness of God. ²¹Wherefore lay apart all filthiness and superfluity of naughtiness, and receive with meekness the engrafted word, which is able to save your souls. ²²But be ye doers of the word, and not hearers only, deceiving your own selves. ²³For if any be a hearer of the word, and not a doer, he is like unto a man beholding his natural face in a glass: ²⁴For he beholdeth himself, and goeth his way, and straightway forgetteth what manner of man he was. ²⁵But whoso looketh into the perfect law of liberty, and continueth *therein*, he being not a forgetful hearer, but a doer of the work, this man shall be blessed in his deed[d]. ²⁶If any man among you seem to be religious, and bridleth not his tongue, but deceiveth his own heart, this man's religion *is* vain. ²⁷Pure religion and undefiled before God and the Father is

---

[a] temptation: or, trials
[b] rejoice: or, glory
[c] evil: or, evils
[d] deed: or, doing

Family Traditions

Supporting Each Other Through Trials

JAMES

When we understand that suffering is a normal part of the Christian life, we can meet it with courage. Establish a "family tradition" of love and support for family members going through difficult times.

George Conroy was his family's primary wage earner when he lost his job. George's wife gently encouraged him to reveal his fears and express his anger. She in turn confided in a friend, who agreed to pray for them and help out in practical ways during periods of extreme stress.

The Conroys' young children were brought into family prayer and asked to be patient about things they wanted that the family couldn't afford right now. The Conroys found their kids rose to the occasion when they were encouraged to contribute to the well-being of the family.

Mona Bermel, a single mom, realized she needed extra support after her own mother had a stroke and needed to be moved to a nursing home. She was visiting her mother every day, juggling household responsibilities, and working full-time. She requested prayer from her church and emotional support from members of her Bible study group. She sat down with her teenage sons and said, "I can't do this by myself. How can you help minimize the trauma for our family?" Mona's older son, John, started attending church again to help get Grandma in and out with her wheelchair, and Mona's friends' husbands rallied to take the younger boy to baseball practices and games. New relationships formed, meeting an unexpressed need in both boys' lives.

Candice Repo was harassed about her faith at her workplace. The jokes, unfriendliness, and verbal stabs from coworkers made her dread going to work, even though she enjoyed what she did. She told her family how hard it was to love those people as Jesus would. As a family, Candice's husband and kids decided to double the amount of time each one spent in personal prayer, using that time to pray for her. This kind of care was like water to a garden, and the Repos' family life took on new vitality. It renewed Candice's faith and gave her deeper spiritual resources to draw from at work. The power in her family's prayer became her support.

Each of these families found there is no substitute for honesty, communication, and prayer when going through trials. When you establish a tradition of meeting crises together, troubles become a stepping-stone to greater family intimacy and love.

this, To visit the fatherless and widows in their affliction, *and* to keep himself unspotted from the world.

2

¹My brethren, have not the faith of our Lord Jesus Christ, *the Lord* of glory, with respect of persons. ²For if there come unto your assembly[a] a man with a gold ring, in goodly apparel, and there come in also a poor man in vile raiment; ³And ye have respect to him that weareth the gay clothing, and say unto him, Sit thou here in a good place; and say to the poor, Stand thou there, or sit here under my footstool: ⁴Are ye not then partial in yourselves, and are become judges of evil thoughts? ⁵Hearken, my beloved brethren, Hath not God chosen the poor of this world rich in faith, and heirs of the kingdom which he hath promised to them that love him? ⁶But ye have despised the poor. Do not rich men oppress you, and draw you before the judgment seats? ⁷Do not they blaspheme[b] that worthy name by the which ye are called?

⁸If ye fulfil the royal law according to the scripture, Thou shalt love thy neighbour as thyself, ye do well: ⁹But if ye have respect to persons, ye commit sin, and are convinced of the law as transgressors. ¹⁰For whosoever shall keep the whole law, and yet offend in one *point*, he is guilty of all. ¹¹For he that said, Do not commit adultery, said also, Do not kill. Now if thou commit no adultery, yet if thou kill, thou art become a transgressor of the law. ¹²So speak ye, and so do, as they that shall be judged by the law of liberty. ¹³For he shall have judgment without mercy, that hath shewed no mercy; and mercy rejoiceth against judgment.

¹⁴What *doth it* profit, my brethren, though a man say he hath faith, and have not works? can faith save him? ¹⁵If a brother or sister be naked, and destitute of daily food, ¹⁶And one of you say unto them, Depart in peace, be *ye* warmed and filled; notwithstanding ye give them not those things which are needful to the body; what *doth it* profit? ¹⁷Even so faith, if it hath not works, is dead, being alone[c]. ¹⁸Yea, a man may say, Thou hast faith, and I have works: shew me thy faith without[d] thy works, and I will shew thee my faith by my works. ¹⁹Thou believest that there is one God; thou doest well: the devils also believe, and tremble. ²⁰But wilt thou know, O vain man, that faith without works is dead? ²¹Was not Abraham our father justified by works, when he had offered Isaac his son upon the altar? ²²Seest thou how faith wrought with his works, and by works was faith made perfect? ²³And the scripture was fulfilled which saith, Abraham believed God, and it was imputed unto him for righteousness: and he was called the Friend of God. ²⁴Ye see then how that by works a man is justified, and not by faith only. ²⁵Likewise also was not Rahab the harlot justified by works, when she had received the messengers, and had sent

---

[a] assembly: Gr. synagogue
[b] blaspheme: or, revile, or, slander
[c] alone: Gr. by itself
[d] without: some copies read, by

them out another way? ²⁶For as the body without the spirit^e is dead, so faith without works is dead also.

3

¹My brethren, be not many masters, knowing that we shall receive the greater condemnation^a. ²For in many things we offend all. If any man offend not in word, the same *is* a perfect man, *and* able also to bridle the whole body. ³Behold, we put bits in the horses' mouths, that they may obey us; and we turn about their whole body. ⁴Behold also the ships, which though *they be* so great, and *are* driven of fierce winds, yet are they turned about with a very small helm, whithersoever the governor listeth. ⁵Even so the tongue is a little member, and boasteth great things. Behold, how great a matter^b a little fire kindleth! ⁶And the tongue *is* a fire, a world of iniquity: so is the tongue among our members, that it defileth the whole body, and setteth on fire the course^c of nature; and it is set on fire of hell. ⁷For every kind^d of beasts, and of birds, and of serpents, and of things in the sea, is tamed, and hath been tamed of mankind: ⁸But the tongue can no man tame; *it is* an unruly evil, full of deadly poison. ⁹Therewith bless we God, even the Father; and therewith curse we men, which are made after the similitude of God. ¹⁰Out of the same mouth proceedeth blessing and cursing.

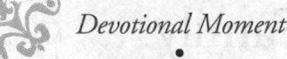

Devotional Moment
•
Wisdom

3:17-18 All of us need the kind of wisdom that James describes in these verses. God's wisdom is quiet and gentle; it doesn't shout or demand or badger. God's wisdom treats people with courtesy—from the checkout person at the grocery store to the teacher at school. God's wisdom allows discussion when people disagree and, if possible, yields to the preferences of others. God's wisdom treats friends with straightforward sincerity. God's wisdom is full of mercy, forgiving those who need forgiveness and helping those who are weak. Ask God for wisdom each day, and then make a commitment to practice it in all your relationships.

My brethren, these things ought not so to be. ¹¹Doth a fountain send forth at the same place^e sweet *water* and bitter? ¹²Can the fig tree, my brethren, bear olive berries? either a vine, figs? so *can* no fountain both yield salt water and fresh.

¹³Who *is* a wise man and endued with knowledge among you? let him shew out of a good conversation his works with meekness of wisdom. ¹⁴But if ye have bitter envying and strife in your hearts, glory not, and lie not against the truth. ¹⁵This wisdom descendeth not from above, but *is* earthly, sensual^f, devilish. ¹⁶For where envying and strife *is*, there *is* confusion^g and every evil work. ¹⁷But the wisdom that

---

^e spirit: or, breath

^a condemnation: or, judgment

^b a matter: or, wood

^c course: Gr. wheel

^d kind: Gr. nature

^e place: or, hole

^f sensual: or, natural

^g confusion: Gr. tumult, unquietness

Family Confessions

by Patricia A. Bigliardi

My son and I had entered a new phase of our lives together. A sophomore in college, Kelly was a strapping, nineteen-year-old six-footer with boundless energy. During his teen years our conversations had revolved around words with no more than three syllables: "Yeah," "No," "I dunno." But suddenly we had reestablished communication.

I was aware of the deep emotional wound my divorce had inflicted on him. I had tried to soothe the pain with love, laughter, and emotional support over the last eleven years.

Now, sharing a late-morning breakfast had become a favorite routine for both of us. I listened with motherly pride as he struggled to maintain his spiritual integrity while pulling all the pieces of life's puzzle together. He was changing, growing, becoming his own person.

Seeing him this mature, I realized our relationship had to change. I would need to begin relating to him as one adult to another. It would mean trusting him in new ways.

It would mean telling him about a painful part of my past that I had suppressed all these years—that I had had an abortion eleven years before.

"How could you do that?" my son shouted, as shock, then anger, crossed his face. "I've always wanted a 'real' brother or sister," he said in a quavering voice, fighting back tears. "I can't believe you took that away from me!"

Now the shock was mine. It had never occurred to me that my decision would deny my only child a heartfelt desire.

"Why, Mom?" Suddenly he was torn between repugnance for sin and love for the sinner.

"I can't justify what I did," I responded. "But your father didn't want another baby. I'd always wanted another child, but the timing never seemed right to your dad. When he said he didn't want this baby, I was afraid of losing him and angry with him at the same time."

"Did you want *me* when I was born?"

"Oh yes, your dad and I were so excited. We'd tried for almost a year before I finally got pregnant. I don't think we stopped smiling the whole nine months I carried you."

"Did Dad know you were doing it—the abortion, I mean?"

"Yes, he went with me to the hospital. Once it was over, we never mentioned it again. Eight months later Dad left anyway.

"When I became a Christian, I realized what I'd done and asked God to forgive me. For months I cried: I hadn't trusted God, not with my life or the life of my baby. I grieved deeply."

As we continued talking, Kelly's anger and pain gave way to his normal gentle, tender manner. His questions were forthright and searching. I tried to answer them as honestly as I could.

"Kelly," I said with tears spilling down my cheeks, "I need to ask your forgiveness. It never occurred to me I wouldn't have another child. I didn't realize I would be hurting you, too. I'm so sorry; please forgive me."

"I'm really trying to understand, Mom," he said, reaching over to hug me. "I do forgive you." We clung to each other tightly and cried—deep, grievous sobs. My son's grief comforted me; we shared a common loss.

That day became a watershed for us. My shame no longer hidden, I was released to mourn and receive God's comfort. My son recognized I was human. But more important, Kelly came to understand God's merciful redemption.

And because I trusted Kelly with my sins, I received an unexpected gift—my son trusted me with his sins, too. We began to speak honestly about our personal struggles, and

I welcomed his insight and wisdom. We prayed for each other in times of need, temptation, and sorrow.

Recently, on one of our breakfast dates, I sat listening to him confess to complacency in his relationship with God. I watched his warm, dark eyes begin to glisten with tears as he shared his disappointment in himself. It was a moment of deep intimacy and trust. And it was then I realized the awesome reward that open confession has brought to our family. Because we are transparent with each other, our prayers are specific, powerful, and effective.

DIGGING DEEPER

1. Read James 5:16 and Psalm 32 slowly, thoughtfully, and carefully. Think about what confession means to you. Why is forgiveness important to you?

2. When was the last time you admitted a mistake to your children? Tell them some of the struggles you are facing, and ask them to pray for you. Then ask if they have any burdens they wish to share with you.

3. Look up Deuteronomy 6:7 and write it out. How often do you just spend time with your children? Plan time for it on a regular basis.

---

is from above is first pure, then peaceable, gentle, *and* easy to be intreated, full of mercy and good fruits, without partiality[h], and without hypocrisy. [18]And the fruit of righteousness is sown in peace of them that make peace.

4

[1]From whence *come* wars and fightings[a] among you? *come they* not hence, *even* of your lusts that war in your members? [2]Ye lust, and have not: ye kill, and desire to have, and cannot obtain: ye fight and war, yet ye have not, because ye ask not. [3]Ye ask, and receive not, because ye ask amiss, that ye may consume *it* upon your lusts[b]. [4]Ye adulterers and adulteresses, know ye not that the friendship of the world is enmity with God? whosoever therefore will be a friend of the world is the enemy of God. [5]Do ye think that the scripture saith in vain, The spirit that dwelleth in us lusteth to envy[c]? [6]But he giveth more grace. Wherefore he saith, God resisteth the proud, but giveth grace unto the humble. [7]Submit yourselves therefore to God. Resist the devil, and he will flee from you. [8]Draw nigh to God, and he will draw nigh to you. Cleanse *your* hands, *ye* sinners; and purify *your* hearts, *ye* double minded. [9]Be afflicted, and mourn, and weep: let your laughter be turned to mourning, and *your* joy to heaviness. [10]Humble yourselves in the sight of the Lord, and he shall lift you up.

[11]Speak not evil one of another, brethren. He that speaketh evil of *his* brother, and judgeth his brother,

---

[h] partiality: or, wrangling
[a] fightings: or, brawlings
[b] lusts: or, pleasures
[c] to envy: or, enviously

speaketh evil of the law, and judgeth the law: but if thou judge the law, thou art not a doer of the law, but a judge. ¹²There is one lawgiver, who is able to save and to destroy: who art thou that judgest another? ¹³Go to now, ye that say, To day or to morrow we will go into such a city, and continue there a year, and buy and sell, and get gain: ¹⁴Whereas ye know not what *shall be* on the morrow. For what *is* your life? It is even a vapour, that appeareth for a little time, and then vanisheth away. ¹⁵For that ye *ought* to say, If the Lord will, we shall live, and do this, or that. ¹⁶But now ye rejoice in your boastings: all such rejoicing is evil. ¹⁷Therefore to him that knoweth to do good, and doeth *it* not, to him it is sin.

5

¹Go to now, *ye* rich men, weep and howl for your miseries that shall come upon *you*. ²Your riches are corrupted, and your garments are motheaten. ³Your gold and silver is cankered; and the rust of them shall be a witness against you, and shall eat your flesh as it were fire. Ye have heaped treasure together for the last days. ⁴Behold, the hire of the labourers who have reaped down your fields, which is of you kept back by fraud, crieth: and the cries of them which have reaped are entered into the ears of the Lord of sabaoth. ⁵Ye have lived in pleasure on the earth, and been wanton; ye have nourished your hearts, as in a day of slaughter. ⁶Ye have condemned *and* killed the just; *and* he doth not resist you. ⁷Be patient therefore, brethren, unto the coming of the Lord. Behold, the husbandman waiteth for the precious fruit of the earth, and hath long patience for it, until he receive the early and latter rain. ⁸Be ye also patient; stablish your hearts: for the coming of the Lord draweth nigh. ⁹Grudge not[a] one against another,

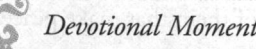

---

[a] Grudge not: or, Groan, or, Grieve not

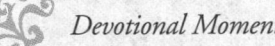

Devotional Moment
•
Prayer

5:16-18 James tells us that we should pray because our prayers have great power. God listens and acts on our requests. Now imagine you are a person who has difficulty balancing your checkbook. One day a certified public accountant moves in next door and says, "If I can ever be of help to you—in any way—don't hesitate to ask." Would you ask him to help you? Or would you struggle on all by yourself? The wise person would jump at the offer. Now suppose that you are a parent—perhaps a single parent—who has a tough time balancing your life. Our heavenly Father has said, "I'm here to help you any way you need, and I listen to your prayers very closely." Would you ask *him* for help or struggle on alone? The wise person will ask.

brethren, lest ye be condemned: behold, the judge standeth before the door. ¹⁰Take, my brethren, the prophets, who have spoken in the name of the Lord, for an example of suffering affliction, and of patience. ¹¹Behold, we count them happy which endure. Ye have heard of the patience of Job, and have seen the end of the Lord; that the Lord is very pitiful, and of tender mercy.

¹²But above all things, my brethren,

swear not, neither by heaven, neither by the earth, neither by any other oath: but let your yea be yea; and *your* nay, nay; lest ye fall into condemnation. ¹³Is any among you afflicted? let him pray. Is any merry? let him sing psalms. ¹⁴Is any sick among you? let him call for the elders of the church; and let them pray over him, anointing him with oil in the name of the Lord: ¹⁵And the prayer of faith shall save the sick, and the Lord shall raise him up; and if he have committed sins, they shall be forgiven him. ¹⁶Confess *your* faults one to another, and pray one for another, that ye may be healed. The effectual fervent prayer of a righteous man availeth much. ¹⁷Elias was a man subject to like passions as we are, and he prayed earnestly[b] that it might not rain: and it rained not on the earth by the space of three years and six months. ¹⁸And he prayed again, and the heaven gave rain, and the earth brought forth her fruit. ¹⁹Brethren, if any of you do err from the truth, and one convert him; ²⁰Let him know, that he which converteth the sinner from the error of his way shall save a soul from death, and shall hide a multitude of sins.

---

[b] earnestly: or, in his prayer

FIRST PETER

Purpose
To offer encouragement to
suffering Christians

Author
Peter

To Whom Written
Jewish Christians who had been
driven out of Jerusalem and
scattered throughout Asia Minor

Date Written
About A.D. 62–64 from Rome

Setting
Throughout the Roman Empire,
Christians were being tortured
and killed for their faith.

Key Verse
"That the trial of your faith . . .
though it be tried with fire, might
be found unto praise and honour
and glory . . ." (1:7).

Key Places
Jerusalem, Rome, and the regions of Pontus, Falatia, Cappadocia, Asia Minor, and Bithynia

Special Features
Peter used several images that
were special to him because Jesus had used them. Peter's
name (which means "stone")
had been given to him by Jesus.
Jesus encouraged Peter to care
for the church as a shepherd
tending the flock. Thus, it is not
surprising to see Peter using the
ideas of living stones (2:5-9) and
sheep (2:25) to describe the
church.

Few Americans wake up each morning thinking about how much suffering the day will hold for them. Unless, of course, a personal crisis is still unresolved or a tragedy has hit us.

Suffering is not the primary focus for most of us. But it was for Peter. He was probably in Rome when the great persecution under Emperor Nero began. (Peter was eventually executed during this persecution.) Count the times he makes reference to suffering in this short letter. The subject is never far from his mind.

Curiously, however, Peter rejects pessimism. As often as suffering comes up, so do a host of attitudes, feelings, and responses that tell us Peter is no doom-and-gloomer. How can this be?

Teaching children to handle suffering may be the hardest lesson on a parent's agenda: first, because we're not so good at it ourselves; second, because every message in the culture around us insists that suffering is to be avoided at all costs.

Peter helps. What pulls us through the hard times? What keeps our hope strong? When the pain gets worse and the pressure follows suit, what resources can we call on?

In fact, many people around the world do wake up to suffering. What does Peter's letter suggest you can do to help?

1

¹Peter, an apostle of Jesus Christ, to the strangers scattered throughout Pontus, Galatia, Cappadocia, Asia, and Bithynia, ²Elect according to the foreknowledge of God the Father, through sanctification of the Spirit, unto obedience and sprinkling of the blood of Jesus Christ: Grace unto you, and peace, be multiplied.

³Blessed *be* the God and Father of our Lord Jesus Christ, which according to his abundant* mercy hath begotten us again unto a lively hope by the resurrection of Jesus Christ from the dead, ⁴To an inheritance incorruptible, and undefiled, and that fadeth not away, reserved in heaven for you*, ⁵Who are kept by the power of God through faith unto salvation ready to be revealed in the last time.

Devotional Moment
•
Baby's First Step

1:3-6 Remember when your baby took his or her first wobbly, faltering step? You clapped and cheered as if it were the first time in history such a thing happened. As exciting as it was, you knew it would not have come to pass without your being there to hold your baby's hands. Peter says that something similar takes place in our journey toward maturity in the faith. Our efforts are often rather feeble; on our own we'd never make it. But a loving heavenly Father lends his supportive hands and enables us. As you help your child learn to walk or fondly recall when you did, remember this: Your heavenly Father is there to make sure *you* make it, too. He will never let you go or let you fail. This is the "priceless gift" God has reserved for you.

---

⁶Wherein ye greatly rejoice, though now for a season, if need be, ye are in heaviness through manifold temptations: ⁷That the trial of your faith, being much more precious than of gold that perisheth, though it be tried with fire, might be found unto praise and honour and glory at the appearing of Jesus Christ: ⁸Whom having not seen, ye love; in whom, though now ye see *him* not, yet believing, ye rejoice with joy unspeakable and full of glory: ⁹Receiving the end of your faith, *even* the salvation of *your* souls.

¹⁰Of which salvation the prophets have enquired and searched diligently, who prophesied of the grace *that should come* unto you: ¹¹Searching what, or what manner of time the Spirit of Christ which was in them did signify, when it testified beforehand the sufferings of Christ, and the glory that should follow. ¹²Unto whom it was revealed, that not unto themselves, but unto us they did minister the things, which are now reported unto you by them that have preached the gospel unto you with the Holy Ghost sent down from heaven; which things the angels desire to look into.

¹³Wherefore gird up the loins of your mind, be sober, and hope to the end* for the grace that is to be brought unto you at the revelation of Jesus Christ; ¹⁴As obedient children, not fashioning yourselves according to the former lusts in your ignorance: ¹⁵But as he which hath called you is holy, so be ye holy in all manner of conversation;

ª abundant: Gr. much
ᵇ for you: or, for us
ᶜ to the end: Gr. perfectly

[16]Because it is written, Be ye holy; for I am holy. [17]And if ye call on the Father, who without respect of persons judgeth according to every man's work, pass the time of your sojourning *here* in fear: [18]Forasmuch as ye know that ye were not redeemed with corruptible things, *as* silver and gold, from your vain conversation *received* by tradition from your fathers; [19]But with the precious blood of Christ, as of a lamb without blemish and without spot: [20]Who verily was foreordained before the foundation of the world, but was manifest in these last times for you, [21]Who by him do believe in God, that raised him up from the dead, and gave him glory; that your faith and hope might be in God. [22]Seeing ye have purified your souls in obeying the truth through the Spirit unto unfeigned love of the brethren, *see that ye* love one another with a pure heart fervently: [23]Being born again, not of corruptible seed, but of incorruptible, by the word of God, which liveth and abideth for ever.

[24]For[d] all flesh *is* as grass, and all the glory of man as the flower of grass. The grass withereth, and the flower thereof falleth away: [25]But the word of the Lord endureth for ever. And this is the word which by the gospel is preached unto you.

2

[1]Wherefore laying aside all malice, and all guile, and hypocrisies, and envies, and all evil speakings, [2]As newborn babes, desire the sincere milk of the word, that ye may grow thereby: [3]If so be ye have tasted that the Lord *is* gracious.

[4]To whom coming, *as unto* a living stone, disallowed indeed of men, but chosen of God, *and* precious, [5]Ye also, as lively stones, are built up a spiritual house, an holy priesthood, to offer up spiritual sacrifices, acceptable to God by Jesus Christ. [6]Wherefore also it is contained in the scripture, Behold, I lay in Sion a chief corner stone, elect, precious: and he that believeth on him shall not be confounded. [7]Unto you therefore which believe *he is* precious[a]: but unto them which be disobedient, the stone which the builders disallowed, the same is made the head of the corner, [8]And a stone of stumbling, and a rock of offence, *even to them* which stumble at the word, being disobedient: whereunto also they were appointed. [9]But ye *are* a chosen generation, a royal priesthood, an holy nation, a peculiar[b] people; that ye should shew forth the praises of him who hath called you out of darkness into his marvellous light: [10]Which in time past *were* not a people, but *are* now the people of God: which had not obtained mercy, but now have obtained mercy. [11]Dearly beloved, I beseech *you* as strangers and pilgrims, abstain from fleshly lusts, which war against the soul; [12]Having your conversation honest among the Gentiles: that, whereas[c] they speak against you as evildoers, they may by *your* good works,

---

[d] For: or, For that
[a] precious: or, an honour
[b] peculiar: or, purchased
[c] whereas: or, wherein

which they shall behold, glorify God in the day of visitation.

[13]Submit yourselves to every ordinance of man for the Lord's sake: whether it be to the king, as supreme; [14]Or unto governors, as unto them that are sent by him for the punishment of evildoers, and for the praise of them that do well. [15]For so is the will of God, that with well doing ye may put to silence the ignorance of foolish men: [16]As free, and not using[d] *your* liberty for a cloke of maliciousness, but as the servants of God. [17]Honour all[e] *men.* Love the brotherhood. Fear God. Honour the king. [18]Servants, *be* subject to *your* masters with all fear; not only to the good and gentle, but also to the froward. [19]For this *is* thankworthy[f], if a man for conscience toward God endure grief, suffering wrongfully. [20]For what glory *is it,* if, when ye be buffeted for your faults, ye shall take it patiently? but if, when ye do well, and suffer *for it,* ye take it patiently, this *is* acceptable[g] with God. [21]For even hereunto were ye called: because Christ also suffered for us[h], leaving us an example, that ye should follow his steps: [22]Who did no sin, neither was guile found in his mouth: [23]Who, when he was reviled, reviled not again; when he suffered, he threatened not; but committed *himself* to him that judgeth righteously: [24]Who his own self bare our sins in his own body on[i] the tree, that we, being dead to sins, should live unto righteousness: by whose stripes ye were healed. [25]For ye were as sheep going astray; but are now returned unto the Shepherd and Bishop of your souls.

3

[1]Likewise, ye wives, *be* in subjection to your own husbands; that, if any obey not the word, they also may without the word be won by the conversation of the wives; [2]While they behold your chaste conversation *coupled* with fear. [3]Whose adorning let it not be that outward *adorning* of plaiting the hair, and of wearing of gold, or of putting on of apparel; [4]But *let it be* the hidden man of

---

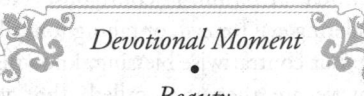

Devotional Moment
•
Beauty

3:3-5 Peter's instructions to wives included a statement about priorities: Be sure to spend time and energy developing inner character, not just outward beauty and attractiveness. It's quite easy to give too much attention to beauty and neglect inner character because physical beauty gains us praise, approval, and acceptance with others. Comparisons are easy to make. The more beautiful you are, the more people like you. Yet taking time for prayer and Bible reading is more important than taking a shower; being self-controlled pays off more than having control of one's curls. Whether or not we spend time, money, and energy on the externals—clothes, makeup, hair, weight, etc.—we must invest in *ourselves.* Praise others for beauty both inside and out.

---

[d] using: Gr. having
[e] Honour all: or, Esteem all
[f] thankworthy: or, thank
[g] acceptable: or, thank
[h] for us: some read, for you
[i] on: or, to

the heart, in that which is not corruptible, *even the ornament* of a meek and quiet spirit, which is in the sight of God of great price. [5]For after this manner in the old time the holy women also, who trusted in God, adorned themselves, being in subjection unto their own husbands: [6]Even as Sara obeyed Abraham, calling him lord: whose daughters[a] ye are, as long as ye do well, and are not afraid with any amazement. [7]Likewise, ye husbands, dwell with *them* according to knowledge, giving honour unto the wife, as unto the weaker vessel, and as being heirs together of the grace of life; that your prayers be not hindered.

[8]Finally, *be ye* all of one mind, having compassion one of another, love as brethren, *be* pitiful, *be* courteous: [9]Not rendering evil for evil, or railing for railing: but contrariwise blessing; knowing that ye are thereunto called, that ye should inherit a blessing. [10]For he that will love life, and see good days, let him refrain his tongue from evil, and his lips that they speak no guile: [11]Let him eschew evil, and do good; let him seek peace, and ensue it. [12]For the eyes of the Lord *are* over the righteous, and his ears *are open* unto their prayers: but the face of the Lord *is* against[b] them that do evil. [13]And who *is* he that will harm you, if ye be followers of that which is good? [14]But and if ye suffer for righteousness' sake, happy *are ye*: and be not afraid of their terror, neither be troubled; [15]But sanctify the Lord God in your hearts: and *be* ready always to *give* an answer to every man that asketh you a reason of

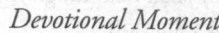

Devotional Moment
•
Family Peace

3:11 It's a secret of many Christian families: They fight like the Hatfields and McCoys all the way to church, but as they pull into the parking lot, they weld on their spiritual smiles and walk in together looking like saints. And you thought your family was the only one! Why is peace so hard to find, even in the family? Some of it is due simply to our self-centered sin nature. But something about being in a family (forced familiarity and intimacy perhaps) brings out the worst in us. That's why this verse says we have to *run after* peace. It doesn't come naturally—quite the opposite. So if your crew is often in training for the next heavyweight bout, remember: If you want peace in your home, you have to run after it and catch it.

the hope that is in you with meekness and fear[c]:

[16]Having a good conscience; that, whereas they speak evil of you, as of evildoers, they may be ashamed that falsely accuse your good conversation in Christ. [17]For *it is* better, if the will of God be so, that ye suffer for well doing, than for evil doing.

[18]For Christ also hath once suffered for sins, the just for the unjust, that he might bring us to God, being put to death in the flesh, but quickened by the Spirit: [19]By which also he went and preached unto the spirits in prison; [20]Which sometime were disobedient, when once the longsuffering of God waited in the days of Noah, while the ark was a preparing, wherein few, that is, eight souls were saved by water.

---

[a] daughters: Gr. children
[b] against: Gr. upon
[c] fear: or, reverence

Breaking Free by John Trent

Breaking Free from Silence

Ye husbands, dwell with them according to knowledge, giving honour unto the wife. 1 Peter 3:7

To understand a woman's needs, hurts, frailties, strengths, goals, hopes, and dreams requires meaningful communication. And the lack of it can create havoc in a home. But in many families, sometimes for generations, men have been taught to be "strong, silent types." Unfortunately, the resulting code of silence negates the command of 1 Peter 3:7 for husbands to be sensitive to their wives.

If you struggle with a code of silence in your home and you'd like to break it, then keep these healthy communication rules in mind.

1. Schedule time for communicating. Our schedules can become so hectic that regular times need to be set aside for talking—even if it's just the last half hour before bedtime. If either or both of you are too exhausted for that to work on a regular basis, you need to find time earlier in the day—maybe breakfast or lunch together—to communicate on a meaningful level.

2. Realize that you're always communicating—even when you're not using words. Those "strong, silent types" are communicating, but it may be 99 percent nonverbal! When left to fill in the blanks left by silence, many people will write in the worst. A lack of verbal expression can leave your spouse feeling insecure and uncertain of your love.

Men who are committed to God's Word and to living with their wife in an understanding way need to realize the deep need in a woman for communication. One counselor reported that in fifteen years of seeing clients, he never saw anyone in his office who, on a scale of one to ten, rated their communication at a six or better. In other words, you may be able to avoid serious marital problems and paying a counselor by increasing the communication level in your home.

3. Don't assume you already know what your spouse has to say. There is an extremely important verse in the book of Proverbs (among many other extremely important verses) that reads, "He that answereth a matter before he heareth it, it is folly and shame unto him" (18:13). Many times, you may feel that you have "heard this all before" and tune out your spouse. Yet if he or she still has the need to process a decision or situation by talking about it, it's important that you listen and not assume you've heard it all. Even if it's a familiar topic, none of us has a crystal ball when it comes to communication. Even if the same old thing is being said, there may be a reason for it. Perhaps your spouse never felt you listened to or understood the issue the first time it came up.

Meaningful communication is an essential part of living with a husband or wife in an understanding way. Each person in a marriage will benefit from growing in this important area and breaking the code of silence.

²¹The like figure whereunto *even* baptism doth also now save us (not the putting away of the filth of the flesh, but the answer of a good conscience toward God,) by the resurrection of Jesus Christ: ²²Who is gone into heaven, and is on the right hand of God; angels and authorities and powers being made subject unto him.

4

¹Forasmuch then as Christ hath suffered for us in the flesh, arm yourselves likewise with the same mind: for he that hath suffered in the flesh hath ceased from sin; ²That he no longer should live the rest of *his* time in the flesh to the lusts of men, but to the will of God. ³For the time past of *our* life may suffice us to have wrought the will of the Gentiles, when we walked in lasciviousness, lusts, excess of wine, revellings, banquetings, and abominable idolatries:

⁴Wherein they think it strange that ye run not with *them* to the same excess of riot, speaking evil of *you*: ⁵Who shall give account to him that is ready to judge the quick and the dead. ⁶For for this cause was the gospel preached also to them that are dead, that they might be judged according to men in the flesh, but live according to God in the spirit.

⁷But the end of all things is at hand: be ye therefore sober, and watch unto prayer. ⁸And above all things have fervent charity among yourselves: for charity shall cover the multitude of sins. ⁹Use hospitality one to another without grudging. ¹⁰As every man hath received the gift, *even so* minister the same one to another, as good stewards of the manifold grace of God. ¹¹If any man speak, *let him speak* as the oracles of God; if any man minister, *let him do it* as of the ability which God giveth: that God in all things may be glorified through Jesus Christ, to whom be praise and dominion for ever and ever. Amen.

¹²Beloved, think it not strange concerning the fiery trial which is to try you, as though some strange thing happened unto you: ¹³But rejoice, inasmuch as ye are partakers of Christ's sufferings; that, when his glory shall be revealed, ye may be glad also with exceeding joy. ¹⁴If ye be reproached for the name of Christ, happy *are ye*; for the spirit of glory and of God resteth upon you: on their part he is evil spoken of, but on your part he is glorified. ¹⁵But let none of you suffer as a murderer, or *as* a thief, or *as* an evildoer, or as a busybody in other men's matters. ¹⁶Yet if *any man suffer* as a Christian, let him not be ashamed; but let him glorify God on this behalf. ¹⁷For the time *is come* that judgment must begin at the house of God: and if *it* first *begin* at us, what shall the end *be* of them that obey not the gospel of God? ¹⁸And if the righteous scarcely be saved, where shall the ungodly and the sinner appear? ¹⁹Wherefore let them that suffer according to the will of God commit the keeping of their souls *to him* in well doing, as unto a faithful Creator.

5

¹The elders which are among you I exhort, who am also an elder, and a witness of the sufferings of Christ, and also a partaker of the glory that shall be revealed: ²Feed the flock of God which is among you, taking the oversight *thereof*, not by constraint, but willingly; not for

filthy lucre, but of a ready mind; ³Neither as being lords over* *God's* heritage, but being ensamples to the flock. ⁴And when the chief Shepherd shall appear, ye shall receive a crown of glory that fadeth not away.

⁵Likewise, ye younger, submit yourselves unto the elder. Yea, all *of you* be subject one to another, and be clothed with humility: for God resisteth the proud, and giveth grace to the humble. ⁶Humble yourselves therefore under the mighty hand of God, that he may exalt you in due time: ⁷Casting all your care upon him; for he careth for you.

⁸Be sober, be vigilant; because your adversary the devil, as a roaring lion, walketh about, seeking whom he may devour: ⁹Whom resist stedfast in the faith, knowing that the same afflictions are accomplished in your brethren that are in the world.

¹⁰But the God of all grace, who hath called us unto his eternal glory by Christ Jesus, after that ye have suffered a while, make you perfect, stablish, strengthen, settle *you.* ¹¹To him *be* glory and dominion for ever and ever. Amen. ¹²By Silvanus, a faithful brother unto you, as I suppose, I have written briefly, exhorting, and testifying that this is the true grace of God wherein ye stand. ¹³The *church that is* at Babylon, elected together with *you,* saluteth you; and *so doth* Marcus my son. ¹⁴Greet ye one another with a kiss of charity. Peace *be* with you all that are in Christ Jesus. Amen.

ᵃ being lords over: or, overruling

SECOND PETER

Purpose
To warn Christians about false teachers and to exhort them to grow in their faith and knowledge of Christ

Author
Peter

To Whom Written
The church at large

Date Written
About A.D. 67, three years after 1 Peter was written, possibly from Rome

Setting
Peter knows that his days on earth are numbered (1:13-14), so he is writing about what is on his heart, warning believers about what will happen when he is gone—especially about false teachers. He reminds them of the unchanging truth of the gospel.

Key Verse
"According as his divine power hath given unto us all things that pertain unto life and godliness, through the knowledge of him that hath called us to glory and virtue" (1:3).

Key People
Peter, Paul

"But Mom, I *saw* it happen!" reports Sheryl.

Mom is skeptical. Sheryl's story just doesn't sound believable. "Well, maybe you imagined it," Mom says, dismissing her gently.

Sheryl is frustrated. She knows what she saw, and she is finding out how tough adults can be to convince. "But Mom, I saw it with my *own eyes,*" Sheryl insists. An eyewitness has absolutely no doubt about the truth. But even an eyewitness faces a skeptical audience when the story is too good (or too awful or too incredible) to be believed.

Like Sheryl's mom, many of us tend to dismiss things too easily. When Peter claims that his letter has the authority of an eyewitness, we should all snap to attention. If he really did see what he writes about, then we had better think twice before we dismiss his report or disregard his advice.

To claim to be an eyewitness is to put all your integrity on the line. It's to say to the world, "Think whatever you will, but I'll tell you what I know." It's risking considerable ridicule from people who believe they're pretty smart already.

Sheryl's story is no less true just because it comes from a child or because it seems unlikely to a jaded adult. Skeptical world, take note: Peter's eyewitness account is a tough claim to dismiss.

Isn't a ball game more exciting in person than on the radio? Doesn't a wedding need eyewitnesses? Isn't God to be loved, honored, and believed because many eyewitnesses confirmed Jesus' message?

1

¹Simon[a] Peter, a servant and an apostle of Jesus Christ, to them that have obtained like precious faith with us through the righteousness of God and our Saviour Jesus Christ: ²Grace and peace be multiplied unto you through the knowledge of God, and of Jesus our Lord, ³According as his divine power hath given unto us all things that *pertain* unto life and godliness, through the knowledge of him that hath called us to[b] glory and virtue: ⁴Whereby are given unto us exceeding great and precious promises: that by these ye might be partakers of the divine nature, having escaped the corruption that is in the world through lust.

⁵And beside this, giving all diligence, add to your faith virtue; and to virtue knowledge; ⁶And to knowledge temperance; and to temperance patience; and to patience godliness; ⁷And to godliness brotherly kindness; and to brotherly kindness charity. ⁸For if these things be in you, and abound, they make *you that ye shall* neither *be* barren[c] nor unfruitful in the knowledge of our Lord Jesus Christ. ⁹But he that lacketh these things is blind, and cannot see afar off, and hath forgotten that he was purged from his old sins. ¹⁰Wherefore the rather, brethren, give diligence to make your calling and election sure: for if ye do these things, ye shall never fall: ¹¹For so an entrance shall be ministered unto you abundantly into the everlasting kingdom of our Lord and Saviour Jesus Christ.

¹²Wherefore I will not be negligent to put you always in remembrance of these things, though ye know *them*, and be established in the present truth. ¹³Yea, I think it meet, as long as I am in this tabernacle, to stir you up by putting *you* in remembrance; ¹⁴Knowing that shortly I must put off *this* my tabernacle, even as our Lord Jesus Christ hath shewed me. ¹⁵Moreover I will endeavour that ye may be able after my decease to have these things always in remembrance.

¹⁶For we have not followed cunningly devised fables, when we made known unto you the power and coming of our Lord Jesus Christ, but were eyewitnesses of his majesty. ¹⁷For he received from God the Father honour and glory, when there came such a voice to him from the excellent glory, This is my beloved Son, in whom I am well pleased. ¹⁸And this voice which came from heaven we heard, when we were with him in the holy mount.

¹⁹We have also a more sure word of prophecy; whereunto ye do well that ye take heed, as unto a light that shineth in a dark place, until the day dawn, and the day star arise in your hearts: ²⁰Knowing this first, that no prophecy of the scripture is of any private interpretation. ²¹For the prophecy came not in old time[d] by the will of

---

[a] Simon: or, Symeon
[b] to: or, by
[c] barren: Gr. idle
[d] in old time: or, at any time

man: but holy men of God spake *as they were* moved by the Holy Ghost.

2

¹But there were false prophets also among the people, even as there shall be false teachers among you, who privily shall bring in damnable heresies, even denying the Lord that bought them, and bring upon themselves swift destruction. ²And many shall follow their pernicious ways[a]; by reason of whom the way of truth shall be evil spoken of.

³And through covetousness shall they with feigned words make merchandise of you: whose judgment now of a long time lingereth not, and their damnation slumbereth not. ⁴For if God spared not the angels that sinned, but cast *them* down to hell, and delivered *them* into chains of darkness, to be reserved unto judgment; ⁵And spared not the old world, but saved Noah the eighth *person*, a preacher of righteousness, bringing in the flood upon the world of the ungodly; ⁶And turning the cities of Sodom and Gomorrha into ashes condemned *them* with an overthrow, making *them* an ensample unto those that after should live ungodly;

⁷And delivered just Lot, vexed with the filthy conversation of the wicked: ⁸(For that righteous man dwelling among them, in seeing and hearing, vexed *his* righteous soul from day to day with *their* unlawful deeds;) ⁹The Lord knoweth how to deliver the godly out of temptations, and to reserve the un-

Devotional Moment

Morality

2:1-2 Peter warned his readers against people who would try to discredit the truth of the Scriptures. The chief error of these false teachers was in telling people what they wanted to hear. Peter urged God's people: *Don't listen to them!* These days, God's standards for morality—sexual or otherwise—often come under attack for being out-of-date or too narrow. Like the false teachers of whom Peter wrote, people who think this way bring destruction on themselves. We break God's laws to our own detriment. Our bodies are not made for sexual promiscuity. In giving us "strict rules," God isn't being "narrow-minded," he's being loving. Remember this next time you are tempted to throw out God's standards.

just unto the day of judgment to be punished:

¹⁰But chiefly them that walk after the flesh in the lust of uncleanness, and despise government[b]. Presumptuous *are they*, selfwilled, they are not afraid to speak evil of dignities. ¹¹Whereas angels, which are greater in power and might, bring not railing accusation against them[c] before the Lord. ¹²But these, as natural brute beasts, made to be taken and destroyed, speak evil of the things that they understand not; and shall utterly perish in their own corruption; ¹³And shall receive the reward of unrighteousness, *as* they that count it pleasure to riot in the day time. Spots *they are* and blemishes, sporting themselves with their own deceivings while they feast with you; ¹⁴Having eyes full of adultery[d], and that cannot cease

---

[a] pernicious ways: or, lascivious ways, as some copies read
[b] government: or, dominion
[c] them: some read, themselves
[d] adultery: Gr. an adulteress

from sin; beguiling unstable souls: an heart they have exercised with covetous practices; cursed children: ¹⁵Which have forsaken the right way, and are gone astray, following the way of Balaam *the son* of Bosor, who loved the wages of unrighteousness; ¹⁶But was rebuked for his iniquity: the dumb ass speaking with man's voice forbad the madness of the prophet. ¹⁷These are wells without water, clouds that are carried with a tempest; to whom the mist of darkness is reserved for ever. ¹⁸For when they speak great swelling *words* of vanity, they allure through the lusts of the flesh, *through much* wantonness, those that were clean^e escaped from them who live in error. ¹⁹While they promise them liberty, they themselves are the servants of corruption: for of whom a man is overcome, of the same is he brought in bondage. ²⁰For if after they have escaped the pollutions of the world through the knowledge of the Lord and Saviour Jesus Christ, they are again entangled therein, and overcome, the latter end is worse with them than the beginning. ²¹For it had been better for them not to have known the way of righteousness, than, after they have known *it*, to turn from the holy commandment delivered unto them. ²²But it is happened unto them according to the true proverb, The dog *is* turned to his own vomit again; and the sow that was washed to her wallowing in the mire.

3

¹This second epistle, beloved, I now write unto you; in *both* which I stir up your pure minds by way of remembrance: ²That ye may be mindful of the words which were spoken before by the holy prophets, and of the commandment of us the apostles of the Lord and Saviour:

³Knowing this first, that there shall come in the last days scoffers, walking after their own lusts, ⁴And saying, Where is the promise of his coming? for since the fathers fell asleep, all things continue as *they were* from the beginning of the creation. ⁵For this they willingly are ignorant of, that by the word of God the heavens were of old, and the earth standing out of the water and in the water: ⁶Whereby the world that then was, being overflowed with water, perished: ⁷But the heavens and the earth, which are now, by the same word are kept in store, reserved unto fire against the day of judgment and perdition of ungodly men.

⁸But, beloved, be not ignorant of this one thing, that one day *is* with the Lord as a thousand years, and a thousand years as one day.

⁹The Lord is not slack concerning his promise, as some men count slackness; but is longsuffering to us-ward, not willing that any should perish, but that all should come to repentance. ¹⁰But the day of the Lord will come as a thief in the night; in the which the heavens shall pass away with a great noise, and the elements shall melt with fervent heat, the earth also and the works that are therein shall be burned up.

¹¹*Seeing* then *that* all these things shall be dissolved, what manner *of persons* ought ye to be in *all* holy conversation and godliness, ¹²Looking for and

---

^e clean: or, for a little, or, a while, as some read

Devotional Moment
•
Priorities

3:10-11 Whenever a house and all its contents are totally destroyed, a reporter will typically appear on the scene to ask the victims, "How do you feel right now?" Those people will often respond, "We're just grateful we all got out alive. That's the truly important thing." A tragedy can focus our sense of what's important more forcefully than anything else. Peter warns us that this world is going to end some day and that we need to get our priorities straight before that happens. It is quite easy to work hard on priorities that ultimately won't matter—education, sports, paying the bills—and neglect what counts for eternity. What is most important to you? Let's straighten out our priorities now while we still have time.

hasting[a] unto the coming of the day of God, wherein the heavens being on fire shall be dissolved, and the elements shall melt with fervent heat? [13]Nevertheless we, according to his promise, look for new heavens and a new earth, wherein dwelleth righteousness. [14]Wherefore, beloved, seeing that ye look for such things, be diligent that ye may be found of him in peace, without spot, and blameless. [15]And account *that* the longsuffering of our Lord *is* salvation; even as our beloved brother Paul also according to the wisdom given unto him hath written unto you; [16]As also in all *his* epistles, speaking in them of these things; in which are some things hard to be understood, which they that are unlearned and unstable wrest, as *they do* also the other scriptures, unto their own destruction. [17]Ye therefore, beloved, seeing ye know *these things* before, beware lest ye also, being led away with the error of the wicked, fall from your own stedfastness. [18]But grow in grace, and *in* the knowledge of our Lord and Saviour Jesus Christ. To him *be* glory both now and for ever. Amen.

---

[a] hasting . . . : or, hasting the coming

FIRST JOHN

Purpose
To reassure Christians in their faith and to counter false teachings

Author
The apostle John

To Whom Written
The letter was written to several Gentile congregations.

Date Written
Probably between A.D. 85 and 90 from Ephesus

Setting
John was an old man and perhaps the only surviving apostle at this time. He had not yet been banished to the island of Patmos, where he would live in exile.

Key Verse
"These things have I written unto you that believe on the name of the Son of God; that ye may know that ye have eternal life. . . ." (5:13).

Special Features
John is known as the apostle of love, and love is mentioned throughout this letter. There are a number of similarities between this letter and John's Gospel—in vocabulary, style, and main ideas. John uses brief statements and simple words, and he features sharp contrasts—light and darkness, truth and error, God and Satan, life and death, love and hate.

Families can become tense with children's jealousy and selfishness. Plenty of siblings in the Bible hated each other. Lots of siblings today of any age cannot bear to speak the other's name. In a family divided by warring siblings, forget fun reunions, holidays, or even calm dinnertimes. Parents take the role of United Nations peacekeepers. Each side sullenly keeps to his or her own turf. There's no fun to this bitterness; it's all grief.

If such turmoil is your family's problem, 1 John will hit home like a whirlwind. John was an emotional guy—an inner-circle disciple and a deep-feeler. But he pulls no punches in this short letter. He hits readers with simple truths that cut no slack and take no prisoners.

You need not be a rocket scientist to see John's point. This book is no puzzle of fancy philosophical paradoxes. It's direct, pointed, and clear.

The dissension that worried John was the terrible teaching infiltrating the church and spoiling the truth about Jesus. But modern family disputes have close parallels. In both cases, John tells us what to do about it.

Parents and adult siblings who know the rivalry problem firsthand should be prepared to trust God for great change as they read this letter. These living words are for you. Pray that they will reach into your hearts. Your life, too, may change in their light.

1

¹That which was from the beginning, which we have heard, which we have seen with our eyes, which we have looked upon, and our hands have handled, of the Word of life; ²(For the life was manifested, and we have seen *it*, and bear witness, and shew unto you that eternal life, which was with the Father, and was manifested unto us;) ³That which we have seen and heard declare we unto you, that ye also may have fellowship with us: and truly our fellowship *is* with the Father, and with his Son Jesus Christ. ⁴And these things write we unto you, that your joy may be full.

⁵This then is the message which we have heard of him, and declare unto you, that God is light, and in him is no darkness at all. ⁶If we say that we have fellowship with him, and walk in darkness, we lie, and do not the truth: ⁷But if we walk in the light, as he is in the light, we have fellowship one with another, and the blood of Jesus Christ his Son cleanseth us from all sin.

⁸If we say that we have no sin, we deceive ourselves, and the truth is not in us. ⁹If we confess our sins, he is faithful and just to forgive us *our* sins, and to cleanse us from all unrighteousness. ¹⁰If we say that we have not sinned, we make him a liar, and his word is not in us.

2

¹My little children, these things write I unto you, that ye sin not. And if any man sin, we have an advocate with the Father, Jesus Christ the righteous: ²And he is the propitiation for our sins: and not for ours only, but also for *the sins of* the whole world.

³And hereby we do know that we know him, if we keep his commandments. ⁴He that saith, I know him, and keepeth not his commandments, is a liar, and the truth is not in him. ⁵But whoso keepeth his word, in him verily is the love of God perfected: hereby know we that we are in him. ⁶He that saith he abideth in him ought himself also so to walk, even as he walked.

⁷Brethren, I write no new commandment unto you, but an old commandment which ye had from the beginning. The old commandment is the word which ye have heard from the beginning. ⁸Again, a new commandment I write unto you, which thing is true in him and in you: because the darkness is past, and the true light now shineth. ⁹He that saith he is in the light, and hateth his brother, is in darkness even until now. ¹⁰He that loveth his brother abideth in the light, and there is none occasion of stumbling in him. ¹¹But he

---

Devotional Moment
•
Confession

1:9 Our part in the forgiveness process is to confess our sin to God, to admit to him that we have done wrong. God responds to our confession in two ways: He forgives us (restoring us to fellowship with him) and cleanses us from the wrong we have done (restoring us to relationship with others). That's what God wants for all our relationships. "Son, it was wrong for me to lash out at you. Please forgive me." "Mom, I was rude to you when you asked me to clear the table. Please forgive me." And we must be willing to extend forgiveness: "Dad, I forgive you. Thanks for letting me know you're sorry." Confession and forgiveness in a family reflect God's character and restore relationships.

Devotional Moment
•
Resentment

2:9-11 This passage tells us that we need to love and respect others, not hate or despise them. Disrespect, cruelty, and especially hatred for other people is simply not an option for a Christian. Yet most of us are tempted to harbor such feelings toward certain people, whether they live in the same house or thousands of miles away, whether they are children, parents, distant relatives, or friends. What can we do about this? If they live in the same house, we can think of ways to speak to them more kindly or to show them more respect; if they live thousands of miles away, we can strive to reopen the lines of communication. We have a great promise from God for reaching out in love to our "enemies," even if we don't feel like it: We will be walking "in the light" and not stumble in life.

that hateth his brother is in darkness, and walketh in darkness, and knoweth not whither he goeth, because that darkness hath blinded his eyes.

¹²I write unto you, little children, because your sins are forgiven you for his name's sake. ¹³I write unto you, fathers, because ye have known him *that is* from the beginning. I write unto you, young men, because ye have overcome the wicked one. I write unto you, little children, because ye have known the Father. ¹⁴I have written unto you, fathers, because ye have known him *that is* from the beginning. I have written unto you, young men, because ye are strong, and the word of God abideth in you, and ye have overcome the wicked one. ¹⁵Love not the world, neither the things *that are* in the world. If any man love the world, the love of the Father is not in him. ¹⁶For all that *is* in the world, the lust of the flesh, and the lust of the eyes, and the pride of life, is not of the Father, but is of the world. ¹⁷And the world passeth away, and the lust thereof: but he that doeth the will of God abideth for ever.

¹⁸Little children, it is the last time: and as ye have heard that antichrist shall come, even now are there many antichrists; whereby we know that it is the last time. ¹⁹They went out from us, but they were not of us; for if they had been of us, they would *no doubt* have continued with us: but *they went out,* that they might be made manifest that they were not all of us.

²⁰But ye have an unction from the Holy One, and ye know all things. ²¹I have not written unto you because ye know not the truth, but because ye know it, and that no lie is of the truth. ²²Who is a liar but he that denieth that Jesus is the Christ? He is antichrist, that denieth the Father and the Son. ²³Whosoever denieth the Son, the same hath not the Father: *(but) he that acknowledgeth the Son hath the Father also.* ²⁴Let that therefore abide in you, which ye have heard from the beginning. If that which ye have heard from the beginning shall remain in you, ye also shall continue in the Son, and in the Father. ²⁵And this is the promise that he hath promised us, *even* eternal life. ²⁶These *things* have I written unto you concerning them that seduce you. ²⁷But the anointing which ye have received of him abideth in you, and ye need not that any man teach you: but as the same anointing teacheth you of all things, and is truth, and is no lie, and even as it hath taught you, ye shall abide in him[a].

---

[a] in him: or, in it

²⁸And now, little children, abide in him; that, when he shall appear, we may have confidence, and not be ashamed before him at his coming. ²⁹If ye know that he is righteous, ye know that every one that doeth righteousness is born of him.

3

¹Behold, what manner of love the Father hath bestowed upon us, that we should be called the sons of God: therefore the world knoweth us not, because it knew him not. ²Beloved, now are we the sons of God, and it doth not yet appear what we shall be: but we know that, when he shall appear, we shall be like him; for we shall see him as he is. ³And every man that hath this hope in him purifieth himself, even as he is pure.

⁴Whosoever committeth sin transgresseth also the law: for sin is the transgression of the law. ⁵And ye know that he was manifested to take away our

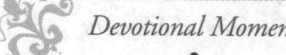

Devotional Moment
•
I Hate You!
3:15 John says that anyone who hates his Christian brother is really a murderer. How can hate make someone a murderer? Hate destroys relationships, teamwork, and reputations, and it can cause a person to deny encouragement to others who need it. Hate can ruin people. That's why we must work hard at rooting it out of our life. Wrongs, slights, criticism, and superior attitudes can make us resent and hate. Make every effort to avoid them. And when they creep in, confess them to each other and start over.

Devotional Moment
•
Generosity
3:17-18 God blesses us so that we can be in a position to help others. If we selfishly hoard all the blessings for ourselves, then we deny the reality of God's love in us. Think about how you can respond to this call to put love into action. Anyone who has a home, education, security, a job, freedom of religion, and freedom from hunger has something to share with others. Discuss ways you can give of whatever God has given to you in abundance. You don't have to save the world from poverty single-handedly—just find a way to share what you have.

sins; and in him is no sin. ⁶Whosoever abideth in him sinneth not: whosoever sinneth hath not seen him, neither known him. ⁷Little children, let no man deceive you: he that doeth righteousness is righteous, even as he is righteous. ⁸He that committeth sin is of the devil; for the devil sinneth from the beginning. For this purpose the Son of God was manifested, that he might destroy the works of the devil. ⁹Whosoever is bornᵃ of God doth not commit sin; for his seed remaineth in him: and he cannot sin, because he is born of God. ¹⁰In this the children of God are manifest, and the children of the devil: whosoever doeth not righteousness is not of God, neither he that loveth not his brother.

¹¹For this is the messageᵇ that ye heard from the beginning, that we should love one another. ¹²Not as Cain, *who* was of that wicked one, and slew his brother. And wherefore slew he him? Because his own works were evil,

ᵃ is born: or, has been born
ᵇ message: or, commandment

Prisoner of Union Square

by Michelle Collings

It is a clear, warm Sunday in Manhattan, one of the last of summer—a perfect day to sit outside, read the paper, and work on my tan. I collect my beach chair, suntan oil, Walkman, and *New York Times* magazine and walk two blocks to Union Square Park, where I join other sunbathers.

Thirty minutes into the crossword puzzle, headphones on, I'm prompted to look up. A man is standing over me, talking to me. He is dirty, dressed in rags, and clearly hostile. I can't hear him, but I know he's asking me for money. Today I don't have the stamina to engage in conversation. I shake my head no.

He doesn't leave; now he's shouting at me.

"Do you want me to kick you in the face?" he yells. I take off my headphones and say no, I don't.

"Do you *see* me?" he asks.

"Yes, I see you," I respond. "But I don't have money to give you."

"I'll kick your face."

He could. Now I'm frightened. As my mind races and I remain still, he walks to the woman next to me just a few feet away who has been watching our encounter. As he addresses her I watch, not sure what to do, hoping he'll give up and go away. He doesn't. I watch him reach down, pick up a pack of cigarettes on her towel, and take a few. "Do you have a problem with this?" he says.

That's enough for me. I get up and go to the edge of the park, looking for a police officer. I find a police car at a stoplight nearby and blurt out what's going on.

"What did you say to *him?*" the officer asks.

I can't believe this. Did he think I was *provoking* the man? Reluctantly he takes the description from me; then a fellow sunbather comes up from behind and says to the officer, "Listen, you'd better come. This guy is out of his mind."

The officer tells me to go into the park and point the guy out. I do, and he heads toward the man. Out of nowhere, five men in blue appear. They talk to him; he leaves after showing his displeasure but just circles the park. Since this man probably knows I'm the one who got the police, and I doubt he'll stay out of the park for long, I collect my things and leave.

I don't *want* to go home. I want to be right there in Union Square Park, minding my own business and sunning myself. It isn't *fair*.

But I don't want to be foolish either, so I go home.

I am angry—angry that I am not free to sit outside in the park on a Sunday afternoon; angry that a police officer won't take me seriously; angry that *I*, not the harasser, have to go home.

Then I realize that the man probably doesn't have a home. He probably lives in the park. I'm angry, but I'll bet he's angry, too. And he may very well have more to be angry about than I do.

Suddenly the issue is complicated. This man is down and out, possibly a drug user. I'm a decent citizen—I pay taxes, put my litter in trash cans, and obey the law. I am also painfully aware that we are all only a few steps from being homeless. So I make an effort to help: I contribute to organizations that help the poor, volunteer, even pass out sandwiches every now and then. But I get tired of being confronted several times every day with hostility, of weaving across streets to avoid people asking for help.

I have no answers. Right now I want only to leave the city and go someplace where there aren't so many homeless people. I want to spare myself the discomfort and frustration of facing a situation that seems chronic and unsolvable. But if we all do that, then New York City will be populated solely by the homeless.

Oddly, now that a few hours have passed, I feel more convicted than abused. I walk around my apartment with its closets full of clothes, refrigerator full of food, and more gadgets than I ever thought I'd own, and I realize that, indeed, life *isn't* fair. I am reminded of the apostle John's admonition for compassion (1 John 3:17) and hope that the next time I'm confronted by someone demanding help, I will remember to try a little harder and help a little more.

DIGGING DEEPER

1. What does God think of the poor? See Luke 4:18; 6:20; 7:22; 14:12-14; 18:22.

2. How were people's physical needs met by the early church? See Acts 4:32-35. What should the church do today?

3. Should a person feel guilty for having enough money or for not being in hardship? Read 2 Corinthians 8:1-15; 1 Timothy 6:7-10, 17-19.

and his brother's righteous. ¹³Marvel not, my brethren, if the world hate you.

¹⁴We know that we have passed from death unto life, because we love the brethren. He that loveth not *his* brother abideth in death. ¹⁵Whosoever hateth his brother is a murderer: and ye know that no murderer hath eternal life abiding in him. ¹⁶Hereby perceive we the love *of God,* because he laid down his life for us: and we ought to lay down *our* lives for the brethren. ¹⁷But whoso hath this world's good, and seeth his brother have need, and shutteth up his bowels *of compassion* from him, how dwelleth the love of God in him? ¹⁸My little children, let us not love in word, neither in tongue; but in deed and in truth. ¹⁹And hereby we know that we are of the truth, and shall assure^c our hearts before him.

²⁰For if our heart condemn us,

God is greater than our heart, and knoweth all things. ²¹Beloved, if our heart condemn us not, *then* have we confidence toward God. ²²And whatsoever we ask, we receive of him, because we keep his commandments, and do those things that are pleasing in his sight.

²³And this is his commandment, That we should believe on the name of his Son Jesus Christ, and love one another, as he gave us commandment. ²⁴And he that keepeth his commandments dwelleth in him, and he in him. And hereby we know that he abideth in us, by the Spirit which he hath given us.

4

¹Beloved, believe not every spirit, but try the spirits whether they are of God: because many false prophets are gone out into the world. ²Hereby know ye

^c assure: Gr. persuade

Family Traditions

Traditions of Everyday Love

1 JOHN 4:7-21

Common, ordinary, everyday expressions of love are the bedrock of a happy family. Every family has originals and favorites. Here are several ideas you can try:

Praise others. Think about the really neat things your spouse and children do, and let them know how much you appreciate them. Talk about the good ideas they have, their timely laughter, the insight, the love for friends, or whatever.

Surprises. Get up early to pick a bouquet for the bathroom, make the coffee, unload the dishwasher, create a fun breakfast.

Plenty o' touch. Warm hugs, playful wrestling, gentle tickles, or pats on the back are physical ways to say, "I love you."

Hidden notes. Written reminders of affection keep life interesting—and they're even more fun when they pop up in unexpected places.

The love jar. Keep a glass jar in the kitchen beside the cookie jar, or better yet, transform the cookie jar. Everybody can write frequent, cheerful, inspiring notes and leave them in the jar. When feeling down, you can dip into the love jar and pull out an encouraging thought from someone in your family.

A shoulder and back rub. After a hard day, such a gesture needs no words.

A smile. Acknowledgment of presence and of welcome in one's own home can easily be forgotten.

A telephone call. Telephone in the middle of the day just to ask, "How ya doin'?"

Homecomings. Sit down together and discuss the day. Share a pot of tea, jug of juice, or piece of fruit. Sharing gives context to the important things on hearts and minds.

Serve each other. Make an extra piece of toast, clean up after someone without being asked, jump up to get the forgotten salt.

Big and little favors, with no strings attached. Open the bedroom window for her when you'd rather have it shut. Bake chocolate chip cookies for him even though your favorite is oatmeal raisin.

Walk together. Suggest a walk in the moonlight, a stroll to the library, or a jog around the block. Walking brings out the talking, often better than face-to-face conversation.

The personal touch. Find out what your loved one especially likes, and do it: fresh flowers on the table, popcorn with a TV special, candlelight in the bedroom, etc.

Create space. Respect the individuality and privacy of other family members. Allow them quiet, uninterrupted time alone.

Forgive. There are few better ways to demonstrate love than by forgiving someone who's wronged you.

the Spirit of God: Every spirit that confesseth that Jesus Christ is come in the flesh is of God: ³And every spirit that confesseth not that Jesus Christ is come in the flesh is not of God: and this is that *spirit* of antichrist, whereof ye have heard that it should come; and even now already is it in the world.

⁴Ye are of God, little children, and have overcome them: because greater is he that is in you, than he that is in the world. ⁵They are of the world: therefore speak they of the world, and the world heareth them. ⁶We are of God: he that knoweth God heareth us; he that is not of God heareth not us. Hereby know we the spirit of truth, and the spirit of error.

⁷Beloved, let us love one another: for love is of God; and every one that loveth is born[a] of God, and knoweth God. ⁸He that loveth not knoweth not God; for God is love. ⁹In this was manifested the love of God toward us, because that God sent his only begotten Son into the world, that we might live through him. ¹⁰Herein is love, not that we loved God, but that he loved us, and sent his Son *to be* the propitiation for our sins. ¹¹Beloved, if God so loved us, we ought also to love one another. ¹²No man hath seen God at any time. If we love one another, God dwelleth in us, and his love is perfected in us. ¹³Hereby know we that we dwell in him, and he in us, because he hath given us of his Spirit.

¹⁴And we have seen and do testify that the Father sent the Son *to be* the Saviour of the world. ¹⁵Whosoever shall confess that Jesus is the Son of God, God dwelleth in him, and he in God. ¹⁶And we have known and believed the love that God hath to us. God is love; and he that dwelleth in love dwelleth in God, and God in him.

¹⁷Herein is our love[b] made perfect, that we may have boldness in the day of judgment: because as he is, so are we in this world. ¹⁸There is no fear in love; but perfect love casteth out fear: because fear hath torment. He that feareth is not made perfect in love. ¹⁹We love him, because he first loved us. ²⁰If a man say, I love God, and hateth his brother, he is a liar: for he that loveth not his brother whom he hath seen, how can he love God whom he hath not seen? ²¹And this commandment have we from him, That he who loveth God love his brother also.

5

¹Whosoever believeth that Jesus is the Christ is born[a] of God: and every one that loveth him that begat loveth him also that is begotten of him. ²By this we know that we love the children of God, when we love God, and keep his commandments. ³For this is the love of God, that we keep his commandments: and his commandments are not grievous. ⁴For whatsoever is born of God overcometh the world: and this is the victory that overcometh the world, *even* our faith. ⁵Who is he that overcometh the world, but he that believeth that Jesus is the Son of God?

---

[a] is born: or, has been born
[b] our love: Gr. love with us
[a] is born: or, has been born

No Fear in Love

by Bruce Narramore

God is our heavenly Father, and as such he is a perfect parent. His love for us is perfect. That is why John wrote, "There is no fear in love; but perfect love casteth out fear. . . . He that feareth is not made perfect in love" (1 John 4:18).

Since Christ has taken the punishment for our sins on the cross, we have absolutely no reason to be afraid of God. God lovingly asks for our obedience. He tells us about consequences of sin and the advantage of obeying him. And he disciplines us. But he doesn't lose his temper or threaten us into conformity. And he doesn't want us to do that with our children.

The Bible sometimes uses the word *fear* in a positive way to mean *respect.* The book of Proverbs says, "The fear of the Lord is the beginning of wisdom" (9:10). This doesn't mean that we should be panicky and anxious before God, but that respect for God and an awareness of his holiness make us more aware of what really matters.

Suppose you want to teach your children to look both ways before crossing the street. You could anxiously yell, "A car's going to hit you!" every time they near the street, but that would only make them fearful. Every visit to a street corner would panic them. Instead, you calmly tell them, "Look both ways before crossing the street so you don't get hit by a car." This teaches your children to be alert to danger without making them unnecessarily afraid. That's the way God works with us.

Or suppose your high schooler sasses you. Since you want him to respect you and your authority, you clearly need to do something. But you have two options. First, you can threaten him, hit him, or attack his character. This might make him behave, and it might scare him, but it *won't* teach him to respect you.

The better way to handle sassing is to hear your children out. Let them tell you how angry or upset they are and why. Be strong enough to listen without retaliating. Afterward, tell them, "I'm sorry you're feeling so upset." If you can do anything to help them feel better, do it. Once you have taken time to understand and be helpful, then tell them, "We all get upset sometimes, and that's OK. I want you to tell me when you're upset, but please tell me in a different way. If you could tell me, 'Mom, I'm mad' instead of 'I hate you' or 'You're so stupid,' it would be easier for me to listen. It's not respectful to say you hate me, and it only makes me want to fight back."

This doesn't mean we should allow unbridled or unkind verbal or physical expression of anger. There are times when each of us, including children, must restrain our feelings. But in an intimate parent-child relationship, your children should feel accepted and loved enough to be honest—even about their negative feelings.

If the situation calls for more discipline than just a brief talk, you can also tell them, "To help you remember not to talk that way, I will ground you for the weekend if you do it again." That's disciplining and being firm without creating fear.

Fear drives people away. Many people have lost a vital relationship with God because they are afraid of him, and many parents have lost a good relationship with their children because they have frightened them away. If you have ever sinned and had that vague thought that "sometime, somehow, God is going to get even," that was fear. Fear operates on a "balanced scale" system. Each time we misbehave, the scale tips to the "bad behavior" side. Once we are punished, the scale evens and again reads, "Accounts even. Paid in full." But for all those who trust in Christ, God has balanced the scale once and for all. That's why we don't need to be afraid that God will punish us. If we discipline our children firmly but in love, they won't be afraid of us either.

DIGGING DEEPER

    1. Read Hebrews 12:5-11. How does God treat his people when they sin? How is this like the actions of a good parent?

    2. Read Romans 8:12-17. Why do God's people not need to fear him? When you correct your children, do you think they feel like sons and daughters or like slaves?

    3. God tells us how to correct our children in love. He also wants us to show love when it becomes necessary for us to correct fellow believers. Read Galatians 6:1-2 and describe how we should correct others.

⁶This is he that came by water and blood, *even* Jesus Christ; not by water only, but by water and blood. And it is the Spirit that beareth witness, because the Spirit is truth. ⁷For there are three that bear record in heaven, the Father, the Word, and the Holy Ghost: and these three are one. ⁸And there are three that bear witness in earth, the Spirit, and the water, and the blood: and these three agree in one. ⁹If we receive the witness of men, the witness of God is greater: for this is the witness of God which he hath testified of his Son.

¹⁰He that believeth on the Son of God hath the witness in himself: he that believeth not God hath made him a liar; because he believeth not the record that God gave of his Son. ¹¹And this is the record, that God hath given to us eternal life, and this life is in his Son. ¹²He that hath the Son hath life; *and* he that hath not the Son of God hath not life. ¹³These things have I written unto you that believe on the name of the Son of God; that ye may know that ye have eternal life, and that ye may believe on the name of the Son of God.

¹⁴And this is the confidence that

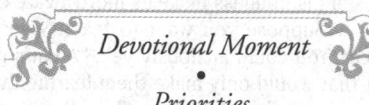

Devotional Moment

Priorities

5:21 John's parting thought in this short letter warns us to stay away from anything that might take God's place in our heart. God understands how easily we can be enticed by things, such as possessions, achievements, power, hatred, recognition, and the like. Consider your greatest ambition: Is it to have power over everyone else? Is it to have a big and beautiful house? Is it to prove your ability to buy things that you don't need or can't afford? Be careful about what motivates you to say what you say, buy what you buy, and do what you do. Make your motive only this: to serve God by serving others. You have nothing to prove to anybody but God.

we have in[b] him, that, if we ask any thing according to his will, he heareth us: ¹⁵And if we know that he hear us, whatsoever we ask, we know that we have the petitions that we desired of him. ¹⁶If any man see his brother sin a sin *which is* not unto death, he shall ask, and he shall give him life for them that sin not unto death. There is a sin unto death: I do not say that he shall pray for it. ¹⁷All unrighteousness is sin: and there is a sin not unto death.

ᵇ in: or, concerning

¹⁸We know that whosoever is born of God sinneth not; but he that is begotten of God keepeth himself, and that wicked one toucheth him not. ¹⁹*And* we know that we are of God, and the whole world lieth in wickedness. ²⁰And we know that the Son of God is come, and hath given us an understanding, that we may know him that is true, and we are in him that is true, *even* in his Son Jesus Christ. This is the true God, and eternal life. ²¹Little children, keep yourselves from idols. Amen.

SECOND JOHN

Purpose
To emphasize the basics
of following Christ—
truth and love—and to
warn against false
teachers

Author
The apostle John

To Whom Written
To a woman called
"Cyria" and her house-
hold—some think that
the greeting refers in-
stead to a local church

Date Written
About the same time as
1 John, around A.D. 90,
from Ephesus

Setting
Evidently the recipients
of this letter were in-
volved in one of the
churches John was
overseeing, and they
had developed a strong
friendship. John was
warning them of the
false teachers who were
becoming prevalent in
some of the churches.

Key Verse
"And this is love, that
we walk after his com-
mandments. This is the
commandment, That, as
ye have heard from the
beginning, ye should
walk in it" (1:6).

"Dear Libby," writes Mom in a note to her teenage daughter. "Your school friend Sarah, the tenth grader, called this morning about nine to say she was back from vacation and would enjoy seeing you. She wants to talk soon. Love, Mom."

Are you kidding? Moms don't write notes like that. Try, "Libby, Sarah called. Wants to talk. Mom."

Or, even more likely: "Lib—Sarah—Mom."

Short notes are a family's communication lifeline. No explanations, just the essentials. Poor Libby has to figure out the meaning of the dashes, but she'll probably get it in three seconds or less.

Second John is brief. No long explanations. No stories or illustrations. Yet his point is strong and vitally important. Love is the key to Christian living, and love means obedience to God's way.

What warning comes in this letter? By what standards can we measure our success at real love? What reasons for loving at all?

Short and sweet, this letter is full of serious purpose and solid help. If these few words become your motto today, the world will be a different place tomorrow.

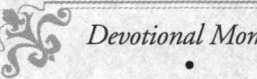

Devotional Moment
•
Teachings

1:7-9 John challenged his readers to pay careful attention to the teachings they followed. The problem was that sometimes false teachers would mislead Christians by teaching ideas contrary to the Scriptures. The believers needed to think about what they heard and read to filter out whatever wasn't true, rather than merely swallowing everything without thought. There is no shortage of advice in this world from many different sources. As we read books and listen to radio and television, we must also be students of God's Word, pray for discernment, and think about what we take in. We can't eliminate the false messages that we hear, but we can be informed, ask God for wisdom, and talk things over with others who are wise.

1

¹The elder unto the elect lady and her children, whom I love in the truth; and not I only, but also all they that have known the truth; ²For the truth's sake, which dwelleth in us, and shall be with us for ever. ³Grace be[a] with you, mercy, *and* peace, from God the Father, and from the Lord Jesus Christ, the Son of the Father, in truth and love. ⁴I rejoiced greatly that I found of thy children walking in truth, as we have received a commandment from the Father.

⁵And now I beseech thee, lady, not as though I wrote a new commandment unto thee, but that which we had from the beginning, that we love one another. ⁶And this is love, that we walk after his commandments. This is the commandment, That, as ye have heard from the beginning, ye should walk in it.

⁷For many deceivers are entered into the world, who confess not that Jesus Christ is come in the flesh. This is a deceiver and an antichrist. ⁸Look to yourselves, that we lose not those things which we have wrought[b], but that we receive a full reward. ⁹Whosoever transgresseth, and abideth not in the doctrine of Christ, hath not God. He that abideth in the doctrine of Christ, he hath both the Father and the Son.

¹⁰If there come any unto you, and bring not this doctrine, receive him not into *your* house, neither bid him God speed: ¹¹For he that biddeth him God speed is partaker of his evil deeds.

¹²Having many things to write unto you, I would not *write* with paper and ink: but I trust to come unto you, and speak face to[c] face, that our joy may be full. ¹³The children of thy elect sister greet thee. Amen.

---

[a] be: Gr. shall be
[b] wrought: or, gained, some copies read, ye have gained, but that ye, etc.
[c] face to . . . : Gr. mouth to mouth

THIRD JOHN

Purpose
To commend Gaius for his hospitality and to encourage him in his Christian life

Author
The apostle John

To Whom Written
Gaius, a prominent Christian in one of the churches known to John

Date Written
About A.D. 90, from Ephesus

Setting
Church leaders traveled from town to town helping to establish new congregations. They depended on the hospitality of fellow believers. Gaius was one who welcomed them into his home.

Key Verse
"Beloved, thou doest faithfully whatsoever thou doest to the brethren, and to strangers" (1:5).

Key People
John, Gaius, Diotrephes, Demetrius

Many people are unaware how much joy they bring to the lives of others. A simple act of kindness to a friend or neighbor can work a miracle. Some elderly people grow old wondering if their acts of love have mattered to anyone. If only they knew.

This heartwarming letter from John to Gaius comes close to telling it like it ought to be told. If more families would read this tiny Bible book at dinnertime devotions, kids might discover how much their eagerness for Christ can make a mom's day, how thoroughly pleased a father can be with each step in a child's walk with God. Not a bad secret to let out, is it?

Let the secret out. Smart members of any family might consider reading this book from time to time, then write similar letters to those who need the news. And even if they quote the letter word for word, they at least can get the main ideas across—"You're a joy to me, and here's why. . . ." Loved ones don't know how they're doing otherwise.

We should also pray a lot for each other, as John doubtless did for Gaius. No one could write a letter with so much feeling and fail to pray often for his or her friend or family.

As you read this letter, aspire to a role you cannot possibly put a price on: that of saying just how much joy others bring to you.

1

¹The elder unto the wellbeloved Gaius, whom I love in^a the truth. ²Beloved, I wish^b above all things that thou mayest prosper and be in health, even as thy soul prospereth.

³For I rejoiced greatly, when the brethren came and testified of the truth that is in thee, even as thou walkest in the truth. ⁴I have no greater joy than to hear that my children walk in truth. ⁵Beloved, thou doest faithfully whatsoever thou doest to the brethren, and to strangers; ⁶Which have borne witness of thy charity before the church: whom if thou bring forward on their journey after^c a godly sort, thou shalt do well: ⁷Because that for his name's sake they went forth, taking nothing of the Gentiles. ⁸We therefore ought to receive such, that we might be fellowhelpers^d to the truth.

⁹I wrote unto the church: but Diotrephes, who loveth to have the preeminence among them, receiveth us not. ¹⁰Wherefore, if I come, I will remember his deeds which he doeth, prating against us with malicious words: and not content therewith, neither doth he himself receive the brethren, and forbiddeth them that would, and casteth *them* out of the church. ¹¹Beloved, follow not that which is evil, but that which is good. He that doeth good is of God: but he that doeth evil hath not seen God.

¹²Demetrius hath good report of all *men*, and of the truth itself: yea, and we *also* bear record; and ye know that our record is true. ¹³I had many things to write, but I will not with ink and pen write unto thee: ¹⁴But I trust I shall shortly see thee, and we shall speak face to^e face. Peace *be* to thee. *Our* friends salute thee. Greet the friends by name.

---

^a in . . . : or, truly
^b wish: or, pray
^c after . . . : Gr. worthy of God
^d fellowhelpers: or, joint-labourers
^e face to . . . : Gr. mouth to mouth

JUDE

Purpose
To remind the church of the need for constant vigilance—to keep strong in the faith and to defend it against heresy

Author
Jude, James's brother and Jesus' half brother

To Whom Written
Jewish Christians

Date Written
About A.D. 65

Setting
From the first century on, the church has been threatened by heresy and false teaching. We must always be on our guard.

Key Verse
"Beloved, when I gave all diligence to write unto you of the common salvation, it was needful for me to write unto you, and exhort you that ye should earnestly contend for the faith which was once delivered unto the saints" (1:3).

Key People
Jude, James, Jesus

Warnings to children are as common as dandelions to lawns and dirty dishes to kitchen sinks. Children get warned about more dangers than a fugitive could ever imagine. Almost everything represents a potential hazard to a child, so a diligent parent has to be encyclopedic in warnings about keeping safe and avoiding mayhem.

Like an ever-watchful parent, Jude warns us about the dangers of following teachers who play loose with God's Word. How do we slip into danger? What kind of a friend would Jude be if he never warned us about anything?

Parents who warn a lot should take a cue from Jude, who concludes by reminding us that God is able to keep us from slipping and falling away. Parents who teach children this strategic fact of life also need to believe it, which isn't always easy.

1

¹Jude, the servant of Jesus Christ, and brother of James, to them that are sanctified by God the Father, and preserved in Jesus Christ, *and* called: ²Mercy unto you, and peace, and love, be multiplied.

³Beloved, when I gave all diligence to write unto you of the common salvation, it was needful for me to write unto you, and exhort *you* that ye should earnestly contend for the faith which was once delivered unto the saints. ⁴For there are certain men crept in unawares, who were before of old ordained to this condemnation, ungodly men, turning the grace of our God into lasciviousness, and denying the only Lord God, and our Lord Jesus Christ. ⁵I will therefore put you in remembrance, though ye once knew this, how that the Lord,

having saved the people out of the land of Egypt, afterward destroyed them that believed not. ⁶And the angels which kept not their first estate[a], but left their own habitation, he hath reserved in everlasting chains under darkness unto the judgment of the great day. ⁷Even as Sodom and Gomorrha, and the cities about them in like manner, giving themselves over to fornication, and going after strange[b] flesh, are set forth for an example, suffering the vengeance of eternal fire.

⁸Likewise also these *filthy* dreamers defile the flesh, despise dominion, and speak evil of dignities. ⁹Yet Michael the archangel, when contending with the devil he disputed about the body of Moses, durst not bring against him a railing accusation, but said, The Lord rebuke thee. ¹⁰But these speak evil of those things which they know not: but what they know naturally, as brute beasts, in those things they corrupt themselves. ¹¹Woe unto them! for they have gone in the way of Cain, and ran greedily after the error of Balaam for reward, and perished in the gainsaying of Core. ¹²These are spots in your feasts of charity, when they feast with you, feeding themselves without fear: clouds *they are* without water, carried about of winds; trees whose fruit withereth, without fruit, twice dead, plucked up by the roots; ¹³Raging waves of the sea, foaming out their own shame; wandering stars, to whom is reserved the blackness of darkness for ever. ¹⁴And Enoch also, the seventh from Adam, prophesied of these, saying, Behold, the Lord

---

[a] first estate: or, principality
[b] strange: Gr. other

cometh with ten thousands of his saints,

¹⁵To execute judgment upon all, and to convince all that are ungodly among them of all their ungodly deeds which they have ungodly committed, and of all their hard *speeches* which ungodly sinners have spoken against him. ¹⁶These are murmurers, complainers, walking after their own lusts; and their mouth speaketh great swelling *words*, having men's persons in admiration because of advantage. ¹⁷But, beloved, remember ye the words which were spoken before of the apostles of our Lord Jesus Christ; ¹⁸How that they told you there should be mockers in the last time, who should walk after their own ungodly lusts. ¹⁹These be they who separate themselves, sensual, having not the Spirit. ²⁰But ye, beloved, building up yourselves on your most holy faith, praying in the Holy Ghost, ²¹Keep yourselves in the love of God, looking for the mercy of our Lord Jesus Christ unto eternal life. ²²And of some have compassion, making a difference: ²³And others save with fear, pulling *them* out of the fire; hating even the garment spotted by the flesh. ²⁴Now unto him that is able to keep you from falling, and to present *you* faultless before the presence of his glory with exceeding joy, ²⁵To the only wise God our Saviour, *be* glory and majesty, dominion and power, both now and ever. Amen.

REVELATION

Purpose
To reveal the full identity
of Christ and to give warning and hope to believers

Author
The apostle John

To Whom Written
The seven churches in Asia
and all believers everywhere

Date Written
About A.D. 95, from Patmos

Setting
Roman authorities had ex-
iled John to the island of
Patmos (off the coast of Asia
Minor). John, who had been
an eyewitness of the incar-
nate Christ, now has a vision
of the glorified Christ.

Key Verse
"Blessed is he that readeth,
and they that hear the
words of this prophecy, and
keep those things which are
written therein: for the time
is at hand" (1:3).

Special Features
Revelation is written in
"apocalyptic" form—a type
of Jewish literature that
uses symbolic imagery to
communicate hope (the ultimate triumph of God) to
those in the middle of persecution. The events are ordered according to literary,
rather than strictly chronological, patterns.

Many parents scarcely get three years under their belt before having to field questions about heaven. "Will there be games in heaven?" "Will there be enough room to run around?" "Will Trooper be there?" "Will it be windy?"

John, the disciple closest to Jesus, gives us quite a picture to ponder. It's a picture about the end of time, a picture that Bible scholars sort and sift in endless efforts to explain and on which few scholars can fully agree. If you come to Revelation with the hope of discovering keys to predicting the future, think twice and take a breather. If you read Revelation to find assurance from God about his special destination for believers—heaven—you're on target. Start reading!

Kids will ask about heaven. At the death of a grand-parent, or even a pet, the questions will arise. Revelation is our best insight into our true home. Revelation de-scribes God's place and helps us see that the end of life on earth is the beginning of what really matters.

Your best efforts at describing heaven may not sat-isfy every curiosity. But Revelation is God's Word about that ultimate place to live, God's home—our *true* home.

1

¹The Revelation of Jesus Christ, which God gave unto him, to shew unto his servants things which must shortly come to pass; and he sent and signified *it* by his angel unto his servant John: ²Who bare record of the word of God, and of the testimony of Jesus Christ, and of all things that he saw.

³Blessed *is* he that readeth, and they that hear the words of this prophecy, and keep those things which are written therein: for the time *is* at hand. ⁴John to the seven churches which are in Asia: Grace *be* unto you, and peace, from him which is, and which was, and which is to come; and from the seven Spirits which are before his throne; ⁵And from Jesus Christ, *who is* the faithful witness, *and* the first begotten of the dead, and the prince of the kings of the earth. Unto him that loved us, and washed us from our sins in his own blood, ⁶And hath made us kings and priests unto God and his Father; to him *be* glory and dominion for ever and ever. Amen. ⁷Behold, he cometh with clouds; and every eye shall see him, and they *also* which pierced him: and all kindreds of the earth shall wail because of him. Even so, Amen. ⁸I am Alpha and Omega, the beginning and the ending, saith the Lord, which is, and which was, and which is to come, the Almighty.

⁹I John, who also am your brother, and companion in tribulation, and in the kingdom and patience of Jesus Christ, was in the isle that is called Patmos, for the word of God, and for the testimony of Jesus Christ. ¹⁰I was in the Spirit on the Lord's day, and heard behind me a great voice, as of a trumpet,

¹¹Saying, I am Alpha and Omega, the first and the last: and, What thou seest, write in a book, and send *it* unto the seven churches which are in Asia; unto Ephesus, and unto Smyrna, and unto Pergamos, and unto Thyatira, and unto Sardis, and unto Philadelphia, and unto Laodicea. ¹²And I turned to see the voice that spake with me. And being turned, I saw seven golden candlesticks; ¹³And in the midst of the seven candlesticks *one* like unto the Son of man, clothed with a garment down to the foot, and girt about the paps with a golden girdle. ¹⁴His head and *his* hairs *were* white like wool, as white as snow; and his eyes *were* as a flame of fire; ¹⁵And his feet like unto fine brass, as if they burned in a furnace; and his voice as the sound of many waters. ¹⁶And he had in his right hand seven stars: and out of his mouth went a sharp twoedged sword: and his countenance *was* as the sun shineth in his strength. ¹⁷And when I saw him, I fell at his feet as dead. And he laid his right hand upon me, saying unto me, Fear not; I am the first and the last: ¹⁸I *am* he that liveth, and was dead; and, behold, I am alive for evermore, Amen; and have the keys of hell and of death. ¹⁹Write the things which thou hast seen, and the things which are, and the things which shall be hereafter; ²⁰The mystery of the seven stars which thou sawest in my right hand, and the seven golden candlesticks. The seven stars are the angels of the seven churches: and the seven candlesticks which thou sawest are the seven churches.

2

¹Unto the angel of the church of Ephesus write; These things saith he that

holdeth the seven stars in his right hand, who walketh in the midst of the seven golden candlesticks; ²I know thy works, and thy labour, and thy patience, and how thou canst not bear them which are evil: and thou hast tried them which say they are apostles, and are not, and hast found them liars: ³And hast borne, and hast patience, and for my name's sake hast laboured, and hast not fainted. ⁴Nevertheless I have *somewhat* against thee, because thou hast left thy first love. ⁵Remember therefore from whence thou art fallen, and repent, and do the first works; or else I will come unto thee quickly, and will remove thy candlestick out of his place, except thou repent. ⁶But this thou hast, that thou hatest the deeds of the Nicolaitans, which I also hate. ⁷He that hath an ear, let him hear what the Spirit saith unto the churches; To him that overcometh will I give to eat of the tree of life, which is in the midst of the paradise of God.

⁸And unto the angel of the church in Smyrna write; These things saith the first and the last, which was dead, and is alive; ⁹I know thy works, and tribulation, and poverty, (but thou art rich) and *I know* the blasphemy of them which say they are Jews, and are not, but *are* the synagogue of Satan. ¹⁰Fear none of those things which thou shalt suffer: behold, the devil shall cast *some* of you into prison, that ye may be tried; and ye shall have tribulation ten days: be thou faithful unto death, and I will give thee a crown of life. ¹¹He that hath an ear, let him hear what the Spirit saith unto the churches; He that overcometh shall not be hurt of the second death.

¹²And to the angel of the church in Pergamos write; These things saith he which hath the sharp sword with two edges; ¹³I know thy works, and where thou dwellest, *even* where Satan's seat *is*: and thou holdest fast my name, and hast not denied my faith, even in those days wherein Antipas *was* my faithful martyr, who was slain among you, where Satan dwelleth. ¹⁴But I have a few things against thee, because thou hast there them that hold the doctrine of Balaam, who taught Balac to cast a stumblingblock before the children of Israel, to eat things sacrificed unto idols, and to commit fornication. ¹⁵So hast thou also them that hold the doctrine of the Nicolaitans, which thing I hate. ¹⁶Repent; or else I will come unto thee quickly, and will fight against them with the sword of my mouth. ¹⁷He that hath an ear, let him hear what the Spirit saith unto the churches; To him that overcometh will I give to eat of the hidden manna, and will give him a white stone, and in the stone a new name written, which no man knoweth saving he that receiveth *it*.

¹⁸And unto the angel of the church in Thyatira write; These things saith the Son of God, who hath his eyes like unto a flame of fire, and his feet *are* like fine brass; ¹⁹I know thy works, and charity, and service, and faith, and thy patience, and thy works; and the last *to be* more than the first. ²⁰Notwithstanding I have a few things against thee, because thou sufferest that woman Jezebel, which calleth herself a prophetess, to teach and to seduce my servants to commit fornication, and to eat things sacrificed unto idols. ²¹And I gave her space to repent of her fornication; and she repented not. ²²Behold, I

Breaking Free from Relational Drift

"I know thy works, and thy labour, and thy patience. . . . Nevertheless I have somewhat against thee, because thou hast left thy first love." Revelation 2:2, 4

Christ's message to the church at Ephesus is telling. This group of believers enjoyed many successes—seven times Jesus praised them for their actions, attitudes, and persistence. Yet they had fallen into a dangerous cycle that often comes with such success: In the process of doing so much good, they had lost the heartfelt reason why they were doing those things. The Lord put it this way: "You don't love me as at first!"

The negative pattern of *relational drift* can, and unfortunately often does, happen in any relationship. It happened to the Christians in Ephesus in their relationship with Christ, and it can happen to husbands and wives, even after they've piled up many successes.

Doug and April met in college at a Campus Crusade function and became fast friends. Committed to Christ and soon to each other, they had a pure, God-honoring courtship and a wonderful marriage. Family members and friends whom they had led to Christ were all shocked when Doug and April suddenly announced—after twenty-two years, two children, and years of faithful ministry together—that they were getting a divorce.

Doug and April had been pillars of the church, models and examples to many others. What happened?

To the surprise of many, it's the successes that often blind couples to the cycle of relational drift, eventually causing them to leave their first love.

How can couples reverse this cycle of drifting away from each other? There are three steps to take that are similar to those that Jesus called the Ephesians to take (Rev. 2:5):

1. **"Remember therefore from whence thou art fallen."** Do you remember when you first came to know Christ and the unbridled joy at learning, growing, and sharing about him? Couples, too, can gain back feelings that may have been forgotten over the years as they think back to their courtship and positive times in their relationship.

Whether it's dragging out old photos or wedding albums, or talking through what attracted us to that other person in the first place, we can begin to rekindle love's flame by recalling the past.

2. **"Repent."** Repentance, carries with it the idea that we not only stop the negative things that we're doing, but that we *turn around* and begin walking in another direction. We need to humble ourselves if we've lost that first-love relationship with our spouse. Ceas-

ing to love a spouse is not merely unfortunate, it's sin. And God calls on us to stop the drifting, turn around, and walk again in love.

3. "Do the first works." How does this help in rekindling love?

Studies have shown that one major difference between couples who are divided by deep conflict and those who are emotionally and physically close is that close couples have continued to do small, specific, caring acts for each other. These aren't great or expensive sacrifices but small acts of love, such as opening the car door, calling from work to check in, writing love notes, holding hands at the mall—small acts that fan the flame of love.

If we've lost our first love with the Person who should be our highest love, then remembering his past faithfulness, turning back to him again, and doing the things we did as new believers can restore that first love. For couples who have lost their first-love relationship, this pattern can help break a negative cycle as well.

---

will cast her into a bed, and them that commit adultery with her into great tribulation, except they repent of their deeds. ²³And I will kill her children with death; and all the churches shall know that I am he which searcheth the reins and hearts: and I will give unto every one of you according to your works. ²⁴But unto you I say, and unto the rest in Thyatira, as many as have not this doctrine, and which have not known the depths of Satan, as they speak; I will put upon you none other burden. ²⁵But that which ye have *already* hold fast till I come. ²⁶And he that overcometh, and keepeth my works unto the end, to him will I give power over the nations: ²⁷And he shall rule them with a rod of iron; as the vessels of a potter shall they be broken to shivers: even as I received of my Father. ²⁸And I will give him the morning star. ²⁹He that hath an ear, let him hear what the Spirit saith unto the churches.

3

¹And unto the angel of the church in Sardis write; These things saith he that hath the seven Spirits of God, and the seven stars; I know thy works, that thou hast a name that thou livest, and art dead. ²Be watchful, and strengthen the things which remain, that are ready to die: for I have not found thy works perfect before God. ³Remember therefore how thou hast received and heard, and hold fast, and repent. If therefore thou shalt not watch, I will come on thee as a thief, and thou shalt not know what hour I will come upon thee. ⁴Thou hast a few names even in Sardis which have not defiled their garments; and they shall walk with me in white: for they are worthy. ⁵He that overcometh, the same shall be clothed in white raiment; and I will not blot out his name out of the book of life, but I will confess his name before my Father, and before his angels. ⁶He that hath an ear, let him hear what the Spirit saith unto the churches.

⁷And to the angel of the church in Philadelphia write; These things saith he that is holy, he that is true, he that hath the key of David, he that openeth, and no man shutteth; and shutteth, and no man openeth; ⁸I know thy works:

behold, I have set before thee an open door, and no man can shut it: for thou hast a little strength, and hast kept my word, and hast not denied my name. [9]Behold, I will make them of the synagogue of Satan, which say they are Jews, and are not, but do lie; behold, I will make them to come and worship before thy feet, and to know that I have loved thee. [10]Because thou hast kept the word of my patience, I also will keep thee from the hour of temptation, which shall come upon all the world, to try them that dwell upon the earth. [11]Behold, I come quickly: hold that fast which thou hast, that no man take thy crown. [12]Him that overcometh will I make a pillar in the temple of my God, and he shall go no more out: and I will write upon him the name of my God, and the name of the city of my God, *which is* new Jerusalem, which cometh down out of heaven from my God: and *I will write upon him* my new name. [13]He that hath an ear, let him hear what the Spirit saith unto the churches.

[14]And unto the angel of the church of the Laodiceans[a] write; These things saith the Amen, the faithful and true witness, the beginning of the creation of God; [15]I know thy works, that thou art neither cold nor hot: I would thou wert cold or hot. [16]So then because thou art lukewarm, and neither cold nor hot, I will spue thee out of my mouth. [17]Because thou sayest, I am rich, and increased with goods, and have need of nothing; and knowest not that thou art wretched, and miserable, and poor, and blind, and naked: [18]I counsel thee to buy of me gold tried in the fire, that thou mayest be rich; and white raiment, that thou mayest be clothed, and *that* the shame of thy nakedness do not appear; and anoint thine eyes with eyesalve, that thou mayest see. [19]As many as I love, I rebuke and chasten: be zealous therefore, and repent. [20]Behold, I stand at the door, and knock: if any man hear my voice, and open the door, I will come in to him, and will sup with him, and he with me. [21]To him that overcometh will I grant to sit with me in my throne, even as I also overcame, and am set down with my Father in his throne. [22]He that hath an ear, let him hear what the Spirit saith unto the churches.

4

[1]After this I looked, and, behold, a door *was* opened in heaven: and the first voice which I heard *was* as it were of a trumpet talking with me; which said, Come up hither, and I will shew thee things which must be hereafter. [2]And immediately I was in the spirit: and, behold, a throne was set in heaven, and *one* sat on the throne. [3]And he that sat was to look upon like a jasper and a sardine stone: and *there was* a rainbow round about the throne, in sight like unto an emerald. [4]And round about the throne *were* four and twenty seats: and upon the seats I saw four and twenty elders sitting, clothed in white raiment; and they had on their heads crowns of gold. [5]And out of the throne proceeded lightnings and thunderings and voices: and *there were* seven lamps of fire burning before the throne, which are the seven Spirits of God. [6]And before the

---

[a] of the Laodiceans: or, in Laodicea

Family Traditions

Keep First Love for Jesus Burning Brightly

REVELATION 2:4-5

What can we do within our families to keep love for Jesus our top priority? These families found a way:

"Once a month, we celebrate what we call 'Our Lord's Supper.' Using our best china and linens, we set an extra place at the table for him to remind us of his invisible presence. We read from the Gospels. Sometimes afterward we watch a video with a Christian theme and message."

"We pray with each of our children, one at a time, before they go to bed. We talk to our heavenly Father about their concerns, and as parents we share our own concerns and lay our own worries before him. Sometimes we break into praise, a chorus, or laughter."

"Our family is go, go, going all the time! Generally it works out all right because we see each other in between. But occasionally my husband or I shout (figuratively), 'Stop!' and force everyone to take another look at family priorities. Sometimes we require everybody to cancel something and sit down long enough to look at each other and talk to each other and pray for each other."

"I'm the kind of person who is energized by time alone, by quietness; I need a lot of personal retreat time. My wife is a people person; she's energized by being with people, talking, exchanging ideas, and so on. To find time for both kinds of pursuits has taken patience, understanding, and coordination. A lot of personal respect goes a long way, but when both of us are fulfilled, our mutual love for the Savior thrives."

"In our family the children never really wanted to pray out loud, so we started the tradition of a family prayer book. We pass it through everyone's hands at least once a week. They write down their prayer needs and sign their names. In a special section in the back, each person writes a prayer for someone else in the family and then passes it on. Our prayer books have become priceless pieces of family spiritual history."

"We have a special minute each day at 9:38 A.M. when no matter where we are, each of us prays for the others. We all set our alarms. The kids say they remember most of the time, especially in math class. I also tape Bible verses inside their textbooks occasionally or stick them in the pages as little bookmarks for surprise inspiration."

throne *there was* a sea of glass like unto crystal: and in the midst of the throne, and round about the throne, *were* four beasts full of eyes before and behind. ⁷And the first beast *was* like a lion, and the second beast like a calf, and the third beast had a face as a man, and the fourth beast *was* like a flying eagle.

⁸And the four beasts had each of them six wings about *him*; and *they were* full of eyes within: and they restᵃ not day and night, saying, Holy, holy, holy, Lord God Almighty, which was, and is, and is to come. ⁹And when those beasts give glory and honour and thanks to him that sat on the throne, who liveth for ever and ever, ¹⁰The four and twenty elders fall down before him that sat on the throne, and worship him that liveth for ever and ever, and cast their crowns before the throne, saying, ¹¹Thou art worthy, O Lord, to receive glory and honour and power: for thou hast created all things, and for thy pleasure they are and were created.

5

¹And I saw in the right hand of him that sat on the throne a book written within and on the backside, sealed with seven seals. ²And I saw a strong angel proclaiming with a loud voice, Who is worthy to open the book, and to loose the seals thereof? ³And no man in heaven, nor in earth, neither under the earth, was able to open the book, neither to look thereon. ⁴And I wept much, because no man was found worthy to open and to read the book, neither to look thereon. ⁵And one of the elders saith

unto me, Weep not: behold, the Lion of the tribe of Juda, the Root of David, hath prevailed to open the book, and to loose the seven seals thereof.

⁶And I beheld, and, lo, in the midst of the throne and of the four beasts, and in the midst of the elders, stood a Lamb as it had been slain, having seven horns and seven eyes, which are the seven Spirits of God sent forth into all the earth. ⁷And he came and took the book out of the right hand of him that sat upon the throne. ⁸And when he had taken the book, the four beasts and four *and* twenty elders fell down before the Lamb, having every one of them harps, and golden vials full of odoursᵃ, which are the prayers of saints. ⁹And they sung a new song, saying, Thou art worthy to take the book, and to open the seals thereof: for thou wast slain, and hast redeemed us to God by thy blood out of every kindred, and tongue, and people, and nation; ¹⁰And hast made us unto our God kings and priests: and we shall reign on the earth. ¹¹And I beheld, and I heard the voice of many angels round about the throne and the beasts and the elders: and the number of them was ten thousand times ten thousand, and thousands of thousands; ¹²Saying with a loud voice, Worthy is the Lamb that was slain to receive power, and riches, and wisdom, and strength, and honour, and glory, and blessing. ¹³And every creature which is in heaven, and on the earth, and under the earth, and such as are in the sea, and all that are in them, heard I saying, Blessing, and honour,

---

ᵃ rest . . . : Gr. have no rest
ᵃ odours: or, incense

and glory, and power, *be* unto him that sitteth upon the throne, and unto the Lamb for ever and ever. ¹⁴And the four beasts said, Amen. And the four *and* twenty elders fell down and worshipped him that liveth for ever and ever.

6

¹And I saw when the Lamb opened one of the seals, and I heard, as it were the noise of thunder, one of the four beasts saying, Come and see. ²And I saw, and behold a white horse: and he that sat on him had a bow; and a crown was given unto him: and he went forth conquering, and to conquer.

³And when he had opened the second seal, I heard the second beast say, Come and see. ⁴And there went out another horse *that was* red: and *power* was given to him that sat thereon to take peace from the earth, and that they should kill one another: and there was given unto him a great sword. ⁵And when he had opened the third seal, I heard the third beast say, Come and see. And I beheld, and lo a black horse; and he that sat on him had a pair of balances in his hand. ⁶And I heard a voice in the midst of the four beasts say, A measureᵃ of wheat for a penny, and three measures of barley for a penny; and *see* thou hurt not the oil and the wine. ⁷And when he had opened the fourth seal, I heard the voice of the fourth beast say, Come and see. ⁸And I looked, and behold a pale horse: and his name that sat on him was Death,

and Hell followed with him. And power was given unto themᵇ over the fourth part of the earth, to kill with sword, and with hunger, and with death, and with the beasts of the earth.

⁹And when he had opened the fifth seal, I saw under the altar the souls of them that were slain for the word of God, and for the testimony which they held: ¹⁰And they cried with a loud voice, saying, How long, O Lord, holy and true, dost thou not judge and avenge our blood on them that dwell on the earth? ¹¹And white robes were given unto every one of them; and it was said unto them, that they should rest yet for a little season, until their fellowservants also and their brethren, that should be killed as they *were*, should be fulfilled. ¹²And I beheld when he had opened the sixth seal, and, lo, there was a great earthquake; and the sun became black as sackcloth of hair, and the moon became as blood; ¹³And the stars of heaven fell unto the earth, even as a fig tree casteth her untimely figsᶜ, when she is shaken of a mighty wind. ¹⁴And the heaven departed as a scroll when it is rolled together; and every mountain and island were moved out of their places. ¹⁵And the kings of the earth, and the great men, and the rich men, and the chief captains, and the mighty men, and every bondman, and every free man, hid themselves in the dens and in the rocks of the mountains; ¹⁶And said to the mountains and rocks, Fall on us, and hide us from the

---

ᵃ A measure: the word choenix signifieth a measure containing one wine quart, and the twelfth part of a quart
ᵇ unto them: or, to him
ᶜ untimely figs: or, green figs

face of him that sitteth on the throne, and from the wrath of the Lamb: ¹⁷For the great day of his wrath is come; and who shall be able to stand?

7

¹And after these things I saw four angels standing on the four corners of the earth, holding the four winds of the earth, that the wind should not blow on the earth, nor on the sea, nor on any tree. ²And I saw another angel ascending from the east, having the seal of the living God: and he cried with a loud voice to the four angels, to whom it was given to hurt the earth and the sea, ³Saying, Hurt not the earth, neither the sea, nor the trees, till we have sealed the servants of our God in their foreheads. ⁴And I heard the number of them which were sealed: *and there were* sealed an hundred *and* forty *and* four thousand of all the tribes of the children of Israel. ⁵Of the tribe of Juda *were* sealed twelve thousand. Of the tribe of Reuben *were* sealed twelve thousand. Of the tribe of Gad *were* sealed twelve thousand. ⁶Of the tribe of Aser *were* sealed twelve thousand. Of the tribe of Nepthalim *were* sealed twelve thousand. Of the tribe of Manasses *were* sealed twelve thousand. ⁷Of the tribe of Simeon *were* sealed twelve thousand. Of the tribe of Levi *were* sealed twelve thousand. Of the tribe of Issachar *were* sealed twelve thousand. ⁸Of the tribe of Zabulon *were* sealed twelve thousand. Of the tribe of Joseph *were* sealed twelve thousand. Of the tribe of Benjamin *were* sealed twelve thousand. ⁹After this I beheld, and, lo, a great multitude, which no man could number, of all nations, and kindreds, and people, and tongues, stood before the throne, and before the Lamb, clothed with white robes, and palms in their hands; ¹⁰And cried with a loud voice, saying, Salvation to our God which sitteth upon the throne, and unto the Lamb. ¹¹And all the angels stood round about the throne, and *about* the elders and the four beasts, and fell before the throne on their faces, and worshipped God, ¹²Saying, Amen: Blessing, and glory, and wisdom, and thanksgiving, and honour, and power, and might, *be* unto our God for ever and ever. Amen.

¹³And one of the elders answered, saying unto me, What are these which are arrayed in white robes? and whence came they? ¹⁴And I said unto him, Sir, thou knowest. And he said to me, These are they which came out of great tribulation, and have washed their robes, and made them white in the blood of the Lamb. ¹⁵Therefore are they before the throne of God, and serve him day and night in his temple: and he that sitteth on the throne shall dwell among them. ¹⁶They shall hunger no more, neither thirst any more; neither shall the sun light on them, nor any heat. ¹⁷For the Lamb which is in the midst of the throne shall feed them, and shall lead them unto living fountains of waters: and God shall wipe away all tears from their eyes.

8

¹And when he had opened the seventh seal, there was silence in heaven about the space of half an hour. ²And I saw the seven angels which stood before God; and to them were given seven trumpets. ³And another angel came and stood at the altar, having a golden

censer; and there was given unto him much incense, that he should offer[a] *it* with the prayers of all saints upon the golden altar which was before the throne. [4]And the smoke of the incense, *which came* with the prayers of the saints, ascended up before God out of the angel's hand. [5]And the angel took the censer, and filled it with fire of the altar, and cast *it* into[b] the earth: and there were voices, and thunderings, and lightnings, and an earthquake. [6]And the seven angels which had the seven trumpets prepared themselves to sound.

[7]The first angel sounded, and there followed hail and fire mingled with blood, and they were cast upon the earth: and the third part of trees was burnt up, and all green grass was burnt up. [8]And the second angel sounded, and as it were a great mountain burning with fire was cast into the sea: and the third part of the sea became blood; [9]And the third part of the creatures which were in the sea, and had life, died; and the third part of the ships were destroyed. [10]And the third angel sounded, and there fell a great star from heaven, burning as it were a lamp, and it fell upon the third part of the rivers, and upon the fountains of waters; [11]And the name of the star is called Wormwood: and the third part of the waters became wormwood; and many men died of the waters, because they were made bitter. [12]And the fourth angel sounded, and the third part of the sun was smitten, and the third part of the moon, and the third part of the stars; so as the third part of them was

darkened, and the day shone not for a third part of it, and the night likewise. [13]And I beheld, and heard an angel flying through the midst of heaven, saying with a loud voice, Woe, woe, woe, to the inhabiters of the earth by reason of the other voices of the trumpet of the three angels, which are yet to sound!

9

[1]And the fifth angel sounded, and I saw a star fall from heaven unto the earth: and to him was given the key of the bottomless pit. [2]And he opened the bottomless pit; and there arose a smoke out of the pit, as the smoke of a great furnace; and the sun and the air were darkened by reason of the smoke of the pit. [3]And there came out of the smoke locusts upon the earth: and unto them was given power, as the scorpions of the earth have power. [4]And it was commanded them that they should not hurt the grass of the earth, neither any green thing, neither any tree; but only those men which have not the seal of God in their foreheads. [5]And to them it was given that they should not kill them, but that they should be tormented five months: and their torment *was* as the torment of a scorpion, when he striketh a man. [6]And in those days shall men seek death, and shall not find it; and shall desire to die, and death shall flee from them. [7]And the shapes of the locusts *were* like unto horses prepared unto battle; and on their heads *were* as it were crowns like gold, and their faces *were* as the faces of men. [8]And they had hair as the hair of women, and their

---

[a] offer . . . : or, add it to the prayers
[b] into: or, upon

teeth were as *the teeth* of lions. ⁹And they had breastplates, as it were breastplates of iron; and the sound of their wings *was* as the sound of chariots of many horses running to battle. ¹⁰And they had tails like unto scorpions, and there were stings in their tails: and their power *was* to hurt men five months. ¹¹And they had a king over them, *which is* the angel of the bottomless pit, whose name in the Hebrew tongue *is* Abaddon, but in the Greek tongue hath *his* name Apollyon[a]. ¹²One woe is past; *and,* behold, there come two woes more hereafter.

¹³And the sixth angel sounded, and I heard a voice from the four horns of the golden altar which is before God, ¹⁴Saying to the sixth angel which had the trumpet, Loose the four angels which are bound in the great river Euphrates. ¹⁵And the four angels were loosed, which were prepared for an hour[b], and a day, and a month, and a year, for to slay the third part of men. ¹⁶And the number of the army of the horsemen *were* two hundred thousand thousand: and I heard the number of them. ¹⁷And thus I saw the horses in the vision, and them that sat on them, having breastplates of fire, and of jacinth, and brimstone: and the heads of the horses *were* as the heads of lions; and out of their mouths issued fire and smoke and brimstone. ¹⁸By these three was the third part of men killed, by the fire, and by the smoke, and by the brimstone, which issued out of their mouths. ¹⁹For their power is in their mouth, and in their tails: for their tails *were* like unto serpents, and had

heads, and with them they do hurt. ²⁰And the rest of the men which were not killed by these plagues yet repented not of the works of their hands, that they should not worship devils, and idols of gold, and silver, and brass, and stone, and of wood: which neither can see, nor hear, nor walk: ²¹Neither repented they of their murders, nor of their sorceries, nor of their fornication, nor of their thefts.

10

¹And I saw another mighty angel come down from heaven, clothed with a cloud: and a rainbow *was* upon his head, and his face *was* as it were the sun, and his feet as pillars of fire: ²And he had in his hand a little book open: and he set his right foot upon the sea, and *his* left *foot* on the earth, ³And cried with a loud voice, as *when* a lion roareth: and when he had cried, seven thunders uttered their voices. ⁴And when the seven thunders had uttered their voices, I was about to write: and I heard a voice from heaven saying unto me, Seal up those things which the seven thunders uttered, and write them not. ⁵And the angel which I saw stand upon the sea and upon the earth lifted up his hand to heaven, ⁶And sware by him that liveth for ever and ever, who created heaven, and the things that therein are, and the earth, and the things that therein are, and the sea, and the things which are therein, that there should be time no longer: ⁷But in the days of the voice of the seventh angel, when he shall begin to sound, the mys-

---

[a] Apollyon: that is to say, A destroyer
[b] for an hour: or, at an hour

tery of God should be finished, as he hath declared to his servants the prophets.

[8]And the voice which I heard from heaven spake unto me again, and said, Go *and* take the little book which is open in the hand of the angel which standeth upon the sea and upon the earth. [9]And I went unto the angel, and said unto him, Give me the little book. And he said unto me, Take *it*, and eat it up; and it shall make thy belly bitter, but it shall be in thy mouth sweet as honey. [10]And I took the little book out of the angel's hand, and ate it up; and it was in my mouth sweet as honey: and as soon as I had eaten it, my belly was bitter. [11]And he said unto me, Thou must prophesy again before many peoples, and nations, and tongues, and kings.

11

[1]And there was given me a reed like unto a rod: and the angel stood, saying, Rise, and measure the temple of God, and the altar, and them that worship therein. [2]But the court which is without the temple leave out[a], and measure it not; for it is given unto the Gentiles: and the holy city shall they tread under foot forty *and* two months.

[3]And I will give[b] *power* unto my two witnesses, and they shall prophesy a thousand two hundred *and* threescore days, clothed in sackcloth. [4]These are the two olive trees, and the two candlesticks standing before the God of the earth. [5]And if any man will hurt them, fire pro-

ceedeth out of their mouth, and devoureth their enemies: and if any man will hurt them, he must in this manner be killed. [6]These have power to shut heaven, that it rain not in the days of their prophecy: and have power over waters to turn them to blood, and to smite the earth with all plagues, as often as they will. [7]And when they shall have finished their testimony, the beast that ascendeth out of the bottomless pit shall make war against them, and shall overcome them, and kill them. [8]And their dead bodies *shall lie* in the street of the great city, which spiritually is called Sodom and Egypt, where also our Lord was crucified. [9]And they of the people and kindreds and tongues and nations shall see their dead bodies three days and an half, and shall not suffer their dead bodies to be put in graves. [10]And they that dwell upon the earth shall rejoice over them, and make merry, and shall send gifts one to another; because these two prophets tormented them that dwelt on the earth. [11]And after three days and an half the Spirit of life from God entered into them, and they stood upon their feet; and great fear fell upon them which saw them. [12]And they heard a great voice from heaven saying unto them, Come up hither. And they ascended up to heaven in a cloud; and their enemies beheld them. [13]And the same hour was there a great earthquake, and the tenth part of the city fell, and in the earthquake were slain of men[c] seven thousand: and the remnant were affrighted, and gave glory to the God of heaven.

---

[a] leave out: Gr. cast out
[b] I will give . . . : or, I will give unto my two witnesses that they may prophesy
[c] of men: Gr. names of men

[14]The second woe is past; *and*, behold, the third woe cometh quickly. [15]And the seventh angel sounded; and there were great voices in heaven, saying, The kingdoms of this world are become *the kingdoms* of our Lord, and of his Christ; and he shall reign for ever and ever. [16]And the four and twenty elders, which sat before God on their seats, fell upon their faces, and worshipped God, [17]Saying, We give thee thanks, O Lord God Almighty, which art, and wast, and art to come; because thou hast taken to thee thy great power, and hast reigned. [18]And the nations were angry, and thy wrath is come, and the time of the dead, that they should be judged, and that thou shouldest give reward unto thy servants the prophets, and to the saints, and them that fear thy name, small and great; and shouldest destroy them which destroy the earth[d]. [19]And the temple of God was opened in heaven, and there was seen in his temple the ark of his testament: and there were lightnings, and voices, and thunderings, and an earthquake, and great hail.

12

[1]And there appeared a great wonder[a] in heaven; a woman clothed with the sun, and the moon under her feet, and upon her head a crown of twelve stars: [2]And she being with child cried, travailing in birth, and pained to be delivered. [3]And there appeared another wonder[b] in heaven; and behold a great red dragon, having seven heads and ten horns, and seven crowns upon his heads. [4]And his tail drew the third part of the stars of heaven, and did cast them to the earth: and the dragon stood before the woman which was ready to be delivered, for to devour her child as soon as it was born. [5]And she brought forth a man child, who was to rule all nations with a rod of iron: and her child was caught up unto God, and *to* his throne. [6]And the woman fled into the wilderness, where she hath a place prepared of God, that they should feed her there a thousand two hundred *and* threescore days. [7]And there was war in heaven: Michael and his angels fought against the dragon; and the dragon fought and his angels, [8]And prevailed not; neither was their place found any more in heaven. [9]And the great dragon was cast out, that old serpent, called the Devil, and Satan, which deceiveth the whole world: he was cast out into the earth, and his angels were cast out with him. [10]And I heard a loud voice saying in heaven, Now is come salvation, and strength, and the kingdom of our God, and the power of his Christ: for the accuser of our brethren is cast down, which accused them before our God day and night. [11]And they overcame him by the blood of the Lamb, and by the word of their testimony; and they loved not their lives unto the death.

[12]Therefore rejoice, *ye* heavens, and ye that dwell in them. Woe to the inhabiters of the earth and of the sea! for the devil is come down unto you, having great wrath, because he knoweth

---

[d] destroy the earth: or, corrupt the earth
[a] wonder: or, sign
[b] wonder: or, sign

that he hath but a short time. ¹³And when the dragon saw that he was cast unto the earth, he persecuted the woman which brought forth the man *child*. ¹⁴And to the woman were given two wings of a great eagle, that she might fly into the wilderness, into her place, where she is nourished for a time, and times, and half a time, from the face of the serpent. ¹⁵And the serpent cast out of his mouth water as a flood after the woman, that he might cause her to be carried away of the flood. ¹⁶And the earth helped the woman, and the earth opened her mouth, and swallowed up the flood which the dragon cast out of his mouth. ¹⁷And the dragon was wroth with the woman, and went to make war with the remnant of her seed, which keep the commandments of God, and have the testimony of Jesus Christ.

13

¹And I stood upon the sand of the sea, and saw a beast rise up out of the sea, having seven heads and ten horns, and upon his horns ten crowns, and upon his heads the name^a of blasphemy. ²And the beast which I saw was like unto a leopard, and his feet were as *the feet* of a bear, and his mouth as the mouth of a lion: and the dragon gave him his power, and his seat, and great authority. ³And I saw one of his heads as it were wounded^b to death; and his deadly wound was healed: and all the world wondered after the beast. ⁴And they worshipped the dragon which gave

power unto the beast: and they worshipped the beast, saying, Who *is* like unto the beast? who is able to make war with him? ⁵And there was given unto him a mouth speaking great things and blasphemies; and power was given unto him to continue^c forty *and* two months. ⁶And he opened his mouth in blasphemy against God, to blaspheme his name, and his tabernacle, and them that dwell in heaven. ⁷And it was given unto him to make war with the saints, and to overcome them: and power was given him over all kindreds, and tongues, and nations. ⁸And all that dwell upon the earth shall worship him, whose names are not written in the book of life of the Lamb slain from the foundation of the world. ⁹If any man have an ear, let him hear. ¹⁰He that leadeth into captivity shall go into captivity: he that killeth with the sword must be killed with the sword. Here is the patience and the faith of the saints.

¹¹And I beheld another beast coming up out of the earth; and he had two horns like a lamb, and he spake as a dragon. ¹²And he exerciseth all the power of the first beast before him, and causeth the earth and them which dwell therein to worship the first beast, whose deadly wound was healed. ¹³And he doeth great wonders, so that he maketh fire come down from heaven on the earth in the sight of men, ¹⁴And deceiveth them that dwell on the earth by *the means of* those miracles which he had power to do in the sight of the beast; saying to them that dwell on the

---

^a name: or, names
^b wounded: Gr. slain
^c to continue: or, to make war

earth, that they should make an image to the beast, which had the wound by a sword, and did live. ¹⁵And he had power to give life[d] unto the image of the beast, that the image of the beast should both speak, and cause that as many as would not worship the image of the beast should be killed. ¹⁶And he causeth all, both small and great, rich and poor, free and bond, to receive[e] a mark in their right hand, or in their foreheads: ¹⁷And that no man might buy or sell, save he that had the mark, or the name of the beast, or the number of his name. ¹⁸Here is wisdom. Let him that hath understanding count the number of the beast: for it is the number of a man; and his number *is* Six hundred threescore *and* six.

14

¹And I looked, and, lo, a Lamb stood on the mount Sion, and with him an hundred forty *and* four thousand, having his Father's name written in their foreheads. ²And I heard a voice from heaven, as the voice of many waters, and as the voice of a great thunder: and I heard the voice of harpers harping with their harps: ³And they sung as it were a new song before the throne, and before the four beasts, and the elders: and no man could learn that song but the hundred *and* forty *and* four thousand, which were redeemed from the earth. ⁴These are they which were not defiled with women; for they are virgins. These are they which follow the Lamb whithersoever he goeth. These

were redeemed[a] from among men, *being* the firstfruits unto God and to the Lamb. ⁵And in their mouth was found no guile: for they are without fault before the throne of God.

⁶And I saw another angel fly in the midst of heaven, having the everlasting gospel to preach unto them that dwell on the earth, and to every nation, and kindred, and tongue, and people, ⁷Saying with a loud voice, Fear God, and give glory to him; for the hour of his judgment is come: and worship him that made heaven, and earth, and the sea, and the fountains of waters. ⁸And there followed another angel, saying, Babylon is fallen, is fallen, that great city, because she made all nations drink of the wine of the wrath of her fornication. ⁹And the third angel followed them, saying with a loud voice, If any man worship the beast and his image, and receive *his* mark in his forehead, or in his hand, ¹⁰The same shall drink of the wine of the wrath of God, which is poured out without mixture into the cup of his indignation; and he shall be tormented with fire and brimstone in the presence of the holy angels, and in the presence of the Lamb: ¹¹And the smoke of their torment ascendeth up for ever and ever: and they have no rest day nor night, who worship the beast and his image, and whosoever receiveth the mark of his name. ¹²Here is the patience of the saints: here *are* they that keep the commandments of God, and the faith of Jesus.

¹³And I heard a voice from heaven

---

[d] life: Gr. breath
[e] to receive: Gr. to give them
[a] redeemed: Gr. bought

saying unto me, Write, Blessed *are* the dead which die in the Lord from henceforth[b]: Yea, saith the Spirit, that they may rest from their labours; and their works do follow them. ¹⁴And I looked, and behold a white cloud, and upon the cloud *one* sat like unto the Son of man, having on his head a golden crown, and in his hand a sharp sickle. ¹⁵And another angel came out of the temple, crying with a loud voice to him that sat on the cloud, Thrust in thy sickle, and reap: for the time is come for thee to reap; for the harvest of the earth is ripe[c]. ¹⁶And he that sat on the cloud thrust in his sickle on the earth; and the earth was reaped. ¹⁷And another angel came out of the temple which is in heaven, he also having a sharp sickle. ¹⁸And another angel came out from the altar, which had power over fire; and cried with a loud cry to him that had the sharp sickle, saying, Thrust in thy sharp sickle, and gather the clusters of the vine of the earth; for her grapes are fully ripe. ¹⁹And the angel thrust in his sickle into the earth, and gathered the vine of the earth, and cast *it* into the great winepress of the wrath of God. ²⁰And the winepress was trodden without the city, and blood came out of the winepress, even unto the horse bridles, by the space of a thousand *and* six hundred furlongs.

15

¹And I saw another sign in heaven, great and marvellous, seven angels having the seven last plagues; for in them is filled up the wrath of God. ²And I saw as it were a sea of glass mingled with fire: and them that had gotten the victory over the beast, and over his image, and over his mark, *and* over the number of his name, stand on the sea of glass, having the harps of God. ³And they sing the song of Moses the servant of God, and the song of the Lamb, saying, Great and marvellous *are* thy works, Lord God Almighty; just and true *are* thy ways, thou King of saints[a]. ⁴Who shall not fear thee, O Lord, and glorify thy name? for *thou* only *art* holy: for all nations shall come and worship before thee; for thy judgments are made manifest.

⁵And after that I looked, and, behold, the temple of the tabernacle of the testimony in heaven was opened: ⁶And the seven angels came out of the temple, having the seven plagues, clothed in pure and white linen, and having their breasts girded with golden girdles. ⁷And one of the four beasts gave unto the seven angels seven golden vials full of the wrath of God, who liveth for ever and ever. ⁸And the temple was filled with smoke from the glory of God, and from his power; and no man was able to enter into the temple, till the seven plagues of the seven angels were fulfilled.

16

¹And I heard a great voice out of the temple saying to the seven angels, Go your ways, and pour out the vials of the wrath of God upon the earth. ²And the first

---

[b] from henceforth . . . : or, from henceforth saith the Spirit, Yea
[c] ripe: or, dried

[a] saints: or, nations, or, ages

went, and poured out his vial upon the earth; and there fell a noisome and grievous sore upon the men which had the mark of the beast, and *upon* them which worshipped his image. ³And the second angel poured out his vial upon the sea; and it became as the blood of a dead *man*: and every living soul died in the sea. ⁴And the third angel poured out his vial upon the rivers and fountains of waters; and they became blood. ⁵And I heard the angel of the waters say, Thou art righteous, O Lord, which art, and wast, and shalt be, because thou hast judged thus. ⁶For they have shed the blood of saints and prophets, and thou hast given them blood to drink; for they are worthy. ⁷And I heard another out of the altar say, Even so, Lord God Almighty, true and righteous *are* thy judgments.

⁸And the fourth angel poured out his vial upon the sun; and power was given unto him to scorch men with fire. ⁹And men were scorchedᵃ with great heat, and blasphemed the name of God, which hath power over these plagues: and they repented not to give him glory. ¹⁰And the fifth angel poured out his vial upon the seat of the beast; and his kingdom was full of darkness; and they gnawed their tongues for pain, ¹¹And blasphemed the God of heaven because of their pains and their sores, and repented not of their deeds.

¹²And the sixth angel poured out his vial upon the great river Euphrates; and the water thereof was dried up, that the way of the kings of the east might be prepared. ¹³And I saw three unclean spirits like frogs *come* out of the mouth of the dragon, and out of the mouth of the beast, and out of the mouth of the false prophet. ¹⁴For they are the spirits of devils, working miracles, *which* go forth unto the kings of the earth and of the whole world, to gather them to the battle of that great day of God Almighty. ¹⁵Behold, I come as a thief. Blessed *is* he that watcheth, and keepeth his garments, lest he walk naked, and they see his shame. ¹⁶And he gathered them together into a place called in the Hebrew tongue Armageddon.

¹⁷And the seventh angel poured out his vial into the air; and there came a great voice out of the temple of heaven, from the throne, saying, It is done. ¹⁸And there were voices, and thunders, and lightnings; and there was a great earthquake, such as was not since men were upon the earth, so mighty an earthquake, *and* so great. ¹⁹And the great city was divided into three parts, and the cities of the nations fell: and great Babylon came in remembrance before God, to give unto her the cup of the wine of the fierceness of his wrath. ²⁰And every island fled away, and the mountains were not found. ²¹And there fell upon men a great hail out of heaven, *every stone* about the weight of a talent: and men blasphemed God because of the plague of the hail; for the plague thereof was exceeding great.

17

¹And there came one of the seven angels which had the seven vials, and talked with me, saying unto me, Come hither; I will shew unto thee the judgment of the great whore that sitteth upon many waters: ²With whom the kings of the

---

ᵃ scorched: or, burned

earth have committed fornication, and the inhabitants of the earth have been made drunk with the wine of her fornication. ³So he carried me away in the spirit into the wilderness: and I saw a woman sit upon a scarlet coloured beast, full of names of blasphemy, having seven heads and ten horns. ⁴And the woman was arrayed in purple and scarlet colour, and deckedᵃ with gold and precious stones and pearls, having a golden cup in her hand full of abominations and filthiness of her fornication: ⁵And upon her forehead *was* a name written, MYSTERY, BABYLON THE GREAT, THE MOTHER OF HARLOTS AND ABOMINATIONS OF THE EARTH. ⁶And I saw the woman drunken with the blood of the saints, and with the blood of the martyrs of Jesus: and when I saw her, I wondered with great admiration.

⁷And the angel said unto me, Wherefore didst thou marvel? I will tell thee the mystery of the woman, and of the beast that carrieth her, which hath the seven heads and ten horns. ⁸The beast that thou sawest was, and is not; and shall ascend out of the bottomless pit, and go into perdition: and they that dwell on the earth shall wonder, whose names were not written in the book of life from the foundation of the world, when they behold the beast that was, and is not, and yet is. ⁹And here *is* the mind which hath wisdom. The seven heads are seven mountains, on which the woman sitteth. ¹⁰And there are seven kings: five are fallen, and one is, *and* the other is not yet come; and when he cometh, he must continue a short space. ¹¹And the beast that was, and is not, even he is the eighth, and is of the seven, and goeth into perdition. ¹²And the ten horns which thou sawest are ten kings, which have received no kingdom as yet; but receive power as kings one hour with the beast. ¹³These have one mind, and shall give their power and strength unto the beast.

¹⁴These shall make war with the Lamb, and the Lamb shall overcome them: for he is Lord of lords, and King of kings: and they that are with him *are* called, and chosen, and faithful. ¹⁵And he saith unto me, The waters which thou sawest, where the whore sitteth, are peoples, and multitudes, and nations, and tongues. ¹⁶And the ten horns which thou sawest upon the beast, these shall hate the whore, and shall make her desolate and naked, and shall eat her flesh, and burn her with fire. ¹⁷For God hath put in their hearts to fulfil his will, and to agree, and give their kingdom unto the beast, until the words of God shall be fulfilled. ¹⁸And the woman which thou sawest is that great city, which reigneth over the kings of the earth.

18

¹And after these things I saw another angel come down from heaven, having great power; and the earth was lightened with his glory. ²And he cried mightily with a strong voice, saying, Babylon the great is fallen, is fallen, and is become the habitation of devils, and the hold of every foul spirit, and a cage of every unclean and hateful bird. ³For all nations have drunk of the wine of the wrath of her fornication, and the

ᵃ decked: Gr. gilded

kings of the earth have committed fornication with her, and the merchants of the earth are waxed rich through the abundance[a] of her delicacies. ⁴And I heard another voice from heaven, saying, Come out of her, my people, that ye be not partakers of her sins, and that ye receive not of her plagues. ⁵For her sins have reached unto heaven, and God hath remembered her iniquities. ⁶Reward her even as she rewarded you, and double unto her double according to her works: in the cup which she hath filled fill to her double. ⁷How much she hath glorified herself, and lived deliciously, so much torment and sorrow give her: for she saith in her heart, I sit a queen, and am no widow, and shall see no sorrow. ⁸Therefore shall her plagues come in one day, death, and mourning, and famine; and she shall be utterly burned with fire: for strong *is* the Lord God who judgeth her.

⁹And the kings of the earth, who have committed fornication and lived deliciously with her, shall bewail her, and lament for her, when they shall see the smoke of her burning, ¹⁰Standing afar off for the fear of her torment, saying, Alas, alas, that great city Babylon, that mighty city! for in one hour is thy judgment come. ¹¹And the merchants of the earth shall weep and mourn over her; for no man buyeth their merchandise any more: ¹²The merchandise of gold, and silver, and precious stones, and of pearls, and fine linen, and purple, and silk, and scarlet, and all thyine[b] wood, and all manner vessels of ivory,

and all manner vessels of most precious wood, and of brass, and iron, and marble, ¹³And cinnamon, and odours, and ointments, and frankincense, and wine, and oil, and fine flour, and wheat, and beasts, and sheep, and horses, and chariots, and slaves[c], and souls of men. ¹⁴And the fruits that thy soul lusted after are departed from thee, and all things which were dainty and goodly are departed from thee, and thou shalt find them no more at all. ¹⁵The merchants of these things, which were made rich by her, shall stand afar off for the fear of her torment, weeping and wailing, ¹⁶And saying, Alas, alas, that great city, that was clothed in fine linen, and purple, and scarlet, and decked with gold, and precious stones, and pearls! ¹⁷For in one hour so great riches is come to nought. And every shipmaster, and all the company in ships, and sailors, and as many as trade by sea, stood afar off, ¹⁸And cried when they saw the smoke of her burning, saying, What *city is* like unto this great city! ¹⁹And they cast dust on their heads, and cried, weeping and wailing, saying, Alas, alas, that great city, wherein were made rich all that had ships in the sea by reason of her costliness! for in one hour is she made desolate. ²⁰Rejoice over her, *thou* heaven, and *ye* holy apostles and prophets; for God hath avenged you on her. ²¹And a mighty angel took up a stone like a great millstone, and cast *it* into the sea, saying, Thus with violence shall that great city Babylon be thrown down, and shall be

---

[a] abundance: or, power

[b] thyine: or, sweet

[c] slaves: or, bodies

found no more at all. ²²And the voice of harpers, and musicians, and of pipers, and trumpeters, shall be heard no more at all in thee; and no craftsman, of whatsoever craft *he be*, shall be found any more in thee; and the sound of a millstone shall be heard no more at all in thee; ²³And the light of a candle shall shine no more at all in thee; and the voice of the bridegroom and of the bride shall be heard no more at all in thee: for thy merchants were the great men of the earth; for by thy sorceries were all nations deceived. ²⁴And in her was found the blood of prophets, and of saints, and of all that were slain upon the earth.

19

¹And after these things I heard a great voice of much people in heaven, saying, Alleluia; Salvation, and glory, and honour, and power, unto the Lord our God: ²For true and righteous *are* his judgments: for he hath judged the great whore, which did corrupt the earth with her fornication, and hath avenged the blood of his servants at her hand. ³And again they said, Alleluia. And her smoke rose up for ever and ever. ⁴And the four and twenty elders and the four beasts fell down and worshipped God that sat on the throne, saying, Amen; Alleluia.

⁵And a voice came out of the throne, saying, Praise our God, all ye his servants, and ye that fear him, both small and great. ⁶And I heard as it were the voice of a great multitude, and as the voice of many waters, and as the voice of mighty thunderings, saying,

Alleluia: for the Lord God omnipotent reigneth. ⁷Let us be glad and rejoice, and give honour to him: for the marriage of the Lamb is come, and his wife hath made herself ready. ⁸And to her was granted that she should be arrayed in fine linen, clean and whiteª: for the fine linen is the righteousness of saints. ⁹And he saith unto me, Write, Blessed *are* they which are called unto the marriage supper of the Lamb. And he saith unto me, These are the true sayings of God. ¹⁰And I fell at his feet to worship him. And he said unto me, See *thou do it* not: I am thy fellowservant, and of thy brethren that have the testimony of Jesus: worship God: for the testimony of Jesus is the spirit of prophecy.

¹¹And I saw heaven opened, and behold a white horse; and he that sat upon him *was* called Faithful and True, and in righteousness he doth judge and make war. ¹²His eyes *were* as a flame of fire, and on his head *were* many crowns; and he had a name written, that no man knew, but he himself. ¹³And he *was* clothed with a vesture dipped in blood: and his name is called The Word of God. ¹⁴And the armies *which were* in heaven followed him upon white horses, clothed in fine linen, white and clean. ¹⁵And out of his mouth goeth a sharp sword, that with it he should smite the nations: and he shall rule them with a rod of iron: and he treadeth the winepress of the fierceness and wrath of Almighty God. ¹⁶And he hath on *his* vesture and on his thigh a name written, KING OF KINGS, AND LORD OF LORDS. ¹⁷And I saw an angel standing in the sun; and he cried with a loud voice, saying to all the fowls that fly in the midst

---

ª white: or, bright

of heaven, Come and gather yourselves together unto the supper of the great God; [18]That ye may eat the flesh of kings, and the flesh of captains, and the flesh of mighty men, and the flesh of horses, and of them that sit on them, and the flesh of all *men, both* free and bond, both small and great. [19]And I saw the beast, and the kings of the earth, and their armies, gathered together to make war against him that sat on the horse, and against his army. [20]And the beast was taken, and with him the false prophet that wrought miracles before him, with which he deceived them that had received the mark of the beast, and them that worshipped his image. These both were cast alive into a lake of fire burning with brimstone. [21]And the remnant were slain with the sword of him that sat upon the horse, which *sword* proceeded out of his mouth: and all the fowls were filled with their flesh.

20

[1]And I saw an angel come down from heaven, having the key of the bottomless pit and a great chain in his hand. [2]And he laid hold on the dragon, that old serpent, which is the Devil, and Satan, and bound him a thousand years, [3]And cast him into the bottomless pit, and shut him up, and set a seal upon him, that he should deceive the nations no more, till the thousand years should be fulfilled: and after that he must be loosed a little season. [4]And I saw thrones, and they sat upon them, and judgment was given unto them: and *I saw* the souls of them that were beheaded for the witness of Jesus, and for the word of God, and which had not worshipped the beast, neither his image, neither had received *his* mark upon their foreheads, or in their hands; and they lived and reigned with Christ a thousand years. [5]But the rest of the dead lived not again until the thousand years were finished. This *is* the first resurrection. [6]Blessed and holy *is* he that hath part in the first resurrection: on such the second death hath no power, but they shall be priests of God and of Christ, and shall reign with him a thousand years. [7]And when the thousand years are expired, Satan shall be loosed out of his prison, [8]And shall go out to deceive the nations which are in the four quarters of the earth, Gog and Magog, to gather them together to battle: the number of whom *is* as the sand of the sea. [9]And they went up on the breadth of the earth, and compassed the camp of the saints about, and the beloved city: and fire came down from God out of heaven, and devoured them. [10]And the devil that deceived them was cast into the lake of fire and brimstone, where the beast and the false prophet *are*, and shall be tormented day and night for ever and ever.

[11]And I saw a great white throne, and him that sat on it, from whose face the earth and the heaven fled away; and there was found no place for them. [12]And I saw the dead, small and great, stand before God; and the books were opened: and another book was opened, which is *the book* of life: and the dead were judged out of those things which were written in the books, according to their works. [13]And the sea gave up the dead which were in it; and death and hell[a] delivered up the dead which were in them: and they were judged every

---

[a] hell: or, the grave

man according to their works. ¹⁴And death and hell were cast into the lake of fire. This is the second death. ¹⁵And whosoever was not found written in the book of life was cast into the lake of fire.

21

¹And I saw a new heaven and a new earth: for the first heaven and the first earth were passed away; and there was no more sea. ²And I John saw the holy city, new Jerusalem, coming down from God out of heaven, prepared as a bride adorned for her husband. ³And I heard a great voice out of heaven saying, Behold, the tabernacle of God *is* with men, and he will dwell with them, and they shall be his people, and God himself shall be with them, *and be* their God. ⁴And God shall wipe away all tears from their eyes; and there shall be no more death, neither sorrow, nor crying, neither shall there be any more pain: for the former things are passed away. ⁵And he that sat upon the throne said, Behold, I make all things new. And he said unto me, Write: for these words are true and faithful. ⁶And he said unto me, It is done. I am Alpha and Omega, the beginning and the end. I will give unto him that is athirst of the fountain of the water of life freely. ⁷He that overcometh shall inherit all things[a]; and I will be his God, and he shall be my son. ⁸But the fearful, and unbelieving, and the abominable, and murderers, and whoremongers, and sorcerers, and idolaters, and all liars, shall have their part in the lake which burneth with fire and brimstone: which is the second death.

⁹And there came unto me one of

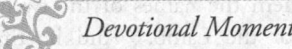

Devotional Moment

Heaven

21:1–22:21 The picture in this passage is of a new heaven and a new earth where God and his people will live forever together. The images paint a picture that we can imagine but only begin to appreciate: What will it really be like to live in this place made of precious gems and gold, of continual light and happiness, of joy and of living with God himself? We can't really know until we get there. We only know from these images that it will be *wonderful*.

Every child eventually has questions about heaven. When they're young, they often want to know if they will get to play their favorite games or eat their favorite foods, if their pets will be there with them, or if Grandma and Grandpa will be there, too. Go ahead and answer, but don't tell them more than the Bible says. The Bible says that all God's people will be there and that living there will be truly wonderful. We will have whatever we need to be happy. Amen.

the seven angels which had the seven vials full of the seven last plagues, and talked with me, saying, Come hither, I will shew thee the bride, the Lamb's wife. ¹⁰And he carried me away in the spirit to a great and high mountain, and shewed me that great city, the holy Jerusalem, descending out of heaven from God, ¹¹Having the glory of God: and her light *was* like unto a stone most precious, even like a jasper stone, clear as crystal; ¹²And had a wall great and high, *and* had twelve gates, and at the gates twelve angels, and names written thereon, which are *the names* of the twelve tribes of the children of Israel: ¹³On the east three gates; on the north three gates; on the south three gates; and on the west three gates. ¹⁴And the wall of the city had twelve foundations,

---

[a] all things: or, these things

and in them the names of the twelve apostles of the Lamb. ¹⁵And he that talked with me had a golden reed to measure the city, and the gates thereof, and the wall thereof. ¹⁶And the city lieth foursquare, and the length is as large as the breadth: and he measured the city with the reed, twelve thousand furlongs. The length and the breadth and the height of it are equal. ¹⁷And he measured the wall thereof, an hundred *and* forty *and* four cubits, *according to* the measure of a man, that is, of the angel. ¹⁸And the building of the wall of it was *of* jasper: and the city *was* pure gold, like unto clear glass. ¹⁹And the foundations of the wall of the city *were* garnished with all manner of precious stones. The first foundation *was* jasper; the second, sapphire; the third, a chalcedony; the fourth, an emerald; ²⁰The fifth, sardonyx; the sixth, sardius; the seventh, chrysolite; the eighth, beryl; the ninth, a topaz; the tenth, a chrysoprasus; the eleventh, a jacinth; the twelfth, an amethyst. ²¹And the twelve gates *were* twelve pearls; every several gate was of one pearl: and the street of the city *was* pure gold, as it were transparent glass. ²²And I saw no temple therein: for the Lord God Almighty and the Lamb are the temple of it. ²³And the city had no need of the sun, neither of the moon, to shine in it: for the glory of God did lighten it, and the Lamb *is* the light thereof. ²⁴And the nations of them which are saved shall walk in the light of it: and the kings of the earth do bring their glory and honour into it. ²⁵And the gates of it shall not be shut at all by day: for there shall be no night there. ²⁶And they shall bring the glory and honour of the nations into it. ²⁷And there shall in no wise enter into it any thing that defileth, neither *whatsoever* worketh abomination, or *maketh* a lie: but they which are written in the Lamb's book of life.

22

¹And he shewed me a pure river of water of life, clear as crystal, proceeding out of the throne of God and of the Lamb. ²In the midst of the street of it, and on either side of the river, *was there* the tree of life, which bare twelve *manner of* fruits, *and* yielded her fruit every month: and the leaves of the tree *were* for the healing of the nations. ³And there shall be no more curse: but the throne of God and of the Lamb shall be in it; and his servants shall serve him: ⁴And they shall see his face; and his name *shall be* in their foreheads. ⁵And there shall be no night there; and they need no candle, neither light of the sun; for the Lord God giveth them light: and they shall reign for ever and ever.

⁶And he said unto me, These sayings *are* faithful and true: and the Lord God of the holy prophets sent his angel to shew unto his servants the things which must shortly be done. ⁷Behold, I come quickly: blessed *is* he that keepeth the sayings of the prophecy of this book. ⁸And I John saw these things, and heard *them*. And when I had heard and seen, I fell down to worship before the feet of the angel which shewed me these things. ⁹Then saith he unto me, See *thou do it* not: for I am thy fellowservant, and of thy brethren the prophets, and of them which keep the sayings of this book: worship God. ¹⁰And he saith unto me, Seal not the sayings of the

prophecy of this book: for the time is at hand. ¹¹He that is unjust, let him be unjust still: and he which is filthy, let him be filthy still: and he that is righteous, let him be righteous still: and he that is holy, let him be holy still. ¹²And, behold, I come quickly; and my reward *is* with me, to give every man according as his work shall be. ¹³I am Alpha and Omega, the beginning and the end, the first and the last. ¹⁴Blessed *are* they that do his commandments, that they may have right to the tree of life, and may enter in through the gates into the city. ¹⁵For without *are* dogs, and sorcerers, and whoremongers, and murderers, and idolaters, and whosoever loveth and maketh a lie. ¹⁶I Jesus have sent mine angel to testify unto you these things in the churches. I am the root and the offspring of David, *and* the bright and morning star. ¹⁷And the Spirit and the bride say, Come. And let him that heareth say, Come. And let him that is athirst come. And whosoever will, let him take the water of life freely. ¹⁸For I testify unto every man that heareth the words of the prophecy of this book, If any man shall add unto these things, God shall add unto him the plagues that are written in this book: ¹⁹And if any man shall take away from the words of the book of this prophecy, God shall take away his part out of the book of life, and out of the holy city, and *from* the things which are written in this book.

²⁰He which testifieth these things saith, Surely I come quickly. Amen. Even so, come, Lord Jesus. ²¹The grace of our Lord Jesus Christ *be* with you all. Amen.

INDEX TO BREAKING FREE

INDEX TO CONTRIBUTORS' ARTICLES

INDEX TO BIBLICAL PROFILES

INDEX TO FAMILY TRADITIONS

Index to Worship in Your Home

Index to Devotional Moments